Account Title	Classification	Financial Statement	Normal Balance
L			
Land	Plant Asset	Balance Sheet	Debit
Loss on Disposal of Plant Assets	Other Expense	Income Statement	Debit
M			
Maintenance and Repairs Expense	Operating Expense	Income Statement	Debit
Mortgage Payable	Long-Term Liability	Balance Sheet	Credit
N			
Notes Payable	Current Liability/ Long-Term Liability	Balance Sheet	Credit
O			
Owner's Capital	Owner's Equity	Owner's Equity and Balance Sheet	Credit
Owner's Drawings	Temporary Account Closed to Owner's Capital	Owner's Equity	Debit
P			
Patent	Intangible Asset	Balance Sheet	Debit
Paid-in Capital in Excess of Par—Common Stock	Stockholders' Equity	Balance Sheet	Credit
Paid-in Capital in Excess of Par—Preferred Stock	Stockholders' Equity	Balance Sheet	Credit
Preferred Stock	Stockholders' Equity	Balance Sheet	Credit
Premium on Bonds Payable	Long-Term Liability—Contra	Balance Sheet	Credit
Prepaid Insurance	Current Asset	Balance Sheet	Debit
Prepaid Rent	Current Asset	Balance Sheet	Debit
R			
Rent Expense	Operating Expense	Income Statement	Debit
Retained Earnings	Stockholders' Equity	Balance Sheet and Retained Earnings Statement	Credit
S			
Salaries and Wages Expense	Operating Expense	Income Statement	Debit
Salaries and Wages Payable	Current Liability	Balance Sheet	Credit
Sales Discounts	Revenue—Contra	Income Statement	Debit
Sales Returns and Allowances	Revenue—Contra	Income Statement	Debit
Sales Revenue	Revenue	Income Statement	Credit
Selling Expenses	Operating Expense	Income Statement	Debit
Service Revenue	Revenue	Income Statement	Credit
Short-Term Investments	Current Asset	Balance Sheet	Debit
Supplies	Current Asset	Balance Sheet	Debit
Supplies Expense	Operating Expense	Income Statement	Debit
T			
Treasury Stock	Stockholders' Equity	Balance Sheet	Debit
U			
Unearned Service Revenue	Current Liability	Balance Sheet	Credit
Utilities Expense	Operating Expense	Income Statement	Debit

(1) The normal balance for Income Summary will be credit when there is a net income, debit when there is a net loss. The Income Summary account does not appear on any financial statement.

(2) If a periodic system is used, Inventory also appears on the income statement in the calculation of cost of goods sold.

The following is a sample chart of accounts. It does not represent a comprehensive chart of all the accounts used in this textbook but rather those accounts that are commonly used. This sample chart of accounts is for a company that generates both service revenue as well as sales revenue. It uses the perpetual approach to inventory. If a periodic system was used, the following temporary accounts would be needed to record inventory purchases: Purchases; Freight-in; Purchase Returns and Allowances; and Purchase Discounts.

CHART OF ACCOUNTS

Assets	Liabilities	Owner's and Stockholders' Equity	Revenues	Expenses
Cash	Notes Payable	Owner's Capital	Service Revenue	Advertising Expense
Accounts Receivable	Accounts Payable	Owner's Drawings	Sales Revenue	Amortization Expense
Allowance for Doubtful Accounts	Unearned Service Revenue	Common Stock	Sales Discounts	Bad Debts Expense
Interest Receivable	Salaries and Wages Payable	Paid-in Capital in Excess of Par—Common Stock	Sales Returns and Allowances	Cost of Goods Sold
Inventory	Unearned Rent Revenue	Preferred Stock	Interest Revenue	Depreciation Expense
Supplies	Interest Payable	Paid-in Capital in Excess of Par—Preferred Stock	Gain on Disposal of Plant Assets	Freight-out
Prepaid Insurance	Dividends Payable		Rent Revenue	Income Tax Expense
Prepaid Rent	Income Taxes Payable	Treasury Stock		Insurance Expense
Land	Bonds Payable	Retained Earnings		Interest Expense
Equipment	Discount on Bonds Payable	Dividends		Loss on Disposal of Plant Assets
Accumulated Depreciation—Equipment	Premium on Bonds Payable	Income Summary		Maintenance and Repairs Expense
Buildings	Mortgage Payable			Rent Expense
Accumulated Depreciation—Buildings				Salaries and Wages Expense
Copyrights				Supplies Expense
Goodwill				Utilities Expense
Patents				

accessible, affordable,
active learning

www.wileyplus.com

WileyPLUS is an innovative, research-based, online environment for effective teaching and learning.

WileyPLUS...

...motivates students with confidence-boosting feedback and proof of progress, 24/7.

...supports instructors with reliable resources that reinforce course goals inside and outside of the classroom.

Includes Interactive Textbook & Resources

WileyPLUS... Learn More.

www.wileyplus.com

www.wileyplus.com

ALL THE HELP, **RESOURCES**, AND PERSONAL **SUPPORT** YOU AND YOUR STUDENTS NEED!

www.wileyplus.com/resources

2-Minute Tutorials and all of the resources you & your students need to get started.

Student support from an experienced student user.

Collaborate with your colleagues, find a mentor, attend virtual and live events, and view resources.
www.WhereFacultyConnect.com

Pre-loaded, ready-to-use assignments and presentations. Created by subject matter experts.

Technical Support 24/7 FAQs, online chat, and phone support.
www.wileyplus.com/support

Your *WileyPLUS* Account Manager. Personal training and implementation support.

weygandt
kimmel
kieso
team for success

ACCOUNTING 10E
PRINCIPLES

Jerry J. Weygandt PhD, CPA
University of Wisconsin—Madison
Madison, Wisconsin

Paul D. Kimmel PhD, CPA
University of Wisconsin—Milwaukee
Milwaukee, Wisconsin

Donald E. Kieso PhD, CPA
Northern Illinois University
DeKalb, Illinois

WILEY

John Wiley & Sons, Inc.

Dedicated to
the **Wiley sales representatives**
who sell our books and service
our adopters in a professional
and ethical manner and to
Enid, Merlynn, and Donna

Vice President & Executive Publisher	George Hoffman
Associate Publisher	Christopher DeJohn
Project Editor	Ed Brislin
Development Editor	Terry Ann Tatro
Project Editor	Yana Mermel
Production Manager	Dorothy Sinclair
Senior Production Editor	Valerie A. Vargas
Production Editor	Erin Bascom
Associate Director of Marketing	Amy Scholz
Senior Marketing Manager	Ramona Sherman
Executive Media Editor	Allison Morris
Media Editor	Greg Chaput
Creative Director	Harry Nolan
Senior Designer	Madelyn Lesure
Production Management Services	Ingrao Associates
Senior Photo Editor	Mary Ann Price
Editorial Assistant	Jacqueline Kepping
Marketing Assistant	Courtney Luzzi
Assistant Marketing Manager	Diane Mars
Cover Design	Maureen Eide
Cover Photo	©Bill Stevenson/Photolibrary

This book was set in Times Ten by Aptara®, Inc. and printed and bound by RR Donnelley. The cover was printed by RR Donnelley.

Copyright © 2007, 2009, 2012 John Wiley & Sons, Inc. All rights reserved. No part of this publication may be reproduced, stored in a retrieval system or transmitted in any form or by any means, electronic, mechanical, photocopying, recording, scanning or otherwise, except as permitted under Sections 107 or 108 of the 1976 United States Copyright Act, without either the prior written permission of the Publisher, or authorization through payment of the appropriate per-copy fee to the Copyright Clearance Center, Inc. 222 Rosewood Drive, Danvers, MA 01923, website www.copyright.com. Requests to the Publisher for permission should be addressed to the Permissions Department, John Wiley & Sons, Inc., 111 River Street, Hoboken, NJ 07030-5774, (201)748-6011, fax (201)748-6008, website http://www.wiley.com/go/permissions.

Founded in 1807, John Wiley & Sons, Inc. has been a valued source of knowledge and understanding for more than 200 years, helping people around the world meet their needs and fulfill their aspirations. Our company is built on a foundation of principles that include responsibility to the communities we serve and where we live and work. In 2008, we launched a Corporate Citizenship Initiative, a global effort to address the environmental, social, economic, and ethical challenges we face in our business. Among the issues we are addressing are carbon impact, paper specifications and procurement, ethical conduct within our business and among our vendors, and community and charitable support. For more information, please visit our website: www.wiley.com/go/citizenship.

Evaluation copies are provided to qualified academics and professionals for review purposes only, for use in their courses during the next academic year. These copies are licensed and may not be sold or transferred to a third party. Upon completion of the review period, please return the evaluation copy to Wiley. Return instructions and a free of charge return shipping label are available at www.wiley.com/go/returnlabel. Outside of the United States, please contact your local representative.

ISBN-13 978-0-470-53479-3 (main textbook)
ISBN-13 978-1-118-00929-1 (BRV edition)

Printed in the United States of America

10 9 8 7 6 5 4 3 2 1

From the Authors

Dear Student,

Why This Course? *Remember your biology course in high school? Did you have one of those "invisible man" models (or maybe something more high-tech than that) that gave you the opportunity to look "inside" the human body? This accounting course offers something similar: To understand a business, you have to understand the financial insides of a business organization. An accounting course will help you understand the essential financial components of businesses. Whether you are looking at a large multinational company like Microsoft or Starbucks or a single-owner software consulting business or coffee shop, knowing the fundamentals of accounting will help you understand what is happening. As an employee, a manager, an investor, a business owner, or a director of your own personal finances—any of which roles you will have at some point in your life—you will be much the wiser for having taken this course.*

Why This Book? *Hundreds of thousands of students have used this textbook. Your instructor has chosen it for you because of its trusted reputation. The authors have worked hard to keep the book fresh, timely, and accurate.*

This textbook contains features to help you learn best, whatever your learning style. To understand what your learning style is, spend about ten minutes to take the learning style quiz at the book's companion website. Then, look at page vii for how you can apply an understanding of your learning style to this course. When you know more about your own learning style, browse through the Student Owner's Manual on pages viii–xi. It shows you the main features you will find in this textbook and explains their purpose.

How To Succeed? *We've asked many students and many instructors whether there is a secret for success in this course. The nearly unanimous answer turns out to be not much of a secret: "Do the homework." This is one course where doing is learning, and the more time you spend on the homework assignments—using the various tools that this textbook provides—the more likely you are to learn the essential concepts, techniques, and methods of accounting. Besides the textbook itself, the book's companion website offers various support resources.*

Good luck in this course. We hope you enjoy the experience and that you put to good use throughout a lifetime of success the knowledge you obtain in this course. We are sure you will not be disappointed.

Jerry J. Weygandt
Paul D. Kimmel
Donald E. Kieso

About the Authors

Jerry Weygandt

Jerry J. Weygandt, PhD, CPA, is Arthur Andersen Alumni Emeritus Professor of Accounting at the University of Wisconsin—Madison. He holds a Ph.D. in accounting from the University of Illinois. Articles by Professor Weygandt have appeared in the Accounting Review. Journal of Accounting Research, Accounting Horizons, Journal of Accountancy, and other academic and professional journals. These articles have examined such financial reporting issues as accounting for price-level adjustments, pensions, convertible securities, stock option contracts, and interim reports. Professor Weygandt is author of other accounting and financial reporting books and is a member of the American Accounting Association, the American Institute of Certified Public Accountants, and the Wisconsin Society of Certified Public Accountants. He has served on numerous committees of the American Accounting Association and as a member of the editorial board of the Accounting Review; he also has served as President and Secretary-Treasurer of the American Accounting Association. In addition, he has been actively involved with the American Institute of Certified Public Accountants and has been a member of the Accounting Standards Executive Committee (AcSEC) of that organization. He has served on the FASB task force that examined the reporting issues related to accounting for income taxes and served as a trustee of the Financial Accounting Foundation. Professor Weygandt has received the Chancellor's Award for Excellence in Teaching and the Beta Gamma Sigma Dean's Teaching Award. He is on the board of directors of M & I Bank of Southern Wisconsin. He is the recipient of the Wisconsin Institute of CPA's Outstanding Educator's Award and the Lifetime Achievement Award. In 2001 he received the American Accounting Association's Outstanding Educator Award.

Paul Kimmel

Paul D. Kimmel, PhD, CPA, received his bachelor's degree from the University of Minnesota and his doctorate in accounting from the University of Wisconsin. He is an Associate Professor at the University of Wisconsin—Milwaukee, and has public accounting experience with Deloitte & Touche (Minneapolis). He was the recipient of the UWM School of Business Advisory Council Teaching Award, the Reggie Taite Excellence in Teaching Award and a three-time winner of the Outstanding Teaching Assistant Award at the University of Wisconsin. He is also a recipient of the Elijah Watts Sells Award for Honorary Distinction for his results on the CPA exam. He is a member of the American Accounting Association and the Institute of Management Accountants and has published articles in Accounting Review, Accounting Horizons, Advances in Management Accounting, Managerial Finance, Issues in Accounting Education, Journal of Accounting Education, as well as other journals. His research interests include accounting for financial instruments and innovation in accounting education. He has published papers and given numerous talks on incorporating critical thinking into accounting education, and helped prepare a catalog of critical thinking resources for the Federated Schools of Accountancy.

Don Kieso

Donald E. Kieso, PhD, CPA, received his bachelor's degree from Aurora University and his doctorate in accounting from the University of Illinois. He has served as chairman of the Department of Accountancy and is currently the KPMG Emeritus Professor of Accountancy at Northern Illinois University. He has public accounting experience with Price Waterhouse & Co. (San Francisco and Chicago) and Arthur Andersen & Co. (Chicago) and research experience with the Research Division of the American Institute of Certified Public Accountants (New York). He has done post doctorate work as a Visiting Scholar at the University of California at Berkeley and is a recipient of NIU's Teaching Excellence Award and four Golden Apple Teaching Awards. Professor Kieso is the author of other accounting and business books and is a member of the American Accounting Association, the American Institute of Certified Public Accountants, and the Illinois CPA Society. He has served as a member of the Board of Directors of the Illinois CPA Society, then AACSB's Accounting Accreditation Committees, the State of Illinois Comptroller's Commission, as Secretary-Treasurer of the Federation of Schools of Accountancy, and as Secretary-Treasurer of the American Accounting Association. Professor Kieso is currently serving on the Board of Trustees and Executive Committee of Aurora University, as a member of the Board of Directors of Kishwaukee Community Hospital, and as Treasurer and Director of Valley West Community Hospital. From 1989 to 1993 he served as a charter member of the national Accounting Education Change Commission. He is the recipient of the Outstanding Accounting Educator Award from the Illinois CPA Society, the FSA's Joseph A. Silvoso Award of Merit, the NIU Foundation's Humanitarian Award for Service to Higher Education, a Distinguished Service Award from the Illinois CPA Society, and in 2003 an honorary doctorate from Aurora University.

What TYPE of learner are you?

	Intake: To take in the information	To make a study package	Text features that may help you the most	Output: To do well on exams
VISUAL	• Pay close attention to charts, drawings, and handouts your instructors use. • Underline. • Use different colors. • Use symbols, flow charts, graphs, different arrangements on the page, white spaces.	Convert your lecture notes into "page pictures." To do this: • Use the "Intake" strategies. • Reconstruct images in different ways. • Redraw pages from memory. • Replace words with symbols and initials. • Look at your pages.	The Navigator/Feature Story/Preview Infographics/Illustrations Accounting Equation Analyses Highlighted words Demonstration Problem/ Action Plan Questions/Exercises/Problems Financial Reporting Problem Comparative Analysis Problem On the Web Tutorials, video, iPod apps	• Recall your "page pictures." • Draw diagrams where appropriate. • Practice turning your visuals back into words.
AURAL	• Attend lectures and tutorials. • Discuss topics with students and instructors. • Explain new ideas to other people. • Use a tape recorder. • Leave spaces in your lecture notes for later recall. • Describe overheads, pictures, and visuals to somebody who was not in class.	You may take poor notes because you prefer to listen. Therefore: • Expand your notes by talking with others and with information from your textbook. • Tape-record summarized notes and listen. • Read summarized notes out loud. • Explain your notes to another "aural" person.	Preview Insight Boxes Review It/Do it!/Action Plan Summary of Study Objectives Glossary Demonstration Problem/Action Plan Self-Test Questions Questions/Exercises/Problems Financial Reporting Problem Comparative Analysis Problem On the Web Decision Making Across the Organization Tutorials, video	Communication Activity Ethics Case • Talk with the instructor. • Spend time in quiet places recalling the ideas. • Practice writing answers to old exam questions. • Say your answers out loud.
READING/WRITING	• Use lists and headings. • Use dictionaries, glossaries, and definitions. • Read handouts, textbooks, and supplementary library readings. • Use lecture notes.	• Write out words again and again. • Reread notes silently. • Rewrite ideas and principles into other words. • Turn charts, diagrams, and other illustrations into statements.	The Navigator/Feature Story/Study Objectives/Preview Review It/Do it!/Action Plan Summary of Study Objectives Glossary/Self-Test Questions Questions/Exercises/Problems Writing Problems Financial Reporting Problem Comparative Analysis Problem "All About You" Activity On the Web Decision Making Across the Organization Communication Activity Flashcards	• Write exam answers. • Practice with multiple-choice questions. • Write paragraphs, beginnings and endings. • Write your lists in outline form. • Arrange your words into hierarchies and points.
KINESTHETIC	• Use all your senses. • Go to labs, take field trips. • Listen to real-life examples. • Pay attention to applications. • Use hands-on approaches. • Use trial-and-error methods.	You may take poor notes because topics do not seem concrete or relevant. Therefore: • Put examples in your summaries. • Use case studies and applications to help with principles and abstract concepts. • Talk about your notes with another "kinesthetic" person. • Use pictures and photographs that illustrate an idea.	The Navigator/Feature Story/Preview Infographics/Illustrations Review It/Do it!/Action Plan Summary of Study Objectives Demonstration Problem/ Action Plan Self-Test Questions Questions/Exercises/Problems Financial Reporting Problem Comparative Analysis Problem On the Web Decision Making Across the Organization Communication Activity "All About You" Activity	• Write practice answers. • Role-play the exam situation.

Student Owner's Manual

Using Your Textbook Effectively

The Navigator guides you through each chapter by pulling learning tools together into one learning system. Throughout the chapter, The Navigator prompts you to use listed learning aids and to set priorities as you study.

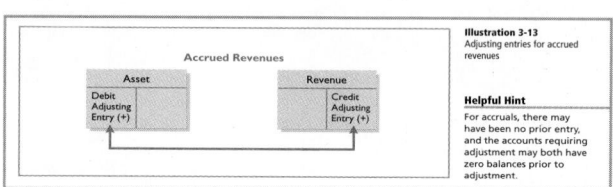

Helpful Hints in the margins further clarify concepts being discussed. They are like having an instructor with you as you read.

Ethics Notes and International Notes point out ethical and international points related to the nearby text discussion.

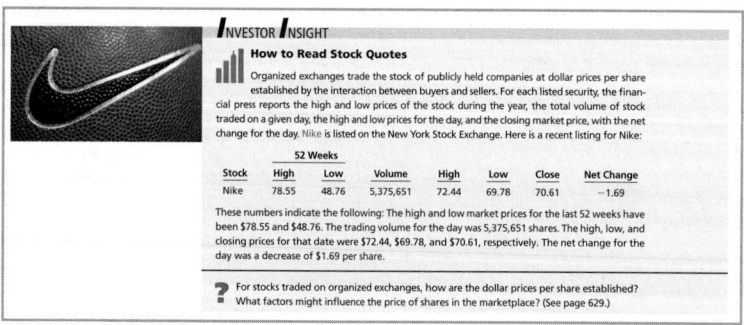

Insight examples give you more glimpses into how actual companies make decisions using accounting information. These high-interest boxes focus on various themes—ethics, international, and investor concerns.

A **critical thinking question** asks you to apply your accounting learning to the story in the example. *Guideline Answers* appear at the end of the chapter.

Accounting Across the Organization examples show the use of accounting by people in non-accounting functions—such as finance, marketing, or management. *Guideline Answers* appear at the end of the chapter.

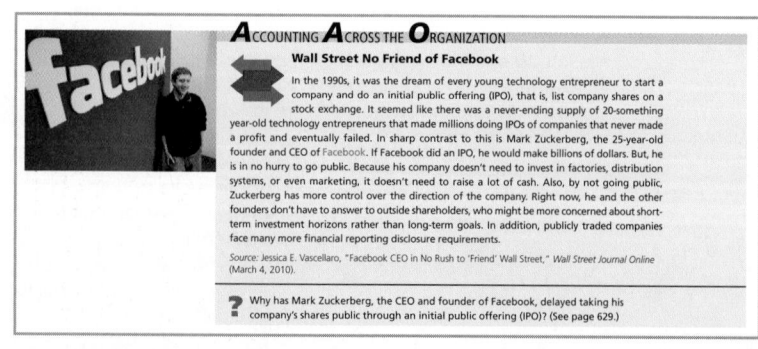

Anatomy of a Fraud boxes illustrate how a lack of specific internal controls resulted in real-world frauds.

ANATOMY OF A FRAUD

Bernie Ebbers was the founder and CEO of the phone company WorldCom. The company engaged in a series of increasingly large, debt-financed acquisitions of other companies. These acquisitions made the company grow quickly, which made the stock price increase dramatically. However, because the acquired companies all had different accounting systems, WorldCom's financial records were a mess. When WorldCom's performance started to flatten out, Bernie coerced WorldCom's accountants to engage in a number of fraudulent activities to make net income look better than it really was and thus prop up the stock price. One of these frauds involved treating $7 billion of line costs as capital expenditures. The line costs, which were rental fees paid to other phone companies to use their phone lines, had always been properly expensed in previous years. Capitalization delayed expense recognition to future periods and thus boosted current-period profits.

Total take: $7 billion

THE MISSING CONTROLS

Documentation procedures. The company's accounting system was a disorganized collection of non-integrated systems, which resulted from a series of corporate acquisitions. Top management took advantage of this disorganization to conceal its fraudulent activities.

Independent internal verification. A fraud of this size should have been detected by a routine comparison of the actual physical assets with the list of physical assets shown in the accounting records.

Do it!

Adjusting Entries for Deferrals

The ledger of Hammond Company, on March 31, 2012, includes these selected accounts before adjusting entries are prepared.

	Debit	Credit
Prepaid Insurance	$ 3,600	
Supplies	2,800	
Equipment	25,000	
Accumulated Depreciation—Equipment		$5,000
Unearned Service Revenue		9,200

An analysis of the accounts shows the following.

1. Insurance expires at the rate of $100 per month.
2. Supplies on hand total $800.

Brief **Do it!** exercises ask you to put to work your newly acquired knowledge. They outline an **Action Plan** necessary to complete the exercise, and they show a **Solution**.

Comprehensive Do it! problem with **Action Plan** gives you an opportunity to see a detailed solution to a representative problem before you do your homework. Coincides with the Do it! problems within the chapter.

COMPREHENSIVE
Do it!

Terry Thomas opens the Green Thumb Lawn Care Company on April 1. At April 30, the trial balance shows the following balances for selected accounts.

Prepaid Insurance	$ 3,600
Equipment	28,000
Notes Payable	20,000
Unearned Service Revenue	4,200
Service Revenue	1,800

Do it! Review problems appear in the homework material and provide another way for you to determine whether you have mastered the content in the chapters.

Do it! Review

Do it! 3-1 Numerous timing concepts are discussed on pages 100–102. A list of concepts is provided below in the left column, with a description of the concept in the right column. There are more descriptions provided than concepts. Match the description of the concept to the concept.

Identify timing concepts. (SO 1, 2)

1. ____ Cash-basis accounting.
2. ____ Fiscal year.
3. ____ Revenue recognition principle.
4. ____ Expense recognition principle.

(a) Monthly and quarterly time periods.
(b) Accountants divide the economic life of a business into artificial time periods.
(c) Efforts (expenses) should be matched with accomplishments (revenues).

What happens when no-par stock does not have a stated value? In that case, the corporation credits the entire proceeds to Common Stock. Thus, if Hydro-Slide does not assign a stated value to its no-par stock, it records the issuance of the 5,000 shares at $8 per share for cash as follows.

A	=	L	+	SE
+40,000				
			+40,000 CS	

Cash Flows
+40,000

Cash		40,000	
Common Stock			40,000
(To record issue of 5,000 shares of no-par stock)			

Accounting equation analyses appear next to key journal entries. They will help you understand the impact of an accounting transaction on the components of the accounting equation, on the stockholders' equity accounts, and on the company's cash flows.

Financial statements appear regularly. Those from actual companies are identified by a company logo or a photo.

Illustration 14-11
Disclosure of restriction

Tektronix Inc.
Notes to the Financial Statements

Certain of the Company's debt agreements require compliance with debt covenants. Management believes that the Company is in compliance with such requirements. The Company had unrestricted retained earnings of $223.8 million after meeting those requirements.

Exercises: Set B are available online at *www.wiley.com/college/weygandt*.

Exercises: Set B

Visit the book's companion website, at **www.wiley.com/college/weygandt**, and choose the Student Companion site to access Exercise Set B.

In the textbook, two similar sets of **Problems—A** and **B**—are keyed to the same study objectives.

Selected problems, identified by this icon, can be solved using the **General Ledger Software (GLS)** package.

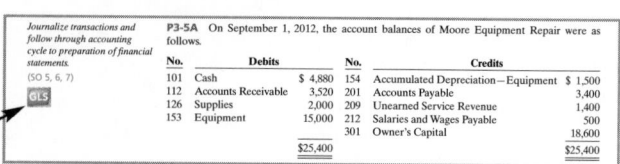

Journalize transactions and follow through accounting cycle to preparation of financial statements.

(SO 5, 6, 7)

GLS

P3-5A On September 1, 2012, the account balances of Moore Equipment Repair were as follows.

No.	Debits		No.	Credits	
101	Cash	$ 4,880	154	Accumulated Depreciation—Equipment	$ 1,500
112	Accounts Receivable	3,520	201	Accounts Payable	3,400
126	Supplies	2,000	209	Unearned Service Revenue	1,400
153	Equipment	15,000	212	Salaries and Wages Payable	500
			301	Owner's Capital	18,600
		$25,400			$25,400

Prepare correct income statement.

(SO 2, 5, 6, 7)

E3-10 The income statement of Brandon Co. for the month of July shows net income of $1,400 based on Service Revenue $5,500, Salaries and Wages Expense $2,300, Supplies Expense $1,200, and Utilities Expense $600. In reviewing the statement, you discover the following.
1. Insurance expired during July of $400 was omitted.
2. Supplies expense includes $250 of supplies that are still on hand at July 31.

An icon identifies **Exercises** and **Problems** that can be solved using Excel templates at the student website.

Those exercises and problems that focus on accounting situations faced by **service companies** are identified by the icon shown here.

Determine cost of jobs and ending balance in work in process and overhead accounts.

(SO 3, 4, 6)

SERVICE

E20-12 Alma Ortiz and Associates, a CPA firm, uses job order costing to capture the costs of its audit jobs. There were no audit jobs in process at the beginning of November. Listed below are data concerning the three audit jobs conducted during November.

	Perez	Rivera	Sota
Direct materials	$600	$400	$200
Auditor labor costs	$5,400	$6,600	$3,375
Auditor hours	72	88	45

Problems: Set C

Visit the book's companion website, at **www.wiley.com/college/weygandt**, and choose the Student Companion site to access Problem Set C.

An additional parallel set of **C Problems** appears at the book's companion website.

Comprehensive Problem: Chapters 3 to 7

CP7 Packard Company has the following opening account balances in its general and subsidiary ledgers on January 1 and uses the periodic inventory system. All accounts have normal debit and credit balances.

General Ledger

Account Number	Account Title	January 1 Opening Balance
101	Cash	$33,750

Comprehensive Problems combine material from the current chapter with previous chapters so that you understand how "it all fits together."

The **Continuing Cookie Chronicle** exercise follows the continuing saga of accounting for a small business begun by an entrepreneurial student.

Continuing Cookie Chronicle

(*Note:* This is a continuation of the Cookie Chronicle from Chapters 1 and 2. Use the information from the previous chapters and follow the instructions below using the general ledger accounts you have already prepared.)

Waterways Continuing Problem

(*Note:* The Waterways Problem begins in Chapter 19 and continues in the remaining chapters. You can also find this problem at the book's Student Companion site.)

The **Waterways Continuing Problem** uses the business activities of a fictional company, to help you apply managerial accounting topics to a realistic entrepreneurial situation.

The **Broadening Your Perspective** section helps to pull together concepts from the chapter and apply them to real-world business situations.

BROADENING YOUR PERSPECTIVE

The **Financial Reporting Problem** focuses on reading and understanding the financial statements of PepsiCo, which are available in Appendix A.

Financial Reporting and Analysis

Financial Reporting Problem: PepsiCo, Inc.

BYP3-1 The financial statements of PepsiCo, Inc. are presented in Appendix A at the end of this textbook.

Instructions
(a) Using the consolidated financial statements and related information, identify items that may result in

PEPSICO

Comparative Analysis Problem: PepsiCo, Inc. vs. The Coca-Cola Company

BYP3-2 PepsiCo's financial statements are presented in Appendix A. Financial statements for The Coca-Cola Company are presented in Appendix B.

A **Comparative Analysis Problem** compares and contrasts the financial reporting of PepsiCo and The Coca-Cola Company.

On the Web

BYP3-3 No financial decision maker should ever rely solely on the financial information reported in the annual report to make decisions. It is important to keep abreast of financial news. This activity demonstrates how to search for financial news on the Web.

Address: http://biz.yahoo.com/i, or go to **www.wiley.com/college/weygandt**

On the Web exercises guide you to websites where you can find and analyze information related to the chapter topic.

Decision Making Across the Organization cases help you build decision-making skills by analyzing accounting information in a less structured situation. These cases require you to work in teams.

Decision Making Across the Organization

BYP20-1 Burgio Parts Company uses a job order cost system. For a number of months, there has been an ongoing rift between the sales department and the production department concerning a special-order product, TC-1. TC-1 is a seasonal product that is manufactured in batches of 1,000 units. TC-1 is sold at cost plus a markup of 40% of cost.

Communication Activity

BYP3-5 In reviewing the accounts of Keri Ann Co. at the end of the year, you discover that adjusting entries have not been made.

Communication Activity problems help you to apply and practice business communication skills.

Ethics Cases ask you to reflect on typical ethical dilemmas, analyze the stakeholders and the issues involved, and decide on an appropriate course of action.

Ethics Case

BYP3-6 Bluestem Company is a pesticide manufacturer. Its sales declined greatly this year due to the passage of legislation outlawing the sale of several of Bluestem's chemical pesticides. In the coming year, Bluestem will have environmentally safe and competitive chemicals to replace these discontinued products. Sales in the next year are expected to greatly exceed any prior year's. The decline in sales and profits appears to be a one-year aberration. But even so, the company president fears a large dip in the current year's profits. He believes that such a dip could cause a significant drop in the market price of Bluestem's stock and make the company a takeover target.

"All About You" Activity

BYP3-7 Companies must report or disclose in their financial statements information about all liabilities, including potential liabilities related to environmental clean-up. There are many situations in which you will be asked to provide personal financial information about your assets, liabilities, revenue, and expenses. Sometimes you will face difficult decisions regarding what to disclose and how to disclose it.

All About You activities are designed to get you thinking and talking about how accounting impacts your personal life.

FASB Codification Activity offers you the opportunity to use this online system, which contains all the authoritative literature related to a particular topic.

FASB Codification Activity

BYP3-8 If your school has a subscription to the FASB Codification, go to *http://aaahq.org/asclogin.cfm* to log in and prepare responses to the following.

Instructions
Access the glossary ("Master Glossary") to answer the following.
(a) What is the definition of revenue?
(b) What is the definition of compensation?

Managerial Analysis

BYP19-2 B.J. King is a fairly large manufacturing company located in the southern United States. The company manufactures tennis rackets, tennis balls, tennis clothing, and tennis shoes, all bearing the company's distinctive logo, a large green question mark on a white-flocked tennis ball. The company's sales have been increasing over the past 10 years.

The tennis racket division has recently implemented several advanced manufacturing techniques. Robot arms hold the tennis rackets in place while glue dries, and machine vision systems check for defects. The engineering and design team uses computerized drafting and testing of new products. The following managers work in the tennis racket division.

Managerial Analysis assignments build analytical and decision-making skills in situations required by managers.

Real World Focus problems require you to apply techniques and concepts learned in the chapter to specific situations faced by actual companies.

Real-World Focus

BYP19-3 Anchor Glass Container Corporation, the third largest manufacturer of glass containers in the United States, supplies beverage and food producers and consumer products manufacturers nationwide. Parent company Consumers Packaging Inc. *(Toronto Stock Exchange: CGC)* is a leading international designer and manufacturer of glass containers.

The following management discussion appeared in a recent annual report of Anchor Glass.

IFRS A Look at IFRS

It is often difficult for companies to determine in what time period they should report particular revenues and expenses. Both the IASB and FASB are working on a joint project to develop a common conceptual framework, as well as a revenue recognition project, that will enable companies to better use the same principles to record transactions consistently over time.

A Look at IFRS provides an overview of the International Financial Reporting Standards (IFRS) that relate to the chapter topics, highlights the differences between GAAP and IFRS, discusses IFRS/GAAP convergence efforts, and tests your understanding through *IFRS Self-Test Questions* and *IFRS Concepts and Application*.

Acknowledgments

Accounting Principles has benefited greatly from the input of focus group participants, manuscript reviewers, those who have sent comments by letter or e-mail, ancillary authors, and proofers. We greatly appreciate the constructive suggestions and innovative ideas of reviewers and the creativity and accuracy of the ancillary authors and checkers.

Prior Editions

Thanks to the following reviewers and focus group participants of prior editions of Accounting Principles:

John Ahmad, *Northern Virginia Community College—Annandale;* Sylvia Allen, *Los Angeles Valley College;* Matt Anderson, *Michigan State University;* Alan Applebaum, *Broward Community College;* Juanita Ardovany, *Los Angeles Valley College;* Yvonne Baker, *Cincinnati State Tech Community College;* Peter Battelle, *University of Vermont;* Colin Battle, *Broward Community College;* Jim Benedum; Beverly Beatty, *Anne Arundel Community College; Milwaukee Area Technical College;* Jaswinder Bhangal, *Chabot College;* Bernard Bieg, *Bucks County College;* Michael Blackett, *National American University;* Barry Bomboy, *J. Sargeant Reynolds Community College;* Kent D. Bowen, *Butler County Community College;* David Boyd, *Arkansas State University;* Greg Brookins, *Santa Monica College;* Kurt H. Buerger, *Angelo State University;* Leroy Bugger, *Edison Community College;* Leon Button, *Scottsdale Community College.*

Ann Cardozo, *Broward Community College;* Steve Carlson, *University of North Dakota;* Fatma Cebenoyan, *Hunter College;* Kimberly Charland, *Kansas State University;* Trudy Chiaravelli, *Lansing Community College;* Shifei Chung, *Rowan University;* Siu Chung, *Los Angeles Valley College;* Lisa Cole, *Johnson County Community College;* Kenneth Couvillion, *San Joaquin Delta College;* Alan B. Czyzewski, *Indiana State University;* Thomas Davies, *University of South Dakota;* Peggy DeJong, *Kirkwood Community College;* John Delaney, *Augustana College;* Tony Dellarte, *Luzerne Community College;* Kevin Dooley, *Kapi'olani Community College;* Pam Donahue, *Northern Essex Community College;* Edmond Douville, *Indiana University Northwest;* Pamela Druger, *Augustana College;* Russell Dunn, *Broward Community College;* John Eagan, *Erie Community College;* Richard Ellison, *Middlesex Community College;* Dora Estes, *Volunteer State Community College;* Mary Falkey, *Prince Georges Community College.*

Raymond Gardner, *Ocean County College;* Lori Grady, *Bucks County Community College;* Richard Ghio, *San Joaquin Delta College;* Joyce Griffin, *Kansas City Community College;* Amy Haas, *Kingsborough Community College, CUNY;* Lester Hall, *Danville Community College;* Becky Hancock, *El Paso Community College;* Jeannie Harrington, *Middle Tennessee State University;* Bonnie Harrison, *College of Southern Maryland;* William Harvey, *Henry Ford Community College;* Michelle Heard, *Metropolitan Community College;* Ruth Henderson, *Union Community College;* Ed Hess, *Butler County Community College;* Kathy Hill, *Leeward Community College;* Patty Holmes, *Des Moines Area Community College;* Zach Holmes, *Oakland Community College;* Paul Holt, *Texas A&M—Kingsville;* Audrey Hunter, *Broward Community College;* Verne Ingram, *Red Rocks Community College;* Joanne Johnson, *Caldwell Community College;* Naomi Karolinski, *Monroe Community College;* Anil Khatri, *Bowie State University;* Shirley Kleiner, *Johnson County Community College;* Jo Koehn, *Central Missouri State University;* Ken Koerber, *Bucks County Community College;* Adriana Kulakowski, *Mynderse Academy.*

Sandra Lang, *McKendree College;* Cathy Xanthaky Larsen, *Middlesex Community College;* David Laurel, *South Texas Community College;* Robert Laycock, *Montgomery College;* Natasha Librizzi, *Madison Area Technical College;* William P. Lovell, *Cayuga Community College;* Melanie Mackey, *Ocean County College;* Jerry Martens, *Community College of Aurora;* Maureen McBeth, *College of DuPage;* Francis McCloskey, *Community College of Philadelphia;* Chris McNamara, *Finger Lakes Community College;* Lori Major, *Luzerne County Community College;* Edwin Mah, *University of Maryland, University College;* Thomas Marsh, *Northern Virginia Community College—Annandale;* Jim Martin, *University of Montevallo;* Suneel Maheshwari, *Marshall University;* Shea Mears, *Des Moines Area Community College;* Pam Meyer, *University of Louisiana—Lafayette;* Cathy Montesarchio, *Broward Community College.*

Robin Nelson, *Community College of Southern Nevada;* Joseph M. Nicassio, *Westmoreland County Community College;* Michael O'Neill, *Seattle Central Community College;* Mike Palma, *Gwinnett Tech;* George Palz, *Erie Community College;* Michael Papke, *Kellogg Community College;* Ruth Parks, *Kellogg Community College;* Al Partington, *Los Angeles Pierce College;* Jennifer Patty, *Des Moines Area Community College;* Yvonne Phang, *Borough of Manhattan Community College;* Jan Pitera, *Broome Community College;* Mike Prockton, *Finger Lakes Community College;* Laura M. Prosser, *Black Hills State University;* Bill Rencher, *Seminole Community College;* Jenny Resnick, *Santa Monica College;* Renee Rigoni, *Monroe Community College;* Kathie Rogers, *SUNY Suffolk;* Al Ruggiero, *SUNY Suffolk;* Jill Russell, *Camden County College.*

Roger Sands, *Milwaukee Area Technical College;* Marcia Sandvold, *Des Moines Area Community College;* Richard Sarkisian, *Camden Community College;* Kent Schneider, *East Tennessee State University;* Karen Searle, Paul J. Shinal, *Cayuga Community College;* Beth Secrest, *Walsh University;* Kevin Sinclair, *Lehigh University;* Alice Sineath, *Forsyth Tech Community College;* Leon Singleton, *Santa Monica College;* Michael S. Skaff, *College of the Sequoias;* Jeff Slater, *North Shore Community College;* Lois Slutsky, *Broward Community College;* Dan Small, *J. Sargeant Reynolds Community College;* Lee Smart, *Southwest Tennessee Community College;* James Smith, *Ivy Tech State College;* Carol Springer, *Georgia State University;* Jeff Spoelman, *Grand Rapids Community College;* Norman Sunderman, *Angelo State University.*

Donald Terpstra, *Jefferson Community College;* Lynda Thompson, *Massasoit Community College;* Shafi Ullah, *Broward Community College;* Sue Van Boven, *Paradise Valley Community College;* Christian Widmer, *Tidewater Community College;* Wanda Wong, *Chabot College;* Pat Walczak, *Lansing Community College;* Kenton Walker, *University of Wyoming;* Patricia Wall, *Middle Tennessee State University;* Carol N. Welsh, *Rowan University;* Idalene Williams, *Metropolitan Community College;* Gloria Worthy, *Southwest Tennessee Community College.*

Thanks also to "perpetual reviewers" Robert Benjamin, *Taylor University;* Charles Malone, Tammy Wend, and Carol Wysocki, all of *Columbia Basin College;* and William Gregg of *Montgomery College.* We appreciate their continuing interest in the textbook and their regular contributions of ideas to improve it.

Tenth Edition

Thanks to the following reviewers, focus group participants, and others who provided suggestions for the Tenth Edition:

Sylvia Allen	*Los Angeles Valley College*
Juanita Ardavany	*Los Angeles Valley College*
Shele Bannon	*Queensborough Community College*
Amy Bentley	*Tallahassee Community College*
Timothy Bergsma	*Davenport University*
Teri Bernstein	*Santa Monica College*
Patrick Borja	*Citrus College*
Stanley Carroll	*New York City College of Technology*
Siu Chung	*Los Angeles Valley College*
Carol Collinsworth	*University of Texas—Brownsville*
Kelly Cranford	*Hinds Community College—Raymond*
Liz Diers	*Black Hills State University*
Samuel A. Duah	*Bowie State University*
Carle Essig	*Montgomery County Community College*
Annette Fisher	*Glendale Community College*
Kelly Ford	*Queensborough Community College*
Lori Grady	*Bucks County Community College*
Mary Halford	*Prince Georges Community College*
Thomas Kam	*Hawaii Pacific University*
Naomi Karolinski	*Monroe Community College*
Lynn Krausse	*Bakersfield College*
David Krug	*Johnson County Community College*
Cathy X. Larson	*Middlesex Community College*
David Laurel	*South Texas College*
Christina Manzo	*Queensborough Community College*
Beverly Mason	*Front Range Community College*
Robert Maxwell	*College of the Canyons*
Jill Mitchell	*Northern Virginia Community College— Annandale*
Ronald O'Brien	*Fayetteville Technical Community College*
Michael Motes	*University of Maryland University College*
Gregory L. Prescott	*University of South Alabama*
Jan Pitera	*Broome Community College*
Debra A. Sills Porter	*Tidewater Community College*
William Prosser	*Cuyuga County Community College*
Ada Rodriguez	*Lehman College, The City University of New York*
Eric Rothenburg	*Kingsborough Community College, The City University of New York*
Al Ruggiero	*Suffolk County Community College*
Marcia Sandvold	*Des Moines Area Community College*
Mary Jane Sauceda	*University of Texas—Brownsville*
Paul J. Shinal	*Cayauga Community College*
Bradley Smith	*Des Moines Area Community College*
Scott Stroher	*Glendale Community College*
Geoffrey Tickell	*Indiana University of Pennsylvania*
Pat Walczak	*Lansing Community College*
Wanda Wong	*Chabot College*
Jack Wiehler	*San Joaquin Delta College*

Ancillary Authors, Contributors, and Proofers

We sincerely thank the following individuals for their hard work in preparing the content that accompanies this textbook:

LuAnn Bean	*Florida Institute of Technology*
John C. Borke	*University of Wisconsin—Platteville*
Richard Campbell	*Rio Grande College*
Siu Chung	*Los Angeles Valley College*
Mel Coe	*DeVry Institute of Technology, Atlanta*
Chris Cole	*Cole Creative Group*
Joan Cook	*Milwaukee Area Technical College*
Larry Falcetto	*Emporia State University*
Mark Gleason	*Metropolitan State University*
Lori Grady	*Bucks County Community College*
Coby Harmon	*University of California, Santa Barbara*
Douglas W. Kieso	*Aurora University*
Yvonne Phang	*Borough of Manhattan Community College*
Rex A. Schildhouse	*San Diego Community College—Miramar*
Eileen Shifflett	*James Madison University*
Diane Tanner	*University of North Florida*
Sheila Viel	*University of Wisconsin—Milwaukee*
Dick Wasson	*Southwestern College*
Bernard Weinrich	*Lindenwood University*
Melanie Yon	

We also greatly appreciate the expert assistance provided by the following individuals in checking the accuracy of the content that accompanies this textbook:

LuAnn Bean	*Florida Institute of Technology*
Jack Borke	*University of Wisconsin—Platteville*
Sandee Cohen	*Columbia College*
Terry Elliott	*Morehead State University*
James Emig	*Villanova University*
Larry Falcetto	*Emporia State University*
Anthony Falgiani	*Western Illinois University*
Lori Grady	*Bucks County Community College*
Kirk Lynch	*Sandhills Community College*
Kevin McNelis	*New Mexico State University*
Jill Misuraca	*Central Connecticut State University*
Barbara Muller	*Arizona State University*
John Plouffe	*California State University—Los Angeles*
Ed Schell	*University of Hawaii*
Rex Schildhouse	*San Diego Community College—Miramar*
Alice Sineath	*Forsyth Tech Community College*
Teresa Speck	*St. Mary's University*
Lynn Stallworth	*Appalachian State University*
Sheila Viel	*University of Wisconsin—Milwaukee*
Dick Wasson	*Southwestern College*
Andrea Weickgenannt	*Xavier University*
Bernie Weinrich	*Lindenwood University*

Our thanks to the publishing "pros" who contribute to our efforts to publish high-quality products that benefit both teachers and students: Terry Ann Tatro, development editor; Ed Brislin, project editor; Yana Mermel, project editor; Allie K. Morris, executive media editor; Greg Chaput, media editor; Jacqueline Kepping, editorial assistant; Valerie A. Vargas, senior production editor; Maddy Lesure, textbook designer; Dorothy Sinclair, managing editor; Erin Bascom, production editor; Pam Kennedy, director of production and manufacturing; Ann Berlin, vice president of higher education production and manufacturing; Mary Ann Price, photo editor; Sandra Rigby, illustration editor; Suzanne Ingrao of Ingrao Associates, project manager; Jo-Anne Naples, permissions editor; Denise Showers of Aptara Inc., project manager at Aptara Inc.; Danielle Urban, project manager at Elm Street Publishing Services; and Cyndy Taylor. They provided innumerable services that helped this project take shape.

We also appreciate the exemplary support and professional commitment given us by Chris DeJohn, associate publisher, and the enthusiasm and ideas that Ramona Sherman, senior marketing manager, brings to the project.

Finally, our thanks to Amy Scholz, Susan Elbe, George Hoffman, Tim Stookesberry, Joe Heider, Bonnie Lieberman, and Will Pesce for their support and leadership in Wiley's College Division.

We thank PepsiCo, Inc. for permitting us the use of its 2009 annual reports for our specimen financial statements and accompanying notes. You can send your thoughts and ideas about the textbook to us via email at: *AccountingAuthors@yahoo.com.*

Jerry J. Weygandt
Madison, Wisconsin

Paul D. Kimmel
Milwaukee, Wisconsin

Donald E. Kieso
DeKalb, Illinois

Brief Contents

APPENDICES

Contents

chapter 18

Financial Statement Analysis 824

chapter 19

Managerial Accounting 876

chapter 20

Job Order Costing 922

chapter 21

Process Costing 964

CHAPTER 1

Accounting in Action

Study Objectives

After studying this chapter, you should be able to:

1 Explain what accounting is.

2 Identify the users and uses of accounting.

3 Understand why ethics is a fundamental business concept.

4 Explain generally accepted accounting principles.

5 Explain the monetary unit assumption and the economic entity assumption.

6 State the accounting equation, and define its components.

7 Analyze the effects of business transactions on the accounting equation.

8 Understand the four financial statements and how they are prepared.

Study Objectives give you a framework for learning the specific concepts covered in the chapter.

✔ The Navigator

The Navigator is a learning system designed to prompt you to use the learning aids in the chapter and set priorities as you study.

Feature Story

KNOWING THE NUMBERS

Many students who take this course do not plan to be accountants. If you are in that group, you might be thinking, "If I'm not going to be an accountant, why do I need to know accounting?" In response, consider the quote from Harold Geneen, the former chairman of IT&T: "To be good at your business, you have to know the numbers—cold." Success in any business comes back to the numbers. You will rely on them to make decisions, and managers will use them to evaluate your performance. That is true whether your job involves marketing, production, management, or information systems.

In business, accounting and financial statements are the means for communicating the numbers. If you don't know how to read financial statements, you can't really know your business.

Many companies spend significant resources teaching their employees basic accounting so

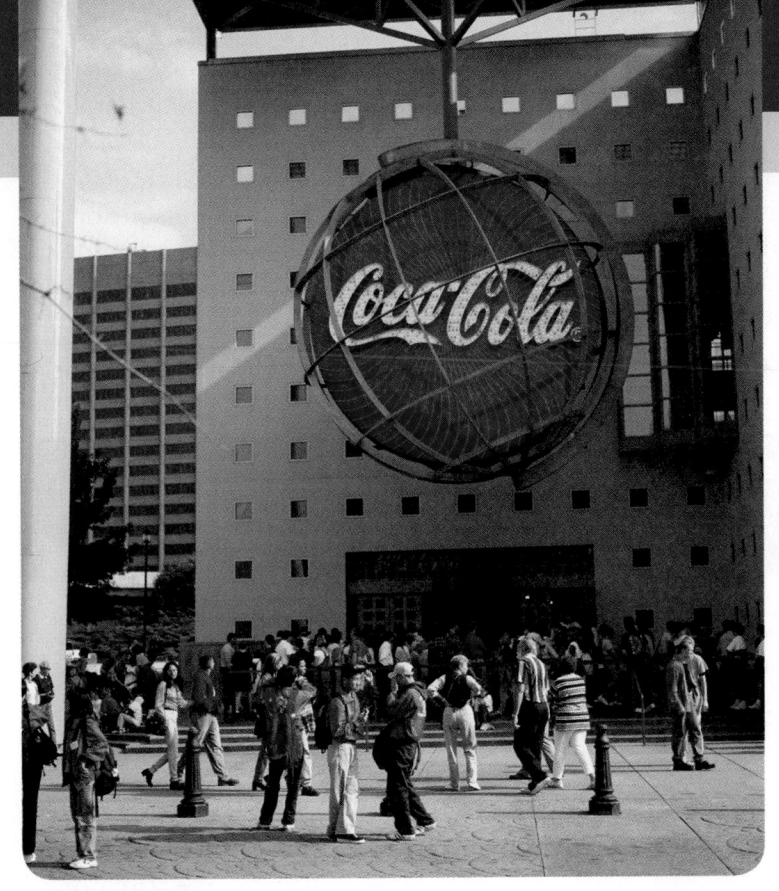

that they can read financial statements and understand how their actions affect the company's financial results. One such company is Springfield ReManufacturing Corporation (SRC). When Jack Stack and 11 other managers purchased SRC for 10 cents a share, it was a failing division of International Harvester. Jack's 119 employees, however, were counting on him for their livelihood. He decided that for the company to survive, every employee needed to think like a businessperson and to act like an owner. To accomplish this, all employees at SRC took basic accounting courses and participated in weekly reviews of the company's financial statements. SRC survived, and eventually thrived. To this day, every employee (now numbering more than 1,000) undergoes this same training.

Many other companies have adopted this approach, which is called "open-book management." Even in companies that do not practice open-book management, employers generally assume that managers in all areas of the company are "financially literate."

Taking this course will go a long way to making you financially literate. In this book, you will learn how to read and prepare financial statements, and how to use basic tools to evaluate financial results. Appendices A and B provide real financial statements of two well-known companies, PepsiCo, Inc. and The Coca-Cola Company. Throughout this textbook, we attempt to increase your familiarity with financial reporting by providing numerous references, questions, and exercises that encourage you to explore these financial statements.

The Feature Story helps you picture how the chapter topic relates to the real world of accounting and business. You will find references to the story throughout the chapter.

Inside**CHAPTER1**

"Inside Chapter x" lists boxes in the chapter that should be of special interest to you.

- ■ *Accounting Across the Organization:* **The Scoop on Accounting** *(p. 6)*
- ■ *Ethics Insight:* **The Numbers Behind Not-for-Profit Organizations** *(p. 8)*
- ■ *International Insight:* **The Korean Discount** *(p. 10)*
- ■ *Accounting Across the Organization:* **Spinning the Career Wheel** *(p. 12)*

PreviewofCHAPTER1

The opening story about Springfield ReManufacturing Corporation highlights the importance of having good financial information to make effective business decisions. Whatever one's pursuits or occupation, the need for financial information is inescapable. You cannot earn a living, spend money, buy on credit, make an investment, or pay taxes without receiving, using, or dispensing financial information. Good decision making depends on good information.

The purpose of this chapter is to show you that accounting is the system used to provide useful financial information. The content and organization of Chapter 1 are as follows.

Accounting in Action

What Is Accounting?	The Building Blocks of Accounting	The Basic Accounting Equation	Using the Accounting Equation	Financial Statements
• Three activities • Who uses accounting data	• Ethics in financial reporting • Generally accepted accounting principles • Measurement principles • Assumptions	• Assets • Liabilities • Owner's equity	• Transaction analysis • Summary of transactions	• Income statement • Owner's equity statement • Balance sheet • Statement of cash flows

The Navigator

*The **Preview** describes and outlines the major topics and subtopics you will see in the chapter.*

What Is Accounting?

Study Objective [1]

Explain what accounting is.

Why is accounting so popular? What consistently ranks as one of the top career opportunities in business? What frequently rates among the most popular majors on campus? What was the undergraduate degree chosen by Nike founder Phil Knight, Home Depot co-founder Arthur Blank, former acting director of the Federal Bureau of Investigation (FBI) Thomas Pickard, and numerous members of Congress? Accounting.[1] Why did these people choose accounting? They wanted to understand what was happening financially to their organizations. Accounting is the financial information system that provides these insights. In short, to understand your organization, you have to know the numbers.

Accounting consists of three basic activities—it **identifies**, **records**, and **communicates** the economic events of an organization to interested users. Let's take a closer look at these three activities.

Three Activities

As a starting point to the accounting process, a company identifies the **economic events relevant to its business**. Examples of economic events are the sale of snack chips by PepsiCo, providing of telephone services by AT&T, and payment of wages by Ford Motor Company.

Once a company like PepsiCo identifies economic events, it **records** those events in order to provide a history of its financial activities. Recording consists of

---

[1]The appendix to this chapter describes job opportunities for accounting majors and explains why accounting is such a popular major.

keeping a **systematic**, **chronological diary of events**, measured in dollars and cents. In recording, PepsiCo also classifies and summarizes economic events.

Finally, PepsiCo **communicates** the collected information to interested users by means of **accounting reports**. The most common of these reports are called **financial statements**. To make the reported financial information meaningful, PepsiCo reports the recorded data in a standardized way. It accumulates information resulting from similar transactions. For example, PepsiCo accumulates all sales transactions over a certain period of time and reports the data as one amount in the company's financial statements. Such data are said to be reported **in the aggregate**. By presenting the recorded data in the aggregate, the accounting process simplifies a multitude of transactions and makes a series of activities understandable and meaningful.

A vital element in communicating economic events is the accountant's ability to **analyze and interpret** the reported information. Analysis involves use of ratios, percentages, graphs, and charts to highlight significant financial trends and relationships. Interpretation involves **explaining the uses**, **meaning**, **and limitations of reported data**. Appendix A of this textbook shows the financial statements of PepsiCo, Inc.; Appendix B illustrates the financial statements of The Coca-Cola Company. We refer to these statements at various places throughout the text. At this point, they probably strike you as complex and confusing. By the end of this course, you'll be surprised at your ability to understand, analyze, and interpret them.

Illustration 1-1 summarizes the activities of the accounting process.

Illustration 1-1
The activities of the accounting process

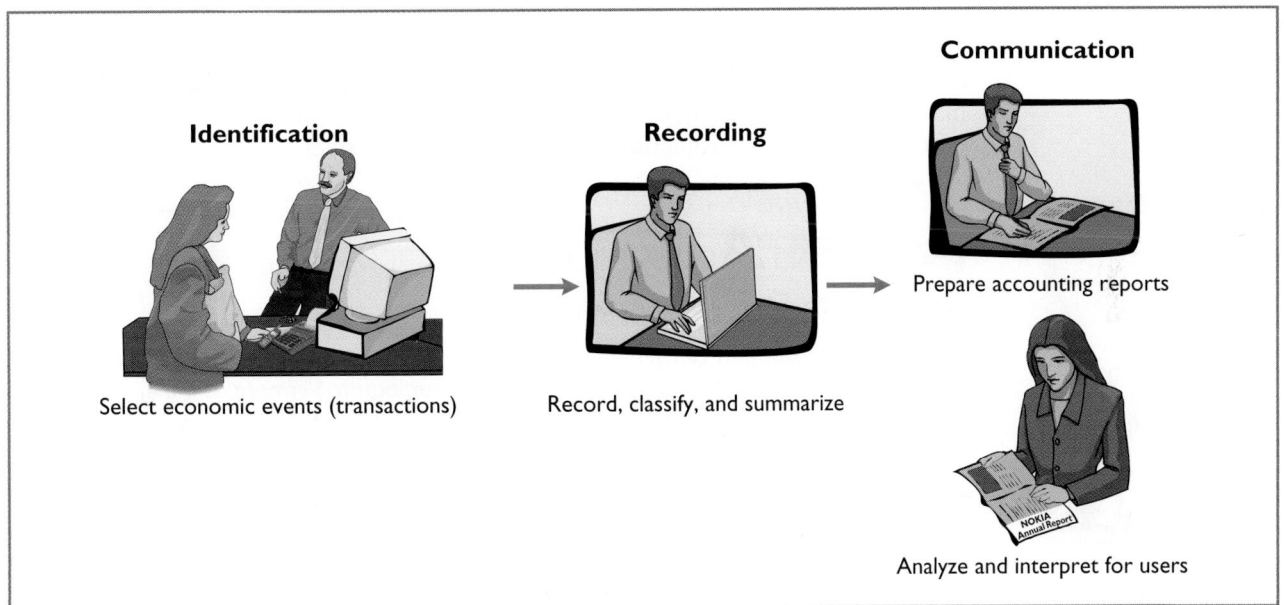

Identification

Select economic events (transactions)

Recording

Record, classify, and summarize

Communication

Prepare accounting reports

Analyze and interpret for users

You should understand that the accounting process **includes** the bookkeeping function. Bookkeeping usually involves **only** the recording of economic events. It is therefore just one part of the accounting process. In total, accounting involves **the entire process of identifying**, **recording**, **and communicating economic events**.[2]

Essential terms are printed in blue when they first appear, and are defined in the end-of-chapter glossary.

---

[2]The origins of accounting are generally attributed to the work of Luca Pacioli, an Italian Renaissance mathematician. Pacioli was a close friend and tutor to Leonardo da Vinci and a contemporary of Christopher Columbus. In his 1494 text *Summa de Arithmetica, Geometria, Proportione et Proportionalite,* Pacioli described a system to ensure that financial information was recorded efficiently and accurately.

Who Uses Accounting Data

Study Objective [2]
Identify the users and
uses of accounting.

The information that a user of financial information needs depends upon the kinds of decisions the user makes. There are two broad groups of users of financial information: internal users and external users.

INTERNAL USERS

Internal users of accounting information are managers who plan, organize, and run the business. These include marketing managers, production supervisors, finance directors, and company officers. In running a business, internal users must answer many important questions, as shown in Illustration 1-2.

Illustration 1-2
Questions that internal users ask

Questions Asked by Internal Users

Finance	**Marketing**	**Human Resources**	**Management**
Is cash sufficient to pay dividends to Microsoft stockholders?	What price for an Apple iPod will maximize the company's net income?	Can we afford to give General Motors employees pay raises this year?	Which PepsiCo product line is the most profitable? Should any product lines be eliminated?

To answer these and other questions, internal users need detailed information on a timely basis. **Managerial accounting** provides internal reports to help users make decisions about their companies. Examples are financial comparisons of operating alternatives, projections of income from new sales campaigns, and forecasts of cash needs for the next year.

Accounting Across the Organization boxes demonstrate applications of accounting information in various business functions.

ACCOUNTING ACROSS THE ORGANIZATION

The Scoop on Accounting

Accounting can serve as a useful recruiting tool even for the human resources department. Rhino Foods, located in Burlington, Vermont, is a manufacturer of specialty ice cream. Its corporate website includes the following:

"Wouldn't it be great to work where you were part of a team? Where your input and hard work made a difference? Where you weren't kept in the dark about what management was thinking? . . . Well—it's not a dream! It's the way we do business . . . Rhino Foods believes in family, honesty and open communication—we really care about and appreciate our employees—and it shows. Operating results are posted and monthly group meetings inform all employees about what's happening in the Company. Employees also share in the Company's profits, in addition to having an excellent comprehensive benefits package."

Source: www.rhinofoods.com/workforus/workforus.html.

? What are the benefits to the company and to the employees of making the financial statements available to all employees? (See page 46.)

EXTERNAL USERS

External users are individuals and organizations outside a company who want financial information about the company. The two most common types of external users are investors and creditors. **Investors** (owners) use accounting information to make decisions to buy, hold, or sell ownership shares of a company. **Creditors** (such as suppliers and bankers) use accounting information to evaluate the risks of granting credit or lending money. Illustration 1-3 shows some questions that investors and creditors may ask.

Questions Asked by External Users

Investors	Investors	Creditors
Is General Electric earning satisfactory income?	How does Disney compare in size and profitability with Time Warner?	Will United Airlines be able to pay its debts as they come due?

Illustration 1-3
Questions that external users ask

Financial accounting answers these questions. It provides economic and financial information for investors, creditors, and other external users. The information needs of external users vary considerably. **Taxing authorities**, such as the Internal Revenue Service, want to know whether the company complies with tax laws. **Regulatory agencies**, such as the Securities and Exchange Commission or the Federal Trade Commission, want to know whether the company is operating within prescribed rules. **Customers** are interested in whether a company like General Motors will continue to honor product warranties and support its product lines. **Labor unions** such as the Major League Baseball Players Association want to know whether the owners have the ability to pay increased wages and benefits.

The Building Blocks of Accounting

A doctor follows certain standards in treating a patient's illness. An architect follows certain standards in designing a building. An accountant follows certain standards in reporting financial information. For these standards to work, a fundamental business concept must be at work—ethical behavior.

Ethics in Financial Reporting

People won't gamble in a casino if they think it is "rigged." Similarly, people won't play the stock market if they think stock prices are rigged. In recent years the financial press has been full of articles about financial scandals at Enron, WorldCom, HealthSouth, AIG, and others. As the scandals came to light, mistrust of financial reporting in general grew. One article in the *Wall Street Journal* noted that "repeated disclosures about questionable accounting practices have bruised investors' faith in the reliability of earnings reports, which in turn has sent stock prices tumbling."[3] Imagine trying to carry on a business or invest money if you could not depend on the financial statements to be honestly prepared. Information would have no credibility. There is no doubt that a sound, well-functioning economy depends on accurate and dependable financial reporting.

United States regulators and lawmakers were very concerned that the economy would suffer if investors lost confidence in corporate accounting because of

Study Objective [3]
Understand why ethics is a fundamental business concept.

---

[3]"U.S. Share Prices Slump," *Wall Street Journal* (February 21, 2002).

unethical financial reporting. In response, Congress passed the **Sarbanes-Oxley Act of 2002** (SOX, or Sarbox). Its intent is to reduce unethical corporate behavior and decrease the likelihood of future corporate scandals. As a result of SOX, top management must now certify the accuracy of financial information. In addition, penalties for fraudulent financial activity are much more severe. Also, SOX increased the independence of the outside auditors who review the accuracy of corporate financial statements and increased the oversight role of boards of directors.

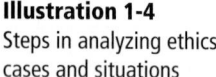

Ethics Note

Circus-founder P.T. Barnum is alleged to have said, "Trust everyone, but cut the deck." What Sarbanes-Oxley does is to provide measures that (like cutting the deck of playing cards) help ensure that fraud will not occur.

Ethics Notes help sensitize you to some of the ethical issues in accounting.

The standards of conduct by which one's actions are judged as right or wrong, honest or dishonest, fair or not fair, are **ethics**. Effective financial reporting depends on sound ethical behavior. To sensitize you to ethical situations in business and to give you practice at solving ethical dilemmas, we address ethics in a number of ways in this book:

1. A number of the *Feature Stories* and other parts of the text discuss the central importance of ethical behavior to financial reporting.
2. *Ethics Insight* boxes and marginal *Ethics Notes* highlight ethics situations and issues in actual business settings.
3. Many of the *All About You* topics (available on the book's companion website) focus on ethical issues you may face in your college and early-career years.
4. At the end of the chapter, an *Ethics Case* simulates a business situation and asks you to put yourself in the position of a decision maker in that case.

Illustration 1-4
Steps in analyzing ethics cases and situations

When analyzing these various ethics cases, as well as experiences in your own life, it is useful to apply the three steps outlined in Illustration 1-4.

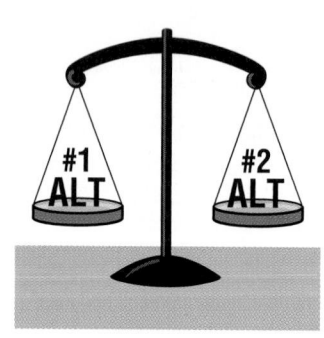

1. Recognize an ethical situation and the ethical issues involved.

Use your personal ethics to identify ethical situations and issues. Some businesses and professional organizations provide written codes of ethics for guidance in some business situations.

2. Identify and analyze the principal elements in the situation.

Identify the *stakeholders*—persons or groups who may be harmed or benefited. Ask the question: What are the responsibilities and obligations of the parties involved?

3. Identify the alternatives, and weigh the impact of each alternative on various stakeholders.

Select the most ethical alternative, considering all the consequences. Sometimes there will be one right answer. Other situations involve more than one right solution; these situations require an evaluation of each and a selection of the best alternative.

Insights provide examples of business situations from various perspectives—ethics, investor, and international.

ETHICS INSIGHT

The Numbers Behind Not-for-Profit Organizations

Accounting plays an important role for a wide range of business organizations worldwide. Just as the integrity of the numbers matters for business, it matters at least as much for not-for-profit organizations. Proper control and reporting help ensure that money is used the way donors intended. Donors are less inclined to give to an organization if they think the organization is subject to waste or theft. The accounting challenges of some large international not-for-profits rival those of the world's largest businesses. For example, after the Haitian earthquake, the Haitian-born musician Wyclef Jean was criticized for the poor accounting controls in a relief fund that he founded. Since then, he has hired a new accountant and improved the transparency regarding funds raised and spent.

? What benefits does a sound accounting system provide to a not-for-profit organization? (See page 46.)

Generally Accepted Accounting Principles

The accounting profession has developed standards that are generally accepted and universally practiced. This common set of standards is called **generally accepted accounting principles (GAAP)**. These standards indicate how to report economic events.

The primary accounting standard-setting body in the United States is the **Financial Accounting Standards Board (FASB)**. The **Securities and Exchange Commission (SEC)** is the agency of the U.S. government that oversees U.S. financial markets and accounting standard-setting bodies. The SEC relies on the FASB to develop accounting standards, which public companies must follow. Many countries outside of the United States have adopted the accounting standards issued by the **International Accounting Standards Board (IASB)**. These standards are called International Financial Reporting Standards (IFRS).

As markets become more global, it is often desirable to compare the result of companies from different countries that report using different accounting standards. In order to increase comparability, in recent years the two standard-setting bodies have made efforts to reduce the differences between U.S. GAAP and IFRS. This process is referred to as **convergence**. As a result of these convergence efforts, it is likely that someday there will be a single set of high-quality accounting standards that are used by companies around the world. Because convergence is such an important issue, we highlight any major differences between GAAP and IFRS in *International Notes* (as shown in the margin here) and provide a more in-depth discussion in the *A Look at IRFS* section at the end of each chapter.

Study Objective [4]
Explain generally accepted accounting principles.

International Note

Over 100 countries use International Financial Reporting Standards (called IFRS). For example, all companies in the European Union follow international standards. The differences between U.S. and international standards are not generally significant.

International Notes highlight differences between U.S. and international accounting standards.

Measurement Principles

GAAP generally uses one of two measurement principles, the cost principle or the fair value principle. Selection of which principle to follow generally relates to trade-offs between relevance and faithful representation. **Relevance** means that financial information is capable of making a difference in a decision. **Faithful representation** means that the numbers and descriptions match what really existed or happened—it if factual.

Helpful Hint

Relevance and *faithful representation* are two primary qualities that make accounting information useful for decision making.

Helpful Hints further clarify concepts being discussed.

COST PRINCIPLE

The **cost principle** (or historical cost principle) dictates that companies record assets at their cost. This is true not only at the time the asset is purchased, but also over the time the asset is held. For example if Best Buy purchases land for $300,000, the company initially reports it in its accounting records at $300,000. But what does Best Buy do if, by the end of the next year, the fair value of the land has increased to $400,000? Under the cost principle, it continues to report the land at $300,000.

FAIR VALUE PRINCIPLE

The **fair value principle** states that assets and liabilities should be reported at fair value (the price received to sell an asset or settle a liability). Fair value information may be more useful than historical cost for certain types of assets and liabilities. For example, certain investment securities are reported at fair value because market value information is usually readily available for these types of assets. In determining which measurement principle to use, companies weigh the factual nature of cost figures versus the relevance of fair value. In general, most companies choose to use cost. Only in situations where assets are actively traded, such as investment securities, do companies apply the fair value principle extensively.

*I*NTERNATIONAL *I*NSIGHT

The Korean Discount

If you think that accounting standards don't matter, consider recent events in South Korea. For many years, international investors complained that the financial reports of South Korean companies were inadequate and inaccurate. Accounting practices there often resulted in huge differences between stated revenues and actual revenues. Because investors did not have faith in the accuracy of the numbers, they were unwilling to pay as much for the shares of these companies relative to shares of comparable companies in different countries. This difference in stock price was often referred to as the "Korean discount."

In response, Korean regulators decided that, beginning in 2011, companies will have to comply with international accounting standards. This change was motivated by a desire to "make the country's businesses more transparent" in order to build investor confidence and spur economic growth. Many other Asian countries, including China, India, Japan, and Hong Kong, have also decided either to adopt international standards or to create standards that are based on the international standards.

Source: Evan Ramstad, "End to 'Korea Discount'?" *Wall Street Journal* (March 16, 2007).

? What is meant by the phrase "make the country's businesses more transparent"? Why would increasing transparency spur economic growth? (See page 46.)

Assumptions

Study Objective [5]
Explain the monetary unit assumption and the economic entity assumption.

Assumptions provide a foundation for the accounting process. Two main assumptions are the **monetary unit assumption** and the **economic entity assumption**.

MONETARY UNIT ASSUMPTION

The **monetary unit assumption** requires that companies include in the accounting records only transaction data that can be expressed in money terms. This assumption enables accounting to quantify (measure) economic events. The monetary unit assumption is vital to applying the cost principle.

This assumption prevents the inclusion of some relevant information in the accounting records. For example, the health of a company's owner, the quality of service, and the morale of employees are not included. The reason: Companies cannot quantify this information in money terms. Though this information is important, companies record only events that can be measured in money.

ECONOMIC ENTITY ASSUMPTION

An economic entity can be any organization or unit in society. It may be a company (such as Crocs, Inc.), a governmental unit (the state of Ohio), a municipality (Seattle), a school district (St. Louis District 48), or a church (Southern Baptist). The **economic entity assumption** requires that the activities of the entity be kept separate and distinct from the activities of its owner and all other economic entities.

Ethics Note

The importance of the economic entity assumption is illustrated by scandals involving Adelphia. In this case, senior company employees entered into transactions that blurred the line between the employees' financial interests and those of the company. For example, Aldephia guaranteed over $2 billion of loans to the founding family.

To illustrate, Sally Rider, owner of Sally's Boutique, must keep her personal living costs separate from the expenses of the Boutique. Similarly, McDonald's, Coca-Cola, and Cadbury-Schweppes are segregated into separate economic entities for accounting purposes.

Proprietorship. A business owned by one person is generally a **proprietorship**. The owner is often the manager/operator of the business. Small service-type businesses (plumbing companies, beauty salons, and auto repair shops), farms, and small retail stores (antique shops, clothing stores, and used-book stores) are often proprietorships. **Usually only a relatively small amount of money (capital) is necessary to start in business as a proprietorship. The owner (proprietor) receives any profits, suffers any losses, and is personally liable for all debts of the business.** There is no legal distinction between the business as an economic unit and the owner, but the accounting records of the business activities are kept separate from the personal records and activities of the owner.

Partnership. A business owned by two or more persons associated as partners is a **partnership.** In most respects a partnership is like a proprietorship except that more than one owner is involved. Typically a partnership agreement (written or oral) sets forth such terms as initial investment, duties of each partner, division of net income (or net loss), and settlement to be made upon death or withdrawal of a partner. Each partner generally has unlimited personal liability for the debts of the partnership. **Like a proprietorship, for accounting purposes the partnership transactions must be kept separate from the personal activities of the partners.** Partnerships are often used to organize retail and service-type businesses, including professional practices (lawyers, doctors, architects, and certified public accountants).

Corporation. A business organized as a separate legal entity under state corporation law and having ownership divided into transferable shares of stock is a **corporation.** The holders of the shares (stockholders) **enjoy limited liability**; that is, they are not personally liable for the debts of the corporate entity. Stockholders **may transfer all or part of their ownership shares to other investors at any time** (i.e., sell their shares). The ease with which ownership can change adds to the attractiveness of investing in a corporation. Because ownership can be transferred without dissolving the corporation, the corporation **enjoys an unlimited life**.

Although the combined number of proprietorships and partnerships in the United States is more than five times the number of corporations, the revenue produced by corporations is eight times greater. Most of the largest enterprises in the United States—for example, ExxonMobil, Ford, Wal-Mart, Citigroup, and Apple—are corporations.

*The **Do it!** exercises ask you to put newly acquired knowledge to work. They outline the Action Plan necessary to complete the exercise, and they show a Solution.*

Do it!

Indicate whether each of the five statements presented below is true or false.

1. The three steps in the accounting process are identification, recording, and communication.

2. The two most common types of external users are investors and company officers.

3. Congress passed the Sarbanes-Oxley Act of 2002 to reduce unethical behavior and decrease the likelihood of future corporate scandals.

4. The primary accounting standard-setting body in the United States is the Financial Accounting Standards Board (FASB).

5. The cost principle dictates that companies record assets at their cost. In later periods, however, the fair value of the asset must be used if fair value is higher than its cost.

Basic Concepts

action plan

✔ Review the basic concepts learned to date.

✔ Develop an understanding of the key terms used.

Solution

1. True   2. False. The two most common types of external users are investors and creditors.   3. True.   4. True.   5. False. The cost principle dictates that companies record assets at their cost. Under the cost principle, the company must also use cost in later periods as well.

Related exercise material: E1-1, E1-2, E1-3, E1-4, and **Do it!** 1-1.

✔
The Navigator

ACCOUNTING ACROSS THE ORGANIZATION

Spinning the Career Wheel

One question that students frequently ask is, "How will the study of accounting help me?" It should help you a great deal, because a working knowledge of accounting is desirable for virtually *every field* of endeavor. Some examples of how accounting is used in other careers include:

General management: Imagine running Ford Motors, Massachusetts General Hospital, Northern Virginia Community College, a Subway franchise, a Trek bike shop. All general managers need to understand accounting data in order to make wise business decisions.

Marketing: A marketing specialist at a company like Procter & Gamble develops strategies to help the sales force be successful. But making a sale is meaningless unless it is a profitable sale. Marketing people must be sensitive to costs and benefits, which accounting helps them quantify and understand.

Finance: Do you want to be a banker for Bank of America, an investment analyst for Goldman Sachs, a stock broker for Merrill Lynch? These fields rely heavily on accounting. In all of them you will regularly examine and analyze financial statements. In fact, it is difficult to get a good finance job without two or three courses in accounting.

Real estate: Are you interested in being a real estate broker for Prudential Real Estate? Because a third party—the bank—is almost always involved in financing a real estate transaction, brokers must understand the numbers involved: Can the buyer afford to make the payments to the bank? Does the cash flow from an industrial property justify the purchase price? What are the tax benefits of the purchase?

 How might accounting help you? (See page 46.)

The Basic Accounting Equation

Study Objective [6]

State the accounting equation, and define its components.

The two basic elements of a business are what it owns and what it owes. **Assets** are the resources a business owns. For example, Google has total assets of approximately $40.5 billion. Liabilities and owner's equity are the rights or claims against these resources. Thus, Google has $40.5 billion of claims against its $40.5 billion of assets. Claims of those to whom the company owes money (creditors) are called **liabilities**. Claims of owners are called **owner's equity**. Google has liabilities of $4.5 billion and owners' equity of $36 billion.

We can express the relationship of assets, liabilities, and owner's equity as an equation, as shown in Illustration 1-5.

Illustration 1-5

The basic accounting equation

Assets	=	Liabilities	+	Owner's Equity

This relationship is the basic accounting equation. Assets must equal the sum of liabilities and owner's equity. Liabilities appear before owner's equity in the basic accounting equation because they are paid first if a business is liquidated.

The accounting equation applies to all **economic entities** regardless of size, nature of business, or form of business organization. It applies to a small proprietorship such as a corner grocery store as well as to a giant corporation such as PepsiCo. The equation provides the **underlying framework** for recording and summarizing economic events.

Let's look in more detail at the categories in the basic accounting equation.

Assets

As noted above, assets are resources a business owns. The business uses its assets in carrying out such activities as production and sales. The common characteristic possessed by all assets is **the capacity to provide future services or benefits**. In a business, that service potential or future economic benefit eventually results in cash inflows (receipts). For example, Campus Pizza owns a delivery truck that provides economic benefits from delivering pizzas. Other assets of Campus Pizza are tables, chairs, jukebox, cash register, oven, tableware, and, of course, cash.

Liabilities

Liabilities are claims against assets—that is, existing debts and obligations. Businesses of all sizes usually borrow money and purchase merchandise on credit. These economic activities result in payables of various sorts:

- Campus Pizza, for instance, purchases cheese, sausage, flour, and beverages on credit from suppliers. These obligations are called **accounts payable**.
- Campus Pizza also has a **note payable** to First National Bank for the money borrowed to purchase the delivery truck.
- Campus Pizza may also have **salaries and wages payable** to employees and **sales and real estate taxes payable** to the local government.

All of these persons or entities to whom Campus Pizza owes money are its **creditors**.

Creditors may legally force the liquidation of a business that does not pay its debts. In that case, the law requires that creditor claims be paid **before** ownership claims.

Owner's Equity

The ownership claim on total assets is **owner's equity**. It is equal to total assets minus total liabilities. Here is why: The assets of a business are claimed by either creditors or owners. To find out what belongs to owners, we subtract the creditors' claims (the liabilities) from assets. The remainder is the owner's claim on the assets—the owner's equity. Since the claims of creditors must be paid **before** ownership claims, owner's equity is often referred to as **residual equity**.

INCREASES IN OWNER'S EQUITY
In a proprietorship, owner's investments and revenues increase owner's equity.

Investments by Owner. **Investments by owner** are the assets the owner puts into the business. These investments increase owner's equity. They are recorded in a category called **owner's capital**.

Revenues. **Revenues** are the **gross increase in owner's equity resulting from business activities entered into for the purpose of earning income**. Generally, revenues result from selling merchandise, performing services, renting property, and lending money. Common sources of revenue are sales, fees, services, commissions, interest, dividends, royalties, and rent.

Revenues usually result in an increase in an asset. They may arise from different sources and are called various names depending on the nature of the business. Campus Pizza, for instance, has two categories of sales revenues—pizza sales and beverage sales.

DECREASES IN OWNER'S EQUITY
In a proprietorship, owner's drawings and expenses decrease owner's equity.

Drawings. An owner may withdraw cash or other assets for personal use. We use a separate classification called **drawings** to determine the total withdrawals for each accounting period. **Drawings decrease owner's equity.** They are recorded in a category called owner's drawings.

Helpful Hint

In some places, we use the term "owner's equity" and in others we use "owners' equity." *Owner's* (singular, possessive) refers to one owner (the case with a sole proprietorship). *Owners'* (plural, possessive) refers to multiple owners (the case with partnerships or corporations).

Expenses. Expenses are the cost of assets consumed or services used in the process of earning revenue. They are **decreases in owner's equity that result from operating the business**. For example, Campus Pizza recognizes the following expenses: cost of ingredients (meat, flour, cheese, tomato paste, mushrooms, etc.); cost of beverages; salaries and wages expense; utilities expense (electric, gas, and water expense); delivery expense (gasoline, repairs, licenses, etc.); supplies expense (napkins, detergents, aprons, etc.); rent expense; interest expense; and property tax expense.

In summary, owner's equity is increased by an owner's investments and by revenues from business operations. Owner's equity is decreased by an owner's withdrawals of assets and by expenses. Illustration 1-6 expands the basic accounting equation by showing the accounts that comprise owner's equity. This format is referred to as the **expanded accounting equation**.

Illustration 1-6
Expanded accounting equation

Basic Equation:	**Assets = Liabilities**	**+**	**Owner's Equity**
Expanded Equation:	**Assets = Liabilities**	**+**	**Owner's Capital − Owner's Drawings + Revenues − Expenses**

Do it!

Owner's Equity Effects

action plan
✔ Understand the sources of revenue.
✔ Understand what causes expenses.
✔ Review the rules for changes in owner's equity: Investments and revenues increase owner's equity. Expenses and drawings decrease owner's equity.
✔ Recognize that drawings are withdrawals of cash or other assets from the business for personal use.

Classify the following items as investment by owner (I), owner's drawings (D), revenues (R), or expenses (E). Then indicate whether each item increases or decreases owner's equity.

(1) Rent Expense   (3) Drawings
(2) Service Revenue   (4) Salaries and Wages Expense

Solution

1. Rent Expense is an expense (E); it decreases owner's equity. 2. Service Revenue is revenue (R); it increases owner's equity. 3. Drawings is owner's drawings (D); it decreases owner's equity. 4. Salaries and Wages Expense is an expense (E); it decreases owner's equity.

Related exercise material: BE1-1, BE1-2, BE1-3, BE1-4, BE1-5, E1-5, E1-6, E1-7, and **Do it!** 1-2.

✔ **The Navigator**

Using the Accounting Equation

Study Objective [7]
Analyze the effects of business transactions on the accounting equation.

Transactions (**business transactions**) are a business's economic events recorded by accountants. Transactions may be external or internal. **External transactions** involve economic events between the company and some outside enterprise. For example, Campus Pizza's purchase of cooking equipment from a supplier, payment of monthly rent to the landlord, and sale of pizzas to customers are external transactions. **Internal transactions** are economic events that occur entirely within one company. The use of cooking and cleaning supplies are internal transactions for Campus Pizza.

Companies carry on many activities that do not represent business transactions. Examples are hiring employees, answering the telephone, talking with customers, and placing merchandise orders. Some of these activities may lead to business transactions: Employees will earn wages, and suppliers will deliver ordered merchandise. The company must analyze each event to find out if it affects the components of the accounting equation. If it does, the company will record the transaction. Illustration 1-7 demonstrates the transaction-identification process.

Illustration 1-7
Transaction-identification process

Each transaction must have a dual effect on the accounting equation. For example, if an asset is increased, there must be a corresponding: (1) decrease in another asset, or (2) increase in a specific liability, or (3) increase in owner's equity.

Two or more items could be affected. For example, as one asset is increased $10,000, another asset could decrease $6,000 and a liability could increase $4,000. Any change in a liability or ownership claim is subject to similar analysis.

Transaction Analysis

The following examples are business transactions for a computer programming business during its first month of operations.

Transaction (1). Investment by Owner. Ray Neal decides to open a computer programming service which he names Softbyte. On September 1, 2012, he invests $15,000 cash in the business. This transaction results in an equal increase in assets and owner's equity.

Helpful Hint

You will want to study these transactions until you are sure you understand them. They are not difficult, but understanding them is important to your success in this course. The ability to analyze transactions in terms of the basic accounting equation is essential in accounting.

Basic Analysis	The asset Cash increases $15,000, and owner's equity identified as Owner's Capital increases $15,000.

	Assets	=	Liabilities	+	Owner's Equity
Equation Analysis	Cash =				Owner's Capital
(1)	+$15,000 =				+$15,000 Initial investment

Observe that the equality of the accounting equation has been maintained. Note that the investments by the owner do not represent revenues, and they are excluded in determining net income. Therefore it is necessary to make clear that the increase is an investment (increasing Owner's Capital) rather than revenue.

Transaction (2). Purchase of Equipment for Cash. Softbyte purchases computer equipment for $7,000 cash. This transaction results in an equal increase and decrease in total assets, though the composition of assets changes. Cash decreases $7,000, and the asset Equipment increases $7,000. The specific effect of this transaction and the cumulative effect of the first two transactions are:

Basic Analysis	Cash decreases $7,000, and the asset Equipment increases $7,000.

	Assets			=	Liabilities	+	Owner's Equity
	Cash	+	Equipment	=			Owner's Capital
Equation Analysis	$15,000						$15,000
(2)	−7,000		+$7,000				
	$ 8,000	+	$7,000	=			$15,000
		$15,000					

Observe that total assets are still $15,000. Neal's equity also remains at $15,000, the amount of his original investment.

Transaction (3). Purchase of Supplies on Credit. Softbyte purchases for $1,600 from Acme Supply Company computer paper and other supplies expected to last several months. Acme agrees to allow Softbyte to pay this bill in October. This transaction is a purchase on account (a credit purchase). Assets increase because of the expected future benefits of using the paper and supplies, and liabilities increase by the amount due Acme Company.

Basic Analysis	The asset Supplies increases $1,600, and the liability Accounts Payable increases by $1,600.

	Assets					=	Liabilities	+	Owner's Equity
	Cash	+	Supplies	+	Equipment	=	Accounts Payable	+	Owner's Capital
Equation Analysis	$8,000				$7,000				$15,000
(3)			+$1,600				+$1,600		
	$8,000	+	$1,600	+	$7,000	=	$1,600	+	$15,000
			$16,600					$16,600	

Total assets are now $16,600. This total is matched by a $1,600 creditor's claim and a $15,000 ownership claim.

Transaction (4). Services Provided for Cash.   Softbyte receives $1,200 cash from customers for programming services it has provided. This transaction represents Softbyte's principal revenue-producing activity. Recall that **revenue increases owner's equity**.

Basic Analysis	Cash increases $1,200, and revenues (specifically, Service Revenue) increase $1,200.

			Assets			=	Liabilities	+	Owner's Equity		
		Cash	+ Supplies	+ Equipment	=	Accounts Payable	+	Owner's Capital	+ Revenues		
		$8,000	$1,600	$7,000		$1,600		$15,000			
Equation Analysis	(4)	+$1,200							+$1,200		Service Revenue
		$9,200 +	$1,600 +	$7,000	=	$1,600	+	$15,000 +	$1,200		
			$17,800					$17,800			

The two sides of the equation balance at $17,800. Service Revenue is included in determining Softbyte's net income.

Note that we do not have room to give details for each individual revenue and expense account in this illustration. Thus, revenues (and expenses when we get to them) are summarized under one column heading for Revenues and one for Expenses. However, it is important to keep track of the category (account) titles affected (e.g., Service Revenue) as they will be needed when we prepare financial statements later in the chapter.

Transaction (5). Purchase of Advertising on Credit. Softbyte receives a bill for $250 from the *Daily News* for advertising but postpones payment until a later date. This transaction results in an increase in liabilities and a decrease in owner's equity. The specific categories involved are Accounts Payable and expenses (specifically, Advertising Expense). The effect on the equation is:

Basic Analysis	Accounts Payable increases $250, and owner's equity decreases $250 due to Advertising Expense.

Equation Analysis											
		Assets			=	Liabilities	+	Owner's Equity			
		Cash	+ Supplies	+ Equipment	=	Accounts Payable	+	Owner's Capital	+ Revenues	− Expenses	
		$9,200	$1,600	$7,000		$1,600		$15,000	$1,200		
(5)						+250				−$250	Advertising Expense
		$9,200 +	$1,600 +	$7,000	=	$1,850	+	$15,000 +	$1,200	− $250	
			$17,800					$17,800			

The two sides of the equation still balance at $17,800. Owner's equity decreases when Softbyte incurs the expense. Expenses are not always paid in cash at the time they are incurred. When Softbyte pays at a later date, the liability Accounts Payable will decrease, and the asset Cash will decrease [see Transaction (8)]. The cost of advertising is an expense (rather than an asset) because the company has *used* the benefits. Advertising Expense is included in determining net income.

Transaction (6). Services Provided for Cash and Credit. Softbyte provides $3,500 of programming services for customers. The company receives cash of $1,500 from customers, and it bills the balance of $2,000 on account. This transaction results in an equal increase in assets and owner's equity.

Basic Analysis	Three specific items are affected: Cash increases $1,500, Accounts Receivable increases $2,000, and Service Revenue increases $3,500.

Equation Analysis

	Assets				=	Liabilities	+	Owner's Equity			
	Cash	+ Accounts Receivable	+ Supplies	+ Equipment =		Accounts Payable	+ Owner's Capital	+ Revenues	− Expenses		
	$9,200		$1,600	$7,000		$1,850	$15,000	$1,200	$250		
(6)	+1,500	+$2,000						+3,500			Service
	$10,700 +	$2,000 +	$1,600 +	$7,000	=	$1,850 +	$15,000 +	$4,700	− $250		Revenue
		$21,300					$21,300				

Softbyte earns revenues when it provides the service, and therefore it recognizes $3,500 in revenue. In exchange for this service, it received $1,500 in Cash and Accounts Receivable of $2,000. This Accounts Receivable represents customers' promise to pay $2,000 to Softbyte in the future. When it later receives collections on account, Softbyte will increase Cash and will decrease Accounts Receivable [see Transaction (9)].

Transaction (7). Payment of Expenses. Softbyte pays the following expenses in cash for September: store rent $600, salaries and wages of employees $900, and utilities $200. These payments result in an equal decrease in assets and expenses. Cash decreases $1,700, and the specific expense categories (Rent Expense, Salaries and Wages Expense, and Utilities Expense) decrease owner's equity by the same amount. The effect of these payments on the equation is:

	Assets				=	Liabilities	+	Owner's Equity			
	Cash	+ Accounts Receivable	+ Supplies	+ Equipment =		Accounts Payable	+ Owner's Capital	+ Revenues	− Expenses		
	$10,700	$2,000	$1,600	$7,000		$1,850	$15,000	$4,700	$ 250		
(7)	−1,700								−600		Rent Expense
									−900		Sal. and Wages Exp.
									−200		Utilities Exp.
	$9,000 +	$2,000	+ $1,600 +	$7,000	=	$1,850 +	$15,000 +	$4,700	− $1,950		
		$19,600					$19,600				

The two sides of the equation now balance at $19,600. Three lines in the analysis indicate the different types of expenses that have been incurred.

Transaction (8). Payment of Accounts Payable. Softbyte pays its $250 *Daily News* bill in cash. The company previously [in Transaction (5)] recorded the bill as an increase in Accounts Payable and a decrease in owner's equity.

Basic Analysis	This cash payment "on account" decreases the asset Cash by $250 and also decreases the liability Accounts Payable by $250.

		Assets			=	Liabilities	+		Owner's Equity		
	Cash	+ Accounts Receivable	+ Supplies	+ Equipment	=	Accounts Payable	+	Owner's Capital	+ Revenues	− Expenses
	$9,000	$2,000	$1,600	$7,000		$1,850		$15,000	$4,700	$1,950
(8)	−250					−250				
	$8,750 +	$2,000 +	$1,600 +	$7,000	=	$1,600	+	$15,000 +	$4,700	− $1,950
			$19,350						$19,350	

Observe that the payment of a liability related to an expense that has previously been recorded does not affect owner's equity. The company recorded this expense in Transaction (5) and should not record it again.

Transaction (9). Receipt of Cash on Account. Softbyte receives $600 in cash from customers who had been billed for services [in Transaction (6)]. This does not change total assets, but it changes the composition of those assets.

Basic Analysis	Cash increases $600, and Accounts Receivable decreases $600.

		Assets			=	Liabilities	+		Owner's Equity		
	Cash	+ Accounts Receivable	+ Supplies	+ Equipment	=	Accounts Payable	+	Owner's Capital	+ Revenues	− Expenses
	$8,750	$2,000	$1,600	$7,000		$1,600		$15,000	$4,700	$1,950
(9)	+600	−600								
	$9,350 +	$1,400 +	$1,600 +	$7,000	=	$1,600	+	$15,000 +	$4,700	− $1,950
			$19,350						$19,350	

Note that the collection of an account receivable for services previously billed and recorded does not affect owner's equity. Softbyte already recorded this revenue in Transaction (6) and should not record it again.

Transaction (10). Withdrawal of Cash by Owner. Ray Neal withdraws $1,300 in cash from the business for his personal use. This transaction results in an equal decrease in assets and owner's equity. Both Cash and Owner's Drawings decrease $1,300, as shown on the next page.

Basic Analysis	Cash decreases $1,300, and Owner's Drawings decreases $1,300 due to owner's withdrawal.

	Assets				=	Liabilities +	Owner's Equity				
	Cash +	Accounts Receivable +	Supplies +	Equipment =		Accounts Payable +	Owner's Capital −	Owner's Drawings +	Revenues −	Expenses	
	$9,350	$1,400	$1,600	$7,000		$1,600	$15,000		$4,700	$1,950	
(10)	−1,300							−$1,300			Drawings
	$8,050 +	$1,400 +	$1,600 +	$7,000 =		$1,600 +	$15,000 −	$1,300 +	$4,700 −	$1,950	
			$18,050					$18,050			

Observe that the effect of a cash withdrawal by the owner is the opposite of the effect of an investment by the owner. **Owner's drawings are not expenses.** Expenses are incurred for the purpose of earning revenue. Drawings do not generate revenue. They are a **disinvestment**. Like owner's investment, the company excludes owner's drawings in determining net income.

Summary of Transactions

Illustration 1-8 summarizes the September transactions of Softbyte to show their cumulative effect on the basic accounting equation. It also indicates the transaction number and the specific effects of each transaction.

	Assets				=	Liabilities +	Owner's Equity				
	Cash +	Accounts Receivable +	Supplies +	Equipment =		Accounts Payable +	Owner's Capital −	Owner's Drawings +	Rev. −	Exp.	
(1)	+$15,000						+ $15,000				Initial inv.
(2)	−7,000			+$7,000							
(3)			+$1,600			+$1,600					
(4)	+1,200								+$1,200		Ser. Rev.
(5)						+250				−$250	Adv. Exp.
(6)	+1,500	+$2,000							+3,500		Ser. Rev.
(7)	−600 ·									−600	Rent Exp.
	−900									−900	Sal./Wages Exp.
	−200									−200	Utilities Exp.
(8)	−250					−250					
(9)	+600	−600									
(10)	−1,300							−$1,300			Drawings
	$ 8,050 +	$1,400 +	$1,600 +	$7,000 =		$1,600 +	$15,000 −	$1,300 +	$4,700 −	$1,950	
			$18,050					$18,050			

Illustration 1-8
Tabular summary of Softbyte transactions

Illustration 1-8 demonstrates some significant facts:

1. Each transaction is analyzed in terms of its effect on:
   (a) the three components of the basic accounting equation.
   (b) specific items within each component.
2. The two sides of the equation must always be equal.

There! You made it through your first transaction analysis. If you feel a bit shaky on any of the transactions, it might be a good idea at this point to get up, take a short break, and come back again for a 10- to 15-minute review of the transactions, to make sure you understand them before you go on to the next section.

Do it!

Transactions made by Virmari & Co., a public accounting firm, for the month of August are shown below. Prepare a tabular analysis which shows the effects of these transactions on the expanded accounting equation, similar to that shown in Illustration 1-8.

1. The owner invested $25,000 cash in the business.
2. The company purchased $7,000 of office equipment on credit.
3. The company received $8,000 cash in exchange for services performed.
4. The company paid $850 for this month's rent.
5. The owner withdrew $1,000 cash for personal use.

Tabular Analysis

action plan

✔ Analyze the effects of each transaction on the accounting equation.

✔ Use appropriate category names (not descriptions).

✔ Keep the accounting equation in balance.

Solution

	Assets			=	Liabilities	+			Owner's Equity			
	Cash	+	Equipment	=	Accounts Payable	+	Owner's Capital	−	Owner's Drawings	+ Revenues	−	Expenses
1.	+$25,000						+$25,000					
2.			+$7,000		+$7,000							
3.	+8,000									+$8,000		
4.	−850											−$850
5.	−1,000								−$1,000			
	$31,150	+	$7,000	=	$7,000	+	$25,000	−	$1,000	+ $8,000	−	$850
		$38,150							$38,150			

Related exercise material: BE1-6, BE1-7, BE1-8, BE1-9, E1-6, E1-7, E1-8, E1-10, E1-11, and **Do it!** 1-3.

✔ **The Navigator**

Financial Statements

Companies prepare four financial statements from the summarized accounting data:

1. An **income statement** presents the revenues and expenses and resulting net income or net loss for a specific period of time.
2. An **owner's equity statement** summarizes the changes in owner's equity for a specific period of time.
3. A **balance sheet** reports the assets, liabilities, and owner's equity at a specific date.
4. A **statement of cash flows** summarizes information about the cash inflows (receipts) and outflows (payments) for a specific period of time.

These statements provide relevant financial data for internal and external users. Illustration 1-9 (page 22) shows the financial statements of Softbyte.

Study Objective [8]
Understand the four financial statements and how they are prepared.

International Note

The primary types of financial statements required by GAAP and IFRS are the same. In practice, some format differences do exist in presentations commonly employed by GAAP companies compared to IFRS companies.

Illustration 1-9
Financial statements and their interrelationships

Helpful Hint

The heading of each statement identifies the company, the type of statement, and the specific date or time period covered by the statement.

Helpful Hint

Note that final sums are double-underlined, and negative amounts (in the statement of cash flows) are presented in parentheses.

Helpful Hint

The arrows in this illustration show the interrelationships of the four financial statements.

1. Net income is computed first and is needed to determine the ending balance in owner's equity.
2. The ending balance in owner's equity is needed in preparing the balance sheet.
3. The cash shown on the balance sheet is needed in preparing the statement of cash flows.

Softbyte
Income Statement
For the Month Ended September 30, 2012

Revenues		
Service revenue		$ 4,700
Expenses		
Salaries and wages expense	$900	
Rent expense	600	
Advertising expense	250	
Utilities expense	200	
Total expenses		1,950
Net income		$ 2,750

Softbyte
Owner's Equity Statement
For the Month Ended September 30, 2012

Owner's capital, September 1		$ –0–
Add: Investments	$15,000	
Net income	2,750	17,750
		17,750
Less: Drawings		1,300
Owner's capital, September 30		$16,450

Softbyte
Balance Sheet
September 30, 2012

Assets

Cash	$ 8,050
Accounts receivable	1,400
Supplies	1,600
Equipment	7,000
Total assets	$18,050

Liabilities and Owner's Equity

Liabilities	
Accounts payable	$ 1,600
Owner's equity	
Owner's capital	16,450
Total liabilities and owner's equity	$18,050

Softbyte
Statement of Cash Flows
For the Month Ended September 30, 2012

Cash flows from operating activities		
Cash receipts from revenues	$ 3,300	
Cash payments for expenses	(1,950)	
Net cash provided by operating activities		1,350
Cash flows from investing activities		
Purchase of equipment		(7,000)
Cash flows from financing activities		
Investments by owner	$15,000)	
Drawings by owner	(1,300)	13,700
Net increase in cash		8,050
Cash at the beginning of the period		0
Cash at the end of the period		$ 8,050

① ② ③

Note that the statements shown in Illustration 1-9 are interrelated:

1. Net income of $2,750 on the **income statement** is added to the beginning balance of owner's capital in the **owner's equity statement**.
2. Owner's capital of $16,450 at the end of the reporting period shown in the **owner's equity statement** is reported on the **balance sheet**.
3. Cash of $8,050 on the **balance sheet** is reported on the **statement of cash flows**.

Also, explanatory notes and supporting schedules are an integral part of every set of financial statements. We illustrate these notes and schedules in later chapters of this textbook.

Be sure to carefully examine the format and content of each statement in Illustration 1-9. We describe the essential features of each in the following sections.

Income Statement

The income statement reports the revenues and expenses for a specific period of time. (In Softbyte's case, this is "For the Month Ended September 30, 2012.") Softbyte's income statement is prepared from the data appearing in the owner's equity columns of Illustration 1-8 (page 20).

The income statement lists revenues first, followed by expenses. Finally the statement shows net income (or net loss). **Net income** results when revenues exceed expenses. A **net loss** occurs when expenses exceed revenues.

Although practice varies, we have chosen in our illustrations and homework solutions to list expenses in order of magnitude. (We will consider alternative formats for the income statement in later chapters.)

Note that the income statement does **not** include investment and withdrawal transactions between the owner and the business in measuring net income. For example, as explained earlier, Ray Neal's withdrawal of cash from Softbyte was not regarded as a business expense.

Owner's Equity Statement

The owner's equity statement reports the changes in owner's equity for a specific period of time. The time period is the same as that covered by the income statement. Data for the preparation of the owner's equity statement come from the owner's equity columns of the tabular summary (Illustration 1-8) and from the income statement. The first line of the statement shows the beginning owner's equity amount (which was zero at the start of the business). Then come the owner's investments, net income (or loss), and the owner's drawings. This statement indicates *why* owner's equity has increased or decreased during the period.

What if Softbyte had reported a net loss in its first month? Let's assume that during the month of September 2012, Softbyte lost $10,000. Illustration 1-10 (page 24) shows the presentation of a net loss in the owner's equity statement.

Illustration 1-10
Presentation of net loss

Softbyte		
Owner's Equity Statement		
For the Month Ended September 30, 2012		
Owner's capital, September 1		$ –0–
Add: Investments		15,000
		15,000
Less: Drawings	$ 1,300	
Net loss	10,000	11,300
Owner's capital, September 30		$ 3,700

If the owner makes any additional investments, the company reports them in the owner's equity statement as investments.

Balance Sheet

Softbyte's balance sheet reports the assets, liabilities, and owner's equity at a specific date (in Softbyte's case, September 30, 2012). The company prepares the balance sheet from the column headings of the tabular summary (Illustration 1-8) and the month-end data shown in its last line.

Observe that the balance sheet lists assets at the top, followed by liabilities and owner's equity. Total assets must equal total liabilities and owner's equity. Softbyte reports only one liability—accounts payable—in its balance sheet. In most cases, there will be more than one liability. When two or more liabilities are involved, a customary way of listing is as follows.

Illustration 1-11
Presentation of liabilities

Liabilities	
Notes payable	$10,000
Accounts payable	63,000
Salaries and wages payable	18,000
Total liabilities	$91,000

The balance sheet is a snapshot of the company's financial condition at a specific moment in time (usually the month-end or year-end).

Statement of Cash Flows

Helpful Hint

Investing activities pertain to investments made by the company, not investments made by the owner.

The statement of cash flows provides information on the cash receipts and payments for a specific period of time. The statement of cash flows reports (1) the cash effects of a company's operations during a period, (2) its investing transactions, (3) its financing transactions, (4) the net increase or decrease in cash during the period, and (5) the cash amount at the end of the period.

Reporting the sources, uses, and change in cash is useful because investors, creditors, and others want to know what is happening to a company's most liquid resource. The statement of cash flows provides answers to the following simple but important questions.

1. Where did cash come from during the period?
2. What was cash used for during the period?
3. What was the change in the cash balance during the period?

As shown in Softbyte's statement of cash flows, cash increased $8,050 during the period. Net cash flow provided from operating activities increased cash $1,350. Cash flow from investing transactions decreased cash $7,000. And cash flow from financing transactions increased cash $13,700. At this time, you need not be concerned with how these amounts are determined. Chapter 17 will examine the statement of cash flows in detail.

Do it!

Presented below is selected information related to Flanagan Company at December 31, 2012. Flanagan reports financial information monthly.

Financial Statement Items

Equipment	$10,000	Utilities Expense	$ 4,000
Cash	8,000	Accounts Receivable	9,000
Service Revenue	36,000	Salaries and Wages Expense	7,000
Rent Expense	11,000	Notes Payable	16,500
Accounts Payable	2,000	Owner's Drawings	5,000

(a) Determine the total assets of Flanagan Company at December 31, 2012.

(b) Determine the net income that Flanagan Company reported for December 2012.

(c) Determine the owner's equity of Flanagan Company at December 31, 2012.

Solution

(a) The total assets are $27,000, comprised of Cash $8,000, Accounts Receivable $9,000, and Equipment $10,000.

(b) Net income is $14,000, computed as follows.

Revenues		
Service revenue		$36,000
Expenses		
Rent expense	$11,000	
Salaries and wages expense	7,000	
Utilities expense	4,000	
Total expenses		22,000
Net income		$14,000

(c) The ending owner's equity of Flanagan Company is $8,500. By rewriting the accounting equation, we can compute owner's equity as assets minus liabilities, as follows:

Total assets [as computed in (a)]		$27,000
Less: Liabilities		
Notes payable	$16,500	
Accounts payable	2,000	18,500
Owner's equity		$ 8,500

Note that it is not possible to determine the company's owner's equity in any other way, because the beginning total for owner's equity is not provided.

action plan

✔ Remember the basic accounting equation: assets must equal liabilities plus owner's equity.

✔ Review previous financial statements to determine how total assets, net income, and owner's equity are computed.

Related exercise material: BE1-10, BE1-11, E1-9, E1-12, E1-13, E1-14, E1-15, E1-16, and **Do it!** 1-4.

The Navigator

COMPREHENSIVE

Do it!

*The **Comprehensive Do it!** is a final review of the chapter. The **Action Plan** gives tips about how to approach the problem, and the **Solution** demonstrates both the form and content of complete answers.*

Joan Robinson opens her own law office on July 1, 2012. During the first month of operations, the following transactions occurred.

1. Joan invested $11,000 in cash in the law practice.
2. Paid $800 for July rent on office space.
3. Purchased office equipment on account $3,000.
4. Provided legal services to clients for cash $1,500.
5. Borrowed $700 cash from a bank on a note payable.
6. Performed legal services for client on account $2,000.
7. Paid monthly expenses: salaries and wages $500, utilities $300, and supplies $100.
8. Joan withdraws $1,000 cash for personal use.

Instructions

(a) Prepare a tabular summary of the transactions.
(b) Prepare the income statement, owner's equity statement, and balance sheet at July 31 for Joan Robinson, Attorney.

Solution to Comprehensive Do it!

(a)

Trans-action	Cash	+	Accounts Receivable	+	Equipment	=	Notes Payable	+	Accounts Payable	+	Owner's Capital	−	Owner's Drawings	+	Revenues	−	Expenses
(1)	+$11,000					=					+$11,000						
(2)	−800																−$800
(3)					+$3,000	=			+$3,000								
(4)	+1,500														+$1,500		
(5)	+700						+$700										
(6)			+$2,000												+2,000		
(7)	−500																−500
	−300																−300
	−100																−100
(8)	−1,000												−$1,000				
	$10,500	+	$2,000	+	$3,000	=	$700	+	$3,000	+	$11,000	−	$1,000	+	$3,500	−	$1,700

Assets $15,500   =   Liabilities + Owner's Equity $15,500

action plan

✔ Make sure that assets equal liabilities plus owner's equity after each transaction.

✔ Investments and revenues increase owner's equity. Withdrawals and expenses decrease owner's equity.

✔ Prepare the financial statements in the order listed.

✔ The income statement shows revenues and expenses for a period of time.

Joan Robinson, Attorney
Income Statement
Month Ended July 31, 2012

Revenues		
Service revenue		$3,500
Expenses		
Rent expense	$800	
Salaries and wages expense	500	
Utilities expense	300	
Supplies expense	100	
Total expenses		1,700
Net income		$1,800

Joan Robinson, Attorney		
Owner's Equity Statement		
Month Ended July 31, 2012		
Owner's capital, July 1		$ 0
Add: Investments	$11,000	
Net income	1,800	12,800
		12,800
Less: Drawings		1,000
Owner's capital, July 31		$11,800

action plan (cont'd)
✔ The owner's equity statement shows the changes in owner's equity for the same period of time as the income statement.

✔ The balance sheet reports assets, liabilities, and owner's equity at a specific date.

Joan Robinson, Attorney	
Balance Sheet	
July 31, 2012	
Assets	
Cash	$10,500
Accounts receivable	2,000
Equipment	3,000
Total assets	$15,500
Liabilities and Owner's Equity	
Liabilities	
Notes payable	$ 700
Accounts payable	3,000
Total liabilities	3,700
Owner's equity	
Owner's capital	11,800
Total liabilities and owner's equity	$15,500

The Navigator

*This would be a good time to return to the **Student Owner's Manual** at the beginning of the book (or look at it for the first time if you skipped it before) to read about the various types of assignment materials that appear at the end of each chapter. Knowing the purpose of the different assignments will help you appreciate what each contributes to your accounting skills and competencies.*

Summary of Study Objectives

[1] Explain what accounting is. Accounting is an information system that identifies, records, and communicates the economic events of an organization to interested users.

[2] Identify the users and uses of accounting. The major users and uses of accounting are as follows: (a) Management uses accounting information to plan, organize, and run the business. (b) Investors (owners) decide whether to buy, hold, or sell their financial interests on the basis of accounting data. (c) Creditors (suppliers and bankers) evaluate the risks of granting credit or lending money on the basis of accounting information. Other groups that use accounting information are taxing authorities, regulatory agencies, customers, and labor unions.

[3] Understand why ethics is a fundamental business concept. Ethics are the standards of conduct by which actions are judged as right or wrong. Effective financial reporting depends on sound ethical behavior.

[4] Explain generally accepted accounting principles. Generally accepted accounting principles are a common set of standards used by accountants.

[5] Explain the monetary unit assumption and the economic entity assumption. The monetary unit assumption requires that companies include in the accounting records only transaction data that can be expressed in terms of money. The economic entity assumption requires that the activities of each economic entity be kept separate from the activities of its owner(s) and other economic entities.

[6] State the accounting equation, and define its components. The basic accounting equation is:

$$\text{Assets} = \text{Liabilities} + \text{Owner's Equity}$$

Assets are resources a business owns. Liabilities are creditorship claims on total assets. Owner's equity is the ownership claim on total assets.

The expanded accounting equation is:

$$\text{Assets} = \text{Liabilities} + \text{Owner's Capital} - \text{Owner's Drawings} + \text{Revenues} - \text{Expenses}$$

Owner's capital is assets the owner puts into the business. Owner's drawings are the assets the owner withdraws for personal use. Revenues are increases in assets resulting from income-earning activities. Expenses are the costs of assets consumed or services used in the process of earning revenue.

[7] Analyze the effects of business transactions on the accounting equation. Each business transaction must have a dual effect on the accounting equation. For example, if an individual asset increases, there must be a corresponding (1) decrease in another asset, or (2) increase in a specific liability, or (3) increase in owner's equity.

[8] Understand the four financial statements and how they are prepared. An income statement presents the revenues and expenses, and resulting net income or net loss, for a specific period of time. An owner's equity statement summarizes the changes in owner's equity for a specific period of time. A balance sheet reports the assets, liabilities, and owner's equity at a specific date. A statement of cash flows summarizes information about the cash inflows (receipts) and outflows (payments) for a specific period of time.

The Navigator

Glossary

Accounting The information system that identifies, records, and communicates the economic events of an organization to interested users. (p. 4).

Assets Resources a business owns. (p. 12).

Balance sheet A financial statement that reports the assets, liabilities, and owner's equity at a specific date. (p. 21).

Basic accounting equation Assets = Liabilities + Owner's Equity. (p. 12).

Bookkeeping A part of accounting that involves only the recording of economic events. (p. 5).

Convergence The process of reducing the differences between GAAP and IFRS. (p. 9).

Corporation A business organized as a separate legal entity under state corporation law, having ownership divided into transferable shares of stock. (p. 11).

Cost principle An accounting principle that states that companies should record assets at their cost. (p. 9).

Drawings Withdrawal of cash or other assets from an unincorporated business for the personal use of the owner(s). (p. 13).

Economic entity assumption An assumption that requires that the activities of the entity be kept separate and distinct from the activities of its owner and all other economic entities. (p. 10).

Ethics The standards of conduct by which one's actions are judged as right or wrong, honest or dishonest, fair or not fair. (p. 8).

Expanded accounting equation Assets = Liabilities + Owner's Capital − Owner's Drawings + Revenues − Expenses. (p. 14).

Expenses The cost of assets consumed or services used in the process of earning revenue. (p. 14).

Fair value principle An accounting principle stating that assets and liabilities should be reported at fair value (the price received to sell an asset or settle a liability). (p. 9).

Faithful representation Numbers and descriptions match what really existed or happened—it is factual. (p. 9).

Financial accounting The field of accounting that provides economic and financial information for investors, creditors, and other external users. (p. 7).

Financial Accounting Standards Board (FASB) A private organization that establishes generally accepted accounting principles (GAAP). (p. 9).

Generally accepted accounting principles (GAAP) Common standards that indicate how to report economic events. (p. 9).

Income statement financial statement that presents the revenues and expenses and resulting net income or net loss of a company for a specific period of time. (p. 21).

International Accounting Standards Board (IASB) An accounting standard-setting body that issues standards adopted by many countries outside of the United States. (p. 9).

Investments by owner The assets an owner puts into the business. (p. 13).

Liabilities Creditor claims on total assets. (p. 13).

Managerial accounting The field of accounting that provides internal reports to help users make decisions about their companies. (p. 6).

Monetary unit assumption An assumption stating that companies include in the accounting records only transaction data that can be expressed in terms of money. (p. 10).

Net income The amount by which revenues exceed expenses. (p. 23).

Net loss The amount by which expenses exceed revenues. (p. 23).

Owner's equity The ownership claim on total assets. (p. 13).

Owner's equity statement A financial statement that summarizes the changes in owner's equity for a specific period of time. (p. 21).

Partnership A business owned by two or more persons associated as partners. (p. 11).

Proprietorship A business owned by one person. (p. 10).

Relevance Financial information that is capable of making a difference in a decision. (p. 9).

Revenues   The gross increase in owner's equity resulting from business activities entered into for the purpose of earning income. (p. 13).

Sarbanes-Oxley Act of 2002 (SOX)   Law passed by Congress in 2002 intended to reduce unethical corporate behavior. (p. 8).

Securities and Exchange Commission (SEC)   A governmental agency that oversees U.S. financial markets and accounting standard-setting bodies. (p. 9).

Statement of cash flows   A financial statement that summarizes information about the cash inflows (receipts) and cash outflows (payments) for a specific period of time. (p. 21).

Transactions   The economic events of a business that are recorded by accountants. (p. 14).

APPENDIX1A

Accounting Career Opportunities

Why is accounting such a popular major and career choice? First, there are a lot of jobs. In many cities in recent years, the demand for accountants exceeded the supply. Not only are there a lot of jobs, but there are a wide array of opportunities. As one accounting organization observed, "accounting is one degree with 360 degrees of opportunity."

Accounting is also hot because it is obvious that accounting matters. Interest in accounting has increased, ironically, because of the attention caused by the accounting failures of companies such as Enron and WorldCom. These widely publicized scandals revealed the important role that accounting plays in society. Most people want to make a difference, and an accounting career provides many opportunities to contribute to society. Finally, the Sarbanes-Oxley Act of 2002 (SOX) (see page 8) significantly increased the accounting and internal control requirements for corporations. This dramatically increased demand for professionals with accounting training.

Accountants are in such demand that it is not uncommon for accounting students to have accepted a job offer a year before graduation. As the following discussion reveals, the job options of people with accounting degrees are virtually unlimited.

> **Study Objective [9]**
> Explain the career opportunities in accounting.

Public Accounting

Individuals in **public accounting** offer expert service to the general public, in much the same way that doctors serve patients and lawyers serve clients. A major portion of public accounting involves **auditing**. In auditing, a certified public accountant (CPA) examines company financial statements and provides an opinion as to how accurately the financial statements present the company's results and financial position. Analysts, investors, and creditors rely heavily on these "audit opinions," which CPAs have the exclusive authority to issue.

Taxation is another major area of public accounting. The work that tax specialists perform includes tax advice and planning, preparing tax returns, and representing clients before governmental agencies such as the Internal Revenue Service.

A third area in public accounting is **management consulting**. It ranges from installing basic accounting software or highly complex enterprise resource planning systems, to providing support services for major marketing projects or merger and acquisition activities.

Many CPAs are entrepreneurs. They form small- or medium-sized practices that frequently specialize in tax or consulting services.

Private Accounting

Instead of working in public accounting, you might choose to be an employee of a for-profit company such as Starbucks, Google, or PepsiCo. In **private** (or **managerial**) **accounting**, you would be involved in activities such as cost accounting (finding the cost of producing specific products), budgeting, accounting information system design and support, or tax planning and preparation. You might also be a member of your company's internal audit team. In response to SOX, the internal auditors' job of reviewing the company's operations to ensure compliance with company policies and to increase efficiency has taken on increased importance.

Alternatively, many accountants work for not-for-profit organizations such as the Red Cross or the Bill and Melinda Gates Foundation, or for museums, libraries, or performing arts organizations.

Opportunities in Government

Another option is to pursue one of the many accounting opportunities in governmental agencies. For example, the Internal Revenue Service (IRS), Federal Bureau of Investigation (FBI), and the Securities and Exchange Commission (SEC) all employ accountants. The FBI has a stated goal that at least 15 percent of its new agents should be CPAs. There is also a very high demand for accounting educators at public colleges and universities and in state and local governments.

Forensic Accounting

Forensic accounting uses accounting, auditing, and investigative skills to conduct investigations into theft and fraud. It is listed among the top 20 career paths of the future. The job of forensic accountants is to catch the perpetrators of the estimated $600 billion per year of theft and fraud occurring at U.S. companies. This includes tracing money-laundering and identity-theft activities as well as tax evasion. Insurance companies hire forensic accountants to detect insurance frauds such as arson, and law offices employ forensic accountants to identify marital assets in divorces. Forensic accountants often have FBI, IRS, or similar government experience.

"Show Me the Money"

How much can a new accountant make? Salary estimates are constantly changing, and salaries vary considerably across the country. At the time this text was written, the following general information was available from Robert Half International.

Illustration 1A-1

Salary estimates for jobs in public and corporate accounting

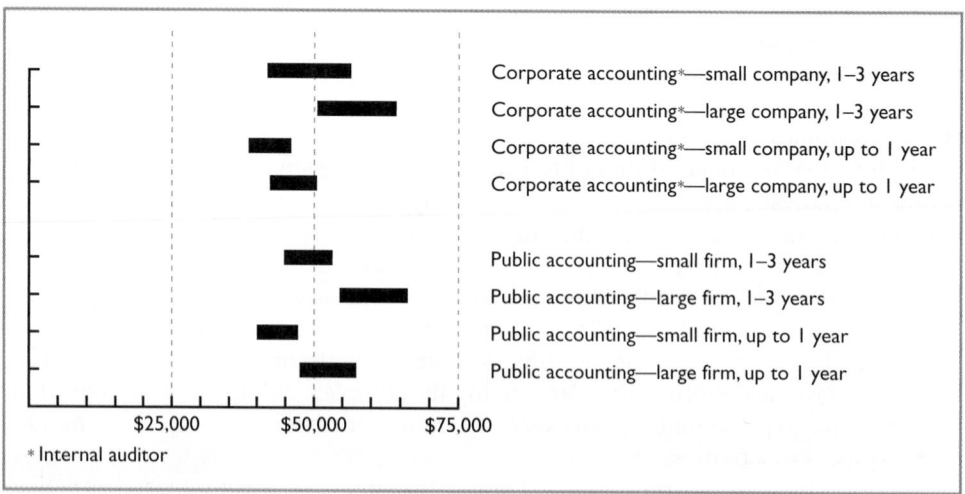

The average salary for a first-year partner in a CPA firm is close to $130,000, with experienced partners often making substantially more. On the corporate side, controllers (the head accountant) can earn $150,000, while chief financial officers can earn as much as $350,000.

For up-to-date salary estimates, as well as a wealth of additional information regarding accounting as a career, check out *www.startheregoplaces.com*.

Summary of Study Objective for Appendix 1A

[9] Explain the career opportunities in accounting. Accounting offers many different jobs in fields such as public and private accounting, government, and forensic accounting.

Accounting is a popular major because there are many different types of jobs, with unlimited potential for career advancement.

Glossary for Appendix 1A

Auditing   The examination of financial statements by a certified public accountant in order to express an opinion as to the fairness of presentation. (p. 29).

Forensic accounting   An area of accounting that uses accounting, auditing, and investigative skills to conduct investigations into theft and fraud. (p. 30).

Management consulting   An area of public accounting ranging from development of accounting and computer systems to support services for marketing projects and merger and acquisition activities. (p. 29).

Private (or managerial) accounting   An area of accounting within a company that involves such activities as cost accounting, budgeting, design and support of accounting information systems, and tax planning and preparation. (p. 29).

Public accounting   An area of accounting in which the accountant offers expert service to the general public. (p. 29).

Taxation   An area of public accounting involving tax advice, tax planning, preparing tax returns, and representing clients before governmental agencies. (p. 29).

Self-Test, Brief Exercises, Exercises, Problem Set A, and many more components are available for practice in *WileyPLUS*

*Note:** All asterisked Questions, Exercises, and Problems relate to material in the appendix to the chapter.

Self-Test Questions

Answers are on page 46.

(SO 1) **1.** Which of the following is *not* a step in the accounting process?
    a. Identification.   **c.** Recording.
    b. Verification.   **d.** Communication.

(SO 2) **2.** Which of the following statements about users of accounting information is *incorrect*?
    a. Management is an internal user.
    b. Taxing authorities are external users.
    c. Present creditors are external users.
    d. Regulatory authorities are internal users.

(SO 4) **3.** The cost principle states that:
    a. assets should be initially recorded at cost and adjusted when the fair value changes.
    b. activities of an entity are to be kept separate and distinct from its owner.
    c. assets should be recorded at their cost.
    d. only transaction data capable of being expressed in terms of money be included in the accounting records.

(SO 5) **4.** Which of the following statements about basic assumptions is *correct*?
    a. Basic assumptions are the same as accounting principles.
    b. The economic entity assumption states that there should be a particular unit of accountability.
    c. The monetary unit assumption enables accounting to measure employee morale.
    d. Partnerships are not economic entities.

5. The three types of business entities are: (SO 5)
    a. proprietorships, small businesses, and partnerships.
    b. proprietorships, partnerships, and corporations.
    c. proprietorships, partnerships, and large businesses.
    d. financial, manufacturing, and service companies.

6. Net income will result during a time period when: (SO 6)
    a. assets exceed liabilities.
    b. assets exceed revenues.
    c. expenses exceed revenues.
    d. revenues exceed expenses.

7. Performing services on account will have the following ef- (SO 7) fects on the components of the basic accounting equation:
    a. increase assets and decrease owner's equity.
    b. increase assets and increase owner's equity.
    c. increase assets and increase liabilities.
    d. increase liabilities and increase owner's equity.

8. As of December 31, 2012, Stoneland Company has assets (SO 7) of $3,500 and owner's equity of $2,000. What are the liabilities for Stoneland Company as of December 31, 2012?
    a. $1,500. **b.** $1,000. **c.** $2,500. **d.** $2,000.

9. Which of the following events is *not* recorded in the (SO 7) accounting records?
    a. Equipment is purchased on account.
    b. An employee is terminated.
    c. A cash investment is made into the business.
    d. The owner withdraws cash for personal use.

(SO 7) **10.** During 2012, Gibson Company's assets decreased $50,000 and its liabilities decreased $90,000. Its owner's equity therefore:
    a. increased $40,000.   **c.** decreased $40,000.
    b. decreased $140,000.   **d.** increased $140,000.

(SO 7) **11.** Payment of an account payable affects the components of the accounting equation in the following way.
    a. Decreases owner's equity and decreases liabilities.
    b. Increases assets and decreases liabilities.
    c. Decreases assets and increases owner's equity.
    d. Decreases assets and decreases liabilities.

(SO 8) **12.** Which of the following statements is *false*?
    a. A statement of cash flows summarizes information about the cash inflows (receipts) and outflows (payments) for a specific period of time.
    b. A balance sheet reports the assets, liabilities, and owner's equity at a specific date.
    c. An income statement presents the revenues, expenses, changes in owner's equity, and resulting net income or net loss for a specific period of time.
    d. An owner's equity statement summarizes the changes in owner's equity for a specific period of time.

13. On the last day of the period, Jim Otto Company buys a (SO 8) $900 machine on credit. This transaction will affect the:
    a. income statement only.
    b. balance sheet only.
    c. income statement and owner's equity statement only.
    d. income statement, owner's equity statement, and balance sheet.

14. The financial statement that reports assets, liabilities, and (SO 8) owner's equity is the:
    a. income statement.
    b. owner's equity statement.
    c. balance sheet.
    d. statement of cash flows.

***15.** Services provided by a public accountant include: (SO 9)
    a. auditing, taxation, and management consulting.
    b. auditing, budgeting, and management consulting.
    c. auditing, budgeting, and cost accounting.
    d. internal auditing, budgeting, and management consulting.

Go to the book's companion website, **www.wiley.com/college/weygandt**, for additional Self-Test Questions.

Questions

1. "Accounting is ingrained in our society and it is vital to our economic system." Do you agree? Explain.

2. Identify and describe the steps in the accounting process.

3. (a) Who are internal users of accounting data? (b) How does accounting provide relevant data to these users?

4. What uses of financial accounting information are made by (a) investors and (b) creditors?

5. "Bookkeeping and accounting are the same." Do you agree? Explain.

6. Eve Myles Travel Agency purchased land for $90,000 cash on December 10, 2012. At December 31, 2012, the land's value has increased to $93,000. What amount should be reported for land on Eve Myles's balance sheet at December 31, 2012? Explain.

7. What is the monetary unit assumption?

8. What is the economic entity assumption?

9. What are the three basic forms of business organizations for profit-oriented enterprises?

10. Maria Contreras is the owner of a successful printing shop. Recently, her business has been increasing, and Maria has been thinking about changing the organization of her business from a proprietorship to a corporation. Discuss some of the advantages Maria would enjoy if she were to incorporate her business.

11. What is the basic accounting equation?

12. (a) Define the terms assets, liabilities, and owner's equity.
    (b) What items affect owner's equity?

13. Which of the following items are liabilities of Karl Jewelry Stores?
    (a) Cash.   (d) Accounts receivable.
    (b) Accounts payable.   (e) Supplies.
    (c) Owner's drawings.   (f) Equipment.

    (g) Salaries and wages payable.
    (h) Service revenue.
    (i) Rent expense.

14. Can a business enter into a transaction in which only the left side of the basic accounting equation is affected? If so, give an example.

15. Are the following events recorded in the accounting records? Explain your answer in each case.
    (a) The owner of the company dies.
    (b) Supplies are purchased on account.
    (c) An employee is fired.
    (d) The owner of the business withdraws cash from the business for personal use.

16. Indicate how the following business transactions affect the basic accounting equation.
    (a) Paid cash for janitorial services.
    (b) Purchased equipment for cash.
    (c) Invested cash in the business.
    (d) Paid accounts payable in full.

17. Listed below are some items found in the financial statements of Dave Ramsey Co. Indicate in which financial statement(s) the following items would appear.
    (a) Service revenue.   (d) Accounts receivable.
    (b) Equipment.   (e) Owner's capital.
    (c) Advertising expense.   (f) Salaries and wages payable.

18. In February 2012, Betty King invested an additional $10,000 in her business, King's Pharmacy, which is organized as a proprietorship. King's accountant, Leroy James, recorded this receipt as an increase in cash and revenues. Is this treatment appropriate? Why or why not?

19. "A company's net income appears directly on the income statement and the owner's equity statement, and it is included indirectly in the company's balance sheet." Do you agree? Explain.

20. Torchwood Enterprises had a capital balance of $168,000 at the beginning of the period. At the end of the accounting period, the capital balance was $198,000.
    (a) Assuming no additional investment or withdrawals during the period, what is the net income for the period?
    (b) Assuming an additional investment of $13,000 but no withdrawals during the period, what is the net income for the period?

21. Summarized operations for J. R. Ewing Co. for the month of July are as follows.

Revenues earned: for cash $20,000; on account $70,000.
Expenses incurred: for cash $26,000; on account $40,000.
Indicate for J. R. Ewing Co. (a) the total revenues, (b) the total expenses, and (c) net income for the month of July.

22. The basic accounting equation is: Assets = Liabilities + Owner's Equity. Replacing the words in that equation with dollar amounts, what is Coca-Cola's accounting equation at December 31, 2009? (*Hint:* Owner's equity is equivalent to shareowners' equity.)

The Navigator

Brief Exercises

BE1-1 Presented below is the basic accounting equation. Determine the missing amounts.

Use basic accounting equation. (SO 6)

Assets	=	Liabilities	+	Owner's Equity
(a) $90,000		$50,000		?
(b) ?		$40,000		$70,000
(c) $94,000		?		$53,000

BE1-2 Given the accounting equation, answer each of the following questions.

Use basic accounting equation. (SO 6)

(a) The liabilities of Buerhle Company are $120,000 and the owner's equity is $232,000. What is the amount of Buerhle Company's total assets?
(b) The total assets of Buerhle Company are $190,000 and its owner's equity is $91,000. What is the amount of its total liabilities?
(c) The total assets of Buerhle Company are $800,000 and its liabilities are equal to one half of its total assets. What is the amount of Buerhle Company's owner's equity?

BE1-3 At the beginning of the year, Danks Company had total assets of $800,000 and total liabilities of $300,000. Answer the following questions.

Use basic accounting equation. (SO 6)

(a) If total assets increased $150,000 during the year and total liabilities decreased $80,000, what is the amount of owner's equity at the end of the year?
(b) During the year, total liabilities increased $100,000 and owner's equity decreased $70,000. What is the amount of total assets at the end of the year?
(c) If total assets decreased $80,000 and owner's equity increased $120,000 during the year, what is the amount of total liabilities at the end of the year?

BE1-4 Use the expanded accounting equation to answer each of the following questions.

Solve expanded accounting equation. (SO 6)

(a) The liabilities of Falk Company are $90,000. Owner's capital account is $150,000; drawings are $40,000; revenues, $450,000; and expenses, $320,000. What is the amount of Falk Company's total assets?
(b) The total assets of Pierogi Company are $57,000. Owner's capital account is $25,000; drawings are $7,000; revenues, $52,000; and expenses, $35,000. What is the amount of the company's total liabilities?
(c) The total assets of Yanko Co. are $600,000 and its liabilities are equal to two-thirds of its total assets. What is the amount of Yanko Co.'s owner's equity?

BE1-5 Indicate whether each of the following items is an asset (A), liability (L), or part of owner's equity (OE).

Identify assets, liabilities, and owner's equity. (SO 6)

_____(a) Accounts receivable
_____(b) Salaries and wages payable
_____(c) Equipment
_____(d) Supplies
_____(e) Owner's capital
_____(f) Notes payable

BE1-6 Presented below are three business transactions. On a sheet of paper, list the letters (a), (b), and (c) with columns for assets, liabilities, and owner's equity. For each column, indicate whether the transactions increased (+), decreased (−), or had no effect (NE) on assets, liabilities, and owner's equity.

Determine effect of transactions on basic accounting equation. (SO 7)

(a) Purchased supplies on account.
(b) Received cash for providing a service.
(c) Paid expenses in cash.

Determine effect of transactions on basic accounting equation.
(SO 7)

BE1-7 Follow the same format as BE1-6 on the previous page. Determine the effect on assets, liabilities, and owner's equity of the following three transactions.

(a) Invested cash in the business.
(b) Withdrawal of cash by owner.
(c) Received cash from a customer who had previously been billed for services provided.

Classify items affecting owner's equity.
(SO 7)

BE1-8 Classify each of the following items as owner's drawings (D), revenue (R), or expense (E).

_____**(a)** Advertising expense   _____**(e)** Owner's drawings
_____**(b)** Service revenue   _____**(f)** Rent revenue
_____**(c)** Insurance expense   _____**(g)** Utilities expense
_____**(d)** Salaries and wages expense

Determine effect of transactions on basic owner's equity.
(SO 7)

BE1-9 Presented below are three transactions. Mark each transaction as affecting owner's investment (I), owner's drawings (D), revenue (R), expense (E), or not affecting owner's equity (NOE).

_____**(a)** Received cash for services performed
_____**(b)** Paid cash to purchase equipment
_____**(c)** Paid employee salaries

Prepare a balance sheet.
(SO 8)

BE1-10 In alphabetical order below are balance sheet items for George Company at December 31, 2012. Kayla George is the owner of George Company. Prepare a balance sheet, following the format of Illustration 1-9.

Accounts payable	$90,000
Accounts receivable	$72,500
Cash	$49,000
Owner's capital	$31,500

Determine where items appear on financial statements.
(SO 8)

BE1-11 Indicate whether the following items would appear on the income statement (IS), balance sheet (BS), or owner's equity statement (OE).

_____**(a)** Notes payable   _____**(d)** Cash
_____**(b)** Advertising expense   _____**(e)** Service revenue
_____**(c)** Owner's capital

Do it! Review

Review basic concepts.
(SO 1, 2, 4)

Do it! 1-1 Indicate whether each of the five statements presented below is true or false.

1. The three steps in the accounting process are identification, recording, and examination.
2. The two most common types of external users are investors and creditors.
3. Congress passed the Sarbanes-Oxley Act of 2002 to ensure that investors invest only in companies that will be profitable.
4. The primary accounting standard-setting body in the United States is the Securities and Exchange Commission (SEC).
5. The cost principle dictates that companies record assets at their cost and continue to report them at their cost over the time the asset is held.

Evaluate effects of transactions on owner's equity.
(SO 6)

Do it! 1-2 Classify the following items as investment by owner (I), owner's drawings (D), revenues (R), or expenses (E). Then indicate whether each item increases or decreases owner's equity.

(1) Drawings   (3) Advertising Expense
(2) Rent Revenue   (4) Owner puts personal assets into the business

Prepare tabular analysis.
(SO 7)

Do it! 1-3 Transactions made by Orlando Bloom and Co., a law firm, for the month of March are shown below. Prepare a tabular analysis which shows the effects of these transactions on the expanded accounting equation, similar to that shown in Illustration 1-8.

1. The company provided $20,000 of services for customers, on credit.
2. The company received $20,000 in cash from customers who had been billed for services [in transaction (1)].
3. The company received a bill for $2,300 of advertising, but will not pay it until a later date.
4. Orlando Bloom withdrew $3,600 cash from the business for personal use.

Do it! 1-4 Presented below is selected information related to Lance Company at December 31, 2012. Lance reports financial information monthly.

Calculate effects of transactions on financial statement items.
(SO 8)

Accounts Payable	$ 3,000	Salaries and Wages Expense	$16,500
Cash	4,500	Notes Payable	25,000
Advertising Expense	6,000	Rent Expense	10,500
Service Revenue	51,500	Accounts Receivable	13,500
Equipment	29,000	Owner's Drawings	7,500

(a) Determine the total assets of Lance Company at December 31, 2012.
(b) Determine the net income that Lance Company reported for December 2012.
(c) Determine the owner's equity of Lance Company at December 31, 2012.

Exercises

E1-1 Jenks Company performs the following accounting tasks during the year.

Classify the three activities of accounting.
(SO 1)

_____Analyzing and interpreting information.
_____Classifying economic events.
_____Explaining uses, meaning, and limitations of data.
_____Keeping a systematic chronological diary of events.
_____Measuring events in dollars and cents.
_____Preparing accounting reports.
_____Reporting information in a standard format.
_____Selecting economic activities relevant to the company.
_____Summarizing economic events.

Accounting is "an information system that **identifies**, **records**, and **communicates** the economic events of an organization to interested users."

Instructions
Categorize the accounting tasks performed by Jenks as relating to either the identification (I), recording (R), or communication (C) aspects of accounting.

E1-2 (a) The following are users of financial statements.

Identify users of accounting information.
(SO 2)

_____Customers
_____Internal Revenue Service
_____Labor unions
_____Marketing manager
_____Production supervisor

_____Securities and Exchange Commission
_____Store manager
_____Suppliers
_____Vice president of finance

Instructions
Identify the users as being either **external users** or **internal users**.

(b) The following questions could be asked by an internal user or an external user.

_____Can we afford to give our employees a pay raise?
_____Did the company earn a satisfactory income?
_____Do we need to borrow in the near future?
_____How does the company's profitability compare to other companies?
_____What does it cost us to manufacture each unit produced?
_____Which product should we emphasize?
_____Will the company be able to pay its short-term debts?

Instructions
Identify each of the questions as being more likely asked by an **internal user** or an **external user**.

E1-3 Lovie Smith, president of Smith Company, has instructed Michelle Martz, the head of the accounting department for Smith Company, to report the company's land in the company's accounting reports at its fair value of $170,000 instead of its cost of $100,000. Smith says, "Showing the land at $170,000 will make our company look like a better investment when we try to attract new investors next month."

Discuss ethics and the cost principle.
(SO 3)

Instructions
Explain the ethical situation involved for Michelle Martz, identifying the stakeholders and the alternatives.

Use accounting concepts.
(SO 4, 5)

E1-4 The following situations involve accounting principles and assumptions.

1. Rex Company owns buildings that are worth substantially more than they originally cost. In an effort to provide more relevant information, Rex reports the buildings at fair value in its accounting reports.
2. Levi Company includes in its accounting records only transaction data that can be expressed in terms of money.
3. Josh Borke, owner of Josh's Photography, records his personal living costs as expenses of the business.

Instructions
For each of the three situations, say if the accounting method used is correct or incorrect. If correct, identify which principle or assumption supports the method used. If incorrect, identify which principle or assumption has been violated.

Classify accounts as assets,
liabilities, and owner's equity.
(SO 6)

E1-5 Garcia Cleaners has the following balance sheet items.

Accounts payable	Accounts receivable
Cash	Notes payable
Equipment	Salaries and wages payable
Supplies	Owner's capital

Instructions
Classify each item as an asset, liability, or owner's equity.

Analyze the effect of
transactions.
(SO 6, 7)

E1-6 Selected transactions for Linebrink Lawn Care Company are listed below.

1. Made cash investment to start business.
2. Paid monthly rent.
3. Purchased equipment on account.
4. Billed customers for services performed.
5. Withdrew cash for owner's personal use.
6. Received cash from customers billed in (4).
7. Incurred advertising expense on account.
8. Purchased additional equipment for cash.
9. Received cash from customers when service was performed.

Instructions
List the numbers of the above transactions and describe the effect of each transaction on assets, liabilities, and owner's equity. For example, the first answer is: (1) Increase in assets and increase in owner's equity.

Analyze the effect of transac-
tions on assets, liabilities, and
owner's equity.
(SO 6, 7)

E1-7 Thornton Computer Timeshare Company entered into the following transactions during May 2012.

1. Purchased computer terminals for $20,000 from Digital Equipment on account.
2. Paid $4,000 cash for May rent on storage space.
3. Received $17,000 cash from customers for contracts billed in April.
4. Provided computer services to Fisher Construction Company for $3,000 cash.
5. Paid Northern States Power Co. $11,000 cash for energy usage in May.
6. Thornton invested an additional $29,000 in the business.
7. Paid Digital Equipment for the terminals purchased in (1) above.
8. Incurred advertising expense for May of $1,200 on account.

Instructions
Indicate with the appropriate letter whether each of the transactions above results in:

(a) An increase in assets and a decrease in assets.
(b) An increase in assets and an increase in owner's equity.
(c) An increase in assets and an increase in liabilities.
(d) A decrease in assets and a decrease in owner's equity.
(e) A decrease in assets and a decrease in liabilities.
(f) An increase in liabilities and a decrease in owner's equity.
(g) An increase in owner's equity and a decrease in liabilities.

E1-8 An analysis of the transactions made by Mark Kotsay & Co., a certified public accounting firm, for the month of August is shown below. The expenses were $650 for rent, $4,800 for salaries and wages, and $500 for utilities.

Analyze transactions and compute net income.
(SO 7)

	Cash	+	Accounts Receivable	+	Supplies	+	Equipment	=	Accounts Payable	+	Owner's Capital	−	Owner's Drawings	+	Revenues	−	Expenses
1.	+$15,000										+$15,000						
2.	−2,000						+$5,000		+$3,000								
3.	−750				+$750												
4.	+4,600		+$3,900												+$8,500		
5.	−1,500								−1,500								
6.	−2,000												−$2,000				
7.	−650																−$650
8.	+450		−450														
9.	−4,800																−4,800
10.									+500								−500

Instructions
(a) Describe each transaction that occurred for the month.
(b) Determine how much owner's equity increased for the month.
(c) Compute the amount of net income for the month.

E1-9 An analysis of transactions for Mark Kotsay & Co. was presented in E1–8.

Prepare financial statements.
(SO 8)

Instructions
Prepare an income statement and an owner's equity statement for August and a balance sheet at August 31, 2012.

E1-10 Andruw Company had the following assets and liabilities on the dates indicated.

Determine net income (or loss).
(SO 7)

December 31	Total Assets	Total Liabilities
2011	$400,000	$250,000
2012	$460,000	$300,000
2013	$590,000	$400,000

Andruw began business on January 1, 2011, with an investment of $100,000.

Instructions
From an analysis of the change in owner's equity during the year, compute the net income (or loss) for:
(a) 2011, assuming Andruw's drawings were $15,000 for the year.
(b) 2012, assuming Andruw made an additional investment of $45,000 and had no drawings in 2012.
(c) 2013, assuming Andruw made an additional investment of $15,000 and had drawings of $25,000 in 2013.

E1-11 Two items are omitted from each of the following summaries of balance sheet and income statement data for two proprietorships for the year 2012, Gavin's Goods and Floyd Enterprises.

Analyze financial statements items.
(SO 6, 7)

	Gavin's Goods	Floyd Enterprises
Beginning of year:		
Total assets	$110,000	$129,000
Total liabilities	85,000	(c)
Total owner's equity	(a)	80,000
End of year:		
Total assets	160,000	180,000
Total liabilities	120,000	50,000
Total owner's equity	40,000	130,000
Changes during year in owner's equity:		
Additional investment	(b)	25,000
Drawings	29,000	(d)
Total revenues	215,000	100,000
Total expenses	175,000	60,000

Instructions
Determine the missing amounts.

Prepare income statement and owner's equity statement.
(SO 8)

E1-12 The following information relates to Jake Peavy Co. for the year 2012.

Owner's capital, January 1, 2012	$48,000	Advertising expense	$ 1,800
Owner's drawings during 2012	6,000	Rent expense	10,400
Service revenue	63,600	Utilities expense	3,100
Salaries and wages expense	29,500		

Instructions

After analyzing the data, prepare an income statement and an owner's equity statement for the year ending December 31, 2012.

Correct an incorrectly prepared balance sheet.
(SO 8)

E1-13 Linda Puff is the bookkeeper for Sajuki Company. Linda has been trying to get the balance sheet of Sajuki Company to balance. Sajuki's balance sheet is shown below.

SAJUKI COMPANY
Balance Sheet
December 31, 2012

Assets		Liabilities	
Cash	$15,000	Accounts payable	$21,000
Supplies	8,000	Accounts receivable	(9,500)
Equipment	46,000	Owner's capital	67,500
Owner's drawings	10,000	Total liabilities and	
Total assets	$79,000	owner's equity	$79,000

Instructions

Prepare a correct balance sheet.

Compute net income and prepare a balance sheet.
(SO 8)

E1-14 Toni Pena is the sole owner of Deer Park, a public camping ground near the Lake Mead National Recreation Area. Toni has compiled the following financial information as of December 31, 2012.

Revenues during 2012—camping fees	$140,000	Fair value of equipment	$140,000
Revenues during 2012—general store	65,000	Notes payable	60,000
Accounts payable	11,000	Expenses during 2012	150,000
Cash on hand	23,000	Supplies on hand	17,500
Original cost of equipment	105,500		

Instructions

(a) Determine Toni Pena's net income from Deer Park for 2012.
(b) Prepare a balance sheet for Deer Park as of December 31, 2012.

Prepare an income statement.
(SO 8)

E1-15 Presented below is financial information related to the 2012 operations of J. J. Putz Cruise Company.

Maintenance and repairs expense	$ 95,000
Supplies expense	10,000
Salaries and wages expense	142,000
Advertising expense	24,500
Ticket revenue	410,000

Instructions

Prepare the 2012 income statement for J. J. Putz Cruise Company.

Prepare an owner's equity statement.
(SO 8)

E1-16 Presented below is information related to the sole proprietorship of Sergio Santos attorney.

Legal service revenue—2012	$335,000
Total expenses—2012	211,000
Assets, January 1, 2012	96,000
Liabilities, January 1, 2012	62,000
Assets, December 31, 2012	168,000
Liabilities, December 31, 2012	100,000
Drawings—2012	?

Instructions

Prepare the 2012 owner's equity statement for Sergio Santos' legal practice.

Exercises: Set B

Visit the book's companion website, at **www.wiley.com/college/weygandt**, and choose the Student Companion site to access Exercise Set B.

Problems: Set A

P1-1A   Threet's Repair Shop was started on May 1 by Erica Threet. A summary of May transactions is presented below.

Analyze transactions and compute net income.
(SO 6, 7)

1. Invested $10,000 cash to start the repair shop.
2. Purchased equipment for $5,000 cash.
3. Paid $400 cash for May office rent.
4. Paid $500 cash for supplies.
5. Incurred $250 of advertising costs in the *Beacon News* on account.
6. Received $6,100 in cash from customers for repair service.
7. Withdrew $1,000 cash for personal use.
8. Paid part-time employee salaries $2,000.
9. Paid utility bills $170.
10. Provided repair service on account to customers $750.
11. Collected cash of $120 for services billed in transaction (10).

Instructions
(a) Prepare a tabular analysis of the transactions, using the following column headings: Cash, Accounts Receivable, Supplies, Equipment, Accounts Payable, Owner's Capital, Owner's Drawings, Revenues, and Expenses.

(a) Total assets $13,280

(b) From an analysis of the owner's equity columns, compute the net income or net loss for May.

(b) Net income $4,030

P1-2A   Ramona Castro opened a veterinary business in Nashville, Tennessee, on August 1. On August 31, the balance sheet showed Cash $9,000, Accounts Receivable $1,700, Supplies $600, Equipment $6,000, Accounts Payable $3,600, and Owner's Capital $13,700. During September, the following transactions occurred.

Analyze transactions and prepare income statement, owner's equity statement, and balance sheet.
(SO 6, 7, 8)

1. Paid $2,900 cash on accounts payable.
2. Collected $1,300 of accounts receivable.
3. Purchased additional office equipment for $2,100, paying $800 in cash and the balance on account.
4. Earned revenue of $7,800, of which $2,500 is received in cash and the balance is due in October.
5. Withdrew $1,100 cash for personal use.
6. Paid salaries $1,700, rent for September $900, and advertising expense $450.
7. Incurred utilities expense for month on account $170.
8. Received $10,000 from Capital Bank (money borrowed on a note payable).

Instructions
(a) Prepare a tabular analysis of the September transactions beginning with August 31 balances. The column headings should be as follows: Cash + Accounts Receivable + Supplies + Equipment = Notes Payable + Accounts Payable + Owner's Capital − Owner's Drawings + Revenues − Expenses.

(a) Total assets $29,350

(b) Prepare an income statement for September, an owner's equity statement for September, and a balance sheet at September 30.

(b) Net income $4,580
Ending capital $17,180

P1-3A   On May 1, A. J. Pierzynski started AJ Flying School, a company that provides flying lessons, by investing $40,000 cash in the business. Following are the assets and liabilities of the company on May 31, 2012, and the revenues and expenses for the month of May.

Prepare income statement, owner's equity statement, and balance sheet.
(SO 8)

Cash	$ 3,400	Notes Payable	$30,000
Accounts Receivable	4,900	Rent Expense	1,200
Equipment	64,000	Maintenance and Repairs Expense	400
Service Revenue	8,100	Gasoline Expense	2,500
Advertising Expense	600	Insurance Expense	400
		Accounts Payable	800

A. J. Pierzynski made no additional investment in May, but he withdrew $1,500 in cash for personal use.

Instructions
(a) Prepare an income statement and owner's equity statement for the month of May and a balance sheet at May 31.
(b) Prepare an income statement and owner's equity statement for May assuming the following data are not included above: (1) $900 of revenue was earned and billed but not collected at May 31, and (2) $1,500 of gasoline expense was incurred but not paid.

(a) Net income $3,000
  Owner's equity $41,500
  Total assets $72,300
(b) Net income $2,400
  Owner's equity $40,900

Analyze transactions and prepare financial statements.
(SO 6, 7, 8)

P1-4A Gordon Beckham started his own delivery service, Beckham Deliveries, on June 1, 2012. The following transactions occurred during the month of June.

June 1 Gordon invested $10,000 cash in the business.
  2 Purchased a used van for deliveries for $12,000. Gordon paid $2,000 cash and signed a note payable for the remaining balance.
  3 Paid $500 for office rent for the month.
  5 Performed $4,400 of services on account.
  9 Withdrew $200 cash for personal use.
  12 Purchased supplies for $150 on account.
  15 Received a cash payment of $1,250 for services provided on June 5.
  17 Purchased gasoline for $200 on account.
  20 Received a cash payment of $1,300 for services provided.
  23 Made a cash payment of $600 on the note payable.
  26 Paid $250 for utilities.
  29 Paid for the gasoline purchased on account on June 17.
  30 Paid $1,000 for employee salaries.

Instructions

(a) Total assets $23,100

(a) Show the effects of the previous transactions on the accounting equation using the following format.

	Assets				Liabilities		Owner's Equity			
Date	Cash +	Accounts Receivable +	Supplies +	Equipment =	Notes Payable +	Accounts Payable +	Owner's Capital −	Owner's Drawings +	Revenues −	Expenses

(b) Net income $3,750
(c) Cash $7,800

(b) Prepare an income statement for the month of June.
(c) Prepare a balance sheet at June 30, 2012.

Determine financial statement amounts and prepare owner's equity statement.
(SO 7, 8)

P1-5A Financial statement information about four different companies is as follows.

	Alexei Company	Ramirez Company	Dayan Company	Viciedo Company
January 1, 2012				
Assets	$ 95,000	$110,000	(g)	$170,000
Liabilities	50,000	(d)	75,000	(j)
Owner's equity	(a)	60,000	45,000	90,000
December 31, 2012				
Assets	(b)	141,000	200,000	(k)
Liabilities	55,000	75,000	(h)	80,000
Owner's equity	63,000	(e)	130,000	162,000
Owner's equity changes in year				
Additional investment	(c)	15,000	10,000	15,000
Drawings	25,000	(f)	14,000	20,000
Total revenues	350,000	420,000	(i)	520,000
Total expenses	320,000	385,000	342,000	(l)

Instructions
(a) Determine the missing amounts. (*Hint:* For example, to solve for (a), Assets − Liabilities = Owner's equity = $45,000.)
(b) Prepare the owner's equity statement for Ramirez Company.
(c) ━━━▶ Write a memorandum explaining the sequence for preparing financial statements and the interrelationship of the owner's equity statement to the income statement and balance sheet.

Problems: Set B

P1-1B On April 1, Vince Morelli established Vince's Travel Agency. The following transactions were completed during the month.

Analyze transactions and compute net income.

(SO 6, 7)

1. Invested $15,000 cash to start the agency.
2. Paid $600 cash for April office rent.
3. Purchased office equipment for $3,000 cash.
4. Incurred $700 of advertising costs in the *Chicago Tribune*, on account.
5. Paid $800 cash for office supplies.
6. Earned $10,000 for services rendered: $3,000 cash is received from customers, and the balance of $7,000 is billed to customers on account.
7. Withdrew $500 cash for personal use.
8. Paid *Chicago Tribune* $500 of the amount due in transaction (4).
9. Paid employees' salaries $2,500.
10. Received $4,000 in cash from customers who have previously been billed in transaction (6).

Instructions
(a) Prepare a tabular analysis of the transactions using the following column headings: Cash, Accounts Receivable, Supplies, Equipment, Accounts Payable, Owner's Capital, Owner's Drawings, Revenues, and Expenses.
(b) From an analysis of the owner's equity columns, compute the net income or net loss for April.

(a) Total assets $20,900

(b) Net income $6,200

P1-2B Juanita Pierre opened a law office, on July 1, 2012. On July 31, the balance sheet showed Cash $5,000, Accounts Receivable $1,500, Supplies $500, Equipment $6,000, Accounts Payable $4,200, and Owner's Capital $8,800. During August, the following transactions occurred.

Analyze transactions and prepare income statement, owner's equity statement, and balance sheet.

(SO 6, 7, 8)

1. Collected $1,200 of accounts receivable.
2. Paid $2,800 cash on accounts payable.
3. Earned revenue of $7,500 of which $3,000 is collected in cash and the balance is due in September.
4. Purchased additional office equipment for $2,000, paying $400 in cash and the balance on account.
5. Paid salaries $2,500, rent for August $900, and advertising expenses $400.
6. Withdrew $700 in cash for personal use.
7. Received $2,000 from Standard Federal Bank—money borrowed on a note payable.
8. Incurred utility expenses for month on account $270.

Instructions
(a) Prepare a tabular analysis of the August transactions beginning with July 31 balances. The column headings should be as follows: Cash + Accounts Receivable + Supplies + Equipment = Notes Payable + Accounts Payable + Owner's Capital − Owner's Drawings + Revenues − Expenses.
(b) Prepare an income statement for August, an owner's equity statement for August, and a balance sheet at August 31.

(a) Total assets $16,800

(b) Net income $3,430
    Ending capital $11,530

P1-3B On June 1, Alexia Rios started Crazy Creations Co., a company that provides craft opportunities, by investing $12,000 cash in the business. Following are the assets and liabilities of the company at June 30 and the revenues and expenses for the month of June.

Prepare income statement, owner's equity statement, and balance sheet.

(SO 8)

Cash	$10,150	Notes Payable	$9,000
Accounts Receivable	3,000	Accounts Payable	1,200
Service Revenue	6,700	Supplies Expense	1,600
Supplies	2,000	Gasoline Expense	200
Advertising Expense	500	Utilities Expense	150
Equipment	10,000		

Alexia made no additional investment in June but withdrew $1,300 in cash for personal use during the month.

Instructions
(a) Prepare an income statement and owner's equity statement for the month of June and a balance sheet at June 30, 2012.
(b) Prepare an income statement and owner's equity statement for June assuming the following data are not included above: (1) $900 of revenue was earned and billed but not collected at June 30, and (2) $150 of gasoline expense was incurred but not paid.

(a) Net income $4,250
    Owner's equity $14,950
    Total assets $25,150
(b) Net income $5,000
    Owner's equity $15,700

Analyze transactions and prepare financial statements.

(SO 6, 7, 8)

P1-4B   Carla Quentin started her own consulting firm, Quentin Consulting, on May 1, 2012. The following transactions occurred during the month of May.

May 1   Carla invested $7,000 cash in the business.
  2   Paid $900 for office rent for the month.
  3   Purchased $600 of supplies on account.
  5   Paid $125 to advertise in the *County News*.
  9   Received $4,000 cash for services provided.
  12   Withdrew $1,000 cash for personal use.
  15   Performed $5,400 of services on account.
  17   Paid $2,500 for employee salaries.
  20   Paid for the supplies purchased on account on May 3.
  23   Received a cash payment of $4,000 for services provided on account on May 15.
  26   Borrowed $5,000 from the bank on a note payable.
  29   Purchased office equipment for $4,200 on account.
  30   Paid $275 for utilities.

Instructions

(a) Total assets $20,800

(a) Show the effects of the previous transactions on the accounting equation using the following format.

		Assets				Liabilities		Owner's Equity				
Date	Cash +	Accounts Receivable +	Supplies +	Equipment =	Notes Payable +	Accounts Payable +	Owner's Capital −	Owner's Drawings +	Revenues −	Expenses

(b) Net income $5,600
(c) Cash $14,600

(b) Prepare an income statement for the month of May.
(c) Prepare a balance sheet at May 31, 2012.

Determine financial statement amounts and prepare owner's equity statement.

(SO 7, 8)

P1-5B   Financial statement information about four different companies is as follows.

	Brent Company	Lillibridge Company	Omar Company	Vizquel Company
January 1, 2012				
Assets	$ 80,000	$ 90,000	(g)	$150,000
Liabilities	48,000	(d)	80,000	(j)
Owner's equity	(a)	40,000	49,000	90,000
December 31, 2012				
Assets	(b)	112,000	180,000	(k)
Liabilities	60,000	72,000	(h)	100,000
Owner's equity	50,000	(e)	82,000	151,000
Owner's equity changes in year				
Additional investment	(c)	8,000	10,000	15,000
Drawings	15,000	(f)	12,000	10,000
Total revenues	350,000	410,000	(i)	500,000
Total expenses	333,000	385,000	350,000	(l)

Instructions

(a) Determine the missing amounts. (*Hint:* For example, to solve for (a), Assets − Liabilities = Owner's equity = $32,000.)
(b) Prepare the owner's equity statement for Brent Company.
(c) ◀━━━━ Write a memorandum explaining the sequence for preparing financial statements and the interrelationship of the owner's equity statement to the income statement and balance sheet.

Problems: Set C

Visit the book's companion website, at **www.wiley.com/college/weygandt**, and choose the Student Companion site to access Problem Set C.

Continuing Cookie Chronicle

CCC1 Natalie Koebel spent much of her childhood learning the art of cookie-making from her grandmother. They passed many happy hours mastering every type of cookie imaginable and later creating new recipes that were both healthy and delicious. Now at the start of her second year in college, Natalie is investigating various possibilities for starting her own business as part of the requirements of the entrepreneurship program in which she is enrolled.

*The **Continuing Cookie Chronicle** starts in this chapter and continues in every chapter. You also can find this problem at the book's Student Companion site.*

A long-time friend insists that Natalie has to somehow include cookies in her business plan. After a series of brainstorming sessions, Natalie settles on the idea of operating a cookie-making school. She will start on a part-time basis and offer her services in people's homes. Now that she has started thinking about it, the possibilities seem endless. During the fall, she will concentrate on holiday cookies. She will offer individual lessons and group sessions (which will probably be more entertainment than education for the participants). Natalie also decides to include children in her target market.

The first difficult decision is coming up with the perfect name for her business. In the end, she settles on "Cookie Creations" and then moves on to more important issues.

Instructions
(a) What form of business organization—proprietorship, partnership, or corporation—do you recommend that Natalie use for her business? Discuss the benefits and weaknesses of each form and give the reasons for your choice.
(b) Will Natalie need accounting information? If yes, what information will she need and why? How often will she need this information?
(c) Identify specific asset, liability, and owner's equity accounts that Cookie Creations will likely use to record its business transactions.
(d) Should Natalie open a separate bank account for the business? Why or why not?

BROADENING YOUR PERSPECTIVE

Financial Reporting and Analysis

Financial Reporting Problem: PepsiCo, Inc.

BYP1-1 The actual financial statements of PepsiCo, Inc., as presented in the company's 2009 annual report, are contained in Appendix A (at the back of the textbook).

Instructions
Refer to PepsiCo's financial statements and answer the following questions.
(a) What were PepsiCo's total assets at December 26, 2009? At December 27, 2008?
(b) How much cash (and cash equivalents) did PepsiCo have on December 26, 2009?
(c) What amount of accounts payable did PepsiCo report on December 26, 2009? On December 27, 2008?
(d) What were PepsiCo's net revenues in 2007? In 2008? In 2009?
(e) What is the amount of the change in PepsiCo's net income from 2008 to 2009?

Comparative Analysis Problem: PepsiCo, Inc. vs. The Coca-Cola Company

BYP1-2 PepsiCo's financial statements are presented in Appendix A. Financial statements of The Coca-Cola Company are presented in Appendix B.

Instructions
(a) Based on the information contained in these financial statements, determine the following for each company.
   (1) Total assets at December 26, 2009, for PepsiCo and for Coca-Cola at December 31, 2009.
   (2) Accounts (notes) receivable, net at December 26, 2009, for PepsiCo and at December 31, 2009, for Coca-Cola.

(3) Net revenues for year ended in 2009.

(4) Net income for year ended in 2009.

(b) What conclusions concerning the two companies can be drawn from these data?

On the Web

BYP1-3 This exercise will familiarize you with skill requirements, job descriptions, and salaries for accounting careers.

Address: www.careers-in-accounting.com, or go to **www.wiley.com/college/weygandt**

Instructions

Go to the site shown above. Answer the following questions.

(a) What are the three broad areas of accounting (from "Skills and Talents")?

(b) List eight skills required in accounting.

(c) How do the three accounting areas differ in terms of these eight required skills?

(d) Explain one of the key job options in accounting.

(e) What is the overall salary range for a junior staff accountant?

Critical Thinking

Decision Making Across the Organization

BYP1-4 Mary and Jack Gray, local golf stars, opened the Chip-Shot Driving Range on March 1, 2012, by investing $25,000 of their cash savings in the business. A caddy shack was constructed for cash at a cost of $8,000, and $800 was spent on golf balls and golf clubs. The Grays leased five acres of land at a cost of $1,000 per month and paid the first month's rent. During the first month, advertising costs totaled $750, of which $150 was unpaid at March 31, and $400 was paid to members of the high-school golf team for retrieving golf balls. All revenues from customers were deposited in the company's bank account. On March 15, Mary and Jack withdrew a total of $1,000 in cash for personal living expenses. A $100 utility bill was received on March 31 but was not paid. On March 31, the balance in the company's bank account was $18,900.

Mary and Jack thought they had a pretty good first month of operations. But, their estimates of profitability ranged from a loss of $6,100 to net income of $2,450.

Instructions

With the class divided into groups, answer the following.

(a) How could the Grays have concluded that the business operated at a loss of $6,100? Was this a valid basis on which to determine net income?

(b) How could the Grays have concluded that the business operated at a net income of $2,450? (*Hint:* Prepare a balance sheet at March 31.) Was this a valid basis on which to determine net income?

(c) Without preparing an income statement, determine the actual net income for March.

(d) What was the revenue earned in March?

Communication Activity

BYP1-5 Lynn Benedict, the bookkeeper for New York Company, has been trying to get the balance sheet to balance. The company's balance sheet is shown below.

New York Company
Balance Sheet
For the Month Ended December 31, 2012

Assets		Liabilities	
Equipment	$25,500	Owner's capital	$26,000
Cash	9,000	Accounts receivable	(6,000)
Supplies	2,000	Owner's drawings	(2,000)
Accounts payable	(8,000)	Notes payable	10,500
	$28,500		$28,500

Instructions

Explain to Lynn Benedict in a memo why the original balance sheet is incorrect, and what should be done to correct it.

Ethics Case

BYP1-6 After numerous campus interviews, Steve Baden, a senior at Great Northern College, received two office interview invitations from the Baltimore offices of two large firms. Both firms offered to cover his out-of-pocket expenses (travel, hotel, and meals). He scheduled the interviews for both firms on the same day, one in the morning and one in the afternoon. At the conclusion of each interview, he submitted to both firms his total out-of-pocket expenses for the trip to Baltimore: mileage $112 (280 miles at $0.40), hotel $130, meals $36, and parking and tolls $18, for a total of $296. He believes this approach is appropriate. If he had made two trips, his cost would have been two times $296. He is also certain that neither firm knew he had visited the other on that same trip. Within ten days, Steve received two checks in the mail, each in the amount of $296.

Instructions

(a) Who are the stakeholders (affected parties) in this situation?

(b) What are the ethical issues in this case?

(c) What would you do in this situation?

"All About You" Activity

BYP1-7 Some people are tempted to make their finances look worse to get financial aid. Companies sometimes also manage their financial numbers in order to accomplish certain goals. Earnings management is the planned timing of revenues, expenses, gains, and losses to smooth out bumps in net income. In managing earnings, companies' actions vary from being within the range of ethical activity, to being both unethical and illegal attempts to mislead investors and creditors.

Instructions

Provide responses for each of the following questions.

(a) Discuss whether you think each of the following actions (adapted from *www.finaid.org/fafsa/ maximize.phtml*) to increase the chances of receiving financial aid is ethical.

  (i) Spend down the student's assets and income first, before spending parents' assets and income.

  (ii) Accelerate necessary expenses to reduce available cash. For example, if you need a new car, buy it before applying for financial aid.

  (iii) State that a truly financially dependent child is independent.

  (iv) Have a parent take an unpaid leave of absence for long enough to get below the "threshold" level of income.

(b) What are some reasons why a *company* might want to overstate its earnings?

(c) What are some reasons why a *company* might want to understate its earnings?

(d) Under what circumstances might an otherwise ethical person decide to illegally overstate or understate earnings?

FASB Codification Activity

BYP1-8 The FASB has developed the Financial Accounting Standards Board Accounting Standards Codification (or more simply "the Codification"). The FASB's primary goal in developing the Codification is to provide in one place all the authoritative literature related to a particular topic. To provide easy access to the Codification, the FASB also developed the Financial Accounting Standards Board Codification Research System (CRS). CRS is an online, real-time database that provides easy access to the Codification. The Codification and the related CRS provide a topically organized structure, subdivided into topic, subtopics, sections, and paragraphs, using a numerical index system.

You may find this system useful in your present and future studies, and so we have provided an opportunity to use this online system as part of the *Broadening Your Perspective* section.

Instructions

Academic access to the FASB Codification is available through university subscriptions, obtained from the American Accounting Association (at *http://aaahq.org/FASB/Access.cfm*), for an annual fee of $150. This subscription covers an unlimited number of students within a single institution. Once this access has been obtained by your school, you should log in (at *http://aaahq.org/ascLogin.cfm*) and familiarize yourself with the resources that are accessible at the FASB Codification site.

Answers to Insight and Accounting Across the Organization Questions

p. 6 The Scoop on Accounting   Q: What are the benefits to the company and to the employees of making the financial statements available to all employees? **A:** If employees can read and use financial reports, a company will benefit in the following ways. The *marketing department* will make better decisions about products to offer and prices to charge. The *finance department* will make better decisions about debt and equity financing and how much to distribute in dividends. The *production department* will make better decisions about when to buy new equipment and how much inventory to produce. The *human resources department* will be better able to determine whether employees can be given raises. Finally, *all employees* will be better informed about the basis on which they are evaluated, which will increase employee morale.

p. 8 The Numbers Behind Not-for-Profit Organizations   Q: What benefits does a sound accounting system provide to a not-for-profit organization? **A:** Accounting provides at least two benefits to not-for-profit organizations. First, it helps to ensure that money is used in the way that donors intended. Second, it assures donors that their money is not going to waste and thus increases the likelihood of future donations.

p. 10 The Korean Discount   Q: What is meant by the phrase "make the country's businesses more transparent"? Why would increasing transparency spur economic growth? **A:** Transparency refers to the extent to which outsiders have knowledge regarding a company's financial performance and financial position. If a company lacks transparency, its financial reports do not adequately inform investors of critical information that is needed to make investment decisions. If corporate transparency is increased, investors will be more willing to supply the financial capital that businesses need in order to grow, which would spur the country's economic growth.

p. 12 Spinning the Career Wheel   Q: How might accounting help you? **A:** You will need to understand financial reports in any enterprise with which you are associated. Whether you become a manager, a doctor, a lawyer, a social worker, a teacher, an engineer, an architect, or an entrepreneur, a working knowledge of accounting is relevant.

Answers to Self-Test Questions

1. b **2.** d **3.** c **4.** b **5.** b **6.** d **7.** b **8.** a ($3,500 − $2,000) **9.** b **10.** a ($90,000 − $50,000) **11.** d **12.** c **13.** b **14.** c *15. a

IFRS A Look at IFRS

Most agree that there is a need for one set of international accounting standards. Here is why:

Multinational corporations. Today's companies view the entire world as their market. For example, Coca-Cola, Intel, and McDonald's generate more than 50% of their sales outside the United States, and many foreign companies, such as Toyota, Nestlé, and Sony, find their largest market to be the United States.

Mergers and acquisitions. The mergers between Fiat/Chrysler and Vodafone/Mannesmann suggest that we will see even more such business combinations in the future.

Information technology. As communication barriers continue to topple through advances in technology, companies and individuals in different countries and markets are becoming more comfortable buying and selling goods and services from one another.

Financial markets. Financial markets are of international significance today. Whether it is currency, equity securities (stocks), bonds, or derivatives, there are active markets throughout the world trading these types of instruments.

Key Points

- International standards are referred to as *International Financial Reporting Standards (IFRS)*, developed by the International Accounting Standards Board (IASB).

- Recent events in the global capital markets have underscored the importance of financial disclosure and transparency not only in the United States but in markets around the world. As a result, many are examining which accounting and financial disclosure rules should be

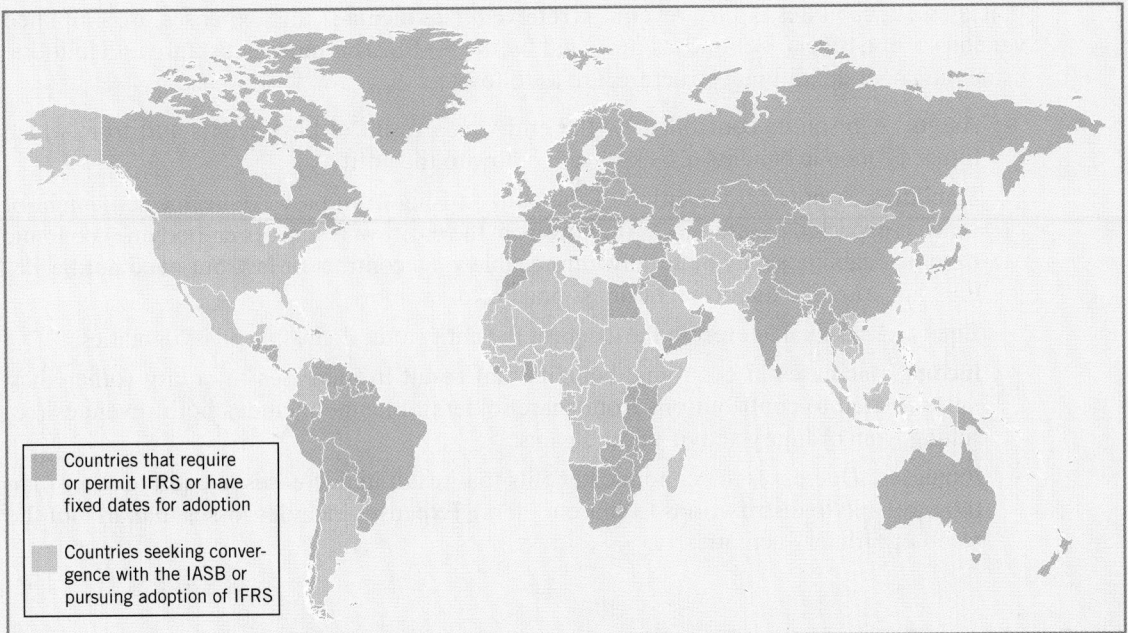

Source: http://www.pwc.com/us/en/issues/ifrs-reporting/country-adoption/index.jhtml.

followed. As indicated in the graphic above, much of the world has voted for the standards issued by the IASB. Over 115 countries require or permit use of IFRS.

- U.S standards, referred to as generally accepted accounting principles (GAAP), are developed by the Financial Accounting Standards Board (FASB). The fact that there are differences between what is in this textbook (which is based on U.S. standards) and IFRS should not be surprising because the FASB and IASB have responded to different user needs. In some countries, the primary users of financial statements are private investors; in others, the primary users are tax authorities or central government planners. It appears that the United States and the international standard-setting environment are primarily driven by meeting the needs of investors and creditors.

- The internal control standards applicable to Sarbanes-Oxley (SOX) apply only to large public companies listed on U.S. exchanges. There is a continuing debate as to whether non-U.S. companies should have to comply with this extra layer of regulation. Debate about international companies (non-U.S.) adopting SOX-type standards centers on whether the benefits exceed the costs. The concern is that the higher costs of SOX compliance are making the U.S. securities markets less competitive.

- The textbook mentions a number of ethics violations, such as Enron, WorldCom, and AIG. These problems have also occurred internationally, for example, at Satyam Computer Services (India), Parmalat (Italy), and Royal Ahold (the Netherlands).

- IFRS tends to be simpler in its accounting and disclosure requirements; some people say more "principles-based." GAAP is more detailed; some people say it is more "rules-based." This difference in approach has resulted in a debate about the merits of "principles-based" versus "rules-based" standards.

- U.S. regulators have recently eliminated the need for foreign companies that trade shares in U.S. markets to reconcile their accounting with GAAP.

- The three most common forms of business organization, proprietorships, partnerships, and corporations, are also found in countries that use IFRS. Because the choice of business organization is influenced by factors such as legal environment, tax rates and regulations, and degree of entrepreneurism, the relative use of each form will vary across countries.

- The conceptual framework that underlies IFRS is very similar to that used to develop GAAP. The basic definitions provided in this textbook for the key elements of financial statements, that is, assets, liabilities, equity, revenues (**referred to as income**), and expenses, are simplified versions of the official definitions provided by the FASB. The more substantive definitions, using the IASB definitional structure, are as follows.

Assets. A resource controlled by the entity as a result of past events and from which future economic benefits are expected to flow to the entity.

Liabilities. A present obligation of the entity arising from past events, the settlement of which is expected to result in an outflow from the entity of resources embodying economic benefits. Liabilities may be legally enforceable via a contract or law, but need not be, i.e., they can arise due to normal business practice or customs.

Equity. A residual interest in the assets of the entity after deducting all its liabilities.

Income. Increases in economic benefits that result in increases in equity (other than those related to contributions from shareholders). Income includes both revenues (resulting from ordinary activities) and gains.

Expenses. Decreases in economic benefits that result in decreases in equity (other than those related to distributions to shareholders). Expenses includes losses that are not the result of ordinary activities.

Looking to the Future

Both the IASB and the FASB are hard at work developing standards that will lead to the elimination of major differences in the way certain transactions are accounted for and reported. In fact, at one time the IASB stated that no new major standards would become effective until 2011. The major reason for this policy was to provide companies the time to translate and implement IFRS into practice, as much has happened in a very short period of time. Consider, for example, that as a result of a joint project on the conceptual framework, the definitions of the most fundamental elements (assets, liabilities, equity, revenues, and expenses) may actually change. However, whether the IASB adopts internal control provisions similar to those in SOX remains to be seen.

IFRS Self-Test Questions

1. Which of the following is *not* a reason why a single set of high-quality international accounting standards would be beneficial?
   (a) Mergers and acquisition activity.
   (b) Financial markets.
   (c) Multinational corporations.
   (d) GAAP is widely considered to be a superior reporting system.

2. The Sarbanes-Oxley Act determines:
   (a) international tax regulations.
   (b) internal control standards as enforced by the IASB.
   (c) internal control standards of U.S. publicly traded companies.
   (d) U.S. tax regulations.

3. IFRS is considered to be more:
   (a) principles-based and less rules-based than GAAP.
   (b) rules-based and less principles-based than GAAP.
   (c) detailed than GAAP.
   (d) None of the above.

4. Which of the following statements is *false*?
   (a) IFRS is based on a conceptual framework that is similar to that used to develop GAAP.
   (b) Assets are defined by the IASB as resources controlled by the entity as a result of past events and from which future economic benefits are expected to flow to the entity.

(c) Non-U.S. companies that trade shares in U.S. markets must reconcile their accounting with GAAP.

(d) Proprietorships, partnerships, and corporations are also found in countries that use IFRS.

5. Which of the following statements is *true*?

(a) Under IFRS, the term income refers to what would be called revenues and gains under GAAP.

(b) The term income is not used under IFRS.

(c) The term income refers only to gains on investments.

(d) Under IFRS, expenses include distributions to owners.

IFRS Concepts and Application

IFRS1-1   Who are the two key international players in the development of international accounting standards? Explain their role.

IFRS1-2   What might explain the fact that different accounting standard-setters have developed accounting standards that are sometimes quite different in nature?

IFRS1-3   What is the benefit of a single set of high-quality accounting standards?

IFRS1-4   Discuss the potential advantages and disadvantages that countries outside the United States should consider before adopting regulations, such as those in the Sarbanes-Oxley Act, that increase corporate internal control requirements.

International Financial Reporting
Problem: Zetar plc

IFRS1-5   The financial statements of Zetar plc are presented in Appendix C. The company's complete annual report, including the notes to its financial statements, is available at *www.zetarplc.com*.

Instructions

Visit Zetar's corporate website and answer the following questions from Zetar's 2009 annual report.

(a) What accounting firm performed the audit of Zetar's financial statements?

(b) What is the address of the company's corporate headquarters?

(c) What is the company's reporting currency?

(d) What two segments does the company operate in, and what were the sales for each segment in the year ended April 30, 2009?

Answers to IFRS Self-Test Questions

1. d   **2.** c   **3.** a   **4.** c   **5.** a

The Navigator

✔   **Remember to go back to the Navigator box on the chapter opening page and check off your completed work.**

CHAPTER2

The Recording Process

Study Objectives

After studying this chapter, you should be able to:

1. Explain what an account is and how it helps in the recording process.
2. Define debits and credits and explain their use in recording business transactions.
3. Identify the basic steps in the recording process.
4. Explain what a journal is and how it helps in the recording process.
5. Explain what a ledger is and how it helps in the recording process.
6. Explain what posting is and how it helps in the recording process.
7. Prepare a trial balance and explain its purposes.

The Navigator

✔ [The Navigator]

Feature Story

ACCIDENTS HAPPEN

How organized are you financially? Take a short quiz. Answer *yes* or *no* to each question:

• Does your wallet contain so many cash machine receipts that you've been declared a walking fire hazard?

• Is your wallet such a mess that it is often faster to fish for money in the crack of your car seat than to dig around in your wallet?

• Was Dwight Howard playing high school basketball the last time you balanced your checkbook?

• Have you ever been tempted to burn down your house so you don't have to try to find all of the receipts and records that you need to fill out your tax return?

If you think it is hard to keep track of the many transactions that make up *your* life, imagine what it is like for a major corporation like Fidelity Investments. Fidelity is one of the largest mutual fund management firms in the world. If you had your life savings invested at Fidelity Investments, you might be just slightly displeased if, when you called to find out your balance, the representative said, "You know, I kind of remember someone with a name like yours sending us some money—now what did we do with that?"

To ensure the accuracy of your balance and the security of your funds, Fidelity Investments, like all other companies large and small, relies on a sophisticated accounting information system. That's not to say that Fidelity or any other company is error-free. In fact, if you've ever really messed up your checkbook register, you may take some comfort from one accountant's mistake at Fidelity Investments. The accountant failed to include a minus sign while doing a calculation, making what was actually a $1.3 billion loss look like a $1.3 billion—yes, *billion*—gain! Fortunately, like most accounting errors, it was detected before any real harm was done.

No one expects that kind of mistake at a company like Fidelity, which has sophisticated computer systems and top investment managers. In explaining the mistake to shareholders, a spokesperson wrote, "Some people have asked how, in this age of technology, such a mistake could be made. While many of our processes are computerized, accounting systems are complex and dictate that some steps must be handled manually by our managers and accountants, and people can make mistakes."

Inside**CHAPTER2**

PreviewofCHAPTER2

In Chapter 1, we analyzed business transactions in terms of the accounting equation, and we presented the cumulative effects of these transactions in tabular form. Imagine a company like Fidelity Investments (as in the Feature Story) using the same tabular format as Softbyte to keep track of its transactions. In a single day, Fidelity engages in thousands of business transactions. To record each transaction this way would be impractical, expensive, and unnecessary. Instead, companies use a set of procedures and records to keep track of transaction data more easily. This chapter introduces and illustrates these basic procedures and records.

The content and organization of Chapter 2 are as follows.

The Recording Process			
The Account	**Steps in the Recording Process**	**The Recording Process Illustrated**	**The Trial Balance**
• Debits and credits • Summary of debit/credit rules	• Journal • Ledger	• Summary illustration of journalizing and posting	• Limitations of a trial balance • Locating errors • Use of dollar signs

The Account

Study Objective [1]

Explain what an account is and how it helps in the recording process.

An **account** is an individual accounting record of increases and decreases in a specific asset, liability, or owner's equity item. For example, Softbyte (the company discussed in Chapter 1) would have separate accounts for Cash, Accounts Receivable, Accounts Payable, Service Revenue, Salaries and Wages Expense, and so on. (Note that whenever we are referring to a specific account, we capitalize the name.)

In its simplest form, an account consists of three parts: (1) a title, (2) a left or debit side, and (3) a right or credit side. Because the format of an account resembles the letter T, we refer to it as a **T account**. Illustration 2-1 shows the basic form of an account.

Illustration 2-1
Basic form of account

We use this form often throughout this book to explain basic accounting relationships.

Study Objective [2]

Define debits and credits and explain how they are used to record business transactions.

Debits and Credits

The term **debit** indicates the left side of an account, and **credit** indicates the right side. They are commonly abbreviated as **Dr.** for debit and **Cr.** for credit. They **do not** mean increase or decrease, as is commonly thought. We use the terms *debit* and *credit* repeatedly in the recording process to describe **where** entries are made in accounts. For example, the act of entering an amount on the left side of an account is called **debiting** the account. Making an entry on the right side is **crediting** the account.

When comparing the totals of the two sides, an account shows a **debit balance** if the total of the debit amounts exceeds the credits. An account shows a **credit balance** if the credit amounts exceed the debits. Note the position of the debit side and credit side in Illustration 2-1.

The procedure of recording debits and credits in an account is shown in Illustration 2-2 for the transactions affecting the Cash account of Softbyte. The data are taken from the Cash column of the tabular summary in Illustration 1-8 (page 20).

Tabular Summary		Account Form			
Cash		**Cash**			
$15,000		(Debits)	15,000	(Credits)	7,000
−7,000			1,200		1,700
1,200			1,500		250
1,500			600		1,300
−1,700		Balance	8,050		
−250		(Debit)			
600					
−1,300					
$ 8,050					

Illustration 2-2
Tabular summary and account form for Softbyte's Cash account

Every positive item in the tabular summary represents a receipt of cash; every negative amount represents a payment of cash. **Notice that in the account form we record the increases in cash as debits, and the decreases in cash as credits.** For example, the $15,000 receipt of cash (in red) is debited to Cash, and the −$7,000 payment of cash (in blue) is credited to Cash.

Having increases on one side and decreases on the other reduces recording errors and helps in determining the totals of each side of the account as well as the account balance. The balance is determined by netting the two sides (subtracting one amount from the other). The account balance, a debit of $8,050, indicates that Softbyte had $8,050 more increases than decreases in cash. That is, since it started with a balance of zero, it has $8,050 in its Cash account.

DEBIT AND CREDIT PROCEDURE

In Chapter 1, you learned the effect of a transaction on the basic accounting equation. Remember that each transaction must affect two or more accounts to keep the basic accounting equation in balance. In other words, for each transaction, debits must equal credits. The equality of debits and credits provides the basis for the double-entry system of recording transactions.

Under the double-entry system, the dual (two-sided) effect of each transaction is recorded in appropriate accounts. This system provides a logical method for recording transactions. The double-entry system also helps ensure the accuracy of the recorded amounts and helps to detect errors such as those at Fidelity Investments as discussed in the Feature Story. If every transaction is recorded with equal debits and credits, the sum of all the debits to the accounts must equal the sum of all the credits.

The double-entry system for determining the equality of the accounting equation is much more efficient than the plus/minus procedure used in Chapter 1. On the following pages, we will illustrate debit and credit procedures in the double-entry system.

International Note

Rules for accounting for specific events sometimes differ across countries. For example, European companies rely less on historical cost and more on fair value than U.S. companies. Despite the differences, the double-entry accounting system is the basis of accounting systems worldwide.

DR./CR. PROCEDURES FOR ASSETS AND LIABILITIES

In Illustration 2-2 for Softbyte, increases in Cash—an asset—were entered on the left side, and decreases in Cash were entered on the right side. We know that both sides of the basic equation (Assets = Liabilities + Owner's Equity) must be equal. It therefore follows that increases and decreases in liabilities will have to be recorded *opposite from* increases and decreases in assets. Thus, increases in liabilities must be entered on the right or credit side, and decreases in liabilities must be entered on the left or debit side. The effects that debits and credits have on assets and liabilities are summarized in Illustration 2-3.

Illustration 2-3
Debit and credit effects—assets and liabilities

Debits	Credits
Increase assets	Decrease assets
Decrease liabilities	Increase liabilities

Asset accounts normally show debit balances. That is, debits to a specific asset account should exceed credits to that account. Likewise, **liability accounts normally show credit balances**. That is, credits to a liability account should exceed debits to that account. The normal balance of an account is on the side where an increase in the account is recorded. Illustration 2-4 shows the normal balances for assets and liabilities.

Illustration 2-4
Normal balances—assets and liabilities

Knowing the normal balance in an account may help you trace errors. For example, a credit balance in an asset account such as Land or a debit balance in a liability account such as Salaries and Wages Payable usually indicates an error. Occasionally, though, an abnormal balance may be correct. The Cash account, for example, will have a credit balance when a company has overdrawn its bank balance (i.e., written a check that "bounced").

DR./CR. PROCEDURES FOR OWNER'S EQUITY

As Chapter 1 indicated, owner's investments and revenues increase owner's equity. Owner's drawings and expenses decrease owner's equity. Companies keep accounts for each of these types of transactions.

Owner's Capital. Investments by owners are credited to the Owner's Capital account. Credits increase this account, and debits decrease it. When an owner invests cash in the business, the company debits (increases) Cash and credits (increases) Owner's Capital. When the owner's investment in the business is reduced, Owner's Capital is debited (decreased).

Illustration 2-5 shows the rules of debit and credit for the Owner's Capital account.

Illustration 2-5
Debit and credit effects—Owner's Capital

Debits	Credits
Decrease Owner's Capital	Increase Owner's Capital

We can diagram the normal balance in Owner's Capital as follows.

Illustration 2-6
Normal balance—Owner's Capital

Owner's Drawings. An owner may withdraw cash or other assets for personal use. Withdrawals could be debited directly to Owner's Capital to indicate a decrease in owner's equity. However, it is preferable to use a separate account, called Owner's Drawings. This separate account makes it easier to determine total withdrawals for each accounting period. Owner's Drawings is increased by debits and decreased by credits. Normally, the drawings account will have a debit balance.

Illustration 2-7 shows the rules of debit and credit for the drawings account.

Debits	**Credits**
Increase Owner's Drawings	Decrease Owner's Drawings

Illustration 2-7
Debit and credit effects—Owner's Drawings

We can diagram the normal balance as follows.

Illustration 2-8
Normal balance—Owner's Drawings

The Owner's Drawings account decreases owner's equity. It is not an income statement account like revenues and expenses.

INVESTOR **I**NSIGHT

Keeping Score

The Chicago Cubs baseball team has these major revenue and expense accounts:

Revenues	Expenses
Admissions (ticket sales)	Players' salaries
Concessions	Administrative salaries
Television and radio	Travel
Advertising	Ballpark maintenance

? Do you think that the Chicago Bears football team would be likely to have the same major revenue and expense accounts as the Cubs? (See page 94.)

Revenues and Expenses. The purpose of earning revenues is to benefit the owner(s) of the business. When a company earns revenues, owner's equity increases. Therefore, **the effect of debits and credits on revenue accounts is the same as their effect on Owner's Capital.** That is, revenue accounts are increased by credits and decreased by debits.

Helpful Hint

Because revenues increase
owner's equity, a revenue
account has the same debit/
credit rules as the Owner's
Capital account. Expenses
have the opposite effect.

Expenses have the opposite effect: Expenses decrease owner's equity. Since expenses decrease net income, and revenues increase it, it is logical that the increase and decrease sides of expense accounts should be the opposite of revenue accounts. Thus, expense accounts are increased by debits and decreased by credits. Illustration 2-9 shows the rules of debits and credits for revenues and expenses.

Illustration 2-9
Debit and credit effects—
revenues and expenses

Debits	Credits
Decrease revenues	Increase revenues
Increase expenses	Decrease expenses

Credits to revenue accounts should exceed debits. Debits to expense accounts should exceed credits. Thus, revenue accounts normally show credit balances, and expense accounts normally show debit balances. We can diagram the normal balances as follows.

Illustration 2-10
Normal balances—revenues
and expenses

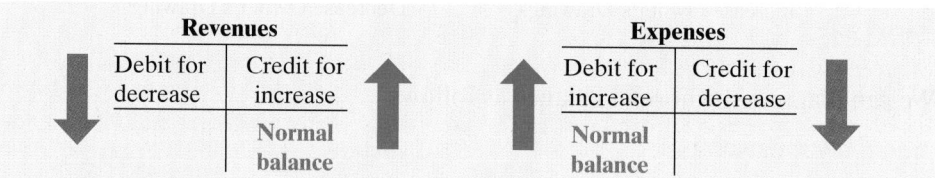

Helpful Hint

You may want to bookmark
Illustration 2-11. You
probably will refer to it
often.

Summary of Debit/Credit Rules

Illustration 2-11 shows a summary of the debit/credit rules and effects on each type of account. Study this diagram carefully. It will help you understand the fundamentals of the double-entry system.

Illustration 2-11
Summary of debit/credit rules

Do it!

Normal Balances

Kate Browne has just rented space in a shopping mall. In this space, she will open a hair salon, to be called "Hair It Is." A friend has advised Kate to set up a double-entry set of accounting records in which to record all of her business transactions.

Identify the balance sheet accounts that Kate will likely need to record the transactions needed to open her business. Indicate whether the normal balance of each account is a debit or a credit.

Solution

Kate would likely need the following accounts in which to record the transactions necessary to ready her hair salon for opening day:

Cash (debit balance)

Equipment (debit balance)

Supplies (debit balance)

Accounts Payable (credit balance)

If she borrows money: Notes Payable (credit balance)

Owner's Capital (credit balance)

Related exercise material: BE2-1, BE2-2, BE2-5, E2-1, E2-2, E2-4, and **Do it!** 2-1.

action plan

✔ Determine the types of accounts needed: Kate will need asset accounts for each different type of asset she invests in the business, and liability accounts for any debts she incurs.

✔ Understand the types of owner's equity accounts: Only Owner's Capital will be needed when Kate begins the business. Other owner's equity accounts will be needed later.

Steps in the Recording Process

Although it is possible to enter transaction information directly into the accounts without using a journal, few businesses do so. Practically every business uses three basic steps in the recording process:

1. Analyze each transaction for its effects on the accounts.
2. Enter the transaction information in a *journal*.
3. Transfer the journal information to the appropriate accounts in the *ledger*.

The recording process begins with the transaction. **Business documents**, such as a sales slip, a check, a bill, or a cash register tape, provide evidence of the transaction. The company analyzes this evidence to determine the transaction's effects on specific accounts. The company then enters the transaction in the journal. Finally, it transfers the journal entry to the designated accounts in the ledger. Illustration 2-12 shows the recording process.

The steps in the recording process occur repeatedly. In Chapter 1, we illustrated the first step, the analysis of transactions, and will give further examples in this and later chapters. The other two steps in the recording process are explained in the next sections.

Study Objective [3]
Identify the basic steps in the recording process.

Ethics Note

Business documents provide evidence that transactions actually occurred. International Outsourcing Services, LLC, was accused of submitting fraudulent documents (store coupons) to companies such as Kraft Foods and PepsiCo for reimbursement of as much as $250 million. Ensuring that all recorded transactions are backed up by proper business documents reduces the likelihood of fraudulent activity.

Analyze each transaction

Enter transaction in a journal

Transfer journal information to ledger accounts

Illustration 2-12
The recording process

The Journal

Study Objective [4]
Explain what a journal is and how it helps in the recording process.

Companies initially record transactions in chronological order (the order in which they occur). Thus, the journal is referred to as the book of original entry. For each transaction the journal shows the debit and credit effects on specific accounts.

Companies may use various kinds of journals, but every company has the most basic form of journal, a general journal. Typically, a general journal has spaces for dates, account titles and explanations, references, and two amount columns. See the format of the journal in Illustration 2-13. *Whenever we use the term "journal" in this textbook without a modifying adjective, we mean the general journal.*

The journal makes several significant contributions to the recording process:

1. It discloses in one place the **complete effects of a transaction**.
2. It provides a **chronological record** of transactions.
3. It helps to **prevent or locate errors** because the debit and credit amounts for each entry can be easily compared.

JOURNALIZING

Entering transaction data in the journal is known as journalizing. Companies make separate journal entries for each transaction. A complete entry consists of (1) the date of the transaction, (2) the accounts and amounts to be debited and credited, and (3) a brief explanation of the transaction.

Illustration 2-13 shows the technique of journalizing, using the first two transactions of Softbyte. On September 1, Ray Neal invested $15,000 cash in the business, and Softbyte purchased computer equipment for $7,000 cash. The number J1 indicates that these two entries are recorded on the first page of the journal. Illustration 2-13 shows the standard form of journal entries for these two transactions. (The boxed numbers correspond to explanations in the list below the illustration.)

Illustration 2-13
Technique of journalizing

Date	Account Titles and Explanation	Ref.	Debit	Credit
2012		[5]		
Sept. 1 [2]	Cash		15,000	
[1] [3]	Owner's Capital			15,000
[4]	(Owner's investment of cash in business)			
1	Equipment		7,000	
	Cash			7,000
	(Purchase of equipment for cash)			

General Journal — J1

[1] The date of the transaction is entered in the Date column.
[2] The debit account title (that is, the account to be debited) is entered first at the extreme left margin of the column headed "Account Titles and Explanation," and the amount of the debit is recorded in the Debit column.
[3] The credit account title (that is, the account to be credited) is indented and entered on the next line in the column headed "Account Titles and Explanation," and the amount of the credit is recorded in the Credit column.

4 A brief explanation of the transaction appears on the line below the credit account title. A space is left between journal entries. The blank space separates individual journal entries and makes the entire journal easier to read.

5 The column titled Ref. (which stands for Reference) is left blank when the journal entry is made. This column is used later when the journal entries are transferred to the ledger accounts.

It is important to use correct and specific account titles in journalizing. Erroneous account titles lead to incorrect financial statements. However, some flexibility exists initially in selecting account titles. The main criterion is that each title must appropriately describe the content of the account. Once a company chooses the specific title to use, it should record under that account title all later transactions involving the account.[1]

SIMPLE AND COMPOUND ENTRIES

Some entries involve only two accounts, one debit and one credit. (See, for example, the entries in Illustration 2-13.) An entry like these is considered a **simple entry**. Some transactions, however, require more than two accounts in journalizing. An entry that requires three or more accounts is a **compound entry**. To illustrate, assume that on July 1, Butler Company purchases a delivery truck costing $14,000. It pays $8,000 cash now and agrees to pay the remaining $6,000 on account (to be paid later). The compound entry is as follows.

General Journal				J1
Date	Account Titles and Explanation	Ref.	Debit	Credit
2012				
July 1	Equipment		14,000	
	Cash			8,000
	Accounts Payable			6,000
	(Purchased truck for cash with balance on account)			

Illustration 2-14
Compound journal entry

In a compound entry, the standard format requires that all debits be listed before the credits.

Do it!

Kate Browne engaged in the following activities in establishing her salon, Hair It Is:

1. Opened a bank account in the name of Hair It Is and deposited $20,000 of her own money in this account as her initial investment.

2. Purchased equipment on account (to be paid in 30 days) for a total cost of $4,800.

3. Interviewed three persons for the position of hair stylist.

In what form (type of record) should Kate record these three activities? Prepare the entries to record the transactions.

Recording Business Activities

---

[1]*In homework problems, you should use specific account titles when they are given.* When account titles are not given, you may select account titles that identify the nature and content of each account. The account titles used in journalizing should not contain explanations such as Cash Paid or Cash Received.

The Navigator

action plan

✔ Understand which activities need to be recorded and which do not. Any that affect assets, liabilities, or owner's capital should be recorded in a journal.

✔ Analyze the effects of transactions on asset, liability, and owner's equity accounts.

Solution

Each transaction that is recorded is entered in the general journal. The three activities would be recorded as follows.

1. Cash	20,000	
Owner's Capital		20,000
(Owner's investment of cash in business)		
2. Equipment	4,800	
Accounts Payable		4,800
(Purchase of equipment on account)		
3. No entry because no transaction has occurred.		

Related exercise material: BE2-3, BE2-6, E2-3, E2-5, E2-6, E2-7, and **Do it!** 2-2.

The Ledger

Study Objective [5]

Explain what a ledger is and how it helps in the recording process.

The entire group of accounts maintained by a company is the **ledger**. The ledger keeps in one place all the information about changes in specific account balances.

Companies may use various kinds of ledgers, but every company has a general ledger. A **general ledger** contains all the asset, liability, and owner's equity accounts, as shown in Illustration 2-15 for J. Lind Company. *Whenever we use the term "ledger" in this textbook, we are referring to the general ledger, unless we specify otherwise.*

Illustration 2-15

The general ledger, which contains all of a company's accounts

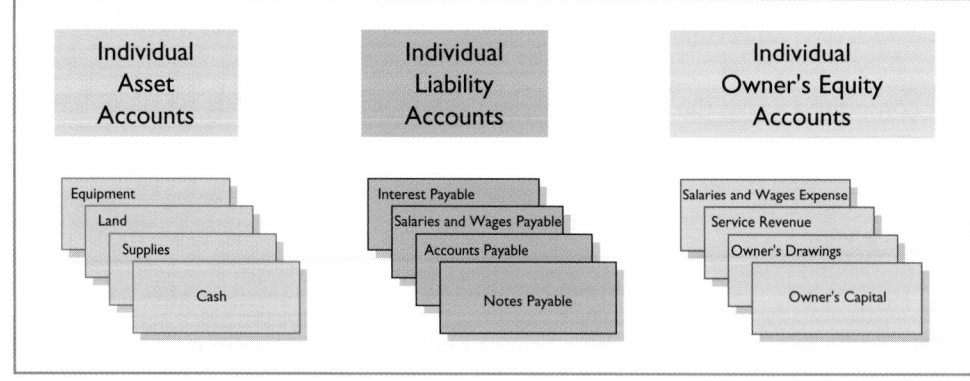

Companies arrange the ledger in the sequence in which they present the accounts in the financial statements, beginning with the balance sheet accounts. First in order are the asset accounts, followed by liability accounts, owner's capital, owner's drawings, revenues, and expenses. Each account is numbered for easier identification.

The ledger provides the balance in each of the accounts. For example, the Cash account shows the amount of cash available to meet current obligations. The Accounts Receivable account shows amounts due from customers. Accounts Payable shows amounts owed to creditors.

ACCOUNTING ACROSS THE ORGANIZATION

What Would Sam Do?

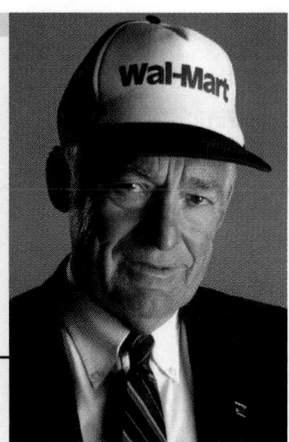

In his autobiography, Sam Walton described the double-entry accounting system he used when Wal-Mart was just getting started: "We kept a little pigeonhole on the wall for the cash receipts and paperwork of each [Wal-Mart] store. I had a blue binder ledger book for each store. When we added a store, we added a pigeonhole. We did this at least up to twenty stores. Then once a month, the bookkeeper and I would enter the merchandise, enter the sales, enter the cash, and balance it."

Source: Sam Walton, *Made in America* (New York: Doubleday, 1992), p. 53.

? Why did Sam Walton keep separate pigeonholes and blue binders? Why bother to keep separate records for each store? (See page 94.)

STANDARD FORM OF ACCOUNT

The simple T-account form used in accounting textbooks is often very useful for illustration purposes. However, in practice, the account forms used in ledgers are much more structured. Illustration 2-16 shows a typical form, using assumed data from a cash account.

Cash					No. 101
Date	**Explanation**	**Ref.**	**Debit**	**Credit**	**Balance**
2012					
June 1			25,000		25,000
2				8,000	17,000
3			4,200		21,200
9			7,500		28,700
17				11,700	17,000
20				250	16,750
30				7,300	9,450

Illustration 2-16
Three-column form of account

This format is called the **three-column form of account**. It has three money columns—debit, credit, and balance. The balance in the account is determined after each transaction. Companies use the explanation space and reference columns to provide special information about the transaction.

POSTING

Transferring journal entries to the ledger accounts is called posting. This phase of the recording process accumulates the effects of journalized transactions into the individual accounts. Posting involves the following steps.

Study Objective [6]

Explain what posting is and how it helps in the recording process.

1. In the **ledger**, in the appropriate columns of the account(s) debited, enter the date, journal page, and debit amount shown in the journal.

2. In the reference column of the **journal**, write the account number to which the debit amount was posted.

3. In the **ledger**, in the appropriate columns of the account(s) credited, enter the date, journal page, and credit amount shown in the journal.

4. In the reference column of the **journal**, write the account number to which the credit amount was posted.

Illustration 2-17 shows these four steps using Softbyte's first journal entry. The boxed numbers indicate the sequence of the steps.

Illustration 2-17

Posting a journal entry

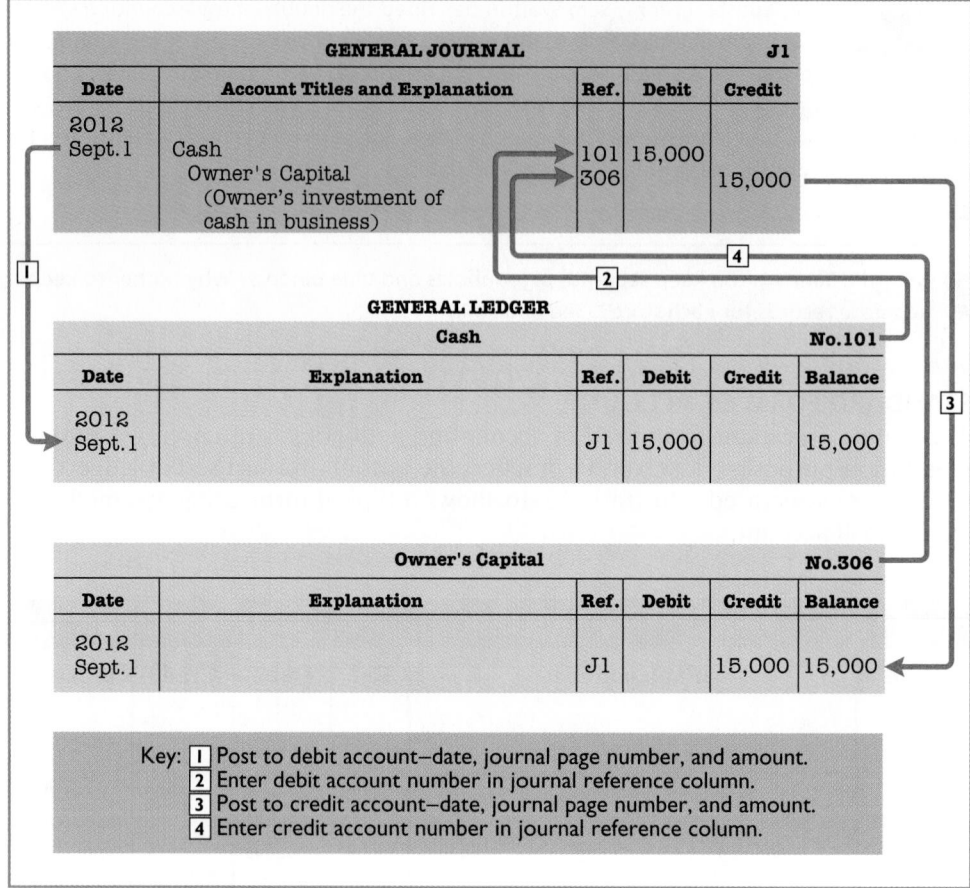

Key: ☐ Post to debit account—date, journal page number, and amount.
2 Enter debit account number in journal reference column.
3 Post to credit account—date, journal page number, and amount.
4 Enter credit account number in journal reference column.

Posting should be performed in chronological order. That is, the company should post all the debits and credits of one journal entry before proceeding to the next journal entry. Postings should be made on a timely basis to ensure that the ledger is up to date.[2]

The reference column of a ledger account indicates the journal page from which the transaction was posted.[3] The explanation space of the ledger account is used infrequently because an explanation already appears in the journal.

CHART OF ACCOUNTS

The number and type of accounts differ for each company. The number of accounts depends on the amount of detail management desires. For example, the management of one company may want a single account for all types of utility expense. Another may keep separate expense accounts for each type of utility, such as gas, electricity, and water. Similarly, a small company like Softbyte will have fewer accounts than a corporate giant like Dell. Softbyte may be able to manage and report its activities in 20 to 30 accounts, while Dell may require thousands of accounts to keep track of its worldwide activities.

---

[2] *In homework problems, you can journalize all transactions before posting any of the journal entries.*
[3] After the last entry has been posted, the accountant should scan the reference column **in the journal**, to confirm that all postings have been made.

Most companies have a **chart of accounts**. This chart lists the accounts and the account numbers that identify their location in the ledger. The numbering system that identifies the accounts usually starts with the balance sheet accounts and follows with the income statement accounts.

In this and the next two chapters, we will be explaining the accounting for Pioneer Advertising Agency (a service company). Accounts 101–199 indicate asset accounts; 200–299 indicate liabilities; 301–350 indicate owner's equity accounts; 400–499, revenues; 601–799, expenses; 800–899, other revenues; and 900–999, other expenses. Illustration 2-18 shows Pioneer's chart of accounts. (C. R. Byrd is Pioneer's owner.) Accounts listed in red are used in this chapter; accounts shown in black are explained in later chapters.

Helpful Hint

On the book's endpapers, you also will find an expanded chart of accounts.

Illustration 2-18
Chart of accounts

Pioneer Advertising Agency
Chart of Accounts

Assets	Owner's Equity
101 Cash	301 Owner's Capital
112 Accounts Receivable	306 Owner's Drawings
126 Supplies	350 Income Summary
130 Prepaid Insurance	
157 Equipment	**Revenues**
158 Accumulated Depreciation—Equipment	400 Service Revenue
Liabilities	**Expenses**
200 Notes Payable	631 Supplies Expense
201 Accounts Payable	711 Depreciation Expense
209 Unearned Service Revenue	722 Insurance Expense
212 Salaries and Wages Payable	726 Salaries and Wages Expense
230 Interest Payable	729 Rent Expense
	905 Interest Expense

You will notice that there are gaps in the numbering system of the chart of accounts for Pioneer Advertising. Companies leave gaps to permit the insertion of new accounts as needed during the life of the business.

The Recording Process Illustrated

Illustrations 2-19 through 2-28 show the basic steps in the recording process, using the October transactions of Pioneer Advertising Agency. Pioneer's accounting period is a month. In these illustrations, a basic analysis, an equation analysis, and a debit-credit analysis precede the journal entry and posting of each transaction. For simplicity, we use the T-account form to show the posting instead of the standard account form.

Study these transaction analyses carefully. **The purpose of transaction analysis is first to identify the type of account involved, and then to determine whether to make a debit or a credit to the account.** You should always perform this type of analysis before preparing a journal entry. Doing so will help you understand the journal entries discussed in this chapter as well as more complex journal entries in later chapters.

Illustration 2-19
Investment of cash by owner

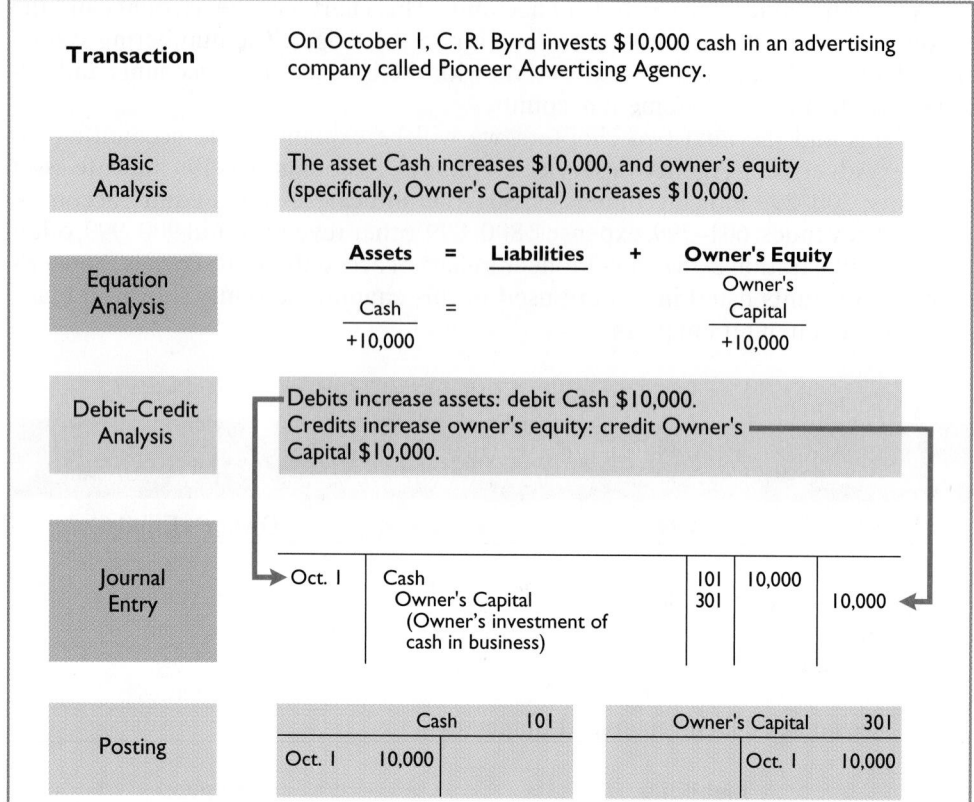

Helpful Hint

Follow these steps:
1. Determine what type of account is involved.
2. Determine what items increased or decreased and by how much.
3. Translate the increases and decreases into debits and credits.

Illustration 2-20
Purchase of office equipment

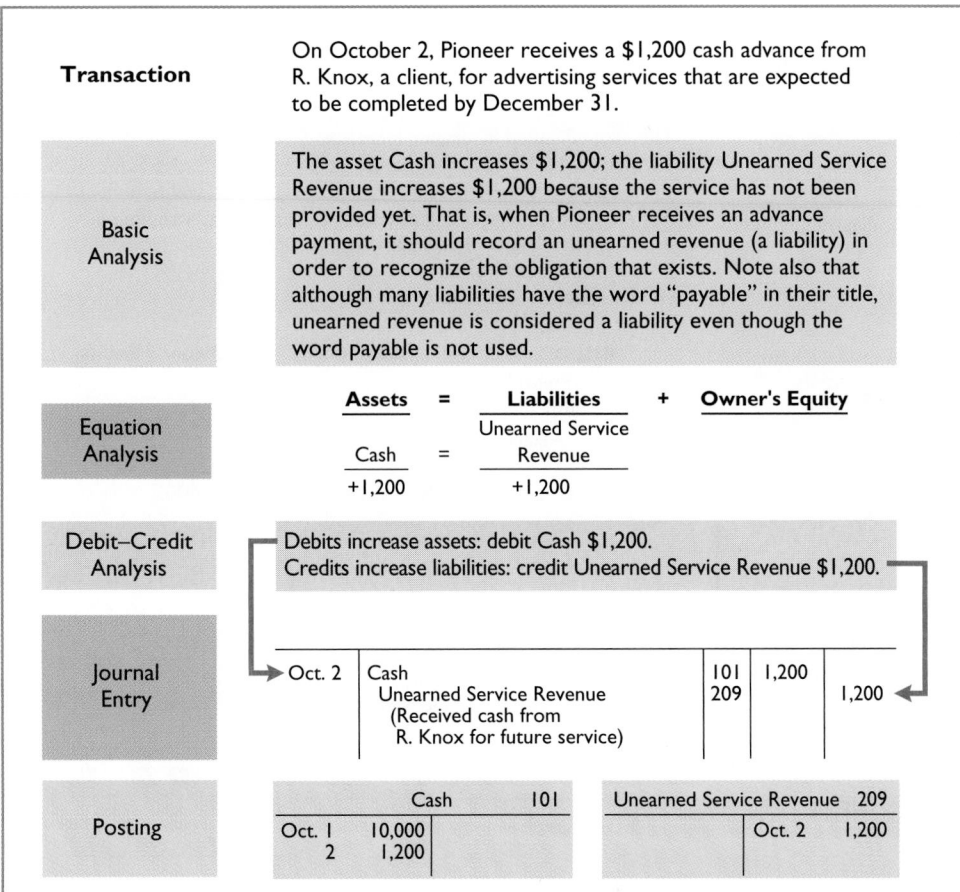

Illustration 2-21
Receipt of cash for future service

Transaction	On October 2, Pioneer receives a $1,200 cash advance from R. Knox, a client, for advertising services that are expected to be completed by December 31.
Basic Analysis	The asset Cash increases $1,200; the liability Unearned Service Revenue increases $1,200 because the service has not been provided yet. That is, when Pioneer receives an advance payment, it should record an unearned revenue (a liability) in order to recognize the obligation that exists. Note also that although many liabilities have the word "payable" in their title, unearned revenue is considered a liability even though the word payable is not used.

Basic Analysis

Equation Analysis

Assets	**=**	**Liabilities**	**+**	**Owner's Equity**
		Unearned Service		
Cash	=	Revenue		
+1,200		+1,200		

Debit–Credit Analysis

Debits increase assets: debit Cash $1,200.
Credits increase liabilities: credit Unearned Service Revenue $1,200.

Journal Entry

Oct. 2	Cash	101	1,200	
	Unearned Service Revenue	209		1,200
	(Received cash from R. Knox for future service)			

Posting

Cash		101		Unearned Service Revenue	209
Oct. 1	10,000			Oct. 2	1,200
2	1,200				

Illustration 2-22
Payment of monthly rent

Transaction	On October 3, Pioneer pays office rent for October in cash, $900.
Basic Analysis	The expense account Rent Expense increases $900 because the payment pertains only to the current month; the asset Cash decreases $900.

Equation Analysis

Assets	**=**	**Liabilities**	**+**	**Owner's Equity**
				Rent
Cash	=			Expense
-900				-900

Debit–Credit Analysis

Debits increase expenses: debit Rent Expense $900.
Credits decrease assets: credit Cash $900.

Journal Entry

Oct. 3	Rent Expense	729	900	
	Cash	101		900
	(Paid October rent)			

Posting

Cash		101			Rent Expense	729	
Oct. 1	10,000	Oct. 3	900	Oct. 3	900		
2	1,200						

Illustration 2-23
Payment for insurance

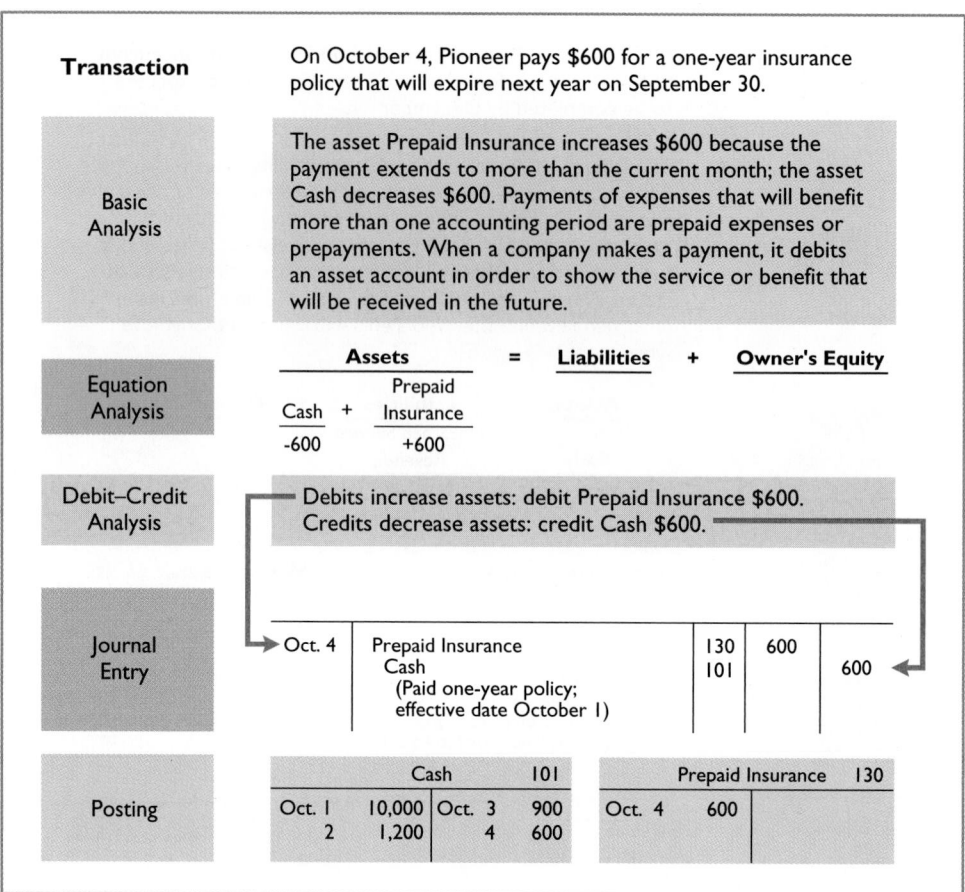

Illustration 2-24
Purchase of supplies on credit

Event	On October 9, Pioneer hires four employees to begin work on October 15. Each employee is to receive a weekly salary of $500 for a 5-day work week, payable every 2 weeks—first payment made on October 26.
Basic Analysis	A business transaction has not occurred. There is only an agreement between the employer and the employees to enter into a business transaction beginning on October 15. Thus, a debit–credit analysis is not needed because there is no accounting entry. (See transaction of October 26 for first entry.)

Illustration 2-25
Hiring of employees

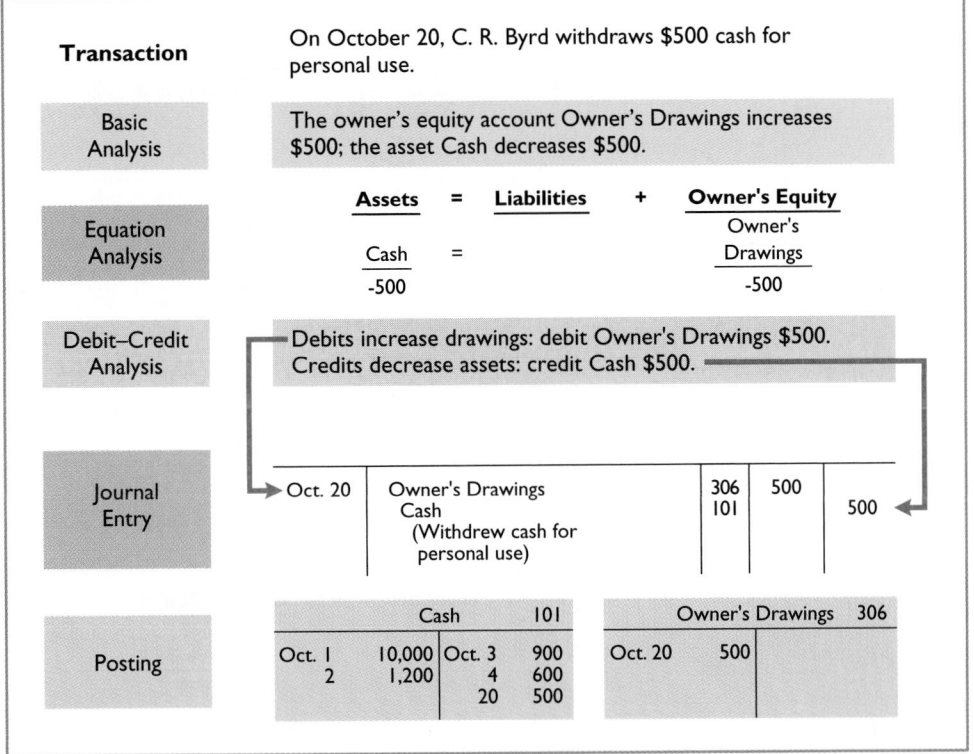

Transaction	On October 20, C. R. Byrd withdraws $500 cash for personal use.
Basic Analysis	The owner's equity account Owner's Drawings increases $500; the asset Cash decreases $500.
Equation Analysis	
Debit–Credit Analysis	Debits increase drawings: debit Owner's Drawings $500. Credits decrease assets: credit Cash $500.
Journal Entry	
Posting	

Illustration 2-26
Withdrawal of cash by owner

Illustration 2-27
Payment of salaries

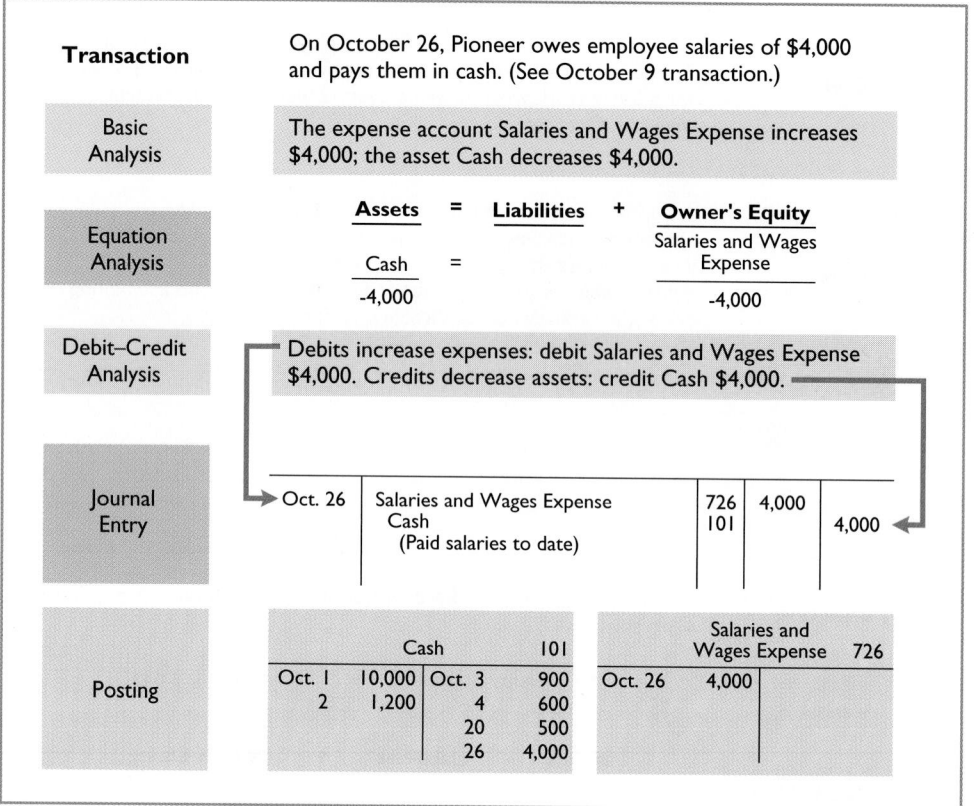

Illustration 2-28
Receipt of cash for services provided

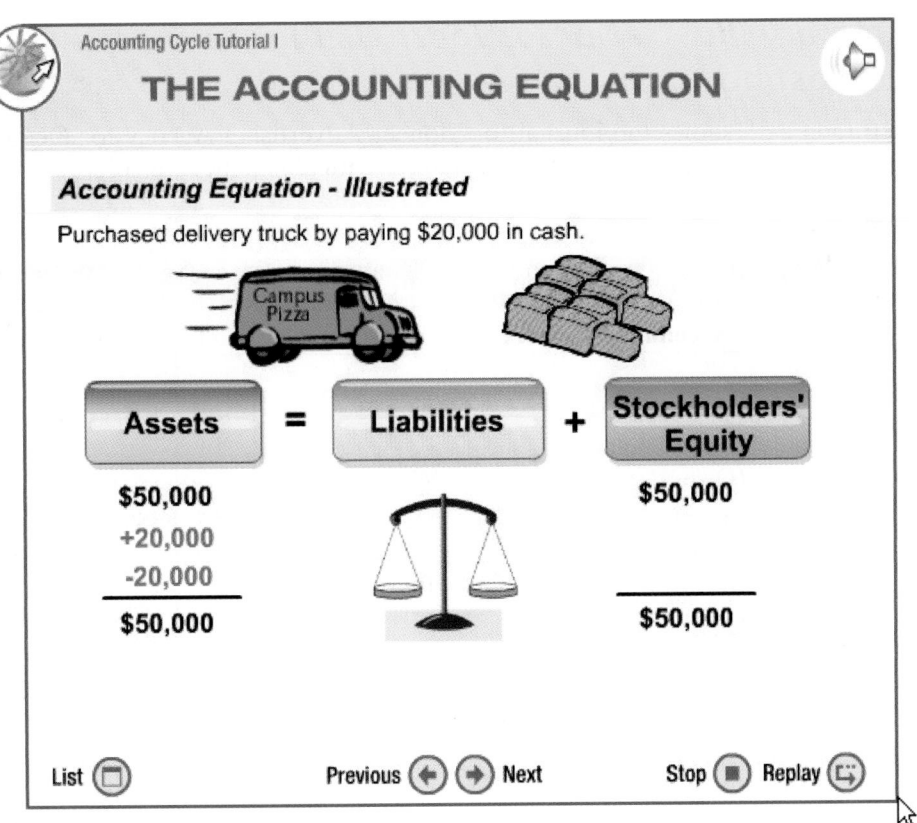

Accounting Cycle Tutorial I

THE ACCOUNTING EQUATION

Accounting Equation - Illustrated

Purchased delivery truck by paying $20,000 in cash.

| Assets | = | Liabilities | + | Stockholders' Equity |

$50,000				$50,000
+20,000				
-20,000				
$50,000				$50,000

List   Previous ← → Next   Stop ■ Replay

Accounting Cycle Tutorial

The diagrams in Illustrations 2-19 to 2-28 review the accounting cycle. If you would like additional practice, an Accounting Cycle Tutorial is available on *WileyPLUS*. The illustration to the left is an example of a screen from the tutorial.

Do it!

Kate Brown recorded the following transactions in a general journal during the month of March.

Posting

Mar.	4	Cash	2,280	
		Service Revenue		2,280
	15	Salaries and Wages Expense	400	
		Cash		400
	19	Utilities Expense	92	
		Cash		92

Post these entries to the Cash account of the general ledger to determine the ending balance in cash. The beginning balance of cash on March 1 was $600.

Solution

Cash			
3/1	600	3/15	400
3/4	2,280	3/19	92
3/31 Bal.	2,388		

action plan

✔ Recall that posting involves transferring the journalized debits and credits to specific accounts in the ledger.

✔ Determine the ending balance by netting the total debits and credits.

Related exercise material: BE2-7, BE2-8, E2-8, E2-12 and **Do it!** 2-3.

The Navigator

Summary Illustration of Journalizing and Posting

Illustration 2-29 shows the journal for Pioneer Advertising Agency for October. Illustration 2-30 (on page 71) shows the ledger, with all balances in color.

Illustration 2-29
General journal entries

Date	Account Titles and Explanation	Ref.	Debit	Credit
2012				
Oct. 1	Cash	101	10,000	
	Owner's Capital	301		10,000
	(Owner's investment of cash in business)			
1	Equipment	157	5,000	
	Notes Payable	200		5,000
	(Issued 3-month, 12% note for office equipment)			
2	Cash	101	1,200	
	Unearned Service Revenue	209		1,200
	(Received cash from R. Knox for future service)			
3	Rent Expense	729	900	
	Cash	101		900
	(Paid October rent)			
4	Prepaid Insurance	130	600	
	Cash	101		600
	(Paid one-year policy; effective date October 1)			
5	Supplies	126	2,500	
	Accounts Payable	201		2,500
	(Purchased supplies on account from Aero Supply)			
20	Owner's Drawings	306	500	
	Cash	101		500
	(Withdrew cash for personal use)			
26	Salaries and Wages Expense	726	4,000	
	Cash	101		4,000
	(Paid salaries to date)			
31	Cash	101	10,000	
	Service Revenue	400		10,000
	(Received cash for services provided)			

General Journal — Page J1

The Trial Balance

Study Objective [7]
Prepare a trial balance and explain its purposes.

A **trial balance** is a list of accounts and their balances at a given time. Customarily, companies prepare a trial balance at the end of an accounting period. They list accounts in the order in which they appear in the ledger. Debit balances appear in the left column and credit balances in the right column.

General Journal

Cash — No. 101

Date	Explanation	Ref.	Debit	Credit	Balance
2012					
Oct. 1		J1	10,000		10,000
2		J1	1,200		11,200
3		J1		900	10,300
4		J1		600	9,700
20		J1		500	9,200
26		J1		4,000	5,200
31		J1	10,000		15,200

Supplies — No. 126

Date	Explanation	Ref.	Debit	Credit	Balance
2012					
Oct. 5		J1	2,500		2,500

Prepaid Insurance — No. 130

Date	Explanation	Ref.	Debit	Credit	Balance
2012					
Oct. 4		J1	600		600

Equipment — No. 157

Date	Explanation	Ref.	Debit	Credit	Balance
2012					
Oct. 1		J1	5,000		5,000

Notes Payable — No. 200

Date	Explanation	Ref.	Debit	Credit	Balance
2012					
Oct. 1		J1		5,000	5,000

Accounts Payable — No. 201

Date	Explanation	Ref.	Debit	Credit	Balance
2012					
Oct. 5		J1		2,500	2,500

Unearned Service Revenue — No. 209

Date	Explanation	Ref.	Debit	Credit	Balance
2012					
Oct. 2		J1		1,200	1,200

Owner's Capital — No. 301

Date	Explanation	Ref.	Debit	Credit	Balance
2012					
Oct. 1		J1		10,000	10,000

Owner's Drawings — No. 306

Date	Explanation	Ref.	Debit	Credit	Balance
2012					
Oct. 20		J1	500		500

Service Revenue — No. 400

Date	Explanation	Ref.	Debit	Credit	Balance
2012					
Oct. 31		J1		10,000	10,000

Salaries and Wages Expense — No. 726

Date	Explanation	Ref.	Debit	Credit	Balance
2012					
Oct. 26		J1	4,000		4,000

Rent Expense — No. 729

Date	Explanation	Ref.	Debit	Credit	Balance
2012					
Oct. 3		J1	900		900

Illustration 2-30
General ledger

The trial balance proves the mathematical equality of debits and credits after posting. Under the double-entry system, this equality occurs when the sum of the debit account balances equals the sum of the credit account balances. **A trial balance may also uncover errors in journalizing and posting.** For example, a trial balance may well have detected the error at Fidelity Investments discussed in the Feature Story. **In addition, a trial balance is useful in the preparation of financial statements**, as we will explain in the next two chapters.

The steps for preparing a trial balance are:

1. List the account titles and their balances in the appropriate debit or credit column.
2. Total the debit and credit columns.
3. Prove the equality of the two columns.

Illustration 2-31 (on the next page) shows the trial balance prepared from Pioneer Advertising's ledger. Note that the total debits equal the total credits.

Illustration 2-31
A trial balance

Helpful Hint

Note that the order of presentation in the trial balance is:
  Assets
  Liabilities
  Owner's equity
  Revenues
  Expenses

Pioneer Advertising Agency Trial Balance October 31, 2012		
	Debit	**Credit**
Cash	$15,200	
Supplies	2,500	
Prepaid Insurance	600	
Equipment	5,000	
Notes Payable		$ 5,000
Accounts Payable		2,500
Unearned Service Revenue		1,200
Owner's Capital		10,000
Owner's Drawings	500	
Service Revenue		10,000
Salaries and Wages Expense	4,000	
Rent Expense	900	
	$28,700	$28,700

A trial balance is a necessary checkpoint for uncovering certain types of errors. For example, if only the debit portion of a journal entry has been posted, the trial balance would bring this error to light.

Limitations of a Trial Balance

Ethics Note

An *error* is the result of an unintentional mistake; it is neither ethical nor unethical. An *irregularity* is an intentional misstatement, which *is* viewed as unethical.

A trial balance does not guarantee freedom from recording errors, however. Numerous errors may exist even though the trial balance columns agree. For example, the trial balance may balance even when:

1. a transaction is not journalized,
2. a correct journal entry is not posted,
3. a journal entry is posted twice,
4. incorrect accounts are used in journalizing or posting, or
5. offsetting errors are made in recording the amount of a transaction.

As long as equal debits and credits are posted, even to the wrong account or in the wrong amount, the total debits will equal the total credits. **The trial balance does not prove that the company has recorded all transactions or that the ledger is correct.**

Locating Errors

Errors in a trial balance generally result from mathematical mistakes, incorrect postings, or simply transcribing data incorrectly. What do you do if you are faced with a trial balance that does not balance? First determine the amount of the difference between the two columns of the trial balance. After this amount is known, the following steps are often helpful:

1. If the error is $1, $10, $100, or $1,000, re-add the trial balance columns and recompute the account balances.
2. If the error is divisible by 2, scan the trial balance to see whether a balance equal to half the error has been entered in the wrong column.

3. If the error is divisible by 9, retrace the account balances on the trial balance to see whether they are incorrectly copied from the ledger. For example, if a balance was $12 and it was listed as $21, a $9 error has been made. Reversing the order of numbers is called a **transposition error**.

4. If the error is not divisible by 2 or 9, scan the ledger to see whether an account balance in the amount of the error has been omitted from the trial balance, and scan the journal to see whether a posting of that amount has been omitted.

Use of Dollar Signs

Note that dollar signs do not appear in journals or ledgers. Dollar signs are typically used only in the trial balance and the financial statements. Generally, a dollar sign is shown only for the first item in the column and for the total of that column. A single line (a totaling rule) is placed under the column of figures to be added or subtracted. Total amounts are double-underlined to indicate they are final sums.

Insight boxes provide examples of business situations from various perspectives—ethics, investor, and international. Guideline answers are provided on the last page of the chapter.

INVESTOR INSIGHT

Why Accuracy Matters

While most companies record transactions very carefully, the reality is that mistakes still happen. For example, bank regulators fined Bank One Corporation (now Chase) $1.8 million because they felt that the unreliability of the bank's accounting system caused it to violate regulatory requirements.

Also, in recent years Fannie Mae, the government-chartered mortgage association, announced a series of large accounting errors. These announcements caused alarm among investors, regulators, and politicians because they fear that the errors may suggest larger, undetected problems. This is important because the home-mortgage market depends on Fannie Mae to buy hundreds of billions of dollars of mortgages each year from banks, thus enabling the banks to issue new mortgages.

Finally, before a major overhaul of its accounting system, the financial records of Waste Management Company were in such disarray that of the company's 57,000 employees, 10,000 were receiving pay slips that were in error.

The Sarbanes-Oxley Act of 2002 was created to minimize the occurrence of errors like these by increasing every employee's responsibility for accurate financial reporting.

? In order for these companies to prepare and issue financial statements, their accounting equations (debits and credits) must have been in balance at year-end. How could these errors or misstatements have occurred? (See page 94.)

Do it!

The following accounts come from the ledger of SnowGo Company at December 31, 2012.

Trial Balance

157	Equipment	$88,000	301	Owner's Capital	$20,000
306	Owner's Drawings	8,000	212	Salaries and Wages	
201	Accounts Payable	22,000		Payable	2,000
726	Salaries and Wages		200	Notes Payable	19,000
	Expense	42,000	722	Insurance Expense	3,000
112	Accounts Receivable	4,000	130	Prepaid Insurance	6,000
400	Service Revenue	95,000	101	Cash	7,000

Prepare a trial balance in good form.

action plan

✔ Determine normal balances and list accounts in the order they appear in the ledger.

✔ Accounts with debit balances appear in the left column, and those with credit balances in the right column.

✔ Total the debit and credit columns to prove equality.

Solution

SNOWGO COMPANY Trial Balance December 31, 2012		
	Debit	**Credit**
Cash	$ 7,000	
Accounts Receivable	4,000	
Prepaid Insurance	6,000	
Equipment	88,000	
Notes Payable		$ 19,000
Accounts Payable		22,000
Salaries and Wages Payable		2,000
Owner's Capital		20,000
Owner's Drawings	8,000	
Service Revenue		95,000
Insurance Expense	3,000	
Salaries and Wages Expense	42,000	
	$158,000	$158,000

Related exercise material: BE2-9, BE2-10, E2-9, E2-10, E2-11, E2-13, E2-14, and **Do it!** 2-4.

The Navigator

COMPREHENSIVE

Do it!

Transactions

Bob Sample opened the Campus Laundromat on September 1, 2012. During the first month of operations, the following transactions occurred.

Sept. 1   Bob invested $20,000 cash in the business.
2   The company paid $1,000 cash for store rent for September.
3   Purchased washers and dryers for $25,000, paying $10,000 in cash and signing a $15,000, 6-month, 12% note payable.
4   Paid $1,200 for a one-year accident insurance policy.
10   Received a bill from the *Daily News* for advertising the opening of the laundromat $200.
20   Bob withdrew $700 cash for personal use.
30   The company determined that cash receipts for laundry services for the month were $6,200.

The chart of accounts for the company is the same as that for Pioneer Advertising Agency plus No. 610 Advertising Expense.

Instructions

(a) Journalize the September transactions. (Use J1 for the journal page number.)
(b) Open ledger accounts and post the September transactions.
(c) Prepare a trial balance at September 30, 2012.

Solution to Comprehensive Do it!

(a)

	GENERAL JOURNAL			J1
Date	Account Titles and Explanation	Ref.	Debit	Credit
2012				
Sept. 1	Cash	101	20,000	
	Owner's Capital	301		20,000
	(Owner's investment of cash in business)			
2	Rent Expense	729	1,000	
	Cash	101		1,000
	(Paid September rent)			
3	Equipment	157	25,000	
	Cash	101		10,000
	Notes Payable	200		15,000
	(Purchased laundry equipment for cash and 6-month, 12% note payable)			
4	Prepaid Insurance	130	1,200	
	Cash	101		1,200
	(Paid one-year insurance policy)			
10	Advertising Expense	610	200	
	Accounts Payable	201		200
	(Received bill from Daily News for advertising)			
20	Owner's Drawings	306	700	
	Cash	101		700
	(Withdrew cash for personal use)			
30	Cash	101	6,200	
	Service Revenue	400		6,200
	(Received cash for services provided)			

action plan

✔ Make separate journal entries for each transaction.

✔ In journalizing, make sure debits equal credits.

✔ In journalizing, use specific account titles taken from the chart of accounts.

✔ Provide appropriate description of each journal entry.

✔ Arrange ledger in statement order, beginning with the balance sheet accounts.

✔ Post in chronological order.

✔ Use numbers in the reference column to indicate the amount has been posted.

✔ In the trial balance, list accounts in the order in which they appear in the ledger.

✔ List debit balances in the left column, and credit balances in the right column.

(b)

GENERAL LEDGER

Cash   No. 101

Date	Explanation	Ref.	Debit	Credit	Balance
2012					
Sept. 1		J1	20,000		20,000
2		J1		1,000	19,000
3		J1		10,000	9,000
4		J1		1,200	7,800
20		J1		700	7,100
30		J1	6,200		13,300

Prepaid Insurance   No. 130

Date	Explanation	Ref.	Debit	Credit	Balance
2012					
Sept. 4		J1	1,200		1,200

Equipment   No. 157

Date	Explanation	Ref.	Debit	Credit	Balance
2012					
Sept. 3		J1	25,000		25,000

Notes Payable   No. 200

Date	Explanation	Ref.	Debit	Credit	Balance
2012					
Sept. 3		J1		15,000	15,000

Accounts Payable   No. 201

Date	Explanation	Ref.	Debit	Credit	Balance
2012					
Sept. 10		J1		200	200

Owner's Capital   No. 301

Date	Explanation	Ref.	Debit	Credit	Balance
2012					
Sept. 1		J1		20,000	20,000

Owner's Drawings   No. 306

Date	Explanation	Ref.	Debit	Credit	Balance
2012					
Sept. 20		J1	700		700

(b)

GENERAL LEDGER (Continued)

Service Revenue   **No. 400**

Date	Explanation	Ref.	Debit	Credit	Balance
2012					
Sept. 30		J1		6,200	6,200

Advertising Expense   **No. 610**

Date	Explanation	Ref.	Debit	Credit	Balance
2012					
Sept. 10		J1	200		200

Rent Expense   **No. 729**

Date	Explanation	Ref.	Debit	Credit	Balance
2012					
Sept. 2		J1	1,000		1,000

(c)

CAMPUS LAUNDROMAT
Trial Balance
September 30, 2012

	Debit	Credit
Cash	$13,300	
Prepaid Insurance	1,200	
Equipment	25,000	
Notes Payable		$15,000
Accounts Payable		200
Owner's Capital		20,000
Owner's Drawings	700	
Service Revenue		6,200
Advertising Expense	200	
Rent Expense	1,000	
	$41,400	$41,400

The Navigator

Summary of Study Objectives

[1] Explain what an account is and how it helps in the recording process. An account is a record of increases and decreases in specific asset, liability, and owner's equity items.

[2] Define debits and credits and explain their use in recording business transactions. The terms debit and credit are synonymous with left and right. Assets, drawings, and expenses are increased by debits and decreased by credits. Liabilities, owner's capital, and revenues are increased by credits and decreased by debits.

[3] Identify the basic steps in the recording process. The basic steps in the recording process are: (a) analyze each transaction for its effects on the accounts, (b) enter the transaction information in a journal, (c) transfer the journal information to the appropriate accounts in the ledger.

[4] Explain what a journal is and how it helps in the recording process. The initial accounting record of a transaction is entered in a journal before the data are entered in the accounts. A journal (a) discloses in one place the complete effects of a transaction, (b) provides a chronological record of transactions, and (c) prevents or locates errors because the debit and credit amounts for each entry can be easily compared.

[5] Explain what a ledger is and how it helps in the recording process. The ledger is the entire group of accounts maintained by a company. The ledger keeps in one place all the information about changes in specific account balances.

[6] Explain what posting is and how it helps in the recording process. Posting is the transfer of journal entries to the ledger accounts. This phase of the recording process accumulates the effects of journalized transactions in the individual accounts.

[7] Prepare a trial balance and explain its purposes. A trial balance is a list of accounts and their balances at a given time. Its primary purpose is to prove the equality of debits and credits after posting. A trial balance also uncovers errors in journalizing and posting and is useful in preparing financial statements.

The Navigator

Glossary

Account A record of increases and decreases in specific asset, liability, or owner's equity items. (p. 52).

Chart of accounts A list of accounts and the account numbers that identify their location in the ledger. (p. 63).

Compound entry A journal entry that involves three or more accounts. (p. 59).

Credit The right side of an account. (p. 52).

Debit The left side of an account. (p. 52).

Double-entry system A system that records in appropriate accounts the dual effect of each transaction. (p. 53).

General journal The most basic form of journal. (p. 58).

General ledger A ledger that contains all asset, liability, and owner's equity accounts. (p. 60).

Journal An accounting record in which transactions are initially recorded in chronological order. (p. 58).

Journalizing The entering of transaction data in the journal. (p. 58).

Ledger The entire group of accounts maintained by a company. (p. 60).

Normal balance An account balance on the side where an increase in the account is recorded. (p. 54).

Posting The procedure of transferring journal entries to the ledger accounts. (p. 61).

Simple entry A journal entry that involves only two accounts. (p. 59).

T account The basic form of an account. (p. 52).

Three-column form of account A form with columns for debit, credit, and balance amounts in an account. (p. 61).

Trial balance A list of accounts and their balances at a given time. (p. 70).

 Self-Test, Brief Exercises, Exercises, Problem Set A, and many more components are available for practice in *WileyPLUS*

Self-Test Questions

Answers are on page 94.

(SO 1) **1.** Which of the following statements about an account is *true*?
  a. In its simplest form, an account consists of two parts.
  b. An account is an individual accounting record of increases and decreases in specific asset, liability, and owner's equity items.
  c. There are separate accounts for specific assets and liabilities but only one account for owner's equity items.
  d. The left side of an account is the credit or decrease side.

(SO 2) **2.** Debits:
  a. increase both assets and liabilities.
  b. decrease both assets and liabilities.
  c. increase assets and decrease liabilities.
  d. decrease assets and increase liabilities.

(SO 2) **3.** A revenue account:
  a. is increased by debits.
  b. is decreased by credits.
  c. has a normal balance of a debit.
  d. is increased by credits.

(SO 2) **4.** Accounts that normally have debit balances are:
  a. assets, expenses, and revenues.
  b. assets, expenses, and owner's capital.
  c. assets, liabilities, and owner's drawings.
  d. assets, owner's drawings, and expenses.

(SO 2) **5.** The expanded accounting equation is:
  a. Assets + Liabilities = Owner's Capital + Owner's Drawings + Revenues + Expenses
  b. Assets = Liabilities + Owner's Capital + Owner's Drawings + Revenues − Expenses

  c. Assets = Liabilities − Owner's Capital − Owner's Drawings − Revenues − Expenses
  d. Assets = Liabilities + Owner's Capital − Owner's Drawings + Revenues − Expenses

(SO 3) **6.** Which of the following is *not* part of the recording process?
  a. Analyzing transactions.
  b. Preparing a trial balance.
  c. Entering transactions in a journal.
  d. Posting transactions.

(SO 4) **7.** Which of the following statements about a journal is *false*?
  a. It is not a book of original entry.
  b. It provides a chronological record of transactions.
  c. It helps to locate errors because the debit and credit amounts for each entry can be readily compared.
  d. It discloses in one place the complete effect of a transaction.

(SO 4) **8.** The purchase of supplies on account should result in:
  a. a debit to Supplies Expense and a credit to Cash.
  b. a debit to Supplies Expense and a credit to Accounts Payable.
  c. a debit to Supplies and a credit to Accounts Payable.
  d. a debit to Supplies and a credit to Accounts Receivable.

(SO 5) **9.** The order of the accounts in the ledger is:
  a. assets, revenues, expenses, liabilities, owner's capital, owner's drawings.
  b. assets, liabilities, owner's capital, owner's drawings, revenues, expenses.
  c. owner's capital, assets, revenues, expenses, liabilities, owner's drawings.
  d. revenues, assets, expenses, liabilities, owner's capital, owner's drawings.

(SO 5) **10.** A ledger:
  a. contains only asset and liability accounts.
  b. should show accounts in alphabetical order.
  c. is a collection of the entire group of accounts maintained by a company.
  d. is a book of original entry.

(SO 6) **11.** Posting:
  a. normally occurs before journalizing.
  b. transfers ledger transaction data to the journal.
  c. is an optional step in the recording process.
  d. transfers journal entries to ledger accounts.

(SO 6) **12.** Before posting a payment of $5,000, the Accounts Payable of Senator Company had a normal balance of $16,000. The balance after posting this transaction was:
  a. $21,000.   **c.** $11,000.
  b. $5,000.   **d.** Cannot be determined.

(SO 7) **13.** A trial balance:
  a. is a list of accounts with their balances at a given time.
  b. proves the mathematical accuracy of journalized transactions.
  c. will not balance if a correct journal entry is posted twice.
  d. proves that all transactions have been recorded.

14. A trial balance will not balance if: (SO 7)
  a. a correct journal entry is posted twice.
  b. the purchase of supplies on account is debited to Supplies and credited to Cash.
  c. a $100 cash drawing by the owner is debited to Owner's Drawings for $1,000 and credited to Cash for $100.
  d. a $450 payment on account is debited to Accounts Payable for $45 and credited to Cash for $45.

15. The trial balance of Clooney Company had accounts with (SO 7) the following normal balances: Cash $5,000, Service Revenue $85,000, Salaries and Wages Payable $4,000, Salaries and Wages Expense $40,000, Rent Expense $10,000, Owner's Capital $42,000; Owner's Drawings $15,000; Equipment $61,000. In preparing a trial balance, the total in the debit column is:
  a. $131,000.   **c.** $91,000.
  b. $216,000.   **d.** $116,000.

Go to the book's companion website, **www.wiley.com/college/weygandt**, for additional Self-Test Questions.

The Navigator

Questions

1. Describe the parts of a T account.

2. "The terms *debit* and *credit* mean increase and decrease, respectively." Do you agree? Explain.

3. Jeff Hiller, a fellow student, contends that the double-entry system means each transaction must be recorded twice. Is Jeff correct? Explain.

4. Maria Alvarez, a beginning accounting student, believes debit balances are favorable and credit balances are unfavorable. Is Maria correct? Discuss.

5. State the rules of debit and credit as applied to (a) asset accounts, (b) liability accounts, and (c) the owner's equity accounts (revenue, expenses, owner's drawings, and owner's capital).

6. What is the normal balance for each of the following accounts? (a) Accounts Receivable. (b) Cash. (c) Owner's Drawings. (d) Accounts Payable. (e) Service Revenue. (f) Salaries and Wages Expense. (g) Owner's Capital.

7. Indicate whether each of the following accounts is an asset, a liability, or an owner's equity account and whether it has a normal debit or credit balance: (a) Accounts Receivable, (b) Accounts Payable, (c) Equipment, (d) Owner's Drawings, (e) Supplies.

8. For the following transactions, indicate the account debited and the account credited.
  (a) Supplies are purchased on account.
  (b) Cash is received on signing a note payable.
  (c) Employees are paid salaries in cash.

9. Indicate whether the following accounts generally will have (a) debit entries only, (b) credit entries only, or (c) both debit and credit entries.

  (1) Cash.   **(5)** Salaries and Wages
  (2) Accounts Receivable.   Expense.
  (3) Owner's Drawings.   **(6)** Service Revenue.
  (4) Accounts Payable.

10. What are the basic steps in the recording process?

11. What are the advantages of using a journal in the recording process?

12. **(a)** When entering a transaction in the journal, should the debit or credit be written first?
  (b) Which should be indented, the debit or credit?

13. Describe a compound entry, and provide an example.

14. **(a)** Should business transaction debits and credits be recorded directly in the ledger accounts?
  (b) What are the advantages of first recording transactions in the journal and then posting to the ledger?

15. The account number is entered as the last step in posting the amounts from the journal to the ledger. What is the advantage of this step?

16. Journalize the following business transactions.
  (a) Hector Molina invests $9,000 cash in the business.
  (b) Insurance of $800 is paid for the year.
  (c) Supplies of $2,000 are purchased on account.
  (d) Cash of $7,500 is received for services rendered.

17. **(a)** What is a ledger?
  (b) What is a chart of accounts and why is it important?

18. What is a trial balance and what are its purposes?

19. Jim Benes is confused about how accounting information flows through the accounting system. He believes the flow of information is as follows.
  (a) Debits and credits posted to the ledger.
  (b) Business transaction occurs.

(c) Information entered in the journal.

(d) Financial statements are prepared.

(e) Trial balance is prepared.

Is Jim correct? If not, indicate to Jim the proper flow of the information.

20. Two students are discussing the use of a trial balance. They wonder whether the following errors, each considered separately, would prevent the trial balance from balancing.

(a) The bookkeeper debited Cash for $600 and credited Salaries and Wages Expense for $600 for payment of wages.

(b) Cash collected on account was debited to Cash for $900 and Service Revenue was credited for $90.

What would you tell them?

21. **PEPSICO** What are the normal balances for PepsiCo's Cash, Accounts Payable, and Interest Expense accounts?

Brief Exercises

BE2-1 For each of the following accounts, indicate the effects of (a) a debit and (b) a credit on the accounts and (c) the normal balance of the account.

1. Accounts Payable.
2. Advertising Expense.
3. Service Revenue.
4. Accounts Receivable.
5. Owner's Capital.
6. Owner's Drawings.

Indicate debit and credit effects and normal balance.
(SO 2)

BE2-2 Transactions for the Daniel Hudson Company for the month of June are presented below. Identify the accounts to be debited and credited for each transaction.

June 1 Dan Hudson invests $5,000 cash in a small welding business of which he is the sole proprietor.

2 Purchases equipment on account for $2,100.

3 $800 cash is paid to landlord for June rent.

12 Bills O. Guillen $300 for welding work done on account.

Identify accounts to be debited and credited.
(SO 2)

BE2-3 Using the data in BE2-2, journalize the transactions. (You may omit explanations.)

Journalize transactions.
(SO 4)

BE2-4 ◖━━━ Kenny Williams a fellow student, is unclear about the basic steps in the recording process. Identify and briefly explain the steps in the order in which they occur.

Identify and explain steps in recording process.
(SO 3)

BE2-5 J. Reinsdorf has the following transactions during August of the current year. Indicate (a) the effect on the accounting equation and (b) the debit-credit analysis illustrated on pages 64–68 of the text.

Aug. 1 Opens an office as a financial advisor, investing $8,000 in cash.

4 Pays insurance in advance for 6 months, $1,800 cash.

16 Receives $3,400 from clients for services provided.

27 Pays secretary $1,000 salary.

Indicate basic and debit-credit analysis.
(SO 2)

BE2-6 Using the data in BE2-5, journalize the transactions. (You may omit explanations.)

Journalize transactions.
(SO 4)

BE2-7 Selected transactions for the Anthony Adams Company are presented in journal form below. Post the transactions to T accounts. Make one T account for each item and determine each account's ending balance.

Post journal entries to T accounts.
(SO 6)

J1

Date	Account Titles and Explanation	Ref.	Debit	Credit
May 5	Accounts Receivable		4,100	
	Service Revenue			4,100
	(Billed for services provided)			
12	Cash		2,400	
	Accounts Receivable			2,400
	(Received cash in payment of account)			
15	Cash		3,000	
	Service Revenue			3,000
	(Received cash for services provided)			

Post journal entries to standard form of account.
(SO 6)

BE2-8   Selected journal entries for the Anthony Adams Company are presented in BE2-7. Post the transactions using the standard form of account.

Prepare a trial balance.
(SO 7)

BE2-9   From the ledger balances given below, prepare a trial balance for the Afalava Company at June 30, 2012. List the accounts in the order shown on page 63 of the text. All account balances are normal.

Accounts Payable $9,000, Cash $5,800, Owner's Capital $15,000, Owner's Drawings $1,200, Equipment $17,000, Service Revenue $10,000, Accounts Receivable $3,000, Salaries and Wages Expense $6,000, and Rent Expense $1,000.

Prepare a correct trial balance.
(SO 7)

BE2-10   An inexperienced bookkeeper prepared the following trial balance. Prepare a correct trial balance, assuming all account balances are normal.

WALTER COMPANY
Trial Balance
December 31, 2012

	Debit	Credit
Cash	$10,800	
Prepaid Insurance		$ 3,500
Accounts Payable		3,000
Unearned Service Revenue	2,200	
Owner's Capital		9,000
Owner's Drawings		4,500
Service Revenue		25,600
Salaries and Wages Expense	18,600	
Rent Expense		2,400
	$31,600	$48,000

Do it! Review

Identify normal balances.
(SO 1, 2)

Do it! 2-1   Joe Seacat has just rented space in a strip mall. In this space, he will open a photography studio, to be called "Picture This!" A friend has advised Joe to set up a double-entry set of accounting records in which to record all of his business transactions.

Identify the balance sheet accounts that Joe will likely need to record the transactions needed to open his business. Indicate whether the normal balance of each account is a debit or credit.

Record business activities.
(SO 4)

Do it! 2-2   Joe Seacat engaged in the following activities in establishing his photography studio, Picture This!:

1. Opened a bank account in the name of Picture This! and deposited $6,300 of his own money into this account as his initial investment.
2. Purchased photography supplies at a total cost of $1,100. The business paid $400 in cash and the balance is on account.
3. Obtained estimates on the cost of photography equipment from three different manufacturers.

In what form (type of record) should Joe record these three activities? Prepare the entries to record the transactions.

Post transactions.
(SO 6)

Do it! 2-3   Joe Seacat recorded the following transactions during the month of April.

April 3	Cash	3,400	
	Service Revenue		3,400
April 16	Rent Expense	700	
	Cash		700
April 20	Salaries and Wages Expense	300	
	Cash		300

Post these entries to the Cash T account of the general ledger to determine the ending balance in cash. The beginning balance in cash on April 1 was $1,600.

Do it! 2-4 The following accounts are taken from the ledger of Angulo Company at December 31, 2012.

Prepare a trial balance.
(SO 7)

200	Notes Payable	$20,000	101	Cash	$ 6,000
301	Owner's Capital	28,000	126	Supplies	6,000
157	Equipment	80,000	631	Supplies Expense	4,000
306	Owner's Drawings	8,000	212	Salaries and Wages Payable	3,000
726	Salaries and Wages Expense	38,000	201	Accounts Payable	11,000
400	Service Revenue	88,000	112	Accounts Receivable	8,000

Prepare a trial balance in good form.

Exercises

E2-1 Johan Aslata has prepared the following list of statements about accounts.

Analyze statements about accounting and the recording process.
(SO 1)

1. An account is an accounting record of either a specific asset or a specific liability.
2. An account shows only increases, not decreases, in the item it relates to.
3. Some items, such as Cash and Accounts Receivable, are combined into one account.
4. An account has a left, or credit side, and a right, or debit side.
5. A simple form of an account consisting of just the account title, the left side, and the right side, is called a T account.

Instructions
Identify each statement as true or false. If false, indicate how to correct the statement.

E2-2 Selected transactions for M. Anderson, an interior decorator, in her first month of business, are as follows.

Identify debits, credits, and normal balances.
(SO 2)

Jan. 2   Invested $10,000 cash in business.
     3   Purchased used car for $4,000 cash for use in business.
     9   Purchased supplies on account for $500.
    11   Billed customers $2,100 for services performed.
    16   Paid $350 cash for advertising.
    20   Received $700 cash from customers billed on January 11.
    23   Paid creditor $300 cash on balance owed.
    28   Withdrew $1,000 cash for personal use by owner.

Instructions
For each transaction, indicate the following.

(a) The basic type of account debited and credited (asset, liability, owner's equity).
(b) The specific account debited and credited (cash, rent expense, service revenue, etc.).
(c) Whether the specific account is increased or decreased.
(d) The normal balance of the specific account.

Use the following format, in which the January 2 transaction is given as an example.

	Account Debited				Account Credited			
Date	**(a)** Basic Type	**(b)** Specific Account	**(c)** Effect	**(d)** Normal Balance	**(a)** Basic Type	**(b)** Specific Account	**(c)** Effect	**(d)** Normal Balance
Jan. 2	Asset	Cash	Increase	Debit	Owner's Equity	Owner's Capital	Increase	Credit

E2-3 Data for M. Anderson, interior decorator, are presented in E2-2.

Journalize transactions.
(SO 4)

Instructions
Journalize the transactions using journal page J1. (You may omit explanations.)

E2-4 Presented below is information related to Aromashodu Real Estate Agency.

Analyze transactions and determine their effect on accounts.
(SO 2)

Oct. 1   Devin Aromashodu begins business as a real estate agent with a cash investment of $15,000.
     2   Hires an administrative assistant.
     3   Purchases office furniture for $1,900, on account.

6   Sells a house and lot for H. Harrelson; bills H. Harrelson $3,600 for realty services provided.
27   Pays $1,100 on the balance related to the transaction of October 3.
30   Pays the administrative assistant $2,500 in salary for October.

Instructions
Prepare the debit-credit analysis for each transaction as illustrated on pages 64–68.

Journalize transactions.
(SO 4)

E2-5   Transaction data for Aromashodu Real Estate Agency are presented in E2-4.

Instructions
Journalize the transactions. (You may omit explanations.)

Analyze transactions and journalize.
(SO 2, 3, 4)

E2-6   Barnes Industries had the following transactions.
1. Borrowed $5,000 from the bank by signing a note.
2. Paid $3,100 cash for a computer.
3. Purchased $850 of supplies on account.

Instructions
(a) Indicate what accounts are increased and decreased by each transaction.
(b) Journalize each transaction. (Omit explanations.)

Analyze transactions and journalize.
(SO 2, 3, 4)

E2-7   Beekman Enterprises had the following selected transactions.
1. Jo Beekman invested $4,000 cash in the business.
2. Paid office rent of $950.
3. Performed consulting services and billed a client $5,200.
4. Jo Beekman withdrew $750 cash for personal use.

Instructions
(a) Indicate the effect each transaction has on the accounting equation (Assets = Liabilities + Owner's Equity), using plus and minus signs.
(b) Journalize each transaction. (Omit explanations.)

Analyze statements about the ledger.
(SO 5)

E2-8   Kahlil Bell has prepared the following list of statements about the general ledger.
1. The general ledger contains all the asset and liability accounts but no owner's equity accounts.
2. The general ledger is sometimes referred to as simply the ledger.
3. The accounts in the general ledger are arranged in alphabetical order.
4. Each account in the general ledger is numbered for easier identification.
5. The general ledger is a book of original entry.

Instructions
Identify each statement as true or false. If false, indicate how to correct the statement.

Post journal entries and prepare a trial balance.
(SO 6, 7)

E2-9   Selected transactions from the journal of Consuela Brown, investment broker, are presented below.

Date	Account Titles and Explanation	Ref.	Debit	Credit
Aug. 1	Cash		5,000	
	Owner's Capital			5,000
	(Owner's investment of cash in business)			
10	Cash		2,400	
	Service Revenue			2,400
	(Received cash for services provided)			
12	Equipment		5,000	
	Cash			3,000
	Notes Payable			2,000
	(Purchased equipment for cash and notes payable)			
25	Accounts Receivable		1,700	
	Service Revenue			1,700
	(Billed clients for services provided)			
31	Cash		900	
	Accounts Receivable			900
	(Receipt of cash on account)			

Instructions
(a) Post the transactions to T accounts.
(b) Prepare a trial balance at August 31, 2012.

E2-10 The T accounts below summarize the ledger of Bennet Landscaping Company at the end of the first month of operations.

Journalize transactions from account data and prepare a trial balance.
(SO 4, 7)

Cash			No. 101
4/1	12,000	4/15	1,300
4/12	900	4/25	1,500
4/29	400		
4/30	1,000		

Unearned Service Revenue		No. 209
	4/30	1,000

Accounts Receivable			No. 112
4/7	3,200	4/29	400

Owner's Capital		No. 301
	4/1	12,000

Supplies		No. 126
4/4	1,800	

Service Revenue		No. 400
	4/7	3,200
	4/12	900

Accounts Payable			No. 201
4/25	1,500	4/4	1,800

Salaries and Wages Expense		No. 726
4/15	1,300	

Instructions
(a) Prepare the complete general journal (including explanations) from which the postings to Cash were made.
(b) Prepare a trial balance at April 30, 2012.

E2-11 Presented below is the ledger for Bowman Co.

Journalize transactions from account data and prepare a trial balance.
(SO 4, 7)

Cash			No. 101
10/1	3,000	10/4	400
10/10	500	10/12	1,500
10/10	4,000	10/15	250
10/20	500	10/30	300
10/25	2,000	10/31	500

Owner's Capital		No. 301
	10/1	3,000
	10/25	2,000

Owner's Drawings		No. 306
10/30	300	

Accounts Receivable			No. 112
10/6	800	10/20	500
10/20	940		

Service Revenue		No. 400
	10/6	800
	10/10	500
	10/20	940

Supplies		No. 126
10/4	400	

Salaries and Wages Expense		No. 726
10/31	500	

Equipment		No. 157
10/3	2,000	

Rent Expense		No. 729
10/15	250	

Notes Payable		No. 200
	10/10	4,000

Accounts Payable			No. 201
10/12	1,500	10/3	2,000

Instructions
(a) Reproduce the journal entries for the transactions that occurred on October 1, 10, and 20, and provide explanations for each.
(b) Determine the October 31 balance for each of the accounts above, and prepare a trial balance at October 31, 2012.

Prepare journal entries and post using standard account form.

(SO 4, 6)

E2-12   Selected transactions for Roberta Garza Company during its first month in business are presented below.

Sept. 1   Invested $10,000 cash in the business.
       5   Purchased equipment for $12,000 paying $4,000 in cash and the balance on account.
      25   Paid $3,000 cash on balance owed for equipment.
      30   Withdrew $700 cash for personal use.

Garza's chart of accounts shows: No. 101 Cash, No. 157 Equipment, No. 201 Accounts Payable, No. 301 Owner's Capital, and No. 306 Owner's Drawings.

Instructions
(a) Journalize the transactions on page J1 of the journal. (Omit explanations.)
(b) Post the transactions using the standard account form.

Analyze errors and their effects on trial balance.

(SO 7)

E2-13   The bookkeeper for Lance Briggs Equipment Repair made a number of errors in journalizing and posting, as described below.

1. A credit posting of $525 to Accounts Receivable was omitted.
2. A debit posting of $750 for Prepaid Insurance was debited to Insurance Expense.
3. A collection from a customer of $100 in payment of its account owed was journalized and posted as a debit to Cash $100 and a credit to Service Revenue $100.
4. A credit posting of $415 to Property Taxes Payable was made twice.
5. A cash purchase of supplies for $250 was journalized and posted as a debit to Supplies $25 and a credit to Cash $25.
6. A debit of $475 to Advertising Expense was posted as $457.

Instructions
For each error:

(a) Indicate whether the trial balance will balance.
(b) If the trial balance will not balance, indicate the amount of the difference.
(c) Indicate the trial balance column that will have the larger total.

Consider each error separately. Use the following form, in which error (1) is given as an example.

Error	**(a)** In Balance	**(b)** Difference	**(c)** Larger Column
(1)	No	$525	debit

Prepare a trial balance.

(SO 2, 7)

E2-14   The accounts in the ledger of Bullucks Delivery Service contain the following balances on July 31, 2012.

Accounts Receivable	$ 7,642	Prepaid Insurance	$ 1,968
Accounts Payable	8,396	Maintenance and Repairs Expense	961
Cash	?	Service Revenue	10,610
Equipment	49,360	Owner's Drawings	700
Gasoline Expense	758	Owner's Capital	42,000
Insurance Expense	523	Salaries and Wages Expense	4,428
Notes Payable	17,000	Salaries and Wages Payable	815

Instructions
Prepare a trial balance with the accounts arranged as illustrated in the chapter and fill in the missing amount for Cash.

Exercises: Set B

Visit the book's companion website, at **www.wiley.com/college/weygandt**, and choose the Student Companion site to access Exercise Set B.

Problems: Set A

Journalize a series of transactions. **GLS**

(SO 2, 4)

P2-1A   Frontier Park was started on April 1 by H. Hillenmeyer. The following selected events and transactions occurred during April.

Apr. 1   Hillenmeyer invested $35,000 cash in the business.
     4   Purchased land costing $27,000 for cash.
     8   Incurred advertising expense of $1,800 on account.
    11   Paid salaries to employees $1,500.
    12   Hired park manager at a salary of $4,000 per month, effective May 1.
    13   Paid $1,650 cash for a one-year insurance policy.
    17   Withdrew $1,000 cash for personal use.
    20   Received $6,800 in cash for admission fees.
    25   Sold 100 coupon books for $25 each. Each book contains 10 coupons that entitle the
         holder to one admission to the park.
    30   Received $8,900 in cash admission fees.
    30   Paid $900 on balance owed for advertising incurred on April 8.

Hillenmeyer uses the following accounts: Cash, Prepaid Insurance, Land, Accounts Payable, Unearned Service Revenue, Owner's Capital, Owner's Drawings, Service Revenue, Advertising Expense, and Salaries and Wages Expense.

Instructions
Journalize the April transactions.

P2-2A   Desiree Clark is a licensed CPA. During the first month of operations of her business, the following events and transactions occurred.

Journalize transactions, post, and prepare a trial balance.
(SO 2, 4, 6, 7)

GLS

May 1   Clark invested $20,000 cash in her business.
    2   Hired a secretary-receptionist at a salary of $2,000 per month.
    3   Purchased $2,500 of supplies on account from Read Supply Company.
    7   Paid office rent of $900 cash for the month.
   11   Completed a tax assignment and billed client $3,200 for services provided.
   12   Received $3,500 advance on a management consulting engagement.
   17   Received cash of $1,200 for services completed for C. Desmond Co.
   31   Paid secretary-receptionist $2,000 salary for the month.
   31   Paid 60% of balance due Read Supply Company.

Desiree uses the following chart of accounts: No. 101 Cash, No. 112 Accounts Receivable, No. 126 Supplies, No. 201 Accounts Payable, No. 209 Unearned Service Revenue, No. 301 Owner's Capital, No. 400 Service Revenue, No. 726 Salaries and Wages Expense, and No. 729 Rent Expense.

Instructions
(a) Journalize the transactions.
(b) Post to the ledger accounts.
(c) Prepare a trial balance on May 31, 2012.

Trial balance totals $28,900

P2-3A   Jay Cutler owns and manages a computer repair service, which had the following trial balance on December 31, 2011 (the end of its fiscal year).

Journalize transactions, post, and prepare a trial balance.
(SO 2, 4, 6, 7)

MEGA REPAIR SERVICE
Trial Balance
December 31, 2011

Cash	$ 8,000	
Accounts Receivable	15,000	
Supplies	13,000	
Prepaid Rent	3,000	
Equipment	20,000	
Accounts Payable		$19,000
Owner's Capital		40,000
	$59,000	$59,000

Summarized transactions for January 2012 were as follows.

1. Advertising costs, paid in cash, $1,000.
2. Additional supplies acquired on account $4,200.
3. Miscellaneous expenses, paid in cash, $2,000.
4. Cash collected from customers in payment of accounts receivable $14,000.
5. Cash paid to creditors for accounts payable due $15,000.

6. Supplies used during January $4,000.
7. Repair services performed during January: for cash $6,000; on account $9,000.
8. Wages for January, paid in cash, $3,500.
9. Jay's drawings during January were $3,000.

Instructions

(a) Open T accounts for each of the accounts listed in the trial balance, and enter the opening balances for 2012.

(b) Prepare journal entries to record each of the January transactions. (Omit explanations.)

(c) Post the journal entries to the accounts in the ledger. (Add accounts as needed.)

Trial balance totals $63,200

(d) Prepare a trial balance as of January 31, 2012.

Prepare a correct trial balance.
(SO 7)

P2-4A   The trial balance of the Kellen Davis Company shown below does not balance.

KELLEN DAVIS COMPANY
Trial Balance
May 31, 2012

	Debit	Credit
Cash	$ 5,850	
Accounts Receivable		$ 2,750
Prepaid Insurance	700	
Equipment	8,000	
Accounts Payable		4,500
Unearned Service Revenue	650	
Owner's Capital		11,700
Service Revenue	6,690	
Salaries and Wages Expense	4,200	
Advertising Expense		1,100
Insurance Expense	890	
	$26,980	$20,050

Your review of the ledger reveals that each account has a normal balance. You also discover the following errors.

1. The totals of the debit sides of Prepaid Insurance, Accounts Payable, and Insurance Expense were each understated $100.

2. Transposition errors were made in Accounts Receivable and Service Revenue. Based on postings made, the correct balances were $2,570 and $6,960, respectively.

3. A debit posting to Salaries and Wages Expense of $200 was omitted.

4. A $1,000 cash drawing by the owner was debited to Owner's Capital for $1,000 and credited to Cash for $1,000.

5. A $520 purchase of supplies on account was debited to Equipment for $520 and credited to Cash for $520.

6. A cash payment of $540 for advertising was debited to Advertising Expense for $54 and credited to Cash for $54.

7. A collection from a customer for $210 was debited to Cash for $210 and credited to Accounts Payable for $210.

Instructions

Trial balance totals $25,020

Prepare a correct trial balance. Note that the chart of accounts includes the following: Owner's Drawings and Supplies. (*Hint:* It helps to prepare the correct journal entry for the transaction described and compare it to the mistake made.)

Journalize transactions, post, and prepare a trial balance.
(SO 2, 4, 6, 7)

P2-5A   The Chicago Theater is owned by Rashied Davis. All facilities were completed on March 31. At this time, the ledger showed: No. 101 Cash $4,000, No. 140 Land $10,000, No. 145 Buildings (concession stand, projection room, ticket booth, and screen) $8,000, No. 157 Equipment $6,000, No. 201 Accounts Payable $2,000, No. 275 Mortgage Payable $8,000, and No. 301 Owner's Capital $18,000. During April, the following events and transactions occurred.

Apr. 2   Paid film rental of $1,100 on first movie.
    3   Ordered two additional films at $1,000 each.
    9   Received $2,800 cash from admissions.
    10   Made $2,000 payment on mortgage and $1,000 for accounts payable due.

11   Chicago Theater contracted with Virginia McCaskey to operate the concession stand. McCaskey is to pay 17% of gross concession receipts (payable monthly) for the rental of the concession stand.

12   Paid advertising expenses $500.

20   Received one of the films ordered on April 3 and was billed $1,000. The film will be shown in April.

25   Received $5,200 cash from admissions.

29   Paid salaries $2,000.

30   Received statement from Virginia McCaskey showing gross concession receipts of $1,000 and the balance due to The Chicago Theater of $170 ($1,000 × 17%) for April. McCaskey paid one-half of the balance due and will remit the remainder on May 5.

30   Prepaid $1,200 rental on special film to be run in May.

In addition to the accounts identified above, the chart of accounts shows: No. 112 Accounts Receivable, No. 136 Prepaid Rent, No. 400 Service Revenue, No. 429 Rent Revenue, No. 610 Advertising Expense, No. 726 Salaries and Wages Expense, and No. 729 Rent Expense.

Instructions

(a) Enter the beginning balances in the ledger as of April 1. Insert a check mark (✓) in the reference column of the ledger for the beginning balance.

Trial balance totals $34,170

(b) Journalize the April transactions. Chicago records admission revenue as service revenue, rental of the concession stand as rent revenue, and film rental expense as rent expense.

(c) Post the April journal entries to the ledger. Assume that all entries are posted from page 1 of the journal.

(d) Prepare a trial balance on April 30, 2012.

Problems: Set B

P2-1B   Forte Disc Golf Course was opened on March 1 by Matt Forte. The following selected events and transactions occurred during March.

Journalize a series of transactions.
(SO 2, 4)

Mar. 1   Invested $20,000 cash in the business.

3   Purchased Heeren's Golf Land for $15,000 cash. The price consists of land $12,000, shed $2,000, and equipment $1,000. (Make one compound entry.)

5   Paid advertising expenses of $700.

6   Paid cash $600 for a one-year insurance policy.

10   Purchased golf discs and other equipment for $1,050 from Innova Company payable in 30 days.

18   Received $1,100 in cash for golf fees earned (Forte records golf fees as service revenue).

19   Sold 150 coupon books for $10 each. Each book contains 4 coupons that enable the holder to play one round of disc golf.

25   Withdrew $800 cash for personal use.

30   Paid salaries of $250.

30   Paid Innova Company in full.

31   Received $2,100 cash for fees earned.

Matt Forte uses the following accounts: Cash, Prepaid Insurance, Land, Buildings, Equipment, Accounts Payable, Unearned Service Revenue, Owner's Capital, Owner's Drawings, Service Revenue, Advertising Expense, and Salaries and Wages Expense.

Instructions

Journalize the March transactions.

P2-2B   Victoria Hall is a licensed dentist. During the first month of the operation of her business, the following events and transactions occurred.

Journalize transactions, post, and prepare a trial balance.
(SO 2, 4, 6, 7)

April 1   Invested $20,000 cash in her business.

1   Hired a secretary-receptionist at a salary of $700 per week payable monthly.

2   Paid office rent for the month $1,100.

3   Purchased dental supplies on account from Smile Company $4,000.

10 Provided dental services and billed insurance companies $5,100.
11 Received $1,000 cash advance from Trudy Borke for an implant.
20 Received $2,100 cash for services completed and delivered to John Carl.
30 Paid secretary-receptionist for the month $2,800.
30 Paid $2,400 to Smile Company for accounts payable due.

Victoria uses the following chart of accounts: No. 101 Cash, No. 112 Accounts Receivable, No. 126 Supplies, No. 201 Accounts Payable, No. 209 Unearned Service Revenue, No. 301 Owner's Capital, No. 400 Service Revenue, No. 726 Salaries and Wages Expense, and No. 729 Rent Expense.

Instructions

Trial balance totals $29,800

(a) Journalize the transactions.
(b) Post to the ledger accounts.
(c) Prepare a trial balance on April 30, 2012.

Journalize transactions, post, and prepare a trial balance.
(SO 2, 4, 6, 7)

P2-3B San Jose Services was formed on May 1, 2012. The following transactions took place during the first month.

Transactions on May 1:

1. Jarron Gilbert invested $40,000 cash in the company, as its sole owner.
2. Hired two employees to work in the warehouse. They will each be paid a salary of $3,050 per month.
3. Signed a 2-year rental agreement on a warehouse; paid $24,000 cash in advance for the first year.
4. Purchased furniture and equipment costing $30,000. A cash payment of $10,000 was made immediately; the remainder will be paid in 6 months.
5. Paid $1,800 cash for a one-year insurance policy on the furniture and equipment.

Transactions during the remainder of the month:

6. Purchased basic office supplies for $500 cash.
7. Purchased more office supplies for $1,500 on account.
8. Total revenues earned were $20,000—$8,000 cash and $12,000 on account.
9. Paid $400 to suppliers for accounts payable due.
10. Received $3,000 from customers in payment of accounts receivable.
11. Received utility bills in the amount of $350, to be paid next month.
12. Paid the monthly salaries of the two employees, totalling $6,100.

Instructions

Trial balance totals $81,450

(a) Prepare journal entries to record each of the events listed. (Omit explanations.)
(b) Post the journal entries to T accounts.
(c) Prepare a trial balance as of May 31, 2012.

Prepare a correct trial balance.
(SO 7)

P2-4B The trial balance of Robbie Gould Co. shown below does not balance.

ROBBIE GOULD CO.
Trial Balance
June 30, 2012

	Debit	Credit
Cash		$ 3,340
Accounts Receivable	$ 2,812	
Supplies	1,200	
Equipment	2,600	
Accounts Payable		3,666
Unearned Service Revenue	1,100	
Owner's Capital		8,000
Owner's Drawings	800	
Service Revenue		2,480
Salaries and Wages Expense	3,200	
Supplies Expense	810	
	$12,522	$17,486

Each of the listed accounts has a normal balance per the general ledger. An examination of the ledger and journal reveals the following errors.

1. Cash received from a customer in payment of its account was debited for $580, and Accounts Receivable was credited for the same amount. The actual collection was for $850.
2. The purchase of a computer on account for $710 was recorded as a debit to Supplies for $710 and a credit to Accounts Payable for $710.
3. Services were performed on account for a client for $980. Accounts Receivable was debited for $980, and Service Revenue was credited for $98.
4. A debit posting to Salaries and Wages Expense of $700 was omitted.
5. A payment of a balance due for $306 was credited to Cash for $306 and credited to Accounts Payable for $360.
6. The withdrawal of $600 cash for Gould's personal use was debited to Salaries and Wages Expense for $600 and credited to Cash for $600.

Instructions

Prepare a correct trial balance. (*Hint:* It helps to prepare the correct journal entry for the transaction described and compare it to the mistake made.)

Trial balance totals $15,462

P2-5B The Cora Theater, owned by Cora Graham, will begin operations in March. The Cora will be unique in that it will show only triple features of sequential theme movies. As of March 1, the ledger of Cora showed: No. 101 Cash $3,000, No. 140 Land $24,000, No. 145 Buildings (concession stand, projection room, ticket booth, and screen) $10,000, No. 157 Equipment $10,000, No. 201 Accounts Payable $7,000, and No. 301 Owner's Capital $40,000. During the month of March the following events and transactions occurred.

Journalize transactions, post, and prepare a trial balance.
(SO 2, 4, 6, 7)

Mar. 2   Rented the three *Indiana Jones* movies to be shown for the first 3 weeks of March. The film rental was $3,500; $1,500 was paid in cash and $2,000 will be paid on March 10.
   3   Ordered the *Lord of the Rings* movies to be shown the last 10 days of March. It will cost $200 per night.
   9   Received $4,000 cash from admissions.
   10   Paid balance due on *Indiana Jones* movies rental and $2,100 on March 1 accounts payable.
   11   Cora Theater contracted with Caleb Hanie to operate the concession stand. Hanie is to pay 15% of gross concession receipts (payable monthly) for the rental of the concession stand.
   12   Paid advertising expenses $800.
   20   Received $5,000 cash from customers for admissions.
   20   Received the *Lord of the Rings* movies and paid the rental fee of $2,000.
   31   Paid salaries of $3,100.
   31   Received statement from Caleb Hanie showing gross receipts from concessions of $6,000 and the balance due to Cora Theater of $900 ($6,000 × 15%) for March. Hanie paid one-half the balance due and will remit the remainder on April 5.
   31   Received $9,000 cash from customers for admissions.

In addition to the accounts identified above, the chart of accounts includes: No. 112 Accounts Receivable, No. 400 Service Revenue, No. 429 Rent Revenue, No. 610 Advertising Expense, No. 726 Salaries and Wages Expense, and No. 729 Rent Expense.

Instructions

(a) Enter the beginning balances in the ledger. Insert a check mark (✓) in the reference column of the ledger for the beginning balance.
(b) Journalize the March transactions. Cora records admission revenue as service revenue, rental of the concession stand as rent revenue, and film rental expense as rent expense.
(c) Post the March journal entries to the ledger. Assume that all entries are posted from page 1 of the journal.
(d) Prepare a trial balance on March 31, 2012.

Trial balance totals $63,800

Problems: Set C

Visit the book's companion website, at **www.wiley.com/college/weygandt**, and choose the Student Companion site to access Problem Set C.

Continuing Cookie Chronicle

(*Note:* This is a continuation of the Cookie Chronicle from Chapter 1.)

CCC2 After researching the different forms of business organization. Natalie Koebel decides to operate "Cookie Creations" as a proprietorship. She then starts the process of getting the business running. In November 2011, the following activities take place.

Nov. 8   Natalie cashes her U.S. Savings Bonds and receives $520, which she deposits in her personal bank account.

8   She opens a bank account under the name "Cookie Creations" and transfers $500 from her personal account to the new account.

11   Natalie pays $65 for advertising.

13   She buys baking supplies, such as flour, sugar, butter, and chocolate chips, for $125 cash. (*Hint:* Use Supplies account.)

14   Natalie starts to gather some baking equipment to take with her when teaching the cookie classes. She has an excellent top-of-the-line food processor and mixer that originally cost her $750. Natalie decides to start using it only in her new business. She estimates that the equipment is currently worth $300. She invests the equipment in the business.

16   Natalie realizes that her initial cash investment is not enough. Her grandmother lends her $2,000 cash, for which Natalie signs a note payable in the name of the business. Natalie deposits the money in the business bank account. (*Hint:* The note does not have to be repaid for 24 months. As a result, the note payable should be reported in the accounts as the last liability and also on the balance sheet as the last liability.)

17   She buys more baking equipment for $900 cash.

20   She teaches her first class and collects $125 cash.

25   Natalie books a second class for December 4 for $150. She receives $30 cash in advance as a down payment.

30   Natalie pays $1,320 for a one-year insurance policy that will expire on December 1, 2011.

Instructions

(a) Prepare journal entries to record the November transactions.

(b) Post the journal entries to general ledger accounts.

(c) Prepare a trial balance at November 30.

BROADENINGYOURPERSPECTIVE

Financial Reporting and Analysis

Financial Reporting Problem: PepsiCo, Inc.

BYP2-1 The financial statements of PepsiCo, Inc. are presented in Appendix A. The notes accompanying the statements contain the following selected accounts, stated in millions of dollars.

Accounts Payable	Income Taxes Payable
Accounts Receivable	Interest Expense
Property, Plant, and Equipment	Inventory

Instructions

(a) Answer the following questions.
  (1) What is the increase and decrease side for each account?
  (2) What is the normal balance for each account?
(b) Identify the probable other account in the transaction and the effect on that account when:
  (1) Accounts Receivable is decreased.
  (2) Accounts Payable is decreased.
  (3) Inventory is increased.
(c) Identify the other account(s) that ordinarily would be involved when:
  (1) Interest Expense is increased.
  (2) Property, Plant, and Equipment is increased.

Comparative Analysis Problem: PepsiCo, Inc. vs. The Coca-Cola Company

BYP2-2 PepsiCo's financial statements are presented in Appendix A. Financial statements of The Coca-Cola Company are presented in Appendix B.

Instructions

(a) Based on the information contained in the financial statements, determine the normal balance of the listed accounts for each company.

PepsiCo	Coca-Cola
1. Inventory	**1.** Accounts Receivable
2. Property, Plant, and Equipment	**2.** Cash and Cash Equivalents
3. Accounts Payable	**3.** Cost of Goods Sold
4. Interest Expense	**4.** Sales (revenue)

(b) Identify the other account ordinarily involved when:
  (1) Accounts Receivable is increased.
  (2) Salaries and Wages Payable is decreased.
  (3) Property, Plant, and Equipment is increased.
  (4) Interest Expense is increased.

On the Web

BYP2-3 Much information about specific companies is available on the Internet. Such information includes basic descriptions of the company's location, activities, industry, financial health, and financial performance.

Address: biz.yahoo.com/i, or go to **www.wiley.com/college/weygandt**

Steps

1. Type in a company name, or use index to find company name.
2. Choose **Profile**. Perform instructions (a)–(c) below.
3. Click on the company's specific industry to identify competitors. Perform instructions (d)–(g) below.

Instructions

Answer the following questions.

(a) What is the company's industry?
(b) What was the company's total sales?
(c) What was the company's net income?
(d) What are the names of four of the company's competitors?
(e) Choose one of these competitors.
(f) What is this competitor's name? What were its sales? What was its net income?
(g) Which of these two companies is larger by size of sales? Which one reported higher net income?

Critical Thinking

Decision Making Across the Organization

BYP2-4 Lisa Ortega operates Ortega Riding Academy. The academy's primary sources of revenue are riding fees and lesson fees, which are paid on a cash basis. Lisa also boards horses for owners, who are billed monthly for boarding fees. In a few cases, boarders pay in advance of expected use. For its revenue transactions, the academy maintains the following accounts: No. 1 Cash, No. 5 Boarding Accounts Receivable, No. 27 Unearned Boarding Revenue, No. 51 Riding Revenue, No. 52 Lesson Revenue, and No. 53 Boarding Revenue.

The academy owns 10 horses, a stable, a riding corral, riding equipment, and office equipment. These assets are accounted for in accounts No. 11 Horses, No. 12 Building, No. 13 Riding Corral, No. 14 Riding Equipment, and No. 15 Office Equipment.

For its expenses, the academy maintains the following accounts: No. 6 Hay and Feed Supplies, No. 7 Prepaid Insurance, No. 21 Accounts Payable, No. 60 Salaries and Wages Expense, No. 61 Advertising Expense, No. 62 Utilities Expense, No. 63 Veterinary Expense, No. 64 Hay and Feed Expense, and No. 65 Insurance Expense.

Lisa makes periodic withdrawals of cash for personal living expenses. To record Lisa's equity in the business and her drawings, two accounts are maintained: No. 50 Owner's Capital, and No. 51 Owner's Drawings.

During the first month of operations an inexperienced bookkeeper was employed. Lisa Ortega asks you to review the following eight entries of the 50 entries made during the month. In each case, the explanation for the entry is correct.

May	1	Cash	18,000	
		Owner's Capital		18,000
		(Invested $18,000 cash in business)		
	5	Cash	250	
		Riding Revenue		250
		(Received $250 cash for lessons provided)		
	7	Cash	300	
		Boarding Revenue		300
		(Received $300 for boarding of horses beginning June 1)		
	14	Riding Equipment	80	
		Cash		800
		(Purchased desk and other office equipment for $800 cash)		
	15	Salaries and Wages Expense	400	
		Cash		400
		(Issued check to Lisa Ortega for personal use)		
	20	Cash	148	
		Riding Revenue		184
		(Received $184 cash for riding fees)		
	30	Veterinary Expense	75	
		Accounts Payable		75
		(Received bill of $75 from veterinarian for services rendered)		
	31	Hay and Feed Expense	1,700	
		Cash		1,700
		(Purchased an estimated 2 months' supply of feed and hay for $1,700 on account)		

Instructions

With the class divided into groups, answer the following.

(a) Identify each journal entry that is correct. For each journal entry that is incorrect, prepare the entry that should have been made by the bookkeeper.

(b) Which of the incorrect entries would prevent the trial balance from balancing?

(c) What was the correct net income for May, assuming the bookkeeper reported net income of $4,500 after posting all 50 entries?

(d) What was the correct cash balance at May 31, assuming the bookkeeper reported a balance of $12,475 after posting all 50 entries (and the only errors occurred in the items listed above)?

Communication Activity

BYP2-5 Woderson's Maid Company offers home-cleaning service. Two recurring transactions for the company are billing customers for services rendered and paying employee salaries. For example, on March 15, bills totaling $6,000 were sent to customers and $2,000 was paid in salaries to employees.

Instructions
Write a memo to your instructor that explains and illustrates the steps in the recording process for each of the March 15 transactions. Use the format illustrated in the text under the heading, "The Recording Process Illustrated" (p. 64).

Ethics Case

BYP2-6 Mary Jansen is the assistant chief accountant at Casey Company, a manufacturer of computer chips and cellular phones. The company presently has total sales of $20 million. It is the end of the first quarter. Mary is hurriedly trying to prepare a general ledger trial balance so that quarterly financial statements can be prepared and released to management and the regulatory agencies. The total credits on the trial balance exceed the debits by $1,000. In order to meet the 4 p.m. deadline, Mary decides to force the debits and credits into balance by adding the amount of the difference to the Equipment account. She chose Equipment because it is one of the larger account balances; percentage-wise, it will be the least misstated. Mary "plugs" the difference! She believes that the difference will not affect anyone's decisions. She wishes that she had another few days to find the error but realizes that the financial statements are already late.

Instructions
(a) Who are the stakeholders in this situation?

(b) What are the ethical issues involved in this case?

(c) What are Mary's alternatives?

"All About You" Activity

BYP2-7 Every company needs to plan in order to move forward. Its top management must consider where it wants the company to be in three to five years. Like a company, you need to think about where you want to be three to five years from now, and you need to start taking steps now in order to get there. With some forethought, you can help yourself avoid a situation, like those described in the **All About You** feature (available online at the book's companion website) in which your résumé seems to need creative writing.

Instructions
Provide responses to each of the following items.

(a) Where would you like to be working in three to five years? Describe your plan for getting there by identifying between five and 10 specific steps that you need to take.

(b) In order to get the job you want, you will need a résumé. Your résumé is the equivalent of a company's annual report. It needs to provide relevant and reliable information about your past accomplishments so that employers can decide whether to "invest" in you. Do a search on the Internet to find a good résumé format. What are the basic elements of a résumé?

(c) A company's annual report provides information about a company's accomplishments. In order for investors to use the annual report, the information must be reliable; that is, users must have faith that the information is accurate and believable. How can you provide assurance that the information on your résumé is reliable?

(d) Prepare a résumé assuming that you have accomplished the five to 10 specific steps you identified in part (a). Also, provide evidence that would give assurance that the information is reliable.

Answers to Insight and Accounting Across the Organization Questions

p. 55 Keeping Score   Q: Do you think that the Chicago Bears football team would be likely to have the same major revenue and expense accounts as the Cubs? **A:** Because their businesses are similar—professional sports—many of the revenue and expense accounts for the baseball and football teams might be similar.

p. 61 What Would Sam Do?   Q: Why did Sam Walton keep separate pigeonholes and blue binders? **A:** Using separate pigeonholes and blue binders for each store enabled Walton to accumulate and track the performance of each individual store easily.   **Q:** Why bother to keep separate records for each store? **A:** Keeping separate records for each store provided Walton with more information about performance of individual stores and managers, and greater control. Walton would want and need the same advantages if he were starting his business today. The difference is that he might now use a computerized system for small businesses.

p. 73 Why Accuracy Matters   Q: In order for these companies to prepare and issue financial statements, their accounting equations (debit and credits) must have been in balance at year-end. How could these errors or misstatements have occurred? **A:** A company's accounting equation (its books) can be in balance yet its financial statements have errors or misstatements because of the following: entire transactions were not recorded; transactions were recorded at wrong amounts; transactions were recorded in the wrong accounts; transactions were recorded in the wrong accounting period. Audits of financial statements uncover some, but obviously not all, errors or misstatements.

Answers to Self-Test Questions
1. b   **2.** c   **3.** d   **4.** d   **5.** d   **6.** b   **7.** a   **8.** c   **9.** b   **10.** c   **11.** d   **12.** c ($16,000 − $5,000)   **13.** a   **14.** c
15. a ($5,000 + $40,000 + $10,000 + $15,000 + $61,000)

IFRS A Look at IFRS

International companies use the same set of procedures and records to keep track of transaction data. Thus, the material in Chapter 2 dealing with the account, general rules of debit and credit, and steps in the recording process—the journal, ledger, and chart of accounts—is the same under both GAAP and IFRS.

Key Points

- Transaction analysis is the same under IFRS and GAAP but, as you will see in later chapters, different standards sometimes impact how transactions are recorded.

- Rules for accounting for specific events sometimes differ across countries. For example, European companies rely less on historical cost and more on fair value than U.S. companies. Despite the differences, the double-entry accounting system is the basis of accounting systems worldwide.

- Both the IASB and FASB go beyond the basic definitions provided in this textbook for the key elements of financial statements, that is, assets, liabilities, equity, revenues, and expenses. The more substantive definitions, using the IASB definitional structure, are provided in the Chapter 1 *A Look at IFRS* discussion.

- A trial balance under IFRS follows the same format as shown in the textbook.

- As shown in the textbook, dollars signs are typically used only in the trial balance and the financial statements. The same practice is followed under IFRS, using the currency of the country that the reporting company is headquartered.

- In February 2010, the SEC expressed a desire to continue working toward a single set of high-quality standards. In deciding whether the United States should adopt IFRS, some of the issues the SEC said should be considered are:

  - Whether IFRS is sufficiently developed and consistent in application.

  - Whether the IASB is sufficiently independent.

  - Whether IFRS is established for the benefit of investors.

  - The issues involved in educating investors about IFRS.

  - The impact of a switch to IFRS on U.S. laws and regulations.

  - The impact on companies including changes to their accounting systems, contractual arrangements, corporate governance, and litigation.

  - The issues involved in educating accountants, so they can prepare statements under IFRS.

Looking to the Future

The basic recording process shown in this textbook is followed by companies across the globe. It is unlikely to change in the future. The definitional structure of assets, liabilities, equity, revenues, and expenses may change over time as the IASB and FASB evaluate their overall conceptual framework for establishing accounting standards.

IFRS Self-Test Questions

1. Which statement is *correct* regarding IFRS?
   (a) IFRS reverses the rules of debits and credits, that is, debits are on the right and credits are on the left.
   (b) IFRS uses the same process for recording transactions as GAAP.
   (c) The chart of accounts under IFRS is different because revenues follow assets.
   (d) None of the above statements are correct.

2. The expanded accounting equation under IFRS is as follows:
   (a) Assets = Liabilities + Owner's Capital + Owner's Drawings + Revenues − Expenses.
   (b) Assets + Liabilities = Owner's Capital + Owner's Drawings + Revenues − Expenses.
   (c) Assets = Liabilities + Owner's Capital − Owner's Drawings + Revenues − Expenses.
   (d) Assets = Liabilities + Owner's Capital + Owner's Drawings − Revenues − Expenses.

3. A trial balance:
   (a) is the same under IFRS and GAAP.
   (b) proves that transactions are recorded correctly.
   (c) proves that all transactions have been recorded.
   (d) will not balance if a correct journal entry is posted twice.

4. One difference between IFRS and GAAP is that:
   (a) GAAP uses accrual-accounting concepts and IFRS uses primarily the cash basis of accounting.
   (b) IFRS uses a different posting process than GAAP.
   (c) IFRS uses more fair value measurements than GAAP.
   (d) the limitations of a trial balance are different between IFRS and GAAP.

5. The general policy for using proper currency signs (dollar, yen, pound, etc.) is the same for both IFRS and this textbook. This policy is as follows:
  (a) Currency signs only appear in ledgers and journal entries.
  (b) Currency signs are only shown in the trial balance.
  (c) Currency signs are shown for all compound journal entries.
  (d) Currency signs are shown in trial balances and financial statements.

IFRS Concepts and Application

IFRS2-1   Describe some of the issues the SEC must consider in deciding whether the United States should adopt IFRS.

International Financial Reporting Problem: Zetar plc

IFRS2-2   The financial statements of Zetar plc are presented in Appendix C. The company's complete annual report, including the notes to its financial statements, is available at *www.zetarplc.com*.

Instructions
Describe in which statement each of the following items is reported, and the position in the statement (e.g., current asset).
  (a) Other administrative expenses.
  (b) Cash at bank.
  (c) Borrowings and overdrafts.
  (d) Finance costs.

Answers to IFRS Self-Test Questions
1. b   **2.** c   **3.** a   **4.** c   **5.** d

The Navigator

✔   **Remember to go back to the Navigator box on the chapter opening page and check off your completed work.**

CHAPTER3

Adjusting the Accounts

Study Objectives

After studying this chapter, you should be able to:

[1] Explain the time period assumption.

[2] Explain the accrual basis of accounting.

[3] Explain the reasons for adjusting entries.

[4] Identify the major types of adjusting entries.

[5] Prepare adjusting entries for deferrals.

[6] Prepare adjusting entries for accruals.

[7] Describe the nature and purpose of an adjusted trial balance.

✔ The Navigator

✔ [The Navigator]

Feature Story

WHAT WAS YOUR PROFIT?

The accuracy of the financial reporting system depends on answers to a few fundamental questions: At what point has revenue been earned? At what point is the earnings process complete? When have expenses really been incurred?

During the 1990s, the stock prices of dot-com companies boomed. Most dot-coms earned most of their revenue from selling advertising space on their websites. To boost reported revenue, some dot-coms began swapping website ad space. Company A would put an ad for its website on company B's website, and company B would put an ad for its website on company A's website. No money changed hands, but each company recorded revenue (for the value of the space that it gave the other company on its site). This practice did little to boost net income, and it resulted in no additional cash flow—but it did boost *reported revenue*.

Regulators eventually put an end to this misleading practice.

Another type of transgression results from companies recording revenues or expenses in the wrong year. In fact, shifting revenues and expenses is one of the most common abuses of financial accounting. Xerox admitted reporting billions of dollars of lease revenue in periods earlier than it should have been reported. And WorldCom stunned the financial markets with its admission that it had boosted net income by billions of dollars by delaying the recognition of expenses until later years.

Unfortunately, revelations such as these have become all too common in the corporate world. It is no wonder that a U.S. Trust survey of affluent Americans reported that 85% of respondents believed that there should be tighter regulation of financial disclosures; 66% said they did not trust the management of publicly traded companies.

Why did so many companies violate basic financial reporting rules and sound ethics? Many speculate that as stock prices climbed, executives were under increasing pressure to meet higher and higher earnings expectations. If actual results weren't as good as hoped for, some gave in to temptation and "adjusted" their numbers to meet market expectations.

InsideCHAPTER3

- *Ethics Insight*: **Cooking the Books?** *(p.102)*
- *Accounting Across the Organization*: **Turning Gift Cards into Revenue** *(p.110)*
- *International Insight*: **Cashing In on Accrual Accounting** *(p.114)*

Preview of CHAPTER 3

In Chapter 1, you learned a neat little formula: Net income = Revenues − Expenses. In Chapter 2, you learned some rules for recording revenue and expense transactions. Guess what? Things are not really that nice and neat. In fact, it is often difficult for companies to determine in what time period they should report some revenues and expenses. In other words, in measuring net income, timing is everything.

The content and organization of Chapter 3 are as follows.

Adjusting the Accounts		
Timing Issues	**The Basics of Adjusting Entries**	**The Adjusted Trial Balance and Financial Statements**
• Fiscal and calendar years • Accrual- vs. cash-basis accounting • Recognizing revenues and expenses	• Types of adjusting entries • Adjusting entries for deferrals • Adjusting entries for accruals • Summary of basic relationships	• Preparing the adjusted trial balance • Preparing financial statements

✔
The Navigator

Timing Issues

Study Objective [1]
Explain the time period assumption.

Time Period Assumption

Year I   Year 10

Year 6

Alternative Terminology

The time period assumption is also called the *periodicity assumption*.

We would need no adjustments if we could wait to prepare financial statements until a company ended its operations. At that point, we could easily determine its final balance sheet and the amount of lifetime income it earned.

However, most companies need immediate feedback about how well they are doing. For example, management usually wants monthly financial statements, and the Internal Revenue Service requires all businesses to file annual tax returns. Therefore, **accountants divide the economic life of a business into artificial time periods.** This convenient assumption is referred to as the **time period assumption**.

Many business transactions affect more than one of these arbitrary time periods. For example, the airplanes purchased by Southwest Airlines five years ago are still in use today. We must determine the relevance of each business transaction to specific accounting periods. (How much of the cost of an airplane contributed to operations this year?)

Fiscal and Calendar Years

Both small and large companies prepare financial statements periodically in order to assess their financial condition and results of operations. **Accounting time periods are generally a month, a quarter, or a year.** Monthly and quarterly time periods are called **interim periods**. Most large companies must prepare both quarterly and annual financial statements.

An accounting time period that is one year in length is a **fiscal year**. A fiscal year usually begins with the first day of a month and ends twelve months later on the last day of a month. Most businesses use the **calendar year** (January 1 to December 31) as their accounting period. Some do not. Companies whose fiscal year differs from the calendar year include Delta Air Lines, June 30, and Walt Disney

Productions, September 30. Sometimes a company's year-end will vary from year to year. For example, PepsiCo's fiscal year ends on the Friday closest to December 31, which was December 30 in 2008 and December 29 in 2009.

Accrual- vs. Cash-Basis Accounting

Study Objective [2]
Explain the accrual basis of accounting.

What you will learn in this chapter is accrual-basis accounting. Under the accrual basis, companies record transactions that change a company's financial statements **in the periods in which the events occur.** For example, using the accrual basis to determine net income means companies recognize revenues when earned (rather than when they receive cash). It also means recognizing expenses when incurred (rather than when paid).

An alternative to the accrual basis is the cash basis. Under cash-basis accounting, companies record revenue when they receive cash. They record an expense when they pay out cash. The cash basis seems appealing due to its simplicity, but it often produces misleading financial statements. It fails to record revenue that a company has earned but for which it has not received the cash. Also, it does not match expenses with earned revenues. **Cash-basis accounting is not in accordance with generally accepted accounting principles (GAAP).**

Individuals and some small companies do use cash-basis accounting. The cash basis is justified for small businesses because they often have few receivables and payables. Medium and large companies use accrual-basis accounting.

Recognizing Revenues and Expenses

It can be difficult to determine the amount of revenues and expenses to report in a given accounting period. Two principles help in this task: the revenue recognition principle and the expense recognition principle.

REVENUE RECOGNITION PRINCIPLE

The revenue recognition principle requires that companies recognize revenue in the accounting period **in which it is earned.** In a service enterprise, revenue is considered to be earned at the time the service is performed. To illustrate, assume that Dave's Dry Cleaning cleans clothing on June 30 but customers do not claim and pay for their clothes until the first week of July. Under the revenue recognition principle, Dave's earns revenue in June when it performed the service, rather than in July when it received the cash. At June 30, Dave's would report a receivable on its balance sheet and revenue in its income statement for the service performed.

Revenue Recognition

Service performed

Customer requests service   Cash received

Revenue should be recognized in the accounting period in which it is earned (generally when service is performed).

EXPENSE RECOGNITION PRINCIPLE

Accountants follow a simple rule in recognizing expenses: "Let the expenses follow the revenues." Thus, expense recognition is tied to revenue recognition. In the dry cleaning example, this means that Dave's should report the salary expense incurred in performing the June 30 cleaning service in the same period in which it recognizes the service revenue. The critical issue in expense recognition is when the expense makes its contribution to revenue. This may or may not be the same period in which the expense is paid. If Dave's does not pay the salary incurred on June 30 until July, it would report salaries payable on its June 30 balance sheet.

This practice of expense recognition is referred to as the expense recognition principle (often referred to as the matching principle). It dictates that efforts (expenses) be matched with results (revenues). Illustration 3-1 (page 102) summarizes the revenue and expense recognition principles.

Matching Revenues

Delivery

AD
Advertising   Utilities

Expenses

Illustration 3-1
GAAP relationships in revenue and expense recognition

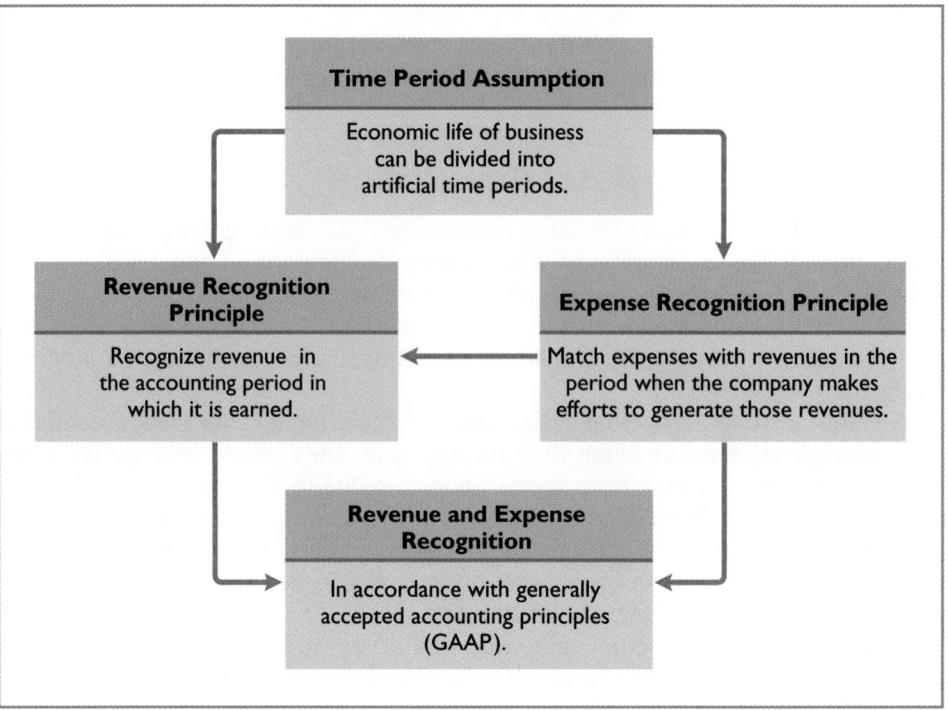

ETHICS INSIGHT

Cooking the Books?

Allegations of abuse of the revenue recognition principle have become all too common in recent years. For example, it was alleged that Krispy Kreme sometimes doubled the number of doughnuts shipped to wholesale customers at the end of a quarter to boost quarterly results. The customers shipped the unsold doughnuts back after the beginning of the next quarter for a refund. Conversely, Computer Associates International was accused of backdating sales—that is, saying that a sale that occurred at the beginning of one quarter occurred at the end of the previous quarter in order to achieve the previous quarter's sales targets.

? What motivates sales executives and finance and accounting executives to participate in activities that result in inaccurate reporting of revenues? (See page 148.)

Do it!

Timing Concepts

Numerous timing concepts are discussed on pages 100–102. A list of concepts is provided in the left column below, with a description of the concept in the right column below and on the next page. There are more descriptions provided than concepts. Match the description of the concept to the concept.

1. ____ Accrual-basis accounting.

2. ____ Calendar year.

3. ____ Time period assumption.

4. ____ Expense recognition principle.

(a) Monthly and quarterly time periods.

(b) Efforts (expenses) should be matched with results (revenues).

(c) Accountants divide the economic life of a business into artificial time periods.

(d) Companies record revenues when they receive cash and record expenses when they pay out cash.

(e) An accounting time period that starts on January 1 and ends on December 31.

(f) Companies record transactions in the period in which the events occur.

action plan

✔ Review the glossary terms identified on page 124.

✔ Study carefully the revenue recognition principle, the expense recognition principle, and the time period assumption.

Solution

1. f **2.** e **3.** c **4.** b

Related exercise material: E3-1, E3-2, E3-3, and **Do it!** 3-1.

✔ **The Navigator**

The Basics of Adjusting Entries

In order for revenues to be recorded in the period in which they are earned, and for expenses to be recognized in the period in which they are incurred, companies make adjusting entries. **Adjusting entries ensure that the revenue recognition and expense recognition principles are followed.**

Adjusting entries are necessary because the **trial balance**—the first pulling together of the transaction data—may not contain up-to-date and complete data. This is true for several reasons:

1. Some events are not recorded daily because it is not efficient to do so. Examples are the use of supplies and the earning of wages by employees.
2. Some costs are not recorded during the accounting period because these costs expire with the passage of time rather than as a result of recurring daily transactions. Examples are charges related to the use of buildings and equipment, rent, and insurance.
3. Some items may be unrecorded. An example is a utility service bill that will not be received until the next accounting period.

Adjusting entries are required every time a company prepares financial statements. The company analyzes each account in the trial balance to determine whether it is complete and up to date for financial statement purposes. **Every adjusting entry will include one income statement account and one balance sheet account.**

Study Objective [3]
Explain the reasons for adjusting entries.

International Note

Internal controls are a system of checks and balances designed to detect and prevent fraud and errors. The Sarbanes-Oxley Act requires U.S. companies to enhance their systems of internal control. However, many foreign companies do not have to meet strict internal control requirements. Some U.S. companies believe that this gives foreign firms an unfair advantage because developing and maintaining internal controls can be very expensive.

Types of Adjusting Entries

Adjusting entries are classified as either **deferrals** or **accruals**. As Illustration 3-2 shows, each of these classes has two subcategories.

Study Objective [4]
Identify the major types of adjusting entries.

Deferrals:
1. Prepaid expenses: Expenses paid in cash and recorded as assets before they are used or consumed.
2. Unearned revenues: Cash received and recorded as liabilities before revenue is earned.

Accruals:
1. Accrued revenues: Revenues earned but not yet received in cash or recorded.
2. Accrued expenses: Expenses incurred but not yet paid in cash or recorded.

Illustration 3-2
Categories of adjusting entries

Subsequent sections give examples of each type of adjustment. Each example is based on the October 31 trial balance of Pioneer Advertising, from Chapter 2, reproduced in Illustration 3-3.

Illustration 3-3
Trial balance

Pioneer Advertising Agency Trial Balance October 31, 2012		
	Debit	**Credit**
Cash	$15,200	
Supplies	2,500	
Prepaid Insurance	600	
Equipment	5,000	
Notes Payable		$ 5,000
Accounts Payable		2,500
Unearned Service Revenue		1,200
Owner's Capital		10,000
Owner's Drawings	500	
Service Revenue		10,000
Salaries and Wages Expense	4,000	
Rent Expense	900	
	$28,700	$28,700

We assume that Pioneer Advertising uses an accounting period of one month. Thus, monthly adjusting entries are made. The entries are dated October 31.

Adjusting Entries For Deferrals

Study Objective [5]
Prepare adjusting entries for deferrals.

To defer means to postpone or delay. **Deferrals** are costs or revenues that are recognized at a date later than the point when cash was originally exchanged. Companies make adjusting entries for deferrals to record the portion of the deferred item that was incurred as an expense or earned as revenue during the current accounting period. The two types of deferrals are prepaid expenses and unearned revenues.

PREPAID EXPENSES

Companies record payments of expenses that will benefit more than one accounting period as assets called prepaid expenses or prepayments. When expenses are prepaid, an asset account is increased (debited) to show the service or benefit that the company will receive in the future. Examples of common prepayments are insurance, supplies, advertising, and rent. In addition, companies make prepayments when they purchase buildings and equipment.

Prepaid expenses are costs that expire either with the passage of time (e.g., rent and insurance) **or through use** (e.g., supplies). The expiration of these costs does not require daily entries, which would be impractical and unnecessary. Accordingly, companies postpone the recognition of such cost expirations until they prepare financial statements. At each statement date, they make adjusting entries to record the expenses applicable to the current accounting period and to show the remaining amounts in the asset accounts.

Prior to adjustment, assets are overstated and expenses are understated. Therefore, as shown in Illustration 3-4, **an adjusting entry for prepaid expenses results in an increase (a debit) to an expense account and a decrease (a credit) to an asset account.**

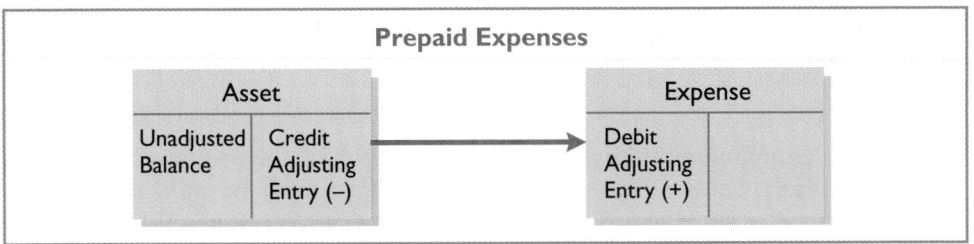

Illustration 3-4
Adjusting entries for prepaid expenses

Let's look in more detail at some specific types of prepaid expenses, beginning with supplies.

Supplies. The purchase of supplies, such as paper and envelopes, results in an increase (a debit) to an asset account. During the accounting period, the company uses supplies. Rather than record supplies expense as the supplies are used, companies recognize supplies expense at the **end** of the accounting period. At the end of the accounting period, the company counts the remaining supplies. The difference between the unadjusted balance in the Supplies (asset) account and the actual cost of supplies on hand represents the supplies used (an expense) for that period (page 106).

Recall from Chapter 2 that Pioneer Advertising purchased supplies costing $2,500 on October 5. Pioneer recorded the purchase by increasing (debiting) the asset Supplies. This account shows a balance of $2,500 in the October 31 trial balance. An inventory count at the close of business on October 31 reveals that $1,000 of supplies are still on hand. Thus, the cost of supplies used is $1,500 ($2,500 − $1,000). This use of supplies decreases an asset, Supplies. It also decreases owner's equity by increasing an expense account, Supplies Expense. This is shown in Illustration 3-5.

Supplies

Oct. 5
Supplies purchased; record asset

Oct. 31
Supplies used; record supplies expense

Illustration 3-5
Adjustment for supplies

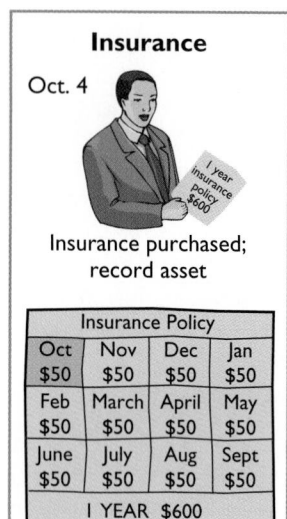

Insurance

Oct. 4

Insurance purchased;
record asset

Insurance Policy			
Oct $50	Nov $50	Dec $50	Jan $50
Feb $50	March $50	April $50	May $50
June $50	July $50	Aug $50	Sept $50
I YEAR $600			

Oct. 31
    Insurance expired;
record insurance expense

After adjustment, the asset account Supplies shows a balance of $1,000, which is equal to the cost of supplies on hand at the statement date. In addition, Supplies Expense shows a balance of $1,500, which equals the cost of supplies used in October. **If Pioneer does not make the adjusting entry, October expenses will be understated and net income overstated by $1,500. Moreover, both assets and owner's equity will be overstated by $1,500 on the October 31 balance sheet.**

Insurance. Companies purchase insurance to protect themselves from losses due to fire, theft, and unforeseen events. Insurance must be paid in advance, often for more than one year. The cost of insurance (premiums) paid in advance is recorded as an increase (debit) in the asset account prepaid insurance. At the financial statement date, companies increase (debit) Insurance expense and decrease (credit) Prepaid insurance for the cost of insurance that has expired during the period.

On October 4, Pioneer Advertising paid $600 for a one-year fire insurance policy. Coverage began on October 1. Pioneer recorded the payment by increasing (debiting) Prepaid Insurance. This account shows a balance of $600 in the October 31 trial balance. Insurance of $50 ($600 ÷ 12) expires each month. The expiration of prepaid insurance decreases an asset, Prepaid Insurance. It also decreases owner's equity by increasing an expense account, Insurance Expense.

As shown in Illustration 3-6, the asset Prepaid Insurance shows a balance of $550, which represents the unexpired cost for the remaining 11 months of coverage. At the same time, the balance in Insurance Expense equals the insurance cost that expired in October. If Pioneer does not make this adjustment, October expenses are understated by $50 and net income is overstated by $50. Moreover, as the accounting equation shows, both assets and owner's equity will be overstated by $50 on the October 31 balance sheet.

Illustration 3-6
Adjustment for insurance

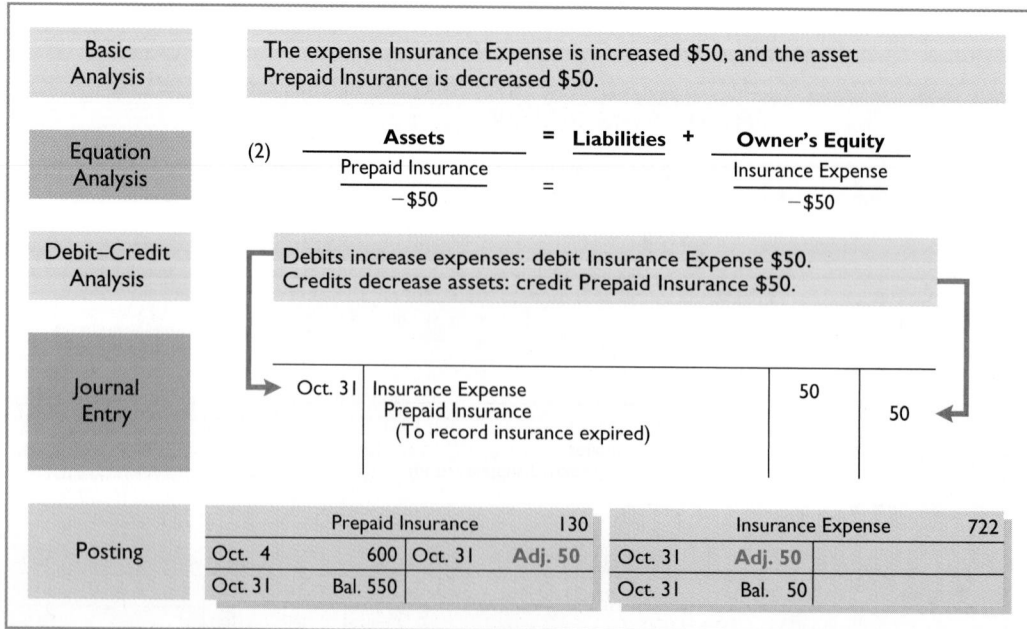

Basic Analysis	The expense Insurance Expense is increased $50, and the asset Prepaid Insurance is decreased $50.
Equation Analysis	(2) $\dfrac{\text{Assets}}{\text{Prepaid Insurance} \atop -\$50}$ = $\dfrac{\text{Liabilities}}{}$ + $\dfrac{\text{Owner's Equity}}{\text{Insurance Expense} \atop -\$50}$
Debit–Credit Analysis	Debits increase expenses: debit Insurance Expense $50. Credits decrease assets: credit Prepaid Insurance $50.

Journal Entry	Oct. 31 Insurance Expense 50
	            Prepaid Insurance 50
	            (To record insurance expired)

Posting

Prepaid Insurance		130
Oct. 4	600	Oct. 31 Adj. 50
Oct. 31	Bal. 550	

Insurance Expense		722
Oct. 31	Adj. 50	
Oct. 31	Bal. 50	

Depreciation. A company typically owns a variety of assets that have long lives, such as buildings, equipment, and motor vehicles. The period of service is referred to as the useful life of the asset. Because a building is expected to provide service for many years, it is recorded as an asset, rather than an expense, on the date it is acquired. As explained in Chapter 1, companies record such assets **at cost**, as required by the cost principle. To follow the expense recognition principle, companies allocate a portion of this cost as an expense during each period of the asset's useful life. Depreciation is the process of allocating the cost of an asset to expense over its useful life.

Need for Adjustment. The acquisition of long-lived assets is essentially a long-term prepayment for the use of an asset. An adjusting entry for depreciation is needed to recognize the cost that has been used (an expense) during the period and to report the unused cost (an asset) at the end of the period. One very important point to understand: **Depreciation is an allocation concept, not a valuation concept.** That is, depreciation **allocates an asset's cost to the periods in which it is used. Depreciation does not attempt to report the actual change in the value of the asset.**

For Pioneer Advertising, assume that depreciation on the equipment is $480 a year, or $40 per month. As shown in Illustration 3-7 below, rather than decrease (credit) the asset account directly, Pioneer instead credits Accumulated Depreciation—Equipment. Accumulated Depreciation is called a contra asset account. Such an account is offset against an asset account on the balance sheet. Thus, the Accumulated Depreciation—Equipment account offsets the asset Equipment. This account keeps track of the total amount of depreciation expense taken over the life of the asset. To keep the accounting equation in balance, Pioneer decreases owner's equity by increasing an expense account, Depreciation Expense.

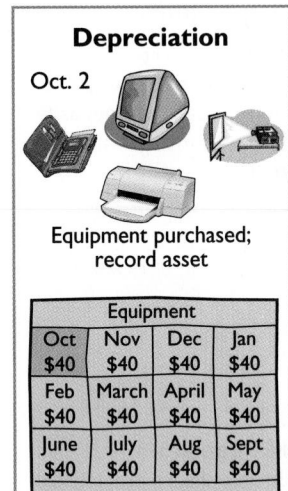

Depreciation

Oct. 2

Equipment purchased; record asset

Equipment			
Oct	Nov	Dec	Jan
$40	$40	$40	$40
Feb	March	April	May
$40	$40	$40	$40
June	July	Aug	Sept
$40	$40	$40	$40
Depreciation = $480/year			

Oct. 31
Depreciation recognized; record depreciation expense

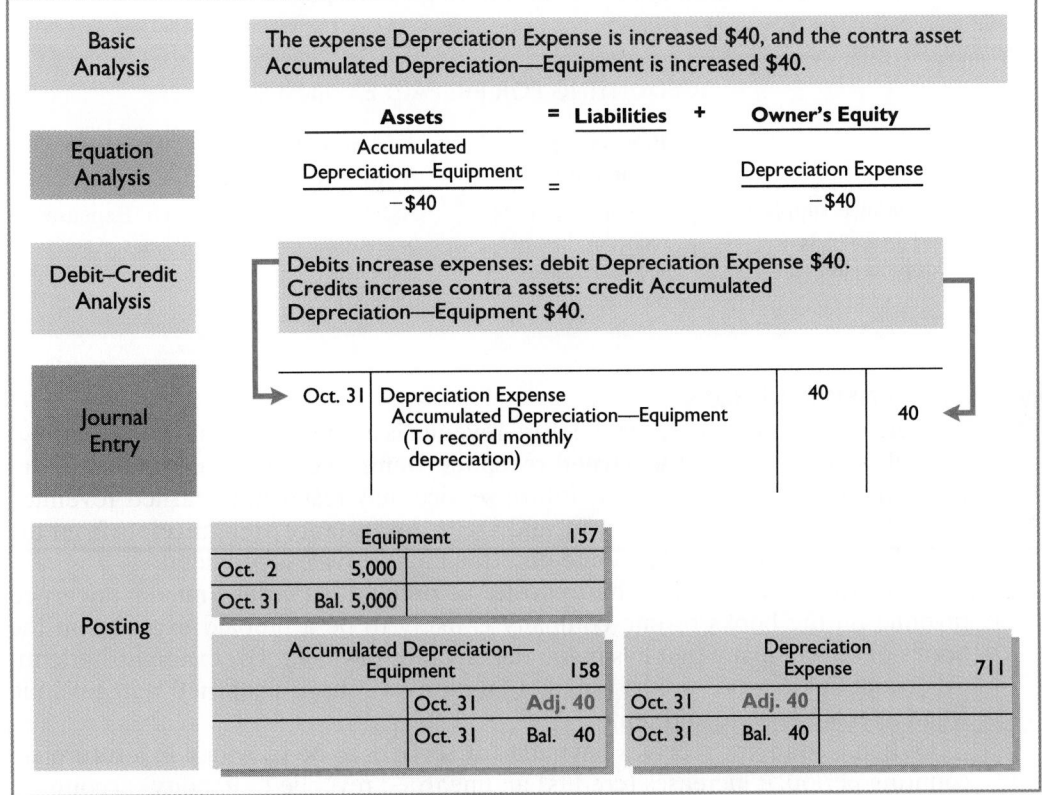

Illustration 3-7
Adjustment for depreciation

Helpful Hint

All contra accounts have increases, decreases, and normal balances **opposite** to the account to which they relate.

The balance in the Accumulated Depreciation—Equipment account will increase $40 each month, and the balance in Equipment remains $5,000.

Statement Presentation. As indicated, Accumulated Depreciation—Equipment is a contra asset account. It is offset against Equipment on the balance sheet. The normal balance of a contra asset account is a credit. A theoretical alternative to using a contra asset account would be to decrease (credit) the asset account by the amount of depreciation each period. But using the contra account is preferable for a simple reason: It discloses *both* the original cost of the equipment *and* the total cost that has expired to date. Thus, in the balance sheet, Pioneer deducts Accumulated Depreciation—Equipment from the related asset account, as shown in Illustration 3-8.

Illustration 3-8
Balance sheet presentation of accumulated depreciation

Equipment	$5,000
Less: Accumulated depreciation—equipment	40
	$4,960

Alternative Terminology

Book value is also referred to as *carrying value*.

Book value is the difference between the cost of any depreciable asset and its related accumulated depreciation. In Illustration 3-8, the book value of the equipment at the balance sheet date is $4,960. The book value and the fair value of the asset are generally two different values. As noted earlier, **the purpose of depreciation is not valuation but a means of cost allocation.**

Depreciation expense identifies the portion of an asset's cost that expired during the period (in this case, in October). The accounting equation shows that without this adjusting entry, total assets, total owner's equity, and net income are overstated by $40 and depreciation expense is understated by $40.

Illustration 3-9 summarizes the accounting for prepaid expenses.

Illustration 3-9
Accounting for prepaid expenses

Unearned Revenues

Oct. 2

Thank you in advance for your work

I will finish by Dec. 31

$1,200

Cash is received in advance; liability is recorded

Oct. 31

Some service has been provided; some revenue is recorded

ACCOUNTING FOR PREPAID EXPENSES

Examples	Reason for Adjustment	Accounts Before Adjustment	Adjusting Entry
Insurance, supplies, advertising, rent, depreciation	Prepaid expenses recorded in asset accounts have been used.	Assets overstated. Expenses understated.	Dr. Expenses Cr. Assets

UNEARNED REVENUES

Companies record cash received before revenue is earned by increasing (crediting) a liability account called **unearned revenues**. Items like rent, magazine subscriptions, and customer deposits for future service may result in unearned revenues. Airlines such as United, American, and Delta, for instance, treat receipts from the sale of tickets as unearned revenue until the flight service is provided.

Unearned revenues are the opposite of prepaid expenses. Indeed, unearned revenue on the books of one company is likely to be a prepaid expense on the books of the company that has made the advance payment. For example, if identical accounting periods are assumed, a landlord will have unearned rent revenue when a tenant has prepaid rent.

When a company receives payment for services to be provided in a future accounting period, it increases (credits) an unearned revenue (a liability) account to recognize the liability that exists. The company subsequently earns revenues by providing service. During the accounting period, it is not practical to make daily entries as the company earns the revenue. Instead, we delay recognition of earned revenue until the adjustment process. Then the company makes an adjusting entry to record the revenue earned during the period and to show the liability that remains at the end of the accounting period. Typically, prior to adjustment, liabilities are overstated and revenues are understated. Therefore, as shown in Illustration 3-10, **the adjusting entry for unearned revenues results in a decrease (a debit) to a liability account and an increase (a credit) to a revenue account.**

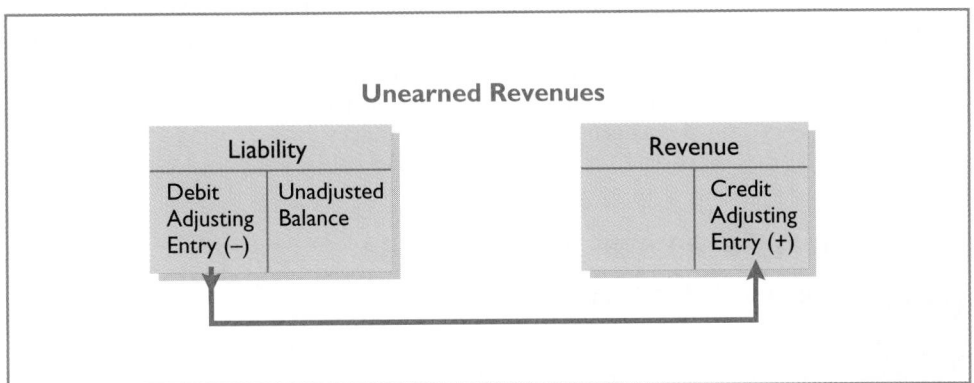

Illustration 3-10
Adjusting entries for unearned revenues

Pioneer Advertising received $1,200 on October 2 from R. Knox for advertising services expected to be completed by December 31. Pioneer credited the payment to Unearned Service Revenue, and this liability account shows a balance of $1,200 in the October 31 trial balance. From an evaluation of the service Pioneer performed for Knox during October, the company determines that it has earned $400 in October. The liability (Unearned Service Revenue) is therefore decreased, and owner's equity (Service Revenue) is increased.

As shown in Illustration 3-11, the liability Unearned Service Revenue now shows a balance of $800. That amount represents the remaining advertising services

Illustration 3-11
Service revenue accounts after adjustment

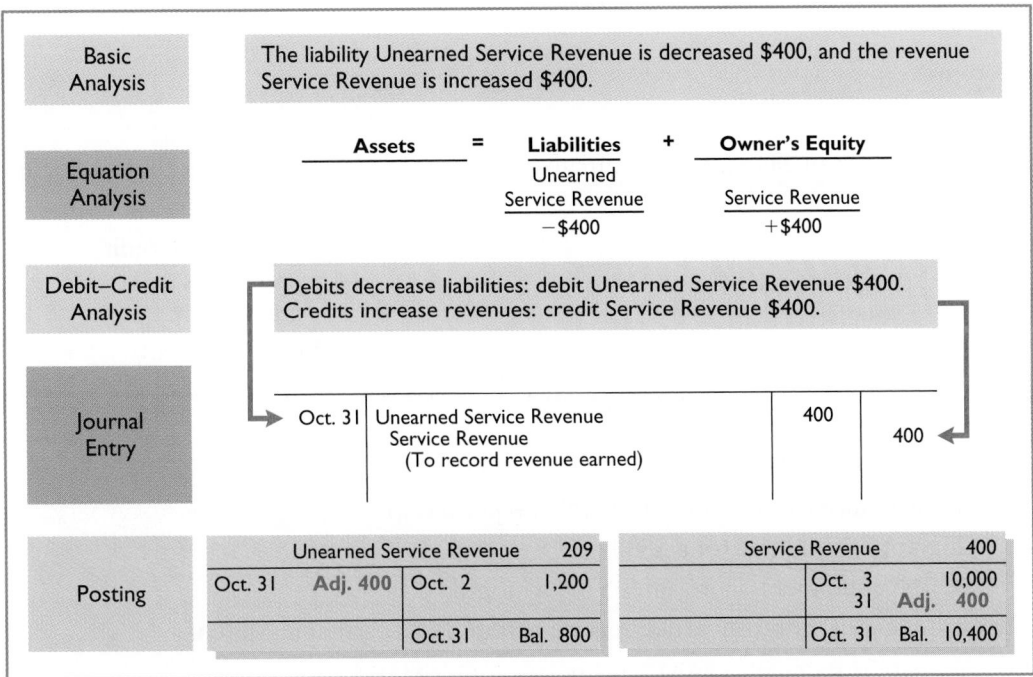

expected to be performed in the future. At the same time, Service Revenue shows total revenue earned in October of $10,400. **Without this adjustment, revenues and net income are understated by $400 in the income statement. Moreover, liabilities are overstated and owner's equity is understated by $400 on the October 31 balance sheet.**

Illustration 3-12 summarizes the accounting for unearned revenues.

Illustration 3-12
Accounting for unearned revenues

ACCOUNTING FOR UNEARNED REVENUES

Examples	Reason for Adjustment	Accounts Before Adjustment	Adjusting Entry
Rent, magazine subscriptions, customer deposits for future service	Unearned revenues recorded in liability accounts have been earned.	Liabilities overstated. Revenues understated.	Dr. Liabilities Cr. Revenues

ACCOUNTING ACROSS THE ORGANIZATION

Turning Gift Cards into Revenue

Those of you who are marketing majors (and even most of you who are not) know that gift cards are among the hottest marketing tools in merchandising today. Customers purchase gift cards and give them to someone for later use. In a recent year, gift-card sales topped $95 billion.

Although these programs are popular with marketing executives, they create accounting questions. Should revenue be recorded at the time the gift card is sold, or when it is exercised? How should expired gift cards be accounted for? In its 2009 balance sheet, Best Buy reported unearned revenue related to gift cards of $479 million.

Source: Robert Berner, "Gift Cards: No Gift to Investors," *BusinessWeek* (March 14, 2005), p. 86.

? Suppose that Robert Jones purchases a $100 gift card at Best Buy on December 24, 2011, and gives it to his wife, Mary Jones, on December 25, 2011. On January 3, 2012, Mary uses the card to purchase $100 worth of CDs. When do you think Best Buy should recognize revenue and why? (See page 148.)

Do it!

Adjusting Entries for Deferrals

The ledger of Hammond Company, on March 31, 2012, includes these selected accounts before adjusting entries are prepared.

	Debit	Credit
Prepaid Insurance	$ 3,600	
Supplies	2,800	
Equipment	25,000	
Accumulated Depreciation—Equipment		$5,000
Unearned Service Revenue		9,200

An analysis of the accounts shows the following.

1. Insurance expires at the rate of $100 per month.
2. Supplies on hand total $800.
3. The equipment depreciates $200 a month.
4. One-half of the unearned service revenue was earned in March.

Prepare the adjusting entries for the month of March.

Solution

1. Insurance Expense	100	
Prepaid Insurance		100
(To record insurance expired)		
2. Supplies Expense	2,000	
Supplies		2,000
(To record supplies used)		
3. Depreciation Expense	200	
Accumulated Depreciation—Equipment		200
(To record monthly depreciation)		
4. Unearned Service Revenue	4,600	
Service Revenue		4,600
(To record revenue earned)		

Related exercise material: BE3-3, BE3-4, BE3-6, and **Do it!** 3-2.

The Navigator

Adjusting Entries for Accruals

Study Objective [6]
Prepare adjusting entries for accruals.

The second category of adjusting entries is **accruals.** Prior to an accrual adjustment, the revenue account (and the related asset account) or the expense account (and the related liability account) are understated. Thus, the adjusting entry for accruals will **increase both a balance sheet and an income statement account.**

ACCRUED REVENUES

Revenues earned but not yet recorded at the statement date are accrued revenues. Accrued revenues may accumulate (accrue) with the passing of time, as in the case of interest revenue. These are unrecorded because the earning of interest does not involve daily transactions. Companies do not record interest revenue on a daily basis because it is often impractical to do so. Accrued revenues also may result from services that have been performed but not yet billed nor collected, as in the case of commissions and fees. These may be unrecorded because only a portion of the total service has been provided and the clients won't be billed until the service has been completed.

An adjusting entry records the receivable that exists at the balance sheet date and the revenue earned during the period. Prior to adjustment, both assets and revenues are understated. As shown in Illustration 3-13, **an adjusting entry for accrued revenues results in an increase (a debit) to an asset account and an increase (a credit) to a revenue account.**

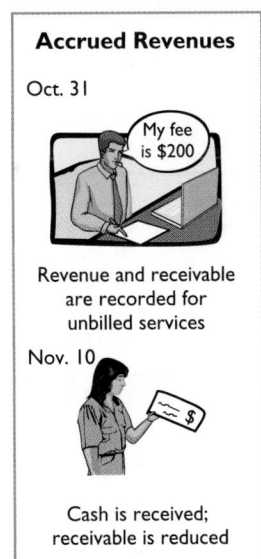

Accrued Revenues

Oct. 31

Revenue and receivable are recorded for unbilled services

Nov. 10

Cash is received; receivable is reduced

Illustration 3-13
Adjusting entries for accrued revenues

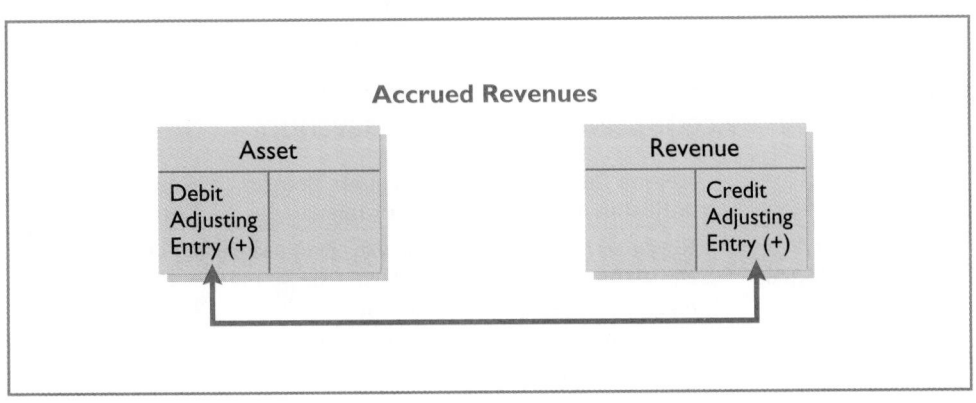

Accrued Revenues

Helpful Hint

For accruals, there may have been no prior entry, and the accounts requiring adjustment may both have zero balances prior to adjustment.

In October, Pioneer Advertising earned $200 for advertising services that were not billed to clients on or before October 31. Because these services are not billed, they are not recorded. The accrual of unrecorded service revenue increases an asset account, Accounts Receivable. It also increases owner's equity by increasing a revenue account, Service Revenue, as shown in Illustration 3-14.

Illustration 3-14
Adjustment for accrued revenue

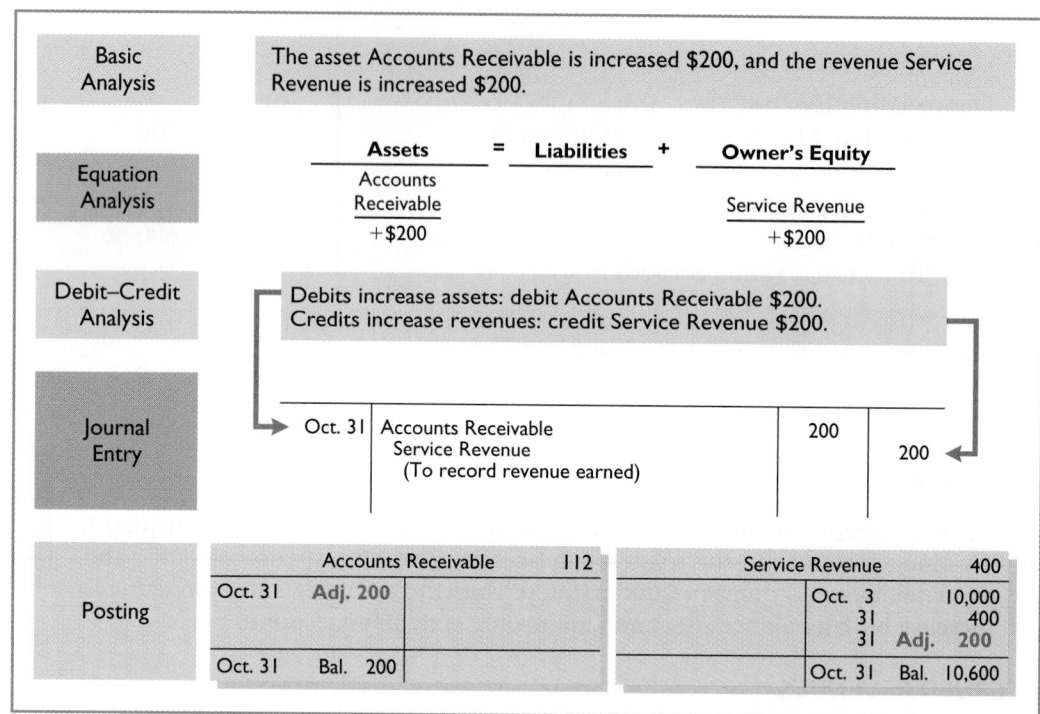

The asset Accounts Receivable shows that clients owe Pioneer $200 at the balance sheet date. The balance of $10,600 in Service Revenue represents the total revenue Pioneer earned during the month ($10,000 + $400 + $200). **Without the adjusting entry, assets and owner's equity on the balance sheet and revenues and net income on the income statement are understated.**

On November 10, Pioneer receives cash of $200 for the services performed in October and makes the following entry.

Equation analyses summarize the effects of transactions on the three elements of the accounting equation, as well as the effect on cash flows.

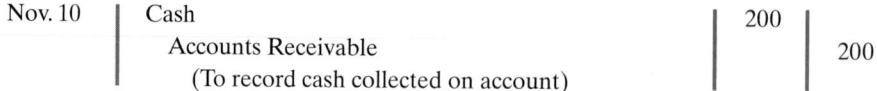

Nov. 10	Cash	200	
	Accounts Receivable		200
	(To record cash collected on account)		

The company records the collection of the receivables by a debit (increase) to Cash and a credit (decrease) to Accounts Receivable.

Illustration 3-15 summarizes the accounting for accrued revenues.

Illustration 3-15
Accounting for accrued revenues

ACCOUNTING FOR ACCRUED REVENUES

Examples	Reason for Adjustment	Accounts Before Adjustment	Adjusting Entry
Interest, rent, services performed but not collected	Revenues have been earned but not yet received in cash or recorded.	Assets understated. Revenues understated.	Dr. Assets Cr. Revenues

ACCRUED EXPENSES

Expenses incurred but not yet paid or recorded at the statement date are called **accrued expenses**. Interest, taxes, and salaries are common examples of accrued expenses.

Companies make adjustments for accrued expenses to record the obligations that exist at the balance sheet date and to recognize the expenses that apply to the current accounting period. Prior to adjustment, both liabilities and expenses are understated. Therefore, as Illustration 3-16 shows, **an adjusting entry for accrued expenses results in an increase (a debit) to an expense account and an increase (a credit) to a liability account.**

> **Ethics Note**
>
> A report released by Fannie Mae's board of directors stated that improper adjusting entries at the mortgage-finance company resulted in delayed recognition of expenses caused by interest-rate changes. The motivation for such accounting apparently was the desire to hit earnings estimates.

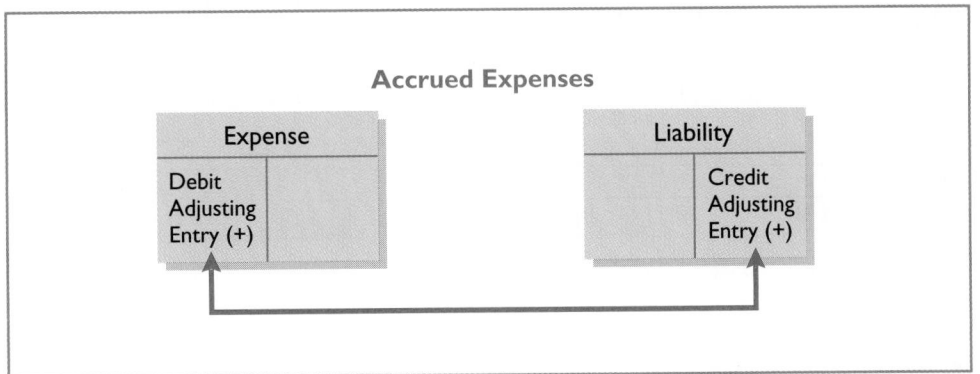

Illustration 3-16
Adjusting entries for accrued expenses

Let's look in more detail at some specific types of accrued expenses, beginning with accrued interest.

Accrued Interest. Pioneer Advertising signed a three-month note payable in the amount of $5,000 on October 1. The note requires Pioneer to pay interest at an annual rate of 12%.

The amount of the interest recorded is determined by three factors: (1) the face value of the note; (2) the interest rate, which is always expressed as an annual rate; and (3) the length of time the note is outstanding. For Pioneer, the total interest due on the $5,000 note at its maturity date three months in the future is $150 ($5,000 $\times$ 12% $\times \frac{3}{12}$), or $50 for one month. Illustration 3-17 shows the formula for computing interest and its application to Pioneer for the month of October.

Face Value of Note	$\times$	Annual Interest Rate	$\times$	Time in Terms of One Year	=	Interest
$5,000	$\times$	12%	$\times$	$\frac{1}{12}$	=	$50

Illustration 3-17
Formula for computing interest

As Illustration 3-18 (page 114) shows, the accrual of interest at October 31 increases a liability account, Interest Payable. It also decreases owner's equity by increasing an expense account, Interest Expense.

Interest Expense shows the interest charges for the month of October. Interest Payable shows the amount of interest the company owes at the statement date. Pioneer will not pay the interest until the note comes due at the end of three months. Companies use the Interest Payable account, instead of crediting Notes Payable, to disclose the two different types of obligations—interest and principal—in the accounts and statements. **Without this adjusting entry, liabilities and interest expense are understated, and net income and owner's equity are overstated.**

Helpful Hint

In computing interest, we express the time period as a fraction of a year.

Illustration 3-18
Adjustment for
accrued interest

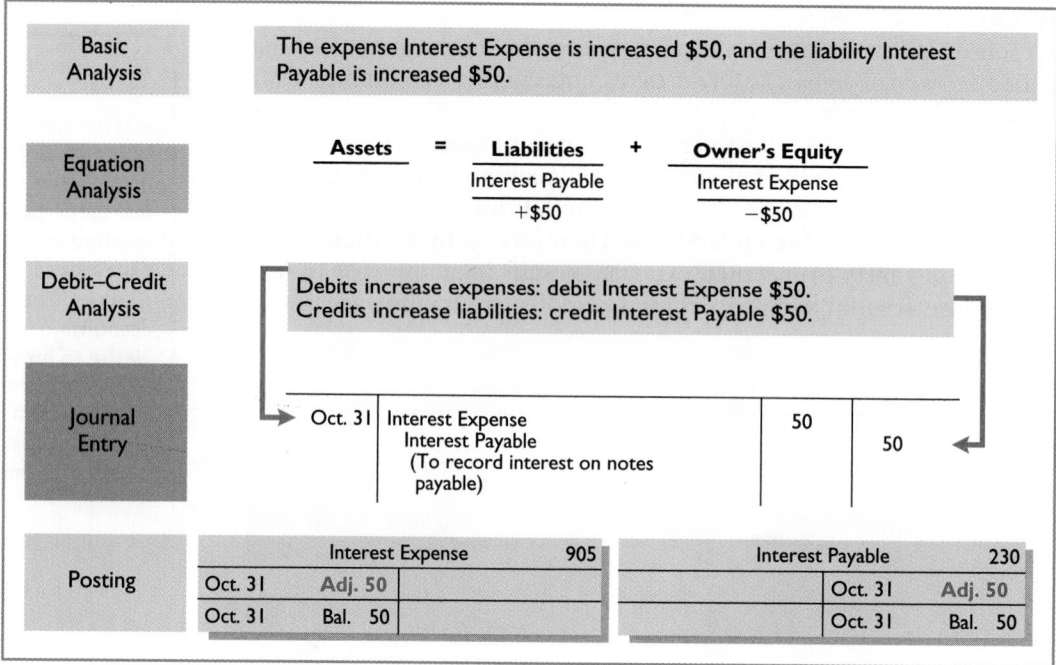

INTERNATIONAL INSIGHT

Cashing In on Accrual Accounting

The Chinese government, like most governments, uses cash accounting. It was therefore interesting when it was recently reported that for about $38 billion of expenditures in a recent budget projection, the Chinese government decided to use accrual accounting versus cash accounting. It decided to expense the amount in the year in which it was originally allocated rather than when the payments would be made. Why did it do this? It enabled the government to keep its projected budget deficit below a 3% threshold. While it was able to keep its projected shortfall below 3%, China did suffer some criticism for its inconsistent accounting. Critics charge that this inconsistent treatment reduces the transparency of China's accounting information. That is, it is not easy for outsiders to accurately evaluate what is really going on.

Source: Andrew Batson, "China Altered Budget Accounting to Reduce Deficit Figure," *Wall Street Journal Online* (March 15, 2010).

?   Accrual accounting is often considered superior to cash accounting. Why, then, were some people critical of China's use of accrual accounting in this instance? (See page 148.)

Accrued Salaries and Wages. Companies pay for some types of expenses, such as employee salaries and wages, after the services have been performed. Pioneer paid salaries and wages on October 26 for its employees' first two weeks of work; the next payment of salaries will not occur until November 9. As Illustration 3-19 shows, three working days remain in October (October 29–31).

At October 31, the salaries and wages for these three days represent an accrued expense and a related liability to Pioneer. The employees receive total salaries and wages of $2,000 for a five-day work week, or $400 per day. Thus, accrued salaries and wages at October 31 are $1,200 ($400 × 3). This accrual increases a liability, Salaries and Wages Payable. It also decreases

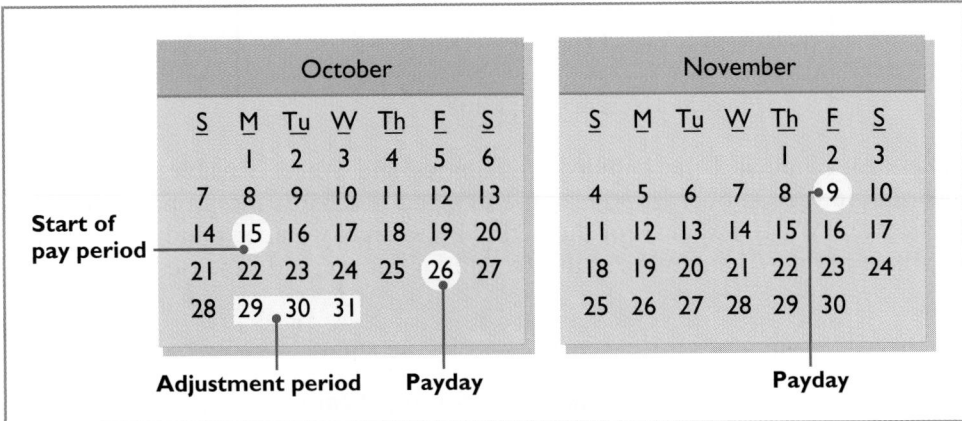

Illustration 3-19
Calendar showing Pioneer's pay periods

owner's equity by increasing an expense account, Salaries and Wages Expense, as shown in Illustration 3-20.

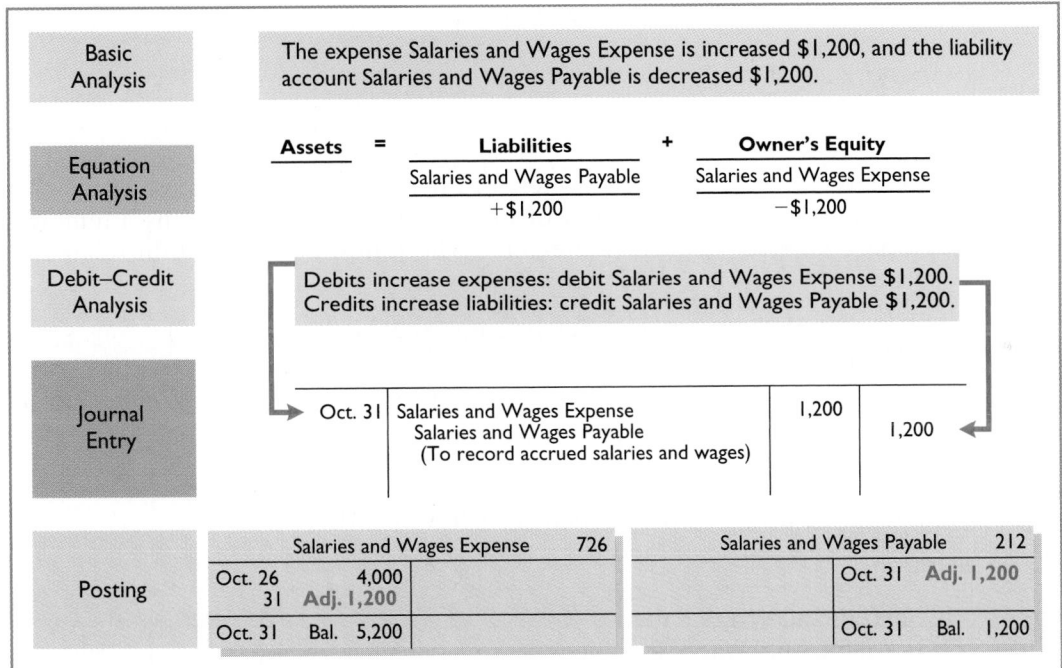

Illustration 3-20
Adjustment for accrued salaries and wages

After this adjustment, the balance in Salaries and Wages Expense of $5,200 (13 days $\times$ $400) is the actual salary and wages expense for October. The balance in Salaries and Wages Payable of $1,200 is the amount of the liability for salaries and wages Pioneer owes as of October 31. **Without the $1,200 adjustment for salaries and wages, Pioneer's expenses are understated $1,200 and its liabilities are understated $1,200.**

Pioneer Advertising pays salaries and wages every two weeks. Consequently, the next payday is November 9, when the company will again pay total salaries and wages of $4,000. The payment consists of $1,200 of salaries and wages payable at October 31 plus $2,800 of salaries and wages expense for November (7 working days, as shown in the November calendar $\times$ $400). Therefore, Pioneer makes the following entry on November 9.

Nov. 9	Salaries and Wages Payable	1,200	
	Salaries and Wages Expense	2,800	
	Cash		4,000
	(To record November 9 payroll)		

This entry eliminates the liability for Salaries and Wages Payable that Pioneer recorded in the October 31 adjusting entry, and it records the proper amount of Salaries and Wages Expense for the period between November 1 and November 9. Illustration 3-21 summarizes the accounting for accrued expenses.

Illustration 3-21
Accounting for accrued expenses

ACCOUNTING FOR ACCRUED EXPENSES

Examples	Reason for Adjustment	Accounts Before Adjustment	Adjusting Entry
Interest, rent, salaries	Expenses have been incurred but not yet paid in cash or recorded.	Expenses understated. Liabilities understated.	Dr. Expenses Cr. Liabilities

Do it!

Adjusting Entries for Accruals

Calvin and Hobbs are the new owners of Micro Computer Services. At the end of August 2012, their first month of operations, Calvin and Hobbs attempted to prepare monthly financial statements. The following information relates to August.

1. At August 31, the company owed its employees $800 in salaries and wages that will be paid on September 1.

2. On August 1, the company borrowed $30,000 from a local bank on a 15-year mortgage. The annual interest rate is 10%.

3. Revenue earned but unrecorded for August totaled $1,100.

Prepare the adjusting entries needed at August 31, 2012.

action plan

✔ Make adjusting entries at the end of the period for revenues earned and expenses incurred in the period.

✔ Don't forget to make adjusting entries for accruals. Adjusting entries for accruals will increase both a balance sheet and an income statement account.

Solution

1. Salaries and Wages Expense		800	
	Salaries and Wages Payable		800
	(To record accrued salaries)		
2. Interest Expense		250	
	Interest Payable		250
	(To record accrued interest: $30,000 \times 10\% \times \frac{1}{12} = \$250$)		
3. Accounts Receivable		1,100	
	Service Revenue		1,100
	(To record revenue earned)		

Related exercise material: BE3-7, E3-5, E3-6, E3-7, E3-8, E3-9, E3-10, E3-11, E3-12, and **Do it!** 3-3.

The Navigator

Summary of Basic Relationships

Illustration 3-22 summarizes the four basic types of adjusting entries. Take some time to study and analyze the adjusting entries. Be sure to note that **each adjusting entry affects one balance sheet account and one income statement account.**

Type of Adjustment	Accounts Before Adjustment	Adjusting Entry
Prepaid expenses	Assets overstated Expenses understated	Dr. Expenses Cr. Assets
Unearned revenues	Liabilities overstated Revenues understated	Dr. Liabilities Cr. Revenues
Accrued revenues	Assets understated Revenues understated	Dr. Assets Cr. Revenues
Accrued expenses	Expenses understated Liabilities understated	Dr. Expenses Cr. Liabilities

Illustration 3-22
Summary of adjusting entries

Illustrations 3-23 (below) and 3-24 (on page 118) show the journalizing and posting of adjusting entries for Pioneer Advertising Agency on October 31. The ledger identifies all adjustments by the reference J2 because they have been recorded on page 2 of the general journal. The company may insert a center caption "Adjusting Entries" between the last transaction entry and the first adjusting entry in the journal. When you review the general ledger in Illustration 3-24, note that the entries highlighted in color are the adjustments.

Illustration 3-23
General journal showing adjusting entries

	General Journal			J2
Date	**Account Titles and Explanation**	**Ref.**	**Debit**	**Credit**

2012
Oct. 31
	Adjusting Entries
	Supplies Expense
	    Supplies
	    (To record supplies used)
		631
		126
			1,500	1,500

31	Insurance Expense
	    Prepaid Insurance
	    (To record insurance expired)
		722
		130
			50	50

31	Depreciation Expense
	    Accumulated Depreciation—Equipment
	    (To record monthly depreciation)
		711
		158
			40	40

31	Unearned Service Revenue
	    Service Revenue
	    (To record revenue for services provided)
		209
		400
			400	400

31	Accounts Receivable
	    Service Revenue
	    (To record revenue for services provided)
		112
		400
			200	200

31	Interest Expense
	    Interest Payable
	    (To record interest on notes payable)
		905
		230
			50	50

31	Salaries and Wages Expense
	    Salaries and Wages Payable
	    (To record accrued salaries and wages)
		726
		212
			1,200	1,200

Helpful Hint

(1) Adjusting entries should not involve debits or credits to cash.
(2) Evaluate whether the adjustment makes sense. For example, an adjustment to recognize supplies used should increase supplies expense.
(3) Double-check all computations.
(4) Each adjusting entry affects one balance sheet account and one income statement account.

Illustration 3-24
General ledger after adjustment

General Journal

Cash — No. 101

Date	Explanation	Ref.	Debit	Credit	Balance
2012					
Oct. 1		J1	10,000		10,000
2		J1	1,200		11,200
3		J1		900	10,300
4		J1		600	9,700
20		J1		500	9,200
26		J1		4,000	5,200
31		J1	10,000		15,200

Accounts Receivable — No. 112

Date	Explanation	Ref.	Debit	Credit	Balance
2012					
Oct. 31	Adj. entry	J2	200		200

Supplies — No. 126

Date	Explanation	Ref.	Debit	Credit	Balance
2012					
Oct. 5		J1	2,500		2,500
31	Adj. entry	J2		1,500	1,000

Prepaid Insurance — No. 130

Date	Explanation	Ref.	Debit	Credit	Balance
2012					
Oct. 4		J1	600		600
31	Adj. entry	J2		50	550

Equipment — No. 157

Date	Explanation	Ref.	Debit	Credit	Balance
2012					
Oct. 1		J1	5,000		5,000

Accumulated Depreciation—Equipment — No. 158

Date	Explanation	Ref.	Debit	Credit	Balance
2012					
Oct. 31	Adj. entry	J2		40	40

Notes Payable — No. 200

Date	Explanation	Ref.	Debit	Credit	Balance
2012					
Oct. 1		J1		5,000	5,000

Accounts Payable — No. 201

Date	Explanation	Ref.	Debit	Credit	Balance
2012					
Oct. 5		J1		2,500	2,500

Unearned Service Revenue — No. 209

Date	Explanation	Ref.	Debit	Credit	Balance
2012					
Oct. 2		J1		1,200	1,200
31	Adj. entry	J2	400		800

Salaries and Wages Payable — No. 212

Date	Explanation	Ref.	Debit	Credit	Balance
2012					
Oct. 31	Adj. entry	J2		1,200	1,200

Interest Payable — No. 230

Date	Explanation	Ref.	Debit	Credit	Balance
2012					
Oct. 31	Adj. entry	J2		50	50

Owner's Capital — No. 301

Date	Explanation	Ref.	Debit	Credit	Balance
2012					
Oct. 1		J1		10,000	10,000

Owner's Drawings — No. 306

Date	Explanation	Ref.	Debit	Credit	Balance
2012					
Oct. 20		J1	500		500

Service Revenue — No. 400

Date	Explanation	Ref.	Debit	Credit	Balance
2012					
Oct. 31		J1		10,000	10,000
31	Adj. entry	J2		400	10,400
31	Adj. entry	J2		200	10,600

Supplies Expense — No. 631

Date	Explanation	Ref.	Debit	Credit	Balance
2012					
Oct. 31	Adj. entry	J2	1,500		1,500

Depreciation Expense — No. 711

Date	Explanation	Ref.	Debit	Credit	Balance
2012					
Oct. 31	Adj. entry	J2	40		40

Insurance Expense — No. 722

Date	Explanation	Ref.	Debit	Credit	Balance
2012					
Oct. 31	Adj. entry	J2	50		50

Salaries and Wages Expense — No. 726

Date	Explanation	Ref.	Debit	Credit	Balance
2012					
Oct. 26		J1	4,000		4,000
31	Adj. entry	J2	1,200		5,200

Rent Expense — No. 729

Date	Explanation	Ref.	Debit	Credit	Balance
2012					
Oct. 3		J1	900		900

Interest Expense — No. 905

Date	Explanation	Ref.	Debit	Credit	Balance
2012					
Oct. 31	Adj. entry	J2	50		50

The Adjusted Trial Balance and Financial Statements

After a company has journalized and posted all adjusting entries, it prepares another trial balance from the ledger accounts. This trial balance is called an adjusted trial balance. It shows the balances of all accounts, including those adjusted, at the end of the accounting period. The purpose of an adjusted trial balance is to **prove the equality** of the total debit balances and the total credit balances in the ledger after all adjustments. Because the accounts contain all data needed for financial statements, the adjusted trial balance is the **primary basis for the preparation of financial statements.**

> **Study Objective [7]**
> Describe the nature and purpose of an adjusted trial balance.

Preparing the Adjusted Trial Balance

Illustration 3-25 presents the adjusted trial balance for Pioneer Advertising Agency prepared from the ledger accounts in Illustration 3-24. The amounts affected by the adjusting entries are highlighted in color. Compare these amounts to those in the unadjusted trial balance in Illustration 3-3 on page 104. In this comparison, you will see that there are more accounts in the adjusted trial balance as a result of the adjusting entries made at the end of the month.

Pioneer Advertising Agency
Adjusted Trial Balance
October 31, 2012

	Dr.	Cr.
Cash	$15,200	
Accounts Receivable	200	
Supplies	1,000	
Prepaid Insurance	550	
Equipment	5,000	
Accumulated Depreciation—Equipment		$ 40
Notes Payable		5,000
Accounts Payable		2,500
Interest Payable		50
Unearned Service Revenue		800
Salaries and Wages Payable		1,200
Owner's Capital		10,000
Owner's Drawings	500	
Service Revenue		10,600
Salaries and Wages Expense	5,200	
Supplies Expense	1,500	
Rent Expense	900	
Insurance Expense	50	
Interest Expense	50	
Depreciation Expense	40	
	$30,190	$30,190

Illustration 3-25
Adjusted trial balance

Preparing Financial Statements

Companies can prepare financial statements directly from the adjusted trial balance. Illustrations 3-26 and 3-27 present the interrelationships of data in the adjusted trial balance and the financial statements.

As Illustration 3-26 shows, companies prepare the income statement from the revenue and expense accounts. Next, they use the owner's capital and drawings accounts and the net income (or net loss) from the income statement to prepare the owner's equity statement. As Illustration 3-27 shows, companies then prepare the balance sheet from the asset and liability accounts and the ending owner's capital balance as reported in the owner's equity statement.

Illustration 3-26

Preparation of the income statement and owner's equity statement from the adjusted trial balance

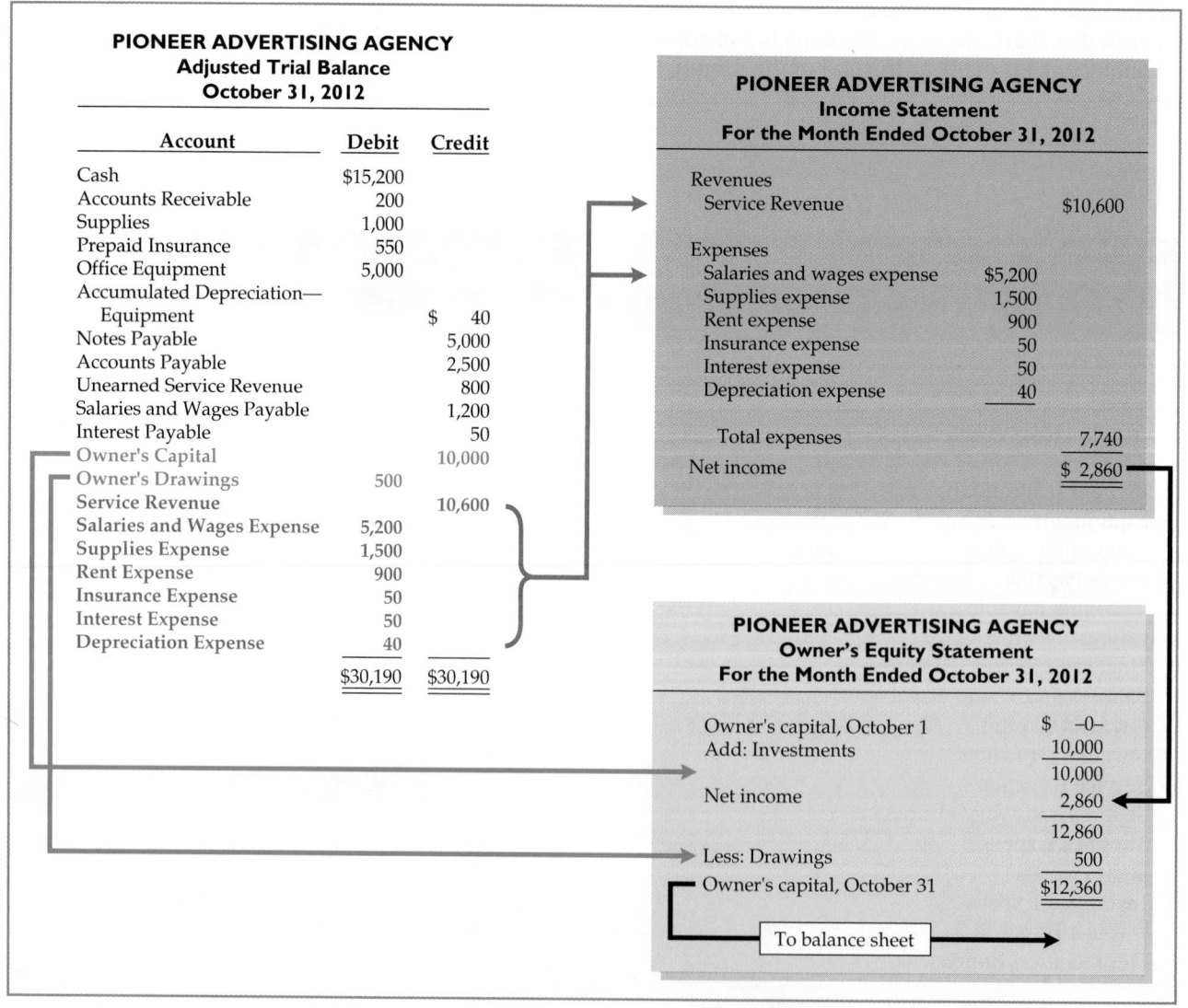

PIONEER ADVERTISING AGENCY
Adjusted Trial Balance
October 31, 2012

Account	Debit	Credit
Cash	$15,200	
Accounts Receivable	200	
Supplies	1,000	
Prepaid Insurance	550	
Office Equipment	5,000	
Accumulated Depreciation—Equipment		$ 40
Notes Payable		5,000
Accounts Payable		2,500
Unearned Service Revenue		800
Salaries and Wages Payable		1,200
Interest Payable		50
Owner's Capital		10,000
Owner's Drawings	500	
Service Revenue		10,600
Salaries and Wages Expense	5,200	
Supplies Expense	1,500	
Rent Expense	900	
Insurance Expense	50	
Interest Expense	50	
Depreciation Expense	40	
	$30,190	$30,190

PIONEER ADVERTISING AGENCY
Income Statement
For the Month Ended October 31, 2012

Revenues		
Service Revenue		$10,600
Expenses		
Salaries and wages expense	$5,200	
Supplies expense	1,500	
Rent expense	900	
Insurance expense	50	
Interest expense	50	
Depreciation expense	40	
Total expenses		7,740
Net income		$ 2,860

PIONEER ADVERTISING AGENCY
Owner's Equity Statement
For the Month Ended October 31, 2012

Owner's capital, October 1		$ –0–
Add: Investments		10,000
		10,000
Net income		2,860
		12,860
Less: Drawings		500
Owner's capital, October 31		$12,360

To balance sheet

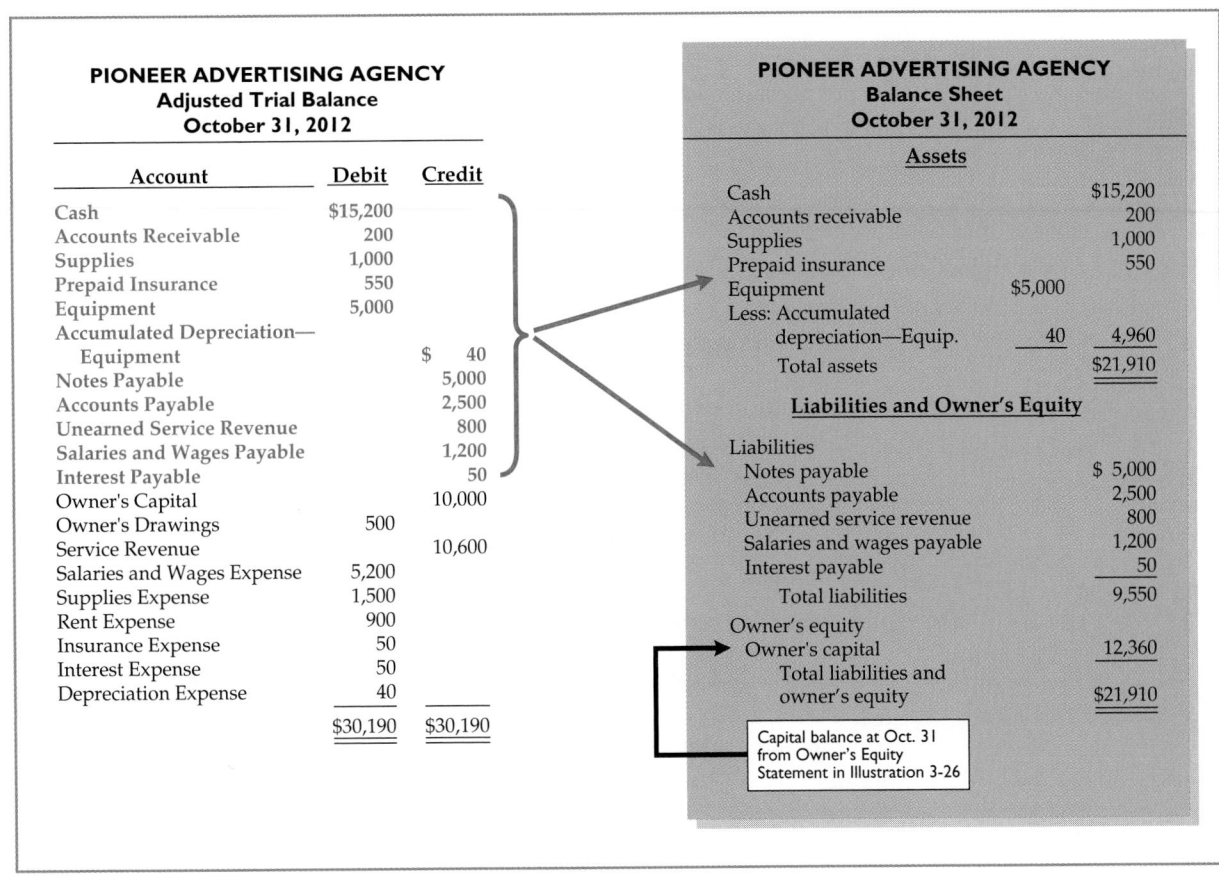

PIONEER ADVERTISING AGENCY
Adjusted Trial Balance
October 31, 2012

Account	Debit	Credit
Cash	$15,200	
Accounts Receivable	200	
Supplies	1,000	
Prepaid Insurance	550	
Equipment	5,000	
Accumulated Depreciation—		
Equipment		$ 40
Notes Payable		5,000
Accounts Payable		2,500
Unearned Service Revenue		800
Salaries and Wages Payable		1,200
Interest Payable		50
Owner's Capital		10,000
Owner's Drawings	500	
Service Revenue		10,600
Salaries and Wages Expense	5,200	
Supplies Expense	1,500	
Rent Expense	900	
Insurance Expense	50	
Interest Expense	50	
Depreciation Expense	40	
	$30,190	$30,190

PIONEER ADVERTISING AGENCY
Balance Sheet
October 31, 2012

Assets

Cash		$15,200
Accounts receivable		200
Supplies		1,000
Prepaid insurance		550
Equipment	$5,000	
Less: Accumulated		
depreciation—Equip.	40	4,960
Total assets		$21,910

Liabilities and Owner's Equity

Liabilities	
Notes payable	$ 5,000
Accounts payable	2,500
Unearned service revenue	800
Salaries and wages payable	1,200
Interest payable	50
Total liabilities	9,550
Owner's equity	
Owner's capital	12,360
Total liabilities and	
owner's equity	$21,910

Capital balance at Oct. 31 from Owner's Equity Statement in Illustration 3-26

Illustration 3-27
Preparation of the balance sheet from the adjusted trial balance

Do it!

Skolnick Co. was organized on April 1, 2012. The company prepares quarterly financial statements. The adjusted trial balance amounts at June 30 are shown below.

Trial Balance

Debits		Credits	
Cash	$ 6,700	Accumulated Depreciation—Equipment	$ 850
Accounts Receivable	600	Notes Payable	5,000
Prepaid Rent	900	Accounts Payable	1,510
Supplies	1,000	Salaries and Wages Payable	400
Equipment	15,000	Interest Payable	50
Owner's Drawings	600	Unearned Rent Revenue	500
Salaries and Wages Expense	9,400	Owner's Capital	14,000
Rent Expense	1,500	Service Revenue	14,200
Depreciation Expense	850	Rent Revenue	800
Supplies Expense	200		
Utilities Expense	510		
Interest Expense	50		
Total debits	$37,310	Total credits	$37,310

(a) Determine the net income for the quarter April 1 to June 30.

(b) Determine the total assets and total liabilities at June 30, 2012, for Skolnick Co.

(c) Determine the amount that appears for Owner's Capital at June 30, 2012.

action plan

✔ In an adjusted trial balance, all asset, liability, revenue, and expense accounts are properly stated.

✔ To determine the ending balance in Owner's Capital, add net income and subtract dividends.

Solution

(a) The net income is determined by adding revenues and subtracting expenses. The net income is computed as follows.

Revenues		
Service revenue	$14,200	
Rent revenue	800	
Total revenues		$15,000
Expenses		
Salaries and wages expense	$ 9,400	
Rent expense	1,500	
Depreciation expense	850	
Utilities expense	510	
Supplies expense	200	
Interest expense	50	
Total expenses		12,510
Net income		$ 2,490

(b) Total assets and liabilities are computed as follows.

Assets			Liabilities	
Cash		$ 6,700	Notes payable	$5,000
Accounts receivable		600	Accounts payable	1,510
Supplies		1,000	Unearned rent	
Prepaid rent		900	revenue	500
			Salaries and wages	
Equipment	15,000		payable	400
Less: Accumulated			Interest payable	50
depreciation—				
equipment	850	14,150		
Total assets		$23,350	Total liabilities	$7,460

(c)
Owner's capital, April 1	$14,000
Add: Net income	2,490
Less: Drawings	600
Owner's capital, June 30	$15,890

Related exercise material: BE3-9, BE3-10, E3-11, E3-13, and **Do it!** 3-4.

The Navigator

COMPREHENSIVE

Do it!

Terry Thomas opens the Green Thumb Lawn Care Company on April 1. At April 30, the trial balance shows the following balances for selected accounts.

Prepaid Insurance	$ 3,600
Equipment	28,000
Notes Payable	20,000
Unearned Service Revenue	4,200
Service Revenue	1,800

Analysis reveals the following additional data.

1. Prepaid insurance is the cost of a 2-year insurance policy, effective April 1.
2. Depreciation on the equipment is $500 per month.
3. The note payable is dated April 1. It is a 6-month, 12% note.
4. Seven customers paid for the company's 6 months' lawn service package of $600 beginning in April. The company performed services for these customers in April.
5. Lawn services provided other customers but not recorded at April 30 totaled $1,500.

Instructions

Prepare the adjusting entries for the month of April. Show computations.

Solution to Comprehensive Do it!

GENERAL JOURNAL   **J1**

Date	Account Titles and Explanation	Ref.	Debit	Credit
	Adjusting Entries			
Apr. 30	Insurance Expense		150	
	Prepaid Insurance			150
	(To record insurance expired: $3,600 ÷ 24 = $150 per month)			
30	Depreciation Expense		500	
	Accumulated Depreciation—Equipment			500
	(To record monthly depreciation)			
30	Interest Expense		200	
	Interest Payable			200
	(To record interest on notes payable: $20,000 × 12% × 1/12 = $200)			
30	Unearned Service Revenue		700	
	Service Revenue			700
	(To record service revenue: $600 ÷ 6 = $100; $100 per month × 7 = $700)			
30	Accounts Receivable		1,500	
	Service Revenue			1,500
	(To record revenue for services provided)			

action plan

✔ Note that adjustments are being made for one month.

✔ Make computations carefully.

✔ Select account titles carefully.

✔ Make sure debits are made first and credits are indented.

✔ Check that debits equal credits for each entry.

The Navigator

Summary of Study Objectives

[1] Explain the time period assumption. The time period assumption assumes that the economic life of a business is divided into artificial time periods.

[2] Explain the accrual basis of accounting. Accrual-basis accounting means that companies record events that change a company's financial statements in the periods in which those events occur, rather than in the periods in which the company receives or pays cash.

[3] Explain the reasons for adjusting entries. Companies make adjusting entries at the end of an accounting period. Such

entries ensure that companies record revenues in the period in which they are earned and that they recognize expenses in the period in which they are incurred.

[4] Identify the major types of adjusting entries. The major types of adjusting entries are deferrals (prepaid expenses and unearned revenues), and accruals (accrued revenues and accrued expenses).

[5] Prepare adjusting entries for deferrals. Deferrals are either prepaid expenses or unearned revenues. Companies make adjusting entries for deferrals to record the portion of the prepayment that represents the expense incurred or the revenue earned in the current accounting period.

[6] Prepare adjusting entries for accruals. Accruals are either accrued revenues or accrued expenses. Companies make adjusting entries for accruals to record revenues earned and expenses incurred in the current accounting period that have not been recognized through daily entries.

[7] Describe the nature and purpose of an adjusted trial balance. An adjusted trial balance shows the balances of all accounts, including those that have been adjusted, at the end of an accounting period. Its purpose is to prove the equality of the total debit balances and total credit balances in the ledger after all adjustments.

The Navigator

Glossary

Accrual-basis accounting Accounting basis in which companies record transactions that change a company's financial statements in the periods in which the events occur. (p. 101).

Accruals Adjusting entries for either accrued revenues or accrued expenses. (p. 103).

Accrued expenses Expenses incurred but not yet paid in cash or recorded. (p. 113).

Accrued revenues Revenues earned but not yet received in cash or recorded. (p. 111).

Adjusted trial balance A list of accounts and their balances after the company has made all adjustments. (p. 119).

Adjusting entries Entries made at the end of an accounting period to ensure that companies follow the revenue recognition and expense recognition principles. (p. 103).

Book value The difference between the cost of a depreciable asset and its related accumulated depreciation. (p. 108).

Calendar year An accounting period that extends from January 1 to December 31. (p. 100).

Cash-basis accounting Accounting basis in which companies record revenue when they receive cash and an expense when they pay cash. (p. 101).

Contra asset account An account offset against an asset account on the balance sheet. (p. 107).

Deferrals Adjusting entries for either prepaid expenses or unearned revenues. (p. 103).

Depreciation The allocation of the cost of an asset to expense over its useful life in a rational and systematic manner. (p. 107).

Expense recognition principle (matching principle) The principle that companies match efforts (expenses) with accomplishments (revenues). (p. 101).

Fiscal year An accounting period that is one year in length. (p. 100).

Interim periods Monthly or quarterly accounting time periods. (p. 100).

Prepaid expenses (prepayments) Expenses paid in cash that benefit more than one accounting period and that are recorded as assets. (p. 104).

Revenue recognition principle The principle that companies recognize revenue in the accounting period in which it is earned. (p. 101).

Time period assumption An assumption that accountants can divide the economic life of a business into artificial time periods. (p. 100).

Unearned revenues Cash received and recorded as liabilities before revenue is earned. (p. 108).

Useful life The length of service of a long-lived asset. (p. 107).

APPENDIX3A

Alternative Treatment of Prepaid Expenses and Unearned Revenues

Study Objective [8]
Prepare adjusting entries for the alternative treatment of deferrals.

In discussing adjusting entries for prepaid expenses and unearned revenues, we illustrated transactions for which companies made the initial entries to balance sheet accounts. In the case of prepaid expenses, the company debited the prepayment to an asset account. In the case of unearned revenue, the company credited a liability account to record the cash received.

Some companies use an alternative treatment: (1) When a company prepays an expense, it debits that amount to an expense account. (2) When it receives payment for future services, it credits the amount to a revenue account. In this appendix, we describe the circumstances that justify such entries and the different adjusting entries that may be required. This alternative treatment of prepaid expenses and unearned revenues has the same effect on the financial statements as the procedures described in the chapter.

Prepaid Expenses

Prepaid expenses become expired costs either through the passage of time (e.g., insurance) or through consumption (e.g., advertising supplies). If, at the time of purchase, the company expects to consume the supplies before the next financial statement date, **it may choose to debit (increase) an expense account rather than an asset account. This alternative treatment is simply more convenient.**

Assume that Pioneer Advertising expects that it will use before the end of the month all of the supplies purchased on October 5. A debit of $2,500 to Supplies Expense (rather than to the asset account Supplies) on October 5 will eliminate the need for an adjusting entry on October 31. At October 31, the Supplies Expense account will show a balance of $2,500, which is the cost of supplies used between October 5 and October 31.

But what if the company does not use all the supplies? For example, what if an inventory of $1,000 of advertising supplies remains on October 31? Obviously, the company would need to make an adjusting entry. Prior to adjustment, the expense account Supplies Expense is overstated $1,000, and the asset account Supplies is understated $1,000. Thus, Pioneer makes the following adjusting entry.

Oct. 31	Supplies	1,000	
	Supplies Expense		1,000
	(To record supplies inventory)		

A	=	L	+	OE
+1,000				
				+1,000 Exp

Cash Flows
no effect

After the company posts the adjusting entry, the accounts show:

Supplies			Supplies Expense			
10/31 Adj.	1,000		10/5	2,500	10/31 Adj.	1,000
			10/31 Bal.	1,500		

Illustration 3A-1
Prepaid expenses accounts after adjustment

After adjustment, the asset account Supplies shows a balance of $1,000, which is equal to the cost of supplies on hand at October 31. In addition, Supplies Expense shows a balance of $1,500. This is equal to the cost of supplies used between October 5 and October 31. Without the adjusting entry expenses are overstated and net income is understated by $1,000 in the October income statement. Also, both assets and owner's equity are understated by $1,000 on the October 31 balance sheet.

Illustration 3A-2 compares the entries and accounts for advertising supplies in the two adjustment approaches.

Prepayment Initially Debited to Asset Account (per chapter)			Prepayment Initially Debited to Expense Account (per appendix)		
Oct. 5 Supplies	2,500		Oct. 5 Supplies Expense	2,500	
Accounts Payable		2,500	Accounts Payable		2,500
Oct. 31 Supplies Expense	1,500		Oct. 31 Supplies	1,000	
Supplies		1,500	Supplies Expense		1,000

Illustration 3A-2
Adjustment approaches—a comparison

After Pioneer posts the entries, the accounts appear as follows.

Illustration 3A-3
Comparison of accounts

(per chapter) Supplies				(per appendix) Supplies			
10/5	2,500	10/31 Adj.	1,500	10/31 Adj.	1,000		
10/31 Bal.	1,000						

Supplies Expense				Supplies Expense			
10/31 Adj.	1,500			10/5	2,500	10/31 Adj.	1,000
				10/31 Bal.	1,500		

Note that the account balances under each alternative are the same at October 31: Supplies $1,000, and Supplies Expense $1,500.

Unearned Revenues

Unearned revenues become earned either through the passage of time (e.g., unearned rent revenue) or through providing the service (e.g., unearned service revenue). Similar to the case for prepaid expenses, companies may credit (increase) a revenue account when they receive cash for future services.

To illustrate, assume that Pioneer Advertising received $1,200 for future services on October 2. Pioneer expects to perform the services before October 31.[1] In such a case, the company credits Service Revenue. If it in fact earns the revenue before October 31, no adjustment is needed.

However, if at the statement date Pioneer has not performed $800 of the services, it would make an adjusting entry. Without the entry, the revenue account Service Revenue is overstated $800, and the liability account Unearned Service Revenue is understated $800. Thus, Pioneer makes the following adjusting entry.

Helpful Hint

The required adjusted balances here are Service Revenue $400 and Unearned Service Revenue $800.

Cash Flows
no effect

Oct. 31	Service Revenue	800	
	Unearned Service Revenue		800
	(To record unearned revenue)		

After Pioneer posts the adjusting entry, the accounts show:

Illustration 3A-4
Unearned service revenue accounts after adjustment

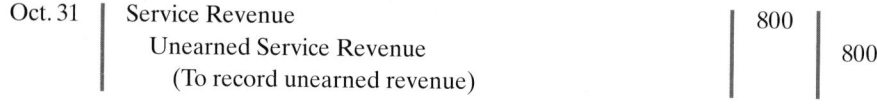

Unearned Service Revenue		Service Revenue			
	10/31 Adj.	800	10/31 Adj.	800	10/2	1,200
					10/31 Bal.	400

The liability account Unearned Service Revenue shows a balance of $800. This equals the services that will be provided in the future. In addition, the balance in Service Revenue equals the services provided in October. Without the adjusting entry, both revenues and net income are overstated by $800 in the October income statement. Also, liabilities are understated by $800, and owner's equity is overstated by $800 on the October 31 balance sheet.

Illustration 3A-5 compares the entries and accounts for service revenue earned and unearned in the two adjustment approaches.

---

[1]This example focuses only on the alternative treatment of unearned revenues. For simplicity, we have ignored the entries to Service Revenue pertaining to the immediate earning of revenue ($10,000) and the adjusting entry for accrued revenue ($200).

Illustration 3A-5
Adjustment approaches—
a comparison

Unearned Service Revenue Initially Credited to Liability Account (per chapter)			Unearned Service Revenue Initially Credited to Revenue Account (per appendix)		
Oct. 2	Cash	1,200	Oct. 2	Cash	1,200
	Unearned Service Revenue	1,200		Service Revenue	1,200
Oct. 31	Unearned Service Revenue	400	Oct. 31	Service Revenue	800
	Service Revenue	400		Unearned Service Revenue	800

After Pioneer posts the entries, the accounts appear as follows.

Illustration 3A-6
Comparison of accounts

(per chapter) Unearned Service Revenue			(per appendix) Unearned Service Revenue		
10/31 Adj. 400	10/2	1,200		10/31 Adj.	800
	10/31 Bal.	800			

Service Revenue			Service Revenue		
	10/31 Adj.	400	10/31 Adj. 800	10/2	1,200
				10/31 Bal.	400

Note that the balances in the accounts are the same under the two alternatives: Unearned Service Revenue $800, and Service Revenue $400.

Summary of Additional Adjustment Relationships

Illustration 3A-7 provides a summary of basic relationships for deferrals.

Illustration 3A-7
Summary of basic relationships for deferrals

Type of Adjustment	Reason for Adjustment	Account Balances before Adjustment	Adjusting Entry
1. Prepaid expenses	(a) Prepaid expenses initially recorded in asset accounts have been used.	Assets overstated Expenses understated	Dr. Expenses Cr. Assets
	(b) Prepaid expenses initially recorded in expense accounts have not been used.	Assets understated Expenses overstated	Dr. Assets Cr. Expenses
2. Unearned revenues	(a) Unearned revenues initially recorded in liability accounts have been earned.	Liabilities overstated Revenues understated	Dr. Liabilities Cr. Revenues
	(b) Unearned revenues initially recorded in revenue accounts have not been earned.	Liabilities understated Revenues overstated	Dr. Revenues Cr. Liabilities

Alternative adjusting entries **do not apply** to accrued revenues and accrued expenses because **no entries occur before companies make these types of adjusting entries.**

Summary of Study Objective for Appendix 3A

[8] Prepare adjusting entries for the alternative treatment of deferrals. Companies may initially debit prepayments to an expense account. Likewise, they may credit unearned revenues to a revenue account. At the end of the period, these accounts may be overstated. The adjusting entries for prepaid expenses are a debit to an asset account and a credit to an expense account. Adjusting entries for unearned revenues are a debit to a revenue account and a credit to a liability account.

Self-Test, Brief Exercises, Exercises, Problem Set A, and many more components are available for practice in *WileyPLUS*

*Note: All asterisked Questions, Exercises, and Problems relate to material in the appendix to the chapter.

Self-Test Questions

Answers are on page 148.

(SO 1) **1.** The time period assumption states that:
   a. revenue should be recognized in the accounting period in which it is earned.
   b. expenses should be matched with revenues.
   c. the economic life of a business can be divided into artificial time periods.
   d. the fiscal year should correspond with the calendar year.

(SO 1) **2.** The time period assumption states that:
   a. companies must wait until the calendar year is completed to prepare financial statements.
   b. companies use the fiscal year to report financial information.
   c. the economic life of a business can be divided into artificial time periods.
   d. companies record information in the time period in which the events occur.

(SO 2) **3.** Which of the following statements about the accrual basis of accounting is *false*?
   a. Events that change a company's financial statements are recorded in the periods in which the events occur.
   b. Revenue is recognized in the period in which it is earned.
   c. This basis is in accord with generally accepted accounting principles.
   d. Revenue is recorded only when cash is received, and expense is recorded only when cash is paid.

(SO 2) **4.** The principle or assumption dictating that efforts (expenses) be matched with accomplishments (revenues) is the:
   a. expense recognition principle.
   b. cost assumption.
   c. time period principle.
   d. revenue recognition principle.

(SO 3) **5.** Adjusting entries are made to ensure that:
   a. expenses are recognized in the period in which they are incurred.
   b. revenues are recorded in the period in which they are earned.
   c. balance sheet and income statement accounts have correct balances at the end of an accounting period.
   d. All of the above.

(SO 4) **6.** Each of the following is a major type (or category) of adjusting entries *except*:
   a. prepaid expenses.
   b. accrued revenues.
   c. accrued expenses.
   d. earned revenues.

(SO 5) **7.** The trial balance shows Supplies $1,350 and Supplies Expense $0. If $600 of supplies are on hand at the end of the period, the adjusting entry is:

a. Supplies	600	
Supplies Expense		600
b. Supplies	750	
Supplies Expense		750
c. Supplies Expense	750	
Supplies		750
d. Supplies Expense	600	
Supplies		600

(SO 5) **8.** Adjustments for prepaid expenses:
   a. decrease assets and increase revenues.
   b. decrease expenses and increase assets.
   c. decrease assets and increase expenses.
   d. decrease revenues and increase assets.

(SO 5) **9.** Accumulated Depreciation is:
   a. a contra asset account.
   b. an expense account.
   c. an owner's equity account.
   d. a liability account.

(SO 5) **10.** Queenan Company computes depreciation on delivery equipment at $1,000 for the month of June. The adjusting entry to record this depreciation is as follows.

a. Depreciation Expense	1,000	
Accumulated Depreciation—		
Queenan Company		1,000
b. Depreciation Expense	1,000	
Equipment		1,000
c. Depreciation Expense	1,000	
Accumulated Depreciation—		
Equipment		1,000
d. Equipment Expense	1,000	
Accumulated Depreciation—		
Equipment		1,000

(SO 5) **11.** Adjustments for unearned revenues:
   a. decrease liabilities and increase revenues.
   b. have an assets and revenues account relationship.
   c. increase assets and increase revenues.
   d. decrease revenues and decrease assets.

(SO 6) **12.** Adjustments for accrued revenues:
   a. have a liabilities and revenues account relationship.
   b. have an assets and revenues account relationship.
   c. decrease assets and revenues.
   d. decrease liabilities and increase revenues.

(SO 6) **13.** Kathy Siska earned a salary of $400 for the last week of September. She will be paid on October 1. The adjusting entry for Kathy's employer at September 30 is:
   a. No entry is required.

b. Salaries and Wages Expense	400	
Salaries and Wages Payable		400

c. Salaries and Wages Expense | 400 |
    Cash | | 400
d. Salaries and Wages Payable | 400 |
    Cash | | 400

d. The adjusted trial balance is prepared after the adjusting entries have been journalized and posted.

(SO 7) **14.** Which of the following statements is *incorrect* concerning the adjusted trial balance?

    a. An adjusted trial balance proves the equality of the total debit balances and the total credit balances in the ledger after all adjustments are made.

    b. The adjusted trial balance provides the primary basis for the preparation of financial statements.

    c. The adjusted trial balance lists the account balances segregated by assets and liabilities.

*15. The trial balance shows Supplies $0 and Supplies Expense $1,500. If $800 of supplies are on hand at the end of the period, the adjusting entry is: (SO 8)

    a. Debit Supplies $800 and credit Supplies Expense $800.

    b. Debit Supplies Expense $800 and credit Supplies $800.

    c. Debit Supplies $700 and credit Supplies Expense $700.

    d. Debit Supplies Expense $700 and credit Supplies $700.

Go to the book's companion website, **www.wiley.com/college/weygandt**, for additional Self-Test Questions.

Questions

1. (a) How does the time period assumption affect an accountant's analysis of business transactions?

    (b) Explain the terms *fiscal year, calendar year,* and *interim periods.*

2. State two generally accepted accounting principles that relate to adjusting the accounts.

3. Chris Harris, a lawyer, accepts a legal engagement in March, performs the work in April, and is paid in May. If Harris's law firm prepares monthly financial statements, when should it recognize revenue from this engagement? Why?

4. Why do accrual-basis financial statements provide more useful information than cash-basis statements?

5. In completing the engagement in question 3, Harris pays no costs in March, $2,000 in April, and $2,500 in May (incurred in April). How much expense should the firm deduct from revenues in the month when it recognizes the revenue? Why?

6. "Adjusting entries are required by the cost principle of accounting." Do you agree? Explain.

7. Why may a trial balance not contain up-to-date and complete financial information?

8. Distinguish between the two categories of adjusting entries, and identify the types of adjustments applicable to each category.

9. What is the debit/credit effect of a prepaid expense adjusting entry?

10. "Depreciation is a valuation process that results in the reporting of the fair value of the asset." Do you agree? Explain.

11. Explain the differences between depreciation expense and accumulated depreciation.

12. T. Harris Company purchased equipment for $18,000. By the current balance sheet date, $6,000 had been depreciated. Indicate the balance sheet presentation of the data.

13. What is the debit/credit effect of an unearned revenue adjusting entry?

14. A company fails to recognize revenue earned but not yet received. Which of the following accounts are involved in the adjusting entry: (a) asset, (b) liability, (c) revenue, or (d) expense? For the accounts selected, indicate whether they would be debited or credited in the entry.

15. A company fails to recognize an expense incurred but not paid. Indicate which of the following accounts is debited and which is credited in the adjusting entry: (a) asset, (b) liability, (c) revenue, or (d) expense.

16. A company makes an accrued revenue adjusting entry for $900 and an accrued expense adjusting entry for $700. How much was net income understated prior to these entries? Explain.

17. On January 9, a company pays $5,000 for salaries, of which $2,000 was reported as Salaries and Wages Payable on December 31. Give the entry to record the payment.

18. For each of the following items before adjustment, indicate the type of adjusting entry (prepaid expense, unearned revenue, accrued revenue, or accrued expense) that is needed to correct the misstatement. If an item could result in more than one type of adjusting entry, indicate each of the types.

    (a) Assets are understated.

    (b) Liabilities are overstated.

    (c) Liabilities are understated.

    (d) Expenses are understated.

    (e) Assets are overstated.

    (f) Revenue is understated.

19. One-half of the adjusting entry is given below. Indicate the account title for the other half of the entry.

    (a) Salaries and Wages Expense is debited.

    (b) Depreciation Expense is debited.

    (c) Interest Payable is credited.

    (d) Supplies is credited.

    (e) Accounts Receivable is debited.

    (f) Unearned Service Revenue is debited.

20. "An adjusting entry may affect more than one balance sheet or income statement account." Do you agree? Why or why not?

21. Why is it possible to prepare financial statements directly from an adjusted trial balance?

*22. M. Harrison Company debits Supplies Expense for all purchases of supplies and credits Rent Revenue for all advanced rentals. For each type of adjustment, give the adjusting entry.

23. ☀ **PEPSICO** What was PepsiCo's depreciation and amortization expense for 2009 and 2008?

Brief Exercises

Indicate why adjusting entries are needed.
(SO 3)

BE3-1 The ledger of Levi Company includes the following accounts. Explain why each account may require adjustment.

(a) Prepaid Insurance
(b) Depreciation Expense
(c) Unearned Service Revenue
(d) Interest Payable

Identify the major types of adjusting entries.
(SO 4, 5, 6)

BE3-2 Horn Company accumulates the following adjustment data at December 31. Indicate (a) the type of adjustment (prepaid expense, accrued revenues and so on), and (b) the status of accounts before adjustment (overstated or understated).

1. Supplies of $100 are on hand.
2. Services provided but not recorded total $900.
3. Interest of $200 has accumulated on a note payable.
4. Rent collected in advance totaling $650 has been earned.

Prepare adjusting entry for supplies.
(SO 5)

BE3-3 Devin Advertising Company's trial balance at December 31 shows Supplies $6,700 and Supplies Expense $0. On December 31, there are $2,500 of supplies on hand. Prepare the adjusting entry at December 31, and using T accounts, enter the balances in the accounts, post the adjusting entry, and indicate the adjusted balance in each account.

Prepare adjusting entry for depreciation.
(SO 5)

BE3-4 At the end of its first year, the trial balance of Hester Company shows Equipment $30,000 and zero balances in Accumulated Depreciation—Equipment and Depreciation Expense. Depreciation for the year is estimated to be $4,000. Prepare the adjusting entry for depreciation at December 31, post the adjustments to T accounts, and indicate the balance sheet presentation of the equipment at December 31.

Prepare adjusting entry for prepaid expense.
(SO 5)

BE3-5 On July 1, 2012, Israel Co. pays $14,400 to Idonije Insurance Co. for a 3-year insurance contract. Both companies have fiscal years ending December 31. For Israel Co., journalize and post the entry on July 1 and the adjusting entry on December 31.

Prepare adjusting entry for unearned revenue.
(SO 5)

BE3-6 Using the data in BE3-5, journalize and post the entry on July 1 and the adjusting entry on December 31 for Idonije Insurance Co. Idonije uses the accounts Unearned Service Revenue and Service Revenue.

Prepare adjusting entries for accruals.
(SO 6)

BE3-7 The bookkeeper for Juaquin Company asks you to prepare the following accrued adjusting entries at December 31.

1. Interest on notes payable of $400 is accrued.
2. Services provided but not recorded total $1,900.
3. Salaries earned by employees of $900 have not been recorded.

Use the following account titles: Service Revenue, Accounts Receivable, Interest Expense, Interest Payable, Salaries and Wages Expense, and Salaries and Wages Payable.

Analyze accounts in an unadjusted trial balance.
(SO 4, 5, 6)

BE3-8 The trial balance of Iglesias Company includes the following balance sheet accounts, which may require adjustment. For each account that requires adjustment, indicate (a) the type of adjusting entry (prepaid expenses, unearned revenues, accrued revenues, and accrued expenses) and (b) the related account in the adjusting entry.

Accounts Receivable
Prepaid Insurance
Accumulated Depreciation—Equipment

Interest Payable
Unearned Service Revenue

Prepare an income statement from an adjusted trial balance.
(SO 7)

BE3-9 The adjusted trial balance of Iwuh Company at December 31, 2012, includes the following accounts: Owner's Capital $15,600; Owner's Drawings $7,000; Service Revenue $37,000; Salaries and Wages Expense $16,000; Insurance Expense $2,000; Rent Expense $4,000; Supplies Expense $1,500; and Depreciation Expense $1,300. Prepare an income statement for the year.

BE3-10 Partial adjusted trial balance data for Iwuh Company is presented in BE3-9. The balance in Owner's Capital is the balance as of January 1. Prepare an owner's equity statement for the year assuming net income is $12,200 for the year.

***BE3-11** Jennings Company records all prepayments in income statement accounts. At April 30, the trial balance shows Supplies Expense $2,800, Service Revenue $9,200, and zero balances in related balance sheet accounts. Prepare the adjusting entries at April 30 assuming (a) $700 of supplies on hand and (b) $3,000 of service revenue should be reported as unearned.

Prepare an owner's equity statement from an adjusted trial balance.
(SO 7)

Prepare adjusting entries under alternative treatment of deferrals.
(SO 8)

Do it! Review

Do it! 3-1 Numerous timing concepts are discussed on pages 100–102. A list of concepts is provided below in the left column, with a description of the concept in the right column. There are more descriptions provided than concepts. Match the description of the concept to the concept.

Identify timing concepts.
(SO 1, 2)

1. ____ Cash-basis accounting.
2. ____ Fiscal year.
3. ____ Revenue recognition principle.
4. ____ Expense recognition principle.

(a) Monthly and quarterly time periods.
(b) Accountants divide the economic life of a business into artificial time periods.
(c) Efforts (expenses) should be matched with accomplishments (revenues).
(d) Companies record revenues when they receive cash and record expenses when they pay out cash.
(e) An accounting time period that is one year in length.
(f) An accounting time period that starts on January 1 and ends on December 31.
(g) Companies record transactions in the period in which the events occur.
(h) Recognize revenue in the accounting period in which it is earned.

Do it! 3-2 The ledger of Lefevour, Inc. on March 31, 2012, includes the following selected accounts before adjusting entries.

Prepare adjusting entries for deferrals.
(SO 5)

	Debit	Credit
Prepaid Insurance	2,400	
Supplies	2,500	
Equipment	30,000	
Unearned Service Revenue		9,000

An analysis of the accounts shows the following.

1. Insurance expires at the rate of $300 per month.
2. Supplies on hand total $1,100.
3. The equipment depreciates $500 per month.
4. 2/5 of the unearned service revenue was earned in March.

Prepare the adjusting entries for the month of March.

Do it! 3-3 Johnny Knox is the new owner of Swift Computer Services. At the end of July 2012, his first month of ownership, Johnny is trying to prepare monthly financial statements. He has the following information for the month.

Prepare adjusting entries for accruals.
(SO 6)

1. At July 31, Knox owed employees $1,300 in salaries that the company will pay in August.
2. On July 1, Knox borrowed $20,000 from a local bank on a 10-year note. The annual interest rate is 12%.
3. Service revenue unrecorded in July totaled $2,400.

Prepare the adjusting entries needed at July 31, 2012.

Do it! 3-4 Kreutz Co. was organized on April 1, 2012. The company prepares quarterly financial statements. The adjusted trial balance amounts at June 30 are shown on the next page.

Calculate amounts from trial balance.
(SO 7)

Debits		Credits	
Cash	$ 5,360	Accumulated Depreciation—	$ 700
Accounts Receivable	480	Equipment	
Prepaid Rent	720	Notes Payable	4,000
Supplies	920	Accounts Payable	790
Equipment	12,000	Salaries and Wages Payable	300
Owner's Drawings	500	Interest Payable	40
Salaries and Wages Expense	7,400	Unearned Rent Revenue	400
Rent Expense	1,200	Owner's Capital	11,200
Depreciation Expense	700	Service Revenue	11,360
Supplies Expense	160	Rent Revenue	1,100
Utilities Expense	410	Total credits	$29,890
Interest Expense	40		
Total debits	$29,890		

(a) Determine the net income for the quarter April 1 to June 30.
(b) Determine the total assets and total liabilities at June 30, 2012 for Kreutz Company.
(c) Determine the amount that appears for Owner's Capital at June 30, 2012.

Exercises

Explain the time period assumption.

(SO 1)

E3-1 Lance Louis has prepared the following list of statements about the time period assumption.

1. Adjusting entries would not be necessary if a company's life were not divided into artificial time periods.
2. The IRS requires companies to file annual tax returns.
3. Accountants divide the economic life of a business into artificial time periods, but each transaction affects only one of these periods.
4. Accounting time periods are generally a month, a quarter, or a year.
5. A time period lasting one year is called an interim period.
6. All fiscal years are calendar years, but not all calendar years are fiscal years.

Instructions
Identify each statement as true or false. If false, indicate how to correct the statement.

Distinguish between cash and accrual basis of accounting.

(SO 2)

E3-2 On numerous occasions, proposals have surfaced to put the federal government on the accrual basis of accounting. This is no small issue. If this basis were used, it would mean that billions in unrecorded liabilities would have to be booked, and the federal deficit would increase substantially.

Instructions
(a) What is the difference between accrual-basis accounting and cash-basis accounting?
(b) Why would politicians prefer the cash basis over the accrual basis?
(c) Write a letter to your senator explaining why the federal government should adopt the accrual basis of accounting.

Compute cash and accrual accounting income.

(SO 2)

E3-3 Malast Industries collected $105,000 from customers in 2012. Of the amount collected, $25,000 was from revenue earned on account in 2011. In addition, Malast earned $40,000 of revenue in 2012, which will not be collected until 2013.

Malast Industries also paid $72,000 for expenses in 2012. Of the amount paid, $30,000 was for expenses incurred on account in 2011. In addition, Malast incurred $42,000 of expenses in 2012, which will not be paid until 2013.

Instructions
(a) Compute 2012 cash-basis net income.
(b) Compute 2012 accrual-basis net income.

Identify the type of adjusting entry needed.

(SO 4, 5, 6)

E3-4 Mannelly Corporation encounters the following situations:

1. Mannelly collects $1,300 from a customer in 2012 for services to be performed in 2013.
2. Mannelly incurs utility expense which is not yet paid in cash or recorded.

3. Mannelly's employees worked 3 days in 2012 but will not be paid until 2013.

4. Mannelly earned service revenue but has not yet received cash or recorded the transaction.

5. Mannelly paid $2,400 rent on December 1 for the 4 months starting December 1.

6. Mannelly received cash for future services and recorded a liability until the revenue was earned.

7. Mannelly performed consulting services for a client in December 2012. On December 31, it had not billed the client for services provided of $1,200.

8. Mannelly paid cash for an expense and recorded an asset until the item was used up.

9. Mannelly purchased $900 of supplies in 2012; at year-end, $400 of supplies remain unused.

10. Mannelly purchased equipment on January 1, 2012; the equipment will be used for 5 years.

11. Mannelly borrowed $10,000 on October 1, 2012, signing an 8% one-year note payable.

Instructions

Identify what type of adjusting entry (prepaid expense, unearned revenue, accrued expense, or accrued revenue) is needed in each situation, at December 31, 2012.

E3-5 Garrett Wolfe Company has the following balances in selected accounts on December 31, 2012.

Prepare adjusting entries from selected data.

(SO 5, 6)

Accounts Receivable	$ -0-
Accumulated Depreciation—Equipment	-0-
Equipment	7,000
Interest Payable	-0-
Notes Payable	10,000
Prepaid Insurance	2,100
Salaries and Wages Payable	-0-
Supplies	2,450
Unearned Service Revenue	30,000

All the accounts have normal balances. The information below has been gathered at December 31, 2012.

1. Garrett Wolfe Company borrowed $10,000 by signing a 12%, one-year note on September 1, 2012.

2. A count of supplies on December 31, 2012, indicates that supplies of $900 are on hand.

3. Depreciation on the equipment for 2012 is $1,000.

4. Garrett Wolfe Company paid $2,100 for 12 months of insurance coverage on June 1, 2012.

5. On December 1, 2012, Garrett Wolfe collected $30,000 for consulting services to be performed from December 1, 2012, through March 31, 2013.

6. Garrett Wolfe performed consulting services for a client in December 2012. The client will be billed $4,200.

7. Garrett Wolfe Company pays its employees total salaries of $9,000 every Monday for the preceding 5-day week (Monday through Friday). On Monday, December 29, employees were paid for the week ending December 26. All employees worked the last 3 days of 2012.

Instructions

Prepare adjusting entries for the seven items described above.

E3-6 J. Marten Company accumulates the following adjustment data at December 31.

Identify types of adjustments and account relationships.

(SO 4, 5, 6)

1. Services provided but not recorded total $1,000.

2. Supplies of $300 have been used.

3. Utility expenses of $225 are unpaid.

4. Unearned service revenue of $260 has been earned.

5. Salaries of $800 are unpaid.

6. Prepaid insurance totaling $350 has expired.

Instructions

For each of the above items indicate the following.

(a) The type of adjustment (prepaid expense, unearned revenue, accrued revenue, or accrued expense).

(b) The status of accounts before adjustment (overstatement or understatement).

E3-7 The ledger of Danieal Rental Agency on March 31 of the current year includes the selected accounts, shown on the next page, before adjusting entries have been prepared.

Prepare adjusting entries from selected account data.

(SO 5, 6)

	Debit	Credit
Prepaid Insurance	$ 3,600	
Supplies	2,800	
Equipment	25,000	
Accumulated		
Depreciation—Equipment		$ 8,400
Notes Payable		20,000
Unearned Rent Revenue		10,200
Rent Revenue		60,000
Interest Expense	–0–	
Salaries and Wages Expense	14,000	

An analysis of the accounts shows the following.

1. The equipment depreciates $400 per month.
2. One-third of the unearned rent revenue was earned during the quarter.
3. Interest of $500 is accrued on the notes payable.
4. Supplies on hand total $900.
5. Insurance expires at the rate of $200 per month.

Instructions

Prepare the adjusting entries at March 31, assuming that adjusting entries are made **quarterly**. Additional accounts are: Depreciation Expense, Insurance Expense, Interest Payable, and Supplies Expense.

Prepare adjusting entries.

(SO 5, 6)

E3-8   Danielle Manning, D.D.S., opened a dental practice on January 1, 2012. During the first month of operations, the following transactions occurred.

1. Performed services for patients who had dental plan insurance. At January 31, $875 of such services was earned but not yet recorded.
2. Utility expenses incurred but not paid prior to January 31 totaled $650.
3. Purchased dental equipment on January 1 for $80,000, paying $20,000 in cash and signing a $60,000, 3-year note payable. The equipment depreciates $400 per month. Interest is $500 per month.
4. Purchased a one-year malpractice insurance policy on January 1 for $24,000.
5. Purchased $1,600 of dental supplies. On January 31, determined that $400 of supplies were on hand.

Instructions

Prepare the adjusting entries on January 31. Account titles are: Accumulated Depreciation—Equipment, Depreciation Expense, Service Revenue, Accounts Receivable, Insurance Expense, Interest Expense, Interest Payable, Prepaid Insurance, Supplies, Supplies Expense, Utilities Expense, and Utilities Payable.

Prepare adjusting entries.

(SO 5, 6)

E3-9   The trial balance for Pioneer Advertising Agency is shown in Illustration 3-3, p. 104. In lieu of the adjusting entries shown in the text at October 31, assume the following adjustment data.

1. Supplies on hand at October 31 total $500.
2. Expired insurance for the month is $100.
3. Depreciation for the month is $50.
4. Unearned service revenue earned in October totals $600.
5. Services provided but not recorded at October 31 are $300.
6. Interest accrued at October 31 is $95.
7. Accrued salaries at October 31 are $1,625.

Instructions

Prepare the adjusting entries for the items above.

Prepare correct income statement.

(SO 2, 5, 6, 7)

E3-10   The income statement of Brandon Co. for the month of July shows net income of $1,400 based on Service Revenue $5,500, Salaries and Wages Expense $2,300, Supplies Expense $1,200, and Utilities Expense $600. In reviewing the statement, you discover the following.

1. Insurance expired during July of $400 was omitted.
2. Supplies expense includes $250 of supplies that are still on hand at July 31.

3. Depreciation on equipment of $150 was omitted.
4. Accrued but unpaid salaries and wages at July 31 of $300 were not included.
5. Services provided but unrecorded totaled $650.

Instructions
Prepare a correct income statement for July 2012.

E3-11 A partial adjusted trial balance of Manumaleuna Company at January 31, 2012, shows the following.

Analyze adjusted data.
(SO 4, 5, 6, 7)

MANUMALEUNA COMPANY
Adjusted Trial Balance
January 31, 2012

	Debit	Credit
Supplies	$ 850	
Prepaid Insurance	2,400	
Salaries and Wages Payable		$ 800
Unearned Service Revenue		750
Supplies Expense	950	
Insurance Expense	400	
Salaries and Wages Expense	2,900	
Service Revenue		2,000

Instructions
Answer the following questions, assuming the year begins January 1.

(a) If the amount in Supplies Expense is the January 31 adjusting entry, and $1,000 of supplies was purchased in January, what was the balance in Supplies on January 1?

(b) If the amount in Insurance Expense is the January 31 adjusting entry, and the original insurance premium was for one year, what was the total premium and when was the policy purchased?

(c) If $3,500 of salaries was paid in January, what was the balance in Salaries and Wages Payable at December 31, 2011?

E3-12 Selected accounts of Tabor Company are shown below.

Journalize basic transactions and adjusting entries.
(SO 5, 6, 7)

Supplies Expense

7/31	800	

Supplies

7/1 Bal.	1,100	7/31	800
7/10	650		

Salaries and Wages Payable

		7/31	1,200

Accounts Receivable

7/31	500	

Unearned Service Revenue

7/31	1,150	7/1 Bal.	1,500
		7/20	1,000

Salaries and Wages Expense

7/15	1,200	
7/31	1,200	

Service Revenue

		7/14	2,000
		7/31	1,150
		7/31	500

Instructions
After analyzing the accounts, journalize **(a)** the July transactions and **(b)** the adjusting entries that were made on July 31. (*Hint:* July transactions were for cash.)

E3-13 The trial balances before and after adjustment for Matthews Company at the end of its fiscal year are presented on the next page.

Prepare adjusting entries from analysis of trial balances.
(SO 5, 6, 7)

MATTHEWS COMPANY
Trial Balance
August 31, 2012

	Before Adjustment		After Adjustment	
	Dr.	**Cr.**	**Dr.**	**Cr.**
Cash	$10,400		$10,400	
Accounts Receivable	8,800		10,800	
Supplies	2,300		900	
Prepaid Insurance	4,000		2,500	
Equipment	14,000		14,000	
Accumulated Depreciation—Equipment		$ 3,600		$ 4,500
Accounts Payable		5,800		5,800
Salaries and Wages Payable		–0–		1,100
Unearned Rent Revenue		1,500		600
Owner's Capital		15,600		15,600
Service Revenue		34,000		36,000
Rent Revenue		11,000		11,900
Salaries and Wages Expense	17,000		18,100	
Supplies Expense	–0–		1,400	
Rent Expense	15,000		15,000	
Insurance Expense	–0–		1,500	
Depreciation Expense	–0–		900	
	$71,500	$71,500	$75,500	$75,500

Instructions

Prepare the adjusting entries that were made.

Prepare financial statements from adjusted trial balance.
(SO 7)

E3-14 The adjusted trial balance for Matthews Company is given in E3-13.

Instructions

Prepare the income and owner's equity statements for the year and the balance sheet at August 31.

Record transactions on accrual basis; convert revenue to cash receipts.
(SO 5, 6)

E3-15 The following data are taken from the comparative balance sheets of Mayberry Billiards Club, which prepares its financial statements using the accrual basis of accounting.

December 31	**2012**	**2011**
Accounts receivable from members	$14,000	$ 9,000
Unearned service revenue	17,000	25,000

Members are billed based upon their use of the club's facilities. Unearned service revenues arise from the sale of gift certificates, which members can apply to their future use of club facilities. The 2012 income statement for the club showed that service revenue of $161,000 was earned during the year.

Instructions

(*Hint:* You will probably find it helpful to use T accounts to analyze these data.)

(a) Prepare journal entries for each of the following events that took place during 2012.
   (1) Accounts receivable from 2011 were all collected.
   (2) Gift certificates outstanding at the end of 2011 were all redeemed.
   (3) An additional $38,000 worth of gift certificates were sold during 2012. A portion of these was used by the recipients during the year; the remainder was still outstanding at the end of 2012.
   (4) Services provided to members for 2012 were billed to members.
   (5) Accounts receivable for 2012 (i.e., those billed in item [4] above) were partially collected.
(b) Determine the amount of cash received by the club, with respect to member services, during 2012.

Journalize adjusting entries.
(SO 8)

*E3-16 Brad Maynard Company has the following balances in selected accounts on December 31, 2012.

Service Revenue	$40,000
Insurance Expense	2,700
Supplies Expense	2,450

All the accounts have normal balances. Brad Maynard Company debits prepayments to expense accounts when paid, and credits unearned revenues to revenue accounts when received. The following information below has been gathered at December 31, 2012.

1. Brad Maynard Company paid $2,700 for 12 months of insurance coverage on June 1, 2012.
2. On December 1, 2012, Brad Maynard Company collected $40,000 for consulting services to be performed from December 1, 2012, through March 31, 2013.
3. A count of supplies on December 31, 2012, indicates that supplies of $900 are on hand.

Instructions
Prepare the adjusting entries needed at December 31, 2012.

*E3-17 At Richmond Company, prepayments are debited to expense when paid, and unearned revenues are credited to revenue when received. During January of the current year, the following transactions occurred.

Journalize transactions and adjusting entries.
(SO 8)

Jan. 2 Paid $1,920 for fire insurance protection for the year.
　10 Paid $1,700 for supplies.
　15 Received $6,100 for services to be performed in the future.

On January 31, it is determined that $2,500 of the services are earned and that there are $650 of supplies on hand.

Instructions
(a) Journalize and post the January transactions. (Use T accounts.)
(b) Journalize and post the adjusting entries at January 31.
(c) Determine the ending balance in each of the accounts.

Exercises: Set B

Visit the book's companion website, at **www.wiley.com/college/weygandt**, and choose the Student Companion site to access Exercise Set B.

Problems: Set A

P3-1A Tony Masasi started his own consulting firm, McGee Company, on June 1, 2012. The trial balance at June 30 is shown below.

Prepare adjusting entries, post to ledger accounts, and prepare adjusted trial balance.
(SO 5, 6, 7)

McGEE COMPANY
Trial Balance
June 30, 2012

Account Number		Debit	Credit
101	Cash	$ 7,150	
112	Accounts Receivable	6,000	
126	Supplies	2,000	
130	Prepaid Insurance	3,000	
157	Equipment	15,000	
201	Accounts Payable		$ 4,500
209	Unearned Service Revenue		4,000
301	Owner's Capital		21,750
400	Service Revenue		7,900
726	Salaries and Wages Expense	4,000	
729	Rent Expense	1,000	
		$38,150	$38,150

In addition to those accounts listed on the trial balance, the chart of accounts for McGee Company also contains the following accounts and account numbers: No. 158 Accumulated Depreciation—Equipment, No. 212 Salaries and Wages Payable, No. 631 Supplies Expense, No. 711 Depreciation Expense, No. 722 Insurance Expense, and No. 732 Utilities Expense.

Other data:

1. Supplies on hand at June 30 are $750.
2. A utility bill for $150 has not been recorded and will not be paid until next month.
3. The insurance policy is for a year.
4. $2,800 of unearned service revenue has been earned at the end of the month.
5. Salaries of $1,900 are accrued at June 30.
6. The equipment has a 5-year life with no salvage value. It is being depreciated at $250 per month for 60 months.
7. Invoices representing $1,200 of services performed during the month have not been recorded as of June 30.

Instructions
(a) Prepare the adjusting entries for the month of June. Use J3 as the page number for your journal.
(b) Post the adjusting entries to the ledger accounts. Enter the totals from the trial balance as beginning account balances and place a check mark in the posting reference column.
(c) Adj. trial balance $41,650   **(c)** Prepare an adjusted trial balance at June 30, 2012.

Prepare adjusting entries, post, and prepare adjusted trial balance, and financial statements.

(SO 5, 6, 7)

P3-2A   Melton River Resort opened for business on June 1 with eight air-conditioned units. Its trial balance before adjustment on August 31 is as follows.

MELTON RIVER RESORT
Trial Balance
August 31, 2012

Account Number		Debit	Credit
101	Cash	$ 19,600	
126	Supplies	3,300	
130	Prepaid Insurance	6,000	
140	Land	25,000	
143	Buildings	125,000	
149	Equipment	26,000	
201	Accounts Payable		$ 6,500
208	Unearned Rent Revenue		7,400
275	Mortgage Payable		80,000
301	Owner's Capital		100,000
306	Owner's Drawings	5,000	
429	Rent Revenue		80,000
622	Maintenance and Repairs Expense	3,600	
726	Salaries and Wages Expense	51,000	
732	Utilities Expense	9,400	
		$273,900	$273,900

In addition to those accounts listed on the trial balance, the chart of accounts for Melton River Resort also contains the following accounts and account numbers: No. 112 Accounts Receivable, No. 144 Accumulated Depreciation—Buildings, No. 150 Accumulated Depreciation—Equipment, No. 212 Salaries and Wages Payable, No. 230 Interest Payable, No. 620 Depreciation Expense, No. 631 Supplies Expense, No. 718 Interest Expense, and No. 722 Insurance Expense.

Other data:

1. Insurance expires at the rate of $300 per month.
2. A count on August 31 shows $800 of supplies on hand.

3. Annual depreciation is $6,000 on buildings and $2,400 on equipment.
4. Unearned rent revenue of $4,800 was earned prior to August 31.
5. Salaries of $400 were unpaid at August 31.
6. Rentals of $4,000 were due from tenants at August 31. (Use Accounts Receivable.)
7. The mortgage interest rate is 9% per year. (The mortgage was taken out on August 1.)

Instructions
(a) Journalize the adjusting entries on August 31 for the 3-month period June 1–August 31.
(b) Prepare a ledger using the three-column form of account. Enter the trial balance amounts and post the adjusting entries. (Use J1 as the posting reference.)
(c) Prepare an adjusted trial balance on August 31.
(d) Prepare an income statement and an owner's equity statement for the 3 months ending August 31 and a balance sheet as of August 31.

*(c) Adj. trial balance
$281,000*
*(d) Net income $18,300
Ending capital balance
$113,300
Total assets $203,400*

P3-3A   Minor Advertising Agency was founded by Brandon Minor in January of 2011. Presented below are both the adjusted and unadjusted trial balances as of December 31, 2012.

Prepare adjusting entries and financial statements.
(SO 5, 6, 7)

MINOR ADVERTISING AGENCY
Trial Balance
December 31, 2012

	Unadjusted		Adjusted	
	Dr.	**Cr.**	**Dr.**	**Cr.**
Cash	$ 11,000		$ 11,000	
Accounts Receivable	20,000		21,500	
Supplies	8,600		4,800	
Prepaid Insurance	3,350		2,500	
Equipment	60,000		60,000	
Accumulated Depreciation—Equipment		$ 28,000		$ 34,000
Accounts Payable		5,000		5,000
Interest Payable		–0–		150
Notes Payable		5,000		5,000
Unearned Service Revenue		7,200		5,900
Salaries and Wages Payable		–0–		2,100
Owner's Capital		25,500		25,500
Owner's Drawings	12,000		12,000	
Service Revenue		58,600		61,400
Salaries and Wages Expense	10,000		12,100	
Insurance Expense			850	
Interest Expense	350		500	
Depreciation Expense			6,000	
Supplies Expense			3,800	
Rent Expense	4,000		4,000	
	$129,300	$129,300	$139,050	$139,050

Instructions
(a) Journalize the annual adjusting entries that were made.
(b) Prepare an income statement and an owner's equity statement for the year ending December 31, 2012, and a balance sheet at December 31.
(c) Answer the following questions.
  (1) If the note has been outstanding 6 months, what is the annual interest rate on that note?
  (2) If the company paid $12,500 in salaries in 2012, what was the balance in Salaries and Wages Payable on December 31, 2011?

*(b) Net income $34,150
Ending capital $47,650
Total assets $65,800*
*(c) (1) 6%
    (2) $2,500*

P3-4A   A review of the ledger of D. J. Moore Company at December 31, 2012, produces the following data pertaining to the preparation of annual adjusting entries.

Preparing adjusting entries.
(SO 5, 6)

1. Salaries and Wages Payable $0. There are eight salaried employees. Salaries are paid every Friday for the current week. Five employees receive a salary of $900 each per week, and three

*1. Salaries and wages
expense $2,640*

employees earn $700 each per week. Assume December 31 is a Tuesday. Employees do not work weekends. All employees worked the last 2 days of December.

2. **Unearned Rent Revenue $354,000.** The company began subleasing office space in its new building on November 1. At December 31, the company had the following rental contracts that are paid in full for the entire term of the lease.

2. Rent revenue $84,000

Date	Term (in months)	Monthly Rent	Number of Leases
Nov. 1	6	$5,000	5
Dec. 1	6	$8,500	4

3. Advertising expense $5,200

3. **Prepaid Advertising $15,600.** This balance consists of payments on two advertising contracts. The contracts provide for monthly advertising in two trade magazines. The terms of the contracts are as follows.

Contract	Date	Amount	Number of Magazine Issues
A650	May 1	$6,000	12
B974	Oct. 1	9,600	24

The first advertisement runs in the month in which the contract is signed.

4. Interest expense $6,300

4. **Notes Payable $120,000.** This balance consists of a note for one year at an annual interest rate of 9%, dated June 1.

Instructions

Prepare the adjusting entries at December 31, 2012. (Show all computations.)

Journalize transactions and follow through accounting cycle to preparation of financial statements.

(SO 5, 6, 7)

GLS

P3-5A On September 1, 2012, the account balances of Moore Equipment Repair were as follows.

No.	Debits		No.	Credits	
101	Cash	$ 4,880	154	Accumulated Depreciation—Equipment	$ 1,500
112	Accounts Receivable	3,520	201	Accounts Payable	3,400
126	Supplies	2,000	209	Unearned Service Revenue	1,400
153	Equipment	15,000	212	Salaries and Wages Payable	500
			301	Owner's Capital	18,600
		$25,400			$25,400

During September, the following summary transactions were completed.

Sept.	8	Paid $1,400 for salaries due employees, of which $900 is for September.
	10	Received $1,200 cash from customers on account.
	12	Received $3,400 cash for services performed in September.
	15	Purchased store equipment on account $3,000.
	17	Purchased supplies on account $1,200.
	20	Paid creditors $4,500 on account.
	22	Paid September rent $500.
	25	Paid salaries $1,250.
	27	Performed services on account and billed customers for services provided $2,100.
	29	Received $650 from customers for future service.

Adjustment data consist of:

1. Supplies on hand $1,300.
2. Accrued salaries payable $300.
3. Depreciation is $100 per month.
4. Unearned service revenue of $1,450 is earned.

Instructions

(a) Enter the September 1 balances in the ledger accounts.
(b) Journalize the September transactions.
(c) Post to the ledger accounts. Use J1 for the posting reference. Use the following additional accounts: No. 407 Service Revenue, No. 615 Depreciation Expense, No. 631 Supplies Expense, No. 726 Salaries and Wages Expense, and No. 729 Rent Expense.

(d) Prepare a trial balance at September 30.

(e) Journalize and post adjusting entries.

(f) Prepare an adjusted trial balance.

(g) Prepare an income statement and an owner's equity statement for September and a balance sheet at September 30.

(d) Trial balance $30,750
(f) Adj. trial balance $31,150
(g) Net income $2,000
    Ending capital $20,600
    Total assets $24,600

*P3-6A Olsen Graphics Company was organized on January 1, 2012, by Gwen Olsen. At the end of the first 6 months of operations, the trial balance contained the accounts shown below.

Prepare adjusting entries, adjusted trial balance, and financial statements using appendix.

(SO 5, 6, 7, 8)

Debits		Credits	
Cash	$ 8,600	Notes Payable	$ 20,000
Accounts Receivable	14,000	Accounts Payable	9,000
Equipment	45,000	Owner's Capital	22,000
Insurance Expense	2,700	Sales Revenue	52,100
Salaries and Wages Expense	30,000	Service Revenue	6,000
Supplies Expense	3,700		
Advertising Expense	1,900		
Rent Expense	1,500		
Utilities Expense	1,700		
	$109,100		$109,100

Analysis reveals the following additional data.

1. The $3,700 balance in Supplies Expense represents supplies purchased in January. At June 30, $1,500 of supplies was on hand.

2. The note payable was issued on February 1. It is a 9%, 6-month note.

3. The balance in Insurance Expense is the premium on a one-year policy, dated March 1, 2012.

4. Service revenues are credited to revenue when received. At June 30, service revenue of $1,300 is unearned.

5. Sales revenue earned but unrecorded at June 30 totals $2,000.

6. Depreciation is $2,250 per year.

Instructions

(a) Journalize the adjusting entries at June 30. (Assume adjustments are recorded every 6 months.)

(b) Prepare an adjusted trial balance.

(c) Prepare an income statement and owner's equity statement for the 6 months ended June 30 and a balance sheet at June 30.

(b) Adj. trial balance $112,975
(c) Net income $18,725
    Ending capital $40,725
    Total assets $71,775

Problems: Set B

P3-1B Fran Omiyale started her own consulting firm, Omiyale Consulting, on May 1, 2012. The trial balance at May 31 is as follows.

Prepare adjusting entries, post to ledger accounts, and prepare an adjusted trial balance.

(SO 5, 6, 7)

OMIYALE CONSULTING
Trial Balance
May 31, 2012

Account Number		Debit	Credit
101	Cash	$ 4,500	
112	Accounts Receivable	6,000	
126	Supplies	1,900	
130	Prepaid Insurance	3,600	
149	Equipment	11,400	
201	Accounts Payable		$ 4,500
209	Unearned Service Revenue		2,000
301	Owner's Capital		17,700
400	Service Revenue		7,500
726	Salaries and Wages Expense	3,400	
729	Rent Expense	900	
		$31,700	$31,700

In addition to those accounts listed on the trial balance, the chart of accounts for Omiyale Consulting also contains the following accounts and account numbers: No. 150 Accumulated Depreciation—Equipment, No. 212 Salaries and Wages Payable, No. 631 Supplies Expense, No. 717 Depreciation Expense, No. 722 Insurance Expense, and No. 736 Utilities Expense.

Other data:

1. $900 of supplies have been used during the month.
2. Utilities expense incurred but not paid on May 31, 2012, $250.
3. The insurance policy is for 2 years.
4. $400 of the balance in the unearned service revenue account remains unearned at the end of the month.
5. May 31 is a Wednesday, and employees are paid on Fridays. Omiyale Consulting has two employees, who are paid $900 each for a 5-day work week.
6. The office furniture has a 5-year life with no salvage value. It is being depreciated at $190 per month for 60 months.
7. Invoices representing $1,700 of services performed during the month have not been recorded as of May 31.

Instructions

(a) Prepare the adjusting entries for the month of May. Use J4 as the page number for your journal.

(b) Post the adjusting entries to the ledger accounts. Enter the totals from the trial balance as beginning account balances and place a check mark in the posting reference column.

(c) Adj. trial balance $34,920   **(c)** Prepare an adjusted trial balance at May 31, 2012.

Prepare adjusting entries, post,   **P3-2B**   The Bear Motel opened for business on May 1, 2012. Its trial balance before adjustment
and prepare adjusted trial   on May 31 is as follows.
balance, and financial
statements.

(SO 5, 6, 7)

BEAR MOTEL
Trial Balance
May 31, 2012

Account Number		Debit	Credit
101	Cash	$ 3,500	
126	Supplies	2,080	
130	Prepaid Insurance	2,400	
140	Land	12,000	
141	Buildings	60,000	
149	Equipment	15,000	
201	Accounts Payable		$ 4,800
208	Unearned Rent Revenue		3,300
275	Mortgage Payable		40,000
301	Owner's Capital		41,380
429	Rent Revenue		10,300
610	Advertising Expense	600	
726	Salaries and Wages Expense	3,300	
732	Utilities Expense	900	
		$99,780	$99,780

In addition to those accounts listed on the trial balance, the chart of accounts for Bear Motel also contains the following accounts and account numbers: No. 142 Accumulated Depreciation—Buildings, No. 150 Accumulated Depreciation—Equipment, No. 212 Salaries and Wages Payable, No. 230 Interest Payable, No. 619 Depreciation Expense, No. 631 Supplies Expense, No. 718 Interest Expense, and No. 722 Insurance Expense.

Other data:

1. Prepaid insurance is a 1-year policy starting May 1, 2012.
2. A count of supplies shows $750 of unused supplies on May 31.
3. Annual depreciation is $3,000 on the buildings and $1,500 on equipment.
4. The mortgage interest rate is 12%. (The mortgage was taken out on May 1.)
5. Two-thirds of the unearned rent revenue has been earned.
6. Salaries of $750 are accrued and unpaid at May 31.

Instructions

(a) Journalize the adjusting entries on May 31.
(b) Prepare a ledger using the three-column form of account. Enter the trial balance amounts and post the adjusting entries. (Use J1 as the posting reference.)
(c) Prepare an adjusted trial balance on May 31.
(d) Prepare an income statement and an owner's equity statement for the month of May and a balance sheet at May 31.

(c) Adj. trial balance $101,305
(d) Net income $4,645
   Ending capital balance $46,025
   Total assets $93,075

P3-3B Peterman Co. was organized on July 1, 2012. Quarterly financial statements are prepared. The unadjusted and adjusted trial balances as of September 30 are shown below.

Prepare adjusting entries and financial statements.
(SO 5, 6, 7)

PETERMAN CO.
Trial Balance
September 30, 2012

	Unadjusted Dr.	Unadjusted Cr.	Adjusted Dr.	Adjusted Cr.
Cash	$ 8,700		$ 8,700	
Accounts Receivable	10,400		11,500	
Supplies	1,500		650	
Prepaid Rent	2,200		1,200	
Equipment	18,000		18,000	
Accumulated Depreciation—Equipment		$ –0–		$ 700
Notes Payable		10,000		10,000
Accounts Payable		2,500		2,500
Salaries and Wages Payable		–0–		725
Interest Payable		–0–		100
Unearned Rent Revenue		1,900		1,050
Owner's Capital		22,000		22,000
Owner's Drawings	1,600		1,600	
Service Revenue		16,000		17,100
Rent Revenue		1,410		2,260
Salaries and Wages Expense	8,000		8,725	
Rent Expense	1,900		2,900	
Depreciation Expense			700	
Supplies Expense			850	
Utilities Expense	1,510		1,510	
Interest Expense			100	
	$53,810	$53,810	$56,435	$56,435

Instructions

(a) Journalize the adjusting entries that were made.
(b) Prepare an income statement and an owner's equity statement for the 3 months ending September 30 and a balance sheet at September 30.
(c) If the note bears interest at 12%, how many months has it been outstanding?

(b) Net income $4,575
   Ending capital $24,975
   Total assets $39,350

P3-4B A review of the ledger of Roach Company at December 31, 2012, produces the following data pertaining to the preparation of annual adjusting entries.

Prepare adjusting entries
(SO 5, 6)
1. Insurance expense $4,890

1. Prepaid Insurance $10,440. The company has separate insurance policies on its buildings and its motor vehicles. Policy B4564 on the building was purchased on April 1, 2011, for $7,920. The policy has a term of 3 years. Policy A2958 on the vehicles was purchased on January 1, 2012, for $4,500. This policy has a term of 2 years.
2. Unearned Rent Revenue $429,000. The company began subleasing office space in its new building on November 1. At December 31, the company had the following rental contracts that are paid in full for the entire term of the lease.

2. Rent revenue $84,000

Date	Term (in months)	Monthly Rent	Number of Leases
Nov. 1	9	$5,000	5
Dec. 1	6	$8,500	4

3. Interest expense $1,800

4. Salaries and wages
   expense $2,000

3. Notes Payable $120,000. This balance consists of a note for 9 months at an annual interest rate of 9%, dated November 1.

4. Salaries and Wages Payable $0. There are eight salaried employees. Salaries are paid every Friday for the current week. Five employees receive a salary of $700 each per week, and three employees earn $500 each per week. Assume December 31 is a Tuesday. Employees do not work weekends. All employees worked the last 2 days of December.

Instructions
Prepare the adjusting entries at December 31, 2012.

Journalize transactions and follow through accounting cycle to preparation of financial statements.

(SO 5, 6, 7)

P3-5B On November 1, 2012, the account balances of Robinson Equipment Repair were as follows.

No.	Debits		No.	Credits	
101	Cash	$ 2,400	154	Accumulated Depreciation—Equipment	$ 2,000
112	Accounts Receivable	4,250	201	Accounts Payable	2,600
126	Supplies	1,800	209	Unearned Service Revenue	1,200
153	Equipment	12,000	212	Salaries and Wages Payable	700
			301	Owner's Capital	13,950
		$20,450			$20,450

During November, the following summary transactions were completed.

Nov.	8	Paid $1,700 for salaries due employees, of which $700 is for October salaries.
	10	Received $3,420 cash from customers on account.
	12	Received $3,100 cash for services performed in November.
	15	Purchased equipment on account $2,000.
	17	Purchased supplies on account $700.
	20	Paid creditors on account $2,700.
	22	Paid November rent $400.
	25	Paid salaries $1,700.
	27	Performed services on account and billed customers for services provided $1,900.
	29	Received $600 from customers for future service.

Adjustment data consist of:

1. Supplies on hand $1,400.
2. Accrued salaries payable $350.
3. Depreciation for the month is $200.
4. Unearned service revenue of $1,250 is earned.

Instructions
(a) Enter the November 1 balances in the ledger accounts.
(b) Journalize the November transactions.
(c) Post to the ledger accounts. Use J1 for the posting reference. Use the following additional accounts: No. 407 Service Revenue, No. 615 Depreciation Expense, No. 631 Supplies Expense, No. 726 Salaries and Wages Expense, and No. 729 Rent Expense.

(d) Trial balance $25,350

(d) Prepare a trial balance at November 30.
(e) Journalize and post adjusting entries.

(f) Adj. trial balance $25,900
(g) Net income $1,500;
    Ending capital $15,450
    Total assets $18,950

(f) Prepare an adjusted trial balance.
(g) Prepare an income statement and an owner's equity statement for November and a balance sheet at November 30.

Problems: Set C

Visit the book's companion website, at **www.wiley.com/college/weygandt**, and choose the Student Companion site to access Problem Set C.

Continuing Cookie Chronicle

(*Note:* This is a continuation of the Cookie Chronicle from Chapters 1 and 2. Use the information from the previous chapters and follow the instructions below using the general ledger accounts you have already prepared.)

CCC3 It is the end of November and Natalie has been in touch with her grandmother. Her grandmother asked Natalie how well things went in her first month of business. Natalie, too, would like to know if she has been profitable or not during November. Natalie realizes that in order to determine Cookie Creations' income, she must first make adjustments.

Natalie puts together the following additional information.

1. A count reveals that $35 of baking supplies were used during November.
2. Natalie estimates that all of her baking equipment will have a useful life of 5 years or 60 months. (Assume Natalie decides to record a full month's worth of depreciation, regardless of when the equipment was obtained by the business.)
3. Natalie's grandmother has decided to charge interest of 6% on the note payable extended on November 16. The loan plus interest is to be repaid in 24 months. (Assume that half a month of interest accrued during November.)
4. On November 30, a friend of Natalie's asks her to teach a class at the neighborhood school. Natalie agrees and teaches a group of 35 first-grade students how to make Santa Claus cookies. The next day, Natalie prepares an invoice for $300 and leaves it with the school principal. The principal says that he will pass the invoice along to the head office, and it will be paid sometime in December.
5. Natalie receives a utilities bill for $45. The bill is for utilities consumed by Natalie's business during November and is due December 15.

Instructions
Using the information that you have gathered through Chapter 2, and based on the new information above, do the following.

(a) Prepare and post the adjusting journal entries.
(b) Prepare an adjusting trial balance.
(c) Using the adjusted trial balance, calculate Cookie Creations' net income or net loss for the month of November. Do not prepare an income statement.

BROADENINGYOURPERSPECTIVE

Financial Reporting and Analysis

Financial Reporting Problem: PepsiCo, Inc.

BYP3-1 The financial statements of PepsiCo, Inc. are presented in Appendix A at the end of this textbook.

Instructions
(a) Using the consolidated financial statements and related information, identify items that may result in adjusting entries for prepayments.
(b) Using the consolidated financial statements and related information, identify items that may result in adjusting entries for accruals.
(c) Using the Selected Financial Data and 5-Year Summary, what has been the trend since 2005 for net income?

Comparative Analysis Problem: PepsiCo, Inc. vs. The Coca-Cola Company

BYP3-2 PepsiCo's financial statements are presented in Appendix A. Financial statements for The Coca-Cola Company are presented in Appendix B.

Instructions
Based on information contained in these financial statements, determine the following for each company.

(a) Net increase (decrease) in property, plant, and equipment (net) from 2008 to 2009.
(b) Increase (decrease) in selling, general, and administrative expenses from 2008 to 2009.

(c) Increase (decrease) in long-term debt (obligations) from 2008 to 2009.

(d) Increase (decrease) in net income from 2008 to 2009.

(e) Increase (decrease) in cash and cash equivalents from 2008 to 2009.

On the Web

BYP3-3   No financial decision maker should ever rely solely on the financial information reported in the annual report to make decisions. It is important to keep abreast of financial news. This activity demonstrates how to search for financial news on the Web.

Address: http://biz.yahoo.com/i, or go to **www.wiley.com/college/weygandt**

Steps:

1. Type in either Wal-Mart, Target Corp., or Kmart.

2. Choose **News**.

3. Select an article that sounds interesting to you and that would be relevant to an investor in these companies.

Instructions

(a) What was the source of the article (e.g., Reuters, Businesswire, Prnewswire)?

(b) Assume that you are a personal financial planner and that one of your clients owns stock in the company. Write a brief memo to your client summarizing the article and explaining the implications of the article for their investment.

Critical Thinking

Decision Making Across the Organization

BYP3-4   Happy Camper Park was organized on April 1, 2011, by Amaya Berge. Amaya is a good manager but a poor accountant. From the trial balance prepared by a part-time bookkeeper, Amaya prepared the following income statement for the quarter that ended March 31, 2012.

HAPPY CAMPER PARK
Income Statement
For the Quarter Ended March 31, 2012

Revenues		
Rent revenue		$90,000
Operating expenses		
Advertising	$ 5,200	
Salaries and wages	29,800	
Utilities	900	
Depreciation	800	
Maintenance and repairs	4,000	
Total operating expenses		40,700
Net income		$49,300

Amaya thought that something was wrong with the statement because net income had never exceeded $20,000 in any one quarter. Knowing that you are an experienced accountant, she asks you to review the income statement and other data.

You first look at the trial balance. In addition to the account balances reported above in the income statement, the ledger contains the following additional selected balances at March 31, 2012.

Supplies	$ 6,200
Prepaid Insurance	7,200
Notes Payable	12,000

You then make inquiries and discover the following.

1. Rent revenues include advanced rentals for summer occupancy $15,000.

2. There were $1,700 of supplies on hand at March 31.

3. Prepaid insurance resulted from the payment of a one-year policy on January 1, 2012.

4. The mail on April 1, 2012, brought the following bills: advertising for week of March 24, $110; repairs made March 10, $260; and utilities, $180.
5. There are four employees, who receive wages totaling $300 per day. At March 31, 2 days' salaries and wages have been incurred but not paid.
6. The note payable is a 3-month, 10% note dated January 1, 2012.

Instructions

With the class divided into groups, answer the following.

(a) Prepare a correct income statement for the quarter ended March 31, 2012.

(b) Explain to Amaya the generally accepted accounting principles that she did not recognize in preparing her income statement and their effect on her results.

Communication Activity

BYP3-5   In reviewing the accounts of Keri Ann Co. at the end of the year, you discover that adjusting entries have not been made.

Instructions

Write a memo to Keri Ann Nickels, the owner of Keri Ann Co., that explains the following: the nature and purpose of adjusting entries, why adjusting entries are needed, and the types of adjusting entries that may be made.

Ethics Case

BYP3-6   Bluestem Company is a pesticide manufacturer. Its sales declined greatly this year due to the passage of legislation outlawing the sale of several of Bluestem's chemical pesticides. In the coming year, Bluestem will have environmentally safe and competitive chemicals to replace these discontinued products. Sales in the next year are expected to greatly exceed any prior year's. The decline in sales and profits appears to be a one-year aberration. But even so, the company president fears a large dip in the current year's profits. He believes that such a dip could cause a significant drop in the market price of Bluestem's stock and make the company a takeover target.

To avoid this possibility, the company president calls in Cathi Bell, controller, to discuss this period's year-end adjusting entries. He urges her to accrue every possible revenue and to defer as many expenses as possible. He says to Cathi, "We need the revenues this year, and next year can easily absorb expenses deferred from this year. We can't let our stock price be hammered down!" Cathi didn't get around to recording the adjusting entries until January 17, but she dated the entries December 31 as if they were recorded then. Cathi also made every effort to comply with the president's request.

Instructions

(a) Who are the stakeholders in this situation?

(b) What are the ethical considerations of (1) the president's request and (2) Cathi's dating the adjusting entries December 31?

(c) Can Cathi accrue revenues and defer expenses and still be ethical?

"All About You" Activity

BYP3-7   Companies must report or disclose in their financial statements information about all liabilities, including potential liabilities related to environmental clean-up. There are many situations in which you will be asked to provide personal financial information about your assets, liabilities, revenue, and expenses. Sometimes you will face difficult decisions regarding what to disclose and how to disclose it.

Instructions

Suppose that you are putting together a loan application to purchase a home. Based on your income and assets, you qualify for the mortgage loan, but just barely. How would you address each of the following situations in reporting your financial position for the loan application? Provide responses for each of the following situations.

(a) You signed a guarantee for a bank loan that a friend took out for $20,000. If your friend doesn't pay, you will have to pay. Your friend has made all of the payments so far, and it appears he will be able to pay in the future.

(b) You were involved in an auto accident in which you were at fault. There is the possibility that you may have to pay as much as $50,000 as part of a settlement. The issue will not be resolved before the bank processes your mortgage request.

(c) The company at which you work isn't doing very well, and it has recently laid off employees. You are still employed, but it is quite possible that you will lose your job in the next few months.

FASB Codification Activity

BYP3-8   If your school has a subscription to the FASB Codification, go to *http://aaahq.org/asclogin.cfm* to log in and prepare responses to the following.

Instructions
Access the glossary ("Master Glossary") to answer the following.

(a) What is the definition of revenue?

(b) What is the definition of compensation?

Answers to Insight and Accounting Across the Organization Questions

p. 102 Cooking the Books?   **Q:** What motivates sales executives and finance and accounting executives to participate in activities that result in inaccurate reporting of revenues? **A:** Sales executives typically receive bonuses based on their ability to meet quarterly sales targets. In addition, they often face the possibility of losing their jobs if they miss those targets. Executives in accounting and finance are very aware of the earnings targets of Wall Street analysts and investors. If they fail to meet these targets, the company's stock price will fall. As a result of these pressures, executives sometimes knowingly engage in unethical efforts to misstate revenues. As a result of the Sarbanes-Oxley Act of 2002, the penalties for such behavior are now much more severe.

p. 110 Turning Gift Cards into Revenue   **Q:** Suppose that Robert Jones purchases a $100 gift card at Best Buy on December 24, 2011, and gives it to his wife, Mary Jones, on December 25, 2011. On January 3, 2012, Mary uses the card to purchase $100 worth of CDs. When do you think Best Buy should recognize revenue and why? **A:** According to the revenue recognition principle, companies should recognize revenue when earned. In this case, revenue is not earned until Best Buy provides the goods. Thus, when Best Buy receives cash in exchange for the gift card on December 24, 2011, it should recognize a liability, Unearned Revenue, for $100. On January 3, 2012, when Mary Jones exchanges the card for merchandise, Best Buy should recognize revenue and eliminate $100 from the balance in the Unearned Revenue account.

p. 114 Cashing In on Accrual Accounting   **Q:** Accrual accounting is often considered superior to cash accounting. Why, then, were some people critical of China's use of accrual accounting in this instance? **A:** In this case, some people were critical because, in general, China uses cash accounting. By switching to accrual accounting for this transaction, China was not being consistent in its accounting practices. Lack of consistency reduces the transparency and usefulness of accounting information.

Answers to Self-Test Questions
1. c   **2.** c   **3.** d   **4.** a   **5.** d   **6.** d   **7.** c ($1,350 − $600)   **8.** c   **9.** a   **10.** c   **11.** a   **12.** b   **13.** b   **14.** c   ***15.** a

IFRS A Look at IFRS

It is often difficult for companies to determine in what time period they should report particular revenues and expenses. Both the IASB and FASB are working on a joint project to develop a common conceptual framework, as well as a revenue recognition project, that will enable companies to better use the same principles to record transactions consistently over time.

Key Points

- In this chapter, you learned accrual-basis accounting applied under GAAP. Companies applying IFRS also use accrual-basis accounting to ensure that they record transactions that change a company's financial statements in the period in which events occur.

- Similar to GAAP, cash-basis accounting is not in accordance with IFRS.

- IFRS also divides the economic life of companies into artificial time periods. Under both GAAP and IFRS, this is referred to as the *time period assumption*.

- IFRS requires that companies present a complete set of financial statements, including comparative information annually.

- GAAP has more than 100 rules dealing with revenue recognition. Many of these rules are industry-specific. In contrast, revenue recognition under IFRS is determined primarily by a single standard. Despite this large disparity in the amount of detailed guidance devoted to revenue recognition, the **general** revenue recognition principles required by GAAP that are used in this textbook are similar to those under IFRS.

- As the Feature Story illustrates, revenue recognition fraud is a major issue in U.S. financial reporting. The same situation occurs in other countries, as evidenced by revenue recognition breakdowns at Dutch software company Baan NV, Japanese electronics giant NEC, and Dutch grocer Ahold NV.

- A specific standard exists for revenue recognition under IFRS *(IAS 18)*. In general, the standard is based on the **probability that the economic benefits associated with the transaction will flow to the company** selling the goods, providing the service, or receiving investment income. In addition, the revenues and costs **must be capable of being measured reliably**. GAAP uses concepts such as *realized, realizable* (that is, it is received, or expected to be received), and *earned* as a basis for revenue recognition.

- Under IFRS, revaluation of items such as land and buildings is permitted. IFRS allows depreciation based on revaluation of assets, which is not permitted under GAAP.

- The terminology used for revenues and gains, and expenses and losses, differs somewhat between IFRS and GAAP. For example, income is defined as:

  Increases in economic benefits during the accounting period in the form of inflows or enhancements of assets or decreases of liabilities that result in increases in equity, other than those relating to contributions from shareholders.

  Income includes *both* revenues, which arise during the normal course of operating activities, and gains, which arise from activities outside of the normal sales of goods and services. The term income is not used this way under GAAP. Instead, under GAAP income refers to the net difference between revenues and expenses. Expenses are defined as:

  Decreases in economic benefits during the accounting period in the form of outflows or depletions of assets or incurrences of liabilities that result in decreases in equity other than those relating to distributions to shareholders.

  Note that under IFRS, expenses include both those costs incurred in the normal course of operations, as well as losses that are not part of normal operations. This is in contrast to GAAP, which defines each separately.

Looking to the Future

The IASB and FASB are now involved in a joint project on revenue recognition. The purpose of this project is to develop comprehensive guidance on when to recognize revenue. Presently, the Boards are considering an approach that focuses on changes in assets and liabilities (rather than on earned and realized) as the basis for revenue recognition. It is hoped that this approach will lead to more consistent accounting in this area. For more on this topic, see *www.fasb.org/project/revenue_recognition.shtml*.

IFRS Self-Test Questions

1. GAAP:
   (a) provides very detailed, industry-specific guidance on revenue recognition, compared to the general guidance provided by IFRS.
   (b) provides only general guidance on revenue recognition, compared to the detailed guidance provided by IFRS.
   (c) allows revenue to be recognized when a customer makes an order.
   (d) requires that revenue not be recognized until cash is received.

2. Which of the following statements is *false*?
   (a) IFRS employs the time period assumption.
   (b) IFRS employs accrual accounting.
   (c) IFRS requires that revenues and costs must be capable of being measured reliably.
   (d) IFRS uses the cash basis of accounting.

3. As a result of the revenue recognition project being undertaken by the FASB and IASB:
   (a) revenue recognition will place more emphasis on when revenue is earned.
   (b) revenue recognition will place more emphasis on when revenue is realized.
   (c) revenue recognition will place more emphasis on when changes occur in assets and liabilities.
   (d) revenue will no longer be recorded unless cash has been received.

4. Which of the following is *false*?
   (a) Under IFRS, the term *income* describes both revenues and gains.
   (b) Under IFRS, the term *expenses* includes losses.
   (c) Under IFRS, firms do not engage in the closing process.
   (d) IFRS has fewer standards than GAAP that address revenue recognition.

5. Accrual-basis accounting:
   (a) is optional under IFRS.
   (b) results in companies recording transactions that change a company's financial statements in the period in which events occur.
   (c) will likely be eliminated as a result of the IASB/FASB joint project on revenue recognition.
   (d) is not consistent with the IASB conceptual framework.

IFRS Concepts and Application

IFRS3-1   Compare and contrast the rules regarding revenue recognition under IFRS versus GAAP.

IFRS3-2   Under IFRS, do the definitions of revenues and expenses include gains and losses? Explain.

International Financial Reporting Problem: Zetar plc

IFRS3-3   The financial statements of Zetar plc are presented in Appendix C. The company's complete annual report, including the notes to its financial statements, is available at *www.zetarplc.com*.

Instructions

Visit Zetar's corporate website and answer the following questions from Zetar's 2009 annual report.

(a) From the notes to the financial statements, how does the company determine the amount of revenue to record at the time of a sale?

(b) From the notes to the financial statements, how does the company determine whether a sale has occurred?

(c) Using the consolidated income statement and consolidated statement of financial position, identify items that may result in adjusting entries for deferrals.

(d) Using the consolidated income statement, identify two items that may result in adjusting entries for accruals.

Answers to IFRS Self-Test Questions

1. a   **2.** d   **3.** c   **4.** c   **5.** b

The Navigator

✔   **Remember to go back to the Navigator box on the chapter opening page and check off your completed work.**

CHAPTER4

Completing the Accounting Cycle

Study Objectives

After studying this chapter, you should be able to:

[1] Prepare a worksheet.

[2] Explain the process of closing the books.

[3] Describe the content and purpose of a post-closing trial balance.

[4] State the required steps in the accounting cycle.

[5] Explain the approaches to preparing correcting entries.

[6] Identify the sections of a classified balance sheet.

✔ The Navigator

✔ [The Navigator]

Feature Story

EVERYONE LIKES TO WIN

When Ted Castle was a hockey coach at the University of Vermont, his players were self-motivated by their desire to win. Hockey was a game you either won or lost. But at Rhino Foods, Inc., a bakery-foods company he founded in Burlington, Vermont, he discovered that manufacturing-line workers were not so self-motivated. Ted thought, what if he turned the food-making business into a game, with rules, strategies, and trophies?

Ted knew that in a game knowing the score is all-important. He felt that only if the employees know the score—know exactly how the business is doing daily, weekly, monthly—could he turn food-making into a game. But Rhino is a closely held, family-owned business, and its financial statements and profits were confidential. Ted wondered, should he open Rhino's books to the employees?

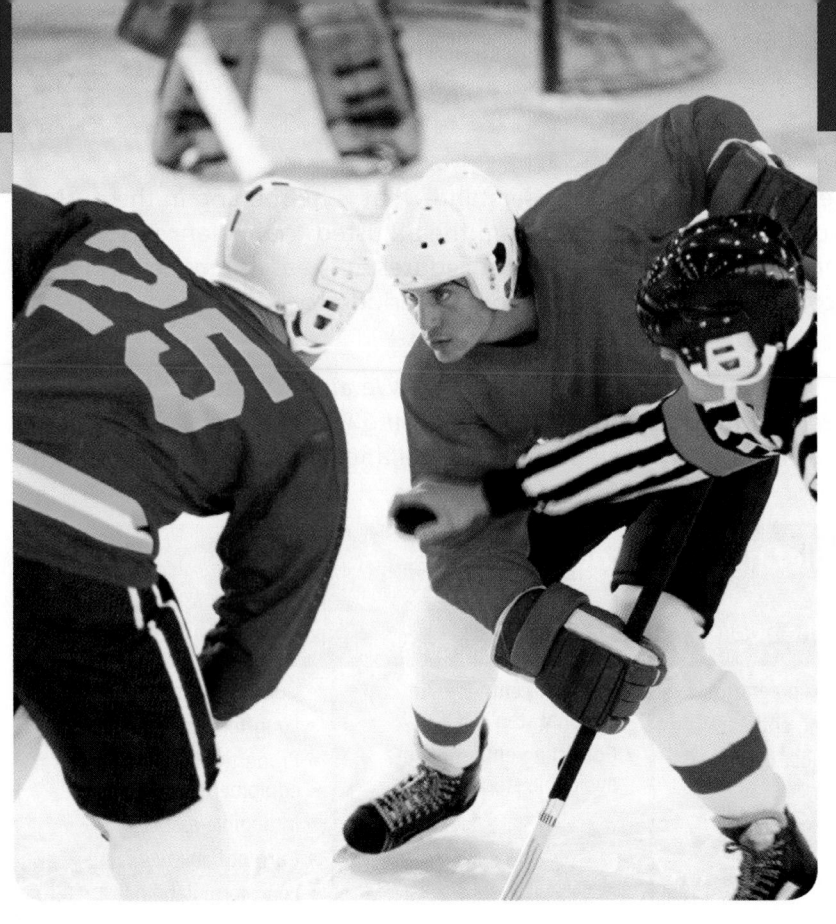

A consultant put Ted's concerns in perspective when he said, "Imagine you're playing touch football. You play for an hour or two, and the whole time I'm sitting there with a book, keeping score. All of a sudden I blow the whistle, and I say, 'OK, that's it. Everybody go home.' I close my book and walk away. How would you feel?" Ted opened his books and revealed the financial statements to his employees.

The next step was to teach employees the rules and strategies of how to "win" at making food. The first lesson: "Your opponent at Rhino is expenses. You must cut and control expenses." Ted and his staff distilled those lessons into daily scorecards—production reports and income statements—that keep Rhino's employees up-to-date on the game. At noon each day, Ted posts the previous day's results at the entrance to the production room. Everyone checks whether they made or lost money on what they produced the day before. And it's not just an academic exercise: There's a bonus check for each employee at the end of every four-week "game" that meets profitability guidelines.

Rhino has flourished since the first game. Employment has increased from 20 to 130 people, while both revenues and profits have grown dramatically.

Inside CHAPTER 4

Preview of CHAPTER 4

At Rhino Foods, Inc., financial statements help employees understand what is happening in the business. In Chapter 3, we prepared financial statements directly from the adjusted trial balance. However, with so many details involved in the end-of-period accounting procedures, it is easy to make errors. One way to minimize errors in the records and to simplify the end-of-period procedures is to use a worksheet.

In this chapter, we will explain the role of the worksheet in accounting. We also will study the remaining steps in the accounting cycle, especially the closing process, again using Pioneer Advertising Agency as an example. Then we will consider correcting entries and classified balance sheets. The content and organization of Chapter 4 are as follows.

Completing the Accounting Cycle

Using a Worksheet	Closing the Books	Summary of Accounting Cycle	Classified Balance Sheet
• Steps in preparation • Preparing financial statements • Preparing adjusting entries	• Preparing closing entries • Posting closing entries • Preparing a post-closing trial balance	• Reversing entries—An optional step • Correcting entries—An avoidable step	• Current assets • Long-term investments • Property, plant, and equipment • Intangible assets • Current liabilities • Long-term liabilities • Owner's equity

✔ The Navigator

Using a Worksheet

Study Objective [1]
Prepare a worksheet.

A **worksheet** is a multiple-column form used in the adjustment process and in preparing financial statements. As its name suggests, the worksheet is a working tool. **It is not a permanent accounting record**; it is neither a journal nor a part of the general ledger. The worksheet is merely a device used in preparing adjusting entries and the financial statements. Companies generally computerize worksheets using an electronic spreadsheet program such as Excel.

Illustration 4-1 shows the basic form of a worksheet and the five steps for preparing it. Each step is performed in sequence. **The use of a worksheet is optional.** When a company chooses to use one, it prepares financial statements from the worksheet. It enters the adjustments in the worksheet columns and then journalizes and posts the adjustments after it has prepared the financial statements. Thus, worksheets make it possible to provide the financial statements to management and other interested parties at an earlier date.

Steps in Preparing a Worksheet

We will use the October 31 trial balance and adjustment data of Pioneer Advertising, from Chapter 3, to illustrate how to prepare a worksheet. We describe each step of the process and demonstrate these steps in Illustration 4-2 (page 156) and transparencies 4-3A, B, C, and D.

Illustration 4-1
Form and procedure for a worksheet

STEP 1. PREPARE A TRIAL BALANCE ON THE WORKSHEET

Enter all ledger accounts with balances in the account titles space. Enter debit and credit amounts from the ledger in the trial balance columns. Illustration 4-2 shows the worksheet trial balance for Pioneer Advertising Agency. This trial balance is the same one that appears in Illustration 2-31 (page 72) and Illustration 3-3 (page 104).

STEP 2. ENTER THE ADJUSTMENTS IN THE ADJUSTMENTS COLUMNS

Turn over the first transparency, Illustration 4-3A. When using a worksheet, enter all adjustments in the adjustments columns. In entering the adjustments, use applicable trial balance accounts. If additional accounts are needed, insert them on the lines immediately below the trial balance totals. A different letter identifies the debit and credit for each adjusting entry. The term used to describe this process is **keying. Companies do not journalize the adjustments until after they complete the worksheet and prepare the financial statements.**

(**Note:** Text continues on page 157, following acetate overlays.)

Illustration 4-2
Preparing a trial balance

Pioneer Advertising.xls											
File Edit View Insert Format Tools Data Window Help											

	A	B	C	D	E	F	G	H	I	J	K
		PIONEER ADVERTISING AGENCY Worksheet For the Month Ended October 31, 2012									
1											
2											
3											
4		Trial Balance		Adjustments		Adjusted Trial Balance		Income Statement		Balance Sheet	
5											
6	Account Titles										
7		Dr.	Cr.	Dr.	Cr.	Dr.	Cr.	Dr.	Cr.	Dr.	Cr.
8	Cash	15,200									
9	Supplies	2,500									
10	Prepaid Insurance	600									
11	Equipment	5,000									
12	Notes Payable		5,000								
13	Accounts Payable		2,500								
14	Unearned Service Revenue		1,200								
15	Owner's Capital		10,000								
16	Owner's Drawings	500									
17	Service Revenue		10,000								
18											
19	Salaries and Wages Expense	4,000									
20	Rent Expense	900									
21	Totals	28,700	28,700								
22											
23											
24											
25											
26											
27											
28											
29											
30											
31											
32											
33											
34											
35											
36											

Include all accounts with balances from ledger.

Trial balance amounts come directly from ledger accounts.

The adjustments for Pioneer Advertising Agency are the same as the adjustments illustrated on page 117. They are keyed in the adjustments columns of the worksheet as follows.

(a) Pioneer debits an additional account, Supplies Expense, $1,500 for the cost of supplies used, and credits Supplies $1,500.

(b) Pioneer debits an additional account, Insurance Expense, $50 for the insurance that has expired, and credits Prepaid Insurance $50.

(c) The company needs two additional depreciation accounts. It debits Depreciation Expense $40 for the month's depreciation, and credits Accumulated Depreciation—Equipment $40.

(d) Pioneer debits Unearned Service Revenue $400 for services provided, and credits Service Revenue $400.

(e) Pioneer debits an additional account, Accounts Receivable, $200 for services provided but not billed, and credits Service Revenue $200.

(f) The company needs two additional accounts relating to interest. It debits Interest Expense $50 for accrued interest, and credits Interest Payable $50.

(g) Pioneer debits Salaries and Wages Expense $1,200 for accrued salaries, and credits an additional account, Salaries and Wages Payable, $1,200.

After Pioneer has entered all the adjustments, the adjustments columns are totaled to prove their equality.

STEP 3. ENTER ADJUSTED BALANCES IN THE ADJUSTED TRIAL BALANCE COLUMNS

Turn over the second transparency, Illustration 4-3B. Pioneer determines the adjusted balance of an account by combining the amounts entered in the first four columns of the worksheet for each account. For example, the Prepaid Insurance account in the trial balance columns has a $600 debit balance and a $50 credit in the adjustments columns. The result is a $550 debit balance recorded in the adjusted trial balance columns. **For each account, the amount in the adjusted trial balance columns is the balance that will appear in the ledger after journalizing and posting the adjusting entries.** The balances in these columns are the same as those in the adjusted trial balance in Illustration 3-25 (page 119).

After Pioneer has entered all account balances in the adjusted trial balance columns, the columns are totaled to prove their equality. If the column totals do not agree, the financial statement columns will not balance and the financial statements will be incorrect.

STEP 4. EXTEND ADJUSTED TRIAL BALANCE AMOUNTS TO APPROPRIATE FINANCIAL STATEMENT COLUMNS

Helpful Hint

Every adjusted trial balance amount must be extended to one of the four statement columns.

Turn over the third transparency, Illustration 4-3C. The fourth step is to extend adjusted trial balance amounts to the income statement and balance sheet columns of the worksheet. Pioneer enters balance sheet accounts in the appropriate balance sheet debit and credit columns. For instance, it enters Cash in the balance sheet debit column, and Notes Payable in the credit column. Pioneer extends Accumulated Depreciation—Equipment to the balance sheet credit column; the reason is that accumulated depreciation is a contra-asset account with a credit balance.

Because the worksheet does not have columns for the owner's equity statement, Pioneer extends the balance in owner's capital to the balance sheet credit column. In addition, it extends the balance in owner's drawings to the balance sheet debit column because it is an owner's equity account with a debit balance.

The company enters the expense and revenue accounts such as Salaries and Wages Expense and Service Revenue in the appropriate income statement columns. Illustration 4-3C shows all of these extensions.

STEP 5. TOTAL THE STATEMENT COLUMNS, COMPUTE THE NET INCOME (OR NET LOSS), AND COMPLETE THE WORKSHEET

Turn over the fourth transparency, Illustration 4-3D. The company now must total each of the financial statement columns. The net income or loss for the period is the difference between the totals of the two income statement columns. If total credits exceed total debits, the result is net income. In such a case, as shown in Illustration 4-3D, the company inserts the words "Net Income" in the account titles space. It then enters the amount in the income statement debit column and the balance sheet credit column. **The debit amount balances the income statement columns; the credit amount balances the balance sheet columns.** In addition, the credit in the balance sheet column indicates the increase in owner's equity resulting from net income.

What if total debits in the income statement columns exceed total credits? In that case, the company has a net loss. It enters the amount of the net loss in the income statement credit column and the balance sheet debit column.

After entering the net income or net loss, the company determines new column totals. The totals shown in the debit and credit income statement columns will match. So will the totals shown in the debit and credit balance sheet columns. If either the income statement columns or the balance sheet columns are not equal after the net income or net loss has been entered, there is an error in the worksheet. Illustration 4-3D shows the completed worksheet for Pioneer Advertising Agency.

Preparing Financial Statements from a Worksheet

After a company has completed a worksheet, it has at hand all the data required for preparation of financial statements. The income statement is prepared from the income statement columns. The balance sheet and owner's equity statement are prepared from the balance sheet columns. Illustration 4-4 (page 159) shows the financial statements prepared from Pioneer's worksheet. At this point, the company has not journalized or posted adjusting entries. Therefore, ledger balances for some accounts are not the same as the financial statement amounts.

The amount shown for owner's capital on the worksheet is the account balance **before considering drawings and net income (or loss).** When the owner has made no additional investments of capital during the period, this worksheet amount for owner's capital is the balance at the beginning of the period.

Using a worksheet, companies can prepare financial statements before they journalize and post adjusting entries. **However, the completed worksheet is not a substitute for formal financial statements.** The format of the data in the financial statement columns of the worksheet is not the same as the format of the financial statements. **A worksheet is essentially a working tool of the accountant;** companies do not distribute it to management and other parties.

Preparing Adjusting Entries from a Worksheet

A worksheet is not a journal, and it cannot be used as a basis for posting to ledger accounts. To adjust the accounts, the company must journalize the adjustments and

Accounting Cycle Tutorial—
Preparing Financial
Statements and Closing the
Books

Helpful Hint

Note that writing the explanation to the adjustment at the bottom of the worksheet is not required.

Illustration 4-4
Financial statements from a worksheet

Pioneer Advertising Agency
Income Statement
For the Month Ended October 31, 2012

Revenues
 Service revenue $10,600
Expenses
 Salaries and wages expense $5,200
 Supplies expense   1,500
 Rent expense   900
 Insurance expense   50
 Interest expense   50
 Depreciation expense   40
  Total expenses   7,740
 Net income $ 2,860

Pioneer Advertising Agency
Owner's Equity Statement
For the Month Ended October 31, 2012

Owner's capital, October 1 $ –0–
Add: Investments $10,000
 Net income   2,860   12,860
                                             12,860
Less: Drawings   500
Owner's capital, October 31 $12,360

Pioneer Advertising Agency
Balance Sheet
October 31, 2012

Assets
Cash $15,200
Accounts receivable   200
Supplies   1,000
Prepaid insurance   550
Office equipment $5,000
Less: Accumulated depreciation—equipment   40   4,960
 Total assets $21,910

Liabilities and Owner's Equity
Liabilities
 Notes payable $5,000
 Accounts payable   2,500
 Interest payable   50
 Unearned service revenue   800
 Salaries and wages payable   1,200
  Total liabilities $ 9,550
Owner's equity
 Owner's capital   12,360
  Total liabilities and owner's equity $21,910

post them to the ledger. **The adjusting entries are prepared from the adjustments columns of the worksheet.** The reference letters in the adjustments columns and the explanations of the adjustments at the bottom of the worksheet help identify the adjusting entries. The journalizing and posting of adjusting entries **follows** the preparation of financial statements when a worksheet is used. The adjusting entries on October 31 for Pioneer Advertising Agency are the same as those shown in Illustration 3-23 (page 117).

Do it!

Worksheet

Susan Elbe is preparing a worksheet. Explain to Susan how she should extend the following adjusted trial balance accounts to the financial statement columns of the worksheet.

> Cash
> Accumulated Depreciation
> Accounts Payable
> Owner's Drawings
> Service Revenue
> Salaries and Wages Expense

action plan

✔ Balance sheet: Extend assets to debit column. Extend liabilities to credit column. Extend contra assets to credit column. Extend drawings account to debit column.

✔ Income statement: Extend expenses to debit column. Extend revenues to credit column.

Solution

Income statement debit column—Salaries and Wages Expense
Income statement credit column—Service Revenue
Balance sheet debit column—Cash; Owner's Drawings
Balance sheet credit column—Accumulated Depreciation; Accounts Payable

Related exercise material: BE4-1, BE4-2, BE4-3, E4-1, E4-2, E4-5, E4-6, and **Do it!** 4-1.

✔
The Navigator

Closing the Books

Study Objective [2]
Explain the process of closing the books.

At the end of the accounting period, the company makes the accounts ready for the next period. This is called **closing the books.** In closing the books, the company distinguishes between temporary and permanent accounts.

Temporary accounts relate only to a given accounting period. They include all income statement accounts and the owner's drawings account. **The company closes all temporary accounts at the end of the period.**

In contrast, permanent accounts relate to one or more future accounting periods. They consist of all balance sheet accounts, including the owner's capital account. **Permanent accounts are not closed from period to period.** Instead, the company carries forward the balances of permanent accounts into the next accounting period. Illustration 4-5 identifies the accounts in each category.

Alternative Terminology

Temporary accounts are sometimes called *nominal accounts,* and permanent accounts are sometimes called *real accounts.*

Illustration 4-5
Temporary versus permanent accounts

Helpful Hint

A contra-asset account, such as accumulated depreciation, is a permanent account also.

Preparing Closing Entries

At the end of the accounting period, the company transfers temporary account balances to the permanent owner's equity account, Owner's Capital, by means of closing entries.[1]

Closing entries formally recognize in the ledger the transfer of net income (or net loss) and owner's drawings to owner's capital. The owner's equity statement shows the results of these entries. **Closing entries also produce a zero balance in each temporary account.** The temporary accounts are then ready to accumulate data in the next accounting period separate from the data of prior periods. Permanent accounts are not closed.

Journalizing and posting closing entries is a required step in the accounting cycle. (See Illustration 4-12 on page 168.) The company performs this step after it has prepared financial statements. In contrast to the steps in the cycle that you have already studied, companies generally journalize and post closing entries **only at the end of the annual accounting period.** Thus, all temporary accounts will contain data for the entire year.

In preparing closing entries, companies could close each income statement account directly to owner's capital. However, to do so would result in excessive detail in the permanent Owner's Capital account. Instead, companies close the revenue and expense accounts to another temporary account, Income Summary, and they transfer the resulting net income or net loss from this account to owner's capital.

Companies **record closing entries in the general journal**. A center caption, Closing Entries, inserted in the journal between the last adjusting entry and the first closing entry, identifies these entries. Then the company posts the closing entries to the ledger accounts.

Companies generally prepare closing entries directly from the adjusted balances in the ledger. They could prepare separate closing entries for each nominal account, but the following four entries accomplish the desired result more efficiently:

1. Debit each revenue account for its balance, and credit Income Summary for total revenues.

2. Debit Income Summary for total expenses, and credit each expense account for its balance.

---

[1]We explain closing entries for a partnership and for a corporation in Chapters 12 and 13, respectively.

Helpful Hint

Owner's Drawings is closed directly to Owner's Capital and *not* to Income Summary; Owner's Drawings is not an expense.

3. Debit Income Summary and credit Owner's Capital for the amount of net income.

4. Debit Owner's Capital for the balance in the Owner's Drawings account, and credit Owner's Drawings for the same amount.

Illustration 4-6 presents a diagram of the closing process. In it, the boxed numbers refer to the four entries required in the closing process.

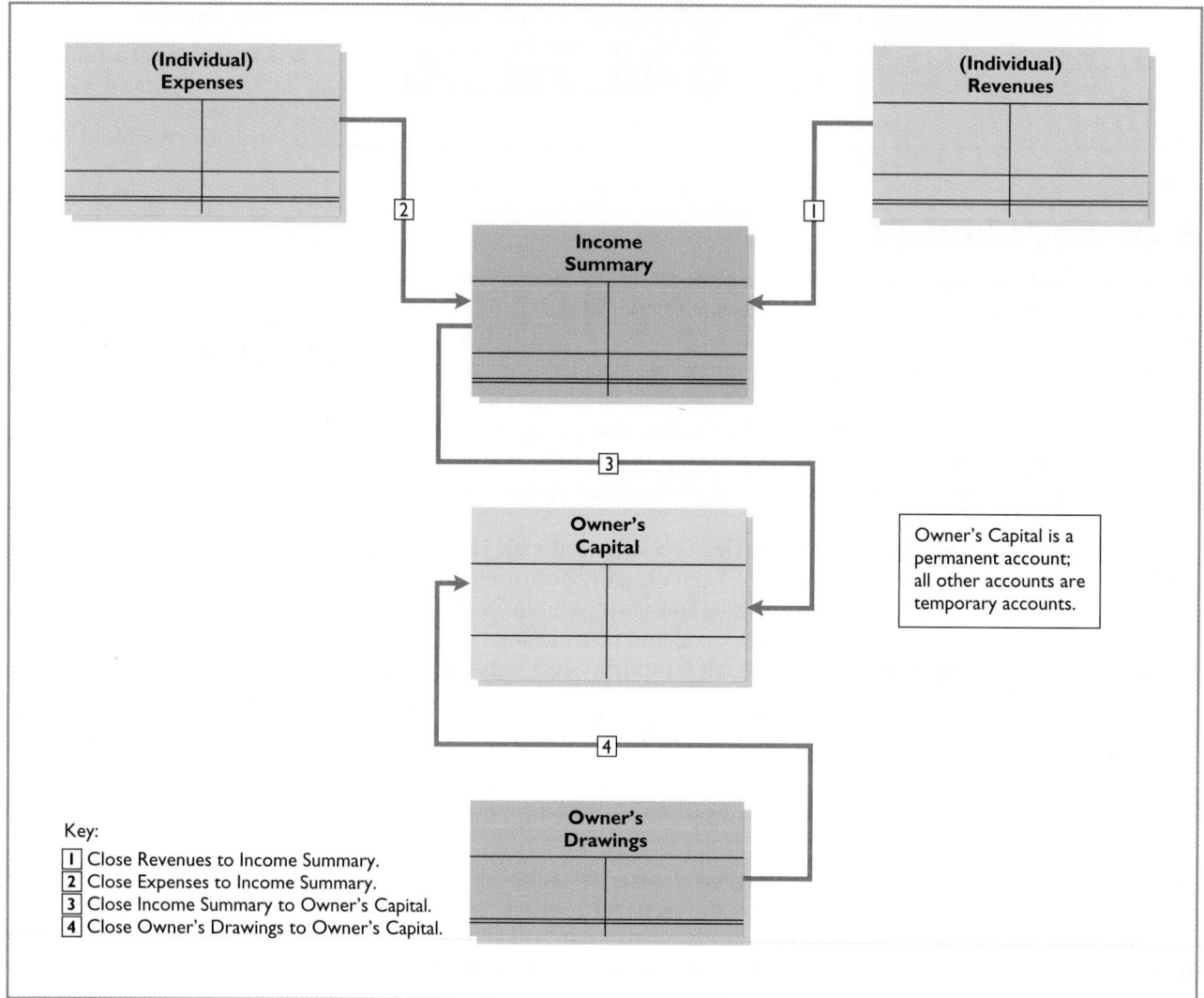

Key:
1 Close Revenues to Income Summary.
2 Close Expenses to Income Summary.
3 Close Income Summary to Owner's Capital.
4 Close Owner's Drawings to Owner's Capital.

Illustration 4-6
Diagram of closing process—proprietorship

If there were a net loss (because expenses exceeded revenues), entry 3 in Illustration 4-6 would be reversed: there would be a credit to Income Summary and a debit to Owner's Capital.

CLOSING ENTRIES ILLUSTRATED

In practice, companies generally prepare closing entries only at the end of the annual accounting period. However, to illustrate the journalizing and posting of closing entries, we will assume that Pioneer Advertising Agency closes its books monthly. Illustration 4-7 shows the closing entries at October 31. (The numbers in parentheses before each entry correspond to the four entries diagrammed in Illustration 4-6.)

Illustration 4-7
Closing entries journalized

General Journal				J3
Date	Account Titles and Explanation	Ref.	Debit	Credit
	Closing Entries			
	(1)			
2012				
Oct. 31	Service Revenue	400	10,600	
	Income Summary	350		10,600
	(To close revenue account)			
	(2)			
31	Income Summary	350	7,740	
	Supplies Expense	631		1,500
	Depreciation Expense	711		40
	Insurance Expense	722		50
	Salaries and Wages Expense	726		5,200
	Rent Expense	729		900
	Interest Expense	905		50
	(To close expense accounts)			
	(3)			
31	Income Summary	350	2,860	
	Owner's Capital	301		2,860
	(To close net income to capital)			
	(4)			
31	Owner's Capital	301	500	
	Owner's Drawings	306		500
	(To close drawings to capital)			

Note that the amounts for Income Summary in entries (1) and (2) are the totals of the income statement credit and debit columns, respectively, in the worksheet.

A couple of cautions in preparing closing entries: (1) Avoid unintentionally doubling the revenue and expense balances rather than zeroing them. (2) Do not close Owner's Drawings through the Income Summary account. **Owner's Drawings is not an expense, and it is not a factor in determining net income.**

Posting Closing Entries

Illustration 4-8 (page 164) shows the posting of the closing entries and the ruling of the accounts. Note that all temporary accounts have zero balances after posting the closing entries. In addition, notice that the balance in owner's capital (Owner's Capital) represents the total equity of the owner at the end of the accounting period. This balance is shown on the balance sheet and is the ending capital reported on the owner's equity statement, as shown in Illustration 4-4 on page 159. Pioneer uses the Income Summary account only in closing. It does not journalize and post entries to this account during the year.

As part of the closing process, Pioneer totals, balances, and double-rules its temporary accounts—revenues, expenses, and owner's drawings, as shown in T account form in Illustration 4-8. It does not close its permanent accounts—assets, liabilities, and owner's capital. Instead, Pioneer draws a single rule beneath the current-period entries for the permanent accounts. The account balance is then entered below the single rule and is carried forward to the next period. (For example, see Owner's Capital.)

Helpful Hint

The balance in Income Summary before it is closed must equal the net income or net loss for the period.

Supplies Expense 631

1,500	(2)	1,500	

Depreciation Expense 711

40	(2)	40	

Insurance Expense 722

50	(2)	50	

Salaries and Wages Expense 726

4,000	(2)	5,200	
1,200			
5,200		5,200	

Rent Expense 729

900	(2)	900	

Interest Expense 905

50	(2)	50	

Service Revenue 400

(1)	10,600	10,000	
		400	
		200	
	10,600	10,600	

Income Summary 350

(2)	7,740	(1)	10,600	
(3)	2,860			
	10,600		10,600	

Owner's Capital 301

(4)	500		10,000	
		(3)	2,860	
		Bal.	12,360	

Owner's Drawings 306

500	(4)	500	

Key:
1 Close Revenues to Income Summary.
2 Close Expenses to Income Summary.
3 Close Income Summary to Owner's Capital.
4 Close Owner's Drawings to Owner's Capital.

Illustration 4-8
Posting of closing entries

Do it!

Closing Entries

action plan

✔ Close Income Summary to Owner's Capital.

✔ Close Owner's Drawings to Owner's Capital.

The worksheet for Hancock Company shows the following in the financial statement columns:

Owner's drawings $15,000

Owner's capital $42,000

Net income $18,000

Prepare the closing entries at December 31 that affect owner's capital.

Solution

Dec. 31	Income Summary	18,000	
	Owner's Capital		18,000
	(To close net income to capital)		
31	Owner's Capital	15,000	
	Owner's Drawings		15,000
	(To close drawings to capital)		

Related exercise material: BE4-4, BE4-5, BE4-6, BE4-7, BE4-8, E4-4, E4-7, E4-8, E4-10, E4-11, and **Do it!** 4-2.

 The Navigator

ACCOUNTING ACROSS THE ORGANIZATION

Cisco Performs the Virtual Close

Technology has dramatically shortened the closing process. Recent surveys have reported that the average company now takes only six to seven days to close, rather than 20 days. But a few companies do much better. Cisco Systems can perform a "virtual close"—closing within 24 hours on any day in the quarter. The same is true at Lockheed Martin Corp., which improved its closing time by 85% in just the last few years. Not very long ago it took 14 to 16 days. Managers at these companies emphasize that this increased speed has not reduced the accuracy and completeness of the data.

This is not just showing off. Knowing exactly where you are financially all of the time allows the company to respond faster than competitors. It also means that the hundreds of people who used to spend 10 to 20 days a quarter tracking transactions can now be more usefully employed on things such as mining data for business intelligence to find new business opportunities.

Source: "Reporting Practices: Few Do It All," *Financial Executive* (November 2003), p. 11.

 Who else benefits from a shorter closing process? (See page 204.)

Preparing a Post-Closing Trial Balance

After Pioneer has journalized and posted all closing entries, it prepares another trial balance, called a **post-closing trial balance**, from the ledger. The post-closing trial balance lists permanent accounts and their balances after journalizing and posting of closing entries. The purpose of the post-closing trial balance is **to prove the equality of the permanent account balances carried forward into the next accounting period.** Since all temporary accounts will have zero balances, **the post-closing trial balance will contain only permanent—balance sheet—accounts**.

Illustration 4-9 shows the post-closing trial balance for Pioneer Advertising Agency.

> **Study Objective [3]**
> Describe the content and purpose of a post-closing trial balance.

Illustration 4-9
Post-closing trial balance

Pioneer Advertising Agency Post-Closing Trial Balance October 31, 2012		
	Debit	**Credit**
Cash	$15,200	
Accounts Receivable	200	
Supplies	1,000	
Prepaid Insurance	550	
Office Equipment	5,000	
Accumulated Depreciation—Equipment		$ 40
Notes Payable		5,000
Accounts Payable		2,500
Unearned Service Revenue		800
Salaries and Wages Payable		1,200
Interest Payable		50
Owner's Capital		12,360
	$21,950	$21,950

Pioneer prepares the post-closing trial balance from the permanent accounts in the ledger. Illustration 4-10 shows the permanent accounts in Pioneer's general ledger.

Illustration 4-10
General ledger, permanent accounts

(Permanent Accounts Only)

General Ledger

Cash — No. 101

Date	Explanation	Ref.	Debit	Credit	Balance
2012					
Oct. 1		J1	10,000		10,000
2		J1	1,200		11,200
3		J1		900	10,300
4		J1		600	9,700
20		J1		500	9,200
26		J1		4,000	5,200
31		J1	10,000		15,200

Accounts Receivable — No. 112

Date	Explanation	Ref.	Debit	Credit	Balance
2012					
Oct. 31	Adj. entry	J2	200		200

Supplies — No. 126

Date	Explanation	Ref.	Debit	Credit	Balance
2012					
Oct. 5		J1	2,500		2,500
31	Adj. entry	J2		1,500	1,000

Prepaid Insurance — No. 130

Date	Explanation	Ref.	Debit	Credit	Balance
2012					
Oct. 4		J1	600		600
31	Adj. entry	J2		50	550

Equipment — No. 157

Date	Explanation	Ref.	Debit	Credit	Balance
2012					
Oct. 1		J1	5,000		5,000

Accumulated Depreciation—Equipment — No. 158

Date	Explanation	Ref.	Debit	Credit	Balance
2012					
Oct. 31	Adj. entry	J2		40	40

Notes Payable — No. 200

Date	Explanation	Ref.	Debit	Credit	Balance
2012					
Oct. 1		J1		5,000	5,000

Accounts Payable — No. 201

Date	Explanation	Ref.	Debit	Credit	Balance
2012					
Oct. 5		J1		2,500	2,500

Unearned Service Revenue — No. 209

Date	Explanation	Ref.	Debit	Credit	Balance
2012					
Oct. 2		J1		1,200	1,200
31	Adj. entry	J2	400		800

Salaries and Wages Payable — No. 212

Date	Explanation	Ref.	Debit	Credit	Balance
2012					
Oct. 31	Adj. entry	J2		1,200	1,200

Interest Payable — No. 230

Date	Explanation	Ref.	Debit	Credit	Balance
2012					
Oct. 31	Adj. entry	J2		50	50

Owner's Capital — No. 301

Date	Explanation	Ref.	Debit	Credit	Balance
2012					
Oct. 1		J1		10,000	10,000
31	Closing entry	J3		2,860	12,860
31	Closing entry	J3	500		12,360

Note: The permanent accounts for Pioneer Advertising Agency are shown here; Illustration 4-11 shows the temporary accounts. Both permanent and temporary accounts are part of the general ledger; they are segregated here to aid in learning.

A post-closing trial balance provides evidence that the company has properly journalized and posted the closing entries. It also shows that the accounting equation is in balance at the end of the accounting period. However, like the trial balance, it does not prove that Pioneer has recorded all transactions or that the ledger is correct.

For example, the post-closing trial balance still will balance even if a transaction is not journalized and posted or if a transaction is journalized and posted twice.

The remaining accounts in the general ledger are temporary accounts, shown in Illustration 4-11. After Pioneer correctly posts the closing entries, each temporary account has a zero balance. These accounts are double-ruled to finalize the closing process.

Illustration 4-11
General ledger, temporary accounts

(Temporary Accounts Only)

General Ledger													

Owner's Drawings   No. 306

Date	Explanation	Ref.	Debit	Credit	Balance
2012					
Oct. 20		J1	500		500
31	Closing entry	J3		500	–0–

Income Summary   No. 350

Date	Explanation	Ref.	Debit	Credit	Balance
2012					
Oct. 31	Closing entry	J3		10,600	10,600
31	Closing entry	J3	7,740		2,860
31	Closing entry	J3	2,860		–0–

Service Revenue   No. 400

Date	Explanation	Ref.	Debit	Credit	Balance
2012					
Oct. 31		J1		10,000	10,000
31	Adj. entry	J2		400	10,400
31	Adj. entry	J2		200	10,600
31	Closing entry	J3	10,600		–0–

Supplies Expense   No. 631

Date	Explanation	Ref.	Debit	Credit	Balance
2012					
Oct. 31	Adj. entry	J2	1,500		1,500
31	Closing entry	J3		1,500	–0–

Depreciation Expense   No. 711

Date	Explanation	Ref.	Debit	Credit	Balance
2012					
Oct. 31	Adj. entry	J2	40		40
31	Closing entry	J3		40	–0–

Insurance Expense   No. 722

Date	Explanation	Ref.	Debit	Credit	Balance
2012					
Oct. 31	Adj. entry	J2	50		50
31	Closing entry	J3		50	–0–

Salaries and Wages Expense   No. 726

Date	Explanation	Ref.	Debit	Credit	Balance
2012					
Oct. 26		J1	4,000		4,000
31	Adj. entry	J2	1,200		5,200
31	Closing entry	J3		5,200	–0–

Rent Expense   No. 729

Date	Explanation	Ref.	Debit	Credit	Balance
2012					
Oct. 3		J1	900		900
31	Closing entry	J3		900	–0–

Interest Expense   No. 905

Date	Explanation	Ref.	Debit	Credit	Balance
2012					
Oct. 31	Adj. entry	J2	50		50
31	Closing entry	J3		50	–0–

Note: The temporary accounts for Pioneer Advertising Agency are shown here; Illustration 4-10 shows the permanent accounts. Both permanent and temporary accounts are part of the general ledger; they are segregated here to aid in learning.

Summary of the Accounting Cycle

Illustration 4-12 (page 168) summarizes the steps in the accounting cycle. You can see that the cycle begins with the analysis of business transactions and ends with the preparation of a post-closing trial balance.

Steps 1–3 may occur daily during the accounting period, as explained in Chapter 2. Companies perform Steps 4–7 on a periodic basis, such as monthly, quarterly, or annually. Steps 8 and 9—closing entries, and a post-closing trial balance—usually take place only at the end of a company's **annual** accounting period.

Study Objective [4]
State the required steps in the accounting cycle.

Illustration 4-12
Steps in the accounting cycle

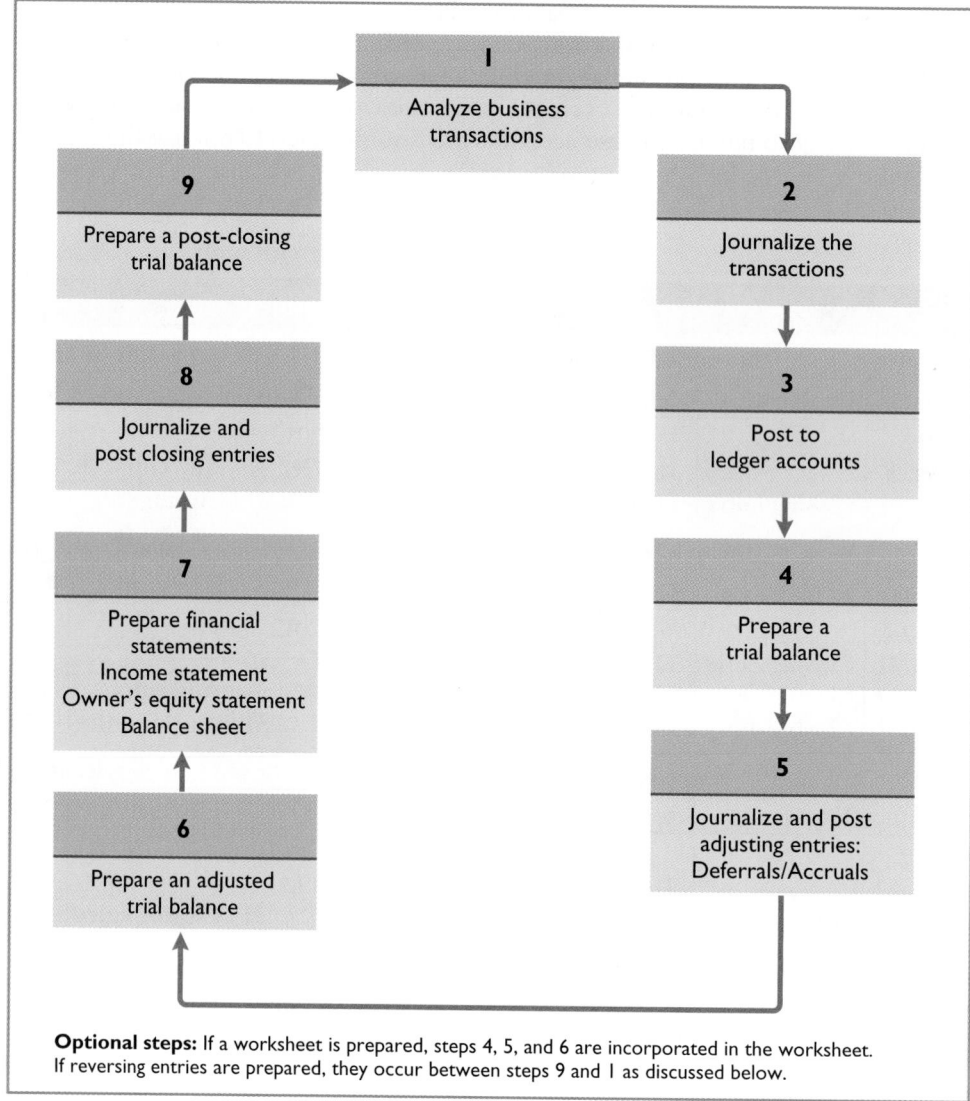

Optional steps: If a worksheet is prepared, steps 4, 5, and 6 are incorporated in the worksheet. If reversing entries are prepared, they occur between steps 9 and 1 as discussed below.

There are also two **optional steps** in the accounting cycle. As you have seen, companies may use a worksheet in preparing adjusting entries and financial statements. In addition, they may use reversing entries, as explained below.

Reversing Entries—An Optional Step

Some accountants prefer to reverse certain adjusting entries by making a **reversing entry** at the beginning of the next accounting period. A reversing entry is the exact opposite of the adjusting entry made in the previous period. **Use of reversing entries is an optional bookkeeping procedure; it is not a required step in the accounting cycle.** Accordingly, we have chosen to cover this topic in an appendix at the end of the chapter.

Study Objective [5]
Explain the approaches to preparing correcting entries.

Correcting Entries—An Avoidable Step

Unfortunately, errors may occur in the recording process. Companies should correct errors, **as soon as they discover them**, by journalizing and posting **correcting entries**. If the accounting records are free of errors, no correcting entries are needed.

You should recognize several differences between correcting entries and adjusting entries. First, adjusting entries are an integral part of the accounting cycle. Correcting entries, on the other hand, are unnecessary if the records are error-free. Second, companies journalize and post adjustments **only at the end of an accounting period**. In contrast, companies make correcting entries **whenever they discover an error**. Finally, adjusting entries always affect at least one balance sheet account and one income statement account. In contrast, correcting entries may involve any combination of accounts in need of correction. **Correcting entries must be posted before closing entries.**

> **Ethics Note**
>
> When companies find errors in previously released income statements, they restate those numbers. Perhaps because of the increased scrutiny caused by Sarbanes-Oxley, in a recent year companies filed a record 1,195 restatements.

To determine the correcting entry, it is useful to compare the incorrect entry with the correct entry. Doing so helps identify the accounts and amounts that should—and should not—be corrected. After comparison, the accountant makes an entry to correct the accounts. The following two cases for Mercato Co. illustrate this approach.

CASE 1

On May 10, Mercato Co. journalized and posted a $50 cash collection on account from a customer as a debit to Cash $50 and a credit to Service Revenue $50. The company discovered the error on May 20, when the customer paid the remaining balance in full.

Illustration 4-13
Comparison of entries

Incorrect Entry (May 10)			Correct Entry (May 10)		
Cash	50		Cash	50	
Service Revenue		50	Accounts Receivable		50

Comparison of the incorrect entry with the correct entry reveals that the debit to Cash $50 is correct. However, the $50 credit to Service Revenue should have been credited to Accounts Receivable. As a result, both Service Revenue and Accounts Receivable are overstated in the ledger. Mercato makes the following correcting entry.

Illustration 4-14
Correcting entry

A = L + OE
−50 Rev
−50

Cash Flows
no effect

	Correcting Entry		
May 20	Service Revenue	50	
	Accounts Receivable		50
	(To correct entry of May 10)		

CASE 2

On May 18, Mercato purchased on account equipment costing $450. The transaction was journalized and posted as a debit to Equipment $45 and a credit to Accounts Payable $45. The error was discovered on June 3, when Mercato received the monthly statement for May from the creditor.

Illustration 4-15
Comparison of entries

Incorrect Entry (May 18)			Correct Entry (May 18)		
Equipment	45		Equipment	450	
Accounts Payable		45	Accounts Payable		450

Comparison of the two entries shows that two accounts are incorrect. Equipment is understated $405, and Accounts Payable is understated $405. Mercato makes the following correcting entry.

A	=	L	+	OE
+405				
		+405		

Cash Flows
no effect

Illustration 4-16
Correcting entry

Correcting Entry

June 3	Equipment	405	
	Accounts Payable		405
	(To correct entry of May 18)		

Instead of preparing a correcting entry, **it is possible to reverse the incorrect entry and then prepare the correct entry**. This approach will result in more entries and postings than a correcting entry, but it will accomplish the desired result.

ACCOUNTING ACROSS THE ORGANIZATION

Yale Express Loses Some Transportation Bills

Yale Express, a short-haul trucking firm, turned over much of its cargo to local truckers to complete deliveries. Yale collected the entire delivery charge; when billed by the local trucker, Yale sent payment for the final phase to the local trucker. Yale used a cutoff period of 20 days into the next accounting period in making its adjusting entries for accrued liabilities. That is, it waited 20 days to receive the local truckers' bills to determine the amount of the unpaid but incurred delivery charges as of the balance sheet date.

On the other hand, Republic Carloading, a nationwide, long-distance freight forwarder, frequently did not receive transportation bills from truckers to whom it passed on cargo until months after the year-end. In making its year-end adjusting entries, Republic waited for months in order to include all of these outstanding transportation bills.

When Yale Express merged with Republic Carloading, Yale's vice president employed the 20-day cutoff procedure for both firms. As a result, millions of dollars of Republic's accrued transportation bills went unrecorded. When the company detected the error and made correcting entries, these and other errors changed a reported profit of $1.14 million into a loss of $1.88 million!

? What might Yale Express's vice president have done to produce more accurate financial statements without waiting months for Republic's outstanding transportation bills? (See page 204.)

The Classified Balance Sheet

Study Objective [6]
Identify the sections of a classified balance sheet.

The balance sheet presents a snapshot of a company's financial position at a point in time. To improve users' understanding of a company's financial position, companies often use a classified balance sheet. A classified balance sheet groups together similar assets and similar liabilities, using a number of standard classifications and sections. This is useful because items within a group have similar economic characteristics. A classified balance sheet generally contains the standard classifications listed in Illustration 4-17.

Illustration 4-17
Standard balance sheet classifications

Assets	Liabilities and Owner's Equity
Current assets	Current liabilities
Long-term investments	Long-term liabilities
Property, plant, and equipment	Owner's (Stockholders') equity
Intangible assets	

These groupings help readers determine such things as (1) whether the company has enough assets to pay its debts as they come due, and (2) the claims of short- and long-term creditors on the company's total assets. Many of these groupings can be seen in the balance sheet of Franklin Company shown in Illustration 4-18 below. In the sections that follow, we explain each of these groupings.

Illustration 4-18
Classified balance sheet

Franklin Company
Balance Sheet
October 31, 2012

Assets

Current assets			
Cash		$ 6,600	
Short-term investments		2,000	
Accounts receivable		7,000	
Notes receivable		1,000	
Inventory		3,000	
Supplies		2,100	
Prepaid insurance		400	
Total current assets			$22,100
Long-term investments			
Investment in stock of Walters Corp.		5,200	
Investment in real estate		2,000	7,200
Property, plant, and equipment			
Land		10,000	
Equipment	$24,000		
Less: Accumulated depreciation— equipment	5,000	19,000	29,000
Intangible assets			
Patents			3,100
Total assets			$61,400

Liabilities and Owner's Equity

Current liabilities		
Notes payable	$11,000	
Accounts payable	2,100	
Salaries and wages payable	1,600	
Unearned service revenue	900	
Interest payable	450	
Total current liabilities		$16,050
Long-term liabilities		
Mortgage payable	10,000	
Notes payable	1,300	
Total long-term liabilities		11,300
Total liabilities		27,350
Owner's equity		
Owner's capital		34,050
Total liabilities and owner's equity		$61,400

Helpful Hint

Recall that the basic accounting equation is Assets = Liabilities + Owner's Equity.

Current Assets

Current assets are assets that a company expects to convert to cash or use up within one year or its operating cycle, whichever is longer. In Illustration 4-18, Franklin Company had current assets of $22,100. For most businesses the cutoff for classification as current assets is one year from the balance sheet date. For example, accounts receivable are current assets because the company will collect them and convert them to cash within one year. Supplies is a current asset because the company expects to use it up in operations within one year.

Some companies use a period longer than one year to classify assets and liabilities as current because they have an operating cycle longer than one year. The operating cycle of a company is the average time that it takes to purchase inventory, sell it on account, and then collect cash from customers. For most businesses this cycle takes less than a year, so they use a one-year cutoff. But, for some businesses, such as vineyards or airplane manufacturers, this period may be longer than a year. **Except where noted, we will assume that companies use one year to determine whether an asset or liability is current or long-term.**

Common types of current assets are (1) cash, (2) short-term investments (such as short-term U.S. government securities), (3) receivables (notes receivable, accounts receivable, and interest receivable), (4) inventories, and (5) prepaid expenses (insurance and supplies). **On the balance sheet, companies usually list these items in the order in which they expect to convert them into cash.**

Illustration 4-19 presents the current assets of Southwest Airlines Co.

Illustration 4-19
Current assets section

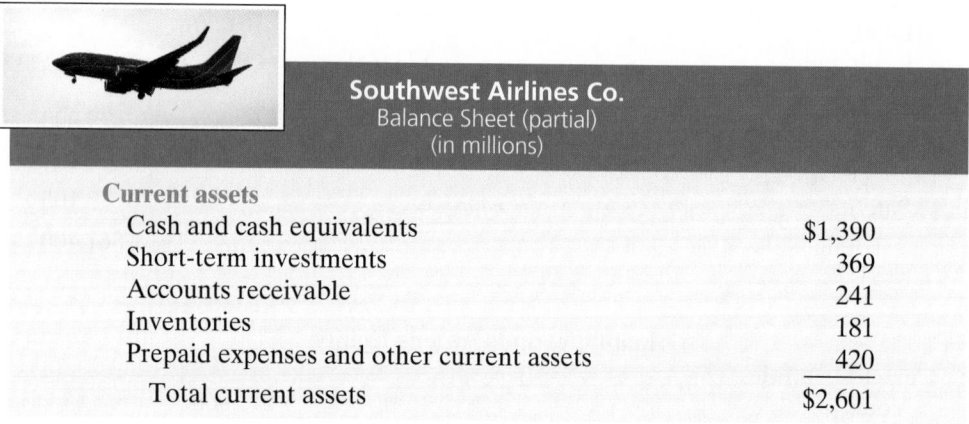

Southwest Airlines Co.
Balance Sheet (partial)
(in millions)

Current assets	
Cash and cash equivalents	$1,390
Short-term investments	369
Accounts receivable	241
Inventories	181
Prepaid expenses and other current assets	420
Total current assets	$2,601

As explained later in the chapter, a company's current assets are important in assessing its short-term debt-paying ability.

Long-Term Investments

Alternative Terminology

Long-term investments are often referred to simply as *investments.*

Long-term investments are generally, (1) investments in stocks and bonds of other companies that are normally held for many years, and (2) long-term assets such as land or buildings that a company is not currently using in its operating activities. In Illustration 4-18, Franklin Company reported total long-term investments of $7,200 on its balance sheet.

Yahoo! Inc. reported long-term investments in its balance sheet as shown in Illustration 4-20.

Yahoo! Inc.
Balance Sheet (partial)
(in thousands)

Illustration 4-20
Long-term investments
section

Long-term investments
    Long-term investments in marketable securities $90,266

Property, Plant, and Equipment

Property, plant, and equipment are assets with relatively long useful lives that a company is currently using in operating the business. This category (sometimes called *fixed assets*) includes land, buildings, machinery and equipment, delivery equipment, and furniture. In Illustration 4-18, Franklin Company reported property, plant, and equipment of $29,000.

    Depreciation is the practice of allocating the cost of assets to a number of years. Companies do this by systematically assigning a portion of an asset's cost as an expense each year (rather than expensing the full purchase price in the year of purchase). The assets that the company depreciates are reported on the balance sheet at cost less accumulated depreciation. The **accumulated depreciation** account shows the total amount of depreciation that the company has expensed thus far in the asset's life. In Illustration 4-18, Franklin Company reported accumulated depreciation of $5,000.

    Illustration 4-21 presents the property, plant, and equipment of Cooper Tire & Rubber Company.

International Note

In 2007 China adopted International Financial Reporting Standards (IFRS). This was done in an effort to reduce fraud and increase investor confidence in financial reports. Under these standards, many items, such as property, plant, and equipment, may be reported at current fair values, rather than historical cost.

Cooper Tire & Rubber Company
Balance Sheet (partial)
(in thousands)

Illustration 4-21
Property, plant, and
equipment section

Property, plant, and equipment		
Land and land improvements	$ 41,553	
Buildings	298,706	
Machinery and equipment	1,636,091	
Molds, cores, and rings	268,158	$2,244,508
Less: Accumulated depreciation		1,252,692
		$ 991,816

Intangible Assets

Many companies have long-lived assets that do not have physical substance yet often are very valuable. We call these assets intangible assets. One common intangible asset is goodwill. Others include patents, copyrights, and trademarks or trade names that give the company **exclusive right** of use for a specified period of time. In Illustration 4-18, Franklin Company reported intangible assets of $3,100.

Helpful Hint

Sometimes intangible assets are reported under a broader heading called *"Other assets."*

Illustration 4-22 shows the intangible assets of media giant Time Warner, Inc.

Illustration 4-22
Intangible assets section

Time Warner, Inc. Balance Sheet (partial) (in millions)	
Intangible assets	
Goodwill	$40,953
Film library	2,690
Customer lists	2,540
Cable television franchises	38,048
Sports franchises	262
Brands, trademarks, and other intangible assets	8,313
	$92,806

Do it!

Asset Section of Balance Sheet

action plan

✔ Present current assets first. Current assets are cash and other resources that the company expects to convert to cash or use up within one year.

✔ Present current assets in the order in which the company expects to convert them into cash.

✔ Subtract accumulated depreciation—equipment from equipment to determine net equipment.

Baxter Hoffman recently received the following information related to Hoffman Company's December 31, 2012, balance sheet.

Prepaid insurance	$ 2,300	Inventory	$3,400
Cash	800	Accumulated depreciation—	
Equipment	10,700	equipment	2,700
		Accounts receivable	1,100

Prepare the asset section of Hoffman Company's balance sheet.

Solution

Assets		
Current assets		
Cash	$ 800	
Accounts receivable	1,100	
Inventory	3,400	
Prepaid insurance	2,300	
Total current assets		$ 7,600
Equipment	10,700	
Less: Accumulated depreciation—equipment	2,700	8,000
Total assets		$15,600

Related exercise material: BE4-10 and **Do it!** 4-3.

The Navigator

Current Liabilities

Ethics Note

A company that has more current assets than current liabilities can increase the ratio of current assets to current liabilities by using cash to pay off some current liabilities. This gives the appearance of being more liquid. Do you think this move is ethical?

In the liabilities and owners' equity section of the balance sheet, the first grouping is current liabilities. **Current liabilities** are obligations that the company is to pay within the coming year or its operating cycle, whichever is longer. Common examples are accounts payable, wages payable, bank loans payable, interest payable, and taxes payable. Also included as current liabilities are current maturities of long-term obligations—payments to be made within the next year on long-term obligations. In Illustration 4-18, Franklin Company reported five different types of current liabilities, for a total of $16,050.

Within the current liabilities section, companies usually list notes payable first, followed by accounts payable. Other items then follow in the order of their magnitude. *In your homework, you should present notes payable first, followed by accounts payable, and then other liabilities in order of magnitude.*

Illustration 4-23 shows the current liabilities section adapted from the balance sheet of Marcus Corporation.

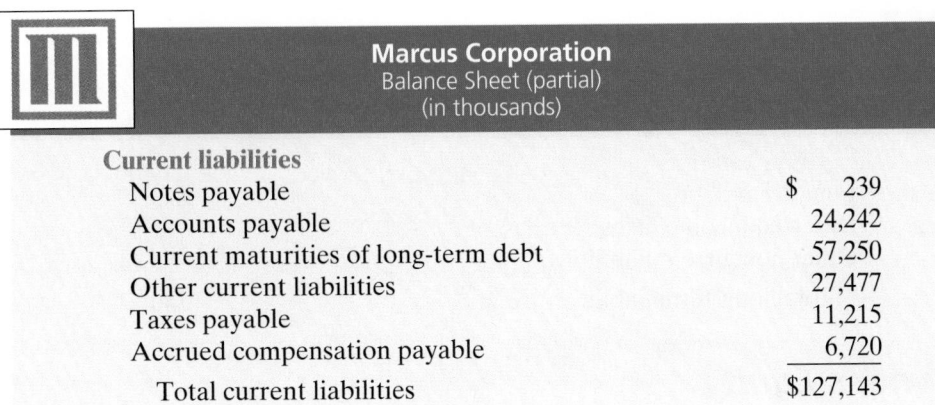

Marcus Corporation
Balance Sheet (partial)
(in thousands)

Current liabilities	
Notes payable	$ 239
Accounts payable	24,242
Current maturities of long-term debt	57,250
Other current liabilities	27,477
Taxes payable	11,215
Accrued compensation payable	6,720
Total current liabilities	$127,143

Illustration 4-23
Current liabilities section

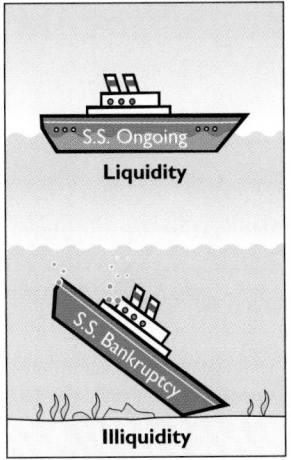

Users of financial statements look closely at the relationship between current assets and current liabilities. This relationship is important in evaluating a company's **liquidity**—its ability to pay obligations expected to be due within the next year. When current assets exceed current liabilities at the balance sheet date, the likelihood for paying the liabilities is favorable. When the reverse is true, short-term creditors may not be paid, and the company may ultimately be forced into bankruptcy.

ACCOUNTING ACROSS THE ORGANIZATION

Can a Company Be Too Liquid?

There actually is a point where a company can be too liquid—that is, it can have too much working capital (current assets less current liabilities). While it is important to be liquid enough to be able to pay short-term bills as they come due, a company does not want to tie up its cash in extra inventory or receivables that are not earning the company money.

By one estimate from the REL Consultancy Group, the thousand largest U.S. companies have on their books cumulative excess working capital of $764 billion. Based on this figure, companies could have reduced debt by 36% or increased net income by 9%. Given that managers throughout a company are interested in improving profitability, it is clear that they should have an eye toward managing working capital. They need to aim for a "Goldilocks solution"—not too much, not too little, but just right.

Source: K. Richardson, "Companies Fall Behind in Cash Management," *Wall Street Journal* (June 19, 2007).

? What can various company managers do to ensure that working capital is managed efficiently to maximize net income? (See page 204.)

Long-Term Liabilities

Long-term liabilities are obligations that a company expects to pay **after** one year. Liabilities in this category include bonds payable, mortgages payable, long-term notes payable, lease liabilities, and pension liabilities. Many companies report long-term debt maturing after one year as a single amount in the balance sheet and show the details of the debt in notes that accompany the financial statements. Others list the various types of long-term liabilities. In Illustration 4-18, Franklin Company reported long-term liabilities of $11,300. *In your homework, list long-term liabilities in the order of their magnitude.*

Illustration 4-24 shows the long-term liabilities that The Procter & Gamble Company reported in its balance sheet.

Illustration 4-24
Long-term liabilities section

The Procter & Gamble Company
Balance Sheet (partial)
(in millions)

Long-term liabilities	
Long-term debt	$23,375
Deferred income taxes	12,015
Other noncurrent liabilities	5,147
Total long-term liabilities	$40,537

Owner's Equity

Alternative Terminology

Common stock is sometimes called *capital stock*.

The content of the owner's equity section varies with the form of business organization. In a proprietorship, there is one capital account. In a partnership, there is a capital account for each partner. Corporations divide owners' equity into two accounts—Common Stock (sometimes referred to as Capital Stock) and Retained Earnings. Corporations record stockholders' investments in the company by debiting an asset account and crediting the Common Stock account. They record in the Retained Earnings account income retained for use in the business. Corporations combine the Common Stock and Retained Earnings accounts and report them on the balance sheet as **stockholders' equity**. (We'll learn more about these corporation accounts in later chapters.) Nordstrom, Inc. recently reported its stockholders' equity section as follows.

Illustration 4-25
Stockholders' equity section

Nordstrom, Inc.
Balance Sheet (partial)
($ in thousands)

Stockholders' equity	
Common stock, 271,331 shares	$ 685,934
Retained earnings	1,406,747
Total stockholders' equity	$2,092,681

Do it!

Balance Sheet Classifications

The following accounts were taken from the financial statements of Callahan Company.

_____ Salaries and wages payable
_____ Service revenue
_____ Interest payable
_____ Goodwill
_____ Short-term investments
_____ Mortgage payable (due in 3 years)

_____ Investment in real estate
_____ Equipment
_____ Accumulated depreciation—equipment
_____ Depreciation expense
_____ Owner's capital
_____ Unearned service revenue

Match each of the following accounts to its proper balance sheet classification, shown below. If the item would not appear on a balance sheet, use "NA."

Current assets (CA)
Long-term investments (LTI)
Property, plant, and equipment (PPE)
Intangible assets (IA)

Current liabilities (CL)
Long-term liabilities (LTL)
Owner's equity (OE)

action plan

✔ Analyze whether each financial statement item is an asset, liability, or owner's equity.

✔ Determine if asset and liability items are short-term or long-term.

Solution

__CL__	Salaries and wages payable	__LTI__	Investment in real estate
__NA__	Service revenue	__PPE__	Equipment
__CL__	Interest payable	__PPE__	Accumulated depreciation— equipment
__IA__	Goodwill		
__CA__	Short-term investments	__NA__	Depreciation expense
__LTL__	Mortgage payable (due in 3 years)	__OE__	Owner's capital
		__CL__	Unearned service revenue

Related exercise material: BE4-11, E4-14, E4-15, E4-16, E4-17, and **Do it!** 4-4.

✔ The Navigator

COMPREHENSIVE

Do it!

At the end of its first month of operations, Watson Answering Service has the following unadjusted trial balance.

WATSON ANSWERING SERVICE
August 31, 2012
Trial Balance

	Debit	Credit
Cash	$ 5,400	
Accounts Receivable	2,800	
Supplies	1,300	
Prepaid Insurance	2,400	
Equipment	60,000	
Notes Payable		$40,000
Accounts Payable		2,400
Owner's Capital		30,000
Owner's Drawings	1,000	
Service Revenue		4,900
Salaries and Wages Expense	3,200	
Utilities Expense	800	
Advertising Expense	400	
	$77,300	$77,300

action plan

✔ In completing the worksheet, be sure to (a) key the adjustments; (b) start at the top of the adjusted trial balance columns and extend adjusted balances to the correct statement columns; and (c) enter net income (or net loss) in the proper columns.

✔ In preparing a classified balance sheet, know the contents of each of the sections.

✔ In journalizing closing entries, remember that there are only four entries and that owner's drawings is closed to owner's capital.

Other data:

1. Insurance expires at the rate of $200 per month.
2. $1,000 of supplies are on hand at August 31.
3. Monthly depreciation on the equipment is $900.
4. Interest of $500 on the notes payable has accrued during August.

Instructions

(a) Prepare a worksheet.

(b) Prepare a classified balance sheet assuming $35,000 of the notes payable are long-term.

(c) Journalize the closing entries.

Solution to Comprehensive Do it!

(a)

WATSON ANSWERING SERVICE
Worksheet for the Month Ended August 31, 2012

Account Titles	Trial Balance Dr.	Trial Balance Cr.	Adjustments Dr.	Adjustments Cr.	Adjusted Trial Balance Dr.	Adjusted Trial Balance Cr.	Income Statement Dr.	Income Statement Cr.	Balance Sheet Dr.	Balance Sheet Cr.
Cash	5,400				5,400				5,400	
Accounts Receivable	2,800				2,800				2,800	
Supplies	1,300			(b) 300	1,000				1,000	
Prepaid Insurance	2,400			(a) 200	2,200				2,200	
Equipment	60,000				60,000				60,000	
Notes Payable		40,000				40,000				40,000
Accounts Payable		2,400				2,400				2,400
Owner's Capital		30,000				30,000				30,000
Owner's Drawings	1,000				1,000				1,000	
Service Revenue		4,900				4,900		4,900		
Salaries and										
Wages Expense	3,200				3,200		3,200			
Utilities Expense	800				800		800			
Advertising Expense	400				400		400			
Totals	77,300	77,300								
Insurance Expense			(a) 200		200		200			
Supplies Expense			(b) 300		300		300			
Depreciation Expense			(c) 900		900		900			
Accumulated Depreciation—										
Equipment				(c) 900		900				900
Interest Expense			(d) 500		500		500			
Interest Payable				(d) 500		500				500
Totals			1,900	1,900	78,700	78,700	6,300	4,900	72,400	73,800
Net Loss								1,400	1,400	
Totals							6,300	6,300	73,800	73,800

Explanation: (a) Insurance expired, (b) Supplies used, (c) Depreciation expensed, (d) Interest accrued.

(b)

WATSON ANSWERING SERVICE
Balance Sheet
August 31, 2012

Assets

Current assets		
Cash	$ 5,400	
Accounts receivable	2,800	
Supplies	1,000	
Prepaid insurance	2,200	
Total current assets		$11,400
Property, plant, and equipment		
Equipment	60,000	
Less: Accumulated depreciation—equipment	900	59,100
Total assets		$70,500

Liabilities and Owner's Equity

Current liabilities		
Notes payable	$ 5,000	
Accounts payable	2,400	
Interest payable	500	
Total current liabilities		$ 7,900
Long-term liabilities		
Notes payable		35,000
Total liabilities		42,900
Owner's equity		
Owner's capital		27,600*
Total liabilities and owner's equity		$70,500

*Owner's capital, $30,000 less drawings $1,000 and net loss $1,400.

(c)

Aug. 31	Service Revenue	4,900	
	Income Summary		4,900
	(To close revenue account)		
31	Income Summary	6,300	
	Salaries and Wages Expense		3,200
	Depreciation Expense		900
	Utilities Expense		800
	Interest Expense		500
	Advertising Expense		400
	Supplies Expense		300
	Insurance Expense		200
	(To close expense accounts)		
31	Owner's Capital	1,400	
	Income Summary		1,400
	(To close net loss to capital)		
31	Owner's Capital	1,000	
	Owner's Drawings		1,000
	(To close drawings to capital)		

The Navigator

Summary of Study Objectives

[1] Prepare a worksheet. The steps in preparing a worksheet are: (a) Prepare a trial balance on the worksheet. (b) Enter the adjustments in the adjustments columns. (c) Enter adjusted balances in the adjusted trial balance columns. (d) Extend adjusted trial balance amounts to appropriate financial statement columns. (e) Total the statement columns, compute net income (or net loss), and complete the worksheet.

[2] Explain the process of closing the books. Closing the books occurs at the end of an accounting period. The process is to journalize and post closing entries and then rule and balance all accounts. In closing the books, companies make separate entries to close revenues and expenses to Income Summary, Income Summary to Owner's Capital, and Owner's Drawings to Owner's Capital. Only temporary accounts are closed.

[3] Describe the content and purpose of a post-closing trial balance. A post-closing trial balance contains the balances in permanent accounts that are carried forward to the next accounting period. The purpose of this trial balance is to prove the equality of these balances.

[4] State the required steps in the accounting cycle. The required steps in the accounting cycle are: (1) analyze business transactions, (2) journalize the transactions, (3) post to ledger accounts, (4) prepare a trial balance, (5) journalize and post adjusting entries, (6) prepare an adjusted trial balance, (7) prepare financial statements, (8) journalize and post closing entries, and (9) prepare a post-closing trial balance.

[5] Explain the approaches to preparing correcting entries. One way to determine the correcting entry is to compare the incorrect entry with the correct entry. After comparison, the company makes a correcting entry to correct the accounts. An alternative to a correcting entry is to reverse the incorrect entry and then prepare the correct entry.

[6] Identify the sections of a classified balance sheet. A classified balance sheet categorizes assets as current assets; long-term investments; property, plant, and equipment; and intangibles. Liabilities are classified as either current or long-term. There is also an owner's (owners') equity section, which varies with the form of business organization.

The Navigator ✔

Glossary

Classified balance sheet A balance sheet that contains standard classifications or sections. (p. 170).

Closing entries Entries made at the end of an accounting period to transfer the balances of temporary accounts to a permanent owner's equity account, Owner's Capital. (p. 161).

Correcting entries Entries to correct errors made in recording transactions. (p. 168).

Current assets Assets that a company expects to convert to cash or use up within one year. (p. 172).

Current liabilities Obligations that a company expects to pay from existing current assets within the coming year. (p. 174).

Income Summary A temporary account used in closing revenue and expense accounts. (p. 161).

Intangible assets Noncurrent assets that do not have physical substance. (p. 173).

Liquidity The ability of a company to pay obligations expected to be due within the next year. (p. 175).

Long-term investments Generally, (1) investments in stocks and bonds of other companies that companies normally hold for many years, and (2) long-term assets, such as land and buildings, not currently being used in operations. (p. 172).

Long-term liabilities Obligations that a company expects to pay after one year. (p. 175).

Operating cycle The average time that it takes to go from cash to cash in producing revenues. (p. 172).

Permanent (real) accounts Accounts that relate to one or more accounting periods. Consist of all balance sheet accounts. Balances are carried forward to next accounting period. (p. 160).

Post-closing trial balance A list of permanent accounts and their balances after a company has journalized and posted closing entries. (p. 165).

Property, plant, and equipment Assets with relatively long useful lives and currently being used in operations. (p. 173).

Reversing entry An entry, made at the beginning of the next accounting period, that is the exact opposite of the adjusting entry made in the previous period. (p. 168).

Stockholders' equity The ownership claim of shareholders on total assets. It is to a corporation what owner's equity is to a proprietorship. (p. 176).

Temporary (nominal) accounts Accounts that relate only to a given accounting period. Consist of all income statement accounts and owner's drawings account. All temporary accounts are closed at end of the accounting period. (p. 160).

Worksheet A multiple-column form that may be used in making adjusting entries and in preparing financial statements. (p. 154).

APPENDIX4A

Reversing Entries

After preparing the financial statements and closing the books, it is often helpful to reverse some of the adjusting entries before recording the regular transactions of the next period. Such entries are **reversing entries**. Companies make **a reversing entry at the beginning of the next accounting period**. Each reversing entry **is the exact opposite of the adjusting entry made in the previous period**. The recording of reversing entries is an **optional step** in the accounting cycle.

Study Objective [7]
Prepare reversing entries.

The purpose of reversing entries is to simplify the recording of a subsequent transaction related to an adjusting entry. For example, in Chapter 3 (page 116), the payment of salaries after an adjusting entry resulted in two debits: one to Salaries and Wages Payable and the other to Salaries and Wages Expense. With reversing entries, the company can debit the entire subsequent payment to Salaries and Wages Expense. **The use of reversing entries does not change the amounts reported in the financial statements.** What it does is simplify the recording of subsequent transactions.

Reversing Entries Example

Companies most often use reversing entries to reverse two types of adjusting entries: accrued revenues and accrued expenses. To illustrate the optional use of reversing entries for accrued expenses, we will use the salaries expense transactions for Pioneer Advertising Agency as illustrated in Chapters 2, 3, and 4. The transaction and adjustment data are as follows.

1. October 26 (initial salary entry): Pioneer pays $4,000 of salaries and wages earned between October 15 and October 26.

2. October 31 (adjusting entry): Salaries and wages earned between October 29 and October 31 are $1,200. The company will pay these in the November 9 payroll.

3. November 9 (subsequent salary entry): Salaries and wages paid are $4,000. Of this amount, $1,200 applied to accrued salaries and wages payable and $2,800 was earned between November 1 and November 9.

Illustration 4A-1 (page 182) shows the entries with and without reversing entries.

The first three entries are the same whether or not Pioneer uses reversing entries. The last two entries are different. The November 1 **reversing entry** eliminates the $1,200 balance in Salaries and Wages Payable created by the October 31 adjusting entry. The reversing entry also creates a $1,200 credit balance in the Salaries and Wages Expense account. As you know, it is unusual for an expense account to have a credit balance. The balance is correct in this instance, though, because it anticipates that the entire amount of the first salaries and wages payment in the new accounting period will be debited to Salaries and Wages Expense. This debit will eliminate the credit balance. The resulting debit balance in the expense account will equal the salaries and wages expense incurred in the new accounting period ($2,800 in this example).

If Pioneer makes reversing entries, it can debit all cash payments of expenses to the expense account. This means that on November 9 (and every payday) Pioneer can debit Salaries and Wages Expense for the amount paid, without regard to any accrued salaries and wages payable. Being able to make the **same entry each time**

Without Reversing Entries **(per chapter)**			**With Reversing Entries** **(per appendix)**		
Initial Salary Entry			*Initial Salary Entry*		
Oct. 26 | Salaries and Wages Expense | Cash	4,000	4,000	Oct. 26 | (Same entry)		
Adjusting Entry			*Adjusting Entry*		
Oct. 31 | Salaries and Wages Expense | Salaries and Wages Payable	1,200	1,200	Oct. 31 | (Same entry)		
Closing Entry			*Closing Entry*		
Oct. 31 | Income Summary | Salaries and Wages Expense	5,200	5,200	Oct. 31 | (Same entry)		
Reversing Entry			*Reversing Entry*		
Nov. 1 | No reversing entry is made.			Nov. 1 | Salaries and Wages Payable | Salaries and Wages Expense	1,200	1,200
Subsequent Salary Entry			*Subsequent Salary Entry*		
Nov. 9 | Salaries and Wages Payable | Salaries and Wages Expense | Cash	1,200 2,800	4,000	Nov. 9 | Salaries and Wages Expense | Cash	4,000	4,000

Illustration 4A-1
Comparative entries—not
reversing vs. reversing

simplifies the recording process: The company can record subsequent transactions as if the related adjusting entry had never been made.

Illustration 4A-2 shows the posting of the entries with reversing entries.

Salaries and Wages Expense				**Salaries and Wages Payable**			
10/26 Paid 31 Adjusting	4,000 1,200	10/31 Closing	5,200	11/1 Reversing	1,200	10/31 Adjusting	1,200
	5,200		5,200				
11/9 Paid	4 ,000	11/1 Reversing	1,200				

Illustration 4A-2
Postings with reversing entries

A = L + OE

−200 Rev
−200

Cash Flows
no effect

A company can also use reversing entries for accrued revenue adjusting entries. For Pioneer Advertising, the adjusting entry was: Accounts Receivable (Dr.) $200 and Service Revenue (Cr.) $200. Thus, the reversing entry on November 1 is:

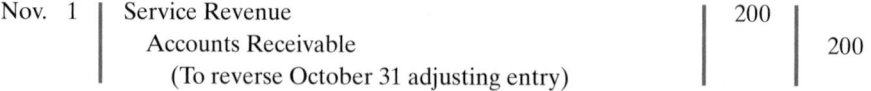

Nov. 1 | Service Revenue | Accounts Receivable | (To reverse October 31 adjusting entry)	200	200

When Pioneer collects the accrued service revenue, it debits Cash and credits Service Revenue.

Summary of Study Objective for Appendix 4A

[7] **Prepare reversing entries.** Reversing entries are the opposite of the adjusting entries made in the preceding period. Some companies choose to make reversing entries at the beginning of a new accounting period to simplify the recording of later transactions related to the adjusting entries. In most cases, only accrued adjusting entries are reversed.

Self-Test, Brief Exercises, Exercises, Problem Set A, and many more components are available for practice in *WileyPLUS*

*****Note:** All asterisked Questions, Exercises, and Problems relate to material in the appendix to the chapter.

Self-Test Questions

Answers are on page 204.

(SO 1)   **1.** Which of the following statements is *incorrect* concerning the worksheet?
  a. The worksheet is essentially a working tool of the accountant.
  b. The worksheet is distributed to management and other interested parties.
  c. The worksheet cannot be used as a basis for posting to ledger accounts.
  d. Financial statements can be prepared directly from the worksheet before journalizing and posting the adjusting entries.

(SO 1)   **2.** In a worksheet, net income is entered in the following columns:
  a. income statement (Dr) and balance sheet (Dr).
  b. income statement (Cr) and balance sheet (Dr).
  c. income statement (Dr) and balance sheet (Cr).
  d. income statement (Cr) and balance sheet (Cr).

(SO 1)   **3.** In the unadjusted trial balance of its worksheet for the year ended December 31, 2012, Taitum Company reported Equipment of $120,000. The year-end adjusting entries require an adjustment of $15,000 for depreciation expense for the equipment. After adjustment, the following adjusted amount should be reported:
  a. A debit of $105,000 for Equipment in the balance sheet column.
  b. A credit of $15,000 for Depreciation Expense—Equipment in the income statement column.
  c. A debit of $120,000 for Equipment in the balance sheet column.
  d. A debit of $15,000 for Accumulated Depreciation—Equipment in the balance sheet column.

(SO 2)   **4.** An account that will have a zero balance after closing entries have been journalized and posted is:
  a. Service Revenue.
  b. Supplies.
  c. Prepaid Insurance.
  d. Accumulated Depreciation—Equipment.

(SO 2)   **5.** When a net loss has occurred, Income Summary is:
  a. debited and Owner's Capital is credited.
  b. credited and Owner's Capital is debited.
  c. debited and Owner's Drawings is credited.
  d. credited and Owner's Drawings is debited.

(SO 2)   **6.** The closing process involves separate entries to close (1) expenses, (2) drawings, (3) revenues, and (4) income summary. The correct sequencing of the entries is:
  a. (4), (3), (2), (1)   **c.** (3), (1), (4), (2)
  b. (1), (2), (3), (4)   **d.** (3), (2), (1), (4)

(SO 3)   **7.** Which types of accounts will appear in the post-closing trial balance?

  a. Permanent (real) accounts.
  b. Temporary (nominal) accounts.
  c. Accounts shown in the income statement columns of a worksheet.
  d. None of the above.

8. All of the following are required steps in the accounting   (SO 4)
cycle *except*:
  a. journalizing and posting closing entries.
  b. preparing financial statements.
  c. journalizing the transactions.
  d. preparing a worksheet.

9. The proper order of the following steps in the accounting   (SO 4)
cycle is:
  a. prepare unadjusted trial balance, journalize transactions, post to ledger accounts, journalize and post adjusting entries.
  b. journalize transactions, prepare unadjusted trial balance, post to ledger accounts, journalize and post adjusting entries.
  c. journalize transactions, post to ledger accounts, prepare unadjusted trial balance, journalize and post adjusting entries.
  d. prepare unadjusted trial balance, journalize and post adjusting entries, journalize transactions, post to ledger accounts.

10. When Alexander Company purchased supplies worth   (SO 5)
$500, it incorrectly recorded a credit to Supplies for $5,000 and a debit to Cash for $5,000. Before correcting this error:
  a. Cash is overstated and Supplies is overstated.
  b. Cash is understated and Supplies is understated.
  c. Cash is understated and Supplies is overstated.
  d. Cash is overstated and Supplies is understated.

11. Cash of $100 received at the time the service was provided   (SO 5)
was journalized and posted as a debit to Cash $100 and a credit to Accounts Receivable $100. Assuming the incorrect entry is not reversed, the correcting entry is:
  a. debit Service Revenue $100 and credit Accounts Receivable $100.
  b. debit Accounts Receivable $100 and credit Service Revenue $100.
  c. debit Cash $100 and credit Service Revenue $100.
  d. debit Accounts Receivable $100 and credit Cash $100.

12. The correct order of presentation in a classified balance   (SO 6)
sheet for the following current assets is:
  a. accounts receivable, cash, prepaid insurance, inventory.
  b. cash, inventory, accounts receivable, prepaid insurance.
  c. cash, accounts receivable, inventory, prepaid insurance.
  d. inventory, cash, accounts receivable, prepaid insurance.

(SO 6) **13.** A company has purchased a tract of land. It expects to build a production plant on the land in approximately 5 years. During the 5 years before construction, the land will be idle. The land should be reported as:

    a. property, plant, and equipment.
    b. land expense.
    c. a long-term investment.
    d. an intangible asset.

(SO 6) **14.** In a classified balance sheet, assets are usually classified using the following categories:

    a. current assets; long-term assets; property, plant, and equipment; and intangible assets.
    b. current assets; long-term investments; property, plant, and equipment; and tangible assets.
    c. current assets; long-term investments; tangible assets; and intangible assets.
    d. current assets; long-term investments; property, plant, and equipment; and intangible assets.

(SO 6) **15.** Current assets are listed:

    a. by expected conversion to cash.
    b. by importance.

    c. by longevity.
    d. alphabetically.

*16. On December 31, Frank Voris Company correctly made (SO 7) an adjusting entry to recognize $2,000 of accrued salaries payable. On January 8 of the next year, total salaries of $3,400 were paid. Assuming the correct reversing entry was made on January 1, the entry on January 8 will result in a credit to Cash $3,400 and the following debit(s):

    a. Salaries and Wages Payable $1,400, and Salaries and Wages Expense $2,000.
    b. Salaries and Wages Payable $2,000 and Salaries and Wages Expense $1,400.
    c. Salaries and Wages Expense $3,400.
    d. Salaries and Wages Payable $3,400.

Go to the book's companion website, **www.wiley.com/college/weygandt**, for additional Self-Test Questions.

Questions

1. "A worksheet is a permanent accounting record and its use is required in the accounting cycle." Do you agree? Explain.

2. Explain the purpose of the worksheet.

3. What is the relationship, if any, between the amount shown in the adjusted trial balance column for an account and that account's ledger balance?

4. If a company's revenues are $125,000 and its expenses are $113,000, in which financial statement columns of the worksheet will the net income of $12,000 appear? When expenses exceed revenues, in which columns will the difference appear?

5. Why is it necessary to prepare formal financial statements if all of the data are in the statement columns of the worksheet?

6. Identify the account(s) debited and credited in each of the four closing entries, assuming the company has net income for the year.

7. Describe the nature of the Income Summary account and identify the types of summary data that may be posted to this account.

8. What are the content and purpose of a post-closing trial balance?

9. Which of the following accounts would not appear in the post-closing trial balance? Interest Payable; Equipment; Depreciation Expense; Owner's Drawings; Unearned Service Revenue; Accumulated Depreciation—Equipment; and Service Revenue.

10. Distinguish between a reversing entry and an adjusting entry. Are reversing entries required?

11. Indicate, in the sequence in which they are made, the three required steps in the accounting cycle that involve journalizing.

12. Identify, in the sequence in which they are prepared, the three trial balances that are often used to report financial information about a company.

13. How do correcting entries differ from adjusting entries?

14. What standard classifications are used in preparing a classified balance sheet?

15. What is meant by the term "operating cycle?"

16. Define current assets. What basis is used for arranging individual items within the current assets section?

17. Distinguish between long-term investments and property, plant, and equipment.

18. (a) What is the term used to describe the owner's equity section of a corporation? (b) Identify the two owners' equity accounts in a corporation and indicate the purpose of each.

19. ⬤ **PEPSICO** Using PepsiCo's annual report, determine its current liabilities at December 26, 2009, and December 27, 2008. Were current liabilities higher or lower than current assets in these two years?

*20. Sanchez Company prepares reversing entries. If the adjusting entry for interest payable is reversed, what type of an account balance, if any, will there be in Interest Payable and Interest Expense after the reversing entry is posted?

*21. At December 31, accrued salaries payable totaled $3,500. On January 10, total salaries of $8,000 are paid. (a) Assume that reversing entries are made at January 1. Give the January 10 entry, and indicate the Salaries and Wages Expense account balance after the entry is posted. (b) Repeat part (a) assuming reversing entries are not made.

Brief Exercises

BE4-1 The steps in using a worksheet are presented in random order below. List the steps in the proper order by placing numbers 1–5 in the blank spaces.

(a) _____ Prepare a trial balance on the worksheet.
(b) _____ Enter adjusted balances.
(c) _____ Extend adjusted balances to appropriate statement columns.
(d) _____ Total the statement columns, compute net income (loss), and complete the worksheet.
(e) _____ Enter adjustment data.

List the steps in preparing a worksheet.
(SO 1)

BE4-2 The ledger of Saddler Company includes the following unadjusted balances: Prepaid Insurance $3,000, Service Revenue $58,000, and Salaries and Wages Expense $25,000. Adjusting entries are required for (a) expired insurance $1,800; (b) services provided $1,100, but unbilled and uncollected; and (c) accrued salaries payable $800. Enter the unadjusted balances and adjustments into a worksheet and complete the worksheet for all accounts. *Note:* You will need to add the following accounts: Accounts Receivable, Salaries and Wages Payable, and Insurance Expense.

Prepare partial worksheet.
(SO 1)

BE4-3 The following selected accounts appear in the adjusted trial balance columns of the worksheet for McQueen Company: Accumulated Depreciation; Depreciation Expense; Owner's Capital; Owner's Drawings; Service Revenue; Supplies; and Accounts Payable. Indicate the financial statement column (income statement Dr., balance sheet Cr., etc.) to which each balance should be extended.

Identify worksheet columns for selected accounts.
(SO 1)

BE4-4 The ledger of Quentin Company contains the following balances: Owner's Capital $30,000; Owner's Drawings $2,000; Service Revenue $50,000; Salaries and Wages Expense $27,000; and Supplies Expense $7,000. Prepare the closing entries at December 31.

Prepare closing entries from ledger balances.
(SO 2)

BE4-5 Using the data in BE4-4, enter the balances in T accounts, post the closing entries, and rule and balance the accounts.

Post closing entries; rule and balance T accounts.
(SO 2)

BE4-6 The income statement for Evergreen Golf Club for the month ending July 31 shows Service Revenue $16,400, Salaries and Wages Expense $8,200, Maintenance and Repairs Expense $2,500, and Net Income $5,700. Prepare the entries to close the revenue and expense accounts. Post the entries to the revenue and expense accounts, and complete the closing process for these accounts using the three-column form of account.

Journalize and post closing entries using the three-column form of account.
(SO 2)

BE4-7 Using the data in BE4-3, identify the accounts that would be included in a post-closing trial balance.

Identify post-closing trial balance accounts.
(SO 3)

BE4-8 The steps in the accounting cycle are listed in random order below. List the steps in proper sequence, assuming no worksheet is prepared, by placing numbers 1–9 in the blank spaces.

(a) _____ Prepare a trial balance.
(b) _____ Journalize the transactions.
(c) _____ Journalize and post closing entries.
(d) _____ Prepare financial statements.
(e) _____ Journalize and post adjusting entries.
(f) _____ Post to ledger accounts.
(g) _____ Prepare a post-closing trial balance.
(h) _____ Prepare an adjusted trial balance.
(i) _____ Analyze business transactions.

List the required steps in the accounting cycle in sequence.
(SO 4)

BE4-9 At Shaffer Company, the following errors were discovered after the transactions had been journalized and posted. Prepare the correcting entries.

1. A collection on account from a customer for $870 was recorded as a debit to Cash $870 and a credit to Service Revenue $870.
2. The purchase of store supplies on account for $1,570 was recorded as a debit to Supplies $1,750 and a credit to Accounts Payable $1,750.

Prepare correcting entries.
(SO 5)

BE4-10 The balance sheet debit column of the worksheet for Shaw Company includes the following accounts: Accounts Receivable $12,500; Prepaid Insurance $3,600; Cash $4,100; Supplies $5,200, and Short-term Investments $6,700. Prepare the current assets section of the balance sheet, listing the accounts in proper sequence.

Prepare the current assets section of a balance sheet.
(SO 6)

Classify accounts on balance sheet.

(SO 6)

BE4-11   The following are the major balance sheet classifications:

Current assets (CA)   Current liabilities (CL)
Long-term investments (LTI)   Long-term liabilities (LTL)
Property, plant, and equipment (PPE)   Owner's equity (OE)
Intangible assets (IA)

Match each of the following accounts to its proper balance sheet classification.

_____ Accounts payable   _____ Income taxes payable
_____ Accounts receivable   _____ Debt investment (long-term)
_____ Accumulated depreciation—buildings   _____ Land
_____ Buildings   _____ Inventory
_____ Cash   _____ Patents
_____ Copyrights   _____ Supplies

Prepare reversing entries.

(SO 7)

*****BE4-12**   At October 31, Steltz Company made an accrued expense adjusting entry of $2,100 for salaries. Prepare the reversing entry on November 1, and indicate the balances in Salaries and Wages Payable and Salaries and Wages Expense after posting the reversing entry.

Do it! Review

Prepare a worksheet.

(SO 1)

Do it! 4-1   Averell Spicer is preparing a worksheet. Explain to Averell how he should extend the following adjusted trial balance accounts to the financial statement columns of the worksheet.

Service Revenue   Accounts Receivable
Notes Payable   Accumulated Depreciation
Owner's Capital   Utilities Expense

Prepare closing entries.

(SO 5)

Do it! 4-2   The worksheet for Ta'ufo'ou Company shows the following in the financial statement columns.

Owner's drawings $22,000
Owner's capital   70,000
Net income   41,000

Prepare the closing entries at December 31 that affect owner's capital.

Prepare assets section of the balance sheet.

(SO 6)

Do it! 4-3   Chester Taylor recently received the following information related to Taylor Company's December 31, 2012, balance sheet.

Inventory $ 2,900   Short-term investments $1,200
Cash   4,300   Accumulated depreciation   5,700
Equipment   21,700   Accounts receivable   4,300
Investments in stock (long-term)   6,500

Prepare the assets section of Taylor Company's classified balance sheet.

Match accounts to balance sheet classifications.

(SO 6)

Do it! 4-4   The following accounts were taken from the financial statements of Tillman Company.

_____ Interest revenue   _____ Owner's capital
_____ Utilities payable   _____ Accumulated depreciation
_____ Accounts payable   _____ Equipment
_____ Supplies   _____ Salaries and wages expense
_____ Bonds payable   _____ Investment in real estate
_____ Trademarks   _____ Unearned rent revenue

Match each of the accounts to its proper balance sheet classification, as shown below. If the item would not appear on a balance sheet, use "NA."

Current assets (CA)   Current liabilities (CL)
Long-term investments (LTI)   Long-term liabilities (LTL)
Property, plant, and equipment (PPE)   Owner's equity (OE)
Intangible assets (IA)

Exercises

E4-1 The trial balance columns of the worksheet for Tinoisamoa Company at June 30, 2012,   *Complete the worksheet.*
are as follows.   (SO 1)

TINOISAMOA COMPANY
Worksheet
For the Month Ended June 30, 2012

Account Titles	Trial Balance Dr.	Trial Balance Cr.
Cash	$2,320	
Accounts Receivable	2,440	
Supplies	1,880	
Accounts Payable		$1,120
Unearned Service Revenue		240
Owner's Capital		3,600
Service Revenue		2,400
Salaries and Wages Expense	560	
Miscellaneous Expense	160	
	$7,360	$7,360

Other data:

1. A physical count reveals $500 of supplies on hand.
2. $100 of the unearned revenue is still unearned at month-end.
3. Accrued salaries are $210.

Instructions
Enter the trial balance on a worksheet and complete the worksheet.

E4-2 The adjusted trial balance columns of the worksheet for Pisa Company are as follows.   *Complete the worksheet.*
(SO 1)

PISA COMPANY
Worksheet (partial)
For the Month Ended April 30, 2012

Account Titles	Adjusted Trial Balance Dr.	Adjusted Trial Balance Cr.	Income Statement Dr.	Income Statement Cr.	Balance Sheet Dr.	Balance Sheet Cr.
Cash	10,000					
Accounts Receivable	7,840					
Prepaid Rent	2,280					
Equipment	23,050					
Accumulated Depreciation—Equip.		4,921				
Notes Payable		5,700				
Accounts Payable		4,920				
Owner's Capital		27,960				
Owner's Drawings	3,650					
Service Revenue		15,590				
Salaries and Wages Expense	10,840					
Rent Expense	760					
Depreciation Expense	671					
Interest Expense	57					
Interest Payable		57				
Totals	59,148	59,148				

Instructions
Complete the worksheet.

Prepare financial statements from worksheet.

(SO 1, 6)

E4-3 Worksheet data for Pisa Company are presented in E4-2. The owner did not make any additional investments in the business in April.

Instructions

Prepare an income statement, an owner's equity statement, and a classified balance sheet.

Journalize and post closing entries and prepare a post-closing trial balance.

(SO 2, 3)

E4-4 Worksheet data for Pisa Company are presented in E4-2.

Instructions

(a) Journalize the closing entries at April 30.
(b) Post the closing entries to Income Summary and Owner's Capital. Use T accounts.
(c) Prepare a post-closing trial balance at April 30.

Prepare adjusting entries from a worksheet, and extend balances to worksheet columns.

(SO 1)

E4-5 The adjustments columns of the worksheet for Toeaina Company are shown below.

	Adjustments	
Account Titles	**Debit**	**Credit**
Accounts Receivable	1,100	
Prepaid Insurance		300
Accumulated Depreciation—Equipment		900
Salaries and Wages Payable		500
Service Revenue		1,100
Salaries and Wages Expense	500	
Insurance Expense	300	
Depreciation Expense	900	
	2,800	2,800

Instructions

(a) Prepare the adjusting entries.
(b) Assuming the adjusted trial balance amount for each account is normal, indicate the financial statement column to which each balance should be extended.

Derive adjusting entries from worksheet data.

(SO 1)

E4-6 Selected worksheet data for Woodny Company are presented below.

Account Titles	**Trial Balance**		**Adjusted Trial Balance**	
	Dr.	**Cr.**	**Dr.**	**Cr.**
Accounts Receivable	?		34,000	
Prepaid Insurance	26,000		20,000	
Supplies	7,000		?	
Accumulated Depreciation—Equipment		12,000		?
Salaries and Wages Payable		?		5,600
Service Revenue		88,000		97,000
Insurance Expense			?	
Depreciation Expense			10,000	
Supplies Expense			4,500	
Salaries and Wages Expense	?		49,000	

Instructions

(a) Fill in the missing amounts.
(b) Prepare the adjusting entries that were made.

Prepare closing entries, and prepare a post-closing trial balance.

(SO 2, 3)

E4-7 Willow Turenne Company had the following adjusted trial balance.

WILLOW TURENNE COMPANY
Adjusted Trial Balance
For the Month Ended June 30, 2012

Account Titles	Adjusted Trial Balance Debits	Credits
Cash	$ 3,712	
Accounts Receivable	3,904	
Supplies	480	
Accounts Payable		$ 1,556
Unearned Service Revenue		160
Owner's Capital		5,760
Owner's Drawings	628	
Service Revenue		4,300
Salaries and Wages Expense	1,344	
Miscellaneous Expense	256	
Supplies Expense	1,900	
Salaries and Wages Payable		448
	$12,224	$12,224

Instructions
(a) Prepare closing entries at June 30, 2012.
(b) Prepare a post-closing trial balance.

E4-8 Turner Company ended its fiscal year on July 31, 2012. The company's adjusted trial balance as of the end of its fiscal year is as shown below.

Journalize and post closing entries, and prepare a post-closing trial balance.
(SO 2, 3)

TURNER COMPANY
Adjusted Trial Balance
July 31, 2012

No.	Account Titles	Debits	Credits
101	Cash	$ 9,840	
112	Accounts Receivable	8,780	
157	Equipment	15,900	
167	Accumulated Depreciation—Equip.		$ 7,400
201	Accounts Payable		4,220
208	Unearned Rent Revenue		1,800
301	Owner's Capital		45,200
306	Owner's Drawings	16,000	
404	Service Revenue		64,000
429	Rent Revenue		6,500
711	Depreciation Expense	8,000	
720	Salaries and Wages Expense	55,700	
732	Utilities Expense	14,900	
		$129,120	$129,120

Instructions
(a) Prepare the closing entries using page J15.
(b) Post to Owner's Capital and No. 350 Income Summary accounts. (Use the three-column form.)
(c) Prepare a post-closing trial balance at July 31.

E4-9 The adjusted trial balance for Turner Company is presented in E4-8.

Prepare financial statements.
(SO 6)

Instructions
(a) Prepare an income statement and an owner's equity statement for the year. Turner did not make any capital investments during the year.
(b) Prepare a classified balance sheet at July 31.

Answer questions related to the accounting cycle.
(SO 4)

E4-10   Vince Vance has prepared the following list of statements about the accounting cycle.

1. "Journalize the transactions" is the first step in the accounting cycle.
2. Reversing entries are a required step in the accounting cycle.
3. Correcting entries do not have to be part of the accounting cycle.
4. If a worksheet is prepared, some steps of the accounting cycle are incorporated into the worksheet.
5. The accounting cycle begins with the analysis of business transactions and ends with the preparation of a post-closing trial balance.
6. All steps of the accounting cycle occur daily during the accounting period.
7. The step of "post to the ledger accounts" occurs before the step of "journalize the transactions."
8. Closing entries must be prepared before financial statements can be prepared.

Instructions
Identify each statement as true or false. If false, indicate how to correct the statement.

Prepare closing entries.
(SO 2)

E4-11   Selected accounts for Brianna's Salon are presented below. All June 30 postings are from closing entries.

Salaries and Wages Expense				Service Revenue				Owner's Capital			
6/10	3,200	6/30	8,800	6/30	18,100	6/15	9,700	6/30	2,500	6/1	12,000
6/28	5,600					6/24	8,400			6/30	5,000
										Bal.	14,500

Supplies Expense				Rent Expense				Owner's Drawings			
6/12	600	6/30	1,300	6/1	3,000	6/30	3,000	6/13	1,000	6/30	2,500
6/24	700							6/25	1,500		

Instructions
(a) Prepare the closing entries that were made.
(b) Post the closing entries to Income Summary.

Prepare correcting entries.
(SO 5)

E4-12   J'Morcus Webb Company discovered the following errors made in January 2012.

1. A payment of Salaries and Wages Expense of $700 was debited to Equipment and credited to Cash, both for $700.
2. A collection of $1,000 from a client on account was debited to Cash $100 and credited to Service Revenue $100.
3. The purchase of equipment on account for $760 was debited to Equipment $670 and credited to Accounts Payable $670.

Instructions
(a) Correct the errors by reversing the incorrect entry and preparing the correct entry.
(b) Correct the errors without reversing the incorrect entry.

Prepare correcting entries.
(SO 5)

E4-13   Williams Company has an inexperienced accountant. During the first 2 weeks on the job, the accountant made the following errors in journalizing transactions. All entries were posted as made.

1. A payment on account of $840 to a creditor was debited to Accounts Payable $480 and credited to Cash $480.
2. The purchase of supplies on account for $560 was debited to Equipment $56 and credited to Accounts Payable $56.
3. A $500 withdrawal of cash for C. Williams' personal use was debited to Salaries and Wages Expense $500 and credited to Cash $500.

Instructions
Prepare the correcting entries.

Prepare a classified balance sheet.
(SO 6)

E4-14   The adjusted trial balance for Wootton Bowling Alley at December 31, 2012, contains the following accounts.

Debits		Credits	
Buildings	$128,800	Owner's Capital	$115,000
Accounts Receivable	14,520	Accumulated Depreciation—Buildings	42,600
Prepaid Insurance	4,680	Accounts Payable	12,300
Cash	18,040	Notes Payable	97,780
Equipment	62,400	Accumulated Depreciation—Equipment	18,720
Land	67,000	Interest Payable	2,600
Insurance Expense	780	Service Revenue	17,180
Depreciation Expense	7,360		$306,180
Interest Expense	2,600		
	$306,180		

Instructions

(a) Prepare a classified balance sheet; assume that $22,000 of the note payable will be paid in 2013.

(b) ➤ Comment on the liquidity of the company.

E4-15 The following are the major balance sheet classifications.

Classify accounts on balance sheet.

(SO 6)

Current assets (CA)   Current liabilities (CL)
Long-term investments (LTI)   Long-term liabilities (LTL)
Property, plant, and equipment (PPE)   Owner's equity (OE)
Intangible assets (IA)

Instructions

Classify each of the following accounts taken from E. Williams Company's balance sheet.

_____ Accounts payable   _____ Accumulated depreciation
_____ Accounts receivable   _____ Buildings
_____ Cash   _____ Land
_____ Owner's capital   _____ Long-term debt
_____ Patents   _____ Supplies
_____ Salaries and wages payable _____ Equipment
_____ Inventory   _____ Prepaid expenses
_____ Investments

E4-16 The following items were taken from the financial statements of M. Wright Company. (All dollars are in thousands.)

Prepare a classified balance sheet.

(SO 6)

Long-term debt	$ 1,000	Accumulated depreciation	5,655
Prepaid insurance	880	Accounts payable	1,444
Equipment	11,500	Notes payable (due after 2013)	400
Long-term investments	264	Owner's capital	12,955
Short-term investments	3,690	Accounts receivable	1,696
Notes payable (due in 2013)	500	Inventory	1,256
Cash	$ 2,668		

Instructions

Prepare a classified balance sheet in good form as of December 31, 2012.

E4-17 These financial statement items are for Major Company at year-end, July 31, 2012.

Prepare financial statements.

(SO 1, 6)

Salaries and wages payable	$ 2,080	Notes payable (long-term)	$ 1,800
Salaries and wages expense	51,700	Cash	14,200
Utilities expense	22,600	Accounts receivable	9,780
Equipment	30,400	Accumulated depreciation—equip.	6,000
Accounts payable	4,100	Owner's drawings	3,000
Service revenue	62,000	Depreciation expense	4,000
Rent revenue	8,500	Owner's Capital (beginning of the year)	51,200

Instructions

(a) Prepare an income statement and an owner's equity statement for the year. The owner did not make any new investments during the year.

(b) Prepare a classified balance sheet at July 31.

Use reversing entries.
(SO 7)

*E4-18 Alexander Company pays salaries of $12,000 every Monday for the preceding 5-day week (Monday through Friday). Assume December 31 falls on a Tuesday, so Alexander's employees have worked 2 days without being paid.

Instructions

(a) Assume the company does not use reversing entries. Prepare the December 31 adjusting entry and the entry on Monday, January 6, when Alexander pays the payroll.

(b) Assume the company does use reversing entries. Prepare the December 31 adjusting entry, the January 1 reversing entry, and the entry on Monday, January 6, when Alexander pays the payroll.

Prepare closing and reversing entries.
(SO 2, 4, 7)

*E4-19 On December 31, the adjusted trial balance of Johnson Employment Agency shows the following selected data.

Accounts Receivable	$24,500	Service Revenue	$92,500
Interest Expense	8,300	Interest Payable	2,000

Analysis shows that adjusting entries were made to (1) accrue $5,000 of service revenue and (2) accrue $2,000 interest expense.

Instructions

(a) Prepare the closing entries for the temporary accounts shown above at December 31.

(b) Prepare the reversing entries on January 1.

(c) Post the entries in (a) and (b). Rule and balance the accounts. (Use T accounts.)

(d) Prepare the entries to record (1) the collection of the accrued revenue on January 10 and (2) the payment of all interest due ($3,000) on January 15.

(e) Post the entries in (d) to the temporary accounts.

Exercises: Set B

Visit the book's companion website, at **www.wiley.com/college/weygandt**, and choose the Student Companion site to access Exercise Set B.

Problems: Set A

Prepare worksheet, financial statements, and adjusting and closing entries.
(SO 1, 2, 3, 6)

P4-1A Omer Asik began operations as a private investigator on January 1, 2012. The trial balance columns of the worksheet for Omer Asik, P.I. at March 31 are as follows.

OMER ASIK, P.I.
Worksheet
For the Quarter Ended March 31, 2012

Account Titles	Trial Balance	
	Dr.	**Cr.**
Cash	11,400	
Accounts Receivable	5,620	
Supplies	1,050	
Prepaid Insurance	2,400	
Equipment	30,000	
Notes Payable		10,000
Accounts Payable		12,350
Owner's Capital		20,000
Owner's Drawings	600	
Service Revenue		13,620
Salaries and Wages Expense	2,200	
Travel Expense	1,300	
Rent Expense	1,200	
Miscellaneous Expense	200	
	55,970	55,970

Other data:

1. Supplies on hand total $480.
2. Depreciation is $800 per quarter.
3. Interest accrued on 6-month note payable, issued January 1, $300.
4. Insurance expires at the rate of $200 per month.
5. Services provided but unbilled at March 31 total $1,030.

Instructions

(a) Enter the trial balance on a worksheet and complete the worksheet.

(b) Prepare an income statement and owner's equity statement for the quarter and a classified balance sheet at March 31. O. Asik did not make any additional investments in the business during the quarter ended March 31, 2012.

(c) Journalize the adjusting entries from the adjustments columns of the worksheet.

(d) Journalize the closing entries from the financial statement columns of the worksheet.

(a) Adjusted trial balance $58,100

(b) Net income $7,480
Total assets $49,530

P4-2A The adjusted trial balance columns of the worksheet for Boozer Company are as follows.

Complete worksheet; prepare financial statements, closing entries, and post-closing trial balance.

(SO 1, 2, 3, 6)

BOOZER COMPANY
Worksheet
For the Year Ended December 31, 2012

Account No.	Account Titles	Adjusted Trial Balance Dr.	Cr.
101	Cash	18,800	
112	Accounts Receivable	16,200	
126	Supplies	2,300	
130	Prepaid Insurance	4,400	
151	Equipment	46,000	
152	Accumulated Depreciation—Equipment		20,000
200	Notes Payable		20,000
201	Accounts Payable		8,000
212	Salaries and Wages Payable		2,600
230	Interest Payable		1,000
301	Owner's Capital		26,000
306	Owner's Drawings	12,000	
400	Service Revenue		87,800
610	Advertising Expense	10,000	
631	Supplies Expense	3,700	
711	Depreciation Expense	8,000	
722	Insurance Expense	4,000	
726	Salaries and Wages Expense	39,000	
905	Interest Expense	1,000	
	Totals	165,400	165,400

Instructions

(a) Complete the worksheet by extending the balances to the financial statement columns.

(b) Prepare an income statement, owner's equity statement, and a classified balance sheet. $5,000 of the notes payable become due in 2013. C. Boozer did not make any additional investments in the business during 2012.

(c) Prepare the closing entries. Use J14 for the journal page.

(d) Post the closing entries. Use the three-column form of account. Income Summary is account No. 350.

(e) Prepare a post-closing trial balance.

(a) Net income $22,100

(b) Current assets $41,700
Current liabilities $16,600

(e) Post-closing trial balance $87,700

Prepare financial statements, closing entries, and post-closing trial balance.

(SO 1, 2, 3, 6)

P4-3A The completed financial statement columns of the worksheet for Carlos Company are shown on the next page.

CARLOS COMPANY
Worksheet
For the Year Ended December 31, 2012

Account No.	Account Titles	Income Statement Dr.	Income Statement Cr.	Balance Sheet Dr.	Balance Sheet Cr.
101	Cash			6,200	
112	Accounts Receivable			7,500	
130	Prepaid Insurance			1,800	
157	Equipment			33,000	
167	Accumulated Depreciation—Equip.				8,600
201	Accounts Payable				11,700
212	Salaries and Wages Payable				3,000
301	Owner's Capital				34,000
306	Owner's Drawings			7,200	
400	Service Revenue		46,000		
622	Maintenance and Repairs Expense	4,400			
711	Depreciation Expense	2,800			
722	Insurance Expense	1,200			
726	Salaries and Wages Expense	35,200			
732	Utilities Expense	4,000			
	Totals	47,600	46,000	55,700	57,300
	Net Loss		1,600	1,600	
		47,600	47,600	57,300	57,300

Instructions

(a) Net loss $1,600
   Ending capital $25,200
   Total assets $39,900

(d Post-closing trial balance
   $48,500

(a) Prepare an income statement, owner's equity statement, and a classified balance sheet. B. Carlos made an additional investment in the business of $4,000 during 2012.

(b) Prepare the closing entries.

(c) Post the closing entries and rule and balance the accounts. Use T accounts. Income Summary is account No. 350.

(d) Prepare a post-closing trial balance.

Complete worksheet; prepare classified balance sheet, entries, and post-closing trial balance.

(SO 1, 2, 3, 6)

P4-4A Noah Amusement Park has a fiscal year ending on September 30. Selected data from the September 30 worksheet are presented below.

NOAH AMUSEMENT PARK
Worksheet
For the Year Ended September 30, 2012

	Trial Balance Dr.	Trial Balance Cr.	Adjusted Trial Balance Dr.	Adjusted Trial Balance Cr.
Cash	41,400		41,400	
Supplies	18,600		2,200	
Prepaid Insurance	31,900		10,900	
Land	80,000		80,000	
Equipment	120,000		120,000	
Accumulated Depreciation—Equip.		36,200		42,200
Accounts Payable		14,600		14,600
Unearned Ticket Revenue		3,700		1,000
Mortgage Payable		50,000		50,000
Owner's Capital		109,700		109,700
Owner's Drawings	14,000		14,000	
Ticket Revenue		277,500		280,200
Salaries and Wages Expense	105,000		105,000	
Maintenance and Repairs Expense	30,500		30,500	
Advertising Expense	9,400		9,400	
Utilities Expense	16,900		16,900	

Property Tax Expense	18,000		21,000
Interest Expense	6,000		10,000
Totals	491,700	491,700	
Insurance Expense			21,000
Supplies Expense			16,400
Interest Payable			4,000
Depreciation Expense		6,000	
Property Taxes Payable			3,000
Totals		504,700	504,700

Instructions

(a) Prepare a complete worksheet.

(b) Prepare a classified balance sheet. (*Note:* $15,000 of the mortgage note payable is due for payment in the next fiscal year.)

(c) Journalize the adjusting entries using the worksheet as a basis.

(d) Journalize the closing entries using the worksheet as a basis.

(e) Prepare a post-closing trial balance.

(a) Net income $44,000

(b) Total current assets $54,500

(e) Post-closing trial balance $254,500

P4-5A   Devine Brown opened Devine's Carpet Cleaners on March 1. During March, the following transactions were completed.

Complete all steps in accounting cycle.

(SO 1, 2, 3, 4, 6)

Mar. 1	Invested $10,000 cash in the business.
1	Purchased used truck for $6,000, paying $3,000 cash and the balance on account.
3	Purchased cleaning supplies for $1,200 on account.
5	Paid $1,200 cash on one-year insurance policy effective March 1.
14	Billed customers $4,800 for cleaning services.
18	Paid $1,500 cash on amount owed on truck and $500 on amount owed on cleaning supplies.
20	Paid $1,800 cash for employee salaries.
21	Collected $1,400 cash from customers billed on March 14.
28	Billed customers $2,500 for cleaning services.
31	Paid gasoline for month on truck $200.
31	Withdrew $700 cash for personal use.

The chart of accounts for Devine's Carpet Cleaners contains the following accounts: No. 101 Cash, No. 112 Accounts Receivable, No. 128 Supplies, No. 130 Prepaid Insurance, No. 157 Equipment, No. 158 Accumulated Depreciation—Equipment, No. 201 Accounts Payable, No. 212 Salaries and Wages Payable, No. 301 Owner's Capital, No. 306 Owner's Drawings, No. 350 Income Summary, No. 400 Service Revenue, No. 633 Gasoline Expense, No. 634 Supplies Expense, No. 711 Depreciation Expense, No. 722 Insurance Expense, and No. 726 Salaries and Wages Expense.

Instructions

(a) Journalize and post the March transactions. Use page J1 for the journal and the three-column form of account.

(b) Prepare a trial balance at March 31 on a worksheet.

(c) Enter the following adjustments on the worksheet and complete the worksheet.

   (1) Earned but unbilled revenue at March 31 was $500.

   (2) Depreciation on equipment for the month was $300.

   (3) One-twelfth of the insurance expired.

   (4) An inventory count shows $250 of cleaning supplies on hand at March 31.

   (5) Accrued but unpaid employee salaries were $550.

(d) Prepare the income statement and owner's equity statement for March and a classified balance sheet at March 31.

(e) Journalize and post adjusting entries. Use page J2 for the journal.

(f) Journalize and post closing entries and complete the closing process. Use page J3 for the journal.

(g) Prepare a post-closing trial balance at March 31.

(b) Trial balance $19,500

(c) Adjusted trial balance $20,850

(d) Net income $3,900
Total assets $15,950

(g) Post-closing trial balance $16,250

P4-6A   Luol Deng CPA, was retained by Acie Cable to prepare financial statements for April 2012. Deng accumulated all the ledger balances per Acie's records and found the following.

Analyze errors and prepare correcting entries and trial balance.

(SO 5)

ACIE CABLE
Trial Balance
April 30, 2012

	Debit	Credit
Cash	$ 4,100	
Accounts Receivable	3,200	
Supplies	800	
Equipment	10,600	
Accumulated Depreciation—Equip.		$ 1,350
Accounts Payable		2,100
Salaries and Wages Payable		700
Unearned Service Revenue		890
Owner's Capital		12,900
Service Revenue		5,450
Salaries and Wages Expense	3,300	
Advertising Expense	600	
Miscellaneous Expense	290	
Depreciation Expense	500	
	$23,390	$23,390

Luol Deng reviewed the records and found the following errors.

1. Cash received from a customer on account was recorded as $950 instead of $590.
2. A payment of $75 for advertising expense was entered as a debit to Miscellaneous Expense $75 and a credit to Cash $75.
3. The first salary payment this month was for $1,900, which included $700 of salaries payable on March 31. The payment was recorded as a debit to Salaries and Wages Expense $1,900 and a credit to Cash $1,900. (No reversing entries were made on April 1.)
4. The purchase on account of a printer costing $310 was recorded as a debit to Supplies and a credit to Accounts Payable for $310.
5. A cash payment of repair expense on equipment for $96 was recorded as a debit to Equipment $69 and a credit to Cash $69.

Instructions

(a) Prepare an analysis of each error showing (1) the incorrect entry, (2) the correct entry, and (3) the correcting entry. Items 4 and 5 occurred on April 30, 2012.

Trial balance $22,690

(b) Prepare a correct trial balance.

Problems: Set B

Prepare a worksheet, financial statements, and adjusting and closing entries.

(SO 1, 2, 3, 6)

P4-1B   The trial balance columns of the worksheet for Gibson Roofing at March 31, 2012, are as follows.

GIBSON ROOFING
Worksheet
For the Month Ended March 31, 2012

Account Titles	Trial Balance	
	Dr.	Cr.
Cash	4,500	
Accounts Receivable	3,200	
Supplies	2,000	
Equipment	11,000	
Accumulated Depreciation—Equipment		1,250
Accounts Payable		2,500
Unearned Service Revenue		550
Owner's Capital		12,900
Owner's Drawings	1,100	
Service Revenue		6,300
Salaries and Wages Expense	1,300	
Miscellaneous Expense	400	
	23,500	23,500

Other data:

1. A physical count reveals only $550 of roofing supplies on hand.
2. Depreciation for March is $250.
3. Unearned revenue amounted to $210 at March 31.
4. Accrued salaries are $700.

Instructions

(a) Enter the trial balance on a worksheet and complete the worksheet.
(b) Prepare an income statement and owner's equity statement for the month of March and a classified balance sheet at March 31. T. Gibson did not make any additional investments in the business in March.
(c) Journalize the adjusting entries from the adjustments columns of the worksheet.
(d) Journalize the closing entries from the financial statement columns of the worksheet.

*(a) Adjusted trial balance
$24,450*

*(b) Net income $2,540
Total assets $17,750*

P4-2B The adjusted trial balance columns of the worksheet for Taj Company, owned by Gabby Taj, are as follows.

Complete worksheet; prepare financial statements, closing entries, and post-closing trial balance.

(SO 1, 2, 3, 6)

TAJ COMPANY
Worksheet
For the Year Ended December 31, 2012

Account No.	Account Titles	Adjusted Trial Balance	
		Dr.	Cr.
101	Cash	5,300	
112	Accounts Receivable	10,800	
126	Supplies	1,500	
130	Prepaid Insurance	2,000	
151	Equipment	27,000	
152	Accumulated Depreciation—Equipment		5,600
200	Notes Payable		15,000
201	Accounts Payable		6,100
212	Salaries and Wages Payable		2,400
230	Interest Payable		600
301	Owner's Capital		13,000
306	Owner's Drawings	7,000	
400	Service Revenue		61,000
610	Advertising Expense	8,400	
631	Supplies Expense	4,000	
711	Depreciation Expense	5,600	
722	Insurance Expense	3,500	
726	Salaries and Wages Expense	28,000	
905	Interest Expense	600	
	Totals	103,700	103,700

Instructions

(a) Complete the worksheet by extending the balances to the financial statement columns.
(b) Prepare an income statement, owner's equity statement, and a classified balance sheet. (*Note:* $5,000 of the notes payable become due in 2013.) Gabby Taj did not make any additional investments in the business during the year.
(c) Prepare the closing entries. Use J14 for the journal page.
(d) Post the closing entries. Use the three-column form of account. Income Summary is No. 350.
(e) Prepare a post-closing trial balance.

(a) Net income $10,900

*(b) Current assets $19,600;
Current liabilities $14,100*

*(e) Post-closing trial balance
$46,600*

Prepare financial statements, closing entries, and post-closing trial balance.

(SO 1, 2, 3, 6)

P4-3B The completed financial statement columns of the worksheet for Korver Company are shown on the next page.

KORVER COMPANY
Worksheet
For the Year Ended December 31, 2012

Account No.	Account Titles	Income Statement Dr.	Income Statement Cr.	Balance Sheet Dr.	Balance Sheet Cr.
101	Cash			8,900	
112	Accounts Receivable			10,800	
130	Prepaid Insurance			2,800	
157	Equipment			24,000	
167	Accumulated Depreciation—Equip.				4,500
201	Accounts Payable				9,000
212	Salaries and Wages Payable				2,400
301	Owner's Capital				19,500
306	Owner's Drawings			11,000	
400	Service Revenue		60,000		
622	Maintenance and Repairs Expense	1,600			
711	Depreciation Expense	3,100			
722	Insurance Expense	1,800			
726	Salaries and Wages Expense	30,000			
732	Utilities Expense	1,400			
	Totals	37,900	60,000	57,500	35,400
	Net Income	22,100			22,100
		60,000	60,000	57,500	57,500

Instructions

(a) Ending capital $30,600;
Total current assets
$22,500

(d) Post-closing trial balance
$46,500

*Complete worksheet; prepare
classified balance sheet, entries,
and post-closing trial balance.*
(SO 1, 2, 3, 6)

(a) Prepare an income statement, an owner's equity statement, and a classified balance sheet.

(b) Prepare the closing entries. Korver did not make any additional investments during the year.

(c) Post the closing entries and rule and balance the accounts. Use T accounts. Income Summary is account No. 350.

(d) Prepare a post-closing trial balance.

P4-4B Law Management Services began business on January 1, 2012, with a capital investment of $120,000. The company manages condominiums for owners (Service Revenue) and rents space in its own office building (Rent Revenue). The trial balance and adjusted trial balance columns of the worksheet at the end of the first year are as follows.

LAW MANAGEMENT SERVICES
Worksheet
For the Year Ended December 31, 2012

Account Titles	Trial Balance Dr.	Trial Balance Cr.	Adjusted Trial Balance Dr.	Adjusted Trial Balance Cr.
Cash	13,800		13,800	
Accounts Receivable	28,300		28,300	
Prepaid Insurance	3,600		2,400	
Land	67,000		67,000	
Buildings	127,000		127,000	
Equipment	59,000		59,000	
Accounts Payable		12,500		12,500
Unearned Rent Revenue		6,000		1,500
Mortgage Payable		120,000		120,000
Owner's Capital		144,000		144,000
Owner's Drawings	22,000		22,000	
Service Revenue		90,700		90,700
Rent Revenue		29,000		33,500
Salaries and Wages Expense	42,000		42,000	
Advertising Expense	20,500		20,500	
Utilities Expense	19,000		19,000	
Totals	402,200	402,200		

Insurance Expense	1,200	
Depreciation Expense	6,600	
Accumulated Depreciation—Buildings		3,000
Accumulated Depreciation—Equipment		3,600
Interest Expense	10,000	
Interest Payable		10,000
Totals	418,800	418,800

Instructions
(a) Prepare a complete worksheet.
(b) Prepare a classified balance sheet. (*Note*: $30,000 of the mortgage note payable is due for payment next year.)
(c) Journalize the adjusting entries.
(d) Journalize the closing entries.
(e) Prepare a post-closing trial balance.

(a) Net income $24,900
(b) Total current assets $44,500

(e) Post-closing trial balance $297,500

P4-5B   Jannero Pargo opened Pargo's Cleaning Service on July 1, 2012. During July the following transactions were completed.

Complete all steps in accounting cycle.
(SO 1, 2, 3, 4, 6)

July	1	Pargo invested $20,000 cash in the business.
	1	Purchased used truck for $9,000, paying $4,000 cash and the balance on account.
	3	Purchased cleaning supplies for $2,100 on account.
	5	Paid $1,800 cash on one-year insurance policy effective July 1.
	12	Billed customers $4,500 for cleaning services.
	18	Paid $1,500 cash on amount owed on truck and $1,400 on amount owed on cleaning supplies.
	20	Paid $2,500 cash for employee salaries.
	21	Collected $3,400 cash from customers billed on July 12.
	25	Billed customers $6,000 for cleaning services.
	31	Paid gasoline for month on truck $350.
	31	Withdraw $5,600 cash for personal use.

The chart of accounts for Pargo's Cleaning Service contains the following accounts: No. 101 Cash, No. 112 Accounts Receivable, No. 128 Supplies, No. 130 Prepaid Insurance, No. 157 Equipment, No. 158 Accumulated Depreciation—Equipment, No. 201 Accounts Payable, No. 212 Salaries and Wages Payable, No. 301 Owner's Capital, No. 306 Owner's Drawings, No. 350 Income Summary, No. 400 Service Revenue, No. 633 Gasoline Expense, No. 634 Supplies Expense, No. 711 Depreciation Expense, No. 722 Insurance Expense, and No. 726 Salaries and Wages Expense.

Instructions
(a) Journalize and post the July transactions. Use page J1 for the journal and the three-column form of account.
(b) Prepare a trial balance at July 31 on a worksheet.
(c) Enter the following adjustments on the worksheet and complete the worksheet.
(1) Services provided but unbilled and uncollected at July 31 were $2,700.
(2) Depreciation on equipment for the month was $500.
(3) One-twelfth of the insurance expired.
(4) An inventory count shows $600 of cleaning supplies on hand at July 31.
(5) Accrued but unpaid employee salaries were $1,000.
(d) Prepare the income statement and owner's equity statement for July and a classified balance sheet at July 31.
(e) Journalize and post adjusting entries. Use page J2 for the journal.
(f) Journalize and post closing entries and complete the closing process. Use page J3 for the journal.
(g) Prepare a post-closing trial balance at July 31.

(b) Trial balance $34,700
(c) Adjusted trial balance $38,900

(d) Net income $7,200; Total assets $26,800
(g) Post-closing trial balance $27,300

Problems: Set C

Visit the book's companion website, at **www.wiley.com/college/weygandt**, and choose the Student Companion site to access Problem Set C.

Comprehensive Problem: Chapters 2 to 4

CP4   Julie Molony opened Julie's Maids Cleaning Service on July 1, 2012. During July, the company completed the following transactions.

July 1	Invested $14,000 cash in the business.
1	Purchased a used truck for $10,000, paying $3,000 cash and the balance on account.
3	Purchased cleaning supplies for $800 on account.
5	Paid $1,800 on a one-year insurance policy, effective July 1.
12	Billed customers $3,800 for cleaning services.
18	Paid $1,000 of amount owed on truck, and $400 of amount owed on cleaning supplies.
20	Paid $1,600 for employee salaries.
21	Collected $1,400 from customers billed on July 12.
25	Billed customers $1,500 for cleaning services.
31	Paid gasoline for the month on the truck, $400.
31	Withdrew $600 cash for personal use.

The chart of accounts for Julie's Maids Cleaning Service contains the following accounts: No. 101 Cash, No. 112 Accounts Receivable, No. 128 Supplies, No. 130 Prepaid Insurance, No. 157 Equipment, No. 158 Accumulated Depreciation—Equipment, No. 201 Accounts Payable, No. 212 Salaries and Wages Payable, No. 301 Owner's Capital, No. 306 Owner's Drawings, No. 350 Income Summary, No. 400 Service Revenue, No. 633 Gasoline Expense, No. 634 Supplies Expense, No. 711 Depreciation Expense, No. 722 Insurance Expense, and No. 726 Salaries and Wages Expense.

Instructions

(a) Journalize and post the July transactions. Use page J1 for the journal.

(b) Trial balance totals $25,700

(b) Prepare a trial balance at July 31 on a worksheet.

(c) Enter the following adjustments on the worksheet, and complete the worksheet.

    (1) Earned but unbilled fees at July 31 were $1,300.

    (2) Depreciation on equipment for the month was $200.

    (3) One-twelfth of the insurance expired.

    (4) An inventory count shows $100 of cleaning supplies on hand at July 31.

    (5) Accrued but unpaid employee salaries were $500.

(d) Net income $3,050
Total assets $23,350

(d) Prepare the income statement and owner's equity statement for July, and a classified balance sheet at July 31, 2012.

(e) Journalize and post the adjusting entries. Use page J2 for the journal.

(f) Journalize and post the closing entries, and complete the closing process. Use page J3 for the journal.

(g) Trial balance totals $23,550

(g) Prepare a post-closing trial balance at July 31.

Continuing Cookie Chronicle

(*Note:* This is a continuation of the Cookie Chronicle from Chapters 1 through 3.)

CCC4   Natalie had a very busy December. At the end of the month, after journalizing and posting the December transactions and adjusting entries, Natalie prepared the following adjusted trial balance.

COOKIE CREATIONS
Adjusted Trial Balance
December 31, 2011

	Debit	Credit
Cash	$1,180	
Accounts Receivable	875	
Supplies	350	
Prepaid Insurance	1,210	
Equipment	1,200	
Accumulated Depreciation—Equipment		$ 40
Accounts Payable		75
Salaries and Wages Payable		56

Interest Payable		15
Unearned Service Revenue		300
Notes Payable		2,000
Owner's Capital		800
Owner's Drawings	500	
Service Revenue		4,515
Salaries and Wages Expense	1,006	
Utilities Expense	125	
Advertising Expense	165	
Supplies Expense	1,025	
Depreciation Expense	40	
Insurance Expense	110	
Interest Expense	15	
	$7,801	$7,801

Instructions

Using the information in the adjusted trial balance, do the following.

(a) Prepare an income statement and an owner's equity statement for the 2 months ended December 31, 2011, and a classified balance sheet as at December 31, 2011. The note payable has a stated interest rate of 6%, and the principal and interest are due on November 16, 2013.

(b) Natalie has decided that her year-end will be December 31, 2011. Prepare and post closing entries as of December 31, 2011.

(c) Prepare a post-closing trial balance.

BROADENING YOUR PERSPECTIVE

Financial Reporting and Analysis

Financial Reporting Problem: PepsiCo, Inc.

BYP4-1 The financial statements of PepsiCo, Inc. are presented in Appendix A at the end of this textbook.

Instructions

Answer the questions on the following page using the Consolidated Balance Sheet and the Notes to Consolidated Financial Statements section.

(a) What were PepsiCo's total current assets at December 26, 2009, and December 27, 2008?
(b) Are assets that PepsiCo included under current assets listed in proper order? Explain.
(c) How are PepsiCo's assets classified?
(d) What are "cash equivalents"?
(e) What were PepsiCo's total current liabilities at December 26, 2009, and December 27, 2008?

Comparative Analysis Problem: PepsiCo, Inc. vs. The Coca-Cola Company

BYP4-2 PepsiCo's financial statements are presented in Appendix A. Financial statements for The Coca-Cola Company are presented in Appendix B.

Instructions

(a) Based on the information contained in these financial statements, determine each of the following for PepsiCo at December 26, 2009, and for Coca-Cola at December 31, 2009.
  (1) Total current assets.
  (2) Net amount of property, plant, and equipment (land, buildings, and equipment).
  (3) Total current liabilities.
  (4) Total equity.
(b) What conclusions concerning the companies' respective financial positions can be drawn?

On the Web

BYP4-3 Numerous companies have established home pages on the Internet, e.g., Capt'n Eli Root Beer Company (*www.captneli.com/rootbeer.php*) and Kodak (*www.kodak.com*).

Instructions

Examine the home pages of any two companies and answer the following questions.

(a) What type of information is available?

(b) Is any accounting-related information presented?

(c) Would you describe the home page as informative, promotional, or both? Why?

Critical Thinking

Decision Making Across the Organization

BYP4-4 Whitegloves Janitorial Service was started 2 years ago by Nancy Kohl. Because business has been exceptionally good, Nancy decided on July 1, 2012, to expand operations by acquiring an additional truck and hiring two more assistants. To finance the expansion, Nancy obtained on July 1, 2012, a $25,000, 10% bank loan, payable $10,000 on July 1, 2013, and the balance on July 1, 2014. The terms of the loan require the borrower to have $10,000 more current assets than current liabilities at December 31, 2012. If these terms are not met, the bank loan will be refinanced at 15% interest. At December 31, 2012, the accountant for Whitegloves Janitorial Service Inc. prepared the balance sheet shown below.

Nancy presented the balance sheet to the bank's loan officer on January 2, 2013, confident that the company had met the terms of the loan. The loan officer was not impressed. She said, "We need financial statements audited by a CPA." A CPA was hired and immediately realized that the balance sheet had been prepared from a trial balance and not from an adjusted trial balance. The adjustment data at the balance sheet date consisted of the following.

(1) Earned but unbilled janitorial services were $3,700.

(2) Janitorial supplies on hand were $2,500.

(3) Prepaid insurance was a 3-year policy dated January 1, 2012.

(4) December expenses incurred but unpaid at December 31, $500.

(5) Interest on the bank loan was not recorded.

(6) The amounts for property, plant, and equipment presented in the balance sheet were reported net of accumulated depreciation (cost less accumulated depreciation). These amounts were $4,000 for cleaning equipment and $5,000 for delivery trucks as of January 1, 2012. Depreciation for 2012 was $2,000 for cleaning equipment and $5,000 for delivery trucks.

WHITEGLOVES JANITORIAL SERVICE
Balance Sheet
December 31, 2012

Assets		Liabilities and Owner's Equity	
Current assets		Current liabilities	
Cash	$ 6,500	Notes payable	$10,000
Accounts receivable	9,000	Accounts payable	2,500
Janitorial supplies	5,200	Total current liabilities	12,500
Prepaid insurance	4,800	Long-term liability	
Total current assets	25,500	Notes payable	15,000
Property, plant, and equipment		Total liabilities	27,500
Cleaning equipment (net)	22,000	Owner's equity	
Delivery trucks (net)	34,000	Owner's capital	54,000
Total property, plant, and equipment	56,000		
Total assets	$81,500	Total liabilities and owner's equity	$81,500

Instructions

With the class divided into groups, answer the following.

(a) Prepare a correct balance sheet.

(b) Were the terms of the bank loan met? Explain.

Communication Activity

BYP4-5   The accounting cycle is important in understanding the accounting process.

Instructions
Write a memo to your instructor that lists the steps of the accounting cycle in the order they should be completed. End with a paragraph that explains the optional steps in the cycle.

Ethics Case

BYP4-6   As the controller of Breathless Perfume Company, you discover a misstatement that overstated net income in the prior year's financial statements. The misleading financial statements appear in the company's annual report which was issued to banks and other creditors less than a month ago. After much thought about the consequences of telling the president, Jerry McNabb, about this misstatement, you gather your courage to inform him. Jerry says, "Hey! What they don't know won't hurt them. But, just so we set the record straight, we'll adjust this year's financial statements for last year's misstatement. We can absorb that misstatement better in this year than in last year anyway! Just don't make such a mistake again."

Instructions
(a) Who are the stakeholders in this situation?
(b) What are the ethical issues in this situation?
(c) What would you do as a controller in this situation?

"All About You" Activity

BYP4-7   Companies prepare balance sheets in order to know their financial position at a specific point in time. This enables them to make a comparison to their position at previous points in time, and gives them a basis for planning for the future. As discussed in the **All About You** feature (available on the book's companion website), in order to evaluate your financial position you need to prepare a personal balance sheet. Assume that you have compiled the following information regarding your finances. (*Hint:* Some of the items might not be used in your personal balance sheet.)

Amount owed on student loan balance (long-term)	$ 5,000
Balance in checking account	1,200
Certificate of deposit (6-month)	3,000
Annual earnings from part-time job	11,300
Automobile	7,000
Balance on automobile loan (current portion)	1,500
Balance on automobile loan (long-term portion)	4,000
Home computer	800
Amount owed to you by younger brother	300
Balance in money market account	1,800
Annual tuition	6,400
Video and stereo equipment	1,250
Balance owed on credit card (current portion)	150
Balance owed on credit card (long-term portion)	1,650

Instructions
Prepare a personal balance sheet using the format you have learned for a classified balance sheet for a company. For the capital account, use Owner's Capital.

FASB Codification Activity

BYP4-8   If your school has a subscription to the FASB Codification, go to *http://aaahq.org/ascLogin.cfm* to log in and prepare responses to the following.

Instructions
(a) Access the glossary ("Master Glossary") at the FASB Codification website to answer the following.
 (1) What is the definition of current assets?
 (2) What is the definition of current liabilities?
(b) A company wants to offset its accounts payable against its cash account and show a cash amount net of accounts payable on its balance sheet. Identify the criteria (found in the FASB Codification) under which a company has the right of set off. Does the company have the right to offset accounts payable against the cash account?

Answers to Insight and Accounting Across the Organization Questions

p. 165 Cisco Performs the Virtual Close   Q: Who else benefits from a shorter closing process? **A:** Investors benefit from a shorter closing process. The shorter the closing, the sooner the company can report its financial results. This means that the financial information is more timely and therefore more relevant to investors.

p. 170 Yale Express Loses Some Transportation Bills   Q: What might Yale Express's vice president have done to produce more accurate financial statements without waiting months for Republic's outstanding transportation bills? **A:** Yale's vice president could have engaged his accountants and auditors to prepare an adjusting entry based on an estimate of the outstanding transportation bills. (The estimate could have been made using past experience and the current volume of business.)

p. 175 Can a Company Be Too Liquid?   Q: What can various company managers do to ensure that working capital is managed efficiently to maximize net income? **A:** Marketing and sales managers must understand that by extending generous repayment terms, they are expanding the company's receivables balance and slowing the company's cash flow. Production managers must strive to minimize the amount of excess inventory on hand. Managers must coordinate efforts to speed up the collection of receivables, while also ensuring that the company pays its payables on time but never too early.

Answers to Self-Test Questions

1. b   **2.** c   **3.** c   **4.** a   **5.** b   **6.** c   **7.** a   **8.** d   **9.** c   **10.** d   **11.** b   **12.** c   **13.** c   **14.** d   **15.** a   *16. c

IFRS A Look at IFRS

The classified balance sheet, although generally required internationally, contains certain variations in format when reporting under IFRS.

Key Points

- The procedures of the closing process are applicable to all companies, whether they are using IFRS or GAAP.

- IFRS recommends but does not require the use of the title "statement of financial position" rather than balance sheet.

- The format of statement of financial position information is often presented differently under IFRS. Although no specific format is required, most companies that follow IFRS present statement of financial position information in this order:

  ◆ Noncurrent assets

  ◆ Current assets

  ◆ Equity

  ◆ Noncurrent liabilities

  ◆ Current liabilities

- IFRS requires a classified statement of financial position except in very limited situations. IFRS follows the same guidelines as this textbook for distinguishing between current and noncurrent assets and liabilities.

- Under IFRS, current assets are usually listed in the reverse order of liquidity. For example, under GAAP cash is listed first, but under IFRS it is listed last.

- Some companies report the subtotal *net assets,* which equals total assets minus total liabilities. See, for example, the statement of financial position of Zetar plc in Appendix C.

- IFRS has many differences in terminology that you will notice in this textbook. For example, in the sample statement of financial position illustrated on the next page, notice in the investment category that stock is called shares.

Franklin Company
Statement of Financial Position
October 31, 2012

Assets

Intangible assets			
Patents			$ 3,100
Property, plant, and equipment			
Land		$10,000	
Equipment	$24,000		
Less: Accumulated depreciation	5,000	19,000	29,000
Long-term investments			
Investment in shares of Walters Corp.		5,200	
Investment in real estate		2,000	7,200
Current assets			
Prepaid insurance		400	
Supplies		2,100	
Inventories		3,000	
Notes receivable		1,000	
Accounts receivable		7,000	
Short-term investments		2,000	
Cash		6,600	22,100
Total assets			$61,400

Equity and Liabilities

Equity			
Owner's capital			$34,050
Non-current liabilities			
Mortgage payable		$10,000	
Notes payable		1,300	11,300
Current liabilities			
Notes payable		11,000	
Accounts payable		2,100	
Salaries payable		1,600	
Unearned service revenue		900	
Interest payable		450	16,050
Total equity and liabilities			$61,400

- Both IFRS and GAAP require disclosures about (1) accounting policies followed, (2) judgments that management has made in the process of applying the entity's accounting policies, and (3) the key assumptions and estimation uncertainty that could result in a material adjustment to the carrying amounts of assets and liabilities within the next financial year.

- Comparative prior-period information must be presented and financial statements must be prepared annually.

- Both GAAP and IFRS are increasing the use of fair value to report assets. However, at this point IFRS has adopted it more broadly. As examples, under IFRS companies can apply fair value to property, plant, and equipment; natural resources; and in some cases intangible assets.

Looking to the Future

The IASB and the FASB are working on a project to converge their standards related to financial statement presentation. A key feature of the proposed framework is that each of the statements will be organized in the same format, to separate an entity's financing activities from its operating and investing activities and, further, to separate financing activities into transactions with owners and creditors. Thus, the same classifications used in the statement of financial position would also be used in the income statement and the statement of cash flows. The project has three phases. You can follow the joint financial presentation project at the following link: *http://www.fasb.org/project/financial_statement_presentation.shtml.*

The IASB and the FASB face a difficult task in attempting to update, modify, and complete a converged conceptual framework. For example, how do companies choose between information that is highly relevant but difficult to verify versus information that is less relevant but easy to verify? How do companies define control when developing a definition of an asset? Is a liability the future sacrifice itself or the obligation to make the sacrifice? Should a single measurement method, such as historical cost or fair value, be used, or does it depend on whether it is an asset or liability that is being measured? It appears that the new document will be a significant improvement over its predecessors and will lead to principles-based standards, which will help financial statement users make better decisions.

IFRS Self-Test Questions

1. Which of the following statements is *false*?
   (a) Assets equals liabilities plus equity.
   (b) Under IFRS, companies sometimes net liabilities against assets to report "net assets."
   (c) The FASB and IASB are working on a joint conceptual framework project.
   (d) Under IFRS, the statement of financial position is usually referred to as the statement of assets and equity.

2. A company has purchased a tract of land and expects to build a production plant on the land in approximately 5 years. During the 5 years before construction, the land will be idle. Under IFRS, the land should be reported as:
   (a) land expense.
   (b) property, plant, and equipment.
   (c) an intangible asset.
   (d) a long-term investment.

3. Current assets under IFRS are listed generally:
   (a) by importance.
   (b) in the reverse order of their expected conversion to cash.
   (c) by longevity.
   (d) alphabetically.

4. Companies that use IFRS:
   (a) may report all their assets on the statement of financial position at fair value.
   (b) may offset assets against liabilities and show net assets and net liabilities on their statement of financial positions, rather than the underlying detailed line items.
   (c) may report noncurrent assets before current assets on the statement of financial position.
   (d) do not have any guidelines as to what should be reported on the statement of financial position.

5. Companies that follow IFRS to prepare a statement of financial position generally use the following order of classification:
   (a) current assets, current liabilities, noncurrent assets, noncurrent liabilities, equity.
   (b) noncurrent assets, noncurrent liabilities, current assets, current liabilities, equity.
   (c) noncurrent assets, current assets, equity, noncurrent liabilities, current liabilities.
   (d) equity, noncurrent assets, current assets, noncurrent liabilities, current liabilities.

IFRS Concepts and Application

IFRS4-1 In what ways does the format of a statement of financial of position under IFRS often differ from a balance sheet presented under GAAP?

IFRS4-2 What term is commonly used under IFRS in reference to the balance sheet?

IFRS4-3 The statement of financial position for Diaz Company includes the following accounts: Accounts Receivable £12,500; Prepaid Insurance £3,600; Cash £15,400; Supplies £5,200; and Short-Term Investments £6,700. Prepare the current assets section of the statement of financial position, listing the accounts in proper sequence.

IFRS4-4 Zurich Company recently received the following information related to the company's December 31, 2012, statement of financial position.

Inventories	CHF 2,900	Short-term investments	CHF 120
Cash	13,400	Accumulated depreciation—	
Equipment	21,700	equipment	5,700
Investments in shares		Accounts receivable	4,300
(long-term)	6,500		

Prepare the assets section of the company's classified statement of financial position.

IFRS4-5 The following information is available for Karr Bowling Alley at December 31, 2012.

Buildings	$128,800	Owner's Capital	$115,000
Accounts Receivable	14,520	Accumulated Depreciation—Buildings	42,600
Prepaid Insurance	4,680	Accounts Payable	12,300
Cash	18,040	Notes Payable	97,780
Equipment	62,400	Accumulated Depreciation—Equipment	18,720
Land	64,000	Interest Payable	2,600
Insurance Expense	780	Bowling Revenues	14,180
Depreciation Expense	7,360		
Interest Expense	2,600		

Prepare a classified statement of financial position; assume that $13,900 of the notes payable will be paid in 2013.

IFRS4-6 Brian Hopkins is interested in comparing the liquidity and solvency of a U.S. software company with a Chinese competitor. Is this possible if the two companies report using different currencies?

International Comparative Analysis
Problem: PepsiCo vs. *Zetar plc*

IFRS4-7 The financial statements of Zetar plc are presented in Appendix C. The company's complete annual report, including the notes to its financial statements, is available at *www.zetarplc.com*.

Instructions
Identify five differences in the format of the statement of financial position used by Zetar plc compared to a company, such as PepsiCo, that follows GAAP. (PepsiCo's financial statements are available in Appendix A.)

Answers to IFRS Self-Test Questions
1. d 2. d 3. b 4. c 5. c

✔
The Navigator

✔ **Remember to go back to the Navigator box on the chapter opening page and check off your completed work.**

CHAPTER5

Accounting for Merchandising Operations

Study Objectives

After studying this chapter, you should be able to:

[1] Identify the differences between service and merchandising companies.

[2] Explain the recording of purchases under a perpetual inventory system.

[3] Explain the recording of sales revenues under a perpetual inventory system.

[4] Explain the steps in the accounting cycle for a merchandising company.

[5] Distinguish between a multiple-step and a single-step income statement.

[6] Explain the computation and importance of gross profit.

✔ **The Navigator**

Feature Story

WHO DOESN'T SHOP AT WAL-MART?

In his book *The End of Work,* Jeremy Rifkin notes that until the 20th century the word *consumption* evoked negative images. To be labeled a "consumer" was an insult. (In fact, one of the deadliest diseases in history, tuberculosis, was often referred to as "consumption.") Twentieth-century merchants realized, however, that in order to prosper, they had to convince people of the need for things not previously needed. For example, General Motors made annual changes in its cars so that people would be discontented with the cars they already owned. Thus began consumerism.

Today, consumption describes the U.S. lifestyle in a nutshell. We consume twice as much today per person as we did at the end of World War II. The amount of U.S. retail space per person is vastly greater than that of any other country. It appears that we live to shop.

The first great retail giant was Sears Roebuck. It started as a catalog company enabling people in rural areas to buy things by mail. For decades, it was the uncontested merchandising leader.

Today, Wal-Mart Stores, Inc. is the undisputed champion provider of basic (and perhaps not-so-basic) human needs. Wal-Mart opened its first store in 1962, and it now has more than 8,000 stores, serving more than 100 million customers every week. A key cause of Wal-Mart's incredible growth is its amazing system of inventory control and distribution. Wal-Mart has a management information system that employs six satellite channels, from which company computers receive 8.4 million updates every minute on what items customers buy and the relationship among items sold to each person.

Measured by sales revenues, Wal-Mart is the largest company in the world. In six years, it went from selling almost no groceries to being America's largest grocery retailer.

It would appear that things have never looked better at Wal-Mart. On the other hand, a *Wall Street Journal* article entitled "How to Sell More to Those Who Think It's Cool to Be Frugal" suggests that consumerism as a way of life might be dying. Don't bet your high-definition 3D TV on it though.

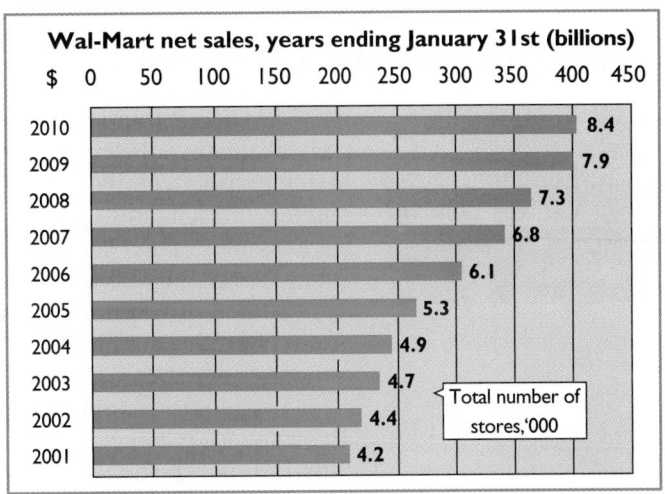

Wal-Mart net sales, years ending January 31st (billions)

Year	Net sales	Total number of stores, '000
2010	~390	8.4
2009	~400	7.9
2008	~375	7.3
2007	~345	6.8
2006	~315	6.1
2005	~285	5.3
2004	~255	4.9
2003	~230	4.7
2002	~215	4.4
2001	~195	4.2

Source: "How Big Can It Grow?" *The Economist* (April 17, 2004), pp. 67–69, and *www.walmart.com* (accessed November 23, 2010).

✔ **The Navigator**

InsideCHAPTER5

PreviewofCHAPTER5

Merchandising is one of the largest and most influential industries in the United States. It is likely that a number of you will work for a merchandiser. Therefore, understanding the financial statements of merchandising companies is important. In this chapter, you will learn the basics about reporting merchandising transactions. In addition, you will learn how to prepare and analyze a commonly used form of the income statement—the multiple-step income statement. The content and organization of the chapter are as follows.

Accounting for Merchandising Operations

Merchandising Operations	Recording Purchases of Merchandise	Recording Sales of Merchandise	Completing the Accounting Cycle	Forms of Financial Statements
• Operating cycles • Flow of costs—perpetual and periodic inventory systems	• Freight costs • Purchase returns and allowances • Purchase discounts • Summary of purchasing transactions	• Sales returns and allowances • Sales discounts	• Adjusting entries • Closing entries • Summary of merchandising entries	• Multiple-step income statement • Single-step income statement • Classified balance sheet

The Navigator

Merchandising Operations

Study Objective [1]

Identify the differences between service and merchandising companies.

Wal-Mart, Kmart, and Target are called merchandising companies because they buy and sell merchandise rather than perform services as their primary source of revenue. Merchandising companies that purchase and sell directly to consumers are called **retailers**. Merchandising companies that sell to retailers are known as **wholesalers**. For example, retailer Walgreens might buy goods from wholesaler McKesson; retailer Office Depot might buy office supplies from wholesaler United Stationers. The primary source of revenues for merchandising companies is the sale of merchandise, often referred to simply as **sales revenue** or **sales**. A merchandising company has two categories of expenses: cost of goods sold and operating expenses.

Cost of goods sold is the total cost of merchandise sold during the period. This expense is directly related to the revenue recognized from the sale of goods. Illustration 5-1 shows the income measurement process for a merchandising

Illustration 5-1
Income measurement process for a merchandising company

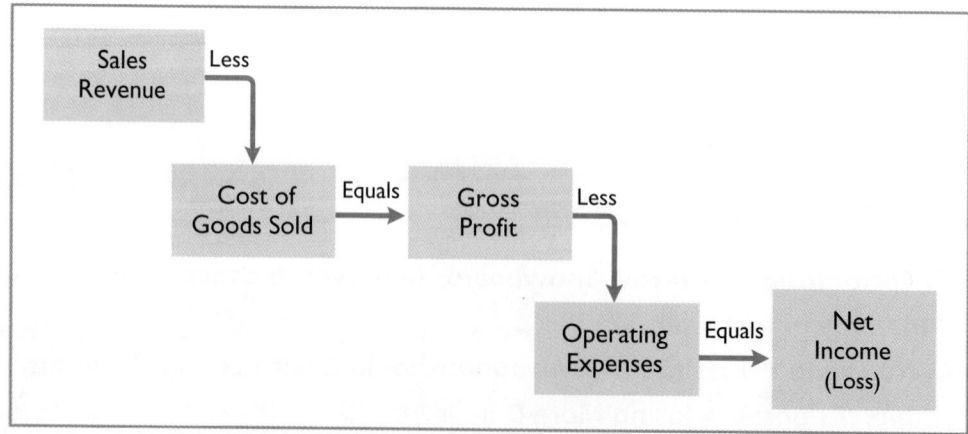

company. The items in the two blue boxes are unique to a merchandising company; they are not used by a service company.

Operating Cycles

The operating cycle of a merchandising company ordinarily is longer than that of a service company. The purchase of merchandise inventory and its eventual sale lengthen the cycle. Illustration 5-2 contrasts the operating cycles of service and merchandising companies. Note that the added asset account for a merchandising company is the Inventory account. Companies report inventory as a current asset on the balance sheet.

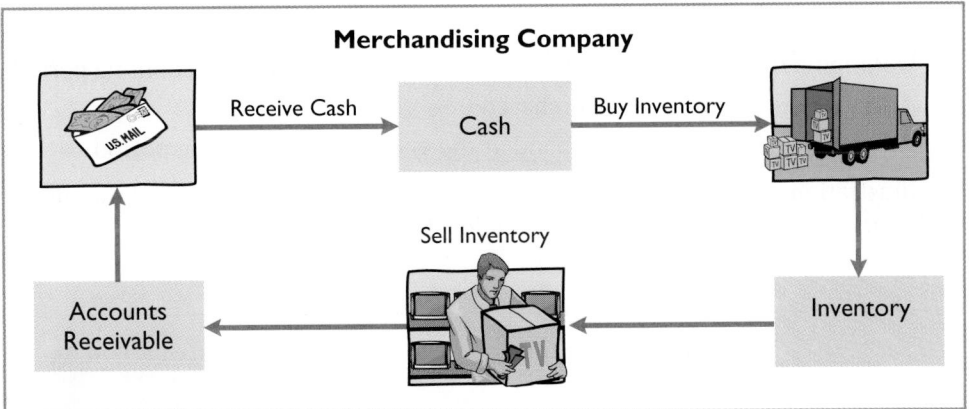

Illustration 5-2
Operating cycles for a service company and a merchandising company

Flow of Costs

The flow of costs for a merchandising company is as follows: Beginning inventory plus the cost of goods purchased is the cost of goods available for sale. As goods are sold, they are assigned to cost of goods sold. Those goods that are not sold by the end of the accounting period represent ending inventory. Illustration 5-3 (page 212) describes these relationships. Companies use one of two systems to account for inventory: a **perpetual inventory system** or a **periodic inventory system**.

PERPETUAL SYSTEM

In a **perpetual inventory system**, companies keep detailed records of the cost of each inventory purchase and sale. These records continuously—perpetually—show the inventory that should be on hand for every item. For example, a Ford dealership has separate inventory records for each automobile, truck, and van on its lot and showroom floor. Similarly, a Kroger grocery store uses bar codes and optical

Helpful Hint

For control purposes, companies take a physical inventory count under the perpetual system, even though it is not needed to determine cost of goods sold.

Illustration 5-3
Flow of costs

scanners to keep a daily running record of every box of cereal and every jar of jelly that it buys and sells. Under a perpetual inventory system, a company determines the cost of goods sold **each time a sale occurs**.

PERIODIC SYSTEM

In a **periodic inventory system**, companies do not keep detailed inventory records of the goods on hand throughout the period. Instead, they determine the cost of goods sold **only at the end of the accounting period**—that is, periodically. At that point, the company takes a physical inventory count to determine the cost of goods on hand.

To determine the cost of goods sold under a periodic inventory system, the following steps are necessary:

1. Determine the cost of goods on hand at the beginning of the accounting period.
2. Add to it the cost of goods purchased.
3. Subtract the cost of goods on hand at the end of the accounting period.

Illustration 5-4 graphically compares the sequence of activities and the timing of the cost of goods sold computation under the two inventory systems.

Illustration 5-4
Comparing perpetual and periodic inventory systems

ADDITIONAL CONSIDERATIONS

Companies that sell merchandise with high unit values, such as automobiles, furniture, and major home appliances, have traditionally used perpetual systems. The growing use of computers and electronic scanners has enabled many more companies to install perpetual inventory systems. The perpetual inventory system is so named because the accounting records continuously—perpetually—show the quantity and cost of the inventory that should be on hand at any time.

A perpetual inventory system provides better control over inventories than a periodic system. Since the inventory records show the quantities that should be on hand, the company can count the goods at any time to see whether the amount of goods actually on hand agrees with the inventory records. If shortages are uncovered, the company can investigate immediately. Although a perpetual inventory system requires additional clerical work and additional cost to maintain the subsidiary records, a computerized system can minimize this cost. As noted in the Feature Story, much of Wal-Mart's success is attributed to its sophisticated inventory system.

Some businesses find it either unnecessary or uneconomical to invest in a computerized perpetual inventory system. Many small merchandising businesses, in particular, find that a perpetual inventory system costs more than it is worth. Managers of these businesses can control their merchandise and manage day-to-day operations using a periodic inventory system.

Because the perpetual inventory system is growing in popularity and use, we illustrate it in this chapter. Appendix 5A describes the journal entries for the periodic system.

_I_NVESTOR _I_NSIGHT

Morrow Snowboards Improves Its Stock Appeal

Investors are often eager to invest in a company that has a hot new product. However, when snowboard maker Morrow Snowboards, Inc., issued shares of stock to the public for the first time, some investors expressed reluctance to invest in Morrow because of a number of accounting control problems. To reduce investor concerns, Morrow implemented a perpetual inventory system to improve its control over inventory. In addition, it stated that it would perform a physical inventory count every quarter until it felt that the perpetual inventory system was reliable.

? If a perpetual system keeps track of inventory on a daily basis, why do companies ever need to do a physical count? (See page 257.)

Recording Purchases of Merchandise

Companies purchase inventory using cash or credit (on account). They normally record purchases when they receive the goods from the seller. Business documents provide written evidence of the transaction. A canceled check or a cash register receipt, for example, indicates the items purchased and amounts paid for each cash purchase. Companies record cash purchases by an increase in Inventory and a decrease in Cash.

A **purchase invoice** should support each credit purchase. This invoice indicates the total purchase price and other relevant information. However, the purchaser does not prepare a separate purchase invoice. Instead, the purchaser uses as a

Study Objective [2]
Explain the recording of purchases under a perpetual inventory system.

purchase invoice a copy of the sales invoice sent by the seller. In Illustration 5-5, for example, Sauk Stereo (the buyer) uses as a purchase invoice the sales invoice prepared by PW Audio Supply, Inc. (the seller).

Illustration 5-5
Sales invoice used as purchase invoice by Sauk Stereo

Helpful Hint

To better understand the contents of this invoice, identify these items:
1. Seller
2. Invoice date
3. Purchaser
4. Salesperson
5. Credit terms
6. Freight terms
7. Goods sold: catalog number, description, quantity, price per unit
8. Total invoice amount

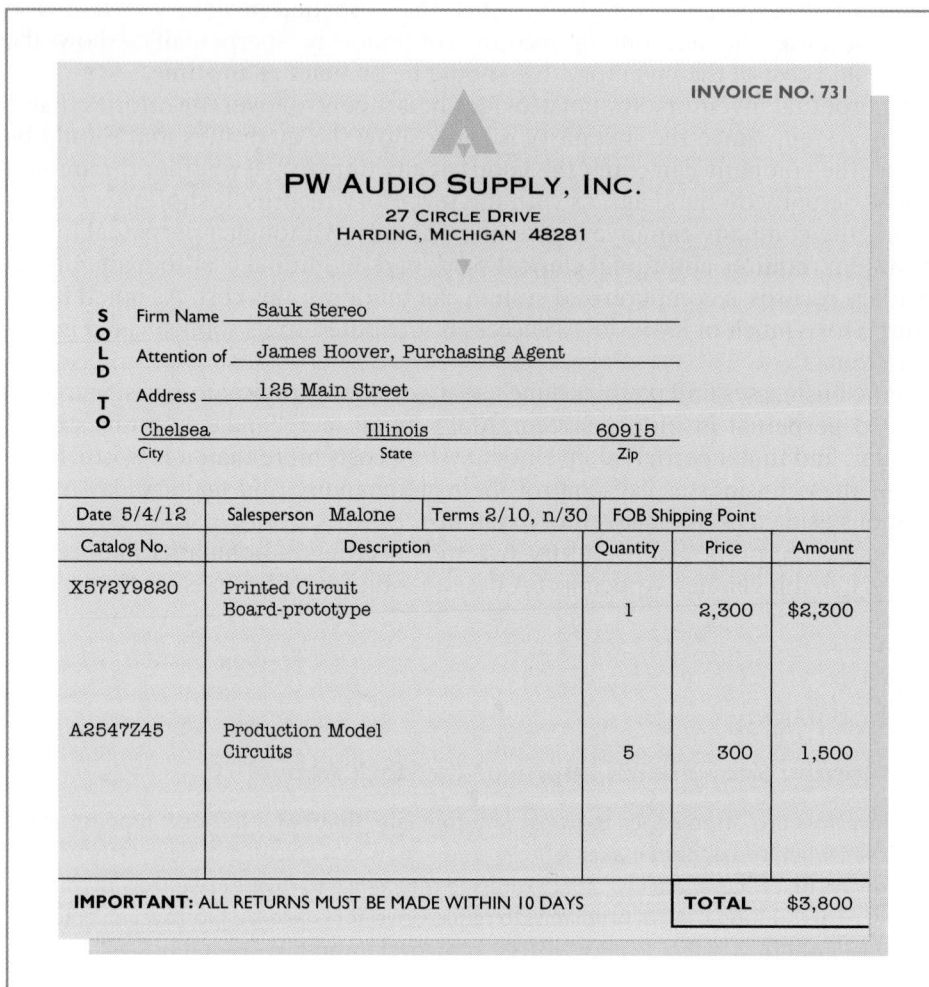

INVOICE NO. 731

PW AUDIO SUPPLY, INC.
27 CIRCLE DRIVE
HARDING, MICHIGAN 48281

SOLD TO

Firm Name ___Sauk Stereo___

Attention of ___James Hoover, Purchasing Agent___

Address ___125 Main Street___

___Chelsea___   ___Illinois___   ___60915___
City   State   Zip

Date 5/4/12	Salesperson Malone		Terms 2/10, n/30	FOB Shipping Point	
Catalog No.	Description		Quantity	Price	Amount
X572Y9820	Printed Circuit Board-prototype		1	2,300	$2,300
A2547Z45	Production Model Circuits		5	300	1,500

IMPORTANT: ALL RETURNS MUST BE MADE WITHIN 10 DAYS   **TOTAL** $3,800

Sauk Stereo makes the following journal entry to record its purchase from PW Audio Supply. The entry increases (debits) Inventory and increases (credits) Accounts Payable.

A = L + OE
+3,800
        +3,800

Cash Flows
no effect

May 4	Inventory	3,800	
	Accounts Payable		3,800
	(To record goods purchased on account from PW Audio Supply)		

Under the perpetual inventory system, companies record purchases of merchandise for sale in the Inventory account. Thus, Wal-Mart would increase (debit) Inventory for clothing, sporting goods, and anything else purchased for resale to customers.

Not all purchases are debited to Inventory, however. Companies record purchases of assets acquired for use and not for resale, such as supplies, equipment, and similar items, as increases to specific asset accounts rather than to Inventory. For example, to record the purchase of materials used to make shelf signs or for cash register receipt paper, Wal-Mart would increase Supplies.

Freight Costs

The sales agreement should indicate who—the seller or the buyer—is to pay for transporting the goods to the buyer's place of business. When a common carrier such as a railroad, trucking company, or airline transports the goods, the carrier prepares a freight bill in accord with the sales agreement.

Freight terms are expressed as either FOB shipping point or FOB destination. The letters FOB mean **free on board**. Thus, FOB shipping point means that the seller places the goods free on board the carrier, and the buyer pays the freight costs. Conversely, FOB destination means that the seller places the goods free on board to the buyer's place of business, and the seller pays the freight. For example, the sales invoice in Illustration 5-5 indicates FOB shipping point. Thus, the buyer (Sauk Stereo) pays the freight charges. Illustration 5-6 illustrates these shipping terms.

Illustration 5-6
Shipping terms

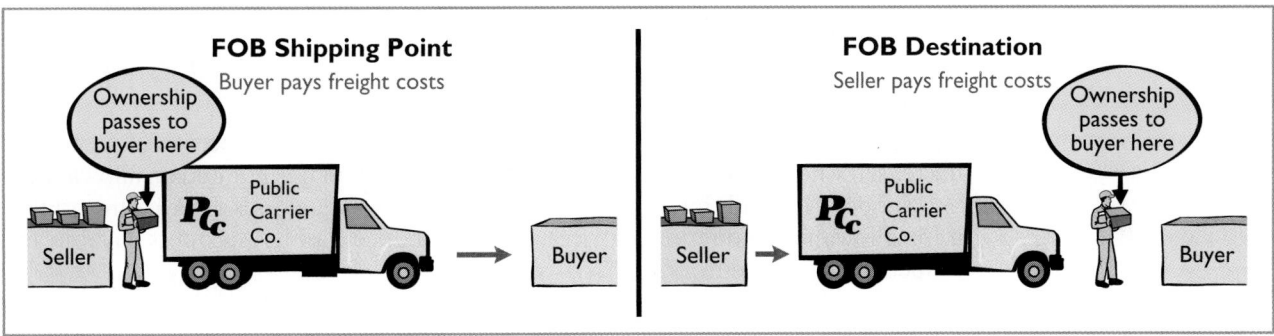

FREIGHT COSTS INCURRED BY THE BUYER
When the buyer incurs the transportation costs, these costs are considered part of the cost of purchasing inventory. Therefore, the buyer debits (increases) the account Inventory. For example, if upon delivery of the goods on May 6, Sauk Stereo (the buyer) pays Acme Freight Company $150 for freight charges, the entry on Sauk Stereo's books is:

May 6	Inventory	150	
	Cash		150
	(To record payment of freight on goods purchased)		

Thus, any freight costs incurred by the buyer are part of the cost of merchandise purchased. The reason: Inventory cost should include any freight charges necessary to deliver the goods to the buyer.

FREIGHT COSTS INCURRED BY THE SELLER
In contrast, **freight costs incurred by the seller on outgoing merchandise are an operating expense to the seller**. These costs increase an expense account titled Freight-out or Delivery Expense. If the freight terms on the invoice had required PW Audio Supply (the seller) to pay the freight charges, the entry by PW Audio Supply would be:

May 4	Freight-out (or Delivery Expense)	150	
	Cash		150
	(To record payment of freight on goods sold)		

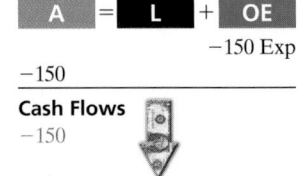

When the seller pays the freight charges, it will usually establish a higher invoice price for the goods to cover the shipping expense.

Purchase Returns and Allowances

A purchaser may be dissatisfied with the merchandise received because the goods are damaged or defective, of inferior quality, or do not meet the purchaser's specifications. In such cases, the purchaser may return the goods to the seller for credit if the sale was made on credit, or for a cash refund if the purchase was for cash. This transaction is known as a **purchase return**. Alternatively, the purchaser may choose to keep the merchandise if the seller is willing to grant an allowance (deduction) from the purchase price. This transaction is known as a **purchase allowance**.

Assume that on May 8 Sauk Stereo returned goods costing $300 to PW Audio Supply. The following entry by Sauk Stereo for the returned merchandise decreases (debits) Accounts Payable and decreases (credits) Inventory.

May 8	Accounts Payable	300	
	Inventory		300
	(To record return of goods purchased		
	from PW Audio Supply)		

Because Sauk Stereo increased Inventory when the goods were received, Inventory is decreased when Sauk Stereo returns the goods (or when it is granted an allowance).

Suppose instead that Sauk Stereo chose to keep the goods after being granted a $50 allowance (reduction in price). It would reduce (debit) Accounts Payable and reduce (credit) Inventory for $50.

Purchase Discounts

The credit terms of a purchase on account may permit the buyer to claim a cash discount for prompt payment. The buyer calls this cash discount a **purchase discount**. This incentive offers advantages to both parties: The purchaser saves money, and the seller shortens the operating cycle by more quickly converting the accounts receivable into cash.

Credit terms specify the amount of the cash discount and time period in which it is offered. They also indicate the time period in which the purchaser is expected to pay the full invoice price. In the sales invoice in Illustration 5-5 (page 214), credit terms are 2/10, n/30, which is read "two-ten, net thirty." This means that the buyer may take a 2% cash discount on the invoice price less ("net of") any returns or allowances, if payment is made within 10 days of the invoice date (the **discount period**). Otherwise, the invoice price, less any returns or allowances, is due 30 days from the invoice date.

Alternatively, the discount period may extend to a specified number of days following the month in which the sale occurs. For example, 1/10 EOM (end of month) means that a 1% discount is available if the invoice is paid within the first 10 days of the next month.

When the seller elects not to offer a cash discount for prompt payment, credit terms will specify only the maximum time period for paying the balance due. For example, the invoice may state the time period as n/30, n/60, or n/10 EOM. This means, respectively, that the buyer must pay the net amount in 30 days, 60 days, or within the first 10 days of the next month.

When the buyer pays an invoice within the discount period, the amount of the discount decreases Inventory. Why? Because companies record inventory at cost and, by paying within the discount period, the merchandiser has reduced that cost. To illustrate, assume Sauk Stereo pays the balance due of $3,500 (gross invoice price of $3,800 less purchase returns and allowances of $300) on May 14, the last

Helpful Hint

The term *net* in "net 30" means the remaining amount due after subtracting any sales returns and allowances and partial payments.

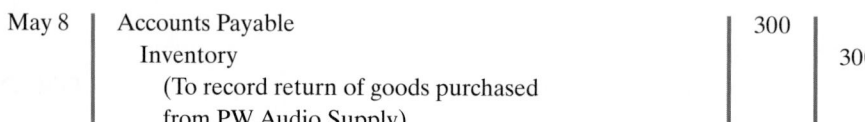

day of the discount period. The cash discount is $70 ($3,500 × 2%), and Sauk Stereo pays $3,430 ($3,500 − $70). The entry Sauk Stereo makes to record its May 14 payment decreases (debits) Accounts Payable by the amount of the gross invoice price, reduces (credits) Inventory by the $70 discount, and reduces (credits) Cash by the net amount owed.

May 14	Accounts Payable	3,500	
	Cash		3,430
	Inventory		70
	(To record payment within discount period)		

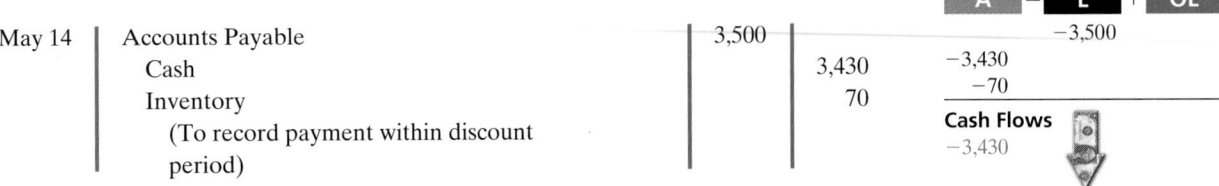

A = L + OE
−3,500
−3,430
−70

Cash Flows
−3,430

If Sauk Stereo failed to take the discount, and instead made full payment of $3,500 on June 3, it would debit Accounts Payable and credit Cash for $3,500 each.

June 3	Accounts Payable	3,500	
	Cash		3,500
	(To record payment with no discount taken)		

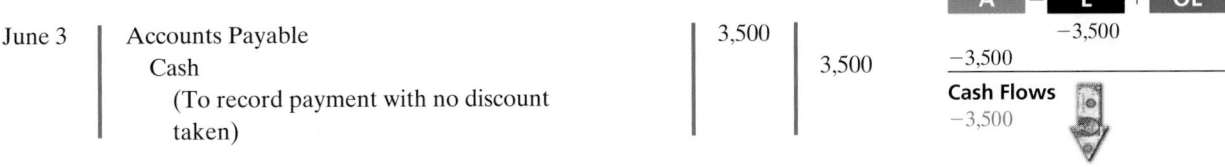

A = L + OE
−3,500
−3,500

Cash Flows
−3,500

A merchandising company usually should take all available discounts. Passing up the discount may be viewed as **paying interest** for use of the money. For example, passing up the discount offered by PW Audio Supply would be comparable to Sauk Stereo paying an interest rate of 2% for the use of $3,500 for 20 days. This is the equivalent of an annual interest rate of approximately 36.5% (2% × 365/20). Obviously, it would be better for Sauk Stereo to borrow at prevailing bank interest rates of 6% to 10% than to lose the discount.

Summary of Purchasing Transactions

The following T account (with transaction descriptions in blue) provides a summary of the effect of the previous transactions on Inventory. Sauk Stereo originally purchased $3,800 worth of inventory for resale. It then returned $300 of goods. It paid $150 in freight charges, and finally, it received a $70 discount off the balance owed because it paid within the discount period. This results in a balance in Inventory of $3,580.

Inventory

Purchase	May 4	3,800	May 8	300	Purchase return	
Freight-in	6	150	14	70	Purchase discount	
		3,580				

Do it!

On September 5, De La Hoya Company buys merchandise on account from Junot Diaz Company. The selling price of the goods is $1,500, and the cost to Diaz Company was $800. On September 8, De La Hoya returns defective goods with a selling price of $200. Record the transactions on the books of De La Hoya Company.

Purchase Transactions

action plan

✔ Purchaser records goods at cost.

✔ When goods are returned, purchaser reduces Inventory.

Solution

Sept. 5	Inventory	1,500	
	Accounts Payable		1,500
	(To record goods purchased on account)		
8	Accounts Payable	200	
	Inventory		200
	(To record return of defective goods)		

Related exercise material: BE5-2, BE5-4, E5-2, E5-3, E5-4, and **Do it!** 5-1.

The Navigator

Recording Sales of Merchandise

Study Objective [3]

Explain the recording of sales revenues under a perpetual inventory system.

Companies record sales revenues, like service revenues, when earned, in compliance with the revenue recognition principle. Typically, companies earn sales revenues when the goods transfer from the seller to the buyer. At this point, the sales transaction is complete and the sales price established.

Sales may be made on credit or for cash. A **business document** should support every sales transaction, to provide written evidence of the sale. **Cash register tapes** provide evidence of cash sales. A sales invoice, like the one shown in Illustration 5-5 (page 214), provides support for a credit sale. The original copy of the invoice goes to the customer, and the seller keeps a copy for use in recording the sale. The invoice shows the date of sale, customer name, total sales price, and other relevant information.

The seller makes two entries for each sale. **The first entry records the sale**: The seller increases (debits) Cash (or Accounts Receivable, if a credit sale), and also increases (credits) Sales Revenue. **The second entry records the cost of the merchandise sold**: The seller increases (debits) Cost of Goods Sold, and also decreases (credits) Inventory for the cost of those goods. As a result, the Inventory account will show at all times the amount of inventory that should be on hand.

To illustrate a credit sales transaction, PW Audio Supply records its May 4 sale of $3,800 to Sauk Stereo (see Illustration 5-5) as follows (assume the merchandise cost PW Audio Supply $2,400).

A = L + OE

+3,800

+3,800 Rev

Cash Flows
no effect

May 4	Accounts Receivable	3,800	
	Sales Revenue		3,800
	(To record credit sale to Sauk Stereo per invoice #731)		

A = L + OE

−2,400 Exp

−2,400

Cash Flows
no effect

4	Cost of Goods Sold	2,400	
	Inventory		2,400
	(To record cost of merchandise sold on invoice #731 to Sauk Stereo)		

For internal decision-making purposes, merchandising companies may use more than one sales account. For example, PW Audio Supply may decide to keep separate sales accounts for its sales of TV sets, DVD recorders, and microwave ovens. Wal-Mart might use separate accounts for sporting goods, children's clothing, and hardware—or it might have even more narrowly defined accounts. By using separate sales accounts for major product lines, rather than a single combined sales account, company management can more closely monitor sales trends and respond more strategically to changes in sales patterns. For example, if TV sales are increasing while microwave oven sales are decreasing, PW Audio Supply might reevaluate both its advertising and pricing policies on these items to ensure they are optimal.

On its income statement presented to outside investors, a merchandising company normally would provide only a single sales figure—the sum of all of its individual sales accounts. This is done for two reasons. First, providing detail on all of its individual sales accounts would add considerable length to its income statement. Second, companies do not want their competitors to know the details of their operating results. However, Microsoft recently expanded its disclosure of revenue from three to five types. The reason: The additional categories will better enable financial statement users to evaluate the growth of the company's consumer and Internet businesses.

Ethics Note

Many companies are trying to improve the quality of their financial reporting. For example, General Electric now provides more detail on its revenues and operating profits.

ANATOMY OF A FRAUD[1]

Holly Harmon was a cashier at a national superstore for only a short while when she began stealing merchandise using three methods. First, her husband or friends took UPC labels from cheaper items and put them on more expensive items. Holly then scanned the goods at the register. Second, Holly rang an item up but then voided the sale and left the merchandise in the shopping cart. A third approach was to put goods into large plastic containers. She rang up the plastic containers but not the goods within them. One day, Holly did not call in sick or show up for work. In such instances, the company reviews past surveillance tapes to look for suspicious activity by employees. This enabled the store to observe the thefts and to identify the participants.

Total take: $12,000

THE MISSING CONTROLS

Human resource controls. A background check would have revealed Holly's previous criminal record. She would not have been hired as a cashier.

Physical controls. Software can flag high numbers of voided transactions or a high number of sales of low-priced goods. Random comparisons of video records with cash register records can ensure that the goods reported as sold on the register are the same goods that are shown being purchased on the video recording. Finally, employees should be aware that they are being monitored.

Source: Adapted from Wells, *Fraud Casebook* (2007), pp. 251–259.

At the end of "Anatomy of a Fraud" stories, which describe some recent real-world frauds, we discuss the missing control activity that would likely have prevented or uncovered the fraud.

Sales Returns and Allowances

We now look at the "flipside" of purchase returns and allowances, which the seller records as **sales returns and allowances**. These are transactions where the seller either accepts goods back from the buyer (a return) or grants a reduction in the purchase price (an allowance) so the buyer will keep the goods. PW Audio Supply's entries to record credit for returned goods involve (1) an increase (debit) in Sales Returns and Allowances (a contra account to Sales Revenue) and a decrease (credit) in Accounts Receivable at the $300 selling price, and (2) an increase (debit) in

---

[1]The "Anatomy of a Fraud" stories in this textbook are adapted from *Fraud Casebook: Lessons from the Bad Side of Business,* edited by Joseph T. Wells (Hoboken, NJ: John Wiley & Sons, Inc., 2007). Used by permission. The names of some of the people and organizations in the stories are fictitious, but the facts in the stories are true.

Inventory (assume a $140 cost) and a decrease (credit) in Cost of Goods Sold, as shown below (assuming that the goods were not defective).

A	=	L	+	OE
				−300 Rev
−300				

Cash Flows
no effect

A	=	L	+	OE
+140				
				+140 Exp

Cash Flows
no effect

May 8	Sales Returns and Allowances	300	
	Accounts Receivable		300
	(To record credit granted to Sauk Stereo		
	for returned goods)		
8	Inventory	140	
	Cost of Goods Sold		140
	(To record cost of goods returned)		

If Sauk Stereo returns goods because they are damaged or defective, then PW Audio Supply's entry to Inventory and Cost of Goods Sold should be for the fair value of the returned goods, rather than their cost. For example, if the returned goods were defective and had a fair value of $50, PW Audio Supply would debit Inventory for $50, and would credit Cost of Goods Sold for $50.

What happens if the goods are not returned but the seller grants the buyer an allowance by reducing the purchase price? In this case, the seller debits Sales Returns and Allowances and credits Accounts Receivable for the amount of the allowance.

As mentioned above, Sales Returns and Allowances is a **contra-revenue account** to Sales Revenue. The normal balance of Sales Returns and Allowances is a debit. Companies use a contra account, instead of debiting Sales Revenue, to disclose in the accounts and in the income statement the amount of sales returns and allowances. Disclosure of this information is important to management: Excessive returns and allowances may suggest problems—inferior merchandise, inefficiencies in filling orders, errors in billing customers, or delivery or shipment mistakes. Moreover, a decrease (debit) recorded directly to Sales Revenue would obscure the relative importance of sales returns and allowances as a percentage of sales. It also could distort comparisons between total sales in different accounting periods.

*A*CCOUNTING *A*CROSS THE *O*RGANIZATION

Should Costco Change Its Return Policy?

In most industries, sales returns are relatively minor. But returns of consumer electronics can really take a bite out of profits. Recently, the marketing executives at Costco Wholesale Corp. faced a difficult decision. Costco has always prided itself on its generous return policy. Most goods have had an unlimited grace period for returns. A new policy will require that certain electronics must be retuned within 90 days of their purchase. The reason? The cost of returned products such as high-definition TVs, computers, and iPods cut an estimated 8¢ per share off Costco's earnings per share, which was $2.30.

Source: Kris Hudson, "Costco Tightens Policy on Returning Electronics," *Wall Street Journal* (February 27, 2007), p. B4.

? If a company expects significant returns, what are the implications for revenue recognition? (See page 257.)

Sales Discounts

As mentioned in our discussion of purchase transactions, the seller may offer the customer a cash discount—called by the seller a **sales discount**—for the prompt payment of the balance due. Like a purchase discount, a sales discount is based on the invoice price less returns and allowances, if any. The seller increases (debits) the Sales Discounts account for discounts that are taken. For example, PW Audio

Supply makes the following entry to record the cash receipt on May 14 from Sauk Stereo within the discount period.

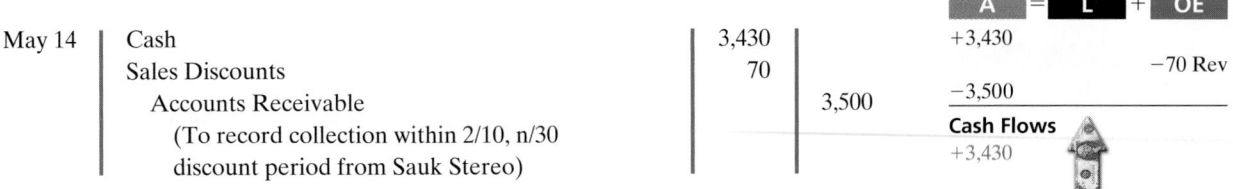

May 14	Cash	3,430	
	Sales Discounts	70	
	Accounts Receivable		3,500
	(To record collection within 2/10, n/30		
	discount period from Sauk Stereo)		

A = L + OE
+3,430
−70 Rev
−3,500

Cash Flows
+3,430

Like Sales Returns and Allowances, Sales Discounts is a **contra-revenue account** to Sales Revenue. Its normal balance is a debit. PW Audio Supply uses this account, instead of debiting Sales Revenue, to disclose the amount of cash discounts taken by customers. If Sauk Stereo does not take the discount, PW Audio Supply increases (debits) Cash for $3,500 and decreases (credits) Accounts Receivable for the same amount at the date of collection.

The following T accounts summarize the three sales-related transactions and show their combined effect on net sales.

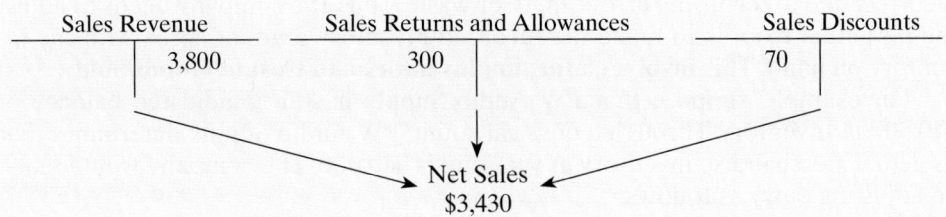

Sales Revenue	Sales Returns and Allowances	Sales Discounts
3,800	300	70

Net Sales
$3,430

Do it!

On September 5, De La Hoya Company buys merchandise on account from Junot Diaz Company. The selling price of the goods is $1,500, and the cost to Diaz Company was $800. On September 8, De La Hoya returns defective goods with a selling price of $200 and a fair value of $30. Record the transactions on the books of Junot Diaz Company.

Sales Transactions

action plan

✔ Seller records both the sale and the cost of goods sold at the time of the sale.

✔ When goods are returned, the seller records the return in a contra account, Sales Returns and Allowances, and reduces Accounts Receivable. Any goods returned increase Inventory and reduce Cost of Goods Sold.

✔ Defective or damaged inventory is recorded at fair value (scrap value).

Solution

Sept. 5	Accounts Receivable	1,500	
	Sales Revenue		1,500
	(To record credit sale)		
5	Cost of Goods Sold	800	
	Inventory		800
	(To record cost of goods sold on		
	account)		
8	Sales Returns and Allowances	200	
	Accounts Receivable		200
	(To record credit granted for receipt of		
	returned goods)		
8	Inventory	30	
	Cost of Goods Sold		30
	(To record fair value of goods		
	returned)		

Related exercise material: BE5-2, BE5-3, E5-3, E5-4, E5-5, and **Do it!** 5-2.

✔
The Navigator

Completing the Accounting Cycle

Study Objective [4]

Explain the steps in the accounting cycle for a merchandising company.

Up to this point, we have illustrated the basic entries for transactions relating to purchases and sales in a perpetual inventory system. Now we consider the remaining steps in the accounting cycle for a merchandising company. Each of the required steps described in Chapter 4 for service companies apply to merchandising companies. Appendix 5B to this chapter shows use of a worksheet by a merchandiser (an optional step).

Adjusting Entries

A merchandising company generally has the same types of adjusting entries as a service company. However, a merchandiser using a perpetual system will require one additional adjustment to make the records agree with the actual inventory on hand. Here's why: At the end of each period, for control purposes, a merchandising company that uses a perpetual system will take a physical count of its goods on hand. The company's unadjusted balance in Inventory usually does not agree with the actual amount of inventory on hand. The perpetual inventory records may be incorrect due to recording errors, theft, or waste. Thus, the company needs to adjust the perpetual records to make the recorded inventory amount agree with the inventory on hand. **This involves adjusting Inventory and Cost of Goods Sold.**

For example, suppose that PW Audio Supply has an unadjusted balance of $40,500 in Inventory. Through a physical count, PW Audio Supply determines that its actual merchandise inventory at year-end is $40,000. The company would make an adjusting entry as follows.

Cost of Goods Sold	500	
Inventory		500
(To adjust inventory to physical count)		

Closing Entries

A merchandising company, like a service company, closes to Income Summary all accounts that affect net income. In journalizing, the company credits all temporary accounts with debit balances, and debits all temporary accounts with credit balances, as shown below for PW Audio Supply. Note that PW Audio Supply closes Cost of Goods Sold to Income Summary.

Helpful Hint

The easiest way to prepare the first two closing entries is to identify the temporary accounts by their balances and then prepare one entry for the credits and one for the debits.

Dec. 31	Sales Revenue	480,000	
	Income Summary		480,000
	(To close income statement accounts with credit balances)		
31	Income Summary	450,000	
	Sales Returns and Allowances		12,000
	Sales Discounts		8,000
	Cost of Goods Sold		316,000
	Salaries and Wages Expense		64,000
	Freight-out		7,000
	Advertising Expense		16,000
	Utilities Expense		17,000
	Depreciation Expense		8,000
	Insurance Expense		2,000
	(To close income statement accounts with debit balances)		

31	Income Summary	30,000	
	Owner's Capital		30,000
	(To close net income to capital)		

31	Owner's Capital	15,000	
	Owner's Drawings		15,000
	(To close drawings to capital)		

After PW Audio Supply has posted the closing entries, all temporary accounts have zero balances. Also, Owner's Capital has a balance that is carried over to the next period.

Summary of Merchandising Entries

Illustration 5-7 summarizes the entries for the merchandising accounts using a perpetual inventory system.

Illustration 5-7
Daily recurring and adjusting and closing entries

	Transactions	Daily Recurring Entries	Dr.	Cr.
Sales Transactions	Selling merchandise to customers.	Cash or Accounts Receivable	XX	
		Sales Revenue		XX
		Cost of Goods Sold	XX	
		Inventory		XX
	Granting sales returns or allowances to customers.	Sales Returns and Allowances	XX	
		Cash or Accounts Receivable		XX
		Inventory	XX	
		Cost of Goods Sold		XX
	Paying freight costs on sales; FOB destination.	Freight-out	XX	
		Cash		XX
	Receiving payment from customers within discount period.	Cash	XX	
		Sales Discounts	XX	
		Accounts Receivable		XX
Purchase Transactions	Purchasing merchandise for resale.	Inventory	XX	
		Cash or Accounts Payable		XX
	Paying freight costs on merchandise purchased; FOB shipping point.	Inventory	XX	
		Cash		XX
	Receiving purchase returns or allowances from suppliers.	Cash or Accounts Payable	XX	
		Inventory		XX
	Paying suppliers within discount period.	Accounts Payable	XX	
		Inventory		XX
		Cash		XX

	Events	Adjusting and Closing Entries		
	Adjust because book amount is higher than the inventory amount determined to be on hand.	Cost of Goods Sold	XX	
		Inventory		XX
	Closing temporary accounts with credit balances.	Sales Revenue	XX	
		Income Summary		XX
	Closing temporary accounts with debit balances.	Income Summary	XX	
		Sales Returns and Allowances		XX
		Sales Discounts		XX
		Cost of Goods Sold		XX
		Freight-out		XX
		Expenses		XX

Do it!

Closing Entries

action plan

✔ Close all temporary accounts with credit balances to Income Summary by debiting these accounts.

✔ Close all temporary accounts with debit balances, except drawings, to Income Summary by crediting these accounts.

The trial balance of Celine's Sports Wear Shop at December 31 shows Inventory $25,000, Sales Revenue $162,400, Sales Returns and Allowances $4,800, Sales Discounts $3,600, Cost of Goods Sold $110,000, Rent Revenue $6,000, Freight-out $1,800, Rent Expense $8,800, and Salaries and Wages Expense $22,000. Prepare the closing entries for the above accounts.

Solution

The two closing entries are:

Dec. 31	Sales Revenue	162,400	
	Rent Revenue	6,000	
	Income Summary		168,400
	(To close accounts with credit balances)		
31	Income Summary	151,000	
	Cost of Goods Sold		110,000
	Sales Returns and Allowances		4,800
	Sales Discounts		3,600
	Freight-out		1,800
	Rent Expense		8,800
	Salaries and Wages Expense		22,000
	(To close accounts with debit balances)		

Related exercise material: BE5-5, BE5-6, E5-6, E5-7, E5-8, and **Do it!** 5-3.

✔
The Navigator

Forms of Financial Statements

Study Objective [5]

Distinguish between a multiple-step and a single-step income statement.

Merchandising companies widely use the classified balance sheet introduced in Chapter 4 and one of two forms for the income statement. This section explains the use of these financial statements by merchandisers.

Multiple-Step Income Statement

The **multiple-step income statement** is so named because it shows several steps in determining net income. Two of these steps relate to the company's principal operating activities. A multiple-step statement also distinguishes between **operating** and **nonoperating activities**. Finally, the statement also highlights intermediate components of income and shows subgroupings of expenses.

INCOME STATEMENT PRESENTATION OF SALES

The multiple-step income statement begins by presenting **sales revenue**. It then deducts contra-revenue accounts—sales returns and allowances, and sales discounts—to arrive at **net sales**. Illustration 5-8 presents the sales revenues section for PW Audio Supply, using assumed data.

This presentation discloses the key data about the company's principal revenue-producing activities.

Illustration 5-8
Computation of net sales

PW Audio Supply		
Income Statement (partial)		
Sales revenues		
Sales revenue		$480,000
Less: Sales returns and allowances	$12,000	
Sales discounts	8,000	20,000
Net sales		$460,000

GROSS PROFIT

From Illustration 5-1, you learned that companies deduct cost of goods sold from sales revenue in order to determine gross profit. For this computation, companies use **net sales** (which takes into consideration Sales Returns and Allowances and Sales Discounts) as the amount of sales revenue. On the basis of the sales data in Illustration 5-8 (net sales of $460,000) and cost of goods sold under the perpetual inventory system (assume $316,000), PW Audio Supply's gross profit is $144,000, computed as follows.

Net sales	$460,000
Cost of goods sold	316,000
Gross profit	$144,000

Illustration 5-9
Computation of gross profit

We also can express a company's gross profit as a percentage, called the gross profit rate. To do so, we divide the amount of gross profit by net sales. For PW Audio Supply, the **gross profit rate** is 31.3%, computed as follows.

Gross Profit	÷	Net Sales	=	Gross Profit Rate
$144,000	÷	$460,000	=	31.3%

Illustration 5-10
Gross profit rate formula and computation

Analysts generally consider the gross profit **rate** to be more useful than the gross profit **amount**. The rate expresses a more meaningful (qualitative) relationship between net sales and gross profit. For example, a gross profit of $1,000,000 may sound impressive. But if it is the result of a gross profit rate of only 7%, it is not so impressive. The gross profit rate tells how many cents of each sales dollar go to gross profit.

Gross profit represents the **merchandising profit** of a company. It is not a measure of the overall profitability, because operating expenses are not yet deducted. But managers and other interested parties closely watch the amount and trend of gross profit. They compare current gross profit with amounts reported in past periods. They also compare the company's gross profit rate with rates of competitors and with industry averages. Such comparisons provide information about the effectiveness of a company's purchasing function and the soundness of its pricing policies.

OPERATING EXPENSES AND NET INCOME

Operating expenses are the next component in measuring net income for a merchandising company. They are the expenses incurred in the process of earning sales revenue. These expenses are similar in merchandising and service companies. At PW Audio Supply, operating expenses were $114,000. The company determines its net income by subtracting operating expenses from gross profit. Thus, net income is $30,000, as shown below.

Gross profit	$144,000
Operating expenses	114,000
Net income	$ 30,000

Illustration 5-11
Operating expenses in computing net income

The net income amount is the so-called "bottom line" of a company's income statement.

Ethics Note

Companies manage earnings in various ways. ConAgra Foods recorded a nonrecurring gain for $186 million from the sale of Pilgrim's Pride stock to help meet an earnings projection for the quarter.

NONOPERATING ACTIVITIES

Nonoperating activities consist of various revenues and expenses and gains and losses that are unrelated to the company's main line of operations. When nonoperating items are included, the label "**Income from operations**" (or "Operating income") precedes them. This label clearly identifies the results of the company's normal operations, an amount determined by subtracting cost of goods sold and operating expenses from net sales. The results of nonoperating activities are shown in the categories "**Other revenues and gains**" and "**Other expenses and losses**." Illustration 5-12 lists examples of each.

Illustration 5-12
Other items of nonoperating activities

Other Revenues and Gains

Interest revenue from notes receivable and marketable securities.

Dividend revenue from investments in common stock.

Rent revenue from subleasing a portion of the store.

Gain from the sale of property, plant, and equipment.

Other Expenses and Losses

Interest expense on notes and loans payable.

Casualty losses from recurring causes, such as vandalism and accidents.

Loss from the sale or abandonment of property, plant, and equipment.

Loss from strikes by employees and suppliers.

Merchandising companies report the nonoperating activities in the income statement immediately after the company's operating activities. Illustration 5-13 shows these sections for PW Audio Supply, Inc., using assumed data.

The distinction between operating and nonoperating activities is crucial to many external users of financial data. These users view operating income as sustainable and many nonoperating activities as nonrecurring. Therefore, when forecasting next year's income, analysts put the most weight on this year's operating income, and less weight on this year's nonoperating activities.

*E*THICS *I*NSIGHT

Disclosing More Details

After Enron, increased investor criticism and regulator scrutiny forced many companies to improve the clarity of their financial disclosures. For example, IBM announced that it would begin providing more detail regarding its "Other gains and losses." It had previously included these items in its selling, general, and administrative expenses, with little disclosure.

Disclosing other gains and losses in a separate line item on the income statement will not have any effect on bottom-line income. However, analysts complained that burying these details in the selling, general, and administrative expense line reduced their ability to fully understand how well IBM was performing. For example previously if IBM sold off one of its buildings at a gain, it would include this gain in the selling, general and administrative expense line item, thus reducing that expense. This made it appear that the company had done a better job of controlling operating expenses than it actually had.

Other companies that also recently announced changes to increase the informativeness of their income statements included PepsiCo and General Electric.

 Why have investors and analysts demanded more accuracy in isolating "Other gains and losses" from operating items? (See page 257.)

Illustration 5-13
Multiple-step income statement

PW Audio Supply, Inc. Income Statement For the Year Ended December 31, 2012			

Calculation of gross profit

Sales revenues			
Sales revenue			$480,000
Less: Sales returns and allowances		$12,000	
Sales discounts		8,000	20,000
Net sales			460,000
Cost of goods sold			316,000
Gross profit			144,000

Calculation of income from operations

Operating expenses			
Salaries and wages expense		64,000	
Utilities expense		17,000	
Advertising expense		16,000	
Depreciation expense		8,000	
Freight-out		7,000	
Insurance expense		2,000	
Total operating expenses			114,000
Income from operations			30,000
Other revenues and gains			
Interest revenue		3,000	
Gain on disposal of plant assets		600	3,600

Results of nonoperating activities

Other expenses and losses			
Interest expense		1,800	
Casualty loss from vandalism		200	2,000
Net income			$ 31,600

Single-Step Income Statement

Another income statement format is the **single-step income statement**. The statement is so named because only one step—subtracting total expenses from total revenues—is required in determining net income.

In a single-step statement, all data are classified into two categories: (1) **revenues**, which include both operating revenues and other revenues and gains; and (2) **expenses**, which include cost of goods sold, operating expenses, and other expenses and losses. Illustration 5-14 (page 228) shows a single-step statement for PW Audio Supply.

There are two primary reasons for using the single-step format: (1) A company does not realize any type of profit or income until total revenues exceed total expenses, so it makes sense to divide the statement into these two categories. (2) The format is simpler and easier to read. *For homework problems, however, you should use the single-step format only when specifically instructed to do so.*

Classified Balance Sheet

In the balance sheet, merchandising companies report inventory as a current asset immediately below accounts receivable. Recall from Chapter 4 that companies generally list current asset items in the order of their closeness to cash

Illustration 5-14
Single-step income statement

PW Audio Supply, Inc. Income Statement For the Year Ended December 31, 2012		
Revenues		
Net sales		$460,000
Interest revenue		3,000
Gain on disposal of plant assets		600
Total revenues		463,600
Expenses		
Cost of goods sold	$316,000	
Operating expenses	114,000	
Interest expense	1,800	
Casualty loss from vandalism	200	
Total expenses		432,000
Net income		$ 31,600

(liquidity). Inventory is less close to cash than accounts receivable because the goods must first be sold and then collection made from the customer. Illustration 5-15 presents the assets section of a classified balance sheet for PW Audio Supply.

Illustration 5-15
Assets section of a classified balance sheet

Helpful Hint

The $40,000 is the cost of the inventory on hand, not its expected selling price.

PW Audio Supply, Inc. Balance Sheet (Partial) December 31, 2012		
Assets		
Current assets		
Cash		$ 9,500
Accounts receivable		16,100
Inventory		40,000
Prepaid insurance		1,800
Total current assets		67,400
Property, plant, and equipment		
Equipment	$80,000	
Less: Accumulated depreciation—equipment	24,000	56,000
Total assets		$123,400

Do it!

Financial Statement Classifications

You are presented with the following list of accounts from the adjusted trial balance for merchandiser Gorman Company. Indicate in which financial statement and under what classification each of the following would be reported.

Accounts Payable
Accounts Receivable
Accumulated Depreciation—Buildings

Accumulated Depreciation—Equipment
Advertising Expense
Buildings

Cash
Depreciation Expense
Equipment
Freight-out
Gain on Disposal of Plant Assets
Insurance Expense
Interest Expense
Interest Payable
Inventory
Land

Notes Payable (due in 3 years)
Owner's Capital (beginning balance)
Owner's Drawings
Property Taxes Payable
Salaries and Wages Expense
Salaries and Wages Payable
Sales Returns and Allowances
Sales Revenue
Utilities Expense

Solution

Account	Financial Statement	Classification
Accounts Payable	Balance sheet	Current liabilities
Accounts Receivable	Balance sheet	Current assets
Accumulated Depreciation— Buildings	Balance sheet	Property, plant, and equipment
Accumulated Depreciation— Equipment	Balance sheet	Property, plant, and equipment
Advertising Expense	Income statement	Operating expenses
Buildings	Balance sheet	Property, plant, and equipment
Cash	Balance sheet	Current assets
Depreciation Expense	Income statement	Operating expenses
Equipment	Balance sheet	Property, plant, and equipment
Freight-out	Income statement	Operating expenses
Gain on Disposal of Plant Assets	Income statement	Other revenues and gains
Insurance Expense	Income statement	Operating expenses
Interest Expense	Income statement	Other expenses and losses
Interest Payable	Balance sheet	Current liabilities
Inventory	Balance sheet	Current assets
Land	Balance sheet	Property, plant, and equipment
Notes Payable	Balance sheet	Long-term liabilities
Owner's Capital	Owner's equity statement	Beginning balance
Owner's Drawings	Owner's equity statement	Deduction section
Property Taxes Payable	Balance sheet	Current liabilities
Salaries and Wages Expense	Income statement	Operating expenses
Salaries and Wages Payable	Balance sheet	Current liabilities
Sales Returns and Allowances	Income statement	Sales revenues
Sales Revenue	Income statement	Sales revenues
Utilities Expense	Income statement	Operating expenses

action plan

✔ Review the major sections of the income statement, sales revenues, cost of goods sold, operating expenses, other revenues and gains, and other expenses and losses.

✔ Add net income and investments to beginning capital and deduct drawings to arrive at ending capital in the owner's equity statement.

✔ Review the major sections of the balance sheet, income statement, and owner's equity statement.

Related exercise material: BE5-7, BE5-8, BE5-9, E5-9, E5-10, E5-12, E5-13, E5-14, and **Do it!** 5-4.

✔
The Navigator

The adjusted trial balance columns of Falcetto Company's worksheet for the year ended December 31, 2012, are as follows.

Debit		Credit	
Cash	14,500	Accumulated Depreciation—Equipment	18,000
Accounts Receivable	11,100	Notes Payable	25,000
Inventory	29,000	Accounts Payable	10,600
Prepaid Insurance	2,500	Owner's Capital	81,000
Equipment	95,000	Sales Revenue	536,800
Owner's Drawings	12,000	Interest Revenue	2,500
Sales Returns and Allowances	6,700		673,900
Sales Discounts	5,000		
Cost of Goods Sold	363,400		
Freight-out	7,600		
Advertising Expense	12,000		
Salaries and Wages Expense	56,000		
Utilities Expense	18,000		
Rent Expense	24,000		
Depreciation Expense	9,000		
Insurance Expense	4,500		
Interest Expense	3,600		
	673,900		

Instructions

Prepare a multiple-step income statement for Falcetto Company.

action plan

✔ Remember that the key components of the income statement are net sales, cost of goods sold, gross profit, total operating expenses, and net income (loss). Report these components in the right-hand column of the income statement.

✔ Put nonoperating items after income from operations.

Solution to Comprehensive Do it!

FALCETTO COMPANY
Income Statement
For the Year Ended December 31, 2012

Sales revenues			
Sales revenue			$536,800
Less: Sales returns and allowances		$ 6,700	
Sales discounts		5,000	11,700
Net sales			525,100
Cost of goods sold			363,400
Gross profit			161,700
Operating expenses			
Salaries and wages expense		56,000	
Rent expense		24,000	
Utilities expense		18,000	
Advertising expense		12,000	
Depreciation expense		9,000	
Freight-out		7,600	
Insurance expense		4,500	
Total operating expenses			131,100
Income from operations			30,600
Other revenues and gains			
Interest revenue		2,500	
Other expenses and losses			
Interest expense		3,600	1,100
Net income			$ 29,500

The Navigator

Summary of Study Objectives

[1] Identify the differences between service and merchandising companies. Because of inventory, a merchandising company has sales revenue, cost of goods sold, and gross profit. To account for inventory, a merchandising company must choose between a perpetual and a periodic inventory system.

[2] Explain the recording of purchases under a perpetual inventory system. The company debits the Inventory account for all purchases of merchandise and freight-in, and credits it for purchase discounts and purchase returns and allowances.

[3] Explain the recording of sales revenues under a perpetual inventory system. When a merchandising company sells inventory, it debits Accounts Receivable (or Cash), and credits Sales Revenue for the **selling price** of the merchandise. At the same time, it debits Cost of Goods Sold, and credits Inventory for the **cost** of the inventory items sold.

[4] Explain the steps in the accounting cycle for a merchandising company. Each of the required steps in the accounting cycle for a service company applies to a merchandising company. A worksheet is again an optional step. Under a perpetual inventory system, the company must adjust the Inventory account to agree with the physical count.

[5] Distinguish between a multiple-step and a single-step income statement. A multiple-step income statement shows numerous steps in determining net income, including nonoperating activities sections. A single-step income statement classifies all data under two categories, revenues or expenses, and determines net income in one step.

[6] Explain the computation and importance of gross profit. Merchandising companies compute gross profit by subtracting cost of goods sold from net sales. Gross profit represents the merchandising profit of a company. Managers and other interested parties closely watch the amount and trend of gross profit and of the gross profit rate.

✔
The Navigator

Glossary

Contra-revenue account An account that is offset against a revenue account on the income statement. (p. 220).

Cost of goods sold The total cost of merchandise sold during the period. (p. 210).

FOB destination Freight terms indicating that the seller places the goods free on board to the buyer's place of business, and the seller pays the freight. (p. 215).

FOB shipping point Freight terms indicating that the seller places goods free on board the carrier, and the buyer pays the freight costs. (p. 215).

Gross profit The excess of net sales over the cost of goods sold. (p. 225).

Gross profit rate Gross profit expressed as a percentage, by dividing the amount of gross profit by net sales. (p. 225).

Income from operations Income from a company's principal operating activity; determined by subtracting cost of goods sold and operating expenses from net sales. (p. 226).

Multiple-step income statement An income statement that shows several steps in determining net income. (p. 224).

Net sales Sales less sales returns and allowances and less sales discounts. (p. 224).

Nonoperating activities Various revenues, expenses, gains, and losses that are unrelated to a company's main line of operations. (p. 226).

Operating expenses Expenses incurred in the process of earning sales revenues. (p. 225).

Other expenses and losses A nonoperating-activities section of the income statement that shows expenses and losses unrelated to the company's main line of operations. (p. 226).

Other revenues and gains A nonoperating-activities section of the income statement that shows revenues and gains unrelated to the company's main line of operations. (p. 226).

Periodic inventory system An inventory system under which the company does not keep detailed inventory records throughout the accounting period but determines the cost of goods sold only at the end of an accounting period. (p. 212).

Perpetual inventory system An inventory system under which the company keeps detailed records of the cost of each inventory purchase and sale, and the records continuously show the inventory that should be on hand. (p. 211).

Purchase allowance A deduction made to the selling price of merchandise, granted by the seller so that the buyer will keep the merchandise. (p. 216).

Purchase discount A cash discount claimed by a buyer for prompt payment of a balance due. (p. 216).

Purchase invoice A document that supports each credit purchase. (p. 213).

Purchase return A return of goods from the buyer to the seller for a cash or credit refund. (p. 216).

Sales discount A reduction given by a seller for prompt payment of a credit sale. (p. 220).

Sales invoice   A document that supports each credit sale. (p. 218).

Sales returns and allowances   Purchase returns and allowances from the seller's perspective. See *Purchase return* and *Purchase allowance*, above. (p. 219).

Sales revenue (Sales)   The primary source of revenue in a merchandising company. (p. 210).

Single-step income statement   An income statement that shows only one step in determining net income. (p. 227).

APPENDIX5A

Periodic Inventory System

Study Objective [7]

Explain the recording of purchases and sales of inventory under a periodic inventory system.

As described in this chapter, companies may use one of two basic systems of accounting for inventories: (1) the perpetual inventory system or (2) the periodic inventory system. In the chapter, we focused on the characteristics of the perpetual inventory system. In this appendix, we discuss and illustrate the **periodic inventory system**. One key difference between the two systems is the point at which the company computes cost of goods sold. For a visual reminder of this difference, refer back to Illustration 5-4 (on page 212).

Determining Cost of Goods Sold Under a Periodic System

Determining cost of goods sold is different when a periodic inventory system is used rather than a perpetual system. As you have seen, a company using a **perpetual system** makes an entry to record cost of goods sold and to reduce inventory *each time a sale is made*. A company using a **periodic system** does not determine cost of goods sold *until the end of the period*. At the end of the period the company performs a count to determine the ending balance of inventory. It then **calculates cost of goods sold by subtracting ending inventory from the goods available for sale**. Goods available for sale is the sum of beginning inventory plus purchases, as shown in Illustration 5A-1.

Illustration 5A-1

Basic formula for cost of goods sold using the periodic system

$$
\begin{array}{l}
\text{Beginning Inventory} \\
\underline{+\;\text{Cost of Goods Purchased}} \\
\text{Cost of Goods Available for Sale} \\
\underline{-\;\text{Ending Inventory}} \\
\text{Cost of Goods Sold}
\end{array}
$$

Another difference between the two approaches is that the perpetual system directly adjusts the Inventory account for any transaction that affects inventory (such as freight costs, returns, and discounts). The periodic system does not do this. Instead, it creates different accounts for purchases, freight costs, returns, and discounts. These various accounts are shown in Illustration 5A-2, which presents the calculation of cost of goods sold for PW Audio Supply using the periodic approach.

Note that the basic elements from Illustration 5A-1 are highlighted in Illustration 5A-2. You will learn more in Chapter 6 about how to determine cost of goods sold using the periodic system.

The use of the periodic inventory system does not affect the form of presentation in the balance sheet. As under the perpetual system, a company reports inventory in the current assets section.

PW Audio Supply, Inc.
Cost of Goods Sold
For the Year Ended December 31, 2012

Cost of goods sold
Inventory, January 1		$ 36,000
Purchases	$325,000	
Less: Purchase returns and allowances	$10,400	
Purchase discounts	6,800	17,200
Net purchases		307,800
Add: Freight-in		12,200
Cost of goods purchased		320,000
Cost of goods available for sale		356,000
Inventory, December 31		40,000
Cost of goods sold		$316,000

Illustration 5A-2
Cost of goods sold for a merchandiser using a periodic inventory system

Helpful Hint

The far right column identifies the primary items that make up cost of goods sold of $316,000. The middle column explains cost of goods purchased of $320,000. The left column reports contra purchase items of $17,200.

Recording Merchandise Transactions

In a **periodic inventory system**, companies record revenues from the sale of merchandise when sales are made, just as in a perpetual system. Unlike the perpetual system, however, companies **do not attempt on the date of sale to record the cost of the merchandise sold**. Instead, they take a physical inventory count at the **end of the period** to determine (1) the cost of the merchandise then on hand and (2) the cost of the goods sold during the period. And, **under a periodic system, companies record purchases of merchandise in the Purchases account rather than the Inventory account**. Also, in a periodic system, purchase returns and allowances, purchase discounts, and freight costs on purchases are recorded in separate accounts.

To illustrate the recording of merchandise transactions under a periodic inventory system, we will use purchase/sale transactions between PW Audio Supply, Inc. and Sauk Stereo, as illustrated for the perpetual inventory system in this chapter.

Recording Purchases of Merchandise

On the basis of the sales invoice (Illustration 5-5, shown on page 214) and receipt of the merchandise ordered from PW Audio Supply, Sauk Stereo records the $3,800 purchase as follows.

May 4	Purchases	3,800	
	Accounts Payable		3,800
	(To record goods purchased on account from PW Audio Supply)		

Helpful Hint
Be careful not to debit purchases of equipment or supplies to a Purchases account.

Purchases is a temporary account whose normal balance is a debit.

FREIGHT COSTS
When the purchaser directly incurs the freight costs, it debits the account Freight-in (or Transportation-in). For example, if Sauk Stereo pays Acme Freight Company $150 for freight charges on its purchase from PW Audio Supply on May 6, the entry on Sauk Stereo's books is:

May 6	Freight-in (Transportation-in)	150	
	Cash		150
	(To record payment of freight on goods purchased)		

Alternative Terminology

Freight-in is also called
transportation-in.

Like Purchases, Freight-in is a temporary account whose normal balance is a debit. **Freight-in is part of cost of goods purchased.** The reason is that cost of goods purchased should include any freight charges necessary to bring the goods to the purchaser. Freight costs are not subject to a purchase discount. Purchase discounts apply only to the invoice cost of the merchandise.

PURCHASE RETURNS AND ALLOWANCES

Sauk Stereo returns $300 of goods to PW Audio Supply and prepares the following entry to recognize the return.

May 8	Accounts Payable	300	
	Purchase Returns and Allowances		300
	(To record return of goods purchased		
	from PW Audio Supply)		

Purchase Returns and Allowances is a temporary account whose normal balance is a credit.

PURCHASE DISCOUNTS

On May 14, Sauk Stereo pays the balance due on account to PW Audio Supply, taking the 2% cash discount allowed by PW Audio Supply for payment within 10 days. Sauk Stereo records the payment and discount as follows.

May 14	Accounts Payable ($3,800 − $300)	3,500	
	Purchase Discounts ($3,500 × .02)		70
	Cash		3,430
	(To record payment within the		
	discount period)		

Purchase Discounts is a temporary account whose normal balance is a credit.

Recording Sales of Merchandise

The seller, PW Audio Supply, records the sale of $3,800 of merchandise to Sauk Stereo on May 4 (sales invoice No. 731, Illustration 5-5, page 214) as follows.

May 4	Accounts Receivable	3,800	
	Sales Revenue		3,800
	(To record credit sales per invoice #731		
	to Sauk Stereo)		

SALES RETURNS AND ALLOWANCES

To record the returned goods received from Sauk Stereo on May 8, PW Audio Supply records the $300 sales return as follows.

May 8	Sales Returns and Allowances	300	
	Accounts Receivable		300
	(To record credit granted to Sauk		
	Stereo for returned goods)		

SALES DISCOUNTS

On May 14, PW Audio Supply receives payment of $3,430 on account from Sauk Stereo. PW Audio Supply honors the 2% cash discount and records the payment of Sauk Stereo's account receivable in full as follows.

May 14	Cash	3,430	
	Sales Discounts ($3,500 × .02)	70	
	Accounts Receivable ($3,800 − $300)		3,500
	(To record collection within 2/10, n/30		
	discount period from Sauk Stereo)		

COMPARISON OF ENTRIES—PERPETUAL VS. PERIODIC

Illustration 5A-3 summarizes the periodic inventory entries shown in this appendix and compares them to the perpetual-system entries from the chapter. Entries that differ in the two systems are shown in color.

Illustration 5A-3
Comparison of entries for perpetual and periodic inventory systems

Entries on Sauk Stereo's Books

Transaction	Perpetual Inventory System		Periodic Inventory System	

May 4 Purchase of merchandise on credit.	Inventory
	  Accounts Payable
		3,800
		  3,800
			Purchases
			  Accounts Payable
				3,800
				  3,800

6 Freight costs on purchases.	Inventory
	  Cash
		150
		  150
			Freight-in
			  Cash
				150
				  150

8 Purchase returns and allowances.	Accounts Payable
	  Inventory
		300
		  300
			Accounts Payable
			  Purchase Returns
			  and Allowances
				300
				
				  300

14 Payment on account with a discount.	Accounts Payable
	  Cash
	  Inventory
		3,500
		  3,430
		  70
			Accounts Payable
			  Cash
			  Purchase Discounts
				3,500
				  3,430
				  70

Entries on PW Audio Supply's Books

Transaction	Perpetual Inventory System		Periodic Inventory System	

May 4 Sale of merchandise on credit.	Accounts Receivable
	  Sales Revenue
		3,800
		  3,800
			Accounts Receivable
			  Sales Revenue
				3,800
				  3,800

	Cost of Goods Sold
	  Inventory
		2,400
		  2,400
			No entry for cost of goods sold	

8 Return of merchandise sold.	Sales Returns and
	Allowances
	  Accounts Receivable
		
		300
		  300
			Sales Returns and
			Allowances
			  Accounts Receivable
				
				300
				  300

	Inventory
	  Cost of Goods Sold
		140
		  140
			No entry	

14 Cash received on account with a discount.	Cash
	Sales Discounts
	  Accounts Receivable
		3,430
		70
		  3,500
			Cash
			Sales Discounts
			  Accounts Receivable
				3,430
				70
				  3,500

Summary of Study Objective for Appendix 5A

[7] **Explain the recording of purchases and sales of inventory under a periodic inventory system.** In recording purchases under a periodic system, companies must make entries for (a) cash and credit purchases, (b) purchase returns and allowances, (c) purchase discounts, and (d) freight costs. In recording sales, companies must make entries for (a) cash and credit sales, (b) sales returns and allowances, and (c) sales discounts.

APPENDIX5B

Worksheet for a Merchandising Company

Using a Worksheet

Study Objective [8]

Prepare a worksheet for a merchandising company.

As indicated in Chapter 4, a worksheet enables companies to prepare financial statements before they journalize and post adjusting entries. The steps in preparing a worksheet for a merchandising company are the same as for a service company (see pages 154–158). Illustration 5B-1 shows the worksheet for PW Audio Supply (excluding nonoperating items). The unique accounts for a merchandiser using a perpetual inventory system are in boldface letters and in red.

PW Audio Supply.xls

File   Edit   View   Insert   Format   Tools   Data   Window   Help

PW AUDIO SUPPLY
Worksheet
For the Year Ended December 31, 2012

Accounts	Trial Balance Dr.	Trial Balance Cr.	Adjustments Dr.	Adjustments Cr.	Adjusted Trial Balance Dr.	Adjusted Trial Balance Cr.	Income Statement Dr.	Income Statement Cr.	Balance Sheet Dr.	Balance Sheet Cr.
Cash	9,500				9,500				9,500	
Accounts Receivable	16,100				16,100				16,100	
Inventory	40,500			(a) 500	40,000				40,000	
Prepaid Insurance	3,800			(b) 2,000	1,800				1,800	
Equipment	80,000				80,000				80,000	
Accumulated Depreciation—Equipment		16,000		(c) 8,000		24,000				24,000
Accounts Payable		20,400				20,400				20,400
Owner's Capital		83,000				83,000				83,000
Owner's Drawings	15,000				15,000				15,000	
Sales Revenue		480,000				480,000		480,000		
Sales Returns and Allowances	12,000				12,000		12,000			
Sales Discounts	8,000				8,000		8,000			
Cost of Goods Sold	315,500		(a) 500		316,000		316,000			
Freight-out	7,000				7,000		7,000			
Advertising Expense	16,000				16,000		16,000			
Salaries and Wages Expense	59,000		(d) 5,000		64,000		64,000			
Utilities Expense	17,000				17,000		17,000			
Totals	599,400	599,400								
Insurance Expense			(b) 2,000		2,000		2,000			
Depreciation Expense			(c) 8,000		8,000		8,000			
Salaries and Wages Payable				(d) 5,000		5,000				5,000
Totals			15,500	15,500	612,400	612,400	450,000	480,000	162,400	132,400
Net Income							30,000			30,000
Totals							480,000	480,000	162,400	162,400

Key: (a) Adjustment to inventory on hand. (b) Insurance expired. (c) Depreciation expense. (d) Salaries accrued.

Illustration 5B-1
Worksheet for merchandising company

TRIAL BALANCE COLUMNS

Data for the trial balance come from the ledger balances of PW Audio Supply at December 31. The amount shown for Inventory, $40,500, is the year-end inventory amount from the perpetual inventory system.

ADJUSTMENTS COLUMNS

A merchandising company generally has the same types of adjustments as a service company. As you see in the worksheet, adjustments (b), (c), and (d) are for insurance, depreciation, and salaries. Pioneer Advertising Agency, as illustrated in Chapters 3 and 4, also had these adjustments. Adjustment (a) was required to adjust the perpetual inventory carrying amount to the actual count.

After PW Audio Supply enters all adjustments data on the worksheet, it establishes the equality of the adjustments column totals. It then extends the balances in all accounts to the adjusted trial balance columns.

ADJUSTED TRIAL BALANCE
The adjusted trial balance shows the balance of all accounts after adjustment at the end of the accounting period.

INCOME STATEMENT COLUMNS
Next, the merchandising company transfers the accounts and balances that affect the income statement from the adjusted trial balance columns to the income statement columns. PW Audio Supply shows sales of $480,000 in the credit column. It shows the contra-revenue accounts Sales Returns and Allowances $12,000 and Sales Discounts $8,000 in the debit column. The difference of $460,000 is the net sales shown on the income statement (Illustration 5-13, page 227).

Finally, the company totals all the credits in the income statement column and compares those totals to the total of the debits in the income statement column. If the credits exceed the debits, the company has net income. PW Audio Supply has net income of $30,000. If the debits exceed the credits, the company would report a net loss.

BALANCE SHEET COLUMNS
The major difference between the balance sheets of a service company and a merchandiser is inventory. PW Audio Supply shows the ending inventory amount of $40,000 in the balance sheet debit column. The information to prepare the owner's equity statement is also found in these columns. That is, the Owner's Capital account is $83,000. Owner's Drawings are $15,000. Net income results when the total of the debit column exceeds the total of the credit column in the balance sheet columns. A net loss results when the total of the credits exceeds the total of the debit balances.

Summary of Study Objective for Appendix 5B

[8] **Prepare a worksheet for a merchandising company.** The steps in preparing a worksheet for a merchandising company are the same as for a service company. The unique accounts for a merchandiser are Inventory, Sales Revenue, Sales Returns and Allowances, Sales Discounts, and Cost of Goods Sold.

Self-Test, Brief Exercises, Exercises, Problem Set A, and many more components are available for practice in WileyPLUS

*Note: All **asterisked** Questions, Exercises, and Problems relate to material in the appendices to the chapter.

Self-Test Questions

Answers are on page 257.

(SO 1) 1. Gross profit will result if:
   a. operating expenses are less than net income.
   b. sales revenues are greater than operating expenses.
   c. sales revenues are greater than cost of goods sold.
   d. operating expenses are greater than cost of goods sold.

(SO 2) 2. Under a perpetual inventory system, when goods are purchased for resale by a company:
   a. purchases on account are debited to Inventory.
   b. purchases on account are debited to Purchases.
   c. purchase returns are debited to Purchase Returns and Allowances.
   d. freight costs are debited to Freight-out.

(SO 3)　**3.** The sales accounts that normally have a debit balance are:
- **a.** Sales Discounts.
- **b.** Sales Returns and Allowances.
- **c.** Both (a) and (b).
- **d.** Neither (a) nor (b).

(SO 3)　**4.** A credit sale of $750 is made on June 13, terms 2/10, net/30. A return of $50 is granted on June 16. The amount received as payment in full on June 23 is:
- **a.** $700.
- **c.** $685.
- **b.** $686.
- **d.** $650.

(SO 2)　**5.** Which of the following accounts will normally appear in the ledger of a merchandising company that uses a perpetual inventory system?
- **a.** Purchases.
- **c.** Cost of Goods Sold.
- **b.** Freight-in.
- **d.** Purchase Discounts.

(SO 3)　**6.** To record the sale of goods for cash in a perpetual inventory system:
- **a.** only one journal entry is necessary to record cost of goods sold and reduction of inventory.
- **b.** only one journal entry is necessary to record the receipt of cash and the sales revenue.
- **c.** two journal entries are necessary: one to record the receipt of cash and sales revenue, and one to record the cost of goods sold and reduction of inventory.
- **d.** two journal entries are necessary: one to record the receipt of cash and reduction of inventory, and one to record the cost of goods sold and sales revenue.

(SO 4)　**7.** The steps in the accounting cycle for a merchandising company are the same as those in a service company *except*:
- **a.** an additional adjusting journal entry for inventory may be needed in a merchandising company.
- **b.** closing journal entries are not required for a merchandising company.
- **c.** a post-closing trial balance is not required for a merchandising company.
- **d.** a multiple-step income statement is required for a merchandising company.

(SO 5)　**8.** The multiple-step income statement for a merchandising company shows each of the following features *except*:
- **a.** gross profit.
- **b.** cost of goods sold.
- **c.** a sales revenue section.
- **d.** investing activities section.

9. If sales revenues are $400,000, cost of goods sold is $310,000, (SO 6) and operating expenses are $60,000, the gross profit is:
- **a.** $30,000.
- **c.** $340,000.
- **b.** $90,000.
- **d.** $400,000.

10. A single-step income statement: (SO 5)
- **a.** reports gross profit.
- **b.** does not report cost of goods sold.
- **c.** reports sales revenues and "Other revenues and gains" in the revenues section of the income statement.
- **d.** reports operating income separately.

11. Which of the following appears on both a single-step and (SO 5) a multiple-step income statement?
- **a.** inventory.
- **b.** gross profit.
- **c.** income from operations.
- **d.** cost of goods sold.

*12. In determining cost of goods sold: (SO 7)
- **a.** purchase discounts are deducted from net purchases.
- **b.** freight-out is added to net purchases.
- **c.** purchase returns and allowances are deducted from net purchases.
- **d.** freight-in is added to net purchases.

*13. If beginning inventory is $60,000, cost of goods purchased (SO 7) is $380,000, and ending inventory is $50,000, cost of goods sold is:
- **a.** $390,000.
- **c.** $330,000.
- **b.** $370,000.
- **d.** $420,000.

*14. When goods are purchased for resale by a company using (SO 7) a periodic inventory system:
- **a.** purchases on account are debited to Inventory.
- **b.** purchases on account are debited to Purchases.
- **c.** purchase returns are debited to Purchase Returns and Allowances.
- **d.** freight costs are debited to Purchases.

*15. In a worksheet, Inventory is shown in the following (SO 8) columns:
- **a.** Adjusted trial balance debit and balance sheet debit.
- **b.** Income statement debit and balance sheet debit.
- **c.** Income statement credit and balance sheet debit.
- **d.** Income statement credit and adjusted trial balance debit.

Go to the book's companion website, **www.wiley.com/college/weygandt**, for additional Self-Test Questions.

✔ **The Navigator**

Questions

1. (a) "The steps in the accounting cycle for a merchandising company are different from the accounting cycle for a service company." Do you agree or disagree? (b) Is the measurement of net income for a merchandising company conceptually the same as for a service company? Explain.

2. Why is the normal operating cycle for a merchandising company likely to be longer than for a service company?

3. (a) How do the components of revenues and expenses differ between merchandising and service companies? (b)

Explain the income measurement process in a merchandising company.

4. How does income measurement differ between a merchandising and a service company?

5. When is cost of goods sold determined in a perpetual inventory system?

6. Distinguish between FOB shipping point and FOB destination. Identify the freight terms that will result in a debit to Inventory by the buyer and a debit to Freight-out by the seller.

7. Explain the meaning of the credit terms 2/10, n/30.

8. Goods costing $2,000 are purchased on account on July 15 with credit terms of 2/10, n/30. On July 18, a $200 credit memo is received from the supplier for damaged goods. Give the journal entry on July 24 to record payment of the balance due within the discount period using a perpetual inventory system.

9. Joan Roland believes revenues from credit sales may be earned before they are collected in cash. Do you agree? Explain.

10. (a) What is the primary source document for recording (1) cash sales, (2) credit sales. (b) Using XXs for amounts, give the journal entry for each of the transactions in part (a).

11. A credit sale is made on July 10 for $900, terms 2/10, n/30. On July 12, $100 of goods are returned for credit. Give the journal entry on July 19 to record the receipt of the balance due within the discount period.

12. Explain why the Inventory account will usually require adjustment at year-end.

13. Prepare the closing entries for the Sales Revenue account, assuming a balance of $200,000 and the Cost of Goods Sold account with a $145,000 balance.

14. What merchandising account(s) will appear in the post-closing trial balance?

15. Reese Co. has sales revenue of $105,000, cost of goods sold of $70,000, and operating expenses of $20,000. What is its gross profit and its gross profit rate?

16. Ann Fort Company reports net sales of $800,000, gross profit of $370,000, and net income of $240,000. What are its operating expenses?

17. Identify the distinguishing features of an income statement for a merchandising company.

18. Identify the sections of a multiple-step income statement that relate to (a) operating activities, and (b) nonoperating activities.

19. How does the single-step form of income statement differ from the multiple-step form?

20. **PEPSICO** Determine PepsiCo's gross profit rate for 2009 and 2008. Indicate whether it increased or decreased from 2008 to 2009.

*21. Identify the accounts that are added to or deducted from Purchases to determine the cost of goods purchased. For each account, indicate whether it is added or deducted.

*22. Goods costing $3,000 are purchased on account on July 15 with credit terms of 2/10, n/30. On July 18, a $200 credit was received from the supplier for damaged goods. Give the journal entry on July 24 to record payment of the balance due within the discount period, assuming a periodic inventory system.

*23. Indicate the columns of the worksheet in which (a) inventory and (b) cost of goods sold will be shown.

Brief Exercises

BE5-1 Presented below are the components in Miller Company's income statement. Determine the missing amounts.

	Sales Revenue	Cost of Goods Sold	Gross Profit	Operating Expenses	Net Income
(a)	$75,000	?	$30,000	?	$10,800
(b)	$108,000	$70,000	?	?	$29,500
(c)	?	$83,900	$79,600	$39,500	?

Compute missing amounts in determining net income.
(SO 1)

BE5-2 Brad Company buys merchandise on account from Murray Company. The selling price of the goods is $780, and the cost of the goods is $470. Both companies use perpetual inventory systems. Journalize the transaction on the books of both companies.

Journalize perpetual inventory entries.
(SO 2, 3)

BE5-3 Prepare the journal entries to record the following transactions on Derrick Company's books using a perpetual inventory system.

(a) On March 2, Derrick Company sold $900,000 of merchandise to Rose Company, terms 2/10, n/30. The cost of the merchandise sold was $620,000.

(b) On March 6, Rose Company returned $90,000 of the merchandise purchased on March 2. The cost of the returned merchandise was $62,000.

(c) On March 12, Derrick Company received the balance due from Rose Company.

Journalize sales transactions.
(SO 3)

BE5-4 From the information in BE5-3, prepare the journal entries to record these transactions on Rose Company's books under a perpetual inventory system.

Journalize purchase transactions.
(SO 2)

BE5-5 At year-end, the perpetual inventory records of Brewer Company showed merchandise inventory of $98,000. The company determined, however, that its actual inventory on hand was $95,700. Record the necessary adjusting entry.

Prepare adjusting entry for merchandise inventory.
(SO 4)

BE5-6 Thibodeau Company has the following merchandise account balances: Sales Revenue $195,000, Sales Discounts $2,000, Cost of Goods Sold $117,000, and Inventory $40,000. Prepare the entries to record the closing of these items to Income Summary.

Prepare closing entries for merchandise accounts.
(SO 4)

Prepare sales revenues section of income statement.

(SO 5)

BE5-7   Myers Company provides the following information for the month ended October 31, 2012: sales on credit $280,000, cash sales $100,000, sales discounts $5,000, sales returns and allowances $11,000. Prepare the sales revenues section of the income statement based on this information.

Contrast presentation in multiple-step and single-step income statements.

(SO 5)

BE5-8   Explain where each of the following items would appear on (1) a multiple-step income statement, and on (2) a single-step income statement: (a) gain on sale of equipment, (b) interest expense, (c) casualty loss from vandalism, and (d) cost of goods sold.

Compute net sales, gross profit, income from operations, and gross profit rate.

(SO 5, 6)

BE5-9   Assume Adams Company has the following reported amounts: Sales revenue $510,000, Sales returns and allowances $15,000, Cost of goods sold $330,000, Operating expenses $110,000. Compute the following: (a) net sales, (b) gross profit, (c) income from operations, and (d) gross profit rate. (Round to one decimal place.)

Compute net purchases and cost of goods purchased.

(SO 7)

*BE5-10   Assume that Byars Company uses a periodic inventory system and has these account balances: Purchases $450,000; Purchase Returns and Allowances $13,000; Purchase Discounts $8,000; and Freight-in $16,000. Determine net purchases and cost of goods purchased.

Compute cost of goods sold and gross profit.

(SO 6, 7)

*BE5-11   Assume the same information as in BE5-10 and also that Byars Company has beginning inventory of $60,000, ending inventory of $90,000, and net sales of $730,000. Determine the amounts to be reported for cost of goods sold and gross profit.

Journalize purchase transactions.

(SO 7)

*BE5-12   Prepare the journal entries to record these transactions on Jerel Company's books using a periodic inventory system.

(a) On March 2, Jerel Company purchased $900,000 of merchandise from McNeal Company, terms 2/10, n/30.

(b) On March 6, Jerel Company returned $130,000 of the merchandise purchased on March 2.

(c) On March 12, Jerel Company paid the balance due to McNeal Company.

Identify worksheet columns for selected accounts.

(SO 8)

*BE5-13   Presented below is the format of the worksheet presented in the chapter.

Trial Balance		Adjustments		Adjusted Trial Balance		Income Statement		Balance Sheet	
Dr.	Cr.	Dr.	Cr.	Dr.	Cr.	Dr.	Cr.	Dr.	Cr.

Indicate where the following items will appear on the worksheet: (a) Cash, (b) Inventory, (c) Sales revenue, and (d) Cost of goods sold.

Example:
Cash: Trial balance debit column; Adjusted trial balance debit column; and Balance sheet debit column.

Do it! Review

Record transactions of purchasing company.

(SO 2)

Do it! 5-1   On October 5, Bouldin Company buys merchandise on account from McClinton Company. The selling price of the goods is $5,000, and the cost to McClinton Company is $3,100. On October 8, Bouldin returns defective goods with a selling price of $650 and a fair value of $100. Record the transactions on the books of Bouldin Company.

Record transactions of selling company.

(SO 3)

Do it! 5-2   Assume information similar to that in **Do it!** 5-1. That is: On October 5, Bouldin Company buys merchandise on account from McClinton Company. The selling price of the goods is $5,000, and the cost to McClinton Company is $3,100. On October 8, Bouldin returns defective goods with a selling price of $650 and a fair value of $100. Record the transactions on the books of McClinton Company.

Prepare closing entries for a merchandising company.

(SO 4)

Do it! 5-3   The trial balance of Ogilvy's Boutique at December 31 shows Inventory $21,000, Sales Revenue $156,000, Sales Returns and Allowances $4,000, Sales Discounts $3,000, Cost of Goods Sold $92,400, Interest Revenue $5,000, Freight-out $1,500, Utilities Expense $7,400, and Salaries and Wages Expense $19,500. Prepare the closing entries for Ogilvy.

Classify financial statement accounts.

(SO 5)

Do it! 5-4   Richard Company is preparing its multiple-step income statement, owner's equity statement, and classified balance sheet. Using the column heads *Account, Financial Statement,* and

Classification, indicate in which financial statement and under what classification each of the following would be reported.

Account	Financial Statement	Classification
Accounts Payable		
Accounts Receivable		
Accumulated Depreciation— Buildings		
Cash		
Casualty Loss from Vandalism		
Cost of Goods Sold		
Depreciation Expense		
Equipment		
Freight-out		
Insurance Expense		
Interest Payable		
Inventory		
Land		
Notes Payable (due in 5 years)		
Owner's Capital (beginning balance)		
Owner's Drawings		
Property Taxes Payable		
Salaries and Wages Expense		
Salaries and Wages Payable		
Sales Returns and Allowances		
Sales Revenue		
Unearned Rent Revenue		
Utilities Expense		

Exercises

E5-1 Mr. Lucas has prepared the following list of statements about service companies and merchandisers.

Answer general questions about merchandisers.
(SO 1)

1. Measuring net income for a merchandiser is conceptually the same as for a service company.
2. For a merchandiser, sales less operating expenses is called gross profit.
3. For a merchandiser, the primary source of revenues is the sale of inventory.
4. Sales salaries and wages is an example of an operating expense.
5. The operating cycle of a merchandiser is the same as that of a service company.
6. In a perpetual inventory system, no detailed inventory records of goods on hand are maintained.
7. In a periodic inventory system, the cost of goods sold is determined only at the end of the accounting period.
8. A periodic inventory system provides better control over inventories than a perpetual system.

Instructions
Identify each statement as true or false. If false, indicate how to correct the statement.

E5-2 Information related to Almond Co. is presented below.

Journalize purchases transactions.
(SO 2)

1. On April 5, purchased merchandise from Morris Company for $23,000, terms 2/10, net/30, FOB shipping point.
2. On April 6, paid freight costs of $900 on merchandise purchased from Morris.
3. On April 7, purchased equipment on account for $26,000.
4. On April 8, returned damaged merchandise to Morris Company and was granted a $3,000 credit for returned merchandise.
5. On April 15, paid the amount due to Morris Company in full.

Instructions
(a) Prepare the journal entries to record these transactions on the books of Almond Co. under a perpetual inventory system.
(b) Assume that Almond Co. paid the balance due to Morris Company on May 4 instead of April 15. Prepare the journal entry to record this payment.

Journalize perpetual inventory entries.

(SO 2, 3)

E5-3   On September 1, Samardo Office Supply had an inventory of 30 calculators at a cost of $18 each. The company uses a perpetual inventory system. During September, the following transactions occurred.

Sept. 6   Purchased 80 calculators at $20 each from Samuels Co. for cash.
       9   Paid freight of $80 on calculators purchased from Samuels Co.
      10   Returned 3 calculators to Samuels Co. for $63 credit (including freight) because they did not meet specifications.
      12   Sold 26 calculators costing $21 (including freight) for $31 each to Trent Book Store, terms n/30.
      14   Granted credit of $31 to Trent Book Store for the return of one calculator that was not ordered.
      20   Sold 30 calculators costing $21 for $32 each to Plaisted's Card Shop, terms n/30.

Instructions

Journalize the September transactions.

Prepare purchase and sale entries.

(SO 2, 3)

E5-4   On June 10, Naveen Company purchased $8,000 of merchandise from Jarrah Company, FOB shipping point, terms 2/10, n/30. Naveen pays the freight costs of $400 on June 11. Damaged goods totaling $300 are returned to Jarrah for credit on June 12. The fair value of these goods is $70. On June 19, Naveen pays Jarrah Company in full, less the purchase discount. Both companies use a perpetual inventory system.

Instructions

(a) Prepare separate entries for each transaction on the books of Naveen Company.
(b) Prepare separate entries for each transaction for Jarrah Company. The merchandise purchased by Naveen on June 10 had cost Jarrah $4,800.

Journalize sales transactions.

(SO 3)

E5-5   Presented below are transactions related to Sayid Company.

1. On December 3, Sayid Company sold $570,000 of merchandise to Shephard Co., terms 2/10, n/30, FOB shipping point. The cost of the merchandise sold was $350,000.
2. On December 8, Shephard Co. was granted an allowance of $20,000 for merchandise purchased on December 3.
3. On December 13, Sayid Company received the balance due from Shephard Co.

Instructions

(a) Prepare the journal entries to record these transactions on the books of Sayid Company using a perpetual inventory system.
(b) Assume that Sayid Company received the balance due from Shephard Co. on January 2 of the following year instead of December 13. Prepare the journal entry to record the receipt of payment on January 2.

Prepare sales revenues section and closing entries.

(SO 4, 5)

E5-6   The adjusted trial balance of Garcia Company shows the following data pertaining to sales at the end of its fiscal year October 31, 2012: Sales Revenue $820,000, Freight-out $16,000, Sales Returns and Allowances $25,000, and Sales Discounts $13,000.

Instructions

(a) Prepare the sales revenues section of the income statement.
(b) Prepare separate closing entries for (1) sales, and (2) the contra accounts to sales.

Prepare adjusting and closing entries.

(SO 4)

E5-7   Hugo Reyes Company had the following account balances at year-end: Cost of Goods Sold $60,000; Inventory $15,000; Operating Expenses $29,000; Sales Revenue $115,000; Sales Discounts $1,200; and Sales Returns and Allowances $1,700. A physical count of inventory determines that merchandise inventory on hand is $13,900.

Instructions

(a) Prepare the adjusting entry necessary as a result of the physical count.
(b) Prepare closing entries.

Prepare adjusting and closing entries.

(SO 4)

E5-8   Presented below is information related to Hurley Co. for the month of January 2012.

Ending inventory per perpetual records	$ 21,600	Insurance expense	$ 12,000
		Rent expense	20,000
Ending inventory actually on hand	21,000	Salaries and wages expense	55,000
		Sales discounts	10,000
Cost of goods sold	218,000	Sales returns and allowances	13,000
Freight-out	7,000	Sales revenue	380,000

Instructions
(a) Prepare the necessary adjusting entry for inventory.
(b) Prepare the necessary closing entries.

E5-9 Presented below is information for Jorge Company for the month of March 2012.

Prepare multiple-step income statement.
(SO 5, 6)

Cost of goods sold	$212,000	Rent expense	$ 32,000
Freight-out	7,000	Sales discounts	8,000
Insurance expense	6,000	Sales returns and allowances	13,000
Salaries and wages expense	58,000	Sales revenue	380,000

Instructions
(a) Prepare a multiple-step income statement.
(b) Compute the gross profit rate.

E5-10 In its income statement for the year ended December 31, 2012, Fox Company reported the following condensed data.

Prepare multiple-step and single-step income statements.
(SO 5)

Operating expenses	$ 725,000	Interest revenue	$ 28,000
Cost of goods sold	1,289,000	Loss on disposal of plant assets	17,000
Interest expense	70,000	Net sales	2,200,000

Instructions
(a) Prepare a multiple-step income statement.
(b) Prepare a single-step income statement.

E5-11 An inexperienced accountant for Sawyer Company made the following errors in recording merchandising transactions.

Prepare correcting entries for sales and purchases.
(SO 2, 3)

1. A $195 refund to a customer for faulty merchandise was debited to Sales Revenue $195 and credited to Cash $195.
2. A $180 credit purchase of supplies was debited to Inventory $180 and credited to Cash $180.
3. A $215 sales discount was debited to Sales Revenue.
4. A cash payment of $20 for freight on merchandise purchases was debited to Freight-out $200 and credited to Cash $200.

Instructions
Prepare separate correcting entries for each error, assuming that the incorrect entry is not reversed. (Omit explanations.)

E5-12 In 2012, James Ford Company had net sales of $900,000 and cost of goods sold of $522,000. Operating expenses were $225,000, and interest expense was $11,000. Ford prepares a multiple-step income statement.

Compute various income measures.
(SO 5, 6)

Instructions
(a) Compute Ford's gross profit.
(b) Compute the gross profit rate. Why is this rate computed by financial statement users?
(c) What is Ford's income from operations and net income?
(d) If Ford prepared a single-step income statement, what amount would it report for net income?
(e) In what section of its classified balance sheet should Ford report merchandise inventory?

E5-13 Presented below is financial information for two different companies.

Compute missing amounts and compute gross profit rate.
(SO 5, 6)

	Dae Company	Kim Company
Sales revenue	$90,000	(d)
Sales returns	(a)	$ 5,000
Net sales	87,000	102,000
Cost of goods sold	56,000	(e)
Gross profit	(b)	41,500
Operating expenses	15,000	(f)
Net income	(c)	15,000

Instructions
(a) Determine the missing amounts.
(b) Determine the gross profit rates. (Round to one decimal place.)

Compute missing amounts.
(SO 5)

E5-14 Financial information is presented below for three different companies.

	Holloway Cosmetics	Jin Grocery	Kwon Wholesalers
Sales revenue	$90,000	$ (e)	$122,000
Sales returns and allowances	(a)	5,000	12,000
Net sales	86,000	95,000	(i)
Cost of goods sold	56,000	(f)	(j)
Gross profit	(b)	38,000	24,000
Operating expenses	15,000	(g)	18,000
Income from operations	(c)	(h)	(k)
Other expenses and losses	4,000	7,000	(l)
Net income	(d)	11,000	5,000

Instructions

Determine the missing amounts.

Prepare cost of goods sold section.
(SO 7)

*E5-15 The trial balance of S. Yunjin Company at the end of its fiscal year, August 31, 2012, includes these accounts: Inventory $17,200; Purchases $149,000; Sales Revenue $190,000; Freight-in $5,000; Sales Returns and Allowances $3,000; Freight-out $1,000; and Purchase Returns and Allowances $2,000. The ending merchandise inventory is $23,000.

Instructions

Prepare a cost of goods sold section for the year ending August 31 (periodic inventory).

Compute various income statement items.
(SO 7)

*E5-16 On January 1, 2012, Evangeline Lilly Corporation had merchandise inventory of $50,000. At December 31, 2012, Evangeline Lilly had the following account balances.

Freight-in	$ 4,000
Purchases	509,000
Purchase discounts	6,000
Purchase returns and allowances	2,000
Sales revenue	840,000
Sales discounts	5,000
Sales returns and allowances	10,000

At December 31, 2012, Evangeline Lilly determines that its ending inventory is $60,000.

Instructions

(a) Compute Evangeline Lilly's 2012 gross profit.

(b) Compute Evangeline Lilly's 2012 operating expenses if net income is $130,000 and there are no nonoperating activities.

Prepare cost of goods sold section.
(SO 7)

*E5-17 Below is a series of cost of goods sold sections for companies B, F, L, and R.

	B	F	L	R
Beginning inventory	$ 150	$ 70	$1,000	$ (j)
Purchases	1,620	1,060	(g)	43,590
Purchase returns and allowances	40	(d)	290	(k)
Net purchases	(a)	1,030	6,210	41,090
Freight-in	110	(e)	(h)	2,240
Cost of goods purchased	(b)	1,280	7,940	(l)
Cost of goods available for sale	1,840	1,350	(i)	49,530
Ending inventory	310	(f)	1,450	6,230
Cost of goods sold	(c)	1,230	7,490	43,300

Instructions

Fill in the lettered blanks to complete the cost of goods sold sections.

Journalize purchase transactions.
(SO 7)

*E5-18 This information relates to Locke Co.

1. On April 5, purchased merchandise from K. Austen Company for $25,000, terms 2/10, net/30, FOB shipping point.

2. On April 6, paid freight costs of $900 on merchandise purchased from K. Austen Company.

3. On April 7, purchased equipment on account for $30,000.

4. On April 8, returned some of April 5 merchandise, which cost $2,800, to K. Austen Company.

5. On April 15, paid the amount due to K. Austen Company in full.

Instructions

(a) Prepare the journal entries to record these transactions on the books of Locke Co. using a periodic inventory system.

(b) Assume that Locke Co. paid the balance due to K. Austen Company on May 4 instead of April 15. Prepare the journal entry to record this payment.

*E5-19   Presented below is information related to Emilie Co.

1. On April 5, purchased merchandise from De Ravin Company for $19,000, terms 2/10, net/30, FOB shipping point.
2. On April 6, paid freight costs of $800 on merchandise purchased from De Ravin.
3. On April 7, purchased equipment on account from Claire Littleton Mfg. Co. for $23,000.
4. On April 8, returned merchandise, which cost $4,000, to De Ravin Company.
5. On April 15, paid the amount due to De Ravin Company in full.

Journalize purchase transactions.
(SO 7)

Instructions

(a) Prepare the journal entries to record these transactions on the books of Emilie Co. using a periodic inventory system.

(b) Assume that Emilie Co. paid the balance due to De Ravin Company on May 4 instead of April 15. Prepare the journal entry to record this payment.

*E5-20   Presented below are selected accounts for Dawson Company as reported in the worksheet at the end of May 2012.

Complete worksheet.
(SO 8)

Accounts	Adjusted Trial Balance		Income Statement		Balance Sheet	
	Dr.	Cr.	Dr.	Cr.	Dr.	Cr.
Cash	11,000					
Inventory	76,000					
Sales Revenue		480,000				
Sales Returns and Allowances	10,000					
Sales Discounts	9,000					
Cost of Goods Sold	300,000					

Instructions

Complete the worksheet by extending amounts reported in the adjusted trial balance to the appropriate columns in the worksheet. Do not total individual columns.

*E5-21   The trial balance columns of the worksheet for Linus Company at June 30, 2012, are as follows.

Prepare a worksheet.
(SO 8)

LINUS COMPANY
Worksheet
For the Month Ended June 30, 2012

	Trial Balance	
Account Titles	Debit	Credit
Cash	$ 1,920	
Accounts Receivable	2,440	
Inventory	11,640	
Accounts Payable		$ 1,120
Owner's Capital		3,500
Sales Revenue		42,500
Cost of Goods Sold	20,560	
Operating Expenses	10,560	
	$47,120	$47,120

Other data:
Operating expenses incurred on account, but not yet recorded, total $1,500.

Instructions

Enter the trial balance on a worksheet and complete the worksheet.

Exercises: Set B

Visit the book's companion website, at **www.wiley.com/college/weygandt**, and choose the Student Companion site to access Exercise Set B.

Problems: Set A

Journalize purchase and sales transactions under a perpetual inventory system.

(SO 2, 3)

P5-1A   O'Quinn Co. distributes suitcases to retail stores and extends credit terms of 1/10, n/30 to all of its customers. At the end of June, O'Quinn's inventory consisted of suitcases costing $1,200. During the month of July, the following merchandising transactions occurred.

July 1   Purchased suitcases on account for $1,800 from Emerson Manufacturers, FOB destination, terms 2/10, n/30. The appropriate party also made a cash payment of $100 for freight on this date.

  3   Sold suitcases on account to Straume Satchels for $2,000. The cost of suitcases sold is $1,200.

  9   Paid Emerson Manufacturers in full.

  12   Received payment in full from Straume Satchels.

  17   Sold suitcases on account to The Going Concern for $1,800. The cost of the suitcases sold was $1,080.

  18   Purchased suitcases on account for $1,900 from Hume Manufacturers, FOB shipping point, terms 1/10, n/30. The appropriate party also made a cash payment of $125 for freight on this date.

  20   Received $300 credit (including freight) for suitcases returned to Hume Manufacturers.

  21   Received payment in full from The Going Concern.

  22   Sold suitcases on account to Desmond's for $2,250. The cost of suitcases sold was $1,350.

  30   Paid Hume Manufacturers in full.

  31   Granted Desmond's $200 credit for suitcases returned costing $120.

O'Quinn's chart of accounts includes the following: No. 101 Cash, No. 112 Accounts Receivable, No. 120 Inventory, No. 201 Accounts Payable, No. 401 Sales Revenue, No. 412 Sales Returns and Allowances, No. 414 Sales Discounts, and No. 505 Cost of Goods Sold.

Instructions

Journalize the transactions for the month of July for O'Quinn using a perpetual inventory system.

Journalize, post, and prepare a partial income statement.

(SO 2, 3, 5, 6)

P5-2A   Pace Distributing Company completed the following merchandising transactions in the month of April. At the beginning of April, the ledger of Pace showed Cash of $9,000 and Owner's Capital of $9,000.

Apr. 2   Purchased merchandise on account from Monaghan Supply Co. $6,900, terms 1/10, n/30.

  4   Sold merchandise on account $6,500, FOB destination, terms 1/10, n/30. The cost of the merchandise sold was $3,900.

  5   Paid $240 freight on April 4 sale.

  6   Received credit from Monaghan Supply Co. for merchandise returned $500.

  11   Paid Monaghan Supply Co. in full, less discount.

  13   Received collections in full, less discounts, from customers billed on April 4.

  14   Purchased merchandise for cash $3,800.

  16   Received refund from supplier for returned goods on cash purchase of April 14, $500.

  18   Purchased merchandise from Dominic Distributors $4,500, FOB shipping point, terms 2/10, n/30.

  20   Paid freight on April 18 purchase $100.

  23   Sold merchandise for cash $7,400. The merchandise sold had a cost of $4,120.

  26   Purchased merchandise for cash $2,300.

  27   Paid Dominic Distributors in full, less discount.

  29   Made refunds to cash customers for defective merchandise $90. The returned merchandise had a fair value of $30.

  30   Sold merchandise on account $3,700, terms n/30. The cost of the merchandise sold was $2,800.

Pace Distributing Company's chart of accounts includes the following: No. 101 Cash, No. 112 Accounts Receivable, No. 120 Inventory, No. 201 Accounts Payable, No. 301 Owner's Capital, No. 401 Sales Revenue, No. 412 Sales Returns and Allowances, No. 414 Sales Discounts, No. 505 Cost of Goods Sold, and No. 644 Freight-out.

Instructions
(a) Journalize the transactions using a perpetual inventory system.
(b) Enter the beginning cash and capital balances, and post the transactions. (Use J1 for the journal reference.)
(c) Prepare the income statement through gross profit for the month of April 2012.

(c) Gross profit $6,655

P5-3A Cusick Department Store is located near the Village Shopping Mall. At the end of the company's calendar year on December 31, 2012, the following accounts appeared in two of its trial balances.

Prepare financial statements and adjusting and closing entries.
(SO 4, 5)

	Unadjusted	Adjusted		Unadjusted	Adjusted
Accounts Payable	$ 79,300	$ 80,300	Inventory	$ 75,000	$ 75,000
Accounts Receivable	50,300	50,300	Mortgage Payable	80,000	80,000
Accumulated Depr.—Buildings	42,100	52,500	Owner's Capital	176,600	176,600
Accumulated Depr.—Equipment	29,600	42,900	Owner's Drawings	28,000	28,000
Buildings	290,000	290,000	Prepaid Insurance	9,600	2,400
Cash	23,800	23,800	Property Tax Expense		4,800
Cost of Goods Sold	412,700	412,700	Property Taxes Payable		4,800
Depreciation Expense		23,700	Salaries and Wages Expense	108,000	108,000
Equipment	110,000	110,000	Sales Revenue	728,000	728,000
Insurance Expense		7,200	Sales Commissions Expense	10,200	14,500
Interest Expense	3,000	12,000	Sales Commissions Payable		4,300
Interest Payable		9,000	Sales Returns and Allowances	8,000	8,000
Interest Revenue	4,000	4,000	Utilities Expense	11,000	12,000

Instructions
(a) Prepare a multiple-step income statement, an owner's equity statement, and a classified balance sheet. $25,000 of the mortgage payable is due for payment next year.
(b) Journalize the adjusting entries that were made.
(c) Journalize the closing entries that are necessary.

(a) Net income $129,100
    Owner's capital $277,700
    Total assets $456,100

P5-4A Juliet Burke, a former professional tennis star, operates Juliet's Tennis Shop at the Mitchell Lake Resort. At the beginning of the current season, the ledger of Juliet's Tennis Shop showed Cash $2,500, Inventory $1,700, and Owner's Capital $4,200. The following transactions were completed during April.

Journalize, post, and prepare a trial balance.
(SO 2, 3, 4)

Apr. 4   Purchased racquets and balls from Miles Co. $840, FOB shipping point, terms 2/10, n/30.
    6   Paid freight on purchase from Miles Co. $40.
    8   Sold merchandise to members $1,150, terms n/30. The merchandise sold had a cost of $790.
   10   Received credit of $40 from Miles Co. for a racquet that was returned.
   11   Purchased tennis shoes from Leung Sports for cash, $420.
   13   Paid Miles Co. in full.
   14   Purchased tennis shirts and shorts from Cyrena's Sportswear $900, FOB shipping point, terms 3/10, n/60.
   15   Received cash refund of $50 from Leung Sports for damaged merchandise that was returned.
   17   Paid freight on Cyrena's Sportswear purchase $30.
   18   Sold merchandise to members $900, terms n/30. The cost of the merchandise sold was $540.
   20   Received $600 in cash from members in settlement of their accounts.
   21   Paid Cyrena's Sportswear in full.
   27   Granted an allowance of $40 to members for tennis clothing that did not fit properly.
   30   Received cash payments on account from members, $710.

The chart of accounts for the tennis shop includes the following: No. 101 Cash, No. 112 Accounts Receivable, No. 120 Inventory, No. 201 Accounts Payable, No. 301 Owner's Capital, No. 401 Sales Revenue, No. 412 Sales Returns and Allowances, and No. 505 Cost of Goods Sold.

Instructions

(a) Journalize the April transactions using a perpetual inventory system.

(b) Enter the beginning balances in the ledger accounts and post the April transactions. (Use J1 for the journal reference.)

(c) Total debits $6,250

(c) Prepare a trial balance on April 30, 2012.

Determine cost of goods sold and gross profit under periodic approach.

(SO 6, 7)

*P5-5A   At the end of Rutherford Department Store's fiscal year on December 31, 2012, these accounts appeared in its adjusted trial balance.

Freight-in	$ 5,600
Inventory	40,500
Purchases	447,000
Purchase Discounts	12,000
Purchase Returns and Allowances	6,400
Sales Revenue	725,000
Sales Returns and Allowances	11,000

Additional facts:

1. Merchandise inventory on December 31, 2012, is $65,000.

2. Rutherford Department Store uses a periodic system.

Instructions

Gross profit $304,300

Prepare an income statement through gross profit for the year ended December 31, 2012.

Calculate missing amounts and assess profitability.

(SO 6, 7)

*P5-6A   Ana Lucia operates a retail clothing operation. She purchases all merchandise inventory on credit and uses a periodic inventory system. The Accounts Payable account is used for recording inventory purchases only; all other current liabilities are accrued in separate accounts. You are provided with the following selected information for the fiscal years 2009–2012.

	2009	**2010**	**2011**	**2012**
Inventory (ending)	$13,000	$ 11,300	$ 14,700	$ 12,200
Accounts payable (ending)	20,000			
Sales revenue		239,000	237,000	235,000
Purchases of merchandise				
inventory on account		146,000	145,000	129,000
Cash payments to suppliers		135,000	161,000	127,000

Instructions

(a) 2011 $141,600

(a) Calculate cost of goods sold for each of the 2010, 2011, and 2012 fiscal years.

(b) Calculate the gross profit for each of the 2010, 2011, and 2012 fiscal years.

(c) 2011 Ending accts payable $15,000

(c) Calculate the ending balance of accounts payable for each of the 2010, 2011, and 2012 fiscal years.

(d) Sales declined in fiscal 2012. Does that mean that profitability, as measured by the gross profit rate, necessarily also declined? Explain, calculating the gross profit rate for each fiscal year to help support your answer. (Round to one decimal place.)

Journalize, post, and prepare trial balance and partial income statement using periodic approach.

(SO 7)

GLS

*P5-7A   At the beginning of the current season, the ledger of Alpert Tennis Shop showed Cash $2,500; Inventory $1,700; and Owner's Capital $4,200. The following transactions were completed during April.

Apr.	4	Purchased racquets and balls from Nestor Co. $740, terms 3/10, n/30.
	6	Paid freight on Nestor Co. purchase $60.
	8	Sold merchandise to members $900, terms n/30.
	10	Received credit of $40 from Nestor Co. for a racquet that was returned.
	11	Purchased tennis shoes from Carbonell Sports for cash $300.
	13	Paid Nestor Co. in full.
	14	Purchased tennis shirts and shorts from Faraday Sportswear $700, terms 2/10, n/60.
	15	Received cash refund of $50 from Carbonell Sports for damaged merchandise that was returned.
	17	Paid freight on Faraday Sportswear purchase $30.

18 Sold merchandise to members $1,000, terms n/30.
20 Received $500 in cash from members in settlement of their accounts.
21 Paid Faraday Sportswear in full.
27 Granted an allowance of $25 to members for tennis clothing that did not fit properly.
30 Received cash payments on account from members $550.

The chart of accounts for the tennis shop includes Cash, Accounts Receivable, Inventory, Accounts Payable, Owner's Capital, Sales Revenue, Sales Returns and Allowances, Purchases, Purchase Returns and Allowances, Purchase Discounts, and Freight-in.

Instructions
(a) Journalize the April transactions using a periodic inventory system.
(b) Using T accounts, enter the beginning balances in the ledger accounts and post the April transactions.
(c) Prepare a trial balance on April 30, 2012.
(d) Prepare an income statement through gross profit, assuming inventory on hand at April 30 is $2,296.

(c) Tot. trial balance $6,225
(d) Gross profit $766

*P5-8A The trial balance of Mr. Eko Fashion Center contained the following accounts at November 30, the end of the company's fiscal year.

Complete accounting cycle beginning with a worksheet.
(SO 4, 5, 6, 8)

MR. EKO FASHION CENTER
Trial Balance
November 30, 2012

	Debit	Credit
Cash	$ 8,700	
Accounts Receivable	30,700	
Inventory	44,700	
Supplies	6,200	
Equipment	133,000	
Accumulated Depreciation—Equipment		$ 28,000
Notes Payable		51,000
Accounts Payable		48,500
Owner's Capital		90,000
Owner's Drawings	12,000	
Sales Revenue		755,200
Sales Returns and Allowances	8,800	
Cost of Goods Sold	497,400	
Salaries and Wages Expense	140,000	
Advertising Expense	24,400	
Utilities Expense	14,000	
Maintenance and Repairs Expense	12,100	
Freight-out	16,700	
Rent Expense	24,000	
Totals	$972,700	$972,700

Adjustment data:
1. Supplies on hand totaled $2,000.
2. Depreciation is $11,500 on the equipment.
3. Interest of $4,000 is accrued on notes payable at November 30.
4. Inventory actually on hand is $44,400.

Instructions
(a) Enter the trial balance on a worksheet, and complete the worksheet.
(b) Prepare a multiple-step income statement and an owner's equity statement for the year, and a classified balance sheet as of November 30, 2012. Notes payable of $20,000 are due in January 2013.
(c) Journalize the adjusting entries.
(d) Journalize the closing entries.
(e) Prepare a post-closing trial balance.

(a) Adj. trial balance $988,200
    Net loss $2,200
(b) Gross profit $248,700
    Total assets $179,300

Problems: Set B

Journalize purchase and sales transactions under a perpetual inventory system.

(SO 2, 3)

P5-1B Jeremy's Book Warehouse distributes hardcover books to retail stores and extends credit terms of 2/10, n/30 to all of its customers. At the end of May, Jeremy's inventory consisted of books purchased for $1,800. During June, the following merchandising transactions occurred.

June 1 Purchased books on account for $1,600 from Davies Publishers, FOB destination, terms 2/10, n/30. The appropriate party also made a cash payment of $50 for the freight on this date.

3 Sold books on account to Reading Rainbow for $2,500. The cost of the books sold was $1,440.

6 Received $100 credit for books returned to Davies Publishers.

9 Paid Davies Publishers in full, less discount.

15 Received payment in full from Reading Rainbow.

17 Sold books on account to Lapidus Books for $1,800. The cost of the books sold was $1,080.

20 Purchased books on account for $1,500 from Fahey Publishers, FOB destination, terms 2/15, n/30. The appropriate party also made a cash payment of $50 for the freight on this date.

24 Received payment in full from Lapidus Books.

26 Paid Fahey Publishers in full, less discount.

28 Sold books on account to Carlyle Bookstore for $1,400. The cost of the books sold was $850.

30 Granted Carlyle Bookstore $120 credit for books returned costing $72.

Jeremy's Book Warehouse's chart of accounts includes the following: No. 101 Cash, No. 112 Accounts Receivable, No. 120 Inventory, No. 201 Accounts Payable, No. 401 Sales Revenue, No. 412 Sales Returns and Allowances, and No. 414 Sales Discounts, and No. 505 Cost of Goods Sold.

Instructions

Journalize the transactions for the month of June for Jeremy's Book Warehouse using a perpetual inventory system.

Journalize, post, and prepare a partial income statement.

(SO 2, 3, 5, 6)

P5-2B Boone Hardware Store completed the following merchandising transactions in the month of May. At the beginning of May, the ledger of Boone showed Cash of $5,000 and Owner's Capital of $5,000.

May 1 Purchased merchandise on account from Adewale's Wholesale Supply $4,200, terms 2/10, n/30.

2 Sold merchandise on account $2,100, terms 1/10, n/30. The cost of the merchandise sold was $1,300.

5 Received credit from Adewale's Wholesale Supply for merchandise returned $300.

9 Received collections in full, less discounts, from customers billed on sales of $2,100 on May 2.

10 Paid Adewale's Wholesale Supply in full, less discount.

11 Purchased supplies for cash $400.

12 Purchased merchandise for cash $1,400.

15 Received refund for poor quality merchandise from supplier on cash purchase $150.

17 Purchased merchandise from Agbaje Distributors $1,300, FOB shipping point, terms 2/10, n/30.

19 Paid freight on May 17 purchase $130.

24 Sold merchandise for cash $3,200. The merchandise sold had a cost of $2,000.

25 Purchased merchandise from Somerhalder, Inc. $620, FOB destination, terms 2/10, n/30.

27 Paid Agbaje Distributors in full, less discount.

29 Made refunds to cash customers for defective merchandise $70. The returned merchandise had a fair value of $30.

31 Sold merchandise on account $1,000 terms n/30. The cost of the merchandise sold was $560.

Boone Hardware's chart of accounts includes the following: No. 101 Cash, No. 112 Accounts Receivable, No. 120 Inventory, No. 126 Supplies, No. 201 Accounts Payable, No. 301 Owner's Capital, No. 401 Sales Revenue, No. 412 Sales Returns and Allowances, No. 414 Sales Discounts, and No. 505 Cost of Goods Sold.

Instructions

(a) Journalize the transactions using a perpetual inventory system.

(b) Enter the beginning cash and capital balances and post the transactions. (Use J1 for the journal reference.)

(c) Prepare an income statement through gross profit for the month of May 2012.

(c) Gross profit $2,379

P5-3B   The Akinnuoye Store is located in midtown Madison. During the past several years, net income has been declining because of suburban shopping centers. At the end of the company's fiscal year on November 30, 2012, the following accounts appeared in two of its trial balances.

Prepare financial statements and adjusting and closing entries.

(SO 4, 5)

	Unadjusted	Adjusted		Unadjusted	Adjusted
Accounts Payable	$ 25,200	$ 25,200	Notes Payable	$ 37,000	$ 37,000
Accounts Receivable	30,500	30,500	Owner's Capital	101,700	101,700
Accumulated Depr.—Equip.	34,000	45,000	Owner's Drawings	10,000	10,000
Cash	26,000	26,000	Prepaid Insurance	10,500	3,500
Cost of Goods Sold	507,000	507,000	Property Tax Expense		2,500
Freight-out	6,500	6,500	Property Taxes Payable		2,500
Equipment	146,000	146,000	Rent Expense	15,000	15,000
Depreciation Expense		11,000	Salaries and Wages Expense	96,000	96,000
Insurance Expense		7,000	Sales Revenue	700,000	700,000
Interest Expense	6,400	6,400	Sales Commissions Expense	6,500	11,000
Interest Revenue	8,000	8,000	Sales Commissions Payable		4,500
Inventory	29,000	29,000	Sales Returns and Allowances	8,000	8,000
			Utilities Expense	8,500	8,500

Instructions

(a) Prepare a multiple-step income statement, an owner's equity statement, and a classified balance sheet. Notes payable are due in 2015.

(b) Journalize the adjusting entries that were made.

(c) Journalize the closing entries that are necessary.

(a) Net income $29,100
Owner's capital $120,800
Total assets $190,000

P5-4B   Ben Borke, a former disc golf star, operates Ben's Discorama. At the beginning of the current season on April 1, the ledger of Ben's Discorama showed Cash $1,800, Inventory $2,500, and Owner's Capital $4,300. The following transactions were completed during April.

Journalize, post, and prepare a trial balance.

(SO 2, 3, 4)

Apr. 5 Purchased golf discs, bags, and other inventory on account from Innova Co. $1,200, FOB shipping point, terms 2/10, n/60.

7 Paid freight on the Innova purchase $50.

9 Received credit from Innova Co. for merchandise returned $100.

10 Sold merchandise on account for $900, terms n/30. The merchandise sold had a cost of $540.

12 Purchased disc golf shirts and other accessories on account from Lightning Sportswear $670, terms 1/10, n/30.

14 Paid Innova Co. in full, less discount.

17 Received credit from Lightning Sportswear for merchandise returned $70.

20 Made sales on account for $610, terms n/30. The cost of the merchandise sold was $370.

21 Paid Lightning Sportswear in full, less discount.

27 Granted an allowance to members for clothing that was flawed $20.

30 Received payments on account from customers $900.

The chart of accounts for the store includes the following: No. 101 Cash, No. 112 Accounts Receivable, No. 120 Inventory, No. 201 Accounts Payable, No. 301 Owner's Capital, No. 401 Sales Revenue, No. 412 Sales Returns and Allowances, and No. 505 Cost of Goods Sold.

Instructions

(a) Journalize the April transactions using a perpetual inventory system.

(b) Enter the beginning balances in the ledger accounts and post the April transactions. (Use J1 for the journal reference.)

(c) Prepare a trial balance on April 30, 2012.

(c) Total debits $5,810

Determine cost of goods sold and gross profit under periodic approach.
(SO 6, 7)

*P5-5B At the end of Cortez Department Store's fiscal year on November 30, 2012, these accounts appeared in its adjusted trial balance.

Freight-in	$ 7,500
Inventory	40,000
Purchases	585,000
Purchase Discounts	6,300
Purchase Returns and Allowances	2,700
Sales Revenue	1,000,000
Sales Returns and Allowances	20,000

Additional facts:

1. Merchandise inventory on November 30, 2012, is $52,600.
2. Cortez Department Store uses a periodic system.

Instructions

Gross profit $409,100

Prepare an income statement through gross profit for the year ended November 30, 2012.

Calculate missing amounts and assess profitability.
(SO 6, 7)

*P5-6B Rodriguez Inc. operates a retail operation that purchases and sells home entertainment products. The company purchases all merchandise inventory on credit and uses a periodic inventory system. The Accounts Payable account is used for recording inventory purchases only; all other current liabilities are accrued in separate accounts. You are provided with the following selected information for the fiscal years 2009 through 2012, inclusive.

	2009	**2010**	**2011**	**2012**
Income Statement Data				
Sales revenue		$55,000	$ (e)	$47,000
Cost of goods sold		(a)	13,800	14,300
Gross profit		38,300	35,200	(i)
Operating expenses		34,900	(f)	28,600
Net income		$ (b)	$ 2,500	$ (j)
Balance Sheet Data				
Inventory	$7,200	$ (c)	$ 8,100	$ (k)
Accounts payable	3,200	3,600	2,500	(l)
Additional Information				
Purchases of merchandise inventory on account		$14,200	$ (g)	$13,200
Cash payments to suppliers		(d)	(h)	13,600

Instructions

(c) $4,700
(g) $17,200
(i) $32,700

(a) Calculate the missing amounts.
(b) Sales declined over the 3-year fiscal period, 2010–2012. Does that mean that profitability necessarily also declined? Explain, computing the gross profit rate and the profit margin ratio for each fiscal year to help support your answer. (Round to one decimal place.)

Journalize, post, and prepare trial balance and partial income statement using periodic approach.
(SO 7)

*P5-7B At the beginning of the current season on April 1, the ledger of Ilana Pro Shop showed Cash $3,000; Inventory $4,000; and Owner's Capital $7,000. These transactions occurred during April 2012.

Apr. 5	Purchased golf bags, clubs, and balls on account from Zuleikha Co. $1,200, FOB shipping point, terms 2/10, n/60.
7	Paid freight on Zuleikha Co. purchases $50.
9	Received credit from Zuleikha Co. for merchandise returned $100.
10	Sold merchandise on account to members $600, terms n/30.
12	Purchased golf shoes, sweaters, and other accessories on account from Libby Sportswear $450, terms 1/10, n/30.
14	Paid Zuleikha Co. in full.
17	Received credit from Libby Sportswear for merchandise returned $50.
20	Made sales on account to members $600, terms n/30.

21   Paid Libby Sportswear in full.
27   Granted credit to members for clothing that had flaws $35.
30   Received payments on account from members $600.

The chart of accounts for the pro shop includes Cash, Accounts Receivable, Inventory, Accounts Payable, Owner's Capital, Sales Revenue, Sales Returns and Allowances, Purchases, Purchase Returns and Allowances, Purchase Discounts, and Freight-in.

Instructions
(a) Journalize the April transactions using a periodic inventory system.
(b) Using T accounts, enter the beginning balances in the ledger accounts and post the April transactions.
(c) Prepare a trial balance on April 30, 2012.
(d) Prepare an income statement through gross profit, assuming merchandise inventory on hand at April 30 is $4,824.

(c) Tot. trial
   balance $8,376
Gross profit $465

Problems: Set C

Visit the book's companion website, at **www.wiley.com/college/weygandt**, and choose the Student Companion site to access Problem Set C.

Comprehensive Problem

CP5   On December 1, 2012, Shiras Distributing Company had the following account balances.

	Debits		**Credits**
Cash	$ 7,200	Accumulated Depreciation—	
Accounts Receivable	4,600	Equipment	$ 2,200
Inventory	12,000	Accounts Payable	4,500
Supplies	1,200	Salaries and Wages Payable	1,000
Equipment	22,000	Owner's Capital	39,300
	$47,000		$47,000

During December, the company completed the following summary transactions.

Dec. 6   Paid $1,600 for salaries and wages due employees, of which $600 is for December and $1,000 is for November salaries and wages payable.
8   Received $1,900 cash from customers in payment of account (no discount allowed).
10   Sold merchandise for cash $6,300. The cost of the merchandise sold was $4,100.
13   Purchased merchandise on account from Gong Co. $9,000, terms 2/10, n/30.
15   Purchased supplies for cash $2,000.
18   Sold merchandise on account $12,000, terms 3/10, n/30. The cost of the merchandise sold was $8,000.
20   Paid salaries $1,800.
23   Paid Gong Co. in full, less discount.
27   Received collections in full, less discounts, from customers billed on December 18.

Adjustment data:
1. Accrued salaries payable $800.
2. Depreciation $200 per month.
3. Supplies on hand $1,500.

Instructions
(a) Journalize the December transactions using a perpetual inventory system.
(b) Enter the December 1 balances in the ledger T accounts and post the December transactions. Use Cost of Goods Sold, Depreciation Expense, Salaries and Wages Expense, Sales Revenue, Sales Discounts, and Supplies Expense.
(c) Journalize and post adjusting entries.
(d) Prepare an adjusted trial balance.
(e) Prepare an income statement and an owner's equity statement for December and a classified balance sheet at December 31.

(d) Totals $65,300
(e) Net income $740

Continuing Cookie Chronicle

(*Note:* This is a continuation of the Cookie Chronicle from Chapters 1 through 4.)

CCC5 Because Natalie has had such a successful first few months, she is considering other opportunities to develop her business. One opportunity is the sale of fine European mixers. The owner of Kzinski Supply Company has approached Natalie to become the exclusive U.S. distributor of these fine mixers in her state. The current cost of a mixer is approximately $525 (U.S.), and Natalie would sell each one for $1,050. Natalie comes to you for advice on how to account for these mixers.

Go to the book's companion website, **www.wiley.com/college/weygandt,** *to see the completion of this problem.*

BROADENINGYOURPERSPECTIVE

Financial Reporting and Analysis

Financial Reporting Problem: PepsiCo, Inc.

BYP5-1 The financial statements of PepsiCo, Inc. are presented in Appendix A at the end of this textbook.

Instructions

Answer the following questions using PepsiCo's Consolidated Statement of Income.

(a) What was the percentage change in (1) sales and in (2) net income from 2007 to 2008 and from 2008 to 2009?

(b) What was the company's gross profit rate in 2007, 2008, and 2009?

(c) What was the company's percentage of net income to net sales in 2007, 2008, and 2009? Comment on any trend in this percentage.

Comparative Analysis Problem: PepsiCo, Inc. vs. The Coca-Cola Company

BYP5-2 PepsiCo's financial statements are presented in Appendix A. Financial statements of The Coca-Cola Company are presented in Appendix B.

Instructions

(a) Based on the information contained in these financial statements, determine each of the following for each company.

  (1) Gross profit for 2009.
  (2) Gross profit rate for 2009.
  (3) Operating income for 2009.
  (4) Percent change in operating income from 2008 to 2009.

(b) What conclusions concerning the relative profitability of the two companies can you draw from these data?

On the Web

BYP5-3 No financial decision maker should ever rely solely on the financial information reported in the annual report to make decisions. It is important to keep abreast of financial news. This activity demonstrates how to search for financial news on the Web.

Address: biz.yahoo.com/i, or go to **www.wiley.com/college/weygandt**

Steps:

1. Type in either PepsiCo or Coca-Cola.

2. Choose **News**.

3. Select an article that sounds interesting to you.

Instructions
(a) What was the source of the article (e.g., Reuters, Businesswire, PR Newswire)?
(b) Assume that you are a personal financial planner and that one of your clients owns stock in the company. Write a brief memo to your client, summarizing the article and explaining the implications of the article for their investment.

Critical Thinking

Decision Making Across the Organization

BYP5-4 Three years ago, Carrie Dungy and her brother-in-law Luke Barber opened FedCo Department Store. For the first two years, business was good, but the following condensed income results for 2011 were disappointing.

FEDCO DEPARTMENT STORE
Income Statement
For the Year Ended December 31, 2011

Net sales		$700,000
Cost of goods sold		553,000
Gross profit		147,000
Operating expenses		
Selling expenses	$100,000	
Administrative expenses	20,000	120,000
Net income		$ 27,000

Carrie believes the problem lies in the relatively low gross profit rate (gross profit divided by net sales) of 21%. Luke believes the problem is that operating expenses are too high.

Carrie thinks the gross profit rate can be improved by making both of the following changes. She does not anticipate that these changes will have any effect on operating expenses.

1. Increase average selling prices by 17%. This increase is expected to lower sales volume so that total sales will increase only 6%.
2. Buy merchandise in larger quantities and take all purchase discounts. These changes are expected to increase the gross profit rate by 3 percentage points.

Luke thinks expenses can be cut by making both of the following changes. He feels that these changes will not have any effect on net sales.

1. Cut 2011 sales salaries of $60,000 in half and give sales personnel a commission of 2% of net sales.
2. Reduce store deliveries to one day per week rather than twice a week; this change will reduce 2011 delivery expenses of $30,000 by 40%.

Carrie and Luke come to you for help in deciding the best way to improve net income.

Instructions
With the class divided into groups, answer the following.
(a) Prepare a condensed income statement for 2012, assuming (1) Carrie's changes are implemented and (2) Luke's ideas are adopted.
(b) What is your recommendation to Carrie and Luke?
(c) Prepare a condensed income statement for 2012, assuming both sets of proposed changes are made.

Communication Activity

BYP5-5 The following situation is in chronological order.

1. Flutie decides to buy a surfboard.
2. He calls Surfing USA Co. to inquire about their surfboards.
3. Two days later, he requests Surfing USA Co. to make him a surfboard.
4. Three days later, Surfing USA Co. sends him a purchase order to fill out.
5. He sends back the purchase order.
6. Surfing USA Co. receives the completed purchase order.

7. Surfing USA Co. completes the surfboard.
8. Flutie picks up the surfboard.
9. Surfing USA Co. bills Flutie.
10. Surfing USA Co. receives payment from Flutie.

Instructions

In a memo to the president of Surfing USA Co., answer the following.

(a) When should Surfing USA Co. record the sale?

(b) Suppose that with his purchase order, Flutie is required to make a down payment. Would that change your answer?

Ethics Case

BYP5-6   Laura McAntee was just hired as the assistant treasurer of Dorchester Stores. The company is a specialty chain store with nine retail stores concentrated in one metropolitan area. Among other things, the payment of all invoices is centralized in one of the departments Laura will manage. Her primary responsibility is to maintain the company's high credit rating by paying all bills when due and to take advantage of all cash discounts.

Danny Feeney, the former assistant treasurer who has been promoted to treasurer, is training Laura in her new duties. He instructs Laura that she is to continue the practice of preparing all checks "net of discount" and dating the checks the last day of the discount period. "But," Danny continues, "we always hold the checks at least 4 days beyond the discount period before mailing them. That way, we get another 4 days of interest on our money. Most of our creditors need our business and don't complain. And, if they scream about our missing the discount period, we blame it on the mail room or the post office. We've only lost one discount out of every hundred we take that way. I think everybody does it. By the way, welcome to our team!"

Instructions

(a) What are the ethical considerations in this case?

(b) Who are the stakeholders that are harmed or benefitted in this situation?

(c) Should Laura continue the practice started by Danny? Does she have any choice?

"All About You" Activity

BYP5-7   There are many situations in business where it is difficult to determine the proper period in which to record revenue. Suppose that after graduation with a degree in finance, you take a job as a manager at a consumer electronics store called Atlantis Electronics. The company has expanded rapidly in order to compete with Best Buy. Atlantis has also begun selling gift cards for its electronic products. The cards are available in any dollar amount and allow the holder of the card to purchase an item for up to 2 years from the time the card is purchased. If the card is not used during that 2 years, it expires.

Instructions

Answer the following questions.

At what point should the revenue from the gift cards be recognized? Should the revenue be recognized at the time the card is sold, or should it be recorded when the card is redeemed? Explain the reasoning to support your answers.

FASB Codification Activity

BYP5-8   If your school has a subscription to the FASB Codification, go to *http://aaahq.org/ascLogin.cfm* to log in and prepare responses to the following

(a) Access the glossary ("Master Glossary") to answer the following.
    (1) What is the definition provided for inventory?
    (2) What is a customer?

(b) What guidance does the Codification provide concerning reporting inventories above cost?

Answers to Insight and Accounting Across the Organization Questions

p. 213 Morrow Snowboards Improves Its Stock Appeal   Q: If a perpetual system keeps track of inventory on a daily basis, why do companies ever need to do a physical count? **A:** A perpetual system keeps track of all sales and purchases on a continuous basis. This provides a constant record of the number of units in the inventory. However, if employees make errors in recording sales or purchases, or if there is theft, the inventory value will not be correct. As a consequence, all companies do a physical count of inventory at least once a year.

p. 220 Should Costco Change Its Return Policy?   Q: If a company expects significant returns, what are the implications for revenue recognition? **A:** If a company expects significant returns, it should make an adjusting entry at the end of the year reducing sales by the estimated amount of sales returns. This is necessary so as not to overstate the amount of revenue recognized in the period.

p. 226 Disclosing More Details   Q: Why have investors and analysts demanded more accuracy in isolating "Other gains and losses" from operating items? **A:** Greater accuracy in the classification of operating versus nonoperating ("Other gains and losses") items permits investors and analysts to judge the real operating margin, the results of continuing operations, and management's ability to control operating expenses.

Answers to Self-Test Questions

1. c **2.** a **3.** c **4.** b (($750 − $50) × .98) **5.** c **6.** c **7.** a **8.** d **9.** b ($400,000 − $310,000) **10.** c **11.** d
*12. d *13. a ($60,000 + $380,000 − $50,000) *14. b *15. a

IFRS A Look at IFRS

The basic accounting entries for merchandising are the same under both GAAP and IFRS. The income statement is a required statement under both sets of standards. The basic format is similar although some differences do exist.

Key Points

- Under both GAAP and IFRS, a company can choose to use either a perpetual or a periodic system.

- Inventories are defined by IFRS as held-for-sale in the ordinary course of business, in the process of production for such sale, or in the form of materials or supplies to be consumed in the production process or in the providing of services.

- Under GAAP, companies generally classify income statement items by function. Classification by function leads to descriptions like administration, distribution, and manufacturing. Under IFRS, companies must classify expenses by either nature or function. Classification by nature leads to descriptions such as the following: salaries, depreciation expense, and utilities expense. If a company uses the functional-expense method on the income statement, disclosure by nature is required in the notes to the financial statements.

- Presentation of the income statement under GAAP follows either a single-step or multiple-step format. IFRS does not mention a single-step or multiple-step approach.

- Under IFRS, revaluation of land, buildings, and intangible assets is permitted. The initial gains and losses resulting from this revaluation are reported as adjustments to equity, often referred to as *other comprehensive income*. The effect of this difference is that the use of IFRS results in more transactions affecting equity (other comprehensive income) but not net income.

- *IAS 1*, "Presentation of Financial Statements," provides general guidelines for the reporting of income statement information. Subsequently, a number of international standards have been issued that provide additional guidance to issues related to income statement presentation.

- Similar to GAAP, comprehensive income under IFRS includes unrealized gains and losses (such as those on so-called "available-for-sale securities") that are not included in the calculation of net income.
- IFRS requires that two years of income statement information be presented, whereas GAAP requires three years.

Looking to the Future

The IASB and FASB are working on a project that would rework the structure of financial statements. Specifically, this project will address the issue of how to classify various items in the income statement. A main goal of this new approach is to provide information that better represents how businesses are run. In addition, this approach draws attention away from just one number—net income. It will adopt major groupings similar to those currently used by the statement of cash flows (operating, investing, and financing), so that numbers can be more readily traced across statements. For example, the amount of income that is generated by operations would be traceable to the assets and liabilities used to generate the income. Finally, this approach would also provide detail, beyond that currently seen in most statements (either GAAP or IFRS), by requiring that line items be presented both by function and by nature. The new financial statement format was heavily influenced by suggestions from financial statement analysts.

IFRS Self-Test Questions

1. Which of the following would *not* be included in the definition of inventory under IFRS?
   (a) Photocopy paper held for sale by an office-supply store.
   (b) Stereo equipment held for sale by an electronics store.
   (c) Used office equipment held for sale by the human relations department of a plastics company.
   (d) All of the above would meet the definition.

2. Which of the following would *not* be a line item of a company reporting costs by nature?
   (a) Depreciation expense.
   (b) Salaries expense.
   (c) Interest expense.
   (d) Manufacturing expense.

3. Which of the following would *not* be a line item of a company reporting costs by function?
   (a) Administration.
   (b) Manufacturing.
   (c) Utilities expense.
   (d) Distribution.

4. Which of the following statements is *false*?
   (a) IFRS specifically requires use of a multiple-step income statement.
   (b) Under IFRS, companies can use either a perpetual or periodic system.
   (c) The proposed new format for financial statements was heavily influenced by the suggestions of financial statement analysts.
   (d) The new income statement format will try to de-emphasize the focus on the "net income" line item.

5. Under the new format for financial statements being proposed under a joint IASB/FASB project:
   (a) all financial statements would adopt headings similar to the current format of the balance sheet.
   (b) financial statements would be presented consistent with the way management usually run companies.

(c) companies would be required to report income statement line items by function only.

(d) the amount of detail shown in the income statement would decrease compared to current presentations.

IFRS Concepts and Application

IFRS5-1 Explain the difference between the "nature-of-expense" and "function-of-expense" classifications.

IFRS5-2 For each of the following income statement line items, state whether the item is a "by nature" expense item or a "by function" expense item.

_____ Cost of goods sold
_____ Depreciation expense
_____ Salaries and wages expense
_____ Selling expenses
_____ Utilities expense
_____ Delivery expense
_____ General and administrative expenses

IFRS5-3 Gribble Company reported the following amounts in 2012: Net income, €150,000; Unrealized gain related to revaluation of buildings, €10,000; and Unrealized loss on available-for-sale securities, €(35,000). Determine Gribble's total comprehensive income for 2012.

International Financial Reporting Problem: Zetar plc

IFRS5-4 The financial statements of Zetar plc are presented in Appendix C. The company's complete annual report, including the notes to its financial statements, is available at *www.zetarplc.com*.

Instructions

(a) Is Zetar using a multiple-step or a single-step income statement format? Explain how you made your determination.

(b) Instead of "interest expense," what label does Zetar use for interest costs that it incurs?

(c) Using the notes to the company's financial statements, explain what each of the following are:

(1) Adjusted results.

(2) One-off items.

Answers to IFRS Self-Test Questions
1. c   **2.** d   **3.** c   **4.** a   **5.** b

✔ **The Navigator**

✔ **Remember to go back to the Navigator box on the chapter opening page and check off your completed work.**

CHAPTER6

Inventories

Study Objectives

After studying this chapter, you should be able to:

[1] Describe the steps in determining inventory quantities.

[2] Explain the accounting for inventories and apply the inventory cost flow methods.

[3] Explain the financial effects of the inventory cost flow assumptions.

[4] Explain the lower-of-cost-or-market basis of accounting for inventories.

[5] Indicate the effects of inventory errors on the financial statements.

[6] Compute and interpret the inventory turnover ratio.

✔ **The Navigator**

✔ [The Navigator]

● Scan Study Objectives	○
● Read Feature Story	○
● Read Preview	○
● Read text and answer **Do it!** p. 265 ○ p. 271 ○ p. 277 ○ p. 280 ○	
● Work Comprehensive **Do it!** 1 p. 280 ○ 2 p. 285 ○	
● Review Summary of Study Objectives	○
● Answer Self-Test Questions	○
● Complete Assignments	○
● Go to *WileyPLUS* for practice and tutorials	○
● Read A Look at IFRS p. 310	○

Feature Story

"WHERE IS THAT SPARE BULLDOZER BLADE?"

Let's talk inventory—big, bulldozer-size inventory. Caterpillar Inc. is the world's largest manufacturer of construction and mining equipment, diesel and natural gas engines, and industrial gas turbines. It sells its products in over 200 countries, making it one of the most successful U.S. exporters. More than 70% of its productive assets are located domestically, and nearly 50% of its sales are foreign.

During the 1980s, Caterpillar's profitability suffered, but today it is very successful. A big part of this turnaround can be attributed to effective management of its inventory. Imagine what it costs Caterpillar to have too many bulldozers sitting around in inventory—a situation the company definitely wants to avoid. Conversely, Caterpillar must make sure it has enough inventory to meet demand.

At one time during a 7-year period, Caterpillar's sales increased by 100%, while its inventory increased by only 50%. To achieve this dramatic reduction in the amount of resources tied up in inventory, while continuing to meet customers' needs, Caterpillar used a two-pronged approach. First, it completed a factory modernization program, which dramatically increased its production efficiency. The program reduced by 60% the amount of inventory the company processed at any one time. It also reduced by an incredible 75% the time it takes to manufacture a part.

Second, Caterpillar dramatically improved its parts distribution system. It ships more than 100,000 items daily from its 23 distribution centers strategically located around the world (10 *million* square feet of warehouse space—remember, we're talking bulldozers). The company can virtually guarantee that it can get any part to anywhere in the world within 24 hours.

After these changes, Caterpillar had record exports, profits, and revenues. It would seem that things couldn't be better. But industry analysts, as well as the company's managers, thought otherwise. In order to maintain Caterpillar's position as the industry leader, management began another major overhaul of inventory production and inventory management processes. The goal: to cut the number of repairs in half, increase productivity by 20%, and increase inventory turnover by 40%.

In short, Caterpillar's ability to manage its inventory has been a key reason for its past success, and inventory management will very likely play a huge part in its ability to succeed in the future.

✔
The Navigator

Inside**CHAPTER6**

Previewof**CHAPTER6**

In the previous chapter, we discussed the accounting for merchandise inventory using a perpetual inventory system. In this chapter, we explain the methods used to calculate the cost of inventory on hand at the balance sheet date and the cost of goods sold.

The content and organization of this chapter are as follows.

Inventories				
Classifying Inventory	**Determining Inventory Quantities**	**Inventory Costing**	**Inventory Errors**	**Statement Presentation and Analysis**
• Finished goods • Work in process • Raw materials	• Taking a physical inventory • Determining ownership of goods	• Specific identification • Cost flow assumptions • Financial statement and tax effects • Consistent use • Lower-of-cost-or-market	• Income statement effects • Balance sheet effects	• Presentation • Analysis

✔
The Navigator

Classifying Inventory

How a company classifies its inventory depends on whether the firm is a merchandiser or a manufacturer. In a *merchandising* company, such as those described in Chapter 5, inventory consists of many different items. For example, in a grocery store, canned goods, dairy products, meats, and produce are just a few of the inventory items on hand. These items have two common characteristics: (1) They are owned by the company, and (2) they are in a form ready for sale to customers in the ordinary course of business. Thus, merchandisers need only one inventory classification, **merchandise inventory**, to describe the many different items that make up the total inventory.

In a *manufacturing* company, some inventory may not yet be ready for sale. As a result, manufacturers usually classify inventory into three categories: finished goods, work in process, and raw materials. Finished goods inventory is manufactured items that are completed and ready for sale. Work in process is that portion of manufactured inventory that has been placed into the production process but is not yet complete. Raw materials are the basic goods that will be used in production but have not yet been placed into production.

For example, Caterpillar classifies earth-moving tractors completed and ready for sale as **finished goods**. It classifies the tractors on the assembly line in various stages of production as **work in process**. The steel, glass, tires, and other components that are on hand waiting to be used in the production of tractors are identified as **raw materials**.

By observing the levels and changes in the levels of these three inventory types, financial statement users can gain insight into management's production plans. For example, low levels of raw materials and high levels of finished goods suggest that management believes it has enough inventory on hand, and production will be slowing down—perhaps in anticipation of a recession. On the other hand, high levels of raw materials and low levels of finished goods probably indicate that management is planning to step up production.

Many companies have significantly lowered inventory levels and costs using just-in-time (JIT) inventory methods. Under a just-in-time method, companies

Helpful Hint

Regardless of the classification, companies report all inventories under Current Assets on the balance sheet.

manufacture or purchase goods just in time for use. Dell is famous for having developed a system for making computers in response to individual customer requests. Even though it makes each computer to meet each customer's particular specifications, Dell is able to assemble the computer and put it on a truck in less than 48 hours. The success of the JIT system depends on reliable suppliers. By integrating its information systems with those of its suppliers, Dell reduced its inventories to nearly zero. This is a huge advantage in an industry where products become obsolete nearly overnight.

The accounting concepts discussed in this chapter apply to the inventory classifications of both merchandising and manufacturing companies. Our focus here is on merchandise inventory.

ACCOUNTING ACROSS THE ORGANIZATION

A Big Hiccup

JIT can save a company a lot of money, but it isn't without risk. An unexpected disruption in the supply chain can cost a company a lot of money. Japanese automakers experienced just such a disruption when a 6.8-magnitude earthquake caused major damage to the company that produces 50% of their piston rings. The rings themselves cost only $1.50, but without them you cannot make a car. No other supplier could quickly begin producing sufficient quantities of the rings to match the desired specifications. As a result, the automakers were forced to shut down production for a few days—a loss of tens of thousands of cars.

Source: Amy Chozick, "A Key Strategy of Japan's Car Makers Backfires," *Wall Street Journal* (July 20, 2007).

? What steps might the companies take to avoid such a serious disruption in the future? (See page 310.)

Determining Inventory Quantities

No matter whether they are using a periodic or perpetual inventory system, all companies need to determine inventory quantities at the end of the accounting period. If using a perpetual system, companies take a physical inventory for two reasons:

1. To check the accuracy of their perpetual inventory records.
2. To determine the amount of inventory lost due to wasted raw materials, shoplifting, or employee theft.

Companies using a periodic inventory system take a physical inventory to determine the inventory on hand at the balance sheet date, and to determine the cost of goods sold for the period.

Determining inventory quantities involves two steps: (1) taking a physical inventory of goods on hand and (2) determining the ownership of goods.

Taking a Physical Inventory

Companies take a physical inventory at the end of the accounting period. Taking a physical inventory involves actually counting, weighing, or measuring each kind of inventory on hand. In many companies, taking an inventory is a formidable task. Retailers such as Target, True Value

Study Objective [1]

Describe the steps in determining inventory quantities.

Ethics Note

In a famous fraud, a salad oil company filled its storage tanks mostly with water. The oil rose to the top, so auditors thought the tanks were full of oil. The company also said it had more tanks than it really did: It repainted numbers on the tanks to confuse auditors.

Hardware, or Home Depot have thousands of different inventory items. An inventory count is generally more accurate when goods are not being sold or received during the counting. Consequently, companies often "take inventory" when the business is closed or when business is slow. Many retailers close early on a chosen day in January—after the holiday sales and returns, when inventories are at their lowest level—to count inventory. Recall from Chapter 5 that Wal-Mart has a year-end of January 31.

*E*THICS *I*NSIGHT

 Falsifying Inventory to Boost Income

Managers at women's apparel maker Leslie Fay were convicted of falsifying inventory records to boost net income—and consequently to boost management bonuses. In another case, executives at Craig Consumer Electronics were accused of defrauding lenders by manipulating inventory records. The indictment said the company classified "defective goods as new or refurbished" and claimed that it owned certain shipments "from overseas suppliers" when, in fact, Craig either did not own the shipments or the shipments did not exist.

? What effect does an overstatement of inventory have on a company's financial statements? (See page 310.)

Determining Ownership of Goods

One challenge in computing inventory quantities is determining what inventory a company owns. To determine ownership of goods, two questions must be answered: Do all of the goods included in the count belong to the company? Does the company own any goods that were not included in the count?

GOODS IN TRANSIT

A complication in determining ownership is **goods in transit** (on board a truck, train, ship, or plane) at the end of the period. The company may have purchased goods that have not yet been received, or it may have sold goods that have not yet been delivered. To arrive at an accurate count, the company must determine ownership of these goods.

Goods in transit should be included in the inventory of the company that has legal title to the goods. Legal title is determined by the terms of the sale, as shown in Illustration 6-1 and described below.

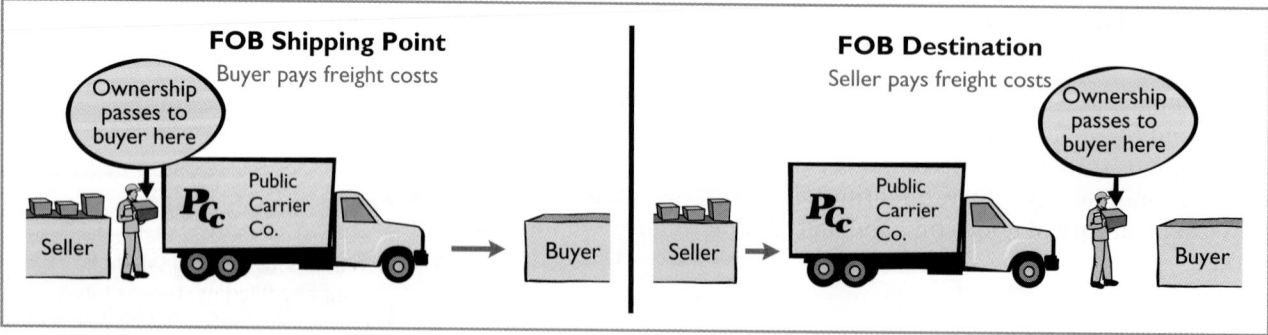

Illustration 6-1
Terms of sale

1. When the terms are FOB (free on board) shipping point, ownership of the goods passes to the buyer when the public carrier accepts the goods from the seller.
2. When the terms are FOB destination, ownership of the goods remains with the seller until the goods reach the buyer.

If goods in transit at the statement date are ignored, inventory quantities may be seriously miscounted. Assume, for example, that Hargrove Company has 20,000 units of inventory on hand on December 31. It also has the following goods in transit:

1. Sales of 1,500 units shipped December 31 FOB destination.
2. Purchases of 2,500 units shipped FOB shipping point by the seller on December 31.

Hargrove has legal title to both the 1,500 units sold and the 2,500 units purchased. If the company ignores the units in transit, it would understate inventory quantities by 4,000 units (1,500 + 2,500).

As we will see later in the chapter, inaccurate inventory counts affect not only the inventory amount shown on the balance sheet but also the cost of goods sold calculation on the income statement.

CONSIGNED GOODS

In some lines of business, it is common to hold the goods of other parties and try to sell the goods for them for a fee, but without taking ownership of the goods. These are called **consigned goods**.

For example, you might have a used car that you would like to sell. If you take the item to a dealer, the dealer might be willing to put the car on its lot and charge you a commission if it is sold. Under this agreement, the dealer **would not take ownership** of the car, which would still belong to you. Therefore, if an inventory count were taken, the car would not be included in the dealer's inventory.

Many car, boat, and antique dealers sell goods on consignment to keep their inventory costs down and to avoid the risk of purchasing an item that they won't be able to sell. Today even some manufacturers are making consignment agreements with their suppliers in order to keep their inventory levels low.

Do it!

Hasbeen Company completed its inventory count. It arrived at a total inventory value of $200,000. As a new member of Hasbeen's accounting department, you have been given the information listed below. Discuss how this information affects the reported cost of inventory.

1. Hasbeen included in the inventory goods held on consignment for Falls Co., costing $15,000.
2. The company did not include in the count purchased goods of $10,000 which were in transit (terms: FOB shipping point).
3. The company did not include in the count sold inventory with a cost of $12,000 which was in transit (terms: FOB shipping point).

Solution

The goods of $15,000 held on consignment should be deducted from the inventory count. The goods of $10,000 purchased FOB shipping point should be added to the inventory count. Sold goods of $12,000 which were in transit FOB shipping point should not be included in the ending inventory. Thus, inventory should be carried at $195,000 ($200,000 − $15,000 + $10,000).

Related exercise material: BE6-1, E6-1, E6-2, and **Do it!** 6-1.

Rules of Ownership

action plan
✔ Apply the rules of ownership to goods held on consignment.
✔ Apply the rules of ownership to goods in transit.

The Navigator

ANATOMY OF A FRAUD

Ted Nickerson, CEO of clock manufacturer Dally Industries, was feared by all of his employees. Ted had expensive tastes. To support his expensive tastes, Ted took out large loans, which he collateralized with his shares of Dally Industries stock. If the price of Dally's stock fell, he was required to provide the bank with more shares of stock. To achieve target net income figures and thus maintain the stock price, Ted coerced employees in the company to alter inventory figures. Inventory quantities were manipulated by changing the amounts on inventory control tags after the year-end physical inventory count. For example, if a tag said there were 20 units of a particular item, the tag was changed to 220. Similarly, the unit costs that were used to determine the value of ending inventory were increased from, for example, $125 per unit to $1,250. Both of these fraudulent changes had the effect of increasing the amount of reported ending inventory. This reduced cost of goods sold and increased net income.

Total take: $245,000

THE MISSING CONTROL

Independent internal verification. The company should have spot-checked its inventory records periodically, verifying that the number of units in the records agreed with the amount on hand and that the unit costs agreed with vendor price sheets.

Source: Adapted from Wells, *Fraud Casebook* (2007), pp. 502–509.

Inventory Costing

Study Objective [2]

Explain the accounting for inventories and apply the inventory cost flow methods.

Inventory is accounted for at cost. Cost includes all expenditures necessary to acquire goods and place them in a condition ready for sale. For example, freight costs incurred to acquire inventory are added to the cost of inventory, but the cost of shipping goods to a customer are a selling expense.

After a company has determined the quantity of units of inventory, it applies unit costs to the quantities to compute the total cost of the inventory and the cost of goods sold. This process can be complicated if a company has purchased inventory items at different times and at different prices.

For example, assume that Crivitz TV Company purchases three identical 50-inch TVs on different dates at costs of $700, $750, and $800. During the year, Crivitz sold two sets at $1,200 each. These facts are summarized in Illustration 6-2.

Illustration 6-2
Data for inventory costing example

Purchases			
February 3	1 TV	at	$700
March 5	1 TV	at	$750
May 22	1 TV	at	$800
Sales			
June 1	2 TVs	for	$2,400 ($1,200 × 2)

Cost of goods sold will differ depending on which two TVs the company sold. For example, it might be $1,450 ($700 + $750), or $1,500 ($700 + $800), or $1,550 ($750 + $800). In this section, we discuss alternative costing methods available to Crivitz.

Specific Identification

If Crivitz can positively identify which particular units it sold and which are still in ending inventory, it can use the **specific identification method** of inventory costing. For example, if Crivitz sold the TVs it purchased on February 3 and May 22, then its cost of goods sold is $1,500 ($700 + $800), and its ending inventory is $750 (see Illustration 6-3). Using this method, companies can accurately determine ending inventory and cost of goods sold.

Illustration 6-3
Specific identification method

Specific identification requires that companies keep records of the original cost of each individual inventory item. Historically, specific identification was possible only when a company sold a limited variety of high-unit-cost items that could be identified clearly from the time of purchase through the time of sale. Examples of such products are cars, pianos, or expensive antiques.

Today, bar coding, electronic product codes, and radio frequency identification make it theoretically possible to do specific identification with nearly any type of product. The reality is, however, that this practice is still relatively rare. Instead, rather than keep track of the cost of each particular item sold, most companies make assumptions, called **cost flow assumptions**, about which units were sold.

Ethics Note

A major disadvantage of the specific identification method is that management may be able to manipulate net income. For example, it can boost net income by selling units purchased at a low cost, or reduce net income by selling units purchased at a high cost.

Cost Flow Assumptions

Because specific identification is often impractical, other cost flow methods are permitted. These differ from specific identification in that they **assume** flows of costs that may be unrelated to the physical flow of goods. There are three assumed cost flow methods:

1. First-in, first-out (FIFO)
2. Last-in, first-out (LIFO)
3. Average-cost

There is no accounting requirement that the cost flow assumption be consistent with the physical movement of the goods. Company management selects the appropriate cost flow method.

To demonstrate the three cost flow methods, we will use a *periodic* inventory system. We assume a periodic system for two main reasons. First, many small companies use periodic rather than perpetual systems. Second, **very few companies use** *perpetual* **LIFO, FIFO, or average-cost** to cost their inventory and related cost of goods sold. Instead, companies that use perpetual systems often use an assumed cost (called a standard cost) to record cost of goods sold at the time of sale. Then, at the end of the period when they count their inventory, they **recalculate cost of** goods sold using *periodic* **FIFO, LIFO, or average-cost** and adjust cost of goods sold to this recalculated number.[1]

To illustrate the three inventory cost flow methods, we will use the data for Houston Electronics' Astro condensers, shown in Illustration 6-4.

Illustration 6-4
Data for Houston Electronics

Houston Electronics Astro Condensers				
Date	**Explanation**	**Units**	**Unit Cost**	**Total Cost**
Jan. 1	Beginning inventory	100	$10	$ 1,000
Apr. 15	Purchase	200	11	2,200
Aug. 24	Purchase	300	12	3,600
Nov. 27	Purchase	400	13	5,200
	Total units available for sale	1,000		$12,000
	Units in ending inventory	450		
	Units sold	550		

The cost of goods sold formula in a periodic system is:

(Beginning Inventory + Purchases) − Ending Inventory = Cost of Goods Sold

Houston Electronics had a total of 1,000 units available to sell during the period (beginning inventory plus purchases). The total cost of these 1,000 units is $12,000, referred to as *cost of goods available for sale.* A physical inventory taken at December 31 determined that there were 450 units in ending inventory. Therefore, Houston sold 550 units (1,000 − 450) during the period. To determine the cost of the 550 units that were sold (the cost of goods sold), we assign a cost to the ending inventory and subtract that value from the cost of goods available for sale. The value assigned to the ending inventory **will depend on which cost flow method we use**. No matter which cost flow assumption we use, though, the sum of cost of goods sold plus the cost of the ending inventory must equal the cost of goods available for sale—in this case, $12,000.

FIRST-IN, FIRST-OUT (FIFO)

The **first-in, first-out (FIFO) method** assumes that the **earliest goods** purchased are the first to be sold. FIFO often parallels the actual physical flow of merchandise; it generally is good business practice to sell the oldest units first. Under the FIFO method, therefore, the **costs** of the earliest goods purchased are the first to be recognized in determining cost of goods sold. (This does not necessarily mean that the oldest units *are* sold first, but that the costs of the oldest units are *recognized* first. In a bin of picture hangers at the hardware store, for example, no one really knows, nor would it matter, which hangers are sold first.) Illustration 6-5 shows the allocation of the cost of goods available for sale at Houston Electronics under FIFO.

---

[1]Also, some companies use a perpetual system to keep track of units, but they do not make an entry for perpetual cost of goods sold. In addition, firms that employ LIFO tend to use *dollar-value LIFO,* a method discussed in upper-level courses. FIFO periodic and FIFO perpetual give the same result; therefore firms should not incur the additional cost to use FIFO perpetual. Few firms use perpetual average-cost because of the added cost of record-keeping. Finally, for instructional purposes, we believe it is easier to demonstrate the cost flow assumptions under the periodic system, which makes it more pedagogically appropriate.

Illustration 6-5
Allocation of costs—FIFO method

Cost of Goods Available for Sale				
Date	**Explanation**	**Units**	**Unit Cost**	**Total Cost**
Jan. 1	Beginning inventory	100	$10	$ 1,000
Apr. 15	Purchase	200	11	2,200
Aug. 24	Purchase	300	12	3,600
Nov. 27	Purchase	400	13	5,200
	Total	1,000		$12,000

Step 1: Ending Inventory				Step 2: Cost of Goods Sold	
Date	**Units**	**Unit Cost**	**Total Cost**		
Nov. 27	400	$13	$5,200	Cost of goods available for sale	$12,000
Aug. 24	50	12	600	Less: Ending inventory	5,800
Total	450		$5,800	Cost of goods sold	$ 6,200

Helpful Hint

Note the sequencing of the allocation:
(1) Compute ending inventory, and
(2) determine cost of goods sold

Helpful Hint

Another way of thinking about the calculation of FIFO ending inventory is the *LISH assumption*—last in still here.

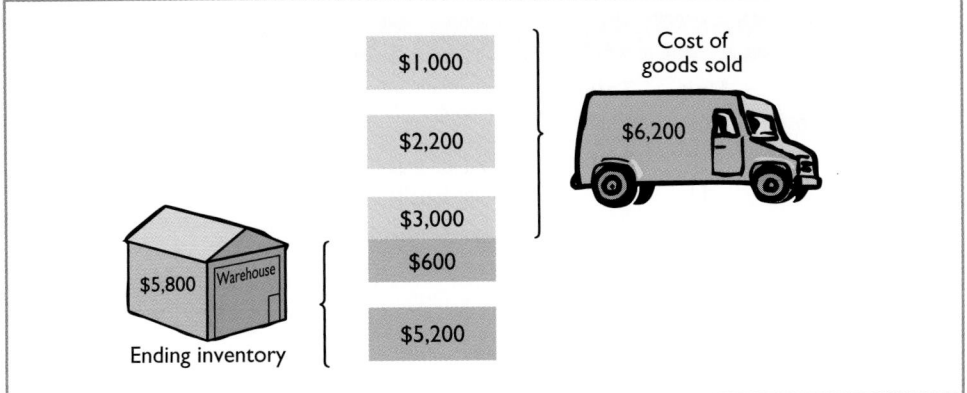

Under FIFO, since it is assumed that the first goods purchased were the first goods sold, ending inventory is based on the prices of the most recent units purchased. That is, **under FIFO, companies obtain the cost of the ending inventory by taking the unit cost of the most recent purchase and working backward until all units of inventory have been costed**. In this example, Houston Electronics prices the 450 units of ending inventory using the *most recent* prices. The last purchase was 400 units at $13 on November 27. The remaining 50 units are priced using the unit cost of the second most recent purchase, $12, on August 24. Next, Houston Electronics calculates cost of goods sold by subtracting the cost of the units **not sold** (ending inventory) from the cost of all goods available for sale.

Illustration 6-6 demonstrates that companies also can calculate cost of goods sold by pricing the 550 units sold using the prices of the first 550 units acquired. Note that of the 300 units purchased on August 24, only 250 units are assumed sold. This agrees with our calculation of the cost of ending inventory, where 50 of these units were assumed unsold and thus included in ending inventory.

Date	**Units**	**Unit Cost**	**Total Cost**
Jan. 1	100	$10	$1,000
Apr. 15	200	11	2,200
Aug. 24	250	12	3,000
Total	550		$6,200

Illustration 6-6
Proof of cost of goods sold

LAST-IN, FIRST-OUT (LIFO)

The last-in, first-out (LIFO) method assumes that the latest goods purchased are the first to be sold. LIFO seldom coincides with the actual physical flow of inventory. (Exceptions include goods stored in piles, such as coal or hay, where goods are removed from the top of the pile as they are sold.) Under the LIFO method, the **costs** of the latest goods purchased are the first to be recognized in determining cost of goods sold. Illustration 6-7 shows the allocation of the cost of goods available for sale at Houston Electronics under LIFO.

Illustration 6-7
Allocation of costs—LIFO method

Cost of Goods Available for Sale				
Date	**Explanation**	**Units**	**Unit Cost**	**Total Cost**
Jan. 1	Beginning inventory	100	$10	$ 1,000
Apr. 15	Purchase	200	11	2,200
Aug. 24	Purchase	300	12	3,600
Nov. 27	Purchase	400	13	5,200
	Total	1,000		$12,000

Step 1: Ending Inventory				Step 2: Cost of Goods Sold	
Date	**Units**	**Unit Cost**	**Total Cost**		
Jan. 1	100	$10	$1,000	Cost of goods available for sale	$12,000
Apr. 15	200	11	2,200	Less: Ending inventory	5,000
Aug. 24	150	12	1,800	Cost of goods sold	$ 7,000
Total	450		$5,000		

Helpful Hint

Another way of thinking about the calculation of LIFO **ending inventory** is the *FISH assumption*—first in still here.

Under LIFO, since it is assumed that the first goods sold were those that were most recently purchased, ending inventory is based on the prices of the oldest units purchased. That is, **under LIFO, companies obtain the cost of the ending inventory by taking the unit cost of the earliest goods available for sale and working forward until all units of inventory have been costed.** In this example, Houston Electronics prices the 450 units of ending inventory using the *earliest* prices. The first purchase was 100 units at $10 in the January 1 beginning inventory. Then 200 units were purchased at $11. The remaining 150 units needed are priced at $12 per unit (August 24 purchase). Next, Houston Electronics calculates cost of goods sold by subtracting the cost of the units **not sold** (ending inventory) from the cost of all goods available for sale.

Illustration 6-8 demonstrates that companies also can calculate cost of goods sold by pricing the 550 units sold using the prices of the last 550 units acquired. Note that of the 300 units purchased on August 24, only 150 units are assumed sold. This agrees with our calculation of the cost of ending inventory, where 150 of these units were assumed unsold and thus included in ending inventory.

Date	Units	Unit Cost	Total Cost
Nov. 27	400	$13	$5,200
Aug. 24	150	12	1,800
Total	550		$7,000

Illustration 6-8
Proof of cost of goods sold

Under a periodic inventory system, which we are using here, **all goods purchased during the period are assumed to be available for the first sale, regardless of the date of purchase**.

AVERAGE-COST

The **average-cost method** allocates the cost of goods available for sale on the basis of the **weighted-average unit cost** incurred. The average-cost method assumes that goods are similar in nature. Illustration 6-9 presents the formula and a sample computation of the weighted-average unit cost.

Cost of Goods Available for Sale	÷	Total Units Available for Sale	=	Weighted-Average Unit Cost
$12,000	÷	1,000	=	$12.00

Illustration 6-9
Formula for weighted-average unit cost

The company then applies the weighted-average unit cost to the units on hand to determine the cost of the ending inventory. Illustration 6-10 (page 272) shows the allocation of the cost of goods available for sale at Houston Electronics using average-cost.

We can verify the cost of goods sold under this method by multiplying the units sold times the weighted-average unit cost (550 × $12 = $6,600). Note that this method does not use the average of the unit costs. That average is $11.50 ($10 + $11 + $12 + $13 = $46; $46 ÷ 4). The average-cost method instead uses the average **weighted by** the quantities purchased at each unit cost.

Do it!

The accounting records of Shumway Ag Implement show the following data.

Beginning inventory	4,000 units at $ 3
Purchases	6,000 units at $ 4
Sales	7,000 units at $12

Determine the cost of goods sold during the period under a periodic inventory system using (a) the FIFO method, (b) the LIFO method, and (c) the average-cost method.

Cost Flow Methods

Solution

Cost of goods available for sale = (4,000 × $3) + (6,000 × $4) = $36,000

Ending inventory = 10,000 − 7,000 = 3,000 units

(a) FIFO: $36,000 − (3,000 × $4) = $24,000

(b) LIFO: $36,000 − (3,000 × $3) = 27,000

(c) Average cost per unit: [(4,000 @ $3) + (6,000 @ $4)] ÷ 10,000 = $3.60
    Average-cost: $36,000 − (3,000 × $3.60) = $25,200

action plan

✔ Understand the periodic inventory system.

✔ Allocate costs between goods sold and goods on hand (ending inventory) for each cost flow method.

✔ Compute cost of goods sold for each method.

Related exercise material: BE6-3, BE6-4, BE6-5, E6-3, E6-4, E6-5, E6-6, E6-7, E6-8, and **Do it!** 6-2.

✔
The Navigator

Illustration 6-10
Allocation of costs—
average-cost method

Cost of Goods Available for Sale				
Date	**Explanation**	**Units**	**Unit Cost**	**Total Cost**
Jan. 1	Beginning inventory	100	$10	$ 1,000
Apr. 15	Purchase	200	11	2,200
Aug. 24	Purchase	300	12	3,600
Nov. 27	Purchase	400	13	5,200
	Total	1,000		$12,000

Step 1: Ending Inventory			Step 2: Cost of Goods Sold	
$12,000 ÷ 1,000 = $12.00			Cost of goods available for sale	$12,000
			Less: Ending inventory	5,400
Units	**Unit Cost**	**Total Cost**	Cost of goods sold	$ 6,600
450	$12.00	$5,400		

$$\frac{\$12,000}{1,000 \text{ units}} = \$12 \text{ per unit}$$

Cost per unit

450 units × $12 = $5,400
Warehouse

Ending inventory

$12,000 − $5,400 = $6,600

Cost of goods sold

Financial Statement and Tax Effects of Cost Flow Methods

Study Objective [3]

Explain the financial effects of the inventory cost flow assumptions.

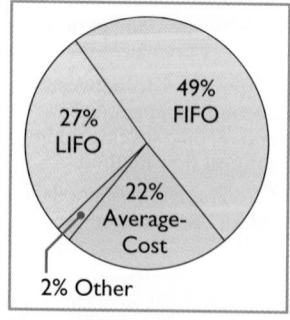

Illustration 6-11
Use of cost flow methods in major U.S. companies

Each of the three assumed cost flow methods is acceptable for use. For example, Reebok International Ltd. and Wendy's International currently use the FIFO method of inventory costing. Campbell Soup Company, Krogers, and Walgreen Drugs use LIFO for part or all of their inventory. Bristol-Myers Squibb, Starbucks, and Motorola use the average-cost method. In fact, a company may also use more than one cost flow method at the same time. Stanley Black & Decker Manufacturing Company, for example, uses LIFO for domestic inventories and FIFO for foreign inventories. Illustration 6-11 (in the margin) shows the use of the three cost flow methods in the 500 largest U.S. companies.

The reasons companies adopt different inventory cost flow methods are varied, but they usually involve one of three factors: (1) income statement effects, (2) balance sheet effects, or (3) tax effects.

INCOME STATEMENT EFFECTS

To understand why companies might choose a particular cost flow method, let's examine the effects of the different cost flow assumptions on the financial statements of Houston Electronics. The condensed income statements in Illustration 6-12 assume that Houston sold its 550 units for $11,500, had operating expenses of $2,000, and is subject to an income tax rate of 30%.

Illustration 6-12
Comparative effects of cost
flow methods

Houston Electronics Condensed Income Statements	FIFO	LIFO	Average-Cost
Sales revenue	$11,500	$11,500	$11,500
Beginning inventory	1,000	1,000	1,000
Purchases	11,000	11,000	11,000
Cost of goods available for sale	12,000	12,000	12,000
Ending inventory	5,800	5,000	5,400
Cost of goods sold	6,200	7,000	6,600
Gross profit	5,300	4,500	4,900
Operating expenses	2,000	2,000	2,000
Income before income taxes[2]	3,300	2,500	2,900
Income tax expense (30%)	990	750	870
Net income	$ 2,310	$ 1,750	$ 2,303

Note the cost of goods available for sale ($12,000) is the same under each of the three inventory cost flow methods. However, the ending inventories and the costs of goods sold are different. This difference is due to the unit costs that the company allocated to cost of goods sold and to ending inventory. Each dollar of difference in ending inventory results in a corresponding dollar difference in income before income taxes. For Houston, an $800 difference exists between FIFO and LIFO cost of goods sold.

In periods of changing prices, the cost flow assumption can have a significant impact on income and on evaluations based on income. In most instances, prices are rising (inflation). In a period of inflation, FIFO produces a higher net income because the lower unit costs of the first units purchased are matched against revenues. In a period of rising prices (as is the case in the Houston example), FIFO reports the highest net income ($2,310) and LIFO the lowest ($1,750); average-cost falls in the middle ($2,030). If prices are falling, the results from the use of FIFO and LIFO are reversed: FIFO will report the lowest net income and LIFO the highest.

To management, higher net income is an advantage: It causes external users to view the company more favorably. In addition, management bonuses, if based on net income, will be higher. Therefore, when prices are rising (which is usually the case), companies tend to prefer FIFO because it results in higher net income.

Some argue that the use of LIFO in a period of inflation enables the company to avoid reporting **paper** (or **phantom**) **profit** as economic gain. To illustrate, assume that Kralik Company buys 200 units of a product at $20 per unit on January 10 and 200 more on December 31 at $24 each. During the year, Kralik sells 200 units at $30 each. Illustration 6-13 shows the results under FIFO and LIFO.

Illustration 6-13
Income statement effects
compared

	FIFO	LIFO
Sales (200 × $30)	$6,000	$6,000
Cost of goods sold	4,000 (200 × $20)	4,800 (200 × $24)
Gross profit	$2,000	$1,200

[2]We are assuming that Houston Electronics is a corporation, and corporations are required to pay income taxes.

Under LIFO, Kralik Company has recovered the current replacement cost ($4,800) of the units sold. Thus, the gross profit in economic terms is real. However, under FIFO, the company has recovered only the January 10 cost ($4,000). To replace the units sold, it must reinvest $800 (200 × $4) of the gross profit. Thus, $800 of the gross profit is said to be phantom or illusory. As a result, reported net income is also overstated in real terms.

BALANCE SHEET EFFECTS

A major advantage of the FIFO method is that in a period of inflation, the costs allocated to ending inventory will approximate their current cost. For example, for Houston Electronics, 400 of the 450 units in the ending inventory are costed under FIFO at the higher November 27 unit cost of $13.

Conversely, a major shortcoming of the LIFO method is that in a period of inflation, the costs allocated to ending inventory may be significantly understated in terms of current cost. The understatement becomes greater over prolonged periods of inflation if the inventory includes goods purchased in one or more prior accounting periods. For example, Caterpillar has used LIFO for 50 years. Its balance sheet shows ending inventory of $6,360 million. But the inventory's actual current cost if FIFO had been used is $9,363 million.

TAX EFFECTS

We have seen that both inventory on the balance sheet and net income on the income statement are higher when companies use FIFO in a period of inflation. Yet, many companies have selected LIFO. Why? The reason is that LIFO results in the lowest income taxes (because of lower net income) during times of rising prices. For example, at Houston Electronics, income taxes are $750 under LIFO, compared to $990 under FIFO. The tax savings of $240 makes more cash available for use in the business.

> **Helpful Hint**
>
> A tax rule, often referred to as the *LIFO conformity rule*, requires that if companies use LIFO for tax purposes they must also use it for financial reporting purposes. This means that if a company chooses the LIFO method to reduce its tax bills, it will also have to report lower net income in its financial statements.

Using Inventory Cost Flow Methods Consistently

Whatever cost flow method a company chooses, it should use that method consistently from one accounting period to another. This approach is often referred to as the **consistency principle**, which means that a company uses the same accounting principles and methods from year to year. Consistent application enhances the comparability of financial statements over successive time periods. In contrast, using the FIFO method one year and the LIFO method the next year would make it difficult to compare the net incomes of the two years.

Although consistent application is preferred, it does not mean that a company may *never* change its inventory costing method. When a company adopts a different method, it should disclose in the financial statements the change and its effects on net income. Illustration 6-14 shows a typical disclosure, using information from financial statements of Quaker Oats (now a unit of PepsiCo).

Illustration 6-14
Disclosure of change in cost flow method

Quaker Oats
Notes to the Financial Statements

Note 1: Effective July 1, the Company adopted the LIFO cost flow assumption for valuing the majority of U.S. Grocery Products inventories. The Company believes that the use of the LIFO method better matches current costs with current revenues. The effect of this change on the current year was to decrease net income by $16.0 million.

INTERNATIONAL INSIGHT

Is LIFO Fair?

ExxonMobil Corporation, like many U.S. companies, uses LIFO to value its inventory for financial reporting and tax purposes. In one recent year, this resulted in a cost of goods sold figure that was $5.6 billion higher than under FIFO. By increasing cost of goods sold, ExxonMobil reduces net income, which reduces taxes. Critics say that LIFO provides an unfair "tax dodge." As Congress looks for more sources of tax revenue, some lawmakers favor the elimination of LIFO. Supporters of LIFO argue that the method is conceptually sound because it matches current costs with current revenues. In addition, they point out that this matching provides protection against inflation.

International accounting standards do not allow the use of LIFO. Because of this, the net income of foreign oil companies such as BP and Royal Dutch Shell are not directly comparable to U.S. companies, which makes analysis difficult.

Source: David Reilly, "Big Oil's Accounting Methods Fuel Criticism," *Wall Street Journal* (August 8, 2006), p. C1.

? What are the arguments for and against the use of LIFO? (See page 310.)

Lower-of-Cost-or-Market

The value of inventory for companies selling high-technology or fashion goods can drop very quickly due to changes in technology or fashions. These circumstances sometimes call for inventory valuation methods other than those presented so far. For example, at one time purchasing managers at Ford decided to make a large purchase of palladium, a precious metal used in vehicle emission devices. They made this purchase because they feared a future shortage. The shortage did not materialize, and by the end of the year the price of palladium had plummeted. Ford's inventory was then worth $1 billion less than its original cost. Do you think Ford's inventory should have been stated at cost, in accordance with the cost principle, or at its lower replacement cost?

As you probably reasoned, this situation requires a departure from the cost basis of accounting. When the value of inventory is lower than its cost, companies can "write down" the inventory to its market value. This is done by valuing the inventory at the **lower-of-cost-or-market (LCM)** in the period in which the price decline occurs. LCM is an example of the accounting concept of **conservatism**, which means that the best choice among accounting alternatives is the method that is least likely to overstate assets and net income.

Companies apply LCM to the items in inventory after they have used one of the cost flow methods (specific identification, FIFO, LIFO, or average-cost) to determine cost. Under the LCM basis, market is defined as **current replacement cost**, not selling price. For a merchandising company, market is the cost of purchasing the same goods at the present time from the usual suppliers in the usual quantities. Current replacement cost is used because a decline in the replacement cost of an item usually leads to a decline in the selling price of the item.

To illustrate the application of LCM, assume that Ken Tuckie TV has the following lines of merchandise with costs and market values as indicated. LCM produces the results shown in Illustration 6-15 (page 276). Note that the amounts shown in the final column are the lower-of-cost-or-market amounts for each item.

Study Objective [4]
Explain the lower-of-cost-or-market basis of accounting for inventories.

International Note

Under U.S. GAAP, companies cannot reverse inventory write-downs if inventory increases in value in subsequent periods. IFRS permits companies to reverse write-downs in some circumstances.

Illustration 6-15
Computation of lower-of-cost-or-market

	Cost	**Market**	**Lower-of-Cost-or-Market**
Flatscreen TVs	$ 60,000	$ 55,000	$ 55,000
Satellite radios	45,000	52,000	45,000
DVD recorders	48,000	45,000	45,000
DVDs	15,000	14,000	14,000
Total inventory			$159,000

Inventory Errors

Study Objective [5]
Indicate the effects of inventory errors on the financial statements.

Unfortunately, errors occasionally occur in accounting for inventory. In some cases, errors are caused by failure to count or price the inventory correctly. In other cases, errors occur because companies do not properly recognize the transfer of legal title to goods that are in transit. When errors occur, they affect both the income statement and the balance sheet.

Income Statement Effects

Under a periodic inventory system, both the beginning and ending inventories appear in the income statement. The ending inventory of one period automatically becomes the beginning inventory of the next period. Thus, inventory errors affect the computation of cost of goods sold and net income in two periods.

The effects on cost of goods sold can be computed by entering incorrect data in the formula in Illustration 6-16 and then substituting the correct data.

Illustration 6-16
Formula for cost of goods sold

Beginning Inventory	+	**Cost of Goods Purchased**	–	**Ending Inventory**	=	**Cost of Goods Sold**

If the error understates *beginning* inventory, cost of goods sold will be understated. If the error understates *ending* inventory, cost of goods sold will be overstated. Illustration 6-17 shows the effects of inventory errors on the current year's income statement.

Illustration 6-17
Effects of inventory errors on current year's income statement

When Inventory Error:	**Cost of Goods Sold Is:**	**Net Income Is:**
Understates beginning inventory	Understated	Overstated
Overstates beginning inventory	Overstated	Understated
Understates ending inventory	Overstated	Understated
Overstates ending inventory	Understated	Overstated

Ethics Note

Inventory fraud increases during recessions. Such fraud includes pricing inventory at amounts in excess of its actual value, or claiming to have inventory when no inventory exists. Inventory fraud usually overstates ending inventory, thereby understating cost of goods sold and creating higher income.

So far, the effects of inventory errors are fairly straightforward. Now, though, comes the (at first) surprising part: An error in the ending inventory of the current period will have a **reverse effect on net income of the next accounting period**. Illustration 6-18 shows this effect. As you study the illustration, you will see that the reverse effect comes from the fact that understating ending inventory in 2011 results in understating beginning inventory in 2012 and overstating net income in 2012.

Over the two years, though, total net income is correct because the errors **offset each other**. Notice that total income using incorrect data is $35,000 ($22,000 + $13,000), which is the same as the total income of

Sample Company
Condensed Income Statements

	2011			2012		
	Incorrect		**Correct**	**Incorrect**		**Correct**
Sales revenue		$80,000	$80,000		$90,000	$90,000
Beginning inventory	$20,000		$20,000	$12,000	$15,000	
Cost of goods purchased	40,000		40,000	68,000	68,000	
Cost of goods available for sale	60,000		60,000	80,000	83,000	
Ending inventory	12,000		15,000	23,000	23,000	
Cost of goods sold		48,000	45,000	57,000		60,000
Gross profit		32,000	35,000	33,000		30,000
Operating expenses		10,000	10,000	20,000		20,000
Net income		$22,000	$25,000	$13,000		$10,000

$(3,000)
Net income
understated

$3,000
Net income
overstated

The errors cancel. Thus the combined total
income for the 2-year period is correct.

Illustration 6-18
Effects of inventory errors on two years' income statements

$35,000 ($25,000 + $10,000) using correct data. Also note in this example that an error in the beginning inventory does not result in a corresponding error in the ending inventory for that period. The correctness of the ending inventory depends entirely on the accuracy of taking and costing the inventory at the balance sheet date under the periodic inventory system.

Balance Sheet Effects

Companies can determine the effect of ending inventory errors on the balance sheet by using the basic accounting equation: Assets = Liabilities + Owner's Equity. Errors in the ending inventory have the effects shown in Illustration 6-19.

Illustration 6-19
Effects of ending inventory errors on balance sheet

Ending Inventory Error	Assets	Liabilities	Owner's Equity
Overstated	Overstated	No effect	Overstated
Understated	Understated	No effect	Understated

The effect of an error in ending inventory on the subsequent period was shown in Illustration 6-18. Recall that if the error is not corrected, the combined total net income for the two periods would be correct. Thus, total owner's equity reported on the balance sheet at the end of 2012 will also be correct.

Do it!

(a) Tracy Company sells three different types of home heating stoves (wood, gas, and pellet). The cost and market value of its inventory of stoves are as follows.

LCM Basis; Inventory Errors

	Cost	Market
Gas	$ 84,000	$ 79,000
Wood	250,000	280,000
Pellet	112,000	101,000

action plan

✔ Determine whether cost or market value is lower for each inventory type.

✔ Sum the lowest value of each inventory type to determine the total value of inventory.

action plan

✔ An ending inventory error in one period will have an equal and opposite effect on cost of goods sold and net income in the next period.

✔ After two years, the errors have offset each other.

Determine the value of the company's inventory under the lower-of-cost-or-market approach.

Solution

> The lowest value for each inventory type is: gas $79,000, wood $250,000, and pellet $101,000. The total inventory value is the sum of these amounts, $430,000.

(b) Visual Company overstated its 2011 ending inventory by $22,000. Determine the impact this error has on ending inventory, cost of goods sold, and owner's equity in 2011 and 2012.

Solution

	2011	**2012**
Ending inventory	$22,000 overstated	No effect
Cost of goods sold	$22,000 understated	$22,000 overstated
Owner's equity	$22,000 overstated	No effect

Related exercise material: BE6-7, BE6-8, E6-9, E6-10, E6-11, E6-12, and **Do it!** 6-3.

The Navigator

Statement Presentation and Analysis

Presentation

As indicated in Chapter 5, inventory is classified in the balance sheet as a current asset immediately below receivables. In a multiple-step income statement, cost of goods sold is subtracted from sales. There also should be disclosure of (1) the major inventory classifications, (2) the basis of accounting (cost, or lower-of-cost-or-market), and (3) the cost method (FIFO, LIFO, or average).

Wal-Mart Stores, Inc., for example, in its January 31, 2010, balance sheet reported inventories of $33,160 million under current assets. The accompanying notes to the financial statements, as shown in Illustration 6-20, disclosed the following information.

Illustration 6-20
Inventory disclosures by Wal-Mart

Wal-Mart Stores, Inc.
Notes to the Financial Statements

Note 1. Summary of Significant Accounting Policies

Inventories

The Company values inventories at the lower of cost or market as determined primarily by the retail method of accounting, using the last-in, first-out ("LIFO") method for substantially all of the Wal-Mart Stores segments' merchandise inventories. SAM'S CLUB merchandise and merchandise in our distribution warehouses are valued based on the weighted average cost using the LIFO method. Inventories of international operations are primarily valued by the retail method of accounting, using the first-in, first-out ("FIFO") method. At January 31, 2010 and 2009, our inventories valued at LIFO approximate those inventories as if they were valued at FIFO.

As indicated in this note, Wal-Mart values its inventories at the lower-of-cost-or-market using LIFO and FIFO.

Analysis

The amount of inventory carried by a company has significant economic consequences. And inventory management is a double-edged sword that requires constant attention. On the one hand, management wants to have a great variety and quantity on hand so that customers have a wide selection and items are always in stock. But such a policy may incur high carrying costs (e.g., investment, storage, insurance, obsolescence, and damage). On the other hand, low inventory levels lead to stockouts and lost sales. Common ratios used to manage and evaluate inventory levels are inventory turnover and a related measure, days in inventory.

Inventory turnover measures the number of times on average the inventory is sold during the period. Its purpose is to measure the liquidity of the inventory. The inventory turnover is computed by dividing cost of goods sold by the average inventory during the period. Unless seasonal factors are significant, average inventory can be computed from the beginning and ending inventory balances. For example, Wal-Mart reported in its 2010 annual report a beginning inventory of $34,511 million, an ending inventory of $33,160 million, and cost of goods sold for the year ended January 31, 2010, of $304,657 million. The inventory turnover formula and computation for Wal-Mart are shown below.

Study Objective [6]
Compute and interpret the inventory turnover ratio.

Cost of Goods Sold	÷	Average Inventory	=	Inventory Turnover
$304,657	÷	$\dfrac{\$33,160 + \$34,511}{2}$	=	9 times

Illustration 6-21
Inventory turnover formula and computation for Wal-Mart

A variant of the inventory turnover ratio is **days in inventory**. This measures the average number of days inventory is held. It is calculated as 365 divided by the inventory turnover ratio. For example, Wal-Mart's inventory turnover of 9 times divided into 365 is approximately 40.6 days. This is the approximate time that it takes a company to sell the inventory once it arrives at the store.

There are typical levels of inventory in every industry. Companies that are able to keep their inventory at lower levels and higher turnovers and still satisfy customer needs are the most successful.

ACCOUNTING ACROSS THE ORGANIZATION

Improving Inventory Control with RFID

Wal-Mart improved its inventory control with the introduction of radio frequency identification (RFID). Much like bar codes, which tell a retailer the number of boxes of a specific product it has, RFID goes a step farther, helping to distinguish one box of a specific product from another. RFID uses technology similar to that used by keyless remotes that unlock car doors.

Companies currently use RFID to track shipments from supplier to distribution center to store. Other potential uses include monitoring product expiration dates and acting quickly on product recalls. Wal-Mart also anticipates faster returns and warranty processing using RFID. This technology will further assist Wal-Mart managers in their efforts to ensure that their store has just the right type of inventory, in just the right amount, in just the right place. Other companies are also interested in RFID. Best Buy has spent millions researching possible applications in its stores.

? Why is inventory control important to managers such as those at Wal-Mart and Best Buy? (See page 310.)

Do it!

Inventory Turnover

Early in 2012, Westmoreland Company switched to a just-in-time inventory system. Its sales, cost of goods sold, and inventory amounts for 2011 and 2012 are shown below.

	2011	2012
Sales revenue	$2,000,000	$1,800,000
Cost of goods sold	1,000,000	910,000
Beginning inventory	290,000	210,000
Ending inventory	210,000	50,000

Determine the inventory turnover and days in inventory for 2011 and 2012. Discuss the changes in the amount of inventory, the inventory turnover and days in inventory, and the amount of sales across the two years.

action plan

✔ To find the inventory turnover ratio, divide cost of goods sold by average inventory.

✔ To determine days in inventory, divide 365 days by the inventory turnover ratio.

✔ Just-in-time inventory reduces the amount of inventory on hand, which reduces carrying costs. Reducing inventory levels by too much has potential negative implications for sales.

Solution

	2011	2012
Inventory turnover ratio	$\frac{\$1,000,000}{(\$290,000 + \$210,000)/2} = 4$	$\frac{\$910,000}{(\$210,000 + \$50,000)/2} = 7$
Days in inventory	$365 \div 4 = 91.3$ days	$365 \div 7 = 52.1$ days

The company experienced a very significant decline in its ending inventory as a result of the just-in-time inventory. This decline improved its inventory turnover ratio and its days in inventory. However, its sales declined by 10%. It is possible that this decline was caused by the dramatic reduction in the amount of inventory that was on hand, which increased the likelihood of "stock-outs." To determine the optimal inventory level, management must weigh the benefits of reduced inventory against the potential lost sales caused by stock-outs.

Related exercise material: BE6-9, E6-13, E6-14, and **Do it!** 6-4.

The Navigator ✔

COMPREHENSIVE

Do it! 1

Gerald D. Englehart Company has the following inventory, purchases, and sales data for the month of March.

Inventory:	March 1	200 units @ $4.00	$ 800
Purchases:			
	March 10	500 units @ $4.50	2,250
	March 20	400 units @ $4.75	1,900
	March 30	300 units @ $5.00	1,500
Sales:			
	March 15	500 units	
	March 25	400 units	

The physical inventory count on March 31 shows 500 units on hand.

Instructions

Under a **periodic inventory system**, determine the cost of inventory on hand at March 31 and the cost of goods sold for March under (a) (FIFO), (b) (LIFO), and (c) average-cost.

action plan

✔ Compute the total goods available for sale, in both units and dollars.

✔ Compute the cost of ending inventory under the periodic FIFO method by allocating to the units on hand the **latest costs**.

✔ Compute the cost of ending inventory under the periodic LIFO method by allocating to the units on hand the **earliest costs**.

✔ Compute the cost of ending inventory under the periodic average-cost method by allocating to the units on hand a **weighted-average cost**.

Solution to Comprehensive Do it! 1

The cost of goods available for sale is $6,450, as follows.

Inventory:		200 units @ $4.00	$ 800
Purchases:			
	March 10	500 units @ $4.50	2,250
	March 20	400 units @ $4.75	1,900
	March 30	300 units @ $5.00	1,500
Total:		1,400	$6,450

Under a **periodic inventory system**, the cost of goods sold under each cost flow method is as follows.

FIFO Method

Ending inventory:

Date	Units	Unit Cost	Total Cost	
March 30	300	$5.00	$1,500	
March 20	200	4.75	950	$2,450

Cost of goods sold: $6,450 − $2,450 = $4,000

LIFO Method

Ending inventory:

Date	Units	Unit Cost	Total Cost	
March 1	200	$4.00	$ 800	
March 10	300	4.50	1,350	$2,150

Cost of goods sold: $6,450 − $2,150 = $4,300

Average-Cost Method

Average unit cost: $6,450 ÷ 1,400 = $4.607
Ending inventory: 500 × $4.607 = $2,303.50

Cost of goods sold: $6,450 − $2,303.50 = $4,146.50

✔ **The Navigator**

Summary of Study Objectives

[1] Describe the steps in determining inventory quantities. The steps are (1) take a physical inventory of goods on hand and (2) determine the ownership of goods in transit or on consignment.

[2] Explain the accounting for inventories and apply the inventory cost flow methods. The primary basis of accounting for inventories is cost. Cost of goods available for sale includes (a) cost of beginning inventory and (b) cost of goods purchased. The inventory cost flow methods are: specific identification and three assumed cost flow methods—FIFO, LIFO, and average-cost.

[3] Explain the financial effects of the inventory cost flow assumptions. Companies may allocate the cost of goods available for sale to cost of goods sold and ending inventory by specific identification or by a method based on an assumed cost flow. When prices are rising, the first-in, first-out (FIFO) method results in lower cost of goods sold and higher net income than the other methods. The reverse is true when prices are falling. In the balance sheet, FIFO results in an ending inventory that is closest to current value; inventory under LIFO is the farthest from current value. LIFO results in the lowest income taxes.

[4] Explain the lower-of-cost-or-market basis of accounting for inventories. Companies may use the lower-of-cost-or-market (LCM) basis when the current replacement cost (market) is less than cost. Under LCM,

companies recognize the loss in the period in which the price decline occurs.

[5] Indicate the effects of inventory errors on the financial statements. *In the income statement of the current year:* (a) An error in beginning inventory will have a reverse effect on net income. (b) An error in ending inventory will have a similar effect on net income. In the following period, its effect on net income for that period is reversed, and total net income for the two years will be correct.

In the balance sheet: Ending inventory errors will have the same effect on total assets and total owner's equity and no effect on liabilities.

[6] Compute and interpret the inventory turnover ratio. The inventory turnover ratio is cost of goods sold divided by average inventory. To convert it to average days in inventory, divide 365 days by the inventory turnover ratio.

Glossary

Average-cost method Inventory costing method that uses the weighted-average unit cost to allocate to ending inventory and cost of goods sold the cost of goods available for sale. (p. 271).

Conservatism Concept that dictates that when in doubt, choose the method that will be least likely to overstate assets and net income. (p. 275).

Consigned goods Goods held for sale by one party although ownership of the goods is retained by another party. (p. 265).

Consistency principle Dictates that a company use the same accounting principles and methods from year to year. (p. 274).

Current replacement cost The current cost to replace an inventory item. (p. 275).

Days in inventory Measure of the average number of days inventory is held; calculated as 365 divided by inventory turnover ratio. (p. 279).

Finished goods inventory Manufactured items that are completed and ready for sale. (p. 262).

First-in, first-out (FIFO) method Inventory costing method that assumes that the costs of the earliest goods purchased are the first to be recognized as cost of goods sold. (p. 268).

FOB (free on board) destination Freight terms indicating that ownership of the goods remains with the seller until the goods reach the buyer. (p. 264).

FOB (free on board) shipping point Freight terms indicating that ownership of the goods passes to the buyer

when the public carrier accepts the goods from the seller. (p. 264).

Inventory turnover A ratio that measures the number of times on average the inventory sold during the period; computed by dividing cost of goods sold by the average inventory during the period. (p. 279).

Just-in-time (JIT) inventory method Inventory system in which companies manufacture or purchase goods just in time for use. (p. 262).

Last-in, first-out (LIFO) method Inventory costing method that assumes the costs of the latest units purchased are the first to be allocated to cost of goods sold. (p. 270).

Lower-of-cost-or-market (LCM) basis A basis whereby inventory is stated at the lower of either its cost or its market value as determined by current replacement cost. (p. 275).

Raw materials Basic goods that will be used in production but have not yet been placed into production. (p. 262).

Specific identification method An actual physical flow costing method in which items still in inventory are specifically costed to arrive at the total cost of the ending inventory. (p. 267).

Weighted-average unit cost Average cost that is weighted by the number of units purchased at each unit cost. (p. 271).

Work in process That portion of manufactured inventory that has been placed into the production process but is not yet complete. (p. 262).

APPENDIX6A

Inventory Cost Flow Methods in Perpetual Inventory Systems

What inventory cost flow methods do companies employ if they use a perpetual inventory system? Simple—they can use any of the inventory cost flow methods described in the chapter. To illustrate the application of the three assumed cost flow methods (FIFO, LIFO, and average-cost), we will use the data shown in Illustration 6A-1 and in this chapter for Houston Electronic's Astro Condenser.

Study Objective [7]

Apply the inventory cost flow methods to perpetual inventory records.

Illustration 6A-1
Inventoriable units and costs

	Houston Electronics Astro Condensers				
Date	Explanation	Units	Units Cost	Total Cost	Balance in Units
1/1	Beginning inventory	100	$10	$ 1,000	100
4/15	Purchases	200	11	2,200	300
8/24	Purchases	300	12	3,600	600
9/10	Sale	550			50
11/27	Purchases	400	13	5,200	450
				$12,000	

First-In, First-Out (FIFO)

Under FIFO, the company charges to cost of goods sold the cost of the earliest goods on hand **prior to each sale**. Therefore, the cost of goods sold on September 10 consists of the units on hand January 1 and the units purchased April 15 and August 24. Illustration 6A-2 shows the inventory under a FIFO method perpetual system.

Illustration 6A-2
Perpetual system—FIFO

Date	Purchases		Cost of Goods Sold	Balance (in units and cost)	
January 1				(100 @ $10)	$1,000
April 15	(200 @ $11)	$2,200		(100 @ $10) (200 @ $11)	$3,200
August 24	(300 @ $12)	$3,600		(100 @ $10) (200 @ $11) (300 @ $12)	$6,800
September 10			(100 @ $10) (200 @ $11) (250 @ $12) $6,200	(50 @ $12)	$ 600
November 27	(400 @ $13)	$5,200		(50 @ $12) (400 @ $13)	$5,800

Cost of goods sold

Ending inventory

The ending inventory in this situation is $5,800, and the cost of goods sold is $6,200 [(100 @ $10) + (200 @ $11) + (250 @ $12)].

Compare Illustrations 6-5 (page 269) and 6A-2. You can see that the results under FIFO in a perpetual system are the **same as in a periodic system**. In both cases, the ending inventory is $5,800 and cost of goods sold is $6,200. Regardless of the system, the first costs in are the costs assigned to cost of goods sold.

Last-In, First-Out (LIFO)

Under the LIFO method using a perpetual system, the company charges to cost of goods sold the cost of the most recent purchase prior to sale. Therefore, the cost of the goods sold on September 10 consists of all the units from the August 24 and April 15 purchases plus 50 of the units in beginning inventory. Illustration 6A-3 shows the computation of the ending inventory under the LIFO method.

Illustration 6A-3
Perpetual system—LIFO

Date	Purchases		Cost of Goods Sold		Balance (in units and cost)	
January 1					(100 @ $10)	$1,000
April 15	(200 @ $11)	$2,200			(100 @ $10) (200 @ $11) }	$3,200
August 24	(300 @ $12)	$3,600			(100 @ $10) (200 @ $11) (300 @ $12) }	$6,800
September 10			(300 @ $12) (200 @ $11) (50 @ $10)	$6,300	(50 @ $10)	$ 500
November 27	(400 @ $13)	$5,200			(50 @ $10) (400 @ $13) }	$5,700

Cost of goods sold ⟶ $6,300

Ending inventory ⟶ $5,700

The use of LIFO in a perpetual system will usually produce cost allocations that differ from those using LIFO in a periodic system. In a perpetual system, the company allocates the latest units purchased *prior to each sale* to cost of goods sold. In contrast, in a periodic system, the latest units purchased *during the period* are allocated to cost of goods sold. Thus, when a purchase is made after the last sale, the LIFO periodic system will apply this purchase to the previous sale. Compare Illustrations 6-7 (page 270) and 6A-3. Illustration 6-7 shows that the 400 units at $13 purchased on November 27 applied to the sale of 550 units on September 10. Under the LIFO perpetual system in Illustration 6A-3, the 400 units at $13 purchased on November 27 are all applied to the ending inventory.

The ending inventory in this LIFO perpetual illustration is $5,700, and cost of goods sold is $6,300, as compared to the LIFO periodic Illustration 6-7 (on page 270) where the ending inventory is $5,000 and cost of goods sold is $7,000.

Average-Cost

The average-cost method in a perpetual inventory system is called the **moving-average method**. Under this method, the company computes a new average **after each purchase**, by dividing the cost of goods available for sale by the units on hand. The average cost is then applied to: (1) the units sold, to determine the cost of goods sold, and (2) the remaining units on hand, to determine the ending inventory amount. Illustration 6A-4 shows the application of the moving-average cost method by Houston Electronics.

Illustration 6A-4
Perpetual system—average-cost method

Date	Purchases		Cost of Goods Sold		Balance (in units and cost)	
January 1					(100 @ $10)	$1,000
April 15	(200 @ $11)	$2,200			(300 @ $10.667)	$3,200
August 24	(300 @ $12)	$3,600			(600 @ $11.333)	$6,800
September 10			(550 @ $11.333)	$6,233	(50 @ $11.333)	$ 567
November 27	(400 @ $13)	$5,200			(450 @ $12.816)	$5,767

Cost of goods sold ⟶ $6,233

Ending inventory ⟶ $5,767

As indicated, Houston Electronics computes **a new average each time it makes a purchase**. On April 15, after it buys 200 units for $2,200, a total of 300 units costing $3,200 ($1,000 + $2,200) are on hand. The average unit cost is $10.667 ($3,200 ÷ 300). On August 24, after Houston Electronics buys 300 units for $3,600, a total of 600 units costing $6,800 ($1,000 + $2,200 + $3,600) are on hand, at an average cost per unit of $11.333 ($6,800 ÷ 600). Houston Electronics uses this unit cost of $11.333 in costing sales until it makes another purchase, when the company computes a new unit cost. Accordingly, the unit cost of the 550 units sold on September 10 is $11.333, and the total cost of goods sold is $6,233. On November 27, following the purchase of 400 units for $5,200, there are 450 units on hand costing $5,767 ($567 + $5,200) with a new average cost of $12.816 ($5,767 ÷ 450).

Compare this moving-average cost under the perpetual inventory system to Illustration 6-10 (on page 272) showing the average-cost method under a periodic inventory system.

COMPREHENSIVE
Do it! 2

Comprehensive Do it! 1 on page 280 showed cost of goods sold computations under a periodic inventory system. Now let's assume that Gerald D. Englehart Company uses a perpetual inventory system. The company has the same inventory, purchases, and sales data for the month of March as shown earlier:

Inventory:	March 1	200 units @ $4.00	$ 800
Purchases:	March 10	500 units @ $4.50	2,250
	March 20	400 units @ $4.75	1,900
	March 30	300 units @ $5.00	1,500
Sales:	March 15	500 units	
	March 25	400 units	

The physical inventory count on March 31 shows 500 units on hand.

Instructions

Under a **perpetual inventory system**, determine the cost of inventory on hand at March 31 and the cost of goods sold for March under (a) FIFO, (b) LIFO, and (c) average-cost.

Solution to Comprehensive Do it! 2

The cost of goods available for sale is $6,450, as follows.

Inventory:		200 units @ $4.00	$ 800
Purchases:	March 10	500 units @ $4.50	2,250
	March 20	400 units @ $4.75	1,900
	March 30	300 units @ $5.00	1,500
	Total:	1,400	$6,450

Under a **perpetual inventory system**, the cost of goods sold under each cost flow method is as follows.

FIFO Method

Date	Purchases	Cost of Goods Sold	Balance	
March 1			(200 @ $4.00)	$ 800
March 10	(500 @ $4.50) $2,250		(200 @ $4.00) (500 @ $4.50)	$3,050

action plan

✔ Compute the cost of goods sold under the perpetual FIFO method by allocating to the goods sold the **earliest** cost of goods purchased.

✔ Compute the cost of goods sold under the perpetual LIFO method by allocating to the goods sold the **latest** cost of goods purchased.

✔ Compute the cost of goods sold under the perpetual average-cost method by allocating to the goods sold a **moving-average** cost.

Date	Purchases		Cost of Goods Sold		Balance	
March 15			(200 @ $4.00)			
			(300 @ $4.50)		(200 @ $4.50)	$ 900
			$2,150			
March 20	(400 @ $4.75)	$1,900			(200 @ $4.50) } (400 @ $4.75) }	$2,800
March 25			(200 @ $4.50)			
			(200 @ $4.75)		(200 @ $4.75)	$ 950
			$1,850			
March 30	(300 @ $5.00)	$1,500			(200 @ $4.75) } (300 @ $5.00) }	$2,450
	Ending inventory, $2,450		Cost of goods sold: $2,150 + $1,850 = $4,000			

LIFO Method

Date	Purchases		Cost of Goods Sold		Balance	
March 1					(200 @ $4.00)	$ 800
March 10	(500 @ $4.50)	$2,250			(200 @ $4.00) } (500 @ $4.50) }	$3,050
March 15			(500 @ $4.50)	$2,250	(200 @ $4.00)	$ 800
March 20	(400 @ $4.75)	$1,900			(200 @ $4.00) } (400 @ $4.75) }	$2,700
March 25			(400 @ $4.75)	$1,900	(200 @ $4.00)	$ 800
March 30	(300 @ $5.00)	$1,500			(200 @ $4.00) } (300 @ $5.00) }	$2,300
	Ending inventory, $2,300		Cost of goods sold: $2,250 + $1,900 = $4,150			

Moving-Average Cost Method

Date	Purchases		Cost of Goods Sold		Balance	
March 1					(200 @ $ 4.00)	$ 800
March 10	(500 @ $4.50)	$2,250			(700 @ $4.357)	$3,050
March 15			(500 @ $4.357)	$ 2,179	(200 @ $4.357)	$ 871
March 20	(400 @ $4.75)	$1,900			(600 @ $4.618)	$2,771
March 25			(400 @ $4.618)	$ 1,847	(200 @ $4.618)	$ 924
March 30	(300 @ $5.00)	$1,500			(500 @ $4.848)	$2,424
	Ending inventory, $2,424		Cost of goods sold: $2,179 + $1,847 = $4,026			

✔
The Navigator

Summary of Study Objective for Appendix 6A

[7] **Apply the inventory cost flow methods to perpetual inventory records.** Under FIFO and a perpetual inventory system, companies charge to cost of goods sold the cost of the earliest goods on hand prior to each sale. Under LIFO and a perpetual system, companies charge to cost of goods sold the cost of the most recent purchase prior to sale. Under the moving-average (average cost) method and a perpetual system, companies compute a new average cost after each purchase.

APPENDIX6B

Estimating Inventories

Study Objective [8]
Describe the two methods of estimating inventories.

In the chapter, we assumed that a company would be able to physically count its inventory. What if it cannot? What if the inventory were destroyed by fire or flood, for example? In that case, the company would use an estimate.

Two circumstances explain why companies sometimes estimate inventories. First, a casualty such as fire, flood, or earthquake may make it impossible to take a physical inventory. Second, managers may want monthly or quarterly financial statements, but a physical inventory is taken only annually. The need for estimating inventories occurs primarily with a periodic inventory system because of the absence of perpetual inventory records.

There are two widely used methods of estimating inventories: (1) the gross profit method, and (2) the retail inventory method.

Gross Profit Method

The **gross profit method** estimates the cost of ending inventory by applying a gross profit rate to net sales. This method is relatively simple, but effective. Accountants, auditors, and managers frequently use the gross profit method to test the reasonableness of the ending inventory amount. It will detect large errors.

To use this method, a company needs to know its net sales, cost of goods available for sale, and gross profit rate. The company then can estimate its gross profit for the period. Illustration 6B-1 shows the formulas for using the gross profit method.

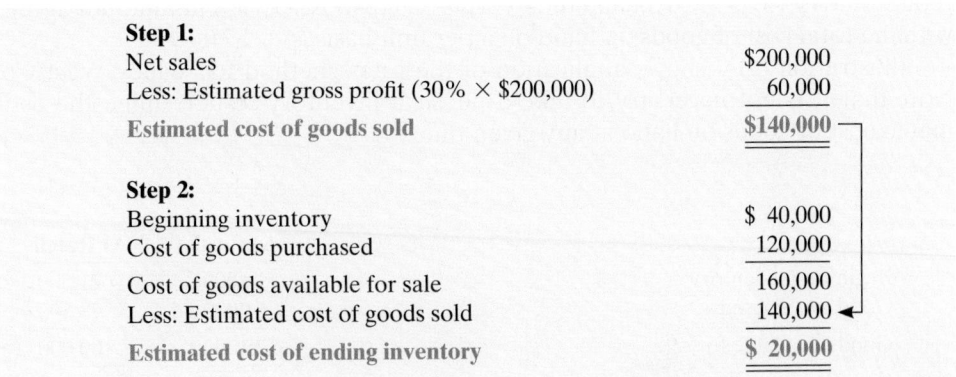

Illustration 6B-1
Gross profit method formulas

To illustrate, assume that Kishwaukee Company wishes to prepare an income statement for the month of January. Its records show net sales of $200,000, beginning inventory $40,000, and cost of goods purchased $120,000. In the preceding year, the company realized a 30% gross profit rate. It expects to earn the same rate this year. Given these facts and assumptions, Kishwaukee can compute the estimated cost of the ending inventory at January 31 under the gross profit method as follows.

Illustration 6B-2
Example of gross profit method

Step 1:	
Net sales	$200,000
Less: Estimated gross profit (30% × $200,000)	60,000
Estimated cost of goods sold	**$140,000**
Step 2:	
Beginning inventory	$ 40,000
Cost of goods purchased	120,000
Cost of goods available for sale	160,000
Less: Estimated cost of goods sold	140,000
Estimated cost of ending inventory	**$ 20,000**

The gross profit method is based on the assumption that the gross profit rate will remain constant. But it may not remain constant, due to a change in merchandising policies or in market conditions. In such cases, the company should adjust the rate to reflect current operating conditions. In some cases, companies can obtain a more accurate estimate by applying this method on a department or product-line basis.

Note that companies should not use the gross profit method to prepare financial statements at the end of the year. These statements should be based on a physical inventory count.

Retail Inventory Method

A retail store such as Home Depot, Ace Hardware, or Wal-Mart has thousands of different types of merchandise at low unit costs. In such cases, it is difficult and time-consuming to apply unit costs to inventory quantities. An alternative is to use the **retail inventory method** to estimate the cost of inventory. Most retail companies can establish a relationship between cost and sales price. The company then applies the cost-to-retail percentage to the ending inventory at retail prices to determine inventory at cost.

Under the retail inventory method, a company's records must show both the cost and retail value of the goods available for sale. Illustration 6B-3 presents the formulas for using the retail inventory method.

Illustration 6B-3
Retail inventory method formulas

		Goods Available for Sale at Retail	−	Net Sales	=	Ending Inventory at Retail
Step 1:						
Step 2:		Goods Available for Sale at Cost	÷	Goods Available for Sale at Retail	=	Cost-to-Retail Ratio
Step 3:		Ending Inventory at Retail	×	Cost-to-Retail Ratio	=	Estimated Cost of Ending Inventory

We can demonstrate the logic of the retail method by using unit-cost data. Assume that Ortiz Inc. has marked 10 units purchased at $7 to sell for $10 per unit. Thus, the cost-to-retail ratio is 70% ($70 ÷ $100). If four units remain unsold, their retail value is $40 (4 × $10), and their cost is $28 ($40 × 70%). This amount agrees with the total cost of goods on hand on a per unit basis (4 × $7).

Illustration 6B-4 shows application of the retail method for Valley West Co. Note that it is not necessary to take a physical inventory to determine the estimated cost of goods on hand at any given time.

Illustration 6B-4
Application of retail inventory method

	At Cost	At Retail
Beginning inventory	$14,000	$ 21,500
Goods purchased	61,000	78,500
Goods available for sale	$75,000	100,000
Net sales		70,000
Step (1) Ending inventory at retail =		$ 30,000

Step (2) Cost-to-retail ratio $75,000 ÷ $100,000 = 75%
Step (3) Estimated cost of ending inventory = $30,000 × 75% = $22,500

The retail inventory method also facilitates taking a physical inventory at the end of the year. Valley West can value the goods on hand at the prices marked on the merchandise, and then apply the cost-to-retail ratio to the goods on hand at retail to determine the ending inventory at cost.

The major disadvantage of the retail method is that it is an averaging technique. Thus, it may produce an incorrect inventory valuation if the mix of the ending inventory is not representative of the mix in the goods available for sale. Assume, for example, that the cost-to-retail ratio of 75% for Valley West Co. consists of equal proportions of inventory items that have cost-to-retail ratios of 70%, 75%, and 80%. If the ending inventory contains only items with a 70% ratio, an incorrect inventory cost will result. Companies can minimize this problem by applying the retail method on a department or product-line basis.

Helpful Hint

In determining inventory at retail, companies use selling prices of the units.

Summary of Study Objective for Appendix 6B

[8] **Describe the two methods of estimating inventories.** The two methods of estimating inventories are the gross profit method and the retail inventory method. Under the gross profit method, companies apply a gross profit rate to net sales to determine estimated cost of goods sold. They then subtract estimated cost of goods sold from cost of goods available for sale to determine the estimated cost of the ending inventory.

Under the retail inventory method, companies compute a cost-to-retail ratio by dividing the cost of goods available for sale by the retail value of the goods available for sale. They then apply this ratio to the ending inventory at retail to determine the estimated cost of the ending inventory.

Glossary for Appendix 6B

Gross profit method A method for estimating the cost of the ending inventory by applying a gross profit rate to net sales and subtracting estimated cost of goods sold from cost of goods available for sale. (p. 287).

Retail inventory method A method for estimating the cost of the ending inventory by applying a cost-to-retail ratio to the ending inventory at retail. (p. 288).

Self-Test, Brief Exercises, Exercises, Problem Set A, and many more components are available for practice in _WileyPLUS_

*Note: All **asterisked** Questions, Exercises, and Problems relate to material in the appendix to the chapter.

Self-Test Questions

Answers are on page 310.

(SO 1) **1.** Which of the following should *not* be included in the physical inventory of a company?
   a. Goods held on consignment from another company.
   b. Goods shipped on consignment to another company.
   c. Goods in transit from another company shipped FOB shipping point.
   d. None of the above.

(SO 1) **2.** As a result of a thorough physical inventory, Railway Company determined that it had inventory worth $180,000 at December 31, 2012. This count did not take into consideration the following facts: Rogers Consignment store currently has goods worth $35,000 on its sales floor that belong to Railway but are being sold on consignment by

Rogers. The selling price of these goods is $50,000. Railway purchased $13,000 of goods that were shipped on December 27, FOB destination, that will be received by Railway on January 3. Determine the correct amount of inventory that Railway should report.
   a. $230,000.   **c.** $228,000.
   b. $215,000.   **d.** $193,000.

3. Cost of goods available for sale consist of two elements: (SO 2) beginning inventory and
   a. ending inventory.
   b. cost of goods purchased.
   c. cost of goods sold.
   d. All of the above.

(SO 2) **4.** Tinker Bell Company has the following:

	Units	Unit Cost
Inventory, Jan. 1	8,000	$11
Purchase, June 19	13,000	12
Purchase, Nov. 8	5,000	13

If Tinker Bell has 9,000 units on hand at December 31, the cost of the ending inventory under FIFO is:
 a. $99,000.   **c.** $113,000.
 b. $108,000.   **d.** $117,000.

(SO 2) **5.** Using the data in Question 4 above, the cost of the ending inventory under LIFO is:
 a. $113,000.   **c.** $99,000.
 b. $108,000.   **d.** $100,000.

(SO 2) **6.** Davidson Electronics has the following:

	Units	Unit Cost
Inventory, Jan. 1	5,000	$ 8
Purchase, April 2	15,000	$10
Purchase, Aug. 28	20,000	$12

If Davidson has 7,000 units on hand at December 31, the cost of ending inventory under the average-cost method is:
 a. $84,000.   **c.** $56,000.
 b. $70,000.   **d.** $75,250.

(SO 3) **7.** In periods of rising prices, LIFO will produce:
 a. higher net income than FIFO.
 b. the same net income as FIFO.
 c. lower net income than FIFO.
 d. higher net income than average costing.

(SO 3) **8.** Factors that affect the selection of an inventory costing method do *not* include:
 a. tax effects.
 b. balance sheet effects.
 c. income statement effects.
 d. perpetual vs. periodic inventory system.

(SO 4) **9.** Rickety Company purchased 1,000 widgets and has 200 widgets in its ending inventory at a cost of $91 each and a current replacement cost of $80 each. The ending inventory under lower-of-cost-or-market is:
 a. $91,000.   **c.** $18,200.
 b. $80,000.   **d.** $16,000.

(SO 5) **10.** Atlantis Company's ending inventory is understated $4,000. The effects of this error on the current year's cost of goods sold and net income, respectively, are:
 a. understated, overstated.
 b. overstated, understated.

 c. overstated, overstated.
 d. understated, understated.

11. Harold Company overstated its inventory by $15,000 at   (SO 4)
December 31, 2011. It did not correct the error in 2011 or 2012. As a result, Harold's owner's equity was:
 a. overstated at December 31, 2011, and understated at December 31, 2012.
 b. overstated at December 31, 2011, and properly stated at December 31, 2012.
 c. understated at December 31, 2011, and understated at December 31, 2012.
 d. overstated at December 31, 2011, and overstated at December 31, 2012.

12. Which of these would cause the inventory turnover ratio   (SO 6)
to increase the most?
 a. Increasing the amount of inventory on hand.
 b. Keeping the amount of inventory on hand constant but increasing sales.
 c. Keeping the amount of inventory on hand constant but decreasing sales.
 d. Decreasing the amount of inventory on hand and increasing sales.

13. Carlos Company had beginning inventory of $80,000, end-   (SO 5)
ing inventory of $110,000, cost of goods sold of $285,000, and sales of $475,000. Carlos's days in inventory is:
 a. 73 days.   **c.** 102.5 days.
 b. 121.7 days.   **d.** 84.5 days.

****14.** Songbird Company has sales of $150,000 and cost of   (SO 8)
goods available for sale of $135,000. If the gross profit rate is 30%, the estimated cost of the ending inventory under the gross profit method is:
 a. $15,000.   **c.** $45,000.
 b. $30,000.   **d.** $75,000.

****15.** In a perpetual inventory system,   (SO 7)
 a. LIFO cost of goods sold will be the same as in a periodic inventory system.
 b. average costs are based entirely on unit cost averages.
 c. a new average is computed under the average-cost method after each sale.
 d. FIFO cost of goods sold will be the same as in a periodic inventory system.

Go to the book's companion website,
www.wiley.com/college/weygandt,
for additional Self-Test Questions.

Questions

1. "The key to successful business operations is effective inventory management." Do you agree? Explain.

2. An item must possess two characteristics to be classified as inventory by a merchandiser. What are these two characteristics?

3. Your friend Tom Witt has been hired to help take the physical inventory in Hawkeye Hardware Store. Explain to Tom Witt what this job will entail.

4. (a) Reeves Company ships merchandise to Cox Company on December 30. The merchandise reaches the buyer on January 6. Indicate the terms of sale that will result in the goods being included in (1) Reeves's December 31 inventory, and (2) Cox's December 31 inventory.

(b) Under what circumstances should Reeves Company include consigned goods in its inventory?

5. Jim's Hat Shop received a shipment of hats for which it paid the wholesaler $2,970. The price of the hats was $3,000 but Jim's was given a $30 cash discount and required to pay freight charges of $50. In addition, Jim's paid $130 to cover the travel expenses of an employee who negotiated the purchase of the hats. What amount will Jim's record for inventory? Why?

6. Explain the difference between the terms FOB shipping point and FOB destination.

7. David Shannon believes that the allocation of inventoriable costs should be based on the actual physical flow of the goods. Explain to David why this may be both impractical and inappropriate.

8. What is a major advantage and a major disadvantage of the specific identification method of inventory costing?

9. "The selection of an inventory cost flow method is a decision made by accountants." Do you agree? Explain. Once a method has been selected, what accounting requirement applies?

10. Which assumed inventory cost flow method:
   (a) usually parallels the actual physical flow of merchandise?
   (b) assumes that goods available for sale during an accounting period are identical?
   (c) assumes that the latest units purchased are the first to be sold?

11. In a period of rising prices, the inventory reported in Plato Company's balance sheet is close to the current cost of the inventory. Cecil Company's inventory is considerably below its current cost. Identify the inventory cost flow method being used by each company. Which company has probably been reporting the higher gross profit?

12. Casey Company has been using the FIFO cost flow method during a prolonged period of rising prices. During the same time period, Casey has been paying out all of its net income as dividends. What adverse effects may result from this policy?

13. Peter Lunde is studying for the next accounting mid-term examination. What should Peter know about (a) departing from the cost basis of accounting for inventories and (b) the meaning of "market" in the lower-of-cost-or-market method?

14. Garitson Music Center has 5 CD players on hand at the balance sheet date. Each cost $400. The current replacement cost is $380 per unit. Under the lower-of-cost-or-market basis of accounting for inventories, what value should be reported for the CD players on the balance sheet? Why?

15. Ruthie Stores has 20 toasters on hand at the balance sheet date. Each cost $27. The current replacement cost is $30 per unit. Under the lower-of-cost-or-market basis of accounting for inventories, what value should Ruthie report for the toasters on the balance sheet? Why?

16. Mintz Company discovers in 2012 that its ending inventory at December 31, 2011, was $7,000 understated. What effect will this error have on (a) 2011 net income, (b) 2012 net income, and (c) the combined net income for the 2 years?

17. Willingham Company's balance sheet shows Inventory $162,800. What additional disclosures should be made?

18. Under what circumstances might inventory turnover be too high? That is, what possible negative consequences might occur?

19. ⬥PEPSICO What inventory cost flow does PepsiCo use for its inventories? (Hint: you will need to examine the notes for PepsiCo's financial statements.)

*20. "When perpetual inventory records are kept, the results under the FIFO and LIFO methods are the same as they would be in a periodic inventory system." Do you agree? Explain.

*21. How does the average-cost method of inventory costing differ between a perpetual inventory system and a periodic inventory system?

*22. When is it necessary to estimate inventories?

*23. Both the gross profit method and the retail inventory method are based on averages. For each method, indicate the average used, how it is determined, and how it is applied.

*24. Maureen Company has net sales of $400,000 and cost of goods available for sale of $300,000. If the gross profit rate is 35%, what is the estimated cost of the ending inventory? Show computations.

*25. Milo Shoe Shop had goods available for sale in 2012 with a retail price of $120,000. The cost of these goods was $84,000. If sales during the period were $80,000, what is the ending inventory at cost using the retail inventory method?

Brief Exercises

BE6-1 Bernard Company identifies the following items for possible inclusion in the taking of a physical inventory. Indicate whether each item should be included or excluded from the inventory taking.

Identify items to be included in taking a physical inventory.

(SO 1)

(a) Goods shipped on consignment by Bernard to another company.
(b) Goods in transit from a supplier shipped FOB destination.
(c) Goods sold but being held for customer pickup.
(d) Goods held on consignment from another company.

BE6-2   The ledger of Charlotte Company includes the following items: (a) Freight-in, (b) Purchase Returns and Allowances, (c) Purchases, (d) Sales Discounts, (e) Purchase Discounts. Identify which items are included in goods available for sale.

BE6-3   In its first month of operations, Danielle Company made three purchases of merchandise in the following sequence: (1) 300 units at $6, (2) 400 units at $7, and (3) 200 units at $8. Assuming there are 360 units on hand, compute the cost of the ending inventory under the (a) FIFO method and (b) LIFO method. Danielle uses a periodic inventory system.

BE6-4   Data for Danielle Company are presented in BE6-3. Compute the cost of the ending inventory under the average-cost method, assuming there are 360 units on hand.

BE6-5   The management of Rousseau Corp. is considering the effects of various inventory-costing methods on its financial statements and its income tax expense. Assuming that the price the company pays for inventory is increasing, which method will:

(a) provide the highest net income?
(b) provide the highest ending inventory?
(c) result in the lowest income tax expense?
(d) result in the most stable earnings over a number of years?

BE6-6   In its first month of operation, Alex Company purchased 100 units of inventory for $6, then 200 units for $7, and finally 150 units for $8. At the end of the month, 180 units remained. Compute the amount of phantom profit that would result if the company used FIFO rather than LIFO. Explain why this amount is referred to as *phantom profit*. The company uses the periodic method.

BE6-7   Tania Appliance Center accumulates the following cost and market data at December 31.

Inventory Categories	Cost Data	Market Data
Cameras	$12,000	$12,100
Camcorders	9,500	9,700
DVD players	14,000	12,800

Compute the lower-of-cost-or-market valuation for the company's total inventory.

BE6-8   Raymonde Company reports net income of $90,000 in 2012. However, ending inventory was understated $10,000. What is the correct net income for 2012? What effect, if any, will this error have on total assets as reported in the balance sheet at December 31, 2012?

BE6-9   At December 31, 2012, the following information was available for C. Widmore Company: ending inventory $40,000, beginning inventory $60,000, cost of goods sold $270,000, and sales revenue $380,000. Calculate inventory turnover and days in inventory for C. Widmore Company.

*BE6-10   Pierre's Department Store uses a perpetual inventory system. Data for product E2-D2 include the following purchases.

Date	Number of Units	Unit Price
May 7	50	$10
July 28	30	13

On June 1, Pierre's sold 30 units, and on August 27, 40 more units. Prepare the perpetual inventory schedule for the above transactions using (a) FIFO, (b) LIFO, and (c) moving-average cost.

*BE6-11   At May 31, Chang Company has net sales of $330,000 and cost of goods available for sale of $230,000. Compute the estimated cost of the ending inventory, assuming the gross profit rate is 35%.

*BE6-12   On June 30, Francois Fabrics has the following data pertaining to the retail inventory method: Goods available for sale: at cost $35,000, at retail $50,000; net sales $40,000, and ending inventory at retail $10,000. Compute the estimated cost of the ending inventory using the retail inventory method.

Do it! Review

Do it! 6-1   Chau Company just took its physical inventory. The count of inventory items on hand at the company's business locations resulted in a total inventory cost of $300,000. In reviewing the details of the count and related inventory transactions, you have discovered the following.

Apply rules of ownership to determine inventory cost.
(SO 1)

1. Chau has sent inventory costing $26,000 on consignment to Nikki Company. All of this inventory was at Nikki's showrooms on December 31.
2. The company did not include in the count inventory (cost, $20,000) that was sold on December 28, terms FOB shipping point. The goods were in transit on December 31.
3. The company did not include in the count inventory (cost, $17,000) that was purchased with terms of FOB shipping point. The goods were in transit on December 31.

Compute the correct December 31 inventory.

Do it! 6-2   The accounting records of Fernandez Electronics show the following data.

Compute cost of goods sold under different cost flow methods.
(SO 2)

Beginning inventory	3,000 units at $5
Purchases	8,000 units at $7
Sales	9,200 units at $10

Determine cost of goods sold during the period under a periodic inventory system using (a) the FIFO method, (b) the LIFO method, and (c) the average-cost method. (Round unit cost to nearest tenth of a cent.)

Do it! 6-3   (a) Kiele Company sells three different categories of tools (small, medium, and large). The cost and fair value of its inventory of tools are as follows.

Compute inventory value under LCM.
(SO 4)

	Cost	Fair Value
Small	$ 64,000	$ 73,000
Medium	290,000	260,000
Large	152,000	171,000

Determine the value of the company's inventory under the lower-of-cost-or-market approach.

(b) Sanchez Company understated its 2011 ending inventory by $31,000. Determine the impact this error has on ending inventory, cost of goods sold, and owner's equity in 2011 and 2012.

Do it! 6-4   Early in 2012, Paulo Company switched to a just-in-time inventory system. Its sales, cost of goods sold, and inventory amounts for 2011 and 2012 are shown below.

Compute inventory turnover ratio and assess inventory level.
(SO 6)

	2011	2012
Sales	$3,120,000	$3,713,000
Cost of goods sold	1,200,000	1,425,000
Beginning inventory	180,000	220,000
Ending inventory	220,000	80,000

Determine the inventory turnover and days in inventory for 2011 and 2012. Discuss the changes in the amount of inventory, the inventory turnover and days in inventory, and the amount of sales across the two years.

Exercises

E6-1   Balboa Bank and Trust is considering giving Rodrigo Company a loan. Before doing so, they decide that further discussions with Rodrigo's accountant may be desirable. One area of particular concern is the inventory account, which has a year-end balance of $297,000. Discussions with the accountant reveal the following.

Determine the correct inventory amount.
(SO 1)

1. Rodrigo sold goods costing $38,000 to Santoro Company, FOB shipping point, on December 28. The goods are not expected to arrive at Santoro until January 12. The goods were not included in the physical inventory because they were not in the warehouse.

2. The physical count of the inventory did not include goods costing $95,000 that were shipped to Rodrigo FOB destination on December 27 and were still in transit at year-end.
3. Rodrigo received goods costing $22,000 on January 2. The goods were shipped FOB shipping point on December 26 by Penelope Co. The goods were not included in the physical count.
4. Rodrigo sold goods costing $35,000 to Naomi Co., FOB destination, on December 30. The goods were received at Naomi on January 8. They were not included in Rodrigo's physical inventory.
5. Rodrigo received goods costing $44,000 on January 2 that were shipped FOB destination on December 29. The shipment was a rush order that was supposed to arrive December 31. This purchase was included in the ending inventory of $297,000.

Instructions
Determine the correct inventory amount on December 31.

*Determine the correct
inventory amount.*

(SO 1)

E6-2   Marsha Thomason, an auditor with Dorrit CPAs, is performing a review of Mikhail Company's inventory account. Mikhail did not have a good year and top management is under pressure to boost reported income. According to its records, the inventory balance at year-end was $740,000. However, the following information was not considered when determining that amount.

1. Included in the company's count were goods with a cost of $250,000 that the company is holding on consignment. The goods belong to Bakunin Corporation.
2. The physical count did not include goods purchased by Mikhail with a cost of $40,000 that were shipped FOB destination on December 28 and did not arrive at Mikhail's warehouse until January 3.
3. Included in the inventory account was $17,000 of office supplies that were stored in the warehouse and were to be used by the company's supervisors and managers during the coming year.
4. The company received an order on December 29 that was boxed and was sitting on the loading dock awaiting pick-up on December 31. The shipper picked up the goods on January 1 and delivered them on January 6. The shipping terms were FOB shipping point. The goods had a selling price of $40,000 and a cost of $30,000. The goods were not included in the count because they were sitting on the dock.
5. On December 29, Mikhail shipped goods with a selling price of $80,000 and a cost of $60,000 to Omar Sales Corporation FOB shipping point. The goods arrived on January 3. Omar Sales had only ordered goods with a selling price of $10,000 and a cost of $8,000. However, a sales manager at Mikhail had authorized the shipment and said that if Omar wanted to ship the goods back next week, it could.
6. Included in the count was $40,000 of goods that were parts for a machine that the company no longer made. Given the high-tech nature of Mikhail's products, it was unlikely that these obsolete parts had any other use. However, management would prefer to keep them on the books at cost, "since that is what we paid for them, after all."

Instructions
Prepare a schedule to determine the correct inventory amount. Provide explanations for each item above, saying why you did or did not make an adjustment for each item.

*Calculate cost of goods sold
using specific identification
and FIFO.*

(SO 2, 3)

E6-3   On December 1, Nadia Electronics Ltd. has three DVD players left in stock. All are identical, all are priced to sell at $150. One of the three DVD players left in stock, with serial #1012, was purchased on June 1 at a cost of $100. Another, with serial #1045, was purchased on November 1 for $90. The last player, serial #1056, was purchased on November 30 for $80.

Instructions
(a) Calculate the cost of goods sold using the FIFO periodic inventory method assuming that two of the three players were sold by the end of December, Nadia Electronics' year-end.
(b) If Nadia Electronics used the specific identification method instead of the FIFO method, how might it alter its earnings by "selectively choosing" which particular players to sell to the two customers? What would Nadia's cost of goods sold be if the company wished to minimize earnings? Maximize earnings?
(c) Which of the two inventory methods do you recommend that Nadia use? Explain why.

*Compute inventory and cost
of goods sold using FIFO
and LIFO.*

(SO 2)

E6-4   Andrea's Boards sells a snowboard, Xpert, that is popular with snowboard enthusiasts. Information relating to Andrea's purchases of Xpert snowboards during September is shown on page 295.

During the same month, 121 Xpert snowboards were sold. Andrea's uses a periodic inventory system.

Date	Explanation	Units	Unit Cost	Total Cost
Sept. 1	Inventory	26	$ 97	$ 2,522
Sept. 12	Purchases	45	102	4,590
Sept. 19	Purchases	20	104	2,080
Sept. 26	Purchases	50	105	5,250
	Totals	141		$14,442

Instructions
(a) Compute the ending inventory at September 30 and cost of goods sold using the FIFO and LIFO methods. Prove the amount allocated to cost of goods sold under each method.
(b) For both FIFO and LIFO, calculate the sum of ending inventory and cost of goods sold. What do you notice about the answers you found for each method?

E6-5   Fionnula Co. uses a periodic inventory system. Its records show the following for the month of May, in which 65 units were sold.

Compute inventory and cost of goods sold using FIFO and LIFO.
(SO 2)

		Units	Unit Cost	Total Cost
May 1	Inventory	30	$ 8	$240
15	Purchases	25	11	275
24	Purchases	35	12	420
	Totals	90		$935

Instructions
Compute the ending inventory at May 31 and cost of goods sold using the FIFO and LIFO methods. Prove the amount allocated to cost of goods sold under each method.

E6-6   Flanagan Company reports the following for the month of June.

Compute inventory and cost of goods sold using FIFO and LIFO.
(SO 2, 3)

		Units	Unit Cost	Total Cost
June 1	Inventory	200	$5	$1,000
12	Purchase	300	6	1,800
23	Purchase	500	7	3,500
30	Inventory	120		

Instructions
(a) Compute the cost of the ending inventory and the cost of goods sold under (1) FIFO and (2) LIFO.
(b) Which costing method gives the higher ending inventory? Why?
(c) Which method results in the higher cost of goods sold? Why?

E6-7   Eloise Company had 100 units in beginning inventory at a total cost of $10,000. The company purchased 200 units at a total cost of $26,000. At the end of the year, Eloise had 80 units in ending inventory.

Compute inventory under FIFO, LIFO, and average-cost.
(SO 2, 3)

Instructions
(a) Compute the cost of the ending inventory and the cost of goods sold under (1) FIFO, (2) LIFO, and (3) average-cost.
(b) Which cost flow method would result in the highest net income?
(c) Which cost flow method would result in inventories approximating current cost in the balance sheet?
(d) Which cost flow method would result in Eloise paying the least taxes in the first year?

E6-8   Inventory data for Flanagan Company are presented in E6-6.

Compute inventory and cost of goods sold using average-cost.
(SO 2, 3)

Instructions
(a) Compute the cost of the ending inventory and the cost of goods sold using the average-cost method.
(b) Will the results in (a) be higher or lower than the results under (1) FIFO and (2) LIFO?
(c) Why is the average unit cost not $6?

Determine ending inventory under LCM.

(SO 4)

E6-9   Venden Camera Shop uses the lower-of-cost-or-market basis for its inventory. The following data are available at December 31.

Item	Units	Unit Cost	Market
Cameras:			
Minolta	5	$170	$156
Canon	6	150	152
Light meters:			
Vivitar	12	125	115
Kodak	14	120	135

Instructions

Determine the amount of the ending inventory by applying the lower-of-cost-or-market basis.

Compute lower-of-cost-or-market.

(SO 4)

E6-10   Radzinsky Company applied FIFO to its inventory and got the following results for its ending inventory.

Cameras	100 units at a cost per unit of $65
DVD players	150 units at a cost per unit of $75
iPods	125 units at a cost per unit of $80

The cost of purchasing units at year-end was cameras $71, DVD players $69, and iPods $78.

Instructions

Determine the amount of ending inventory at lower-of-cost-or-market.

Determine effects of inventory errors.

(SO 5)

E6-11   Jacob's Hardware reported cost of goods sold as follows.

	2011	2012
Beginning inventory	$ 20,000	$ 30,000
Cost of goods purchased	150,000	175,000
Cost of goods available for sale	170,000	205,000
Ending inventory	30,000	35,000
Cost of goods sold	$140,000	$170,000

Jacob's made two errors: (1) 2011 ending inventory was overstated $3,000, and (2) 2012 ending inventory was understated $6,000.

Instructions

Compute the correct cost of goods sold for each year.

Prepare correct income statements.

(SO 5)

E6-12   Pellegrino Watch Company reported the following income statement data for a 2-year period.

	2011	2012
Sales revenue	$210,000	$250,000
Cost of goods sold		
Beginning inventory	32,000	44,000
Cost of goods purchased	173,000	202,000
Cost of goods available for sale	205,000	246,000
Ending inventory	44,000	52,000
Cost of goods sold	161,000	194,000
Gross profit	$ 49,000	$ 56,000

Pellegrino uses a periodic inventory system. The inventories at January 1, 2011, and December 31, 2012, are correct. However, the ending inventory at December 31, 2011, was overstated $5,000.

Instructions

(a) Prepare correct income statement data for the 2 years.

(b) What is the cumulative effect of the inventory error on total gross profit for the 2 years?

(c)   ✎   Explain in a letter to the president of Pellegrino Company what has happened—i.e., the nature of the error and its effect on the financial statements.

E6-13   This information is available for Paik's Photo Corporation for 2010, 2011, and 2012.

Compute inventory turnover, days in inventory, and gross profit rate.
(SO 6)

	2010	**2011**	**2012**
Beginning inventory	$ 100,000	$ 300,000	$ 400,000
Ending inventory	300,000	400,000	480,000
Cost of goods sold	900,000	1,120,000	1,300,000
Sales revenue	1,200,000	1,600,000	1,900,000

Instructions

Calculate inventory turnover, days in inventory, and gross profit rate (from Chapter 5) for Paik's Photo Corporation for 2010, 2011, and 2012. Comment on any trends.

E6-14   The cost of goods sold computations for Target Company and Caesar Company are shown below.

Compute inventory turnover and days in inventory.
(SO 6)

	Target Company	**Caesar Company**
Beginning inventory	$ 45,000	$ 71,000
Cost of goods purchased	200,000	290,000
Cost of goods available for sale	245,000	361,000
Ending inventory	55,000	69,000
Cost of goods sold	$190,000	$292,000

Instructions

(a) Compute inventory turnover and days in inventory for each company.
(b) Which company moves its inventory more quickly?

*E6-15   Hiroyuki Appliance uses a perpetual inventory system. For its flat-screen television sets, the January 1 inventory was 3 sets at $600 each. On January 10, Hiroyuki purchased 6 units at $660 each. The company sold 2 units on January 8 and 4 units on January 15.

Apply cost flow methods to perpetual records.
(SO 7)

Instructions

Compute the ending inventory under (1) FIFO, (2) LIFO, and (3) moving-average cost.

*E6-16   Flanagan Company reports the following for the month of June.

Calculate inventory and cost of goods sold using three cost flow methods in a perpetual inventory system.
(SO 7)

Date	Explanation	Units	Unit Cost	Total Cost
June 1	Inventory	200	$5	$1,000
12	Purchase	300	6	1,800
23	Purchase	500	7	3,500
30	Inventory	120		

Instructions

(a) Calculate the cost of the ending inventory and the cost of goods sold for each cost flow assumption, using a perpetual inventory system. Assume a sale of 400 units occurred on June 15 for a selling price of $8 and a sale of 480 units on June 27 for $9.
(b) How do the results differ from E6-6 and E6-8?
(c) Why is the average unit cost not $6 [($5 + $6 + $7) ÷ 3 = $6]?

*E6-17   Information about Andrea's Boards is presented in E6-4. Additional data regarding Andrea's sales of Xpert snowboards are provided below. Assume that Andrea's uses a perpetual inventory system.

Apply cost flow methods to perpetual records.
(SO 7)

Date		Units	Unit Price	Total Cost
Sept. 5	Sale	12	$199	$ 2,388
Sept. 16	Sale	50	199	9,950
Sept. 29	Sale	59	209	12,331
	Totals	121		$24,669

Instructions

(a) Compute ending inventory at September 30 using FIFO, LIFO, and moving-average cost.
(b) Compare ending inventory using a perpetual inventory system to ending inventory using a periodic inventory system (from E6-4).
(c) Which inventory cost flow method (FIFO, LIFO) gives the same ending inventory value under both periodic and perpetual? Which method gives different ending inventory values?

Use the gross profit method to estimate inventory.
(SO 8)

*E6-18 Sanada Company reported the following information for November and December 2012.

	November	December
Cost of goods purchased	$500,000	$ 610,000
Inventory, beginning-of-month	100,000	120,000
Inventory, end-of-month	120,000	????
Sales revenue	800,000	1,000,000

Sanada's ending inventory at December 31 was destroyed in a fire.

Instructions
(a) Compute the gross profit rate for November.
(b) Using the gross profit rate for November, determine the estimated cost of inventory lost in the fire.

Determine merchandise lost using the gross profit method of estimating inventory.
(SO 8)

*E6-19 The inventory of Dogen Company was destroyed by fire on March 1. From an examination of the accounting records, the following data for the first 2 months of the year are obtained: Sales Revenue $51,000, Sales Returns and Allowances $1,000, Purchases $31,200, Freight-in $1,200, and Purchase Returns and Allowances $1,400.

Instructions
Determine the merchandise lost by fire, assuming:

(a) A beginning inventory of $20,000 and a gross profit rate of 40% on net sales.
(b) A beginning inventory of $30,000 and a gross profit rate of 30% on net sales.

Determine ending inventory at cost using retail method.
(SO 8)

*E6-20 Seamus Shoe Store uses the retail inventory method for its two departments, Women's Shoes and Men's Shoes. The following information for each department is obtained.

Item	Women's Shoes	Men's Shoes
Beginning inventory at cost	$ 32,000	$ 45,000
Cost of goods purchased at cost	148,000	136,300
Net sales	178,000	185,000
Beginning inventory at retail	46,000	60,000
Cost of goods purchased at retail	179,000	185,000

Instructions
Compute the estimated cost of the ending inventory for each department under the retail inventory method.

Exercises: Set B

Visit the book's companion website, at **www.wiley.com/college/weygandt**, and choose the Student Companion site to access Exercise Set B.

Problems: Set A

Determine items and amounts to be recorded in inventory.
(SO 1)

P6-1A Toledo Limited is trying to determine the value of its ending inventory at February 28, 2012, the company's year-end. The accountant counted everything that was in the warehouse as of February 28, which resulted in an ending inventory valuation of $48,000. However, she didn't know how to treat the following transactions so she didn't record them.

(a) On February 26, Toledo shipped to a customer goods costing $800. The goods were shipped FOB shipping point, and the receiving report indicates that the customer received the goods on March 2.
(b) On February 26, Grisel Inc. shipped goods to Toledo FOB destination. The invoice price was $350. The receiving report indicates that the goods were received by Toledo on March 2.
(c) Toledo had $500 of inventory at a customer's warehouse "on approval." The customer was going to let Toledo know whether it wanted the merchandise by the end of the week, March 4.
(d) Toledo also had $400 of inventory on consignment at a Balboa craft shop.
(e) On February 26, Toledo ordered goods costing $750. The goods were shipped FOB shipping point on February 27. Toledo received the goods on March 1.

(f) On February 28, Toledo packaged goods and had them ready for shipping to a customer FOB destination. The invoice price was $350; the cost of the items was $250. The receiving report indicates that the goods were received by the customer on March 2.

(g) Toledo had damaged goods set aside in the warehouse because they are no longer saleable. These goods originally cost $400 and, originally, Toledo expected to sell these items for $600.

Instructions

For each of the above transactions, specify whether the item in question should be included in ending inventory, and if so, at what amount. For each item that is not included in ending inventory, indicate who owns it and what account, if any, it should have been recorded in.

P6-2A Kyoto Distribution markets CDs of the performing artist A. A. Bondy. At the beginning of March, Kyoto had in beginning inventory 1,500 Bondy CDs with a unit cost of $7. During March Kyoto made the following purchases of Bondy CDs.

| March 5 | 3,000 @ $8 | March 21 | 4,000 @ $10 |
| March 13 | 5,500 @ $9 | March 26 | 2,000 @ $11 |

During March 12,500 units were sold. Kyoto uses a periodic inventory system.

Determine cost of goods sold and ending inventory using FIFO, LIFO, and average-cost with analysis.

(SO 2, 3)

Instructions

(a) Determine the cost of goods available for sale.

(b) Determine (1) the ending inventory and (2) the cost of goods sold under each of the assumed cost flow methods (FIFO, LIFO, and average-cost). Prove the accuracy of the cost of goods sold under the FIFO and LIFO methods.

(c) Which cost flow method results in (1) the highest inventory amount for the balance sheet and (2) the highest cost of goods sold for the income statement?

(b)(2) Cost of goods sold:
FIFO $109,000
LIFO $119,500
Average $114,062

P6-3A Lu Company had a beginning inventory of 400 units of Product Ribo at a cost of $8 per unit. During the year, purchases were:

| Feb. 20 | 600 units at $9 | Aug. 12 | 300 units at $11 |
| May 5 | 500 units at $10 | Dec. 8 | 200 units at $12 |

Lu Company uses a periodic inventory system. Sales totaled 1,500 units.

Determine cost of goods sold and ending inventory using FIFO, LIFO, and average-cost with analysis.

(SO 2, 3)

Instructions

(a) Determine the cost of goods available for sale.

(b) Determine (1) the ending inventory, and (2) the cost of goods sold under each of the assumed cost flow methods (FIFO, LIFO, and average). Prove the accuracy of the cost of goods sold under the FIFO and LIFO methods.

(c) Which cost flow method results in (1) the lowest inventory amount for the balance sheet, and (2) the lowest cost of goods sold for the income statement?

(b) Cost of goods sold:
FIFO $13,600
LIFO $15,200
Average $14,475

P6-4A The management of Reiko Co. is reevaluating the appropriateness of using its present inventory cost flow method, which is average-cost. They request your help in determining the results of operations for 2012 if either the FIFO method or the LIFO method had been used. For 2012, the accounting records show the following data.

Compute ending inventory, prepare income statements, and answer questions using FIFO and LIFO.

(SO 2, 3)

Inventories		Purchases and Sales	
Beginning (15,000 units)	$32,000	Total net sales (215,000 units)	$865,000
Ending (30,000 units)		Total cost of goods purchased	
		(230,000 units)	595,000

Purchases were made quarterly as follows.

Quarter	Units	Unit Cost	Total Cost
1	60,000	$2.40	$144,000
2	50,000	2.50	125,000
3	50,000	2.60	130,000
4	70,000	2.80	196,000
	230,000		$595,000

Operating expenses were $147,000, and the company's income tax rate is 34%.

Instructions

(a) Net income
FIFO $115,500
LIFO $104,940
(b)(4) $5,440

(a) Prepare comparative condensed income statements for 2012 under FIFO and LIFO. (Show computations of ending inventory.)

(b) ▬▬▬ Answer the following questions for management.

(1) Which cost flow method (FIFO or LIFO) produces the more meaningful inventory amount for the balance sheet? Why?

(2) Which cost flow method (FIFO or LIFO) produces the more meaningful net income? Why?

(3) Which cost flow method (FIFO or LIFO) is more likely to approximate actual physical flow of the goods? Why?

(4) How much additional cash will be available for management under LIFO than under FIFO? Why?

(5) Will gross profit under the average-cost method be higher or lower than (i) FIFO and (ii) LIFO? (*Note:* It is not necessary to quantify your answer.)

Calculate ending inventory, cost of goods sold, gross profit, and gross profit rate under periodic method; compare results.
(SO 2, 3)

P6-5A You are provided with the following information for Aylesworth Inc. for the month ended October 31, 2012. Aylesworth uses a periodic method for inventory.

Date	Description	Units	Unit Cost or Selling Price
October 1	Beginning inventory	60	$25
October 9	Purchase	120	26
October 11	Sale	100	35
October 17	Purchase	70	27
October 22	Sale	60	40
October 25	Purchase	80	28
October 29	Sale	110	40

Instructions

(a)(iii) Gross profit:
LIFO $3,050
FIFO $3,230
Average $3,141

(a) Calculate (i) ending inventory, (ii) cost of goods sold, (iii) gross profit, and (iv) gross profit rate under each of the following methods.

(1) LIFO.
(2) FIFO.
(3) Average-cost.

(b) Compare results for the three cost flow assumptions.

Compare specific identification, FIFO and LIFO under periodic method; use cost flow assumption to influence earnings.
(SO 2, 3)

P6-6A You have the following information for Goodspeed Diamonds. Goodspeed Diamonds uses the periodic method of accounting for its inventory transactions. Goodspeed only carries one brand and size of diamonds—all are identical. Each batch of diamonds purchased is carefully coded and marked with its purchase cost.

March 1 Beginning inventory 150 diamonds at a cost of $300 per diamond.
March 3 Purchased 200 diamonds at a cost of $350 each.
March 5 Sold 180 diamonds for $600 each.
March 10 Purchased 350 diamonds at a cost of $375 each.
March 25 Sold 400 diamonds for $650 each.

Instructions

(a) Gross profit:
(1) Maximum $166,750
(2) Minimum $157,750

(a) Assume that Goodspeed Diamonds uses the specific identification cost flow method.

(1) Demonstrate how Goodspeed Diamonds could maximize its gross profit for the month by specifically selecting which diamonds to sell on March 5 and March 25.

(2) Demonstrate how Goodspeed Diamonds could minimize its gross profit for the month by selecting which diamonds to sell on March 5 and March 25.

(b) Assume that Goodspeed Diamonds uses the FIFO cost flow assumption. Calculate cost of goods sold. How much gross profit would Goodspeed Diamonds report under this cost flow assumption?

(c) Assume that Goodspeed Diamonds uses the LIFO cost flow assumption. Calculate cost of goods sold. How much gross profit would the company report under this cost flow assumption?

(d) Which cost flow method should Goodspeed Diamonds select? Explain.

Compute ending inventory, prepare income statements, and answer questions using FIFO and LIFO.
(SO 2, 3)

P6-7A The management of Hillary Inc. asks your help in determining the comparative effects of the FIFO and LIFO inventory cost flow methods. For 2012, the accounting records provide the data shown on page 301.

Inventory, January 1 (10,000 units)	$ 35,000
Cost of 120,000 units purchased	504,500
Selling price of 100,000 units sold	665,000
Operating expenses	130,000

Units purchased consisted of 35,000 units at $4.00 on May 10; 60,000 units at $4.20 on August 15; and 25,000 units at $4.50 on November 20. Income taxes are 28%.

Instructions

(a) Prepare comparative condensed income statements for 2012 under FIFO and LIFO. (Show computations of ending inventory.)

(b) ━━━━━➤ Answer the following questions for management in the form of a business letter.

Gross profit:
FIFO $259,000
LIFO $240,500

  (1) Which inventory cost flow method produces the most meaningful inventory amount for the balance sheet? Why?

  (2) Which inventory cost flow method produces the most meaningful net income? Why?

  (3) Which inventory cost flow method is most likely to approximate the actual physical flow of the goods? Why?

  (4) How much more cash will be available for management under LIFO than under FIFO? Why?

  (5) How much of the gross profit under FIFO is illusionary in comparison with the gross profit under LIFO?

*P6-8A Yemi Ltd. is a retailer operating in Edmonton, Alberta. Yemi uses the perpetual inventory method. All sales returns from customers result in the goods being returned to inventory; the inventory is not damaged. Assume that there are no credit transactions; all amounts are settled in cash. You are provided with the following information for Yemi Ltd. for the month of January 2012.

Calculate cost of goods sold and ending inventory for FIFO, moving-average cost, and LIFO under the perpetual system; compare gross profit under each assumption.

(SO 7)

Date	Description	Quantity	Unit Cost or Selling Price
December 31	Ending inventory	150	$17
January 2	Purchase	100	21
January 6	Sale	150	40
January 9	Sale return	10	40
January 9	Purchase	75	24
January 10	Purchase return	15	24
January 10	Sale	50	45
January 23	Purchase	100	28
January 30	Sale	110	50

Instructions

(a) For each of the following cost flow assumptions, calculate (i) cost of goods sold, (ii) ending inventory, and (iii) gross profit.

  (1) LIFO.   (2) FIFO.   (3) Moving-average cost.

(b) Compare results for the three cost flow assumptions.

Gross profit:
LIFO $6,330
FIFO $7,500
Average $7,090

*P6-9A Farman Appliance Mart began operations on May 1. It uses a perpetual inventory system. During May, the company had the following purchases and sales for its Model 25 Sureshot camera.

Determine ending inventory under a perpetual inventory system.

(SO 7)

	Purchases		
Date	Units	Unit Cost	Sales Units
May 1	7	$150	
4			4
8	8	$170	
12			5
15	6	$185	
20			3
25			4

Instructions

(a) Determine the ending inventory under a perpetual inventory system using (1) FIFO, (2) moving-average cost, and (3) LIFO.

(b) Which costing method produces (1) the highest ending inventory valuation and (2) the lowest ending inventory valuation?

(a) FIFO $925
Average $874
LIFO $790

Estimate inventory loss using gross profit method.
(SO 8)

*P6-10A   Jae Company lost 70% of its inventory in a fire on March 25, 2012. The accounting records showed the following gross profit data for February and March.

	February	March (to 3/25)
Net sales	$300,000	$250,000
Net purchases	197,800	191,000
Freight-in	2,900	4,000
Beginning inventory	4,500	13,200
Ending inventory	13,200	?

Jae Company is fully insured for fire losses but must prepare a report for the insurance company.

Instructions
(a) Compute the gross profit rate for the month of February.
(b) Using the gross profit rate for February, determine both the estimated total inventory and inventory lost in the fire in March.

Compute ending inventory using retail method.
(SO 8)

*P6-11A   Marin Department Store uses the retail inventory method to estimate its monthly ending inventories. The following information is available for two of its departments at August 31, 2012.

	Sporting Goods		Jewelry and Cosmetics	
	Cost	Retail	Cost	Retail
Net sales		$1,000,000		$1,160,000
Purchases	$675,000	1,066,000	$741,000	1,158,000
Purchase returns	(26,000)	(40,000)	(12,000)	(20,000)
Purchase discounts	(12,360)	—	(2,440)	—
Freight-in	9,000	—	14,000	—
Beginning inventory	47,360	74,000	39,440	62,000

At December 31, Marin Department Store takes a physical inventory at retail. The actual retail values of the inventories in each department are Sporting Goods $95,000, and Jewelry and Cosmetics $44,000.

Instructions
(a) Determine the estimated cost of the ending inventory for each department on **August 31**, 2012, using the retail inventory method.
(b) Compute the ending inventory at cost for each department at **December 31**, assuming the cost-to-retail ratios are 60% for Sporting Goods and 64% for Jewelry and Cosmetics.

Problems: Set B

Determine items and amounts to be recorded in inventory.
(SO 1)

P6-1B   Titus Manin Black Limited is trying to determine the value of its ending inventory as of February 28, 2012, the company's year-end. The following transactions occurred, and the accountant asked your help in determining whether they should be recorded or not.

(a) On February 26, Titus shipped goods costing $800 to a customer and charged the customer $1,000. The goods were shipped with terms FOB shipping point and the receiving report indicates that the customer received the goods on March 2.
(b) On February 26, Welliver Inc. shipped goods to Titus under terms FOB shipping point. The invoice price was $450 plus $30 for freight. The receiving report indicates that the goods were received by Titus on March 2.
(c) Titus had $650 of inventory isolated in the warehouse. The inventory is designated for a customer who has requested that the goods be shipped on March 10.
(d) Also included in Titus's warehouse is $700 of inventory that Ishii Producers shipped to Titus on consignment.
(e) On February 26, Titus issued a purchase order to acquire goods costing $900. The goods were shipped with terms FOB destination on February 27. Titus received the goods on March 2.

(f) On February 26, Titus shipped goods to a customer under terms FOB destination. The invoice price was $350; the cost of the items was $200. The receiving report indicates that the goods were received by the customer on March 2.

Instructions
For each of the above transactions, specify whether the item in question should be included in ending inventory, and if so, at what amount.

P6-2B   Achilles Distribution markets CDs of the performing artist Vandyver. At the beginning of October, Achilles had in beginning inventory 2,000 of Vandyver's CDs with a unit cost of $7. During October Achilles made the following purchases of Vandyver's CDs.

Determine cost of goods sold and ending inventory using FIFO, LIFO, and average-cost with analysis.

(SO 2, 3)

Oct. 3	3,000 @ $8	Oct. 19	3,000 @ $10
Oct. 9	3,500 @ $9	Oct. 25	3,500 @ $11

During October, 11,400 units were sold. Achilles uses a periodic inventory system.

Instructions
(a) Determine the cost of goods available for sale.
(b) Determine (1) the ending inventory and (2) the cost of goods sold under each of the assumed cost flow methods (FIFO, LIFO, and average-cost). Prove the accuracy of the cost of goods sold under the FIFO and LIFO methods.
(c) Which cost flow method results in (1) the highest inventory amount for the balance sheet and (2) the highest cost of goods sold for the income statement?

(b)(2) Cost of goods sold:
FIFO $98,500
LIFO $111,200
Average $104,880

P6-3B   Gacis Company had a beginning inventory on January 1 of 150 units of Product 4-18-15 at a cost of $20 per unit. During the year, the following purchases were made.

Determine cost of goods sold and ending inventory, using FIFO, LIFO, and average-cost with analysis.

(SO 2, 3)

Mar. 15	400 units at $23	Sept. 4	350 units at $26
July 20	250 units at $24	Dec. 2	100 units at $29

1,000 units were sold. Gacis Company uses a periodic inventory system.

Instructions
(a) Determine the cost of goods available for sale.
(b) Determine (1) the ending inventory, and (2) the cost of goods sold under each of the assumed cost flow methods (FIFO, LIFO, and average-cost). Prove the accuracy of the cost of goods sold under the FIFO and LIFO methods.
(c) Which cost flow method results in (1) the highest inventory amount for the balance sheet, and (2) the highest cost of goods sold for the income statement?

(b)(2) Cost of goods sold:
FIFO $23,400
LIFO $24,900
Average $24,160

P6-4B   The management of Perrineau Inc. is reevaluating the appropriateness of using its present inventory cost flow method, which is average-cost. The company requests your help in determining the results of operations for 2012 if either the FIFO or the LIFO method had been used. For 2012, the accounting records show these data:

Compute ending inventory, prepare income statements, and answer questions using FIFO and LIFO.

(SO 2, 3)

Inventories		Purchases and Sales	
Beginning (8,000 units)	$16,000	Total net sales (180,000 units)	$747,000
Ending (18,000 units)		Total cost of goods purchased (190,000 units)	468,000

Purchases were made quarterly as follows.

Quarter	Units	Unit Cost	Total Cost
1	50,000	$2.20	$110,000
2	40,000	2.40	96,000
3	40,000	2.50	100,000
4	60,000	2.70	162,000
	190,000		$468,000

Operating expenses were $130,000, and the company's income tax rate is 40%.

Instructions
(a) Prepare comparative condensed income statements for 2012 under FIFO and LIFO. (Show computations of ending inventory.)

(a) Gross profit:
FIFO $311,600
LIFO $301,000

(b) ◀━━━ Answer the following questions for management.
   (1) Which cost flow method (FIFO or LIFO) produces the more meaningful inventory amount for the balance sheet? Why?
   (2) Which cost flow method (FIFO or LIFO) produces the more meaningful net income? Why?
   (3) Which cost flow method (FIFO or LIFO) is more likely to approximate the actual physical flow of goods? Why?
   (4) How much more cash will be available for management under LIFO than under FIFO? Why?
   (5) Will gross profit under the average-cost method be higher or lower than FIFO? Than LIFO? (*Note:* It is not necessary to quantify your answer.)

Calculate ending inventory, cost of goods sold, gross profit, and gross profit rate under periodic method; compare results.

(SO 2, 3)

P6-5B   You are provided with the following information for Guillaume Inc. for the month ended June 30, 2012. Guillaume uses the periodic method for inventory.

Date	Description	Quantity	Unit Cost or Selling Price
June 1	Beginning inventory	40	$40
June 4	Purchase	135	44
June 10	Sale	110	70
June 11	Sale return	15	70
June 18	Purchase	55	46
June 18	Purchase return	10	46
June 25	Sale	65	75
June 28	Purchase	30	50

(a)(iii) Gross profit:
LIFO $4,215
FIFO $4,645
Average $4,414.60

Instructions
(a) Calculate (i) ending inventory, (ii) cost of goods sold, (iii) gross profit, and (iv) gross profit rate under each of the following methods.
   (1) LIFO.   **(2)** FIFO.   **(3)** Average-cost.
(b) Compare results for the three cost flow assumptions.

Compare specific identification, FIFO, and LIFO under periodic method; use cost flow assumption to justify price increase.

(SO 2, 3)

P6-6B   You are provided with the following information for Dabinpons Inc. Dabinpons Inc. uses the periodic method of accounting for its inventory transactions.

March 1   Beginning inventory 2,000 liters at a cost of 60¢ per liter.
March 3   Purchased 2,500 liters at a cost of 65¢ per liter.
March 5   Sold 2,200 liters for $1.05 per liter.
March 10   Purchased 4,000 liters at a cost of 72¢ per liter.
March 20   Purchased 2,500 liters at a cost of 80¢ per liter.
March 30   Sold 5,000 liters for $1.25 per liter.

Instructions
(a) Prepare partial income statements through gross profit, and calculate the value of ending inventory that would be reported on the balance sheet, under each of the following cost flow assumptions. Round ending inventory and cost of goods sold to the nearest dollar.

(a)(1) Gross profit:
Specific identification
$3,590

   (1) Specific identification method assuming:
      (i) The March 5 sale consisted of 1,100 liters from the March 1 beginning inventory and 1,100 liters from the March 3 purchase; and
      (ii) The March 30 sale consisted of the following number of units sold from beginning inventory and each purchase: 450 liters from March 1; 550 liters from March 3; 2,900 liters from March 10; 1,100 liters from March 20.

(2) FIFO $3,791
(3) LIFO $3,225

   (2) FIFO.
   (3) LIFO.
(b) How can companies use a cost flow method to justify price increases? Which cost flow method would best support an argument to increase prices?

Compute ending inventory, prepare income statements, and answer questions using FIFO and LIFO.

(SO 2, 3)

P6-7B   The management of Tamara Co. asks your help in determining the comparative effects of the FIFO and LIFO inventory cost flow methods. For 2012, the accounting records provide the data shown on page 305.

Inventory, January 1 (10,000 units)	$ 45,000
Cost of 100,000 units purchased	532,000
Selling price of 80,000 units sold	700,000
Operating expenses	140,000

Units purchased consisted of 35,000 units at $5.10 on May 10; 35,000 units at $5.30 on August 15; and 30,000 units at $5.60 on November 20. Income taxes are 30%.

Instructions

(a) Prepare comparative condensed income statements for 2012 under FIFO and LIFO. (Show computations of ending inventory.)

(b) ➤ Answer the following questions for management.
 (1) Which inventory cost flow method produces the most meaningful inventory amount for the balance sheet? Why?
 (2) Which inventory cost flow method produces the most meaningful net income? Why?
 (3) Which inventory cost flow method is most likely to approximate actual physical flow of the goods? Why?
 (4) How much additional cash will be available for management under LIFO than under FIFO? Why?
 (5) How much of the gross profit under FIFO is illusory in comparison with the gross profit under LIFO?

(a) Net income
FIFO $105,700
LIFO $91,000

*P6-8B Ticotin Inc. is a retailer operating in British Columbia. Ticotin uses the perpetual inventory method. All sales returns from customers result in the goods being returned to inventory; the inventory is not damaged. Assume that there are no credit transactions; all amounts are settled in cash. You are provided with the following information for Ticotin Inc. for the month of January 2012.

Calculate cost of goods sold and ending inventory under LIFO, FIFO, and moving-average cost under the perpetual system; compare gross profit under each assumption.
(SO 7)

Date	Description	Quantity	Unit Cost or Selling Price
January 1	Beginning inventory	100	$15
January 5	Purchase	150	18
January 8	Sale	110	28
January 10	Sale return	10	28
January 15	Purchase	55	20
January 16	Purchase return	5	20
January 20	Sale	80	32
January 25	Purchase	30	22

Instructions

(a) For each of the following cost flow assumptions, calculate (i) cost of goods sold, (ii) ending inventory, and (iii) gross profit.
 (1) LIFO.   **(2)** FIFO.   **(3)** Moving-average cost.

(b) Compare results for the three cost flow assumptions.

Gross profit:
LIFO $2,020
FIFO $2,420
Average $2,272

*P6-9B Cortez Co. began operations on July 1. It uses a perpetual inventory system. During July, the company had the following purchases and sales.

Determine ending inventory under a perpetual inventory system.
(SO 7)

	Purchases		
Date	Units	Unit Cost	Sales Units
July 1	5	$120	
July 6			4
July 11	7	$136	
July 14			3
July 21	8	$147	
July 27			6

Instructions

(a) Determine the ending inventory under a perpetual inventory system using (1) FIFO, (2) moving-average cost, and (3) LIFO.

(b) Which costing method produces the highest ending inventory valuation?

(a) Ending inventory
FIFO $1,029
Avg. $994
LIFO $958

Compute gross profit rate and inventory loss using gross profit method.

(SO 8)

*P6-10B   Bottitta Company lost all of its inventory in a fire on December 26, 2012. The accounting records showed the following gross profit data for November and December.

	November	December (to 12/26)
Net sales	$600,000	$700,000
Beginning inventory	32,000	36,000
Purchases	377,000	424,000
Purchase returns and allowances	13,300	14,900
Purchase discounts	8,500	9,500
Freight-in	8,800	9,900
Ending inventory	36,000	?

Bottitta is fully insured for fire losses but must prepare a report for the insurance company.

Instructions

(a) Compute the gross profit rate for November.

(b) Using the gross profit rate for November, determine the estimated cost of the inventory lost in the fire.

Compute ending inventory using retail method.

(SO 8)

*P6-11B   Farooqui Books uses the retail inventory method to estimate its monthly ending inventories. The following information is available for two of its departments at October 31, 2012.

	Hardcovers		Paperbacks	
	Cost	Retail	Cost	Retail
Beginning inventory	$ 420,000	$ 700,000	$ 280,000	$ 360,000
Purchases	2,135,000	3,200,000	1,155,000	1,540,000
Freight-in	24,000		12,000	
Purchase discounts	44,000		22,000	
Net sales		3,100,000		1,570,000

At December 31, Farooqui Books takes a physical inventory at retail. The actual retail values of the inventories in each department are Hardcovers $790,000 and Paperbacks $335,000.

Instructions

(a) Determine the estimated cost of the ending inventory for each department at **October 31, 2012**, using the retail inventory method.

(b) Compute the ending inventory at cost for each department at **December 31**, assuming the cost-to-retail ratios for the year are 65% for hardcovers and 75% for paperbacks.

Problems: Set C

Visit the book's companion website, at **www.wiley.com/college/weygandt**, and choose the Student Companion site to access Problem Set C.

Comprehensive Problem

CP6   On December 1, 2012, Ruggiero Company had the account balances shown below.

	Debits		Credits
Cash	$ 4,800	Accumulated Depreciation—Equipment	$ 1,500
Accounts Receivable	3,900	Accounts Payable	3,000
Inventory	1,800*	Owner's Capital	27,000
Equipment	21,000		
	$31,500		$31,500

*(3,000 × $0.60)

The following transactions occurred during December.

Dec. 3 Purchased 4,000 units of inventory on account at a cost of $0.72 per unit.
    5 Sold 4,400 units of inventory on account for $0.90 per unit. (It sold 3,000 of the $0.60 units and 1,400 of the $0.72.)
    7 Granted the December 5 customer $180 credit for 200 units of inventory returned costing $150. These units were returned to inventory.
  17 Purchased 2,200 units of inventory for cash at $0.80 each.
  22 Sold 2,000 units of inventory on account for $0.95 per unit. (It sold 2,000 of the $0.72 units.)

Adjustment data:

1. Accrued salaries payable $400.
2. Depreciation $200 per month.

Instructions

(a) Journalize the December transactions and adjusting entries, assuming Ruggiero uses the perpetual inventory method.
(b) Enter the December 1 balances in the ledger T accounts and post the December transactions. In addition to the accounts mentioned above, use the following additional accounts: Cost of Goods Sold, Depreciation Expense, Salaries and Wages Expense, Salaries and Wages Payable, Sales Revenue, and Sales Returns and Allowances.
(c) Prepare an adjusted trial balance as of December 31, 2012.
(d) Prepare an income statement for December 2012 and a classified balance sheet at December 31, 2012.
(e) Compute ending inventory and cost of goods sold under FIFO, assuming Ruggiero Company uses the periodic inventory system.
(f) Compute ending inventory and cost of goods sold under LIFO, assuming Ruggiero Company uses the periodic inventory system.

Continuing Cookie Chronicle

(*Note:* This is a continuation of the Cookie Chronicle from Chapters 1 through 5.)

CCC6 Natalie is busy establishing both divisions of her business (cookie classes and mixer sales) and completing her business degree. Her goals for the next 11 months are to sell one mixer per month and to give two to three classes per week.

The cost of the fine European mixers is expected to increase. Natalie has just negotiated new terms with Kzinski that include shipping costs in the negotiated purchase price (mixers will be shipped FOB destination). Natalie must choose a cost flow assumption for her mixer inventory.

Go to the book's companion website, **www.wiley.com/college/weygandt**, *to see the completion of this problem.*

BROADENINGYOURPERSPECTIVE

Financial Reporting and Analysis

Financial Reporting Problem: PepsiCo, Inc.

BYP6-1 The notes that accompany a company's financial statements provide informative details that would clutter the amounts and descriptions presented in the statements. Refer to the financial statements of PepsiCo, Inc. and the Notes to Consolidated Financial Statements in Appendix A.

Instructions

Answer the following questions. Complete the requirements in millions of dollars, as shown in PepsiCo's annual report.

(a) What did PepsiCo report for the amount of inventories in its consolidated balance sheet at December 26, 2009? At December 27, 2008?

(b) Compute the dollar amount of change and the percentage change in inventories between 2008 and 2009. Compute inventory as a percentage of current assets at December 26, 2009.

(c) How does PepsiCo value its inventories? Which inventory cost flow method does PepsiCo use? (See Notes to the Financial Statements.)

(d) What is the cost of sales (cost of goods sold) reported by PepsiCo for 2009, 2008, and 2007? Compute the percentage of cost of sales to net sales in 2009.

Comparative Analysis Problem: PepsiCo, Inc. vs. The Coca-Cola Company

BYP6-2   PepsiCo's financial statements are presented in Appendix A. Financial statements of The Coca-Cola Company are presented in Appendix B.

Instructions

(a) Based on the information contained in these financial statements, compute the following 2009 ratios for each company.

  (1) Inventory turnover ratio

  (2) Days in inventory

(b) What conclusions concerning the management of the inventory can you draw from these data?

On the Web

BYP6-3   A company's annual report usually will identify the inventory method used. Knowing that, you can analyze the effects of the inventory method on the income statement and balance sheet.

Address: www.cisco.com, or go to **www.wiley.com/college/weygandt**

Instructions

Answer the following questions based on the current year's annual report on Cisco's website.

(a) At Cisco's fiscal year-end, what was the inventory on the balance sheet?

(b) How has this changed from the previous fiscal year-end?

(c) How much of the inventory was finished goods?

(d) What inventory method does Cisco use?

Critical Thinking

Decision Making Across the Organization

BYP6-4   On April 10, 2012, fire damaged the office and warehouse of Inwood Company. Most of the accounting records were destroyed, but the following account balances were determined as of March 31, 2012: Inventory (January 1), 2012, $80,000; Sales Revenue (January 1–March 31, 2012), $180,000; Purchases (January 1–March 31, 2012), $94,000.

The company's fiscal year ends on December 31. It uses a periodic inventory system.

From an analysis of the April bank statement, you discover cancelled checks of $4,200 for cash purchases during the period April 1–10. Deposits during the same period totaled $18,500. Of that amount, 60% were collections on accounts receivable, and the balance was cash sales.

Correspondence with the company's principal suppliers revealed $12,400 of purchases on account from April 1 to April 10. Of that amount, $1,600 was for merchandise in transit on April 10 that was shipped FOB destination.

Correspondence with the company's principal customers produced acknowledgments of credit sales totaling $37,000 from April 1 to April 10. It was estimated that $5,600 of credit sales will never be acknowledged or recovered from customers.

Inwood Company reached an agreement with the insurance company that its fire-loss claim should be based on the average of the gross profit rates for the preceding 2 years. The financial statements for 2010 and 2011 showed the following data.

	2011	2010
Net sales	$600,000	$480,000
Cost of goods purchased	404,000	356,000
Beginning inventory	60,000	40,000
Ending inventory	80,000	60,000

Inventory with a cost of $17,000 was salvaged from the fire.

Instructions

With the class divided into groups, answer the following.

(a) Determine the balances in (1) Sales Revenue and (2) Purchases at April 10.

*(b) Determine the average gross profit rate for the years 2010 and 2011. (*Hint:* Find the gross profit rate for each year and divide the sum by 2.)

*(c) Determine the inventory loss as a result of the fire, using the gross profit method.

Communication Activity

BYP6-5 You are the controller of Small Toys Inc. Janice LeMay, the president, recently mentioned to you that she found an error in the 2011 financial statements which she believes has corrected itself. She determined, in discussions with the Purchasing Department, that 2011 ending inventory was overstated by $1 million. Janice says that the 2012 ending inventory is correct. Thus, she assumes that 2012 income is correct. Janice says to you, "What happened has happened—there's no point in worrying about it anymore."

Instructions

You conclude that Janice is incorrect. Write a brief, tactful memo to Janice, clarifying the situation.

Ethics Case

BYP6-6 B. J. Ortiz Wholesale Corp. uses the LIFO method of inventory costing. In the current year, profit at B. J. Ortiz is running unusually high. The corporate tax rate is also high this year, but it is scheduled to decline significantly next year. In an effort to lower the current year's net income and to take advantage of the changing income tax rate, the president of B. J. Ortiz Wholesale instructs the plant accountant to recommend to the purchasing department a large purchase of inventory for delivery 3 days before the end of the year. The price of the inventory to be purchased has doubled during the year, and the purchase will represent a major portion of the ending inventory value.

Instructions

(a) What is the effect of this transaction on this year's and next year's income statement and income tax expense? Why?

(b) If B. J. Ortiz Wholesale had been using the FIFO method of inventory costing, would the president give the same directive?

(c) Should the plant accountant order the inventory purchase to lower income? What are the ethical implications of this order?

"All About You" Activity

BYP6-7 Some of the largest business frauds ever perpetrated have involved the misstatement of inventory. Two classics were at Leslie Fay Cos, and McKesson Corporation.

Instructions

There is considerable information regarding inventory frauds available on the Internet. Search for information about one of the two cases mentioned above, or inventory fraud at any other company, and prepare a short explanation of the nature of the inventory fraud.

FASB Codification Activity

BYP6-8   If your school has a subscription to the FASB Codification, go to *http://aaahq.org/ascLogin. cfm* to log in and prepare responses to the following.

(a) The primary basis for accounting for inventories is cost. How is cost defined in the Codification?

(b) What does the Codification state regarding the use of consistency in the selection or employment of a basis for inventory?

(c) What does the Codification indicate is a justification for the use of the lower-of-cost-or-market for inventory valuation?

Answers to Insight and Accounting Across the Organization Questions

p. 263 A Big Hiccup   Q: What steps might the companies take to avoid such a serious disruption in the future? **A:** The manufacturer of the piston rings should spread its manufacturing facilities across a few locations that are far enough apart that they would not all be at risk at once. In addition, the automakers might consider becoming less dependent on a single supplier.

p. 264 Falsifying Inventory to Boost Income   Q: What effect does an overstatement of inventory have on a company's financial statements? **A:** The balance sheet looks stronger because inventory and retained earnings are overstated. The income statement looks better because cost of goods sold is understated and income is overstated.

p. 275 Is LIFO Fair?   Q: What are the arguments for and against the use of LIFO? **A:** Proponents of LIFO argue that it is conceptually superior because it matches the most recent cost with the most recent selling price. Critics contend that it artificially understates the company's net income and consequently reduces tax payments. Also, because most foreign companies are not allowed to use LIFO, its use by U.S. companies reduces the ability of investors to compare U.S. companies with foreign companies.

p. 279 Improving Inventory Control with RFID   Q: Why is inventory control important to managers such as those at Wal-Mart and Best Buy? **A:** In the very competitive environment of discount retailing, where Wal-Mart and Best Buy are major players, small differences in price matter to the customer. Wal-Mart sells a high volume of inventory at a low gross profit rate. When operating in a high-volume, low-margin environment, small cost savings can mean the difference between being profitable or going out of business.

Answers to Self-Test Questions

1. a   **2.** b ($180,000 + $35,000)   **3.** b   **4.** c [(5,000 × $13) + (4,000 × $12)]   **5.** d [(8,000 × $11) + (1,000 × $12)]   **6.** d ((5,000 × $8) + (15,000 × $10) + (20,000 × $12)) ÷ 40,000 = $10.75; $10.75 × 7,000   **7.** c   **8.** d   **9.** d (200 × $80)   **10.** b   **11.** b   **12.** d   **13.** b $285,000 ÷ [($80,000 + $110,000) ÷ 2] = 3; 365 ÷ 3   ***14.** b [$150,000 − (30% × $150,000)] = $105,000; $135,000 − $105,000   ***15.** d

IFRS A Look at IFRS

The major IFRS requirements related to accounting and reporting for inventories are the same as GAAP. The major differences are that IFRS prohibits the use of the LIFO cost flow assumption and determines market in the lower-of-cost-or-market inventory valuation differently.

Key Points

- The requirements for accounting for and reporting inventories are more principles-based under IFRS. That is, GAAP provides more detailed guidelines in inventory accounting.

- The definitions for inventory are essentially similar under IFRS and GAAP. Both define inventory as assets held-for-sale in the ordinary course of business, in the process of production for sale (work in process), or to be consumed in the production of goods or services (e.g., raw materials).

- Who owns the goods—goods in transit or consigned goods—as well as the costs to include in inventory, are accounted for the same under IFRS and GAAP.

- Both GAAP and IFRS permit specific identification where appropriate. IFRS actually requires that the specific identification method be used where the inventory items are not interchangeable (i.e., can be specifically identified). If the inventory items are not specifically identifiable, a cost flow assumption is used. GAAP does not specify situations in which specific identification must be used.

- A major difference between IFRS and GAAP relates to the LIFO cost flow assumption. GAAP permits the use of LIFO for inventory valuation. IFRS prohibits its use. FIFO and average-cost are the only two acceptable cost flow assumptions permitted under IFRS.

- IFRS requires companies to use the same cost flow assumption for all goods of a similar nature. GAAP has no specific requirement in this area.

- In the lower-of-cost-or-market test for inventory valuation, IFRS defines market as net realizable value. Net realizable value is the estimated selling price in the ordinary course of business, less the estimated costs of completion and estimated selling expenses. In other words, net realizable value is the best estimate of the net amounts that inventories are expected to realize. GAAP, on the other hand, defines market as essentially replacement cost.

- Under GAAP, if inventory is written down under the lower-of-cost-or-market valuation, the new basis is now considered its cost. As a result, the inventory may not be written back up to its original cost in a subsequent period. Under IFRS, the write-down may be reversed in a subsequent period up to the amount of the previous write-down. Both the write-down and any subsequent reversal should be reported on the income statement as an expense. An item-by-item approach is generally followed under IFRS.

- An example of the use of lower-of-cost-or-net realizable value under IFRS follows.

Mendel Company has the following four items in its ending inventory as of December 31, 2012. The company uses the lower-of-cost-or-net realizable value approach for inventory valuation following IFRS.

Item No.	Cost	Net Realizable Value
1320	$3,600	$3,400
1333	4,000	4,100
1428	2,800	2,100
1510	5,000	4,700

The computation of the ending inventory value to be reported in the financial statements at December 31, 2012, is as follows.

Item No.	Cost	Net Realizable Value	LCNRV
1320	$ 3,600	$ 3,400	$ 3,400
1333	4,000	4,100	4,000
1428	2,800	2,100	2,100
1510	5,000	4,700	4,700
Total	$15,400	$14,300	$14,200

- Unlike property, plant, and equipment, IFRS does not permit the option of valuing inventories at fair value. As indicated above, IFRS requires inventory to be written down, but inventory cannot be written up above its original cost.

- Similar to GAAP, certain agricultural products and mineral products can be reported at net realizable value using IFRS.

Looking to the Future

One convergence issue that will be difficult to resolve relates to the use of the LIFO cost flow assumption. As indicated, IFRS specifically prohibits its use. Conversely, the LIFO cost flow assumption is widely used in the United States because of its favorable tax advantages. In addition, many argue that LIFO from a financial reporting point of view provides a better matching of current costs against revenue and, therefore, enables companies to compute a more realistic income.

With a new conceptual framework being developed, it is highly probable that the use of the concept of conservatism will be eliminated. Similarly, the concept of "prudence" in the IASB literature will also be eliminated. This may ultimately have implications for the application of the lower-of-cost-or-net realizable value.

IFRS Self-Test Questions

1. Which of the following should *not* be included in the inventory of a company using IFRS?
   (a) Goods held on consignment from another company.
   (b) Goods shipped on consignment to another company.
   (c) Goods in transit from another company shipped FOB shipping point.
   (d) None of the above.

2. Which method of inventory costing is prohibited under IFRS?
   (a) Specific identification.   (c) FIFO.
   (b) LIFO.   (d) Average-cost.

3. Yang Company purchased 2,000 widgets and has 400 widgets in its ending inventory at a cost of $90 each and a current replacement cost of $80 each. The net realizable value of each unit in the ending inventory is $70. The ending inventory under lower-of-cost-or-net realizable value is:
   (a) $36,000.   (c) $28,000.
   (b) $32,000.   (d) None of the above.

4. Specific identification:
   (a) must be used under IFRS if the inventory items are not interchangeable.
   (b) cannot be used under IFRS.
   (c) cannot be used under GAAP.
   (d) must be used under IFRS if it would result in the most conservative net income.

5. IFRS requires the following:
   (a) Ending inventory is written up and down to net realizable value each reporting period.
   (b) Ending inventory is written down to net realizable value but cannot be written up.
   (c) Ending inventory is written down to net realizable value and may be written up in future periods to its net realizable value but not above its original cost.
   (d) Ending inventory is written down to net realizable value and may be written up in future periods to its net realizable value.

IFRS Concepts and Application

IFRS6-1   Briefly describe some of the similarities and differences between GAAP and IFRS with respect to the accounting for inventories.

IFRS6-2   LaTour Inc. is based in France and prepares its financial statements in accordance with IFRS. In 2012, it reported cost of goods sold of €578 million and average inventory of €154 million. Briefly discuss how analysis of LaTour's inventory turnover ratio (and comparisons to a company using GAAP) might be affected by differences in inventory accounting between IFRS and GAAP.

IFRS6-3   Franklin Company has the following four items in its ending inventory as of December 31, 2012. The company uses the lower-of-cost-or-net realizable value approach for inventory valuation following IFRS.

Item No.	Cost	Net Realizable Value
AB	$1,700	$1,400
TRX	2,200	2,300
NWA	7,800	7,100
SGH	3,000	3,700

Compute the lower-of-cost-or-net realizable value.

International Financial Reporting
Problem: *Zetar plc*

IFRS6-4   The financial statements of Zetar plc are presented in Appendix C. The company's complete annual report, including the notes to its financial statements, is available at *www.zetarplc.com.*

Instructions

Using the notes to the company's financial statements, answer the following questions.

(a) What cost flow assumption does the company use to value inventory?

(b) What was the amount of expense that the company reported for inventory write-downs during 2009?

(c) What amount of raw materials, work in process, and finished goods inventory did the company report at April 30, 2009?

Answers to IFRS Self-Test Questions
1. a   2. b   3. c   4. a   5. c

✔
The Navigator

✔ Remember to go back to the Navigator box on the chapter opening page and check off your completed work.

CHAPTER 7

Accounting Information Systems

Study Objectives

After studying this chapter, you should be able to:

[1] Identify the basic concepts of an accounting information system.

[2] Describe the nature and purpose of a subsidiary ledger.

[3] Explain how companies use special journals in journalizing.

[4] Indicate how companies post a multi-column journal.

The Navigator

✔ [The Navigator]

● Scan Study Objectives	○
● Read Feature Story	○
● Read Preview	○
● Read text and answer **Do it!** p. 321 ○ p. 335 ○	
● Work Comprehensive **Do it!** p. 335	○
● Review Summary of Study Objectives	○
● Answer Self-Test Questions	○
● Complete Assignments	○
● Go to *WileyPLUS* for practice and tutorials	○
● Read A Look at IFRS p. 357	○

Feature Story

QUICKBOOKS® HELPS THIS RETAILER SELL GUITARS

Starting a small business requires many decisions. For example, you have to decide where to locate, how much space you need, how much inventory to have, how many employees to hire, and where to advertise. Small business owners are typically so concerned about the product and sales side of their business that they often do not give enough thought to something that is critical to their success—how to keep track of financial results.

Small business owners today can choose either manual or computerized accounting systems. For example, Paul and Laura West are the owners of the first independent dealership of Carvin guitars and professional audio equipment. When they founded their company, in Sacramento, California, they decided to purchase a computerized accounting system that would integrate

314

many aspects of their retail operations. They wanted their accounting software to manage their inventory of guitars and amplifiers, ring up sales, record and report financial data, and process credit card and debit card transactions. They evaluated a number of options and chose QuickBooks® by Intuit Inc.

QuickBooks®, like most other popular software packages, has programs designed for the needs of a specific business, which in this case is retailing. This QuickBooks® retailing package automatically collects sales information from its point-of-sale scanning devices. It also keeps track of inventory levels and automatically generates purchase orders for popular items when re-order points are reached. It even supports sales efforts by compiling a customer database from which the Wests send out targeted direct mailings to potential customers. The computerized system enables data files to be emailed to the company's accountant. This keeps costs down and makes it easier and more efficient to generate financial reports as needed. The Wests believe that the investment in the computerized system has saved them time and money, and allowed them to spend more time on other aspects of their business.

Source: Intuit Inc., "QuickBooks® and ProAdvisor® Help Make Guitar Store a Hit," *Journal of Accountancy* (May 2006), p. 101.

The Navigator

Inside**CHAPTER7**

PreviewofCHAPTER7

As you see from the Feature Story, a reliable information system is a necessity for any company. Whether companies use pen, pencil, or computers in maintaining accounting records, certain principles and procedures apply. The purpose of this chapter is to explain and illustrate these features.

The content and organization of Chapter 7 are as follows.

Accounting Information Systems

Basic Concepts of Accounting Information Systems	Subsidiary Ledgers	Special Journals
• Computerized accounting systems • Manual accounting systems	• Example • Advantages	• Sales journal • Cash receipts journal • Purchases journal • Cash payments journal • Effects of special journals on general journal

Basic Concepts of Accounting Information Systems

Study Objective [1]

Identify the basic concepts of an accounting information system.

The **accounting information system** collects and processes transaction data and communicates financial information to decision makers. It includes each of the steps in the accounting cycle that you studied in earlier chapters. It also includes the documents that provide evidence of the transactions, and the records, trial balances, worksheets, and financial statements that result. An **accounting system** may be either manual or computerized. Most businesses these days use some sort of computerized accounting system, whether it is an off-the-shelf system for small businesses, like QuickBooks or Peachtree, or a more complex custom-made system.

Efficient and effective accounting information systems are based on certain basic principles. These principles, as described in Illustration 7-1, are (1) cost-effectiveness, (2) usefulness, and (3) flexibility. If the accounting system is cost-effective, provides useful output, and has the flexibility to meet future needs, it can contribute to both individual and organizational goals.

Computerized Accounting Systems

Many small businesses eventually replace their manual accounting system with a computerized general ledger accounting system. **General ledger accounting systems** are software programs that integrate the various accounting functions related to sales, purchases, receivables, payables, cash receipts and disbursements, and payroll. They also generate financial statements. Computerized systems have a number of advantages over manual systems. First, the company typically enters data only once in a computerized system. Second, because the computer does most steps automatically, many errors resulting from human intervention in a manual system,

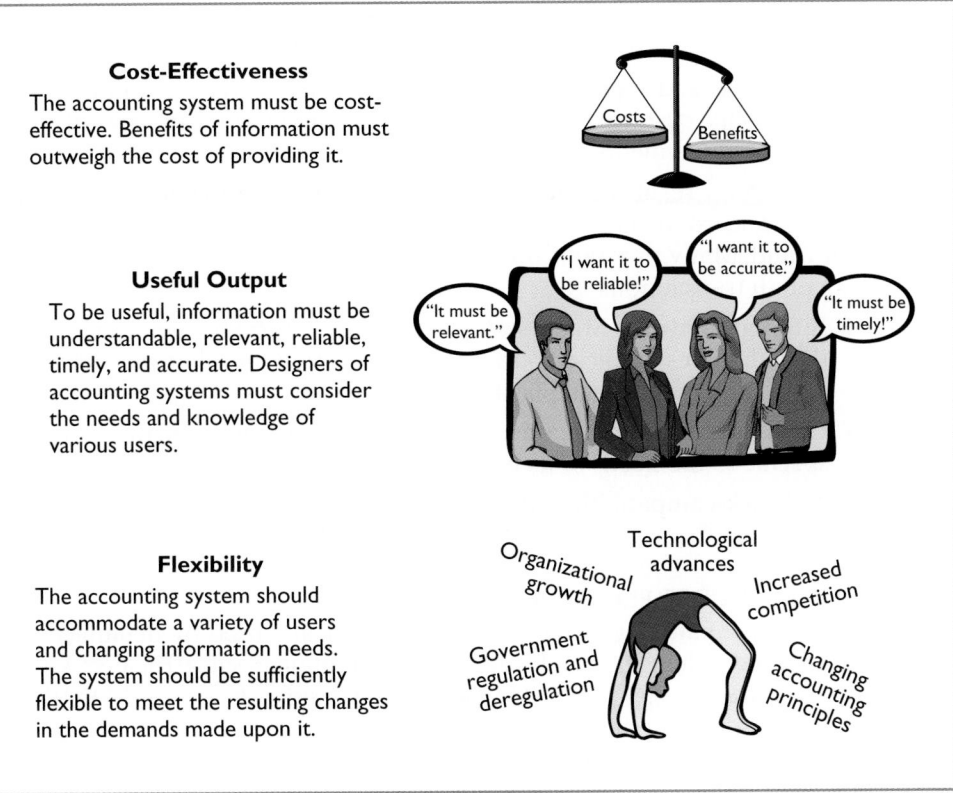

Illustration 7-1
Principles of an efficient and effective accounting information system

such as errors in posting or preparation of financial statements, are eliminated. Computerized systems also provide information up-to-the-minute. More timely information results in better business decisions. Many different general ledger software packages are available.

CHOOSING A SOFTWARE PACKAGE

To identify the right software for your business, you must understand your company's operations. For example, consider its needs with regard to inventory, billing, payroll, and cash management. In addition, the company might have specific needs that are not supported by all software systems. For example, you might want to track employees' hours on individual jobs or to extract information for determining sales commissions. Choosing the right system is critical because installation of even a basic system is time-consuming, and learning a new system will require many hours of employee time.

ENTRY-LEVEL SOFTWARE

Software publishers tend to classify businesses into groups based on revenue and the number of employees. Companies with revenues of less than $5 million and up to 20 employees generally use **entry-level programs**. The two leading entry-level programs are Intuit's QuickBooks and Sage Software's Peachtree. These programs control more than 90% of the market. Each of these entry-level programs comes in many different industry-specific versions. For example, some are designed for very specific industry applications such as restaurants, retailing, construction, manufacturing, or nonprofit. *(This textbook's general ledger system can be used in working many of the problems in this textbook.)*

Quality entry-level packages typically involve more than recording transactions and preparing financial statements. Here are some common features and benefits:

- **Easy data access and report preparation.** Users can easily access information related to specific customers or suppliers. For example, you can view all transactions, invoices, payments, as well as contact information for a specific client.

- **Audit trail.** As a result of the Sarbanes-Oxley Act, companies are now far more concerned that their accounting system minimizes opportunities for fraud. Many programs provide an "audit trail" that enables the tracking of all transactions.

- **Internal controls.** Some systems have an internal accounting review that identifies suspicious transactions or likely mistakes such as wrong account numbers or duplicate transactions.

- **Customization.** This feature enables the company to create data fields specific to the needs of its business.

- **Network-compatibility.** Multiple users in the company can access the system at the same time.

Ethics Note

Entire books and movies have used computer-system tampering as a major theme. Most programmers would agree that tamper-proofing and debugging programs are the most difficult and time-consuming phases of their jobs.

ENTERPRISE RESOURCE PLANNING SYSTEMS

Enterprise resource planning (ERP) systems are typically used by manufacturing companies with more than 500 employees and $500 million in sales. The best-known of these systems are SAPAG's SAP (the most widely used), J.D. Edwards' ERP, and Oracle's Financials. ERP systems go far beyond the functions of an entry-level general ledger package. They integrate all aspects of the organization, including accounting, sales, human resource management, and manufacturing. Because of the complexity of an ERP system, implementation can take three years and cost five times as much as the purchase price of the system. Purchase and implementation of ERP systems can cost from $250,000 to as much as $50 million for the largest multinational corporations.

*E*THICS *I*NSIGHT

Curbing Fraudulent Activity with Software

The Sarbanes-Oxley Act (SOX) requires that companies demonstrate that they have adequate controls in place to detect significant fraudulent behavior by employees. Recently, about 15% of publicly traded companies reported at least one material weakness in their controls that needed to be remedied.

The SOX requirements have created a huge market for software that can monitor and trace every recorded transaction and adjusting entry. This enables companies to pinpoint who used the accounting system and when they used it. These systems also require "electronic signatures" by employees for all significant transactions. Such signatures verify that employees have followed all required procedures, and that all actions are properly authorized. SOX-related technology spending was estimated to be approximately $2 billion at one time. One firm that specializes in compliance software had 10 clients prior to SOX and 250 after SOX.

Source: W. M. Bulkeley and C. Forelle, "Anti-Crime Program: How Corporate Scandals Gave Tech Firms a New Business Line," *Wall Street Journal* (December 9, 2005), p. A1.

 Why might this software help reduce fraudulent activity by employees? (See page 357.)

Manual Accounting Systems

Manual accounting systems perform each of the steps in the accounting cycle by hand. For example, someone manually enters each accounting transaction in the journal and manually posts each to the ledger. Other manual computations must be made to obtain ledger account balances and to prepare a trial balance and financial statements. In the remainder of this chapter, we illustrate the use of a manual system.

You might be wondering, "Why cover manual accounting systems if the real world uses computerized systems?" First, small businesses still abound. Most of them begin operations with manual accounting systems and convert to computerized systems as the business grows. You may work in a small business, or start your own someday, so it is useful to know how a manual system works. Second, to understand what computerized accounting systems do, you also need to understand manual accounting systems.

The manual accounting system represented in the first six chapters of this textbook is satisfactory in a company with a low volume of transactions. However, in most companies, it is necessary to add additional ledgers and journals to the accounting system to record transaction data efficiently.

Subsidiary Ledgers

Imagine a business that has several thousand charge (credit) customers and shows the transactions with these customers in only one general ledger account—Accounts Receivable. It would be nearly impossible to determine the balance owed by an individual customer at any specific time. Similarly, the amount payable to one creditor would be difficult to locate quickly from a single Accounts Payable account in the general ledger.

Study Objective [2]
Describe the nature and purpose of a subsidiary ledger.

Instead, companies use subsidiary ledgers to keep track of individual balances. A **subsidiary ledger** is a group of accounts with a common characteristic (for example, all accounts receivable). It is an addition to, and an expansion of, the general ledger. The subsidiary ledger frees the general ledger from the details of individual balances.

Two common subsidiary ledgers are:

1. The **accounts receivable** (or **customers'**) **subsidiary ledger**, which collects transaction data of individual customers.

2. The **accounts payable** (or **creditors'**) **subsidiary ledger**, which collects transaction data of individual creditors.

In each of these subsidiary ledgers, companies usually arrange individual accounts in alphabetical order.

A general ledger account summarizes the detailed data from a subsidiary ledger. For example, the detailed data from the accounts receivable subsidiary ledger are summarized in Accounts Receivable in the general ledger. The general ledger account that summarizes subsidiary ledger data is called a **control account**. Illustration 7-2 (page 320) presents an overview of the relationship of subsidiary ledgers to the general ledger. There, the general ledger control accounts and subsidiary ledger accounts are in green. Note that cash and owner's capital in this illustration are not control accounts because there are no subsidiary ledger accounts related to these accounts.

At the end of an accounting period, each general ledger control account balance must equal the composite balance of the individual accounts in the related subsidiary ledger. For example, the balance in Accounts Payable in Illustration 7-2 must equal the total of the subsidiary balances of Creditors X + Y + Z.

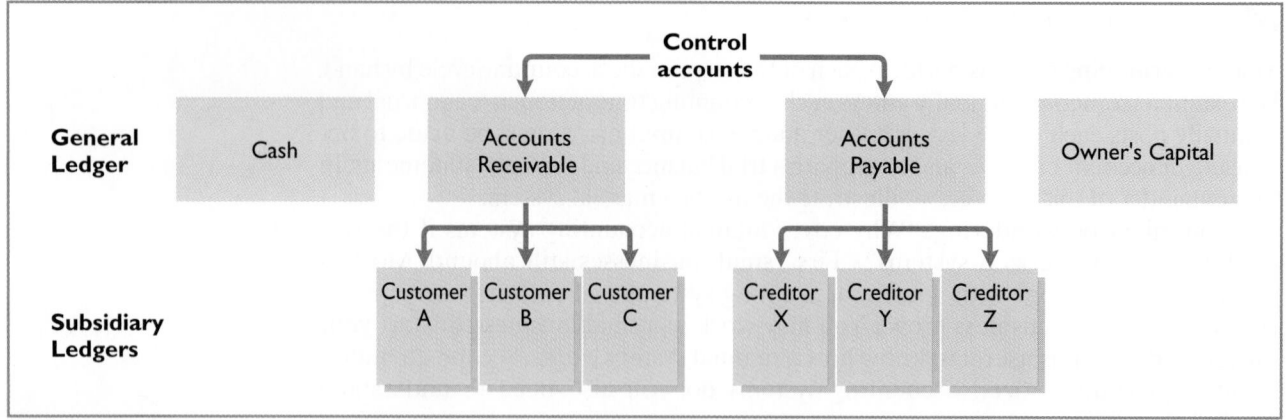

Illustration 7-2
Relationship of general ledger and subsidiary ledgers

Illustration 7-3
Relationship between general and subsidiary ledgers

Subsidiary Ledger Example

Illustration 7-3 provides an example of a control account and subsidiary ledger for Pujols Enterprises. (Due to space considerations, the explanation column in these accounts is not shown in this and subsequent illustrations.) Illustration 7-3 is based on the transactions listed in Illustration 7-4.

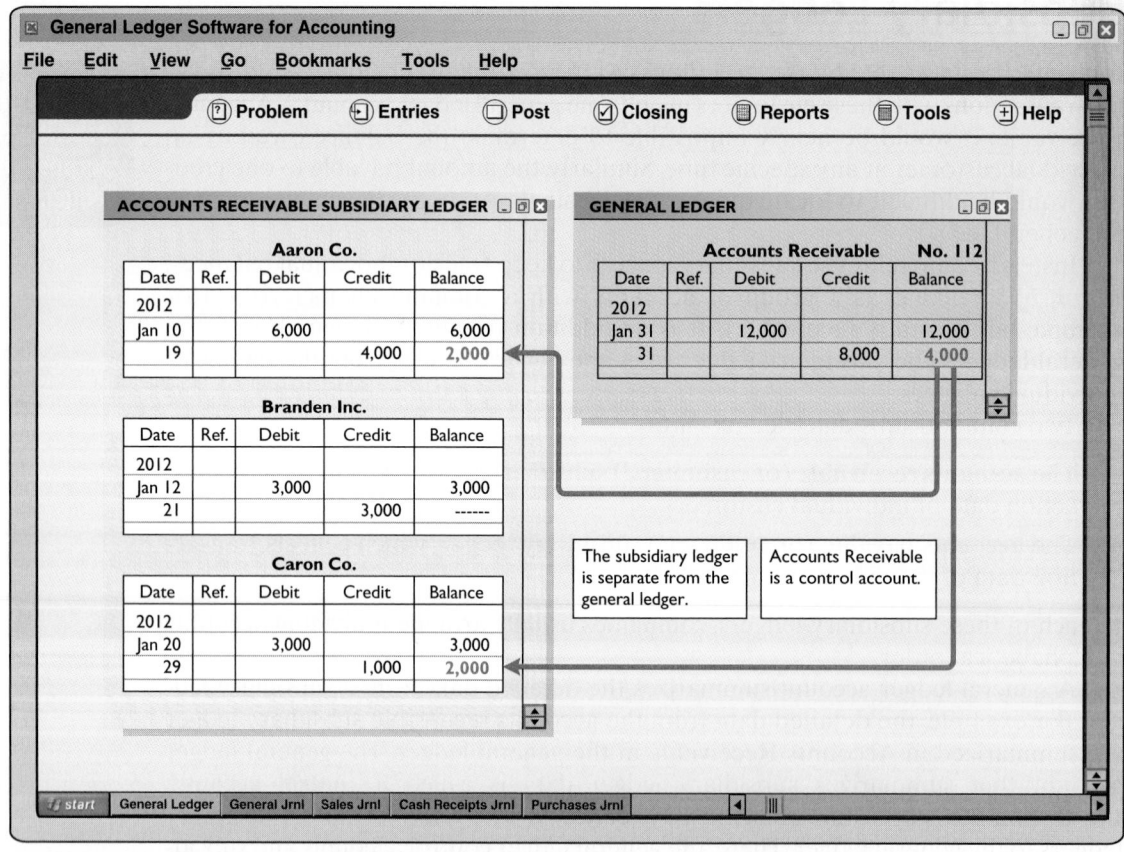

Illustration 7-4
Sales and collection transactions

	Credit Sales				Collections on Account	
Jan. 10	Aaron Co.	$ 6,000		Jan. 19	Aaron Co.	$4,000
12	Branden Inc.	3,000		21	Branden Inc.	3,000
20	Caron Co.	3,000		29	Caron Co.	1,000
		$12,000				$8,000

Pujols can reconcile the total debits ($12,000) and credits ($8,000) in Accounts Receivable in the general ledger to the detailed debits and credits in the subsidiary accounts. Also, the balance of $4,000 in the control account agrees with the total of the balances in the individual accounts (Aaron Co. $2,000 + Branden Inc. $0 + Caron Co. $2,000) in the subsidiary ledger.

As Illustration 7-3 shows, companies make monthly postings to the control accounts in the general ledger. This practice allows them to prepare monthly financial statements. Companies post to the individual accounts in the subsidiary ledger daily. Daily posting ensures that account information is current. This enables the company to monitor credit limits, bill customers, and answer inquiries from customers about their account balances.

Advantages of Subsidiary Ledgers

Subsidiary ledgers have several advantages:

1. **They show in a single account transactions affecting one customer or one creditor**, thus providing up-to-date information on specific account balances.
2. **They free the general ledger of excessive details.** As a result, a trial balance of the general ledger does not contain vast numbers of individual account balances.
3. **They help locate errors in individual accounts** by reducing the number of accounts in one ledger and by using control accounts.
4. **They make possible a division of labor** in posting. One employee can post to the general ledger while someone else posts to the subsidiary ledgers.

ACCOUNTING **A**CROSS THE **O**RGANIZATION

"I'm John Smith, a.k.a. 13695071642"

Rather than relying on customer or creditor names in a subsidiary ledger, a computerized system expands the account number of the control account in a pre-specified manner. For example, if Accounts Receivable was numbered 10010, the first account in the accounts receivable subsidiary ledger might be numbered 10010–0001. Most systems allow inquiries about specific accounts in the subsidiary ledger (by account number) or about the control account. With the latter, the system would automatically total all the subsidiary accounts whenever an inquiry to the control account was made.

 Why use numbers to identify names in a computerized system? (See page 357.)

Do it!

Presented below is information related to Sims Company for its first month of operations. Determine the balances that appear in the accounts payable subsidiary ledger. What Accounts Payable balance appears in the general ledger at the end of January?

Subsidiary Ledgers

Credit Purchases			Cash Paid		
Jan. 5	Devon Co.	$11,000	Jan. 9	Devon Co.	$7,000
11	Shelby Co.	7,000	14	Shelby Co.	2,000
22	Taylor Co.	14,000	27	Taylor Co.	9,000

action plan

✔ Subtract cash paid from credit purchases to determine the balances in the accounts payable subsidiary ledger.

✔ Sum the individual balances to determine the Accounts Payable balance.

Solution

Subsidiary ledger balances:

Devon Co. $4,000 ($11,000 − $7,000)

Shelby Co. $5,000 ($7,000 − $2,000)

Taylor Co. $5,000 ($14,000 − $9,000)

General ledger Accounts Payable balance: $14,000 ($4,000 + $5,000 + $5,000)

Related exercise material: BE7-4, BE7-5, E7-1, E7-2, E7-4, E7-5, and **Do it!** 7-1.

✔
The Navigator

Special Journals

Study Objective [3]

Explain how companies use special journals in journalizing.

So far you have learned to journalize transactions in a two-column general journal and post each entry to the general ledger. This procedure is satisfactory in only the very smallest companies. To expedite journalizing and posting, most companies use special journals **in addition to the general journal**.

Companies use special journals to record similar types of transactions. Examples are all sales of merchandise on account, or all cash receipts. The types of transactions that occur frequently in a company determine what special journals the company uses. Most merchandising enterprises record daily transactions using the journals shown in Illustration 7-5.

Illustration 7-5
Use of special journals and the general journal

Sales Journal	Cash Receipts Journal	Purchases Journal	Cash Payments Journal	General Journal
Used for:	Used for:	Used for:	Used for:	Used for:
All sales of merchandise on account	All cash received (including cash sales)	All purchases of merchandise on account	All cash paid (including cash purchases)	Transactions that cannot be entered in a special journal, including correcting, adjusting, and closing entries

If a transaction cannot be recorded in a special journal, the company records it in the general journal. For example, if a company had special journals for only the four types of transactions listed above, it would record purchase returns and allowances in the general journal. Similarly, **correcting, adjusting, and closing entries are recorded in the general journal**. In some situations, companies might use special journals other than those listed above. For example, when sales returns and allowances are frequent, a company might use a special journal to record these transactions.

Special journals **permit greater division of labor** because several people can record entries in different journals at the same time. For example, one employee may journalize all cash receipts, and another may journalize all credit sales. Also, the use of special journals **reduces the time needed to complete the posting process**. With special journals, companies may post some accounts monthly, instead of daily, as we will illustrate later in the chapter. On the following pages, we discuss the four special journals shown in Illustration 7-5.

Sales Journal

In the sales journal, companies record **sales of merchandise on account**. Cash sales of merchandise go in the cash receipts journal. Credit sales of assets other than merchandise go in the general journal.

JOURNALIZING CREDIT SALES

To demonstrate use of a sales journal, we will use data for Karns Wholesale Supply, which uses a **perpetual inventory system**. Under this system, each entry in the sales journal results in one entry **at selling price** and another entry **at cost**. The entry at selling price is a debit to Accounts Receivable (a control account) and a credit of equal amount to Sales Revenue. The entry at cost is a debit to Cost of Goods Sold and a credit of equal amount to Inventory (a control account). Using a sales journal with two amount columns, the company can show on only one line a sales transaction at both selling price and cost. Illustration 7-6 shows this two-column sales journal of Karns Wholesale Supply, using assumed credit sales transactions (for sales invoices 101–107).

Helpful Hint

Postings are also made daily to individual ledger accounts in the inventory subsidiary ledger to maintain a perpetual inventory.

General Ledger Software for Accounting

File　Edit　View　Go　Bookmarks　Tools　Help

? Problem　⊞ Entries　☐ Post　☑ Closing　▦ Reports　▤ Tools　⊞ Help

SALES JOURNAL　S1

Date	Account Debited	Invoice No.	Ref.	Accts. Receivable Dr. Sales Revenue Cr.	Cost of Goods Sold Dr. Inventory Cr.
2012					
May　3	Abbot Sisters	101		10,600	6,360
7	Babson Co.	102		11,350	7,370
14	Carson Bros.	103		7,800	5,070
19	Deli Co.	104		9,300	6,510
21	Abbot Sisters	105		15,400	10,780
24	Deli Co.	106		21,210	15,900
27	Babson Co.	107		14,570	10,200
				90,230	62,190

start　General Ledger　General Jrnl　Sales Jrnl　Cash Receipts Jrnl　Purchases Jrnl

Illustration 7-6
Journalizing the sales journal—perpetual inventory system

Note that, unlike the general journal, an explanation is not required for each entry in a special journal. Also, note that use of prenumbered invoices ensures that all invoices are journalized. Finally, note that the reference (Ref.) column is not used in journalizing. It is used in posting the sales journal, as explained in the next section.

POSTING THE SALES JOURNAL

Companies make daily postings from the sales journal **to the individual accounts receivable** in the subsidiary ledger. Posting **to the general ledger** is done **monthly**. Illustration 7-7 (page 324) shows both the daily and monthly postings.

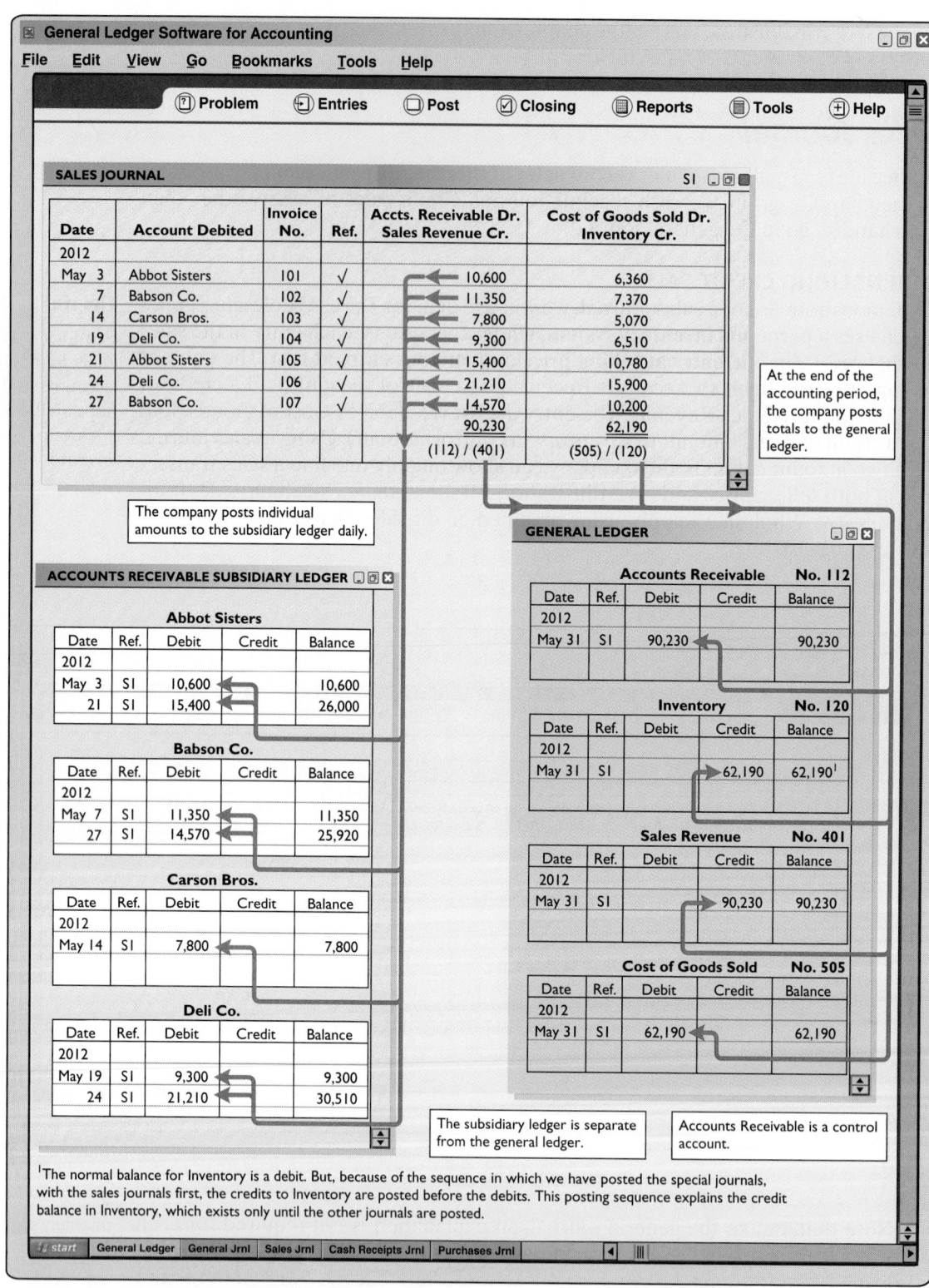

Illustration 7-7
Posting the sales journal

A check mark (✓) is inserted in the reference posting column to indicate that the daily posting to the customer's account has been made. If the subsidiary ledger accounts were numbered, the account number would be entered in place of the check mark. At the end of the month, Karns posts the column totals of the sales journal to the general ledger. Here, the column totals are as follows: From the selling-price column, a debit of $90,230 to Accounts Receivable (account No. 112), and a credit of $90,230 to Sales Revenue (account No. 401). From the cost column, a debit of $62,190 to Cost of Goods Sold (account No. 505), and a credit of $62,190 to Inventory (account No. 120). Karns inserts the account numbers below the column totals to indicate that the postings have been made. In both the general ledger and subsidiary ledger accounts, the reference **S1** indicates that the posting came from page 1 of the sales journal.

PROVING THE LEDGERS

The next step is to "prove" the ledgers. To do so, Karns must determine two things: (1) The total of the general ledger debit balances must equal the total of the general ledger credit balances. (2) The sum of the subsidiary ledger balances must equal the balance in the control account. Illustration 7-8 shows the proof of the postings from the sales journal to the general and subsidiary ledgers.

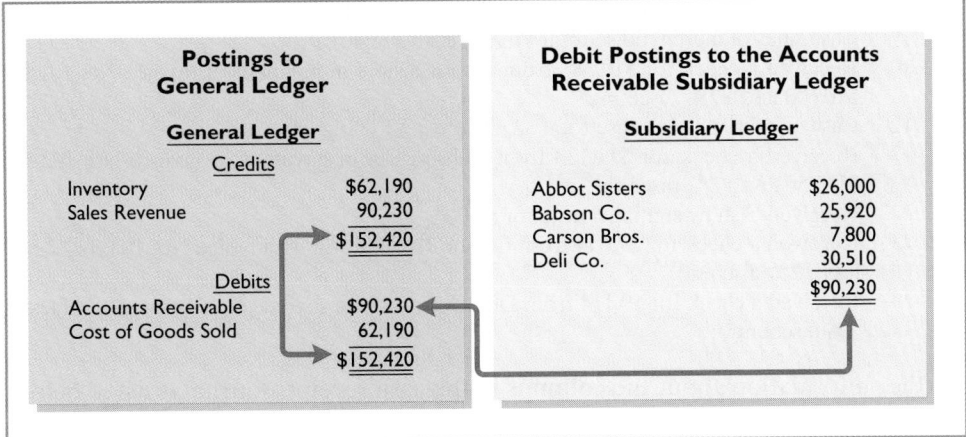

Illustration 7-8
Proving the equality of the postings from the sales journal

ADVANTAGES OF THE SALES JOURNAL

The use of a special journal to record sales on account has a number of advantages. First, the one-line entry for each sales transaction saves time. In the sales journal, it is not necessary to write out the four account titles for each transaction. Second, only totals, rather than individual entries, are posted to the general ledger. This saves posting time and reduces the possibilities of errors in posting. Finally, a division of labor results because one individual can take responsibility for the sales journal.

Cash Receipts Journal

In the **cash receipts journal**, companies record all receipts of cash. The most common types of cash receipts are cash sales of merchandise and collections of accounts receivable. Many other possibilities exist, such as receipt of money from bank loans and cash proceeds from disposal of equipment. A one- or two-column cash receipts journal would not have space enough for all possible cash receipt transactions. Therefore, companies use a multiple-column cash receipts journal.

Generally, a cash receipts journal includes the following columns: debit columns for Cash and Sales Discounts, and credit columns for Accounts Receivable, Sales Revenue, and "Other Accounts." Companies use the "Other Accounts" category when the cash receipt does not involve a cash sale or a collection of accounts receivable. Under a perpetual inventory system, each sales entry also is accompanied by an entry that debits Cost of Goods Sold and credits Inventory for the cost of the merchandise sold. Illustration 7-9 shows a six-column cash receipts journal.

Companies may use additional credit columns if these columns significantly reduce postings to a specific account. For example, a loan company, such as Household International, receives thousands of cash collections from customers. Using separate credit columns for Loans Receivable and Interest Revenue, rather than the Other Accounts credit column, would reduce postings.

JOURNALIZING CASH RECEIPTS TRANSACTIONS

To illustrate the journalizing of cash receipts transactions, we will continue with the May transactions of Karns Wholesale Supply. Collections from customers relate to the entries recorded in the sales journal in Illustration 7-6. The entries in the cash receipts journal are based on the following cash receipts.

May	1	D. A. Karns makes an investment of $5,000 in the business.
	7	Cash sales of merchandise total $1,900 (cost, $1,240).
	10	Received a check for $10,388 from Abbot Sisters in payment of invoice No. 101 for $10,600 less a 2% discount.
	12	Cash sales of merchandise total $2,600 (cost, $1,690).
	17	Received a check for $11,123 from Babson Co. in payment of invoice No. 102 for $11,350 less a 2% discount.
	22	Received cash by signing a note for $6,000.
	23	Received a check for $7,644 from Carson Bros. in full for invoice No. 103 for $7,800 less a 2% discount.
	28	Received a check for $9,114 from Deli Co. in full for invoice No. 104 for $9,300 less a 2% discount.

Further information about the columns in the cash receipts journal is listed below.

Debit Columns:

1. **Cash.** Karns enters in this column the amount of cash actually received in each transaction. The column total indicates the total cash receipts for the month.

2. **Sales Discounts.** Karns includes a Sales Discounts column in its cash receipts journal. By doing so, it does not need to enter sales discount items in the general journal. As a result, the cash receipts journal shows on one line the collection of an account receivable within the discount period.

Credit Columns:

3. **Accounts Receivable.** Karns uses the Accounts Receivable column to record cash collections on account. The amount entered here is the amount to be credited to the individual customer's account.

4. **Sales Revenue.** The Sales Revenue column records all cash sales of merchandise. Cash sales of other assets (plant assets, for example) are not reported in this column.

5. **Other Accounts.** Karns uses the Other Accounts column whenever the credit is other than to Accounts Receivable or Sales Revenue. For example, in the first entry, Karns enters $5,000 as a credit to Owner's Capital. This column is often referred to as the sundry accounts column.

Debit and Credit Column:

6. **Cost of Goods Sold and Inventory.** This column records debits to Cost of Goods Sold and credits to Inventory.

Helpful Hint

When is an account title entered in the "Account Credited" column of the cash receipts journal? Answer: A *subsidiary ledger* account is entered when the entry involves a collection of accounts receivable. A *general ledger* account is entered when the account is not shown in a special column (and an amount must be entered in the Other Accounts column). Otherwise, no account is shown in the "Account Credited" column.

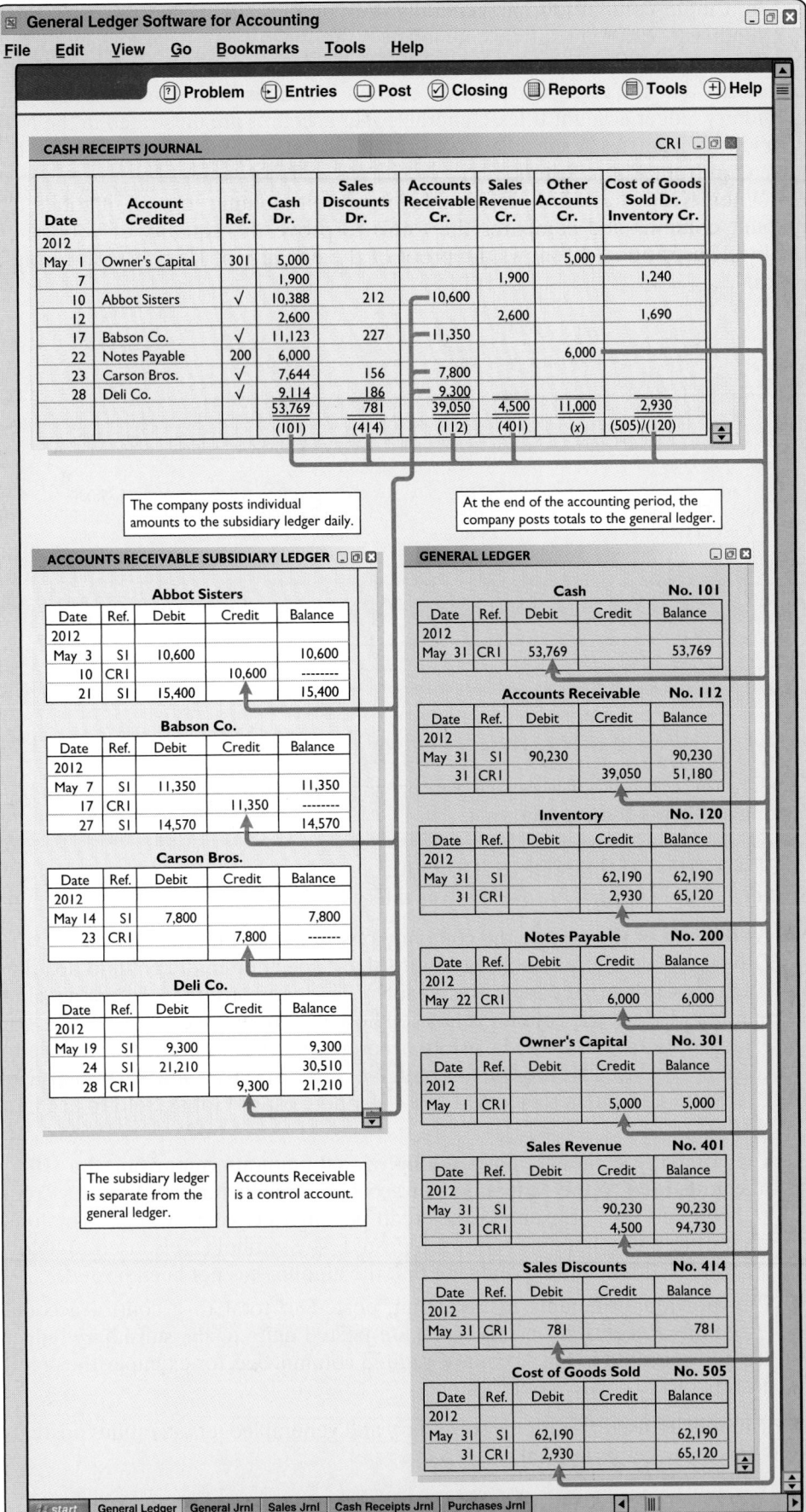

Illustration 7-9
Journalizing and posting the
cash receipts journal

In a multi-column journal, generally only one line is needed for each entry. Debit and credit amounts for each line must be equal. When Karns journalizes the collection from Abbot Sisters on May 10, for example, three amounts are indicated. Note also that the Account Credited column identifies both general ledger and subsidiary ledger account titles. General ledger accounts are illustrated in the May 1 and May 22 entries. A subsidiary account is illustrated in the May 10 entry for the collection from Abbot Sisters.

When Karns has finished journalizing a multi-column journal, it totals the amount columns and compares the totals to prove the equality of debits and credits. Illustration 7-10 shows the proof of the equality of Karns's cash receipts journal.

Illustration 7-10

Proving the equality of the cash receipts journal

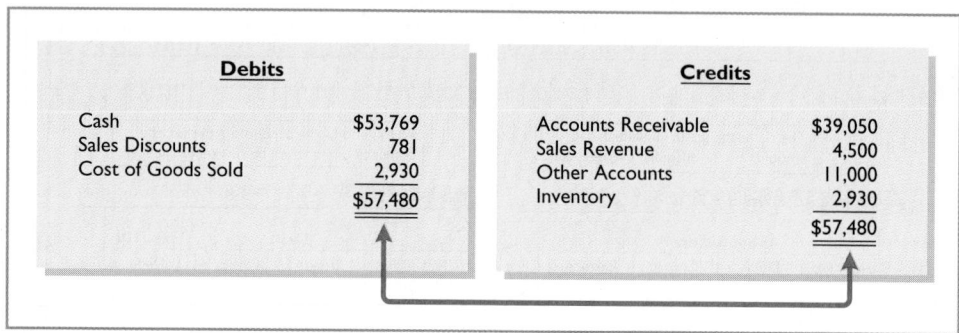

Totaling the columns of a journal and proving the equality of the totals is called **footing** and **cross-footing** a journal.

POSTING THE CASH RECEIPTS JOURNAL

Posting a multi-column journal involves the following steps.

Study Objective [4]

Indicate how companies post a multi-column journal.

1. **At the end of the month**, the company posts all column totals, except for the Other Accounts total, to the account title(s) specified in the column heading (such as Cash or Accounts Receivable). The company then enters account numbers below the column totals to show that they have been posted. For example, Karns has posted Cash to account No. 101, Accounts Receivable to account No. 112, Inventory to account No. 120, Sales Revenue to account No. 401, Sales Discounts to account No. 414, and Cost of Goods Sold to account No. 505.

2. The company **separately posts the individual amounts comprising the Other Accounts total** to the general ledger accounts specified in the Account Credited column. See, for example, the credit posting to Owner's Capital. The total amount of this column has not been posted. The symbol (X) is inserted below the total to this column to indicate that the amount has not been posted.

3. The individual amounts in a column, posted in total to a control account (Accounts Receivable, in this case), are posted **daily to the subsidiary ledger** account specified in the Account Credited column. See, for example, the credit posting of $10,600 to Abbot Sisters.

The symbol **CR**, used in both the subsidiary and general ledgers, identifies postings from the cash receipts journal.

PROVING THE LEDGERS
After posting of the cash receipts journal is completed, Karns proves the ledgers. As shown in Illustration 7-11, the general ledger totals agree. Also, the sum of the subsidiary ledger balances equals the control account balance.

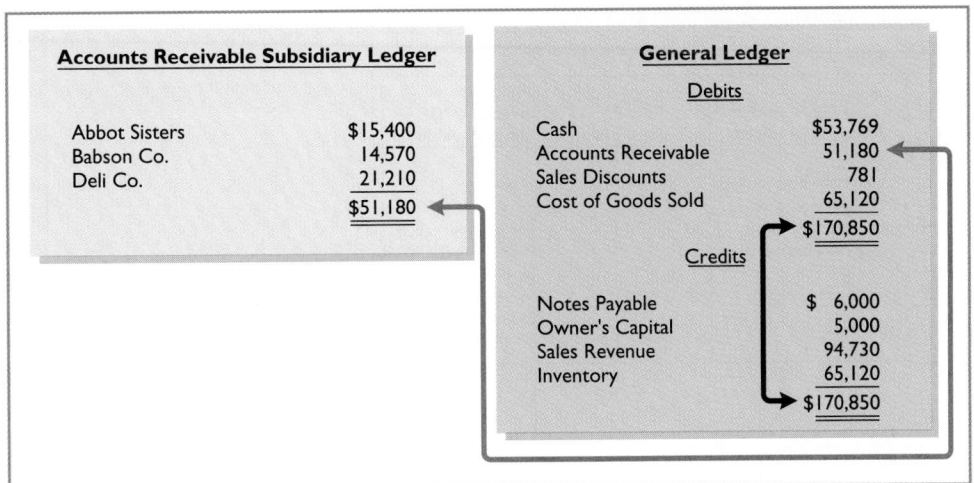

Illustration 7-11
Proving the ledgers after posting the sales and the cash receipts journals

Purchases Journal

In the **purchases journal**, companies record all purchases of merchandise on account. Each entry in this journal results in a debit to Inventory and a credit to Accounts Payable. Illustration 7-13 (on page 330) shows the purchases journal for Karns Wholesale Supply.

When using a one-column purchases journal (as in Illustration 7-13), a company cannot journalize other types of purchases on account or cash purchases in it. For example, in the purchases journal in Illustration 7-13, Karns would have to record credit purchases of equipment or supplies in the general journal. Likewise, all cash purchases would be entered in the cash payments journal. As illustrated later, companies that make numerous credit purchases for items other than merchandise often expand the purchases journal to a multi-column format. (See Illustration 7-15 on page 331.)

JOURNALIZING CREDIT PURCHASES OF MERCHANDISE
The journalizing procedure is similar to that for a sales journal. Companies make entries in the purchases journal from purchase invoices. In contrast to the sales journal, the purchases journal may not have an invoice number column, because invoices received from different suppliers will not be in numerical sequence. To ensure that they record all purchase invoices, some companies consecutively number each invoice upon receipt and then use an internal document number column in the purchases journal. The entries for Karns Wholesale Supply are based on the assumed credit purchases listed in Illustration 7-12.

Date	Supplier	Amount
5/6	Jasper Manufacturing Inc.	$11,000
5/10	Eaton and Howe Inc.	7,200
5/14	Fabor and Son	6,900
5/19	Jasper Manufacturing Inc.	17,500
5/26	Fabor and Son	8,700
5/29	Eaton and Howe Inc.	12,600

Illustration 7-12
Credit purchases transactions

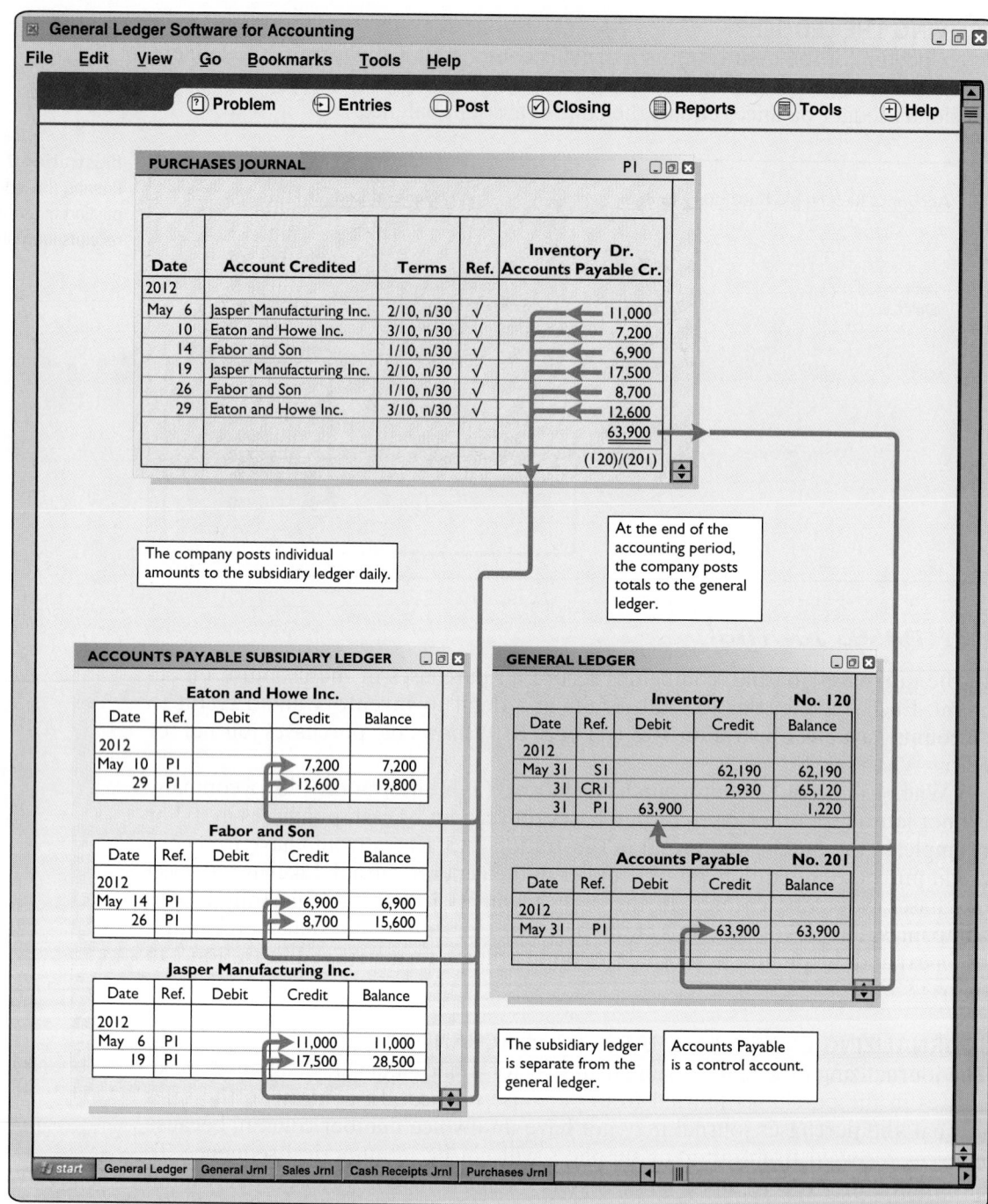

Illustration 7-13
Journalizing and posting the purchases journal

Helpful Hint

Postings to subsidiary ledger accounts are done daily because it is often necessary to know a current balance for the subsidiary accounts.

POSTING THE PURCHASES JOURNAL

The procedures for posting the purchases journal are similar to those for the sales journal. In this case, Karns makes **daily** postings to the **accounts payable ledger**; it makes **monthly** postings to Inventory and Accounts Payable in the general ledger. In both ledgers, Karns uses **P1** in the reference column to show that the postings are from page 1 of the purchases journal.

Proof of the equality of the postings from the purchases journal to both ledgers is shown in Illustration 7-14.

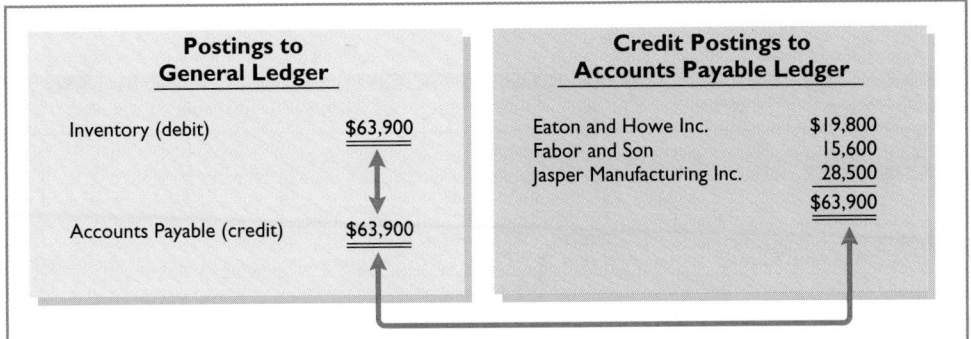

Illustration 7-14
Proving the equality of the
purchases journal

EXPANDING THE PURCHASES JOURNAL

As noted earlier, some companies expand the purchases journal to include all types of purchases on account. Instead of one column for inventory and accounts payable, they use a multiple-column format. This format usually includes a credit column for Accounts Payable and debit columns for purchases of Inventory, Supplies, and Other Accounts. Illustration 7-15 shows a multi-column purchases journal for Hanover Co. The posting procedures are similar to those shown earlier for posting the cash receipts journal.

Helpful Hint

A single-column purchases journal needs only to be footed to prove the equality of debits and credits.

Illustration 7-15
Multi-column purchases journal

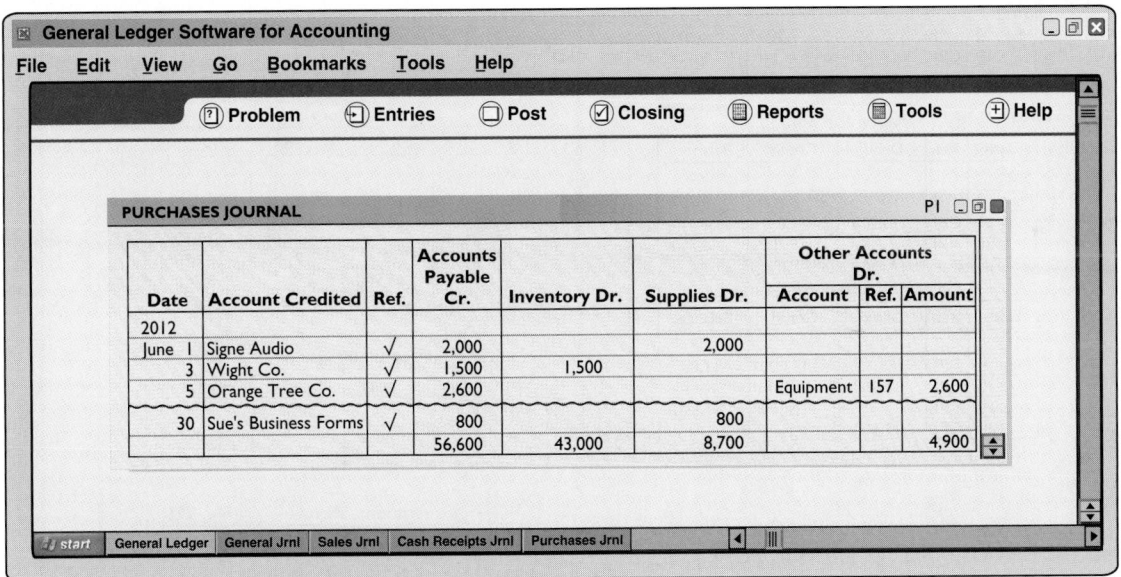

Cash Payments Journal

In a **cash payments (cash disbursements) journal**, companies record all disbursements of cash. Entries are made from prenumbered checks. Because companies make cash payments for various purposes, the cash payments journal has multiple columns. Illustration 7-16 (page 332) shows a four-column journal.

JOURNALIZING CASH PAYMENTS TRANSACTIONS

The procedures for journalizing transactions in this journal are similar to those for the cash receipts journal. Karns records each transaction on one line, and for each line there must be equal debit and credit amounts. The entries in the cash payments

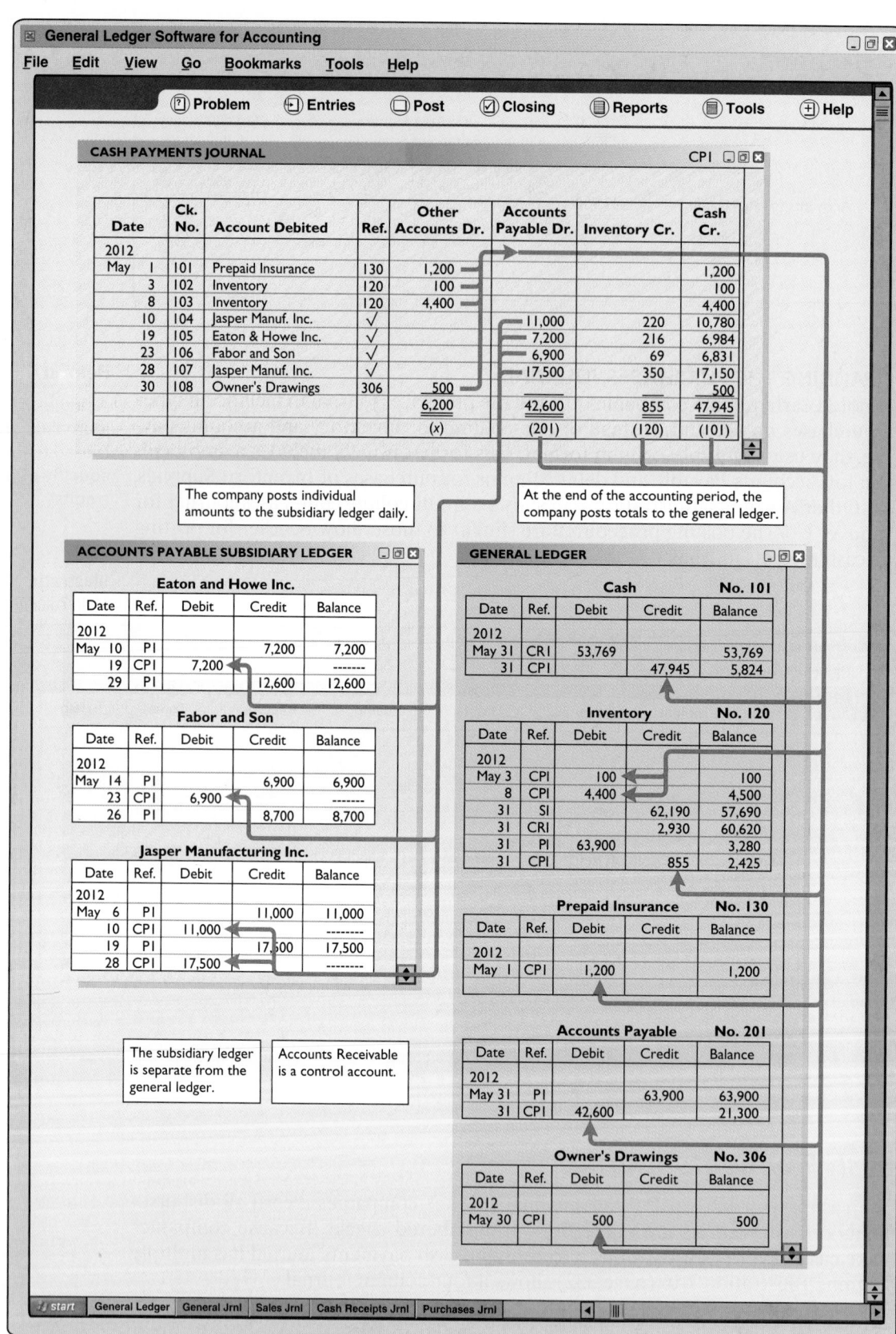

Illustration 7-16
Journalizing and posting the
cash payments journal

journal in Illustration 7-16 are based on the following transactions for Karns Wholesale Supply.

May 1   Issued check No. 101 for $1,200 for the annual premium on a fire insurance policy.
      3   Issued check No. 102 for $100 in payment of freight when terms were FOB shipping
          point.
      8   Issued check No. 103 for $4,400 for the purchase of merchandise.
     10   Sent check No. 104 for $10,780 to Jasper Manufacturing Inc. in payment of May 6
          invoice for $11,000 less a 2% discount.
     19   Mailed check No. 105 for $6,984 to Eaton and Howe Inc. in payment of May 10 invoice
          for $7,200 less a 3% discount.
     23   Sent check No. 106 for $6,831 to Fabor and Son in payment of May 14 invoice for
          $6,900 less a 1% discount.
     28   Sent check No. 107 for $17,150 to Jasper Manufacturing Inc. in payment of May 19
          invoice for $17,500 less a 2% discount.
     30   Issued check No. 108 for $500 to D. A. Karns as a cash withdrawal for personal use.

Note that whenever Karns enters an amount in the Other Accounts column, it must
identify a specific general ledger account in the Account Debited column. The entries for checks No. 101, 102, 103, and 108 illustrate this situation. Similarly, Karns
must identify a subsidiary account in the Account Debited column whenever it
enters an amount in the Accounts Payable column. See, for example, the entry for
check No. 104.

   After Karns journalizes the cash payments journal, it totals the columns. The
totals are then balanced to prove the equality of debits and credits.

POSTING THE CASH PAYMENTS JOURNAL

The procedures for posting the cash payments journal are similar to those for the
cash receipts journal. Karns posts the amounts recorded in the Accounts Payable
column individually to the subsidiary ledger and in total to the control account. It
posts Inventory and Cash only in total at the end of the month. Transactions in the
Other Accounts column are posted individually to the appropriate account(s)
affected. The company does not post totals for the Other Accounts column.

   Illustration 7-16 shows the posting of the cash payments journal. Note that
Karns uses the symbol **CP** as the posting reference. After postings are completed,
the company proves the equality of the debit and credit balances in the general
ledger. In addition, the control account balances should agree with the subsidiary
ledger total balance. Illustration 7-17 shows the agreement of these balances.

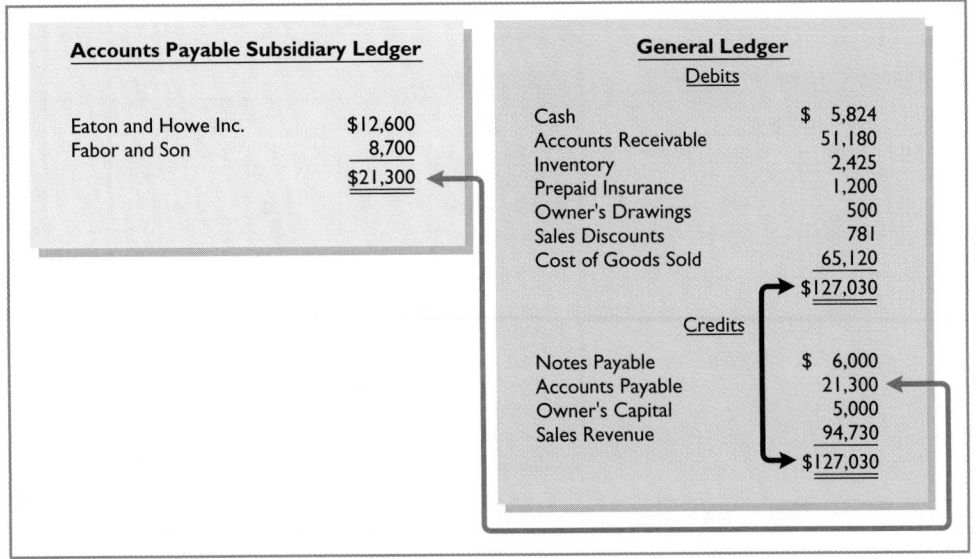

Illustration 7-17
Proving the ledgers after
postings from the sales, cash
receipts, purchases, and cash
payments journals

Effects of Special Journals on the General Journal

Special journals for sales, purchases, and cash substantially reduce the number of entries that companies make in the general journal. **Only transactions that cannot be entered in a special journal are recorded in the general journal.** For example, a company may use the general journal to record such transactions as granting of credit to a customer for a sales return or allowance, granting of credit from a supplier for purchases returned, acceptance of a note receivable from a customer, and purchase of equipment by issuing a note payable. Also, **correcting, adjusting, and closing entries are made in the general journal**.

The general journal has columns for date, account title and explanation, reference, and debit and credit amounts. When control and subsidiary accounts are not involved, the procedures for journalizing and posting of transactions are the same as those described in earlier chapters. When control and subsidiary accounts *are* involved, companies make two changes from the earlier procedures:

1. In **journalizing**, they identify both the control and the subsidiary accounts.
2. In **posting**, there must be a **dual posting**: once to the control account and once to the subsidiary account.

To illustrate, assume that on May 31, Karns Wholesale Supply returns $500 of merchandise for credit to Fabor and Son. Illustration 7-18 shows the entry in the general journal and the posting of the entry. Note that if Karns receives cash instead of credit on this return, then it would record the transaction in the cash receipts journal.

Illustration 7-18
Journalizing and posting the general journal

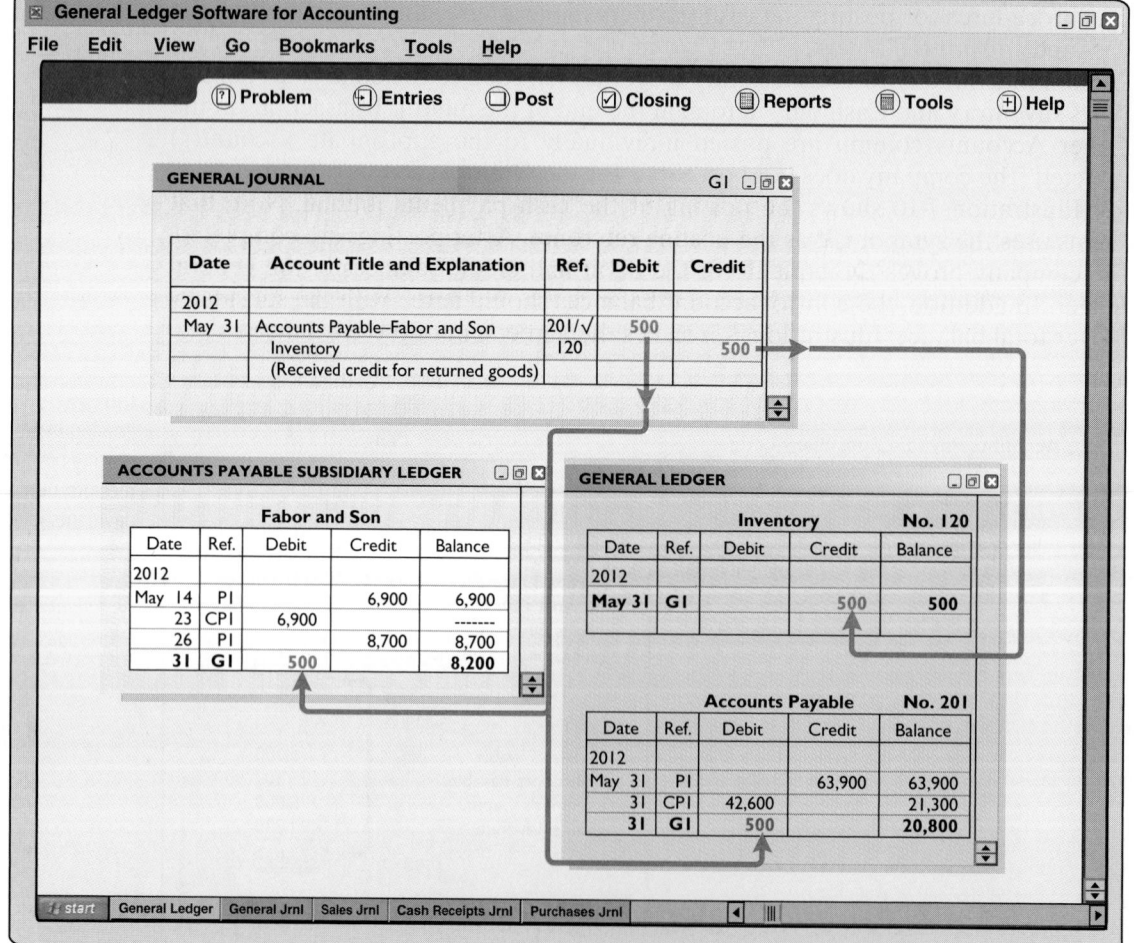

Note that the general journal indicates two accounts (Accounts Payable, and Fabor and Son) for the debit, and two postings ("201/✓") in the reference column. One debit is posted to the control account and another debit to the creditor's account in the subsidiary ledger.

Do it!

Swisher Company had the following transactions during March.

1. Collected cash on account from Oakland Company.
2. Purchased equipment by signing a note payable.
3. Sold merchandise on account.
4. Purchased merchandise on account.
5. Paid $2,400 for a 2-year insurance policy.

Identify the journal in which each of the transactions above is recorded.

Solution

1. Collected cash on account from Oakland Company.	Cash receipts journal
2. Purchased equipment by signing a note payable.	General journal
3. Sold merchandise on account.	Sales journal
4. Purchased merchandise on account.	Purchases journal
5. Paid $2,400 for a 2-year insurance policy.	Cash payments journal

Related exercise material: BE7-6, BE7-7, BE7-8, BE7-9, E7-6, E7-7, E7-8, E7-10, and **Do it!** 7-2.

Special Journals

action plan
✔ Determine if the transaction involves the receipt of cash (cash receipts journal) or the payment of cash (cash payments journal).
✔ Determine if the transaction is a sale of merchandise on account (sales journal) or a purchase of merchandise on account (purchases journal).
✔ All other transactions are recorded in the general journal.

✔
The Navigator

COMPREHENSIVE
Do it!

Cassandra Wilson Company uses a six-column cash receipts journal with the following columns.

Cash (Dr.)   Other Accounts (Cr.)
Sales Discounts (Dr.)   Cost of Goods Sold (Dr.) and
Accounts Receivable (Cr.)   Inventory (Cr.)
Sales Revenue (Cr.)

Cash receipts transactions for the month of July 2012 are as follows.

July   3   Cash sales total $5,800 (cost, $3,480).
       5   Received a check for $6,370 from Jeltz Company in payment of an invoice dated June 26 for $6,500, terms 2/10, n/30.
       9   Cassandra Wilson, the proprietor, made an additional investment of $5,000 in cash in the business.
      10   Cash sales total $12,519 (cost, $7,511).
      12   Received a check for $7,275 from R. Eliot & Co. in payment of a $7,500 invoice dated July 3, terms 3/10, n/30.
      15   Received an advance of $700 cash for future services.
      20   Cash sales total $15,472 (cost, $9,283).
      22   Received a check for $5,880 from Beck Company in payment of $6,000 invoice dated July 13, terms 2/10, n/30.
      29   Cash sales total $17,660 (cost, $10,596).
      31   Received cash of $200 on interest earned for July.

action plan
✔ Record all cash receipts in the cash receipts journal.
✔ The "account credited" indicates items posted individually to the subsidiary ledger or to the general ledger.
✔ Record cash sales in the cash receipts journal—not in the sales journal.
✔ The total debits must equal the total credits.

Instructions

(a) Journalize the transactions in the cash receipts journal.

(b) Contrast the posting of the Accounts Receivable and Other Accounts columns.

Solution to Comprehensive Do it!

(a)

CASSANDRA WILSON COMPANY

Cash Receipts Journal   CR1

Date	Account Credited	Ref.	Cash Dr.	Sales Discounts Dr.	Accounts Receivable Cr.	Sales Revenue Cr.	Other Accounts Cr.	Cost of Goods Sold Dr. Inventory Cr.
2012								
7/3			5,800			5,800		3,480
5	Jeltz Company		6,370	130	6,500			
9	Owner's Capital		5,000				5,000	
10			12,519			12,519		7,511
12	R. Eliot & Co.		7,275	225	7,500			
15	Unearned Service Revenue		700				700	
20			15,472			15,472		9,283
22	Beck Company		5,880	120	6,000			
29			17,660			17,660		10,596
31	Interest Revenue		200				200	
			76,876	475	20,000	51,451	5,900	30,870

(b) The Accounts Receivable column total is posted as a credit to Accounts Receivable. The individual amounts are credited to the customers' accounts identified in the Account Credited column, which are maintained in the accounts receivable subsidiary ledger.

The amounts in the Other Accounts column are posted individually. They are credited to the account titles identified in the Account Credited column.

The Navigator

Summary of Study Objectives

[1] Identify the basic concepts of an accounting information system. The basic principles in developing an accounting information system are cost-effectiveness, useful output, and flexibility. Most companies use a computerized accounting system. Smaller companies use entry-level software such as QuickBooks or Peachtree. Larger companies use custom-made software packages, which often integrate all aspects of the organization.

[2] Describe the nature and purpose of a subsidiary ledger. A subsidiary ledger is a group of accounts with a common characteristic. It facilitates the recording process by freeing the general ledger from details of individual balances.

[3] Explain how companies use special journals in journalizing. Companies use special journals to group similar types of transactions. In a special journal, generally only one line is used to record a complete transaction.

[4] Indicate how companies post a multi-column journal. In posting a multi-column journal:

(a) Companies post all column totals except for the Other Accounts column once at the end of the month to the account title specified in the column heading.

(b) Companies do not post the total of the Other Accounts column. Instead, the individual amounts comprising the total are posted separately to the general ledger accounts specified in the Account Credited (Debited) column.

(c) The individual amounts in a column posted in total to a control account are posted daily to the subsidiary ledger accounts specified in the Account Credited (Debited) column.

The Navigator

Glossary

Accounting information system A system that collects and processes transaction data, and communicates financial information to decision makers. (p. 316).

Accounts payable (creditors') subsidiary ledger A subsidiary ledger that collects transaction data of individual creditors. (p. 319).

Accounts receivable (customers') subsidiary ledger A subsidiary ledger that collects transaction data of individual customers. (p. 319).

Cash payments (disbursements) journal A special journal that records all disbursements of cash. (p. 331).

Cash receipts journal A special journal that records all cash received. (p. 325).

Control account An account in the general ledger that summarizes subsidiary ledger data. (p. 319).

Manual accounting system A system in which someone performs each of the steps in the accounting cycle by hand. (p. 319).

Purchases journal A special journal that records all purchases of merchandise on account. (p. 329).

Sales journal A special journal that records all sales of merchandise on account. (p. 323).

Special journal A journal that records similar types of transactions, such as all credit sales. (p. 322).

Subsidiary ledger A group of accounts with a common characteristic. (p. 319).

 Self-Test, Brief Exercises, Exercises, Problem Set A, and many more components are available for practice in *WileyPLUS*

Self-Test Questions

Answers are on page 357.

(SO 1) **1.** The basic principles of an accounting information system include all of the following except:
  a. cost-effectiveness. **c.** useful output.
  b. flexibility. **d.** periodicity.

(SO 1) **2.** Which of the following is *not* an advantage of computerized accounting systems?
  a. Data is entered only once in computerized accounting systems.
  b. Computerized accounting systems provide up-to-date information.
  c. Computerized accounting systems eliminate entering of transaction information.
  d. Computerized accounting systems eliminate many errors resulting from human intervention.

(SO 2) **3.** Which of the following is *incorrect* concerning subsidiary ledgers?
  a. The purchases ledger is a common subsidiary ledger for creditor accounts.
  b. The accounts receivable ledger is a subsidiary ledger.
  c. A subsidiary ledger is a group of accounts with a common characteristic.
  d. An advantage of the subsidiary ledger is that it permits a division of labor in posting.

(SO 2) **4.** Two common subsidiary ledgers are:
  a. accounts receivable and cash receipts.
  b. accounts payable and cash payments.
  c. accounts receivable and accounts payable.
  d. sales and cost of goods sold.

(SO 2) **5.** At the beginning of the month, the accounts receivable subsidiary ledger showed balances for Apple Company $5,000 and Berry Company $7,000. During the month, credit sales were made to Apple $6,000, Berry $4,500, and Cantaloupe $8,500. Cash was collected on account from Berry $11,500 and Cantaloupe $3,000. At the end of the month, the control account Accounts Receivable in the general ledger should have a balance of:
  a. $11,000. **c.** $16,500.
  b. $12,000. **d.** $31,000.

(SO 3) **6.** A sales journal will be used for:

	Credit Sales	Cash Sales	Sales Discounts
a.	no	yes	yes
b.	yes	no	yes
c.	yes	no	no
d.	yes	yes	no

(SO 3) **7.** A purchase of equipment on account is recorded in the:
  a. cash receipts journal. **c.** cash payments journal.
  b. purchases journal. **d.** general journal.

(SO 3) **8.** A purchase of equipment using cash is recorded in the:
  a. cash receipts journal. **c.** cash payments journal.
  b. purchases journal. **d.** general journal.

(SO 3, 4) **9.** Which of the following statements is *correct*?
  a. The sales discount column is included in the cash receipts journal.
  b. The purchases journal records all purchases of merchandise whether for cash or on account.
  c. The cash receipts journal records sales on account.
  d. Merchandise returned by the buyer is recorded by the seller in the purchases journal.

(SO 4) **10.** Dotel Company's cash receipts journal includes an Accounts Receivable column and an Other Accounts column. At the end of the month, these columns are posted to the general ledger as:

	Accounts Receivable	Other Accounts
a.	a column total	a column total
b.	individual amounts	a column total
c.	individual amounts	individual amounts
d.	a column total	individual amounts

(SO 4) **11.** Which of the following is *incorrect* concerning the posting of the cash receipts journal?

    a. The total of the Other Accounts column is not posted.

    b. All column totals except the total for the Other Accounts column are posted once at the end of the month to the account title(s) specified in the column heading.

    c. The totals of all columns are posted daily to the accounts specified in the column heading.

    d. The individual amounts in a column posted in total to a control account are posted daily to the subsidiary ledger account specified in the Account Credited column.

(SO 4) **12.** Postings from the purchases journal to the subsidiary ledger are generally made:

    a. yearly.   **c.** weekly.

    b. monthly.   **d.** daily.

(SO 3) **13.** Which statement is *incorrect* regarding the general journal?

    a. Only transactions that cannot be entered in a special journal are recorded in the general journal.

    b. Dual postings are always required in the general journal.

    c. The general journal may be used to record acceptance of a note receivable in payment of an account receivable.

    d. Correcting, adjusting, and closing entries are made in the general journal.

14. When companies use special journals: (SO 3)

    a. they record all purchase transactions in the purchases journal.

    b. they record all cash received, except from cash sales, in the cash receipts journal.

    c. they record all cash disbursements in the cash payments journal.

    d. a general journal is not necessary.

15. If a customer returns goods for credit, the selling company (SO 3) normally makes an entry in the:

    a. cash payments journal.   **c.** general journal.

    b. sales journal.   **d.** cash receipts journal.

Go to the book's companion website, **www.wiley.com/college/weygandt**, for additional Self-Test Questions.

The Navigator

Questions

1. (a) What is an accounting information system? (b) "An accounting information system applies only to a manual system." Do you agree? Explain.

2. Certain principles should be followed in the development of an accounting information system. Identify and explain each of the principles.

3. What are common features of computerized accounting packages beyond recording transactions and preparing financial statements?

4. How does an enterprise resource planning (ERP) system differ from an entry-level computerized accounting system?

5. What are the advantages of using subsidiary ledgers?

6. (a) When do companies normally post to (1) the subsidiary accounts and (2) the general ledger control accounts? (b) Describe the relationship between a control account and a subsidiary ledger.

7. Identify and explain the four special journals discussed in the chapter. List an advantage of using each of these journals rather than using only a general journal.

8. Thogmartin Company uses special journals. It recorded in a sales journal a sale made on account to R. Peters for $435. A few days later, R. Peters returns $70 worth of merchandise for credit. Where should Thogmartin Company record the sales return? Why?

9. A $500 purchase of merchandise on account from Lore Company was properly recorded in the purchases journal. When posted, however, the amount recorded in the subsidiary ledger was $50. How might this error be discovered?

10. Why would special journals used in different businesses not be identical in format? What type of business would maintain a cash receipts journal but not include a column for accounts receivable?

11. The cash and the accounts receivable columns in the cash receipts journal were mistakenly overadded by $4,000 at the end of the month. (a) Will the customers' ledger agree with the Accounts Receivable control account? (b) Assuming no other errors, will the trial balance totals be equal?

12. One column total of a special journal is posted at month-end to only two general ledger accounts. One of these two accounts is Accounts Receivable. What is the name of this special journal? What is the other general ledger account to which that same month-end total is posted?

13. In what journal would the following transactions be recorded? (Assume that a two-column sales journal and a single-column purchases journal are used.)

    (a) Recording of depreciation expense for the year.

    (b) Credit given to a customer for merchandise purchased on credit and returned.

    (c) Sales of merchandise for cash.

    (d) Sales of merchandise on account.

    (e) Collection of cash on account from a customer.

    (f) Purchase of office supplies on account.

14. In what journal would the following transactions be recorded? (Assume that a two-column sales journal and a single-column purchases journal are used.)

    (a) Cash received from signing a note payable.

    (b) Investment of cash by the owner of the business.

    (c) Closing of the expense accounts at the end of the year.

(d) Purchase of merchandise on account.
(e) Credit received for merchandise purchased and returned to supplier.
(f) Payment of cash on account due a supplier.

15. What transactions might be included in a multiple-column purchases journal that would not be included in a single-column purchases journal?

16. Give an example of a transaction in the general journal that causes an entry to be posted twice (i.e., to two accounts), one in the general ledger, the other in the subsidiary ledger. Does this affect the debit/credit equality of the general ledger?

17. Give some examples of appropriate general journal transactions for an organization using special journals.

Brief Exercises

BE7-1 Indicate whether each of the following statements is true or false.
1. When designing an accounting system, we need to think about the needs and knowledge of both the top managers and various other users.
2. When the environment changes as a result of technological advances, increased competition, or government regulation, an accounting system does not have to be sufficiently flexible to meet the changes in order to save money.
3. In developing an accounting system, cost is relevant. The benefits obtained from the information disseminated must outweigh the cost of providing it.

Identify basic concepts of an accounting information system.
(SO 1)

BE7-2 Here is a list of words or phrases related to computerized accounting systems.
1. Entry-level software.
2. Enterprise resource planning systems.
3. Network-compatible.
4. Audit trail.
5. Internal control.

Identify basic concepts of an accounting information system.
(SO 1)

Instructions
Match each word or phrase with the best description of it.
_____**(a)** Allows multiple users to access the system at the same time.
_____**(b)** Enables the tracking of all transactions.
_____**(c)** Identifies suspicious transactions or likely mistakes such as wrong account numbers or duplicate transactions.
_____**(d)** Large-scale computer systems that integrate all aspects of the organization including accounting, sales, human resource management, and manufacturing.
_____**(e)** System for companies with revenues of less than $5 million and up to 20 employees.

BE7-3 Benji Borke has prepared the following list of statements about accounting information systems.
1. The accounting information system includes each of the steps of the accounting cycle, the documents that provide evidence of transactions that have occurred, and the accounting records.
2. The benefits obtained from information provided by the accounting information system need not outweigh the cost of providing that information.
3. Designers of accounting systems must consider the needs and knowledge of various users.
4. If an accounting information system is cost-effective and provides useful output, it does not need to be flexible.

Identify basic concepts of an accounting information system.
(SO 1)

Instructions
Identify each statement as true or false. If false, indicate how to correct the statement.

BE7-4 Presented below is information related to Montand Company for its first month of operations. Identify the balances that appear in the accounts receivable subsidiary ledger and the accounts receivable balance that appears in the general ledger at the end of January.

Identify subsidiary ledger balances.
(SO 2)

Credit Sales		Cash Collections	
Jan. 7 Ahuna Co.	$10,000	Jan. 17 Ahuna Co.	$7,000
15 Aldo Co.	6,000	24 Aldo Co.	4,000
23 Tito Co.	9,000	29 Tito Co.	9,000

Identify subsidiary ledger accounts.

(SO 2)

BE7-5   Identify in what ledger (general or subsidiary) each of the following accounts is shown.

1. Rent Expense
2. Accounts Receivable—Obileye
3. Notes Payable
4. Accounts Payable—Kolawole

Identify special journals.

(SO 3)

BE7-6   Identify the journal in which each of the following transactions is recorded.

1. Cash sales
2. Owner withdrawal of cash
3. Cash purchase of land
4. Credit sales
5. Purchase of merchandise on account
6. Receipt of cash for services performed

Identify entries to cash receipts journal.

(SO 3)

BE7-7   Indicate whether each of the following debits and credits is included in the cash receipts journal. (Use "Yes" or "No" to answer this question.)

1. Debit to Sales Revenue.
2. Credit to Inventory.
3. Credit to Accounts Receivable.
4. Debit to Accounts Payable.

Identify transactions for special journals.

(SO 3)

BE7-8   Olekan Co. uses special journals and a general journal. Identify the journal in which each of the following transactions is recorded.

(a) Purchased equipment on account.
(b) Purchased merchandise on account.
(c) Paid utility expense in cash.
(d) Sold merchandise on account.

Identify transactions for special journals.

(SO 3)

BE7-9   Identify the special journal(s) in which the following column headings appear.

1. Sales Discounts Dr.
2. Accounts Receivable Cr.
3. Cash Dr.
4. Sales Revenue Cr.
5. Inventory Dr.

Indicate postings for cash receipts journal.

(SO 4)

BE7-10   Bruni Computer Components Inc. uses a multi-column cash receipts journal. Indicate which column(s) is/are posted only in total, only daily, or both in total and daily.

1. Accounts Receivable
2. Sales Discounts
3. Cash
4. Other Accounts

Do it! Review

Determine subsidiary and general ledger balances.

(SO 2)

Do it! 7-1   Presented below is information related to Chung Company for its first month of operations. Determine the balances that appear in the accounts payable subsidiary ledger. What Accounts Payable balance appears in the general ledger at the end of January?

Credit Purchases			Cash Paid		
Jan. 6	Shada Company	$ 9,000	Jan. 11	Shada Company	$ 6,500
Jan. 10	Liam Company	12,000	Jan. 16	Liam Company	12,000
Jan. 23	Esmond Company	10,000	Jan. 29	Esmond Company	7,700

Identify special journals.

(SO 3)

Do it! 7-2   Tomiko Company had the following transactions during April.

1. Sold merchandise on account.
2. Purchased merchandise on account.
3. Collected cash from a sale to Kahale Company.
4. Recorded accrued interest on a note payable.
5. Paid $2,000 for supplies.

Identify the journal in which each of the transactions above is recorded.

Exercises

Determine control account balances, and explain posting of special journals.

(SO 2, 4)

E7-1   Ruz Company uses both special journals and a general journal as described in this chapter. On June 30, after all monthly postings had been completed, the Accounts Receivable control account in the general ledger had a debit balance of $320,000; the Accounts Payable control account had a credit balance of $77,000.

The July transactions recorded in the special journals are summarized below. No entries affecting accounts receivable and accounts payable were recorded in the general journal for July.

Sales journal	Total sales $161,400
Purchases journal	Total purchases $56,400
Cash receipts journal	Accounts receivable column total $131,000
Cash payments journal	Accounts payable column total $47,500

Instructions

(a) What is the balance of the Accounts Receivable control account after the monthly postings on July 31?

(b) What is the balance of the Accounts Payable control account after the monthly postings on July 31?

(c) To what account(s) is the column total of $161,400 in the sales journal posted?

(d) To what account(s) is the accounts receivable column total of $131,000 in the cash receipts journal posted?

E7-2 Presented below is the subsidiary accounts receivable account of Lana Parilla.

Explain postings to subsidiary ledger.

(SO 2)

Date	Ref.	Debit	Credit	Balance
2012				
Sept. 2	S31	61,000		61,000
9	G4		14,000	47,000
27	CR8		47,000	—

Instructions

Write a memo to Maya Henssens, chief financial officer, that explains each transaction.

E7-3 On September 1, the balance of the Accounts Receivable control account in the general ledger of Joss Whedon Company was $10,960. The customers' subsidiary ledger contained account balances as follows: Gareth $1,440, Gillum $2,640, Minear $2,060, Edlund $4,820. At the end of September, the various journals contained the following information.

Post various journals to control and subsidiary accounts.

(SO 2, 4)

Sales journal: Sales to Edlund $800; to Gareth $1,260; to Molina $1,330; to Minear $1,100.

Cash receipts journal: Cash received from Minear $1,310; from Edlund $2,300; from Molina $380; from Gillum $1,800; from Gareth $1,240.

General journal: An allowance is granted to Edlund $220.

Instructions

(a) Set up control and subsidiary accounts and enter the beginning balances. Do not construct the journals.

(b) Post the various journals. Post the items as individual items or as totals, whichever would be the appropriate procedure. (No sales discounts given.)

(c) Prepare a list of customers and prove the agreement of the controlling account with the subsidiary ledger at September 30, 2012.

E7-4 Malcolnn Reynolds Company has a balance in its Accounts Receivable control account of $11,000 on January 1, 2012. The subsidiary ledger contains three accounts: Nathan Company, balance $4,000; Fillion Company, balance $2,500; and Lassak Company. During January, the following receivable-related transactions occurred.

Determine control and subsidiary ledger balances for accounts receivable.

(SO 2)

	Credit Sales	Collections	Returns
Nathan Company	$9,000	$8,000	$ -0-
Fillion Company	7,000	2,500	3,000
Lassak Company	8,500	9,000	-0-

Instructions

(a) What is the January 1 balance in the Lassak Company subsidiary account?

(b) What is the January 31 balance in the control account?

(c) Compute the balances in the subsidiary accounts at the end of the month.

(d) Which January transaction would not be recorded in a special journal?

Determine control and subsidiary ledger balances for accounts payable.

(SO 2)

E7-5   Zoe Washburne Company has a balance in its Accounts Payable control account of $8,250 on January 1, 2012. The subsidiary ledger contains three accounts: Gina Company, balance $3,000; Torres Company, balance $1,875; and Wankum Company. During January, the following payable-related transactions occurred.

	Purchases	Payments	Returns
Gina Company	$6,750	$6,000	$ -0-
Torres Company	5,250	1,875	2,250
Wankum Company	6,375	6,750	-0-

Instructions
(a) What is the January 1 balance in the Wankum Company subsidiary account?
(b) What is the January 31 balance in the control account?
(c) Compute the balances in the subsidiary accounts at the end of the month.
(d) Which January transaction would not be recorded in a special journal?

Record transactions in sales and purchases journal.

(SO 2, 3)

E7-6   Hoban Company uses special journals and a general journal. The following transactions occurred during September 2012.

Sept. 2   Sold merchandise on account to H. Wash, invoice no. 101, $720, terms n/30. The cost of the merchandise sold was $420.
   10   Purchased merchandise on account from A. Tudyk $600, terms 2/10, n/30.
   12   Purchased office equipment on account from R. Press $6,500.
   21   Sold merchandise on account to G. Edmonson, invoice no. 102 for $800, terms 2/10, n/30. The cost of the merchandise sold was $480.
   25   Purchased merchandise on account from D. Boyd $860, terms n/30.
   27   Sold merchandise to S. Miller for $700 cash. The cost of the merchandise sold was $400.

Instructions
(a) Prepare a sales journal (see Illustration 7-7) and a single-column purchases journal (see Illustration 7-13). (Use page 1 for each journal.)
(b) Record the transaction(s) for September that should be journalized in the sales journal and the purchases journal.

Record transactions in cash receipts and cash payments journal.

(SO 2, 3)

E7-7   Inara Serra Co. uses special journals and a general journal. The following transactions occurred during May 2012.

May 1   I. Serra invested $50,000 cash in the business.
   2   Sold merchandise to Morena Co. for $6,300 cash. The cost of the merchandise sold was $4,200.
   3   Purchased merchandise for $7,200 from J. DeLeon using check no. 101.
   14   Paid salary to H. Potter $700 by issuing check no. 102.
   16   Sold merchandise on account to K. Kimbell for $900, terms n/30. The cost of the merchandise sold was $630.
   22   A check of $9,000 is received from M. Baccarin in full for invoice 101; no discount given.

Instructions
(a) Prepare a multiple-column cash receipts journal (see Illustration 7-9) and a multiple-column cash payments journal (see Illustration 7-16). (Use page 1 for each journal.)
(b) Record the transaction(s) for May that should be journalized in the cash receipts journal and cash payments journal.

Explain journalizing in cash journals.

(SO 3)

E7-8   Blue Glove Company uses the columnar cash journals illustrated in the textbook. In April, the following selected cash transactions occurred.

1. Made a refund to a customer as an allowance for damaged goods.
2. Received collection from customer within the 3% discount period.
3. Purchased merchandise for cash.
4. Paid a creditor within the 3% discount period.
5. Received collection from customer after the 3% discount period had expired.
6. Paid freight on merchandise purchased.
7. Paid cash for office equipment.
8. Received cash refund from supplier for merchandise returned.
9. Withdrew cash for personal use of owner.
10. Made cash sales.

Instructions
Indicate (a) the journal, and (b) the columns in the journal that should be used in recording each transaction.

E7-9   Jayne Cobb Company has the following selected transactions during March.

Journalize transactions in general journal and explain postings.
(SO 2, 4)

Mar. 2   Purchased equipment costing $9,400 from Adam Company on account.
    5   Received credit of $410 from Baldwin Company for merchandise damaged in shipment to Jayne Cobb.
    7   Issued credit of $400 to Cockrum Company for merchandise the customer returned. The returned merchandise had a cost of $260.

Jayne Cobb Company uses a one-column purchases journal, a sales journal, the columnar cash journals used in the text, and a general journal.

Instructions
(a) Journalize the transactions in the general journal.
(b) ◂▬▬▬ In a brief memo to the president of Jayne Cobb Company, explain the postings to the control and subsidiary accounts from each type of journal.

E7-10   Below are some typical transactions incurred by Ricketts Company.

Indicate journalizing in special journals.
(SO 3)

1. Payment of creditors on account.
2. Return of merchandise sold for credit.
3. Collection on account from customers.
4. Sale of land for cash.
5. Sale of merchandise on account.
6. Sale of merchandise for cash.
7. Received credit for merchandise purchased on credit.
8. Sales discount taken on goods sold.
9. Payment of employee wages.
10. Income summary closed to owner's capital.
11. Depreciation on building.
12. Purchase of office supplies for cash.
13. Purchase of merchandise on account.

Instructions
For each transaction, indicate whether it would normally be recorded in a cash receipts journal, cash payments journal, sales journal, single-column purchases journal, or general journal.

E7-11   The general ledger of Fairman Company contained the following Accounts Payable control account (in T-account form). Also shown is the related subsidiary ledger.

Explain posting to control account and subsidiary ledger.
(SO 2, 4)

GENERAL LEDGER

Accounts Payable

Feb. 15	General journal	1,400	Feb. 1	Balance	26,025
28	?	?	5	General journal	265
			11	General journal	550
			28	Purchases	13,400
			Feb. 28	Balance	9,500

ACCOUNTS PAYABLE LEDGER

Adelai			**Niska**		
	Feb. 28	Bal. 4,600		Feb. 28	Bal. ?

Badger		
	Feb. 28	Bal. 2,300

Instructions
(a) Indicate the missing posting reference and amount in the control account, and the missing ending balance in the subsidiary ledger.
(b) Indicate the amounts in the control account that were dual-posted (i.e., posted to the control account and the subsidiary accounts).

Prepare purchases and general journals.
(SO 2, 3)

E7-12   Selected accounts from the ledgers of Kaylee Frye Company at July 31 showed the following.

GENERAL LEDGER

Equipment					No. 153
Date	Explanation	Ref.	Debit	Credit	Balance
July 1		G1	3,900		3,900

Accounts Payable					No. 201
Date	Explanation	Ref.	Debit	Credit	Balance
July 1		G1		3,900	3,900
15		G1		400	4,300
18		G1	100		4,200
25		G1	200		4,000
31		P1		8,300	12,300

Inventory					No. 120
Date	Explanation	Ref.	Debit	Credit	Balance
July 15		G1	400		400
18		G1		100	300
25		G1		200	100
31		P1	8,300		8,400

ACCOUNTS PAYABLE LEDGER

De Rovin Equipment Co.					
Date	Explanation	Ref.	Debit	Credit	Balance
July 1		G1		3,900	3,900

Staite Co.					
Date	Explanation	Ref.	Debit	Credit	Balance
July 14		P1		1,100	1,100
25		G1	200		900

Jewel Co.					
Date	Explanation	Ref.	Debit	Credit	Balance
July 3		P1		2,400	2,400
20		P1		700	3,100

Sunny Co.					
Date	Explanation	Ref.	Debit	Credit	Balance
July 12		P1		500	500
21		P1		600	1,100

Hodge Corp					
Date	Explanation	Ref.	Debit	Credit	Balance
July 17		P1		1,400	1,400
18		G1	100		1,300
29		P1		1,600	2,900

Bernardo Inc.					
Date	Explanation	Ref.	Debit	Credit	Balance
July 15		G1		400	400

Instructions

From the data prepare:

(a) The single-column purchases journal for July.

(b) The general journal entries for July.

Determine correct posting amount to control account.
(SO 4)

E7-13   Simon Products uses both special journals and a general journal as described in this chapter. Simon also posts customers' accounts in the accounts receivable subsidiary ledger. The postings for the most recent month are included in the subsidiary T accounts below.

Tam			Doctor		
Bal.	340	250	Bal.	150	150
	200			240	

Sean			Maher		
Bal.	–0–	145	Bal.	120	120
	145			190	
				150	

Instructions

Determine the correct amount of the end-of-month posting from the sales journal to the Accounts Receivable control account.

Compute balances in various accounts.
(SO 4)

E7-14   Selected account balances for R. Tam Company at January 1, 2012, are presented below.

Accounts Payable	$14,000
Accounts Receivable	22,000
Cash	17,000
Inventory	13,500

R. Tam's sales journal for January shows a total of $100,000 in the selling price column, and its one-column purchases journal for January shows a total of $72,000.

The column totals in R. Tam's cash receipts journal are: Cash Dr. $61,000; Sales Discounts Dr. $1,100; Accounts Receivable Cr. $45,000; Sales Revenue Cr. $6,000; and Other Accounts Cr. $11,100.

The column totals in R. Tam's cash payments journal for January are: Cash Cr. $55,000; Inventory Cr. $1,000; Accounts Payable Dr. $46,000; and Other Accounts Dr. $10,000. R. Tam's total cost of goods sold for January is $63,600.

Accounts Payable, Accounts Receivable, Cash, Inventory, and Sales Revenue are not involved in the "Other Accounts" column in either the cash receipts or cash payments journal, and are not involved in any general journal entries.

Instructions

Compute the January 31 balance for R. Tam in the following accounts.

(a) Accounts Payable.
(b) Accounts Receivable.
(c) Cash.
(d) Inventory.
(e) Sales Revenue.

Exercises: Set B

Visit the book's companion website, at **www.wiley.com/college/weygandt**, and choose the Student Companion site to access Exercise Set B.

Problems: Set A

P7-1A   River Company's chart of accounts includes the following selected accounts.

101	Cash	401	Sales Revenue
112	Accounts Receivable	414	Sales Discounts
120	Inventory	505	Cost of Goods Sold
301	Owner's Capital		

Journalize transactions in cash receipts journal; post to control account and subsidiary ledger.

(SO 2, 3, 4)

On April 1 the accounts receivable ledger of River Company showed the following balances: Summer $1,550, Glav $1,200, Sheppard Co. $2,900, and Book $1,800. The April transactions involving the receipt of cash were as follows.

Apr.	1	The owner, T. River, invested additional cash in the business $7,200.
	4	Received check for payment of account from Book less 2% cash discount.
	5	Received check for $920 in payment of invoice no. 307 from Sheppard Co.
	8	Made cash sales of merchandise totaling $7,245. The cost of the merchandise sold was $4,347.
	10	Received check for $600 in payment of invoice no. 309 from Summer.
	11	Received cash refund from a supplier for damaged merchandise $740.
	23	Received check for $1,500 in payment of invoice no. 310 from Sheppard Co.
	29	Received check for payment of account from Glav.

Instructions

(a) Journalize the transactions above in a six-column cash receipts journal with columns for Cash Dr., Sales Discounts Dr., Accounts Receivable Cr., Sales Revenue Cr., Other Accounts Cr., and Cost of Goods Sold Dr./Inventory Cr. Foot and crossfoot the journal.

(b) Insert the beginning balances in the Accounts Receivable control and subsidiary accounts, and post the April transactions to these accounts.

(c) Prove the agreement of the control account and subsidiary account balances.

(a) Balancing totals $21,205

(c) Accounts Receivable $1,430

P7-2A   Saffron Company's chart of accounts includes the following selected accounts.

101	Cash	201	Accounts Payable
120	Inventory	306	Owner's Drawings
130	Prepaid Insurance	505	Cost of Goods Sold
157	Equipment		

Journalize transactions in cash payments journal; post to control account and subsidiary ledgers.

(SO 2, 3, 4)

On October 1, the accounts payable ledger of Saffron Company showed the following balances: Glass Company $2,700, Ron Co. $2,500, Hendricks Co. $1,800, and Christina Company $3,700. The October transactions involving the payment of cash were as follows.

Oct. 1   Purchased merchandise, check no. 63, $300.
      3   Purchased equipment, check no. 64, $800.
      5   Paid Glass Company balance due of $2,700, less 2% discount, check no. 65, $2,646.
      10   Purchased merchandise, check no. 66, $2,250.
      15   Paid Hendricks Co. balance due of $1,800, check no. 67.
      16   C. Saffron, the owner, pays his personal insurance premium of $400, check no. 68.
      19   Paid Ron Co. in full for invoice no. 610, $1,600 less 2% cash discount, check no. 69, $1,568.
      29   Paid Christina Company in full for invoice no. 264, $2,500, check no. 70.

Instructions

(a) Balancing totals $12,350

(a) Journalize the transactions above in a four-column cash payments journal with columns for Other Accounts Dr., Accounts Payable Dr., Inventory Cr., and Cash Cr. Foot and crossfoot the journal.

(b) Insert the beginning balances in the Accounts Payable control and subsidiary accounts, and post the October transactions to these accounts.

(c) Accounts Payable $2,100

(c) Prove the agreement of the control account and the subsidiary account balances.

Journalize transactions in multi-column purchases journal and sales journal; post to the general and subsidiary ledgers.

(SO 2, 3, 4)

GLS

P7-3A   The chart of accounts of IT Company includes the following selected accounts.

112	Accounts Receivable	401	Sales Revenue
120	Inventory	412	Sales Returns and Allowances
126	Supplies	505	Cost of Goods Sold
157	Equipment	610	Advertising Expense
201	Accounts Payable		

In July, the following selected transactions were completed. All purchases and sales were on account. The cost of all merchandise sold was 70% of the sales price.

July 1   Purchased merchandise from Roy Company $8,000.
      2   Received freight bill from Moss Shipping on Roy purchase $400.
      3   Made sales to Jen Company $1,300, and to O'Dowd Bros. $1,500.
      5   Purchased merchandise from Moon Company $3,200.
      8   Received credit on merchandise returned to Moon Company $300.
      13   Purchased store supplies from Cress Supply $720.
      15   Purchased merchandise from Roy Company $3,600 and from Anton Company $3,300.
      16   Made sales to Sager Company $3,450 and to O'Dowd Bros. $1,570.
      18   Received bill for advertising from Lynda Advertisements $600.
      21   Sales were made to Jen Company $310 and to Haddad Company $2,800.
      22   Granted allowance to Jen Company for merchandise damaged in shipment $40.
      24   Purchased merchandise from Moon Company $3,000.
      26   Purchased equipment from Cress Supply $900.
      28   Received freight bill from Moss Shipping on Moon purchase of July 24, $380.
      30   Sales were made to Sager Company $5,600.

Instructions

(a) Purchases journal—
   Accounts Payable $24,100
   Sales column total $16,530

(c) Accounts Receivable
   $16,490
   Accounts Payable $23,800

(a) Journalize the transactions above in a purchases journal, a sales journal, and a general journal. The purchases journal should have the following column headings: Date, Account Credited (Debited), Ref., Accounts Payable Cr., Inventory Dr., and Other Accounts Dr.

(b) Post to both the general and subsidiary ledger accounts. (Assume that all accounts have zero beginning balances.)

(c) Prove the agreement of the control and subsidiary accounts.

Journalize transactions in special journals.

(SO 2, 3, 4)

GLS

P7-4A   Selected accounts from the chart of accounts of Ayoade Company are shown below.

101	Cash	126	Supplies
112	Accounts Receivable	157	Equipment
120	Inventory	201	Accounts Payable

401 Sales Revenue
412 Sales Returns and Allowances
414 Sales Discounts

505 Cost of Goods Sold
726 Salaries and Wages Expense

The cost of all merchandise sold was 60% of the sales price. During January, Ayoade completed the following transactions.

Jan. 3   Purchased merchandise on account from Parkinson Co. $10,000.
4   Purchased supplies for cash $80.
4   Sold merchandise on account to Douglas $5,250, invoice no. 371, terms 1/10, n/30.
5   Returned $300 worth of damaged goods purchased on account from Parkinson Co. on January 3.
6   Made cash sales for the week totaling $3,150.
8   Purchased merchandise on account from Denholm Co. $4,500.
9   Sold merchandise on account to Connor Corp. $6,400, invoice no. 372, terms 1/10, n/30.
11   Purchased merchandise on account from Betz Co. $3,700.
13   Paid in full Parkinson Co. on account less a 2% discount.
13   Made cash sales for the week totaling $6,260.
15   Received payment from Connor Corp. for invoice no. 372.
15   Paid semi-monthly salaries of $14,300 to employees.
17   Received payment from Douglas for invoice no. 371.
17   Sold merchandise on account to Bullock Co. $1,200, invoice no. 373, terms 1/10, n/30.
19   Purchased equipment on account from Murphy Corp. $5,500.
20   Cash sales for the week totaled $3,200.
20   Paid in full Denholm Co. on account less a 2% discount.
23   Purchased merchandise on account from Parkinson Co. $7,800.
24   Purchased merchandise on account from Forgetta Corp. $5,100.
27   Made cash sales for the week totaling $4,230.
30   Received payment from Bullock Co. for invoice no. 373.
31   Paid semi-monthly salaries of $13,200 to employees.
31   Sold merchandise on account to Douglas $9,330, invoice no. 374, terms 1/10, n/30.

Ayoade Company uses the following journals.

1. Sales journal.
2. Single-column purchases journal.
3. Cash receipts journal with columns for Cash Dr., Sales Discounts Dr., Accounts Receivable Cr., Sales Revenue Cr., Other Accounts Cr., and Cost of Goods Sold Dr./Inventory Cr.
4. Cash payments journal with columns for Other Accounts Dr., Accounts Payable Dr., Inventory Cr., and Cash Cr.
5. General journal.

Instructions
Using the selected accounts provided:

(a) Record the January transactions in the appropriate journal noted.
(b) Foot and crossfoot all special journals.
(c) Show how postings would be made by placing ledger account numbers and checkmarks as needed in the journals. (Actual posting to ledger accounts is not required.)

(a) Sales journal $22,180
    Purchases journal $31,100
    Cash receipts journal
      balancing total $29,690
    Cash payments journal
      balancing total $41,780

P7-5A   Presented below and on page 348 are the purchases and cash payments journals for Richmond Co. for its first month of operations.

Journalize in sales and cash receipts journals; post; prepare a trial balance; prove control to subsidiary; prepare adjusting entries; prepare an adjusted trial balance.

(SO 2, 3, 4)

PURCHASES JOURNAL			P1
Date	Account Credited	Ref.	Inventory Dr. Accounts Payable Cr.
July 4	N. Fielding		6,800
5	F. Noel		8,100
11	J. Shaggy		5,920
13	C. Tabor		15,300
20	M. Sneezy		7,900
			44,020

CASH PAYMENTS JOURNAL CP1

Date	Account Debited	Ref	Other Accounts Dr.	Accounts Payable Dr.	Inventory Cr.	Cash Cr.
July 4	Supplies		600			600
10	F. Noel			8,100	81	8,019
11	Prepaid Rent		6,000			6,000
15	N. Fielding			6,800		6,800
19	Owner's Drawings		2,500			2,500
21	C. Tabor			15,300	153	15,147
			9,100	30,200	234	39,066

In addition, the following transactions have not been journalized for July. The cost of all merchandise sold was 65% of the sales price.

July 1   The founder, N. Richmond, invests $80,000 in cash.
    6   Sell merchandise on account to Abi Co. $6,200 terms 1/10, n/30.
    7   Make cash sales totaling $6,000.
    8   Sell merchandise on account to S. Beauty $3,600, terms 1/10, n/30.
   10   Sell merchandise on account to W. Pitts $4,900, terms 1/10, n/30.
   13   Receive payment in full from S. Beauty.
   16   Receive payment in full from W. Pitts.
   20   Receive payment in full from Abi Co.
   21   Sell merchandise on account to H. Prince $5,000, terms 1/10, n/30.
   29   Returned damaged goods to N. Fielding and received cash refund of $420.

Instructions
(a) Open the following accounts in the general ledger.

101   Cash
112   Accounts Receivable
120   Inventory
127   Supplies
131   Prepaid Rent
201   Accounts Payable
301   Owner's Capital
306   Owner's Drawings
401   Sales Revenue
414   Sales Discounts
505   Cost of Goods Sold
631   Supplies Expense
729   Rent Expense

(b) Sales journal total $19,700
Cash receipts journal balancing totals $101,120

(e) Totals $119,520
(f) Accounts Receivable $5,000
Accounts Payable $13,820
(h) Totals $119,520

Journalize in special journals; post; prepare a trial balance.
(SO 2, 3, 4)   GLS

(b) Journalize the transactions that have not been journalized in the sales journal, the cash receipts journal (see Illustration 7-9), and the general journal.
(c) Post to the accounts receivable and accounts payable subsidiary ledgers. Follow the sequence of transactions as shown in the problem.
(d) Post the individual entries and totals to the general ledger.
(e) Prepare a trial balance at July 31, 2012.
(f) Determine whether the subsidiary ledgers agree with the control accounts in the general ledger.
(g) The following adjustments at the end of July are necessary.
   (1) A count of supplies indicates that $140 is still on hand.
   (2) Recognize rent expense for July, $500.
   Prepare the necessary entries in the general journal. Post the entries to the general ledger.
(h) Prepare an adjusted trial balance at July 31, 2012.

P7-6A The post-closing trial balance for Bugeja Co. is shown on page 349.

BUGEJA CO.
Post-Closing Trial Balance
December 31, 2012

	Debit	Credit
Cash	$ 41,500	
Accounts Receivable	15,000	
Notes Receivable	45,000	
Inventory	23,000	
Equipment	6,450	
Accumulated Depreciation—Equipment		$ 1,500
Accounts Payable		43,000
Owner's Capital		86,450
	$130,950	$130,950

The subsidiary ledgers contain the following information: (1) accounts receivable—B. Cordelia $2,500, I. Togo $7,500, T. Dudley $5,000; (2) accounts payable—T. Igawa $10,000, D. Miranda $18,000, and K. Inwood $15,000. The cost of all merchandise sold was 60% of the sales price.

The transactions for January 2013 are as follows.

Jan. 3   Sell merchandise to M. Rensing $5,000, terms 2/10, n/30.
   5   Purchase merchandise from E. Vietti $2,000, terms 2/10, n/30.
   7   Receive a check from T. Dudley $3,500.
   11 Pay freight on merchandise purchased $300.
   12 Pay rent of $1,000 for January.
   13 Receive payment in full from M. Rensing.
   14 Post all entries to the subsidiary ledgers. Issued credit of $300 to B. Cordelia for returned merchandise.
   15 Send K. Inwood a check for $14,850 in full payment of account, discount $150.
   17 Purchase merchandise from G. Marley $1,600, terms 2/10, n/30.
   18 Pay sales salaries of $2,800 and office salaries $2,000.
   20 Give D. Miranda a 60-day note for $18,000 in full payment of account payable.
   23 Total cash sales amount to $9,100.
   24 Post all entries to the subsidiary ledgers. Sell merchandise on account to I. Togo $7,400, terms 1/10, n/30.
   27 Send E. Vietti a check for $950.
   29 Receive payment on a note of $40,000 from B. Lemke.
   30 Post all entries to the subsidiary ledgers. Return merchandise of $300 to G. Marley for credit.

Instructions
(a) Open general and subsidiary ledger accounts for the following.

101	Cash	301	Owner's Capital
112	Accounts Receivable	401	Sales Revenue
115	Notes Receivable	412	Sales Returns and Allowances
120	Inventory	414	Sales Discounts
157	Equipment	505	Cost of Goods Sold
158	Accumulated Depreciation—Equipment	726	Salaries and Wages Expense
200	Notes Payable	729	Rent Expense
201	Accounts Payable		

(b) Record the January transactions in a sales journal, a single-column purchases journal, a cash receipts journal (see Illustration 7-9), a cash payments journal (see Illustration 7-16), and a general journal.
(c) Post the appropriate amounts to the general ledger.
(d) Prepare a trial balance at January 31, 2013.
(e) Determine whether the subsidiary ledgers agree with controlling accounts in the general ledger.

(b) Sales journal $12,400
   Purchases journal $3,600
   Cash receipts journal (balancing) $57,600
   Cash payments journal (balancing) $22,050
(d) Totals $139,800
(e) Accounts Receivable $18,600
   Accounts Payable $12,350

Problems: Set B

Journalize transactions in cash receipts journal; post to control account and subsidiary ledger.

(SO 2, 3, 4)

P7-1B   Feig Company's chart of accounts includes the following selected accounts.

101	Cash	401	Sales Revenue
112	Accounts Receivable	414	Sales Discounts
120	Inventory	505	Cost of Goods Sold
301	Owner's Capital		

On June 1, the accounts receivable ledger of Feig Company showed the following balances: Kwapis & Son $3,500, Einhorn Co. $2,800, Randall Bros. $2,400, and Daniels Co. $2,000. The June transactions involving the receipt of cash were as follows.

June 1   The owner, Paul Feig, invested additional cash in the business $12,000.
       3   Received check in full from Daniels Co. less 2% cash discount.
       6   Received check in full from Einhorn Co. less 2% cash discount.
       7   Made cash sales of merchandise totaling $8,700. The cost of the merchandise sold was $5,000.
       9   Received check in full from Kwapis & Son less 2% cash discount.
      11   Received cash refund from a supplier for damaged merchandise $450.
      15   Made cash sales of merchandise totaling $6,500. The cost of the merchandise sold was $4,000.
      20   Received check in full from Randall Bros. $2,400.

Instructions

(a) Balancing totals $38,350

(a) Journalize the transactions above in a six-column cash receipts journal with columns for Cash Dr., Sales Discounts Dr., Accounts Receivable Cr., Sales Revenue Cr., Other Accounts Cr., and Cost of Goods Sold Dr./Inventory Cr. Foot and crossfoot the journal.

(b) Insert the beginning balances in the Accounts Receivable control and subsidiary accounts, and post the June transactions to these accounts.

(c) Accounts Receivable $0

(c) Prove the agreement of the control account and subsidiary account balances.

Journalize transactions in cash payments journal and sales journal; post to the general and subsidiary ledgers.

(SO 2, 3, 4)

P7-2B   Dunder Mifflin Company's chart of accounts includes the following selected accounts.

101	Cash	157	Equipment
120	Inventory	201	Accounts Payable
130	Prepaid Insurance	306	Owner's Drawings

On November 1, the accounts payable ledger of Dunder Mifflin Company showed the following balances: S. Carell $4,000, D. Schrute $2,100, R. Wilson $800, and W. Rainn $1,300. The November transactions involving the payment of cash were as follows.

Nov. 1   Purchased merchandise, check no. 11, $950.
       3   Purchased store equipment, check no. 12, $1,400.
       5   Paid W. Rainn balance due of $1,300, less 1% discount, check no. 13, $1,287.
      11   Purchased merchandise, check no. 14, $1,700.
      15   Paid R. Wilson balance due of $800, less 3% discount, check no. 15, $776.
      16   M. Scott, the owner, withdrew $400 cash for own use, check no. 16.
      19   Paid D. Schrute in full for invoice no. 1245, $2,100 less 2% discount, check no. 17, $2,058.
      25   Paid premium due on one-year insurance policy, check no. 18, $2,400.
      30   Paid S. Carell in full for invoice no. 832, $2,900, check no. 19.

Instructions

(a) Balancing totals $13,950

(a) Journalize the transactions above in a four-column cash payments journal with columns for Other Accounts Dr., Accounts Payable Dr., Inventory Cr., and Cash Cr. Foot and crossfoot the journal.

(b) Insert the beginning balances in the Accounts Payable control and subsidiary accounts, and post the November transactions to these accounts.

(c) Accounts Payable $1,100

(c) Prove the agreement of the control account and the subsidiary account balances.

Journalize transactions in multi-column purchases journal; post to the general and subsidiary ledgers.

(SO 2, 3, 4)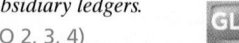

P7-3B   The chart of accounts of Sabre Company includes the following selected accounts.

112	Accounts Receivable	401	Sales Revenue
120	Inventory	412	Sales Returns and Allowances
126	Supplies	505	Cost of Goods Sold
157	Equipment	610	Advertising Expense
201	Accounts Payable		

In May, the following selected transactions were completed. All purchases and sales were on account except as indicated. The cost of all merchandise sold was 60% of the sales price.

May 2   Purchased merchandise from Halpert Company $5,000.
      3   Received freight bill from Fast Freight on Halpert purchase $250.
      5   Sales were made to Krasinski Company $1,300, Coen Bros. $1,800, and Lucy Company $1,000.
      8   Purchased merchandise from Beesly Company $5,400 and Fischer Company $3,000.
     10   Received credit on merchandise returned to Fischer Company $350.
     15   Purchased supplies from Jenna's Supplies $600.
     16   Purchased merchandise from Halpert Company $3,100, and Beesly Company $4,800.
     17   Returned supplies to Jenna's Supplies, receiving credit $70. (*Hint:* Credit Supplies.)
     18   Received freight bills on May 16 purchases from Fast Freight $325.
     20   Returned merchandise to Halpert Company receiving credit $200.
     23   Made sales to Coen Bros. $1,600 and to Lucy Company $2,500.
     25   Received bill for advertising from Ole Advertising $620.
     26   Granted allowance to Lucy Company for merchandise damaged in shipment $140.
     28   Purchased equipment from Jenna's Supplies $400.

Instructions

(a) Journalize the transactions above in a purchases journal, a sales journal, and a general journal. The purchases journal should have the following column headings: Date, Account Credited (Debited), Ref., Accounts Payable Cr., Inventory Dr., and Other Accounts Dr.

(b) Post to both the general and subsidiary ledger accounts. (Assume that all accounts have zero beginning balances.)

(c) Prove the agreement of the control and subsidiary accounts.

P7-4B   Selected accounts from the chart of accounts of Malone Company are shown below.

101	Cash	201	Accounts Payable
112	Accounts Receivable	401	Sales Revenue
120	Inventory	414	Sales Discounts
126	Supplies	505	Cost of Goods Sold
140	Land	610	Advertising Expense
145	Buildings		

The cost of all merchandise sold was 65% of the sales price. During October, Malone Company completed the following transactions.

Oct. 2   Purchased merchandise on account from Ryan Company $12,000.
      4   Sold merchandise on account to Howard Co. $5,600. Invoice no. 204, terms 2/10, n/30.
      5   Purchased supplies for cash $60.
      7   Made cash sales for the week totaling $6,700.
      9   Paid in full the amount owed Ryan Company less a 2% discount.
     10   Purchased merchandise on account from Arduino Corp. $2,600.
     12   Received payment from Howard Co. for invoice no. 204.
     13   Returned $150 worth of damaged goods purchased on account from Arduino Corp. on October 10.
     14   Made cash sales for the week totaling $6,000.
     16   Sold a parcel of land for $20,000 cash, the land's original cost.
     17   Sold merchandise on account to BJ's Warehouse $3,900, invoice no. 205, terms 2/10, n/30.
     18   Purchased merchandise for cash $1,600.
     21   Made cash sales for the week totaling $6,000.
     23   Paid in full the amount owed Arduino Corp. for the goods kept (no discount).
     25   Purchased supplies on account from Paul Martin Co. $190.
     25   Sold merchandise on account to David Corp. $3,800, invoice no. 206, terms 2/10, n/30.
     25   Received payment from BJ's Warehouse for invoice no. 205.
     26   Purchased for cash a small parcel of land and a building on the land to use as a storage facility. The total cost of $26,000 was allocated $16,000 to the land and $10,000 to the building.
     27   Purchased merchandise on account from Novak Co. $6,200.
     28   Made cash sales for the week totaling $5,500.
     30   Purchased merchandise on account from Ryan Company $10,000.
     30   Paid advertising bill for the month from the *Gazette*, $290.
     30   Sold merchandise on account to BJ's Warehouse $3,400, invoice no. 207, terms 2/10, n/30.

(a) Purchases journal—
Accounts Payable, Cr.
$23,495
Sales column total $8,200
(c) Accounts Receivable
$8,060
Accounts Payable $22,875

Journalize transactions in special journals.

(SO 2, 3, 4)

Malone Company uses the following journals.

1. Sales journal.
2. Single-column purchases journal.
3. Cash receipts journal with columns for Cash Dr., Sales Discounts Dr., Accounts Receivable Cr., Sales Revenue Cr., Other Accounts Cr., and Cost of Goods Sold Dr./Inventory Cr.
4. Cash payments journal with columns for Other Accounts Dr., Accounts Payable Dr., Inventory Cr., and Cash Cr.
5. General journal.

(b) Sales journal $16,700
   Purchases journal
   $30,800
   Cash receipts journal—
     Cash, Dr. $53,510
   Cash payments journal,
     Cash, Cr. $42,160

Instructions
Using the selected accounts provided:

(a) Record the October transactions in the appropriate journals.
(b) Foot and crossfoot all special journals.
(c) Show how postings would be made by placing ledger account numbers and check marks as needed in the journals. (Actual posting to ledger accounts is not required.)

Journalize in purchases and cash payments journals; post; prepare a trial balance; prove control to subsidiary; prepare adjusting entries; prepare an adjusted trial balance.

(SO 2, 3, 4)

P7-5B Presented below are the sales and cash receipts journals for Hudson Co. for its first month of operations.

SALES JOURNAL   S1

Date	Account Debited	Ref.	Accounts Receivable Dr. Sales Revenue Cr.	Cost of Goods Sold Dr. Inventory Cr.
Feb. 3	C. Leslie		4,000	2,400
9	S. David		5,000	3,000
12	T. Baker		6,500	3,900
26	W. Oz		5,500	3,300
			21,000	12,600

CASH RECEIPTS JOURNAL   CR1

Date	Owner's Account Credited	Ref.	Cash Dr.	Sales Discounts Dr.	Accounts Receivable Cr.	Sales Revenue Cr.	Other Accounts Cr.	Cost of Goods Sold Dr. Inventory Cr.
Feb. 1	Owner's Capital		23,000				23,000	
2			4,500			4,500		2,700
13	C. Leslie		3,960	40	4,000			
18	Inventory		120				120	
26	S. David		5,000		5,000			
			36,580	40	9,000	4,500	23,120	2,700

In addition, the following transactions have not been journalized for February 2012.

Feb. 2   Purchased merchandise on account from B. Baumgartner for $3,600, terms 2/10, n/30.
     7   Purchased merchandise on account from A. Martin for $23,000, terms 1/10, n/30.
     9   Paid cash of $980 for purchase of supplies.
   12   Paid $3,528 to B. Baumgartner in payment for $3,600 invoice, less 2% discount.
   15   Purchased equipment for $5,500 cash.
   16   Purchased merchandise on account from D. Gale $1,900, terms 2/10, n/30.
   17   Paid $22,770 to A. Martin in payment of $23,000 invoice, less 1% discount.
   20   S. Hudson withdrew cash of $800 from the business for personal use.
   21   Purchased merchandise on account from Kansas Company for $6,000, terms 1/10, n/30.
   28   Paid $1,900 to D. Gale in payment of $1,900 invoice.

Instructions

(a) Open the following accounts in the general ledger.

101	Cash	301	Owner's Capital
112	Accounts Receivable	306	Owner's Drawings
120	Inventory	401	Sales Revenue
126	Supplies	414	Sales Discounts
157	Equipment	505	Cost of Goods Sold
158	Accumulated Depreciation—Equipment	631	Supplies Expense
201	Accounts Payable	711	Depreciation Expense

(b) Journalize the transactions that have not been journalized in a one-column purchases journal and the cash payments journal (see Illustration 7-16).

(c) Post to the accounts receivable and accounts payable subsidiary ledgers. Follow the sequence of transactions as shown in the problem.

(d) Post the individual entries and totals to the general ledger.

(e) Prepare a trial balance at February 28, 2012.

(f) Determine that the subsidiary ledgers agree with the control accounts in the general ledger.

(g) The following adjustments at the end of February are necessary.
   (1) A count of supplies indicates that $200 is still on hand.
   (2) Depreciation on equipment for February is $150.
   Prepare the adjusting entries and then post the adjusting entries to the general ledger.

(h) Prepare an adjusted trial balance at February 28, 2012.

(b) Purchases journal total
   $34,500
   Cash payments journal—
   Cash, Cr. $35,478

(e) Totals $54,500

(f) Accounts Receivable
   $12,000
   Accounts Payable $6,000

(h) Totals $54,650

Problems: Set C

Visit the book's companion website, at **www.wiley.com/college/weygandt**, and choose the Student Companion site to access Problem Set C.

Comprehensive Problem: Chapters 3 to 7

CP7   Packard Company has the following opening account balances in its general and subsidiary ledgers on January 1 and uses the periodic inventory system. All accounts have normal debit and credit balances.

General Ledger

Account Number	Account Title	January 1 Opening Balance
101	Cash	$33,750
112	Accounts Receivable	13,000
115	Notes Receivable	39,000
120	Inventory	20,000
125	Supplies	1,000
130	Prepaid Insurance	2,000
157	Equipment	6,450
158	Accumulated Depreciation—Equip.	1,500
201	Accounts Payable	35,000
301	Owner's Capital	78,700

Accounts Receivable Subsidiary Ledger

Customer	January 1 Opening Balance
R. Draves	$1,500
B. Hachinski	7,500
S. Ingles	4,000

Accounts Payable Subsidiary Ledger

Creditor	January 1 Opening Balance
S. Kosko	$ 9,000
R. Mikush	15,000
D. Moreno	11,000

Jan. 3   Sell merchandise on account to B. Remy $3,100, invoice no. 510, and J. Fine $1,800, invoice no. 511.

   5   Purchase merchandise on account from S. Yost $3,000 and D. Laux $2,700.

7	Receive checks for $4,000 from S. Ingles and $2,000 from B. Hachinski.	
8	Pay freight on merchandise purchased $180.	
9	Send checks to S. Kosko for $9,000 and D. Moreno for $11,000.	
9	Issue credit of $300 to J. Fine for merchandise returned.	
10	Summary cash sales total $15,500.	
11	Sell merchandise on account to R. Draves for $1,900, invoice no. 512, and to S. Ingles $900, invoice no. 513.	

Post all entries to the subsidiary ledgers.

12	Pay rent of $1,000 for January.
13	Receive payment in full from B. Remy and J. Fine.
15	Withdraw $800 cash by I. Packard for personal use.
16	Purchase merchandise on account from D. Moreno for $15,000, from S. Kosko for $13,900, and from S. Yost for $1,500.
17	Pay $400 cash for supplies.
18	Return $200 of merchandise to S. Kosko and receive credit.
20	Summary cash sales total $17,500.
21	Issue $15,000 note to R. Mikush in payment of balance due.
21	Receive payment in full from S. Ingles.

Post all entries to the subsidiary ledgers.

22	Sell merchandise on account to B. Remy for $3,700, invoice no. 514, and to R. Draves for $800, invoice no. 515.
23	Send checks to D. Moreno and S. Kosko in full payment.
25	Sell merchandise on account to B. Hachinski for $3,500, invoice no. 516, and to J. Fine for $6,100, invoice no. 517.
27	Purchase merchandise on account from D. Moreno for $12,500, from D. Laux for $1,200, and from S. Yost for $2,800.
28	Pay $200 cash for office supplies.
31	Summary cash sales total $22,920.
31	Pay sales salaries of $4,300 and office salaries of $3,600.

Instructions

(a) Record the January transactions in the appropriate journal—sales, purchases, cash receipts, cash payments, and general.

(b) Post the journals to the general and subsidiary ledgers. Add and number new accounts in an orderly fashion as needed.

(c) Trial balance totals
$196,820;
Adj. T/B totals $196,975

(c) Prepare a trial balance at January 31, 2012, using a worksheet. Complete the worksheet using the following additional information.

(1) Supplies at January 31 total $700.
(2) Insurance coverage expires on October 31, 2012.
(3) Annual depreciation on the equipment is $1,500.
(4) Interest of $30 has accrued on the note payable.
(5) Inventory at January 31 is $15,000.

(d) Net income $9,685
Total assets $126,315

(d) Prepare a multiple-step income statement and an owner's equity statement for January and a classified balance sheet at the end of January.

(e) Prepare and post the adjusting and closing entries.

(f) Post-closing T/B totals
$127,940

(f) Prepare a post-closing trial balance, and determine whether the subsidiary ledgers agree with the control accounts in the general ledger.

BROADENINGYOURPERSPECTIVE

Financial Reporting and Analysis

Financial Reporting Problem—Mini Practice Set

BYP7-1 **(You may use the working papers that accompany this textbook to work this mini practice set.)**
Bluma Co. uses a perpetual inventory system and both an accounts receivable and an accounts payable subsidiary ledger. Balances related to both the general ledger and the subsidiary ledger for Bluma are indicated in the working papers. Presented on the next page are a series of transactions for Bluma Co. for the month of January. Credit sales terms are 2/10, n/30. The cost of all merchandise sold was 60% of the sales price.

Jan. 3   Sell merchandise on account to B. Richey $3,100, invoice no. 510, and to J. Forbes $1,800, invoice no. 511.
      5   Purchase merchandise from S. Vogel $5,000 and D. Lynch $2,200, terms n/30.
      7   Receive checks from S. LaDew $4,000 and B. Garcia $2,000 after discount period has lapsed.
      8   Pay freight on merchandise purchased $235.
      9   Send checks to S. Hoyt for $9,000 less 2% cash discount, and to D. Omara for $11,000 less 1% cash discount.
      9   Issue credit of $300 to J. Forbes for merchandise returned.
     10   Summary daily cash sales total $15,500.
     11   Sell merchandise on account to R. Dvorak $1,600, invoice no. 512, and to S. LaDew $900, invoice no. 513.
     12   Pay rent of $1,000 for January.
     13   Receive payment in full from B. Richey and J. Forbes less cash discounts.
     15   Withdraw $800 cash by M. Bluma for personal use.
     15   Post all entries to the subsidiary ledgers.
     16   Purchase merchandise from D. Omara $18,000, terms 1/10, n/30; S. Hoyt $14,200, terms 2/10, n/30; and S. Vogel $1,500, terms n/30.
     17   Pay $400 cash for office supplies.
     18   Return $200 of merchandise to S. Hoyt and receive credit.
     20   Summary daily cash sales total $20,100.
     21   Issue $15,000 note, maturing in 90 days, to R. Moses in payment of balance due.
     21   Receive payment in full from S. LaDew less cash discount.
     22   Sell merchandise on account to B. Richey $2,700, invoice no. 514, and to R. Dvorak $1,300, invoice no. 515.
     22   Post all entries to the subsidiary ledgers.
     23   Send checks to D. Omara and S. Hoyt in full payment less cash discounts.
     25   Sell merchandise on account to B. Garcia $3,500, invoice no. 516, and to J. Forbes $6,100, invoice no. 517.
     27   Purchase merchandise from D. Omara $14,500, terms 1/10, n/30; D. Lynch $1,200, terms n/30; and S. Vogel $5,400, terms n/30.
     27   Post all entries to the subsidiary ledgers.
     28   Pay $200 cash for office supplies.
     31   Summary daily cash sales total $21,300.
     31   Pay sales salaries $4,300 and office salaries $3,800.

Instructions

(a) Record the January transactions in a sales journal, a single-column purchases journal, a cash receipts journal as shown on page 327, a cash payments journal as shown on page 332, and a two-column general journal.
(b) Post the journals to the general ledger.
(c) Prepare a trial balance at January 31, 2012, in the trial balance columns of the worksheet. Complete the worksheet using the following additional information.
    (1) Office supplies at January 31 total $900.
    (2) Insurance coverage expires on October 31, 2012.
    (3) Annual depreciation on the equipment is $1,500.
    (4) Interest of $50 has accrued on the note payable.
(d) Prepare a multiple-step income statement and an owner's equity statement for January and a classified balance sheet at the end of January.
(e) Prepare and post adjusting and closing entries.
(f) Prepare a post-closing trial balance, and determine whether the subsidiary ledgers agree with the control accounts in the general ledger.

On the Web

BYP7-2 Intuit provides some of the leading accounting software packages. Information related to its products are found at its website.

Address: http://quickbooks.intuit.com or go to **www.wiley.com/college/weygandt**

Instructions

Look under product and services for the product QuickBooks Premier for Accountants. Be ready to discuss its new features with the class.

Critical Thinking

Decision Making Across the Organization

BYP7-3   Hughey & Payne is a wholesaler of small appliances and parts. Hughey & Payne is operated by two owners, Rich Hughey and Kristen Payne. In addition, the company has one employee, a repair specialist, who is on a fixed salary. Revenues are earned through the sale of appliances to retailers (approximately 75% of total revenues), appliance parts to do-it-yourselfers (10%), and the repair of appliances brought to the store (15%). Appliance sales are made on both a credit and cash basis. Customers are billed on prenumbered sales invoices. Credit terms are always net/30 days. All parts sales and repair work are cash only.

Merchandise is purchased on account from the manufacturers of both the appliances and the parts. Practically all suppliers offer cash discounts for prompt payments, and it is company policy to take all discounts. Most cash payments are made by check. Checks are most frequently issued to suppliers, to trucking companies for freight on merchandise purchases, and to newspapers, radio, and TV stations for advertising. All advertising bills are paid as received. Rich and Kristen each make a monthly drawing in cash for personal living expenses. The salaried repairman is paid twice monthly. Hughey & Payne currently has a manual accounting system.

Instructions

With the class divided into groups, answer the following.

(a) Identify the special journals that Hughey & Payne should have in its manual system. List the column headings appropriate for each of the special journals.

(b) What control and subsidiary accounts should be included in Hughey & Payne's manual system? Why?

Communication Activity

BYP7-4   Barb Doane, a classmate, has a part-time bookkeeping job. She is concerned about the inefficiencies in journalizing and posting transactions. Jim Houser is the owner of the company where Barb works. In response to numerous complaints from Barb and others, Jim hired two additional bookkeepers a month ago. However, the inefficiencies have continued at an even higher rate. The accounting information system for the company has only a general journal and a general ledger. Jim refuses to install a computerized accounting system.

Instructions

Now that Barb is an expert in manual accounting information systems, she decides to send a letter to Jim Houser explaining (1) why the additional personnel did not help and (2) what changes should be made to improve the efficiency of the accounting department. Write the letter that you think Barb should send.

Ethics Case

BYP7-5   Roniger Products Company operates three divisions, each with its own manufacturing plant and marketing/sales force. The corporate headquarters and central accounting office are in Roniger, and the plants are in Freeport, Rockport, and Bayport, all within 50 miles of Roniger. Corporate management treats each division as an independent profit center and encourages competition among them. They each have similar but different product lines. As a competitive incentive, bonuses are awarded each year to the employees of the fastest-growing and most-profitable division.

Jose Molina is the manager of Roniger's centralized computerized accounting operation that enters the sales transactions and maintains the accounts receivable for all three divisions. Jose came up in the accounting ranks from the Bayport division where his wife, several relatives, and many friends still work.

As sales documents are entered into the computer, the originating division is identified by code. Most sales documents (95%) are coded, but some (5%) are not coded or are coded incorrectly. As the manager, Jose has instructed the data-entry personnel to assign the Bayport code to all uncoded and incorrectly coded sales documents. This is done he says, "in order to expedite processing and to keep the computer files current since they are updated daily." All receivables and cash collections for all three divisions are handled by Roniger as one subsidiary accounts receivable ledger.

Instructions

(a) Who are the stakeholders in this situation?

(b) What are the ethical issues in this case?

(c) How might the system be improved to prevent this situation?

"All About You" Activity

BYP7-6 In this chapter, you learned about a basic manual accounting information system. Computerized accounting systems range from the very basic and inexpensive to the very elaborate and expensive. However, even the most sophisticated systems are based on the fundamental structures and relationships that you learned in this chapter.

Instructions
Go to the book companion site for this text, **www.wiley.com/college/weygandt**, and review the demonstration that is provided for the general ledger software package that is used with this text. Prepare a brief explanation of how the general ledger system works—that is, how it is used, and what information it provides.

Answers to Insight and Accounting Across the Organization Questions
p. 318 Curbing Fraudulent Activity with Software Q: Why might this software help reduce fraudulent activity by employees? **A:** By pinpointing who used the accounting system and when they used it, the software can hold employees more accountable for their actions. Companies hope that this will reduce efforts by employees to enter false accounting entries, change the dates of transactions, or create unauthorized expenditures. If employees do engage in these activities, there will be significant evidence of their activities.
p. 321 "I'm John Smith, a.k.a. 13695071642" Q: Why use numbers to identify names in a computerized system? **A:** Computerized systems process numbers faster than letters. Also, letters sometimes cause problems because you may have two people with the same name. Computerized systems avoid this problem by giving different customers, including those with the same names, different account numbers.

Answers to Self-Test Questions
1. d **2.** c **3.** a **4.** c **5.** c ($5,000 + $7,000 + $6,000 + $4,500 + $8,500 − $11,500 − $3,000) **6.** c **7.** d
8. c **9.** a **10.** d **11.** c **12.** d **13.** b **14.** c **15.** c

IFRS A Look at IFRS

As discussed in Chapter 1, IFRS is growing in acceptance around the world. For example, recent statistics indicate 40% of the Global Fortune 500 companies use IFRS. And the chair of the IASB predicts that IFRS adoption will grow from its current level of 115 countries to nearly 150 countries in the near future.

When countries accept IFRS for use as accepted accounting policies, companies need guidance to ensure that their first IFRS financial statements contain high-quality information. Specifically, *IFRS 1* requires that information in a company's first IFRS statements (1) be transparent, (2) provide a suitable starting point, and (3) have a cost that does not exceed the benefits.

Key Points

- The basic concepts related to an accounting information system are the same under GAAP and IFRS.
- The use of subsidiary ledgers and control accounts, as well as the system used for recording transactions, are the same under GAAP and IFRS.
- Many companies will be going through a substantial conversion process to switch from their current reporting standards to IFRS.
- The overriding principle in converting to IFRS is full retrospective application of IFRS. Retrospective application—recasting prior financial statements on the basis of IFRS—provides financial statement users with comparable information.
- As indicated, the objective of the conversion process is to present a set of IFRS statements as if the company always reported under IFRS. To achieve this objective, a company follows these steps.
  1. Identify the timing of its first IFRS statements.
  2. Prepare an opening balance sheet at the date of transition to IFRS.

3. Select accounting principles that comply with IFRS, and apply these principles retrospectively.

4. Make extensive disclosures to explain the transition to IFRS.

- Once a company decides to convert to IFRS, it must decide on the transition date and the reporting date. The transition date is the beginning of the earliest period for which full comparative IFRS information is presented. The reporting date is the closing balance sheet date for the first IFRS financial statements.

- To illustrate, assume that FirstChoice Company plans to provide its first IFRS statements for the year ended December 31, 2014. FirstChoice decides to present comparative information for one year only. Therefore, its date of transition to IFRS is January 1, 2013, and its reporting date is December 31, 2014.

- The timeline for first-time adoption is presented in the following graphic.

The graphic shows the following.

1. The opening IFRS statement of financial position for FirstChoice on January 1, 2013, serves as the starting point (date of transition) for the company's accounting under IFRS.

2. The first full IFRS statements are shown for FirstChoice for December 31, 2014. In other words, a minimum of two years of IFRS statements must be presented before a conversion to IFRS occurs. As a result, FirstChoice must prepare at least one year of comparative financial statements for 2013 using IFRS.

3. FirstChoice presents financial statements in accordance with U.S. GAAP annually to December 31, 2013.

Following this conversion process, FirstChoice provides users of the financial statements with comparable IFRS statements for 2013 and 2014.

- Upon first-time adoption of IFRS, a company must present at least one year of comparative information under IFRS.

Looking to the Future

The basic recording process shown in this textbook is followed by companies around the globe. It is unlikely to change in the future. The definitional structure of assets, liabilities, equity, revenues, and expenses may change over time as the IASB and FASB evaluate their overall conceptual framework for establishing accounting standards. In addition, high-quality international accounting requires both high-quality accounting standards and high-quality auditing. Similar to the convergence of U.S. GAAP and IFRS, there is a movement to improve international auditing standards. The International Auditing and Assurance Standards Board (IAASB) functions as an independent standard-setting body. It works to establish high-quality auditing and assurance and quality-control standards throughout the world. Whether the IAASB adopts internal control provisions similar to those in SOX remains to be seen. You can follow developments in the international audit arena at *http://www.ifac.org/laasb/*.

Self-Test Questions

1. Information in a company's first IFRS statements must:
   (a) have a cost that does not exceed the benefits.
   (b) be transparent.
   (c) provide a suitable starting point.
   (d) All the above.

2. Indicate which of these statements is *false*.
   (a) The use of subsidiary ledgers is the same under IFRS and GAAP.
   (b) GAAP and IFRS use the same accounting principles.
   (c) The use of special journals is the same under IFRS and GAAP.
   (d) At conversion, companies should retrospectively adjust the financial statements presented following IFRS.

3. The transition date is the date:
   (a) when a company no longer reports under its national standards.
   (b) when the company issues its most recent financial statement under IFRS.
   (c) three years prior to the reporting date.
   (d) None of the above.

4. When converting to IFRS, a company must:
   (a) recast previously issued financial statements in accordance with IFRS.
   (b) use U.S. GAAP in the reporting period but subsequently use IFRS.
   (c) prepare at least three years of comparative statements.
   (d) use U.S. GAAP in the transition year, but IFRS in the reporting year.

5. The purpose of presenting comparative information in the transition to IFRS is:
   (a) to ensure that the information is reliable.
   (b) in accordance with the Sarbanes-Oxley Act.
   (c) to provide users of the financial statements with information on U.S. GAAP in one period and IFRS in the other period.
   (d) to provide users of the financial statements with information on IFRS for at least two periods.

IFRS Concepts and Applications

IFRS7-1   How is the date of transition and the date of reporting determined in first-time adoption of IFRS?

IFRS7-2   What are the characteristics of high-quality information in a company's first IFRS financial statements?

IFRS7-3   What are the steps to be completed in preparing the opening IFRS statement of financial position?

IFRS7-4   Becker Ltd. is planning to adopt IFRS and prepare its first IFRS financial statements at December 31, 2013. What is the date of Becker's opening balance sheet assuming one year of comparative information? What periods will be covered in Becker's first IFRS financial statements?

IFRS7-5   Stengel plc is preparing its opening IFRS balance sheet on January 1, 2012. Under its previous GAAP, Stengel used the LIFO inventory method. Under LIFO, its inventory is reported at £250,000; under FIFO, which Stengel will use upon adoption of IFRS, the inventory is valued at £265,000. Explain what Stengel must do.

Answers to IFRS Self-Test Questions
1. d   2. b   3. d   4. a   5. d

The Navigator

✔ **Remember to go back to the Navigator box on the chapter opening page and check off your completed work.**

CHAPTER8

Fraud, Internal Control, and Cash

Study Objectives

After studying this chapter, you should be able to:

[1] Define fraud and internal control.

[2] Identify the principles of internal control activities.

[3] Explain the applications of internal control principles to cash receipts.

[4] Explain the applications of internal control principles to cash disbursements.

[5] Describe the operation of a petty cash fund.

[6] Indicate the control features of a bank account.

[7] Prepare a bank reconciliation.

[8] Explain the reporting of cash.

The Navigator

✔ [The Navigator]

- Scan Study Objectives ○
- Read Feature Story ○
- Read Preview ○
- Read text and answer **Do it!** p. 372 ○ p. 375 ○ p. 380 ○ p. 387 ○
- Work Comprehensive **Do it!** p. 389 ○
- Review Summary of Study Objectives ○
- Answer Self-Test Questions ○
- Complete Assignments ○
- Go to *WileyPLUS* for practice and tutorials ○
- Read A Look at IFRS p. 410 ○

Feature Story

MINDING THE MONEY IN MOOSE JAW

If you're ever looking for a cappuccino in Moose Jaw, Saskatchewan, stop by Stephanie's Gourmet Coffee and More, located on Main Street. Staff there serve, on average, 650 cups of coffee a day, including both regular and specialty coffees, not to mention soups, Italian sandwiches, and a wide assortment of gourmet cheesecakes.

"We've got high school students who come here, and students from the community college," says owner/manager Stephanie Mintenko, who has run the place since opening it in 1995. "We have customers who are retired, and others who are working people and have only 30 minutes for lunch. We have to be pretty quick."

That means that the cashiers have to be efficient. Like most businesses where purchases are low-cost and high-volume, cash control has to be simple.

"We have an electronic cash register, but it's not the fancy new kind where you just punch in the item," explains Ms. Mintenko. "You have to punch in the prices." The machine does keep track of sales in several categories, however. Cashiers punch a button to indicate whether each item is a beverage, a meal, or a charge for the cafe's Internet connections. An internal tape in the machine keeps a record of all transactions; the customer receives a receipt only upon request.

There is only one cash register. "Up to three of us might operate it on any given shift, including myself," says Ms. Mintenko.

She and her staff do two "cashouts" each day—one with the shift change at 5:00 p.m. and one when the shop closes at 10:00 p.m. At each cashout, they count the cash in the register drawer. That amount, minus the cash change carried forward (the float), should match the shift total on the register tape. If there's a discrepancy, they do another count. Then, if necessary, "we go through the whole tape to find the mistake," she explains. "It usually turns out to be someone who punched in $18 instead of $1.80, or something like that."

Ms. Mintenko sends all the cash tapes and float totals to a bookkeeper, who double-checks everything and provides regular reports. "We try to keep the accounting simple, so we can concentrate on making great coffee and food."

Inside CHAPTER 8

As the story about recording cash sales at Stephanie's Gourmet Coffee and More indicates, control of cash is important to ensure that fraud does not occur. Companies also need controls to safeguard other types of assets. For example, Stephanie's undoubtedly has controls to prevent the theft of food and supplies, and controls to prevent the theft of tableware and dishes from its kitchen.

In this chapter, we explain the essential features of an internal control system and how it prevents fraud. We also describe how those controls apply to a specific asset—cash. The applications include some controls with which you may be already familiar, such as the use of a bank.

The content and organization of Chapter 8 are as follows.

Fraud, Internal Control, and Cash

Fraud and Internal Control	Cash Controls	Control Features: Use of a Bank	Reporting Cash
• Fraud • The Sarbanes-Oxley Act • Internal control • Principles of internal control activities • Limitations	• Cash receipts controls • Cash disbursements controls	• Making deposits • Writing checks • Bank statements • Reconciling the bank account • Electronic funds transfer (EFT) system	• Cash equivalents • Restricted cash

✔
The Navigator

Fraud and Internal Control

Study Objective [1]
Define fraud and internal control.

The Feature Story describes many of the internal control procedures used by Stephanie's Gourmet Coffee and More. These procedures are necessary to discourage employees from fraudulent activities.

Fraud

A **fraud** is a dishonest act by an employee that results in personal benefit to the employee at a cost to the employer. Examples of fraud reported in the financial press include:

- A bookkeeper in a small company diverted $750,000 of bill payments to a personal bank account over a three-year period.

- A shipping clerk with 28 years of service shipped $125,000 of merchandise to himself.

- A computer operator embezzled $21 million from Wells Fargo Bank over a two-year period.

- A church treasurer "borrowed" $150,000 of church funds to finance a friend's business dealings.

Why does fraud occur? The three main factors that contribute to fraudulent activity are depicted by the **fraud triangle** in Illustration 8-1.

The most important element of the fraud triangle is **opportunity**. For an employee to commit fraud, the workplace environment must provide opportunities that an employee can take advantage of. Opportunities occur when the workplace lacks sufficient controls to deter and detect fraud. For example, inadequate monitoring of employee actions can create opportunities for theft and can embolden employees because they believe they will not be caught.

A second factor that contributes to fraud is **financial pressure**. Employees sometimes commit fraud because of personal financial problems caused by too much debt. Or they might commit fraud because they want to lead a lifestyle that they cannot afford on their current salary.

The third factor that contributes to fraud is **rationalization**. In order to justify their fraud, employees rationalize their dishonest actions. For example, employees sometimes justify fraud because they believe they are underpaid while the employer is making lots of money. Employees feel justified in stealing because they believe they deserve to be paid more.

Illustration 8-1
Fraud triangle

The Sarbanes-Oxley Act

What can be done to prevent or to detect fraud? After numerous corporate scandals came to light in the early 2000s, Congress addressed this issue by passing the Sarbanes-Oxley Act of 2002 (SOX). Under SOX, all publicly traded U.S. corporations are required to maintain an adequate system of internal control. Corporate executives and boards of directors must ensure that these controls are reliable and effective. In addition, independent outside auditors must attest to the adequacy of the internal control system. Companies that fail to comply are subject to fines, and company officers can be imprisoned. SOX also created the Public Company Accounting Oversight Board (PCAOB), to establish auditing standards and regulate auditor activity.

One poll found that 60% of investors believe that SOX helps safeguard their stock investments. Many say they would be unlikely to invest in a company that fails to follow SOX requirements. Although some corporate executives have criticized the time and expense involved in following the SOX requirements, SOX appears to be working well. For example, the chief accounting officer of Eli Lily noted that SOX triggered a comprehensive review of how the company documents controls. This review uncovered redundancies and pointed out controls that needed to be added. In short, it added up to time and money well spent. And the finance chief at General Electric noted, "We have seen value in SOX. It helps build investors' trust and gives them more confidence."[1]

Internal Control

Internal control consists of all the related methods and measures adopted within an organization to safeguard its assets, enhance the reliability of its accounting records, increase efficiency of operations, and ensure compliance with laws and regulations. Internal control systems have five primary components as listed below.[2]

- **A control environment.** It is the responsibility of top management to make it clear that the organization values integrity and that unethical activity will not be tolerated. This component is often referred to as the "tone at the top."

[1]"Corporate Regulation Must Be Working—There's a Backlash," *Wall Street Journal,* June 16, 2004, p. C1; and Judith Burns, "Is Sarbanes-Oxley Working?" *Wall Street Journal,* June 21, 2004, pp. R8–R9.

[2]The Committee of Sponsoring Organizations of the Treadway Commission, "Internal Control—Integrated Framework," *www.coso.org/publications/executive_summary_integrated_framework.htm* (accessed March 2008).

- **Risk assessment.** Companies must identify and analyze the various factors that create risk for the business and must determine how to manage these risks.
- **Control activities.** To reduce the occurrence of fraud, management must design policies and procedures to address the specific risks faced by the company.
- **Information and communication.** The internal control system must capture and communicate all pertinent information both down and up the organization, as well as communicate information to appropriate external parties.
- **Monitoring.** Internal control systems must be monitored periodically for their adequacy. Significant deficiencies need to be reported to top management and/ or the board of directors.

Principles of Internal Control Activities

Study Objective [2]
Identify the principles of internal control activities.

Each of the five components of an internal control system is important. Here, we will focus on one component, the control activities. The reason? These activities are the backbone of the company's efforts to address the risks it faces, such as fraud. The specific control activities used by a company will vary, depending on management's assessment of the risks faced. This assessment is heavily influenced by the size and nature of the company.

The six principles of control activities are as follows.

- Establishment of responsibility
- Segregation of duties
- Documentation procedures
- Physical controls
- Independent internal verification
- Human resource controls

We explain these principles in the following sections. You should recognize that they apply to most companies and are relevant to both manual and computerized accounting systems.

ESTABLISHMENT OF RESPONSIBILITY

An essential principle of internal control is to assign responsibility to specific employees. **Control is most effective when only one person is responsible for a given task.**

To illustrate, assume that the cash on hand at the end of the day in a Safeway supermarket is $10 short of the cash rung up on the cash register. If only one person has operated the register, the shift manager can quickly determine responsibility for the shortage. If two or more individuals have worked the register, it may be impossible to determine who is responsible for the error. In the Feature Story, the principle of establishing responsibility does not appear to be strictly applied by Stephanie's, since three people operate the cash register on any given shift.

Establishing responsibility often requires limiting access only to authorized personnel, and then identifying those personnel. For example, the automated systems used by many companies have mechanisms such as identifying passcodes that keep track of who made a journal entry, who rang up a sale, or who entered an inventory storeroom at a particular time. Use of identifying passcodes enables the company to establish responsibility by identifying the particular employee who carried out the activity.

It's your shift now. I'm turning in my cash drawer and heading home.

Transfer of cash drawers

ANATOMY OF A FRAUD

Maureen Frugali was a training supervisor for claims processing at Colossal Healthcare. As a standard part of the claims processing training program, Maureen created fictitious claims for use by trainees. These fictitious claims were then sent to the accounts payable department. After the training claims had been processed, she was to notify Accounts Payable of all fictitious claims, so that they would not be paid. However, she did not inform Accounts Payable about every fictitious claim. She created some fictitious claims for entities that she controlled (that is, she would receive the payment), and she let Accounts Payable pay her.

Total take: $11 million

THE MISSING CONTROL

Establishment of responsibility. The healthcare company did not adequately restrict the responsibility for authoring and approving claims transactions. The training supervisor should not have been authorized to create claims in the company's "live" system.

Source: Adapted from Wells, *Fraud Casebook* (2007), pp. 61–70.

SEGREGATION OF DUTIES

Segregation of duties is indispensable in an internal control system. There are two common applications of this principle:

1. Different individuals should be responsible for related activities.

2. The responsibility for record-keeping for an asset should be separate from the physical custody of that asset.

The rationale for segregation of duties is this: **The work of one employee should, without a duplication of effort, provide a reliable basis for evaluating the work of another employee.** For example, the personnel that design and program computerized systems should not be assigned duties related to day-to-day use of the system. Otherwise, they could design the system to benefit them personally and conceal the fraud through day-to-day use.

Segregation of Related Activities.   **Making one individual responsible for related activities increases the potential for errors and irregularities**. For example, companies should assign related *purchasing activities* to different individuals. Related purchasing activities include ordering merchandise, order approval, receiving goods, authorizing payment, and paying for goods or services. Various frauds are possible when one person handles related purchasing activities. For example:

- If a purchasing agent is allowed to order goods without obtaining supervisory approval, the likelihood of the purchasing agent receiving kickbacks from suppliers increases.

- If an employee who orders goods also handles receipt of the goods and invoice, as well as payment authorization, he or she might authorize payment for a fictitious invoice.

These abuses are less likely to occur when companies divide the purchasing tasks.

Similarly, companies should assign related *sales activities* to different individuals. Related selling activities include making a sale, shipping (or delivering) the goods to the customer, billing the customer, and receiving payment. Various frauds are possible when one person handles related sales transactions. For example:

- If a salesperson can make a sale without obtaining supervisory approval, he or she might make sales at unauthorized prices to increase sales commissions.
- A shipping clerk who also has access to accounting records could ship goods to himself.
- A billing clerk who handles billing and receipt could understate the amount billed for sales made to friends and relatives.

These abuses are less likely to occur when companies divide the sales tasks: The salespeople make the sale; the shipping department ships the goods on the basis of the sales order; and the billing department prepares the sales invoice after comparing the sales order with the report of goods shipped.

ANATOMY OF A FRAUD

Lawrence Fairbanks, the assistant vice-chancellor of communications at Aesop University, was allowed to make purchases of under $2,500 for his department without external approval. Unfortunately, he also sometimes bought items for himself, such as expensive antiques and other collectibles. How did he do it? He replaced the vendor invoices he received with fake vendor invoices that he created. The fake invoices had descriptions that were more consistent with the communications department's purchases. He submitted these fake invoices to the accounting department as the basis for their journal entries and to the accounts payable department as the basis for payment.

Total take: $475,000

THE MISSING CONTROL

Segregation of duties. The university had not properly segregated related purchasing activities. Lawrence was ordering items, receiving the items, and receiving the invoice. By receiving the invoice, he had control over the documents that were used to account for the purchase and thus was able to substitute a fake invoice.

Source: Adapted from Wells, *Fraud Casebook* (2007), pp. 3–15.

Segregation of Record-Keeping from Physical Custody. The accountant should have neither physical custody of the asset nor access to it. Likewise, the custodian of the asset should not maintain or have access to the accounting records. **The custodian of the asset is not likely to convert the asset to personal use when one employee maintains the record of the asset, and a different employee has physical custody of the asset.** The separation of accounting responsibility from the custody of assets is especially important for cash and inventories because these assets are very vulnerable to fraud.

Accounting Employee A
Maintains cash balances per books

Segregation of Duties
(Accountability for assets)

Assistant Cashier B
Maintains custody of cash on hand

ANATOMY OF A FRAUD

Angela Bauer was an accounts payable clerk for Aggasiz Construction Company. She prepared and issued checks to vendors and reconciled bank statements. She perpetrated a fraud in this way: She wrote checks for costs that the company had not actually incurred (e.g., fake taxes). A supervisor then approved and signed the checks. Before issuing the check, though, she would "white-out" the payee line on the check and change it to personal accounts that she controlled. She was able to conceal the theft because she also reconciled the bank account. That is, nobody else ever saw that the checks had been altered.

Total take: $570,000

THE MISSING CONTROL

Segregation of duties. Aggasiz Construction Company did not properly segregate record-keeping from physical custody. Angela had physical custody of the checks, which essentially was control of the cash. She also had record-keeping responsibility because she prepared the bank reconciliation.

Source: Adapted from Wells, *Fraud Casebook* (2007), pp. 100–107.

DOCUMENTATION PROCEDURES

Documents provide evidence that transactions and events have occurred. At Stephanie's Gourmet Coffee and More, the cash register tape is the restaurant's documentation for the sale and the amount of cash received. Similarly, a shipping document indicates that the goods have been shipped, and a sales invoice indicates that the company has billed the customer for the goods. By requiring signatures (or initials) on the documents, the company can identify the individual(s) responsible for the transaction or event. Companies should document transactions when the transaction occurs.

Companies should establish procedures for documents. First, whenever possible, companies should use **prenumbered documents, and all documents should be accounted for**. Prenumbering helps to prevent a transaction from being recorded more than once, or conversely, from not being recorded at all. Second, the control system should require that employees **promptly forward source documents for accounting entries to the accounting department**. **This control measure helps to ensure timely recording of the transaction** and contributes directly to the accuracy and reliability of the accounting records.

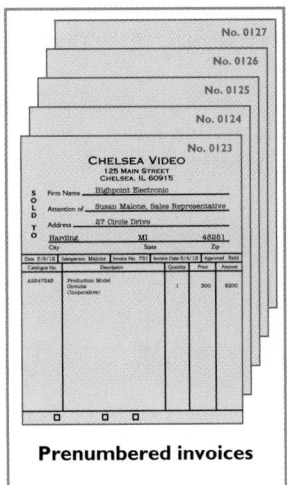

Prenumbered invoices

ANATOMY OF A FRAUD

To support their reimbursement requests for travel costs incurred, employees at Mod Fashions Corporation's design center were required to submit receipts. The receipts could include the detailed bill provided for a meal, or the credit card receipt provided when the credit card payment is made, or a copy of the employee's monthly credit card bill that listed the item. A number of the designers who frequently traveled together came up with a fraud scheme: They submitted claims for the same expenses. For example, if they had a meal together that cost $200, one person submitted the detailed meal bill, another submitted the credit card receipt, and a third submitted a monthly credit card bill showing the meal as a line item. Thus, all three received a $200 reimbursement.

Total take: $75,000

THE MISSING CONTROL

Documentation procedures. Mod Fashions should require the original, detailed receipt. It should not accept photocopies, and it should not accept credit card statements. In addition, documentation procedures could be further improved by requiring the use of a corporate credit card (rather than a personal credit card) for all business expenses.

Source: Adapted from Wells, *Fraud Casebook* (2007), pp. 79–90.

PHYSICAL CONTROLS

Use of physical controls is essential. *Physical controls* relate to the safeguarding of assets and enhance the accuracy and reliability of the accounting records. Illustration 8-2 shows examples of these controls.

Physical Controls

Safes, vaults, and safety deposit boxes for cash and business papers	Locked warehouses and storage cabinets for inventories and records	Computer facilities with pass key access or fingerprint or eyeball scans	Alarms to prevent break-ins	Television monitors and garment sensors to deter theft	Time clocks for recording time worked

Illustration 8-2
Physical controls

ANATOMY OF A FRAUD

At Centerstone Health, a large insurance company, the mailroom each day received insurance applications from prospective customers. Mailroom employees scanned the applications into electronic documents before the applications were processed. Once the applications are scanned they can be accessed online by authorized employees.

Insurance agents at Centerstone Health earn commissions based upon successful applications. The sales agent's name is listed on the application. However, roughly 15% of the applications are from customers who did not work with a sales agent. Two friends—Alex, an employee in record keeping, and Parviz, a sales agent—thought up a way to perpetrate a fraud. Alex identified scanned applications that did not list a sales agent. After business hours, he entered the mailroom and found the hardcopy applications that did not show a sales agent. He wrote in Parviz's name as the sales agent and then rescanned the application for processing. Parviz received the commission, which the friends then split.

Total take: $240,000

THE MISSING CONTROL

Physical controls. Centerstone Health lacked two basic physical controls that could have prevented this fraud. First, the mailroom should have been locked during nonbusiness hours, and access during business hours should have been tightly controlled. Second, the scanned applications supposedly could be accessed only by authorized employees using their passwords. However, the password for each employee was the same as the employee's user ID. Since employee user-ID numbers were available to all other employees, all employees knew all other employees' passwords. Unauthorized employees could access the scanned applications. Thus, Alex could enter the system using another employee's password and access the scanned applications.

Source: Adapted from Wells, *Fraud Casebook* (2007), pp. 316–326.

INDEPENDENT INTERNAL VERIFICATION

Most internal control systems provide for **independent internal verification**. This principle involves the review of data prepared by employees. To obtain maximum benefit from independent internal verification:

1. Companies should verify records periodically or on a surprise basis.

2. An employee who is independent of the personnel responsible for the information should make the verification.

3. Discrepancies and exceptions should be reported to a management level that can take appropriate corrective action.

Independent internal verification is especially useful in comparing recorded accountability with existing assets. The reconciliation of the cash register tape with the cash in the register at Stephanie's Gourmet Coffee and More is an example of this internal control principle. Another common example is the reconciliation of a company's cash balance per books with the cash balance per bank and the verification of the perpetual inventory records through a count of physical inventory. Illustration 8-3 shows the relationship between this principle and the segregation of duties principle.

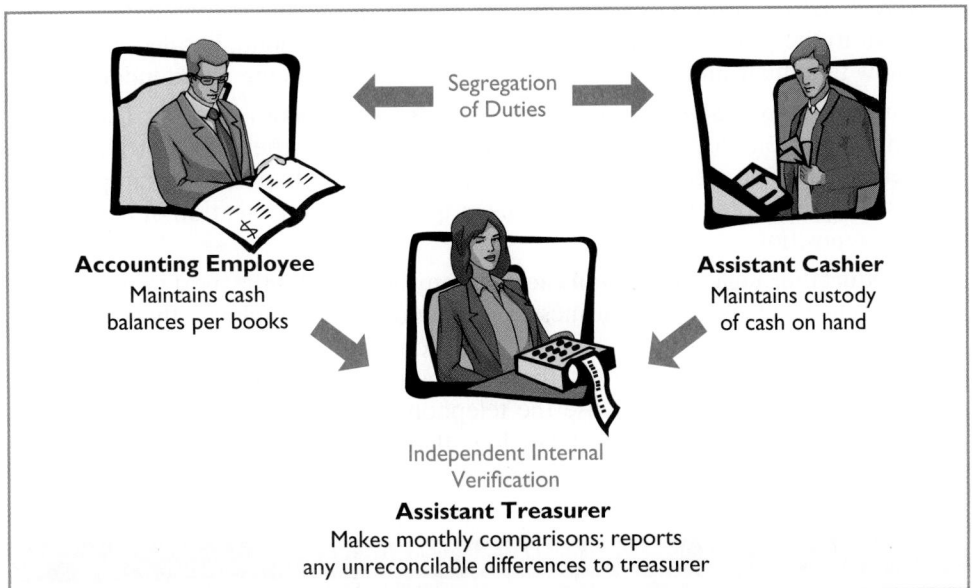

Accounting Employee
Maintains cash
balances per books

Segregation
of Duties

Assistant Cashier
Maintains custody
of cash on hand

Independent Internal
Verification
Assistant Treasurer
Makes monthly comparisons; reports
any unreconcilable differences to treasurer

Illustration 8-3
Comparison of segregation of duties principle with independent internal verification principle

ANATOMY OF A FRAUD

Bobbi Jean Donnelly, the office manager for Mod Fashions Corporations design center, was responsible for preparing the design center budget and reviewing expense reports submitted by design center employees. Her desire to upgrade her wardrobe got the better of her, and she enacted a fraud that involved filing expense-reimbursement requests for her own personal clothing purchases. She was able to conceal the fraud because she was responsible for reviewing all expense reports, including her own. In addition, she sometimes was given ultimate responsibility for signing off on the expense reports when her boss was "too busy." Also, because she controlled the budget, when she submitted her expenses, she coded them to budget items that she knew were running under budget, so that they would not catch anyone's attention.

Total take: $275,000

THE MISSING CONTROL

Independent internal verification. Bobbi Jean's boss should have verified her expense reports. When asked what he thought her expenses for a year were, the boss said about $10,000. At $115,000 per year, her actual expenses were more than ten times what would have been expected. However, because he was "too busy" to verify her expense reports or to review the budget, he never noticed.

Source: Adapted from Wells, *Fraud Casebook* (2007), pp. 79–90.

Large companies often assign independent internal verification to internal auditors. **Internal auditors** are company employees who continuously evaluate the effectiveness of the company's internal control systems. They review the activities of departments and individuals to determine whether prescribed internal controls are being followed. They also recommend improvements when needed. In fact, most fraud is discovered by the company through internal mechanisms such as existing internal controls and internal audits. For example, the alleged fraud at WorldCom, involving billions of dollars, was uncovered by an internal auditor.

HUMAN RESOURCE CONTROLS

Human resource control activities include the following.

1. **Bond employees who handle cash.** Bonding involves obtaining insurance protection against theft by employees. It contributes to the safeguarding of cash in two ways: First, the insurance company carefully screens all individuals before adding them to the policy and may reject risky applicants. Second, bonded employees know that the insurance company will vigorously prosecute all offenders.

2. **Rotate employees' duties and require employees to take vacations.** These measures deter employees from attempting thefts since they will not be able to permanently conceal their improper actions. Many banks, for example, have discovered employee thefts when the employee was on vacation or assigned to a new position.

3. **Conduct thorough background checks.** Many believe that the most important and inexpensive measure any business can take to reduce employee theft and fraud is for the human resources department to conduct thorough background checks. Two tips: (1) Check to see whether job applicants actually graduated from the schools they list. (2) Never use the telephone numbers for previous employers given on the reference sheet; always look them up yourself.

ANATOMY OF A FRAUD

Ellen Lowry was the desk manager and Josephine Rodriquez was the head of housekeeping at the Excelsior Inn, a luxury hotel. The two best friends were so dedicated to their jobs that they never took vacations, and they frequently filled in for other employees. In fact, Ms. Rodriquez, whose job as head of housekeeping did not include cleaning rooms, often cleaned rooms herself, "just to help the staff keep up." These two "dedicated" employees, working as a team, found a way to earn a little more cash. Ellen, the desk manager, provided significant discounts to guests who paid with cash. She kept the cash and did not register the guest in the hotel's computerized system. Instead, she took the room out of circulation "due to routine maintenance." Because the room did not show up as being used, it did not receive a normal housekeeping assignment. Instead, Josephine, the head of housekeeping, cleaned the rooms during the guests' stay.

Total take: $95,000

THE MISSING CONTROL

Human resource controls. Ellen, the desk manager, had been fired by a previous employer after being accused of fraud. If the Excelsior Inn had conducted a thorough background check, it would not have hired her. The hotel fraud was detected when Ellen missed work for a few days due to illness. A system of mandatory vacations and rotating days off would have increased the chances of detecting the fraud before it became so large.

Source: Adapted from Wells, *Fraud Casebook* (2007), pp. 145–155.

ACCOUNTING ACROSS THE ORGANIZATION

SOX Boosts the Role of Human Resources

Under SOX, a company needs to keep track of employees' degrees and certifications to ensure that employees continue to meet the specified requirements of a job. Also, to ensure proper employee supervision and proper separation of duties, companies must develop and monitor an organizational chart. When one corporation went through this exercise, it found that out of 17,000 employees, there were 400 people who did not report to anyone, and they had 35 people who reported to each other. In addition, if an employee complains of an unfair firing and mentions financial issues at the company, HR must refer the case to the company audit committee and possibly to its legal counsel.

? Why would unsupervised employees or employees who report to each other represent potential internal control threats? (See page 410.)

Limitations of Internal Control

Companies generally design their systems of internal control to provide **reasonable assurance** of proper safeguarding of assets and reliability of the accounting records. The concept of reasonable assurance rests on the premise that the costs of establishing control procedures should not exceed their expected benefit.

To illustrate, consider shoplifting losses in retail stores. Stores could eliminate such losses by having a security guard stop and search customers as they leave the store. But store managers have concluded that the negative effects of such a procedure cannot be justified. Instead, stores have attempted to control shoplifting losses by less costly procedures: They post signs saying, "We reserve the right to inspect all packages" and "All shoplifters will be prosecuted." They use hidden TV cameras and store detectives to monitor customer activity, and they install sensor equipment at exits.

The **human element** is an important factor in every system of internal control. A good system can become ineffective as a result of employee fatigue, carelessness, or indifference. For example, a receiving clerk may not bother to count goods received and may just "fudge" the counts. Occasionally, two or more individuals may work together to get around prescribed controls. Such **collusion** can significantly reduce the effectiveness of a system, eliminating the protection offered by segregation of duties. No system of internal control is perfect.

The size of the business also may impose limitations on internal control. A small company, for example, may find it difficult to segregate duties or to provide for independent internal verification.

> **Helpful Hint**
>
> Controls may vary with the risk level of the activity. For example, management may consider cash to be high risk and maintaining inventories in the stockroom as low risk. Thus, management would have stricter controls for cash.

ETHICS INSIGHT

Big Theft at Small Companies

A study by the Association of Certified Fraud Examiners indicates that businesses with fewer than 100 employees are most at risk for employee theft. In fact, 38% of frauds occurred at companies with fewer than 100 employees. The median loss at small companies was $200,000, which was higher than the median fraud at companies with more than 10,000 employees ($147,000). A $200,000 loss can threaten the very existence of a small company.

Source: 2008 Report to the Nation on Occupational Fraud and Abuse, Association of Certified Fraud Examiners, www.acfe.com/documents/2008-rttn.pdf, p. 26.

? Why are small companies more susceptible to employee theft? (See page 410.)

Do it!

Control Activities

Identify which control activity is violated in each of the following situations, and explain how the situation creates an opportunity for a fraud.

1. The person with primary responsibility for reconciling the bank account is also the company's accountant and makes all bank deposits.
2. Wellstone Company's treasurer received an award for distinguished service because he had not taken a vacation in 30 years.
3. In order to save money spent on order slips, and to reduce time spent keeping track of order slips, a local bar/restaurant does not buy prenumbered order slips.

action plan

✔ Familiarize yourself with each of the control activities summarized on page xxx.

✔ Understand the nature of the frauds that each control activity is intended to address.

Solution

1. Violates the control activity of segregation of duties. Record-keeping should be separate from physical custody. As a consequence, the employee could embezzle cash and make journal entries to hide the theft.
2. Violates the control activity of human resource controls. Key employees must take vacations. Otherwise, the treasurer, who manages the company's cash, might embezzle cash and use his position to conceal the theft.
3. Violates the control activity of documentation procedures. If pre-numbered documents are not used, then it is virtually impossible to account for the documents. As a consequence, an employee could write up a dinner sale, receive the cash from the customer, and then throw away the order slip and keep the cash.

Related exercise material: **BE8-1, BE8-2, BE8-3, E8-1,** and **Do it! 8-1.**

The Navigator

Cash Controls

Cash is the one asset that is readily convertible into any other type of asset. It also is easily concealed and transported, and is highly desired. Because of these characteristics, **cash is the asset most susceptible to fraudulent activities**. In addition, because of the large volume of cash transactions, numerous errors may occur in executing and recording them. To safeguard cash and to ensure the accuracy of the accounting records for cash, effective internal control over cash is critical.

Cash Receipts Controls

Study Objective [3]
Explain the applications of internal control principles to cash receipts.

Illustration 8-4 shows how the internal control principles explained earlier apply to cash receipts transactions. As you might expect, companies vary considerably in how they apply these principles. To illustrate internal control over cash receipts, we will examine control activities for a retail store with both over-the-counter and mail receipts.

OVER-THE-COUNTER RECEIPTS

In retail businesses, control of over-the-counter receipts centers on cash registers that are visible to customers. A cash sale is rung up on a cash register, with the amount clearly visible to the customer. This activity prevents the cashier from ringing up a lower amount and pocketing the difference. The customer receives an itemized cash register receipt slip and is expected to count the change received. The

Cash Receipts Controls

Establishment of Responsibility

Only designated personnel are authorized to handle cash receipts (cashiers)

Segregation of Duties

Different individuals receive cash, record cash receipts, and hold the cash

Documentation Procedures

Use remittance advice (mail receipts), cash register tapes, and deposit slips

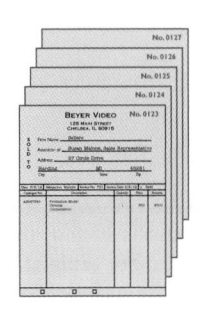

Physical Controls

Store cash in safes and bank vaults; limit access to storage areas; use cash registers

Independent Internal Verification

Supervisors count cash receipts daily; treasurer compares total receipts to bank deposits daily

Human Resource Controls

Bond personnel who handle cash; require employees to take vacations; conduct background checks

Illustration 8-4
Application of internal control principles to cash receipts

cash register's tape is locked in the register until a supervisor removes it. This tape accumulates the daily transactions and totals.

At the end of the clerk's shift, the clerk counts the cash and sends the cash and the count to the cashier. The cashier counts the cash, prepares a deposit slip, and deposits the cash at the bank. The cashier also sends a duplicate of the deposit slip to the accounting department to indicate cash received. The supervisor removes the cash register tape and sends it to the accounting department as the basis for a journal entry to record the cash received. Illustration 8-5 (page 374) summarizes this process.

This system for handling cash receipts uses an important internal control principle—segregation of record-keeping from physical custody. The supervisor has access to the cash register tape, but **not** to the cash. The clerk and the cashier have access to the cash, but **not** to the register tape. In addition, the cash register tape provides documentation and enables independent internal verification. Use of these three principles of internal control (segregation of record-keeping from physical custody, documentation, and independent internal verification) provides an effective system of internal control. Any attempt at fraudulent activity should be detected unless there is collusion among the employees.

In some instances, the amount deposited at the bank will not agree with the cash recorded in the accounting records based on the cash register tape. These differences often result because the clerk hands incorrect change back to the retail customer. In this case, the difference between the actual cash and the amount reported on the cash register tape is reported in a Cash Over and Short account. For example, suppose that the cash register tape indicated sales of $6,956.20 but the amount of cash was only $6,946.10. A cash shortfall of $10.10 exists. To account for this cash shortfall and related cash, the company makes the following entry.

Illustration 8-5
Control of over-the-counter
receipts

Helpful Hint

Flowcharts such as this one
enhance the understanding
of the flow of documents,
the processing steps, and
the internal control
procedures.

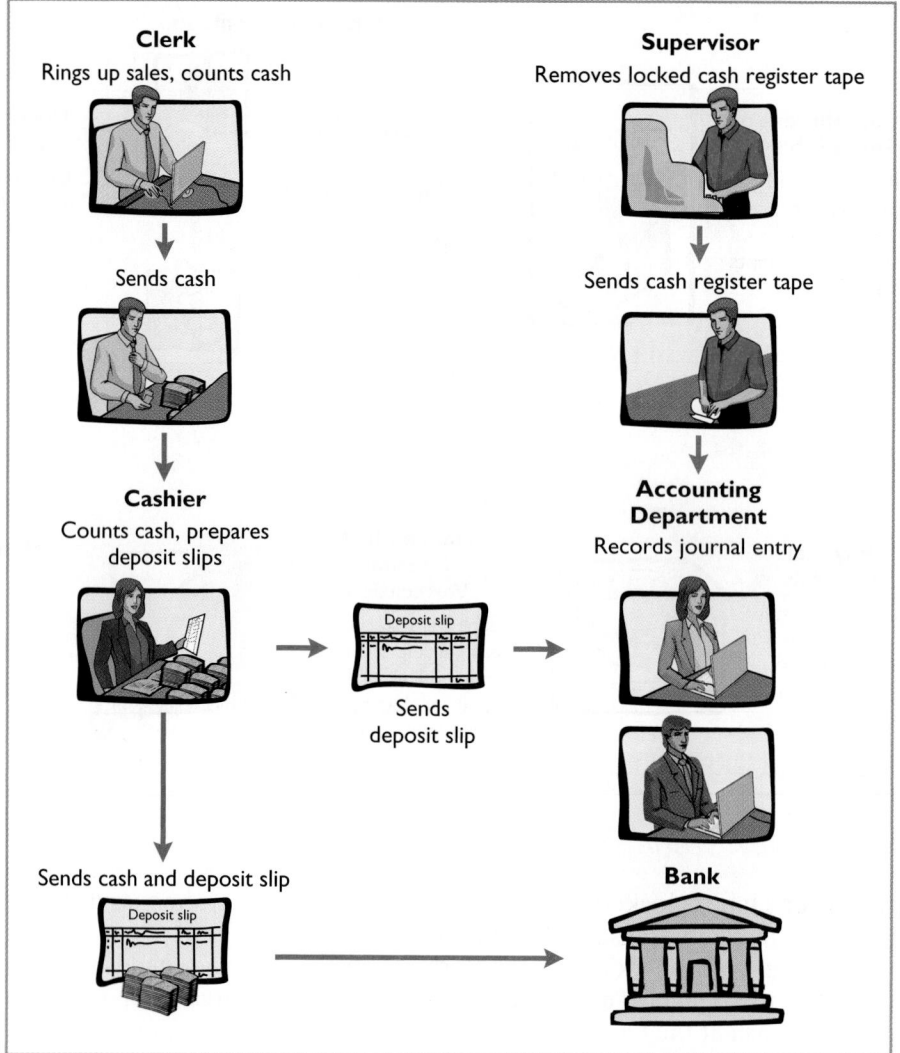

Clerk
Rings up sales, counts cash

Sends cash

Cashier
Counts cash, prepares
deposit slips

Sends
deposit slip

Sends cash and deposit slip

Supervisor
Removes locked cash register tape

Sends cash register tape

**Accounting
Department**
Records journal entry

Bank

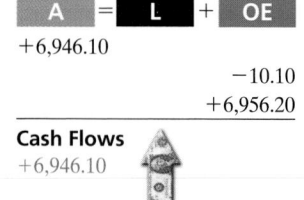

A	=	L	+	OE

+6,946.10

−10.10

+6,956.20

Cash Flows
+6,946.10

Cash	6,946.10	
Cash Over and Short	10.10	
Sales Revenue		6,956.20
(To record cash shortfall)		

Cash Over and Short is an income statement item. It is reported as miscellaneous expense when there is a cash shortfall, and as miscellaneous revenue when there is an overage. Clearly, the amount should be small. Any material amounts in this account should be investigated.

MAIL RECEIPTS

All mail receipts should be opened in the presence of at least two mail clerks. These receipts are generally in the form of checks. A mail clerk should endorse each check "For Deposit Only." This restrictive endorsement reduces the likelihood that someone could divert the check to personal use. Banks will not give an individual cash when presented with a check that has this type of endorsement.

The mail-receipt clerks prepare, in triplicate, a list of the checks received each day. This list shows the name of the check issuer, the purpose of the payment, and the amount of the check. Each mail clerk signs the list to establish responsibility for the data. The original copy of the list, along with the checks, is then sent to the cashier's department. A copy of the list is sent to the accounting department for recording in the accounting records. The clerks also keep a copy.

This process provides excellent internal control for the company. By employing two clerks, the chance of fraud is reduced; each clerk knows he or she is being observed by the other clerk(s). To engage in fraud, they would have to collude. The customers who submit payments also provide control, because they will contact the company with a complaint if they are not properly credited for payment. Because the cashier has access to cash but not the records, and the accounting department has access to records but not cash, neither can engage in undetected fraud.

Do it!

L. R. Cortez is concerned about the control over cash receipts in his fast-food restaurant, Big Cheese. The restaurant has two cash registers. At no time do more than two employees take customer orders and ring up sales. Work shifts for employees range from 4 to 8 hours. Cortez asks your help in installing a good system of internal control over cash receipts.

Solution

Cortez should assign a cash register to each employee at the start of each work shift, with register totals set at zero. Each employee should be instructed to use only the assigned register and to ring up all sales. Each customer should be given a receipt. At the end of the shift, the employee should do a cash count. A separate employee should compare the cash count with the register tape, to be sure they agree. In addition, Cortez should install an automated system that would enable the company to compare orders rung up on the register to orders processed by the kitchen.

Related exercise material: BE8-5, E8-2, and **Do it!** 8-2.

Control over Cash Receipts

action plan

✔ Differentiate among the internal control principles of (1) establishing responsibility, (2) using physical controls, and (3) independent internal verification.

✔ Design an effective system of internal control over cash receipts.

✔
The Navigator

Cash Disbursements Controls

Companies disburse cash for a variety of reasons, such as to pay expenses and liabilities or to purchase assets. **Generally, internal control over cash disbursements is more effective when companies pay by check, rather than by cash.** One exception is **for incidental amounts that are paid out of petty cash.**[3]

Companies generally issue checks only after following specified control procedures. Illustration 8-6 (page 376) shows how principles of internal control apply to cash disbursements.

VOUCHER SYSTEM CONTROLS

Most medium and large companies use vouchers as part of their internal control over cash disbursements. A **voucher system** is a network of approvals by authorized individuals, acting independently, to ensure that all disbursements by check are proper.

Study Objective [4]
Explain the applications of internal control principles to cash disbursements.

---

[3]We explain the operation of a petty cash fund on pages 377–380.

Cash Disbursements Controls

Establishment of Responsibility

Only designated personnel are authorized to sign checks (treasurer) and approve vendors

Physical Controls

Store blank checks in safes, with limited access; print check amounts by machine in indelible ink

Segregation of Duties

Different individuals approve and make payments; check signers do not record disbursements

Independent Internal Verification

Compare checks to invoices; reconcile bank statement monthly

Documentation Procedures

Use prenumbered checks and account for them in sequence; each check must have an approved invoice; require employees to use corporate credit cards for reimbursable expenses; stamp invoices "paid"

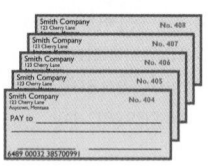

Human Resource Controls

Bond personnel who handle cash; require employees to take vacations; conduct background checks

Illustration 8-6
Application of internal control principles to cash disbursements

The system begins with the authorization to incur a cost or expense. It ends with the issuance of a check for the liability incurred. A **voucher** is an authorization form prepared for each expenditure. Companies require vouchers for all types of cash disbursements except those from petty cash.

The starting point in preparing a voucher is to fill in the appropriate information about the liability on the face of the voucher. The vendor's invoice provides most of the needed information. Then, an employee in accounts payable records the voucher (in a journal called a **voucher register**) and files it according to the date on which it is to be paid. The company issues and sends a check on that date, and stamps the voucher "paid." The paid voucher is sent to the accounting department for recording (in a journal called the **check register**). A voucher system involves two journal entries, one to record the liability when the voucher is issued and a second to pay the liability that relates to the voucher.

The use of a voucher system improves internal control over cash disbursements. First, the authorization process inherent in a voucher system establishes responsibility. Each individual has responsibility to review the underlying documentation to ensure that it is correct. In addition, the voucher system keeps track of the documents that back up each transaction. By keeping these documents in one place, a supervisor can independently verify the authenticity of each transaction. Consider, for example, the case of Aesop University presented on page 366. Aesop did not use a voucher system for transactions under $2,500. As a consequence, there was no independent verification of the documents, which enabled the employee to submit fake invoices to hide his unauthorized purchases.

PETTY CASH FUND CONTROLS

As you learned earlier in the chapter, better internal control over cash disbursements is possible when companies make payments by check. However, using checks to pay small amounts is both impractical and a nuisance. For instance, a company would not want to write checks to pay for postage due, working lunches, or taxi fares. A common way of handling such payments, while maintaining satisfactory control, is to use a petty cash fund to pay relatively small amounts. The operation of a petty cash fund, often called an **imprest system**, involves (1) establishing the fund, (2) making payments from the fund, and (3) replenishing the fund.[4]

Study Objective [5]
Describe the operation of a petty cash fund.

Establishing the Petty Cash Fund.   Two essential steps in establishing a petty cash fund are: (1) appointing a petty cash custodian who will be responsible for the fund, and (2) determining the size of the fund. Ordinarily, a company expects the amount in the fund to cover anticipated disbursements for a three- to four-week period.

To establish the fund, a company issues a check payable to the petty cash custodian for the stipulated amount. For example, if Laird Company decides to establish a $100 fund on March 1, the general journal entry is:

Mar. 1	Petty Cash	100	
	Cash		100
	(To establish a petty cash fund)		

A = L + OE
+100
−100

Cash Flows
no effect

The fund custodian cashes the check and places the proceeds in a locked petty cash box or drawer. Most petty cash funds are established on a fixed-amount basis. The company will make no additional entries to the Petty Cash account unless management changes the stipulated amount of the fund. For example, if Laird Company decides on July 1 to increase the size of the fund to $250, it would debit Petty Cash $150 and credit Cash $150.

Ethics Note
Petty cash funds are authorized and legitimate. In contrast, "slush" funds are unauthorized and hidden (under the table).

Making Payments from the Petty Cash Fund.   The petty cash fund custodian has the authority to make payments from the fund that conform to prescribed management policies. Usually, management limits the size of expenditures that come from petty cash. Likewise, it may not permit use of the fund for certain types of transactions (such as making short-term loans to employees).

Each payment from the fund must be documented on a prenumbered petty cash receipt (or petty cash voucher), as shown in Illustration 8-7 (page 378). The signatures of both the fund custodian and the person receiving payment are required on the receipt. If other supporting documents such as a freight bill or invoice are available, they should be attached to the petty cash receipt.

Helpful Hint

The petty cash receipt satisfies two internal control procedures: (1) establishing responsibility (signature of custodian), and (2) documentation procedures.

---
[4]The term "imprest" means an advance of money for a designated purpose.

Illustration 8-7
Petty cash receipt

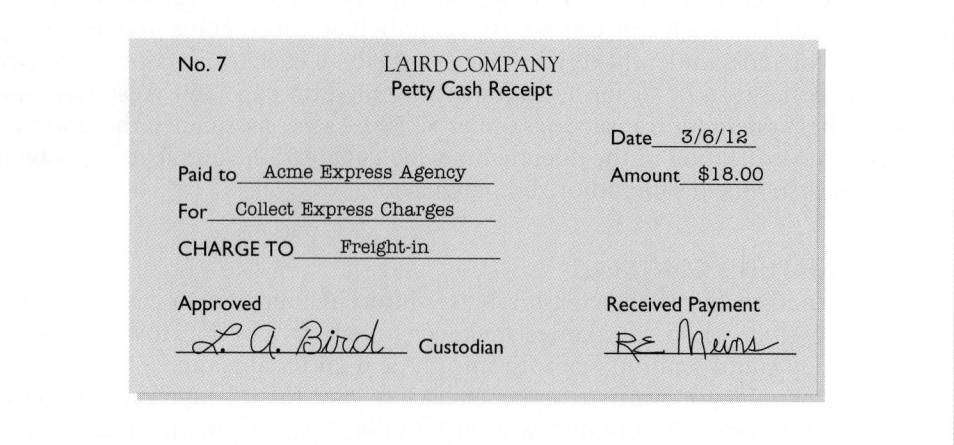

Ethics Note

Internal control over a petty cash fund is strengthened by: (1) having a supervisor make surprise counts of the fund to confirm whether the paid petty cash receipts and fund cash equal the imprest amount, and (2) canceling or mutilating the paid petty cash receipts so they cannot be resubmitted for reimbursement.

The fund custodian keeps the receipts in the petty cash box until the fund is replenished. The sum of the petty cash receipts and the money in the fund should equal the established total at all times. Management can (and should) make surprise counts at any time to determine whether the fund is being maintained correctly.

The company does not make an accounting entry to record a payment when it is made from petty cash. It is considered both inexpedient and unnecessary to do so. Instead, the company recognizes the accounting effects of each payment when it replenishes the fund.

Replenishing the Petty Cash Fund. When the money in the petty cash fund reaches a minimum level, the company replenishes the fund. The petty cash custodian initiates a request for reimbursement. The individual prepares a schedule (or summary) of the payments that have been made and sends the schedule, supported by petty cash receipts and other documentation, to the treasurer's office. The treasurer's office examines the receipts and supporting documents to verify that proper payments from the fund were made. The treasurer then approves the request and issues a check to restore the fund to its established amount. At the same time, all supporting documentation is stamped "paid" so that it cannot be submitted again for payment.

To illustrate, assume that on March 15 Laird's petty cash custodian requests a check for $87. The fund contains $13 cash and petty cash receipts for postage $44, freight-out $38, and miscellaneous expenses $5. The general journal entry to record the check is:

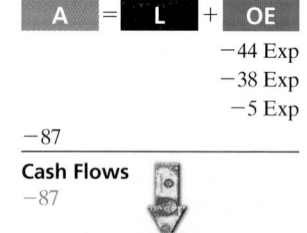

A	=	L	+	OE
				−44 Exp
				−38 Exp
				−5 Exp
−87				

Cash Flows
−87

Mar. 15	Postage Expense		44	
	Freight-out		38	
	Miscellaneous Expense		5	
	Cash			87
	(To replenish petty cash fund)			

Note that the reimbursement entry does not affect the Petty Cash account. Replenishment changes the composition of the fund by replacing the petty cash receipts with cash. It does not change the balance in the fund.

Occasionally, in replenishing a petty cash fund, the company may need to recognize a cash shortage or overage. This results when the total of the cash plus receipts in the petty cash box does not equal the established amount of the petty cash fund. To illustrate, assume that Laird's petty cash custodian has only $12 in cash in the fund plus the receipts as listed. The request for reimbursement would therefore be for $88, and Laird would make the following entry.

Mar. 15	Postage Expense	44	
	Freight-out	38	
	Miscellaneous Expense	5	
	Cash Over and Short	1	
	Cash		88
	(To replenish petty cash fund)		

A = L + OE
−44 Exp
−38 Exp
−5 Exp
−1 Exp
−88
Cash Flows
−88

Conversely, if the custodian has $14 in cash, the reimbursement request would be for $86, and the company would credit Cash Over and Short for $1 (overage). A company reports a debit balance in Cash Over and Short in the income statement as miscellaneous expense. It reports a credit balance in the account as miscellaneous revenue. The company closes Cash Over and Short to Income Summary at the end of the year.

Companies should replenish a petty cash fund at the end of the accounting period, regardless of the cash in the fund. Replenishment at this time is necessary in order to recognize the effects of the petty cash payments on the financial statements.

Helpful Hint

Cash over and short situations result from mathematical errors or from failure to keep accurate records.

*E*THICS *I*NSIGHT

How Employees Steal

A recent study by the Association of Certified Fraud Examiners found that two-thirds of all employee thefts involved a fraudulent disbursement by an employee. The most common form (28.3% of cases) was fraudulent billing schemes. In these, the employee causes the company to issue a payment to the employee by submitting a bill for nonexistent goods or services, purchases of personal goods by the employee, or inflated invoices. The following graph shows various types of fraudulent disbursements and the median loss from each.

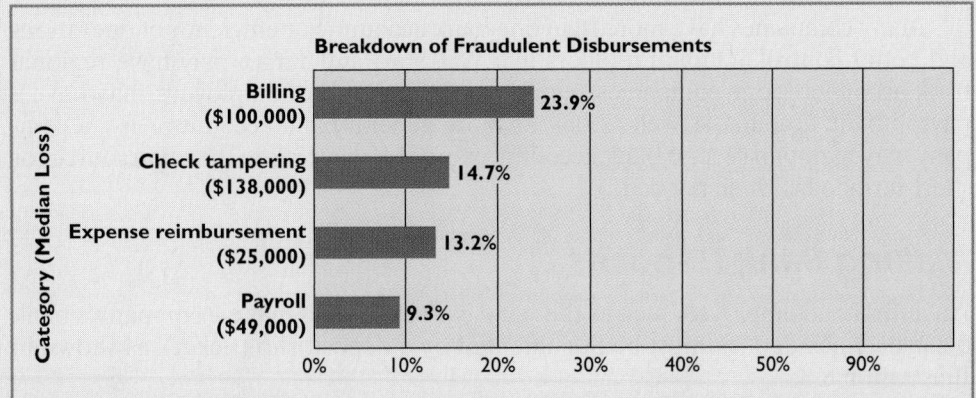

Breakdown of Fraudulent Disbursements

Category (Median Loss)

- Billing ($100,000): 23.9%
- Check tampering ($138,000): 14.7%
- Expense reimbursement ($25,000): 13.2%
- Payroll ($49,000): 9.3%

Source: 2008 Report to the Nation on Occupational Fraud and Abuse, Association of Certified Fraud Examiners, www.acfe.com/documents/2008_rttn.pdf, p.13.

? How can companies reduce the likelihood of fraudulent disbursements? (See page 410.)

Do it!

Petty Cash Fund

action plan

✔ To establish the fund, set up a separate general ledger account.

✔ Determine how much cash is needed to replenish the fund: subtract the cash remaining from the petty cash fund balance.

✔ Total the petty cash receipts. Determine any cash over or short—the difference between the cash needed to replenish the fund and the total of the petty cash receipts.

✔ Record the expenses incurred according to the petty cash receipts when replenishing the fund.

Bateer Company established a $50 petty cash fund on July 1. On July 30, the fund had $12 cash remaining and petty cash receipts for postage $14, office supplies $10, and delivery expense $15. Prepare journal entries to establish the fund on July 1 and to replenish the fund on July 30.

Solution

July 1	Petty Cash		50	
	Cash			50
	(To establish petty cash fund)			
30	Postage Expense		14	
	Supplies		10	
	Delivery Expense		15	
	Cash Over and Short			1
	Cash ($50 – $12)			38
	(To replenish petty cash)			

Related exercise material: BE8-9, E8-7, E8-8, and **Do it!** 8-3.

The Navigator

Control Features: Use of a Bank

Study Objective [6]

Indicate the control features of a bank account.

The use of a bank contributes significantly to good internal control over cash. A company can safeguard its cash by using a bank as a depository and as a clearing house for checks received and written. Use of a bank minimizes the amount of currency that a company must keep on hand. Also, use of a bank facilitates the control of cash because it creates a double record of all bank transactions—one by the company and the other by the bank. The asset account Cash maintained by the company should have the same balance as the bank's liability account for that company. A **bank reconciliation** compares the bank's balance with the company's balance and explains any differences to make them agree.

Many companies have more than one bank account. For efficiency of operations and better control, national retailers like Wal-Mart and Target may have regional bank accounts. Large companies, with tens of thousands of employees, may have a payroll bank account, as well as one or more general bank accounts. Also, a company may maintain several bank accounts in order to have more than one source for short-term loans when needed.

Making Bank Deposits

An authorized employee, such as the head cashier, should make a company's bank deposits. Each deposit must be documented by a deposit slip (ticket), as shown in Illustration 8-8.

Deposit slips are prepared in duplicate. The bank retains the original; the depositor keeps the duplicate, machine-stamped by the bank to establish its authenticity.

Writing Checks

Most of us write checks, without thinking very much about them. A **check** is a written order signed by the depositor directing the bank to pay a specified sum of money to

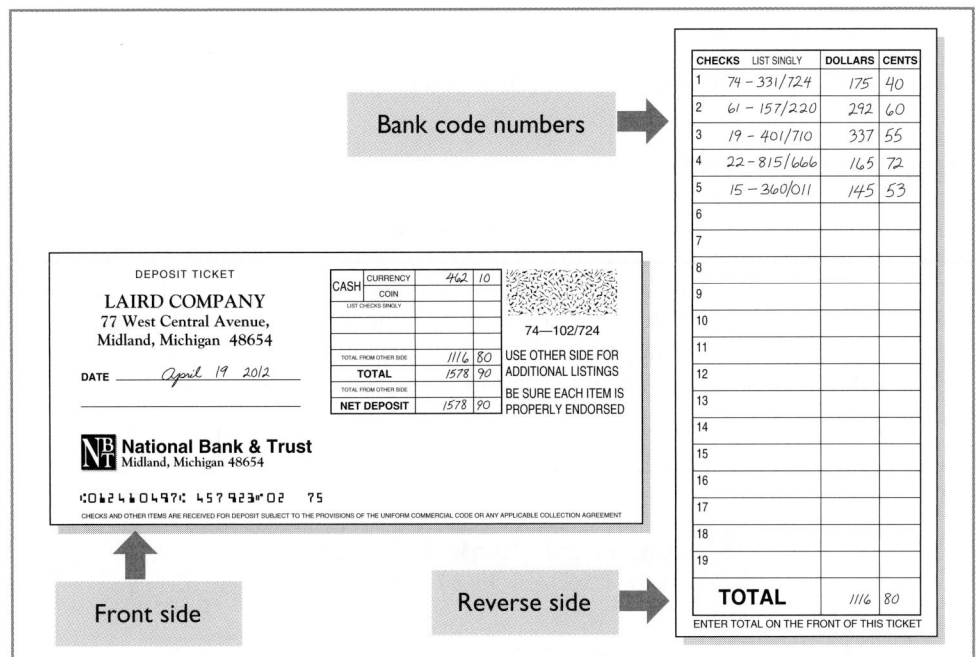

Illustration 8-8
Deposit slip

a designated recipient. There are three parties to a check: (1) the **maker** (or drawer) who issues the check, (2) the **bank** (or payer) on which the check is drawn, and (3) the **payee** to whom the check is payable. A check is a **negotiable instrument** that one party can transfer to another party by endorsement. Each check should be accompanied by an explanation of its purpose. In many companies, a remittance advice attached to the check, as shown in Illustration 8-9 explains the check's purpose.

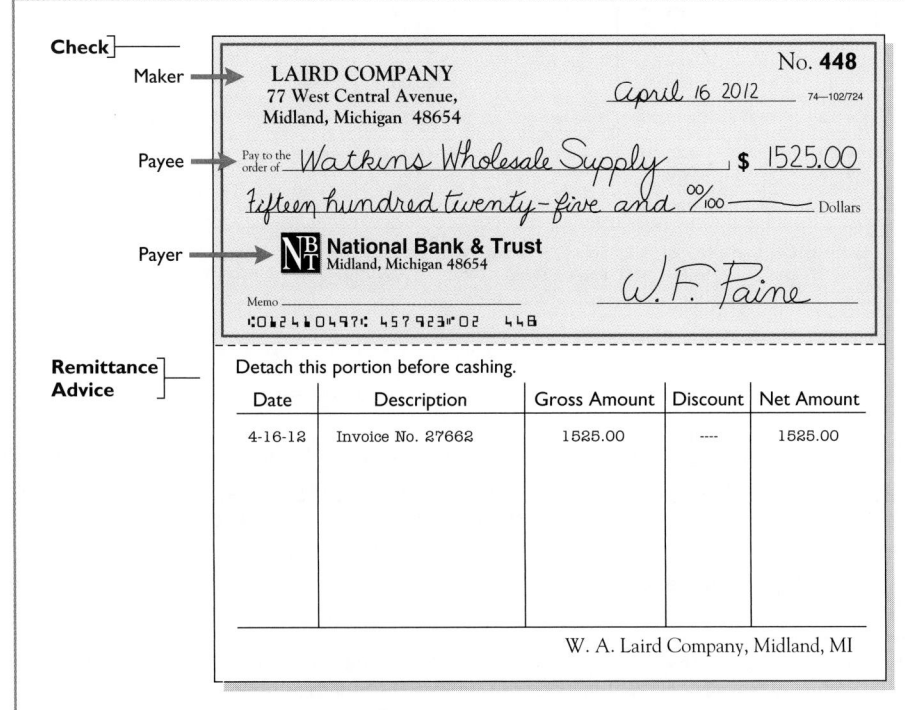

Illustration 8-9
Check with remittance advice

It is important to know the balance in the checking account at all times. To keep the balance current, the depositor should enter each deposit and check on running-balance memo forms provided by the bank or on the check stubs in the checkbook.

Bank Statements

Helpful Hint

Essentially, the bank statement is a copy of the bank's records sent to the customer for periodic review.

Illustration 8-10
Bank statement

If you have a personal checking account, you are probably familiar with bank statements. A **bank statement** shows the depositor's bank transactions and balances.[5] Each month, a depositor receives a statement from the bank. Illustration 8-10 presents a typical bank statement. It shows: (1) checks paid and other debits that reduce the balance in the depositor's account, (2) deposits and other credits that increase the balance in the account, and (3) the account balance after each day's transactions.

Helpful Hint

The bank *credits* to the customer's account every deposit it receives. The reverse occurs when the bank "pays" a check issued by a company on its checking account balance: Payment reduces the bank's liability. Thus the bank *debits* check payments to the customer's account with the bank.

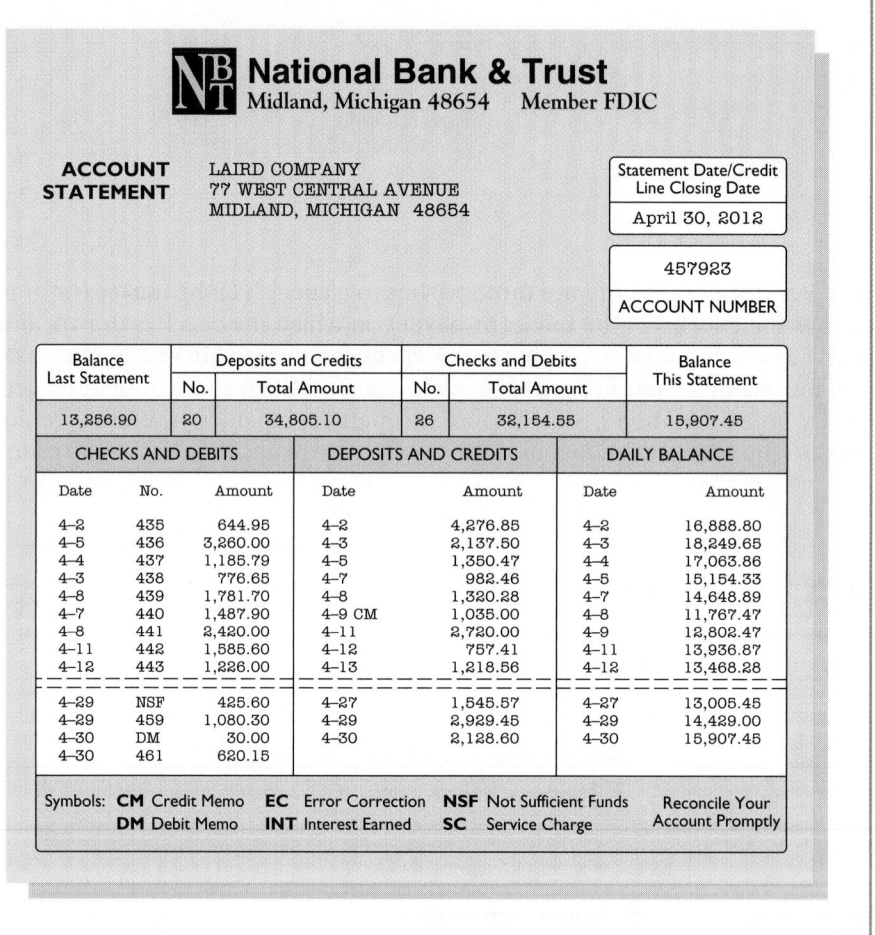

The bank statement lists in numerical sequence all "paid" checks, along with the date the check was paid and its amount. Upon paying a check, the bank stamps the check "paid"; a paid check is sometimes referred to as a **canceled** check. On the statement the bank also includes memoranda explaining other debits and credits it made to the depositor's account.

---

[5]Our presentation assumes that the depositor makes all adjustments at the end of the month. In practice, a company may also make journal entries during the month as it receives information from the bank regarding its account.

DEBIT MEMORANDUM

Some banks charge a monthly fee for their services. Often they charge this fee only when the average monthly balance in a checking account falls below a specified amount. They identify the fee, called a **bank service charge**, on the bank statement by a symbol such as **SC**. The bank also sends with the statement a debit memorandum explaining the charge noted on the statement. Other debit memoranda may also be issued for other bank services such as the cost of printing checks, issuing traveler's checks, and wiring funds to other locations. The symbol **DM** is often used for such charges.

Banks also use a debit memorandum when a deposited check from a customer "bounces" because of insufficient funds. For example, assume that Scott Company, a customer of Laird Company, sends a check for $800 to Laird Company for services provided. Unfortunately, Scott does not have sufficient funds at its bank to pay for these services. In such a case, Scott's bank marks the check **NSF** (not sufficient funds) and returns it to Laird's (the depositor's) bank. Laird's bank then debits Laird's account, as shown by the symbol NSF on the bank statement in Illustration 8-10. The bank sends the NSF check and debit memorandum to Laird as notification of the charge. Laird then records an Account Receivable from Scott Company (the writer of the bad check) and reduces cash for the NSF check.

CREDIT MEMORANDUM

Sometimes a depositor asks the bank to collect its notes receivable. In such a case, the bank will credit the depositor's account for the cash proceeds of the note. This is illustrated by the symbol **CM** on the Laird Company bank statement. The bank issues and sends with the statement a credit memorandum to explain the entry. Many banks also offer interest on checking accounts. The interest earned may be indicated on the bank statement by the symbol **CM** or **INT**.

Reconciling the Bank Account

The bank and the depositor maintain independent records of the depositor's checking account. People tend to assume that the respective balances will always agree. In fact, the two balances are seldom the same at any given time, and both balances differ from the "correct" or "true" balance. Therefore, it is necessary to make the balance per books and the balance per bank agree with the correct or true amount—a process called **reconciling the bank account**. The need for agreement has two causes:

Study Objective [7]
Prepare a bank reconciliation.

1. **Time lags** that prevent one of the parties from recording the transaction in the same period as the other party.
2. **Errors** by either party in recording transactions.

Time lags occur frequently. For example, several days may elapse between the time a company mails a check to a payee and the date the bank pays the check. Similarly, when the depositor uses the bank's night depository to make its deposits, there will be a difference of at least one day between the time the depositor records the deposit and the time the bank does so. A time lag also occurs whenever the bank mails a debit or credit memorandum to the depositor.

The incidence of errors depends on the effectiveness of the internal controls of the depositor and the bank. Bank errors are infrequent. However, either party could accidentally record a $450 check as $45 or $540. In addition, the bank might mistakenly charge a check to a wrong account by keying in an incorrect account name or number.

RECONCILIATION PROCEDURE

The bank reconciliation should be prepared by an employee who has no other responsibilities pertaining to cash. If a company fails to follow this internal control principle of independent internal verification, cash embezzlements may go unnoticed. For example, a cashier who prepares the reconciliation can embezzle cash and conceal the embezzlement by misstating the reconciliation. Thus, the bank accounts would reconcile, and the embezzlement would not be detected.

In reconciling the bank account, it is customary to reconcile the balance per books and balance per bank to their adjusted (correct or true) cash balances. The starting point in preparing the reconciliation is to enter the balance per bank statement and balance per books on the reconciliation schedule. The company then makes various adjustments, as shown in Illustration 8-11.

The following steps should reveal all the reconciling items that cause the difference between the two balances.

Helpful Hint

Deposits in transit and outstanding checks are reconciling items because of time lags.

Step 1. Deposits in transit. Compare the individual deposits listed on the bank statement with deposits in transit from the preceding bank reconciliation and with the deposits per company records or duplicate deposit slips. Deposits recorded by the depositor that have not been recorded by the bank are the **deposits in transit.** Add these deposits to the balance per bank.

Step 2. Outstanding checks. Compare the paid checks shown on the bank statement with (a) checks outstanding from the previous bank reconciliation,

Illustration 8-11
Bank reconciliation adjustments

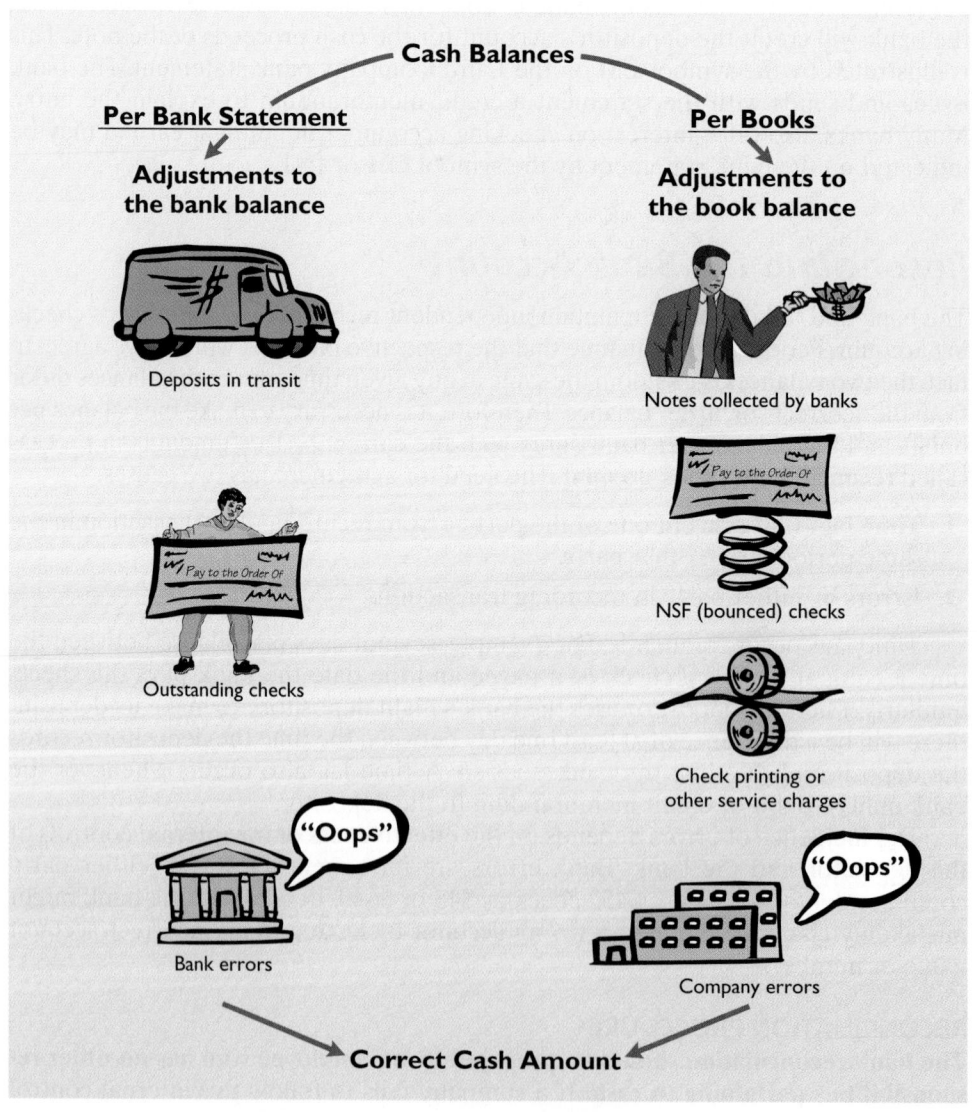

and (b) checks issued by the company as recorded in the cash payments journal (or in the check register in your personal checkbook). Issued checks recorded by the company but that have not yet been paid by the bank are **outstanding checks**. Deduct outstanding checks from the balance per the bank.

Step 3. Errors. Note any errors discovered in the foregoing steps and list them in the appropriate section of the reconciliation schedule. For example, if the company mistakenly recorded as $169 a paid check correctly written for $196, it would deduct the error of $27 from the balance per books. All errors made by the depositor are reconciling items in determining the adjusted cash balance per books. In contrast, all errors made by the bank are reconciling items in determining the adjusted cash balance per the bank.

Step 4. Bank memoranda. Trace bank memoranda to the depositor's records. List in the appropriate section of the reconciliation schedule any unrecorded memoranda. For example, the company would deduct from the balance per books a $5 debit memorandum for bank service charges. Similarly, it would add to the balance per books $32 of interest earned.

BANK RECONCILIATION ILLUSTRATED

The bank statement for Laird Company, in Illustration 8-10, shows a balance per bank of $15,907.45 on April 30, 2012. On this date the balance of cash per books is $11,589.45. Using the four reconciliation steps, Laird determines the following reconciling items.

Helpful Hint

Note in the bank statement on page 382 that checks no. 459 and 461 have been paid but check no. 460 is not listed. Thus, this check is outstanding. If a complete bank statement were provided, checks no. 453 and 457 would also not be listed. The amounts for these three checks are obtained from the company's cash payments records.

Step 1. Deposits in transit: April 30 deposit (received by bank on May 1). $2,201.40

Step 2. Outstanding checks: No. 453, $3,000.00; no. 457, $1,401.30; no. 460, $1,502.70.   5,904.00

Step 3. Errors: Laird wrote check no. 443 for $1,226.00 and the bank correctly paid that amount. However, Laird recorded the check as $1,262.00.   36.00

Step 4. Bank memoranda:
   a. Debit—NSF check from J. R. Baron for $425.60   425.60
   b. Debit—Charge for printing company checks $30.00   30.00
   c. Credit—Collection of note receivable for $1,000
      plus interest earned $50, less bank collection fee $15.00   1,035.00

Illustration 8-12 (page 386) shows Laird's bank reconciliation.

ENTRIES FROM BANK RECONCILIATION

The company records each reconciling item used to determine the **adjusted cash balance per books. If the company does not journalize and post these items, the Cash account will not show the correct balance.** Laird Company would make the following entries on April 30.

Helpful Hint

The entries that follow are adjusting entries. In prior chapters, Cash was an account that did not require adjustment. That was a simplifying assumption for learning purposes, because we had not yet explained a bank reconciliation.

Collection of Note Receivable. This entry involves four accounts. Assuming that the interest of $50 has not been accrued and the collection fee is charged to Miscellaneous Expense, the entry is:

Apr. 30	Cash	1,035.00	
	Miscellaneous Expense	15.00	
	Notes Receivable		1,000.00
	Interest Revenue		50.00
	(To record collection of note receivable by bank)		

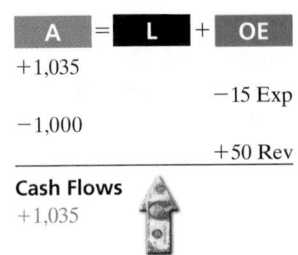

A = L + OE
+1,035
−1,000
                                  −15 Exp
                                  +50 Rev

Cash Flows
+1,035

Illustration 8-12
Bank reconciliation

Laird Company		
Bank Reconciliation		
April 30, 2012		
Cash balance per bank statement		$ 15,907.45
Add: Deposits in transit		2,201.40
		18,108.85
Less: Outstanding checks		
No. 453	$3,000.00	
No. 457	1,401.30	
No. 460	1,502.70	5,904.00
Adjusted cash balance per bank		**$12,204.85** ←
Cash balance per books		$11,589.45
Add: Collection of note receivable $1,000, plus		
interest earned $50, less collection fee $15	$1,035.00	
Error in recording check no. 443	36.00	1,071.00
		12,660.45
Less: NSF check	425.60	
Bank service charge	30.00	455.60
Adjusted cash balance per books		**$12,204.85** ←

Alternative Terminology

The terms *adjusted cash balance, true cash balance,* and *correct cash balance* are used interchangeably.

Book Error.   The cash disbursements journal shows that check no. 443 was a payment on account to Andrea Company, a supplier. The correcting entry is:

A = L + OE
+36
         +36
Cash Flows
+36

Apr. 30	Cash	36.00	
	Accounts Payable—Andrea Company		36.00
	(To correct error in recording check		
	no. 443)		

NSF Check.   As indicated earlier, an NSF check becomes an account receivable to the depositor. The entry is:

A = L + OE
+425.60
−425.60
Cash Flows
−425.60

Apr. 30	Accounts Receivable—J. R. Baron	425.60	
	Cash		425.60
	(To record NSF check)		

Bank Service Charges.   Depositors debit check printing charges (DM) and other bank service charges (SC) to Miscellaneous Expense because they are usually nominal in amount. The entry is:

A = L + OE
             −30 Exp
−30
Cash Flows
−30

Apr. 30	Miscellaneous Expense	30.00	
	Cash		30.00
	(To record charge for printing company		
	checks)		

Instead of making four separate entries, Laird could combine them into one compound entry.

After Laird has posted the entries, the Cash account will show the following.

Illustration 8-13
Adjusted balance in cash account

Cash				
Apr. 30 Bal.	11,589.45	Apr. 30	425.60
30	1,035.00	30	30.00
30	36.00		
Apr. 30 Bal.	12,204.85		

The adjusted cash balance in the ledger should agree with the adjusted cash balance per books in the bank reconciliation in Illustration 8-12 (page 386).

What entries does the bank make? If the company discovers any bank errors in preparing the reconciliation, it should notify the bank. The bank then can make the necessary corrections in its records. The bank does not make any entries for deposits in transit or outstanding checks. Only when these items reach the bank will the bank record these items.

Electronic Funds Transfer (EFT) System

It is not surprising that companies and banks have developed approaches to transfer funds among parties without the use of paper (deposit tickets, checks, etc.). Such procedures, called **electronic funds transfers (EFT)**, are disbursement systems that use wire, telephone, or computers to transfer cash balances from one location to another. Use of EFT is quite common. For example, many employees receive no formal payroll checks from their employers. Instead, employers send electronic payroll data to the appropriate banks. Also, individuals now frequently make regular payments such as those for house, car, and utilities by EFT.

EFT transfers normally result in better internal control since no cash or checks are handled by company employees. This does not mean that opportunities for fraud are eliminated. In fact, the same basic principles related to internal control apply to EFT transfers. For example, without proper segregation of duties and authorizations, an employee might be able to redirect electronic payments into a personal bank account and conceal the theft with fraudulent accounting entries.

INVESTOR INSIGHT

Madoff's Ponzi Scheme

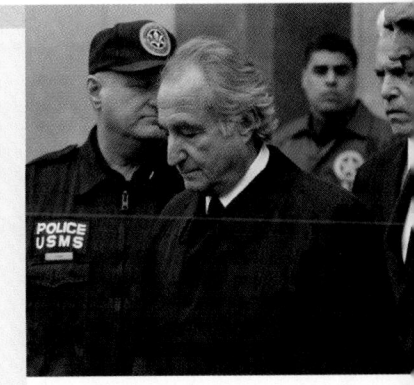

No recent fraud has generated more interest and rage than the one perpetrated by Bernard Madoff. Madoff was an elite New York investment fund manager who was highly regarded by securities regulators. Investors flocked to him because he delivered very steady returns of between 10% and 15%, no matter whether the market was going up or going down. However, for many years, Madoff did not actually invest the cash that people gave to him. Instead, he was running a Ponzi scheme: He paid returns to existing investors using cash received from new investors. As long as the size of his investment fund continued to grow from new investments at a rate that exceeded the amounts that he needed to pay out in returns, Madoff was able to operate his fraud smoothly. To conceal his misdeeds, he fabricated false investment statements that were provided to investors. In addition, Madoff hired an auditor that never verified the accuracy of the investment records but automatically issued unqualified opinions each year. Although a competing fund manager warned the SEC a number of times over a nearly 10-year period that he thought Madoff was engaged in fraud, the SEC never aggressively investigated the allegations. Investors, many of which were charitable organizations, lost more than $18 billion. Madoff was sentenced to a jail term of 150 years.

? How was Madoff able to conceal such a giant fraud? (See page 410.)

Do it!

Sally Kist owns Linen Kist Fabrics. Sally asks you to explain how she should treat the following reconciling items when reconciling the company's bank account: (1) a debit memorandum for an NSF check, (2) a credit memorandum for a note collected by the bank, (3) outstanding checks, and (4) a deposit in transit.

Bank Reconciliation

action plan

✔ Understand the purpose of a bank reconciliation.

✔ Identify time lags and explain how they cause reconciling items.

Solution

Sally should treat the reconciling items as follows.

(1) NSF check: Deduct from balance per books.

(2) Collection of note: Add to balance per books.

(3) Outstanding checks: Deduct from balance per bank.

(4) Deposit in transit: Add to balance per bank.

Related exercise material: BE8-11, BE8-12, BE8-13, BE8-14, E8-9, E8-10, E8-11, E8-12, E8-13, and **Do it!** 8-4.

The Navigator

Reporting Cash

Study Objective [8]

Explain the reporting of cash.

Cash consists of coins, currency (paper money), check, money orders, and money on hand or on deposit in a bank or similar depository. Companies report cash in two different statements: the balance sheet and the statement of cash flows. The balance sheet reports the amount of cash available at a given point in time. The statement of cash flows shows the sources and uses of cash during a period of time. The cash flow statement was introduced in Chapter 1 and will be discussed in much detail in Chapter 17. In this section, we discuss some important points regarding the presentation of cash in the balance sheet.

When presented in a balance sheet, cash on hand, cash in banks, and petty cash are often combined and reported simply as **Cash**. Because it is the most liquid asset owned by the company, cash is listed first in the current assets section of the balance sheet.

Cash Equivalents

Many companies use the designation "Cash and cash equivalents" in reporting cash. (See Illustration 8-14 for an example.) **Cash equivalents** are short-term, highly liquid investments that are both:

1. Readily convertible to known amounts of cash, and

2. So near their maturity that their market value is relatively insensitive to changes in interest rates.

Illustration 8-14

Balance sheet presentation of cash

Delta Air Lines, Inc.	
Balance Sheet (partial)	
December 31, 2009 (in millions)	
Assets	
Current assets	
Cash and cash equivalents	$4,607
Short-term investments	71
Restricted cash	423
Accounts receivable and other net	1,360
Parts inventories	327
Prepaid expenses and other	953
Total current assets	$7,741

Examples of cash equivalents are Treasury bills, commercial paper (short-term corporate notes), and money market funds. All typically are purchased with cash that is in excess of immediate needs.

Occasionally, a company will have a net negative balance in its bank account. In this case, the company should report the negative balance among current liabilities. For example, farm equipment manufacturer Ag-Chem recently reported "Checks outstanding in excess of cash balances" of $2,145,000 among its current liabilities.

Ethics Note

Recently, some companies were forced to restate their financial statements because they had too broadly interpreted which types of investments could be treated as cash equivalents. By reporting these items as cash equivalents, the companies made themselves look more liquid.

Restricted Cash

A company may have **restricted cash**, cash that is not available for general use but rather is restricted for a special purpose. For example, landfill companies are often required to maintain a fund of restricted cash to ensure they will have adequate resources to cover closing and clean-up costs at the end of a landfill site's useful life. McKessor Corp. recently reported restricted cash of $962 million to be paid out as the result of investor lawsuits.

Cash restricted in use should be reported separately on the balance sheet as restricted cash. If the company expects to use the restricted cash within the next year, it reports the amount as a current asset. When this is not the case, it reports the restricted funds as a noncurrent asset.

Illustration 8-14 shows restricted cash reported in the financial statements of Delta Air Lines. The company is required to maintain restricted cash as collateral to support insurance obligations related to workers' compensation claims. Delta does not have access to these funds for general use, and so it must report them separately, rather than as part of cash and cash equivalents.

COMPREHENSIVE

Do it!

Poorten Company's bank statement for May 2012 shows the following data.

Balance 5/1	$12,650	Balance 5/31	$14,280
Debit memorandum:		Credit memorandum:	
NSF check	$175	Collection of note receivable	$505

The cash balance per books at May 31 is $13,319. Your review of the data reveals the following.

1. The NSF check was from Copple Co., a customer.
2. The note collected by the bank was a $500, 3-month, 12% note. The bank charged a $10 collection fee. No interest has been accrued.
3. Outstanding checks at May 31 total $2,410.
4. Deposits in transit at May 31 total $1,752.
5. A Poorten Company check for $352, dated May 10, cleared the bank on May 25. The company recorded this check, which was a payment on account, for $325.

Instructions

(a) Prepare a bank reconciliation at May 31.

(b) Journalize the entries required by the reconciliation.

action plan

✔ Follow the four steps in the reconciliation procedure (pp. 384–385).

✔ Work carefully to minimize mathematical errors in the reconciliation.

✔ Prepare entries from reconciling items per books.

✔ Make sure the cash ledger balance after posting the reconciling entries agrees with the adjusted cash balance per books.

Solution to Comprehensive Do it!

(a)

POORTEN COMPANY
Bank Reconciliation
May 31, 2012

Cash balance per bank statement		$14,280
Add: Deposits in transit		1,752
		16,032
Less: Outstanding checks		2,410
Adjusted cash balance per bank		$13,622
Cash balance per books		$13,319
Add: Collection of note receivable $500, plus $15		
interest, less collection fee $10		505
		13,824
Less: NSF check	$175	
Error in recording check	27	202
Adjusted cash balance per books		$13,622

(b)

Date	Account	Debit	Credit
May 31	Cash	505	
	Miscellaneous Expense	10	
	Notes Receivable		500
	Interest Revenue		15
	(To record collection of note by bank)		
31	Accounts Receivable—Copple Co.	175	
	Cash		175
	(To record NSF check from Copple Co.)		
31	Accounts Payable	27	
	Cash		27
	(To correct error in recording check)		

✔ **The Navigator**

Summary of Study Objectives

[1] Define fraud and internal control. A fraud is a dishonest act by an employee that results in personal benefit to the employee at a cost to the employer. The fraud triangle refers to the three factors that contribute to fraudulent activity by employees: opportunity, financial pressure, and rationalization. Internal control consists of all the related methods and measures adopted within an organization to safeguard its assets, enhance the reliability of its accounting records, increase efficiency of operations, and ensure compliance with laws and regulations.

[2] Identify the principles of internal control activities. The principles of internal control are: establishment of responsibility; segregation of duties; documentation procedures; physical controls; independent internal verification; and human resource controls such as bonding and requiring employees to take vacations.

[3] Explain the applications of internal control principles to cash receipts. Internal controls over cash receipts include: (a) designating specific personnel to handle cash; (b) assigning different individuals to receive cash, record cash, and maintain custody of cash; (c) using remittance advices for mail receipts, cash register tapes for over-the-counter receipts, and deposit slips for bank deposits; (d) using company safes and bank vaults to store cash with access limited to authorized personnel, and using cash registers in executing over-the-counter receipts; (e) making independent daily counts of register receipts and daily comparison of total receipts with total deposits; and (f) bonding personnel that handle cash and requiring them to take vacations.

[4] Explain the applications of internal control principles to cash disbursements. Internal controls over cash disbursements include: (a) having specific individuals such as the treasurer authorized to sign checks and approve invoices; (b) assigning different individuals to approve items for payment, pay the items, and record the payment; (c) using prenumbered checks and accounting for all checks, with each check supported by an approved invoice; (d) storing blank checks in a safe or vault with access restricted to authorized personnel, and using a checkwriting machine to imprint amounts on checks; (e) comparing each check with the approved invoice before issuing the check, and making monthly reconciliations of bank and book balances; and (f) bonding personnel who handle cash, requiring employees to take vacations, and conducting background checks.

[5] Describe the operation of a petty cash fund. Companies operate a petty cash fund to pay relatively small amounts of cash. They must establish the fund, make payments from the fund, and replenish the fund when the cash in the fund reaches a minimum level.

[6] Indicate the control features of a bank account. A bank account contributes to good internal control by providing physical controls for the storage of cash. It minimizes the amount of currency that a company must keep on hand, and it creates a double record of a depositor's bank transactions.

[7] Prepare a bank reconciliation. It is customary to reconcile the balance per books and balance per bank to their adjusted balances. The steps in the reconciling process are to determine deposits in transit, outstanding checks, errors by the depositor or the bank, and unrecorded bank memoranda.

[8] Explain the reporting of cash. Companies list cash first in the current assets section of the balance sheet. In some cases, they report cash together with cash equivalents. Cash restricted for a special purpose is reported separately as a current asset or as a noncurrent asset, depending on when the cash is expected to be used.

The Navigator

Glossary

Bank reconciliation The process of comparing the bank's balance of an account with the company's balance and explaining any differences to make them agree. (p. 380).

Bank service charge A fee charged by a bank for the use of its services. (p. 383).

Bank statement A monthly statement from the bank that shows the depositor's bank transactions and balances. (p. 382).

Bonding Obtaining insurance protection against misappropriation of assets by employees. (p. 370).

Cash Resources that consist of coins, currency, checks, money orders, and money on hand or on deposit in a bank or similar depository. (p. 388).

Cash equivalents Short-term, highly liquid investments that can be converted to a specific amount of cash. (p. 388).

Check A written order signed by a bank depositor, directing the bank to pay a specified sum of money to a designated recipient. (p. 380).

Deposits in transit Deposits recorded by the depositor but not yet been recorded by the bank. (p. 384).

Electronic funds transfer (EFT) A disbursement system that uses wire, telephone, or computers to transfer funds from one location to another. (p. 387).

Fraud A dishonest act by an employee that results in personal benefit to the employee at a cost to the employer. (p. 362).

Fraud triangle The three factors that contribute to fraudulent activity by employees: opportunity, financial pressure, and rationalization. (p. 362).

Internal auditors Company employees who continuously evaluate the effectiveness of the company's internal control system. (p. 370).

Internal control All of the related methods and activities adopted within an organization to safeguard its assets and enhance the accuracy and reliability of its accounting records. (p. 363).

NSF check A check that is not paid by a bank because of insufficient funds in a customer's bank account. (p. 383).

Outstanding checks Checks issued and recorded by a company but not yet paid by the bank. (p. 385).

Petty cash fund A cash fund used to pay relatively small amounts. (p. 377).

Restricted cash Cash that must be used for a special purpose. (p. 389).

Sarbanes-Oxley Act of 2002 (SOX) Regulations passed by Congress to try to reduce unethical corporate behavior. (p. 363).

Voucher An authorization form prepared for each payment in a voucher system. (p. 376).

Voucher system A network of approvals by authorized individuals acting independently to ensure that all disbursements by check are proper. (p. 375).

WILEY PLUS   **Self-Test, Brief Exercises, Exercises, Problem Set A, and many more components are available for practice in *WileyPLUS***

Self-Test Questions

Answers are on page 410.

(SO 1) **1.** Which of the following is *not* an element of the fraud triangle?
  a. Rationalization.   **c.** Segregation of duties.
  b. Financial pressure.   **d.** Opportunity.

2. An organization uses internal control to enhance the (SO 1) accuracy and reliability of its accounting records and to:
  a. safeguard its assets.
  b. prevent fraud.

c. produce correct financial statements.

d. deter employee dishonesty.

(SO 1) **3.** Which of the following was *not* a result of the Sarbanes-Oxley Act?

a. Companies must file financial statements with the Internal Revenue Service.

b. All publicly traded companies must maintain adequate internal controls.

c. The Public Company Accounting Oversight Board was created to establish auditing standards and regulate auditor activity.

d. Corporate executives and board of directors must ensure that controls are reliable and effective, and they can be fined or imprisoned for failure to do so.

(SO 2) **4.** The principles of internal control do *not* include:

a. establishment of responsibility.

b. documentation procedures.

c. management responsibility.

d. independent internal verification.

(SO 2) **5.** Physical controls do *not* include:

a. safes and vaults to store cash.

b. independent bank reconciliations.

c. locked warehouses for inventories.

d. bank safety deposit boxes for important papers.

(SO 3) **6.** Permitting only designated personnel to handle cash receipts is an application of the principle of:

a. segregation of duties.

b. establishment of responsibility.

c. independent check.

d. human resource controls.

(SO 3) **7.** Which of the following control activities is *not* relevant to when a company uses a computerized (rather than manual) accounting system?

a. Establishment of responsibility.

b. Segregation of duties.

c. Independent internal verification.

d. All of these control activities are relevant to a computerized system.

(SO 4) **8.** The use of prenumbered checks in disbursing cash is an application of the principle of:

a. establishment of responsibility.

b. segregation of duties.

c. physical controls.

d. documentation procedures.

(SO 5) **9.** A company writes a check to replenish a $100 petty cash fund when the fund contains receipts of $94 and $4 in cash. In recording the check, the company should:

a. debit Cash Over and Short for $2.

b. debit Petty Cash for $94.

c. credit Cash for $94.

d. credit Petty Cash for $2.

(SO 6) **10.** The control features of a bank account do *not* include:

a. having bank auditors verify the correctness of the bank balance per books.

b. minimizing the amount of cash that must be kept on hand.

c. providing a double record of all bank transactions.

d. safeguarding cash by using a bank as a depository.

(SO 7) **11.** In a bank reconciliation, deposits in transit are:

a. deducted from the book balance.

b. added to the book balance.

c. added to the bank balance.

d. deducted from the bank balance.

(SO 7) **12.** The reconciling item in a bank reconciliation that will result in an adjusting entry by the depositor is:

a. outstanding checks.   c. a bank error.

b. deposit in transit.   d. bank service charges.

(SO 8) **13.** Which of the following items in a cash drawer at November 30 is *not* cash?

a. Money orders.

b. Coins and currency.

c. A customer check dated December 1.

d. A customer check dated November 28.

(SO 8) **14.** Which of the following statements correctly describes the reporting of cash?

a. Cash cannot be combined with cash equivalents.

b. Restricted cash funds may be combined with Cash.

c. Cash is listed first in the current assets section.

d. Restricted cash funds cannot be reported as a current asset.

Go to the book's companion website, **www.wiley.com/college/weygandt**, for additional Self-Test Questions.

The Navigator

Questions

1. A local bank reported that it lost $150,000 as the result of an employee fraud. Randal Smith is not clear on what is meant by an "employee fraud." Explain the meaning of fraud to Randal and give an example of frauds that might occur at a bank.

2. Fraud experts often say that there are three primary factors that contribute to employee fraud. Identify the three factors and explain what is meant by each.

3. Identify and describe the five components of a good internal control system.

4. "Internal control is concerned only with enhancing the accuracy of the accounting records." Do you agree? Explain.

5. What principles of internal control apply to most organizations?

6. At the corner grocery store, all sales clerks make change out of one cash register drawer. Is this a violation of internal control? Why?

7. Meg Lucas is reviewing the principle of segregation of duties. What are the two common applications of this principle?

8. How do documentation procedures contribute to good internal control?

9. What internal control objectives are met by physical controls?

10. (a) Explain the control principle of independent internal verification. (b) What practices are important in applying this principle?

11. The management of Sewell Company asks you, as the company accountant, to explain (a) the concept of reasonable assurance in internal control and (b) the importance of the human factor in internal control.

12. McCartney Fertilizer Co. owns the following assets at the balance sheet date.

Cash in bank savings account	$ 8,000
Cash on hand	850
Cash refund due from the IRS	1,000
Checking account balance	12,000
Postdated checks	500

What amount should McCartney report as cash in the balance sheet?

13. What principle(s) of internal control is (are) involved in making daily cash counts of over-the-counter receipts?

14. Jacobs Department Stores has just installed new electronic cash registers in its stores. How do cash registers improve internal control over cash receipts?

15. At Hummel Wholesale Company, two mail clerks open all mail receipts. How does this strengthen internal control?

16. "To have maximum effective internal control over cash disbursements, all payments should be made by check." Is this true? Explain.

17. Joe Griswold Company's internal controls over cash disbursements provide for the treasurer to sign checks imprinted by a check-writing machine in indelible ink after comparing the check with the approved invoice. Identify the internal control principles that are present in these controls.

18. How do the principles of (a) physical controls and (b) documentation controls apply to cash disbursements?

19. (a) What is a voucher system? (b) What principles of internal control apply to a voucher system?

20. What is the essential feature of an electronic funds transfer (EFT) procedure?

21. (a) Identify the three activities that pertain to a petty cash fund, and indicate an internal control principle that is applicable to each activity. (b) When are journal entries required in the operation of a petty cash fund?

22. "The use of a bank contributes significantly to good internal control over cash." Is this true? Why or why not?

23. Lori Figgs is confused about the lack of agreement between the cash balance per books and the balance per the bank. Explain the causes for the lack of agreement to Lori, and give an example of each cause.

24. What are the four steps involved in finding differences between the balance per books and balance per bank?

25. Kristen Hope asks your help concerning an NSF check. Explain to Kristen (a) what an NSF check is, (b) how it is treated in a bank reconciliation, and (c) whether it will require an adjusting entry.

26. (a) "Cash equivalents are the same as cash." Do you agree? Explain. (b) How should restricted cash funds be reported on the balance sheet?

27. **PEPSICO** At what amount does PepsiCo report cash and cash equivalents in its 2009 consolidated balance sheet?

Brief Exercises

BE8-1 Match each situation with the fraud triangle factor—opportunity, financial pressure, or rationalization—that best describes it.

Identify fraud triangle concepts.
(SO 1)

1. An employee's monthly credit card payments are nearly 75% of his or her monthly earnings.
2. An employee earns minimum wage at a firm that has reported record earnings for each of the last five years.
3. An employee has an expensive gambling habit.
4. An employee has check-writing and signing responsibilities for a small company, as well as reconciling the bank account.

BE8-2 Angela Kinsey has prepared the following list of statements about internal control.

Indicate internal control concepts.
(SO 1)

1. One of the objectives of internal control is to safeguard assets from employee theft, robbery, and unauthorized use.
2. One of the objectives of internal control is to enhance the accuracy and reliability of the accounting records.
3. No laws require U.S. corporations to maintain an adequate system of internal control.

Identify each statement as true or false. If false, indicate how to correct the statement.

BE8-3 Phyllis Lapin is the new owner of Ready Parking. She has heard about internal control but is not clear about its importance for her business. Explain to Phyllis the four purposes of internal control and give her one application of each purpose for Ready Parking.

Explain the importance of internal control.
(SO 1)

Identify internal control principles.

(SO 2)

BE8-4   The internal control procedures in Meredith Palmer Company provide that:

1. Employees who have physical custody of assets do not have access to the accounting records.
2. Each month the assets on hand are compared to the accounting records by an internal auditor.
3. A prenumbered shipping document is prepared for each shipment of goods to customers.

Identify the principles of internal control that are being followed.

Identify the internal control principles applicable to cash receipts.

(SO 3)

BE8-5   Kate Flannery Company has the following internal control procedures over cash receipts. Identify the internal control principle that is applicable to each procedure.

1. All over-the-counter receipts are registered on cash registers.
2. All cashiers are bonded.
3. Daily cash counts are made by cashier department supervisors.
4. The duties of receiving cash, recording cash, and custody of cash are assigned to different individuals.
5. Only cashiers may operate cash registers.

Make journal entries for cash overage and shortfall.

(SO 3)

BE8-6   The cash register tape for Kelly Kapoor Industries reported sales of $6,891.50. Record the journal entry that would be necessary for each of the following situations. (a) Cash to be accounted for exceeds cash on hand by $50.75. (b) Cash on hand exceeds cash to be accounted for by $28.32.

Make journal entry using cash count sheet.

(SO 3)

BE8-7   While examining cash receipts information, the accounting department determined the following information: opening cash balance $150, cash on hand $1,125.74, and cash sales per register tape $990.83. Prepare the required journal entry based upon the cash count sheet.

Identify the internal control principles applicable to cash disbursements.

(SO 4)

BE8-8   Mindy Kaliny Company has the following internal control procedures over cash disbursements. Identify the internal control principle that is applicable to each procedure.

1. Company checks are prenumbered.
2. The bank statement is reconciled monthly by an internal auditor.
3. Blank checks are stored in a safe in the treasurer's office.
4. Only the treasurer or assistant treasurer may sign checks.
5. Check signers are not allowed to record cash disbursement transactions.

Prepare entry to replenish a petty cash fund.

(SO 5)

BE8-9   On March 20, Toby's petty cash fund of $100 is replenished when the fund contains $7 in cash and receipts for postage $52, freight-out $26, and travel expense $10. Prepare the journal entry to record the replenishment of the petty cash fund.

Identify the control features of a bank account.

(SO 6)

BE8-10   Creed Bratton is uncertain about the control features of a bank account. Explain the control benefits of (a) a check and (b) a bank statement.

Indicate location of reconciling items in a bank reconciliation.

(SO 7)

BE8-11   The following reconciling items are applicable to the bank reconciliation for Flenderson Company: (1) outstanding checks, (2) bank debit memorandum for service charge, (3) bank credit memorandum for collecting a note for the depositor, (4) deposits in transit. Indicate how each item should be shown on a bank reconciliation.

Identify reconciling items that require adjusting entries.

(SO 7)

BE8-12   Using the data in BE8-11, indicate (a) the items that will result in an adjustment to the depositor's records and (b) why the other items do not require adjustment.

Prepare partial bank reconciliation.

(SO 7)

BE8-13   At July 31, Martinez Company has the following bank information: cash balance per bank $7,420, outstanding checks $762, deposits in transit $1,120, and a bank service charge $20. Determine the adjusted cash balance per bank at July 31.

Prepare partial bank reconciliation.

(SO 7)

BE8-14   At August 31, Oscar Company has a cash balance per books of $8,500 and the following additional data from the bank statement: charge for printing Oscar Company checks $35, interest earned on checking account balance $40, and outstanding checks $800. Determine the adjusted cash balance per books at August 31.

Explain the statement presentation of cash balances.

(SO 8)

BE8-15   Nunez Company has the following cash balances: Cash in Bank $15,742, Payroll Bank Account $6,000, and Plant Expansion Fund Cash $25,000. Explain how each balance should be reported on the balance sheet.

Do it! Review

Do it! 8-1 Identify which control activity is violated in each of the following situations, and explain how the situation creates an opportunity for fraud or inappropriate accounting practices.

1. Once a month, the sales department sends sales invoices to the accounting department to be recorded.
2. Leah Hutcherson orders merchandise for Rice Lake Company; he also receives merchandise and authorizes payment for merchandise.
3. Several clerks at Pig Foods use the same cash register drawer.

Identify violations of control activities.
(SO 2)

Do it! 8-2 Andy Bernard is concerned with control over mail receipts at Andy's Sporting Goods. All mail receipts are opened by Ed Helms. Ed sends the checks to the accounting department, where they are stamped "For Deposit Only." The accounting department records and deposits the mail receipts weekly. Andy asks for your help in installing a good system of internal control over mail receipts.

Design system of internal control over cash receipts.
(SO 3)

Do it! 8-3 Craig Robinson Company established a $100 petty cash fund on August 1. On August 30, the fund had $9 cash remaining and petty cash receipts for postage $31, office supplies $42, and miscellaneous expense $16. Prepare journal entries to establish the fund on August 1 and replenish the fund on August 30.

Make journal entries for petty cash fund.
(SO 5)

Do it! 8-4 Daryl Philbin owns Philbin Blankets. Philbin asks you to explain how he should treat the following reconciling items when reconciling the company's bank account.

1. Outstanding checks
2. A deposit in transit
3. The bank charged to our account a check written by another company
4. A debit memorandum for a bank service charge

Explain treatment of items in bank reconciliation.
(SO 7)

Exercises

E8-1 Jan Levinson is the owner of Levinson's Pizza. Levinson's is operated strictly on a carryout basis. Customers pick up their orders at a counter where a clerk exchanges the pizza for cash. While at the counter, the customer can see other employees making the pizzas and the large ovens in which the pizzas are baked.

Identify the principles of internal control.
(SO 2)

Instructions
Identify the six principles of internal control and give an example of each principle that you might observe when picking up your pizza. (*Note:* It may not be possible to observe all the principles.)

E8-2 The following control procedures are used at Melora Company for over-the-counter cash receipts.

1. To minimize the risk of robbery, cash in excess of $100 is stored in an unlocked attaché case in the stock room until it is deposited in the bank.
2. All over-the-counter receipts are registered by three clerks who use a cash register with a single cash drawer.
3. The company accountant makes the bank deposit and then records the day's receipts.
4. At the end of each day, the total receipts are counted by the cashier on duty and reconciled to the cash register total.
5. Cashiers are experienced; they are not bonded.

Identify internal control weaknesses over cash receipts and suggest improvements.
(SO 2, 3)

Instructions
(a) For each procedure, explain the weakness in internal control, and identify the control principle that is violated.
(b) For each weakness, suggest a change in procedure that will result in good internal control.

Identify internal control weaknesses over cash disbursements and suggest improvements.
(SO 2, 4)

E8-3 The following control procedures are used in Kelly Erin's Boutique Shoppe for cash disbursements.

1. The company accountant prepares the bank reconciliation and reports any discrepancies to the owner.
2. The store manager personally approves all payments before signing and issuing checks.
3. Each week, Kelly leaves 100 company checks in an unmarked envelope on a shelf behind the cash register.
4. After payment, bills are filed in a paid invoice folder.
5. The company checks are unnumbered.

Instructions

(a) For each procedure, explain the weakness in internal control, and identify the internal control principle that is violated.

(b) For each weakness, suggest a change in the procedure that will result in good internal control.

Identify internal control weaknesses for cash disbursements and suggest improvements.
(SO 4)

E8-4 At Hannon Company, checks are not prenumbered because both the purchasing agent and the treasurer are authorized to issue checks. Each signer has access to unissued checks kept in an unlocked file cabinet. The purchasing agent pays all bills pertaining to goods purchased for resale. Prior to payment, the purchasing agent determines that the goods have been received and verifies the mathematical accuracy of the vendor's invoice. After payment, the invoice is filed by the vendor, and the purchasing agent records the payment in the cash disbursements journal. The treasurer pays all other bills following approval by authorized employees. After payment, the treasurer stamps all bills PAID, files them by payment date, and records the checks in the cash disbursements journal. Hannon Company maintains one checking account that is reconciled by the treasurer.

Instructions

(a) List the weaknesses in internal control over cash disbursements.

(b) ▬▬▬▬ Write a memo to the company treasurer indicating your recommendations for improvement.

Indicate whether procedure is good or weak internal control.
(SO 2, 3, 4)

E8-5 Listed below are five procedures followed by Ellie Kempet Company.

1. Several individuals operate the cash register using the same register drawer.
2. A monthly bank reconciliation is prepared by someone who has no other cash responsibilities.
3. Roy Anderson writes checks and also records cash payment journal entries.
4. One individual orders inventory, while a different individual authorizes payments.
5. Unnumbered sales invoices from credit sales are forwarded to the accounting department every four weeks for recording.

Instructions

Indicate whether each procedure is an example of good internal control or of weak internal control. If it is an example of good internal control, indicate which internal control principle is being followed. If it is an example of weak internal control, indicate which internal control principle is violated. Use the table below.

Procedure	IC Good or Weak?	Related Internal Control Principle
1.		
2.		
3.		
4.		
5.		

Indicate whether procedure is good or weak internal control.
(SO 2, 3, 4)

E8-6 Listed below are five procedures followed by Wallace Company.

1. Employees are required to take vacations.
2. Any member of the sales department can approve credit sales.
3. Andy Buckley ships goods to customers, bills customers, and receives payment from customers.
4. Total cash receipts are compared to bank deposits daily by someone who has no other cash responsibilities.
5. Time clocks are used for recording time worked by employees.

Instructions

Indicate whether each procedure is an example of good internal control or of weak internal control. If it is an example of good internal control, indicate which internal control principle is being followed. If it is an example of weak internal control, indicate which internal control principle is violated. Use the table below.

Procedure	IC Good or Weak?	Related Internal Control Principle
1.		
2.		
3.		
4.		
5.		

E8-7 Karen Filippelli Company established a petty cash fund on May 1, cashing a check for $100. The company reimbursed the fund on June 1 and July 1 with the following results.

Prepare journal entries for a petty cash fund.
(SO 5)

June 1: Cash in fund $2.75. Receipts: delivery expense $31.25; postage expense $39.00; and miscellaneous expense $25.00.

July 1: Cash in fund $3.25. Receipts: delivery expense $21.00; entertainment expense $51.00; and miscellaneous expense $24.75.

On July 10, Karen Filippelli increased the fund from $100 to $150.

Instructions

Prepare journal entries for Karen Filippelli Company for May 1, June 1, July 1, and July 10.

E8-8 Rashida Company uses an imprest petty cash system. The fund was established on March 1 with a balance of $100. During March, the following petty cash receipts were found in the petty cash box.

Prepare journal entries for a petty cash fund.
(SO 5)

Date	Receipt No.	For	Amount
3/5	1	Stamp Inventory	$39
7	2	Freight-out	21
9	3	Miscellaneous Expense	6
11	4	Travel Expense	24
14	5	Miscellaneous Expense	5

The fund was replenished on March 15 when the fund contained $3 in cash. On March 20, the amount in the fund was increased to $150.

Instructions

Journalize the entries in March that pertain to the operation of the petty cash fund.

E8-9 Bob Vance is unable to reconcile the bank balance at January 31. Bob's reconciliation is as follows.

Prepare bank reconciliation and adjusting entries.
(SO 7)

Cash balance per bank	$3,560.20
Add: NSF check	690.00
Less: Bank service charge	25.00
Adjusted balance per bank	$4,225.20
Cash balance per books	$3,875.20
Less: Deposits in transit	530.00
Add: Outstanding checks	930.00
Adjusted balance per books	$4,275.20

Instructions

(a) Prepare a correct bank reconciliation.

(b) Journalize the entries required by the reconciliation.

E8-10 On April 30, the bank reconciliation of Gabe Lewis Company shows three outstanding checks: no. 254, $650; no. 255, $820; and no. 257, $410. The May bank statement and the May cash payments journal show the following.

Determine outstanding checks.
(SO 7)

Bank Statement			Cash Payments Journal		
Checks Paid			**Checks Issued**		
Date	**Check No.**	**Amount**	**Date**	**Check No.**	**Amount**
5/4	254	650	5/2	258	159
5/2	257	410	5/5	259	275
5/17	258	159	5/10	260	890
5/12	259	275	5/15	261	500
5/20	261	500	5/22	262	750
5/29	263	480	5/24	263	480
5/30	262	750	5/29	264	560

Instructions

Using step 2 in the reconciliation procedure, list the outstanding checks at May 31.

Prepare bank reconciliation and adjusting entries.

(SO 7)

E8-11   The following information pertains to Miner Video Company.

1. Cash balance per bank, July 31, $7,263.
2. July bank service charge not recorded by the depositor $28.
3. Cash balance per books, July 31, $7,284.
4. Deposits in transit, July 31, $1,500.
5. Bank collected $900 note for Miner in July, plus interest $36, less fee $20. The collection has not been recorded by Miner, and no interest has been accrued.
6. Outstanding checks, July 31, $591.

Instructions

(a) Prepare a bank reconciliation at July 31.
(b) Journalize the adjusting entries at July 31 on the books of Miner Video Company.

Prepare bank reconciliation and adjusting entries.

(SO 7)

E8-12   The information below relates to the Cash account in the ledger of Porter Company.

Balance September 1—$17,150; Cash deposited—$64,000.
Balance September 30—$17,404; Checks written—$63,746.

The September bank statement shows a balance of $16,422 on September 30 and the following memoranda.

Credits		**Debits**	
Collection of $1,500 note plus interest $30	$1,530	NSF check: Charles Esten	$425
Interest earned on checking account	$45	Safety deposit box rent	$65

At September 30, deposits in transit were $4,450, and outstanding checks totaled $2,383.

Instructions

(a) Prepare the bank reconciliation at September 30.
(b) Prepare the adjusting entries at September 30, assuming (1) the NSF check was from a customer on account, and (2) no interest had been accrued on the note.

Compute deposits in transit and outstanding checks for two bank reconciliations.

(SO 7)

E8-13   The cash records of Holly Company show the following four situations.

1. The June 30 bank reconciliation indicated that deposits in transit total $720. During July, the general ledger account Cash shows deposits of $15,750, but the bank statement indicates that only $15,600 in deposits were received during the month.
2. The June 30 bank reconciliation also reported outstanding checks of $680. During the month of July, Holly Company books show that $17,200 of checks were issued. The bank statement showed that $16,400 of checks cleared the bank in July.
3. In September, deposits per the bank statement totaled $26,700, deposits per books were $25,400, and deposits in transit at September 30 were $2,100.
4. In September, cash disbursements per books were $23,700, checks clearing the bank were $25,000, and outstanding checks at September 30 were $2,100.

There were no bank debit or credit memoranda. No errors were made by either the bank or Holly Company.

Instructions

Answer the following questions.

(a) In situation (1), what were the deposits in transit at July 31?
(b) In situation (2), what were the outstanding checks at July 31?
(c) In situation (3), what were the deposits in transit at August 31?
(d) In situation (4), what were the outstanding checks at August 31?

E8-14   Flax Company has recorded the following items in its financial records.

Cash in bank	$ 47,000
Cash in plant expansion fund	100,000
Cash on hand	12,000
Highly liquid investments	34,000
Petty cash	500
Receivables from customers	89,000
Stock investments	61,000

Show presentation of cash in financial statements.

(SO 8)

The cash in bank is subject to a compensating balance of $5,000. The highly liquid investments had maturities of 3 months or less when they were purchased. The stock investments will be sold in the next 6 to 12 months. The plant expansion project will begin in 3 years.

Instructions

(a) What amount should Flax report as "Cash and cash equivalents" on its balance sheet?
(b) Where should the items not included in part (a) be reported on the balance sheet?
(c) What disclosures should Flax make in its financial statements concerning "cash and cash equivalents"?

Exercises: Set B

Visit the book's companion website, at **www.wiley.com/college/weygandt**, and choose the Student Companion site to access Exercise Set B.

Problems: Set A

P8-1A   Mose Office Supply Company recently changed its system of internal control over cash disbursements. The system includes the following features.

Instead of being unnumbered and manually prepared, all checks must now be prenumbered and written by using the new checkwriting machine purchased by the company. Before a check can be issued, each invoice must have the approval of Linda Purl, the purchasing agent, and Idris Elba, the receiving department supervisor. Checks must be signed by either Vivianne Collins, the treasurer, or Nick D'Agosto, the assistant treasurer. Before signing a check, the signer is expected to compare the amount of the check with the amount on the invoice.

After signing a check, the signer stamps the invoice PAID and inserts within the stamp, the date, check number, and amount of the check. The "paid" invoice is then sent to the accounting department for recording.

Blank checks are stored in a safe in the treasurer's office. The combination to the safe is known only by the treasurer and assistant treasurer. Each month, the bank statement is reconciled with the bank balance per books by the assistant chief accountant. All employees who handle or account for cash are bonded.

Identify internal control principles over cash disbursements.

(SO 2, 4)

Instructions

Identify the internal control principles and their application to cash disbursements of Mose Office Supply Company.

P8-2A   Ursula Company maintains a petty cash fund for small expenditures. The following transactions occurred over a 2-month period.

Journalize and post petty cash fund transactions.

(SO 5)

July 1   Established petty cash fund by writing a check on Scranton Bank for $200.
     15   Replenished the petty cash fund by writing a check for $196.00. On this date the fund consisted of $4.00 in cash and the following petty cash receipts: freight-out $94.00, postage expense $42.40, entertainment expense $46.60, and miscellaneous expense $11.20.

> 31 Replenished the petty cash fund by writing a check for $192.00. At this date, the fund consisted of $8.00 in cash and the following petty cash receipts: freight-out $82.10, charitable contributions expense $45.00, postage expense $25.50, and miscellaneous expense $39.40.
>
> Aug. 15 Replenished the petty cash fund by writing a check for $187.00. On this date, the fund consisted of $13.00 in cash and the following petty cash receipts: freight-out $75.60, entertainment expense $43.00, postage expense $33.00, and miscellaneous expense $37.00.
>
> 16 Increased the amount of the petty cash fund to $300 by writing a check for $100.
>
> 31 Replenished petty cash fund by writing a check for $284.00. On this date, the fund consisted of $16 in cash and the following petty cash receipts: postage expense $140.00, travel expense $95.60, and freight-out $47.10.

Instructions

(a) July 15, Cash short $1.80

(b) Aug. 31 balance $300

(a) Journalize the petty cash transactions.

(b) Post to the Petty Cash account.

(c) What internal control features exist in a petty cash fund?

Prepare a bank reconciliation and adjusting entries.

(SO 7)

P8-3A On May 31, 2012, Sabre Company had a cash balance per books of $6,781.50. The bank statement from New York State Bank on that date showed a balance of $6,404.60. A comparison of the statement with the cash account revealed the following facts.

1. The statement included a debit memo of $40 for the printing of additional company checks.
2. Cash sales of $836.15 on May 12 were deposited in the bank. The cash receipts journal entry and the deposit slip were incorrectly made for $886.15. The bank credited Sabre Company for the correct amount.
3. Outstanding checks at May 31 totaled $576.25. Deposits in transit were $1,916.15.
4. On May 18, the company issued check No. 1181 for $685 to Carol Stills on account. The check, which cleared the bank in May, was incorrectly journalized and posted by Sabre Company for $658.
5. A $2,500 note receivable was collected by the bank for Sabre Company on May 31 plus $80 interest. The bank charged a collection fee of $20. No interest has been accrued on the note.
6. Included with the cancelled checks was a check issued by Rapier Company to Tom Lujak for $800 that was incorrectly charged to Sabre Company by the bank.
7. On May 31, the bank statement showed an NSF charge of $680 for a check issued by Jo Bennett, a customer, to Sabre Company on account.

Instructions

(a) Adjusted cash balance per bank $8,544.50

(a) Prepare the bank reconciliation at May 31, 2012.

(b) Prepare the necessary adjusting entries for Sabre Company at May 31, 2012.

Prepare a bank reconciliation and adjusting entries from detailed data.

(SO 7)

P8-4A The bank portion of the bank reconciliation for Helene Company at November 30, 2012, was as follows.

HELENE COMPANY
Bank Reconciliation
November 30, 2012

Cash balance per bank		$14,367.90
Add: Deposits in transit		2,530.20
		16,898.10

Less: Outstanding checks

Check Number	Check Amount	
3451	$2,260.40	
3470	720.10	
3471	844.50	
3472	1,426.80	
3474	1,050.00	6,301.80
Adjusted cash balance per bank		$10,596.30

The adjusted cash balance per bank agreed with the cash balance per books at November 30.

The December bank statement showed the following checks and deposits.

Bank Statement				
Checks			**Deposits**	
Date	Number	Amount	Date	Amount
12-1	3451	$ 2,260.40	12-1	$ 2,530.20
12-2	3471	844.50	12-4	1,211.60
12-7	3472	1,426.80	12-8	2,365.10
12-4	3475	1,640.70	12-16	2,672.70
12-8	3476	1,300.00	12-21	2,945.00
12-10	3477	2,130.00	12-26	2,567.30
12-15	3479	3,080.00	12-29	2,836.00
12-27	3480	600.00	12-30	1,025.00
12-30	3482	475.50	Total	$18,152.90
12-29	3483	1,140.00		
12-31	3485	540.80		
	Total	$15,438.70		

The cash records per books for December showed the following.

Cash Payments Journal							Cash Receipts Journal	
Date	Number	Amount	Date	Number	Amount		Date	Amount
12-1	3475	$1,640.70	12-20	3482	$ 475.50		12-3	$ 1,211.60
12-2	3476	1,300.00	12-22	3483	1,140.00		12-7	2,365.10
12-2	3477	2,130.00	12-23	3484	798.00		12-15	2,672.70
12-4	3478	621.30	12-24	3485	450.80		12-20	2,954.00
12-8	3479	3,080.00	12-30	3486	1,889.50		12-25	2,567.30
12-10	3480	600.00	Total		$14,933.20		12-28	2,836.00
12-17	3481	807.40					12-30	1,025.00
							12-31	1,690.40
							Total	$17,322.10

The bank statement contained two memoranda:

1. A credit of $4,145 for the collection of a $4,000 note for Helene Company plus interest of $160 and less a collection fee of $15. Helene Company has not accrued any interest on the note.
2. A debit of $572.80 for an NSF check written by L. Purl, a customer. At December 31, the check had not been redeposited in the bank.

At December 31, the cash balance per books was $12,485.20, and the cash balance per the bank statement was $20,154.30. The bank did not make any errors, but two errors were made by Helene Company.

Instructions

(a) Using the four steps in the reconciliation procedure, prepare a bank reconciliation at December 31.
(b) Prepare the adjusting entries based on the reconciliation. (*Hint:* The correction of any errors pertaining to recording checks should be made to Accounts Payable. The correction of any errors relating to recording cash receipts should be made to Accounts Receivable.)

(a) Adjusted balance per books $15,958.40

Prepare a bank reconciliation and adjusting entries.

(SO 7)

P8-5A   Hidetoshi Company maintains a checking account at the Imura Bank. At July 31, selected data from the ledger balance and the bank statement are shown below.

	Cash in Bank	
	Per Books	**Per Bank**
Balance, July 1	$17,600	$16,800
July receipts	81,400	
July credits		82,470
July disbursements	77,150	
July debits		74,756
Balance, July 31	$21,850	$24,514

Analysis of the bank data reveals that the credits consist of $79,000 of July deposits and a credit memorandum of $3,470 for the collection of a $3,400 note plus interest revenue of $70. The July debits per bank consist of checks cleared $74,700 and a debit memorandum of $56 for printing additional company checks.

You also discover the following errors involving July checks: (1) A check for $230 to a creditor on account that cleared the bank in July was journalized and posted as $320. (2) A salary check to an employee for $255 was recorded by the bank for $155.

The June 30 bank reconciliation contained only two reconciling items: deposits in transit $7,000 and outstanding checks of $6,200.

Instructions

(a) Adjusted balance per books $25,354

(a) Prepare a bank reconciliation at July 31, 2012.

(b) Journalize the adjusting entries to be made by Hidetoshi Company. Assume that interest on the note has not been accrued.

Identify internal control weaknesses in cash receipts and cash disbursements.

(SO 2, 3, 4)

P8-6A   Hasagama Middle School wants to raise money for a new sound system for its auditorium. The primary fund-raising event is a dance at which the famous disc jockey D.J. Rivet will play classic and not-so-classic dance tunes. Will Schuester, the music and theater instructor, has been given the responsibility for coordinating the fund-raising efforts. This is Will's first experience with fund-raising. He decides to put the eighth-grade choir in charge of the event; he will be a relatively passive observer.

Will had 500 unnumbered tickets printed for the dance. He left the tickets in a box on his desk and told the choir students to take as many tickets as they thought they could sell for $5 each. In order to ensure that no extra tickets would be floating around, he told them to dispose of any unsold tickets. When the students received payment for the tickets, they were to bring the cash back to Will and he would put it in a locked box in his desk drawer.

Some of the students were responsible for decorating the gymnasium for the dance. Will gave each of them a key to the money box and told them that if they took money out to purchase materials, they should put a note in the box saying how much they took and what it was used for. After 2 weeks the money box appeared to be getting full, so Will asked Luke Gilmor to count the money, prepare a deposit slip, and deposit the money in a bank account Will had opened.

The day of the dance, Will wrote a check from the account to pay the DJ. D.J. Rivet, however, said that he accepted only cash and did not give receipts. So Will took $200 out of the cash box and gave it to D.J. At the dance Will had Mel Harris working at the entrance to the gymnasium, collecting tickets from students, and selling tickets to those who had not prepurchased them. Will estimated that 400 students attended the dance.

The following day Will closed out the bank account, which had $250 in it, and gave that amount plus the $180 in the cash box to Principal Foran. Principal Foran seemed surprised that, after generating roughly $2,000 in sales, the dance netted only $430 in cash. Will did not know how to respond.

Instructions

Identify as many internal control weaknesses as you can in this scenario, and suggest how each could be addressed.

Problems: Set B

P8-1B Magical Elves Theater is located in the Brooklyn Mall. A cashier's booth is located near the entrance to the theater. Three cashiers are employed. One works from 1–5 P.M., another from 5–9 P.M. The shifts are rotated among the three cashiers. The cashiers receive cash from customers and operate a machine that ejects serially numbered tickets. The rolls of tickets are inserted and locked into the machine by the theater manager at the beginning of each cashier's shift.

Identify internal control weaknesses over cash receipts.
(SO 2, 3)

After purchasing a ticket, the customer takes the ticket to an usher stationed at the entrance of the theater lobby some 60 feet from the cashier's booth. The usher tears the ticket in half, admits the customer, and returns the ticket stub to the customer. The other half of the ticket is dropped into a locked box by the usher.

At the end of each cashier's shift, the theater manager removes the ticket rolls from the machine and makes a cash count. The cash count sheet is initialed by the cashier. At the end of the day, the manager deposits the receipts in total in a bank night deposit vault located in the mall. The manager also sends copies of the deposit slip and the initialed cash count sheets to the theater company treasurer for verification and to the company's accounting department. Receipts from the first shift are stored in a safe located in the manager's office.

Instructions
(a) Identify the internal control principles and their application to the cash receipts transactions of the Magical Elves Theater.
(b) If the usher and cashier decide to collaborate to misappropriate cash, what actions might they take?

P8-2B Chow Company maintains a petty cash fund for small expenditures. The following transactions occurred over a 2-month period.

Journalize and post petty cash find transactions.
(SO 5)

July	1	Established petty cash fund by writing a check on China Bank for $100.
	15	Replenished the petty cash fund by writing a check for $96.90. On this date, the fund consisted of $3.10 in cash and the following petty cash receipts: freight-out $51.00, postage expense $20.50, entertainment expense $23.10, and miscellaneous expense $4.10.
	31	Replenished the petty cash fund by writing a check for $95.90. At this date, the fund consisted of $4.10 in cash and the following petty cash receipts: freight-out $43.50, charitable contributions expense $20.00, postage expense $20.10, and miscellaneous expense $12.30.
Aug.	15	Replenished the petty cash fund by writing a check for $98.00. On this date, the fund consisted of $2.00 in cash and the following petty cash receipts: freight-out $40.20, entertainment expense $21.00, postage expense $14.00, and miscellaneous expense $19.80.
	16	Increased the amount of the petty cash fund to $150 by writing a check for $50.
	31	Replenished the petty cash fund by writing a check for $137.00. On this date, the fund consisted of $13 in cash and the following petty cash receipts: freight-out $74.00, entertainment expense $43.20, and postage expense $17.70.

Instructions
(a) Journalize the petty cash transactions.
(b) Post to the Petty Cash account.
(c) What internal control features exist in a petty cash fund?

(a) July 15 Cash over $1.80
(b) Aug. 31 balance $150

P8-3B Rohatyn Genetics Company of Lancaster, Wisconsin, spreads herbicides and applies liquid fertilizer for local farmers. On May 31, 2012, the company's Cash account per its general ledger showed the following balance.

Prepare a bank reconciliation and adjusting entries.
(SO 7)

	CASH				NO. 101
Date	Explanation	Ref.	Debit	Credit	Balance
May 31	Balance				13,287

The bank statement from Lancaster State Bank on that date showed the following balance.

LANCASTER STATE BANK

Checks and Debits	Deposits and Credits	Daily Balance
XXX	XXX	5/31 13,332

A comparison of the details on the bank statement with the details in the cash account revealed the following facts.

1. The statement included a debit memo of $35 for the printing of additional company checks.
2. Cash sales of $1,720 on May 12 were deposited in the bank. The cash receipts journal entry and the deposit slip were incorrectly made for $1,820. The bank credited Rohatyn Genetics Company for the correct amount.
3. Outstanding checks at May 31 totaled $1,225, and deposits in transit were $2,100.
4. On May 18, the company issued check no. 1181 for $911 to J. Greenberg on account. The check, which cleared the bank in May, was incorrectly journalized and posted by Rohatyn Genetics Company for $119.
5. A $4,000 note receivable was collected by the bank for Rohatyn Genetics Company on May 31 plus $80 interest. The bank charged a collection fee of $25. No interest has been accrued on the note.
6. Included with the cancelled checks was a check issued by Powers Company to Jerry Saltz for $900 that was incorrectly charged to Rohatyn Genetics Company by the bank.
7. On May 31, the bank statement showed an NSF charge of $1,308 for a check issued by Simon de Pury, a customer, to Rohatyn Genetics Company on account.

Instructions

(a) Adj. cash bal. $15,107

(a) Prepare the bank reconciliation at May 31, 2012.
(b) Prepare the necessary adjusting entries for Rohatyn Genetics Company at May 31, 2012.

Prepare a bank reconciliation and adjusting entries from detailed data.
(SO 7)

P8-4B The bank portion of the bank reconciliation for Williams Company at October 31, 2012, was as follows.

WILLIAMS COMPANY
Bank Reconciliation
October 31, 2012

Cash balance per bank		$6,000
Add: Deposits in transit		842
		6,842
Less: Outstanding checks		

Check Number	Check Amount	
2451	$700	
2470	396	
2471	464	
2472	270	
2474	578	2,408
Adjusted cash balance per bank		$4,434

The adjusted cash balance per bank agreed with the cash balance per books at October 31. The November bank statement showed the following checks and deposits:

Bank Statement					
Checks			**Deposits**		
Date	Number	Amount	Date	Amount	
11-1	2470	$ 396	11-1	$ 842	
11-2	2471	464	11-4	666	
11-5	2474	578	11-8	545	
11-4	2475	903	11-13	1,416	
11-8	2476	1,556	11-18	810	
11-10	2477	330	11-21	1,624	
11-15	2479	980	11-25	1,412	
11-18	2480	714	11-28	908	
11-27	2481	382	11-30	652	
11-30	2483	317	Total	$8,875	
11-29	2486	495			
	Total	$7,115			

The cash records per books for November showed the following.

Cash Payments Journal							**Cash Receipts Journal**	
Date	Number	Amount	Date	Number	Amount		Date	Amount
11-1	2475	$ 903	11-20	2483	$ 317		11-3	$ 666
11-2	2476	1,556	11-22	2484	460		11-7	545
11-2	2477	330	11-23	2485	525		11-12	1,416
11-4	2478	300	11-24	2486	495		11-17	810
11-8	2479	890	11-29	2487	210		11-20	1,642
11-10	2480	714	11-30	2488	635		11-24	1,412
11-15	2481	382	Total		$8,067		11-27	908
11-18	2482	350					11-29	652
							11-30	1,541
							Total	$9,592

The bank statement contained two bank memoranda:

1. A credit of $1,375 for the collection of a $1,300 note for Williams Company plus interest of $91 and less a collection fee of $16. Williams Company has not accrued any interest on the note.
2. A debit for the printing of additional company checks $34.

At November 30, the cash balance per books was $5,958, and the cash balance per the bank statement was $9,100. The bank did not make any errors, but two errors were made by Williams Company.

Instructions

(a) Using the four steps in the reconciliation procedure described on pages 384–385, prepare a bank reconciliation at November 30.
(b) Prepare the adjusting entries based on the reconciliation. (*Hint:* The correction of any errors pertaining to recording checks should be made to Accounts Payable. The correction of any errors relating to recording cash receipts should be made to Accounts Receivable).

(a) Adjusted cash balance per bank $7,191

P8-5B Trong Company's bank statement from Nguyen National Bank at August 31, 2012, shows the information below.

Prepare a bank reconciliation and adjusting entries.
(SO 7)

Balance, August 1	$11,284	Bank credit memoranda:	
August deposits	47,521	Collection of note	
Checks cleared in August	46,475	receivable plus $105	
Balance, August 31	16,856	interest	$4,505
		Interest earned	41
		Bank debit memorandum:	
		Safety deposit box rent	20

A summary of the Cash account in the ledger for August shows: Balance, August 1, $10,959; receipts $50,050; disbursements $47,794; and balance, August 31, $13,215. Analysis reveals that the only reconciling items on the July 31 bank reconciliation were a deposit in transit for $2,600 and outstanding checks of $2,925. The deposit in transit was the first deposit recorded by the bank in August. In addition, you determine that there were two errors involving company checks drawn in August: (1) A check for $340 to a creditor on account that cleared the bank in August was journalized and posted for $430. (2) A salary check to an employee for $275 was recorded by the bank for $277.

Instructions

(a) Adjusted balance per books $17,831

(a) Prepare a bank reconciliation at August 31.

(b) Journalize the adjusting entries to be made by Trong Company at August 31. Assume that interest on the note has not been accrued by the company.

Prepare a comprehensive bank reconciliation with theft and internal control deficiencies.

(SO 2, 3, 4, 7)

P8-6B Braun Company is a very profitable small business. It has not, however, given much consideration to internal control. For example, in an attempt to keep clerical and office expenses to a minimum, the company has combined the jobs of cashier and bookkeeper. As a result, Judith Tan handles all cash receipts, keeps the accounting records, and prepares the monthly bank reconciliations.

The balance per the bank statement on October 31, 2012, was $15,453. Outstanding checks were: no. 62 for $107.74, no. 183 for $127.50, no. 284 for $215.26, no. 862 for $162.10, no. 863 for $192.78, and no. 864 for $140.49. Included with the statement was a credit memorandum of $340 indicating the collection of a note receivable for Braun Company by the bank on October 25. This memorandum has not been recorded by Braun Company.

The company's ledger showed one cash account with a balance of $18,608.81. The balance included undeposited cash on hand. Because of the lack of internal controls, Tan took for personal use all of the undeposited receipts in excess of $3,226.18. She then prepared the following bank reconciliation in an effort to conceal her theft of cash.

BANK RECONCILIATION

Cash balance per books, October 31		$18,608.81
Add: Outstanding checks		
No. 862	$162.10	
No. 863	192.78	
No. 864	140.49	410.37
		19,019.18
Less: Undeposited receipts		3,226.18
Unadjusted balance per bank, October 31		15,793.00
Less: Bank credit memorandum		340.00
Cash balance per bank statement, October 31		$15,453.00

Instructions

(a) Adjusted balance per books $17,733.31

(a) Prepare a correct bank reconciliation. (*Hint:* Deduct the amount of the theft from the adjusted balance per books.)

(b) Indicate the three ways that Tan attempted to conceal the theft and the dollar amount pertaining to each method.

(c) What principles of internal control were violated in this case?

Problems: Set C

Visit the book's companion website, at **www.wiley.com/college/weygandt**, and choose the Student Companion site to access Problem Set C.

Comprehensive Problem

CP8   On December 1, 2012, Bluemound Company had the following account balances.

	Debits		Credits
Cash	$18,200	Accumulated Depreciation—	
Notes Receivable	2,200	Equipment	$ 3,000
Accounts Receivable	7,500	Accounts Payable	6,100
Inventory	16,000	Owner's Capital	64,400
Prepaid Insurance	1,600		$73,500
Equipment	28,000		
	$73,500		

During December, the company completed the following transactions.

Dec. 7   Received $3,600 cash from customers in payment of account (no discount allowed).
   12   Purchased merchandise on account from Klump Co. $12,000, terms 1/10, n/30.
   17   Sold merchandise on account $15,000, terms 2/10, n/30. The cost of the merchandise sold was $10,000.
   19   Paid salaries $2,500.
   22   Paid Klump Co. in full, less discount.
   26   Received collections in full, less discounts, from customers billed on December 17.

Adjustment data:

1. Depreciation $200 per month.
2. Insurance expired $400.

Instructions

(a) Journalize the December transactions. (Assume a perpetual inventory system.)
(b) Enter the December 1 balances in the ledger T accounts and post the December transactions. Use Cost of Goods Sold, Depreciation Expense, Insurance Expense, Salaries and Wages Expense, Sales Revenue, and Sales Discounts.
(c) The statement from Jackson County Bank on December 31 showed a balance of $21,994. A comparison of the bank statement with the Cash account revealed the following facts.
   1. The bank collected a note receivable of $2,200 for Bluemound Company on December 15.
   2. The December 31 receipts of $2,736 were not included in the bank deposits for December. The company deposited these receipts in a night deposit vault on December 31.
   3. Checks outstanding on December 31 totaled $1,210.
   4. On December 31, the bank statement showed a NSF charge of $800 for a check received by the company from L. Shur, a customer, on account.

   Prepare a bank reconciliation as of December 31 based on the available information. (*Hint:* The cash balance per books is $22,120. This can be proven by finding the balance in the Cash account from parts (a) and (b).)
(d) Journalize the adjusting entries resulting from the bank reconciliation and adjustment data.
(e) Post the adjusting entries to the ledger T accounts.
(f) Prepare an adjusted trial balance.
(g) Prepare an income statement for December and a classified balance sheet at December 31.

Continuing Cookie Chronicle

(*Note:* This is a continuation of the Cookie Chronicle from Chapters 1 through 7.)

CCC8   Part 1   Natalie is struggling to keep up with the recording of her accounting transactions. She is spending a lot of time marketing and selling mixers and giving her cookie classes. Her friend John is an accounting student who runs his own accounting service. He has asked Natalie if she would like to have him do her accounting. John and Natalie meet and discuss her business.

Part 2   Natalie decides that she cannot afford to hire John to do her accounting. One way that she can ensure that her cash account does not have any errors and is accurate and up-to-date is to prepare a bank reconciliation at the end of each month. Natalie would like you to help her.

Go to the book's companion website, **www.wiley.com/college/weygandt**, *to see the completion of this problem.*

BROADENINGYOURPERSPECTIVE

Financial Reporting and Analysis

Financial Reporting Problem: PepsiCo, Inc.

BYP8-1   The financial statements of PepsiCo, Inc. are presented in Appendix A at the end of this textbook.

Instructions

(a) What comments, if any, are made about cash in the report of the independent registered public accounting firm?

(b) What data about cash and cash equivalents are shown in the consolidated balance sheet?

(c) In its notes to Consolidated Financial Statements, how does PepsiCo define cash equivalents?

(d) In management's letter that assumes "Responsibility for Financial Reporting," what does PepsiCo's management say about internal control? (See page A31 in Appendix A of the back of the book.)

Comparative Analysis Problem: PepsiCo, Inc. vs. The Coca-Cola Company

BYP8-2   PepsiCo's financial statements are presented in Appendix A. Financial statements of The Coca-Cola Company are presented in Appendix B.

Instructions

(a) Based on the information contained in these financial statements, determine each of the following for each company:

   (1) Cash and cash equivalents balance at December 26, 2009, for PepsiCo and at December 31, 2009, for Coca-Cola.

   (2) Increase (decrease) in cash and cash equivalents from 2008 to 2009.

   (3) Cash provided by operating activities during the year ended December 2009 (from statement of cash flows).

(b) What conclusions concerning the management of cash can be drawn from these data?

On the Web

BYP8-3   All organizations should have systems of internal control. Universities are no exception. This site discusses the basics of internal control in a university setting.

Address: www.bc.edu/offices/audit/controls, or go to **www.wiley.com/college/weygandt**

Steps: Go to the site shown above.

Instructions

The front page of this site provides links to pages that answer six critical questions. Use these links to answer the following questions.

(a) In a university setting, who has responsibility for evaluating the adequacy of the system of internal control?

(b) What do reconciliations ensure in the university setting? Who should review the reconciliation?

(c) What are some examples of physical controls?

(d) What are two ways to accomplish inventory counts?

Critical Thinking

Decision Making Across the Organization

BYP8-4   The board of trustees of a local church is concerned about the internal accounting controls for the offering collections made at weekly services. The trustees ask you to serve on a three-person audit team with the internal auditor of a local college and a CPA who has just joined the church.

At a meeting of the audit team and the board of trustees, you learn the following.

1. The church's board of trustees has delegated responsibility for the financial management and audit of the financial records to the finance committee. This group prepares the annual budget and approves major disbursements. It is not involved in collections or record-keeping. No audit has been made in recent years because the same trusted employee has kept church records and served as financial secretary for 15 years. The church does not carry any fidelity insurance.

2. The collection at the weekly service is taken by a team of ushers who volunteer to serve one month. The ushers take the collection plates to a basement office at the rear of the church. They hand their plates to the head usher and return to the church service. After all plates have been turned in, the head usher counts the cash received. The head usher then places the cash in the church safe along with a notation of the amount counted. The head usher volunteers to serve for 3 months.

3. The next morning, the financial secretary opens the safe and recounts the collection. The secretary withholds $150–$200 in cash, depending on the cash expenditures expected for the week, and deposits the remainder of the collections in the bank. To facilitate the deposit, church members who contribute by check are asked to make their checks payable to "Cash."

4. Each month, the financial secretary reconciles the bank statement and submits a copy of the reconciliation to the board of trustees. The reconciliations have rarely contained any bank errors and have never shown any errors per books.

Instructions

With the class divided into groups, answer the following.

(a) Indicate the weaknesses in internal accounting control over the handling of collections.

(b) List the improvements in internal control procedures that you plan to make at the next meeting of the audit team for (1) the ushers, (2) the head usher, (3) the financial secretary, and (4) the finance committee.

(c) What church policies should be changed to improve internal control?

Communication Activity

BYP8-5   As a new auditor for the CPA firm of Croix, Marais, and Kale, you have been assigned to review the internal controls over mail cash receipts of Manhattan Company. Your review reveals the following: Checks are promptly endorsed "For Deposit Only," but no list of the checks is prepared by the person opening the mail. The mail is opened either by the cashier or by the employee who maintains the accounts receivable records. Mail receipts are deposited in the bank weekly by the cashier.

Instructions

Write a letter to Jerry Mays, owner of Manhattan Company, explaining the weaknesses in internal control and your recommendations for improving the system.

Ethics Case

BYP8-6   You are the assistant controller in charge of general ledger accounting at Riverside Bottling Company. Your company has a large loan from an insurance company. The loan agreement requires that the company's cash account balance be maintained at $200,000 or more, as reported monthly.

At June 30, the cash balance is $80,000, which you report to Gena Schmitt, the financial vice president. Gena excitedly instructs you to keep the cash receipts book open for one additional day for purposes of the June 30 report to the insurance company. Gena says, "If we don't get that cash balance over $200,000, we'll default on our loan agreement. They could close us down, put us all out of our jobs!" Gena continues, "I talked to Oconto Distributors (one of Riverside's largest customers) this morning. They said they sent us a check for $150,000 yesterday. We should receive it tomorrow. If we include just that one check in our cash balance, we'll be in the clear. It's in the mail!"

Instructions

(a) Who will suffer negative effects if you do not comply with Gena Schmitt's instructions? Who will suffer if you do comply?

(b) What are the ethical considerations in this case?

(c) What alternatives do you have?

"All About You" Activity

BYP8-7   The **All About You** feature (available on the book's companion website) indicates potential security risks that may arise from your personal computer. It is important to keep in mind, however, that there are also many other ways that your identity can be stolen other than from your computer. The federal government provides many resources to help protect you from identity thieves.

Instructions
Go to **http://onguardonline.gov/idtheft.html**, and click on **ID Theft Faceoff**. Complete the quiz provided there.

FASB Codification Activity

BYP8-8   If your school has a subscription to the FASB Codification, go to *http://aaahq.org/ascLogin.cfm* to log in and prepare responses to the following.
(a) How is cash defined in the Codification?
(b) How are cash equivalents defined in the Codification?
(c) What are the disclosure requirements related to cash and cash equivalents?

Answers to Insight and Accounting Across the Organization Questions

p. 371 SOX Boosts the Role of Human Resources   Q: Why would unsupervised employees or employees who report to each other represent potential internal control threats? **A:** An unsupervised employee may have a fraudulent job (or may even be a fictitious person), e.g., a person drawing a paycheck without working. Or, if two employees supervise each other, there is no real separation of duties, and they can conspire to defraud the company.

p. 371 Big Theft at Small Companies   Q: Why are small companies more susceptible to employee theft? **A:** The high degree of trust often found in small companies makes them more vulnerable. Also, small companies tend to have less sophisticated systems of internal control, and they usually lack internal auditors. In addition, it is very hard to achieve some internal control features, such as segregation of duties, when you have very few employees.

p. 379 How Employees Steal   Q: How can companies reduce the likelihood of fraudulent disbursements? **A:** To reduce the occurrence of fraudulent disbursements, a company should follow the procedures discussed in this chapter. These include having only designated personnel sign checks; having different personnel approve payments and make payments; ensuring that check signers do not record disbursements; using prenumbered checks and matching each check to an approved invoice; storing blank checks securely; reconciling the bank statement; and stamping invoices PAID.

p. 387 Madoff's Ponzi Scheme   Q: How was Madoff able to conceal such a giant fraud? **A:** Madoff fabricated false investment statements that were provided to investors. In addition, his auditor never verified these investment statements even though the auditor gave him an unqualified opinion each year.

Answers to Self-Test Questions
1. c   **2.** a   **3.** a   **4.** c   **5.** b   **6.** b   **7.** d   **8.** d   **9.** a ($100 − ($94 + $4))   **10.** a   **11.** c   **12.** d   **13.** c   **14.** c

IFRS   A Look at IFRS

Fraud can occur anywhere. And because the three main factors that contribute to fraud are universal in nature, the principles of internal control activities are used globally by companies. While Sarbanes-Oxley (SOX) does not apply to international companies, most large international companies have internal controls similar to those indicated in the chapter. IFRS and GAAP are very similar in accounting for cash. *IAS No. 1 (revised)*, "Presentation of Financial Statements," is the only standard that discusses issues specifically related to cash.

Key Points

- The fraud triangle discussed in this chapter is applicable to all international companies. Some of the major frauds on an international basis are Parmalat (Italy), Royal Ahold (the Netherlands), and Satyam Computer Services (India).

- Rising economic crime poses a growing threat to companies, with nearly half of all organizations worldwide being victims of fraud in a recent two-year period (*PricewaterhouseCoopers' Global Economic Crime Survey,* 2005). Specifically, 44% of Romanian companies surveyed experienced fraud in the past two years.

- Globally, the number of companies reporting fraud increased from 37% to 45% since 2003, a 22% increase. The cost to companies was an average US$1.7 million in losses from "tangible frauds," that is, those that result in an immediate and direct financial loss. These include asset misappropriation, false pretenses, and counterfeiting (*PricewaterhouseCoopers' Global Economic Crime Survey,* 2005).

- Accounting scandals both in the United States and internationally have re-ignited the debate over the relative merits of GAAP, which takes a "rules-based" approach to accounting, versus IFRS, which takes a "principles-based" approach. The FASB announced that it intends to introduce more principles-based standards.

- On a lighter note, at one time Ig Nobel Prize in Economics went to the CEOs of those companies involved in the corporate accounting scandals of that year for "adapting the mathematical concept of imaginary numbers for use in the business world." The Ig Nobel Prizes (read Ignoble, as not noble) are a parody of the Nobel Prizes and are given each year in early October for 10 achievements that "first make people laugh, and then make them think." Organized by the scientific humor magazine *Annals of Improbable Research* (*AIR*), they are presented by a group that includes genuine Nobel laureates at a ceremony at Harvard University's Sanders Theater. (See *en.wikipedia.org/wiki/Ig_Nobel_Prize.*)

- Internal controls are a system of checks and balances designed to prevent and detect fraud and errors. While most companies have these systems in place, many have never completely documented them, nor had an independent auditor attest to their effectiveness. Both of these actions are required under SOX.

- Companies find that internal control review is a costly process but badly needed. One study estimates the cost of SOX compliance for U.S. companies at over $35 billion, with audit fees doubling in the first year of compliance. At the same time, examination of internal controls indicates lingering problems in the way companies operate. One study of first compliance with the internal-control testing provisions documented material weaknesses for about 13% of companies reporting in a two-year period (*PricewaterhouseCoopers' Global Economic Crime Survey,* 2005).

- The SOX internal control standards apply only to companies listed on U.S. exchanges. There is continuing debate over whether foreign issuers should have to comply with this extra layer of regulation.

- The accounting and internal control procedures related to cash are essentially the same under both IFRS and this textbook. In addition, the definition used for cash equivalents is the same.

- Most companies report cash and cash equivalents together under IFRS, as shown in this textbook. In addition, IFRS follows the same accounting policies related to the reporting of restricted cash.

- IFRS defines cash and cash equivalents as follows.

  - **Cash** is comprised of cash on hand and demand deposits.

  - **Cash equivalents** are short-term, highly liquid investments that are readily convertible to known amounts of cash and which are subject to an insignificant risk of changes in value.

Looking to the Future

Ethics has become a very important aspect of reporting. Different cultures have different perspectives on bribery and other questionable activities, and consequently penalties for engaging in such activities vary considerably across countries.

High-quality international accounting requires both high-quality accounting standards and high-quality auditing. Similar to the convergence of GAAP and IFRS, there is movement to improve international auditing standards. The International Auditing and Assurance Standards Board (IAASB) functions as an independent standard-setting body. It works to establish high-quality auditing and assurance and quality-control standards throughout the world. Whether the IAASB adopts internal control provisions similar to those in SOX remains to be seen. You can follow developments in the international audit arena at *http://www.ifac.org/iaasb/*.

Under proposed new standards for financial statements, companies would not be allowed to combine cash equivalents with cash.

IFRS Self-Test Questions

1. Non-U.S companies that follow IFRS:
   (a) do not normally use the principles of internal control activities used in this textbook.
   (b) often offset cash with accounts payable on the balance sheet.
   (c) are not required to follow SOX.
   (d) None of the above.

2. Which of the following is the correct accounting under IFRS for cash?
   (a) Cash cannot be combined with cash equivalents.
   (b) Restricted cash funds may be reported as a current or non-current asset depending on the circumstances.
   (c) Restricted cash funds cannot be reported as a current asset.
   (d) Cash on hand is not reported on the balance sheet as Cash.

3. The Sarbanes-Oxley Act of 2002 applies to:
   (a) all U.S. companies listed on U.S. exchanges.
   (b) all companies that list stock on any stock exchange in any country.
   (c) all European companies listed on European exchanges.
   (d) Both (a) and (c).

4. High-quality international accounting requires both high-quality accounting standards and:
   (a) a reconsideration of SOX to make it less onerous.
   (b) high-quality auditing standards.
   (c) government intervention to ensure that the public interest is protected.
   (d) the development of new principles of internal control activities.

5. Cash equivalents under IFRS:
   (a) are significantly different than the cash equivalents discussed in the textbook.
   (b) are generally disclosed separately from cash.
   (c) may be required to be reported separately from cash in the future.
   (d) None of the above.

IFRS Concepts and Application

IFRS8-1   Some people argue that the internal control requirements of the Sarbanes-Oxley Act (SOX) put U.S. companies at a competitive disadvantage to companies outside the United States. Discuss the competitive implications (both pros and cons) of SOX.

IFRS8-2   State whether each of the following is true or false. For those that are false, explain why.

(a) A proposed new financial accounting standard would not allow cash equivalents to be reported in combination with cash.

(b) Perspectives on bribery and penalties for engaging in bribery are the same across all countries.

(c) Cash equivalents are comprised of cash on hand and demand deposits.

(d) SOX was created by the International Accounting Standards Board.

International Financial Reporting Problem: *Zetar plc*

IFRS8-3   The financial statements of Zetar plc are presented in Appendix C. The company's complete annual report, including the notes to its financial statements, is available at *www.zetarplc.com.*

Instructions

Using the notes to the company's financial statements, answer the following questions.

(a) Which committee of the board of directors is responsible for considering management's reports on internal control?

(b) What are the company's key control procedures?

(c) Does the company have an internal audit department?

(d) In what section or sections does Zetar report its bank overdrafts?

Answers to IFRS Self-Test Questions
1. c   **2.** b   **3.** a   **4.** b   **5.** c

The Navigator

✔ **Remember to go back to the Navigator box on the chapter opening page and check off your completed work.**

CHAPTER9

Accounting for Receivables

Study Objectives

After studying this chapter, you should be able to:

[1] Identify the different types of receivables.

[2] Explain how companies recognize accounts receivable.

[3] Distinguish between the methods and bases companies use to value accounts receivable.

[4] Describe the entries to record the disposition of accounts receivable.

[5] Compute the maturity date of and interest on notes receivable.

[6] Explain how companies recognize notes receivable.

[7] Describe how companies value notes receivable.

[8] Describe the entries to record the disposition of notes receivable.

[9] Explain the statement presentation and analysis of receivables.

✔ The Navigator

✔ [The Navigator]

- ● Scan Study Objectives ○
- ● Read Feature Story ○
- ● Read Preview ○
- ● Read text and answer **Do it!** p. 425 ○ p. 427 ○ p. 433 ○ p. 434 ○
- ● Work Comprehensive **Do it!** p. 435 ○
- ● Review Summary of Study Objectives ○
- ● Answer Self-Test Questions ○
- ● Complete Assignments ○
- ● Go to *WileyPLUS* for practice and tutorials ○
- ● Read A Look at IFRS p. 453 ○

Feature Story

A DOSE OF CAREFUL MANAGEMENT KEEPS RECEIVABLES HEALTHY

"Sometimes you have to know when to be very tough, and sometimes you can give them a bit of a break," says Vivi Su. She's not talking about her children, but about the customers of a subsidiary of pharmaceutical company Whitehall-Robins, where she works as supervisor of credit and collections.

For example, while the company's regular terms are 1/15, n/30 (1% discount if paid within 15 days), a customer might ask for and receive a few days of grace and still get the discount. Or a customer might place orders above its credit limit, in which case, depending on its payment history and the circumstances, Ms. Su might authorize shipment of the goods anyway.

"It's not about drawing a line in the sand, and that's all," she explains. "You want a good relationship with your customers—but you also need to bring in the money."

"The money," in Whitehall-Robins's case, amounts to some $170 million in sales a year. Nearly all of it comes in through the credit accounts Ms. Su manages. The process starts with the decision to grant a customer an account in the first place, Ms. Su explains. The sales rep gives the customer a credit application. "My department reviews this application very carefully; a customer needs to supply three good references, and we also run a check with a credit firm like Equifax. If we accept them, then based on their size and history, we assign a credit limit."

Once accounts are established, the company supervises them very carefully. "I get an aging report every single day," says Ms. Su.

"The rule of thumb is that we should always have at least 85% of receivables current—meaning they were billed less than 30 days ago," she continues. "But we try to do even better than that—I like to see 90%." Similarly, her guideline is never to have more than 5% of receivables at over 90 days. But long before that figure is reached, "we jump on it," she says firmly.

At 15 days overdue, Whitehall-Robins phones the client. Often there's a reasonable explanation for the delay—an invoice may have gone astray, or the payables clerk is away. "But if a customer keeps on delaying, and tells us several times that it'll only be a few more days, we know there's a problem," says Ms. Su. After 45 days, "I send a letter. Then a second notice is sent in writing. After the third and final notice, the client has 10 days to pay, and then I hand it over to a collection agency, and it's out of my hands."

Ms. Su's boss, Terry Norton, records an estimate for bad debts every year, based on a percentage of receivables. The percentage depends on the current aging history. He also calculates and monitors the company's receivables turnover ratio, which the company reports in its financial statements. "I think of it in terms of collection period of DSO—days of sales outstanding," he explains.

Ms. Su knows that she and Mr. Norton are crucial to the profitability of Whitehall-Robins. "Receivables are generally the second-largest asset of any company (after its capital assets)," she points out. "So it's no wonder we keep a very close eye on them."

✔
The Navigator

PreviewofCHAPTER9

As indicated in the Feature Story, receivables are a significant asset for many pharmaceutical companies. Because a significant portion of sales in the United States are done on credit, receivables are significant to companies in other industries as well. As a consequence, companies must pay close attention to their receivables and manage them carefully. In this chapter you will learn what journal entries companies make when they sell products, when they collect cash from those sales, and when they write off accounts they cannot collect.

The content and organization of the chapter are as follows.

Accounting for Receivables

Types of Receivables	Accounts Receivable	Notes Receivable	Statement Presentation and Analysis
• Accounts receivable • Notes receivable • Other receivables	• Recognizing accounts receivable • Valuing accounts receivable • Disposing of accounts receivable	• Determining maturity date • Computing interest • Recognizing notes receivable • Valuing notes receivable • Disposing of notes receivable	• Presentation • Analysis

The Navigator

Types of Receivables

Study Objective [1]
Identify the different types of receivables.

The term **receivables** refers to amounts due from individuals and companies. Receivables are claims that are expected to be collected in cash. The management of receivables is a very important activity for any company that sells goods or services on credit.

Receivables are important because they represent one of a company's most liquid assets. For many companies, receivables are also one of the largest assets. For example, receivables represented 30.8% of the current assets of pharmaceutical giant Rite Aid in 2009. Illustration 9-1 lists receivables as a percentage of total assets for five other well-known companies in a recent year.

Illustration 9-1
Receivables as a percentage of assets

Company	Receivables as a Percentage of Total Assets
General Electric	52%
Ford Motor Company	42%
Minnesota Mining and Manufacturing Company (3M)	14%
DuPont Co.	17%
Intel Corporation	5%

The relative significance of a company's receivables as a percentage of its assets depends on various factors: its industry, the time of year, whether it extends long-term financing, and its credit policies. To reflect important differences among receivables, they are frequently classified as (1) accounts receivable, (2) notes receivable, and (3) other receivables.

Accounts receivable are amounts customers owe on account. They result from the sale of goods and services. Companies generally expect to collect accounts receivable within 30 to 60 days. They are usually the most significant type of claim held by a company.

Notes receivable represent claims for which formal instruments of credit are issued as evidence of the debt. The credit instrument normally requires the debtor to pay interest and extends for time periods of 60–90 days or longer. Notes and accounts receivable that result from sales transactions are often called **trade receivables**.

Other receivables include nontrade receivables such as interest receivable, loans to company officers, advances to employees, and income taxes refundable. These do not generally result from the operations of the business. Therefore, they are generally classified and reported as separate items in the balance sheet.

Ethics Note

Companies report receivables from employees separately in the financial statements. The reason: Sometimes those assets are not the result of an "arm's-length" transaction.

Accounts Receivable

Three accounting issues associated with accounts receivable are:

1. Recognizing accounts receivable.
2. Valuing accounts receivable.
3. Disposing of accounts receivable.

Recognizing Accounts Receivable

Recognizing accounts receivable is relatively straightforward. A service organization records a receivable when it provides service on account. A merchandiser records accounts receivable at the point of sale of merchandise on account. When a merchandiser sells goods, it increases (debits) Accounts Receivable and increases (credits) Sales Revenue.

The seller may offer terms that encourage early payment by providing a discount. Sales returns also reduce receivables. The buyer might find some of the goods unacceptable and choose to return the unwanted goods.

To review, assume that Jordache Co. on July 1, 2012, sells merchandise on account to Polo Company for $1,000, terms 2/10, n/30. On July 5, Polo returns merchandise worth $100 to Jordache Co. On July 11, Jordache receives payment from Polo Company for the balance due. The journal entries to record these transactions on the books of Jordache Co. are as follows. **(Cost of goods sold entries are omitted.)**

Study Objective [2]
Explain how companies recognize accounts receivable.

Ethics Note

In exchange for lower interest rates, some companies have eliminated the 25-day grace period before finance charges kick in. Be sure you read the fine print in any credit agreement you sign.

July 1	Accounts Receivable—Polo Company	1,000	
	Sales Revenue		1,000
	(To record sales on account)		
July 5	Sales Returns and Allowances	100	
	Accounts Receivable—Polo Company		100
	(To record merchandise returned)		
July 11	Cash ($900 − $18)	882	
	Sales Discounts ($900 × .02)	18	
	Accounts Receivable—Polo Company		900
	(To record collection of accounts receivable)		

Helpful Hint

These entries are the same as those described in Chapter 5. For simplicity, we have omitted inventory and cost of goods sold from this set of journal entries and from end-of-chapter material.

Some retailers issue their own credit cards. When you use a retailer's credit card (JCPenney, for example), the retailer charges interest on the balance due if not paid within a specified period (usually 25–30 days).

To illustrate, assume that you use your JCPenney Company credit card to purchase clothing with a sales price of $300. JCPenney will increase (debit) Accounts Receivable for $300 and increase (credit) Sales Revenue for $300 (cost of goods sold entry omitted) as follows.

Accounts Receivable	300	
Sales Revenue		300
(To record sale of merchandise)		

Cash Flows
no effect

Assuming that you owe $300 at the end of the month, and JCPenney charges 1.5% per month on the balance due, the adjusting entry that JCPenney makes to record interest revenue of $4.50 ($300 × 1.5%) is as follows.

Accounts Receivable	4.50	
Interest Revenue		4.50
(To record interest on amount due)		

Cash Flows
no effect

Interest revenue is often substantial for many retailers.

ANATOMY OF A FRAUD

Tasanee was the accounts receivable clerk for a large non-profit foundation that provided performance and exhibition space for the performing and visual arts. Her responsibilities included activities normally assigned to an accounts receivable clerk, such as recording revenues from various sources that included donations, facility rental fees, ticket revenue, and bar receipts. However, she was also responsible for handling all cash and checks from the time they were received until the time she deposited them, as well as preparing the bank reconciliation. Tasanee took advantage of her situation by falsifying bank deposits and bank reconciliations so that she could steal cash from the bar receipts. Since nobody else logged the donations or matched the donation receipts to pledges prior to Tasanee receiving them, she was able to offset the cash that was stolen against donations that she received but didn't record. Her crime was made easier by the fact that her boss, the company's controller, only did a very superficial review of the bank reconciliation and thus didn't notice that some numbers had been cut out from other documents and taped onto the bank reconciliation.

Total take: $1.5 million

THE MISSING CONTROL

Segregation of duties. The foundation should not have allowed an accounts receivable clerk, whose job was to record receivables, to also handle cash, record cash, make deposits, and especially prepare the bank reconciliation.

Independent internal verification. The controller was supposed to perform a thorough review of the bank reconciliation. Because he did not, he was terminated from his position.

Source: Adapted from Wells, *Fraud Casebook* (2007), pp. 183–194.

Study Objective [3]
Distinguish between the methods and bases companies use to value accounts receivable.

Valuing Accounts Receivable

Once companies record receivables in the accounts, the next question is: How should they report receivables in the financial statements? Companies report accounts receivable on the balance sheet as an asset. But determining the **amount** to report is sometimes difficult because some receivables will become uncollectible.

Each customer must satisfy the credit requirements of the seller before the credit sale is approved. Inevitably, though, some accounts receivable become uncollectible. For example, a customer may not be able to pay because of a decline in its sales revenue due to a downturn in the economy. Similarly, individuals may be laid off from their jobs or faced with unexpected hospital bills. Companies record credit losses as debits to **Bad Debts Expense** (or Uncollectible Accounts Expense). Such losses are a normal and necessary risk of doing business on a credit basis.

Recently, when U.S. home prices fell, home foreclosures rose, and the economy in general slowed, lenders experienced huge increases in their bad debts expense. For example, during a recent quarter Wachovia, the fourth largest U.S. bank, increased bad debts expense from $108 million to $408 million. Similarly, American Express increased its bad debts expense by 70%.

Two methods are used in accounting for uncollectible accounts: (1) the direct write-off method and (2) the allowance method. The following sections explain these methods.

DIRECT WRITE-OFF METHOD FOR UNCOLLECTIBLE ACCOUNTS

Under the **direct write-off method**, when a company determines a particular account to be uncollectible, it charges the loss to Bad Debts Expense. Assume, for example, that Warden Co. writes off as uncollectible M. E. Doran's $200 balance on December 12. Warden's entry is:

Dec. 12	Bad Debts Expense	200	
	Accounts Receivable—M. E. Doran		200
	(To record write-off of M. E. Doran account)		

Cash Flows
no effect

Under this method, Bad Debts Expense will show only **actual losses** from uncollectibles. The company will report accounts receivable at its gross amount.

Although this method is simple, its use can reduce the usefulness of both the income statement and balance sheet. Consider the following example. Assume that in 2012, Quick Buck Computer Company decided it could increase its revenues by offering computers to college students without requiring any money down and with no credit-approval process. On campuses across the country, it distributed one million computers with a selling price of $800 each. This increased Quick Buck's revenues and receivables by $800 million. The promotion was a huge success! The 2012 balance sheet and income statement looked great. Unfortunately, during 2013, nearly 40% of the customers defaulted on their loans. This made the 2013 income statement and balance sheet look terrible. Illustration 9-2 shows the effect of these events on the financial statements if the direct write-off method is used.

Alternative Terminology

You will sometimes see *Bad Debts Expense* called *Uncollectible Accounts Expense*.

Illustration 9-2
Effects of direct write-off method

Year 2012	Year 2013
Net income	Net income
Huge sales promotion. Sales increase dramatically. Accounts receivable increases dramatically.	Customers default on loans. Bad debts expense increases dramatically. Accounts receivable plummets.

Under the direct write-off method, companies often record bad debts expense in a period different from the period in which they record the revenue. The method does not attempt to match bad debts expense to sales revenues in the income statement. Nor does the direct write-off method show accounts receivable in the balance sheet at the amount the company actually expects to receive. **Consequently, unless bad debts losses are insignificant, the direct write-off method is not acceptable for financial reporting purposes.**

ALLOWANCE METHOD FOR UNCOLLECTIBLE ACCOUNTS

The **allowance method** of accounting for bad debts involves estimating uncollectible accounts at the end of each period. This provides better matching on the income statement. It also ensures that companies state receivables on the balance sheet at their cash (net) realizable value. **Cash (net) realizable value** is the net amount the company expects to receive in cash. It excludes amounts that the company estimates it will not collect. Thus, this method reduces receivables in the balance sheet by the amount of estimated uncollectible receivables.

GAAP requires the allowance method for financial reporting purposes when bad debts are material in amount. This method has three essential features:

Helpful Hint

In this context, *material* means significant or important to financial statement users.

1. Companies **estimate** uncollectible accounts receivable. They match this estimated expense **against revenues** in the same accounting period in which they record the revenues.

2. Companies debit estimated uncollectibles to Bad Debts Expense and credit them to Allowance for Doubtful Accounts through an adjusting entry at the end of each period. Allowance for Doubtful Accounts is a contra account to Accounts Receivable.

3. When companies write off a specific account, they debit actual uncollectibles to Allowance for Doubtful Accounts and credit that amount to Accounts Receivable.

Recording Estimated Uncollectibles.   To illustrate the allowance method, assume that Hampson Furniture has credit sales of $1,200,000 in 2012. Of this amount, $200,000 remains uncollected at December 31. The credit manager estimates that $12,000 of these sales will be uncollectible. The adjusting entry to record the estimated uncollectibles increases (debits) Bad Debts Expense and increases (credits) Allowance for Doubtful Accounts, as follows.

A = L + OE

−12,000 Exp

−12,000

Cash Flows
no effect

Dec. 31	Bad Debts Expense	12,000	
	Allowance for Doubtful Accounts		12,000
	(To record estimate of uncollectible		
	accounts)		

Hampson reports Bad Debts Expense in the income statement as an operating expense (usually as a selling expense). Thus, the estimated uncollectibles are matched with sales in 2012. Hampson records the expense in the same year it made the sales.

Allowance for Doubtful Accounts shows the estimated amount of claims on customers that the company expects will become uncollectible in the future. Companies use a contra account instead of a direct credit to Accounts Receivable because they do not know *which* customers will not pay. The credit balance in the allowance account will absorb the specific write-offs when they occur. As Illustration 9-3 shows, the company deducts the allowance account from accounts receivable in the current assets section of the balance sheet.

Helpful Hint

Cash realizable value is sometimes referred to as *accounts receivable (net)*.

The amount of $188,000 in Illustration 9-3 represents the expected **cash realizable value** of the accounts receivable at the statement date. **Companies do not close Allowance for Doubtful Accounts at the end of the fiscal year.**

Illustration 9-3
Presentation of allowance for doubtful accounts

Hampson Furniture
Balance Sheet (partial)

Current assets		
Cash		$ 14,800
Accounts receivable	$200,000	
Less: Allowance for doubtful accounts	12,000	188,000
Inventory		310,000
Supplies		25,000
Total current assets		$537,800

Recording the Write-Off of an Uncollectible Account. As described in the Feature Story, companies use various methods of collecting past-due accounts, such as letters, calls, and legal action. When they have exhausted all means of collecting a past-due account and collection appears impossible, the company should write off the account. In the credit card industry, for example, it is standard practice to write off accounts that are 210 days past due. To prevent premature or unauthorized write-offs, authorized management personnel should formally approve each write-off. To maintain good internal control, companies should not authorize someone to write off accounts who also has daily responsibilities related to cash or receivables.

To illustrate a receivables write-off, assume that the financial vice president of Hampson Furniture authorizes a write-off of the $500 balance owed by R. A. Ware on March 1, 2013. The entry to record the write-off is:

Mar. 1	Allowance for Doubtful Accounts	500	
	Accounts Receivable—R. A. Ware		500
	(Write-off of R. A. Ware account)		

A = L + OE
+500
−500

Cash Flows
no effect

Bad Debts Expense does not increase when the write-off occurs. **Under the allowance method, companies debit every bad debt write-off to the allowance account rather than to Bad Debts Expense.** A debit to Bad Debts Expense would be incorrect because the company has already recognized the expense when it made the adjusting entry for estimated bad debts. Instead, the entry to record the write-off of an uncollectible account reduces both Accounts Receivable and Allowance for Doubtful Accounts. After posting, the general ledger accounts will appear as in Illustration 9-4.

Illustration 9-4
General ledger balances after write-off

Accounts Receivable				Allowance for Doubtful Accounts			
Jan. 1 Bal.	200,000	Mar. 1	500	Mar. 1	500	Jan. 1 Bal.	12,000
Mar. 1 Bal.	199,500					Mar. 1 Bal.	11,500

A write-off affects **only balance sheet accounts**—not income statement accounts. The write-off of the account reduces both Accounts Receivable and Allowance for Doubtful Accounts. Cash realizable value in the balance sheet, therefore, remains the same, as Illustration 9-5 shows.

Illustration 9-5
Cash realizable value comparison

	Before Write-Off	After Write-Off
Accounts receivable	$200,000	$199,500
Allowance for doubtful accounts	12,000	11,500
Cash realizable value	$188,000	$188,000

Recovery of an Uncollectible Account. Occasionally, a company collects from a customer after it has written off the account as uncollectible. The company makes two entries to record the recovery of a bad debt: (1) It reverses the entry made in writing off the account. This reinstates the customer's account. (2) It journalizes the collection in the usual manner.

To illustrate, assume that on July 1, R. A. Ware pays the $500 amount that Hampson had written off on March 1. Hampson makes these entries:

A = L + OE
+500
−500
Cash Flows
no effect

	(1)		
July 1	Accounts Receivable—R. A. Ware	500	
	Allowance for Doubtful Accounts		500
	(To reverse write-off of R. A. Ware		
	account)		

A = L + OE
+500
−500
Cash Flows
+500

	(2)		
July 1	Cash	500	
	Accounts Receivable—R. A. Ware		500
	(To record collection from R. A. Ware)		

Note that the recovery of a bad debt, like the write-off of a bad debt, affects **only balance sheet accounts**. The net effect of the two entries above is a debit to Cash and a credit to Allowance for Doubtful Accounts for $500. Accounts Receivable and the Allowance for Doubtful Accounts both increase in entry (1) for two reasons: First, the company made an error in judgment when it wrote off the account receivable. Second, after R. A. Ware did pay, Accounts Receivable in the general ledger and Ware's account in the subsidiary ledger should show the collection for possible future credit purposes.

Estimating the Allowance. For Hampson Furniture in Illustration 9-3, the amount of the expected uncollectibles was given. However, in "real life," companies must estimate that amount when they use the allowance method. Two bases are used to determine this amount: **(1) percentage of sales**, and **(2) percentage of receivables**. Both bases are generally accepted. The choice is a management decision. It depends on the relative emphasis that management wishes to give to expenses and revenues on the one hand or to cash realizable value of the accounts receivable on the other. The choice is whether to emphasize income statement or balance sheet relationships. Illustration 9-6 compares the two bases.

Illustration 9-6
Comparison of bases for estimating uncollectibles

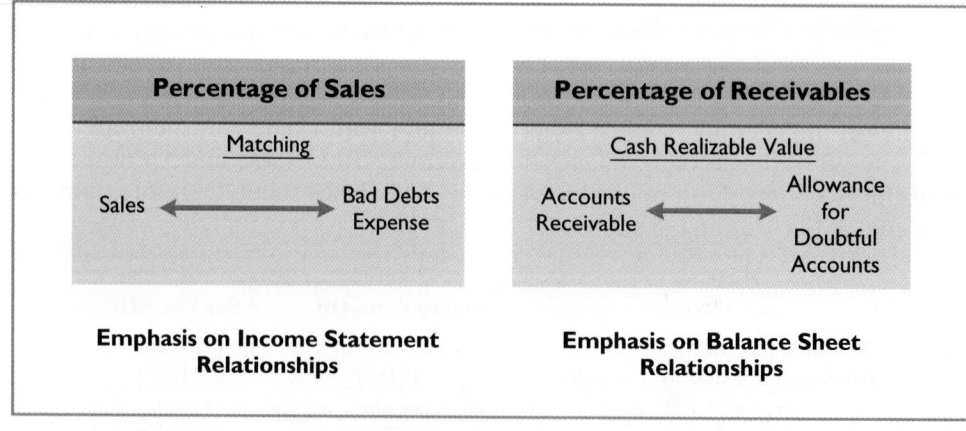

The percentage-of-sales basis results in a better matching of expenses with revenues—an income statement viewpoint. The percentage-of-receivables basis produces the better estimate of cash realizable value—a balance sheet viewpoint. Under both bases, the company must determine its past experience with bad debt losses.

Percentage-of-Sales. In the percentage-of-sales basis, management estimates what percentage of credit sales will be uncollectible. This percentage is based on past experience and anticipated credit policy.

The company applies this percentage to either total credit sales or net credit sales of the current year. To illustrate, assume that Gonzalez Company elects to use the percentage-of-sales basis. It concludes that 1% of net credit sales will become uncollectible. If net credit sales for 2012 are $800,000, the estimated bad debts expense is $8,000 (1% × $800,000). The adjusting entry is:

Dec. 31	Bad Debts Expense	8,000	
	Allowance for Doubtful Accounts		8,000
	(To record estimated bad debts for year)		

A = L + OE
−8,000 Exp
−8,000

Cash Flows
no effect

After the adjusting entry is posted, assuming the allowance account already has a credit balance of $1,723, the accounts of Gonzalez Company will show the following:

Bad Debts Expense		**Allowance for Doubtful Accounts**	
Dec. 31 Adj. 8,000		Jan. 1 Bal. 1,723	
		Dec. 31 Adj. 8,000	
		Dec. 31 Bal. 9,723	

Illustration 9-7
Bad debts accounts after posting

This basis of estimating uncollectibles emphasizes the matching of expenses with revenues. As a result, Bad Debts Expense will show a direct percentage relationship to the sales base on which it is computed. **When the company makes the adjusting entry, it disregards the existing balance in Allowance for Doubtful Accounts.** The adjusted balance in this account should be a reasonable approximation of the realizable value of the receivables. If actual write-offs differ significantly from the amount estimated, the company should modify the percentage for future years.

Percentage-of-Receivables. Under the percentage-of-receivables basis, management estimates what percentage of receivables will result in losses from uncollectible accounts. The company prepares an **aging schedule**, in which it classifies customer balances by the length of time they have been unpaid. Because of its emphasis on time, the analysis is often called aging the accounts receivable. In the Feature Story, Whitehall-Robins prepared an aging report daily.

After the company arranges the accounts by age, it determines the expected bad debt losses. It applies percentages based on past experience to the totals in each category. The longer a receivable is past due, the less likely it is to be collected. Thus, the estimated percentage of uncollectible debts increases as the number of days past due increases. Illustration 9-8 (page 424) shows an aging schedule for Dart Company. Note that the estimated percentage uncollectible increases from 2 to 40% as the number of days past due increases.

Illustration 9-8
Aging schedule

Worksheet.xls						
File Edit View Insert Format Tools Data Window Help						

	A	B	C	D	E	F	G
1					**Number of Days Past Due**		
2			**Not**				
3	**Customer**	**Total**	**Yet Due**	**1–30**	**31–60**	**61–90**	**Over 90**
4	T. E. Adert	$ 600		$ 300		$ 200	$ 100
5	R. C. Bortz	300	$ 300				
6	B. A. Carl	450		200	$ 250		
7	O. L. Diker	700	500			200	
8	T. O. Ebbet	600			300		300
9	Others	36,950	26,200	5,200	2,450	1,600	1,500
10		$39,600	$27,000	$5,700	$3,000	$2,000	$1,900
11	Estimated Percentage Uncollectible		2%	4%	10%	20%	40%
12	Total Estimated Bad Debts	$ 2,228	$ 540	$ 228	$ 300	$ 400	$ 760
13							

Helpful Hint

The older categories have higher percentages because the longer an account is past due, the less likely it is to be collected.

Total estimated bad debts for Dart Company ($2,228) represent the amount of existing customer claims the company expects will become uncollectible in the future. This amount represents the **required balance** in Allowance for Doubtful Accounts at the balance sheet date. **The amount of the bad debt adjusting entry is the difference between the required balance and the existing balance in the allowance account.** If the trial balance shows Allowance for Doubtful Accounts with a credit balance of $528, the company will make an adjusting entry for $1,700 ($2,228 − $528), as shown here.

A = L + OE
−1,700 Exp
−1,700

Cash Flows
no effect

Dec. 31	Bad Debts Expense	1,700	
	Allowance for Doubtful Accounts		1,700
	(To adjust allowance account to total estimated uncollectibles)		

After Dart posts its adjusting entry, its accounts will appear as follows.

Illustration 9-9
Bad debts accounts after posting

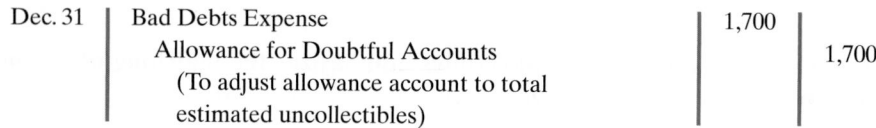

Bad Debts Expense		Allowance for Doubtful Accounts	
Dec. 31 Adj. **1,700**		Bal. 528	
		Dec. 31 Adj. **1,700**	
		Bal. 2,228	

Occasionally, the allowance account will have a **debit balance** prior to adjustment. This occurs when write-offs during the year have exceeded previous provisions for bad debts. In such a case, the company **adds the debit balance to the required balance** when it makes the adjusting entry. Thus, if there had been a $500 debit balance in the allowance account before adjustment, the adjusting entry would have been for $2,728 ($2,228 + $500) to arrive at a credit balance of $2,228. The percentage-of-receivables basis will normally result in the better approximation of cash realizable value.

Do it!

Brule Co. has been in business five years. The ledger at the end of the current year shows:

Accounts Receivable	$30,000 Dr.
Sales Revenue	$180,000 Cr.
Allowance for Doubtful Accounts	$2,000 Dr.

Bad debts are estimated to be 10% of receivables. Prepare the entry to adjust Allowance for Doubtful Accounts.

Solution

The following entry should be made to bring the balance in Allowance for Doubtful Accounts up to a balance of $3,000 (0.1 × $30,000):

Bad Debts Expense [(0.1 × $30,000) + $2,000]	5,000	
Allowance for Doubtful Accounts		5,000
(To record estimate of uncollectible accounts)		

Related exercise material: BE9-3, BE9-4, BE9-5, BE9-6, BE9-7, E9-3, E9-4, E9-5, E9-6, and **Do it!** 9-1.

Uncollectible Accounts Receivable

action plan

✔ Report receivables at their cash (net) realizable value.

✔ Estimate the amount the company does not expect to collect.

✔ Consider the existing balance in the allowance account when using the percentage-of-receivables basis.

The Navigator

Disposing of Accounts Receivable

In the normal course of events, companies collect accounts receivable in cash and remove the receivables from the books. However, as credit sales and receivables have grown in significance, the "normal course of events" has changed. Companies now frequently sell their receivables to another company for cash, thereby shortening the cash-to-cash operating cycle.

Companies sell receivables for two major reasons. First, **they may be the only reasonable source of cash**. When money is tight, companies may not be able to borrow money in the usual credit markets. Or, if money is available, the cost of borrowing may be prohibitive.

A second reason for selling receivables is that **billing and collection are often time-consuming and costly**. It is often easier for a retailer to sell the receivables to another party with expertise in billing and collection matters. Credit card companies such as MasterCard, Visa, and Discover specialize in billing and collecting accounts receivable.

Study Objective [4]
Describe the entries to record the disposition of accounts receivable.

SALE OF RECEIVABLES

A common sale of receivables is a sale to a factor. A **factor** is a finance company or bank that buys receivables from businesses and then collects the payments directly from the customers. Factoring is a multibillion dollar business.

Factoring arrangements vary widely. Typically the factor charges a commission to the company that is selling the receivables. This fee ranges from 1–3% of the amount of receivables purchased. To illustrate, assume that Hendredon Furniture factors $600,000 of receivables to Federal Factors. Federal Factors assesses a service charge of 2% of the amount of receivables sold. The journal entry to record the sale by Hendredon Furniture is as follows.

Cash	588,000	
Service Charge Expense (2% × $600,000)	12,000	
Accounts Receivable		600,000
(To record the sale of accounts receivable)		

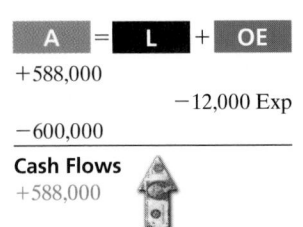

A = L + OE
+588,000
−12,000 Exp
−600,000
Cash Flows
+588,000

If the company often sells its receivables, it records the service charge expense (such as that incurred by Hendredon) as selling expense. If the company infrequently sells receivables, it may report this amount in the "Other expenses and losses" section of the income statement.

CREDIT CARD SALES

Over one billion credit cards are in use in the United States—more than three credit cards for every man, woman, and child in this country. Visa, MasterCard, and American Express are the national credit cards that most individuals use. Three parties are involved when national credit cards are used in retail sales: (1) the credit card issuer, who is independent of the retailer, (2) the retailer, and (3) the customer. A retailer's acceptance of a national credit card is another form of selling (factoring) the receivable.

Illustration 9-10 shows the major advantages of national credit cards to the retailer. In exchange for these advantages, the retailer pays the credit card issuer a fee of 2–6% of the invoice price for its services.

Illustration 9-10
Advantages of credit cards to the retailer

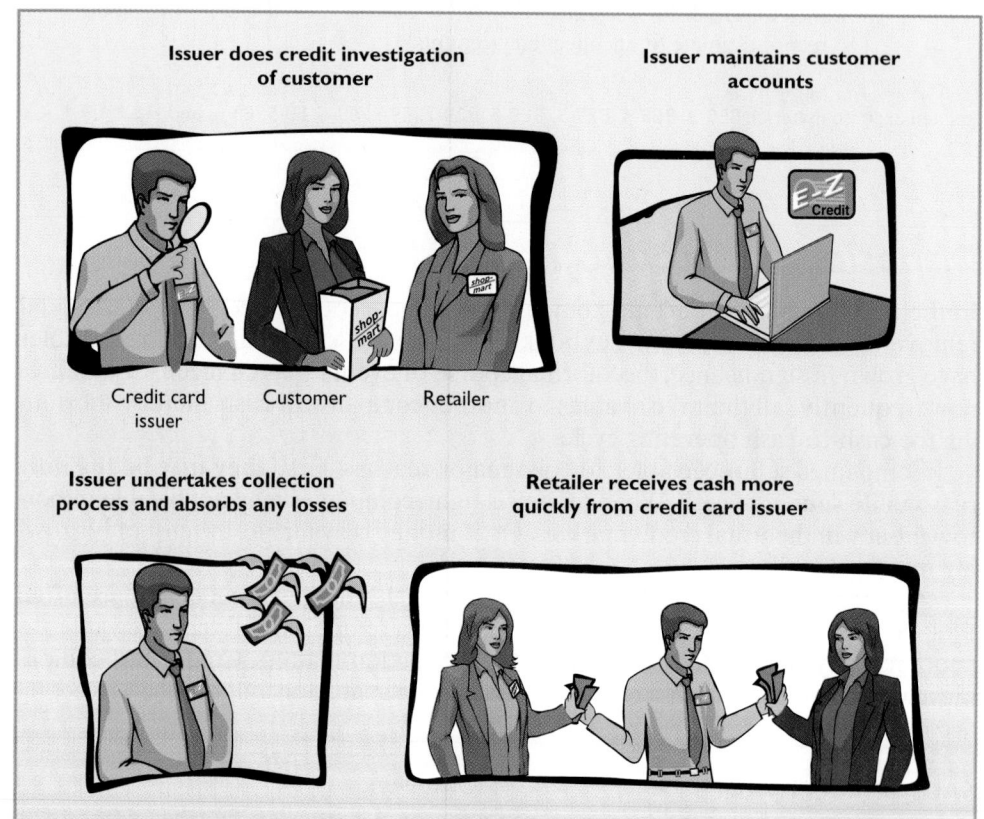

Accounting for Credit Card Sales.   The retailer generally considers sales from the use of national credit card sales as *cash sales*. The retailer must pay to the bank that issues the card a fee for processing the transactions. The retailer records the credit card slips in a similar manner as checks deposited from a cash sale.

To illustrate, Anita Ferreri purchases $1,000 of compact discs for her restaurant from Karen Kerr Music Co., using her Visa First Bank Card. First Bank charges a service fee of 3%. The entry to record this transaction by Karen Kerr Music is as follows.

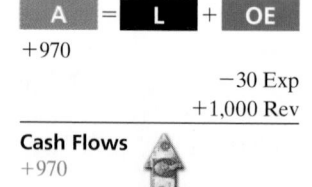

A = L + OE
+970

−30 Exp
+1,000 Rev

Cash Flows
+970

Cash	970	
Service Charge Expense	30	
Sales Revenue		1,000
(To record Visa credit card sales)		

ACCOUNTING ACROSS THE ORGANIZATION

How Does a Credit Card Work?

Most of you know how to *use* a credit card, but do you know what happens in the transaction and how the transaction is processed? Suppose that you use a Visa card to purchase some new ties at Nordstrom. The salesperson swipes your card, and the swiping machine reads the information on the magnetic strip on the back of the card. The salesperson then types in the amount of the purchase. The machine contacts the Visa computer, which routes the call back to the bank that issued your Visa card. The issuing bank verifies that the account exists, that the card is not stolen, and that you have not exceeded your credit limit. At this point, the slip is printed, which you sign.

Visa acts as the clearing agent for the transaction. It transfers funds from the issuing bank to Nordstrom's bank account. Generally this transfer of funds, from sale to the receipt of funds in the merchant's account, takes two to three days.

In the meantime, Visa puts a pending charge on your account for the amount of the tie purchase; that amount counts immediately against your available credit limit. At the end of the billing period, Visa sends you an invoice (your credit card bill) which shows the various charges you made, and the amounts that Visa expended on your behalf, for the month. You then must "pay the piper" for your stylish new ties.

? Assume that Nordstrom prepares a bank reconciliation at the end of each month. If some credit card sales have not been processed by the bank, how should Nordstrom treat these transactions on its bank reconciliation? (See page 453.)

Do it!

Mehl Wholesalers Co. has been expanding faster than it can raise capital. According to its local banker, the company has reached its debt ceiling. Mehl's suppliers (creditors) are demanding payment within 30 days of the invoice date for goods acquired, but Mehl's customers are slow in paying (60–90 days). As a result, Mehl has a cash flow problem.

Mehl needs $120,000 in cash to safely cover next Friday's payroll. Its balance of outstanding accounts receivables totals $750,000. What might Mehl do to alleviate this cash crunch? Record the entry that Mehl would make when it raises the needed cash.

Solution

Assuming that Mehl Wholesalers factors $125,000 of its accounts receivable at a 1% service charge, it would make the following entry.

Cash	123,750	
Service Charge Expense	1,250	
Accounts Receivable		125,000
(To record sale of receivables to factor)		

Related exercise material: BE9-8, E9-7, E9-8, E9-9, and **Do it!** 9-2.

Disposition of Accounts Receivable

action plan

✔ To speed up the collection of cash, sell receivables to a factor.

✔ Calculate service charge expense as a percentage of the factored receivables.

✔
The Navigator

Notes Receivable

Companies may also grant credit in exchange for a formal credit instrument known as a **promissory note**. A **promissory note** is a written promise to pay a specified amount of money on demand or at a definite time. Promissory notes may be used

(1) when individuals and companies lend or borrow money, (2) when the amount of the transaction and the credit period exceed normal limits, or (3) in settlement of accounts receivable.

In a promissory note, the party making the promise to pay is called the **maker**. The party to whom payment is to be made is called the **payee**. The note may specifically identify the payee by name or may designate the payee simply as the bearer of the note.

In the note shown in Illustration 9-11, Calhoun Company is the maker, Wilma Company is the payee. To Wilma Company, the promissory note is a note receivable; to Calhoun Company, it is a note payable.

Illustration 9-11
Promissory note

Helpful Hint

Who are the two key parties to a note, and what entry does each party make when the note is issued?

Answer:
1. The maker, Calhoun Company, credits Notes Payable.
2. The payee, Wilma Company, debits Notes Receivable.

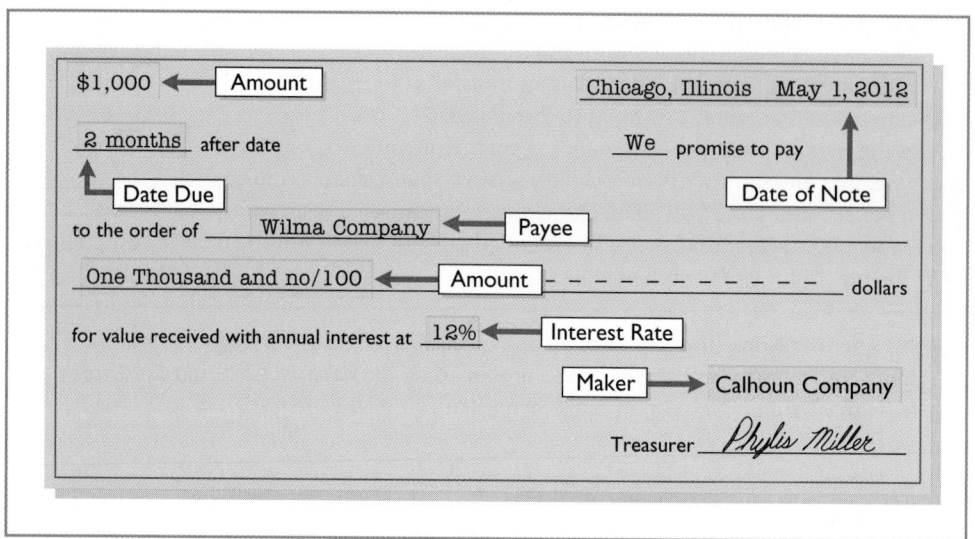

Notes receivable give the holder a stronger legal claim to assets than do accounts receivable. Like accounts receivable, notes receivable can be readily sold to another party. Promissory notes are negotiable instruments (as are checks), which means that they can be transferred to another party by endorsement.

Companies frequently accept notes receivable from customers who need to extend the payment of an outstanding account receivable. They often require such notes from high-risk customers. In some industries (such as the pleasure and sport boat industry), all credit sales are supported by notes. The majority of notes, however, originate from loans.

The basic issues in accounting for notes receivable are the same as those for accounts receivable:

1. **Recognizing** notes receivable.
2. **Valuing** notes receivable.
3. **Disposing of** notes receivable.

On the following pages, we will look at these issues. Before we do, we need to consider two issues that did not apply to accounts receivable: maturity date and computing interest.

Determining the Maturity Date

Study Objective [5]
Compute the maturity date of and interest on notes receivable.

When the life of a note is expressed in terms of months, you find the date when it matures by counting the months from the date of issue. For example, the maturity date of a three-month note dated May 1 is August 1. A note drawn on the last day of a month matures on the last day of a subsequent month. That is, a July 31 note due in two months matures on September 30.

When the due date is stated in terms of days, you need to count the exact number of days to determine the maturity date. In counting, **omit the date the note is issued but include the due date**. For example, the maturity date of a 60-day note dated July 17 is September 15, computed as follows.

Term of note		60 days
July (31 − 17)	14	
August	31	45
Maturity date: September		15

Illustration 9-12
Computation of maturity date

Illustration 9-13 shows three ways of stating the maturity date of a promissory note.

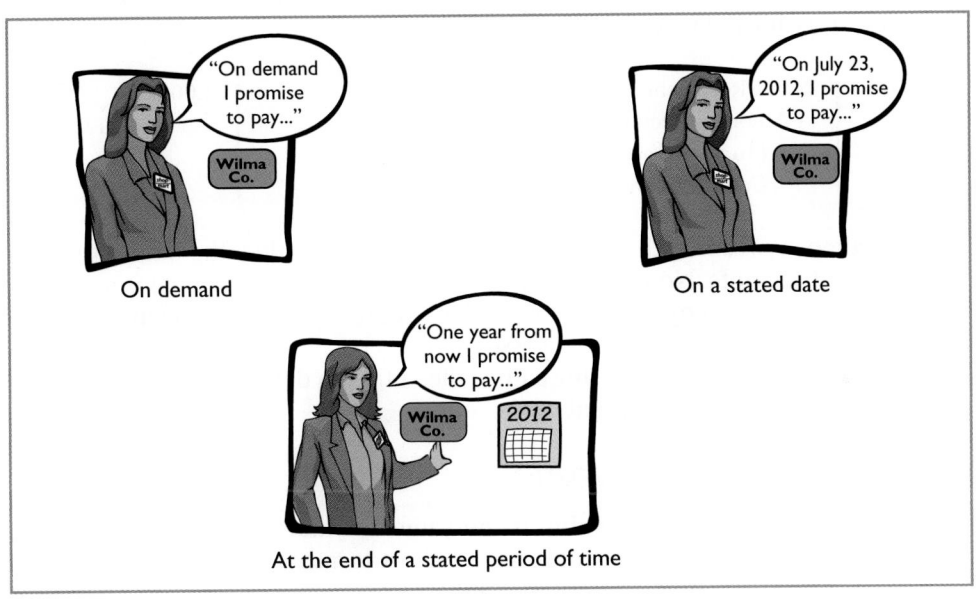

At the end of a stated period of time

Illustration 9-13
Maturity date of different notes

Computing Interest

Illustration 9-14 gives the basic formula for computing interest on an interest-bearing note.

Face Value of Note	×	Annual Interest Rate	×	Time in Terms of One Year	=	Interest

Illustration 9-14
Formula for computing interest

Helpful Hint

The interest rate specified is the *annual* rate.

The interest rate specified in a note is an **annual** rate of interest. The time factor in the computation in Illustration 9-14 expresses the fraction of a year that the note is outstanding. When the maturity date is stated in days, the time factor is often the number of days divided by 360. When counting days, omit the date that the note is issued but include the due date. When the due date is stated in months, the time factor is the number of months divided by 12. Illustration 9-15 (page 430) shows computation of interest for various time periods.

Illustration 9-15
Computation of interest

Terms of Note	Interest Computation
	Face × Rate × Time = Interest
$ 730, 18%, 120 days	$ 730 × 18% × 120/360 = $ 43.80
$1,000, 15%, 6 months	$1,000 × 15% × 6/12 = $ 75.00
$2,000, 12%, 1 year	$2,000 × 12% × 1/1 = $240.00

There are different ways to calculate interest. For example, the computation in Illustration 9-15 assumed 360 days for the length of the year. Most financial instruments use 365 days to compute interest. *For homework problems, assume 360 days to simplify computations.*

Recognizing Notes Receivable

Study Objective [6]
Explain how companies recognize notes receivable.

To illustrate the basic entry for notes receivable, we will use Calhoun Company's $1,000, two-month, 12% promissory note dated May 1. Assuming that Calhoun Company wrote the note to settle an open account, Wilma Company makes the following entry for the receipt of the note.

May 1	Notes Receivable	1,000	
	Accounts Receivable—Calhoun Company		1,000
	(To record acceptance of Calhoun Company note)		

A = L + OE
+1,000
−1,000

Cash Flows
no effect

The company records the note receivable at its **face value**, the amount shown on the face of the note. No interest revenue is reported when the note is accepted, because the revenue recognition principle does not recognize revenue until earned. Interest is earned (accrued) as time passes.

If a company lends money using a note, the entry is a debit to Notes Receivable and a credit to Cash in the amount of the loan.

Valuing Notes Receivable

Study Objective [7]
Describe how companies value notes receivable.

Valuing short-term notes receivable is the same as valuing accounts receivable. Like accounts receivable, companies report short-term notes receivable at their **cash (net) realizable value**. The notes receivable allowance account is Allowance for Doubtful Accounts. The estimations involved in determining cash realizable value and in recording bad debts expense and the related allowance are done similarly to accounts receivable.

INTERNATIONAL INSIGHT

Can Fair Value Be Unfair?

The FASB and the International Accounting Standards Board (IASB) are considering proposals for how to account for financial instruments. The FASB has proposed that loans and receivables be accounted for at their fair value (the amount they could currently be sold for), as are most investments. The FASB believes that this would provide a more accurate view of a company's financial position. It might be especially useful as an early warning when a bank is in trouble because of poor-quality loans. But, banks argue that fair values are difficult to estimate accurately. They are also concerned that volatile fair values could cause large swings in a bank's reported net income.

Source: David Reilly, "Banks Face a Mark-to-Market Challenge," *Wall Street Journal Online* (March 15, 2010).

? What are the arguments in favor of and against fair value accounting for loans and receivables? (See page 453.)

Disposing of Notes Receivable

Notes may be held to their maturity date, at which time the face value plus accrued interest is due. In some situations, the maker of the note defaults, and the payee must make an appropriate adjustment. In other situations, similar to accounts receivable, the holder of the note speeds up the conversion to cash by selling the receivables as described later in this chapter.

Study Objective [8]
Describe the entries to record the disposition of notes receivable.

HONOR OF NOTES RECEIVABLE

A note is **honored** when its maker pays in full at its maturity date. For each interest-bearing note, the **amount due at maturity** is the face value of the note plus interest for the length of time specified on the note.

To illustrate, assume that Wolder Co. lends Higley Co. $10,000 on June 1, accepting a five-month, 9% interest note. In this situation, interest is $375 ($10,000 \times 9\% \times \frac{5}{12}$). The amount due, the maturity value, is $10,375 ($10,000 + $375). To obtain payment, Wolder (the payee) must present the note either to Higley Co. (the maker) or to the maker's agent, such as a bank. If Wolder presents the note to Higley Co. on November 1, the maturity date, Wolder's entry to record the collection is:

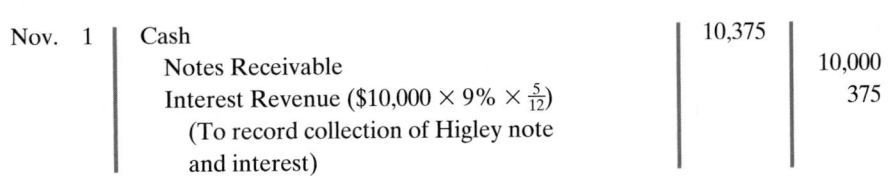

Nov. 1	Cash	10,375	
	Notes Receivable		10,000
	Interest Revenue ($10,000 \times 9\% \times \frac{5}{12}$)		375
	(To record collection of Higley note and interest)		

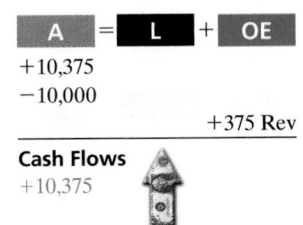

ACCRUAL OF INTEREST RECEIVABLE

Suppose instead that Wolder Co. prepares financial statements as of September 30. The timeline in Illustration 9-16 presents this situation.

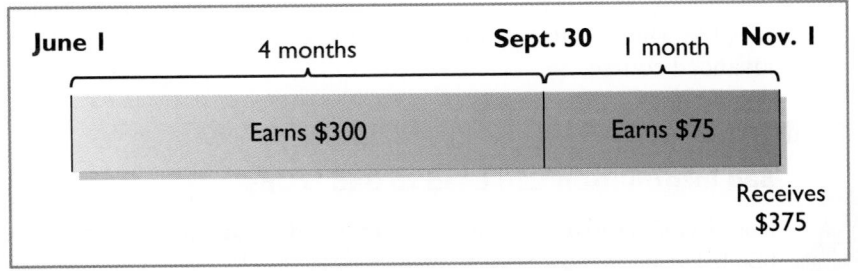

Illustration 9-16
Timeline of interest earned

To reflect interest earned but not yet received, Wolder must accrue interest on September 30. In this case, the adjusting entry by Wolder is for four months of interest, or $300, as shown below.

Sept. 30	Interest Receivable ($10,000 \times 9\% \times \frac{4}{12}$)	300	
	Interest Revenue		300
	(To accrue 4 months' interest on Higley note)		

At the note's maturity on November 1, Wolder receives $10,375. This amount represents repayment of the $10,000 note as well as five months of interest, or $375, as shown on the next page. The $375 is comprised of the $300 Interest Receivable accrued on September 30 plus $75 earned during October. Wolder's entry to record the honoring of the Higley note on November 1 is:

	A	=	L	+	OE	
+10,375						
−10,000						
−300						
					+75 Rev	

Cash Flows
+10,375

Nov. 1	Cash [$10,000 + ($10,000 × 9% × $\frac{5}{12}$)]	10,375	
	Notes Receivable		10,000
	Interest Receivable		300
	Interest Revenue ($10,000 × 9% × $\frac{1}{12}$)		75
	(To record collection of Higley note and interest)		

In this case, Wolder credits Interest Receivable because the receivable was established in the adjusting entry on September 30.

DISHONOR OF NOTES RECEIVABLE

A **dishonored note** is a note that is not paid in full at maturity. A dishonored note receivable is no longer negotiable. However, the payee still has a claim against the maker of the note for both the note and the interest. Therefore the note holder usually transfers the Notes Receivable account to an Account Receivable.

To illustrate, assume that Higley Co. on November 1 indicates that it cannot pay at the present time. The entry to record the dishonor of the note depends on whether Wolder Co. expects eventual collection. If it does expect eventual collection, Wolder Co. debits the amount due (face value and interest) on the note to Accounts Receivable. It would make the following entry at the time the note is dishonored (assuming no previous accrual of interest).

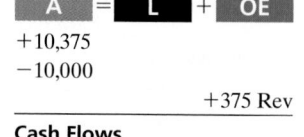

	A	=	L	+	OE	
+10,375						
−10,000						
					+375 Rev	

Cash Flows
no effect

Nov. 1	Accounts Receivable—Higley	10,375	
	Notes Receivable		10,000
	Interest Revenue		375
	(To record the dishonor of Higley note)		

If instead, on November 1, there is no hope of collection, the note holder would write off the face value of the note by debiting Allowance for Doubtful Accounts. No interest revenue would be recorded because collection will not occur.

SALE OF NOTES RECEIVABLE

The accounting for the sale of notes receivable is recorded similarly to the sale of accounts receivable. The accounting entries for the sale of notes receivable are left for a more advanced course.

ACCOUNTING ACROSS THE ORGANIZATION

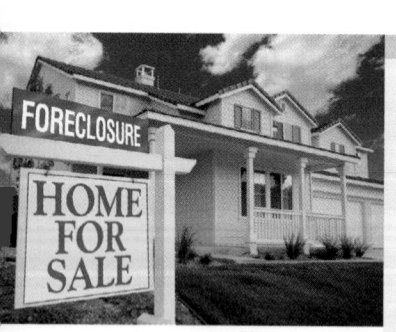

Bad Information Can Lead to Bad Loans

Many factors have contributed to the recent credit crisis. One significant factor that resulted in many bad loans was a failure by lenders to investigate loan customers sufficiently. For example, Countrywide Financial Corporation wrote many loans under its "Fast and Easy" loan program. That program allowed borrowers to provide little or no documentation for their income or their assets. Other lenders had similar programs, which earned the nickname "liars' loans." One study found that in these situations 60% of applicants overstated their incomes by more than 50% in order to qualify for a loan. Critics of the banking industry say that because loan officers were compensated for loan volume, and because banks were selling the loans to investors rather than holding them, the lenders had little incentive to investigate the borrowers' creditworthiness.

Source: Glenn R. Simpson and James R. Hagerty, "Countrywide Loss Focuses Attention on Underwriting," *Wall Street Journal* (April 30, 2008), p. B1; and Michael Corkery, "Fraud Seen as Driver in Wave of Foreclosures," *Wall Street Journal* (December 21, 2007), p. A1.

? What steps should the banks have taken to ensure the accuracy of financial information provided on loan applications? (See page 453.)

Do it!

Gambit Stores accepts from Leonard Co. a $3,400, 90-day, 6% note dated May 10 in settlement of Leonard's overdue account. (a) What is the maturity date of the note? (b) What entry does Gambit make at the maturity date, assuming Leonard pays the note and interest in full at that time?

Solution

(a) The maturity date is August 8, computed as follows.

Term of note:		90 days
May (31−10)	21	
June	30	
July	31	82
Maturity date: August		8

(b) The interest payable at the maturity date is $51, computed as follows.

$$\text{Face} \times \text{Rate} \times \text{Time} = \text{Interest}$$
$$\$3,400 \times 6\% \times 90/360 = \$51$$

The entry recorded by Gambit Stores at the maturity date is:

Cash	3,451	
Notes Receivable		3,400
Interest Revenue		51
(To record collection of Leonard note)		

Related exercise material: BE9-9, BE9-10, BE9-11, E9-10, E9-11, E9-12, E9-13, and **Do it!** 9-3.

Notes Receivable

action plan

✔ Count the exact number of days to determine the maturity date. Omit the date the note is issued, but include the due date.

✔ Determine whether interest was accrued.

✔ Compute the accrued interest.

✔ Prepare the entry for payment of the note and interest.

✔ The entry to record interest at maturity in this solution assumes no interest has been previously accrued on this note.

✔
The Navigator

Statement Presentation and Analysis

Presentation

Companies should identify in the balance sheet or in the notes to the financial statements each of the major types of receivables. Short-term receivables appear in the current assets section of the balance sheet. Short-term investments appear before short-term receivables because these investments are more liquid (nearer to cash). Companies report both the gross amount of receivables and the allowance for doubtful accounts.

In a multiple-step income statement, companies report bad debts expense and service charge expense as selling expenses in the operating expenses section. Interest revenue appears under "Other revenues and gains" in the nonoperating activities section of the income statement.

Study Objective [9]
Explain the statement presentation and analysis of receivables.

Analysis

Investors and corporate managers compute financial ratios to evaluate the liquidity of a company's accounts receivable. They use the **accounts receivable turnover ratio** to assess the liquidity of the receivables. This ratio measures the number of times, on average, the company collects accounts receivable during the period. It is computed by dividing net credit sales (net sales less cash sales) by the average net accounts receivable during the year. Unless seasonal factors are significant, average net accounts receivable outstanding can be computed from the beginning and ending balances of net accounts receivable.

For example, in 2009 Cisco Systems had net sales of $29,131 million for the year. It had a beginning accounts receivable (net) balance of $3,821 million and an ending accounts receivable (net) balance of $3,177 million. Assuming that Cisco's sales were all on credit, its accounts receivable turnover ratio is computed as follows.

Illustration 9-17
Accounts receivable turnover ratio and computation

Net Credit Sales	÷	Average Net Accounts Receivable	=	Accounts Receivable Turnover
$29,131	÷	$\dfrac{\$3,821 + \$3,177}{2}$	=	8.3 times

The result indicates an accounts receivable turnover ratio of 8.3 times per year. The higher the turnover ratio the more liquid the company's receivables.

A variant of the accounts receivable turnover ratio that makes the liquidity even more evident is its conversion into an **average collection period** in terms of days. This is done by dividing the turnover ratio into 365 days. For example, Cisco's turnover of 8.3 times is divided into 365 days, as shown in Illustration 9-18, to obtain approximately 44 days. This means that it takes Cisco 44 days to collect its accounts receivable.

Illustration 9-18
Average collection period for receivables formula and computation

Days in Year	÷	Accounts Receivable Turnover	=	Average Collection Period in Days
365 days	÷	8.3 times	=	44 days

Companies frequently use the average collection period to assess the effectiveness of a company's credit and collection policies. The general rule is that the collection period should not greatly exceed the credit term period (that is, the time allowed for payment).

Do it!

Analysis of Receivables

action plan

✔ Review the formula to compute the accounts receivable turnover.

✔ Make sure that both the beginning and ending accounts receivable balances are considered in the computation.

✔ Review the formula to compute the average collection period in days.

In 2012, Phil Mickelson Company has net credit sales of $923,795 for the year. It had a beginning accounts receivable (net) balance of $38,275 and an ending accounts receivable (net) balance of $35,988. Compute Phil Mickelson Company's (a) accounts receivable turnover and (b) average collection period in days.

Solution

(a)

Net credit sales	÷	Average net accounts receivable	=	Accounts receivable turnover
$923,795	÷	$\dfrac{38,275 + 35,988}{2}$	=	24.9 times

(b)

Days in year	÷	Accounts receivable turnover	=	Average collection period in days
365	÷	24.9 times	=	14.7 days

Related exercise material: BE9-12, E9-14, and **Do it!** 9-4.

✔
The Navigator

COMPREHENSIVE
Do it!

The following selected transactions relate to Dylan Company.

Mar. 1   Sold $20,000 of merchandise to Potter Company, terms 2/10, n/30.
11   Received payment in full from Potter Company for balance due.
12   Accepted Juno Company's $20,000, 6-month, 12% note for balance due.
13   Made Dylan Company credit card sales for $13,200.
15   Made Visa credit card sales totaling $6,700. A 3% service fee is charged by Visa.

Apr. 11   Sold accounts receivable of $8,000 to Harcot Factor. Harcot Factor assesses a service charge of 2% of the amount of receivables sold.
13   Received collections of $8,200 on Dylan Company credit card sales and added finance charges of 1.5% to the remaining balances.

May 10   Wrote off as uncollectible $16,000 of accounts receivable. Dylan uses the percentage-of-sales basis to estimate bad debts.

June 30   Credit sales recorded during the first 6 months total $2,000,000. The bad debt percentage is 1% of credit sales. At June 30, the balance in the allowance account is $3,500.

July 16   One of the accounts receivable written off in May was from J. Simon, who pays the amount due, $4,000, in full.

Instructions

Prepare the journal entries for the transactions.

action plan

✔ Generally, record accounts receivable at invoice price.

✔ Recognize that sales returns and allowances and cash discounts reduce the amount received on accounts receivable.

✔ Record service charge expense on the seller's books when accounts receivable are sold.

✔ Prepare an adjusting entry for bad debts expense.

✔ Ignore any balance in the allowance account under the percentage-of-sales basis. Recognize the balance in the allowance account under the percentage-of-receivables basis.

✔ Record write-offs of accounts receivable only in balance sheet accounts.

Solution to Comprehensive Do it!

Date	Account	Debit	Credit
Mar. 1	Accounts Receivable–Potter	20,000	
	Sales Revenue		20,000
	(To record sales on account)		
11	Cash	19,600	
	Sales Discounts (2% × $20,000)	400	
	Accounts Receivable—Potter		20,000
	(To record collection of accounts receivable)		
12	Notes Receivable	20,000	
	Accounts Receivable—Juno		20,000
	(To record acceptance of Juno Company note)		
13	Accounts Receivable	13,200	
	Sales Revenue		13,200
	(To record company credit card sales)		
15	Cash	6,499	
	Service Charge Expense (3% × $6,700)	201	
	Sales		6,700
	(To record credit card sales)		
Apr. 11	Cash	7,840	
	Service Charge Expense (2% × $8,000)	160	
	Accounts Receivable		8,000
	(To record sale of receivables to factor)		
13	Cash	8,200	
	Accounts Receivable		8,200
	(To record collection of accounts receivable)		
	Accounts Receivable [($13,200 − $8,200) × 1.5%]	75	
	Interest Revenue		75
	(To record interest on amount due)		
May 10	Allowance for Doubtful Accounts	16,000	
	Accounts Receivable		16,000
	(To record write-off of accounts receivable)		

June 30	Bad Debts Expense ($2,000,000 × 1%)		20,000	
	Allowance for Doubtful Accounts			20,000
	(To record estimate of uncollectible accounts)			
July 16	Accounts Receivable—J. Simon		4,000	
	Allowance for Doubtful Accounts			4,000
	(To reverse write-off of accounts receivable)			
	Cash		4,000	
	Accounts Receivable—J. Simon			4,000
	(To record collection of accounts receivable)			

✔ **The Navigator**

Summary of Study Objectives

[1] Identify the different types of receivables. Receivables are frequently classified as (1) accounts, (2) notes, and (3) other. Accounts receivable are amounts customers owe on account. Notes receivable are claims for which lenders issue formal instruments of credit as proof of the debt. Other receivables include nontrade receivables such as interest receivable, loans to company officers, advances to employees, and income taxes refundable.

[2] Explain how companies recognize accounts receivable. Companies record accounts receivable at invoice price. They are reduced by sales returns and allowances. Cash discounts reduce the amount received on accounts receivable. When interest is charged on a past due receivable, the company adds this interest to the accounts receivable balance and recognizes it as interest revenue.

[3] Distinguish between the methods and bases companies use to value accounts receivable. There are two methods of accounting for uncollectible accounts: the allowance method and the direct write-off method. Companies may use either the percentage-of-sales or the percentage-of-receivables basis to estimate uncollectible accounts using the allowance method. The percentage-of-sales basis emphasizes the expense recognition (matching) principle. The percentage-of-receivables basis emphasizes the cash realizable value of the accounts receivable. An aging schedule is often used with this basis.

[4] Describe the entries to record the disposition of accounts receivable. When a company collects an account receivable, it credits Accounts Receivable. When a company sells (factors) an account receivable, a service charge expense reduces the amount received.

[5] Compute the maturity date of and interest on notes receivable. For a note stated in months, the maturity date is found by counting the months from the date of issue. For a note stated in days, the number of days is counted, omitting the issue date and counting the due date. The formula for computing interest is: Face value × Interest rate × Time.

[6] Explain how companies recognize notes receivable. Companies record notes receivable at face value. In some cases, it is necessary to accrue interest prior to maturity. In this case, companies debit Interest Receivable and credit Interest Revenue.

[7] Describe how companies value notes receivable. As with accounts receivable, companies report notes receivable at their cash (net) realizable value. The notes receivable allowance account is Allowance for Doubtful Accounts. The computation and estimations involved in valuing notes receivable at cash realizable value, and in recording the proper amount of bad debts expense and related allowance are similar to those for accounts receivable.

[8] Describe the entries to record the disposition of notes receivable. Notes can be held to maturity. At that time the face value plus accrued interest is due, and the note is removed from the accounts. In many cases, the holder of the note speeds up the conversion by selling the receivable to another party (a factor). In some situations, the maker of the note dishonors the note (defaults), in which case the company transfers the note and accrued interest to an account receivable or writes off the note.

[9] Explain the statement presentation and analysis of receivables. Companies should identify in the balance sheet or in the notes to the financial statements each major type of receivable. Short-term receivables are considered current assets. Companies report the gross amount of receivables and the allowance for doubtful accounts. They report bad debts and service charge expenses in the multiple-step income statement as operating (selling) expenses; interest revenue appears under other revenues and gains in the nonoperating activities section of the statement. Managers and investors evaluate accounts receivable for liquidity by computing a turnover ratio and an average collection period.

✔ **The Navigator**

Glossary

Accounts receivable   Amounts owed by customers on account. (p. 416).

Accounts receivable turnover ratio   A measure of the liquidity of accounts receivable; computed by dividing net credit sales by average net accounts receivable. (p. 433).

Aging the accounts receivable   The analysis of customer balances by the length of time they have been unpaid. (p. 423).

Allowance method   A method of accounting for bad debts that involves estimating uncollectible accounts at the end of each period. (p. 420).

Average collection period   The average amount of time that a receivable is outstanding; calculated by dividing 365 days by the accounts receivables turnover ratio. (p. 434).

Bad Debts Expense   An expense account to record uncollectible receivables. (p. 419).

Cash (net) realizable value   The net amount a company expects to receive in cash. (p. 420).

Direct write-off method   A method of accounting for bad debts that involves expensing accounts at the time they are determined to be uncollectible. (p. 419).

Dishonored note   A note that is not paid in full at maturity. (p. 432).

Factor   A finance company or bank that buys receivables from businesses and then collects the payments directly from the customers. (p. 425).

Maker   The party in a promissory note who is making the promise to pay. (p. 428).

Notes receivable   Claims for which formal instruments of credit are issued as proof of the debt. (p. 417).

Other receivables   Various forms of nontrade receivables, such as interest receivable and income taxes refundable. (p. 417).

Payee   The party to whom payment of a promissory note is to be made. (p. 428).

Percentage-of-receivables basis   Management estimates what percentage of receivables will result in losses from uncollectible accounts. (p. 423).

Percentage-of-sales basis   Management estimates what percentage of credit sales will be uncollectible. (p. 423).

Promissory note   A written promise to pay a specified amount of money on demand or at a definite time. (p. 427).

Receivables   Amounts due from individuals and other companies. (p. 416).

Trade receivables   Notes and accounts receivable that result from sales transactions. (p. 417).

Self-Test, Brief Exercises, Exercises, Problem Set A, and many more components are available for practice in *WileyPLUS*

Self-Test Questions

Answers are on page 453.

(SO 1)   **1.** Receivables are frequently classified as:
   a. accounts receivable, company receivables, and other receivables.
   b. accounts receivable, notes receivable, and employee receivables.
   c. accounts receivable and general receivables.
   d. accounts receivable, notes receivable, and other receivables.

(SO 2)   **2.** Buehler Company on June 15 sells merchandise on account to Chaz Co. for $1,000, terms 2/10, n/30. On June 20, Chaz Co. returns merchandise worth $300 to Buehler Company. On June 24, payment is received from Chaz Co. for the balance due. What is the amount of cash received?
   a. $700.   **c.** $686.
   b. $680.   **d.** None of the above.

(SO 3)   **3.** Which of the following approaches for bad debts is best described as a balance sheet method?
   a. Percentage-of-receivables basis.
   b. Direct write-off method.
   c. Percentage-of-sales basis.
   d. Both a and b.

(SO 3)   **4.** Hughes Company has a credit balance of $5,000 in its Allowance for Doubtful Accounts before any adjustments are made at the end of the year. Based on review and aging of its accounts receivable at the end of the year, Hughes estimates that $60,000 of its receivables are uncollectible. The amount of bad debts expense which should be reported for the year is:
   a. $5,000.   **c.** $60,000.
   b. $55,000.   **d.** $65,000.

(SO 3)   **5.** Use the same information as in question 4, except that Hughes has a debit balance of $5,000 in its Allowance for Doubtful Accounts before any adjustments are made at the end of the year. In this situation, the amount of bad debts expense that should be reported for the year is:
   a. $5,000.   **c.** $60,000.
   b. $55,000.   **d.** $65,000.

(SO 3)   **6.** Net sales for the month are $800,000, and bad debts are expected to be 1.5% of net sales. The company uses the percentage-of-sales basis. If Allowance for Doubtful Accounts has a credit balance of $15,000 before adjustment, what is the balance after adjustment?
   a. $15,000.   **c.** $23,000.
   b. $27,000.   **d.** $31,000.

(SO 3)   **7.** In 2012, Roso Carlson Company had net credit sales of $750,000. On January 1, 2012, Allowance for Doubtful Accounts had a credit balance of $18,000. During 2012, $30,000 of uncollectible accounts receivable were written off. Past experience indicates that 3% of net credit sales become uncollectible. What should be the adjusted balance of Allowance for Doubtful Accounts at December 31, 2012?

a. $10,050.   **c.** $22,500.
b.. $10,500.   **d.** $40,500.

(SO 3) **8.** An analysis and aging of the accounts receivable of Prince Company at December 31 reveals the following data.

Accounts receivable	$800,000
Allowance for doubtful accounts per books before adjustment	50,000
Amounts expected to become uncollectible	65,000

The cash realizable value of the accounts receivable at December 31, after adjustment, is:

a. $685,000.   **c.** $800,000.
b. $750,000.   **d.** $735,000.

(SO 6) **9.** One of the following statements about promissory notes is incorrect. The *incorrect* statement is:

a. The party making the promise to pay is called the maker.
b. The party to whom payment is to be made is called the payee.
c. A promissory note is not a negotiable instrument.
d. A promissory note is often required from high-risk customers.

(SO 4) **10.** Which of the following statements about Visa credit card sales is *incorrect*?

a. The credit card issuer makes the credit investigation of the customer.
b. The retailer is not involved in the collection process.
c. Two parties are involved.
d. The retailer receives cash more quickly than it would from individual customers on account.

(SO 4) **11.** Blinka Retailers accepted $50,000 of Citibank Visa credit card charges for merchandise sold on July 1. Citibank charges 4% for its credit card use. The entry to record this transaction by Blinka Retailers will include a credit to Sales Revenue of $50,000 and a debit(s) to:

a. Cash $48,000
and Service Charge Expense $2,000
b. Accounts Receivable $48,000
and Service Charge Expense $2,000

c. Cash $50,000
d. Accounts Receivable $50,000

12. Foti Co. accepts a $1,000, 3-month, 6% promissory note (SO 6) in settlement of an account with Bartelt Co. The entry to record this transaction is as follows.

a. Notes Receivable	1,015		
Accounts Receivable			1,015
b. Notes Receivable	1,000		
Accounts Receivable			1,000
c. Notes Receivable	1,000		
Sales Revenue			1,000
d. Notes Receivable	1,030		
Accounts Receivable			1,030

13. Ginter Co. holds Kolar Inc.'s $10,000, 120-day, 9% note. (SO 8) The entry made by Ginter Co. when the note is collected, assuming no interest has been previously accrued, is:

a. Cash	10,300		
Notes Receivable			10,300
b. Cash	10,000		
Notes Receivable			10,000
c. Accounts Receivable	10,300		
Notes Receivable			10,000
Interest Revenue			300
d. Cash	10,300		
Notes Receivable			10,000
Interest Revenue			300

14. Accounts and notes receivable are reported in the current (SO 9) assets section of the balance sheet at:

a. cash (net) realizable value
b. net book value.
c. lower-of-cost-or-market value.
d. invoice cost.

15. Oliveras Company had net credit sales during the year of (SO 9) $800,000 and cost of goods sold of $500,000. The balance in accounts receivable at the beginning of the year was $100,000, and the end of the year it was $150,000. What were the accounts receivable turnover ratio and the average collection period in days?

a. 4.0 and 91.3 days.   **c.** 6.4 and 57 days.
b. 5.3 and 68.9 days.   **d.** 8.0 and 45.6 days.

Go to the book's companion website, **www.wiley.com/college/weygandt**, for additional Self-Test Questions.

The Navigator

Questions

1. What is the difference between an account receivable and a note receivable?

2. What are some common types of receivables other than accounts receivable and notes receivable?

3. Texaco Oil Company issues its own credit cards. Assume that Texaco charges you $40 interest on an unpaid balance. Prepare the journal entry that Texaco makes to record this revenue.

4. What are the essential features of the allowance method of accounting for bad debts?

5. Jerry Gatewood cannot understand why cash realizable value does not decrease when an uncollectible account is

written off under the allowance method. Clarify this point for Jerry Gatewood.

6. Distinguish between the two bases that may be used in estimating uncollectible accounts.

7. Eaton Company has a credit balance of $3,500 in Allowance for Doubtful Accounts. The estimated bad debts expense under the percentage-of-sales basis is $4,100. The total estimated uncollectibles under the percentage-of-receivables basis is $5,800. Prepare the adjusting entry under each basis.

8. How are bad debts accounted for under the direct write-off method? What are the disadvantages of this method?

9. DeVito Company accepts both its own credit cards and national credit cards. What are the advantages of accepting both types of cards?

10. An article recently appeared in the *Wall Street Journal* indicating that companies are selling their receivables at a record rate. Why are companies selling their receivables?

11. Pinkston Textiles decides to sell $600,000 of its accounts receivable to First Factors Inc. First Factors assesses a service charge of 3% of the amount of receivables sold. Prepare the journal entry that Pinkston Textiles makes to record this sale.

12. Your roommate is uncertain about the advantages of a promissory note. Compare the advantages of a note receivable with those of an account receivable.

13. How may the maturity date of a promissory note be stated?

14. Indicate the maturity date of each of the following promissory notes:

Date of Note	Terms
(a) March 13	one year after date of note
(b) May 4	3 months after date
(c) June 20	30 days after date
(d) July 1	60 days after date

15. Compute the missing amounts for each of the following notes.

	Principal	Annual Interest Rate	Time	Total Interest
(a)	?	9%	120 days	$ 600
(b)	$30,000	10%	3 years	?
(c)	$60,000	?	5 months	$2,000
(d)	$45,000	8%	?	$1,200

16. In determining interest revenue, some financial institutions use 365 days per year and others use 360 days. Why might a financial institution use 360 days?

17. Cain Company dishonors a note at maturity. What are the options available to the lender?

18. General Motors Corporation has accounts receivable and notes receivable. How should the receivables be reported on the balance sheet?

19. The accounts receivable turnover ratio is 8.14, and average net receivables during the period are $400,000. What is the amount of net credit sales for the period?

20. **PEPSICO** What percentage does PepsiCo's allowance for doubtful accounts represent as a percent of its gross receivables?

Brief Exercises

BE9-1   Presented below are three receivables transactions. Indicate whether these receivables are reported as accounts receivable, notes receivable, or other receivables on a balance sheet.

(a) Sold merchandise on account for $64,000 to a customer.
(b) Received a promissory note of $57,000 for services performed.
(c) Advanced $10,000 to an employee.

Identify different types of receivables.
(SO 1)

BE9-2   Record the following transactions on the books of Nao Co.

(a) On July 1, Nao Co. sold merchandise on account to Bustamante Inc. for $15,200, terms 2/10, n/30.
(b) On July 8, Bustamante Inc. returned merchandise worth $3,800 to Nao Co.
(c) On July 11, Bustamante Inc. paid for the merchandise.

Record basic accounts receivable transactions.
(SO 2)

BE9-3   During its first year of operations, Parot Company had credit sales of $3,000,000; $600,000 remained uncollected at year-end. The credit manager estimates that $35,000 of these receivables will become uncollectible.

(a) Prepare the journal entry to record the estimated uncollectibles.
(b) Prepare the current assets section of the balance sheet for Parot Company. Assume that in addition to the receivables it has cash of $90,000, inventory of $130,000, and prepaid insurance of $7,500.

Prepare entry for allowance method and partial balance sheet.
(SO 3, 9)

BE9-4   At the end of 2012, Henderson Co. has accounts receivable of $700,000 and an allowance for doubtful accounts of $54,000. On January 24, 2013, the company learns that its receivable from Jaime Lynn is not collectible, and management authorizes a write-off of $5,400.

(a) Prepare the journal entry to record the write-off.
(b) What is the cash realizable value of the accounts receivable (1) before the write-off and (2) after the write-off?

Prepare entry for write-off; determine cash realizable value.
(SO 3)

BE9-5   Assume the same information as BE9-4. On March 4, 2013, Henderson Co. receives payment of $5,400 in full from Jaime Lynn. Prepare the journal entries to record this transaction.

Prepare entries for collection of bad debts write-off.
(SO 3)

BE9-6   Erik Co. elects to use the percentage-of-sales basis in 2012 to record bad debts expense. It estimates that 2% of net credit sales will become uncollectible. Sales revenues are $800,000 for 2012, sales returns and allowances are $45,000, and the allowance for doubtful accounts has a credit balance of $9,000. Prepare the adjusting entry to record bad debts expense in 2012.

Prepare entry using percentage-of-sales method.
(SO 3)

Prepare entry using percentage-of-receivables method.
(SO 3)

BE9-7 Johnson Co. uses the percentage-of-receivables basis to record bad debts expense. It estimates that 1% of accounts receivable will become uncollectible. Accounts receivable are $450,000 at the end of the year, and the allowance for doubtful accounts has a credit balance of $1,500.

(a) Prepare the adjusting journal entry to record bad debts expense for the year.

(b) If the allowance for doubtful accounts had a debit balance of $800 instead of a credit balance of $1,500, determine the amount to be reported for bad debts expense.

Prepare entries to dispose of accounts receivable.
(SO 4)

BE9-8 Presented below are two independent transactions.

(a) Ryan's Restaurant accepted a Visa card in payment of a $150 lunch bill. The bank charges a 4% fee. What entry should Ryan's make?

(b) Shultz Company sold its accounts receivable of $60,000. What entry should Shultz make, given a service charge of 3% on the amount of receivables sold?

Compute interest and determine maturity dates on notes.
(SO 5)

BE9-9 Compute interest and find the maturity date for the following notes.

	Date of Note	Principal	Interest Rate (%)	Terms
(a)	June 10	$80,000	6%	60 days
(b)	July 14	$50,000	7%	90 days
(c)	April 27	$12,000	8%	75 days

Determine maturity dates and compute interest and rates on notes.
(SO 5)

BE9-10 Presented below are data on three promissory notes. Determine the missing amounts.

	Date of Note	Terms	Maturity Date	Principal	Annual Interest Rate	Total Interest
(a)	April 1	60 days	?	$600,000	9%	?
(b)	July 2	30 days	?	90,000	?	$600
(c)	March 7	6 months	?	120,000	10%	?

Prepare entry for notes receivable exchanged for account receivable.
(SO 6)

BE9-11 On January 10, 2012, Honig Co. sold merchandise on account to Peregrine Co. for $13,600, n/30. On February 9, Peregrine Co. gave Honig Co. a 10% promissory note in settlement of this account. Prepare the journal entry to record the sale and the settlement of the account receivable.

Compute ratios to analyze receivables.
(SO 9)

BE9-12 The financial statements of Minnesota Mining and Manufacturing Company (3M) report net sales of $20.0 billion. Accounts receivable (net) are $2.7 billion at the beginning of the year and $2.8 billion at the end of the year. Compute 3M's receivables turnover ratio. Compute 3M's average collection period for accounts receivable in days.

Do it! Review

Prepare entry for uncollectible accounts.
(SO 3)

Do it! 9-1 Valasquez Company has been in business several years. At the end of the current year, the ledger shows:

Accounts Receivable	$ 310,000 Dr.
Sales Revenue	2,200,000 Cr.
Allowance for Doubtful Accounts	6,100 Cr.

Bad debts are estimated to be 7% of receivables. Prepare the entry to adjust Allowance for Doubtful Accounts.

Prepare entry for factored accounts.
(SO 4)

Do it! 9-2 Mark Distributors is a growing company whose ability to raise capital has not been growing as quickly as its expanding assets and sales. Mark's local banker has indicated that the company cannot increase its borrowing for the foreseeable future. Mark's suppliers are demanding payment for goods acquired within 30 days of the invoice date, but Mark's customers are slow in paying for their purchases (60–90 days). As a result, Mark has a cash flow problem.

Mark needs $160,000 to cover next Friday's payroll. Its balance of outstanding accounts receivable totals $1,000,000. What might Mark do to alleviate this cash crunch? Record the entry that Mark would make when it raises the needed cash. (Assume a 2% service charge.)

Prepare entries for notes receivable.
(SO 5, 8)

Do it! 9-3 Nadeau Wholesalers accepts from Nicole Stores a $6,200, 4-month, 12% note dated May 31 in settlement of Nicole's overdue account. (a) What is the maturity date of the note?

(b) What is the entry made by Nadeau at the maturity date, assuming Nicole pays the note and interest in full at that time?

Do it! 9-4   In 2012, Abdi Farah Company has net credit sales of $1,600,000 for the year. It had a beginning accounts receivable (net) balance of $101,000 and an ending accounts receivable (net) balance of $107,000. Compute Abdi Farah Company's (a) accounts receivable turnover and (b) average collection period in days.

Compute ratios for receivables.
(SO 9)

Exercises

E9-1   Presented below are selected transactions of Santos Company. Santos sells in large quantities to other companies and also sells its product in a small retail outlet.

Journalize entries related to accounts receivable.
(SO 2)

March	1	Sold merchandise on account to Jaclyn Company for $3,000, terms 2/10, n/30.
	3	Jaclyn Company returned merchandise worth $500 to Santos.
	9	Santos collected the amount due from Jaclyn Company from the March 1 sale.
	15	Santos sold merchandise for $400 in its retail outlet. The customer used his Santos credit card.
	31	Santos added 1.5% monthly interest to the customer's credit card balance.

Instructions
Prepare journal entries for the transactions above.

E9-2   Presented below are two independent situations.

Journalize entries for recognizing accounts receivable.
(SO 2)

(a) On January 6, Mendenhall Co. sells merchandise on account to Miles Inc. for $9,000, terms 2/10, n/30. On January 16, Miles Inc. pays the amount due. Prepare the entries on Mendenhall's books to record the sale and related collection.

(b) On January 10, Markus Klinko uses his Indrani Co. credit card to purchase merchandise from Indrani Co. for $9,000. On February 10, Klinko is billed for the amount due of $9,000. On February 12, Klinko pays $5,000 on the balance due. On March 10, Klinko is billed for the amount due, including interest at 2% per month on the unpaid balance as of February 12. Prepare the entries on Indrani Co.'s books related to the transactions that occurred on January 10, February 12, and March 10.

E9-3   The ledger of G.K. Reid Company at the end of the current year shows Accounts Receivable $120,000, Sales Revenue $840,000, and Sales Returns and Allowances $30,000.

Journalize entries to record allowance for doubtful accounts using two different bases.
(SO 3)

Instructions
(a) If G.K. Reid uses the direct write-off method to account for uncollectible accounts, journalize the adjusting entry at December 31, assuming G.K. Reid determines that L. Gaga's $1,400 balance is uncollectible.
(b) If Allowance for Doubtful Accounts has a credit balance of $2,100 in the trial balance, journalize the adjusting entry at December 31, assuming bad debts are expected to be (1) 1% of net sales, and (2) 10% of accounts receivable.
(c) If Allowance for Doubtful Accounts has a debit balance of $200 in the trial balance, journalize the adjusting entry at December 31, assuming bad debts are expected to be (1) 0.75% of net sales and (2) 6% of accounts receivable.

E9-4   Lohan Company has accounts receivable of $93,100 at March 31. An analysis of the accounts shows the following information.

Determine bad debts expense; prepare the adjusting entry for bad debts expense.
(SO 3)

Month of Sale	Balance, March 31
March	$60,000
February	17,600
January	8,500
Prior to January	7,000
	$93,100

Credit terms are 2/10, n/30. At March 31, Allowance for Doubtful Accounts has a credit balance of $1,200 prior to adjustment. The company uses the percentage-of-receivables basis for estimating uncollectible accounts. The company's estimate of bad debts is shown on the next page.

Age of Accounts	Estimated Percentage Uncollectible
1–30 days	2.0%
31–60 days	5.0%
61–90 days	30.0%
Over 90 days	50.0%

Instructions

(a) Determine the total estimated uncollectibles.

(b) Prepare the adjusting entry at March 31 to record bad debts expense.

Journalize write-off and recovery.

(SO 3)

E9-5   At December 31, 2011, Kardashian Company had a balance of $15,000 in Allowance for Doubtful Accounts. During 2012, Kardashian wrote off accounts totaling $13,000. One of those accounts ($1,800) was later collected. At December 31, 2012, an aging schedule indicated that the balance in Allowance for Doubtful Accounts should be $19,000.

Instructions

Prepare journal entries to record the 2012 transactions of Kardashian Company.

Journalize percentage of sales basis, write-off, recovery.

(SO 3)

E9-6   On December 31, 2012, Dita Co. estimated that 2% of its net sales of $400,000 will become uncollectible. The company recorded this amount as an addition to Allowance for Doubtful Accounts. On May 11, 2013, Dita Co. determined that the Alex Lundquist account was uncollectible and wrote off $1,100. On June 12, 2013, Lundquist paid the amount previously written off.

Instructions

Prepare the journal entries on December 31, 2012, May 11, 2013, and June 12, 2013.

Journalize entries for the sale of accounts receivable.

(SO 4)

E9-7   Presented below are two independent situations.

(a) On March 3, Van Teese Appliances sells $680,000 of its receivables to Naomi Factors Inc. Naomi Factors assesses a finance charge of 3% of the amount of receivables sold. Prepare the entry on Van Teese Appliances' books to record the sale of the receivables.

(b) On May 10, Campbell Company sold merchandise for $3,500 and accepted the customer's America Bank MasterCard. America Bank charges a 4% service charge for credit card sales. Prepare the entry on Campbell Company's books to record the sale of merchandise.

Journalize entries for credit card sales.

(SO 4)

E9-8   Presented below are two independent situations.

(a) On April 2, Brooklyn Decker uses her J. C. Penney Company credit card to purchase merchandise from a J. C. Penney store for $1,500. On May 1, Decker is billed for the $1,500 amount due. Decker pays $700 on the balance due on May 3. On June 1, Decker receives a bill for the amount due, including interest at 1.0% per month on the unpaid balance as of May 3. Prepare the entries on J. C. Penney Co.'s books related to the transactions that occurred on April 2, May 3, and June 1.

(b) On July 4, Vanderloo's Restaurant accepts a Visa card for a $200 dinner bill. Visa charges a 3% service fee. Prepare the entry on Vanderloo's books related to this transaction.

Journalize credit card sales, and indicate the statement presentation of financing charges and service charge expense.

(SO 4)

E9-9   Bowie Stores accepts both its own and national credit cards. During the year, the following selected summary transactions occurred.

Jan. 15   Made Bowie credit card sales totaling $18,000. (There were no balances prior to January 15.)

20   Made Visa credit card sales (service charge fee 2%) totaling $4,300.

Feb. 10   Collected $10,000 on Bowie credit card sales.

15   Added finance charges of 1% to Bowie credit card balance.

Instructions

(a) Journalize the transactions for Bowie Stores.

(b) Indicate the statement presentation of the financing charges and the credit card service charge expense for Bowie Stores.

Journalize entries for notes receivable transactions.

(SO 5, 6)

E9-10   Stroup Supply Co. has the following transactions related to notes receivable during the last 2 months of 2012.

Nov. 1   Loaned $15,000 cash to Jorge Perez on a 1-year, 10% note.

Dec. 11   Sold goods to Armle Hammer, Inc., receiving a $6,750, 90-day, 8% note.

16   Received a $4,000, 6-month, 9% note in exchange for Max Weinberg's outstanding accounts receivable.

31   Accrued interest revenue on all notes receivable.

Instructions

(a) Journalize the transactions for Stroup Supply Co.

(b) Record the collection of the Perez note at its maturity in 2013.

E9-11   Record the following transactions for Conando Co. in the general journal.

Journalize entries for notes receivable.

(SO 5, 6)

2012

May 1   Received a $7,500, 1-year, 10% note in exchange for Andy Richter's outstanding accounts receivable.

Dec.31   Accrued interest on the Richter note.

Dec.31   Closed the interest revenue account.

2013

May 1   Received principal plus interest on the Richter note. (No interest has been accrued in 2013.)

E9-12   La Bamba Company had the following select transactions.

Prepare entries for note receivable transactions.

(SO 5, 6, 8)

Apr. 1, 2012	Accepted Shatner Company's 1-year, 12% note in settlement of a $20,000 account receivable.
July 1, 2012	Loaned $25,000 cash to Richie Rosenberg on a 9-month, 10% note.
Dec. 31, 2012	Accrued interest on all notes receivable.
Apr. 1, 2013	Received principal plus interest on the Shatner note.
Apr. 1, 2013	Richie Rosenberg dishonored its note; La Bamba expects it will eventually collect.

Instructions

Prepare journal entries to record the transactions. La Bamba prepares adjusting entries once a year on December 31.

E9-13   On May 2, George Company lends $7,600 to Takei, Inc., issuing a 6-month, 9% note. At the maturity date, November 2, Takei indicates that it cannot pay.

Journalize entries for dishonor of notes receivable.

(SO 5, 8)

Instructions

(a) Prepare the entry to record the issuance of the note.

(b) Prepare the entry to record the dishonor of the note, assuming that George Company expects collection will occur.

(c) Prepare the entry to record the dishonor of the note, assuming that George Company does not expect collection in the future.

E9-14   Nachito Company had accounts receivable of $100,000 on January 1, 2012. The only transactions that affected accounts receivable during 2012 were net credit sales of $1,000,000, cash collections of $900,000, and accounts written off of $30,000.

Compute receivables turnover and average collection period.

(SO 9)

Instructions

(a) Compute the ending balance of accounts receivable.

(b) Compute the accounts receivable turnover ratio for 2012.

(c) Compute the average collection period in days.

Exercises: Set B

Visit the book's companion website, at **www.wiley.com/college/weygandt**, and choose the Student Companion site to access Exercise Set B.

Problems: Set A

P9-1A   At December 31, 2011, Mernt Co. reported the following information on its balance sheet.

Prepare journal entries related to bad debts expense.

(SO 2, 3, 9)

Accounts receivable	$960,000
Less: Allowance for doubtful accounts	80,000

During 2012, the company had the following transactions related to receivables.

1. Sales on account $3,200,000
2. Sales returns and allowances   50,000
3. Collections of accounts receivable   2,810,000
4. Write-offs of accounts receivable deemed uncollectible   90,000
5. Recovery of bad debts previously written off as uncollectible 24,000

Instructions

(a) Prepare the journal entries to record each of these five transactions. Assume that no cash discounts were taken on the collections of accounts receivable.

(b) Enter the January 1, 2012, balances in Accounts Receivable and Allowance for Doubtful Accounts, post the entries to the two accounts (use T accounts), and determine the balances.

(c) Prepare the journal entry to record bad debts expense for 2012, assuming that an aging of accounts receivable indicates that expected bad debts are $115,000.

(d) Compute the accounts receivable turnover ratio for 2012.

(b) Accounts receivable
$1,210,000
ADA $14,000
(c) Bad debts expense
$101,000

Compute bad debts amounts.
(SO 3)

P9-2A Information related to Jordan Schlansky Company for 2012 is summarized below.

Total credit sales	$2,200,000
Accounts receivable at December 31	825,000
Bad debts written off	33,000

Instructions

(a) What amount of bad debts expense will Jordan Schlansky Company report if it uses the direct write-off method of accounting for bad debts?

(b) Assume that Jordan Schlansky Company estimates its bad debts expense to be 2% of credit sales. What amount of bad debts expense will Jordan Schlansky record if it has an Allowance for Doubtful Accounts credit balance of $4,000?

(c) Assume that Jordan Schlansky Company estimates its bad debts expense based on 6% of accounts receivable. What amount of bad debts expense will Jordan Schlansky record if it has an Allowance for Doubtful Accounts credit balance of $3,000?

(d) Assume the same facts as in (c), except that there is a $3,000 debit balance in Allowance for Doubtful Accounts. What amount of bad debts expense will Jordan Schlansky record?

(e) ◀━━━ What is the weakness of the direct write-off method of reporting bad debts expense?

Journalize entries to record transactions related to bad debts.
(SO 2, 3)

P9-3A Presented below is an aging schedule for McCann Company.

Worksheet.xls

File Edit View Insert Format Tools Data Window Help

	A	B	C	D	E	F	G
1				Number of Days Past Due			
2			Not				
3	Customer	Total	Yet Due	1–30	31–60	61–90	Over 90
4	Amos	$ 22,000		$10,000	$12,000		
5	Brian	40,000	$ 40,000				
6	Chevy	57,000	16,000	6,000		$35,000	
7	Drake	34,000					$34,000
8	Others	132,000	96,000	16,000	14,000		6,000
9		$285,000	$152,000	$32,000	$26,000	$35,000	$40,000
10	Estimated Percentage Uncollectible		3%	6%	13%	25%	60%
11	Total Estimated Bad Debts	$ 42,610	$ 4,560	$ 1,920	$ 3,380	$ 8,750	$24,000
12							

At December 31, 2012, the unadjusted balance in Allowance for Doubtful Accounts is a credit of $12,000.

Instructions

(a) Journalize and post the adjusting entry for bad debts at December 31, 2012.

(b) Journalize and post to the allowance account the following events and transactions in the year 2013.

(a) Bad debts expense
$30,610

(1) On March 31, a $1,000 customer balance originating in 2012 is judged uncollectible.
(2) On May 31, a check for $1,000 is received from the customer whose account was written off as uncollectible on March 31.

(c) Journalize the adjusting entry for bad debts on December 31, 2013, assuming that the unadjusted balance in Allowance for Doubtful Accounts is a debit of $800 and the aging schedule indicates that total estimated bad debts will be $28,600.

(c) Bad debts expense
$29,400

P9-4A   Pender Inc. uses the allowance method to estimate uncollectible accounts receivable. The company produced the following aging of the accounts receivable at year-end.

Journalize transactions related to bad debts.
(SO 2, 3)

Worksheet.xls

File   Edit   View   Insert   Format   Tools   Data   Window   Help

	A	B	C	D	E	F	G
1				Number of Days Outstanding			
2							
3		Total	0–30	31–60	61–90	91–120	Over 120
4	Accounts receivable	200,000	77,000	46,000	39,000	23,000	$15,000
5	% uncollectible		1%	4%	5%	8%	10%
6	Estimated bad debts						
7							

Instructions
(a) Calculate the total estimated bad debts based on the above information.
(b) Prepare the year-end adjusting journal entry to record the bad debts using the aged uncollectible accounts receivable determined in (a). Assume the current balance in Allowance for Doubtful Accounts is a $8,000 debit.
(c) Of the above accounts, $5,000 is determined to be specifically uncollectible. Prepare the journal entry to write off the uncollectible account.
(d) The company collects $5,000 subsequently on a specific account that had previously been determined to be uncollectible in (c). Prepare the journal entry(ies) necessary to restore the account and record the cash collection.
(e) Comment on how your answers to (a)–(d) would change if Pender Inc. used 3% of *total* accounts receivable, rather than aging the accounts receivable. What are the advantages to the company of aging the accounts receivable rather than applying a percentage to total accounts receivable?

(a) Tot. est.
bad debts $11,510

P9-5A   At December 31, 2012, the trial balance of Stack Company contained the following amounts before adjustment.

Journalize entries to record transactions related to bad debts.
(SO 3)

	Debits	Credits
Accounts Receivable	$385,000	
Allowance for Doubtful Accounts		$ 2,000
Sales Revenue		950,000

Instructions
(a) Based on the information given, which method of accounting for bad debts is Stack Company using—the direct write-off method or the allowance method? How can you tell?
(b) Prepare the adjusting entry at December 31, 2012, for bad debts expense under each of the following independent assumptions.
(1) An aging schedule indicates that $11,750 of accounts receivable will be uncollectible.
(2) The company estimates that 1% of sales will be uncollectible.
(c) Repeat part (b) assuming that instead of a credit balance there is an $2,000 debit balance in Allowance for Doubtful Accounts.
(d) During the next month, January 2013, a $3,000 account receivable is written off as uncollectible. Prepare the journal entry to record the write-off.
(e) Repeat part (d) assuming that Stack uses the direct write-off method instead of the allowance method in accounting for uncollectible accounts receivable.
(f) What type of account is Allowance for Doubtful Accounts? How does it affect how accounts receivable is reported on the balance sheet at the end of the accounting period?

(b) (2) $9,500

Prepare entries for various notes receivable transactions.

(SO 2, 4, 5, 8, 9)

GLS

P9-6A Manatee Company closes its books monthly. On September 30, selected ledger account balances are:

Notes Receivable	$33,000
Interest Receivable	170

Notes Receivable include the following.

Date	Maker	Face	Term	Interest
Aug. 16	M. Bear Inc.	$ 8,000	60 days	8%
Aug. 25	Pope Co.	9,000	60 days	10%
Sept. 30	Quackers Corp.	16,000	6 months	9%

Interest is computed using a 360-day year. During October, the following transactions were completed.

Oct.   7   Made sales of $6,900 on Manatee credit cards.
     12   Made sales of $900 on MasterCard credit cards. The credit card service charge is 3%.
     15   Added $460 to Manatee customer balance for finance charges on unpaid balances.
     15   Received payment in full from M. Bear Inc. on the amount due.
     24   Received notice that the Pope note has been dishonored. (Assume that Pope is expected to pay in the future.)

Instructions
(a) Journalize the October transactions and the October 31 adjusting entry for accrued interest receivable.

(b) Accounts receivable $16,510

(c) Total receivables $32,630

(b) Enter the balances at October 1 in the receivable accounts. Post the entries to all of the receivable accounts.
(c) Show the balance sheet presentation of the receivable accounts at October 31.

Prepare entries for various receivable transactions.

(SO 2, 4, 5, 6, 7, 8)

P9-7A On January 1, 2012, Pierre Company had Accounts Receivable $139,000, Notes Receivable $25,000, and Allowance for Doubtful Accounts $13,200. The note receivable is from Stacy Richter Company. It is a 4-month, 12% note dated December 31, 2011. Pierre Company prepares financial statements annually. During the year, the following selected transactions occurred.

Jan.   5   Sold $20,000 of merchandise to Bernard Company, terms n/15.
     20   Accepted Bernard Company's $20,000, 3-month, 9% note for balance due.
Feb. 18   Sold $8,000 of merchandise to LaBamba Company and accepted LaBamba's $8,000, 6-month, 9% note for the amount due.
Apr. 20   Collected Bernard Company note in full.
     30   Received payment in full from Stacy Richter Company on the amount due.
May 25   Accepted Cloppy Inc.'s $4,000, 3-month, 7% note in settlement of a past-due balance on account.
Aug. 18   Received payment in full from LaBamba Company on note due.
     25   The Cloppy Inc. note was dishonored. Cloppy Inc. is not bankrupt; future payment is anticipated.
Sept. 1   Sold $12,000 of merchandise to Bessie Lou Company and accepted a $12,000, 6-month, 10% note for the amount due.

Instructions
Journalize the transactions.

Problems: Set B

Prepare journal entries related to bad debts expense.

(SO 2, 3, 9)

P9-1B At December 31, 2011, Artie Kendall Imports reported the following information on its balance sheet.

Accounts receivable	$250,000
Less: Allowance for doubtful accounts	15,000

During 2012, the company had the following transactions related to receivables.

1. Sales on account	$2,400,000
2. Sales returns and allowances	45,000

3. Collections of accounts receivable   2,250,000
4. Write-offs of accounts receivable deemed uncollectible   12,000
5. Recovery of bad debts previously written off as uncollectible   3,000

Instructions
(a) Prepare the journal entries to record each of these five transactions. Assume that no cash discounts were taken on the collections of accounts receivable.
(b) Enter the January 1, 2012, balances in Accounts Receivable and Allowance for Doubtful Accounts. Post the entries to the two accounts (use T accounts), and determine the balances.
(c) Prepare the journal entry to record bad debts expense for 2012, assuming that an aging of accounts receivable indicates that estimated bad debts are $22,000.
(d) Compute the accounts receivable turnover ratio for the year 2012.

(b) Accounts receivable
  $343,000
  ADA $6,000
(c) Bad debts expense
  $16,000

P9-2B Information related to Gustavo Company for 2012 is summarized below.

Compute bad debts amounts.
(SO 3)

Total credit sales	$1,100,000
Accounts receivable at December 31	369,000
Bad debts written off	22,150

Instructions
(a) What amount of bad debts expense will Gustavo Company report if it uses the direct write-off method of accounting for bad debts?
(b) Assume that Gustavo Company decides to estimate its bad debts expense to be 2% of credit sales. What amount of bad debts expense will Gustavo record if Allowance for Doubtful Accounts has a credit balance of $3,000?
(c) Assume that Gustavo Company decides to estimate its bad debts expense based on 6% of accounts receivable. What amount of bad debts expense will Gustavo Company record if Allowance for Doubtful Accounts has a credit balance of $4,000?
(d) Assume the same facts as in (c), except that there is a $2,000 debit balance in Allowance for Doubtful Accounts. What amount of bad debts expense will Gustavo record?
(e) ◄━━━━ What is the weakness of the direct write-off method of reporting bad debts expense?

P9-3B Presented below is an aging schedule for Stol Company.

Journalize entries to record transactions related to bad debts.
(SO 2, 3)

Worksheet.xls ▢▣☒

File   Edit   View   Insert   Format   Tools   Data   Window   Help

	A	B	C	D	E	F	G
1					**Number of Days Past Due**		
2			**Not**				
3	**Customer**	**Total**	**Yet Due**	**1–30**	**31–60**	**61–90**	**Over 90**
4	Ang	$ 30,000		$ 13,500	$16,500		
5	Bistro	45,000	$ 45,000				
6	Conesie	75,000	22,500	7,500		$45,000	
7	Dagova	57,000					$57,000
8	Others	189,000	138,000	22,500	19,500		9,000
9		$396,000	$205,500	$43,500	$36,000	$45,000	$66,000
10	Estimated Percentage Uncollectible		2%	6%	10%	25%	50%
11	Total Estimated Bad Debts	$ 54,570	$ 4,110	$ 2,610	$ 3,600	$ 11,250	$33,000
12							

At December 31, 2012, the unadjusted balance in Allowance for Doubtful Accounts is a credit of $16,000.

Instructions
(a) Journalize and post the adjusting entry for bad debts at December 31, 2012.
(b) Journalize and post to the allowance account the following events and transactions in the year 2013.
  (1) March 1, a $1,900 customer balance originating in 2012 is judged uncollectible.
  (2) May 1, a check for $1,900 is received from the customer whose account was written off as uncollectible on March 1.

(a) Bad debts expense
  $38,570

(c) Bad debts expense
$44,300

(c) Journalize the adjusting entry for bad debts on December 31, 2013. Assume that the unadjusted balance in Allowance for Doubtful Accounts is a debit of $2,000, and the aging schedule indicates that total estimated bad debts will be $42,300.

Journalize transactions related to bad debts.
(SO 2, 3)

P9-4B The following represents selected information taken from a company's aging schedule to estimate uncollectible accounts receivable at year-end.

⊠ Worksheet.xls							
🖫 **File** **Edit** **View** **Insert** **Format** **Tools** **Data** **Window** **Help**							
	A	**B**	**C**	**D**	**E**	**F**	**G**
1				**Number of Days Outstanding**			
2							
3		**Total**	**0–30**	**31–60**	**61–90**	**91–120**	**Over 120**
4	Accounts receivable	$375,000	$220,000	$90,000	$40,000	$10,000	$15,000
5	% uncollectible		1%	4%	5%	8%	10%
6	Estimated bad debts						
7							

Instructions

(a) Tot. est.
bad debts $10,100

(a) Calculate the total estimated bad debts based on the above information.

(b) Prepare the year-end adjusting journal entry to record the bad debts using the allowance method and the aged uncollectible accounts receivable determined in (a). Assume the current balance in Allowance for Doubtful Accounts is a $3,000 credit.

(c) Of the above accounts, $1,600 is determined to be specifically uncollectible. Prepare the journal entry to write off the uncollectible accounts.

(d) The company subsequently collects $700 on a specific account that had previously been determined to be uncollectible in (c). Prepare the journal entry(ies) necessary to restore the account and record the cash collection.

(e) Explain how establishing an allowance account satisfies the expense recognition principle.

Journalize entries to record transactions related to bad debts.
(SO 3)

P9-5B At December 31, 2012, the trial balance of Flexenfusser Company contained the following amounts before adjustment.

	Debits	**Credits**
Accounts Receivable	$250,000	
Allowance for Doubtful Accounts		$ 1,100
Sales Revenue		600,000

Instructions

(a) (2) $12,000

(a) Prepare the adjusting entry at December 31, 2012, to record bad debts expense under each of the following independent assumptions.

   (1) An aging schedule indicates that $12,500 of accounts receivable will be uncollectible.

   (2) The company estimates that 2% of sales will be uncollectible.

(b) Repeat part (a) assuming that instead of a credit balance, there is a $1,100 debit balance in Allowance for Doubtful Accounts.

(c) During the next month, January 2013, a $3,200 account receivable is written off as uncollectible. Prepare the journal entry to record the write-off.

(d) Repeat part (c) assuming that Flexenfusser Company uses the direct write-off method instead of the allowance method in accounting for uncollectible accounts receivable.

(e) What are the advantages of using the allowance method in accounting for uncollectible accounts as compared to the direct write-off method?

Prepare entries for various notes receivable transactions.
(SO 2, 4, 5, 8, 9)

GLS

P9-6B Mr. T Co. closes its books monthly. On June 30, selected ledger account balances are:

Notes Receivable	$57,000
Interest Receivable	420

Notes Receivable include the following.

Date	Maker	Face	Term	Interest
May 16	Abe Inc.	$12,000	60 days	10%
May 26	Vigoda Co.	30,000	60 days	9%
June 30	Lipton Corp.	15,000	6 months	12%

During July, the following transactions were completed.

July 5 Made sales of $7,200 on Mr. T Co. credit cards.
14 Made sales of $1,000 on Visa credit cards. The credit card service charge is 3%.
14 Added $510 to Mr. T Co. credit card customer balances for finance charges on unpaid balances.
15 Received payment in full from Abe Inc. on the amount due.
25 Received notice that the Vigoda Co. note has been dishonored. (Assume that Vigoda Co. is expected to pay in the future.)

Instructions

(a) Journalize the July transactions and the July 31 adjusting entry for accrued interest receivable. (Interest is computed using 360 days.)

(b) Enter the balances at July 1 in the receivable accounts. Post the entries to all of the receivable accounts.

(b) Accounts receivable $38,160

(c) Show the balance sheet presentation of the receivable accounts at July 31.

(c) Total receivables $53,310

P9-7B On January 1, 2012, DeCarlo Company had Accounts Receivable $98,000 and Allowance for Doubtful Accounts $8,100. DeCarlo Company prepares financial statements annually. During the year, the following selected transactions occurred.

Prepare entries for various receivable transactions.

(SO 2, 4, 5, 6, 7, 8)

Jan. 5 Sold $10,800 of merchandise to Kelly Company, terms n/30.
Feb. 2 Accepted a $10,800, 4-month, 10% promissory note from Kelly Company for the balance due.
12 Sold $13,500 of merchandise to Raymond Company and accepted Raymond's $13,500, 2-month, 10% note for the balance due.
26 Sold $7,000 of merchandise to Ringspin Co., terms n/10.
Apr. 5 Accepted a $7,000, 3-month, 8% note from Ringspin Co. for the balance due.
12 Collected Raymond Company note in full.
June 2 Collected Kelly Company note in full.
July 5 Ringspin Co. dishonors its note of April 5. It is expected that Ringspin will eventually pay the amount owed.
15 Sold $12,000 of merchandise to Butter Co. and accepted Butter's $12,000, 3-month, 12% note for the amount due.
Oct. 15 Butter Co.'s note was dishonored. Butter Co. is bankrupt, and there is no hope of future settlement.

Instructions

Journalize the transactions.

Problems: Set C

Visit the book's companion website, at **www.wiley.com/college/weygandt**, and choose the Student Companion site to access Problem Set C.

Comprehensive Problem

CP9 Porter Company's balance sheet at December 31, 2011, is presented below.

PORTER COMPANY
Balance Sheet
December 31, 2011

Cash	$13,100	Accounts payable	$ 8,750
Accounts receivable	19,780	Owner's capital	32,730
Allowance for doubtful accounts	(800)		$41,480
Inventory	9,400		
	$41,480		

During January 2012, the following transactions occurred. Porter uses the perpetual inventory method.

Jan. 1　Porter accepted a 4-month, 8% note from Anderko Company in payment of Anderko's $1,200 account.

3　Porter wrote off as uncollectible the accounts of Elrich Corporation ($450) and Rios Company ($280).

8　Porter purchased $17,200 of inventory on account.

11　Porter sold for $25,000 on account inventory that cost $17,500.

15　Porter sold inventory that cost $700 to Fred Berman for $1,000. Berman charged this amount on his Visa First Bank card. The service fee charged Porter by First Bank is 3%.

17　Porter collected $22,900 from customers on account.

21　Porter paid $16,300 on accounts payable.

24　Porter received payment in full ($280) from Rios Company on the account written off on January 3.

27　Porter purchased advertising supplies for $1,400 cash.

31　Porter paid other operating expenses, $3,218.

Adjustment data:

1. Interest is recorded for the month on the note from January 1.
2. Bad debts are expected to be 6% of the January 31, 2012, accounts receivable.
3. A count of advertising supplies on January 31, 2012, reveals that $560 remains unused.

Instructions

(You may want to set up T accounts to determine ending balances.)

(a) Prepare journal entries for the transactions listed above and adjusting entries. (Include entries for cost of goods sold using the perpetual system.)

(b) Prepare an adjusted trial balance at January 31, 2012.

(c) Prepare an income statement and an owner's equity statement for the month ending January 31, 2012, and a classified balance sheet as of January 31, 2012.

Continuing Cookie Chronicle

(*Note:* This is a continuation of the Cookie Chronicle from Chapters 1 through 8.)

CCC9　One of Natalie's friends, Curtis Lesperance, runs a coffee shop where he sells specialty coffees and prepares and sells muffins and cookies. He is eager to buy one of Natalie's fine European mixers, which would enable him to make larger batches of muffins and cookies. However, Curtis cannot afford to pay for the mixer for at least 30 days. He asks Natalie if she would be willing to sell him the mixer on credit. Natalie comes to you for advice.

Go to the book's companion website, **www.wiley.com/college/weygandt,** *to see the completion of this problem.*

BROADENINGYOURPERSPECTIVE

Financial Reporting and Analysis

Financial Reporting Problem: SEK Company

BYP9-1　SEK Company sells office equipment and supplies to many organizations in the city and surrounding area on contract terms of 2/10, n/30. In the past, over 75% of the credit customers have taken advantage of the discount by paying within 10 days of the invoice date.

The number of customers taking the full 30 days to pay has increased within the last year. Current indications are that less than 60% of the customers are now taking the discount. Bad debts as a percentage of gross credit sales have risen from the 2.5% provided in past years to about 4.5% in the current year.

The company's Finance Committee has requested more information on the collections of accounts receivable. The controller responded to this request with the report reproduced below.

SEK COMPANY
Accounts Receivable Collections
May 31, 2012

The fact that some credit accounts will prove uncollectible is normal. Annual bad debts write-offs have been 2.5% of gross credit sales over the past 5 years. During the last fiscal year, this percentage increased to slightly less than 4.5%. The current Accounts Receivable balance is $1,400,000. The condition of this balance in terms of age and probability of collection is as follows.

Proportion of Total	Age Categories	Probability of Collection
62%	not yet due	98%
20%	less than 30 days past due	96%
9%	30 to 60 days past due	94%
5%	61 to 120 days past due	91%
$2^1/_2$%	121 to 180 days past due	75%
$1^1/_2$%	over 180 days past due	30%

Allowance for Doubtful Accounts had a credit balance of $29,500 on June 1, 2011. SEK has provided for a monthly bad debts expense accrual during the current fiscal year based on the assumption that 4.5% of gross credit sales will be uncollectible. Total gross credit sales for the 2011–2012 fiscal year amounted to $2,900,000. Write-offs of bad accounts during the year totaled $102,000.

Instructions
(a) Prepare an accounts receivable aging schedule for SEK Company using the age categories identified in the controller's report to the Finance Committee showing the following.
  (1) The amount of accounts receivable outstanding for each age category and in total.
  (2) The estimated amount that is uncollectible for each category and in total.
(b) Compute the amount of the year-end adjustment necessary to bring Allowance for Doubtful Accounts to the balance indicated by the age analysis. Then prepare the necessary journal entry to adjust the accounting records.
(c) In a recessionary environment with tight credit and high interest rates:
  (1) Identify steps SEK Company might consider to improve the accounts receivable situation.
  (2) Then evaluate each step identified in terms of the risks and costs involved.

Comparative Analysis Problem: PepsiCo, Inc. vs. The Coca-Cola Company

BYP9-2 PepsiCo, Inc.'s financial statements are presented in Appendix A. Financial statements of The Coca-Cola Company are presented in Appendix B.

PEPSICO

Instructions
(a) Based on the information in these financial statements, compute the following 2009 ratios for each company. (Assume all sales are credit sales and that PepsiCo's receivables on its balance sheet are all trade receivables.)
  (1) Accounts receivable turnover ratio.
  (2) Average collection period for receivables.
(b) What conclusions about managing accounts receivable can you draw from these data?

On the Web

BYP9-3 **Purpose:** To learn more about factoring services.

Address: www.invoicebankers.com, or go to **www.wiley.com/college/weygandt**

Steps: Go to the website and answer the following questions.
(a) What are some of the benefits of factoring?
(b) What is the range of the percentages of the typical discount rate?
(c) If a company factors its receivables, what percentage of the value of the receivables can it expect to receive from the factor in the form of cash, and how quickly will it receive the cash?

Critical Thinking

Decision Making Across the Organization

BYP9-4 Molly and Joe Mayne own Campus Fashions. From its inception Campus Fashions has sold merchandise on either a cash or credit basis, but no credit cards have been accepted. During the past several months, the Maynes have begun to question their sales policies. First, they have lost some sales because of refusing to accept credit cards. Second, representatives of two metropolitan banks have been persuasive in almost convincing them to accept their national credit cards. One bank, City National Bank, has stated that its credit card fee is 4%.

The Maynes decide that they should determine the cost of carrying their own credit sales. From the accounting records of the past 3 years, they accumulate the following data.

	2012	2011	2010
Net credit sales	$500,000	$600,000	$400,000
Collection agency fees for slow-paying			
customers	2,450	2,500	2,400
Salary of part-time accounts receivable clerk	4,100	4,100	4,100

Credit and collection expenses as a percentage of net credit sales are: uncollectible accounts 1.6%, billing and mailing costs 0.5%, and credit investigation fee on new customers 0.15%.

Molly and Joe also determine that the average accounts receivable balance outstanding during the year is 5% of net credit sales. The Maynes estimate that they could earn an average of 8% annually on cash invested in other business opportunities.

Instructions
With the class divided into groups, answer the following.

(a) Prepare a table showing, for each year, total credit and collection expenses in dollars and as a percentage of net credit sales.

(b) Determine the net credit and collection expense in dollars and as a percentage of sales after considering the revenue not earned from other investment opportunities.

(c) Discuss both the financial and nonfinancial factors that are relevant to the decision.

Communication Activity

BYP9-5 Rene Mai, a friend of yours, overheard a discussion at work about changes her employer wants to make in accounting for uncollectible accounts. Rene knows little about accounting, and she asks you to help make sense of what she heard. Specifically, she asks you to explain the differences between the percentage-of-sales, percentage-of-receivables, and the direct write-off methods for uncollectible accounts.

Instructions
In a letter of one page (or less), explain to Rene the three methods of accounting for uncollectibles. Be sure to discuss differences among these methods.

Ethics Case

BYP9-6 The controller of Ruiz Co. believes that the yearly allowance for doubtful accounts for Ruiz Co. should be 2% of net credit sales. The president of Ruiz Co., nervous that the stockholders might expect the company to sustain its 10% growth rate, suggests that the controller increase the allowance for doubtful accounts to 4%. The president thinks that the lower net income, which reflects a 6% growth rate, will be a more sustainable rate for Ruiz Co.

Instructions
(a) Who are the stakeholders in this case?

(b) Does the president's request pose an ethical dilemma for the controller?

(c) Should the controller be concerned with Ruiz Co.'s growth rate? Explain your answer.

"All About You" Activity

BYP9-7 As the **All About You** feature (available on the book's companion website) indicates, credit card usage in the United States is substantial. Many startup companies use credit cards as a way to help meet short-term financial needs. The most common forms of debt for startups are use of credit cards and loans from relatives.

Suppose that you start up Brothers Sandwich Shop. You invested your savings of $20,000 and borrowed $70,000 from your relatives. Although sales in the first few months are good, you see that you may not have sufficient cash to pay expenses and maintain your inventory at acceptable levels, at least in the short term. You decide you may need to use one or more credit cards to fund the possible cash shortfall.

Instructions

(a) Go to the Internet and find two sources that provide insight into how to compare credit card terms.

(b) Develop a list, in descending order of importance, as to what features are most important to you in selecting a credit card for your business.

(c) Examine the features of your present credit card. (If you do not have a credit card, select a likely one online for this exercise.) Given your analysis above, what are the three major disadvantages of your present credit card?

FASB Codification Activity

BYP9-8 If your school has a subscription to the FASB Codification, go to *http://aaahq.org/ascLogin.cfm* to log in and prepare responses to the following.

(a) How are receivables defined in the Codification?

(b) What are the conditions under which losses from uncollectible receivables (Bad Debts Expense) should be reported?

Answers to Insight and Accounting Across the Organization Questions

p. 427 How Does a Credit Card Work? **Q:** Assume that Nordstrom prepares a bank reconciliation at the end of each month. If some credit card sales have not been processed by the bank, how should Nordstrom treat these transactions on its bank reconciliation? **A:** Nordstrom would treat the credit card receipts as deposits in transit. It has already recorded the receipts as cash. Its bank will increase Nordstrom's cash account when it receives the receipts.

p. 430 Can Fair Value Be Unfair? **Q:** What are the arguments in favor of and against fair value accounting for loans and receivables? **A:** Arguments in favor of fair value accounting for loans and receivables are that fair value would provide a more accurate view of a company's financial position. This might provide a useful early warning of when a bank or other financial institution was in trouble because its loans were of poor quality. But, banks argue that estimating fair values is very difficult to do accurately. They are also concerned that volatile fair values could cause large swings in a bank's reported net income.

p. 432 Bad Information Can Lead to Bad Loans **Q:** What steps should the banks have taken to ensure the accuracy of financial information provided on loan applications? **A:** At a minimum, the bank should have requested copies of recent income tax forms and contacted the supposed employer to verify income. To verify ownership and value of assets, it should have examined bank statements, investment statements, and title documents and should have employed appraisers.

Answers to Self-Test Questions

1. d **2.** c ($1,000 − $300) × (100% − 2%) **3.** a **4.** b ($60,000 − $5,000) **5.** d ($60,000 + $5,000) **6.** b ($800,000 × 1.5%) + $15,000 **7.** b ($750,000 × 3%) + ($18,000 − $30,000) **8.** d ($800,000 − $65,000) **9.** c **10.** c **11.** a **12.** b **13.** d $10,000 + ($10,000 × 120/360 × 9%) **14.** a **15.** c $800,000 ÷ [($100,000 + $15,000) ÷ 2]

IFRS A Look at IFRS

The basic accounting and reporting issues related to recognition and measurement of receivables, such as the use of allowance accounts, how to record discounts, use of the allowance method to account for bad debts, and factoring, are essentially the same between IFRS and GAAP.

Key Points

- IFRS requires that loans and receivables be accounted for at amortized cost, adjusted for allowances for doubtful accounts. IFRS sometimes refers to these allowances as *provisions*. The entry to record the allowance would be:

Bad Debts Expense	xxxxxx	
Allowance for Doubtful Accounts		xxxxxx

- Although IFRS implies that receivables with different characteristics should be reported separately, there is no standard that mandates this segregation.

- The FASB and IASB have worked to implement fair value measurement (the amount they currently could be sold for) for financial instruments. Both Boards have faced bitter opposition from various factions. As a consequence, the Boards have adopted a piecemeal approach; the first step is disclosure of fair value information in the notes. The second step is the fair value option, which permits, but does not require, companies to record some types of financial instruments at fair values in the financial statements.

- IFRS requires a two-tiered approach to test whether the value of loans and receivables are impaired. First, a company should look at specific loans and receivables to determine whether they are impaired. Then, the loans and receivables as a group should be evaluated for impairment. GAAP does not prescribe a similar two-tiered approach.

- IFRS and GAAP differ in the criteria used to determine how to record a factoring transaction. IFRS is a combination of an approach focused on risks and rewards and loss of control. GAAP uses loss of control as the primary criterion. In addition, IFRS permits partial derecognition of receivables; GAAP does not.

Looking to the Future

It appears likely that the question of recording fair values for financial instruments will continue to be an important issue to resolve as the Boards work toward convergence. Both the IASB and the FASB have indicated that they believe that financial statements would be more transparent and understandable if companies recorded and reported all financial instruments at fair value. That said, in *IFRS 9*, which was issued in 2009, the IASB created a split model, where some financial instruments are recorded at fair value, but other financial assets, such as loans and receivables, can be accounted for at amortized cost if certain criteria are met. Critics say that this can result in two companies with identical securities accounting for those securities in different ways. A proposal by the FASB would require that nearly all financial instruments, including loans and receivables, be accounted for at fair value. It has been suggested that *IFRS 9* will likely be changed or replaced as the FASB and IASB continue to deliberate the best treatment for financial instruments. In fact, one past member of the IASB said that companies should ignore *IFRS 9* and continue to report under the old standard, because in his opinion, it was extremely likely that it would be changed before the mandatory adoption date of the standard arrived in 2013.

IFRS Self-Test Questions

1. Under IFRS, loans and receivables are to be reported on the balance sheet at:
 (a) amortized cost.
 (b) amortized cost adjusted for estimated loss provisions.
 (c) historical cost.
 (d) replacement cost.

2. Which of the following statements is *false*?
 (a) Loans and receivables include equity securities purchased by the company.
 (b) Loans and receivables include credit card receivables.

(c) Loans and receivables include amounts owed by employees as a result of company loans to employees.

(d) Loans and receivables include amounts resulting from transactions with customers.

3. In recording a factoring transaction:
   (a) IFRS focuses on loss of control.
   (b) GAAP focuses on loss of control and risks and rewards.
   (c) IFRS and GAAP allow partial derecognition.
   (d) IFRS allows partial derecognition

4. Under IFRS:
   (a) the entry to record estimated uncollected accounts is the same as GAAP.
   (b) loans and receivables should only be tested for impairment as a group.
   (c) it is always acceptable to use the direct write-off method.
   (d) all financial instruments are recorded at fair value.

5. Which of the following statements is *true*?
   (a) The fair value option requires that some types of financial instruments be recorded at fair value.
   (b) The fair value option allows, but does not require, that some types of financial instruments be recorded at amortized cost.
   (c) The fair value option allows, but does not require, that some types of financial instruments be recorded at fair value.
   (d) The FASB and IASB would like to reduce the reliance on fair value accounting for financial instruments in the future.

IFRS Concepts and Application

IFRS9-1 What are some steps taken by both the FASB and IASB to move to fair value measurement for financial instruments? In what ways have some of the approaches differed?

International Financial Reporting Problem: Zetar plc

IFRS9-2 The financial statements of Zetar plc are presented in Appendix C. The company's complete annual report, including the notes to its financial statements, is available at *www.zetarplc.com*.

Instructions
Use the company's annual report to answer the following questions.

(a) According to the Operational Review of Financial Performance, what was one reason why the balance in receivables increased relative to the previous year?

(b) According to the notes to the financial statements, how are loans and receivables defined?

(c) In the notes to the financial statements, the company reports a "one off item" related to receivables. Explain what this item was.

(d) Using information in the notes to the financial statements, determine what percentage the provision for impairment of receivables was as a percentage of total trade receivables for 2009 and 2008. How did the ratio change from 2008 to 2009, and what does this suggest about the company's receivables?

Answers to IFRS Self-Test Questions
1. b   **2.** a   **3.** d   **4.** a   **5.** c

The Navigator

✔ **Remember to go back to the Navigator box on the chapter opening page and check off your completed work.**

CHAPTER10

Plant Assets, Natural Resources, and Intangible Assets

Feature Story

HOW MUCH FOR A RIDE TO THE BEACH?

It's spring break. Your plane has landed, you've finally found your bags, and you're dying to hit the beach—but first you need a "vehicular unit" to get you there. As you turn away from baggage claim you see a long row of rental agency booths. Many are names you are familiar with—Hertz, Avis, and Budget. But a booth at the far end catches your eye—Rent-A-Wreck. Now there's a company making a clear statement!

Any company that relies on equipment to generate revenues must make decisions about what kind of equipment to buy, how long to keep it, and how vigorously to maintain it. Rent-A-Wreck has decided to rent used rather than new cars and trucks. It rents these vehicles across the United States, Europe, and Asia. While the big-name agencies push vehicles with that "new car smell," Rent-A-Wreck competes on price. The message is simple: Rent a used car and save some cash. It's not a message that appeals to everyone. If you're a marketing executive wanting to impress a big client, you probably don't want to pull up in a Rent-A-Wreck car. But if you want to get from point A to point B for the minimum cash per mile, then they are playing your tune. The company's message seems to be getting across to the right clientele. Revenues have increased significantly.

When you rent a car from Rent-A-Wreck, you are renting from an independent business person who has paid a "franchise fee" for the right to use the Rent-A-Wreck name. In order to gain a franchise, he or she must meet financial and other criteria, and must agree to run the rental agency according to rules prescribed by Rent-A-Wreck. Some of these rules require that each franchise maintain its cars in a reasonable fashion. This ensures that, though you won't be cruising down Daytona Beach's Atlantic Avenue in a Mercedes convertible, you can be reasonably assured that you won't be calling a towtruck.

The Navigator ✔

Inside**CHAPTER10**

Previewof**CHAPTER10**

The accounting for long-term assets has important implications for a company's reported results. In this chapter, we explain the application of the cost principle of accounting to property, plant, and equipment, such as Rent-A-Wreck vehicles, as well as to natural resources and intangible assets such as the "Rent-A-Wreck" trademark. We also describe the methods that companies may use to allocate an asset's cost over its useful life. In addition, we discuss the accounting for expenditures incurred during the useful life of assets, such as the cost of replacing tires and brake pads on rental cars.

The content and organization of Chapter 10 are as follows.

Plant Assets, Natural Resources, and Intangible Assets

Plant Assets	Natural Resources	Intangible Assets	Statement Presentation and Analysis
• Determining the cost of plant assets • Depreciation • Expenditures during useful life • Plant asset disposals	• Depletion	• Accounting for intangibles • Research and development costs	• Presentation • Analysis

✔ **The Navigator**

SECTION1 PLANT ASSETS

Plant assets are resources that have three characteristics: they have a physical substance (a definite size and shape), are used in the operations of a business, and are not intended for sale to customers. They are also called **property, plant, and equipment; plant and equipment;** and **fixed assets**. These assets are expected to provide services to the company for a number of years. Except for land, plant assets decline in service potential over their useful lives.

Because plant assets play a key role in ongoing operations, companies keep plant assets in good operating condition. They also replace worn-out or outdated plant assets, and expand productive resources as needed. Many companies have substantial investments in plant assets. Illustration 10-1 shows the

Illustration 10-1
Percentages of plant assets in relation to total assets

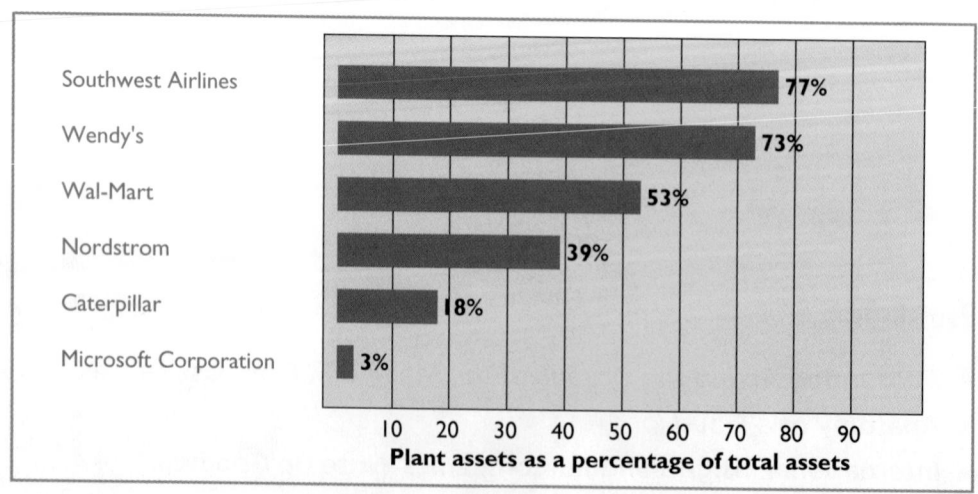

percentages of plant assets in relation to total assets of companies in a number of industries.

Determining the Cost of Plant Assets

The cost principle requires that companies record plant assets at cost. Thus Rent-A-Wreck records its vehicles at cost. **Cost consists of all expenditures necessary to acquire the asset and make it ready for its intended use**. For example, the cost of factory machinery includes the purchase price, freight costs paid by the purchaser, and installation costs. Once cost is established, the company uses that amount as the basis of accounting for the plant asset over its useful life.

In the following sections, we explain the application of the cost principle to each of the major classes of plant assets.

Study Objective [1]
Describe how the cost principle applies to plant assets.

Land

Companies often use **land** as a building site for a manufacturing plant or office site. The cost of land includes (1) the cash purchase price, (2) closing costs such as title and attorney's fees, (3) real estate brokers' commissions, and (4) accrued property taxes and other liens assumed by the purchaser. For example, if the cash price is $50,000 and the purchaser agrees to pay accrued taxes of $5,000, the cost of the land is $55,000.

Companies record as debits (increases) to the Land account all necessary costs incurred to make land **ready for its intended use**. When a company acquires vacant land, these costs include expenditures for clearing, draining, filling, and grading. Sometimes the land has a building on it that must be removed before construction of a new building. In this case, the company debits to the Land account all demolition and removal costs, less any proceeds from salvaged materials.

To illustrate, assume that Hayes Manufacturing Company acquires real estate at a cash cost of $100,000. The property contains an old warehouse that is razed at a net cost of $6,000 ($7,500 in costs less $1,500 proceeds from salvaged materials). Additional expenditures are the attorney's fee, $1,000, and the real estate broker's commission, $8,000. The cost of the land is $115,000, computed as shown in Illustration 10-2.

Helpful Hint
Management's intended use is important in applying the cost principle.

Land	
Cash price of property	$100,000
Net removal cost of warehouse	6,000
Attorney's fee	1,000
Real estate broker's commission	8,000
Cost of land	$115,000

Illustration 10-2
Computation of cost of land

When Hayes records the acquisition, it debits Land for $115,000 and credits Cash for $115,000.

Land Improvements

Land improvements are structural additions made to land. Examples are driveways, parking lots, fences, landscaping, and underground sprinklers. The cost of land improvements includes all expenditures necessary to make the improvements ready for their intended use. For example, the cost of a new parking lot for Home Depot includes the amount paid for paving, fencing, and lighting. Thus, Home Depot debits to Land Improvements the total of all of these costs.

Land improvements have limited useful lives, and their maintenance and replacement are the responsibility of the company. Because of their limited useful life, companies expense (depreciate) the cost of land improvements over their useful lives.

Buildings

Buildings are facilities used in operations, such as stores, offices, factories, warehouses, and airplane hangars. Companies debit to the Buildings account all necessary expenditures related to the purchase or construction of a building. When a building is **purchased**, such costs include the purchase price, closing costs (attorney's fees, title insurance, etc.) and real estate broker's commission. Costs to make the building ready for its intended use include expenditures for remodeling and replacing or repairing the roof, floors, electrical wiring, and plumbing. When a new building is **constructed**, cost consists of the contract price plus payments for architects' fees, building permits, and excavation costs.

In addition, companies charge certain interest costs to the Buildings account: Interest costs incurred to finance the project are included in the cost of the building when a significant period of time is required to get the building ready for use. In these circumstances, interest costs are considered as necessary as materials and labor. However, the inclusion of interest costs in the cost of a constructed building is **limited to the construction period**. When construction has been completed, the company records subsequent interest payments on funds borrowed to finance the construction as debits (increases) to Interest Expense.

Equipment

Equipment includes assets used in operations, such as store check-out counters, office furniture, factory machinery, delivery trucks, and airplanes. The cost of equipment, such as Rent-A-Wreck vehicles, consists of the **cash purchase price, sales taxes, freight charges, and insurance during transit paid by the purchaser**. It also includes expenditures required in assembling, installing, and testing the unit. However, Rent-A-Wreck does not include motor vehicle licenses and accident insurance on company vehicles in the cost of equipment. These costs **represent annual recurring expenditures and do not benefit future periods**. Thus, they are treated as expenses as they are incurred.

To illustrate, assume Merten Company purchases factory machinery at a cash price of $50,000. Related expenditures are for sales taxes $3,000, insurance during shipping $500, and installation and testing $1,000. The cost of the factory machinery is $54,500, computed in Illustration 10-3.

Illustration 10-3
Computation of cost of factory machinery

Factory Machinery	
Cash price	$50,000
Sales taxes	3,000
Insurance during shipping	500
Installation and testing	1,000
Cost of factory machinery	**$54,500**

Merten makes the following summary entry to record the purchase and related expenditures.

Equipment	54,500	
Cash		54,500
(To record purchase of factory machine)		

A = L + OE
+54,500
−54,500

Cash Flows
−54,500

For another example, assume that Lenard Company purchases a delivery truck at a cash price of $22,000. Related expenditures consist of sales taxes $1,320, painting and lettering $500, motor vehicle license $80, and a three-year accident insurance policy $1,600. The cost of the delivery truck is $23,820, computed as follows.

Delivery Truck	
Cash price	$22,000
Sales taxes	1,320
Painting and lettering	500
Cost of delivery truck	**$23,820**

Illustration 10-4
Computation of cost of delivery truck

Lenard treats the cost of the motor vehicle license as an expense, and the cost of the insurance policy as a prepaid asset. Thus, Lenard makes the following entry to record the purchase of the truck and related expenditures:

Equipment	23,820	
License Expense	80	
Prepaid Insurance	1,600	
Cash		25,500
(To record purchase of delivery truck and related expenditures)		

A = L + OE
+23,820
                −80 Exp
+1,600
−25,500

Cash Flows
−25,500

ACCOUNTING ACROSS THE ORGANIZATION

Many U.S. Firms Use Leases

Leasing is big business for U.S. companies. For example, business investment in equipment in a recent year totaled $709 billion. Leasing accounted for about 31% of all business investment ($218 billion).

Who does the most leasing? Interestingly major banks, such as Continental Bank, J.P. Morgan Leasing, and US Bancorp Equipment Finance, are the major lessors. Also, many companies have established separate leasing companies, such as Boeing Capital Corporation, Dell Financial Services, and John Deere Capital Corporation. And, as an excellent example of the magnitude of leasing, leased planes account for nearly 40% of the U.S. fleet of commercial airlines. In addition, leasing is becoming increasingly common in the hotel industry. Marriott, Hilton, and InterContinental are increasingly choosing to lease hotels that are owned by someone else.

? Why might airline managers choose to lease rather than purchase their planes?
(See page 503.)

Do it!

Cost of Plant Assets

action plan

✔ Identify expenditures made in order to get delivery equipment ready for its intended use.

✔ Treat operating costs as expenses.

Assume that Drummond Heating and Cooling Co. purchases a delivery truck for $15,000 cash, plus sales taxes of $900 and delivery costs of $500. The buyer also pays $200 for painting and lettering, $600 for an annual insurance policy, and $80 for a motor vehicle license. Explain how each of these costs would be accounted for.

Solution

The first four payments ($15,000, $900, $500, and $200) are expenditures necessary to make the truck ready for its intended use. Thus, the cost of the truck is $16,600. The payments for insurance and the license are operating costs and therefore are expensed.

Related exercise material: BE10-1, BE10-2, E10-1, E10-2, E10-3, and **Do it!** 10-1.

The Navigator

Depreciation

Study Objective [2]
Explain the concept of depreciation.

As explained in Chapter 3, depreciation **is the process of allocating to expense the cost of a plant asset over its useful (service) life in a rational and systematic manner**. Cost allocation enables companies to properly match expenses with revenues in accordance with the expense recognition principle (see Illustration 10-5).

Illustration 10-5
Depreciation as a cost allocation concept

It is important to understand that **depreciation is a process of cost allocation. It is not a process of asset valuation**. No attempt is made to measure the change in an asset's fair value during ownership. So, the **book value** (cost less accumulated depreciation) of a plant asset may be quite different from its fair value. In fact, if an asset is fully depreciated, it can have a zero book value but still have a significant fair value.

Depreciation applies to three classes of plant assets: land improvements, buildings, and equipment. Each asset in these classes is considered to be a **depreciable asset**. Why? Because the usefulness to the company and revenue-producing ability of each asset will decline over the asset's useful life. Depreciation **does not apply to land** because its usefulness and revenue-producing ability generally remain intact over time. In fact, in many cases, the usefulness of land is greater over time because of the scarcity of good land sites. Thus, **land is not a depreciable asset**.

Ethics Note

When a business is acquired, proper allocation of the purchase price to various asset classes is important, since different depreciation treatment can materially affect income. For example, buildings are depreciated, but land is not.

During a depreciable asset's useful life, its revenue-producing ability declines because of **wear and tear**. A delivery truck that has been driven 100,000 miles will be less useful to a company than one driven only 800 miles.

Revenue-producing ability may also decline because of obsolescence. **Obsolescence** is the process of becoming out of date before the asset physically wears out. For example, major airlines moved from Chicago's Midway Airport to Chicago-O'Hare International Airport because Midway's runways were too short for jumbo jets. Similarly, many companies replace their computers long before they originally planned to do so because improvements in new computing technology make the old computers obsolete.

Recognizing depreciation on an asset does not result in an accumulation of cash for replacement of the asset. The balance in Accumulated Depreciation represents the total amount of the asset's cost that the company has charged to expense. It is not a cash fund.

Note that the concept of depreciation is consistent with the going-concern assumption. The going-concern assumption states that the company will continue in operation for the foreseeable future. If a company does not use a going-concern assumption, then plant assets should be stated at their fair value. In that case, depreciation of these assets is not needed.

Factors in Computing Depreciation

Three factors affect the computation of depreciation, as shown in Illustration 10-6.

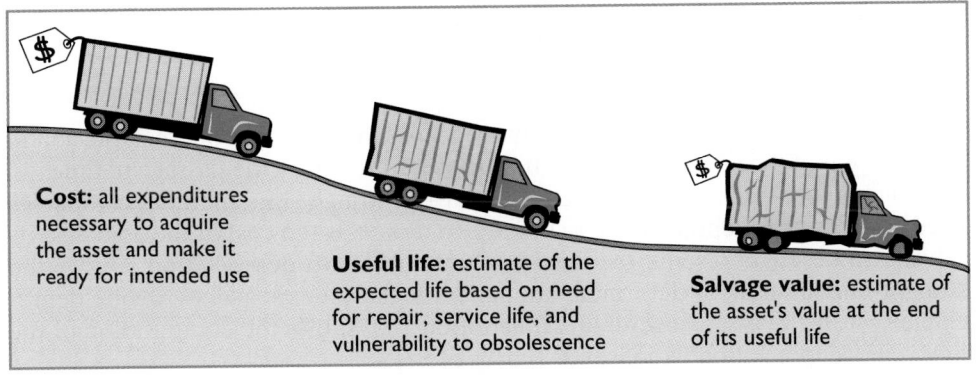

Cost: all expenditures necessary to acquire the asset and make it ready for intended use

Useful life: estimate of the expected life based on need for repair, service life, and vulnerability to obsolescence

Salvage value: estimate of the asset's value at the end of its useful life

Illustration 10-6
Three factors in computing depreciation

Helpful Hint

Depreciation expense is reported on the income statement. Accumulated depreciation is reported on the balance sheet as a deduction from plant assets.

1. **Cost.** Earlier, we explained the issues affecting the cost of a depreciable asset. Recall that companies record plant assets at cost, in accordance with the cost principle.

2. **Useful life.** Useful life is an estimate of the expected *productive life*, also called *service life*, of the asset for its owner. Useful life may be expressed in terms of time, units of activity (such as machine hours), or units of output. Useful life is an estimate. In making the estimate, management considers such factors as the intended use of the asset, its expected repair and maintenance, and its vulnerability to obsolescence. Past experience with similar assets is often helpful in deciding on expected useful life. We might reasonably expect Rent-A-Wreck and Avis to use different estimated useful lives for their vehicles.

3. **Salvage value.** Salvage value is an estimate of the asset's value at the end of its useful life. This value may be based on the asset's worth as scrap or on its expected trade-in value. Like useful life, salvage value is an estimate. In making the estimate, management considers how it plans to dispose of the asset and its experience with similar assets.

Alternative Terminology

Another term sometimes used for salvage value is *residual value*.

Depreciation Methods

Study Objective [3]
Compute periodic depreciation using different methods.

Depreciation is generally computed using one of the following methods:

1. Straight-line
2. Units-of-activity
3. Declining-balance

Each method is acceptable under generally accepted accounting principles. Management selects the method(s) it believes to be appropriate. The objective is to select the method that best measures an asset's contribution to revenue over its useful life. Once a company chooses a method, it should apply it consistently over the useful life of the asset. Consistency enhances the comparability of financial statements. Depreciation affects the balance sheet through accumulated depreciation and the income statement through depreciation expense.

We will compare the three depreciation methods using the following data for a small delivery truck purchased by Barb's Florists on January 1, 2012.

Illustration 10-7
Delivery truck data

Cost	$13,000
Expected salvage value	$ 1,000
Estimated useful life in years	5
Estimated useful life in miles	100,000

Illustration 10-8 (in the margin) shows the use of the primary depreciation methods in 600 of the largest companies in the United States.

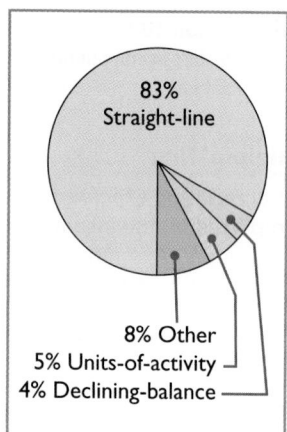

STRAIGHT-LINE

Under the **straight-line method**, companies expense the same amount of depreciation for each year of the asset's useful life. It is measured solely by the passage of time.

To compute depreciation expense under the straight-line method, companies need to determine depreciable cost. **Depreciable cost** is the cost of the asset less its salvage value. It represents the total amount subject to depreciation. Under the straight-line method, to determine annual depreciation expense, we divide depreciable cost by the asset's useful life. Illustration 10-9 shows the computation of the first year's depreciation expense for Barb's Florists.

Illustration 10-8
Use of depreciation methods in 600 large U.S. companies

Illustration 10-9
Formula for straight-line method

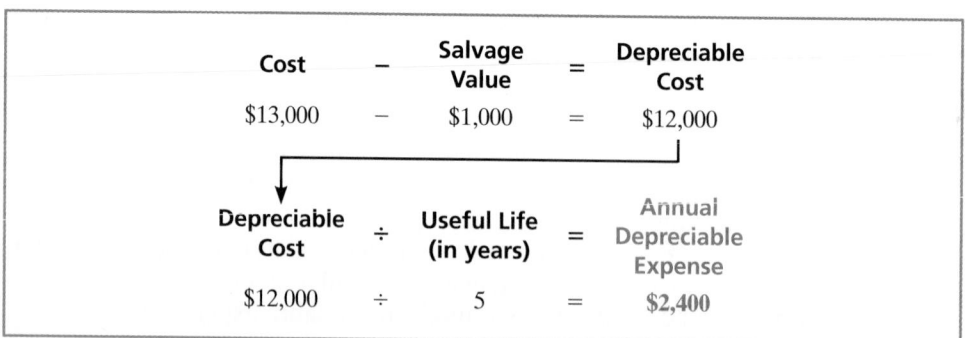

Alternatively, we also can compute an annual **rate** of depreciation. In this case, the rate is 20% (100% ÷ 5 years). When a company uses an annual straight-line rate, it applies the percentage rate to the depreciable cost of the asset. Illustration 10-10 shows a **depreciation schedule** using an annual rate.

Illustration 10-10
Straight-line depreciation schedule

Barb's Florists

	Computation				Annual	End of Year	
Year	Depreciable Cost	×	Depreciation Rate	=	Depreciation Expense	Accumulated Depreciation	Book Value
2012	$12,000		20%		$2,400	$ 2,400	$10,600*
2013	12,000		20		2,400	4,800	8,200
2014	12,000		20		2,400	7,200	5,800
2015	12,000		20		2,400	9,600	3,400
2016	12,000		20		2,400	12,000	1,000

*Book Value = Cost − Accumulated depreciation = ($13,000 − $2,400).

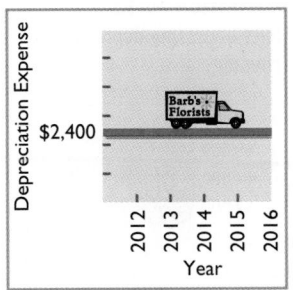

Note that the depreciation expense of $2,400 is the same each year. The book value (computed as cost minus accumulated depreciation) at the end of the useful life is equal to the expected $1,000 salvage value.

What happens to these computations for an asset purchased **during** the year, rather than on January 1? In that case, it is necessary to **prorate the annual depreciation** on a time basis. If Barb's Florists had purchased the delivery truck on April 1, 2012, the company would own the truck for nine months of the first year (April–December). Thus, depreciation for 2012 would be $1,800 ($12,000 × 20% × 9/12 of a year).

The straight-line method predominates in practice. Such large companies as Campbell Soup, Marriott, and General Mills use the straight-line method. It is simple to apply, and it matches expenses with revenues when the use of the asset is reasonably uniform throughout the service life.

UNITS-OF-ACTIVITY

Under the **units-of-activity method**, useful life is expressed in terms of the total units of production or use expected from the asset, rather than as a time period. The units-of-activity method is ideally suited to factory machinery. Manufacturing companies can measure production in units of output or in machine hours. This method can also be used for such assets as delivery equipment (miles driven) and airplanes (hours in use). The units-of-activity method is generally not suitable for buildings or furniture, because depreciation for these assets is more a function of time than of use.

To use this method, companies estimate the total units of activity for the entire useful life, and then divide these units into depreciable cost. The resulting number represents the depreciation cost per unit. The depreciation cost per unit is then applied to the units of activity during the year to determine the annual depreciation expense.

To illustrate, assume that Barb's Florists drives its delivery truck 15,000 miles in the first year. Illustration 10-11 shows the units-of-activity formula and the computation of the first year's depreciation expense.

Alternative Terminology

Another term often used is the *units-of-production method*.

Helpful Hint

Under any method, depreciation stops when the asset's book value equals expected salvage value.

Illustration 10-11
Formula for units-of-activity method

Depreciable Cost	÷	Total Units of Activity	=	Depreciable Cost per Unit
$12,000	÷	100,000 miles	=	$0.12

Depreciable Cost per Unit	×	Units of Activity during the Year	=	Annual Depreciable Expense
$0.12	×	15,000 miles	=	$1,800

The units-of-activity depreciation schedule, using assumed mileage, is as follows.

Illustration 10-12
Units-of-activity depreciation schedule

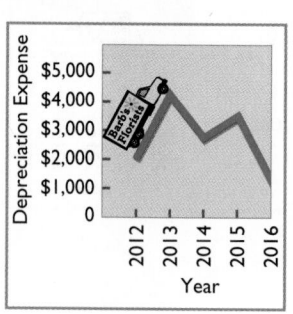

	Barb's Florists				
	Computation		**Annual**	**End of Year**	
Year	**Units of Activity** ×	**Depreciation Cost/Unit** =	**Depreciation Expense**	**Accumulated Depreciation**	**Book Value**
2012	15,000	$0.12	**$1,800**	$ 1,800	$11,200*
2013	30,000	0.12	**3,600**	5,400	7,600
2014	20,000	0.12	**2,400**	7,800	5,200
2015	25,000	0.12	**3,000**	10,800	2,200
2016	10,000	0.12	**1,200**	12,000	**1,000**

*($13,000 − $1,800).

This method is easy to apply for assets purchased mid-year. In such a case, the company computes the depreciation using the productivity of the asset for the partial year.

The units-of-activity method is not nearly as popular as the straight-line method (see Illustration 10-8, page 464), primarily because it is often difficult for companies to reasonably estimate total activity. However, some very large companies, such as Chevron and Boise Cascade (a forestry company), do use this method. When the productivity of an asset varies significantly from one period to another, the units-of-activity method results in the best matching of expenses with revenues.

DECLINING-BALANCE

The **declining-balance method** produces a decreasing annual depreciation expense over the asset's useful life. The method is so named because the periodic depreciation is based on a **declining book value** (cost less accumulated depreciation) of the asset. With this method, companies compute annual depreciation expense by multiplying the book value at the beginning of the year by the declining-balance depreciation rate. **The depreciation rate remains constant from year to year, but the book value to which the rate is applied declines each year.**

At the beginning of the first year, book value is the cost of the asset. This is so because the balance in accumulated depreciation at the beginning of the asset's useful life is zero. In subsequent years, book value is the difference between cost and accumulated depreciation to date. Unlike the other depreciation methods, the declining-balance method does not use depreciable cost. That is, **it ignores salvage value in determining the amount to which the declining-balance rate is applied**. Salvage value, however, does limit the total depreciation that can be taken. Depreciation stops when the asset's book value equals expected salvage value.

A common declining-balance rate is double the straight-line rate. The method is often called the **double-declining-balance method**. If Barb's Florists uses the double-declining-balance method, it uses a depreciation rate of 40% (2 × the straight-line rate of 20%). Illustration 10-13 shows the declining-balance formula and the computation of the first year's depreciation on the delivery truck.

Illustration 10-13
Formula for declining-balance method

Book Value at Beginning of Year	×	**Declining-Balance Rate**	=	**Annual Depreciation Expense**
$13,000	×	40%	=	$5,200

The depreciation schedule under this method is as follows.

	Computation			Annual	End of Year	
Year	Book Value Beginning of Year	× Depreciation Rate	=	Depreciation Expense	Accumulated Depreciation	Book Value
2012	$13,000	40%		$5,200	$ 5,200	$7,800
2013	7,800	40		3,120	8,320	4,680
2014	4,680	40		1,872	10,192	2,808
2015	2,808	40		1,123	11,315	1,685
2016	1,685	40		685*	12,000	1,000

Barb's Florists (table title)

*Computation of $674 ($1,685 × 40%) is adjusted to $685 in order for book value to equal salvage value.

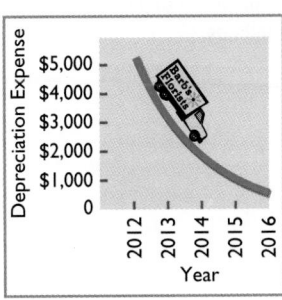

Illustration 10-14
Double-declining-balance depreciation schedule

The delivery equipment is 69% depreciated ($8,320 ÷ $12,000) at the end of the second year. Under the straight-line method, the truck would be depreciated 40% ($4,800 ÷ $12,000) at that time. Because the declining-balance method produces higher depreciation expense in the early years than in the later years, it is considered an **accelerated-depreciation method**. The declining-balance method is compatible with the expense recognition principle. It matches the higher depreciation expense in early years with the higher benefits received in these years. It also recognizes lower depreciation expense in later years, when the asset's contribution to revenue is less. Some assets lose usefulness rapidly because of obsolescence. In these cases, the declining-balance method provides the most appropriate depreciation amount.

When a company purchases an asset during the year, it must prorate the first year's declining-balance depreciation on a time basis. For example, if Barb's Florists had purchased the truck on April 1, 2012, depreciation for 2012 would become $3,900 ($13,000 × 40% × 9/12). The book value at the beginning of 2013 is then $9,100 ($13,000 − $3,900), and the 2013 depreciation is $3,640 ($9,100 × 40%). Subsequent computations would follow from those amounts.

Helpful Hint

The method recommended for an asset that is expected to be significantly more productive in the first half of its useful life is the declining-balance method.

Do it!

On January 1, 2012, Iron Mountain Ski Corporation purchased a new snow-grooming machine for $50,000. The machine is estimated to have a 10-year life with a $2,000 salvage value. What journal entry would Iron Mountain Ski Corporation make at December 31, 2012, if it uses the straight-line method of depreciation?

Solution

$$\text{Depreciation expense} = \frac{\text{Cost} - \text{Salvage value}}{\text{Useful life}} = \frac{\$50,000 - \$2,000}{10} = \$4,800$$

The entry to record the first year's depreciation would be:

Dec. 31	Depreciation Expense	4,800	
	Accumulated Depreciation—Equipment		4,800
	(To record annual depreciation on snow-grooming machine)		

Straight-Line Depreciation

action plan

✔ Calculate depreciable cost (Cost − Salvage value).

✔ Divide the depreciable cost by the asset's estimated useful life.

Related exercise material: BE10-3, BE10-4, BE10-5, BE10-6, BE10-7, E10-5, E10-6, E10-7, E10-8, and **Do it!** 10-2.

✔ The Navigator

COMPARISON OF METHODS

Illustration 10-15 compares annual and total depreciation expense under each of the three methods for Barb's Florists.

Illustration 10-15
Comparison of depreciation methods

Year	Straight-Line	Units-of-Activity	Declining-Balance
2012	$ 2,400	$ 1,800	$ 5,200
2013	2,400	3,600	3,120
2014	2,400	2,400	1,872
2015	2,400	3,000	1,123
2016	2,400	1,200	685
	$12,000	**$12,000**	**$12,000**

Annual depreciation varies considerably among the methods, but **total depreciation is the same for the five-year period** under all three methods. Each method is acceptable in accounting because each recognizes in a rational and systematic manner the decline in service potential of the asset. Illustration 10-16 graphs the depreciation expense pattern under each method.

Illustration 10-16
Patterns of depreciation

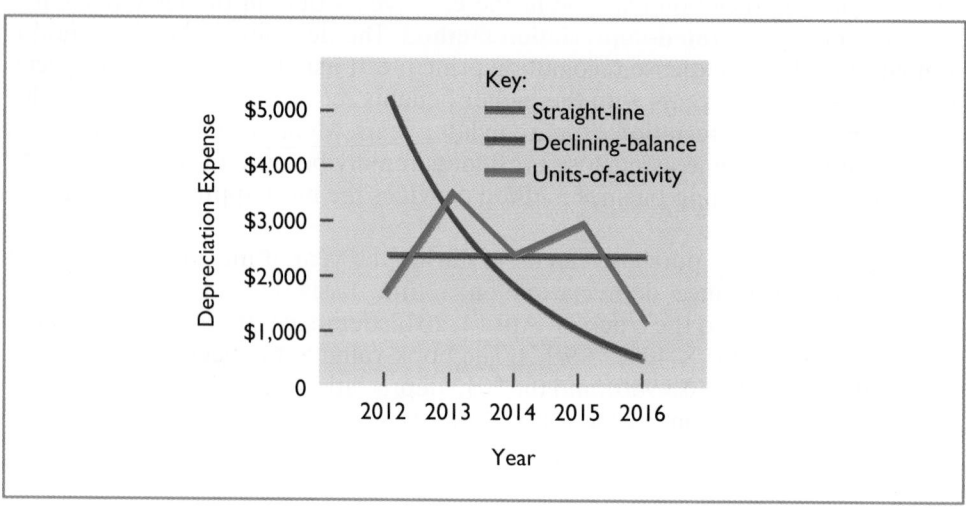

Depreciation and Income Taxes

The Internal Revenue Service (IRS) allows corporate taxpayers to deduct depreciation expense when they compute taxable income. However, the IRS does not require the taxpayer to use the same depreciation method on the tax return that is used in preparing financial statements.

Many corporations use straight-line in their financial statements to maximize net income. At the same time, they use a special accelerated-depreciation method on their tax returns to minimize their income taxes. Taxpayers must use on their tax returns either the straight-line method or a special accelerated-depreciation method called the **Modified Accelerated Cost Recovery System** (MACRS).

Revising Periodic Depreciation

Study Objective [4]

Describe the procedure for revising periodic depreciation.

Depreciation is one example of the use of estimation in the accounting process. Management should periodically review annual depreciation expense. If wear and tear or obsolescence indicate that annual depreciation estimates are inadequate or excessive, the company should change the amount of depreciation expense.

When a change in an estimate is required, the company makes the change in **current and future years**. **It does not change depreciation in prior periods.** The rationale is that continual restatement of prior periods would adversely affect confidence in financial statements.

To determine the new annual depreciation expense, the company first computes the asset's depreciable cost at the time of the revision. It then allocates the revised depreciable cost to the remaining useful life.

To illustrate, assume that Barb's Florists decides on January 1, 2015, to extend the useful life of the truck one year (a total life of six years) and increase its salvage value to $2,200. The company has used the straight-line method to depreciate the asset to date. Depreciation per year was $2,400 (($13,000 − $1,000) ÷ 5). Accumulated depreciation after three years (2012–2014) is $7,200 ($2,400 × 3), and book value is $5,800 ($13,000 − $7,200). The new annual depreciation is $1,200, computed as follows.

Book value, 1/1/15	$ 5,800
Less: Salvage value	2,200
Depreciable cost	$ 3,600
Remaining useful life	3 years (2015–2017)
Revised annual depreciation ($3,600 ÷ 3)	$ 1,200

Helpful Hint
Use a step-by-step approach: (1) determine new depreciable cost; (2) divide by remaining useful life.

Illustration 10-17
Revised depreciation computation

Barb's Florists makes no entry for the change in estimate. On December 31, 2015, during the preparation of adjusting entries, it records depreciation expense of $1,200. Companies must describe in the financial statements significant changes in estimates.

Do it!

Chambers Corporation purchased a piece of equipment for $36,000. It estimated a 6-year life and $6,000 salvage value. Thus, straight-line depreciation was $5,000 per year (($36,000 − $6,000) ÷ 6). At the end of year three (before the depreciation adjustment), it estimated the new total life to be 10 years and the new salvage value to be $2,000. Compute the revised depreciation.

Solution

Original depreciation expense = [($36,000 − $6,000) ÷ 6] = $5,000
Accumulated depreciation after 2 years = 2 × $5,000 = $10,000
Book value = $36,000 − $10,000 = $26,000

Book value after 2 years of depreciation	$26,000
Less: New salvage value	2,000
Depreciable cost	24,000
Remaining useful life	8 years
Revised annual depreciation ($24,000 ÷ 8)	$ 3,000

Related exercise material: BE10-7, E10-8, and **Do it!** 10-3.

Revised Depreciation

action plan
✔ Calculate remaining depreciable cost.
✔ Divide remaining depreciable cost by new remaining life.

The Navigator

Expenditures During Useful Life

Study Objective [5]
Distinguish between revenue and capital expenditures, and explain the entries for each.

During the useful life of a plant asset, a company may incur costs for ordinary repairs, additions, or improvements. **Ordinary repairs** are expenditures to **maintain** the operating efficiency and productive life of the unit. They usually are fairly small amounts that occur frequently. Examples are motor tune-ups and oil changes, the painting of buildings, and the replacing of worn-out gears on machinery. Companies record such repairs as debits to Maintenance and Repairs Expense as they are incurred. Because they are immediately charged as an expense against revenues, these costs are often referred to as **revenue expenditures**.

In contrast, **additions and improvements** are costs incurred to **increase** the operating efficiency, productive capacity, or useful life of a plant asset. They are usually material in amount and occur infrequently. Additions and improvements increase the company's investment in productive facilities. Companies generally debit these amounts to the plant asset affected. They are often referred to as **capital expenditures**.

Companies must use good judgment in deciding between a revenue expenditure and capital expenditure. For example, assume that Rodriguez Co. purchases a number of wastepaper baskets. Although the proper accounting would appear to be to capitalize and then depreciate these wastepaper baskets over their useful life, it would be more usual for Rodriguez to expense them immediately. This practice is justified on the basis of **materiality**. Materiality refers to the impact of an item's size on a company's financial operations. The **materiality principle** states that if an item would not make a difference in decision making, the company does not have to follow GAAP in reporting that item.

ANATOMY OF A FRAUD

Bernie Ebbers was the founder and CEO of the phone company WorldCom. The company engaged in a series of increasingly large, debt-financed acquisitions of other companies. These acquisitions made the company grow quickly, which made the stock price increase dramatically. However, because the acquired companies all had different accounting systems, WorldCom's financial records were a mess. When WorldCom's performance started to flatten out, Bernie coerced WorldCom's accountants to engage in a number of fraudulent activities to make net income look better than it really was and thus prop up the stock price. One of these frauds involved treating $7 billion of line costs as capital expenditures. The line costs, which were rental fees paid to other phone companies to use their phone lines, had always been properly expensed in previous years. Capitalization delayed expense recognition to future periods and thus boosted current-period profits.

Total take: $7 billion

THE MISSING CONTROLS

Documentation procedures. The company's accounting system was a disorganized collection of non-integrated systems, which resulted from a series of corporate acquisitions. Top management took advantage of this disorganization to conceal its fraudulent activities.

Independent internal verification. A fraud of this size should have been detected by a routine comparison of the actual physical assets with the list of physical assets shown in the accounting records.

Plant Asset Disposals

Companies dispose of plant assets that are no longer useful to them. Illustration 10-18 below shows the three ways in which companies make plant asset disposals.

Whatever the disposal method, the company must determine the book value of the plant asset at the disposal date to determine the gain or loss. Recall that the book value is the difference between the cost of the plant asset and the accumulated depreciation to date. If the disposal occurs at any time during the year, the company must record depreciation for the fraction of the year to the date of disposal. The company then eliminates the book value by reducing (debiting) Accumulated Depreciation for the total depreciation associated with that asset to the date of disposal and reducing (crediting) the asset account for the cost of the asset.

Study Objective [6]

Explain how to account for the disposal of a plant asset.

Sale	Retirement	Exchange
Equipment is sold to another party.	Equipment is scrapped or discarded.	Existing equipment is traded for new equipment.

Illustration 10-18
Methods of plant asset disposal

In this chapter, we examine the accounting for the retirement and sale of plant assets. In the appendix to the chapter, we discuss and illustrate the accounting for exchanges of plant assets.

Retirement of Plant Assets

To illustrate the retirement of plant assets, assume that Hobart Enterprises retires its computer printers, which cost $32,000. The accumulated depreciation on these printers is $32,000. The equipment, therefore, is fully depreciated (zero book value). The entry to record this retirement is as follows.

Accumulated Depreciation—Equipment	32,000	
Equipment		32,000
(To record retirement of fully depreciated equipment)		

+32,000
−32,000

Cash Flows
no effect

What happens if a fully depreciated plant asset is still useful to the company? In this case, the asset and its accumulated depreciation continue to be reported on the balance sheet, without further depreciation adjustment, until the company retires the asset. Reporting the asset and related accumulated depreciation on the balance sheet informs the financial statement reader that the asset is still in use. Once fully depreciated, no additional depreciation should be taken, even if an asset is still being used. In no situation can the accumulated depreciation on a plant asset exceed its cost.

If a company retires a plant asset before it is fully depreciated, and no cash is received for scrap or salvage value, a loss on disposal occurs. For example, assume

Helpful Hint

When a company disposes of a plant asset, the company must remove from the accounts all amounts related to the asset. This includes the original cost in the asset account and the total depreciation to date in the accumulated depreciation account.

that Sunset Company discards delivery equipment that cost $18,000 and has accumulated depreciation of $14,000. The entry is as follows.

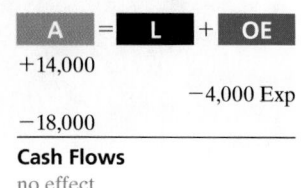

Accumulated Depreciation—Equipment	14,000	
Loss on Disposal of Plant Assets	4,000	
Equipment		18,000
(To record retirement of delivery equipment at a loss)		

Companies report a loss on disposal of plant assets in the "Other expenses and losses" section of the income statement.

Sale of Plant Assets

In a disposal by sale, the company compares the book value of the asset with the proceeds received from the sale. If the proceeds of the sale **exceed** the book value of the plant asset, **a gain on disposal occurs**. If the proceeds of the sale **are less than** the book value of the plant asset sold, **a loss on disposal occurs**.

Only by coincidence will the book value and the fair value of the asset be the same when the asset is sold. Gains and losses on sales of plant assets are therefore quite common. For example, Delta Airlines reported a $94,343,000 gain on the sale of five Boeing B727-200 aircraft and five Lockheed L-1011-1 aircraft.

GAIN ON SALE

To illustrate a gain on sale of plant assets, assume that on July 1, 2012, Wright Company sells office furniture for $16,000 cash. The office furniture originally cost $60,000. As of January 1, 2012, it had accumulated depreciation of $41,000. Depreciation for the first six months of 2012 is $8,000. Wright records depreciation expense and updates accumulated depreciation to July 1 with the following entry.

July 1	Depreciation Expense	8,000	
	Accumulated Depreciation—Equipment		8,000
	(To record depreciation expense for the first		
	6 months of 2012)		

After the accumulated depreciation balance is updated, the company computes the gain or loss. The gain or loss is the difference between the proceeds from the sale and the book value at the date of disposal. Illustration 10-19 shows this computation for Wright Company, which has a gain on disposal of $5,000.

Illustration 10-19
Computation of gain on disposal

Cost of office furniture	$60,000
Less: Accumulated depreciation ($41,000 + $8,000)	49,000
Book value at date of disposal	11,000
Proceeds from sale	16,000
Gain on disposal of plant asset	**$ 5,000**

Wright records the sale and the gain on disposal of the plant asset as follows.

July 1	Cash	16,000	
	Accumulated Depreciation—Equipment	49,000	
	Equipment		60,000
	Gain on Disposal of Plant Assets		5,000
	(To record sale of office furniture		
	at a gain)		

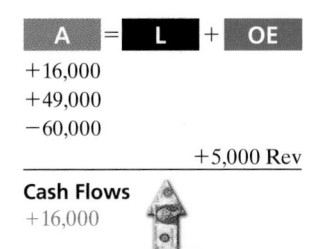

A = L + OE

+16,000
+49,000
−60,000
         +5,000 Rev

Cash Flows
+16,000

Companies report a gain on disposal of plant assets in the "Other revenues and gains" section of the income statement.

LOSS ON SALE

Assume that instead of selling the office furniture for $16,000, Wright sells it for $9,000. In this case, Wright computes a loss of $2,000 as follows.

Cost of office furniture	$60,000
Less: Accumulated depreciation	49,000
Book value at date of disposal	11,000
Proceeds from sale	9,000
Loss on disposal of plant asset	**$ 2,000**

Illustration 10-20
Computation of loss on disposal

Wright records the sale and the loss on disposal of the plant asset as follows.

July 1	Cash	9,000	
	Accumulated Depreciation—Equipment	49,000	
	Loss on Disposal of Plant Assets	2,000	
	Equipment		60,000
	(To record sale of office furniture at a loss)		

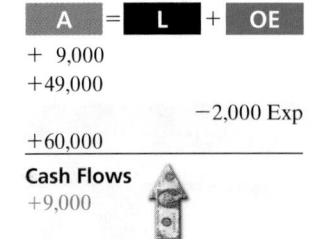

A = L + OE

+ 9,000
+49,000
         −2,000 Exp
+60,000

Cash Flows
+9,000

Companies report a loss on disposal of plant assets in the "Other expenses and losses" section of the income statement.

Do it!

Overland Trucking has an old truck that cost $30,000, and it has accumulated depreciation of $16,000 on this truck. Overland has decided to sell the truck. (a) What entry would Overland Trucking make to record the sale of the truck for $17,000 cash? (b) What entry would Overland trucking make to record the sale of the truck for $10,000 cash?

Solution

(a) Sale of truck for cash at a gain:

Cash	17,000	
Accumulated Depreciation—Equipment	16,000	
Equipment		30,000
Gain on Disposal of Plant Assets [$17,000 − ($30,000 − $16,000)]		3,000
(To record sale of truck at a gain)		

Plant Asset Disposal

action plan

✔ At the time of disposal, determine the book value of the asset.

✔ Compare the asset's book value with the proceeds received to determine whether a gain or loss has occurred.

(b) Sale of truck for cash at a loss:

Cash	10,000	
Loss on Disposal of Plant Assets [$10,000 − ($30,000 − $16,000)]	4,000	
Accumulated Depreciation—Equipment	16,000	
Equipment		30,000
(To record sale of truck at a loss)		

Related exercise material: BE10-9, BE10-10, E10-9, E10-10, and **Do it!** 10-3.

The Navigator

SECTION2 NATURAL RESOURCES

Helpful Hint

On a balance sheet, natural resources may be described more specifically as *timberlands*, *mineral deposits*, *oil reserves*, and so on.

Natural resources consist of standing timber and underground deposits of oil, gas, and minerals. These long-lived productive assets have two distinguishing characteristics: (1) They are physically extracted in operations (such as mining, cutting, or pumping). (2) They are replaceable only by an act of nature.

The acquisition cost of a natural resource is the price needed to acquire the resource **and** prepare it for its intended use. For an already-discovered resource, such as an existing coal mine, cost is the price paid for the property.

The allocation of the cost of natural resources to expense in a rational and systematic manner over the resource's useful life is called **depletion**. (That is, *depletion* is to natural resources as *depreciation* is to plant assets.) **Companies generally use the units-of-activity method** (learned earlier in the chapter) **to compute depletion**. The reason is that **depletion generally is a function of the units extracted during the year**.

Under the units-of-activity method, companies divide the total cost of the natural resource minus salvage value by the number of units estimated to be in the resource. The result is a **depletion cost per unit of product**. They then multiply the depletion cost per unit by the number of units extracted and sold. The result is the **annual depletion expense**. Illustration 10-21 shows the formula to compute depletion expense.

Study Objective [7]

Compute periodic depletion of natural resources.

Illustration 10-21
Formula to compute depletion expense

Ethics Note

Investors were stunned at news that Royal Dutch/Shell Group had significantly overstated its reported oil reserves—and perhaps had done so intentionally.

To illustrate, assume that Lane Coal Company invests $5 million in a mine estimated to have 10 million tons of coal and no salvage value. In the first year, Lane extracts and sells 800,000 tons of coal. Using the formulas above, Lane computes the depletion expense as follows:

$$\$5,000,000 \div 10,000,000 = \$0.50 \text{ depletion cost per ton}$$

$$\$0.50 \times 800,000 = \$400,000 \text{ annual depletion expense}$$

Lane records depletion expense for the first year of operation as follows.

Dec. 31	Depletion Expense		400,000	
	Accumulated Depletion			400,000
	(To record depletion expense on coal			
	deposits)			

A = L + OE
−400,000 Exp
−400,000

Cash Flows
no effect

The company reports the account Depletion Expense as a part of the cost of producing the product. Accumulated Depletion is a contra-asset account, similar to accumulated depreciation. It is deducted from the cost of the natural resource in the balance sheet, as Illustration 10-22 shows.

Illustration 10-22
Statement presentation of accumulated depletion

Lane Coal Company
Balance Sheet (partial)

Coal mine	$5,000,000	
Less: Accumulated depletion	400,000	$4,600,000

Many companies do not use an Accumulated Depletion account. In such cases, the company credits the amount of depletion directly to the natural resources account.

Sometimes, a company will extract natural resources in one accounting period but not sell them until a later period. In this case, the company does not expense the depletion until it sells the resource. It reports the amount not sold as inventory in the current assets section.

SECTION3 INTANGIBLE ASSETS

Intangible assets are rights, privileges, and competitive advantages that result from the ownership of long-lived assets that do not possess physical substance. Evidence of intangibles may exist in the form of contracts or licenses. Intangibles may arise from the following sources:

1. Government grants, such as patents, copyrights, licenses, trademarks, and trade names.
2. Acquisition of another business, in which the purchase price includes a payment for *goodwill*.
3. Private monopolistic arrangements arising from contractual agreements, such as franchises and leases.

Some widely known intangibles are Microsoft's patents, McDonald's franchises, Apple's trade name iPod, J.K. Rowlings' copyrights on the Harry Potter books, and the trademark Rent-A-Wreck in the Feature Story.

Accounting for Intangible Assets

Companies record intangible assets at cost. Intangibles are categorized as having either a limited life or an indefinite life. If an intangible has a **limited life**, the company allocates its cost over the asset's useful life using a process similar to depreciation. The process of allocating the cost of intangibles is referred to as amortization. The cost of intangible assets with **indefinite lives should not be amortized**.

Study Objective [8]
Explain the basic issues related to accounting for intangible assets.

Helpful Hint

Amortization is to intangibles what *depreciation* is to plant assets and *depletion* is to natural resources.

To record amortization of an intangible asset, a company increases (debits) Amortization Expense, and decreases (credits) the specific intangible asset. (Unlike depreciation, no contra account, such as Accumulated Amortization, is usually used.)

Intangible assets are typically amortized on a straight-line basis. For example, the legal life of a patent is 20 years. Companies **amortize the cost of a patent over its 20-year life or its useful life, whichever is shorter**. To illustrate the computation of patent amortization, assume that National Labs purchases a patent at a cost of $60,000. If National estimates the useful life of the patent to be eight years, the annual amortization expense is $7,500 ($60,000 ÷ 8). National records the annual amortization as follows.

−7,500 Exp

−7,500

Cash Flows
no effect

Dec. 31	Amortization Expense	7,500	
	Patents		7,500
	(To record patent amortization)		

Companies classify Amortization Expense as an operating expense in the income statement.

There is a difference between intangible assets and plant assets in determining cost. For plant assets, cost includes both the purchase price of the asset and the costs incurred in designing and constructing the asset. In contrast, cost for an intangible asset includes **only the purchase price**. Companies expense any costs incurred in developing an intangible asset.

Patents

A patent is an exclusive right issued by the U.S. Patent Office that enables the recipient to manufacture, sell, or otherwise control an invention for a period of 20 years from the date of the grant. A patent is nonrenewable. But companies can extend the legal life of a patent by obtaining new patents for improvements or other changes in the basic design. **The initial cost of a patent is the cash or cash equivalent price paid to acquire the patent.**

The saying, "A patent is only as good as the money you're prepared to spend defending it" is very true. Most patents are subject to litigation by competitors. Any legal costs an owner incurs in successfully defending a patent in an infringement suit are considered necessary to establish the patent's validity. **The owner adds those costs to the Patents account and amortizes them over the remaining life of the patent.**

The patent holder amortizes the cost of a patent over its 20-year legal life or its useful life, whichever is shorter. Companies consider obsolescence and inadequacy in determining useful life. These factors may cause a patent to become economically ineffective before the end of its legal life.

Copyrights

The federal government grants copyrights which give the owner the exclusive right to reproduce and sell an artistic or published work. Copyrights extend for the life of the creator plus 70 years. The cost of a copyright is the **cost of acquiring and defending it**. The cost may be only the small fee paid to the U.S. Copyright Office. Or it may amount to much more if an infringement suit is involved.

The useful life of a copyright generally is significantly shorter than its legal life. Therefore, copyrights usually are amortized over a relatively short period of time.

Trademarks and Trade Names

A trademark or trade name is a word, phrase, jingle, or symbol that identifies a particular enterprise or product. Trade names like Wheaties, Monopoly, Big Mac,

Kleenex, Coca-Cola, and Jeep create immediate product identification. They also generally enhance the sale of the product. The creator or original user may obtain exclusive legal right to the trademark or trade name by registering it with the U.S. Patent Office. Such registration provides 20 years of protection. The registration may be renewed indefinitely as long as the trademark or trade name is in use.

If a company purchases the trademark or trade name, its cost is the purchase price. If a company develops and maintains the trademark or trade name, any costs related to these activities are expensed as incurred. Because trademarks and trade names have indefinite lives, they are not amortized.

Franchises and Licenses

When you fill up your tank at the corner Shell station, eat lunch at Subway, or rent a car from Rent-A-Wreck, you are dealing with franchises. A **franchise** is a contractual arrangement between a franchisor and a franchisee. The franchisor grants the franchisee the right to sell certain products, provide specific services, or use certain trademarks or trade names, usually within a designated geographical area.

Another type of franchise is that entered into between a governmental body (commonly municipalities) and a company. This franchise permits the company to use public property in performing its services. Examples are the use of city streets for a bus line or taxi service, use of public land for telephone and electric lines, and the use of airwaves for radio or TV broadcasting. Such operating rights are referred to as **licenses**. Franchises and licenses may by granted for a definite period of time, an indefinite period, or perpetually.

When a company can identify costs with the purchase of a franchise or license, it should recognize an intangible asset. Companies should amortize the cost of a limited-life franchise (or license) over its useful life. If the life is indefinite, the cost is not amortized. Annual payments made under a franchise agreement are recorded as **operating expenses** in the period in which they are incurred.

Goodwill

Usually, the largest intangible asset that appears on a company's balance sheet is goodwill. **Goodwill** represents the value of all favorable attributes that relate to a company that are not attributable to any other specific asset. These include exceptional management, desirable location, good customer relations, skilled employees, high-quality products, and harmonious relations with labor unions. Goodwill is unique: Unlike assets such as investments and plant assets, which can be sold *individually* in the marketplace, goodwill can be identified only with the business as a whole.

If goodwill can be identified only with the business as a whole, how can its amount be determined? One could try to put a dollar value on the factors listed above (exceptional management, desirable location, and so on). But the results would be very subjective, and such subjective valuations would not contribute to the reliability of financial statements. **Therefore, companies record goodwill only when an entire business is purchased. In that case, goodwill is the excess of cost over the fair value of the net assets (assets less liabilities) acquired.**

In recording the purchase of a business, the company debits (increases) the identifiable acquired assets, and credits liabilities at their fair values, credits cash for the purchase price, and records the difference as goodwill. **Goodwill is not amortized** because it is considered to have an indefinite life. Companies report goodwill in the balance sheet under intangible assets.

*I*NTERNATIONAL *I*NSIGHT

Should Companies Write Up Goodwill?

Softbank Corp. is Japan's biggest Internet company. At one time, it boosted the profit margin of its mobile-phone unit from 3.2% to 11.2% through what appeared to some as accounting tricks. What did it do? It wrote down the value of its mobile-phone-unit assets by half. This would normally result in a huge loss. But rather than take a loss, the company wrote up goodwill by the same amount. How did this move increase earnings? The assets were being depreciated over 10 years, but the company amortizes goodwill over 20 years. (Amortization of goodwill was allowed under the accounting standards it followed at that time.) While the new treatment did not break any rules, the company was criticized by investors for not providing sufficient justification or a detailed explanation for the sudden shift in policy.

Source: Andrew Morse and Yukari Iwatani Kane, "Softbank's Accounting Shift Raises Eyebrows," *Wall Street Journal* (August 28, 2007), p. C1.

? Do you think that this treatment would be allowed under U.S. GAAP? (See page 503.)

Research and Development Costs

Helpful Hint

Research and development (R&D) costs are not intangible assets. But because they may lead to patents and copyrights, we discuss them in this section.

Research and development costs are expenditures that may lead to patents, copyrights, new processes, and new products. Many companies spend considerable sums of money on research and development (R&D). For example, in a recent year IBM spent over $5.1 billion on R&D.

Research and development costs present accounting problems. For one thing, it is sometimes difficult to assign the costs to specific projects. Also, there are uncertainties in identifying the extent and timing of future benefits. As a result, companies usually record R&D costs **as an expense when incurred**, whether the research and development is successful or not.

To illustrate, assume that Laser Scanner Company spent $3 million on R&D that resulted in two highly successful patents. It spent $20,000 on legal fees for the patents. The company would add the lawyers' fees to the patent account. The R&D costs, however, cannot be included in the cost of the patent. Instead, the company would record the R&D costs as an expense when incurred.

Many disagree with this accounting approach. They argue that expensing R&D costs leads to understated assets and net income. Others, however, argue that capitalizing these costs will lead to highly speculative assets on the balance sheet. Who is right is difficult to determine.

Do it!

Classification Concepts

Match the statement with the term most directly associated with it.

Copyrights   Depletion
Intangible assets   Franchises
Research and development costs

1. _____ The allocation of the cost of a natural resource to expense in a rational and systematic manner.

2. _____ Rights, privileges, and competitive advantages that result from the ownership of long-lived assets that do not possess physical substance.

3. _____ An exclusive right granted by the federal government to reproduce and sell an artistic or published work.

4. _____ A right to sell certain products or services or to use certain trademarks or trade names within a designated geographic area.

5. _____ Costs incurred by a company that often lead to patents or new products. These costs must be expensed as incurred.

action plan

✔ Know that the accounting for intangibles often depends on whether the item has a finite or indefinite life.

✔ Recognize the many similarities and differences between the accounting for natural resources, plant assets, and intangible assets.

Solution

1. Depletion
2. Intangible assets
3. Copyrights
4. Franchises
5. Research and development costs

Related exercise material: BE10-11, BE10-12, E10-11, E10-12, E10-13, and **Do it!** 10-4.

The Navigator

Statement Presentation and Analysis

Presentation

Usually, companies combine plant assets and natural resources under "Property, plant, and equipment" in the balance sheet. They show intangibles separately. Companies disclose either in the balance sheet or the notes the balances of the major classes of assets, such as land, buildings, and equipment, and accumulated depreciation by major classes or in total. In addition, they should describe the depreciation and amortization methods that were used, as well as disclose the amount of depreciation and amortization expense for the period.

Illustration 10-23 shows a typical financial statement presentation of property, plant, and equipment and intangibles for The Procter & Gamble Company

Study Objective [9]
Indicate how plant assets, natural resources, and intangible assets are reported.

Illustration 10-23
P&G's presentation of property, plant, and equipment, and intangible assets

P&G

The Procter & Gamble Company
Balance Sheet (partial)
(in millions)

	June 30 2009	June 30 2008
Property, plant, and equipment		
Buildings	$ 6,724	$ 7,052
Machinery and equipment	29,042	30,145
Land	885	889
	36,651	38,086
Accumulated depreciation	(17,189)	(17,446)
Net property, plant, and equipment	19,462	20,640
Goodwill and other intangible assets		
Goodwill	56,512	59,767
Trademarks and other intangible assets, net	32,606	34,233
Net goodwill and other intangible assets	$89,118	$94,000

(P&G) in its 2009 balance sheet. The notes to P&G's financial statements present greater details about the accounting for its long-term tangible and intangible assets.

Illustration 10-24 shows another comprehensive presentation of property, plant, and equipment, from the balance sheet of Owens-Illinois. The notes to the financial statements of Owens-Illinois identify the major classes of property, plant, and equipment. They also indicate that depreciation and amortization are by the straight-line method, and depletion is by the units-of-activity method.

Illustration 10-24
Owens-Illinois' presentation of property, plant, and equipment, and intangible assets

Owens-Illinois, Inc.
Balance Sheet (partial)
(in millions)

Property, plant, and equipment		
Timberlands, at cost, less accumulated depletion		$ 95.4
Buildings and equipment, at cost	$2,207.1	
Less: Accumulated depreciation	1,229.0	978.1
Total property, plant, and equipment		$1,073.5
Intangibles		
Patents		410.0
Total		$1,483.5

Analysis

Using ratios, we can analyze how efficiently a company uses its assets to generate sales. The **asset turnover ratio** analyzes the productivity of a company's assets. It tells us how many dollars of sales a company generates for each dollar invested in assets. This ratio is computed by dividing net sales by average total assets for the period. The formula in Illustration 10-25 shows the computation of the asset turnover ratio for The Procter & Gamble Company. P&G's net sales for 2009 were $79,029 million. Its total ending assets were $134,833 million, and beginning assets were $143,992 million.

Illustration 10-25
Asset turnover formula and computation

$$\text{Net Sales} \div \text{Average Total Assets} = \text{Asset Turnover Ratio}$$

$$\$79{,}029 \div \frac{\$134{,}833 + \$143{,}992}{2} = .57 \text{ times}$$

Thus, each dollar invested in assets produced $0.57 in sales for P&G. If a company is using its assets efficiently, each dollar of assets will create a high amount of sales. This ratio varies greatly among different industries—from those that are asset intensive (utilities) to those that are not (services).

COMPREHENSIVE
Do it! 1

DuPage Company purchases a factory machine at a cost of $18,000 on January 1, 2012. DuPage expects the machine to have a salvage value of $2,000 at the end of its 4-year useful life.

During its useful life, the machine is expected to be used 160,000 hours. Actual annual hourly use was: 2012, 40,000; 2013, 60,000; 2014, 35,000; and 2015, 25,000.

Instructions

Prepare depreciation schedules for the following methods: (a) straight-line, (b) units-of-activity, and (c) declining-balance using double the straight-line rate.

action plan

✔ Under the straight-line method, apply the depreciation rate to depreciable cost.

✔ Under the units-of-activity method, compute the depreciation cost per unit by dividing depreciable cost by total units of activity.

✔ Under the declining-balance method, apply the depreciation rate to **book value** at the beginning of the year.

Solution to Comprehensive Do it! 1

(a)

Straight-Line Method

| | Computation | | | Annual | End of Year | |
| | Depreciable | | Depreciation | Depreciation | Accumulated | Book |
Year	Cost*	×	Rate	= Expense	Depreciation	Value
2012	$16,000		25%	$4,000	$ 4,000	$14,000**
2013	16,000		25%	4,000	8,000	10,000
2014	16,000		25%	4,000	12,000	6,000
2015	16,000		25%	4,000	16,000	2,000

*$18,000 − $2,000.
**$18,000 − $4,000.

(b)

Units-of-Activity Method

| | Computation | | | Annual | End of Year | |
| | Units of | | Depreciation | Depreciation | Accumulated | Book |
Year	Activity	×	Cost/Unit	= Expense	Depreciation	Value
2012	40,000		$0.10*	$4,000	$ 4,000	$14,000
2013	60,000		0.10	6,000	10,000	8,000
2014	35,000		0.10	3,500	13,500	4,500
2015	25,000		0.10	2,500	16,000	2,000

*($18,000 − $2,000) ÷ 160,000.

(c)

Declining-Balance Method

| | Computation | | | Annual | End of Year | |
| | Book Value Beginning of | | Depreciation | Depreciation | Accumulated | Book |
Year	Year	×	Rate*	= Expense	Depreciation	Value
2012	$18,000		50%	$9,000	$ 9,000	$9,000
2013	9,000		50%	4,500	13,500	4,500
2014	4,500		50%	2,250	15,750	2,250
2015	2,250		50%	250**	16,000	2,000

*¼ × 2.
**Adjusted to $250 because ending book value should not be less than expected salvage value.

The Navigator

COMPREHENSIVE
Do it! 2

On January 1, 2012, Skyline Limousine Co. purchased a limo at an acquisition cost of $28,000. The vehicle has been depreciated by the straight-line method using a 4-year service life and a $4,000 salvage value. The company's fiscal year ends on December 31.

Instructions

Prepare the journal entry or entries to record the disposal of the limousine assuming that it was:

(a) Retired and scrapped with no salvage value on January 1, 2016.

(b) Sold for $5,000 on July 1, 2015.

action plan

✔ At the time of disposal, determine the book value of the asset.

✔ Recognize any gain or loss from disposal of the asset.

✔ Remove the book value of the asset from the records by debiting Accumulated Depreciation for the total depreciation to date of disposal and crediting the asset account for the cost of the asset.

Solution to Comprehensive Do it! 2			
(a) 1/1/16	Accumulated Depreciation—Equipment	24,000	
	Loss on Disposal of Plant Assets	4,000	
	Equipment		28,000
	(To record retirement of limousine)		
(b) 7/1/15	Depreciation Expense	3,000	
	Accumulated Depreciation—Equipment		3,000
	(To record depreciation to date of disposal)		
	Cash	5,000	
	Accumulated Depreciation—Equipment	21,000	
	Loss on Disposal of Plant Assets	2,000	
	Equipment		28,000
	(To record sale of limousine)		

✔ The Navigator

Summary of Study Objectives

[1] Describe how the cost principle applies to plant assets. The cost of plant assets includes all expenditures necessary to acquire the asset and make it ready for its intended use. Cost is measured by the cash or cash equivalent price paid.

[2] Explain the concept of depreciation. Depreciation is the allocation of the cost of a plant asset to expense over its useful (service) life in a rational and systematic manner. Depreciation is not a process of valuation, nor is it a process that results in an accumulation of cash.

[3] Compute periodic depreciation using different methods. Three depreciation methods are:

Method	Effect on Annual Depreciation	Formula
Straight-line	Constant amount	Depreciable cost ÷ Useful life (in years)
Units-of-activity	Varying amount	Depreciation cost per unit × Units of activity during the year
Declining-balance	Decreasing amount	Book value at beginning of year × Declining-balance rate

[4] Describe the procedure for revising periodic depreciation. Companies make revisions of periodic depreciation in present and future periods, not retroactively. They determine the new annual depreciation by dividing the depreciable cost at the time of the revision by the remaining useful life.

[5] Distinguish between revenue and capital expenditures, and explain the entries for each. Companies incur revenue expenditures to maintain the operating efficiency and productive life of an asset. They debit these expenditures to Maintenance and Repairs Expense as incurred. Capital expenditures increase the operating efficiency, productive capacity, or expected useful life of the asset. Companies generally debit these expenditures to the plant asset affected.

[6] Explain how to account for the disposal of a plant asset. The accounting for disposal of a plant asset through retirement or sale is as follows.

(a) Eliminate the book value of the plant asset at the date of disposal.

(b) Record cash proceeds, if any.

(c) Account for the difference between the book value and the cash proceeds as a gain or loss on disposal.

[7] **Compute periodic depletion of natural resources.** Companies compute depletion cost per unit by dividing the total cost of the natural resource minus salvage value by the number of units estimated to be in the resource. They then multiply the depletion cost per unit by the number of units extracted and sold.

[8] **Explain the basic issues related to accounting for intangible assets.** The process of allocating the cost of an intangible asset is referred to as amortization. The cost of intangible assets with indefinite lives are not amortized. Companies normally use the straight-line method for amortizing intangible assets.

[9] **Indicate how plant assets, natural resources, and intangible assets are reported.** Companies usually combine plant assets and natural resources under property, plant, and equipment; they show intangibles separately under intangible assets. Either within the balance sheet or in the notes, companies should disclose the balances of the major classes of assets, such as land, buildings, and equipment, and accumulated depreciation by major classes or in total. They also should describe the depreciation and amortization methods used, and should disclose the amount of depreciation and amortization expense for the period. The asset turnover ratio measures the productivity of a company's assets in generating sales.

Glossary

Accelerated-depreciation method Depreciation method that produces higher depreciation expense in the early years than in the later years. (p. 467).

Additions and improvements Costs incurred to increase the operating efficiency, productive capacity, or useful life of a plant asset. (p. 470).

Amortization The allocation of the cost of an intangible asset to expense over its useful life in a systematic and rational manner. (p. 475).

Asset turnover ratio A measure of how efficiently a company uses its assets to generate sales; calculated as net sales divided by average total assets. (p. 480).

Capital expenditures Expenditures that increase the company's investment in productive facilities. (p. 470).

Copyrights Exclusive grant from the federal government that allows the owner to reproduce and sell an artistic or published work. (p. 476).

Declining-balance method Depreciation method that applies a constant rate to the declining book value of the asset and produces a decreasing annual depreciation expense over the useful life of the asset. (p. 466).

Depletion The allocation of the cost of a natural resource to expense in a rational and systematic manner over the resource's useful life. (p. 474).

Depreciation The process of allocating to expense the cost of a plant asset over its useful (service) life in a rational and systematic manner. (p. 462).

Depreciable cost The cost of a plant asset less its salvage value. (p. 464).

Franchise (license) A contractual arrangement under which the franchisor grants the franchisee the right to sell certain products, provide specific services, or use certain trademarks or trade names, usually within a designated geographical area. (p. 477).

Going-concern assumption States that the company will continue in operation for the foreseeable future. (p. 463).

Goodwill The value of all favorable attributes that relate to a company that is not attributable to any other specific asset. (p. 477).

Intangible assets Rights, privileges, and competitive advantages that result from the ownership of long-lived assets that do not possess physical substance. (p. 475).

Licenses Operating rights to use public property, granted to a business by a governmental agency. (p. 477).

Materiality principle If an item would not make a difference in decision making, a company does not have to follow GAAP in reporting it. (p. 470).

Natural resources Assets that consist of standing timber and underground deposits of oil, gas, or minerals. (p. 474).

Ordinary repairs Expenditures to maintain the operating efficiency and productive life of the unit. (p. 470).

Patent An exclusive right issued by the U.S. Patent Office that enables the recipient to manufacture, sell, or otherwise control an invention for a period of 20 years from the date of the grant. (p. 476).

Plant assets Tangible resources that are used in the operations of the business and are not intended for sale to customers. (p. 458).

Research and development (R&D) costs Expenditures that may lead to patents, copyrights, new processes, or new products. (p. 478).

Revenue expenditures Expenditures that are immediately charged against revenues as an expense. (p. 470).

Salvage value An estimate of an asset's value at the end of its useful life. (p. 463).

Straight-line method Depreciation method in which periodic depreciation is the same for each year of the asset's useful life. (p. 464).

Trademark (trade name) A word, phrase, jingle, or symbol that identifies a particular enterprise or product. (p. 476).

Units-of-activity method Depreciation method in which useful life is expressed in terms of the total units of production or use expected from an asset. (p. 465).

Useful life An estimate of the expected productive life, also called service life, of an asset. (p. 463).

APPENDIX10A

Exchange of Plant Assets

Study Objective [10]

Explain how to account for the exchange of plant assets.

Ordinarily, companies record a gain or loss on the exchange of plant assets. The rationale for recognizing a gain or loss is that most exchanges have **commercial substance**. An exchange has commercial substance if the future cash flows change as a result of the exchange.

To illustrate, Ramos Co. exchanges some of its equipment for land held by Brodhead Inc. It is likely that the timing and amount of the cash flows arising from the land will differ significantly from the cash flows arising from the equipment. As a result, both Ramos and Brodhead are in different economic positions. Therefore **the exchange has commercial substance**, and the companies recognize a gain or loss in the exchange. Because most exchanges have commercial substance (even when similar assets are exchanged), we illustrate only this type of situation, for both a loss and a gain.

Loss Treatment

To illustrate an exchange that results in a loss, assume that Roland Company exchanged a set of used trucks plus cash for a new semi-truck. The used trucks have a combined book value of $42,000 (cost $64,000 less $22,000 accumulated depreciation). Roland's purchasing agent, experienced in the second-hand market, indicates that the used trucks have a fair value of $26,000. In addition to the trucks, Roland must pay $17,000 for the semi-truck. Roland computes the cost of the semi-truck as follows.

Illustration 10A-1
Cost of semi-truck

Fair value of used trucks	$26,000
Cash paid	17,000
Cost of semi-truck	$43,000

Roland incurs a loss on disposal of plant assets of $16,000 on this exchange. The reason is that the book value of the used trucks is greater than the fair value of these trucks. The computation is as follows.

Illustration 10A-2
Computation of loss on disposal

Book value of used trucks ($64,000 − $22,000)	$42,000
Fair value of used trucks	26,000
Loss on disposal of plant assets	**$16,000**

In recording an exchange at a loss, three steps are required: (1) Eliminate the book value of the asset given up, (2) record the cost of the asset acquired, and (3) recognize the loss on disposal of plant assets. Roland Company thus records the exchange on the loss as follows.

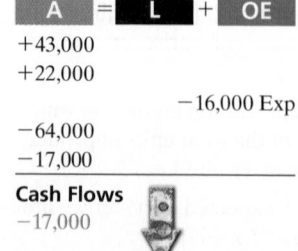

A	=	L	+	OE
+43,000				
+22,000				
				−16,000 Exp
−64,000				
−17,000				

Cash Flows
−17,000

Equipment (new)	43,000	
Accumulated Depreciation—Equipment	22,000	
Loss on Disposal of Plant Assets	16,000	
Equipment (old)		64,000
Cash		17,000
(To record exchange of used trucks for semi-truck)		

Gain Treatment

To illustrate a gain situation, assume that Mark Express Delivery decides to exchange its old delivery equipment plus cash of $3,000 for new delivery equipment. The book value of the old delivery equipment is $12,000 (cost $40,000 less accumulated depreciation $28,000). The fair value of the old delivery equipment is $19,000.

The cost of the new asset is the fair value of the old asset exchanged plus any cash paid (or other consideration given up). The cost of the new delivery equipment is $22,000, computed as follows.

Fair value of old delivery equipment	$19,000
Cash paid	3,000
Cost of new delivery equipment	$22,000

Illustration 10A-3
Cost of new delivery equipment

A gain results when the fair value of the old delivery equipment is greater than its book value. For Mark Express, there is a gain of $7,000 on disposal of plant assets, computed as follows.

Fair value of old delivery equipment	$19,000
Book value of old delivery equipment ($40,000 − $28,000)	12,000
Gain on disposal of plant assets	$ 7,000

Illustration 10A-4
Computation of gain on disposal

Mark Express Delivery records the exchange as follows.

Equipment (new)	22,000	
Accumulated Depreciation—Equipment (old)	28,000	
Equipment (old)		40,000
Gain on Disposal of Plant Assets		7,000
Cash		3,000
(To record exchange of old delivery equipment for new delivery equipment)		

A	=	L	+	OE
+22,000				
+28,000				
−40,000				
				+7,000 Rev
−3,000				

Cash Flows
−3,000

In recording an exchange at a gain, the following three steps are involved: (1) Eliminate the book value of the asset given up, (2) record the cost of the asset acquired, and (3) recognize the gain on disposal of plant assets. Accounting for exchanges of plant assets becomes more complex if the transaction does not have commercial substance. This issue is discussed in more advanced accounting classes.

Summary of Study Objective for Appendix 10A

[10] Explain how to account for the exchange of plant assets. Ordinarily, companies record a gain or loss on the exchange of plant assets. The rationale for recognizing a gain or loss is that most exchanges have commercial substance. An exchange has commercial substance if the future cash flows change as a result of the exchange.

Self-Test, Brief Exercises, Exercises, Problem Set A, and many
more components are available for practice in *WileyPLUS*

Note: All **asterisked** Questions, Exercises, and Problems relate to material in the appendix to the chapter.

Self-Test Questions

Answers are on page 503.

(SO 1) **1.** Erin Danielle Company purchased equipment and incurred the following costs.

Cash price	$24,000
Sales taxes	1,200
Insurance during transit	200
Installation and testing	400
Total costs	$25,800

What amount should be recorded as the cost of the equipment?
- **a.** $24,000.
- **b.** $25,200.
- **c.** $25,400.
- **d.** $25,800.

(SO 2) **2.** Depreciation is a process of:
- **a.** valuation.
- **b.** cost allocation.
- **c.** cash accumulation.
- **d.** appraisal.

(SO 3) **3.** Micah Bartlett Company purchased equipment on January 1, 2011, at a total invoice cost of $400,000. The equipment has an estimated salvage value of $10,000 and an estimated useful life of 5 years. The amount of accumulated depreciation at December 31, 2012, if the straight-line method of depreciation is used, is:
- **a.** $80,000.
- **b.** $160,000.
- **c.** $78,000.
- **d.** $156,000.

(SO 3) **4.** Ann Torbert purchased a truck for $11,000 on January 1, 2011. The truck will have an estimated salvage value of $1,000 at the end of 5 years. Using the units-of-activity method, the balance in accumulated depreciation at December 31, 2012, can be computed by the following formula:
- **a.** ($11,000 ÷ Total estimated activity) × Units of activity for 2012.
- **b.** ($10,000 ÷ Total estimated activity) × Units of activity for 2012.
- **c.** ($11,000 ÷ Total estimated activity) × Units of activity for 2011 and 2012.
- **d.** ($10,000 ÷ Total estimated activity) × Units of activity for 2011 and 2012.

(SO 3) **5.** Jefferson Company purchased a piece of equipment on January 1, 2012. The equipment cost $60,000 and has an estimated life of 8 years and a salvage value of $8,000. What was the depreciation expense for the asset for 2013 under the double-declining-balance method?
- **a.** $6,500.
- **b.** $11,250.
- **c.** $15,000.
- **d.** $6,562.

6. When there is a change in estimated depreciation: (SO 4)
- **a.** previous depreciation should be corrected.
- **b.** current and future years' depreciation should be revised.
- **c.** only future years' depreciation should be revised.
- **d.** None of the above.

7. Able Towing Company purchased a tow truck for $60,000 (SO 4) on January 1, 2010. It was originally depreciated on a straight-line basis over 10 years with an assumed salvage value of $12,000. On December 31, 2012, before adjusting entries had been made, the company decided to change the remaining estimated life to 4 years (including 2012) and the salvage value to $2,000. What was the depreciation expense for 2012?
- **a.** $6,000.
- **b.** $4,800.
- **c.** $15,000.
- **d.** $12,100.

8. Additions to plant assets are: (SO 5)
- **a.** revenue expenditures.
- **b.** debited to the Maintenance and Repairs Expense account.
- **c.** debited to the Purchases account.
- **d.** capital expenditures.

9. Bennie Razor Company has decided to sell one of its old (SO 6) manufacturing machines on June 30, 2012. The machine was purchased for $80,000 on January 1, 2008, and was depreciated on a straight-line basis for 10 years assuming no salvage value. If the machine was sold for $26,000, what was the amount of the gain or loss recorded at the time of the sale?
- **a.** $18,000.
- **b.** $54,000.
- **c.** $22,000.
- **d.** $46,000.

10. Maggie Sharrer Company expects to extract 20 million (SO 7) tons of coal from a mine that cost $12 million. If no salvage value is expected and 2 million tons are mined and sold in the first year, the entry to record depletion will include a:
- **a.** debit to Accumulated Depletion of $2,000,000.
- **b.** credit to Depletion Expense of $1,200,000.
- **c.** debit to Depletion Expense of $1,200,000.
- **d.** credit to Accumulated Depletion of $2,000,000.

11. Which of the following statements is *false*?   (SO 8)
- **a.** If an intangible asset has a finite life, it should be amortized.
- **b.** The amortization period of an intangible asset can exceed 20 years.
- **c.** Goodwill is recorded only when a business is purchased.
- **d.** Research and development costs are expensed when incurred, except when the research and development expenditures result in a successful patent.

(SO 8) **12.** Martha Beyerlein Company incurred $150,000 of research and development costs in its laboratory to develop a patent granted on January 2, 2012. On July 31, 2012, Beyerlein paid $35,000 for legal fees in a successful defense of the patent. The total amount debited to Patents through July 31, 2012, should be:
a. $150,000.   c. $185,000.
b. $35,000.   d. $170,000.

(SO 9) **13.** Indicate which of the following statements is *true*.
a. Since intangible assets lack physical substance, they need be disclosed only in the notes to the financial statements.
b. Goodwill should be reported as a contra-account in the owner's equity section.
c. Totals of major classes of assets can be shown in the balance sheet, with asset details disclosed in the notes to the financial statements.
d. Intangible assets are typically combined with plant assets and natural resources and shown in the property, plant, and equipment section.

(SO 9) **14.** Lake Coffee Company reported net sales of $180,000, net income of $54,000, beginning total assets of $200,000, and ending total assets of $300,000. What was the company's asset turnover ratio?
a. 0.90   c. 0.72
b. 0.20   d. 1.39

*15. Schopenhauer Company exchanged an old machine, with (SO 10) a book value of $39,000 and a fair value of $35,000, and paid $10,000 cash for a similar new machine. The transaction has commercial substance. At what amount should the machine acquired in the exchange be recorded on Schopenhauer's books?
a. $45,000.   c. $49,000.
b. $46,000.   d. $50,000.

*16. In exchanges of assets in which the exchange has commer- (SO 10) cial substance:
a. neither gains nor losses are recognized immediately.
b. gains, but not losses, are recognized immediately.
c. losses, but not gains, are recognized immediately.
d. both gains and losses are recognized immediately.

Go to the book's companion website, **www.wiley.com/college/weygandt**, for additional Self-Test Questions.

Questions

1. Tim Hoover is uncertain about the applicability of the cost principle to plant assets. Explain the principle to Tim.
2. What are some examples of land improvements?
3. Dain Company acquires the land and building owned by Corrs Company. What types of costs may be incurred to make the asset ready for its intended use if Dain Company wants to use (a) only the land, and (b) both the land and the building?
4. In a recent newspaper release, the president of Keene Company asserted that something has to be done about depreciation. The president said, "Depreciation does not come close to accumulating the cash needed to replace the asset at the end of its useful life." What is your response to the president?
5. Robert is studying for the next accounting examination. He asks your help on two questions: (a) What is salvage value? (b) Is salvage value used in determining periodic depreciation under each depreciation method? Answer Robert's questions.
6. Contrast the straight-line method and the units-of-activity method as to (a) useful life, and (b) the pattern of periodic depreciation over useful life.
7. Contrast the effects of the three depreciation methods on annual depreciation expense.
8. In the fourth year of an asset's 5-year useful life, the company decides that the asset will have a 6-year service life. How should the revision of depreciation be recorded? Why?
9. Distinguish between revenue expenditures and capital expenditures during useful life.

10. How is a gain or loss on the sale of a plant asset computed?
11. Mendez Corporation owns a machine that is fully depreciated but is still being used. How should Mendez account for this asset and report it in the financial statements?
12. What are natural resources, and what are their distinguishing characteristics?
13. Explain what depletion is and how it is computed.
14. What are the similarities and differences between the terms depreciation, depletion, and amortization?
15. Pendergrass Company hires an accounting intern who says that intangible assets should always be amortized over their legal lives. Is the intern correct? Explain.
16. Goodwill has been defined as the value of all favorable attributes that relate to a business. What types of attributes could result in goodwill?
17. Kenny Sain, a business major, is working on a case problem for one of his classes. In the case problem, the company needs to raise cash to market a new product it developed. Joe Morris, an engineering major, takes one look at the company's balance sheet and says, "This company has an awful lot of goodwill. Why don't you recommend that they sell some of it to raise cash?" How should Kenny respond to Joe?
18. Under what conditions is goodwill recorded?
19. Often research and development costs provide companies with benefits that last a number of years. (For example, these costs can lead to the development of a patent that will increase the company's income for many years.) However, generally accepted accounting principles require that such costs be recorded as an expense when incurred. Why?

20. McDonald's Corporation reports total average assets of $28.9 billion and net sales of $20.5 billion. What is the company's asset turnover ratio?

21. Resco Corporation and Yapan Corporation operate in the same industry. Resco uses the straight-line method to account for depreciation; Yapan uses an accelerated method. Explain what complications might arise in trying to compare the results of these two companies.

22. Lopez Corporation uses straight-line depreciation for financial reporting purposes but an accelerated method for tax purposes. Is it acceptable to use different methods for the two purposes? What is Lopez's motivation for doing this?

23. You are comparing two companies in the same industry. You have determined that May Corp. depreciates its plant assets over a 40-year life, whereas Won Corp. depreciates its plant assets over a 20-year life. Discuss the implications this has for comparing the results of the two companies.

24. Wade Company is doing significant work to revitalize its warehouses. It is not sure whether it should capitalize these costs or expense them. What are the implications for current-year net income and future net income of expensing versus capitalizing these costs?

25. ⊕ **PEPSICO** What classifications and amounts are shown in PepsiCo's Note 4 to explain its total property, plant, and equipment (net) of $12,671 million?

26. When assets are exchanged in a transaction involving commercial substance, how is the gain or loss on disposal of plant assets computed?

*27. Tatum Refrigeration Company trades in an old machine on a new model when the fair value of the old machine is greater than its book value. The transaction has commercial substance. Should Tatum recognize a gain on disposal of plant assets? If the fair value of the old machine is less than its book value, should Tatum recognize a loss on disposal of plant assets?

Brief Exercises

Determine the cost of land.
(SO 1)

BE10-1 The following expenditures were incurred by Krunk Company in purchasing land: cash price $70,000, accrued taxes $3,000, attorneys' fees $2,500, real estate broker's commission $2,000, and clearing and grading $3,500. What is the cost of the land?

Determine the cost of a truck.
(SO 1)

BE10-2 Mick Ferguson Company incurs the following expenditures in purchasing a truck: cash price $30,000, accident insurance $2,000, sales taxes $1,500, motor vehicle license $100, and painting and lettering $400. What is the cost of the truck?

Compute straight-line depreciation.
(SO 3)

BE10-3 Tomorry Company acquires a delivery truck at a cost of $42,000. The truck is expected to have a salvage value of $6,000 at the end of its 4-year useful life. Compute annual depreciation for the first and second years using the straight-line method.

Compute depreciation and evaluate treatment.
(SO 3)

BE10-4 String Dance Company purchased land and a building on January 1, 2012. Management's best estimate of the value of the land was $100,000 and of the building $200,000. But management told the accounting department to record the land at $220,000 and the building at $80,000. The building is being depreciated on a straight-line basis over 20 years with no salvage value. Why do you suppose management requested this accounting treatment? Is it ethical?

Compute declining-balance depreciation.
(SO 3)

BE10-5 Depreciation information for Tomorry Company is given in BE10-3. Assuming the declining-balance depreciation rate is double the straight-line rate, compute annual depreciation for the first and second years under the declining-balance method.

Compute depreciation using the units-of-activity method.
(SO 3)

BE10-6 Koman Taxi Service uses the units-of-activity method in computing depreciation on its taxicabs. Each cab is expected to be driven 150,000 miles. Taxi no. 10 cost $33,500 and is expected to have a salvage value of $500. Taxi no. 10 is driven 30,000 miles in year 1 and 20,000 miles in year 2. Compute the depreciation for each year.

Compute revised depreciation.
(SO 4)

BE10-7 On January 1, 2012, the Dancing Gorillas Company ledger shows Equipment $29,000 and Accumulated Depreciation—Equipment $9,000. The depreciation resulted from using the straight-line method with a useful life of 10 years and salvage value of $2,000. On this date, the company concludes that the equipment has a remaining useful life of only 4 years with the same salvage value. Compute the revised annual depreciation.

Prepare entries for delivery truck costs.
(SO 5)

BE10-8 Euro Guy Company had the following two transactions related to its delivery truck.
1. Paid $45 for an oil change.
2. Paid $400 to install special gear unit, which increases the operating efficiency of the truck.

Prepare Euro Guy's journal entries to record these two transactions.

Prepare entries for disposal by retirement.
(SO 6)

BE10-9 Prepare journal entries to record the following.
(a) Twitter Tracker Company retires its delivery equipment, which cost $41,000. Accumulated depreciation is also $41,000 on this delivery equipment. No salvage value is received.
(b) Assume the same information as (a), except that accumulated depreciation is $39,000, instead of $41,000, on the delivery equipment.

BE10-10   Wing Pang Company sells equipment on September 30, 2012, for $20,000 cash. The equipment originally cost $72,000 and as of January 1, 2012, had accumulated depreciation of $42,000. Depreciation for the first 9 months of 2012 is $5,250. Prepare the journal entries to (a) update depreciation to September 30, 2012, and (b) record the sale of the equipment.

Prepare entries for disposal by sale.
(SO 6)

BE10-11   Deon Cole Mining Co. purchased for $7 million a mine that is estimated to have 35 million tons of ore and no salvage value. In the first year, 6 million tons of ore are extracted and sold.
(a) Prepare the journal entry to record depletion expense for the first year.
(b) Show how this mine is reported on the balance sheet at the end of the first year.

Prepare depletion expense entry and balance sheet presentation for natural resources.
(SO 7)

BE10-12   Pevensie Company purchases a patent for $120,000 on January 2, 2012. Its estimated useful life is 10 years.
(a) Prepare the journal entry to record amortization expense for the first year.
(b) Show how this patent is reported on the balance sheet at the end of the first year.

Prepare amortization expense entry and balance sheet presentation for intangibles.
(SO 8)

BE10-13   Information related to plant assets, natural resources, and intangibles at the end of 2012 for Lucy Company is as follows: buildings $1,100,000; accumulated depreciation—buildings $650,000; goodwill $410,000; coal mine $500,000; accumulated depletion—coal mine $108,000. Prepare a partial balance sheet of Lucy Company for these items.

Classify long-lived assets on balance sheet.
(SO 9)

BE10-14   In its 2009 annual report, Target reported beginning total assets of $44.1 billion; ending total assets of $44.5 billion; and net sales of $63.4 billion. Compute Target's asset turnover ratio.

Analyze long-lived assets.
(SO 9)

*BE10-15   Edmund Company exchanges old delivery equipment for new delivery equipment. The book value of the old delivery equipment is $31,000 (cost $61,000 less accumulated depreciation $30,000). Its fair value is $19,000, and cash of $5,000 is paid. Prepare the entry to record the exchange, assuming the transaction has commercial substance.

Prepare entry for disposal by exchange.
(SO 10)

*BE10-16   Assume the same information as BE10-15, except that the fair value of the old delivery equipment is $38,000. Prepare the entry to record the exchange.

Prepare entry for disposal by exchange.
(SO 10)

Do it! Review

Do it! 10-1   Henley Company purchased a delivery truck. The total cash payment was $27,900, including the following items.

Explain accounting for cost of plant assets.
(SO 1)

Negotiated purchase price	$24,000
Installation of special shelving	1,100
Painting and lettering	900
Motor vehicle license	100
Annual insurance policy	500
Sales tax	1,300
Total paid	$27,900

Explain how each of these costs would be accounted for.

Do it! 10-2   On January 1, 2012, Skandar Country Club purchased a new riding mower for $15,000. The mower is expected to have an 8-year life with a $1,000 salvage value. What journal entry would Skandar make at December 31, 2012, if it uses straight-line depreciation?

Calculate depreciation expense and make journal entry.
(SO 2)

Do it! 10-3   Whistler Corporation purchased a piece of equipment for $50,000. It estimated an 8-year life and $2,000 salvage value. At the end of year four (before the depreciation adjustment), it estimated the new total life to be 10 years and the new salvage value to be $4,000. Compute the revised depreciation.

Calculated revised depreciation
(SO 4)

Do it! 10-4   Keynes Manufacturing has old equipment that cost $50,000. The equipment has accumulated depreciation of $28,000 and a fair value of $26,000. Keynes has decided to sell the equipment.
(a) What entry would Keynes make to record the sale of the equipment for $26,000 cash?
(b) What entry would Keynes make to record the sale of the equipment for $15,000 cash?

Make journal entries to record plant asset disposal.
(SO 6)

Match intangibles classifications concepts.

(SO 7, 8)

Do it! 10-5   Match the statement with the term most directly associated with it.

Goodwill   Amortization
Intangible assets   Franchises
Research and development costs

1. _____ Rights, privileges, and competitive advantages that result from the ownership of long-lived assets that do not possess physical substance.
2. _____ The allocation of the cost of an intangible asset to expense in a rational and systematic manner.
3. _____ A right to sell certain products or services, or use certain trademarks or trade names within a designated geographic area.
4. _____ Costs incurred by a company that often lead to patents or new products. These costs must be expensed as incurred.
5. _____ The excess of the cost of a company over the fair value of the net assets acquired.

Exercises

Determine cost of plant acquisitions.

(SO 1)

E10-1   The following expenditures relating to plant assets were made by Georgie Company during the first 2 months of 2012.

1. Paid $5,000 of accrued taxes at time plant site was acquired.
2. Paid $200 insurance to cover possible accident loss on new factory machinery while the machinery was in transit.
3. Paid $850 sales taxes on new delivery truck.
4. Paid $17,500 for parking lots and driveways on new plant site.
5. Paid $250 to have company name and advertising slogan painted on new delivery truck.
6. Paid $8,000 for installation of new factory machinery.
7. Paid $900 for one-year accident insurance policy on new delivery truck.
8. Paid $75 motor vehicle license fee on the new truck.

Instructions

(a) _____ Explain the application of the cost principle in determining the acquisition cost of plant assets.
(b) List the numbers of the foregoing transactions, and opposite each indicate the account title to which each expenditure should be debited.

Determine property, plant, and equipment costs.

(SO 1)

E10-2   Moseley Company incurred the following costs.

1. Sales tax on factory machinery purchased	$ 5,000
2. Painting of and lettering on truck immediately upon purchase	700
3. Installation and testing of factory machinery	2,000
4. Real estate broker's commission on land purchased	3,500
5. Insurance premium paid for first year's insurance on new truck	880
6. Cost of landscaping on property purchased	7,200
7. Cost of paving parking lot for new building constructed	17,900
8. Cost of clearing, draining, and filling land	13,300
9. Architect's fees on self-constructed building	10,000

Instructions

Indicate to which account Moseley would debit each of the costs.

Determine acquisition costs of land.

(SO 1)

E10-3   On March 1, 2012, Popplewell Company acquired real estate on which it planned to construct a small office building. The company paid $80,000 in cash. An old warehouse on the property was razed at a cost of $8,600; the salvaged materials were sold for $1,700. Additional expenditures before construction began included $1,100 attorney's fee for work concerning the land purchase, $5,000 real estate broker's fee, $7,800 architect's fee, and $14,000 to put in driveways and a parking lot.

Instructions

(a) Determine the amount to be reported as the cost of the land.
(b) For each cost not used in part (a), indicate the account to be debited.

E10-4 Jim McAvoy has prepared the following list of statements about depreciation.

1. Depreciation is a process of asset valuation, not cost allocation.
2. Depreciation provides for the proper matching of expenses with revenues.
3. The book value of a plant asset should approximate its fair value.
4. Depreciation applies to three classes of plant assets: land, buildings, and equipment.
5. Depreciation does not apply to a building because its usefulness and revenue-producing ability generally remain intact over time.
6. The revenue-producing ability of a depreciable asset will decline due to wear and tear and to obsolescence.
7. Recognizing depreciation on an asset results in an accumulation of cash for replacement of the asset.
8. The balance in accumulated depreciation represents the total cost that has been charged to expense.
9. Depreciation expense and accumulated depreciation are reported on the income statement.
10. Four factors affect the computation of depreciation: cost, useful life, salvage value, and residual value.

Understand depreciation concepts.
(SO 2)

Instructions
Identify each statement as true or false. If false, indicate how to correct the statement.

E10-5 Tilda Bus Lines uses the units-of-activity method in depreciating its buses. One bus was purchased on January 1, 2012, at a cost of $168,000. Over its 4-year useful life, the bus is expected to be driven 100,000 miles. Salvage value is expected to be $8,000.

Compute depreciation under units-of-activity method.
(SO 3)

Instructions
(a) Compute the depreciation cost per unit.
(b) Prepare a depreciation schedule assuming actual mileage was: 2012, 26,000; 2013, 32,000; 2014, 25,000; and 2015, 17,000.

E10-6 Swinton Company purchased a new machine on October 1, 2012, at a cost of $120,000. The company estimated that the machine will have a salvage value of $12,000. The machine is expected to be used for 10,000 working hours during its 5-year life.

Determine depreciation for partial periods.
(SO 3)

Instructions
Compute the depreciation expense under the following methods for the year indicated.
(a) Straight-line for 2012.
(b) Units-of-activity for 2012, assuming machine usage was 1,700 hours.
(c) Declining-balance using double the straight-line rate for 2012 and 2013.

E10-7 Tumnus Company purchased a delivery truck for $30,000 on January 1, 2012. The truck has an expected salvage value of $2,000, and is expected to be driven 100,000 miles over its estimated useful life of 8 years. Actual miles driven were 15,000 in 2012 and 12,000 in 2013.

Compute depreciation using different methods.
(SO 3)

Instructions
(a) Compute depreciation expense for 2012 and 2013 using (1) the straight-line method, (2) the units-of-activity method, and (3) the double-declining-balance method.
(b) Assume that Tumnus uses the straight-line method.
   (1) Prepare the journal entry to record 2012 depreciation.
   (2) Show how the truck would be reported in the December 31, 2012, balance sheet.

E10-8 Kiran Shah, the new controller of Ginarrbrik Company, has reviewed the expected useful lives and salvage values of selected depreciable assets at the beginning of 2012. His findings are as follows.

Compute revised annual depreciation.
(SO 4)

Type of Asset	Date Acquired	Cost	Accumulated Depreciation 1/1/12	Useful Life in Years		Salvage Value	
				Old	Proposed	Old	Proposed
Building	1/1/06	$800,000	$114,000	40	50	$40,000	$37,000
Warehouse	1/1/07	100,000	19,000	25	20	5,000	3,600

All assets are depreciated by the straight-line method. Ginarrbrik Company uses a calendar year in preparing annual financial statements. After discussion, management has agreed to accept Kiran's proposed changes.

Instructions
(a) Compute the revised annual depreciation on each asset in 2012. (Show computations.)
(b) Prepare the entry (or entries) to record depreciation on the building in 2012.

Journalize entries for disposal of plant assets.
(SO 6)

E10-9   Presented below are selected transactions at Kirke Company for 2012.

Jan.   1   Retired a piece of machinery that was purchased on January 1, 2002. The machine cost $62,000 on that date. It had a useful life of 10 years with no salvage value.

June 30   Sold a computer that was purchased on January 1, 2009. The computer cost $40,000. It had a useful life of 5 years with no salvage value. The computer was sold for $14,000.

Dec. 31   Discarded a delivery truck that was purchased on January 1, 2008. The truck cost $39,000. It was depreciated based on a 6-year useful life with a $3,000 salvage value.

Instructions
Journalize all entries required on the above dates, including entries to update depreciation, where applicable, on assets disposed of. Kirke Company uses straight-line depreciation. (Assume depreciation is up to date as of December 31, 2011.)

Journalize entries for disposal of equipment.
(SO 6)

E10-10   Cosmo Company owns equipment that cost $50,000 when purchased on January 1, 2009. It has been depreciated using the straight-line method based on estimated salvage value of $5,000 and an estimated useful life of 5 years.

Instructions
Prepare Cosmo Company's journal entries to record the sale of the equipment in these four independent situations.

(a) Sold for $28,000 on January 1, 2012.
(b) Sold for $28,000 on May 1, 2012.
(c) Sold for $11,000 on January 1, 2012.
(d) Sold for $11,000 on October 1, 2012.

Journalize entries for natural resources depletion.
(SO 7)

E10-11   On July 1, 2012, Macready Inc. invested $720,000 in a mine estimated to have 800,000 tons of ore of uniform grade. During the last 6 months of 2012, 100,000 tons of ore were mined and sold.

Instructions
(a) Prepare the journal entry to record depletion expense.
(b) Assume that the 100,000 tons of ore were mined, but only 80,000 units were sold. How are the costs applicable to the 20,000 unsold units reported?

Prepare adjusting entries for amortization.
(SO 8)

E10-12   The following are selected 2012 transactions of Oveius Corporation.

Jan. 1   Purchased a small company and recorded goodwill of $150,000. Its useful life is indefinite.
May 1   Purchased for $90,000 a patent with an estimated useful life of 5 years and a legal life of 20 years.

Instructions
Prepare necessary adjusting entries at December 31 to record amortization required by the events above.

Prepare entries to set up appropriate accounts for different intangibles; amortize intangible assets.
(SO 8)

E10-13   Kake Company, organized in 2012, has the following transactions related to intangible assets.

1/2/12	Purchased patent (7-year life)	$560,000
4/1/12	Goodwill purchased (indefinite life)	360,000
7/1/12	10-year franchise; expiration date 7/1/2022	440,000
9/1/12	Research and development costs	185,000

Instructions
Prepare the necessary entries to record these intangibles. All costs incurred were for cash. Make the adjusting entries as of December 31, 2012, recording any necessary amortization and reflecting all balances accurately as of that date.

Calculate asset turnover ratio.
(SO 9)

E10-14   During 2012 Otmin Corporation reported net sales of $4,900,000 and net income of $1,500,000. Its balance sheet reported average total assets of $1,400,000.

Instructions
Calculate the asset turnover ratio.

*E10-15 Presented below are two independent transactions. Both transactions have commercial substance.

Journalize entries for exchanges.
(SO 10)

1. Rangi Co. exchanged old trucks (cost $64,000 less $22,000 accumulated depreciation) plus cash of $17,000 for new trucks. The old trucks had a fair value of $36,000.
2. Dryad Inc. trades its used machine (cost $12,000 less $4,000 accumulated depreciation) for a new machine. In addition to exchanging the old machine (which had a fair value of $9,000), Dryad also paid cash of $3,000.

Instructions
(a) Prepare the entry to record the exchange of assets by Rangi Co.
(b) Prepare the entry to record the exchange of assets by Dryad Inc.

*E10-16 Jaxin's Delivery Company and Felicity's Express Delivery exchanged delivery trucks on January 1, 2012. Jaxin's truck cost $22,000. It has accumulated depreciation of $15,000 and a fair value of $4,000. Felicity's truck cost $10,000. It has accumulated depreciation of $8,000 and a fair value of $4,000. The transaction has commercial substance.

Journalize entries for the exchange of plant assets.
(SO 10)

Instructions
(a) Journalize the exchange for Jaxin's Delivery Company.
(b) Journalize the exchange for Felicity's Express Delivery.

Exercises: Set B

Visit the book's companion website, at **www.wiley.com/college/weygandt**, and choose the Student Companion site to access Exercise Set B.

Problems: Set A

P10-1A Rumblebuffin Company was organized on January 1. During the first year of operations, the following plant asset expenditures and receipts were recorded in random order.

Determine acquisition costs of land and building.
(SO 1)

Debits

1. Cost of filling and grading the land	$ 4,000
2. Full payment to building contractor	700,000
3. Real estate taxes on land paid for the current year	5,000
4. Cost of real estate purchased as a plant site (land $100,000 and building $45,000)	145,000
5. Excavation costs for new building	35,000
6. Architect's fees on building plans	10,000
7. Accrued real estate taxes paid at time of purchase of real estate	2,000
8. Cost of parking lots and driveways	14,000
9. Cost of demolishing building to make land suitable for construction of new building	15,000
	$930,000

Credit

10. Proceeds from salvage of demolished building	$ 3,500

Instructions
Analyze the foregoing transactions using the following column headings. Insert the number of each transaction in the Item space, and insert the amounts in the appropriate columns. For amounts entered in the Other Accounts column, also indicate the account titles.

Totals
Land $162,500
Buildings $745,000

Item	Land	Buildings	Other Accounts

P10-2A In recent years, Sonya Transportation purchased three used buses. Because of frequent turnover in the accounting department, a different accountant selected the depreciation method for each bus, and various methods were selected. Information concerning the buses is summarized on page 494.

Compute depreciation under different methods.
(SO 3)

Bus	Acquired	Cost	Salvage Value	Useful Life in Years	Depreciation Method
1	1/1/10	$ 96,000	$ 6,000	5	Straight-line
2	1/1/10	120,000	10,000	4	Declining-balance
3	1/1/11	80,000	8,000	5	Units-of-activity

For the declining-balance method, the company uses the double-declining rate. For the units-of-activity method, total miles are expected to be 120,000. Actual miles of use in the first 3 years were: 2011, 24,000; 2012, 34,000; and 2013, 30,000.

Instructions

(a) Bus 2, 2011, $90,000

(a) Compute the amount of accumulated depreciation on each bus at December 31, 2012.

(b) If bus no. 2 was purchased on April 1 instead of January 1, what is the depreciation expense for this bus in (1) 2010 and (2) 2011?

Compute depreciation under different methods.
(SO 3)

P10-3A On January 1, 2012, Tiggy Company purchased the following two machines for use in its production process.

Machine A: The cash price of this machine was $38,000. Related expenditures included: sales tax $1,700, shipping costs $150, insurance during shipping $80, installation and testing costs $70, and $100 of oil and lubricants to be used with the machinery during its first year of operations. Tiggy estimates that the useful life of the machine is 5 years with a $5,000 salvage value remaining at the end of that time period. Assume that the straight-line method of depreciation is used.

Machine B: The recorded cost of this machine was $160,000. Tiggy estimates that the useful life of the machine is 4 years with a $10,000 salvage value remaining at the end of that time period.

Instructions

(a) Prepare the following for Machine A.
  (1) The journal entry to record its purchase on January 1, 2012.
  (2) The journal entry to record annual depreciation at December 31, 2012.

(b) (2) 2012 DDB depreciation $80,000

(b) Calculate the amount of depreciation expense that Tiggy should record for machine B each year of its useful life under the following assumptions.
  (1) Tiggy uses the straight-line method of depreciation.
  (2) Tiggy uses the declining-balance method. The rate used is twice the straight-line rate.
  (3) Tiggy uses the units-of-activity method and estimates that the useful life of the machine is 125,000 units. Actual usage is as follows: 2012, 45,000 units; 2013, 35,000 units; 2014, 25,000 units; 2015, 20,000 units.

(c) Which method used to calculate depreciation on machine B reports the highest amount of depreciation expense in year 1 (2012)? The highest amount in year 4 (2015)? The highest total amount over the 4-year period?

Calculate revisions to depreciation expense.
(SO 3, 4)

P10-4A At the beginning of 2010, Sarofim Company acquired equipment costing $90,000. It was estimated that this equipment would have a useful life of 6 years and a residual value of $9,000 at that time. The straight-line method of depreciation was considered the most appropriate to use with this type of equipment. Depreciation is to be recorded at the end of each year.

During 2012 (the third year of the equipment's life), the company's engineers reconsidered their expectations, and estimated that the equipment's useful life would probably be 7 years (in total) instead of 6 years. The estimated residual value was not changed at that time. However, during 2015 the estimated residual value was reduced to $5,000.

Instructions

Indicate how much depreciation expense should be recorded each year for this equipment, by completing the following table.

Year	Depreciation Expense	Accumulated Depreciation
2010		
2011		
2012		
2013		
2014		
2015		
2016		

2016 depreciation expense, $12,800

P10-5A At December 31, 2012, Alina Company reported the following as plant assets.

Land		$ 4,000,000
Buildings	$28,500,000	
Less: Accumulated depreciation—buildings	12,100,000	16,400,000
Equipment	48,000,000	
Less: Accumulated depreciation—equipment	5,000,000	43,000,000
Total plant assets		$63,400,000

Journalize a series of equipment transactions related to purchase, sale, retirement, and depreciation.

(SO 3, 6, 9)

During 2013, the following selected cash transactions occurred.

April 1 Purchased land for $2,130,000.
May 1 Sold equipment that cost $780,000 when purchased on January 1, 2009. The equipment was sold for $450,000.
June 1 Sold land purchased on June 1, 2003 for $1,500,000. The land cost $400,000.
July 1 Purchased equipment for $2,000,000.
Dec. 31 Retired equipment that cost $500,000 when purchased on December 31, 2003. No salvage value was received.

Instructions

(a) Journalize the above transactions. The company uses straight-line depreciation for buildings and equipment. The buildings are estimated to have a 50-year life and no salvage value. The equipment is estimated to have a 10-year useful life and no salvage value. Update depreciation on assets disposed of at the time of sale or retirement.

(b) Record adjusting entries for depreciation for 2013.

(c) Prepare the plant assets section of Alina's balance sheet at December 31, 2013.

(b) Depreciation Expense—Buildings $570,000; Equipment $4,772,000

(c) Total plant assets $61,270,000

P10-6A Faun Co. has equipment that cost $75,000 and that has been depreciated $50,000. Record the disposal under the following assumptions.

(a) It was scrapped as having no value.
(b) It was sold for $21,000.
(c) It was sold for $31,000.

Record disposals.

(SO 6)

P10-7A The intangible assets section of Centaur Company at December 31, 2012, is presented below.

Patents ($70,000 cost less $7,000 amortization)	$63,000
Franchises ($48,000 cost less $19,200 amortization)	28,800
Total	$91,800

Prepare entries to record transactions related to acquisition and amortization of intangibles; prepare the intangible assets section.

(SO 8, 9)

The patent was acquired in January 2012 and has a useful life of 10 years. The franchise was acquired in January 2009 and also has a useful life of 10 years. The following cash transactions may have affected intangible assets during 2013.

Jan. 2 Paid $45,000 legal costs to successfully defend the patent against infringement by another company.
Jan.–June Developed a new product, incurring $140,000 in research and development costs. A patent was granted for the product on July 1. Its useful life is equal to its legal life.
Sept. 1 Paid $50,000 to an extremely large defensive lineman to appear in commercials advertising the company's products. The commercials will air in September and October.
Oct. 1 Acquired a franchise for $100,000. The franchise has a useful life of 50 years.

Instructions

(a) Prepare journal entries to record the transactions above.
(b) Prepare journal entries to record the 2013 amortization expense.
(c) Prepare the intangible assets section of the balance sheet at December 31, 2013.

(b) Amortization Expense (patents) $12,000 Amortization Expense (franchises) $5,300

(c) Total intangible assets $219,500

P10-8A Due to rapid turnover in the accounting department, a number of transactions involving intangible assets were improperly recorded by the Satyr Company in 2012.

1. Satyr developed a new manufacturing process, incurring research and development costs of $136,000. The company also purchased a patent for $60,000. In early January, Satyr capitalized $196,000 as the cost of the patents. Patent amortization expense of $9,800 was recorded based on a 20-year useful life.

Prepare entries to correct errors made in recording and amortizing intangible assets.

(SO 8)

2. On July 1, 2012, Satyr purchased a small company and as a result acquired goodwill of $92,000. Satyr recorded a half-year's amortization in 2012, based on a 50-year life ($920 amortization). The goodwill has an indefinite life.

Instructions

1. R&D Exp. $136,000

Prepare all journal entries necessary to correct any errors made during 2012. Assume the books have not yet been closed for 2012.

Calculate and comment on asset turnover ratio.

(SO 9)

P10-9A Ratilal Company and Navi Corporation, two corporations of roughly the same size, are both involved in the manufacture of in-line skates. Each company depreciates its plant assets using the straight-line approach. An investigation of their financial statements reveals the following information.

	Ratilal Co.	Navi Corp.
Net income	$ 800,000	$1,000,000
Sales revenue	1,200,000	1,080,000
Average total assets	2,500,000	2,000,000
Average plant assets	1,800,000	1,000,000

Instructions

(a) For each company, calculate the asset turnover ratio.

(b) ━━◀ Based on your calculations in part (a), comment on the relative effectiveness of the two companies in using their assets to generate sales and produce net income.

Problems: Set B

Determine acquisition costs of land and building.

(SO 1)

P10-1B Bhaja Company was organized on January 1. During the first year of operations, the following plant asset expenditures and receipts were recorded in random order.

Debits

1. Accrued real estate taxes paid at time of purchase of real estate	$ 5,000
2. Real estate taxes on land paid for the current year	7,500
3. Full payment to building contractor	500,000
4. Excavation costs for new building	19,000
5. Cost of real estate purchased as a plant site (land $75,000 and building $25,000)	100,000
6. Cost of parking lots and driveways	18,000
7. Architect's fees on building plans	9,000
8. Installation cost of fences around property	6,000
9. Cost of demolishing building to make land suitable for construction of new building	17,000
	$681,500

Credit

10. Proceeds from salvage of demolished building	$ 3,500

Instructions

Analyze the foregoing tranactions using the following column headings. Insert the number of each transaction in the Item space, and insert the amounts in the appropriate columns. For amounts entered in the Other Accounts column, also indicate the account title.

Totals

Land $118,500
Buildings $528,000

Item	Land	Buildings	Other Accounts

Compute depreciation under different methods.

(SO 3)

P10-2B In recent years, Kannada Company purchased three machines. Because of heavy turnover in the accounting department, a different accountant was in charge of selecting the depreciation method for each machine, and each selected a different method. Information concerning the machines is summarized below.

Machine	Acquired	Cost	Salvage Value	Useful Life in Years	Depreciation Method
1	1/1/09	$105,000	$ 5,000	10	Straight-line
2	1/1/10	150,000	10,000	8	Declining-balance
3	11/1/12	100,000	15,000	6	Units-of-activity

For the declining-balance method, the company uses the double-declining rate. For the units-of-activity method, total machine hours are expected to be 25,000. Actual hours of use in the first 3 years were: 2012, 2,000; 2013, 4,500; and 2014, 5,500.

Instructions

(a) Compute the amount of accumulated depreciation on each machine at December 31, 2012.

(a) Machine 2, 2011, $28,125

(b) If machine 2 had been purchased on May 1 instead of January 1, what would be the depreciation expense for this machine in (1) 2010 and (2) 2011?

P10-3B On January 1, 2012, Zakiuddin Company purchased the following two machines for use in its production process.

Compute depreciation under different methods.

(SO 3)

Machine A: The cash price of this machine was $55,000. Related expenditures included: sales tax $2,750, shipping costs $100, insurance during shipping $75, installation and testing costs $75, and $90 of oil and lubricants to be used with the machinery during its first year of operation. Zakiuddin estimates that the useful life of the machine is 4 years with a $5,000 salvage value remaining at the end of that time period.

Machine B: The recorded cost of this machine was $100,000. Zakiuddin estimates that the useful life of the machine is 4 years with a $10,000 salvage value remaining at the end of that time period.

Instructions

(a) Prepare the following for Machine A.
  (1) The journal entry to record its purchase on January 1, 2012.
  (2) The journal entry to record annual depreciation at December 31, 2012, assuming the straight-line method of depreciation is used.

(a) (2) $13,250

(b) Calculate the amount of depreciation expense that Zakiuddin should record for machine B each year of its useful life under the following assumption.
  (1) Zakiuddin uses the straight-line method of depreciation.
  (2) Zakiuddin uses the declining-balance method. The rate used is twice the straight-line rate.
  (3) Zakiuddin uses the units-of-activity method and estimates the useful life of the machine is 25,000 units. Actual usage is as follows: 2012, 5,500 units; 2013, 7,000 units; 2014, 8,000 units; 2015, 4,500 units.

(c) Which method used to calculate depreciation on machine B reports the lowest amount of depreciation expense in year 1 (2012)? The lowest amount in year 4 (2015)? The lowest total amount over the 4-year period?

P10-4B At the beginning of 2010, Farooque Company acquired equipment costing $200,000. It was estimated that this equipment would have a useful life of 6 years and a residual value of $20,000 at that time. The straight-line method of depreciation was considered the most appropriate to use with this type of equipment. Depreciation is to be recorded at the end of each year.

Calculate revisions to depreciation expense.

(SO 3, 4)

During 2012 (the third year of the equipment's life), the company's engineers reconsidered their expectations, and estimated that the equipment's useful life would probably be 7 years (in total) instead of 6 years. The estimated residual value was not changed at that time. However, during 2015 the estimated residual value was reduced to $5,000.

Instructions

Indicate how much depreciation expense should be recorded for this equipment each year by completing the following table.

Year	Depreciation Expense	Accumulated Depreciation
2010		
2011		
2012		
2013		
2014		
2015		
2016		

2016 depreciation expense, $31,500

Journalize a series of equipment transactions related to purchase, sale, retirement, and depreciation.

(SO 3, 6, 9)

P10-5B At December 31, 2012, Ramaswami Company reported the following as plant assets.

Land		$ 2,000,000
Buildings	$20,000,000	
Less: Accumulated depreciation—buildings	8,000,000	12,000,000
Equipment	30,000,000	
Less: Accumulated depreciation—equipment	4,000,000	26,000,000
Total plant assets		$40,000,000

During 2013, the following selected cash transactions occurred.

April 1	Purchased land for $1,200,000.
May 1	Sold equipment that cost $420,000 when purchased on January 1, 2009. The equipment was sold for $240,000.
June 1	Sold land purchased on June 1, 2003, for $1,000,000. The land cost $340,000.
July 1	Purchased equipment for $1,100,000.
Dec. 31	Retired equipment that cost $300,000 when purchased on December 31, 2003. No salvage value was received.

Instructions

(a) Journalize the above transactions. Ramaswami uses straight-line depreciation for buildings and equipment. The buildings are estimated to have a 50-year useful life and no salvage value. The equipment is estimated to have a 10-year useful life and no salvage value. Update depreciation on assets disposed of at the time of sale or retirement.

(b) Record adjusting entries for depreciation for 2013.

(c) Prepare the plant assets section of Ramaswami's balance sheet at December 31, 2013.

(b) Depreciation Expense— Buildings $400,000; Equipment $2,983,000

(c) Total plant assets $38,295,000

Record disposals.

(SO 6)

P10-6B Nikhom's has equipment that cost $40,000 and that has been depreciated $26,000. Record the disposal under the following assumptions.

(a) It was scrapped as having no value.

(b) It was sold for $29,000.

(c) It was sold for $10,000.

Prepare entries to record transactions related to acquisition and amortization of intangibles; prepare the intangible assets section.

(SO 8, 9)

P10-7B The intangible assets section of Praphaphorn Company at December 31, 2012, is presented below.

Patents ($100,000 cost less $10,000 amortization)	$ 90,000
Copyrights ($60,000 cost less $24,000 amortization)	36,000
Total	$126,000

The patent was acquired in January 2012 and has a useful life of 10 years. The copyright was acquired in January 2009 and also has a useful life of 10 years. The following cash transactions may have affected intangible assets during 2013.

Jan. 2	Paid $45,000 legal costs to successfully defend the patent against infringement by another company.
Jan.–June	Developed a new product, incurring $230,000 in research and development costs. A patent was granted for the product on July 1. Its useful life is equal to its legal life.
Sept. 1	Paid $125,000 to an Xgames star to appear in commercials advertising the company's products. The commercials will air in September and October.
Oct. 1	Acquired a copyright for $200,000. The copyright has a useful life of 50 years.

Instructions

(a) Prepare journal entries to record the transactions above.

(b) Prepare journal entries to record the 2013 amortization expense for intangible assets.

(c) Prepare the intangible assets section of the balance sheet at December 31, 2013.

(d) ◄══════ Prepare the note to the financials on Praphaphorn's intangibles as of December 31, 2013.

(b) Amortization Expense (patents) $15,000; Amortization Expense (copyrights) $7,000

(c) Total intangible assets, $349,000

Prepare entries to correct errors made in recording and amortizing intangible assets.

(SO 8)

P10-8B Due to rapid turnover in the accounting department, a number of transactions involving intangible assets were improperly recorded by Chansantor Company in 2012.

1. Chansantor developed a new manufacturing process, incurring research and development costs of $110,000. The company also purchased a patent for $50,000. In early January, Chansantor capitalized $160,000 as the cost of the patents. Patent amortization expense of $8,000 was recorded based on a 20-year useful life.

2. On July 1, 2012, Chansantor purchased a small company and as a result acquired goodwill of $200,000. Chansantor recorded a half-year's amortization in 2012, based on a 50-year life ($2,000 amortization). The goodwill has an indefinite life.

Instructions

Prepare all journal entries necessary to correct any errors made during 2012. Assume the books have not yet been closed for 2012.

R&D Exp. $110,000

P10-9B Liam Corporation and Aslan Corporation, two corporations of roughly the same size, are both involved in the manufacture of canoes and sea kayaks. Each company depreciates its plant assets using the straight-line approach. An investigation of their financial statements reveals the following information.

Calculate and comment on asset turnover ratio.
(SO 9)

	Liam Corp.	Aslan Corp.
Net income	$ 300,000	$ 325,000
Sales revenue	1,100,000	990,000
Average total assets	1,000,000	1,050,000
Average plant assets	750,000	770,000

Instructions

(a) For each company, calculate the asset turnover ratio.
(b) ⬛━━▶ Based on your calculations in part (a), comment on the relative effectiveness of the two companies in using their assets to generate sales and produce net income.

Problems: Set C

Visit the book's companion website, at **www.wiley.com/college/weygandt**, and choose the Student Companion site to access Problem Set C.

Comprehensive Problem: Chapters 3 to 10

CP10 Winterschid Company's trial balance at December 31, 2012, is presented below. All 2012 transactions have been recorded except for the items described on page 500.

	Debit	Credit
Cash	$ 28,000	
Accounts Receivable	36,800	
Notes Receivable	10,000	
Interest Receivable	–0–	
Inventory	36,200	
Prepaid Insurance	3,600	
Land	20,000	
Buildings	150,000	
Equipment	60,000	
Patents	9,000	
Allowance for Doubtful Accounts		$ 500
Accumulated Depreciation—Buildings		50,000
Accumulated Depreciation—Equipment		24,000
Accounts Payable		27,300
Salaries and Wages Payable		–0–
Unearned Rent Revenue		6,000
Notes Payable (due in 2013)		11,000
Interest Payable		–0–
Notes Payable (due after 2013)		35,000
Owner's Capital		113,600
Owner's Drawings	12,000	

	Debit	Credit
Sales Revenue		900,000
Interest Revenue		–0–
Rent Revenue		–0–
Gain on Disposal of Plant Assets		–0–
Bad Debts Expense	–0–	
Cost of Goods Sold	630,000	
Depreciation Expense	–0–	
Insurance Expense	–0–	
Interest Expense	–0–	
Other Operating Expenses	61,800	
Amortization Expense	–0–	
Salaries and Wages Expense	110,000	
Total	$1,167,400	$1,167,400

Unrecorded transactions:

1. On May 1, 2012, Winterschid purchased equipment for $13,200 plus sales taxes of $600 (all paid in cash).
2. On July 1, 2012, Winterschid sold for $3,500 equipment which originally cost $5,000. Accumulated depreciation on this equipment at January 1, 2012, was $1,800; 2012 depreciation prior to the sale of the equipment was $450.
3. On December 31, 2012, Winterschid sold for $9,000 on account inventory that cost $6,300.
4. Winterschid estimates that uncollectible accounts receivable at year-end is $4,000.
5. The note receivable is a one-year, 8% note dated April 1, 2012. No interest has been recorded.
6. The balance in prepaid insurance represents payment of a $3,600 6-month premium on September 1, 2012.
7. The building is being depreciated using the straight-line method over 30 years. The salvage value is $30,000.
8. The equipment owned prior to this year is being depreciated using the straight-line method over 5 years. The salvage value is 10% of cost.
9. The equipment purchased on May 1, 2012, is being depreciated using the straight-line method over 5 years, with a salvage value of $1,800.
10. The patent was acquired on January 1, 2012, and has a useful life of 10 years from that date.
11. Unpaid salaries and wages at December 31, 2012, total $2,200.
12. The unearned rent revenue of $6,000 was received on December 1, 2012, for 3 months rent.
13. Both the short-term and long-term notes payable are dated January 1, 2012, and carry a 9% interest rate. All interest is payable in the next 12 months.

Instructions

(a) Prepare journal entries for the transactions listed above.

(b) Totals $1,201,290   (b) Prepare an updated December 31, 2012, trial balance.

(c) Prepare a 2012 income statement and an owner's equity statement.

(d) Total assets $260,400   (d) Prepare a December 31, 2012, classified balance sheet.

Continuing Cookie Chronicle

(*Note:* This is a continuation of the Cookie Chronicle from Chapters 1 through 9.)

CCC10   Natalie is also thinking of buying a van that will be used only for business. Natalie is concerned about the impact of the van's cost on her income statement and balance sheet. She has come to you for advice on calculating the van's depreciation.

Go to the book's companion website, **www.wiley.com/college/weygandt**, *to see the completion of this problem.*

BROADENINGYOURPERSPECTIVE

Financial Reporting and Analysis

Financial Reporting Problem: PepsiCo, Inc.

BYP10-1   The financial statements and the Notes to Consolidated Financial Statements of PepsiCo, Inc. are presented in Appendix A.

Instructions
Refer to PepsiCo's financial statements and answer the following questions.

(a) What was the total cost and book value of property, plant, and equipment at December 26, 2009?
(b) What method or methods of depreciation are used by the company for financial reporting purposes?
(c) What was the amount of depreciation and amortization expense for each of the three years 2007–2009?
(d) Using the statement of cash flows, what is the amount of capital spending in 2009 and 2008?
(e) Where does the company disclose its intangible assets, and what types of intangibles did it have at December 26, 2009?

Comparative Analysis Problem: PepsiCo, Inc. vs. The Coca-Cola Company

BYP10-2   PepsiCo's financial statements are presented in Appendix A. Financial statements of The Coca-Cola Company are presented in Appendix B.

Instructions
(a) Compute the asset turnover ratio for each company for 2009.
(b) What conclusions concerning the efficiency of assets can be drawn from these data?

On the Web

BYP10-3   A company's annual report identifies the amount of its plant assets and the depreciation method used.

Address: www.reportgallery.com, or go to **www.wiley.com/college/weygandt**

Steps
1. From Report Gallery Homepage, choose **Search by Alphabet**, and pick a letter.
2. Select a particular company.
3. Choose the most recent **Annual Report**.
4. Follow instructions below.

Instructions
(a) What is the name of the company?
(b) At fiscal year-end, what is the net amount of its plant assets?
(c) What is the accumulated depreciation?
(d) Which method of depreciation does the company use?

Critical Thinking

Decision Making Across the Organization

BYP10-4   Reimer Company and Lingo Company are two proprietorships that are similar in many respects. One difference is that Reimer Company uses the straight-line method and Lingo Company uses the declining-balance method at double the straight-line rate. On January 2, 2010, both companies acquired the depreciable assets shown on page 502.

Asset	Cost	Salvage Value	Useful Life
Buildings	$320,000	$20,000	40 years
Equipment	110,000	10,000	10 years

Including the appropriate depreciation charges, annual net income for the companies in the years 2010, 2011, and 2012 and total income for the 3 years were as follows.

	2010	2011	2012	Total
Reimer Company	$84,000	$88,400	$90,000	$262,400
Lingo Company	68,000	76,000	85,000	229,000

At December 31, 2012, the balance sheets of the two companies are similar except that Lingo Company has more cash than Reimer Company.

Sally Vogts is interested in buying one of the companies. She comes to you for advice.

Instructions

With the class divided into groups, answer the following.

(a) Determine the annual and total depreciation recorded by each company during the 3 years.

(b) Assuming that Lingo Company also uses the straight-line method of depreciation instead of the declining-balance method as in (a), prepare comparative income data for the 3 years.

(c) Which company should Sally Vogts buy? Why?

Communication Activity

BYP10-5 The following was published with the financial statements to American Exploration Company.

American Exploration Company
Notes to the Financial Statements

Property, Plant, and Equipment—The Company accounts for its oil and gas exploration and production activities using the successful efforts method of accounting. Under this method, acquisition costs for proved and unproved properties are capitalized when incurred.... The costs of drilling exploratory wells are capitalized pending determination of whether each well has discovered proved reserves. If proved reserves are not discovered, such drilling costs are charged to expense.... Depletion of the cost of producing oil and gas properties is computed on the units-of-activity method.

Instructions

Write a brief memo to your instructor discussing American Exploration Company's note regarding property, plant, and equipment. Your memo should address what is meant by the "successful efforts method" and "units-of-activity method."

Ethics Case

BYP10-6 Buster Container Company is suffering declining sales of its principal product, nonbiodegradable plastic cartons. The president, Dennis Harwood, instructs his controller, Shelly McGlone, to lengthen asset lives to reduce depreciation expense. A processing line of automated plastic extruding equipment, purchased for $3.1 million in January 2012, was originally estimated to have a useful life of 8 years and a salvage value of $300,000. Depreciation has been recorded for 2 years on that basis. Dennis wants the estimated life changed to 12 years total, and the straight-line method continued. Shelly is hesitant to make the change, believing it is unethical to increase net income in this manner. Dennis says, "Hey, the life is only an estimate, and I've heard that our competition uses a 12-year life on their production equipment."

Instructions

(a) Who are the stakeholders in this situation?

(b) Is the change in asset life unethical, or is it simply a good business practice by an astute president?

(c) What is the effect of Dennis Harwood's proposed change on income before taxes in the year of change?

"All About You" Activity

BYP10-7   Both the **All About You** feature (available at the book's companion website) and the Feature Story at the beginning of the chapter discussed the company Rent-A-Wreck. Note that the trade name Rent-A-Wreck is a very important asset to the company, as it creates immediate product identification. As indicated in the chapter, companies invest substantial sums to ensure that their product is well-known to the consumer. Test your knowledge of who owns some famous brands and their impact on the financial statements.

Instructions
(a) Provide an answer to the five multiple-choice questions below.
  (1) Which company owns both Taco Bell and Pizza Hut?
   (a) McDonald's.
   (b) CKE.
   (c) Yum Brands.
   (d) Wendy's.
  (2) Dairy Queen belongs to:
   (a) Breyer.
   (b) Berkshire Hathaway.
   (c) GE.
   (d) The Coca-Cola Company.
  (3) Phillip Morris, the cigarette maker, is owned by:
   (a) Altria.
   (b) GE.
   (c) Boeing.
   (d) ExxonMobil.
  (4) AOL, a major Internet provider, belongs to:
   (a) Microsoft.
   (b) Cisco.
   (c) NBC.
   (d) Time Warner.
  (5) ESPN, the sports broadcasting network, is owned by:
   (a) Procter & Gamble.
   (b) Altria.
   (c) Walt Disney.
   (d) The Coca-Cola Company.
(b) How do you think the value of these brands is reported on the appropriate company's balance sheet?

FASB Codification Activity

BYP10-8   If your school has a subscription to the FASB Codification, go to *http://aaahq.org/ascLogin.cfm* to log in and prepare responses to the following.
(a) What does it mean to capitalize an item?
(b) What is the definition provided for an intangible asset?
(c) Your great-uncle, who is a CPA, is impressed that you are taking an accounting class. Based on his experience, he believes that depreciation is something that companies do based on past practice, not on the basis of authoritative guidance. Provide the authoritative literature to support the practice of fixed-asset depreciation.

Answers to Insight and Accounting Across the Organization Questions
p. 461 Many U.S. Firms Use Leases   **Q:** Why might airline managers choose to lease rather than purchase their planes? **A:** The reasons for leasing include favorable tax treatment, better financing options, increased flexibility, reduced risk of obsolescence, and low airline income.
p. 478 Should Companies Write Up Goodwill?   **Q:** Do you think that this treatment would be allowed under U.S. GAAP? **A:** The write-down of assets would have been allowed if it could be shown that the assets had declined in value (an impairment). However, the creation of goodwill to offset the write-down would not have been allowed. Goodwill can be recorded only when it results from the acquisition of a business. It cannot be recorded as the result of being created internally.

Answers to Self-Test Questions
1. d ($24,000 + $1,200 + $200 + $400)   **2.** b   **3.** d [($400,000 − $10,000) ÷ 5] × 2   **4.** d   **5.** b $60,000 × 25% = $15,000; ($60,000 − $15,000) × 25% = $11,250   **6.** b   **7.** d [($60,000 − $12,000) ÷ 10] × 2 = $9,600; ($60,000 − $9,600 − $2,000) ÷ 4   **8.** d   **9.** a [($80,000 ÷ 10) × 4.5] = $36,000; ($80,000 − $36,000) − $26,000   **10.** c ($12 million ÷ 20 million) × 2 million   **11.** d   **12.** b   **13.** c   **14.** c $180,000 ÷ [($200,000 + $300,000) ÷ 2]   ***15.** a ($35,000 + $10,000)   ***16.** d

IFRS   A Look at IFRS

IFRS follows most of the same principles as GAAP in the accounting for property, plant, and equipment. There are, however, some significant differences in the implementation: IFRS allows the use of revaluation of property, plant, and equipment, and it also requires the use of component depreciation. In addition, there are some significant differences in the accounting for both intangible assets and impairments.

Key Points

- The definition for plant assets for both IFRS and GAAP is essentially the same.

- Both international standards and GAAP follow the cost principle when accounting for property, plant, and equipment at date of acquisition. Cost consists of all expenditures necessary to acquire the asset and make it ready for its intended use.

- Under both IFRS and GAAP, interest costs incurred during construction are capitalized. Recently, IFRS converged to GAAP requirements in this area.

- IFRS, like GAAP, capitalizes all direct costs in self-constructed assets such as raw materials and labor. IFRS does not address the capitalization of fixed overhead, although in practice these costs are generally capitalized.

- IFRS also views depreciation as an allocation of cost over an asset's useful life. IFRS permits the same depreciation methods (e.g., straight-line, accelerated, and units-of-activity) as GAAP. However, a major difference is that IFRS requires component depreciation. *Component depreciation* specifies that any significant parts of a depreciable asset that have different estimated useful lives should be separately depreciated. Component depreciation is allowed under GAAP but is seldom used.

    To illustrate, assume that Lexure Construction builds an office building for $4,000,000, not including the cost of the land. If the $4,000,000 is allocated over the 40-year useful life of the building, Lexure reports $100,000 of depreciation per year, assuming straight-line depreciation and no disposal value. However, assume that $320,000 of the cost of the building relates to personal property and $600,000 relates to land improvements. The personal property has a depreciable life of 5 years, and the land improvements have a depreciable life of 10 years. In accordance with IFRS, Lexure must use component depreciation. It must reclassify $320,000 of the cost of the building to personal property and $600,000 to the cost of land improvements. Assuming that Lexure uses straight-line depreciation, component depreciation for the first year of the office building is computed as follows.

Building cost adjusted ($4,000,000 − $320,000 − $600,000)	$3,080,000
Building cost depreciation per year ($3,080,000/40)	$ 77,000
Personal property depreciation ($320,000/5)	64,000
Land improvements depreciation ($600,000/10)	60,000
Total component depreciation in first year	$ 201,000

- IFRS uses the term *residual value*, rather than salvage value, to refer to an owner's estimate of an asset's value at the end of its useful life for that owner.

- IFRS allows companies to revalue plant assets to fair value at the reporting date. Companies that choose to use the revaluation framework must follow revaluation procedures. If revaluation is used, it must be applied to all assets in a class of assets. Assets that are experiencing rapid price changes must be revalued on an annual basis, otherwise less frequent revaluation is acceptable.

    To illustrate asset revaluation accounting, assume that Pernice Company applies revaluation to plant assets with a carrying value of $1,000,000, a useful life of 5 years, and no residual value. Pernice makes the following journal entries in year 1, assuming straight-line depreciation.

Depreciation Expense	200,000	
Accumulated Depreciation—Plant Assets		200,000
(To record depreciation expense in year 1)		

After this entry, Pernice's plant assets have a carrying amount of $800,000 ($1,000,000 − $200,000). At the end of year 1, independent appraisers determine that the asset has a fair value of $850,000. To report the plant assets at fair value, or $850,000, Pernice eliminates the Accumulated Depreciation—Plant Assets account, reduces Plant Assets to its fair value of $850,000, and records Revaluation Surplus of $50,000. The entry to record the revaluation is as follows.

Accumulated Depreciation—Plant Assets	200,000	
Plant Assets		150,000
Revaluation Surplus		50,000
(To record adjusting the plant assets to fair value)		

Thus, Pernice follows a two-step process. First, Pernice records depreciation based on the cost basis of $1,000,000. As a result, it reports depreciation expense of $200,000 on the income statement. Second, it records the revaluation. It does this by eliminating any accumulated depreciation, adjusting the recorded value of the plant assets to fair value, and debiting or crediting the Revaluation Surplus account. In this example, the revaluation surplus is $50,000, which is the difference between the fair value of $850,000 and the book value of $800,000. Revaluation surplus is an example of an item reported as other comprehensive income, as discussed in the *A Look at IFRS* section of Chapter 5. Pernice now reports the following information in its statement of financial position at the end of year 1.

Plant assets ($1,000,000 − $150,000)	$850,000
Accumulated depreciation—plant assets	0
	$850,000
Revaluation surplus (equity)	$ 50,000

As indicated, $850,000 is the new basis of the asset. Pernice reports depreciation expense of $200,000 in the income statement and $50,000 in other comprehensive income. Assuming no change in the total useful life, depreciation in year 2 will be $212,500 ($850,000 ÷ 4).

- Under both GAAP and IFRS, changes in the depreciation method used and changes in useful life are handled in current and future periods. Prior periods are not affected. GAAP recently conformed to international standards in the accounting for changes in depreciation methods.

- The accounting for subsequent expenditures, such as ordinary repairs and additions, are essentially the same under IFRS and GAAP.

- The accounting for plant asset disposals is essentially the same under IFRS and GAAP.

- Initial costs to acquire natural resources are essentially the same under IFRS and GAAP.

- The definition of intangible assets is essentially the same under IFRS and GAAP.

- As in GAAP, under IFRS the costs associated with research and development are segregated into the two components. Costs in the research phase are always expensed under both IFRS and GAAP. Under IFRS, however, costs in the development phase are capitalized as Development Costs once technological feasibility is achieved.

To illustrate, assume that Laser Scanner Company spent $1 million on research and $2 million on development of new products. Of the $2 million in development costs, $500,000 was incurred prior to technological feasibility and $1,500,000 was incurred after technological feasibility had been demonstrated. The company would record these costs as follows.

Research Expense	1,000,000	
Development Expense	500,000	
Development Costs	1,500,000	
Cash		3,000,000
(To record research and development costs)		

- IFRS permits revaluation of intangible assets (except for goodwill). GAAP prohibits revaluation of intangible assets.

- IFRS requires an impairment test at each reporting date for plant assets and intangibles and records an impairment if the asset's carrying amount exceeds its recoverable amount. The recoverable amount is the higher of the asset's fair value less costs to sell or its value-in-use. Value-in-use is the future cash flows to be derived from the particular asset, discounted to present value. Under GAAP, impairment loss is measured as the excess of the carrying amount over the asset's fair value.

- IFRS allows reversal of impairment losses when there has been a change in economic conditions or in the expected use of the asset. Under GAAP, impairment losses cannot be reversed for assets to be held and used; the impairment loss results in a new cost basis for the asset. IFRS and GAAP are similar in the accounting for impairments of assets held for disposal.

- The accounting for exchanges of nonmonetary assets has recently converged between IFRS and GAAP. GAAP now requires that gains on exchanges of nonmonetary assets be recognized if the exchange has commercial substance. This is the same framework used in IFRS.

Looking to the Future

With respect to revaluations, as part of the conceptual framework project, the Boards will examine the measurement bases used in accounting. It is too early to say whether a converged conceptual framework will recommend fair value measurement (and revaluation accounting) for plant assets and intangibles. However, this is likely to be one of the more contentious issues, given the long-standing use of historical cost as a measurement basis in GAAP.

The IASB and FASB have identified a project that would consider expanded recognition of internally generated intangible assets. IFRS permits more recognition of intangibles compared to GAAP. Thus, it will be challenging to develop converged standards for intangible assets, given the long-standing prohibition on capitalizing internally generated intangible assets and research and development costs in GAAP.

IFRS Self-Test Questions

1. Which of the following statements is *correct*?
   (a) Both IFRS and GAAP permit revaluation of property, plant, and equipment and intangible assets (except for goodwill).
   (b) IFRS permits revaluation of property, plant, and equipment and intangible assets (except for goodwill).
   (c) Both IFRS and GAAP permit revaluation of property, plant, and equipment but not intangible assets.
   (d) GAAP permits revaluation of property, plant, and equipment but not intangible assets.

2. International Company has land that cost $450,000 but now has a fair value of $600,000. International Company decides to use the revaluation method specified in IFRS to account for the land. Which of the following statements is *correct*?
   (a) International Company must continue to report the land at $450,000.
   (b) International Company would report a net income increase of $150,000 due to an increase in the value of the land.
   (c) International Company would debit Revaluation Surplus for $150,000.
   (d) International Company would credit Revaluation Surplus by $150,000.

3. Francisco Corporation is constructing a new building at a total initial cost of $10,000,000. The building is expected to have a useful live of 50 years with no residual value. The building's finished surfaces (e.g., roof cover and floor cover) are 5% of this cost and have a useful life of 20 years. Building services systems (e.g., electric, heating, and plumbing) are 20% of the cost and have a useful life of 25 years. The depreciation in the first year using component depreciation, assuming straight-line depreciation with no residual value, is:
   (a) $200,000.   (c) $255,000.
   (b) $215,000.   (d) None of the above.

4. Research and development costs are:
- **(a)** expensed under GAAP.
- **(b)** expensed under IFRS.
- **(c)** expensed under both GAAP and IFRS.
- **(d)** None of the above.

5. Under IFRS, value-in-use is defined as:
- **(a)** net realizable value.
- **(b)** fair value.
- **(c)** future cash flows discounted to present value.
- **(d)** total future undiscounted cash flows.

IFRS Concepts and Application

IFRS10-1   What is component depreciation, and when must it be used?

IFRS10-2   What is revaluation of plant assets? When should revaluation be applied?

IFRS10-3   Some product development expenditures are recorded as development expenses and others as development costs. Explain the difference between these accounts and how a company decides which classification is appropriate.

IFRS10-4   Mandall Company constructed a warehouse for $280,000. Mandall estimates that the warehouse has a useful life of 20 years and no residual value. Construction records indicate that $40,000 of the cost of the warehouse relates to its heating, ventilation, and air conditioning (HVAC) system, which has an estimated useful life of only 10 years. Compute the first year of depreciation expense using straight-line component depreciation.

IFRS10-5   At the end of its first year of operations, Brianna Company chose to use the revaluation framework allowed under IFRS. Brianna's ledger shows Plant Assets $480,000 and Accumulated Depreciation—Plant Assets $60,000. Prepare journal entries to record the following.
(a) Independent appraisers determine that the plant assets have a fair value of $460,000.
(b) Independent appraisers determine that the plant assets have a fair value of $400,000.

IFRS10-6   Newell Industries spent $300,000 on research and $600,000 on development of a new product. Of the $600,000 in development costs, $400,000 was incurred prior to technological feasibility and $200,000 after technological feasibility had been demonstrated. Prepare the journal entry to record research and development costs.

International Financial Statement Analysis: *Zetar plc*

IFRS10-7   The financial statements of Zetar plc are presented in Appendix C.

Instructions
Use the company's annual report, available at *www.zetarplc.com*, to answer the following questions.

(a) According to the notes to the financial statements, what method or methods does the company use to depreciate "plant and equipment?" What rate does it use to depreciate plant and equipment?

(b) According to the notes to the financial statements, how often is goodwill tested for impairment?

(c) Using the notes to the financial statements, as well as information from the statement of cash flows, prepare the journal entry to record the disposal of property, plant, and equipment during 2009. (Round your amounts to the nearest thousand.)

Answers to IFRS Self-Test Questions
1. b   **2.** d   **3.** c ($10,000,000 × .05/20) + ($10,000,000 × .20/25) + ($10,000,000 × .75/50)   **4.** a   **5.** c

The Navigator

✔   **Remember to go back to the Navigator box on the chapter opening page and check off your completed work.**

CHAPTER11

Current Liabilities and Payroll Accounting

Study Objectives

After studying this chapter, you should be able to:

[1] Explain a current liability, and identify the major types of current liabilities.

[2] Describe the accounting for notes payable.

[3] Explain the accounting for other current liabilities.

[4] Explain the financial statement presentation and analysis of current liabilities.

[5] Describe the accounting and disclosure requirements for contingent liabilities.

[6] Compute and record the payroll for a pay period.

[7] Describe and record employer payroll taxes.

[8] Discuss the objectives of internal control for payroll.

✔ **The Navigator**

✔ The Navigator

Feature Story

FINANCING HIS DREAMS

What would you do if you had a great idea for a new product, but couldn't come up with the cash to get the business off the ground? Small businesses often cannot attract investors. Nor can they obtain traditional debt financing through bank loans or bond issuances. Instead, they often resort to unusual, and costly, forms of nontraditional financing.

Such was the case for Wilbert Murdock. Murdock grew up in a New York housing project, and always had great ambitions. This ambitious spirit led him into some business ventures that failed: a medical diagnostic tool, a device to eliminate carpal-tunnel syndrome, custom-designed sneakers, and a device to keep people from falling asleep while driving.

Another idea was computerized golf clubs that analyze a golfer's swing and provide immediate feedback. Murdock saw great potential in the idea: Many golfers are willing to shell out considerable sums of money for devices that might improve their game. But Murdock had no cash to develop his product, and banks and other lenders had shied away. Rather than give up, Murdock resorted to credit cards—in a big way. He quickly owed $25,000 to credit card companies.

While funding a business with credit cards might sound unusual, it isn't. A recent study found that one-third of businesses with fewer than 20 employees financed at least part of their operations with credit cards. As Murdock explained, credit cards are an appealing way to finance a start-up because "credit-card companies don't care how the money is spent." However, they do care how they are paid. And so Murdock faced high interest charges and a barrage of credit card collection letters.

Murdock's debt forced him to sacrifice nearly everything in order to keep his business afloat. His car stopped running, he barely had enough money to buy food, and he lived and worked out of a dimly lit apartment in his mother's basement. Through it all he tried to maintain a positive spirit, joking that, if he becomes successful, he might some day get to appear in an American Express commercial.

Source: Rodney Ho, "Banking on Plastic: To Finance a Dream, Many Entrepreneurs Binge on Credit Cards," *Wall Street Journal* (March 9, 1998), p. A1.

The Navigator

Inside CHAPTER 11

PreviewofCHAPTER11

Inventor-entrepreneur Wilbert Murdock, as you can tell from the Feature Story, had to use multiple credit cards to finance his business ventures. Murdock's credit card debts would be classified as *current liabilities* because they are due every month. Yet by making minimal payments and paying high interest each month, Murdock used this credit source long-term. Some credit card balances remain outstanding for years as they accumulate interest.

Earlier, we defined liabilities as creditors' claims on total assets and as existing debts and obligations. These claims, debts, and obligations must be settled or paid at some time **in the future** by the transfer of assets or services. The future date on which they are due or payable (maturity date) is a significant feature of liabilities. This "future date" feature gives rise to two basic classifications of liabilities: (1) current liabilities and (2) long-term liabilities. We will explain current liabilities, along with payroll accounting, in this chapter. We will explain long-term liabilities in Chapter 15.

The content and organization of Chapter 11 are as follows.

Current Liabilities and Payroll Accounting		
Accounting for Current Liabilities	**Contingent Liabilities**	**Payroll Accounting**
• Notes payable • Sales taxes payable • Unearned revenues • Current maturities of long-term debt • Statement presentation and analysis	• Recording • Disclosure	• Determining payroll • Recording payroll • Employer payroll taxes • Filing and remitting payroll taxes • Internal control for payroll

The Navigator

Accounting for Current Liabilities

Study Objective [1]
Explain a current liability, and identify the major types of current liabilities.

As explained in Chapter 4, a **current liability** is a debt with two key features: (1) The company reasonably expects to pay the debt from existing current assets or through the creation of other current liabilities. (2) The company will pay the debt within one year or the operating cycle, whichever is longer. Debts that do not meet **both criteria** are classified as long-term liabilities.

Companies must carefully monitor the relationship of current liabilities to current assets. This relationship is critical in evaluating a company's short-term debt-paying ability. A company that has more current liabilities than current assets may not be able to meet its current obligations when they become due.

Current liabilities include notes payable, accounts payable, and unearned revenues. They also include accrued liabilities such as taxes, salaries and wages, and interest payable. In the sections that follow, we discuss a few of the common types of current liabilities.

Notes Payable

Study Objective [2]
Describe the accounting for notes payable.

Companies record obligations in the form of written notes as notes payable. Notes payable are often used instead of accounts payable because they give the lender formal proof of the obligation in case legal remedies are needed to collect the debt. Companies frequently issue notes payable to meet short-term financing needs. Notes payable usually require the borrower to pay interest.

Notes are issued for varying periods of time. **Those due for payment within one year of the balance sheet date are usually classified as current liabilities.**

To illustrate the accounting for notes payable, assume that First National Bank agrees to lend $100,000 on September 1, 2012, if Cole Williams Co. signs a $100,000, 12%, four-month note maturing on January 1. When a company issues an interest-bearing note, the amount of assets it receives upon issuance of the note generally equals the note's face value. Cole Williams Co. therefore will receive $100,000 cash and will make the following journal entry.

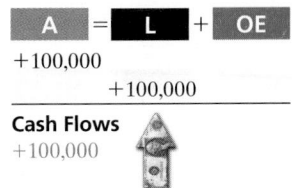

Sept. 1	Cash	100,000	
	Notes Payable		100,000
	(To record issuance of 12%, 4-month note		
	to First National Bank)		

A = L + OE
+100,000
        +100,000
Cash Flows
+100,000

Interest accrues over the life of the note, and the company must periodically record that accrual. If Cole Williams Co. prepares financial statements annually, it makes an adjusting entry at December 31 to recognize interest expense and interest payable of $4,000 ($100,000 × 12% × 4/12). Illustration 11-1 shows the formula for computing interest, and its application to Cole Williams Co.'s note.

Face Value of Note	×	Annual Interest Rate	×	Time in Terms of One Year	=	Interest
$100,000	×	12%	×	4/12	=	**$4,000**

Illustration 11-1
Formula for computing interest

Cole Williams makes an adjusting entry as follows:

Dec. 31	Interest Expense	4,000	
	Interest Payable		4,000
	(To accrue interest for 4 months on		
	First National Bank note)		

A = L + OE
           −4,000 Exp
    +4,000
Cash Flows
no effect

In the December 31 financial statements, the current liabilities section of the balance sheet will show notes payable $100,000 and interest payable $4,000. In addition, the company will report interest expense of $4,000 under "Other expenses and losses" in the income statement. If Cole Williams Co. prepared financial statements monthly, the adjusting entry at the end of each month would have been $1,000 ($100,000 × 12% × 1/12).

At maturity (January 1, 2013), Cole Williams Co. must pay the face value of the note ($100,000) plus $4,000 interest ($100,000 × 12% × 4/12). It records payment of the note and accrued interest as follows.

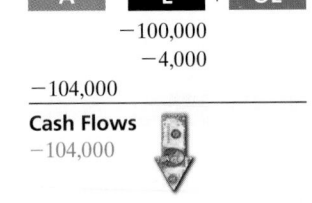

Jan. 1	Notes Payable	100,000	
	Interest Payable	4,000	
	Cash		104,000
	(To record payment of First National Bank		
	interest-bearing note and accrued interest		
	at maturity)		

A = L + OE
        −100,000
        −4,000
−104,000
Cash Flows
−104,000

Sales Taxes Payable

As a consumer, you know that many of the products you purchase at retail stores are subject to sales taxes. Many states also are now collecting sales taxes on purchases made on the Internet as well. Sales taxes are expressed as a percentage of the sales price. The selling company collects the tax from the customer when the

Study Objective [3]
Explain the accounting for other current liabilities.

sale occurs. Periodically (usually monthly), the retailer remits the collections to the state's department of revenue.

Under most state sales tax laws, the selling company must ring up separately on the cash register the amount of the sale and the amount of the sales tax collected. (Gasoline sales are a major exception.) The company then uses the cash register readings to credit Sales Revenue and Sales Taxes Payable. For example, if the March 25 cash register reading for Cooley Grocery shows sales of $10,000 and sales taxes of $600 (sales tax rate of 6%), the journal entry is:

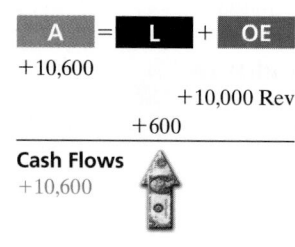

Mar. 25	Cash	10,600	
	Sales Revenue		10,000
	Sales Taxes Payable		600
	(To record daily sales and sales taxes)		

When the company remits the taxes to the taxing agency, it debits Sales Taxes Payable and credits Cash. The company does not report sales taxes as an expense. It simply forwards to the government the amount paid by the customers. Thus, Cooley Grocery serves only as a **collection agent** for the taxing authority.

Sometimes, companies do not ring up sales taxes separately on the cash register. To determine the amount of sales in such cases, divide total receipts by 100% plus the sales tax percentage. To illustrate, assume that in the above example Cooley Grocery rings up total receipts of $10,600. The receipts from the sales are equal to the sales price (100%) plus the tax percentage (6% of sales), or 1.06 times the sales total. We can compute the sales amount as follows.

$$\$10,600 \div 1.06 = \$10,000$$

Helpful Hint

Alternatively, Cooley could find the tax by multiplying sales by the sales tax rate ($10,000 × .06).

Thus, Cooley Grocery could find the sales tax amount it must remit to the state ($600) by subtracting sales from total receipts ($10,600 − $10,000).

Unearned Revenues

A magazine publisher, such as Sports Illustrated, receives customers' checks when they order magazines. An airline company, such as American Airlines, often receives cash when it sells tickets for future flights. Season tickets for concerts, sporting events, and theater programs are also paid for in advance. How do companies account for unearned revenues that are received before goods are delivered or services are provided?

1. When a company receives the advance payment, it debits Cash, and credits a current liability account identifying the source of the unearned revenue.

2. When the company earns the revenue, it debits an unearned revenue account, and credits an earned revenue account.

To illustrate, assume that Superior University sells 10,000 season football tickets at $50 each for its five-game home schedule. The university makes the following entry for the sale of season tickets.

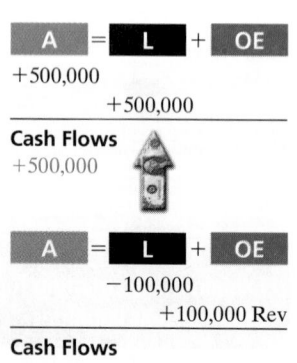

Aug. 6	Cash	500,000	
	Unearned Ticket Revenue		500,000
	(To record sale of 10,000 season tickets)		

As each game is completed, Superior records the earning of revenue with the following entry.

Sept. 7	Unearned Ticket Revenue	100,000	
	Ticket Revenue		100,000
	(To record football ticket revenue earned)		

The account Unearned Ticket Revenue represents unearned revenue, and Superior reports it as a current liability. As the school earns the revenue, it reclassifies the amount from unearned revenue to earned revenue. Unearned revenue is material for some companies. In the airline industry, for example, tickets sold for future flights represent almost 50% of total current liabilities. At United Air Lines, unearned ticket revenue was its largest current liability, recently amounting to over $1 billion.

Illustration 11-2 shows specific unearned and earned revenue accounts used in selected types of businesses.

Illustration 11-2
Unearned and earned revenue accounts

Type of Business	Account Title	
	Unearned Revenue	**Earned Revenue**
Airline	Unearned Ticket Revenue	Ticket Revenue
Magazine publisher	Unearned Subscription Revenue	Subscription Revenue
Hotel	Unearned Rent Revenue	Rent Revenue

Current Maturities of Long-Term Debt

Companies often have a portion of long-term debt that comes due in the current year. That amount is considered a current liability. As an example, assume that Wendy Construction issues a five-year interest-bearing $25,000 note on January 1, 2011. This note specifies that each January 1, starting January 1, 2012, Wendy should pay $5,000 of the note. When the company prepares financial statements on December 31, 2011, it should report $5,000 as a current liability and $20,000 as a long-term liability. (The $5,000 amount is the portion of the note that is due to be paid within the next 12 months.) Companies often identify current maturities of long-term debt on the balance sheet as **long-term debt due within one year**.

It is not necessary to prepare an adjusting entry to recognize the current maturity of long-term debt. At the balance sheet date, all obligations due within one year are classified as current, and all other obligations as long-term.

Do it!

You and several classmates are studying for the next accounting examination. They ask you to answer the following questions.

1. If cash is borrowed on a $50,000, 6-month, 12% note on September 1, how much interest expense would be incurred by December 31?
2. How is the sales tax amount determined when the cash register total includes sales taxes?
3. If $15,000 is collected in advance on November 1 for 3-months' rent, what amount of rent revenue is earned by December 31?

Solution

1. $50,000 × 12% × 4/12 = $2,000
2. First, divide the total cash register receipts by 100% plus the sales tax percentage to find the sales amount. Second, subtract the sales amount from the total cash register receipts to determine the sales taxes.
3. $15,000 × 2/3 = $10,000

Current Liabilities

action plan

✔ Use the interest formula: Face value of note × Annual interest rate × Time in terms of one year.

✔ Divide total receipts by 100% plus the tax rate to determine sales; then subtract sales from the total receipts.

✔ Determine what fraction of the total unearned rent was earned this year.

Related exercise material: BE11-2, BE11-3, BE11-4, E11-1, E11-2, E11-3, E11-4, and **Do it!** 11-1.

✔
The Navigator

Study Objective [4]

Explain the financial statement presentation and analysis of current liabilities.

Statement Presentation and Analysis

PRESENTATION

As indicated in Chapter 4, current liabilities are the first category under liabilities on the balance sheet. Each of the principal types of current liabilities is listed separately. In addition, companies disclose the terms of notes payable and other key information about the individual items in the notes to the financial statements.

Companies seldom list current liabilities in the order of liquidity. The reason is that varying maturity dates may exist for specific obligations such as notes payable. A more common method of presenting current liabilities is to list them by **order of magnitude**, with the largest ones first. Or, as a matter of custom, many companies show notes payable first, and then accounts payable, regardless of amount. Then the remaining current liabilities are listed by magnitude. (*Use this approach in your homework.*) The following adapted excerpt from the balance sheet of Caterpillar Inc. illustrates its order of presentation.

Illustration 11-3
Balance sheet presentation of current liabilities

Caterpillar Inc. Balance Sheet December 31, 2009 (in millions)	
Assets	
Current assets	$26,789
Property, plant and equipment (net)	12,386
Other long-term assets	20,863
Total assets	$60,038
Liabilities and Stockholders' Equity	
Current liabilities	
Short-term borrowings (notes payable)	$ 4,083
Accounts payable	2,993
Accrued expenses	3,351
Accrued wages, salaries, and employee benefits	797
Customer advances	1,217
Dividends payable	262
Other current liabilities	888
Long-term debt due within one year	5,701
Total current liabilities	19,292
Noncurrent liabilities	31,446
Total liabilities	50,738
Stockholders' equity	9,300
Total liabilities and stockholders' equity	$60,038

Helpful Hint

For other examples of current liabilities sections, refer to the PepsiCo and Coca-Cola balance sheets in Appendixes A and B.

ANALYSIS

Use of current and noncurrent classifications makes it possible to analyze a company's liquidity. **Liquidity** refers to the ability to pay maturing obligations and meet unexpected needs for cash. The relationship of current assets to current liabilities is critical in analyzing liquidity. We can express this relationship as a dollar amount (working capital) and as a ratio (the current ratio).

The excess of current assets over current liabilities is **working capital**. Illustration 11-4 shows the formula for the computation of Caterpillar's working capital (dollar amounts in millions).

Current Assets	−	Current Liabilities	=	Working Capital
$26,789	−	$19,292	=	$7,497

Illustration 11-4
Working capital formula and computation

As an absolute dollar amount, working capital offers limited informational value. For example, $1 million of working capital may be far more than needed for a small company but be inadequate for a large corporation. Also, $1 million of working capital may be adequate for a company at one time but inadequate at another time.

The **current ratio** permits us to compare the liquidity of different-sized companies and of a single company at different times. The current ratio is calculated as current assets divided by current liabilities. The formula for this ratio is illustrated below, along with its computation using Caterpillar's current asset and current liability data (dollar amounts in millions).

Current Assets	÷	Current Liabilities	=	Current Ratio
$26,789	÷	$19,292	=	1.39:1

Illustration 11-5
Current ratio formula and computation

Historically, companies and analysts considered a current ratio of 2:1 to be the standard for a good credit rating. In recent years, however, many healthy companies have maintained ratios well below 2:1 by improving management of their current assets and liabilities. Caterpillar's ratio of 1.39:1 is adequate but certainly below the standard of 2:1.

Contingent Liabilities

With notes payable, interest payable, accounts payable, and sales taxes payable, we know that an obligation to make a payment exists. But suppose that your company is involved in a dispute with the Internal Revenue Service (IRS) over the amount of its income tax liability. Should you report the disputed amount as a liability on the balance sheet? Or suppose your company is involved in a lawsuit which, if you lose, might result in bankruptcy. How should you report this major contingency? The answers to these questions are difficult, because these liabilities are dependent—contingent—upon some future event. In other words, a **contingent liability** is a potential liability that may become an actual liability in the future.

How should companies report contingent liabilities? They use the following guidelines:

Study Objective [5]
Describe the accounting and disclosure requirements for contingent liabilities.

1. If the contingency is **probable** (if it is *likely* to occur) **and** the amount can be **reasonably estimated**, the liability should be recorded in the accounts.

2. If the contingency is only **reasonably possible** (if it *could* happen), then it needs to be disclosed only in the notes that accompany the financial statements.

3. If the contingency is **remote** (if it is *unlikely* to occur), it need not be recorded or disclosed.

Accounting Across the Organization

Contingencies: How Big Are They?

Contingent liabilities abound in the real world. Consider the following: Manville Corp. filed for bankruptcy when it was hit by billions of dollars in asbestos product-liability claims. Companies having multiple toxic waste sites are faced with cleanup costs that average $10 to $30 million and can reach as high as $500 million depending on the type of waste. For life and health insurance companies and their stockholders, the cost of diseases such as diabetes, Alzheimer's, and AIDS is like an iceberg: Everyone wonders how big such costs really are and what damage they might do in the future. And frequent-flyer programs are so popular that airlines at one time owed participants more than 3 million round-trip domestic tickets. That's enough to fly at least 5.4 billion miles—free for the passengers, but at what future cost to the airlines?

? Why do you think most companies disclose, but do not record, contingent liabilities? (See page 549.)

Recording a Contingent Liability

Product warranties are an example of a contingent liability that companies should record in the accounts. Warranty contracts result in future costs that companies may incur in replacing defective units or repairing malfunctioning units. Generally, a manufacturer, such as Stanley Black & Decker, knows that it will incur some warranty costs. From prior experience with the product, the company usually can reasonably estimate the anticipated cost of servicing (honoring) the warranty.

The accounting for warranty costs is based on the expense recognition principle. **The estimated cost of honoring product warranty contracts should be recognized as an expense in the period in which the sale occurs.** To illustrate, assume that in 2012 Denson Manufacturing Company sells 10,000 washers and dryers at an average price of $600 each. The selling price includes a one-year warranty on parts. Denson expects that 500 units (5%) will be defective and that warranty repair costs will average $80 per unit. In 2012, the company honors warranty contracts on 300 units, at a total cost of $24,000.

At December 31, it is necessary to accrue the estimated warranty costs on the 2012 sales. Denson computes the estimated warranty liability as follows.

Illustration 11-6
Computation of estimated product warranty liability

Number of units sold	10,000
Estimated rate of defective units	× 5%
Total estimated defective units	500
Average warranty repair cost	× $80
Estimated product warranty liability	**$40,000**

The company makes the following adjusting entry.

A	=	L	+	OE
				−40,000 Exp
		+40,000		

Cash Flows
no effect

Dec. 31	Warranty Expense	40,000	
	Warranty Liability		40,000
	(To accrue estimated warranty costs)		

Denson records those repair costs incurred in 2012 to honor warranty contracts on 2012 sales as shown below.

Jan. 1– Dec. 31	Warranty Liability	24,000	
	Repair Parts		24,000
	(To record honoring of 300 warranty contracts on 2012 sales)		

A = L + OE
−24,000
−24,000
Cash Flows
no effect

The company reports warranty expense of $40,000 under selling expenses in the income statement. It classifies warranty liability of $16,000 ($40,000 − $24,000) as a current liability on the balance sheet.

In the following year, Denson should debit to Warranty Liability all expenses incurred in honoring warranty contracts on 2012 sales. To illustrate, assume that the company replaces 20 defective units in January 2013, at an average cost of $80 in parts and labor. The summary entry for the month of January 2013 is:

Jan. 31	Warranty Liability	1,600	
	Repair Parts		1,600
	(To record honoring of 20 warranty contracts on 2012 sales)		

A = L + OE
−1,600
−1,600
Cash Flows
no effect

Disclosure of Contingent Liabilities

When it is probable that a company will incur a contingent liability but it cannot reasonably estimate the amount, or when the contingent liability is only reasonably possible, only disclosure of the contingency is required. Examples of contingencies that may require disclosure are pending or threatened lawsuits and assessment of additional income taxes pending an IRS audit of the tax return.

The disclosure should identify the nature of the item and, if known, the amount of the contingency and the expected outcome of the future event. Disclosure is usually accomplished through a note to the financial statements, as illustrated by the following.

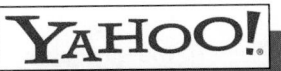

Yahoo! Inc.
Notes to the Financial Statements

Illustration 11-7
Disclosure of contingent liability

Contingencies. From time to time, third parties assert patent infringement claims against the company. Currently the company is engaged in several lawsuits regarding patent issues and has been notified of a number of other potential patent disputes. In addition, from time to time the company is subject to other legal proceedings and claims in the ordinary course of business, including claims for infringement of trademarks, copyrights and other intellectual property rights.... The Company does not believe, based on current knowledge, that any of the foregoing legal proceedings or claims are likely to have a material adverse effect on the financial position, results of operations or cash flows.

The required disclosure for contingencies is a good example of the use of the full-disclosure principle. The **full-disclosure principle** requires that companies disclose all circumstances and events that would make a difference to financial statement users. Some important financial information, such as contingencies, is not easily reported in the financial statements. Reporting information on contingencies in the notes to the financial statements will help investors be aware of events that can affect the financial health of a company.

Do it!

Current Liabilities

Lepid Company has the following account balances at December 31, 2012.

Notes payable ($80,000 due after 12/31/13)	$200,000
Unearned service revenue	75,000
Other long-term debt ($30,000 due in 2013)	150,000
Salaries and wages payable	22,000
Other accrued expenses	15,000
Accounts payable	100,000

In addition, Lepid is involved in a lawsuit. Legal counsel feels it is probable Lepid will pay damages of $38,000 in 2013.

(a) Prepare the current liability section of Lepid's December 31, 2012, balance sheet.

(b) Lepid's current assets are $504,000. Compute Lepid's working capital and current ratio.

action plan

✔ Determine which liabilities will be paid within one year or the operating cycle and include those as current liabilities.

✔ If the contingent liability is probable and reasonably estimable, include it as a current liability.

✔ Use the formula for working capital: Current assets − Current liabilities.

✔ Use the formula for the current ratio: Current assets ÷ Current liabilities.

Solution

(a) Current liabilities

Notes payable	$120,000
Accounts payable	100,000
Unearned service revenue	75,000
Lawsuit liability	38,000
Salaries and wages payable	22,000
Other accrued expenses	15,000
Long-term debt due within one year	30,000
Total current liabilities	$400,000

(b) Working capital = Current assets − Current liabilities = $504,000 − $400,000 = $104,000
Current ratio: Current assets ÷ Current liabilities = $504,000 ÷ $400,000 = 1.26:1

Related exercise material: **BE11-5, E11-7, E11-8, E11-9, and Do it! 11-2.**

✔
The Navigator

Payroll Accounting

Payroll and related fringe benefits often make up a large percentage of current liabilities. Employee compensation is often the most significant expense that a company incurs. For example, Costco recently reported total employees of 103,000 and labor and fringe benefits costs which approximated 70% of the company's total cost of operations.

Payroll accounting involves more than paying employees' wages. Companies are required by law to maintain payroll records for each employee, to file and pay payroll taxes, and to comply with state and federal tax laws related to employee compensation.

The term "payroll" **pertains to both salaries and wages of employees**. Managerial, administrative, and sales personnel are generally paid salaries. Salaries are often expressed in terms of a specified amount per month or per year rather than an hourly rate. Store clerks, factory employees, and manual laborers are normally paid wages.

Wages are based on a rate per hour or on a piecework basis (such as per unit of product). Frequently, people use the terms "salaries" and "wages" interchangeably.

The term "payroll" **does not apply to payments made for services of professionals** such as certified public accountants, attorneys, and architects. Such professionals are independent contractors rather than salaried employees. Payments to them are called fees. This distinction is important because government regulations relating to the payment and reporting of payroll taxes apply only to employees.

Determining the Payroll

Determining the payroll involves computing three amounts: (1) gross earnings, (2) payroll deductions, and (3) net pay.

Study Objective [6]
Compute and record the payroll for a pay period.

GROSS EARNINGS

Gross earnings is the total compensation earned by an employee. It consists of wages or salaries, plus any bonuses and commissions.

Companies determine total **wages** for an employee by multiplying the hours worked by the hourly rate of pay. In addition to the hourly pay rate, most companies are required by law to pay hourly workers a minimum of 1½ times the regular hourly rate for overtime work in excess of eight hours per day or 40 hours per week. In addition, many employers pay overtime rates for work done at night, on weekends, and on holidays.

For example, assume that Michael Jordan, an employee of Academy Company, worked 44 hours for the weekly pay period ending January 14. His regular wage is $12 per hour. For any hours in excess of 40, the company pays at one-and-a-half times the regular rate. Academy computes Jordan's gross earnings (total wages) as follows.

Type of Pay	Hours	×	Rate	=	Gross Earnings
Regular	40	×	$12	=	$480
Overtime	4	×	18	=	72
Total wages					$552

Illustration 11-8
Computation of total wages

This computation assumes that Jordan receives 1½ times his regular hourly rate ($12 × 1.5) for his overtime hours. Union contracts often require that overtime rates be as much as twice the regular rates.

An employee's **salary** is generally based on a monthly or yearly rate. The company then prorates these rates to its payroll periods (e.g., biweekly or monthly). Most executive and administrative positions are salaried. Federal law does not require overtime pay for employees in such positions.

Many companies have bonus agreements for employees. One survey found that over 94% of the largest U.S. manufacturing companies offer annual bonuses to key executives. Bonus arrangements may be based on such factors as increased sales or net income. Companies may pay bonuses in cash and/or by granting employees the opportunity to acquire shares of company stock at favorable prices (called stock option plans).

Ethics Note

Bonuses often reward outstanding individual performance, but successful corporations also need considerable teamwork. A challenge is to motivate individuals while preventing an unethical employee from taking another's idea for his or her own advantage.

PAYROLL DEDUCTIONS

As anyone who has received a paycheck knows, gross earnings are usually very different from the amount actually received. The difference is due to payroll deductions.

Payroll deductions may be mandatory or voluntary. **Mandatory deductions are required by law and consist of FICA taxes and income taxes.** Voluntary deductions are at the option of the employee. Illustration 11-9 (page 520) summarizes common

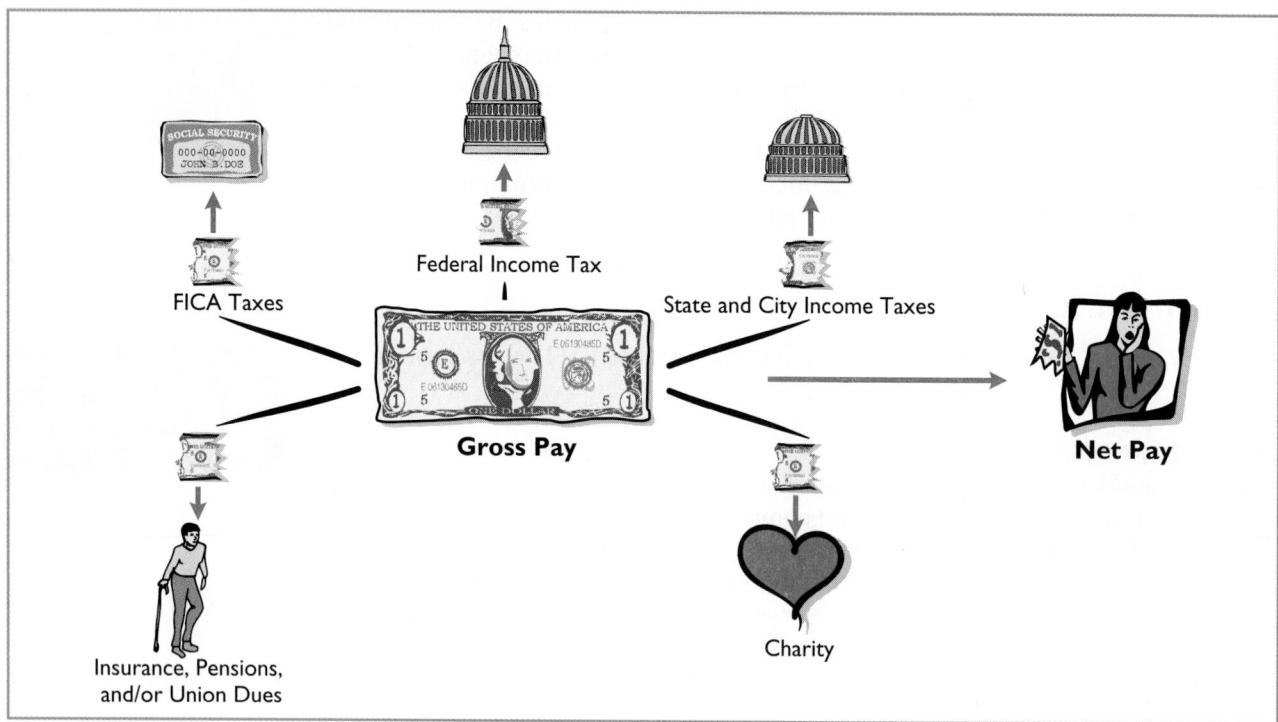

Illustration 11-9
Payroll deductions

types of payroll deductions. Such deductions do not result in payroll tax expense to the employer. The employer is merely a collection agent, and subsequently transfers the deducted amounts to the government and designated recipients.

FICA Taxes.   In 1937, Congress enacted the Federal Insurance Contribution Act (FICA). **FICA taxes are designed to provide workers with supplemental retirement, employment disability, and medical benefits.** In 1965, Congress extended benefits to include Medicare for individuals over 65 years of age. The benefits are financed by a tax levied on employees' earnings. FICA taxes are commonly referred to as **Social Security taxes**.

Congress sets the tax rate and the tax base for FICA taxes. When FICA taxes were first imposed, the rate was 1% on the first $3,000 of gross earnings, or a maximum of $30 per year. The rate and base have changed dramatically since that time! In 2010, the rate was 7.65% (6.2% Social Security plus 1.45% Medicare) on the first $106,800 of gross earnings for each employee.[1] For purpose of illustration in this chapter, we will assume a rate of 8% on the first $100,000 of gross earnings, or a maximum of $8,000. Using the 8% rate, the FICA withholding for Jordan for the weekly pay period ending January 14 is $44.16 ($552 × 8%).

Income Taxes.   Under the U.S. pay-as-you-go system of federal income taxes, employers are required to withhold income taxes from employees each pay period. Three variables determine the amount to be withheld: (1) the employee's gross earnings; (2) the number of allowances claimed by the employee; and (3) the length of the pay period. The number of allowances claimed typically includes the employee, his or her spouse, and other dependents.

---

[1]The Medicare provision also includes a tax of 1.45% on gross earnings in excess of $106,800. In the interest of simplification, we ignore this 1.45% charge in our end-of-chapter assignment material. We assume zero FICA withholdings on gross earnings above $100,000.

Withholding tables furnished by the Internal Revenue Service indicate the amount of income tax to be withheld. Withholding amounts are based on gross wages and the number of allowances claimed. Separate tables are provided for weekly, biweekly, semimonthly, and monthly pay periods. Illustration 11-10 shows the withholding tax table for Michael Jordan (assuming he earns $552 per week and claims two allowances). For a weekly salary of $552 with two allowances, the income tax to be withheld is $49.

Illustration 11-10
Withholding tax table

MARRIED Persons — **WEEKLY** Payroll Period
(For Wages Paid in 2010)

If the wages are —		And the number of withholding allowances claimed is —										
At least	But less than	0	1	2	3	4	5	6	7	8	9	10
		The amount of income tax to be withheld is —										
490	500	56	48	40	32	24	17	9	1	0	0	0
500	510	57	49	42	34	26	18	10	3	0	0	0
510	520	59	51	43	35	27	20	12	4	0	0	0
520	530	60	52	45	37	29	21	13	6	0	0	0
530	540	62	54	46	38	30	23	15	7	0	0	0
540	550	63	55	48	40	32	24	16	9	1	0	0
550	560	65	57	49	41	33	26	18	10	2	0	0
560	570	66	58	51	43	35	27	19	12	4	0	0
570	580	68	60	52	44	36	29	21	13	5	0	0
580	590	69	61	54	46	38	30	22	15	7	0	0
590	600	71	63	55	47	39	32	24	16	8	1	0
600	610	72	64	57	49	41	33	25	18	10	2	0
610	620	74	66	58	50	42	35	27	19	11	4	0
620	630	75	67	60	52	44	36	28	21	13	5	0
630	640	77	69	61	53	45	38	30	22	14	7	0
640	650	78	70	63	55	47	39	31	24	16	8	0
650	660	80	72	64	56	48	41	33	25	17	10	2
660	670	81	73	66	58	50	42	34	27	19	11	3
670	680	83	75	67	59	51	44	36	28	20	13	5
680	690	84	76	69	61	53	45	37	30	22	14	6

In addition, most states (and some cities) require **employers** to withhold income taxes from employees' earnings. As a rule, the amounts withheld are a percentage (specified in the state revenue code) of the amount withheld for the federal income tax. Or they may be a specified percentage of the employee's earnings. For the sake of simplicity, we have assumed that Jordan's wages are subject to state income taxes of 2%, or $11.04 (2% × $552) per week.

There is no limit on the amount of gross earnings subject to income tax withholdings. In fact, under our progressive system of taxation, the higher the earnings, the higher the percentage of income withheld for taxes.

Other Deductions.   Employees may voluntarily authorize withholdings for charitable organizations, retirement, and other purposes. All voluntary deductions from gross earnings should be authorized in writing by the employee. The authorization(s) may be made individually or as part of a group plan. Deductions for charitable organizations, such as the United Fund, or for financial arrangements, such as U.S. savings bonds and repayment of loans from company credit unions, are made individually. Deductions for union dues, health and life insurance, and pension plans are often made on a group basis. We will assume that Jordan has weekly voluntary deductions of $10 for the United Fund and $5 for union dues.

Alternative Terminology

Net pay is also called *take-home pay.*

NET PAY

Academy determines **net pay** by subtracting payroll deductions from gross earnings. Illustration 11-11 shows the computation of Jordan's net pay for the pay period.

Illustration 11-11
Computation of net pay

Gross earnings		$552.00
Payroll deductions:		
FICA taxes	$44.16	
Federal income taxes	49.00	
State income taxes	11.04	
United Fund	10.00	
Union dues	5.00	119.20
Net pay		**$432.80**

Assuming that Michael Jordan's wages for each week during the year are $552, total wages for the year are $28,704 (52 × $552). Thus, all of Jordan's wages are subject to FICA tax during the year. In comparison, let's assume that Jordan's department head earns $2,000 per week, or $104,000 for the year. Since we assume that only the first $100,000 is subject to FICA taxes, the maximum FICA withholdings on the department head's earnings would be $8,000 ($100,000 × 8%).

Recording the Payroll

Recording the payroll involves maintaining payroll department records, recognizing payroll expenses and liabilities, and recording payment of the payroll.

MAINTAINING PAYROLL DEPARTMENT RECORDS

To comply with state and federal laws, an employer must keep a cumulative record of each employee's gross earnings, deductions, and net pay during the year. The record that provides this information is the **employee earnings record**. Illustration 11-12 (page 523) shows Michael Jordan's employee earnings record.

Companies keep a separate earnings record for each employee, and update these records after each pay period. The employer uses the cumulative payroll data on the earnings record to: (1) determine when an employee has earned the maximum earnings subject to FICA taxes, (2) file state and federal payroll tax returns (as explained later), and (3) provide each employee with a statement of gross earnings and tax withholdings for the year. Illustration 11-16 on page 529 shows this statement.

In addition to employee earnings records, many companies find it useful to prepare a **payroll register**. This record accumulates the gross earnings, deductions, and net pay by employee for each pay period. Illustration 11-13 (page 523) presents Academy Company's payroll register. It provides the documentation for preparing a paycheck for each employee. For example, it shows the data for Michael Jordan in the wages section. In this example, Academy Company's total weekly payroll is $17,210, as shown in the gross earnings column (column E, row 24).

Note that this record is a listing of each employee's payroll data for the pay period. In some companies, a payroll register is a journal or book of original entry. Postings are made from it directly to ledger accounts. In other companies, the payroll register is a memorandum record that provides the data for a general journal entry and subsequent posting to the ledger accounts. At Academy Company, the latter procedure is followed.

Academy Company.xls

File   Edit   View   Insert   Format   Tools   Data   Window   Help

ACADEMY COMPANY
Employee Earnings Record
For the Year 2012

Name	Michael Jordan	Address	2345 Mifflin Ave.
Social Security Number	329-35-9547		Hampton, Michigan 48292
Date of Birth	December 24, 1964	Telephone	555-238-9051
Date Employed	September 1, 2005	Date Employment Ended	
Sex	Male	Exemptions	2
Single _____	Married x		

2012	Total	Gross Earnings				Deductions						Payment	
Period Ending	Hours	Regular	Overtime	Total	Cumulative	FICA	Fed. Inc. Tax	State Inc. Tax	United Fund	Union Dues	Total	Net Amount	Check No.
1/7	42	480.00	36.00	516.00	516.00	41.28	43.00	10.32	10.00	5.00	109.60	406.40	974
1/14	44	480.00	72.00	552.00	1,068.00	44.16	49.00	11.04	10.00	5.00	119.20	432.80	1028
1/21	43	480.00	54.00	534.00	1,602.00	42.72	46.00	10.68	10.00	5.00	114.40	419.60	1077
1/28	42	480.00	36.00	516.00	2,118.00	41.28	43.00	10.32	10.00	5.00	109.60	406.40	1133
Jan. Total		1,920.00	198.00	2,118.00		169.44	181.00	42.36	40.00	20.00	452.80	1,665.20	

Illustration 11-12

Employee earnings record

Illustration 11-13

Payroll register

Academy Company.xls

File   Edit   View   Insert   Format   Tools   Data   Window   Help

ACADEMY COMPANY
Payroll Register
For the Week Ending January 14, 2012

Employee	Total Hours	Earnings			Deductions						Paid		Account Debited
		Regular	Over-time	Gross	FICA	Federal Income Tax	State Income Tax	United Fund	Union Dues	Total	Net Pay	Check No.	Salaries and Wages Expense
Arnold, Patricia	40	580.00		580.00	46.40	61.00	11.60	15.00		134.00	446.00	998	580.00
Canton, Matthew	40	590.00		590.00	47.20	63.00	11.80	20.00		142.00	448.00	999	590.00
Mueller, William	40	530.00		530.00	42.40	54.00	10.60	11.00		118.00	412.00	1000	530.00
Bennett, Robin	42	480.00	36.00	516.00	41.28	43.00	10.32	18.00	5.00	117.60	398.40	1025	516.00
Jordan, Michael	44	480.00	72.00	552.00	44.16	49.00	11.04	10.00	5.00	119.20	432.80	1028	552.00
Milroy, Lee	43	480.00	54.00	534.00	42.72	46.00	10.68	10.00	5.00	114.40	419.60	1029	534.00
Total		16,200.00	1,010.00	17,210.00	1,376.80	3,490.00	344.20	421.50	115.00	5,747.50	11,462.50		17,210.00

RECOGNIZING PAYROLL EXPENSES AND LIABILITIES

From the payroll register in Illustration 11-13, Academy Company makes a journal entry to record the payroll. For the week ending January 14, the entry is:

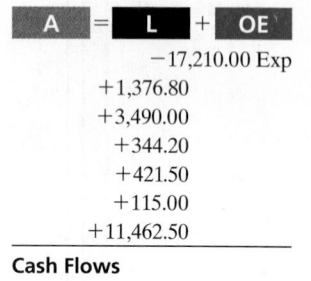

A = L + OE
−17,210.00 Exp
+1,376.80
+3,490.00
+344.20
+421.50
+115.00
+11,462.50

Cash Flows
no effect

Jan. 14	Salaries and Wages Expense	17,210.00	
	FICA Taxes Payable		1,376.80
	Federal Income Taxes Payable		3,490.00
	State Income Taxes Payable		344.20
	United Fund Payable		421.50
	Union Dues Payable		115.00
	Salaries and Wages Payable		11,462.50
	(To record payroll for the week ending January 14)		

The company credits specific liability accounts for the mandatory and voluntary deductions made during the pay period. In the example, Academy debits Salaries and Wages Expense for the gross earnings of its employees. The amount credited to Salaries and Wages Payable is the sum of the individual checks the employees will receive.

RECORDING PAYMENT OF THE PAYROLL

A company makes payments by check (or electronic funds transfer) either from its regular bank account or a payroll bank account. Each paycheck is usually accompanied by a detachable statement of earnings document. This shows the employee's gross earnings, payroll deductions, and net pay, both for the period and for the year-to-date. Academy Company uses its regular bank account for payroll checks. Illustration 11-14 shows the paycheck and statement of earnings for Michael Jordan.

Illustration 11-14
Paycheck and statement of earnings

Helpful Hint

Do any of the income tax liabilities result in payroll tax expense for the employer?

Answer: No. The employer is acting only as a collection agent for the government.

AC

ACADEMY COMPANY   No. 1028
19 Center St.
Hampton, MI 48291

January 14, 2012   62—1113 / 610

Pay to the order of   *Michael Jordan* $ 432.80

Four Hundred Thirty-two and 80/100   Dollars

City Bank & Trust
P.O. Box 3000
Hampton, MI 48291

For   *Payroll*   *Randall E. Barnes*

⑈003244??⑈ ⑈1028

- -

DETACH AND RETAIN THIS PORTION FOR YOUR RECORDS

NAME				SOC. SEC. NO.	EMPL. NUMBER	NO. EXEMP	PAY PERIOD ENDING
Michael Jordan				329-35-9547		2	1/14/12

REG. HRS.	O.T. HRS.	OTH. HRS. (1)	OTH. HRS. (2)	REG. EARNINGS	O.T. EARNINGS	OTH. EARNINGS (1)	OTH. EARNINGS (2)	GROSS
40	4			480.00	72.00			$552.00

FED. W/H TAX	FICA	STATE TAX	LOCAL TAX	OTHER DEDUCTIONS				NET PAY
49.00	44.16	11.04		(1) 10.00	(2) 5.00	(3)	(4)	432.80

YEAR TO DATE								
FED. W/H TAX	FICA	STATE TAX	LOCAL TAX	OTHER DEDUCTIONS				NET PAY
92.00	85.44	21.36		(1) 20.00	(2) 10.00	(3)	(4)	$839.20

Following payment of the payroll, the company enters the check numbers in the payroll register. Academy Company records payment of the payroll as follows.

Jan. 14	Salaries and Wages Payable	11,462.50	
	Cash		11,462.50
	(To record payment of payroll)		

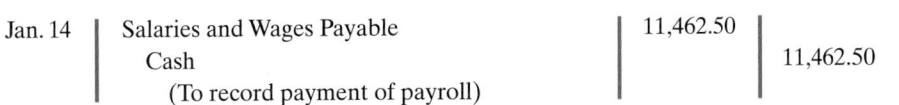

A = L + OE
−11,462.50
−11,462.50

Cash Flows
−11,462.50

Many medium- and large-size companies use a payroll processing center that provides payroll record-keeping services. Companies send the center payroll information about employee pay rates and hours worked. The center maintains the payroll records and prepares the payroll checks. In most cases, it costs less to process the payroll through the center than if the company did so internally.

Do it!

In January, gross earnings in Ramirez Company were $40,000. All earnings are subject to 8% FICA taxes. Federal income tax withheld was $9,000, and state income tax withheld was $1,000. (a) Calculate net pay for January, and (b) record the payroll.

Solution

(a) Net pay: $40,000 − (8% × $40,000) − $9,000 − $1,000 = $26,800

(b) Salaries and Wages Expense	40,000	
FICA Taxes Payable		3,200
Federal Income Taxes Payable		9,000
State Income Taxes Payable		1,000
Salaries and Wages Payable		26,800
(To record payroll)		

Related exercise material: BE11-7, BE11-8, E11-10, E11-11, E11-12, E11-13, and **Do it!** 11-3.

Payroll

action plan

✔ Determine net pay by subtracting payroll deductions from gross earnings.

✔ Record gross earnings as Salaries and Wages Expense, record payroll deductions as liabilities, and record net pay as Salaries and Wages Payable.

✔
The Navigator

Employer Payroll Taxes

Payroll tax expense for businesses results from three taxes that governmental agencies levy **on employers**. These taxes are: (1) FICA, (2) federal unemployment tax, and (3) state unemployment tax. These taxes plus such items as paid vacations and pensions (discussed in the appendix to this chapter) are collectively referred to as **fringe benefits**. As indicated earlier, the cost of fringe benefits in many companies is substantial. The pie chart in the margin shows the pieces of the benefits "pie."

FICA TAXES

Each employee must pay FICA taxes. In addition, employers must match each employee's FICA contribution. This means the employer must remit to the federal government 12.4% of each employee's first $106,800 of taxable earnings, plus 2.9% of each employee's earnings, regardless of amount. The matching contribution results in **payroll tax expense** to the employer. The employer's tax is subject to the same rate and maximum earnings as the employee's. The company uses the same account, FICA Taxes Payable, to record both the employee's and the employer's FICA contributions. For the January 14 payroll, Academy Company's FICA tax contribution is $1,376.80 ($17,210.00 × 8%).

Study Objective [7]
Describe and record employer payroll taxes.

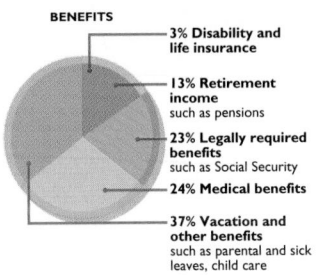

BENEFITS
- 3% Disability and life insurance
- 13% Retirement income such as pensions
- 23% Legally required benefits such as Social Security
- 24% Medical benefits
- 37% Vacation and other benefits such as parental and sick leaves, child care

FEDERAL UNEMPLOYMENT TAXES

Helpful Hint

Both the employer and employee pay FICA taxes. Federal unemployment taxes and (in most states) the state unemployment taxes are borne entirely by the employer.

The Federal Unemployment Tax Act (FUTA) is another feature of the federal Social Security program. **Federal unemployment taxes** provide benefits for a limited period of time to employees who lose their jobs through no fault of their own. The FUTA tax rate is 6.2% of taxable wages. The taxable wage base is the first $7,000 of wages paid to each employee in a calendar year. Employers who pay the state unemployment tax on a timely basis will receive an offset credit of up to 5.4%. Therefore, the net federal tax rate is generally 0.8% (6.2%–5.4%). This rate would equate to a maximum of $56 of federal tax per employee per year (0.8% × $7,000). State tax rates are based on state law.

The **employer** bears the entire federal unemployment tax. There is no deduction or withholding from employees. Companies use the account Federal Unemployment Taxes Payable to recognize this liability. The federal unemployment tax for Academy Company for the January 14 payroll is $137.68 ($17,210.00 × 0.8%).

STATE UNEMPLOYMENT TAXES

All states have unemployment compensation programs under state unemployment tax acts (SUTA). Like federal unemployment taxes, **state unemployment taxes** provide benefits to employees who lose their jobs. These taxes are levied on employers.[2] The basic rate is usually 5.4% on the first $7,000 of wages paid to an employee during the year. The state adjusts the basic rate according to the employer's experience rating: Companies with a history of stable employment may pay less than 5.4%. Companies with a history of unstable employment may pay more than the basic rate. Regardless of the rate paid, the company's credit on the federal unemployment tax is still 5.4%.

Companies use the account State Unemployment Taxes Payable for this liability. The state unemployment tax for Academy Company for the January 14 payroll is $929.34 ($17,210.00 × 5.4%). Illustration 11-15 summarizes the types of employer payroll taxes.

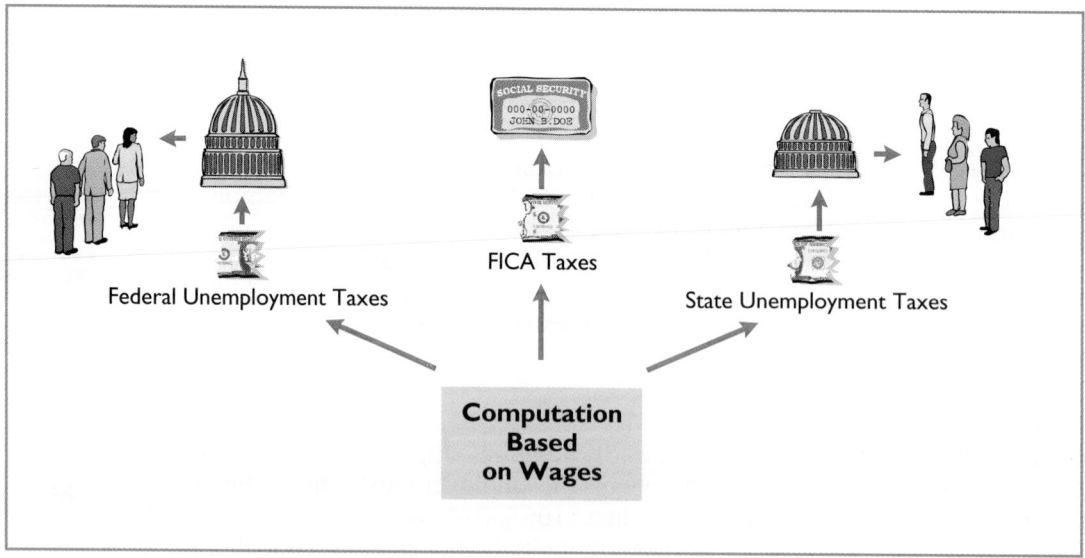

Illustration 11-15
Employer payroll taxes

---

[2]In a few states, the employee is also required to make a contribution. *In this textbook, including the homework, we will assume that the tax is only on the employer.*

RECORDING EMPLOYER PAYROLL TAXES

Companies usually record employer payroll taxes at the same time they record the payroll. The entire amount of gross pay ($17,210.00) shown in the payroll register in Illustration 11-13 is subject to each of the three taxes mentioned above. Accordingly, Academy records the payroll tax expense associated with the January 14 payroll with the following entry.

Jan. 14	Payroll Tax Expense	2,443.82	
	FICA Taxes Payable		1,376.80
	Federal Unemployment Taxes Payable		137.68
	State Unemployment Taxes Payable		929.34
	(To record employer's payroll taxes on January 14 payroll)		

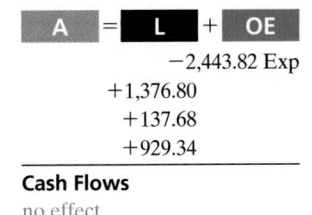

A = L + OE

−2,443.82 Exp
+1,376.80
+137.68
+929.34

Cash Flows
no effect

Note that Academy uses separate liability accounts instead of a single credit to Payroll Taxes Payable. Why? Because these liabilities are payable to different taxing authorities at different dates. Companies classify the liability accounts in the balance sheet as current liabilities since they will be paid within the next year. They classify Payroll Tax Expense on the income statement as an operating expense.

ACCOUNTING ACROSS THE ORGANIZATION

It Costs $74,000 to Put $44,000 in Sally's Pocket

Sally works for Bogan Communications, a small company in New Jersey that provides audio systems. She makes $59,000 a year but only nets $44,000. What happened to the other $15,000? Well, $2,376 goes for Sally's share of the medical and dental insurance that Bogan provides, $126 for state unemployment insurance, $149 for disability insurance, and $856 for Medicare. New Jersey takes $1,893 in income taxes, and the federal government gets $3,661 for Social Security and another $6,250 for income tax withholding. All of this adds up to some 22% of Sally's gross pay going to Washington or Trenton.

Employing Sally costs Bogan plenty too. Bogan has to write checks for $74,000 so Sally can receive her $59,000 in base pay. Health insurance is the biggest cost: While Sally pays nearly $2,400 for coverage, Bogan pays the rest—$9,561. Then, the federal and state governments take $56 for federal unemployment coverage, $149 for disability insurance, $300 for workers' comp, and $505 for state unemployment insurance. Finally, the government requires Bogan to pay $856 for Sally's Medicare and $3,661 for her Social Security.

When you add it all up, it costs $74,000 to put $44,000 in Sally's pocket and to give her $12,000 in benefits.

Source: Michael P. Fleischer, "Why I'm Not Hiring," *Wall Street Journal* (August 9, 2010), p. A17.

? How are the Social Security and Medicare taxes computed for Sally's salary?
(See page 549.)

Do it!

In January, the payroll supervisor determines that gross earnings for Halo Company are $70,000. All earnings are subject to 8% FICA taxes, 5.4% state unemployment taxes, and 0.8% federal unemployment taxes. Halo asks you to record the employer's payroll taxes.

Employer's Payroll Taxes

action plan

✔ Compute the employer's payroll taxes on the period's gross earnings.

✔ Identify the expense account(s) to be debited.

✔ Identify the liability account(s) to be credited.

Solution

The entry to record the employer's payroll taxes is:

Payroll Tax Expense	9,940	
FICA Taxes Payable ($70,000 × 8%)		5,600
Federal Unemployment Taxes Payable ($70,000 × 0.8%)		560
State Unemployment Taxes Payable ($70,000 × 5.4%)		3,780
(To record employer's payroll taxes		
on January payroll)		

Related exercise material: **BE11-9, E11-12, E11-14**, and **Do it!** **11-4.**

✔ **The Navigator**

Filing and Remitting Payroll Taxes

Preparation of payroll tax returns is the responsibility of the payroll department. The treasurer's department makes the tax payment. Much of the information for the returns is obtained from employee earnings records.

For purposes of reporting and remitting to the IRS, the company combines the FICA taxes and federal income taxes that it withheld. **Companies must report the taxes quarterly**, no later than one month following the close of each quarter. The remitting requirements depend on the amount of taxes withheld and the length of the pay period. Companies remit funds through deposits in either a Federal Reserve bank or an authorized commercial bank.

Companies generally file and remit federal unemployment taxes **annually** on or before January 31 of the subsequent year. Earlier payments are required when the tax exceeds a specified amount. Companies usually must file and pay state unemployment taxes by the **end of the month following each quarter**. When payroll taxes are paid, companies debit payroll liability accounts, and credit Cash.

ANATOMY OF A FRAUD

Art was a custodial supervisor for a large school district. The district was supposed to employ between 35 and 40 regular custodians, as well as 3 or 4 substitute custodians to fill in when regular custodians were missing. Instead, in addition to the regular custodians, Art "hired" 77 substitutes. In fact, almost none of these people worked for the district. Instead, Art submitted time cards for these people, collected their checks at the district office, and personally distributed the checks to the "employees." If a substitute's check was for $1,200, that person would cash the check, keep $200, and pay Art $1,000.

Total take: $150,000

THE MISSING CONTROLS

Human Resource Controls. Thorough background checks should be performed. No employees should begin work until they have been approved by the Board of Education and entered into the payroll system. No employees should be entered into the payroll system until they have been approved by a supervisor. All paychecks should be distributed directly to employees at the official school locations by designated employees.

Independent internal verification. Budgets should be reviewed monthly to identify situations where actual costs significantly exceed budgeted amounts.

Source: Adapted from Wells, *Fraud Casebook* (2007), pp. 164–171.

Employers also must provide each employee with a **Wage and Tax Statement (Form W-2)** by January 31 following the end of a calendar year. This statement shows gross earnings, FICA taxes withheld, and income taxes withheld for the year. The required W-2 form for Michael Jordan, using assumed annual data, is shown in Illustration 11-16. The employer must send a copy of each employee's Wage and Tax Statement (Form W-2) to the Social Security Administration. This agency subsequently furnishes the Internal Revenue Service with the income data required.

22222	Void ☐	**a** Employee's social security number 329-35-9547	For Official Use Only ▶ OMB No. 1545-0008	
b Employer identification number (EIN) 36-2167852			**1** Wages, tips, other compensation 26,300.00	**2** Federal income tax withheld 2,248.00
c Employer's name, address, and ZIP code Academy Company 19 Center St. Hampton, MI 48291			**3** Social security wages 26,300.00	**4** Social security tax withheld 2,104.00
			5 Medicare wages and tips 26,300.00	**6** Medicare tax withheld
			7 Social security tips	**8** Allocated tips
d Control number			**9** Advance EIC payment	**10** Dependent care benefits
e Employee's first name and initial Michael	Last name Jordan	Suff.	**11** Nonqualified plans	**12a** See instructions for box 12
2345 Mifflin Ave. Hampton, MI 48292			**13** Statutory employee ☐ Retirement plan ☐ Third-party sick pay ☐	**12b**
			14 Other	**12c**
				12d
f Employee's address and ZIP code				

15 State Employer's state ID number MI 423-1466-3	**16** State wages, tips, etc. 26,300.00	**17** State income tax 526.00	**18** Local wages, tips, etc.	**19** Local income tax	**20** Locality name

Form **W-2** Wage and Tax Statement   **2010**   Department of the Treasury—Internal Revenue Service

Copy A For Social Security Administration — Send this entire page with Form W-3 to the Social Security Administration; photocopies are **not** acceptable.

For Privacy Act and Paperwork Reduction Act Notice, see back of Copy D.

Cat. No. 10134D

Illustration 11-16
W-2 form

Internal Control for Payroll

Chapter 8 introduced internal control. As applied to payrolls, the objectives of internal control are (1) to safeguard company assets against unauthorized payments of payrolls, and (2) to ensure the accuracy and reliability of the accounting records pertaining to payrolls.

Irregularities often result if internal control is lax. Frauds involving payroll include overstating hours, using unauthorized pay rates, adding fictitious employees to the payroll, continuing terminated employees on the payroll, and distributing duplicate payroll checks. Moreover, inaccurate records will result in incorrect paychecks, financial statements, and payroll tax returns.

Payroll activities involve four functions: hiring employees, timekeeping, preparing the payroll, and paying the payroll. For effective internal control, companies should assign these four functions to different departments or individuals. Illustration 11-17 (page 530) highlights these functions and illustrates their internal control features.

Study Objective [8]
Discuss the objectives of internal control for payroll.

Payroll Function

Hiring Employees

Human Resources

Internal control feature:
Human Resources department documents and authorizes employment.

Fraud prevented:
Fictitious employees are not added to payroll.

Timekeeping

Internal control feature:
Supervisors monitor hours worked through time cards and time reports.

Fraud prevented:
Employee works appropriate hours.

Payroll Function

Preparing the Payroll

Internal control feature:
Two (or more) employees verify payroll amounts; supervisor approves.

Fraud prevented:
Payroll calculations are accurate and relevant.

Paying the Payroll

Internal control feature:
Treasurer signs and distributes prenumbered checks.

Fraud prevented:
Checks are not lost from theft; endorsed check provides proof of payment.

Illustration 11-17
Internal control for payroll

COMPREHENSIVE

Do it!

Indiana Jones Company had the following selected transactions.

Feb. 1   Signs a $50,000, 6-month, 9%-interest-bearing note payable to CitiBank and receives $50,000 in cash.

10   Cash register sales total $43,200, which includes an 8% sales tax.

28   The payroll for the month consists of salaries and wages of $50,000. All wages are subject to 8% FICA taxes. A total of $8,900 federal income taxes are withheld. The salaries are paid on March 1.

28   The company develops the following adjustment data.
1. Interest expense of $375 has been incurred on the note.
2. Employer payroll taxes include 8% FICA taxes, a 5.4% state unemployment tax, and a 0.8% federal unemployment tax.
3. Some sales were made under warranty. Of the units sold under warranty, 350 are expected to become defective. Repair costs are estimated to be $40 per unit.

Instructions

(a) Journalize the February transactions.

(b) Journalize the adjusting entries at February 28.

action plan

✔ To determine sales, divide the cash register total by 100% plus the sales tax percentage.

✔ Base payroll taxes on gross earnings.

✔ Expense warranty costs in the period in which the sale occurs.

Solution to Comprehensive Do it!

(a) Feb. 1	Cash		50,000	
	Notes Payable			50,000
	(Issued 6-month, 9%-interest-bearing note to CitiBank)			
10	Cash		43,200	
	Sales Revenue ($43,200 ÷ 1.08)			40,000
	Sales Taxes Payable ($40,000 × 8%)			3,200
	(To record sales and sales taxes payable)			

28	Salaries and Wages Expense	50,000	
	FICA Taxes Payable (8% × $50,000)		4,000
	Federal Income Taxes Payable		8,900
	Salaries and Wages Payable		37,100
	(To record February salaries)		
(b) Feb. 28	Interest Expense	375	
	Interest Payable		375
	(To record accrued interest for February)		
28	Payroll Tax Expense	7,100	
	FICA Taxes Payable		4,000
	Federal Unemployment Taxes Payable		400
	(0.8% × $50,000)		
	State Unemployment Taxes Payable		2,700
	(5.4% × $50,000)		
	(To record employer's payroll taxes on		
	February payroll)		
28	Warranty Expense (350 × $40)	14,000	
	Warranty Liability		14,000
	(To record estimated product warranty		
	liability)		

Summary of Study Objectives

[1] Explain a current liability, and identify the major types of current liabilities. A current liability is a debt that a company can reasonably expect to pay (1) from existing current assets or through the creation of other current liabilities, and (2) within one year or the operating cycle, whichever is longer. The major types of current liabilities are notes payable, accounts payable, sales taxes payable, unearned revenues, and accrued liabilities such as taxes, salaries and wages, and interest payable.

[2] Describe the accounting for notes payable. When a promissory note is interest-bearing, the amount of assets received upon the issuance of the note is generally equal to the face value of the note. Interest expense accrues over the life of the note. At maturity, the amount paid equals the face value of the note plus accrued interest.

[3] Explain the accounting for other current liabilities. Companies record sales taxes payable at the time the related sales occur. The company serves as a collection agent for the taxing authority. Sales taxes are not an expense to the company. Companies initially record unearned revenues in an Unearned Revenue account. As the company earns the revenue, a transfer from unearned revenue to earned revenue occurs. Companies report the current maturities of long-term debt as a current liability in the balance sheet.

[4] Explain the financial statement presentation and analysis of current liabilities. Companies should report the nature and amount of each current liability in the balance sheet or in schedules in the notes accompanying the statements. The liquidity of a company may be analyzed by computing working capital and the current ratio.

[5] Describe the accounting and disclosure requirements for contingent liabilities. If the contingency is *probable* (likely to occur) and the amount is reasonably estimable, the company should record the liability in the accounts. If the contingency is only *reasonably possible* (it could happen), then it should be disclosed only in the notes to the financial statements. If the possibility that the contingency will happen is *remote* (unlikely to occur), it need not be recorded or disclosed.

[6] Compute and record the payroll for a pay period. The computation of the payroll involves gross earnings, payroll deductions, and net pay. In recording the payroll, companies debit salaries (or wages) expense for gross earnings, credit individual tax and other liability accounts for payroll deductions, and credit salaries (wages) payable for net pay. When the payroll is paid, companies debit Salaries and Wages Payable, and credit Cash.

[7] Describe and record employer payroll taxes. Employer payroll taxes consist of FICA, federal unemployment taxes, and state unemployment taxes. The taxes are usually accrued at the time the company records the payroll, by debiting Payroll Tax Expense and crediting separate liability accounts for each type of tax.

[8] Discuss the objectives of internal control for payroll. The objectives of internal control for payroll are (1) to safeguard company assets against unauthorized payments of payrolls, and (2) to ensure the accuracy of the accounting records pertaining to payrolls.

Glossary

Bonus   Compensation to management and other personnel, based on factors such as increased sales or the amount of net income. (p. 519).

Contingent liability   A potential liability that may become an actual liability in the future. (p. 515).

Current ratio   A measure of a company's liquidity; computed as current assets divided by current liabilities. (p. 515).

Employee earnings record   A cumulative record of each employee's gross earnings, deductions, and net pay during the year. (p. 522).

Federal unemployment taxes   Taxes imposed on the employer by the federal government that provide benefits for a limited time period to employees who lose their jobs through no fault of their own. (p. 526).

Fees   Payments made for the services of professionals. (p. 519).

FICA taxes   Taxes designed to provide workers with supplemental retirement, employment disability, and medical benefits. (p. 520).

Full-disclosure principle   Requires that companies disclose all circumstances and events that would make a difference to financial statement users. (p. 517).

Gross earnings   Total compensation earned by an employee. (p. 519).

Net pay   Gross earnings less payroll deductions. (p. 522).

Notes payable   Obligations in the form of written notes. (p. 510).

Payroll deductions   Deductions from gross earnings to determine the amount of a paycheck. (p. 519).

Payroll register   A payroll record that accumulates the gross earnings, deductions, and net pay by employee for each pay period. (p. 522).

Salaries   Employee pay based on a specified amount rather than an hourly rate. (p. 518).

Statement of earnings   A document attached to a paycheck that indicates the employee's gross earnings, payroll deductions, and net pay. (p. 524).

State unemployment taxes   Taxes imposed on the employer by states that provide benefits to employees who lose their jobs. (p. 526).

Wage and Tax Statement (Form W-2)   A form showing gross earnings, FICA taxes withheld, and income taxes withheld, prepared annually by an employer for each employee. (p. 528).

Wages   Amounts paid to employees based on a rate per hour or on a piecework basis. (p. 518).

Working capital   A measure of a company's liquidity; computed as current assets minus current liabilities. (p. 515).

APPENDIX11A

Additional Fringe Benefits

Study Objective [9]
Identify additional fringe benefits associated with employee compensation.

In addition to the three payroll-tax fringe benefits, employers incur other substantial fringe benefit costs. Two of the most important are paid absences and post-retirement benefits.

Paid Absences

Employees often are given rights to receive compensation for absences when they meet certain conditions of employment. The compensation may be for paid vacations, sick pay benefits, and paid holidays. When the payment for such absences is **probable** and the amount can be **reasonably estimated**, the company should accrue a liability for paid future absences. When the amount cannot be reasonably estimated, the company should instead disclose the potential liability. Ordinarily, vacation pay is the only paid absence that is accrued. The other types of paid absences are only disclosed.

To illustrate, assume that Academy Company employees are entitled to one day's vacation for each month worked. If 30 employees earn an average of $110 per day in a given month, the accrual for vacation benefits in one month is $3,300. Academy records the liability at the end of the month by the following adjusting entry.

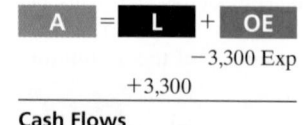

−3,300 Exp
+3,300

Cash Flows
no effect

Jan. 31	Vacation Benefits Expense	3,300	
	Vacation Benefits Payable		3,300
	(To accrue vacation benefits expense)		

This accrual is required by the expense recognition principle. Academy would report Vacation Benefits Expense as an operating expense in the income statement, and Vacation Benefits Payable as a current liability in the balance sheet.

Later, when Academy pays vacation benefits, it debits Vacation Benefits Payable and credits Cash. For example, if employees take 10 days of vacation in July, the entry is:

July 31	Vacation Benefits Payable	1,100	
	Cash		1,100
	(To record payment of vacation benefits)		

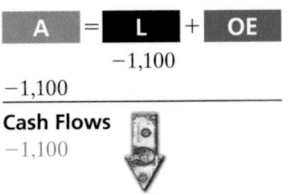

The magnitude of unpaid absences has gained employers' attention. Consider the case of an assistant superintendent of schools who worked for 20 years and rarely took a vacation or sick day. A month or so before she retired, the school district discovered that she was due nearly $30,000 in accrued benefits. Yet the school district had never accrued the liability.

Post-Retirement Benefits

Post-retirement benefits are benefits that employers provide to retired employees for (1) pensions and (2) health care and life insurance. Companies account for both types of post-retirement benefits on the accrual basis. The cost of post-retirement benefits is getting steep. For example, states and localities must deal with a $1 trillion deficit in public employees' retirement benefit funds. The shortfall amounts to more than $8,800 for every household in the nation.

The average American has debt of approximately $10,000 (not counting the mortgage on their home) and has little in the way of savings. What will happen at retirement for these people? The picture is not pretty—people are living longer, the future of Social Security is unclear, and companies are cutting back on post-retirement benefits. This situation may lead to one of the great social and moral dilemmas this country faces in the next 40 years. The more you know about post-retirement benefits, the better you will understand the issues involved in this dilemma.

PENSIONS

A **pension plan** is an agreement whereby employers provide benefits (payments) to employees after they retire. The most popular type of pension plan used is the 401(k) plan. A 401(k) plan works as follows: As an employee, you can contribute up to a certain percentage of your pay into a 401(k) plan, and your employer will match a percentage of your contribution. These contributions are then generally invested in stocks and bonds through mutual funds. These funds will grow without being taxed and can be withdrawn beginning at age 59-1/2. If you must access the funds earlier, you may be able to do so, but a penalty usually occurs along with a payment of tax on the proceeds. Any time you have the opportunity to be involved in a 401(k) plan, you should avail yourself of this benefit!

The accounting for a 401(k) plan by the company is straightforward. When the company makes a contribution on behalf of the employee, it debits Pension Expense and credits Cash for the amount contributed. For example, Mark Hatfield, an employee of Veri Company, contributes $11,000 to his 401(k) plan. Veri Company matches this contribution, and records the expense with the following entry.

Pension Expense	11,000	
Cash		11,000
(To record contribution to 401(k) plan)		

If the pension expense is not funded during the year, the company credits Pension Liability.

A 401(k) plan is often referred to as a **defined-contribution plan**. In a defined-contribution plan, the plan defines the contribution that an employer will make but not the benefit that the employee will receive at retirement.

The other type of pension plan is a **defined-benefit plan**. In a defined-benefit plan, the employer agrees to pay a defined amount to retirees, based on employees meeting certain eligibility standards. The amount of the benefit is usually based on years of service and average salary over a period of years. Employers are at risk with defined-benefit plans because they must contribute enough to meet the cost of benefits that the plan defines. Many large companies have defined-benefit plans. The accounting for these plans is complex. Many companies are starting to utilize 401(k) plans more extensively instead.

POST-RETIREMENT HEALTH-CARE AND LIFE INSURANCE BENEFITS

Providing medical and related health-care benefits for retirees was at one time an inexpensive and highly effective way of generating employee goodwill. This practice has now turned into one of corporate America's most worrisome financial problems. Runaway medical costs, early retirement, and increased longevity are sending the liability for retiree health plans through the roof.

Companies estimate and expense post-retirement costs during the working years of the employee because the company benefits from the employee's services during this period. However, the company rarely sets up funds to meet the cost of the future benefits. It follows a pay-as-you-go basis for these costs. The major reason is that the company does not receive a tax deduction until it actually pays the medical bill.

Summary of Study Objective for Appendix 11A

[9] **Identify additional fringe benefits associated with employee compensation.** Additional fringe benefits associated with wages are paid absences (paid vacations, sick pay benefits, and paid holidays), and post-retirement benefits (pensions, health care, and life insurance).

Glossary for Appendix 11A

Pension plan   An agreement whereby an employer provides benefits to employees after they retire. (p. 533).

Post-retirement benefits   Payments by employers to retired employees for health care, life insurance, and pensions. (p. 533).

 Self-Test, Brief Exercises, Exercises Problem Set A, and many more components are available for practice in *WileyPLUS*

*Note: All **asterisked** Questions, Exercises, and Problems relate to material in the appendix to the chapter.

Self-Test Questions

Answers are on page 549.

(SO 1)   1. The time period for classifying a liability as current is one year or the operating cycle, whichever is:
  a. longer.
  b. shorter.
  c. probable.
  d. possible.

2. To be classified as a current liability, a debt must be ex-   (SO 1) pected to be paid:
  a. out of existing current assets.
  b. by creating other current liabilities.
  c. within 2 years.
  d. Both (a) and (b).

(SO 2)   **3.** Maggie Sharrer Company borrows $88,500 on September 1, 2012, from Sandwich State Bank by signing an $88,500, 12%, one-year note. What is the accrued interest at December 31, 2012?
   a. $2,655.
   b. $3,540.
   c. $4,425.
   d. $10,620.

(SO 2)   **4.** RS Company borrowed $70,000 on December 1 on a 6-month, 6% note. At December 31:
   a. neither the note payable nor the interest payable is a current liability.
   b. the note payable is a current liability, but the interest payable is not.
   c. the interest payable is a current liability but the note payable is not.
   d. both the note payable and the interest payable are current liabilities.

(SO 3)   **5.** Becky Sherrick Company has total proceeds from sales of $4,515. If the proceeds include sales taxes of 5%, the amount to be credited to Sales Revenue is:
   a. $4,000.
   b. $4,300.
   c. $4,289.25.
   d. No correct answer given.

(SO 3)   **6.** Sensible Insurance Company collected a premium of $18,000 for a 1-year insurance policy on April 1. What amount should Sensible report as a current liability for Unearned Insurance Premiums at December 31?
   a. $0.
   b. $4,500.
   c. $13,500.
   d. $18,000.

(SO 4)   **7.** Working capital is calculated as:
   a. current assets minus current liabilities.
   b. total assets minus total liabilities.
   c. long-term liabilities minus current liabilities.
   d. Both (b) and (c).

(SO 4)   **8.** The current ratio is computed as:
   a. total assets divided by total liabilities.
   b. total assets divided by current liabilities.
   c. current assets divided by total liabilities.
   d. current assets divided by current liabilities.

(SO 5)   **9.** A contingent liability should be recorded in the accounts when:
   a. it is probable the contingency will happen, but the amount cannot be reasonably estimated.
   b. it is reasonably possible the contingency will happen, and the amount can be reasonably estimated.
   c. it is probable the contingency will happen, and the amount can be reasonably estimated.

   d. it is reasonably possible the contingency will happen, but the amount cannot be reasonably estimated.

(SO 5)   **10.** At December 31, Hanes Company prepares an adjusting entry for a product warranty contract. Which of the following accounts is/are included in the entry?
   a. Miscellaneous Expense.
   b. Warranty Liability.
   c. Repair Parts.
   d. Both (a) and (b).

(SO 6)   **11.** Andy Manion earns $14 per hour for a 40-hour week and $21 per hour for any overtime work. If Manion works 45 hours in a week, gross earnings are:
   a. $560.
   b. $630.
   c. $650.
   d. $665.

(SO 6)   **12.** When recording payroll:
   a. gross earnings are recorded as salaries and wages payable.
   b. net pay is recorded as salaries and wages expense.
   c. payroll deductions are recorded as liabilities.
   d. More than one of the above.

(SO 7)   **13.** Employer payroll taxes do *not* include:
   a. federal unemployment taxes.
   b. state unemployment taxes.
   c. federal income taxes.
   d. FICA taxes.

(SO 7)   **14.** FICA Taxes Payable was credited for $7,500 in the entry when Antonio Company recorded payroll. When Antonio Company records employer's payroll taxes, FICA Taxes Payable should be credited for:
   a. $0.
   b. $7,500.
   c. $15,000.
   d. Some other amount.

(SO 8)   **15.** The department that should pay the payroll is the:
   a. timekeeping department.
   b. human resources department.
   c. payroll department.
   d. treasurer's department.

*(SO 9)   ***16.** Which of the following is *not* an additional fringe benefit?
   a. Post-retirement pensions.
   b. Paid absences.
   c. Paid vacations.
   d. Salaries.

Go to the book's companion website, **www.wiley.com/college/weygandt**, for additional Self-Test Questions.

The Navigator

Questions

1. Jill Loomis believes a current liability is a debt that can be expected to be paid in one year. Is Jill correct? Explain.

2. Frederickson Company obtains $40,000 in cash by signing a 9%, 6-month, $40,000 note payable to First Bank on July 1. Frederickson's fiscal year ends on September 30. What information should be reported for the note payable in the annual financial statements?

3. (a) Your roommate says, "Sales taxes are reported as an expense in the income statement." Do you agree? Explain.

(b) Planet Hollywood has cash proceeds from sales of $7,400. This amount includes $400 of sales taxes. Give the entry to record the proceeds.

4. Baylor University sold 10,000 season football tickets at $80 each for its five-game home schedule. What entries should be made (a) when the tickets were sold, and (b) after each game?

5. What is liquidity? What are two measures of liquidity?

6. What is a contingent liability? Give an example of a contingent liability that is usually recorded in the accounts.

7. Under what circumstances is a contingent liability disclosed only in the notes to the financial statements? Under what circumstances is a contingent liability not recorded in the accounts nor disclosed in the notes to the financial statements?

8. What is the difference between gross pay and net pay? Which amount should a company record as wages and salaries expense?

9. Which payroll tax is levied on both employers and employees?

10. Are the federal and state income taxes withheld from employee paychecks a payroll tax expense for the employer? Explain your answer.

11. What do the following acronyms stand for: FICA, FUTA, and SUTA?

12. What information is shown in a W-2 statement?

13. Distinguish between the two types of payroll deductions and give examples of each.

14. What are the primary uses of the employee earnings record?

15. (a) Identify the three types of employer payroll taxes.
    (b) How are tax liability accounts and payroll tax expense accounts classified in the financial statements?

16. You are a newly hired accountant with Batista Company. On your first day, the controller asks you to identify the main internal control objectives related to payroll accounting. How would you respond?

17. What are the four functions associated with payroll activities?

*18. Identify two additional types of fringe benefits associated with employees' compensation.

*19. Often during job interviews, the candidate asks the potential employer about the firm's paid absences policy. What are paid absences? How are they accounted for?

*20. What are two types of post-retirement benefits?

*21. Explain how a 401(k) plan works.

*22. What is the difference between a defined-contribution pension plan and a defined-benefit pension plan?

Brief Exercises

Identify whether obligations are current liabilities.
(SO 1)

BE11-1 Sanford Company has the following obligations at December 31: (a) a note payable for $100,000 due in 2 years, (b) a 10-year mortgage payable of $300,000 payable in ten $30,000 annual payments, (c) interest payable of $15,000 on the mortgage, and (d) accounts payable of $60,000. For each obligation, indicate whether it should be classified as a current liability. (Assume an operating cycle of less than one year.)

Prepare entries for an interest-bearing note payable.
(SO 2)

BE11-2 Douglas Company borrows $80,000 on July 1 from the bank by signing a $80,000, 10%, one-year note payable.

(a) Prepare the journal entry to record the proceeds of the note.

(b) Prepare the journal entry to record accrued interest at December 31, assuming adjusting entries are made only at the end of the year.

Compute and record sales taxes payable.
(SO 3)

BE11-3 Savango Auto Supply does not segregate sales and sales taxes at the time of sale. The register total for March 16 is $15,540. All sales are subject to a 5% sales tax. Compute sales taxes payable, and make the entry to record sales taxes payable and sales.

Prepare entries for unearned revenues.
(SO 3)

BE11-4 Frost University sells 4,000 season basketball tickets at $180 each for its 12-game home schedule. Give the entry to record (a) the sale of the season tickets and (b) the revenue earned by playing the first home game.

Analyze liquidity.
(SO 4)

BE11-5 Yahoo! Inc.'s 2009 financial statements contain the following selected data (in thousands).

Current assets	$ 4,594,772	Current liabilities	$1,717,728
Total assets	14,936,030	Total liabilities	2,417,394

Compute (a) working capital and (b) current ratio.

Prepare adjusting entry for warranty costs.
(SO 5)

BE11-6 On December 1, Beaver Company introduces a new product that includes a one-year warranty on parts. In December, 1,000 units are sold. Management believes that 5% of the units will be defective and that the average warranty costs will be $80 per unit. Prepare the adjusting entry at December 31 to accrue the estimated warranty cost.

Compute gross earnings and net pay.
(SO 6)

BE11-7 Dawn French's regular hourly wage rate is $16, and she receives an hourly rate of $24 for work in excess of 40 hours. During a January pay period, Dawn works 47 hours. Dawn's federal income tax withholding is $95, and she has no voluntary deductions. Compute Dawn French's gross earnings and net pay for the pay period.

Record a payroll and the payment of wages.
(SO 6)

BE11-8 Data for Dawn French are presented in BE11-7. Prepare the journal entries to record (a) Dawn's pay for the period and (b) the payment of Dawn's wages. Use January 15 for the end of the pay period and the payment date.

BE11-9   In January, gross earnings in Gyro Company totaled $70,000. All earnings are subject to 8% FICA taxes, 5.4% state unemployment taxes, and 0.8% federal unemployment taxes. Prepare the entry to record January payroll tax expense.

Record employer payroll taxes.
(SO 7)

BE11-10   Vardan Company has the following payroll procedures.

(a) Supervisor approves overtime work.
(b) The human resources department prepares hiring authorization forms for new hires.
(c) A second payroll department employee verifies payroll calculations.
(d) The treasurer's department pays employees.

Identify the payroll function to which each procedure pertains.

Identify payroll functions.
(SO 8)

*BE11-11   At Wolf Company, employees are entitled to one day's vacation for each month worked. In January, 80 employees worked the full month. Record the vacation pay liability for January assuming the average daily pay for each employee is $120.

Record estimated vacation benefits.
(SO 9)

Do it! Review

Do it! 11-1   You and several classmates are studying for the next accounting examination. They ask you to answer the following questions:

1. If cash is borrowed on a $70,000, 9-month, 12% note on August 1, how much interest expense would be incurred by December 31?
2. The cash register total including sales taxes is $42,000, and the sales tax rate is 5%. What is the sales taxes payable?
3. If $42,000 is collected in advance on November 1 for 6-month magazine subscriptions, what amount of subscription revenue is earned by December 31?

Answer questions about current liabilities.
(SO 2, 3)

Do it! 11-2   Goblin Company, has the following account balances at December 31, 2012.

Notes payable ($60,000 due after 12/31/13)	$100,000
Unearned service revenue	70,000
Other long-term debt ($90,000 due in 2013)	250,000
Salaries and wages payable	32,000
Accounts payable	63,000

Prepare current liabilities section and compute liquidity measures.
(SO 4, 5)

In addition, Goblin is involved in a lawsuit. Legal counsel feels it is probable Goblin will pay damages of $85,000 in 2013.

(a) Prepare the current liability section of Goblin's 12/31/12 balance sheet.
(b) Goblin's current assets are $570,000. Compute Goblin's working capital and current ratio.

Do it! 11-3   In January, gross earnings in Centaur Company were $60,000. All earnings are subject to 8% FICA taxes. Federal income tax withheld was $14,000, and state income tax withheld was $1,600. (a) Calculate net pay for January, and (b) record the payroll.

Calculate net pay and record payroll.
(SO 6)

Do it! 11-4   In January, the payroll supervisor determines that gross earnings for Maugrim Company are $110,000. All earnings are subject to 8% FICA taxes, 5.4% state unemployment taxes, and 0.8% federal unemployment taxes. Bond asks you to record the employer's payroll taxes.

Record employer's payroll taxes.
(SO 7)

Exercises

E11-1   C.S. Lewis Company had the following transactions involving notes payable.

Prepare entries for interest-bearing notes.
(SO 2)

July 1, 2012	Borrows $50,000 from Fourth National Bank by signing a 9-month, 12% note.
Nov. 1, 2012	Borrows $60,000 from Livingston State Bank by signing a 3-month, 10% note.
Dec. 31, 2012	Prepares adjusting entries.
Feb. 1, 2013	Pays principal and interest to Livingston State Bank.
Apr. 1, 2013	Pays principal and interest to Fourth National Bank.

Instructions
Prepare journal entries for each of the transactions.

E11-2   On June 1, Caspian Company borrows $90,000 from First Bank on a 6-month, $90,000, 12% note.

Prepare entries for interest-bearing notes.
(SO 2)

Instructions

(a) Prepare the entry on June 1.
(b) Prepare the adjusting entry on June 30.
(c) Prepare the entry at maturity (December 1), assuming monthly adjusting entries have been made through November 30.
(d) What was the total financing cost (interest expense)?

Journalize sales and related taxes.

(SO 3)

E11-3 In providing accounting services to small businesses, you encounter the following situations pertaining to cash sales.

1. Miraz Company rings up sales and sales taxes separately on its cash register. On April 10, the register totals are sales $30,000 and sales taxes $1,500.
2. Trumpkin Company does not segregate sales and sales taxes. Its register total for April 15 is $23,540, which includes a 7% sales tax.

Instructions

Prepare the entry to record the sales transactions and related taxes for each client.

Journalize unearned subscription revenue.

(SO 3)

E11-4 Sergio Company publishes a monthly sports magazine, *Fishing Preview*. Subscriptions to the magazine cost $20 per year. During November 2012, Sergio sells 12,000 subscriptions beginning with the December issue. Sergio prepares financial statements quarterly and recognizes subscription revenue earned at the end of the quarter. The company uses the accounts Unearned Subscription Revenue and Subscription Revenue.

Instructions

(a) Prepare the entry in November for the receipt of the subscriptions.
(b) Prepare the adjusting entry at December 31, 2012, to record sales revenue earned in December 2012.
(c) Prepare the adjusting entry at March 31, 2013, to record sales revenue earned in the first quarter of 2013.

Record estimated liability and expense for warranties.

(SO 5)

E11-5 Castellitto Company sells automatic can openers under a 75-day warranty for defective merchandise. Based on past experience, Castellitto estimates that 3% of the units sold will become defective during the warranty period. Management estimates that the average cost of replacing or repairing a defective unit is $20. The units sold and units defective that occurred during the last 2 months of 2012 are as follows.

Month	Units Sold	Units Defective Prior to December 31
November	30,000	600
December	32,000	400

Instructions

(a) Determine the estimated warranty liability at December 31 for the units sold in November and December.
(b) Prepare the journal entries to record the estimated liability for warranties and the costs incurred in honoring 1,000 warranty claims. (Assume actual costs of $20,000.)
(c) Give the entry to record the honoring of 500 warranty contracts in January at an average cost of $20.

Record and disclose contingent liabilities.

(SO 5)

E11-6 Nikabrik Co. is involved in a lawsuit as a result of an accident that took place September 5, 2012. The lawsuit was filed on November 1, 2012, and claims damages of $1,000,000.

Instructions

(a) At December 31, 2012, Nikabrik's attorneys feel it is remote that Nikabrik will lose the lawsuit. How should the company account for the effects of the lawsuit?
(b) Assume instead that at December 31, 2012, Nikabrik's attorneys feel it is probable that Nikabrik will lose the lawsuit and be required to pay $1,000,000. How should the company account for this lawsuit?
(c) Assume instead that at December 31, 2012, Nikabrik's attorneys feel it is reasonably possible that Nikabrik could lose the lawsuit and be required to pay $1,000,000. How should the company account for this lawsuit?

Prepare the current liability section of the balance sheet.

(SO 1, 2, 3, 4, 5)

E11-7 Warwick Online Company has the following liability accounts after posting adjusting entries: Accounts Payable $63,000, Unearned Ticket Revenue $24,000, Estimated Warranty Liability $18,000, Interest Payable $8,000, Mortgage Payable $120,000, Notes Payable $80,000, and Sales Taxes Payable $10,000. Assume the company's operating cycle is less than 1 year, ticket revenue will be earned within 1 year, warranty costs are expected to be incurred within 1 year, and the notes mature in 3 years.

Instructions

(a) Prepare the current liabilities section of the balance sheet, assuming $30,000 of the mortgage is payable next year.

(b) Comment on Warwick Online Company's liquidity, assuming total current assets are $300,000.

E11-8   Kroger Co.'s 2009 financial statements contained the following data (in millions).

Calculate liquidity ratios.
(SO 4)

Current assets	$ 7,450	Accounts receivable	$909
Total assets	23,093	Interest expense	502
Current liabilities	7,714	Income tax expense	532
Total liabilities	18,187	Net income	70
Cash	424		

Instructions

Compute these values:

(a) Working capital.   **(b)** Current ratio.

E11-9   The following financial data were reported by 3M Company for 2008 and 2009 (dollars in millions).

Calculate current ratio and working capital before and after paying accounts payable.
(SO 4)

3M Company Balance Sheets (partial)		
	2009	**2008**
Current assets		
Cash and cash equivalents	$ 3,040	$1,849
Accounts receivable, net	3,250	3,195
Inventories	2,639	3,013
Other current assets	1,866	1,541
Total current assets	$10,795	$9,598
Current liabilities	$ 4,897	$5,839

Instructions

(a) Calculate the current ratio and working capital for 3M for 2008 and 2009.

(b) Suppose that at the end of 2009, 3M management used $200 million cash to pay off $200 million of accounts payable. How would its current ratio and working capital have changed?

E11-10   Pedja Belic's regular hourly wage rate is $15, and she receives a wage of 1½ times the regular hourly rate for work in excess of 40 hours. During a March weekly pay period, Pedja worked 42 hours. Her gross earnings prior to the current week were $6,000. Pedja is married and claims three withholding allowances. Her only voluntary deduction is for group hospitalization insurance at $25 per week.

Compute net pay and record pay for one employee.
(SO 6)

Instructions

(a) Compute the following amounts for Pedja's wages for the current week.

　(1) Gross earnings.

　(2) FICA taxes. (Assume an 8% rate on maximum of $90,000.)

　(3) Federal income taxes withheld. (Use the withholding table in the text, page 521.)

　(4) State income taxes withheld. (Assume a 2.0% rate.)

　(5) Net pay.

(b) Record Pedja's pay.

E11-11   Employee earnings records for Cornelius Company reveal the following gross earnings for four employees through the pay period of December 15.

Compute maximum FICA deductions.
(SO 6)

J. Glozelle	$93,500	L. Schooler	$96,100
R. Jen	$97,600	T. Crier	$104,000

For the pay period ending December 31, each employee's gross earnings is $4,000. The FICA tax rate is 8% on gross earnings of $100,000.

Instructions

Compute the FICA withholdings that should be made for each employee for the December 31 pay period. (Show computations.)

Prepare payroll register and record payroll and payroll tax expense.

(SO 6, 7)

E11-12   Alvarez Company has the following data for the weekly payroll ending January 31.

Employee	M	T	W	T	F	S	Hourly Rate	Federal Income Tax Withholding	Health Insurance
L. Donnon	8	8	9	8	10	3	$12	$34	$10
L. Gregoire	8	8	8	8	8	2	13	37	25
D. Alcazar	9	10	8	8	9	0	15	58	25

Employees are paid 1½ times the regular hourly rate for all hours worked in excess of 40 hours per week. FICA taxes are 8% on the first $100,000 of gross earnings. Alvarez Company is subject to 5.4% state unemployment taxes and 0.8% federal unemployment taxes on the first $7,000 of gross earnings.

Instructions

(a) Prepare the payroll register for the weekly payroll.

(b) Prepare the journal entries to record the payroll and Alvarez's payroll tax expense.

Compute missing payroll amounts and record payroll.

(SO 6)

E11-13   Selected data from a February payroll register for Favino Company are presented below. Some amounts are intentionally omitted.

Gross earnings:		State income taxes	$ (3)
Regular	$8,900	Union dues	100
Overtime	(1)	Total deductions	(4)
Total	(2)	Net pay	$7,660
Deductions:		Account debited:	
FICA taxes	$ 800	Salaries and wages expense	(5)
Federal income taxes	1,140		

FICA taxes are 8%. State income taxes are 3% of gross earnings.

Instructions

(a) Fill in the missing amounts.

(b) Journalize the February payroll and the payment of the payroll.

Determine employer's payroll taxes; record payroll tax expense.

(SO 7)

E11-14   According to a payroll register summary of Pierfrancesco Company, the amount of employees' gross pay in December was $850,000, of which $90,000 was not subject to FICA tax and $750,000 was not subject to state and federal unemployment taxes.

Instructions

(a) Determine the employer's payroll tax expense for the month, using the following rates: FICA 8%, state unemployment 5.4%, federal unemployment 0.8%.

(b) Prepare the journal entry to record December payroll tax expense.

Prepare adjusting entries for fringe benefits.

(SO 9)

*E11-15   Borrachero Company has two fringe benefit plans for its employees:

1. It grants employees 2 days' vacation for each month worked. Ten employees worked the entire month of March at an average daily wage of $120 per employee.

2. In its pension plan, the company recognizes 10% of gross earnings as a pension expense. Gross earnings in March were $40,000. No contribution has been made to the pension fund.

Instructions

Prepare the adjusting entries at March 31.

Prepare journal entries for fringe benefits.

(SO 9)

*E11-16   Glenstorm Corporation has 20 employees who each earn $120 a day. The following information is available.

1. At December 31, Glenstorm recorded vacation benefits. Each employee earned 5 vacation days during the year.

2. At December 31, Glenstorm recorded pension expense of $100,000, and made a contribution of $70,000 to the pension plan.

3. In January, 18 employees used one vacation day each.

Instructions

Prepare Glenstorm's journal entries to record these transactions.

Exercises: Set B

Visit the book's companion website, at **www.wiley.com/college/weygandt**, and choose the Student Companion site to access Exercise Set B.

Problems: Set A

P11-1A On January 1, 2012, the ledger of Montoya Company contains the following liability accounts.

Accounts Payable	$52,000
Sales Taxes Payable	7,700
Unearned Service Revenue	16,000

During January, the following selected transactions occurred.

Jan. 5   Sold merchandise for cash totaling $22,680, which includes 8% sales taxes.
     12   Provided services for customers who had made advance payments of $10,000. (Credit Service Revenue.)
     14   Paid state revenue department for sales taxes collected in December 2011 ($7,700).
     20   Sold 800 units of a new product on credit at $50 per unit, plus 8% sales tax. This new product is subject to a 1-year warranty.
     21   Borrowed $18,000 from DeKalb Bank on a 3-month, 8%, $18,000 note.
     25   Sold merchandise for cash totaling $12,420, which includes 8% sales taxes.

Instructions

(a) Journalize the January transactions.

(b) Journalize the adjusting entries at January 31 for (1) the outstanding notes payable, and (2) estimated warranty liability, assuming warranty costs are expected to equal 7% of sales of the new product. (*Hint:* Use one-third of a month for the DeKalb Bank note.)

(c) Prepare the current liabilities section of the balance sheet at January 31, 2012. Assume no change in accounts payable.

Prepare current liability entries, adjusting entries, and current liabilities section.
(SO 1, 2, 3, 4, 5)

(c) Current liability total $84,640

P11-2A The following are selected transactions of Andreu Company. Andreu prepares financial statements quarterly.

Jan. 2   Purchased merchandise on account from Diego Company, $30,000, terms 2/10, n/30. (Andreu uses the perpetual inventory system.)
Feb. 1   Issued a 9%, 2-month, $30,000 note to Diego in payment of account.
Mar. 31   Accrued interest for 2 months on Diego note.
Apr. 1   Paid face value and interest on Diego note.
July 1   Purchased equipment from Garcia Equipment paying $11,000 in cash and signing a 10%, 3-month, $40,000 note.
Sept. 30   Accrued interest for 3 months on Garcia note.
Oct. 1   Paid face value and interest on Garcia note.
Dec. 1   Borrowed $15,000 from the Isova Bank by issuing a 3-month, 8% note with a face value of $15,000.
Dec. 31   Recognized interest expense for 1 month on Isova Bank note.

Instructions

(a) Prepare journal entries for the listed transactions and events.

(b) Post to the accounts Notes Payable, Interest Payable, and Interest Expense.

(c) Show the balance sheet presentation of notes and interest payable at December 31.

(d) What is total interest expense for the year?

Journalize and post note transactions; show balance sheet presentation.
(SO 2)

(d) $1,550

Prepare payroll register and payroll entries.

(SO 6, 7)

P11-3A Hira Hardware has four employees who are paid on an hourly basis plus time-and-a half for all hours worked in excess of 40 a week. Payroll data for the week ended March 15, 2012, are presentd below.

Employee	Hours Worked	Hourly Rate	Federal Income Tax Withholdings	United Fund
Joe Hana	40	$15.00	$?	$5.00
Mary Alina	42	15.00	?	5.00
Andy Silva	44	13.00	60	8.00
Kim Gomez	46	13.00	61	5.00

Hana and Alina are married. They claim 0 and 4 withholding allowances, respectively. The following tax rates are applicable: FICA 8%, state income taxes 3%, state unemployment taxes 5.4%, and federal unemployment 0.8%.

Instructions

(a) Net pay $1,944.20

(a) Prepare a payroll register for the weekly payroll. (Use the wage-bracket withholding table in the text for federal income tax withholdings.)

(b) Payroll tax expense $352.16

(b) Journalize the payroll on March 15, 2012, and the accrual of employer payroll taxes.

(d) Cash paid $636.80

(c) Journalize the payment of the payroll on March 16, 2012.

(d) Journalize the deposit in a Federal Reserve bank on March 31, 2012, of the FICA and federal income taxes payable to the government.

Journalize payroll transactions and adjusting entries.

(SO 6, 7, 9)

P11-4A The following payroll liability accounts are included in the ledger of Wimble Company on January 1, 2012.

FICA Taxes Payable	$ 760.00
Federal Income Taxes Payable	1,204.60
State Income Taxes Payable	108.95
Federal Unemployment Taxes Payable	288.95
State Unemployment Taxes Payable	1,954.40
Union Dues Payable	870.00
U.S. Savings Bonds Payable	360.00

In January, the following transactions occurred.

Jan. 10 Sent check for $870.00 to union treasurer for union dues.
　12 Remitted check for $1,964.60 to the Federal Reserve bank for FICA taxes and federal income taxes withheld.
　15 Purchased U.S. Savings Bonds for employees by writing check for $360.00.
　17 Paid state income taxes withheld from employees.
　20 Paid federal and state unemployment taxes.
　31 Completed monthly payroll register, which shows office salaries $26,600, store wages $28,400, FICA taxes withheld $4,400, federal income taxes payable $2,158, state income taxes payable $454, union dues payable $400, United Fund contributions payable $1,888, and net pay $45,700.
　31 Prepared payroll checks for the net pay and distributed checks to employees.

At January 31, the company also makes the following accrued adjustments pertaining to employee compensation.

1. Employer payroll taxes: FICA taxes 8%, federal unemployment taxes 0.8%, and state unemployment taxes 5.4%.

*2. Vacation pay: 6% of gross earnings.

(b) Payroll tax expense $7,810; Vacation benefits expense $3,300

Instructions

(a) Journalize the January transactions.

(b) Journalize the adjustments pertaining to employee compensation at January 31.

Prepare entries for payroll and payroll taxes; prepare W-2 data.

(SO 6, 7)

P11-5A For the year ended December 31, 2012, Telmarine Electrical Repair Company reports the following summary payroll data.

Gross earnings:

Administrative salaries	$200,000
Electricians' wages	370,000
Total	$570,000

Deductions:

FICA taxes	$ 38,800
Federal income taxes withheld	174,400
State income taxes withheld (3%)	17,100
United Fund contributions payable	27,500
Health insurance premiums	17,200
Total	$275,000

Telmarine Company's payroll taxes are: FICA 8%, state unemployment 2.5% (due to a stable employment record), and 0.8% federal unemployment. Gross earnings subject to FICA taxes total $485,000, and gross earnings subject to unemployment taxes total $135,000.

Instructions

(a) Prepare a summary journal entry at December 31 for the full year's payroll.

(b) Journalize the adjusting entry at December 31 to record the employer's payroll taxes.

(c) The W-2 Wage and Tax Statement requires the following dollar data.

(a) Salaries and wages payable $295,000

(b) Payroll tax expense $43,255

Wages, Tips, Other Compensation	Federal Income Tax Withheld	State Income Tax Withheld	FICA Wages	FICA Tax Withheld

Complete the required data for the following employees.

Employee	Gross Earnings	Federal Income Tax Withheld
Lucie Solarava	$59,000	$28,500
Kristina Madericova	26,000	10,200

Problems: Set B

P11-1B On January 1, 2012, the ledger of Tyrus Company contains the following liability accounts.

Accounts Payable	$30,000
Sales Taxes Payable	5,000
Unearned Service Revenue	12,000

Prepare current liability entries, adjusting entries, and current liabilities section.

(SO 1, 2, 3, 4, 5)

During January, the following selected transactions occurred.

Jan.	1	Borrowed $20,000 in cash from Platteville Bank on a 4-month, 6%, $20,000 note.
	5	Sold merchandise for cash totaling $9,752, which includes 6% sales taxes.
	12	Provided services for customers who had made advance payments of $8,000. (Credit Service Revenue.)
	14	Paid state treasurer's department for sales taxes collected in December 2011, $5,000.
	20	Sold 900 units of a new product on credit at $44 per unit, plus 6% sales tax. This new product is subject to a 1-year warranty.
	25	Sold merchandise for cash totaling $16,536, which includes 6% sales taxes.

Instructions

(a) Journalize the January transactions.

(b) Journalize the adjusting entries at January 31 for (1) the outstanding notes payable, and (2) estimated warranty liability, assuming warranty costs are expected to equal 5% of sales of the new product.

(c) Prepare the current liabilities section of the balance sheet at January 31, 2012. Assume no change in accounts payable.

(c) Current liability total $59,944

P11-2B The following are selected transactions of Karolina Company. Karolina prepares financial statements *quarterly*.

Journalize and post note transactions and show balance sheet presentation.

(SO 2)

Jan.	2	Purchased merchandise on account from Pavel Company, $20,000, terms 2/10, n/30. (Karolina uses the perpetual inventory system.)

Feb.   1   Issued a 12%, 2-month, $20,000 note to Pavel in payment of account.
Mar. 31   Accrued interest for 2 months on Pavel note.
Apr.   1   Paid face value and interest on Pavel note.
July   1   Purchased equipment from Filipensky Equipment paying $12,000 in cash and signing a 10%, 3-month, $25,000 note.
Sept. 30   Accrued interest for 3 months on Filipensky note.
Oct.   1   Paid face value and interest on Filipensky note.
Dec.   1   Borrowed $15,000 from the Federated Bank by issuing a 3-month, 12% note with a face value of $15,000.
Dec. 31   Recognized interest expense for 1 month on Federated Bank note.

Instructions
(a) Prepare journal entries for the above transactions and events.
(b) Post to the accounts, Notes Payable, Interest Payable, and Interest Expense.
(c) Show the balance sheet presentation of notes and interest payable at December 31.

(d) $1,175

(d) What is total interest expense for the year?

Prepare payroll register and payroll entries.
(SO 6, 7)

P11-3B   Yemi's Drug Store has four employees who are paid on an hourly basis plus time-and-a-half for all hours worked in excess of 40 a week. Payroll data for the week ended February 15, 2012, are shown below.

Employee	Hours Worked	Hourly Rate	Federal Income Tax Withholdings	United Fund Contributions
M. Dvorska	39	$12.00	$34	$ –0–
D. Mottl	42	11.00	20	10.00
L. Abbasova	44	10.00	51	5.00
A. Lee	46	10.00	36	5.00

The following tax rates are applicable: FICA 8%, state income taxes 3%, state unemployment taxes 5.4%, and federal unemployment 0.8%. The first three employees are sales clerks (store wages expense). The fourth employee performs administrative duties (office wages expense).

Instructions

(a) Net pay $1,521.99

(b) Payroll tax expense $268.52

(d) Cash paid $443.56

(a) Prepare a payroll register for the weekly payroll.
(b) Journalize the payroll on February 15, 2012, and the accrual of employer payroll taxes.
(c) Journalize the payment of the payroll on February 16, 2012.
(d) Journalize the remittance to the Federal Reserve bank on February 28, 2012, of the FICA and federal income taxes payable to the government.

Journalize payroll transactions and adjusting entries.
(SO 6, 7, 9)

P11-4B   The following payroll liability accounts are included in the ledger of Patteri Company on January 1, 2012.

FICA Taxes Payable	$ 540
Federal Income Taxes Payable	1,100
State Income Taxes Payable	210
Federal Unemployment Taxes Payable	54
State Unemployment Taxes Payable	365
Union Dues Payable	200
U.S. Savings Bonds Payable	300

In January, the following transactions occurred.

Jan. 10   Sent check for $200 to union treasurer for union dues.
     12   Remitted check for $1,640 to the Federal Reserve bank for FICA taxes and federal income taxes withheld.
     15   Purchased U.S. Savings Bonds for employees by writing check for $300.
     17   Paid state income taxes withheld from employees.
     20   Paid federal and state unemployment taxes.
     31   Completed monthly payroll register, which shows office salaries $17,400, store wages $22,500, FICA taxes withheld $3,192, federal income taxes payable $2,540, state income taxes payable $500, union dues payable $300, United Fund contributions payable $1,300, and net pay $32,068.
     31   Prepared payroll checks for the net pay and distributed checks to employees.

At January 31, the company also makes the following accruals pertaining to employee compensation.

1. Employer payroll taxes: FICA taxes 8%, state unemployment taxes 5.4%, and federal unemployment taxes 0.8%.
*2. Vacation pay: 5% of gross earnings.

Instructions
(a) Journalize the January transactions.
(b) Journalize the adjustments pertaining to employee compensation at January 31.

(b) Payroll tax expense $5,665.80; Vacation benefits expense $1,995

P11-5B For the year ended December 31, 2012, Radar Company reports the following summary payroll data.

Prepare entries for payroll and payroll taxes; prepare W-2 data.
(SO 6, 7)

Gross earnings:		Deductions:	
Administrative salaries	$150,000	FICA taxes	$ 29,600
Electricians' wages	240,000	Federal income taxes withheld	78,000
Total	$390,000	State income taxes withheld (3%)	11,700
		United Fund contributions payable	17,000
		Health insurance premiums	12,000
		Total	$148,300

Radar Company's payroll taxes are: FICA 8%, state unemployment 2.5% (due to a stable employment record), and 0.8% federal unemployment. Gross earnings subject to FICA taxes total $370,000, and gross earnings subject to unemployment taxes total $90,000.

Instructions
(a) Prepare a summary journal entry at December 31 for the full year's payroll.
(b) Journalize the adjusting entry at December 31 to record the employer's payroll taxes.
(c) The W-2 Wage and Tax Statement requires the dollar data shown below.

(a) Salaries and wages payable $241,700
(b) Payroll tax expense $32,570

Wages, Tips, Other Compensation	Federal Income Tax Withheld	State Income Tax Withheld	FICA Wages	FICA Tax Withheld

Complete the required data for the following employees.

Employee	Gross Earnings	Federal Income Tax Withheld
A. Valdez	$50,000	$18,300
E. Izzard	24,000	4,800

Problems: Set C

Visit the book's companion website, at **www.wiley.com/college/weygandt**, and choose the Student Companion site to access Problem Set C.

Comprehensive Problem

CP11 Wright Company's balance sheet at December 31, 2011, is presented below.

WRIGHT COMPANY
Balance Sheet
December 31, 2011

Cash	$ 30,000	Accounts Payable	$ 13,750
Inventory	30,750	Interest Payable	250
Prepaid Insurance	6,000	Notes Payable	50,000
Equipment	38,000	Owner's Capital	40,750
	$104,750		$104,750

During January 2012, the following transactions occurred. (Wright Company uses the perpetual inventory system.)

1. Wright paid $250 interest on the note payable on January 1, 2012. The note is due December 31, 2013.

2. Wright purchased $241,100 of inventory on account.
3. Wright sold for $480,000 cash, inventory which cost $265,000. Wright also collected $28,800 in sales taxes.
4. Wright paid $230,000 in accounts payable.
5. Wright paid $17,000 in sales taxes to the state.
6. Paid other operating expenses of $20,000.
7. On January 31, 2012, the payroll for the month consists of salaries and wages of $60,000. All salaries and wages are subject to 8% FICA taxes. A total of $8,900 federal income taxes are withheld. The salaries and wages are paid on February 1.

Adjustment data:

8. Interest expense of $250 has been incurred on the notes payable.
9. The insurance for the year 2012 was prepaid on December 31, 2011.
10. The equipment was acquired on December 31, 2011, and will be depreciated on a straight-line basis over 5 years with a $2,000 salvage value.
11. Employer's payroll taxes include 8% FICA taxes, a 5.4% state unemployment tax, and an 0.8% federal unemployment tax.

Instructions
(You may need to set up T accounts to determine ending balances.)

(a) Prepare journal entries for the transactions listed above and the adjusting entries.
(b) Prepare an adjusted trial balance at January 31, 2012.
(c) Prepare an income statement, an owner's equity statement for the month ending January 31, 2012, and a classified balance sheet as of January 31, 2012.

Continuing Cookie Chronicle

(*Note:* This is a continuation of the Cookie Chronicle from Chapters 1 through 10.)

CCC11   Recall that Cookie Creations sells fine European mixers that it purchases from Kzinski Supply Co. Kzinski warrants the mixers to be free of defects in material and workmanship for a period of one year from the date of original purchase. If the mixer has such a defect, Kzinski will repair or replace the mixer free of charge for parts and labor.

Go to the book's companion website, **www.wiley.com/college/weygandt**, *to see the completion of this problem.*

BROADENINGYOURPERSPECTIVE

Financial Reporting and Analysis

Financial Reporting Problem: PepsiCo, Inc.

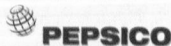

BYP11-1   The financial statements of PepsiCo, Inc. and the notes to consolidated financial statements appear in Appendix A.

Instructions
Refer to PepsiCo's financial statements and answer the following questions about current and contingent liabilities and payroll costs.

(a) What were PepsiCo's total current liabilities at December 26, 2009? What was the increase/decrease in PepsiCo's total current liabilities from the prior year?
(b) In PepsiCo's Note 2 ("Our Significant Accounting Policies"), the company explains the nature of its contingencies. Under what conditions does PepsiCo recognize (record and report) liabilities for contingencies?
(c) What were the components of total current liabilities on December 26, 2009?

Comparative Analysis Problem: PepsiCo, Inc. vs. The Coca-Cola Company

BYP11-2   PepsiCo, Inc.'s financial statements are presented in Appendix A. Financial statements of The Coca-Cola Company are presented in Appendix B.

Instructions
(a) At December 26, 2009, what was PepsiCo's largest current liability account? What were its total current liabilities? At December 31, 2009, what was Coca-Cola's largest current liability account? What were its total current liabilities?
(b) Based on information contained in those financial statements, compute the following 2009 values for each company.
    (1) Working capital.
    (2) Current ratio.
(c) What conclusions concerning the relative liquidity of these companies can be drawn from these data?

On the Web

BYP11-3   The Internal Revenue Service provides considerable information over the Internet. The following site answers payroll tax questions faced by employers.

Address: www.irs.ustreas.gov/formspubs/index.html, or go to **www.wiley.com/college/weygandt**

Steps
1. Go to the site shown above.
2. Choose **View Online, Tax Publications**.
3. Choose **Publication 15, Circular E, Employer's Tax Guide**.

Instructions
Answer each of the following questions.
(a) How does the government define "employees"?
(b) What are the special rules for Social Security and Medicare regarding children who are employed by their parents?
(c) How can an employee obtain a Social Security card if he or she doesn't have one?
(d) Must employees report to their employer tips received from customers? If so, how?
(e) Where should the employer deposit Social Security taxes withheld or contributed?

Critical Thinking

Decision Making Across the Organization

BYP11-4   Kensingtown Processing Company provides word-processing services for business clients and students in a university community. The work for business clients is fairly steady throughout the year. The work for students peaks significantly in December and May as a result of term papers, research project reports, and dissertations.

Two years ago, the company attempted to meet the peak demand by hiring part-time help. This led to numerous errors and much customer dissatisfaction. A year ago, the company hired four experienced employees on a permanent basis in place of part-time help. This proved to be much better in terms of productivity and customer satisfaction. But, it has caused an increase in annual payroll costs and a significant decline in annual net income.

Recently, Valarie Flynn, a sales representative of Metcalfe Services Inc., has made a proposal to the company. Under her plan, Metcalfe will provide up to four experienced workers at a daily rate of $75 per person for an 8-hour workday. Metcalfe workers are not available on an hourly basis. Kensingtown would have to pay only the daily rate for the workers used.

The owner of Kensingtown Processing, Donna Bell, asks you, as the company's accountant, to prepare a report on the expenses that are pertinent to the decision. If the Metcalfe plan is adopted, Donna will terminate the employment of two permanent employees and will keep two permanent employees. At the moment, each employee earns an annual income of $21,000. Kensingtown pays 8% FICA taxes, 0.8% federal unemployment taxes, and 5.4% state unemployment taxes. The unemployment taxes apply to only the first $7,000 of gross earnings. In addition, Kensingtown pays $40 per month for each employee for medical and dental insurance. Donna indicates that if the Metcalfe Services plan is accepted, her needs for temporary workers will be as follows.

Months	Number of Employees	Working Days per Month
January–March	2	20
April–May	3	25
June–October	2	18
November–December	3	23

Instructions

With the class divided into groups, answer the following.

(a) Prepare a report showing the comparative payroll expense of continuing to employ permanent workers compared to adopting the Metcalfe Services Inc. plan.

(b) What other factors should Donna consider before finalizing her decision?

Communication Activity

BYP11-5   Jack Quaney, president of the Ramsberg Company, has recently hired a number of additional employees. He recognizes that additional payroll taxes will be due as a result of this hiring, and that the company will serve as the collection agent for other taxes.

Instructions

In a memorandum to Jack Quaney, explain each of the taxes, and identify the taxes that result in payroll tax expense to Ramsberg Company.

Ethics Case

BYP11-6   Daniel Longan owns and manages Daniel's Restaurant, a 24-hour restaurant near the city's medical complex. Daniel employs 9 full-time employees and 16 part-time employees. He pays all of the full-time employees by check, the amounts of which are determined by Daniel's public accountant, Gina Watt. Daniel pays all of his part-time employees in currency. He computes their wages and withdraws the cash directly from his cash register.

Gina has repeatedly urged Daniel to pay all employees by check. But as Daniel has told his competitor and friend, Steve Hill, who owns the Greasy Diner, "My part-time employees prefer the currency over a check. Also, I don't withhold or pay any taxes or worker's compensation insurance on those cash wages because they go totally unrecorded and unnoticed."

Instructions

(a) Who are the stakeholders in this situation?

(b) What are the legal and ethical considerations regarding Daniel's handling of his payroll?

(c) Gina Watt is aware of Daniel's payment of the part-time payroll in currency. What are her ethical responsibilities in this case?

(d) What internal control principle is violated in this payroll process?

"All About You" Activity

BYP11-7   As indicated in the **All About You** feature (available on the book's companion website), medical costs are substantial and rising. But will they be the most substantial expense over your lifetime? Not likely. Will it be housing or food? Again, not likely. The answer is taxes. On average, Americans work 99 days to afford their taxes. Companies, too, have large tax burdens. They look very hard at tax issues in deciding where to build their plants and where to locate their administrative headquarters.

Instructions

(a) Determine what your state income taxes are if your taxable income is $60,000 and you file as a single taxpayer in the state in which you live.

(b) Assume that you own a home worth $200,000 in your community and the tax rate is 2.1%. Compute the property taxes you would pay.

(c) Assume that the total gasoline bill for your automobile is $1,200 a year (300 gallons at $4 per gallon). What are the amounts of state and federal taxes that you pay on the $1,200?

(d) Assume that your purchases for the year total $9,000. Of this amount, $5,000 was for food and prescription drugs. What is the amount of sales tax you would pay on these purchases? (Many states do not levy a sales tax on food or prescription drugs. Does yours?)

(e) Determine what your Social Security taxes are if your income is $60,000.

(f) Determine what your federal income taxes are if your taxable income is $60,000 and you file as a single taxpayer.

(g) Determine your total taxes paid based on the above calculations, and determine the percentage of income that you would pay in taxes based on the following formula: Total taxes paid ÷ Total income.

FASB Codification Activity

BYP11-8 If your school has a subscription to the FASB Codification, go to *http://aaahq.org/ascLogin.cfm* to log in and prepare responses to the following.

(a) What is the definition of current liabilities?

(b) What is the definition of a *contingent liability*?

(c) What guidance does the Codification provide for the disclosure of contingent liabilities?

Answers to Accounting Across the Organization Questions

p. 516 Contingencies: How Big Are They? **Q:** Why do you think most companies disclose, but do not record, contingent liabilities? **A:** A contingent liability may be probable, but often its amount is difficult to determine. If it cannot be determined, the company is not required to accrue it as a liability.

p. 527 It Costs $74,000 to Put $44,000 in Sally's Pocket **Q:** How are the Social Security and Medicare taxes computed for Sally's salary? **A:** As indicated in the story, Sally's gross earnings were $59,000. The Social Security tax is 6.2% for both employee and employer up to gross earnings of $106,800 (2010 guidelines). As shown, both Sally and Bogan pay $3,661, which is 6.2% × $59,000. In addition, the Medicare tax is 1.45% on all gross earnings for both employee and employer. As shown, both Sally and Bogan pay $856, which is 1.45% × $59,000.

Answers to Self-Test Questions

1. a **2.** d **3.** b ($88,500 × 12% × 4/12) **4.** d **5.** b ($4,515 ÷ 1.05) **6.** b ($18,000 × 3/12) **7.** a **8.** d **9.** c **10.** b **11.** d ($14 × 40) + ($21 × 5) **12.** c **13.** c **14.** b **15.** d ***16.** d

IFRS A Look at IFRS

IFRS and GAAP have similar definitions of liabilities. IFRS related to reporting and recognition of liabilities are found in *IAS 1 (revised)* ("Presentation of Financial Statements") and *IAS 37* ("Provisions, Contingent Liabilities, and Contingent Assets"). The general recording procedures for payroll are similar, although differences occur depending on the types of benefits that are provided in different countries. For example, companies in other countries often have different forms of pensions, unemployment benefits, welfare payments, and so on. The accounting for various forms of compensation plans under IFRS is found in *IAS 19* ("Employee Benefits") and *IFRS 2* ("Share-based Payments"). *IAS 19* addresses the accounting for a wide range of compensation elements, including wages, bonuses, post-employment benefits, and compensated absences. Both of these standards were recently amended, resulting in significant convergence between IFRS and GAAP.

Key Points

- The basic definition of a liability under GAAP and IFRS is very similar. In a more technical way, liabilities are defined by the IASB as a present obligation of the entity arising from past events, the settlement of which is expected to result in an outflow from the entity of resources embodying economic benefits. Liabilities may be legally enforceable via a contract or law but need not be; that is, they can arise due to normal business practice or customs.

- IFRS requires that companies classify liabilities as current or noncurrent on the face of the statement of financial position (balance sheet), except in industries where a *presentation* based on liquidity would be considered to provide more useful information (such as financial institutions). When current liabilities (also called short-term liabilities) are presented, they are generally presented in order of liquidity.

- Under IFRS, liabilities are classified as current if they are expected to be paid within 12 months.

- Similar to GAAP, items are normally reported in order of liquidity. Companies sometimes show liabilities before assets. Also, they will sometimes show long-term liabilities before current liabilities.

- Under IFRS, companies sometimes will net current liabilities against current assets to show working capital on the face of the statement of financial position. (This is evident in the Zetar financial statements in Appendix C.)

- Under GAAP, some contingent liabilities are recorded in the financial statements, others are disclosed, and in some cases no disclosure is required. Unlike GAAP, IFRS reserves the use of the term *contingent liability* to refer only to possible obligations that are *not* recognized in the financial statements but may be disclosed if certain criteria are met. Contingent liabilities are defined in *IAS 37* as being:

  ♦ A possible obligation that arises from past events and whose existence will be confirmed only by the occurrence or nonoccurrence of one or more uncertain future events not wholly within the control of the entity; or

  ♦ A present obligation that arises from past events but is not recognized because:

    • It is not probable that an outflow of resources embodying economic benefits will be required to settle the obligation; or

    • The amount of the obligation cannot be measured with sufficient reliability.

- For those items that GAAP would treat as recordable contingent liabilities, IFRS instead uses the term *provisions*. **Provisions** are defined as liabilities of uncertain timing or amount. Examples of provisions would be provisions for warranties, employee vacation pay, or anticipated losses. Under IFRS, the measurement of a provision related to an uncertain obligation is based on the best estimate of the expenditure required to settle the obligation.

- IFRS and GAAP separate plans into defined benefit and defined contribution. The accounting for defined contribution plans is similar. For defined benefit plans, there are still some significant technical differences in the reporting between GAAP and IFRS. However, the IASB and FASB are working on a joint project on pensions that will most likely eliminate the differences between the two, while dramatically changing the approach used by both.

Looking to the Future

The FASB and IASB are currently involved in two projects, each of which has implications for the accounting for liabilities. One project is investigating approaches to differentiate between debt and equity instruments. The other project, the elements phase of the conceptual framework project, will evaluate the definitions of the fundamental building blocks of accounting. The results of these projects could change the classification of many debt and equity securities.

IFRS Self-Test Questions

1. Which of the following is *false*?
   (a) Under IFRS, current liabilities must always be presented before noncurrent liabilities.
   (b) Under IFRS, an item is a current liability if it will be paid within the next 12 months.
   (c) Under IFRS, current liabilities are shown in order of liquidity.
   (d) Under IFRS, a liability is only recognized if it is a present obligation.

2. Under IFRS, a contingent liability is:
   (a) disclosed in the notes if certain criteria are met.
   (b) reported on the face of the financial statements if certain criteria are met.
   (c) the same as a provision.
   (d) not covered by IFRS.

3. Under IFRS, obligations related to warranties are considered:
   (a) contingent liabilities.
   (b) provisions.
   (c) possible obligations.
   (d) None of these.

4. Which of the following statements is *true*?
   (a) Under IFRS, the accounting for issues related to payroll are not covered in any IFRS.
   (b) The accounting for payrolls is similar under IFRS and U.S. GAAP.
   (c) Salary and wages payable is considered a contingent liability under IFRS.
   (d) IFRS does not normally report liabilities in order of liquidity.

5. The joint projects of the FASB and IASB could potentially:
   (a) change the definition of liabilities.
   (b) change the definition of equity.
   (c) change the definition of assets.
   (d) All of the above.

IFRS Concepts and Application

IFRS11-1 Define a provision and give an example.

IFRS11-2 Define a contingent liability and give an example.

IFRS11-3 Briefly describe some of the similarities and differences between GAAP and IFRS with respect to the accounting for liabilities.

International Financial Statement Analysis: Zetar plc

IFRS11-4 The financial statements of Zetar plc are presented in Appendix C.

Instructions
Use the company's complete annual report, available at *www.zetarplc.com*, to answer the following questions.
(a) According to the notes to the financial statements, what types of transactions do trade payables relate to? What was the average amount of time it took the company to pay its payables?
(b) Note 2(B) discusses provisions that the company records for certain types of activities. What do the provisions relate to, what are the estimates based on, and what could cause those estimates to change in subsequent periods?
(c) What was the average interest rate paid on bank loans and overdrafts?

Answers to IFRS Self-Test Questions
1. a   2. a   3. b   4. b   5. d

The Navigator

✔ **Remember to go back to the Navigator box on the chapter opening page and check off your completed work.**

CHAPTER 12

Accounting for Partnerships

Study Objectives

After studying this chapter, you should be able to:

1 Identify the characteristics of the partnership form of business organization.

2 Explain the accounting entries for the formation of a partnership.

3 Identify the bases for dividing net income or net loss.

4 Describe the form and content of partnership financial statements.

5 Explain the effects of the entries to record the liquidation of a partnership.

✔ The Navigator

Feature Story

FROM TRIALS TO THE TOP TEN

In 1990, Cliff Chenfield and Craig Balsam gave up the razors, ties, and six-figure salaries they had become accustomed to as New York lawyers. Instead, they set up a partnership, Razor & Tie Music, in Cliff's living room. Ten years later, it became the only record company in the country that had achieved success in selling music both on television and in stores. Razor & Tie's entertaining and effective TV commercials have yielded unprecedented sales for multi-artist music compilations. At the same time, its hot retail label has been behind some of the most recent original, progressive releases from artists such as Kelly Sweet, All That Remains, EndeverafteR, Angelique Kidjo, Ryan Shaw, Dave Barnes, Twisted Sister, Dar Williams, Danko Jones, and Yerba Buena.

Razor & Tie may be best known for its wildly popular *Kidz Bop* CD series, the top-selling children's audio product in the United States. Advertised on Nickelodeon, the

Cartoon Network, and elsewhere, *Kidz Bop* titles have sold millions of copies. Many of its releases in the series have "gone Gold."

Razor & Tie got its start with its first TV release, *Those Fabulous '70s* (100,000 copies sold), followed by *Disco Fever* (over 300,000 sold).

After restoring the respectability of the oft-maligned music of the 1970s, the partners forged into the musical '80s with the same zeal that elicited success with their first releases. In 1993, Razor & Tie released *Totally '80s*, a collection of Top-10 singles from the 1980s that has sold over 450,000 units. Featuring the tag line, "The greatest hits from the decade when communism died and music videos were born," *Totally '80s* was the best-selling direct-response album in the country in 1993.

In 1995, Razor & Tie broke into the contemporary music world with *Living in the '90s*, the most successful record in the history of the company. Featuring a number of songs that were still hits on the radio at the time the package initially aired, *Living in the '90s* was a blockbuster. It received Gold certification in less than nine months and rewrote the rules on direct-response albums. For the first time, contemporary music was available through an album offered only through direct-response spots. Razor & Tie pursued that same strategy with its 2002 introduction of the *Kidz Bop* titles.

In fact, Razor & Tie is now a vertically integrated business that includes a music company with major label distribution, a music publishing business, a media buying company, a home video company, a direct marketing operation, and a growing database of entertainment consumers.

Razor & Tie has carved out a sizable piece of the market through the complementary talents of the two partners. Their imagination and savvy, along with exciting new releases planned for the coming years, ensure Razor & Tie's continued growth.

The Navigator

Inside**CHAPTER12**

It is not surprising that when Cliff Chenfield and Craig Balsam began Razor & Tie, they decided to use the partnership form of organization. Both saw the need for hands-on control of their product and its promotion. In this chapter, we will discuss reasons why businesses select the partnership form of organization. We also will explain the major issues in accounting for partnerships.

The content and organization of Chapter 12 are as follows.

Accounting for Partnerships		
Partnership Form of Organization	**Basic Partnership Accounting**	**Liquidation of a Partnership**
• Characteristics • Organizations with partnership characteristics • Advantages/disadvantages • Partnership agreement	• Forming a partnership • Dividing net income/loss • Financial statements	• No capital deficiency • Capital deficiency

✔
The Navigator

Partnership Form of Organization

A **partnership** is an association of two or more persons to carry on as co-owners of a business for profit. Partnerships are sometimes used in small retail, service, or manufacturing companies. Also accountants, lawyers, and doctors find it desirable to form partnerships with other professionals in the field.

Study Objective [1]

Identify the characteristics of the partnership form of business organization.

Characteristics of Partnerships

Partnerships are fairly easy to form. People form partnerships simply by a verbal agreement, or more formally, by written agreement. We explain the principal characteristics of partnerships in the following sections.

ASSOCIATION OF INDIVIDUALS

A partnership is a legal entity. A partnership can own property (land, buildings, equipment), and can sue or be sued. **A partnership also is an accounting entity.** Thus, the personal assets, liabilities, and transactions of the partners are excluded from the accounting records of the partnership, just as they are in a proprietorship.

The net income of a partnership is not taxed as a separate entity. But, a partnership must file an information tax return showing partnership net income and each partner's share of that net income. Each partner's share is taxable at **personal tax rates**, regardless of the amount of net income each withdraws from the business during the year.

Association of Individuals

MUTUAL AGENCY

Mutual agency means that each partner acts on behalf of the partnership when engaging in partnership business. The act of any partner is binding on all other partners. This is true even when partners act beyond the scope of their authority, so long as the act appears to be appropriate for the partnership. For example, a partner of a

Mutual Agency

grocery store who purchases a delivery truck creates a binding contract in the name of the partnership, even if the partnership agreement denies this authority. On the other hand, if a partner in a law firm purchased a snowmobile for the partnership, such an act would not be binding on the partnership. The purchase is clearly outside the scope of partnership business.

LIMITED LIFE

Corporations have unlimited life. Partnerships do not. A partnership may be ended voluntarily at any time through the acceptance of a new partner or the withdrawal of a partner. It may be ended involuntarily by the death or incapacity of a partner. **Partnership dissolution** occurs whenever a partner withdraws or a new partner is admitted. Dissolution does not necessarily mean that the business ends. If the continuing partners agree, operations can continue without interruption by forming a new partnership.

Limited Life

UNLIMITED LIABILITY

Each partner is **personally and individually liable** for all partnership liabilities. Creditors' claims attach first to partnership assets. If these are insufficient, the claims then attach to the personal resources of any partner, irrespective of that partner's equity in the partnership. Because each partner is responsible for all the debts of the partnership, each partner is said to have **unlimited liability**.

Unlimited Liability

CO-OWNERSHIP OF PROPERTY

Partners jointly own partnership assets. If the partnership is dissolved, each partner has a claim on total assets equal to the balance in his or her respective capital account. This claim does not attach to **specific assets** that an individual partner contributed to the firm. Similarly, if a partner invests a building in the partnership valued at $100,000 and the building is later sold at a gain of $20,000, the partners all share in the gain.

Partnership net income (or net loss) is also co-owned. **If the partnership contract does not specify to the contrary, all net income or net loss is shared equally by the partners.** As you will see later, though, partners may agree to unequal sharing of net income or net loss.

Co-ownership of Property

Organizations with Partnership Characteristics

If you are starting a business with a friend and each of you has little capital and your business is not risky, you probably want to use a partnership. As indicated above, the partnership is easy to establish and its cost is minimal. These types of partnerships are often called **regular partnerships**. However if your business is risky—say, roof repair or providing some type of professional service—you will want to limit your liability and not use a regular partnership. As a result, special forms of business organizations with partnership characteristics are now often used to provide protection from unlimited liability for people who wish to work together in some activity.

The special partnership forms are: limited partnerships, limited liability partnerships, and limited liability companies. These special forms use the same accounting procedures as those described for a regular partnership. In addition, for taxation purposes, all the profits and losses pass through these organizations (similar to the regular partnership) to the owners, who report their share of partnership net income or losses on their personal tax returns.

LIMITED PARTNERSHIPS

In a **limited partnership**, one or more partners have **unlimited liability** and one or more partners have **limited liability** for the debts of the firm. Those with unlimited

International Note

Much of the funding for successful new U.S. businesses comes from "venture capital" firms, which are organized as limited partnerships. To develop its own venture capital industry, China believes that it needs the limited liability form. Therefore, China has taken steps to model its partnership laws to allow for limited partnerships like those in the United States.

Helpful Hint

In an LLP, *all* partners have limited liability. There are no general partners.

liability are general partners. Those with limited liability are limited partners. Limited partners are responsible for the debts of the partnership up to the limit of their investment in the firm.

The words "Limited Partnership," or "Ltd.," or "LP" identify this type of organization. For the privilege of limited liability, the limited partner usually accepts less compensation than a general partner and exercises less influence in the affairs of the firm. If the limited partners get involved in management, they risk their liability protection.

LIMITED LIABILITY PARTNERSHIP

Most states allow professionals such as lawyers, doctors, and accountants to form a limited liability partnership or "LLP." The LLP is designed to protect innocent partners from malpractice or negligence claims resulting from the acts of another partner. LLPs generally carry large insurance policies as protection against malpractice suits. These professional partnerships vary in size from a medical partnership of three to five doctors, to 150 to 200 partners in a large law firm, to more than 2,000 partners in an international accounting firm.

LIMITED LIABILITY COMPANIES

A hybrid form of business organization with certain features like a corporation and others like a limited partnership is the limited liability company, or "LLC." An LLC usually has a limited life. The owners, called **members**, have limited liability like owners of a corporation. Whereas limited partners do not actively participate in the management of a limited partnership (LP), the members of a limited liability company (LLC) can assume an active management role. For income tax purposes, the IRS usually classifies an LLC as a partnership.

ACCOUNTING ACROSS THE ORGANIZATION

Limited Liability Companies Gain in Popularity

The proprietorship form of business organization is still the most popular, followed by the corporate form. But whenever a group of individuals wants to form a partnership, the limited liability company is usually the popular choice.

One other form of business organization is a *subchapter S corporation*. A subchapter S corporation has many of the characteristics of a partnership—especially, taxation as a partnership—but it is losing its popularity. The reason: It involves more paperwork and expense than a limited liability company, which in most cases offers similar advantages.

 Why do you think that the use of the limited liability company is gaining in popularity? (See page 591.)

Illustration 12-1 summarizes different forms of organizations that have partnership characteristics.

Advantages and Disadvantages of Partnerships

Why do people choose partnerships? One major advantage of a partnership is to combine the skills and resources of two or more individuals. In addition, partnerships are easily formed and are relatively free from government regulations and restrictions. A partnership does not have to contend with the "red tape" that a

	Major Advantages	Major Disadvantages
Regular Partnership General Partners	Simple and inexpensive to create and operate.	Owners (partners) personally liable for business debts.
Limited Partnership General Partners Limited Partners	Limited partners have limited personal liability for business debts as long as they do not participate in management. General partners can raise cash without involving outside investors in management of business.	General partners personally liable for business debts. More expensive to create than regular partnership. Suitable mainly for companies that invest in real estate.
Limited Liability Partnership	Mostly of interest to partners in old-line professions such as law, medicine, and accounting. Owners (partners) are not personally liable for the malpractice of other partners.	Unlike a limited liability company, owners (partners) remain personally liable for many types of obligations owed to business creditors, lenders, and landlords. Often limited to a short list of professions.
Limited Liability Company	Owners have limited personal liability for business debts even if they participate in management.	More expensive to create than regular partnership.

Illustration 12-1
Different forms of organizations with partnership characteristics

Source: www.nolo.com (accessed June 2010).

corporation must face. Also, partners generally can make decisions quickly on substantive business matters without having to consult a board of directors.

On the other hand, partnerships also have some major disadvantages. **Unlimited liability** is particularly troublesome. Many individuals fear they may lose not only their initial investment but also their personal assets, if those assets are needed to pay partnership creditors.

Illustration 12-2 summarizes the advantages and disadvantages of the regular partnership form of business organization. As indicated in the previous section,

Advantages	Disadvantages
Combining skills and resources of two or more individuals	Mutual agency
Ease of formation	Limited life
Freedom from governmental regulations and restrictions	Unlimited liability
Ease of decision making	

Illustration 12-2
Advantages and disadvantages of a partnership

different types of partnership forms have evolved to reduce some of the disadvantages.

Do it!

Partnership Organization

action plan

✔ When forming a business, carefully consider what type of organization would best suit the needs of the business.

✔ Keep in mind the new, "hybrid" organizational forms that have many of the best characteristics of partnerships and corporations.

Indicate whether each of the following statements is true or false.

_____ **1.** Partnerships have unlimited life. Corporations do not.

_____ **2.** Partners jointly own partnership assets. A partner's claim on partnership assets does not attach to specific assets.

_____ **3.** In a limited partnership, the general partners have unlimited liability.

_____ **4.** The members of a limited liability company have limited liability, like shareholders of a corporation, and they are taxed like corporate shareholders.

_____ **5.** Because of mutual agency, the act of any partner is binding on all other partners.

Solution

1. False. Corporations have unlimited life. Partnerships do not.
2. True.
3. True.
4. False. The members of a limited liability company are taxed like partners in a partnership.
5. True.

Related exercise material: E12-1 and **Do it!** 12-1.

✔
The Navigator

Ethics Note

A well-developed partnership agreement reduces ethical conflict among partners. It specifies in clear and concise language the process by which the partners will resolve ethical and legal problems. This issue is especially significant when the partnership experiences financial distress.

The Partnership Agreement

Ideally, the agreement of two or more individuals to form a partnership should be expressed in a written contract, called the **partnership agreement** or **articles of co-partnership**. The partnership agreement contains such basic information as the name and principal location of the firm, the purpose of the business, and date of inception. In addition, it should specify relationships among the partners, such as:

1. Names and capital contributions of partners.
2. Rights and duties of partners.
3. Basis for sharing net income or net loss.
4. Provision for withdrawals of assets.
5. Procedures for submitting disputes to arbitration.
6. Procedures for the withdrawal or addition of a partner.
7. Rights and duties of surviving partners in the event of a partner's death.

We cannot overemphasize the importance of a written contract. The agreement should attempt to anticipate all possible situations, contingencies, and disagreements. The help of a lawyer is highly desirable in preparing the agreement.

ACCOUNTING ACROSS THE ORGANIZATION

How to Part Ways Nicely

What should you do when you and your business partner do not agree on things, to the point where you are no longer on speaking terms? Given how heated business situations can get, this is not an unusual occurrence. Unfortunately, in many instances the partners do everything they can to undermine the other partner, eventually destroying the business. In some instances people even steal from the partnership because they either feel that they "deserve it" or they assume that the other partners are stealing from them.

It would be much better to follow the example of Jennifer Appel and her partner. They found that after opening a successful bakery and writing a cookbook, they couldn't agree on how the business should be run. The other partner bought out Ms. Appel's share of the business, and Ms. Appel went on to start her own style of bakery, which she ultimately franchised.

Source: Paulette Thomas, "As Partnership Sours, Parting Is Sweet," *Wall Street Journal*, (July 6, 2004), p. A20.

 How can partnership conflicts be minimized and more easily resolved? (See page 591.)

Basic Partnership Accounting

We now turn to the basic accounting for partnerships. The major accounting issues relate to forming the partnership, dividing income or loss, and preparing financial statements.

Study Objective [2]
Explain the accounting entries for the formation of a partnership.

Forming a Partnership

Each partner's initial investment in a partnership is entered in the partnership records. The partnership should record these investments at the **fair value of the assets at the date of their transfer to the partnership**. All partners must agree to the values assigned.

To illustrate, assume that A. Rolfe and T. Shea combine their proprietorships to start a partnership named U.S. Software. The firm will specialize in developing financial modeling software packages. Rolfe and Shea have the following assets prior to the formation of the partnership.

	Book Value		Fair Value	
	A. Rolfe	T. Shea	A. Rolfe	T. Shea
Cash	$ 8,000	$ 9,000	$ 8,000	$ 9,000
Equipment	5,000		4,000	
Accumulated depreciation	(2,000)			
Accounts receivable		4,000		4,000
Allowance for doubtful accounts		(700)		(1,000)
	$11,000	$12,300	$12,000	$12,000

Illustration 12-3
Book and fair values of assets invested

*Items under **owners' equity** (OE) in the accounting equation analyses (in margins) are not labeled in this partnership chapter. Nearly all affect partners' **capital** accounts.*

The partnership records the investments as follows.

Investment of A. Rolfe

Cash	8,000	
Equipment	4,000	
A. Rolfe, Capital		12,000
(To record investment of Rolfe)		

A = L + OE
+8,000
+4,000
+12,000

Cash Flows
+8,000

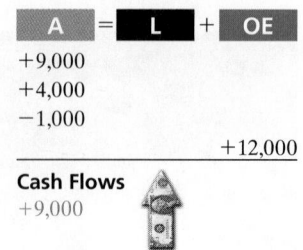

A	=	L	+	OE
+9,000				
+4,000				
−1,000				
				+12,000

Cash Flows
+9,000

International Note

Partnership accounting under GAAP and IFRS are essentially the same.

Investment of T. Shea

Cash	9,000	
Accounts Receivable	4,000	
Allowance for Doubtful Accounts		1,000
T. Shea, Capital		12,000
(To record investment of Shea)		

Note that the partnership records neither the original cost of the office equipment ($5,000) nor its book value ($5,000 − $2,000). It records the equipment at its fair value, $4,000. The partnership does not carry forward any accumulated depreciation from the books of previous entities (in this case, the two proprietorships).

In contrast, the gross claims on customers ($4,000) are carried forward to the partnership. The partnership adjusts the allowance for doubtful accounts to $1,000, to arrive at a cash (net) realizable value of $3,000. A partnership may start with an allowance for doubtful accounts because it will continue to collect existing accounts receivable, some of which are expected to be uncollectible. In addition, this procedure maintains the control and subsidiary relationship between Accounts Receivable and the accounts receivable subsidiary ledger.

After formation of the partnership, the accounting for transactions is similar to any other type of business organization. For example, the partners record all transactions with outside parties, such as the purchase or sale of merchandise inventory and the payment or receipt of cash, the same as would a sole proprietor.

The steps in the accounting cycle described in Chapter 4 for a proprietorship also apply to a partnership. For example, the partnership prepares a trial balance and journalizes and posts adjusting entries. A worksheet may be used. There are minor differences in journalizing and posting closing entries and in preparing financial statements, as we explain in the following sections. The differences occur because there is more than one owner.

Dividing Net Income or Net Loss

Partners equally share partnership net income or net loss unless the partnership contract indicates otherwise. The same basis of division usually applies to both net income and net loss. It is customary to refer to this basis as the **income ratio**, the **income and loss ratio**, or the **profit and loss (P&L) ratio.** Because of its wide acceptance, we will use the term income ratio to identify the basis for dividing net income and net loss. The partnership recognizes a partner's share of net income or net loss in the accounts through closing entries.

CLOSING ENTRIES

As in the case of a proprietorship, a partnership must make four entries in preparing closing entries. The entries are:

1. Debit each revenue account for its balance, and credit Income Summary for total revenues.

2. Debit Income Summary for total expenses, and credit each expense account for its balance.

3. Debit Income Summary for its balance, and credit each partner's capital account for his or her share of net income. Or, credit Income Summary, and debit each partner's capital account for his or her share of net loss.

4. Debit each partner's capital account for the balance in that partner's drawing account, and credit each partner's drawing account for the same amount.

The first two entries are the same as in a proprietorship. The last two entries are different because (1) there are two or more owners' capital and drawing accounts, and (2) it is necessary to divide net income (or net loss) among the partners.

To illustrate the last two closing entries, assume that AB Company has net income of $32,000 for 2012. The partners, L. Arbor and D. Barnett, share net income and net loss equally. Drawings for the year were Arbor $8,000 and Barnett $6,000. The last two closing entries are:

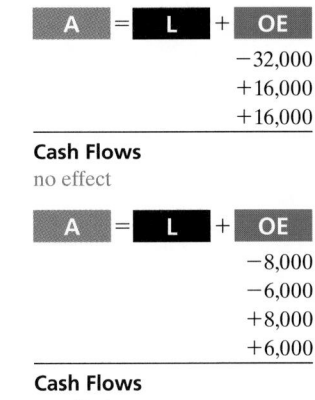

Dec. 31	Income Summary	32,000	
	L. Arbor, Capital ($32,000 × 50%)		16,000
	D. Barnett, Capital ($32,000 × 50%)		16,000
	(To transfer net income to partners' capital accounts)		
Dec. 31	L. Arbor, Capital	8,000	
	D. Barnett, Capital	6,000	
	L. Arbor, Drawings		8,000
	D. Barnett, Drawings		6,000
	(To close drawing accounts to capital accounts)		

A = L + OE
−32,000
+16,000
+16,000

Cash Flows
no effect

A = L + OE
−8,000
−6,000
+8,000
+6,000

Cash Flows
no effect

Assume that the beginning capital balance is $47,000 for Arbor and $36,000 for Barnett. After posting the closing entries, the capital and drawing accounts will appear as shown in Illustration 12-4.

L. Arbor, Capital				**D. Barnett, Capital**			
12/31 Clos.	8,000	1/1 Bal.	47,000	12/31 Clos.	6,000	1/1 Bal.	36,000
		12/31 Clos.	16,000			12/31 Clos.	16,000
		12/31 Bal.	55,000			12/31 Bal.	46,000
L. Arbor, Drawings				**D. Barnett, Drawings**			
12/31 Bal.	8,000	12/31 Clos.	8,000	12/31 Bal.	6,000	12/31 Clos.	6,000

Illustration 12-4
Partners' capital and drawing accounts after closing

As in a proprietorship, the partners' capital accounts are permanent accounts; their drawing accounts are temporary accounts. Normally, the capital accounts will have credit balances, and the drawing accounts will have debit balances. Drawing accounts are debited when partners withdraw cash or other assets from the partnership for personal use.

INCOME RATIOS

As noted earlier, the partnership agreement should specify the basis for sharing net income or net loss. The following are typical income ratios.

1. A fixed ratio, expressed as a proportion (6:4), a percentage (70% and 30%), or a fraction (2/3 and 1/3).
2. A ratio based either on capital balances at the beginning of the year or on average capital balances during the year.
3. Salaries to partners and the remainder on a fixed ratio.
4. Interest on partners' capital balances and the remainder on a fixed ratio.
5. Salaries to partners, interest on partners' capital, and the remainder on a fixed ratio.

Study Objective [3]
Identify the bases for dividing net income or net loss.

The objective is to settle on a basis that will equitably reflect the partners' capital investment and service to the partnership.

A **fixed ratio** is easy to apply, and it may be an equitable basis in some circumstances. Assume, for example, that Hughes and Lane are partners. Each contributes the same amount of capital, but Hughes expects to work full-time in the partnership and Lane expects to work only half-time. Accordingly, the partners agree to a fixed ratio of 2/3 to Hughes and 1/3 to Lane.

A **ratio based on capital balances** may be appropriate when the funds invested in the partnership are considered the critical factor. Capital ratios may also be equitable when the partners hire a manager to run the business and do not plan to take an active role in daily operations.

The three remaining ratios (items 3, 4, and 5) give specific recognition to differences among partners. These ratios provide salary allowances for time worked and interest allowances for capital invested. Then, the partnership allocates any remaining net income or net loss on a fixed ratio.

Salaries to partners and interest on partners' capital are not expenses of the partnership. Therefore, these items do not enter into the matching of expenses with revenues and the determination of net income or net loss. For a partnership, as for other entities, salaries and wages expense pertains to the cost of services performed by employees. Likewise, interest expense relates to the cost of borrowing from creditors. But partners, as owners, are not considered either **employees** or **creditors**. When the partnership agreement permits the partners to make monthly withdrawals of cash based on their "salary," the partnership debits these withdrawals to the partner's drawing account.

SALARIES, INTEREST, AND REMAINDER ON A FIXED RATIO

Under income ratio (5) in the list above, the partnership must apply salaries and interest **before** it allocates the remainder on the specified fixed ratio. **This is true even if the provisions exceed net income. It is also true even if the partnership has suffered a net loss for the year.** The partnership's income statement should show, below net income, detailed information concerning the division of net income or net loss.

To illustrate, assume that King and Lee are co-partners in the Kingslee Company. The partnership agreement provides for: (1) salary allowances of $8,400 to King and $6,000 to Lee, (2) interest allowances of 10% on capital balances at the beginning of the year, and (3) the remainder equally. Capital balances on January 1 were King $28,000, and Lee $24,000. In 2012, partnership net income is $22,000. The division of net income is as follows.

Illustration 12-5
Division of net income schedule

Kingslee Company
Division of Net Income
For the Year Ended December 31, 2012

Net income $ 22,000

Division of Net Income

	Sara King	Ray Lee	Total
Salary allowance	$ 8,400	$6,000	$14,400
Interest allowance on partners' capital			
Sara King ($28,000 × 10%)	2,800		
Ray Lee ($24,000 × 10%)		2,400	
Total interest allowance			5,200
Total salaries and interest	11,200	8,400	19,600
Remaining income, $2,400			
($22,000 − $19,600)			
Sara King ($2,400 × 50%)	1,200		
Ray Lee ($2,400 × 50%)		1,200	
Total remainder			2,400
Total division of net income	$12,400	$9,600	$22,000

Kingslee records the division of net income as follows.

Dec. 31	Income Summary	22,000	
	Sara King, Capital		12,400
	Ray Lee, Capital		9,600
	(To close net income to partners' capital)		

A	=	L	+	OE
				−22,000
				+12,000
				+9,600

Cash Flows
no effect

Now let's look at a situation in which the salary and interest allowances *exceed* net income. Assume that Kingslee Company's net income is only $18,000. In this case, the salary and interest allowances will create a deficiency of $1,600 ($19,600 − $18,000). The computations of the allowances are the same as those in the preceding example. Beginning with total salaries and interest, we complete the division of net income as shown in Illustration 12-6.

	Sara King	Ray Lee	Total
Total salaries and interest	$11,200	$8,400	$19,600
Remaining deficiency ($1,600)			
($18,000 − $19,600)			
Sara King ($1,600 × 50%)	(800)		
Ray Lee ($1,600 × 50%)		(800)	
Total remainder			(1,600)
Total division	$10,400	$7,600	$18,000

Illustration 12-6
Division of net income—income deficiency

Partnership Financial Statements

The financial statements of a partnership are similar to those of a proprietorship. The differences are due to the number of owners involved. The income statement for a partnership is identical to the income statement for a proprietorship except for the division of net income, as shown earlier.

The owners' equity statement for a partnership is called the **partners' capital statement**. It explains the changes in each partner's capital account and in total partnership capital during the year. Illustration 12-7 shows the partners' capital statement for Kingslee Company. It is based on the division of $22,000 of net income in Illustration 12-5. The statement includes assumed data for the additional investment and drawings. The partnership prepares the partners' capital statement from the income statement and the partners' capital and drawing accounts.

Study Objective [4]
Describe the form and content of partnership financial statements.

Kingslee Company
Partners' Capital Statement
For the Year Ended December 31, 2012

	Sara King	Ray Lee	Total
Capital, January 1	$28,000	$24,000	$52,000
Add: Additional investment	2,000		2,000
Net income	12,400	9,600	22,000
	42,400	33,600	76,000
Less: Drawings	7,000	5,000	12,000
Capital, December 31	$35,400	$28,600	$64,000

Illustration 12-7
Partners' capital statement

Helpful Hint

As in a proprietorship, partners' capital may change due to (1) additional investment, (2) drawings, and (3) net income or net loss.

The balance sheet for a partnership is the same as for a proprietorship except for the owner's equity section. For a partnership, the balance sheet shows the capital balances of each partner. The owners' equity section for Kingslee Company would show the following.

Illustration 12-8
Owners' equity section of a partnership balance sheet

Kingslee Company Balance Sheet (partial) December 31, 2012		
Total liabilities (assumed amount)		$115,000
Owners' equity		
Sara King, capital	$35,400	
Ray Lee, capital	28,600	
Total owners' equity		64,000
Total liabilities and owners' equity		$179,000

Do it!

Division of Net Income

action plan

✔ Compute net income exclusive of any salaries to partners and interest on partners' capital.

✔ Deduct salaries to partners from net income.

✔ Apply the partners' income ratios to the remaining net income.

✔ Prepare the closing entry distributing net income or net loss among the partners' capital accounts.

LeeMay Company reports net income of $57,000. The partnership agreement provides for salaries of $15,000 to L. Lee and $12,000 to R. May. They will share the remainder on a 60:40 basis (60% to Lee). L. Lee asks your help to divide the net income between the partners and to prepare the closing entry.

Solution

The division of net income is as follows.

	L. Lee	R. May	Total
Salary allowance	$15,000	$12,000	$27,000
Remaining income $30,000 ($57,000 − $27,000)			
L. Lee (60% × $30,000)	18,000		
R. May (40% × $30,000)		12,000	
Total remaining income			30,000
Total division of net income	$33,000	$24,000	$57,000

The closing entry for net income therefore is:

Income Summary	57,000	
L. Lee, Capital		33,000
R. May, Capital		24,000
(To close net income to partners' capital accounts)		

Related exercise material: BE12-3, BE12-4, BE12-5, E12-4, E12-5, and **Do it!** 12-2.

✔ **The Navigator**

Liquidation of a Partnership

Study Objective [5]
Explain the effects of the entries to record the liquidation of a partnership.

Liquidation of a business involves selling the assets of the firm, paying liabilities, and distributing any remaining assets. Liquidation may result from the sale of the business by mutual agreement of the partners, from the death of a partner, or from bankruptcy. **Partnership liquidation** ends both the legal and economic life of the entity.

From an accounting standpoint, the partnership should complete the accounting cycle for the final operating period prior to liquidation. This includes preparing adjusting entries and financial statements. It also involves preparing closing entries and a post-closing trial balance. Thus, only balance sheet accounts should be open as the liquidation process begins.

In liquidation, the sale of noncash assets for cash is called **realization**. Any difference between book value and the cash proceeds is called the **gain or loss on realization**. To liquidate a partnership, it is necessary to:

1. Sell noncash assets for cash and recognize a gain or loss on realization.
2. Allocate gain/loss on realization to the partners based on their income ratios.
3. Pay partnership liabilities in cash.
4. Distribute remaining cash to partners on the basis of their **capital balances**.

Each of the steps must be performed in sequence. The partnership must pay creditors **before** partners receive any cash distributions. Also, an accounting entry must record each step.

When a partnership is liquidated, all partners may have credit balances in their capital accounts. This situation is called no capital deficiency. Or, one or more partners may have a debit balance in the capital account. This situation is termed a capital deficiency. To illustrate each of these conditions, assume that Ace Company is liquidated when its ledger shows the following assets, liabilities, and owners' equity accounts.

> **Ethics Note**
>
> The process of selling noncash assets and then distributing the cash reduces the likelihood of partner disputes. If, instead, the partnership distributes noncash assets to partners to liquidate the firm, the partners would need to agree on the value of the noncash assets, which can be very difficult to determine.

Assets		Liabilities and Owners' Equity	
Cash	$ 5,000	Notes payable	$15,000
Accounts receivable	15,000	Accounts payable	16,000
Inventory	18,000	R. Arnet, capital	15,000
Equipment	35,000	P. Carey, capital	17,800
Accum. depr.—equipment	(8,000)	W. Eaton, capital	1,200
	$65,000		$65,000

Illustration 12-9
Account balances prior to liquidation

No Capital Deficiency

The partners of Ace Company agree to liquidate the partnership on the following terms: (1) The partnership will sell its noncash assets to Jackson Enterprises for $75,000 cash. (2) The partnership will pay its partnership liabilities. The income ratios of the partners are 3:2:1, respectively. The steps in the liquidation process are as follows.

1. Ace sells the noncash assets (accounts receivable, inventory, and equipment) for $75,000. The book value of these assets is $60,000 ($15,000 + $18,000 + $35,000 − $8,000). Thus, Ace realizes a gain of $15,000 on the sale. The entry is:

(1)		
Cash	75,000	
Accumulated Depreciation–Equipment	8,000	
Accounts Receivable		15,000
Inventory		18,000
Equipment		35,000
Gain on Realization		15,000
(To record realization of noncash assets)		

A = L + OE
+75,000
+8,000
−15,000
−18,000
−35,000
+15,000

Cash Flows
+75,000

2. Ace allocates the $15,000 gain on realization to the partners based on their income ratios, which are 3:2:1. The entry is:

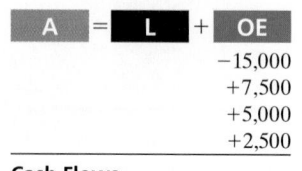

Cash Flows
no effect

(2)

Gain on Realization	15,000	
R. Arnet, Capital ($15,000 × 3/6)		7,500
P. Carey, Capital ($15,000 × 2/6)		5,000
W. Eaton, Capital ($15,000 × 1/6)		2,500
(To allocate gain to partners' capital accounts)		

3. Partnership liabilities consist of Notes Payable $15,000 and Accounts Payable $16,000. Ace pays creditors in full by a cash payment of $31,000. The entry is:

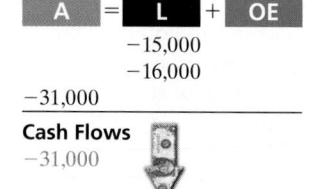

Cash Flows
−31,000

(3)

Notes Payable	15,000	
Accounts Payable	16,000	
Cash		31,000
(To record payment of partnership liabilities)		

4. Ace distributes the remaining cash to the partners on the basis of **their capital balances**. After posting the entries in the first three steps, all partnership accounts, including Gain on Realization, will have zero balances except for four accounts: Cash $49,000; R. Arnet, Capital $22,500; P. Carey, Capital $22,800; and W. Eaton, Capital $3,700, as shown below.

Cash				R. Arnet, Capital		P. Carey, Capital		W. Eaton, Capital	
Bal.	5,000	(3)	31,000	Bal.	15,000	Bal.	17,800	Bal.	1,200
(1)	75,000			(2)	7,500	(2)	5,000	(2)	2,500
Bal.	**49,000**			**Bal.**	**22,500**	**Bal.**	**22,800**	**Bal.**	**3,700**

Illustration 12-10
Ledger balances before distribution of cash

Ace records the distribution of cash as follows.

Cash Flows
−49,000

(4)

R. Arnet, Capital	22,500	
P. Carey, Capital	22,800	
W. Eaton, Capital	3,700	
Cash		49,000
(To record distribution of cash to partners)		

After posting this entry, all partnership accounts will have zero balances.

A word of caution: **Partnerships should not distribute remaining cash to partners on the basis of their income-sharing ratios.** On this basis, Arnet would receive three-sixths, or $24,500, which would produce an erroneous debit balance of $2,000. The income ratio is the proper basis for allocating net income or loss. **It is not a proper basis for making the final distribution of cash to the partners.**

Alternative Terminology

The schedule of cash payments is sometimes called a *safe cash payments schedule*.

SCHEDULE OF CASH PAYMENTS

The **schedule of cash payments** shows the distribution of cash to the partners in a partnership liquidation. A cash payments schedule is sometimes prepared to determine the distribution of cash to the partners in the liquidation of a partnership.

The schedule of cash payments is organized around the basic accounting equation. Illustration 12-11 shows the schedule for Ace Company. The numbers in parentheses refer to the four required steps in the liquidation of a partnership. They also identify the accounting entries that Ace must make. The cash payments schedule is especially useful when the liquidation process extends over a period of time.

ACE COMPANY
Schedule of Cash Payments

Item		Cash	+	Noncash Assets	=	Liabilities	+	R. Arnet, Capital	+	P. Carey, Capital	+	W. Eaton, Capital
Balances before liquidation		5,000	+	60,000	=	31,000	+	15,000	+	17,800	+	1,200
Sale of noncash assets and allocation of gain	(1)&(2)	75,000	+	(60,000)	=			7,500	+	5,000	+	2,500
New balances		80,000	+	–0–	=	31,000	+	22,500	+	22,800	+	3,700
Pay liabilities	(3)	(31,000)			=	(31,000)						
New balances		49,000	+	–0–	=	–0–	+	22,500	+	22,800	+	3,700
Cash distribution to partners	(4)	(49,000)			=			(22,500)	+	(22,800)	+	(3,700)
Final balances		–0–		–0–		–0–		–0–		–0–		–0–

Illustration 12-11
Schedule of cash payments, no capital deficiency

Do it!

The partners of Grafton Company have decided to liquidate their business. Noncash assets were sold for $115,000. The income ratios of the partners Kale D., Croix D., and Marais K. are 2:3:3, respectively. Complete the following schedule of cash payments for Grafton Company.

Item	Cash	+	Noncash Assets	=	Liabilities	+	Kale D., Capital	+	Croix D., Capital	+	Marais K., Capital
Balances before liquidation	10,000		85,000		40,000		15,000		35,000		5,000
Sale of noncash assets and allocation of gain											
New balances											
Pay liabilities											
New balances											
Cash distribution to partners											
Final balances											

Partnership Liquidation

action plan

✔ First, sell the noncash assets and determine the gain.

✔ Allocate the gain to the partners based on their income ratios.

✔ Use cash to pay off liabilities.

✔ Distribute remaining cash on the basis of their capital balances.

Solution

GRAFTON Company.xls

File Edit View Insert Format Tools Data Window Help

	A	B	C	D	E	F	G	H	I	J	K	L
1	Item	Cash	+	Noncash Assets	=	Liabilities	+	Kale D., Capital	+	Croix D., Capital	+	Marais K., Capital
2	Balances before liquidation	10,000		85,000		40,000		15,000		35,000		5,000
3	Sale of noncash assets and allocation of gain	115,000		(85,000)				7,500ᵃ		11,250ᵇ		11,250ᵇ
4	New balances	125,000		–0–		40,000		22,500		46,250		16,250
5	Pay liabilities	(40,000)				(40,000)						
6	New balances	85,000		–0–		–0–		22,500		46,250		16,250
7	Cash distribution to partners	85,000						(22,500)		(46,250)		(16,250)
8	Final balances	–0–		–0–		–0–		–0–		–0–		–0–

ᵃ$30,000 \times 2/8$
ᵇ$30,000 \times 3/8$

Related exercise material: **BE12-6, E12-8, E12-9, E12-10,** and **Do it!** 12-3.

Capital Deficiency

A capital deficiency may result from recurring net losses, excessive drawings, or losses from realization suffered during liquidation. To illustrate, assume that Ace Company is on the brink of bankruptcy. The partners decide to liquidate by having a "going-out-of-business" sale. They sell merchandise at substantial discounts, and sell the equipment at auction. Cash proceeds from these sales and collections from customers total only $42,000. Thus, the loss from liquidation is $18,000 ($60,000 − $42,000). The steps in the liquidation process are as follows.

1. The entry for the realization of noncash assets is:

(1)

Cash	42,000	
Accumulated Depreciation—Equipment	8,000	
Loss on Realization	18,000	
Accounts Receivable		15,000
Inventory		18,000
Equipment		35,000
(To record realization of noncash assets)		

2. Ace allocates the loss on realization to the partners on the basis of their income ratios. The entry is:

(2)

A = L + OE
−9,000
−6,000
−3,000
+18,000

Cash Flows
no effect

R. Arnet, Capital ($18,000 \times 3/6$)	9,000	
P. Carey, Capital ($18,000 \times 2/6$)	6,000	
W. Eaton, Capital ($18,000 \times 1/6$)	3,000	
Loss on Realization		18,000
(To allocate loss on realization to partners)		

3. Ace pays the partnership liabilities. This entry is the same as the previous one.

(3)

Notes Payable	15,000	
Accounts Payable	16,000	
Cash		31,000
(To record payment of partnership liabilities)		

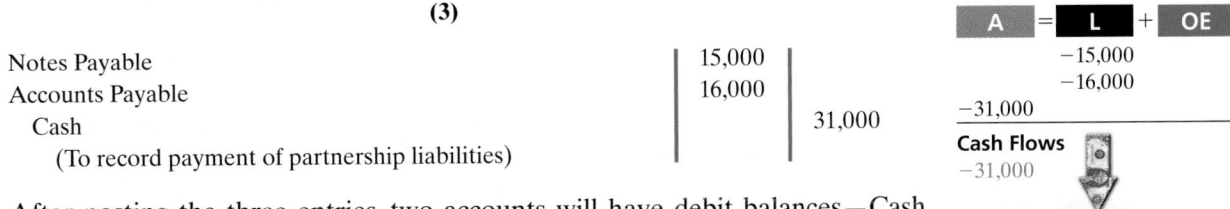

A = L + OE
−15,000
−16,000
−31,000

Cash Flows
−31,000

4. After posting the three entries, two accounts will have debit balances—Cash $16,000, and W. Eaton, Capital $1,800. Two accounts will have credit balances— R. Arnet, Capital $6,000, and P. Carey, Capital $11,800. All four accounts are shown below.

Cash				R. Arnet, Capital				P. Carey, Capital				W. Eaton, Capital			
Bal.	5,000	(3)	31,000	(2)	9,000	Bal.	15,000	(2)	6,000	Bal.	17,800	(2)	3,000	Bal.	1,200
(1)	42,000					Bal.	6,000			Bal.	11,800	Bal.	1,800		
Bal.	16,000														

Illustration 12-12
Ledger balances before distribution of cash

Eaton has a capital deficiency of $1,800, and so owes the partnership $1,800. Arnet and Carey have a legally enforceable claim for that amount against Eaton's personal assets. Note that the distribution of cash is still made on the basis of capital balances. But the amount will vary depending on how Eaton settles the deficiency. Two alternatives are presented in the following sections.

PAYMENT OF DEFICIENCY

If the partner with the capital deficiency pays the amount owed the partnership, the deficiency is eliminated. To illustrate, assume that Eaton pays $1,800 to the partnership. The entry is:

(a)

Cash	1,800	
W. Eaton, Capital		1,800
(To record payment of capital deficiency by Eaton)		

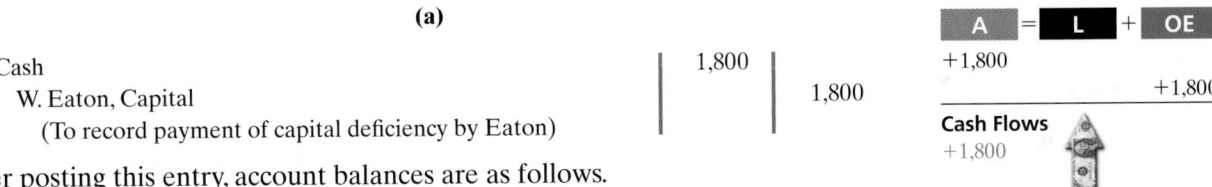

A = L + OE
+1,800
+1,800

Cash Flows
+1,800

After posting this entry, account balances are as follows.

Cash				R. Arnet, Capital				P. Carey, Capital				W. Eaton, Capital			
Bal.	5,000	(3)	31,000	(2)	9,000	Bal.	15,000	(2)	6,000	Bal.	17,800	(2)	3,000	Bal.	1,200
(1)	42,000					Bal.	6,000			Bal.	11,800			(a)	1,800
(a)	1,800													Bal.	—0—
Bal.	17,800														

Illustration 12-13
Ledger balances after paying capital deficiency

The cash balance of $17,800 is now equal to the credit balances in the capital accounts (Arnet $6,000 + Carey $11,800). Ace now distributes cash on the basis of these balances. The entry is:

R. Arnet, Capital	6,000	
P. Carey, Capital	11,800	
Cash		17,800
(To record distribution of cash to the partners)		

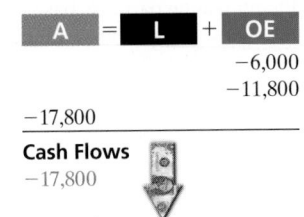

A = L + OE
−6,000
−11,800
−17,800

Cash Flows
−17,800

After posting this entry, all accounts will have zero balances.

NONPAYMENT OF DEFICIENCY

If a partner with a capital deficiency is unable to pay the amount owed to the partnership, the partners with credit balances must absorb the loss. The partnership allocates the loss on the basis of the income ratios that exist between the partners with credit balances.

The income ratios of Arnet and Carey are 3:2, or 3/5 and 2/5, respectively. Thus, Ace would make the following entry to remove Eaton's capital deficiency.

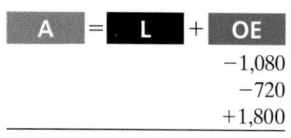

A = L + OE
−1,080
−720
+1,800

Cash Flows
no effect

(a)

R. Arnet, Capital ($1,800 × 3/5)	1,080	
P. Carey, Capital ($1,800 × 2/5)	720	
W. Eaton, Capital		1,800
(To record write-off of capital deficiency)		

After posting this entry, the cash and capital accounts will have the following balances.

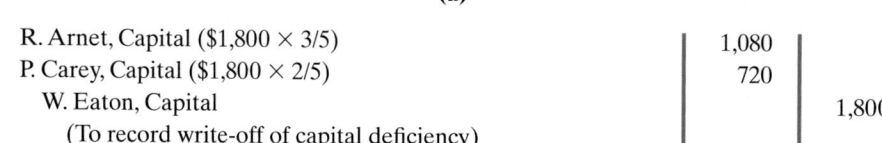

Cash				R. Arnet, Capital				P. Carey, Capital				W. Eaton, Capital			
Bal.	5,000	(3)	31,000	(2)	9,000	Bal.	15,000	(2)	6,000	Bal.	17,800	(2)	3,000	Bal.	1,200
(1)	42,000			(a)	1,080			(a)	720					(a)	1,800
Bal.	16,000					Bal.	4,920			Bal.	11,080			Bal.	—0—

Illustration 12-14
Ledger balances after nonpayment of capital deficiency

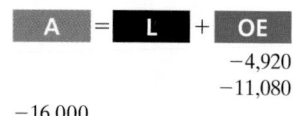

A = L + OE
−4,920
−11,080

−16,000

Cash Flows
−16,000

The cash balance ($16,000) now equals the sum of the credit balances in the capital accounts (Arnet $4,920 + Carey $11,080). Ace records the distribution of cash as:

R. Arnet, Capital	4,920	
P. Carey, Capital	11,080	
Cash		16,000
(To record distribution of cash to the partners)		

After posting this entry, all accounts will have zero balances.

Do it!

Partnership Liquidation

action plan

✔ Allocate any unpaid capital deficiency to the partners with credit balances, based on their income ratios.

✔ After distribution of the deficiency, distribute cash to the remaining partners, based on their capital balances.

Kessington Company wishes to liquidate the firm by distributing the company's cash to the three partners. Prior to the distribution of cash, the company's balances are: Cash $45,000; Rollings, Capital (Cr.) $28,000; Havens, Capital (Dr.) $12,000; and Ostergard, Capital (Cr.) $29,000. The income ratios of the three partners are 4:4:2, respectively. Prepare the entry to record the absorption of Havens' capital deficiency by the other partners and the distribution of cash to the partners with credit balances.

Solution

Rollings, Capital ($12,000 × 4/6)	8,000	
Ostergard, Capital ($12,000 × 2/6)	4,000	
Havens, Capital		12,000
(To record write-off of capital deficiency)		
Rollings, Capital ($28,000 − $8,000)	20,000	
Ostergard, Capital ($29,000 − $4,000)	25,000	
Cash		45,000
(To record distribution of cash to partners)		

Related exercise material: E12-10 and **Do it!** 12-4.

The Navigator

COMPREHENSIVE

Do it!

On January 1, 2012, the capital balances in Hollingsworth Company are Lois Holly $26,000, and Jim Worth $24,000. In 2012 the partnership reports net income of $30,000. The income ratio provides for salary allowances of $12,000 for Holly and $10,000 to Worth and the remainder equally. Neither partner had any drawings in 2012.

Instructions

(a) Prepare a schedule showing the distribution of net income in 2012.

(b) Journalize the division of 2012 net income to the partners.

action plan

✔ Compute the net income of the partnership.

✔ Allocate the partners' salaries.

✔ Divide the remaining net income among the partners, applying the income/loss ratio.

✔ Journalize the division of net income in a closing entry.

Solution to Comprehensive Do it!

(a)   Net income   30,000

Division of Net Income

	Lois Holly	Jim Worth	Total
Salary allowance	$12,000	$10,000	$22,000
Remaining income $8,000 ($30,000 − $22,000)			
Lois Holly ($8,000 × 50%)	4,000		
Jim Worth ($8,000 × 50%)		4,000	
Total remainder			8,000
Total division of net income	$16,000	$14,000	$30,000

(b) 12/31/12

Income Summary	30,000	
Lois Holly, Capital		16,000
Jim Worth, Capital		14,000
(To close net income to partners' capital)		

The Navigator

Summary of Study Objectives

[1] Identify the characteristics of the partnership form of business organization. The principal characteristics of a partnership are: (a) association of individuals, (b) mutual agency, (c) limited life, (d) unlimited liability, and (e) co-ownership of property.

[2] Explain the accounting entries for the formation of a partnership. When formed, a partnership records each partner's initial investment at the fair value of the assets at the date of their transfer to the partnership.

[3] Identify the bases for dividing net income or net loss. Partnerships divide net income or net loss on the basis of the income ratio, which may be (a) a fixed ratio, (b) a ratio based on beginning or average capital balances, (c) salaries to partners and the remainder on a fixed ratio, (d) interest on partners' capital and the remainder on a fixed ratio, and (e) salaries to partners, interest on partners' capital, and the remainder on a fixed ratio.

[4] Describe the form and content of partnership financial statements. The financial statements of a partnership are similar to those of a proprietorship. The principal differences are: (a) The partnership shows the division of net income on the income statement. (b) The owners' equity statement is called a partners' capital statement. (c) The partnership reports each partner's capital on the balance sheet.

[5] Explain the effects of the entries to record the liquidation of a partnership. When a partnership is liquidated, it is necessary to record the (a) sale of noncash assets, (b) allocation of the gain or loss on realization, (c) payment of partnership liabilities, and (d) distribution of cash to the partners on the basis of their capital balances.

✔
The Navigator

Glossary

Capital deficiency   A debit balance in a partner's capital account after allocation of gain or loss. (p. 565).

General partners   Partners who have unlimited liability for the debts of the firm. (p. 556).

Income ratio   The basis for dividing net income and net loss in a partnership. (p. 560).

Limited liability company   A form of business organization, usually classified as a partnership for tax purposes and usually with limited life, in which partners, who are called *members*, have limited liability. (p. 556).

Limited liability partnership   A partnership of professionals in which partners are given limited liability and the public is protected from malpractice by insurance carried by the partnership. (p. 556).

Limited partners   Partners whose liability for the debts of the firm is limited to their investment in the firm. (p. 556).

Limited partnership   A partnership in which one or more general partners have unlimited liability and one or more partners have limited liability for the obligations of the firm. (p. 555).

No capital deficiency   All partners have credit balances after allocation of gain or loss. (p. 565).

Partners' capital statement   The owners' equity statement for a partnership which shows the changes in each partner's capital account and in total partnership capital during the year. (p. 563).

Partnership   An association of two or more persons to carry on as co-owners of a business for profit. (p. 554).

Partnership agreement   A written contract expressing the voluntary agreement of two or more individuals in a partnership. (p. 558).

Partnership dissolution   A change in partners due to withdrawal or admission, which does not necessarily terminate the business. (p. 555).

Partnership liquidation   An event that ends both the legal and economic life of a partnership. (p. 564).

Schedule of cash payments   A schedule showing the distribution of cash to the partners in a partnership liquidation. (p. 566).

APPENDIX12A

Admission and Withdrawal of Partners

The chapter explained how the basic accounting for a partnership works. We now look at how to account for a common occurrence in partnerships—the addition or withdrawal of a partner.

Admission of a Partner

Study Objective [6]
Explain the effects of the entries when a new partner is admitted.

Helpful Hint

In a purchase of an interest, the partnership is not a participant in the transaction. In this transaction, the new partner contributes *no* cash to the partnership.

The admission of a new partner results in the **legal dissolution** of the existing partnership and the beginning of a new one. From an economic standpoint, however, the admission of a new partner (or partners) may be of minor significance in the continuity of the business. For example, in large public accounting or law firms, partners are admitted annually without any change in operating policies. **To recognize the economic effects, it is necessary only to open a capital account for each new partner.** In the entries illustrated in this appendix, we assume that the accounting records of the predecessor firm will continue to be used by the new partnership.

A new partner may be admitted either by (1) purchasing the interest of one or more existing partners or (2) investing assets in the partnership. The former affects only the capital accounts of the partners who are parties to the transaction. The latter increases both net assets and total capital of the partnership.

PURCHASE OF A PARTNER'S INTEREST

The **admission** of a partner **by purchase of an interest** is a personal transaction between one or more existing partners and the new partner. Each party acts as an individual separate from the partnership entity. The individuals involved negotiate the price paid. It may be equal to or different from the capital equity acquired. The purchase price passes directly from the new partner to the partners who are giving up part or all of their ownership claims.

Any money or other consideration exchanged is the personal property of the participants and **not** the property of the partnership. Upon purchase of an interest, the new partner acquires each selling partner's capital interest and income ratio.

Accounting for the purchase of an interest is straightforward. The partnership records record only the changes in partners' capital. **Partners' capital accounts are debited for any ownership claims sold.** At the same time, the new partner's capital account is credited for the capital equity purchased. Total assets, total liabilities, and total capital remain unchanged, as do all individual asset and liability accounts.

To illustrate, assume that L. Carson agrees to pay $10,000 each to C. Ames and D. Barker for 33⅓% (one-third) of their interest in the Ames–Barker partnership. At the time of the admission of Carson, each partner has a $30,000 capital balance. Both partners, therefore, give up $10,000 of their capital equity. The entry to record the admission of Carson is:

C. Ames, Capital	10,000	
D. Barker, Capital	10,000	
L. Carson, Capital		20,000
(To record admission of Carson by purchase)		

The effect of this transaction on net assets and partners' capital is shown below.

Illustration 12A-1
Ledger balances after purchase of a partner's interest

Net Assets	C. Ames, Capital		D. Barker, Capital		L. Carson, Capital
60,000	10,000	30,000	10,000	30,000	20,000
		Bal. 20,000		Bal. 20,000	

Note that net assets remain unchanged at $60,000, and each partner has a $20,000 capital balance. Ames and Barker continue as partners in the firm, but the capital interest of each has changed. The cash paid by Carson goes directly to the individual partners and not to the partnership.

Regardless of the amount paid by Carson for the one-third interest, the entry is exactly the same. If Carson pays $12,000 each to Ames and Barker for one-third of the partnership, the partnership still makes the entry shown above.

INVESTMENT OF ASSETS IN A PARTNERSHIP

The admission of a partner by an investment of assets is a transaction between the new partner and the partnership. Often referred to simply as admission by investment, the transaction **increases both the net assets and total capital of the partnership**.

Assume, for example, that instead of purchasing an interest, Carson invests $30,000 in cash in the Ames–Barker partnership for a 33⅓% capital interest. In such a case, the entry is:

Cash	30,000	
L. Carson, Capital		30,000
(To record admission of Carson by investment)		

The effects of this transaction on the partnership accounts would be:

Illustration 12A-2
Ledger balances after investment of assets

Net Assets	C. Ames, Capital	D. Barker, Capital	L. Carson, Capital
60,000	30,000	30,000	30,000
30,000			
Bal. 90,000			

Note that both net assets and total capital have increased by $30,000.

Remember that Carson's one-third capital interest might not result in a one-third income ratio. The new partnership agreement should specify Carson's income ratio, and it may or may not be equal to the one-third capital interest.

The comparison of the net assets and capital balances in Illustration 12A-3 shows the different effects of the purchase of an interest and admission by investment.

Illustration 12A-3
Comparison of purchase of an interest and admission by investment

Purchase of an Interest			Admission by Investment		
Net assets		$60,000	Net assets		$90,000
Capital			Capital		
C. Ames	$20,000		C. Ames	$30,000	
D. Barker	20,000		D. Barker	30,000	
L. Carson	20,000		L. Carson	30,000	
Total capital		$60,000	Total capital		$90,000

When a new partner purchases an interest, the total net assets and total capital of the partnership *do not change*. When a partner is admitted by investment, both the total net assets and the total capital *change*.

In the case of admission by investment, further complications occur when the new partner's investment differs from the capital equity acquired. When those amounts are not the same, the difference is considered a **bonus** either to (1) the existing (old) partners or (2) the new partner.

Bonus to Old Partners.   For both personal and business reasons, the existing partners may be unwilling to admit a new partner without receiving a bonus. In an established firm, existing partners may insist on a bonus as compensation for the work they have put into the company over the years. Two accounting factors underlie the business reason: First, total partners' capital equals the **book value** of the recorded net assets of the partnership. When the new partner is admitted, the fair values of assets such as land and buildings may be higher than their book values. The bonus will help make up the difference between fair value and book value. Second, when the partnership has been profitable, goodwill may exist. But, the partnership balance sheet does not report goodwill. The new partner is usually willing to pay the bonus to become a partner.

A bonus to old partners results when the new partner's investment in the firm is greater than the capital credit on the date of admittance. The bonus results in **an increase in the capital balances of the old partners**. **The partnership allocates the bonus to them on the basis of their income ratios before the admission of the new partner.** To illustrate, assume that the Bart–Cohen partnership, owned by Sam Bart and Tom Cohen, has total capital of $120,000. Lea Eden acquires a 25% ownership (capital) interest in the partnership by making a cash investment of $80,000. The procedure for determining Eden's capital credit and the bonus to the old partners is as follows.

1. **Determine the total capital of the new partnership:** Add the new partner's investment to the total capital of the old partnership. In this case, the total capital of the new firm is $200,000, computed as follows.

Total capital of existing partnership	$120,000
Investment by new partner, Eden	80,000
Total capital of new partnership	$200,000

2. **Determine the new partner's capital credit:** Multiply the total capital of the new partnership by the new partner's ownership interest. Eden's capital credit is $50,000 ($200,000 × 25%).

3. **Determine the amount of bonus:** Subtract the new partner's capital credit from the new partner's investment. The bonus in this case is $30,000 ($80,000 − $50,000).

4. **Allocate the bonus to the old partners on the basis of their income ratios:** Assuming the ratios are Bart 60%, and Cohen 40%, the allocation is: Bart $18,000 ($30,000 × 60%) and Cohen $12,000 ($30,000 × 40%).

The entry to record the admission of Eden is:

Cash	80,000	
Sam Bart, Capital		18,000
Tom Cohen, Capital		12,000
Lea Eden, Capital		50,000
(To record admission of Eden and bonus to old partners)		

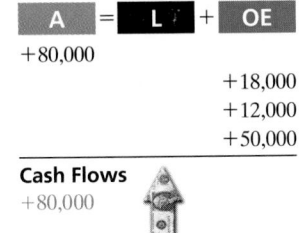

Bonus to New Partner.   A bonus to a new partner results when the new partner's investment in the firm is less than his or her capital credit. This may occur when the new partner possesses special attributes that the partnership wants. For example, the new partner may be able to supply cash that the firm needs for expansion or to meet maturing debts. Or the new partner may be a recognized expert in a relevant field. Thus, an engineering firm may be willing to give a renowned engineer a bonus to join the firm. The partners of a restaurant may offer a bonus to a sports celebrity in order to add the athlete's name to the partnership. A bonus to a new partner may also result when recorded book values on the partnership books are higher than their fair values.

A bonus to a new partner results in a **decrease in the capital balances of the old partners. The amount of the decrease for each partner is based on the income ratios before the admission of the new partner.** To illustrate, assume that Lea Eden invests $20,000 in cash for a 25% ownership interest in the Bart–Cohen partnership. The computations for Eden's capital credit and the bonus are as follows, using the four procedures described in the preceding section.

1. Total capital of Bart–Cohen partnership		$120,000
Investment by new partner, Eden		20,000
Total capital of new partnership		$140,000
2. **Eden's capital credit** (25% × $140,000)		$ 35,000
3. **Bonus to Eden** ($35,000 − $20,000)		$ 15,000
4. Allocation of bonus to old partners:		
Bart ($15,000 × 60%)	$9,000	
Cohen ($15,000 × 40%)	6,000	$ 15,000

Illustration 12A-4
Computation of capital credit and bonus to new partner

The partnership records the admission of Eden as follows.

Cash	20,000	
Sam Bart, Capital	9,000	
Tom Cohen, Capital	6,000	
Lea Eden, Capital		35,000
(To record Eden's admission and bonus)		

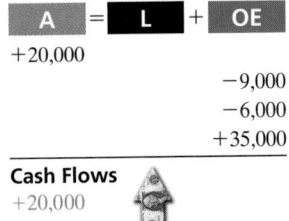

Withdrawal of a Partner

Study Objective [7]
Describe the effects of the entries when a partner withdraws from the firm.

Now let's look at the opposite situation—the withdrawal of a partner. A partner may withdraw from a partnership **voluntarily**, by selling his or her equity in the firm. Or, he or she may withdraw **involuntarily**, by reaching mandatory retirement age or by dying. The withdrawal of a partner, like the admission of a partner, legally dissolves the partnership. The legal effects may be recognized by dissolving the firm. However, it is customary to record only the economic effects of the partner's withdrawal, while the firm continues to operate and reorganizes itself legally.

As indicated earlier, the partnership agreement should specify the terms of withdrawal. The withdrawal of a partner may be accomplished by (1) payment from partners' personal assets or (2) payment from partnership assets. The former affects only the partners' capital accounts. The latter decreases total net assets and total capital of the partnership.

PAYMENT FROM PARTNERS' PERSONAL ASSETS

Withdrawal by payment from partners' personal assets is a personal transaction between the partners. **It is the direct opposite of admitting a new partner who purchases a partner's interest.** The remaining partners pay the retiring partner directly from their personal assets. **Partnership assets are not involved in any way, and total capital does not change.** The effect on the partnership is limited to changes in the partners' capital balances.

To illustrate, assume that partners Morz, Nead, and Odom have capital balances of $25,000, $15,000, and $10,000, respectively. Morz and Nead agree to buy out Odom's interest. Each of them agrees to pay Odom $8,000 in exchange for one-half of Odom's total interest of $10,000. The entry to record the withdrawal is:

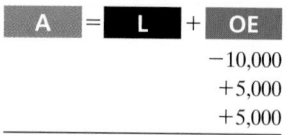

A = L + OE
−10,000
+5,000
+5,000

Cash Flows
no effect

	Debit	Credit
J. Odom, Capital	10,000	
A. Morz, Capital		5,000
M. Nead, Capital		5,000
(To record purchase of Odom's interest)		

The effect of this entry on the partnership accounts is shown below.

Net Assets		A. Morz, Capital		M. Nead, Capital		J. Odom, Capital	
50,000			25,000		15,000	10,000	10,000
			5,000		5,000		
			Bal. 30,000		Bal. 20,000	Bal.	–0–

Illustration 12A-5
Ledger balances after payment from partners' personal assets

Note that net assets and total capital remain the same at $50,000.

What about the $16,000 paid to Odom? You've probably noted that it is not recorded. The entry debited Odom's capital only for $10,000, not for the $16,000 that she received. Similarly, both Morz and Nead credit their capital accounts for only $5,000, not for the $8,000 they each paid.

After Odom's withdrawal, Morz and Nead will share net income or net loss equally unless they indicate another income ratio in the partnership agreement.

PAYMENT FROM PARTNERSHIP ASSETS

Withdrawal by payment from partnership assets is a transaction that involves the partnership. **Both partnership net assets and total capital decrease as a result.** Using partnership assets to pay for a withdrawing partner's interest is the **reverse** of admitting a partner through the investment of assets in the partnership.

Many partnership agreements provide that the amount paid should be based on the fair value of the assets at the time of the partner's withdrawal. When this basis is required, some maintain that any differences between recorded asset balances and their fair values should be (1) recorded by an adjusting entry, and (2) allocated to all partners on the basis of their income ratios. This position has serious flaws. Recording the revaluations violates the cost principle, which requires that assets be stated at original cost. It also violates the going-concern assumption, which assumes the entity will continue indefinitely. The terms of the partnership contract should not dictate the accounting for this event.

In accounting for a withdrawal by payment from partnership assets, the partnership should not record asset revaluations. Instead, it should consider any difference between the amount paid and the withdrawing partner's capital balance as **a bonus** to the retiring partner or to the remaining partners.

Bonus to Retiring Partner.
A partnership may pay a bonus to a retiring partner when:

1. The fair value of partnership assets is more than their book value,
2. There is unrecorded goodwill resulting from the partnership's superior earnings record, or
3. The remaining partners are eager to remove the partner from the firm.

The partnership deducts the bonus from the remaining partners' capital balances on the basis of their income ratios at the time of the withdrawal.

To illustrate, assume that the following capital balances exist in the RST partnership: Roman $50,000, Sand $30,000, and Terk $20,000. The partners share income in the ratio of 3 : 2 : 1, respectively. Terk retires from the partnership and receives a cash payment of $25,000 from the firm. The procedure for determining the bonus to the retiring partner and the allocation of the bonus to the remaining partners is as follows.

1. **Determine the amount of the bonus:** Subtract the retiring partner's capital balance from the cash paid by the partnership. The bonus in this case is $5,000 ($25,000 − $20,000).

2. **Allocate the bonus to the remaining partners on the basis of their income ratios:** The ratios of Roman and Sand are 3 : 2. Thus, the allocation of the $5,000 bonus is: Roman $3,000 ($5,000 × 3/5) and Sand $2,000 ($5,000 × 2/5).

The partnership records the withdrawal of Terk as follows.

B. Terk, Capital	20,000	
F. Roman, Capital	3,000	
D. Sand, Capital	2,000	
Cash		25,000
(To record withdrawal of and bonus to Terk)		

Helpful Hint
Compare this entry to the one on page 578.

The remaining partners, Roman and Sand, will recover the bonus given to Terk as the partnership sells or uses the undervalued assets.

Bonus to Remaining Partners.
The retiring partner may give a bonus to the remaining partners when:

1. Recorded assets are overvalued,
2. The partnership has a poor earnings record, or
3. The partner is eager to leave the partnership.

In such cases, the cash paid to the retiring partner will be less than the retiring partner's capital balance. **The partnership allocates (credits) the bonus to the capital accounts of the remaining partners on the basis of their income ratios.**

To illustrate, assume instead that the partnership pays Terk only $16,000 for her $20,000 equity when she withdraws from the partnership. In that case:

1. The bonus to remaining partners is $4,000 ($20,000 − $16,000).
2. The allocation of the $4,000 bonus is: Roman $2,400 ($4,000 × 3/5) and Sand $1,600 ($4,000 × 2/5).

Under these circumstances, the entry to record the withdrawal is:

Helpful Hint

Compare this entry to the one on page 577.

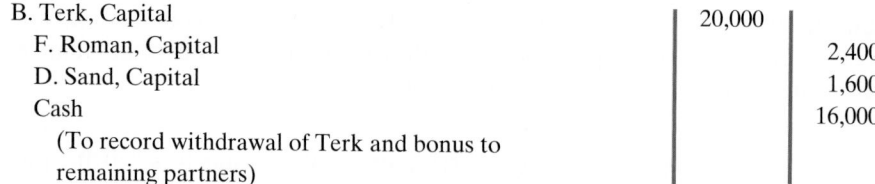

A = L + OE
−20,000
+2,400
+1,600
−16,000

Cash Flows
−16,000

B. Terk, Capital	20,000	
F. Roman, Capital		2,400
D. Sand, Capital		1,600
Cash		16,000
(To record withdrawal of Terk and bonus to remaining partners)		

Note that if Sand had withdrawn from the partnership, Roman and Terk would divide any bonus on the basis of their income ratio, which is 3 : 1 or 75% and 25%.

DEATH OF A PARTNER

The death of a partner dissolves the partnership. But partnership agreements usually contain a provision for the surviving partners to continue operations. When a partner dies, it usually is necessary to determine the partner's equity at the date of death. This is done by (1) determining the net income or loss for the year to date, (2) closing the books, and (3) preparing financial statements. The partnership agreement may also require an independent audit and a revaluation of assets.

The surviving partners may agree to purchase the deceased partner's equity from their personal assets. Or they may use partnership assets to settle with the deceased partner's estate. In both instances, the entries to record the withdrawal of the partner are similar to those presented earlier.

To facilitate payment from partnership assets, some partnerships obtain life insurance policies on each partner, with the partnership named as the beneficiary. The partnership then uses the proceeds from the insurance policy on the deceased partner to settle with the estate.

Summary of Study Objectives for Appendix 12A

[6] **Explain the effects of the entries when a new partner is admitted.** The entry to record the admittance of a new partner by purchase of a partner's interest affects only partners' capital accounts. The entries to record the admittance by investment of assets in the partnership (a) increase both net assets and total capital and (b) may result in recognition of a bonus to either the old partners or the new partner.

[7] **Describe the effects of the entries when a partner withdraws from the firm.** The entry to record a withdrawal from the firm when the partners pay from their personal assets affects only partners' capital accounts. The entry to record a withdrawal when payment is made from partnership assets (a) decreases net assets and total capital and (b) may result in recognizing a bonus either to the retiring partner or the remaining partners.

Glossary for Appendix 12A

Admission by investment Admission of a partner by investing assets in the partnership, causing both partnership net assets and total capital to increase. (p. 573).

Admission by purchase of an interest Admission of a partner in a personal transaction between one or more existing partners and the new partner; does not change total partnership assets or total capital. (p. 572).

Withdrawal by payment from partners' personal assets Withdrawal of a partner in a personal transaction between partners; does not change total partnership assets or total capital. (p. 576).

Withdrawal by payment from partnership assets Withdrawal of a partner in a transaction involving the partnership, causing both partnership net assets and total capital to decrease. (p. 576).

Self-Test, Brief Exercises, Exercises, Problem Set A, and many more components are available for practice in *WileyPLUS*

*Note: All **asterisked** Questions, Exercises, and Problems relate to material in the appendix to the chapter.

Self-Test Questions

Answers are on page 591.

(SO 1) 1. Which of the following is *not* a characteristic of a partnership?
    a. Taxable entity.
    b. Co-ownership of property.
    c. Mutual agency.
    d. Limited life.

(SO 1) 2. A partnership agreement should include each of the following except:
    a. names and capital contributions of partners.
    b. rights and duties of partners as well as basis for sharing net income or loss.
    c. basis for splitting partnership income taxes.
    d. provision for withdrawal of assets.

(SO 1) 3. The advantages of a partnership do *not* include:
    a. ease of formation.
    b. unlimited liability.
    c. freedom from government regulation.
    d. ease of decision making.

(SO 2) 4. Upon formation of a partnership, each partner's initial investment of assets should be recorded at their:
    a. book values.
    b. cost.
    c. fair values.
    d. appraised values.

(SO 2) 5. Ben and Sam Jenkins formed a partnership. Ben contributed $8,000 cash and a used truck that originally cost $35,000 and had accumulated depreciation of $15,000. The truck's fair value was $16,000. Sam, a builder, contributed a new storage garage. His cost of construction was $40,000. The garage has a fair value of $55,000. What is the combined total capital that would be recorded on the partnership books for the two partners?
    a. $79,000.
    b. $60,000.
    c. $75,000.
    d. $90,000.

(SO 3) 6. The NBC Company reports net income of $60,000. If partners N, B, and C have an income ratio of 50%, 30%, and 20%, respectively, C's share of the net income is:
    a. $30,000.
    b. $12,000.
    c. $18,000.
    d. No correct answer is given.

(SO 3) 7. Using the data in (6) above, what is B's share of net income if the percentages are applicable after each partner receives a $10,000 salary allowance?
    a. $12,000.
    b. $20,000.
    c. $19,000.
    d. $21,000.

(SO 3) 8. To close a partner's drawing account, an entry must be made that:
    a. debits that partner's drawing account and credits Income Summary.
    b. debits that partner's drawing account and credits that partner's capital account.

    c. credits that partner's drawing account and debits that partner's capital account.
    d. credits that partner's drawing account and debits the firm's dividend account.

9. Which of the following statements about partnership **(SO 4)** financial statements is *true*?
    a. Details of the distribution of net income are shown in the owners' equity statement.
    b. The distribution of net income is shown on the balance sheet.
    c. Only the total of all partner capital balances is shown in the balance sheet.
    d. The owners' equity statement is called the partners' capital statement.

10. In the liquidation of a partnership, it is necessary to (1) **(SO 5)** distribute cash to the partners, (2) sell noncash assets, (3) allocate any gain or loss on realization to the partners, and (4) pay liabilities. These steps should be performed in the following order:
    a. (2), (3), (4), (1).
    b. (2), (3), (1), (4).
    c. (3), (2), (1), (4).
    d. (3), (2), (4), (1).

Use the following account balance information for Creekville Partnership to answer questions 11 and 12. Income ratios are 2 : 4 : 4 for Harriet, Mike, and Elly, respectively.

Assets		Liabilities and Owners' Equity	
Cash	$ 9,000	Accounts payable	$ 21,000
Accounts		Harriet, capital	23,000
receivable	22,000	Mike, capital	8,000
Inventory	73,000	Elly, capital	52,000
	$104,000		$104,000

11. Assume that, as part of liquidation proceedings, **(SO 5)** Creekville sells its noncash assets for $85,000. The amount of cash that would ultimately be distributed to Elly would be:
    a. $52,000.
    b. $48,000.
    c. $34,000.
    d. $86,000.

12. Assume that, as part of liquidation proceedings, Creekville **(SO 5)** sells its noncash assets for $60,000. As a result, one of the partners has a capital deficiency which that partner decides not to repay. The amount of cash that would ultimately be distributed to Elly would be:
    a. $52,000.
    b. $38,000.
    c. $24,000.
    d. $34,000.

13. Louisa Santiago purchases 50% of Leo Lemon's capital **(SO 6)** interest in the K & L partnership for $22,000. If the capital

balance of Kate Kildare and Leo Lemon are $40,000 and $30,000, respectively, Santiago's capital balance following the purchase is:

a. $22,000.   c. $20,000.

b. $35,000.   d. $15,000.

(SO 6) *14. Capital balances in the MEM partnership are Mary, Capital $60,000; Ellen, Capital $50,000; and Mills, Capital $40,000, and income ratios are 5 : 3 : 2, respectively. The MEMO partnership is formed by admitting Oleg to the firm with a cash investment of $60,000 for a 25% capital interest. The bonus to be credited to Mills, Capital in admitting Oleg is:

a. $10,000.   c. $3,750.

b. $7,500.   d. $1,500.

*15. Capital balances in the MURF partnership are Molly, (SO 7) Capital $50,000; Ursula, Capital $40,000; Ray, Capital $30,000; and Fred, Capital $20,000, and income ratios are 4 : 3 : 2 : 1, respectively. Fred withdraws from the firm following payment of $29,000 in cash from the partnership. Ursula's capital balance after recording the withdrawal of Fred is:

a. $36,000.   c. $38,000.

b. $37,000.   d. $40,000.

Go to the book's companion website, **www.wiley.com/college/weygandt**, for additional Self-Test Questions.

Questions

1. The characteristics of a partnership include the following: (a) association of individuals, (b) limited life, and (c) co-ownership of property. Explain each of these terms.

2. Jerry Kerwin is confused about the partnership characteristics of (a) mutual agency and (b) unlimited liability. Explain these two characteristics for Jerry.

3. Brent Houghton and Dick Kreibach are considering a business venture. They ask you to explain the advantages and disadvantages of the partnership form of organization.

4. Why might a company choose to use a limited partnership?

5. Sampson and Stevens form a partnership. Sampson contributes land with a book value of $50,000 and a fair value of $65,000. Sampson also contributes equipment with a book value of $52,000 and a fair value of $57,000. The partnership assumes a $20,000 mortgage on the land. What should be the balance in Sampson's capital account upon formation of the partnership?

6. W. Mantle, N. Cash, and W. DiMaggio have a partnership called Outlaws. A dispute has arisen among the partners. Mantle has invested twice as much in assets as the other two partners, and he believes net income and net losses should be shared in accordance with the capital ratios. The partnership agreement does not specify the division of profits and losses. How will net income and net loss be divided?

7. Blue and Grey are discussing how income and losses should be divided in a partnership they plan to form. What factors should be considered in determining the division of net income or net loss?

8. M. Carson and R. Leno have partnership capital balances of $40,000 and $80,000, respectively. The partnership agreement indicates that net income or net loss should be shared equally. If net income for the partnership is $36,000, how should the net income be divided?

9. S. McMurray and F. Kohl share net income and net loss equally. (a) Which account(s) is (are) debited and credited to record the division of net income between the partners? (b) If S. McMurray withdraws $30,000 in cash for personal use in lieu of salary, which account is debited and which is credited?

10. Partners T. Evans and R. Meloy are provided salary allowances of $30,000 and $25,000, respectively. They divide the remainder of the partnership income in a ratio of 3 : 2. If partnership net income is $45,000, how much is allocated to Evans and Meloy?

11. Are the financial statements of a partnership similar to those of a proprietorship? Discuss.

12. How does the liquidation of a partnership differ from the dissolution of a partnership?

13. Bobby Donal and Bill Spader are discussing the liquidation of a partnership. Bobby maintains that all cash should be distributed to partners on the basis of their income ratios. Is he correct? Explain.

14. In continuing their discussion from Question 13, Bill says that even in the case of a capital deficiency, all cash should still be distributed on the basis of capital balances. Is Bill correct? Explain.

15. Lowery, Keegan, and Feeney have income ratios of 5 : 3 : 2 and capital balances of $34,000, $31,000, and $28,000, respectively. Noncash assets are sold at a gain. After creditors are paid, $109,000 of cash is available for distribution to the partners. How much cash should be paid to Keegan?

16. Before the final distribution of cash, account balances are: Cash $23,000; S. Penn, Capital $19,000 (Cr.); L. Pattison, Capital $12,000 (Cr.); and M. Jeter, Capital $8,000 (Dr.). Jeter is unable to pay any of the capital deficiency. If the income-sharing ratios are 5 : 3 : 2, respectively, how much cash should be paid to L. Pattison?

*17. Linda Ratzlaff decides to purchase from an existing partner for $50,000 a one-third interest in a partnership. What effect does this transaction have on partnership net assets?

*18. Steve Renn decides to invest $25,000 in a partnership for a one-sixth capital interest. How much do the partnership's net assets increase? Does Renn also acquire a one-sixth income ratio through this investment?

*19. Kate Robidou purchases for $72,000 Grant's interest in the Sharon-Grant partnership. Assuming that Grant has a $66,000 capital balance in the partnership, what journal entry is made by the partnership to record this transaction?

*20. Tracy Harper has a $39,000 capital balance in a partnership. She sells her interest to Kim Remington for $45,000 cash. What entry is made by the partnership for this transaction?

*21. Debbie Perry retires from the partnership of Garland, Newlin, and Perry. She receives $85,000 of partnership assets in settlement of her capital balance of $77,000. Assuming that the income-sharing ratios are 5 : 3 : 2,

respectively, how much of Perry's bonus is debited to Newlin's capital account?

*22. Your roommate argues that partnership assets should be revalued in situations like those in question 21. Why is this generally not done?

*23. How is a deceased partner's equity determined?

24. ⬡**PEPSICO** Why is PepsiCo not a partnership?

Brief Exercises

BE12-1 Eustace Scrubb and Will Poulter decide to organize the ALL-Star partnership. Scrubb invests $15,000 cash, and Poulter contributes $10,000 cash and equipment having a book value of $3,500. Prepare the entry to record Poulter's investment in the partnership, assuming the equipment has a fair value of $5,000.

Journalize entries in forming a partnership.
(SO 2)

BE12-2 Rhince and Rynelf decide to merge their proprietorships into a partnership called Dawn Treader Company. The balance sheet of Rynelf Co. shows:

Accounts receivable	$16,000	
Less: Allowance for doubtful accounts	1,200	$14,800
Equipment	20,000	
Less: Accumulated depreciation—equip.	7,000	13,000

Prepare portion of opening balance sheet for partnership.
(SO 2)

The partners agree that the net realizable value of the receivables is $13,500 and that the fair value of the equipment is $11,000. Indicate how the accounts should appear in the opening balance sheet of the partnership.

BE12-3 Pug Bern Co. reports net income of $70,000. The income ratios are Pug 60% and Bern 40%. Indicate the division of net income to each partner, and prepare the entry to distribute the net income.

Journalize the division of net income using fixed income ratios.
(SO 3)

BE12-4 SDT Co. reports net income of $55,000. Partner salary allowances are Sweet $15,000, Drinian $5,000, and Tavros $5,000. Indicate the division of net income to each partner, assuming the income ratio is 50 : 30 : 20, respectively.

Compute division of net income with a salary allowance and fixed ratios.
(SO 3)

BE12-5 Lill & Dil Co. reports net income of $28,000. Interest allowances are Lill $7,000 and Dil $5,000; salary allowances are Lill $15,000 and Dil $10,000; the remainder is shared equally. Show the distribution of income on the income statement.

Show division of net income when allowances exceed net income.
(SO 3)

BE12-6 After liquidating noncash assets and paying creditors, account balances in the Kidz Co. are Cash $19,000, A Capital (Cr.) $8,000, B Capital (Cr.) $7,000, and C Capital (Cr.) $4,000. The partners share income equally. Journalize the final distribution of cash to the partners.

Journalize final cash distribution in liquidation.
(SO 5)

*BE12-7** Beta Co. capital balances are: Ace $30,000, Bly $25,000, and Gumpus $20,000. The partners share income equally. Rhoop is admitted to the firm by purchasing one-half of Gumpus's interest for $13,000. Journalize the admission of Rhoop to the partnership.

Journalize admission by purchase of an interest.
(SO 6)

*BE12-8** In Coriakin Co., capital balances are Gael $40,000 and Nausus $50,000. The partners share income equally. Slaver is admitted to the firm with a 45% interest by an investment of cash of $52,000. Journalize the admission of Slaver.

Journalize admission by investment.
(SO 6)

*BE12-9** Capital balances in Midway Co. are Mirko $40,000, Neil $30,000, and Grillini $18,000. Mirko and Neil each agree to pay Grillini $12,000 from their personal assets. Mirko and Neil each receive 50% of Grillini's equity. The partners share income equally. Journalize the withdrawal of Grillini.

Journalize withdrawal paid by personal assets.
(SO 7)

*BE12-10** Data pertaining to Midway Co. are presented in BE12-9. Instead of payment from personal assets, assume that Grillini receives $24,000 from partnership assets in withdrawing from the firm. Journalize the withdrawal of Grillini.

Journalize withdrawal paid by partnership assets.
(SO 7)

Do it! Review

Analyze statements about partnership organization.
(SO 1)

Do it! 12-1   Indicate whether each of the following statements is true or false.

_____ **1.** Each partner is personally and individually liable for all partnership liabilities.
_____ **2.** If a partnership dissolves, each partner has a claim to the specific assets he/she contributed to the firm.
_____ **3.** In a limited partnership, all partners have limited liability.
_____ **4.** A major advantage of regular partnership is that it is simple and inexpensive to create and operate.
_____ **5.** Members of a limited liability company can take an active management role.

Divide net income and prepare closing entry.
(SO 3)

Do it! 12-2   Villa America Company reported net income of $85,000. The partnership agreement provides for salaries of $25,000 to Kibra and $18,000 to Devrish. They divide the remainder 40% to Kibra and 60% to Devrish. Kibra asks your help to divide the net income between the partners and to prepare the closing entry.

Complete schedule of partnership liquidation payments.
(SO 5)

Do it! 12-3   The partners of CS Company have decided to liquidate their business. Noncash assets were sold for $125,000. The income ratios of the partners Arabella, Dufflepud, and Davies are 3 : 2 : 3, respectively. Complete the following schedule of cash payments for CS Company

	A	B	C	D	E	F	G	H	I	J	K	L
1	Item	Cash	+	Noncash Assets	=	Liabilities	+	Arabella, Capital	+	Dufflepud, Capital	+	Davies, Capital
2	Balances before liquidation	15,000		90,000		40,000		20,000		32,000		13,000
3	Sale of noncash assets and allocation of gain											
4	New balances											
5	Pay liabilities											
6	New balances											
7	Cash distribution to partners											
8	Final balances											

Prepare entries to record absorption of capital deficiency and distribution of cash.
(SO 5)

Do it! 12-4   Granger Company wishes to liquidate the firm by distributing the company's cash to the three partners. Prior to the distribution of cash, the company's balances are: Cash $66,000; Moffit, Capital (Cr.) $47,000; Nation, Capital (Dr.) $21,000; and Davis, Capital (Cr.) $40,000. The income ratios of the three partners are 3 : 3 : 4, respectively. Prepare the entry to record the absorption of Nation's capital deficiency by the other partners and the distribution of cash to the partners with credit balances.

Exercises

Identify characteristics of partnership.
(SO 1)

E12-1   David Tennant has prepared the following list of statements about partnerships.

1. A partnership is an association of three or more persons to carry on as co-owners of a business for profit.
2. The legal requirements for forming a partnership can be quite burdensome.
3. A partnership is not an entity for financial reporting purposes.
4. The net income of a partnership is taxed as a separate entity.
5. The act of any partner is binding on all other partners, even when partners perform business acts beyond the scope of their authority.
6. Each partner is personally and individually liable for all partnership liabilities.
7. When a partnership is dissolved, the assets legally revert to the original contributor.

8. In a limited partnership, one or more partners have unlimited liability and one or more partners have limited liability for the debts of the firm.

9. Mutual agency is a major advantage of the partnership form of business.

Instructions

Identify each statement as true or false. If false, indicate how to correct the statement.

E12-2 K. Billie, S. Piper, and E. Rose are forming a partnership. Billie is transferring $50,000 of personal cash to the partnership. Piper owns land worth $15,000 and a small building worth $80,000, which she transfers to the partnership. Rose transfers to the partnership cash of $9,000, accounts receivable of $32,000 and equipment worth $19,000. The partnership expects to collect $29,000 of the accounts receivable.

Journalize entry for formation of a partnership.
(SO 2)

Instructions

(a) Prepare the journal entries to record each of the partners' investments.

(b) What amount would be reported as total owners' equity immediately after the investments?

E12-3 Rose Tyler has owned and operated a proprietorship for several years. On January 1, she decides to terminate this business and become a partner in the firm of Tyler and Sigma. Tyler's investment in the partnership consists of $12,000 in cash, and the following assets of the proprietorship: accounts receivable $14,000 less allowance for doubtful accounts of $2,000, and equipment $20,000 less accumulated depreciation of $4,000. It is agreed that the allowance for doubtful accounts should be $3,000 for the partnership. The fair value of the equipment is $13,500.

Journalize entry for formation of a partnership.
(SO 2)

Instructions

Journalize Tyler's admission to the firm of Tyler and Sigma.

E12-4 Martha and Jones have capital balances on January 1 of $50,000 and $40,000, respectively. The partnership income-sharing agreement provides for (1) annual salaries of $20,000 for Martha and $12,000 for Jones, (2) interest at 10% on beginning capital balances, and (3) remaining income or loss to be shared 60% by Martha and 40% by Jones.

Prepare schedule showing distribution of net income and closing entry.
(SO 3)

Instructions

(a) Prepare a schedule showing the distribution of net income, assuming net income is (1) $50,000 and (2) $36,000.

(b) Journalize the allocation of net income in each of the situations above.

E12-5 Aikman (beginning capital, $60,000) and Rory (beginning capital $90,000) are partners. During 2012, the partnership earned net income of $70,000, and Aikman made drawings of $18,000 while Rory made drawings of $24,000.

Prepare journal entries to record allocation of net income.
(SO 3)

Instructions

(a) Assume the partnership income-sharing agreement calls for income to be divided 45% to Aikman and 55% to Rory. Prepare the journal entry to record the allocation of net income.

(b) Assume the partnership income-sharing agreement calls for income to be divided with a salary of $30,000 to Aikman and $25,000 to Rory, with the remainder divided 45% to Aikman and 55% to Rory. Prepare the journal entry to record the allocation of net income.

(c) Assume the partnership income-sharing agreement calls for income to be divided with a salary of $40,000 to Aikman and $35,000 to Rory, interest of 10% on beginning capital, and the remainder divided 50%–50%. Prepare the journal entry to record the allocation of net income.

(d) Compute the partners' ending capital balances under the assumption in part (c).

E12-6 For Starrite Co., beginning capital balances on January 1, 2012, are Donna Noble $20,000 and Amy Bond $18,000. During the year, drawings were Noble $8,000 and Bond $5,000. Net income was $30,000, and the partners share income equally.

Prepare partners' capital statement and partial balance sheet.
(SO 4)

Instructions

(a) Prepare the partners' capital statement for the year.

(b) Prepare the owners' equity section of the balance sheet at December 31, 2012.

E12-7 David, Matt, and Chris are forming The Doctor Partnership. David is transferring $30,000 of personal cash and equipment worth $25,000 to the partnership. Matt owns land worth $18,000 and a small building worth $75,000, which he transfers to the partnership. There is a long-term mortgage of $20,000 on the land and building, which the partnership assumes. Chris transfers cash of $7,000, accounts receivable of $36,000, supplies worth $3,000, and equipment

Prepare a classified balance sheet of a partnership.
(SO 4)

worth $22,000 to the partnership. The partnership expects to collect $32,000 of the accounts receivable.

Instructions

Prepare a classified balance sheet for the partnership after the partners' investments on December 31, 2012.

Prepare cash payments schedule.

(SO 5)

E12-8   The Freema Company at December 31 has cash $20,000, noncash assets $100,000, liabilities $55,000, and the following capital balances: Dalek $45,000 and Briggs $20,000. The firm is liquidated, and $110,000 in cash is received for the noncash assets. Dalek and Briggs income ratios are 60% and 40%, respectively.

Instructions

Prepare a schedule of cash payments.

Journalize transactions in a liquidation.

(SO 5)

E12-9   Data for The Freema Company are presented in E12-8.

Instructions

Prepare the entries to record:

(a) The sale of noncash assets.
(b) The allocation of the gain or loss on realization to the partners.
(c) Payment of creditors.
(d) Distribution of cash to the partners.

Journalize transactions with a capital deficiency.

(SO 5)

E12-10   Prior to the distribution of cash to the partners, the accounts in the TSM Company are: Cash $28,000; Tyler, Capital (Cr.) $17,000; Smith, Capital (Cr.) $15,000; and Mott, Capital (Dr.) $4,000. The income ratios are 5 : 3 : 2, respectively.

Instructions

(a) Prepare the entry to record (1) Mott's payment of $4,000 in cash to the partnership and (2) the distribution of cash to the partners with credit balances.
(b) Prepare the entry to record (1) the absorption of Mott's capital deficiency by the other partners and (2) the distribution of cash to the partners with credit balances.

Journalize admission of a new partner by purchase of an interest.

(SO 6)

***E12-11**   K. Gillan, C. Coduri, and C. Tate share income on a 5 : 3 : 2 basis. They have capital balances of $30,000, $26,000, and $18,000, respectively, when Cap Harkness is admitted to the partnership.

Instructions

Prepare the journal entry to record the admission of Cap Harkness under each of the following assumptions.

(a) Purchase of 50% of Gillan's equity for $19,000.
(b) Purchase of 50% of Coduri's equity for $12,000.
(c) Purchase of 33⅓% of Tate's equity for $9,000.

Journalize admission of a new partner by investment.

(SO 6)

***E12-12**   S. Noble and T. Wells share income on a 6 : 4 basis. They have capital balances of $100,000 and $70,000, respectively, when W. Trinity is admitted to the partnership.

Instructions

Prepare the journal entry to record the admission of W. Trinity under each of the following assumptions.

(a) Investment of $90,000 cash for a 30% ownership interest with bonuses to the existing partners.
(b) Investment of $50,000 cash for a 30% ownership interest with a bonus to the new partner.

Journalize withdrawal of a partner with payment from partners' personal assets.

(SO 7)

***E12-13**   N. Clark, C. Camille, and C. Eccleston have capital balances of $50,000, $40,000, and $32,000, respectively. Their income ratios are 5 : 3 : 2. Eccleston withdraws from the partnership under each of the following independent conditions.

1. Clark and Camille agree to purchase Eccleston's equity by paying $17,000 each from their personal assets. Each purchaser receives 50% of Eccleston's equity.
2. Camille agrees to purchase all of Eccleston's equity by paying $22,000 cash from her personal assets.
3. Clark agrees to purchase all of Eccleston's equity by paying $26,000 cash from his personal assets.

Instructions

Journalize the withdrawal of Eccleston under each of the assumptions above.

*E12-14 B. Edwards, J. King, and N. Pegg have capital balances of $95,000, $75,000, and $60,000, respectively. They share income or loss on a 5 : 3 : 2 basis. Pegg withdraws from the partnership under each of the following conditions.

1. Pegg is paid $68,000 in cash from partnership assets, and a bonus is granted to the retiring partner.
2. Pegg is paid $56,000 in cash from partnership assets, and bonuses are granted to the remaining partners.

Instructions
Journalize the withdrawal of Pegg under each of the assumptions above.

Journalize withdrawal of a partner with payment from partnership assets.
(SO 7)

*E12-15 Carl, Barrowman, and Cribbins are partners who share profits and losses 50%, 30%, and 20%, respectively. Their capital balances are $100,000, $60,000, and $40,000, respectively.

Instructions
(a) Assume Darvill joins the partnership by investing $80,000 for a 25% interest with bonuses to the existing partners. Prepare the journal entry to record his investment.
(b) Assume instead that Carl leaves the partnership. Carl is paid $120,000 with a bonus to the retiring partner. Prepare the journal entry to record Carl's withdrawal.

Journalize entry for admission and withdrawal of partners.
(SO 6, 7)

Exercises: Set B

Visit the book's companion website, at **www.wiley.com/college/weygandt**, and choose the Student Companion site to access Exercise Set B.

Problems: Set A

P12-1A The post-closing trial balances of two proprietorships on January 1, 2012, are presented below.

Prepare entries for formation of a partnership and a balance sheet.
(SO 2, 4)

GLS

	Williams Company		Jones Company	
	Dr.	Cr.	Dr.	Cr.
Cash	$ 14,000		$12,000	
Accounts receivable	17,500		26,000	
Allowance for doubtful accounts		$ 3,000		$ 4,400
Inventory	26,500		18,400	
Equipment	45,000		29,000	
Accumulated depreciation—equipment		24,000		11,000
Notes payable		18,000		15,000
Accounts payable		22,000		31,000
Williams, capital		36,000		
Jones, capital				24,000
	$103,000	$103,000	$85,400	$85,400

Williams and Jones decide to form a partnership, Wijo Company, with the following agreed upon valuations for noncash assets.

	Williams Company	Jones Company
Accounts receivable	$17,500	$26,000
Allowance for doubtful accounts	4,500	4,000
Inventory	28,000	20,000
Equipment	23,000	16,000

All cash will be transferred to the partnership, and the partnership will assume all the liabilities of the two proprietorships. Further, it is agreed that Williams will invest an additional $5,000 in cash, and Jones will invest an additional $19,000 in cash.

Instructions
(a) Prepare separate journal entries to record the transfer of each proprietorship's assets and liabilities to the partnership.
(b) Journalize the additional cash investment by each partner.
(c) Prepare a classified balance sheet for the partnership on January 1, 2012.

(a) Williams, Capital $38,000
    Jones, Capital $24,000

(c) Total assets $172,000

Journalize divisions of net income and prepare a partners' capital statement.
(SO 3, 4)

P12-2A   At the end of its first year of operations on December 31, 2012, LAD Company's accounts show the following.

Partner	Drawings	Capital
Rory Lachelle	$23,000	$48,000
Andy Andoh	14,000	30,000
Francine Dalek	10,000	25,000

The capital balance represents each partner's initial capital investment. Therefore, net income or net loss for 2012 has not been closed to the partners' capital accounts.

Instructions

(a) Journalize the entry to record the division of net income for the year 2012 under each of the following independent assumptions.

(a) (1) Lachelle $18,000
    (2) Lachelle $19,000
    (3) Lachelle $15,700

 (1) Net income is $30,000. Income is shared 6 : 3 : 1.
 (2) Net income is $37,000. Lachelle and Andoh are given salary allowances of $15,000 and $10,000, respectively. The remainder is shared equally.
 (3) Net income is $19,000. Each partner is allowed interest of 10% on beginning capital balances. Lachelle is given a $12,000 salary allowance. The remainder is shared equally.

(b) Prepare a schedule showing the division of net income under assumption (3) above.

(c) Lachelle $40,700

(c) Prepare a partners' capital statement for the year under assumption (3) above.

Prepare entries with a capital deficiency in liquidation of a partnership.
(SO 5)

P12-3A   The partners in River Song Company decide to liquidate the firm when the balance sheet shows the following.

RIVER SONG COMPANY
Balance Sheet
May 31, 2012

Assets		Liabilities and Owners' Equity	
Cash	$ 27,500	Notes payable	$ 13,500
Accounts receivable	25,000	Accounts payable	27,000
Allowance for doubtful accounts	(1,000)	Salaries and wages payable	4,000
Inventory	34,500	A. Mangold, capital	33,000
Equipment	21,000	S. Otis, capital	21,000
Accumulated depreciation—equipment	(5,500)	P. Tyler, capital	3,000
Total	$101,500	Total	$101,500

The partners share income and loss 5 : 3 : 2. During the process of liquidation, the following transactions were completed in the following sequence.

1. A total of $55,000 was received from converting noncash assets into cash.
2. Gain or loss on realization was allocated to partners.
3. Liabilities were paid in full.
4. P. Tyler paid his capital deficiency.
5. Cash was paid to the partners with credit balances.

Instructions

(a) Loss on realization
    $19,000
    Cash paid: to Mangold
    $23,500; to Otis
    $15,300

(a) Prepare the entries to record the transactions.
(b) Post to the cash and capital accounts.
(c) Assume that Tyler is unable to pay the capital deficiency.
 (1) Prepare the entry to allocate Tyler's debit balance to Mangold and Otis.
 (2) Prepare the entry to record the final distribution of cash.

Journalize admission of a partner under different assumptions.
(SO 6)

*P12-4A**   At April 30, partners' capital balances in SCJ Company are: G. Cooper $52,000, C. Jones $54,000, and J. Simmonds $18,000. The income sharing ratios are 5 : 4 : 1, respectively. On May 1, the SCJR Company is formed by admitting J. Redfern to the firm as a partner.

Instructions

(a) Journalize the admission of Redfern under each of the following independent assumptions.

(a) (1) Redfern $9,000
    (2) Redfern $18,000
    (3) Redfern $57,000
    (4) Redfern $51,000

 (1) Redfern purchases 50% of Simmonds's ownership interest by paying Simmonds $16,000 in cash.
 (2) Redfern purchases 33⅓% of Jones's ownership interest by paying Jones $15,000 in cash.

(3) Redfern invests $66,000 for a 30% ownership interest, and bonuses are given to the old partners.

(4) Redfern invests $46,000 for a 30% ownership interest, which includes a bonus to the new partner.

(b) Jones's capital balance is $32,000 after admitting Redfern to the partnership by investment. If Jones's ownership interest is 20% of total partnership capital, what were (1) Redfern's cash investment and (2) the bonus to the new partner?

*P12-5A On December 31, the capital balances and income ratios in SAR Company are as follows.

Journalize withdrawal of a partner under different assumptions.
(SO 7)

Partner	Capital Balance	Income Ratio
Spargo	$60,000	50%
Ames	40,000	30%
Ruscoe	26,000	20%

Instructions

(a) Journalize the withdrawal of Ruscoe under each of the following assumptions.

(1) Each of the continuing partners agrees to pay $18,000 in cash from personal funds to purchase Ruscoe's ownership equity. Each receives 50% of Ruscoe's equity.

(2) Ames agrees to purchase Ruscoe's ownership interest for $25,000 cash.

(3) Ruscoe is paid $34,000 from partnership assets, which includes a bonus to the retiring partner.

(4) Ruscoe is paid $22,000 from partnership assets, and bonuses to the remaining partners are recognized.

(b) If Ames's capital balance after Ruscoe's withdrawal is $42,400, what were (1) the total bonus to the remaining partners and (2) the cash paid by the partnership to Ruscoe?

(a) (1) Ames, Capital
$13,000
(2) Ames, Capital
$26,000
(3) Bonus $8,000
(4) Bonus $4,000

Problems: Set B

P12-1B The post-closing trial balances of two proprietorships on January 1, 2012, are presented below.

Prepare entries for formation of a partnership and a balance sheet.
(SO 2, 4)

	Skorr Company		Crane Company	
	Dr.	Cr.	Dr.	Cr.
Cash	$ 10,000		$ 8,000	
Accounts receivable	18,000		30,000	
Allowance for doubtful accounts		$ 2,000		$ 3,000
Inventory	35,000		20,000	
Equipment	60,000		35,000	
Accumulated depreciation—equipment		28,000		15,000
Notes payable		20,000		
Accounts payable		30,000		40,000
Skorr, capital		43,000		
Crane, capital				35,000
	$123,000	$123,000	$93,000	$93,000

Skorr and Crane decide to form a partnership, Commander Company, with the following agreed upon valuations for noncash assets.

	Skorr Company	Crane Company
Accounts receivable	$18,000	$30,000
Allowance for doubtful accounts	2,500	4,000
Inventory	38,000	25,000
Equipment	40,000	22,000

All cash will be transferred to the partnership, and the partnership will assume all the liabilities of the two proprietorships. Further, it is agreed that Skorr will invest an additional $3,500 in cash, and Crane will invest an additional $16,000 in cash.

(a) Skorr, Capital $53,500
Crane, Capital $41,000

(c) Total assets $204,000

Journalize divisions of net income and prepare a partners' capital statement.

(SO 3, 4)

(a) (1) Staal $25,000
(2) Staal $20,000
(3) Staal $27,000

(c) Staal $52,000

Prepare entries and schedule of cash payments in liquidation of a partnership

(SO 5)

(a) Loss on realization
$13,000
Cash paid: to Laszlo
$21,500; to Octavian
$3,250

Journalize admission of a partner under different assumptions.

(SO 6)

(a) (1) Chantho, Capital
$7,500
(2) Chantho $8,000
(3) Chantho $36,000

Instructions

(a) Prepare separate journal entries to record the transfer of each proprietorship's assets and liabilities to the partnership.

(b) Journalize the additional cash investment by each partner.

(c) Prepare a classified balance sheet for the partnership on January 1, 2012.

P12-2B At the end of its first year of operations on December 31, 2012, SHB Company's accounts show the following.

Partner	Drawings	Capital
Staal	$15,000	$40,000
Harris	10,000	25,000
Blaine	5,000	15,000

The capital balance represents each partner's initial capital investment. Therefore, net income or net loss for 2012 has not been closed to the partners' capital accounts.

Instructions

(a) Journalize the entry to record the division of net income for 2012 under each of the independent assumptions shown on the next page.

 (1) Net income is $50,000. Income is shared 5 : 3 : 2.

 (2) Net income is $40,000. Staal and Harris are given salary allowances of $15,000 and $10,000, respectively. The remainder is shared equally.

 (3) Net income is $37,000. Each partner is allowed interest of 10% on beginning capital balances. Staal is given a $20,000 salary allowance. The remainder is shared equally.

(b) Prepare a schedule showing the division of net income under assumption (3) above.

(c) Prepare a partners' capital statement for the year under assumption (3) above.

P12-3B The partners in Tallis Company decide to liquidate the firm when the balance sheet shows the following.

TALLIS COMPANY
Balance Sheet
April 30, 2012

Assets		Liabilities and Owners' Equity	
Cash	$30,000	Notes payable	$20,000
Accounts receivable	25,000	Accounts payable	30,000
Allowance for doubtful accounts	(2,000)	Salaries and wages payable	2,500
Inventory	35,000	Laszlo, capital	28,000
Equipment	20,000	Alaya, capital	13,650
Accumulated depreciation—equipment	(8,000)	Octavian, capital	5,850
Total	$100,000	Total	$100,000

The partners share income and loss 5 : 3 : 2. During the process of liquidation, the transactions below were completed in the following sequence.

1. A total of $57,000 was received from converting noncash assets into cash.

2. Gain or loss on relization was allocated to partners.

3. Liabilities were paid in full.

4. Cash was paid to the partners with credit balances.

Instructions

(a) Prepare a schedule of cash payments.

(b) Prepare the entries to record the transactions.

(c) Post to the cash and capital accounts.

*P12-4B At April 30, partners' capital balances in ZCF Company are: Zachary $30,000. Cross $16,000, and Flane $15,000. The income-sharing ratios are 5 : 3 : 2, respectively. On May 1, the ZCFC Company is formed by admitting Chantho to the firm as a partner.

Instructions

(a) Journalize the admission of Chantho under each of the following independent assumptions.

 (1) Chantho purchases 50% of Flane's ownership interest by paying Flane $6,000 in cash.

 (2) Chantho purchases 50% of Cross's ownership interest by paying Cross $10,000 in cash.

 (3) Chantho invests $29,000 cash in the partnership for a 40% ownership interest that includes a bonus to the new partner.

(4) Chantho invests $24,000 in the partnership for a 20% ownership interest, and bonuses are given to the old partners.

(4) Chantho $17,000

(b) Cross's capital balance is $24,000 after admitting Chantho to the partnership by investment. If Cross's ownership interest is 24% of total partnership capital, what were (1) Chantho's cash investment and (2) the total bonus to the old partners?

*P12-5B On December 31, the capital balances and income ratios in Noma Company are as follows.

Journalize withdrawal of a partner under different assumptions.

(SO 7)

Partner	Capital Balance	Income Ratio
Morgan	$100,000	60%
White	51,000	30
Ogden	25,000	10

Instructions

(a) Journalize the withdrawal of Ogden under each of the following independent assumptions.

(1) Each of the remaining partners agrees to pay $15,000 in cash from personal funds to purchase Ogden's ownership equity. Each receives 50% of Ogden's equity.

(2) White agrees to purchase Ogden's ownership interest for $22,000 in cash.

(3) From partnership assets, Ogden is paid $34,000, which includes a bonus to the retiring partner.

(4) Ogden is paid $19,000 from partnership assets. Bonuses to the remaining partners are recognized.

(a) (1) White, Capital $12,500
(2) White, Capital $25,000
(3) Bonus $9,000
(4) Bonus $6,000

(b) If White's capital balance after Ogden's withdrawal is $55,000, what were (1) the total bonus to the remaining partners and (2) the cash paid by the partnership to Ogden?

Problems: Set C

Visit the book's companion website, at **www.wiley.com/college/weygandt**, and choose the Student Companion site to access Problem Set C.

Continuing Cookie Chronicle

(*Note:* This is a continuation of the Cookie Chronicle from Chapters 1 through 11.)

CCC12 Natalie's high school friend, Katy Peterson, has been operating a bakery for approximately 18 months. Because Natalie has been so successful operating Cookie Creations, Katy would like to have Natalie become her partner. Katy believes that together they will create a thriving cookie-making business. Natalie is quite happy with her current business set-up. Up until now, she had not considered joining forces with anyone. However, Natalie thinks that it may be a good idea to establish a partnership with Katy, and decides to look into it.

Go to the book's companion website, **www.wiley.com/college/weygandt**, *to see the completion of this problem.*

BROADENING YOUR PERSPECTIVE

Financial Reporting and Analysis

On the Web

BYP12-1 This exercise is an introduction to the Big Four accounting firms, all of which are partnerships.

Addresses

Deloitte & Touche	**www.deloitte.com/**
Ernst & Young	**www.ey.com/**
KPMG	**www.us.kpmg.com/**
PricewaterhouseCoopers	**www.pw.com/**
	or go to **www.wiley.com/college/weygandt**

Steps

1. Select a firm that is of interest to you.
2. Go to the firm's homepage.

Instructions

(a) Name two services provided by the firm.
(b) What is the firm's total annual revenue?
(c) How many clients does it service?
(d) How many people are employed by the firm?
(e) How many partners are there in the firm?

Critical Thinking

Decision Making Across the Organization

BYP12-2   Richard Powers and Jane Keckley, two professionals in the finance area, have worked for Eberhart Leasing for a number of years. Eberhart Leasing is a company that leases high-tech medical equipment to hospitals. Richard and Jane have decided that, with their financial expertise, they might start their own company to provide consulting services to individuals interested in leasing equipment. One form of organization they are considering is a partnership.

If they start a partnership, each individual plans to contribute $50,000 in cash. In addition, Richard has a used IBM computer that originally cost $3,700, which he intends to invest in the partnership. The computer has a present fair value of $1,500.

Although both Richard and Jane are financial wizards, they do not know a great deal about how a partnership operates. As a result, they have come to you for advice.

Instructions

With the class divided into groups, answer the following.

(a) What are the major disadvantages of starting a partnership?
(b) What type of document is needed for a partnership, and what should this document contain?
(c) Both Richard and Jane plan to work full-time in the new partnership. They believe that net income or net loss should be shared equally. However, they are wondering how they can provide compensation to Richard Powers for his additional investment of the computer. What would you tell them?
(d) Richard is not sure how the computer equipment should be reported on his tax return. What would you tell him?
(e) As indicated above, Richard and Jane have worked together for a number of years. Richard's skills complement Jane's and vice versa. If one of them dies, it will be very difficult for the other to maintain the business, not to mention the difficulty of paying the deceased partner's estate for his or her partnership interest. What would you advise them to do?

Communication Activity

BYP12-3   You are an expert in the field of forming partnerships. Daniel Ortman and Sue Stafford want to establish a partnership to start "Pasta Shop," and they are going to meet with you to discuss their plans. Prior to the meeting, you will send them a memo discussing the issues they need to consider before their visit.

Instructions

Write a memo in good form to be sent to Ortman and Stafford.

Ethics Case

BYP12-4   Elizabeth and Laurie operate a beauty salon as partners who share profits and losses equally. The success of their business has exceeded their expectations; the salon is operating quite profitably. Laurie is anxious to maximize profits and schedules appointments from 8 a.m. to 6 p.m. daily, even sacrificing some lunch hours to accommodate regular customers. Elizabeth schedules her appointments from 9 a.m. to 5 p.m. and takes long lunch hours. Elizabeth regularly makes significantly larger withdrawals of

cash than Laurie does, but, she says, "Laurie, you needn't worry, I never make a withdrawal without you knowing about it, so it is properly recorded in my drawing account and charged against my capital at the end of the year." Elizabeth's withdrawals to date are double Laurie's.

Instructions
(a) Who are the stakeholders in this situation?
(b) Identify the problems with Elizabeth's actions and discuss the ethical considerations of her actions.
(c) How might the partnership agreement be revised to accommodate the differences in Elizabeth's and Laurie's work and withdrawal habits?

"All About You" Activity

BYP12-5   As the text in this chapter indicates, the partnership form of organization has advantages and disadvantages. The chapter noted that different types of partnerships have been developed to minimize some of these disadvantages. Alternatively, an individual or company can choose the proprietorship or corporate form of organization.

Instructions
Go to two local businesses that are different, such as a restaurant, a retailer, a construction company, or a professional office (dentist, doctor, etc.), and find the answers to the following questions.

(a) What form of organization do you use in your business?
(b) What do you believe are the two major advantages of this form of organization for your business?
(c) What do you believe are the two major disadvantages of this form of organization for your business?
(d) Do you believe that eventually you may choose another form of organization?
(e) Did you have someone help you form this organization (attorney, accountant, relative, etc.)?

Answers to Insight and Accounting Across the Organization Questions
p. 556 Limited Liability Companies Gain in Popularity   Q: Why do you think that the use of the limited liability company is gaining in popularity? **A:** The LLC is gaining in popularity because owners in such companies have limited liability for business debts even if they participate in management. As a result, the LLC form has a distinct advantage over regular partnerships. In addition, the other limited-type partnerships discussed in Illustration 12-1 are restrictive as to their use. As a result, it is not surprising that limited liability companies are now often used as the form of organization when individuals want to set up a partnership.
p. 559 How to Part Ways Nicely   Q: How can partnership conflicts be minimized and more easily resolved? **A:** First, it is important to develop a business plan that all parties agree to. Second, it is vital to have a well-thought-out partnership agreement. Third, it can be useful to set up a board of mutually agreed upon and respected advisors to consult when making critical decisions.

Answers to Self-Test Questions
1. a   **2.** c   **3.** b   **4.** c   **5.** a ($8,000 + $16,000 + $55,000)   **6.** b ($60,000 × 20%)   **7.** c [$60,000 − ($10,000 × 3)] × 30% = $9,000   **8.** c   **9.** d   **10.** a   **11.** b ($22,000 + $73,000) − $85,000 = $10,000 loss; Ely $52,000 − (40% × 10,000)   **12.** d ($22,000 + $73,000) − $60,000 = $35,000 loss; loss allocation Harriett $23,000 − (20% × 35,000); Mike $8,000 − (40% × 35,000); Elly $52,000 − (40% × 35,000); Mike deficiency is $6,000; allocated to Elly $38,000 − ($6,000 × 4/6)   *****13.** d ($30,000 × 50%)   *****14.** d ($60,000 + $50,000 + $40,000 + $60,000) = $210,000; $210,000 × 25% = $52,500; ($60,000 − $52,500) × 20%   *****15.** b ($29,000 − $20,000) = $9,000 loss; $40,000 − ($9,000 × 3/9)

✔ **The Navigator**

✔ **Remember to go back to the Navigator box on the chapter opening page and check off your completed work.**

CHAPTER13

Corporations: Organization and Capital Stock Transactions

Study Objectives

After studying this chapter, you should be able to:

1 Identify the major characteristics of a corporation.

2 Differentiate between paid-in capital and retained earnings.

3 Record the issuance of common stock.

4 Explain the accounting for treasury stock.

5 Differentiate preferred stock from common stock.

6 Prepare a stockholders' equity section.

✔ The Navigator

Feature Story

WHAT'S COOKING?

What major U.S. corporation got its start 38 years ago with a waffle iron? *Hint:* It doesn't sell food. *Another hint:* Swoosh. *Another hint:* "Just do it." That's right, Nike. In 1971 Nike co-founder Bill Bowerman put a piece of rubber into a kitchen waffle iron, and the trademark waffle sole was born. It seems fair to say that at Nike, "They don't make 'em like they used to."

Nike was co-founded by Bowerman and Phil Knight, a member of Bowerman's University of Oregon track team. Each began in the shoe business independently during the early 1960s. Bowerman got his start by making hand-crafted running shoes for his University of Oregon track team. Knight, after completing graduate school, started a small business importing low-cost, high-quality shoes from Japan. In 1964, the two joined forces, each contributing $500, and formed Blue Ribbon Sports, a partnership that marketed Japanese shoes.

It wasn't until 1971 that the company began manufacturing its own line of shoes. With the new shoes came a new corporate name–Nike–the Greek goddess of victory. It is hard to imagine that the company that now boasts a stable full of world-class athletes as promoters at one time had part-time employees selling shoes out of car trunks at track meets. Nike has achieved its success through relentless innovation combined with unbridled promotion.

By 1980, Nike was sufficiently established that it was able to issue its first stock to the public. In that same year, it also created a stock ownership program for its employees, allowing them to share in the company's success. Since then, Nike has enjoyed phenomenal growth, with 2009 sales reaching $19.2 billion and total dividends paid of $467 million.

Nike is not alone in its quest for the top of the sport shoe world. Reebok used to be Nike's arch rival (get it? "arch"), but then Reebok was acquired by the German company adidas. Now adidas pushes Nike every step of the way.

The shoe market is fickle, with new styles becoming popular almost daily and vast international markets still lying untapped. Whether one of these two giants does eventually take control of the pedi-planet remains to be seen. Meanwhile, the shareholders sit anxiously in the stands as this Olympic-size drama unfolds.

Inside CHAPTER 13

Preview of CHAPTER 13

Corporations like Nike and adidas have substantial resources at their disposal. In fact, the corporation is the dominant form of business organization in the United States in terms of sales, earnings, and number of employees. All of the 500 largest companies in the United States are corporations. In this chapter, we will explain the essential features of a corporation and the accounting for a corporation's capital stock transactions. In Chapter 14, we will look at other issues related to accounting for corporations.

The content and organization of Chapter 13 are as follows.

Corporations: Organization and Capital Stock Transactions

The Corporate Form of Organization	Accounting for Issues of Common Stock	Accounting for Treasury Stock	Preferred Stock	Statement Presentation
• Characteristics • Formation • Stockholder rights • Stock issue considerations • Corporate capital	• Issuing par value stock • Issuing no-par stock • Issuing stock for services or noncash assets	• Purchase of treasury stock • Disposal of treasury stock	• Dividend preferences • Liquidation preference	• Capital stock • Additional paid-in capital • Retained earnings

The Navigator

The Corporate Form of Organization

In 1819, Chief Justice John Marshall defined a corporation as "an artificial being, invisible, intangible, and existing only in contemplation of law." This definition is the foundation for the prevailing legal interpretation that a **corporation** is an **entity separate and distinct from its owners**.

A corporation is created by law, and its continued existence depends upon the statutes of the state in which it is incorporated. As a legal entity, a corporation has most of the rights and privileges of a person. The major exceptions relate to privileges that only a living person can exercise, such as the right to vote or to hold public office. A corporation is subject to the same duties and responsibilities as a person. For example, it must abide by the laws, and it must pay taxes.

Two common ways to classify corporations are by **purpose** and by **ownership**. A corporation may be organized for the purpose of making a profit, or it may be not-for-profit. For-profit corporations include such well-known companies as McDonald's, Nike, PepsiCo, and Google. Not-for-profit corporations are organized for charitable, medical, or educational purposes. Examples are the Salvation Army and the American Cancer Society.

Classification by ownership differentiates publicly held and privately held corporations. A **publicly held corporation** may have thousands of stockholders. Its stock is regularly traded on a national securities exchange such as the New York Stock Exchange. Examples are IBM, Caterpillar, and General Electric.

Alternative Terminology

Privately held corporations are also referred to as *closely held corporations*.

In contrast, a **privately held corporation** usually has only a few stockholders, and does not offer its stock for sale to the general public. Privately held companies are generally much smaller than publicly held companies, although some notable exceptions exist. Cargill Inc., a private corporation that trades in grain and other commodities, is one of the largest companies in the United States.

Characteristics of a Corporation

In 1964, when Nike's founders, Knight and Bowerman, were just getting started in the running shoe business, they formed their original organization as a partnership. In 1968, they reorganized the company as a corporation. A number of characteristics distinguish corporations from proprietorships and partnerships. We explain the most important of these characteristics below.

SEPARATE LEGAL EXISTENCE

As an entity separate and distinct from its owners, the corporation acts under its own name rather than in the name of its stockholders. Nike may buy, own, and sell property. It may borrow money, and may enter into legally binding contracts in its own name. It may also sue or be sued, and it pays its own taxes.

Remember that in a partnership the acts of the owners (partners) bind the partnership. In contrast, the acts of its owners (stockholders) do not bind the corporation unless such owners are **agents** of the corporation. For example, if you owned shares of Nike stock, you would not have the right to purchase inventory for the company unless you were designated as an agent of the corporation.

Stockholders
Legal existence separate from owners

LIMITED LIABILITY OF STOCKHOLDERS

Since a corporation is a separate legal entity, creditors have recourse only to corporate assets to satisfy their claims. The liability of stockholders is normally limited to their investment in the corporation. Creditors have no legal claim on the personal assets of the owners unless fraud has occurred. Even in the event of bankruptcy, stockholders' losses are generally limited to their capital investment in the corporation.

Stockholders
Limited liability of stockholders

TRANSFERABLE OWNERSHIP RIGHTS

Shares of capital stock give ownership in a corporation. These shares are transferable units. Stockholders may dispose of part or all of their interest in a corporation simply by selling their stock. Remember that the transfer of an ownership interest in a partnership requires the consent of each owner. In contrast, the transfer of stock is entirely at the discretion of the stockholder. It does not require the approval of either the corporation or other stockholders.

The transfer of ownership rights between stockholders normally has no effect on the daily operating activities of the corporation. Nor does it affect the corporation's assets, liabilities, and total ownership equity. The transfer of these ownership rights is a transaction between individual owners. After it first issues the capital stock, the company does not participate in such transfers.

Transferable ownership rights

ABILITY TO ACQUIRE CAPITAL

It is relatively easy for a corporation to obtain capital through the issuance of stock. Investors buy stock in a corporation to earn money over time as the share price grows, and because a stockholder has limited liability and shares of stock are readily transferable. Also, individuals can become stockholders by investing relatively small amounts of money. In sum, the ability of a successful corporation to obtain capital is virtually unlimited.

Ability to acquire capital

CONTINUOUS LIFE

The life of a corporation is stated in its charter. The life may be perpetual, or it may be limited to a specific number of years. If it is limited, the company can extend the life through renewal of the charter. Since a corporation is a separate legal entity, its continuance as a going concern is not affected by the withdrawal, death, or incapacity of a stockholder, employee, or officer. As a result, a successful company can have a continuous and perpetual life.

Continuous life

CORPORATION MANAGEMENT

Stockholders legally own the corporation. However, they manage the corporation indirectly through a board of directors they elect. Philip Knight is the chairman of Nike. The board, in turn, formulates the operating policies for the company. The board also selects officers, such as a president and one or more vice presidents, to execute policy and to perform daily management functions. As a result of the Sarbanes-Oxley Act, the board is now required to monitor management's actions more closely. Many feel that the failures of Enron and WorldCom could have been avoided by more diligent boards.

Illustration 13-1 presents a typical organization chart showing the delegation of responsibility.

Illustration 13-1
Corporation organization chart

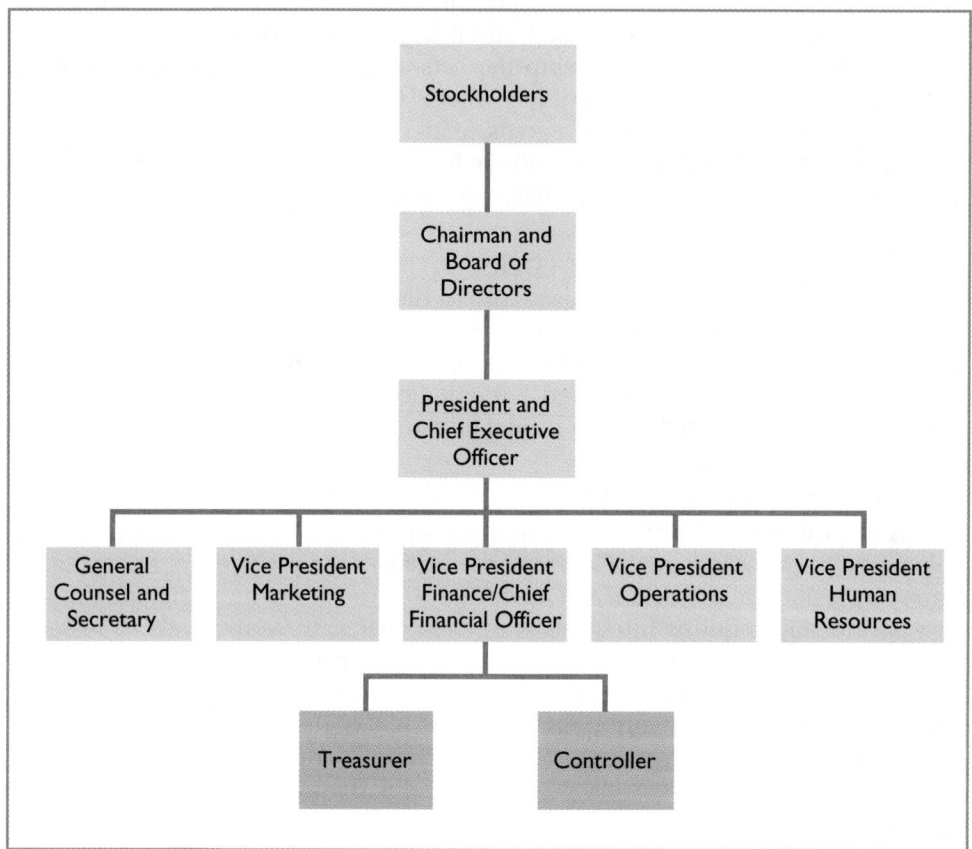

The chief executive officer (CEO) has overall responsibility for managing the business. As the organization chart shows, the CEO delegates responsibility to other officers. The chief accounting officer is the **controller**. The controller's responsibilities include (1) maintaining the accounting records, (2) maintaining an adequate system of internal control, and (3) preparing financial statements, tax returns, and internal reports. The **treasurer** has custody of the corporation's funds and is responsible for maintaining the company's cash position.

The organizational structure of a corporation enables a company to hire professional managers to run the business. On the other hand, the separation of ownership and management often reduces an owner's ability to actively manage the company.

Ethics Note

Managers who are not owners are often compensated based on the performance of the firm. They thus may be tempted to exaggerate firm performance by inflating income figures.

GOVERNMENT REGULATIONS

A corporation is subject to numerous state and federal regulations. For example, state laws usually prescribe the requirements for issuing stock, the distributions of earnings permitted to stockholders, and the effects of retiring stock. Federal securities laws govern the sale of capital stock to the general public. Also, most publicly held corporations are required to make extensive disclosure of their financial affairs to the Securities and Exchange Commission (SEC) through quarterly and annual reports. In addition, when a corporation lists its stock on organized securities exchanges, it must comply with the reporting requirements of these exchanges. Government regulations are designed to protect the owners of the corporation.

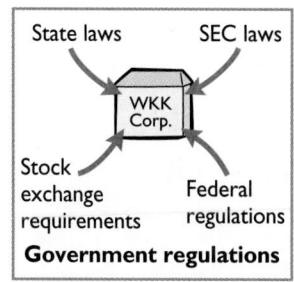
Government regulations

ADDITIONAL TAXES

Owners of proprietorships and partnerships report their share of earnings on their personal income tax returns. The individual owner then pays taxes on this amount. Corporations, on the other hand, must pay federal and state income taxes **as a separate legal entity**. These taxes are substantial.

In addition, stockholders must pay taxes on cash dividends (pro rata distributions of net income). Thus, many argue that the government taxes corporate income **twice (double taxation)**—once at the corporate level, and again at the individual level.

In summary, Illustration 13-2 shows the advantages and disadvantages of a corporation compared to a proprietorship and a partnership.

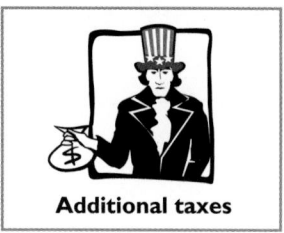
Additional taxes

Advantages	Disadvantages
Separate legal existence	Corporation management—separation of ownership and management
Limited liability of stockholders	
Transferable ownership rights	Government regulations
Ability to acquire capital	Additional taxes
Continuous life	
Corporation management—professional managers	

Illustration 13-2
Advantages and disadvantages of a corporation

Forming a Corporation

A corporation is formed by grant of a state charter. The charter is a document that describes the name and purpose of the corporation, the types and number of shares of stock that are authorized to be issued, the names of the individuals that formed the company, and the number of shares that these individuals agreed to purchase. Regardless of the number of states in which a corporation has operating divisions, it is incorporated in only one state.

It is to the company's advantage to incorporate in a state whose laws are favorable to the corporate form of business organization. For example, although General Motors has its headquarters in Michigan, it is incorporated in New Jersey. In fact, more and more corporations have been incorporating in states with rules that favor existing management. For example, Gulf Oil changed its state of incorporation to Delaware to thwart possible unfriendly takeovers. There, certain defensive tactics against takeovers can be approved by the board of directors alone, without a vote by shareholders.

Upon receipt of its charter from the state of incorporation, the corporation establishes **by-laws**. The by-laws establish the internal rules and procedures for conducting the affairs of the corporation. Corporations engaged in interstate commerce must also obtain a **license** from each state in which they do business. The license subjects the corporation's operating activities to the general corporation laws of the state.

Costs incurred in the formation of a corporation are called organization costs. These costs include legal and state fees, and promotional expenditures involved in the organization of the business. **Corporations expense organization costs as incurred.** To determine the amount and timing of future benefits is so difficult that it is standard procedure to take a conservative approach of expensing these costs immediately.

Alternative Terminology

The charter is often referred to as the *articles of incorporation*.

Wall Street No Friend of Facebook

In the 1990s, it was the dream of every young technology entrepreneur to start a company and do an initial public offering (IPO), that is, list company shares on a stock exchange. It seemed like there was a never-ending supply of 20-something year-old technology entrepreneurs that made millions doing IPOs of companies that never made a profit and eventually failed. In sharp contrast to this is Mark Zuckerberg, the 25-year-old founder and CEO of Facebook. If Facebook did an IPO, he would make billions of dollars. But, he is in no hurry to go public. Because his company doesn't need to invest in factories, distribution systems, or even marketing, it doesn't need to raise a lot of cash. Also, by not going public, Zuckerberg has more control over the direction of the company. Right now, he and the other founders don't have to answer to outside shareholders, who might be more concerned about short-term investment horizons rather than long-term goals. In addition, publicly traded companies face many more financial reporting disclosure requirements.

Source: Jessica E. Vascellaro, "Facebook CEO in No Rush to 'Friend' Wall Street," *Wall Street Journal Online* (March 4, 2010).

 Why has Mark Zuckerberg, the CEO and founder of Facebook, delayed taking his company's shares public through an initial public offering (IPO)? (See page 629.)

Ownership Rights of Stockholders

When chartered, the corporation may begin selling ownership rights in the form of shares of stock. When a corporation has only one class of stock, it is **common stock**. Each share of common stock gives the stockholder the ownership rights pictured in Illustration 13-3. The articles of incorporation or the by-laws state the ownership rights of a share of stock.

Proof of stock ownership is evidenced by a form known as a **stock certificate**. As Illustration 13-4 shows, the face of the certificate shows the name of the corporation, the stockholder's name, the class and special features of the stock, the number of shares owned, and the signatures of authorized corporate officials. Prenumbered certificates facilitate accountability. They may be issued for any quantity of shares.

Stock Issue Considerations

In considering the issuance of stock, a corporation must resolve a number of basic questions: How many shares should it authorize for sale? How should it issue the stock? At what price should it issue the shares? What value should the corporation assign to the stock? These questions are addressed in the following sections.

AUTHORIZED STOCK

The charter indicates the amount of stock that a corporation is **authorized** to sell. The total amount of authorized stock at the time of incorporation normally anticipates both initial and subsequent capital needs. As a result, the number of shares authorized generally exceeds the number initially sold. If it sells all authorized stock, a corporation must obtain consent of the state to amend its charter before it can issue additional shares.

The authorization of capital stock does not result in a formal accounting entry. This event has no immediate effect on either corporate assets or stockholders' equity. However, the number of authorized shares is often reported in the stockholders' equity section. It is then simple to determine the number of unissued shares that the corporation can issue without amending the charter: subtract the total shares issued from the total authorized. For example, if Advanced Micro was authorized to sell 100,000 shares of common stock and issued 80,000 shares, 20,000 shares would remain unissued.

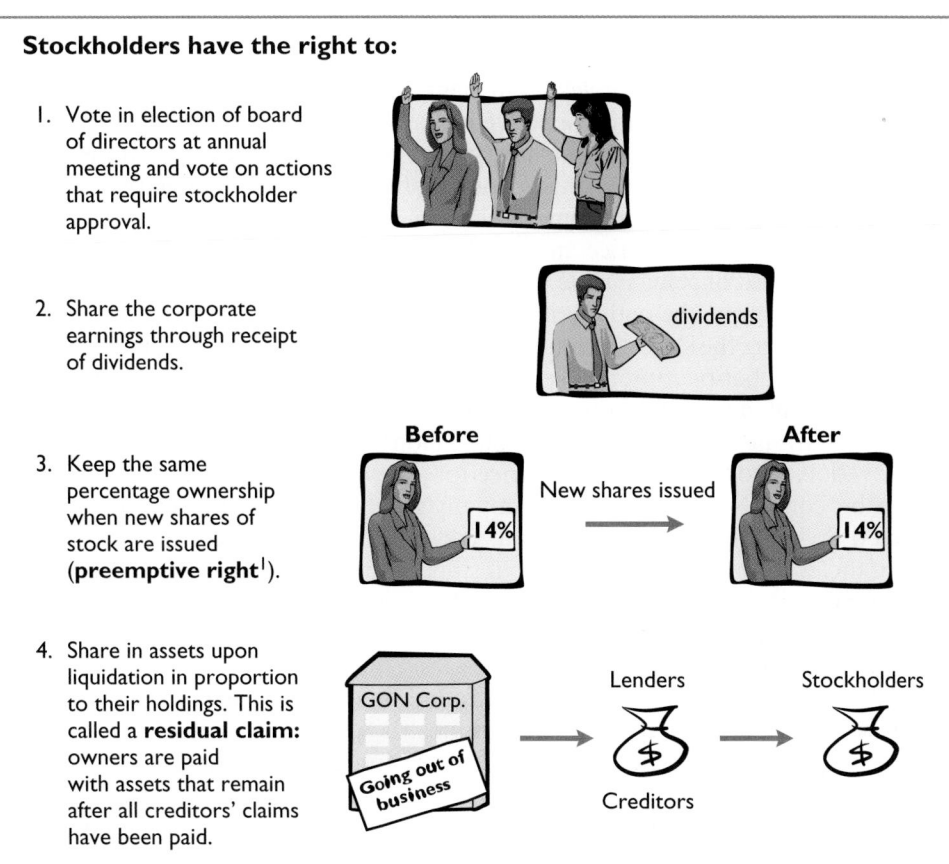

Illustration 13-3
Ownership rights of stockholders

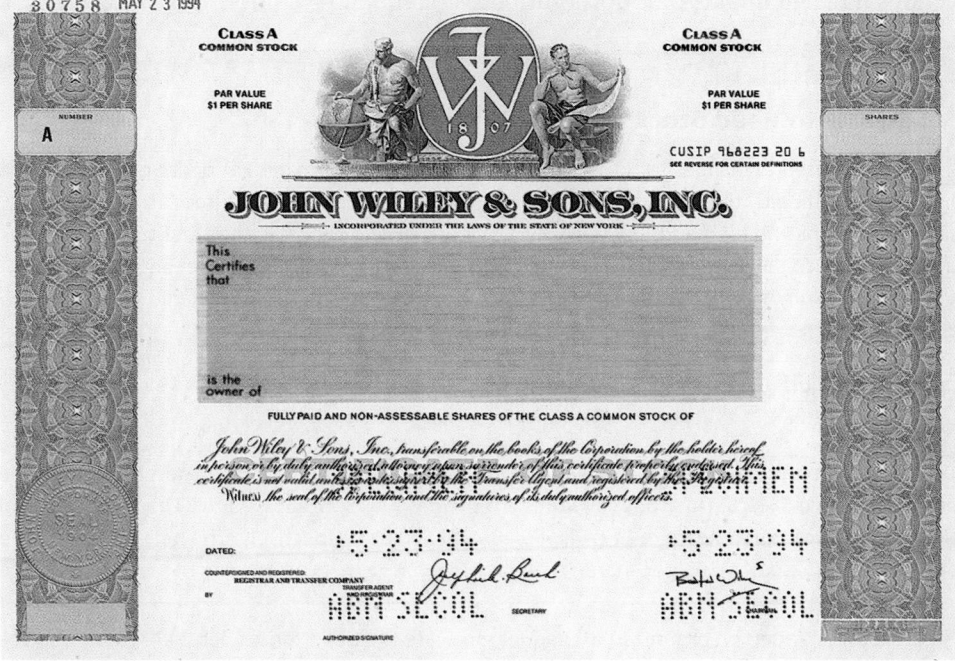

Illustration 13-4
A stock certificate

---

[1] A number of companies have eliminated the preemptive right, because they believe it makes an unnecessary and cumbersome demand on management. For example, by stockholder approval, IBM has dropped its preemptive right for stockholders.

ISSUANCE OF STOCK

A corporation can issue common stock **directly** to investors. Or, it can issue the stock **indirectly** through an investment banking firm that specializes in bringing securities to the attention of prospective investors. Direct issue is typical in closely held companies. Indirect issue is customary for a publicly held corporation.

In an indirect issue, the investment banking firm may agree to **underwrite** the entire stock issue. In this arrangement, the investment banker buys the stock from the corporation at a stipulated price and resells the shares to investors. The corporation thus avoids any risk of being unable to sell the shares. Also, it obtains immediate use of the cash received from the underwriter. The investment banking firm, in turn, assumes the risk of reselling the shares, in return for an underwriting fee.[2] For example, Google (the world's number-one Internet search engine) used underwriters when it issued a highly successful initial public offering, raising $1.67 billion. The underwriters charged a 3% underwriting fee (approximately $50 million) on Google's stock offering.

How does a corporation set the price for a new issue of stock? Among the factors to be considered are: (1) the company's anticipated future earnings, (2) its expected dividend rate per share, (3) its current financial position, (4) the current state of the economy, and (5) the current state of the securities market. The calculation can be complex and is properly the subject of a finance course.

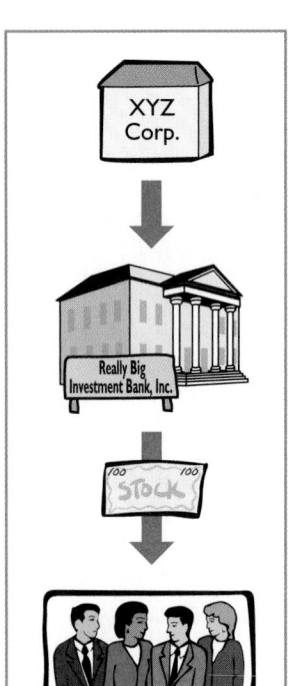

Indirect Issuance

MARKET VALUE OF STOCK

The stock of publicly held companies is traded on organized exchanges. The interaction between buyers and sellers determines the prices per share. In general, the prices set by the marketplace tend to follow the trend of a company's earnings and dividends. But, factors beyond a company's control, such as an oil embargo, changes in interest rates, and the outcome of a presidential election, may cause day-to-day fluctuations in market prices.

The trading of capital stock on securities exchanges involves the transfer of **already issued shares** from an existing stockholder to another investor. These transactions have **no impact** on a corporation's stockholders' equity.

*I*NVESTOR *I*NSIGHT

How to Read Stock Quotes

Organized exchanges trade the stock of publicly held companies at dollar prices per share established by the interaction between buyers and sellers. For each listed security, the financial press reports the high and low prices of the stock during the year, the total volume of stock traded on a given day, the high and low prices for the day, and the closing market price, with the net change for the day. Nike is listed on the New York Stock Exchange. Here is a recent listing for Nike:

| Stock | 52 Weeks | | Volume | High | Low | Close | Net Change |
	High	Low					
Nike	78.55	48.76	5,375,651	72.44	69.78	70.61	−1.69

These numbers indicate the following: The high and low market prices for the last 52 weeks have been $78.55 and $48.76. The trading volume for the day was 5,375,651 shares. The high, low, and closing prices for that date were $72.44, $69.78, and $70.61, respectively. The net change for the day was a decrease of $1.69 per share.

? For stocks traded on organized exchanges, how are the dollar prices per share established? What factors might influence the price of shares in the marketplace? (See page 629.)

---

[2]Alternatively, the investment banking firm may agree only to enter into a **best-efforts** contract with the corporation. In such cases, the banker agrees to sell as many shares as possible at a specified price. The corporation bears the risk of unsold stock. Under a best-efforts arrangement, the banking firm is paid a fee or commission for its services.

PAR AND NO-PAR VALUE STOCKS

Par value stock is capital stock to which the charter has assigned a value per share. Years ago, par value determined the **legal capital** per share that a company must retain in the business for the protection of corporate creditors; that amount was not available for withdrawal by stockholders. Thus, in the past, most states required the corporation to sell its shares at par or above.

However, par value was often immaterial relative to the value of the company's stock—even at the time of issue. Thus, its usefulness as a protective device to creditors was questionable. For example, Loews Corporation's par value is $0.01 per share, yet a new issue in 2010 would have sold at a **market value** in the $35 per share range. Thus, par has no relationship with market value; in the vast majority of cases, it is an immaterial amount. As a consequence, today many states do not require a par value. Instead, they use other means to protect creditors.

No-par value stock is capital stock to which the charter has not assigned a value. No-par value stock is fairly common today. For example, Nike and Procter & Gamble both have no-par stock. In many states, the board of directors assigns a **stated value** to no-par shares.

Do it!

Indicate whether each of the following statements is true or false.

_____ **1.** Similar to partners in a partnership, stockholders of a corporation have unlimited liability.

_____ **2.** It is relatively easy for a corporation to obtain capital through the issuance of stock.

_____ **3.** The separation of ownership and management is an advantage of the corporate form of business.

_____ **4.** The journal entry to record the authorization of capital stock includes a credit to the appropriate capital stock account.

_____ **5.** All states require a par value per share for capital stock.

Corporate Organization

Solution

1. False. The liability of stockholders is normally limited to their investment in the corporation.

2. True.

3. False. The separation of ownership and management is a disadvantage of the corporate form of business.

4. False. The authorization of capital stock does not result in a formal accounting entry.

5. False. Many states do not require a par value.

action plan

✔ Review the characteristics of a corporation and understand which are advantages and which are disadvantages.

✔ Understand that corporations raise capital through the issuance of stock, which can be par or no-par.

Related exercise material: BE13-1, E13-1, E13-2, and **Do it!** 13-1.

✔
The Navigator

Corporate Capital

Owners' equity is identified by various names: **stockholders' equity**, **shareholders' equity**, or **corporate capital**. The stockholders' equity section of a corporation's balance sheet consists of two parts: (1) paid-in (contributed) capital and (2) retained earnings (earned capital).

Study Objective [2]
Differentiate between paid-in capital and retained earnings.

The distinction between **paid-in capital** and **retained earnings** is important from both a legal and a financial point of view. Legally, corporations can make distributions of earnings (declare dividends) out of retained earnings in all states. However, in many states they cannot declare dividends out of paid-in capital. Management, stockholders, and others often look to retained earnings for the continued existence and growth of the corporation.

PAID-IN CAPITAL

Paid-in capital is the total amount of cash and other assets paid in to the corporation by stockholders in exchange for capital stock. As noted earlier, when a corporation has only one class of stock, it is **common stock**.

RETAINED EARNINGS

Retained earnings is net income that a corporation retains for future use. Net income is recorded in Retained Earnings by a closing entry that debits Income Summary and credits Retained Earnings. For example, assuming that net income for Delta Robotics in its first year of operations is $130,000, the closing entry is:

−130,000 Inc
+130,000 RE

Cash Flows
no effect

Income Summary	130,000	
Retained Earnings		130,000
(To close Income Summary and transfer net income		
to retained earnings)		

If Delta Robotics has a balance of $800,000 in common stock at the end of its first year, its stockholders' equity section is as follows.

Illustration 13-5
Stockholders' equity section

Delta Robotics
Balance Sheet (partial)

Stockholders' equity		
Paid-in capital		
Common stock	$800,000	
Retained earnings	130,000	
Total stockholders' equity		$930,000

The following illustration compares the owners' equity (stockholders' equity) accounts reported on a balance sheet for a proprietorship, a partnership, and a corporation.

Illustration 13-6
Comparison of owners' equity accounts

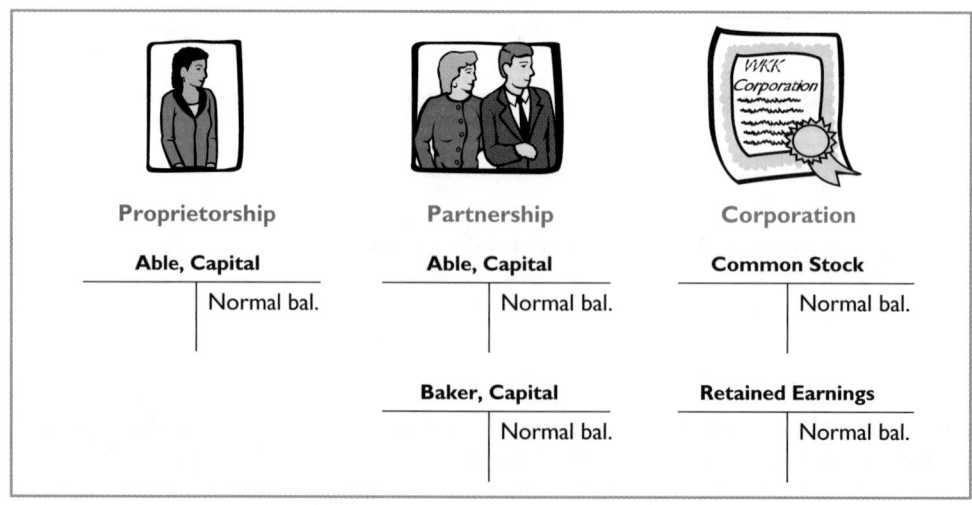

Do it!

At the end of its first year of operation, Doral Corporation has $750,000 of common stock and net income of $122,000. Prepare (a) the closing entry for net income and (b) the stockholders' equity section at year-end.

Corporate Capital

action plan

✔ Record net income in Retained Earnings by a closing entry in which Income Summary is debited and Retained Earnings is credited.

✔ In the stockholders' equity section, show (1) paid-in capital and (2) retained earnings.

Solution

(a) Income Summary		122,000	
Retained Earnings			122,000
(To close Income Summary and transfer net income to retained earnings)			
(b) Stockholders' equity			
Paid-in capital			
Common stock	$750,000		
Retained earnings	122,000		
Total stockholders' equity	$872,000		

Related exercise material: BE13-2 and **Do it!** 13-2.

The Navigator

Accounting for Issues of Common Stock

Let's now look at how to account for issues of common stock. The primary objectives in accounting for the issuance of common stock are: (1) to identify the specific sources of paid-in capital, and (2) to maintain the distinction between paid-in capital and retained earnings. **The issuance of common stock affects only paid-in capital accounts.**

Study Objective [3]
Record the issuance of common stock.

Issuing Par Value Common Stock for Cash

As discussed earlier, par value does not indicate a stock's market value. Therefore, the cash proceeds from issuing par value stock may be equal to, greater than, or less than par value. When the company records issuance of common stock for cash, it credits to Common Stock the par value of the shares. It records in a separate paid-in capital account the portion of the proceeds that is above or below par value.

To illustrate, assume that Hydro-Slide, Inc. issues 1,000 shares of $1 par value common stock at par for cash. The entry to record this transaction is:

Cash	1,000	
Common Stock		1,000
(To record issuance of 1,000 shares of $1 par common stock at par)		

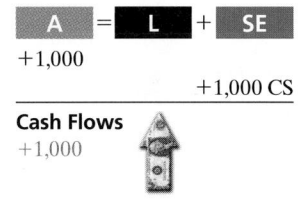

Now assume that Hydro-Slide issues an additional 1,000 shares of the $1 par value common stock for cash at $5 per share. The amount received above the par value, in this case $4 ($5 − $1), is credited to Paid-in Capital in Excess of Par—Common Stock. The entry is:

Cash	5,000	
Common Stock		1,000
Paid-in Capital in Excess of Par—Common Stock		4,000
(To record issuance of 1,000 shares of $1 par common stock)		

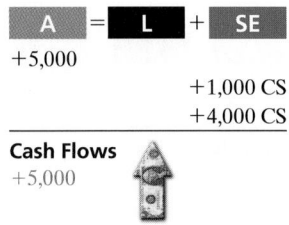

The total paid-in capital from these two transactions is $6,000, and the legal capital is $2,000. Assuming Hydro-Slide, Inc. has retained earnings of $27,000, Illustration 13-7 shows the company's stockholders' equity section.

Illustration 13-7
Stockholders' equity—paid-in capital in excess of par

Hydro-Slide, Inc.	
Balance Sheet (partial)	
Stockholders' equity	
Paid-in capital	
Common stock	$ 2,000
Paid-in capital in excess of par—	
common stock	4,000
Total paid-in capital	6,000
Retained earnings	27,000
Total stockholders' equity	$33,000

Alternative Terminology

Paid-in Capital in Excess of Par is also called *Premium on Stock*.

When a corporation issues stock for less than par value, it debits the account Paid-in Capital in Excess of Par—Common Stock if a credit balance exists in this account. If a credit balance does not exist, then the corporation debits to Retained Earnings the amount less than par. This situation occurs only rarely: Most states do not permit the sale of common stock below par value, because stockholders may be held personally liable for the difference between the price paid upon original sale and par value.

Issuing No-Par Common Stock for Cash

When no-par common stock has a stated value, the entries are similar to those illustrated for par value stock. The corporation credits the stated value to Common Stock. Also, when the selling price of no-par stock exceeds stated value, the corporation credits the excess to Paid-in Capital in Excess of Stated Value—Common Stock.

For example, assume that instead of $1 par value stock, Hydro-Slide, Inc. has $5 stated value no-par stock and the company issues 5,000 shares at $8 per share for cash. The entry is:

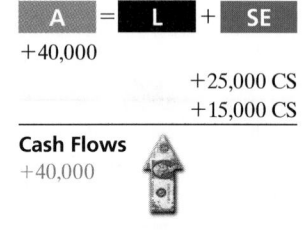

A = L + SE
+40,000
        +25,000 CS
        +15,000 CS

Cash Flows
+40,000

Cash	40,000	
Common Stock		25,000
Paid-in Capital in Excess of Stated Value—Common Stock		15,000
(To record issue of 5,000 shares of $5 stated		
value no-par stock)		

Hydro-Slide, Inc. reports Paid-in Capital in Excess of Stated Value—Common Stock as part of paid-in capital in the stockholders' equity section.

What happens when no-par stock does not have a stated value? In that case, the corporation credits the entire proceeds to Common Stock. Thus, if Hydro-Slide does not assign a stated value to its no-par stock, it records the issuance of the 5,000 shares at $8 per share for cash as follows.

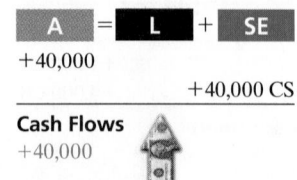

A = L + SE
+40,000
        +40,000 CS

Cash Flows
+40,000

Cash	40,000	
Common Stock		40,000
(To record issue of 5,000 shares of no-par stock)		

Issuing Common Stock for Services or Noncash Assets

Corporations also may issue stock for services (compensation to attorneys or consultants) or for noncash assets (land, buildings, and equipment). In such cases, what cost should be recognized in the exchange transaction? To comply with the **cost principle**, in a noncash transaction **cost is the cash equivalent price**. Thus, **cost is either the fair value of the consideration given up, or the fair value of the consideration received**, whichever is more clearly determinable.

To illustrate, assume that attorneys have helped Jordan Company incorporate. They have billed the company $5,000 for their services. They agree to accept 4,000 shares of $1 par value common stock in payment of their bill. At the time of the exchange, there is no established market price for the stock. In this case, the fair value of the consideration received, $5,000, is more clearly evident. Accordingly, Jordan Company makes the following entry.

Organization Expense	5,000	
Common Stock		4,000
Paid-in Capital in Excess of Par—Common Stock		1,000
(To record issuance of 4,000 shares of $1 par value		
stock to attorneys)		

A = L + SE
−5,000 Exp
+4,000 CS
+1,000 CS

Cash Flows
no effect

As explained on page 597, organization costs are expensed as incurred.

In contrast, assume that Athletic Research Inc. is an existing publicly held corporation. Its $5 par value stock is actively traded at $8 per share. The company issues 10,000 shares of stock to acquire land recently advertised for sale at $90,000. The most clearly evident value in this noncash transaction is the market price of the consideration given, $80,000. The company records the transaction as follows.

Land	80,000	
Common Stock		50,000
Paid-in Capital in Excess of Par—Common Stock		30,000
(To record issuance of 10,000 shares of $5 par value		
stock for land)		

A = L + SE
+80,000
+50,000 CS
+30,000 CS

Cash Flows
no effect

As illustrated in these examples, **the par value of the stock is never a factor in determining the cost of the assets received**. This is also true of the stated value of no-par stock.

ANATOMY OF A FRAUD

The president, chief operating officer, and chief financial officer of SafeNet, a software encryption company, were each awarded employee stock options by the company's board of directors as part of their compensation package. Stock options enable an employee to buy a company's stock sometime in the future at the price that existed when the stock option was awarded. For example, suppose that you received stock options today, when the stock price of your company was $30. Three years later, if the stock price rose to $100, you could "exercise" your options and buy the stock for $30 per share, thereby making $70 per share. After being awarded their stock options, the three employees changed the award dates in the company's records to dates in the past, when the company's stock was trading at historical lows. For example, using the previous example, they would choose a past date when the stock was selling for $10 per share, rather than the $30 price on the actual award date. In our example, this would increase the profit from exercising the options to $90 per share.

Total take: $1.7 million

THE MISSING CONTROL

Independent internal verification. The company's board of directors should have ensured that the awards were properly administered. For example, the date on the minutes from the board meeting could be compared to the dates that were recorded for the awards. In addition, the dates should again be confirmed upon exercise.

Do it!

Issuance of Stock

action plan

✔ In issuing shares for cash, credit Common Stock for par value per share.

✔ Credit any additional proceeds in excess of par to a separate paid-in capital account.

✔ When stock is issued for services, use the cash equivalent price.

✔ For the cash equivalent price use either the fair value of what is given up or the fair value of what is received, whichever is more clearly determinable.

Cayman Corporation begins operations on March 1 by issuing 100,000 shares of $10 par value common stock for cash at $12 per share. On March 15, it issues 5,000 shares of common stock to attorneys in settlement of their bill of $50,000 for organization costs. Journalize the issuance of the shares, assuming the stock is not publicly traded.

Solution

Mar. 1	Cash	1,200,000	
	Common Stock		1,000,000
	Paid-in Capital in Excess of Par—		
	Common Stock		200,000
	(To record issuance of 100,000 shares		
	at $12 per share)		
Mar. 15	Organization Expense	50,000	
	Common Stock		50,000
	(To record issuance of 5,000 shares		
	for attorneys' fees)		

Related exercise material: BE13-3, BE13-4, BE13-5, E13-3, E13-4, E13-6, and **Do it!** 13-3.

✔
The Navigator

Accounting for Treasury Stock

Study Objective [4]
Explain the accounting for treasury stock.

Helpful Hint

Treasury shares do not have dividend rights or voting rights.

Treasury stock is a corporation's own stock that it has issued and subsequently re-acquired from shareholders, but not retired. A corporation may acquire treasury stock for various reasons:

1. To reissue the shares to officers and employees under bonus and stock compensation plans.

2. To signal to the stock market that management believes the stock is underpriced, in the hope of enhancing its market value.

3. To have additional shares available for use in the acquisition of other companies.

4. To reduce the number of shares outstanding and thereby increase earnings per share.

Another infrequent reason for purchasing shares is that management may want to eliminate hostile shareholders by buying them out.

Many corporations have treasury stock. For example, in the United States approximately 70% of companies have treasury stock.[3] In a recent year, Nike purchased more than 6 million treasury shares.

---
[3] *Accounting Trends & Techniques 2009* (New York: American Institute of Certified Public Accountants).

Purchase of Treasury Stock

Companies generally account for treasury stock by **the cost method**. This method uses the cost of the shares purchased to value the treasury stock. Under the cost method, the company debits **Treasury Stock** for the **price paid to reacquire the shares**. When the company disposes of the shares, it credits to Treasury Stock **the same amount** it paid to reacquire the shares.

To illustrate, assume that on January 1, 2012, the stockholders' equity section of Mead, Inc. has 100,000 shares of $5 par value common stock outstanding (all issued at par value) and Retained Earnings of $200,000. The stockholders' equity section before purchase of treasury stock is as follows.

Illustration 13-8
Stockholders' equity with no treasury stock

Mead, Inc.	
Balance Sheet (partial)	
Stockholders' equity	
Paid-in capital	
Common stock, $5 par value, 100,000 shares	
issued and outstanding	$500,000
Retained earnings	200,000
Total stockholders' equity	$700,000

On February 1, 2012, Mead acquires 4,000 shares of its stock at $8 per share. The entry is:

Feb. 1	Treasury Stock	32,000	
	Cash		32,000
	(To record purchase of 4,000 shares of		
	treasury stock at $8 per share)		

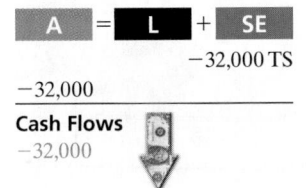

A = L + SE
−32,000 TS
−32,000
Cash Flows
−32,000

Note that Mead debits Treasury Stock for the cost of the shares purchased. Is the original paid-in capital account, Common Stock, affected? No, because the number of issued shares does not change. In the stockholders' equity section of the balance sheet, Mead deducts treasury stock from total paid-in capital and retained earnings. Treasury Stock is a **contra stockholders' equity account**. Thus, the acquisition of treasury stock reduces stockholders' equity.

The stockholders' equity section of Mead, Inc. after purchase of treasury stock is as follows.

Illustration 13-9
Stockholders' equity with treasury stock

Mead, Inc.	
Balance Sheet (partial)	
Stockholders' equity	
Paid-in capital	
Common stock, $5 par value, 100,000 shares issued	
and 96,000 shares outstanding	$500,000
Retained earnings	200,000
Total paid-in capital and retained earnings	700,000
Less: Treasury stock (4,000 shares)	32,000
Total stockholders' equity	$668,000

Ethics Note

The purchase of treasury stock reduces the cushion for creditors and preferred stockholders. A restriction for the cost of treasury stock purchased is often required. The restriction is usually applied to retained earnings.

Mead discloses in the balance sheet both the number of shares issued (100,000) and the number in the treasury (4,000). The difference is the number of shares of stock outstanding (96,000). The term **outstanding stock** means the number of shares of issued stock that are being held by stockholders.

Some maintain that companies should report treasury stock as an asset because it can be sold for cash. Under this reasoning, companies should also show unissued stock as an asset, clearly an erroneous conclusion. Rather than being an asset, treasury stock reduces stockholder claims on corporate assets. This effect is correctly shown by reporting treasury stock as a deduction from total paid-in capital and retained earnings.

ACCOUNTING ACROSS THE ORGANIZATION

Why Did Reebok Buy Its Own Stock?

In a bold (and some would say risky) move, Reebok at one time bought back nearly a *third* of its shares. This repurchase of shares dramatically reduced Reebok's available cash. In fact, the company borrowed significant funds to accomplish the repurchase. In a press release, management stated that it was repurchasing the shares because it believed its stock was severely underpriced. The repurchase of so many shares was meant to signal management's belief in good future earnings.

Skeptics, however, suggested that Reebok's management was repurchasing shares to make it less likely that another company would acquire Reebok (in which case Reebok's top managers would likely lose their jobs). By depleting its cash, Reebok became a less likely acquisition target. Acquiring companies like to purchase companies with large cash balances so they can pay off debt used in the acquisition.

? What signal might a large stock repurchase send to investors regarding management's belief about the company's growth opportunities? (See page 629.)

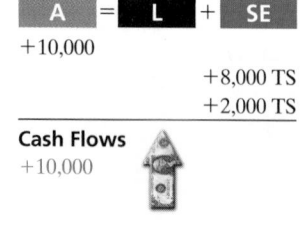

Disposal of Treasury Stock

Treasury stock is usually sold or retired. The accounting for its sale differs when treasury stock is sold above cost than when it is sold below cost.

SALE OF TREASURY STOCK ABOVE COST

If the selling price of the treasury shares is equal to their cost, the company records the sale of the shares by a debit to Cash and a credit to Treasury Stock. When the selling price of the shares is greater than their cost, the company credits the difference to Paid-in Capital from Treasury Stock.

To illustrate, assume that on July 1, Mead sells for $10 per share the 1,000 shares of its treasury stock, previously acquired at $8 per share. The entry is as follows.

Helpful Hint

Treasury stock transactions are classified as capital stock transactions. As in the case when stock is issued, the income statement is not involved.

A	=	L	+	SE
+10,000				
				+8,000 TS
				+2,000 TS

Cash Flows
+10,000

July 1	Cash	10,000	
	Treasury Stock		8,000
	Paid-in Capital from Treasury Stock		2,000
	(To record sale of 1,000 shares of treasury stock above cost)		

Mead does not record a $2,000 gain on sale of treasury stock for two reasons: (1) Gains on sales occur when **assets** are sold, and treasury stock is not an asset. (2) A corporation does not realize a gain or suffer a loss from stock transactions with its own stockholders. Thus, companies should not include in net income any paid-in capital arising from the sale of treasury stock. Instead, they report Paid-in Capital from Treasury Stock separately on the balance sheet, as a part of paid-in capital.

SALE OF TREASURY STOCK BELOW COST

When a company sells treasury stock below its cost, it usually debits to Paid-in Capital from Treasury Stock the excess of cost over selling price. Thus, if Mead, Inc. sells an additional 800 shares of treasury stock on October 1 at $7 per share, it makes the following entry.

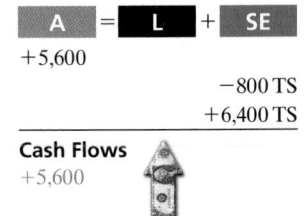

Oct. 1	Cash	5,600	
	Paid-in Capital from Treasury Stock	800	
	Treasury Stock		6,400
	(To record sale of 800 shares of treasury		
	stock below cost)		

Observe the following from the two sales entries: (1) Mead credits Treasury Stock at cost in each entry. (2) Mead uses Paid-in Capital from Treasury Stock for the difference between cost and the resale price of the shares. (3) The original paid-in capital account, Common Stock, is not affected. **The sale of treasury stock increases both total assets and total stockholders' equity.**

After posting the foregoing entries, the treasury stock accounts will show the following balances on October 1.

Illustration 13-10
Treasury stock accounts

	Treasury Stock				Paid-in Capital from Treasury Stock		
Feb. 1	32,000	July 1	8,000	Oct. 1	800	July 1	2,000
		Oct. 1	6,400			Oct. 1 Bal.	1,200
Oct. 1 Bal.	17,600						

When a company fully depletes the credit balance in Paid-in Capital from Treasury Stock, it debits to Retained Earnings any additional excess of cost over selling price. To illustrate, assume that Mead, Inc. sells its remaining 2,200 shares at $7 per share on December 1. The excess of cost over selling price is $2,200 [2,200 × ($8 − $7)]. In this case, Mead debits $1,200 of the excess to Paid-in Capital from Treasury Stock. It debits the remainder to Retained Earnings. The entry is:

Dec. 1	Cash	15,400	
	Paid-in Capital from Treasury Stock	1,200	
	Retained Earnings	1,000	
	Treasury Stock		17,600
	(To record sale of 2,200 shares of treasury		
	stock at $7 per share)		

Do it!

Santa Anita Inc. purchases 3,000 shares of its $50 par value common stock for $180,000 cash on July 1. It will hold the shares in the treasury until resold. On November 1, the corporation sells 1,000 shares of treasury stock for cash at $70 per share. Journalize the treasury stock transactions.

Solution

July 1	Treasury Stock	180,000	
	Cash		180,000
	(To record the purchase of 3,000 shares at		
	$60 per share)		

Treasury Stock

action plan

✔ Record the purchase of treasury stock at cost.

✔ When treasury stock is sold above its cost, credit the excess of the selling price over cost to Paid-in Capital from Treasury Stock.

action plan (cont'd)

✔ When treasury stock is sold below its cost, debit the excess of cost over selling price to Paid-in Capital from Treasury Stock.

Nov. 1	Cash	70,000	
	Treasury Stock		60,000
	Paid-in Capital from Treasury Stock		10,000
	(To record the sale of 1,000 shares at $70 per share)		

Related exercise material: BE13-6, E13-5, E13-7, E13-8, and **Do it!** 13-4.

✔
The Navigator

Preferred Stock

Study Objective [5]
Differentiate preferred stock from common stock.

To appeal to more investors, a corporation may issue an additional class of stock, called preferred stock. **Preferred stock** has contractual provisions that give it some preference or priority over common stock. Typically, preferred stockholders have a priority as to (1) distributions of earnings (dividends) and (2) assets in the event of liquidation. However, they generally do not have voting rights.

Like common stock, corporations may issue preferred stock for cash or for noncash assets. The entries for these transactions are similar to the entries for common stock. When a corporation has more than one class of stock, each paid-in capital account title should identify the stock to which it relates. A company might have the following accounts: Preferred Stock, Common Stock, Paid-in Capital in Excess of Par—Preferred Stock, and Paid-in Capital in Excess of Par—Common Stock. For example, if Stine Corporation issues 10,000 shares of $10 par value preferred stock for $12 cash per share, the entry to record the issuance is:

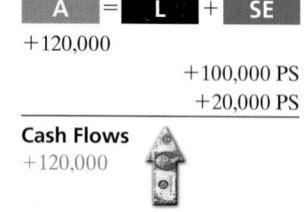

A = L + SE
+120,000
+100,000 PS
+20,000 PS

Cash Flows
+120,000

	Cash	120,000	
	Preferred Stock		100,000
	Paid-in Capital in Excess of Par—Preferred Stock		20,000
	(To record the issuance of 10,000 shares of $10 par value preferred stock)		

Preferred stock may have either a par value or no-par value. In the stockholders' equity section of the balance sheet, companies list preferred stock first because of its dividend and liquidation preferences over common stock.

We discuss various features associated with the issuance of preferred stock on the following pages.

Dividend Preferences

I hope there is some money left when it's my turn.

Preferred   Common
stockholders stockholders

Dividend Preference

As indicated above, **preferred stockholders have the right to receive dividends before common stockholders**. For example, if the dividend rate on preferred stock is $5 per share, common shareholders will not receive any dividends in the current year until preferred stockholders have received $5 per share. The first claim to dividends does not, however, guarantee the payment of dividends. Dividends depend on many factors, such as adequate retained earnings and availability of cash. If a company does not pay dividends to preferred stockholders, it cannot of course pay dividends to common stockholders.

For preferred stock, companies state the per share dividend amount as a percentage of the par value or as a specified amount. For example, Earthlink specifies a 3% dividend on its $100 par value preferred, whereas PepsiCo pays $4.56 per share on its no-par value stock.

CUMULATIVE DIVIDEND

Preferred stock often contains a **cumulative dividend** feature. This means that preferred stockholders must be paid both current-year dividends and any unpaid prior-year dividends before common stockholders receive dividends. When preferred stock is cumulative, preferred dividends not declared in a given period are called **dividends in arrears**.

To illustrate, assume that Scientific Leasing has 5,000 shares of 7%, $100 par value, cumulative preferred stock outstanding. Each $100 share pays a $7 dividend (.07 × $100). The annual dividend is $35,000 (5,000 × $7 per share). If dividends are two years in arrears, preferred stockholders are entitled to receive the following dividends in the current year.

Dividends in arrears ($35,000 × 2)	$ 70,000
Current-year dividends	35,000
Total preferred dividends	**$105,000**

Illustration 13-11
Computation of total dividends to preferred stock

The company cannot pay dividends to common stockholders until it pays the entire preferred dividend. In other words, companies cannot pay dividends to common stockholders while any preferred dividends are in arrears.

Are dividends in arrears considered a liability? **No—no payment obligation exists until the board of directors declares a dividend**. However, companies should disclose in the notes to the financial statements the amount of dividends in arrears. Doing so enables investors to assess the potential impact of this commitment on the corporation's financial position.

Companies that are unable to meet their dividend obligations are not looked upon favorably by the investment community. As a financial officer noted in discussing one company's failure to pay its cumulative preferred dividend for a period of time, "Not meeting your obligations on something like that is a major black mark on your record." The accounting entries for preferred stock dividends are explained in Chapter 14.

Payment of a Cumulative Dividend

Dividend in arrears

Current dividend

Preferred stockholders

Liquidation Preference

Most preferred stocks also have a preference on corporate assets if the corporation fails. This feature provides security for the preferred stockholder. The preference to assets may be for the par value of the shares or for a specified liquidating value. For example, Commonwealth Edison's preferred stock entitles its holders to receive $31.80 per share, plus accrued and unpaid dividends, in the event of liquidation. The liquidation preference establishes the respective claims of creditors and preferred stockholders in litigation involving bankruptcy lawsuits.

Statement Presentation

Companies report paid-in capital and retained earnings in the stockholders' equity section of the balance sheet. They identify the specific sources of paid-in capital, using the following classifications.

Study Objective [6]
Prepare a stockholders' equity section.

1. **Capital stock.** This category consists of preferred and common stock. Preferred stock appears before common stock because of its preferential rights. Companies report par value, shares authorized, shares issued, and shares outstanding for each class of stock.

2. **Additional paid-in capital.** This category includes the excess of amounts paid in over par or stated value and paid-in capital from treasury stock.

Alternative Terminology

Paid-in capital is sometimes called *contributed capital.*

The stockholders' equity section of Connally Inc. in Illustration 13-12 includes most of the accounts discussed in this chapter. The disclosures pertaining to Connally's common stock indicate that: the company issued 400,000 shares; 100,000 shares are unissued (500,000 authorized less 400,000 issued); and 390,000 shares are outstanding (400,000 issued less 10,000 shares in treasury).

Illustration 13-12
Stockholders' equity section

Connally Inc. Balance Sheet (partial)		
Stockholders' equity		
Paid-in capital		
Capital stock		
9% preferred stock, $100 par value cumulative, 10,000 shares authorized, 6,000 shares issued and outstanding		$ 600,000
Common stock, no par, $5 stated value, 500,000 shares authorized, 400,000 shares issued, and 390,000 outstanding		2,000,000
Total capital stock		2,600,000
Additional paid-in capital		
In excess of par—preferred stock	$ 30,000	
In excess of stated—common stock	860,000	
From treasury stock	140,000	
Total additional paid-in capital		1,030,000
Total paid-in capital		3,630,000
Retained earnings		1,058,000
Total paid-in capital and retained earnings		4,688,000
Less: Treasury stock (10,000 common shares) (at cost)		(80,000)
Total stockholders' equity		$4,608,000

Published annual reports often combine and report as a single amount the individual sources of additional paid-in capital, as shown in Illustration 13-13. In addition, authorized shares are sometimes not reported.

Illustration 13-13
Published stockholders' equity section

Kellogg Company Balance Sheet (partial) ($ in millions)	
Stockholders' equity	
Common stock, $0.25 par value, 1,000,000,000 shares authorized	
Issued: 418,669,193 shares	$ 105
Capital in excess of par value	388
Retained earnings	4,217
Treasury stock, at cost	
28,618,052 shares	(1,357)
Accumulated other comprehensive income (loss)	(827)
Total stockholders' equity	$2,526

In practice, companies sometimes use the term "Capital surplus" in place of "Additional paid-in capital," and "Earned surplus" in place of "Retained earnings." The use of the term "surplus" suggests that the company has available an excess amount of funds. Such is not necessarily the case. Therefore, **the term "surplus" should not be employed in accounting**. Unfortunately, a number of companies still do use it.

Vivi Corporation
Balance Sheet (partial)

Stockholder's Equity
   Paid-in capital
      Capital Stock
         Common stock, $10 par value, 5000 shares
         issued $50000
   — Additional paid-in capital
      In excess of par - common stock $ 20000
      From Treasury Stock   1000
         Total Additional Paid in Capital $ 21000
         Total Paid-in Capital   71000
Retained Earnings   45000
                    Paid-in
   Total Capital + Retained Earnings   116000
   Total Equity $116000

13-2	Dec 31	Income Summary 450,000	
		Retained Earnings (capital)	450,000
		(To close Income Summary + transfer to	
		retained earnings)	
3		Cash 36000	
		Common Stock	20000
		Paid in Capital in Excess of Par - Common Stock	16000
		(to record issuance of 2,000 shares of $10 par common stock)	
4		Cash 18000	
		Common Stock	3000
		Paid in Capital in Excess of Stated Value - Common Stock	15000
		(to record issue of 3000 shares of $1 stated value no-par stock)	
6	July 1	Treasury Stock 4000	
		Cash	4000
		(to record purchase of treasury stock 500 at 8 per share)	
	Sep 1	Cash 3300	
		Treasury Stock	2400
		Paid - in Capital from Treasury Stock	900
		(to record sale of 300 shares of treasury stock above cost)	
7		Cash 650 000	
		Preferred Stock	500000
		Paid in Capital in Excess of Par - Preferred Stock	150000
		(to record issuance of 5000 shares of $100 par value preferred stock)	

Do it!

Stockholders'
Equity Section

Jennifer Corporation has issued 300,000 shares of $3 par value common stock. It authorized 600,000 shares. The paid-in capital in excess of par on the common stock is $380,000. The corporation has reacquired 15,000 shares at a cost of $50,000 and is currently holding those shares. Treasury stock was reissued in prior years for $72,000 more than its cost.

The corporation also has 4,000 shares issued and outstanding of 8%, $100 par-value preferred stock. It authorized 10,000 shares. The paid-in capital in excess of par on the preferred stock is $25,000. Retained earnings is $610,000.

Prepare the stockholders' equity section of the balance sheet.

action plan

✔ Present capital stock first; list preferred stock before common stock.

✔ Present additional paid-in capital after capital stock.

✔ Report retained earnings after capital stock and additional paid-in capital.

✔ Deduct treasury stock from total paid-in capital and retained earnings.

Solution

JENNIFER CORPORATION
Balance Sheet (partial)

Stockholders' equity		
Paid-in capital		
Capital stock		
8% preferred stock, $100 par value, 10,000 shares authorized, 4,000 shares issued and outstanding		$ 400,000
Common stock, $3 par value, 600,000 shares authorized, 300,000 shares issued, and 285,000 shares outstanding		900,000
Total capital stock		1,300,000
Additional paid-in capital		
In excess of par—preferred stock	$ 25,000	
In excess of par—common stock	380,000	
From treasury stock	72,000	
Total additional paid-in capital		477,000
Total paid-in capital		1,777,000
Retained earnings		610,000
Total paid-in capital and retained earnings		2,387,000
Less: Treasury stock (15,000 common shares) (at cost)		(50,000)
Total stockholders' equity		$2,337,000

Related exercise material: BE13-8, E13-9, E13-12, E13-13, E13-14, E13-15, and **Do it!** 13-5.

The Navigator

COMPREHENSIVE

Do it!

The Rolman Corporation is authorized to issue 1,000,000 shares of $5 par value common stock. In its first year, the company has the following stock transactions.

Jan. 10	Issued 400,000 shares of stock at $8 per share.
July 1	Issued 100,000 shares of stock for land. The land had an asking price of $900,000. The stock is currently selling on a national exchange at $8.25 per share.
Sept. 1	Purchased 10,000 shares of common stock for the treasury at $9 per share.
Dec. 1	Sold 4,000 shares of the treasury stock at $10 per share.

Instructions

(a) Journalize the transactions.

(b) Prepare the stockholders' equity section assuming the company had retained earnings of $200,000 at December 31.

action plan

✔ When common stock has a par value, credit Common Stock for par value.

✔ Use fair value in a noncash transaction.

✔ Debit and credit the Treasury Stock account at cost.

✔ Record differences between the cost and selling price of treasury stock in stockholders' equity accounts, not as gains or losses.

Solution to Comprehensive Do it!

(a)

Jan. 10	Cash		3,200,000	
	Common Stock			2,000,000
	Paid-in Capital in Excess of Par— Common Stock			1,200,000
	(To record issuance of 400,000 shares of $5 par value stock)			
July 1	Land		825,000	
	Common Stock			500,000
	Paid-in Capital in Excess of Par— Common Stock			325,000
	(To record issuance of 100,000 shares of $5 par value stock for land)			
Sept. 1	Treasury Stock		90,000	
	Cash			90,000
	(To record purchase of 10,000 shares of treasury stock at cost)			
Dec. 1	Cash		40,000	
	Treasury Stock			36,000
	Paid-in Capital from Treasury Stock			4,000
	(To record sale of 4,000 shares of treasury stock above cost)			

(b)

ROLMAN CORPORATION
Balance Sheet (partial)

Stockholders' equity		
Paid-in capital		
Capital stock		
Common stock, $5 par value, 1,000,000 shares authorized, 500,000 shares issued, 494,000 shares outstanding		$2,500,000
Additional paid-in capital		
In excess of par—common stock	$1,525,000	
From treasury stock	4,000	
Total additional paid-in capital		1,529,000
Total paid-in capital		4,029,000
Retained earnings		200,000
Total paid-in capital and retained earnings		4,229,000
Less: Treasury stock (6,000 shares)		(54,000)
Total stockholders' equity		$4,175,000

The Navigator

Summary of Study Objectives

[1] Identify the major characteristics of a corporation. The major characteristics of a corporation are separate legal existence, limited liability of stockholders, transferable ownership rights, ability to acquire capital, continuous life, corporation management, government regulations, and additional taxes.

[2] Differentiate between paid-in capital and retained earnings. Paid-in capital is the total amount paid in on capital stock. It is often called contributed capital. Retained earnings is net income retained in a corporation. It is often called earned capital.

[3] Record the issuance of common stock. When companies record the issuance of common stock for cash, they credit the par value of the shares to Common Stock. They record in a separate paid-in capital account the portion of the proceeds that is above or below par value. When no-par common stock has a stated value, the entries are similar to those for par value stock. When no-par stock does not have a stated value, companies credit the entire proceeds to Common Stock.

[4] Explain the accounting for treasury stock. The cost method is generally used in accounting for treasury stock. Under this approach, companies debit Treasury Stock at the price paid to reacquire the shares. They credit the same amount to Treasury Stock when they sell the shares. The difference between the sales price and cost is recorded in stockholders' equity accounts, not in income statement accounts.

[5] Differentiate preferred stock from common stock. Preferred stock has contractual provisions that give it priority over common stock in certain areas. Typically, preferred stockholders have preferences (1) to dividends and (2) to assets in liquidation. They usually do not have voting rights.

[6] Prepare a stockholders' equity section. In the stockholders' equity section, companies report paid-in capital and retained earnings and identify specific sources of paid-in capital. Within paid-in capital, two classifications are shown: capital stock and additional paid-in capital. If a corporation has treasury stock, it deducts the cost of treasury stock from total paid-in capital and retained earnings to obtain total stockholders' equity.

✔ **The Navigator**

Glossary

Authorized stock   The amount of stock that a corporation is authorized to sell as indicated in its charter. (p. 598).

Charter   A document that creates a corporation. (p. 597).

Corporation   A business organized as a legal entity separate and distinct from its owners under state corporation law. (p. 594).

Cumulative dividend   A feature of preferred stock entitling the stockholder to receive current and unpaid prior-year dividends before common stockholders receive dividends. (p. 611).

No-par value stock   Capital stock that has not been assigned a value in the corporate charter. (p. 601).

Organization costs   Costs incurred in the formation of a corporation. (p. 597).

Outstanding stock   Capital stock that has been issued and is being held by stockholders. (p. 608).

Paid-in capital   Total amount of cash and other assets paid in to the corporation by stockholders in exchange for capital stock. (p. 602).

Par value stock   Capital stock that has been assigned a value per share in the corporate charter. (p. 601).

Preferred stock   Capital stock that has some preferences over common stock. (p. 610).

Privately held corporation   A corporation that has only a few stockholders and whose stock is not available for sale to the general public. (p. 594).

Publicly held corporation   A corporation that may have thousands of stockholders and whose stock is regularly traded on a national securities exchange. (p. 594).

Retained earnings   Net income that is retained in the corporation for future use. (p. 602).

Stated value   The amount per share assigned by the board of directors to no-par stock. (p. 601).

Treasury stock   A corporation's own stock that has been issued and subsequently reacquired from shareholders by the corporation but not retired. (p. 606).

 Self-Test, Brief Exercises, Exercises, Problem Set A, and many more components are available for practice in *WileyPLUS*

Self-Test Questions

Answers are on page 629.

(SO 1)   **1.** Which of the following is *not* a major advantage of a corporation?
  a. Separate legal existence.
  b. Continuous life.
  c. Government regulations.
  d. Transferable ownership rights.

(SO 1)   **2.** A major disadvantage of a corporation is:
  a. limited liability of stockholders.
  b. additional taxes.
  c. transferable ownership rights.
  d. None of the above.

3. Costs incurred in the formation of a corporation: (SO 1)
  a. do not include legal fees.
  b. are expensed as incurred.
  c. are recorded as an asset.
  d. provide future benefits whose amounts and timing are easily determined.

4. Which of the following statements is *false*?   (SO 1)
  a. Ownership of common stock gives the owner a voting right.
  b. The stockholders' equity section begins with paid-in capital.
  c. The authorization of capital stock does not result in a formal accounting entry.

d. Legal capital per share applies to par value stock but not to no-par value stock.

(SO 2) **5.** Total stockholders' equity (in the absence of treasury stock) equals:
   a. Total paid-in capital + Retained earnings.
   b. Paid-in capital + Capital stock + Retained earnings.
   c. Capital stock + Additional paid-in capital − Retained earnings.
   d. Common stock + Retained earnings.

(SO 2) **6.** The account Retained Earnings is:
   a. a subdivision of paid-in capital.
   b. net income retained in the corporation.
   c. reported as an expense in the income statement.
   d. closed to capital stock.

(SO 3) **7.** A-Team Corporation issued 1,000 shares of $5 par value stock for land. The stock is actively traded at $9 per share. The land was advertised for sale at $10,500. The land should be recorded at:
   a. $4,000.   **c.** $9,000.
   b. $5,000.   **d.** $10,500.

(SO 3) **8.** ABC Corporation issues 1,000 shares of $10 par value common stock at $12 per share. In recording the transaction, credits are made to:
   a. Common Stock $10,000 and Paid-in Capital in Excess of Stated Value $2,000.
   b. Common Stock $12,000.
   c. Common Stock $10,000 and Paid-in Capital in Excess of Par $2,000.
   d. Common Stock $10,000 and Retained Earnings $2,000.

(SO 4) **9.** Treasury stock may be repurchased:
   a. to reissue the shares to officers and employees under bonus and stock compensation plans.
   b. to signal to the stock market that management believes the stock is underpriced.
   c. to have additional shares available for use in the acquisition of other companies.
   d. More than one of the above.

(SO 4) **10.** XYZ, Inc. sells 100 shares of $5 par value treasury stock at $13 per share. If the cost of acquiring the shares was $10 per share, the entry for the sale should include credits to:

a. Treasury Stock $1,000 and Paid-in Capital from Treasury Stock $300.
b. Treasury Stock $500 and Paid-in Capital from Treasury Stock $800.
c. Treasury Stock $1,000 and Retained Earnings $300.
d. Treasury Stock $500 and Paid-in Capital in Excess of Par $800.

11. In the stockholders' equity section, the cost of treasury (SO 4) stock is deducted from:
   a. total paid-in capital and retained earnings.
   b. retained earnings.
   c. total stockholders' equity.
   d. common stock in paid-in capital.

12. Preferred stock may have priority over common stock (SO 5) *except* in:
   a. dividends.
   b. assets in the event of liquidation.
   c. cumulative dividend features.
   d. voting.

13. Which of the following is *not* reported under additional (SO 6) paid-in capital?
   a. Paid-in capital in excess of par.
   b. Common stock.
   c. Paid-in capital in excess of stated value.
   d. Paid-in capital from treasury stock.

14. M-Bot Corporation has 10,000 shares of 8%, $100 par value, (SO 5) cumulative preferred stock outstanding at December 31, 2012. No dividends were declared in 2010 or 2011. If M-Bot wants to pay $375,000 of dividends in 2012, common stockholders will receive:
   a. $0.   **c.** $215,000.
   b. $295,000.   **d.** $135,000.

15. In the stockholders' equity section of the balance sheet, (SO 6) common stock:
   a. is listed before preferred stock.
   b. is added to total capital stock.
   c. is part of paid-in capital.
   d. is part of additional paid-in capital.

Go to the book's companion website, **www.wiley.com/college/weygandt**, for additional Self-Test Questions.

The Navigator

Questions

1. Eric Fink, a student, asks your help in understanding the following characteristics of a corporation: (a) separate legal existence, (b) limited liability of stockholders, and (c) transferable ownership rights. Explain these characteristics to Eric.

2. **(a)** Your friend Vicky Biel cannot understand how the characteristic of corporation management is both an advantage and a disadvantage. Clarify this problem for Vicky.
   (b) Identify and explain two other disadvantages of a corporation.

3. **(a)** The following terms pertain to the forming of a corporation: (1) charter, (2) by-laws, and (3) organization costs. Explain the terms.
   (b) Linda Merando believes a corporation must be incorporated in the state in which its headquarters office is located. Is Linda correct? Explain.

4. What are the basic ownership rights of common stockholders in the absence of restrictive provisions?

5. **(a)** What are the two principal components of stockholders' equity?
   (b) What is paid-in capital? Give three examples.

6. How do the financial statements for a corporation differ from the statements for a proprietorship?

7. The corporate charter of Hawes Corporation allows the issuance of a maximum of 100,000 shares of common stock. During its first two years of operations, Hawes sold 70,000 shares to shareholders and reacquired 7,000 of these shares. After these transactions, how many shares are authorized, issued, and outstanding?

8. Which is the better investment—common stock with a par value of $5 per share, or common stock with a par value of $20 per share? Why?

9. What factors help determine the market value of stock?

10. What effect does the issuance of stock at a price above par value have on the issuer's net income? Explain.

11. Why is common stock usually not issued at a price that is less than par value?

12. Land appraised at $80,000 is purchased by issuing 1,000 shares of $20 par value common stock. The market price of the shares at the time of the exchange, based on active trading in the securities market, is $95 per share. Should the land be recorded at $20,000, $80,000, or $95,000? Explain.

13. For what reasons might a company like IBM repurchase some of its stock (treasury stock)?

14. Kwun, Inc. purchases 1,000 shares of its own previously issued $5 par common stock for $12,000. Assuming the shares are held in the treasury, what effect does this transaction have on (a) net income, (b) total assets, (c) total paid-in capital, and (d) total stockholders' equity?

15. The treasury stock purchased in question 14 is resold by Kwun, Inc. for $18,000. What effect does this transaction have on (a) net income, (b) total assets, (c) total paid-in capital, and (d) total stockholders' equity?

16. (a) What are the principal differences between common stock and preferred stock?

(b) Preferred stock may be cumulative. Discuss this feature.

(c) How are dividends in arrears presented in the financial statements?

17. Ruiz Inc.'s common stock has a par value of $1 and a current market value of $15. Explain why these amounts are different.

18. Indicate how each of the following accounts should be classified in the stockholders' equity section.
   (a) Common stock
   (b) Paid-in capital in excess of par—common stock
   (c) Retained earnings
   (d) Treasury stock
   (e) Paid-in capital from treasury stock
   (f) Paid-in capital in excess of stated value—common stock
   (g) Preferred stock

19. PEPSICO How many shares of treasury stock did PepsiCo have at December 26, 2009, and at December 27, 2008?

Brief Exercises

BE13-1   Trudy Borke is studying for her accounting midterm examination. Identify for Trudy the advantages and disadvantages of the corporate form of business organization.

List the advantages and disadvantages of a corporation.
(SO 1)

BE13-2   At December 31, Jimbo Corporation reports net income of $450,000. Prepare the entry to close net income.

Prepare closing entries for a corporation. (SO 2)

BE13-3   On May 10, Jack Corporation issues 2,000 shares of $10 par value common stock for cash at $18 per share. Journalize the issuance of the stock.

Prepare entries for issuance of par value common stock.
(SO 3)

BE13-4   On June 1, Donkey Inc. issues 3,000 shares of no-par common stock at a cash price of $6 per share. Journalize the issuance of the shares assuming the stock has a stated value of $1 per share.

Prepare entries for issuance of no-par value common stock.
(SO 3)

BE13-5   Jer Inc.'s $10 par value common stock is actively traded at a market value of $15 per share. Jer issues 5,000 shares to purchase land advertised for sale at $85,000. Journalize the issuance of the stock in acquiring the land.

Prepare entries for issuance of stock in a noncash transaction.
(SO 3)

BE13-6   On July 1, Laura Corporation purchases 500 shares of its $5 par value common stock for the treasury at a cash price of $8 per share. On September 1, it sells 300 shares of the treasury stock for cash at $11 per share. Journalize the two treasury stock transactions.

Prepare entries for treasury stock transactions.
(SO 4)

BE13-7   Cora Inc. issues 5,000 shares of $100 par value preferred stock for cash at $130 per share. Journalize the issuance of the preferred stock.

Prepare entries for issuance of preferred stock.
(SO 5)

BE13-8   Vivi Corporation has the following accounts at December 31: Common Stock, $10 par, 5,000 shares issued, $50,000; Paid-in Capital in Excess of Par—Common Stock $20,000; Retained Earnings $45,000; and Treasury Stock, 500 shares, $11,000. Prepare the stockholders' equity section of the balance sheet.

Prepare stockholders' equity section.
(SO 6)

Do it! Review

Analyze statements about corporate organization.
(SO 1)

Do it! 13-1   Indicate whether each of the following statements is true or false.

_____ **1.** The corporation is an entity separate and distinct from its owners.

_____ **2.** The liability of stockholders is normally limited to their investment in the corporation.

_____ **3.** The relative lack of government regulation is an advantage of the corporate form of business.

_____ **4.** There is no journal entry to record the authorization of capital stock.

_____ **5.** No-par value stock is quite rare today.

Close net income and prepare stockholders' equity section.
(SO 2)

Do it! 13-2   At the end of its first year of operation, Jane Corporation has $1,000,000 of common stock and net income of $216,000. Prepare (a) the closing entry for net income and (b) the stockholders' equity section at year-end.

Journalize issuance of stock.
(SO 3)

Do it! 13-3   Balboa Island Corporation began operations on April 1 by issuing 60,000 shares of $5 par value common stock for cash at $13 per share. On April 19, it issued 2,000 shares of common stock to attorneys in settlement of their bill of $27,500 for organization costs. Journalize both issuances, assuming the stock is not publicly traded.

Journalize treasury stock transactions.
(SO 4)

Do it! 13-4   Caleb Corporation purchased 2,000 shares of its $10 par value common stock for $120,000 on August 1. It will hold these shares in the treasury until resold. On December 1, the corporation sold 1,200 shares of treasury stock for cash at $72 per share. Journalize the treasury stock transactions.

Prepare stockholders' equity section.
(SO 6)

Do it! 13-5   Doreen Corporation has issued 100,000 shares of $5 par value common stock. It authorized 500,000 shares. The paid-in capital in excess of par on the common stock is $240,000. The corporation has reacquired 7,000 shares at a cost of $46,000 and is currently holding those shares. Treasury stock was reissued in prior years for $47,000 more than its cost.

The corporation also has 2,000 shares issued and outstanding of 7%, $100 par-value preferred stock. It authorized 10,000 shares. The paid-in capital in excess of par on the preferred stock is $23,000.

Retained earnings is $372,000.

Prepare the stockholders' equity section of the balance sheet.

Exercises

Identify characteristics of a corporation.
(SO 1)

E13-1   Angela has prepared the following list of statements about corporations.

1. A corporation is an entity separate and distinct from its owners.

2. As a legal entity, a corporation has most of the rights and privileges of a person.

3. Most of the largest U.S. corporations are privately held corporations.

4. Corporations may buy, own, and sell property; borrow money; enter into legally binding contracts; and sue and be sued.

5. The net income of a corporation is not taxed as a separate entity.

6. Creditors have a legal claim on the personal assets of the owners of a corporation if the corporation does not pay its debts.

7. The transfer of stock from one owner to another requires the approval of either the corporation or other stockholders.

8. The board of directors of a corporation legally owns the corporation.

9. The chief accounting officer of a corporation is the controller.

10. Corporations are subject to less state and federal regulations than partnerships or proprietorships.

Instructions

Identify each statement as true or false. If false, indicate how to correct the statement.

Identify characteristics of a corporation.
(SO 1, 2)

E13-2   Angela (see E13-1) has studied the information you gave her in that exercise and has come to you with more statements about corporations.

1. Corporation management is both an advantage and a disadvantage of a corporation compared to a proprietorship or a partnership.

2. Limited liability of stockholders, government regulations, and additional taxes are the major disadvantages of a corporation.
3. When a corporation is formed, organization costs are recorded as an asset.
4. Each share of common stock gives the stockholder the ownership rights to vote at stockholder meetings, share in corporate earnings, keep the same percentage ownership when new shares of stock are issued, and share in assets upon liquidation.
5. The number of issued shares is always greater than or equal to the number of authorized shares.
6. A journal entry is required for the authorization of capital stock.
7. Publicly held corporations usually issue stock directly to investors.
8. The trading of capital stock on a securities exchange involves the transfer of already issued shares from an existing stockholder to another investor.
9. The market value of common stock is usually the same as its par value.
10. Retained earnings is the total amount of cash and other assets paid in to the corporation by stockholders in exchange for capital stock.

Instructions
Identify each statement as true or false. If false, indicate how to correct the statement.

E13-3 During its first year of operations, Benji Corporation had the following transactions pertaining to its common stock.

Journalize issuance of common stock.

(SO 3)

Jan. 10	Issued 70,000 shares for cash at $5 per share.
July 1	Issued 40,000 shares for cash at $7 per share.

Instructions
(a) Journalize the transactions, assuming that the common stock has a par value of $5 per share.
(b) Journalize the transactions, assuming that the common stock is no-par with a stated value of $1 per share.

E13-4 Jake Corporation issued 1,000 shares of stock.

Journalize issuance of common stock.

(SO 3)

Instructions
Prepare the entry for the issuance under the following assumptions.
(a) The stock had a par value of $5 per share and was issued for a total of $52,000.
(b) The stock had a stated value of $5 per share and was issued for a total of $52,000.
(c) The stock had no par or stated value and was issued for a total of $52,000.
(d) The stock had a par value of $5 per share and was issued to attorneys for services during incorporation valued at $52,000.
(e) The stock had a par value of $5 per share and was issued for land worth $52,000.

E13-5 Laci Co. had the following transactions during the current period.

Journalize issuance of common and preferred stock and purchase of treasury stock.

(SO 3, 4, 5)

Mar. 2	Issued 5,000 shares of $5 par value common stock to attorneys in payment of a bill for $30,000 for services provided in helping the company to incorporate.
June 12	Issued 60,000 shares of $5 par value common stock for cash of $375,000.
July 11	Issued 1,000 shares of $100 par value preferred stock for cash at $110 per share.
Nov. 28	Purchased 2,000 shares of treasury stock for $80,000.

Instructions
Journalize the transactions.

E13-6 As an auditor for the CPA firm of Valente and Ardvino, you encounter the following situations in auditing different clients.

Journalize noncash common stock transactions.

(SO 3)

1. PM Corporation is a closely held corporation whose stock is not publicly traded. On December 5, the corporation acquired land by issuing 5,000 shares of its $20 par value common stock. The owners' asking price for the land was $120,000, and the fair value of the land was $115,000.
2. Paul Corporation is a publicly held corporation whose common stock is traded on the securities markets. On June 1, it acquired land by issuing 20,000 shares of its $10 par value stock. At the time of the exchange, the land was advertised for sale at $250,000. The stock was selling at $12 per share.

Instructions
Prepare the journal entries for each of the situations above.

Journalize treasury stock transactions.
(SO 4)

E13-7 On January 1, 2012, the stockholders' equity section of Joshua Corporation shows: Common stock ($5 par value) $1,500,000; paid-in capital in excess of par $1,000,000; and retained earnings $1,200,000. During the year, the following treasury stock transactions occurred.

Mar. 1 Purchased 50,000 shares for cash at $15 per share.
July 1 Sold 10,000 treasury shares for cash at $17 per share.
Sept. 1 Sold 8,000 treasury shares for cash at $14 per share.

Instructions
(a) Journalize the treasury stock transactions.
(b) Restate the entry for September 1, assuming the treasury shares were sold at $12 per share.

Journalize treasury stock transactions.
(SO 4)

E13-8 Michaela Corporation purchased from its stockholders 5,000 shares of its own previously issued stock for $250,000. It later resold 2,000 shares for $54 per share, then 2,000 more shares for $49 per share, and finally 1,000 shares for $40 per share.

Instructions
Prepare journal entries for the purchase of the treasury stock and the three sales of treasury stock.

Journalize preferred stock transactions and indicate statement presentation.
(SO 5, 6)

E13-9 Paul Corporation is authorized to issue both preferred and common stock. The par value of the preferred is $50. During the first year of operations, the company had the following events and transactions pertaining to its preferred stock.

Feb. 1 Issued 20,000 shares for cash at $53 per share.
July 1 Issued 12,000 shares for cash at $57 per share.

Instructions
(a) Journalize the transactions.
(b) Post to the stockholders' equity accounts.
(c) Indicate the financial statement presentation of the related accounts.

Differentiate between preferred and common stock.
(SO 5)

E13-10 David Corporation issued 100,000 shares of $20 par value, cumulative, 8% preferred stock on January 1, 2011, for $2,100,000. In December 2013, David declared its first dividend of $500,000.

Instructions
(a) Prepare David's journal entry to record the issuance of the preferred stock.
(b) If the preferred stock is *not* cumulative, how much of the $500,000 would be paid to **common** stockholders?
(c) If the preferred stock is cumulative, how much of the $500,000 would be paid to **common** stockholders?

Prepare correct entries for capital stock transactions.
(SO 3, 4, 5)

E13-11 Carolyn Corporation recently hired a new accountant with extensive experience in accounting for partnerships. Because of the pressure of the new job, the accountant was unable to review his textbooks on the topic of corporation accounting. During the first month, the accountant made the following entries for the corporation's capital stock.

May 2	Cash		130,000	
	Capital Stock			130,000
	(Issued 10,000 shares of $10 par value common stock at $13 per share)			
10	Cash		600,000	
	Capital Stock			600,000
	(Issued 10,000 shares of $50 par value preferred stock at $60 per share)			
15	Capital Stock		15,000	
	Cash			15,000
	(Purchased 1,000 shares of common stock for the treasury at $15 per share)			

31	Cash	8,000	
	Capital Stock		5,000
	Gain on Sale of Stock		3,000
	(Sold 500 shares of treasury stock at $16 per share)		

Instructions
On the basis of the explanation for each entry, prepare the entry that should have been made for the capital stock transactions.

E13-12 The following stockholders' equity accounts, arranged alphabetically, are in the ledger of Borkowski Corporation at December 31, 2012.

Prepare a stockholders' equity section.
(SO 6)

Common Stock ($5 stated value)	$1,700,000
Paid-in Capital in Excess of Par—Preferred Stock	280,000
Paid-in Capital in Excess of Stated Value—Common Stock	900,000
Preferred Stock (8%, $100 par, noncumulative)	500,000
Retained Earnings	1,134,000
Treasury Stock (10,000 common shares)	120,000

Instructions
Prepare the stockholders' equity section of the balance sheet at December 31, 2012.

E13-13 The stockholders' equity section of Erik Corporation at December 31 is as follows.

Answer questions about stockholders' equity section.
(SO 3, 4, 5, 6)

ERIK CORPORATION
Balance Sheet (partial)

Paid-in capital	
Preferred stock, cumulative, 10,000 shares authorized, 6,000 shares issued and outstanding	$ 300,000
Common stock, no par, 750,000 shares authorized, 600,000 shares issued	1,200,000
Total paid-in capital	1,500,000
Retained earnings	1,858,000
Total paid-in capital and retained earnings	3,358,000
Less: Treasury stock (10,000 common shares)	(64,000)
Total stockholders' equity	$3,294,000

Instructions
From a review of the stockholders' equity section, as chief accountant, write a memo to the president of the company answering the following questions.
(a) How many shares of common stock are outstanding?
(b) Assuming there is a stated value, what is the stated value of the common stock?
(c) What is the par value of the preferred stock?
(d) If the annual dividend on preferred stock is $30,000, what is the dividend rate on preferred stock?
(e) If dividends of $60,000 were in arrears on preferred stock, what would be the balance in Retained Earnings?

E13-14 In a recent year, the stockholders' equity section of Aluminum Company of America (Alcoa) showed the following (in alphabetical order): additional paid-in capital $6,101, common stock $925, preferred stock $55, retained earnings $7,428, and treasury stock 2,828. All dollar data are in millions.

Prepare a stockholders' equity section.
(SO 6)

The preferred stock has 557,740 shares authorized, with a par value of $100 and an annual $3.75 per share cumulative dividend preference. At December 31, 557,649 shares of preferred are issued and 546,024 shares are outstanding. There are 1.8 billion shares of $1 par value common stock authorized, of which 924.6 million are issued and 844.8 million are outstanding at December 31.

Instructions
Prepare the stockholders' equity section, including disclosure of all relevant data.

Classify stockholders' equity accounts.

(SO 6)

E13-15 The ledger of Hickory Hills Corporation contains the following accounts: Common Stock, Preferred Stock, Treasury Stock, Paid-in Capital in Excess of Par—Preferred Stock, Paid-in Capital in Excess of Stated Value—Common Stock, Paid-in Capital from Treasury Stock, and Retained Earnings.

Instructions
Classify each account using the following table headings.

	Paid-in Capital			
	Capital		Retained	
Account	Stock	Additional	Earnings	Other

Exercises: Set B

Visit the book's companion website, at **www.wiley.com/college/weygandt**, and choose the Student Companion site to access Exercise Set B.

Problems: Set A

Journalize stock transactions, post, and prepare paid-in capital section.

(SO 3, 5, 6)

P13-1A Alexia Corporation was organized on January 1, 2012. It is authorized to issue 10,000 shares of 8%, $100 par value preferred stock, and 500,000 shares of no-par common stock with a stated value of $2 per share. The following stock transactions were completed during the first year.

Jan. 10   Issued 80,000 shares of common stock for cash at $4 per share.
Mar. 1   Issued 5,000 shares of preferred stock for cash at $105 per share.
Apr. 1   Issued 24,000 shares of common stock for land. The asking price of the land was $90,000. The fair value of the land was $85,000.
May 1   Issued 80,000 shares of common stock for cash at $4.50 per share.
Aug. 1   Issued 10,000 shares of common stock to attorneys in payment of their bill of $30,000 for services provided in helping the company organize.
Sept. 1   Issued 10,000 shares of common stock for cash at $5 per share.
Nov. 1   Issued 1,000 shares of preferred stock for cash at $109 per share.

Instructions
(a) Journalize the transactions.

(c) Total paid-in capital
$1,479,000

(b) Post to the stockholders' equity accounts. (Use J5 as the posting reference.)
(c) Prepare the paid-in capital section of stockholders' equity at December 31, 2012.

Journalize and post treasury stock transactions, and prepare stockholders' equity section.

(SO 4, 6)

P13-2A Brandon Corporation had the following stockholders' equity accounts on January 1, 2012: Common Stock ($5 par) $500,000, Paid-in Capital in Excess of Par—Common Stock $200,000, and Retained Earnings $100,000. In 2012, the company had the following treasury stock transactions.

Mar. 1   Purchased 5,000 shares at $9 per share.
June 1   Sold 1,000 shares at $12 per share.
Sept. 1   Sold 2,000 shares at $10 per share.
Dec. 1   Sold 1,000 shares at $6 per share.

Brandon Corporation uses the cost method of accounting for treasury stock. In 2012, the company reported net income of $30,000.

Instructions
(a) Journalize the treasury stock transactions, and prepare the closing entry at December 31, 2012, for net income.

(b) Treasury Stock $9,000
(c) Total stockholders' equity
$823,000

(b) Open accounts for (1) Paid-in Capital from Treasury Stock, (2) Treasury Stock, and (3) Retained Earnings. Post to these accounts using J10 as the posting reference.
(c) Prepare the stockholders' equity section for Jacobsen Corporation at December 31, 2012.

Journalize and post transactions, prepare stockholders' equity section.

(SO 2, 3, 4, 5, 6)

P13-3A The stockholders' equity accounts of Ashley Corporation on January 1, 2012, were as follows.

Preferred Stock (8%, $50 par, cumulative, 10,000 shares authorized)	$ 400,000
Common Stock ($1 stated value, 2,000,000 shares authorized)	1,000,000
Paid-in Capital in Excess of Par—Preferred Stock	100,000
Paid-in Capital in Excess of Stated Value—Common Stock	1,450,000
Retained Earnings	1,816,000
Treasury Stock (10,000 common shares)	50,000

During 2012, the corporation had the following transactions and events pertaining to its stockholders' equity.

Feb. 1   Issued 25,000 shares of common stock for $120,000.
Apr. 14   Sold 6,000 shares of treasury stock—common for $33,000.
Sept. 3   Issued 5,000 shares of common stock for a patent valued at $35,000.
Nov. 10   Purchased 1,000 shares of common stock for the treasury at a cost of $6,000.
Dec. 31   Determined that net income for the year was $452,000.

No dividends were declared during the year.

Instructions
(a) Journalize the transactions and the closing entry for net income.
(b) Enter the beginning balances in the accounts, and post the journal entries to the stockholders' equity accounts. (Use J5 for the posting reference.)
(c) Prepare a stockholders' equity section at December 31, 2012, including the disclosure of the preferred dividends in arrears.

(c) Total stockholders' equity $5,350,000

P13-4A   Mary Corporation is authorized to issue 20,000 shares of $50 par value, 10% preferred stock and 125,000 shares of $3 par value common stock. On January 1, 2012, the ledger contained the following stockholders' equity balances.

Journalize and post stock transactions, and prepare stockholders' equity section.
(SO 2, 3, 5, 6)

Preferred Stock (10,000 shares)	$500,000
Paid-in Capital in Excess of Par—Preferred Stock	75,000
Common Stock (70,000 shares)	210,000
Paid-in Capital in Excess of Par—Common Stock	700,000
Retained Earnings	300,000

During 2012, the following transactions occurred.

Feb. 1   Issued 2,000 shares of preferred stock for land having a fair value of $125,000.
Mar. 1   Issued 1,000 shares of preferred stock for cash at $65 per share.
July 1   Issued 16,000 shares of common stock for cash at $7 per share.
Sept. 1   Issued 400 shares of preferred stock for a patent. The asking price of the patent was $30,000. Market values were preferred stock $70 and patent indeterminable.
Dec. 1   Issued 8,000 shares of common stock for cash at $7.50 per share.
Dec. 31   Net income for the year was $260,000. No dividends were declared.

Instructions
(a) Journalize the transactions and the closing entry for net income.
(b) Enter the beginning balances in the accounts, and post the journal entries to the stockholders' equity accounts. (Use J2 for the posting reference.)
(c) Prepare a stockholders' equity section at December 31, 2012.

(c) Total stockholders' equity $2,435,000

P13-5A   The following stockholders' equity accounts arranged alphabetically are in the ledger of Desiree Corporation at December 31, 2012.

Prepare stockholders' equity section.
(SO 6)

Common Stock ($5 stated value)	$2,000,000
Paid-in Capital from Treasury Stock	10,000
Paid-in Capital in Excess of Stated Value—Common Stock	1,600,000
Paid-in Capital in Excess of Par—Preferred Stock	679,000
Preferred Stock (8%, $50 par, noncumulative)	800,000
Retained Earnings	1,748,000
Treasury Stock (10,000 common shares)	130,000

Instructions
Prepare a stockholders' equity section at December 31, 2012.

Total stockholders' equity $6,707,000

P13-6A   Leigh Corporation has been authorized to issue 20,000 shares of $100 par value, 10%, noncumulative preferred stock and 1,000,000 shares of no-par common stock. The corporation assigned a $2.50 stated value to the common stock. At December 31, 2012, the ledger contained the following balances pertaining to stockholders' equity.

Prepare entries for stock transactions and prepare stockholders' equity section.
(SO 3, 4, 5, 6)

Preferred Stock	$ 120,000
Paid-in Capital in Excess of Par—Preferred Stock	20,000
Common Stock	1,000,000
Paid-in Capital in Excess of Stated Value—Common Stock	1,800,000

Treasury Stock (1,000 common shares)	13,000
Paid-in Capital from Treasury Stock	500
Retained Earnings	82,000

The preferred stock was issued for land having a fair value of $140,000. All common stock issued was for cash. In November, 1,500 shares of common stock were purchased for the treasury at a per share cost of $13. In December, 500 shares of treasury stock were sold for $14 per share. No dividends were declared in 2012.

Instructions
(a) Prepare the journal entries for the:
    (1) Issuance of preferred stock for land.
    (2) Issuance of common stock for cash.
    (3) Purchase of common treasury stock for cash.
(b) Total stockholders' equity
$3,009,500
    (4) Sale of treasury stock for cash.
(b) Prepare the stockholders' equity section at December 31, 2012.

Problems: Set B

Journalize stock transactions, post, and prepare paid-in capital section.
(SO 3, 5, 6)

P13-1B Joanjim Corporation was organized on January 1, 2012. It is authorized to issue 20,000 shares of 6%, $40 par value preferred stock, and 500,000 shares of no-par common stock with a stated value of $2 per share. The following stock transactions were completed during the first year.

Jan.	10	Issued 100,000 shares of common stock for cash at $3 per share.
Mar.	1	Issued 10,000 shares of preferred stock for cash at $55 per share.
Apr.	1	Issued 25,000 shares of common stock for land. The asking price of the land was $90,000. The company's estimate of fair value of the land was $75,000.
May	1	Issued 75,000 shares of common stock for cash at $4 per share.
Aug.	1	Issued 10,000 shares of common stock to attorneys in payment of their bill for $50,000 for services provided in helping the company organize.
Sept.	1	Issued 5,000 shares of common stock for cash at $6 per share.
Nov.	1	Issued 2,000 shares of preferred stock for cash at $60 per share.

Instructions
(a) Journalize the transactions.
(c) Total paid-in capital
$1,425,000
(b) Post to the stockholders' equity accounts. (Use J1 as the posting reference.)
(c) Prepare the paid-in capital section of stockholders' equity at December 31, 2012.

Journalize and post treasury stock transactions, and prepare stockholders' equity section.
(SO 4, 6)

P13-2B Dougherty Corporation had the following stockholders' equity accounts on January 1, 2012: Common Stock ($1 par) $400,000, Paid-in Capital in Excess of Par—Common Stock $500,000, and Retained Earnings $100,000. In 2012, the company had the following treasury stock transactions.

Mar.	1	Purchased 5,000 shares at $7 per share.
June	1	Sold 1,000 shares at $10 per share.
Sept.	1	Sold 2,000 shares at $9 per share.
Dec.	1	Sold 1,000 shares at $5 per share.

Dougherty Corporation uses the cost method of accounting for treasury stock. In 2012, the company reported net income of $80,000.

Instructions
(a) Journalize the treasury stock transactions, and prepare the closing entry at December 31, 2012, for net income.
(b) Treasury Stock $7,000
(b) Open accounts for (1) Paid-in Capital from Treasury Stock, (2) Treasury Stock, and (3) Retained Earnings. Post to these accounts using J12 as the posting reference.
(c) Total stockholders' equity
$1,078,000
(c) Prepare the stockholders' equity section for Dougherty Corporation at December 31, 2012.

P13-3B The stockholders' equity accounts of Joey Corporation on January 1, 2012, were as follows.

Preferred Stock (10%, $100 par, noncumulative, 5,000 shares authorized)	$ 300,000
Common Stock ($5 stated value, 300,000 shares authorized)	1,000,000
Paid-in Capital in Excess of Par—Preferred Stock	20,000
Paid-in Capital in Excess of Stated Value—Common Stock	425,000
Retained Earnings	488,000
Treasury Stock (5,000 common shares)	40,000

Journalize and post transactions, prepare stockholders' equity section.

(SO 2, 3, 4, 5, 6)

During 2012, the corporation had the following transactions and events pertaining to its stockholders' equity.

Feb. 1	Issued 3,000 shares of common stock for $25,500.
Mar. 20	Purchased 1,500 additional shares of common treasury stock at $8 per share.
June 14	Sold 4,000 shares of treasury stock—common for $36,000.
Sept. 3	Issued 2,000 shares of common stock for a patent valued at $19,000.
Dec. 31	Determined that net income for the year was $350,000.

Instructions
(a) Journalize the transactions and the closing entry for net income.
(b) Enter the beginning balances in the accounts and post the journal entries to the stockholders' equity accounts. (Use J1 as the posting reference.)
(c) Prepare a stockholders' equity section at December 31, 2012.

(c) Total stockholders' equity $2,611,500

P13-4B Dominick Corporation is authorized to issue 10,000 shares of $40 par value, 10% preferred stock and 200,000 shares of $5 par value common stock. On January 1, 2012, the ledger contained the following stockholders' equity balances.

Preferred Stock (5,000 shares)	$200,000
Paid-in Capital in Excess of Par—Preferred Stock	60,000
Common Stock (70,000 shares)	350,000
Paid-in Capital in Excess of Par—Common Stock	700,000
Retained Earnings	300,000

Journalize and post stock transactions, and prepare stockholders' equity section.

(SO 2, 3, 5, 6)

During 2012, the following transactions occurred.

Feb. 1	Issued 1,000 shares of preferred stock for land having a fair value of $65,000.
Mar. 1	Issued 2,000 shares of preferred stock for cash at $60 per share.
July 1	Issued 20,000 shares of common stock for cash at $5.80 per share.
Sept. 1	Issued 800 shares of preferred stock for a patent. The asking price of the patent was $60,000. Market values were preferred stock $65 and patent, indeterminable.
Dec. 1	Issued 10,000 shares of common stock for cash at $6 per share.
Dec. 31	Net income for the year was $210,000. No dividends were declared.

Instructions
(a) Journalize the transactions and the closing entry for net income.
(b) Enter the beginning balances in the accounts, and post the journal entries to the stockholders' equity accounts. (Use J2 as the posting reference.)
(c) Prepare a stockholders' equity section at December 31, 2012.

(c) Total stockholders' equity $2,233,000

P13-5B The following stockholders' equity accounts arranged alphabetically are in the ledger of Dillon Corporation at December 31, 2012.

Common Stock ($10 stated value)	$1,200,000
Paid-in Capital from Treasury Stock	6,000
Paid-in Capital in Excess of Stated Value—Common Stock	690,000
Paid-in Capital in Excess of Par—Preferred Stock	288,400
Preferred Stock (8%, $100 par, noncumulative)	300,000
Retained Earnings	826,000
Treasury Stock (8,000 common shares)	88,000

Prepare stockholders' equity section.

(SO 6)

Instructions
Prepare a stockholders' equity section at December 31, 2012.

Total stockholders' equity $3,222,400

Prepare entries for stock transactions and prepare stockholders' equity section.

(SO 3, 4, 5, 6)

P13-6B　Geoffery Corporation has been authorized to issue 40,000 shares of $100 par value, 8%, noncumulative preferred stock and 2,000,000 shares of no-par common stock. The corporation assigned a $5 stated value to the common stock. At December 31, 2012, the ledger contained the following balances pertaining to stockholders' equity.

Preferred Stock	$ 240,000
Paid-in Capital in Excess of Par—Preferred Stock	56,000
Common Stock	2,000,000
Paid-in Capital in Excess of Stated Value—Common Stock	4,400,000
Treasury Stock (1,000 common shares)	22,000
Paid-in Capital from Treasury Stock	3,000
Retained Earnings	560,000

The preferred stock was issued for land having a fair value of $296,000. All common stock issued was for cash. In November, 1,500 shares of common stock were purchased for the treasury at a per share cost of $22. In December, 500 shares of treasury stock were sold for $28 per share. No dividends were declared in 2012.

Instructions

(a) Prepare the journal entries for the:

    (1) Issuance of preferred stock for land.

    (2) Issuance of common stock for cash.

    (3) Purchase of common treasury stock for cash.

(b) Total stockholders' equity $7,237,000

    (4) Sale of treasury stock for cash.

(b) Prepare the stockholders' equity section at December 31, 2012.

Problems: Set C

Visit the book's companion website, at **www.wiley.com/college/weygandt**, and choose the Student Companion site to access Problem Set C.

Continuing Cookie Chronicle

(Note: This is a continuation of the Cookie Chronicle from Chapters 1 through 12.)

CCC13　Natalie's friend, Curtis Lesperance, decides to meet with Natalie after hearing that her discussions about a possible business partnership with her friend Katy Peterson have failed. Because Natalie has been so successful with Cookie Creations and Curtis has been just as successful with his coffee shop, they both conclude that they could benefit from each other's business expertise. Curtis and Natalie next evaluate the different types of business organization, and because of the advantage of limited personal liability, decide to form a corporation. Natalie and Curtis are very excited about this new business venture. They come to you with information about their businesses and with a number of questions.

Go to the book's companion website, **www.wiley.com/college/weygandt**, *to see the completion of this problem.*

BROADENINGYOURPERSPECTIVE

Financial Reporting and Analysis

Financial Reporting Problem: PepsiCo

BYP13-1　The stockholders' equity section for PepsiCo, Inc. is shown in Appendix A. You will also find data relative to this problem on other pages of the appendix.

Instructions

(a) What is the par or stated value per share of PepsiCo's common stock?

(b) What percentage of PepsiCo's authorized common stock was issued at December 26, 2009?

(c) How many shares of common stock were outstanding at December 26, 2009, and at December 27, 2008?

(d) What was the high and low market price per share in the fourth quarter of fiscal 2009, as reported under Selected Financial Data?

Comparative Analysis Problem: PepsiCo vs. Coca-Cola

BYP13-2 PepsiCo, Inc.'s financial statements are presented in Appendix A. Financial statements of The Coca-Cola Company are presented in Appendix B.

Instructions

(a) What is the par or stated value of Coca-Cola's and PepsiCo's common of capital, stock?

(b) What percentage of authorized shares was issued by Coca-Cola at December 31, 2009, and by PepsiCo at December 26, 2009?

(c) How many shares are held as treasury stock by Coca-Cola at December 31, 2009, and by PepsiCo at December 26, 2009?

(d) How many Coca-Cola common shares are outstanding at December 31, 2009? How many PepsiCo shares of capital stock are outstanding at December 26, 2009?

On the Web

BYP13-3 SEC filings of publicly traded companies are available to view online.

Address: http://biz.yahoo.com/i, or go to **www.wiley.com/college/weygandt**

Steps

1. Pick a company and type in the company's name.
2. Choose **Quote**.

Instructions

Answer the following questions.

(a) What company did you select?

(b) What is its stock symbol?

(c) What was the stock's trading range today?

(d) What was the stock's trading range for the year?

Critical Thinking

Decision Making Across the Organization

BYP13-4 The stockholders' meeting for Strauder Corporation has been in progress for some time. The chief financial officer for Strauder is presently reviewing the company's financial statements and is explaining the items that comprise the stockholders' equity section of the balance sheet for the current year. The stockholders' equity section of Strauder Corporation at December 31, 2012, is as follows.

STRAUDER CORPORATION
Balance Sheet (partial)
December 31, 2012

Paid-in capital
  Capital stock
    Preferred stock, authorized 1,000,000 shares
      cumulative, $100 par value, $8 per share, 6,000

shares issued and outstanding		$ 600,000
Common stock, authorized 5,000,000 shares, $1 par		
value, 3,000,000 shares issued, and 2,700,000		
outstanding		3,000,000
Total capital stock		3,600,000
Additional paid-in capital		
In excess of par—preferred stock	$ 50,000	
In excess of par—common stock	25,000,000	

Total additional paid-in capital	25,050,000
Total paid-in capital	28,650,000
Retained earnings	900,000
Total paid-in capital and retained earnings	29,550,000
Less: Treasury stock (300,000 common shares)	9,300,000
Total stockholders' equity	$20,250,000

At the meeting, stockholders have raised a number of questions regarding the stockholders' equity section.

Instructions

With the class divided into groups, answer the following questions as if you were the chief financial officer for Strauder Corporation.

(a) "What does the cumulative provision related to the preferred stock mean?"

(b) "I thought the common stock was presently selling at $29.75, but the company has the stock stated at $1 per share. How can that be?"

(c) "Why is the company buying back its common stock? Furthermore, the treasury stock has a debit balance because it is subtracted from stockholders' equity. Why is treasury stock not reported as an asset if it has a debit balance?"

Communication Activity

BYP13-5   Sid Hosey, your uncle, is an inventor who has decided to incorporate. Uncle Sid knows that you are an accounting major at U.N.O. In a recent letter to you, he ends with the question, "I'm filling out a state incorporation application. Can you tell me the difference in the following terms: (1) authorized stock, (2) issued stock, (3) outstanding stock, (4) preferred stock?"

Instructions

In a brief note, differentiate for Uncle Sid among the four different stock terms. Write the letter to be friendly, yet professional.

Ethics Case

BYP13-6   The R&D division of Marco Chemical Corp. has just developed a chemical for sterilizing the vicious Brazilian "killer bees" which are invading Mexico and the southern states of the United States. The president of Marco is anxious to get the chemical on the market to boost Marco's profits. He believes his job is in jeopardy because of decreasing sales and profits. Marco has an opportunity to sell this chemical in Central American countries, where the laws are much more relaxed than in the United States.

The director of Marco's R&D division strongly recommends further testing in the laboratory for side-effects of this chemical on other insects, birds, animals, plants, and even humans. He cautions the president, "We could be sued from all sides if the chemical has tragic side-effects that we didn't even test for in the labs." The president answers, "We can't wait an additional year for your lab tests. We can avoid losses from such lawsuits by establishing a separate wholly owned corporation to shield Marco Corp. from such lawsuits. We can't lose any more than our investment in the new corporation, and we'll invest just the patent covering this chemical. We'll reap the benefits if the chemical works and is safe, and avoid the losses from lawsuits if it's a disaster." The following week Marco creates a new wholly owned corporation called Brecht Inc., sells the chemical patent to it for $10, and watches the spraying begin.

Instructions

(a) Who are the stakeholders in this situation?

(b) Are the president's motives and actions ethical?

(c) Can Marco shield itself against losses of Brecht Inc.?

"All About You" Activity

BYP13-7   A high percentage of Americans own stock in corporations. As a shareholder in a corporation, you will receive an annual report. One of the goals of this course is for you to learn how to navigate your way around an annual report.

Instructions

Use the annual report provided in Appendix A to answer the following questions.

(a) What CPA firm performed the audit of PepsiCo's financial statements?

(b) What was the amount of PepsiCo's earnings per share in 2009?

(c) What was net revenue in 2009?

(d) How many shares of treasury stock did the company have at the end of 2009?

(e) How much cash did PepsiCo spend on capital expenditures in 2009?

(f) Over what life does the company depreciate its buildings?

(g) What was the total amount of dividends paid in 2009?

FASB Codification Activity

BYP13-8 If your school has a subscription to the FASB Codification, go to *http://aaahq.org/ascLogin.cfm* to log in and prepare responses to the following.

(a) How is *common stock* defined?

(b) How is *preferred stock* defined?

(c) What is the meaning of the term *shares*?

Answers to Insight and Accounting Across the Organization Questions

p. 598 Wall Street No Friend of Facebook **Q:** Why has Mark Zuckerberg, the CEO and founder of Facebook, delayed taking his company's shares public through an initial public offering (IPO)? **A:** Facebook doesn't need to invest in factories, distribution systems, or even marketing, so it doesn't need to raise a lot of cash. Also, by not going public, Zuckerberg has more control over the direction of the company. In addition, publicly traded companies face many more financial reporting disclosure requirements.

p. 600 How to Read Stock Quotes **Q:** For stocks traded on organized stock exchanges, how are the dollar prices per share established? **A:** The dollar prices per share are established by the interaction between buyers and sellers of the shares. **Q:** What factors might influence the price of shares in the marketplace? **A:** The price of shares is influenced by a company's earnings and dividends as well as by factors beyond a company's control, such as changes in interest rates, labor strikes, scarcity of supplies or resources, and politics. The number of willing buyers and sellers (demand and supply) also plays a part in the price of shares.

p. 608 Why Did Reebok Buy Its Own Stock? **Q:** What signal might a large stock repurchase send to investors regarding management's belief about the company's growth opportunities? **A:** When a company has many growth opportunities it will normally conserve its cash in order to be better able to fund expansion. A large use of cash to buy back stock (and essentially shrink the company) would suggest that management was not optimistic about its growth opportunities.

Answers to Self-Test Questions

1. c **2.** b **3.** b **4.** d **5.** a **6.** b **7.** c $(1,000 \times \$9)$ **8.** c **9.** d **10.** a **11.** a **12.** d **13.** b **14.** d **15.** c

IFRS A Look at IFRS

The accounting for transactions related to stockholders' equity, such as issuance of shares and purchase of treasury stock, are similar under both IFRS and GAAP. Major differences relate to terminology used, introduction of items such as revaluation surplus, and presentation of stockholders' equity information.

Key Points

- Under IFRS, the term *reserves* is used to describe all equity accounts other than those arising from contributed (paid-in) capital. This would include, for example, reserves related to retained earnings, asset revaluations, and fair value differences.

- Many countries have a different mix of investor groups than in the United States. For example, in Germany, financial institutions like banks are not only major creditors of corporations but often are the largest corporate stockholders as well. In the United States, Asia, and the United Kingdom, many companies rely on substantial investment from private investors.

- There are often terminology differences for equity accounts. The following summarizes some of the common differences in terminology.

GAAP	IFRS
Common stock	Share capital—ordinary
Stockholders	Shareholders
Par value	Nominal or face value
Authorized stock	Authorized share capital
Preferred stock	Share capital—preference
Paid-in capital	Issued/allocated share capital
Paid-in capital in excess of par—common stock	Share premium—ordinary
Paid-in capital in excess of par—preferred stock	Share premium—preference
Retained earnings	Retained earnings or Retained profits
Retained earnings deficit	Accumulated losses
Accumulated other comprehensive income	General reserve and other reserve accounts

As an example of how similar transactions use different terminology under IFRS, consider the accounting for the issuance of 1,000 shares of $1 par value common stock for $5 per share. Under IFRS, the entry is as follows.

Cash	5,000	
Share Capital—Ordinary		1,000
Share Premium—Ordinary		4,000

- The accounting for treasury stock differs somewhat between IFRS and GAAP. (However, many of the differences are beyond the scope of this course.) Like GAAP, IFRS does not allow a company to record gains or losses on purchases of its own shares. One difference worth noting is that, when a company purchases its own shares, IFRS treats it as a reduction of stockholders' equity, but it does not specify which particular stockholders' equity accounts are to be affected. Therefore, it could be shown as an increase to a contra equity account (Treasury Stock) or a decrease to retained earnings or share capital.

- A major difference between IFRS and GAAP relates to the account Revaluation Surplus. Revaluation surplus arises under IFRS because companies are permitted to revalue their property, plant, and equipment to fair value under certain circumstances. This account is part of general reserves under IFRS and is not considered contributed capital.

- IFRS often uses terms such as *retained profits* or *accumulated profit or loss* to describe retained earnings. The term *retained earnings* is also often used.

- Equity is given various descriptions under IFRS, such as shareholders' equity, owners' equity, capital and reserves, and shareholders' funds.

Looking to the Future

As indicated in earlier discussions, the IASB and the FASB are currently working on a project related to financial statement presentation. An important part of this study is to determine whether certain line items, subtotals, and totals should be clearly defined and required to be displayed in the financial statements.

IFRS Self-Test Questions

1. Under IFRS, a purchase by a company of its own shares is recorded by:
   (a) an increase in Treasury Stock.
   (b) a decrease in contributed capital.
   (c) a decrease in share capital.
   (d) All of these are acceptable treatments.

2. Which of the following is *true*?
   (a) In the United States, the primary corporate stockholders are financial institutions.
   (b) Share capital means total assets under IFRS.
   (c) The IASB and FASB are presently studying how financial statement information should be presented.
   (d) The accounting for treasury stock differs extensively between GAAP and IFRS.

3. Under IFRS, the amount of capital received in excess of par value would be credited to:
   (a) Retained Earnings.
   (b) Contributed Capital.
   (c) Share Premium.
   (d) Par value is not used under IFRS.

4. Which of the following is *false*?
   (a) Under GAAP, companies cannot record gains on transactions involving their own shares.
   (b) Under IFRS, companies cannot record gains on transactions involving their own shares.
   (c) Under IFRS, the statement of stockholders' equity is a required statement.
   (d) Under IFRS, a company records a revaluation surplus when it experiences an increase in the price of its common stock.

5. Which of the following does *not* represent a pair of GAAP/IFRS-comparable terms?
   (a) Additional paid-in capital/Share premium.
   (b) Treasury stock/Repurchase reserve.
   (c) Common stock/Share capital.
   (d) Preferred stock/Preference shares.

IFRS Concepts and Application

IFRS13-1   On May 10, Romano Corporation issues 1,000 shares of $10 par value ordinary shares for cash at $18 per share. Journalize the issuance of the shares.

IFRS13-2   Ingram Corporation has the following accounts at December 31: Share Capital—Ordinary, €10 par, 5,000 shares issued, €50,000; Share Premium—Ordinary €10,000; Retained Earnings €45,000; and Treasury Shares—Ordinary, 500 shares, €11,000. Prepare the equity section of the statement of financial position.

IFRS13-3   Sorocaba Co. had the following transactions during the current period.

Mar. 2	Issued 5,000 shares of $1 par value ordinary shares to attorneys in payment of a bill for $30,000 for services provided in helping the company to incorporate.
June 12	Issued 60,000 shares of $1 par value ordinary shares for cash of $375,000.
July 11	Issued 1,000 shares of $100 par value preference shares for cash at $110 per share.
Nov. 28	Purchased 2,000 treasury shares for $80,000.

Instructions
Journalize the above transactions.

International Financial Reporting Problem: *Zetar plc*

IFRS13-4   The financial statements of Zetar plc are presented in Appendix C. The company's complete annual report, including the notes to its financial statements, is available at *www.zetarplc.com*.

Instructions
Use the company's annual report to answer the following questions.

(a) Using the information in the statement of changes in equity, prepare the journal entry to record the issuance of ordinary shares during the year ended April 30, 2009.

(b) Examine the equity section of the company's balance sheet. For each item in the equity section, provide the comparable label that would be used under GAAP.

Answers to IFRS Self-Test Questions
1. d   2. c   3. c   4. d   5. b

✔
The Navigator

✔ Remember to go back to the Navigator box on the chapter opening page and check off your completed work.

CHAPTER14

Corporations: Dividends, Retained Earnings, and Income Reporting

Study Objectives

After studying this chapter, you should be able to:

1 Prepare the entries for cash dividends and stock dividends.

2 Identify the items reported in a retained earnings statement.

3 Prepare and analyze a comprehensive stock-holders' equity section.

4 Describe the form and content of corporation income statements.

5 Compute earnings per share.

The Navigator

Feature Story

OWNING A PIECE OF THE ACTION

Van Meter Industrial, Inc., an electrical-parts distributor in Cedar Rapids, Iowa, is 100% employee-owned. For many years the company has issued bonuses in the form of shares of company stock to all of its employees. These bonus distributions typically have a value equal to several weeks of pay. Top management always thought that this was a great program. Therefore, it came as quite a surprise a few years ago when an employee stood up at a company-wide meeting and said that he did not see any real value in receiving the company's shares. Instead, he wanted "a few hundred extra bucks for beer and cigarettes."

As it turned out, many of the company's 340 employees felt this way. Rather than end the stock bonus program, however, the company decided to educate its employees on the value of share ownership. The employees now are taught how to determine the worth of their shares, the rights that come with share owner-ship, and what they can do to help increase the value of those shares.

As part of the education program, management developed a slogan, "Work ten, get five free." The idea is that after working 10 years, an employee's shares would be worth the equivalent of about five years' worth of salary. For example, a person earning a $30,000 salary would earn $300,000 in wages over a 10-year period. During that same 10-year period, it was likely that the value of the employee's shares would accumulate to about $150,000 (five years' worth of salary). This demonstrates in more concrete terms why employees should be excited about share ownership.

A 12-member employee committee has the responsibility of educating new employees about the program. The committee also runs training programs so that employees understand how their cost-saving actions improve the company's results—and its stock price. It appears that the company's education program to encourage employees to act like owners is working. Profitability has increased rapidly, and employee turnover has fallen from 18% to 8%. Given Van Meter's success, many of the 10,000 other employee-owned companies in the United States might want to investigate whether their employees understand the benefits of share ownership.

Source: Adapted from Simona Covel, "How to Get Workers to Think and Act Like Owners," *Wall Street Journal Online* (February 15, 2008).

The Navigator

Inside**CHAPTER14**

PreviewofCHAPTER14

As indicated in the Feature Story, a profitable corporation like Van Meter Industrial, Inc. can provide real benefits to employees through its stock bonus plan. And as employees learn more about the role of dividends, retained earnings, and earnings per share, they develop an understanding and appreciation for what the company is providing to them.

The content and organization of Chapter 14 are as follows.

Corporations: Dividends, Retained Earnings, and Income Reporting

Dividends	Retained Earnings	Statement Presentation and Analysis
• Cash dividends • Stock dividends • Stock splits	• Retained earnings restrictions • Prior period adjustments • Retained earnings statement	• Stockholders' equity presentation • Stockholders' equity analysis • Income statement presentation • Income statement analysis

The Navigator

Dividends

Study Objective [1]
Prepare the entries for cash dividends and stock dividends.

A dividend is a corporation's distribution of cash or stock to its stockholders on a pro rata (proportional to ownership) basis. Pro rata means that if you own 10% of the common shares, you will receive 10% of the dividend. Dividends can take four forms: cash, property, scrip (a promissory note to pay cash), or stock. Cash dividends predominate in practice. Also, companies declare stock dividends with some frequency. These two forms of dividends will be the focus of discussion in this chapter.

Investors are very interested in a company's dividend practices. In the financial press, **dividends are generally reported quarterly as a dollar amount per share.** (Sometimes they are reported on an annual basis.) For example, Nike's **quarterly** dividend rate in the fourth quarter of 2010 was 27 cents per share; the dividend rate for the fourth quarter of 2010 for GE was 12 cents, and for ConAgra Foods it was 28 cents.

Cash Dividends

A **cash dividend** is a pro rata distribution of cash to stockholders. For a corporation to pay a cash dividend, it must have:

1. **Retained earnings.** The legality of a cash dividend depends on the laws of the state in which the company is incorporated. Payment of cash dividends from retained earnings is legal in all states. In general, cash dividend distributions from only the balance in common stock (legal capital) are illegal.

   A dividend declared out of paid-in capital is termed a **liquidating dividend**. Such a dividend reduces or "liquidates" the amount originally paid in by stockholders. Statutes vary considerably with respect to cash dividends based on paid-in capital in excess of par or stated value. Many states permit such dividends.

2. **Adequate cash.** The legality of a dividend and the ability to pay a dividend are two different things. For example, Nike, with retained earnings of over $4.8 billion,

could legally declare a dividend of at least $4.8 billion. But Nike's cash balance is only $1.8 billion.

Before declaring a cash dividend, a company's board of directors must carefully consider both current and future demands on the company's cash resources. In some cases, current liabilities may make a cash dividend inappropriate. In other cases, a major plant expansion program may warrant only a relatively small dividend.

3. **A declaration of dividends.** A company does not pay dividends unless its board of directors decides to do so, at which point the board "declares" the dividend. The board of directors has full authority to determine the amount of income to distribute in the form of a dividend and the amount to retain in the business. Dividends do not accrue like interest on a note payable, and they are not a liability until declared.

The amount and timing of a dividend are important issues for management to consider. The payment of a large cash dividend could lead to liquidity problems for the company. On the other hand, a small dividend or a missed dividend may cause unhappiness among stockholders. Many stockholders expect to receive a reasonable cash payment from the company on a periodic basis. Many companies declare and pay cash dividends quarterly. On the other hand, a number of high-growth companies pay no dividends, preferring to conserve cash to finance future capital expenditures.

ENTRIES FOR CASH DIVIDENDS

Three dates are important in connection with dividends: (1) the declaration date, (2) the record date, and (3) the payment date. Normally, there are two to four weeks between each date. Companies make accounting entries on the declaration date and the payment date.

On the **declaration date**, the board of directors formally declares (authorizes) the cash dividend and announces it to stockholders. Declaration of a cash dividend **commits the corporation to a legal obligation**. The obligation is binding and cannot be rescinded. The company makes an entry to recognize the increase in Cash Dividends and the increase in the liability Dividends Payable.

To illustrate, assume that on December 1, 2012, the directors of Media General declare a 50¢ per share cash dividend on 100,000 shares of $10 par value common stock. The dividend is $50,000 (100,000 × 50¢). The entry to record the declaration is:

Declaration Date

Dec. 1	Cash Dividends	50,000	
	Dividends Payable		50,000
	(To record declaration of cash dividend)		

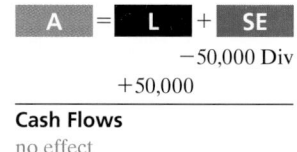

−50,000 Div
+50,000

Cash Flows
no effect

Media General debits the account Cash Dividends. Cash dividends decrease retained earnings. We use the specific title Cash Dividends to differentiate it from other types of dividends, such as stock dividends. Dividends Payable is a current liability: It will normally be paid within the next several months.

When using a dividend account, the company transfers the balance of that account to Retained Earnings at the end of the year by a closing entry. Whichever account is used for the dividend declaration, the effect is the same: Retained earnings decreases, and a current liability increases. *For homework problems, you should use the Cash Dividends account for recording dividend declarations.*

At the **record date**, the company determines ownership of the outstanding shares for dividend purposes. The stockholders' records maintained by the corporation supply this information. In the interval between the declaration date and the record date, the corporation updates its stock ownership records. For Media General, the record date is December 22. No entry is required on this date because the corporation's liability recognized on the declaration date is unchanged.

Helpful Hint

The purpose of the record date is to identify the persons or entities that will receive the dividend, not to determine the amount of the dividend liability.

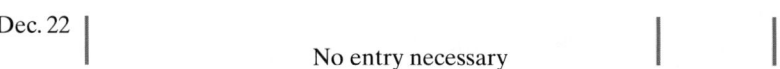

Record Date

Dec. 22 | No entry necessary

On the **payment date**, the company makes cash dividend payments to the stockholders of record (as of December 22) and records the payment of the dividend. If January 20 is the payment date for Media General, the entry on that date is:

Payment Date

Jan. 20 | Dividends Payable | 50,000 |
| | Cash | | 50,000
| | (To record payment of cash dividend) | |

Note that payment of the dividend reduces both current assets and current liabilities. It has no effect on stockholders' equity. The **cumulative effect** of the **declaration and payment** of a cash dividend is to **decrease both stockholders' equity and total assets**. Illustration 14-1 summarizes the three important dates associated with dividends for Media General.

Illustration 14-1
Key dividend dates

ALLOCATING CASH DIVIDENDS BETWEEN PREFERRED AND COMMON STOCK

As explained in Chapter 13, preferred stock has priority over common stock in regard to dividends. Holders of cumulative preferred stock must be paid any unpaid prior-year dividends and its current year's dividend before common stockholders receive dividends.

To illustrate, assume that at December 31, 2012, IBR Inc. has 1,000 shares of 8%, $100 par value cumulative preferred stock. It also has 50,000 shares of $10 par value common stock outstanding. The dividend per share for preferred stock is $8 ($100 par value × 8%). The required annual dividend for preferred stock is therefore $8,000 (1,000 × $8). At December 31, 2012, the directors declare a $6,000 cash dividend. In this case, the entire dividend amount goes to preferred stockholders because of their dividend preference. The entry to record the declaration of the dividend is:

Dec. 31 | Cash Dividends | 6,000 |
| | Dividends Payable | | 6,000
| | (To record $6 per share cash dividend | |
| | to preferred stockholders) | |

Because of the cumulative feature, dividends of $2 ($8 − $6) per share are in arrears on preferred stock for 2012. IBR must pay these dividends to preferred stockholders before it can pay any future dividends to common stockholders. IBR should disclose dividends in arrears in the financial statements.

At December 31, 2013, IBR declares a $50,000 cash dividend. The allocation of the dividend to the two classes of stock is as follows.

Illustration 14-2
Allocating dividends to preferred and common stock

Total dividend		$50,000
Allocated to preferred stock		
Dividends in arrears, 2012 (1,000 × $2)	$2,000	
2013 dividend (1,000 × $8)	8,000	10,000
Remainder allocated to common stock		$40,000

The entry to record the declaration of the dividend is:

Dec. 31	Cash Dividends	50,000	
	Dividends Payable		50,000
	(To record declaration of cash dividends of $10,000 to preferred stock and $40,000 to common stock)		

A = L + SE
−50,000 Div
+50,000
Cash Flows
no effect

If IBR's preferred stock is not cumulative, preferred stockholders receive only $8,000 in dividends in 2013. Common stockholders receive $42,000.

ACCOUNTING ACROSS THE ORGANIZATION

Up, Down, and ??

The decision whether to pay a dividend, and how much to pay, is a very important management decision. As the chart below shows, from 2002 to 2007, many companies substantially increased their dividends, and total dividends paid by U.S. companies hit record levels. One reason for the increase is that Congress lowered, from 39% to 15%, the tax rate paid by investors on dividends received, making dividends more attractive to investors.

Then the financial crisis of 2008 occurred. As result, in 2009, 804 companies cut their dividends (see chart), the highest level since the S&P started collecting data in 1995. In 2010, more companies are again starting to increase their dividends. However, potential higher taxes on dividends coming in 2011 and the possibility of a low-growth economy may stall any significant increase.

Source: Matt Phillips and Jay Miller, "Last Year's Dividend Slash Was $58 Billion," *Wall Street Journal* (January 8, 2010), p. C5.

? What factors must management consider in deciding how large a dividend to pay? (See page 665.)

Do it!

Dividends on Preferred and Common Stock

MasterMind Corporation has 2,000 shares of 6%, $100 par value preferred stock outstanding at December 31, 2012. At December 31, 2012, the company declared a $60,000 cash dividend. Determine the dividend paid to preferred stockholders and common stockholders under each of the following scenarios.

1. The preferred stock is noncumulative, and the company has not missed any dividends in previous years.

2. The preferred stock is noncumulative, and the company did not pay a dividend in each of the two previous years.

3. The preferred stock is cumulative, and the company did not pay a dividend in each of the two previous years.

action plan

✔ Determine dividends on preferred shares by multiplying the dividend rate times the par value of the stock times the number of preferred shares.

✔ Understand the cumulative feature: If preferred stock is cumulative, then any missed dividends (dividends in arrears) and the current year's dividend must be paid to preferred stockholders before dividends are paid to common stockholders.

Solution

1. The company has not missed past dividends and the preferred stock is noncumulative; thus, the preferred stockholders are paid only this year's dividend. The dividend paid to preferred stockholders would be $12,000 (2,000 × .06 × $100). The dividend paid to common stockholders would be $48,000 ($60,000 − $12,000).

2. The preferred stock is noncumulative; thus, past unpaid dividends do not have to be paid. The dividend paid to preferred stockholders would be $12,000 (2,000 × .06 × $100). The dividend paid to common stockholders would be $48,000 ($60,000 − $12,000).

3. The preferred stock is cumulative; thus, dividends that have been missed (dividends in arrears) must be paid. The dividend paid to preferred stockholders would be $36,000 (3 × 2,000 × .06 × $100). The dividend paid to common stockholders would be $24,000 ($60,000 − $36,000).

Related exercise material: E14-2, E14-17, and **Do it!** 14-1.

✔
The Navigator

Stock Dividends

A **stock dividend** is a pro rata distribution to stockholders of the corporation's own stock. Whereas a company pays cash in a cash dividend, a company issues shares of stock in a stock dividend. **A stock dividend results in a decrease in retained earnings and an increase in paid-in capital.** Unlike a cash dividend, a stock dividend does not decrease total stockholders' equity or total assets.

To illustrate, assume that you have a 2% ownership interest in Cetus Inc.; you own 20 of its 1,000 shares of common stock. If Cetus declares a 10% stock dividend, it would issue 100 shares (1,000 × 10%) of stock. You would receive two shares (2% × 100). Would your ownership interest change? No, it would remain at 2% (22 ÷ 1,100). **You now own more shares of stock, but your ownership interest has not changed.** Illustration 14-3 (next page) shows the effect of a stock dividend for stockholders.

Cetus has disbursed no cash, and has assumed no liabilities. What, then, are the purposes and benefits of a stock dividend? Corporations issue stock dividends generally for one or more of the following reasons.

1. To satisfy stockholders' dividend expectations without spending cash.

2. To increase the marketability of the corporation's stock. When the number of shares outstanding increases, the market price per share decreases. Decreasing

Illustration 14-3
Effect of stock dividend
for stockholders

Number of shares owned increases, but
percentage of company owned remains the same.

the market price of the stock makes it easier for smaller investors to purchase
the shares.

3. To emphasize that a portion of stockholders' equity has been permanently
reinvested in the business (and is unavailable for cash dividends).

When the dividend is declared, the board of directors determines the size of the
stock dividend and the value assigned to each dividend.

Generally, if the company issues a **small stock dividend** (less than 20–25% of
the corporation's issued stock), the value assigned to the dividend is the fair value
per share. This treatment is based on the assumption that a small stock dividend
will have little effect on the market price of the shares previously outstanding. Thus,
many stockholders consider small stock dividends to be distributions of earnings
equal to the fair market value of the shares distributed. If a company issues a **large
stock dividend** (greater than 20–25%), the value assigned to the dividend is the par
or stated value. Small stock dividends predominate in practice. Thus, we will illustrate only entries for small stock dividends.

ENTRIES FOR STOCK DIVIDENDS
To illustrate the accounting for small stock dividends, assume that Medland Corporation has a balance of $300,000 in retained earnings. It declares a 10% stock
dividend on its 50,000 shares of $10 par value common stock. The current fair
market value of its stock is $15 per share. The number of shares to be issued is 5,000
(10% × 50,000). Therefore the total amount to be debited to Stock Dividends is
$75,000 (5,000 × $15). The entry to record the declaration of the stock dividend is
as follows.

Stock Dividends	75,000	
Common Stock Dividends Distributable		50,000
Paid-in Capital in Excess of Par—Common Stock		25,000
(To record declaration of 10% stock dividend)		

−75,000 Div
+50,000 CS
+25,000 CS

Cash Flows
no effect

Medland debits Stock Dividends for the fair market value of the stock issued ($15 ×
5,000). (Similar to Cash Dividends, Stock Dividends decrease retained earnings.)
Medland also credits Common Stock Dividends Distributable for the par value of
the dividend shares ($10 × 5,000), and credits Paid-in Capital in Excess of Par—
Common Stock for the excess over par ($5 × 5,000).

Common Stock Dividends Distributable is a **stockholders' equity account**. It is
not a liability because assets will not be used to pay the dividend. If the company
prepares a balance sheet before it issues the dividend shares, it reports the distributable account under Paid-in capital as shown in Illustration 14-4 (next page).

Illustration 14-4
Statement presentation of common stock dividends distributable

Paid-in capital		
Common stock	$500,000	
Common stock dividends distributable	50,000	$550,000

When Medland issues the dividend shares, it debits Common Stock Dividends Distributable and credits Common Stock, as follows.

A	=	L	+	SE
				−50,000 CS
				+50,000 CS

Cash Flows
no effect

Common Stock Dividends Distributable	50,000	
Common Stock		50,000
(To record issuance of 5,000 shares in a stock dividend)		

EFFECTS OF STOCK DIVIDENDS

How do stock dividends affect stockholders' equity? They **change the composition of stockholders' equity**, because they transfer to paid-in capital a portion of retained earnings. However, **total stockholders' equity remains the same**. Stock dividends also have no effect on the par or stated value per share. But the number of shares outstanding increases. Illustration 14-5 shows these effects for Medland Corporation.

Illustration 14-5
Stock dividend effects

	Before Dividend	After Dividend
Stockholders' equity		
Paid-in capital		
Common stock, $10 par	$500,000	$550,000
Paid-in capital in excess of par—common stock	—	25,000
Total paid-in capital	500,000	575,000
Retained earnings	300,000	225,000
Total stockholders' equity	$800,000	$800,000
Outstanding shares	50,000	55,000
Par value per share	$10.00	$10.00

In this example, total paid-in capital increases by $75,000 (50,000 shares × 10% × $15) and retained earnings decreases by the same amount. Note also that total stockholders' equity remains unchanged at $800,000. The number of shares increases by 5,000 (50,000 × 10%).

Stock Splits

A **stock split**, like a stock dividend, involves issuance of additional shares to stockholders according to their percentage ownership. **However, a stock split results in a reduction in the par or stated value per share.** The purpose of a stock split is to increase the marketability of the stock by lowering its market value per share. This, in turn, makes it easier for the corporation to issue additional stock.

The effect of a split on market value is generally *inversely proportional* to the size of the split. For example, after a recent 2-for-1 stock split, the market value of Nike's stock fell from $111 to approximately $55. The lower market value stimulated market activity, and within one year the stock was trading above $100 again.

In a stock split, the number of shares increases in the same proportion that par or stated value per share decreases. For example, in a 2-for-1 split, one share of $10 par value stock is exchanged for two shares of $5 par value stock. **A stock split does**

Helpful Hint

A stock split changes the par value per share but does not affect any balances in stockholders' equity.

not have any effect on total paid-in capital, retained earnings, or total stockholders' equity. But the number of shares outstanding increases, and par value per share decreases. Illustration 14-6 shows these effects for Medland Corporation, assuming that it splits its 50,000 shares of common stock on a 2-for-1 basis.

Illustration 14-6
Stock split effects

	Before Stock Split	After Stock Split
Stockholders' equity		
Paid-in capital		
Common stock	$500,000	$500,000
Paid-in capital in excess of par value	–0–	–0–
Total paid-in capital	500,000	500,000
Retained earnings	300,000	300,000
Total stockholders' equity	$800,000	$800,000
Outstanding shares	50,000	100,000
Par value per share	$10.00	$5.00

A stock split does not affect the balances in any stockholders' equity accounts. Therefore **it is not necessary to journalize a stock split.**

Illustration 14-7 summarizes the differences between stock splits and stock dividends.

Illustration 14-7
Differences between the effects of stock splits and stock dividends

Item	Stock Split	Stock Dividend
Total paid-in capital	No change	Increase
Total retained earnings	No change	Decrease
Total par value (common stock)	No change	Increase
Par value per share	Decrease	No change
Total stockholders' equity	No change	No change

INVESTOR INSIGHT

A No-Split Philosophy

Warren Buffett's company, Berkshire Hathaway, has two classes of shares. Until recently, the company had never split either class of stock. As a result, the class A stock had a market price of $97,000 and the class B sold for about $3,200 per share. Because the price per share is so high, the stock does not trade as frequently as the stock of other companies. Mr. Buffett has always opposed stock splits because he feels that a lower stock price attracts short-term investors. He appears to be correct. For example, while more than 6 million shares of IBM are exchanged on the average day, only about 1,000 class A shares of Berkshire are traded. Despite Mr. Buffett's aversion to splits, in order to accomplish a recent acquisition, Berkshire decided to split its class B shares 50 to 1.

Source: Scott Patterson, "Berkshire Nears Smaller Baby B's," *Wall Street Journal Online* (January 19, 2010).

? Why does Warren Buffett usually oppose stock splits? (See page 665.)

Do it!

Sing CD Company has had five years of record earnings. Due to this success, the market price of its 500,000 shares of $2 par value common stock has tripled from $15 per share to $45. During this period, paid-in capital remained the same at $2,000,000. Retained earnings increased from $1,500,000 to $10,000,000. President

Stock Dividends and Stock Splits

Joan Elbert is considering either a 10% stock dividend or a 2-for-1 stock split. She asks you to show the before-and-after effects of each option on retained earnings and total stockholders' equity.

action plan

✔ Calculate the stock dividend's effect on retained earnings by multiplying the number of new shares times the market price of the stock (or par value for a large stock dividend).

✔ Recall that a stock dividend increases the number of shares without affecting total stockholders' equity.

✔ Recall that a stock split only increases the number of shares outstanding and decreases the par value per share.

Solution

The stock dividend amount is $2,250,000 [(500,000 × 10%) × $45]. The new balance in retained earnings is $7,750,000 ($10,000,000 − $2,250,000). The retained earnings balance after the stock split is the same as it was before the split: $10,000,000. Total stockholders' equity does not change. The effects on the stockholders' equity accounts are as follows.

	Original Balances	After Dividend	After Split
Paid-in capital	$ 2,000,000	$ 4,250,000	$ 2,000,000
Retained earnings	10,000,000	7,750,000	10,000,000
Total stockholders' equity	$12,000,000	$12,000,000	$12,000,000
Shares outstanding	500,000	550,000	1,000,000

Related exercise material: BE14-3, E14-4, E14-5, E14-6, E14-7, and **Do it!** 14-2.

✔ **The Navigator**

Retained Earnings

Study Objective [2]
Identify the items reported in a retained earnings statement.

As you learned in Chapter 13, **retained earnings** is net income that a company retains in the business. The balance in retained earnings is part of the stockholders' claim on the total assets of the corporation. It does not, though, represent a claim on any specific asset. Nor can the amount of retained earnings be associated with the balance of any asset account. For example, a $100,000 balance in retained earnings does not mean that there should be $100,000 in cash. The reason is that the company may have used the cash resulting from the excess of revenues over expenses to purchase buildings, equipment, and other assets.

To demonstrate that retained earnings and cash may be quite different, Illustration 14-8 shows recent amounts of retained earnings and cash in selected companies.

Illustration 14-8
Retained earnings and cash balances

Company	Retained Earnings	Cash
	(in millions)	
Disney Co.	$24,207	$3,670
Intel Corp.	28,984	6,598
Kellogg Co.	4,217	1,026
Amazon.com	(1,837)	1,022

Helpful Hint

Remember that Retained Earnings is a stockholders' equity account, whose normal balance is a credit.

Remember from Chapter 13 that when a company has net income, it closes net income to retained earnings. The closing entry is a debit to Income Summary and a credit to Retained Earnings.

When a company has a **net loss** (expenses exceed revenues), it also closes this amount to retained earnings. The closing entry in this case is a debit to Retained Earnings and a credit to Income Summary. This is done even if it results in a debit balance in Retained Earnings. **Companies do not debit net losses to paid-in capital accounts.** To do so would destroy the distinction between paid-in and earned capital. If cumulative losses exceed cumulative income over a company's life, a debit balance in Retained Earnings results. A debit balance in Retained Earnings is identified as a **deficit**. A company reports a deficit as a deduction in the stockholders' equity section, as shown in Illustration 14-9.

Illustration 14-9
Stockholders' equity with deficit

Balance Sheet (partial)

Stockholders' equity
  Paid-in capital
    Common stock $800,000
    Retained earnings (deficit) ... (50,000)
      Total stockholders' equity ... $750,000

Retained Earnings Restrictions

The balance in retained earnings is generally available for dividend declarations. Some companies state this fact. For example, Lockheed Martin Corporation states the following in the notes to its financial statements.

Lockheed Martin Corporation
Notes to the Financial Statements

Illustration 14-10
Disclosure of unrestricted retained earnings

At December 31, retained earnings were unrestricted and available for dividend payments.

In some cases, there may be **retained earnings restrictions**. These make a portion of the retained earnings balance currently unavailable for dividends. Restrictions result from one or more of the following causes.

1. **Legal restrictions.** Many states require a corporation to restrict retained earnings for the cost of treasury stock purchased. The restriction keeps intact the corporation's legal capital that is being temporarily held as treasury stock. When the company sells the treasury stock, the restriction is lifted.

2. **Contractual restrictions.** Long-term debt contracts may restrict retained earnings as a condition for the loan. The restriction limits the use of corporate assets for payment of dividends. Thus, it increases the likelihood that the corporation will be able to meet required loan payments.

3. **Voluntary restrictions.** The board of directors may voluntarily create retained earnings restrictions for specific purposes. For example, the board may authorize a restriction for future plant expansion. By reducing the amount of retained earnings available for dividends, the company makes more cash available for the planned expansion.

Companies generally disclose **retained earnings restrictions** in the notes to the financial statements. For example, Tektronix Inc., a manufacturer of electronic measurement devices, had total retained earnings of $774 million, but the unrestricted portion was only $223.8 million.

Illustration 14-11
Disclosure of restriction

Tektronix Inc.
Notes to the Financial Statements

Certain of the Company's debt agreements require compliance with debt covenants. Management believes that the Company is in compliance with such requirements. The Company had unrestricted retained earnings of $223.8 million after meeting those requirements.

Prior Period Adjustments

Suppose that a corporation has closed its books and issued financial statements. The corporation then discovers that it made a material error in reporting net income of a prior year. How should the company record this situation in the accounts and report it in the financial statements?

The correction of an error in previously issued financial statements is known as a **prior period adjustment**. The company makes the correction directly to Retained Earnings, because the effect of the error is now in this account. The net income for the prior period has been recorded in retained earnings through the journalizing and posting of closing entries.

To illustrate, assume that General Microwave discovers in 2012 that it understated depreciation expense on equipment in 2011 by $300,000 due to computational errors. These errors overstated both net income for 2011 and the current balance in retained earnings. The entry for the prior period adjustment, ignoring all tax effects, is as follows.

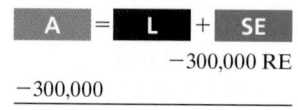

−300,000
Cash Flows
no effect

Retained Earnings	300,000	
Accumulated Depreciation—Equipment		300,000
(To adjust for understatement of depreciation in a prior period)		

A debit to an income statement account in 2012 is incorrect because the error pertains to a prior year.

Companies report prior period adjustments in the retained earnings statement.[1] They add (or deduct, as the case may be) these adjustments from the beginning retained earnings balance. This results in an adjusted beginning balance. For example, assuming a beginning balance of $800,000 in retained earnings, General Microwave reports the prior period adjustment as follows.

Illustration 14-12
Statement presentation of prior period adjustments

General Microwave	
Retained Earnings Statement (partial)	
Balance, January 1, as reported	$ 800,000
Correction for overstatement of net income **in prior period (depreciation error)**	(300,000)
Balance, January 1, as adjusted	$ 500,000

Again, reporting the correction in the current year's income statement would be incorrect because it applies to a prior year's income statement.

---

[1] A complete retained earnings statement is shown in Illustration 14-14 on the next page.

Retained Earnings Statement

The **retained earnings statement** shows the changes in retained earnings during the year. The company prepares the statement from the Retained Earnings account. Illustration 14-13 shows (in account form) transactions that affect retained earnings.

Illustration 14-13
Debits and credits to retained earnings

Retained Earnings	
1. Net loss	1. Net income
2. Prior period adjustments for overstatement of net income	2. Prior period adjustments for understatement of net income
3. Cash dividends and stock dividends	
4. Some disposals of treasury stock	

As indicated, net income increases retained earnings, and a net loss decreases retained earnings. Prior period adjustments may either increase or decrease retained earnings. Both cash dividends and stock dividends decrease retained earnings. The circumstances under which treasury stock transactions decrease retained earnings are explained in Chapter 13, page 609.

A complete retained earnings statement for Graber Inc., based on assumed data, is as follows.

Illustration 14-14
Retained earnings statement

Graber Inc. Retained Earnings Statement For the Year Ended December 31, 2012		
Balance, January 1, as reported		$1,050,000
Correction for understatement of net income in prior period (inventory error)		50,000
Balance, January 1, as adjusted		1,100,000
Add: Net income		360,000
		1,460,000
Less: Cash dividends	$100,000	
Stock dividends	200,000	300,000
Balance, December 31		$1,160,000

Do it!

Vega Corporation has retained earnings of $5,130,000 on January 1, 2012. During the year, Vega earned $2,000,000 of net income. It declared and paid a $250,000 cash dividend. In 2012, Vega recorded an adjustment of $180,000 due to the understatement (from a mathematical error) of 2011 depreciation expense. Prepare a retained earnings statement for 2012.

Retained Earnings Statement

action plan

✔ Recall that a retained earnings statement begins with retained earnings, as reported at the end of the previous year.

✔ Add or subtract any prior period adjustments to arrive at the adjusted beginning figure.

✔ Add net income and subtract dividends declared to arrive at the ending balance in retained earnings.

Solution

VEGA CORPORATION Retained Earnings Statement For the Year Ended December 31, 2012	
Balance, January 1, as reported	$5,130,000
Correction for overstatement of net income in prior period (depreciation error)	(180,000)
Balance, January 1, as adjusted	4,950,000
Add: Net income	2,000,000
	6,950,000
Less: Cash dividends	250,000
Balance, December 31	$6,700,000

Related exercise material: BE14-4, BE14-5, E14-8, E14-9, and **Do it!** 14-3.

Statement Presentation and Analysis

Stockholders' Equity Presentation

Study Objective [3]
Prepare and analyze a comprehensive stockholders' equity section.

Illustration 14-15 presents the stockholders' equity section of Graber Inc.'s balance sheet. Note the following: (1) "Common stock dividends distributable" is shown under "Capital stock," in "Paid-in capital." (2) A note (Note R) discloses a retained earnings restriction.

Illustration 14-15
Comprehensive stockholders' equity section

Graber Inc. Balance Sheet (partial)		
Stockholders' equity		
Paid-in capital		
Capital stock		
9% Preferred stock, $100 par value, cumulative, callable at $120, 10,000 shares authorized, 6,000 shares issued and outstanding		$ 600,000
Common stock, no par, $5 stated value, 500,000 shares authorized, 400,000 shares issued and 390,000 outstanding	$2,000,000	
Common stock dividends distributable	50,000	2,050,000
Total capital stock		2,650,000
Additional paid-in capital		
In excess of par—preferred stock	30,000	
In excess of stated value—common stock	1,050,000	
Total additional paid-in capital		1,080,000
Total paid-in capital		3,730,000
Retained earnings (see Note R)		1,160,000
Total paid-in capital and retained earnings		4,890,000
Less: Treasury stock (10,000 common shares)		80,000
Total stockholders' equity		$4,810,000

Note R: Retained earnings is restricted for the cost of treasury stock, $80,000.

Instead of presenting a detailed stockholders' equity section in the balance sheet and a retained earnings statement, many companies prepare a **stockholders' equity statement**. This statement shows the changes (1) in each stockholders' equity account and (2) in total that occurred during the year. An example of a stockholders' equity statement appears in PepsiCo's financial statements in Appendix A (page A7).

Stockholders' Equity Analysis

Investors and analysts can measure profitability from the viewpoint of the common stockholder by the **return on common stockholders' equity**. This ratio shows how many dollars of net income the company earned for each dollar invested by the common stockholders. It is computed by dividing **net income available to common stockholders** (which is net income minus preferred stock dividends) by average common stockholders' equity.

To illustrate, Walt Disney Company's beginning-of-the-year and end-of-the-year common stockholders' equity were $31,820 and $30,753 million respectively. Its net income was $4,687 million, and no preferred stock was outstanding. The return on common stockholders' equity ratio is computed as follows.

Net Income Available to Common Stockholders	÷	Average Common Stockholders' Equity	=	Return on Common Stockholders' Equity
($4,687 − $0)	÷	$\dfrac{(\$31,820 + \$30,753)}{2}$	=	15.0%

Illustration 14-16
Return on common stockholders' equity ratio and computation

As shown above, if a company has preferred stock, we would deduct the amount of **preferred dividends** from the company's net income to compute income available to common stockholders. Also, the par value of preferred stock is deducted from total average stockholders' equity to arrive at the amount of common stockholders' equity.

Income Statement Presentation

Income statements for **corporations are the same as the statements for proprietorships or partnerships except for one thing: the reporting of income taxes**. For income tax purposes, corporations are a separate legal entity. As a result, corporations report **income tax expense** in a separate section of the corporation income statement, before net income. The condensed income statement for Leads Inc. in Illustration 14-17 shows a typical presentation. Note that the

Study Objective [4]
Describe the form and content of corporation income statements.

Illustration 14-17
Income statement with income taxes

Leads Inc. Income Statement For the Year Ended December 31, 2012	
Sales revenue	$800,000
Cost of goods sold	600,000
Gross profit	200,000
Operating expenses	50,000
Income from operations	150,000
Other revenues and gains	10,000
Other expenses and losses	(4,000)
Income before income taxes	156,000
Income tax expense	46,800
Net income	$109,200

corporation reports income before income taxes as one line item and income tax expense as another.

Companies record income tax expense and the related liability for income taxes payable as part of the adjusting process. Using the data for Leads Inc., in Illustration 14-17, the adjusting entry for income tax expense at December 31, 2012, is:

A = L + SE
        −46,800 Exp
        +46,800

Cash Flows
no effect

Income Tax Expense	46,800	
Income Taxes Payable		46,800
(To record income taxes for 2012)		

The income statement of PepsiCo, in Appendix A presents another illustration of income taxes.

Income Statement Analysis

Study Objective [5]
Compute earnings per share.

The financial press frequently reports earnings data. Stockholders and potential investors widely use these data in evaluating the profitability of a company. A convenient measure of earnings is **earnings per share (EPS)**, which indicates the net income earned by each share of outstanding **common stock**.

EPS AND PREFERRED DIVIDENDS

The existence of preferred dividends slightly complicates the calculation of EPS. When a corporation has both preferred and common stock, we must subtract the current year's preferred dividend from net income, to arrive at **income available to common stockholders**. Illustration 14-18 shows the formula for computing EPS.

Illustration 14-18
Formula for earnings per share

Net Income minus Preferred Dividends	÷	Weighted-Average of Common Shares Outstanding	=	Earnings per Share

Ethics Note

In order to meet market expectations for EPS, some managers engage in elaborate treasury stock transactions. These transactions can be very costly for the remaining shareholders.

To illustrate, assume that Rally Inc. reports net income of $211,000 on its 102,500 weighted-average common shares.[2] During the year it also declares a $6,000 dividend on its preferred stock. Therefore, the amount Rally has available for common stock dividends is $205,000 ($211,000 − $6,000). Earnings per share is $2 ($205,000 ÷ 102,500). If the preferred stock is cumulative, Rally deducts the dividend for the current year, whether or not it is declared. Remember that companies report **earnings per share only for common stock**.

Investors often attempt to link earnings per share to the market price per share of a company's stock.[3] Because of the importance of earnings per share, most companies must report it on the face of the income statement. Generally companies simply report this amount below net income on the statement. For Rally Inc. the presentation is as follows.

Illustration 14-19
Basic earnings per share disclosure

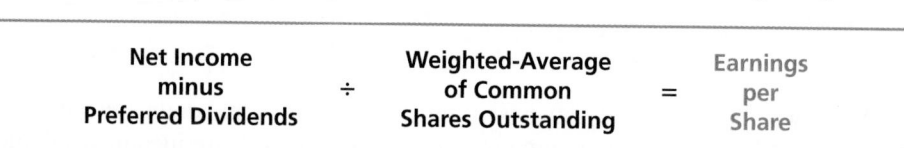

Rally Inc.
Income Statement (partial)

Net income	$211,000
Earnings per share	$2.00

---

[2]The calculation of the weighted average of common shares outstanding is discussed in advanced accounting courses.

[3]The ratio of the market price per share to the earnings per share is called the *price/earnings (P/E) ratio*. The financial media report this ratio for common stocks listed on major stock exchanges.

Do it!

On January 1, 2012, Siena Corporation purchased 2,000 shares of treasury stock. Other information regarding Siena Corporation is provided below.

Stockholders' Equity and EPS

	2011	2012
Net income	$110,000	$110,000
Dividends on preferred stock	$10,000	$10,000
Dividends on common stock	$2,000	$1,600
Weighted-average number of shares outstanding	10,000	8,000*
Common stockholders' equity, beginning of year	$500,000	$400,000*
Common stockholders' equity, end of year	$500,000	$400,000

*Adjusted for purchase of treasury stock.

Compute (a) return on common stockholders' equity for each year and (b) earnings per share for each year, and (c) discuss the changes in each.

action plan

✔ Determine return on common stockholders' equity by dividing net income available to common stockholders by the average common stockholders' equity.

✔ Determine earnings per share by dividing net income available to common stockholders by the weighted-average number of common shares outstanding.

Solution

(a)

	2011	2012
Return on common stockholders' equity	$\dfrac{(\$110,000 - \$10,000)}{(\$500,000 + \$500,000)/2} = 20\%$	$\dfrac{(\$110,000 - \$10,000)}{(\$400,000 + \$400,000)/2} = 25\%$

(b)

	2011	2012
Earnings per share	$\dfrac{(\$110,000 - \$10,000)}{10,000} = \$10$	$\dfrac{(\$110,000 - \$10,000)}{8,000} = \$12.50$

(c) Between 2011 and 2012, return on common stockholders' equity improved from 20% to 25%. Earnings per share increased from $10 to $12.50. While this would appear to be good news for the company's common stockholders, these increases should be carefully evaluated. It is important to note that net income did not change during this period. The increase in both ratios was due to the purchase of treasury shares, which reduced the denominator of each ratio. As the company repurchases its own shares, it becomes more reliant on debt and thus increases its risk.

Related exercise material: BE14-6, BE14-7, BE14-9, BE14-10, E14-12, E14-13, E14-14, E14-15, E14-16, E14-17, and Do it! 14-4.

The Navigator

COMPREHENSIVE

Do it!

On January 1, 2012, Hayslett Corporation had the following stockholders' equity accounts.

Common Stock ($10 par value, 260,000 shares issued and outstanding)	$2,600,000
Paid-in Capital in Excess of Par—Common Stock	1,500,000
Retained Earnings	3,200,000

During the year, the following transactions occurred.

April 1   Declared a $1.50 cash dividend per share to stockholders of record on April 15, payable May 1.
May 1   Paid the dividend declared in April.
June 1   Announced a 2-for-1 stock split. Prior to the split, the market price per share was $24.
Aug. 1   Declared a 10% stock dividend to stockholders of record on August 15, distributable August 31. On August 1, the market price of the stock was $10 per share.
       31   Issued the shares for the stock dividend.

Dec. 1 Declared a $1.50 per share dividend to stockholders of record on December 15, payable January 5, 2011.

    31 Determined that net income for the year was $600,000.

Instructions

(a) Journalize the transactions and the closing entry for net income.

(b) Prepare a stockholders' equity section at December 31.

action plan

✔ Award dividends to outstanding shares only.

✔ Adjust the par value and number of shares for stock splits, but make no journal entry.

✔ Use fair value of stock to determine the value of a small stock dividend.

✔ Close Income Summary to Retained Earnings.

Solution to Comprehensive Do it!

(a)

			Debit	Credit
Apr. 1	Cash Dividends (260,000 × $1.50)		390,000	
	Dividends Payable			390,000
May 1	Dividends Payable		390,000	
	Cash			390,000
June 1	Memo—two-for-one stock split increases number of shares to 520,000 (260,000 × 2) and reduces par value to $5 per share.			
Aug. 1	Stock Dividends (52,000* × $10)		520,000	
	Common Stock Dividends Distributable (52,000 × $5)			260,000
	Paid-in Capital in Excess of Par—Common Stock (52,000 × $5)			260,000
	*520,000 × .10			
31	Common Stock Dividends Distributable		260,000	
	Common Stock			260,000
Dec. 1	Cash Dividends (572,000** × $1.50)		858,000	
	Dividends Payable			858,000
	**(260,000 × 2) + 52,000			
31	Income Summary		600,000	
	Retained Earnings			600,000

(b)

HAYSLETT CORPORATION

Stockholders' equity
  Paid-in capital
    Capital stock
      Common stock, $5 par value, 572,000

shares issued and outstanding	$2,860,000
Paid-in capital in excess of par—common stock	1,760,000
Total paid-in capital	4,620,000
Retained earnings	2,032,000*
Total stockholders' equity	$6,652,000

*$3,200,000 + $600,000 − $390,000 − $520,000 − $858,000

✔ **The Navigator**

Summary of Study Objectives

[1] Prepare the entries for cash dividends and stock dividends. Companies make entries for both cash and stock dividends at the declaration date and at the payment date. At the *declaration date*, the entries are: cash dividend—debit Cash Dividends, and credit Dividends Payable; small stock dividend—debit Stock Dividends, credit Paid-in Capital in Excess of Par (or Stated) Value—Common Stock, and credit Common Stock Dividends Distributable. At the *payment date*, the entries for cash and stock dividends are: cash dividend—debit Dividends Payable and credit Cash; small stock dividend—debit Common Stock Dividends Distributable and credit Common Stock.

[2] Identify the items reported in a retained earnings statement. Companies report each of the individual debits and credits to retained earnings in the retained earnings statement. Additions consist of net income and prior period adjustments to correct understatements of prior years' net income. Deductions consist of net loss, adjustments to correct overstatements of prior years' net income, cash and stock dividends, and some disposals of treasury stock.

[3] Prepare and analyze a comprehensive stockholders' equity section. A comprehensive stockholders' equity section includes all stockholders' equity accounts. It consists of two sections: paid-in capital and retained earnings. It should also include notes to the financial statements that explain any restrictions on retained earnings and any dividends in arrears. One measure of profitability is the return on common stockholders' equity. It is calculated by dividing net income minus preferred stock dividends by average common stockholders' equity.

[4] Describe the form and content of corporation income statements. The form and content of corporation income statements are similar to the statements of proprietorships and partnerships with one exception: Corporations must report income taxes or income tax expense in a separate section before net income in the income statement.

[5] Compute earnings per share. Companies compute earnings per share by dividing net income by the weighted-average number of common shares outstanding during the period. When preferred stock dividends exist, they must be deducted from net income in order to calculate EPS.

The Navigator

Glossary

Cash dividend A pro rata distribution of cash to stockholders. (p. 634).

Declaration date The date the board of directors formally declares a dividend and announces it to stockholders. (p. 635).

Deficit A debit balance in retained earnings. (p. 643).

Dividend A corporation's distribution of cash or stock to its stockholders on a pro rata (proportional) basis. (p. 634).

Earnings per share The net income earned by each share of outstanding common stock. (p. 648).

Liquidating dividend A dividend declared out of paid-in capital. (p. 634).

Payment date The date dividend checks are mailed to stockholders. (p. 636).

Prior period adjustment The correction of an error in previously issued financial statements. (p. 644).

Record date The date when ownership of outstanding shares is determined for dividend purposes. (p. 635).

Retained earnings Net income that is retained in the business. (p. 642).

Retained earnings restrictions Circumstances that make a portion of retained earnings currently unavailable for dividends. (p. 643).

Retained earnings statement A financial statement that shows the changes in retained earnings during the year. (p. 645).

Return on common stockholders' equity A measure of profitability that shows how many dollars of net income were earned for each dollar invested by the owners; computed as net income minus preferred dividends divided by average common stockholders' equity. (p. 647).

Stock dividend A pro rata distribution to stockholders of the corporation's own stock. (p. 638).

Stockholders' equity statement A statement that shows the changes in each stockholders' equity account and in total stockholders' equity during the year. (p. 647).

Stock split The issuance of additional shares of stock to stockholders according to their percentage ownership; is accompanied by a reduction in the par or stated value per share. (p. 640).

Self-Test, Brief Exercises, Exercises, Problem Set A, and many more components are available for practice in *WileyPLUS*

Self-Test Questions

Answers are on page 665.

(SO 1) **1.** Entries for cash dividends are required on the:
  a. declaration date and the payment date.
  b. record date and the payment date.
  c. declaration date, record date, and payment date.
  d. declaration date and the record date.

(SO 1) **2.** Which of the following statements about small stock dividends is *true*?

  a. A debit to Retained Earnings for the par value of the shares issued should be made.
  b. A small stock dividend decreases total stockholders' equity.
  c. Market value per share should be assigned to the dividend shares.
  d. A small stock dividend ordinarily will have an effect on par value per share of stock.

(SO 1) **3.** Which of the following statements about a 3-for-1 stock split is *true*?
  a. It will triple the market value of the stock.
  b. It will triple the amount of total stockholders' equity.
  c. It will have no effect on total stockholders' equity.
  d. It requires the company to distribute cash.

(SO 1) **4.** Encore Inc. declared an $80,000 cash dividend. It currently has 3,000 shares of 7%, $100 par value cumulative preferred stock outstanding. It is one year in arrears on its preferred stock. How much cash will Encore distribute to the common stockholders?
  a. $38,000.   **c.** $59,000.
  b. $42,000.   **d.** None.

(SO 1) **5.** Raptor Inc. has retained earnings of $500,000 and total stockholders' equity of $2,000,000. It has 100,000 shares of $8 par value common stock outstanding, which is currently selling for $30 per share. If Raptor declares a 10% stock dividend on its common stock:
  a. net income will decrease by $80,000.
  b. retained earnings will decrease by $80,000 and total stockholders' equity will increase by $80,000.
  c. retained earnings will decrease by $300,000 and total stockholders' equity will increase by $300,000.
  d. retained earnings will decrease by $300,000 and total paid-in capital will increase by $300,000.

(SO 2) **6.** Which of the following can cause a restriction in retained earnings?
  a. State laws regarding treasury stock.
  b. Long-term debt contract terms.
  c. Authorizations by the board of directors in light of planned expansion of corporate facilities.
  d. All of the above.

(SO 2) **7.** All *but one* of the following is reported in a retained earnings statement. The exception is:
  a. cash and stock dividends.
  b. net income and net loss.
  c. sales revenue.
  d. prior period adjustments.

(SO 2) **8.** A prior period adjustment is:
  a. reported in the income statement as a nontypical item.
  b. a correction of an error that is recorded directly to retained earnings.
  c. reported directly in the stockholders' equity section.
  d. reported in the retained earnings statement as an adjustment of the ending balance of retained earnings.

(SO 3) **9.** In the stockholders' equity section, Common Stock Dividends Distributable is reported as a(n):

  a. deduction from total paid-in capital and retained earnings.
  b. addition to additional paid-in capital.
  c. deduction from retained earnings.
  d. addition to capital stock.

10. Katie Inc. reported net income of $186,000 during 2012 (SO 3) and paid dividends of $26,000 on common stock. It also has 10,000 shares of 6%, $100 par value, noncumulative preferred stock outstanding. Common stockholders' equity was $1,200,000 on January 1, 2012, and $1,600,000 on December 31, 2012. The company's return on common stockholders' equity for 2012 is:
  a. 10.0%.   **c.** 7.1%.
  b. 9.0%.   **d.** 13.3%.

11. Corporation income statements may be the same as the in- (SO 4) come statements for unincorporated companies *except* for:
  a. gross profit.   **c.** operating income.
  b. income tax expense.   **d.** net sales.

12. During 2012, Talon Inc. had sales revenue $376,000, (SO 4) gross profit $176,000, operating expenses $66,000, cash dividends $30,000, other expenses and losses $20,000. Its corporate tax rate is 30%. What was Talon's income tax expense for the year?
  a. $18,000.   **c.** $112,800.
  b. $52,800.   **d.** $27,000.

13. The return on common stockholders' equity is defined as: (SO 3)
  a. net income divided by total assets.
  b. cash dividends divided by average common stockholders' equity.
  c. income available to common stockholders divided by average common stockholders' equity.
  d. None of these is correct.

14. If everything else is held constant, earnings per share is (SO 5) increased by:
  a. the payment of a cash dividend to common shareholders.
  b. the payment of a cash dividend to preferred shareholders.
  c. the issuance of new shares of common stock.
  d. the purchase of treasury stock.

15. The income statement for Nadeen, Inc. shows income before (SO 5) income taxes $700,000, income tax expense $210,000, and net income $490,000. If Nadeen has 100,000 shares of common stock outstanding throughout the year, earnings per share is:
  a. $7.00.   **c.** $2.10.
  b. $4.90.   **d.** No correct answer is given.

Go to the book's companion website,
www.wiley.com/college/weygandt,
for additional Self-Test Questions.

The Navigator

Questions

1. (a) What is a dividend? (b) "Dividends must be paid in cash." Do you agree? Explain.

2. Sue DeVine maintains that adequate cash is the only requirement for the declaration of a cash dividend. Is Sue correct? Explain.

3. (a) Three dates are important in connection with cash dividends. Identify these dates, and explain their significance to the corporation and its stockholders.
  (b) Identify the accounting entries that are made for a cash dividend and the date of each entry.

4. Conger Inc. declares a $45,000 cash dividend on December 31, 2012. The required annual dividend on preferred stock is $10,000. Determine the allocation of the dividend to preferred and common stockholders assuming the preferred stock is cumulative and dividends are 1 year in arrears.

5. Contrast the effects of a cash dividend and a stock dividend on a corporation's balance sheet.

6. Todd Huebner asks, "Since stock dividends don't change anything, why declare them?" What is your answer to Todd?

7. Meenen Corporation has 30,000 shares of $10 par value common stock outstanding when it announces a 2-for-1 stock split. Before the split, the stock had a market price of $120 per share. After the split, how many shares of stock will be outstanding? What will be the approximate market price per share?

8. The board of directors is considering either a stock split or a stock dividend. They understand that total stockholders' equity will remain the same under either action. However, they are not sure of the different effects of the two types of actions on other aspects of stockholders' equity. Explain the differences to the directors.

9. What is a prior period adjustment, and how is it reported in the financial statements?

10. KSU Corporation has a retained earnings balance of $210,000 on January 1. During the year, a prior period adjustment of $50,000 is recorded because of the under-statement of depreciation in the prior period. Show the retained earnings statement presentation of these data.

11. What is the purpose of a retained earnings restriction? Identify the possible causes of retained earnings restrictions.

12. How are retained earnings restrictions generally reported in the financial statements?

13. Identify the events that result in debits and credits to retained earnings.

14. Juan Ortega believes that both the beginning and ending balances in retained earnings are shown in the stockholders' equity section. Is Juan correct? Discuss.

15. Gene Remington, who owns many investments in common stock, says, "I don't care what a company's net income is. The stock price tells me everything I need to know!" How do you respond to Gene?

16. What is the unique feature of a corporation income statement? Illustrate this feature, using assumed data.

17. Why must preferred stock dividends be subtracted from net income in computing earnings per share?

18. ● **PEPSICO** What were the amounts of the dividends PepsiCo declared per share of common stock in the years 2005 to 2009? Is the trend in dividends consistent with the company's net income trend during the period?

✔
The Navigator

Brief Exercises

BE14-1 Charmaine Corporation has 80,000 shares of common stock outstanding. It declares a $1 per share cash dividend on November 1 to stockholders of record on December 1. The dividend is paid on December 31. Prepare the entries on the appropriate dates to record the declaration and payment of the cash dividend.

Prepare entries for a cash dividend.
(SO 1)

BE14-2 Willand Corporation has 50,000 shares of $10 par value common stock outstanding. It declares a 10% stock dividend on December 1 when the market value per share is $16. The dividend shares are issued on December 31. Prepare the entries for the declaration and payment of the stock dividend.

Prepare entries for a stock dividend.
(SO 1)

BE14-3 The stockholders' equity section of Melanie Corporation consists of common stock ($10 par) $2,000,000 and retained earnings $500,000. A 10% stock dividend (20,000 shares) is declared when the market value per share is $14. Show the before and after effects of the dividend on the following.

Show before and after effects of a stock dividend.
(SO 1)

(a) The components of stockholders' equity.
(b) Shares outstanding.
(c) Par value per share.

BE14-4 For the year ending December 31, 2012, Vail Inc. reports net income $140,000 and dividends $85,000. Prepare the retained earnings statement for the year assuming the balance in retained earnings on January 1, 2012, was $220,000.

Prepare a retained earnings statement.
(SO 2)

BE14-5 The balance in retained earnings on January 1, 2012, for Thomas Inc, was $800,000. During the year, the corporation paid cash dividends of $90,000 and distributed a stock dividend of $8,000. In addition, the company determined that it had understated its depreciation expense in prior years by $50,000. Net income for 2012 was $120,000. Prepare the retained earnings statement for 2012.

Prepare a retained earnings statement.
(SO 2)

BE14-6 SUPERVALU, one of the largest grocery retailers in the United States, is head-quartered in Minneapolis. The following financial information (in millions) was taken from the

Calculate the return on common stockholders' equity.
(SO 3)

company's 2009 annual report. Net sales $40,597; net income $393; beginning stockholders' equity $2,581; ending stockholders' equity $2,887. Compute the return on common stockholders' equity ratio.

Compute return on common stockholders' equity.

(SO 3)

BE14-7   Stanley Corporation reported net income of $152,000, declared dividends on common stock of $50,000, and had an ending balance in retained earnings of $360,000. Stockholders' equity was $700,000 at the beginning of the year and $820,000 at the end of the year. Compute the return on common stockholders' equity.

Prepare a corporate income statement.

(SO 4)

BE14-8   The following information is available for Mildred Corporation for the year ended December 31, 2012: Cost of goods sold $205,000; Sales revenue $450,000; Other revenues and gains $50,000; and Operating expenses $75,000. Assuming a corporate tax rate of 30%, prepare an income statement for the company.

Compute earnings per share.

(SO 5)

BE14-9   Wegrzyn Corporation reports net income of $380,000 and a weighted-average of 200,000 shares of common stock outstanding for the year. Compute the earnings per share of common stock.

Compute earnings per share with cumulative preferred stock.

(SO 5)

BE14-10   Income and common stock data for Wegrzyn Corporation are presented in BE14-9. Assume also that Wegrzyn has cumulative preferred stock dividends for the current year of $20,000 that were declared and paid. Compute the earnings per share of common stock.

Do it! Review

Determine dividends paid to preferred and common stockholders.

(SO 1)

Do it! 14-1   Erik Corporation has 3,000 shares of 7%, $100 par value preferred stock outstanding at December 31, 2012. At December 31, 2012, the company declared a $105,000 cash dividend. Determine the dividend paid to preferred stockholders and common stockholders under each of the following scenarios.

1. The preferred stock is noncumulative, and the company has not missed any dividends in previous years.
2. The preferred stock is noncumulative, and the company did not pay a dividend in each of the two previous years.
3. The preferred stock is cumulative, and the company did not pay a dividend in each of the two previous years.

Determine effects of stock dividend and stock split.

(SO 1)

Do it! 14-2   Ekedahl Company has had 4 years of retained earnings. Due to this success, the market price of its 400,000 shares of $3 par value common stock has increased from $12 per share to $51. During this period, paid-in capital remained the same at $2,400,000. Retained earnings increased from $1,800,000 to $12,000,000. President E. Ofey is considering either a 15% stock dividend or a 2-for-1 stock split. He asks you to show the before-and-after effects of each option on (a) retained earnings and (b) total stockholders' equity.

Prepare a retained earnings statement.

(SO 2)

Do it! 14-3   Jason Corporation has retained earnings of $3,100,000 on January 1, 2012. During the year, Jason earned $1,200,000 of net income. It declared and paid a $150,000 cash dividend. In 2012, Jason recorded an adjustment of $110,000 due to the overstatement (from mathematical error) of 2011 depreciation expense. Prepare a retained earnings statement for 2012.

Compute return on stockholders' equity and EPS and discuss changes in each.

(SO 3, 5)

Do it! 14-4   On January 1, 2012, Raczynski Corporation purchased 1,000 shares of treasury stock. Other information regarding Raczynski Corporation is provided below.

	2011	2012
Net income	$200,000	$210,000
Dividends on preferred stock	$30,000	$30,000
Dividends on common stock	$20,000	$25,000
Weighted-average number of common shares outstanding	10,000	9,000
Common stockholders' equity beginning of year	$600,000	$750,000
Common stockholders' equity end of year	$750,000	$830,000

Compute (a) return on common stockholders' equity for each year and (b) earnings per share for each year, and (c) discuss the changes in each.

14-1 Nov 1 | Cash Dividends   80,000
                 Dividends Payable   80,000
               (to record declaration of cash dividend)

      Dec 31 | Dividends Payable   80000
                  Cash   80000

               (to record payment of cash dividend)

14-6   393 ÷ $\frac{2581 + 2887}{2}$ = 14.37 %

14-8   Mildred Corporation
                         Income Statement
                  For the year ended Dec 31, 2012

       Sales Revenue $450,000
       Cost of goods Sold   205,000
       Gross Profit   245,000
       Operating Expenses   75,000
       Income from operations   170,000
       Other Revenues + Gains   50,000
       Other Expenses + Losses   0
       Income before taxes   220000
       Income tax expense   66000
       Net Income   154000

14-9   380000 ÷ 200,000 = $1.90 EPS

Exercises

E14-1 On January 1, Chreesh Corporation had 95,000 shares of no-par common stock issued and outstanding. The stock has a stated value of $5 per share. During the year, the following occurred.

Apr. 1	Issued 25,000 additional shares of common stock for $17 per share.
June 15	Declared a cash dividend of $1 per share to stockholders of record on June 30.
July 10	Paid the $1 cash dividend.
Dec. 1	Issued 2,000 additional shares of common stock for $19 per share.
15	Declared a cash dividend on outstanding shares of $1.20 per share to stockholders of record on December 31.

Journalize cash dividends; indicate statement presentation.
(SO 1)

Instructions
(a) Prepare the entries, if any, on each of the three dividend dates.
(b) How are dividends and dividends payable reported in the financial statements prepared at December 31?

E14-2 Griseta Corporation was organized on January 1, 2011. During its first year, the corporation issued 2,000 shares of $50 par value preferred stock and 100,000 shares of $10 par value common stock. At December 31, the company declared the following cash dividends: 2011, $6,000; 2012, $12,000; and 2013, $28,000.

Allocate cash dividends to preferred and common stock.
(SO 1)

Instructions
(a) Show the allocation of dividends to each class of stock, assuming the preferred stock dividend is 7% and not cumulative.
(b) Show the allocation of dividends to each class of stock, assuming the preferred stock dividend is 8% and cumulative.
(c) Journalize the declaration of the cash dividend at December 31, 2013, under part (b).

E14-3 On January 1, 2012, Brittany Corporation had $1,000,000 of common stock outstanding that was issued at par. It also had retained earnings of $750,000. The company issued 40,000 shares of common stock at par on July 1 and earned net income of $400,000 for the year.

Journalize stock dividends.
(SO 1)

Instructions
Journalize the declaration of a 15% stock dividend on December 10, 2012, for the following independent assumptions.

1. Par value is $10, and market value is $18.
2. Par value is $5, and market value is $20.

E14-4 On October 31, the stockholders' equity section of Ennis Company consists of common stock $300,000 and retained earnings $900,000. Ennis is considering the following two courses of action: (1) declaring a 5% stock dividend on the 30,000, $10 par value shares outstanding, or (2) effecting a 2-for-1 stock split that will reduce par value to $5 per share. The current market price is $14 per share.

Compare effects of a stock dividend and a stock split.
(SO 1)

Instructions
Prepare a tabular summary of the effects of the alternative actions on the components of stockholders' equity, outstanding shares, and par value per share. Use the following column headings: Before Action, After Stock Dividend, and After Stock Split.

E14-5 On October 1, Little Tommy Corporation's stockholders' equity is as follows.

Indicate account balances after a stock dividend.
(SO 1, 3)

Common stock, $5 par value	$400,000
Paid-in capital in excess of par—common stock	25,000
Retained earnings	155,000
Total stockholders' equity	$580,000

On October 1, Little Tommy declares and distributes a 10% stock dividend when the market value of the stock is $15 per share.

Instructions
(a) Compute the par value per share (1) before the stock dividend and (2) after the stock dividend.
(b) Indicate the balances in the three stockholders' equity accounts after the stock dividend shares have been distributed.

*Indicate the effects on
stockholders' equity
components.*

(SO 1, 2, 3)

E14-6 During 2012, Margan Corporation had the following transactions and events.
1. Declared a cash dividend.
2. Issued par value common stock for cash at par value.
3. Completed a 2-for-1 stock split in which $10 par value stock was changed to $5 par value stock.
4. Declared a small stock dividend when the market value was higher than par value.
5. Made a prior period adjustment for overstatement of net income.
6. Issued the shares of common stock required by the stock dividend declaration in item no. 4 above.
7. Paid the cash dividend in item no. 1 above.
8. Issued par value common stock for cash above par value.

Instructions
Indicate the effect(s) of each of the foregoing items on the subdivisions of stockholders' equity. Present your answer in tabular form with the following columns. Use (I) for increase, (D) for decrease, and (NE) for no effect. Item no. 1 is given as an example.

	Paid-in Capital		
Item	**Capital Stock**	**Additional**	**Retained Earnings**
1	NE	NE	D

*Prepare correcting entries for
dividends and a stock split.*

(SO 1)

E14-7 Before preparing financial statements for the current year, the chief accountant for Paul Company discovered the following errors in the accounts.
1. The declaration and payment of $50,000 cash dividend was recorded as a debit to Interest Expense $50,000 and a credit to Cash $50,000.
2. A 10% stock dividend (1,000 shares) was declared on the $10 par value stock when the market value per share was $18. The only entry made was: Stock Dividends (Dr.) $10,000 and Dividend Payable (Cr.) $10,000. The shares have not been issued.
3. A 4-for-1 stock split involving the issue of 400,000 shares of $5 par value common stock for 100,000 shares of $20 par value common stock was recorded as a debit to Retained Earnings $2,000,000 and a credit to Common Stock $2,000,000.

Instructions
Prepare the correcting entries at December 31.

*Prepare a retained earnings
statement.*

(SO 2)

E14-8 On January 1, 2012, Barb Corporation had retained earnings of $550,000. During the year, Barb had the following selected transactions.
1. Declared cash dividends $120,000.
2. Corrected overstatement of 2011 net income because of depreciation error $40,000.
3. Earned net income $350,000.
4. Declared stock dividends $60,000.

Instructions
Prepare a retained earnings statement for the year.

*Prepare a retained earnings
statement.*

(SO 2)

E14-9 Jayleah Company reported retained earnings at December 31, 2011, of $310,000. Jayleah had 200,000 shares of common stock outstanding throughout 2012.
  The following transactions occurred during 2012.
1. An error was discovered: in 2010, depreciation expense was recorded at $70,000, but the correct amount was $50,000.
2. A cash dividend of $0.50 per share was declared and paid.
3. A 5% stock dividend was declared and distributed when the market price per share was $15 per share.
4. Net income was $285,000.

Instructions
Prepare a retained earnings statement for 2012.

*Prepare stockholders' equity
section.*

(SO 3)

E14-10 Beck Company reported the following balances at December 31, 2011: common stock $400,000; paid-in capital in excess of par value—common stock $100,000; and retained earnings $250,000. During 2012, the following transactions affected stockholder's equity.

1. Issued preferred stock with a par value of $125,000 for $200,000.
2. Purchased treasury stock (common) for $40,000.
3. Earned net income of $140,000.
4. Declared and paid cash dividends of $56,000.

Instructions
Prepare the stockholders' equity section of Beck Company's December 31, 2012, balance sheet.

E14-11 The following accounts appear in the ledger of Kallie Inc. after the books are closed at December 31.

Prepare a stockholders' equity section.
(SO 3)

Common Stock, no par, $1 stated value, 400,000 shares authorized;	
300,000 shares issued	$ 300,000
Common Stock Dividends Distributable	30,000
Paid-in Capital in Excess of Stated Value—Common Stock	1,200,000
Preferred Stock, $5 par value, 8%, 40,000 shares authorized;	
30,000 shares issued	150,000
Retained Earnings	800,000
Treasury Stock (10,000 common shares)	74,000
Paid-in Capital in Excess of Par—Preferred Stock	344,000

Instructions
Prepare the stockholders' equity section at December 31, assuming retained earnings is restricted for plant expansion in the amount of $100,000.

E14-12 The following information is available for Kelsey Corporation for the year ended December 31, 2012: Sales $800,000; Other revenues and gains $92,000; Operating expenses $110,000; Cost of goods sold $465,000; Other expenses and losses $32,000; Preferred stock dividends $30,000. The company's tax rate was 20%, and it had 50,000 shares outstanding during the entire year.

Prepare an income statement and compute earnings per share.
(SO 4, 5)

Instructions
(a) Prepare a corporate income statement.
(b) Calculate earnings per share.

E14-13 In 2012, Stone Pony Corporation had net sales of $600,000 and cost of goods sold of $360,000. Operating expenses were $153,000, and interest expense was $7,500. The corporation's tax rate is 30%. The corporation declared preferred dividends of $15,000 in 2012, and its average common stockholders' equity during the year was $200,000.

Prepare an income statement and compute return on equity.
(SO 3, 4)

Instructions
(a) Prepare an income statement for Stone Pony Corporation.
(b) Compute Stone Pony Corporation's return on common stockholders' equity for 2012.

E14-14 Nikennis Corporation has outstanding at December 31, 2012, 50,000 shares of $20 par value, cumulative, 8% preferred stock and 200,000 shares of $5 par value common stock. All shares were outstanding the entire year. During 2012, Nikennis earned total revenues of $2,000,000 and incurred total expenses (except income taxes) of $1,200,000. Nikennis's income tax rate is 30%.

Compute EPS.
(SO 4, 5)

Instructions
Compute Nikennis's 2012 earnings per share.

E14-15 The following financial information is available for Monique Corporation.

Calculate ratios to evaluate earnings performance.
(SO 3, 5)

	2012	2011
Average common stockholders' equity	$1,200,000	$900,000
Dividends paid to common stockholders	50,000	30,000
Dividends paid to preferred stockholders	20,000	20,000
Net income	290,000	200,000
Market price of common stock	20	15

The weighted-average number of shares of common stock outstanding was 80,000 for 2011 and 100,000 for 2012.

Instructions

Calculate earnings per share and return on common stockholders' equity for 2012 and 2011.

Calculate ratios to evaluate earnings performance.

(SO 3, 5)

E14-16 This financial information is available for Hoyle Corporation.

	2012	**2011**
Average common stockholders' equity	$1,800,000	$1,900,000
Dividends paid to common stockholders	90,000	70,000
Dividends paid to preferred stockholders	20,000	20,000
Net income	290,000	248,000
Market price of common stock	20	25

The weighted-average number of shares of common stock outstanding was 180,000 for 2011 and 150,000 for 2012.

Instructions

Calculate earnings per share and return on common stockholders' equity for 2012 and 2011.

Compute earnings per share under different assumptions.

(SO 5)

E14-17 At December 31, 2012, Jennyfer Corporation has 2,000 shares of $100 par value, 8%, preferred stock outstanding and 100,000 shares of $10 par value common stock issued. Jennyfer's net income for the year is $241,000.

Instructions

Compute the earnings per share of common stock under the following independent situations. (Round to two decimals.)

(a) The dividend to preferred stockholders was declared. There has been no change in the number of shares of common stock outstanding during the year.

(b) The dividend to preferred stockholders was not declared. The preferred stock is cumulative. Jennyfer held 10,000 shares of common treasury stock throughout the year.

Exercises: Set B

Visit the book's companion website, at **www.wiley.com/college/weygandt**, and choose the Student Companion site to access Exercise Set B.

Problems: Set A

Prepare dividend entries and stockholders' equity section.

(SO 1, 3)

GLS

P14-1A On January 1, 2012, Kristen Corporation had the following stockholders' equity accounts.

Common Stock ($20 par value, 60,000 shares issued and outstanding)	$1,200,000
Paid-in Capital in Excess of Par—Common Stock	200,000
Retained Earnings	600,000

During the year, the following transactions occurred.

Feb. 1 Declared a $1 cash dividend per share to stockholders of record on February 15, payable March 1.

Mar. 1 Paid the dividend declared in February.

Apr. 1 Announced a 2-for-1 stock split. Prior to the split, the market price per share was $36.

July 1 Declared a 10% stock dividend to stockholders of record on July 15, distributable July 31. On July 1, the market price of the stock was $13 per share.

31 Issued the shares for the stock dividend.

Dec. 1 Declared a $0.50 per share dividend to stockholders of record on December 15, payable January 5, 2013.

31 Determined that net income for the year was $350,000.

Instructions

(a) Journalize the transactions and the closing entry for net income.

(b) Enter the beginning balances, and post the entries to the stockholders' equity accounts. (*Note:* Open additional stockholders' equity accounts as needed.)

(c) Total stockholders' equity
$2,224,000

(c) Prepare a stockholders' equity section at December 31.

P14-2A   The stockholders' equity accounts of Falk Company at January 1, 2012, are as follows.

Preferred Stock, 6%, $50 par	$600,000
Common Stock, $5 par	800,000
Paid-in Capital in Excess of Par—Preferred Stock	200,000
Paid-in Capital in Excess of Par—Common Stock	300,000
Retained Earnings	800,000

Journalize and post transactions; prepare retained earnings statement and stockholders' equity section.

(SO 1, 2, 3)

There were no dividends in arrears on preferred stock. During 2012, the company had the following transactions and events.

July	1	Declared a $0.50 cash dividend on common stock.
Aug.	1	Discovered $25,000 understatement of 2011 depreciation on equipment. Ignore income taxes.
Sept.	1	Paid the cash dividend declared on July 1.
Dec.	1	Declared a 10% stock dividend on common stock when the market value of the stock was $18 per share.
	15	Declared a 6% cash dividend on preferred stock payable January 15, 2013.
	31	Determined that net income for the year was $355,000.
	31	Recognized a $200,000 restriction of retained earnings for plant expansion.

Instructions
(a) Journalize the transactions, events, and closing entry.
(b) Enter the beginning balances in the accounts, and post to the stockholders' equity accounts. (*Note:* Open additional stockholders' equity accounts as needed.)
(c) Prepare a retained earnings statement for the year.
(d) Prepare a stockholders' equity section at December 31, 2012.

(c) Ending balance $726,000
(d) Total stockholders' equity $2,914,000

P14-3A   The post-closing trial balance of Violet Corporation at December 31, 2012, contains the following stockholders' equity accounts.

Preferred Stock (15,000 shares issued)	$ 750,000
Common Stock (250,000 shares issued)	2,500,000
Paid-in Capital in Excess of Par—Preferred Stock	250,000
Paid-in Capital in Excess of Par—Common Stock	400,000
Common Stock Dividends Distributable	250,000
Retained Earnings	1,042,000

Prepare retained earnings statement and stockholders' equity section, and compute earnings per share.

(SO 1, 2, 3, 5)

A review of the accounting records reveals the following.

1. No errors have been made in recording 2012 transactions or in preparing the closing entry for net income.
2. Preferred stock is $50 par, 6%, and cumulative; 15,000 shares have been outstanding since January 1, 2011.
3. Authorized stock is 20,000 shares of preferred, 500,000 shares of common with a $10 par value.
4. The January 1 balance in Retained Earnings was $1,170,000.
5. On July 1, 20,000 shares of common stock were issued for cash at $16 per share.
6. On September 1, the company discovered an understatement error of $90,000 in computing depreciation in 2011. The net of tax effect of $63,000 was properly debited directly to Retained Earnings.
7. A cash dividend of $250,000 was declared and properly allocated to preferred and common stock on October 1. No dividends were paid to preferred stockholders in 2011.
8. On December 31, a 10% common stock dividend was declared out of retained earnings on common stock when the market price per share was $16.
9. Net income for the year was $585,000.
10. On December 31, 2012, the directors authorized disclosure of a $200,000 restriction of retained earnings for plant expansion. (Use Note X.)

Instructions
(a) Reproduce the Retained Earnings account for 2012.
(b) Prepare a retained earnings statement for 2012.
(c) Prepare a stockholders' equity section at December 31, 2012.
(d) Compute the allocation of the cash dividend to preferred and common stock.
(e) Compute the earnings per share of common stock using 240,000 as the weighted-average shares outstanding for the year.

(c) Total stockholders' equity, $5,192,000

Prepare the stockholders' equity section, reflecting dividends and stock split.

(SO 1, 2, 3)

P14-4A On January 1, 2012, Saa Corporation had the following stockholders' equity accounts.

Common Stock (no par value, 90,000 shares issued and outstanding)	$1,400,000
Retained Earnings	500,000

During the year, the following transactions occurred.

Feb.	1	Declared a $1 cash dividend per share to stockholders of record on February 15, payable March 1.
Mar.	1	Paid the dividend declared in February.
Apr.	1	Announced a 4-for-1 stock split. Prior to the split, the market price per share was $36.
July	1	Declared a 5% stock dividend to stockholders of record on July 15, distributable July 31. On July 1, the market price of the stock was $13 per share.
	31	Issued the shares for the stock dividend.
Dec.	1	Declared a $0.50 per share dividend to stockholders of record on December 15, payable January 5, 2013.
	31	Determined that net income for the year was $350,000.

Instructions

(d) Total stockholders' equity $1,971,000

Prepare the stockholders' equity section of the balance sheet at: (a) March 31, (b) June 30, (c) September 30, and (d) December 31, 2012.

Prepare the stockholders' equity section, reflecting various events.

(SO 1, 3)

P14-5A On January 1, 2012, Hammermeister Inc. had the following stockholders' equity account balances.

Common Stock, no-par value (500,000 shares issued)	$1,500,000
Common Stock Dividends Distributable	200,000
Retained Earnings	600,000

During 2012, the following transactions and events occurred.

1. Issued 50,000 shares of common stock as a result of a 10% stock dividend declared on December 15, 2009.
2. Issued 30,000 shares of common stock for cash at $6 per share.
3. Corrected an error that had understated the net income for 2010 by $70,000.
4. Declared and paid a cash dividend of $80,000.
5. Earned net income of $300,000.

Total stockholders' equity $2,770,000

Instructions
Prepare the stockholders' equity section of the balance sheet at December 31, 2012.

Problems: Set B

Prepare dividend entries and stockholders' equity section.

(SO 1, 3)

P14-1B On January 1, 2012, Syed Corporation had the following stockholders' equity accounts.

Common Stock ($5 par value, 200,000 shares issued and outstanding)	$1,000,000
Paid-in Capital in Excess of Par—Common Stock	200,000
Retained Earnings	840,000

During the year, the following transactions occurred.

Jan.	15	Declared a $1 cash dividend per share to stockholders of record on January 31, payable February 15.
Feb.	15	Paid the dividend declared in January.
Apr.	15	Declared a 10% stock dividend to stockholders of record on April 30, distributable May 15. On April 15, the market price of the stock was $15 per share.
May	15	Issued the shares for the stock dividend.
July	1	Announced a 2-for-1 stock split. The market price per share prior to the announcement was $17. (The new par value is $2.50.)
Dec.	1	Declared a $0.50 per share cash dividend to stockholders of record on December 15, payable January 10, 2013.
	31	Determined that net income for the year was $250,000.

Instructions
(a) Journalize the transactions and the closing entry for net income.
(b) Enter the beginning balances, and post the entries to the stockholders' equity accounts. (*Note:* Open additional stockholders' equity accounts as needed.)
(c) Prepare a stockholders' equity section at December 31.

(c) Total stockholders' equity
   $1,870,000

P14-2B   The stockholders' equity accounts of Motz Inc., at January 1, 2012, are as follows.

Journalize and post transactions; prepare retained earnings statement and stockholders' equity section.

(SO 1, 2, 3)

Preferred Stock, $100 par, 7%	$600,000
Common Stock, $10 par	900,000
Paid-in Capital in Excess of Par—Preferred Stock	100,000
Paid-in Capital in Excess of Par—Common Stock	200,000
Retained Earnings	500,000

There were no dividends in arrears on preferred stock. During 2012, the company had the following transactions and events.

July	1	Declared a $0.50 cash dividend on common stock.
Aug.	1	Discovered a $72,000 overstatement of 2011 depreciation on equipment. Ignore income taxes.
Sept.	1	Paid the cash dividend declared on July 1.
Dec.	1	Declared a 10% stock dividend on common stock when the market value of the stock was $16 per share.
	15	Declared a 7% cash dividend on preferred stock payable January 31, 2013.
	31	Determined that net income for the year was $350,000.

Instructions
(a) Journalize the transactions and the closing entry for net income.
(b) Enter the beginning balances in the accounts and post to the stockholders' equity accounts. (*Note:* Open additional stockholders' equity accounts as needed.)
(c) Prepare a retained earnings statement for the year.
(d) Prepare a stockholders' equity section at December 31, 2012.

(c) Ending balance $691,000
(d) Total stockholders' equity
   $2,635,000

P14-3B   The ledger of Conway Corporation at December 31, 2012, after the books have been closed, contains the following stockholders' equity accounts.

Prepare retained earnings statement and stockholders' equity section, and compute earnings per share.

(SO 1, 2, 3, 5)

Preferred Stock (10,000 shares issued)	$1,000,000
Common Stock (400,000 shares issued)	2,000,000
Paid-in Capital in Excess of Par—Preferred Stock	200,000
Paid-in Capital in Excess of Stated—Common Stock	1,180,000
Common Stock Dividends Distributable	200,000
Retained Earnings	2,560,000

A review of the accounting records reveals the following.

1. No errors have been made in recording 2012 transactions or in preparing the closing entry for net income.
2. Preferred stock is 6%, $100 par value, noncumulative, and callable at $125. Since January 1, 2011, 10,000 shares have been outstanding; 20,000 shares are authorized.
3. Common stock is no-par with a stated value of $5 per share; 600,000 shares are authorized.
4. The January 1 balance in Retained Earnings was $2,450,000.
5. On October 1, 100,000 shares of common stock were sold for cash at $8 per share.
6. A cash dividend of $500,000 was declared and properly allocated to preferred and common stock on November 1. No dividends were paid to preferred stockholders in 2011.
7. On December 31, a 10% common stock dividend was declared out of retained earnings on common stock when the market price per share was $9.
8. Net income for the year was $970,000.
9. On December 31, 2012, the directors authorized disclosure of a $100,000 restriction of retained earnings for plant expansion. (Use Note A.)

Instructions
(a) Reproduce the Retained Earnings account (T account) for 2012.
(b) Prepare a retained earnings statement for 2012.

(c) Total stockholders' equity:
$7,140,000

(c) Prepare a stockholders' equity section at December 31, 2012.
(d) Compute the allocation of the cash dividend to preferred and common stock.
(e) Compute the earnings per share of common stock using 325,000 as the weighted-average shares outstanding for the year.

Prepare the stockholders' equity section, reflecting dividends and stock split.

(SO 1, 2, 3)

P14-4B On January 1, 2012, Acierno Corporation had the following stockholders' equity accounts.

Common Stock (no-par value, 100,000 shares issued and outstanding)	$2,800,000
Retained Earnings	1,000,000

During the year, the following transactions occurred.

Feb. 1 Declared a $1 cash dividend per share to stockholders of record on February 15, payable March 1.

Mar. 1 Paid the dividend declared in February.

Apr. 1 Announced a 4-for-1 stock split. Prior to the split, the market price per share was $36.

July 1 Declared a 5% stock dividend to stockholders of record on July 15, distributable July 31. On July 1, the market price of the stock was $13 per share.

31 Issued the shares for the stock dividend.

Dec. 1 Declared a $0.50 per share dividend to stockholders of record on December 15, payable January 5, 2013.

31 Determined that net income for the year was $700,000.

Instructions

(d) Total, stockholders' equity
$4,190,000

Prepare the stockholders' equity section of the balance sheet at: (a) March 31, (b) June 30, (c) September 30, and (d) December 31, 2012.

Prepare the stockholders' equity section, reflecting various events.

(SO 1, 3)

P14-5B On January 1, 2012, Beacham Inc. had the following shareholders' equity balances.

Common Stock, no-par value (1,000,000 shares issued)	$3,000,000
Common Stock Dividends Distributable	400,000
Retained Earnings	1,200,000

During 2012, the following transactions and events occurred.

1. Issued 100,000 shares of common stock as a result of a 10% stock dividend declared on December 15, 2011.

2. Issued 60,000 shares of common stock for cash at $5 per share.

3. Corrected an error that had understated the net income for 2010 by $140,000.

4. Declared and paid a cash dividend of $300,000.

5. Earned net income of $600,000.

Total stockholders' equity
$5,340,000

Instructions

Prepare the stockholders' equity section of the balance sheet at December 31, 2012.

Problems: Set C

Visit the book's companion website, at **www.wiley.com/college/weygandt**, and choose the Student Companion site to access Problem Set C.

Continuing Cookie Chronicle

(*Note:* This is a continuation of the Cookie Chronicle from Chapters 1 through 13.)

CCC14 After establishing their company's fiscal year-end to be October 31, Natalie and Curtis began operating Cookie & Coffee Creations Inc. on November 1, 2012. On that date, they issued both preferred and common stock. After the first year of operations, Natalie and Curtis want to prepare financial information for the year.

Go to the book's companion website, **www.wiley.com/college/weygandt**, *to see the completion of this problem.*

BROADENING YOUR PERSPECTIVE

Financial Reporting and Analysis

Financial Reporting Problem: PepsiCo, Inc.

BYP14-1   The financial statements of PepsiCo, Inc. are presented in Appendix A.

Instructions
Refer to PepsiCo's financial statements and answer the following questions.
(a) What amount did PepsiCo declare in dividends on common stock in the year ended December 26, 2009?
(b) How does this amount compare with dividends declared on common stock in the year ended December 27, 2008?

Comparative Analysis Problem: PepsiCo, Inc. vs. The Coca-Cola Company

BYP14-2   PepsiCo's financial statements are presented in Appendix A. Financial statements of The Coca-Cola Company are presented in Appendix B.

Instructions
(a) Compute earnings per share and return on common stockholders' equity for both companies for 2009. Assume PepsiCo's weighted-average shares were 1,560 million and Coca-Cola's weighted-average shares were 2,314 million. Can these measures be used to compare the profitability of the two companies? Why or why not?
(b) What was the total amount of dividends paid by each company in 2009?

On the Web

BYP14-3   Use the stockholders' equity section of an annual report and identify the major components.

Address: www.reportgallery.com, or go to **www.wiley.com/college/weygandt**

Steps
1. From Report Gallery Homepage, choose **Search by Alphabet**, and choose a letter.
2. Select a particular company.
3. Choose Annual Report.
4. Follow instructions below.

Instructions
Answer the following questions.
(a) What is the company's name?
(b) What classes of capital stock has the company issued?
(c) For each class of stock:
   (1) How many shares are authorized, issued, and/or outstanding?
   (2) What is the par value?
(d) What are the company's retained earnings?
(e) Has the company acquired treasury stock? How many shares?

Critical Thinking

Decision Making Across the Organization

BYP14-4   The stockholders' equity accounts of Fernandez, Inc., at January 1, 2012, are as follows.

Preferred Stock, no par, 4,000 shares issued	$400,000
Common Stock, no par, 140,000 shares issued	700,000
Retained Earnings	500,000

During 2012, the company had the following transactions and events.

July   1   Declared a $0.50 cash dividend on common stock.
Aug.   1   Discovered a $72,000 overstatement of 2011 depreciation expense. (Ignore income taxes.)
Sept. 1   Paid the cash dividend declared on July 1.
Dec.   1   Declared a 10% stock dividend on common stock when the market value of the stock was $12 per share.
        15   Declared a $9 per share cash dividend on preferred stock, payable January 31, 2013.
        31   Determined that net income for the year was $320,000.

Instructions
With the class divided into groups, answer the following questions.

(a) Prepare a retained earnings statement for the year. There are no preferred dividends in arrears.
(b) Discuss why the overstatement of 2011 depreciation expense is not treated as an adjustment of the current year's income.
(c) Discuss the reasons why a company might decide to issue a stock dividend rather than a cash dividend.

Communication Activity

BYP14-5   In the past year, Cormier Corporation declared a 10% stock dividend, and Fegan, Inc. announced a 2-for-1 stock split. Your parents own 100 shares of each company's $50 par value common stock. During a recent phone call, your parents ask you, as an accounting student, to explain the differences between the two events.

Instructions
Write a letter to your parents that explains the effects of the two events to them as stockholders and the effects of each event on the financial statements of each corporation.

Ethics Case

BYP14-6   Garcia Corporation has paid 60 consecutive quarterly cash dividends (15 years). The last 6 months, however, have been a cash drain on the company, as profit margins have been greatly narrowed by increasing competition. With a cash balance sufficient to meet only day-to-day operating needs, the president, Tom Henson, has decided that a stock dividend instead of a cash dividend should be declared. He tells Garcia's financial vice president, Andrea Lane, to issue a press release stating that the company is extending its consecutive dividend record with the issuance of a 5% stock dividend. "Write the press release convincing the stockholders that the stock dividend is just as good as a cash dividend," he orders. "Just watch our stock rise when we announce the stock dividend; it must be a good thing if that happens."

Instructions
(a) Who are the stakeholders in this situation?
(b) Is there anything unethical about Henson's intentions or actions?
(c) What is the effect of a stock dividend on a corporation's stockholders' equity accounts? Which would you rather receive as a stockholder—a cash dividend or a stock dividend? Why?

"All About You" Activity

BYP14-7   In the **All About You** feature (available at the book's companion website), you learned that in response to the Sarbanes-Oxley Act, many companies have implemented formal ethics codes. Many other organizations also have ethics codes.

Instructions
Obtain the ethics code from an organization that you belong to (e.g., student organization, business school, employer, or a volunteer organization). Evaluate the ethics code based on how clearly it identifies proper and improper behavior. Discuss its strengths, and how it might be improved.

FASB Codification Activity

BYP14-8   If your school has a subscription to the FASB Codification, go to *http://aaahq.org/ascLogin.cfm* to log in and prepare responses to the following.
(a) What is the stock dividend?
(b) What is a stock split?
(c) At what percentage point does the issuance of additional shares qualify as a stock dividend, as opposed to a stock split?

Answers to Insight and Accounting Across the Organization Questions

p. 637 Up, Down, and ?? **Q:** What factors must management consider in deciding how large a dividend to pay? **A:** Management must consider the size of the company's retained earnings balance, the amount of available cash, the company's expected near-term cash needs, the company's growth opportunities, and what level of dividend the company will be able to sustain based upon its expected future earnings.

p. 641 A No-Split Philosophy **Q:** Why does Warren Buffett usually oppose stock splits? **A:** Mr. Buffett prefers to attract shareholders that make a long-term commitment to his company, as opposed to traders that only hold their investment for a short period of time. He believes that a high stock price discourages short-term investment.

Answers to Self-Test Questions

1. a **2.** c **3.** c **4.** a $\$80,000 - [(3,000 \times 7\% \times \$100) \times 2]$ **5.** d $(100,000 \times 10\% \times \$30)$ **6.** d **7.** c
8. b **9.** d **10.** b $\$186,000 - (6\% \times \$100 \times 10,000) = \$126,000; (\$1,200,000 + \$1,600,000) \div 2 = \$1,400,000; (\$126,000 \div \$1,400,000)$ **11.** b **12.** d $(\$176,000 - \$66,000 - \$20,000) \times 30\%$ **13.** c
14. d **15.** b $(\$490,000 \div 100,000)$

IFRS A Look at IFRS

The basic accounting for cash and stock dividends is essentially the same under both GAAP and IFRS. IFRS terminology is something different, but the recording of the transaction is the same.

Key Points

- The term *reserves* is used in IFRS to indicate all non–contributed (non–paid-in) capital. Reserves include retained earnings and other comprehensive income items, such as revaluation surplus and unrealized gains or losses on available-for sale securities.

- IFRS often uses terms such as *retained profits* or *accumulated profit or loss* to describe retained earnings. The term *retained earnings* is also often used.

- The accounting related to prior period adjustment is essentially the same under IFRS and GAAP. IFRS addresses the accounting for errors in *IAS 8* ("Accounting Policies, Changes in Accounting Estimates, and Errors"). One area where IFRS and GAAP differ in reporting relates to error corrections in previously issued financial statements. While IFRS requires restatement with some exceptions, GAAP does not permit any exceptions.

- The stockholders' equity section is essentially the same under IFRS and GAAP. However, terminology used to describe certain components is often different. These differences are discussed in Chapter 13.

- Equity is given various descriptions under IFRS, such as shareholder's equity, owners' equity, capital and reserves, and shareholders' funds.

- The income statement using IFRS is called the *statement of comprehensive income.* A statement of comprehensive income is presented in a one- or two-statement format. The single-statement approach includes all items of income and expense, as well as each component of other comprehensive income or loss by its individual characteristic. In the two-statement approach, a traditional income statement is prepared. It is then followed by a statement of comprehensive income, which starts with net income or loss and then adds other comprehensive income or loss items. Regardless of which approach is reported, income tax expense is required to be reported.

- The computations related to earnings per share are essentially the same under IFRS and GAAP.

Looking to the Future

The IASB and the FASB are currently working on a project related to financial statement presentation. An important part of this study is to determine whether certain line items, subtotals, and totals should be clearly defined and required to be displayed in the financial statements. For example, it is likely that the statement of stockholders' equity and its presentation will be examined closely.

Both the IASB and FASB are working toward a convergence of any remaining differences related to earnings per share computations. This convergence will deal with highly technical changes beyond the scope of this textbook.

IFRS Self-Test Questions

1. The basic accounting for cash dividends and stock dividends:
   a. is different under IFRS versus GAAP.
   b. is the same under IFRS and GAAP.
   c. differs only for the accounting for cash dividends between GAAP and IFRS.
   d. differs only for the accounting for stock dividends between GAAP and IFRS.

2. Which item in *not* considered part of reserves?
   a. Unrealized loss on available-for-sale investments.
   b. Revaluation surplus.
   c. Retained earnings.
   d. Issued shares.

3. Under IFRS, a statement of comprehensive income must include:
   a. accounts payable.
   b. retained earnings.
   c. income tax expense.
   d. preference stock.

4. Which set of terms can be used to describe total stockholders' equity under IFRS?
   a. Shareholders' equity, capital and reserves, other comprehensive income.
   b. Capital and reserves, shareholders' equity, shareholders' funds.
   c. Capital and reserves, retained earnings, shareholders' equity.
   d. All of the above.

5. Earnings per share computations related to IFRS and GAAP:
   a. are essentially similar.
   b. result in an amount referred to as earnings per share.
   c. must deduct preferred (preference) dividends when computing earnings per share.
   d. All of the above.

IFRS Concepts and Application

International Financial Reporting Problem: Zetar plc

IFRS14-1 The financial statements of Zetar plc are presented in Appendix C. The company's complete annual report, including the notes to its financial statements, is available at *www.zetarplc.com*.

Instructions
Use the company's annual report to answer the following questions.

(a) Did the company declare and pay any dividends for the year ended April 30, 2009?
(b) Compute the company's return on ordinary shareholders' equity for the year ended April 30, 2009.
(c) What was Zetar's earnings per share for the year ended April 30, 2009?

Answers to IFRS Self-Test Questions
1. b **2.** d **3.** c **4.** b **5.** d

The Navigator

> ✔ **Remember to go back to the Navigator box on the chapter opening page and check off your completed work.**

CHAPTER15

Long-Term Liabilities

Study Objectives

After studying this chapter, you should be able to:

[1] Explain why bonds are issued.

[2] Prepare the entries for the issuance of bonds and interest expense.

[3] Describe the entries when bonds are redeemed or converted.

[4] Describe the accounting for long-term notes payable.

[5] Contrast the accounting for operating and capital leases.

[6] Identify the methods for the presentation and analysis of long-term liabilities.

✔ The Navigator

✔ [The Navigator]

● Scan Study Objectives	○
● Read Feature Story	○
● Read Preview	○
● Read text and answer **Do it!** p. 674 ○ p. 678 ○ p. 680 ○ p. 681 ○ p. 686 ○	
● Work Comprehensive **Do it!** p. 686	○
● Review Summary of Study Objectives	○
● Answer Self-Test Questions	○
● Complete Assignments	○
● Go to *WileyPLUS* for practice and tutorials	○
● Read A Look at IFRS p. 718	○

Feature Story

THANK GOODNESS FOR BANKRUPTCY

One piece of baggage America's first settlers carried with them from England was the belief that not repaying one's debts was a moral failure. As in England, the colonists' penalty for such wickedness was often prison.

The theory behind jailing debtors was that the threat of incarceration might persuade them to reveal hidden assets. Or their families might take pity and pay their ransom. But if the debtor was truly penniless, he could be sentenced to what amounted to life in prison. Unlike murderers, rapists, and thieves, the debtors were also responsible for paying their own upkeep, thus putting them even further into debt. . . .

The colonies gradually developed more forgiving laws on debt, recognizing that owing money could be the result of bad luck rather than evidence of fraud or indolence. "Crops fail, prices fall, ships sink, warehouses burn, owners die, partners steal, pirates pillage, wars ravage, and people simply make mistakes," wrote Bruce Mann in his 2002 book *Republic of Debtors*. "Failure was the down side of entrepreneurial risk. This made failure the potential common fate of all merchants." . . .

Colonial lawmakers began taking a more charitable view toward debtors, but they were likelier to excuse a rich defaulter than a poor one. . . . Indeed, when some large speculative financial schemes collapsed after the Revolutionary War, many wealthy men were suddenly bankrupt. One of them, Robert Morris, who had signed the Declaration of Independence and provided critical financing for the war, lost his fortune speculating on land. Sentenced to debtors' prison in Philadelphia, Morris rented the best room in the jail and outfitted it with a settee, writing desks, a bed, a trunk of clothes and other comforts of home.

However lavishly they could outfit their prison cells, though, rich and poor faced the same dim future. There was no way an insolvent could get a fresh start—the "holy grail of debt relief," as Mr. Mann put it. In prison or out, debtors were expected to repay every penny they owed their creditors, even if it took them the rest of their lives. . . .

Congress passed a bankruptcy law in 1800 but then repealed it three years later. Not until 1831 did New York abolish prison for most debtors; Pennsylvania kept its debtors' prisons open until 1842. . . .

Source: Excerpted from Cynthia Crossen, "Early Debtors Faced Jail at Own Expense Until All Was Repaid," *Wall Street Journal* (January 30, 2006), p. B1. By permission.

The Navigator

Inside CHAPTER 15

Preview of CHAPTER 15

As you can see from the Feature Story, having liabilities can be dangerous in difficult economic times. In this chapter we will explain the accounting for the major types of long-term liabilities reported on the balance sheet. Long-term liabilities are obligations that are expected to be paid after one year. These liabilities may be bonds, long-term notes, or lease obligations.

The content and organization of Chapter 15 are as follows.

Long-Term Liabilities				
Bond Basics	**Bond Issuances**	**Bond Retirements**	**Other Long-Term Liabilities**	**Statement Presentation and Analysis**
• Types of bonds • Issuing procedures • Market value	• Issuing bonds at face value • Discount or premium • Issuing bonds at a discount • Issuing bonds at a premium	• Redeeming bonds at maturity • Redeeming bonds before maturity • Converting bonds into common stock	• Long-term notes payable • Lease liabilities	• Presentation • Analysis

The Navigator

Bond Basics

Study Objective [1]
Explain why bonds are issued.

Bonds are a form of interest-bearing notes payable. To obtain **large amounts of long-term capital**, corporate management usually must decide whether to issue common stock (equity financing) or bonds. Bonds offer three advantages over common stock, as shown in Illustration 15-1.

Illustration 15-1
Advantages of bond financing over common stock

Bond Financing	Advantages
[Ballot Box]	1. **Stockholder control is not affected.** Bondholders do not have voting rights, so current owners (stockholders) retain full control of the company.
[Tax Bill]	2. **Tax savings result.** Bond interest is deductible for tax purposes; dividends on stock are not.
[$ / Stock]	3. **Earnings per share may be higher.** Although bond interest expense reduces net income, earnings per share on common stock often is higher under bond financing because no additional shares of common stock are issued.

As the illustration shows, one reason to issue bonds is that they do not affect stockholder control. Because bondholders do not have voting rights, owners can raise capital with bonds and still maintain corporate control. In addition, bonds are attractive to corporations because the cost of bond interest is tax-deductible.

As a result of this tax treatment, which stock dividends do not offer, bonds may result in lower cost of capital than equity financing.

To illustrate the third advantage, on earnings per share, assume that Microsystems, Inc. is considering two plans for financing the construction of a new $5 million plant. Plan A involves issuance of 200,000 shares of common stock at the current market price of $25 per share. Plan B involves issuance of $5 million, 8% bonds at face value. Income before interest and taxes on the new plant will be $1.5 million. Income taxes are expected to be 30%. Microsystems currently has 100,000 shares of common stock outstanding. Illustration 15-2 shows the alternative effects on earnings per share.

	Plan A Issue Stock	Plan B Issue Bonds
Income before interest and taxes	$1,500,000	$1,500,000
Interest (8% × $5,000,000)	—	400,000
Income before income taxes	1,500,000	1,100,000
Income tax expense (30%)	450,000	330,000
Net income	$1,050,000	$ 770,000
Outstanding shares	300,000	100,000
Earnings per share	$3.50	$7.70

Illustration 15-2
Effects on earnings per share—stocks vs. bonds

Note that net income is $280,000 less ($1,050,000 − $770,000) with long-term debt financing (bonds). However, earnings per share is higher because there are 200,000 fewer shares of common stock outstanding.

One disadvantage in using bonds is that the company must **pay interest** on a periodic basis. In addition, the company must also **repay the principal** at the due date. A company with fluctuating earnings and a relatively weak cash position may have great difficulty making interest payments when earnings are low.

A corporation may also obtain long-term financing from notes payable and leasing. However, notes payable and leasing are seldom sufficient to furnish the amount of funds needed for plant expansion and major projects like new buildings.

Bonds are sold in relatively small denominations (usually $1,000 multiples). As a result of their size, and the variety of their features, bonds attract many investors.

Helpful Hint

Besides corporations, governmental agencies and universities also issue bonds to raise capital.

Types of Bonds

Bonds may have many different features. In the following sections, we describe the types of bonds commonly issued.

SECURED AND UNSECURED BONDS

Secured bonds have specific assets of the issuer pledged as collateral for the bonds. A bond secured by real estate, for example, is called a mortgage bond. A bond secured by specific assets set aside to retire the bonds is called a sinking fund bond.

Unsecured bonds, also called debenture bonds, are issued against the general credit of the borrower. Companies with good credit ratings use these bonds extensively. For example, at one time, DuPont reported over $2 billion of debenture bonds outstanding.

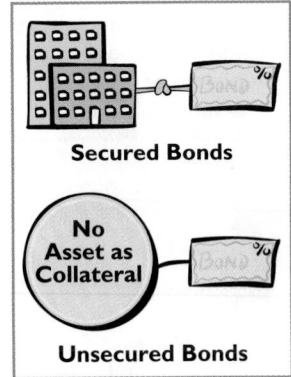

Secured Bonds

No Asset as Collateral

Unsecured Bonds

TERM AND SERIAL BONDS

Bonds that mature—are due for payment—at a single specified future date are **term bonds**. In contrast, bonds that mature in installments are **serial bonds**.

REGISTERED AND BEARER BONDS

Bonds issued in the name of the owner are **registered bonds**. Interest payments on registered bonds are made by check to bondholders of record. Bonds not registered are **bearer** (or **coupon**) **bonds**. Holders of bearer bonds must send in coupons to receive interest payments. Most bonds issued today are registered bonds.

CONVERTIBLE AND CALLABLE BONDS

Convertible Bonds

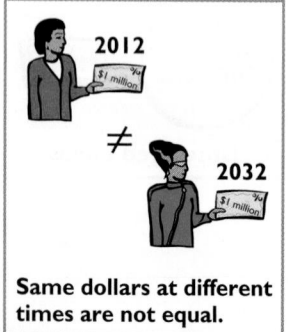

Callable Bonds

Bonds that can be converted into common stock at the bondholder's option are **convertible bonds**. The conversion feature generally is attractive to bond buyers. Bonds that the issuing company can retire at a stated dollar amount prior to maturity are **callable bonds**. A call feature is included in nearly all corporate bond issues.

Issuing Procedures

State laws grant corporations the power to issue bonds. Both the board of directors and stockholders usually must approve bond issues. **In authorizing the bond issue, the board of directors must stipulate the number of bonds to be authorized, total face value, and contractual interest rate**. The total bond authorization often exceeds the number of bonds the company originally issues. This gives the corporation the flexibility to issue more bonds, if needed, to meet future cash requirements.

The **face value** is the amount of principal the issuing company must pay at the maturity date. The **maturity date** is the date that the final payment is due to the investor from the issuing company. The **contractual interest rate**, often referred to as the **stated rate**, is the rate used to determine the amount of cash interest the borrower pays and the investor receives. Usually the contractual rate is stated as an annual rate. Interest is generally paid semiannually.

Ethics Note

Some companies try to minimize the amount of debt reported on their balance sheet by not reporting certain types of commitments as liabilities. This subject is of intense interest in the financial community.

The terms of the bond issue are set forth in a legal document called a **bond indenture**. The indenture shows the terms and summarizes the rights of the bondholders and their trustees, and the obligations of the issuing company. The **trustee** (usually a financial institution) keeps records of each bondholder, maintains custody of unissued bonds, and holds conditional title to pledged property.

In addition, the issuing company arranges for the printing of **bond certificates**. The indenture and the certificate are separate documents. As shown in Illustration 15-3, a bond certificate provides the following information: name of the issuer, face value, contractual interest rate, and maturity date. An investment company that specializes in selling securities generally sells the bonds for the issuing company.

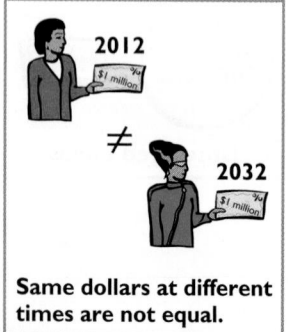

2012

≠

2032

Same dollars at different times are not equal.

Determining the Market Value of Bonds

If you were an investor wanting to purchase a bond, how would you determine how much to pay? To be more specific, assume that Coronet, Inc. issues a **zero-interest bond** (pays no interest) with a face value of $1,000,000 due in 20 years. For this bond, the only cash you receive is a million dollars at the end of 20 years. Would you pay a million dollars for this bond? We hope not! A million dollars received 20 years from now is not the same as a million dollars received today.

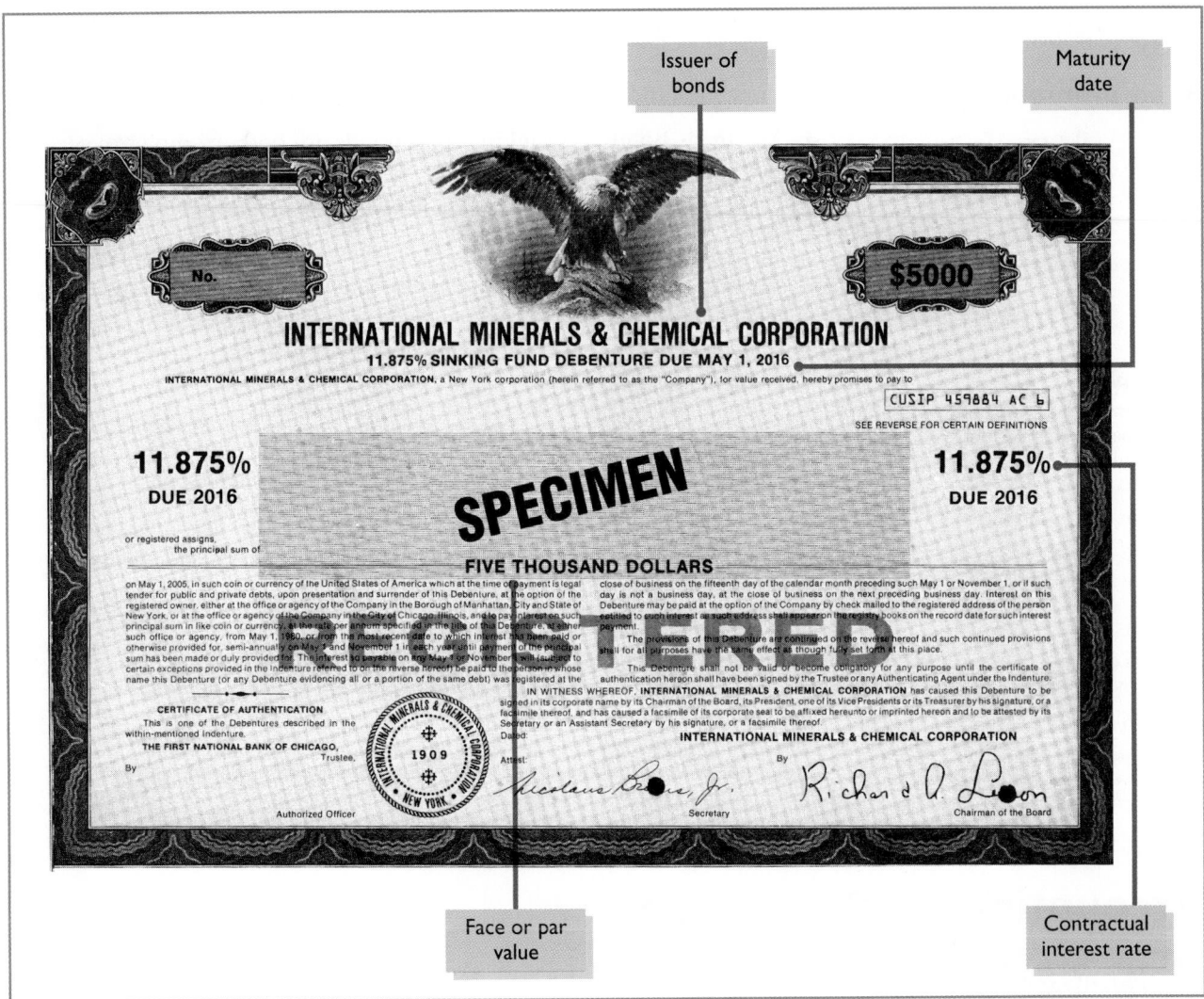

Illustration 15-3
Bond certificate

The term **time value of money** is used to indicate the relationship between time and money—that a dollar received today is worth more than a dollar promised at some time in the future. If you had a million dollars today, you would invest it. From that investment, you would earn interest such that at the end of 20 years, you would have much more than a million dollars. If someone is going to pay you a million dollars 20 years from now, you would want to find its equivalent today, in other words, you would want to determine how much you must invest today at current interest rates to have a million dollars in 20 years. The amount that must be invested today at a given rate of interest over a specified time is called **present value**.

The present value of a bond is the value at which it should sell in the marketplace. Market value therefore is a function of the three factors that determine present value: (1) the dollar amounts to be received, (2) the length of time until the amounts are received, and (3) the market rate of interest. The **market interest rate** is the rate investors demand for loaning funds. Appendix 15A discusses the process of finding the present value for bonds. Appendix C near the end of the book also provides additional material for time value of money computations.

Do it!

Bond Terminology

State whether each of the following statements is true or false.

_____ **1.** Mortgage bonds and sinking fund bonds are both examples of secured bonds.

_____ **2.** Unsecured bonds are also known as debenture bonds.

_____ **3.** The stated rate is the rate investors demand for loaning funds.

_____ **4.** The face value is the amount of principal the issuing company must pay at the maturity date.

_____ **5.** The bond issuer must make journal entries to record transfers of its bonds among investors.

action plan

✔ Review the types of bonds and the basic terms associated with bonds.

Solution

1. True.

2. True.

3. False.   The stated rate is the contractual interest rate used to determine the amount of cash interest the borrower pays.

4. True.

5. False.   The bond issuer makes journal entries only when it issues or buys back bonds, when it records interest, and when bonds are converted.

Related exercise material: BE15-1, E15-1, E15-2, and **Do it!** 15-1.

The Navigator

Accounting for Bond Issues

Study Objective [2]
Prepare the entries for the issuance of bonds and interest expense.

A corporation records bond transactions when it issues (sells) or retires (buys back) bonds and when bondholders convert bonds into common stock. If bondholders sell their bond investments to other investors, the issuing firm receives no further money on the transaction, **nor does the issuing corporation journalize the transaction** (although it does keep records of the names of bondholders in some cases).

Bonds may be issued at face value, below face value (discount), or above face value (premium). Bond prices for both new issues and existing bonds are quoted as **a percentage of the face value of the bond. Face value is usually $1,000.** Thus, a $1,000 bond with a quoted price of 97 means that the selling price of the bond is 97% of face value, or $970.

Issuing Bonds at Face Value

To illustrate the accounting for bonds issued at face value, assume that on January 1, 2012, Candlestick Corporation issues $100,000, five-year, 10% bonds at 100 (100% of face value). The entry to record the sale is:

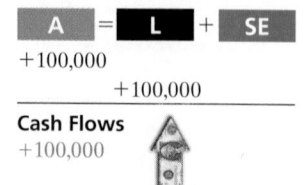

A = L + SE
+100,000
　　　+100,000
Cash Flows
+100,000

Jan. 1	Cash	100,000	
	Bonds Payable		100,000
	(To record sale of bonds at face value)		

Candlestick reports bonds payable in the long-term liabilities section of the balance sheet because the maturity date is January 1, 2017 (more than one year away).

Over the term (life) of the bonds, companies make entries to record bond interest. Interest on bonds payable is computed in the same manner as interest on notes payable, as explained in Chapter 11 (page 511). Assume that interest is payable semiannually on January 1 and July 1 on the Candlestick bonds. In that case, Candlestick must pay interest of $5,000 ($100,000 × 10% × 6/12) on July 1, 2012. The entry for the payment, assuming no previous accrual of interest, is:

July 1	Interest Expense	5,000	
	Cash		5,000
	(To record payment of bond interest)		

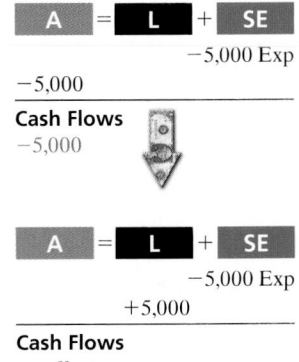

A = L + SE

−5,000 Exp

−5,000

Cash Flows
−5,000

At December 31, Candlestick recognizes the $5,000 of interest expense incurred since July 1 with the following adjusting entry:

Dec. 31	Interest Expense	5,000	
	Interest Payable		5,000
	(To accrue bond interest)		

A = L + SE

−5,000 Exp

+5,000

Cash Flows
no effect

Companies classify interest payable as a current liability because it is scheduled for payment within the next year. When Candlestick pays the interest on January 1, 2013, it debits (decreases) Interest Payable and credits (decreases) Cash for $5,000.

Candlestick records the payment on January 1 as follows.

Jan. 1	Interest Payable	5,000	
	Cash		5,000
	(To record payment of bond interest)		

Discount or Premium on Bonds

In the Candlestick illustrations above, we assumed that the contractual (stated) interest rate and the market (effective) interest rate paid on the bonds were the same. Recall that the **contractual interest rate** is the rate applied to the face (par) value to arrive at the interest paid in a year. The **market interest rate** is the rate investors demand for loaning funds to the corporation. When the contractual interest rate and the market interest rate are the same, bonds sell **at face value (par value)**.

However, market interest rates change daily. The type of bond issued, the state of the economy, current industry conditions, and the company's performance all affect market interest rates. As a result, contractual and market interest rates often differ. To make bonds salable when the two rates differ, bonds sell below or above face value.

To illustrate, suppose that a company issues 10% bonds at a time when other bonds of similar risk are paying 12%. Investors will not be interested in buying the 10% bonds, so their value will fall below their face value. When a bond is sold for less than its face value, the difference between the face value of a bond and its selling price is called a discount. As a result of the decline in the bonds' selling price, the actual interest rate incurred by the company increases to the level of the current market interest rate.

Conversely, if the market rate of interest is **lower than** the contractual interest rate, investors will have to pay more than face value for the bonds. That is, if the market rate of interest is 8% but the contractual interest rate on the bonds is 10%, the price of the bonds will be bid up. When a bond is sold for more than its face value, the difference between the face value and its selling price is called a premium. Illustration 15-4 (page 676) shows these relationships graphically.

Illustration 15-4
Interest rates and bond prices

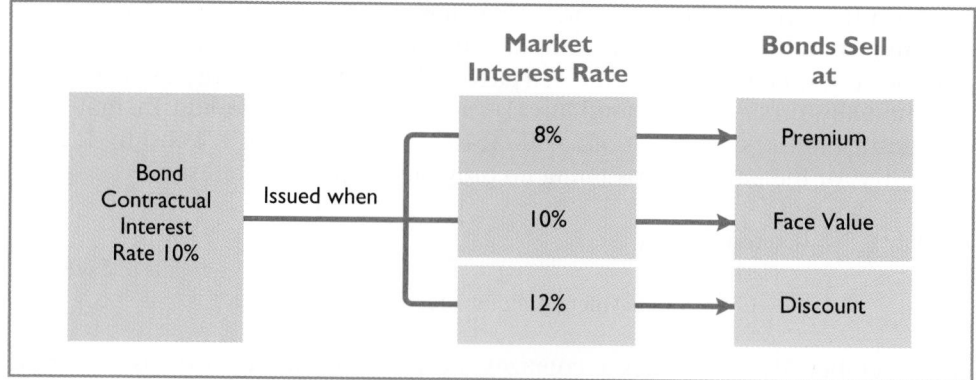

Issuance of bonds at an amount different from face value is quite common. By the time a company prints the bond certificates and markets the bonds, it will be a coincidence if the market rate and the contractual rate are the same. Thus, the issuance of bonds at a discount does not mean that the issuer's financial strength is suspect. Conversely, the sale of bonds at a premium does not indicate that the financial strength of the issuer is exceptional.

Issuing Bonds at a Discount

To illustrate issuance of bonds at a discount, assume that on January 1, 2012, Candlestick, Inc. sells $100,000, five-year, 10% bonds for $92,639 (92.639% of face value). Interest is payable on July 1 and January 1. The entry to record the issuance is:

Helpful Hint

Discount on Bonds Payable	
Increase	Decrease
Debit	Credit
↓	
Normal Balance	

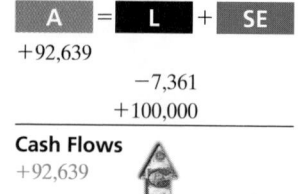

Jan. 1	Cash	92,639	
	Discount on Bonds Payable	7,361	
	Bonds Payable		100,000
	(To record sale of bonds at a discount)		

+92,639
−7,361
+100,000

Cash Flows
+92,639

Although Discount on Bonds Payable has a debit balance, **it is not an asset**. Rather, it is a **contra account**. This account is **deducted from bonds payable** on the balance sheet, as shown in Illustration 15-5.

Illustration 15-5
Statement presentation of discount on bonds payable

Candlestick, Inc.		
Balance Sheet (partial)		
Long-term liabilities		
Bonds payable	$100,000	
Less: Discount on bonds payable	7,361	$92,639

Helpful Hint

Carrying value (book value) of bonds issued at a discount is determined by subtracting the balance of the discount account from the balance of the Bonds Payable account.

The $92,639 represents the **carrying (or book) value** of the bonds. On the date of issue this amount equals the market price of the bonds.

The issuance of bonds below face value—at a discount—causes the total cost of borrowing to differ from the bond interest paid. That is, the issuing corporation must pay not only the contractual interest rate over the term of the bonds, but also the face value (rather than the issuance price) at maturity. Therefore, the difference between the issuance price and face value of the bonds—the discount—is an

additional cost of borrowing. The company records this additional cost as **interest expense** over the life of the bonds. Appendices 15B and 15C show the procedures for recording this additional cost.

The total cost of borrowing $92,639 for Candlestick, Inc. is $57,361, computed as follows.

<table>
<tr><td colspan="2" align="center">**Bonds Issued at a Discount**</td></tr>
<tr><td>Semiannual interest payments</td><td></td></tr>
<tr><td>   ($100,000 × 10% × ½ = $5,000; $5,000 × 10)</td><td>$50,000</td></tr>
<tr><td>Add: Bond discount ($100,000 − $92,639)</td><td>7,361</td></tr>
<tr><td>   **Total cost of borrowing**</td><td>$57,361</td></tr>
</table>

Illustration 15-6
Total cost of borrowing—bonds issued at a discount

Alternatively, we can compute the total cost of borrowing as follows.

<table>
<tr><td colspan="2" align="center">**Bonds Issued at a Discount**</td></tr>
<tr><td>Principal at maturity</td><td>$100,000</td></tr>
<tr><td>Semiannual interest payments ($5,000 × 10)</td><td>50,000</td></tr>
<tr><td>Cash to be paid to bondholders</td><td>150,000</td></tr>
<tr><td>Cash received from bondholders</td><td>92,639</td></tr>
<tr><td>   **Total cost of borrowing**</td><td>$ 57,361</td></tr>
</table>

Illustration 15-7
Alternative computation of total cost of borrowing—bonds issued at a discount

Issuing Bonds at a Premium

To illustrate the issuance of bonds at a premium, we now assume the Candlestick, Inc. bonds described above sell for $108,111 (108.111% of face value) rather than for $92,639. The entry to record the sale is:

Jan. 1	Cash	108,111	
	Bonds Payable		100,000
	Premium on Bonds Payable		8,111
	(To record sale of bonds at a premium)		

A = L + SE
+108,111
+100,000
+8,111

Cash Flows
+108,111

Candlestick adds the premium on bonds payable **to the bonds payable amount** on the balance sheet, as shown in Illustration 15-8.

<table>
<tr><td colspan="3" align="center">**Candlestick, Inc.**
Balance Sheet (partial)</td></tr>
<tr><td>Long-term liabilities</td><td></td><td></td></tr>
<tr><td>   Bonds payable</td><td>$100,000</td><td></td></tr>
<tr><td>   Add: Premium on bonds payable</td><td>8,111</td><td>$108,111</td></tr>
</table>

Illustration 15-8
Statement presentation of bond premium

The sale of bonds above face value causes the total cost of borrowing to be less **than the bond interest paid**. The reason: The borrower is not required to pay the bond premium at the maturity date of the bonds. Thus, the bond premium is considered to be **a reduction in the cost of borrowing**. The company credits the bond premium to Interest Expense over the life of the bonds. Appendices 15B and 15C

Helpful Hint

Premium on Bonds Payable	
Decrease Debit	Increase Credit
	↓
	Normal Balance

show the procedures for recording this reduction in the cost of borrowing. The total cost of borrowing $108,111 for Candlestick, Inc. is computed as follows.

Illustration 15-9
Total cost of borrowing—bonds issued at a premium

Bonds Issued at a Premium	
Semiannual interest payments	
($100,000 × 10% × ½ = $5,000; $5,000 × 10)	$50,000
Less: Bond premium ($108,111 − $100,000)	8,111
Total cost of borrowing	**$41,889**

Alternatively, we can compute the cost of borrowing as follows.

Illustration 15-10
Alternative computation of total cost of borrowing—bonds issued at a premium

Bonds Issued at a Premium	
Principal at maturity	$100,000
Semiannual interest payments ($5,000 × 10)	50,000
Cash to be paid to bondholders	150,000
Cash received from bondholders	108,111
Total cost of borrowing	**$ 41,889**

Do it!

Bond Issuance

action plan

✔ Record cash received, bonds payable at face value, and the difference as a discount or premium.

✔ Report discount as a deduction from bonds payable and premium as an addition to bonds payable.

Giant Corporation issues $200,000 of bonds for $189,000. (a) Prepare the journal entry to record the issuance of the bonds, and (b) show how the bonds would be reported on the balance sheet at the date of issuance.

Solution

(a)
Cash	189,000	
Discount on Bonds Payable	11,000	
Bonds Payable		200,000
(To record sale of bonds at a discount)		

(b)
Long-term liabilities
Bonds payable	$200,000	
Less: Discount on bonds payable	(11,000)	
		$189,000

Related exercise material: BE15-2, BE15-3, BE15-4, E15-6, E15-7, and **Do it!** 15-2.

✔ **The Navigator**

Accounting for Bond Retirements

Study Objective [3]
Describe the entries when bonds are redeemed or converted.

An issuing corporation retires bonds either when it buys back (redeems) the bonds or when bondholders convert them into common stock. We explain the entries for these transactions in the following sections.

Redeeming Bonds at Maturity

Regardless of the issue price of bonds, the book value of the bonds at maturity will equal their face value. Assuming that the company pays and records separately the interest for the last interest period, Candlestick records the redemption of its bonds at maturity as follows:

Bonds Payable	100,000	
Cash		100,000
(To record redemption of bonds at maturity)		

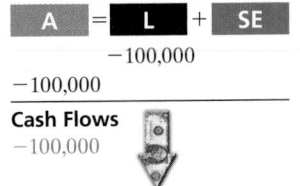

Redeeming Bonds before Maturity

Bonds also may be redeemed before maturity. A company may decide to retire bonds before maturity to reduce interest cost and to remove debt from its balance sheet. A company should retire debt early only if it has sufficient cash resources.

When a company retires bonds before maturity, it is necessary to: (1) eliminate the carrying value of the bonds at the redemption date; (2) record the cash paid; and (3) recognize the gain or loss on redemption. The **carrying value** of the bonds is the face value of the bonds less any remaining bond discount or plus any remaining bond premium at the redemption date.

To illustrate, assume that Candlestick, Inc. has sold its bonds at a premium. At the end of the eighth period, Candlestick retires these bonds at 103 after paying the semiannual interest. Assume also that the carrying value of the bonds at the redemption date is $101,623. Candlestick makes the following entry to record the redemption at the end of the eighth interest period (January 1, 2016):

Helpful Hint

Question: A bond is redeemed prior to its maturity date. Its carrying value exceeds its redemption price. Will the retirement result in a gain or a loss on redemption? Answer: Gain.

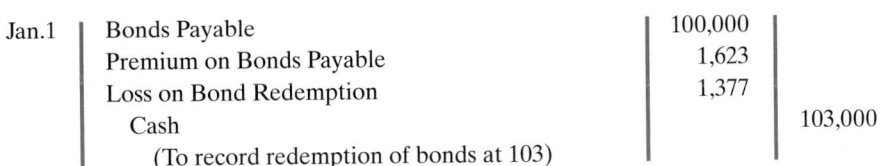

Jan.1	Bonds Payable	100,000	
	Premium on Bonds Payable	1,623	
	Loss on Bond Redemption	1,377	
	Cash		103,000
	(To record redemption of bonds at 103)		

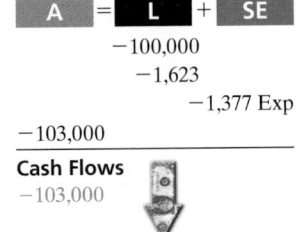

Note that the loss of $1,377 is the difference between the cash paid of $103,000 and the carrying value of the bonds of $101,623.

Converting Bonds into Common Stock

Convertible bonds have features that are attractive both to bondholders and to the issuer. The conversion often gives bondholders an opportunity to benefit if the market price of the common stock increases substantially. Until conversion, though, the bondholder receives interest on the bond. For the issuer of convertible bonds, the bonds sell at a higher price and pay a lower rate of interest than comparable debt securities without the conversion option. Many corporations, such as Intel, Ford, and Wells Fargo, have convertible bonds outstanding.

When the issuing company records a conversion, the company ignores the current market prices of the bonds and stock. Instead, the company transfers the **carrying value** of the bonds to paid-in capital accounts. **No gain or loss is recognized.**

To illustrate, assume that on July 1 Saunders Associates converts $100,000 bonds sold at face value into 2,000 shares of $10 par value common stock. Both the bonds and the common stock have a market value of $130,000. Saunders makes the following entry to record the conversion:

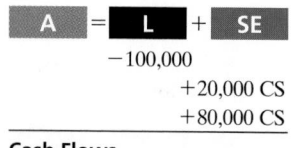

−100,000
+20,000 CS
+80,000 CS

Cash Flows
no effect

July 1	Bonds Payable	100,000	
	Common Stock		20,000
	Paid-in Capital in Excess of Par—		
	Common Stock		80,000
	(To record bond conversion)		

Note that the company does not consider the current market price of the bonds and stock ($130,000) in making the entry. This method of recording the bond conversion is often referred to as the **carrying (or book) value method**.

Do it!

Bond Redemption

action plan

✔ Determine and eliminate the carrying value of the bonds.

✔ Record the cash paid.

✔ Compute and record the gain or loss (the difference between the first two items).

R & B Inc. issued $500,000, 10-year bonds at a premium. Prior to maturity, when the carrying value of the bonds is $508,000, the company retires the bonds at 102. Prepare the entry to record the redemption of the bonds.

Solution

There is a loss on redemption: The cash paid, $510,000 ($500,000 × 102%), is greater than the carrying value of $508,000. The entry is:

Bonds Payable	500,000	
Premium on Bonds Payable	8,000	
Loss on Bond Redemption	2,000	
Cash		510,000
(To record redemption of bonds at 102)		

Related exercise material: BE15-5, E15-5, E15-6, E15-8, E15-9, and **Do it!** 15-3.

The Navigator

Accounting for Other Long-Term Liabilities

Other common types of long-term obligations are notes payable and lease liabilities. The accounting for these liabilities is explained in the following sections.

Long-Term Notes Payable

Study Objective [4]

Describe the accounting for long-term notes payable.

The use of notes payable in long-term debt financing is quite common. **Long-term notes payable** are similar to short-term interest-bearing notes payable except that the term of the notes exceeds one year. In periods of unstable interest rates, lenders may tie the interest rate on long-term notes to changes in the market rate for comparable loans. Examples are the 8.03% adjustable rate notes issued by General Motors and the floating-rate notes issued by American Express Company.

A long-term note may be secured by a **mortgage** that pledges title to specific assets as security for a loan. Individuals widely use **mortgage notes payable** to purchase homes, and many small and some large companies use them to acquire plant assets. At one time, approximately 18% of McDonald's long-term debt related to mortgage notes on land, buildings, and improvements.

Like other long-term notes payable, the mortgage loan terms may stipulate either a **fixed** or an **adjustable** interest rate. The interest rate on a fixed-rate mortgage remains the same over the life of the mortgage. The interest rate on an adjustable-rate mortgage is adjusted periodically to reflect changes in the market rate of interest. Typically, the terms require the borrower to make equal installment payments over the term of the loan. Each payment consists of (1) interest on the unpaid balance of the loan and (2) a reduction of loan principal. While the total amount of the payment remains constant, the interest decreases each period, while the portion applied to the loan principal increases.

Companies initially record mortgage notes payable at face value. They subsequently make entries for each installment payment. To illustrate, assume that Porter Technology Inc. issues a $500,000, 12%, 20-year mortgage note on December 31, 2012, to obtain needed financing for a new research laboratory. The terms provide for semiannual installment payments of $33,231 (not including real estate taxes and insurance). The installment payment schedule for the first two years is as follows.

Semiannual Interest Period	(A) Cash Payment	(B) Interest Expense (D) × 6%	(C) Reduction of Principal (A) − (B)	(D) Principal Balance (D) − (C)
12/31/12				$500,000
06/30/13	$33,231	$30,000	$3,231	496,769
12/31/13	33,231	29,806	3,425	493,344
06/30/14	33,231	29,601	3,630	489,714
12/31/14	33,231	29,383	3,848	485,866

Illustration 15-11
Mortgage installment payment schedule

Porter records the mortgage loan and first installment payment as follows.

Dec. 31	Cash	500,000	
	Mortgage Payable		500,000
	(To record mortgage loan)		

A = L + SE
+500,000
+500,000

Cash Flows
+500,000

June 30	Interest Expense	30,000	
	Mortgage Payable	3,231	
	Cash		33,231
	(To record semiannual payment on mortgage)		

A = L + SE
−30,000 Exp
−3,231
−33,231

Cash Flows
−33,231

In the balance sheet, the company reports the reduction in principal for the next year as a current liability, and it classifies the remaining unpaid principal balance as a long-term liability. At December 31, 2013, the total liability is $493,344. Of that amount, $7,478 ($3,630 + $3,848) is current, and $485,866 ($493,344 − $7,478) is long-term.

Do it!

Cole Research issues a $250,000, 8%, 20-year mortgage note to obtain needed financing for a new lab. The terms call for semiannual payments of $12,631 each. Prepare the entries to record the mortgage loan and the first installment payment.

Long-Term Note

action plan

✔ Record the issuance of the note as a cash receipt and a liability.

✔ Each installment payment consists of interest and payment of principal.

Solution

Cash	250,000	
Mortgage Payable		250,000
(To record mortgage loan)		
Interest Expense	10,000*	
Mortgage Payable	2,361	
Cash		12,361
(To record semiannual payment on mortgage)		

*Interest expense = $250,000 × 8% × 6/12.

Related exercise material: BE15-6, E15-10, E15-11, and **Do it!** 15-4.

The Navigator ✔

ACCOUNTING ACROSS THE ORGANIZATION

Bonds Versus Notes?

Companies have a choice in the form of long-term borrowing they undertake—issue bonds or issue notes. Notes are generally issued to a single lender (usually through a loan from a bank). Bonds, on the other hand, allow the company to divide the borrowing into many small investing units, thereby enabling more than one investor to participate in the borrowing. As indicated in the graph below, companies are recently borrowing more from bond investors than from banks and other loan providers in a bid to lock in cheap, long-term funding.

Corporate Bonds/Corporate Loans
Global volumes ($ in billions)

Bonds / Loans

2000 02 04 06 08 09
*Excluding financial issuance   Year-to-date

Why this trend? For one thing, low interest rates and rising inflows into fixed-income funds have triggered record bond issuances as banks cut back lending. In addition, for some high-rated companies, it can be riskier to borrow from a bank than the bond markets. The reason: High-rated companies tended to rely on short-term financing to fund working capital but were left stranded when these markets froze up. Some are now financing themselves with longer-term bonds instead.

Source: A. Sakoui and N. Bullock, "Companies Choose Bonds for Cheap Funds," *Financial Times* (October 12, 2009).

? Why might companies prefer bond financing instead of short-term financing? (See page 718.)

Lease Liabilities

A lease is a contractual arrangement between a lessor (owner of the property) and a lessee (renter of the property). It grants the right to use specific property for a period of time in return for cash payments. Leasing is big business. The global leasing market has recently been between $600 to $700 billion for capital equipment. This represents approximately one-third of equipment financed in a year. The two most common types of leases are operating leases and capital leases.

Study Objective [5]
Contrast the accounting for operating and capital leases.

OPERATING LEASES

The renting of an apartment and the rental of a car at an airport are examples of **operating leases. In an** operating lease **the intent is temporary use of the property by the lessee, while the lessor continues to own the property.**

In an operating lease, the lessee records the lease (or rental) payments as an expense. The lessor records the payments as revenue. For example, assume that a sales representative for Western Inc. leases a car from Hertz Car Rental at the Los Angeles airport and that Hertz charges a total of $275. Western, the lessee, records the rental as follows:

Car Rental Expense	275	
Cash		275
(To record payment of lease rental charge)		

A	=	L	+	SE
				−275 Exp

−275
_____
Cash Flows
−275

The lessee may incur other costs during the lease period. For example, in the case above, Western will generally incur costs for gas. Western would report these costs as an expense.

CAPITAL LEASES

In most lease contracts, the lessee makes a periodic payment and records that payment in the income statement as rent expense. In some cases, however, the lease contract transfers to the lessee substantially all the benefits and risks of ownership. Such a lease is in effect a purchase of the property. This type of lease is a **capital lease**. Its name comes from the fact that the company capitalizes the present value of the cash payments for the lease and records that amount as an asset. Illustration 15-12 indicates the major difference between operating and capital leases.

Operating lease

"Have it back by 6:00 Sunday."
"OK!"
U-Drive Corp.

Lessor has substantially all of the benefits and risks of ownership

Capital lease

"Only 3 more payments and this baby is ours!"

Lessee has substantially all of the benefits and risks of ownership

Illustration 15-12
Types of leases

Helpful Hint

A capital lease situation is one that, although legally a rental case, is *in substance* an installment purchase by the lessee. Accounting standards require that substance over form be used in such a situation.

If **any one** of the following conditions exists, the lessee must record a lease **as an asset**—that is, as a capital lease:

1. **The lease transfers ownership of the property to the lessee.** *Rationale:* If during the lease term the lessee receives ownership of the asset, the lessee should report the leased item as an asset on its books.

2. **The lease contains a bargain purchase option.** *Rationale:* If during the term of the lease the lessee can purchase the asset at a price substantially below its fair market value, the lessee will exercise this option. Thus, the lessee should report the leased item as an asset on its books.

3. **The lease term is equal to 75% or more of the economic life of the leased property.** *Rationale:* If the lease term is for much of the asset's useful life, the lessee should report the leased item as an asset on its books.

4. **The present value of the lease payments equals or exceeds 90% of the fair market value of the leased property.** *Rationale:* If the present value of the lease payments is equal to or almost equal to the fair market value of the asset, the lessee has essentially purchased the asset. As a result, the lessee should report the leased item as an asset on its books.

To illustrate, assume that Gonzalez Company decides to lease new equipment. The lease period is four years; the economic life of the leased equipment is estimated to be five years. The present value of the lease payments is $190,000, which is equal to the fair market value of the equipment. There is no transfer of ownership during the lease term, nor is there any bargain purchase option.

In this example, Gonzalez has essentially purchased the equipment. Conditions 3 and 4 have been met. First, the lease term is 75% or more of the economic life of the asset. Second, the present value of cash payments is equal to the equipment's fair market value. Gonzalez records the transaction as follows.

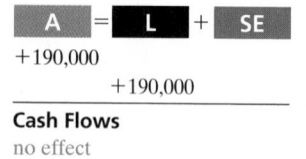

+190,000

+190,000

Cash Flows

no effect

Leased Asset—Equipment	190,000	
Lease Liability		190,000
(To record leased asset and lease liability)		

The lessee reports a leased asset on the balance sheet under plant assets. It reports the lease liability on the balance sheet as a liability. **The portion of the lease liability expected to be paid in the next year is a current liability. The remainder is classified as a long-term liability.**

Most lessees do not like to report leases on their balance sheets. Why? Because the lease liability increases the company's total liabilities. This, in turn, may make it more difficult for the company to obtain needed funds from lenders. As a result, companies attempt to keep leased assets and lease liabilities off the balance sheet by structuring leases so as not to meet any of the four conditions discussed earlier. The practice of keeping liabilities off the balance sheet is referred to as **off–balance-sheet financing**.

Ethics Note

Accounting standard setters are attempting to rewrite rules on lease accounting because of concerns that abuse of the current standards is reducing the usefulness of financial statements.

Statement Presentation and Analysis

Study Objective [6]

Identify the methods for the presentation and analysis of long-term liabilities.

Presentation

Companies report long-term liabilities in a separate section of the balance sheet immediately following current liabilities, as shown in Illustration 15-13. Alternatively, companies may present summary data in the balance sheet, with detailed data (interest rates, maturity dates, conversion privileges, and assets pledged as collateral) shown in a supporting schedule.

Illustration 15-13
Balance sheet presentation
of long-term liabilities

Lax Corporation		
Balance Sheet (partial)		
Long-term liabilities		
Bonds payable 10% due in 2017	$1,000,000	
Less: Discount on bonds payable	80,000	$ 920,000
Mortgage payable, 11%, due in 2023		
and secured by plant assets		500,000
Lease liability		440,000
Total long-term liabilities		$1,860,000

Companies report the current maturities of long-term debt under current liabilities if they are to be paid from current assets.

Analysis

Long-term creditors and stockholders are interested in a company's long-run solvency. Of particular interest is the company's ability to pay interest as it comes due and to repay the face value of the debt at maturity. Here we look at two ratios that provide information about debt-paying ability and long-run solvency.

The **debt to total assets ratio** measures the percentage of the total assets provided by creditors. As shown in the formula in Illustration 15-14, it is computed by dividing total debt (both current and long-term liabilities) by total assets. The higher the percentage of debt to total assets, the greater the risk that the company may be unable to meet its maturing obligations.

The **times interest earned ratio** indicates the company's ability to meet interest payments as they come due. It is computed by dividing income before income taxes and interest expense by interest expense.

To illustrate these ratios, we will use data from Kellogg Company's recent annual report. The company had total liabilities of $8,925 million, total assets of $11,200 million, interest expense of $295 million, income taxes of $476 million, and net income of $1,208 million. Kellogg's debt to total assets ratio and times interest earned ratio are shown below.

Illustration 15-14
Debt to total assets and times
interest earned ratios, with
computations

Total Debt	÷	Total Assets	=	Debt to Total Assets
$8,925	÷	$11,200	=	79.7%

Income before Income Taxes and Interest Expenses	÷	Interest Expense	=	Times Interest Earned
$1,208 + $476 + $295	÷	$295	=	6.71 times

Kellogg has a relatively high debt to total assets percentage of 79.7%. Its interest coverage of 6.71 times is considered safe.

Do it!

Lease Liability; Analysis of Long-Term Liabilities

action plan

✔ Record the present value of the lease payments as an asset and a liability.

✔ Use the formula for the debt to total assets ratio (total debt divided by total assets).

FX Corporation leases new equipment on December 31, 2012. The lease transfers ownership to FX at the end of the lease. The present value of the lease payments is $240,000. After recording this lease, FX has assets of $2,000,000, liabilities of $1,200,000, and stockholders' equity of $800,000. (a) Prepare the entry to record the lease, and (b) compute and discuss the debt to total assets ratio at year-end.

Solution

(a)

Leased Asset—Equipment	240,000	
Lease Liability		240,000
(To record leased asset and lease liability)		

(b) The debt to total assets ratio = $1,200,000 ÷ $2,000,000 = 60%. This means that 60% of the total assets were provided by creditors. The higher the percentage of debt to total assets, the greater the risk that the company may be unable to meet its maturing obligations.

Related exercise material: BE15-7, E15-12, E15-14, and **Do it!** 15-5.

The Navigator

*I*NVESTOR *I*NSIGHT

"Covenant-Lite" Debt

In many corporate loans and bond issuances the lending agreement specifies debt covenants. These covenants typically are specific financial measures, such as minimum levels of retained earnings, cash flows, times interest earned ratios, or other measures that a company must maintain during the life of the loan. If the company violates a covenant it is considered to have violated the loan agreement; the creditors can demand immediate repayment, or they can renegotiate the loan's terms. Covenants protect lenders because they enable lenders to step in and try to get their money back before the borrower gets too deep into trouble.

During the 1990s most traditional loans specified between three to six covenants or "triggers." In more recent years, when lots of cash was available, lenders began reducing or completely eliminating covenants from loan agreements in order to be more competitive with other lenders. When the economy declined, lenders lost big money when companies defaulted.

Source: Cynthia Koons, "Risky Business: Growth of 'Covenant-Lite' Debt," *Wall Street Journal* (June 18, 2007), p. C2.

? How can financial ratios such as those covered in this chapter provide protection for creditors? (See page 718.)

COMPREHENSIVE

Do it!

Snyder Software Inc. has successfully developed a new spreadsheet program. To produce and market the program, the company needed $2 million of additional financing. On January 1, 2012, Snyder borrowed money as follows.

1. Snyder issued $500,000, 11%, 10-year convertible bonds. The bonds sold at face value and pay semiannual interest on January 1 and July 1. Each $1,000 bond is convertible into 30 shares of Snyder's $20 par value common stock.

2. Snyder issued $1 million, 10%, 10-year bonds at face value. Interest is payable semiannually on January 1 and July 1.

3. Snyder also issued a $500,000, 12%, 15-year mortgage payable. The terms provide for semiannual installment payments of $36,324 on June 30 and December 31.

Instructions

1. For the convertible bonds, prepare journal entries for:
   (a) The issuance of the bonds on January 1, 2012.
   (b) Interest expense on July 1 and December 31, 2012.
   (c) The payment of interest on January 1, 2013.
   (d) The conversion of all bonds into common stock on January 1, 2013, when the market value of the common stock was $67 per share.

2. For the 10-year, 10% bonds:
   (a) Journalize the issuance of the bonds on January 1, 2012.
   (b) Prepare the journal entries for interest expense in 2012. Assume no accrual of interest on July 1.
   (c) Prepare the entry for the redemption of the bonds at 101 on January 1, 2015, after paying the interest due on this date.

3. For the mortgage note payable:
   (a) Prepare the entry for the issuance of the note on January 1, 2012.
   (b) Prepare a payment schedule for the first four installment payments.
   (c) Indicate the current and noncurrent amounts for the mortgage note payable at December 31, 2012.

action plan

✔ Compute interest semiannually (six months).

✔ Record the accrual and payment of interest on appropriate dates.

✔ Record the conversion of the bonds into common stock by removing the book (carrying) value of the bonds from the liability account.

Solution to Comprehensive Do it!

1. (a) 2012

Jan. 1	Cash	500,000	
	Bonds Payable		500,000
	(To record issue of 11%, 10-year convertible bonds at face value)		

(b) 2012

July 1	Interest Expense	27,500	
	Cash ($500,000 × 0.055)		27,500
	(To record payment of semiannual interest)		
Dec. 31	Interest Expense	27,500	
	Interest Payable		27,500
	(To record accrual of semiannual bond interest)		

(c) 2013

Jan. 1	Interest Payable	27,500	
	Cash		27,500
	(To record payment of accrued interest)		

(d) Jan. 1

	Bonds Payable	500,000	
	Common Stock		300,000*
	Paid-in Capital in Excess of Par—Common Stock		200,000
	(To record conversion of bonds into common stock)		
	*($500,000 ÷ $1,000 = 500 bonds; 500 × 30 = 15,000 shares; 15,000 × $20 = $300,000)		

action plan

✔ Record the issuance of the bonds.

✔Compute interest expense for each period.

✔ Compute the loss on bond redemption as the excess of the cash paid over the carrying value of the redeemed bonds.

2. (a) 2012

Jan. 1	Cash	1,000,000	
	Bonds Payable		1,000,000
	(To record issuance of bonds)		

(b) 2012

July 1	Interest Expense	50,000	
	Cash		50,000
	(To record payment of semiannual interest)		
Dec. 31	Interest Expense	50,000	
	Interest Payable		50,000
	(To record accrual of semiannual interest)		

(c) 2015

Jan. 1	Bonds Payable	1,000,000	
	Loss on Bond Redemption	10,000*	
	Cash		1,010,000
	(To record redemption of bonds at 101)		
	*($1,010,000 − $1,000,000)		

action plan

✔ Compute periodic interest expense on a mortgage note, recognizing that as the principal amount decreases, so does the interest expense.

✔ Record mortgage payments, recognizing that each payment consists of (1) interest on the unpaid loan balance and (2) a reduction of the loan principal.

3. (a) 2012

Jan. 1	Cash	500,000	
	Mortgage Payable		500,000
	(To record issuance of mortgage note payable)		

(b)

Semiannual Interest Period	Cash Payment	Interest Expense	Reduction of Principal	Principal Balance
Issue date				$500,000
1	$36,324	$30,000	$6,324	493,676
2	36,324	29,621	6,703	486,973
3	36,324	29,218	7,106	479,867
4	36,324	28,792	7,532	472,335

(c) Current liability $14,638 ($7,106 + $7,532)
Long-term liability $472,335

✔ **The Navigator**

Summary of Study Objectives

[1] **Explain why bonds are issued.** Companies may sell bonds to investors to raise long-term capital. Bonds offer the following advantages over common stock: (a) stockholder control is not affected, (b) tax savings result, (c) earnings per share of common stock may be higher.

[2] **Prepare the entries for the issuance of bonds and interest expense.** When companies issue bonds, they debit Cash for the cash proceeds, and credit Bonds Payable for the face value of the bonds. The account Premium on Bonds

Payable shows a bond premium; Discount on Bonds Payable shows a bond discount.

[3] **Describe the entries when bonds are redeemed or converted.** When bondholders redeem bonds at maturity, the issuing company credits Cash and debits Bonds Payable for the face value of the bonds. When bonds are redeemed before maturity, the issuing company (a) eliminates the carrying value of the bonds at the redemption date, (b) records the cash paid, and (c) recognizes the gain or loss on

redemption. When bonds are converted to common stock, the issuing company transfers the carrying (or book) value of the bonds to appropriate paid-in capital accounts; no gain or loss is recognized.

[4] Describe the accounting for long-term notes payable. Each payment consists of (1) interest on the unpaid balance of the loan and (2) a reduction of loan principal. The interest decreases each period, while the portion applied to the loan principal increases.

[5] Contrast the accounting for operating and capital leases. For an operating lease, the lessee (renter) records lease (rental) payments as an expense. For a capital lease, the lessee records the asset and related obligation at the present value of the future lease payments.

[6] Identify the methods for the presentation and analysis of long-term liabilities. Companies should report the nature and amount of each long-term debt in the balance sheet or in the notes accompanying the financial statements. Stockholders and long-term creditors are interested in a company's long-run solvency. Debt to total assets and times interest earned are two ratios that provide information about debt-paying ability and long-run solvency.

The Navigator

Glossary

Bearer (coupon) bonds Bonds not registered in the name of the owner. (p. 672).

Bond certificate A legal document that indicates the name of the issuer, the face value of the bonds, the contractual interest rate and maturity date of the bonds. (p. 672).

Bond indenture A legal document that sets forth the terms of the bond issue. (p. 672).

Bonds A form of interest-bearing notes payable issued by corporations, universities, and governmental entities. (p. 670).

Callable bonds Bonds that are subject to retirement at a stated dollar amount prior to maturity at the option of the issuer. (p. 672).

Capital lease A contractual arrangement that transfers substantially all the benefits and risks of ownership to the lessee so that the lease is in effect a purchase of the property. (p. 683).

Contractual interest rate Rate used to determine the amount of cash interest the borrower pays and the investor receives. (p. 672).

Convertible bonds Bonds that permit bondholders to convert them into common stock at the bondholders' option. (p. 672).

Debenture bonds Bonds issued against the general credit of the borrower. Also called unsecured bonds. (p. 671).

Debt to total assets ratio A solvency measure that indicates the percentage of total assets provided by creditors; computed as total debt divided by total assets. (p. 685).

Discount (on a bond) The difference between the face value of a bond and its selling price, when the bond is sold for less than its face value. (p. 675).

Face value (par value) Amount of principal the issuer must pay at the maturity date of the bond. (p. 672).

Long-term liabilities Obligations expected to be paid after one year. (p. 670).

Market interest rate The rate investors demand for loaning funds to the corporation. (p. 673).

Maturity date The date on which the final payment on the bond is due from the bond issuer to the investor. (p. 672).

Mortgage bond A bond secured by real estate. (p. 671).

Mortgage notes payable A long-term note secured by a mortgage that pledges title to specific assets as security for a loan. (p. 680).

Operating lease A contractual arrangement giving the lessee temporary use of the property, with continued ownership of the property by the lessor. (p. 683).

Premium (on a bond) The difference between the selling price and the face value of a bond, when the bond is sold for more than its face value. (p. 675).

Registered bonds Bonds issued in the name of the owner. (p. 672).

Secured bonds Bonds that have specific assets of the issuer pledged as collateral. (p. 671).

Serial bonds Bonds that mature in installments. (p. 672).

Sinking fund bonds Bonds secured by specific assets set aside to retire them. (p. 671).

Term bonds Bonds that mature at a single specified future date. (p. 672).

Times interest earned ratio A solvency measure that indicates a company's ability to meet interest payments; computed by dividing income before income taxes and interest expense by interest expense. (p. 685).

Time value of money The relationship between time and money. A dollar received today is worth more than a dollar promised at some time in the future. (p. 673).

Unsecured bonds Bonds issued against the general credit of the borrower. Also called debenture bonds. (p. 671).

APPENDIX15A

Present Value Concepts Related to Bond Pricing

Congratulations! You have a winning lottery ticket and the state has provided you with three possible options for payment. They are:

1. Receive $10,000,000 in three years.
2. Receive $7,000,000 immediately.
3. Receive $3,500,000 at the end of each year for three years.

Which of these options would you select? The answer is not easy to determine at a glance. To make a dollar-maximizing choice, you must perform present value computations. A present value computation is based on the concept of time value of money. Time value of money concepts are useful for the lottery situation and for pricing other amounts to be received in the future. This appendix discusses how to use present value concepts to price bonds. It also will tell you how to determine what option you should take as a lottery winner.

Present Value of Face Value

Study Objective [7]
Compute the market price of a bond.

To illustrate present value concepts, assume that you are willing to invest a sum of money that will yield $1,000 at the end of one year. In other words, what amount would you need to invest today to have $1,000 one year from now? If you want to earn 10%, the investment (or present value) is $909.09 ($1,000 ÷ 1.10). Illustration 15A-1 shows the computation.

Illustration 15A-1
Present value computation—$1,000 discounted at 10% for one year

Present value	×	(1 + Interest rate)	=	Future amount
Present value	×	(1 + 10%)	=	$1,000
Present value			=	$1,000 ÷ 1.10
Present value			=	$909.09

The future amount ($1,000), the interest rate (10%), and the number of periods (1) are known. We can depict the variables in this situation as shown in the time diagram in Illustration 15A-2.

Illustration 15A-2
Finding present value if discounted for one period

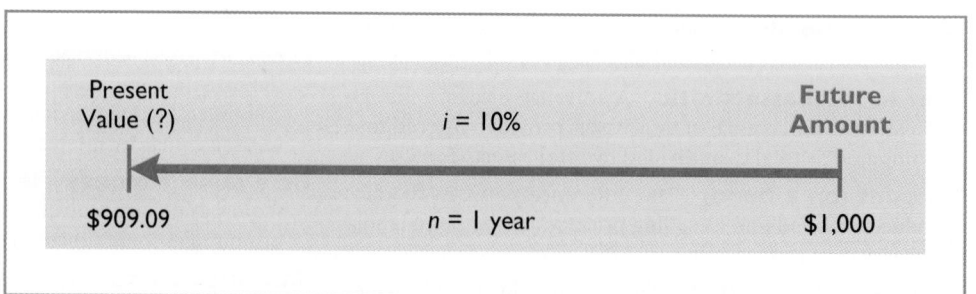

If you are to receive the single future amount of $1,000 **in two years**, discounted at 10%, its present value is $826.45 [($1,000 ÷ 1.10) ÷ 1.10], depicted as follows.

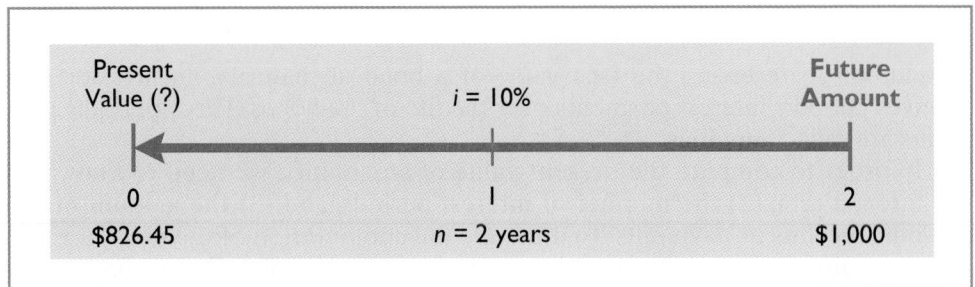

Illustration 15A-3
Finding present value if
discounted for two periods

We also can determine the present value of 1 through tables that show the present value of 1 for *n* periods. In Table 15A-1, *n* is the number of discounting periods involved. The percentages are the periodic interest rates, and the 5-digit decimal numbers in the respective columns are the factors for the present value of 1.

When using Table 15A-1, we multiply the future amount by the present value factor specified at the intersection of the number of periods and the interest rate. For example, the present value factor for 1 period at an interest rate of 10% is .90909, which equals the $909.09 ($1,000 × .90909) computed in Illustration 15A-1.

Table 15A-1
Present Value of 1

(*n*) Periods	4%	5%	6%	8%	9%	10%	11%	12%	15%
1	.96154	.95238	.94340	.92593	.91743	.90909	.90090	.89286	.86957
2	.92456	.90703	.89000	.85734	.84168	.82645	.81162	.79719	.75614
3	.88900	.86384	.83962	.79383	.77218	.75132	.73119	.71178	.65752
4	.85480	.82270	.79209	.73503	.70843	.68301	.65873	.63552	.57175
5	.82193	.78353	.74726	.68058	.64993	.62092	.59345	.56743	.49718
6	.79031	.74622	.70496	.63017	.59627	.56447	.53464	.50663	.43233
7	.75992	.71068	.66506	.58349	.54703	.51316	.48166	.45235	.37594
8	.73069	.67684	.62741	.54027	.50187	.46651	.43393	.40388	.32690
9	.70259	.64461	.59190	.50025	.46043	.42410	.39092	.36061	.28426
10	.67556	.61391	.55839	.46319	.42241	.38554	.35218	.32197	.24719

For two periods at an interest rate of 10%, the present value factor is .82645, which equals the $826.45 ($1,000 × .82645) computed previously.

Let's now go back to our lottery example. Given the present value concepts just learned, we can determine whether receiving $10,000,000 in three years is better than receiving $7,000,000 today, assuming the appropriate discount rate is 9%. The computation is as follows.

Illustration 15A-4
Present value of $10,000,000
to be received in three years

$10,000,000 × PV of 1 due in 3 years at 9% =	
$10,000,000 × .77218 (Table 15A-1)	$7,721,800
Amount to be received from state immediately	7,000,000
Difference	$ 721,800

What this computation shows you is that you would be $721,800 better off receiving the $10,000,000 at the end of three years rather than taking $7,000,000 immediately.

Present Value of Interest Payments (Annuities)

In addition to receiving the face value of a bond at maturity, an investor also receives periodic interest payments over the life of the bonds. These periodic payments are called **annuities**.

In order to compute the present value of an annuity, we need to know: (1) the interest rate, (2) the number of interest periods, and (3) the amount of the periodic receipts or payments. To illustrate the computation of the present value of an annuity, assume that you will receive $1,000 cash annually for three years and the interest rate is 10%. The time diagram in Illustration 15A-5 depicts this situation.

Illustration 15A-5
Time diagram for a three-year annuity

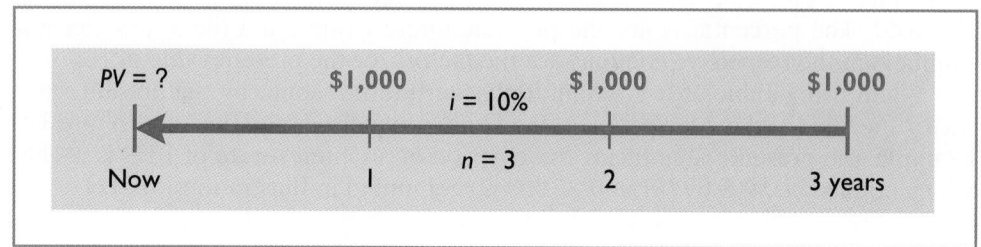

The present value in this situation may be computed as follows.

Illustration 15A-6
Present value of a series of future amounts computation

Future Amount	×	Present Value of 1 Factor at 10%	=	Present Value
$1,000 (1 year away)		.90909		$ 909.09
1,000 (2 years away)		.82645		826.45
1,000 (3 years away)		.75132		751.32
		2.48686		$2,486.86

We also can use annuity tables to value annuities. As illustrated in Table 15A-2 below, these tables show the present value of 1 to be received periodically for a given number of periods.

Table 15A-2
Present Value of an Annuity of 1

(n) Periods	4%	5%	6%	8%	9%	10%	11%	12%	15%
1	.96154	.95238	.94340	.92593	.91743	.90909	.90090	.89286	.86957
2	1.88609	1.85941	1.83339	1.78326	1.75911	1.73554	1.71252	1.69005	1.62571
3	2.77509	2.72325	2.67301	2.57710	2.53130	2.48685	2.44371	2.40183	2.28323
4	3.62990	3.54595	3.46511	3.31213	3.23972	3.16986	3.10245	3.03735	2.85498
5	4.45182	4.32948	4.21236	3.99271	3.88965	3.79079	3.69590	3.60478	3.35216
6	5.24214	5.07569	4.91732	4.62288	4.48592	4.35526	4.23054	4.11141	3.78448
7	6.00205	5.78637	5.58238	5.20637	5.03295	4.86842	4.71220	4.56376	4.16042
8	6.73274	6.46321	6.20979	5.74664	5.53482	5.33493	5.14612	4.96764	4.48732
9	7.43533	7.10782	6.80169	6.24689	5.99525	5.75902	5.53705	5.32825	4.77158
10	8.11090	7.72173	7.36009	6.71008	6.41766	6.14457	5.88923	5.65022	5.01877

From Table 15A-2 you can see that the present value factor of an annuity of 1 for three periods at 10% is 2.48685.[1] This present value factor is the total of the three individual present value factors as shown in Illustration 15A-6. Applying this amount to the annual cash flow of $1,000 produces a present value of $2,486.85.

Let's now go back to our lottery example. We determined that you would get more money if you wait and take the $10,000,000 in three years rather than take $7,000,000 immediately. But there is still another option—to receive $3,500,000 at the end of **each year** for three years (an annuity). The computation to evaluate this option (again assuming a 9% discount rate) is as follows.

$3,500,000 × PV of 1 due yearly for 3 years at 9% =	
$3,500,000 × 2.53130 (Table 15A-2)	$8,859,550
Present value of $10,000,000 to be received in 3 years	7,721,800
Difference	$1,137,750

Illustration 15A-7
Present value of lottery payments to be received over three years

If you take the annuity of $3,500,000 for each of 3 years, you will be $1,137,750 richer as a result.

Time Periods and Discounting

We have used an **annual** interest rate to determine present value. Present value computations may also be done over shorter periods of time, such as monthly, quarterly, or semiannually. When the time frame is less than one year, it is necessary to convert the annual interest rate to the shorter time frame.

Assume, for example, that the investor in Illustration 15A-6 received $500 **semiannually** for three years instead of $1,000 annually. In this case, the number of periods becomes 6 (3 × 2), the interest rate is 5% (10% ÷ 2), the present value factor from Table 15A-2 is 5.07569, and the present value of the future cash flows is $2,537.85 (5.07569 × $500). This amount is slightly higher than the $2,486.86 computed in Illustration 15A-6 because interest is computed twice during the same year. That is, interest is earned on the first half year's interest.

Computing the Present Value of a Bond

The present value (or market price) of a bond is a function of three variables: (1) the payment amounts, (2) the length of time until the amounts are paid, and (3) the interest (discount) rate.

The first variable (dollars to be paid) is made up of two elements: (1) a series of interest payments (an annuity), and (2) the principal amount (a single sum). To compute the present value of the bond, we must discount both the interest payments and the principal amount.

When the investor's interest (discount) rate is equal to the bond's contractual interest rate, the present value of the bonds will equal the face value of the bonds. To illustrate, assume a bond issue of 10%, five-year bonds with a face value of $100,000 with interest payable **semiannually** on January 1 and July 1. If the discount rate is the same as the contractual rate, the bonds will sell **at face value**. In this case, the investor will receive: (1) $100,000 at maturity and (2) a series of ten $5,000 interest payments [$100,000 × (10% ÷ 2)] over the term of the bonds. The length of time is expressed in terms of interest periods (in this case, 10) and the discount rate per interest period (5%). The time diagram in Illustration 15A-8 (page 694) depicts the variables involved in this discounting situation.

---

[1] The difference of .00001 between 2.48686 and 2.48685 is due to rounding.

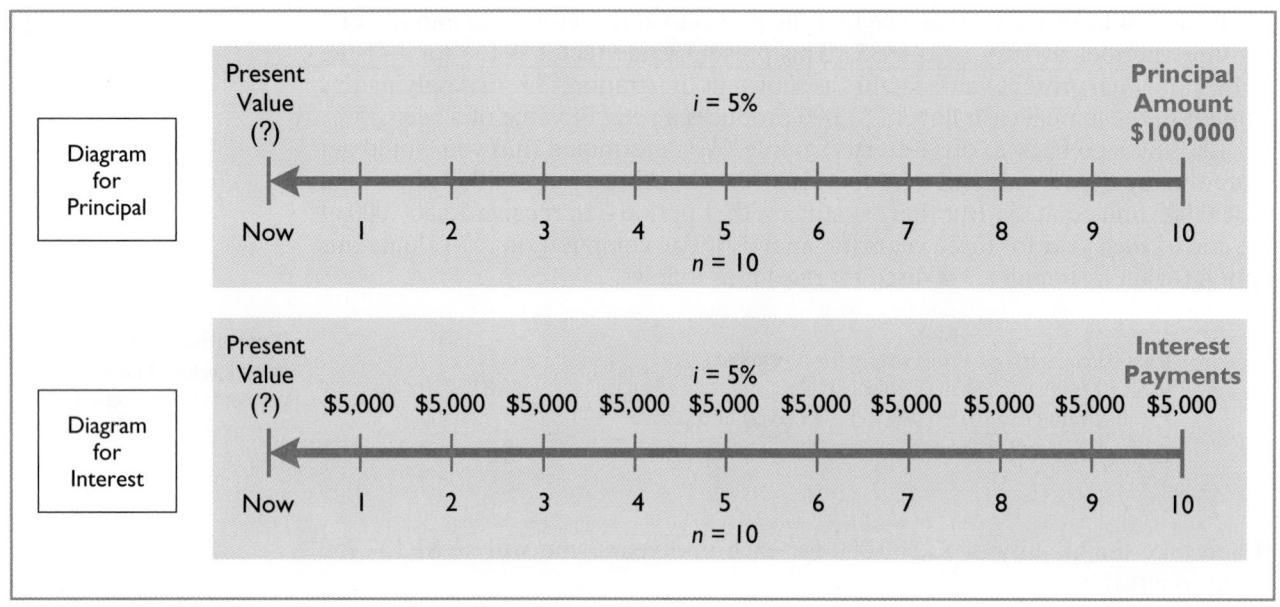

Illustration 15A-8
Time diagram for the present value of a 10%, five-year bond paying interest semiannually

The computation of the present value of Candlestick's bonds, assuming they were issued at face value (page 674), is shown below.

Illustration 15A-9
Present value of principal and interest (face value)

10% Contractual Rate—10% Discount Rate

Present value of principal to be received at maturity	
$100,000 × PV of 1 due in 10 periods at 5%	
$100,000 × .61391 (Table 15A-1)	$ 61,391
Present value of interest to be received periodically	
over the term of the bonds	
$5,000 × PV of 1 due periodically for 10 periods at 5%	
$5,000 × 7.72173 (Table 15A-2)	38,609*
Present value of bonds	**$100,000**

*(Rounded).

Now assume that the investor's required rate of return is 12%, not 10%. The future amounts are again $100,000 and $5,000, respectively. But now we must use a discount rate of 6% (12% ÷ 2). The present value of Candlestick's bonds issued at a discount (page 676) is $92,639 as computed below.

Illustration 15A-10
Present value of principal and interest (discount)

10% Contractual Rate—12% Discount Rate

Present value of principal to be received at maturity	
$100,000 × .55839 (Table 15A-1)	$55,839
Present value of interest to be received periodically	
over the term of the bonds	
$5,000 × 7.36009 (Table 15A-2)	36,800
Present value of bonds	**$92,639**

If the discount rate is 8% and the contractual rate is 10%, the present value of Candlestick's bonds issued at a premium (page 677) is $108,111, computed as follows.

10% Contractual Rate—8% Discount Rate

Present value of principal to be received at maturity	
$100,000 × .67556 (Table 15A-1)	$ 67,556
Present value of interest to be received periodically	
over the term of the bonds	
$5,000 × 8.11090 (Table 15A-2)	40,555
Present value of bonds	**$108,111**

Illustration 15A-11
Present value of principal and interest (premium)

Summary of Study Objective for Appendix 15A

[7] **Compute the market price of a bond.** Time value of money concepts are useful for pricing bonds. The present value (or market price) of a bond is a function of three variables: (1) the payment amounts, (2) the length of time until the amounts are paid, and (3) the interest rate.

APPENDIX15B

Effective-Interest Method of Bond Amortization

Under the **effective-interest method**, the amortization of bond discount or bond premium results in periodic interest expense equal to a **constant percentage** of the carrying value of the bonds. The effective-interest method results in varying amounts of amortization and interest expense per period but **a constant percentage rate**.

The following steps are required under the effective-interest method.

1. Compute the **bond interest expense**. To do so, multiply the carrying value of the bonds at the beginning of the interest period by the effective-interest rate.

2. Compute the **bond interest paid** (or accrued). To do so, multiply the face value of the bonds by the contractual interest rate.

3. Compute the **amortization amount**. To do so, determine the difference between the amounts computed in steps (1) and (2).

Illustration 15B-1 depicts these steps.

> **Study Objective [8]**
> Apply the effective-interest method of amortizing bond discount and bond premium.

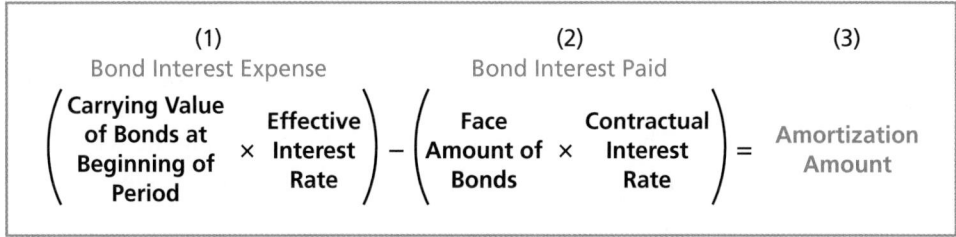

Illustration 15B-1
Computation of amortization—effective-interest method

When the difference between the straight-line method of amortization (Appendix 15C) and the effective-interest method is material, GAAP requires the use of the effective-interest method.

Amortizing Bond Discount

To illustrate the effective-interest method of bond discount amortization, assume that Candlestick, Inc. issues $100,000 of 10%, five-year bonds on January 1, 2012, with interest payable each July 1 and January 1 (pages 676–677). The bonds sell for $92,639 (92.639% of face value). This sales price results in bond discount of $7,361 ($100,000 − $92,639) and an effective-interest rate of 12%. A bond discount amortization schedule, as shown in Illustration 15B-2 (page 696), facilitates the recording of interest expense and the discount amortization. Note that interest expense as a percentage of carrying value remains constant at 6%.

Candlestick Inc.xls

| File | Edit | View | Insert | Format | Tools | Data | Window | Help |

	A	B	C	D	E	F
			CANDLESTICK, INC.			
			Bond Discount Amortization			
			Effective-Interest Method—Semiannual Interest Payments			
			10% Bonds Issued at 12%			
			(B)			
			Interest Expense	**(C)**	**(D)**	**(E)**
	Semiannual	**(A)**	**to Be Recorded**	**Discount**	**Unamortized**	**Bond**
	Interest	**Interest to Be Paid**	**(6% × Preceding Bond**	**Amortization**	**Discount**	**Carrying Value**
	Periods	**(5% × $100,000)**	**Carrying Value)**	**(B) − (A)**	**(D) − (C)**	**($100,000 − D)**
9	Issue date				$7,361	$92,639
10	1	$ 5,000	$ 5,558 (6% × $92,639)	$ 558	6,803	93,197
11	2	5,000	5,592 (6% × $93,197)	592	6,211	93,789
12	3	5,000	5,627 (6% × $93,789)	627	5,584	94,416
13	4	5,000	5,665 (6% × $94,416)	665	4,919	95,081
14	5	5,000	5,705 (6% × $95,081)	705	4,214	95,786
15	6	5,000	5,747 (6% × $95,786)	747	3,467	96,533
16	7	5,000	5,792 (6% × $96,533)	792	2,675	97,325
17	8	5,000	5,840 (6% × $97,325)	840	1,835	98,165
18	9	5,000	5,890 (6% × $98,165)	890	945	99,055
19	10	5,000	5,945* (6% × $99,055)	945	−0−	100,000
20		$50,000	$57,361	$7,361		
22	Column (A) remains constant because the face value of the bonds ($100,000) is multiplied by the semiannual contractual interest rate					
23	(5%) each period.					
24	Column (B) is computed as the preceding bond carrying value times the semiannual effective-interest rate (6%).					
25	Column (C) indicates the discount amortization each period.					
26	Column (D) decreases each period until it reaches zero at maturity.					
27	Column (E) increases each period until it equals face value at maturity.					
29	*$2 difference due to rounding.					

Illustration 15B-2
Bond discount amortization schedule

We have highlighted columns (A), (B), and (C) in the amortization schedule to emphasize their importance. These three columns provide the numbers for each period's journal entries. They are the primary reason for preparing the schedule.

For the first interest period, the computations of interest expense and the bond discount amortization are:

Illustration 15B-3
Computation of bond discount amortization

Interest expense ($92,639 × 6%)	$5,558
Contractual interest ($100,000 × 5%)	5,000
Bond discount amortization	$ 558

Candlestick records the payment of interest and amortization of bond discount on July 1, 2012, as follows.

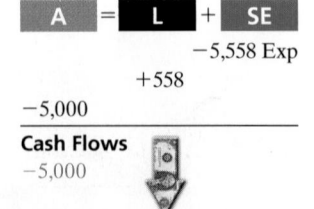

A = L + SE
−5,558 Exp
+558
−5,000

Cash Flows
−5,000

July 1	Interest Expense	5,558	
	Discount on Bonds Payable		558
	Cash		5,000
	(To record payment of bond interest and amortization of bond discount)		

For the second interest period, bond interest expense will be $5,592 ($93,197 × 6%), and the discount amortization will be $592. At December 31, Candlestick makes the following adjusting entry.

Dec. 31	Interest Expense	5,592	
	Discount on Bonds Payable		592
	Interest Payable		5,000
	(To record accrued interest and		
	amortization of bond discount)		

A = **L** + **SE**

              −5,592 Exp
    +592
    +5,000

Cash Flows
no effect

Total interest expense for 2012 is $11,150 ($5,558 + $5,592). On January 1, Candlestick records payment of the interest by a debit to Interest Payable and a credit to Cash.

Amortizing Bond Premium

The amortization of bond premium by the effective-interest method is similar to the procedures described for bond discount. For example, assume that Candlestick, Inc. issues $100,000, 10%, five-year bonds on January 1, 2012, with interest payable on July 1 and January 1 (pages 677–678). In this case, the bonds sell for $108,111. This sales price results in bond premium of $8,111 and an effective-interest rate of 8%. Illustration 15B-4 shows the bond premium amortization schedule.

Helpful Hint

When a bond sells for $108,111, it is quoted as 108.111% of face value. Note that $108,111 can be proven as shown in Appendix 15A.

Illustration 15B-4
Bond premium amortization schedule

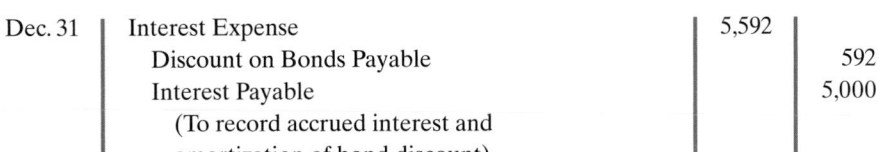

Candlestick Inc.xls

File   Edit   View   Insert   Format   Tools   Data   Window   Help

CANDLESTICK, INC.
Bond Premium Amortization
Effective-Interest Method—Semiannual Interest Payments
10% Bonds Issued at 8%

Semiannual Interest Periods	(A) Interest to Be Paid (5% × $100,000)	(B) Interest Expense to Be Recorded (4% × Preceding Bond Carrying Value)	(C) Premium Amortization (A) − (B)	(D) Unamortized Premium (D) − (C)	(E) Bond Carrying Value ($100,000 + D)
Issue date				$8,111	$108,111
1	$ 5,000	$ 4,324 (4% × $108,111)	$ 676	7,435	107,435
2	5,000	4,297 (4% × $107,435)	703	6,732	106,732
3	5,000	4,269 (4% × $106,732)	731	6,001	106,001
4	5,000	4,240 (4% × $106,001)	760	5,241	105,241
5	5,000	4,210 (4% × $105,241)	790	4,451	104,451
6	5,000	4,178 (4% × $104,451)	822	3,629	103,629
7	5,000	4,145 (4% × $103,629)	855	2,774	102,774
8	5,000	4,111 (4% × $102,774)	889	1,885	101,885
9	5,000	4,075 (4% × $101,885)	925	960	100,960
10	5,000	4,040* (4% × $100,960)	960	–0–	100,000
	$50,000	$41,889	$8,111		

Column **(A)** remains constant because the face value of the bonds ($100,000) is multiplied by the semiannual contractual interest rate (5%) each period.
Column **(B)** is computed as the carrying value of the bonds times the semiannual effective-interest rate (4%).
Column **(C)** indicates the premium amortization each period.
Column **(D)** decreases each period until it reaches zero at maturity.
Column **(E)** decreases each period until it equals face value at maturity.

*$2 difference due to rounding.

For the first interest period, the computations of interest expense and the bond premium amortization are:

Illustration 15B-5
Computation of bond premium amortization

Interest expense ($108,111 × 4%)	$4,324
Contractual interest ($100,000 × 5%)	5,000
Bond premium amortization	**$ 676**

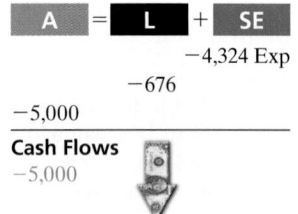

A	=	L	+	SE
				−4,324 Exp
		−676		
−5,000				

Cash Flows
−5,000

Candlestick records payments on the first interest date as follows.

July 1	Interest Expense	4,324	
	Premium on Bonds Payable	676	
	Cash		5,000
	(To record payment of bond interest and amortization of bond premium)		

For the second interest period, interest expense will be $4,297, and the premium amortization will be $703. Total bond interest expense for 2012 is $8,621 ($4,324 + $4,297).

Do it!

Gardner Corporation issues $1,750,000, 10-year, 12% bonds on January 1, 2012, at $1,968,090, to yield 10%. The bonds pay semiannual interest July 1 and January 1. Gardner uses the effective-interest method of amortization.

Instructions

action plan

✔ Compute interest expense by multiplying bond carrying value at the beginning of the period by the effective-interest rate.

✔ Compute credit to cash (or bond interest payable) by multiplying the face value of the bonds by the contractual interest rate.

✔ Compute bond premium or discount amortization, which is the difference between interest expense and cash paid.

✔ Interest expense decreases when the effective-interest method is used for bonds issued at a premium. The reason is that a constant percentage is applied to a decreasing book value to compute interest expense.

(a) Prepare the journal entry to record the issuance of the bonds.

(b) Prepare the journal entry to record the payment of interest on July 1, 2012.

Solution to Comprehensive Do it! for Appendix 15B

(a) 2012

Jan. 1	Cash	1,968,090	
	Bonds Payable		1,750,000
	Premium on Bonds Payable		218,090
	(To record issuance of bonds at a premium)		

(b) 2012

July 1	Interest Expense	98,405*	
	Premium on Bonds Payable	6,595**	
	Cash		105,000
	(To record payment of semiannual interest and amortization of bond premium)		
	*($1,968,090 × 5%)		
	**($105,000 − $98,405)		

✔ **The Navigator**

Summary of Study Objective for Appendix 15B

[8] **Apply the effective-interest method of amortizing bond discount and bond premium.** The effective-interest method results in varying amounts of amortization and interest expense per period but a *constant percentage rate* of interest. When the difference between the straight-line and effective-interest method is material, GAAP requires the use of the effective-interest method.

Glossary for Appendix 15B

Effective-interest method of amortization A method of amortizing bond discount or bond premium that results in periodic interest expense equal to a constant percentage of the carrying value of the bonds. (p. 695).

APPENDIX15C

Straight-Line Amortization

Amortizing Bond Discount

Under the **straight-line method of amortization**, the amortization of bond discount or bond premium results in periodic interest expense of the same amount in each interest period. In other words, the straight-line method results in a constant amount of amortization and interest expense per period. The amount is determined using the formula in Illustration 15C-1.

> **Bond Discount** ÷ **Number of Interest Periods** = **Bond Discount Amortization**

Study Objective [9]
Apply the straight-line method of amortizing bond discount and bond premium.

Illustration 15C-1
Formula for straight-line method of bond discount amortization

In the Candlestick, Inc. example (pages 676–677), the company sold $100,000, five-year, 10% bonds on January 1, 2012, for $92,639. This price resulted in a $7,361 bond discount ($100,000 − $92,639). Interest is payable on July 1 and January 1. The bond discount amortization for each interest period is $736 ($7,361 ÷ 10). Candlestick records the payment of bond interest and the amortization of bond discount on the first interest date (July 1, 2012) as follows.

July 1	Interest Expense	5,736	
	Discount on Bonds Payable		736
	Cash		5,000
	(To record payment of bond interest and amortization of bond discount)		

At December 31, Candlestick makes the following adjusting entry.

Dec. 31	Interest Expense	5,736	
	Discount on Bonds Payable		736
	Interest Payable		5,000
	(To record accrued bond interest and amortization of bond discount)		

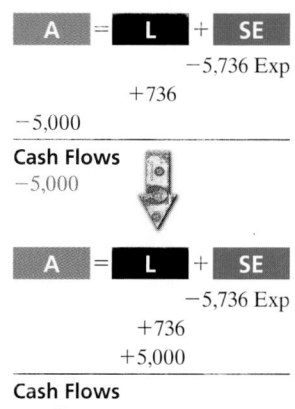

Over the term of the bonds, the balance in Discount on Bonds Payable will decrease annually by the **same amount** until it has a zero balance at the maturity date of the bonds. Thus, the carrying value of the bonds at maturity will be equal to the face value.

It is useful to prepare a bond discount amortization schedule as shown in Illustration 15C-2 (page 700). The schedule shows interest expense, discount amortization, and the carrying value of the bond for each interest period. As indicated, the interest expense recorded **each period** for the Candlestick bond is $5,736. Also note that the carrying value of the bond increases $736 each period until it reaches its face value $100,000 at the end of period 10.

Illustration 15C-2
Bond discount amortization schedule

	Candlestick Inc.xls					□ ▫ ⊠
	🗐 File Edit View Insert Format Tools Data Window Help					

	A	B	C	D	E	F
1			**CANDLESTICK, INC.**			
2			**Bond Discount Amortization**			
3			**Straight-Line Method—Semiannual Interest Payments**			
4						
5		**(A)**	**(B)**	**(C)**	**(D)**	**(E)**
6	**Semiannual**	**Interest to**	**Interest Expense**	**Discount**	**Unamortized**	**Bond**
7	**Interest**	**Be Paid**	**to Be Recorded**	**Amortization**	**Discount**	**Carrying Value**
8	**Periods**	**(5% × $100,000)**	**(A) + (C)**	**($7,361 ÷ 10)**	**(D) − (C)**	**($100,000 − D)**
9	Issue date				$7,361	$92,639
10	1	$ 5,000	$ 5,736	$ 736	6,625	93,375
11	2	5,000	5,736	736	5,889	94,111
12	3	5,000	5,736	736	5,153	94,847
13	4	5,000	5,736	736	4,417	95,583
14	5	5,000	5,736	736	3,681	96,319
15	6	5,000	5,736	736	2,945	97,055
16	7	5,000	5,736	736	2,209	97,791
17	8	5,000	5,736	736	1,473	98,527
18	9	5,000	5,736	736	737	99,263
19	10	5,000	5,737*	737*	–0–	100,000
20		$50,000	$57,361	$7,361		
21						
22	Column **(A)** remains constant because the face value of the bonds ($100,000) is multiplied by the					
23	semiannual contractual interest rate (5%) each period.					
24	Column **(B)** is computed as the interest paid (Column A) plus the discount amortization (Column C).					
25	Column **(C)** indicates the discount amortization each period.					
26	Column **(D)** decreases each period by the same amount until it reaches zero at maturity.					
27	Column **(E)** increases each period by the same amount of discount amortization until it equals the					
28	face value at maturity.					
29	*One dollar difference due to rounding.					

We have highlighted columns (A), (B), and (C) in the amortization schedule to emphasize their importance. These three columns provide the numbers for each period's journal entries. They are the primary reason for preparing the schedule.

Amortizing Bond Premium

The amortization of bond premium parallels that of bond discount. Illustration 15C-3 presents the formula for determining bond premium amortization under the straight-line method.

Illustration 15C-3
Formula for straight-line method of bond premium amortization

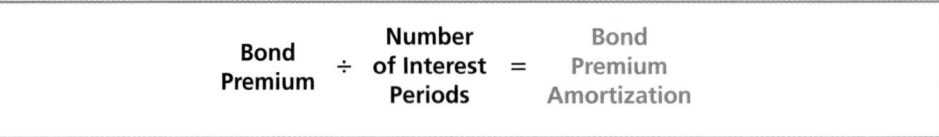

$$\text{Bond Premium} \div \text{Number of Interest Periods} = \text{Bond Premium Amortization}$$

Continuing our example, assume that Candlestick sells the bonds for $108,111, rather than $92,639 (pages 677–678). This sale price results in a bond premium of $8,111 ($108,111 − $100,000). The bond premium amortization for each interest period is $811 ($8,111 ÷ 10). Candlestick records the first payment of interest on July 1 as follows.

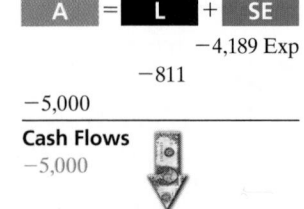

A = L + SE
−4,189 Exp
−811
−5,000

Cash Flows
−5,000

July 1	Interest Expense		4,189	
	Premium on Bonds Payable		811	
	Cash			5,000
	(To record payment of bond interest and			
	amortization of bond premium)			

At December 31, the company makes the following adjusting entry.

Dec. 31	Interest Expense	4,189	
	Premium on Bonds Payable	811	
	Interest Payable		5,000
	(To record accrued bond interest and		
	amortization of bond premium)		

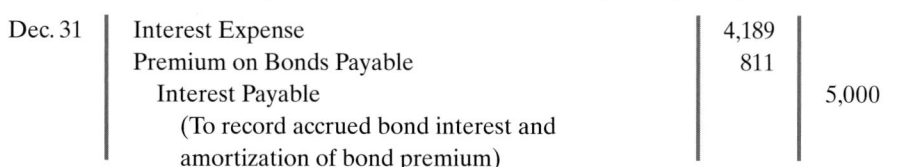

A = L + SE
−4,189 Exp
−811
+5,000

Cash Flows
no effect

Over the term of the bonds, the balance in Premium on Bonds Payable will decrease annually **by the same amount** until it has a zero balance at maturity.

It is useful to prepare a bond premium amortization schedule as shown in Illustration 15C-4. It shows interest expense, premium amortization, and the carrying value of the bond. The interest expense recorded each period for the Candlestick bond is $4,189. Also note that the carrying value of the bond decreases $811 each period until it reaches its face value $100,000 at the end of period 10.

Illustration 15C-4
Bond premium amortization schedule

Candlestick Inc.xls

File Edit View Insert Format Tools Data Window Help

CANDLESTICK, INC.
Bond Premium Amortization
Straight-Line Method—Semiannual Interest Payments

Semiannual Interest Periods	(A) Interest to Be Paid (5% × $100,000)	(B) Interest Expense to Be Recorded (A) − (C)	(C) Premium Amortization ($8,111 ÷ 10)	(D) Unamortized Premium (D) − (C)	(E) Bond Carrying Value ($100,000 + D)
Issue date				$8,111	$108,111
1	$ 5,000	$ 4,189	$ 811	7,300	107,300
2	5,000	4,189	811	6,489	106,489
3	5,000	4,189	811	5,678	105,678
4	5,000	4,189	811	4,867	104,867
5	5,000	4,189	811	4,056	104,056
6	5,000	4,189	811	3,245	103,245
7	5,000	4,189	811	2,434	102,434
8	5,000	4,189	811	1,623	101,623
9	5,000	4,189	811	812	100,812
10	5,000	4,188*	812*	−0−	100,000
	$50,000	$41,889	$8,111		

Column (A) remains constant because the face value of the bonds ($100,000) is multiplied by the semiannual contractual interest rate (5%) each period.
Column (B) is computed as the interest paid (Column A) less the premium amortization (Column C).
Column (C) indicates the premium amortization each period.
Column (D) decreases each period by the same amount until it reaches zero at maturity.
Column (E) decreases each period by the amount of premium amortization until it equals the face value at maturity.
*One dollar difference due to rounding.

Do it!

Glenda Corporation issues $1,750,000, 10-year, 12% bonds on January 1, 2012, for $1,968,090 to yield 10%. The bonds pay semiannual interest July 1 and January 1. Glenda uses the straight-line method of amortization.

Instructions

(a) Prepare the journal entry to record the issuance of the bonds.

(b) Prepare the journal entry to record the payment of interest on July 1, 2012.

action plan

✔ Compute credit to cash (or interest payable) by multiplying the face value of the bonds by the contractual interest rate.

✔ Compute bond premium or discount amortization by dividing bond premium or discount by the total number of periods.

✔ Understand that interest expense decreases when bonds are issued at a premium. The reason is that the amortization of premium reduces the total cost of borrowing.

Solution to Comprehensive Do it! for Appendix 15C

(a) 2012

Jan. 1	Cash	1,968,090	
	Bonds Payable		1,750,000
	Premium on Bonds Payable		218,090

(b) 2012

July 1	Interest Expense	94,095.50**	
	Premium on Bonds Payable	10,904.50*	
	Cash		105,000

*$218,090 ÷ 20
**$105,000 − $10,904.50

The Navigator

Summary of Study Objective for Appendix 15C

[9] Apply the straight-line method of amortizing bond discount and bond premium. The straight-line method of amortization results in a *constant amount* of amortization and interest expense per period.

Glossary for Appendix 15C

Straight-line method of amortization. A method of amortizing bond discount or bond premium that results in allocating the same amount to interest expense in each interest period. (p. 699)

Self-Test, Brief Exercises, Exercises, Problem Set A, and many more components are available for practice in *WileyPLUS*

---

*Note: All **asterisked** Questions, Exercises, and Problems relate to material in the appendices to the chapter.

Self-Test Questions

Answers are on page 718.

(SO 1) **1.** The term used for bonds that are unsecured is:
   a. callable bonds.
   b. indenture bonds.
   c. debenture bonds.
   d. bearer bonds.

(SO 1) **2.** The market interest rate:
   a. is the contractual interest rate used to determine the amount of cash interest paid by the borrower.
   b. is listed in the bond indenture.
   c. is the rate investors demand for loaning funds.
   d. More than one of the above is true.

(SO 2) **3.** Karson Inc. issues 10-year bonds with a maturity value of $200,000. If the bonds are issued at a premium, this indicates that:
   a. the contractual interest rate exceeds the market interest rate.
   b. the market interest rate exceeds the contractual interest rate.

   c. the contractual interest rate and the market interest rate are the same.
   d. no relationship exists between the two rates.

(SO 2) **4.** Four-Nine Corporation issued bonds that pay interest every July 1 and January 1. The entry to accrue bond interest at December 31 includes a:
   a. debit to Interest Payable.
   b. credit to Cash.
   c. credit to Interest Expense.
   d. credit to Interest Payable.

(SO 3) **5.** Gester Corporation retires its $100,000 face value bonds at 105 on January 1, following the payment of semiannual interest. The carrying value of the bonds at the redemption date is $103,745. The entry to record the redemption will include a:
   a. credit of $3,745 to Loss on Bond Redemption.
   b. debit of $3,745 to Premium on Bonds Payable.
   c. credit of $1,255 to Gain on Bond Redemption.
   d. debit of $5,000 to Premium on Bonds Payable.

(SO 3) **6.** Colson Inc. converts $600,000 of bonds sold at face value into 10,000 shares of common stock, par value $1. Both the bonds and the stock have a market value of $760,000. What amount should be credited to Paid-in Capital in Excess of Par—Common Stock as a result of the conversion?
- **a.** $10,000.
- **b.** $160,000.
- **c.** $600,000.
- **d.** $590,000.

(SO 4) **7.** Howard Corporation issued a 20-year mortgage note payable on January 1, 2012. At December 31, 2012, the unpaid principal balance will be reported as:
- **a.** a current liability.
- **b.** a long-term liability.
- **c.** part current and part long-term liability.
- **d.** interest payable.

(SO 4) **8.** Andrews Inc. issues a $497,000, 10% 3-year mortgage note on January 1. The note will be paid in three annual installments of $200,000, each payable at the end of the year. What is the amount of interest expense that should be recognized by Andrews Inc. in the second year?
- **a.** $16,567.
- **b.** $49,700.
- **c.** $34,670.
- **d.** $346,700.

(SO 5) **9.** Lease A does not contain a bargain purchase option, but the lease term is equal to 90 percent of the estimated economic life of the leased property. Lease B does not transfer ownership of the property to the lessee by the end of the lease term, but the lease term is equal to 75 percent of the estimated economic life of the leased property. How should the lessee classify these leases?

	Lease A	Lease B
a.	Operating lease	Capital lease
b.	Operating lease	Operating lease
c.	Capital lease	Operating lease
d.	Capital lease	Capital lease

(SO 6) **10.** For 2012, Corn Flake Corporation reported net income of $300,000. Interest expense was $40,000 and income taxes were $100,000. The times interest earned ratio was:
- **a.** 3 times.
- **b.** 4.4 times.
- **c.** 7.5 times.
- **d.** 11 times.

*11. The market price of a bond is dependent on: (SO 7)
- **a.** the payment amounts.
- **b.** the length of time until the amounts are paid.
- **c.** the interest rate.
- **d.** All of the above.

*12. On January 1, Besalius Inc. issued $1,000,000, 9% bonds (SO 8) for $938,554. The market rate of interest for these bonds is 10%. Interest is payable annually on December 31. Besalius uses the effective-interest method of amortizing bond discount. At the end of the first year, Besalius should report unamortized bond discount of:
- **a.** $54,900.
- **b.** $57,591.
- **c.** $51,610.
- **d.** $51,000.

*13. On January 1, Dias Corporation issued $1,000,000, 10%, (SO 8) 5-year bonds with interest payable on July 1 and January 1. The bonds sold for $1,081,105. The market rate of interest for these bonds was 8%. On the first interest date, using the effective-interest method, the debit entry to Interest Expense is for:
- **a.** $50,000.
- **b.** $54,055.
- **c.** $43,244.
- **d.** $100,811.

*14. On January 1, Hurley Corporation issues $500,000, 5-year, (SO 9) 12% bonds at 96 with interest payable on July 1 and January 1. The entry on July 1 to record payment of bond interest and the amortization of bond discount using the straight-line method will include a:
- **a.** debit to Interest Expense $30,000.
- **b.** debit to Interest Expense $60,000.
- **c.** credit to Discount on Bonds Payable $4,000.
- **d.** credit to Discount on Bonds Payable $2,000.

*15. For the bonds issued in question 14 above, what is the carrying (SO 9) value of the bonds at the end of the third interest period?
- **a.** $486,000.
- **b.** $488,000.
- **c.** $472,000.
- **d.** $464,000.

Go to the book's companion website, **www.wiley.com/college/weygandt**, for additional Self-Test Questions.

The Navigator

Questions

1. (a) What are long-term liabilities? Give three examples. (b) What is a bond?

2. (a) As a source of long-term financing, what are the major advantages of bonds over common stock? (b) What are the major disadvantages in using bonds for long-term financing?

3. Contrast the following types of bonds: (a) secured and unsecured, (b) term and serial, (c) registered and bearer, and (d) convertible and callable.

4. The following terms are important in issuing bonds: (a) face value, (b) contractual interest rate, (c) bond indenture, and (d) bond certificate. Explain each of these terms.

5. Describe the two major obligations incurred by a company when bonds are issued.

6. Assume that Koslowski Inc. sold bonds with a face value of $100,000 for $104,000. Was the market interest rate equal to, less than, or greater than the bonds' contractual interest rate? Explain.

7. If a 7%, 10-year, $800,000 bond is issued at face value and interest is paid semiannually, what is the amount of the interest payment at the end of the first semiannual period?

8. If the Bonds Payable account has a balance of $900,000 and the Discount on Bonds Payable account has a balance of $40,000, what is the carrying value of the bonds?

9. Which accounts are debited and which are credited if a bond issue originally sold at a premium is redeemed before maturity at 97 immediately following the payment of interest?

10. Henricks Corporation is considering issuing a convertible bond. What is a convertible bond? Discuss the advantages of a convertible bond from the standpoint of (a) the bondholders and (b) the issuing corporation.

11. Tim Brown, a friend of yours, has recently purchased a home for $125,000, paying $25,000 down and the remainder financed by a 10.5%, 20-year mortgage, payable at $998.38 per month. At the end of the first month, Tim receives a statement from the bank indicating that only $123.38 of principal was paid during the month. At this rate, he calculates that it will take over 67 years to pay off the mortgage. Is he right? Discuss.

12. (a) What is a lease agreement? (b) What are the two most common types of leases? (c) Distinguish between the two types of leases.

13. Clooney Company rents a warehouse on a month-to-month basis for the storage of its excess inventory. The company periodically must rent space when its production greatly exceeds actual sales. What is the nature of this type of lease agreement, and what accounting treatment should be used?

14. Rondelli Company entered into an agreement to lease 12 computers from Estes Electronics Inc. The present value of the lease payments is $186,300. Assuming that this is a capital lease, what entry would Rondelli Company make on the date of the lease agreement?

15. In general, what are the requirements for the financial statement presentation of long-term liabilities?

*16. Laura Hiatt is discussing the advantages of the effective-interest method of bond amortization with her accounting staff. What do you think Laura is saying?

*17. Markham Corporation issues $500,000 of 9%, 5-year bonds on January 1, 2012, at 104. If Markham uses the effective-interest method in amortizing the premium, will the annual interest expense increase or decrease over the life of the bonds? Explain.

*18. Tina Cruz and Dale Commons are discussing how the market price of a bond is determined. Tina believes that the market price of a bond is solely a function of the amount of the principal payment at the end of the term of a bond. Is she right? Discuss.

*19. Explain the straight-line method of amortizing discount and premium on bonds payable.

*20. DeWeese Corporation issues $400,000 of 8%, 5-year bonds on January 1, 2012, at 105. Assuming that the straight-line method is used to amortize the premium, what is the total amount of interest expense for 2012?

21. **PEPSICO** Did PepsiCo redeem any of its debt during the fiscal year ended December 26, 2009? (*Hint:* Examine PepsiCo's statement of cash flows.)

Brief Exercises

Compare bond versus stock financing.
(SO 1)

BE15-1 Laci Inc. is considering two alternatives to finance its construction of a new $2 million plant.

(a) Issuance of 200,000 shares of common stock at the market price of $10 per share.
(b) Issuance of $2 million, 8% bonds at face value.

Complete the following table, and indicate which alternative is preferable.

	Issue Stock	Issue Bond
Income before interest and taxes	$700,000	$700,000
Interest expense from bonds	_____	_____
Income before income taxes	$	$
Income tax expense (30%)	_____	_____
Net income	$	$
Outstanding shares	_____	500,000
Earnings per share	_____	_____

Prepare entries for bonds issued at face value.
(SO 2)

BE15-2 Xenia Corporation issued 3,000, 8%, 5-year, $1,000 bonds dated January 1, 2012, at 100.
(a) Prepare the journal entry to record the sale of these bonds on January 1, 2012.
(b) Prepare the journal entry to record the first interest payment on July 1, 2012 (interest payable semiannually), assuming no previous accrual of interest.
(c) Prepare the adjusting journal entry on December 31, 2012, to record interest expense.

Prepare entries for bonds sold at a discount and a premium.
(SO 2)

BE15-3 Robbell Company issues $2 million, 10-year, 8% bonds at 97, with interest payable on July 1 and January 1.
(a) Prepare the journal entry to record the sale of these bonds on January 1, 2012.
(b) Assuming instead that the above bonds sold for 104, prepare the journal entry to record the sale of these bonds on January 1, 2012.

Prepare entries for bonds issued.
(SO 2)

BE15-4 Beetown Company has issued three different bonds during 2012. Interest is payable semiannually on each of these bonds.

1. On January 1, 2012, 1,000, 8%, 5-year, $1,000 bonds dated January 1, 2012, were issued at face value.
2. On July 1, $800,000, 9%, 5-year bonds dated July 1, 2012, were issued at 102.
3. On September 1, $200,000, 7%, 5-year bonds dated September 1, 2012, were issued at 98.

Prepare the journal entry to record each bond transaction at the date of issuance.

BE15-5 The balance sheet for Focus Consulting reports the following information on July 1, 2012.

Prepare entry for redemption of bonds.
(SO 3)

Long-term liabilities
Bonds payable $1,000,000
Less: Discount on bonds payable 60,000 $940,000

Focus decides to redeem these bonds at 101 after paying semiannual interest. Prepare the journal entry to record the redemption on July 1, 2012.

BE15-6 Bondorf Inc. issues a $600,000, 10%, 10-year mortgage note on December 31, 2012, to obtain financing for a new building. The terms provide for semiannual installment payments of $48,145. Prepare the entry to record the mortgage loan on December 31, 2012, and the first installment payment.

Prepare entries for long-term notes payable.
(SO 4)

BE15-7 Prepare the journal entries that the lessee should make to record the following transactions.

Contrast accounting for operating and capital leases.
(SO 5)

1. The lessee makes a lease payment of $80,000 to the lessor in an operating lease transaction.
2. Bethel Company leases a new building from Sasse Construction, Inc. The present value of the lease payments is $700,000. The lease qualifies as a capital lease.

BE15-8 Presented below are long-term liability items for Beun Company at December 31, 2012. Prepare the long-term liabilities section of the balance sheet for Beun Company.

Prepare statement presentation of long-term liabilities.
(SO 6)

Bonds payable, due 2014 $500,000
Lease liability 70,000
Notes payable, due 2017 80,000
Discount on bonds payable 45,000

***BE15-9** (a) What is the present value of $10,000 due 8 periods from now, discounted at 10%?
(b) What is the present value of $20,000 to be received at the end of each of 6 periods, discounted at 8%?

Determine present value.
(SO 7)

***BE15-10** Presented below is the partial bond discount amortization schedule for Bilder Corp. Bilder uses the effective-interest method of amortization.

Use effective-interest method of bond amortization.
(SO 8)

Semiannual Interest Periods	Interest to Be Paid	Interest Expense to Be Recorded	Discount Amortization	Unamortized Discount	Bond Carrying Value
Issue date				$62,311	$937,689
1	$45,000	$46,884	$1,884	60,427	939,573
2	45,000	46,979	1,979	58,448	941,552

Instructions
(a) Prepare the journal entry to record the payment of interest and the discount amortization at the end of period 1.
(b) Explain why interest expense is greater than interest paid.
(c) Explain why interest expense will increase each period.

***BE15-11** Pagewynne Company issues $5 million, 10-year, 9% bonds at 96, with interest payable on July 1 and January 1. The straight-line method is used to amortize bond discount.

Prepare entries for bonds issued at a discount.
(SO 9)

(a) Prepare the journal entry to record the sale of these bonds on January 1, 2012.
(b) Prepare the journal entry to record interest expense and bond discount amortization on July 1, 2012, assuming no previous accrual of interest.

***BE15-12** Binger Inc. issues $3 million, 5-year, 10% bonds at 102, with interest payable on July 1 and January 1. The straight-line method is used to amortize bond premium.

Prepare entries for bonds issued at a premium.
(SO 9)

(a) Prepare the journal entry to record the sale of these bonds on January 1, 2012.
(b) Prepare the journal entry to record interest expense and bond premium amortization on July 1, 2012, assuming no previous accrual of interest.

Do it! Review

Evaluate statements about bonds.

(SO 1)

Do it! 15-1   State whether each of the following statements is true or false.

_____ **1.** Mortgage bonds and sinking fund bonds are both examples of debenture bonds.

_____ **2.** Convertible bonds are also known as callable bonds.

_____ **3.** The market rate is the rate investors demand for loaning funds.

_____ **4.** Semiannual interest on bonds is equal to the face value times the stated rate times 6/12.

_____ **5.** The present value of a bond is the value at which it should sell in the market.

Prepare journal entry for bond issuance and show balance sheet presentation.

(SO 2)

Do it! 15-2   Biskup Corporation issues $300,000 of bonds for $312,000. (a) Prepare the journal entry to record the issuance of the bonds, and (b) show how the bonds would be reported on the balance sheet at the date of issuance.

Prepare entry for bond redemption.

(SO 3)

Do it! 15-3   Venice Corporation issued $400,000 of 10-year bonds at a discount. Prior to maturity, when the carrying value of the bonds was $390,000, the company retired the bonds at 99. Prepare the entry to record the redemption of the bonds.

Prepare entries for mortgage note and installment payment on note.

(SO 4)

Do it! 15-4   Bluebell Orchard issues a $350,000, 6%, 15-year mortgage note to obtain needed financing for a new lab. The terms call for semiannual payments of $17,857 each. Prepare the entries to record the mortgage loan and the first installment payment.

Prepare entry for lease, and compute debt to total assets ratio.

(SO 5)

Do it! 15-5   Seipple Corporation leases new equipment on December 31, 2012. The lease transfers ownership of the equipment to Seipple at the end of the lease. The present value of the lease payments is $192,000. After recording this lease, Seipple has assets of $1,800,000, liabilities of $1,100,000, and stockholders' equity of $700,000. (a) Prepare the entry to record the lease, and (b) compute and discuss the debt to total assets ratio at year-end.

Exercises

Evaluate statements about bonds.

(SO 1)

E15-1   Jeff Bly has prepared the following list of statements about bonds.

1. Bonds are a form of interest-bearing notes payable.
2. When seeking long-term financing, an advantage of issuing bonds over issuing common stock is that stockholder control is not affected.
3. When seeking long-term financing, an advantage of issuing common stock over issuing bonds is that tax savings result.
4. Secured bonds have specific assets of the issuer pledged as collateral for the bonds.
5. Secured bonds are also known as debenture bonds.
6. Bonds that mature in installments are called term bonds.
7. A conversion feature may be added to bonds to make them more attractive to bond buyers.
8. The rate used to determine the amount of cash interest the borrower pays is called the stated rate.
9. Bond prices are usually quoted as a percentage of the face value of the bond.
10. The present value of a bond is the value at which it should sell in the marketplace.

Instructions

Identify each statement as true or false. If false, indicate how to correct the statement.

Compare two alternatives of financing—issuance of common stock vs. issuance of bonds.

(SO 1)

E15-2   Bohlander Airlines is considering two alternatives for the financing of a purchase of a fleet of airplanes. These two alternatives are:

1. Issue 60,000 shares of common stock at $45 per share. (Cash dividends have not been paid nor is the payment of any contemplated).
2. Issue 10%, 10-year bonds at face value for $2,700,000.

It is estimated that the company will earn $800,000 before interest and taxes as a result of this purchase. The company has an estimated tax rate of 30% and has 90,000 shares of common stock outstanding prior to the new financing.

Instructions

Determine the effect on net income and earnings per share for these two methods of financing.

E15-3   On January 1, Camel Cove Company issued $500,000, 10%, 10-year bonds at face value. Interest is payable semiannually on July 1 and January 1.

Prepare entries for issuance of bonds, and payment and accrual of bond interest.

(SO 2)

Instructions
Present journal entries to record the following.

(a) The issuance of the bonds.
(b) The payment of interest on July 1, assuming that interest was not accrued on June 30.
(c) The accrual of interest on December 31.

E15-4   On January 1, Borgstrom Company issued $300,000, 8%, 5-year bonds at face value. Interest is payable semiannually on July 1 and January 1.

Prepare entries for bonds issued at face value.

(SO 2)

Instructions
Prepare journal entries to record the following events.

(a) The issuance of the bonds.
(b) The payment of interest on July 1, assuming no previous accrual of interest.
(c) The accrual of interest on December 31.

E15-5   Reffue Company issued $400,000 of 9%, 10-year bonds on January 1, 2012, at face value. Interest is payable semiannually on July 1 and January 1.

Prepare entries for bonds issued at face value.

(SO 2, 3)

Instructions
Prepare the journal entries to record the following events.

(a) The issuance of the bonds.
(b) The payment of interest on July 1, assuming no previous accrual of interest.
(c) The accrual of interest on December 31.
(d) The redemption of bonds at maturity, assuming interest for the last interest period has been paid and recorded.

E15-6   Pas Company issued $1,000,000 of bonds on January 1, 2012.

Prepare entries for issuance, retirement, and conversion of bonds.

(SO 2, 3)

Instructions
(a) Prepare the journal entry to record the issuance of the bonds if they are issued at (1) 100, (2) 98, and (3) 103.
(b) Prepare the journal entry to record the retirement of the bonds at maturity, assuming the bonds were issued at 100.
(c) Prepare the journal entry to record the retirement of the bonds before maturity at 98. Assume the balance in Premium on Bonds Payable is $9,000.
(d) Prepare the journal entry to record the conversion of the bonds into 30,000 shares of $10 par value common stock. Assume the bonds were issued at par.

E15-7   Jacobson Company issued $500,000 of 5-year, 8% bonds at 97 on January 1, 2012. The bonds pay interest twice a year.

Prepare entries to record issuance of bonds at discount and premium.

(SO 2)

Instructions
(a) (1) Prepare the journal entry to record the issuance of the bonds.
       (2) Compute the total cost of borrowing for these bonds.
(b) Repeat the requirements from part (a), assuming the bonds were issued at 105.

E15-8   The following section is taken from Koster Corp.'s balance sheet at December 31, 2011.

Prepare entries for bond interest and redemption.

(SO 2, 3)

Current liabilities		
Interest payable	$	72,000
Long-term liabilities		
Bonds payable, 9%, due January 1, 2016		1,600,000

Bond interest is payable semiannually on January 1 and July 1. The bonds are callable on any interest date.

Instructions
(a) Journalize the payment of the bond interest on January 1, 2012.
(b) Assume that on January 1, 2012, after paying interest, Koster calls bonds having a face value of $600,000. The call price is 104. Record the redemption of the bonds.
(c) Prepare the entry to record the payment of interest on July 1, 2012, assuming no previous accrual of interest on the remaining bonds.

Prepare entries for redemption of bonds and conversion of bonds into common stock.

(SO 3)

E15-9   Presented below are three independent situations.

1. Wakarusa Corporation retired $130,000 face value, 12% bonds on June 30, 2012, at 102. The carrying value of the bonds at the redemption date was $117,500. The bonds pay semiannual interest, and the interest payment due on June 30, 2012, has been made and recorded.
2. Pin Oak Inc. retired $150,000 face value, 12.5% bonds on June 30, 2012, at 98. The carrying value of the bonds at the redemption date was $151,000. The bonds pay semiannual interest, and the interest payment due on June 30, 2012, has been made and recorded.
3. Mishawaka Company has $80,000, 8%, 12-year convertible bonds outstanding. These bonds were sold at face value and pay semiannual interest on June 30 and December 31 of each year. The bonds are convertible into 30 shares of Mishawaka $5 par value common stock for each $1,000 worth of bonds. On December 31, 2012, after the bond interest has been paid, $20,000 face value bonds were converted. The market value of Mishawaka common stock was $44 per share on December 31, 2012.

Instructions

For each independent situation above, prepare the appropriate journal entry for the redemption or conversion of the bonds.

Prepare entries to record mortgage note and installment payments.

(SO 4)

E15-10   Bay Front Co. receives $240,000 when it issues a $240,000, 10%, mortgage note payable to finance the construction of a building at December 31, 2012. The terms provide for semiannual installment payments of $20,000 on June 30 and December 31.

Instructions

Prepare the journal entries to record the mortgage loan and the first two installment payments.

Prepare entries to record mortgage note and installment payments.

(SO 4)

E15-11   Amethyst Company borrowed $300,000 on January 1, 2012, by issuing a $300,000, 8% mortgage note payable. The terms call for semiannual installment payments of $20,000 on June 30 and December 31.

Instructions

(a) Prepare the journal entries to record the mortgage loan and the first two installment payments.
(b) Indicate the amount of mortgage note payable to be reported as a current liability and as a long-term liability at December 31, 2012.

Prepare entries for operating lease and capital lease.

(SO 5)

E15-12   Presented below are two independent situations.

1. Sunny Isles Car Rental leased a car to Emmaus Company for one year. Terms of the operating lease agreement call for monthly payments of $500.
2. On January 1, 2012, Wruck Inc. entered into an agreement to lease 20 computers from Braskich Electronics. The terms of the lease agreement require three annual rental payments of $30,000 (including 10% interest) beginning December 31, 2012. The present value of the three rental payments is $74,606. Wruck considers this a capital lease.

Instructions

(a) Prepare the appropriate journal entry to be made by Emmaus Company for the first lease payment.
(b) Prepare the journal entry to record the lease agreement on the books of Wruck Inc. on January 1, 2012.

Prepare long-term liabilities section.

(SO 6)

E15-13   The adjusted trial balance for Olde Farm Corporation at the end of the current year contained the following accounts.

Interest Payable	$ 9,000
Lease Liability	89,500
Bonds Payable, due 2017	180,000
Premium on Bonds Payable	32,000

Instructions

Prepare the long-term liabilities section of the balance sheet.

E15-14   Brasswood Corporation reports the following amounts in its 2012 financial statements:

Compute debt to total assets and times interest earned ratios.
(SO 6)

	At December 31, 2012	For the Year 2012
Total assets	$1,000,000	
Total liabilities	620,000	
Total stockholders' equity	?	
Interest expense		$ 7,000
Income tax expense		100,000
Net income		150,000

Instructions
(a) Compute the December 31, 2012, balance in stockholders' equity.
(b) Compute the debt to total assets ratio at December 31, 2012.
(c) Compute times interest earned for 2012.

*E15-15   Brislin Corporation is issuing $200,000 of 8%, 5-year bonds when potential bond investors want a return of 10%. Interest is payable semiannually.

Compute market price of bonds.
(SO 7)

Instructions
Compute the market price (present value) of the bonds.

*E15-16   Hoboken Corporation issued $600,000, 9%, 10-year bonds on January 1, 2012, for $562,613. This price resulted in an effective-interest rate of 10% on the bonds. Interest is payable semiannually on July 1 and January 1. Hoboken uses the effective-interest method to amortize bond premium or discount.

Prepare entries for issuance of bonds, payment of interest, and amortization of discount using effective-interest method.
(SO 8)

Instructions
Prepare the journal entries to record the following. (Round to the nearest dollar.)
(a) The issuance of the bonds.
(b) The payment of interest and the discount amortization on July 1, 2012, assuming that interest was not accrued on June 30.
(c) The accrual of interest and the discount amortization on December 31, 2012.

*E15-17   WJTY Company issued $300,000, 11%, 10-year bonds on January 1, 2012, for $318,694. This price resulted in an effective-interest rate of 10% on the bonds. Interest is payable semiannually on July 1 and January 1. WJTY uses the effective-interest method to amortize bond premium or discount.

Prepare entries for issuance of bonds, payment of interest, and amortization of premium using effective-interest method.
(SO 8)

Instructions
Prepare the journal entries to record the following. (Round to the nearest dollar.)
(a) The issuance of the bonds.
(b) The payment of interest and the premium amortization on July 1, 2012, assuming that interest was not accrued on June 30.
(c) The accrual of interest and the premium amortization on December 31, 2012.

*E15-18   Caruba Company issued $400,000, 9%, 20-year bonds on January 1, 2012, at 103. Interest is payable semiannually on July 1 and January 1. Caruba uses straight-line amortization for bond premium or discount.

Prepare entries to record issuance of bonds, payment of interest, amortization of premium, and redemption at maturity.
(SO 3, 9)

Instructions
Prepare the journal entries to record the following.
(a) The issuance of the bonds.
(b) The payment of interest and the premium amortization on July 1, 2012, assuming that interest was not accrued on June 30.
(c) The accrual of interest and the premium amortization on December 31, 2012.
(d) The redemption of the bonds at maturity, assuming interest for the last interest period has been paid and recorded.

*E15-19   Caygill Company issued $800,000, 11%, 10-year bonds on December 31, 2011, for $730,000. Interest is payable semiannually on June 30 and December 31. Caygill Company uses the straight-line method to amortize bond premium or discount.

Prepare entries to record issuance of bonds, payment of interest, amortization of discount, and redemption at maturity.
(SO 3, 9)

Instructions
Prepare the journal entries to record the following.

(a) The issuance of the bonds.
(b) The payment of interest and the discount amortization on June 30, 2012.
(c) The payment of interest and the discount amortization on December 31, 2012.
(d) The redemption of the bonds at maturity, assuming interest for the last interest period has been paid and recorded.

Exercises: Set B

Visit the book's companion website, at **www.wiley.com/college/weygandt**, and choose the Student Companion site to access Exercise Set B.

Problems: Set A

Prepare entries to record issuance of bonds, interest accrual, and bond redemption.
(SO 2, 3, 6)

P15-1A On May 1, 2012, Chance Corp. issued $600,000, 9%, 5-year bonds at face value. The bonds were dated May 1, 2012, and pay interest semiannually on May 1 and November 1. Financial statements are prepared annually on December 31.

Instructions
(a) Prepare the journal entry to record the issuance of the bonds.
(b) Prepare the adjusting entry to record the accrual of interest on December 31, 2012.
(c) Show the balance sheet presentation on December 31, 2012.

(d) Int. exp. $18,000

(d) Prepare the journal entry to record payment of interest on May 1, 2013, assuming no accrual of interest from January 1, 2013, to May 1, 2013.
(e) Prepare the journal entry to record payment of interest on November 1, 2013.

(f) Loss $12,000

(f) Assume that on November 1, 2013, Chance calls the bonds at 102. Record the redemption of the bonds.

Prepare entries to record issuance of bonds, interest accrual, and bond redemption.
(SO 2, 3, 6)

P15-2A Cherney Electric sold $500,000, 10%, 10-year bonds on January 1, 2012. The bonds were dated January 1 and paid interest on January 1 and July 1. The bonds were sold at 104.

Instructions
(a) Prepare the journal entry to record the issuance of the bonds on January 1, 2012.
(b) At December 31, 2012, the balance in the Premium on Bonds Payable account is $18,000. Show the balance sheet presentation of accrued interest and the bond liability at December 31, 2012.

(c) Loss $9,000

(c) On January 1, 2014, when the carrying value of the bonds was $516,000, the company redeemed the bonds at 105. Record the redemption of the bonds assuming that interest for the period has already been paid.

Prepare installment payments schedule and journal entries for a mortgage note payable.
(SO 4)

P15-3A Dutch Hollow Electronics issues a $400,000, 8%, 10-year mortgage note on December 31, 2011. The proceeds from the note are to be used in financing a new research laboratory. The terms of the note provide for semiannual installment payments, exclusive of real estate taxes and insurance, of $29,433. Payments are due June 30 and December 31.

Instructions

(b) June 30 Mortgage Payable $13,433

(a) Prepare an installment payments schedule for the first 2 years.
(b) Prepare the entries for (1) the loan and (2) the first two installment payments.

(c) Current liability—2012 $29,639

(c) Show how the total mortgage liability should be reported on the balance sheet at December 31, 2012.

Analyze three different lease situations and prepare journal entries.
(SO 5)

P15-4A Presented below are three different lease transactions that occurred for Manitoba Inc. in 2012. Assume that all lease contracts start on January 1, 2012. In no case does Manitoba receive title to the properties leased during or at the end of the lease term.

	Lessor		
	Farrey Delivery	**DiBell Co.**	**Diederich Auto**
Type of property	Computer	Delivery equipment	Automobile
Yearly rental	$ 6,000	$ 4,200	$ 3,700
Lease term	6 years	4 years	2 years
Estimated economic life	7 years	7 years	5 years
Fair value of lease asset	$33,000	$19,000	$11,000
Present value of the lease rental payments	$31,000	$13,000	$ 6,400
Bargain purchase option	None	None	None

Instructions

(a) Which of the leases are operating leases and which are capital leases? Explain.

(b) How should the lease transaction for DiBell Co. be recorded in 2012?

(c) How should the lease transaction for Farrey Delivery be recorded on January 1, 2012?

*P15-5A   On July 1, 2012, Charisse Corporation issued $2,000,000 face value, 10%, 10-year bonds at $2,271,813. This price resulted in an effective-interest rate of 8% on the bonds. Charisse uses the effective-interest method to amortize bond premium or discount. The bonds pay semiannual interest July 1 and January 1.

Prepare entries to record issuance of bonds, payment of interest, and amortization of bond premium using effective-interest method.
(SO 2, 8)

Instructions

(Round all computations to the nearest dollar.)

(a) Prepare the journal entry to record the issuance of the bonds on July 1, 2012.

(b) Prepare an amortization table through December 31, 2013 (3 interest periods) for this bond issue.

(c) Prepare the journal entry to record the accrual of interest and the amortization of the premium on December 31, 2012.

(c) Amortization $9,127

(d) Prepare the journal entry to record the payment of interest and the amortization of the premium on July 1, 2013, assuming no accrual of interest on June 30.

(d) Amortization $9,493

(e) Prepare the journal entry to record the accrual of interest and the amortization of the premium on December 31, 2013.

(e) Amortization $9,872

*P15-6A   On July 1, 2012, Francesca Company issued $4,000,000 face value, 8%, 10-year bonds at $3,501,514. This price resulted in an effective-interest rate of 10% on the bonds. Francesca uses the effective-interest method to amortize bond premium or discount. The bonds pay semiannual interest July 1 and January 1.

Prepare entries to record issuance of bonds, payment of interest, and amortization of discount using effective-interest method. In addition, answer questions.
(SO 2, 8)

Instructions

(Round all computations to the nearest dollar.)

(a) Prepare the journal entries to record the following transactions.

　(1) The issuance of the bonds on July 1, 2012.

　(2) The accrual of interest and the amortization of the discount on December 31, 2012.

　(3) The payment of interest and the amortization of the discount on July 1, 2013, assuming no accrual of interest on June 30.

(a) (3) Amortization $15,830

　(4) The accrual of interest and the amortization of the discount on December 31, 2013.

(a) (4) Amortization $16,621

(b) Show the proper balance sheet presentation for the liability for bonds payable on the December 31, 2013, balance sheet.

(b) Bond carrying value $3,549,041

(c) ━━━━▶ Provide the answers to the following questions in letter form.

　(1) What amount of interest expense is reported for 2013?

　(2) Would the bond interest expense reported in 2013 be the same as, greater than, or less than the amount that would be reported if the straight-line method of amortization were used?

　(3) Determine the total cost of borrowing over the life of the bond.

　(4) Would the total bond interest expense be greater than, the same as, or less than the total interest expense that would be reported if the straight-line method of amortization were used?

*P15-7A   Brown Deer Electric sold $3,000,000, 10%, 10-year bonds on January 1, 2012. The bonds were dated January 1 and pay interest July 1 and January 1. Brown Deer Electric uses the straight-line method to amortize bond premium or discount. The bonds were sold at 104. Assume no interest is accrued on June 30.

Prepare entries to record issuance of bonds, interest accrual, and straight-line amortization for 2 years.
(SO 6, 9)

Instructions

(a) Prepare the journal entry to record the issuance of the bonds on January 1, 2012.

(b) Prepare a bond premium amortization schedule for the first 4 interest periods.

(b) Amortization $6,000

(c) Prepare the journal entries for interest and the amortization of the premium in 2012 and 2013.

(d) Show the balance sheet presentation of the bond liability at December 31, 2013.

(d) Premium on bonds payable $96,000

*P15-8A   Canyon Run Company sold $2,500,000, 8%, 10-year bonds on July 1, 2012. The bonds were dated July 1, 2012, and pay interest July 1 and January 1. Canyon Run Company uses the straight-line method to amortize bond premium or discount. Assume no interest is accrued on June 30.

Prepare entries to record issuance of bonds, interest, and straight-line amortization of bond premium and discount.
(SO 6, 9)

(a) Amortization $5,000
(b) Amortization $2,500
(c) Premium on bonds
     payable $95,000
     Discount on bonds
     payable $47,500

Prepare entries to record interest payments, straight-line premium amortization, and redemption of bonds.

(SO 2, 3, 9)

Instructions

(a) Prepare all the necessary journal entries to record the issuance of the bonds and bond interest expense for 2012, assuming that the bonds sold at 104.

(b) Prepare journal entries as in part (a) assuming that the bonds sold at 98.

(c) Show balance sheet presentation for each bond issue at December 31, 2012.

*P15-9A   The following is taken from the Gajda Company balance sheet.

GAJDA COMPANY
Balance Sheet (partial)
December 31, 2012

Current liabilities		
Interest payable (for 6 months from July 1 to December 31)		$ 105,000
Long-term liabilities		
Bonds payable, 7% due January 1, 2023	$3,000,000	
Add: Premium on bonds payable	200,000	$3,200,000

Interest is payable semiannually on January 1 and July 1. The bonds are callable on any semiannual interest date. Gajda uses straight-line amortization for any bond premium or discount. From December 31, 2012, the bonds will be outstanding for an additional 10 years (120 months).

Instructions

(a) Journalize the payment of bond interest on January 1, 2013.

(b) Amortization $10,000

(b) Prepare the entry to amortize bond premium and to pay the interest due on July 1, 2013, assuming no accrual of interest on June 30.

(c) Gain $64,000

(c) Assume that on July 1, 2013, after paying interest, Gajda Company calls bonds having a face value of $1,200,000. The call price is 101. Record the redemption of the bonds.

(d) Amortization $6,000

(d) Prepare the adjusting entry at December 31, 2013, to amortize bond premium and to accrue interest on the remaining bonds.

Problems: Set B

Prepare entries to record issuance of bonds, interest accrual, and bond redemption.

(SO 2, 3, 6)

P15-1B   On June 1, 2012, Lublin Corp. issued $2,000,000, 9%, 5-year bonds at face value. The bonds were dated June 1, 2012, and pay interest semiannually on June 1 and December 1. Financial statements are prepared annually on December 31.

Instructions

(a) Prepare the journal entry to record the issuance of the bonds.

(b) Prepare the adjusting entry to record the accrual of interest on December 31, 2012.

(c) Show the balance sheet presentation on December 31, 2012.

(d) Int. exp. $75,000

(d) Prepare the journal entry to record payment of interest on June 1, 2013, assuming no accrual of interest from January 1, 2013, to June 1, 2013.

(e) Prepare the journal entry to record payment of interest on December 1, 2013.

(f) Loss $40,000

(f) Assume that on December 1, 2013, Lublin calls the bonds at 102. Record the redemption of the bonds.

Prepare entries to record issuance of bonds, interest accrual, and bond redemption.

(SO 2, 3, 6)

P15-2B   Petoskey Co. sold $800,000, 9%, 10-year bonds on January 1, 2012. The bonds were dated January 1, and interest is paid on January 1 and July 1. The bonds were sold at 105.

Instructions

(a) Prepare the journal entry to record the issuance of the bonds on January 1, 2012.

(b) At December 31, 2012, the balance in the Premium on Bonds Payable account is $36,000. Show the balance sheet presentation of accrued interest and the bond liability at December 31, 2012.

(c) Loss $8,000

(c) On January 1, 2014, when the carrying value of the bonds was $832,000, the company redeemed the bonds at 105. Record the redemption of the bonds assuming that interest for the period has already been paid.

Prepare installment payments schedule and journal entries for a mortgage note payable.

(SO 4)

P15-3B   Giordano's Electronics issues a $600,000, 8%, 10-year mortgage note on December 31, 2012, to help finance a plant expansion program. The terms provide for semiannual installment payments, not including real estate taxes and insurance, of $44,149. Payments are due June 30 and December 31.

Instructions
(a) Prepare an installment payments schedule for the first 2 years.
(b) Prepare the entries for (1) the mortgage loan and (2) the first two installment payments.
(c) Show how the total mortgage liability should be reported on the balance sheet at December 31, 2013.

(b) June 30 Mortgage
Payable $20,149
(c) Current liability—2013:
$44,458

P15-4B Presented below are three different lease transactions in which Kristi Enterprises engaged in 2012. Assume that all lease transactions start on January 1, 2012. In no case does Kristi receive title to the properties leased during or at the end of the lease term.

Analyze three different lease situations and prepare journal entries.
(SO 5)

	Lessor		
	Denham Springs Co.	**Hofmeister Co.**	**Janca Inc.**
Type of property	Bulldozer	Truck	Furniture
Bargain purchase option	None	None	None
Lease term	4 years	6 years	3 years
Estimated economic life	8 years	7 years	5 years
Yearly rental	$13,000	$20,000	$ 3,000
Fair value of leased asset	$80,000	$96,000	$20,500
Present value of the lease rental payments	$48,000	$82,000	$ 9,000

Instructions
(a) Identify the leases above as operating or capital leases. Explain.
(b) How should the lease transaction for Hofmeister Co. be recorded on January 1, 2012?
(c) How should the lease transaction for Janca Inc. be recorded in 2012?

P15-5B On July 1, 2012, Sagittarius Satellites issued $4,500,000 face value, 9%, 10-year bonds at $4,219,600. This price resulted in an effective-interest rate of 10% on the bonds. Sagittarius uses the effective-interest method to amortize bond premium or discount. The bonds pay semiannual interest July 1 and January 1.

Prepare entries to record issuance of bonds, payment of interest, and amortization of bond discount using effective-interest method.
(SO 2, 8)

Instructions
(Round all computations to the nearest dollar.)
(a) Prepare the journal entry to record the issuance of the bonds on July 1, 2012.
(b) Prepare an amortization table through December 31, 2013 (3 interest periods) for this bond issue.
(c) Prepare the journal entry to record the accrual of interest and the amortization of the discount on December 31, 2012.
(d) Prepare the journal entry to record the payment of interest and the amortization of the discount on July 1, 2013, assuming that interest was not accrued on June 30.
(e) Prepare the journal entry to record the accrual of interest and the amortization of the discount on December 31, 2013.

(c) Amortization $8,480

(d) Amortization $8,904

(e) Amortization $9,349

P15-6B On July 1, 2012, Dacotah Chemical Company issued $4,000,000 face value, 10%, 10-year bonds at $4,543,627. This price resulted in an 8% effective-interest rate on the bonds. Dacotah uses the effective-interest method to amortize bond premium or discount. The bonds pay semiannual interest on each July 1 and January 1.

Prepare entries to record issuance of bonds, payment of interest, and amortization of premium using effective-interest method. In addition, answer questions.
(SO 2, 8)

Instructions
(Round all computations to the nearest dollar.)
(a) Prepare the journal entries to record the following transactions.
   (1) The issuance of the bonds on July 1, 2012.
   (2) The accrual of interest and the amortization of the premium on December 31, 2012.
   (3) The payment of interest and the amortization of the premium on July 1, 2013, assuming no accrual of interest on June 30.
   (4) The accrual of interest and the amortization of the premium on December 31, 2013.
(b) Show the proper balance sheet presentation for the liability for bonds payable on the December 31, 2013, balance sheet.
(c) ➤ Provide the answers to the following questions in letter form.
   (1) What amount of interest expense is reported for 2013?
   (2) Would the bond interest expense reported in 2013 be the same as, greater than, or less than the amount that would be reported if the straight-line method of amortization were used?

(a) (2) Amortization $18,255
(a) (3) Amortization $18,985

(a) (4) Amortization $19,745
(b) Bond carrying value
$4,486,642

(3) Determine the total cost of borrowing over the life of the bond.
(4) Would the total bond interest expense be greater than, the same as, or less than the total interest expense if the straight-line method of amortization were used?

Prepare entries to record issuance of bonds, interest accrual, and straight-line amortization for 2 years.

(SO 6, 9)

(b) Amortization $6,000

(d) Discount on bonds payable $216,000

*P15-7B Somonauk Company sold $6,000,000, 9%, 20-year bonds on January 1, 2012. The bonds were dated January 1, 2012, and pay interest on January 1 and July 1. Somonauk Company uses the straight-line method to amortize bond premium or discount. The bonds were sold at 96. Assume no interest is accrued on June 30.

Instructions
(a) Prepare the journal entry to record the issuance of the bonds on January 1, 2012.
(b) Prepare a bond discount amortization schedule for the first 4 interest periods.
(c) Prepare the journal entries for interest and the amortization of the discount in 2012 and 2013.
(d) Show the balance sheet presentation of the bond liability at December 31, 2013.

Prepare entries to record issuance of bonds, interest, and straight-line amortization of bond premium and discount.

(SO 6, 9)

(a) Amortization $6,000
(b) Amortization $8,000
(c) Premium on bonds payable $108,000
Discount on bonds payable $144,000

*P15-8B Gabriel Corporation sold $4,000,000, 8%, 10-year bonds on January 1, 2012. The bonds were dated January 1, 2012, and pay interest on July 1 and January 1. Gabriel Corporation uses the straight-line method to amortize bond premium or discount. Assume no interest is accrued on June 30.

Instructions
(a) Prepare all the necessary journal entries to record the issuance of the bonds and bond interest expense for 2012, assuming that the bonds sold at 103.
(b) Prepare journal entries as in part (a) assuming that the bonds sold at 96.
(c) Show balance sheet presentation for each bond issue at December 31, 2012.

Prepare entries to record interest payments, straight-line discount amortization, and redemption of bonds.

(SO 2, 3, 9)

*P15-9B The following is taken from the Kijak Corp. balance sheet.

KIJAK CORPORATION
Balance Sheet (partial)
December 31, 2012

Current liabilities		
Interest payable (for 6 months from July 1 to December 31)		$ 108,000
Long-term liabilities		
Bonds payable, 9%, due January 1, 2023	$2,400,000	
Less: Discount on bonds payable	90,000	2,310,000

Interest is payable semiannually on January 1 and July 1. The bonds are callable on any semiannual interest date. Kijak uses straight-line amortization for any bond premium or discount. From December 31, 2012, the bonds will be outstanding for an additional 10 years (120 months).

Instructions
(Round all computations to the nearest dollar).
(a) Journalize the payment of bond interest on January 1, 2013.

(b) Amortization $4,500

(c) Loss $44,500

(d) Amortization $3,000

(b) Prepare the entry to amortize bond discount and to pay the interest due on July 1, 2013, assuming that interest was not accrued on June 30.
(c) Assume that on July 1, 2013, after paying interest, Kijak Corp. calls bonds having a face value of $800,000. The call price is 102. Record the redemption of the bonds.
(d) Prepare the adjusting entry at December 31, 2013, to amortize bond discount and to accrue interest on the remaining bonds.

Problems: Set C

Comprehensive Problem: Chapters 13–15

CP15   Nordham Corporation's trial balance at December 31, 2012, is presented below. All 2012 transactions have been recorded except for the items described below.

	Debit	Credit
Cash	$ 23,000	
Accounts Receivable	51,000	
Inventory	22,700	
Land	65,000	
Buildings	95,000	
Equipment	40,000	
Allowance for Doubtful Accounts		$ 450
Accumulated Depreciation—Buildings		30,000
Accumulated Depreciation—Equipment		14,400
Accounts Payable		19,300
Interest Payable		–0–
Dividends Payable		–0–
Unearned Rent Revenue		8,000
Bonds Payable (10%)		50,000
Common Stock ($10 par)		30,000
Paid-in Capital in Excess of Par—Common Stock		6,000
Preferred Stock ($20 par)		–0–
Paid-in Capital in Excess of Par—Preferred Stock		–0–
Retained Earnings		75,050
Treasury Stock	–0–	
Cash Dividends	–0–	
Sales Revenue		570,000
Rent Revenue		–0–
Bad Debts Expense	–0–	
Interest Expense	2,500	
Cost of Goods Sold	400,000	
Depreciation Expense	–0–	
Other Operating Expenses	39,000	
Salaries and Wages Expense	65,000	
Total	$803,200	$803,200

Unrecorded transactions

1. On January 1, 2012, Nordham issued 1,000 shares of $20 par, 6% preferred stock for $22,000.
2. On January 1, 2012, Nordham also issued 1,000 shares of common stock for $23,000.
3. Nordham reacquired 300 shares of its common stock on July 1, 2012, for $49 per share.
4. On December 31, 2012, Nordham declared the annual preferred stock dividend and a $1.50 per share dividend on the outstanding common stock, all payable on January 15, 2013.
5. Nordham estimates that uncollectible accounts receivable at year-end is $5,100.
6. The building is being depreciated using the straight-line method over 30 years. The salvage value is $5,000.
7. The equipment is being depreciated using the straight-line method over 10 years. The salvage value is $4,000.
8. The unearned rent was collected on October 1, 2012. It was receipt of 4 months' rent in advance (October 1, 2012 through January 31, 2013).
9. The 10% bonds payable pay interest every January 1 and July 1. The interest for the 6 months ended December 31, 2012, has not been paid or recorded.

Instructions

(Ignore income taxes.)

(a) Prepare journal entries for the transactions listed above.
(b) Prepare an updated December 31, 2012, trial balance, reflecting the unrecorded transactions.   *(b) Total $868,700*
(c) Prepare a multiple-step income statement for the year ending December 31, 2012.
(d) Prepare a retained earnings statement for the year ending December 31, 2012.
(e) Prepare a classified balance sheet as of December 31, 2012.   *(e) Total assets $270,900*

Continuing Cookie Chronicle

(*Note:* This is a continuation of the Cookie Chronicle from Chapters 1 through 14.)

CCC15   Natalie and Curtis have been experiencing great demand for their cookies and muffins. As a result, they are now thinking about buying a commercial oven. They know which oven they want and how much it will cost. They have some cash set aside for the purchase and will need to borrow the rest. They met with a bank manager to discuss their options.

Go to the book's companion website, **www.wiley.com/college/weygandt,** *to see the completion of this problem.*

BROADENING**YOUR**PERSPECTIVE

Financial Reporting and Analysis

Financial Reporting Problem: PepsiCo, Inc.

BYP15-1   Refer to the financial statements of PepsiCo, Inc. and the Notes to Consolidated Financial Statements in Appendix A.

Instructions

(a) What was PepsiCo's total long-term debt at December 26, 2009? What was the increase/decrease in total long-term debt from the prior year? What does Note 9 to the financial statements indicate about the composition of PepsiCo's long-term debt obligation?

(b) What type of leases, operating or capital, does PepsiCo report? (See Note 9.) Are these leases reported on PepsiCo's financial statements?

(c) What are the total long-term contractual commitments that PepsiCo reports as of December 26, 2009? (See Note 9.)

Comparative Analysis Problem: PepsiCo, Inc. vs. The Coca-Cola Company

BYP15-2   PepsiCo's financial statements are presented in Appendix A. Financial statements of The Coca-Cola Company are presented in Appendix B.

Instructions

(a) Based on the information contained in these financial statements, compute the following 2009 ratios for each company.
  (1) Debt to total assets.
  (2) Times interest earned.

(b) What conclusions concerning the companies' long-run solvency can be drawn from these ratios?

(c) Which company has reported the greater amount of future long-term commitments for the 5 succeeding years?

On the Web

BYP15-3   Bond or debt securities pay a stated rate of interest. This rate of interest is dependent on the risk associated with the investment. Moody's Investment Service provides ratings for companies that issue debt securities.

Address: www.moodys.com, or go to **www.wiley.com/college/weygandt**

Steps: From Moody's homepage, choose **About Moody's**.

Instructions

(a) What year did Moody's introduce the first bond rating? (See **Moody's History**.)

(b) What is the total amount of debt securities that Moody's analysts "track"? (See **An Introduction**.)

(c) What characteristics must debt ratings have in order to be useful to the capital markets? (See **Understand Risk: The Truth About Credit Ratings**.)

Critical Thinking

Decision Making Across the Organization

*BYP15-4   On January 1, 2010, Carlin Corporation issued $2,400,000 of 5-year, 8% bonds at 95; the bonds pay interest semiannually on July 1 and January 1. By January 1, 2012, the market rate of interest for bonds of risk similar to those of Carlin Corporation had risen. As a result, the market value of these bonds was $2,000,000 on January 1, 2012—below their carrying value. Andrea Carlin, president of the company, suggests repurchasing all of these bonds in the open market at the $2,000,000 price. To do so the company will have to issue $2,000,000 (face value) of new 10-year, 11% bonds at par. The president asks you, as controller, "What is the feasibility of my proposed repurchase plan?"

Instructions

With the class divided into groups, answer the following.

(a) What is the carrying value of the outstanding Carlin Corporation 5-year bonds on January 1, 2012? (Assume straight-line amortization.)

(b) Prepare the journal entry to retire the 5-year bonds on January 1, 2012. Prepare the journal entry to issue the new 10-year bonds.

(c) Prepare a short memo to the president in response to her request for advice. List the economic factors that you believe should be considered for her repurchase proposal.

Communication Activity

BYP15-5   Joe Penner, president of Penner Corporation, is considering the issuance of bonds to finance an expansion of his business. He has asked you to (1) discuss the advantages of bonds over common stock financing, (2) indicate the types of bonds he might issue, and (3) explain the issuing procedures used in bond transactions.

Instructions

Write a memo to the president, answering his request.

Ethics Case

BYP15-6   Sam Farr is the president, founder, and majority owner of Galena Medical Corporation, an emerging medical technology products company. Galena is in dire need of additional capital to keep operating and to bring several promising products to final development, testing, and production. Sam, as owner of 51% of the outstanding stock, manages the company's operations. He places heavy emphasis on research and development and on long-term growth. The other principal stockholder is Jill Hutton who, as a nonemployee investor, owns 40% of the stock. Jill would like to deemphasize the R&D functions and emphasize the marketing function, to maximize short-run sales and profits from existing products. She believes this strategy would raise the market price of Galena's stock.

All of Sam's personal capital and borrowing power is tied up in his 51% stock ownership. He knows that any offering of additional shares of stock will dilute his controlling interest because he won't be able to participate in such an issuance. But, Jill has money and would likely buy enough shares to gain control of Galena. She then would dictate the company's future direction, even if it meant replacing Sam as president and CEO.

The company already has considerable debt. Raising additional debt will be costly, will adversely affect Galena's credit rating, and will increase the company's reported losses due to the growth in interest expense. Jill and the other minority stockholders express opposition to the assumption of additional debt, fearing the company will be pushed to the brink of bankruptcy. Wanting to maintain his control and to preserve the direction of "his" company, Sam is doing everything to avoid a stock issuance. He is contemplating a large issuance of bonds, even if it means the bonds are issued with a high effective-interest rate.

Instructions

(a) Who are the stakeholders in this situation?

(b) What are the ethical issues in this case?

(c) What would you do if you were Sam?

"All About You" Activity

BYP15-7   Numerous articles have been written that identify early warning signs that you might be getting into trouble with your personal debt load. You can find many good articles on this topic on the Internet.

Instructions
Find an article that identifies early warning signs of personal debt trouble. Write a summary of the article and bring your summary and the article to class to share.

FASB Codification Activity

BYP15-8   If your school has a subscription to the FASB Codification, go to *http://aaahq.org/ascLogin.cfm* to log in and prepare responses to the following:

(a) What is the long-term obligation?
(b) What guidance does the Codification provide for the disclosure of long-term obligations?

Answers to Insight and Accounting Across the Organization Questions
p. 682 Bonds Versus Notes?   Q: Why might companies prefer bond financing instead of short-term financing? **A:** In some cases, it is difficult to get loans from banks. In addition, low interest rates have encouraged companies to go more long-term and fix their rate. Recently, short-term loans suddenly froze, leading to liquidity problems for certain companies.

p. 686 "Covenant-Lite" Debt   Q: How can financial ratios such as those covered in this chapter provide protection for creditors? **A:** Financial ratios such as the current ratio, debt to total assets ratio, and the times interest earned ratio provide indications of a company's liquidity and solvency. By specifying minimum levels of liquidity and solvency, as measured by these ratios, a creditor creates triggers that enable it to step in before a company's financial situation becomes too dire.

Answers to Self-Test Questions
1. c **2.** c **3.** a **4.** d **5.** b **6.** d $600,000 - (10,000 \times \$1)$ **7.** c **8.** c $\$200,000 - (10\% \times \$497,000) = \$150,300$; $(\$497,000 - \$150,300) \times 10\%$ **9.** d **10.** d $(\$300,000 + \$40,000 + \$100,000) \div \$40,000$ ***11.** d ***12.** b $[(\$938,554 \times 10\%) - (\$1,000,000 \times 9\%)] = \$3,855$; $(\$1,000,000 - \$938,554) - \$3,855$ ***13.** c $(\$1,081,105 \times 8\%) \div 2$ **14.** d $[\$500,000 - (96\% \times \$500,000)] = \$20,000$; $(\$20,000 \div 10)$ **15.** a $500,000 \times .96) = 480,000$; $(\$480,000 + \$2,000 + \$2,000 + \$2,000)$

IFRS A Look at IFRS

IFRS and GAAP have similar definitions of liabilities. IFRSs related to reporting and recognition of liabilities are found in *IAS I (revised)* ("Presentation of Financial Statements") and *IAS 37* ("Provisions, Contingent Liabilities, and Contingent Assets").

Key Points

- As indicated in Chapter 11, in general GAAP and IFRS define liabilities similarly.

- IFRS requires that companies classify liabilities as current or noncurrent on the face of the statement of financial position (balance sheet), except in industries where a *presentation* based on liquidity would be considered to provide more useful information (such as financial institutions). When current liabilities (also called short-term liabilities) are presented, they are generally presented in order of liquidity.

- Under IFRS, liabilities are classified as current if they are expected to be paid within 12 months.

- Similar to GAAP, items are normally reported in order of liquidity. Companies sometimes show liabilities before assets. Also, they will sometimes show noncurrent (long-term) liabilities before current liabilities.

- Under both GAAP and IFRS, preferred stock that is required to be redeemed at a specific point in time in the future must be reported as debt, rather than being presented as either equity or in a "mezzanine" area between debt and equity.

- The basic calculation for bond valuation is the same under GAAP and IFRS. In addition, the accounting for bond liability transactions is essentially the same between GAAP and IFRS.

- IFRS requires use of the effective-interest method for amortization of bond discounts and premiums. GAAP also requires the effective-interest method, except that it allows use of the straight-line method where the difference is not material. Under IFRS, companies do not use a premium or discount account but instead show the bond at its net amount. For example, if a $100,000 bond was issued at 97, under IFRS a company would record:

Cash	97,000	
Bonds Payable		97,000

- The accounting for convertible bonds differs between IFRS and GAAP. Unlike GAAP, IFRS splits the proceeds from the convertible bond between an equity component and a debt component. The equity conversion rights are reported in equity.

  To illustrate, assume that Harris Corp. issues convertible 7% bonds with a face value of $1,000,000 and receives $1,000,000. Comparable bonds without a conversion feature would have required a 9% rate of interest. To determine how much of the proceeds would be allocated to debt and how much to equity, the promised payments of the bond obligation would be discounted at the market rate of 9%. Suppose that this results in a present value of $850,000. The entry to record the issuance would be:

Cash	1,000,000	
Bonds Payable		850,000
Share Premium—Conversion Equity		150,000

- The IFRS leasing standard is *IAS 17*. Both Boards share the same objective of recording leases by lessees and lessors according to their economic substance—that is, according to the definitions of assets and liabilities. However, GAAP for leases is much more "rules-based" with specific bright-line criteria (such as the "90% of fair value" test) to determine if a lease arrangement transfers the risks and rewards of ownership; IFRS is more conceptual in its provisions. Rather than a 90% cut-off, it asks whether the agreement transfers substantially all of the risks and rewards associated with ownership.

Looking to the Future

The FASB and IASB are currently involved in two projects, each of which has implications for the accounting for liabilities. One project is investigating approaches to differentiate between debt and equity instruments. The other project, the elements phase of the conceptual framework project, will evaluate the definitions of the fundamental building blocks of accounting. The results of these projects could change the classification of many debt and equity securities.

In addition to these projects, the FASB and IASB have also identified leasing as one of the most problematic areas of accounting. A joint project is now focused on lessee accounting. One of the first areas studied is, "What are the assets and liabilities to be recognized related to a lease contract?" Should the focus remain on the leased item or the right to use the leased item? This question is tied to the Boards' joint project on the conceptual framework—defining an "asset" and a "liability."

IFRS Self-Test Questions

1. The accounting for bonds payable is:
   (a) essentially the same under IFRS and GAAP.
   (b) differs in that GAAP requires use of the straight-line method for amortization of bond premium and discount.
   (c) the same except that market prices may be different because the present value calculations are different between IFRS and GAAP.
   (d) not covered by IFRS.

2. Stevens Corporation issued 5% convertible bonds with a total face value of $3,000,000 for $3,000,000. If the bonds had not had a conversion feature, they would have sold for $2,600,000. Under IFRS, the entry to record the transaction would require a credit to:
   (a) Bonds Payable for $3,000,000.
   (b) Bonds Payable for $400,000.
   (c) Share Premium—Conversion Equity for $400,000.
   (d) Discount on Bonds Payable for $400,000.

3. Under IFRS, if preference shares (preferred stock) have a requirement to be redeemed at a specific point in time in the future, they are treated:
   (a) as a type of asset account.
   (b) as ordinary shares (common stock).
   (c) in the same fashion as other types of preference shares.
   (d) as a liability.

4. The leasing standards employed by IFRS:
   (a) rely more heavily on interpretation of the conceptual meaning of assets and liabilities than GAAP.
   (b) are more "rules based" than those of GAAP.
   (c) employ the same "bright-line test" as GAAP.
   (d) are identical to those of GAAP.

5. The joint projects of the FASB and IASB could potentially:
   (a) change the definition of liabilities.
   (b) change the definition of equity.
   (c) change the definition of assets.
   (d) All of the above.

IFRS Concepts and Application

IFRS15-1 Briefly describe some of the similarities and differences between GAAP and IFRS with respect to the accounting for liabilities.

IFRS15-2 Ratzlaff Company issues €2 million, 10-year, 8% bonds at 97, with interest payable on July 1 and January 1.

Instructions
(a) Prepare the journal entry to record the sale of these bonds on January 1, 2012.
(b) Assuming instead that the above bonds sold for 104, prepare the journal entry to record the sale of these bonds on January 1, 2012.

IFRS15-3 Archer Company issued £4,000,000 par value, 7% convertible bonds at 99 for cash. The net present value of the debt without the conversion feature is £3,800,000. Prepare the journal entry to record the issuance of the convertible bonds.

International Financial Statement Analysis: *Zetar plc*

IFRS15-4 The financial statements of Zetar plc are presented on Appendix C. The company's complete annual report, including the notes to its financial statements, is available at *www.zetarplc.com.*

Instructions

Use the company's annual report to answer the following questions.

(a) According to the notes to the financial statements, what types of transactions do trade payables relate to? What was the average amount of time it took the company to pay its payables?

(b) Note 2 (B) discusses provisions that the company records for certain types of activities. What do the provisions relate to, what are the estimates based on, and what could cause those estimates to change in subsequent periods?

(c) What was the average interest rate paid on bank loans and overdrafts?

Answers to IFRS Self-Test Questions

1. a **2.** c **3.** d **4.** a **5.** d

✔ The Navigator

✔ **Remember to go back to the Navigator box on the chapter opening page and check off your completed work.**

CHAPTER16

Investments

Study Objectives

After studying this chapter, you should be able to:

[1] Discuss why corporations invest in debt and stock securities.

[2] Explain the accounting for debt investments.

[3] Explain the accounting for stock investments.

[4] Describe the use of consolidated financial statements.

[5] Indicate how debt and stock investments are reported in financial statements.

[6] Distinguish between short-term and long-term investments.

✔ **The Navigator**

Feature Story

"IS THERE ANYTHING ELSE WE CAN BUY?"

In a rapidly changing world, you must change rapidly or suffer the consequences. In business, change requires investment.

A case in point is found in the entertainment industry. Technology is bringing about innovations so quickly that it is nearly impossible to guess which technologies will last and which will soon fade away. For example, will both satellite TV and cable TV survive, or will just one succeed, or will both be replaced by something else? Or consider the publishing industry. Will paper newspapers and magazines be replaced by online news via the World Wide Web? If you are a publisher, you have to make your best guess about what the future holds and invest accordingly.

Time Warner, Inc. lives at the center of this arena. It is not an environment for the timid, and Time Warner's philosophy is anything but timid. It might be characterized as, "If we can't beat you, we will buy you." Its mantra is "invest, invest, invest." A list of Time Warner's holdings gives an idea of its reach. Magazines: *People, Time, Life, Sports Illustrated, Fortune.* Book publishers: Time-Life Books, Book-of-the-Month Club, Little, Brown & Co, Sunset Books. Television and movies: Warner Bros. ("ER," "Without a Trace," the WB Network), HBO, and movies like *Harry Potter and the Goblet of Fire, and Batman Begins.* Broadcasting: TNT, CNN news, and Turner's library of thousands of classic movies. Internet: America Online, and AOL Anywhere. Time Warner owns more information and entertainment copyrights and brands than any other company in the world.

The merger of America Online (AOL) with Time Warner, one of the biggest mergers ever, was originally perceived by many as the gateway to the future. In actuality, it was a financial disaster. It is largely responsible for much of the decline in Time Warner's stock price, from a high of $95.80 to a recent level of $14.07. Ted Turner, who was at one time Time Warner's largest shareholder, lost billions of dollars on the deal and eventually sold most of his shares.

✔
The Navigator

Inside CHAPTER 16

PreviewofCHAPTER16

Time Warner's management believes in aggressive growth through investing in the stock of existing companies. Besides purchasing stock, companies also purchase other securities such as bonds issued by corporations or by governments. Companies can make investments for a short or long period of time, as a passive investment, or with the intent to control another company. As you will see in this chapter, the way in which a company accounts for its investments is determined by a number of factors.

The content and organization of Chapter 16 are as follows.

Investments			
Why Corporations Invest	**Accounting for Debt Investments**	**Accounting for Stock Investments**	**Valuing and Reporting Investments**
• Cash management • Investment income • Strategic reasons	• Recording acquisition of bonds • Recording bond interest • Recording sale of bonds	• Holdings of less than 20% • Holdings between 20% and 50% • Holdings of more than 50%	• Categories of securities • Balance sheet presentation • Realized and unrealized gain or loss • Classified balance sheet

✔
The Navigator

Why Corporations Invest

Study Objective [1]

Discuss why corporations invest in debt and stock securities.

Corporations purchase investments in debt or stock securities generally for one of three reasons. First, a corporation may **have excess cash** that it does not need for the immediate purchase of operating assets. For example, many companies experience seasonal fluctuations in sales. A Cape Cod marina has more sales in the spring and summer than in the fall and winter. (The reverse is true for an Aspen ski shop.) At the end of an operating cycle, the marina may have cash on hand that is temporarily idle until the start of another operating cycle. It may invest the excess funds to earn a greater return—interest and dividends—than it would get by just holding the funds in the bank. Illustration 16-1 depicts the role that such temporary investments play in the operating cycle.

Illustration 16-1
Temporary investments and the operating cycle

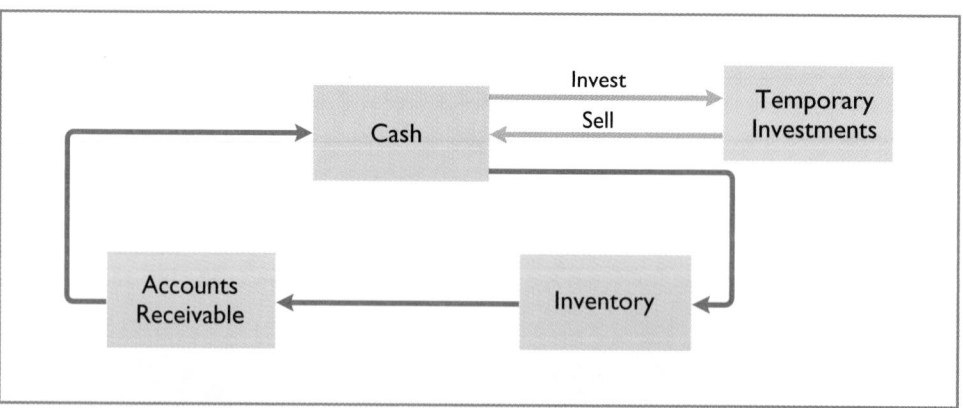

Excess cash may also result from economic cycles. For example, when the economy is booming, General Electric generates considerable excess cash. It uses some of this cash to purchase new plant and equipment and pays out some of the cash in dividends. But it may also invest excess cash in liquid assets in anticipation of a future downturn in the economy. It can then liquidate these investments during a recession, when sales slow and cash is scarce.

When investing excess cash for short periods of time, corporations invest in low-risk, highly liquid securities—most often short-term government securities. It is generally not wise to invest short-term excess cash in shares of common stock because stock investments can experience rapid price changes. If you did invest your short-term excess cash in stock and the price of the stock declined significantly just before you needed cash again, you would be forced to sell your stock investment at a loss.

A second reason some companies purchase investments is to generate **earnings from investment income**. For example, banks make most of their earnings by lending money, but they also generate earnings by investing in debt. Conversely, mutual stock funds invest primarily in equity securities in order to benefit from stock-price appreciation and dividend revenue.

Third, companies also invest for **strategic reasons**. A company can exercise some influence over a customer or supplier by purchasing a significant, but not controlling, interest in that company. Or, a company may purchase a noncontrolling interest in another company in a related industry in which it wishes to establish a presence. For example, Time Warner initially purchased an interest of less than 20% in Turner Broadcasting to have a stake in Turner's expanding business opportunities. At a later date Time Warner acquired the remaining 80%. Subsequently, Time Warner merged with AOL and became AOL Time Warner, Inc. Now, it is again just Time Warner, Inc., having dropped the "AOL" from its name in late 2003.

A corporation may also choose to purchase a controlling interest in another company. For example, as the *Accounting Across the Organization* box on page 731 shows, Procter & Gamble purchased Gillette. Such purchases might be done to enter a new industry without incurring the tremendous costs and risks associated with starting from scratch. Or a company might purchase another company in its same industry.

In summary, businesses invest in other companies for the reasons shown in Illustration 16-2.

Illustration 16-2
Why corporations invest

Reason	Typical Investment
To house excess cash until needed	Low-risk, high-liquidity, short-term securities such as government-issued securities
To generate earnings	Debt securities (banks and other financial institutions) and stock securities (mutual funds and pension funds)
To meet strategic goals	Stocks of companies in a related industry or in an unrelated industry that the company wishes to enter

Accounting for Debt Investments

Debt investments are investments in government and corporation bonds. In accounting for debt investments, companies make entries to record (1) the acquisition, (2) the interest revenue, and (3) the sale.

Study Objective [2]
Explain the accounting for debt investments.

Recording Acquisition of Bonds

At acquisition, the cost principle applies. Cost includes all expenditures necessary to acquire these investments, such as the price paid plus brokerage fees (commissions), if any.

Assume, for example, that Kuhl Corporation acquires 50 Doan Inc. 8%, 10-year, $1,000 bonds on January 1, 2012, for $54,000, including brokerage fees of $1,000. The entry to record the investment is:

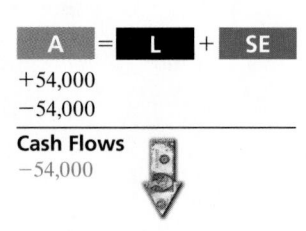

Jan. 1	Debt Investments	54,000	
	Cash		54,000
	(To record purchase of 50 Doan Inc. bonds)		

Recording Bond Interest

The Doan, Inc. bonds pay interest of $2,000 semiannually on July 1 and January 1 ($50,000 × 8% × ½). The entry for the receipt of interest on July 1 is:

July 1	Cash	2,000	
	Interest Revenue		2,000
	(To record receipt of interest on Doan Inc. bonds		

If Kuhl Corporation's fiscal year ends on December 31, it accrues the interest of $2,000 earned since July 1. The adjusting entry is:

Dec. 31	Interest Receivable	2,000	
	Interest Revenue		2,000
	(To accrue interest on Doan Inc. bonds)		

Kuhl reports Interest Receivable as a current asset in the balance sheet. It reports Interest Revenue under "Other revenues and gains" in the income statement.

Kuhl reports receipt of the interest on January 1 as follows.

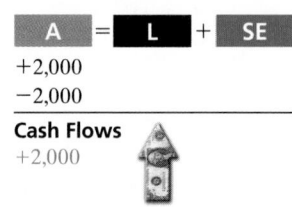

Jan. 1	Cash	2,000	
	Interest Receivable		2,000
	(To record receipt of accrued interest)		

A credit to Interest Revenue at this time is incorrect because the company earned and accrued interest revenue in the *preceding* accounting period.

Recording Sale of Bonds

When Kuhl sells the bonds, it credits the investment account for the cost of the bonds. Kuhl records as a gain or loss any difference between the net proceeds from the sale (sales price less brokerage fees) and the cost of the bonds.

Assume, for example, that Kuhl Corporation receives net proceeds of $58,000 on the sale of the Doan Inc. bonds on January 1, 2013, after receiving the interest due. Since the securities cost $54,000, the company realizes a gain of $4,000. It records the sale as:

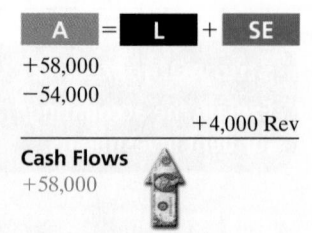

Jan. 1	Cash	58,000	
	Debt Investments		54,000
	Gain on Sale of Debt Investments		4,000
	(To record sale of Doan Inc. bonds)		

Kuhl reports the gain on sale of debt investments under "Other revenues and gains" in the income statement and reports losses under "Other expenses and losses."

Do it!

Waldo Corporation had the following transactions pertaining to debt investments.

Debt Investments

Jan. 1   Purchased 30, $1,000 Hillary Co. 10% bonds for $30,000, plus brokerage fees of $900. Interest is payable semiannually on July 1 and January 1.

July 1   Received semiannual interest on Hillary Co. bonds.

July 1   Sold 15 Hillary Co. bonds for $15,000, less $400 brokerage fees.

(a) Journalize the transactions, and (b) prepare the adjusting entry for the accrual of interest on December 31.

action plan

✔ Record bond investments at cost.

✔ Record interest when received and/or accrued.

✔ When bonds are sold, credit the investment account for the cost of the bonds.

✔ Record any difference between the cost and the net proceeds as a gain or loss.

Solution

(a) Jan. 1	Debt Investments		30,900	
	Cash			30,900
	(To record purchase of 30 Hillary Co. bonds)			
July 1	Cash		1,500	
	Interest Revenue ($30,000 × .10 × 6/12)			1,500
	(To record receipt of interest on Hillary Co. bonds)			
July 1	Cash		14,600	
	Loss on Sale of Debt Investments		850	
	Debt Investments ($30,900 × 15/30)			15,450
	(To record sale of 15 Hillary Co. bonds)			
(b) Dec. 31	Interest Receivable		750	
	Interest Revenue ($15,000 × .10 × 6/12)			750
	(To accrue interest on Hillary Co. bonds)			

Related exercise material: BE16-1, E16-2, E16-3, and **Do it!** 16-1.

The Navigator

Accounting for Stock Investments

Stock investments are investments in the capital stock of other corporations. When a company holds stock (and/or debt) of several different corporations, the group of securities is identified as an investment portfolio.

The accounting for investments in common stock depends on the extent of the investor's influence over the operating and financial affairs of the issuing corporation (the **investee**). Illustration 16-3 (page 728) shows the general guidelines.

Companies are required to use judgment instead of blindly following the guidelines.[1] On the following pages we will explain the application of each guideline.

Study Objective [3]
Explain the accounting for stock investments.

---

[1] Among the questions that are considered in determining an investor's influence are these: (1) Does the investor have representation on the investee's board? (2) Does the investor participate in the investee's policy-making process? (3) Are there material transactions between the investor and investee? (4) Is the common stock held by other stockholders concentrated or dispersed?

Illustration 16-3
Accounting guidelines for
stock investments

Investor's Ownership Interest in Investee's Common Stock	Presumed Influence on Investee	Accounting Guidelines
Less than 20%	Insignificant	Cost method
Between 20% and 50%	Significant	Equity method
More than 50%	Controlling	Consolidated financial statements

Helpful Hint

The entries for investments in common stock also apply to investments in preferred stock.

Holdings of Less than 20%

In accounting for stock investments of less than 20%, companies use the cost method. Under the **cost method**, companies record the investment at cost, and recognize revenue only when cash dividends are received.

RECORDING ACQUISITION OF STOCK INVESTMENTS

At acquisition, the cost principle applies. Cost includes all expenditures necessary to acquire these investments, such as the price paid plus any brokerage fees (commissions).

Assume, for example, that on July 1, 2012, Sanchez Corporation acquires 1,000 shares (10% ownership) of Beal Corporation common stock. Sanchez pays $40 per share plus brokerage fees of $500. The entry for the purchase is:

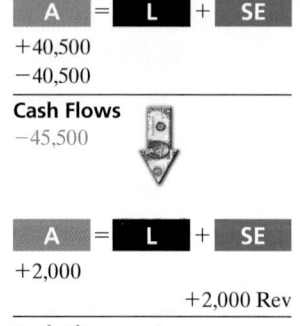

A = L + SE
+40,500
−40,500

Cash Flows
−45,500

July 1	Stock Investments	40,500	
	Cash		40,500
	(To record purchase of 1,000 shares of Beal Corporation common stock)		

RECORDING DIVIDENDS

During the time Sanchez owns the stock, it makes entries for any cash dividends received. If Sanchez receives a $2 per share dividend on December 31, the entry is:

A = L + SE
+2,000
        +2,000 Rev

Cash Flows
+2,000

Dec. 31	Cash (1,000 × $2)	2,000	
	Dividend Revenue		2,000
	(To record receipt of a cash dividend)		

Sanchez reports Dividend Revenue under "Other revenues and gains" in the income statement. Unlike interest on notes and bonds, dividends do not accrue. Therefore, companies do not make adjusting entries to accrue dividends.

RECORDING SALE OF STOCK

When a company sells a stock investment, it recognizes as a gain or a loss the difference between the net proceeds from the sale (sales price less brokerage fees) and the cost of the stock.

Assume that Sanchez Corporation receives net proceeds of $39,500 on the sale of its Beal stock on February 10, 2013. Because the stock cost $40,500, Sanchez incurred a loss of $1,000. The entry to record the sale is:

Feb. 10	Cash	39,500	
	Loss on Sale of Stock Investments	1,000	
	Stock Investments		40,500
	(To record sale of Beal common stock)		

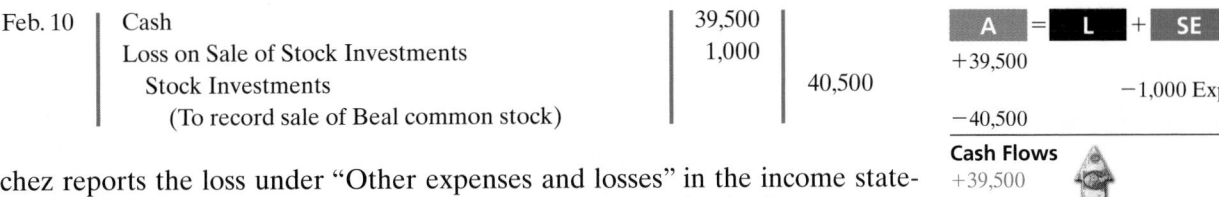

A = L + SE

+39,500

−1,000 Exp

−40,500

Cash Flows
+39,500

Sanchez reports the loss under "Other expenses and losses" in the income statement. It would show a gain on sale under "Other revenues and gains."

Holdings Between 20% and 50%

When an investor company owns only a small portion of the shares of stock of another company, the investor cannot exercise control over the investee. But, when an investor owns between 20% and 50% of the common stock of a corporation, it is presumed that the investor has significant influence over the financial and operating activities of the investee. The investor probably has a representative on the investee's board of directors, and through that representative, may exercise some control over the investee. The investee company in some sense becomes part of the investor company.

For example, even prior to purchasing all of Turner Broadcasting, Time Warner owned 20% of Turner. Because it exercised significant control over major decisions made by Turner, Time Warner used an approach called the equity method. Under the equity method, **the investor records its share of the net income of the investee in the year when it is earned**. An alternative might be to delay recognizing the investor's share of net income until the investee declares a cash dividend. But that approach would ignore the fact that the investor and investee are, in some sense, one company, making the investor better off by the investee's earned income.

Under the equity method, the investor company initially records the investment in common stock at cost. After that, it **adjusts** the investment account annually to show the investor's equity in the investee. Each year, the investor does the following: (1) It increases (debits) the investment account and increases (credits) revenue for its share of the investee's net income.[2] (2) The investor also decreases (credits) the investment account for the amount of dividends received. The investment account is reduced for dividends received, because payment of a dividend decreases the net assets of the investee.

Helpful Hint

Under the equity method, the investor recognizes revenue on the accrual basis—i.e., when it is earned by the investee.

RECORDING ACQUISITION OF STOCK INVESTMENTS

Assume that Milar Corporation acquires 30% of the common stock of Beck Company for $120,000 on January 1, 2012. The entry to record this transaction is:

Jan. 1	Stock Investments	120,000	
	Cash		120,000
	(To record purchase of Beck common stock)		

A = L + SE

+120,000
−120,000

Cash Flows
−120,000

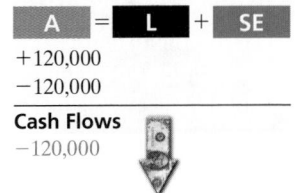

RECORDING REVENUE AND DIVIDENDS

For 2012, Beck reports net income of $100,000. It declares and pays a $40,000 cash dividend. Milar records (1) its share of Beck's income, $30,000 (30% × $100,000)

---

[2]Or, the investor increases (debits) a loss account and decreases (credits) the investment account for its share of the investee's net loss.

and (2) the reduction in the investment account for the dividends received, $12,000 ($40,000 × 30%). The entries are:

A = L + SE

+30,000

+30,000 Rev

Cash Flows
no effect

(1)

Dec. 31	Stock Investments	30,000	
	Revenue from Stock Investments		30,000
	(To record 30% equity in Beck's 2012		
	net income)		

A = L + SE

+12,000

−12,000

Cash Flows
+12,000

(2)

Dec. 31	Cash	12,000	
	Stock Investments		12,000
	(To record dividends received)		

After Milar posts the transactions for the year, its investment and revenue accounts will show the following.

Illustration 16-4
Investment and revenue accounts after posting

Stock Investments					Revenue from Stock Investments		
Jan. 1	120,000	Dec. 31	12,000			Dec. 31	30,000
Dec. 31	30,000						
Dec. 31 Bal.	138,000						

During the year, the net increase in the investment account was $18,000. As indicated above, the investment account increased by $30,000 due to Milar's share of Beck's income, and it decreased by $12,000 due to dividends received from Beck. In addition, Milar reports $30,000 of revenue from its investment, which is 30% of Beck's net income of $100,000.

Note that the difference between reported revenue under the cost method and reported revenue under the equity method can be significant. For example, Milar would report only $12,000 of dividend revenue (30% × $40,000) if it used the cost method.

Holdings of More than 50%

Study Objective [4]
Describe the use of consolidated financial statements.

Helpful Hint

If parent (A) has three wholly owned subsidiaries (B, C, & D), there are four separate legal entities. From the viewpoint of the shareholders of the parent company, there is only one economic entity.

A company that owns more than 50% of the common stock of another entity is known as the **parent company**. The entity whose stock the parent company owns is called the **subsidiary (affiliated) company**. Because of its stock ownership, the parent company has a **controlling interest** in the subsidiary.

When a company owns more than 50% of the common stock of another company, it usually prepares **consolidated financial statements**. These statements present the total assets and liabilities controlled by the parent company. They also present the total revenues and expenses of the subsidiary companies. Companies prepare consolidated statements **in addition to** the financial statements for the parent and individual subsidiary companies.

As noted earlier, when Time Warner had a 20% investment in Turner, it reported this investment in a single line item—Other Investments. After the merger, Time Warner instead consolidated Turner's results with its own. Under this approach, Time Warner included Turner's individual assets and liabilities with its own: its plant and equipment were added to Time Warner's plant and equipment, its receivables were added to Time Warner's receivables, and so on.

ACCOUNTING ACROSS THE ORGANIZATION

How Procter & Gamble Accounts for Gillette

Recently, Procter & Gamble Company acquired Gillette Company for $53.4 billion. The common stockholders of Procter & Gamble elect the board of directors of the company, who, in turn, select the officers and managers of the company. Procter & Gamble's board of directors controls the property owned by the corporation, which includes the common stock of Gillette. Thus, they are in a position to elect the board of directors of Gillette and, in effect, control its operations. These relationships are graphically illustrated here.

? Where on Procter & Gamble's balance sheet will you find its investment in Gillette Company? (See page 756.)

Consolidated statements are useful to the stockholders, board of directors, and managers of the parent company. These statements indicate the magnitude and scope of operations of the companies under common control. For example, regulators and the courts undoubtedly used the consolidated statements of AT&T to determine whether a breakup of AT&T was in the public interest. Listed below are three companies that prepare consolidated statements and some of the companies they have owned. One, Disney, is Time Warner's arch rival.

PepsiCo	Cendant	The Disney Company
Frito-Lay	Howard Johnson	Capital Cities/ABC, Inc.
Tropicana	Ramada Inn	Disneyland, Disney World
Quaker Oats	Century 21	Mighty Ducks
Pepsi-Cola	Coldwell Banker	Anaheim Angels
Gatorade	Avis	ESPN

Illustration 16-5
Examples of consolidated companies and their subsidiaries

Do it!

Presented below are two independent situations.

Stock Investments

1. Rho Jean Inc. acquired 5% of the 400,000 shares of common stock of Stillwater Corp. at a total cost of $6 per share on May 18, 2012. On August 30, Stillwater declared and paid a $75,000 dividend. On December 31, Stillwater reported net income of $244,000 for the year.

2. Debbie, Inc. obtained significant influence over North Sails by buying 40% of North Sails' 60,000 outstanding shares of common stock at a cost of $12 per share on January 1, 2012. On April 15, North Sails declared and paid a cash dividend of $45,000. On December 31, North Sails reported net income of $120,000 for the year.

Prepare all necessary journal entries for 2012 for (1) Rho Jean Inc. and (2) Debbie, Inc.

action plan

✔ Presume that the investor has relatively little influence over the investee when an investor owns less than 20% of the common stock of another corporation. In this case, net income earned by the investee is not considered a proper basis for recognizing income from the investment by the investor.

✔ Presume significant influence for investments of 20%–50%. Therefore, record the investor's share of the net income of the investee.

Solution

(1) May 18	Stock Investments (20,000 × $6)		120,000	
	Cash			120,000
	(To record purchase of 20,000 shares of			
	Stillwater Co. stock)			
Aug. 30	Cash		3,750	
	Dividend Revenue ($75,000 × 5%)			3,750
	(To record receipt of cash dividend)			
(2) Jan. 1	Stock Investments (60,000 × 40% × $12)		288,000	
	Cash			288,000
	(To record purchase of 24,000 shares of			
	North Sails' stock)			
Apr. 15	Cash		18,000	
	Stock Investments ($45,000 × 40%)			18,000
	(To record receipt of cash dividend)			
Dec. 31	Stock Investments ($120,000 × 40%)		48,000	
	Revenue from Stock Investments			48,000
	(To record 40% equity in North Sails'			
	net income)			

Related exercise material: BE16-2, BE16-3, E16-4, E16-5, E16-6, E16-7, E16-8, and **Do it!** 16-2.

The Navigator

Valuing and Reporting Investments

Study Objective [5]

Indicate how debt and stock investments are reported in financial statements.

The value of debt and stock investments may fluctuate greatly during the time they are held. For example, in one 12-month period, the stock price of Time Warner hit a high of $58.50 and a low of $9. In light of such price fluctuations, how should companies value investments at the balance sheet date? Valuation could be at cost, at fair value, or at the lower-of-cost-or-market value.

Many people argue that fair value offers the best approach because it represents the expected cash realizable value of securities. **Fair value** is the amount for which a security could be sold in a normal market. Others counter that, unless a security is going to be sold soon, the fair value is not relevant because the price of the security will likely change again.

Categories of Securities

For purposes of valuation and reporting at a financial statement date, companies classify debt and stock investments into three categories:

1. **Trading securities** are bought and held primarily for sale in the near term to generate income on short-term price differences.

2. **Available-for-sale securities** are held with the intent of selling them sometime in the future.

3. **Held-to-maturity securities** are debt securities that the investor has the intent and ability to hold to maturity.[3]

> **International Note**
>
> A recent U.S. accounting standard gives companies the "option" of applying fair value accounting, rather than historical cost, to certain types of assets and liabilities. This makes U.S. accounting more similar to international standards.

Illustration 16-6 shows the valuation guidelines for these securities. **These guidelines apply to all debt securities and all stock investments in which the holdings are less than 20%.**

Illustration 16-6
Valuation guidelines

Trading

"We'll sell within ten days."

At fair value with changes reported in net income

Available-for-sale

"We'll hold the stock for a while to see how it performs."

At fair value with changes reported in the stockholders' equity section

Held-to-maturity

"We intend to hold until maturity."

At amortized cost

TRADING SECURITIES

Companies hold trading securities with the intention of selling them in a short period (generally less than a month). *Trading* means frequent buying and selling. As indicated in Illustration 16-7, companies adjust trading securities to fair value at the end of each period, and report changes from cost as part of net income. The changes are reported as **unrealized gains or losses** because the securities have not been sold. The unrealized gain or loss is the difference between the **total cost** of trading securities and their **total fair value**. Companies classify trading securities as current assets.

Illustration 16-7 shows the cost and fair values for investments Pace Corporation classified as trading securities on December 31, 2012. Pace has an unrealized gain of $7,000 because total fair value of $147,000 is $7,000 greater than total cost of $140,000.

> **Helpful Hint**
>
> The fact that trading securities are short-term investments increases the likelihood that they will be sold at fair value (the company may not be able to time their sale) and the likelihood that there will be realized gains or losses.

Illustration 16-7
Valuation of trading securities

Trading Securities, December 31, 2012			
Investments	Cost	Fair Value	Unrealized Gain (Loss)
Yorkville Company bonds	$ 50,000	$ 48,000	$(2,000)
Kodak Company stock	90,000	99,000	9,000
Total	$140,000	$147,000	$ 7,000

---

[3]This category is provided for completeness. The accounting and valuation issues related to held-to-maturity securities are discussed in more advanced accounting courses.

Pace records fair value and unrealized gain or loss through an adjusting entry at the time it prepares financial statements. In this entry, the company uses a valuation allowance account, Market Adjustment—Trading, to record the difference between the total cost and the total fair value of the securities. The adjusting entry for Pace Corporation is:

A	=	L	+	SE
+7,000				
				+7,000 Rev

Cash Flows
no effect

Dec. 31	Market Adjustment—Trading	7,000	
	Unrealized Gain—Income		7,000
	(To record unrealized gain on trading securities)		

The use of a Market Adjustment—Trading account enables Pace to maintain a record of the investment cost. It needs actual cost to determine the gain or loss realized when it sells the securities. Pace adds the debit balance (or subtracts a credit balance) of the Market Adjustment—Trading balance to the cost of the investments to arrive at a fair value for the trading securities.

The fair value of the securities is the amount Pace reports on its balance sheet. It reports the unrealized gain in the income statement in the "Other revenues and gains" section. The term "Income" in the account title indicates that the gain affects net income.

If the total cost of the trading securities is greater than total fair value, an unrealized loss has occurred. In such a case, the adjusting entry is a debit to Unrealized Loss—Income and a credit to Market Adjustment—Trading. Companies report the unrealized loss under "Other expenses and losses" in the income statement.

The market adjustment account is carried forward into future accounting periods. The company does not make any entry to the account until the end of each reporting period. At that time, the company adjusts the balance in the account to the difference between cost and fair value. For trading securities, it closes the Unrealized Gain (Loss)—Income account at the end of the reporting period.

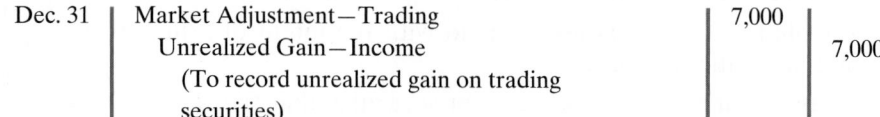

ACCOUNTING ACROSS THE ORGANIZATION

And the Correct Way to Report Investments Is...?

The accompanying graph presents an estimate of the percentage of companies on the major exchanges that have investments in the equity of other entities.

As the graph indicates, many companies have equity investments of some type. These investments can be substantial. For example, the total amount of equity-method investments appearing on company balance sheets is approximately $403 billion, and the amount shown in the income statements in any one year for all companies is approximately $38 billion.

Source: "Report and Recommendations Pursuant to Section 401(c) of the Sarbanes-Oxley Act of 2002 on Arrangements with Off-Balance Sheet Implications, Special Purpose Entities, and Transparency of Filings by Issuers," United States Securities and Exchange Commission—Office of Chief Accountant, Office of Economic Analyses, Division of Corporation Finance (June 2005), pp. 36–39.

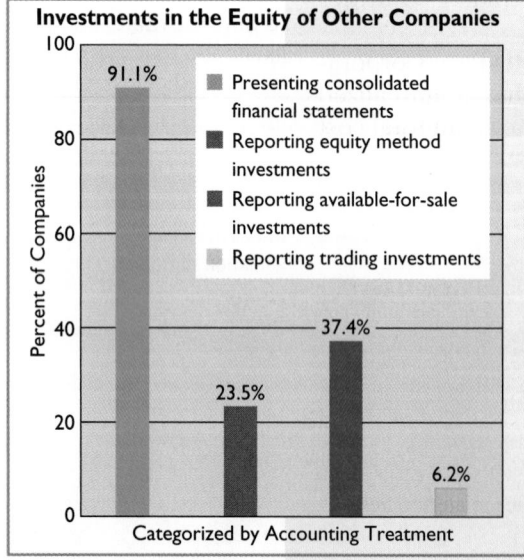

Investments in the Equity of Other Companies

- Presenting consolidated financial statements
- Reporting equity method investments
- Reporting available-for-sale investments
- Reporting trading investments

91.1% 23.5% 37.4% 6.2%

Percent of Companies

Categorized by Accounting Treatment

? Why might the use of the equity method not lead to full disclosure in the financial statements? (See page 756.)

AVAILABLE-FOR-SALE SECURITIES

As indicated earlier, companies hold available-for-sale securities with the intent of selling these investments sometime in the future. If the intent is to sell the securities within the next year or operating cycle, the investor classifies the securities as current assets in the balance sheet. Otherwise, it classifies them as long-term assets in the investments section of the balance sheet.

Ethics Note

Some managers seem to hold their available-for-sale securities that have experienced losses, while selling those that have gains, thus increasing income. Do you think this is ethical?

Companies report available-for-sale securities at fair value. The procedure for determining fair value and the unrealized gain or loss for these securities is the same as for trading securities. To illustrate, assume that Ingrao Corporation has two securities that it classifies as available-for-sale. Illustration 16-8 provides information on the cost, fair value, and amount of the unrealized gain or loss on December 31, 2012. There is an unrealized loss of $9,537 because total cost of $293,537 is $9,537 more than total fair value of $284,000.

Available-for-Sale Securities, December 31, 2012			
Investments	Cost	Fair Value	Unrealized Gain (Loss)
Campbell Soup Corporation 8% bonds	$ 93,537	$103,600	$10,063
Hershey Company stock	200,000	180,400	(19,600)
Total	$293,537	$284,000	$(9,537)

Illustration 16-8
Valuation of available-for-sale securities

Both the adjusting entry and the reporting of the unrealized gain or loss for Ingrao's available-for-sale securities differ from those illustrated for trading securities. The differences result because Ingrao does not expect to sell these securities in the near term. Thus, prior to actual sale it is more likely that changes in fair value may change either unrealized gains or losses. Therefore, Ingrao does not report an unrealized gain or loss in the income statement. Instead, it reports it as a **separate component of stockholders' equity**.

In the adjusting entry, Ingrao identifies the market adjustment account with available-for-sale securities, and it identifies the unrealized gain or loss account with stockholders' equity. Ingrao records the unrealized loss of $9,537 as follows.

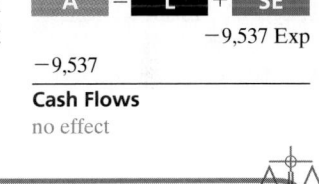

	A	=	L	+	SE
					−9,537 Exp
	−9,537				

Cash Flows
no effect

Dec. 31	Unrealized Gain or Loss—Equity	9,537	
	Market Adjustment—Available-for-Sale		9,537
	(To record unrealized loss on available-for-sale securities)		

If total fair value exceeds total cost, Ingrao debits Market Adjustment—Available-for-Sale and credits Unrealized Gain or Loss—Equity.

For available-for-sale securities, the company carries forward the Unrealized Gain or Loss—Equity account to future periods. At each future balance sheet date, Ingrao adjusts the market adjustment and the Unrealized Gain or Loss—Equity account to show the difference between cost and fair value at that time.

Ethics Note

At one time, the SEC accused investment bank Morgan Stanley of overstating the value of certain bond investments by $75 million. The SEC stated that, in applying market value accounting, Morgan Stanley used its own more-optimistic assumptions rather than relying on external pricing sources.

Do it!

Some of Powderhorn Corporation's investment securities are classified as trading securities and some are classified as available-for-sale. The cost and fair value of each category at December 31, 2012, are shown on page 736.

Trading and Available-for-Sale Securities

	Cost	Fair Value	Unrealized Gain (Loss)
Trading securities	$93,600	$94,900	$1,300
Available-for-sale securities	$48,800	$51,400	$2,600

At December 31, 2011, the Market Adjustment—Trading account had a debit balance of $9,200, and the Market Adjustment—Available-for-Sale account had a credit balance of $5,750. Prepare the required journal entries for each group of securities for December 31, 2012.

Solution

Trading securities:

Unrealized Loss—Income	7,900*	
Market Adjustment—Trading		7,900
(To record unrealized loss on trading securities)		
*$9,200 − $1,300		

Available-for-sale securities:

Market Adjustment—Available-for-Sale	8,350**	
Unrealized Gain or Loss—Equity		8,350
(To record unrealized gain on available-for-sale securities)		
**$5,750 + $2,600		

Related exercise material: BE16-4, BE16-5, BE16-6, BE16-7, E16-10, E16-11, E16-12, and **Do it!** 16-3.

✔ **The Navigator**

Balance Sheet Presentation

Study Objective [6]
Distinguish between short-term and long-term investments.

In the balance sheet, companies classify investments as either short-term or long-term.

SHORT-TERM INVESTMENTS

Short-term investments (also called **marketable securities**) are securities held by a company that are (1) **readily marketable** and (2) **intended to be converted into cash** within the next year or operating cycle, whichever is longer. Investments that do not meet **both criteria** are classified as long-term investments.

Helpful Hint

Trading securities are always classified as short-term. Available-for-sale securities can be either short-term or long-term.

Readily Marketable. **An investment is readily marketable when it can be sold easily whenever the need for cash arises.** Short-term paper[4] meets this criterion. It can be readily sold to other investors. Stocks and bonds traded on organized securities exchanges, such as the New York Stock Exchange, are readily marketable. They can be bought and sold daily. In contrast, there may be only a limited market for the securities issued by small corporations, and no market for the securities of a privately held company.

Intent to Convert. **Intent to convert means that management intends to sell the investment within the next year or operating cycle, whichever is longer.** Generally, this criterion is satisfied when the investment is considered a resource that the investor will use whenever the need for cash arises. For example, a ski resort may invest idle cash during the summer months with the intent to sell the securities to buy supplies and equipment shortly before the winter season. This investment is

---

[4]**Short-term paper** includes (1) certificates of deposit (CDs) issued by banks, (2) money market certificates issued by banks and savings and loan associations, (3) Treasury bills issued by the U.S. government, and (4) commercial paper (notes) issued by corporations with good credit ratings.

considered short-term even if lack of snow cancels the next ski season and eliminates the need to convert the securities into cash as intended.

Because of their high liquidity, short-term investments appear immediately below Cash in the "Current assets" section of the balance sheet. They are reported at fair value. For example, Pace Corporation would report its trading securities as shown in Illustration 16-9.

Pace Corporation Balance Sheet (partial)	
Current assets	
Cash	$ 21,000
Short-term investments, at fair value	147,000

Illustration 16-9
Presentation of short-term investments

LONG-TERM INVESTMENTS

Companies generally report long-term investments in a separate section of the balance sheet immediately below "Current assets," as shown later in Illustration 16-12 (page 739). Long-term investments in available-for-sale securities are reported at fair value. Investments in common stock accounted for under the equity method are reported at equity.

Presentation of Realized and Unrealized Gain or Loss

Companies must present in the financial statements gains and losses on investments, whether realized or unrealized. In the income statement, companies report gains and losses in the nonoperating activities section under the categories listed in Illustration 16-10. Interest and dividend revenue are also reported in that section.

Other Revenue and Gains	**Other Expenses and Losses**
Interest Revenue	Loss on Sale of Investments
Dividend Revenue	Unrealized Loss—Income
Gain on Sale of Investments	
Unrealized Gain—Income	

Illustration 16-10
Nonoperating items related to investments

As indicated earlier, companies report an unrealized gain or loss on available-for-sale securities as a separate component of stockholders' equity. To illustrate, assume that Dawson Inc. has common stock of $3,000,000, retained earnings of $1,500,000, and an unrealized loss on available-for-sale securities of $100,000. Illustration 16-11 shows the balance sheet presentation of the unrealized loss.

Dawson Inc. Balance Sheet (partial)	
Stockholders' equity	
Common stock	$3,000,000
Retained earnings	1,500,000
Total paid-in capital and retained earnings	4,500,000
Less: Unrealized loss on available-for-sale securities	100,000
Total stockholders' equity	$4,400,000

Illustration 16-11
Unrealized loss in stockholders' equity section

Note that the loss decreases stockholders' equity. An unrealized gain is added to stockholders' equity. Reporting the unrealized gain or loss in the stockholders' equity section serves two purposes: (1) It reduces the volatility of net income due to fluctuations in fair value. (2) It informs the financial statement user of the gain or loss that would occur if the securities were sold at fair value.

Companies must report items such as this, which affect stockholders' equity but are not included in the calculation of net income, as part of a more inclusive measure called *comprehensive income.* We discuss comprehensive income more fully in Chapter 18.

Classified Balance Sheet

We have presented many sections of classified balance sheets in this and preceding chapters. The classified balance sheet in Illustration 16-12 includes, in one place, key topics from previous chapters: the issuance of par value common stock, restrictions of retained earnings, and issuance of long-term bonds. From this chapter, the statement includes (highlighted in red) short-term and long-term investments. The investments in short-term securities are considered trading securities. The long-term investments in stock of less than 20% owned companies are considered available-for-sale securities. Illustration 16-12 also includes a long-term investment reported at equity and descriptive notations within the statement, such as the basis for valuing merchandise inventory and one note to the statement.

Do it!

Financial Statement Presentation of Investments

Identify where each of the following items would be reported in the financial statements.

1. Interest earned on investments in bonds.
2. Market adjustment—available-for-sale.
3. Unrealized loss on available-for-sale securities.
4. Gain on sale of investments in stock.
5. Unrealized gain on trading securities.

Use the following possible categories:

Balance sheet:

Current assets	Current liabilities
Investments	Long-term liabilities
Property, plant, and equipment	Stockholders' equity
Intangible assets	

Income statement:

Other revenues and gains	Other expenses and losses

action plan

✔ Classify investments as current assets if they will be held for less than one year.

✔ Report unrealized gains or losses on trading securities in income.

✔ Report unrealized gains or losses on available-for-sale securities in equity.

✔ Report realized earnings on investments in the income statement as "Other revenues and gains" or as "Other expenses and losses."

Solution

Item	Financial Statement	Category
1. Interest earned on investments in bonds.	Income statement	Other revenues and gains
2. Market adjustment—available-for-sale	Balance sheet	Investments
3. Unrealized loss on available-for-sale securities	Balance sheet	Stockholders' equity
4. Gain on sale of investments in stock.	Income statement	Other revenues and gains
5. Unrealized gain on trading securities	Income statement	Other revenues and gains

Related exercise material: BE16-6, BE16-7, BE16-8, E16-10, E16-11, E16-12, and **Do it!** 16-4.

✔
The Navigator

Illustration 16-12
Classified balance sheet

Pace Corporation
Balance Sheet
December 31, 2012

Assets

Current assets			
Cash			$ 21,000
Short-term investments, at fair value			147,000
Accounts receivable		$ 84,000	
Less: Allowance for doubtful accounts		4,000	80,000
Inventory, at FIFO cost			43,000
Prepaid insurance			23,000
Total current assets			314,000
Investments			
Investments in stock of less than 20% owned companies, at fair value		50,000	
Investment in stock of 20–50% owned company, at equity		150,000	
Total investments			200,000
Property, plant, and equipment			
Land			200,000
Buildings	$800,000		
Less: Accumulated depreciation—buildings	200,000	600,000	
Equipment	180,000		
Less: Accumulated depreciation—equipment	54,000	126,000	
Total property, plant, and equipment			926,000
Intangible assets			
Goodwill			270,000
Total assets			$1,710,000

Liabilities and Stockholders' Equity

Current liabilities			
Accounts payable			$ 185,000
Federal income taxes payable			60,000
Interest payable			10,000
Total current liabilities			255,000
Long-term liabilities			
Bonds payable, 10%, due 2021		$ 300,000	
Less: Discount on bonds		10,000	
Total long-term liabilities			290,000
Total liabilities			545,000
Stockholders' equity			
Paid-in capital			
Common stock, $10 par value, 200,000 shares authorized, 80,000 shares issued and outstanding		800,000	
Paid-in capital in excess of par— common stock		100,000	
Total paid-in capital		900,000	
Retained earnings (Note 1)		255,000	
Total paid-in capital and retained earnings		1,155,000	
Add: Unrealized gain on available-for-sale securities		10,000	
Total stockholders' equity			1,165,000
Total liabilities and stockholders' equity			$1,710,000

Note 1. Retained earnings of $100,000 is restricted for plant expansion.

COMPREHENSIVE

Do it!

In its first year of operations, DeMarco Company had the following selected transactions in stock investments that are considered trading securities.

June 1   Purchased for cash 600 shares of Sanburg common stock at $24 per share, plus $300 brokerage fees.
July 1   Purchased for cash 800 shares of Cey common stock at $33 per share, plus $600 brokerage fees.
Sept. 1   Received a $1 per share cash dividend from Cey Corporation.
Nov. 1   Sold 200 shares of Sanburg common stock for cash at $27 per share, less $150 brokerage fees.
Dec. 15   Received a $0.50 per share cash dividend on Sanburg common stock.

At December 31, the fair values per share were Sanburg $25 and Cey $30.

Instructions

(a) Journalize the transactions.

(b) Prepare the adjusting entry at December 31 to report the securities at fair value.

action plan

✔ Include the price paid plus brokerage fees in the cost of the investment.

✔ Compute the gain or loss on sales as the difference between net selling price and the cost of the securities.

✔ Base the adjustment to fair value on the total difference between the cost and the fair value of the securities.

Solution to Comprehensive Do it!

(a) June 1 | Stock Investments | 14,700 | |
| Cash (600 × $24) + $300 | | 14,700 |
| (To record purchase of 600 shares of Sanburg common stock) | | |

July 1 | Stock Investments | 27,000 | |
| Cash (800 × $33) + $600 | | 27,000 |
| (To record purchase of 800 shares of Cey common stock) | | |

Sept. 1 | Cash (800 × $1.00) | 800 | |
| Dividend Revenue | | 800 |
| (To record receipt of $1 per share cash dividend from Cey Corporation) | | |

Nov. 1 | Cash (200 × $27) − $150 | 5,250 | |
Stock Investments ($14,700 × 200/600)		4,900
Gain on Sale of Stock Investments		350
(To record sale of 200 shares of Sanburg common stock)		

Dec. 15 | Cash (600 − 200) × $0.50 | 200 | |
| Dividend Revenue | | 200 |
| (To record receipt of $0.50 per share dividend from Sanburg Corporation) | | |

(b) Dec. 31 | Unrealized Loss—Income | 2,800 | |
| Market Adjustment—Trading | | 2,800 |
| (To record unrealized loss on trading securities) | | |

Investment	Cost	Fair Value	Unrealized Gain (Loss)
Sanburg common stock	$ 9,800	$10,000	$ 200
Cey common stock	27,000	24,000	(3,000)
Totals	$36,800	$34,000	$(2,800)

✔
The Navigator

Summary of Study Objectives

[1] Discuss why corporations invest in debt and stock securities. Corporations invest for three primary reasons: (a) They have excess cash. (b) They view investments as a significant revenue source. (c) They have strategic goals such as gaining control of a competitor or moving into a new line of business.

[2] Explain the accounting for debt investments. Companies record investments in debt securities when they purchase bonds, receive or accrue interest, and sell the bonds. They report gains or losses on the sale of bonds in the "Other revenues and gains" or "Other expenses and losses" sections of the income statement.

[3] Explain the accounting for stock investments. Companies record investments in common stock when they purchase the stock, receive dividends, and sell the stock. When ownership is less than 20%, the cost method is used. When ownership is between 20% and 50%, the equity method should be used. When ownership is more than 50%, companies prepare consolidated financial statements.

[4] Describe the use of consolidated financial statements. When a company owns more than 50% of the common stock of another company, it usually prepares consolidated financial statements. These statements indicate the magnitude and scope of operations of the companies under common control.

[5] Indicate how debt and stock investments are reported in financial statements. Investments in debt and stock securities are classified as trading, available-for-sale, or held-to-maturity securities for valuation and reporting purposes. Trading securities are reported as current assets at fair value, with changes from cost reported in net income. Available-for-sale securities are also reported at fair value, with the changes from cost reported in stockholders' equity. Available-for-sale securities are classified as short-term or long-term, depending on their expected future sale date.

[6] Distinguish between short-term and long-term investments. Short-term investments are securities that are (a) readily marketable and (b) intended to be converted to cash within the next year or operating cycle, whichever is longer. Investments that do not meet both criteria are classified as long-term investments.

The Navigator

Glossary

Available-for-sale securities Securities that are held with the intent of selling them sometime in the future. (p. 733).

Consolidated financial statements Financial statements that present the assets and liabilities controlled by the parent company and the total revenues and expenses of the subsidiary companies. (p. 730).

Controlling interest Ownership of more than 50% of the common stock of another entity. (p. 730).

Cost method An accounting method in which the investment in common stock is recorded at cost, and revenue is recognized only when cash dividends are received. (p. 728).

Debt investments Investments in government and corporation bonds. (p. 725).

Equity method An accounting method in which the investment in common stock is initially recorded at cost, and the investment account is then adjusted annually to show the investor's equity in the investee. (p. 729).

Fair value Amount for which a security could be sold in a normal market. (p. 732).

Held-to-maturity securities Debt securities that the investor has the intent and ability to hold to their maturity date. (p. 733).

Investment portfolio A group of stocks and/or debt securities in different corporations held for investment purposes. (p. 727).

Long-term investments Investments that are not readily marketable or that management does not intend to convert into cash within the next year or operating cycle, whichever is longer. (p. 736).

Parent company A company that owns more than 50% of the common stock of another entity. (p. 730).

Short-term investments Investments that are readily marketable and intended to be converted into cash within the next year or operating cycle, whichever is longer. (p. 736).

Stock investments Investments in the capital stock of other corporations. (p. 727).

Subsidiary (affiliated) company A company in which more than 50% of its stock is owned by another company. (p. 730).

Trading securities Securities bought and held primarily for sale in the near term to generate income on short-term price differences. (p. 733).

Self-Test, Brief Exercises, Exercises, Problem Set A, and many more components are available for practice in *WileyPLUS*

Self-Test Questions

Answers are on page 756.

(SO 1) **1.** Which of the following is *not* a primary reason why corporations invest in debt and equity securities?
   a. They wish to gain control of a competitor.
   b. They have excess cash.
   c. They wish to move into a new line of business.
   d. They are required to by law.

(SO 2) **2.** Debt investments are initially recorded at:
   a. cost.
   b. cost plus accrued interest.
   c. fair value.
   d. None of the above.

(SO 2) **3.** Hanes Company sells debt investments costing $26,000 for $28,000, plus accrued interest that has been recorded. In journalizing the sale, credits are to:
   a. Debt Investments and Loss on Sale of Debt Investments.
   b. Debt Investments, Gain on Sale of Debt Investments, and Bond Interest Receivable.
   c. Stock Investments and Bond Interest Receivable.
   d. No correct answer is given.

(SO 3) **4.** Pryor Company receives net proceeds of $42,000 on the sale of stock investments that cost $39,500. This transaction will result in reporting in the income statement a:
   a. loss of $2,500 under "Other expenses and losses."
   b. loss of $2,500 under "Operating expenses."
   c. gain of $2,500 under "Other revenues and gains."
   d. gain of $2,500 under "Operating revenues."

(SO 3) **5.** The equity method of accounting for long-term investments in stock should be used when the investor has significant influence over an investee and owns:
   a. between 20% and 50% of the investee's common stock.
   b. 20% or more of the investee's common stock.
   c. more than 50% of the investee's common stock.
   d. less than 20% of the investee's common stock.

(SO 3) **6.** Assume that Horicon Corp acquired 25% of the common stock of Sheboygan Corp. on January 1, 2012, for $300,000. During 2012, Sheboygan Corp. reported net income of $160,000 and paid total dividends of $60,000. If Horicon uses the equity method to account for its investment, the balance in the investment account on December 31, 2012, will be:
   a. $300,000.
   b. $325,000.
   c. $400,000.
   d. $340,000.

(SO 3) **7.** Using the information in question 6, what entry would Horicon make to record the receipt of the dividend from Sheboygan?

   a. Debit Cash and credit Revenue from Stock Investments.
   b. Debit Cash Dividends and credit Revenue from Stock Investments.
   c. Debit Cash and credit Stock Investments.
   d. Debit Cash and credit Dividend Revenue.

8. You have a controlling interest if: (SO 3)
   a. you own more than 20% of a company's stock.
   b. you are the president of the company.
   c. you use the equity method.
   d. you own more than 50% of a company's stock.

9. Which of the following statements is *not true*? Consoli- (SO 4) dated financial statements are useful to:
   a. determine the profitability of specific subsidiaries.
   b. determine the total profitability of enterprises under common control.
   c. determine the breadth of a parent company's operations.
   d. determine the full extent of total obligations of enterprises under common control.

10. At the end of the first year of operations, the total cost of (SO 5) the trading securities portfolio is $120,000. Total fair value is $115,000. The financial statements should show:
   a. a reduction of an asset of $5,000 and a realized loss of $5,000.
   b. a reduction of an asset of $5,000 and an unrealized loss of $5,000 in the stockholders' equity section.
   c. a reduction of an asset of $5,000 in the current assets section and an unrealized loss of $5,000 in "Other expenses and losses."
   d. a reduction of an asset of $5,000 in the current assets section and a realized loss of $5,000 in "Other expenses and losses."

11. At December 31, 2012, the fair value of available-for-sale (SO 5) securities is $41,300 and the cost is $39,800. At January 1, 2012, there was a credit balance of $900 in the Market Adjustment—Available-for-Sale account. The required adjusting entry would be:
   a. Debit Market Adjustment—Available-for-Sale for $1,500 and credit Unrealized Gain or Loss—Equity for $1,500.
   b. Debit Market Adjustment—Available-for-Sale for $600 and credit Unrealized Gain or Loss—Equity for $600.
   c. Debit Market Adjustment—Available-for-Sale for $2,400 and credit Unrealized Gain or Loss—Equity for $2,400.
   d. Debit Unrealized Gain or Loss—Equity for $2,400 and credit Market Adjustment—Available-for-Sale for $2,400.

(SO 5) **12.** In the balance sheet, a debit balance in Unrealized Gain or Loss—Equity is reported as a(n):
   a. increase to stockholders' equity.
   b. decrease to stockholders' equity.
   c. loss in the income statement.
   d. loss in the retained earnings statement.

(SO 6) **13.** Short-term debt investments must be readily marketable and expected to be sold within:

a. 3 months from the date of purchase.
b. the next year or operating cycle, whichever is shorter.
c. the next year or operating cycle, whichever is longer.
d. the operating cycle.

Go to the book's companion website, **www.wiley.com/college/weygandt**, for additional Self-Test Questions.

 The Navigator

Questions

1. What are the reasons that corporations invest in securities?

2. (a) What is the cost of an investment in bonds?
   (b) When is interest on bonds recorded?

3. Tino Martinez is confused about losses and gains on the sale of debt investments. Explain to Tino (a) how the gain or loss is computed, and (b) the statement presentation of the gains and losses.

4. Olindo Company sells Gish's bonds costing $40,000 for $45,000, including $500 of accrued interest. In recording the sale, Olindo books a $5,000 gain. Is this correct? Explain.

5. What is the cost of an investment in stock?

6. To acquire Kinston Corporation stock, R. Neal pays $62,000 in cash, plus $1,200 broker's fees. What entry should be made for this investment?

7. (a) When should a long-term investment in common stock be accounted for by the equity method? (b) When is revenue recognized under this method?

8. Rijo Corporation uses the equity method to account for its ownership of 30% of the common stock of Pippen Packing. During 2012, Pippen reported a net income of $80,000 and declares and pays cash dividends of $10,000. What recognition should Rijo Corporation give to these events?

9. What constitutes "significant influence" when an investor's financial interest is below the 50% level?

10. Distinguish between the cost and equity methods of accounting for investments in stocks.

11. What are consolidated financial statements?

12. What are the valuation guidelines for investments at a balance sheet date?

13. Tina Eddings is the controller of Mendez Inc. At December 31, the company's investments in trading securities cost $74,000. They have a fair value of $70,000. Indicate how Tina would report these data in the financial statements prepared on December 31.

14. Using the data in question 13, how would Tina report the data if the investment were long-term and the securities were classified as available-for-sale?

15. Hashmi Company's investments in available-for-sale securities at December 31 show total cost of $195,000 and total fair value of $205,000. Prepare the adjusting entry.

16. Using the data in question 15, prepare the adjusting entry assuming the securities are classified as trading securities.

17. What is the proper statement presentation of the account Unrealized Loss—Equity?

18. What purposes are served by reporting Unrealized Gains (Losses)—Equity in the stockholders' equity section?

19. Altoona Wholesale Supply owns stock in Key Corporation. Altoona intends to hold the stock indefinitely because of some negative tax consequences if sold. Should the investment in Key be classified as a short-term investment? Why or why not?

20. 🌐 **PEPSICO** What does PepsiCo state regarding its accounting policy involving consolidated financial statements?

Brief Exercises

BE16-1 Kimmel Corporation purchased debt investments for $52,000 on January 1, 2012. On July 1, 2012, Kimmel received cash interest of $2,340. Journalize the purchase and the receipt of interest. Assume that no interest has been accrued.

Journalize entries for debt investments.
(SO 2)

BE16-2 On August 1, Paul Company buys 1,000 shares of Merlynn common stock for $35,000 cash, plus brokerage fees of $700. On December 1, Paul sells the stock investments for $40,000 in cash. Journalize the purchase and sale of the common stock.

Journalize entries for stock investments.
(SO 3)

BE16-3 Texas Company owns 25% of Plano Company. For the current year, Plano reports net income of $180,000 and declares and pays a $50,000 cash dividend. Record Texas's equity in Plano's net income and the receipt of dividends from Plano.

Record transactions under the equity method of accounting.
(SO 3)

BE16-4 The cost of the trading securities of Hardy Company at December 31, 2012, is $62,000. At December 31, 2012, the fair value of the securities is $59,000. Prepare the adjusting entry to record the securities at fair value.

Prepare adjusting entry using fair value.
(SO 5)

BE16-5 For the data presented in BE16-4, show the financial statement presentation of the trading securities and related accounts.

Indicate statement presentation using fair value.
(SO 5, 6)

Prepare adjusting entry using fair value.
(SO 5)

BE16-6   Latrobe Corporation holds as a long-term investment available-for-sale stock securities costing $72,000. At December 31, 2012, the fair value of the securities is $66,000. Prepare the adjusting entry to record the securities at fair value.

Indicate statements presentation using fair value.
(SO 5, 6)

BE16-7   For the data presented in BE16-6, show the financial statement presentation of the available-for-sale securities and related accounts. Assume the available-for-sale securities are noncurrent.

Prepare investments section of balance sheet.
(SO 5, 6)

BE16-8   Gurnee Corporation has the following long-term investments: (1) Common stock of Kornas Co. (10% ownership) held as available-for-sale securities, cost $108,000, fair value $115,000. (2) Common stock of Kozanecki Inc. (30% ownership), cost $210,000, equity $270,000. Prepare the investments section of the balance sheet.

Do it! Review

Make journal entry for bond purchase and adjusting entry for interest accrual.
(SO 2)

Do it! 16-1   Kurtyka Corporation had the following transactions relating to debt investments:

Jan. 1   Purchased 50, $1,000, 12% Nordica Company bonds for $50,000 plus broker's fees of $1,500. Interest is payable semiannually on January 1 and July 1.
July 1   Received semiannual interest from Nordica Company bonds.
July 1   Sold 30 Nordica Company bonds for $30,000, less $800 broker's fees.

(a) Journalize the transactions, and (b) prepare the adjusting entry for the accrual of interest on December 31.

Make journal entries for stock investments.
(SO 3)

Do it! 16-2   Presented below are two independent situations:

1. Lorfeld Inc. acquired 10% of the 500,000 shares of common stock of Northbrook Corporation at a total cost of $11 per share on June 17, 2012. On September 3, Northbrook declared and paid a $160,000 dividend. On December 31, Northbrook reported net income of $550,000 for the year.
2. Saa Corporation obtained significant influence over McCarthy Company by buying 30% of McCarthy's 100,000 outstanding shares of common stock at a cost of $18 per share on January 1, 2012. On May 15, McCarthy declared and paid a cash dividend of $150,000. On December 31, McCarthy reported net income of $270,000 for the year.

Prepare all necessary journal entries for 2012 for (1) Lorfeld and (2) Saa.

Make journal entries for trading and available-for-sale securities.
(SO 5)

Do it! 16-3   Some of McEleveen Corporation's investment securities are classified as trading securities and some are classified as available-for-sale. The cost and fair value of each category at December 31, 2012, was as follows.

	Cost	Fair Value	Unrealized Gain (Loss)
Trading securities	$96,300	$84,900	$(11,400)
Available-for-sale securities	$59,000	$63,200	$ 4,200

At December 31, 2011, the Market Adjustment—Trading account had a debit balance of $2,200, and the Market Adjustment—Available-for-Sale account had a credit balance of $7,750. Prepare the required journal entries for each group of securities for December 31, 2012.

Indicate financial statement presentation of investments.
(SO 6)

Do it! 16-4   Identify where each of the following items would be reported in the financial statements.

1. Loss on sale of investments in stock.
2. Unrealized gain on available-for-sale securities.
3. Market adjustment—trading.
4. Interest earned on investments in bonds.
5. Unrealized loss on trading securities.

Use the following possible categories:
Balance sheet:

Current assets	Current liabilities
Investments	Long-term liabilities
Property, plant, and equipment	Stockholders' equity
Intangible assets	

Income statement:

Other revenues and gains	Other expenses and losses

Exercises

E16-1   Mr. Wellington is studying for an accounting test and has developed the following questions about investments.

1. What are three reasons why companies purchase investments in debt or stock securities?
2. Why would a corporation have excess cash that it does not need for operations?
3. What is the typical investment when investing cash for short periods of time?
4. What are the typical investments when investing cash to generate earnings?
5. Why would a company invest in securities that provide no current cash flows?
6. What is the typical stock investment when investing cash for strategic reasons?

Understand debt and stock investments.
(SO 1)

Instructions
Provide answers for Mr. Wellington.

E16-2   Floyd Corporation had the following transactions pertaining to debt investments.

Jan. 1   Purchased 50 8%, $1,000 Petal Co. bonds for $50,000 cash plus brokerage fees of $900. Interest is payable semiannually on July 1 and January 1.
July 1   Received semiannual interest on Petal Co. bonds.
July 1   Sold 30 Petal Co. bonds for $34,000 less $500 brokerage fees.

Journalize debt investment transactions and accrue interest.
(SO 2)

Instructions
(a) Journalize the transactions.
(b) Prepare the adjusting entry for the accrual of interest at December 31.

E16-3   Brook Company purchased 70 Meissner Company 12%, 10-year, $1,000 bonds on January 1, 2012, for $73,000. Brook Company also had to pay $500 of broker's fees. The bonds pay interest semiannually on July 1 and January 1. On January 1, 2013, after receipt of interest, Brook Company sold 40 of the bonds for $40,100.

Journalize debt investment transactions, accrue interest, and record sale.
(SO 2)

Instructions
Prepare the journal entries to record the transactions described above.

E16-4   Diann Company had the following transactions pertaining to stock investments.

Feb. 1   Purchased 600 shares of Ronn common stock (2%) for $6,000 cash, plus brokerage fees of $200.
July 1   Received cash dividends of $1 per share on Ronn common stock.
Sept. 1   Sold 300 shares of Ronn common stock for $4,400, less brokerage fees of $100.
Dec. 1   Received cash dividends of $1 per share on Ronn common stock.

Journalize stock investment transactions.
(SO 3)

Instructions
(a) Journalize the transactions.
(b) Explain how dividend revenue and the gain (loss) on sale should be reported in the income statement.

E16-5   Spring Inc. had the following transactions pertaining to investments in common stock.

Jan. 1   Purchased 2,500 shares of Angeltide Corporation common stock (5%) for $140,000 cash plus $2,100 broker's commission.
July 1   Received a cash dividend of $3 per share.
Dec. 1   Sold 500 shares of Angeltide Corporation common stock for $32,000 cash, less $800 broker's commission.
Dec. 31   Received a cash dividend of $3 per share.

Journalize transactions for investments in stocks.
(SO 3)

Instructions
Journalize the transactions.

E16-6   On February 1, Minitori Company purchased 500 shares (2% ownership) of Becker Company common stock for $30 per share plus brokerage fees of $400. On March 20, Minitori Company sold 100 shares of Becker stock for $2,900, less a $50 brokerage fee. Minitori received a dividend of $1.00 per share on April 25. On June 15, Minitori sold 200 shares of Becker stock for $7,400, less a $90 brokerage fee. On July 28, Minitori received a dividend of $1.25 per share.

Journalize transactions for investments in stocks.
(SO 3)

Instructions
Prepare the journal entries to record the transactions described above.

Journalize and post transac-
tions, and contrast cost and
equity method results.
(SO 3)

E16-7   On January 1, Vince Corporation purchased a 25% equity in Morelli Corporation for $180,000. At December 31, Morelli declared and paid a $60,000 cash dividend and reported net income of $200,000.

Instructions
(a) Journalize the transactions.
(b) Determine the amount to be reported as an investment in Morelli stock at December 31.

Journalize entries under cost
and equity methods.
(SO 3, 5)

E16-8   Presented below are two independent situations.
1. Chicory Cosmetics acquired 15% of the 200,000 shares of common stock of Racine Fashion at a total cost of $13 per share on March 18, 2012. On June 30, Racine declared and paid a $60,000 dividend. On December 31, Racine reported net income of $122,000 for the year. At December 31, the market price of Racine Fashion was $15 per share. The stock is classified as available-for-sale.
2. Frank, Inc., obtained significant influence over Nowak Corporation by buying 30% of Nowak's 30,000 outstanding shares of common stock at a total cost of $9 per share on January 1, 2012. On June 15, Nowak declared and paid a cash dividend of $30,000. On December 31, Nowak reported a net income of $80,000 for the year.

Instructions
Prepare all the necessary journal entries for 2012 for (1) Chicory Cosmetics and (2) Frank, Inc.

Understand the usefulness of
consolidated statements.
(SO 4)

E16-9   Edna Company purchased 70% of the outstanding common stock of Damen Corporation.

Instructions
(a) Explain the relationship between Edna Company and Damen Corporation.
(b) How should Edna account for its investment in Damen?
(c) Why is the accounting treatment described in (b) useful?

Prepare adjusting entry to
record fair value, and indicate
statement presentation.
(SO 5, 6)

E16-10   At December 31, 2012, the trading securities for Oglesbee, Inc. are as follows.

Security	Cost	Fair Value
A	$17,500	$16,000
B	12,500	14,000
C	23,000	19,000
	$53,000	$49,000

Instructions
(a) Prepare the adjusting entry at December 31, 2012, to report the securities at fair value.
(b) Show the balance sheet and income statement presentation at December 31, 2012, after adjustment to fair value.

Prepare adjusting entry to
record fair value, and indicate
statement presentation.
(SO 5, 6)

E16-11   Data for investments in stock classified as trading securities are presented in E16-10. Assume instead that the investments are classified as available-for-sale securities. They have the same cost and fair value. The securities are considered to be a long-term investment.

Instructions
(a) Prepare the adjusting entry at December 31, 2012, to report the securities at fair value.
(b) Show the statement presentation at December 31, 2012, after adjustment to fair value.
(c) ━━━ E. Devonshire, a member of the board of directors, does not understand the reporting of the unrealized gains or losses. Write a letter to Ms. Devonshire explaining the reporting and the purposes that it serves.

Prepare adjusting entries
for fair value, and indicate
statement presentation for two
classes of securities.
(SO 5, 6)

E16-12   Zippydah Company has the following data at December 31, 2012.

Securities	Cost	Fair Value
Trading	$120,000	$124,000
Available-for-sale	100,000	94,000

The available-for-sale securities are held as a long-term investment.

Instructions
(a) Prepare the adjusting entries to report each class of securities at fair value.
(b) Indicate the statement presentation of each class of securities and the related unrealized gain (loss) accounts.

Exercises: Set B

Visit the book's companion website, at **www.wiley.com/college/weygandt**, and choose the Student Companion site to access Exercise Set B.

Problems: Set A

P16-1A Pagnucci Carecenters Inc. provides financing and capital to the health-care industry, with a particular focus on nursing homes for the elderly. The following selected transactions relate to bonds acquired as an investment by Pagnucci, whose fiscal year ends on December 31.

Journalize debt investment transactions and show financial statement presentation.
(SO 2, 5, 6)

2012

Jan.	1	Purchased at face value $2,000,000 of Franco Nursing Centers, Inc., 10-year, 8% bonds dated January 1, 2012, directly from Franco.
July	1	Received the semiannual interest on the Franco bonds.
Dec.	31	Accrual of interest at year-end on the Franco bonds.

(Assume that all intervening transactions and adjustments have been properly recorded and that the number of bonds owned has not changed from December 31, 2012, to December 31, 2014.)

2015

Jan.	1	Received the semiannual interest on the Franco bonds.
Jan.	1	Sold $1,000,000 Franco bonds at 106. The broker deducted $6,000 for commissions and fees on the sale.
July	1	Received the semiannual interest on the Franco bonds.
Dec.	31	Accrual of interest at year-end on the Franco bonds.

Instructions

(a) Journalize the listed transactions for the years 2012 and 2015.
(b) Assume that the fair value of the bonds at December 31, 2012, was $2,200,000. These bonds are classified as available-for-sale securities. Prepare the adjusting entry to record these bonds at fair value.
(c) Based on your analysis in part (b), show the balance sheet presentation of the bonds and interest receivable at December 31, 2012. Assume the investments are considered long-term. Indicate where any unrealized gain or loss is reported in the financial statements.

(a) Gain on sale of debt investment $54,000

P16-2A In January 2012, the management of Stefan Company concludes that it has sufficient cash to permit some short-term investments in debt and stock securities. During the year, the following transactions occurred.

Journalize investment transactions, prepare adjusting entry, and show statement presentation.
(SO 2, 3, 5, 6)

Feb.	1	Purchased 600 shares of Superior common stock for $31,800, plus brokerage fees of $600.
Mar.	1	Purchased 800 shares of Pawlik common stock for $20,000, plus brokerage fees of $400.
Apr.	1	Purchased 50 $1,000, 7% Venice bonds for $50,000, plus $1,000 brokerage fees. Interest is payable semiannually on April 1 and October 1.
July	1	Received a cash dividend of $0.60 per share on the Superior common stock.
Aug.	1	Sold 200 shares of Superior common stock at $58 per share less brokerage fees of $200.
Sept.	1	Received a $1 per share cash dividend on the Pawlik common stock.
Oct.	1	Received the semiannual interest on the Venice bonds.
Oct.	1	Sold the Venice bonds for $50,000 less $1,000 brokerage fees.

At December 31, the fair value of the Superior common stock was $55 per share. The fair value of the Pawlik common stock was $24 per share.

Instructions

(a) Journalize the transactions and post to the accounts Debt Investments and Stock Investments. (Use the T-account form.)
(b) Prepare the adjusting entry at December 31, 2012, to report the investment securities at fair value. All securities are considered to be trading securities.

(a) Gain on stock sale $600

(c) Show the balance sheet presentation of investment securities at December 31, 2012.

(d) Identify the income statement accounts and give the statement classification of each account.

Journalize transactions and adjusting entry for stock investments.

(SO 3, 5, 6)

P16-3A On December 31, 2012, Ogallala Associates owned the following securities, held as a long-term investment. The securities are not held for influence or control of the investee.

Common Stock	Shares	Cost
Carlene Co.	2,000	$60,000
Riverdale Co.	5,000	45,000
Raczynski Co.	1,500	30,000

On December 31, 2012, the total fair value of the securities was equal to its cost. In 2013, the following transactions occurred.

July 1 Received $1 per share semiannual cash dividend on Riverdale Co. common stock.
Aug. 1 Received $0.50 per share cash dividend on Carlene Co. common stock.
Sept. 1 Sold 1,500 shares of Riverdale Co. common stock for cash at $8 per share, less brokerage fees of $300.
Oct. 1 Sold 800 shares of Carlene Co. common stock for cash at $33 per share, less brokerage fees of $500.
Nov. 1 Received $1 per share cash dividend on Raczynski Co. common stock.
Dec. 15 Received $0.50 per share cash dividend on Carlene Co. common stock.
    31 Received $1 per share semiannual cash dividend on Riverdale Co. common stock.

At December 31, the fair values per share of the common stocks were: Carlene Co. $32, Riverdale Co. $8, and Raczynski Co. $18.

Instructions

(a) Journalize the 2013 transactions and post to the account Stock Investments. (Use the T-account form.)

(b) Unrealized loss $4,100

(b) Prepare the adjusting entry at December 31, 2013, to show the securities at fair value. The stock should be classified as available-for-sale securities.

(c) Show the balance sheet presentation of the investments at December 31, 2013. At this date, Ogallala Associates has common stock $1,500,000 and retained earnings $1,000,000.

Prepare entries under the cost and equity methods, and tabulate differences.

(SO 3)

P16-4A Control Alt Design acquired 30% of the outstanding common stock of Walter Company on January 1, 2012, by paying $800,000 for the 45,000 shares. Walter declared and paid $0.30 per share cash dividends on March 15, June 15, September 15, and December 15, 2012. Walter reported net income of $320,000 for the year. At December 31, 2012, the market price of Walter common stock was $24 per share.

Instructions

(a) Total dividend revenue $54,000

(a) Prepare the journal entries for Control Alt Design for 2012 assuming Control Alt Design cannot exercise significant influence over Walter. (Use the cost method and assume that Walter common stock should be classified as a trading security.)

(b) Revenue from investments $96,000

(b) Prepare the journal entries for Control Alt Design for 2012, assuming Control Alt Design can exercise significant influence over Walter. Use the equity method.

(c) Indicate the balance sheet and income statement account balances at December 31, 2012, under each method of accounting.

Journalize stock investment transactions and show statement presentation.

(SO 3, 5, 6)

P16-5A The following securities are in Amberwood Company's portfolio of long-term available-for-sale securities at December 31, 2012.

	Cost
1,000 shares of Reginald Corporation common stock	$52,000
1,400 shares of Elderberry Corporation common stock	84,000
1,200 shares of Mattoon Corporation preferred stock	33,600

On December 31, 2012, the total cost of the portfolio equaled total fair value. Amberwood had the following transactions related to the securities during 2013.

Jan. 20 Sold all 1,000 shares of Reginald Corporation common stock at $55 per share less brokerage fees of $600.
    28 Purchased 400 shares of $70 par value common stock of Hachito Corporation at $78 per share, plus brokerage fees of $480.
    30 Received a cash dividend of $1.15 per share on Elderberry Corp. common stock.

Feb. 8   Received cash dividends of $0.40 per share on Mattoon Corp. preferred stock.
      18   Sold all 1,200 shares of Mattoon Corp. preferred stock at $27 per share less brokerage fees of $360.
July 30   Received a cash dividend of $1.00 per share on Elderberry Corp. common stock.
Sept. 6   Purchased an additional 900 shares of $10 par value common stock of Hachito Corporation at $82 per share, plus brokerage fees of $1,200.
Dec. 1   Received a cash dividend of $1.50 per share on Hachito Corporation common stock.

At December 31, 2013, the fair values of the securities were:

| Elderberry Corporation common stock | $64 per share |
| Hachito Corporation common stock | $72 per share |

Instructions

(a) Prepare journal entries to record the transactions.
(b) Post to the investment accounts. (Use T accounts.)
(c) Prepare the adjusting entry at December 31, 2013 to report the portfolio at fair value.
(d) Show the balance sheet presentation at December 31, 2013, for the investment-related accounts.

(a) Loss on sale of stock investment $1,560
(c) Unrealized loss $7,480

P16-6A The following data, presented in alphabetical order, are taken from the records of Radar Corporation.

Prepare a balance sheet.
(SO 5, 6)

Accounts payable	$ 240,000
Accounts receivable	140,000
Accumulated depreciation—buildings	180,000
Accumulated depreciation—equipment	52,000
Allowance for doubtful accounts	6,000
Bonds payable (10%, due 2020)	500,000
Buildings	950,000
Cash	42,000
Common stock ($10 par value; 500,000 shares authorized, 150,000 shares issued)	1,500,000
Dividends payable	80,000
Equipment	275,000
Goodwill	200,000
Income taxes payable	120,000
Inventory	170,000
Investment in Sasse common stock (10% ownership), at cost	278,000
Investment in Mara common stock (30% ownership), at equity	380,000
Land	390,000
Market adjustment—available-for-sale securities (Dr)	8,000
Notes payable (due 2013)	70,000
Paid-in capital in excess of par—common stock	130,000
Premium on bonds payable	40,000
Prepaid insurance	16,000
Retained earnings	103,000
Short-term investments, at fair value (and cost)	180,000
Unrealized gain—available-for-sale securities	8,000

The investment in Sasse common stock is considered to be a long-term available-for-sale security.

Instructions

Prepare a classified balance sheet at December 31, 2012.

Total assets $2,791,000

Problems: Set B

P16-1B Cheese Farms is a grower of hybrid seed corn for Steenbergen Genetics Corporation. It has had two exceptionally good years and has elected to invest its excess funds in bonds. The selected transactions, shown on the next page, relate to bonds acquired as an investment by Cheese Farms, whose fiscal year ends on December 31.

Journalize debt investment transactions and show financial statement presentation.
(SO 2, 5, 6)

2012

Jan. 1   Purchased at face value $400,000 of Stombaugh Corporation 10-year, 9% bonds dated January 1, 2012, directly from the issuing corporation.
July 1   Received the semiannual interest on the Stombaugh bonds.
Dec. 31   Accrual of interest at year-end on the Stombaugh bonds.

(Assume that all intervening transactions and adjustments have been properly recorded and the number of bonds owned has not changed from December 31, 2012, to December 31, 2014.)

2015

Jan. 1   Received the semiannual interest on the Stombaugh bonds.
Jan. 1   Sold $200,000 of Stombaugh bonds at 114. The broker deducted $7,000 for commissions and fees on the sale.
July 1   Received the semiannual interest on the Stombaugh bonds.
Dec. 31   Accrual of interest at year-end on the Stombaugh bonds.

Instructions

(a) Gain on sale of debt investments $21,000

(a) Journalize the listed transactions for the years 2012 and 2015.
(b) Assume that the fair value of the bonds at December 31, 2012, was $385,000. These bonds are classified as available-for-sale securities. Prepare the adjusting entry to record these bonds at fair value.
(c) Based on your analysis in part (b), show the balance sheet presentation of the bonds and interest receivable at December 31, 2012. Assume the investments are considered long-term. Indicate where any unrealized gain or loss is reported in the financial statements.

Journalize investment transactions, prepare adjusting entry, and show statement presentation.

(SO 2, 3, 5, 6)

P16-2B In January 2012, the management of Gina Company concludes that it has sufficient cash to purchase some short-term investments in debt and stock securities. During the year, the following transactions occurred.

Feb. 1   Purchased 500 shares of Joy common stock for $30,000, plus brokerage fees of $800.
Mar. 1   Purchased 600 shares of Aurelius common stock for $20,000, plus brokerage fees of $300.
Apr. 1   Purchased 40 $1,000, 9% Sikich bonds for $40,000, plus $1,200 brokerage fees. Interest is payable semiannually on April 1 and October 1.
July 1   Received a cash dividend of $0.60 per share on the Joy common stock.
Aug. 1   Sold 300 shares of Joy common stock at $69 per share, less brokerage fees of $350.
Sept. 1   Received a $1 per share cash dividend on the Aurelius common stock.
Oct. 1   Received the semiannual interest on the Sikich bonds.
Oct. 1   Sold the Sikich bonds for $45,000, less $1,000 brokerage fees.

At December 31, the fair value of the Joy common stock was $66 per share. The fair value of the Aurelius common stock was $29 per share.

Instructions

(b) Unrealized loss $2,020

(a) Journalize the transactions and post to the accounts Debt Investments and Stock Investments. (Use the T-account form.)
(b) Prepare the adjusting entry at December 31, 2012, to report the investments at fair value. All securities are considered to be trading securities.
(c) Show the balance sheet presentation of investment securities at December 31, 2012.
(d) Identify the income statement accounts and give the statement classification of each account.

Journalize transactions and adjusting entry for stock investments.

(SO 3, 5, 6)

P16-3B On December 31, 2012, Eli Associates owned the following securities, held as long-term investments.

Common Stock	Shares	Cost
Trowbridge Co.	4,000	$100,000
Holly Co.	5,000	30,000
Oriental Motors Co.	3,000	60,000

On this date, the total fair value of the securities was equal to its cost. The securities are not held for influence or control over the investees. In 2013, the following transactions occurred.

July 1   Received $1 per share semiannual cash dividend on Holly Co. common stock.
Aug. 1   Received $0.50 per share cash dividend on Trowbridge Co. common stock.

Sept. 1   Sold 1,500 shares of Holly Co. common stock for cash at $8 per share, less brokerage fees of $300.
Oct.   1   Sold 600 shares of Trowbridge Co. common stock for cash at $30 per share, less brokerage fees of $600.
Nov. 1   Received $1 per share cash dividend on Oriental Motor Co. common stock.
Dec. 15   Received $0.50 per share cash dividend on Trowbridge Co. common stock.
     31   Received $1 per share semiannual cash dividend on Holly Co. common stock.

At December 31, the fair values per share of the common stocks were: Trowbridge Co. $23, Holly Co. $7, and Oriental Motors Co. $19.

Instructions
(a) Journalize the 2013 transactions and post to the account Stock Investments. (Use the T-account form.)
(b) Prepare the adjusting entry at December 31, 2013, to show the securities at fair value. The stock should be classified as available-for-sale securities.
(c) Show the balance sheet presentation of the investment-related accounts at December 31, 2013. At this date, Eli Associates has common stock $2,000,000 and retained earnings $1,200,000.

(a) Gain on sale, $2,700 and $2,400

P16-4B Tuecke's Concrete acquired 20% of the outstanding common stock of Drew, Inc. on January 1, 2012, by paying $1,100,000 for 40,000 shares. Drew declared and paid a $0.50 per share cash dividend on June 30 and again on December 31, 2012. Drew reported net income of $600,000 for the year. At December 31, 2012, the market price of Drew's common stock was $30 per share.

Prepare entries under the cost and equity methods, and tabulate differences.
(SO 3)

Instructions
(a) Prepare the journal entries for Tuecke's Concrete for 2012, assuming Tuecke's cannot exercise significant influence over Drew. (Use the cost method and assume Drew common stock should be classified as available-for-sale.)
(b) Prepare the journal entries for Tuecke's Concrete for 2012, assuming Tuecke's can exercise significant influence over Drew. (Use the equity method.)
(c) Indicate the balance sheet and income statement account balances at December 31, 2012, under each method of accounting.

(a) Total dividend revenue $40,000

(b) Revenue from investment $120,000

P16-5B The following are in Verbitsky's Company's portfolio of long-term available-for-sale securities at December 31, 2012.

Journalize stock investment transactions and show statement presentation.
(SO 3, 5, 6)

	Cost
700 shares of Sasha Corporation common stock	$35,000
900 shares of Ukraine Corporation common stock	42,000
800 shares of Zaba Corporation preferred stock	22,400

On December 31, the total cost of the portfolio equaled total fair value. Verbitsky's Company had the following transactions related to the securities during 2013.

Jan. 7   Sold 700 shares of Sasha Corporation common stock at $56 per share, less brokerage fees of $700.
     10   Purchased 300 shares, $70 par value common stock of Vanucci Corporation at $78 per share, plus brokerage fees of $240.
     26   Received a cash dividend of $1.15 per share on Ukraine Corporation common stock.
Feb. 2   Received cash dividends of $0.40 per share on Zaba Corporation preferred stock.
     10   Sold all 800 shares of Zaba Corporation preferred stock at $26 per share less brokerage fees of $180.
July 1   Received a cash dividend of $1.00 per share on Ukraine Corporation common stock.
Sept. 1   Purchased an additional 800 shares of the $70 par value common stock of Vanucci Corporation at $75 per share, plus brokerage fees of $900.
Dec. 15   Received a cash dividend of $1.50 per share on Vanucci Corporation common stock.

At December 31, 2013, the fair values of the securities were:

Ukraine Corporation common stock	$48 per share
Vanucci Corporation common stock	$72 per share

(a) Loss on sale $1,780

(c) Unrealized loss $4,140

Instructions

(a) Prepare journal entries to record the transactions.

(b) Post to the investment accounts. (Use T accounts.)

(c) Prepare the adjusting entry at December 31, 2013, to report the portfolio at fair value.

(d) Show the balance sheet presentation at December 31, 2013, for the investment-related accounts.

Prepare a balance sheet.
(SO 5, 6)

P16-6B The following data, presented in alphabetical order, are taken from the records of Redlands Corporation.

Accounts payable	$ 375,000
Accounts receivable	135,000
Accumulated depreciation—buildings	270,000
Accumulated depreciation—equipment	80,000
Allowance for doubtful accounts	10,000
Bonds payable (10%, due 2022)	600,000
Buildings	1,350,000
Cash	210,000
Common stock ($5 par value; 500,000 shares authorized, 440,000 shares issued)	2,200,000
Discount on bonds payable	30,000
Dividends payable	75,000
Equipment	415,000
Goodwill	300,000
Income taxes payable	180,000
Inventory	255,000
Investment in Bonita Inc. stock (30% ownership), at equity	900,000
Land	780,000
Notes payable (due 2013)	110,000
Paid-in capital in excess of par—common stock	300,000
Prepaid insurance	25,000
Retained earnings	480,000
Short-term investments, at fair value (and cost)	280,000

Total assets $4,290,000

Instructions

Prepare a classified balance sheet at December 31, 2012.

Problems: Set C

Visit the book's companion website, at **www.wiley.com/college/weygandt**, and choose the Student Companion site to access Problem Set C.

Comprehensive Problem: Chapters 12 to 16

CP16 **Part I** Mindy Feldkamp and her two colleagues, Oscar Lopez and Lori Melton, are personal trainers at an upscale health spa/resort in Tampa, Florida. They want to start a health club that specializes in health plans for people in the 50+ age range. The growing population in this age range and strong consumer interest in the health benefits of physical activity have convinced them they can profitably operate their own club. In addition to many other decisions, they need to determine what type of business organization they want. Oscar believes there are more advantages to the corporate form than a partnership, but he hasn't yet convinced Mindy and Lori. They have come to you, a small-business consulting specialist, seeking information and advice regarding the choice of starting a partnership versus a corporation.

Instructions

(a) Prepare a memo (dated May 26, 2011) that describes the advantages and disadvantages of both partnerships and corporations. Advise Mindy, Oscar, and Lori regarding which organizational form you believe would better serve their purposes. Make sure to include reasons supporting your advice.

Part II   After deciding to incorporate, each of the three investors receives 20,000 shares of $2 par common stock on June 12, 2011, in exchange for their co-owned building ($200,000 fair value) and $100,000 total cash they contributed to the business. The next decision that Mindy, Oscar, and Lori need to make is how to obtain financing for renovation and equipment. They understand the difference between equity securities and debt securities, but do not understand the tax, net income, and earnings per share consequences of equity versus debt financing on the future of their business.

Instructions

(b) Prepare notes for a discussion with the three entrepreneurs in which you will compare the consequences of using equity versus debt financing. As part of your notes, show the differences in interest and tax expense assuming $1,400,000 is financed with common stock, and then alternatively with debt. Assume that when common stock is used, 140,000 shares will be issued. When debt is used, assume the interest rate on debt is 9%, the tax rate is 32%, and income before interest and taxes is $300,000. (You may want to use an electronic spreadsheet.)

Part III   During the discussion about financing, Lori mentions that one of her clients, Roberto Marino, has approached her about buying a significant interest in the new club. Having an interested investor sways the three to issue equity securities to provide the financing they need. On July 21, 2011, Mr. Marino buys 90,000 shares at a price of $10 per share.

   The club, LifePath Fitness, opens on January 12, 2012, and after a slow start, begins to produce the revenue desired by the owners. The owners decide to pay themselves a stock dividend, since cash has been less than abundant since they opened their doors. The 10% stock dividend is declared by the owners on July 27, 2012. The market price of the stock is $3 on the declaration date. The date of record is July 31, 2012 (there have been no changes in stock ownership since the initial issuance), and the issue date is August 15, 2012. By the middle of the fourth quarter of 2012, the cash flow of LifePath Fitness has improved to the point that the owners feel ready to pay themselves a cash dividend. They declare a $0.05 cash dividend on December 4, 2012. The record date is December 14, 2012, and the payment date is December 24, 2012.

Instructions

(c) (1) Record all of the transactions related to the common stock of LifePath Fitness during the years 2011 and 2012. (2) Indicate how many shares are issued and outstanding after the stock dividend is issued.

Part IV   Since the club opened, a major concern has been the pool facilities. Although the existing pool is adequate, Mindy, Oscar, and Lori all desire to make LifePath a cutting-edge facility. Until the end of 2012, financing concerns prevented this improvement. However, because there has been steady growth in clientele, revenue, and income since the fourth quarter of 2012, the owners have explored possible financing options. They are hesitant to issue stock and change the ownership mix because they have been able to work together as a team with great effectiveness. They have formulated a plan to issue secured term bonds to raise the needed $600,000 for the pool facilities. By the end of April 2013, everything was in place for the bond issue to go ahead. On June 1, 2013, the bonds were issued for $548,000. The bonds pay semiannual interest of 3% (6% annual) on December 1 and June 1 of each year. The bonds mature in 10 years, and amortization is computed using the straight-line method.

Instructions

(d) Record (1) the issuance of the secured bonds, (2) the interest payment made on December 1, 2013, (3) the adjusting entry required at December 31, 2013, and (4) the interest payment made on June 1, 2014.

Part V   Mr. Marino's purchase of the stock of LifePath Fitness was done through his business. The stock investment has always been accounted for using the cost method on his firm's books. However, early in 2014 he decided to take his company public. He is preparing an IPO (initial public offering), and he needs to have the firm's financial statements audited. One of the issues to be resolved is to restate the stock investment in LifePath Fitness using the equity method, since Mr. Marino's ownership percentage is greater than 20%.

Instructions

(e) (1) Give the entries that would have been made on Marino's books if the equity method of accounting for investments had been used since the initial investment. Assume the following data for LifePath.

	2011	2012	2013
Net income	$30,000	$70,000	$105,000
Total cash dividends	$ 2,100	$20,000	$ 50,000

(2) Compute the balance in the Stock Investment account (as it relates to LifePath Fitness) at the end of 2013.

Continuing Cookie Chronicle

(*Note:* This is a continuation of the Cookie Chronicle from Chapters 1 through 15.)

CCC16   Natalie has been approached by Ken Thornton, a shareholder of The Beanery Coffee Inc. Ken wants to retire and would like to sell his 1,000 shares in The Beanery Coffee, which represents 20% of all shares issued. The Beanery is currently operated by Ken's twin daughters, who each own 40% of the common shares. The Beanery not only operates a coffee shop but also roasts and sells beans to retailers, under the name "Rocky Mountain Beanery."

Ken has met with Curtis and Natalie to discuss the business operation. All have concluded that there would be many advantages for Cookie & Coffee Creations Inc. to acquire an interest in The Beanery Coffee. Despite the apparent advantages, however, Natalie and Curtis are still not convinced that they should participate in this business venture.

Go to the book's companion website, **www.wiley.com/college/weygandt,** *to see the completion of this problem.*

BROADENINGYOURPERSPECTIVE

Financial Reporting and Analysis

Financial Reporting Problem: Pepsico, Inc.

BYP16-1   The annual report of PepsiCo. is presented in Appendix A.

Instructions

(a) See Note 1 to the financial statements and indicate what the consolidated financial statements include.

(b) Using PepsiCo's consolidated statement of cash flows, determine how much was spent for capital acquisitions during the current year.

Comparative Analysis Problem: PepsiCo, Inc. vs. The Coca-Cola Company

BYP16-2   PepsiCo's financial statements are presented in Appendix A. Financial statements of The Coca-Cola Company are presented in Appendix B.

Instructions

(a) Based on the information contained in these financial statements, determine each of the following for each company.

  (1) Net cash used for investing (investment) activities for the current year (from the statement of cash flows).

  (2) Cash used for capital expenditures during the current year.

(b) Each of PepsiCo's financial statements is labeled "consolidated." What has been consolidated? That is, from the contents of PepsiCo's annual report, identify by name the corporations that have been consolidated (parent and subsidiaries).

On the Web

BYP16-3   Most publicly traded companies are analyzed by numerous analysts. These analysts often don't agree about a company's future prospects. In this exercise, you will find analysts' ratings about companies and make comparisons over time and across companies in the same industry. You will also see to what extent the analysts experienced "earnings surprises." Earnings surprises can cause changes in stock prices.

Address: biz.yahoo.com/i, or go to **www.wiley.com/college/weygandt**

Steps
1. Choose a company.
2. Use the index to find the company's name.
3. Choose **Research**.

Instructions
(a) How many analysts rated the company?
(b) What percentage rated it a strong buy?
(c) What was the average rating for the week?
(d) Did the average rating improve or decline relative to the previous week?
(e) What was the amount of the earnings surprise percentage during the last quarter?

Critical Thinking

Decision Making Across the Organization

BYP16-4   At the beginning of the question and answer portion of the annual stockholders' meeting of Kemper Corporation, stockholder Mike Kerwin asks, "Why did management sell the holdings in UMW Company at a loss when this company has been very profitable during the period its stock was held by Kemper?"

Since president Tony Chavez has just concluded his speech on the recent success and bright future of Kemper, he is taken aback by this question and responds, "I remember we paid $1,300,000 for that stock some years ago, and I am sure we sold that stock at a much higher price. You must be mistaken."

Kerwin retorts, "Well, right here in footnote number 7 to the annual report it shows that 240,000 shares, a 30% interest in UMW, were sold on the last day of the year. Also, it states that UMW earned $520,000 this year and paid out $160,000 in cash dividends. Further, a summary statement indicates that in past years, while Kemper held UMW stock, UMW earned $1,240,000 and paid out $440,000 in dividends. Finally, the income statement for this year shows a loss on the sale of UMW stock of $180,000. So, I doubt that I am mistaken."

Red-faced, president Chavez turns to you.

Instructions
With the class divided into groups, answer the following.

(a) What dollar amount did Kemper receive upon the sale of the UMW stock?
(b) Explain why both stockholder Kerwin and president Chavez are correct.

Communication Activity

BYP16-5   Bunge Corporation has purchased two securities for its portfolio. The first is a stock investment in Longley Corporation, one of its suppliers. Bunge purchased 10% of Longley with the intention of holding it for a number of years, but has no intention of purchasing more shares. The second investment was a purchase of debt securities. Bunge purchased the debt securities because its analysts believe that changes in market interest rates will cause these securities to increase in value in a short period of time. Bunge intends to sell the securities as soon as they have increased in value.

Instructions
Write a memo to Max Scholes, the chief financial officer, explaining how to account for each of these investments. Explain what the implications for reported income are from this accounting treatment.

Ethics Case

BYP16-6   Bartlet Financial Services Company holds a large portfolio of debt and stock securities as an investment. The total fair value of the portfolio at December 31, 2012, is greater than total cost. Some securities have increased in value and others have decreased. Deb Faust, the financial vice president, and Jan McCabe, the controller, are in the process of classifying for the first time the securities in the portfolio.

Faust suggests classifying the securities that have increased in value as trading securities in order to increase net income for the year. She wants to classify the securities that have decreased in value as long-term available-for-sale securities, so that the decreases in value will not affect 2012 net income.

McCabe disagrees. She recommends classifying the securities that have decreased in value as trading securities and those that have increased in value as long-term available-for-sale securities. McCabe argues that the company is having a good earnings year and that recognizing the losses now will help to smooth income for this year. Moreover, for future years, when the company may not be as profitable, the company will have built-in gains.

Instructions

(a) Will classifying the securities as Faust and McCabe suggest actually affect earnings as each says it will?

(b) Is there anything unethical in what Faust and McCabe propose? Who are the stakeholders affected by their proposals?

(c) Assume that Faust and McCabe properly classify the portfolio. Assume, at year-end, that Faust proposes to sell the securities that will increase 2012 net income, and that McCabe proposes to sell the securities that will decrease 2012 net income. Is this unethical?

"All About You" Activity

BYP16-7   The Securities and Exchange Commission (SEC) is the primary regulatory agency of U.S. financial markets. Its job is to ensure that the markets remain fair for all investors. The following SEC sites provide useful information for investors.

Address: www.sec.gov/answers.shtml and **http://www.sec.gov/investor/tools/quiz.htm,** or go to **www.wiley.com/college/weygandt**.

Instructions

(a) Go to the first SEC site and find the definition of the following terms.

  (i)   Ask price.

  (ii) Margin account.

  (iii) Prospectus.

  (iv) Index fund.

(b) Go to the second SEC site and take the short quiz.

FASB Codification Activity

BYP16-8   If your school has a subscription to the FASB Codification, go to *http://aaahq.org/ascLogin.cfm* to log in and prepare responses to the following.

(a) What is the definition of a trading security?

(b) What is the definition of an available-for-sale security?

(c) What is definition of a holding gain or loss?

Answers to Insight and Accounting Across the Organization Questions

p. 731 How Procter & Gamble Accounts for Gillette   **Q:** Where on Procter & Gamble's balance sheet will you find its investment in Gillette Company? **A:** Because Procter & Gamble owns 9% of Gillette, Procter & Gamble does not report Gillette in the investment section of its balance sheet. Instead, Gillette's assets and liabilities are included and commingled with the assets and liabilities of Procter & Gamble.

p. 734 And the Correct Way to Report Investments Is... ?   **Q:** Why might the use of the equity method not lead to full disclosure in the financial statements? **A:** Under the equity method, the investment in common stock of another company is initially recorded at cost. After that, the investment account is adjusted at each reporting date to show the investor's equity in the investee. However, on the investor's balance sheet, only the investment account is shown. The pro-rata share of the investee's assets and liabilities are not reported. Because the pro-rata share of the investee's assets and liabilities are not shown, some argue that the full disclosure principle is violated.

Answers to Self-Test Questions

1. d **2.** a **3.** b **4.** c **5.** a **6.** b $300,000 + [25\% \times (\$160,000 - \$60,000)]$ **7.** c **8.** d **9.** a **10.** c **11.** c ($41,300 - \$39,800) + \$900)   **12.** b **13.** c

IFRS A Look at IFRS

Until recently, when the IASB issued *IFRS 9,* the accounting and reporting for investments under IFRS and GAAP were for the most part very similar. However, *IFRS 9* introduces new investment classifications and increases the situations when investments are accounted for at fair value, with gains and losses recorded in income.

Key Points

- The basic accounting entries to record the acquisition of debt securities, the receipt of interest, and the sale of debt securities are the same under IFRS and GAAP.

- The basic accounting entries to record the acquisition of stock investments, the receipt of dividends, and the sale of stock securities are the same under IFRS and GAAP.

- Both IFRS and GAAP use the same criteria to determine whether the equity method of accounting should be used—that is, significant influence with a general guide of over 20 percent ownership, IFRS uses the term *associate investment* rather than equity investment to describe its investment under the equity method.

- Under IFRS, both the investor and an associate company should follow the same accounting policies. As a result, in order to prepare financial information, adjustments are made to the associate's policies to conform to the investor's books. GAAP does not have that requirement.

- The basis for consolidation under IFRS is control. Under GAAP, a bipolar approach is used, which is a risk-and-reward model (often referred to as a variable-entity approach) and a voting-interest approach. However, under both systems, for consolidation to occur, the investor company must generally own 50 percent of another company.

- In general, IFRS requires that companies determine how to measure their financial assets based on two criteria:
  - The company's business model for managing their financial assets; and
  - The contractual cash flow characteristics of the financial asset.

  If a company has (1) a business model whose objective is to hold assets in order to collect contractual cash flows and (2) the contractual terms of the financial asset gives specified dates to cash flows that are solely payments of principal and interest on the principal amount outstanding, then the company should use cost (often referred to as amortized cost).

  For example, assume that Mitsubishi purchases a bond investment that it intends to hold to maturity. Its business model for this type of investment is to collect interest and then principal at maturity. The payment dates for the interest rate and principal are stated on the bond. In this case, Mitsubishi accounts for the investment at cost. If, on the other hand, Mitsubishi purchased the bonds as part of a trading strategy to speculate on interest rate changes (a trading investment), then the debt investment is reported at fair value. As a result, only debt investments such as receivables, loans, and bond investments that meet the two criteria above are recorded at amortized cost. All other debt investments are recorded and reported at fair value.

- Equity investments are generally recorded and reported at fair value under IFRS. Equity investments do not have a fixed interest or principal payment schedule and therefore cannot be accounted for at amortized cost. In general, equity investments are valued at fair value, with all gains and losses reported in income.

- GAAP classifies investments as trading, available-for-sale (both debt and equity investments), and held-to-maturity (only for debt investments). IFRS uses held-for-collection (debt investments), trading (both debt and equity investments), and non-trading equity investment classifications. GAAP classifications are based on management's intent with respect to the investment. IFRS classifications are based on the business model used to manage the investments and the type of security.

- The accounting for trading investments is the same between GAAP and IFRS. Held-to-maturity (GAAP) and held-for-collection (IFRS) investments are accounted for at amortized cost. Gains and losses related to available-for-sale securities (GAAP) and non-trading equity investments (IFRS) are reported in other comprehensive income.

- Unrealized gains and losses related to available-for-sale securities are reported in other comprehensive income under GAAP and IFRS. These gains and losses that accumulate are then reported in the balance sheet.

- IFRS does not use Other Revenues and Gains or Other Expenses and Losses in its income statement presentation. It will generally classify these items as unusual items or financial items.

Looking to the Future

As indicated earlier, both the FASB and IASB have indicated that they believe that all financial instruments should be reported at fair value and that changes in fair value should be reported as part of net income. It seems likely, as more companies choose the fair value option for financial instruments, that we will eventually arrive at fair value measurement for all financial instruments.

IFRS Self-Test Questions

1. The following asset is *not* considered a financial asset under IFRS:
   a. trading securities.
   b. equity securities.
   c. held-for-collection securities.
   d. inventories.

2. Under IFRS, the equity method of accounting for long-term investments in common stock should be used when the investor has significant influence over an investee and owns:
   a. between 20% and 50% of the investee's common stock.
   b. 30% or more of the investee's common stock.
   c. more than 50% of the investee's common stock.
   d. less than 20% of the investee's common stock.

3. Under IFRS, at the end of the first year of operations, the total cost of the trading investments portfolio is $120,000. Total fair value is $115,000. The financial statement should show:
   a. a reduction of an asset of $5,000 and an unrealized loss of $5,000 in the income statement.
   b. a reduction of an asset of $5,000 and an unrealized loss of $5,000 in the stockholders' equity section.
   c. a reduction of an asset of $5,000 in the current assets section and an unrealized loss of $5,000 in other comprehensive income.
   d. a reduction of an asset of $5,000 in the current assets section and a realized loss of $5,000 in the other expenses and losses.

4. Under IFRS, unrealized gains on non-trading stock investments should:
   a. be reported as other revenues and gains in the income statement as part of net income.
   b. be reported as other gains on the income statement as part of net income.
   c. not be reported on the income statement or balance sheet.
   d. be reported as other comprehensive income.

5. Under IFRS, the unrealized loss on trading investments should be reported:
   a. as part of other comprehensive loss reducing net income.
   b. on the income statement reducing net income.
   c. as part of other comprehensive loss not affecting net income.
   d. directly to stockholders' equity bypassing the income statement.

Answers to IFRS Self-Test Questions
1. d   **2.** a   **3.** a   **4.** d   **5.** b

The Navigator

✔ **Remember to go back to the Navigator box on the chapter opening page and check off your completed work.**

CHAPTER 17

Statement of Cash Flows

Study Objectives

After studying this chapter, you should be able to:

[1] Indicate the usefulness of the statement of cash flows.

[2] Distinguish among operating, investing, and financing activities.

[3] Prepare a statement of cash flows using the indirect method.

[4] Analyze the statement of cash flows.

The Navigator

Feature Story

GOT CASH?

In today's environment, companies must be ready to respond to changes quickly in order to survive and thrive. This requires that they manage their cash very carefully. One company that managed cash successfully in its early years was Microsoft. During those years, the company paid much of its payroll with stock options (rights to purchase company stock in the future at a given price) instead of cash. This strategy conserved cash and turned more than a thousand of its employees into millionaires during the company's first 20 years of business.

In recent years, Microsoft has had a different kind of cash problem. Now that it has reached a more "mature" stage in life, it generates so much cash—roughly $1 billion per month—that it cannot always figure out what to do with it. At one time, Microsoft had accumulated $60 billion.

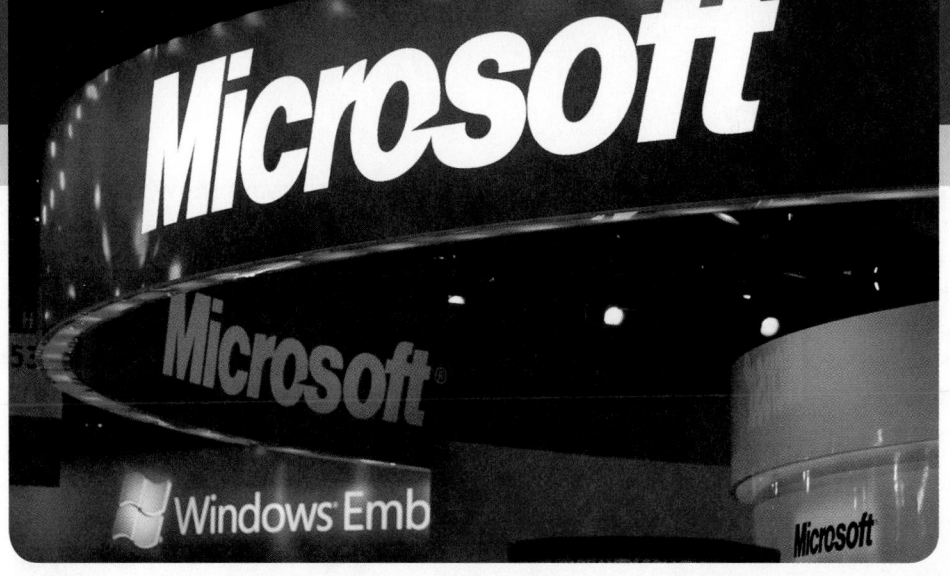

The company said it was accumulating cash to invest in new opportunities, buy other companies, and pay off pending lawsuits. But for many years, the federal government blocked attempts by Microsoft to buy anything other than small firms because it feared that purchase of a large firm would only increase Microsoft's monopolistic position.

Microsoft's stockholders have complained for years that holding all this cash was putting a drag on the company's profitability. Why? Because Microsoft had the cash invested in very low-yielding government securities. Stockholders felt that the company either should find new investment projects that would bring higher returns, or return some of the cash to stockholders.

Finally, Microsoft announced a plan to return cash to stockholders, by paying a special one-time $32 billion dividend. This special dividend was so large that, according to the U.S. Commerce Department, it caused total personal income in the United States to rise by 3.7% in one month—the largest increase ever recorded by the agency. (It also made the holiday season brighter, especially for retailers in the Seattle area.) Microsoft also doubled its regular annual dividend to $3.50 per share. Further, it announced that it would spend another $30 billion buying treasury stock. In addition, Microsoft more recently offered to buy Yahoo! for $44.6 billion (Yahoo! declined the offer). Dividends, stock buybacks, and acquisitions will help to deplete some of its massive cash horde, but as you will see in this chapter, for a cash-generating machine like Microsoft, the company will be anything but cash-starved.

Interestingly, in 2010 Google found itself in a position similar to Microsoft's. Its cash pile of $26.5 billion was nearly 20% of the company's value. That's enough to pay a dividend of $80 per share. Unless it can find large, worthwhile projects to invest in, Google will also need to return a big chunk of its cash to shareholders.

Source: "Business: An End to Growth? Microsoft's Cash Bonanza," *The Economist* (July 23, 2005), p. 61.

InsideCHAPTER17

PreviewofCHAPTER17

The balance sheet, income statement, and retained earnings statement do not always show the whole picture of the financial condition of a company or institution. In fact, looking at the financial statements of some well-known companies, a thoughtful investor might ask questions like these: How did Eastman Kodak finance cash dividends of $649 million in a year in which it earned only $17 million? How could United Airlines purchase new planes that cost $1.9 billion in a year in which it reported a net loss of over $2 billion? How did the companies that spent a combined fantastic $3.4 trillion on mergers and acquisitions in a recent year finance those deals? Answers to these and similar questions can be found in this chapter, which presents the statement of cash flows.

The content and organization of this chapter are as follows.

Statement of Cash Flows		
The Statement of Cash Flows: Usefulness and Format	**Preparing the Statement of Cash Flows—Indirect Method**	**Using Cash Flows to Evaluate a Company**
• Usefulness • Classifications • Significant noncash activities • Format • Preparation • Indirect and direct methods	• Step 1: Operating activities • Step 2: Investing and financing activities • Step 3: Net change in cash	• Free cash flow

The Navigator

The Statement of Cash Flows: Usefulness and Format

The balance sheet, income statement, and retained earnings statement provide only limited information about a company's cash flows (cash receipts and cash payments). For example, comparative balance sheets show the increase in property, plant, and equipment during the year. But they do not show how the additions were financed or paid for. The income statement shows net income. But it does not indicate the amount of cash generated by operating activities. The retained earnings statement shows cash dividends declared but not the cash dividends paid during the year. None of these statements presents a detailed summary of where cash came from and how it was used.

Usefulness of the Statement of Cash Flows

Study Objective [1]
Indicate the usefulness of the statement of cash flows.

The **statement of cash flows** reports the cash receipts, cash payments, and net change in cash resulting from operating, investing, and financing activities during a period. The information in a statement of cash flows should help investors, creditors, and others assess:

1. **The entity's ability to generate future cash flows.** By examining relationships between items in the statement of cash flows, investors can make predictions of the amounts, timing, and uncertainty of future cash flows better than they can from accrual basis data.

2. **The entity's ability to pay dividends and meet obligations.** If a company does not have adequate cash, it cannot pay employees, settle debts, or pay dividends.

Employees, creditors, and stockholders should be particularly interested in this statement, because it alone shows the flows of cash in a business.

3. **The reasons for the difference between net income and net cash provided (used) by operating activities.** Net income provides information on the success or failure of a business enterprise. However, some financial statement users are critical of accrual-basis net income because it requires many estimates. As a result, users often challenge the reliability of the number. Such is not the case with cash. Many readers of the statement of cash flows want to know the reasons for the difference between net income and net cash provided by operating activities. Then they can assess for themselves the reliability of the income number.

4. **The cash investing and financing transactions during the period.** By examining a company's investing and financing transactions, a financial statement reader can better understand why assets and liabilities changed during the period.

Ethics Note

Though we would discourage reliance on cash flows to the exclusion of accrual accounting, comparing cash from operations to net income can reveal important information about the "quality" of reported net income. Such a comparison can reveal the extent to which net income provides a good measure of actual performance.

Classification of Cash Flows

The statement of cash flows classifies cash receipts and cash payments as operating, investing, and financing activities. Transactions and other events characteristic of each kind of activity are as follows.

Study Objective [2]
Distinguish among operating, investing, and financing activities.

1. **Operating activities** include the cash effects of transactions that create revenues and expenses. They thus enter into the determination of net income.
2. **Investing activities** include (a) acquiring and disposing of investments and property, plant, and equipment, and (b) lending money and collecting the loans.
3. **Financing activities** include (a) obtaining cash from issuing debt and repaying the amounts borrowed, and (b) obtaining cash from stockholders, repurchasing shares, and paying dividends.

The operating activities category is the most important. It shows the cash provided by company operations. This source of cash is generally considered to be the best measure of a company's ability to generate sufficient cash to continue as a going concern.

Illustration 17-1 (page 764) lists typical cash receipts and cash payments within each of the three classifications. **Study the list carefully.** It will prove very useful in solving homework exercises and problems.

Note the following general guidelines:

1. Operating activities involve income statement items.
2. Investing activities involve cash flows resulting from changes in investments and long-term asset items.
3. Financing activities involve cash flows resulting from changes in long-term liability and stockholders' equity items.

Companies classify as operating activities some cash flows related to investing or financing activities. For example, receipts of investment revenue (interest and dividends) are classified as operating activities. So are payments of interest to lenders. Why are these considered operating activities? **Because companies report these items in the income statement, where results of operations are shown.**

Illustration 17-1
Typical receipt and payment classifications

Operating activities

Investing activities

Financing activities

TYPES OF CASH INFLOWS AND OUTFLOWS

Operating activities—Income statement items
Cash inflows:
  From sale of goods or services.
  From interest received and dividends received.
Cash outflows:
  To suppliers for inventory.
  To employees for services.
  To government for taxes.
  To lenders for interest.
  To others for expenses.

Investing activities—Changes in investments and long-term assets
Cash inflows:
  From sale of property, plant, and equipment.
  From sale of investments in debt or equity securities of other entities.
  From collection of principal on loans to other entities.
Cash outflows:
  To purchase property, plant, and equipment.
  To purchase investments in debt or equity securities of other entities.
  To make loans to other entities.

Financing activities—Changes in long-term liabilities and stockholders' equity
Cash inflows:
  From sale of common stock.
  From issuance of long-term debt (bonds and notes).
Cash outflows:
  To stockholders as dividends.
  To redeem long-term debt or reacquire capital stock (treasury stock).

Significant Noncash Activities

Not all of a company's significant activities involve cash. Examples of significant noncash activities are:

1. Direct issuance of common stock to purchase assets.
2. Conversion of bonds into common stock.
3. Direct issuance of debt to purchase assets.
4. Exchanges of plant assets.

Helpful Hint

Do not include noncash investing and financing activities in the body of the statement of cash flows. Report this information in a separate schedule.

Companies do not report in the body of the statement of cash flows significant financing and investing activities that do not affect cash. Instead, they report these activities in either a **separate schedule** at the bottom of the statement of cash flows or in a **separate note or supplementary schedule** to the financial statements. The reporting of these noncash activities in a separate schedule satisfies the **full disclosure principle**.

In solving homework assignments you should present significant noncash investing and financing activities in a separate schedule at the bottom of the statement of cash flows. (See the last entry in Illustration 17-2, at the bottom of page 765, for an example.)

ACCOUNTING ACROSS THE ORGANIZATION

Net *What*?

Net income is not the same as net cash provided by operating activities. Below are some results from recent annual reports (dollars in millions). Note the wide disparity among these companies, all of which engaged in retail merchandising.

Company	Net Income	Net Cash Provided by Operating Activities
Kohl's Corporation	$ 1,083	$ 1,234
Wal-Mart Stores, Inc.	11,284	20,169
J. C. Penney Company, Inc.	1,153	1,255
Costco Wholesale Corp.	1,082	2,076
Target Corporation	2,849	4,125

? In general, why do differences exist between net income and net cash provided by operating activities? (See page 819.)

Format of the Statement of Cash Flows

The general format of the statement of cash flows presents the results of the three activities discussed previously—operating, investing, and financing—plus the significant noncash investing and financing activities. Illustration 17-2 shows a widely used form of the statement of cash flows.

Illustration 17-2
Format of statement of cash flows

Company Name
Statement of Cash Flows
Period Covered

Cash flows from operating activities
(List of individual items)   XX
    Net cash provided (used) by operating activities   XXX
Cash flows from investing activities
(List of individual inflows and outflows)   XX
    Net cash provided (used) by investing activities   XXX
Cash flows from financing activities
(List of individual inflows and outflows)   XX
    Net cash provided (used) by financing activities   XXX
Net increase (decrease) in cash   XXX
Cash at beginning of period   XXX
Cash at end of period   XXX

Noncash investing and financing activities
(List of individual noncash transactions)   XXX

The cash flows from operating activities section always appears first, followed by the investing activities section and then the financing activities section. The sum of the operating, investing, and financing sections equals the net increase or decrease in cash for the period. This amount is added to the beginning cash balance to arrive at the ending cash balance—the same amount reported on the balance sheet.

Do it!

Classification of Cash Flows

action plan

✔ Identify the three types of activities used to report all cash inflows and outflows.

✔ Report as operating activities the cash effects of transactions that create revenues and expenses and enter into the determination of net income.

✔ Report as investing activities transactions that (a) acquire and dispose of investments and long-term assets and (b) lend money and collect loans.

✔ Report as financing activities transactions that (a) obtain cash from issuing debt and repay the amounts borrowed and (b) obtain cash from stockholders and pay them dividends.

During its first week, Duffy & Stevenson Company had these transactions.

1. Issued 100,000 shares of $5 par value common stock for $800,000 cash.
2. Borrowed $200,000 from Castle Bank, signing a 5-year note bearing 8% interest.
3. Purchased two semi-trailer trucks for $170,000 cash.
4. Paid employees $12,000 for salaries and wages.
5. Collected $20,000 cash for services provided.

Classify each of these transactions by type of cash flow activity.

Solution

1. Financing activity	4. Operating activity
2. Financing activity	5. Operating activity
3. Investing activity	

Related exercise material: BE17-1, BE17-2, BE17-3, E17-1, E17-2, E17-3, and **Do it!** 17-1.

The Navigator

Preparing the Statement of Cash Flows

Companies prepare the statement of cash flows differently from the three other basic financial statements. First, it is not prepared from an adjusted trial balance. It requires detailed information concerning the changes in account balances that occurred between two points in time. An adjusted trial balance will not provide the necessary data. Second, the statement of cash flows deals with cash receipts and payments. As a result, the company **must adjust** the effects of the use of accrual accounting **to determine cash flows**.

The information to prepare this statement usually comes from three sources:

- **Comparative balance sheets.** Information in the comparative balance sheets indicates the amount of the changes in assets, liabilities, and stockholders' equities from the beginning to the end of the period.

- **Current income statement.** Information in this statement helps determine the amount of cash provided or used by operations during the period.

- **Additional information.** Such information includes transaction data that are needed to determine how cash was provided or used during the period.

Preparing the statement of cash flows from these data sources involves three major steps, explained in Illustration 17-3 on the next page.

Illustration 17-3
Three major steps in preparing
the statement of cash flows

> **Step 1: Determine net cash provided/used by operating activities by converting net income from an accrual basis to a cash basis.**

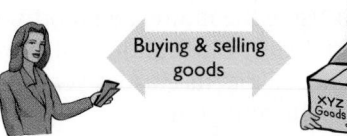 Buying & selling goods

This step involves analyzing not only the current year's income statement but also comparative balance sheets and selected additional data.

> **Step 2: Analyze changes in noncurrent asset and liability accounts and record as investing and financing activities, or disclose as noncash transactions.**

 Investing   Financing

This step involves analyzing comparative balance sheet data and selected additional information for their effects on cash.

> **Step 3: Compare the net change in cash on the statement of cash flows with the change in the cash account reported on the balance sheet to make sure the amounts agree.**

The difference between the beginning and ending cash balances can be easily computed from comparative balance sheets.

Indirect and Direct Methods

In order to perform step 1, a company **must convert net income from an accrual basis to a cash basis**. This conversion may be done by either of two methods: (1) the indirect method or (2) the direct method. **Both methods arrive at the same total amount** for "Net cash provided by operating activities." They differ in **how** they arrive at the amount.

The indirect method adjusts net income for items that do not affect cash. A great majority of companies (99%) use this method, as shown in the nearby chart.[1] Companies favor the indirect method for two reasons: (1) It is easier and less costly to prepare, and (2) it focuses on the differences between net income and net cash flow from operating activities.

The direct method shows operating cash receipts and payments, making it more consistent with the objective of a statement of cash flows. The FASB has expressed a preference for the direct method, but allows the use of either method.

The next section illustrates the more popular indirect method. Appendix 17B illustrates the direct method.

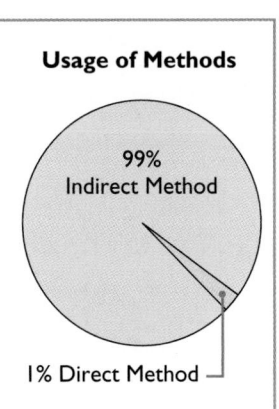

Usage of Methods

99% Indirect Method

1% Direct Method

[1] *Accounting Trends and Techniques—2009* (New York: American Institute of Certified Public Accountants, 2009).

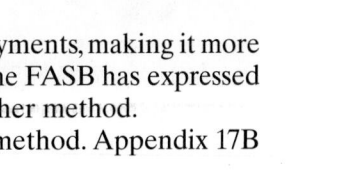

Preparing the Statement of Cash Flows—Indirect Method

Study Objective [3]

Prepare a statement of cash flows using the indirect method.

To explain how to prepare a statement of cash flows using the indirect method, we use financial information from Computer Services Company. Illustration 17-4 presents Computer Services' current and previous-year balance sheets, its current-year income statement, and related financial information for the current year.

Illustration 17-4
Comparative balance sheets, income statement, and additional information for Computer Services Company

Computer Services Company
Comparative Balance Sheets
December 31

Assets	2012	2011	Change in Account Balance Increase/Decrease
Current assets			
Cash	$ 55,000	$ 33,000	$ 22,000 Increase
Accounts receivable	20,000	30,000	10,000 Decrease
Inventory	15,000	10,000	5,000 Increase
Prepaid expenses	5,000	1,000	4,000 Increase
Property, plant, and equipment			
Land	130,000	20,000	110,000 Increase
Buildings	160,000	40,000	120,000 Increase
Accumulated depreciation—buildings	(11,000)	(5,000)	6,000 Increase
Equipment	27,000	10,000	17,000 Increase
Accumulated depreciation—equipment	(3,000)	(1,000)	2,000 Increase
Total assets	$398,000	$138,000	

Liabilities and Stockholders' Equity	2012	2011	
Current liabilities			
Accounts payable	$ 28,000	$ 12,000	$ 16,000 Increase
Income taxes payable	6,000	8,000	2,000 Decrease
Long-term liabilities			
Bonds payable	130,000	20,000	110,000 Increase
Stockholders' equity			
Common stock	70,000	50,000	20,000 Increase
Retained earnings	164,000	48,000	116,000 Increase
Total liabilities and stockholders' equity	$398,000	$138,000	

Computer Services Company
Income Statement
For the Year Ended December 31, 2012

Sales revenue		$507,000
Cost of goods sold	$150,000	
Operating expenses (excluding depreciation)	111,000	
Depreciation expense	9,000	
Loss on sale of equipment	3,000	
Interest expense	42,000	315,000
Income before income tax		192,000
Income tax expense		47,000
Net income		$145,000

Illustration 17-4
(continued)

Additional information for 2012:
1. The company declared and paid a $29,000 cash dividend.
2. Issued $110,000 of long-term bonds in direct exchange for land.
3. A building costing $120,000 was purchased for cash. Equipment costing $25,000 was also purchased for cash.
4. The company sold equipment with a book value of $7,000 (cost $8,000, less accumulated depreciation $1,000) for $4,000 cash.
5. Issued common stock for $20,000 cash.
6. Depreciation expense was comprised of $6,000 for building and $3,000 for equipment.

We will now apply the three steps to the information provided for Computer Services Company.

Step 1: Operating Activities

DETERMINE NET CASH PROVIDED/USED BY OPERATING ACTIVITIES BY CONVERTING NET INCOME FROM AN ACCRUAL BASIS TO A CASH BASIS

To determine net cash provided by operating activities under the indirect method, companies **adjust net income in numerous ways**. A useful starting point is to understand **why** net income must be converted to net cash provided by operating activities.

Under generally accepted accounting principles, most companies use the accrual basis of accounting. This basis requires that companies record revenue when earned and record expenses when incurred. Earned revenues may include credit sales for which the company has not yet collected cash. Expenses incurred may include some items that it has not yet paid in cash. Thus, under the accrual basis, net income is not the same as net cash provided by operating activities.

Therefore, under the indirect method, companies must adjust net income to convert certain items to the cash basis. The indirect method (or reconciliation method) starts with net income and converts it to net cash provided by operating activities. Illustration 17-5 lists the three types of adjustments.

Net Income	+/−	Adjustments	=	Net Cash Provided/Used by Operating Activities
		• **Add back noncash expenses**, such as depreciation expense, amortization, or depletion.		
		• **Deduct gains and add losses** that resulted from investing and financing activities.		
		• **Analyze changes** to noncash current asset and current liability accounts.		

Illustration 17-5
Three types of adjustments to convert net income to net cash provided by operating activities

Helpful Hint

Depreciation is similar to any other expense in that it reduces net income. It differs in that it does not involve a current cash outflow; that is why it must be *added back* to net income to arrive at cash provided by operating activities.

We explain the three types of adjustments in the next three sections.

DEPRECIATION EXPENSE

Computer Services' income statement reports depreciation expense of $9,000. Although depreciation expense reduces net income, it does not reduce cash. In other words, depreciation expense is a noncash charge. The company must add it back to net income to arrive at net cash provided by operating activities. Computer Services reports depreciation expense in the statement of cash flows as shown below.

Illustration 17-6
Adjustment for depreciation

Cash flows from operating activities	
Net income	$145,000
Adjustments to reconcile net income to net cash provided by operating activities:	
Depreciation expense	**9,000**
Net cash provided by operating activities	$154,000

As the first adjustment to net income in the statement of cash flows, companies frequently list depreciation and similar noncash charges such as amortization of intangible assets, depletion expense, and bad debt expense.

LOSS ON SALE OF EQUIPMENT

Illustration 17-1 states that the investing activities section should report cash received from the sale of plant assets. Because of this, **companies must eliminate from net income all gains and losses related to the disposal of plant assets, to arrive at cash provided by operating activities**.

In our example, Computer Services' income statement reports a $3,000 loss on the sale of equipment (book value $7,000, less $4,000 cash received from sale of equipment). The company's loss of $3,000 should not be included in the operating activities section of the statement of cash flows. Illustration 17-7 shows that the $3,000 loss is eliminated by adding $3,000 back to net income to arrive at net cash provided by operating activities.

Illustration 17-7
Adjustment for loss on sale of equipment

Cash flows from operating activities		
Net income		$145,000
Adjustments to reconcile net income to net cash provided by operating activities:		
Depreciation expense	$9,000	
Loss on sale of equipment	**3,000**	12,000
Net cash provided by operating activities		$157,000

If a gain on sale occurs, the company deducts the gain from its net income in order to determine net cash provided by operating activities. **In the case of either a gain or a loss, companies report as a source of cash in the investing activities section of the statement of cash flows the actual amount of cash received from the sale.**

CHANGES TO NONCASH CURRENT ASSET AND CURRENT LIABILITY ACCOUNTS

A final adjustment in reconciling net income to net cash provided by operating activities involves examining all changes in current asset and current liability accounts. The accrual accounting process records revenues in the period earned and expenses in the period incurred. For example, companies use Accounts Receivable to record amounts owed to the company for sales that have been made but for which cash collections have not yet been received. They use the Prepaid Insurance account to reflect insurance that has been paid for, but which has not yet expired, and therefore has not been expensed. Similarly, the Salaries and Wages Payable account reflects salaries and wages expense that has been incurred by the company but has not been paid.

As a result, we need to adjust net income for these accruals and prepayments to determine net cash provided by operating activities. Thus, we must analyze the change in each current asset and current liability account to determine its impact on net income and cash.

CHANGES IN NONCASH CURRENT ASSETS. The adjustments required for changes in noncash current asset accounts are as follows: **Deduct from net income increases in current asset accounts, and add to net income decreases in current asset accounts, to arrive at net cash provided by operating activities.** We can observe these relationships by analyzing the accounts of Computer Services Company.

Decrease in Accounts Receivable. Computer Services Company's accounts receivable decreased by $10,000 (from $30,000 to $20,000) during the period. For Computer Services, this means that cash receipts were $10,000 higher than sales revenue. The Accounts Receivable account in Illustration 17-8 shows that Computer Services Company had $507,000 in sales revenue (as reported on the income statement), but it collected $517,000 in cash.

Accounts Receivable				
1/1/10	Balance	30,000	Receipts from customers	517,000
	Sales revenue	507,000		
12/31/10	Balance	20,000		

Illustration 17-8
Analysis of accounts receivable

To adjust net income to net cash provided by operating activities, the company adds to net income the decrease of $10,000 in accounts receivable (see Illustration 17-9, page 772). When the Accounts Receivable balance increases, cash receipts are lower than sales revenue earned under the accrual basis. Therefore, the company deducts from net income the amount of the increase in accounts receivable, to arrive at net cash provided by operating activities.

Increase in Inventory. Computer Services Company's Inventory balance increased $5,000 (from $10,000 to $15,000) during the period. The change in the Inventory account reflects the difference between the amount of inventory purchased and the amount sold. For Computer Services, this means that the cost of merchandise purchased exceeded the cost of goods sold by $5,000. As a result, cost of goods sold does not reflect $5,000 of cash payments made for merchandise. The company deducts from net income this inventory increase of $5,000 during the period, to arrive at net cash provided by operating activities (see Illustration 17-9, page 772). If inventory decreases, the company adds to net income the amount of the change, to arrive at net cash provided by operating activities.

Increase in Prepaid Expenses. Computer Services' prepaid expenses increased during the period by $4,000. This means that cash paid for expenses is higher than expenses reported on an accrual basis. In other words, the company has made cash payments in the current period, but will not charge expenses to income until future periods (as charges to the income statement). To adjust net income to net cash provided by operating activities, the company deducts from net income the $4,000 increase in prepaid expenses (see Illustration 17-9, page 772).

Illustration 17-9
Adjustments for changes in current asset accounts

Cash flows from operating activities		
Net income		$145,000
Adjustments to reconcile net income to net cash provided by operating activities:		
Depreciation expense	$ 9,000	
Loss on sale of equipment	3,000	
Decrease in accounts receivable	10,000	
Increase in inventory	(5,000)	
Increase in prepaid expenses	(4,000)	13,000
Net cash provided by operating activities		$158,000

If prepaid expenses decrease, reported expenses are higher than the expenses paid. Therefore, the company adds to net income the decrease in prepaid expenses, to arrive at net cash provided by operating activities.

CHANGES IN CURRENT LIABILITIES. The adjustments required for changes in current liability accounts are as follows: **Add to net income increases in current liability accounts, and deduct from net income decreases in current liability accounts, to arrive at net cash provided by operating activities.**

Increase in Accounts Payable. For Computer Services Company, Accounts Payable increased by $16,000 (from $12,000 to $28,000) during the period. That means the company received $16,000 more in goods than it actually paid for. As shown in Illustration 17-10 (below), to adjust net income to determine net cash provided by operating activities, the company adds to net income the $16,000 increase in Accounts Payable.

Decrease in Income Taxes Payable. When a company incurs income tax expense but has not yet paid its taxes, it records income tax payable. A change in the Income Taxes Payable account reflects the difference between income tax expense incurred and income tax actually paid. Computer Services' Income Taxes Payable account decreased by $2,000. That means the $47,000 of income tax expense reported on the income statement was $2,000 less than the amount of taxes paid during the period of $49,000. As shown in Illustration 17-10, to adjust net income to a cash basis, the company must reduce net income by $2,000.

Illustration 17-10
Adjustments for changes in current liability accounts

Cash flows from operating activities		
Net income		$145,000
Adjustments to reconcile net income to net cash provided by operating activities:		
Depreciation expense	$ 9,000	
Loss on sale of equipment	3,000	
Decrease in accounts receivable	10,000	
Increase in inventory	(5,000)	
Increase in prepaid expenses	(4,000)	
Increase in accounts payable	16,000	
Decrease in income taxes payable	(2,000)	27,000
Net cash provided by operating activities		$172,000

Illustration 17-10 shows that, after starting with net income of $145,000, the sum of all of the adjustments to net income was $27,000. This resulted in net cash provided by operating activities of $172,000.

Summary of Conversion to Net Cash Provided by Operating Activities—Indirect Method

As shown in the previous illustrations, the statement of cash flows prepared by the indirect method starts with net income. It then adds or deducts items to arrive at net cash provided by operating activities. The required adjustments are of three types:

1. Noncash charges such as depreciation, amortization, and depletion.
2. Gains and losses on the sale of plant assets.
3. Changes in noncash current asset and current liability accounts.

Illustration 17-11 provides a summary of these changes.

		Adjustments Required to Convert Net Income to Net Cash Provided by Operating Activities
Noncash Charges	Depreciation expense	Add
	Patent amortization expense	Add
	Depletion expense	Add
Gains and Losses	Loss on disposal of plant assets	Add
	Gain on disposal of plant assets	Deduct
Changes in Current Assets and Current Liabilities	Increase in current asset account	Deduct
	Decrease in current asset account	Add
	Increase in current liability account	Add
	Decrease in current liability account	Deduct

Illustration 17-11
Adjustments required to convert net income to net cash provided by operating activities

Ethics Insight

Cash Flow Isn't Always What It Seems

Some managers have taken actions that artificially increase cash flow from operating activities. They do this by moving negative amounts out of the operating section and into the investing or financing section.

For example, WorldCom, Inc. disclosed that it had improperly capitalized expenses: It had moved $3.8 billion of cash outflows from the "Cash from operating activities" section of the cash flow statement to the "Investing activities" section, thereby greatly enhancing cash provided by operating activities. Similarly, Dynegy, Inc. restated its cash flow statement because it had improperly included in operating activities, instead of in financing activities, $300 million from natural gas trading. The restatement resulted in a drop of 37% in cash flow from operating activities.

Source: Henny Sender, "Sadly, These Days Even Cash Flow Isn't Always What It Seems to Be," *Wall Street Journal* (May 8, 2002).

? For what reasons might managers at WorldCom and at Dynegy take the actions noted above? (See page 820.)

Do it!

Josh's PhotoPlus reported net income of $73,000 for 2012. Included in the income statement were depreciation expense of $7,000 and a gain on sale of equipment of $2,500. Josh's comparative balance sheets show the following balances.

Cash From Operating Activities

	12/31/11	12/31/12
Accounts receivable	$17,000	$21,000
Accounts payable	6,000	2,200

action plan

✔ Add noncash charges such as depreciation back to net income to compute net cash provided by operating activities.

✔ Deduct from net income gains on the sale of plant assets, or add losses back to net income, to compute net cash provided by operating activities.

✔ Use changes in noncash current asset and current liability accounts to compute net cash provided by operating activities.

Calculate net cash provided by operating activities for Josh's PhotoPlus.

Solution

Cash flows from operating activities		
Net income		$73,000
Adjustments to reconcile net income to net cash provided by operating activities:		
Depreciation expense	$ 7,000	
Gain on sale of equipment	(2,500)	
Increase in accounts receivable	(4,000)	
Decrease in accounts payable	(3,800)	(3,300)
Net cash provided by operating activities		$69,700

Related exercise material: **BE17-4, BE17-5, BE17-6, BE17-7, E17-4, E17-5, E17-6, E17-7, E17-8,** and **Do it!** 17-2.

✔ **The Navigator**

Step 2: Investing and Financing Activities

ANALYZE CHANGES IN NONCURRENT ASSET AND LIABILITY ACCOUNTS AND RECORD AS INVESTING AND FINANCING ACTIVITIES, OR AS NONCASH INVESTING AND FINANCING ACTIVITIES

Increase in Land.   As indicated from the change in the Land account and the additional information, the company purchased land of $110,000 through the issuance of long-term bonds. The issuance of bonds payable for land has no effect on cash. But it is a significant noncash investing and financing activity that merits disclosure in a separate schedule. (See Illustration 17-13 on page 775.)

Increase in Buildings.   As the additional data indicate, Computer Services Company acquired an office building for $120,000 cash. This is a cash outflow reported in the investing section. (See Illustration 17-13 on page 775.)

Increase in Equipment.   The Equipment account increased $17,000. The additional information explains that this was a net increase that resulted from two transactions: (1) a purchase of equipment of $25,000, and (2) the sale for $4,000 of equipment costing $8,000. These transactions are investing activities. The company should report each transaction separately. Thus, it reports the purchase of equipment as an outflow of cash for $25,000. It reports the sale as an inflow of cash for $4,000. The T account below shows the reasons for the change in this account during the year.

Illustration 17-12
Analysis of equipment

Equipment			
1/1/12 Balance	10,000	Cost of equipment sold	8,000
Purchase of equipment	25,000		
12/31/12 Balance	27,000		

The following entry shows the details of the equipment sale transaction.

Cash	4,000	
Accumulated Depreciation—Equipment	1,000	
Loss on Sale of Equipment	3,000	
Equipment		8,000

Increase in Bonds Payable. The Bonds Payable account increased $110,000. As indicated in the additional information, the company acquired land from the issuance of these bonds. It reports this noncash transaction in a separate schedule at the bottom of the statement.

Increase in Common Stock. The balance sheet reports an increase in Common Stock of $20,000. The additional information section notes that this increase resulted from the issuance of new shares of stock. This is a cash inflow reported in the financing section.

Increase in Retained Earnings. Retained earnings increased $116,000 during the year. This increase can be explained by two factors: (1) Net income of $145,000 increased retained earnings. (2) Dividends of $29,000 decreased retained earnings. The company adjusts net income to net cash provided by operating activities in the operating activities section. Payment of the dividends (not the declaration) is a **cash outflow that the company reports as a financing activity**.

STATEMENT OF CASH FLOWS—2012

Using the previous information, we can now prepare a statement of cash flows for 2012 for Computer Services Company as shown in Illustration 17-13.

Step 3: Net Change in Cash

COMPARE THE NET CHANGE IN CASH ON THE STATEMENT OF CASH FLOWS WITH THE CHANGE IN THE CASH ACCOUNT REPORTED ON THE BALANCE SHEET TO MAKE SURE THE AMOUNTS AGREE

Illustration 17-13 indicates that the net change in cash during the period was an increase of $22,000. This agrees with the change in Cash account reported on the balance sheet in Illustration 17-4 (page 768).

Computer Services Company		
Statement of Cash Flows—Indirect Method		
For the Year Ended December 31, 2012		
Cash flows from operating activities		
Net income		$145,000
Adjustments to reconcile net income to net cash		
provided by operating activities:		
Depreciation expense	$ 9,000	
Loss on sale of equipment	3,000	
Decrease in accounts receivable	10,000	
Increase in inventory	(5,000)	
Increase in prepaid expenses	(4,000)	
Increase in accounts payable	16,000	
Decrease in income taxes payable	(2,000)	27,000
Net cash provided by operating activities		172,000

Helpful Hint

When companies issue stocks or bonds for cash, the actual proceeds will appear in the statement of cash flows as a financing inflow (rather than the par value of the stocks or face value of bonds).

Illustration 17-13
Statement of cash flows, 2012—indirect method

Helpful Hint

Note that in the investing and financing activities sections, positive numbers indicate cash inflows (receipts), and negative numbers indicate cash outflows (payments).

Cash flows from investing activities		
Purchase of building	(120,000)	
Purchase of equipment	(25,000)	
Sale of equipment	4,000	
Net cash used by investing activities		(141,000)
Cash flows from financing activities		
Issuance of common stock	20,000	
Payment of cash dividends	(29,000)	
Net cash used by financing activities		(9,000)
Net increase in cash		22,000
Cash at beginning of period		33,000
Cash at end of period		$ 55,000
Noncash investing and financing activities		
Issuance of bonds payable to purchase land		$110,000

Do it!

Indirect Method

action plan

✔ Determine net cash provided/used by operating activities by adjusting net income for items that did not affect cash.

✔ Determine net cash provided/used by investing activities and financing activities.

✔ Determine the net increase/decrease in cash.

Use the information below and on page 777 to prepare a statement of cash flows using the indirect method.

Reynolds Company
Comparative Balance Sheets
December 31

Assets	2012	2011	Change Increase/Decrease
Cash	$ 54,000	$ 37,000	$ 17,000 Increase
Accounts receivable	68,000	26,000	42,000 Increase
Inventory	54,000	–0–	54,000 Increase
Prepaid expenses	4,000	6,000	2,000 Decrease
Land	45,000	70,000	25,000 Decrease
Buildings	200,000	200,000	–0–
Accumulated depreciation—buildings	(21,000)	(11,000)	10,000 Increase
Equipment	193,000	68,000	125,000 Increase
Accumulated depreciation—equipment	(28,000)	(10,000)	18,000 Increase
Totals	$569,000	$386,000	
Liabilities and Stockholders' Equity			
Accounts payable	$ 23,000	$ 40,000	$ 17,000 Decrease
Accrued expenses payable	10,000	–0–	10,000 Increase
Bonds payable	110,000	150,000	40,000 Decrease
Common stock ($1 par)	220,000	60,000	160,000 Increase
Retained earnings	206,000	136,000	70,000 Increase
Totals	$569,000	$386,000	

Reynolds Company
Income Statement
For the Year Ended December 31, 2012

Sales revenue		$890,000
Cost of goods sold	$465,000	
Operating expenses	221,000	
Interest expense	12,000	
Loss on sale of equipment	2,000	700,000
Income before income taxes		190,000
Income tax expense		65,000
Net income		$125,000

Additional information:

1. Operating expenses include depreciation expense of $33,000 and charges from prepaid expenses of $2,000.
2. Land was sold at its book value for cash.
3. Cash dividends of $55,000 were declared and paid in 2012.
4. Interest expense of $12,000 was paid in cash.
5. Equipment with a cost of $166,000 was purchased for cash. Equipment with a cost of $41,000 and a book value of $36,000 was sold for $34,000 cash.
6. Bonds of $10,000 were redeemed at their face value for cash. Bonds of $30,000 were converted into common stock.
7. Common stock ($1 par) of $130,000 was issued for cash.
8. Accounts payable pertain to merchandise suppliers.

Solution

Reynolds Company
Statement of Cash Flows—Indirect Method
For the Year Ended December 31, 2012

Cash flows from operating activities		
Net income		$ 125,000
Adjustments to reconcile net income to net		
cash provided by operating activities:		
Depreciation expense	$ 33,000	
Loss on sale of equipment	2,000	
Increase in accounts receivable	(42,000)	
Increase in inventory	(54,000)	
Decrease in prepaid expenses	2,000	
Decrease in accounts payable	(17,000)	
Increase in accrued expenses payable	10,000	(66,000)
Net cash provided by operating activities		59,000
Cash flows from investing activities		
Sale of land	25,000	
Sale of equipment	34,000	
Purchase of equipment	(166,000)	
Net cash used by investing activities		(107,000)
Cash flows from financing activities		
Redemption of bonds	(10,000)	
Sale of common stock	130,000	

Helpful Hint

1. Determine net cash provided/used by operating activities, recognizing that operating activities generally relate to changes in current assets and current liabilities.
2. Determine net cash provided/used by investing activities, recognizing that investing activities generally relate to changes in noncurrent assets.
3. Determine net cash provided/used by financing activities, recognizing that financing activities generally relate to changes in long-term liabilities and stockholders' equity accounts.

Payment of dividends	(55,000)	
Net cash provided by financing activities		65,000
Net increase in cash		17,000
Cash at beginning of period		37,000
Cash at end of period		$ 54,000
Noncash investing and financing activities		
Conversion of bonds into common stock		$ 30,000

Related exercise material: BE17-4, BE17-5, BE17-6, BE17-7, E17-4, E17-5, E17-6, E17-7, E17-8, and E17-9.

✔ The Navigator

ANATOMY OF A FRAUD

For more than a decade, the top executives at the Italian dairy products company Parmalat engaged in multiple frauds which overstated cash and other assets by more than $1 billion while understating liabilities by between $8 and $12 billion. Much of the fraud involved creating fictitious sources and uses of cash. Some of these activities incorporated sophisticated financial transactions with subsidiaries created with the help of large international financial institutions. However, much of the fraud employed very basic, even sloppy, forgery of documents. For example, when outside auditors requested confirmation of bank accounts (such as a fake $4.8 billion account in the Cayman Islands), documents were created on scanners, with signatures that were cut and pasted from other documents. These were then passed through a fax machine numerous times to make them look real (if difficult to read). Similarly, fictitious bills were created in order to divert funds to other businesses owned by the Tanzi family (who controlled Parmalat).

Total take: Billions of dollars

THE MISSING CONTROL

Independent internal verification. Internal auditors at the company should have independently verified bank accounts and major transfers of cash to outside companies that were controlled by the Tanzi family.

Using Cash Flows to Evaluate a Company

Study Objective [4]
Analyze the statement of cash flows.

Traditionally, investors and creditors have most commonly used ratios based on accrual accounting. These days, cash-based ratios are gaining increased acceptance among analysts.

Free Cash Flow

In the statement of cash flows, cash provided by operating activities is intended to indicate the cash-generating capability of the company. Analysts have noted, however, that **cash provided by operating activities fails to take into account**

that a company must invest in new fixed assets just to maintain its current level of operations. Companies also must at least **maintain dividends at current levels** to satisfy investors. The measurement of free cash flow provides additional insight regarding a company's cash-generating ability. Free cash flow describes the cash remaining from operations after adjustment for capital expenditures and dividends.

Consider the following example: Suppose that MPC produced and sold 10,000 personal computers this year. It reported $100,000 cash provided by operating activities. In order to maintain production at 10,000 computers, MPC invested $15,000 in equipment. It chose to pay $5,000 in dividends. Its free cash flow was $80,000 ($100,000 − $15,000 − $5,000). The company could use this $80,000 either to purchase new assets to expand the business or to pay an $80,000 dividend and continue to produce 10,000 computers. In practice, free cash flow is often calculated with the formula in Illustration 17-14. (Alternative definitions also exist.)

Free Cash Flow	=	Cash Provided by Operating Activities	−	Capital Expenditures	−	Cash Dividends

Illustration 17-14
Free cash flow

Illustration 17-15 provides basic information (in billions) excerpted from the 2009 statement of cash flows of Microsoft Corporation.

Illustration 17-15
Microsoft cash flow information ($ in millions)

Microsoft Corporation
Statement of Cash Flows (partial)
2009

Cash provided by operating activities		$19,037
Cash flows from investing activities		
Additions to property and equipment	$ (3,119)	
Purchases of investments	(36,850)	
Sales of investments	19,806	
Acquisitions of companies	(868)	
Maturities of investments	6,191	
Other	(930)	
Cash used by investing activities		(15,770)
Cash paid for dividends		(4,468)

Microsoft's free cash flow is calculated as shown in Illustration 17-16.

Illustration 17-16
Calculation of Microsoft's free cash flow ($ in millions)

Cash provided by operating activities	$19,037
Less: Expenditures on property, plant, and equipment	3,119
Dividends paid	4,468
Free cash flow	**$11,450**

Microsoft generated approximately $11.4 billion of free cash flow. This is a tremendous amount of cash generated in a single year. It is available for the acquisition of new assets, the retirement of stock or debt, or the payment of dividends.

Also note that Microsoft's cash from operations of $19 billion exceeds its 2009 net income of $14.6 billion. This lends additional credibility to Microsoft's income number as an indicator of potential future performance. If anything, Microsoft's net income might understate its actual performance.

Oracle Corporation is one of the world's largest sellers of database software and information management services. Like Microsoft, its success depends on continuing to improve its existing products while developing new products to keep pace with rapid changes in technology. Oracle's free cash flow for 2009 was $7.5 billion. This is impressive but significantly less than Microsoft's amazing ability to generate cash.

Do it!

Free Cash Flow

Chicago Corporation issued the following statement of cash flows for 2012.

Chicago Corporation Statement of Cash Flows—Indirect Method For the Year Ended December 31, 2012		
Cash flows from operating activities		
Net income		$19,000
Adjustments to reconcile net income to net cash provided by operating activities:		
Depreciation expense	$ 8,100	
Loss on disposal of plant assets	1,300	
Decrease in accounts receivable	6,900	
Increase in inventory	(4,000)	
Decrease in accounts payable	(2,000)	10,300
Net cash provided by operating activities		29,300
Cash flows from investing activities		
Sale of investments	1,100	
Purchase of equipment	(19,000)	
Net cash used by investing activities		(17,900)
Cash flows from financing activities		
Issuance of stock	10,000	
Payment on long-term note payable	(5,000)	
Payment for dividends	(9,000)	
Net cash used by financing activities		(4,000)
Net increase in cash		7,400
Cash at beginning of year		10,000
Cash at end of year		$ 17,400

(a) Compute free cash flow for Chicago Corporation. (b) Explain why free cash flow often provides better information than "Net cash provided by operating activities."

Solution

(a) Free cash flow = $29,300 − $19,000 − $9,000 = $1,300

(b) Cash provided by operating activities fails to take into account that a company must invest in new plant assets just to maintain the current level of operations. Companies must also maintain dividends at current levels to satisfy investors. The measurement of free cash flow provides additional insight regarding a company's cash-generating ability.

action plan

✔ Compute free cash flow as: Cash provided by operating activities − Capital expenditures − Cash dividends.

Related exercise material: BE17-8, BE17-9, BE17-10, BE17-11, E17-7, E17-9, and **Do it!** 17-3.

The Navigator

COMPREHENSIVE
Do it! 1

The income statement for the year ended December 31, 2012, for Kosinski Manufacturing Company contains the following condensed information.

KOSINSKI MANUFACTURING COMPANY
Income Statement
For the Year Ended December 31, 2012

Sales revenue		$6,583,000
Operating expenses (excluding depreciation)	$4,920,000	
Depreciation expense	880,000	5,800,000
Income before income taxes		783,000
Income tax expense		353,000
Net income		$ 430,000

Included in operating expenses is a $24,000 loss resulting from the sale of machinery for $270,000 cash. Machinery was purchased at a cost of $750,000.

The following balances are reported on Kosinski's comparative balance sheets at December 31.

KOSINSKI MANUFACTURING COMPANY
Comparative Balance Sheets (partial)

	2012	2011
Cash	$672,000	$130,000
Accounts receivable	775,000	610,000
Inventory	834,000	867,000
Accounts payable	521,000	501,000

Income tax expense of $353,000 represents the amount paid in 2012. Dividends declared and paid in 2012 totaled $200,000.

action plan

✔ Determine net cash from operating activities. Operating activities generally relate to changes in current assets and current liabilities.

✔ Determine net cash from investing activities. Investing activities generally relate to changes in noncurrent assets.

✔ Determine net cash from financing activities. Financing activities generally relate to changes in long-term liabilities and stockholders' equity accounts.

Instructions

Prepare the statement of cash flows using the indirect method.

Solution to Comprehensive Do it! 1

KOSINSKI MANUFACTURING COMPANY
Statement of Cash Flows—Indirect Method
For the Year Ended December 31, 2012

Cash flows from operating activities		
Net income		$ 430,000
Adjustments to reconcile net income to net cash		
provided by operating activities:		
Depreciation expense	$ 880,000	
Loss on sale of machinery	24,000	
Increase in accounts receivable	(165,000)	
Decrease in inventory	33,000	
Increase in accounts payable	20,000	792,000
Net cash provided by operating activities		1,222,000
Cash flows from investing activities		
Sale of machinery	270,000	
Purchase of machinery	(750,000)	
Net cash used by investing activities		(480,000)
Cash flows from financing activities		
Payment of cash dividends		(200,000)
Net increase in cash		542,000
Cash at beginning of period		130,000
Cash at end of period		$ 672,000

✔ **The Navigator**

Summary of Study Objectives

[1] Indicate the usefulness of the statement of cash flows. The statement of cash flows provides information about the cash receipts, cash payments, and net change in cash resulting from the operating, investing, and financing activities of a company during the period.

[2] Distinguish among operating, investing, and financing activities. Operating activities include the cash effects of transactions that enter into the determination of net income. Investing activities involve cash flows resulting from changes in investments and long-term asset items. Financing activities involve cash flows resulting from changes in long-term liability and stockholders' equity items.

[3] Prepare a statement of cash flows using the indirect method. The preparation of a statement of cash

flows involves three major steps: (1) Determine net cash provided/used by operating activities by converting net income from an accrual basis to a cash basis. (2) Analyze changes in noncurrent asset and liability accounts and record as investing and financing activities, or disclose as noncash transactions. (3) Compare the net change in cash on the statement of cash flows with the change in the cash account reported on the balance sheet to make sure the amounts agree.

[4] Analyze the statement of cash flows. Free cash flow indicates the amount of cash a company generated during the current year that is available for the payment of additional dividends or for expansion.

✔ **The Navigator**

Glossary

Direct method   A method of determining net cash provided by operating activities by adjusting each item in the income statement from the accrual basis to the cash basis and which shows operating cash recipts and payments. (p. 767)

Financing activities   Cash flow activities that include (a) obtaining cash from issuing debt and repaying the amounts borrowed and (b) obtaining cash from stockholders, repurchasing shares, and paying dividends. (p. 763).

Free cash flow   Cash provided by operating activities adjusted for capital expenditures and dividends paid. (p. 779).

Indirect method   A method of preparing a statement of cash flows in which net income is adjusted for items that do not affect cash, to determine net cash provided by operating activities. (pp. 767, 769).

Investing activities   Cash flow activities that include (a) purchasing and disposing of investments and property, plant, and equipment using cash and (b) lending money and collecting the loans. (p. 763).

Operating activities   Cash flow activities that include the cash effects of transactions that create revenues and expenses and thus enter into the determination of net income. (p. 763).

Statement of cash flows   A basic financial statement that provides information about the cash receipts, cash payments, and net change in cash during a period, resulting from operating, investing, and financing activities. (p. 762).

APPENDIX17A

Using a Worksheet to Prepare the Statement of Cash Flows—Indirect Method

When preparing a statement of cash flows, companies may need to make numerous adjustments of net income. In such cases, they often use **a worksheet to assemble and classify the data that will appear on the statement**. The worksheet is merely an aid in preparing the statement. Its use is optional. Illustration 17A-1 shows the skeleton format of the worksheet for preparation of the statement of cash flows.

The following guidelines are important in preparing a worksheet.

1. In the balance sheet accounts section, **list accounts with debit balances separately from those with credit balances**. This means, for example, that Accumulated Depreciation appears under credit balances and not as a contra account under debit balances. Enter the beginning and ending balances of each account in the

Study Objective [5]
Explain how to use a worksheet to prepare the statement of cash flows using the indirect method.

Illustration 17A-1
Format of worksheet

appropriate columns. Enter as reconciling items in the two middle columns the transactions that caused the change in the account balance during the year.

After all reconciling items have been entered, each line pertaining to a balance sheet account should "foot across." That is, the beginning balance plus or minus the reconciling item(s) must equal the ending balance. When this agreement exists for all balance sheet accounts, all changes in account balances have been reconciled.

2. The bottom portion of the worksheet consists of the operating, investing, and financing activities sections. It provides the information necessary to prepare the formal statement of cash flows. **Enter inflows of cash as debits in the reconciling columns. Enter outflows of cash as credits in the reconciling columns.** Thus, in this section, the sale of equipment for cash at book value appears as a debit under investing activities. Similarly, the purchase of land for cash appears as a credit under investing activities.

3. **The reconciling items shown in the worksheet are not entered in any journal or posted to any account.** They do not represent either adjustments or corrections of the balance sheet accounts. They are used only to facilitate the preparation of the statement of cash flows.

Preparing the Worksheet

As in the case of worksheets illustrated in earlier chapters, preparing a worksheet involves a series of prescribed steps. The steps in this case are:

1. Enter in the balance sheet accounts section the balance sheet accounts and their beginning and ending balances.

2. Enter in the reconciling columns of the worksheet the data that explain the changes in the balance sheet accounts other than cash and their effects on the statement of cash flows.

3. Enter on the cash line and at the bottom of the worksheet the increase or decrease in cash. This entry should enable the totals of the reconciling columns to be in agreement.

To illustrate the preparation of a worksheet, we will use the 2012 data for Computer Services Company. Your familiarity with these data (from the chapter) should help you understand the use of a worksheet. For ease of reference, the comparative balance sheets, income statement, and selected data for 2012 are presented in Illustration 17A-2.

DETERMINING THE RECONCILING ITEMS

Companies can use one of several approaches to determine the reconciling items. For example, they can first complete the changes affecting net cash provided by operating activities, and then can determine the effects of financing and investing transactions. Or, they can analyze the balance sheet accounts in the order in which they are listed on the worksheet. We will follow this latter approach for Computer Services, except for cash. As indicated in step 3, **cash is handled last**.

Accounts Receivable. The decrease of $10,000 in accounts receivable means that cash collections from sales revenue are higher than the sales revenue reported in the income statement. To convert net income to net cash provided by operating activities, we add the decrease of $10,000 to net income. The entry in the reconciling columns of the worksheet is:

| (a) | Operating—Decrease in Accounts Receivable | 10,000 | |
| | Accounts Receivable | | 10,000 |

Illustration 17A-2

Comparative balance sheets, income statement, and additional information for Computer Services Company

```
┌─────────────────────────────────────────────────────────────────────────┐
│ ⊠ Computer Services Company.xls                                  ⬜◻⊠      │
│ 📄 File   Edit   View   Insert   Format   Tools   Data   Window   Help     │
```

	A	B	C	D
1	**COMPUTER SERVICES COMPANY**			
2	**Comparative Balance Sheets**			
3	**December 31**			
4				**Change in Account Balance Increase/Decrease**
5		**2012**	**2011**	
6	**Assets**			
7	Current assets			
8	Cash	$ 55,000	$ 33,000	$ 22,000 Increase
9	Accounts receivable	20,000	30,000	10,000 Decrease
10	Inventory	15,000	10,000	5,000 Increase
11	Prepaid expenses	5,000	1,000	4,000 Increase
12	Property, plant, and equipment			
13	Land	130,000	20,000	110,000 Increase
14	Buildings	160,000	40,000	120,000 Increase
15	Accumulated depreciation—buildings	(11,000)	(5,000)	6,000 Increase
16	Equipment	27,000	10,000	17,000 Increase
17	Accumulated depreciation—equipment	(3,000)	(1,000)	2,000 Increase
18	Total	$398,000	$138,000	
19				
20	**Liabilities and Stockholders' Equity**			
21	Current liabilities			
22	Accounts payable	$ 28,000	$ 12,000	$ 16,000 Increase
23	Income taxes payable	6,000	8,000	2,000 Decrease
24	Long-term liabilities			
25	Bonds payable	130,000	20,000	110,000 Increase
26	Stockholders' equity			
27	Common stock	70,000	50,000	20,000 Increase
28	Retained earnings	164,000	48,000	116,000 Increase
29	Total liabilities and stockholders' equity	$398,000	$138,000	

```
│ ◀ ▏▥ Sheet 1 / Sheet 2 /                                           ▶      │
└─────────────────────────────────────────────────────────────────────────┘
```

```
┌─────────────────────────────────────────────────────────────────────────┐
│ ⊠ Computer Services Company.xls                                  ⬜◻⊠      │
│ 📄 File   Edit   View   Insert   Format   Tools   Data   Window   Help     │
```

	A	B	C	D
1	**COMPUTER SERVICES COMPANY**			
2	**Income Statement**			
3	**For the Year Ended December 31, 2012**			
4				
5	Sales revenue			$507,000
6	Cost of goods sold		$150,000	
7	Operating expenses (excluding depreciation)		111,000	
8	Depreciation expense		9,000	
9	Loss on sale of equipment		3,000	
10	Interest expense		42,000	315,000
11	Income before income tax			192,000
12	Income tax expense			47,000
13	Net income			$145,000
14				

```
│ ◀ ▏▥ Sheet 1 / Sheet 2 /                                           ▶      │
└─────────────────────────────────────────────────────────────────────────┘
```

Additional information for 2012:

1. The company declared and paid a $29,000 cash dividend.
2. Issued $110,000 of long-term bonds in direct exchange for land.
3. A building costing $120,000 was purchased for cash. Equipment costing $25,000 was also purchased for cash.
4. The company sold equipment with a book value of $7,000 (cost $8,000, less accumulated depreciation $1,000) for $4,000 cash.
5. Issued common stock for $20,000 cash.
6. Depreciation expense was comprised of $6,000 for building and $3,000 for equipment.

Inventory.   Computer Services Company's inventory balance increases $5,000 during the period. The Inventory account reflects the difference between the amount of inventory that the company purchased and the amount that it sold. For Computer Services, this means that the cost of merchandise purchased exceeds the cost of goods sold by $5,000. As a result, cost of goods sold does not reflect $5,000 of cash payments made for merchandise. We deduct this inventory increase of $5,000 during the period from net income to arrive at net cash provided by operating activities. The worksheet entry is:

| (b) | Inventory | 5,000 | |
| | Operating—Increase in Inventory | | 5,000 |

Prepaid Expenses.   An increase of $4,000 in prepaid expenses means that expenses deducted in determining net income are less than expenses that were paid in cash. We deduct the increase of $4,000 from net income in determining net cash provided by operating activities. The worksheet entry is:

| (c) | Prepaid Expenses | 4,000 | |
| | Operating—Increase in Prepaid Expenses | | 4,000 |

Helpful Hint

These amounts are asterisked in the worksheet to indicate that they result from a significant noncash transaction.

Land.   The increase in land of $110,000 resulted from a purchase through the issuance of long-term bonds. The company should report this transaction as a significant noncash investing and financing activity. The worksheet entry is:

| (d) | Land | 110,000 | |
| | Bonds Payable | | 110,000 |

Buildings.   The cash purchase of a building for $120,000 is an investing activity cash outflow. The entry in the reconciling columns of the worksheet is:

| (e) | Buildings | 120,000 | |
| | Investing—Purchase of Building | | 120,000 |

Equipment.   The increase in equipment of $17,000 resulted from a cash purchase of $25,000 and the sale of equipment costing $8,000. The book value of the equipment was $7,000, the cash proceeds were $4,000, and a loss of $3,000 was recorded. The worksheet entries are:

| (f) | Equipment | 25,000 | |
| | Investing—Purchase of Equipment | | 25,000 |

(g)	Investing—Sale of Equipment	4,000	
	Operating—Loss on Sale of Equipment	3,000	
	Accumulated Depreciation—Equipment	1,000	
	Equipment		8,000

Accounts Payable.   We must add the increase of $16,000 in accounts payable to net income to determine net cash provided by operating activities. The worksheet entry is:

| (h) | Operating—Increase in Accounts Payable | 16,000 | |
| | Accounts Payable | | 16,000 |

Income Taxes Payable.   When a company incurs income tax expense but has not yet paid its taxes, it records income taxes payable. A change in the Income Taxes Payable account reflects the difference between income tax expense incurred and income tax actually paid. Computer Services' Income Taxes Payable account decreases by $2,000.

That means the $47,000 of income tax expense reported on the income statement was $2,000 less than the amount of taxes paid during the period of $49,000. To adjust net income to a cash basis, we must reduce net income by $2,000. The worksheet entry is:

| (i) | Income Taxes Payable | 2,000 | |
| | Operating—Decrease in Income Taxes Payable | | 2,000 |

Bonds Payable. The increase of $110,000 in this account resulted from the issuance of bonds for land. This is a significant noncash investing and financing activity. Worksheet entry (d) above is the only entry necessary.

Common Stock. The balance sheet reports an increase in Common Stock of $20,000. The additional information section notes that this increase resulted from the issuance of new shares of stock. This is a cash inflow reported in the financing section. The worksheet entry is:

| (j) | Financing—Issuance of Common Stock | 20,000 | |
| | Common Stock | | 20,000 |

Accumulated Depreciation—Buildings, and Accumulated Depreciation—Equipment. Increases in these accounts of $6,000 and $3,000, respectively, resulted from depreciation expense. Depreciation expense is a **noncash charge that we must add to net income** to determine net cash provided by operating activities. The worksheet entries are:

| (k) | Operating—Depreciation Expense | 6,000 | |
| | Accumulated Depreciation—Buildings | | 6,000 |

| (l) | Operating—Depreciation Expense | 3,000 | |
| | Accumulated Depreciation—Equipment | | 3,000 |

Retained Earnings. The $116,000 increase in retained earnings resulted from net income of $145,000 and the declaration and payment of a $29,000 cash dividend. Net income is included in net cash provided by operating activities, and the dividends are a financing activity cash outflow. The entries in the reconciling columns of the worksheet are:

| (m) | Operating—Net Income | 145,000 | |
| | Retained Earnings | | 145,000 |

| (n) | Retained Earnings | 29,000 | |
| | Financing—Payment of Dividends | | 29,000 |

Disposition of Change in Cash. The firm's cash increased $22,000 in 2012. The final entry on the worksheet, therefore, is:

| (o) | Cash | 22,000 | |
| | Increase in Cash | | 22,000 |

As shown in the worksheet, we enter the increase in cash in the reconciling credit column as a **balancing** amount. This entry should complete the reconciliation of the changes in the balance sheet accounts. Also, it should permit the totals of the reconciling columns to be in agreement. When all changes have been explained and the reconciling columns are in agreement, the reconciling columns are ruled to complete the worksheet. The completed worksheet for Computer Services Company is shown in Illustration 17A-3 (page 788).

Illustration 17A-3
Completed worksheet—
indirect method

Computer Services Company.xls

| File | Edit | View | Insert | Format | Tools | Data | Window | Help |

COMPUTER SERVICES COMPANY
Worksheet
Statement of Cash Flows For the Year Ended December 31, 2012

	Balance 12/31/11	Reconciling Items		Balance 12/31/12
Balance Sheet Accounts		Debit	Credit	
Debits				
Cash	33,000	(o) 22,000		55,000
Accounts Receivable	30,000		(a) 10,000	20,000
Inventory	10,000	(b) 5,000		15,000
Prepaid Expenses	1,000	(c) 4,000		5,000
Land	20,000	(d) 110,000*		130,000
Buildings	40,000	(e) 120,000		160,000
Equipment	10,000	(f) 25,000	(g) 8,000	27,000
Total	144,000			412,000
Credits				
Accounts Payable	12,000		(h) 16,000	28,000
Income Taxes Payable	8,000	(i) 2,000		6,000
Bonds Payable	20,000		(d) 110,000*	130,000
Accumulated Depreciation—Buildings	5,000		(k) 6,000	11,000
Accumulated Depreciation—Equipment	1,000	(g) 1,000	(l) 3,000	3,000
Common Stock	50,000		(j) 20,000	70,000
Retained Earnings	48,000	(n) 29,000	(m) 145,000	164,000
Total	144,000			412,000
Statement of Cash Flows Effects				
Operating activities				
Net income		(m) 145,000		
Decrease in accounts receivable		(a) 10,000		
Increase in inventory			(b) 5,000	
Increase in prepaid expenses			(c) 4,000	
Increase in accounts payable		(h) 16,000		
Decrease in income taxes payable			(i) 2,000	
Depreciation expense		⌠(k) 6,000		
		⌡(l) 3,000		
Loss on sale of equipment		(g) 3,000		
Investing activities				
Purchase of building			(e) 120,000	
Purchase of equipment			(f) 25,000	
Sale of equipment		(g) 4,000		
Financing activities				
Issuance of common stock		(j) 20,000		
Payment of dividends			(n) 29,000	
Totals		525,000	503,000	
Increase in cash			(o) 22,000	
Totals		525,000	525,000	

* Significant noncash investing and financing activity.

Summary of Study Objective for Appendix 17A

[5] **Explain how to use a worksheet to prepare the statement of cash flows using the indirect method.** When there are numerous adjustments, a worksheet can be a helpful tool in preparing the statement of cash flows. Key guidelines for using a worksheet are: (1) List accounts with debit balances separately from those with credit balances. (2) In the reconciling columns in the bottom portion of the work- sheet, show cash inflows as debits and cash outflows as credits. (3) Do not enter reconciling items in any journal or account, but use them only to help prepare the statement of cash flows.

The steps in preparing the worksheet are: (1) Enter begin- ning and ending balances of balance sheet accounts. (2) Enter debits and credits in reconciling columns. (3) Enter the increase or decrease in cash in two places as a balancing amount.

APPENDIX 17B

Statement of Cash Flows—Direct Method

To explain and illustrate the direct method, we will use the transactions of Juarez Company for 2012, to prepare a statement of cash flows. Illustration 17B-1 presents information related to 2012 for Juarez Company.

Study Objective [6]
Prepare a statement of cash flows using the direct method.

Illustration 17B-1
Comparative balance sheets, income statement, and additional information for Juarez Company

Juarez Company
Comparative Balance Sheets
December 31

Assets	2012	2011	Change Increase/Decrease
Cash	$191,000	$159,000	$32,000 Increase
Accounts receivable	12,000	15,000	3,000 Decrease
Inventory	170,000	160,000	10,000 Increase
Prepaid expenses	6,000	8,000	2,000 Decrease
Land	140,000	80,000	60,000 Increase
Equipment	160,000	–0–	160,000 Increase
Accumulated depreciation—equipment	(16,000)	–0–	16,000 Increase
Total	$663,000	$422,000	

Liabilities and Stockholders' Equity	2012	2011	Change Increase/Decrease
Accounts payable	$ 52,000	$ 60,000	$ 8,000 Decrease
Accrued expenses payable	15,000	20,000	5,000 Decrease
Income taxes payable	12,000	–0–	12,000 Increase
Bonds payable	130,000	–0–	130,000 Increase
Common stock	360,000	300,000	60,000 Increase
Retained earnings	94,000	42,000	52,000 Increase
Total	$663,000	$422,000	

Juarez Company
Income Statement
For the Year Ended December 31, 2012

Sales revenue		$975,000
Cost of goods sold	$660,000	
Operating expenses (excluding depreciation)	176,000	
Depreciation expense	18,000	
Loss on sale of equipment	1,000	855,000
Income before income taxes		120,000
Income tax expense		36,000
Net income		$ 84,000

Additional information:
1. In 2012, the company declared and paid a $32,000 cash dividend.
2. Bonds were issued at face value for $130,000 in cash.
3. Equipment costing $180,000 was purchased for cash.
4. Equipment costing $20,000 was sold for $17,000 cash when the book value of the equipment was $18,000.
5. Common stock of $60,000 was issued to acquire land.

To prepare a statement of cash flows under the direct approach, we will apply the three steps outlined in Illustration 17-3 (page 767).

Step 1: Operating Activities

DETERMINE NET CASH PROVIDED/USED BY OPERATING ACTIVITIES BY CONVERTING NET INCOME FROM AN ACCRUAL BASIS TO A CASH BASIS

Under the direct method, companies compute net cash provided by operating activities by **adjusting each item in the income statement** from the accrual basis to the cash basis. To simplify and condense the operating activities section, companies **report only major classes of operating cash receipts and cash payments**. For these major classes, the difference between cash receipts and cash payments is the net cash provided by operating activities. These relationships are as shown in Illustration 17B-2.

Illustration 17B-2
Major classes of cash receipts and payments

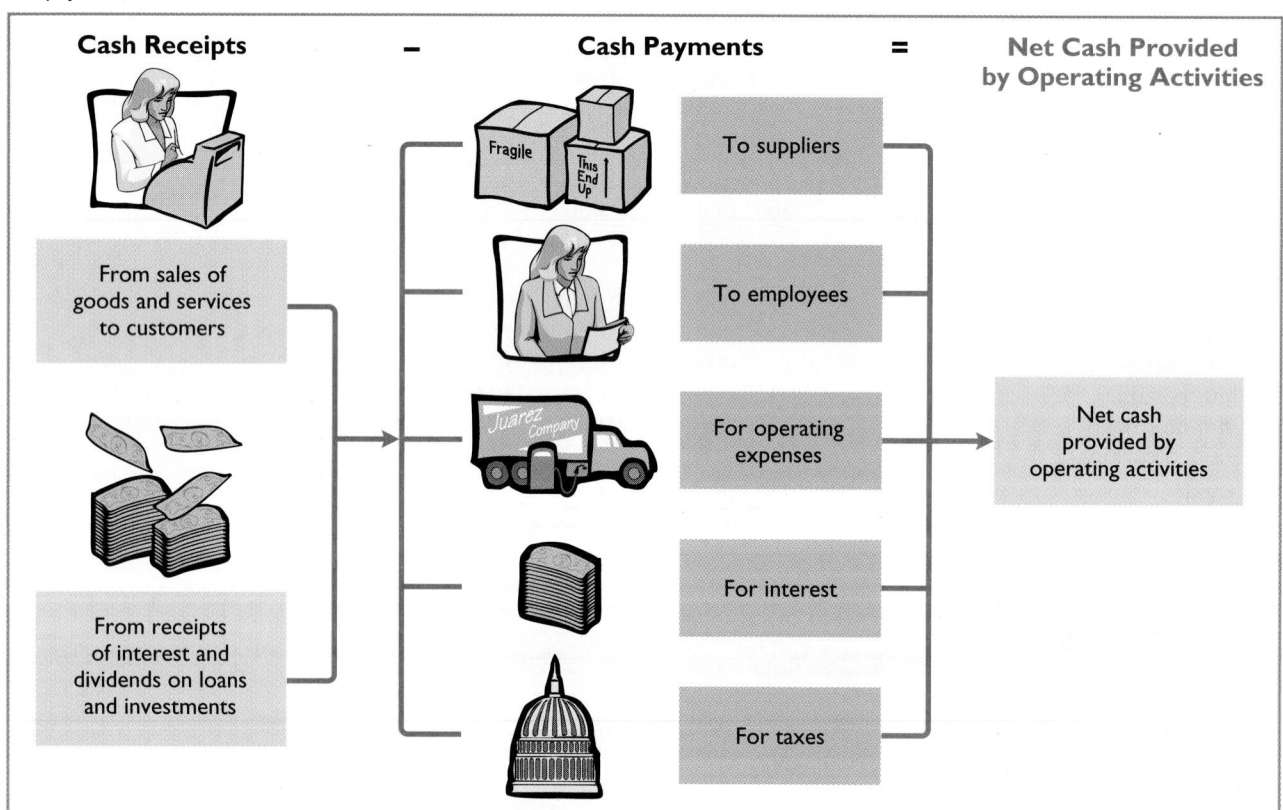

An efficient way to apply the direct method is to analyze the items reported in the income statement in the order in which they are listed. We then determine cash receipts and cash payments related to these revenues and expenses. The following pages present the adjustments required to prepare a statement of cash flows for Juarez Company using the direct approach.

Cash Receipts from Customers.   The income statement for Juarez Company reported revenues from customers of $975,000. How much of that was cash receipts? To answer that, companies need to consider the change in accounts receivable during the year. When accounts receivable increase during the year, sales revenue on an accrual basis is higher than cash receipts from customers. Operations led to sales revenue, but not all of this revenue resulted in cash receipts.

To determine the amount of cash receipts, the company deducts from sales revenues the increase in accounts receivable. On the other hand, there may be a decrease in accounts receivable. That would occur if cash receipts from customers exceeded sales revenues. In that case, the company adds to sales revenues the decrease in accounts receivable.

For Juarez Company, accounts receivable decreased $3,000. Thus, cash receipts from customers were $978,000, computed as shown in Illustration 17B-3.

Sales revenue	$975,000
Add: Decrease in accounts receivable	3,000
Cash receipts from customers	**$978,000**

Illustration 17B-3
Computation of cash receipts from customers

Juarez can also determine cash receipts from customers from an analysis of the Accounts Receivable account, as shown in Illustration 17B-4.

Accounts Receivable			
1/1/12 Balance	15,000	**Receipts from customers**	978,000
Sales revenue	975,000		
12/31/12 Balance	12,000		

Illustration 17B-4
Analysis of accounts receivable

Helpful Hint

The T account shows that sales revenue plus decrease in receivables equals cash receipts.

Illustration 17B-5 shows the relationships among cash receipts from customers, sales revenue, and changes in accounts receivable.

Cash Receipts from Customers	=	Sales Revenue	+ Decrease in Accounts Receivable or − Increase in Accounts Receivable

Illustration 17B-5
Formula to compute cash receipts from customers—direct method

Cash Payments to Suppliers.   Juarez Company reported cost of goods sold of $660,000 on its income statement. How much of that was cash payments to suppliers? To answer that, it is first necessary to find purchases for the year. To find purchases, companies adjust cost of goods sold for the change in inventory. When inventory increases during the year, purchases for the year have exceeded cost of goods sold. As a result, to determine the amount of purchases, the company adds to cost of goods sold the increase in inventory.

In 2012, Juarez Company's inventory increased $10,000. It computes purchases as follows.

Cost of goods sold	$660,000
Add: Increase in inventory	10,000
Purchases	**$670,000**

Illustration 17B-6
Computation of purchases

After computing purchases, a company can determine cash payments to suppliers. This is done by adjusting purchases for the change in accounts payable. When accounts payable increase during the year, purchases on an accrual basis are higher than they are on a cash basis. As a result, to determine cash payments to suppliers, a company deducts from purchases the increase in accounts payable. On the other hand, if cash payments to suppliers exceed purchases, there will be a decrease in accounts payable. In that case, a company adds to purchases the decrease in accounts payable.

For Juarez Company, cash payments to suppliers were $678,000, computed as follows.

Illustration 17B-7
Computation of cash payments to suppliers

Purchases	$670,000
Add: Decrease in accounts payable	8,000
Cash payments to suppliers	**$678,000**

Juarez also can determine cash payments to suppliers from an analysis of the Accounts Payable account, as shown in Illustration 17B-8.

Illustration 17B-8
Analysis of accounts payable

Accounts Payable					
Payments to suppliers	678,000	1/1/12	Balance		60,000
			Purchase		670,000
		12/31/12	Balance		52,000

Helpful Hint

The T account shows that purchases plus decrease in accounts payable equals payments to suppliers.

Illustration 17B-9 shows the relationships among cash payments to suppliers, cost of goods sold, changes in inventory, and changes in accounts payable.

Illustration 17B-9
Formula to compute cash payments to suppliers—direct method

Cash Payments to Suppliers	=	Cost of Goods Sold	{ + Increase in Inventory or − Decrease in Inventory	{ + Decrease in Accounts Payable or − Increase in Accounts Payable

Cash Payments for Operating Expenses. Juarez reported on its income statement operating expenses of $176,000. How much of that amount was cash paid for operating expenses? To answer that, we need to adjust this amount for any changes in prepaid expenses and accrued expenses payable. For example, if prepaid expenses increased during the year, cash paid for operating expenses is higher than operating expenses reported on the income statement. To convert operating expenses to cash payments for operating expenses, a company adds the increase to operating expenses. On the other hand, if prepaid expenses decrease during the year, it deducts the decrease from operating expenses.

Companies must also adjust operating expenses for changes in accrued expenses payable. When accrued expenses payable increase during the year, operating expenses on an accrual basis are higher than they are in a cash basis. As a result, to determine cash payments for operating expenses, a company deducts from operating expenses an increase in accrued expenses payable. On the other hand, a company adds to operating expenses a decrease in accrued expenses payable because cash payments exceed operating expenses.

Juarez Company's cash payments for operating expenses were $179,000, computed as follows.

Illustration 17B-10
Computation of cash payments for operating expenses

Operating expenses	$176,000
Deduct: Decrease in prepaid expenses	(2,000)
Add: Decrease in accrued expenses payable	5,000
Cash payments for operating expenses	**$179,000**

Illustration 17B-11 shows the relationships among cash payments for operating expenses, changes in prepaid expenses, and changes in accrued expenses payable.

| Cash Payments for Operating Expenses | = | Operating Expenses | $\left\{\begin{array}{c}\text{+ Increase in}\\ \text{Prepaid Expense}\\ \text{or}\\ \text{– Decrease in}\\ \text{Prepaid Expense}\end{array}\right.$ | $\left\{\begin{array}{c}\text{+ Decrease in Accrued}\\ \text{Expenses Payable}\\ \text{or}\\ \text{– Increase in Accrued}\\ \text{Expenses Payable}\end{array}\right.$ |

Illustration 17B-11
Formula to compute cash payments for operating expenses—direct method

Depreciation Expense and Loss on Sale of Equipment.   Companies show operating expenses exclusive of depreciation. Juarez's depreciation expense in 2012 was $18,000. Depreciation expense is not shown on a statement of cash flows because it is a noncash charge. If the amount for operating expenses includes depreciation expense, the company must reduce operating expenses by the amount of depreciation to determine cash payments for operating expenses.

The loss on sale of equipment of $1,000 is also a noncash charge. The loss on sale of equipment reduces net income, but it does not reduce cash. Thus, companies do not report on a statement of cash flows the loss on sale of equipment.

Other charges to expense that do not require the use of cash, such as the amortization of intangible assets, depletion expense, and bad debt expense, are treated in the same manner as depreciation.

Cash Payments for Income Taxes.   Juarez reported income tax expense of $36,000 on the income statement. Income taxes payable, however, increased $12,000. This increase means that the company has not yet paid $12,000 of the income taxes. As a result, income taxes paid were less than income taxes reported in the income statement. Cash payments for income taxes were, therefore, $24,000 as shown below.

Income tax expense	$36,000
Deduct: Increase in income taxes payable	12,000
Cash payments for income taxes	**$24,000**

Illustration 17B-12
Computation of cash payments for income taxes

Illustration 17B-13 shows the relationships among cash payments for income taxes, income tax expense, and changes in income taxes payable.

| Cash Payments for Income Taxes | = | Income Tax Expense | $\left\{\begin{array}{c}\text{+ Decrease in Income Taxes Payable}\\ \text{or}\\ \text{– Increase in Income Taxes Payable}\end{array}\right.$ |

Illustration 17B-13
Formula to compute cash payments for income taxes—direct method

The operating activities section of the statement of cash flows of Juarez Company is shown in Illustration 17B-14.

Cash flows from operating activities		
Cash receipts from customers		$978,000
Less: Cash payments:		
To suppliers	$678,000	
For operating expenses	179,000	
For income taxes	24,000	881,000
Net cash provided by operating activities		$ 97,000

Illustration 17B-14
Operating activities section of the statement of cash flows

When a company uses the direct method, it must also provide in a **separate schedule** (not shown here) the net cash flows from operating activities as computed under the indirect method.

Step 2: Investing and Financing Activities

ANALYZE CHANGES IN NONCURRENT ASSET AND LIABILITY ACCOUNTS AND RECORD AS INVESTING AND FINANCING ACTIVITIES, OR AS SIGNIFICANT NONCASH TRANSACTIONS

Increase in Land. Juarez's land increased $60,000. The additional information section indicates that the company issued common stock to purchase the land. The issuance of common stock for land has no effect on cash. But it is a **significant non-cash investing and financing transaction**. This transaction requires disclosure in a separate schedule at the bottom of the statement of cash flows.

Increase in Equipment. The comparative balance sheets show that equipment increased $160,000 in 2012. The additional information in Illustration 17B-1 indicated that the increase resulted from two investing transactions: (1) Juarez purchased for cash equipment costing $180,000. And (2) it sold for $17,000 cash equipment costing $20,000, whose book value was $18,000. The relevant data for the statement of cash flows is the cash paid for the purchase and the cash proceeds from the sale. For Juarez Company, the investing activities section will show the following: The $180,000 purchase of equipment as an outflow of cash, and the $17,000 sale of equipment as an inflow of cash. The company **should not net** the two amounts. **Both individual outflows and inflows of cash should be shown.**

The analysis of the changes in equipment should include the related Accumulated Depreciation account. These two accounts for Juarez Company are shown in Illustration 17B-15.

Illustration 17B-15
Analysis of equipment and related accumulated depreciation

Equipment

1/1/12	Balance	–0–	Cost of equipment sold	20,000
	Cash purchase	180,000		
12/31/12	Balance	160,000		

Accumulated Depreciation — Equipment

Sale of equipment	2,000	1/1/12	Balance	–0–
			Depreciation expense	18,000
		12/31/12	Balance	16,000

Increase in Bonds Payable. Bonds Payable increased $130,000. The additional information in Illustration 17B-1 indicated that Juarez issued, for $130,000 cash, bonds with a face value of $130,000. The issuance of bonds is a financing activity. For Juarez Company, there is an inflow of cash of $130,000 from the issuance of bonds.

Increase in Common Stock. The Common Stock account increased $60,000. The additional information indicated that Juarez acquired land from the issuance of common stock. This transaction is a **significant noncash investing and financing**

transaction which the company should report separately at the bottom of the statement.

Increase in Retained Earnings.   The $52,000 net increase in Retained Earnings resulted from net income of $84,000 and the declaration and payment of a cash dividend of $32,000. Companies **do not report net income in the statement of cash flows under the direct method**. Cash dividends paid of $32,000 are reported in the financing activities section as an outflow of cash.

STATEMENT OF CASH FLOWS—2012

Illustration 17B-16 shows the statement of cash flows for Juarez.

Juarez Company Statement of Cash Flows—Direct Method For the Year Ended December 31, 2012		
Cash flows from operating activities		
Cash receipts from customers		$978,000
Less: Cash payments:		
To suppliers	$ 678,000	
For operating expenses	179,000	
For income taxes	24,000	881,000
Net cash provided by operating activities		97,000
Cash flows from investing activities		
Purchase of equipment	(180,000)	
Sale of equipment	17,000	
Net cash used by investing activities		(163,000)
Cash flows from financing activities		
Issuance of bonds payable	130,000	
Payment of cash dividends	(32,000)	
Net cash provided by financing activities		98,000
Net increase in cash		32,000
Cash at beginning of period		159,000
Cash at end of period		$191,000
Noncash investing and financing activities		
Issuance of common stock to purchase land		$ 60,000

Step 3: Net Change in Cash

COMPARE THE NET CHANGE IN CASH ON THE STATEMENT OF CASH FLOWS WITH THE CHANGE IN THE CASH ACCOUNT REPORTED ON THE BALANCE SHEET TO MAKE SURE THE AMOUNTS AGREE

Illustration 17B-16 indicates that the net change in cash during the period was an increase of $32,000. This agrees with the change in balances in the cash account reported on the balance sheets in Illustration 17B-1 (page 789).

Summary of Study Objective for Appendix 17B

[6] Prepare a statement of cash flows using the direct method. The preparation of the statement of cash flows involves three major steps: (1) Determine net cash provided/used by operating activities by converting net income from an accrual basis to a cash basis. (2) Analyze changes in noncurrent asset and liability accounts and record as invest- ing and financing activities, or disclose as noncash transactions. (3) Compare the net change in cash on the statement of cash flows with the change in the cash account reported on the balance sheet to make sure the amounts agree. The direct method reports cash receipts less cash payments to arrive at net cash provided by operating activities.

Glossary for Appendix 17B

Direct method A method of determining net cash pro- vided by operating activities by adjusting each item in the income statement from the accrual basis to the cash basis. (p. 790)

COMPREHENSIVE

Do it! 2

The income statement for Kosinski Manufacturing Company contains the follow- ing condensed information.

KOSINSKI MANUFACTURING COMPANY
Income Statement
For the Year Ended December 31, 2012

Sales revenue		$6,583,000
Operating expenses, excluding depreciation	$4,920,000	
Depreciation expense	880,000	5,800,000
Income before income taxes		783,000
Income tax expense		353,000
Net income		$ 430,000

Included in operating expenses is a $24,000 loss resulting from the sale of machinery for $270,000 cash. Machinery was purchased at a cost of $750,000. The following balances are reported on Kosinski's comparative balance sheet at December 31.

KOSINSKI MANUFACTURING COMPANY
Comparative Balance Sheets (partial)

	2012	2011
Cash	$672,000	$130,000
Accounts receivable	775,000	610,000
Inventory	834,000	867,000
Accounts payable	521,000	501,000

Income tax expense of $353,000 represents the amount paid in 2012. Dividends declared and paid in 2012 totaled $200,000.

Instructions

Prepare the statement of cash flows using the direct method.

Solution to Comprehensive Do it! 2

KOSINSKI MANUFACTURING COMPANY
Statement of Cash Flows—Direct Method
For the Year Ended December 31, 2012

Cash flows from operating activities		
Cash collections from customers		$6,418,000*
Cash payments:		
For operating expenses	$4,843,000**	
For income taxes	353,000	5,196,000
Net cash provided by operating activities		1,222,000
Cash flows from investing activities		
Sale of machinery	270,000	
Purchase of machinery	(750,000)	
Net cash used by investing activities		(480,000)
Cash flows from financing activities		
Payment of cash dividends	(200,000)	
Net cash used by financing activities		(200,000)
Net increase in cash		542,000
Cash at beginning of period		130,000
Cash at end of period		$ 672,000

Direct-Method Computations:

*Computation of cash collections from customers:	
Sales revenue per the income statement	$6,583,000
Deduct: Increase in accounts receivable	(165,000)
Cash collections from customers	$6,418,000
**Computation of cash payments for operating expenses:	
Operating expenses per the income statement	$4,920,000
Deduct: Loss from sale of machinery	(24,000)
Deduct: Decrease in inventories	(33,000)
Deduct: Increase in accounts payable	(20,000)
Cash payments for operating expenses	$4,843,000

action plan

✔ Determine net cash from operating activities. Each item in the income statement must be adjusted to the cash basis.

✔ Determine net cash from investing activities. Investing activities generally relate to changes in noncurrent assets.

✔ Determine net cash from financing activities. Financing activities generally relate to changes in long-term liabilities and stockholders' equity accounts.

The Navigator

Self-Test, Brief Exercises, Exercises, Problem Set A, and many more components are available for practice in WileyPLUS

Note: All Questions, Exercises, and Problems marked with an asterisk relate to material in the appendices to the chapter.

Self-Test Questions

Answers are on page 820.

(SO 1) **1.** Which of the following is *incorrect* about the statement of cash flows?
   a. It is a fourth basic financial statement.
   b. It provides information about cash receipts and cash payments of an entity during a period.
   c. It reconciles the ending cash account balance to the balance per the bank statement.
   d. It provides information about the operating, investing, and financing activities of the business.

2. Which of the following will *not* be reported in the statement of cash flows? (SO 1)

a. The net change in plant assets during the year.
b. Cash payments for plant assets during the year.
c. Cash receipts from sales of plant assets during the year.
d. How acquisitions of plant assets during the year were financed.

(SO 2) **3.** The statement of cash flows classifies cash receipts and cash payments by these activities:
a. operating and nonoperating.
b. investing, financing, and operating.
c. financing, operating, and nonoperating.
d. investing, financing, and nonoperating.

(SO 2) **4.** Which is an example of a cash flow from an operating activity?
a. Payment of cash to lenders for interest.
b. Receipt of cash from the sale of capital stock.
c. Payment of cash dividends to the company's stockholders.
d. None of the above.

(SO 2) **5.** Which is an example of a cash flow from an investing activity?
a. Receipt of cash from the issuance of bonds payable.
b. Payment of cash to repurchase outstanding capital stock.
c. Receipt of cash from the sale of equipment.
d. Payment of cash to suppliers for inventory.

(SO 2) **6.** Cash dividends paid to stockholders are classified on the statement of cash flows as:
a. operating activities.
b. investing activities.
c. a combination of (a) and (b).
d. financing activities.

(SO 2) **7.** Which is an example of a cash flow from a financing activity?
a. Receipt of cash from sale of land.
b. Issuance of debt for cash.
c. Purchase of equipment for cash.
d. None of the above

(SO 2) **8.** Which of the following is *incorrect* about the statement of cash flows?
a. The direct method may be used to report cash provided by operations.
b. The statement shows the cash provided (used) for three categories of activity.
c. The operating section is the last section of the statement.
d. The indirect method may be used to report cash provided by operations.

Questions 9 through 11 apply only to the indirect method.

(SO 3) **9.** Net income is $132,000, accounts payable increased $10,000 during the year, inventory decreased $6,000 during the year, and accounts receivable increased $12,000 during the year. Under the indirect method, what is net cash provided by operating activities?
a. $102,000.   **c.** $124,000.
b. $112,000.   **d.** $136,000.

(SO 3) **10.** Items that are added back to net income in determining cash provided by operating activities under the indirect method do *not* include:

a. depreciation expense.   **c.** amortization expense.
b. an increase in inventory. **d.** loss on sale of equipment.

11. The following data are available for Allen Clapp (SO 3) Corporation.

Net income	$200,000
Depreciation expense	40,000
Dividends paid	60,000
Gain on sale of land	10,000
Decrease in accounts receivable	20,000
Decrease in accounts payable	30,000

Net cash provided by operating activities is:
a. $160,000.   **c.** $240,000.
b. $220,000.   **d.** $280,000.

12. The following data are available for Orange Peels (SO 3) Corporation.

Sale of land	$100,000
Sale of equipment	50,000
Issuance of common stock	70,000
Purchase of equipment	30,000
Payment of cash dividends	60,000

Net cash provided by investing activities is:
a. $120,000.   **c.** $150,000.
b. $130,000.   **d.** $190,000.

13. The following data are available for Something Strange! (SO 3)

Increase in accounts payable	$ 40,000
Increase in bonds payable	100,000
Sale of investment	50,000
Issuance of common stock	60,000
Payment of cash dividends	30,000

Net cash provided by financing activities is:
a. $90,000.   **c.** $160,000.
b. $130,000.   **d.** $170,000.

14. The statement of cash flows should *not* be used to evalu- (SO 4) ate an entity's ability to:
a. earn net income.
b. generate future cash flows.
c. pay dividends.
d. meet obligations.

15. Free cash flow provides an indication of a company's abil- (SO 4) ity to:
a. generate net income.
b. generate cash to pay dividends.
c. generate cash to invest in new capital expenditures.
d. Both (b) and (c).

16. In a worksheet for the statement of cash flows, a decrease (SO 5) in accounts receivable is entered in the reconciling columns as a credit to Accounts Receivable and a debit in the:
a. investing activities section.
b. operating activities section.
c. financing activities section.
d. None of the above.

17. In a worksheet for the statement of cash flows, a work- (SO 5) sheet entry that includes a credit to accumulated depreciation will also include a:
a. credit in the operating section and a debit in another section.
b. debit in the operating section.

c. debit in the investing section.

d. debit in the financing section.

a. Loss on sale of building.

b. Increase in accounts receivable.

c. Depreciation expense.

d. Cash payments to suppliers.

Questions 18 and 19 apply only to the direct method.

(SO 6) *18. The beginning balance in accounts receivable is $44,000, the ending balance is $42,000, and sales during the period are $129,000. What are cash receipts from customers?

 a. $127,000. **c.** $131,000.

 b. $129,000. **d.** $141,000.

(SO 6) *19. Which of the following items is reported on a cash flow statement prepared by the direct method?

Go to the book's companion website, **www.wiley.com/college/weygandt**, for additional Self-Test Questions.

 The Navigator

Questions

1. **(a)** What is a statement of cash flows?

 (b) John Norris maintains that the statement of cash flows is an optional financial statement. Do you agree? Explain.

2. What questions about cash are answered by the statement of cash flows?

3. Distinguish among the three types of activities reported in the statement of cash flows.

4. **(a)** What are the major sources (inflows) of cash in a statement of cash flows?

 (b) What are the major uses (outflows) of cash?

5. Why is it important to disclose certain noncash transactions? How should they be disclosed?

6. Wilma Flintstone and Barny Rublestone were discussing the format of the statement of cash flows of Hart Candy Co. At the bottom of Hart Candy's statement of cash flows was a separate section entitled "Noncash investing and financing activities." Give three examples of significant noncash transactions that would be reported in this section.

7. Why is it necessary to use comparative balance sheets, a current income statement, and certain transaction data in preparing a statement of cash flows?

8. Contrast the advantages and disadvantages of the direct and indirect methods of preparing the statement of cash flows. Are both methods acceptable? Which method is preferred by the FASB? Which method is more popular?

9. When the total cash inflows exceed the total cash outflows in the statement of cash flows, how and where is this excess identified?

10. Describe the indirect method for determining net cash provided (used) by operating activities.

11. Why is it necessary to convert accrual-based net income to cash-basis income when preparing a statement of cash flows?

12. The president of Ferneti Company is puzzled. During the last year, the company experienced a net loss of $800,000, yet its cash increased $300,000 during the same period of time. Explain to the president how this could occur.

13. Identify five items that are adjustments to convert net income to net cash provided by operating activities under the indirect method.

14. Why and how is depreciation expense reported in a statement prepared using the indirect method?

15. Why is the statement of cash flows useful?

16. During 2012, Doubleday Company converted $1,700,000 of its total $2,000,000 of bonds payable into common stock. Indicate how the transaction would be reported on a statement of cash flows, if at all.

*17. Why is it advantageous to use a worksheet when preparing a statement of cash flows? Is a worksheet required to prepare a statement of cash flows?

*18. Describe the direct method for determining net cash provided by operating activities.

*19. Give the formulas under the direct method for computing (a) cash receipts from customers and (b) cash payments to suppliers.

*20. Garcia Inc. reported sales of $2 million for 2012. Accounts receivable decreased $200,000 and accounts payable increased $300,000. Compute cash receipts from customers, assuming that the receivable and payable transactions related to operations.

*21. In the direct method, why is depreciation expense not reported in the cash flows from operating activities section?

22. **PEPSICO** In its 2009 statement of cash flows, what amount did PepsiCo report for net cash (a) provided by operating activities, (b) used for investing activities, and (c) used for financing activities?

Brief Exercises

BE17-1 Each of the items on the next page must be considered in preparing a statement of cash flows for Alpha-Omega Co. for the year ended December 31, 2012. For each item, state how it should be shown in the statement of cash flows for 2012.

Indicate statement presentation of selected transactions.

(SO 2)

(a) Issued bonds for $200,000 cash.
(b) Purchased equipment for $150,000 cash.
(c) Sold land costing $20,000 for $20,000 cash.
(d) Declared and paid a $50,000 cash dividend.

Classify items by activities.
(SO 2)

BE17-2   Classify each item as an operating, investing, or financing activity. Assume all items involve cash unless there is information to the contrary.

(a) Purchase of equipment.   (d) Depreciation.
(b) Sale of building.   (e) Payment of dividends.
(c) Redemption of bonds.   (f) Issuance of capital stock.

Identify financing activity
transactions.
(SO 2)

BE17-3   The following T account is a summary of the cash account of Wiegman Company.

Cash (Summary Form)			
Balance, Jan. 1	8,000		
Receipts from customers	364,000	Payments for goods	200,000
Dividends on stock investments	6,000	Payments for operating expenses	140,000
Proceeds from sale of equipment	36,000	Interest paid	10,000
Proceeds from issuance of		Taxes paid	8,000
bonds payable	300,000	Dividends paid	50,000
Balance, Dec. 31	306,000		

What amount of net cash provided (used) by financing activities should be reported in the statement of cash flows?

Compute cash provided by
operating activities—indirect
method.   *(SO 3)*

BE17-4   Mokena, Inc. reported net income of $2.5 million in 2012. Depreciation for the year was $160,000, accounts receivable decreased $350,000, and accounts payable decreased $280,000. Compute net cash provided by operating activities using the indirect method.

Compute cash provided by
operating activities—indirect
method.   *(SO 3)*

BE17-5   The net income for Lodi Co. for 2012 was $280,000. For 2012, depreciation on plant assets was $70,000, and the company incurred a loss on sale of plant assets of $12,000. Compute net cash provided by operating activities under the indirect method.

Compute net cash provided by
operating activities—indirect
method.
(SO 3)

BE17-6   The comparative balance sheets for Tobemory Company show these changes in non-cash current asset accounts: accounts receivable decrease $80,000, prepaid expenses increase $28,000, and inventories increase $30,000. Compute net cash provided by operating activities using the indirect method assuming that net income is $200,000.

Determine cash received from
sale of equipment.
(SO 3)

BE17-7   The T accounts for Equipment and the related Accumulated Depreciation—Equipment for Ada Company at the end of 2012 are shown here.

Equipment				Accumulated Depreciation—Equipment			
Beg. bal.	80,000	Disposals	22,000	Disposals	5,500	Beg. bal.	44,500
Acquisitions	41,600					Depr. exp.	12,000
End. bal.	99,600					End. bal.	51,000

In addition, Ada Company's income statement reported a loss on the sale of equipment of $5,500. What amount was reported on the statement of cash flows as "cash flow from sale of equipment"?

Calculate free cash flow.
(SO 4)

BE17-8   In a recent year, Cypress Semiconductor Corporation reported cash provided by operating activities of $155,793,000, cash used in investing of $207,826,000, and cash used in financing of $33,372,000. In addition, cash spent for fixed assets during the period was $132,280,000. No dividends were paid. Calculate free cash flow.

Calculate free cash flow.
(SO 4)

BE17-9   Wruck Corporation reported cash provided by operating activities of $360,000, cash used by investing activities of $250,000, and cash provided by financing activities of $70,000. In addition, cash spent for capital assets during the period was $200,000. No dividends were paid. Calculate free cash flow.

Calculate free cash flow.
(SO 4)

BE17-10   In a recent quarter, Alliance Atlantis Communications Inc. reported cash provided by operating activities of $45,600,000 and revenues of $264,800,000. Cash spent on plant asset additions during the quarter was $1,600,000. Calculate free cash flow.

Calculate and analyze free
cash flow.
(SO 4)

BE17-11   The management of Russel Inc. is trying to decide whether it can increase its dividend. During the current year, it reported net income of $875,000. It had cash provided by operating activities of $734,000, paid cash dividends of $70,000, and had capital expenditures of

$280,000. Compute the company's free cash flow, and discuss whether an increase in the dividend appears warranted. What other factors should be considered?

Indicate entries in worksheet.
(SO 5)

*BE17-12 During the year, prepaid expenses decreased $6,600, and accrued expenses increased $2,400. Indicate how the changes in prepaid expenses and accrued expenses payable should be entered in the reconciling columns of a worksheet. Assume that beginning balances were: Prepaid expenses $18,600 and Accrued expenses payable $8,200.

Compute receipts from customers—direct method.
(SO 6)

*BE17-13 Columbia Sportswear Company had accounts receivable of $206,024,000 at the beginning of a recent year, and $267,653,000 at year-end. Sales revenues were $1,095,307,000 for the year. What is the amount of cash receipts from customers?

Compute cash payments for income taxes—direct method.
(SO 6)

*BE17-14 Kinsey Corporation reported income taxes of $340,000,000 on its 2012 income statement and income taxes payable of $277,000,000 at December 31, 2011, and $522,000,000 at December 31, 2012. What amount of cash payments were made for income taxes during 2012?

Compute cash payments for operating expenses—direct method.
(SO 6)

*BE17-15 Yaddof Corporation reports operating expenses of $80,000 excluding depreciation expense of $15,000 for 2012. During the year, prepaid expenses decreased $6,600 and accrued expenses payable increased $4,400. Compute the cash payments for operating expenses in 2012.

Do it! Review

Classify transactions by type of cash flow activity.
(SO 2)

Do it! 17-1 Piekarski Corporation had the following transactions.

1. Issued $200,000 of bonds payable.
2. Paid utilities expense.
3. Issued 500 shares of preferred stock for $45,000.
4. Sold land and a building for $250,000.
5. Lent $30,000 to Zarembski Corporation, receiving Zarembski's 1-year, 12% note.

Classify each of these transactions by type of cash flow activity (operating, investing, or financing).

Calculate net cash from operating activities.
(SO 3)

Do it! 17-2 Jojo Photography reported net income of $100,000 for 2012. Included in the income statement were depreciation expense of $6,000, amortization expense of $2,000, and a gain on sale of equipment of $3,600. Jojo's comparative balance sheets show the following balances.

	12/31/11	12/31/12
Accounts receivable	$27,000	$21,000
Accounts payable	6,000	9,200

Calculate net cash provided by operating activities for Jojo Photography.

Compute and discuss free cash flow.
(SO 4)

Do it! 17-3 Zielinski Corporation issued the following statement of cash flows for 2012.

ZIELINSKI CORPORATION
Statement of Cash Flows—Indirect Method
For the Year Ended December 31, 2012

Cash flows from operating activities		
Net income		$59,000
Adjustments to reconcile net income to net cash provided by operating activities:		
Depreciation expense	$ 9,100	
Decrease in accounts receivable	9,500	
Loss on sale of equipment	3,300	
Increase in inventory	(5,000)	
Decrease in accounts payable	(2,200)	14,700
Net cash provided by operating activities		73,700
Cash flows from investing activities		
Sale of investments	3,100	
Purchase of equipment	(27,000)	
Net cash used by investing activities		(23,900)

Cash flows from financing activities
Issuance of stock	20,000	
Payment on long-term note payable	(10,000)	
Payment for dividends	(15,000)	
Net cash used by financing activities		(5,000)
Net increase in cash		44,800
Cash at beginning of year		13,000
Cash at end of year		$57,800

(a) Compute free cash flow for Zielinski Corporation. (b) Explain why free cash flow often provides better information than "Net cash provided by operating activities."

Exercises

Classify transactions by type of activity.

(SO 2)

E17-1 Quarshee Corporation had these transactions during 2012.

(a) Issued $50,000 par value common stock for cash.
(b) Purchased a machine for $30,000, giving a long-term note in exchange.
(c) Issued $200,000 par value common stock upon conversion of bonds having a face value of $200,000.
(d) Declared and paid a cash dividend of $18,000.
(e) Sold a long-term investment with a cost of $15,000 for $15,000 cash.
(f) Collected $16,000 of accounts receivable.
(g) Paid $18,000 on accounts payable.

Instructions
Analyze the transactions and indicate whether each transaction resulted in a cash flow from operating activities, investing activities, financing activities, or noncash investing and financing activities.

Classify transactions by type of activity.

(SO 2)

E17-2 An analysis of comparative balance sheets, the current year's income statement, and the general ledger accounts of Solomon Corp. uncovered the following items. Assume all items involve cash unless there is information to the contrary.

(a) Payment of interest on notes payable.
(b) Exchange of land for patent.
(c) Sale of building at book value.
(d) Payment of dividends.
(e) Depreciation.
(f) Receipt of dividends on investment in stock.
(g) Receipt of interest on notes receivable.
(h) Issuance of capital stock.
(i) Amortization of patent.
(j) Issuance of bonds for land.
(k) Purchase of land.
(l) Conversion of bonds into common stock.
(m) Loss on sale of land.
(n) Retirement of bonds.

Instructions
Indicate how each item should be classified in the statement of cash flows using these four major classifications: operating activity (indirect method), investing activity, financing activity, and significant noncash investing and financing activity.

Prepare journal entry and determine effect on cash flows.

(SO 2)

E17-3 Tim Latimer Corporation had the following transactions.

1. Sold land (cost $12,000) for $15,000.
2. Issued common stock for $20,000.
3. Recorded depreciation on buildings for $17,000.
4. Paid salaries of $9,000.
5. Issued 1,000 shares of $1 par value common stock for equipment worth $8,000.
6. Sold equipment (cost $10,000, accumulated depreciation $7,000) for $1,200.

Instructions
For each transaction above, (a) prepare the journal entry, and (b) indicate how it would affect the statement of cash flows.

E17-4   Bracewell Company reported net income of $195,000 for 2012. Bracewell also reported depreciation expense of $45,000 and a loss of $5,000 on the sale of equipment. The comparative balance sheet shows a decrease in accounts receivable of $15,000 for the year, a $17,000 increase in accounts payable, and a $4,000 decrease in prepaid expenses.

Prepare the operating activities section—indirect method.

(SO 3)

Instructions
Prepare the operating activities section of the statement of cash flows for 2012. Use the indirect method.

E17-5   The current sections of Nasreen Inc.'s balance sheets at December 31, 2011 and 2012, are presented here.

Nasreen's net income for 2012 was $153,000. Depreciation expense was $24,000.

Prepare the operating activities section—indirect method.

(SO 3)

	2012	2011
Current assets		
Cash	$105,000	$ 99,000
Accounts receivable	110,000	89,000
Inventory	158,000	172,000
Prepaid expenses	27,000	22,000
Total current assets	$400,000	$382,000
Current liabilities		
Accrued expenses payable	$ 15,000	$ 5,000
Accounts payable	85,000	92,000
Total current liabilities	$100,000	$ 97,000

Instructions
Prepare the net cash provided by operating activities section of the company's statement of cash flows for the year ended December 31, 2012, using the indirect method.

E17-6   The three accounts shown below appear in the general ledger of Chaudry Corp. during 2012.

Prepare partial statement of cash flows—indirect method.

(SO 3)

Equipment

Date		Debit	Credit	Balance
Jan. 1	Balance			160,000
July 31	Purchase of equipment	70,000		230,000
Sept. 2	Cost of equipment constructed	53,000		283,000
Nov. 10	Cost of equipment sold		49,000	234,000

Accumulated Depreciation—Equipment

Date		Debit	Credit	Balance
Jan. 1	Balance			71,000
Nov. 10	Accumulated depreciation on equipment sold	30,000		41,000
Dec. 31	Depreciation for year		28,000	69,000

Retained Earnings

Date		Debit	Credit	Balance
Jan. 1	Balance			105,000
Aug. 23	Dividends (cash)	14,000		91,000
Dec. 31	Net income		67,000	158,000

Instructions
From the postings in the accounts, indicate how the information is reported on a statement of cash flows using the indirect method. The loss on sale of equipment was $5,000. (*Hint:* Cost of equipment constructed is reported in the investing activities section as a decrease in cash of $53,000.)

Prepare statement of cash flows and compute free cash flow.

(SO 3, 4)

E17-7   Meera Corporation's comparative balance sheets are presented below.

MEERA CORPORATION
Comparative Balance Sheets
December 31

	2012	2011
Cash	$ 14,300	$ 10,700
Accounts receivable	21,200	23,400
Land	20,000	26,000
Buildings	70,000	70,000
Accumulated depreciation—buildings	(15,000)	(10,000)
Total	$110,500	$120,100
Accounts payable	$ 12,370	$ 31,100
Common stock	75,000	69,000
Retained earnings	23,130	20,000
Total	$110,500	$120,100

Additional information:

1. Net income was $22,630. Dividends declared and paid were $19,500.
2. All other changes in noncurrent account balances had a direct effect on cash flows, except the change in accumulated depreciation. The land was sold for $4,900.

Instructions

(a) Prepare a statement of cash flows for 2012 using the indirect method.
(b) Compute free cash flow.

Prepare a statement of cash flows—indirect method.

(SO 3)

E17-8   Here are comparative balance sheets for Syal Company.

SYAL COMPANY
Comparative Balance Sheets
December 31

Assets	2012	2011
Cash	$ 73,000	$ 22,000
Accounts receivable	85,000	76,000
Inventory	170,000	189,000
Land	75,000	100,000
Equipment	260,000	200,000
Accumulated depreciation—equipment	(66,000)	(32,000)
Total	$597,000	$555,000
Liabilities and Stockholders' Equity		
Accounts payable	$ 39,000	$ 47,000
Bonds payable	150,000	200,000
Common stock ($1 par)	216,000	174,000
Retained earnings	192,000	134,000
Total	$597,000	$555,000

Additional information:

1. Net income for 2012 was $103,000.
2. Cash dividends of $45,000 were declared and paid.
3. Bonds payable amounting to $50,000 were redeemed for cash $50,000.
4. Common stock was issued for $42,000 cash.
5. No equipment was sold during 2012, but land was sold at cost.

Instructions

Prepare a statement of cash flows for 2012 using the indirect method.

E17-9 Cassandra Corporation's comparative balance sheets are presented below.

Prepare statement of cash flows and compute free cash flow.
(SO 3, 4)

CASSANDRA CORPORATION
Comparative Balance Sheets
December 31

	2012	2011
Cash	$ 15,200	$ 17,700
Accounts receivable	25,200	22,300
Investments	20,000	16,000
Equipment	60,000	70,000
Accumulated depreciation—equipment	(14,000)	(10,000)
Total	$106,400	$116,000
Accounts payable	$ 14,600	$ 11,100
Bonds payable	10,000	30,000
Common stock	50,000	45,000
Retained earnings	31,800	29,900
Total	$106,400	$116,000

Additional information:
1. Net income was $18,300. Dividends declared and paid were $16,400.
2. Equipment which cost $10,000 and had accumulated depreciation of $1,200 was sold for $3,300.
3. All other changes in noncurrent account balances had a direct effect on cash flows, except the change in accumulated depreciation.

Instructions
(a) Prepare a statement of cash flows for 2012 using the indirect method.
(b) Compute free cash flow.

*E17-10 Comparative balance sheets for Erisa Magambo Company are presented below.

Prepare a worksheet.
(SO 5)

ERISA MAGAMBO COMPANY
Comparative Balance Sheets
December 31

Assets	2012	2011
Cash	$ 63,000	$ 22,000
Accounts receivable	85,000	76,000
Inventory	180,000	189,000
Land	75,000	100,000
Equipment	260,000	200,000
Accumulated depreciation—equipment	(66,000)	(42,000)
Total	$597,000	$545,000
Liabilities and Stockholders' Equity		
Accounts payable	$ 34,000	$ 47,000
Bonds payable	150,000	200,000
Common stock ($1 par)	214,000	164,000
Retained earnings	199,000	134,000
Total	$597,000	$545,000

Additional information:
1. Net income for 2012 was $125,000.
2. Cash dividends of $60,000 were declared and paid.
3. Bonds payable amounting to $50,000 were redeemed for cash $50,000.
4. Common stock was issued for $50,000 cash.
5. Depreciation expense was $24,000.
6. Sales for the year were $978,000.

Instructions

Prepare a worksheet for a statement of cash flows for 2012 using the indirect method. Enter the reconciling items directly on the worksheet, using letters to cross-reference each entry.

Compute cash provided by operating activities—direct method.
(SO 6)

*E17-11   Dumezweni Company completed its first year of operations on December 31, 2012. Its initial income statement showed that Dumezweni had revenues of $192,000 and operating expenses of $78,000. Accounts receivable and accounts payable at year-end were $60,000 and $23,000, respectively. Assume that accounts payable related to operating expenses. Ignore income taxes.

Instructions

Compute net cash provided by operating activities using the direct method.

Compute cash payments—direct method.
(SO 6)

*E17-12   A recent income statement for McDonald's Corporation shows cost of goods sold $4,852.7 million and operating expenses (including depreciation expense of $1,201 million) $10,671.5 million. The comparative balance sheet for the year shows that inventory increased $18.1 million, prepaid expenses increased $56.3 million, accounts payable (merchandise suppliers) increased $136.9 million, and accrued expenses payable increased $160.9 million.

Instructions

Using the direct method, compute (a) cash payments to suppliers and (b) cash payments for operating expenses.

Compute cash flow from operating activities—direct method.
(SO 6)

*E17-13   The 2012 accounting records of Liz Ten Transport reveal these transactions and events.

Payment of interest	$ 10,000	Collection of accounts receivable	$182,000
Cash sales	48,000	Payment of salaries and wages	53,000
Receipt of dividend revenue	18,000	Depreciation expense	16,000
Payment of income taxes	12,000	Proceeds from sale of vehicles	12,000
Net income	38,000	Purchase of equipment for cash	22,000
Payment of accounts payable		Loss on sale of vehicles	3,000
for merchandise	115,000	Payment of dividends	14,000
Payment for land	74,000	Payment of operating expenses	28,000

Instructions

Prepare the cash flows from operating activities section using the direct method. (Not all of the items will be used.)

Calculate cash flows—direct method.
(SO 6)

*E17-14   The following information is taken from the 2012 general ledger of Okonedo Company.

Rent	Rent expense	$ 40,000
	Prepaid rent, January 1	5,900
	Prepaid rent, December 31	9,000
Salaries	Salaries and wages expense	$ 54,000
	Salaries and wages payable, January 1	10,000
	Salaries and wages payable, December 31	8,000
Sales	Sales revenue	$170,000
	Accounts receivable, January 1	16,000
	Accounts receivable, December 31	7,000

Instructions

In each case, compute the amount that should be reported in the operating activities section of the statement of cash flows under the direct method.

Exercises: Set B

Visit the book's companion website, at **www.wiley.com/college/weygandt**, and choose the Student Companion site to access Exercise Set B.

Problems: Set A

Distinguish among operating, investing, and financing activities.   *(SO 2)*

P17-1A   You are provided with the following transactions that took place during a recent fiscal year.

Transaction	Statement of Cash Flow Activity Affected	Cash Inflow, Outflow, or No Effect?
(a) Recorded depreciation expense on the plant assets.		
(b) Recorded and paid interest expense.		
(c) Recorded cash proceeds from a sale of plant assets.		
(d) Acquired land by issuing common stock.		
(e) Paid a cash dividend to preferred stockholders.		
(f) Paid a cash dividend to common stockholders.		
(g) Recorded cash sales.		
(h) Recorded sales on account.		
(i) Purchased inventory for cash.		
(j) Purchased inventory on account.		

Instructions

Complete the table indicating whether each item (1) affects operating (O) activities, investing (I) activities, financing (F) activities, or is a noncash (NC) transaction reported in a separate schedule, and (2) represents a cash inflow or cash outflow or has no cash flow effect. Assume use of the indirect approach.

P17-2A The following account balances relate to the stockholders' equity accounts of Chipo Corp. at year-end.

Determine cash flow effects of changes in equity accounts.

(SO 3)

	2012	2011
Common stock, 10,500 and 10,000 shares, respectively, for 2012 and 2011	$160,000	$140,000
Preferred stock, 5,000 shares	125,000	125,000
Retained earnings	300,000	260,000

A small stock dividend was declared and issued in 2012. The market value of the shares was $10,500. Cash dividends were $15,000 in both 2012 and 2011. The common stock has no par or stated value.

Instructions

(a) What was the amount of net income reported by Chipo Corp. in 2012?

(b) Determine the amounts of any cash inflows or outflows related to the common stock and dividend accounts in 2012.

(c) Indicate where each of the cash inflows or outflows identified in (b) would be classified on the statement of cash flows.

(a) Net income $65,500

P17-3A The income statement of Toby Zed Company is presented here.

Prepare the operating activities section—indirect method.

(SO 3)

TOBY ZED COMPANY
Income Statement
For the Year Ended November 30, 2012

Sales revenue		$7,700,000
Cost of goods sold		
Beginning inventory	$1,900,000	
Purchases	4,400,000	
Goods available for sale	6,300,000	
Ending inventory	1,400,000	
Total cost of goods sold		4,900,000
Gross profit		2,800,000
Operating expenses		1,150,000
Net income		$1,650,000

Additional information:

1. Accounts receivable increased $250,000 during the year, and inventory decreased $500,000.
2. Prepaid expenses increased $150,000 during the year.

3. Accounts payable to suppliers of merchandise decreased $340,000 during the year.
4. Accrued expenses payable decreased $100,000 during the year.
5. Operating expenses include depreciation expense of $90,000.

Instructions

Prepare the operating activities section of the statement of cash flows for the year ended November 30, 2012, for Toby Zed Company, using the indirect method.

Cash from operations
$1,400,000

Prepare the operating activities section—direct method.
(SO 6)

Cash from operations
$1,400,000

Prepare the operating activities section—indirect method.
(SO 3)

*P17-4A   Data for Toby Zed Company are presented in P17-3A.

Instructions

Prepare the operating activities section of the statement of cash flows using the direct method.

P17-5A   Rattigan Company's income statement contained the condensed information below.

RATTIGAN COMPANY
Income Statement
For the Year Ended December 31, 2012

Sales revenue		$970,000
Operating expenses, excluding depreciation	$624,000	
Depreciation expense	60,000	
Loss on sale of equipment	16,000	700,000
Income before income taxes		270,000
Income tax expense		40,000
Net income		$230,000

Rattigan's balance sheet contained the comparative data at December 31, shown below.

	2012	2011
Accounts receivable	$75,000	$60,000
Accounts payable	41,000	28,000
Income taxes payable	11,000	7,000

Accounts payable pertain to operating expenses.

Cash from operations
$308,000

Instructions

Prepare the operating activities section of the statement of cash flows using the indirect method.

Prepare the operating activities section—direct method.
(SO 6)   *Cash from operations $308,000*

*P17-6A   Data for Rattigan Company are presented in P17-5A.

Instructions

Prepare the operating activities section of the statement of cash flows using the direct method.

Prepare a statement of cash flows—indirect method, and compute free cash flow.
(SO 3, 4)

P17-7A   Presented below are the financial statements of Rajesh Company.

RAJESH COMPANY
Comparative Balance Sheets
December 31

Assets	2012	2011
Cash	$ 35,000	$ 20,000
Accounts receivable	33,000	14,000
Inventory	27,000	20,000
Equipment	60,000	78,000
Accumulated depreciation—equipment	(29,000)	(24,000)
Total	$126,000	$108,000

Liabilities and Stockholders' Equity	2012	2011
Accounts payable	$ 29,000	$ 15,000
Income taxes payable	7,000	8,000
Bonds payable	27,000	33,000
Common stock	18,000	14,000
Retained earnings	45,000	38,000
Total	$126,000	$108,000

RAJESH COMPANY
Income Statement
For the Year Ended December 31, 2012

Sales revenue	$242,000
Cost of goods sold	175,000
Gross profit	67,000
Operating expenses	24,000
Income from operations	43,000
Interest expense	3,000
Income before income taxes	40,000
Income tax expense	8,000
Net income	$ 32,000

Additional data:

1. Dividends declared and paid were $25,000.
2. During the year equipment was sold for $8,500 cash. This equipment cost $18,000 originally and had a book value of $8,500 at the time of sale.
3. All depreciation expense, $14,500, is in the operating expenses.
4. All sales and purchases are on account.

Instructions

(a) Prepare a statement of cash flows using the indirect method.
(b) Compute free cash flow.

*(a) Cash from operations
$33,500*

*P17-8A Data for Rajesh Company are presented in P17-7A. Further analysis reveals the following.

1. Accounts payable pertain to merchandise suppliers.
2. All operating expenses except for depreciation were paid in cash.

*Prepare a statement of cash flows—direct method, and compute free cash flow.
(SO 4, 6)*

Instructions

(a) Prepare a statement of cash flows for Rajesh Company using the direct method.
(b) Compute free cash flow.

*(a) Cash from operations
$33,500*

P17-9A Condensed financial data of Sinjh Inc. follow.

*Prepare a statement of cash flows—indirect method.
(SO 3)*

SINJH INC.
Comparative Balance Sheets
December 31

Assets	2012	2011
Cash	$ 90,800	$ 48,400
Accounts receivable	92,800	33,000
Inventory	112,500	102,850
Prepaid expenses	28,400	26,000
Investments	138,000	114,000
Plant assets	270,000	242,500
Accumulated depreciation	(50,000)	(52,000)
Total	$682,500	$514,750

Liabilities and Stockholders' Equity		
Accounts payable	$112,000	$ 67,300
Accrued expenses payable	16,500	17,000
Bonds payable	110,000	150,000
Common stock	220,000	175,000
Retained earnings	224,000	105,450
Total	$682,500	$514,750

SINJH INC.
Income Statement
For the Year Ended December 31, 2012

Sales		$392,780
Less:		
Cost of goods sold	$135,460	
Operating expenses, excluding depreciation	12,410	
Depreciation expense	46,500	
Income taxes	27,280	
Interest expense	4,730	
Loss on sale of plant assets	7,500	233,880
Net income		$158,900

Additional information:

1. New plant assets costing $85,000 were purchased for cash during the year.
2. Old plant assets having an original cost of $57,500 were sold for $1,500 cash.
3. Bonds matured and were paid off at face value for cash.
4. A cash dividend of $40,350 was declared and paid during the year.

Instructions

Cash from operations
$185,250

Prepare a statement of cash flows using the indirect method.

Prepare a statement of cash flows—direct method.
(SO 6)

*P17-10A   Data for Sinjh Inc. are presented in P17-9A. Further analysis reveals that accounts payable pertain to merchandise creditors.

Instructions

Cash from operations
$185,250

Prepare a statement of cash flows for Sinjh Inc. using the direct method.

Prepare a statement of cash flows—indirect method.
(SO 3)

P17-11A   The comparative balance sheets for Strackman Lux Company as of December 31 are presented below.

STRACKMAN LUX COMPANY
Comparative Balance Sheets
December 31

Assets	2012	2011
Cash	$ 71,000	$ 45,000
Accounts receivable	44,000	62,000
Inventory	151,450	142,000
Prepaid expenses	15,280	21,000
Land	105,000	130,000
Equipment	228,000	155,000
Accumulated depreciation—equipment	(45,000)	(35,000)
Buildings	200,000	200,000
Accumulated depreciation—buildings	(60,000)	(40,000)
Total	$709,730	$680,000

Liabilities and Stockholders' Equity	2012	2011
Accounts payable	$ 47,730	$ 40,000
Bonds payable	260,000	300,000
Common stock, $1 par	200,000	160,000
Retained earnings	202,000	180,000
Total	$709,730	$680,000

Additional information:

1. Operating expenses include depreciation expense of $42,000 and charges from prepaid expenses of $5,720.
2. Land was sold for cash at book value.

3. Cash dividends of $15,000 were paid.
4. Net income for 2012 was $37,000.
5. Equipment was purchased for $95,000 cash. In addition, equipment costing $22,000 with a book value of $10,000 was sold for $6,000 cash.
6. Bonds were converted at face value by issuing 40,000 shares of $1 par value common stock.

Cash from operations
$105,000

Instructions
Prepare a statement of cash flows for the year ended December 31, 2012, using the indirect method.

P17-12A   Condensed financial data of Jhutti Company appear below.

Prepare a worksheet—indirect method.
(SO 5)

JHUTTI COMPANY
Comparative Balance Sheets
December 31

Assets	2012	2011
Cash	$ 92,700	$ 47,250
Accounts receivable	90,800	57,000
Inventory	121,900	102,650
Investments	84,500	87,000
Equipment	250,000	205,000
Accumulated depreciation—buildings	(49,500)	(40,000)
	$590,400	$458,900

Liabilities and Stockholders' Equity		
Accounts payable	$ 57,700	$ 48,280
Accrued expenses payable	12,100	18,830
Bonds payable	100,000	70,000
Common stock	250,000	200,000
Retained earnings	170,600	121,790
	$590,400	$458,900

JHUTTI COMPANY
Income Statement
For the Year Ended December 31, 2012

Sales revenue		$297,500
Gain on sale of equipment		8,750
		306,250
Less:		
Cost of goods sold	$99,460	
Operating expenses (excluding depreciation expense)	14,670	
Depreciation expense	49,700	
Income taxes	7,270	
Interest expense	2,940	174,040
Net income		$132,210

Additional information:
1. Equipment costing $92,000 was purchased for cash during the year.
2. Investments were sold at cost.
3. Equipment costing $47,000 was sold for $15,550, resulting in gain of $8,750.
4. A cash dividend of $83,400 was declared and paid during the year.

Instructions
Prepare a worksheet for the statement of cash flows using the indirect method. Enter the reconciling items directly in the worksheet columns, using letters to cross-reference each entry.

Reconciling items total
$610,210

Problems: Set B

Distinguish among operating, investing, and financing activities.

(SO 2)

P17-1B   You are provided with the following transactions that took place during a recent fiscal year.

Transaction	Statement of Cash Flow Activity Affected	Cash Inflow, Outflow, or No Effect?
(a) Recorded depreciation expense on the plant assets.		
(b) Incurred a loss on disposal of plant assets.		
(c) Acquired a building by paying cash.		
(d) Made principal repayments on a mortgage.		
(e) Issued common stock.		
(f) Purchased shares of another company to be held as a long-term equity investment.		
(g) Paid cash dividends to common stockholders.		
(h) Sold inventory on credit. The company uses a perpetual inventory system.		
(i) Purchased inventory on credit.		
(j) Paid wages to employees.		

Instructions

Complete the table indicating whether each item (1) affects operating (O) activities, investing (I) activities, financing (F) activities, or is a noncash (NC) transaction reported in a separate schedule, and (2) represents a cash inflow or cash outflow or has no cash flow effect. Assume use of the indirect approach.

Determine cash flow effects of changes in plant asset accounts.

(SO 3)

P17-2B   The following selected account balances relate to the plant asset accounts of Raji Inc. at year-end.

	2012	2011
Accumulated depreciation—buildings	$337,500	$300,000
Accumulated depreciation—equipment	144,000	96,000
Buildings	750,000	750,000
Depreciation expense	101,500	85,500
Equipment	300,000	240,000
Land	100,000	70,000
Loss on sale of equipment	8,000	0

Additional information:

1. Raji purchased $95,000 of equipment and $30,000 of land for cash in 2012.
2. Raji also sold equipment in 2012.
3. Depreciation expense in 2012 was $37,500 on building and $64,000 on equipment.

Instructions

(a) Cash proceeds $11,000

(a) Determine the amounts of any cash inflows or outflows related to the plant asset accounts in 2012.

(b) Indicate where each of the cash inflows or outflows identified in (a) would be classified on the statement of cash flows.

Prepare the operating activities section—indirect method.

(SO 3)

P17-3B   The income statement of Asquith Company is presented on the next page.

Additional information:

1. Accounts receivable decreased $320,000 during the year, and inventory increased $120,000.
2. Prepaid expenses increased $175,000 during the year.

3. Accounts payable to merchandise suppliers increased $50,000 during the year.
4. Accrued expenses payable increased $155,000 during the year.

ASQUITH COMPANY
Income Statement
For the Year Ended December 31, 2012

Sales revenue		$5,400,000
Cost of goods sold		
Beginning inventory	$1,780,000	
Purchases	3,430,000	
Goods available for sale	5,210,000	
Ending inventory	1,900,000	
Total cost of goods sold		3,310,000
Gross profit		2,090,000
Operating expenses		
Depreciation expense	105,000	
Amortization expense	20,000	
Other expenses	945,000	1,070,000
Net income		$1,020,000

Instructions
Prepare the operating activities section of the statement of cash flows for the year ended December 31, 2012, for Asquith Company, using the indirect method.

Cash from operations
$1,375,000

P17-4B Data for Asquith Company are presented in P17-3B.

Prepare the operating activities section—direct method.
(SO 6)

Instructions
Prepare the operating activities section of the statement of cash flows using the direct method.

Cash from operations
$1,375,000

P17-5B The income statement of Anne Droid Inc. reported the following condensed information.

Prepare the operating activities section—indirect method.
(SO 3)

ANNE DROID INC.
Income Statement
For the Year Ended December 31, 2012

Sales revenue	$545,000
Operating expenses	400,000
Income from operations	145,000
Income tax expense	36,000
Net income	$109,000

Anne Droid's balance sheet contained these comparative data at December 31.

	2012	2011
Accounts receivable	$50,000	$70,000
Accounts payable	30,000	51,000
Income taxes payable	10,000	4,000

Anne Droid has no depreciable assets. Accounts payable pertain to operating expenses.

Instructions
Prepare the operating activities section of the statement of cash flows using the indirect method.

Cash from operations
$114,000

P17-6B Data for Anne Droid Inc. are presented in P17-5B.

Prepare the operating activities section—direct method.
(SO 6)

Instructions
Prepare the operating activities section of the statement of cash flows using the direct method.

Cash from operations
$114,000

Prepare a statement of cash flows—indirect method, and compute free cash flow.

(SO 3, 4)

P17-7B   Presented below are the financial statements of Rocastle Company.

ROCASTLE COMPANY
Comparative Balance Sheets
December 31

Assets		2012		2011
Cash		$ 24,000		$ 33,000
Accounts receivable		25,000		14,000
Inventory		41,000		25,000
Equipment	$ 70,000		$ 78,000	
Less: Accumulated depreciation— equipment	(27,000)	43,000	(24,000)	54,000
Total		$133,000		$126,000

Liabilities and Stockholders' Equity		2012		2011
Accounts payable		$ 31,000		$ 43,000
Income taxes payable		24,000		20,000
Bonds payable		20,000		10,000
Common stock		25,000		25,000
Retained earnings		33,000		28,000
Total		$133,000		$126,000

ROCASTLE COMPANY
Income Statement
For the Year Ended December 31, 2012

Sales revenue	$286,000
Cost of goods sold	204,000
Gross profit	82,000
Operating expenses	37,000
Income from operations	45,000
Interest expense	7,000
Income before income taxes	38,000
Income tax expense	10,000
Net income	$ 28,000

Additional data:

1. Dividends of $23,000 were declared and paid.
2. During the year equipment was sold for $10,000 cash. This equipment cost $15,000 originally and had a book value of $10,000 at the time of sale.
3. All depreciation expense, $8,000, is in the operating expenses.
4. All sales and purchases are on account.
5. Additional equipment was purchased for $7,000 cash.

Instructions

(a) Cash from operations
$1,000

(a) Prepare a statement of cash flows using the indirect method.
(b) Compute free cash flow.

Prepare a statement of cash flows—direct method, and compute free cash flow.

(SO 4, 6)

*P17-8B   Data for Rocastle Company are presented in P17-7B. Further analysis reveals the following.

1. Accounts payable pertains to merchandise creditors.
2. All operating expenses except for depreciation are paid in cash.

Instructions

(a) Cash from operations
$1,000

(a) Prepare a statement of cash flows using the direct method.
(b) Compute free cash flow.

P17-9B   Condensed financial data of Minnie Hooper Company are shown below.

Prepare a statement of cash flows — indirect method.

(SO 3)

MINNIE HOOPER COMPANY
Comparative Balance Sheets
December 31

Assets	2012	2011
Cash	$102,700	$ 33,400
Accounts receivable	60,800	37,000
Inventory	126,900	102,650
Investments	79,500	107,000
Plant assets	315,000	205,000
Accumulated depreciation	(44,500)	(40,000)
Total	$640,400	$445,050

Liabilities and Stockholders' Equity		
Accounts payable	$ 57,700	$ 48,280
Accrued expenses payable	15,100	18,830
Bonds payable	145,000	70,000
Common stock	250,000	200,000
Retained earnings	172,600	107,940
Total	$640,400	$445,050

MINNIE HOOPER COMPANY
Income Statement
For the Year Ended December 31, 2012

Sales revenue		$297,500
Gain on sale of plant assets		5,000
		302,500
Less:		
Cost of goods sold	$99,460	
Operating expenses, excluding depreciation expense	19,670	
Depreciation expense	30,500	
Income taxes	37,270	
Interest expense	2,940	189,840
Net income		$112,660

Additional information:

1. New plant assets costing $146,000 were purchased for cash during the year.
2. Investments were sold at cost.
3. Plant assets costing $36,000 were sold for $15,000, resulting in a gain of $5,000.
4. A cash dividend of $48,000 was declared and paid during the year.

Cash from operations $95,800

Instructions
Prepare a statement of cash flows using the indirect method.

P17-10B   Data for Minnie Hooper Company are presented in P17-9B. Further analysis reveals that accounts payable pertain to merchandise creditors.

Prepare a statement of cash flows — direct method.

(SO 6)

Instructions
Prepare a statement of cash flows for Minnie Hooper Company using the direct method.

Cash from operations $95,800

P17-11B   Presented on next page are the comparative balance sheets for Vernet Company at December 31.

Prepare a statement of cash flows — indirect method.

(SO 3)

VERNET COMPANY
Comparative Balance Sheets
December 31

Assets	2012	2011
Cash	$ 41,000	$ 57,000
Accounts receivable	77,000	64,000
Inventory	172,000	140,000
Prepaid expenses	12,140	16,540
Land	110,000	150,000
Equipment	215,000	175,000
Accumulated depreciation—equipment	(70,000)	(42,000)
Buildings	250,000	250,000
Accumulated depreciation—buildings	(70,000)	(50,000)
Total	$737,140	$760,540

Liabilities and Stockholders' Equity		
Accounts payable	$ 58,000	$ 45,000
Bonds payable	235,000	265,000
Common stock, $1 par	280,000	250,000
Retained earnings	164,140	200,540
Total	$737,140	$760,540

Additional information:

1. Operating expenses include depreciation expense $55,000 and charges from prepaid expenses of $4,400.
2. Land was sold for cash at cost.
3. Cash dividends of $84,290 were paid.
4. Net income for 2012 was $47,890.
5. Equipment was purchased for $80,000 cash. In addition, equipment costing $40,000 with a book value of $33,000 was sold for $37,000 cash.
6. Bonds were converted at face value by issuing 30,000 shares of $1 par value common stock.

Cash from operations
$71,290

Instructions
Prepare a statement of cash flows for 2012 using the indirect method.

Problems: Set C

Visit the book's companion website, at **www.wiley.com/college/weygandt**, and choose the Student Companion site to access Problem Set C.

Continuing Cookie Chronicle

(*Note:* This is a continuation of the Cookie Chronicle from Chapters 1 through 16.)

CCC17   Natalie has prepared the balance sheet and income statement of Cookie & Coffee Creations Inc. and would like you to prepare the cash flow statement.

Go to the book's companion website, **www.wiley.com/college/weygandt,** *to see the completion of this problem.*

BROADENING**YOUR**PERSPECTIVE

Financial Reporting and Analysis

Financial Reporting Problem: PepsiCo, Inc.

BYP17-1   Refer to the financial statements of PepsiCo's, presented in Appendix A, and answer the following questions.

(a) What was the amount of net cash provided by operating activities for the year ended December 26, 2009? For the year ended December 27, 2008?

(b) What was the amount of increase or decrease in cash and cash equivalents for the year ended December 26, 2009? For the year ended December 27, 2008?

(c) Which method of computing net cash provided by operating activities does PepsiCo use?

(d) From your analysis of the 2009 statement of cash flows, did the change in accounts and notes receivable require or provide cash? Did the change in inventories require or provide cash? Did the change in accounts payable and other current liabilities require or provide cash?

(e) What was the net outflow or inflow of cash from investing activities for the year ended December 26, 2009?

(f) What was the amount of interest paid in the year ended December 26, 2009? What was the amount of income taxes paid in the year ended December 26, 2009? (See Note 14.)

Comparative Analysis Problem: PepsiCo, Inc. vs. The Coca-Cola Company

BYP17-2   PepsiCo's financial statements are presented in Appendix A. Financial statements of The Coca-Cola Company are presented in Appendix B.

Instructions

(a) Based on the information contained in these financial statements, compute free cash flow for each company.

(b) What conclusions concerning the management of cash can be drawn from these data?

On the Web

BYP17-3   Purpose: Learn about the SEC.

Address: www.sec.gov/index.html, or go to **www.wiley.com/college/weygandt**

From the SEC homepage, choose **About the SEC**.

Instructions

Answer the following questions.

(a) How many enforcement actions does the SEC take each year against securities law violators? What are typical infractions?

(b) After the Depression, Congress passed the Securities Acts of 1933 and 1934 to improve investor confidence in the markets. What two "common sense" notions are these laws based on?

(c) Who was the President of the United States at the time of the creation of the SEC? Who was the first SEC Chairperson?

BYP17-4   Purpose: Use the Internet to view SEC filings.

Address: biz.yahoo.com/i, or go to **www.wiley.com/college/weygandt**

Steps:

1. Type in a company name.
2. Choose **Profile**.
3. Choose **SEC Filings**. (This will take you to Yahoo-Edgar Online.)

Instructions

Answer the following questions.

(a) What company did you select?

(b) Which filing is the most recent? What is the date?

(c) What other recent SEC filings are available for your viewing?

Critical Thinking

Decision Making Across the Organization

BYP17-5 Ron Nord and Lisa Smith are examining the following statement of cash flows for Carpino Company for the year ended January 31, 2012.

CARPINO COMPANY
Statement of Cash Flows
For the Year Ended January 31, 2012

Sources of cash	
From sales of merchandise	$380,000
From sale of capital stock	420,000
From sale of investment (purchased below)	80,000
From depreciation	55,000
From issuance of note for truck	20,000
From interest on investments	6,000
Total sources of cash	961,000
Uses of cash	
For purchase of fixtures and equipment	330,000
For merchandise purchased for resale	258,000
For operating expenses (including depreciation)	160,000
For purchase of investment	75,000
For purchase of truck by issuance of note	20,000
For purchase of treasury stock	10,000
For interest on note payable	3,000
Total uses of cash	856,000
Net increase in cash	$105,000

Ron claims that Carpino's statement of cash flows is an excellent portrayal of a superb first year with cash increasing $105,000. Lisa replies that it was not a superb first year. Rather, she says, the year was an operating failure, that the statement is presented incorrectly, and that $105,000 is not the actual increase in cash. The cash balance at the beginning of the year was $140,000.

Instructions

With the class divided into groups, answer the following.

(a) Using the data provided, prepare a statement of cash flows in proper form using the indirect method. The only noncash items in the income statement are depreciation and the gain from the sale of the investment.

(b) With whom do you agree, Ron or Lisa? Explain your position.

Communication Activity

BYP17-6 Kyle Benson, the owner-president of Computer Services Company, is unfamiliar with the statement of cash flows that you, as his accountant, prepared. He asks for further explanation.

Instructions

Write him a brief memo explaining the form and content of the statement of cash flows as shown in Illustration 17-13 (page 775).

Ethics Case

BYP17-7 Tappit Corp. is a medium-sized wholesaler of automotive parts. It has 10 stockholders who have been paid a total of $1 million in cash dividends for 8 consecutive years. The board's policy requires that, for this dividend to be declared, net cash provided by operating activities as reported in Tappit's current year's statement of cash flows must exceed $1 million. President and CEO Willie Morton's job is secure so long as he produces annual operating cash flows to support the usual dividend.

At the end of the current year, controller Robert Jennings presents president Willie Morton with some disappointing news: The net cash provided by operating activities is calculated by the indirect method to be only $970,000. The president says to Robert, "We must get that amount above $1 million. Isn't there some way to increase operating cash flow by another $30,000?" Robert answers, "These figures were prepared by my assistant. I'll go back to my office and see what I can do." The president replies, "I know you won't let me down, Robert."

Upon close scrutiny of the statement of cash flows, Robert concludes that he can get the operating cash flows above $1 million by reclassifying a $60,000, 2-year note payable listed in the financing activities section as "Proceeds from bank loan—$60,000." He will report the note instead as "Increase in payables—$60,000" and treat it as an adjustment of net income in the operating activities section. He returns to the president, saying, "You can tell the board to declare their usual dividend. Our net cash flow provided by operating activities is $1,030,000." "Good man, Robert! I knew I could count on you," exults the president.

Instructions

(a) Who are the stakeholders in this situation?

(b) Was there anything unethical about the president's actions? Was there anything unethical about the controller's actions?

(c) Are the board members or anyone else likely to discover the misclassification?

"All About You" Activity

BYP17-8   In this chapter, you learned that companies prepare a statement of cash flows in order to keep track of their sources and uses of cash and to help them plan for their future cash needs. Planning for your own short- and long-term cash needs is every bit as important as it is for a company.

Instructions

Read the article ("Financial Uh-Oh? No Problem") provided at **www.fool.com/personal-finance/saving/index.aspx**, and answer the following questions.

(a) Describe the three factors that determine how much money you should set aside for short-term needs.

(b) How many months of living expenses does the article suggest to set aside?

(c) Estimate how much you should set aside based upon your current situation. Are you closer to Cliff's scenario or to Prudence's?

FASB Codification Activity

BYP17-9   If your school has a subscription to the FASB Codification, go to *http://aaahq.org/ascLogin.cfm* to log in and prepare responses to the following. Use the Master Glossary to determine the proper definitions.

(a) What are cash equivalents?

(b) What are financing activities?

(c) What are investing activities?

(d) What are operating activities?

(e) What is the primary objective for the statement of cash flow? Is working capital the basis for meeting this objective?

(f) Do companies need to disclose information about investing and financing activities that do not affect cash receipts or cash payments? If so, how should such information be disclosed?

Answers to Insight and Accounting Across the Organization Questions

p. 765 Net *What*?   Q: In general, why do differences exist between net income and net cash provided by operating activities?   **A:** The differences are explained by differences in the timing of the reporting of revenues and expenses under accrual accounting versus cash. Under accrual accounting, companies report revenues when earned, even if cash hasn't been received, and they report expenses when incurred, even if cash hasn't been paid.

p. 773 Cash Flow Isn't Always What It Seems **Q:** For what reasons might managers at WorldCom and at Dynegy take the actions noted above? **A:** Analysts increasingly use cash flow-based measures of income, such as cash flow provided by operations, in addition to net income. More investors now focus on cash flow from operations, and some compensation contracts now have bonuses tied to cash flow numbers. Thus, some managers have taken actions that artificially increase cash flow from operations.

Answers to Self-Test Questions

1. c **2.** a **3.** b **4.** a **5.** c **6.** d **7.** b **8.** c **9.** d ($132,000 + $10,000 + $6,000 − $12,000)
10. b **11.** b ($200,000 + $40,000 − $10,000 + $20,000 − $30,000) **12.** a ($100,000 + $50,000 − $30,000)
13. b ($100,000 + $60,000 − $30,000) **14.** a **15.** d *16. b *17. b *18. c [$129,000 + ($44,000 − $42,000)] *19. d

IFRS A Look at IFRS

As in GAAP, the statement of cash flows is a required statement for IFRS. In addition, the content and presentation of an IFRS statement of cash flows is similar to the one used for GAAP. However, the disclosure requirements related to the statement of cash flows are more extensive under GAAP. *IAS 7* ("Cash Flow Statements") provides the overall IFRS requirements for cash flow information.

Key Points

- Companies preparing financial statements under IFRS must prepare a statement of cash flows as an integral part of the financial statements.

- Both IFRS and GAAP require that the statement of cash flows should have three major sections—operating, investing, and financing—along with changes in cash and cash equivalents.

- Similar to GAAP, the cash flow statement can be prepared using either the indirect or direct method under IFRS. In both U.S. and international settings, companies choose for the most part to use the indirect method for reporting net cash flows from operating activities.

- The definition of cash equivalents used in IFRS is similar to that used in GAAP. A major difference is that in certain situations, bank overdrafts are considered part of cash and cash equivalents under IFRS (which is not the case in GAAP). Under GAAP, bank overdrafts are classified as financing activities in the statement of cash flows and are reported as liabilities on the balance sheet.

- IFRS requires that noncash investing and financing activities be excluded from the statement of cash flows. Instead, these noncash activities should be reported elsewhere. This requirement is interpreted to mean that noncash investing and financing activities should be disclosed in the notes to the financial statements instead of in the financial statements. Under GAAP, companies may present this information on the face of the cash flow statement.

- One area where there can be substantial differences between IFRS and GAAP relates to the classification of interest, dividends, and taxes. The following table indicates the differences between the two approaches.

Item	IFRS	GAAP
Interest paid	Operating or financing	Operating
Interest received	Operating or investing	Operating
Dividends paid	Operating or financing	Financing
Dividends received	Operating or investing	Operating
Taxes paid	Operating—unless specific identification with financing or investing activity	Operating

- Under IFRS, some companies present the operating section in a single line item, with a full reconciliation provided in the notes to the financial statements. This presentation is not seen under GAAP.

- Similar to GAAP, under IFRS companies must disclose the amount of taxes and interest paid. Under GAAP, companies disclose this in the notes to the financial statements. Under IFRS, some companies disclose this information in the notes, but others provide individual line items on the face of the statement. In order to provide this information on the face of the statement, companies first add back the amount of interest expense and tax expense (similar to adding back depreciation expense) and then further down the statement they subtract the cash amount paid for interest and taxes. This treatment can be seen in the statement of cash flows provided for Zetar in Appendix C.

Looking to the Future

Presently, the FASB and the IASB are involved in a joint project on the presentation and organization of information in the financial statements. One interesting approach, revealed in a published proposal from that project, is that in the future the income statement and balance sheet would adopt headings similar to those of the statement of cash flows. That is, the income statement and balance sheet would be broken into operating, investing, and financing sections.

With respect to the cash flow statement specifically, the notion of *cash equivalents* will probably not be retained. That is, cash equivalents will not be combined with cash but instead will be reported as a form of highly liquid, low-risk investment. The definition of cash in the existing literature would be retained, and the statement of cash flows would present information on changes in cash only. In addition, the FASB favors presentation of operating cash flows using the direct method only. However, the majority of IASB members express a preference for not requiring use of the direct method of reporting operating cash flows. The two Boards will have to resolve their differences in this area in order to issue a converged standard for the statement of cash flows.

IFRS Self-Test Questions

1. Under IFRS, interest paid can be reported as:
   (a) only a financing element.
   (b) a financing element or an investing element.
   (c) a financing element or an operating element.
   (d) only an operating element.

2. IFRS requires that noncash items:
   (a) be reported in the section to which they relate, that is, a noncash investing activity would be reported in the investing section.
   (b) be disclosed in the notes to the financial statements.
   (c) do not need to be reported.
   (d) be treated in a fashion similar to cash equivalents.

3. In the future, it appears likely that:
   (a) the income statement and balance sheet will have headings of operating, investing, and financing, much like the statement of cash flows.
   (b) cash and cash equivalents will be combined in a single line item.
   (c) the IASB will not allow companies to use the direct approach to the statement of cash flows.
   (d) None of the above.

4. Under IFRS:
   (a) taxes are always treated as an operating item.
   (b) the income statement uses the headings operating, investing, and financing.
   (c) dividends received can be either an operating or investing item.
   (d) dividends paid can be either an operating or investing item.

5. Which of the following is *correct*?
   (a) Under IFRS, the statement of cash flows is optional.
   (b) IFRS requires use of the direct approach in preparing the statement of cash flows.
   (c) The majority of companies following GAAP and the majority following IFRS employ the indirect approach to the statement of cash flows.
   (d) Cash and cash equivalents are reported as separate line items under IFRS.

IFRS Concepts and Application

IFRS17-1   Discuss the differences that exist in the treatment of bank overdrafts under GAAP and IFRS.

IFRS17-2   Describe the treatment of each of the following items under IFRS versus GAAP.
(a) Interest paid.
(b) Interest received.
(c) Dividends paid.
(d) Dividends received.

IFRS17-3   Explain how the treatment of cash equivalents will probably change in the future.

International Financial Reporting Problem: Zetar plc

IFRS17-4   The financial statements of Zetar plc are presented in Appendix C. The company's complete annual report, including the notes to its financial statements, is available at *www.zetarplc.com*.

Instructions
Use the company's annual report to answer the following questions.
(a) In which section (operating, investing, or financing) does Zetar report interest paid?
(b) Explain why the amount that Zetar reports for cash and cash equivalents in its statement of cash flows is negative.
(c) If Zetar reported under GAAP rather than IFRS, how would its treatment of bank overdrafts differ?
(d) Zetar's statement of cash flows reports negative "net movement in working capital" in 2009 of £2,469 (in thousands). According to the statement of cash flows, what were the components of this "net movement"?

Answers to IFRS Self-Test Questions
1. c   2. b   3. a   4. c   5. c

The Navigator

✔ **Remember to go back to the Navigator box on the chapter opening page and check off your completed work.**

CHAPTER18

Financial Statement Analysis

Study Objectives

After studying this chapter, you should be able to:

[1] Discuss the need for comparative analysis.

[2] Identify the tools of financial statement analysis.

[3] Explain and apply horizontal analysis.

[4] Describe and apply vertical analysis.

[5] Identify and compute ratios used in analyzing a firm's liquidity, profitability, and solvency.

[6] Understand the concept of earning power, and how irregular items are presented.

[7] Understand the concept of quality of earnings.

✔ **The Navigator**

✔ [The Navigator]

● Scan Study Objectives	○
● Read Feature Story	○
● Read Preview	○
● Read text and answer **Do it!** p. 831 ○ p. 844 ○ p. 849 ○ p. 851 ○	
● Work Comprehensive **Do it!** p. 852	○
● Review Summary of Study Objectives	○
● Answer Self-Test Questions	○
● Complete Assignments	○
● Go to *WileyPLUS* for practice and tutorials	○
● Read A Look at IFRS p. 874	○

Feature Story

IT PAYS TO BE PATIENT

A recent issue of *Forbes* magazine listed Warren Buffett as the richest person in the world. His estimated wealth was $62 billion, give or take a few million. How much is $62 billion? If you invested $62 billion in an investment earning just 4%, you could spend $6.8 million per day—every day—forever. How did Mr. Buffett amass this wealth? Through careful investing.

However, if you think you might want to follow Mr. Buffett's example and transform your humble nest-egg into a mountain of cash, be warned: His techniques have been widely circulated and emulated, but never practiced with the same degree of success.

Mr. Buffett epitomizes a "value investor." To this day, he applies the same basic techniques he learned in the 1950s from the great value investor Benjamin Graham. That means he spends his time looking for companies that have good long-term potential but are currently underpriced. He invests in companies that have low exposure to debt and that reinvest their earnings for future growth. He does not get caught up in fads or the latest trend.

Instead, he looks for companies in industries with sound economics and ones that have high returns on stockholders' equity. He looks for steady earnings trends and high margins.

Mr. Buffett sat out on the dot-com mania in the 1990s. When other investors put lots of money into fledgling high-tech firms, Mr. Buffett did not bite because he did not find dot-com companies that met his criteria. He didn't get to enjoy the stock price boom on the way up, but on the other hand, he didn't have to ride the price back down to Earth. Instead, when the dot-com bubble burst, and nearly everyone else was suffering from investment shock, he swooped in and scooped up deals on companies that he had been following for years.

So, how does Mr. Buffett spend his money? Basically, he doesn't! He still lives in the same house that he purchased in Omaha, Nebraska, in 1958 for $31,500. He still drives his own car (a Cadillac DTS). And in case you were thinking that his kids are riding the road to Easy Street, think again. Mr. Buffett has committed to giving virtually all of his money to charity before he dies.

So, given that neither you nor anyone else will be inheriting Mr. Buffett's riches, you should probably start honing your financial analysis skills. A good way for you to begin your career as a successful investor is to master the fundamentals of financial analysis discussed in this chapter.

PreviewofCHAPTER18

We can learn an important lesson from Warren Buffett. The lesson: Study companies carefully if you wish to invest. Do not get caught up in fads but instead find companies that are financially healthy. Using some of the basic decision tools presented in this book, you can perform a rudimentary analysis on any U.S. company and draw basic conclusions about its financial health. Although it would not be wise for you to bet your life savings on a company's stock relying solely on your current level of knowledge, we strongly encourage you to practice your new skills wherever possible. Only with practice will you improve your ability to interpret financial numbers.

Before unleashing you on the world of high finance, we will present a few more important concepts and techniques, as well as provide you with one more comprehensive review of corporate financial statements. We use all of the decision tools presented in this text to analyze a single company—J.C. Penney Company, one of the country's oldest and largest retail store chains.

The content and organization of Chapter 18 are as follows.

Financial Statement Analysis				
Basics of Financial Statement Analysis	**Horizontal and Vertical Analysis**	**Ratio Analysis**	**Earning Power and Irregular Items**	**Quality of Earnings**
• Need for comparative analysis • Tools of analysis	• Balance sheet • Income statement • Retained earnings statement	• Liquidity • Profitability • Solvency • Summary	• Discontinued operations • Extraordinary items • Changes in accounting principle • Comprehensive income	• Alternative accounting methods • Pro forma income • Improper recognition

The Navigator

Basics of Financial Statement Analysis

Analyzing financial statements involves evaluating three characteristics: a company's liquidity, profitability, and solvency. A **short-term creditor**, such as a bank, is primarily interested in liquidity—the ability of the borrower to pay obligations when they come due. The liquidity of the borrower is extremely important in evaluating the safety of a loan. A **long-term creditor**, such as a bondholder, looks to profitability and solvency measures that indicate the company's ability to survive over a long period of time. Long-term creditors consider such measures as the amount of debt in the company's capital structure and its ability to meet interest payments. Similarly, **stockholders** look at the profitability and solvency of the company. They want to assess the likelihood of dividends and the growth potential of the stock.

Need for Comparative Analysis

Study Objective [1]
Discuss the need for comparative analysis.

Every item reported in a financial statement has significance. When J.C. Penney Company, Inc. reports cash and cash equivalents of $3 billion on its balance sheet, we know the company had that amount of cash on the balance sheet date. But, we do not know whether the amount represents an increase over prior years, or whether it is adequate in relation to the company's need for cash. To obtain such information, we need to compare the amount of cash with other financial statement data.

Comparisons can be made on a number of different bases. Three are illustrated in this chapter.

1. **Intracompany basis.** Comparisons within a company are often useful to detect changes in financial relationships and significant trends. For example, a comparison of J.C. Penney's current year's cash amount with the prior year's cash amount shows either an increase or a decrease. Likewise, a comparison of J.C. Penney's year-end cash amount with the amount of its total assets at year-end shows the proportion of total assets in the form of cash.

2. **Industry averages.** Comparisons with industry averages provide information about a company's relative position within the industry. For example, financial statement readers can compare J.C. Penney's financial data with the averages for its industry compiled by financial rating organizations such as Dun & Bradstreet, Moody's, and Standard & Poor's, or with information provided on the Internet by organizations such as Yahoo! on its financial site.

3. **Intercompany basis.** Comparisons with other companies provide insight into a company's competitive position. For example, investors can compare J.C. Penney's total sales for the year with the total sales of its competitors in retail, such as Sears.

Tools of Analysis

We use various tools to evaluate the significance of financial statement data. Three commonly used tools are these:

- **Horizontal analysis** evaluates a series of financial statement data over a period of time.
- **Vertical analysis** evaluates financial statement data by expressing each item in a financial statement as a percent of a base amount.
- **Ratio analysis** expresses the relationship among selected items of financial statement data.

Study Objective [2]
Identify the tools of financial statement analysis.

Horizontal analysis is used primarily in intracompany comparisons. Two features in published financial statements facilitate this type of comparison: First, each of the basic financial statements presents comparative financial data for a minimum of two years. Second, a summary of selected financial data is presented for a series of five to ten years or more. *Vertical analysis* is used in both intra- and intercompany comparisons. *Ratio analysis* is used in all three types of comparisons. In the following sections, we explain and illustrate each of the three types of analysis.

Horizontal Analysis

Horizontal analysis, also called **trend analysis**, is a technique for evaluating a series of financial statement data over a period of time. Its purpose is to determine the increase or decrease that has taken place. This change may be expressed as either an amount or a percentage. For example, Illustration 18-1 (page 828) shows the recent net sales figures of J.C. Penney Company.

Study Objective [3]
Explain and apply horizontal analysis.

Illustration 18-1
J.C. Penney Company's
Net Sales

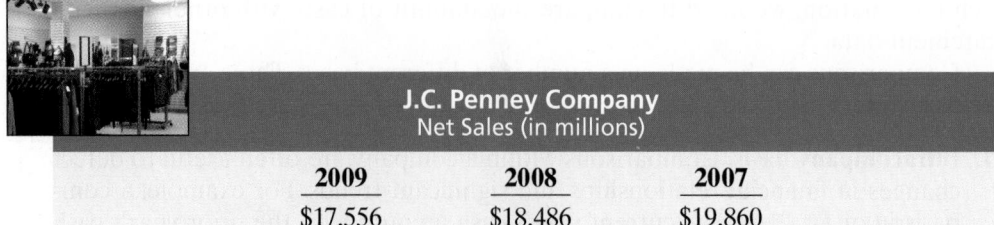

J.C. Penney Company Net Sales (in millions)		
2009	**2008**	**2007**
$17,556	$18,486	$19,860

If we assume that 2007 is the base year, we can measure all percentage increases or decreases from this base period amount as follows.

Illustration 18-2
Formula for horizontal analysis
of changes since base period

$$\text{Change Since Base Period} = \frac{\text{Current Year Amount} - \text{Base Year Amount}}{\text{Base Year Amount}}$$

For example, we can determine that net sales for J.C. Penney decreased from 2007 to 2008 approximately 6.9% [($18,486 − $19,860) ÷ $19,860]. Similarly, we can determine that net sales decreased from 2007 to 2009 approximately 11.6% [($17,556 − $19,860) ÷ $19,860].

Alternatively, we can express current year sales as a percentage of the base period. We do this by dividing the current year amount by the base year amount, as shown below.

Illustration 18-3
Formula for horizontal analysis
of current year in relation to
base year

$$\text{Current Results in Relation to Base Period} = \frac{\text{Current Year Amount}}{\text{Base Year Amount}}$$

Illustration 18-4 presents this analysis for J.C. Penney for a three-year period using 2007 as the base period.

Illustration 18-4
Horizontal analysis of
J.C. Penney Company's
net sales in relation to base
period

J.C. Penney Company Net Sales (in millions) in relation to base period 2007		
2009	**2008**	**2007**
$17,556	$18,486	$19,860
88.4%	93.1%	100%

Balance Sheet

To further illustrate horizontal analysis, we will use the financial statements of Quality Department Store Inc., a fictional retailer. Illustration 18-5 presents a horizontal analysis of its two-year condensed balance sheets, showing dollar and percentage changes.

Illustration 18-5
Horizontal analysis of
balance sheets

Quality Department Store Inc.
Condensed Balance Sheets
December 31

	2009	2008	Increase or (Decrease) during 2009 Amount	Percent
Assets				
Current assets	$1,020,000	$ 945,000	$ 75,000	7.9%
Plant assets (net)	800,000	632,500	167,500	26.5%
Intangible assets	15,000	17,500	(2,500)	(14.3%)
Total assets	$1,835,000	$1,595,000	$240,000	15.0%
Liabilities				
Current liabilities	$ 344,500	$ 303,000	$ 41,500	13.7%
Long-term liabilities	487,500	497,000	(9,500)	(1.9%)
Total liabilities	832,000	800,000	32,000	4.0%
Stockholders' Equity				
Common stock, $1 par	275,400	270,000	5,400	2.0%
Retained earnings	727,600	525,000	202,600	38.6%
Total stockholders' equity	1,003,000	795,000	208,000	26.2%
Total liabilities and stockholders' equity	$1,835,000	$1,595,000	$240,000	15.0%

The comparative balance sheets in Illustration 18-5 show that a number of significant changes have occurred in Quality Department Store's financial structure from 2008 to 2009:

- In the assets section, plant assets (net) increased $167,500, or 26.5%.
- In the liabilities section, current liabilities increased $41,500, or 13.7%.
- In the stockholders' equity section, retained earnings increased $202,600, or 38.6%.

These changes suggest that the company expanded its asset base during 2009 and **financed this expansion primarily by retaining income** rather than assuming additional long-term debt.

Income Statement

Illustration 18-6 (page 830) presents a horizontal analysis of the two-year condensed income statements of Quality Department Store Inc. for the years 2009 and 2008. Horizontal analysis of the income statements shows the following changes:

- Net sales increased $260,000, or 14.2% ($260,000 ÷ $1,837,000).
- Cost of goods sold increased $141,000, or 12.4% ($141,000 ÷ $1,140,000).
- Total operating expenses increased $37,000, or 11.6% ($37,000 ÷ $320,000).

Overall, gross profit and net income were up substantially. Gross profit increased 17.1%, and net income, 26.5%. Quality's profit trend appears favorable.

Illustration 18-6
Horizontal analysis of
income statements

			Increase or (Decrease) during 2009	
Quality Department Store Inc. Condensed Income Statements For the Years Ended December 31				
	2009	**2008**	**Amount**	**Percent**
Sales revenue	$2,195,000	$1,960,000	$235,000	12.0%
Sales returns and allowances	98,000	123,000	(25,000)	(20.3%)
Net sales	2,097,000	1,837,000	260,000	14.2%
Cost of goods sold	1,281,000	1,140,000	141,000	12.4%
Gross profit	816,000	697,000	119,000	17.1%
Selling expenses	253,000	211,500	41,500	19.6%
Administrative expenses	104,000	108,500	(4,500)	(4.1%)
Total operating expenses	357,000	320,000	37,000	11.6%
Income from operations	459,000	377,000	82,000	21.8%
Other revenues and gains				
Interest and dividends	9,000	11,000	(2,000)	(18.2%)
Other expenses and losses				
Interest expense	36,000	40,500	(4,500)	(11.1%)
Income before income taxes	432,000	347,500	84,500	24.3%
Income tax expense	168,200	139,000	29,200	21.0%
Net income	$ 263,800	$ 208,500	$ 55,300	26.5%

Helpful Hint

Note that though the amount column is additive (the total is $55,300), the percentage column is not additive (26.5% is not the total). A separate percentage has been calculated for each item.

Retained Earnings Statement

Illustration 18-7 presents a horizontal analysis of Quality Department Store's comparative retained earnings statements. Analyzed horizontally, net income increased $55,300, or 26.5%, whereas dividends on the common stock increased only $1,200, or 2%. We saw in the horizontal analysis of the balance sheet that ending retained earnings increased 38.6%. As indicated earlier, the company retained a significant portion of net income to finance additional plant facilities.

Illustration 18-7
Horizontal analysis of retained
earnings statements

			Increase or (Decrease) during 2009	
Quality Department Store Inc. Retained Earnings Statements For the Years Ended December 31				
	2009	**2008**	**Amount**	**Percent**
Retained earnings, Jan. 1	$525,000	$376,500	$148,500	39.4%
Add: Net income	263,800	208,500	55,300	26.5%
	788,800	585,000	203,800	
Deduct: Dividends	61,200	60,000	1,200	2.0%
Retained earnings, Dec. 31	$727,600	$525,000	$202,600	38.6%

Horizontal analysis of changes from period to period is relatively straightforward and is quite useful. But complications can occur in making the computations. If an item has no value in a base year or preceding year but does have a value in the next year, we cannot compute a percentage change. Similarly, if a negative amount appears in the base or preceding period and a positive amount exists the following year (or vice versa), no percentage change can be computed.

Do it!

Summary financial information for Rosepatch Company is as follows.

	December 31, 2012	December 31, 2011
Current assets	$234,000	$180,000
Plant assets (net)	756,000	420,000
Total assets	$990,000	$600,000

Compute the amount and percentage changes in 2012 using horizontal analysis, assuming 2011 is the base year.

Solution

	Increase in 2012	
	Amount	Percent
Current assets	$ 54,000	30% [($234,000 − $180,000) ÷ $180,000]
Plant assets (net)	336,000	80% [($756,000 − $420,000) ÷ $420,000]
Total assets	$390,000	65% [($990,000 − $600,000) ÷ $600,000]

Related exercise material: BE18-2, BE18-3, BE18-5, BE18-6, BE18-7, E18-1, E18-3, E18-4, and **Do it!** 18-1.

Horizontal Analysis

action plan
✔ Find the percentage change by dividing the amount of the increase by the 2011 amount (base year).

The Navigator

Vertical Analysis

Vertical analysis, also called **common-size analysis**, is a technique that expresses each financial statement item as a percent of a base amount. On a balance sheet we might say that current assets are 22% of total assets—*total assets* being the base amount. Or on an income statement, we might say that selling expenses are 16% of net sales—net sales being the base amount.

Study Objective [4]
Describe and apply vertical analysis.

Balance Sheet

Illustration 18-8 (page 832) presents the vertical analysis of Quality Department Store Inc.'s comparative balance sheets. The base for the asset items is **total assets**. The base for the liability and stockholders' equity items is **total liabilities and stockholders' equity**.

Vertical analysis shows the relative size of each category in the balance sheet. It also can show the **percentage change** in the individual asset, liability, and stockholders' equity items. For example, we can see that current assets decreased from 59.2% of total assets in 2008 to 55.6% in 2009 (even though the absolute dollar amount increased $75,000 in that time). Plant assets (net) have increased from 39.7% to 43.6% of total assets. Retained earnings have increased from 32.9% to 39.7% of total liabilities and stockholders' equity. These results reinforce the earlier observations that **Quality is choosing to finance its growth through retention of earnings rather than through issuing additional debt**.

Income Statement

Illustration 18-9 (page 832) shows vertical analysis of Quality's income statements. Cost of goods sold as a percentage of net sales declined 1% (62.1% vs. 61.1%), and

Illustration 18-8
Vertical analysis of balance sheets

Quality Department Store Inc.
Condensed Balance Sheets
December 31

	2009		**2008**	
	Amount	**Percent**	**Amount**	**Percent**
Assets				
Current assets	$1,020,000	55.6%	$ 945,000	59.2%
Plant assets (net)	800,000	43.6%	632,500	39.7%
Intangible assets	15,000	0.8%	17,500	1.1%
Total assets	$1,835,000	100.0%	$1,595,000	100.0%
Liabilities				
Current liabilities	$ 344,500	18.8%	$ 303,000	19.0%
Long-term liabilities	487,500	26.5%	497,000	31.2%
Total liabilities	832,000	45.3%	800,000	50.2%
Stockholders' Equity				
Common stock, $1 par	275,400	15.0%	270,000	16.9%
Retained earnings	727,600	39.7%	525,000	32.9%
Total stockholders' equity	1,003,000	54.7%	795,000	49.8%
Total liabilities and stockholders' equity	$1,835,000	100.0%	$1,595,000	100.0%

Helpful Hint

The formula for calculating these balance sheet percentages is:

$$\frac{\text{Each item on B/S}}{\text{Total assets}} = \%$$

Illustration 18-9
Vertical analysis of income statements

Quality Department Store Inc.
Condensed Income Statements
For the Years Ended December 31

	2009		**2008**	
	Amount	**Percent**	**Amount**	**Percent**
Sales revenue	$2,195,000	104.7%	$1,960,000	106.7%
Sales returns and allowances	98,000	4.7%	123,000	6.7%
Net sales	2,097,000	100.0%	1,837,000	100.0%
Cost of goods sold	1,281,000	61.1%	1,140,000	62.1%
Gross profit	816,000	38.9%	697,000	37.9%
Selling expenses	253,000	12.0%	211,500	11.5%
Administrative expenses	104,000	5.0%	108,500	5.9%
Total operating expenses	357,000	17.0%	320,000	17.4%
Income from operations	459,000	21.9%	377,000	20.5%
Other revenues and gains				
Interest and dividends	9,000	0.4%	11,000	0.6%
Other expenses and losses				
Interest expense	36,000	1.7%	40,500	2.2%
Income before income taxes	432,000	20.6%	347,500	18.9%
Income tax expense	168,200	8.0%	139,000	7.5%
Net income	$ 263,800	12.6%	$ 208,500	11.4%

Helpful Hint

The formula for calculating these income statement percentages is:

$$\frac{\text{Each item on I/S}}{\text{Net sales}} = \%$$

total operating expenses declined 0.4% (17.4% vs. 17.0%). As a result, it is not surprising to see net income as a percent of net sales increase from 11.4% to 12.6%. Quality appears to be a profitable business that is becoming even more successful.

An associated benefit of vertical analysis is that it enables you to compare companies of different sizes. For example, Quality's main competitor is a JC Penney store in a nearby town. Using vertical analysis, we can compare the condensed income statements of Quality Department Store Inc. (a small retail company) with J.C. Penney Company, Inc. (a giant international retailer), as shown in Illustration 18-10.

Condensed Income Statements (in thousands)				
	Quality Department Store Inc.		**J.C. Penney Company**[1]	
	Dollars	**Percent**	**Dollars**	**Percent**
Net sales	$2,097	100.0%	$17,556,000	100.0%
Cost of goods sold	1,281	61.1%	10,646,000	60.6%
Gross profit	816	38.9%	6,910,000	39.4%
Selling and administrative expenses	357	17.0%	6,247,000	35.7%
Income from operations	459	21.9%	663,000	3.7%
Other expenses and revenues (including income taxes)	195	9.3%	412,000	2.3%
Net income	$ 264	12.6%	$ 251,000	1.4%

Illustration 18-10
Intercompany income statement comparison

J.C. Penney's net sales are 8,372 times greater than the net sales of relatively tiny Quality Department Store. But vertical analysis eliminates this difference in size. The percentages show that Quality's and J.C. Penney's gross profit rates were comparable at 38.9% and 39.4%. However, the percentages related to income from operations were significantly different at 21.9% and 3.7%. This disparity can be attributed to Quality's selling and administrative expense percentage (17%) which is much lower than J.C. Penney's (35.7%). Although J.C. Penney earned net income more than 951 times larger than Quality's, J.C. Penney's net income as a **percent of each sales dollar** (1.4%) is only 11% of Quality's (12.6%).

Ratio Analysis

Ratio analysis expresses the relationship among selected items of financial statement data. A ratio expresses the mathematical relationship between one quantity and another. The relationship is expressed in terms of either a percentage, a rate, or a simple proportion. To illustrate, in 2010 Nike, Inc., had current assets of $10,959.2 million and current liabilities of $3,364.2 million. We can find the relationship between these two measures by dividing current assets by current liabilities. The alternative means of expression are:

Study Objective [5]
Identify and compute ratios used in analyzing a firm's liquidity, profitability, and solvency.

Percentage:	Current assets are 326% of current liabilities.
Rate:	Current assets are 3.26 times current liabilities.
Proportion:	The relationship of current assets to liabilities is 3.26:1.

To analyze the primary financial statements, we can use ratios to evaluate liquidity, profitability, and solvency. Illustration 18-11 (page 834) describes these classifications.

---

[1]*2009 Annual Report* J.C. Penney Company, Inc. (Dallas, Texas).

Illustration 18-11
Financial ratio classifications

Liquidity Ratios

Measure short-term ability of the company to pay its maturing obligations and to meet unexpected needs for cash

Profitability Ratios

Measure the income or operating success of a company for a given period of time

Solvency Ratios

Measure the ability of the company to survive over a long period of time

Ratios can provide clues to underlying conditions that may not be apparent from individual financial statement components. However, a single ratio by itself is not very meaningful. Thus, in the discussion of ratios we will use the following types of comparisons.

1. **Intracompany comparisons** for two years for Quality Department Store.
2. **Industry average comparisons** based on median ratios for department stores.
3. **Intercompany comparisons** based on J.C. Penney Company as Quality Department Store's principal competitor.

ANATOMY OF A FRAUD

This final *Anatomy of a Fraud* box demonstrates that sometimes relationships between numbers can be used by companies to detect fraud. The numeric relationships that can reveal fraud can be such things as financial ratios that appear abnormal, or statistical abnormalities in the numbers themselves. For example, the fact that WorldCom's line costs, as a percentage of either total expenses or revenues, differed very significantly from its competitors should have alerted people to the possibility of fraud. Or, consider the case of a bank manager, who cooperated with a group of his friends to defraud the bank's credit card department. The manager's friends would apply for credit cards and then run up balances of slightly less than $5,000. The bank had a policy of allowing bank personnel to write-off balances of less than $5,000 without seeking supervisor approval. The fraud was detected by applying statistical analysis based on Benford's Law. Benford's Law states that in a random collection of numbers, the frequency of lower digits (e.g., 1, 2, or 3) should be much higher than higher digits (e.g., 7, 8, or 9). In this case, bank auditors analyzed the first two digits of amounts written off. There was a spike at 48 and 49, which was not consistent with what would be expected if the numbers were random.

Total take: Thousands of dollars

THE MISSING CONTROL

Independent internal verification. While it might be efficient to allow employees to write off accounts below a certain level, it is important that these write-offs be reviewed and verified periodically. Such a review would likely call attention to an employee with large amounts of write-offs, or in this case, write-offs that were frequently very close to the approval threshold.

Source: Mark J. Nigrini, "I've Got Your Number," *Journal of Accountancy Online* (May 1999).

Liquidity Ratios

Liquidity ratios measure the short-term ability of the company to pay its maturing obligations and to meet unexpected needs for cash. Short-term creditors such as bankers and suppliers are particularly interested in assessing liquidity. The ratios we can use to determine the company's short-term debt-paying ability are the current ratio, the acid-test ratio, receivables turnover, and inventory turnover.

> **International Note**
>
> As more countries adopt international accounting standards, the ability of analysts to compare companies from different countries should improve. However, international standards are open to widely varying interpretations. In addition, some countries adopt international standards "with modifications." As a consequence, most cross-country comparisons are still not as transparent as within-country comparisons.

1. CURRENT RATIO

The **current ratio** is a widely used measure for evaluating a company's liquidity and short-term debt-paying ability. The ratio is computed by dividing current assets by current liabilities. Illustration 18-12 shows the 2009 and 2008 current ratios for Quality Department Store and comparative data.

$$\text{Current Ratio} = \frac{\text{Current Assets}}{\text{Current Liabilities}}$$

Quality Department Store

2009	2008
$\dfrac{\$1,020,000}{\$344,500} = 2.96{:}1$	$\dfrac{\$945,000}{\$303,000} = 3.12{:}1$
Industry average	J.C. Penney Company
1.70:1	**2.05:1**

Illustration 18-12
Current ratio

What does the ratio actually mean? The 2009 ratio of 2.96:1 means that for every dollar of current liabilities, Quality has $2.96 of current assets. Quality's current ratio has decreased in the current year. But, compared to the industry average of 1.70:1, Quality appears to be reasonably liquid. J.C. Penney has a current ratio of 2.05:1, which indicates it has adequate current assets relative to its current liabilities.

The current ratio is sometimes referred to as the **working capital ratio**; **working capital** is current assets minus current liabilities. The current ratio is a more dependable indicator of liquidity than working capital. Two companies with the same amount of working capital may have significantly different current ratios.

The current ratio is only one measure of liquidity. It does not take into account the **composition** of the current assets. For example, a satisfactory current ratio does not disclose the fact that a portion of the current assets may be tied up in slow-moving inventory. A dollar of cash would be more readily available to pay the bills than a dollar of slow-moving inventory.

> **Helpful Hint**
>
> Can any company operate successfully without working capital? Yes, if it has very predictable cash flows and solid earnings. A number of companies (e.g., Whirlpool, American Standard, and Campbell's Soup) are pursuing this goal. The rationale: Less money tied up in working capital means more money to invest in the business.

2. ACID-TEST RATIO

The **acid-test (quick) ratio** is a measure of a company's immediate short-term liquidity. We compute this ratio by dividing the sum of cash, short-term investments, and net receivables by current liabilities. Thus, it is an important complement to the current ratio. For example, assume that the current assets of Quality Department Store for 2009 and 2008 consist of the items shown in Illustration 18-13 (page 836).

Illustration 18-13
Current assets of Quality
Department Store

Quality Department Store Inc. Balance Sheet (partial)		
	2009	**2008**
Current assets		
Cash	$ 100,000	$155,000
Short-term investments	20,000	70,000
Receivables (net*)	230,000	180,000
Inventory	620,000	500,000
Prepaid expenses	50,000	40,000
Total current assets	$1,020,000	$945,000

*Allowance for doubtful accounts is $10,000 at the end of each year.

Cash, short-term investments, and receivables (net) are highly liquid compared to inventory and prepaid expenses. The inventory may not be readily saleable, and the prepaid expenses may not be transferable to others. Thus, the acid-test ratio measures **immediate** liquidity. The 2009 and 2008 acid-test ratios for Quality Department Store and comparative data are as follows.

Illustration 18-14
Acid-test ratio

$$\text{Acid-Test Ratio} = \frac{\text{Cash + Short-Term Investments + Receivables (Net)}}{\text{Current Liabilities}}$$

Quality Department Store

2009

$$\frac{\$100,000 + \$20,000 + \$230,000}{\$344,500} = 1.02:1$$

Industry average
0.70:1

2008

$$\frac{\$155,000 + \$70,000 + \$180,000}{\$303,000} = 1.34:1$$

J.C. Penney Company
1.05:1

The ratio has declined in 2009. Is an acid-test ratio of 1.02:1 adequate? This depends on the industry and the economy. When compared with the industry average of 0.70:1 and J.C. Penney's of 1.05:1, Quality's acid-test ratio seems adequate.

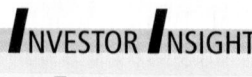

INVESTOR INSIGHT

How to Manage the Current Ratio

The apparent simplicity of the current ratio can have real-world limitations because adding equal amounts to both the numerator and the denominator causes the ratio to decrease.

Assume, for example, that a company has $2,000,000 of current assets and $1,000,000 of current liabilities; its current ratio is 2:1. If it purchases $1,000,000 of inventory on account, it will have $3,000,000 of current assets and $2,000,000 of current liabilities; its current ratio decreases to 1.5:1. If, instead, the company pays off $500,000 of its current liabilities, it will have $1,500,000 of current assets and $500,000 of current liabilities; its current ratio increases to 3:1. Thus, any trend analysis should be done with care because the ratio is susceptible to quick changes and is easily influenced by management.

? How might management influence a company's current ratio? (See page 873.)

3. RECEIVABLES TURNOVER

We can measure liquidity by how quickly a company can convert certain assets to cash. How liquid, for example, are the receivables? The ratio used to assess the liquidity of the receivables is **receivables turnover**. It measures the number of times, on average, the company collects receivables during the period. We compute receivables turnover by dividing net credit sales (net sales less cash sales) by the average net receivables. Unless seasonal factors are significant, average net receivables can be computed from the beginning and ending balances of the net receivables.[2]

Assume that all sales are credit sales. The balance of net receivables at the beginning of 2008 is $200,000. Illustration 18-15 shows the receivables turnover for Quality Department Store and comparative data. Quality's receivables turnover improved in 2009. The turnover of 10.2 times is substantially lower than J.C. Penney's 37.2 times, and is also lower than the department store industry's average of 46.4 times.

Illustration 18-15
Receivables turnover

Average Collection Period.   A popular variant of the receivables turnover ratio is to convert it to an **average collection period** in terms of days. To do so, we divide the receivables turnover ratio into 365 days. For example, the receivables turnover of 10.2 times divided into 365 days gives an average collection period of approximately 36 days. This means that receivables are collected on average every 36 days, or about every 5 weeks. Analysts frequently use the average collection period to assess the effectiveness of a company's credit and collection policies. The general rule is that the collection period should not greatly exceed the credit term period (the time allowed for payment).

4. INVENTORY TURNOVER

Inventory turnover measures the number of times, on average, the inventory is sold during the period. Its purpose is to measure the liquidity of the inventory. We compute the inventory turnover by dividing cost of goods sold by the average inventory. Unless seasonal factors are significant, we can use the beginning and ending inventory balances to compute average inventory.

Assuming that the inventory balance for Quality Department Store at the beginning of 2008 was $450,000, its inventory turnover and comparative data are as shown in Illustration 18-16 (page 838). Quality's inventory turnover declined slightly in

[2]If seasonal factors are significant, the average receivables balance might be determined by using monthly amounts.

2009. The turnover of 2.3 times is low compared with the industry average of 4.3 and J.C. Penney's 3.1. Generally, the faster the inventory turnover, the less cash a company has tied up in inventory and the less the chance of inventory obsolescence.

Illustration 18-16
Inventory turnover

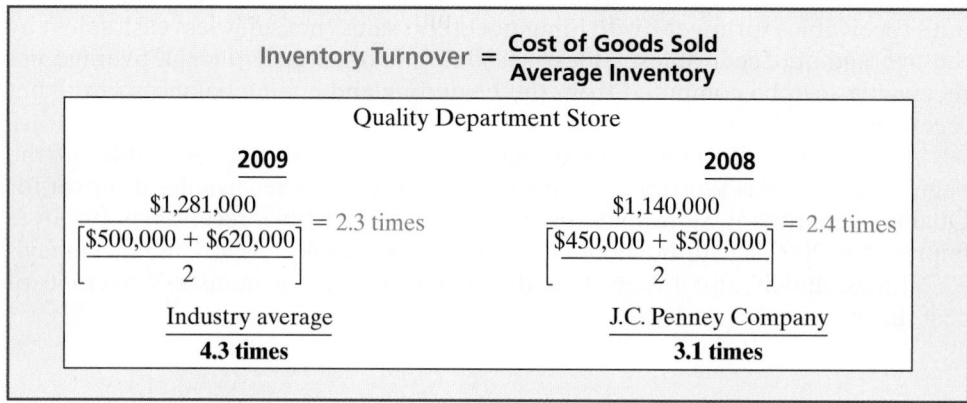

Days in Inventory.   A variant of inventory turnover is the **days in inventory**. We calculate it by dividing the inventory turnover into 365. For example, Quality's 2009 inventory turnover of 2.3 times divided into 365 is approximately 159 days. An average selling time of 159 days is also high compared with the industry average of 84.9 days (365 ÷ 4.3) and J.C. Penney's 117.7 days (365 ÷ 3.1).

Inventory turnover ratios vary considerably among industries. For example, grocery store chains have a turnover of 17.1 times and an average selling period of 21 days. In contrast, jewelry stores have an average turnover of 0.80 times and an average selling period of 456 days.

Profitability Ratios

Profitability ratios measure the income or operating success of a company for a given period of time. Income, or the lack of it, affects the company's ability to obtain debt and equity financing. It also affects the company's liquidity position and the company's ability to grow. As a consequence, both creditors and investors are interested in evaluating earning power—profitability. Analysts frequently use profitability as the ultimate test of management's operating effectiveness.

5. PROFIT MARGIN

Alternative Terminology

Profit margin is also called the *rate of return on sales*.

Profit margin is a measure of the percentage of each dollar of sales that results in net income. We can compute it by dividing net income by net sales. Illustration 18-17 shows Quality Department Store's profit margin and comparative data.

Illustration 18-17
Profit margin

Quality experienced an increase in its profit margin from 2008 to 2009. Its profit margin is unusually high in comparison with the industry average of 8% and J.C. Penney's 1.4%.

High-volume (high inventory turnover) businesses, such as grocery stores (Safeway or Kroger) and discount stores (Kmart or Wal-Mart), generally experience low profit margins. In contrast, low-volume businesses, such as jewelry stores (Tiffany & Co.) or airplane manufacturers (Boeing Co.), have high profit margins.

6. ASSET TURNOVER

Asset turnover measures how efficiently a company uses its assets to generate sales. It is determined by dividing net sales by average assets. The resulting number shows the dollars of sales produced by each dollar invested in assets. Unless seasonal factors are significant, we can use the beginning and ending balance of total assets to determine average total assets. Assuming that total assets at the beginning of 2008 were $1,446,000, the 2009 and 2008 asset turnover for Quality Department Store and comparative data are shown in Illustration 18-18.

Illustration 18-18
Asset turnover

Asset turnover shows that in 2009 Quality generated sales of $1.22 for each dollar it had invested in assets. The ratio changed very little from 2008 to 2009. Quality's asset turnover is below both the industry average of 1.40 times and J.C. Penney's ratio of 1.40 times.

Asset turnover ratios vary considerably among industries. For example, a large utility company like Consolidated Edison (New York) has a ratio of 0.40 times, and the large grocery chain Kroger Stores has a ratio of 3.4 times.

7. RETURN ON ASSETS

An overall measure of profitability is **return on assets**. We compute this ratio by dividing net income by average assets. The 2009 and 2008 return on assets for Quality Department Store and comparative data are shown below.

Illustration 18-19
Return on assets

Quality's return on assets improved from 2008 to 2009. Its return of 15.4% is very high compared with the department store industry average of 8.9% and J.C. Penney's 2.4%.

8. RETURN ON COMMON STOCKHOLDERS' EQUITY

Another widely used profitability ratio is **return on common stockholders' equity**. It measures profitability from the common stockholders' viewpoint. This ratio shows how many dollars of net income the company earned for each dollar invested by the owners. We compute it by dividing net income by average common stockholders' equity. Assuming that common stockholders' equity at the beginning of 2008 was $667,000, Illustration 18-20 shows the 2009 and 2008 ratios for Quality Department Store and comparative data.

Illustration 18-20
Return on common stockholders' equity

Quality's rate of return on common stockholders' equity is high at 29.3%, considering an industry average of 18.3% and a rate of 6.4% for J.C. Penney.

With Preferred Stock.   When a company has preferred stock, we must deduct **preferred dividend** requirements from net income to compute income available to common stockholders. Similarly, we deduct the par value of preferred stock (or call price, if applicable) from total stockholders' equity to determine the amount of common stockholders' equity used in this ratio. The ratio then appears as follows.

Illustration 18-21
Return on common stockholders' equity with preferred stock

$$\text{Return on Common Stockholders' Equity} = \frac{\text{Net Income} - \text{Preferred Dividends}}{\text{Average Common Stockholders' Equity}}$$

Note that Quality's rate of return on stockholders' equity (29.3%) is substantially higher than its rate of return on assets (15.4%). The reason is that Quality has made effective use of **leverage**. **Leveraging** or **trading on the equity** at a gain means that the company has borrowed money at a lower rate of interest than it is able to earn by using the borrowed money. Leverage enables Quality Department Store to use money supplied by nonowners to increase the return to the owners. A comparison of the rate of return on total assets with the rate of interest paid for borrowed money indicates the profitability of trading on the equity. Quality Department Store earns more on its borrowed funds than it has to pay in the form of interest. Thus, the return to stockholders exceeds the return on the assets, due to benefits from the positive leveraging.

9. EARNINGS PER SHARE (EPS)

Earnings per share (EPS) is a measure of the net income earned on each share of common stock. It is computed by dividing net income by the number of weighted-average common shares outstanding during the year. A measure of net income earned on a per share basis provides a useful perspective for determining profitability. Assuming that there is no change in the number of outstanding shares during 2008 and that the 2009 increase occurred midyear, Illustration 18-22 shows the net income per share for Quality Department Store for 2009 and 2008.

Illustration 18-22
Earnings per share

Note that no industry or J.C. Penney data are presented. Such comparisons are not meaningful because of the wide variations in the number of shares of outstanding stock among companies. The only meaningful EPS comparison is an intracompany trend comparison: Quality's earnings per share increased 20 cents per share in 2009. This represents a 26% increase over the 2008 earnings per share of 77 cents.

The terms "earnings per share" and "net income per share" refer to the amount of net income applicable to each share of **common stock**. Therefore, in computing EPS, if there are preferred dividends declared for the period, we must deduct them from net income to determine income available to the common stockholders.

10. PRICE-EARNINGS RATIO

The **price-earnings (P-E) ratio** is an oft-quoted measure of the ratio of the market price of each share of common stock to the earnings per share. The price-earnings (P-E) ratio reflects investors' assessments of a company's future earnings. We compute it by dividing the market price per share of the stock by earnings per share. Assuming that the market price of Quality Department Store Inc. stock is $8 in 2008 and $12 in 2009, the price-earnings ratio computation is as follows.

Illustration 18-23
Price-earnings ratio

In 2009, each share of Quality's stock sold for 12.4 times the amount that the company earned on each share. Quality's price-earnings ratio is lower than the industry average of 21.3 times, and also lower than the ratio of 17.2 times for J.C. Penney. The average price-earnings ratio for the stocks that constitute the Standard and Poor's 500 Index (500 largest U.S. firms) in early 2009 was approximately 19.1 times.

11. PAYOUT RATIO

The **payout ratio** measures the percentage of earnings distributed in the form of cash dividends. We compute it by dividing cash dividends by net income. Companies that have high growth rates generally have low payout ratios because they reinvest most of their net income into the business. The 2009 and 2008 payout ratios for Quality Department Store are computed as shown in Illustration 18-24.

Illustration 18-24
Payout ratio

$$\text{Payout Ratio} = \frac{\text{Cash Dividends}}{\text{Net Income}}$$

Quality Department Store

2009	2008
$\frac{\$61,200}{\$263,800} = 23.2\%$	$\frac{\$60,000}{\$208,500} = 28.8\%$
Industry average	J.C. Penney Company
16.1%	**63.0%**

Quality's payout ratio is higher than the industry average payout ratio of 16.1%. J.C. Penney's ratio is very high because its net income in 2009 was quite low.

Solvency Ratios

Solvency ratios measure the ability of a company to survive over a long period of time. Long-term creditors and stockholders are particularly interested in a company's ability to pay interest as it comes due and to repay the face value of debt at maturity. Debt to total assets and times interest earned are two ratios that provide information about debt-paying ability.

12. DEBT TO TOTAL ASSETS RATIO

The **debt to total assets ratio** measures the percentage of the total assets that creditors provide. We compute it by dividing total debt (both current and long-term liabilities) by total assets. This ratio indicates the company's degree of leverage. It also provides some indication of the company's ability to withstand losses without impairing the interests of creditors. The higher the percentage of debt to total assets, the greater the risk that the company may be unable to meet its maturing obligations. The 2009 and 2008 ratios for Quality Department Store and comparative data are as follows.

Illustration 18-25
Debt to total assets ratio

$$\text{Debt to Total Assets Ratio} = \frac{\text{Total Debt}}{\text{Total Assets}}$$

Quality Department Store

2009	2008
$\frac{\$832,000}{\$1,835,000} = 45.3\%$	$\frac{\$800,000}{\$1,595,000} = 50.2\%$
Industry average	J.C. Penney Company
34.2%	**62.0%**

A ratio of 45.3% means that creditors have provided 45.3% of Quality Department Store's total assets. Quality's 45.3% is above the industry average of 34.2%. It is considerably below the high 62.0% ratio of J.C. Penney. The lower the ratio, the more equity "buffer" there is available to the creditors. Thus, from the creditors' point of view, a low ratio of debt to total assets is usually desirable.

The adequacy of this ratio is often judged in the light of the company's earnings. Generally, companies with relatively stable earnings (such as public utilities) have higher debt to total assets ratios than cyclical companies with widely fluctuating earnings (such as many high-tech companies).

13. TIMES INTEREST EARNED

Times interest earned provides an indication of the company's ability to meet interest payments as they come due. We compute it by dividing income before interest expense and income taxes by interest expense. Illustration 18-26 shows the 2009 and 2008 ratios for Quality Department Store and comparative data. Note that times interest earned uses income before income taxes and interest expense. This represents the amount available to cover interest. For Quality Department Store, the 2009 amount of $468,000 is computed by taking the income before income taxes of $432,000 and adding back the $36,000 of interest expense.

Alternative Terminology

Times interest earned is also called *interest coverage*.

$$\text{Times Interest Earned} = \frac{\text{Income before Income Taxes and Interest Expense}}{\text{Interest Expense}}$$

Quality Department Store

2009	**2008**
$\dfrac{\$468,000}{\$36,000} = 13 \text{ times}$	$\dfrac{\$388,000}{\$40,500} = 9.6 \text{ times}$
Industry average	J.C. Penney Company
16.1 times	**2.9 times**

Illustration 18-26
Times interest earned

Quality's interest expense is well covered at 13 times, compared with the industry average of 16.1 times and J.C. Penney's 2.9 times.

Summary of Ratios

Illustration 18-27 summarizes the ratios discussed in this chapter. The summary includes the formula and purpose or use of each ratio.

Illustration 18-27
Summary of liquidity, profitability, and solvency ratios

Ratio	Formula	Purpose or Use
Liquidity Ratios		
1. Current ratio	$\dfrac{\text{Current assets}}{\text{Current liabilities}}$	Measures short-term debt-paying ability.
2. Acid-test (quick) ratio	$\dfrac{\text{Cash + Short-term investments + Receivables (net)}}{\text{Current liabilities}}$	Measures immediate short-term liquidity.
3. Receivables turnover	$\dfrac{\text{Net credit sales}}{\text{Average net receivables}}$	Measures liquidity of receivables.
4. Inventory turnover	$\dfrac{\text{Cost of goods sold}}{\text{Average inventory}}$	Measures liquidity of inventory.
Profitability Ratios		
5. Profit margin	$\dfrac{\text{Net income}}{\text{Net sales}}$	Measures net income generated by each dollar of sales.
6. Asset turnover	$\dfrac{\text{Net sales}}{\text{Average assets}}$	Measures how efficiently assets are used to generate sales.

Ratio	Formula	Purpose or Use
7. Return on assets	$\dfrac{\text{Net income}}{\text{Average assets}}$	Measures overall profitability of assets.
8. Return on common stockholders' equity	$\dfrac{\text{Net income} - \text{Preferred dividends}}{\text{Average common stockholders' equity}}$	Measures profitability of owners' investment.
9. Earnings per share (EPS)	$\dfrac{\text{Net income} - \text{Preferred dividends}}{\text{Weighted-average common shares outstanding}}$	Measures net income earned on each share of common stock.
10. Price-earnings (P-E) ratio	$\dfrac{\text{Market price per share of stock}}{\text{Earnings per share}}$	Measures the ratio of the market price per share to earnings per share.
11. Payout ratio	$\dfrac{\text{Cash dividends}}{\text{Net income}}$	Measures percentage of earnings distributed in the form of cash dividends.
Solvency Ratios		
12. Debt to total assets ratio	$\dfrac{\text{Total debt}}{\text{Total assets}}$	Measures the percentage of total assets provided by creditors.
13. Times interest earned	$\dfrac{\text{Income before income taxes and interest expense}}{\text{Interest expense}}$	Measures ability to meet interest payments as they come due.

Illustration 18-27
(continued)

Do it!

Ratio Analysis

The condensed financial statements of John Cully Company, for the years ended June 30, 2012 and 2011, are presented below.

John Cully Company
Balance Sheets
June 30

	(in thousands)	
Assets	**2012**	**2011**
Current assets		
Cash and cash equivalents	$ 553.3	$ 611.6
Accounts receivable (net)	776.6	664.9
Inventory	768.3	653.5
Prepaid expenses and other current assets	204.4	269.2
Total current assets	2,302.6	2,199.2
Property, plant, and equipment (net)	694.2	647.0
Investments	12.3	12.6
Intangibles and other assets	876.7	849.3
Total assets	$3,885.8	$3,708.1
Liabilities and Stockholders' Equity		
Current liabilities	$1,497.7	$1,322.0
Long-term liabilities	679.5	637.1
Stockholders' equity—common	1,708.6	1,749.0
Total liabilities and stockholders' equity	$3,885.8	$3,708.1

John Cully Company
Income Statements
For the Year Ended June 30

	(in thousands)	
	2012	**2011**
Sales revenue	$6,336.3	$5,790.4
Costs and expenses		
Cost of goods sold	1,617.4	1,476.3
Selling and administrative expenses	4,007.6	3,679.0
Interest expense	13.9	27.1
Total costs and expenses	5,638.9	5,182.4
Income before income taxes	697.4	608.0
Income tax expense	291.3	232.6
Net income	$ 406.1	$ 375.4

Compute the following ratios for 2012 and 2011.

(a) Current ratio.

(b) Inventory turnover. (Inventory on 6/30/10 was $599.0.)

(c) Profit margin ratio.

(d) Return on assets. (Assets on 6/30/10 were $3,349.9.)

(e) Return on common stockholders' equity. (Stockholders' equity on 6/30/10 was $1,795.9.)

(f) Debt to total assets ratio.

(g) Times interest earned.

Solution

	2012	2011
(a) Current ratio:		
$2,302.6 ÷ $1,497.7 =	1.5:1	
$2,199.2 ÷ $1,322.0 =		1.7:1
(b) Inventory turnover:		
$1,617.4 ÷ [($768.3 + $653.5) ÷ 2] =	2.3 times	
$1,476.3 ÷ [($653.5 + $599.0) ÷ 2] =		2.4 times
(c) Profit margin:		
$406.1 ÷ $6,336.3	6.4%	
$375.4 ÷ $5,790.4		6.5%
(d) Return on assets:		
$406.1 ÷ [($3,885.8 + $3,708.1) ÷ 2] =	10.7%	
$375.4 ÷ [($3,708.1 + $3,349.9) ÷ 2] =		10.6%
(e) Return on common stockholders' equity:		
$406.1 ÷ [($1,708.6 + $1,749.0) ÷ 2] =	23.5%	
$375.4 ÷ [($1,749.0 + $1,795.9) ÷ 2] =		21.2%
(f) Debt to total assets ratio:		
($1,497.7 + $679.5) ÷ $3,885.8 =	56.0%	
($1,322.0 + $637.1) ÷ $3,708.1 =		52.8%
(g) Times interest earned:		
($406.1 + $291.3 + $13.9) ÷ $13.9 =	51.2 times	
($375.4 + $232.6 + $27.1) ÷ $27.1 =		23.4 times

action plan

✔ Remember that the current ratio includes all current assets. The acid-test ratio uses only cash, short-term investments, and net receivables.

✔ Use average balances for turnover ratios like inventory, receivables, and assets.

Related exercise material: BE18-9, BE18-10, BE18-12, BE18-13, E18-5, E18-7, E18-8, E18-9, E18-11, and **Do it!** 18-2.

The Navigator

Earning Power and Irregular Items

Study Objective [6]
Understand the concept of earning power, and how irregular items are presented.

Users of financial statements are interested in the concept of earning power. **Earning power** means the normal level of income to be obtained in the future. Earning power differs from actual net income by the amount of irregular revenues, expenses, gains, and losses. Users are interested in earning power because it helps them derive an estimate of future earnings without the "noise" of irregular items.

For users of financial statements to determine earning power or regular income, the "irregular" items are separately identified on the income statement. Companies report two types of "irregular" items.

1. Discontinued operations.
2. Extraordinary items.

These "irregular" items are reported net of income taxes. That is, the income statement first reports income tax on the income before "irregular" items. Then the amount of tax for each of the listed "irregular" items is computed. The general concept is "let the tax follow income or loss."

Discontinued Operations

Discontinued operations refers to the disposal of a **significant component** of a business, such as the elimination of a major class of customers, or an entire activity. For example, to downsize its operations, General Dynamics Corp. sold its missile business to Hughes Aircraft Co. for $450 million. In its income statement, General Dynamics reported the sale in a separate section entitled "Discontinued operations."

Following the disposal of a significant component, the company should report on its income statement both income from continuing operations and income (or loss) from discontinued operations. **The income (loss) from discontinued operations consists of two parts: the income (loss) from operations** and **the gain (loss) on disposal of the segment**.

To illustrate, assume that during 2012 Acro Energy Inc. has income before income taxes of $800,000. During 2012, Acro discontinued and sold its unprofitable chemical division. The loss in 2012 from chemical operations (net of $60,000 taxes) was $140,000. The loss on disposal of the chemical division (net of $30,000 taxes) was $70,000. Assuming a 30% tax rate on income, Illustration 18-28 shows Acro's income statement presentation.

Illustration 18-28
Statement presentation of discontinued operations

Helpful Hint

Observe the dual disclosures: (1) The results of operations of the discontinued division must be eliminated from the results of continuing operations. (2) The company must also report the disposal of the operation.

Acro Energy Inc. Income Statement (partial) For the Year Ended December 31, 2012		
Income before income taxes		$800,000
Income tax expense		240,000
Income from continuing operations		560,000
Discontinued operations		
Loss from operations of chemical division, net of $60,000 income tax saving	$140,000	
Loss from disposal of chemical division, net of $30,000 income tax saving	70,000	210,000
Net income		$350,000

Note that the statement uses the caption "Income from continuing operations," and adds a new section "Discontinued operations." **The new section reports both**

the operating loss and the loss on disposal net of applicable income taxes. This presentation clearly indicates the separate effects of continuing operations and discontinued operations on net income.

Extraordinary Items

Extraordinary items are events and transactions that meet two conditions: They are (1) **unusual in nature,** and (2) **infrequent in occurrence**. To be *unusual*, the item should be abnormal and only incidentally related to the company's customary activities. To be *infrequent*, the item should not be reasonably expected to recur in the foreseeable future.

A company must evaluate both criteria in terms of its operating environment. Thus, Weyerhaeuser Co. reported the $36 million in damages to its timberland caused by the volcanic eruption of Mount St. Helens as an extraordinary item. The eruption was both unusual and infrequent. In contrast, Florida Citrus Company does not report frost damage to its citrus crop as an extraordinary item, because frost damage is not infrequent. Illustration 18-29 shows the classification of extraordinary and ordinary items.

<table>
<tr><th>Extraordinary items</th><th>Ordinary items</th></tr>
<tr>
<td>1. Effects of major natural casualties, if rare in the area. </td>
<td>1. Effects of major natural casualties, not uncommon in the area. </td>
</tr>
<tr>
<td>2. Expropriation (takeover) of property by a foreign government. 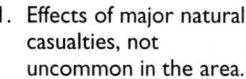</td>
<td>2. Write-down of inventories or write-off of receivables. 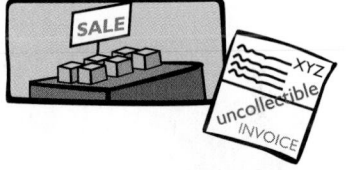</td>
</tr>
<tr>
<td>3. Effects of a newly enacted law or regulation, such as a property condemnation action. </td>
<td>3. Losses attributable to labor strikes. </td>
</tr>
<tr>
<td></td>
<td>4. Gains or losses from sales of property, plant, or equipment. </td>
</tr>
</table>

Illustration 18-29
Examples of extraordinary and ordinary items

Companies report extraordinary items net of taxes in a separate section of the income statement, immediately below discontinued operations. To illustrate, assume that in 2012 a foreign government expropriated property held as an investment by Acro Energy Inc. If the loss is $70,000 before applicable income taxes of $21,000, the income statement will report a deduction of $49,000, as shown in Illustration 18-30 (page 848). When there is an extraordinary item to report, the company adds the caption "Income before extraordinary item" immediately before the section for the extraordinary item. This presentation clearly indicates the effect of the extraordinary item on net income.

Illustration 18-30
Statement presentation of extraordinary items

Acro Energy Inc. Income Statement (partial) For the Year Ended December 31, 2012		
Income before income taxes		$800,000
Income tax expense		240,000
Income from continuing operations		560,000
Discontinued operations		
Loss from operations of chemical division,		
net of $60,000 income tax saving	$140,000	
Loss from disposal of chemical division,		
net of $30,000 income tax saving	70,000	210,000
Income before extraordinary item		350,000
Extraordinary item		
Expropriation of investment, net of		
$21,000 income tax saving		49,000
Net income		$301,000

Helpful Hint

If there are no discontinued operations, the third line of the income statement would be labeled "Income before extraordinary item."

What if a transaction or event meets one (but not both) of the criteria for an extraordinary item? In that case, the company reports it under either "Other revenues and gains" or "Other expenses and losses" at its gross amount (not net of tax). This is true, for example, of gains (losses) resulting from the sale of property, plant, and equipment, as explained in Chapter 10. It is quite common for companies to use the label "Non-recurring charges" for losses that do not meet the extraordinary item criteria.

_I_NVESTOR _I_NSIGHT

What Does "Non-Recurring" Really Mean?

Many companies incur restructuring charges as they attempt to reduce costs. They often label these items in the income statement as "non-recurring" charges to suggest that they are isolated events which are unlikely to occur in future periods. The question for analysts is, are these costs really one-time, "non-recurring" events, or do they reflect problems that the company will be facing for many periods in the future? If they are one-time events, they can be largely ignored when trying to predict future earnings.

But some companies report "one-time" restructuring charges over and over again. For example, toothpaste and other consumer-goods giant Procter & Gamble Co. reported a restructuring charge in 12 consecutive quarters. Motorola had "special" charges in 14-consecutive quarters. On the other hand, other companies have a restructuring charge only once in a five- or ten-year period. There appears to be no substitute for careful analysis of the numbers that comprise net income.

? If a company takes a large restructuring charge, what is the effect on the company's current income statement versus future ones? (See page 873.)

Changes in Accounting Principle

For ease of comparison, users of financial statements expect companies to prepare such statements on a basis **consistent** with the preceding period. A **change in accounting principle** occurs when the principle used in the current year is different from the one used in the preceding year. Accounting rules permit a change when management can show that the new principle is preferable to the old principle. An example is a change in inventory costing methods (such as FIFO to average cost).

Companies report most changes in accounting principle retroactively. That is, they report both the current period and previous periods using the new principle. As a result the same principle applies in all periods. This treatment improves the ability to compare results across years.

Comprehensive Income

> **Ethics Note**
>
> Changes in accounting principle should result in financial statements that are more informative for statement users. They should *not* be used to artificially improve the reported performance or financial position of the corporation.

The income statement reports most revenues, expenses, gains, and losses recognized during the period. However, over time, specific exceptions to this general practice have developed. Certain items now bypass income and are reported directly in stockholders' equity.

For example, in Chapter 16 you learned that companies do not include in income any unrealized gains and losses on available-for-sale securities. Instead, they report such gains and losses in the balance sheet as adjustments to stockholders' equity. Why are these gains and losses on available-for-sale securities excluded from net income? Because disclosing them separately (1) reduces the volatility of net income due to fluctuations in fair value, yet (2) informs the financial statement user of the gain or loss that would be incurred if the securities were sold at fair value.

Many analysts have expressed concern over the significant increase in the number of items that bypass the income statement. They feel that such reporting has reduced the usefulness of the income statement. To address this concern, in addition to reporting net income, a company must also report comprehensive income. Comprehensive income includes all changes in stockholders' equity during a period except those resulting from investments by stockholders and distributions to stockholders. A number of alternative formats for reporting comprehensive income are allowed. These formats are discussed in advanced accounting courses.

Do it!

In its proposed 2012 income statement, AIR Corporation reports income before income taxes $400,000, extraordinary loss due to earthquake $100,000, income taxes $120,000 (not including irregular items), loss on operation of discontinued flower division $50,000, and loss on disposal of discontinued flower division $90,000. The income tax rate is 30%. Prepare a correct income statement, beginning with "Income before income taxes."

Solution

Irregular Items

action plan

✔ Recall that a loss is extraordinary if it is both unusual and infrequent.

✔ Disclose the income tax effect of each component of income, beginning with income before any irregular items.

✔ Show discontinued operations before extraordinary items.

AIR CORPORATION
Income Statement (partial)
For the Year Ended December 31, 2012

Income before income taxes		$400,000
Income tax expense		120,000
Income from continuing operations		280,000
Discontinued operations		
Loss from operation of flower division, net of $15,000 tax saving	$35,000	
Loss on disposal of flower division, net of $27,000 tax saving	63,000	98,000
Income before extraordinary item		182,000
Extraordinary earthquake loss, net of $30,000 tax saving		70,000
Net income		$112,000

Related exercise material: BE18-14, BE18-15, E18-12, E18-13, and **Do it!** 18-3.

✔
The Navigator

Quality of Earnings

Study Objective [7]
Understand the concept of quality of earnings.

In evaluating the financial performance of a company, the quality of a company's earnings is of extreme importance to analysts. A company that has a high **quality of earnings** provides full and transparent information that will not confuse or mislead users of the financial statements.

The issue of quality of earnings has taken on increasing importance because recent accounting scandals suggest that some companies are spending too much time managing their income and not enough time managing their business. Here are some of the factors affecting quality of earnings.

Alternative Accounting Methods

Variations among companies in the application of generally accepted accounting principles may hamper comparability and reduce quality of earnings. For example, one company may use the FIFO method of inventory costing, while another company in the same industry may use LIFO. If inventory is a significant asset to both companies, it is unlikely that their current ratios are comparable. For example, if General Motors Corporation had used FIFO instead of LIFO for inventory valuation, its inventories in a recent year would have been 26% higher, which significantly affects the current ratio (and other ratios as well).

In addition to differences in inventory costing methods, differences also exist in reporting such items as depreciation, depletion, and amortization. Although these differences in accounting methods might be detectable from reading the notes to the financial statements, adjusting the financial data to compensate for the different methods is often difficult, if not impossible.

Pro Forma Income

Companies whose stock is publicly traded are required to present their income statement following generally accepted accounting principles (GAAP). In recent years, many companies have also reported a second measure of income, called pro forma income. **Pro forma income** usually excludes items that the company thinks are unusual or nonrecurring. For example, at one time, Cisco Systems (a high-tech company) reported a quarterly net loss under GAAP of $2.7 billion. Cisco reported pro forma income for the same quarter as a profit of $230 million. This large difference in profits between GAAP income numbers and pro forma income is not unusual these days. For example, during one 9-month period the 100 largest firms on the Nasdaq stock exchange reported a total pro forma income of $19.1 billion, but a total loss as measured by GAAP of $82.3 billion—a difference of about $100 billion!

To compute pro forma income, companies generally can exclude any items they deem inappropriate for measuring their performance. Many analysts and investors are critical of the practice of using pro forma income because these numbers often make companies look better than they really are. As the financial press noted, pro forma numbers might be called EBS, which stands for "earnings before bad stuff." Companies, on the other hand, argue that pro forma numbers more clearly indicate sustainable income because they exclude unusual and nonrecurring expenses. "Cisco's technique gives readers of financial statements a clear picture of Cisco's normal business activities," the company said in a statement issued in response to questions about its pro forma income accounting.

The SEC has provided some guidance on how companies should present pro forma information. Stay tuned: Everyone seems to agree that pro forma numbers can be useful if they provide insights into determining a company's sustainable income. However, many companies have abused the flexibility that pro forma numbers allow and have used the measure as a way to put their companies in a good light.

Improper Recognition

Because some managers have felt pressure from Wall Street to continually increase earnings, they have manipulated the earnings numbers to meet these expectations. The most common abuse is the improper recognition of revenue. One practice that companies are using is *channel stuffing*: Offering deep discounts on their products to customers, companies encourage their customers to buy early (stuff the channel) rather than later. This lets the company report good earnings in the current period, but it often leads to a disaster in subsequent periods because customers have no need for additional goods. To illustrate, Bristol-Myers Squibb at one time indicated that it used sales incentives to encourage wholesalers to buy more drugs than needed to meet patients' demands. As a result, the company had to issue revised financial statements showing corrected revenues and income.

Another practice is the improper capitalization of operating expenses. The classic case is WorldCom. It capitalized over $7 billion dollars of operating expenses so that it would report positive net income. In other situations, companies fail to report all their liabilities. Enron had promised to make payments on certain contracts if financial difficulty developed, but these guarantees were not reported as liabilities. In addition, disclosure was so lacking in transparency that it was impossible to understand what was happening at the company.

Do it!

Match each of the following terms with the phrase that it best matches.

Comprehensive income   Vertical analysis
Quality of earnings   Pro forma income
Solvency ratio   Extraordinary item

Quality of Earnings, Financial Statement Analysis

1. _____ Measures the ability of the company to survive over a long period of time.
2. _____ Usually excludes items that a company thinks are unusual or non-recurring.
3. _____ Includes all changes in stockholders' equity during a period except those resulting from investments by stockholders and distributions to stockholders.
4. _____ Indicates the level of full and transparent information provided to users of the financial statements.
5. _____ Describes events and transactions that are unusual in nature and infrequent in occurrence.
6. _____ Expresses each item within a financial statement as a percent of a base amount.

action plan
✔ Develop a sound understanding of basic methods used for financial reporting.
✔ Understand the use of fundamental analysis techniques.

Solution

1. Solvency ratio: Measures the ability of the company to survive over a long period of time.
2. Pro forma income: Usually excludes items that a company thinks are unusual or non-recurring.
3. Comprehensive income: Includes all changes in stockholders' equity during a period except those resulting from investments by stockholders and distributions to stockholders.
4. Quality of earnings: Indicates the level of full and transparent information provided to users of the financial statements.

5. Extraordinary item: Describes events and transactions that are unusual in nature and infrequent in occurrence.

6. Vertical analysis: Expresses each item within a financial statement as a percent of a base amount.

Related exercise material: **Do it!** 18-4.

COMPREHENSIVE
Do it!

The events and transactions of Dever Corporation for the year ending December 31, 2012, resulted in the following data.

Cost of goods sold	$2,600,000
Net sales	4,400,000
Other expenses and losses	9,600
Other revenues and gains	5,600
Selling and administrative expenses	1,100,000
Income from operations of plastics division	70,000
Gain from disposal of plastics division	500,000
Loss from tornado disaster (extraordinary loss)	600,000

Analysis reveals that:

1. All items are before the applicable income tax rate of 30%.
2. The plastics division was sold on July 1.
3. All operating data for the plastics division have been segregated.

Instructions

Prepare an income statement for the year.

action plan

✔ Report material items not typical of continuing operations in separate sections, net of taxes.

✔ Associate income taxes with the item that affects the taxes.

✔ Apply the corporate tax rate to income before income taxes to determine tax expense.

✔ Recall that all data presented in determining income before income taxes are the same as for unincorporated companies.

Solution to Comprehensive Do it!

DEVER CORPORATION
Income Statement
For the Year Ended December 31, 2012

Net sales		$4,400,000
Cost of goods sold		2,600,000
Gross profit		1,800,000
Selling and administrative expenses		1,100,000
Income from operations		700,000
Other revenues and gains	$ 5,600	
Other expenses and losses	9,600	4,000
Income before income taxes		696,000
Income tax expense ($696,000 × 30%)		208,800
Income from continuing operations		487,200
Discontinued operations		
Income from operations of plastics division, net of		
$21,000 income taxes ($70,000 × 30%)	49,000	
Gain from disposal of plastics division, net of $150,000		
income taxes ($500,000 × 30%)	350,000	399,000
Income before extraordinary item		886,200
Extraordinary item		
Tornado loss, net of $180,000 income tax saving		
($600,000 × 30%)		420,000
Net income		$ 466,200

Summary of Study Objectives

[1] Discuss the need for comparative analysis. There are three bases of comparison: (1) Intracompany, which compares an item or financial relationship with other data within a company. (2) Industry, which compares company data with industry averages. (3) Intercompany, which compares an item or financial relationship of a company with data of one or more competing companies.

[2] Identify the tools of financial statement analysis. Financial statements can be analyzed horizontally, vertically, and with ratios.

[3] Explain and apply horizontal analysis. Horizontal analysis is a technique for evaluating a series of data over a period of time to determine the increase or decrease that has taken place, expressed as either an amount or a percentage.

[4] Describe and apply vertical analysis. Vertical analysis is a technique that expresses each item within a financial statement in terms of a percentage of a relevant total or a base amount.

[5] Identify and compute ratios used in analyzing a firm's liquidity, profitability, and solvency. The formula and purpose of each ratio was presented in Illustration 18-27 (page 843).

[6] Understand the concept of earning power, and how irregular items are presented. Earning power refers to a company's ability to sustain its profits from operations. "Irregular items"—discontinued operations and extraordinary items—are presented net of tax below income from continuing operations to highlight their unusual nature.

[7] Understand the concept of quality of earnings. A high quality of earnings provides full and transparent information that will not confuse or mislead users of the financial statements. Issues related to quality of earnings are (1) alternative accounting methods, (2) pro forma income, and (3) improper recognition.

The Navigator

Glossary

Acid-test (quick) ratio A measure of a company's immediate short-term liquidity; computed by dividing the sum of cash, short-term investments, and net receivables by current liabilities. (p. 835).

Asset turnover A measure of how efficiently a company uses its assets to generate sales; computed by dividing net sales by average assets. (p. 839).

Change in accounting principle The use of a principle in the current year that is different from the one used in the preceding year. (p. 848).

Comprehensive income Includes all changes in stockholders' equity during a period except those resulting from investments by stockholders and distributions to stockholders. (p. 849).

Current ratio A measure used to evaluate a company's liquidity and short-term debt-paying ability; computed by dividing current assets by current liabilities. (p. 835).

Debt to total assets ratio Measures the percentage of total assets provided by creditors; computed by dividing total debt by total assets. (p. 842).

Discontinued operations The disposal of a significant segment of a business. (p. 846).

Earnings per share (EPS) The net income earned on each share of common stock; computed by dividing net income minus preferred dividends (if any) by the number of weighted-average common shares outstanding. (p. 841).

Extraordinary items Events and transactions that are unusual in nature and infrequent in occurrence. (p. 847).

Horizontal analysis A technique for evaluating a series of financial statement data over a period of time, to determine the increase (decrease) that has taken place, expressed as either an amount or a percentage. (p. 827).

Inventory turnover A measure of the liquidity of inventory; computed by dividing cost of goods sold by average inventory. (p. 837).

Leveraging See *Trading on the equity*. (p. 840).

Liquidity ratios Measures of the short-term ability of the company to pay its maturing obligations and to meet unexpected needs for cash. (p. 835).

Payout ratio Measures the percentage of earnings distributed in the form of cash dividends; computed by dividing cash dividends by net income. (p. 842).

Price-earnings (P-E) ratio Measures the ratio of the market price of each share of common stock to the earnings per share; computed by dividing the market price of the stock by earnings per share. (p. 841).

Profit margin Measures the percentage of each dollar of sales that results in net income; computed by dividing net income by net sales. (p. 838).

Profitability ratios Measures of the income or operating success of a company for a given period of time. (p. 838).

Pro forma income A measure of income that usually excludes items that a company thinks are unusual or nonrecurring. (p. 850).

Quality of earnings Indicates the level of full and transparent information provided to users of the financial statements. (p. 850).

Ratio An expression of the mathematical relationship between one quantity and another. The relationship may be expressed either as a percentage, a rate, or a simple proportion. (p. 833).

Ratio analysis A technique for evaluating financial statements that expresses the relationship between selected financial statement data. (p. 833).

Receivables turnover A measure of the liquidity of receivables; computed by dividing net credit sales by average net receivables. (p. 837).

Return on assets An overall measure of profitability; computed by dividing net income by average assets. (p. 839).

Return on common stockholders' equity Measures the dollars of net income earned for each dollar invested by the owners; computed by dividing net income minus preferred dividends (if any) by average common stock-holders' equity. (p. 840).

Solvency ratios Measures of the ability of the company to survive over a long period of time. (p. 842).

Times interest earned Measures a company's ability to meet interest payments as they come due; computed by dividing income before interest expense and income taxes by interest expense. (p. 843).

Trading on the equity Borrowing money at a lower rate of interest than can be earned by using the borrowed money. (p. 840).

Vertical analysis A technique for evaluating financial statement data that expresses each item within a financial statement as a percent of a base amount. (p. 831).

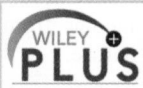 **Self-Test, Brief Exercises, Exercises, Problem Set A, and many more components are available for practice in *WileyPLUS***

Self-Test Questions

Answers are on page 873.

(SO 1) **1.** Comparisons of data within a company are an example of the following comparative basis:
 a. Industry averages.
 b. Intracompany.
 c. Intercompany.
 d. Both (b) and (c).

(SO 3) **2.** In horizontal analysis, each item is expressed as a percent-age of the:
 a. net income amount.
 b. stockholders' equity amount.
 c. total assets amount.
 d. base year amount.

(SO 4) **3.** In vertical analysis, the base amount for depreciation expense is generally:
 a. net sales.
 b. depreciation expense in a previous year.
 c. gross profit.
 d. fixed assets.

(SO 4) **4.** The following schedule is a display of what type of analysis?

	Amount	Percent
Current assets	$200,000	25%
Property, plant, and equipment	600,000	75%
Total assets	$800,000	

 a. Horizontal analysis.   **c.** Vertical analysis.
 b. Differential analysis.   **d.** Ratio analysis.

(SO 3) **5.** Sammy Corporation reported net sales of $300,000, $330,000, and $360,000 in the years, 2010, 2011, and 2012, respectively. If 2010 is the base year, what is the trend per-centage for 2012?
 a. 77%.   **c.** 120%.
 b. 108%.   **d.** 130%.

(SO 5) **6.** Which of the following measures is an evaluation of a firm's ability to pay current liabilities?
 a. Acid-test ratio.   **c.** Both (a) and (b).
 b. Current ratio.   **d.** None of the above.

7. A measure useful in evaluating the efficiency in managing (SO 5) inventories is:
 a. inventory turnover.
 b. average days to sell inventory.
 c. Both (a) and (b).
 d. None of the above.

Use the following financial statement information as of the end of each year to answer Self-Test Questions 8–12.

	2012	2011
Inventory	$ 54,000	$ 48,000
Current assets	81,000	106,000
Total assets	382,000	326,000
Current liabilities	27,000	36,000
Total liabilities	102,000	88,000
Preferred stock	40,000	40,000
Common stockholders' equity	240,000	198,000
Net sales	784,000	697,000
Cost of goods sold	306,000	277,000
Net income	134,000	90,000
Tax expense	22,000	18,000
Interest expense	12,000	12,000
Dividends paid to preferred stockholders	4,000	4,000
Dividends paid to common stockholders	15,000	10,000

8. Compute the days in inventory for 2012.   (SO 5)
 a. 64.4 days.   **c.** 6 days.
 b. 60.8 days.   **d.** 24 days.

9. Compute the current ratio for 2012.   (SO 5)
 a. 1.26:1.   **c.** .80:1.
 b. 3.0:1.   **d.** 3.75:1.

10. Compute the profit margin ratio for 2012.   (SO 5)
 a. 17.1%.   **c.** 37.9%.
 b. 18.1%.   **d.** 5.9%.

11. Compute the return on common stockholders' equity for (SO 5) 2012.
 a. 47.9%.   **c.** 61.2%.
 b. 51.7%.   **d.** 59.4%.

(SO 5) **12.** Compute the times interest earned for 2012.
    a. 11.2 times.   **c.** 14.0 times.
    b. 65.3 times.   **d.** 13.0 times.

(SO 6) **13.** In reporting discontinued operations, the income statement should show in a special section:
    a. gains and losses on the disposal of the discontinued segment.
    b. gains and losses from operations of the discontinued segment.
    c. Both (a) and (b).
    d. Neither (a) nor (b).

(SO 6) **14.** Scout Corporation has income before taxes of $400,000 and an extraordinary loss of $100,000. If the income tax rate is 25% on all items, the income statement should show income before extraordinary items and extraordinary items, respectively, of:

    a. $325,000 and $100,000.
    b. $325,000 and $75,000.
    c. $300,000 and $100,000
    d. $300,000 and $75,000.

15. Which situation below might indicate a company has a (SO 7) low quality of earnings?
    a. The same accounting principles are used each year.
    b. Revenue is recognized when earned.
    c. Maintenance costs are expensed as incurred.
    d. The company is continually reporting pro forma income numbers.

Go to the book's companion website, **www.wiley.com/college/weygandt**, for additional Self-Test Questions.

Questions

1. (a) Juan Marichal believes that the analysis of financial statements is directed at two characteristics of a company: liquidity and profitability. Is Juan correct? Explain.
    (b) Are short-term creditors, long-term creditors, and stockholders interested primarily in the same characteristics of a company? Explain.

2. (a) Distinguish among the following bases of comparison: (1) intracompany, (2) industry averages, and (3) intercompany.
    (b) Give the principal value of using each of the three bases of comparison.

3. Two popular methods of financial statement analysis are horizontal analysis and vertical analysis. Explain the difference between these two methods.

4. (a) If Leonard Company had net income of $360,000 in 2012 and it experienced a 24.5% increase in net income for 2013, what is its net income for 2013?
    (b) If six cents of every dollar of Leonard revenue is net income in 2012, what is the dollar amount of 2012 revenue?

5. What is a ratio? What are the different ways of expressing the relationship of two amounts? What information does a ratio provide?

6. Name the major ratios useful in assessing (a) liquidity and (b) solvency.

7. Raphael Ochoa is puzzled. His company had a profit margin of 10% in 2012. He feels that this is an indication that the company is doing well. Cindy Lore, his accountant, says that more information is needed to determine the firm's financial well-being. Who is correct? Why?

8. What do the following classes of ratios measure? (a) Liquidity ratios. (b) Profitability ratios. (c) Solvency ratios.

9. What is the difference between the current ratio and the acid-test ratio?

10. Donte Company, a retail store, has a receivables turnover of 4.5 times. The industry average is 12.5 times. Does Donte have a collection problem with its receivables?

11. Which ratios should be used to help answer the following questions?
    (a) How efficient is a company in using its assets to produce sales?
    (b) How near to sale is the inventory on hand?
    (c) How many dollars of net income were earned for each dollar invested by the owners?
    (d) How able is a company to meet interest charges as they fall due?

12. The price-earnings ratio of General Motors (automobile builder) was 8, and the price-earnings ratio of Microsoft (computer software) was 38. Which company did the stock market favor? Explain.

13. What is the formula for computing the payout ratio? Would you expect this ratio to be high or low for a growth company?

14. Holding all other factors constant, indicate whether each of the following changes generally signals good or bad news about a company.
    (a) Increase in profit margin.
    (b) Decrease in inventory turnover.
    (c) Increase in the current ratio.
    (d) Decrease in earnings per share.
    (e) Increase in price-earnings ratio.
    (f) Increase in debt to total assets ratio.
    (g) Decrease in times interest earned.

15. The return on assets for Tresh Corporation is 7.6%. During the same year, Tresh's return on common stockholders' equity is 12.8%. What is the explanation for the difference in the two rates?

16. Which two ratios do you think should be of greatest interest to:
    (a) A pension fund considering the purchase of 20-year bonds?
    (b) A bank contemplating a short-term loan?
    (c) A common stockholder?

17. Why must preferred stock dividends be subtracted from net income in computing earnings per share?

18. (a) What is meant by trading on the equity?
    (b) How would you determine the profitability of trading on the equity?

19. Hillman Inc. has net income of $160,000, weighted-average shares of common stock outstanding of 50,000, and preferred dividends for the period of $40,000. What is Hillman's earnings per share of common stock? Kate Hillman, the president of Hillman Inc., believes the computed EPS of the company is high. Comment.

20. Why is it important to report discontinued operations separately from income from continuing operations?

21. You are considering investing in Shawnee Transportation. The company reports 2012 earnings per share of $6.50 on income before extraordinary items and $4.75 on net income. Which EPS figure would you consider more relevant to your investment decision? Why?

22. STL Inc. reported 2011 earnings per share of $3.20 and had no extraordinary items. In 2012, EPS on income before extraordinary items was $2.99, and EPS on net income was $3.49. Is this a favorable trend?

23. Indicate which of the following items would be reported as an extraordinary item in Mordica Corporation's income statement.
    (a) Loss from damages caused by volcano eruption.
    (b) Loss from sale of temporary investments.
    (c) Loss attributable to a labor strike.
    (d) Loss caused when manufacture of a product was prohibited by the Food and Drug Administration.
    (e) Loss from flood damage. (The nearby Black River floods every 2 to 3 years.)
    (f) Write-down of obsolete inventory.
    (g) Expropriation of a factory by a foreign government.

24. Identify and explain factors that affect quality of earnings.

25. 🌐 **PEPSICO** Identify the specific sections in PepsiCo's 2009 annual report where horizontal and vertical analyses of financial data are presented.

Brief Exercises

Follow the rounding procedures used in the chapter.

Discuss need for comparative analysis.
(SO 1)

BE18-1 You recently received a letter from your Uncle Jimbo. A portion of the letter is presented below.

You know that I have a significant amount of money I saved over the years. I am thinking about starting an investment program. I want to do the investing myself, based on my own research and analysis of financial statements. I know that you are studying accounting, so I have a couple of questions for you. I have heard that different users of financial statements are interested in different characteristics of companies. Is this true, and, if so, why? Also, some of my friends, who are already investing, have told me that comparisons involving a company's financial data can be made on a number of different bases. Can you explain these bases to me?

Instructions

➤ Write a letter to your Uncle Jimbo which answers his questions.

Identify and use tools of financial statement analysis.
(SO 2, 3, 4, 5)

BE18-2 Abigail Naismith Corporation reported the following amounts in 2011, 2012, and 2013.

	2011	**2012**	**2013**
Current assets	$200,000	$230,000	$240,000
Current liabilities	$160,000	$168,000	$184,000
Total assets	$500,000	$600,000	$620,000

Instructions

(a) Identify and describe the three tools of financial statement analysis. (b) Perform each of the three types of analysis on Abigail Naismith's current assets.

Prepare horizontal analysis.
(SO 3)

BE18-3 Using the following data from the comparative balance sheet of Doabe Company, illustrate horizontal analysis.

	December 31, 2013	**December 31, 2012**
Accounts receivable	$ 520,000	$ 400,000
Inventory	$ 840,000	$ 600,000
Total assets	$3,000,000	$2,500,000

Prepare vertical analysis.
(SO 4)

BE18-4 Using the same data presented above in BE18-3 for Doabe Company, illustrate vertical analysis.

Calculate percentage of change.
(SO 3)

BE18-5 Net income was $500,000 in 2011, $450,000 in 2012, and $522,000 in 2013. What is the percentage of change from (a) 2011 to 2012 and (b) 2012 to 2013? Is the change an increase or a decrease?

Calculate net income.
(SO 3)

BE18-6 If Vansittart Company had net income of $585,000 in 2013 and it experienced a 30% increase in net income over 2012, what was its 2012 net income?

BE18-7 Horizontal analysis (trend analysis) percentages for Algy Company's sales, cost of goods sold, and expenses are shown below.

Calculate change in net income.
(SO 3)

Horizontal Analysis	2013	2012	2011
Sales	96.2	106.8	100.0
Cost of goods sold	102.0	97.0	100.0
Expenses	109.6	98.4	100.0

Did Algy's net income increase, decrease, or remain unchanged over the 3-year period?

BE18-8 Vertical analysis (common size) percentages for Fagbenle Company's sales, cost of goods sold, and expenses are shown below.

Calculate change in net income.
(SO 4)

Vertical Analysis	2013	2012	2011
Sales	100.0	100.0	100.0
Cost of goods sold	59.2	62.4	64.5
Expenses	25.0	25.6	27.5

Did Fagbenle's net income as a percent of sales increase, decrease, or remain unchanged over the 3-year period? Provide numerical support for your answer.

BE18-9 Selected condensed data taken from a recent balance sheet of Evangelista Inc. are as follows.

Calculate liquidity ratios.
(SO 5)

EVANGELISTA INC.
Balance Sheet (partial)

Cash	$ 8,041,000
Short-term investments	4,947,000
Accounts receivable	12,545,000
Inventory	14,814,000
Other current assets	5,571,000
Total current assets	$45,918,000
Total current liabilities	$40,644,000

What are the (a) working capital, (b) current ratio, and (c) acid-test ratio?

BE18-10 Constantine Corporation has net income of $11.44 million and net revenue of $80 million in 2012. Its assets are $14 million at the beginning of the year and $18 million at the end of the year. What are Constantine's (a) asset turnover and (b) profit margin?

Calculate profitability ratios.
(SO 5)

BE18-11 The following data are taken from the financial statements of Morganstern Company.

Evaluate collection of accounts receivable.
(SO 5)

	2013	2012
Accounts receivable (net), end of year	$ 550,000	$ 520,000
Net sales on account	3,960,000	3,100,000
Terms for all sales are 1/10, n/60.		

(a) Compute for each year (1) the receivables turnover and (2) the average collection period. At the end of 2011, accounts receivable (net) was $480,000.

(b) ▬▬▬ What conclusions about the management of accounts receivable can be drawn from these data?

BE18-12 The following data are from the income statements of Davros Company.

Evaluate management of inventory.
(SO 5)

	2013	2012
Sales	$6,420,000	$6,240,000
Beginning inventory	980,000	860,000
Purchases	4,340,000	4,661,000
Ending inventory	1,020,000	980,000

(a) Compute for each year (1) the inventory turnover and (2) the average days to sell the inventory.

(b) ▬▬▬ What conclusions concerning the management of the inventory can be drawn from these data?

BE18-13 Boe Company has owners' equity of $400,000 and net income of $66,000. It has a payout ratio of 20% and a rate of return on assets of 15%. How much did Boe pay in cash dividends, and what were its average assets?

Calculate profitability ratios.
(SO 5)

Prepare income statement including extraordinary items.
(SO 6)

BE18-14 An inexperienced accountant for Nerys Corporation showed the following in the income statement: income before income taxes and extraordinary item $400,000, and extraordinary loss from flood (before taxes) $70,000. The extraordinary loss and taxable income are both subject to a 30% tax rate. Prepare a correct income statement.

Prepare discontinued operations section of income statement.
(SO 6)

BE18-15 On June 30, Malohkeh Corporation discontinued its operations in Europe. During the year, the operating loss was $300,000 before taxes. On September 1, Malohkeh disposed of its European facilities at a pretax loss of $120,000. The applicable tax rate is 30%. Show the discontinued operations section of the income statement.

Do it! Review

Prepare horizontal analysis.
(SO 3)

Do it! 18-1 Summary financial information for Talulah Company is as follows.

	December 31, 2013	December 31, 2012
Current assets	$ 199,000	$ 220,000
Plant assets	821,000	780,000
Total assets	$1,020,000	$1,000,000

Compute the amount and percentage changes in 2013 using horizontal analysis, assuming 2012 is the base year.

Compute ratios.
(SO 5)

Do it! 18-2 The condensed financial statements of Ifeachor Company for the years 2011 and 2012 are presented below.

IFEACHOR COMPANY
Balance Sheets
December 31

	2012	2011
Current assets		
Cash and cash equivalents	$ 330	$ 360
Accounts receivable (net)	470	400
Inventory	460	390
Prepaid expenses	120	160
Total current assets	1,380	1,310
Property, plant, and equipment	420	380
Investments	10	10
Intangibles and other assets	530	510
Total assets	$2,340	$2,210
Current liabilities	$ 900	$ 790
Long-term liabilities	410	380
Stockholders' equity—common	1,030	1,040
Total liabilities and stockholders' equity	$2,340	$2,210

IFEACHOR COMPANY
Income Statements
For the Years Ended December 31

	2012	2011
Sales revenue	$3,800	$3,460
Costs and expenses		
Cost of goods sold	970	890
Selling & administrative expenses	2,400	2,330
Interest expense	10	20
Total costs and expenses	3,380	3,240
Income before income taxes	420	220
Income tax expense	168	132
Net income	$ 252	$ 88

Compute the following ratios for 2012 and 2011.
(a) Current ratio.
(b) Inventory turnover. (Inventory on 12/31/10 was $340.)
(c) Profit margin ratio.
(d) Return on assets. (Assets on 12/31/10 were $1,900.)
(e) Return on common stockholders' equity. (Equity on 12/31/10 was $900.)
(f) Debt to total assets ratio.
(g) Times interest earned.

Do it! 18-3 In its proposed 2012 income statement, DuToit Corporation reports income before income taxes $500,000, extraordinary loss due to earthquake $150,000, income taxes $200,000 (not including irregular items), loss on operation of discontinued music division $60,000, and gain on disposal of discontinued music division $40,000. The income tax rate is 40%. Prepare a correct income statement, beginning with income before income taxes.

Prepare income statement, including irregular items.
(SO 6)

Do it! 18-4 Match each of the following terms with the phrase that it best matches.

Match terms relating to quality of earnings and financial statement analysis.
(SO 3, 4, 5, 6, 7)

Quality of earnings	Pro forma income
Current ratio	Discontinued operations
Horizontal analysis	Comprehensive income

1. _____ A measure used to evaluate a company's liquidity.
2. _____ Usually excludes items that a company thinks are unusual or nonrecurring.
3. _____ Indicates the level of full and transparent information provided to users of the financial statements.
4. _____ The disposal of a significant segment of a business.
5. _____ Determines increases or decreases in a series of financial statement data.
6. _____ Includes all changes in stockholders' equity during a period except those resulting from investments by stockholders and distributions to stockholders.

Exercises

Follow the rounding procedures used in the chapter.

E18-1 Financial information for Sinead Inc. is presented below.

Prepare horizontal analysis.
(SO 3)

	December 31, 2013	December 31, 2012
Current assets	$125,000	$100,000
Plant assets (net)	396,000	330,000
Current liabilities	91,000	70,000
Long-term liabilities	133,000	95,000
Common stock, $1 par	161,000	115,000
Retained earnings	136,000	150,000

Instructions
Prepare a schedule showing a horizontal analysis for 2013 using 2012 as the base year.

E18-2 Operating data for Krystal Corporation are presented below.

Prepare vertical analysis.
(SO 4)

	2013	2012
Net sales	$750,000	$600,000
Cost of goods sold	465,000	390,000
Selling expenses	120,000	72,000
Administrative expenses	60,000	54,000
Income tax expense	33,000	24,000
Net income	72,000	60,000

Instructions
Prepare a schedule showing a vertical analysis for 2013 and 2012.

Prepare horizontal and vertical analyses.
(SO 3, 4)

E18-3   The comparative condensed balance sheets of Monero Corporation are presented below.

MONERO CORPORATION
Comparative Condensed Balance Sheets
December 31

	2013	2012
Assets		
Current assets	$ 74,000	$ 80,000
Property, plant, and equipment (net)	99,000	90,000
Intangibles	27,000	40,000
Total assets	$200,000	$210,000
Liabilities and stockholders' equity		
Current liabilities	$ 42,000	$ 48,000
Long-term liabilities	143,000	150,000
Stockholders' equity	15,000	12,000
Total liabilities and stockholders' equity	$200,000	$210,000

Instructions
(a) Prepare a horizontal analysis of the balance sheet data for Monero Corporation using 2012 as a base.
(b) Prepare a vertical analysis of the balance sheet data for Monero Corporation in columnar form for 2013.

Prepare horizontal and vertical analyses.
(SO 3, 4)

E18-4   The comparative condensed income statements of Indra Corporation are shown below.

INDRA CORPORATION
Comparative Condensed Income Statements
For the Years Ended December 31

	2013	2012
Net sales	$600,000	$500,000
Cost of goods sold	483,000	420,000
Gross profit	117,000	80,000
Operating expenses	57,200	44,000
Net income	$ 59,800	$ 36,000

Instructions
(a) Prepare a horizontal analysis of the income statement data for Indra Corporation using 2012 as a base. (Show the amounts of increase or decrease.)
(b) Prepare a vertical analysis of the income statement data for Indra Corporation in columnar form for both years.

Compute liquidity ratios and compare results.
(SO 5)

E18-5   Nordstrom, Inc. operates department stores in numerous states. Selected financial statement data for the year ending January 30, 2010, are shown below.

Nordstrom, Inc. Balance Sheet (partial)		
(in millions)	**End-of-Year**	**Beginning-of-Year**
Cash and cash equivalents	$ 795	$ 72
Accounts receivable (net)	2,035	1,942
Merchandise inventory	898	900
Prepaid expenses	88	93
Other current assets	238	210
Total current assets	$4,054	$3,217
Total current liabilities	$2,014	$1,601

For the year, net sales were $8,258 and cost of goods sold was $5,328 (in millions).

Instructions

(a) Compute the four liquidity ratios at the end of the year.

(b) Using the data in the chapter, compare Nordstrom's liquidity with (1) that of J.C. Penney Company, and (2) the industry averages for department stores.

E18-6 Ganesh Incorporated had the following transactions occur involving current assets and current liabilities during February 2012.

Perform current and acid-test ratio analysis.

(SO 5)

Feb. 3 Accounts receivable of $15,000 are collected.
7 Equipment is purchased for $28,000 cash.
11 Paid $3,000 for a 3-year insurance policy.
14 Accounts payable of $12,000 are paid.
18 Cash dividends of $5,000 are declared.

Additional information:

1. As of February 1, 2012, current assets were $130,000, and current liabilities were $50,000.

2. As of February 1, 2012, current assets included $15,000 of inventory and $2,000 of prepaid expenses.

Instructions

(a) Compute the current ratio as of the beginning of the month and after each transaction.

(b) Compute the acid-test ratio as of the beginning of the month and after each transaction.

E18-7 Bella Company has the following comparative balance sheet data.

Compute selected ratios.

(SO 5)

BELLA COMPANY
Balance Sheets
December 31

	2013	**2012**
Cash	$ 15,000	$ 30,000
Receivables (net)	70,000	60,000
Inventory	60,000	50,000
Plant assets (net)	200,000	180,000
	$345,000	$320,000
Accounts payable	$50,000	$60,000
Mortgage payable (15%)	100,000	100,000
Common stock, $10 par	140,000	120,000
Retained earnings	55,000	40,000
	$345,000	$320,000

Additional information for 2013:

1. Net income was $25,000.

2. Sales on account were $410,000. Sales returns and allowances were $20,000.

3. Cost of goods sold was $198,000.

Instructions

Compute the following ratios at December 31, 2013.

(a) Current.

(b) Acid-test.

(c) Receivables turnover.

(d) Inventory turnover.

E18-8 Selected comparative statement data for Navin Products Company are presented on the next page. All balance sheet data are as of December 31.

Compute selected ratios.

(SO 5)

	2013	2012
Net sales	$760,000	$720,000
Cost of goods sold	480,000	440,000
Interest expense	7,000	5,000
Net income	50,000	42,000
Accounts receivable	120,000	100,000
Inventory	85,000	75,000
Total assets	580,000	500,000
Total common stockholders' equity	430,000	325,000

Instructions

Compute the following ratios for 2013.

(a) Profit margin.

(b) Asset turnover.

(c) Return on assets.

(d) Return on common stockholders' equity.

Compute selected ratios.
(SO 5)

E18-9   The income statement for Mary Hatch, Inc., appears below.

MARY HATCH, INC.
Income Statement
For the Year Ended December 31, 2012

Net sales	$400,000
Cost of goods sold	230,000
Gross profit	170,000
Expenses (including $16,000 interest and $24,000 income taxes)	105,000
Net income	$ 65,000

Additional information:

1. The weighted-average common shares outstanding in 2012 were 30,000 shares.

2. The market price of Mary Hatch, Inc. stock was $13 in 2012.

3. Cash dividends of $26,000 were paid, $5,000 of which were to preferred stockholders.

Instructions

Compute the following ratios for 2012.

(a) Earnings per share.

(b) Price-earnings.

(c) Payout.

(d) Times interest earned.

Compute amounts from ratios.
(SO 5)

E18-10   George Bailey Corporation experienced a fire on December 31, 2013, in which its financial records were partially destroyed. It has been able to salvage some of the records and has ascertained the following balances.

	December 31, 2013	December 31, 2012
Cash	$ 30,000	$ 10,000
Receivables (net)	72,500	126,000
Inventory	200,000	180,000
Accounts payable	50,000	90,000
Notes payable	30,000	60,000
Common stock, $100 par	400,000	400,000
Retained earnings	113,500	101,000

Additional information:

1. The inventory turnover is 3.5 times.

2. The return on common stockholders' equity is 24%. The company had no additional paid-in capital.

3. The receivables turnover is 8.8 times.

4. The return on assets is 20%.

5. Total assets at December 31, 2012, were $605,000.

Instructions

Compute the following for George Bailey Corporation.

(a) Cost of goods sold for 2013.

(b) Net sales (credit) for 2013.

(c) Net income for 2013.

(d) Total assets at December 31, 2013.

E18-11 Stewart Corporation's comparative balance sheets are presented below.

Compute ratios.
(SO 5)

STEWART CORPORATION
Balance Sheets
December 31

	2012	2011
Cash	$ 4,300	$ 3,700
Accounts receivable	21,200	23,400
Inventory	10,000	7,000
Land	20,000	26,000
Buildings	70,000	70,000
Accumulated depreciation—buildings	(15,000)	(10,000)
Total	$110,500	$120,100
Accounts payable	$ 12,370	$ 31,100
Common stock	75,000	69,000
Retained earnings	23,130	20,000
Total	$110,500	$120,100

Stewart's 2012 income statement included net sales of $100,000, cost of goods sold of $60,000, and net income of $15,000.

Instructions

Compute the following ratios for 2012.

(a) Current ratio.

(b) Acid-test ratio.

(c) Receivables turnover.

(d) Inventory turnover.

(e) Profit margin.

(f) Asset turnover.

(g) Return on assets.

(h) Return on common stockholders' equity.

(i) Debt to total assets ratio.

E18-12 For its fiscal year ending October 31, 2012, Reed Corporation reports the following partial data shown below.

Prepare a correct income statement.
(SO 6)

Income before income taxes	$540,000
Income tax expense (30% × $390,000)	117,000
Income before extraordinary items	423,000
Extraordinary loss from flood	150,000
Net income	$273,000

The flood loss is considered an extraordinary item. The income tax rate is 30% on all items.

Instructions

(a) Prepare a correct income statement, beginning with income before income taxes.

(b) ◄━━━━━ Explain in memo form why the income statement data are misleading.

E18-13 Potter Corporation has income from continuing operations of $290,000 for the year ended December 31, 2012. It also has the following items (before considering income taxes).

Prepare income statement.
(SO 6)

1. An extraordinary loss of $80,000.

2. A gain of $30,000 on the discontinuance of a division.

3. A correction of an error in last year's financial statements that resulted in a $20,000 under-statement of 2011 net income.

Assume all items are subject to income taxes at a 30% tax rate.

Instructions
(a) Prepare an income statement, beginning with income from continuing operations.
(b) Indicate the statement presentation of any item not included in (a) above.

Exercises: Set B

Visit the book's companion website, at **www.wiley.com/college/weygandt**, and choose the Student Companion site to access Exercise Set B.

Problems

Follow the rounding procedures used in the chapter.

Prepare vertical analysis and comment on profitability.
(SO 4, 5)

P18-1   Comparative statement data for Lionel Company and Barrymore Company, two competitors, appear below. All balance sheet data are as of December 31, 2013, and December 31, 2012.

	Lionel Company		Barrymore Company	
	2013	**2012**	**2013**	**2012**
Net sales	$1,549,035		$339,038	
Cost of goods sold	1,080,490		241,000	
Operating expenses	302,275		79,000	
Interest expense	8,980		2,252	
Income tax expense	54,500		6,650	
Current assets	325,975	$312,410	83,336	$ 79,467
Plant assets (net)	521,310	500,000	139,728	125,812
Current liabilities	65,325	75,815	35,348	30,281
Long-term liabilities	108,500	90,000	29,620	25,000
Common stock, $10 par	500,000	500,000	120,000	120,000
Retained earnings	173,460	146,595	38,096	29,998

Instructions
(a) Prepare a vertical analysis of the 2013 income statement data for Lionel Company and Barrymore Company in columnar form.
(b) ➤ Comment on the relative profitability of the companies by computing the return on assets and the return on common stockholders' equity ratios for both companies.

Compute ratios from balance sheet and income statement.
(SO 5)

P18-2   The comparative statements of Larker Tool Company are presented below.

LARKER TOOL COMPANY
Income Statement
For the Years Ended December 31

	2013	**2012**
Net sales	$1,818,500	$1,750,500
Cost of goods sold	1,011,500	996,000
Gross profit	807,000	754,500
Selling and administrative expense	516,000	479,000
Income from operations	291,000	275,500
Other expenses and losses		
Interest expense	18,000	14,000
Income before income taxes	273,000	261,500
Income tax expense	81,000	77,000
Net income	$ 192,000	$ 184,500

LARKER TOOL COMPANY
Balance Sheets
December 31

Assets	2013	2012
Current assets		
Cash	$ 60,100	$ 64,200
Short-term investments	69,000	50,000
Accounts receivable (net)	117,800	102,800
Inventory	123,000	115,500
Total current assets	369,900	332,500
Plant assets (net)	600,300	520,300
Total assets	$970,200	$852,800
Liabilities and Stockholders' Equity		
Current liabilities		
Accounts payable	$160,000	$145,400
Income taxes payable	43,500	42,000
Total current liabilities	203,500	187,400
Bonds payable	200,000	200,000
Total liabilities	403,500	387,400
Stockholders' equity		
Common stock ($5 par)	280,000	300,000
Retained earnings	286,700	165,400
Total stockholders' equity	566,700	465,400
Total liabilities and stockholders' equity	$970,200	$852,800

All sales were on account.

Instructions

Compute the following ratios for 2013. (Weighted-average common shares in 2013 were 57,000.)

(a) Earnings per share.
(b) Return on common stockholders' equity.
(c) Return on assets.
(d) Current.
(e) Acid-test.
(f) Receivables turnover.
(g) Inventory turnover.
(h) Times interest earned.
(i) Asset turnover.
(j) Debt to total assets.

P18-3 Condensed balance sheet and income statement data for Clarence Corporation appear below and on page 866.

Perform ratio analysis, and evaluate financial position and operating results.

(SO 5)

CLARENCE CORPORATION
Balance Sheets
December 31

	2013	2012	2011
Cash	$ 25,000	$ 20,000	$ 18,000
Receivables (net)	50,000	45,000	48,000
Other current assets	90,000	95,000	64,000
Investments	75,000	70,000	45,000
Plant and equipment (net)	400,000	370,000	358,000
	$640,000	$600,000	$533,000
Current liabilities	$ 75,000	$ 80,000	$ 70,000
Long-term debt	80,000	85,000	50,000
Common stock, $10 par	340,000	310,000	300,000
Retained earnings	145,000	125,000	113,000
	$640,000	$600,000	$533,000

CLARENCE CORPORATION
Income Statement
For the Years Ended December 31

	2013	2012
Sales revenue	$740,000	$700,000
Less: Sales returns and allowances	40,000	50,000
Net sales	700,000	650,000
Cost of goods sold	420,000	400,000
Gross profit	280,000	250,000
Operating expenses (including income taxes)	235,000	220,000
Net income	$ 45,000	$ 30,000

Additional information:

1. The market price of Clarence's common stock was $4.00, $5.00, and $8.00 for 2011, 2012, and 2013, respectively.
2. All dividends were paid in cash.

Instructions

(a) Compute the following ratios for 2012 and 2013.
   (1) Profit margin.
   (2) Asset turnover.
   (3) Earnings per share. (Weighted-average common shares in 2013 were 32,000 and in 2012 were 31,000.)
   (4) Price-earnings.
   (5) Payout.
   (6) Debt to total assets.
(b) ━━━ Based on the ratios calculated, discuss briefly the improvement or lack thereof in financial position and operating results from 2012 to 2013 of Clarence Corporation.

Compute ratios, and comment on overall liquidity and profitability.
(SO 5)

P18-4 Financial information for Ernie Bishop Company is presented below.

ERNIE BISHOP COMPANY
Balance Sheets
December 31

Assets	**2013**	**2012**
Cash	$ 70,000	$ 65,000
Short-term investments	52,000	40,000
Receivables (net)	98,000	80,000
Inventory	125,000	135,000
Prepaid expenses	29,000	23,000
Land	130,000	130,000
Building and equipment (net)	180,000	175,000
	$684,000	$648,000

Liabilities and Stockholders' Equity		
Notes payable	$100,000	$100,000
Accounts payable	48,000	42,000
Accrued liabilities	50,000	40,000
Bonds payable, due 2014	150,000	150,000
Common stock, $10 par	200,000	200,000
Retained earnings	136,000	116,000
	$684,000	$648,000

ERNIE BISHOP COMPANY
Income Statement
For the Years Ended December 31

	2013	2012
Net sales	$850,000	$790,000
Cost of goods sold	620,000	575,000
Gross profit	230,000	215,000
Operating expenses	187,000	173,000
Net income	$ 43,000	$ 42,000

Additional information:
1. Inventory at the beginning of 2012 was $118,000.
2. Total assets at the beginning of 2012 were $630,000.
3. No common stock transactions occurred during 2012 or 2013.
4. All sales were on account.

Instructions
(a) Indicate, by using ratios, the change in liquidity and profitability of Ernie Bishop Company from 2012 to 2013. (*Note:* Not all profitability ratios can be computed.)
(b) Given below are three independent situations and a ratio that may be affected. For each situation, compute the affected ratio (1) as of December 31, 2013, and (2) as of December 31, 2014, after giving effect to the situation. Net income for 2014 was $50,000. Total assets on December 31, 2014, were $700,000.

Situation	Ratio
(1) 18,000 shares of common stock were sold at par on July 1, 2014.	Return on common stockholders' equity
(2) All of the notes payable were paid in 2014. The only change in liabilities was that the notes payable were paid.	Debt to total assets
(3) Market price of common stock was $9 on December 31, 2013, and $12.80 on December 31, 2014.	Price-earnings ratio

P18-5 Selected financial data of Target and Wal-Mart for a recent year are presented here (in millions).

Compute selected ratios, and compare liquidity, profitability, and solvency for two companies.
(SO 5)

	Target Corporation	Wal-Mart Stores, Inc.
Income Statement Data for Year		
Net sales	$61,471	$374,526
Cost of goods sold	41,895	286,515
Selling and administrative expenses	16,200	70,847
Interest expense	647	1,798
Other income (expense)	1,896	4,273
Income tax expense	1,776	6,908
Net income	$ 2,849	$ 12,731
Balance Sheet Data (End of Year)		
Current assets	$18,906	$ 47,585
Noncurrent assets	25,654	115,929
Total assets	$44,560	$163,514
Current liabilities	$11,782	$ 58,454
Long-term debt	17,471	40,452
Total stockholders' equity	15,307	64,608
Total liabilities and stockholders' equity	$44,560	$163,514

	Target Corporation	Wal-Mart Stores, Inc.
	Beginning-of-Year Balances	
Total assets	$37,349	$151,587
Total stockholders' equity	15,633	61,573
Current liabilities	11,117	52,148
Total liabilities	21,716	90,014
	Other Data	
Average net receivables	$ 7,124	$ 3,247
Average inventory	6,517	34,433
Net cash provided by operating activities	4,125	20,354

Instructions

(a) For each company, compute the following ratios.

(1) Current.	(7) Asset turnover.
(2) Receivables turnover.	(8) Return on assets.
(3) Average collection period.	(9) Return on common stockholders' equity.
(4) Inventory turnover.	(10) Debt to total assets.
(5) Days in inventory.	(11) Times interest earned.
(6) Profit margin.	

(b) Compare the liquidity, profitability, and solvency of the two companies.

Compute numerous ratios.
(SO 5)

P18-6 The comparative statements of Beulah Company are presented below.

BEULAH COMPANY
Income Statement
For the Years Ended December 31

	2013	2012
Net sales (all on account)	$600,000	$520,000
Expenses		
Cost of goods sold	415,000	354,000
Selling and administrative	120,800	114,800
Interest expense	7,800	6,000
Income tax expense	18,000	14,000
Total expenses	561,600	488,800
Net income	$ 38,400	$ 31,200

BEULAH COMPANY
Balance Sheets
December 31

Assets	2013	2012
Current assets		
Cash	$ 21,000	$ 18,000
Short-term investments	18,000	15,000
Accounts receivable (net)	86,000	74,000
Inventory	90,000	70,000
Total current assets	215,000	177,000
Plant assets (net)	423,000	383,000
Total assets	$638,000	$560,000

Liabilities and Stockholders' Equity

Current liabilities		
Accounts payable	$122,000	$110,000
Income taxes payable	23,000	20,000
Total current liabilities	145,000	130,000
Long-term liabilities		
Bonds payable	120,000	80,000
Total liabilities	265,000	210,000
Stockholders' equity		
Common stock ($5 par)	150,000	150,000
Retained earnings	223,000	200,000
Total stockholders' equity	373,000	350,000
Total liabilities and stockholders' equity	$638,000	$560,000

Additional data:

The common stock recently sold at $19.50 per share.

Instructions

Compute the following ratios for 2013.

(a) Current.	**(h)** Return on common stockholders' equity.
(b) Acid-test.	**(i)** Earnings per share.
(c) Receivables turnover.	**(j)** Price-earnings.
(d) Inventory turnover.	**(k)** Payout.
(e) Profit margin.	**(l)** Debt to total assets.
(f) Asset turnover.	**(m)** Times interest earned.
(g) Return on assets.	

P18-7 Presented below is an incomplete income statement and an incomplete comparative balance sheet of Bondi Corporation.

Compute missing information given a set of ratios.

(SO 5)

BONDI CORPORATION
Income Statement
For the Year Ended December 31, 2013

Net sales	$11,000,000
Cost of goods sold	?
Gross profit	?
Operating expenses	1,665,000
Income from operations	?
Other expenses and losses	
Interest expense	?
Income before income taxes	?
Income tax expense	560,000
Net income	$?

BONDI CORPORATION
Balance Sheets
December 31

Assets	2013	2012
Current assets		
Cash	$ 450,000	$ 375,000
Accounts receivable (net)	?	950,000
Inventory	?	1,720,000
Total current assets	?	3,045,000
Plant assets (net)	4,620,000	3,955,000
Total assets	$?	$7,000,000

Assets	2013	2012
Liabilities and Stockholders' Equity		
Current liabilities	$?	$ 825,000
Long-term notes payable	?	2,800,000
Total liabilities	?	3,625,000
Common stock, $1 par	3,000,000	3,000,000
Retained earnings	400,000	375,000
Total stockholders' equity	3,400,000	3,375,000
Total liabilities and stockholders' equity	$?	$7,000,000

Additional information:

1. The receivables turnover for 2013 is 10 times.
2. All sales are on account.
3. The profit margin for 2013 is 14.5%.
4. Return on assets is 22% for 2013.
5. The current ratio on December 31, 2013, is 3.0.
6. The inventory turnover for 2013 is 4.8 times.

Instructions

Compute the missing information given the ratios above. Show computations. (*Note:* Start with one ratio and derive as much information as possible from it before trying another ratio. List all missing amounts under the ratio used to find the information.)

Prepare income statement with discontinued operations and extraordinary loss.

(SO 6)

P18-8   Violet Bick Corporation owns a number of cruise ships and a chain of hotels. The hotels, which have not been profitable, were discontinued on September 1, 2012. The 2012 operating results for the company were as follows.

Operating revenues	$12,850,000
Operating expenses	8,700,000
Operating income	$ 4,150,000

Analysis discloses that these data include the operating results of the hotel chain, which were: operating revenues $2,000,000 and operating expenses $2,400,000. The hotels were sold at a gain of $200,000 before taxes. This gain is not included in the operating results. During the year, Violet Bick suffered an extraordinary loss of $800,000 before taxes, which is not included in the operating results. In 2012, the company had other revenues and gains of $100,000, which are not included in the operating results. The corporation is in the 30% income tax bracket.

Instructions

Prepare a condensed income statement.

Prepare income statement with nontypical items.

(SO 6)

P18-9   The ledger of Gower Corporation at December 31, 2012, contains the following summary data.

Net sales	$1,700,000	Cost of goods sold	$1,100,000
Selling expenses	120,000	Administrative expenses	150,000
Other revenues and gains	20,000	Other expenses and losses	28,000

Your analysis reveals the following additional information that is not included in the above data.

1. The entire puzzles division was discontinued on August 31. The income from operations for this division before income taxes was $20,000. The puzzles division was sold at a loss of $90,000 before income taxes.
2. On May 15, company property was expropriated for an interstate highway. The settlement resulted in an extraordinary gain of $120,000 before income taxes.
3. The income tax rate on all items is 30%.

Instructions

Prepare an income statement for the year ended December 31, 2012. Use the format illustrated in the Comprehensive **Do it!** (p. 852).

Problems: Set B

Visit the book's companion website, at **www.wiley.com/college/weygandt**, and choose the Student Companion site to access Problem Set B.

Continuing Cookie Chronicle

(*Note:* This is a continuation of the Cookie Chronicle from Chapters 1 through 17.)

CCC18   Natalie and Curtis have comparative balance sheets and income statements for Cookie & Coffee Creations Inc. They have been told that they can use these financial statements to prepare horizontal and vertical analyses, and to calculate financial ratios, to analyze how their business is doing and to make some decisions they have been considering.

Go to the book's companion website, **www.wiley.com/college/weygandt**, *to see the completion of this problem.*

BROADENINGYOURPERSPECTIVE

Financial Reporting and Analysis

Financial Reporting Problem: PepsiCo, Inc.

BYP18-1   Your parents are considering investing in PepsiCo common stock. They ask you, as an accounting expert, to make an analysis of the company for them. Fortunately, excerpts from a current annual report of PepsiCo are presented in Appendix A of this textbook. Note that all dollar amounts are in millions.

Instructions
(Follow the approach in the chapter for rounding numbers.)

(a) Make a 5-year trend analysis, using 2005 as the base year, of (1) net sales and (2) net income. Comment on the significance of the trend results.

(b) Compute for 2009 and 2008 the (1) profit margin, (2) asset turnover, (3) return on assets, and (4) return on common stockholders' equity. How would you evaluate PepsiCo's profitability? Total assets at December 31, 2007, were $34,628 and total stockholders' equity at December 31, 2007, was $17,325.

(c) Compute for 2009 and 2008 the (1) debt to total assets and (2) times interest earned ratio. How would you evaluate PepsiCo's long-term solvency?

(d) What information outside the annual report may also be useful to your parents in making a decision about PepsiCo, Inc.?

Comparative Analysis Problem:
PepsiCo, Inc. vs. The Coca-Cola Company

BYP18-2   PepsiCo's financial statements are presented in Appendix A. Financial statements of The Coca-Cola Company are presented in Appendix B.

Instructions
(a) Based on the information contained in these financial statements, determine each of the following for each company.
  (1) The percentage increase (decrease) in (i) net sales and (ii) net income from 2008 to 2009.
  (2) The percentage increase in (i) total assets and (ii) total common stockholders' (shareholders') equity from 2008 to 2009.
  (3) The basic earnings per share and price-earnings ratio for 2009. (For both PepsiCo and Coca-Cola, use the basic earnings per share.) Coca-Cola's common stock had a market price of $56.06 at the end of fiscal-year 2009, and PepsiCo's common stock had a market price of $60.07.
(b) What conclusions concerning the two companies can be drawn from these data?

On the Web

BYP18-3   The Management Discussion and Analysis section of an annual report addresses corporate performance for the year, and sometimes uses financial ratios to support its claims.

Address: www.ibm.com/investor/tools/index.phtml or go to **www.wiley.com/college/weygandt**

Steps
1. Choose **How to read annual reports** (in the Guides section).
2. Choose **Anatomy**.

Instructions
Using the information from the above site, answer the following questions.

(a) What are the optional elements that are often included in an annual report?
(b) What are the elements of an annual report that are required by the SEC?
(c) Describe the contents of the Management Discussion.
(d) Describe the contents of the Auditors' Report.
(e) Describe the contents of the Selected Financial Data.

Critical Thinking

Decision Making Across the Organization

BYP18-4   As the CPA for Carismo Manufacturing Inc., you have been asked to develop some key ratios from the comparative financial statements. This information is to be used to convince creditors that the company is solvent and will continue as a going concern. The data requested and the computations developed from the financial statements follow.

	2012	2011
Current ratio	3.1 times	2.1 times
Acid-test ratio	.8 times	1.4 times
Asset turnover	2.8 times	2.2 times
Net income	Up 32%	Down 8%
Earnings per share	$3.30	$2.50

Instructions
With the class divided into groups, complete the following.

Carismo Manufacturing Inc. asks you to prepare a list of brief comments stating how each of these items supports the solvency and going-concern potential of the business. The company wishes to use these comments to support its presentation of data to its creditors. You are to prepare the comments as requested, giving the implications and the limitations of each item separately. Then prepare a collective inference that may be drawn from the individual items about Carismo's solvency and going-concern potential.

Communication Activity

BYP18-5   Beth Harlan is the CEO of Lafferty's Electronics. Harlan is an expert engineer but a novice in accounting. She asks you to explain (1) the bases for comparison in analyzing Lafferty's financial statements, and (2) the factors affecting quality of earnings.

Instructions
Write a letter to Beth Harlan that explains the bases for comparison and factors affecting quality of earnings.

Ethics Case

BYP18-6   Jack McClintock, president of McClintock Industries, wishes to issue a press release to bolster his company's image and maybe even its stock price, which has been gradually falling. As controller, you have been asked to provide a list of 20 financial ratios along with some other operating statistics relative to McClintock Industries' first quarter financials and operations.

Two days after you provide the ratios and data requested, Jeremy Phelps, the public relations director of McClintock, asks you to prove the accuracy of the financial and operating data contained in the press release written by the president and edited by Jeremy. In the press release, the president highlights the sales increase of 25% over last year's first quarter and the positive change in the current ratio from 1.5:1 last year to 3:1 this year. He also emphasizes that production was up 50% over the prior year's first quarter.

You note that the press release contains only positive or improved ratios and none of the negative or deteriorated ratios. For instance, no mention is made that the debt to total assets ratio has increased from 35% to 55%, that inventories are up 89%, and that while the current ratio improved, the acid-test ratio fell from 1:1 to. 5:1. Nor is there any mention that the reported profit for the quarter would have been a loss had not the estimated lives of McClintock's plant and machinery been increased by 30%. Jeremy emphasized, "The prez wants this release by early this afternoon."

Instructions
(a) Who are the stakeholders in this situation?
(b) Is there anything unethical in president McClintock's actions?
(c) Should you as controller remain silent? Does Jeremy have any responsibility?

"All About You" Activity

BYP18-7   In this chapter, you learned how to use many tools for performing a financial analysis of a company. When making personal investments, however, it is most likely that you won't be buying stocks and bonds in individual companies. Instead, when most people want to invest in stock, they buy mutual funds. By investing in a mutual fund, you reduce your risk because the fund diversifies by buying the stock of a variety of different companies, bonds, and other investments, depending on the stated goals of the fund.

Before you invest in a fund, you will need to decide what type of fund you want. For example, do you want a fund that has the potential of high growth (but also high risk), or are you looking for lower risk and a steady stream of income? Do you want a fund that invests only in U.S. companies, or do you want one that invests globally? Many resources are available to help you with these types of decisions.

Instructions
Go to **http://web.archive.org/web/20050210200843/http://www.cnb1.com/invallocmdl.htm** and complete the investment allocation questionnaire. Add up your total points to determine the type of investment fund that would be appropriate for you.

FASB Codification Activity

BYP18-8   If your school has a subscription to the FASB Codification, go to *http://aaahq.org/ascLogin.cfm* to log in and prepare responses to the following. Use the Master Glossary for determining the proper definitions.

(a) Discontinued operations.
(b) Extraordinary items.
(c) Comprehensive income.

Answers to Insight and Accounting Across the Organization Questions
p. 836 How to Manage the Current Ratio   Q: How might management influence a company's current ratio? **A:** Management can affect the current ratio by speeding up or withholding payments on accounts payable just before the balance sheet date. Management can alter the cash balance by increasing or decreasing long-term assets or long-term debt, or by issuing or purchasing common stock.
p. 848 What Does "Non-Recurring" Really Mean?   Q: If a company takes a large restructuring charge, what is the effect on the company's current income statement versus future ones? **A:** The current period's net income can be greatly diminished by a large restructuring charge. The net incomes in future periods can be enhanced because they are relieved of costs (i.e., depreciation and labor expenses) that would have been charged to them.

Answers to Self-Test Questions
1. b   **2.** d   **3.** a   **4.** c   **5.** c ($360,000 ÷ 300,000)   **6.** c   **7.** c   **8.** b $306,000 ÷ [($54,000 + $48,000) ÷ 2] = 6; 365 ÷ 6   **9.** b ($81,000 ÷ $27,000)   **10.** a $134,000 ÷ $784,000   **11.** d ($134,000 − $4,000) ÷ [($240,000 + $198,000) ÷ 2]   **12.** c ($134,000 + $22,000 + $12,000) ÷ $12,000   **13.** c   **14.** d ($400,000 − (25% × $400,000); $100,000 − (25% × $100,000)   **15.** d

IFRS A Look at IFRS

The first sections of this chapter, dealing with the tools of financial analysis, are the same throughout the world. Techniques such as vertical and horizontal analysis, for example, are tools used by analysts regardless of whether GAAP- or IFRS-related financial statements are being evaluated. In addition, the ratios provided in the textbook are the same ones that are used internationally.

The latter part of this chapter relates to the income statement and irregular items. As in GAAP, the income statement is a required statement under IFRS. In addition, the content and presentation of an IFRS income statement is similar to the one used for GAAP. *IAS 1* (revised), "Presentation of Financial Statements," provides general guidelines for the reporting of income statement information. In general, the differences in the presentation of financial statement information are relatively minor.

IFRS Additions to the Textbook

- The tools of financial statement analysis covered in this chapter are universal and therefore no significant differences exist in the analysis methods used.

- The basic objectives of the income statement are the same under both GAAP and IFRS. As indicated in the textbook, a very important objective is to ensure that users of the income statement can evaluate the earning power of the company. Earning power is the normal level of income to be obtained in the future. Thus, both the IASB and the FASB are interested in distinguishing normal levels of income from irregular items in order to better predict a company's future profitability.

- The basic accounting for discontinued operations is the same under IFRS and GAAP.

- Under IFRS, there is no classification for extraordinary items. In other words, extraordinary item treatment is prohibited under IFRS. All revenue and expense items are considered ordinary in nature. Disclosure, however, is extensive for items that are considered material to the financial results. Examples are write-downs of inventory or plant assets, or gains and losses on the sale of plant assets.

- The accounting for changes in accounting principles and changes in accounting estimates are the same for both GAAP and IFRS.

- The income statement under IFRS is referred to as a *statement of comprehensive income*. The statement of comprehensive income can be prepared under the one-statement approach or the two-statement approach.

- The issues related to quality of earnings are the same under both GAAP and IFRS. It is hoped that by adopting a more principles-based approach, as found in IFRS, that many of the earnings' quality issues will disappear.

Looking to the Future

The FASB and the IASB are working on a project that would rework the structure of financial statements. Recently, the IASB decided to require a statement of comprehensive income, similar to what was required under GAAP. In addition, another part of this project addresses the issue of how to classify various items in the income statement. A main goal of this new approach is to provide information that better represents how businesses are run. In addition, the approach draws attention away from one number—net income.

IFRS Self-Test Questions

1. The basic tools of financial analysis are the same under both GAAP and IFRS *except* that:
   (a) horizontal analysis cannot be done because the format of the statements is sometimes different.

(b) analysis is different because vertical analysis cannot be done under IFRS.

(c) the current ratio cannot be computed because current liabilities are often reported before current assets in IFRS statements of position.

(d) None of the above.

2. Under IFRS:

(a) the reporting of discontinued items is different than GAAP.

(b) the reporting of extraordinary items is prohibited.

(c) the reporting of changes in accounting principles is different than under GAAP.

(d) None of the above.

3. Presentation of comprehensive income must be reported under IFRS in:

(a) the statement of stockholders' equity.

(b) the income statement ending with net income.

(c) the notes to the financial statements.

(d) a statement of comprehensive income.

4. In preparing its income statement for 2012, Parmalane assembles the following information:

Sales revenue	$500,000
Cost of goods sold	300,000
Operating expenses	40,000
Loss on discontinued operations	20,000
Loss from flood disaster (an extraordinary item under GAAP)	10,000

Ignoring income taxes, what is Parmalane's income from continuing operations for 2012 under IFRS?

(a) $260,000.   (c) $240,000.

(b) $250,000   (d) $160,000.

5. Using the same information as question 4, which statement is *incorrect*?

(a) Net income under GAAP and IFRS are the same.

(b) Under GAAP, special reporting is provided for extraordinary items.

(c) Both GAAP and IFRS report the same amount for income from continuing operations.

(d) IFRS would not provide separate disclosure for discontinued operations.

International Financial Reporting Problem: *Zetar plc*

IFRS18-1 The financial statements of Zetar plc are presented in Appendix C. The company's complete annual report, including the notes to its financial statements, is available at *www.zetarplc.com*.

Instructions

Use the company's annual report to answer the following questions.

(a) The company's income statement reports a loss on discontinued operations. What business did the company discontinue, and why did it choose to discontinue the business?

(b) For the year ended April 30, 2009, what amount did the company lose on the operation of the discontinued business, and what amount did it lose on disposal?

(c) What was the total recorded value of the net assets at the date of disposal, and what was the amount of costs incurred to dispose of the business?

Answers to IFRS Self-Test Questions

1. d   2. b   3. d   4. d   5. d

✔
The Navigator

✔ **Remember to go back to the Navigator box on the chapter opening page and check off your completed work.**

CHAPTER19

Managerial Accounting

Study Objectives

After studying this chapter, you should be able to:

[1] Explain the distinguishing features of managerial accounting.

[2] Identify the three broad functions of management.

[3] Define the three classes of manufacturing costs.

[4] Distinguish between product and period costs.

[5] Explain the difference between a merchandising and a manufacturing income statement.

[6] Indicate how cost of goods manufactured is determined.

[7] Explain the difference between a merchandising and a manufacturing balance sheet.

[8] Identify trends in managerial accounting.

✔ **The Navigator**

✔ The Navigator

- Scan Study Objectives ○
- Read Feature Story ○
- Read Preview ○
- Read text and answer **Do it!** p. 883 ○
  p. 887 ○ p. 890 ○ p. 898 ○
- Work Comprehensive **Do it! 1** p. 898 ○
  2 p. 900 ○
- Review Summary of Study Objectives ○
- Answer Self-Test Questions ○
- Complete Assignments ○
- Go to *WileyPLUS* for practice and tutorials ○

Feature Story

THINK FAST

The business world changes rapidly. To survive you must make well-informed, quick decisions. Consider this. In January 1998, Compaq Computer was the largest seller of personal computers and *Forbes* magazine's "company of the year." During the next two years, it lost $2 billion and its CEO was out of a job.

Compaq fell victim to Dell Computer. Dell pioneered a new way of making and selling computers. It reengineered its supply chain so that it could produce computers with the exact features that customers ordered, ship them within 24 hours of taking the order, and invest almost no money in inventory. Compaq was not able to respond quickly enough. Ultimately, it merged with Hewlett-Packard (HP).

After the merger of HP and Compaq, HP lost significant market share in the PC market to Dell because its cost structure made it hard to compete with Dell on price. To make matters worse for HP, Dell then began selling computer printers, a business that HP had always dominated. Many people predicted that Dell would soon reign supreme over the printer business as well.

Just when it appeared that Dell could not be beat, HP regained its footing and Dell stumbled. By June 2008, HP had accomplished a remarkable three-year turnaround. With more than $100 billion in sales, HP had become the biggest technology company in the world. How did it do it? HP adopted "lean" manufacturing practices so it could compete with Dell on price. In addition, it developed exciting design innovations that it marketed successfully in retail stores, as compared to Dell's online sales approach.

Perhaps most importantly, HP has expanded its consulting and data storage services. You can only sell a piece of equipment once. But consulting services provide ongoing, high-margin revenue that frequently results in additional hardware sales. To further expand its service revenue opportunities, in 2008 HP acquired Electronic Data Services (EDS) for $13.9 billion. Although many industry analysts questioned the decision, HP says the move was based on a sound strategy. Now management must prove that it was the correct decision for the future.

✔
The Navigator

Inside CHAPTER 19

This chapter focuses on issues illustrated in the Feature Story about Compaq Computer, Hewlett-Packard, and Dell. These include determining and controlling the costs of material, labor, and overhead and the relationship between costs and profits. In previous chapters, you learned about the form and content of **financial statements for external users** of financial information, such as stockholders and creditors. These financial statements represent the principal product of financial accounting. Managerial accounting focuses primarily on the preparation of **reports for internal users** of financial information, such as the managers and officers of a company. In today's rapidly changing global environment, managers often make decisions that determine their company's fate—and their own. Managers are evaluated on the results of their decisions. Managerial accounting provides tools for assisting management in making decisions and for evaluating the effectiveness of those decisions.

The content and organization of this chapter are as follows.

Managerial Accounting			
Managerial Accounting Basics	**Managerial Cost Concepts**	**Manufacturing Costs in Financial Statements**	**Managerial Accounting Today**
• Comparing managerial and financial accounting • Management functions • Organizational structure • Business ethics	• Manufacturing costs • Product vs. period costs	• Income statement • Cost of goods manufactured • Balance sheet • Cost concepts—A review • Product costing for service industries	• Value chain • Technological change • JIT • Quality • Activity-based costing • Theory of constraints • Balanced scorecard

The Navigator

Managerial Accounting Basics

Managerial accounting, also called **management accounting**, is a field of accounting that provides economic and financial information for managers and other internal users. The activities that are part of managerial accounting (and the chapters in which they are discussed in this textbook) are as follows.

1. Explaining manufacturing and nonmanufacturing costs and how they are reported in the financial statements (Chapter 19).

2. Computing the cost of providing a service or manufacturing a product (Chapters 20 and 21).

3. Determining the behavior of costs and expenses as activity levels change and analyzing cost–volume–profit relationships within a company (Chapter 22).

4. Assisting management in profit planning and formalizing these plans in the form of budgets (Chapter 23).

5. Providing a basis for controlling costs and expenses by comparing actual results with planned objectives and standard costs (Chapters 24 and 25).

6. Accumulating and presenting data for management decision making (Chapter 26).

Managerial accounting applies to all types of businesses—service, merchandising, and manufacturing. It also applies to all forms of business organizations—proprietorships, partnerships, and corporations. Not-for-profit entities as well as profit-oriented enterprises need managerial accounting.

In the past, managerial accountants were primarily engaged in cost accounting—collecting and reporting costs to management. Recently that role has changed significantly. First as the business environment has become more automated, methods to determine the amount and type of cost in a product have changed. Second, managerial accountants are now held responsible for strategic cost management; that is, they assist in evaluating how well the company is employing its resources. As a result, managerial accountants now serve as team members alongside personnel from production, marketing, and engineering when the company makes critical strategic decisions.

Opportunities for managerial accountants to advance within the company are considerable. Financial executives must have a background that includes an understanding of managerial accounting concepts. Whatever your position in the company—marketing, sales, or production, knowledge of managerial accounting greatly improves your opportunities for advancement. As the CEO of Microsoft noted: "If you're supposed to be making money in business and supposed to be satisfying customers and building market share, there are numbers that characterize those things. And if somebody can't sort of speak to me quantitatively about it, then I'm nervous."

Comparing Managerial and Financial Accounting

There are both similarities and differences between managerial and financial accounting. First, each field of accounting deals with the economic events of a business. Thus, their interests overlap. For example, *determining* the unit cost of manufacturing a product is part of managerial accounting. *Reporting* the total cost of goods manufactured and sold is part of financial accounting. In addition, both managerial and financial accounting require that a company's economic events be quantified and communicated to interested parties.

Illustration 19-1 illustrates the principal differences between financial accounting and managerial accounting. The need for various types of economic data is responsible for many of the differences.

> **Study Objective [1]**
> Explain the distinguishing features of managerial accounting.

Illustration 19-1
Differences between financial and managerial accounting

Financial Accounting		Managerial Accounting
• External users: stockholders, creditors, and regulators.	**Primary Users of Reports**	• Internal users: officers and managers.
• Financial statements. • Quarterly and annually.	**Types and Frequency of Reports**	• Internal reports. • As frequently as needed.
• General-purpose.	**Purpose of Reports**	• Special-purpose for specific decisions.
• Pertains to business as a whole. • Highly aggregated (condensed). • Limited to double-entry accounting and cost data. • Generally accepted accounting principles.	**Content of Reports**	• Pertains to subunits of the business. • Very detailed. • Extends beyond double-entry accounting to any relevant data. • Standard is relevance to decisions.
• Audit by CPA.	**Verification Process**	• No independent audits.

Management Functions

Study Objective [2]

Identify the three broad functions of management.

Managers' activities and responsibilities can be classified into three broad functions:

1. Planning.
2. Directing.
3. Controlling.

In performing these functions, managers make decisions that have a significant impact on the organization.

Planning requires managers to look ahead and to establish objectives. These objectives are often diverse: maximizing short-term profits and market share, maintaining a commitment to environmental protection, and contributing to social programs. For example, Hewlett-Packard, in an attempt to gain a stronger foothold in the computer industry, has greatly reduced its prices to compete with Dell. A key objective of management is to add **value** to the business under its control. Value is usually measured by the trading price of the company's stock and by the potential selling price of the company.

Directing involves coordinating a company's diverse activities and human resources to produce a smooth-running operation. This function relates to implementing planned objectives and providing necessary incentives to motivate employees. For example, manufacturers such as Campbell Soup Company, General Motors, and Dell must coordinate purchasing, manufacturing, warehousing, and selling. Service corporations such as American Airlines, FedEx, and AT&T must coordinate scheduling, sales, service, and acquisitions of equipment and supplies. Directing also involves selecting executives, appointing managers and supervisors, and hiring and training employees.

MANAGEMENT **I**NSIGHT

Even the Best Have to Get Better

Louis Vuitton is a French manufacturer of high-end handbags, wallets, and suitcases.

Its reputation for quality and style allows it to charge extremely high prices—for example, $700 for a tote bag. But often in the past, when demand was hot, supply was nonexistent—shelves were empty, and would-be buyers left empty-handed.

Luxury-goods manufacturers used to consider stock-outs to be a good thing, but recently Louis Vuitton changed its attitude. The company adopted "lean" processes used by car manufacturers and electronics companies to speed up production of "hot" products. Work is done by flexible teams, with jobs organized based on how long a task takes. By reducing wasted time and eliminating bottlenecks, what used to take 20 to 30 workers eight days to do now takes 6 to 12 workers one day. Also, production employees who used to specialize on a single task on a single product are now multiskilled. This allows them to quickly switch products to meet demand.

To make sure that the factory is making the right products, within a week of a product launch, Louis Vuitton stores around the world feed sales information to the headquarters in France, and production is adjusted accordingly. Finally, the new production processes have also improved quality. Returns of some products are down by two-thirds, which makes quite a difference to the bottom line when the products are pricey.

Source: Christina Passariello, "Louis Vuitton Tries Modern Methods on Factory Lines," *Wall Street Journal* (October 9, 2006).

 What are some of the steps that this company has taken in order to ensure that production meets demand? (See page 921.)

The third management function, **controlling**, is the process of keeping the company's activities on track. In controlling operations, managers determine whether planned goals are being met. When there are deviations from targeted objectives, managers must decide what changes are needed to get back on track. Scandals at companies like Enron, Lucent, and Xerox attest to the fact that companies must have adequate controls to ensure that the company develops and distributes accurate information.

How do managers achieve control? A smart manager in a small operation can make personal observations, ask good questions, and know how to evaluate the answers. But using this approach in a large organization would result in chaos. Unless there is some record of what has happened and what is expected to occur, imagine the president of Dell attempting to determine whether the company is meeting its planned objectives. Thus, large businesses typically use a formal system of evaluation. These systems include such features as budgets, responsibility centers, and performance evaluation reports—all of which are features of managerial accounting.

Decision making is not a separate management function. Rather, it is the outcome of the exercise of good judgment in planning, directing, and controlling.

Organizational Structure

In order to assist in carrying out management functions, most companies prepare **organization charts** to show the interrelationships of activities and the delegation of authority and responsibility within the company. Illustration 19-2 shows a typical organization chart, which outlines the delegation of responsibility.

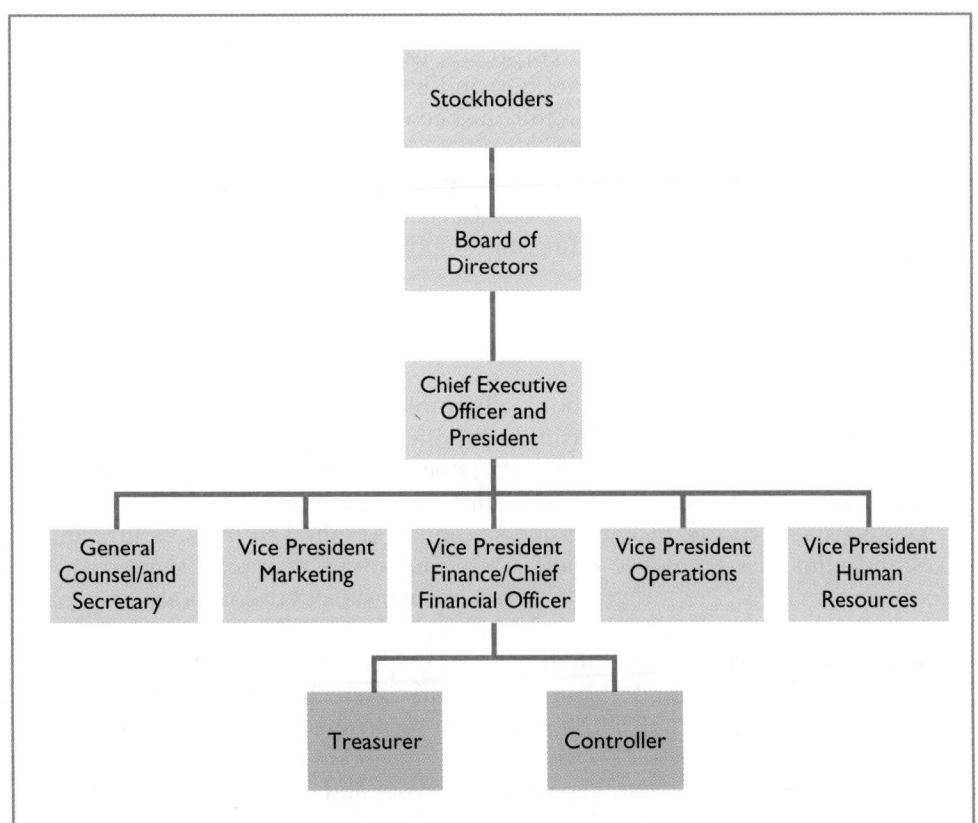

Illustration 19-2
Corporation's organization chart

Stockholders own the corporation, but they manage it indirectly through a **board of directors** they elect. Even not-for-profit organizations have boards of directors. The board formulates the operating policies for the company or organization.

The board also selects officers, such as a president and one or more vice presidents, to execute policy and to perform daily management functions.

The **chief executive officer (CEO)** has overall responsibility for managing the business. Obviously, even in a small business, in order to accomplish organizational objectives, the company relies on delegation of responsibilities. As the organization chart in Illustration 19-2 (page 881) shows, the CEO delegates responsibilities to other officers. Each member of the organization has a clearly defined role to play.

Responsibilities within the company are frequently classified as either line or staff positions. Employees with **line positions** are directly involved in the company's primary revenue-generating operating activities. Examples of line positions include the vice president of operations, vice president of marketing, plant managers, supervisors, and production personnel. Employees with **staff positions** are involved in activities that support the efforts of the line employees. In a firm like General Electric or ExxonMobile, employees in finance, legal, and human resources have staff positions. While activities of staff employees are vital to the company, these employees are nonetheless there to serve the line employees who engage in the company's primary operations.

The **chief financial officer (CFO)** is responsible for all of the accounting and finance issues the company faces. The CFO is supported by the **controller** and the **treasurer**. The controller's responsibilities include (1) maintaining the accounting records, (2) maintaining an adequate system of internal control, and (3) preparing financial statements, tax returns, and internal reports. The treasurer has custody of the corporation's funds and is responsible for maintaining the company's cash position.

Also serving the CFO is the internal audit staff. The staff's responsibilities include reviewing the reliability and integrity of financial information provided by the controller and treasurer. Staff members also ensure that internal control systems are functioning properly to safeguard corporate assets. In addition, they investigate compliance with policies and regulations, and in many companies they determine whether resources are being used in the most economical and efficient fashion.

The vice president of operations oversees employees with line positions. For example, the company might have multiple plant managers, each of whom would report to the vice president of operations. Each plant would also have department managers, such as fabricating, painting, and shipping, each of whom would report to the plant manager.

Business Ethics

As indicated throughout the textbook, all employees within an organization are expected to act ethically in their business activities. Given the importance of ethical behavior to corporations and their owners (stockholders), an increasing number of organizations provide codes of business ethics for their employees.

Despite these efforts, recent business scandals resulted in massive investment losses and numerous employee layoffs. A recent survey of fraud by international accounting firm KPMG reported a 13% increase in instances of corporate fraud compared to five years earlier. It noted that while employee fraud (such things as expense-account abuse, payroll fraud, and theft of assets) represented 60% of all instances of fraud, financial reporting fraud (the intentional misstatement of financial reports) was the most costly to companies. That should not be surprising given the long list of companies such as Enron, Global Crossing, WorldCom, and others that engaged in massive financial frauds which led to huge financial losses and thousands of lost jobs.

CREATING PROPER INCENTIVES
Companies like Motorola, IBM, and Nike use complex systems to control and evaluate the actions of managers. They dedicate substantial resources to monitor and effectively evaluate the actions of employees. Unfortunately, these systems and

controls sometimes unwittingly create incentives for managers to take unethical actions. For example, companies prepare budgets to provide direction. Because the budget is also used as an evaluation tool, some managers try to "game" the budgeting process by underestimating their division's predicted performance so that it will be easier to meet their performance targets. On the other hand, if the budget is set at unattainable levels, managers sometimes take unethical actions to meet the targets in order to receive higher compensation or, in some cases, to keep their jobs.

For example, in recent years, airline manufacturer Boeing was plagued by a series of scandals including charges of over-billing, corporate espionage, and illegal conflicts of interest. Some long-time employees of Boeing blame the decline in ethics on a change in the corporate culture that took place after Boeing merged with McDonnell Douglas. They suggest that evaluation systems implemented after the merger to monitor results and evaluate employee performance made employees believe they needed to succeed no matter what.

As another example, manufacturing companies need to establish production goals for their processes. Again, if controls are not effective and realistic, problems develop. To illustrate, Schering-Plough, a pharmaceutical manufacturer, found that employees were so concerned with meeting production standards that they failed to monitor the quality of the product, and as a result the dosages were often wrong.

CODE OF ETHICAL STANDARDS

In response to ethical scandals in 2000 and 2001, the U.S. Congress enacted legislation to help prevent lapses in internal control. This legislation, referred to as the **Sarbanes-Oxley Act of 2002 (SOX)**, has important implications for the financial community. One result of SOX was to clarify top management's responsibility for the company's financial statements. CEOs and CFOs must now certify that financial statements give a fair presentation of the company's operating results and its financial condition. In addition, top managers must certify that the company maintains an adequate system of internal controls to safeguard the company's assets and ensure accurate financial reports.

Another result of Sarbanes-Oxley is that companies now pay more attention to the composition of the board of directors. In particular, the audit committee of the board of directors must be comprised entirely of independent members (that is, nonemployees) and must contain at least one financial expert.

Finally, to increase the likelihood of compliance with the rules that are part of the new legislation, the law substantially increases the penalties for misconduct.

To provide guidance for managerial accountants, the Institute of Management Accountants (IMA) has developed a code of ethical standards, entitled *IMA Statement of Ethical Professional Practice*. Management accountants should not commit acts in violation of these standards. Nor should they condone such acts by others within their organizations. We include the IMA code of ethical standards in Appendix F at the end of the book. Throughout the chapters on managerial accounting, we will address various ethical issues faced by managers.

Do it!

Indicate whether the following statements are true or false.

1. Managerial accountants have a single role within an organization, collecting and reporting costs to management.
2. Financial accounting reports are general-purpose and intended for external users.
3. Managerial accounting reports are special-purpose and issued as frequently as needed.

Managerial Accounting Concepts

4. Managers' activities and responsibilities can be classified into three broad functions: cost accounting, budgeting, and internal control.

5. As a result of the Sarbanes-Oxley Act of 2002, managerial accounting reports must now comply with generally accepted accounting principles (GAAP).

6. Top managers must certify that a company maintains an adequate system of internal controls.

action plan

✔ Understand that managerial accounting is a field of accounting that provides economic and financial information for managers and other internal users.

✔ Understand that financial accounting provides information for external users.

✔ Analyze which users require which different types of information.

Solution

1. False. Managerial accounts today must help determine the amount and type of a cost in product. In addition, managerial accountants are now held responsible for evaluating how well the company is employing its resources. As a result, when the company makes critical strategic decisions, managerial accountants now serve as team members alongside personnel from production, marketing, and engineering.

2. True.

3. True.

4. False. Managers' activities are classified into three broad functions: planning, directing, and controlling. Planning requires managers to look ahead to establish objectives. Directing involves coordinating a company's diverse activities and human resources to produce a smooth-running operation. Controlling is keeping the company's activities on track.

5. False. SOX clarifies top management's responsibility for the company's financial statements. In addition, top managers must certify that the company maintains an adequate system of internal control to safeguard the company's assets and ensure accurate financial reports.

6. True.

Related exercise material: BE19-1, BE19-2, BE19-3, E19-1, and **Do it!** 19-1.

The Navigator

Managerial Cost Concepts

In order for managers at companies like Dell or Hewlett-Packard to plan, direct, and control operations effectively, they need good information. One very important type of information is related to costs. Managers should ask questions such as the following.

1. What costs are involved in making a product or providing a service?

2. If we decrease production volume, will costs decrease?

3. What impact will automation have on total costs?

4. How can we best control costs?

To answer these questions, managers need reliable and relevant cost information. We now explain and illustrate the various cost categories that companies use.

Manufacturing Costs

Study Objective [3]
Define the three classes of manufacturing costs.

Manufacturing consists of activities and processes that convert raw materials into finished goods. Contrast this type of operation with merchandising, which sells merchandise in the form in which it is purchased. Manufacturing costs are typically classified as shown in Illustration 19-3.

Manufacturing Costs

Direct Materials   Direct Labor   Manufacturing Overhead

Illustration 19-3
Classifications of manufacturing costs

DIRECT MATERIALS

To obtain the materials that will be converted into the finished product, the manufacturer purchases raw materials. **Raw materials** are the basic materials and parts used in the manufacturing process. For example, auto manufacturers such as General Motors, Ford, and Toyota use steel, plastics, and tires as raw materials in making cars.

Direct Materials

Raw materials that can be physically and directly associated with the finished product during the manufacturing process are **direct materials**. Examples include flour in the baking of bread, syrup in the bottling of soft drinks, and steel in the making of automobiles. Direct materials for Hewlett-Packard and Dell Computer include plastic, glass, hard drives, and processing chips.

But some raw materials cannot be easily associated with the finished product. These are called indirect materials. **Indirect materials** have one of two characteristics: (1) They do not physically become part of the finished product (such as lubricants and polishing compounds). Or (2) they cannot be traced because their physical association with the finished product is too small in terms of cost (such as cotter pins and lock washers). Companies account for indirect materials as part of **manufacturing overhead**.

DIRECT LABOR

The work of factory employees that can be physically and directly associated with converting raw materials into finished goods is **direct labor**. Bottlers at Coca-Cola, bakers at Sara Lee, and typesetters at Aptara Corp. are employees whose activities are usually classified as direct labor. **Indirect labor** refers to the work of employees that has no physical association with the finished product, or for which it is impractical to trace costs to the goods produced. Examples include wages of maintenance people, time-keepers, and supervisors. Like indirect materials, companies classify indirect labor as **manufacturing overhead**.

Direct Labor

MANUFACTURING OVERHEAD

Manufacturing overhead consists of costs that are indirectly associated with the manufacture of the finished product. These costs may also be manufacturing costs that cannot be classified as direct materials or direct labor. Manufacturing overhead includes indirect materials, indirect labor, depreciation on factory buildings and machines, and insurance, taxes, and maintenance on factory facilities.

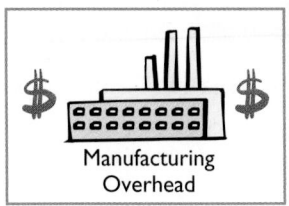

Manufacturing Overhead

One study found the following magnitudes of the three different product costs as a percentage of the total product cost: direct materials 54%, direct labor 13%, and manufacturing overhead 33%. Note that the direct labor component is the smallest. This component of product cost is dropping substantially because of automation. Companies are working hard to increase productivity by decreasing labor.

A Nissan Motor plant in Tennessee produces Altima automobiles using only 15.74 labor hours per vehicle compared to 26 to 28 hours per vehicle at Ford and Daimler plants, for example. In some companies, direct labor has become as little as 5% of the total cost.

Allocating materials and labor costs to specific products is fairly straightforward. Good record keeping can tell a company how much plastic it used in making each type of gear, or how many hours of factory labor it took to assemble a part. But allocating overhead costs to specific products presents problems. How much of the purchasing agent's salary is attributable to the hundreds of different products made in the same plant? What about the grease that keeps the machines humming, or the computers that make sure paychecks come out on time? Boiled down to its simplest form, the question becomes: Which products cause the incurrence of which costs? In subsequent chapters, we show various methods of allocating overhead to products.

Alternative Terminology

Some companies use terms such as *factory overhead, indirect manufacturing costs,* and *burden* instead of manufacturing overhead.

MANAGEMENT INSIGHT

How Many Labor Hours to Build a Car?

Nissan and Toyota were number 1 and 2 in a recent annual study of labor productivity in the auto industry. But U.S. auto manufacturers showed improvements. Labor represents about 15% of the total cost to make a vehicle. Since Nissan required only 28.46 labor hours per vehicle, it saves about $300 to $450 in labor costs to build a car relative to Ford, the least-efficient manufacturer. General Motors (GM) has shown steady improvement over the years. In 1998 it needed almost 17 more hours of labor than Toyota to build a car; it now needs only 4 more hours than Toyota. Chrysler says that much of its improvement in labor productivity has come from designing cars that are easier to build. For example, Chrysler noted that its Toledo Jeep Wrangler plant used 12.69 man-hours to produce the sport utility vehicles made there in 2008. That was an improvement over the prior year's figure of 13.57 man-hours.

Source: Rick Popely, "Japanese Automakers Lead Big Three in Productivity Review," *Knight Ridder Tribune News Service* (June 1, 2006), p. 1, and Larry P. Vellequette, "3 Metro Automotive Plants Again Tops in Productivity: But Industry Study Limits Touting of Performance," *Tribune Business News* (September 1, 2009).

? Why might Nissan production require significantly fewer labor hours? (See page 921.)

Product versus Period Costs

Study Objective [4]
Distinguish between product and period costs.

Alternative Terminology

Product costs are also called *inventoriable costs.*

Each of the manufacturing cost components—direct materials, direct labor, and manufacturing overhead—are product costs. As the term suggests, **product costs** are costs that are a necessary and integral part of producing the finished product. Companies record product costs, when incurred, as inventory. Under the matching principle, these costs do not become expenses until the company sells the finished goods inventory. At that point, the company records the expense as cost of goods sold.

Period costs are costs that are matched with the revenue of a specific time period rather than included as part of the cost of a salable product. These are nonmanufacturing costs. Period costs include selling and administrative expenses. In order to determine net income, companies deduct these costs from revenues in the period in which they are incurred.

Illustration 19-4 summarizes these relationships and cost terms. Our main concern in this chapter is with product costs.

Illustration 19-4
Product versus period costs

Do it!

A bicycle company has these costs: tires, salaries of employees who put tires on the wheels, factory building depreciation, lubricants, spokes, salary of factory manager, handlebars, and salaries of factory maintenance employees. Classify each cost as direct materials, direct labor, or overhead.

Solution

> Tires, spokes, and handlebars are direct materials. Salaries of employees who put tires on the wheels are direct labor. All of the other costs are manufacturing overhead.

Related exercise material: BE19-4, BE19-5, BE19-6, BE19-7, E19-2, E19-3, E19-4, E19-5, E19-6, E19-7, and **Do it!** 19-2.

Managerial Cost Concepts

action plan

✔ Classify as direct materials any raw materials that can be physically and directly associated with the finished product.

✔ Classify as direct labor the work of factory employees that can be physically and directly associated with the finished product.

✔ Classify as manufacturing overhead any costs that are indirectly associated with the finished product.

Manufacturing Costs in Financial Statements

The financial statements of a manufacturer are very similar to those of a merchandiser. For example, you will find many of the same sections and same accounts in the financial statements of Procter & Gamble that you find in the financial statements of Dick's Sporting Goods. The principal differences between their financial statements occur in two places: the cost of goods sold section in the income statement and the current assets section in the balance sheet.

Study Objective [5]

Explain the difference between a merchandising and a manufacturing income statement.

Income Statement

Under a periodic inventory system, the income statements of a merchandiser and a manufacturer differ in the cost of goods sold section. Merchandisers compute cost of goods sold by adding the beginning inventory to the **cost of goods purchased** and subtracting the ending inventory. Manufacturers compute cost of goods sold by adding the beginning finished goods inventory to the **cost of goods manufactured** and subtracting the ending finished goods inventory. Illustration 19-5 shows these different methods.

Illustration 19-5
Cost of goods sold components

Helpful Hint

We assume a periodic inventory system in this illustration.

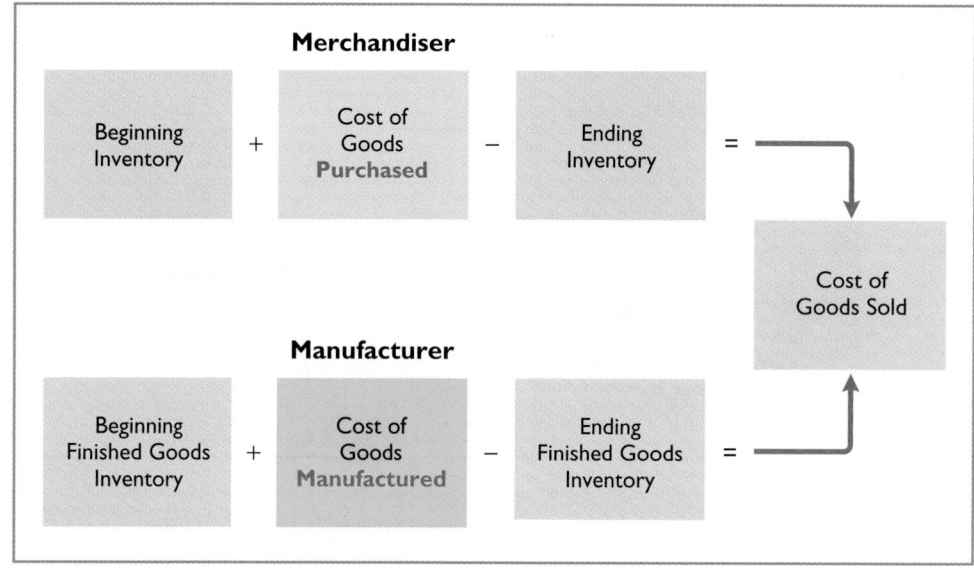

A number of accounts are involved in determining the cost of goods manufactured. To eliminate excessive detail, income statements typically show only the total cost of goods manufactured. A separate statement, called a Cost of Goods Manufactured Schedule, presents the details. (For more information, see the discussion on page 889 and Illustration 19-8.)

Illustration 19-6
Cost of goods sold sections of merchandising and manufacturing income statements

Illustration 19-6 shows the different presentations of the cost of goods sold sections for merchandising and manufacturing companies. The other sections of an income statement are similar for merchandisers and manufacturers.

Merchandising Company Income Statement (partial) For the Year Ended December 31, 2012		Manufacturing Company Income Statement (partial) For the Year Ended December 31, 2012	
Cost of goods sold		Cost of goods sold	
Inventory, January 1	$ 70,000	Finished goods inventory, January 1	$ 90,000
Cost of goods purchased	650,000	Cost of goods manufactured (see Illustration 19-8)	370,000
Cost of goods available for sale	720,000	Cost of goods available for sale	460,000
Inventory, December 31	400,000	Finished goods inventory, December 31	80,000
Cost of goods sold	$320,000	Cost of goods sold	$380,000

Cost of Goods Manufactured

Study Objective [6]
Indicate how cost of goods manufactured is determined.

An example may help show how companies determine the cost of goods manufactured. Assume that HP has a number of computers in various stages of production on January 1. In total, these partially completed units are called **beginning work in process inventory**. The costs the company assigns to beginning work in process inventory are based on the **manufacturing costs incurred in the prior period**.

HP first uses the manufacturing costs incurred in the current year to complete the work that was in process on January 1. It then incurs manufacturing costs for production of new orders. The sum of the direct materials costs, direct labor costs, and manufacturing overhead incurred in the current year is the **total manufacturing costs** for the current period.

We now have two cost amounts: (1) the cost of the beginning work in process and (2) the total manufacturing costs for the current period. The sum of these costs is the **total cost of work in process** for the year.

At the end of the year, HP may have some computers that are only partially completed. The costs of these units become the cost of the **ending work in process inventory**. To find the **cost of goods manufactured**, we subtract this cost from the total cost of work in process. Illustration 19-7 shows the formula for determining the cost of goods manufactured.

Illustration 19-7
Cost of goods manufactured formula

COST OF GOODS MANUFACTURED SCHEDULE

The **cost of goods manufactured schedule** reports cost elements used in calculating cost of goods manufactured. Illustration 19-8 shows the schedule for Olsen Manufacturing Company (using assumed data). The schedule presents detailed data for direct materials and for manufacturing overhead.

Review Illustration 19-7 and then examine the cost of goods manufactured schedule in Illustration 19-8. You should be able to distinguish between "Total

Illustration 19-8
Cost of goods manufactured schedule

Olsen Manufacturing Company
Cost of Goods Manufactured Schedule
For the Year Ended December 31, 2012

Work in process, January 1		$ 18,400
Direct materials		
Raw materials inventory, January 1	$ 16,700	
Raw materials purchases	152,500	
Total raw materials available for use	169,200	
Less: Raw materials inventory, December 31	22,800	
Direct materials used		$146,400
Direct labor		175,600
Manufacturing overhead		
Indirect labor	14,300	
Factory repairs	12,600	
Factory utilities	10,100	
Factory depreciation	9,440	
Factory insurance	8,360	
Total manufacturing overhead		54,800
Total manufacturing costs		376,800
Total cost of work in process		395,200
Less: Work in process, December 31		25,200
Cost of goods manufactured		$370,000

manufacturing costs" and "Cost of goods manufactured." The difference is the effect of the change in work in process during the period.

Do it!

Cost of Goods Manufactured

The following information is available for Keystone Manufacturing Company.

	March 1	March 31
Raw material inventory	$12,000	$10,000
Work in process inventory	2,500	4,000
Materials purchased in March	$ 90,000	
Direct labor in March	75,000	
Manufacturing overhead in March	220,000	

Prepare the cost of goods manufactured schedule for the month of March.

action plan

✔ Start with beginning work in process as the first item in the cost of goods manufactured schedule.

✔ Sum direct materials used, direct labor, and total manufacturing overhead to determine total manufacturing costs.

✔ Sum beginning work in process and total manufacturing costs to determine total cost of work in process.

✔ Cost of goods manufactured is the total cost of work in process less ending work in process.

Solution

KEYSTONE MANUFACTURING COMPANY Cost of Goods Manufactured Schedule For the Month Ended March 31			
Work in process, March 1			$ 2,500
Direct materials			
Raw materials, March 1	$ 12,000		
Raw material purchases	90,000		
Total raw materials available for use	102,000		
Less: Raw materials, March 31	10,000		
Direct materials used		$ 92,000	
Direct labor		75,000	
Manufacturing overhead		220,000	
Total manufacturing costs			387,000
Total cost of work in process			389,500
Less: Work in process, March 31			4,000
Cost of goods manufactured			$385,500

Related exercise material: BE19-8, BE19-10, BE19-11, E19-8, E19-9, E19-10, E19-11, E19-12, E19-13, E19-14, E19-15, E19-16, E19-17, and **Do it!** 19-3.

✔
The Navigator

Balance Sheet

Study Objective [7]

Explain the difference between a merchandising and a manufacturing balance sheet.

The balance sheet for a merchandising company shows just one category of inventory. In contrast, the balance sheet for a manufacturer may have three inventory accounts, as shown in Illustration 19-9.

Raw Materials Inventory

Shows the cost of raw materials on hand.

Work in Process Inventory

Shows the cost applicable to units that have been started into production but are only partially completed.

Finished Goods Inventory

Shows the cost of completed goods on hand.

Illustration 19-9

Inventory accounts for a manufacturer

Finished Goods Inventory is to a manufacturer what Inventory is to a merchandiser. Each of these classifications represents the goods that are available for sale.

The current assets sections presented in Illustration 19-10 contrast the presentations of inventories for merchandising and manufacturing companies. Manufacturing companies generally list their inventories in the order of their liquidity—the order in which they are expected to be realized in cash. Thus, finished goods inventory comes first. The remainder of the balance sheet is similar for the two types of companies.

Merchandising Company Balance Sheet December 31, 2012		Manufacturing Company Balance Sheet December 31, 2012		
Current assets		Current assets		
Cash	$100,000	Cash		$180,000
Receivables (net)	210,000	Receivables (net)		210,000
Inventory	400,000	Inventories		
Prepaid expenses	22,000	Finished goods	$80,000	
Total current assets	$732,000	Work in process	25,200	
		Raw materials	22,800	128,000
		Prepaid expenses		18,000
		Total current assets		$536,000

Illustration 19-10
Current assets sections of merchandising and manufacturing balance sheets

Each step in the accounting cycle for a merchandiser applies to a manufacturer. For example, prior to preparing financial statements, manufacturers make adjusting entries. The adjusting entries are essentially the same as those of a merchandiser. The closing entries are also similar for manufacturers and merchandisers. *For expanded coverage, go to the Student Companion site and select Chapter 19, Accounting Cycle (Worksheet) for a Manufacturing Company.*

Cost Concepts—A Review

You have learned a number of cost concepts in this chapter. Because many of these concepts are new, we provide here an extended example for review. Suppose you started your own snowboard factory, Terrain Park Boards. Think that's impossible? Burton Snowboards was started by Jake Burton Carpenter, when he was only 23 years old. Jake initially experimented with 100 different prototype designs before settling on a final design. Then Jake, along with two relatives and a friend, started making 50 boards per day in Londonderry, Vermont. Unfortunately, while they made a lot of boards in their first year, they were only able to sell 300 of them. To get by during those early years, Jake taught tennis and tended bar to pay the bills.

Here are some of the costs that your snowboard factory would incur.

1. The materials cost of each snowboard (wood cores, fiberglass, resins, metal screw holes, metal edges, and ink) is $30.

2. The labor costs (for example, to trim and shape each board using jig saws and band saws) are $40.

3. Depreciation on the factory building and equipment (for example, presses, grinding machines, and lacquer machines) used to make the snowboards is $25,000 per year.

4. Property taxes on the factory building (where the snowboards are made) are $6,000 per year.

5. Advertising costs (mostly online and catalogue) are $60,000 per year.

6. Sales commissions related to snowboard sales are $20 per snowboard.

7. Salaries for maintenance employees are $45,000 per year.

8. The salary of the plant manager is $70,000.

9. The cost of shipping is $8 per snowboard.

Illustration 19-11 shows how Terrain Park Boards would assign these manufacturing and selling costs to the various categories.

Illustration 19-11

Assignment of costs to cost categories

	Product Costs			
Cost Item	Direct Materials	Direct Labor	Manufacturing Overhead	Period Costs
1. Material cost ($30) per board	X			
2. Labor costs ($40) per board		X		
3. Depreciation on factory equipment ($25,000 per year)			X	
4. Property taxes on factory building ($6,000 per year)			X	
5. Advertising costs ($60,000 per year)				X
6. Sales commissions ($20 per board)				X
7. Maintenance salaries (factory facilities) ($45,000 per year)			X	
8. Salary of plant manager ($70,000)			X	
9. Cost of shipping boards ($8 per board)				X

Remember that total manufacturing costs are the sum of the **product costs**—direct materials, direct labor, and manufacturing overhead. If Terrain Park Boards produces 10,000 snowboards the first year, the total manufacturing costs would be $846,000 as shown in Illustration 19-12.

Illustration 19-12

Computation of total manufacturing costs

Cost Number and Item	Manufacturing Cost
1. Material cost ($30 × 10,000)	$300,000
2. Labor cost ($40 × 10,000)	400,000
3. Depreciation on factory equipment	25,000
4. Property taxes on factory building	6,000
7. Maintenance salaries (factory facilities)	45,000
8. Salary of plant manager	70,000
Total manufacturing costs	$846,000

Knowing the total manufacturing costs, Terrain Park Boards can compute the manufacturing cost per unit. Assuming 10,000 units, the cost to produce one snowboard is $84.60 ($846,000 ÷ 10,000 units).

In subsequent chapters, we will use extensively the cost concepts discussed in this chapter. Study Illustration 19-11 carefully. If you do not understand any of these classifications, go back and reread the appropriate section in this chapter.

Product Costing for Service Industries

The Feature Story notes HP's belief that its greatest opportunities for growth are in technology services, not hardware. In fact, much of the U.S. economy has shifted toward an emphasis on services. Today, more than 50% of U.S. workers are employed by service companies. Airlines, marketing agencies, cable companies, and governmental agencies are just a few examples of service companies. How do service companies differ from manufacturing companies? One good way to differentiate these two different types of companies is by how quickly the product is used or consumed by the customer—services are consumed immediately. For example, when a restaurant produces a meal, that meal is not put in inventory, but it is instead consumed immediately. An airline uses special equipment to provide its product, but again, the output of that equipment is consumed immediately by the customer in the form of a flight. And a marketing agency performs services for its clients that are immediately consumed by the customer in the form of a marketing plan. For a manufacturing company, like Boeing, it often has a long lead time before its airplane is used or consumed by the customer.

In presenting our initial examples, we used manufacturing companies because accounting for the manufacturing environment requires the use of the broadest range of accounts. That is, the accounts used by service companies represent a subset of those used by manufacturers because service companies are not producing inventory. Neither the restaurant, the airline, or the marketing agency discussed above produces an inventoriable product. However, just like a manufacturer, each needs to keep track of the costs of its services in order to know whether it is generating a profit. A successful restaurateur needs to know the cost of each offering on the menu, an airline needs to know the cost of flight service to each destination, and a marketing agency needs to know the cost to develop a marketing plan. Thus, the techniques shown in this chapter, to accumulate manufacturing costs to determine manufacturing inventory, are equally useful for determining the costs of providing services.

Ethics Note

Do telecommunications companies have an obligation to provide service to remote or low-user areas for a fee that may be less than the cost of the service?

For example, let's consider the costs that HP might incur on a consulting engagement. A significant portion of its costs would be salaries of consulting personnel. It might also incur travel costs, materials, software costs, and depreciation charges on equipment used by the employees to provide the consulting service. In the same way that it needs to keep track of the cost of manufacturing its computers and printers, HP needs to know what its costs are on each consulting job. It could prepare a cost of services provided schedule similar to the cost of goods manufactured schedule in Illustration 19-8. The structure would be essentially the same as the cost of goods manufactured schedule, but section headings would be reflective of the costs of the particular service organization.

Managers of service companies look to managerial accounting to answer many questions. In some instances, the managerial accountant may need to develop new systems for measuring the cost of serving individual customers. In others, companies may need new operating controls to improve the quality and efficiency of specific services. Many of the examples we present in subsequent chapters will be based on service companies. To highlight the relevance of the techniques used in this course for service companies, we have placed a service company icon next to those items in the text and end-of-chapter materials that relate to nonmanufacturing companies.

SERVICE COMPANY INSIGHT

Low Fares but Decent Profits

During 2008, when other airlines were cutting flight service due to the recession, Allegiant Airlines increased capacity by 21%. Sounds crazy, doesn't it? But it must know something, because while the other airlines were losing money, it was generating profits. Consider also that its average one-way fare is only $83. So how does it make money? As a low-budget airline, it focuses on controlling costs. It purchases used planes for $4 million each rather than new planes for $40 million. It flies out of small towns, so wages are low and competition is nonexistent. It only flies a route if its 150-passenger planes are nearly full (it averages about 90% of capacity). If a route isn't filling up, it quits flying it as often or cancels it altogether. It adjusts its prices weekly. The bottom line is that it knows its costs to the penny. Knowing what your costs are might not be glamorous, but it sure beats losing money.

Source: Susan Carey, "For Allegiant, Getaways Mean Profits," *Wall Street Journal Online* (February 18, 2009).

? What are some of the line items that would appear in the cost of services provided schedule of an airline? (See page 921.)

Managerial Accounting Today

Study Objective [8]
Identify trends in managerial accounting.

In recent years, the competitive environment for U.S. business has changed significantly. For example, the airline, financial services, and telecommunications industries have been deregulated. Global competition has intensified. The world economy now has the European Union (EU), North American Free Trade Agreement (NAFTA), and Association of Southeast Asian Nations (ASEAN). Countries like China and India are becoming economic powerhouses. As indicated earlier, managerial accountants must be forward-looking, acting as advisors and information providers to different parts of the organization. Some of the issues they face are discussed below.

The Value Chain

The **value chain** refers to all activities associated with providing a product or service. For a manufacturer these include research and development, product design, acquisition of raw materials, production, sales and marketing, delivery, customer relations, and subsequent service. Illustration 19-13 depicts the value chain for a manufacturer. In recent years, companies have made huge strides in analyzing all stages of the value chain in an effort to improve productivity and eliminate waste. Japanese automobile manufacturer Toyota pioneered many of these innovations.

Illustration 19-13
A manufacturer's value chain

| Research & development and product design | Acquisition of raw materials | Production | Sales & marketing | Delivery | Customer relations and subsequent services |

In the 1980s, many companies purchased giant machines to replace humans in the manufacturing process. These machines were designed to produce large batches of products. In recent years these large-batch manufacturing processes have been recognized as wasteful. They require vast amounts of inventory storage capacity and considerable movement of materials. Consequently, many companies have reengineered their manufacturing processes. As one example, the manufacturing company Pratt and Whitney has replaced many large machines with smaller, more flexible ones and has begun reorganizing its plants for more efficient flow of goods. Pratt and Whitney was able to reduce the time that its turbine engine blades spend in the grinding section of its factory from 10 days down to 2 hours. It cut the total amount of time spent making a blade from 22 days to 7 days. Analysis of the value chain has made companies far more responsive to customer needs and has improved profitability.

Technological Change

Technology has played a large role in the value chain. Computerization and automation have permitted companies to be more effective in streamlining production and thus enhancing the value chain. For example, many companies now employ **enterprise resource planning (ERP)** software systems to manage their value chain. ERP systems provide a comprehensive, centralized, integrated source of information that companies can use to manage all major business processes, from purchasing to manufacturing to human resources.

In large companies, an ERP system might replace as many as 200 individual software packages. For example, an ERP system can eliminate the need for individual software packages for personnel, inventory management, receivables, and payroll. Because the value chain extends beyond the walls of the company, ERP systems enable a two-way flow of information between a company and its major suppliers, customers, and business partners. Such systems both collect and disperse information throughout the value chain. The largest ERP provider, German corporation SAP AG, has more than 36,000 customers worldwide.

Another example of technological change is **computer-integrated manufacturing (CIM)**. Using CIM, many companies can now manufacture products that are untouched by human hands. An example is the use of robotic equipment in the steel and automobile industries. Workers monitor the manufacturing process by watching instrument panels. Automation significantly reduces direct labor costs in many cases.

Also, the widespread use of computers has greatly reduced the cost of accumulating, storing, and reporting managerial accounting information. Computers now make it possible to do more detailed costing of products, processes, and services than was possible under manual processing.

Technology is also affecting the value chain through business-to-business (B2B) e-commerce on the Internet. The Internet has dramatically changed the way corporations do business with one another. Interorganizational information systems connected over the Internet enable suppliers to share information nearly instantaneously. The Internet has also changed the marketplace, often cutting out intermediaries. Industries such as the automobile, airline, hotel, and electronics industries have made commitments to purchase some or all of their supplies and raw materials in the huge B2B electronic marketplaces. For example, Hilton Hotels recently agreed to purchase as much as $1.5 billion of bed sheets, pest control services, and other items from an online supplier, PurchasePro.com.

Just-in-Time Inventory Methods

Many companies have significantly lowered inventory levels and costs using **just-in-time (JIT) inventory** methods. Under a just-in-time method, goods are manufactured or purchased just in time for use. As noted in the Feature Story, Dell is

Ethics Note

Does just-in-time inventory justify "just-in-time" employees obtained through temporary employment services?

famous for having developed a system for making computers in response to individual customer requests. Even though each computer is custom-made to meet each customer's specifications, it takes Dell less than 48 hours to assemble the computer and put it on a truck. By integrating its information systems with those of its suppliers, Dell reduced its inventories to nearly zero. This is a huge advantage in an industry where products become obsolete nearly overnight.

Quality

JIT inventory systems require an increased emphasis on product quality. If products are produced only as they are needed, it is very costly for the company to have to stop production because of defects or machine breakdowns. Many companies have installed **total quality management (TQM)** systems to reduce defects in finished products. The goal is to achieve zero defects. These systems require timely data on defective products, rework costs, and the cost of honoring warranty contracts. Often, companies use this information to help redesign the product in a way that makes it less prone to defect. Or they may use the information to reengineer the production process to reduce setup time and decrease the potential for error. TQM systems also provide information on nonfinancial measures such as customer satisfaction, number of service calls, and time to generate reports. Attention to these measures, which employees can control, leads to increased profitability.

Activity-Based Costing

As discussed earlier, overhead costs have become an increasingly large component of product and service costs. By definition, overhead costs cannot be directly traced to individual products. But to determine each product's cost, overhead must be **allocated** to the various products. In order to obtain more accurate product costs, many companies now allocate overhead using **activity-based costing (ABC)**. Under ABC, companies allocate overhead based on each product's use of activities in making the product. For example, companies can keep track of their cost of setting up machines for each batch of a production process. Then companies can allocate part of the total set-up cost to a particular product based on the number of set-ups that product required.

Activity-based costing is beneficial because it results in more accurate product costing and in more careful scrutiny of all activities in the value chain. For example, if a product's cost is high because it requires a high number of set-ups, management will be motivated to determine how to produce the product using the optimal number of machine set-ups. Both manufacturing and service companies now widely use ABC. Allied Signal and Coca-Cola have both enjoyed improved results from ABC. Fidelity Investments uses ABC to identify which customers cost the most to serve.

Theory of Constraints

All companies have certain aspects of their business that create "bottlenecks"— constraints that limit the company's potential profitability. An important aspect of managing the value chain is identifying these constraints. The **theory of constraints** is a specific approach used to identify and manage constraints in order to achieve the company's goals. Automobile manufacturer General Motors has implemented the theory of constraints in all of its North American plants. GM has found that it is most profitable when it focuses on fixing bottlenecks, rather than worrying about whether all aspects of the company are functioning at full capacity. It has greatly improved the company's ability to effectively use overtime labor while meeting customer demand.

MANAGEMENT INSIGHT

Bananas Receive Special Treatment

When it comes to total quality management, few companies can compare with Chiquita Brands International. Grocery store customers are very picky about bananas— bad bananas are consistently the number one grocery store complaint. Because bananas often account for up to 3% of a grocery store's sales, Chiquita goes to great lengths to protect the popular fruit. While bananas are in transit from Central America, "black box" recording devices attached to shipping crates ensure that they are kept in an environment of 90% humidity and an unvarying 55-degree temperature. Upon arrival in the U.S., bananas are ripened in airtight warehouses that use carefully monitored levels of ethylene gas. Regular checks are made of each warehouse using ultrasonic detectors that can detect leaks the size of a pinhole. Says one grocery store executive, "No other item in the store has this type of attention and resources devoted to it."

Source: Devon Spurgeon, "When Grocers in U.S. Go Bananas Over Bad Fruit, They Call Laubenthal," *Wall Street Journal* (August 14, 2000), p. A1.

? Why is it important to keep track of costs that are incurred to improve product quality? (See page 921.)

Balanced Scorecard

As companies implement various business practice innovations, managers sometimes focus too enthusiastically on the latest innovation, to the detriment of other areas of the business. For example, in focusing on improving quality, companies sometimes have lost sight of cost/benefit considerations. Similarly, in focusing on reducing inventory levels through just-in-time, companies sometimes have lost sales due to inventory shortages. The **balanced scorecard** is a performance-measurement approach that uses both financial and nonfinancial measures to evaluate all aspects of a company's operations in an **integrated** fashion. The performance measures are linked in a cause-and-effect fashion to ensure that they all tie to the company's overall objectives.

For example, the company may desire to increase its return on assets, a common financial performance measure (calculated as net income divided by average total assets). It will then identify a series of linked goals. If the company accomplishes each goal, the ultimate result will be an increase in return on assets. For example, in order to increase return on assets, sales must increase. In order to increase sales, customer satisfaction must be increased. In order to increase customer satisfaction, product defects must be reduced. In order to reduce product defects, employee training must be increased. Note the linkage, which starts with employee training and ends with return on assets. Each objective will have associated performance measures.

The use of the balanced scorecard is widespread among well-known and respected companies. For example, Hilton Hotels Corporation uses the balanced scorecard to evaluate the performance of employees at all of its hotel chains. Wal-Mart employs the balanced scorecard, and actually extends its use to evaluation of its suppliers. For example, Wal-Mart recently awarded Welch Company the "Dry Grocery Division Supplier of the Year Award" for its balanced scorecard results. We discuss the balanced scorecard further in Chapter 25.

Do it!

Match the descriptions that follow with the corresponding terms.

Descriptions:

1. _____ All activities associated with providing a product or service.

2. _____ A method of allocating overhead based on each product's use of activities in making the product.

3. _____ Systems implemented to reduce defects in finished products with the goal of achieving zero defects.

4. _____ A performance-measurement approach that uses both financial and nonfinancial measures, tied to company objectives, to evaluate a company's operations in an integrated fashion.

5. _____ Inventory system in which goods are manufactured or purchased just as they are needed for use.

Terms:

a. Activity-based costing

b. Balanced scorecard

c. Just-in-time (JIT) inventory

d. Total quality management (TQM)

e. Value chain

action plan

✔ Develop a forward-looking view, in order to advise and provide information to various members of the organization.

✔ Understand current business trends and issues.

Solution

1. e	2. a	3. d	4. b	5. c

Related exercise material: E19-18 and **Do it!** 19-4.

The Navigator

COMPREHENSIVE

Do it! 1

Giant Manufacturing Co. specializes in manufacturing different models of bicycles. Assume that the market has responded enthusiastically to a new model, the Jaguar. As a result, the company has established a separate manufacturing facility to produce these bicycles. The company produces 1,000 of these bicycles per month. Giant's monthly manufacturing cost and other expenses data related to these bicycles are as follows.

1.	Rent on manufacturing equipment (lease cost)	$2,000/month
2.	Insurance on manufacturing building	$750/month
3.	Raw materials (frames, tires, etc.)	$80/bicycle
4.	Utility costs for manufacturing facility	$1,000/month
5.	Supplies for administrative office	$800/month
6.	Wages for assembly line workers in manufacturing facility	$30/bicycle
7.	Depreciation on office equipment	$650/month
8.	Miscellaneous materials (lubricants, solders, etc.)	$1.20/bicycle
9.	Property taxes on manufacturing building	$2,400/year
10.	Manufacturing supervisor's salary	$3,000/month
11.	Advertising for bicycles	$30,000/year
12.	Sales commissions	$10/bicycle
13.	Depreciation on manufacturing building	$1,500/month

Instructions

(a) Prepare an answer sheet with the following column headings.

	Product Costs			
Cost Item	Direct Materials	Direct Labor	Manufacturing Overhead	Period Costs

Enter each cost item on your answer sheet, placing an "X" under the appropriate headings.

(b) Compute total manufacturing costs for the month.

Solution to Comprehensive Do it! 1

(a)

Cost Item	Direct Materials	Direct Labor	Manufacturing Overhead	Period Costs
1. Rent on manufacturing equipment ($2,000/month)			X	
2. Insurance on manufacturing building ($750/month)			X	
3. Raw materials ($80/bicycle)	X			
4. Manufacturing utilities ($1,000/month)			X	
5. Office supplies ($800/month)				X
6. Wages for workers ($30/bicycle)		X		
7. Depreciation on office equipment ($650/month)				X
8. Miscellaneous materials ($1.20/bicycle)			X	
9. Property taxes on manufacturing building ($2,400/year)			X	
10. Manufacturing supervisor's salary ($3,000/month)			X	
11. Advertising cost ($30,000/year)				X
12. Sales commissions ($10/bicycle)				X
13. Depreciation on manufacturing building ($1,500/month)			X	

(b)

Cost Item	Manufacturing Cost
Rent on manufacturing equipment	$ 2,000
Insurance on manufacturing building	750
Raw materials ($80 × 1,000)	80,000
Manufacturing utilities	1,000
Labor ($30 × 1,000)	30,000
Miscellaneous materials ($1.20 × 1,000)	1,200
Property taxes on manufacturing building ($2,400 ÷ 12)	200
Manufacturing supervisor's salary	3,000
Depreciation on manufacturing building	1,500
Total manufacturing costs	$119,650

The Navigator

COMPREHENSIVE

Do it! 2

Superior Manufacturing Company has the following cost and expense data for the year ending December 31, 2012.

Raw materials, 1/1/12	$ 30,000	Insurance, factory	$ 14,000
Raw materials, 12/31/12	20,000	Property taxes, factory building	6,000
Raw materials purchases	205,000	Sales (net)	1,500,000
Indirect materials	15,000	Delivery expenses	100,000
Work in process, 1/1/12	80,000	Sales commissions	150,000
Work in process, 12/31/12	50,000	Indirect labor	90,000
Finished goods, 1/1/12	110,000	Factory machinery rent	40,000
Finished goods, 12/31/12	120,000	Factory utilities	65,000
Direct labor	350,000	Depreciation, factory building	24,000
Factory manager's salary	35,000	Administrative expenses	300,000

Instructions

(a) Prepare a cost of goods manufactured schedule for Superior Company for 2012.

(b) Prepare an income statement for Superior Company for 2012.

(c) Assume that Superior Company's ledgers show the balances of the following current asset accounts: Cash $17,000, Accounts Receivable (net) $120,000, Prepaid Expenses $13,000, and Short-term Investments $26,000. Prepare the current assets section of the balance sheet for Superior Company as of December 31, 2012.

action plan

✔ Start with beginning work in process as the first item in the cost of goods manufactured schedule.

✔ Sum direct materials used, direct labor, and total manufacturing overhead to determine total manufacturing costs.

✔ Sum beginning work in process and total manufacturing costs to determine total cost of work in process.

✔ Cost of goods manufactured is the total cost of work in process less ending work in process.

✔ In the cost of goods sold section of the income statement, show beginning and ending finished goods inventory and cost of goods manufactured.

✔ In the balance sheet, list manufacturing inventories in the order of their expected realization in cash, with finished goods first.

Solution to Comprehensive Do it! 2

(a)
SUPERIOR MANUFACTURING COMPANY
Cost of Goods Manufactured Schedule
For the Year Ended December 31, 2012

Work in process, 1/1			$ 80,000
Direct materials			
Raw materials inventory, 1/1	$ 30,000		
Raw materials purchases	205,000		
Total raw materials available for use	235,000		
Less: Raw materials inventory, 12/31	20,000		
Direct materials used		$215,000	
Direct labor		350,000	
Manufacturing overhead			
Indirect labor	90,000		
Factory utilities	65,000		
Factory machinery rent	40,000		
Factory manager's salary	35,000		
Depreciation on building	24,000		
Indirect materials	15,000		
Factory insurance	14,000		
Property taxes	6,000		
Total manufacturing overhead		289,000	
Total manufacturing costs			854,000
Total cost of work in process			934,000
Less: Work in process, 12/31			50,000
Cost of goods manufactured			$884,000

(b)

SUPERIOR MANUFACTURING COMPANY
Income Statement
For the Year Ended December 31, 2012

Sales (net)		$1,500,000
Cost of goods sold		
Finished goods inventory, January 1	$110,000	
Cost of goods manufactured	884,000	
Cost of goods available for sale	994,000	
Finished goods inventory, December 31	120,000	
Cost of goods sold		874,000
Gross profit		626,000
Operating expenses		
Administrative expenses	300,000	
Sales commissions	150,000	
Delivery expenses	100,000	
Total operating expenses		550,000
Net income		$ 76,000

(c)

SUPERIOR MANUFACTURING COMPANY
Balance Sheet (partial)
December 31, 2012

Current assets		
Cash		$ 17,000
Short-term investments		26,000
Accounts receivable (net)		120,000
Inventories		
Finished goods	$120,000	
Work in process	50,000	
Raw materials	20,000	190,000
Prepaid expenses		13,000
Total current assets		$366,000

The Navigator

Summary of Study Objectives

[1] Explain the distinguishing features of managerial accounting. The *primary users* of managerial accounting reports are internal users, who are officers, department heads, managers, and supervisors in the company. Managerial accounting issues internal reports as frequently as the need arises. The purpose of these reports is to provide special-purpose information for a particular user for a specific decision. The content of managerial accounting reports pertains to subunits of the business, may be very detailed, and may extend beyond the double-entry accounting system. The reporting standard is relevance to the decision being made. No independent audits are required in managerial accounting.

[2] Identify the three broad functions of management. The three functions are planning, directing, and controlling. Planning requires management to look ahead and to establish objectives. Directing involves coordinating the diverse activities and human resources of a company to produce a smooth-running operation. Controlling is the process of keeping the activities on track.

[3] Define the three classes of manufacturing costs. Manufacturing costs are typically classified as either (1) direct materials, (2) direct labor, or (3) manufacturing overhead. Raw materials that can be physically and directly associated with the finished product during the manufacturing process are called direct materials. The work of factory employees that can be physically and directly associated with converting raw materials into finished goods is considered direct labor. Manufacturing overhead consists of costs that are indirectly associated with the manufacture of the finished product.

[4] Distinguish between product and period costs. Product costs are costs that are a necessary and integral part of producing the finished product. Product costs are also called inventoriable costs. Under the matching principle, these costs do not become expenses until the company sells the finished goods inventory. Period costs are costs that are identified with a specific time period rather than with a salable product. These costs relate to nonmanufacturing costs and therefore are not inventoriable costs.

[5] Explain the difference between a merchandising and a manufacturing income statement. The difference between a merchandising and a manufacturing income statement is in the cost of goods sold section. A manufacturing cost of goods sold section shows beginning and ending finished goods inventories and the cost of goods manufactured.

[6] Indicate how cost of goods manufactured is determined. Companies add the cost of the beginning work in process to the total manufacturing costs for the current year to arrive at the total cost of work in process for the year. They then subtract the ending work in process from the total cost of work in process to arrive at the cost of goods manufactured.

[7] Explain the difference between a merchandising and a manufacturing balance sheet. The difference between a merchandising and a manufacturing balance sheet

is in the current assets section. The current assets section of a manufacturing company's balance sheet presents three inventory accounts: finished goods inventory, work in process inventory, and raw materials inventory.

[8] Identify trends in managerial accounting. Managerial accounting has experienced many changes in recent years. Among these are a shift toward addressing the needs of service companies and improving practices to better meet the needs of managers. Improved practices include a focus on managing the value chain through techniques such as just-in-time inventory and technological applications such as enterprise resource management, computer-integrated manufacturing, and B2B e-commerce. In addition, techniques such as just-in-time inventory, total quality management, activity-based costing, and theory of constraints are improving decision making. Finally, the balanced scorecard is now used by many companies in order to attain a more comprehensive view of the company's operations.

Glossary

Activity-based costing (ABC)   A method of allocating overhead based on each product's use of activities in making the product. (p. 896).

Balanced scorecard   A performance-measurement approach that uses both financial and nonfinancial measures, tied to company objectives, to evaluate a company's operations in an integrated fashion. (p. 897).

Board of directors   The group of officials elected by the stockholders of a corporation to formulate operating policies, select officers, and otherwise manage the company. (p. 881).

Chief executive officer (CEO)   Corporate officer who has overall responsibility for managing the business and delegates responsibilities to other corporate officers. (p. 882).

Chief financial officer (CFO)   Corporate officer who is responsible for all of the accounting and finance issues of the company. (p. 882).

Controller   Financial officer responsible for a company's accounting records, system of internal control, and preparation of financial statements, tax returns, and internal reports. (p. 882).

Cost of goods manufactured   Total cost of work in process less the cost of the ending work in process inventory. (p. 889).

Direct labor   The work of factory employees that can be physically and directly associated with converting raw materials into finished goods. (p. 885).

Direct materials   Raw materials that can be physically and directly associated with manufacturing the finished product. (p. 885).

Enterprise resource planning (ERP) system   Software that provides a comprehensive, centralized, integrated

source of information used to manage all major business processes. (p. 895).

Indirect labor   Work of factory employees that has no physical association with the finished product, or for which it is impractical to trace the costs to the goods produced. (p. 885).

Indirect materials   Raw materials that do not physically become part of the finished product or cannot be traced because their physical association with the finished product is too small. (p. 885).

Just-in-time (JIT) inventory   Inventory system in which goods are manufactured or purchased just in time for use. (p. 895).

Line positions   Jobs that are directly involved in a company's primary revenue-generating operating activities. (p. 882).

Managerial accounting   A field of accounting that provides economic and financial information for managers and other internal users. (p. 878).

Manufacturing overhead   Manufacturing costs that are indirectly associated with the manufacture of the finished product. (p. 885).

Period costs   Costs that are matched with the revenue of a specific time period and charged to expense as incurred. (p. 886).

Product costs   Costs that are a necessary and integral part of producing the finished product. (p. 886).

Sarbanes-Oxley Act of 2002 (SOX)   Law passed by Congress in 2002, intended to reduce unethical corporate behavior. (p. 883).

Staff positions   Jobs that support the efforts of line employees. (p. 882).

Theory of constraints   A specific approach used to identify and manage constraints in order to achieve the company's goals. (p. 896).

Total cost of work in process   Cost of the beginning work in process plus total manufacturing costs for the current period. (p. 889).

Total manufacturing costs   The sum of direct materials, direct labor, and manufacturing overhead incurred in the current period. (p. 889).

Total quality management (TQM)   Systems implemented to reduce defects in finished products with the goal of achieving zero defects. (p. 896).

Treasurer   Financial officer who has custody of the corporation's funds and is responsible for maintaining the company's cash position. (p. 882).

Value chain   All activities associated with providing a product or service. (p. 894).

 Self-Test, Brief Exercises, Exercises, Problem Set A, and many more components are available for practice in _WileyPLUS_

Self-Test Questions

Answers are on page 921.

(SO 1)   **1.** Managerial accounting:
   a. is governed by generally accepted accounting principles.
   b. places emphasis on special-purpose information.
   c. pertains to the entity as a whole and is highly aggregated.
   d. is limited to cost data.

(SO 2)   **2.** The management of an organization performs several broad functions. They are:
   a. planning, directing, and selling.
   b. planning, directing, and controlling.
   c. planning, manufacturing, and controlling.
   d. directing, manufacturing, and controlling.

(SO 2)   **3.** After passage of the Sarbanes-Oxley Act of 2002:
   a. reports prepared by managerial accountants must be audited by CPAs.
   b. CEOs and CFOs must certify that financial statements give a fair presentation of the company's operating results.
   c. the audit committee, rather than top management, is responsible for the company's financial statements.
   d. reports prepared by managerial accountants must comply with generally accepted accounting principles (GAAP).

(SO 3)   **4.** Direct materials are a:

	Product Cost	Manufacturing Overhead	Period Cost
a.	Yes	Yes	No
b.	Yes	No	No
c.	Yes	Yes	Yes
d.	No	No	No

(SO 3)   **5.** Which of the following costs would a computer manufacturer include in manufacturing overhead?
   a. The cost of the disk drives.
   b. The wages earned by computer assemblers.
   c. The cost of the memory chips.
   d. Depreciation on testing equipment.

(SO 3)   **6.** Which of the following is *not* an element of manufacturing overhead?
   a. Sales manager's salary.
   b. Plant manager's salary.
   c. Factory repairman's wages.
   d. Product inspector's salary.

(SO 4)   **7.** Indirect labor is a:
   a. nonmanufacturing cost.
   b. raw material cost.
   c. product cost.
   d. period cost.

(SO 4)   **8.** Which of the following costs are classified as a period cost?
   a. Wages paid to a factory custodian.
   b. Wages paid to a production department supervisor.
   c. Wages paid to a cost accounting department supervisor.
   d. Wages paid to an assembly worker.

(SO 5)   **9.** For the year, Redder Company has cost of goods manufactured of $600,000, beginning finished goods inventory of $200,000, and ending finished goods inventory of $250,000. The cost of goods sold is:
   a. $450,000.   **c.** $550,000.
   b. $500,000.   **d.** $600,000.

(SO 5)   **10.** Cost of goods available for sale is reported on the income statement of:
   a. a merchandising company but not a manufacturing company.
   b. a manufacturing company but not a merchandising company.
   c. a merchandising company and a manufacturing company.
   d. neither a manufacturing company nor a merchandising company.

(SO 6)   **11.** A cost of goods manufactured schedule shows beginning and ending inventories for:
   a. raw materials and work in process only.
   b. work in process only.
   c. raw materials only.
   d. raw materials, work in process, and finished goods.

(SO 6)   **12.** The formula to determine the cost of goods manufactured is:
   a. Beginning raw materials inventory + Total manufacturing costs − Ending work in process inventory.
   b. Beginning work in process inventory + Total manufacturing costs − Ending finished goods inventory.
   c. Beginning finished good inventory + Total manufacturing costs − Ending finished goods inventory.
   d. Beginning work in process inventory + Total manufacturing costs − Ending work in process inventory.

(SO 7) **13.** A manufacturer may report three inventories in its balance sheet: (1) raw materials, (2) work in process, and (3) finished goods. Indicate in what sequence these inventories generally appear on a balance sheet.

    a. (1), (2), (3)   **c.** (3), (1), (2)
    b. (2), (3), (1)   **d.** (3), (2), (1)

(SO 8) **14.** Which of the following managerial accounting techniques attempts to allocate manufacturing overhead in a more meaningful fashion?
    a. Just-in-time inventory.
    b. Total-quality management.
    c. Balanced scorecard.
    d. Activity-based costing.

(SO 8) **15.** Examples of recent trends in the economic environment of U.S. businesses are:

    a. increasing deregulation, decreasing global competition, and a shift toward providing services rather than goods.
    b. increasing deregulation, increasing global competition, and a shift toward providing goods rather than services.
    c. decreasing deregulation, decreasing global competition, and a shift toward providing services rather than goods.
    d. increasing deregulation, increasing global competition, and a shift toward providing services rather than goods.

Go to the book's companion website, **www.wiley.com/college/weygandt**, for additional Self-Test Questions.

 The Navigator

Questions

1. (a) "Managerial accounting is a field of accounting that provides economic information for all interested parties." Do you agree? Explain.
    (b) Jenny Gardner believes that managerial accounting serves only manufacturing firms. Is Jenny correct? Explain.

2. Distinguish between managerial and financial accounting as to (a) primary users of reports, (b) types and frequency of reports, and (c) purpose of reports.

3. How does the content of reports and the verification of reports differ between managerial and financial accounting?

4. In what ways can the budgeting process create incentives for unethical behavior?

5. Carla Pietro is studying for the next accounting mid-term examination. Summarize for Carla what she should know about management functions.

6. "Decision making is management's most important function." Do you agree? Why or why not?

7. What new rules were enacted under the Sarbanes-Oxley Act to address unethical accounting practices?

8. Ken Taser is studying for his next accounting examination. Explain to Ken what he should know about the differences between the income statements for a manufacturing and for a merchandising company.

9. Sheri Laine is unclear as to the difference between the balance sheets of a merchandising company and a manufacturing company. Explain the difference to Sheri.

10. How are manufacturing costs classified?

11. Vinh Yen claims that the distinction between direct and indirect materials is based entirely on physical association with the product. Is Vinh correct? Why?

12. Sarah Limoges is confused about the differences between a product cost and a period cost. Explain the differences to Sarah.

13. Identify the differences in the cost of goods sold section of an income statement between a merchandising company and a manufacturing company.

14. The determination of the cost of goods manufactured involves the following factors: (A) beginning work in process inventory, (B) total manufacturing costs, and (C) ending work in process inventory. Identify the meaning of x in the following formulas:
    (a) $A + B = x$
    (b) $A + B - C = x$

15. Hammen Manufacturing has beginning raw materials inventory $12,000, ending raw materials inventory $15,000, and raw materials purchases $170,000. What is the cost of direct materials used?

16. Conrad Manufacturing Inc. has beginning work in process $26,000, direct materials used $240,000, direct labor $200,000, total manufacturing overhead $180,000, and ending work in process $32,000. What are total manufacturing costs?

17. Using the data in question 16, what are (a) the total cost of work in process and (b) the cost of goods manufactured?

18. In what order should manufacturing inventories be listed in a balance sheet?

19. How do the products of manufacturing operations differ from those of service operations?

20. Discuss whether the product costing techniques discussed in this chapter apply equally well to manufacturers and service companies.

21. What is the value chain? Describe, in sequence, the main components of a manufacturer's value chain.

22. What is an enterprise resource planning (ERP) system? What are its primary benefits?

23. Why is product quality important for companies that implement a just-in-time inventory system?

24. Explain what is meant by "balanced" in the balanced scorecard approach.

25. What is activity-based costing, and what are its potential benefits?

Brief Exercises

BE19-1 Complete the following comparison table between managerial and financial accounting.

	Financial Accounting	**Managerial Accounting**
Primary users		
Types of reports		
Frequency of reports		
Purpose of reports		
Content of reports		
Verification		

Distinguish between managerial and financial accounting.
(SO 1)

BE19-2 The Sarbanes-Oxley Act of 2002 (SOX) has important implications for the financial community. Explain two implications of SOX.

Identify important regulatory changes.
(SO 2)

BE19-3 Listed below are the three functions of the management of an organization.

1. Planning   2. Directing   3. Controlling

Identify which of the following statements best describes each of the above functions.

(a) ____ requires management to look ahead and to establish objectives. A key objective of management is to add value to the business.

(b) ____ involves coordinating the diverse activities and human resources of a company to produce a smooth-running operation. This function relates to the implementation of planned objectives.

(c) ____ is the process of keeping the activities on track. Management must determine whether goals are being met and what changes are necessary when there are deviations.

Identify the three management functions.
(SO 2)

BE19-4 Determine whether each of the following costs should be classified as direct materials (DM), direct labor (DL), or manufacturing overhead (MO).

(a) ____Frames and tires used in manufacturing bicycles.
(b) ____Wages paid to production workers.
(c) ____Insurance on factory equipment and machinery.
(d) ____Depreciation on factory equipment.

Classify manufacturing costs.
(SO 3)

BE19-5 Indicate whether each of the following costs of an automobile manufacturer would be classified as direct materials, direct labor, or manufacturing overhead.

(a) ____Windshield.
(b) ____Engine.
(c) ____Wages of assembly line worker.
(d) ____Depreciation of factory machinery.
(e) ____Factory machinery lubricants.
(f) ____Tires.
(g) ____Steering wheel.
(h) ____Salary of painting supervisor.

Classify manufacturing costs.
(SO 3)

BE19-6 Identify whether each of the following costs should be classified as product costs or period costs.

(a) ____Manufacturing overhead.
(b) ____Selling expenses.
(c) ____Administrative expenses.
(d) ____Advertising expenses.
(e) ____Direct labor.
(f) ____Direct material.

Identify product and period costs.
(SO 4)

BE19-7 Presented below are Bennett Company's monthly manufacturing cost data related to its personal computer products.

(a) Utilities for manufacturing equipment $116,000
(b) Raw material (CPU, chips, etc.) $ 85,000
(c) Depreciation on manufacturing building $880,000
(d) Wages for production workers $191,000

Enter each cost item in the following table, placing an "X" under the appropriate headings.

Classify manufacturing costs.
(SO 3)

	Product Costs		
	Direct Materials	**Direct Labor**	**Manufacturing Overhead**
(a)			
(b)			
(c)			
(d)			

Compute total manufacturing costs and total cost of work in process.
(SO 6)

BE19-8   Stahl Manufacturing Company has the following data: direct labor $229,000, direct materials used $180,000, total manufacturing overhead $208,000, and beginning work in process $25,000. Compute (a) total manufacturing costs and (b) total cost of work in process.

Prepare current assets section.
(SO 7)

BE19-9   In alphabetical order below are current asset items for Wallace Company's balance sheet at December 31, 2012. Prepare the current assets section (including a complete heading).

Accounts receivable	$200,000
Cash	62,000
Finished goods	71,000
Prepaid expenses	38,000
Raw materials	73,000
Work in process	87,000

Determine missing amounts in computing total manufacturing costs.
(SO 6)

BE19-10   Presented below are incomplete manufacturing cost data. Determine the missing amounts for three different situations.

	Direct Materials Used	Direct Labor Used	Manufacturing Overhead	Total Manufacturing Costs
(1)	$25,000	$61,000	$ 50,000	?
(2)	?	$75,000	$140,000	$296,000
(3)	$55,000	?	$111,000	$310,000

Determine missing amounts in computing cost of goods manufactured.
(SO 6)

BE19-11   Use the same data from BE19–10 above and the data below. Determine the missing amounts.

	Total Manufacturing Costs	Work in Process (1/1)	Work in Process (12/31)	Cost of Goods Manufactured
(1)	?	$120,000	$82,000	?
(2)	$296,000	?	$98,000	$321,000
(3)	$310,000	$463,000	?	$715,000

Do it! Review

Identify managerial accounting concepts.
(SO 1, 2)

Do it! 19-1   Indicate whether the following statements are true or false.

1. Managerial accountants explain and report manufacturing and nonmanufacturing costs, determine cost behaviors, and perform cost-volume-profit analysis, but are not involved in the budget process.
2. Financial accounting reports pertain to subunits of the business and are very detailed.
3. Managerial accounting reports must follow GAAP and are audited by CPAs.
4. Managers' activities and responsibilities can be classified into three broad functions: planning, directing, and controlling.
5. As a result of the Sarbanes-Oxley Act of 2002 (SOX), top managers must certify that the company maintains an adequate system of internal control.
6. Management accountants follow a code of ethics developed by the Institute of Management Accountants.

Identify managerial cost concepts.
(SO 3, 4)

Do it! 19-2   A music company has these costs:

Advertising	Paper inserts for CD cases
Blank CDs	CD plastic cases
Depreciation of CD image burner	Salaries of sales representatives
Salary of factory manager	Salaries of factory maintenance employees
Factory supplies used	Salaries of employees who burn music onto CDs

Classify each cost as a period or a product cost. Within the product cost category, indicate if the cost is part of direct materials (DM), direct labor (DL), or manufacturing overhead (MO).

Do it! 19-3   The following information is available for Sanchez Manufacturing Company.

Prepare cost of goods manufactured schedule.

(SO 6)

	April 1	April 31
Raw material inventory	$10,000	$14,000
Work in process inventory	5,000	3,500

Materials purchased in April	$ 98,000
Direct labor in April	60,000
Manufacturing overhead in April	180,000

Prepare the cost of goods manufactured schedule for the month of April.

Do it! 19-4   Match the descriptions that follow with the corresponding terms.

Identify trends in managerial accounting.

(SO 8)

Descriptions:

1. _____ Inventory system in which goods are manufactured or purchased just as they are needed for use.
2. _____ A method of allocating overhead based on each product's use of activities in making the product.
3. _____ Systems that are especially important to firms adopting just-in-time inventory methods.
4. _____ One part of the value chain for a manufacturing company.
5. _____ The U.S. economy is trending toward this.
6. _____ A performance-measurement approach that uses both financial and nonfinancial measures, tied to company objectives, to evaluate a company's operations in an integrated fashion.

Terms:

(a) Activity-based costing
(b) Balanced scorecard
(c) Total quality management (TQM)
(d) Research and development, and product design
(e) Service industries
(f) Just-in-time (JIT) inventory

Exercises

E19-1   Denis Mayer has prepared the following list of statements about managerial accounting and financial accounting.

Identify distinguishing features of managerial accounting.

(SO 1)

1. Financial accounting focuses on providing information to internal users.
2. Analyzing cost-volume-profit relationships is part of managerial accounting.
3. Preparation of budgets is part of financial accounting.
4. Managerial accounting applies only to merchandising and manufacturing companies.
5. Both managerial accounting and financial accounting deal with many of the same economic events.
6. Managerial accounting reports are prepared only quarterly and annually.
7. Financial accounting reports are general-purpose reports.
8. Managerial accounting reports pertain to subunits of the business.
9. Managerial accounting reports must comply with generally accepted accounting principles.
10. Although managerial accountants are expected to behave ethically, there is no code of ethical standards for managerial accountants.

Instructions

Identify each statement as true or false. If false, indicate how to correct the statement.

E19-2   Presented below is a list of costs and expenses usually incurred by Gurule Corporation, a manufacturer of furniture, in its factory.

Classify costs into three classes of manufacturing costs.

(SO 3)

1. Salaries for assembly line inspectors.
2. Insurance on factory machines.
3. Property taxes on the factory building.
4. Factory repairs.
5. Upholstery used in manufacturing furniture.

6. Wages paid to assembly line workers.
7. Factory machinery depreciation.
8. Glue, nails, paint, and other small parts used in production.
9. Factory supervisors' salaries.
10. Wood used in manufacturing furniture.

Instructions

Classify the above items into the following categories: (a) direct materials, (b) direct labor, and (c) manufacturing overhead.

Identify types of cost and explain their accounting.

(SO 3, 4)

E19-3   Bacala Corporation incurred the following costs while manufacturing its product.

Materials used in product	$100,000	Advertising expense	$45,000
Depreciation on plant	60,000	Property taxes on plant	14,000
Property taxes on store	7,500	Delivery expense	21,000
Labor costs of assembly-line workers	110,000	Sales commissions	35,000
Factory supplies used	13,000	Salaries paid to sales clerks	50,000

Instructions

(a) Identify each of the costs as direct materials, direct labor, manufacturing overhead, or period costs.

(b) Explain the basic difference in accounting for product costs and period costs.

Determine the total amount of various types of costs.

(SO 3, 4)

E19-4   Drew Company reports the following costs and expenses in May.

Factory utilities	$ 11,500	Direct labor	$69,100
Depreciation on factory equipment	12,650	Sales salaries	46,400
Depreciation on delivery trucks	3,800	Property taxes on factory building	2,500
Indirect factory labor	48,900	Repairs to office equipment	1,300
Indirect materials	80,800	Factory repairs	2,000
Direct materials used	137,600	Advertising	18,000
Factory manager's salary	8,000	Office supplies used	2,640

Instructions

From the information, determine the total amount of:

(a) Manufacturing overhead.

(b) Product costs.

(c) Period costs.

Classify various costs into different cost categories.

(SO 3, 4)

E19-5   Sami Company is a manufacturer of personal computers. Various costs and expenses associated with its operations are as follows.

1. Property taxes on the factory building.
2. Production superintendents' salaries.
3. Memory boards and chips used in assembling computers.
4. Depreciation on the factory equipment.
5. Salaries for assembly line quality control inspectors.
6. Sales commissions paid to sell personal computers.
7. Electrical components used in assembling computers.
8. Wages of workers assembling personal computers.
9. Soldering materials used on factory assembly lines.
10. Salaries for the night security guards for the factory building.

The company intends to classify these costs and expenses into the following categories: (a) direct materials, (b) direct labor, (c) manufacturing overhead, and (d) period costs.

Instructions

List the items (1) through (10). For each item, indicate the cost category to which it belongs.

Classify various costs into different cost categories.

(SO 3)

E19-6   The administrators of San Mateo County's Memorial Hospital are interested in identifying the various costs and expenses that are incurred in producing a patient's X-ray. A list of such costs and expenses is presented below.

1. Salaries for the X-ray machine technicians.
2. Wages for the hospital janitorial personnel.
3. Film costs for the X-ray machines.
4. Property taxes on the hospital building.

	DM	DL	Manufacturing Overhead	Total MF Cost
1	25,000	61,000	55,000	141,000
2	81,000	75,000	140,000	296,000
3	55,000	194,000	111,000	310,000

Total MF Cost	Work In Progress 1/1	Work in Progress 12/31	COG Manufactured
81,000	120,000	82,000	284,000
296,000	123,000	98,000	321,000
310,000	463,000	773,000	715,000

$$120 + x = x - 82$$

5. Salary of the X-ray technicians' supervisor.
6. Electricity costs for the X-ray department.
7. Maintenance and repairs on the X-ray machines.
8. X-ray department supplies.
9. Depreciation on the X-ray department equipment.
10. Depreciation on the hospital building.

The administrators want these costs and expenses classified as: (a) direct materials, (b) direct labor, or (c) service overhead.

Instructions
List the items (1) through (10). For each item, indicate the cost category to which the item belongs.

E19-7 Speedi Delivery Service reports the following costs and expenses in June 2012.

Classify various costs into different cost categories.

(SO 4)

Indirect materials	$ 5,400	Drivers' salaries	$11,000
Depreciation on delivery equipment	11,200	Advertising	1,600
Dispatcher's salary	5,000	Delivery equipment repairs	300
Property taxes on office building	870	Office supplies	650
CEO's salary	12,000	Office utilities	990
Gas and oil for delivery trucks	2,200	Repairs on office equipment	180

Instructions
Determine the total amount of (a) delivery service (product) costs and (b) period costs.

E19-8 Craig Corporation incurred the following costs while manufacturing its product.

Compute cost of goods manufactured and sold.

(SO 5, 6)

Materials used in product	$100,000	Advertising expense	$45,000
Depreciation on plant	60,000	Property taxes on plant	14,000
Property taxes on store	7,500	Delivery expense	21,000
Labor costs of assembly-line workers	110,000	Sales commissions	35,000
Factory supplies used	23,000	Salaries paid to sales clerks	50,000

Work in process inventory was $12,000 at January 1 and $15,500 at December 31. Finished goods inventory was $60,000 at January 1 and $55,600 at December 31.

Instructions
(a) Compute cost of goods manufactured.
(b) Compute cost of goods sold.

E19-9 An incomplete cost of goods manufactured schedule is presented below.

Determine missing amounts in cost of goods manufactured schedule.

(SO 6)

ORLANDO MANUFACTURING COMPANY
Cost of Goods Manufactured Schedule
For the Year Ended December 31, 2012

Work in process (1/1)			$210,000
Direct materials			
Raw materials inventory (1/1)	$?		
Add: Raw materials purchases	158,000		
Total raw materials available for use	?		
Less: Raw materials inventory (12/31)	12,500		
Direct materials used		$190,000	
Direct labor		?	
Manufacturing overhead			
Indirect labor	$ 18,000		
Factory depreciation	36,000		
Factory utilities	68,000		
Total overhead		122,000	
Total manufacturing costs			?
Total cost of work in process			?
Less: Work in process (12/31)			81,000
Cost of goods manufactured			$510,000

Instructions
Complete the cost of goods manufactured schedule for Orlando Manufacturing Company.

Determine the missing amount of different cost items.
(SO 6)

E19-10   Manufacturing cost data for Fortney Company are presented below.

	Case A	Case B	Case C
Direct materials used	(a)	$58,400	$130,000
Direct labor	$ 57,000	86,000	(g)
Manufacturing overhead	46,500	81,600	102,000
Total manufacturing costs	185,650	(d)	253,700
Work in process 1/1/12	(b)	16,500	(h)
Total cost of work in process	221,500	(e)	337,000
Work in process 12/31/12	(c)	11,000	70,000
Cost of goods manufactured	185,275	(f)	(i)

Instructions
Indicate the missing amount for each letter (a) through (i).

Determine the missing amount of different cost items, and prepare a condensed cost of goods manufactured schedule.
(SO 6)

E19-11   Incomplete manufacturing cost data for Juego Company for 2012 are presented as follows for four different situations.

	Direct Materials Used	Direct Labor Used	Manufacturing Overhead	Total Manufacturing Costs	Work in Process 1/1	Work in Process 12/31	Cost of Goods Manufactured
(1)	$127,000	$140,000	$ 77,000	(a)	$33,000	(b)	$360,000
(2)	(c)	200,000	132,000	$450,000	(d)	$40,000	470,000
(3)	80,000	100,000	(e)	245,000	60,000	80,000	(f)
(4)	70,000	(g)	75,000	288,000	45,000	(h)	270,000

Instructions
(a) Indicate the missing amount for each letter.
(b) Prepare a condensed cost of goods manufactured schedule for situation (1) for the year ended December 31, 2012.

Prepare a cost of goods manufactured schedule and a partial income statement.
(SO 5, 6)

E19-12   Troy Corporation has the following cost records for June 2012.

Indirect factory labor	$ 4,500	Factory utilities	$ 400
Direct materials used	20,000	Depreciation, factory equipment	1,400
Work in process, 6/1/12	3,000	Direct labor	30,000
Work in process, 6/30/12	3,800	Maintenance, factory equipment	1,800
Finished goods, 6/1/12	5,000	Indirect materials	2,200
Finished goods, 6/30/12	7,500	Factory manager's salary	3,000

Instructions
(a) Prepare a cost of goods manufactured schedule for June 2012.
(b) Prepare an income statement through gross profit for June 2012 assuming net sales are $87,100.

Classify various costs into different categories and prepare cost of services provided schedule.
(SO 4, 5, 6)

E19-13   Tiffany Pratt, the bookkeeper for Bush, Clinton, and Obama, a political consulting firm, has recently completed an accounting course at her local college. One of the topics covered in the course was the cost of goods manufactured schedule. Tiffany wondered if such a schedule could be prepared for her firm. She realized that, as a service-oriented company, it would have no work in process inventory to consider.

Listed below are the costs her firm incurred for the month ended August 31, 2012.

Supplies used on consulting contracts	$ 1,200
Supplies used in the administrative offices	1,500
Depreciation on equipment used for contract work	900
Depreciation used on administrative office equipment	1,050
Salaries of professionals working on contracts	12,600
Salaries of administrative office personnel	7,700
Janitorial services for professional offices	400
Janitorial services for administrative offices	500
Insurance on contract operations	800
Insurance on administrative operations	900
Utilities for contract operations	1,400
Utilities for administrative offices	1,300

Instructions

(a) Prepare a schedule of cost of contract services provided (similar to a cost of goods manufactured schedule) for the month.

(b) For those costs not included in (a), explain how they would be classified and reported in the financial statements.

E19-14 The following information is available for Xotchil Company.

Prepare a cost of goods manufactured schedule and a partial income statement.

(SO 5, 6, 7)

	January 1, 2012	2012	December 31, 2012
Raw materials inventory	$21,000		$30,000
Work in process inventory	13,500		17,200
Finished goods inventory	27,000		21,000
Materials purchased		$150,000	
Direct labor		200,000	
Manufacturing overhead		180,000	
Sales		900,000	

Instructions

(a) Compute cost of goods manufactured.

(b) Prepare an income statement through gross profit.

(c) Show the presentation of the ending inventories on the December 31, 2012, balance sheet.

(d) How would the income statement and balance sheet of a merchandising company be different from Xotchil's financial statements?

E19-15 Yacob Manufacturing Company produces blankets. From its accounting records it prepares the following schedule and financial statements on a yearly basis.

(a) Cost of goods manufactured schedule.

(b) Income statement.

(c) Balance sheet.

Indicate in which schedule or financial statement(s) different cost items will appear.

(SO 5, 6, 7)

The following items are found in its ledger and accompanying data.

1. Direct labor
2. Raw materials inventory, 1/1
3. Work in process inventory, 12/31
4. Finished goods inventory, 1/1
5. Indirect labor
6. Depreciation on factory machinery
7. Work in process, 1/1
8. Finished goods inventory, 12/31

9. Factory maintenance salaries
10. Cost of goods manufactured
11. Depreciation on delivery equipment
12. Cost of goods available for sale
13. Direct materials used
14. Heat and electricity for factory
15. Repairs to roof of factory building
16. Cost of raw materials purchases

Instructions

List the items (1)–(16). For each item, indicate by using the appropriate letter or letters, the schedule and/or financial statement(s) in which the item will appear.

E19-16 An analysis of the accounts of Zuniga Manufacturing reveals the following manufacturing cost data for the month ended June 30, 2012.

Prepare a cost of goods manufactured schedule, and present the ending inventories of the balance sheet.

(SO 6, 7)

Inventories	Beginning	Ending
Raw materials	$9,000	$13,100
Work in process	5,000	7,000
Finished goods	9,000	6,000

Costs incurred: Raw materials purchases $54,000, direct labor $57,000, manufacturing overhead $19,900. The specific overhead costs were: indirect labor $5,500, factory insurance $4,000, machinery depreciation $4,000, machinery repairs $1,800, factory utilities $3,100, miscellaneous factory costs $1,500. Assume that all raw materials used were direct materials.

Instructions

(a) Prepare the cost of goods manufactured schedule for the month ended June 30, 2012.

(b) Show the presentation of the ending inventories on the June 30, 2012, balance sheet.

E19-17 Pohl Motor Company manufactures automobiles. During September 2012 the company purchased 5,000 head lamps at a cost of $9 per lamp. Todd withdrew 4,650 lamps from the warehouse during the month. Fifty of these lamps were used to replace the head lamps in autos

Determine the amount of cost to appear in various accounts, and indicate in which financial statements these accounts would appear.

(SO 5, 6, 7)

used by traveling sales staff. The remaining 4,600 lamps were put in autos manufactured during the month.

Of the autos put into production during September 2012, 90% were completed and transferred to the company's storage lot. Of the cars completed during the month, 75% were sold by September 30.

Instructions

(a) Determine the cost of head lamps that would appear in each of the following accounts at September 30, 2012: Raw Materials, Work in Process, Finished Goods, Cost of Goods Sold, and Selling Expenses.

(b) ◄▬▬▬ Write a short memo to the chief accountant, indicating whether and where each of the accounts in (a) would appear on the income statement or on the balance sheet at September 30, 2012.

Identify various managerial accounting practices.

(SO 8)

E19-18   The following is a list of terms related to managerial accounting practices.

1. Activity-based costing.
2. Just-in-time inventory.
3. Balanced scorecard.
4. Value chain.

Instructions

Match each of the terms with the statement below that best describes the term.

(a) ____ A performance-measurement technique that attempts to consider and evaluate all aspects of performance using financial and nonfinancial measures in an integrated fashion.

(b) ____ The group of activities associated with providing a product or service.

(c) ____ An approach used to reduce the cost associated with handling and holding inventory by reducing the amount of inventory on hand.

(d) ____ A method used to allocate overhead to products based on each product's use of the activities that cause the incurrence of the overhead cost.

Exercises: Set B

Visit the book's companion website, at **www.wiley.com/college/weygandt**, and choose the Student Companion site to access Exercise Set B.

Problems: Set A

Classify manufacturing costs into different categories and compute the unit cost.

(SO 3, 4)

P19-1A   Fabila Company specializes in manufacturing a unique model of bicycle helmet. The model is well accepted by consumers, and the company has enough orders to keep the factory production at 10,000 helmets per month (80% of its full capacity). Fabila's monthly manufacturing cost and other expense data are as follows.

Rent on factory equipment	$ 7,000
Insurance on factory building	1,500
Raw materials (plastics, polystyrene, etc.)	75,000
Utility costs for factory	900
Supplies for general office	300
Wages for assembly line workers	43,000
Depreciation on office equipment	800
Miscellaneous materials (glue, thread, etc.)	1,100
Factory manager's salary	5,700
Property taxes on factory building	400
Advertising for helmets	14,000
Sales commissions	7,000
Depreciation on factory building	1,500

Instructions

(a) Prepare an answer sheet with the following column headings.

	Product Costs			
Cost Item	Direct Materials	Direct Labor	Manufacturing Overhead	Period Costs

(a) DM $75,000
DL $43,000
MO $18,100
PC $22,100

Enter each cost item on your answer sheet, placing the dollar amount under the appropriate headings. Total the dollar amounts in each of the columns.

(b) Compute the cost to produce one helmet.

P19-2A Kabana Company, a manufacturer of stereo systems, started its production in October 2012. For the preceding 3 years Kabana had been a retailer of stereo systems. After a thorough survey of stereo system markets, Kabana decided to turn its retail store into a stereo equipment factory.

Classify manufacturing costs into different categories and compute the unit cost.

(SO 3, 4)

Raw materials cost for a stereo system will total $74 per unit. Workers on the production lines are on average paid $12 per hour. A stereo system usually takes 5 hours to complete. In addition, the rent on the equipment used to assemble stereo systems amounts to $4,900 per month. Indirect materials cost $5 per system. A supervisor was hired to oversee production; her monthly salary is $3,000.

Factory janitorial costs are $1,300 monthly. Advertising costs for the stereo system will be $8,500 per month. The factory building depreciation expense is $7,200 per year. Property taxes on the factory building will be $9,000 per year.

Instructions

(a) Prepare an answer sheet with the following column headings.

	Product Costs			
Cost Item	Direct Materials	Direct Labor	Manufacturing Overhead	Period Costs

(a) DM $96,200
DL $78,000
MO $17,050
PC $ 8,500

Assuming that Kabana manufactures, on average, 1,300 stereo systems per month, enter each cost item on your answer sheet, placing the dollar amount per month under the appropriate headings. Total the dollar amounts in each of the columns.

(b) Compute the cost to produce one stereo system.

P19-3A Incomplete manufacturing costs, expenses, and selling data for two different cases are as follows.

Indicate the missing amount of different cost items, and prepare a condensed cost of goods manufactured schedule, an income statement, and a partial balance sheet.

(SO 5, 6, 7)

	Case	
	1	**2**
Direct Materials Used	$ 7,600	$ (g)
Direct Labor	5,000	8,000
Manufacturing Overhead	8,000	4,000
Total Manufacturing Costs	(a)	18,000
Beginning Work in Process Inventory	1,000	(h)
Ending Work in Process Inventory	(b)	3,000
Sales	24,500	(i)
Sales Discounts	2,500	1,400
Cost of Goods Manufactured	17,000	22,000
Beginning Finished Goods Inventory	(c)	3,300
Goods Available for Sale	18,000	(j)
Cost of Goods Sold	(d)	(k)
Ending Finished Goods Inventory	3,400	2,500
Gross Profit	(e)	7,000
Operating Expenses	2,500	(l)
Net Income	(f)	5,000

Instructions

(a) Indicate the missing amount for each letter.

(b) Prepare a condensed cost of goods manufactured schedule for Case 1.

(c) Prepare an income statement and the current assets section of the balance sheet for Case 1. Assume that in Case 1 the other items in the current assets section are as follows: Cash $4,000, Receivables (net) $15,000, Raw Materials $600, and Prepaid Expenses $400.

(b) Ending WIP $4,600
(c) Current assets $28,000

*Prepare a cost of goods manu-
factured schedule, a partial
income statement, and a partial
balance sheet.*

(SO 5, 6, 7)

P19-4A The following data were taken from the records of Blumbey Manufacturing Company for the fiscal year ended June 30, 2012.

Raw Materials		Factory Insurance	$ 4,600
Inventory 7/1/11	$ 48,000	Factory Machinery	
Raw Materials		Depreciation	16,000
Inventory 6/30/12	39,600	Factory Utilities	27,600
Finished Goods		Office Utilities Expense	8,650
Inventory 7/1/11	96,000	Sales	554,000
Finished Goods		Sales Discounts	4,200
Inventory 6/30/12	95,900	Plant Manager's Salary	29,000
Work in Process		Factory Property Taxes	9,600
Inventory 7/1/11	19,800	Factory Repairs	1,400
Work in Process		Raw Materials Purchases	96,400
Inventory 6/30/12	18,600	Cash	32,000
Direct Labor	149,250		
Indirect Labor	24,460		
Accounts Receivable	27,000		

Instructions

(a) CGM $367,910

(a) Prepare a cost of goods manufactured schedule. (Assume all raw materials used were direct materials.)

(b) Gross profit $181,790

(b) Prepare an income statement through gross profit.

(c) Current assets $213,100

(c) Prepare the current assets section of the balance sheet at June 30, 2012.

*Prepare a cost of goods manu-
factured schedule and a correct
income statement.*

(SO 5, 6)

P19-5A Dibene Company is a manufacturer of computers. Its controller resigned in October 2012. An inexperienced assistant accountant has prepared the following income statement for the month of October 2012.

DIBENE COMPANY
Income Statement
For the Month Ended October 31, 2012

Sales (net)		$780,000
Less: Operating expenses		
Raw materials purchases	$264,000	
Direct labor cost	190,000	
Advertising expense	90,000	
Selling and administrative salaries	75,000	
Rent on factory facilities	60,000	
Depreciation on sales equipment	45,000	
Depreciation on factory equipment	31,000	
Indirect labor cost	28,000	
Utilities expense	12,000	
Insurance expense	8,000	803,000
Net loss		$(23,000)

Prior to October 2012, the company had been profitable every month. The company's president is concerned about the accuracy of the income statement. As her friend, you have been asked to review the income statement and make necessary corrections. After examining other manufacturing cost data, you have acquired additional information as follows.

1. Inventory balances at the beginning and end of October were:

	October 1	October 31
Raw materials	$18,000	$34,000
Work in process	16,000	14,000
Finished goods	30,000	48,000

2. Only 70% of the utilities expense and 60% of the insurance expense apply to factory operations. The remaining amounts should be charged to selling and administrative activities.

Instructions

(a) CGM $572,200

(a) Prepare a schedule of cost of goods manufactured for October 2012.

(b) NI $ 9,000

(b) Prepare a correct income statement for October 2012.

Problems: Set B

P19-1B Gazca Company specializes in manufacturing motorcycle helmets. The company has enough orders to keep the factory production at 1,000 motorcycle helmets per month. Gazca's monthly manufacturing cost and other expense data are as follows.

Classify manufacturing costs into different categories and compute the unit cost.
(SO 3, 4)

Maintenance costs on factory building	$ 1,500
Factory manager's salary	4,000
Advertising for helmets	8,000
Sales commissions	5,000
Depreciation on factory building	700
Rent on factory equipment	6,000
Insurance on factory building	3,000
Raw materials (plastic, polystyrene, etc.)	20,000
Utility costs for factory	800
Supplies for general office	200
Wages for assembly line workers	54,000
Depreciation on office equipment	500
Miscellaneous materials (glue, thread, etc.)	2,000

Instructions
(a) Prepare an answer sheet with the following column headings.

(a) DM $20,000
DL $54,000
MO $18,000
PC $13,700

Cost Item	Product Costs Direct Materials	Direct Labor	Manufacturing Overhead	Period Costs

Enter each cost item on your answer sheet, placing the dollar amount under the appropriate headings. Total the dollar amounts in each of the columns.

(b) Compute the cost to produce one motorcycle helmet.

P19-2B Vanessa Williams Company, a manufacturer of tennis rackets, started production in November 2012. For the preceding 5 years, Williams had been a retailer of sports equipment. After a thorough survey of tennis racket markets, Williams decided to turn its retail store into a tennis racket factory.

Classify manufacturing costs into different categories and compute the unit cost.
(SO 3, 4)

Raw materials cost for a tennis racket will total $23 per racket. Workers on the production lines are paid on average $13 per hour. A racket usually takes 2 hours to complete. In addition, the rent on the equipment used to produce rackets amounts to $1,300 per month. Indirect materials cost $3 per racket. A supervisor was hired to oversee production; her monthly salary is $3,500.

Janitorial costs are $1,400 monthly. Advertising costs for the rackets will be $6,000 per month. The factory building depreciation expense is $8,400 per year. Property taxes on the factory building will be $7,200 per year.

Instructions
(a) Prepare an answer sheet with the following column headings.

(a) DM $57,500
DL $65,000
MO $15,000
PC $ 6,000

Cost Item	Product Costs Direct Materials	Direct Labor	Manufacturing Overhead	Period Costs

Assuming that Williams manufactures, on average, 2,500 tennis rackets per month, enter each cost item on your answer sheet, placing the dollar amount per month under the appropriate headings. Total the dollar amounts in each of the columns.

(b) Compute the cost to produce one racket.

P19-3B Incomplete manufacturing costs, expenses, and selling data for two different cases are as follows.

Indicate the missing amount of different cost items, and prepare a condensed cost of goods manufactured schedule, an income statement, and a partial balance sheet.
(SO 5, 6, 7)

	Case A	Case B
Direct Materials Used	$ 6,300	$ (g)
Direct Labor	3,000	4,000
Manufacturing Overhead	6,000	5,000
Total Manufacturing Costs	(a)	16,000
Beginning Work in Process Inventory	1,000	(h)

Ending Work in Process Inventory	(b)	2,000
Sales	22,500	(i)
Sales Discounts	1,500	1,200
Cost of Goods Manufactured	15,800	20,000
Beginning Finished Goods Inventory	(c)	5,000
Goods Available for Sale	18,300	(j)
Cost of Goods Sold	(d)	(k)
Ending Finished Goods Inventory	1,200	2,500
Gross Profit	(e)	6,000
Operating Expenses	2,700	(l)
Net Income	(f)	2,200

Instructions

(a) Indicate the missing amount for each letter.

(b) Prepare a condensed cost of goods manufactured schedule for Case A.

(c) Current assets $15,600

(c) Prepare an income statement and the current assets section of the balance sheet for Case A. Assume that in Case A the other items in the current assets section are as follows: Cash $3,000, Receivables (net) $10,000, Raw Materials $700, and Prepaid Expenses $200.

Prepare a cost of goods manufactured schedule, a partial income statement, and a partial balance sheet.

(SO 5, 6, 7)

P19-4B   The following data were taken from the records of Goodman Manufacturing Company for the year ended December 31, 2012.

Raw Materials		Factory Insurance	$ 7,400
Inventory 1/1/12	$ 47,000	Factory Machinery	
Raw Materials		Depreciation	7,700
Inventory 12/31/12	44,200	Factory Utilities	12,900
Finished Goods		Office Utilities Expense	8,600
Inventory 1/1/12	85,000	Sales	465,000
Finished Goods		Sales Discounts	2,500
Inventory 12/31/12	67,800	Plant Manager's Salary	40,000
Work in Process		Factory Property Taxes	6,100
Inventory 1/1/12	9,500	Factory Repairs	800
Work in Process		Raw Materials Purchases	62,500
Inventory 12/31/12	8,000	Cash	28,000
Direct Labor	145,100		
Indirect Labor	18,100		
Accounts Receivable	27,000		

Instructions

(a) CGM $304,900

(a) Prepare a cost of goods manufactured schedule. (Assume all raw materials used were direct materials.)

(b) Gross profit $140,400
(c) Current assets $175,000

(b) Prepare an income statement through gross profit.

(c) Prepare the current assets section of the balance sheet at December 31.

Prepare a cost of goods manufactured schedule and a correct income statement.

(SO 5, 6)

P19-5B   Quintana Company is a manufacturer of toys. Its controller resigned in August 2012. An inexperienced assistant accountant has prepared the following income statement for the month of August 2012.

QUINTANA COMPANY
Income Statement
For the Month Ended August 31, 2012

Sales (net)		$675,000
Less: Operating expenses		
Raw materials purchases	$220,000	
Direct labor cost	160,000	
Advertising expense	75,000	
Selling and administrative salaries	70,000	
Rent on factory facilities	60,000	
Depreciation on sales equipment	50,000	
Depreciation on factory equipment	35,000	
Indirect labor cost	20,000	
Utilities expense	10,000	
Insurance expense	5,000	705,000
Net loss		$(30,000)

Prior to August 2012 the company had been profitable every month. The company's president is concerned about the accuracy of the income statement. As her friend, you have been asked to review the income statement and make necessary corrections. After examining other manufacturing cost data, you have acquired additional information as follows.

1. Inventory balances at the beginning and end of August were:

	August 1	August 31
Raw materials	$19,500	$30,000
Work in process	25,000	21,000
Finished goods	40,000	59,000

2. Only 50% of the utilities expense and 70% of the insurance expense apply to factory operations; the remaining amounts should be charged to selling and administrative activities.

Instructions

(a) Prepare a cost of goods manufactured schedule for August 2012.

(b) Prepare a correct income statement for August 2012.

(a) CGM $497,000

(b) NL $ (4,500)

Problems: Set C

Visit the book's companion website, at **www.wiley.com/college/weygandt**, and choose the Student Companion site to access Problem Set C.

Waterways Continuing Problem

(*Note:* The Waterways Problem begins in Chapter 19 and continues in the remaining chapters. You can also find this problem at the book's Student Companion site.)

WCP19 Waterways Corporation is a private corporation formed for the purpose of providing the products and the services needed to irrigate farms, parks, commercial projects, and private lawns. It has a centrally located factory in a U.S. city that manufactures the products it markets to retail outlets across the nation. It also maintains a division that provides installation and warranty servicing in six metropolitan areas.

*The **Waterways Problem** starts in this chapter and continues in the remaining chapters. You will find the complete problem for each chapter at the book's companion website.*

The mission of Waterways is to manufacture quality parts that can be used for effective irrigation projects that also conserve water. By that effort, the company hopes to satisfy its customers, provide rapid and responsible service, and serve the community and the employees who represent them in each community.

The company has been growing rapidly, so management is considering new ideas to help the company continue its growth and maintain the high quality of its products.

Waterways was founded by Will Winkman, who is the company president and chief executive officer (CEO). Working with him from the company's inception was Will's brother, Ben, whose sprinkler designs and ideas about the installation of proper systems have been a major basis of the company's success. Ben is the vice president who oversees all aspects of design and production in the company.

The factory itself is managed by Todd Senter who hires his line managers to supervise the factory employees. The factory makes all of the parts for the irrigation systems. The purchasing department is managed by Hector Hines.

The installation and training division is overseen by vice president Henry Writer, who supervises the managers of the six local installation operations. Each of these local managers hires his or her own local service people. These service employees are trained by the home office under Henry Writer's direction because of the uniqueness of the company's products.

There is a small human resources department under the direction of Sally Fenton, a vice president who handles the employee paperwork, though hiring is actually performed by the separate departments. Sam Totter is the vice president who heads the sales and marketing area; he oversees 10 well-trained salespeople.

The accounting and finance division of the company is headed by Abe Headman, who is the chief financial officer (CFO) and a company vice president; he is a member of the Institute of Management Accountants and holds a certificate in management accounting. He has a small staff of Certified Public Accountants, including a controller and a treasurer, and a staff of accounting input operators who maintain the financial records.

A partial list of Waterways' accounts and their balances for the month of November follows.

Accounts Receivable	$290,000
Advertising Expenses	54,000
Cash	260,000
Depreciation—Factory Equipment	16,800
Depreciation—Office Equipment	2,400
Direct Labor	22,000
Factory Supplies Used	16,000
Factory Utilities	10,200
Finished Goods Inventory, November 30	68,800
Finished Goods Inventory, October 31	72,550
Indirect Labor	48,000
Office Supplies Expense	1,600
Other Administrative Expenses	72,000
Prepaid Expenses	42,150
Raw Materials Inventory, November 30	52,700
Raw Materials Inventory, October 31	38,000
Raw Materials Purchases	184,500
Rent—Factory Equipment	47,000
Repairs—Factory Equipment	4,500
Salaries Expense (administrative)	325,000
Sales	1,350,000
Sales Commissions	40,500
Work in Process Inventory, October 31	52,900
Work in Process Inventory, November 30	42,000

Instructions
(a) Based on the information given, construct an organizational chart of Waterways Corporation.
(b) A list of accounts and their values are given above. From this information, prepare a cost of goods manufactured schedule, an income statement, and a partial balance sheet for Waterways Corporation for the month of November.

BROADENING YOUR PERSPECTIVE

Decision Making Across the Organization

BYP19-1   Katy Perry Manufacturing Company specializes in producing fashion outfits. On July 31, 2012, a tornado touched down at its factory and general office. The inventories in the warehouse and the factory were completely destroyed as was the general office nearby. Next morning, through a careful search of the disaster site, however, Jim Craig, the company's controller, and Teresa Perry, the cost accountant, were able to recover a small part of manufacturing cost data for the current month.

"What a horrible experience," sighed Jim. "And the worst part is that we may not have enough records to use in filing an insurance claim."

"It was terrible," replied Teresa. "However, I managed to recover some of the manufacturing cost data that I was working on yesterday afternoon. The data indicate that our direct labor cost in July totaled $240,000 and that we had purchased $345,000 of raw materials. Also, I recall that the amount of raw materials used for July was $350,000. But I'm not sure this information will help. The rest of our records are blown away."

"Well, not exactly," said Jim. "I was working on the year-to-date income statement when the tornado warning was announced. My recollection is that our sales in July were $1,260,000 and our gross profit ratio has been 40% of sales. Also, I can remember that our cost of goods available for sale was $770,000 for July."

"Maybe we can work something out from this information!" exclaimed Teresa. "My experience tells me that our manufacturing overhead is usually 60% of direct labor."

"Hey, look what I just found," cried Teresa. "It's a copy of this June's balance sheet, and it shows that our inventories as of June 30 are Finished Goods $38,000, Work in Process $25,000, and Raw Materials $19,000."

"Super," yelled Jim. "Let's go work something out."

In order to file an insurance claim, Katy Perry Company must determine the amount of its inventories as of July 31, 2012, the date of the tornado touchdown.

Instructions

With the class divided into groups, determine the amount of cost in the Raw Materials, Work in Process, and Finished Goods inventory accounts as of the date of the tornado touchdown.

Managerial Analysis

BYP19-2 B.J. King is a fairly large manufacturing company located in the southern United States. The company manufactures tennis rackets, tennis balls, tennis clothing, and tennis shoes, all bearing the company's distinctive logo, a large green question mark on a white-flocked tennis ball. The company's sales have been increasing over the past 10 years.

The tennis racket division has recently implemented several advanced manufacturing techniques. Robot arms hold the tennis rackets in place while glue dries, and machine vision systems check for defects. The engineering and design team uses computerized drafting and testing of new products. The following managers work in the tennis racket division.

Andre Agassi, Sales Manager (supervises all sales representatives).
Serena Williams, technical specialist (supervises computer programmers).
Pete Sampras, cost accounting manager (supervises cost accountants).
Andy Roddick, production supervisor (supervises all manufacturing employees).
Venus Williams, engineer (supervises all new-product design teams).

Instructions

(a) What are the primary information needs of each manager?

(b) Which, if any, financial accounting report(s) is each likely to use?

(c) Name one special-purpose management accounting report that could be designed for each manager. Include the name of the report, the information it would contain, and how frequently it should be issued.

Real-World Focus

BYP19-3 Anchor Glass Container Corporation, the third largest manufacturer of glass containers in the United States, supplies beverage and food producers and consumer products manufacturers nationwide. Parent company Consumers Packaging Inc. *(Toronto Stock Exchange: CGC)* is a leading international designer and manufacturer of glass containers.

The following management discussion appeared in a recent annual report of Anchor Glass.

Anchor Glass Container Corporation
Management Discussion

Cost of Products Sold Cost of products sold as a percentage of net sales was 89.3% in the current year compared to 87.6% in the prior year. The increase in cost of products sold as a percentage of net sales principally reflected the impact of operational problems during the second quarter of the current year at a major furnace at one of the Company's plants, higher downtime, and costs and expenses associated with an increased number of scheduled capital improvement projects, increases in labor, and certain other manufacturing costs (with no corresponding selling price increases in the current year). Reduced fixed costs from the closing of the Streator, Illinois, plant in June of the current year and productivity and efficiency gains partially offset these cost increases.

Instructions
What factors affect the costs of products sold at Anchor Glass Container Corporation?

On the Web

BYP19-4 The Institute of Management Accountants (IMA) is an organization dedicated to excellence in the practice of management accounting and financial management.

Address: www.imanet.org, or go to **www.wiley.com/college/weygandt**

Instructions
At the IMA's home page, locate the answers to the following questions.

(a) How many members does the IMA have, and what are their job titles?

(b) What are some of the benefits of joining the IMA as a student?

(c) Use the chapter locator function to locate the IMA chapter nearest you, and find the name of the chapter president.

Communication Activity

BYP19-5 Refer to Problem 19–5A and add the following requirement.
    Prepare a letter to the president of the company, Gina Dibene, describing the changes you made. Explain clearly why net income is different after the changes. Keep the following points in mind as you compose your letter.

1. This is a letter to the president of a company, who is your friend. The style should be generally formal, but you may relax some requirements. For example, you may call the president by her first name.

2. Executives are very busy. Your letter should tell the president your main results first (for example, the amount of net income).

3. You should include brief explanations so that the president can understand the changes you made in the calculations.

Ethics Case

BYP19-6 Steve Joyce, controller for Prather Industries, was reviewing production cost reports for the year. One amount in these reports continued to bother him—advertising. During the year, the company had instituted an expensive advertising campaign to sell some of its slower-moving products. It was still too early to tell whether the advertising campaign was successful.
    There had been much internal debate as how to report advertising cost. The vice president of finance argued that advertising costs should be reported as a cost of production, just like direct materials and direct labor. He therefore recommended that this cost be identified as manufacturing overhead and reported as part of inventory costs until sold. Others disagreed. Joyce believed that this cost should be reported as an expense of the current period, based on the conservatism principle. Others argued that it should be reported as Prepaid Advertising and reported as a current asset.
    The president finally had to decide the issue. He argued that these costs should be reported as inventory. His arguments were practical ones. He noted that the company was experiencing financial difficulty and expensing this amount in the current period might jeopardize a planned bond offering. Also, by reporting the advertising costs as inventory rather than as prepaid advertising, less attention would be directed to it by the financial community.

Instructions

(a) Who are the stakeholders in this situation?

(b) What are the ethical issues involved in this situation?

(c) What would you do if you were Steve Joyce?

"All About You" Activity

BYP19-7 The primary purpose of managerial accounting is to provide information useful for management decisions. Many of the managerial accounting techniques that you learn in this course will be useful for decisions you make in your everyday life.

Instructions

For each of the following managerial accounting techniques, read the definition provided and then provide an example of a personal situation that would benefit from use of this technique.

(a) Break-even analysis (page 1023).
(b) Budgeting (page 1054).
(c) Balanced scorecard (page 897).
(d) Capital budgeting (page 1205).

Answers to Insight and Accounting Across the Organization Questions

p. 880 Even the Best Have to Get Better   Q: What are some of the steps that this company has taken in order to ensure that production meets demand? **A:** The company has organized flexible teams, with jobs arranged by the amount of time a task takes. Employees now are multiskilled, so they can switch between tasks and products. Also, the stores now provide sales data more quickly to the manufacturing facility, so that production levels can be changed more quickly to respond to demand.

p. 886 How Many Labor Hours to Build a Car?   Q: Why might Nissan production require significantly fewer labor hours? **A:** Nissan's U.S. factories are probably newer than those of Daimler-Chrysler and Ford. Newer factories tend to be more highly automated with less reliance on production-line employees.

p. 894 Low Fares but Decent Profits   Q: What are some of the cost items that would appear in the cost of services provided schedule of an airline? **A:** Some of the cost items that would appear in the cost of services provided schedule of an airline would be fuel, flight crew salaries, maintenance wages, depreciation on equipment, airport gate fees, and food-service costs.

p. 897 Bananas Receive Special Treatment   Q: Why is it important to keep track of costs that are incurred to improve product quality? **A:** Most companies are concerned about product quality, but managers need to consider the cost/benefit trade-off. If you spend too much on improving product quality, your customers might not be willing to pay the price needed to recover costs. Therefore it is very important that Chiquita closely track all of the costs that it incurs to protect the bananas, to ensure that these costs are factored into the price that it ultimately charges for the bananas.

Answers to Self-Test Questions

1. b   **2.** b   **3.** b   **4.** b   **5.** d   **6.** a   **7.** c   **8.** c   **9.** c ($200,000 + $600,000 − $250,000)   **10.** c
11. a   **12.** d   **13.** d   **14.** d   **15.** d

✔
The Navigator

✔ **Remember to go back to the Navigator box on the chapter opening page and check off your completed work.**

CHAPTER20

Job Order Costing

Study Objectives

After studying this chapter, you should be able to:

[1] Explain the characteristics and purposes of cost accounting.

[2] Describe the flow of costs in a job order costing system.

[3] Explain the nature and importance of a job cost sheet.

[4] Indicate how the predetermined overhead rate is determined and used.

[5] Prepare entries for jobs completed and sold.

[6] Distinguish between under- and overapplied manufacturing overhead.

✔ The Navigator

✔ The Navigator

- Scan Study Objectives — ○
- Read Feature Story — ○
- Read Preview — ○
- Read text and answer **Do it!** p. 929 ○ p. 935 ○ p. 940 ○ p. 943 ○
- Work Comprehensive **Do it!** p. 943 — ○
- Review Summary of Study Objectives — ○
- Answer Self-Test Questions — ○
- Complete Assignments — ○
- Go to *WileyPLUS* for practice and tutorials — ○

Feature Story

" . . . AND WE'D LIKE IT IN RED"

Western States Fire Apparatus, Inc., of Cornelius, Oregon, is one of the few U.S. companies that makes fire trucks. The company builds about 25 trucks per year. Founded in 1941, the company is run by the children and grandchildren of the original founder.

"We buy the chassis, which is the cab and the frame," says Susan Scott, the company's bookkeeper. "In our computer, we set up an account into which all of the direct material that is purchased for that particular job is charged." Other direct materials include the water pump—which can cost $10,000—the lights, the siren, ladders, and hoses.

As for direct labor, the production workers fill out time tickets that tell what jobs they worked on. Usually, the company is building four trucks at any one time. On payday, the controller allocates the payroll to the appropriate job record.

The company allocates indirect materials, such as nuts and bolts, wiring, lubricants, and abrasives, to each job in proportion to direct material dollars. It allocates other costs, such as insurance and supervisors' salaries, based on direct labor hours. "We need to allocate overhead in order to know what kind of price we have to charge when we submit our bids," she says.

Western gets orders through a "blind-bidding" process. That is, Western submits its bid without knowing the bid prices made by its competitors. "If we bid too low, we won't make a profit. If we bid too high, we don't get the job."

Regardless of the final price for the truck, the quality had better be first-rate. "The fire departments let you know if they don't like what you did, and you usually end up fixing it."

Inside CHAPTER 20

The Feature Story about Western States Fire Apparatus describes the manufacturing costs used in making a fire truck. It demonstrates that accurate costing is critical to the company's success. For example, in order to submit accurate bids on new jobs and to know whether it profited from past jobs, the company needs a good costing system. This chapter illustrates how these manufacturing costs are assigned to specific jobs, such as the manufacture of individual fire trucks. We begin the discussion in this chapter with an overview of the flow of costs in a job order cost accounting system. We then use a case study to explain and illustrate the documents, entries, and accounts in this type of cost accounting system.

The content and organization of Chapter 20 are as follows.

Job Order Costing

Cost Accounting Systems	Job Order Cost Flow	Reporting Job Cost Data
• Job order cost system • Process cost system	• Accumulating manufacturing costs • Assigning manufacturing costs to work in process • Assigning costs to finished goods • Assigning costs to cost of goods sold • Job order costing for service companies • Summary of job order cost flows • Advantages and disadvantages of job order costing	• Cost of goods manufactured schedule • Income statement presentation • Under- or overapplied manufacturing overhead

The Navigator

Cost Accounting Systems

Study Objective [1]

Explain the characteristics and purposes of cost accounting.

Cost accounting involves the measuring, recording, and reporting of product costs. From the data accumulated, companies determine both the total cost and the unit cost of each product. The accuracy of the product cost information produced by the cost accounting system is critical to the success of the company. Companies use this information to determine which products to produce, what price to charge, and the amounts to produce. Accurate product cost information is also vital for effective evaluation of employee performance.

A **cost accounting system** consists of accounts for the various manufacturing costs. These accounts are fully integrated into the general ledger of a company. An important feature of a cost accounting system is the use of **a perpetual inventory system.** Such a system **provides immediate, up-to-date information on the cost of a product.**

There are two basic types of cost accounting systems: (1) a job order cost system and (2) a process cost system. Although cost accounting systems differ widely from company to company, most involve one of these two traditional product costing systems.

Job Order Cost System

Under a **job order cost system,** the company assigns costs to each **job** or to each **batch** of goods. An example of a job is the manufacture of a mainframe computer by IBM, the production of a movie by Disney, or the making of a fire truck by Western States. An example of a batch is the printing of 225 wedding invitations by a local print shop, or the printing of a weekly issue of *Fortune* magazine by a hi-tech printer such as Quad Graphics. Companies may complete jobs or batches to fill a specific customer order or to replenish inventory.

An important feature of job order costing is that each job or batch has its own distinguishing characteristics. For example, each house is custom built, each consulting engagement by a CPA firm is unique, and each printing job is different. **The objective is to compute the cost per job.** At each point in manufacturing a product or providing a service, the company can identify the job and its associated costs. A job order cost system measures costs for each completed job, rather than for set time periods. Illustration 20-1 shows the recording of costs in a job order cost system.

Illustration 20-1
Job order cost system

Job Order Cost System
Two jobs: Wedding Invitations and Menus

Black ink $
Typesetting $
225 Invitations $
225 Envelopes $
Vellum stock, pure white $
Job # 9501

Typesetting $
Lamination $
MENU
Colored ink $
Yellow stock $
50 Copies $
Job # 9502

Each job has distinguishing characteristics and related costs.

Process Cost System

A company uses a **process cost system** when it manufactures a large volume of similar products. Production is continuous. Examples of a process cost system are the manufacture of cereal by Kellogg, the refining of petroleum by ExxonMobil, and the production of automobiles by General Motors. Process costing accumulates product-related costs **for a period of time** (such as a week or a month) instead of assigning costs to specific products or job orders. In process costing, companies assign the costs to departments or processes for the specified period of time. Illustration 20-2 shows examples of the use of a process cost system. We will discuss the process cost system further in Chapter 21.

Illustration 20-2
Process cost system

Process Cost System
Compact Disc Production

1. Oil is pumped.
2. Benzene is removed.
3. The benzene is made into pellets...
4. ...from which compact discs are produced.

Similar products are produced over a specified time period.

Can a company use both types of cost systems? Yes. For example, General Motors uses process cost accounting for its standard model cars, such as Buicks and Corvettes, and job order cost accounting for a custom-made limousine for the President of the United States. The objective of both cost accounting systems is to provide unit cost information for product pricing, cost control, inventory valuation, and financial statement presentation.

MANAGEMENT INSIGHT

Jobs Won, Money Lost

Many companies suffer from poor cost accounting. As a result, they sometimes make products they should not be selling at all, or they buy other products that they could more profitably make themselves. Also, inaccurate cost data lead companies to misallocate capital and frustrate efforts by plant managers to improve efficiency.

For example, consider the case of a diversified company in the business of rebuilding diesel locomotives. The managers thought they were making money, but a consulting firm found that the company had seriously underestimated costs. The company bailed out of the business, and not a moment too soon. Says the consultant who advised the company, "The more contracts it won, the more money it lost." Given that situation, a company cannot stay in business very long!

 What type of costs do you think the company had been underestimating? (See page 962.)

Job Order Cost Flow

Study Objective [2]

Describe the flow of costs in a job order costing system.

The flow of costs (direct materials, direct labor, and manufacturing overhead) in job order cost accounting parallels the physical flow of the materials as they are converted into finished goods. As shown in Illustration 20-3, companies assign manufacturing costs to the Work in Process Inventory account. When a job is completed, the company transfers the cost of the job to Finished Goods Inventory. Later, when the goods are sold, the company transfers their cost to Cost of Goods Sold.

Illustration 20-3
Flow of costs in job order costing

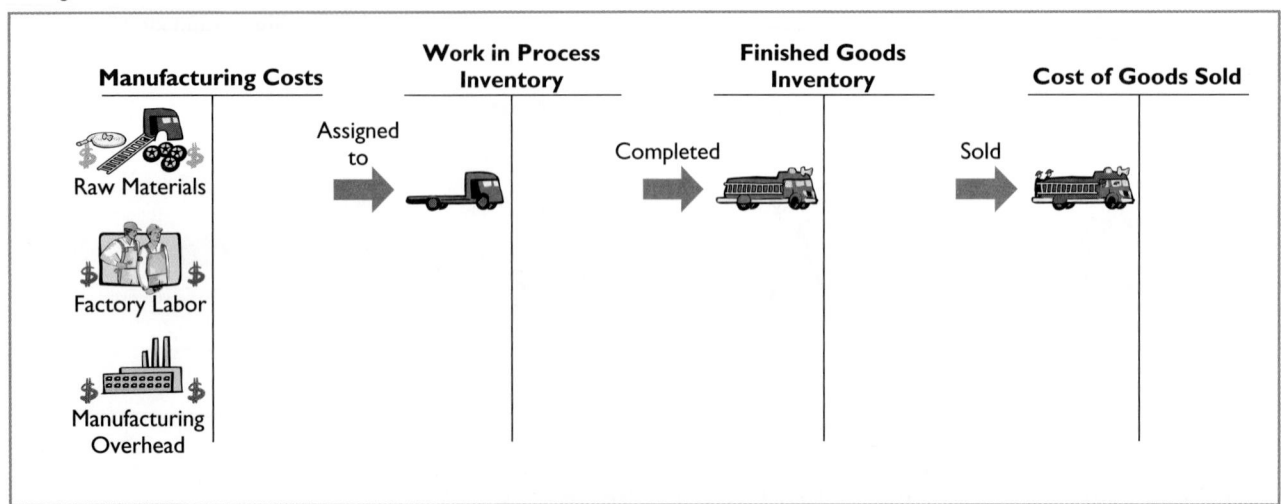

Illustration 20-3 provides a basic overview of the flow of costs in a manufacturing setting. A more detailed presentation of the flow of costs is shown in Illustration 20-4. The box in the lower-right corner of Illustration 20-4 indicates

Illustration 20-4
Job order costing system

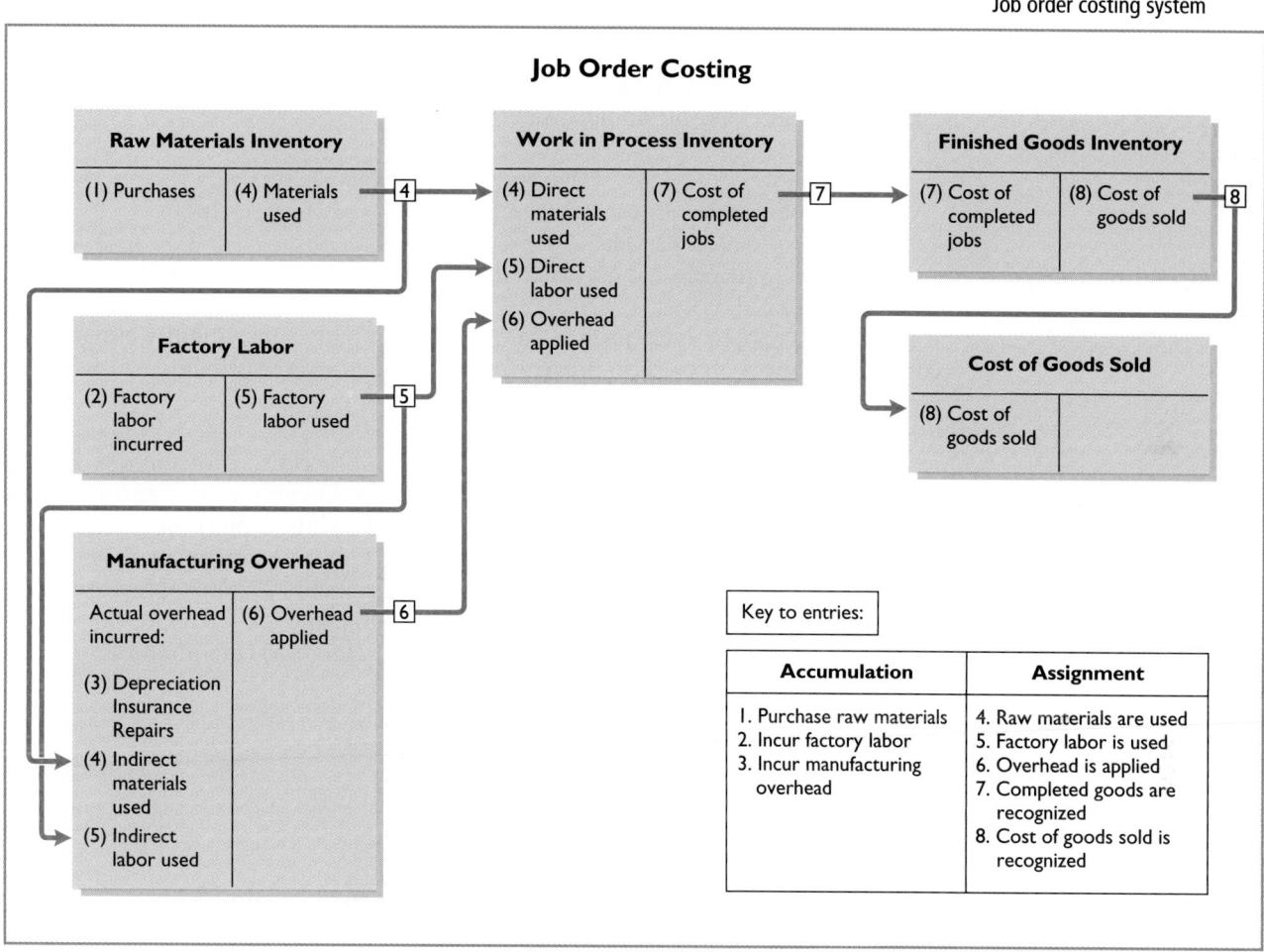

two major steps in the flow of costs: (1) *accumulating* the manufacturing costs incurred, and (2) *assigning* the accumulated costs to the work done. As shown, the company accumulates manufacturing costs incurred in entries 1–3 by debits to Raw Materials Inventory, Factory Labor, and Manufacturing Overhead. When the company incurs these costs, it does not attempt to associate the costs with specific jobs. The remaining entries (entries 4–8) assign manufacturing costs incurred. In the remainder of this chapter, we will use a case study to explain how a job order system operates.

Accumulating Manufacturing Costs

To illustrate a job order cost system, we will use the January transactions of Wallace Manufacturing Company, which makes machine tools.

RAW MATERIALS COSTS

When Wallace receives the raw materials it has purchased, **it debits the costs of the materials to Raw Materials Inventory**. The company would debit this account for the invoice cost of the raw materials and freight costs chargeable to the purchaser. It would credit the account for purchase discounts taken and purchase returns and allowances. Wallace makes **no effort at this point to associate the cost of materials with specific jobs or orders**.

To illustrate, assume that Wallace Manufacturing purchases 2,000 handles (Stock No. AA2746) at $5 per unit ($10,000) and 800 modules (Stock No. AA2850) at $40 per unit ($32,000) for a total cost of $42,000 ($10,000 + $32,000). The entry to record this purchase on January 4 is:

	(1)		
Jan. 4	Raw Materials Inventory	42,000	
	Accounts Payable		42,000
	(Purchase of raw materials on account)		

As we will explain later in the chapter, the company subsequently assigns raw materials inventory to work in process and manufacturing overhead.

FACTORY LABOR COSTS

In a manufacturing company, the cost of factory labor consists of three costs: (1) gross earnings of factory workers, (2) employer payroll taxes on these earnings, and (3) fringe benefits (such as sick pay, pensions, and vacation pay) incurred by the employer. **Companies debit labor costs to Factory Labor as they incur those costs**.

To illustrate, assume that Wallace Manufacturing incurs $32,000 of factory labor costs. Of that amount, $27,000 relates to wages payable and $5,000 relates to payroll taxes payable in January. The entry to record factory labor for the month is:

	(2)		
Jan. 31	Factory Labor	32,000	
	Factory Wages Payable		27,000
	Employer Payroll Taxes Payable		5,000
	(To record factory labor costs)		

The company subsequently assigns factory labor to work in process and manufacturing overhead.

MANUFACTURING OVERHEAD COSTS

A company has many types of overhead costs. It may recognize these costs **daily**, as in the case of machinery repairs and the use of indirect materials and indirect labor. Or, it may record overhead costs **periodically** through adjusting entries. Companies record property taxes, depreciation, and insurance periodically, for example. This is done using a summary entry, which summarizes the totals from multiple transactions.

Using assumed data, the summary entry for manufacturing overhead in Wallace Manufacturing Company is:

	(3)		
Jan. 31	Manufacturing Overhead	13,800	
	Utilities Payable		4,800
	Prepaid Insurance		2,000
	Accounts Payable (for repairs)		2,600
	Accumulated Depreciation—Equipment		3,000
	Property Taxes Payable		1,400
	(To record overhead costs)		

The company subsequently assigns manufacturing overhead to work in process.

Do it!

During the current month, Ringling Company incurs the following manufacturing costs:

(a) Raw material purchases of $4,200 on account.

(b) Incurs factory labor of $18,000. Of that amount, $15,000 relates to wages payable and $3,000 relates to payroll taxes payable.

(c) Factory utilities of $2,200 are payable, prepaid factory insurance of $1,800 has expired, and depreciation on the factory building is $3,500.

Prepare journal entries for each type of manufacturing cost.

Manufacturing Costs

Solution

(a) Raw Materials Inventory	42,000	
Accounts Payable		4,200
(Purchases of raw materials on account)		
(b) Factory Labor	18,000	
Factory Wages Payable		15,000
Employer Payroll Taxes Payable		3,000
(To record factory labor costs)		
(c) Manufacturing Overhead	7,500	
Utilities Payable		2,200
Prepaid Insurance		1,800
Accumulated Depreciation		3,500
(To record overhead costs)		

action plan

✔ In accumulating manufacturing costs, debit at least one of three accounts: Raw Materials Inventory, Factory Labor, and Manufacturing Overhead.

✔ Manufacturing overhead costs may be recognized daily. Or manufacturing overhead may be recorded periodically through a summary entry.

Related exercise material: BE20-1, BE20-2, E20-1, E20-7, E20-8, E20-11, and **Do it!** 20-1.

The Navigator

Assigning Manufacturing Costs to Work in Process

As Illustration 20-4 (page 927) shows, assigning manufacturing costs to work in process results in the following entries:

1. **Debits** made to Work in Process Inventory.
2. **Credits** made to Raw Materials Inventory, Factory Labor, and Manufacturing Overhead.

Study Objective [3]
Explain the nature and importance of a job cost sheet.

An essential accounting record in assigning costs to jobs is a **job cost sheet**, shown in Illustration 20-5 (page 930). A job cost sheet is a form used to record the costs chargeable to a specific job and to determine the total and unit costs of the completed job.

Companies keep a separate job cost sheet for each job. The job cost sheets constitute the subsidiary ledger for the Work in Process Inventory account. A **subsidiary ledger** consists of individual records for each individual item—in this case, each job. The Work in Process account is referred to as a **control account** because it summarizes the detailed data regarding specific jobs contained in the job cost sheets. **Each entry to Work in Process Inventory must be accompanied by a corresponding posting to one or more job cost sheets.**

Illustration 20-5
Job cost sheet

Job Cost Sheet

Job No. _____   Quantity _____
Item _____   Date Requested _____
For _____   Date Completed _____

Date	Direct Materials	Direct Labor	Manufacturing Overhead

Cost of completed job
  Direct materials $ _____
  Direct labor   _____
  Manufacturing overhead   _____
Total cost $ _____
Unit cost (total dollars ÷ quantity) $ _____

Helpful Hint

In today's electronic environment, companies typically maintain job cost sheets as computer files.

RAW MATERIALS COSTS

Companies assign raw materials costs when their materials storeroom issues the materials. Requests for issuing raw materials are made on a prenumbered materials requisition slip. The materials issued may be used directly on a job, or they may be considered indirect materials. As Illustration 20-6 shows, the requisition should indicate the quantity and type of materials withdrawn and the account to be charged. The company will charge direct materials to Work in Process Inventory, and indirect materials to Manufacturing Overhead.

Illustration 20-6
Materials requisition slip

Wallace Manufacturing Company
Materials Requisition Slip

Deliver to: _____Assembly Department_____   Req. No.   R247
Charge to: ___Work in Process—Job No. 101___   Date: 1/6/12

Quantity	Description	Stock No.	Cost per Unit	Total
200	Handles	AA2746	$5.00	$1,000

Requested by _Bruce Howart_   Received by _Herb Crowley_
Approved by _Kap Shin_   Costed by _Heather Remmers_

The company may use any of the inventory costing methods (FIFO, LIFO, or average-cost) in costing the requisitions **to the individual job cost sheets**.

Periodically, the company journalizes the requisitions. For example, if Wallace Manufacturing uses $24,000 of direct materials and $6,000 of indirect materials in January, the entry is:

> **Ethics Note**
>
> The internal control principle of documentation includes prenumbering to enhance accountability.

(4)

Jan. 31	Work in Process Inventory	24,000	
	Manufacturing Overhead	6,000	
	Raw Materials Inventory		30,000
	(To assign materials to jobs and overhead)		

Illustration 20-7 shows the posting of requisition slip R247 and other assumed postings to the job cost sheets for materials. The requisition slips provide the basis for total direct materials costs of $12,000 for Job No. 101, $7,000 for Job No. 102, and $5,000 for Job No. 103. After the company has completed all postings, the sum of the direct materials columns of the job cost sheets (the subsidiary accounts) should equal the direct materials debited to Work in Process Inventory (the control account).

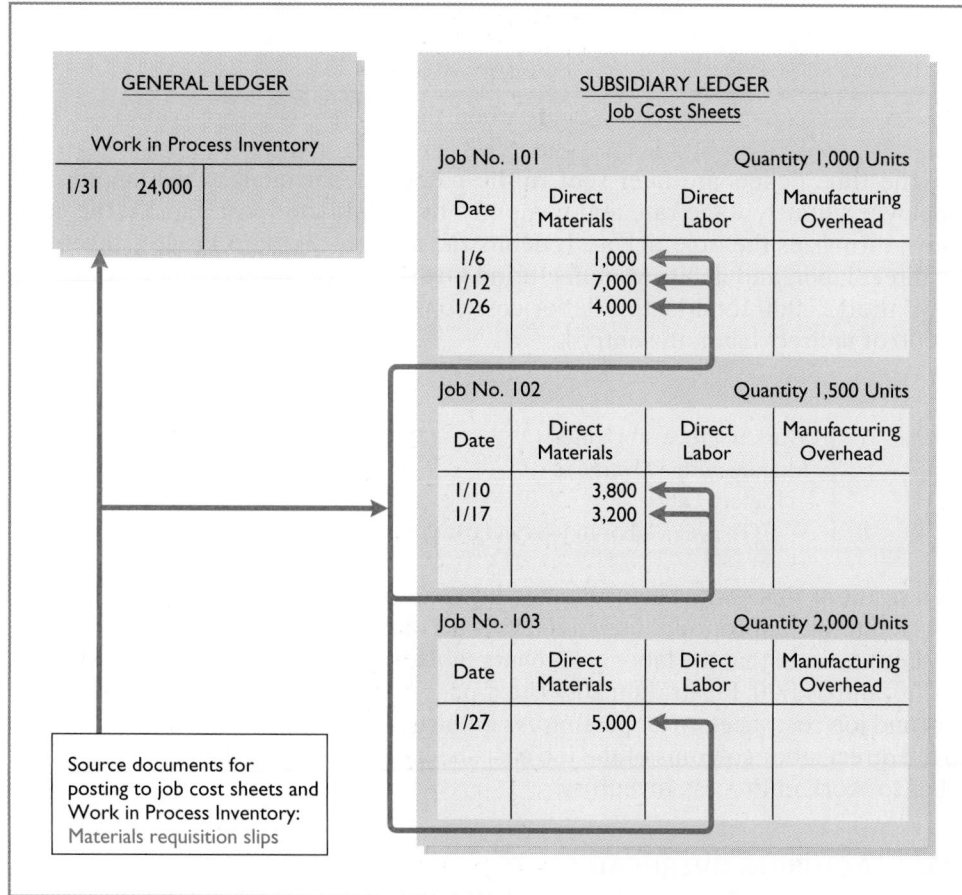

Illustration 20-7
Job cost sheets—direct materials

Helpful Hint

Companies post to control accounts monthly and post to job cost sheets daily.

FACTORY LABOR COSTS

Companies assign factory labor costs to jobs on the basis of time tickets prepared when the work is performed. The time ticket indicates the employee, the hours worked, the account and job to be charged, and the total labor cost. Many companies accumulate these data through the use of bar coding and scanning devices. When they start and end work, employees scan bar codes on their identification badges and bar codes associated with each job they work on. When direct labor is involved, the time ticket must indicate the job number, as shown in Illustration 20-8. The employee's supervisor should approve all time tickets.

Illustration 20-8
Time ticket

Helpful Hint

Some companies use different colored time tickets for direct and for indirect labor.

Wallace Manufacturing Company					
Time Ticket					
				Date:	1/6/12
Employee	John Nash			Employee No.	124
Charge to:	Work in Process			Job No.	101

Time			Hourly Rate	Total Cost
Start	Stop	Total Hours		
0800	1200	4	10.00	40.00

Approved by _Bob Kadler_   Costed by _M. Cher_

The time tickets are later sent to the payroll department, which applies the employee's hourly wage rate and computes the total labor cost. Finally, the company journalizes the time tickets. It debits the account Work in Process Inventory for direct labor, and debits Manufacturing Overhead for indirect labor. For example, if the $32,000 total factory labor cost consists of $28,000 of direct labor and $4,000 of indirect labor, the entry is:

	(5)		
Jan. 31	Work in Process Inventory	28,000	
	Manufacturing Overhead	4,000	
	Factory Labor		32,000
	(To assign labor to jobs and overhead)		

As a result of this entry, Factory Labor has a zero balance, and gross earnings are assigned to the appropriate manufacturing accounts.

Let's assume that the labor costs chargeable to Wallace's three jobs are $15,000, $9,000, and $4,000. Illustration 20-9 (next page) shows the Work in Process Inventory and job cost sheets after posting. As in the case of direct materials, the postings to the direct labor columns of the job cost sheets should equal the posting of direct labor to Work in Process Inventory.

MANUFACTURING OVERHEAD COSTS

Study Objective [4]
Indicate how the predetermined overhead rate is determined and used.

Companies charge the actual costs of direct materials and direct labor to specific jobs. In contrast, manufacturing **overhead** relates to production operations **as a whole**. As a result, overhead costs cannot be assigned to specific jobs on the basis of actual costs incurred. Instead, companies assign manufacturing overhead to work in process and to specific jobs **on an estimated basis through the use of a predetermined overhead rate.**

Illustration 20-9
Job cost sheets—direct labor

Helpful Hint

Prove the $28,000 by totaling the charges by jobs:

101	$15,000
102	9,000
103	4,000
	$28,000

The **predetermined overhead rate** is based on the relationship between estimated annual overhead costs and expected annual operating activity, expressed in terms of a common **activity base**. The company may state the activity in terms of direct labor costs, direct labor hours, machine hours, or any other measure that will provide an equitable basis for applying overhead costs to jobs. Companies establish the predetermined overhead rate at the beginning of the year. Small companies often use a single, company-wide predetermined overhead rate. Large companies often use rates that vary from department to department. The formula for a predetermined overhead rate is as follows.

$$\begin{array}{c}\text{Estimated Annual}\\\text{Overhead Costs}\end{array} \div \begin{array}{c}\text{Expected Annual}\\\text{Operating Activity}\end{array} = \begin{array}{c}\text{Predetermined}\\\text{Overhead Rate}\end{array}$$

Illustration 20-10
Formula for predetermined overhead rate

Overhead relates to production operations as a whole. To know what "the whole" is, the logical thing is to wait until the end of the year's operations. At that time the company knows all of its costs for the period. As a practical matter, though, managers cannot wait until the end of the year. To price products accurately, they need information about product costs of specific jobs completed during the year. Using a predetermined overhead rate enables a cost to be determined for the job immediately. Illustration 20-11 indicates how manufacturing overhead is assigned to work in process.

Illustration 20-11
Using predetermined overhead rates

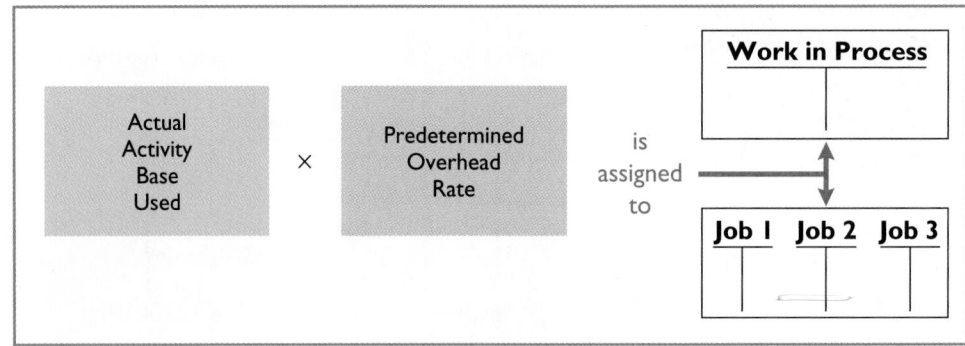

Wallace Manufacturing uses direct labor cost as the activity base. Assuming that the company expects annual overhead costs to be $280,000 and direct labor costs for the year to be $350,000, the overhead rate is 80% of direct labor costs, computed as follows:

$$\$280,000 \div \$350,000 = 80\%$$

This means that for every dollar of direct labor, Wallace will assign 80 cents of manufacturing overhead to a job. The use of a predetermined overhead rate enables the company to determine the approximate total cost of each job **when it completes the job**.

Historically, companies used direct labor costs or direct labor hours as the activity base. The reason was the relatively high correlation between direct labor and manufacturing overhead. Today more companies are using **machine hours as the activity base, due to increased reliance on automation in manufacturing operations**. Or, as mentioned in Chapter 19, many companies now use activity-based costing in an attempt to more accurately allocate overhead costs based on the activities that give rise to the costs.

A company may use more than one activity base. For example, if a job is manufactured in more than one factory department, each department may have its own overhead rate. In the Feature Story about fire trucks, Western States Fire Apparatus uses two bases in assigning overhead to jobs: direct materials dollars for indirect materials, and direct labor hours for such costs as insurance and supervisors' salaries.

Wallace Manufacturing applies manufacturing overhead to work in process when it assigns direct labor costs. It also applies manufacturing overhead to specific jobs at the same time. For Wallace Manufacturing, overhead applied for January is $22,400 (direct labor cost of $28,000 × 80%). The following entry records this application.

	(6)		
Jan. 31	Work in Process Inventory	22,400	
	Manufacturing Overhead		22,400
	(To assign overhead to jobs)		

The overhead that Wallace applies to each job will be 80% of the direct labor cost of the job for the month. Illustration 20-12 shows the Work in Process Inventory account and the job cost sheets after posting. Note that the debit of $22,400 to Work in Process Inventory equals the sum of the overhead applied to jobs: Job 101 $12,000 + Job 102 $7,200 + Job 103 $3,200.

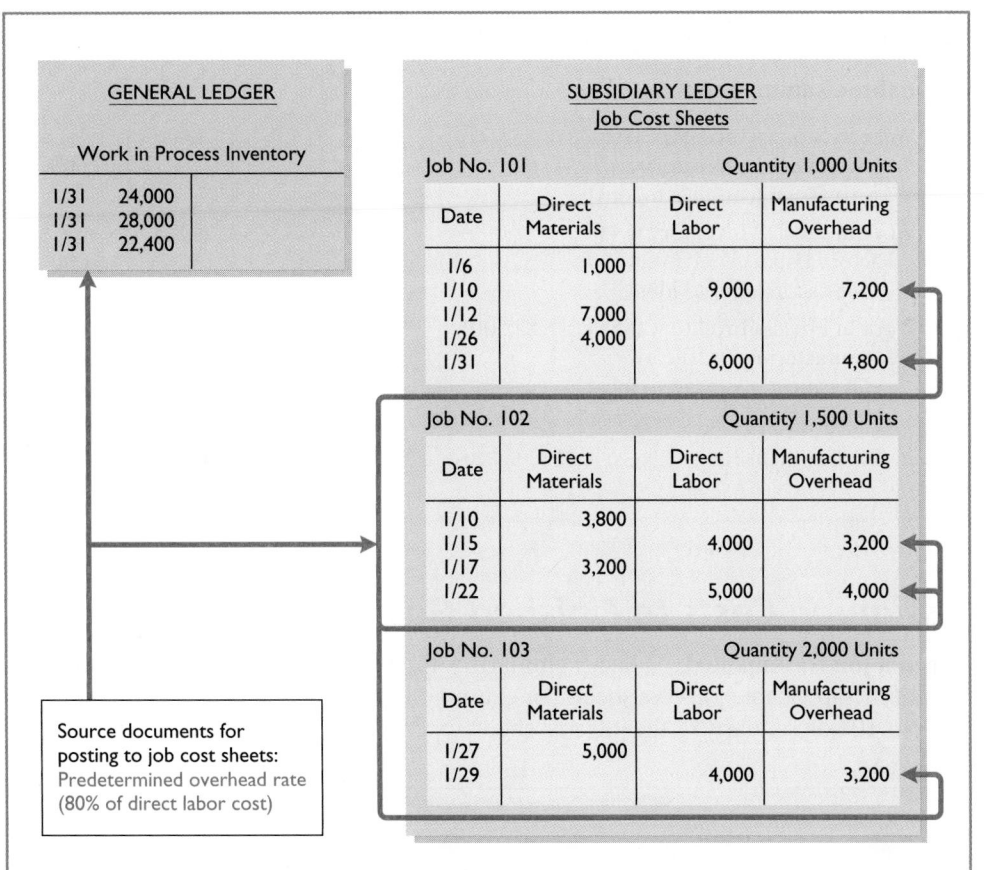

Illustration 20-12
Job cost sheets—
manufacturing overhead
applied

At the end of each month, **the balance in Work in Process Inventory should equal the sum of the costs shown on the job cost sheets of unfinished jobs**. Illustration 20-13 presents proof of the agreement of the control and subsidiary accounts in Wallace Manufacturing. (It assumes that all jobs are still in process.)

Work in Process Inventory			Job Cost Sheets	
Jan. 31	24,000		No. 101	$39,000
31	28,000		102	23,200
31	22,400		103	12,200
	74,400	←		**$74,400**

Illustration 20-13
Proof of job cost sheets to
work in process inventory

Do it!

Danielle Company is working on two job orders. The job cost sheets show the following:

Work in Process

Direct materials—Job 120 $6,000, Job 121 $3,600
Direct labor—Job 120 $4,000, Job 121 $2,000
Manufacturing overhead—Job 120 $5,000, Job 121 $2,500

Prepare the three summary entries to record the assignment of costs to Work in Process from the data on the job cost sheets.

action plan

✔ Recognize that Work in Process Inventory is the control account for all unfinished job cost sheets.

✔ Debit Work in Process Inventory for the materials, labor, and overhead charged to the job cost sheets.

✔ Credit the accounts that were debited when the manufacturing costs were accumulated.

Solution

The three summary entries are:

Work in Process Inventory ($6,000 + $3,600)	9,600	
Raw Materials Inventory		9,600
(To assign materials to jobs)		
Work in Process Inventory ($4,000 + $2,000)	6,000	
Factory Labor		6,000
(To assign labor to jobs)		
Work in Process Inventory ($5,000 + $2,500)	7,500	
Manufacturing Overhead		7,500
(To assign overhead to jobs)		

Related exercise material: BE20-3, BE20-4, BE20-5, E20-1, E20-2, E20-7, E20-8, and **Do it!** 20-2.

The Navigator

Assigning Costs to Finished Goods

Study Objective [5]
Prepare entries for jobs completed and sold.

When a job is completed, Wallace summarizes the costs and completes the lower portion of the applicable job cost sheet. For example, if we assume that Wallace completes Job No. 101 on January 31, the job cost sheet appears as shown in Illustration 20-14.

Illustration 20-14
Completed job cost sheet

Job Cost Sheet

Job No. _____ 101 _____   Quantity _____ 1,000 _____
Item _____ Magnetic Sensors _____   Date Requested _____ February 5 _____
For _____ Tanner Company _____   Date Completed _____ January 31 _____

Date	Direct Materials	Direct Labor	Manufacturing Overhead
1/6	$ 1,000		
1/10		$ 9,000	$ 7,200
1/12	7,000		
1/26	4,000		
1/31		6,000	4,800
	$12,000	$15,000	$12,000

Cost of completed job
Direct materials	$	12,000
Direct labor		15,000
Manufacturing overhead		12,000
Total cost	$	39,000
Unit cost ($39,000 ÷ 1,000)	$	39.00

When a job is finished, Wallace makes an entry to transfer its total cost to finished goods inventory. The entry is as follows:

(7)

Jan. 31	Finished Goods Inventory	39,000	
	Work in Process Inventory		39,000
	(To record completion of Job No. 101)		

Finished Goods Inventory is a control account. It controls individual finished goods records in a finished goods subsidiary ledger. The company posts directly from completed job cost sheets to the receipts columns. Illustration 20-15 shows the finished goods inventory record for Job No. 101.

Illustration 20-15
Finished goods record

Finished Goods.xls										
File Edit View Insert Format Tools Data Window Help										
	A	B	C	D	E	F	G	H	I	J
1	Item: Magnetic Sensors								Job No: 101	
2										
3		**Receipts**			**Issues**			**Balance**		
4	Date	Units	Cost	Total	Units	Cost	Total	Units	Cost	Total
5	1/31	1,000	$39	$39,000				1,000	$39	$39,000
6	1/31				1,000	$39	$39,000			– 0 –
7										

Assigning Costs to Cost of Goods Sold

Companies recognize cost of goods sold when each sale occurs. To illustrate the entries a company makes when it sells a completed job, assume that on January 31 Wallace Manufacturing sells on account Job 101. The job cost $39,000, and it sold for $50,000. The entries to record the sale and recognize cost of goods sold are:

		(8)		
Jan. 31	Accounts Receivable		50,000	
	Sales			50,000
	(To record sale of Job No. 101)			
31	Cost of Goods Sold		39,000	
	Finished Goods Inventory			39,000
	(To record cost of Job No. 101)			

As Illustration 20-15 above shows, Wallace records, in the issues section of the finished goods record, the units sold, the cost per unit, and the total cost of goods sold for each job sold.

Job Order Costing for Service Companies

Our extended job order costing example focuses on a manufacturer so that you see the flow of costs through the inventory accounts. It is important to understand, however, that job order costing is also commonly used by service companies. While service companies do not have inventory, the techniques of job order costing are still quite useful in many service-industry environments. Consider, for example, the Mayo Clinic (health care), PriceWaterhouseCoopers (accounting firm), and Goldman Sachs (financial services firm). These companies need to keep track of the cost of jobs performed for specific customers to evaluate the profitability of medical treatments, audits, or consulting engagements.

Many service organizations bill their customers using cost-plus contracts. Cost-plus contracts mean that the customer's bill is the sum of the costs incurred on the job, plus a profit amount that is calculated as a percentage of the costs incurred. In order to minimize conflict with customers and reduce potential contract disputes, service companies that use cost-plus contracts must maintain accurate and up-to-date costing records. Up-to-date cost records enable a service company to immediately notify a customer of cost overruns due to customer requests for changes to the original plan or unexpected complications. Timely record-keeping allows the contractor and customer to consider alternatives before it is too late.

A service company that uses a job order costing system does not have inventory accounts. It does, however, use an account (often called Service Contracts in Process) to record job costs prior to completion. Job cost sheets for a service company keep track of the materials, labor, and overhead used on a particular job similar to a manufacturer. A number of the exercises at the end this chapter apply job order costing to service companies.

SERVICE COMPANY INSIGHT

Sales Are Nice, but Service Revenue Pays the Bills

Jet engines are one of the many products made by the industrial operations division of General Electric (GE). At prices as high as $30 million per engine, you can bet that GE does its best to keep track of costs. It might surprise you that GE doesn't make much profit on the sale of each engine. So why does it bother making them? Service revenue—during one recent year, about 75% of the division's revenues came from servicing its own products. One estimate is that the $13 billion in aircraft engines sold during a recent three-year period will generate about $90 billion in service revenue over the 30-year life of the engines. Because of the high product costs, both the engines themselves and the subsequent service are most likely accounted for using job order costing. Accurate service cost records are important because GE needs to generate high profit margins on its service jobs to make up for the low margins on the original sale. It also needs good cost records for its service jobs in order to control its costs. Otherwise, a competitor, such as Pratt and Whitney, might submit lower bids for service contracts and take lucrative jobs away from GE.

Source: Paul Glader, "GE's Focus on Service Faces Test," *Wall Street Journal Online* (March 3, 2009).

? Explain why GE would use job order costing to keep track of the cost of repairing a malfunctioning engine for a major airline. (See page 962.)

Summary of Job Order Cost Flows

Illustration 20-16 shows a completed flow chart for a job order cost accounting system. All postings are keyed to entries 1–8 in Wallace Manufacturing's accounts presented in the cost flow graphic in Illustration 20-4 (page 927).

The cost flows in the diagram can be categorized as one of four types:

- **Accumulation:** The company first accumulates costs by (1) purchasing raw materials, (2) incurring labor costs, and (3) incurring manufacturing overhead costs.

- **Assignment to Jobs:** Once the company has incurred manufacturing costs, it must assign them to specific jobs. For example, as it uses raw materials on specific jobs (4), it assigns them to work in process, or treats them as manufacturing overhead if the raw materials cannot be associated with a specific job. Similarly, it either assigns factory labor (5) to work in process, or treats it as manufacturing overhead if the factory labor cannot be associated with a specific job. Finally it assigns manufacturing overhead (6) to work in process using a *predetermined overhead rate*. This deserves emphasis: **Do not assign overhead using actual overhead costs, but instead use a predetermined rate.**

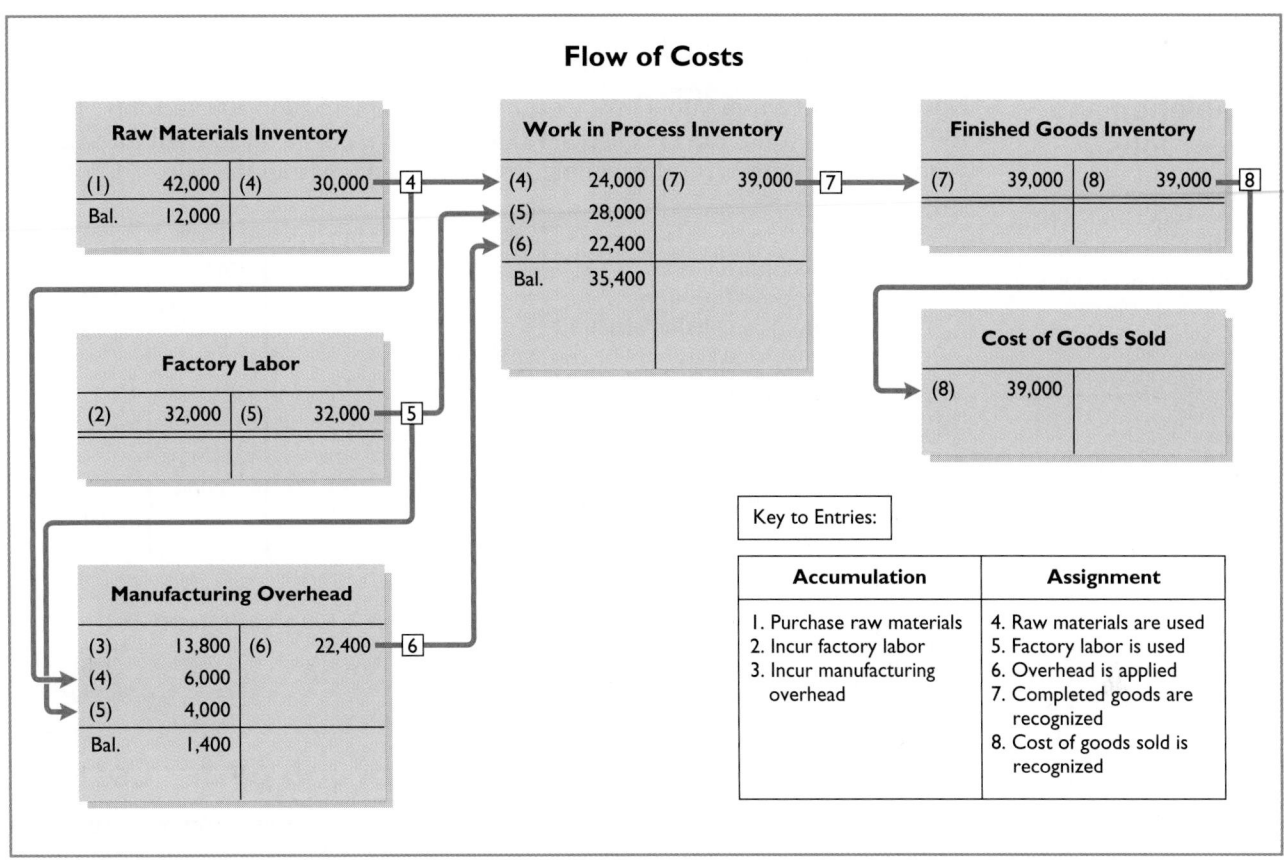

Illustration 20-16
Flow of costs in a job order cost system

- **Completed Jobs:** As jobs are completed (7), the company transfers the cost of the completed job out of work in process inventory into finished goods inventory.
- **When Goods Are Sold:** As specific items are sold (8), the company transfers their cost out of finished goods inventory into cost of goods sold.

Illustration 20-17 summarizes the flow of documents in a job order cost system.

Illustration 20-17
Flow of documents in a job order cost system

Do it!

Completion and Sale of Jobs

action plan

✔ Debit Finished Goods for the cost of completed jobs.

✔ Debit Cost of Goods Sold for the cost of jobs sold.

During the current month, Onyx Corporation completed Job 109 and Job 112. Job 109 cost $19,000 and Job 112 costs $27,000. Job 112 was sold on account for $42,000. Journalize the entries for the completion of the two jobs and the sale of Job 112.

Solution

Finished Goods Inventory	46,000	
Work in Process Inventory		46,000
(To record completion of Job 109,		
costing $19,000 and Job 112, costing $27,000)		
Accounts Receivable	42,000	
Sales		42,000
(To record sale of Job 112)		
Cost of Goods Sold	27,000	
Finished Goods Inventory		27,000
(To record cost of goods sold for Job 112)		

Related exercise material: BE20-8, E20-2, E20-3, E20-4, E20-6, E20-7, E20-10, and **Do it!** 20-3.

✔ **The Navigator**

Advantages and Disadvantages of Job Order Costing

An advantage of job order costing is it is more precise in assignment of costs to projects than process costing. For example, assume that Juan Company (home manufacturer) builds 10 custom homes a year at a total cost of $2,000,000. One way to determine the cost of the homes is to divide the total construction cost incurred during the year by the number of homes produced during the year. For Juan Company, an average cost of $200,000 ($2,000,000 ÷ 10) is computed. If the homes are identical, then this approach is adequate for purposes of determining profit per home. But if the homes vary in terms of size, style, and material types, using the average cost of $200,000 to determine profit per home is inappropriate. Instead, Juan Company should use a job order costing system to determine the specific cost incurred to build each home and the amount of profit made on each. Thus, job order costing provides more useful information for determining the profitability of particular projects and for estimating costs when preparing bids on future jobs.

One disadvantage of job order costing is that it requires a significant amount of data entry. For Juan Company, it is much easier to simply keep track of total costs incurred during the year than it is to keep track of the costs incurred on each job (home built). Recording this information is time-consuming, and if the data is not entered accurately, then the product costs are not accurate. In recent years, technological advances, such as bar-coding devices for both labor costs and materials, have increased the accuracy and reduced the effort needed to record costs on specific jobs. These innovations expand the opportunities to apply job order costing in a wider variety of business settings, thus improving management's ability to control costs and make better informed decisions.

A common problem of all costing systems is how to allocate overhead to the finished product. Overhead often represents more than 50% of a product's cost, and this cost is often difficult to allocate meaningfully to the product. How, for example, is the salary of Juan Company's president allocated to the various homes that may differ in size, style, and materials used? The accuracy of the job order costing system is largely dependent on the accuracy of the overhead allocation process. Even if the company does a good job of keeping track of the specific amounts of materials and labor used on each job, if the overhead costs are not allocated to individual jobs in a meaningful way, the product costing information is not useful.

Reporting Job Cost Data

At the end of a period, companies prepare financial statements that present aggregate data on all jobs manufactured and sold. The cost of goods manufactured schedule in job order costing is the same as in Chapter 19 with one exception: **The schedule shows manufacturing overhead applied, rather than actual overhead costs. The company adds manufacturing overhead applied to direct materials and direct labor to determine total manufacturing costs.**

Companies prepare the cost of goods manufactured schedule directly from the Work in Process Inventory account. Illustration 20-18 shows a condensed schedule for Wallace Manufacturing Company for January.

Helpful Hint

Monthly financial statements are usually prepared for management use only.

Wallace Manufacturing Company Cost of Goods Manufactured Schedule For the Month Ended January 31, 2012		
Work in process, January 1		$ –0–
Direct materials used	$24,000	
Direct labor	28,000	
Manufacturing overhead applied	22,400	
Total manufacturing costs		74,400
Total cost of work in process		74,400
Less: Work in process, January 31		35,400
Cost of goods manufactured		$39,000

Illustration 20-18
Cost of goods manufactured schedule

Note that the cost of goods manufactured ($39,000) agrees with the amount transferred from Work in Process Inventory to Finished Goods Inventory in journal entry no. 7 in Illustration 20-16 (page 939).

The income statement and balance sheet are the same as those illustrated in Chapter 19. For example, Illustration 20-19 shows the partial income statement for Wallace Manufacturing for the month of January.

Wallace Manufacturing Company Income Statement (partial) For the Month Ending January 31, 2012		
Sales		$50,000
Cost of goods sold		
Finished goods inventory, January 1	$ –0–	
Cost of goods manufactured (See Illustration 20-18)	39,000	
Cost of goods available for sale	39,000	
Less: Finished goods inventory, January 31	–0–	
Cost of goods sold		39,000
Gross profit		$11,000

Illustration 20-19
Partial income statement

Under- or Overapplied Manufacturing Overhead

When Manufacturing Overhead has a **debit balance**, overhead is said to be underapplied. Underapplied overhead means that the overhead assigned to work in process is less than the overhead incurred. Conversely, when manufacturing overhead has a **credit balance**, overhead is overapplied. Overapplied overhead means that the overhead assigned to work in process is greater than the overhead incurred. Illustration 20-20 (page 942) shows these concepts.

Study Objective [6]
Distinguish between under- and overapplied manufacturing overhead.

Manufacturing Overhead		If actual is *greater* than applied, manufacturing overhead is underapplied.
Actual (Costs incurred)	Applied (Costs assigned)	If actual is *less* than applied, manufacturing overhead is overapplied.

Illustration 20-20
Under- and overapplied overhead

YEAR-END BALANCE

At the end of the year, all manufacturing overhead transactions are complete. There is no further opportunity for offsetting events to occur. At this point, Wallace eliminates any balance in Manufacturing Overhead by an adjusting entry. It considers under- or overapplied overhead to be an **adjustment to cost of goods sold**. Thus, Wallace **debits underapplied overhead to Cost of Goods Sold**. It **credits overapplied overhead to Cost of Goods Sold**.

To illustrate, assume that Wallace Manufacturing has a $2,500 credit balance in Manufacturing Overhead at December 31. The adjusting entry for the overapplied overhead is:

Dec. 31	Manufacturing Overhead	2,500	
	Cost of Goods Sold		2,500
	(To transfer overapplied overhead to cost of goods sold)		

After Wallace posts this entry, Manufacturing Overhead has a zero balance. In preparing an income statement for the year, Wallace reports cost of goods sold **after adjusting it** for either under- or overapplied overhead.

Conceptually, some argue, under- or overapplied overhead at the end of the year should be allocated among ending work in process, finished goods, and cost of goods sold. The discussion of this possible allocation approach is left to more advanced courses.

*E*THICS *I*NSIGHT

Working a 25-Hour Day

In some industries, companies bill jobs on a "cost plus profit" basis. For example, law offices bill their customers based upon the "billable hours" incurred by their legal staff. This creates an incentive for law offices to pad their bills—that is, to overstate the costs incurred on particular jobs so as to inflate their bills. In one survey, two-thirds of attorneys reported knowledge of bill padding.

Similarly, suppliers to the government have often been accused of overbilling by misstating their cost accounting records. For example, the government recently filed a lawsuit against Northrop Grumman. This suit accused the company of intentionally concealing cost-accounting and material-tracking problems related to radar-jamming devices that the company made for the U.S. government more than 20 years before. These problems, the suit alleged, resulted in the government overpaying by $27 million. Company memos discussed strategies for training cost-accounting managers on how to conceal the problem from the government. One memo stated, "We can't tell the truth."

Sources: Nathan Koppel, "Lawyer's Charge Opens Window on Bill Padding," *Wall Street Journal* (August 30, 2006); and Andy Pasztor and Jonathan Karp, "Northrop Papers Indicate Coverup," *Wall Street Journal* (April 19, 2004).

 What feature of these businesses creates an incentive to misstate cost accounting data on particular jobs? What can customers do to protect themselves from overbilling? (See page 962.)

Do it!

For Karr Company, the predetermined overhead rate is 140% of direct labor cost. During the month, Karr incurred $90,000 of factory labor costs, of which $80,000 is direct labor and $10,000 is indirect labor. Actual overhead incurred was $119,000.

Compute the amount of manufacturing overhead applied during the month. Determine the amount of under- or overapplied manufacturing overhead.

Solution

Manufacturing overhead applied = (140% × $80,000) = $112,000
Underapplied manufacturing overhead = ($119,000 − $112,000) = $7,000

Related exercise material: BE20-9, E20-5, E20-12, E20-13, and **Do it!** 20-4.

Applied Manufacturing Overhead

action plan

✔ Calculate the amount of overhead applied by multiplying the predetermined overhead rate by actual activity.

✔ If actual manufacturing overhead is greater than applied, manufacturing overhead is underapplied.

✔ If actual manufacturing overhead is less than applied, manufacturing overhead is overapplied.

✔
The Navigator

COMPREHENSIVE

Do it!

During February, Cardella Manufacturing works on two jobs: A16 and B17. Summary data concerning these jobs are as follows.

Manufacturing Overhead

Cardella Manufacturing uses a predetermined overhead rate with direct labor costs as the activity base. It expects annual overhead costs to be $760,000 and direct labor costs for the year to be $950,000.

Manufacturing Costs Incurred

Purchased $54,000 of raw materials on account.
Factory labor $76,000, plus $4,000 employer payroll taxes.
Manufacturing overhead exclusive of indirect materials and indirect labor $59,800.

Assignment of Costs

Direct materials:	Job A16 $27,000, Job B17 $21,000
Indirect materials:	$3,000
Direct labor:	Job A16 $52,000, Job B17 $26,000
Indirect labor:	$2,000

Job A16 was completed and sold on account for $150,000. Job B17 was only partially completed.

Instructions

(a) Compute the predetermined overhead rate.
(b) Journalize the February transactions in the sequence followed in the chapter.
(c) What was the amount of under- or overapplied manufacturing overhead?

action plan

✔ Predetermined overhead rate = Estimated annual overhead costs ÷ Expected annual operating activity.

✔ In accumulating costs, debit three accounts: Raw Materials Inventory, Factory Labor, and Manufacturing Overhead.

✔ When Work in Process Inventory is debited, credit one of the three accounts listed above.

✔ Debit Finished Goods Inventory for the cost of completed jobs. Debit Cost of Goods Sold for the cost of jobs sold.

✔ Overhead is underapplied when Manufacturing Overhead has a debit balance.

Solution to Comprehensive Do it!

(a) Estimated annual overhead costs	÷	Expected annual operating activity	=	Predetermined overhead rate
$760,000	÷	$950,000	=	80%

(b)

1.

Feb. 28	Raw Materials Inventory	54,000	
	Accounts Payable		54,000
	(Purchase of raw materials on account)		

2.

28	Factory Labor	80,000	
	Factory Wages Payable		76,000
	Employer Payroll Taxes Payable		4,000
	(To record factory labor costs)		

3.

28	Manufacturing Overhead	59,800	
	Accounts Payable, Accumulated		
	Depreciation, and Prepaid Insurance		59,800
	(To record overhead costs)		

4.

28	Work in Process Inventory	48,000	
	Manufacturing Overhead	3,000	
	Raw Materials Inventory		51,000
	(To assign raw materials to production)		

5.

Feb. 28	Work in Process Inventory	78,000	
	Manufacturing Overhead	2,000	
	Factory Labor		80,000
	(To assign factory labor to production)		

6.

28	Work in Process Inventory	62,400	
	Manufacturing Overhead		62,400
	(To assign overhead to jobs—		
	80% × $78,000)		

7.

28	Finished Goods Inventory	120,600	
	Work in Process Inventory		120,600
	(To record completion of Job A16: direct		
	materials $27,000, direct labor $52,000,		
	and manufacturing overhead $41,600)		

8.

28	Accounts Receivable	150,000	
	Sales		150,000
	(To record sale of Job A16)		
28	Cost of Goods Sold	120,600	
	Finished Goods Inventory		120,600
	(To record cost of sale for Job A16)		

(c) Manufacturing Overhead has a debit balance of $2,400 as shown below.

Manufacturing Overhead

(3)	59,800	(6)		62,400
(4)	3,000			
(5)	2,000			
Bal.	2,400			

Thus, manufacturing overhead is underapplied for the month.

The Navigator ✔

Summary of Study Objectives

[1] Explain the characteristics and purposes of cost accounting. Cost accounting involves the procedures for measuring, recording, and reporting product costs. From the data accumulated, companies determine the total cost and the unit cost of each product. The two basic types of cost accounting systems are job order cost and process cost.

[2] Describe the flow of costs in a job order costing system. In job order costing, manufacturing costs are first accumulated in three accounts: Raw Materials Inventory, Factory Labor, and Manufacturing Overhead. The accumulated costs are then assigned to Work in Process Inventory and eventually to Finished Goods Inventory and Cost of Goods Sold.

[3] Explain the nature and importance of a job cost sheet. A job cost sheet is a form used to record the costs chargeable to a specific job and to determine the total and unit costs of the completed job. Job cost sheets constitute the subsidiary ledger for the Work in Process Inventory control account.

[4] Indicate how the predetermined overhead rate is determined and used. The predetermined overhead rate is based on the relationship between estimated annual overhead costs and expected annual operating activity. This is expressed in terms of a common activity base, such as direct labor cost. The rate is used in assigning overhead costs to work in process and to specific jobs.

[5] Prepare entries for jobs completed and sold. When jobs are completed, the cost is debited to Finished Goods Inventory and credited to Work in Process Inventory. When a job is sold the entries are: (a) Debit Cash or Accounts Receivable and credit Sales for the selling price. And (b) debit Cost of Goods Sold and credit Finished Goods Inventory for the cost of the goods.

[6] Distinguish between under- and overapplied manufacturing overhead. Underapplied manufacturing overhead means that the overhead assigned to work in process is less than the overhead incurred. Overapplied overhead means that the overhead assigned to work in process is greater than the overhead incurred.

✔ **The Navigator**

Glossary

Cost accounting An area of accounting that involves measuring, recording, and reporting product costs. (p. 924).

Cost accounting system Manufacturing cost accounts that are fully integrated into the general ledger of a company. (p. 924).

Job cost sheet A form used to record the costs chargeable to a specific job and to determine the total and unit costs of the completed job. (p. 929).

Job order cost system A cost accounting system in which costs are assigned to each job or batch. (p. 924).

Materials requisition slip A document authorizing the issuance of raw materials from the storeroom to production. (p. 930).

Overapplied overhead A situation in which overhead assigned to work in process is greater than the overhead incurred. (p. 941).

Predetermined overhead rate A rate based on the relationship between estimated annual overhead costs and expected annual operating activity, expressed in terms of a common activity base. (p. 933).

Process cost system A system of accounting used when a large quantity of similar products are manufactured. (p. 925).

Summary entry A journal entry that summarizes the totals from multiple transactions. (p. 928).

Time ticket A document that indicates the employee, the hours worked, the account and job to be charged, and the total labor cost. (p. 931).

Underapplied overhead A situation in which overhead assigned to work in process is less than the overhead incurred. (p. 941).

Self-Test, Brief Exercises, Exercises, Problem Set A, and many more components are available for practice in *WileyPLUS*

Self-Test Questions

Answers are on page 962.

(SO 1) **1.** Cost accounting involves the measuring, recording, and reporting of:
   a. product costs.
   b. future costs.
   c. manufacturing processes.
   d. managerial accounting decisions.

(SO 1) **2.** A company is more likely to use a job costing system if:
   a. it manufactures a large volume of similar products.
   b. its production is continuous.
   c. it manufactures products with unique characteristics.
   d. it uses a periodic inventory system.

(SO 2) **3.** In accumulating raw materials costs, the cost of raw materials purchased in a perpetual system is debited to:

a. Raw Materials Purchases.
b. Raw Materials Inventory.
c. Purchases.
d. Work in Process.

(SO 2) **4.** When incurred, factory labor costs are debited to:
   a. Work in Process.
   b. Factory Wages Expense.
   c. Factory Labor.
   d. Factory Wages Payable.

(SO 2) **5.** The flow of costs in job order costing:
   a. begins with work in process inventory and ends with finished goods inventory.
   b. begins as soon as a sale occurs.
   c. parallels the physical flow of materials as they are converted into finished goods.
   d. is necessary to prepare the cost of goods manufactured schedule.

(SO 3) **6.** Raw materials are assigned to a job when:
   a. the job is sold.
   b. the materials are purchased.
   c. the materials are received from the vendor.
   d. the materials are issued by the materials storeroom.

(SO 3) **7.** The source documents for assigning costs to job cost sheets are:
   a. invoices, time tickets, and the predetermined overhead rate.
   b. materials requisition slips, time tickets, and the actual overhead costs.
   c. materials requisition slips, payroll register, and the predetermined overhead rate.
   d. materials requisition slips, time tickets, and the predetermined overhead rate.

(SO 3) **8.** In recording the issuance of raw materials in a job order cost system, it would be *incorrect* to:
   a. debit Work in Process Inventory.
   b. debit Finished Goods Inventory.
   c. debit Manufacturing Overhead.
   d. credit Raw Materials Inventory.

(SO 3) **9.** The entry when direct factory labor is assigned to jobs is a debit to:
   a. Work in Process Inventory and a credit to Factory Labor.
   b. Manufacturing Overhead and a credit to Factory Labor.
   c. Factory Labor and a credit to Manufacturing Overhead.
   d. Factory Labor and a credit to Work in Process Inventory.

(SO 4) **10.** The formula for computing the predetermined manufacturing overhead rate is estimated annual overhead costs divided by an expected annual operating activity, expressed as:
   a. direct labor cost.
   b. direct labor hours.
   c. machine hours.
   d. Any of the above.

(SO 4) **11.** In Crawford Company, the predetermined overhead rate is 80% of direct labor cost. During the month, $210,000 of factory labor costs are incurred, of which $180,000 is direct labor and $30,000 is indirect labor. Actual overhead incurred was $200,000. The amount of overhead debited to Work in Process Inventory should be:
   a. $120,000.
   c. $168,000.
   b. $144,000.
   d. $160,000.

(SO 5) **12.** In Mynex Company, Job No. 26 is completed at a cost of $4,500 and later sold for $7,000 cash. A correct entry is:
   a. Debit Finished Goods Inventory $7,000 and credit Work in Process Inventory $7,000.
   b. Debit Cost of Goods Sold $7,000 and credit Finished Goods Inventory $7,000.
   c. Debit Finished Goods Inventory $4,500 and credit Work in Process Inventory $4,500.
   d. Debit Accounts Receivable $7,000 and credit Sales $7,000.

(SO 5) **13.** At the end of an accounting period, a company using a job costing system prepares the cost of goods manufactured schedule:
   a. from the job cost sheet.
   b. from the Work in Process Inventory account.
   c. by adding direct materials used, direct labor incurred, and manufacturing overhead incurred.
   d. from the Cost of Goods Sold account.

(SO 6) **14.** At end of the year, a company has a $1,200 debit balance in Manufacturing Overhead. The company:
   a. makes an adjusting entry by debiting Manufacturing Overhead Applied for $1,200 and crediting Manufacturing Overhead for $1,200.
   b. makes an adjusting entry by debiting Manufacturing Overhead Expense for $1,200 and crediting Manufacturing Overhead for $1,200.
   c. makes an adjusting entry by debiting Cost of Goods Sold for $1,200 and crediting Manufacturing Overhead for $1,200.
   d. makes no adjusting entry because differences between actual overhead and the amount applied are a normal part of job costing and will average out over the next year.

(SO 6) **15.** Manufacturing overhead is underapplied if:
   a. actual overhead is less than applied.
   b. actual overhead is greater than applied.
   c. the predetermined rate equals the actual rate.
   d. actual overhead equals applied overhead.

Go to the book's companion website, **www.wiley.com/college/weygandt**, for additional Self-Test Questions.

Questions

1. (a) Bill Meyer is not sure about the difference between cost accounting and a cost accounting system. Explain the difference to Bill. (b) What is an important feature of a cost accounting system?

2. (a) Distinguish between the two types of cost accounting systems. (b) May a company use both types of cost accounting systems?

3. What type of industry is likely to use a job order cost system? Give some examples.

4. What type of industry is likely to use a process cost system? Give some examples.

5. Your roommate asks your help in understanding the major steps in the flow of costs in a job order cost system. Identify the steps for your roommate.

6. There are two inventory control accounts in a job order system. Identify the control accounts and their subsidiary ledgers.

7. What source documents are used in accumulating direct labor costs?

8. "Entries to Manufacturing Overhead normally are only made daily." Do you agree? Explain.

9. Yuan Li is confused about the source documents used in assigning materials and labor costs. Identify the documents and give the entry for each document.

10. What is the purpose of a job cost sheet?

11. Indicate the source documents that are used in charging costs to specific jobs.

12. Explain how a "materials requisition slip" is used in a job order cost system.

13. Pham Hannah believes actual manufacturing overhead should be charged to jobs. Do you agree? Why or why not?

14. What relationships are involved in computing a predetermined overhead rate?

15. How can the agreement of Work in Process Inventory and job cost sheets be verified?

16. Tia Conn believes that the cost of goods manufactured schedule in job order cost accounting is the same as shown in Chapter 19. Is Tia correct? Explain.

17. Jeff Gillum is confused about under- and overapplied manufacturing overhead. Define the terms for Jeff, and indicate the balance in the manufacturing overhead account applicable to each term.

18. "At the end of the year, under- or overapplied overhead is closed to Income Summary." Is this correct? If not, indicate the customary treatment of this amount.

Brief Exercises

BE20-1 Alomar Tool & Die begins operations on January 1. Because all work is done to customer specifications, the company decides to use a job order cost accounting system. Prepare a flow chart of a typical job order system with arrows showing the flow of costs. Identify the eight transactions.

Prepare a flowchart of a job order cost accounting system, and identify transactions.
(SO 2)

BE20-2 During January, its first month of operations, Alomar Tool & Die accumulated the following manufacturing costs: raw materials $4,000 on account, factory labor $5,000 of which $4,200 relates to factory wages payable and $800 relates to payroll taxes payable, and utilities payable $2,000. Prepare separate journal entries for each type of manufacturing cost.

Prepare entries in accumulating manufacturing costs.
(SO 2)

BE20-3 In January, Alomar Tool & Die requisitions raw materials for production as follows: Job 1 $900, Job 2 $1,200, Job 3 $700, and general factory use $600. Prepare a summary journal entry to record raw materials used.

Prepare entry for the assignment of raw materials costs.
(SO 3)

BE20-4 Factory labor data for Alomar Tool & Die is given in BE20-2. During January, time tickets show that the factory labor of $5,000 was used as follows: Job 1 $1,200, Job 2 $1,600, Job 3 $1,400, and general factory use $800. Prepare a summary journal entry to record factory labor used.

Prepare entry for the assignment of factory labor costs.
(SO 3)

BE20-5 Data pertaining to job cost sheets for Alomar Tool & Die are given in BE20-3 and BE20-4. Prepare the job cost sheets for each of the three jobs. (*Note:* You may omit the column for Manufacturing Overhead.)

Prepare job cost sheets.
(SO 3)

BE20-6 Formu Company estimates that annual manufacturing overhead costs will be $800,000. Estimated annual operating activity bases are: direct labor cost $500,000, direct labor hours 50,000, and machine hours 100,000. Compute the predetermined overhead rate for each activity base.

Compute predetermined overhead rates.
(SO 4)

BE20-7 During the first quarter, McKay Company incurs the following direct labor costs: January $40,000, February $30,000, and March $50,000. For each month, prepare the entry to assign overhead to production using a predetermined rate of 90% of direct labor cost.

Assign manufacturing overhead to production.
(SO 4)

BE20-8 In March, Samani Company completes Jobs 10 and 11. Job 10 cost $25,000 and Job 11 $30,000. On March 31, Job 10 is sold to the customer for $35,000 in cash. Journalize the entries for the completion of the two jobs and the sale of Job 10.

Prepare entries for completion and sale of completed jobs.
(SO 5)

BE20-9 At December 31, balances in Manufacturing Overhead are: Mair Company—debit $1,500, Gitau Company—credit $900. Prepare the adjusting entry for each company at December 31, assuming the adjustment is made to cost of goods sold.

Prepare adjusting entries for under- and overapplied overhead.
(SO 6)

Do it! Review

Prepare journal entries for manufacturing costs.
(SO 2)

Do it! 20-1   During the current month, Brady Company incurs the following manufacturing costs:

a. Purchased raw materials of $13,000 on account.

b. Incurred factory labor of $40,000. Of that amount, $31,000 relates to wages payable and $9,000 relates to payroll taxes payable.

c. Factory utilities of $3,100 are payable, prepaid factory property taxes of $2,400 have expired, and depreciation on the factory building is $9,500.

Prepare journal entries for each type of manufacturing cost. (Use a summary entry to record manufacturing overhead.)

Assign costs to work in process.
(SO 3, 4)

Do it! 20-2   Francisco Company is working on two job orders. The job cost sheets show the following:

	Job 201	Job 202
Direct materials	$7,200	$9,000
Direct labor	4,000	6,000
Manufacturing overhead	5,200	7,800

Prepare the three summary entries to record the assignment of costs to Work in Process from the data on the job cost sheets.

Prepare entries for completion and sale of jobs.
(SO 5)

Do it! 20-3   During the current month, Weller Corporation completed Job 310 and Job 312. Job 310 cost $60,000 and Job 312 cost $40,000. Job 312 was sold on account for $90,000. Journalize the entries for the completion of the two jobs and the sale of Job 312.

Apply manufacturing overhead and determine under- or overapplication.
(SO 6)

Do it! 20-4   For FreeFall Company, the predetermined overhead rate is 150% of direct labor cost. During the month, FreeFall incurred $100,000 of factory labor costs, of which $85,000 is direct labor and $15,000 is indirect labor. Actual overhead incurred was $120,000.

Compute the amount of manufacturing overhead applied during the month. Determine the amount of under- or overapplied manufacturing overhead.

Exercises

Prepare entries for factory labor.
(SO 2, 3)

E20-1   The gross earnings of the factory workers for Zorn Company during the month of January are $60,000. The employer's payroll taxes for the factory payroll are $8,000. The fringe benefits to be paid by the employer on this payroll are $4,000. Of the total accumulated cost of factory labor, 85% is related to direct labor and 15% is attributable to indirect labor.

Instructions
(a) Prepare the entry to record the factory labor costs for the month of January.
(b) Prepare the entry to assign factory labor to production.

Prepare journal entries for manufacturing costs.
(SO 3, 4, 5)

E20-2   Tiet Manufacturing uses a job order cost accounting system. On May 1, the company has a balance in Work in Process Inventory of $3,200 and two jobs in process: Job No. 429 $2,000, and Job No. 430 $1,200. During May, a summary of source documents reveals the following.

Job Number	Materials Requisition Slips		Labor Time Tickets	
429	$2,500		$1,900	
430	3,500		3,000	
431	4,400	$10,400	7,600	$12,500
General use		800		1,200
		$11,200		$13,700

Tiet Manufacturing applies manufacturing overhead to jobs at an overhead rate of 80% of direct labor cost. Job No. 429 is completed during the month.

Instructions
(a) Prepare summary journal entries on May 31 to record: (i) the requisition slips, (ii) the time tickets, (iii) the assignment of manufacturing overhead to jobs, and (iv) the completion of Job No. 429.
(b) Post the entries to Work in Process Inventory, and prove the agreement of the control account with the job cost sheets of the unfinished jobs.

E20-3 A job order cost sheet for Renshaw Company is shown below.

Analyze a job cost sheet and prepare entries for manufacturing costs.
(SO 3, 4, 5)

Job No. 92			For 2,000 Units
Date	Direct Materials	Direct Labor	Manufacturing Overhead
Beg. bal. Jan. 1	5,000	6,000	4,500
8	6,000		
12		8,000	6,400
25	2,000		
27		4,000	3,200
	13,000	18,000	14,100

Cost of completed job:	
Direct materials	$13,000
Direct labor	18,000
Manufacturing overhead	14,100
Total cost	$45,100
Unit cost ($45,100 ÷ 2,000)	$22.55

Instructions
(a) On the basis of the foregoing data answer the following questions.
  (1) What was the balance in Work in Process Inventory on January 1 if this was the only unfinished job?
  (2) If manufacturing overhead is applied on the basis of direct labor cost, what overhead rate was used in each year?
(b) Prepare summary entries at January 31 to record the current year's transactions pertaining to Job No. 92.

E20-4 Manufacturing cost data for Meneses Company, which uses a job order cost system, are presented below.

Analyze costs of manufacturing and determine missing amounts.
(SO 5)

	Case A	Case B	Case C
Direct materials used	$ (a)	$ 83,000	$ 63,150
Direct labor	50,000	120,000	(h)
Manufacturing overhead applied	42,500	(d)	(i)
Total manufacturing costs	155,650	(e)	213,000
Work in process 1/1/12	(b)	15,500	18,000
Total cost of work in process	201,500	(f)	(j)
Work in process 12/31/12	(c)	11,800	(k)
Cost of goods manufactured	192,300	(g)	222,000

Instructions
Indicate the missing amount for each letter. Assume that in all cases manufacturing overhead is applied on the basis of direct labor cost and the rate is the same.

E20-5 Hodgkiss Company applies manufacturing overhead to jobs on the basis of machine hours used. Overhead costs are expected to total $305,000 for the year, and machine usage is estimated at 125,000 hours.
  For the year, $322,000 of overhead costs are incurred and 130,000 hours are used.

Compute the manufacturing overhead rate and under- or overapplied overhead.
(SO 4, 6)

Instructions

(a) Compute the manufacturing overhead rate for the year.

(b) What is the amount of under- or overapplied overhead at December 31?

(c) Assuming the under- or overapplied overhead for the year is not allocated to inventory accounts, prepare the adjusting entry to assign the amount to cost of goods sold.

Analyze job cost sheet and prepare entry for completed job.

(SO 2, 3, 4, 5)

E20-6 A job cost sheet of Fenter Company is given below.

Job Cost Sheet			
JOB NO. 469		Quantity 2,000	
ITEM Snow Leopard Cages		Date Requested 7/2	
FOR Mensa Company		Date Completed 7/31	

Date	Direct Materials	Direct Labor	Manufacturing Overhead
7/10	825		
12	900		
15		440	550
22		380	475
24	1,600		
27	1,500		
31		540	675

Cost of completed job:

Direct materials _____

Direct labor _____

Manufacturing overhead _____

Total cost _____

Unit cost _____

Instructions

(a) ◄▬▬▬ Answer the following questions.

  (1) What are the source documents for direct materials, direct labor, and manufacturing overhead costs assigned to this job?

  (2) What is the predetermined manufacturing overhead rate?

  (3) What are the total cost and the unit cost of the completed job?

(b) Prepare the entry to record the completion of the job.

Prepare entries for manufacturing costs.

(SO 2, 3, 4, 5)

E20-7 Cooke Corporation incurred the following transactions.

1. Purchased raw materials on account $46,300.

2. Raw Materials of $36,000 were requisitioned to the factory. An analysis of the materials requisition slips indicated that $6,800 was classified as indirect materials.

3. Factory labor costs incurred were $53,900, of which $49,000 pertained to factory wages payable and $4,900 pertained to employer payroll taxes payable.

4. Time tickets indicated that $48,000 was direct labor and $5,900 was indirect labor.

5. Overhead costs incurred on account were $80,500.

6. Manufacturing overhead was applied at the rate of 150% of direct labor cost.

7. Goods costing $88,000 were completed and transferred to finished goods.

8. Finished goods costing $75,000 to manufacture were sold on account for $103,000.

Instructions

Journalize the transactions. (Omit explanations.)

Prepare entries for manufacturing costs.

(SO 2, 3, 4, 5)

E20-8 Benton Printing Corp. uses a job order cost system. The following data summarize the operations related to the first quarter's production.

1. Materials purchased on account $192,000, and factory wages incurred $87,300.

2. Materials requisitioned and factory labor used by job:

Job Number	Materials	Factory Labor
A20	$ 35,240	$18,000
A21	42,920	22,000
A22	36,100	15,000
A23	39,270	25,000
General factory use	4,470	7,300
	$158,000	$87,300

3. Manufacturing overhead costs incurred on account $39,500.
4. Depreciation on equipment $14,550.
5. Manufacturing overhead rate is 80% of direct labor cost.
6. Jobs completed during the quarter: A20, A21, and A23.

Instructions
Prepare entries to record the operations summarized above. (Prepare a schedule showing the individual cost elements and total cost for each job in item 6.)

E20-9   At May 31, 2012, the accounts of Contreras Manufacturing Company show the following.

Prepare a cost of goods manufactured schedule and partial financial statements.
(SO 2, 5)

1. May 1 inventories—finished goods $12,600, work in process $14,700, and raw materials $8,200.
2. May 31 inventories—finished goods $9,500, work in process $17,900, and raw materials $7,100.
3. Debit postings to work in process were: direct materials $62,400, direct labor $32,000, and manufacturing overhead applied $40,000.
4. Sales totaled $200,000.

Instructions
(a) Prepare a condensed cost of goods manufactured schedule.
(b) Prepare an income statement for May through gross profit.
(c) Indicate the balance sheet presentation of the manufacturing inventories at May 31, 2012.

E20-10   Forte Company begins operations on April 1. Information from job cost sheets shows the following.

Compute work in process and finished goods from job cost sheets.
(SO 3, 5)

Job Number		Manufacturing Costs Assigned		Month Completed
	April	May	June	
10	$5,200	$4,400		May
11	4,100	3,900	$3,000	June
12	1,200			April
13		4,700	4,500	June
14		4,900	3,600	Not complete

Job 12 was completed in April. Job 10 was completed in May. Jobs 11 and 13 were completed in June. Each job was sold for 25% above its cost in the month following completion.

Instructions
(a) What is the balance in Work in Process Inventory at the end of each month?
(b) What is the balance in Finished Goods Inventory at the end of each month?
(c) What is the gross profit for May, June, and July?

E20-11   Shown below are the job cost related accounts for the law firm of Han, Kung, and Ming and their manufacturing-company equivalents:

Prepare entries for costs of services provided.
(SO 2, 4, 5)

Law Firm Accounts	Manufacturing-Company Accounts
Supplies	Raw Materials
Salaries and Wages Payable	Factory Wages Payable
Operating Overhead	Manufacturing Overhead
Service Contracts in Process	Work in Process
Cost of Completed Service Contracts	Cost of Goods Sold

Cost data for the month of March follow.

1. Purchased supplies on account $1,500.
2. Issued supplies $1,200 (60% direct and 40% indirect).
3. Time cards for the month indicated labor costs of $50,000 (80% direct and 20% indirect).
4. Operating overhead costs incurred for cash totaled $40,000.
5. Operating overhead is applied at a rate of 90% of direct attorney cost.
6. Work completed totaled $70,000.

Instructions
(a) Journalize the transactions for March. Omit explanations.
(b) Determine the balance of the Work in Process account. Use a T account.

Determine cost of jobs and ending balance in work in process and overhead accounts.
(SO 3, 4, 6)

E20-12   Alma Ortiz and Associates, a CPA firm, uses job order costing to capture the costs of its audit jobs. There were no audit jobs in process at the beginning of November. Listed below are data concerning the three audit jobs conducted during November.

	Perez	**Rivera**	**Sota**
Direct materials	$600	$400	$200
Auditor labor costs	$5,400	$6,600	$3,375
Auditor hours	72	88	45

Overhead costs are applied to jobs on the basis of auditor hours, and the predetermined overhead rate is $55 per auditor hour. The Perez job is the only incomplete job at the end of November. Actual overhead for the month was $12,000.

Instructions
(a) Determine the cost of each job.
(b) Indicate the balance of the Work in Process account at the end of November.
(c) Calculate the ending balance of the Manufacturing Overhead account for November.

Determine predetermined overhead rate, apply overhead, and determine whether balance is under- or overapplied.
(SO 4, 6)

E20-13   Irma's Interiors uses a job order costing system to collect the costs of its interior decorating business. Each client's consultation is treated as a separate job. Overhead is applied to each job based on the number of decorator hours incurred. Listed below are data for the current year.

Budgeted overhead	$960,000
Actual overhead	$982,800
Budgeted decorator hours	40,000
Actual decorator hours	40,500

The company uses Operating Overhead in place of Manufacturing Overhead.

Instructions
(a) Compute the predetermined overhead rate.
(b) Prepare the entry to apply the overhead for the year.
(c) Determine whether the overhead was under- or overapplied and by how much.

Exercises: Set B

Visit the book's companion website, at **www.wiley.com/college/weygandt**, and choose the Student Companion site to access Exercise Set B.

Problems: Set A

Prepare entries in a job cost system and job cost sheets.
(SO 2, 3, 4, 5, 6)

P20-1A   Bynum Manufacturing uses a job order cost system and applies overhead to production on the basis of direct labor costs. On January 1, 2012, Job No. 50 was the only job in process. The costs incurred prior to January 1 on this job were as follows: direct materials $20,000, direct labor $12,000, and manufacturing overhead $16,000. As of January 1, Job No. 49 had been completed at a cost of $90,000 and was part of finished goods inventory. There was a $15,000 balance in the Raw Materials Inventory account.

During the month of January, Bynum Manufacturing began production on Jobs 51 and 52, and completed Jobs 50 and 51. Jobs 49 and 50 were also sold on account during the month for $122,000 and $158,000, respectively. The following additional events occurred during the month.

1. Purchased additional raw materials of $90,000 on account.
2. Incurred factory labor costs of $65,000. Of this amount, $16,000 related to employer payroll taxes.
3. Incurred manufacturing overhead costs as follows: indirect materials $17,000; indirect labor $15,000; depreciation expense on equipment $19,000; and various other manufacturing overhead costs on account $20,000.
4. Assigned direct materials and direct labor to jobs as follows.

Job No.	Direct Materials	Direct Labor
50	$10,000	$ 5,000
51	39,000	25,000
52	30,000	20,000

Instructions

(a) Calculate the predetermined overhead rate for 2012, assuming Bynum Manufacturing estimates total manufacturing overhead costs of $1,050,000, direct labor costs of $700,000, and direct labor hours of 20,000 for the year.
(b) Open job cost sheets for Jobs 50, 51, and 52. Enter the January 1 balances on the job cost sheet for Job No. 50.
(c) Prepare the journal entries to record the purchase of raw materials, the factory labor costs incurred, and the manufacturing overhead costs incurred during the month of January.
(d) Prepare the journal entries to record the assignment of direct materials, direct labor, and manufacturing overhead costs to production. In assigning manufacturing overhead costs, use the overhead rate calculated in (a). Post all costs to the job cost sheets as necessary.
(e) Total the job cost sheets for any job(s) completed during the month. Prepare the journal entry (or entries) to record the completion of any job(s) during the month.
(f) Prepare the journal entry (or entries) to record the sale of any job(s) during the month.
(g) What is the balance in the Finished Goods Inventory account at the end of the month? What does this balance consist of?
(h) What is the amount of over- or underapplied overhead?

*(e) Job 50, $70,500
Job 51, $101,500*

P20-2A For the year ended December 31, 2012, the job cost sheets of Heimer Company contained the following data.

*Prepare entries in a job cost system and partial income statement.
(SO 2, 3, 4, 5, 6)*

Job Number	Explanation	Direct Materials	Direct Labor	Manufacturing Overhead	Total Costs
7640	Balance 1/1	$25,000	$24,000	$28,800	$ 77,800
	Current year's costs	30,000	36,000	43,200	109,200
7641	Balance 1/1	11,000	18,000	21,600	50,600
	Current year's costs	43,000	48,000	57,600	148,600
7642	Current year's costs	48,000	55,000	66,000	169,000

Other data:

1. Raw materials inventory totaled $15,000 on January 1. During the year, $140,000 of raw materials were purchased on account.
2. Finished goods on January 1 consisted of Job No. 7638 for $87,000 and Job No. 7639 for $92,000.
3. Job No. 7640 and Job No. 7641 were completed during the year.
4. Jobs 7638, 7639, and 7641 were sold on account for $530,000.
5. Manufacturing overhead incurred on account totaled $120,000.
6. Other manufacturing overhead consisted of indirect materials $14,000, indirect labor $20,000, and depreciation on factory machinery $8,000.

Instructions

(a) Prove the agreement of Work in Process Inventory with job cost sheets pertaining to unfinished work. (*Hint:* Use a single T account for Work in Process Inventory.) Calculate each of the following, then post each to the T account: (1) beginning balance, (2) direct materials, (3) direct labor, (4) manufacturing overhead, and (5) completed jobs.

*(a) $169,000; Job 7642:
$169,000*

(b) Amount = $4,800

(c) $156,600

Prepare entries in a job cost system and cost of goods manufactured schedule.

(SO 2, 3, 4, 5)

(b) Prepare the adjusting entry for manufacturing overhead, assuming the balance is allocated entirely to cost of goods sold.

(c) Determine the gross profit to be reported for 2012.

P20-3A Skop Inc. is a construction company specializing in custom patios. The patios are constructed of concrete, brick, fiberglass, and lumber, depending upon customer preference. On June 1, 2012, the general ledger for Skop Inc. contains the following data.

Raw Materials Inventory	$4,200	Manufacturing Overhead Applied	$32,640
Work in Process Inventory	$5,540	Manufacturing Overhead Incurred	$31,650

Subsidiary data for Work in Process Inventory on June 1 are as follows.

Job Cost Sheets

	Customer Job		
Cost Element	Gomes	Innes	Larsen
Direct materials	$ 600	$ 800	$ 900
Direct labor	320	540	580
Manufacturing overhead	400	675	725
	$1,320	$2,015	$2,205

During June, raw materials purchased on account were $3,900, and all wages were paid. Additional overhead costs consisted of depreciation on equipment $700 and miscellaneous costs of $400 incurred on account.

A summary of materials requisition slips and time tickets for June shows the following.

Customer Job	Materials Requisition Slips	Time Tickets
Gomes	$ 800	$ 450
Franz	2,000	800
Innes	500	360
Larsen	1,300	1,600
Gomes	300	390
	4,900	3,600
General use	1,500	1,200
	$6,400	$4,800

Overhead was charged to jobs at the same rate of $1.25 per dollar of direct labor cost. The patios for customers Gomes, Innes, and Larsen were completed during June and sold for a total of $18,900. Each customer paid in full.

Instructions

(a) Journalize the June transactions: (i) for purchase of raw materials, factory labor costs incurred, and manufacturing overhead costs incurred; (ii) assignment of raw materials, labor, and overhead to production; and (iii) completion of jobs and sale of goods.

(b) Post the entries to Work in Process Inventory.

(d) Cost of goods manufactured $14,740

(c) Reconcile the balance in Work in Process Inventory with the costs of unfinished jobs.

(d) Prepare a cost of goods manufactured schedule for June.

Compute predetermined overhead rates, apply overhead, and calculate under- or overapplied overhead.

(SO 4, 6)

P20-4A Hsung Manufacturing Company uses a job order cost system in each of its three manufacturing departments. Manufacturing overhead is applied to jobs on the basis of direct labor cost in Department E, direct labor hours in Department G, and machine hours in Department I.

In establishing the predetermined overhead rates for 2012, the following estimates were made for the year.

	Department		
	E	G	I
Manufacturing overhead	$1,050,000	$1,500,000	$840,000
Direct labor costs	$1,500,000	$1,250,000	$450,000
Direct labor hours	100,000	125,000	40,000
Machine hours	400,000	500,000	120,000

During January, the job cost sheets showed the following costs and production data.

	Department		
	E	**G**	**I**
Direct materials used	$140,000	$126,000	$78,000
Direct labor costs	$120,000	$110,000	$37,500
Manufacturing overhead incurred	$ 89,000	$124,000	$74,000
Direct labor hours	8,000	11,000	3,500
Machine hours	34,000	45,000	10,400

Instructions

(a) Compute the predetermined overhead rate for each department.
(b) Compute the total manufacturing costs assigned to jobs in January in each department.
(c) Compute the under- or overapplied overhead for each department at January 31.

(a) 70%, $12, $7.00
(b) $344,000, $368,000,
* $188,300*
(c) $5,000, $(8,000), $1,200

P20-5A Sveta Corporation's fiscal year ends on November 30. The following accounts are found in its job order cost accounting system for the first month of the new fiscal year.

Analyze manufacturing accounts and determine missing amounts.
(SO 2, 3, 4, 5, 6)

Raw Materials Inventory

Dec. 1	Beginning balance	(a)	Dec. 31	Requisitions	18,850
31	Purchases	19,225			
Dec. 31	Ending balance	7,975			

Work in Process Inventory

Dec. 1	Beginning balance	(b)	Dec. 31	Jobs completed	(f)
31	Direct materials	(c)			
31	Direct labor	8,800			
31	Overhead	(d)			
Dec. 31	Ending balance	(e)			

Finished Goods Inventory

Dec. 1	Beginning balance	(g)	Dec. 31	Cost of goods sold	(i)
31	Completed jobs	(h)			
Dec. 31	Ending balance	(j)			

Factory Labor

Dec. 31	Factory wages	12,465	Dec. 31	Wages assigned	(k)

Manufacturing Overhead

Dec. 31	Indirect materials	1,900	Dec. 31	Overhead applied	(m)
31	Indirect labor	(l)			
31	Other overhead	1,245			

Other data:

1. On December 1, two jobs were in process: Job No. 154 and Job No. 155. These jobs had combined direct materials costs of $9,750 and direct labor costs of $15,000. Overhead was applied at a rate that was 80% of direct labor cost.
2. During December, Job Nos. 156, 157, and 158 were started. On December 31, Job No. 158 was unfinished. This job had charges for direct materials $3,800 and direct labor $4,800, plus manufacturing overhead. All jobs, except for Job No. 158, were completed in December.
3. On December 1, Job No. 153 was in the finished goods warehouse. It had a total cost of $5,000. On December 31, Job No. 157 was the only job finished that was not sold. It had a cost of $4,000.
4. Manufacturing overhead was $230 overapplied in December.

Instructions

List the letters (a) through (m) and indicate the amount pertaining to each letter.

(c) $16,950
(f) $57,100
(i) $58,100

Problems: Set B

P20-1B Saeed Manufacturing uses a job order cost system and applies overhead to production on the basis of direct labor hours. On January 1, 2012, Job No. 25 was the only job in process. The costs incurred prior to January 1 on this job were as follows: direct materials $10,000; direct

Prepare entries in a job cost system and job cost sheets.
(SO 2, 3, 4, 5, 6)

labor $6,000; and manufacturing overhead $9,000. Job No. 23 had been completed at a cost of $42,000 and was part of finished goods inventory. There was a $5,000 balance in the Raw Materials Inventory account.

During the month of January, the company began production on Jobs 26 and 27, and completed Jobs 25 and 26. Jobs 23 and 25 were sold on account during the month for $63,000 and $74,000, respectively. The following additional events occurred during the month.

1. Purchased additional raw materials of $40,000 on account.
2. Incurred factory labor costs of $31,500. Of this amount, $7,500 related to employer payroll taxes.
3. Incurred manufacturing overhead costs as follows: indirect materials $10,000; indirect labor $7,500; depreciation expense on equipment $12,000; and various other manufacturing overhead costs on account $11,000.
4. Assigned direct materials and direct labor to jobs as follows.

Job No.	Direct Materials	Direct Labor
25	$ 5,000	$ 3,000
26	17,000	12,000
27	13,000	9,000

5. The company uses direct labor hours as the activity base to assign overhead. Direct labor hours incurred on each job were as follows: Job No. 25, 200; Job No. 26, 800; and Job No. 27, 600.

Instructions

(a) Calculate the predetermined overhead rate for the year 2012, assuming Saeed Manufacturing estimates total manufacturing overhead costs of $480,000, direct labor costs of $300,000, and direct labor hours of 20,000 for the year.
(b) Open job cost sheets for Jobs 25, 26, and 27. Enter the January 1 balances on the job cost sheet for Job No. 25.
(c) Prepare the journal entries to record the purchase of raw materials, the factory labor costs incurred, and the manufacturing overhead costs incurred during the month of January.
(d) Prepare the journal entries to record the assignment of direct materials, direct labor, and manufacturing overhead costs to production. In assigning manufacturing overhead costs, use the overhead rate calculated in (a). Post all costs to the job cost sheets as necessary.

(e) Job 25, $37,800
  Job 26, $48,200

(e) Total the job cost sheets for any job(s) completed during the month. Prepare the journal entry (or entries) to record the completion of any job(s) during the month.
(f) Prepare the journal entry (or entries) to record the sale of any job(s) during the month.
(g) What is the balance in the Work in Process Inventory account at the end of the month? What does this balance consist of?
(h) What is the amount of over- or underapplied overhead?

Prepare entries in a job cost system and partial income statement.

(SO 2, 3, 4, 5, 6)

P20-2B For the year ended December 31, 2012, the job cost sheets of Guo Company contained the following data.

Job Number	Explanation	Direct Materials	Direct Labor	Manufacturing Overhead	Total Costs
7650	Balance 1/1	$18,000	$20,000	$25,000	$ 63,000
	Current year's costs	32,000	36,000	45,000	113,000
7651	Balance 1/1	12,000	16,000	20,000	48,000
	Current year's costs	30,000	40,000	50,000	120,000
7652	Current year's costs	45,000	68,000	85,000	198,000

Other data:

1. Raw materials inventory totaled $20,000 on January 1. During the year, $100,000 of raw materials were purchased on account.
2. Finished goods on January 1 consisted of Job No. 7648 for $93,000 and Job No. 7649 for $62,000.
3. Job No. 7650 and Job No. 7651 were completed during the year.
4. Job Nos. 7648, 7649, and 7650 were sold on account for $490,000.
5. Manufacturing overhead incurred on account totaled $135,000.
6. Other manufacturing overhead consisted of indirect materials $12,000, indirect labor $18,000, and depreciation on factory machinery $19,500.

Instructions

(a) Prove the agreement of Work in Process Inventory with job cost sheets pertaining to unfinished work. (*Hint:* Use a single T account for Work in Process Inventory.) Calculate each of the following, then post each to the T account: (1) beginning balance, (2) direct materials, (3) direct labor, (4) manufacturing overhead, and (5) completed jobs.

(b) Prepare the adjusting entry for manufacturing overhead, assuming the balance is allocated entirely to cost of goods sold.

(c) Determine the gross profit to be reported for 2012.

(a) (1) $111,000
(4) $180,000
Unfinished job 7652, $198,000

(b) Amount = $4,500

(c) $154,500

P20-3B Nami Yee is a contractor specializing in custom-built jacuzzis. On May 1, 2012, her ledger contains the following data.

Raw Materials Inventory	$30,000
Work in Process Inventory	12,200
Manufacturing Overhead	2,500 (dr.)

Prepare entries in a job cost system and cost of goods manufactured schedule.

(SO 2, 3, 4, 5)

The Manufacturing Overhead account has debit totals of $12,500 and credit totals of $10,000. Subsidiary data for Work in Process Inventory on May 1 include:

Job Cost Sheets

Job by Customer	Direct Materials	Direct Labor	Manufacturing Overhead
Scott	$2,500	$2,000	$1,400
Condon	2,000	1,200	840
Keefe	900	800	560
	$5,400	$4,000	$2,800

During May, the following costs were incurred: (a) raw materials purchased on account $4,000, (b) labor paid $7,600, and (c) manufacturing overhead paid $1,400.

A summary of materials requisition slips and time tickets for the month of May reveals the following.

Job by Customer	Materials Requisition Slips	Time Tickets
Scott	$ 500	$ 400
Condon	600	1,000
Keefe	2,300	1,300
Tarr	1,900	2,900
	5,300	5,600
General use	1,500	2,000
	$6,800	$7,600

Overhead was charged to jobs on the basis of $0.70 per dollar of direct labor cost.

The jacuzzis for customers Scott, Condon, and Keefe were completed during May. Each jacuzzi was sold for $12,000 cash.

Instructions

(a) Prepare journal entries for the May transactions: (i) for purchase of raw materials, factory labor costs incurred, and manufacturing overhead costs incurred; (ii) assignment of raw materials, labor, and overhead to production; and (iii) completion of jobs and sale of goods.

(b) Post the entries to Work in Process Inventory.

(c) Reconcile the balance in Work in Process Inventory with the costs of unfinished jobs.

(d) Prepare a cost of goods manufactured schedule for May.

(d) Cost of goods manufactured $20,190.

P20-4B Lyon Manufacturing uses a job order cost system in each of its three manufacturing departments. Manufacturing overhead is applied to jobs on the basis of direct labor cost in Department F, direct labor hours in Department G, and machine hours in Department H.

In establishing the predetermined overhead rates for 2012, the following estimates were made for the year.

Compute predetermined overhead rates, apply overhead, and calculate under- or overapplied overhead.

(SO 4, 6)

	Department		
	F	G	H
Manufacturing overhead	$780,000	$640,000	$750,000
Direct labor cost	$600,000	$100,000	$600,000
Direct labor hours	50,000	40,000	40,000
Machine hours	100,000	120,000	150,000

During January, the job cost sheets showed the following costs and production data.

| | Department | | |
	F	G	H
Direct materials used	$92,000	$86,000	$64,000
Direct labor cost	$48,000	$35,000	$50,400
Manufacturing overhead incurred	$66,000	$60,000	$62,100
Direct labor hours	4,000	3,500	4,200
Machine hours	8,000	10,500	12,600

(a) 130%, $16, $5
(b) $202,400, $177,000,
$177,400
(c) $3,600, $4,000, $(900)

Instructions
(a) Compute the predetermined overhead rate for each department.
(b) Compute the total manufacturing costs assigned to jobs in January in each department.
(c) Compute the under- or overapplied overhead for each department at January 31.

*Analyze manufacturing
accounts and determine
missing amounts.*
(SO 2, 3, 4, 5, 6)

P20-5B Angel Company's fiscal year ends on June 30. The following accounts are found in its job order cost accounting system for the first month of the new fiscal year.

Raw Materials Inventory

July	1	Beginning balance	19,000	July 31	Requisitions	(a)
	31	Purchases	90,400			
July	31	Ending balance	(b)			

Work in Process Inventory

July	1	Beginning balance	(c)	July 31	Jobs completed	(f)
	31	Direct materials	75,000			
	31	Direct labor	(d)			
	31	Overhead	(e)			
July	31	Ending balance	(g)			

Finished Goods Inventory

July	1	Beginning balance	(h)	July 31	Cost of goods sold	(j)
	31	Completed jobs	(i)			
July	31	Ending balance	(k)			

Factory Labor

July	31	Factory wages	(l)	July 31	Wages assigned	(m)

Manufacturing Overhead

July	31	Indirect materials	8,900	July 31	Overhead applied	114,000
	31	Indirect labor	16,000			
	31	Other overhead	(n)			

Other data:
1. On July 1, two jobs were in process: Job No. 4085 and Job No. 4086, with costs of $19,000 and $13,200, respectively.
2. During July, Job Nos. 4087, 4088, and 4089 were started. On July 31, only Job No. 4089 was unfinished. This job had charges for direct materials $2,000 and direct labor $1,500, plus manufacturing overhead. Manufacturing overhead was applied at the rate of 120% of direct labor cost.
3. On July 1, Job No. 4084, costing $145,000, was in the finished goods warehouse. On July 31, Job No. 4088, costing $138,000, was in finished goods.
4. Overhead was $3,000 underapplied in July.

(d) $ 95,000
(f) $310,900
(l) $111,000

Instructions
List the letters (a) through (n) and indicate the amount pertaining to each letter. Show computations.

Problems: Set C

Visit the book's companion website, at **www.wiley.com/college/weygandt**, and choose the Student Companion site to access Problem Set C.

Waterways Continuing Problem

(*Note:* This is a continuation of the Waterways Problem from Chapter 19.)

WCP20 Waterways has two major public-park projects to provide with comprehensive irrigation in one of its service locations this month. Job J57 and Job K52 involve 15 acres of landscaped terrain which will require special-order sprinkler heads to meet the specifications of the project. This problem asks you to help Waterways use a job cost system to account for production of these parts.

Go to the book's companion website, **www.wiley.com/college/weygandt**, *to see the completion of this problem.*

BROADENINGYOURPERSPECTIVE

Decision Making Across the Organization

BYP20-1 Burgio Parts Company uses a job order cost system. For a number of months, there has been an ongoing rift between the sales department and the production department concerning a special-order product, TC-1. TC-1 is a seasonal product that is manufactured in batches of 1,000 units. TC-1 is sold at cost plus a markup of 40% of cost.

The sales department is unhappy because fluctuating unit production costs significantly affect selling prices. Sales personnel complain that this has caused excessive customer complaints and the loss of considerable orders for TC-1.

The production department maintains that each job order must be fully costed on the basis of the costs incurred during the period in which the goods are produced. Production personnel maintain that the only real solution to the problem is for the sales department to increase sales in the slack periods.

Alona Macarty, president of the company, asks you as the company accountant to collect quarterly data for the past year on TC-1. From the cost accounting system, you accumulate the following production quantity and cost data.

Costs	Quarter			
	1	2	3	4
Direct materials	$100,000	$220,000	$ 80,000	$200,000
Direct labor	60,000	132,000	48,000	120,000
Manufacturing overhead	105,000	123,000	97,000	125,000
Total	$265,000	$475,000	$225,000	$445,000
Production in batches	5	11	4	10
Unit cost (per batch)	$ 53,000	$ 43,182	$ 56,250	$ 44,500

Instructions

With the class divided into groups, answer the following questions.

(a) What manufacturing cost element is responsible for the fluctuating unit costs? Why?

(b) What is your recommended solution to the problem of fluctuating unit cost?

(c) Restate the quarterly data on the basis of your recommended solution.

Managerial Analysis

BYP20-2 In the course of routine checking of all journal entries prior to preparing year-end reports, Maria Ferreira discovered several strange entries. She recalled that the president's son Tom had come in to help out during an especially busy time and that he had recorded some journal entries. She was relieved that there were only a few of his entries, and even more relieved that he had included rather lengthy explanations. The entries Tom made were:

(1)

Work in Process Inventory	25,000	
Cash		25,000

(This is for materials put into process. I didn't find the record that we paid for these, so I'm crediting Cash, because I know we'll have to pay for them sooner or later.)

(2)

Manufacturing Overhead	12,000	
Cash		12,000

(This is for bonuses paid to salespeople. I know they're part of overhead, and I can't find an account called "Non-factory Overhead" or "Other Overhead" so I'm putting it in Manufacturing Overhead. I have the check stubs, so I know we paid these.)

(3)

Wages Expense	120,000	
Cash		120,000

(This is for the factory workers' wages. I have a note that payroll taxes are $15,000. I still think that's part of wages expense, and that we'll have to pay it all in cash sooner or later, so I credited Cash for the wages and the taxes.)

(4)

Work in Process Inventory	3,000	
Raw Materials Inventory		3,000

(This is for the glue used in the factory. I know we used this to make the products, even though we didn't use very much on any one of the products. I got it out of inventory, so I credited an inventory account.)

Instructions

(a) How should Tom have recorded each of the four events?

(b) If the entry was not corrected, which financial statements (income statement or balance sheet) would be affected? What balances would be overstated or understated?

Real-World Focus

BYP20-3 Founded in 1970, Parlex Corporation is a world leader in the design and manufacture of flexible interconnect products. Utilizing proprietary and patented technologies, Parlex produces custom flexible interconnects including flexible circuits, polymer thick film, laminated cables, and value-added assemblies for sophisticated electronics used in automotive, telecommunications, computer, diversified electronics, and aerospace applications. In addition to manufacturing sites in Methuen, Massachusetts; Salem, New Hampshire; Cranston, Rhode Island; San Jose, California; Shanghai, China; Isle of Wight, UK; and Empalme, Mexico, Parlex has logistic support centers and strategic alliances throughout North America, Asia, and Europe.

The following information was provided in the company's annual report.

Parlex Company
Notes to the Financial Statements

The Company's products are manufactured on a job order basis to customers' specifications. Customers submit requests for quotations on each job, and the Company prepares bids based on its own cost estimates. The Company attempts to reflect the impact of changing costs when establishing prices. However, during the past several years, the market conditions for flexible circuits and the resulting price sensitivity haven't always allowed this to transpire. Although still not satisfactory, the Company was able to reduce the cost of products sold as a percentage of sales to 85% this year versus 87% that was experienced in the two immediately preceding years. Management continues to focus on improving operational efficiency and further reducing costs.

Instructions
(a) Parlex management discusses the job order cost system employed by their company. What are several advantages of using the job order approach to costing?
(b) Contrast the products produced in a job order environment, like Parlex, to those produced when process cost systems are used.

On the Web

BYP20-4 The Institute of Management Accountants sponsors a certification for management accountants, allowing them to obtain the title of Certified Management Accountant.

Address: www.imanet.org, or go to **www.wiley.com/college/weygandt**

Steps
1. Go to the site shown above.
2. Choose **Certification**, and then, **Getting Started**.

Instructions
(a) What is the experience qualification requirement?
(b) How many hours of continuing education are required, and what types of activities qualify?

Communication Activity

BYP20-5 You are the management accountant for Knowles Manufacturing. Your company does custom carpentry work and uses a job order cost accounting system. Knowles sends detailed job cost sheets to its customers, along with an invoice. The job cost sheets show the date materials were used, the dollar cost of materials, and the hours and cost of labor. A predetermined overhead application rate is used, and the total overhead applied is also listed.

Saira Ortiz is a customer who recently had custom cabinets installed. Along with her check in payment for the work done, she included a letter. She thanked the company for including the detailed cost information but questioned why overhead was estimated. She stated that she would be interested in knowing exactly what costs were included in overhead, and she thought that other customers would, too.

Instructions
Prepare a letter to Ms. Ortiz (address: 456 Maple Avenue, Boise, Idaho 83702) and tell her why you did not send her information on exact costs of overhead included in her job. Respond to her suggestion that you provide this information.

Ethics Case

BYP20-6 TKE Catering provides catering services to many different corporate clients. Although TKE bids most jobs, some jobs, particularly new ones, are negotiated on a "cost-plus" basis. Cost-plus means that the buyer is willing to pay the actual cost plus a return (profit) on these costs to TKE.

Anna Tsing, controller for TKE, has recently returned from a meeting where TKE's president stated that he wanted her to find a way to charge most costs to any project that was on a cost-plus basis. The president noted that the company needed more profits to meet its stated goals this period. By charging more costs to the cost-plus projects and therefore fewer costs to the jobs that were bid, the company should be able to increase its profit for the current year.

Anna knew why the president wanted to take this action. Rumors were that he was looking for a new position and if the company reported strong profit, the president's opportunities would be enhanced. Anna also recognized that she could probably increase the cost of certain jobs by changing the basis used to allocate manufacturing overhead.

Instructions
(a) Who are the stakeholders in this situation?
(b) What are the ethical issues in this situation?
(c) What would you do if you were Anna Tsing?

"All About You" Activity

BYP20-7   Many of you will work for a small business. As noted in the **All About You** feature (available on the book's companion website), some of you will even own your own business. In order to operate a small business you will need a good understanding of managerial accounting, as well as many other skills. Much information is available to assist people who are interested in starting a new business. A great place to start is the website provided by the Small Business Administration, which is an agency of the federal government whose purpose is to support small business.

Instructions
Go to **www.sba.gov** and in the "Starting Your Business" link, review the material under the "Are You Ready?" Answer the following questions.

(a) What are some of the characteristics required of a small business owner?
(b) What are the top 10 reasons given for business failure?

Answers to Insight and Accounting Across the Organization Questions
p. 926 Jobs Won, Money Lost   Q: What type of costs do you think the company had been underestimating? **A:** It is most likely that the company failed to estimate and track overhead. In a highly diversified company, overhead associated with the diesel locomotive jobs may have been "lost" in the total overhead pool for the entire company.
p. 938 Sales Are Nice, but Service Revenue Pays the Bills   Q: Explain why GE would use job order costing to keep track of the cost of repairing a malfunctioning engine for a major airline. **A:** GE operates in a competitive environment. Other companies offer competing bids to win service contracts on GE airplane engines. GE needs to know what it costs to repair engines, so that it can present competitive bids while still generating a reasonable profit.
p. 942 Working a 25-Hour Day   Q: What feature of these businesses creates an incentive to misstate cost accounting data on particular jobs? What can customers do to protect themselves from overbilling? **A:** In these business situations, the compensation to the supplier depends on the costs incurred by the supplier. This so-called "cost-plus" arrangement creates an incentive for the supplier to overstate costs. Customers should stipulate that they have the right to have the suppliers' records audited.

Answers to Self-Test Questions
1. a **2.** c **3.** b **4.** c **5.** c **6.** d **7.** d **8.** b **9.** a **10.** d **11.** b (80% × $180,000) **12.** c **13.** b **14.** c **15.** b

✔
The Navigator

✔ **Remember to go back to the Navigator box on the chapter opening page and check off your completed work.**

CHAPTER21

Process Costing

Study Objectives

After studying this chapter, you should be able to:

[1] Understand who uses process cost systems.

[2] Explain the similarities and differences between job order cost and process cost systems.

[3] Explain the flow of costs in a process cost system.

[4] Make the journal entries to assign manufacturing costs in a process cost system.

[5] Compute equivalent units.

[6] Explain the four steps necessary to prepare a production cost report.

[7] Prepare a production cost report.

[8] Explain just-in-time (JIT) processing.

[9] Explain activity-based costing (ABC).

✔ The Navigator

✔ The Navigator

- Scan Study Objectives ○
- Read Feature Story ○
- Read Preview ○
- Read text and answer **Do it!** p. 969 ○ p. 972 ○ p. 975 ○ p. 981 ○ p. 985 ○
- Work Comprehensive **Do it!** p. 985 ○
- Review Summary of Study Objectives ○
- Answer Self-Test Questions ○
- Complete Assignments ○
- Go to *WileyPLUS* for practice and tutorials ○

Feature Story

BEN & JERRY'S TRACKS ITS MIX-UPS

Ben & Jerry's Homemade, Inc. is one of the "hottest" and "coolest" U.S. companies. Based in Waterbury, Vermont, the ice cream company that started out of a garage in 1978 is now a public company.

Making ice cream is a process—a movement of product from a mixing department to a prepping department to a pint department. The mixing department is where the ice cream is created. In the prep area the production process adds extras such as cherries and walnuts to make plain ice cream into "Cherry Garcia," Ben & Jerry's most popular flavor, or fudge-covered waffle cone pieces and a swirl of caramel for "Stephen Colbert's Americone Dream," one of B & J's newest flavors. The pint department is where the ice cream is actually put into containers. As the product is processed from one department to the next, the appropriate materials, labor, and overhead are added to it.

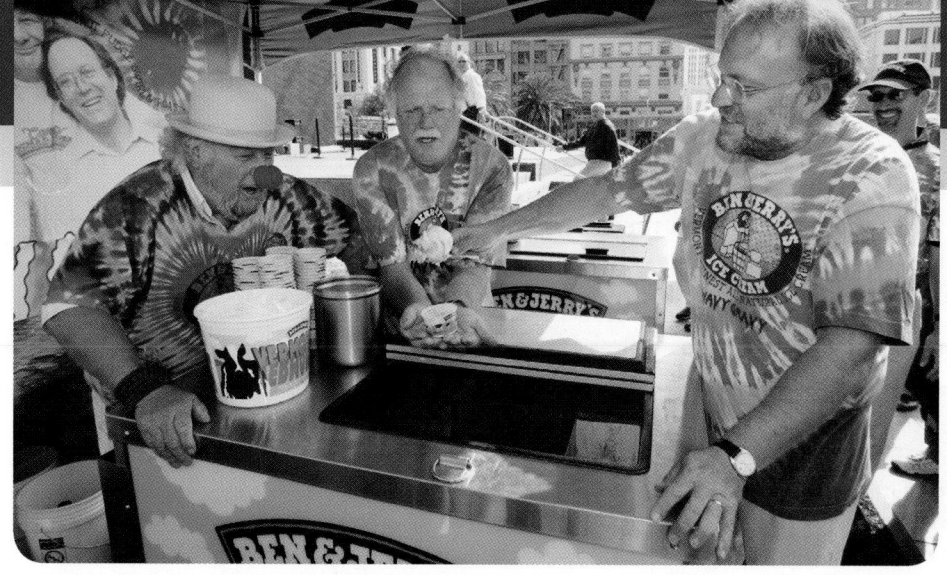

"The incoming ingredients from the shipping and receiving departments are stored in certain locations, either in a freezer or dry warehouse," says Beecher Eurich, staff accountant.

"As ingredients get added, so do the costs associated with them." How much ice cream is produced? Running plants around the clock, the company produces 18 million gallons a year.

With the company's process costing system, Eurich can tell you how much a certain batch of ice cream costs to make—its materials, labor, and overhead in each of the production departments. She generates reports for the production department heads, but makes sure not to overdo it. "You can get bogged down in numbers," says Eurich. "If you're generating a report that no one can use, then that's a waste of time."

It's more likely, though, Ben & Jerry's production people want to know how efficient they are. Why? Many own stock in the company.

Inside**CHAPTER21**

The cost accounting system used by companies such as Ben & Jerry's is **process cost accounting**. In contrast to job order cost accounting, which focuses on the individual job, process cost accounting focuses on the *processes* involved in mass-producing products that are identical or very similar in nature. The primary objective of the chapter is to explain and illustrate process costing.

The content and organization of this chapter are as follows.

Process Costing			
Nature of Process Cost Systems	**Equivalent Units**	**Comprehensive Example of Process Costing**	**Contemporary Developments**
• Uses • Service companies • Similarities and differences • Process cost flow • Assigning manufacturing costs	• Weighted-average method • Refinements • Production cost report	• Physical units • Equivalent units of production • Unit production costs • Cost reconciliation schedule • Production cost report • Costing systems—Final comments	• Just-in-time processing • Activity-based costing

The Navigator ✔

The Nature of Process Cost Systems

Study Objective [1]
Understand who uses process cost systems.

Uses of Process Cost Systems

Companies use **process cost systems** to apply costs to similar products that are mass-produced in a continuous fashion. Ben & Jerry's uses a process cost system: Production of the ice cream, once it begins, continues until the ice cream emerges, and the processing is the same for the entire run—with precisely the same amount of materials, labor, and overhead. Each finished pint of ice cream is indistinguishable from another.

A company such as USX uses process costing in the manufacturing of steel. Kellogg and General Mills use process costing for cereal production; ExxonMobil uses process costing for its oil refining; Sherwin Williams uses process costing for its paint products. At a bottling company like Coca-Cola, the manufacturing process begins with the blending of ingredients. Next, automated machinery moves the bottles into position and fills them. The production process then caps, packages, and forwards the bottles to the finished goods warehouse. Illustration 21-1 shows this process.

Illustration 21-1
Manufacturing processes

Manufacturing Processes → Blending → Filling → Packaging (COLA)

For Coca-Cola, as well as the other companies just mentioned, once the production begins, it continues until the finished product emerges, and each unit of finished product is like every other unit.

In comparison, in a job order cost system companies assign costs to a *specific job*. Examples are the construction of a customized home, the making of a motion picture, or the manufacturing of a specialized machine. Illustration 21-2 provides examples of companies that primarily use either a process cost system or a job order cost system.

Illustration 21-2
Process cost and job order cost companies and products

Process Cost System Company	Product		Job Order Cost System Company	Product	
Coca-Cola, PepsiCo	Soft drinks		Young & Rubicam, Omnicom	Advertising	
ExxonMobil, Royal Dutch Shell	Oil		Walt Disney, Warner Brothers	Motion pictures	
Intel, Advanced Micro Devices	Computer chips		Center Ice Consultants, Ice Rink Events	Ice rinks	
Dow Chemical, DuPont	Chemicals		Kaiser Permanente, Mayo Clinic	Patient health care	

Process Costing for Service Companies

Frequently, when we think of service companies, we think of specific, nonroutine tasks, such as rebuilding an automobile engine, providing consulting services on a business acquisition, or working on a major lawsuit. However, many service companies specialize in performing repetitive, routine aspects of a particular business. For example, auto-care vendors such as Jiffy Lube focus on the routine aspects of car care. H&R Block focuses on the routine aspects of basic tax practice, and many large law firms focus on routine legal services, such as uncomplicated divorces. Service companies that provide specific, nonroutine services will probably benefit from using a job order cost system. Those that perform routine, repetitive services will probably be better off with a process cost system.

Similarities and Differences Between Job Order Cost and Process Cost Systems

In a job order cost system, companies assign costs to each job. In a process cost system, companies track costs through a series of connected manufacturing processes or departments, rather than by individual jobs. Thus, companies use process cost systems when they produce a large volume of uniform or relatively homogeneous products. Illustration 21-3 (page 968) shows the basic flow of costs in these two systems.

Study Objective [2]

Explain the similarities and differences between job order cost and process cost systems.

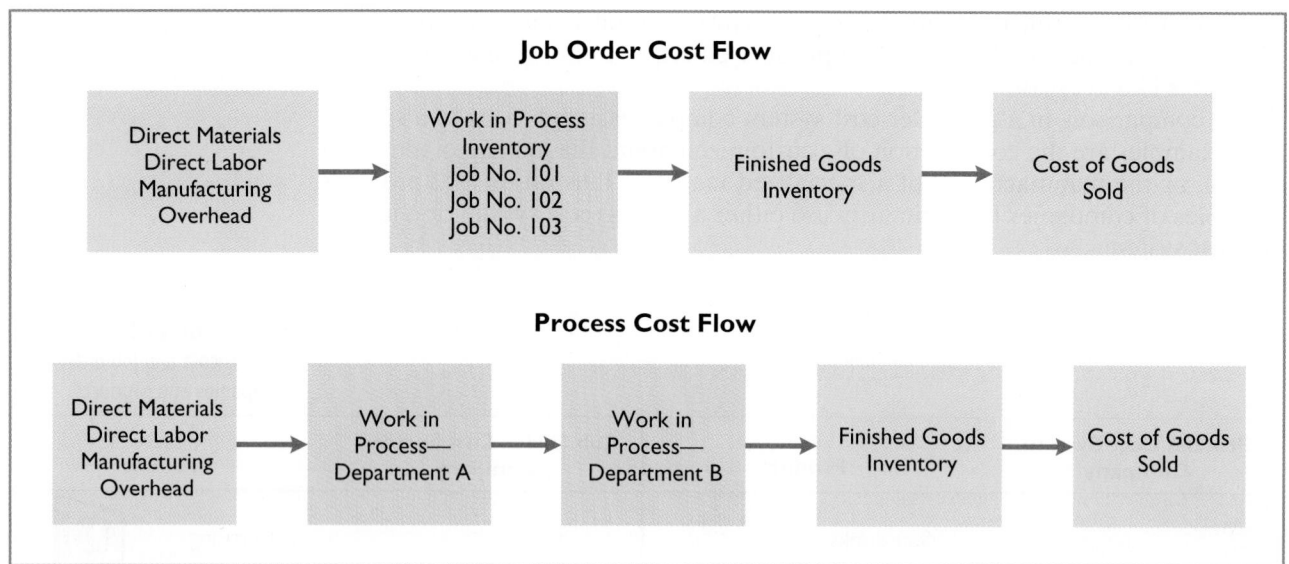

Illustration 21-3
Job order cost and process cost flow

SIMILARITIES

Job order cost and process cost systems are similar in three ways:

1. **The manufacturing cost elements.** Both costing systems track three manufacturing cost elements—direct materials, direct labor, and manufacturing overhead.

2. **The accumulation of the costs of materials, labor, and overhead.** Both costing systems debit raw materials to Raw Materials Inventory; factory labor to Factory Labor; and manufacturing overhead costs to Manufacturing Overhead.

3. **The flow of costs.** As noted above, both systems accumulate all manufacturing costs by debits to Raw Materials Inventory, Factory Labor, and Manufacturing Overhead. Both systems then assign these costs to the same accounts—Work in Process, Finished Goods Inventory, and Cost of Goods Sold. **The methods of assigning costs, however, differ significantly.** These differences are explained and illustrated later in the chapter.

DIFFERENCES

The differences between a job order cost and a process cost system are as follows.

1. **The number of work in process accounts used.** A job order cost system uses only one Work in Process account. A process cost system uses multiple work in process accounts.

2. **Documents used to track costs.** A job order cost system charges costs to individual jobs and summarizes them in a job cost sheet. A process cost system summarizes costs in a production cost report for each department.

3. **The point at which costs are totaled.** A job order cost system totals costs when the job is completed. A process cost system totals costs at the end of a period of time.

4. **Unit cost computations.** In a job order cost system, the unit cost is the total cost per job divided by the units produced. In a process cost system, the unit cost is total manufacturing costs for the period divided by the units produced during the period.

Illustration 21-4 summarizes the major differences between a job order cost and a process cost system.

Illustration 21-4
Job order versus process
cost systems

Features	Job Order Cost System	Process Cost System
Work in process accounts	• One work in process account	• Multiple work in process accounts
Documents used	• Job cost sheets	• Production cost reports
Determination of total manufacturing costs	• Each job	• Each period
Unit-cost computations	• Cost of each job ÷ Units produced for the job	• Total manufacturing costs ÷ Units produced during the period

Do it!

Indicate whether each of the following statements is true or false.

1. A law firm is likely to use process costing for major lawsuits.
2. A manufacturer of paintballs is likely to use process costing.
3. Both job order and process costing determine total costs at the end of a period of time.
4. Process costing does not keep track of manufacturing overhead.

Solution

1. false.	2. true.	3. false.	4. false.

Related exercise material: E21-1 and **Do it!** 21-1.

**Compare Job
Order and Process
Cost Systems**

action plan

✔ Use job order costing in situations where unit costs are high, unit volume is low, and products are unique.

✔ Use process costing when there is a large volume of relatively homogeneous products.

Process Cost Flow

Illustration 21-5 shows the flow of costs in the process cost system for Tyler Company. Tyler Company manufactures automatic can openers that it sells to retail outlets. Manufacturing consists of two processes: machining and assembly. The Machining Department shapes, hones, and drills the raw materials. The Assembly Department assembles and packages the parts.

Study Objective [3]
Explain the flow of costs in a process cost system.

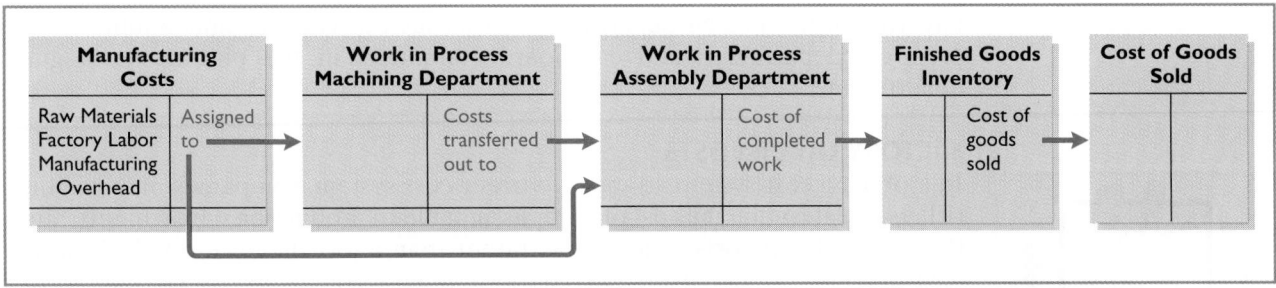

Illustration 21-5
Flow of costs in process cost system

As the flow of costs indicates, the company can add materials, labor, and manufacturing overhead in both the Machining and Assembly departments. When it finishes its work, the Machining Department transfers the partially completed units to the Assembly Department. The Assembly Department finishes the goods and then transfers them to the finished goods inventory. Upon sale, Tyler removes the goods from the finished goods inventory. Within each department, a similar set of activities is performed on each unit processed.

Assigning Manufacturing Costs—Journal Entries

Study Objective [4]
Make the journal entries to assign manufacturing costs in a process cost system.

As indicated, the accumulation of the costs of materials, labor, and manufacturing overhead is the same in a process cost system as in a job order cost system. That is, both systems follow these procedures:

- Companies debit all raw materials to Raw Materials Inventory at the time of purchase.
- They debit all factory labor to Factory Labor as the labor costs are incurred.
- They debit overhead costs to Manufacturing Overhead as these costs are incurred.

However, the assignment of the three manufacturing cost elements to Work in Process in a process cost system is different from a job order cost system. Here we'll look at how companies assign these manufacturing cost elements in a process cost system.

MATERIALS COSTS

All raw materials issued for production are a materials cost to the producing department. A process cost system may use materials requisition slips, but **it generally requires fewer requisitions than in a job order cost system, because the materials are used for processes rather than for specific jobs** and therefore typically are for larger quantities.

At the beginning of the first process, a company usually adds most of the materials needed for production. However, other materials may be added at various points. For example, in the manufacture of Hershey candy bars, the chocolate and other ingredients are added at the beginning of the first process, and the wrappers and cartons are added at the end of the packaging process. Tyler Company adds materials at the beginning of each process. Tyler makes the following entry to record the materials used:

Work in Process—Machining	XXXX	
Work in Process—Assembly	XXXX	
Raw Materials Inventory		XXXX
(To record materials used)		

Ice cream maker Ben & Jerry's adds materials in three departments: milk and flavoring in the mixing department; extras such as cherries and walnuts in the prepping department; and cardboard containers in the pinting (packaging) department.

FACTORY LABOR COSTS

In a process cost system, as in a job order cost system, companies may use time tickets to determine the cost of labor assignable to production departments. Since they assign labor costs to a process rather than a job, they can obtain from the payroll register or departmental payroll summaries the labor cost chargeable to a process.

Labor costs for the Machining Department will include the wages of employees who shape, hone, and drill the raw materials. The entry to assign these costs for Tyler Company is:

Factory Labor

Work in Process—Machining	XXXX	
Work in Process—Assembly	XXXX	
Factory Labor		XXXX
(To assign factory labor to production)		

MANUFACTURING OVERHEAD COSTS

The objective in assigning overhead in a process cost system is to allocate the overhead costs to the production departments on an objective and equitable basis. That basis is the activity that "drives" or causes the costs. A primary driver of overhead costs in continuous manufacturing operations is **machine time used**, not direct labor. Thus, companies **widely use machine hours** in allocating manufacturing overhead costs. Tyler's entry to allocate overhead to the two processes is:

Manufacturing Overhead

Work in Process—Machining	XXXX	
Work in Process—Assembly	XXXX	
Manufacturing Overhead		XXXX
(To assign overhead to production)		

MANAGEMENT INSIGHT

Choosing a Cost Driver

In one of its automated cost centers, Caterpillar feeds work into the cost center, where robotic machines process it and transfer the finished job to the next cost center without human intervention. One person tends all of the machines and spends more time maintaining machines than operating them. In such cases, overhead rates based on direct labor hours may be misleading. Some companies continue to assign manufacturing overhead on the basis of direct labor despite the fact that there is no cause-and-effect relationship between labor and overhead.

 What is the result if a company uses the wrong "cost driver" to assign manufacturing overhead? (See page 1009.)

TRANSFER TO NEXT DEPARTMENT

At the end of the month, Tyler needs an entry to record the cost of the goods transferred out of the department. In this case, the transfer is to the Assembly Department, and Tyler makes the following entry.

Work in Process—Assembly	XXXXX	
Work in Process—Machining		XXXXX
(To record transfer of units to the		
Assembly Department)		

TRANSFER TO FINISHED GOODS

When the Assembly Department completes the units, it transfers them to the finished goods warehouse. The entry for this transfer is as follows.

Finished Goods Inventory	XXXXX	
Work in Process—Assembly		XXXXX
(To record transfer of units to finished goods)		

TRANSFER TO COST OF GOODS SOLD

When Tyler sells the finished goods, it records the cost of goods sold as follows.

Cost of Goods Sold	XXXXX	
Finished Goods Inventory		XXXXX
(To record cost of units sold)		

Do it!

Manufacturing Costs in Process Costing

action plan

✔ In process cost accounting, keep separate work in process accounts for each process.

✔ When the costs are assigned to production, debit the separate work in process accounts.

✔ Transfer cost of completed units to the next process or to Finished Goods.

Ruth Company manufactures ZEBO through two processes: blending and bottling. In June, raw materials used were Blending $18,000 and Bottling $4,000. Factory labor costs were Blending $12,000 and Bottling $5,000. Manufacturing overhead costs were Blending $6,000 and Bottling $2,500. The company transfers units completed at a cost of $19,000 in the Blending Department to the Bottling Department. The Bottling Department transfers units completed at a cost of $11,000 to Finished Goods. Journalize the assignment of these costs to the two processes and the transfer of units as appropriate.

Solution

The entries are:

Work in Process—Blending	18,000	
Work in Process—Bottling	4,000	
Raw Materials Inventory		22,000
(To record materials used)		
Work in Process—Blending	12,000	
Work in Process—Bottling	5,000	
Factory Labor		17,000
(To assign factory labor to production)		
Work in Process—Blending	6,000	
Work in Process—Bottling	2,500	
Manufacturing Overhead		8,500
(To assign overhead to production)		
Work in Process—Bottling	19,000	
Work in Process—Blending		19,000
(To record transfer of units to the Bottling Department)		
Finished Goods Inventory	11,000	
Work in Process—Bottling		11,000
(To record transfer of units to finished goods)		

Related exercise material: BE21-1, BE21-2, BE21-3, E21-2, E21-4, and **Do it!** 21-1.

✔ **The Navigator**

Equivalent Units

Study Objective [5]
Compute equivalent units.

Suppose you have a work-study job in the office of your college's president, and she asks you to compute the cost of instruction per full-time equivalent student at your college. The college's vice president for finance provides the following information.

Costs:

Total cost of instruction	$9,000,000
Student population:	
Full-time students	900
Part-time students	1,000

Illustration 21-6
Information for full-time
student example

Part-time students take 60% of the classes of a full-time student during the year. To compute the number of full-time equivalent students per year, you would make the following computation.

Full-time Students	+	Equivalent Units of Part-time Students	=	Full-time Equivalent Students
900	+	(60% × 1,000)	=	1,500

Illustration 21-7
Full-time equivalent unit
computation

The cost of instruction per full-time equivalent student is therefore the total cost of instruction ($9,000,000) divided by the number of full-time equivalent students (1,500), which is $6,000 ($9,000,000 ÷ 1,500).

A process cost system uses the same idea, called equivalent units of production. **Equivalent units of production** measure the work done during the period, expressed in fully completed units. Companies use this measure to determine the cost per unit of completed product.

Weighted-Average Method

The formula to compute equivalent units of production is as follows.

Units Completed and Transferred Out	+	Equivalent Units of Ending Work in Process	=	Equivalent Units of Production

Illustration 21-8
Equivalent units of production
formula

To better understand this concept of equivalent units, consider the following two separate examples.

Example 1: In a specific period the entire output of Sullivan Company's Blending Department consists of ending work in process of 4,000 units which are 60% complete as to materials, labor, and overhead. The equivalent units of production for the Blending Department are therefore 2,400 units (4,000 × 60%).

Example 2: The output of Kori Company's Packaging Department during the period consists of 10,000 units completed and transferred out, and 5,000 units in ending work in process which are 70% completed. The equivalent units of production are therefore 13,500 [10,000 + (5,000 × 70%)].

This method of computing equivalent units is referred to as the **weighted-average method**. It considers the degree of completion (weighting) of the units completed and transferred out and the ending work in process. *Use the weighted-average method to compute equivalent units in the homework.*

Refinements on the Weighted-Average Method

Kellogg Company has produced Eggo® Waffles since 1970. Three departments produce these waffles: Mixing, Baking, and Freezing/Packaging. The Mixing Department combines dry ingredients, including flour, salt, and baking powder, with liquid ingredients, including eggs and vegetable oil, to make waffle batter. Illustration 21-9 provides information related to the Mixing Department at the end of June.

Illustration 21-9
Information for Mixing Department

Mixing Department			
		Percentage Complete	
	Physical Units	**Materials**	**Conversion Costs**
Work in process, June 1	100,000	100%	70%
Started into production	800,000		
Total units	900,000		
Units transferred out	700,000		
Work in process, June 30	200,000	100%	60%
Total units	900,000		

Illustration 21-9 indicates that the beginning work in process is 100% complete as to materials cost and 70% complete as to conversion costs. **Conversion costs are the sum of labor costs and overhead costs**. In other words, Kellogg adds both the dry and liquid ingredients (materials) at the beginning of the waffle-making process. The conversion costs (labor and overhead) related to the mixing of these ingredients are incurred uniformly and are 70% complete. The ending work in process is 100% complete as to materials cost and 60% complete as to conversion costs.

We then use the Mixing Department information to determine equivalent units. **In computing equivalent units, the beginning work in process is not part of the equivalent-units-of-production formula.** The units transferred out to the Baking Department are fully complete as to both materials and conversion costs. The ending work in process is fully complete as to materials, but only 60% complete as to conversion costs. We therefore need to make **two equivalent unit computations**: one for materials, and the other for conversion costs. Illustration 21-10 shows these computations.

Illustration 21-10
Computation of equivalent units—Mixing Department

Mixing Department		
	Equivalent Units	
	Materials	**Conversion Costs**
Units transferred out	700,000	700,000
Work in process, June 30		
200,000 × 100%	200,000	
200,000 × 60%		120,000
Total equivalent units	900,000	820,000

We can refine the earlier formula used to compute equivalent units of production (Illustration 21-8) (page 973) to show the computations for materials and for conversion costs, as follows.

Units Completed and Transferred Out— Materials	+	Equivalent Units of Ending Work in Process—Materials	=	Equivalent Units of Production— Materials
Units Completed and Transferred Out— Conversion Costs	+	Equivalent Units of Ending Work in Process—Conversion Costs	=	Equivalent Units of Production— Conversion Costs

Illustration 21-11
Refined equivalent units of production formula

Do it!

The fabricating department has the following production and cost data for the current month.

Beginning Work in Process	Units Transferred Out	Ending Work in Process
–0–	15,000	10,000

Materials are entered at the beginning of the process. The ending work in process units are 30% complete as to conversion costs. Compute the equivalent units of production for (a) materials and (b) conversion costs.

Equivalent Units

Solution

(a) Since materials are entered at the beginning of the process, the equivalent units of ending work in process are 10,000. Thus, 15,000 units + 10,000 units = 25,000 equivalent units of production for materials.

(b) Since ending work in process is only 30% complete as to conversion costs, the equivalent units of ending work in process are 3,000 (30% × 10,000 units). Thus, 15,000 units + 3,000 units = 18,000 equivalent units of production for conversion costs.

Related exercise material: BE21-5, BE21-10, E21-5, E21-6, E21-7, E21-8, E21-9, E21-10, E21-11, E21-13, and **Do it!** 21-2.

action plan

✔ To measure the work done during the period, expressed in fully completed units, compute equivalent units of production.

✔ Use the appropriate formula: Units completed and transferred out + Equivalent units of ending work in process = Equivalent units of production.

✔
The Navigator

Production Cost Report

As mentioned earlier, companies prepare a production cost report for each department. A **production cost report** is the key document that management uses to understand the activities in a department; it shows the production quantity and cost data related to that department. For example, in producing Eggo® Waffles, Kellogg Company uses three production cost reports: Mixing, Baking, and Freezing/Packaging. Illustration 21-12 (page 976) shows the flow of costs to make an Eggo® Waffle and the related production cost reports for each department.

In order to complete a production cost report, the company must perform four steps, which as a whole, make up the process costing system.

1. Compute the physical unit flow.
2. Compute the equivalent units of production.

Study Objective [6]
Explain the four steps necessary to prepare a production cost report.

Illustration 21-12
Flow of costs in making Eggo®
Waffles

3. Compute unit production costs.
4. Prepare a cost reconciliation schedule.

The next section explores these steps in an extended example.

MANAGEMENT INSIGHT

Keeping Score for the Xbox

When you are as big and as profitable as Microsoft, you get to a point where continued rapid growth is very difficult. For example, many believe it is unlikely that Microsoft will see much growth in software sales. As a result, the company is looking for new markets, such as the video game market with its Xbox player.

Profitability in the video-game hardware market has been elusive. Microsoft has struggled to control the costs of both manufacturing and distribution. One analyst predicted that Microsoft's "snowballing" costs in the next period could exceed budget by $2.4 billion. Microsoft's Chief Financial Officer blamed the high costs on unexpectedly high volumes, saying, "We pushed market volumes very high in the Xbox business. As a result of that we incurred some costs in the supply chain." Given these issues and, despite its incredible success as a software company, some observers question whether Microsoft will be able to make the changes that are required to become a successful hardware manufacturer.

Source: Robert A. Guth, "Microsoft Net Rises 16%, but Costs Damp Results," *Wall Street Journal Online* (April 28, 2006).

 In what ways has cost accounting probably become more critical for Microsoft in recent years? (See page 1009.)

Comprehensive Example of Process Costing

Illustration 21-13 shows assumed data for the Mixing Department at Kellogg Company for the month of June. We will use this information to complete a production cost report for the Mixing Department.

Illustration 21-13
Unit and cost data—Mixing Department

Mixing Department	
Units	
Work in process, June 1	100,000
Direct materials: 100% complete	
Conversion costs: 70% complete	
Units started into production during June	800,000
Units completed and transferred out to Baking Department	700,000
Work in process, June 30	200,000
Direct materials: 100% complete	
Conversion costs: 60% complete	
Costs	
Work in process, June 1	
Direct materials: 100% complete	$ 50,000
Conversion costs: 70% complete	35,000
Cost of work in process, June 1	$ 85,000
Costs incurred during production in June	
Direct materials	$400,000
Conversion costs	170,000
Costs incurred in June	$570,000

Compute the Physical Unit Flow (Step 1)

Physical units are the actual units to be accounted for during a period, irrespective of any work performed. To keep track of these units, add the units started (or transferred) into production during the period to the units in process at the beginning of the period. This amount is referred to as the total units to be accounted for.

The total units then are accounted for by the output of the period. The output consists of units transferred out during the period and any units in process at the end of the period. This amount is referred to as the total units accounted for. Illustration 21-14 shows the flow of physical units for Kellogg's Mixing Department for the month of June.

Illustration 21-14
Physical unit flow—Mixing Department

Mixing Department	Physical Units
Units to be accounted for	
Work in process, June 1	100,000
Started (transferred) into production	800,000
Total units	900,000
Units accounted for	
Completed and transferred out	700,000
Work in process, June 30	200,000
Total units	900,000

The records indicate that the Mixing Department must account for 900,000 units. Of this sum, 700,000 units were transferred to the Baking Department and 200,000 units were still in process.

Compute Equivalent Units of Production (Step 2)

Helpful Hint

Materials are not always added at the beginning of the process. For example, materials are sometimes added uniformly during the process and at the end of the process.

Once the physical flow of the units is established, Kellogg must measure the Mixing Department's productivity in terms of equivalent units of production. The Mixing Department adds materials at the beginning of the process, and incurs conversion costs uniformly during the process. Thus, we need two computations of equivalent units: one for materials and one for conversion costs. The equivalent unit computation is as follows.

Illustration 21-15
Computation of equivalent units—Mixing Department

Helpful Hint

Remember that we ignore the beginning work in process in this computation.

	Equivalent Units	
	Materials	**Conversion Costs**
Units transferred out	700,000	700,000
Work in process, June 30		
200,000 × 100%	200,000	
200,000 × 60%		120,000
Total equivalent units	900,000	820,000

Compute Unit Production Costs (Step 3)

Armed with the knowledge of the equivalent units of production, we can now compute the unit production costs. **Unit production costs** are costs expressed in terms of equivalent units of production. When equivalent units of production are different for materials and conversion costs, we compute three unit costs: (1) materials, (2) conversion, and (3) total manufacturing.

The computation of total materials cost related to Eggo® Waffles is as follows.

Illustration 21-16
Total materials cost computation

Work in process, June 1	
Direct materials cost	$ 50,000
Costs added to production during June	
Direct materials cost	400,000
Total materials cost	$450,000

The computation of unit materials cost is as follows.

Illustration 21-17
Unit materials cost computation

Total Materials Cost	÷	**Equivalent Units of Materials**	=	Unit Materials Cost
$450,000	÷	900,000	=	$0.50

Illustration 21-18 shows the computation of total conversion costs.

Illustration 21-18
Total conversion costs computation

Work in process, June 1	
Conversion costs	$ 35,000
Costs added to production during June	
Conversion costs	170,000
Total conversion costs	$205,000

The computation of unit conversion cost is as follows.

Illustration 21-19
Unit conversion cost computation

Total Conversion Costs	÷	Equivalent Units of Conversion Costs	=	Unit Conversion Cost
$205,000	÷	820,000	=	$0.25

Total manufacturing cost per unit is therefore computed as shown in Illustration 21-20.

Illustration 21-20
Total manufacturing cost per unit

Unit Materials Cost	+	Unit Conversion Cost	=	Total Manufacturing Cost per Unit
$0.50	+	$0.25	=	$0.75

Prepare a Cost Reconciliation Schedule (Step 4)

We are now ready to determine the cost of goods transferred out of the Mixing Department to the Baking Department and the costs in ending work in process. Kellogg charged total costs of $655,000 to the Mixing Department in June, calculated as follows.

Illustration 21-21
Costs charged to Mixing Department

Costs to be accounted for	
Work in process, June 1	$ 85,000
Started into production	570,000
Total costs	$655,000

The company then prepares a cost reconciliation schedule to assign these costs to (a) units transferred out to the Baking Department and (b) ending work in process.

Illustration 21-22
Cost reconciliation schedule—Mixing Department

Mixing Department
Cost Reconciliation Schedule

Costs accounted for		
Transferred out (700,000 × $0.75)		$525,000
Work in process, June 30		
Materials (200,000 × $0.50)	$100,000	
Conversion costs (120,000 × $0.25)	30,000	130,000
Total costs		$655,000

Kellogg uses the total manufacturing cost per unit, $0.75, in costing the **units completed** and transferred to the Baking Department. In contrast, the unit cost of materials and the unit cost of conversion are needed in costing **units in process**. The **cost reconciliation schedule** shows that the **total costs accounted for** (Illustration 21-22) equal the **total costs to be accounted for** (see Illustration 21-21).

Preparing the Production Cost Report

Study Objective [7]
Prepare a production cost report.

At this point, Kellogg is ready to prepare the production cost report for the Mixing Department. As indicated earlier, this report is an internal document for management that shows production quantity and cost data for a production department.

There are four steps in preparing a production cost report. They are:

(1) Prepare a physical unit schedule.

(2) Compute equivalent units.

(3) Compute unit costs.

(4) Prepare a cost reconciliation schedule.

Illustration 21-23 shows the production cost report for the Mixing Department. The report identifies the four steps.

Illustration 21-23
Production cost report

Mixing Department.xls

Mixing Department
Production Cost Report
For the Month Ended June 30, 2012

	A	B	C Physical Units	D Materials	E Conversion Costs	F Total
				Equivalent Units		
6	**QUANTITIES**		Step 1	Step 2		
7	Units to be accounted for					
8	Work in process, June 1		100,000			
9	Started into production		800,000			
10	Total units		900,000			
11	Units accounted for					
12	Transferred out		700,000	700,000	700,000	
13	Work in process, June 30		200,000	200,000	120,000 (200,000 × 60%)	
14	Total units		900,000	900,000	820,000	
15	**COSTS** Unit costs		Step 3	Materials	Conversion Costs	Total
16	Costs in June	(a)		$450,000	$205,000	$655,000
17	Equivalent units	(b)		900,000	820,000	
18	Unit costs [(a) ÷ (b)]			$0.50	$0.25	$0.75
19	Costs to be accounted for					
20	Work in process, June 1					$85,000
21	Started into production					570,000
22	Total costs					$655,000
23	**Cost Reconciliation Schedule**		Step 4			
24	Costs accounted for					
25	Transferred out (700,000 × $0.75)					$525,000
26	Work in process, June 30					
27	Materials (200,000 × $0.50)				$100,000	
28	Conversion costs (120,000 × $0.25)				30,000	130,000
29	Total costs					$655,000

Production cost reports provide a basis for evaluating the productivity of a department. In addition, managers can use the cost data to assess whether unit costs and total costs are reasonable. By comparing the quantity and cost data with predetermined goals, top management can also judge whether current performance is meeting planned objectives.

Do it!

In March, Rodayo Manufacturing had the following unit production costs: materials $6 and conversion costs $9. On March 1, it had zero work in process. During March, Rodayo transferred out 12,000 units. As of March 31, 800 units that were 25% complete as to conversion costs and 100% complete as to materials were in ending work in process. Total costs to be accounted for are $186,600.

(a) Compute the total units to be accounted for.

(b) Compute the equivalent units of production.

(c) Prepare a cost reconciliation schedule, including the costs of materials transferred out and the costs of materials in process.

Solution

(a) 0 (work in process, March 1) + 12,800 (started into production) = 12,800 units

(b) Equivalent units of production:

	Materials	Conversion
Units transferred out	12,000	12,000
Work in process, March 31	800	200 (800 × 25%)
Total	12,800	12,200

(c) Cost reconciliation schedule:

Costs accounted for			
Transferred out (12,000 × $15)			$180,000
Work in process, March 31			
Materials (800 × $6)		$4,800	
Conversion costs (200 × $9)		1,800	6,600
Total costs			$186,600

Related exercise material: BE21-4, BE21-5, BE21-6, BE21-7, BE21-8, BE21-9, BE21-10, E21-5, E21-6, E21-8, E21-9, E21-10, E21-11, E21-12, E21-14, E21-15, E21-16, and **Do it!** 21-3.

Cost Reconciliation Schedule

action plan

✔ To find units to be accounted for, add the units started into production during the month to the units in process at the beginning of the month.

✔ Realize that equivalent units of production for materials will differ from equivalent units of production for conversion costs. The units in ending work in process are 100% complete as to materials but only 25% complete as to conversion costs.

✔ Assign the total manufacturing cost of $15 per unit to the 12,000 units transferred out.

✔ Assign the materials cost and conversion costs based on equivalent units of production to units in process.

✔ **The Navigator**

Costing Systems—Final Comments

Companies often use a combination of a process cost and a job order cost system. Called **operations costing**, this hybrid system is similar to process costing in its assumption that standardized methods are used to manufacture the product. At the same time, the product may have some customized, individual features that require the use of a job order cost system.

Consider, for example, the automobile manufacturer Ford Motor Company. Each vehicle at a given plant goes through the same assembly line, but Ford uses different materials (such as seat coverings, paint, and tinted glass) for different vehicles. Similarly, Kellogg's Pop-Tarts Toaster Pastries® go through numerous standardized processes—mixing, filling, baking, frosting, and packaging. The pastry dough, though, comes in different flavors—plain, chocolate, and graham—and fillings include Smucker's® real fruit, chocolate fudge, vanilla creme, brown sugar cinnamon, and S'mores.

A cost-benefit tradeoff occurs as a company decides which costing system to use. A job order system, for example, provides detailed information related to the cost of the product. Because each job has its own distinguishing characteristics, the system can provide an accurate cost per job. This information is useful in controlling costs and pricing products. However, the cost of implementing a job order cost system is often expensive because of the accounting costs involved.

On the other hand, for a company like Intel, which makes computer chips, is there a benefit in knowing whether the cost of the one hundredth chip produced is different from the one thousandth chip produced? Probably not. An average cost of the product will suffice for control and pricing purposes.

In summary, when deciding to use one of these systems, or a combination system, a company must weigh the costs of implementing the system against the benefits from the additional information provided.

Contemporary Developments

As indicated in Chapter 19, two contemporary developments in managerial accounting are just-in-time processing and activity-based costing. We explain these innovations in the following sections.

Just-In-Time Processing

Study Objective [8]

Explain just-in-time (JIT) processing.

Traditionally, continuous process manufacturing has been based on a **just-in-case** philosophy: Companies hold inventories of raw materials *just in case* some items are of poor quality or a key supplier is shut down by a strike. They manufacture and store subassembly parts *just in case* these parts are needed later in the manufacturing process. Companies complete and store finished goods *just in case* they receive unexpected and rush customer orders. This philosophy often results in a **"push approach"**: Raw materials and subassembly parts are pushed through each process. Traditional processing often results in the buildup of extensive manufacturing inventories.

Primarily in response to foreign competition, many U.S. firms have switched to **just-in-time (JIT) processing**. JIT manufacturing is dedicated to having the right amount of materials, parts, or products just as they are needed. JIT first hit the United States in the early 1980s when automobile companies adopted it to compete with foreign automakers. Many companies, including Dell, Caterpillar, and Harley-Davidson now successfully use JIT. Under JIT processing, companies receive raw materials *just in time* for use in production, they complete subassembly parts *just in time* for use in finished goods, and they complete finished goods *just in time* to be sold. Illustration 21-24 shows the sequence of activities in just-in-time processing.

OBJECTIVE OF JIT PROCESSING

A primary objective of JIT is to eliminate all manufacturing inventories. Inventories have an adverse effect on net income because they tie up funds and storage space that could be put to more productive uses. JIT strives to eliminate inventories by using a **"pull approach"** in manufacturing. This approach begins with the customer placing an order with the company, which starts the process of pulling the product through the manufacturing process. A computer at the final work station sends a signal to the preceding work station. This signal indicates the exact materials (parts and subassemblies) needed to complete the production of a specified product for a specified time period, such as an eight-hour shift. The next preceding process, in turn, sends its signal to other processes back up the line. The goal is a smooth continuous flow in the manufacturing process and no buildup of inventories at any point.

ELEMENTS OF JIT PROCESSING

There are three important elements in JIT processing:

1. **Dependable suppliers.** Suppliers must be willing to deliver on short notice exact quantities of raw materials according to precise quality specifications

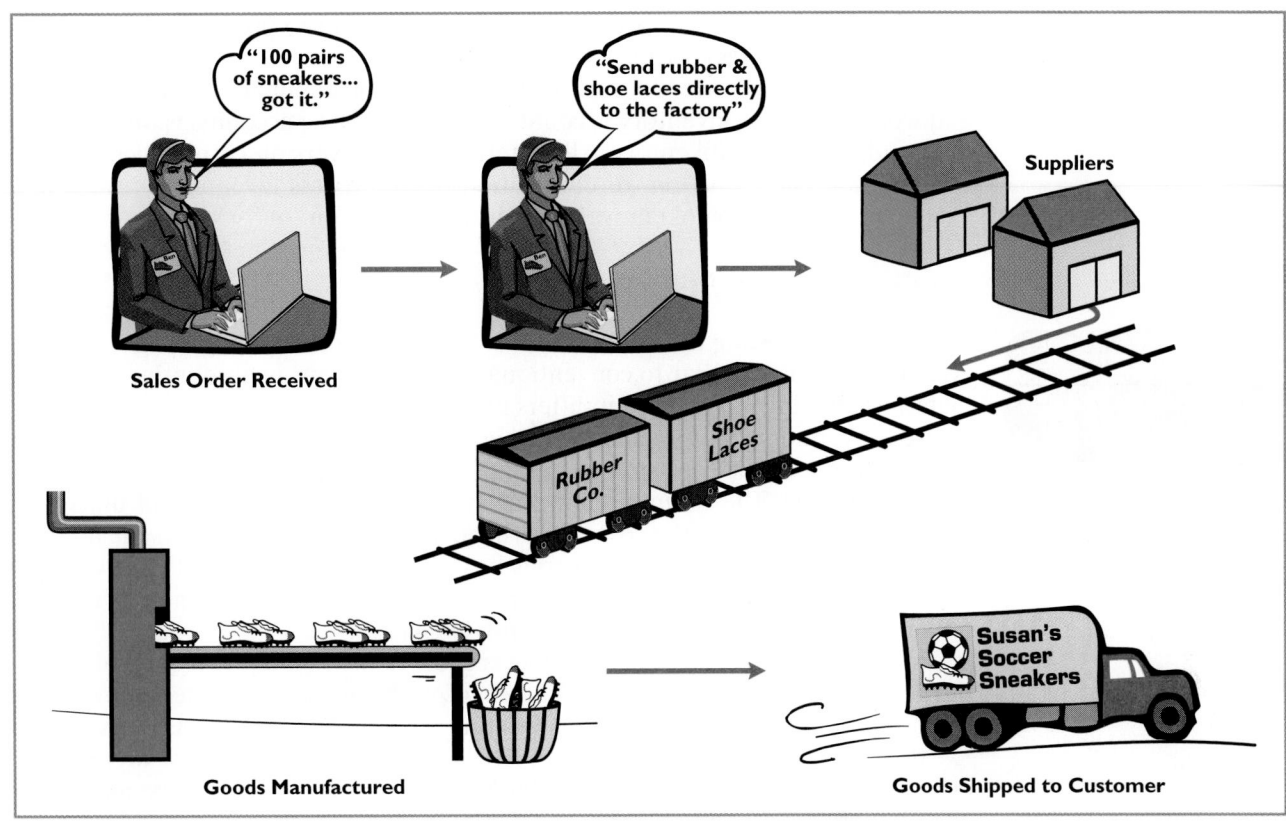

Illustration 21-24
Just-in-time processing

(even including multiple deliveries within the same day). Suppliers must also be willing to deliver the raw materials at specified work stations rather than at a central receiving department. This type of purchasing requires constant and direct communication. Such communication is facilitated by an online computer linkage between the company and its suppliers.

2. **A multiskilled workforce.** Under JIT, machines are often strategically grouped around work cells or work stations. Much of the work is automated. As a result, one worker may have the responsibility to operate and maintain several different types of machines.

3. **A total quality control system.** The company must establish total quality control throughout the manufacturing operations. Total quality control means **no defects**. Since the **pull approach** signals only required quantities, any defects at any work station will shut down operations at subsequent work stations. Total quality control requires continuous monitoring by both employees and supervisors at each work station.

BENEFITS OF JIT PROCESSING

The major benefits of JIT processing are:

1. Significant reduction or elimination of manufacturing inventories.
2. Enhanced product quality.
3. Reduction or elimination of rework costs and inventory storage costs.
4. Production cost savings from the improved flow of goods through the processes.

The effects in many cases have been dramatic. For example, after using JIT for two years, a major division of Hewlett-Packard found that work in process inventories (in dollars) were down 82%, scrap/rework costs were down 30%, space utilization improved by 40%, and labor efficiency improved 50%. As indicated, JIT not only reduces inventory but also enables a manufacturer to produce a better product faster and with less waste.

One of the major accounting benefits of JIT is the elimination of raw materials and work in process inventory accounts. In place of these accounts is **one account**, Raw and In-Process Inventory. All materials and conversion costs are charged to this account. The reduction (or elimination) of in-process inventories results in a simplified computation of equivalent units of production.

Activity-Based Costing

Study Objective [9]
Explain activity-based costing (ABC).

Activity-based costing focuses on the activities performed in producing a product. An ABC system is similar to conventional costing systems in accounting for direct materials and direct labor, but it differs in regard to manufacturing overhead.

A conventional cost system uses a **single unit-level** basis to allocate overhead costs to products. The basis may be direct labor or machine hours used to manufacture the product. The assumption in this approach is that as volume of units produced increases, so does the cost of overhead. However, in recent years the amount of direct labor used in many industries has greatly *decreased*, and total overhead costs resulting from depreciation on expensive equipment and machinery, utilities, repairs, and maintenance have significantly *increased*.

In ABC costing, the cost of a product is equal to the sum of the costs of all activities performed to manufacture it. ABC recognizes that to have accurate and meaningful cost data, **more than one basis** of allocating activity costs to products is needed.

In selecting the allocation basis, ABC seeks to identify the **cost drivers** that measure the activities performed on the product. A cost driver may be any factor or activity that has a direct cause–effect relationship with the resources consumed. Examples of activities and possible cost drivers are as follows.

Illustration 21-25
Activities and cost drivers in ABC

Activity	Cost Driver
Ordering raw materials	Ordering hours; number of orders
Receiving raw materials	Receiving hours; number of shipments
Materials handling	Number of requisitions; weight of materials; handling hours
Production scheduling	Number of orders
Machine setups	Setup hours; number of setups
Machining (fabricating, assembling, etc.)	Machine hours
Quality control inspections	Number of inspections
Factory supervision	Number of employees

Two important assumptions must be met in order to obtain accurate product costs under ABC:

1. All overhead costs related to the activity must be driven by the cost driver used to assign costs to products.

2. All overhead costs related to the activity should respond proportionally to changes in the activity level of the cost driver.

For example, if there is little or no correlation between changes in the cost driver and consumption of the overhead cost, inaccurate product costs are inevitable. An example of the use of ABC is illustrated in the appendix at the end of this chapter.

Activity-based costing may be used with either a job order or a process cost accounting system. The primary benefit of ABC is more accurate and meaningful product costing. Also, improved cost data about an activity can lead to reduced costs for the activity. In sum, ABC makes managers realize that it is *activities*, and not products, that determine the profitability of a company—a realization that should lead to better management decisions.

Do it!

Indicate whether each of the following statements is true or false.

1. Continuous process manufacturing often results in a reduction of inventory.
2. Companies that use just-in-time processing complete and store finished goods all the time to meet rush orders from customers.
3. A major benefit of just-in-time processing is production cost savings from the improved flow of goods through the processes.
4. An ABC system is similar to traditional costing systems in accounting for manufacturing costs but differs in regard to period costs.
5. The primary benefit of ABC is more accurate and meaningful costs.
6. In recent years, the amount of direct labor used in many industries has greatly increased and total overhead costs have significantly decreased.

Solution

| 1. False. | 2. False. | 3. True. | 4. False. | 5. True. | 6. False. |

Related exercise material: BE21-11 and **Do it!** 21-4.

JIT and ABC

action plan

✔ JIT manufacturing is dedicated to having the right amounts of materials, parts, or products just as they are needed.

✔ ABC focuses on the activities performed in producing a product. It recognizes that to have accurate and meaningful cost data, more than one basis of allocating costs to products is needed.

✔ **The Navigator**

COMPREHENSIVE

Do it!

Essence Company manufactures a high-end after-shave lotion, called Eternity, in 10-ounce plastic bottles. Because the market for after-shave lotion is highly competitive, the company is very concerned about keeping its costs under control. Eternity is manufactured through three processes: mixing, filling, and corking. Materials are added at the beginning of each of the processes, and labor and overhead are incurred uniformly throughout each process. The company uses a weighted-average method to cost its product. A partially completed production cost report for the month of May for the Mixing Department is shown below.

ESSENCE COMPANY
Mixing Department
Production Cost Report
For the Month Ended May 31, 2012

| | | Equivalent Units | |
QUANTITIES	Physical Units	Materials	Conversion Costs
Units to be accounted for	Step 1	Step 2	
Work in process, May 1	1,000		
Started into production	2,000		
Total units	3,000		
Units accounted for			
Transferred out	2,200	?	?
Work in process, May 31	800	?	?
Total units	3,000	?	?

COSTS		Materials	Conversion Costs	Total
Unit costs Step 3				
Costs in May	(a)	?	?	?
Equivalent units	(b)	?	?	
Unit costs [(a) ÷ (b)]		?	?	?
Costs to be accounted for				
Work in process, May 1				$ 56,300
Started into production				119,320
Total costs				$175,620

COST RECONCILIATION SCHEDULE Step 4

Costs accounted for		
Transferred out		?
Work in process, May 31		
Materials	?	
Conversion costs	?	?
Total costs		?

Additional information:

Work in process, May 1, 1,000 units

Materials cost, 1,000 units (100% complete)	$49,100	
Conversion costs, 1,000 units (70% complete)	7,200	$56,300
Materials cost for May, 2,000 units		$100,000
Conversion costs for May		$19,320

Work in process, May 31, 800 units, 100% complete as to materials and 50% complete as to conversion costs.

Instructions

(a) Prepare a production cost report for the Mixing Department for the month of May.

(b) Prepare the journal entry to record the transfer of goods from the Mixing Department to the Filling Department.

(c) Explain why Essence Company is using a process cost system to account for its costs.

action plan

✔ Compute the physical unit flow—that is, the total units to be accounted for.

✔ Compute the equivalent units of production.

✔ Compute the unit production costs, expressed in terms of equivalent units of production.

✔ Prepare a cost reconciliation schedule, which shows that the total costs accounted for equal the total costs to be accounted for.

Solution to Comprehensive Do it!

(a) A completed production cost report for the Mixing Department is shown below. Computations to support the amounts reported follow the report.

ESSENCE COMPANY
Mixing Department
Production Cost Report
For the Month Ended May 31, 2012

	Physical Units	Equivalent Units	
QUANTITIES		Materials	Conversion Costs
Units to be accounted for	Step 1		Step 2
Work in process, May 1	1,000		
Started into production	2,000		
Total units	3,000		

QUANTITIES		Equivalent Units	
	Physical Units	Materials	Conversion Costs
Units accounted for			
Transferred out	2,200	2,200	2,200
Work in process, May 31	800	800	400 (800 × 50%)
Total units	3,000	3,000	2,600

COSTS			Conversion	
Unit costs Step 3		Materials	Costs	Total
Costs in May	(a)	$149,100	$26,520	$175,620
Equivalent units	(b)	3,000	2,600	
Unit costs [(a) ÷ (b)]		$49.70	$10.20	$59.90
Costs to be accounted for				
Work in process, May 1				$ 56,300
Started into production				119,320
Total costs				$175,620

COST RECONCILIATION SCHEDULE Step 4

Costs accounted for		
Transferred out (2,200 × $59.90)		$131,780
Work in process, May 31		
Materials (800 × $49.70)	$39,760	
Conversion costs (400 × $10.20)	4,080	43,840
Total costs		$175,620

Additional computations to support production cost report data:
Materials cost—$49,100 + $100,000
Conversion costs—$7,200 + $19,320 ($119,320 − $100,000)

(b) Work in Process—Filling   131,780
      Work in Process—Mixing   131,780

(c) Companies use process cost systems to apply costs to similar products that are mass-produced in a continuous fashion. Essence Company uses a process cost system because production of the after-shave lotion, once it begins, continues until the after-shave lotion emerges. The processing is the same for the entire run—with precisely the same amount of materials, labor, and overhead. Each bottle of Eternity after-shave lotion is indistinguishable from another.

The Navigator

Summary of Study Objectives

[1] Understand who uses process cost systems. Companies that mass-produce similar products in a continuous fashion use process cost systems. Once production begins, it continues until the finished product emerges. Each unit of finished product is indistinguishable from every other unit.

[2] Explain the similarities and differences between job order cost and process cost systems. Job order cost systems are similar to process cost systems in three ways: (1) Both systems track the same cost elements—direct materials, direct labor, and manufacturing overhead. (2) Both accumulate costs in the same accounts—Raw Materials Inventory, Factory Labor, and Manufacturing Overhead. (3) Both assign

accumulated costs to the same accounts—Work in Process, Finished Goods Inventory, and Cost of Goods Sold. However, the method of assigning costs differs significantly.

There are four main differences between the two cost systems: (1) A process cost system uses separate accounts for each department or manufacturing process, rather than only one work in process account used in a job order cost system. (2) A process cost system summarizes costs in a production cost report for each department. A job cost system charges costs to individual jobs and summarizes them in a job cost sheet. (3) Costs are totaled at the end of a time period in a process cost system, but at the completion of a job in a job cost system. (4) A process cost system calculates unit cost as: Total manufacturing costs for the period ÷ Units produced during the period. A job cost system calculates unit cost as: Total cost per job ÷ Units produced.

[3] Explain the flow of costs in a process cost system. A process cost system assigns manufacturing costs for raw materials, labor, and overhead to work in process accounts for various departments or manufacturing processes. It transfers the costs of units completed from one department to another as those units move through the manufacturing process. The system transfers the costs of completed work to Finished Goods Inventory. Finally, when inventory is sold, the system transfers costs to Cost of Goods Sold.

[4] Make the journal entries to assign manufacturing costs in a process cost system. Entries to assign the costs of raw materials, labor, and overhead consist of a credit to Raw Materials Inventory, Factory Labor, and Manufacturing Overhead, and a debit to Work in Process for each department. Entries to record the cost of goods transferred to another department are a credit to Work in Process for the department whose work is finished and a debit to the department to which the goods are transferred. The entry to record units completed and transferred to the warehouse is a credit for the department whose work is finished and a debit to Finished Goods Inventory. The entry to record the sale of goods is a credit to Finished Goods Inventory and a debit to Cost of Goods Sold.

[5] Compute equivalent units. Equivalent units of production measure work done during a period, expressed in fully completed units. Companies use this measure to determine

the cost per unit of completed product. Equivalent units are the sum of units completed and transferred out plus equivalent units of ending work in process.

[6] Explain the four steps necessary to prepare a production cost report. The four steps to complete a production cost report are: (1) Compute the physical unit flow—that is, the total units to be accounted for. (2) Compute the equivalent units of production. (3) Compute the unit production costs, expressed in terms of equivalent units of production. (4) Prepare a cost reconciliation schedule, which shows that the total costs accounted for equal the total costs to be accounted for.

[7] Prepare a production cost report. The production cost report contains both quantity and cost data for a production department. There are four sections in the report: (1) number of physical units, (2) equivalent units determination, (3) unit costs, and (4) cost reconciliation schedule.

[8] Explain just-in-time (JIT) processing. JIT is a manufacturing technique dedicated to producing the right products at the right time as needed. One of the principal accounting effects is that a Raw and In-Process Inventory account replaces both the raw materials and work in process inventory accounts.

[9] Explain activity-based costing (ABC). ABC is a method of product costing that focuses on the activities performed to produce products. It assigns the cost of the activities to products by using cost drivers that measure the activities performed. The primary objective of ABC is accurate and meaningful product costs.

✔
The Navigator

Glossary

Activity-based costing A cost accounting system that focuses on the activities performed in manufacturing a specific product. (p. 984).

Conversion costs The sum of labor costs and overhead costs. (p. 974).

Cost driver Any factor or activity that has a direct cause–effect relationship with the resources consumed. (p. 984).

Cost reconciliation schedule A schedule that shows that the total costs accounted for equal the total costs to be accounted for. (p. 979).

Equivalent units of production A measure of the work done during the period, expressed in fully completed units. (p. 973).

Just-in-time processing A processing system dedicated to producing the right products (or parts) as they are needed. (p. 982).

Operations costing A combination of a process cost and a job order cost system, in which products are manufactured primarily by standardized methods, with some customization. (p. 981).

Physical units Actual units to be accounted for during a period, irrespective of any work performed. (p. 977).

Process cost systems An accounting system used to apply costs to similar products that are mass-produced in a continuous fashion. (p. 966).

Production cost report An internal report for management that shows both production quantity and cost data for a production department. (p. 975).

Total units (costs) accounted for The sum of the units (costs) transferred out during the period plus the units (costs) in process at the end of the period. (pp. 977, 979).

Total units (costs) to be accounted for The sum of the units (costs) started (or transferred) into production during the period plus the units (costs) in process at the beginning of the period. (pp. 977, 979).

Unit production costs Costs expressed in terms of equivalent units of production. (p. 978).

Weighted-average method Method used to compute equivalent units of production which considers the degree of completion (weighting) of the units completed and transferred out and the ending work in process. (p. 973).

APPENDIX21A

Example of Traditional Costing versus Activity-Based Costing

Production and Cost Data

In this appendix we present an example that compares activity-based costing to traditional costing. Assume that Atlas Company produces two products, The Boot and The Club. The Boot is a high-volume item totaling 25,000 units annually. The Club is a low-volume item totaling only 5,000 units per year. Each product requires one hour of direct labor for completion. Therefore, total annual direct labor hours are 30,000 (25,000 + 5,000). Expected annual manufacturing overhead costs are $900,000. The predetermined overhead rate is $30 ($900,000 ÷ 30,000) per direct labor hour.

The direct materials cost per unit is $40 for The Boot and $30 for The Club. The direct labor cost is $12 per unit for each product.

Study Objective [10]
Apply activity-based costing to specific company data.

Unit Costs Under Traditional Costing

Illustration 21A-1 shows the unit cost for each product under traditional costing.

	Product	
Manufacturing Costs	**The Boot**	**The Club**
Direct materials	$40	$30
Direct labor	12	12
Overhead	30*	30*
Total unit cost	$82	$72

*Predetermined overhead rate × Direct labor hours ($30 × 1 hr = $30)

Illustration 21A-1
Units costs—traditional costing

Unit Costs Under ABC

Let's now calculate unit costs under ABC, in order to compare activity-based costing with a traditional costing system. The first step is to determine overhead rates under ABC.

DETERMINING OVERHEAD RATES UNDER ABC

Analysis reveals that Atlas Company's expected annual overhead costs of $900,000 relate to three activities—machine setups, machining, and inspections. Illustration 21A-2 shows the cost driver and overhead rate for each activity.

Activity	Cost Driver	Total Expected Overhead Cost	Total Expected Use of Driver	Activity Based Overhead Rate
Machine setups	Number of setups	$300,000	1,500	$200 per setup
Machining	Machine hours	500,000	50,000	$10 per machine hour
Inspections	Number of inspections	100,000	2,000	$50 per inspection

Illustration 21A-2
Computing overhead rates—ABC

ASSIGNING OVERHEAD COSTS TO PRODUCTS UNDER ABC

In assigning costs, it is necessary to know the expected number of cost drivers for each product. Because of its low volume, The Club requires more setups and inspections than The Boot. The expected number of cost drivers for each product is as follows.

Cost Driver	The Boot	The Club	Total Usage
	Product		
Number of machine setups	500	1,000	1,500
Machine hours	30,000	20,000	50,000
Number of inspections	500	1,500	2,000

Using these data, Atlas can assign the expected annual overhead cost to each product as follows.

Activity	The Boot Number	The Boot Cost	The Club Number	The Club Cost	Total Cost
Machine setups ($200)	500	$100,000	1,000	$200,000	$300,000
Machining ($10)	30,000	300,000	20,000	200,000	500,000
Inspections ($50)	500	25,000	1,500	75,000	100,000
Total assigned costs (a)		$425,000		$475,000	$900,000
Units produced (b)		25,000		5,000	
Overhead cost per unit [(a) ÷ (b)]		$17		$95	

These data show that under ABC, overhead costs are shifted from the high-volume product (The Boot) to the low-volume product (The Club). This shift results in more accurate costing for two reasons:

1. Low-volume products often require more special handling, such as more machine setups and inspections, than high-volume products. This is true for Atlas Company. Thus, the low-volume product frequently is responsible for more overhead costs per unit than a high-volume product.

2. Assigning overhead using ABC will usually increase the cost per unit for low-volume products as compared to a traditional overhead allocation. Therefore, traditional cost drivers such as direct labor hours are usually not appropriate for assigning overhead costs to low-volume products.

Comparing Unit Costs

A comparison of unit manufacturing costs under traditional costing and ABC shows the following significant differences.

Manufacturing Costs	The Boot Traditional Costing	The Boot ABC	The Club Traditional Costing	The Club ABC
Direct materials	$40	$40	$30	$ 30
Direct labor	12	12	12	12
Overhead	30	17	30	95
Total cost per unit	$82	$69	$72	$137
	Overstated		Understated	
	$13		$65	

The comparison shows that unit costs under traditional costing have been significantly distorted. The cost of The Boot has been overstated $13 per unit ($82 − $69). The cost of The Club has been understated $65 per unit ($137 − $72). The differences are attributable to how Atlas Company assigns manufacturing overhead. A likely consequence of the differences is that Atlas has been overpricing The Boot and possibly losing market share to competitors. It also has been sacrificing profitability by underpricing The Club.

As illustrated in the above case, ABC involves the following steps.

1. Identify the major activities that pertain to the manufacture of specific products.
2. Accumulate manufacturing overhead costs by activities.
3. Identify the cost driver(s) that accurately measure(s) each activity's contribution to the finished product.
4. Assign manufacturing overhead costs for each activity to products, using the cost driver(s).

Benefits and Limitations of Activity-Based Costing

We have already seen that a primary benefit of ABC is more accurate product costing. In addition, ABC offers the following other benefits:

1. **Enhanced control over overhead costs.** Under ABC, companies can trace many overhead costs directly to activities—allowing some indirect costs to be identified as direct costs. Thus, managers have become more aware of their responsibility to control the activities that generate the costs.
2. **Better management decisions.** More accurate product costing should contribute to setting selling prices that can help achieve desired product profitability levels. In addition, more accurate cost data could be helpful in deciding whether to make or buy a component, and sometimes even whether to discontinue or expand a product.

The principal disadvantages of ABC generally focus on two factors. First, **the expense of obtaining the cost data** required by the system is relatively high. ABC requires data that are not normally generated within a company. Examples of such data are the number of setups, inspections, orders placed, and orders received. In addition, many computations are involved in assigning overhead costs to individual products.

Second, **ABC does not eliminate arbitrary assignments** of overhead. For example, plant-wide overhead costs such as depreciation, insurance, and property taxes on the factory building should be allocated to the activity centers in determining the cost of a product. With ABC, these allocations may be more difficult to do accurately because of the increased number of activity centers. As a result, accuracy of product costs could be adversely affected.

Summary of Study Objective for Appendix 21A

[10] Apply activity-based costing to specific company data. In applying ABC, it is necessary to compute the overhead rate for each activity by dividing total expected overhead by the total expected usage of the cost driver. The overhead cost for each activity is then assigned to products on the basis of each product's use of the cost driver.

Self-Test, Brief Exercises, Exercises, Problem Set A, and many more components are available for practice in *WileyPLUS*

Note: All **asterisked** Questions, Exercises, and Problems relate to material contained in the appendix to the chapter.

Self-Test Questions

Answers are on page 1009.

(SO 1) 1. Which of the following items is *not* characteristic of a process cost system?

a. Once production begins, it continues until the finished product emerges.
b. The products produced are heterogeneous in nature.

c. The focus is on continually producing homogeneous products.

d. When the finished product emerges, all units have precisely the same amount of materials, labor, and overhead.

(SO 2)   2. Indicate which of the following statements is *not* correct.

a. Both a job order and a process cost system track the same three manufacturing cost elements—direct materials, direct labor, and manufacturing overhead.

b. A job order cost system uses only one work in process account, whereas a process cost system uses multiple work in process accounts.

c. Manufacturing costs are accumulated the same way in a job order and in a process cost system.

d. Manufacturing costs are assigned the same way in a job order and in a process cost system.

(SO 3)   3. In a process cost system, costs are assigned only:

a. to one work in process account.

b. to work in process and finished goods inventory.

c. to work in process, finished goods, and cost of goods sold.

d. to work in process accounts.

(SO 4)   4. In making the journal entry to assign raw materials costs, a company:

a. debits Finished Goods Inventory.

b. often debits two or more work in process accounts.

c. generally credits two or more work in process accounts.

d. credits Finished Goods Inventory.

(SO 4)   5. In a process cost system, manufacturing overhead:

a. is assigned to finished goods at the end of each accounting period.

b. is assigned to a work in process account for each job as the job is completed.

c. is assigned to a work in process account for each production department on the basis of a predetermined overhead rate.

d. is assigned to a work in process account for each production department as overhead costs are incurred.

(SO 5)   6. Conversion costs are the sum of:

a. fixed and variable overhead costs.

b. labor costs and overhead costs.

c. direct material costs and overhead costs.

d. direct labor and indirect labor costs.

(SO 5)   7. The Mixing Department's output during the period consists of 20,000 units completed and transferred out, and 5,000 units in ending work in process 60% complete as to materials and conversion costs. Beginning inventory is 1,000 units, 40% complete as to materials and conversion costs. The equivalent units of production are:

a. 22,600.   c. 24,000.

b. 23,000.   d. 25,000.

(SO 6)   8. In RYZ Company, there are zero units in beginning work in process, 7,000 units started into production, and 500 units in ending work in process 20% completed. The physical units to be accounted for are:

a. 7,000.   c. 7,600.

b. 7,360.   d. 7,340.

(SO 6)   9. Stock Company has 2,000 units in beginning work in process, 20% complete as to conversion costs, 23,000 units transferred out to finished goods, and 3,000 units in ending work in process 33⅓% complete as to conversion costs. The beginning and ending inventory is fully complete as to materials costs. Equivalent units for materials and conversion costs are, respectively:

a. 22,000, 24,000.   c. 26,000, 24,000.

b. 24,000, 26,000.   d. 26,000, 26,000.

(SO 6)   10. Fortner Company has no beginning work in process; 9,000 units are transferred out and 3,000 units in ending work in process are one-third finished as to conversion costs and fully complete as to materials cost. If total materials cost is $60,000, the unit materials cost is:

a. $5.00.   c. $6.00.

b. $5.45 rounded.   d. No correct answer is given.

(SO 6)   11. Largo Company has unit costs of $10 for materials and $30 for conversion costs. If there are 2,500 units in ending work in process, 40% complete as to conversion costs, and fully complete as to materials cost, the total cost assignable to the ending work in process inventory is:

a. $45,000.   c. $75,000.

b. $55,000.   d. $100,000.

(SO 7)   12. A production cost report

a. is an external report.

b. shows costs charged to a department and costs accounted for.

c. shows equivalent units of production but not physical units.

d. contains six sections.

(SO 7)   13. In a production cost report, units to be accounted for are calculated as:

a. Units started into production + Units in ending work in process.

b. Units started into production − Units in beginning work in process.

c. Units transferred out + Units in beginning work in process.

d. Units started into production + Units in beginning work in process.

(SO 8)   14. Just-in-time processing (JIT):

a. strives to eliminate inventories.

b. uses a pull approach in manufacturing.

c. Neither of the above.

d. Both (a) and (b).

(SO 8)   15. The sequence of activities in just-in-time processing begins when the manufacturer:

a. orders raw materials from a supplier.

b. issues raw materials to work in process inventory.

c. receives a sales order from a customer.

d. calculates its predetermined overhead rates.

(SO 9)   16. Activity-based costing:

a. assumes that the cost of a product is equal to the sum of the costs of all activities performed to manufacture it.

b. has become more widespread as overhead costs have been decreasing relative to materials and labor costs.

c. is similar to a conventional cost accounting system in accounting for direct labor and manufacturing overhead but differs in regard to direct materials.

d. uses a single unit-level basis to allocate overhead costs to products.

(SO 9) 17. Activity-based costing (ABC):

a. can be used only in a process cost system.

b. focuses on units of production.

c. focuses on activities performed to produce a product.

d. uses only a single basis of allocation.

*18. The overhead rate for Machine Setups is $100 per setup. (SO 10) Products A and B have 80 and 60 setups, respectively. The overhead assigned to each product is:

a. Product A $8,000, Product B $8,000.

b. Product A $8,000, Product B $6,000.

c. Product A $6,000, Product B $6,000.

d. Product A $6,000, Product B $8,000.

Go to the book's companion website, **www.wiley.com/college/weygandt,** for additional Self-Test Questions.

 The Navigator

Questions

1. Identify which costing system—job order or process cost—the following companies would primarily use: (a) Quaker Oats, (b) Ford Motor Company, (c) Kinko's Print Shop, and (d) Warner Bros. Motion Pictures.

2. Contrast the primary focus of job order cost accounting and of process cost accounting.

3. What are the similarities between a job order and a process cost system?

4. Your roommate is confused about the features of process cost accounting. Identify and explain the distinctive features for your roommate.

5. Sal Torre believes there are no significant differences in the flow of costs between job order cost accounting and process cost accounting. Is Torre correct? Explain.

6. (a) What source documents are used in assigning (1) materials and (2) labor to production in a process cost system?

(b) What criterion and basis are commonly used in allocating overhead to processes?

7. At Dos Company, overhead is assigned to production departments at the rate of $5 per machine hour. In July, machine hours were 3,000 in the Machining Department and 2,400 in the Assembly Department. Prepare the entry to assign overhead to production.

8. Mary Watters is uncertain about the steps used to prepare a production cost report. State the procedures that are required in the sequence in which they are performed.

9. Mitch Chorro is confused about computing physical units. Explain to Mitch how physical units to be accounted for and physical units accounted for are determined.

10. What is meant by the term "equivalent units of production"?

11. How are equivalent units of production computed?

12. Samson Company had zero units of beginning work in process. During the period, 9,000 units were completed, and there were 600 units of ending work in process. What were the units started into production?

13. Gratle Co. had zero units of beginning work in process. During the period, 12,000 units were completed, and there were 800 units of ending work in process one-fifth complete as to conversion cost and 100% complete as to materials cost. What were the equivalent units of production for (a) materials and (b) conversion costs?

14. Mays Co. started 3,000 units during the period. Its beginning inventory is 500 units one-fourth complete as to conversion costs and 100% complete as to materials cost. Its ending inventory is 200 units one-fifth complete as to conversion cost and 100% complete as to materials costs. How many units were transferred out this period?

15. Kira Company transfers out 14,000 units and has 2,000 units of ending work in process that are 25% complete. Materials are entered at the beginning of the process and there is no beginning work in process. Assuming unit materials costs of $3 and unit conversion costs of $6, what are the costs to be assigned to units (a) transferred out and (b) in ending work in process?

16. (a) Adam Vadim believes the production cost report is an external report for stockholders. Is Adam correct? Explain.

(b) Identify the sections in a production cost report.

17. What purposes are served by a production cost report?

18. At Stan Company, there are 800 units of ending work in process that are 100% complete as to materials and 40% complete as to conversion costs. If the unit cost of materials is $4 and the costs assigned to the 800 units is $6,000, what is the per-unit conversion cost?

19. What is the difference between operations costing and a process costing system?

20. How does a company decide whether to use a job order or a process cost system?

21. (a) Describe the philosophy and approach of just-in-time processing.

(b) Identify the major elements of JIT processing.

22. (a) What are the principal differences between activity-based costing (ABC) and traditional product costing?

(b) What assumptions must be met for ABC costing to be useful?

23. Chopra Co. identifies the following activities that pertain to manufacturing overhead: Materials Handling, Machine Setups, Factory Machine Maintenance, Factory Supervision, and Quality Control. For each activity, identify an appropriate cost driver.

*24. (a) Identify the steps that pertain to activity-based costing.

(b) What are the advantages of ABC costing?

Brief Exercises

Journalize entries for accumulating costs.
(SO 4)

BE21-1 Mendez Manufacturing purchases $45,000 of raw materials on account, and it incurs $50,000 of factory labor costs. Journalize the two transactions on March 31 assuming the labor costs are not paid until April.

Journalize the assignment of materials and labor costs.
(SO 4)

BE21-2 Data for Mendez Manufacturing are given in BE21-1. Supporting records show that (a) the Assembly Department used $24,000 of raw materials and $30,000 of the factory labor, and (b) the Finishing Department used the remainder. Journalize the assignment of the costs to the processing departments on March 31.

Journalize the assignment of overhead costs.
(SO 4)

BE21-3 Factory labor data for Mendez Manufacturing are given in BE21-2. Manufacturing overhead is assigned to departments on the basis of 200% of labor costs. Journalize the assignment of overhead to the Assembly and Finishing Departments.

Compute physical units of production.
(SO 6)

BE21-4 Sawyer Manufacturing Company has the following production data for selected months.

Month	Beginning Work in Process	Units Transferred Out	Ending Work in Process	
			Units	% Complete as to Conversion Cost
January	–0–	30,000	10,000	40%
March	–0–	40,000	8,000	75
July	–0–	40,000	16,000	25

Compute the physical units for each month.

Compute equivalent units of production.
(SO 5)

BE21-5 Using the data in BE21-4, compute equivalent units of production for materials and conversion costs, assuming materials are entered at the beginning of the process.

Compute unit costs of production.
(SO 6)

BE21-6 In Boca Company, total material costs are $32,000, and total conversion costs are $54,000. Equivalent units of production are materials 10,000 and conversion costs 12,000. Compute the unit costs for materials, conversion costs, and total manufacturing costs.

Assign costs to units transferred out and in process.
(SO 6)

BE21-7 Prya Company has the following production data for April: units transferred out 40,000, and ending work in process 5,000 units that are 100% complete for materials and 40% complete for conversion costs. If unit materials cost is $4 and unit conversion cost is $9, determine the costs to be assigned to the units transferred out and the units in ending work in process.

Compute unit costs.
(SO 6)

BE21-8 Production costs chargeable to the Finishing Department in June in Huang Company are materials $15,000, labor $29,500, and overhead $18,000. Equivalent units of production are materials 20,000 and conversion costs 19,000. Compute the unit costs for materials and conversion costs.

Prepare cost reconciliation schedule.
(SO 6)

BE21-9 Data for Huang Company are given in BE21-8. Production records indicate that 18,000 units were transferred out, and 2,000 units in ending work in process were 50% complete as to conversion cost and 100% complete as to materials. Prepare a cost reconciliation schedule.

Compute equivalent units of production.
(SO 5)

BE21-10 The Smelting Department of Caruso Manufacturing Company has the following production and cost data for November.

Production: Beginning work in process 2,000 units that are 100% complete as to materials and 20% complete as to conversion costs; units transferred out 8,000 units; and ending work in process 5,000 units that are 100% complete as to materials and 40% complete as to conversion costs.

Compute the equivalent units of production for (a) materials and (b) conversion costs for the month of November.

Understand contemporary developments.
(SO 8, 9)

BE21-11 Sam Snead has formulated the following list of statements about contemporary developments in managerial accounting.

1. Just-in-time processing results in a push approach; that is, raw materials are pushed through each process.
2. A primary objective of just-in-time processing is to eliminate all manufacturing inventories.

3. A major disadvantage of just-in-time processing is lower product quality.
4. A primary benefit of activity-based costing is more accurate and meaningful product costing.
5. A major advantage of activity-based costing is that it uses a single unit-level basis, such as direct labor or machine hours, to allocate overhead.

Identify each statement as true or false. If false, indicate how to correct the statement to make it true.

*BE21-12 Meyers Company identifies three activities in its manufacturing process: machine setups, machining, and inspections. Estimated annual overhead cost for each activity is $120,000, $300,000, and $70,000, respectively. The cost driver for each activity and the expected annual usage are: number of setups 1,000, machine hours 25,000, and number of inspections 2,000. Compute the overhead rate for each activity.

Compute overhead rates for activities.
(SO 10)

Do it! Review

Do it! 21-1 Hutto Company manufactures CH-21 through two processes: Mixing and Packaging. In July, the following costs were incurred.

Assign and journalize manufacturing costs.
(SO 4)

	Mixing	**Packaging**
Raw Materials used	$10,000	$24,000
Factory Labor costs	8,000	36,000
Manufacturing Overhead costs	12,000	54,000

Units completed at a cost of $21,000 in the Mixing Department are transferred to the Packaging Department. Units completed at a cost of $102,000 in the Packaging Department are transferred to Finished Goods. Journalize the assignment of these costs to the two processes and the transfer of units as appropriate.

Do it! 21-2 The assembly department has the following production and cost data for the current month.

Compute equivalent units.
(SO 5)

Beginning Work in Process	**Units Transferred Out**	**Ending Work in Process**
–0–	20,000	16,000

Materials are entered at the beginning of the process. The ending work in process units are 70% complete as to conversion costs. Compute the equivalent units of production for (a) materials and (b) conversion costs.

Do it! 21-3 In March, Viren Manufacturing had the following unit production costs: materials $10 and conversion costs $8. On March 1, it had zero work in process. During March, Viren transferred out 22,000 units. As of March 31, 2,000 units that were 40% complete as to conversion costs and 100% complete as to materials were in ending work in process.

Prepare cost reconciliation schedule.
(SO 6, 7)

(a) Compute the total units to be accounted for.
(b) Compute the equivalent units of production.
(c) Prepare a cost reconciliation schedule, including the costs of units transferred out and the costs of units in process.

Do it! 21-4 Indicate whether each of the following statements is true or false.

Answer questions about JIT and ABC.
(SO 8, 9)

1. Just-in-time processing is also known as just-in-case processing.
2. Companies that use just-in-time processing complete finished goods just in time to be sold.
3. A major benefit of just-in-time processing is enhanced product quality.
4. An ABC system is similar to conventional costing systems in accounting for period costs but differs in regard to manufacturing costs.
5. The primary benefit of ABC is significant reduction or elimination of manufacturing inventories.
6. In recent years, the amount of direct labor used in many industries has greatly decreased and total overhead costs have significantly increased.

Exercises

E21-1   Greg Reid has prepared the following list of statements about process cost accounting.

1. Process cost systems are used to apply costs to similar products that are mass-produced in a continuous fashion.
2. A process cost system is used when each finished unit is indistinguishable from another.
3. Companies that produce soft drinks, motion pictures, and computer chips would all use process cost accounting.
4. In a process cost system, costs are tracked by individual jobs.
5. Job order costing and process costing track different manufacturing cost elements.
6. Both job order costing and process costing account for direct materials, direct labor, and manufacturing overhead.
7. Costs flow through the accounts in the same basic way for both job order costing and process costing.
8. In a process cost system, only one work in process account is used.
9. In a process cost system, costs are summarized in a job cost sheet.
10. In a process cost system, the unit cost is total manufacturing costs for the period divided by the units produced during the period.

Instructions
Identify each statement as true or false. If false, indicate how to correct the statement.

E21-2   Lamas Company manufactures pizza sauce through two production departments: Cooking and Canning. In each process, materials and conversion costs are incurred evenly throughout the process. For the month of April, the work in process accounts show the following debits.

	Cooking	**Canning**
Beginning work in process	$ –0–	$ 4,000
Materials	21,000	6,000
Labor	8,500	7,000
Overhead	29,500	25,800
Costs transferred in		53,000

Instructions
Journalize the April transactions.

E21-3   The ledger of Penland Company has the following work in process account.

Work in Process—Painting						
5/1	Balance	3,590	5/31	Transferred out		?
5/31	Materials	5,160				
5/31	Labor	2,740				
5/31	Overhead	1,650				
5/31	Balance	?				

Production records show that there were 400 units in the beginning inventory, 30% complete, 1,100 units started, and 1,200 units transferred out. The beginning work in process had materials cost of $2,040 and conversion costs of $1,550. The units in ending inventory were 40% complete. Materials are entered at the beginning of the painting process.

Instructions
(a) How many units are in process at May 31?
(b) What is the unit materials cost for May?
(c) What is the unit conversion cost for May?
(d) What is the total cost of units transferred out in May?
(e) What is the cost of the May 31 inventory?

E21-4 Kirk Manufacturing Company has two production departments: Cutting and Assembly. July 1 inventories are Raw Materials $4,200, Work in Process—Cutting $2,900, Work in Process—Assembly $10,600, and Finished Goods $31,000. During July, the following transactions occurred.

Journalize transactions for two processes.
(SO 4)

1. Purchased $62,500 of raw materials on account.
2. Incurred $56,000 of factory labor. (Credit Wages Payable.)
3. Incurred $70,000 of manufacturing overhead; $40,000 was paid and the remainder is unpaid.
4. Requisitioned materials for Cutting $15,700 and Assembly $8,900.
5. Used factory labor for Cutting $29,000 and Assembly $27,000.
6. Applied overhead at the rate of $15 per machine hour. Machine hours were Cutting 1,680 and Assembly 1,720.
7. Transferred goods costing $67,600 from the Cutting Department to the Assembly Department.
8. Transferred goods costing $134,900 from Assembly to Finished Goods.
9. Sold goods costing $150,000 for $200,000 on account.

Instructions
Journalize the transactions. (Omit explanations.)

E21-5 In Macadoo Company, materials are entered at the beginning of each process. Work in process inventories, with the percentage of work done on conversion costs, and production data for its Sterilizing Department in selected months during 2012 are as follows.

Compute physical units and equivalent units of production.
(SO 5, 6)

	Beginning Work in Process			Ending Work in Process	
Month	Units	Conversion Cost%	Units Transferred Out	Units	Conversion Cost%
January	–0–	—	7,000	2,000	60
March	–0–	—	12,000	3,000	30
May	–0–	—	16,000	5,000	80
July	–0–	—	10,000	1,500	40

Instructions
(a) Compute the physical units for January and May.
(b) Compute the equivalent units of production for (1) materials and (2) conversion costs for each month.

E21-6 The Cutting Department of Hong Manufacturing has the following production and cost data for July.

Determine equivalent units, unit costs, and assignment of costs.
(SO 5, 6)

Production	Costs	
1. Transferred out 9,000 units.	Beginning work in process	$ –0–
2. Started 3,000 units that are 60%	Materials	45,000
complete as to conversion	Labor	16,200
costs and 100% complete as	Manufacturing overhead	18,900
to materials at July 31.		

Materials are entered at the beginning of the process. Conversion costs are incurred uniformly during the process.

Instructions
(a) Determine the equivalent units of production for (1) materials and (2) conversion costs.
(b) Compute unit costs and prepare a cost reconciliation schedule.

E21-7 The Sanding Department of Saez Furniture Company has the following production and manufacturing cost data for March 2012, the first month of operation.

Prepare a production cost report.
(SO 5, 6, 7)

Production: 12,000 units finished and transferred out; 3,000 units started that are 100% complete as to materials and 20% complete as to conversion costs.
Manufacturing costs: Materials $33,000; labor $27,000; overhead $36,000.

Instructions

Prepare a production cost report.

Determine equivalent units, unit costs, and assignment of costs.

(SO 5, 6)

E21-8 The Blending Department of Peacock Company has the following cost and production data for the month of April.

Costs:	
Work in process, April 1	
Direct materials: 100% complete	$100,000
Conversion costs: 20% complete	70,000
Cost of work in process, April 1	$170,000
Costs incurred during production in April	
Direct materials	$ 800,000
Conversion costs	362,000
Costs incurred in April	$1,162,000

Units transferred out totaled 14,000. Ending work in process was 1,000 units that are 100% complete as to materials and 40% complete as to conversion costs.

Instructions

(a) Compute the equivalent units of production for (1) materials and (2) conversion costs for the month of April.

(b) Compute the unit costs for the month.

(c) Determine the costs to be assigned to the units transferred out and in ending work in process.

Determine equivalent units, unit costs, and assignment of costs.

(SO 5, 6)

E21-9 Eleby Company has gathered the following information.

Units in beginning work in process	–0–
Units started into production	36,000
Units in ending work in process	6,000
Percent complete for conversion costs in ending work in process	40%
Costs incurred:	
Direct materials	$72,000
Direct labor	$81,000
Overhead	$97,200

Instructions

(All materials added at the beginning of the process.)

(a) Compute equivalent units of production for materials and for conversion costs.

(b) Determine the unit costs of production.

(c) Show the assignment of costs to units transferred out and in process.

Determine equivalent units, unit costs, and assignment of costs.

(SO 5, 6)

E21-10 Red Sky Company has gathered the following information.

Units in beginning work in process	20,000
Units started into production	72,000
Units in ending work in process	24,000
Percent complete for conversion costs in ending work in process	60%
Costs incurred (includes beginning work in process):	
Direct materials	$101,200
Direct labor	$164,800
Overhead	$123,600

Instructions

(All materials added at the beginning of the process.)

(a) Compute equivalent units of production for materials and for conversion costs.

(b) Determine the unit costs of production.

(c) Show the assignment of costs to units transferred out and in process.

E21-11 The Polishing Department of Burgoa Manufacturing Company has the following production and manufacturing cost data for September. Materials are entered at the beginning of the process.

Compute equivalent units, unit costs, and costs assigned.
(SO 5, 6)

> *Production:* Beginning inventory 1,600 units that are 100% complete as to materials and 30% complete as to conversion costs; units started during the period are 18,400; ending inventory of 5,000 units 10% complete as to conversion costs.
>
> *Manufacturing costs:* Beginning inventory costs, comprised of $20,000 of materials and $43,180 of conversion costs; materials costs added in Polishing during the month, $177,200; labor and overhead applied in Polishing during the month, $102,680 and $257,140, respectively.

Instructions
(a) Compute the equivalent units of production for materials and conversion costs for the month of September.
(b) Compute the unit costs for materials and conversion costs for the month.
(c) Determine the costs to be assigned to the units transferred out and in process.

E21-12 Sid Vicious has recently been promoted to production manager, and so he has just started to receive various managerial reports. One of the reports he has received is the production cost report that you prepared. It showed that his department had 2,000 equivalent units in ending inventory. His department has had a history of not keeping enough inventory on hand to meet demand. He has come to you, very angry, and wants to know why you credited him with only 2,000 units when he knows he had at least twice that many on hand.

Explain the production cost report.
(SO 7)

Instructions

         Explain to him why his production cost report showed only 2,000 equivalent units in ending inventory. Write an informal memo. Be kind and explain very clearly why he is mistaken.

E21-13 The Welding Department of Castro Manufacturing Company has the following production and manufacturing cost data for February 2012. All materials are added at the beginning of the process.

Prepare a production cost report.
(SO 5, 6, 7)

Manufacturing Costs			Production Data	
Beginning work in process			Beginning work in process	15,000 units
Materials	$18,000			1/10 complete
Conversion costs	14,175	$32,175	Units transferred out	49,000
Materials		180,000	Units started	60,000
Labor		32,780	Ending work in process	26,000 units
Overhead		61,445		1/5 complete

Instructions
Prepare a production cost report for the Welding Department for the month of February.

E21-14 Debrozzo Shipping, Inc. is contemplating the use of process costing to track the costs of its operations. The operation consists of three segments (departments): receiving, shipping, and delivery. Containers are received at Debrozzo's docks and sorted according to the ship they will be carried on. The containers are loaded onto a ship, which carries them to the appropriate port of destination. The containers are then off-loaded and delivered to the receiving company.

Compute physical units and equivalent units of production.
(SO 5, 6)

    Debrozzo Shipping wants to begin using process costing in the shipping department. Direct materials represent the fuel costs to run the ship, and "Containers in transit" represents work in process. Listed below is information about the shipping department's first month's activity.

Containers in transit, April 1	0	
Containers loaded	800	
Containers in transit, April 30	350	40% of direct materials and 30% of conversion costs

Instructions
(a) Determine the physical flow of containers for the month.
(b) Calculate the equivalent units for direct materials and conversion costs.

*Determine equivalent units,
unit costs, and assignment
of costs.*
(SO 5, 6)

E21-15   Verber Mortgage Company uses a process costing system to accumulate costs in its loan application department. When an application is completed, it is forwarded to the loan department for final processing. The following processing and cost data pertain to September.

1. Applications in process on September 1, 100	Beginning WIP:
	Direct materials $ 1,000
2. Applications started in September, 900	Conversion costs 4,000
	September costs:
3. Completed applications during September, 800	Direct materials $ 4,000
	Direct labor 12,000
4. Applications still in process at September 30 were 100% complete as to materials (forms) and 60% complete as to conversion costs	Overhead 9,400

Materials are the forms used in the application process, and these costs are incurred at the beginning of the process. Conversion costs are incurred uniformly during the process.

Instructions
(a) Determine the equivalent units of service (production) for materials and conversion costs.
(b) Compute the unit costs and prepare a cost reconciliation schedule.

*Compute overhead rates and
assign overhead using ABC.*
(SO 10)

*E21-16   Imelda Instrument Inc. manufactures two products: missile range instruments and space pressure gauges. During January, 50 range instruments and 300 pressure gauges were produced, and overhead costs of $81,000 were incurred. An analysis of overhead costs reveals the following activities.

Activity	Cost Driver	Total Cost
1. Materials handling	Number of requisitions	$30,000
2. Machine setups	Number of setups	27,000
3. Quality inspections	Number of inspections	24,000

The cost driver volume for each product was as follows.

Cost Driver	Instruments	Gauges	Total
Number of requisitions	400	600	1,000
Number of setups	150	300	450
Number of inspections	200	400	600

Instructions
(a) Determine the overhead rate for each activity.
(b) Assign the manufacturing overhead costs for January to the two products using activity-based costing.
(c) Write a memo to the president of Imelda Instrument, explaining the benefits of activity-based costing.

*Compute product cost using
traditional costing and ABC.*
(SO 10)

*E21-17   Mathias Company manufactures a number of specialized machine parts. Part Bunkka-22 uses $35 of direct materials and $15 of direct labor per unit.

Mathias' estimated manufacturing overhead is as follows:

Materials handling	$100,000
Machining	200,000
Factory supervision	150,000
Total	$450,000

Overhead is applied based on direct labor costs, which were estimated at $200,000.

Mathias is considering adopting activity-based costing. The cost drivers are estimated at:

Activity	Cost Driver	Expected Use
Materials handling	Weight of materials	50,000 pounds
Machining	Machine hours	20,000 hours
Factory supervision	Direct labor hours	12,000 hours

Instructions

(a) Compute the cost of 1,000 units of Bunkka-22 using the current traditional costing system.

(b) Compute the cost of 1,000 units of Bunkka-22 using the proposed activity-based costing system. Assume the 1,000 units use 2,500 pounds of materials, 500 machine hours, and 1,000 direct labor hours.

Exercises: Set B

Visit the book's companion website, at **www.wiley.com/college/weygandt**, and choose the Student Companion site to access Exercise Set B.

Problems: Set A

P21-1A Zou Company manufactures bowling balls through two processes: Molding and Packaging. In the Molding Department, the urethane, rubber, plastics, and other materials are molded into bowling balls. In the Packaging Department, the balls are placed in cartons and sent to the finished goods warehouse. All materials are entered at the beginning of each process. Labor and manufacturing overhead are incurred uniformly throughout each process. Production and cost data for the Molding Department during June 2012 are presented below.

Complete four steps necessary to prepare a production cost report.
(SO 5, 6, 7)

Production Data	June
Beginning work in process units	–0–
Units started into production	20,000
Ending work in process units	2,000
Percent complete—ending inventory	60%

Cost Data	
Materials	$198,000
Labor	50,400
Overhead	112,800
Total	$361,200

Instructions

(a) Prepare a schedule showing physical units of production.

(b) Determine the equivalent units of production for materials and conversion costs.

(c) Compute the unit costs of production.

(d) Determine the costs to be assigned to the units transferred and in process for June.

(e) Prepare a production cost report for the Molding Department for the month of June.

P21-2A Chakos Industries Inc. manufactures in separate processes furniture for homes. In each process, materials are entered at the beginning, and conversion costs are incurred uniformly. Production and cost data for the first process in making two products in two different manufacturing plants are as follows.

Complete four steps necessary to prepare a production cost report.
(SO 5, 6, 7)

	Cutting Department	
	Plant 1	Plant 2
Production Data—July	T12-Tables	C10-Chairs
Work in process units, July 1	–0–	–0–
Units started into production	20,000	16,000
Work in process units, July 31	3,000	500
Work in process percent complete	60	80

Cost Data—July		
Work in process, July 1	$ –0–	$ –0–
Materials	380,000	288,000
Labor	234,400	125,900
Overhead	104,000	96,700
Total	$718,400	$510,600

Instructions
(a) For each plant:
    (1) Compute the physical units of production.
    (2) Compute equivalent units of production for materials and for conversion costs.
    (3) Determine the unit costs of production.
    (4) Show the assignment of costs to units transferred out and in process.
(b) Prepare the production cost report for Plant 1 for July 2012.

Journalize transactions.
(SO 3, 4)

P21-3A   Dees Company manufactures its product, Vitadrink, through two manufacturing processes: Mixing and Packaging. All materials are entered at the beginning of each process. On October 1, 2012, inventories consisted of Raw Materials $26,000, Work in Process—Mixing $0, Work in Process—Packaging $250,000, and Finished Goods $289,000. The beginning inventory for Packaging consisted of 10,000 units that were 50% complete as to conversion costs and fully complete as to materials. During October, 50,000 units were started into production in the Mixing Department and the following transactions were completed.

1. Purchased $300,000 of raw materials on account.
2. Issued raw materials for production: Mixing $210,000 and Packaging $45,000.
3. Incurred labor costs of $248,900.
4. Used factory labor: Mixing $182,500 and Packaging $66,400.
5. Incurred $790,000 of manufacturing overhead on account.
6. Applied manufacturing overhead on the basis of $22 per machine hour. Machine hours were 28,000 in Mixing and 6,000 in Packaging.
7. Transferred 45,000 units from Mixing to Packaging at a cost of $979,000.
8. Transferred 53,000 units from Packaging to Finished Goods at a cost of $1,315,000.
9. Sold goods costing $1,604,000 for $2,500,000 on account.

Instructions
Journalize the October transactions.

Assign costs and prepare
production cost report.
(SO 5, 6, 7)

P21-4A   Estrella Company has several processing departments. Costs charged to the Assembly Department for November 2012 totaled $2,229,000 as follows.

Work in process, November 1		
Materials	$69,000	
Conversion costs	48,150	$117,150
Materials added		1,548,000
Labor		225,920
Overhead		337,930

Production records show that 35,000 units were in beginning work in process 30% complete as to conversion costs, 700,000 units were started into production, and 25,000 units were in ending work in process 40% complete as to conversion costs. Materials are entered at the beginning of each process.

Instructions
(a) Determine the equivalent units of production and the unit production costs for the Assembly Department.
(b) Determine the assignment of costs to goods transferred out and in process.
(c) Prepare a production cost report for the Assembly Department.

Determine equivalent units and
unit costs and assign costs.
(SO 5, 6, 7)

P21-5A   Fong Company manufactures basketballs. Materials are added at the beginning of the production process and conversion costs are incurred uniformly. Production and cost data for the month of July 2012 are as follows.

Production Data—Basketballs	Units	Percent Complete
Work in process units, July 1	500	60%
Units started into production	1,000	
Work in process units, July 31	600	30%

Cost Data—Basketballs		
Work in process, July 1		
Materials	$750	
Conversion costs	600	$1,350
Direct materials		2,400
Direct labor		1,580
Manufacturing overhead		1,060

Instructions

(a) Calculate the following.

    (1) The equivalent units of production for materials and conversion.

    (2) The unit costs of production for materials and conversion costs.

    (3) The assignment of costs to units transferred out and in process at the end of the accounting period.

(b) Prepare a production cost report for the month of July for the basketballs.

P21-6A Martine Processing Company uses a weighted-average process costing system and manufactures a single product—a premium rug shampoo and cleaner. The manufacturing activity for the month of October has just been completed. A partially completed production cost report for the month of October for the mixing and cooking department is shown below.

Compute equivalent units and complete production cost report.

(SO 5, 7)

Instructions

(a) Prepare a schedule that shows how the equivalent units were computed so that you can complete the "Quantities: Units accounted for" equivalent units section shown in the production cost report, and compute October unit costs.

(b) Complete the "Cost Reconciliation Schedule" part of the production cost report below.

MARTINE PROCESSING COMPANY
Mixing and Cooking Department
Production Cost Report
For the Month Ended October 31

		Equivalent Units	
QUANTITIES	Physical Units	Materials	Conversion Costs
Units to be accounted for			
Work in process, October 1	20,000		
Started into production	160,000		
Total units	180,000		
Units accounted for			
Transferred out	130,000	?	?
Work in process, October 31			
(60% materials, 40%			
conversion costs)	50,000	?	?
Total units	180,000	?	?

COSTS		Conversion	
Unit costs	Materials	Costs	Total
Costs in October	$240,000	$105,000	$345,000
Equivalent units	?	?	
Unit costs	$? +	$? =	$?
Costs to be accounted for			
Work in process, October 1			$ 30,000
Started into production			315,000
Total costs			$345,000

COST RECONCILIATION SCHEDULE

Costs accounted for		
Transferred out		$?
Work in process, October 31		
Materials	?	
Conversion costs	?	?
Total costs		?

*P21-7A Gerber Electronics manufactures two large-screen television models: the Royale, which sells for $1,500, and a new model, the Majestic, which sells for $1,200. The production cost per unit for each model in 2012 is shown on the next page.

Assign overhead to products using ABC.

(SO 10)

	Royale	Majestic
Direct materials	$ 700	$420
Direct labor ($20 per hour)	100	80
Manufacturing overhead ($40 per DLH)	200	160
Total per unit cost	$1,000	$660

In 2012, Gerber manufactured 30,000 units of the Royale and 10,000 units of the Majestic. The overhead rate of $40 per direct labor hour was determined by dividing total expected manufacturing overhead of $7,600,000 by the total direct labor hours (190,000) for the two models.

The gross profit on the model was: Royale $500 ($1,500 − $1,000) and Majestic $540 ($1,200 − $660). Because of this difference, management is considering phasing out the Royale model and increasing the production of the Majestic model.

Before finalizing its decision, management asks the controller, Sally Fields, to prepare an analysis using activity-based costing. Sally accumulates the following information about overhead for the year ended December 31, 2012.

Activity	Cost Driver	Total Cost	Cost Driver Volume	Overhead Rate
Purchase orders	Number of orders	$1,200,000	30,000	$40
Machine setups	Number of setups	900,000	15,000	60
Machining	Machine hours	4,800,000	160,000	30
Quality control	Number of inspections	700,000	35,000	20

The cost driver volume for each product was:

Cost Driver	Royale	Majestic	Total
Purchase orders	16,000	14,000	30,000
Machine setups	5,000	10,000	15,000
Machine hours	100,000	60,000	160,000
Inspections	10,000	25,000	35,000

Instructions

(a) Assign the total 2012 manufacturing overhead costs to the two products using activity-based costing (ABC).

(b) What was the cost per unit and gross profit of each model using ABC costing?

(c) Are management's future plans for the two models sound?

Problems: Set B

Complete four steps necessary to prepare a production cost report.

(SO 5, 6, 7)

P21-1B Rivers Corporation manufactures water skis through two processes: Molding and Packaging. In the Molding Department, fiberglass is heated and shaped into the form of a ski. In the Packaging Department, the skis are placed in cartons and sent to the finished goods warehouse. Materials are entered at the beginning of both processes. Labor and manufacturing overhead are incurred uniformly throughout each process. Production and cost data for the Molding Department for January 2012 are presented below.

Production Data	January
Beginning work in process units	–0–
Units started into production	42,500
Ending work in process units	2,500
Percent complete—ending inventory	40%

Cost Data	
Materials	$510,000
Labor	96,000
Overhead	150,000
Total	$756,000

Instructions
(a) Compute the physical units of production.
(b) Determine the equivalent units of production for materials and conversion costs.
(c) Compute the unit costs of production.
(d) Determine the costs to be assigned to the units transferred out and in process.
(e) Prepare a production cost report for the Molding Department for the month of January.

P21-2B Klein Corporation manufactures in separate processes refrigerators and freezers for homes. In each process, materials are entered at the beginning and conversion costs are incurred uniformly. Production and cost data for the first process in making two products in two different manufacturing plants are as follows.

Complete four steps necessary to prepare a production cost report.
(SO 5, 6, 7)

	Stamping Department	
Production Data—June	**Plant A** **R12 Refrigerators**	**Plant B** **F24 Freezers**
Work in process units, June 1	–0–	–0–
Units started into production	21,000	20,000
Work in process units, June 30	4,000	2,500
Work in process percent complete	75	60
Cost Data—June		
Work in process, June 1	$ –0–	$ –0–
Materials	840,000	720,000
Labor	220,000	221,000
Overhead	420,000	292,000
Total	$1,480,000	$1,233,000

Instructions
(a) For each plant:
   (1) Compute the physical units of production.
   (2) Compute equivalent units of production for materials and for conversion costs.
   (3) Determine the unit costs of production.
   (4) Show the assignment of costs to units transferred out and in process.
(b) Prepare the production cost report for Plant A for June 2012.

P21-3B Forrest Company manufactures a nutrient, Everlife, through two manufacturing processes: Blending and Packaging. All materials are entered at the beginning of each process. On August 1, 2012, inventories consisted of Raw Materials $5,000, Work in Process—Blending $0, Work in Process—Packaging $3,945, and Finished Goods $7,500. The beginning inventory for Packaging consisted of 500 units, two-fifths complete as to conversion costs and fully complete as to materials. During August, 9,000 units were started into production in Blending, and the following transactions were completed.

Journalize transactions.
(SO 3, 4)

1. Purchased $25,000 of raw materials on account.
2. Issued raw materials for production: Blending $18,930 and Packaging $9,140.
3. Incurred labor costs of $23,770.
4. Used factory labor: Blending $13,320 and Packaging $10,450.
5. Incurred $41,500 of manufacturing overhead on account.
6. Applied manufacturing overhead at the rate of $25 per machine hour. Machine hours were Blending 900 and Packaging 300.
7. Transferred 8,200 units from Blending to Packaging at a cost of $44,940.
8. Transferred 8,600 units from Packaging to Finished Goods at a cost of $67,490.
9. Sold goods costing $62,000 for $90,000 on account.

Instructions
Journalize the August transactions.

P21-4B Ignatenko Company has several processing departments. Costs charged to the Assembly Department for October 2012 totaled $1,249,500 as follows.

Assign costs and prepare production cost report.
(SO 5, 6, 7)

Work in process, October 1		
Materials	$29,000	
Conversion costs	16,500	$ 45,500
Materials added		1,006,000
Labor		90,000
Overhead		108,000

Production records show that 25,000 units were in beginning work in process 40% complete as to conversion cost, 425,000 units were started into production, and 35,000 units were in ending work in process 40% complete as to conversion costs. Materials are entered at the beginning of each process.

Instructions
(a) Determine the equivalent units of production and the unit production costs for the Assembly Department.
(b) Determine the assignment of costs to goods transferred out and in process.
(c) Prepare a production cost report for the Assembly Department.

Determine equivalent units and unit costs and assign costs.
(SO 5, 6, 7)

P21-5B   Forte Company manufactures bicycles and tricycles. For both products, materials are added at the beginning of the production process, and conversion costs are incurred uniformly. Production and cost data for the month of May are as follows.

Production Data—Bicycles	Units	Percent Complete
Work in process units, May 1	500	80%
Units started in production	1,500	
Work in process units, May 31	800	25%

Cost Data—Bicycles		
Work in process, May 1		
Materials	$15,000	
Conversion costs	18,000	$33,000
Direct materials		50,000
Direct labor		18,320
Manufacturing overhead		33,680

Instructions
(a) Calculate the following.
   (1) The equivalent units of production for materials and conversion.
   (2) The unit costs of production for materials and conversion costs.
   (3) The assignment of costs to units transferred out and in process at the end of the accounting period.
(b) Prepare a production cost report for the month of May for the bicycles.

Compute equivalent units and complete production cost report.
(SO 5, 7)

P21-6B   Thang Cleaner Company uses a weighted-average process costing system and manufactures a single product—an all-purpose liquid cleaner. The manufacturing activity for the month of March has just been completed. A partially completed production cost report for the month of March for the mixing and blending department is shown below.

THANG CLEANER COMPANY
Mixing and Blending Department
Production Cost Report
For the Month Ended March 31

		Equivalent Units	
QUANTITIES	Physical Units	Materials	Conversion Costs
Units to be accounted for			
Work in process, March 1	10,000		
Started into production	100,000		
Total units	110,000		
Units accounted for			
Transferred out	95,000	?	?
Work in process, March 31			
(60% materials, 20%			
conversion costs)	15,000	?	?
Total units	110,000	?	?

COSTS		Conversion	
Unit costs	**Materials**	**Costs**	**Total**
Costs in March	$156,000	$ 98,000	$254,000
Equivalent units	?	?	
Unit costs	$? +	$? =	$?

Costs to be accounted for		
Work in process, March 1		$ 8,700
Started into production		245,300
Total costs		$254,000

COST RECONCILIATION SCHEDULE

Costs accounted for		
Transferred out		$?
Work in process, March 31		
Materials	?	
Conversion costs	?	?
Total costs		?

Instructions

(a) Prepare a schedule that shows how the equivalent units were computed so that you can complete the "Quantities: Units accounted for" equivalent units section shown in the production cost report above, and compute March unit costs.

(b) Complete the "Cost Reconciliation Schedule" part of the production cost report above.

Problems: Set C

Visit the book's companion website, at **www.wiley.com/college/weygandt**, and choose the Student Companion site to access Problem Set C.

Waterways Continuing Problem

(*Note:* This is a continuation of the Waterways Problem from Chapters 19 and 20.)

WCP21 Because most of the parts for its irrigation systems are standard, Waterways handles the majority of its manufacturing as a process cost system. There are multiple process departments. Three of these departments are the Molding, Cutting, and Welding departments. All items eventually end up in the Packaging department which prepares items for sale in kits or individually. This problem asks you to help Waterways calculate equivalent units and prepare a production cost report.

Go to the book's companion website, **www.wiley.com/college/weygandt**, *to find the remainder of this problem.*

BROADENINGYOURPERSPECTIVE

Decision Making Across the Organization

BYP21-1 Sea Breeze Beach Company manufactures suntan lotion, called Surtan, in 11-ounce plastic bottles. Surtan is sold in a competitive market. As a result, management is very cost-conscious. Surtan is manufactured through two processes: mixing and filling. Materials are entered at the beginning of each process and labor and manufacturing overhead occur uniformly throughout each process. Unit costs are based on the cost per gallon of Surtan using the weighted-average costing approach.

On June 30, 2012, Rita Jenz, the chief accountant for the past 20 years, opted to take early retirement. Her replacement, Neil Benton, had extensive accounting experience with motels in the area but only limited contact with manufacturing accounting. During July, Neil correctly accumulated the following production quantity and cost data for the Mixing Department.

Production quantities: Work in process, July 1, 8,000 gallons 75% complete; started into production 91,000 gallons; work in process, July 31, 5,000 gallons 20% complete. Materials are added at the beginning of the process.

Production costs: Beginning work in process $88,000, comprised of $21,000 of materials costs and $67,000 of conversion costs; incurred in July: materials $573,000, conversion costs $769,000.

Neil then prepared a production cost report on the basis of physical units started into production. His report showed a production cost of $15.71 per gallon of Surtan. The management of Sea Breeze Beach was surprised at the high unit cost. The president comes to you, as Rita's top assistant, to review Neil's report and prepare a correct report if necessary.

Instructions

With the class divided into groups, answer the following questions.

(a) Show how Neil arrived at the unit cost of $15.71 per gallon of Surtan.
(b) What error(s) did Neil make in preparing his production cost report?
(c) Prepare a correct production cost report for July.

Managerial Analysis

BYP21-2   Lorena Furniture Company manufactures living room furniture through two departments: Framing and Upholstering. Materials are entered at the beginning of each process. For May, the following cost data are obtained from the two work in process accounts.

	Framing	Upholstering
Work in process, May 1	$ –0–	$?
Materials	420,000	?
Conversion costs	280,000	330,000
Costs transferred in	–0–	600,000
Costs transferred out	600,000	?
Work in process, May 31	100,000	?

Instructions

Answer the following questions.

(a) If 3,000 sofas were started into production on May 1 and 2,500 sofas were transferred to Upholstering, what was the unit cost of materials for May in the Framing Department?
(b) Using the data in (a) above, what was the per unit conversion cost of the sofas transferred to Upholstering?
(c) Continuing the assumptions in (a) above, what is the percentage of completion of the units in process at May 31 in the Framing Department?

On the Web

BYP21-3   Search the Internet and find the websites of two manufacturers that you think are likely to use process costing. Are there any specifics included in their websites that confirm the use of process costing for each of these companies?

Communication Activity

BYP21-4   Meg Ryan was a good friend of yours in high school and is from your home town. While you chose to major in accounting when you both went away to college, she majored in marketing and management. You have recently been promoted to accounting manager for the Snack Foods Division of Tranh Enterprises, and your friend was promoted to regional sales manager for the same division of Tranh. Meg recently telephoned you. She explained that she was familiar with job cost sheets, which had been used by the Special Projects division where she had formerly worked. She was, however, very uncomfortable with the production cost reports prepared by your division. She emailed you a list of her particular questions:

1. Since Tranh occasionally prepares snack foods for special orders in the Snack Foods Division, why don't we track costs of the orders separately?
2. What is an equivalent unit?
3. Why am I getting four production cost reports? Isn't there one Work in Process account?

Instructions

Prepare a memo to Meg. Answer her questions, and include any additional information you think would be helpful. You may write informally, but do use proper grammar and punctuation.

Ethics Case

BYP21-5 E. E. Cummings Company manufactures a high-tech component that passes through two production processing departments, Molding and Assembly. Department managers are partially compensated
on the basis of units of products completed and transferred out relative to units of product put into production. This was intended as encouragement to be efficient and to minimize waste.

Wendy Soo is the department head in the Molding Department, and Bart Fender is her quality control inspector. During the month of June, Wendy had three new employees who were not yet technically
skilled. As a result, many of the units produced in June had minor molding defects. In order to maintain the
department's normal high rate of completion, Wendy told Bart to pass through inspection and on to the
Assembly Department all units that had defects nondetectable to the human eye. "Company and industry
tolerances on this product are too high anyway," says Wendy. "Less than 2% of the units we produce are
subjected in the market to the stress tolerance we've designed into them. The odds of those 2% being any
of this month's units are even less. Anyway, we're saving the company money."

Instructions
(a) Who are the potential stakeholders involved in this situation?
(b) What alternatives does Bart have in this situation? What might the company do to prevent this situation from occurring?

"All About You" Activity

BYP21-6 Many of you ultimately will work in service environments, such as medical facilities. Many
service organizations have adopted activity-based management systems, which incorporate activity-based
costing concepts throughout the organization.

Mt. Walton Hospital is a primary medical health-care facility and trauma center that serves 11 small,
rural Midwestern communities within a 40-mile radius. The hospital offers all the medical/surgical services
of a typical small hospital. It has a staff of 18 full-time doctors and 20 part-time visiting specialists. Mt. Walton
has a payroll of 150 employees, consisting of nurses, technicians, therapists, dieticians, managers, directors,
administrators, secretaries, data processors, and janitors.

Instructions
(a) Using your existing knowledge (however limited, moderate, or in-depth) of a hospital's operations,
identify as many *activities* as you can that would serve as the basis for implementing an activity-based
costing system.
(b) For each of the activities listed in **(a)**, identify a *cost driver* that would serve as a valid measure of the
resources consumed in the activity.

Answers to Insight and Accounting Across the Organization Questions

p. 971 Choosing a Cost Driver   Q: What is the result if a company uses the wrong "cost driver" to assign
manufacturing overhead? **A:** Incorrect application of manufacturing overhead will result in some products receiving too much overhead and others receiving too little.

p. 976 Keeping Score for the Xbox   Q: In what ways has cost accounting probably become more critical
for Microsoft in recent years? **A:** In the past Microsoft enjoyed very high profit margins on its software
sales. As a consequence, it could afford to be less cost-conscious than most companies. In addition, in
producing software, manufacturing costs represented a very small part of its total product cost. But the
video-game hardware market is very competitive. In order to achieve its profitability goals, Microsoft will
have to manufacture its product efficiently in order to meet its cost targets to ensure adequate margins.
The information provided by process cost accounting will be critical to its efforts.

Answers to Self-Test Questions

1. b **2.** d **3.** c **4.** b **5.** c **6.** b **7.** b $20,000 + (60\% \times 5,000)$ **8.** a $(0 + 7,000)$ **9.** c $(23,000 + 3,000)$;
$(23,000 + 1,000)$ **10.** a $\$60,000 \div (9,000 + 3,000)$ **11.** b $[(2,500 \times 40\%) \times \$30] + (2,500 \times \$10)$
12. b **13.** d **14.** d **15.** c **16.** a **17.** c **18.** b $(\$100 \times 80)$; $(\$100 \times 60)$

The Navigator

✔ **Remember to go back to the Navigator box on the chapter
opening page and check off your completed work.**

CHAPTER22

Cost-Volume-Profit

Study Objectives

After studying this chapter, you should be able to:

[1] Distinguish between variable and fixed costs.

[2] Explain the significance of the relevant range.

[3] Explain the concept of mixed costs.

[4] List the five components of cost-volume-profit analysis.

[5] Indicate what contribution margin is and how it can be expressed.

[6] Identify the three ways to determine the break-even point.

[7] Give the formulas for determining sales required to earn target net income.

[8] Define margin of safety, and give the formulas for computing it.

[9] Describe the essential features of a cost-volume-profit income statement.

The Navigator

✔ The Navigator

Feature Story

UNDERSTANDING MEDICAL COSTS MIGHT LEAD TO BETTER HEALTH CARE

Dr. Brian Forrest was frustrated with the standard approach to the practice of medicine. He was forced to see too many patients for too few minutes per patient—so he did something about it. He started a small medical practice that flew directly in the face of virtually every accepted assumption of modern medicine. Today, his practice can break even on 4 patients per day.

How did he do it? First, he identified all non–value-adding expenditures. A normal medical practice needs lots of employees to collect money from insurance companies or from past-due accounts. Dr. Forrest completely eliminated the need for these employees (and thus eliminated these costs) by requiring patients to pay cash at the time of service.

Dr. Forrest's fees are significantly lower than a standard clinic. He charges a flat $45 office visit fee (no matter how long he is with a patient), plus patients pay for lab and supply costs, which average $37 per visit. To keep his rate so low and still spend a lot of time with patients, he has to keep tight control of his costs. That is, to lower his break-even point, he needs to keep his fixed costs down. His overhead costs average just 25 percent of revenue, compared to 40 to 60 percent of revenue for a standard practice. He buys his equipment from a hospital surplus store (e.g., $100 for an exam table versus $1,500 new) and tries to keep his office space to a minimum. Dr. Forrest saves about $10,000 per year by not hiring a janitorial service. Instead, he and the other two employees share the cleaning tasks, and he takes out his own trash.

To increase his ability to service more patients, Dr. Forrest hired a nurse-practitioner. To keep his fixed costs down, she was hired on a "productivity basis," that is, she is paid per patient. Thus, her cost to the practice represents a variable cost, as her wages are paid out of the incremental revenue that she produces. Interestingly, the nurse-practitioner has found that under this approach, she is able to spend more time with her patients than she did in other practices. Yet, she actually makes more money. This is an unusual approach because in most medical practices, nearly all of the labor costs are fixed.

Dr. Forrest originally anticipated that most of his patients would be people without insurance, since he is unwilling to accept payments from insurance companies. He expected that people with insurance would not be willing to incur out-of-pocket expenses for health care. However, because his patients appreciate that he spends much more time with them than a traditional doctor, more than 50% of his patients have insurance. He is happy, and so are his patients.

Source: Brian R. Forrest, M.D., "Breaking Even on 4 Visits Per Day," Family Practice Management website (*www.aafp.org/fpm*, 2007). (*Note:* Copyrights are available at copyrights@aafp.org.)

Inside**CHAPTER22**

PreviewofCHAPTER22

As the Feature Story indicates, to manage any size business you must understand how costs respond to changes in sales volume and the effect of costs and revenues on profits. A prerequisite to understanding cost-volume-profit (CVP) relationships is knowledge of how costs behave. In this chapter, we first explain the considerations involved in cost behavior analysis. Then we discuss and illustrate CVP analysis.

The content and organization of Chapter 22 are as follows.

Cost-Volume-Profit	
Cost Behavior Analysis	**Cost-Volume-Profit Analysis**
• Variable costs • Fixed costs • Relevant range • Mixed costs • Identifying variable and fixed costs	• Basic components • CVP income statement • Break-even analysis • Target net income • Margin of safety • Changes in business environment • CVP income statement revisited

The Navigator

Cost Behavior Analysis

Cost behavior analysis is the study of how specific costs respond to changes in the level of business activity. As you might expect, some costs change, and others remain the same. For example, for an airline company such as Southwest or United, the longer the flight the higher the fuel costs. On the other hand, Massachusetts General Hospital's costs to staff the emergency room on any given night are relatively constant regardless of the number of patients treated. A knowledge of cost behavior helps management plan operations and decide between alternative courses of action. Cost behavior analysis applies to all types of entities, as the Feature Story about Dr. Forrest's medical practice indicates.

The starting point in cost behavior analysis is measuring the key business activities. Activity levels may be expressed in terms of sales dollars (in a retail company), miles driven (in a trucking company), room occupancy (in a hotel), or dance classes taught (by a dance studio). Many companies use more than one measurement base. A manufacturer, for example, may use direct labor hours or units of output for manufacturing costs and sales revenue or units sold for selling expenses.

For an activity level to be useful in cost behavior analysis, changes in the level or volume of activity should be correlated with changes in costs. The activity level selected is referred to as the activity (or volume) index. The **activity index** identifies the activity that causes changes in the behavior of costs. With an appropriate activity index, companies can classify the behavior of costs in response to changes in activity levels into three categories: variable, fixed, or mixed.

Variable Costs

Study Objective [1]
Distinguish between variable and fixed costs.

Variable costs are costs that vary **in total** directly and proportionately with changes in the activity level. If the level increases 10%, total variable costs will increase 10%. If the level of activity decreases by 25%, variable costs will decrease 25%.

Examples of variable costs include direct materials and direct labor for a manufacturer; cost of goods sold, sales commissions, and freight-out for a merchandiser; and gasoline in airline and trucking companies. A variable cost may also be defined as a cost that **remains the same *per unit* at every level of activity**.

To illustrate the behavior of a variable cost, assume that Damon Company manufactures radios that contain a $10 digital clock. The activity index is the number of radios produced. As Damon manufactures each radio, the total cost of the clocks increases by $10. As part (a) of Illustration 22-1 shows, total cost of the clocks will be $20,000 if Damon produces 2,000 radios, and $100,000 when it produces 10,000 radios. We also can see that a variable cost remains the same per unit as the level of activity changes. As part (b) of Illustration 22-1 shows, the unit cost of $10 for the clocks is the same whether Damon produces 2,000 or 10,000 radios.

Illustration 22-1
Behavior of total and unit variable costs

Helpful Hint

True or false: Variable cost per unit changes directly and proportionately with changes in activity. Answer: False. Per unit cost remains constant at all levels of activity.

Companies that rely heavily on labor to manufacture a product, such as Nike or Reebok, or to provide a service, such as Hilton or Marriott, are likely to have many variable costs. In contrast, companies that use a high proportion of machinery and equipment in producing revenue, such as AT&T or Duke Energy Co., may have few variable costs.

Fixed Costs

Fixed costs are costs that **remain the same in total** regardless of changes in the activity level. Examples include property taxes, insurance, rent, supervisory salaries, and depreciation on buildings and equipment. Because total fixed costs remain constant as activity changes, it follows that **fixed costs *per unit* vary inversely with activity: As volume increases, unit cost declines, and vice versa**.

To illustrate the behavior of fixed costs, assume that Damon Company leases its productive facilities at a cost of $10,000 per month. Total fixed costs of the facilities will remain constant at every level of activity, as part (a) of Illustration 22-2 (page 1014) shows. But, on a per unit basis, the cost of rent will decline as activity increases, as part (b) of Illustration 22-2 shows. At 2,000 units, the unit cost is $5 ($10,000 ÷ 2,000). When Damon produces 10,000 radios, the unit cost is only $1 ($10,000 ÷ 10,000).

Illustration 22-2
Behavior of total and unit
fixed costs

(a)
Total Fixed Costs
(Rent Expense)

(b)
Fixed Costs per Unit
(Rent Expense)

The trend for many manufacturers is to have more fixed costs and fewer variable costs. This trend is the result of increased use of automation and less use of employee labor. As a result, depreciation and lease charges (fixed costs) increase, whereas direct labor costs (variable costs) decrease.

Management Insight

Woodworker Runs an Efficient Operation for Producing Furniture

When Thomas Moser quit teaching communications at Bates College 25 years ago, he turned to what he loved doing—furniture woodworking. Today he has over 120 employees. In a business where profit margins are seldom thicker than wood shavings, cost control is everything. Moser keeps no inventory; he uses customers' 50% deposits on orders to buy the wood. Because computer-driven machines cut most of the standardized parts and joints, "we're free to be inefficient in assembly and finishing work, where the craft is most obviously expressed," says Moser. Direct labor costs are a manageable 30% of revenues. By keeping a tight lid on costs and running an efficient operation, Moser is free to spend most of his time doing what he enjoys most—designing furniture.

Source: Excerpts from "Out of the Woods," *Forbes* (April 5, 1999), p. 74.

 Are the costs associated with use of the computer-driven cutting machines fixed or variable? (See page 1050.)

Relevant Range

Study Objective [2]

Explain the significance of the relevant range.

In Illustration 22-1, part (a) (page 1013), a straight line is drawn throughout the entire range of the activity index for total variable costs. In essence, the assumption is that the costs are **linear**. If a relationship is linear (that is, straight-line), then changes in the activity index will result in a direct, proportional change in the variable cost. For example, if the activity level doubles, the cost doubles.

It is now necessary to ask: Is the straight-line relationship realistic? Does the linear assumption produce useful data for CVP analysis?

In most business situations, a straight-line relationship **does not exist** for variable costs throughout the entire range of possible activity. At abnormally low levels of activity, it may be impossible to be cost-efficient. Small-scale operations may not allow the company to obtain quantity discounts for raw materials or to use specialized labor. In contrast, at abnormally high levels of activity, labor costs may increase sharply because of overtime pay. Also at high activity levels, materials costs may jump significantly because of excess spoilage caused by worker fatigue.

As a result, in the real world, the relationship between the behavior of a variable cost and changes in the activity level is often **curvilinear**, as shown in part (a) of Illustration 22-3. In the curved sections of the line, a change in the activity index will not result in a direct, proportional change in the variable cost. That is, a doubling of the activity index will not result in an exact doubling of the variable cost. The variable cost may more than double, or it may be less than double.

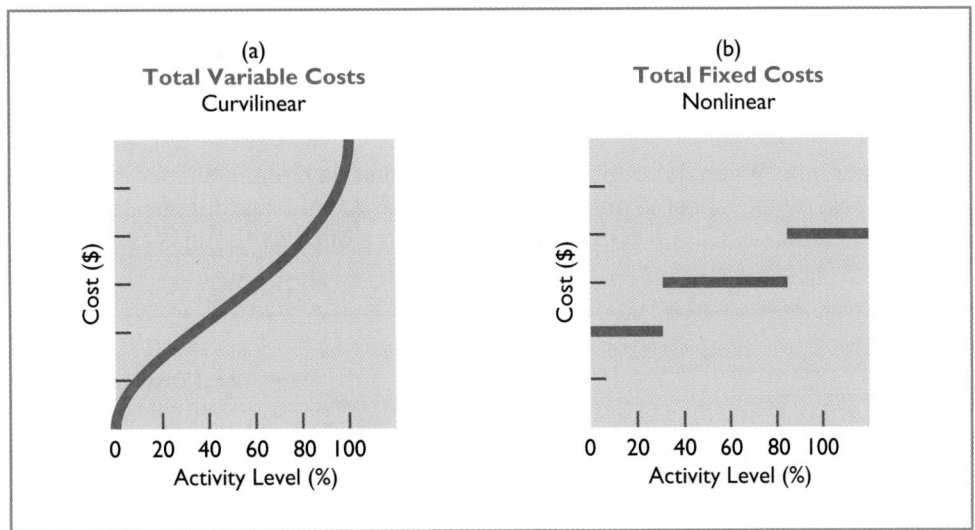

Illustration 22-3
Nonlinear behavior of variable and fixed costs

Total fixed costs also do not have a straight-line relationship over the entire range of activity. Some fixed costs will not change. But it is possible for management to change other fixed costs. For example, in the Feature Story, Dr. Forrest changed the nurse-practitioner's pay from a fixed cost to a variable cost. Illustration 22-3, part (b), shows an example of the behavior of total fixed costs through all potential levels of activity.

For most companies, operating at almost zero or at 100% capacity is the exception rather than the rule. Instead, companies often operate over a somewhat narrower range, such as 40–80% of capacity. The range over which a company expects to operate during a year is called the **relevant range** of the activity index. Within the relevant range, as both diagrams in Illustration 22-4 (page 1016) show, a straight-line relationship generally exists for both variable and fixed costs.

As you can see, although the linear (straight-line) relationship may not be completely realistic, **the linear assumption produces useful data for CVP analysis as long as the level of activity remains within the relevant range.**

Helpful Hint

Fixed costs that may be changeable include research, such as new product development, and management training programs.

Alternative Terminology

The relevant range is also called the *normal* or *practical range*.

Mixed Costs

Mixed costs are costs that contain both a variable element and a fixed element. **Mixed costs, therefore, change in total but not proportionately with changes in the activity level.**

The rental of a U-Haul truck is a good example of a mixed cost. Assume that local rental terms for a 17-foot truck, including insurance, are $50 per day plus

Study Objective [3]
Explain the concept of mixed costs.

Illustration 22-4
Linear behavior within
relevant range

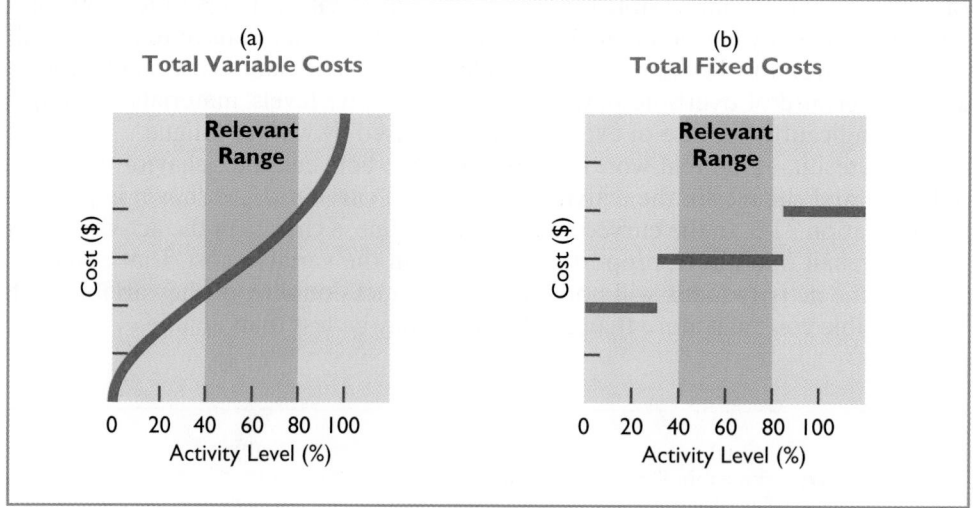

50 cents per mile. When determining the cost of a one-day rental, the per day charge is a fixed cost (with respect to miles driven), whereas the mileage charge is a variable cost. The graphic presentation of the rental cost for a one-day rental is as follows.

Illustration 22-5
Behavior of a mixed cost

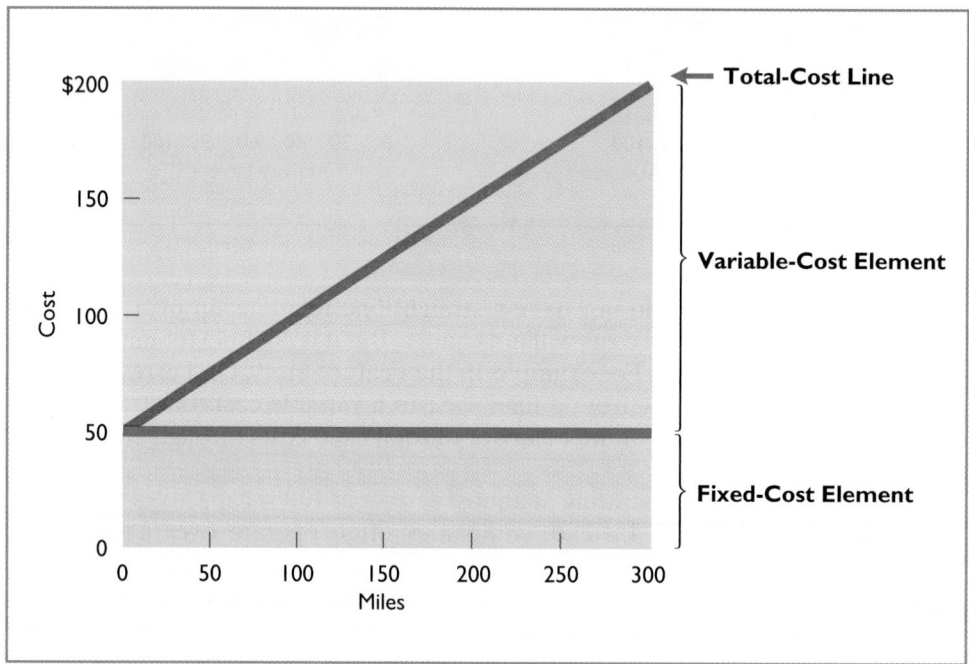

In this case, the fixed-cost element is the cost of having the service available. The variable-cost element is the cost of actually using the service. Another example of a mixed cost is utility costs (electric, telephone, and so on), where there is a flat service fee plus a usage charge.

For purposes of CVP analysis, **mixed costs must be classified into their fixed and variable elements**. How does management make the classification? One possibility is to determine the variable and fixed components each time a mixed cost is incurred. But because of time and cost constraints, this approach is rarely followed. Instead, the usual approach is to collect data on the behavior of the mixed costs at various levels of activity. Analysts then identify the fixed and variable cost components. Companies use various types of analysis. One type of analysis, called the **high-low method**, is discussed in the next section. Other methods, such as the scatter diagram method and least squares regression analysis, are more appropriately explained in cost accounting courses.

Do it!

Helena Company reports the following total costs at two levels of production.

Types of Costs

	10,000 Units	20,000 Units
Direct materials	$20,000	$40,000
Maintenance	8,000	10,000
Direct labor	17,000	34,000
Indirect materials	1,000	2,000
Depreciation	4,000	4,000
Utilities	3,000	5,000
Rent	6,000	6,000

Classify each cost as variable, fixed, or mixed.

action plan

✔ Recall that a variable cost varies in total directly and proportionately with each change in activity.

✔ Recall that a fixed cost remains the same in total with each change in activity.

✔ Recall that a mixed cost changes in total but not proportionately with each change in activity.

Solution

> Variable costs: Direct materials, direct labor, and indirect materials are variable costs.
>
> Fixed costs: Depreciation and rent are fixed costs.
>
> Mixed costs: Maintenance and utilities are mixed costs.

Related exercise material: BE22-1, BE22-2, E22-1, E22-2, E22-3, and **Do it!** 22-1.

The Navigator

HIGH-LOW METHOD

The **high-low method** uses the total costs incurred at the high and low levels of activity to classify mixed costs into fixed and variable components. The difference in costs between the high and low levels represents variable costs, since only the variable cost element can change as activity levels change.

The steps in computing fixed and variable costs under this method are as follows.

1. **Determine variable cost per unit from the following formula.**

Change in Total Costs	÷	High minus Low Activity Level	=	Variable Cost per Unit

Illustration 22-6
Formula for variable cost per unit using high-low method

To illustrate, assume that Metro Transit Company has the following maintenance costs and mileage data for its fleet of buses over a 4-month period.

Illustration 22-7
Assumed maintenance costs and mileage data

Month	Miles Driven	Total Cost	Month	Miles Driven	Total Cost
January	20,000	$30,000	March	35,000	$49,000
February	40,000	48,000	April	50,000	63,000

The high and low levels of activity are 50,000 miles in April and 20,000 miles in January. The maintenance costs at these two levels are $63,000 and $30,000, respectively. The difference in maintenance costs is $33,000 ($63,000 − $30,000), and the difference in miles is 30,000 (50,000 − 20,000). Therefore, for Metro Transit, variable cost per unit is $1.10, computed as follows.

$$\$33,000 \div 30,000 = \$1.10$$

2. **Determine the fixed cost by subtracting the total variable cost at either the high or the low activity level from the total cost at that activity level.**

For Metro Transit, the computations are shown in Illustration 22-8.

Illustration 22-8
High-low method computation of fixed costs

Metro Transit.xls				
File Edit View Insert Format Tools Data Window Help Acrobat				
	A	B	C	D
1		METRO TRANSIT		
2			Activity Level	
3			High	Low
4	Total cost		$63,000	$30,000
5	Less:	Variable costs		
6		50,000 × $1.10	55,000	
7		20,000 × $1.10		22,000
8	Total fixed costs		$ 8,000	$ 8,000

Maintenance costs are therefore $8,000 per month plus $1.10 per mile. This is represented by the following formula:

$$\text{Maintenance costs} = \text{Fixed costs} + (\$1.10 \times \text{miles driven})$$

For example, at 45,000 miles, estimated maintenance costs would be $8,000 fixed and $49,500 variable ($1.10 × 45,000) for a total of $57,500.

The high-low method generally produces a reasonable estimate for analysis. However, it does not produce a precise measurement of the fixed and variable elements in a mixed cost because it ignores other activity levels in the computation.

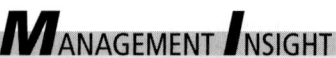

MANAGEMENT INSIGHT

Skilled Labor Is Truly Essential

The recession that started in 2008 had devastating implications for employment. But one surprise was that for some manufacturers, the number of jobs lost was actually lower than in previous recessions. One of the main explanations for this was that between 2000 and 2008, many factories adopted lean manufacturing practices. This meant that production relied less on large numbers of low-skilled workers, and more on machines and a few highly skilled workers. As a result of this approach, a single employee was supporting far more dollars in sales. Thus, it would require a larger decline in sales before an employee would need to be laid-off in order to continue to break even. Also, because the employees are highly skilled, employers are reluctant to lose them. Instead of lay-offs, many manufacturers have resorted to cutting employees hours.

Source: Timothy Aeppel and Justin Lahart, "Lean Factories Find It Hard to Cut Jobs Even in a Slump," *Wall Street Journal Online* (March 9, 2009).

 Would you characterize labor costs as being a fixed cost, a variable cost, or something else in this situation? (See page 1050.)

Importance of Identifying Variable and Fixed Costs

Why is it important to segregate costs into variable and fixed elements? The answer may become apparent if we look at the following four business decisions.

1. If American Airlines is to make a profit when it reduces all domestic fares by 30%, what reduction in costs or increase in passengers will be required?
   Answer: To make a profit when it cuts domestic fares by 30%, American Airlines will have to increase the number of passengers or cut its variable costs for those flights. Its fixed costs will not change.

2. If Ford Motor Company meets workers' demands for higher wages, what increase in sales revenue will be needed to maintain current profit levels?
   Answer: Higher wages at Ford Motor Company will increase the variable costs of manufacturing automobiles. To maintain present profit levels, Ford will have to cut other variable costs or increase the price of its automobiles.

3. If United States Steel Corp.'s program to modernize plant facilities through significant equipment purchases reduces the work force by 50%, what will be the effect on the cost of producing one ton of steel?
   Answer: The modernizing of plant facilities at United States Steel Corp. changes the proportion of fixed and variable costs of producing one ton of steel. Fixed costs increase because of higher depreciation charges, whereas variable costs decrease due to the reduction in the number of steelworkers.

4. What happens if Kellogg Company increases its advertising expenses but cannot increase prices because of competitive pressure?
   Answer: Sales volume must be increased to cover the increase in fixed advertising costs.

Do it!

Byrnes Company accumulates the following data concerning a mixed cost, using units produced as the activity level.

High-Low Method

	Units Produced	Total Cost
March	9,800	$14,740
April	8,500	13,250
May	7,000	11,100
June	7,600	12,000
July	8,100	12,460

(a) Compute the variable and fixed cost elements using the high-low method.

(b) Estimate the total cost if the company produces 6,000 units.

Solution

(a) Variable cost: ($14,740 − $11,100) ÷ (9,800 − 7,000) = $1.30 per unit
  Fixed cost: $14,740 − $12,740 ($1.30 × 9,800 units) = $2,000
      or $11,100 − $9,100 ($1.30 × 7,000) = $2,000

(b) Total cost to produce 6,000 units: $2,000 + $7,800 ($1.30 × 6,000) = $9,800

action plan

✔ Determine the highest and lowest levels of activity.

✔ Compute variable cost per unit as: Change in total costs ÷ High − Low activity level = Variable cost per unit.

✔ Compute fixed cost as: Total cost − (Variable cost per unit × Units produced) = Fixed cost.

Related exercise material: BE22-3, BE22-4, E22-1, E22-2, E22-3, and **Do it!** 22-2.

The Navigator

Cost-Volume-Profit Analysis

Cost-volume-profit (CVP) analysis is the study of the effects of changes in costs and volume on a company's profits. CVP analysis is important in profit planning. It also is a critical factor in such management decisions as setting selling prices, determining product mix, and maximizing use of production facilities.

Basic Components

CVP analysis considers the interrelationships among the components shown in Illustration 22-9.

Illustration 22-9
Components of CVP analysis

| Volume or level of activity | Unit selling prices | Variable cost per unit | Total fixed costs | Sales mix |

The following assumptions underlie each CVP analysis.

1. The behavior of both costs and revenues is linear throughout the relevant range of the activity index.
2. Costs can be classified accurately as either variable or fixed.
3. Changes in activity are the only factors that affect costs.
4. All units produced are sold.
5. When more than one type of product is sold, the sales mix will remain constant. That is, the percentage that each product represents of total sales will stay the same. Sales mix complicates CVP analysis because different products will have different cost relationships. In this chapter we assume a single product.

When these assumptions are not valid, the CVP analysis may be inaccurate.

CVP Income Statement

Study Objective [5]

Indicate what contribution margin is and how it can be expressed.

Because CVP is so important for decision making, management often wants this information reported in a **CVP income statement** format for internal use. The CVP income statement classifies costs as variable or fixed and computes a contribution margin. **Contribution margin** is the amount of revenue remaining after deducting variable costs. It is often stated both as a total amount and on a per unit basis.

We will use Vargo Video Company to illustrate a CVP income statement. Vargo Video produces a high-definition digital camcorder with a 15× optical zoom and a wide-screen, high-resolution LCD monitor. Relevant data for the camcorders sold by the company in June 2012 are as follows.

Illustration 22-10
Assumed selling and cost data for Vargo Video

Unit selling price of camcorder	$500
Unit variable costs	$300
Total monthly fixed costs	$200,000
Units sold	1,600

The CVP income statement for Vargo Video therefore would be reported as follows.

Illustration 22-11
CVP income statement, with net income

Vargo Video Company
CVP Income Statement
For the Month Ended June 30, 2012

	Total	Per Unit
Sales (1,600 camcorders)	$800,000	$500
Variable costs	480,000	300
Contribution margin	320,000	$200
Fixed costs	200,000	
Net income	$120,000	

A traditional income statement and a CVP income statement both report the same net income of $120,000. However, a traditional income statement does not classify costs as variable or fixed, and therefore it does not report a contribution margin. In addition, both a total and a per unit amount are often shown on a CVP income statement to facilitate CVP analysis.

In the applications of CVP analysis that follow, we assume that the term "cost" includes all costs and expenses related to production and sale of the product. That is, cost includes manufacturing costs plus selling and administrative expenses.

CONTRIBUTION MARGIN PER UNIT

Vargo Video's CVP income statement shows a contribution margin of $320,000, and a contribution margin per unit of $200 ($500 − $300). The formula for **contribution margin per unit** and the computation for Vargo Video are:

Illustration 22-12
Formula for contribution margin per unit

Unit Selling Price	−	Unit Variable Costs	=	Contribution Margin Per Unit
$500	−	$300	=	$200

Contribution margin per unit indicates that for every camcorder sold, Vargo has $200 to cover fixed costs and contribute to net income. Because Vargo Video has fixed costs of $200,000, it must sell 1,000 camcorders ($200,000 ÷ $200) before it earns any net income. Vargo's CVP income statement, assuming a zero net income, is as follows.

Illustration 22-13
CVP income statement, with zero net income

Vargo Video Company
CVP Income Statement
For the Month Ended June 30, 2012

	Total	Per Unit
Sales (1,000 camcorders)	$500,000	$500
Variable costs	300,000	300
Contribution margin	200,000	$200
Fixed costs	200,000	
Net income	$ –0–	

It follows that for every camcorder sold above 1,000 units, net income increases $200. For example, assume that Vargo sold one more camcorder, for a total of 1,001 camcorders sold. In this case Vargo reports net income of $200 as shown in Illustration 22-14.

Illustration 22-14
CVP income statement, with net income

Vargo Video Company		
CVP Income Statement		
For the Month Ended June 30, 2012		
	Total	**Per Unit**
Sales (1,001 camcorders)	$500,500	$500
Variable costs	300,300	300
Contribution margin	200,200	$200
Fixed costs	200,000	
Net income	$ 200	

CONTRIBUTION MARGIN RATIO

Some managers prefer to use a contribution margin ratio in CVP analysis. The **contribution margin ratio** is the contribution margin per unit divided by the unit selling price. For Vargo Video, the ratio is shown in Illustration 22-15.

Illustration 22-15
Formula for contribution margin ratio

Contribution Margin per Unit	÷	Unit Selling Price	=	Contribution Margin Ratio
$200	÷	$500	=	40%

The contribution margin ratio of 40% means that $0.40 of each sales dollar ($1 × 40%) is available to apply to fixed costs and to contribute to net income.

This expression of contribution margin is very helpful in determining the effect of changes in sales dollars on net income. For example, if sales increase $100,000, net income will increase $40,000 (40% × $100,000). Thus, by using the contribution margin ratio, managers can quickly determine increases in net income from any change in sales dollars.

We can also see this effect through a CVP income statement. Assume that Vargo Video's current sales are $500,000 and it wants to know the effect of a $100,000 increase in sales. Vargo prepares a comparative CVP income statement analysis as follows.

Illustration 22-16
Comparative CVP income statements

Vargo Video Company				
CVP Income Statement				
For the Month Ended June 30, 2012				
	No Change		**With Change**	
	Total	**Per Unit**	**Total**	**Per Unit**
Sales	$500,000	$500	$600,000	$500
Variable costs	300,000	300	360,000	300
Contribution margin	200,000	$200	240,000	$200
Fixed costs	200,000		200,000	
Net income	$ –0–		$ 40,000	

Study these CVP income statements carefully. The concepts presented in these statements are used extensively in this and later chapters.

Break-even Analysis

A key relationship in CVP analysis is the level of activity at which total revenues equal total costs (both fixed and variable). This level of activity is called the **break-even point**. At this volume of sales, the company will realize no income but will suffer no loss. The process of finding the break-even point is called **break-even analysis**. Knowledge of the break-even point is useful to management when it decides whether to introduce new product lines, change sales prices on established products, or enter new market areas.

The break-even point can be:

1. Computed from a mathematical equation.
2. Computed by using contribution margin.
3. Derived from a cost-volume-profit (CVP) graph.

The break-even point can be expressed either in **sales units** or **sales dollars**.

Study Objective [6]
Identify the three ways to determine the break-even point.

MATHEMATICAL EQUATION
Illustration 22-17 shows a common equation used for CVP analysis.

$$\text{Sales} = \text{Variable Costs} + \text{Fixed Costs} + \text{Net Income}$$

Illustration 22-17
Basic CVP equation

Identifying the break-even point is a special case of CVP analysis. Because at the break-even point net income is zero, **break-even occurs where total sales equal variable costs plus fixed costs**.

We can compute the break-even point **in units** directly from the equation by **using unit selling prices** and **unit variable costs**. The computation for Vargo Video is:

$$\text{Sales} = \text{Variable Costs} + \text{Fixed Costs} + \text{Net Income}$$

$$\$500Q = \$300Q + \$200,000 + \$0$$

$$\$200Q = \$200,000$$

$$Q = \textbf{1,000 units}$$

where

$$Q = \text{sales volume in units}$$
$$\$500 = \text{selling price}$$
$$\$300 = \text{variable costs per unit}$$
$$\$200,000 = \text{total fixed costs}$$

Illustration 22-18
Computation of break-even point

Thus, Vargo Video must sell 1,000 units to break even.

To find **sales dollars** required to break even, we multiply the units sold at the break-even point times the selling price per unit, as shown below.

$$1,000 \times \$500 = \$500,000 \text{ (break-even sales dollars)}$$

CONTRIBUTION MARGIN TECHNIQUE

We know that contribution margin equals total revenues less variable costs. It follows that at the break-even point, **contribution margin must equal total fixed costs**. On the basis of this relationship, we can compute the break-even point using either the contribution margin per unit or the contribution margin ratio.

When a company uses the contribution margin per unit, the formula to compute break-even point in units is fixed costs divided by contribution margin per unit. For Vargo Video, the computation is as follows.

Illustration 22-19
Formula for break-even point in units using contribution margin

Fixed Cost	÷	Contribution Margin per Unit	=	Break-even Point in Units
$200,000	÷	$200	=	1,000 units

One way to interpret this formula is that Vargo Video generates $200 of contribution margin with each unit that it sells. This $200 goes to pay off fixed costs. Therefore, the company must sell 1,000 units to pay off $200,000 in fixed costs.

When a company uses the contribution margin ratio, the formula to compute break-even point in dollars is fixed costs divided by the contribution margin ratio. We know that the contribution margin ratio for Vargo Video is 40% ($200 ÷ $500), which means that every dollar of sales generates 40 cents to pay off fixed costs. Thus, the break-even point in dollars is:

Illustration 22-20
Formula for break-even point in dollars using contribution margin ratio

Fixed Costs	÷	Contribution Margin Ratio	=	Break-even Point in Dollars
$200,000	÷	40%	=	$500,000

SERVICE COMPANY INSIGHT

Charter Flights Offer a Good Deal

The Internet is wringing inefficiencies out of nearly every industry. While commercial aircraft spend roughly 4,000 hours a year in the air, chartered aircraft spend only 500 hours flying. That means that they are sitting on the ground—not making any money—about 90% of the time. One company, FlightServe, saw a business opportunity in that fact. For about the same cost as a first-class ticket, FlightServe decided to match up executives with charter flights in small "private jets." The executive would get a more comfortable ride and could avoid the hassle of big airports. FlightServe noted that the average charter jet has eight seats. When all eight seats were full, the company would have an 80% profit margin. It would break even at an average of 3.3 full seats per flight.

Source: "Jet Set Go," *The Economist* (March 18, 2000), p. 68.

? How did FlightServe determine that it would break even with 3.3 seats full per flight? (See page 1050.)

GRAPHIC PRESENTATION

An effective way to find the break-even point is to prepare a break-even graph. Because this graph also shows costs, volume, and profits, it is referred to as a **cost-volume-profit (CVP) graph**.

As the CVP graph in Illustration 22-21 shows, sales volume is recorded along the horizontal axis. This axis should extend to the maximum level of expected sales. Both total revenues (sales) and total costs (fixed plus variable) are recorded on the vertical axis.

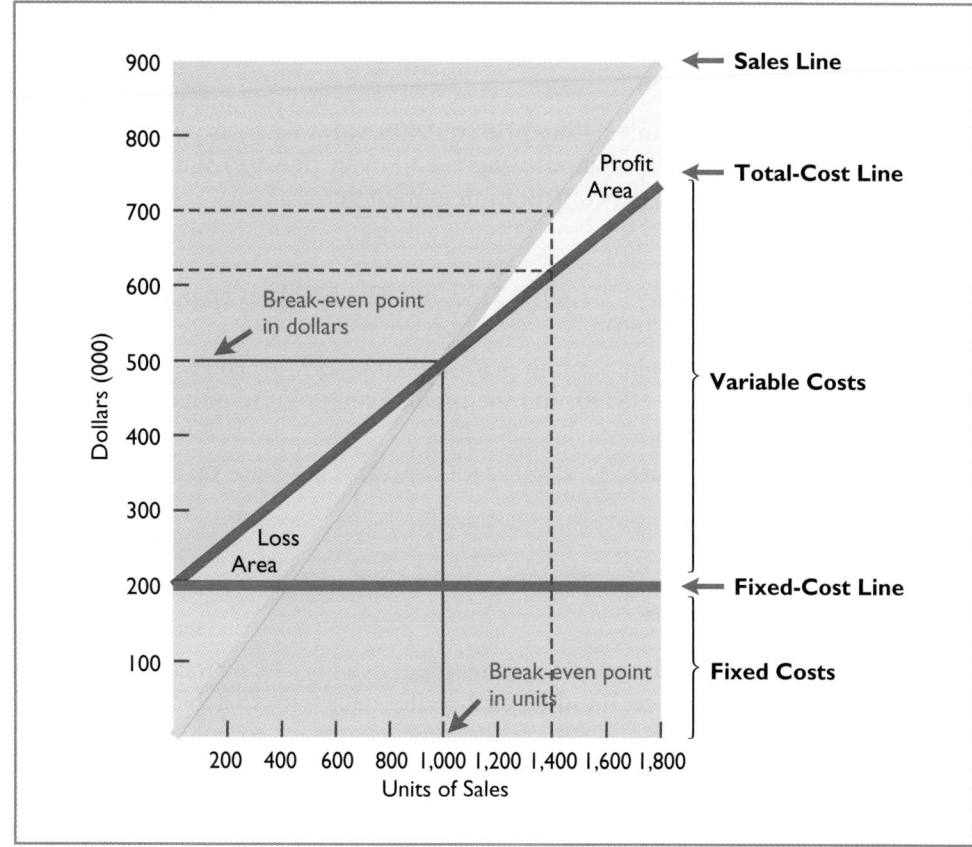

Illustration 22-21
CVP graph

The construction of the graph, using the data for Vargo Video, is as follows.

1. Plot the total-sales line, starting at the zero activity level. For every camcorder sold, total revenue increases by $500. For example, at 200 units, sales are $100,000. At the upper level of activity (1,800 units), sales are $900,000. The revenue line is assumed to be linear through the full range of activity.

2. Plot the total fixed cost using a horizontal line. For the camcorders, this line is plotted at $200,000. The fixed cost is the same at every level of activity.

3. Plot the total-cost line. This starts at the fixed-cost line at zero activity. It increases by the variable cost at each level of activity. For each camcorder, variable costs are $300. Thus, at 200 units, total variable cost is $60,000, and the total cost is $260,000. At 1,800 units total variable cost is $540,000, and total cost is $740,000. On the graph, the amount of the variable cost can be derived from the difference between the total cost and fixed cost lines at each level of activity.

4. Determine the break-even point from the intersection of the total-cost line and the total-revenue line. The break-even point in dollars is found by drawing a horizontal line from the break-even point to the vertical axis. The break-even point in units is found by drawing a vertical line from the break-even point to the horizontal axis. For the camcorders, the break-even point is $500,000 of sales, or 1,000 units. At this sales level, Vargo Video will cover costs but make no profit.

The CVP graph also shows both the net income and net loss areas. Thus, the amount of income or loss at each level of sales can be derived from the total sales and total cost lines.

A CVP graph is useful because the effects of a change in any element in the CVP analysis can be quickly seen. For example, a 10% increase in selling price will change the location of the total revenue line. Likewise, the effects on total costs of wage increases can be quickly observed.

Do it!

Break-Even Analysis

action plan

✔ Apply the formula: Sales = Variable costs + Fixed costs + Net income.

✔ Apply the formula: Fixed costs ÷ Contribution margin per unit = Break-even point in units.

Lombardi Company has a unit selling price of $400, variable costs per unit of $240, and fixed costs of $180,000. Compute the break-even point in units using (a) a mathematical equation and (b) contribution margin per unit.

Solution

(a) The formula is $400Q = $240Q + $180,000. The break-even point in units is 1,125 ($180,000 ÷ $160).

(b) The contribution margin per unit is $160 ($400 − $240). The formula therefore is $180,000 ÷ $160, and the break-even point in units is 1,125.

Related exercise material: BE22-5, BE22-6, E22-4, E22-5, E22-6, E22-7, E22-8, and **Do it!** 22-3.

The Navigator

Target Net Income

Study Objective [7]

Give the formulas for determining sales required to earn target net income.

Rather than simply "breaking even," management usually sets an income objective often called **target net income**. It indicates the sales necessary to achieve a specified level of income. Companies determine the sales necessary to achieve target net income by using one of the three approaches discussed earlier.

MATHEMATICAL EQUATION

We know that at the break-even point no profit or loss results for the company. By adding an amount for target net income to the same basic equation, we obtain the following formula for determining required sales.

Illustration 22-22
Formula for required sales to meet target net income

Required Sales	=	Variable Costs	+	Fixed Costs	+	Target Net Income

Required sales may be expressed in either **sales units** or **sales dollars**. Assuming that target net income is $120,000 for Vargo Video, the computation of required sales in units is as follows.

Illustration 22-23
Computation of required unit sales

Required Sales	=	Variable Costs	+	Fixed Costs	+	Target Net Income
$500Q	=	$300Q	+	$200,000	+	$120,000

$$200Q = $320,000$$
$$Q = 1,600$$

where

$$Q = \text{sales volume}$$
$$\$500 = \text{selling price}$$
$$\$300 = \text{variable cost per unit}$$
$$\$200,000 = \text{total fixed costs}$$
$$\$120,000 = \text{target net income}$$

The sales dollars required to achieve the target net income is found by multiplying the units sold by the unit selling price [(1,600 × $500) = $800,000].

CONTRIBUTION MARGIN TECHNIQUE

As in the case of break-even sales, we can compute in either units or dollars the sales required to meet a target net income. The formula to compute required sales in units for Vargo Video using the contribution margin per unit is as follows.

Fixed Costs + Target Net Income	÷	Contribution Margin Per Unit	=	Required Sales in Units
($200,000 + $120,000)	÷	$200	=	1,600 units

Illustration 22-24
Formula for required sales in units using contribution margin per unit

This computation tells Vargo that to achieve its desired target net income of $120,000, it must sell 1,600 camcorders.

The formula to compute the required sales in dollars for Vargo Video using the contribution margin ratio is as follows.

Fixed Costs + Target Net Income	÷	Contribution Margin Ratio	=	Required Sales in Dollars
($200,000 + $120,000)	÷	40%	=	$800,000

Illustration 22-25
Formula for required sales in dollars using contribution margin ratio

This computation tells Vargo that to achieve its desired target net income of $120,000, it must generate sales of $800,000.

GRAPHIC PRESENTATION

We also can use the CVP graph in Illustration 22-21 (on page 1025) to find the sales required to meet target net income. In the profit area of the graph, the distance between the sales line and the total cost line at any point equals net income. We can find required sales by analyzing the differences between the two lines until the desired net income is found.

For example, suppose Vargo Video sells 1,400 camcorders. Illustration 22-21 shows that a vertical line drawn at 1,400 units intersects the sales line at $700,000 and the total cost line at $620,000. The difference between the two amounts represents the net income (profit) of $80,000.

Margin of Safety

The margin of safety is another relationship used in CVP analysis. **Margin of safety** is the difference between actual or expected sales and sales at the break-even point. This relationship measures the "cushion" that management has, allowing it to still break even if expected sales fail to materialize. The margin of safety is expressed in dollars or as a ratio.

The formula for stating the **margin of safety in dollars** is actual (or expected) sales minus break-even sales. Assuming that actual (expected) sales for Vargo Video are $750,000, the computation is:

Study Objective [8]
Define margin of safety, and give the formulas for computing it.

Actual (Expected) Sales	−	Break-even Sales	=	Margin of Safety in Dollars
$750,000	−	$500,000	=	$250,000

Illustration 22-26
Formula for margin of safety in dollars

Vargo's margin of safety is $250,000. Its sales must fall $250,000 before it operates at a loss.

The **margin of safety ratio** is the margin of safety in dollars divided by actual (or expected) sales. The formula and computation for determining the margin of safety ratio are:

Illustration 22-27
Formula for margin of safety ratio

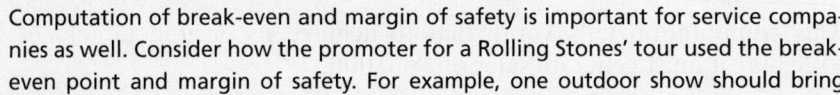

Margin of Safety in Dollars	÷	Actual (Expected) Sales	=	Margin of Safety Ratio
$250,000	÷	$750,000	=	33%

This means that the company's sales could fall by 33% before it would be operating at a loss.

The higher the dollars or the percentage, the greater the margin of safety. Management continuously evaluates the adequacy of the margin of safety in terms of such factors as the vulnerability of the product to competitive pressures and to downturns in the economy.

SERVICE COMPANY INSIGHT

How a Rolling Stones' Tour Makes Money

Computation of break-even and margin of safety is important for service companies as well. Consider how the promoter for a Rolling Stones' tour used the break-even point and margin of safety. For example, one outdoor show should bring 70,000 individuals for a gross of $2.45 million. The promoter guarantees $1.2 million to the Rolling Stones. In addition, 20% of gross goes to the stadium in which the performance is staged. Add another $400,000 for other expenses such as ticket takers, parking attendants, advertising, and so on. The promoter also shares in sales of T-shirts and memorabilia for which the promoter will net over $7 million during the tour. From a successful Rolling Stones' tour, the promoter could make $35 million!

? What amount of sales dollars are required for the promoter to break even? (See page 1050.)

CVP and Changes in the Business Environment

When the personal computer was introduced, it sold for $2,500; today similar computers sell for much less. Recently, when oil prices rose, the break-even point for airline companies such as American and Northwest rose dramatically. Because of lower prices for imported steel, the demand for domestic steel dropped significantly. The point should be clear: Business conditions change rapidly, and management must respond intelligently to these changes. CVP analysis can help.

To better understand how CVP analysis works, let's look at three independent situations that might occur at Vargo Video. Each case uses the original camcorder sales and cost data, which were:

Illustration 22-28
Original camcorder sales and cost data

Unit selling price	$500
Unit variable cost	$300
Total fixed costs	$200,000
Break-even sales	$500,000 or 1,000 units

Case 1. A competitor is offering a 10% discount on the selling price of its camcorders. Management must decide whether to offer a similar discount.

Question: What effect will a 10% discount on selling price have on the break-even point for camcorders?

Answer: A 10% discount on selling price reduces the selling price per unit to $450 [$500 − ($500 × 10%)]. Variable costs per unit remain unchanged at $300. Thus, the contribution margin per unit is $150. Assuming no change in fixed costs, break-even point is 1,333 units, computed as follows.

Fixed Costs	÷	Contribution Margin per Unit	=	Break-even Point in Units
$200,000	÷	$150	=	1,333 units (rounded)

Illustration 22-29
Computation of break-even sales in units

For Vargo Video, this change requires monthly sales to increase by 333 units, or $33\frac{1}{3}$%, in order to break even. In reaching a conclusion about offering a 10% discount to customers, management must determine how likely it is to achieve the increased sales. Also, management should estimate the possible loss of sales if the competitor's discount price is not matched.

Case 2. To meet the threat of foreign competition, management invests in new robotic equipment that will lower the amount of direct labor required to make camcorders. The company estimates that total fixed costs will increase 30% and that variable cost per unit will decrease 30%.

Question: What effect will the new equipment have on the sales volume required to break even?

Answer: Total fixed costs become $260,000 [$200,000 + (30% × $200,000)]. The variable cost per unit becomes $210 [$300 − (30% × $300)]. The new break-even point is approximately 897 units, computed as follows.

Fixed Costs	÷	Contribution Margin per Unit	=	Break-even Point in Units
$260,000	÷	($500 − $210)	=	897 units (rounded)

Illustration 22-30
Computation of break-even sales in units

These changes appear to be advantageous for Vargo Video. The break-even point is reduced by approximately 10%, or 100 units.

Case 3. Vargo's principal supplier of raw materials has just announced a price increase. The higher cost is expected to increase the variable cost of camcorders by $25 per unit. Management decides to hold the line on the selling price of the camcorders. It plans a cost-cutting program that will save $17,500 in fixed costs per month. Vargo is currently realizing monthly net income of $80,000 on sales of 1,400 camcorders.

Question: What increase in units sold will be needed to maintain the same level of net income?

Answer: The variable cost per unit increases to $325 ($300 + $25). Fixed costs are reduced to $182,500 ($200,000 − $17,500). Because of the change in variable cost, the contribution margin per unit becomes $175 ($500 − $325). The required number of units sold to achieve the target net income is computed as follows.

Illustration 22-31
Computation of required sales

Fixed Costs + Target Net Income	÷	Contribution Margin per Unit	=	Required Sales in Units
($182,500 + $80,000)	÷	$175	=	1,500

To achieve the required sales, Vargo will have to sell 1,500 camcorders, an increase of 100 units. If this does not seem to be a reasonable expectation, management will either have to make further cost reductions or accept less net income if the selling price remains unchanged.

CVP Income Statement Revisited

Study Objective [9]
Describe the essential features of a cost-volume-profit income statement.

Earlier in the chapter we presented a simple CVP income statement. When companies prepare a CVP income statement, they provide more detail about specific variable and fixed-cost items.

To illustrate a more detailed CVP income statement, we will assume that Vargo Video reaches its target net income of $120,000 (see Illustration 22-23 on page 1026). The following information is obtained on the $680,000 of costs that were incurred in June to produce and sell 1,600 units.

Illustration 22-32
Assumed cost and expense data

	Variable	Fixed	Total
Cost of goods sold	$400,000	$120,000	$520,000
Selling expenses	60,000	40,000	100,000
Administrative expenses	20,000	40,000	60,000
	$480,000	$200,000	$680,000

The detailed CVP income statement for Vargo is shown below.

Illustration 22-33
Detailed CVP income statement

Vargo Video Company
CVP Income Statement
For the Month Ended June 30, 2012

		Total	Per Unit
Sales		$800,000	$500
Variable expenses			
Cost of goods sold	$400,000		
Selling expenses	60,000		
Administrative expenses	20,000		
Total variable expenses		480,000	300
Contribution margin		320,000	$200
Fixed expenses			
Cost of goods sold	120,000		
Selling expenses	40,000		
Administrative expenses	40,000		
Total fixed expenses		200,000	
Net Income		$120,000	

Do it!

Mabo Company makes calculators that sell for $20 each. For the coming year, management expects fixed costs to total $220,000 and variable costs to be $9 per unit.

(a) Compute break-even point in units using the mathematical equation.

(b) Compute break-even point in dollars using the contribution margin (CM) ratio.

(c) Compute the margin of safety percentage assuming actual sales are $500,000.

(d) Compute the sales required in dollars to earn net income of $165,000 using the mathematical equation.

Margin of Safety; Required Sales

action plan

✔ Know the formulas.

✔ Recognize that variable costs change with sales volume; fixed costs do not.

✔ Avoid computational errors.

Solution

(a) Sales = Variable costs + Fixed costs + Net income
$20Q = $9Q + $220,000 + $0
$11Q = $220,000
   Q = 20,000 units

(b) Contribution margin per unit = Unit selling price − Unit variable costs
        $11 = $20 − $9
   Contribution margin ratio = Contribution margin per unit ÷ Unit selling price
        55% = $11 ÷ $20
   Break-even point in dollars = Fixed cost ÷ Contribution margin ratio
        = $220,000 ÷ 55%
        = $400,000

(c) Margin of safety = $\dfrac{\text{Actual sales} - \text{Break-even sales}}{\text{Actual sales}}$

   $= \dfrac{\$500,000 - \$400,000}{\$500,000}$

   = 20%

(d) Required sales = Variable costs + Fixed costs + Net income
        $20Q = $9Q + $220,000 + $165,000
        $11Q = $385,000
           Q = 35,000 units
   35,000 units × $20 = $700,000 required sales

Related exercise material: **BE22-6, BE22-7, BE22-8, E22-5, E22-6, E22-7, E22-8, E22-9, E22-10, E22-11, E22-12, E22-13,** and **Do it! 22-4.**

✔
The Navigator

COMPREHENSIVE

Do it!

B.T. Hernandez Company, maker of high-quality flashlights, has experienced steady growth over the last 6 years. However, increased competition has led Mr. Hernandez, the president, to believe that an aggressive campaign is needed next year to maintain the company's present growth. The company's accountant has presented Mr. Hernandez with the following data for the current year, 2012, for use in preparing next year's advertising campaign.

Cost Schedules

Variable costs		
Direct labor per flashlight		$ 8.00
Direct materials		4.00
Variable overhead		3.00
Variable cost per flashlight		$15.00
Fixed costs		
Manufacturing		$ 25,000
Selling		40,000
Administrative		70,000
Total fixed costs		$135,000
Selling price per flashlight		$25.00
Expected sales, 2012 (20,000 flashlights)		$500,000

Mr. Hernandez has set the sales target for the year 2013 at a level of $550,000 (22,000 flashlights).

Instructions

(Ignore any income tax considerations.)

(a) What is the projected operating income for 2012?

(b) What is the contribution margin per unit for 2012?

(c) What is the break-even point in units for 2012?

(d) Mr. Hernandez believes that to attain the sales target in the year 2013, the company must incur an additional selling expense of $10,000 for advertising in 2013, with all other costs remaining constant. What will be the break-even point in dollar sales for 2013 if the company spends the additional $10,000?

(e) If the company spends the additional $10,000 for advertising in 2013, what is the sales level in dollars required to equal 2012 operating income?

action plan

✔ Know the formulas.

✔ Recognize that variable costs change with sales volume; fixed costs do not.

✔ Avoid computational errors.

Solution to Comprehensive Do it!

(a)

Expected sales		$500,000
Less:		
Variable cost (20,000 flashlights × $15)	$300,000	
Fixed costs	135,000	435,000
Projected operating income		$ 65,000

(b)

Selling price per flashlight	$25
Variable cost per flashlight	15
Contribution margin per unit	$10

(c) Fixed costs ÷ Contribution margin per unit = Break-even point in units
$135,000 ÷ $10 = 13,500 units

(d) Fixed costs ÷ Contribution margin ratio = Break-even point in dollars
$145,000 ÷ 40% = $362,500

Fixed costs (from 2012)	$135,000
Additional advertising expense	10,000
Fixed costs (2013)	$145,000

Contribution margin per unit (b) $10
Contribution margin ratio = Contribution margin per unit ÷ Unit selling price
40% = $10 ÷ $25

(e) Required sales = (Fixed costs + Target net income) ÷ Contribution margin ratio
$525,000 = ($145,000 + $65,000) ÷ 40%

The Navigator

Summary of Study Objectives

[1] Distinguish between variable and fixed costs. Variable costs are costs that vary in total directly and proportionately with changes in the activity index. Fixed costs are costs that remain the same in total regardless of changes in the activity index.

[2] Explain the significance of the relevant range. The relevant range is the range of activity in which a company expects to operate during a year. It is important in CVP analysis because the behavior of costs is assumed to be linear throughout the relevant range.

[3] Explain the concept of mixed costs. Mixed costs increase in total but not proportionately with changes in the activity level. For purposes of CVP analysis, mixed costs must be classified into their fixed and variable elements. One method that management may use to classify these costs is the high-low method.

[4] List the five components of cost-volume-profit analysis. The five components of CVP analysis are (a) volume or level of activity, (b) unit selling prices, (c) variable cost per unit, (d) total fixed costs, and (e) sales mix.

[5] Indicate what contribution margin is and how it can be expressed. Contribution margin is the amount of revenue remaining after deducting variable costs. It is identified in a CVP income statement, which classifies costs as variable or fixed. It can be expressed as a per unit amount or as a ratio.

[6] Identify the three ways to determine the break-even point. The break-even point can be (a) computed from a mathematical equation, (b) computed by using a contribution margin technique, and (c) derived from a CVP graph.

[7] Give the formulas for determining sales required to earn target net income. The general formula is: Required sales = Variable costs + Fixed costs + Target net income. Two other formulas are: Required sales in units = (Fixed costs + Target net income) ÷ Contribution margin per unit, and Required sales in dollars = (Fixed costs + Target net income) ÷ Contribution margin ratio.

[8] Define margin of safety, and give the formulas for computing it. Margin of safety is the difference between actual or expected sales and sales at the break-even point. The formulas for margin of safety are: Actual (expected) sales − Break-even sales = Margin of safety in dollars; Margin of safety in dollars ÷ Actual (expected) sales = Margin of safety ratio.

[9] Describe the essential features of a cost-volume-profit income statement. The CVP income statement classifies costs and expenses as variable or fixed and reports contribution margin in the body of the statement.

The Navigator

Glossary

Activity index The activity that causes changes in the behavior of costs. (p. 1012).

Break-even point The level of activity at which total revenues equal total costs. (p. 1023).

Contribution margin (CM) The amount of revenue remaining after deducting variable costs. (p. 1020).

Contribution margin per unit The amount of revenue remaining per unit after deducting variable costs; calculated as unit selling price minus unit variable cost. (p. 1021).

Contribution margin ratio The percentage of each dollar of sales that is available to apply to fixed costs and contribute to net income; calculated as contribution margin per unit divided by unit selling price. (p. 1022).

Cost behavior analysis The study of how specific costs respond to changes in the level of business activity. (p. 1012).

Cost-volume-profit (CVP) analysis The study of the effects of changes in costs and volume on a company's profits. (p. 1020).

Cost-volume-profit (CVP) graph A graph showing the relationship between costs, volume, and profits. (p. 1024).

Cost-volume-profit (CVP) income statement A statement for internal use that classifies costs as fixed or variable and reports contribution margin in the body of the statement. (p. 1020).

Fixed costs Costs that remain the same in total regardless of changes in the activity level. (p. 1013).

High-low method A mathematical method that uses the total costs incurred at the high and low levels of activity to classify mixed costs into fixed and variable components. (p. 1017).

Margin of safety The difference between actual or expected sales and sales at the break-even point. (p. 1027).

Mixed costs Costs that contain both a variable and a fixed cost element and change in total but not proportionately with changes in the activity level. (p. 1015).

Relevant range The range of the activity index over which the company expects to operate during the year. (p. 1015).

Target net income The income objective set by management. (p. 1026).

Variable costs Costs that vary in total directly and proportionately with changes in the activity level. (p. 1012).

APPENDIX22A

Variable Costing

Study Objective [10]

Explain the difference between absorption costing and variable costing.

In earlier chapters, we classified both variable and fixed manufacturing costs as product costs. In job order costing, for example, a job is assigned the costs of direct materials, direct labor, and both variable and fixed manufacturing overhead. This costing approach is called **absorption costing** (or **full costing**). It is so named because all manufacturing costs are charged to, or absorbed by, the product. Absorption costing is the approach used for external reporting under GAAP.

An alternative approach is to use variable costing. Under **variable costing** only direct materials, direct labor, and variable manufacturing overhead costs are considered product costs. Companies recognize fixed manufacturing overhead costs as period costs (expenses) when incurred. Illustration 22A-1 shows the difference between absorption costing and variable costing.

Illustration 22A-1

Difference between absorption costing and variable costing

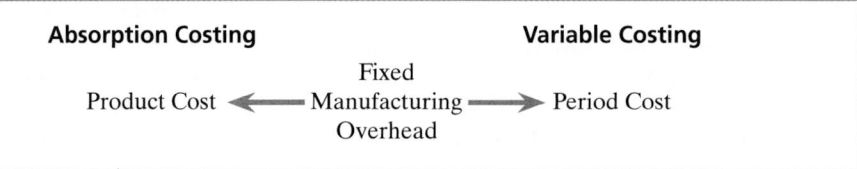

Absorption Costing		Variable Costing
	Fixed	
Product Cost ⟵	Manufacturing ⟶	Period Cost
	Overhead	

Under both absorption and variable costing selling and administrative expenses are period costs. Companies may not use variable costing for external financial reports because GAAP requires that fixed manufacturing overhead be accounted for as a product cost.

To illustrate the computation of unit production cost under absorption and variable costing, assume that Premium Products Corporation manufactures a polyurethane sealant, called Fix-It, for car windshields. Relevant data for Fix-It in January 2012, the first month of production, are as follows.

Illustration 22A-2

Sealant sales and cost data for Premium Products Corporation

Selling price	$20 per unit.
Units	Produced 30,000; sold 20,000; beginning inventory zero.
Variable unit costs	Manufacturing $9 (direct materials $5, direct labor $3, and variable overhead $1). Selling and administrative expenses $2.
Fixed costs	Manufacturing overhead $120,000. Selling and administrative expenses $15,000.

The per unit production cost of Fix-It under each costing approach is:

Illustration 22A-3

Computation of per unit production cost

Type of Cost	Absorption Costing	Variable Costing
Direct materials	$ 5	$5
Direct labor	3	3
Variable manufacturing overhead	1	1
Fixed manufacturing overhead		
($120,000 ÷ 30,000 units produced)	4	0
Total unit cost	$13	$9

The total unit cost is $4 higher ($13 – $9) for absorption costing. This occurs because fixed manufacturing costs are a product cost under absorption costing. Under variable costing, they are, instead, a period cost, and so are expensed. Based on these data, each unit sold and each unit remaining in inventory is costed at $13 under absorption costing and at $9 under variable costing.

Effects of Variable Costing on Income

Illustrations 22A-4 and 22A-5 show the income statements under the two costing approaches. Absorption costing uses the traditional income statement format. Variable costing uses the cost-volume-profit format. We have inserted computations parenthetically in the statements to facilitate your understanding of the amounts.

Premium Products Corporation
Income Statement
For the Month Ended January 31, 2012
(Absorption Costing)

Sales (20,000 units × $20)		$400,000
Cost of goods sold		
Inventory, January 1	$ –0–	
Cost of goods manufactured (30,000 units × $13)	390,000	
Cost of goods available for sale	390,000	
Inventory, January 31 (10,000 units × $13)	130,000	
Cost of goods sold (20,000 units × $13)		260,000
Gross profit		140,000
Selling and administrative expenses		
(Variable 20,000 units × $2 + fixed $15,000)		55,000
Income from operations		**$ 85,000**

Illustration 22A-4
Absorption costing income statement

Helpful Hint

This is the traditional statement that would result from job order and processing costing explained in Chapters 20 and 21.

Premium Products Corporation
Income Statement
For the Month Ended January 31, 2012
(Variable Costing)

Sales (20,000 units × $20)		$400,000
Variable expenses		
Variable cost of goods sold		
Inventory, January 1	$ –0–	
Variable manufacturing costs (30,000 units × $9)	270,000	
Cost of goods available for sale	270,000	
Inventory, January 31 (10,000 units × $9)	90,000	
Variable cost of goods sold	180,000	
Variable selling and administrative expenses		
(20,000 units × $2)	40,000	
Total variable expenses		220,000
Contribution margin		180,000
Fixed expenses		
Manufacturing overhead	120,000	
Selling and administrative expenses	15,000	
Total fixed expenses		135,000
Income from operations		**$ 45,000**

Illustration 22A-5
Variable costing income statement

Helpful Hint

Note the difference in the computation of the ending inventory: $9 per unit here, $13 per unit in Illustration 22A-4.

Income from operations under absorption costing (Illustration 22A-4) is $40,000 ($85,000 − $45,000) higher than under variable costing (Illustration 22A-5). The reason: There is a $40,000 difference in the ending inventories ($130,000 under absorption costing versus $90,000 under variable costing). Under absorption costing, the company defers $40,000 of the fixed overhead costs (10,000 units × $4) to a future period as a product cost. In contrast, under variable costing the company expenses the entire fixed manufacturing costs when incurred.

The following relationships apply:

- When units produced exceed units sold (as shown), income from operations under absorption costing is higher than variable costing.
- When units produced are less than units sold, income from operations under absorption costing is lower than variable costing.
- When units produced and sold are the same, income from operations will be equal under the two costing approaches. In this case, there is no increase in ending inventory. So fixed overhead costs of the current period are not deferred to future periods through the ending inventory.

Illustration 22A-6 summarizes the foregoing effects of the two costing approaches on income from operations.

Illustration 22A-6
Summary of income effects

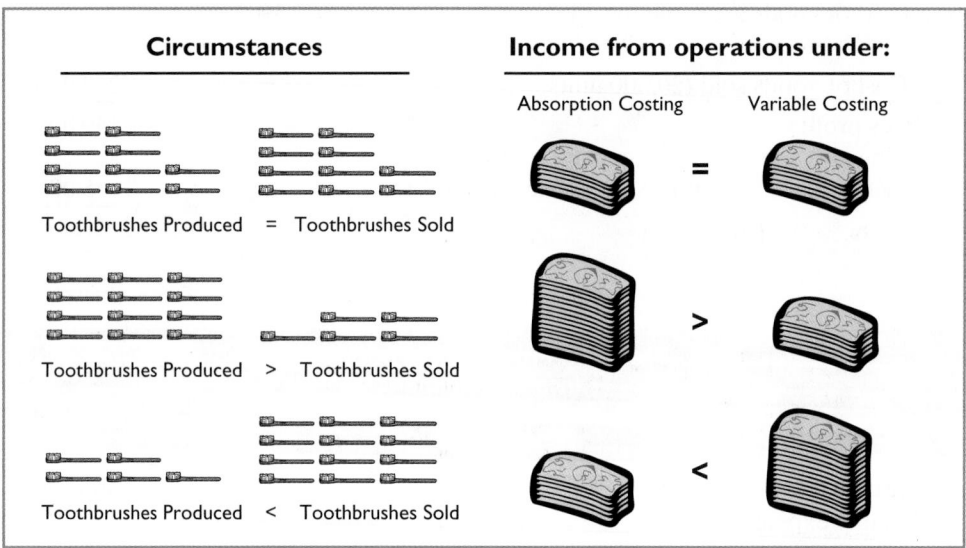

Rationale for Variable Costing

The purpose of fixed manufacturing costs is **to have productive facilities available for use**. A company incurs these costs whether it operates at zero or at 100% of capacity. Thus, proponents of variable costing argue that these costs are period costs and therefore should be expensed when incurred.

Supporters of absorption costing defend the assignment of fixed manufacturing overhead costs to inventory. They say that these costs are as much a cost of getting a product ready for sale as direct materials or direct labor. Accordingly, they contend, these costs should not be matched with revenues until the product is sold.

The use of variable costing is acceptable **only for internal use by management**. It cannot be used in determining product costs in financial statements prepared in accordance with generally accepted accounting principles because it understates inventory costs. To comply with the matching principle, a company must use absorption costing for its work in process and finished goods inventories. Similarly, companies must use absorption costing for income tax purposes.

Summary of Study Objective for Appendix 22A

[10] **Explain the difference between absorption costing and variable costing.** Under absorption costing, fixed manufacturing costs are product costs. Under variable costing, fixed manufacturing costs are period costs.

Glossary for Appendix 22A

Absorption costing A costing approach in which all manufacturing costs are charged to the product. (p. 1034).

Variable costing A costing approach in which only variable manufacturing costs are product costs, and fixed manufacturing costs are period costs (expenses). (p. 1034).

 Self-Test, Brief Exercises, Exercises, Problem Set A, and many more components are available for practice in *WileyPLUS*

*Note: All **asterisked** Questions, Exercises, and Problems relate to material in the appendix to the chapter.

Self-Test Questions

Answers are on page 1050.

(SO 1) **1.** Variable costs are costs that:
    a. vary in total directly and proportionately with changes in the activity level.
    b. remain the same per unit at every activity level.
    c. Neither of the above.
    d. Both (a) and (b) above.

(SO 2) **2.** The relevant range is:
    a. the range of activity in which variable costs will be curvilinear.
    b. the range of activity in which fixed costs will be curvilinear.
    c. the range over which the company expects to operate during a year.
    d. usually from zero to 100% of operating capacity.

(SO 3) **3.** Mixed costs consist of a:
    a. variable cost element and a fixed cost element.
    b. fixed cost element and a controllable cost element.
    c. relevant cost element and a controllable cost element.
    d. variable cost element and a relevant cost element.

(SO 3) **4.** Your phone service provider offers a plan that is classified as a mixed cost. The cost per month for 1,000 minutes is $50. If you use 2,000 minutes this month, your cost will be:
    a. $50.   **c.** more than $100.
    b. $100.   **d.** between $50 and $100.

(SO 4) **5.** One of the following is *not* involved in CVP analysis. That factor is:
    a. sales mix.   **c.** fixed costs per unit.
    b. unit selling prices.   **d.** volume or level of activity.

(SO 5) **6.** Contribution margin:
    a. is revenue remaining after deducting variable costs.
    b. may be expressed as contribution margin per unit.
    c. is selling price less cost of goods sold.
    d. Both (a) and (b) above.

7. When comparing a traditional income statement to a CVP **(SO 5)** income statement:
    a. net income will always be greater on the traditional statement.
    b. net income will always be less on the traditional statement.
    c. net income will always be identical on both.
    d. net income will be greater or less depending on the sales volume.

8. Brownstone Company's contribution margin ratio is 30%. **(SO 6)** If Brownstone's sales revenue is $100 greater than its break-even sales in dollars, its net income:
    a. will be $100.
    b. will be $70.
    c. will be $30.
    d. cannot be determined without knowing fixed costs.

9. Gossen Company is planning to sell 200,000 pliers for $4 per **(SO 6)** unit. The contribution margin ratio is 25%. If Gossen will break even at this level of sales, what are the fixed costs?
    a. $100,000.   **c.** $200,000.
    b. $160,000.   **d.** $300,000.

10. The mathematical equation for computing required sales **(SO 7)** to obtain target net income is: Required sales =
    a. Variable costs + Target net income.
    b. Variable costs + Fixed costs + Target net income.
    c. Fixed costs + Target net income.
    d. No correct answer is given.

11. Marshall Company had actual sales of $600,000 when break- **(SO 8)** even sales were $420,000. What is the margin of safety ratio?
    a. 25%.   **c.** 33⅓%.
    b. 30%.   **d.** 45%.

12. Margin of safety is computed as: **(SO 8)**
    a. Actual sales − Break-even sales.
    b. Contribution margin − Fixed costs.
    c. Break-even sales − Variable costs.
    d. Actual sales − Contribution margin.

(SO 9) **13.** On a CVP income statement:
  a. Sales − Cost of goods sold = Contribution margin.
  b. Sales − Variable costs − Fixed costs = Contribution margin.
  c. Sales − Variable costs = Contribution margin.
  d. Sales − Fixed costs = Contribution margin.

(SO 9) **14.** Cournot Company sells 100,000 wrenches for $12 a unit. Fixed costs are $300,000, and net income is $200,000. What should be reported as variable expenses in the CVP income statement?

  a. $700,000.   **c.** $500,000.
  b. $900,000.   **d.** $1,000,000.

*15. Under variable costing, fixed manufacturing costs are (SO 10) classified as:
  a. period costs.   **c.** both (a) and (b).
  b. product costs.   **d.** neither (a) nor (b).

Go to the book's companion website, **www.wiley.com/college/weygandt,** for additional Self-Test Questions.

The Navigator

Questions

1. (a) What is cost behavior analysis?
  (b) Why is cost behavior analysis important to management?

2. (a) Kenny Jerrad asks your help in understanding the term "activity index." Explain the meaning and importance of this term for Kenny.
  (b) State the two ways that variable costs may be defined.

3. Contrast the effects of changes in the activity level on total fixed costs and on unit fixed costs.

4. S.V. Ayala claims that the relevant range concept is important only for variable costs.
  (a) Explain the relevant range concept.
  (b) Do you agree with S.V.'s claim? Explain.

5. "The relevant range is indispensable in cost behavior analysis." Is this true? Why or why not?

6. Rick Yotts is confused. He does not understand why rent on his apartment is a fixed cost and rent on a Hertz rental truck is a mixed cost. Explain the difference to Rick.

7. How should mixed costs be classified in CVP analysis? What approach is used to determine the appropriate classification?

8. At the high and low levels of activity during the month, direct labor hours are 90,000 and 40,000, respectively. The related costs are $160,000 and $100,000. What are the fixed and variable costs at any level of activity?

9. "Cost-volume-profit (CVP) analysis is based entirely on unit costs." Do you agree? Explain.

10. Bob Barker defines contribution margin as the amount of profit available to cover operating expenses. Is there any truth in this definition? Discuss.

11. Tech Company's Speedo calculator sells for $40. Variable costs per unit are estimated to be $28. What are the contribution margin per unit and the contribution margin ratio?

12. "Break-even analysis is of limited use to management because a company cannot survive by just breaking even." Do you agree? Explain.

13. Total fixed costs are $25,000 for Daaz Inc. It has a contribution margin per unit of $15, and a contribution margin ratio of 25%. Compute the break-even sales in dollars.

14. Peggy Sutton asks your help in constructing a CVP graph. Explain to Peggy (a) how the break-even point is plotted, and (b) how the level of activity and dollar sales at the break-even point are determined.

15. Define the term "margin of safety." If Cortez Company expects to sell 1,250 units of its product at $12 per unit, and break-even sales for the product are $12,000, what is the margin of safety ratio?

16. Salsa Company's break-even sales are $600,000. Assuming fixed costs are $180,000, what sales volume is needed to achieve a target net income of $60,000?

17. The traditional income statement for Eaton Company shows sales $900,000, cost of goods sold $500,000, and operating expenses $200,000. Assuming all costs and expenses are 70% variable and 30% fixed, prepare a CVP income statement through contribution margin.

*18. Distinguish between absorption costing and variable costing.

*19. **(a)** What is the major rationale for the use of variable costing? (b) Discuss why variable costing may not be used for financial reporting purposes.

Brief Exercises

Classify costs as variable, fixed, or mixed.
(SO 1, 3)

BE22-1 Monthly production costs in Provenza Company for two levels of production are as follows.

Cost	3,000 units	6,000 units
Indirect labor	$10,000	$20,000
Supervisory salaries	5,000	5,000
Maintenance	4,000	7,000

Indicate which costs are variable, fixed, and mixed, and give the reason for each answer.

Diagram the behavior of costs within the relevant range.
(SO 2)

BE22-2 For Brenda Company, the relevant range of production is 40–80% of capacity. At 40% of capacity, a variable cost is $4,000 and a fixed cost is $6,000. Diagram the behavior of each cost within the relevant range assuming the behavior is linear.

BE22-3 For Lamar Company, a mixed cost is $20,000 plus $16 per direct labor hour. Diagram the behavior of the cost using increments of 500 hours up to 2,500 hours on the horizontal axis and increments of $20,000 up to $80,000 on the vertical axis.

Diagram the behavior of a mixed cost.
(SO 3)

BE22-4 Moines Company accumulates the following data concerning a mixed cost, using miles as the activity level.

Determine variable and fixed cost elements using the high-low method.
(SO 3)

	Miles Driven	Total Cost		Miles Driven	Total Cost
January	8,000	$14,150	March	8,500	$15,000
February	7,500	13,600	April	8,200	14,490

Compute the variable and fixed cost elements using the high-low method.

BE22-5 Determine the missing amounts.

Determine missing amounts for contribution margin.
(SO 5)

	Unit Selling Price	Unit Variable Costs	Contribution Margin per Unit	Contribution Margin Ratio
1.	$250	$170	(a)	(b)
2.	$500	(c)	$200	(d)
3.	(e)	(f)	$300	30%

BE22-6 Leon Company has a unit selling price of $400, variable costs per unit of $260, and fixed costs of $210,000. Compute the break-even point in units using (a) the mathematical equation and (b) contribution margin per unit.

Compute the break-even point.
(SO 6)

BE22-7 For Longeis Company, variable costs are 70% of sales, and fixed costs are $210,000. Management's net income goal is $60,000. Compute the required sales needed to achieve management's target net income of $60,000. (Use the mathematical equation approach.)

Compute sales for target net income.
(SO 7)

BE22-8 For Amos Company, actual sales are $1,200,000 and break-even sales are $900,000. Compute (a) the margin of safety in dollars and (b) the margin of safety ratio.

Compute the margin of safety and the margin of safety ratio.
(SO 8)

BE22-9 Sylvia Manufacturing Inc. had sales of $1,800,000 for the first quarter of 2012. In making the sales, the company incurred the following costs and expenses.

Prepare CVP income statement.
(SO 9)

	Variable	Fixed
Cost of goods sold	$760,000	$540,000
Selling expenses	95,000	60,000
Administrative expenses	79,000	66,000

Prepare a CVP income statement for the quarter ended March 31, 2012.

*BE22-10 Alton Company's fixed overhead costs are $3 per unit, and its variable overhead costs are $8 per unit. In the first month of operations, 50,000 units are produced and 47,000 units are sold. Write a short memo to the chief financial officer explaining which costing approach will produce the higher income and what the difference will be.

Compute net income under absorption and variable costing.
(SO 10)

Do it! Review

Do it! 22-1 Wyoming Company reports the following total costs at two levels of production.

Classify types of costs.
(SO 1, 3)

	5,000 Units	10,000 Units
Indirect labor	$ 3,000	$ 6,000
Property taxes	7,000	7,000
Direct labor	27,000	54,000
Direct materials	22,000	44,000
Depreciation	4,000	4,000
Utilities	3,000	5,000
Maintenance	9,000	11,000

Classify each cost as variable, fixed, or mixed.

Compute costs using high-low method and estimate total cost.
(SO 3)

Do it! 22-2   Blakely Company accumulates the following data concerning a mixed cost, using units produced as the activity level.

	Units Produced	Total Cost
March	10,000	$18,000
April	9,000	16,650
May	10,500	18,750
June	8,800	16,200
July	9,500	17,100

(a) Compute the variable and fixed cost elements using the high-low method.
(b) Estimate the total cost if the company produces 8,500 units.

Compute break-even point in units.
(SO 6)

Do it! 22-3   Lombardi Company has a unit selling price of $250, variable cost per unit of $160, and fixed costs of $135,000. Compute the break-even point in units using (a) a mathematical equation and (b) contribution margin per unit.

Compute margin of safety percentage and required sales.
(SO 8, 9)

Do it! 22-4   Wales Company makes radios that sell for $30 each. For the coming year, management expects fixed costs to total $200,000 and variable costs to be $20 per unit.
(a) Compute the break-even point in dollars using the contribution margin (CM) ratio.
(b) Compute the margin of safety percentage assuming actual sales are $750,000.
(c) Compute the sales required in dollars to earn net income of $120,000.

Exercises

Define and classify variable, fixed, and mixed costs.
(SO 1, 3)

E22-1   Pyle Company manufactures a single product. Annual production costs incurred in the manufacturing process are shown below for two levels of production.

	Costs Incurred			
Production in Units	**5,000**		**10,000**	
Production Costs	**Total Cost**	**Cost/ Unit**	**Total Cost**	**Cost/ Unit**
Direct materials	$8,250	$1.65	$16,500	$1.65
Direct labor	9,500	1.90	19,000	1.90
Utilities	1,500	0.30	2,500	0.25
Rent	4,000	0.80	4,000	0.40
Maintenance	800	0.16	1,100	0.11
Supervisory salaries	1,000	0.20	1,000	0.10

Instructions
(a) Define the terms variable costs, fixed costs, and mixed costs.
(b) Classify each cost above as either variable, fixed, or mixed.

Determine fixed and variable costs using the high-low method and prepare graph.
(SO 1, 3)

E22-2   The controller of Loran Industries has collected the following monthly expense data for use in analyzing the cost behavior of maintenance costs.

Month	Total Maintenance Costs	Total Machine Hours
January	$2,400	300
February	3,000	400
March	3,600	600
April	4,500	790
May	3,200	500
June	4,900	800

Instructions
(a) Determine the fixed and variable cost components using the high-low method.
(b) Prepare a graph showing the behavior of maintenance costs, and identify the fixed and variable cost elements. Use 200 unit increments and $1,000 cost increments.

Classify variable, fixed, and mixed costs.
(SO 1, 3)

E22-3   Blue's Sisters Furniture Corporation incurred the following costs.
1. Wood used in the production of furniture.
2. Fuel used in delivery trucks.

3. Straight-line depreciation on factory building.
4. Screws used in the production of furniture.
5. Sales staff salaries.
6. Sales commissions.
7. Property taxes.
8. Insurance on buildings.
9. Hourly wages of furniture craftsmen.
10. Salaries of factory supervisors.
11. Utilities expense.
12. Telephone bill.

Instructions
Identify the costs above as variable, fixed, or mixed.

E22-4 Vic Taley wants Taley Company to use CVP analysis to study the effects of changes in costs and volume on the company. Taley has heard that certain assumptions must be valid in order for CVP analysis to be useful.

Explain assumptions underlying CVP analysis.

(SO 4)

Instructions
Prepare a memo to Vic Taley concerning the assumptions that underlie CVP analysis.

E22-5 In the month of June, Bonita Beauty Salon gave 2,700 haircuts, shampoos, and permanents at an average price of $30. During the month, fixed costs were $18,000 and variable costs were 70% of sales.

Compute contribution margin, break-even point, and margin of safety.

(SO 5, 6, 8)

Instructions
(a) Determine the contribution margin in dollars, per unit, and as a ratio.
(b) Using the contribution margin technique, compute the break-even point in dollars and in units.
(c) Compute the margin of safety in dollars and as a ratio.

E22-6 Stuart Company estimates that variable costs will be 60% of sales, and fixed costs will total $800,000. The selling price of the product is $4.

Prepare a CVP graph and compute break-even point and margin of safety.

(SO 6, 8)

Instructions
(a) Prepare a CVP graph, assuming maximum sales of $3,200,000. (*Note:* Use $400,000 increments for sales and costs and 100,000 increments for units.)
(b) Compute the break-even point in (1) units and (2) dollars.
(c) Compute the margin of safety in (1) dollars and (2) as a ratio, assuming actual sales are $2.5 million.

E22-7 Green with Envy provides environmentally friendly lawn services for homeowners. Its operating costs are as follows.

Compute break-even point in units and dollars.

(SO 5, 6)

Depreciation	$1,500 per month
Advertising	$200 per month
Insurance	$ 2,000 per month
Weed and feed materials	$13 per lawn
Direct labor	$12 per lawn
Fuel	$2 per lawn

Green with Envy charges $60 per treatment for the average single-family lawn.

Instructions
Determine the company's break-even point in (a) number of lawns serviced per month and (b) dollars.

E22-8 The Lake Shore Inn is trying to determine its break-even point. The inn has 50 rooms that it rents at $60 a night. Operating costs are as follows.

Compute break-even point.

(SO 5, 6)

Salaries	$7,200 per month
Utilities	$1,500 per month
Depreciation	$1,200 per month
Maintenance	$300 per month
Maid service	$8 per room
Other costs	$28 per room

Instructions
Determine the inn's break-even point in (a) number of rented rooms per month and (b) dollars.

Compute contribution margin and break-even point.

(SO 5, 6)

E22-9 In the month of March, New Day Spa services 570 clients at an average price of $120. During the month, fixed costs were $21,000 and variable costs were 65% of sales.

Instructions

(a) Determine the contribution margin in dollars, per unit, and as a ratio.

(b) Using the contribution margin technique, compute the break-even point in dollars and in units.

Compute break-even point.

(SO 5, 6)

E22-10 Airport Connection provides shuttle service between four hotels near a medical center and an international airport. Airport Connection uses two 10-passenger vans to offer 12 round trips per day. A recent month's activity in the form of a cost-volume-profit income statement is shown below.

Fare revenues (1,440 fares)		$36,000
Variable costs		
Fuel	$ 5,040	
Tolls and parking	3,100	
Maintenance	500	8,640
Contribution margin		27,360
Fixed costs		
Salaries	13,000	
Depreciation	1,300	
Insurance	1,128	15,428
Net income		$11,932

Instructions

(a) Calculate the break-even point in (1) dollars and (2) number of fares.

(b) Without calculations, determine the contribution margin at the break-even point.

Compute variable cost per unit, contribution margin ratio, and increase in fixed costs.

(SO 5, 6)

E22-11 In 2012, Paterno Company had a break-even point of $350,000 based on a selling price of $7 per unit and fixed costs of $105,000. In 2013, the selling price and the variable cost per unit did not change, but the break-even point increased to $420,000.

Instructions

(a) Compute the variable cost per unit and the contribution margin ratio for 2012.

(b) Compute the increase in fixed costs for 2013.

Prepare CVP income statements.

(SO 5, 6)

E22-12 CTU Company has the following information available for September 2012.

Unit selling price of video game consoles	$ 400
Unit variable costs	$ 270
Total fixed costs	$52,000
Units sold	620

Instructions

(a) Prepare a CVP income statement that shows both total and per unit amounts.

(b) Compute CTU's break-even point in units.

(c) Prepare a CVP income statement for the break-even point that shows both total and per unit amounts.

Compute various components to derive target net income under different assumptions.

(SO 6, 7)

E22-13 Manx Company had $150,000 of net income in 2012 when the selling price per unit was $150, the variable costs per unit were $90, and the fixed costs were $570,000. Management expects per unit data and total fixed costs to remain the same in 2013. The president of Manx Company is under pressure from stockholders to increase net income by $60,000 in 2013.

Instructions

(a) Compute the number of units sold in 2012.

(b) Compute the number of units that would have to be sold in 2013 to reach the stockholders' desired profit level.

(c) Assume that Manx Company sells the same number of units in 2013 as it did in 2012. What would the selling price have to be in order to reach the stockholders' desired profit level?

Compute net income under different alternatives.

(SO 7)

E22-14 Erin Company reports the following operating results for the month of August: Sales $350,000 (units 5,000); variable costs $210,000; and fixed costs $90,000. Management is considering the following independent courses of action to increase net income.

1. Increase selling price by 10% with no change in total variable costs.

2. Reduce variable costs to 55% of sales.

3. Reduce fixed costs by $10,000.

Instructions
Compute the net income to be earned under each alternative. Which course of action will produce the highest net income?

E22-15 Yeltsin Company had sales in 2012 of $1,500,000 on 60,000 units. Variable costs totaled $840,000, and fixed costs totaled $500,000.

    A new raw material is available that will decrease the variable costs per unit by 20% (or $2.80). However, to process the new raw material, fixed operating costs will increase by $60,000. Management feels that one-half of the decline in the variable costs per unit should be passed on to customers in the form of a sales price reduction. The marketing department expects that this sales price reduction will result in a 7% increase in the number of units sold.

Prepare a CVP income statement before and after changes in business environment.
(SO 9)

Instructions
Prepare a CVP income statement for 2012, assuming the changes are made as described.

*E22-16 Titus Company manufactures and distributes industrial air compressors. The following costs are available for the year ended December 31, 2012. The company has no beginning inventory. In 2012, 1,500 units were produced, but only 1,300 units were sold. The unit selling price was $4,500. Costs and expenses were:

Compute total product cost and prepare an income statement using variable costing.
(SO 10)

Variable costs per unit	
Direct materials	$ 1,000
Direct labor	1,500
Variable manufacturing overhead	300
Variable selling and administrative expenses	70
Annual fixed costs and expenses	
Manufacturing overhead	$1,400,000
Selling and administrative expenses	100,000

Instructions
(a) Compute the manufacturing cost of one unit of product using variable costing.
(b) Prepare a 2012 income statement for Titus Company using variable costing.

*E22-17 Symond Corporation produces one product. Its cost includes direct materials ($10 per unit), direct labor ($8 per unit), variable overhead ($6 per unit), fixed manufacturing ($250,000), and fixed selling and administrative ($30,000). In October 2012, Symond produced 25,000 units and sold 20,000 at $50 each.

Prepare absorption cost and variable cost income statements.
(SO 10)

Instructions
(a) Prepare an absorption costing income statement.
(b) Prepare a variable costing income statement.
(c) Explain the difference in net income in the two income statements.

Exercises: Set B

Visit the book's companion website, at **www.wiley.com/college/weygandt**, and choose the Student Companion site to access Exercise Set B.

Problems: Set A

P22-1A Stan Loy owns the Vista Barber Shop. He employs five barbers and pays each a base rate of $1,000 per month. One of the barbers serves as the manager and receives an extra $500 per month. In addition to the base rate, each barber also receives a commission of $5.50 per haircut.

    Other costs are as follows.

Determine variable and fixed costs, compute break-even point, prepare a CVP graph, and determine net income.
(SO 1, 3, 5, 6)

Advertising	$200 per month
Rent	$900 per month
Barber supplies	$0.30 per haircut
Utilities	$175 per month plus $0.20 per haircut
Magazines	$25 per month

Stan currently charges $10 per haircut.

Instructions

(a) Determine the variable cost per haircut and the total monthly fixed costs.

(b) Compute the break-even point in units and dollars.

(c) Prepare a CVP graph, assuming a maximum of 1,800 haircuts in a month. Use increments of 300 haircuts on the horizontal axis and $3,000 on the vertical axis.

(d) Determine net income, assuming 1,900 haircuts are given in a month.

Prepare a CVP income statement, compute break-even point, contribution margin ratio, margin of safety ratio, and sales for target net income.
(SO 5, 6, 7, 8, 9)

P22-2A   Hytek Company bottles and distributes Livit, a diet soft drink. The beverage is sold for 50 cents per 16-ounce bottle to retailers, who charge customers 75 cents per bottle. For the year 2012, management estimates the following revenues and costs.

Net sales	$1,800,000	Selling expenses—variable	$70,000
Direct materials	430,000	Selling expenses—fixed	65,000
Direct labor	352,000	Administrative expenses—	
Manufacturing overhead—		variable	20,000
variable	316,000	Administrative expenses—	
Manufacturing overhead—		fixed	60,000
fixed	283,000		

Instructions

(a) Prepare a CVP income statement for 2012 based on management's estimates.

(b) Compute the break-even point in (1) units and (2) dollars.

(c) Compute the contribution margin ratio and the margin of safety ratio. (Round to full percents.)

(d) Determine the sales dollars required to earn net income of $238,000.

Compute break-even point under alternative courses of action.
(SO 5, 6)

P22-3A   Magic Manufacturing's sales slumped badly in 2012. For the first time in its history, it operated at a loss. The company's income statement showed the following results from selling 600,000 units of product: Net sales $2,400,000; total costs and expenses $2,540,000; and net loss $140,000. Costs and expenses consisted of the amounts shown below.

	Total	Variable	Fixed
Cost of goods sold	$2,100,000	$1,440,000	$660,000
Selling expenses	240,000	72,000	168,000
Administrative expenses	200,000	48,000	152,000
	$2,540,000	$1,560,000	$980,000

Management is considering the following independent alternatives for 2013.

1. Increase unit selling price 20% with no change in costs, expenses, and sales volume.

2. Change the compensation of salespersons from fixed annual salaries totaling $150,000 to total salaries of $60,000 plus a 3% commission on net sales.

3. Purchase new automated equipment that will change the proportion between variable and fixed cost of goods sold to 54% variable and 46% fixed.

Instructions

(a) Compute the break-even point in dollars for 2012.

(b) Compute the break-even point in dollars under each of the alternative courses of action. (Round all ratios to nearest full percent.) Which course of action do you recommend?

Compute break-even point and margin of safety ratio, and prepare a CVP income statement before and after changes in business environment.
(SO 6, 8, 9)

P22-4A   Svetlana Pace is the advertising manager for Bargain Shoe Store. She is currently working on a major promotional campaign. Her ideas include the installation of a new lighting system and increased display space that will add $34,000 in fixed costs to the $270,000 currently spent. In addition, Svetlana is proposing that a 5% price decrease ($40 to $38) will produce a 20% increase in sales volume (20,000 to 24,000). Variable costs will remain at $22 per pair of shoes. Management is impressed with Svetlana's ideas but concerned about the effects that these changes will have on the break-even point and the margin of safety.

Instructions

(a) Compute the current break-even point in units, and compare it to the break-even point in units if Svetlana's ideas are used.

(b) Compute the margin of safety ratio for current operations and after Svetlana's changes are introduced. (Round to nearest full percent.)

(c) Prepare a CVP income statement for current operations and after Svetlana's changes are introduced. Would you make the changes suggested?

P22-5A Lopez Corporation has collected the following information after its first year of sales. Net sales were $1,600,000 on 100,000 units; selling expenses $240,000 (40% variable and 60% fixed); direct materials $511,000; direct labor $285,000; administrative expenses $280,000 (20% variable and 80% fixed); manufacturing overhead $360,000 (70% variable and 30% fixed). Top management has asked you to do a CVP analysis so that it can make plans for the coming year. It has projected that unit sales will increase by 10% next year.

Compute break-even point and margin of safety ratio, and prepare a CVP income statement before and after changes in business environment.
(SO 5, 6, 7, 8)

Instructions

(a) Compute (1) the contribution margin for the current year and the projected year, and (2) the fixed costs for the current year. (Assume that fixed costs will remain the same in the projected year.)

(b) Compute the break-even point in units and sales dollars for the current year.

(c) The company has a target net income of $310,000. What is the required sales in dollars for the company to meet its target?

(d) If the company meets its target net income number, by what percentage could its sales fall before it is operating at a loss? That is, what is its margin of safety ratio?

(e) The company is considering a purchase of equipment that would reduce its direct labor costs by $104,000 and would change its manufacturing overhead costs to 30% variable and 70% fixed (assume total manufacturing overhead cost is $360,000, as above). It is also considering switching to a pure commission basis for its sales staff. This would change selling expenses to 90% variable and 10% fixed (assume total selling expense is $240,000, as above). Assuming that net sales remain at first-year levels, compute (1) the contribution margin and (2) the contribution margin ratio, and recompute (3) the break-even point in sales dollars. Comment on the effect each of management's proposed changes has on the break-even point.

*P22-6A BLT produces plastic that is used for injection molding applications such as gears for small motors. In 2012, the first year of operations, BLT produced 6,000 tons of plastic and sold 5,000 tons. In 2013, the production and sales results were exactly reversed. In each year, selling price per ton was $1,000, variable manufacturing costs were 15% of the sales price of units produced, variable selling expenses were 10% of the selling price of units sold, fixed manufacturing costs were $2,100,000, and fixed administrative expenses were $500,000.

Prepare income statements under absorption and variable costing.
(SO 10)

Instructions

(a) Prepare comparative income statements for each year using variable costing.

(b) Prepare comparative income statements for each year using absorption costing.

(c) Reconcile the differences each year in income from operations under the two costing approaches.

(d) Comment on the effects of production and sales on net income under the two costing approaches.

Problems: Set B

P22-1B The All Cuts Barber Shop employs four barbers. One barber, who also serves as the manager, is paid a salary of $3,900 per month. The other barbers are paid $1,900 per month. In addition, each barber is paid a commission of $2 per haircut. Other monthly costs are: store rent $700 plus 60 cents per haircut, depreciation on equipment $500, barber supplies 40 cents per haircut, utilities $300, and advertising $100. The price of a haircut is $10.

Determine variable and fixed costs, compute break-even point, prepare a CVP graph, and determine net income.
(SO 1, 3, 5, 6)

Instructions

(a) Determine the variable cost per haircut and the total monthly fixed costs.

(b) Compute the break-even point in units and dollars.

(c) Prepare a CVP graph, assuming a maximum of 1,800 haircuts in a month. Use increments of 300 haircuts on the horizontal axis and $3,000 increments on the vertical axis.

(d) Determine the net income, assuming 1,700 haircuts are given in a month.

P22-2B Mobley Company bottles and distributes No-FIZZ, a fruit drink. The beverage is sold for 50 cents per 16-ounce bottle to retailers, who charge customers 70 cents per bottle. For the year 2012, management estimates the following revenues and costs.

Prepare a CVP income statement, compute break-even point, contribution margin ratio, margin of safety ratio, and sales for target net income.
(SO 5, 6, 7, 8, 9)

Net sales	$2,000,000	Selling expenses—variable	$ 80,000
Direct materials	360,000	Selling expenses—fixed	150,000
Direct labor	450,000	Administrative expenses—	
Manufacturing overhead—		variable	40,000
variable	270,000	Administrative expenses—	
Manufacturing overhead—		fixed	70,000
fixed	280,000		

Instructions

(a) Prepare a CVP income statement for 2012 based on management's estimates.

(b) Compute the break-even point in (1) units and (2) dollars.

(c) Compute the contribution margin ratio and the margin of safety ratio.

(d) Determine the sales dollars required to earn net income of $390,000.

Compute break-even point under alternative courses of action.

(SO 5, 6)

P22-3B Werner Manufacturing had a bad year in 2012. For the first time in its history, it operated at a loss. The company's income statement showed the following results from selling 60,000 units of product: Net sales $1,500,000; total costs and expenses $1,890,000; and net loss $390,000. Costs and expenses consisted of the amounts shown below.

	Total	Variable	Fixed
Cost of goods sold	$1,350,000	$ 930,000	$420,000
Selling expenses	420,000	65,000	355,000
Administrative expenses	120,000	55,000	65,000
	$1,890,000	$1,050,000	$840,000

Management is considering the following independent alternatives for 2013.

1. Increase unit selling price 40% with no change in costs, expenses, and sales volume.

2. Change the compensation of salespersons from fixed annual salaries totaling $200,000 to total salaries of $30,000 plus a 4% commission on net sales.

3. Purchase new high-tech factory machinery that will change the proportion between variable and fixed cost of goods sold to 50:50.

Instructions

(a) Compute the break-even point in dollars for 2012.

(b) Compute the break-even point in dollars under each of the alternative courses of action. Which course of action do you recommend?

Compute break-even point and margin of safety ratio, and prepare a CVP income statement before and after changes in business environment.

(SO 6, 8, 9)

P22-4B Kay Jo is the advertising manager for Costless Shoe Store. She is currently working on a major promotional campaign. Her ideas include the installation of a new lighting system and increased display space that will add $24,000 in fixed costs to the $210,000 currently spent. In addition, Kay is proposing that a 6⅔% price decrease (from $30 to $28) will produce an increase in sales volume from 16,000 to 20,000 units. Variable costs will remain at $15 per pair of shoes. Management is impressed with Kay's ideas but concerned about the effects that these changes will have on the break-even point and the margin of safety.

Instructions

(a) Compute the current break-even point in units, and compare it to the break-even point in units if Kay's ideas are used.

(b) Compute the margin of safety ratio for current operations and after Kay's changes are introduced. (Round to nearest full percent.)

(c) Prepare a CVP income statement for current operations and after Kay's changes are introduced. Would you make the changes suggested?

Compute break-even point and margin of safety ratio, and prepare a CVP income statement before and after changes in business environment.

(SO 5, 6, 7, 8)

P22-5B Perkins Corporation has collected the following information after its first year of sales. Net sales were $2,000,000 on 100,000 units; selling expenses $400,000 (30% variable and 70% fixed); direct materials $600,000; direct labor $340,000; administrative expenses $500,000 (30% variable and 70% fixed); manufacturing overhead $480,000 (20% variable and 80% fixed). Top management has asked you to do a CVP analysis so that it can make plans for the coming year. It has projected that unit sales will increase by 20% next year.

Instructions

(a) Compute (1) the contribution margin for the current year and the projected year, and (2) the fixed costs for the current year. (Assume that fixed costs will remain the same in the projected year.)

(b) Compute the break-even point in units and sales dollars.

(c) The company has a target net income of $374,000. What is the required sales in dollars for the company to meet its target?

(d) If the company meets its target net income number, by what percentage could its sales fall before it is operating at a loss? That is, what is its margin of safety ratio?

(e) The company is considering a purchase of equipment that would reduce its direct labor costs by $140,000 and would change its manufacturing overhead costs to 10% variable and 90% fixed (assume total manufacturing overhead cost is $480,000, as above). It is also considering switching to a pure commission basis for its sales staff. This would change selling expenses to 80% variable and 20% fixed (assume total selling expense is $400,000, as above). Compute (1) the contribution margin and (2) the contribution margin ratio, and recompute (3) the break-even point in sales dollars. Comment on the effect each of management's proposed changes has on the break-even point.

*P22-6B Azul Metal Company produces the steel wire that goes into the production of paper clips. In 2012, the first year of operations, Azul produced 50,000 miles of wire and sold 45,000 miles. In 2013, the production and sales results were exactly reversed. In each year, selling price per mile was $60, variable manufacturing costs were 20% of the sales price, variable selling expenses were $8.00 per mile sold, fixed manufacturing costs were $1,200,000, and fixed administrative expenses were $230,000.

Prepare income statements under absorption and variable costing.
(SO 10)

Instructions

(a) Prepare comparative income statements for each year using variable costing.

(b) Prepare comparative income statements for each year using absorption costing.

(c) Reconcile the differences each year in income from operations under the two costing approaches.

(d) Comment on the effects of production and sales on net income under the two costing approaches.

Problems: Set C

Visit the book's companion website, at **www.wiley.com/college/weygandt**, and choose the Student Companion site to access Problem Set C.

Waterways Continuing Problem

(*Note:* This is a continuation of the Waterways Problem from Chapters 19 through 21.)

WCP22 The Vice President for Sales and Marketing at Waterways Corporation is planning for production needs to meet sales demand in the coming year. He is also trying to determine how the company's profits might be increased in the coming year. This problem asks you to use cost-volume-profit concepts to help Waterways understand contribution margins of some of its products and to decide whether to mass-produce certain products.

Go to the book's companion website, **www.wiley.com/college/weygandt**, *to see the completion of this problem.*

BROADENINGYOURPERSPECTIVE

Decision Making Across the Organization

BYP22-1 Zumello Company has decided to introduce a new product. The new product can be manufactured by either a capital-intensive method or a labor-intensive method. The manufacturing method will not affect the quality of the product. The estimated manufacturing costs by the two methods are as follows.

	Capital-Intensive	Labor-Intensive
Direct materials	$5 per unit	$5.50 per unit
Direct labor	$6 per unit	$8.00 per unit
Variable overhead	$3 per unit	$4.50 per unit
Fixed manufacturing costs	$2,508,000	$1,538,000

Zumello's market research department has recommended an introductory unit sales price of $30. The incremental selling expenses are estimated to be $502,000 annually plus $2 for each unit sold, regardless of manufacturing method.

Instructions

With the class divided into groups, answer the following.

(a) Calculate the estimated break-even point in annual unit sales of the new product if Zumello Company uses the:
   (1) Capital-intensive manufacturing method.
   (2) Labor-intensive manufacturing method.
(b) Determine the annual unit sales volume at which Zumello Company would be indifferent between the two manufacturing methods.
(c) Explain the circumstance under which Zumello should employ each of the two manufacturing methods.

(CMA adapted)

Managerial Analysis

BYP22-2 The condensed income statement for the Penn and Stiller partnership for 2012 is as follows.

PENN AND STILLER COMPANY
Income Statement
For the Year Ended December 31, 2012

Sales (200,000 units)		$1,200,000
Cost of goods sold		800,000
Gross profit		400,000
Operating expenses		
Selling	$280,000	
Administrative	160,000	440,000
Net loss		($40,000)

A cost behavior analysis indicates that 75% of the cost of goods sold are variable, 50% of the selling expenses are variable, and 25% of the administrative expenses are variable.

Instructions

(Round to nearest unit, dollar, and percentage, where necessary. Use the CVP income statement format in computing profits.)

(a) Compute the break-even point in total sales dollars and in units for 2012.
(b) Penn has proposed a plan to get the partnership "out of the red" and improve its profitability. She feels that the quality of the product could be substantially improved by spending $0.25 more per unit on better raw materials. The selling price per unit could be increased to only $6.25 because of competitive pressures. Penn estimates that sales volume will increase by 30%. What effect would Penn's plan have on the profits and the break-even point in dollars of the partnership? (Round the contribution margin ratio to two decimal places.)
(c) Stiller was a marketing major in college. She believes that sales volume can be increased only by intensive advertising and promotional campaigns. She therefore proposed the following plan as an alternative to Penn's. (1) Increase variable selling expenses to $0.79 per unit, (2) lower the selling price per unit by $0.30, and (3) increase fixed selling expenses by $35,000. Stiller quoted an old marketing research report that said that sales volume would increase by 60% if these changes were made. What effect would Stiller's plan have on the profits and the break-even point in dollars of the partnership?
(d) Which plan should be accepted? Explain your answer.

Real-World Focus

BYP22-3 The Coca-Cola Company hardly needs an introduction. A line taken from the cover of a recent annual report says it all: If you measured time in servings of Coca-Cola, "a billion Coca-Cola's ago was yesterday morning." On average, every U.S. citizen drinks 363 8-ounce servings of Coca-Cola products each year. Coca-Cola's primary line of business is the making and selling of syrup to bottlers. These bottlers then sell the finished bottles and cans of Coca-Cola to the consumer.

The annual report of Coca-Cola provided the following information.

The Coca-Cola Company
Management Discussion

Our gross margin declined to 61 percent this year from 62 percent in the prior year, primarily due to costs for materials such as sweeteners and packaging.

The increases [in selling expenses] in the last two years were primarily due to higher marketing expenditures in support of our Company's volume growth.

We measure our sales volume in two ways: (1) gallon shipments of concentrates and syrups and (2) unit cases of finished product (bottles and cans of Coke sold by bottlers).

Instructions

Answer the following questions.

(a) Are sweeteners and packaging a variable cost or a fixed cost? What is the impact on the contribution margin of an increase in the per unit cost of sweeteners or packaging? What are the implications for profitability?

(b) In your opinion, are marketing expenditures a fixed cost, variable cost, or mixed cost to The Coca-Cola Company? Give justification for your answer.

(c) Which of the two measures cited for measuring volume represents the activity index as defined in this chapter? Why might Coca-Cola use two different measures?

On the Web

BYP22-4   Ganong Bros. Ltd., located in St. Stephen, New Brunswick, is Canada's oldest independent candy company. Its products are distributed worldwide. In 1885, Ganong invented the popular "chicken bone," a cinnamon-flavored, pink, hard candy jacket over a chocolate center. The home page of Ganong, listed below, includes information about the company and its products.

Address: www.ganong.com/retail/chicken_bones.html, or go to **www.wiley.com/college/weygandt**

Instructions

Read the description of "chicken bones" and answer the following.

(a) Describe the steps in making "chicken bones."

(b) Identify at least two variable and two fixed costs that are likely to affect the production of "chicken bones."

Communication Activity

BYP22-5   Your roommate asks your help on the following questions about CVP analysis formulas.

(a) How can the mathematical equation for break-even sales show both sales units and sales dollars?

(b) How do the formulas differ for contribution margin per unit and contribution margin ratio?

(c) How can contribution margin be used to determine break-even sales in units and in dollars?

Instructions

Write a memo to your roommate stating the relevant formulas and answering each question.

Ethics Case

BYP22-6   Harry Plimpton is an accountant for Handley Company. Early this year, Harry made a highly favorable projection of sales and profits over the next 3 years for Handley's hot-selling computer PLEX. As a result of the projections Harry presented to senior management, the company decided to expand production in this area. This decision led to dislocations of some plant personnel who were reassigned to one of the company's newer plants in another state. However, no one was fired, and in fact the company expanded its work force slightly.

Unfortunately, Harry rechecked his computations on the projections a few months later and found that he had made an error that would have reduced his projections substantially. Luckily, sales of PLEX have exceeded projections so far, and management is satisfied with its decision. Harry, however, is not sure what to do. Should he confess his honest mistake and jeopardize his possible promotion? He suspects that no one will catch the error because sales of PLEX have exceeded his projections, and it appears that profits will materialize close to his projections.

Instructions

(a) Who are the stakeholders in this situation?

(b) Identify the ethical issues involved in this situation.

(c) What are the possible alternative actions for Harry? What would you do in Harry's position?

"All About You" Activity

BYP22-7   In the **All About You** feature (available on the book's companion website), you learned that cost-volume-profit analysis can be used in making personal financial decisions. The purchase of a new car is one of your biggest personal expenditures. It is important that you carefully analyze your options.

Suppose that you are considering the purchase of a hybrid vehicle. Let's assume the following facts: The hybrid will initially cost an additional $3,000 above the cost of a traditional vehicle. The hybrid will get 40 miles per gallon of gas, and the traditional car will get 25 miles per gallon. Also, assume that the cost of gas is $4 per gallon.

Instructions

Using the facts above, answer the following questions.

(a) What is the variable gasoline cost of going one mile in the hybrid car? What is the variable cost of going one mile in the traditional car?

(b) Using the information in part (a), if "miles" is your unit of measure, what is the "contribution margin" of the hybrid vehicle relative to the traditional vehicle? That is, express the variable cost savings on a per-mile basis.

(c) How many miles would you have to drive in order to break even on your investment in the hybrid car?

(d) What other factors might you want to consider?

Answers to Insight and Accounting Across the Organization Questions

p. 1014 Woodworker Runs an Efficient Operation for Producing Furniture   Q: Are the costs associated with use of the computer-driven cutting machine fixed or variable? **A:** The cost of the cutting machine that is recognized through depreciation expense is a fixed cost. The costs of operating (electricity) and maintaining the machine are variable.

p. 1018 Skilled Labor Is Truly Essential   Q: Would you characterize labor costs as being a fixed cost, a variable cost, or something else in this situation? **A:** Because these labor costs are essentially unchanged for most levels of production, they are primarily fixed. However, it could be described as being a "step function." If production gets too far outside the normal range, workers' hours will change. If production goes too low, hours are cut, and if it goes too high, overtime hours are needed.

p. 1024 Charter Flights Offer a Good Deal   Q: How did FlightServe determine that it would break even with 3.3 seats full per flight? **A:** FlightServe determined its break-even point with the following formula: Fixed costs ÷ Contribution margin per seat occupied = Break-even point in seats.

p. 1028 How a Rolling Stones' Tour Makes Money   Q: What amount of sales dollars are required for the promoter to break even? **A:** Fixed costs = $1,200,000 + $400,000 = $1,600,000; contribution margin ratio = 80%; and break-even sales = $1,600,000 ÷ .80 = $2,000,000.

Answers to Self-Test Questions

1. d   **2.** c   **3.** a   **4.** d   **5.** c   **6.** d   **7.** c   **8.** c ($100 × 30%)   **9.** c ($800,000 × 25%)   **10.** b   **11.** b $600,000 − $420,000 = $180,000; $180,000 ÷ $600,000 = 30%   **12.** a   **13.** c   **14.** a ($100,000 × $12) − ($300,000 + $200,000)   **15.** a

✔
The Navigator

✔   **Remember to go back to the Navigator box on the chapter opening page and check off your completed work.**

CHAPTER23

Budgetary Planning

Study Objectives

After studying this chapter, you should be able to:

[1] Indicate the benefits of budgeting.

[2] State the essentials of effective budgeting.

[3] Identify the budgets that comprise the master budget.

[4] Describe the sources for preparing the budgeted income statement.

[5] Explain the principal sections of a cash budget.

[6] Indicate the applicability of budgeting in nonmanufacturing companies.

The Navigator

✔ [The Navigator]

- Scan Study Objectives ○
- Read Feature Story ○
- Read Preview ○
- Read text and answer **Do it!** p. 1058 ○ p. 1062 ○ p. 1066 ○ p. 1071 ○
- Work Comprehensive **Do it!** **1** p. 1074 ○ **2** p. 1076 ○
- Review Summary of Study Objectives ○
- Answer Self-Test Questions ○
- Complete Assignments ○
- Go to *WileyPLUS* for practice and tutorials ○

Feature Story

THE NEXT AMAZON.COM? NOT QUITE

The bursting of the dot-com bubble resulted in countless stories of dot-com failures. Many of these ventures were half-baked, get-rich-quick schemes, rarely based on sound business practices. Initially they saw money flowing in faster than they knew what to do with—which was precisely the problem. Without proper planning and budgeting, much of the money went to waste. In some cases, failure was actually brought on by rapid, uncontrolled growth.

One such example was online discount bookseller www.Positively-You.com. One of the website's co-founders, Lyle Bowline, had never run a business. However, his experience as an assistant director of an entrepreneurial center had provided him with knowledge about the do's and don'ts of small business. To minimize costs, he started the company small and simple. He invested $5,000 in computer equipment and ran the business out of his basement. In the early months, even though sales were only about $2,000 a month, the company actually made a profit because it kept its costs low (a feat few other dot-coms could boast of).

Things changed dramatically when the company received national publicity in the financial press. Suddenly the company's sales increased to $50,000 a month—fully 25 times the previous level. The "simple" little business suddenly needed a business plan, a strategic plan, and a budget. It needed to rent office space and to hire employees.

Initially, members of a local book club donated time to help meet the sudden demand. Some put in so much time that eventually the company hired them. Quickly the number of paid employees ballooned. The sudden growth necessitated detailed planning and budgeting. The need for a proper budget was accentuated by the fact that the company's gross profit was only 16 cents on each dollar of goods sold. This meant that after paying for its inventory, the company had only 16 cents of every dollar to cover its remaining operating costs.

Unfortunately, the company never got things under control. Within a few months, sales had plummeted to $12,000 per month. At this level of sales the company could not meet the mountain of monthly expenses that it had accumulated in trying to grow. Ironically, the company's sudden success, and the turmoil it created, appears to have been what eventually caused the company to fail.

InsideCHAPTER23

PreviewofCHAPTER23

As the Feature Story about Positively-You.com indicates, budgeting is critical to financial well-being. As a student, you budget your study time and your money. Families budget income and expenses. Governmental agencies budget revenues and expenditures. Business enterprises use budgets in planning and controlling their operations.

Our primary focus in this chapter is budgeting—specifically, how budgeting is used as a *planning tool* by management. Through budgeting, it should be possible for management to maintain enough cash to pay creditors, to have sufficient raw materials to meet production requirements, and to have adequate finished goods to meet expected sales.

The content and organization of Chapter 23 are as follows.

Budgetary Planning			
Budgeting Basics	**Preparing the Operating Budgets**	**Preparing the Financial Budgets**	**Budgeting in Nonmanufacturing Companies**
• Budgeting and accounting • Benefits • Essentials of effective budgeting • Length of budget period • Budgeting process • Budgeting and human behavior • Budgeting and long-range planning • The master budget	• Sales • Production • Direct materials • Direct labor • Manufacturing overhead • Selling and administrative expense • Budgeted income statement	• Cash • Budgeted balance sheet	• Merchandisers • Service • Not-for-profit

✔ **The Navigator**

Budgeting Basics

One of management's major responsibilities is planning. As explained in Chapter 19, **planning** is the process of establishing enterprise-wide objectives. A successful organization makes both long-term and short-term plans. These plans set forth the objectives of the company and the proposed way of accomplishing them.

A **budget** is a formal written statement of management's plans for a specified future time period, expressed in financial terms. It normally represents the primary method of communicating agreed-upon objectives throughout the organization. Once adopted, a budget becomes an important basis for evaluating performance. It promotes efficiency and serves as a deterrent to waste and inefficiency. We consider the role of budgeting as a **control device** in Chapter 24.

Budgeting and Accounting

Accounting information makes major contributions to the budgeting process. From the accounting records, companies can obtain historical data on revenues, costs, and expenses. These data are helpful in formulating future budget goals.

Normally, accountants have the responsibility for presenting management's budgeting goals in financial terms. In this role, they translate management's plans and communicate the budget to employees throughout the company. They prepare periodic budget reports that provide the basis for measuring performance and comparing actual results with planned objectives. The budget itself, and the administration of the budget, however, are entirely management responsibilities.

The Benefits of Budgeting

The primary benefits of budgeting are:

Study Objective [1]
Indicate the benefits of budgeting.

1. It requires all levels of management to **plan ahead** and to formalize goals on a recurring basis.
2. It provides **definite objectives** for evaluating performance at each level of responsibility.
3. It creates an **early warning system** for potential problems so that management can make changes before things get out of hand.
4. It facilitates the **coordination of activities** within the business. It does this by correlating the goals of each segment with overall company objectives. Thus, the company can integrate production and sales promotion with expected sales.
5. It results in greater **management awareness** of the entity's overall operations and the impact on operations of external factors, such as economic trends.
6. It **motivates personnel** throughout the organization to meet planned objectives.

A budget is an aid to management; it is not a *substitute* for management. A budget cannot operate or enforce itself. Companies can realize the benefits of budgeting only when managers carefully administer budgets.

Essentials of Effective Budgeting

Effective budgeting depends on a **sound organizational structure**. In such a structure, authority and responsibility for all phases of operations are clearly defined. Budgets based on **research and analysis** should result in realistic goals that will contribute to the growth and profitability of a company. And, the effectiveness of a budget program is directly related to its **acceptance by all levels of management**.

Study Objective [2]
State the essentials of effective budgeting.

Once adopted, the budget should be an important tool for evaluating performance. Managers should systematically and periodically review variations between actual and expected results to determine their cause(s). However, individuals should not be held responsible for variations that are beyond their control.

Length of the Budget Period

The budget period is not necessarily one year in length. **A budget may be prepared for any period of time.** Various factors influence the length of the budget period. These factors include the type of budget, the nature of the organization, the need for periodic appraisal, and prevailing business conditions. For example, cash may be budgeted monthly, whereas a plant expansion budget may cover a 10-year period.

The budget period should be long enough to provide an attainable goal under normal business conditions. Ideally, the time period should minimize the impact of seasonal or cyclical fluctuations. On the other hand, the budget period should not be so long that reliable estimates are impossible.

The **most common budget period is one year**. The annual budget, in turn, is often supplemented by monthly and quarterly budgets. Many companies use **continuous 12-month budgets**. These budgets drop the month just ended and add a future month. One advantage of continuous budgeting is that it keeps management planning a full year ahead.

The Budgeting Process

The development of the budget for the coming year generally starts several months before the end of the current year. The budgeting process usually begins with the collection of data from each organizational unit of the company. Past performance is often the starting point from which future budget goals are formulated.

The budget is developed within the framework of a **sales forecast**. This forecast shows potential sales for the industry and the company's expected share of such sales. Sales forecasting involves a consideration of various factors: (1) general economic conditions, (2) industry trends, (3) market research studies, (4) anticipated advertising and promotion, (5) previous market share, (6) changes in prices, and (7) technological developments. The input of sales personnel and top management is essential to the sales forecast.

In small companies like Positively-You.com, the budgeting process is often informal. In larger companies, a **budget committee** has responsibility for coordinating the preparation of the budget. The committee ordinarily includes the president, treasurer, chief accountant (controller), and management personnel from each of the major areas of the company, such as sales, production, and research. The budget committee serves as a review board where managers can defend their budget goals and requests. Differences are reviewed, modified if necessary, and reconciled. The budget is then put in its final form by the budget committee, approved, and distributed.

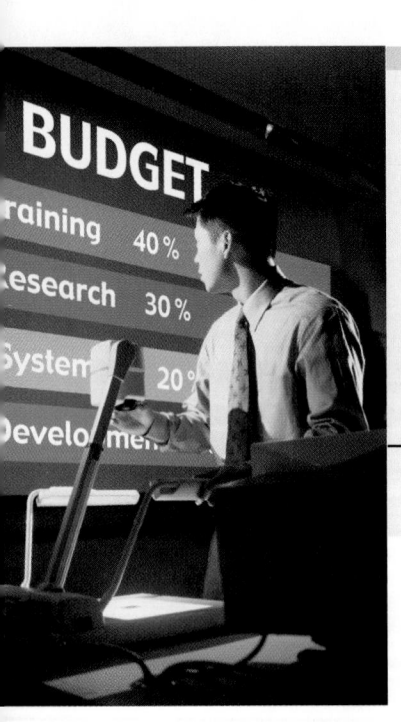

ACCOUNTING ACROSS THE ORGANIZATION

Businesses Often Feel Too Busy to Plan for the Future

A study by Willard & Shullman Group Ltd. found that fewer than 14% of businesses with fewer than 500 employees prepare an annual budget or have a written business plan. In all, nearly 60% of these businesses have no plans on paper at all. For many small businesses the basic assumption is that, "As long as I sell as much as I can, and keep my employees paid, I'm doing OK." A few small business owners even say that they see no need for budgeting and planning. Most small business owners, though, say that they understand that budgeting and planning are critical for survival and growth. But given the long hours that they already work addressing day-to-day challenges, they also say that they are "just too busy to plan for the future."

? Describe a situation in which a business "sells as much as it can" but cannot "keep its employees paid." (See page 1095.)

Budgeting and Human Behavior

A budget can have a significant impact on human behavior. It may inspire a manager to higher levels of performance. Or, it may discourage additional effort and pull down the morale of a manager. Why do these diverse effects occur? The answer is found in how the budget is developed and administered.

In developing the budget, each level of management should be invited to participate. This "bottom-to-top" approach is referred to as **participative budgeting**. The advantages of participative budgeting are, first, that lower-level managers have more detailed knowledge of their specific area and thus are able to provide more accurate budgetary estimates. Second, when lower-level managers participate in the budgeting process, they are more likely to perceive the resulting budget as fair. The overall goal is to reach agreement on a budget that the managers consider fair and achievable, but which also meets the corporate goals set by top management. When this goal is met, the budget will provide positive motivation for the managers. In contrast, if the managers view the budget as being unfair and unrealistic, they may feel discouraged and uncommitted to budget goals. The risk of having unrealistic budgets is generally greater when the budget is developed from top management down to lower management than vice versa.

Participative budgeting does, however, have potential disadvantages. First, it is more time-consuming (and thus more costly) than a "top-down" approach, in which the budget is simply dictated to lower-level managers. A second disadvantage is that participative budgeting can foster budgetary "gaming" through budgetary slack. **Budgetary slack** occurs when managers intentionally underestimate budgeted revenues or overestimate budgeted expenses in order to make it easier to achieve budgetary goals. To minimize budgetary slack, higher-level managers must carefully review and thoroughly question the budget projections provided to them by employees whom they supervise. Illustration 23-1 graphically displays the appropriate flow of budget data from bottom to top in an organization.

> **Ethics Note**
>
> Unrealistic budgets can lead to unethical employee behavior such as cutting corners on the job or distorting internal financial reports.

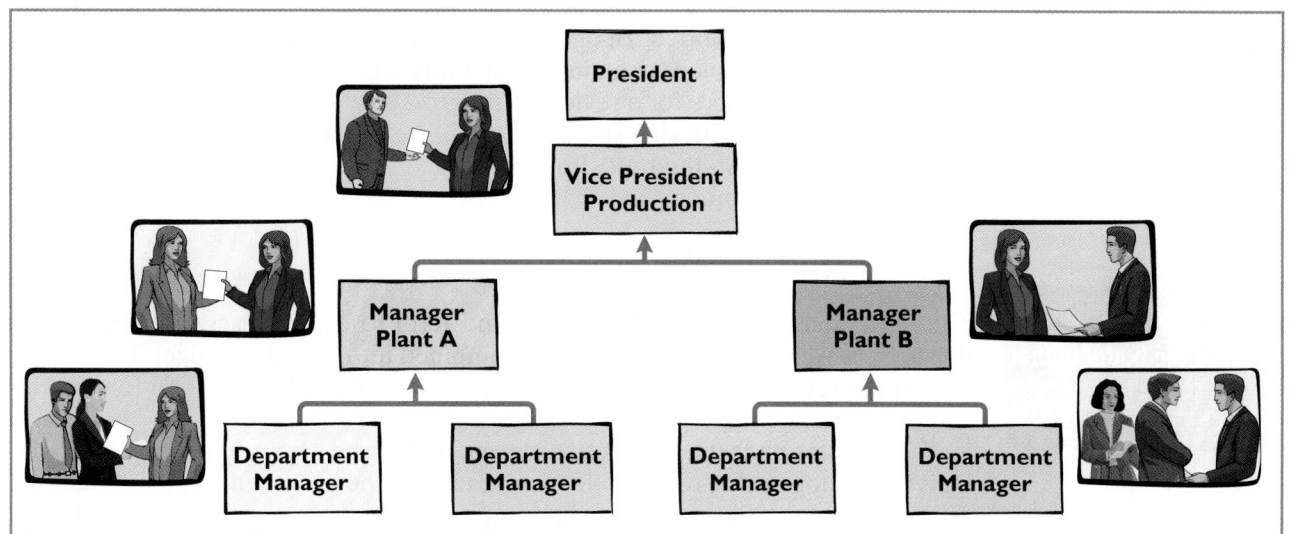

Illustration 23-1
Flow of budget data from lower levels of management to top levels

For the budget to be effective, top management must completely support the budget. The budget is an important basis for evaluating performance. It also can be used as a positive aid in achieving projected goals. The effect of an evaluation is positive when top management tempers criticism with advice and assistance. In contrast, a manager is likely to respond negatively if top management uses the budget exclusively to assess blame. A budget should not be used as a pressure device to force improved performance. In sum, a budget can be a manager's friend or a foe.

ACCOUNTING ACROSS THE ORGANIZATION

Which Budget Approach Do You Prefer?

At one time, in an effort to revive its plummeting stock, Time Warner's top management determined and publicly announced bold new financial goals for the coming year. Unfortunately, these goals were not reached.

The next year the company got a new CEO who promised, "We will not over promise, and we will deliver." The new budgets were developed with each operating unit setting what it felt were optimistic but attainable goals. In the words of one manager, using this approach created a sense of teamwork: "We're all going forward with our arms locked together."

Source: Carol J. Loomis, "AOL Time Warner's New Math," *Fortune* (February 4, 2002), pp. 98–102.

 What approach did Time Warner use to prepare the old budget? What approach did it use to prepare the new budget? (See page 1095.)

Budgeting and Long-Range Planning

Helpful Hint

In comparing a budget with a long-range plan:
(1) Which has more detail?
(2) Which is done for a longer period of time?
(3) Which is more concerned with short-term goals?
Answers: (1) Budget.
(2) Long-range plan.
(3) Budget.

Budgeting and long-range planning are not the same. One important difference is the **time period involved**. The maximum length of a budget is usually one year, and budgets are often prepared for shorter periods of time, such as a month or a quarter. In contrast, long-range planning usually encompasses a period of at least five years.

A second significant difference is in **emphasis**. Budgeting focuses on achieving specific short-term goals, such as meeting annual profit objectives. Long-range planning, on the other hand, identifies long-term goals, selects strategies to achieve those goals, and develops policies and plans to implement the strategies. In long-range planning, management also considers anticipated trends in the economic and political environment and how the company should cope with them.

The final difference between budgeting and long-range planning relates to the **amount of detail presented**. Budgets, as you will see in this chapter, can be very detailed. Long-range plans contain considerably less detail. The data in long-range plans are intended more for a review of progress toward long-term goals than as a basis of control for achieving specific results. The primary objective of long-range planning is to develop the best strategy to maximize the company's performance over an extended future period.

The Master Budget

Study Objective [3]

Identify the budgets that comprise the master budget.

The term "budget" is actually a shorthand term to describe a variety of budget documents. All of these documents are combined into a master budget. The **master budget** is a set of interrelated budgets that constitutes a plan of action for a specified time period.

The master budget contains two classes of budgets. **Operating budgets** are the individual budgets that result in the preparation of the budgeted income statement. These budgets establish goals for the company's sales and production personnel. In contrast, **financial budgets** are the capital expenditure budget, the cash budget, and the budgeted balance sheet. These budgets focus primarily on the cash resources needed to fund expected operations and planned capital expenditures.

Illustration 23-2 pictures the individual budgets included in a master budget, and the sequence in which they are prepared. The company first develops the operating budgets, beginning with the sales budget. Then it prepares the financial budgets. We will explain and illustrate each budget shown in Illustration 23-2 except the capital expenditure budget. That budget is discussed under the topic of capital budgeting in Chapter 26.

Do it!

Budget Terminology

Use this list of terms to complete the sentences that follow.

Long-range planning	Participative budgeting
Sales forecast	Operating budgets
Master budget	Financial budgets

1. A _____ shows potential sales for the industry and a company's expected share of such sales.

2. _____ are used as the basis for the preparation of the budgeted income statement.

3. The _____ is a set of interrelated budgets that constitutes a plan of action for a specified time period.

4. _____ identifies long-term goals, selects strategies to achieve these goals, and develops policies and plans to implement the strategies.

Illustration 23-2
Components of the master budget

5. Lower-level managers are more likely to perceive results as fair and achievable under a _____ approach.

6. _____ focus primarily on the cash resources needed to fund expected operations and planned capital expenditures.

Solution

1. Sales forecast.	**4.** Long-range planning.
2. Operating budgets.	**5.** Participative budgeting.
3. Master budget.	**6.** Financial budgets.

Related exercise material: BE23-1, E23-1, and **Do it!** 23-1.

action plan

✔ Understand the budgeting process, including the importance of the sales forecast.

✔ Understand the difference between an operating and a financial budget.

✔ Differentiate budgeting from long-range planning.

✔ Realize that the master budget is a set of interrelated budgets.

The Navigator

Preparing the Operating Budgets

We use a case study of Hayes Company in preparing the operating budgets. Hayes manufactures and sells a single product, Kitchen-Mate. The budgets are prepared by quarters for the year ending December 31, 2012. Hayes Company begins its annual budgeting process on September 1, 2011, and it completes the budget for 2012 by December 1, 2011.

Sales Budget

As shown in the master budget in Illustration 23-2, **the sales budget is the first budget prepared**. Each of the other budgets depends on the sales budget. The sales budget

Helpful Hint

For a retail or manufacturing company, what is the starting point in preparing the master budget, and why?
Answer: The sales budget is the starting point for the master budget. It sets the level of activity for other functions such as production and purchasing.

is derived from the sales forecast. It represents management's best estimate of sales revenue for the budget period. An inaccurate sales budget may adversely affect net income. For example, an overly optimistic sales budget may result in excessive inventories that may have to be sold at reduced prices. In contrast, an unduly conservative budget may result in loss of sales revenue due to inventory shortages.

For example, at one time Amazon significantly underestimated demand for its e-book reader, the Kindle. As a consequence, it did not produce enough units and was completely sold out well before the holiday shopping season. Not only did this represent a huge lost opportunity for Amazon, but it exposed it to potential competitors, who were eager to provide customers with alternatives to the Kindle.

Forecasting sales is challenging. For example, consider the forecasting challenges faced by major sports arenas, whose revenues depend on the success of the home team. Madison Square Garden's revenues from April to June were $193 million when the Knicks made the NBA playoffs. But revenues were only $133.2 million a couple of years later when the team did not make the playoffs. Or consider the challenges faced by Hollywood movie producers in predicting the complicated revenue stream produced by a new movie. Movie theater ticket sales represent only 20% of total revenue. The bulk of revenue comes from global sales, DVDs, video-on-demand, merchandising products, and videogames, all of which are difficult to forecast.

The sales budget is prepared by multiplying the expected unit sales volume for each product by its anticipated unit selling price. Hayes Company expects sales volume to be 3,000 units in the first quarter, with 500-unit increases in each succeeding quarter. Illustration 23-3 shows the sales budget for the year, by quarters, based on a sales price of $60 per unit.

Illustration 23-3
Sales budget

Some companies classify the anticipated sales revenue as cash or credit sales and by geographical regions, territories, or salespersons.

Production Budget

The **production budget** shows the units to produce to meet anticipated sales. Production requirements are determined from the following formula.[1]

Illustration 23-4
Production requirements formula

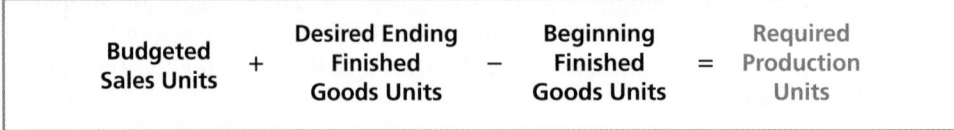

[1]This formula ignores any work in process inventories, which are assumed to be nonexistent in Hayes Company.

A realistic estimate of ending inventory is essential in scheduling production requirements. Excessive inventories in one quarter may lead to cutbacks in production and employee layoffs in a subsequent quarter. On the other hand, inadequate inventories may result either in added costs for overtime work or in lost sales. Hayes Company believes it can meet future sales requirements by maintaining an ending inventory equal to 20% of the next quarter's budgeted sales volume. For example, the ending finished goods inventory for the first quarter is 700 units (20% × anticipated second-quarter sales of 3,500 units). Illustration 23-5 shows the production budget.

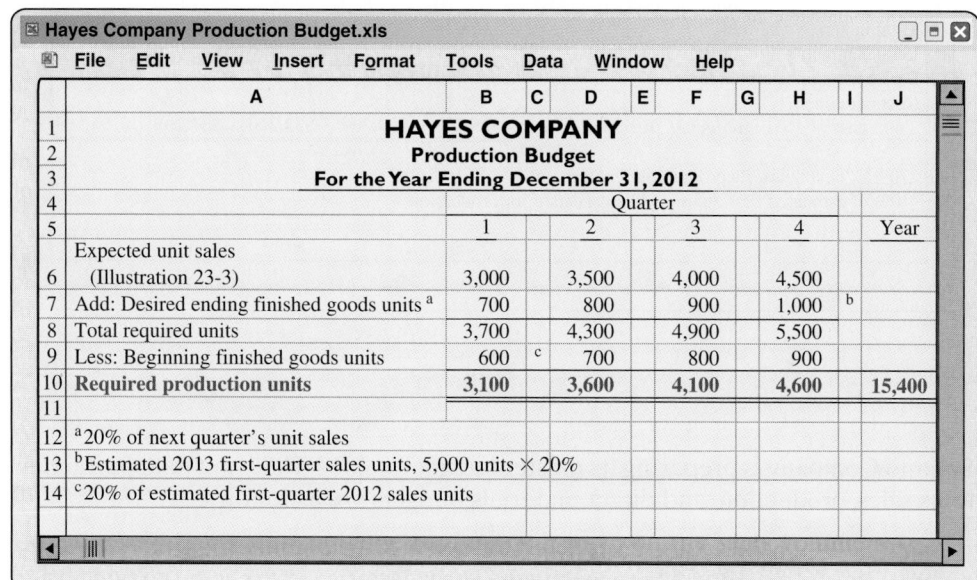

Illustration 23-5
Production budget

The production budget, in turn, provides the basis for the budgeted costs for each manufacturing cost element, as explained in the following pages.

Direct Materials Budget

The **direct materials budget** shows both the quantity and cost of direct materials to be purchased. The quantities of direct materials are derived from the following formula.

Illustration 23-6
Formula for direct materials quantities

The company then computes the budgeted cost of direct materials to be purchased by multiplying the required units of direct materials by the anticipated cost per unit.

The desired ending inventory is again a key component in the budgeting process. For example, inadequate inventories could result in temporary shutdowns of production. Because of its close proximity to suppliers, Hayes Company maintains an ending inventory of raw materials equal to 10% of the next quarter's production requirements. The manufacture of each Kitchen-Mate requires 2 pounds of raw materials, and the expected cost per pound is $4. Illustration 23-7 (page 1062) shows the direct materials budget. Assume that the desired ending direct materials amount is 1,020 pounds for the fourth quarter of 2012.

Illustration 23-7
Direct materials budget

Hayes Company Direct Materials Budget.xls

File   Edit   View   Insert   Format   Tools   Data   Window   Help

HAYES COMPANY
Direct Materials Budget
For the Year Ending December 31, 2012

	Quarter				
	1	2	3	4	Year
Units to be produced (Illustration 23-5)	3,100	3,600	4,100	4,600	
Direct materials per unit	× 2	× 2	× 2	× 2	
Total pounds needed for production	6,200	7,200	8,200	9,200	
Add: Desired ending direct materials (pounds)[a]	720	820	920	1,020	
Total materials required	6,920	8,020	9,120	10,220	
Less: Beginning direct materials (pounds)	620 [b]	720	820	920	
Direct materials purchases	6,300	7,300	8,300	9,300	
Cost per pound	× $4	× $4	× $4	× $4	
Total cost of direct materials purchases	$25,200	$29,200	$33,200	$37,200	$124,800
[a]10% of next quarter's production requirements					
[b]10% of estimated first-quarter pounds needed for production					

Do it!

Master Budget

Soriano Company is preparing its master budget for 2012. Relevant data pertaining to its sales, production, and direct materials budgets are as follows:

Sales: Sales for the year are expected to total 1,200,000 units. Quarterly sales are 20%, 25%, 30%, and 25% respectively. The sales price is expected to be $50 per unit for the first three quarters and $55 per unit beginning in the fourth quarter. Sales in the first quarter of 2013 are expected to be 10% higher than the budgeted sales for the first quarter of 2012.

Production: Management desires to maintain the ending finished goods inventories at 25% of the next quarter's budgeted sales volume.

Direct materials: Each unit requires 3 pounds of raw materials at a cost of $5 per pound. Management desires to maintain raw materials inventories at 5% of the next quarter's production requirements. Assume the production requirements for the first quarter of 2013 are 810,000 pounds.

Prepare the sales, production, and direct materials budgets by quarters for 2012.

action plan

✔ Know the form and content of the sales budget.

✔ Prepare the sales budget first, as the basis for the other budgets.

✔ Determine the units that must be produced to meet anticipated sales.

✔ Know how to compute the beginning and ending finished goods units.

✔ Determine the materials required to meet production needs.

✔ Know how to compute the beginning and ending direct materials units.

Solution

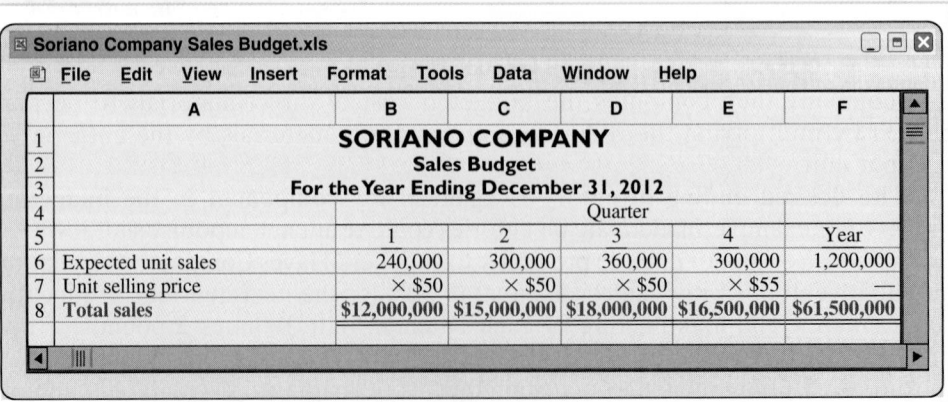

Soriano Company Sales Budget.xls

File   Edit   View   Insert   Format   Tools   Data   Window   Help

SORIANO COMPANY
Sales Budget
For the Year Ending December 31, 2012

	Quarter				
	1	2	3	4	Year
Expected unit sales	240,000	300,000	360,000	300,000	1,200,000
Unit selling price	× $50	× $50	× $50	× $55	—
Total sales	$12,000,000	$15,000,000	$18,000,000	$16,500,000	$61,500,000

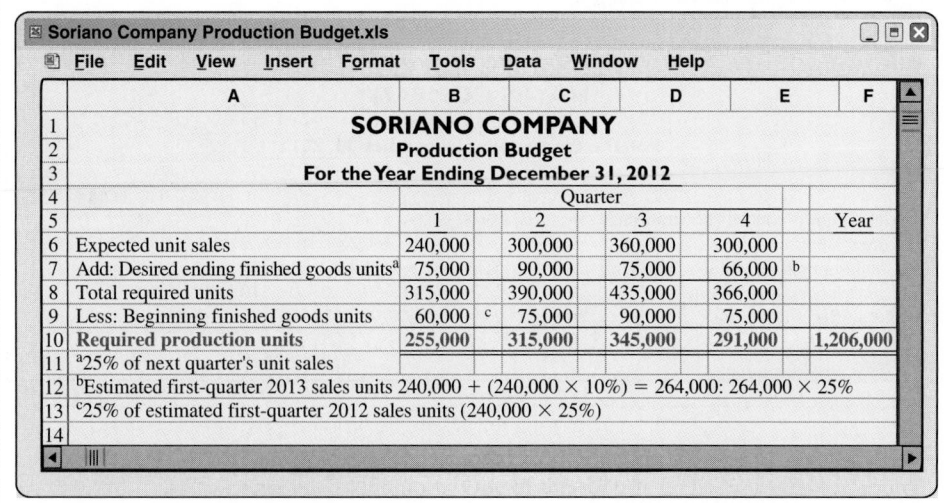

Soriano Company Production Budget.xls

File Edit View Insert Format Tools Data Window Help

	A	B	C	D	E	F
1			SORIANO COMPANY			
2			Production Budget			
3			For the Year Ending December 31, 2012			
4				Quarter		
5		1	2	3	4	Year
6	Expected unit sales	240,000	300,000	360,000	300,000	
7	Add: Desired ending finished goods units[a]	75,000	90,000	75,000	66,000 [b]	
8	Total required units	315,000	390,000	435,000	366,000	
9	Less: Beginning finished goods units	60,000 [c]	75,000	90,000	75,000	
10	**Required production units**	**255,000**	**315,000**	**345,000**	**291,000**	**1,206,000**
11	[a]25% of next quarter's unit sales					
12	[b]Estimated first-quarter 2013 sales units 240,000 + (240,000 × 10%) = 264,000: 264,000 × 25%					
13	[c]25% of estimated first-quarter 2012 sales units (240,000 × 25%)					
14						

Soriano Company Direct Materials Budget.xls

File Edit View Insert Format Tools Data Window Help

	A	B	C	D	E	F	G	H
1				SORIANO COMPANY				
2				Direct Materials Budget				
3				For the Year Ending December 31, 2012				
4					Quarter			
5		1		2	3	4		Year
6	Units to be produced	255,000		315,000	345,000	291,000		
7	Direct materials per unit	× 3		× 3	× 3	× 3		
8	Total pounds needed for production	765,000		945,000	1,035,000	873,000		
9	Add: Desired ending direct materials (pounds)	47,250		51,750	43,650	40,500 [a]		
10	Total materials required	812,250		996,750	1,078,650	913,500		
11	Less: Beginning direct materials (pounds)	38,250 [b]		47,250	51,750	43,650		
12	Direct materials purchases	774,000		949,500	1,026,900	869,850		
13	Cost per pound	× $5		× $5	× $5	× $5		
14	Total cost of direct materials purchases	$3,870,000		$4,747,500	$5,134,500	$4,349,250		$18,101,250
15								
16	[a]Estimated first-quarter 2013 production requirements 810,000 × 5% = 40,500							
17	[b]5% of estimated first-quarter pounds needed for production							
18								

Related exercise material: BE23-2, BE23-3, BE23-4, E23-2, E23-3, E23-4, E23-5, E23-6, E23-10, and **Do it!** 23-2.

The Navigator

Direct Labor Budget

Like the direct materials budget, the **direct labor budget** contains the quantity (hours) and cost of direct labor necessary to meet production requirements. The total direct labor cost is derived from the following formula.

Units to Be Produced	×	**Direct Labor Time per Unit**	×	**Direct Labor Cost per Hour**	=	Total Direct Labor Cost

Illustration 23-8
Formula for direct labor cost

Direct labor hours are determined from the production budget. At Hayes Company, two hours of direct labor are required to produce each unit of finished goods. The anticipated hourly wage rate is $10. Illustration 23-9 (page 1064) shows these data.

Illustration 23-9
Direct labor budget

Hayes Company Direct Labor Budget.xls										
File Edit View Insert Format Tools Data Window Help										

	A	B	C	D	E	F	G	H	I	J
1	**HAYES COMPANY**									
2	**Direct Labor Budget**									
3	**For the Year Ending December 31, 2012**									
4					Quarter					
5			1		2		3		4	Year
6	Units to be produced (Illustration 23-5)		3,100		3,600		4,100		4,600	
7	Direct labor time (hours) per unit		× 2		× 2		× 2		× 2	
8	Total required direct labor hours		6,200		7,200		8,200		9,200	
9	Direct labor cost per hour		× $10		× $10		× $10		× $10	
10	Total direct labor cost		$62,000		$72,000		$82,000		$92,000	$308,000
11										

Helpful Hint

An important assumption in Illustration 23-9 is that the company can add to and subtract from its work force as needed so that the $10 per hour labor cost applies to a wide range of possible production activity.

The direct labor budget is critical in maintaining a labor force that can meet the expected levels of production.

Manufacturing Overhead Budget

The **manufacturing overhead budget** shows the expected manufacturing overhead costs for the budget period. As Illustration 23-10 shows, **this budget distinguishes between variable and fixed overhead costs**. Hayes Company expects variable costs to fluctuate with production volume on the basis of the following rates per direct labor hour: indirect materials $1.00, indirect labor $1.40, utilities $0.40, and maintenance $0.20. Thus, for the 6,200 direct labor hours to produce 3,100 units, budgeted indirect materials are $6,200 (6,200 × $1), and budgeted indirect labor is $8,680 (6,200 × $1.40). Hayes also recognizes that some maintenance is fixed. The amounts reported for fixed costs are assumed for our example. The accuracy of budgeted fixed overhead cost estimates can be greatly improved by employing activity-based costing.

Illustration 23-10
Manufacturing overhead budget

Hayes Company Manufacturing Overhead Budget.xls						
File Edit View Insert Format Tools Data Window Help						

	A	B	C	D	E	F
1	**HAYES COMPANY**					
2	**Manufacturing Overhead Budget**					
3	**For the Year Ending December 31, 2012**					
4				Quarter		
5		1	2	3	4	Year
6	Variable costs					
7	Indirect materials ($1.00/hour)	$ 6,200	$ 7,200	$ 8,200	$ 9,200	$ 30,800
8	Indirect labor ($1.40/hour)	8,680	10,080	11,480	12,880	43,120
9	Utilities ($0.40/hour)	2,480	2,880	3,280	3,680	12,320
10	Maintenance ($0.20/hour)	1,240	1,440	1,640	1,840	6,160
11	Total variable costs	18,600	21,600	24,600	27,600	92,400
12	Fixed costs					
13	Supervisory salaries	20,000	20,000	20,000	20,000	80,000
14	Depreciation	3,800	3,800	3,800	3,800	15,200
15	Property taxes and insurance	9,000	9,000	9,000	9,000	36,000
16	Maintenance	5,700	5,700	5,700	5,700	22,800
17	Total fixed costs	38,500	38,500	38,500	38,500	154,000
18	Total manufacturing overhead	$57,100	$60,100	$63,100	$66,100	$246,400
19	Direct labor hours (Illustration 23-9)	6,200	7,200	8,200	9,200	30,800
20	Manufacturing overhead rate per direct labor hour ($246,400 ÷ 30,800)					$ 8
21						

At Hayes Company, overhead is applied to production on the basis of direct labor hours. Thus, as Illustration 23-10 shows, the annual rate is $8 per hour ($246,400 ÷ 30,800).

Selling and Administrative Expense Budget

Hayes Company combines its operating expenses into one budget, the **selling and administrative expense budget**. This budget projects anticipated selling and administrative expenses for the budget period. This budget (Illustration 23-11) also classifies expenses as either variable or fixed. In this case, the variable expense rates per unit of sales are sales commissions $3 and freight-out $1. Variable expenses per quarter are based on the unit sales from the sales budget (Illustration 23-3). For example, Hayes expects sales in the first quarter to be 3,000 units. Thus, Sales Commissions Expense is $9,000 (3,000 × $3), and Freight-out is $3,000 (3,000 × $1). Fixed expenses are based on assumed data. Illustration 23-11 shows the selling and administrative expense budget.

Illustration 23-11
Selling and administrative expense budget

Hayes Company Manufacturing Selling and Administrative Expense Budget.xls

File Edit View Insert Format Tools Data Window Help

	A	B	C	D	E	F
1	**HAYES COMPANY**					
2	**Selling and Administrative Expense Budget**					
3	**For the Year Ending December 31, 2012**					
4		Quarter				
5		1	2	3	4	Year
6	Budgeted sales in units (Illustration 23-3)	3,000	3,500	4,000	4,500	15,000
7	Variable expenses					
8	Sales commissions ($3 per unit)	$ 9,000	$10,500	$12,000	$13,500	$ 45,000
9	Freight-out ($1 per unit)	3,000	3,500	4,000	4,500	15,000
10	Total variable expenses	12,000	14,000	16,000	18,000	60,000
11	Fixed expenses					
12	Advertising	5,000	5,000	5,000	5,000	20,000
13	Sales salaries	15,000	15,000	15,000	15,000	60,000
14	Office salaries	7,500	7,500	7,500	7,500	30,000
15	Depreciation	1,000	1,000	1,000	1,000	4,000
16	Property taxes and insurance	1,500	1,500	1,500	1,500	6,000
17	Total fixed expenses	30,000	30,000	30,000	30,000	120,000
18	Total selling and administrative expenses	$42,000	$44,000	$46,000	$48,000	$180,000
19						

Budgeted Income Statement

The **budgeted income statement** is the important end-product of the operating budgets. This budget indicates the expected profitability of operations for the budget period. The budgeted income statement provides the basis for evaluating company performance. Budgeted income statements often act as a call to action. For example, a board member at XM Satellite Radio Holdings felt that budgeted costs were too high relative to budgeted revenues. When management refused to cut its marketing and programming costs, the board member resigned; he felt that without the cuts, the company risked financial crisis.

As you would expect, the budgeted income statement is prepared from the various operating budgets. For example, to find the cost of goods sold, it is first necessary to determine the total unit cost of producing one Kitchen-Mate, as follows.

Study Objective [4]
Describe the sources for preparing the budgeted income statement.

Illustration 23-12
Computation of total unit cost

Cost Element	Cost of One Kitchen-Mate Illustration	Quantity	Unit Cost	Total
Direct materials	23-7	2 pounds	$ 4.00	$ 8.00
Direct labor	23-9	2 hours	$10.00	20.00
Manufacturing overhead	23-10	2 hours	$ 8.00	16.00
Total unit cost				**$44.00**

Hayes Company then determines cost of goods sold by multiplying the units sold by the unit cost. Its budgeted cost of goods sold is $660,000 (15,000 × $44). All data for the statement come from the individual operating budgets except the following: (1) interest expense is expected to be $100, and (2) income taxes are estimated to be $12,000. Illustration 23-13 shows the budgeted income statement.

Illustration 23-13
Budgeted income statement

Hayes Company
Budgeted Income Statement
For the Year Ending December 31, 2012

Sales (Illustration 23-3)	$900,000
Cost of goods sold (15,000 × $44)	660,000
Gross profit	240,000
Selling and administrative expenses (Illustration 23-11)	180,000
Income from operations	60,000
Interest expense	100
Income before income taxes	59,900
Income tax expense	12,000
Net income	$ 47,900

Do it!

Budgeted Income Statement

Soriano Company is preparing its budgeted income statement for 2012. Relevant data pertaining to its sales, production, and direct materials budgets can be found in the **Do it!** exercise on page 1062.

In addition, Soriano budgets 0.5 hours of direct labor per unit, labor costs at $15 per hour, and manufacturing overhead at $25 per direct labor hour. Its budgeted selling and administrative expenses for 2012 are $12,000,000.

(a) Calculate the budgeted total unit cost.

(b) Prepare the budgeted income statement for 2012.

action plan

✔ Recall that total unit cost consists of direct materials, direct labor, and manufacturing overhead.

✔ Recall that direct materials costs are included in the direct materials budget.

✔ Know the form and content of the income statement.

✔ Use the total unit sales information from the sales budget to compute annual sales and cost of goods sold.

Solution

(a)

Cost Element	Quantity	Unit Cost	Total
Direct materials	3.0 pounds	$ 5	$15.00
Direct labor	0.5 hours	$15	7.50
Manufacturing overhead	0.5 hours	$25	12.50
Total unit cost			**$35.00**

(b)

Soriano Company	
Budgeted Income Statement	
For the Year Ending December 31, 2012	
Sales (1,200,000 units from sales budget, page 1062)	$61,500,000
Cost of goods sold (1,200,000 × $35.00/unit)	42,000,000
Gross profit	19,500,000
Selling and administrative expenses	12,000,000
Net income	$ 7,500,000

Related exercise material: BE23-8, E23-11, and **Do it!** 23-3.

The Navigator

Preparing the Financial Budgets

As shown in Illustration 23-2 (page 1059), the financial budgets consist of the capital expenditure budget, the cash budget, and the budgeted balance sheet. We will discuss the capital expenditure budget in Chapter 26; the other budgets are explained in the following sections.

Cash Budget

The **cash budget** shows anticipated cash flows. Because cash is so vital, this budget is often considered to be the most important financial budget.

The cash budget contains three sections (cash receipts, cash disbursements, and financing) and the beginning and ending cash balances, as shown in Illustration 23-14.

Study Objective [5]

Explain the principal sections of a cash budget.

Illustration 23-14
Basic form of a cash budget

Any Company	
Cash Budget	
Beginning cash balance	$X,XXX
Add: Cash receipts (Itemized)	X,XXX
Total available cash	X,XXX
Less: Cash disbursements (Itemized)	X,XXX
Excess (deficiency) of available cash over cash disbursements	X,XXX
Financing	X,XXX
Ending cash balance	$X,XXX

The **cash receipts section** includes expected receipts from the company's principal source(s) of revenue. These are usually cash sales and collections from customers on credit sales. This section also shows anticipated receipts of interest and dividends, and proceeds from planned sales of investments, plant assets, and the company's capital stock.

Helpful Hint

Why is the cash budget prepared after the other budgets are prepared? Answer: Because the information generated by the other budgets dictates the expected inflows and outflows of cash.

The **cash disbursements section** shows expected cash payments. Such payments include direct materials, direct labor, manufacturing overhead, and selling and administrative expenses. This section also includes projected payments for income taxes, dividends, investments, and plant assets.

The **financing section** shows expected borrowings and the repayment of the borrowed funds plus interest. Companies need this section when there is a cash deficiency or when the cash balance is below management's minimum required balance.

Data in the cash budget are prepared in sequence. The ending cash balance of one period becomes the beginning cash balance for the next period. Companies obtain data for preparing the cash budget from other budgets and from information provided by management. In practice, cash budgets are often prepared for the year on a monthly basis.

To minimize detail, we will assume that Hayes Company prepares an annual cash budget by quarters. Hayes Company's cash budget is based on the following assumptions.

1. The January 1, 2012, cash balance is expected to be $38,000.
2. Sales (Illustration 23-3, page 1060): 60% are collected in the quarter sold and 40% are collected in the following quarter. Accounts receivable of $60,000 at December 31, 2011, are expected to be collected in full in the first quarter of 2012.
3. Short-term investments are expected to be sold for $2,000 cash in the first quarter.
4. Direct materials (Illustration 23-7, page 1062): 50% are paid in the quarter purchased and 50% are paid in the following quarter. Accounts payable of $10,600 at December 31, 2011, are expected to be paid in full in the first quarter of 2012.
5. Direct labor (Illustration 23-9, page 1064): 100% is paid in the quarter incurred.
6. Manufacturing overhead (Illustration 23-10, page 1064) and selling and administrative expenses (Illustration 23-11, page 1065): All items except depreciation are paid in the quarter incurred.
7. Management plans to purchase a truck in the second quarter for $10,000 cash.
8. Hayes makes equal quarterly payments of its estimated annual income taxes.
9. Loans are repaid in the earliest quarter in which there is sufficient cash (that is, when the cash on hand exceeds the $15,000 minimum required balance).

In preparing the cash budget, it is useful to prepare schedules for collections from customers (assumption No. 2, above) and cash payments for direct materials (assumption No. 4, above). These schedules are shown in Illustrations 23-15 and 23-16.

Illustration 23-15
Collections from customers

Hayes Company
Schedule of Expected Collections from Customers

	Quarter			
	1	2	3	4
Accounts receivable, 12/31/11	$ 60,000			
First quarter ($180,000)	108,000	$ 72,000		
Second quarter ($210,000)		126,000	$ 84,000	
Third quarter ($240,000)			144,000	$ 96,000
Fourth quarter ($270,000)				162,000
Total collections	$168,000	$198,000	$228,000	$258,000

Illustration 23-16
Payments for direct materials

Hayes Company				
Schedule of Expected Payments for Direct Materials				
	Quarter			
	1	**2**	**3**	**4**
Accounts payable, 12/31/11	$10,600			
First quarter ($25,200)	12,600	$12,600		
Second quarter ($29,200)		14,600	$14,600	
Third quarter ($33,200)			16,600	$16,600
Fourth quarter ($37,200)				18,600
Total payments	$23,200	$27,200	$31,200	$35,200

Illustration 23-17 shows the cash budget for Hayes Company. The budget indicates that Hayes will need $3,000 of financing in the second quarter to maintain a minimum cash balance of $15,000. Since there is an excess of available cash over disbursements of $22,500 at the end of the third quarter, the borrowing, plus $100 interest, is repaid in this quarter.

Illustration 23-17
Cash budget

Hayes Company Cash Budget.xls

File　Edit　View　Insert　Format　Tools　Data　Window　Help

	A	B	C	D	E	F	G	H	I	J
1			**HAYES COMPANY**							
2			Cash Budget							
3			For the Year Ending December 31, 2012							
4					Quarter					
5		Assumption	1		2		3		4	
6	Beginning cash balance	1	$ 38,000		$ 25,500		$ 15,000		$ 19,400	
7	**Add: Receipts**									
8	Collections from customers	2	168,000		198,000		228,000		258,000	
9	Sale of securities	3	2,000		0		0		0	
10	Total receipts		170,000		198,000		228,000		258,000	
11	Total available cash		208,000		223,500		243,000		277,400	
12	**Less: Disbursements**									
13	Direct materials	4	23,200		27,200		31,200		35,200	
14	Direct labor	5	62,000		72,000		82,000		92,000	
15	Manufacturing overhead	6	53,300	a	56,300		59,300		62,300	
16	Selling and administrative expenses	6	41,000	b	43,000		45,000		47,000	
17	Purchase of truck	7	0		10,000		0		0	
18	Income tax expense	8	3,000		3,000		3,000		3,000	
19	Total disbursements		182,500		211,500		220,500		239,500	
20	Excess (deficiency) of available cash over cash disbursements		25,500		12,000		22,500		37,900	
21	**Financing**									
22	Borrowings		0		3,000		0		0	
23	Repayments-plus $100 interest	9	0		0		3,100		0	
24	Ending cash balance		$ 25,500		$ 15,000		$ 19,400		$ 37,900	
25										
26	a$57,100-$3,800 depreciation									
27	b$42,000-$1,000 depreciation									

A cash budget contributes to more effective cash management. It shows managers when additional financing is necessary well before the actual need arises. And, it indicates when excess cash is available for investments or other purposes.

SERVICE COMPANY INSIGHT

Without a Budget, Can the Games Begin?

Behind the grandeur of the Olympic Games lies a huge financial challenge—how to keep budgeted costs in line with revenues. For example, the 2006 Winter Olympics in Turin, Italy, narrowly avoided going into bankruptcy before the Games even started. In order for the event to remain solvent, organizers cancelled glitzy celebrations and shifted promotional responsibilities to an Italian state-run agency. Despite these efforts, after the Games were over, the Italian government created a lottery game to cover its financial losses.

As another example, organizers of the 2002 Winter Olympics in Salt Lake City cut budgeted costs by $200 million shortly before the events began. According to the chief operating and financial officer, the organizers went through every line item in the budget, sorting each one into "must have" versus "nice to have." As a result, the Salt Lake City Games produced a surplus of $100 million.

Source: Gabriel Kahn and Roger Thurow, "In Turin, Paying for Games Went Down to the Wire," *Wall Street Journal* (February 10, 2006).

 Why does it matter whether the Olympic Games exceed their budget? (See page 1095.)

Budgeted Balance Sheet

The **budgeted balance sheet** is a projection of financial position at the end of the budget period. This budget is developed from the budgeted balance sheet for the preceding year and the budgets for the current year. Pertinent data from the budgeted balance sheet at December 31, 2011, are as follows.

Buildings and equipment	$182,000	Common stock	$225,000
Accumulated depreciation	$ 28,800	Retained earnings	$ 46,480

Illustration 23-18 shows Hayes Company's budgeted balance sheet at December 31, 2012.

The computations and sources of the amounts are explained below.

Cash: Ending cash balance $37,900, shown in the cash budget (Illustration 23-17, page 1069).

Accounts receivable: 40% of fourth-quarter sales $270,000, shown in the schedule of expected collections from customers (Illustration 23-15, page 1068).

Finished goods inventory: Desired ending inventory 1,000 units, shown in the production budget (Illustration 23-5, page 1061) times the total unit cost $44 (shown in Illustration 23-12, page 1066).

Raw materials inventory: Desired ending inventory 1,020 pounds, times the cost per pound $4, shown in the direct materials budget (Illustration 23-7, page 1062).

Buildings and equipment: December 31, 2011, balance $182,000, plus purchase of truck for $10,000.

Illustration 23-18
Budgeted balance sheet

Hayes Company
Budgeted Balance Sheet
December 31, 2012

Assets

Cash		$ 37,900
Accounts receivable		108,000
Finished goods inventory		44,000
Raw materials inventory		4,080
Buildings and equipment	$192,000	
Less: Accumulated depreciation	48,000	144,000
Total assets		$337,980

Liabilities and Stockholders' Equity

Accounts payable	$ 18,600
Common stock	225,000
Retained earnings	94,380
Total liabilities and stockholders' equity	$337,980

Accumulated depreciation: December 31, 2011, balance $28,800, plus $15,200 depreciation shown in manufacturing overhead budget (Illustration 23-10, page 1064) and $4,000 depreciation shown in selling and administrative expense budget (Illustration 23-11, page 1065).

Accounts payable: 50% of fourth-quarter purchases $37,200, shown in schedule of expected payments for direct materials (Illustration 23-16, page 1069).

Common stock: Unchanged from the beginning of the year.

Retained earnings: December 31, 2011, balance $46,480, plus net income $47,900, shown in budgeted income statement (Illustration 23-13, page 1066).

After budget data are entered into the computer, Hayes prepares the various budgets (sales, cash, etc.), as well as the budgeted financial statements. Using spreadsheets, management can also perform "what if" (sensitivity) analyses based on different hypothetical assumptions. For example, suppose that sales managers project that sales will be 10% higher in the coming quarter. What impact does this change have on the rest of the budgeting process and the financing needs of the business? The impact of the various assumptions on the budget is quickly determined by the spreadsheet. Armed with these analyses, managers make more informed decisions about the impact of various projects. They also anticipate future problems and business opportunities. As seen in this chapter, budgeting is an excellent use of electronic spreadsheets.

Do it!

Martian Company management wants to maintain a minimum monthly cash balance of $15,000. At the beginning of March, the cash balance is $16,500, expected cash receipts for March are $210,000, and cash disbursements are expected to be $220,000. How much cash, if any, must be borrowed to maintain the desired minimum monthly balance?

Cash Budget

action plan

✔ Write down the basic form of the cash budget, starting with the beginning cash balance, adding cash receipts for the period, deducting cash disbursements, and identifying the needed financing to achieve the desired minimum ending cash balance.

✔ Insert the data given into the outlined form of the cash budget.

Solution

MARTIAN COMPANY
Cash Budget
For the Month Ending March 31, 2012

Beginning cash balance	$ 16,500
Add: Cash receipts for March	210,000
Total available cash	226,500
Less: Cash disbursements for March	220,000
Excess of available cash over cash disbursements	6,500
Financing	8,500
Ending cash balance	$ 15,000

To maintain the desired minimum cash balance of $15,000, Martian Company must borrow $8,500 cash.

Related exercise material: BE23-9, E23-12, E23-13, E23-16, and **Do it!** 23-4.

Budgeting in Nonmanufacturing Companies

Study Objective [6]

Indicate the applicability of budgeting in nonmanufacturing companies.

Budgeting is not limited to manufacturers. Budgets are also used by merchandisers, service enterprises, and not-for-profit organizations.

Merchandisers

As in manufacturing operations, the sales budget for a merchandiser is both the starting point and the key factor in the development of the master budget. The major differences between the master budgets of a merchandiser and a manufacturer are these:

1. A merchandiser **uses a merchandise purchases budget instead of a production budget**.

2. A merchandiser **does not use the manufacturing budgets (direct materials, direct labor, and manufacturing overhead)**.

The merchandise purchases budget shows the estimated cost of goods to be purchased to meet expected sales. The formula for determining budgeted merchandise purchases is:

Illustration 23-19
Merchandise purchases formula

Budgeted Cost of Goods Sold		Desired Ending Merchandise Inventory		Beginning Merchandise Inventory		Required Merchandise Purchases
	+		−		=	

To illustrate, assume that the budget committee of Lima Company is preparing the merchandise purchases budget for July 2012. It estimates that budgeted sales will be $300,000 in July and $320,000 in August. Cost of goods sold is expected to be 70% of sales—that is, $210,000 in July (.70 × $300,000) and $224,000 in August (.70 × $320,000). Lima's desired ending inventory is 20% of the following month's cost of goods sold. Required merchandise purchases for July are $212,800, as shown in Illustration 23-20.

Lima Company Merchandise Purchases Budget For the Month Ending July 31, 2012	
Budgeted cost of goods sold ($300,000 × 70%)	$210,000
Add: Desired ending merchandise inventory ($224,000 × 20%)	44,800
Total	254,800
Less: Beginning merchandise inventory ($210,000 × 20%)	42,000
Required merchandise purchases for July	**$212,800**

Illustration 23-20
Merchandise purchases budget

When a merchandiser is departmentalized, it prepares separate budgets for each department. For example, a grocery store prepares sales budgets and purchases budgets for each of its major departments, such as meats, dairy, and produce. The store then combines these budgets into a master budget for the store. When a retailer has branch stores, it prepares separate master budgets for each store. Then it incorporates these budgets into master budgets for the company as a whole.

Departmentalized budgets

Service Enterprises

In a service enterprise, such as a public accounting firm, a law office, or a medical practice, the critical factor in budgeting is **coordinating professional staff needs with anticipated services**. If a firm is overstaffed, several problems may result: Labor costs are disproportionately high. Profits are lower because of the additional salaries. Staff turnover sometimes increases because of lack of challenging work. In contrast, if a service enterprise is understaffed, it may lose revenue because existing and prospective client needs for service cannot be met. Also, professional staff may seek other jobs because of excessive work loads.

Service enterprises can obtain budget data for service revenue from **expected output** or **expected input**. When output is used, it is necessary to determine the expected billings of clients for services provided. In a public accounting firm, for example, output is the sum of its billings in auditing, tax, and consulting services. When input data are used, each professional staff member projects his or her billable time. The firm then applies billing rates to billable time to produce expected service revenue.

Not-for-Profit Organizations

Budgeting is just as important for not-for-profit organizations as for profit-oriented enterprises. The budget process, however, is different. In most cases, not-for-profit entities budget **on the basis of cash flows (expenditures and receipts), rather than on a revenue and expense basis**. Further, the starting point in the process is usually expenditures, not receipts. For the not-for-profit entity, management's task generally is to find the receipts needed to support the planned expenditures. The activity index is also likely to be significantly different. For example, in a not-for-profit entity, such as a university, budgeted faculty positions may be based on full-time equivalent students or credit hours expected to be taught in a department.

For some governmental units, voters approve the budget. In other cases, such as state governments and the federal government, legislative approval is required. After the budget is adopted, it must be followed. Overspending is often illegal.

In governmental budgets, authorizations tend to be on a line-by-line basis. That is, the budget for a municipality may have a specified authorization for police and fire protection, garbage collection, street paving, and so on. The line-item authorization of governmental budgets significantly limits the amount of discretion management can exercise. The city manager often cannot use savings from one line item, such as street paving, to cover increased spending in another line item, such as snow removal.

SERVICE COMPANY INSIGHT

Budget Shortfalls as Far as the Eye Can See

All organizations need to stick to budgets. The Museum of Contemporary Art in Los Angeles learned this the hard way. Over a 10-year period, its endowment shrunk from $50 million to $6 million as its newly hired director strove to build the museum's reputation through spending. The director consistently ran budget deficits, which eventually threatened the museum's survival.

The most recent recession has created budgeting challenges for nearly all governmental agencies. Tax revenues dropped rapidly as earnings declined and unemployment skyrocketed. At the same time, sources of debt financing dried up. To meet a projected shortfall of nearly $50 billion, California proposed to cut the school year by five days, give state workers two unpaid days off per month, and raise the state's sales tax percentage. Even Princeton University, with the largest endowment per student of any U.S. university ($2 million per student), experienced a 25% drop in the value of its endowment when the financial markets plunged. Because the endowment supports 45% of the university's $1.25 billion budget, when the endowment fell the university had to make cuts. Many raises were capped at $2,000, administrative budgets were cut by 5%, and major construction projects were put on hold.

Sources: Edward Wyatt and Jori Finkel, "Soaring in Art, Museum Trips Over Finances," *Wall Street Journal Online* (December 4, 2008); Stu Woo, "California's Plans to Close Gap Become More Drastic," *Wall Street Journal Online* (January 8, 2009); John Hechinger, "Princeton Cuts Budget as Endowment Slides," *Wall Street Journal Online* (January 9, 2009).

? Why would a university's budgeted scholarships probably fall when the stock market suffers a serious drop? (See page 1095.)

COMPREHENSIVE
Do it! 1

Barrett Company has completed all operating budgets other than the income statement for 2012. Selected data from these budgets follow.

Sales: $300,000
Purchases of raw materials: $145,000
Ending inventory of raw materials: $15,000
Direct labor: $40,000
Manufacturing overhead: $73,000, including $3,000 of depreciation expense
Selling and administrative expenses: $36,000 including depreciation expense of $1,000
Interest expense: $1,000
Principal payment on note: $2,000
Dividends declared: $2,000
Income tax rate: 30%

Other information:

Year-end accounts receivable: 4% of 2012 sales

Year-end accounts payable: 50% of ending inventory of raw materials

Interest, direct labor, manufacturing overhead, and selling and administrative expenses other than depreciation are paid as incurred.

Dividends declared and income taxes for 2012 will not be paid until 2013.

Barrett Company
Balance Sheet
December 31, 2011

Assets

Cash		$20,000
Raw materials inventory		10,000
Equipment	$40,000	
Less: Accumulated depreciation	4,000	36,000
Total assets		$66,000

Liabilities and Stockholders' Equity

Accounts payable	$ 5,000	
Notes payable	22,000	
Total liabilities		$27,000
Common stock	25,000	
Retained earnings	14,000	39,000
Total liabilities and stockholders' equity		$66,000

action plan

✔ Recall that beginning raw materials inventory plus purchases less ending raw materials inventory equals direct materials used.

✔ Prepare the budgeted income statement before the budgeted balance sheet.

✔ Use the standard form of a cash budget to determine cash on the budgeted balance sheet.

✔ Add budgeted depreciation expense to accumulated depreciation at the beginning of the year to determine accumulated depreciation on the budgeted balance sheet.

✔ Add budgeted net income to retained earnings from the beginning of the year and subtract dividends declared to determine retained earnings on the budgeted balance sheet.

✔ Verify that total assets equal total liabilities and stockholders' equity on the budgeted balance sheet.

Instructions

(a) Calculate budgeted cost of goods sold.

(b) Prepare a budgeted income statement for the year ending December 31, 2012.

(c) Prepare a budgeted balance sheet as of December 31, 2012.

Solution to Comprehensive Do it! 1

(a) Beginning raw materials + Purchases − Ending raw materials = Cost of direct materials used ($10,000 + $145,000 − $15,000 = $140,000)

Direct materials used + Direct labor + Manufacturing overhead = Cost of goods sold ($140,000 + $40,000 + $73,000 = $253,000)

(b)

Barrett Company
Budgeted Income Statement
For the Year Ending December 31, 2012

Sales		$300,000
Cost of goods sold		253,000
Gross profit		47,000
Selling and administrative expenses	$36,000	
Interest expense	1,000	37,000
Income before income tax expense		10,000
Income tax expense (30%)		3,000
Net income		$ 7,000

(c)

Barrett Company
Budgeted Balance Sheet
December 31, 2012

Assets

Cash[1]		$17,500
Accounts receivable (4% × $300,000)		12,000
Raw materials inventory		15,000
Equipment	$40,000	
Less: Accumulated depreciation	8,000	32,000
Total assets		$76,500

Liabilities and Stockholders' Equity

Accounts payable (50% × $15,000)	$ 7,500	
Income taxes payable	3,000	
Dividends payable	2,000	
Note payable	20,000	
Total liabilities		$32,500
Common stock	25,000	
Retained earnings[2]	19,000	44,000
Total liabilities and stockholders' equity		$76,500

[1]Beginning cash balance		$ 20,000
Add: Collections from customers		
(96% × $300,000 sales)		288,000
Total available cash		308,000
Less: Disbursements		
Direct materials ($5,000 + $145,000 − $7,500)	$142,500	
Direct labor	40,000	
Manufacturing overhead	70,000	
Selling and administrative expenses	35,000	
Total disbursements		287,500
Excess of available cash over cash disbursements		20,500
Financing		
Repayments of principal	2,000	
Interest payments	1,000	3,000
Ending cash balance		$ 17,500

[2]Beginning retained earnings + Net income − Dividends declared = Ending retained earnings ($14,000 + $7,000 − $2,000 = $19,000)

The Navigator

COMPREHENSIVE

Do it! 2

Asheville Company is preparing its master budget for 2012. Relevant data pertaining to its sales and production budgets are as follows:

Sales: Sales for the year are expected to total 1,200,000 units. Quarterly sales, as a percentage of total sales, are 20%, 25%, 30%, and 25%, respectively. The sales price is expected to be $50 per unit for the first three quarters and $55 per unit beginning in the fourth quarter. Sales in the first quarter of 2013 are expected to be 10% higher than the budgeted sales volume for the first quarter of 2012.

Production: Management desires to maintain ending finished goods inventories at 25% of the next quarter's budgeted sales volume.

Instructions

Prepare the sales budget and production budget by quarters for 2012.

action plan

✔ Know the form and content of the sales budget.

✔ Prepare the sales budget first as the basis for the other budgets.

✔ Determine the units that must be produced to meet anticipated sales.

✔ Know how to compute the beginning and ending finished goods units.

Solution to Comprehensive Do it! 2

ASHEVILLE COMPANY
Sales Budget
For the Year Ending December 31, 2012

	Quarter				
	1	2	3	4	Year
Expected unit sales	240,000	300,000	360,000	300,000	1,200,000
Unit selling price	× $50	× $50	× $50	× $55	—
Total sales	$12,000,000	$15,000,000	$18,000,000	$16,500,000	$61,500,000

ASHEVILLE COMPANY
Production Budget
For the Year Ending December 31, 2012

	Quarter				
	1	2	3	4	Year
Expected unit sales	240,000	300,000	360,000	300,000	
Add: Desired ending finished goods units	75,000	90,000	75,000	66,000[1]	
Total required units	315,000	390,000	435,000	366,000	
Less: Beginning finished goods units	60,000[2]	75,000	90,000	75,000	
Required production units	255,000	315,000	345,000	291,000	1,206,000

[1]Estimated first-quarter 2013 sales volume 240,000 + (240,000 × 10%) = 264,000; 264,000 × 25%.
[2]25% of estimated first-quarter 2012 sales units (240,000 × 25%).

✔ The Navigator

Summary of Study Objectives

[1] Indicate the benefits of budgeting. The primary advantages of budgeting are that it (a) requires management to plan ahead, (b) provides definite objectives for evaluating performance, (c) creates an early warning system for potential problems, (d) facilitates coordination of activities, (e) results in greater management awareness, and (f) motivates personnel to meet planned objectives.

[2] State the essentials of effective budgeting. The essentials of effective budgeting are (a) sound organizational structure, (b) research and analysis, and (c) acceptance by all levels of management.

[3] Identify the budgets that comprise the master budget. The master budget consists of the following budgets: (a) sales, (b) production, (c) direct materials, (d) direct labor, (e) manufacturing overhead, (f) selling and administrative expense, (g) budgeted income statement, (h) capital expenditure budget, (i) cash budget, and (j) budgeted balance sheet.

[4] Describe the sources for preparing the budgeted income statement. The budgeted income statement is prepared from (a) the sales budget, (b) the budgets for direct materials, direct labor, and manufacturing overhead, and (c) the selling and administrative expense budget.

[5] Explain the principal sections of a cash budget. The cash budget has three sections (receipts, disbursements, and financing) and the beginning and ending cash balances.

[6] Indicate the applicability of budgeting in nonmanufacturing companies. Budgeting may be used by merchandisers for development of a master budget. In service enterprises budgeting is a critical factor in coordinating staff needs with anticipated services. In not-for-profit organizations, the starting point in budgeting is usually expenditures, not receipts.

✔ The Navigator

Glossary

Budget A formal written statement of management's plans for a specified future time period, expressed in financial terms. (p. 1054).

Budget committee A group responsible for coordinating the preparation of the budget. (p. 1056).

Budgetary slack The amount by which a manager intentionally underestimates budgeted revenues or overestimates budgeted expenses in order to make it easier to achieve budgetary goals. (p. 1057).

Budgeted balance sheet A projection of financial position at the end of the budget period. (p. 1070).

Budgeted income statement An estimate of the expected profitability of operations for the budget period. (p. 1065).

Cash budget A projection of anticipated cash flows. (p. 1067).

Direct labor budget A projection of the quantity and cost of direct labor necessary to meet production requirements. (p. 1063).

Direct materials budget An estimate of the quantity and cost of direct materials to be purchased. (p. 1061).

Financial budgets Individual budgets that focus primarily on the cash resources needed to fund expected operations and planned capital expenditures. (p. 1058).

Long-range planning A formalized process of selecting strategies to achieve long-term goals and developing policies and plans to implement the strategies. (p. 1058).

Manufacturing overhead budget An estimate of expected manufacturing overhead costs for the budget period. (p. 1064).

Master budget A set of interrelated budgets that constitutes a plan of action for a specific time period. (p. 1058).

Merchandise purchases budget The estimated cost of goods to be purchased by a merchandiser to meet expected sales. (p. 1072).

Operating budgets Individual budgets that result in a budgeted income statement. (p. 1058).

Participative budgeting A budgetary approach that starts with input from lower-level managers and works upward so that managers at all levels participate. (p. 1056).

Production budget A projection of the units that must be produced to meet anticipated sales. (p. 1060).

Sales budget An estimate of expected sales revenue for the budget period. (p. 1059).

Sales forecast The projection of potential sales for the industry and the company's expected share of such sales. (p. 1056).

Selling and administrative expense budget A projection of anticipated selling and administrative expenses for the budget period. (p. 1065).

 Self-Test, Brief Exercises, Exercises, Problem Set A, and many more components are available for practice in *WileyPLUS*

Self-Test Questions

Answers are on page 1095.

(SO 1) **1.** Which of the following is *not* a benefit of budgeting?
  a. Management can plan ahead.
  b. An early warning system is provided for potential problems.
  c. It enables disciplinary action to be taken at every level of responsibility.
  d. The coordination of activities is facilitated.

(SO 1) **2.** A budget:
  a. is the responsibility of management accountants.
  b. is the primary method of communicating agreed-upon objectives throughout an organization.
  c. ignores past performance because it represents management's plans for a future time period.
  d. may promote efficiency but has no role in evaluating performance.

(SO 2) **3.** The essentials of effective budgeting do *not* include:
  a. top-down budgeting.
  b. management acceptance.
  c. research and analysis.
  d. sound organizational structure.

4. Compared to budgeting, long-range planning generally (SO 2) has the:
  a. same amount of detail.
  b. longer time period.
  c. same emphasis.
  d. same time period.

5. A sales budget is: (SO 3)
  a. derived from the production budget.
  b. management's best estimate of sales revenue for the year.
  c. not the starting point for the master budget.
  d. prepared only for credit sales.

6. The formula for the production budget is budgeted sales (SO 3) in units plus:
  a. desired ending merchandise inventory less beginning merchandise inventory.
  b. beginning finished goods units less desired ending finished goods units.
  c. desired ending direct materials units less beginning direct materials units.
  d. desired ending finished goods units less beginning finished goods units.

(SO 3) 7. Direct materials inventories are kept in pounds in Byrd Company, and the total pounds of direct materials needed for production is 9,500. If the beginning inventory is 1,000 pounds and the desired ending inventory is 2,200 pounds, the total pounds to be purchased is:
   a. 9,400.   c. 9,700.
   b. 9,500.   d. 10,700.

(SO 4) 8. The formula for computing the direct labor budget is to multiply the direct labor cost per hour by the:
   a. total required direct labor hours.
   b. physical units to be produced.
   c. equivalent units to be produced.
   d. No correct answer is given.

(SO 4) 9. Each of the following budgets is used in preparing the budgeted income statement *except* the:
   a. sales budget.
   b. selling and administrative budget.
   c. capital expenditure budget.
   d. direct labor budget.

(SO 4) 10. The budgeted income statement is:
   a. the end-product of the operating budgets.
   b. the end-product of the financial budgets.
   c. the starting point of the master budget.
   d. dependent on cash receipts and cash disbursements.

(SO 5) 11. The budgeted balance sheet is:
   a. developed from the budgeted balance sheet for the preceding year and the budgets for the current year.
   b. the last operating budget prepared.
   c. used to prepare the cash budget.
   d. All of the above.

(SO 5) 12. The format of a cash budget is:
   a. Beginning cash balance + Cash receipts + Cash from financing − Cash disbursements = Ending cash balance.

   b. Beginning cash balance + Cash receipts − Cash disbursements +/− Financing = Ending cash balance.
   c. Beginning cash balance + Net income − Cash dividends = Ending cash balance.
   d. Beginning cash balance + Cash revenues − Cash expenses = Ending cash balance.

13. Expected direct materials purchases in Read Company (SO 5) are $70,000 in the first quarter and $90,000 in the second quarter. Forty percent of the purchases are paid in cash as incurred, and the balance is paid in the following quarter. The budgeted cash payments for purchases in the second quarter are:
   a. $96,000.   c. $78,000.
   b. $90,000.   d. $72,000.

14. The budget for a merchandiser differs from a budget for a (SO 6) manufacturer because:
   a. a merchandise purchases budget replaces the production budget.
   b. the manufacturing budgets are not applicable.
   c. None of the above.
   d. Both (a) and (b) above.

15. In most cases, not-for-profit entities: (SO 6)
   a. prepare budgets using the same steps as those used by profit-oriented enterprises.
   b. know budgeted cash receipts at the beginning of a time period, so they budget only for expenditures.
   c. begin the budgeting process by budgeting expenditures rather than receipts.
   d. can ignore budgets because they are not expected to generate net income.

Go to the book's companion website, **www.wiley.com/college/weygandt**, for additional Self-Test Questions.

The Navigator

Questions

1. (a) What is a budget?
   (b) How does a budget contribute to good management?

2. Alex Mashiri and Dana Mendel are discussing the benefits of budgeting. They ask you to identify the primary advantages of budgeting. Comply with their request.

3. June Hizemann asks your help in understanding the essentials of effective budgeting. Identify the essentials for June.

4. (a) "Accounting plays a relatively unimportant role in budgeting." Do you agree? Explain.
   (b) What responsibilities does management have in budgeting?

5. What criteria are helpful in determining the length of the budget period? What is the most common budget period?

6. Denise Cruz maintains that the only difference between budgeting and long-range planning is time. Do you agree? Why or why not?

7. What is participative budgeting? What are its potential benefits? What are its potential shortcomings?

8. What is budgetary slack? What incentive do managers have to create budgetary slack?

9. Distinguish between a master budget and a sales forecast.

10. What budget is the starting point in preparing the master budget? What may result if this budget is inaccurate?

11. "The production budget shows both unit production data and unit cost data." Is this true? Explain.

12. Lima Company has 15,000 beginning finished goods units. Budgeted sales units are 160,000. If management desires 20,000 ending finished goods units, what are the required units of production?

13. In preparing the direct materials budget for Rudder Company, management concludes that required purchases are 64,000 units. If 52,000 direct materials units are required in production and there are 7,000 units of beginning direct materials, what is the desired units of ending direct materials?

14. The production budget of Artest Company calls for 80,000 units to be produced. If it takes 30 minutes to make one

unit and the direct labor rate is $16 per hour, what is the total budgeted direct labor cost?

15. Ichiro Company's manufacturing overhead budget shows total variable costs of $198,000 and total fixed costs of $162,000. Total production in units is expected to be 160,000. It takes 15 minutes to make one unit, and the direct labor rate is $15 per hour. Express the manufacturing overhead rate as (a) a percentage of direct labor cost, and (b) an amount per direct labor hour.

16. Phat Company's variable selling and administrative expenses are 10% of net sales. Fixed expenses are $50,000 per quarter. The sales budget shows expected sales of $200,000 and $250,000 in the first and second quarters, respectively. What are the total budgeted selling and administrative expenses for each quarter?

17. For Nikoli Company, the budgeted cost for one unit of product is direct materials $10, direct labor $20, and manufacturing overhead 90% of direct labor cost. If 25,000 units are expected to be sold at $69 each, what is the budgeted gross profit?

18. Indicate the supporting schedules used in preparing a budgeted income statement through gross profit for a manufacturer.

19. Identify the three sections of a cash budget. What balances are also shown in this budget?

20. Bill Blass Company has credit sales of $500,000 in January. Past experience suggests that 45% is collected in the month of sale, 50% in the month following the sale, and 5% in the second month following the sale. Compute the cash collections from January sales in January, February, and March.

21. What is the formula for determining required merchandise purchases for a merchandiser?

22. How may expected revenues in a service enterprise be computed?

Brief Exercises

Prepare a diagram of a master budget.
(SO 3)

BE23-1   Royalty Manufacturing Company uses the following budgets: Balance Sheet, Capital Expenditure, Cash, Direct Labor, Direct Materials, Income Statement, Manufacturing Overhead, Production, Sales, and Selling and Administrative. Prepare a diagram of the interrelationships of the budgets in the master budget. Indicate whether each budget is an operating or a financial budget.

Prepare a sales budget.
(SO 3)

BE23-2   Moon Company estimates that unit sales will be 10,000 in quarter 1; 12,000 in quarter 2; 14,000 in quarter 3; and 18,000 in quarter 4. Using a sales price of $80 per unit, prepare the sales budget by quarters for the year ending December 31, 2012.

Prepare a production budget for 2 quarters.
(SO 3)

BE23-3   Sales budget data for Moon Company are given in BE23-2. Management desires to have an ending finished goods inventory equal to 20% of the next quarter's expected unit sales. Prepare a production budget by quarters for the first 6 months of 2012.

Prepare a direct materials budget for 1 month.
(SO 3)

BE23-4   Gutierrez Company has 1,600 pounds of raw materials in its December 31, 2012, ending inventory. Required production for January and February of 2013 are 4,000 and 5,500 units, respectively. Two pounds of raw materials are needed for each unit, and the estimated cost per pound is $6. Management desires an ending inventory equal to 20% of next month's materials requirements. Prepare the direct materials budget for January.

Prepare a direct labor budget for 2 quarters.
(SO 3)

BE23-5   For Pickney Company, units to be produced are 5,000 in quarter 1 and 6,000 in quarter 2. It takes 1.5 hours to make a finished unit, and the expected hourly wage rate is $14 per hour. Prepare a direct labor budget by quarters for the 6 months ending June 30, 2012.

Prepare a manufacturing overhead budget.
(SO 3)

BE23-6   For Orville Inc., variable manufacturing overhead costs are expected to be $20,000 in the first quarter of 2012 with $4,000 increments in each of the remaining three quarters. Fixed overhead costs are estimated to be $35,000 in each quarter. Prepare the manufacturing overhead budget by quarters and in total for the year.

Prepare a selling and administrative expense budget.
(SO 3)

BE23-7   Jeter Company classifies its selling and administrative expense budget into variable and fixed components. Variable expenses are expected to be $25,000 in the first quarter, and $5,000 increments are expected in the remaining quarters of 2012. Fixed expenses are expected to be $40,000 in each quarter. Prepare the selling and administrative expense budget by quarters and in total for 2012.

Prepare a budgeted income statement for the year.
(SO 4)

BE23-8   Hawke Company has completed all of its operating budgets. The sales budget for the year shows 50,000 units and total sales of $2,000,000. The total unit cost of making one unit of sales is $22. Selling and administrative expenses are expected to be $300,000. Income taxes are estimated to be $150,000. Prepare a budgeted income statement for the year ending December 31, 2012.

Prepare data for a cash budget.
(SO 5)

BE23-9   Apogee Industries expects credit sales for January, February, and March to be $200,000, $260,000, and $310,000, respectively. It is expected that 70% of the sales will be collected in the month of sale, and 30% will be collected in the following month. Compute cash collections from customers for each month.

BE23-10   Naples Wholesalers is preparing its merchandise purchases budget. Budgeted sales are $400,000 for April and $475,000 for May. Cost of goods sold is expected to be 60% of sales. The company's desired ending inventory is 20% of the following month's cost of goods sold. Compute the required purchases for April.

Determine required merchandise purchases for 1 month.
(SO 6)

Do it! Review

Do it! 23-1   Use this list of terms to complete the sentences that follow.

Identify budget terminology.
(SO 2, 3)

Long-range plans	Participative budgeting
Sales forecast	Operating budgets
Master budget	Financial budgets

1. _____ establish goals for the company's sales and production personnel.
2. The _____ is a set of interrelated budgets that constitutes a plan of action for a specified time period.
3. _____ reduces the risk of having unrealistic budgets.
4. _____ include the cash budget and the budgeted balance sheet.
5. The budget is formed within the framework of a _____.
6. _____ contain considerably less detail than budgets.

Do it! 23-2   Green River Company is preparing its master budget for 2012. Relevant data pertaining to its sales, production, and direct materials budgets are as follows.

Prepare sales, production, and direct materials budgets.
(SO 3)

Sales: Sales for the year are expected to total 1,000,000 units. Quarterly sales are 20%, 25%, 25%, and 30%, respectively. The sales price is expected to be $40 per unit for the first three quarters and $45 per unit beginning in the fourth quarter. Sales in the first quarter of 2013 are expected to be 10% higher than the budgeted sales for the first quarter of 2012.

Production: Management desires to maintain the ending finished goods inventories at 20% of the next quarter's budgeted sales volume.

Direct materials: Each unit requires 2 pounds of raw materials at a cost of $10 per pound. Management desires to maintain raw materials inventories at 10% of the next quarter's production requirements. Assume the production requirements for first quarter of 2013 are 500,000 pounds.

Prepare the sales, production, and direct materials budgets by quarters for 2012.

Do it! 23-3   Green River Company is preparing its budgeted income statement for 2012. Relevant data pertaining to its sales, production, and direct materials budgets can be found in Do it! 23-2 above.

Calculate budgeted total unit cost and prepare budgeted income statement.
(SO 4)

   In addition, Green River budgets 0.3 hours of direct labor per unit, labor costs at $14 per hour, and manufacturing overhead at $20 per direct labor hour. Its budgeted selling and administrative expenses for 2012 are $7,000,000.

(a) Calculate the budgeted total unit cost.
(b) Prepare the budgeted income statement for 2012.

Do it! 23-4   Algerian Company management wants to maintain a minimum monthly cash balance of $20,000. At the beginning of April, the cash balance is $22,000, expected cash receipts for April are $245,000, and cash disbursements are expected to be $256,000. How much cash, if any, must be borrowed to maintain the desired minimum monthly balance?

Determine amount of financing needed.
(SO 5)

Exercises

E23-1   ━━━━━▶ Rolling Stone Company has always done some planning for the future, but the company has never prepared a formal budget. Now that the company is growing larger, it is considering preparing a budget.

Explain the concept of budgeting.
(SO 1, 2, 3)

Instructions

Write a memo to Mick Jagger, the president of Rolling Stone Company, in which you define budgeting, identify the budgets that comprise the master budget, identify the primary benefits of budgeting, and discuss the essentials of effective budgeting.

Prepare a sales budget for 2 quarters.

(SO 3)

E23-2   Antwon Electronics Inc. produces and sells two models of pocket calculators, XQ-103 and XQ-104. The calculators sell for $12 and $25, respectively. Because of the intense competition Antwon faces, management budgets sales semiannually. Its projections for the first 2 quarters of 2012 are as follows.

	Unit Sales	
Product	**Quarter 1**	**Quarter 2**
XQ-103	20,000	25,000
XQ-104	12,000	15,000

No changes in selling prices are anticipated.

Instructions

Prepare a sales budget for the 2 quarters ending June 30, 2012. List the products and show for each quarter and for the 6 months, units, selling price, and total sales by product and in total.

Prepare a sales budget for four quarters.

(SO 3, 6)

E23-3   Ernst and Anderson, CPAs, are preparing their service revenue (sales) budget for the coming year (2012). The practice is divided into three departments: auditing, tax, and consulting. Billable hours for each department, by quarter, are provided below.

Department	**Quarter 1**	**Quarter 2**	**Quarter 3**	**Quarter 4**
Auditing	2,200	1,600	2,000	2,400
Tax	3,000	2,400	2,000	2,500
Consulting	1,500	1,500	1,500	1,500

Average hourly billing rates are: auditing $80, tax $90, and consulting $100.

Instructions

Prepare the service revenue (sales) budget for 2012 by listing the departments and showing for each quarter and the year in total, billable hours, billable rate, and total revenue.

Prepare quarterly production budgets.

(SO 3)

E23-4   Paulina Company produces and sells automobile batteries, the heavy-duty HD-240. The 2012 sales budget is as follows.

Quarter	**HD-240**
1	5,000
2	7,000
3	8,000
4	10,000

The January 1, 2012, inventory of HD-240 is 2,500 units. Management desires an ending inventory each quarter equal to 50% of the next quarter's sales. Sales in the first quarter of 2013 are expected to be 30% higher than sales in the same quarter in 2012.

Instructions

Prepare quarterly production budgets for each quarter and in total for 2012.

Prepare a direct materials purchases budget.

(SO 3)

E23-5   Paseo Industries has adopted the following production budget for the first 4 months of 2013.

Month	**Units**	**Month**	**Units**
January	10,000	March	5,000
February	8,000	April	4,000

Each unit requires 3 pounds of raw materials costing $2 per pound. On December 31, 2012, the ending raw materials inventory was 9,000 pounds. Management wants to have a raw materials inventory at the end of the month equal to 30% of next month's production requirements.

Instructions

Prepare a direct materials purchases budget by month for the first quarter.

E23-6 On January 1, 2013 the Jorge Company budget committee has reached agreement on the following data for the 6 months ending June 30, 2013.

Prepare production and direct materials budgets by quarters for 6 months.
(SO 3)

Sales units:	First quarter 5,000; second quarter 6,000; third quarter 7,000
Ending raw materials inventory:	50% of the next quarter's production requirements
Ending finished goods inventory:	30% of the next quarter's expected sales units
Third-quarter production:	7,250 units

The ending raw materials and finished goods inventories at December 31, 2012, follow the same percentage relationships to production and sales that occur in 2013. Three pounds of raw materials are required to make each unit of finished goods. Raw materials purchased are expected to cost $4 per pound.

Instructions

(a) Prepare a production budget by quarters for the 6-month period ended June 30, 2013.

(b) Prepare a direct materials budget by quarters for the 6-month period ended June 30, 2013.

E23-7 Chung, Inc., is preparing its direct labor budget for 2012 from the following production budget based on a calendar year.

Prepare a direct labor budget.
(SO 3)

Quarter	Units	Quarter	Units
1	20,000	3	35,000
2	25,000	4	30,000

Each unit requires 1.6 hours of direct labor.

Instructions

Prepare a direct labor budget for 2012. Wage rates are expected to be $15 for the first 2 quarters and $16 for quarters 3 and 4.

E23-8 Tye Company is preparing its manufacturing overhead budget for 2012. Relevant data consist of the following.

Prepare a manufacturing overhead budget for the year.
(SO 3)

Units to be produced (by quarters): 10,000, 12,000, 14,000, 16,000.

Direct labor: Time is 1.5 hours per unit.

Variable overhead costs per direct labor hour: Indirect materials $0.70; indirect labor $1.20; and maintenance $0.50.

Fixed overhead costs per quarter: Supervisory salaries $35,000; depreciation $16,000; and maintenance $12,000.

Instructions

Prepare the manufacturing overhead budget for the year, showing quarterly data.

E23-9 Duke Company combines its operating expenses for budget purposes in a selling and administrative expense budget. For the first 6 months of 2012, the following data are available.

Prepare a selling and administrative expense budget for 2 quarters.
(SO 3)

1. Sales: 20,000 units quarter 1; 22,000 units quarter 2.

2. Variable costs per dollar of sales: Sales commissions 5%, delivery expense 2%, and advertising 3%.

3. Fixed costs per quarter: Sales salaries $10,000, office salaries $6,000, depreciation $4,200, insurance $1,500, utilities $800, and repairs expense $600.

4. Unit selling price: $20.

Instructions

Prepare a selling and administrative expense budget by quarters for the first 6 months of 2012.

E23-10 Buddy Holly Company's sales budget projects unit sales of part 198Z of 10,000 units in January, 12,000 units in February, and 13,000 units in March. Each unit of part 198Z requires 2 pounds of materials, which cost $3 per pound. Buddy Holly Company desires its ending raw materials inventory to equal 40% of the next month's production requirements, and its ending

Prepare a production and a direct materials budget.
(SO 3)

finished goods inventory to equal 25% of the next month's expected unit sales. These goals were met at December 31, 2011.

Instructions
(a) Prepare a production budget for January and February 2012.
(b) Prepare a direct materials budget for January 2012.

Prepare a budgeted income statement for the year.
(SO 3, 4)

E23-11   Stan Company has accumulated the following budget data for the year 2012.
1. Sales: 30,000 units, unit selling price $80.
2. Cost of one unit of finished goods: Direct materials 2 pounds at $5 per pound, direct labor 3 hours at $12 per hour, and manufacturing overhead $6 per direct labor hour.
3. Inventories (raw materials only): Beginning, 10,000 pounds; ending, 15,000 pounds.
4. Raw materials cost: $5 per pound.
5. Selling and administrative expenses: $200,000.
6. Income taxes: 30% of income before income taxes.

Instructions
(a) Prepare a schedule showing the computation of cost of goods sold for 2012.
(b) Prepare a budgeted income statement for 2012.

Prepare a cash budget for 2 months.
(SO 5)

E23-12   Ming Company expects to have a cash balance of $46,000 on January 1, 2012. Relevant monthly budget data for the first 2 months of 2012 are as follows.

Collections from customers: January $85,000, February $150,000.

Payments for direct materials: January $50,000, February $70,000.

Direct labor: January $30,000, February $45,000. Wages are paid in the month they are incurred.

Manufacturing overhead: January $21,000, February $25,000. These costs include depreciation of $1,000 per month. All other overhead costs are paid as incurred.

Selling and administrative expenses: January $15,000, February $20,000. These costs are exclusive of depreciation. They are paid as incurred.

Sales of marketable securities in January are expected to realize $10,000 in cash. Ming Company has a line of credit at a local bank that enables it to borrow up to $25,000. The company wants to maintain a minimum monthly cash balance of $20,000.

Instructions
Prepare a cash budget for January and February.

Prepare a cash budget.
(SO 5)

E23-13   Blue Lagoon Corporation is projecting a cash balance of $31,000 in its December 31, 2011, balance sheet. Blue Lagoon's schedule of expected collections from customers for the first quarter of 2012 shows total collections of $180,000. The schedule of expected payments for direct materials for the first quarter of 2012 shows total payments of $41,000. Other information gathered for the first quarter of 2012 is: sale of equipment $3,500, direct labor $70,000, manufacturing overhead $35,000, selling and administrative expenses $45,000, and purchase of securities $12,000. Blue Lagoon wants to maintain a balance of at least $25,000 cash at the end of each quarter.

Instructions
Prepare a cash budget for the first quarter.

Prepare schedules of expected collections and payments.
(SO 5)

E23-14   AIM Company's budgeted sales and direct materials purchases are as follows.

	Budgeted Sales	**Budgeted D.M. Purchases**
January	$200,000	$30,000
February	220,000	35,000
March	270,000	41,000

AIM's sales are 40% cash and 60% credit. Credit sales are collected 10% in the month of sale, 50% in the month following sale, and 36% in the second month following sale; 4% are uncollectible. AIM's purchases are 50% cash and 50% on account. Purchases on account are paid 40% in the month of purchase, and 60% in the month following purchase.

Instructions
(a) Prepare a schedule of expected collections from customers for March.
(b) Prepare a schedule of expected payments for direct materials for March.

E23-15 Home Exteriors Inc. is preparing its budget for the first quarter of 2012. The next step in the budgeting process is to prepare a cash receipts schedule and a cash payments schedule. To that end, the following information has been collected.

Prepare schedules for cash receipts and cash payments, and determine ending balances for balance sheet.
(SO 5, 6)

Clients usually pay 60% of their fee in the month that service is provided, 30% the month after, and 10% the second month after receiving service.

Actual service revenue for 2011 and expected service revenues for 2012 are: November 2011, $90,000; December 2011, $80,000; January 2012, $100,000; February 2012, $120,000; March 2012, $130,000.

Purchases of landscaping supplies (direct materials) are paid 40% in the month of purchase and 60% the following month. Actual purchases for 2011 and expected purchases for 2012 are: December 2011, $14,000; January 2012, $12,000; February 2012, $15,000; March 2012, $18,000.

Instructions
(a) Prepare the following schedules for each month in the first quarter of 2012 and for the quarter in total:
   (1) Expected collections from clients.
   (2) Expected payments for landscaping supplies.
(b) Determine the following balances at March 31, 2012:
   (1) Accounts receivable.
   (2) Accounts payable.

E23-16 Medina Dental Clinic is a medium-sized dental service specializing in family dental care. The clinic is currently preparing the master budget for the first 2 quarters of 2012. All that remains in this process is the cash budget. The following information has been collected from other portions of the master budget and elsewhere.

Prepare a cash budget for two quarters.
(SO 5, 6)

Beginning cash balance	$ 30,000
Required minimum cash balance	25,000
Payment of income taxes (2nd quarter)	4,000
Professional salaries:	
1st quarter	140,000
2nd quarter	140,000
Interest from investments (2nd quarter)	5,000
Overhead costs:	
1st quarter	75,000
2nd quarter	100,000
Selling and administrative costs, including	
$3,000 depreciation:	
1st quarter	50,000
2nd quarter	70,000
Purchase of equipment (2nd quarter)	50,000
Sale of equipment (1st quarter)	15,000
Collections from clients:	
1st quarter	230,000
2nd quarter	380,000
Interest payments (2nd quarter)	300

Instructions
Prepare a cash budget for each of the first two quarters of 2012.

E23-17 In May 2012, the budget committee of Moseby Stores assembles the following data in preparation of budgeted merchandise purchases for the month of June.

Prepare a purchases budget and budgeted income statement for a merchandiser.
(SO 6)

1. Expected sales: June $500,000, July $600,000.
2. Cost of goods sold is expected to be 70% of sales.
3. Desired ending merchandise inventory is 40% of the following (next) month's cost of goods sold.
4. The beginning inventory at June 1 will be the desired amount.

Instructions
(a) Compute the budgeted merchandise purchases for June.
(b) Prepare the budgeted income statement for June through gross profit.

Exercises: Set B

Visit the book's companion website, at **www.wiley.com/college/weygandt**, and choose the Student Companion site to access Exercise Set B.

Problems: Set A

Prepare budgeted income statement and supporting budget.

(SO 3, 4)

P23-1A Greene Farm Supply Company manufactures and sells a pesticide called Snare. The following data are available for preparing budgets for Snare for the first 2 quarters of 2013.

1. Sales: Quarter 1, 28,000 bags; quarter 2, 42,000 bags. Selling price is $60 per bag.
2. Direct materials: Each bag of Snare requires 4 pounds of Gumm at a cost of $4 per pound and 6 pounds of Tarr at $1.50 per pound.
3. Desired inventory levels:

Type of Inventory	January 1	April 1	July 1
Snare (bags)	8,000	12,000	18,000
Gumm (pounds)	9,000	10,000	13,000
Tarr (pounds)	14,000	20,000	25,000

4. Direct labor: Direct labor time is 15 minutes per bag at an hourly rate of $14 per hour.
5. Selling and administrative expenses are expected to be 15% of sales plus $175,000 per quarter.
6. Income taxes are expected to be 30% of income from operations.

Your assistant has prepared two budgets: (1) The manufacturing overhead budget shows expected costs to be 150% of direct labor cost. (2) The direct materials budget for Tarr shows the cost of Tarr purchases to be $297,000 in quarter 1 and $421,500 in quarter 2.

Instructions

Net income $600,250
Cost per bag $33.75

Prepare the budgeted income statement for the first 6 months and all required supporting budgets by quarters. (*Note:* Use variable and fixed in the selling and administrative expense budget.) Do not prepare the manufacturing overhead budget or the direct materials budget for Tarr.

Prepare sales, production, direct materials, direct labor, and income statement budgets.

(SO 3, 4)

P23-2A Tranh Inc. is preparing its annual budgets for the year ending December 31, 2013. Accounting assistants furnish the data shown below.

	Product JB 50	Product JB 60
Sales budget:		
Anticipated volume in units	400,000	200,000
Unit selling price	$20	$25
Production budget:		
Desired ending finished goods units	25,000	15,000
Beginning finished goods units	30,000	10,000
Direct materials budget:		
Direct materials per unit (pounds)	2	3
Desired ending direct materials pounds	30,000	15,000
Beginning direct materials pounds	40,000	10,000
Cost per pound	$3	$4
Direct labor budget:		
Direct labor time per unit	0.4	0.6
Direct labor rate per hour	$12	$12
Budgeted income statement:		
Total unit cost	$12	$21

An accounting assistant has prepared the detailed manufacturing overhead budget and the selling and administrative expense budget. The latter shows selling expenses of $660,000 for product JB 50 and $360,000 for product JB 60, and administrative expenses of $540,000 for product JB 50 and $340,000 for product JB 60. Income taxes are expected to be 30%.

Instructions

Prepare the following budgets for the year. Show data for each product. You do not need to prepare quarterly budgets.

(a) Sales
(b) Production
(c) Direct materials
(d) Direct labor
(e) Income statement (*Note:* Income taxes are not allocated to the products.)

P23-3A Remington Industries had sales in 2012 of $6,400,000 and gross profit of $1,100,000. Management is considering two alternative budget plans to increase its gross profit in 2013.

Plan A would increase the selling price per unit from $8.00 to $8.40. Sales volume would decrease by 5% from its 2012 level. Plan B would decrease the selling price per unit by $0.50. The marketing department expects that the sales volume would increase by 150,000 units.

At the end of 2012, Remington has 40,000 units of inventory on hand. If Plan A is accepted, the 2013 ending inventory should be equal to 5% of the 2013 sales. If Plan B is accepted, the ending inventory should be equal to 50,000 units. Each unit produced will cost $1.80 in direct labor, $2.00 in direct materials, and $1.20 in variable overhead. The fixed overhead for 2013 should be $1,895,000.

Instructions

(a) Prepare a sales budget for 2013 under each plan.
(b) Prepare a production budget for 2013 under each plan.
(c) Compute the production cost per unit under each plan. Why is the cost per unit different for each of the two plans? (Round to two decimals.)
(d) Which plan should be accepted? (*Hint:* Compute the gross profit under each plan.)

P23-4A Singh Company prepares monthly cash budgets. Relevant data from operating budgets for 2013 are:

	January	February
Sales	$350,000	$400,000
Direct materials purchases	110,000	130,000
Direct labor	90,000	100,000
Manufacturing overhead	70,000	75,000
Selling and administrative expenses	79,000	86,000

All sales are on account. Collections are expected to be 50% in the month of sale, 30% in the first month following the sale, and 20% in the second month following the sale. Sixty percent (60%) of direct materials purchases are paid in cash in the month of purchase, and the balance due is paid in the month following the purchase. All other items above are paid in the month incurred except for selling and administrative expenses that include $1,000 of depreciation per month.

Other data:

1. Credit sales: November 2012, $260,000; December 2012, $320,000.
2. Purchases of direct materials: December 2012, $100,000.
3. Other receipts: January—Collection of December 31, 2012, notes receivable $15,000; February—Proceeds from sale of securities $6,000.
4. Other disbursements: February—Withdrawal of $5,000 cash for personal use of owner, Dwight Yocum.

The company's cash balance on January 1, 2013, is expected to be $60,000. The company wants to maintain a minimum cash balance of $50,000.

Instructions

(a) Prepare schedules for (1) expected collections from customers and (2) expected payments for direct materials purchases.
(b) Prepare a cash budget for January and February in columnar form.

P23-5A The budget committee of Earnhart Company collects the following data for its Del Fuego Store in preparing budgeted income statements for May and June 2013.

1. Sales for May are expected to be $800,000. Sales in June and July are expected to be 10% higher than the preceding month.
2. Cost of goods sold is expected to be 75% of sales.
3. Company policy is to maintain ending merchandise inventory at 20% of the following month's cost of goods sold.

(a) Total sales $13,000,000
(b) Required production units: JB 50, 395,000 JB 60, 205,000
(c) Total cost of direct materials purchases $4,820,000
(d) Total direct labor cost $3,372,000
(e) Net income $1,470,000

Prepare sales and production budgets and compute cost per unit under two plans.
(SO 3, 4)

(c) Unit cost: Plan A $7.50, Plan B $6.97
(d) Gross profit:
   Plan A $684,000
   Plan B $503,500

Prepare cash budget for 2 months.
(SO 5)

(a) January: collections $323,000 payments $106,000
(b) Ending cash balance: January $54,000 February $50,000

Prepare purchases and income statement budgets for a merchandiser.
(SO 6)

4. Operating expenses are estimated to be:

Sales salaries	$30,000 per month
Advertising	5% of monthly sales
Delivery expense	3% of monthly sales
Sales commissions	4% of monthly sales
Rent expense	$5,000 per month
Depreciation	$800 per month
Utilities	$600 per month
Insurance	$500 per month

5. Income taxes are estimated to be 30% of income from operations.

Instructions

(a) Prepare the merchandise purchases budget for each month in columnar form.

(b) Prepare budgeted income statements for each month in columnar form. Show in the statements the details of cost of goods sold.

(a) Purchases:
May $612,000
June $673,200
(b) Net income:
May $46,970
June $54,250

Prepare budgeted income statement and balance sheet.
(SO 4, 5)

P23-6A   Putin Industries' balance sheet at December 31, 2012, is presented below.

PUTIN INDUSTRIES
Balance Sheet
December 31, 2012

Assets

Current assets		
Cash		$ 7,500
Accounts receivable		82,500
Finished goods inventory (2,000 units)		30,000
Total current assets		120,000
Property, plant, and equipment		
Equipment	$40,000	
Less: Accumulated depreciation—equip.	10,000	30,000
Total assets		$150,000

Liabilities and Stockholders' Equity

Liabilities		
Notes payable		$ 25,000
Accounts payable		45,000
Total liabilities		70,000
Stockholders' equity		
Common stock	$50,000	
Retained earnings	30,000	
Total stockholders' equity		80,000
Total liabilities and stockholders' equity		$150,000

Additional information accumulated for the budgeting process is as follows.
Budgeted data for the year 2013 include the following.

	4th Qtr. of 2013	Year 2013 Total
Sales budget (8,000 units at $35)	$84,000	$280,000
Direct materials used	17,000	69,400
Direct labor	12,500	56,600
Manufacturing overhead applied	10,000	54,000
Selling and administrative expenses	18,000	76,000

To meet sales requirements and to have 3,000 units of finished goods on hand at December 31, 2013, the production budget shows 9,000 required units of output. The total unit cost of production is expected to be $20. Putin Industries uses the first-in, first-out (FIFO) inventory costing method. Selling and administrative expenses include $4,000 for depreciation on equipment. Interest expense is expected to be $3,500 for the year. Income taxes are expected to be 30% of income before income taxes.

All sales and purchases are on account. It is expected that 60% of quarterly sales are collected in cash within the quarter and the remainder is collected in the following quarter. Direct materials purchased from suppliers are paid 50% in the quarter incurred and the remainder in the following quarter. Purchases in the fourth quarter were the same as the materials used. In 2013, the company expects to purchase additional equipment costing $19,000. It expects to pay $8,000 on notes payable plus all interest due and payable to December 31 (included in interest expense $3,500, above). Accounts payable at December 31, 2013, includes amounts due suppliers (see above) plus other accounts payable of $5,700. In 2013, the company expects to declare and pay a $5,000 cash dividend. Unpaid income taxes at December 31 will be $5,000. The company's cash budget shows an expected cash balance of $7,950 at December 31, 2013.

Instructions

Prepare a budgeted income statement for 2013 and a budgeted balance sheet at December 31, 2013. In preparing the income statement, you will need to compute cost of goods manufactured (direct materials + direct labor + manufacturing overhead) and finished goods inventory (December 31, 2013).

Net income $35,350
Total assets $146,550

Problems: Set B

P23-1B Myagi Farm Supply Company manufactures and sells a fertilizer called Basic II. The following data are available for preparing budgets for Basic II for the first 2 quarters of 2012.

1. Sales: Quarter 1, 40,000 bags; quarter 2, 50,000 bags. Selling price is $65 per bag.
2. Direct materials: Each bag of Basic II requires 6 pounds of Crup at a cost of $4 per pound and 10 pounds of Dert at $1.50 per pound.
3. Desired inventory levels:

Prepare budgeted income statement and supporting budgets.

(SO 3, 4)

Type of Inventory	January 1	April 1	July 1
Basic II (bags)	10,000	15,000	20,000
Crup (pounds)	9,000	12,000	15,000
Dert (pounds)	15,000	20,000	25,000

4. Direct labor: Direct labor time is 15 minutes per bag at an hourly rate of $10 per hour.
5. Selling and administrative expenses are expected to be 10% of sales plus $160,000 per quarter.
6. Income taxes are expected to be 30% of income from operations.

Your assistant has prepared two budgets: (1) The manufacturing overhead budget shows expected costs to be 100% of direct labor cost. (2) The direct materials budget for Dert which shows the cost of Dert to be $682,500 in quarter 1 and $825,00 in quarter 2.

Instructions

Prepare the budgeted income statement for the first 6 months of 2012 and all required supporting budgets by quarters. (*Note:* Use variable and fixed in the selling and administrative expense budget.) Do not prepare the manufacturing overhead budget or the direct materials budget for Dert.

Net income $689,500
Cost per bag $44.00

P23-2B Raleigh Inc. is preparing its annual budgets for the year ending December 31, 2012. Accounting assistants furnish the following data.

Prepare sales, production, direct materials, direct labor, and income statement budgets.

(SO 3, 4)

	Product LN 35	Product LN 40
Sales budget:		
Anticipated volume in units	400,000	240,000
Unit selling price	$25	$35
Production budget:		
Desired ending finished goods units	30,000	25,000
Beginning finished goods units	20,000	15,000

Direct materials budget:

Direct materials per unit (pounds)	2	3
Desired ending direct materials pounds	50,000	20,000
Beginning direct materials pounds	40,000	10,000
Cost per pound	$2	$3

Direct labor budget:

Direct labor time per unit	0.5	0.75
Direct labor rate per hour	$12	$12

Budgeted income statement:

Total unit cost	$11	$20

An accounting assistant has prepared the detailed manufacturing overhead budget and the selling and administrative expense budget. The latter shows selling expenses of $750,000 for product LN 35 and $590,000 for product LN 40, and administrative expenses of $420,000 for product LN 35 and $380,000 for product LN 40. Income taxes are expected to be 30%.

(a) Total sales $18,400,000

(b) Required production units: LN 35, 410,000

(c) Total cost of direct materials purchases $3,940,000

(d) Total direct labor cost $4,710,000

(e) Net income $4,942,000

Instructions

Prepare the following budgets for the year. Show data for each product. You do not need to prepare quarterly budgets.

(a) Sales
(b) Production
(c) Direct materials
(d) Direct labor
(e) Income statement (*Note:* Income taxes are not allocated to the products.)

Prepare sales and production budgets and compute cost per unit under two plans.

(SO 3, 4)

P23-3B   Mintz Industries has sales in 2012 of $5,600,000 (800,000 units) and gross profit of $1,344,000. Management is considering two alternative budget plans to increase its gross profit in 2013.

Plan A would increase the selling price per unit from $7.00 to $7.60. Sales volume would decrease by 10% from its 2012 level. Plan B would decrease the selling price per unit by 5%. The marketing department expects that the sales volume would increase by 100,000 units.

At the end of 2012, Mintz has 70,000 units on hand. If Plan A is accepted, the 2013 ending inventory should be equal to 90,000 units. If Plan B is accepted, the ending inventory should be equal to 100,000 units. Each unit produced will cost $2.00 in direct materials, $1.50 in direct labor, and $0.50 in variable overhead. The fixed overhead for 2013 should be $925,000.

Instructions

(c) Unit cost: Plan A $5.25
    Plan B $4.99

(d) Gross profit:
    Plan A $1,692,000
    Plan B $1,494,000

(a) Prepare a sales budget for 2013 under (1) Plan A and (2) Plan B.
(b) Prepare a production budget for 2013 under (1) Plan A and (2) Plan B.
(c) Compute the cost per unit under (1) Plan A and (2) Plan B. Explain why the cost per unit is different for each of the two plans. (Round to two decimals.)
(d) Which plan should be accepted? (*Hint:* Compute the gross profit under each plan.)

Prepare cash budget for 2 months.

(SO 5)

P23-4B   Weiss Company prepares monthly cash budgets. Relevant data from operating budgets for 2013 are:

	January	February
Sales	$350,000	$400,000
Direct materials purchases	120,000	110,000
Direct labor	85,000	115,000
Manufacturing overhead	60,000	75,000
Selling and administrative expenses	75,000	80,000

All sales are on account. Collections are expected to be 60% in the month of sale, 30% in the first month following the sale, and 10% in the second month following the sale. Thirty percent (30%) of direct materials purchases are paid in cash in the month of purchase, and the balance due is paid in the month following the purchase. All other items above are paid in the month incurred. Depreciation has been excluded from manufacturing overhead and selling and administrative expenses.

Other data:

1. Credit sales: November 2012, $200,000; December 2012, $280,000.
2. Purchases of direct materials: December 2012, $90,000.
3. Other receipts: January—Collection of December 31, 2012, interest receivable $3,000; February—Proceeds from sale of securities $5,000.
4. Other disbursements: February—payment of $20,000 for land.

The company's cash balance on January 1, 2013, is expected to be $50,000. The company wants to maintain a minimum cash balance of $40,000.

Instructions

(a) Prepare schedules for (1) expected collections from customers and (2) expected payments for direct materials purchases.

(b) Prepare a cash budget for January and February in columnar form.

(a) January: collections
$314,000
payments $99,000
(b) Ending cash balance:
January $48,000
February $40,000

P23-5B The budget committee of Georg Company collects the following data for its Northgate Store in preparing budgeted income statements for July and August 2012.

Prepare purchases and income statement budgets for a merchandiser.

(SO 6)

1. Expected sales: July $400,000, August $450,000, September $500,000.
2. Cost of goods sold is expected to be 60% of sales.
3. Company policy is to maintain ending merchandise inventory at 20% of the following month's cost of goods sold.
4. Operating expenses are estimated to be:

Sales salaries	$50,000 per month
Advertising	4% of monthly sales
Delivery expense	2% of monthly sales
Sales commissions	3% of monthly sales
Rent expense	$3,000 per month
Depreciation	$700 per month
Utilities	$500 per month
Insurance	$300 per month

5. Income taxes are estimated to be 30% of income from operations.

Instructions

(a) Prepare the merchandise purchases budget for each month in columnar form.

(b) Prepare budgeted income statements for each month in columnar form. Show the details of cost of goods sold in the statements.

(a) Purchases: July $246,000
August $276,000
(b) Net income: July $48,650
August $59,500

Problems: Set C

Visit the book's companion website, at **www.wiley.com/college/weygandt**, and choose the Student Companion site to access Problem Set C.

Waterways Continuing Problem

(This is a continuation of the Waterways Problem from Chapters 19 through 22.)

WCP23 Waterways Corporation is preparing its budget for the coming year, 2013. The first step is to plan for the first quarter of that coming year. The company has gathered information from its managers in preparation of the budgeting process. This problem asks you to prepare the various budgets that comprise the master budget for 2013.

Go to the book's companion website, **www.wiley.com/college/weygandt**, *to find the remainder of this problem.*

BROADENINGYOURPERSPECTIVE

Decision Making Across the Organization

BYP23-1 Bryant Corporation operates on a calendar-year basis. It begins the annual budgeting process in late August when the president establishes targets for the total dollar sales and net income before taxes for the next year.

The sales target is given first to the marketing department. The marketing manager formulates a sales budget by product line in both units and dollars. From this budget, sales quotas by product line in units and dollars are established for each of the corporation's sales districts. The marketing manager also estimates the cost of the marketing activities required to support the target sales volume and prepares a tentative marketing expense budget.

The executive vice president uses the sales and profit targets, the sales budget by product line, and the tentative marketing expense budget to determine the dollar amounts that can be devoted to manufacturing and corporate office expense. The executive vice president prepares the budget for corporate expenses. She then forwards to the production department the product-line sales budget in units and the total dollar amount that can be devoted to manufacturing.

The production manager meets with the factory managers to develop a manufacturing plan that will produce the required units when needed within the cost constraints set by the executive vice president. The budgeting process usually comes to a halt at this point because the production department does not consider the financial resources allocated to be adequate.

When this standstill occurs, the vice president of finance, the executive vice president, the marketing manager, and the production manager meet together to determine the final budgets for each of the areas. This normally results in a modest increase in the total amount available for manufacturing costs and cuts in the marketing expense and corporate office expense budgets. The total sales and net income figures proposed by the president are seldom changed. Although the participants are seldom pleased with the compromise, these budgets are final. Each executive then develops a new detailed budget for the operations in his or her area.

None of the areas has achieved its budget in recent years. Sales often run below the target. When budgeted sales are not achieved, each area is expected to cut costs so that the president's profit target can be met. However, the profit target is seldom met because costs are not cut enough. In fact, costs often run above the original budget in all functional areas (marketing, production, and corporate office).

The president is disturbed that Bryant has not been able to meet the sales and profit targets. He hired a consultant with considerable experience with companies in Bryant's industry. The consultant reviewed the budgets for the past 4 years. He concluded that the product line sales budgets were reasonable and that the cost and expense budgets were adequate for the budgeted sales and production levels.

Instructions
With the class divided into groups, answer the following.

(a) Discuss how the budgeting process employed by Bryant Corporation contributes to the failure to achieve the president's sales and profit targets.

(b) Suggest how Bryant Corporation's budgeting process could be revised to correct the problems.

(c) Should the functional areas be expected to cut their costs when sales volume falls below budget? Explain your answer.   (CMA adapted.)

Managerial Analysis

BYP23-2 Blog & Twitter Inc. manufactures ergonomic devices for computer users. Some of their more popular products include glare screens (for computer monitors), keyboard stands with wrist rests, and carousels that allow easy access to magnetic disks. Over the past 5 years, it experienced rapid growth, with sales of all products increasing 20% to 50% each year.

Last year, some of the primary manufacturers of computers began introducing new products with some of the ergonomic designs, such as glare screens and wrist rests, already built in. As a result, sales of Blog & Twitter's accessory devices have declined somewhat. The company believes that the disk carousels will probably continue to show growth, but that the other products will probably continue to decline. When the next year's budget was prepared, increases were built in to research and development so that replacement products could be developed or the company could expand into some other product line. Some product lines being considered are general-purpose ergonomic devices including back supports, foot rests, and sloped writing pads.

The most recent results have shown that sales decreased more than was expected for the glare screens. As a result, the company may have a shortage of funds. Top management has therefore asked that all expenses be reduced 10% to compensate for these reduced sales. Summary budget information is as follows.

Direct materials	$240,000
Direct labor	110,000
Insurance	50,000
Depreciation	90,000
Machine repairs	30,000
Sales salaries	50,000
Office salaries	80,000
Factory salaries (indirect labor)	50,000
Total	$700,000

Instructions

Using the information above, answer the following questions.

(a) What are the implications of reducing each of the costs? For example, if the company reduces direct materials costs, it may have to do so by purchasing lower-quality materials. This may affect sales in the long run.

(b) Based on your analysis in (a), what do you think is the best way to obtain the $70,000 in cost savings requested? Be specific. Are there any costs that cannot or should not be reduced? Why?

Real-World Focus

BYP23-3 Network Computing Devices, Inc. was founded in 1988 in Mountain View, California. The company develops software products such as X-terminals, Z-mail, PC X-ware, and related hardware products. Presented below is a discussion by management in its annual report.

> ### Network Computing Devices, Inc.
> #### Management Discussion
>
> The Company's operating results have varied significantly, particularly on a quarterly basis, as a result of a number of factors, including general economic conditions affecting industry demand for computer products, the timing and market acceptance of new product introductions by the Company and its competitors, the timing of significant orders from large customers, periodic changes in product pricing and discounting due to competitive factors, and the availability of key components, such as video monitors and electronic subassemblies, some of which require substantial order lead times. The Company's operating results may fluctuate in the future as a result of these and other factors, including the Company's success in developing and introducing new products, its product and customer mix, and the level of competition which it experiences. The Company operates with a small backlog. Sales and operating results, therefore, generally depend on the volume and timing of orders received, which are difficult to forecast. The Company has experienced slowness in orders from some customers during the first quarter of each calendar year due to budgeting cycles common in the computer industry. In addition, sales in Europe typically are adversely affected in the third calendar quarter as many European customers reduce their business activities during the month of August.
>
> Due to the Company's rapid growth rate and the effect of new product introductions on quarterly revenues, these seasonal trends have not materially impacted the Company's results of operations to date. However, as the Company's product lines mature and its rate of revenue growth declines, these seasonal factors may become more evident. Additionally, the Company's international sales are denominated in U.S. dollars, and an increase or decrease in the value of the U.S. dollar relative to foreign currencies could make the Company's products less or more competitive in those markets.

Instructions

(a) Identify the factors that affect the budgeting process at Network Computing Devices, Inc.

(b) Explain the additional budgeting concerns created by the international operations of the company.

Communication Activity

BYP23-4 In order to better serve their rural patients, Drs. Greg and Don Kaye (brothers) began giving safety seminars. Especially popular were their "emergency-preparedness" talks given to farmers. Many people asked whether the "kit" of materials the doctors recommended for common farm emergencies was commercially available.

After checking with several suppliers, the doctors realized that no other company offered the supplies they recommended in their seminars, packaged in the way they described. Their wives, Jo and Jan, agreed to make a test package by ordering supplies from various medical supply companies and assembling them into a "kit" that could be sold at the seminars. When these kits proved a runaway success, the sisters-in-law decided to market them. At the advice of their accountant, they organized this venture as a separate company, called First Aid Products (FAP), with Jo Kaye as CEO and Jan Kaye as Secretary-Treasurer.

FAP soon started receiving requests for the kits from all over the country, as word spread about their availability. Even without advertising, FAP was able to sell its full inventory every month. However, the company was becoming financially strained. Jo and Jan had about $100,000 in savings, and they invested about half that amount initially. They believed that this venture would allow them to make money. However, at the present time, only about $30,000 of the cash remains, and the company is constantly short of cash.

Jo has come to you for advice. She does not understand why the company is having cash flow problems. She and Jan have not even been withdrawing salaries. However, they have rented a local building and have hired two more full-time workers to help them cope with the increasing demand. They do not think they could handle the demand without this additional help.

Jo is also worried that the cash problems mean that the company may not be able to support itself. She has prepared the cash budget shown below. All seminar customers pay for their products in full at the time of purchase. In addition, several large companies have ordered the kits for use by employees who work in remote sites. They have requested credit terms and have been allowed to pay in the month following the sale. These large purchasers amount to about 25% of the sales at the present time. FAP purchases the materials for the kits about 2 months ahead of time. Jo and Jan are considering slowing the growth of the company by simply purchasing less materials, which will mean selling fewer kits.

The workers are paid in cash weekly. Jo and Jan need about $15,000 cash on hand at the beginning of the month to pay for purchases of raw materials. Right now they have been using cash from their savings, but as noted, only $30,000 is left.

Instructions

Write a response to Jo Kaye. Explain why FAP is short of cash. Will this company be able to support itself? Explain your answer. Make any recommendations you deem appropriate.

FIRST AID PRODUCTS
Cash Budget
For the Quarter Ending June 30, 2013

	April	**May**	**June**
Cash balance, beginning	$15,000	$15,000	$15,000
Cash received			
From prior month sales	5,000	7,500	12,500
From current sales	15,000	22,500	37,500
Total cash on hand	35,000	45,000	65,000
Cash payments			
To employees	3,000	3,000	3,000
For products	25,000	35,000	45,000
Miscellaneous expenses	5,000	6,000	7,000
Postage	1,000	1,000	1,000
Total cash payments	34,000	45,000	56,000
Cash balance	$ 1,000	$ 0	$ 9,000
Borrow from savings	$14,000	$15,000	$ 1,000
Borrow from bank?	$ 0	$ 0	$ 5,000

Ethics Case

BYP23-5 You are an accountant in the budgetary, projections, and special projects department of Tech Components, Inc., a large manufacturing company. The president, Sam White, asks you on very short notice to prepare some sales and income projections covering the next 2 years of the company's much heralded new product lines. He wants these projections for a series of speeches he is making while on a 2-week trip to eight East Coast brokerage firms. The president hopes to bolster Tech's stock sales and price.

You work 23 hours in 2 days to compile the projections, hand deliver them to the president, and are swiftly but graciously thanked as he departs. A week later, you find time to go over some of your computations and discover a miscalculation that makes the projections grossly overstated. You quickly inquire about the president's itinerary and learn that he has made half of his speeches and has half yet to make. You are in a quandary as to what to do.

Instructions
(a) What are the consequences of telling the president of your gross miscalculations?
(b) What are the consequences of not telling the president of your gross miscalculations?
(c) What are the ethical considerations to you and the president in this situation?

"All About You" Activity

BYP23-6 The **All About You** feature (available on the book's companion website) emphasizes that in order to get your personal finances under control, you need to prepare a personal budget. Assume that you have compiled the following information regarding your expected cash flows for a typical month.

Rent payment	$ 400	Miscellaneous costs	$110
Interest income	50	Savings	50
Income tax withheld	300	Eating out	150
Electricity bill	22	Telephone and Internet costs	90
Groceries	80	Student loan payments	275
Wages earned	2,000	Entertainment costs	250
Insurance	100	Transportation costs	150

Instructions
Using the information above, prepare a personal budget. In preparing this budget, use the format found at **http://financialplan.about.com/cs/budgeting/l/blbudget.htm**. Just skip any unused line items.

Answers to Insight and Accounting Across the Organization Questions
p. 1056 Businesses Often Feel Too Busy to Plan for the Future   Q: Describe a situation in which a business "sells as much as it can" but cannot "keep its employees paid." **A:** If sales are made to customers on credit and collection is slow, the company may find that it does not have enough cash to pay employees or suppliers. Without these resources, the company will fail to survive.
p. 1057 Which Budget Approach Do You Prefer?   Q: What approach did Time Warner use to prepare the old budget? What approach did it use to prepare the new budget? **A:** Time Warner used a "top-down" approach to prepare the old budget since its goals were determined by top management. It used a participative approach to prepare the new budget since each operating unit set goals.
p. 1070 Without a Budget, Can the Games Begin?   Q: Why does it matter whether the Olympic Games exceed their budget? **A:** If the Olympic Games exceed their budget, taxpayers of the sponsoring community and country will end up footing the bill. Depending on the size of the losses, and the resources of the community, this could produce a substantial burden. As a result, other communities might be reluctant to host the Olympics in the future.
p. 1074 Budget Shortfalls as Far as the Eye Can See   Q: Why would a university's budgeted scholarships probably fall when the stock market suffers a serious drop? **A:** Scholarships typically cannot be paid out of the "principal" portion of donations made to scholarship endowment funds. Instead, scholarships are usually funded through earnings generated by endowment investments. Any excess earnings above current-year scholarship needs can be used for scholarships in subsequent years. But a serious drop in the value of endowment investments can wipe out previous earnings, in some cases completely eliminating funds available for scholarships.

Answers to Self-Test Questions
1. c **2.** b **3.** a **4.** b **5.** b **6.** d **7.** d $(9,500 + 2,200 - 1,000)$ **8.** a **9.** c **10.** a **11.** a **12.** b **13.** c $(60\% \times \$70,000) + (40\% \times \$90,000)$ **14.** d **15.** c

✔
The Navigator

✔   **Remember to go back to the Navigator box on the chapter opening page and check off your completed work.]**

CHAPTER24

Budgetary Control and Responsibility Accounting

Study Objectives

After studying this chapter, you should be able to:

[1] Describe the concept of budgetary control.

[2] Evaluate the usefulness of static budget reports.

[3] Explain the development of flexible budgets and the usefulness of flexible budget reports.

[4] Describe the concept of responsibility accounting.

[5] Indicate the features of responsibility reports for cost centers.

[6] Identify the content of responsibility reports for profit centers.

[7] Explain the basis and formula used in evaluating performance in investment centers.

✔ **The Navigator**

✔ [The Navigator]

- Scan Study Objectives ○
- Read Feature Story ○
- Read Preview ○
- Read text and answer **Do it!** p. 1106 ○ p. 1108 ○ p. 1116 ○ p. 1121 ○
- Work Comprehensive **Do it!** **1** p. 1122 ○ **2** p. 1123 ○
- Review Summary of Study Objectives ○
- Answer Self-Test Questions ○
- Complete Assignments ○
- Go to *WileyPLUS* for practice and tutorials ○

Feature Story

TURNING TRASH INTO TREASURE

Vancouver teenager Brian Scudamore needed to raise money to pay his way through college. With $700 and a strong desire to do it on his own, he established his own junk-removal company. Fifteen years later, 1-800-GOT-JUNK? had 113 franchise partners across Canada and the United States, and projected revenues of more than $60 million.

"It was a high-school business project that was out of control," says Cameron Herold, vice president of operations.

While the exponential growth of 1-800-GOT-JUNK? may seem unwieldy (at one point it had five consecutive years of 100-percent compounded growth), it has in fact involved sound financial planning, budgeting, and cash management. The company follows a "zero-based budget," says Mr. Herold. That is, it only spends money it has; it has no outside investors or debt.

Managing this growth involves forecasting everything by creating a "painted picture" of what the company will look like in three years. The company knows its staffing plans, training requirements, and overhead and office-space needs well in advance. "That filters back to our budgeting process," Mr. Herold says. "We'll sit down and say, 'If this is where we're going, what are all the components of that?' . . . Then we bring it back to zero and say, 'What's it going to cost us? Where does it fit into the budget?'"

Key to the company's growth management was the introduction of franchising. "We chose franchising because our franchise partners would actually finance our growth," Mr. Herold says. In addition to the initial franchise fee, franchisees pay the head office 8 percent of their sales, plus another 7 percent to run the centralized call center.

While the company has used franchising to manage growth, a frugal approach to day-to-day costs has also been integral to its budgeting success. "We're always looking for ways to cut costs," Mr. Herold says. This includes establishing strategic relationships with the local coffee shop, doing regular cost analyses of office equipment and changing suppliers when needed, and buying office furniture in bulk from liquidators at 10 cents on the dollar. "All those little things start to really add up," he says.

InsideCHAPTER24

- *Service Company Insight:* **Budgets and the Exotic Newcastle Disease** *(p. 1107)*
- *Management Insight:* **Competition versus Collaboration** *(p. 1110)*
- *Accounting Across the Organization:* **Does Hollywood Look at ROI?** *(p. 1119)*
- *Management Insight:* **Flexible Manufacturing Requires Flexible Accounting** *(p. 1121)*

In contrast to Chapter 23, we now consider how budgets are used by management to control operations. In the Feature Story on 1-800-GOT-JUNK?, we saw that management tries to use the budget to adapt to the business environment. This chapter focuses on two aspects of management control: (1) budgetary control and (2) responsibility accounting.

The content and organization of Chapter 24 are as follows.

Budgetary Control and Responsibility Accounting				
The Concept of Budgetary Control	**Static Budget Reports**	**Flexible Budgets**	**The Concept of Responsibility Accounting**	**Types of Responsibility Centers**
• Budget reports • Control activities • Reporting systems	• Examples • Uses and limitations	• Why flexible budgets? • Development • Case study • Reports • Management by exception	• Controllable vs. noncontrollable • Reporting system	• Cost centers • Profit centers • Investment centers • Performance evaluation

✔ **The Navigator**

The Concept of Budgetary Control

Study Objective [1]
Describe the concept of budgetary control.

One of management's major functions is to control company operations. Control consists of the steps taken by management to see that planned objectives are met. We now ask: How do budgets contribute to control of operations?

The use of budgets in controlling operations is known as budgetary control. Such control takes place by means of **budget reports** that compare actual results with planned objectives. The use of budget reports is based on the belief that planned objectives lose much of their potential value without some monitoring of progress along the way. Just as your professors give midterm exams to evaluate your progress, so top management requires periodic reports on the progress of department managers toward their planned objectives.

Budget reports provide management with feedback on operations. The feedback for a crucial objective, such as having enough cash on hand to pay bills, may be made daily. For other objectives, such as meeting budgeted annual sales and operating expenses, monthly budget reports may suffice. Budget reports are prepared as frequently as needed. From these reports, management analyzes any differences between actual and planned results and determines their causes. Management then takes corrective action, or it decides to modify future plans.

Budgetary control involves activities shown in Illustration 24-1. Budgetary control works best when a company has a formalized reporting system. The system does the following:

1. Identifies the name of the budget report, such as the sales budget or the manufacturing overhead budget.
2. States the frequency of the report, such as weekly or monthly.
3. Specifies the purpose of the report.
4. Indicates the primary recipient(s) of the report.

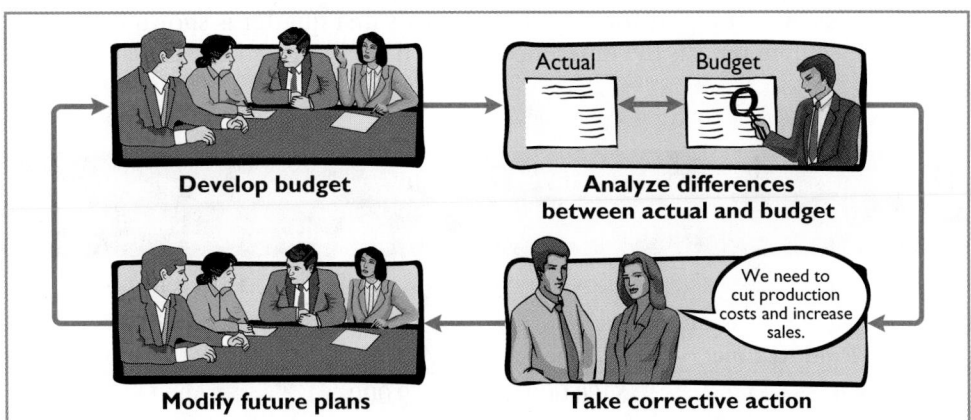

Illustration 24-1
Budgetary control activities

Illustration 24-2 provides a partial budgetary control system for a manufacturing company. Note the frequency of the reports and their emphasis on control. For example, there is a daily report on scrap and a weekly report on labor.

Illustration 24-2
Budgetary control reporting system

Name of Report	Frequency	Purpose	Primary Recipient(s)
Sales	Weekly	Determine whether sales goals are being met	Top management and sales manager
Labor	Weekly	Control direct and indirect labor costs	Vice president of production and production department managers
Scrap	Daily	Determine efficient use of materials	Production manager
Departmental overhead costs	Monthly	Control overhead costs	Department manager
Selling expenses	Monthly	Control selling expenses	Sales manager
Income statement	Monthly and quarterly	Determine whether income objectives are being met	Top management

Static Budget Reports

You learned in Chapter 23 that the master budget formalizes management's planned objectives for the coming year. When used in budgetary control, each budget included in the master budget is considered to be static. A **static budget** is a projection of budget data at **one level of activity**. These budgets do not consider data for different levels of activity. As a result, companies always compare actual results with budget data at the activity level that was used in developing the master budget.

Study Objective [2]
Evaluate the usefulness of static budget reports.

Examples

To illustrate the role of a static budget in budgetary control, we will use selected data prepared for Hayes Company in Chapter 23. Budget and actual sales data for the Kitchen-Mate product in the first and second quarters of 2012 are as follows.

Illustration 24-3
Budget and actual sales data

Sales	First Quarter	Second Quarter	Total
Budgeted	$180,000	$210,000	$390,000
Actual	179,000	199,500	378,500
Difference	$ 1,000	$ 10,500	$ 11,500

The sales budget report for Hayes Company's first quarter is shown below. The right-most column reports the difference between the budgeted and actual amounts.

Illustration 24-4
Sales budget report—first quarter

Alternative Terminology

The difference between budget and actual is sometimes called a *budget variance*.

Hayes Company
Sales Budget Report
For the Quarter Ended March 31, 2012

Product Line	Budget	Actual	Difference Favorable F Unfavorable U
Kitchen-Mate[a]	$180,000	$179,000	$1,000 U

[a]In practice, each product line would be included in the report.

The report shows that sales are $1,000 under budget—an unfavorable result. This difference is less than 1% of budgeted sales ($1,000 ÷ $180,000 = .0056). Top management's reaction to unfavorable differences is often influenced by the materiality (significance) of the difference. Since the difference of $1,000 is immaterial in this case, we assume that Hayes Company management takes no specific corrective action.

Illustration 24-5 shows the budget report for the second quarter. It contains one new feature: cumulative year-to-date information. This report indicates that sales for the second quarter are $10,500 below budget. This is 5% of budgeted sales ($10,500 ÷ $210,000). Top management may now conclude that the difference between budgeted and actual sales requires investigation.

Illustration 24-5
Sales budget report—second quarter

Hayes Company
Sales Budget Report
For the Quarter Ended June 30, 2012

Product Line	Second Quarter Budget	Actual	Difference Favorable F Unfavorable U	Year-to-Date Budget	Actual	Difference Favorable F Unfavorable U
Kitchen-Mate	$210,000	$199,500	$10,500 U	$390,000	$378,500	$11,500 U

Management's analysis should start by asking the sales manager the cause(s) of the shortfall. Managers should consider the need for corrective action. For example, management may decide to spur sales by offering sales incentives to customers or by increasing the advertising of Kitchen-Mates. Or, if management concludes that a downturn in the economy is responsible for the lower sales, it may modify planned sales and profit goals for the remainder of the year.

Uses and Limitations

From these examples, you can see that a master sales budget is useful in evaluating the performance of a sales manager. It is now necessary to ask: Is the master budget appropriate for evaluating a manager's performance in controlling costs? Recall that in a static budget, data are not modified or adjusted, regardless of changes in activity. It follows, then, that a static budget is appropriate in evaluating a manager's effectiveness in controlling costs when:

1. The actual level of activity closely approximates the master budget activity level, and/or

2. The behavior of the costs in response to changes in activity is fixed.

A static budget report is, therefore, appropriate for **fixed manufacturing costs** and for **fixed selling and administrative expenses**. But, as you will see shortly, static budget reports may not be a proper basis for evaluating a manager's performance in controlling variable costs.

Static budgets report a single level of activity

Flexible Budgets

In contrast to a static budget, which is based on one level of activity, a flexible budget projects budget data for various levels of activity. In essence, **the flexible budget is a series of static budgets at different levels of activity**. The flexible budget recognizes that the budgetary process is more useful if it is adaptable to changed operating conditions.

Flexible budgets can be prepared for each of the types of budgets included in the master budget. For example, Marriott Hotels can budget revenues and net income on the basis of 60%, 80%, and 100% of room occupancy. Similarly, American Van Lines can budget its operating expenses on the basis of various levels of truck miles driven. Duke Energy can budget revenue and net income on the basis of estimated billions of kwh (kilowatt hours) of residential, commercial, and industrial electricity generated. In the following pages, we will illustrate a flexible budget for manufacturing overhead.

Study Objective [3]

Explain the development of flexible budgets and the usefulness of flexible budget reports.

Flexible budgets are static budgets at different activity levels

Why Flexible Budgets?

Assume that you are the manager in charge of manufacturing overhead in the Forging Department of Barton Steel. In preparing the manufacturing overhead budget for 2012, you prepare the following static budget based on a production volume of 10,000 units of steel ingots.

Illustration 24-6
Static overhead budget

Barton Steel Manufacturing Overhead Static Budget Forging Department For the Year Ended December 31, 2012	
Budgeted production in units (steel ingots)	10,000
Budgeted costs	
Indirect materials	$ 250,000
Indirect labor	260,000
Utilities	190,000
Depreciation	280,000
Property taxes	70,000
Supervision	50,000
	$1,100,000

Helpful Hint

The static budget is the master budget described in Chapter 23.

Fortunately for the company, the demand for steel ingots has increased, and Barton produces and sells 12,000 units during the year, rather than 10,000. You are elated: Increased sales means increased profitability, which should mean a bonus or a raise for you and the employees in your department. Unfortunately, a comparison of Forging Department actual and budgeted costs has put you on the spot. The budget report is shown below.

Illustration 24-7
Static overhead budget report

	A	B	C	D	E
		BARTON STEEL			
1					
2		Manufacturing Overhead Static Budget Report			
3		For the Year Ended December 31, 2012			
4				Difference	
5		Budget	Actual	Favorable - F Unfavorable - U	
6	Production in units	10,000	12,000		
7					
8	Costs				
9	Indirect materials	$ 250,000	$ 295,000	$ 45,000	U
10	Indirect labor	260,000	312,000	52,000	U
11	Utilities	190,000	225,000	35,000	U
12	Depreciation	280,000	280,000	0	
13	Property taxes	70,000	70,000	0	
14	Supervision	50,000	50,000	0	
15		$1,100,000	$1,232,000	$132,000	U
16					

Helpful Hint

A static budget is not useful for performance evaluation if a company has substantial variable costs.

This comparison uses budget data based on the original activity level (10,000 steel ingots). It indicates that the Forging Department is significantly **over budget** for three of the six overhead costs. And, there is a total unfavorable difference of $132,000, which is 12% over budget ($132,000 ÷ $1,100,000). Your supervisor is very unhappy! Instead of sharing in the company's success, you may find yourself looking for another job. What went wrong?

When you calm down and carefully examine the manufacturing overhead budget, you identify the problem: The budget data are not relevant! At the time the budget was developed, the company anticipated that only 10,000 units of steel ingots would be produced, **not** 12,000. Comparing actual with budgeted variable costs is meaningless. As production increases, the budget allowances for variable costs should increase proportionately. The variable costs in this example are indirect materials, indirect labor, and utilities.

Analyzing the budget data for these costs at 10,000 units, you arrive at the following per unit results.

Illustration 24-8
Variable costs per unit

Item	Total Cost	Per Unit
Indirect materials	$250,000	$25
Indirect labor	260,000	26
Utilities	190,000	19
	$700,000	$70

Illustration 24-9 calculates the budgeted variable costs at 12,000 units.

Item	Computation	Total
Indirect materials	$25 × 12,000	$300,000
Indirect labor	26 × 12,000	312,000
Utilities	19 × 12,000	228,000
		$840,000

Illustration 24-9
Budgeted variable costs, 12,000 units

Because fixed costs do not change in total as activity changes, the budgeted amounts for these costs remain the same. Illustration 24-10 shows the budget report based on the flexible budget for **12,000 units** of production. (Compare this with Illustration 24-7, on page 1102.)

Illustration 24-10
Flexible overhead budget report

Barton Steel.xls

File Edit View Insert Format Tools Data Window Help

BARTON STEEL
Manufacturing Overhead Flexible Budget Report
For the Year Ended December 31, 2012

	A	B	C	D	E
				Difference	
				Favorable - F	
5		Budget	Actual	Unfavorable - U	
6	Production in units	12,000	12,000		
7					
8	Variable costs				
9	Indirect materials	$ 300,000	$ 295,000	$5,000	F
10	Indirect labor	312,000	312,000	0	
11	Utilities	228,000	225,000	3,000	F
12	Total variable costs	840,000	832,000	8,000	F
13					
14	Fixed costs				
15	Depreciation	280,000	280,000	0	
16	Property taxes	70,000	70,000	0	
17	Supervision	50,000	50,000	0	
18	Total fixed costs	400,000	400,000	0	
19	Total costs	$1,240,000	$1,232,000	$8,000	F
20					

This report indicates that the Forging Department is *below budget*—a favorable difference. Instead of worrying about being fired, you may be in line for a bonus or a raise after all! As this analysis shows, the only appropriate comparison is between actual costs at 12,000 units of production and budgeted costs at 12,000 units. Flexible budget reports provide this comparison.

Developing the Flexible Budget

The flexible budget uses the master budget as its basis. To develop the flexible budget, management uses the following steps.

1. Identify the activity index and the relevant range of activity.
2. Identify the variable costs, and determine the budgeted variable cost per unit of activity for each cost.
3. Identify the fixed costs, and determine the budgeted amount for each cost.
4. Prepare the budget for selected increments of activity within the relevant range.

The activity index chosen should significantly influence the costs being budgeted. For manufacturing overhead costs, for example, the activity index is usually the same as the index used in developing the predetermined overhead rate—that is, direct labor hours or machine hours. For selling and administrative expenses, the activity index usually is sales or net sales.

The choice of the increment of activity is largely a matter of judgment. For example, if the relevant range is 8,000 to 12,000 direct labor hours, increments of 1,000 hours may be selected. The flexible budget is then prepared for each increment within the relevant range.

Flexible Budget—A Case Study

To illustrate the flexible budget, we use Fox Manufacturing Company. Fox's management uses a **flexible budget for monthly comparisons** of actual and budgeted manufacturing overhead costs of the Finishing Department. The master budget for the year ending December 31, 2012, shows expected annual operating capacity of 120,000 direct labor hours and the following overhead costs.

Illustration 24-11
Master budget data

Variable Costs		Fixed Costs	
Indirect materials	$180,000	Depreciation	$180,000
Indirect labor	240,000	Supervision	120,000
Utilities	60,000	Property taxes	60,000
Total	$480,000	Total	$360,000

The four steps for developing the flexible budget are applied as follows.

STEP 1. **Identify the activity index and the relevant range of activity.** The activity index is direct labor hours. The relevant range is 8,000–12,000 direct labor hours per month.

STEP 2. **Identify the variable costs, and determine the budgeted variable cost per unit of activity for each cost.** There are three variable costs. The variable cost per unit is found by dividing each total budgeted cost by the direct labor hours used in preparing the master budget (120,000 hours). For Fox Manufacturing, the computations are:

Illustration 24-12
Computation of variable costs per direct labor hour

Variable Cost	Computation	Variable Cost per Direct Labor Hour
Indirect materials	$180,000 ÷ 120,000	$1.50
Indirect labor	$240,000 ÷ 120,000	2.00
Utilities	$ 60,000 ÷ 120,000	0.50
Total		$4.00

STEP 3. **Identify the fixed costs, and determine the budgeted amount for each cost.** There are three fixed costs. Since Fox desires **monthly budget data**, it divides each annual budgeted cost by 12 to find the monthly amounts. For Fox Manufacturing, the monthly budgeted fixed costs are: depreciation $15,000, supervision $10,000, and property taxes $5,000.

STEP 4. **Prepare the budget for selected increments of activity within the relevant range.** Management prepares the budget in increments of 1,000 direct labor hours.

Illustration 24-13 shows Fox's flexible budget.

Illustration 24-13
Monthly overhead flexible budget

```
🔲 Fox Manufacturing Company.xls                              ▢▣▣
   File    Edit    View    Insert    Format    Tools    Data    Window    Help
```

	A	B	C	D	E	F
1	**FOX MANUFACTURING COMPANY**					
2	**Monthly Manufacturing Overhead Flexible Budget**					
3	**Finishing Department**					
4	**For the Year 2012**					
5	Activity level					
6	Direct labor hours	8,000	9,000	10,000	11,000	12,000
7	Variable costs					
8	Indirect materials	$12,000	$13,500	$15,000	$16,500	$18,000
9	Indirect labor	16,000	18,000	20,000	22,000	24,000
10	Utilities	4,000	4,500	5,000	5,500	6,000
11	Total variable costs	32,000	36,000	40,000	44,000	48,000
12	Fixed costs					
13	Depreciation	15,000	15,000	15,000	15,000	15,000
14	Supervision	10,000	10,000	10,000	10,000	10,000
15	Property taxes	5,000	5,000	5,000	5,000	5,000
16	Total fixed costs	30,000	30,000	30,000	30,000	30,000
17	Total costs	$62,000	$66,000	$70,000	$74,000	$78,000
18						

Fox uses the formula below to determine total budgeted costs at any level of activity.

Illustration 24-14
Formula for total budgeted costs

$$\underset{\text{Fixed Costs}}{} + \underset{\text{Variable Costs*}}{} = \underset{\text{Total Budgeted Costs}}{}$$

*Total variable cost per unit of activity × Activity level.

For Fox, fixed costs are $30,000, and total variable cost per direct labor hour is $4. At 9,000 direct labor hours, total budgeted costs are $66,000 [$30,000 + ($4 × 9,000)]. At 8,622 direct labor hours, total budgeted costs are $64,488 [$30,000 + ($4 × 8,622)].

Total budgeted costs can also be shown graphically, as in Illustration 24-15.

Helpful Hint

Using the data given for Fox, what amount of total costs would be budgeted for 10,600 direct labor hours?
Answer: $30,000 fixed + $42,400 variable (10,600 × $4) = $72,400 total.

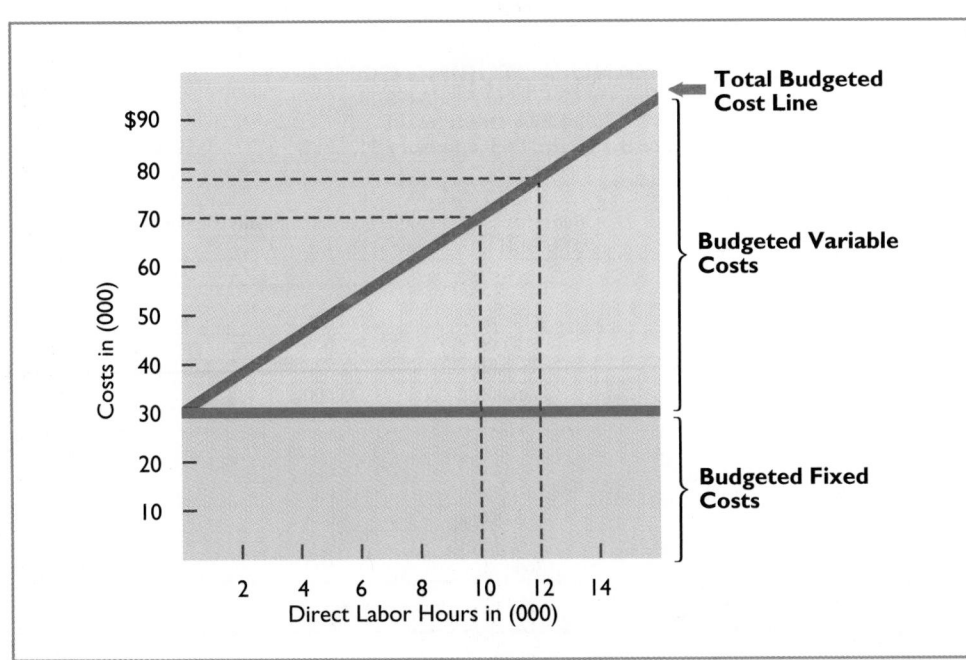

Illustration 24-15
Flexible budget graph high-lighting 10,000 and 12,000 hours of activity levels

In the graph, the horizontal axis represents the activity index, and costs are indicated on the vertical axis. The graph highlights two activity levels (10,000 and 12,000). As shown, total budgeted costs at these activity levels are $70,000 [$30,000 + ($4 × 10,000)] and $78,000 [$30,000 + ($4 × 12,000)], respectively.

Do it!

Flexible Budgets

action plan

✔ Apply the formula: Fixed costs + Variable costs (Total variable costs per unit × Activity level) = Total budgeted costs.

In Strassel Company's flexible budget graph, the fixed cost line and the total budgeted cost line intersect the vertical axis at $36,000. The total budgeted cost line is $186,000 at an activity level of 50,000 direct labor hours. Compute total budgeted costs at 30,000 direct labor hours.

Solution

Using the graph, fixed costs are $36,000, and variable costs are $3 per direct labor hour [($186,000 − $36,000) ÷ 50,000]. Thus, at 30,000 direct labor hours, total budgeted costs are $126,000 [$36,000 + ($3 × 30,000)].

Related exercise material: BE24-4, E24-3, E24-5, E24-10, and **Do it!** 24-1.

✔ **The Navigator**

Flexible Budget Reports

As shown in Illustration 24-10 (page 1103), the flexible budget report consists of two sections: (1) production data for a selected activity index, such as direct labor hours, and (2) cost data for variable and fixed costs. The report provides a basis for evaluating a manager's performance in two areas: production control and cost control. Flexible budget reports are widely used in production and service departments.

Illustration 24-16 shows a budget report for the Finishing Department of Fox Company for the month of January. In this month, 9,000 hours are worked.

Illustration 24-16
Overhead flexible budget report

Fox Manufacturing Company.xls				
File Edit View Insert Format Tools Data Window Help				
	A	**B**	**C**	**D** E
FOX MANUFACTURING COMPANY				
1				
2	Manufacturing Overhead Flexible Budget Report			
3	Finishing Department			
4	For the Month Ended January 31, 2012			
5				Difference
6		Budget at	Actual costs at	Favorable - F Unfavorable - U
7	Direct labor hours (DLH)	9,000 DLH	9,000 DLH	
8				
9	Variable costs			
10	Indirect materials	$13,500	$14,000	$ 500 U
11	Indirect labor	18,000	17,000	1,000 F
12	Utilities	4,500	4,600	100 U
13	Total variable costs	36,000	35,600	400 F
14				
15	Fixed costs			
16	Depreciation	15,000	15,000	0
17	Supervision	10,000	10,000	0
18	Property taxes	5,000	5,000	0
19	Total fixed costs	30,000	30,000	0
20	Total costs	$66,000	$65,600	$ 400 F
21				

The budget data are therefore based on the flexible budget for 9,000 hours in Illustration 24-13 (page 1105). The actual cost data are assumed.

How appropriate is this report in evaluating the Finishing Department manager's performance in controlling overhead costs? The report clearly provides a reliable basis. Both actual and budget costs are based on the activity level worked during January. Since variable costs generally are incurred directly by the department, the difference between the budget allowance for those hours and the actual costs is the responsibility of the department manager.

In subsequent months, Fox Manufacturing will prepare other flexible budget reports. For each month, the budget data are based on the actual activity level attained. In February that level may be 11,000 direct labor hours, in July 10,000, and so on.

Note that this flexible budget is based on a single cost driver. A more accurate budget often can be developed using the activity-based costing concepts explained in Chapter 21.

SERVICE COMPANY INSIGHT

Budgets and the Exotic Newcastle Disease

Exotic Newcastle Disease, one of the most infectious bird diseases in the world, kills so swiftly that many victims die before any symptoms appear. When it broke out in Southern California in 2003, it could have spelled disaster for the San Diego Zoo. "We have one of the most valuable collections of birds in the world, if not *the* most valuable," says Paula Brock, CFO of the Zoological Society of San Diego, which operates the zoo.

Bird exhibits were closed to the public for several months (the disease, which is harmless to humans, can be carried on clothes and shoes). The tires of arriving delivery trucks were sanitized, as were the shoes of anyone visiting the zoo's nonpublic areas. Zookeeper uniforms had to be changed and cleaned daily. And ultimately, the zoo, with $150 million in revenues, spent almost half a million dollars on quarantine measures in 2003.

It worked: No birds got sick. Better yet, the damage to the rest of the zoo's budget was minimized by another protective measure: the monthly budget reforecast. "When we get a hit like this, we still have to find a way to make our bottom line," says Brock. Thanks to a new planning process Brock had introduced a year earlier, the zoo's scientists were able to raise the financial alarm as they redirected resources to ward off the disease. "Because we had timely awareness," she says, "we were able to make adjustments to weather the storm."

Budget reforecasting is nothing new. (The San Diego Zoo's annual static budget was behind the times before Brock took over as CFO in 2001.) But the reaction of the zoo's staff shows the benefits of Brock's immediate efforts to link strategy to the process. It's a move long touted by consultants as a key way to improve people's involvement in budgeting.

"To keep your company on a path, it has to have some kind of map," says Brock. "The budgeting-and-planning process is that map. I cannot imagine an organization feeling in control if it didn't have that sort of discipline."

Source: Tim Reason, "Budgeting in the Real World," *CFO Magazine* (July 12, 2005), *www.cfodirect.com/ cfopublic.nsf/vContentPrint/649A82C8FF8AB06B85257037004* (accessed July 2005).

? What is the major benefit of tying a budget to the overall goals of the company?
(See page 1145.)

Management by Exception

Management by exception means that top management's review of a budget report is focused either entirely or primarily on differences between actual results and planned objectives. This approach enables top management to focus on problem areas. For example, many companies now use online reporting systems for employees to file their travel and entertainment expense reports. In addition to cutting reporting time in half, the online system enables managers to quickly analyze variances from travel budgets. This enables companies to cut down on expense account "padding" such as spending too much on meals or falsifying documents for costs that were never actually incurred.

Management by exception does not mean that top management will investigate every difference. For this approach to be effective, there must be guidelines for identifying an exception. The usual criteria are materiality and controllability.

MATERIALITY

Without quantitative guidelines, management would have to investigate every budget difference regardless of the amount. Materiality is usually expressed as a percentage difference from budget. For example, management may set the percentage difference at 5% for important items and 10% for other items. Managers will investigate all differences either over or under budget by the specified percentage. Costs over budget warrant investigation to determine why they were not controlled. Likewise, costs under budget merit investigation to determine whether costs critical to profitability are being curtailed. For example, if maintenance costs are budgeted at $80,000 but only $40,000 is spent, major unexpected breakdowns in productive facilities may occur in the future.

Alternatively, a company may specify a single percentage difference from budget for all items and supplement this guideline with a minimum dollar limit. For example, the exception criteria may be stated at 5% of budget or more than $10,000.

CONTROLLABILITY OF THE ITEM

Exception guidelines are more restrictive for controllable items than for items the manager cannot control. In fact, there may be no guidelines for noncontrollable items. For example, a large unfavorable difference between actual and budgeted property tax expense may not be flagged for investigation because the only possible causes are an unexpected increase in the tax rate or in the assessed value of the property. An investigation into the difference would be useless: the manager cannot control either cause.

Do it!

Flexible Budget Reports

Lawler Company expects to produce 40,000 units of product CV93 during the current year. Budgeted variable manufacturing costs per unit are direct materials $6, direct labor $15, and overhead $24. Annual budgeted fixed manufacturing overhead costs are $120,000 for depreciation and $60,000 for supervision.

In the current month, Lawler produced 5,000 units and incurred the following costs: direct materials $33,900, direct labor $74,200, variable overhead $120,500, depreciation $10,000, and supervision $5,000.

Prepare a flexible budget report. (*Note:* You do not have to prepare the heading.) Were costs controlled?

Solution

action plan

✔ Use budget for actual units produced.

✔ Classify each cost as variable or fixed.

✔ Determine monthly fixed costs by dividing annual amounts by 12.

✔ Classify the difference as favorable or unfavorable.

✔ Determine the difference in total variable costs, total fixed costs, and total costs.

⊠ Lawler Company.xls

| | File | Edit | View | Insert | Format | Tools | Data | Window | Help | | |

	A	B	C	D	E
1				Difference	
2		Budget at 5,000 units	Actual costs at 5,000 units	Favorable - F Unfavorable - U	
3	Units produced	5,000 units	5,000 units		
4					
5	Variable costs				
6	Direct materials	$ 30,000	$ 33,900	$3,900	U
7	Direct labor	75,000	74,200	800	F
8	Overhead	120,000	120,500	500	U
9	Total variable costs	225,000	228,600	3,600	U
10					
11	Fixed costs				
12	Depreciation	10,000	10,000	0	
13	Supervision	5,000	5,000	0	
14	Total fixed costs	15,000	15,000	0	
15	Total costs	$240,000	$243,600	$3,600	U
16					
17					

The responsibility report indicates that actual direct labor was only about 1% different from the budget, and overhead was less than half a percent different. Both appear to have been well controlled.

This was not the case for direct materials. Its 13% unfavorable difference should probably be investigated.

Actual fixed costs had no difference from budget and were well controlled.

Related exercise material: BE24-5, E24-4, E24-6, E24-7, E24-8, and **Do it!** 24-2.

 The Navigator

The Concept of Responsibility Accounting

Study Objective [4]
Describe the concept of responsibility accounting.

Like budgeting, responsibility accounting is an important part of management accounting. **Responsibility accounting** involves accumulating and reporting costs (and revenues, where relevant) on the basis of the manager who has the authority to make the day-to-day decisions about the items. Under responsibility accounting, a manager's performance is evaluated on matters directly under that manager's control. Responsibility accounting can be used at every level of management in which the following conditions exist.

1. Costs and revenues can be directly associated with the specific level of management responsibility.

2. The costs and revenues can be controlled by employees at the level of responsibility with which they are associated.

3. Budget data can be developed for evaluating the manager's effectiveness in controlling the costs and revenues.

Illustration 24-17 (page 1110) depicts levels of responsibility for controlling costs.

Under responsibility accounting, any individual who controls a specified set of activities can be a responsibility center. Thus, responsibility accounting may extend from the lowest level of control to the top strata of management. Once responsibility is established, the company first measures and reports the effectiveness of the individual's performance for the specified activity. It then reports that measure upward throughout the organization.

Responsibility accounting is especially valuable in a decentralized company. **Decentralization** means that the control of operations is delegated to many

Helpful Hint

All companies use responsibility accounting. Without some form of responsibility accounting, there would be chaos in discharging management's control function.

Illustration 24-17
Responsibility for controllable costs at varying levels of management

managers throughout the organization. The term segment is sometimes used to identify an area of responsibility in decentralized operations. Under responsibility accounting, companies prepare segment reports periodically, such as monthly, quarterly, and annually, to evaluate managers' performance.

Responsibility accounting is an essential part of any effective system of budgetary control. The reporting of costs and revenues under responsibility accounting differs from budgeting in two respects:

1. A distinction is made between controllable and noncontrollable items.
2. Performance reports either emphasize or include only items controllable by the individual manager.

Responsibility accounting applies to both profit and not-for-profit entities. For-profit entities seek to maximize net income. Not-for-profit entities wish to provide services as efficiently as possible.

MANAGEMENT INSIGHT

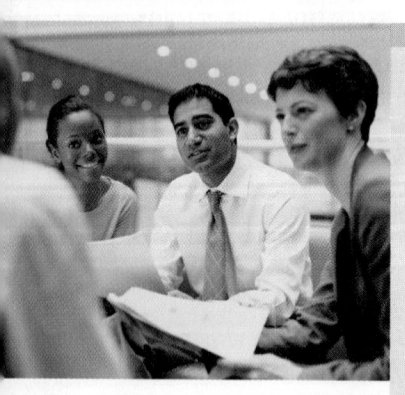

Competition versus Collaboration

Many compensation and promotion programs encourage competition among employees for pay raises. To get ahead you have to perform better than your fellow employees. While this may encourage hard work, it does not foster collaboration, and it can lead to distrust and disloyalty. Such results have led some companies to believe that cooperation and collaboration are essential in order to succeed in today's environment. For example, division managers might increase collaboration (and reduce costs) by sharing design and marketing resources or by jointly negotiating with suppliers. In addition, companies can reduce the need to hire and lay off employees by sharing employees across divisions as human resource needs increase and decrease.

As a consequence, many companies now explicitly include measures of collaboration in their performance measures. For example, Procter & Gamble measures collaboration in employees' annual performance reviews. At Cisco Systems the assessment of an employee's teamwork can affect the annual bonus by as much as 20%.

Source: Carol Hymowitz, "Rewarding Competitors Over Collaboration No Longer Makes Sense," *Wall Street Journal* (February 13, 2006).

? How might managers of separate divisions be able to reduce division costs through collaboration? (See page 1145.)

Controllable versus Noncontrollable Revenues and Costs

All costs and revenues are controllable at some level of responsibility within a company. This truth underscores the adage by the CEO of any organization that "the buck stops here." Under responsibility accounting, the critical issue is **whether the cost or revenue is controllable at the level of responsibility with which it is associated**. A cost over which a manager has control is called a controllable cost. From this definition, it follows that:

1. All costs are controllable by top management because of the broad range of its authority.
2. Fewer costs are controllable as one moves down to each lower level of managerial responsibility because of the manager's decreasing authority.

In general, **costs incurred directly by a level of responsibility are controllable at that level**. In contrast, costs incurred indirectly and allocated to a responsibility level are noncontrollable costs at that level.

Responsibility Reporting System

A responsibility reporting system involves the preparation of a report for each level of responsibility in the company's organization chart. To illustrate such a system, we use the partial organization chart and production departments of Francis Chair Company in Illustration 24-18.

Helpful Hint
Are there more or fewer controllable costs as you move to higher levels of management?
Answer: More.

Helpful Hint
The longer the time span, the more likely that the cost becomes controllable.

Illustration 24-18
Partial organization chart

Report A
President sees summary data of vice presidents.

Report B
Vice president sees summary of controllable costs in his/her functional area.

Report C
Plant manager sees summary of controllable costs for each department in the plant.

Report D
Department manager sees controllable costs of his/her department.

Detroit plant Chicago plant St. Louis plant

Fabricating Assembly Enameling

The responsibility reporting system begins with the lowest level of responsibility for controlling costs and moves upward to each higher level. Illustration 24-19 (page 1113) details the connections between levels. A brief description of the four reports for Francis Chair Company is as follows.

1. **Report D** is typical of reports that go to managers at the lowest level of responsibility shown in the organization chart—department managers. Similar reports are prepared for the managers of the Fabricating, Assembly, and Enameling Departments.

2. **Report C** is an example of reports that are sent to plant managers. It shows the costs of the Chicago plant that are controllable at the second level of responsibility. In addition, Report C shows summary data for each department that is controlled by the plant manager. Similar reports are prepared for the Detroit and St. Louis plant managers.

3. **Report B** illustrates the reports at the third level of responsibility. It shows the controllable costs of the vice president of production and summary data on the three assembly plants for which this officer is responsible. Similar reports are prepared for the vice presidents of sales and finance.

4. **Report A** is typical of reports that go to the top level of responsibility—the president. It shows the controllable costs and expenses of this office and summary data on the vice presidents that are accountable to the president.

A responsibility reporting system permits management by exception at each level of responsibility. And, each higher level of responsibility can obtain the detailed report for each lower level of responsibility. For example, the vice president of production in the Francis Chair Company may request the Chicago plant manager's report because this plant is $5,300 over budget.

This type of reporting system also permits comparative evaluations. In Illustration 24-19, the Chicago plant manager can easily rank the department managers' effectiveness in controlling manufacturing costs. Comparative rankings provide further incentive for a manager to control costs.

Types of Responsibility Centers

There are three basic types of responsibility centers: cost centers, profit centers, and investment centers. These classifications indicate the degree of responsibility the manager has for the performance of the center.

A **cost center** incurs costs (and expenses) but does not directly generate revenues. Managers of cost centers have the authority to incur costs. They are evaluated on their ability to control costs. **Cost centers are usually either production departments or service departments.** Production departments participate directly in making the product. Service departments provide only support services. In a Ford Motor Company automobile plant, the welding, painting, and assembling departments are production departments. Ford's maintenance, cafeteria, and human resources departments are service departments. All of them are cost centers.

A **profit center** incurs costs (and expenses) and also generates revenues. Managers of profit centers are judged on the profitability of their centers. Examples of profit centers include the individual departments of a retail store, such as clothing, furniture, and automotive products, and branch offices of banks.

Like a profit center, an **investment center** incurs costs (and expenses) and generates revenues. In addition, an investment center has control over decisions regarding the assets available for use. Investment center managers are evaluated on both the profitability of the center and the rate of return earned on the funds invested. Investment centers are often associated with subsidiary companies. Utility Duke Energy

Helpful Hint

(1) Is the jewelry department of Macy's department store a profit center or a cost center? (2) Is the props department of a movie studio a profit center or a cost center?
Answers: (1) Profit center. (2) Cost center.

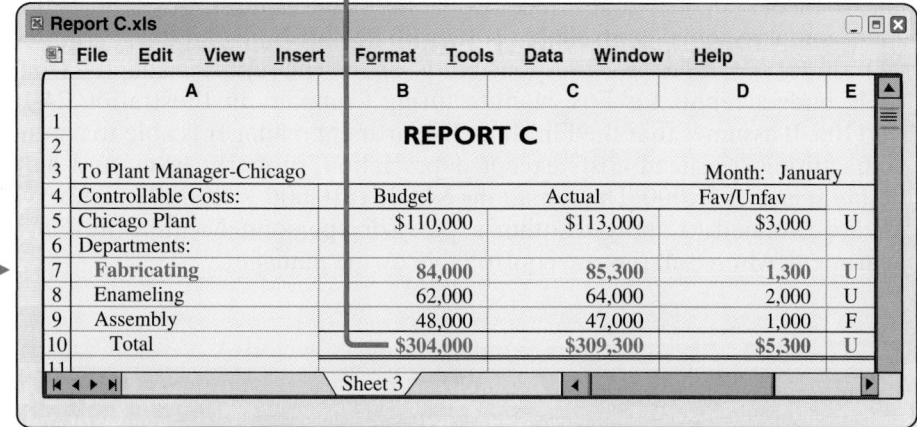

Illustration 24-19
Responsibility reporting system

Report A
President sees summary data of vice presidents.

Report B
Vice president sees summary of controllable costs in his/her functional area.

Report C
Plant manager sees summary of controllable costs for each department in the plant.

Report D
Department manager sees controllable costs of his/her department.

has operating divisions such as electric utility, energy trading, and natural gas. Investment center managers control or significantly influence investment decisions related to such matters as plant expansion and entry into new market areas. Illustration 24-20 depicts these three types of responsibility centers.

Illustration 24-20
Types of responsibility centers

Responsibility Accounting for Cost Centers

Study Objective [5]
Indicate the features of responsibility reports for cost centers.

The evaluation of a manager's performance for cost centers is based on his or her ability to meet budgeted goals for controllable costs. **Responsibility reports for cost centers compare actual controllable costs with flexible budget data.**

Illustration 24-21 shows a responsibility report. The report is adapted from the flexible budget report for Fox Manufacturing Company in Illustration 24-16 on page 1106. It assumes that the Finishing Department manager is able to control all manufacturing overhead costs except depreciation, property taxes, and his own monthly salary of $6,000. The remaining $4,000 ($10,000 − $6,000) of supervision costs are assumed to apply to other supervisory personnel within the Finishing Department, whose salaries are controllable by the manager.

Illustration 24-21
Responsibility report for a cost center

Fox Manufacturing Company.xls

File Edit View Insert Format Tools Data Window Help

	A	B	C	D	E
1	**FOX MANUFACTURING COMPANY**				
2	Finishing Department				
3	Responsibility Report				
4	For the Month Ended January 31, 2012				
5				Difference	
6	Controllable Cost	Budget	Actual	Favorable - F Unfavorable - U	
7	Indirect materials	$13,500	$14,000	$ 500	U
8	Indirect labor	18,000	17,000	$1,000	F
9	Utilities	4,500	4,600	100	U
10	**Supervision**	**4,000**	**4,000**	**0**	
11		$40,000	$39,600	$ 400	F
12					

The report in Illustration 24-21 includes **only controllable costs**, and no distinction is made between variable and fixed costs. The responsibility report continues the concept of management by exception. In this case, top management may request an explanation of the $1,000 favorable difference in indirect labor and/or the $500 unfavorable difference in indirect materials.

Responsibility Accounting for Profit Centers

To evaluate the performance of a profit center manager, upper management needs detailed information about both controllable revenues and controllable costs. The operating revenues earned by a profit center, such as sales, are controllable by the manager. All variable costs (and expenses) incurred by the center are also controllable by the manager because they vary with sales. However, to determine the controllability of fixed costs, it is necessary to distinguish between direct and indirect fixed costs.

Study Objective [6]
Identify the content of responsibility reports for profit centers.

DIRECT AND INDIRECT FIXED COSTS

A profit center may have both direct and indirect fixed costs. Direct fixed costs relate specifically to one center and are incurred for the sole benefit of that center. Examples of such costs include the salaries established by the profit center manager for supervisory personnel and the cost of a timekeeping department for the center's employees. Since these fixed costs can be traced directly to a center, they are also called **traceable costs**. **Most direct fixed costs are controllable by the profit center manager.**

In contrast, indirect fixed costs pertain to a company's overall operating activities and are incurred for the benefit of more than one profit center. Management allocates indirect fixed costs to profit centers on some type of equitable basis. For example, property taxes on a building occupied by more than one center may be allocated on the basis of square feet of floor space used by each center. Or, the costs of a company's human resources department may be allocated to profit centers on the basis of the number of employees in each center. Because these fixed costs apply to more than one center, they are also called **common costs**. **Most indirect fixed costs are not controllable by the profit center manager.**

RESPONSIBILITY REPORT

The responsibility report for a profit center shows budgeted and actual **controllable revenues and costs**. The report is prepared using the cost-volume-profit income statement explained in Chapter 22. In the report:

1. Controllable fixed costs are deducted from contribution margin.
2. The excess of contribution margin over controllable fixed costs is identified as controllable margin.
3. Noncontrollable fixed costs are not reported.

Illustration 24-22 (page 1116) shows the responsibility report for the manager of the Marine Division, a profit center of Mantle Manufacturing Company. For the year, the Marine Division also had $60,000 of indirect fixed costs that were not controllable by the profit center manager.

Controllable margin is considered to be the best measure of the manager's performance **in controlling revenues and costs**. The report in Illustration 24-22 shows that the manager's performance was below budgeted expectations by 10% ($36,000 ÷ $360,000). Top management would likely investigate the causes of this unfavorable result. Note that the report does not show the Marine Division's noncontrollable fixed costs of $60,000. These costs would be included in a report on the profitability of the profit center.

Illustration 24-22
Responsibility report for profit center

	Mantle Manufacturing Company.xls					
	File Edit View Insert Format Tools Data Window Help					
	A	B	C	D	E	

	A	B	C	D	E
1	**MANTLE MANUFACTURING COMPANY**				
2	**Marine Division**				
3	**Responsibility Report**				
4	**For the Year Ended December 31, 2012**				
5				Difference	
6		Budget	Actual	Favorable - F Unfavorable - U	
7	Sales	$1,200,000	$1,150,000	$50,000	U
8	Variable costs				
9	Cost of goods sold	500,000	490,000	10,000	F
10	Selling and administrative	160,000	156,000	4,000	F
11	Total	660,000	646,000	14,000	F
12	Contribution margin	540,000	504,000	36,000	U
13	Controllable fixed costs				
14	Cost of goods sold	100,000	100,000	0	
15	Selling and administrative	80,000	80,000	0	
16	Total	180,000	180,000	0	
17	Controllable margin	$ 360,000	$ 324,000	$36,000	U
18					

Management also may choose to see monthly responsibility reports for profit centers. In addition, responsibility reports may include cumulative year-to-date results.

Do it!

Responsibility Reports for Profit Centers

Midwest Division operates as a profit center. It reports the following for the year.

	Budgeted	Actual
Sales	$1,500,000	$1,700,000
Variable costs	700,000	800,000
Controllable fixed costs	400,000	400,000
Noncontrollable fixed costs	200,000	200,000

Prepare a responsibility report for the Midwest Division for December 31, 2012.

action plan

✔ Deduct variable costs from sales to show contribution margin.

✔ Deduct controllable fixed costs from the contribution margin to show controllable margin.

✔ Do not report noncontrollable fixed costs.

Solution

MIDWEST DIVISION
Responsibility Report
For the Year Ended December 31, 2012

	Budget	Actual	Difference Favorable F Unfavorable U
Sales	$1,500,000	$1,700,000	$200,000 F
Variable costs	700,000	800,000	100,000 U
Contribution margin	800,000	900,000	100,000 F
Controllable fixed costs	400,000	400,000	–0–
Controllable margin	$ 400,000	$ 500,000	$100,000 F

Related exercise material: BE24-7, E24-9, E24-13, and **Do it!** 24-3.

The Navigator

Responsibility Accounting for Investment Centers

As explained earlier, an investment center manager can control or significantly influence the investment funds available for use. Thus, the primary basis for evaluating the performance of a manager of an investment center is **return on investment (ROI)**. The return on investment is considered to be a useful performance measurement because it shows the **effectiveness of the manager in utilizing the assets at his or her disposal**.

Study Objective [7]
Explain the basis and formula used in evaluating performance in investment centers.

RETURN ON INVESTMENT (ROI)

The formula for computing ROI for an investment center, together with assumed illustrative data, is shown in Illustration 24-23.

Controllable Margin	÷	Average Operating Assets	=	Return on Investment (ROI)
$1,000,000	÷	$5,000,000	=	20%

Illustration 24-23
ROI formula

Both factors in the formula are controllable by the investment center manager. Operating assets consist of current assets and plant assets used in operations by the center and controlled by the manager. Nonoperating assets such as idle plant assets and land held for future use are excluded. Average operating assets are usually based on the cost or book value of the assets at the beginning and end of the year.

RESPONSIBILITY REPORT

The scope of the investment center manager's responsibility significantly affects the content of the performance report. Since an investment center is an independent entity for operating purposes, **all fixed costs are controllable by its manager**. For example, the manager is responsible for depreciation on investment center assets. Therefore, more fixed costs are identified as controllable in the performance report for an investment center manager than in a performance report for a profit center manager. The report also shows budgeted and actual ROI below controllable margin.

To illustrate this responsibility report, we will now assume that the Marine Division of Mantle Manufacturing Company is an investment center. It has budgeted and actual average operating assets of $2,000,000. The manager can control $60,000 of fixed costs that were not controllable when the division was a profit center. Illustration 24-24 (page 1118) shows the division's responsibility report.

The report shows that the manager's performance based on ROI was below budget expectations by 1.8% (15.0% versus 13.2%). Top management would likely want an explanation of the reasons for this unfavorable result.

JUDGMENTAL FACTORS IN ROI

The return on investment approach includes two judgmental factors:

1. **Valuation of operating assets.** Operating assets may be valued at acquisition cost, book value, appraised value, or fair value. The first two bases are readily available from the accounting records.
2. **Margin (income) measure.** This measure may be controllable margin, income from operations, or net income.

Each of the alternative values for operating assets can provide a reliable basis for evaluating a manager's performance as long as it is consistently applied between reporting periods. However, the use of income measures other than controllable

Illustration 24-24
Responsibility report for investment center

```
┌─────────────────────────────────────────────────────────────────────────┐
│ ⊠ Mantle Manufacturing Company.xls                                □ ▫ ☒   │
│ 🗐 File   Edit   View   Insert   Format   Tools   Data   Window   Help     │
├─────────────────────────────────────────────────────────────────────────┤
```

	A	B	C	D	E
1	**MANTLE MANUFACTURING COMPANY**				
2	Marine Division				
3	Responsibility Report				
4	For the Year Ended December 31, 2012				
5				Difference	
6		Budget	Actual	Favorable - F Unfavorable - U	
7	Sales	$1,200,000	$1,150,000	$ 50,000	U
8	Variable costs				
9	Cost of goods sold	500,000	490,000	10,000	F
10	Selling and administrative	160,000	156,000	4,000	F
11	Total	660,000	646,000	14,000	F
12	Contribution margin	540,000	504,000	36,000	U
13	**Controllable fixed costs**				
14	Cost of goods sold	100,000	100,000	0	
15	Selling and administrative	80,000	80,000	0	
16	**Other fixed costs**	60,000	60,000	0	
17	Total	240,000	240,000	0	
18	**Controllable margin**	$ 300,000	$ 264,000	$ 36,000	U
19	**Return on investment**	15.0%	13.2%	1.8%	U
20		(a)	(b)	(c)	
21					
22		(a) $ 300,000 / $2,000,000	(b) $ 264,000 / $2,000,000	(c) $ 36,000 / $2,000,000	
23					

margin will not result in a valid basis for evaluating the performance of an investment center manager.

IMPROVING ROI

The manager of an investment center can improve ROI in two ways: (1) increase controllable margin, and/or (2) reduce average operating assets. To illustrate, we will use the following assumed data for the Laser Division of Berra Manufacturing.

Illustration 24-25
Assumed data for Laser Division

Sales	$2,000,000
Variable costs	1,100,000
Contribution margin (45%)	900,000
Controllable fixed costs	300,000
Controllable margin (a)	$ 600,000
Average operating assets (b)	$5,000,000
Return on investment (a) ÷ (b)	12%

Increasing Controllable Margin. Controllable margin can be increased by increasing sales or by reducing variable and controllable fixed costs as follows.

1. **Increase sales 10%.** Sales will increase $200,000 ($2,000,000 × .10). Assuming no change in the contribution margin percentage of 45%, contribution margin will increase $90,000 ($200,000 × .45). Controllable margin will increase by the same amount because controllable fixed costs will not change. Thus, controllable margin becomes $690,000 ($600,000 + $90,000). The new ROI is 13.8%, computed as follows.

Illustration 24-26
ROI computation—increase in sales

$$\text{ROI} = \frac{\text{Controllable margin}}{\text{Average operating assets}} = \frac{\$690,000}{\$5,000,000} = 13.8\%$$

An increase in sales benefits both the investment center and the company if it results in new business. It would not benefit the company if the increase was achieved at the expense of other investment centers.

2. **Decrease variable and fixed costs 10%.** Total costs decrease $140,000 [($1,100,000 + $300,000) × .10]. This reduction results in a corresponding increase in controllable margin. Thus, controllable margin becomes $740,000 ($600,000 + $140,000). The new ROI is 14.8%, computed as follows.

$$\text{ROI} = \frac{\text{Controllable margin}}{\text{Average operating assets}} = \frac{\$740,000}{\$5,000,000} = 14.8\%$$

Illustration 24-27
ROI computation—decrease in costs

This course of action is clearly beneficial when waste and inefficiencies are eliminated. But, a reduction in vital costs such as required maintenance and inspections is not likely to be acceptable to top management.

Reducing Average Operating Assets. Assume that average operating assets are reduced 10% or $500,000 ($5,000,000 × .10). Average operating assets become $4,500,000 ($5,000,000 − $500,000). Since controllable margin remains unchanged at $600,000, the new ROI is 13.3%, computed as follows.

$$\text{ROI} = \frac{\text{Controllable margin}}{\text{Average operating assets}} = \frac{\$600,000}{\$4,500,000} = 13.3\%$$

Illustration 24-28
ROI computation—decrease in operating assets

Reductions in operating assets may or may not be prudent. It is beneficial to eliminate overinvestment in inventories and to dispose of excessive plant assets. However, it is unwise to reduce inventories below expected needs or to dispose of essential plant assets.

ACCOUNTING ACROSS THE ORGANIZATION

Does Hollywood Look at ROI?

If Hollywood were run like a real business, where things like return on investment mattered, there would be one unchallenged, sacred principle that studio chieftains would never violate: Make lots of G-rated movies.

No matter how you slice the movie business—by star vehicles, by budget levels, by sequels or franchises—by far the best return on investment comes from the not-so-glamorous world of G-rated films. The problem is, these movies represent only 3% of the total films made in a typical year.

Take 2003: According to Motion Picture Association of America statistics, of the 940 movies released that year, only 29 were G-rated. Yet the highest-grossing movie of the year, *Finding Nemo*, was G-rated. . . . On the flip side are the R-rated films, which dominate the total releases and yet yield the worst return on investment. A whopping 646 R-rated films were released in 2003—69% of the total output—but only four of the top-20 grossing movies of the year were R-rated films.

This trend—G-rated movies are good for business but underproduced; R-rated movies are bad for business, and yet overdone—is something that has been driving economists batty for the past several years.

Source: Grainger, David, "The Dysfunctional Family-Film Business," *Fortune* (January 10, 2005), pp. 20–21.

? What might be the reason that movie studios do not produce G-rated movies as often as R-rated ones? (See page 1145.)

Principles of Performance Evaluation

Performance evaluation is at the center of responsibility accounting. **Performance evaluation** is a management function that compares actual results with budget goals. It involves both behavioral and reporting principles.

BEHAVIORAL PRINCIPLES

The human factor is critical in evaluating performance. Behavioral principles include the following.

1. **Managers of responsibility centers should have direct input into the process of establishing budget goals of their area of responsibility.** Without such input, managers may view the goals as unrealistic or arbitrarily set by top management. Such views adversely affect the managers' motivation to meet the targeted objectives.

2. **The evaluation of performance should be based entirely on matters that are controllable by the manager being evaluated.** Criticism of a manager on matters outside his or her control reduces the effectiveness of the evaluation process. It leads to negative reactions by a manager and to doubts about the fairness of the company's evaluation policies.

3. **Top management should support the evaluation process.** As explained earlier, the evaluation process begins at the lowest level of responsibility and extends upward to the highest level of management. Managers quickly lose faith in the process when top management ignores, overrules, or bypasses established procedures for evaluating a manager's performance.

4. **The evaluation process must allow managers to respond to their evaluations.** Evaluation is not a one-way street. Managers should have the opportunity to defend their performance. Evaluation without feedback is both impersonal and ineffective.

5. **The evaluation should identify both good and poor performance.** Praise for good performance is a powerful motivating factor for a manager. This is especially true when a manager's compensation includes rewards for meeting budget goals.

REPORTING PRINCIPLES

Performance evaluation under responsibility accounting should be based on certain reporting principles. These principles pertain primarily to the internal reports that provide the basis for evaluating performance. Performance reports should:

1. Contain only data that are controllable by the manager of the responsibility center.

2. Provide accurate and reliable budget data to measure performance.

3. Highlight significant differences between actual results and budget goals.

4. Be tailor-made for the intended evaluation.

5. Be prepared at reasonable intervals.

In recent years companies have come under increasing pressure from influential shareholder groups to do a better job of linking executive pay to corporate performance. For example, software maker Siebel Systems unveiled a new incentive plan after lengthy discussions with the California Public Employees' Retirement System. One unique feature of the plan is that managers' targets will be publicly disclosed at the beginning of each year for investors to evaluate.

MANAGEMENT INSIGHT

Flexible Manufacturing Requires Flexible Accounting

Flexible budgeting is useful because it enables managers to evaluate performance in light of changing conditions. But the ability to react quickly to changing conditions is even more important. Among automobile manufacturing facilities in the U.S., nobody has more flexible plants than Honda. The manufacturing facilities of some auto companies can make slight alterations to the features of a vehicle in response to changes in demand for particular features. But for most plants, to switch from production of one type of vehicle to a completely different type of vehicle, when demand for types of vehicles shifts, typically takes months and costs hundreds of millions of dollars. But at the Honda plant, the switch takes minutes. For example, it takes about five minutes to install different hand-like parts on the robots so they can switch from making Civic compacts to the longer, taller CR-V crossover. This ability to adjust quickly to changing demand gave Honda a huge advantage when gas prices surged and demand for more fuel-efficient cars increased quickly.

Source: Kate Linebaugh, "Honda's Flexible Plants Provide Edge," *Wall Street Journal Online* (September 23, 2008).

? What implications do these improvements in production capabilities have for management accounting information and performance evaluation within the organization? (See page 1145.)

Do it!

The service division of Metro Industries reported the following results for 2012.

Sales	$400,000
Variable costs	320,000
Controllable fixed costs	40,800
Average operating assets	280,000

Performance Evaluation

Management is considering the following independent courses of action in 2013 in order to maximize the return on investment for this division.

1. Reduce average operating assets by $80,000, with no change in controllable margin.
2. Increase sales $80,000, with no change in the contribution margin percentage.

(a) Compute the controllable margin and the return on investment for 2012.

(b) Compute the controllable margin and the expected return on investment for each proposed alternative.

Solution

(a) Return on investment for 2012

Sales	$400,000
Variable costs	320,000
Contribution margin	80,000
Controllable fixed costs	40,800
Controllable margin	$ 39,200

Return on investment $\frac{\$39,200}{\$280,000} = 14\%$

action plan

✔ Recall key formulas: Sales – Variable costs = Contribution margin.

✔ Contribution margin ÷ Sales = Contribution margin percentage.

✔ Contribution margin – Controllable fixed costs = Controllable margin.

✔ Return on investment = Controllable margin ÷ Average operating assets.

(b) Expected return on investment for alternative 1:

$$\frac{\$39,200}{\$200,000} = 19.6\%$$

Expected return on investment for alternative 2:

Sales ($400,000 + 80,000)	$480,000
Variable costs ($320,000/400,000 × $480,000)	384,000
Contribution margin	96,000
Controllable fixed costs	40,800
Controllable margin	$ 55,200
Return on investment	$\dfrac{\$55,200}{\$280,000} = 19.7\%$

Related exercise material: BE24-8, BE24-9, BE24-10, E24-14, E24-15, E24-16, E24-17, and **Do it!** 24-4.

COMPREHENSIVE

Do it! 1

action plan

✔ Compute the cost per direct labor hour for all variable costs.

✔ Use budget data for actual direct labor hours worked.

✔ Classify each cost as variable or fixed.

✔ Determine the difference between budgeted and actual costs.

✔ Identify the difference as favorable or unfavorable.

✔ Determine the difference in total variable costs, total fixed costs, and total costs.

Glenda Company uses a flexible budget for manufacturing overhead based on direct labor hours. For 2012, the master overhead budget for the Packaging Department based on 300,000 direct labor hours was as follows.

Variable Costs		Fixed Costs	
Indirect labor	$360,000	Supervision	$ 60,000
Supplies and lubricants	150,000	Depreciation	24,000
Maintenance	210,000	Property taxes	18,000
Utilities	120,000	Insurance	12,000
	$840,000		$114,000

During July, 24,000 direct labor hours were worked. The company incurred the following variable costs in July: indirect labor $30,200, supplies and lubricants $11,600, maintenance $17,500, and utilities $9,200. Actual fixed overhead costs were the same as monthly budgeted fixed costs.

Instructions

Prepare a flexible budget report for the Packaging Department for July.

Solution to Comprehensive Do it! 1

GLENDA COMPANY
Manufacturing Overhead Flexible Budget Report
Packaging Department
For the Month Ended July 31, 2012

	Budget	Actual Costs	Difference
			Favorable F
Direct labor hours (DLH)	**24,000 DLH**	**24,000 DLH**	**Unfavorable U**
Variable costs			
Indirect labor ($1.20)	$28,800	$30,200	$1,400 U
Supplies and lubricants ($0.50)	12,000	11,600	400 F
Maintenance ($0.70)	16,800	17,500	700 U
Utilities ($0.40)	9,600	9,200	400 F
Total variable	67,200	68,500	1,300 U

Fixed costs			
Supervision	$ 5,000	$ 5,000	–0–
Depreciation	2,000	2,000	–0–
Property taxes	1,500	1,500	–0–
Insurance	1,000	1,000	–0–
Total fixed	9,500	9,500	–0–
Total costs	$76,700	$78,000	$1,300 U

✔ **The Navigator**

COMPREHENSIVE

Do it! 2

The manufacturing overhead budget for Reebles Company contains the following items:

Variable costs	
Indirect materials	$25,000
Indirect labor	12,000
Maintenance expenses	10,000
Manufacturing supplies	6,000
Total variable	$53,000
Fixed costs	
Supervision	$17,000
Inspection costs	1,000
Insurance expenses	2,000
Depreciation	15,000
Total fixed	$35,000

The budget was based on an estimated 2,000 units being produced. During November, 1,500 units were produced, and the following costs incurred.

Variable costs	
Indirect materials	$25,000
Indirect labor	13,500
Maintenance expenses	8,200
Manufacturing supplies	5,100
Total variable	$52,000
Fixed costs	
Supervision	$19,300
Inspection costs	1,200
Insurance expenses	2,200
Depreciation	14,700
Total fixed	$37,400

Instructions

(a) Determine which items would be controllable by Ed Lopat, the production manager. (Assume "supervision" excludes Lopat's own salary.)

(b) How much should have been spent during the month for the manufacture of the 1,500 units?

(c) Prepare a flexible manufacturing overhead budget report for Mr. Lopat.

(d) Prepare a responsibility report. Include only the costs that would have been controllable by Mr. Lopat. In an attached memo, describe clearly for Mr. Lopat the areas in which his performance needs to be improved.

Solution to Comprehensive Do it! 2

(a) Ed Lopat should be able to control all the variable costs and the fixed costs of supervision and inspection. Insurance and depreciation ordinarily are not the responsibility of the department manager.

(b) The total variable cost per unit is $26.50 ($53,000 ÷ 2,000). The total budgeted cost during the month to manufacture 1,500 units is variable costs $39,750 (1,500 × $26.50) plus fixed costs ($35,000), for a total of $74,750 ($39,750 + $35,000).

(c)

REEBLES COMPANY
Production Department
Manufacturing Overhead Flexible Budget Report
For the Month Ended November 30, 2012

	Budget at 1,500 Units	Actual at 1,500 Units	Difference Favorable F Unfavorable U
Variable costs			
Indirect materials ($12.50)	$18,750	$25,200	$ 6,450 U
Indirect labor ($6)	9,000	13,500	4,500 U
Maintenance ($5)	7,500	8,200	700 U
Manufacturing supplies ($3)	4,500	5,100	600 U
Total variable	39,750	52,000	12,250 U
Fixed costs			
Supervision	17,000	19,300	2,300 U
Inspection	1,000	1,200	200 U
Insurance	2,000	2,200	200 U
Depreciation	15,000	14,700	300 F
Total fixed	35,000	37,400	2,400 U
Total costs	$74,750	$89,400	$14,650 U

(d) Because a production department is a cost center, the responsibility report should include only the costs that are controllable by the production manager. In this type of report, no distinction is made between variable and fixed costs. Budget data in the report should be based on the units actually produced.

REEBLES COMPANY
Production Department
Manufacturing Overhead Responsibility Report
For the Month Ended November 30, 2012

Controllable Cost	Budget	Actual	Difference Favorable F Unfavorable U
Indirect materials	$18,750	$25,200	$ 6,450 U
Indirect labor	9,000	13,500	4,500 U
Maintenance	7,500	8,200	700 U
Manufacturing supplies	4,500	5,100	600 U
Supervision	17,000	19,300	2,300 U
Inspection	1,000	1,200	200 U
Total	$57,750	$72,500	$14,750 U

To: Mr. Ed Lopat, Production Manager

From: _____, Vice President of Production

Subject: Performance Evaluation for the Month of November

Your performance in controlling costs that are your responsibility was very disappointing in the month of November. As indicated in the accompanying responsibility report, total costs were $14,750 over budget. On a percentage basis, costs were 26% over budget. As you can see, actual costs were over budget for every cost item. In three instances, costs were significantly over budget (indirect materials 34%, indirect labor 50%, and supervision 14%).

Ed, it is imperative that you get costs under control in your department as soon as possible.

I think we need to talk about ways to implement more effective cost control measures. I would like to meet with you in my office at 9 a.m. on Wednesday to discuss possible alternatives.

The Navigator

Summary of Study Objectives

[1] **Describe the concept of budgetary control.** Budgetary control consists of (a) preparing periodic budget reports that compare actual results with planned objectives, (b) analyzing the differences to determine their causes, (c) taking appropriate corrective action, and (d) modifying future plans, if necessary.

[2] **Evaluate the usefulness of static budget reports.** Static budget reports are useful in evaluating the progress toward planned sales and profit goals. They are also appropriate in assessing a manager's effectiveness in controlling costs when (a) actual activity closely approximates the master budget activity level, and/or (b) the behavior of the costs in response to changes in activity is fixed.

[3] **Explain the development of flexible budgets and the usefulness of flexible budget reports.** To develop the flexible budget it is necessary to: (a) Identify the activity index and the relevant range of activity. (b) Identify the variable costs, and determine the budgeted variable cost per unit of activity for each cost. (c) Identify the fixed costs, and determine the budgeted amount for each cost. (d) Prepare the budget for selected increments of activity within the relevant range. Flexible budget reports permit an evaluation of a manager's performance in controlling production and costs.

[4] **Describe the concept of responsibility accounting.** Responsibility accounting involves accumulating and reporting revenues and costs on the basis of the individual manager who has the authority to make the day-to-day decisions about the items. The evaluation of a manager's performance is based on the matters directly under the manager's control. In responsibility accounting, it is necessary to distinguish between controllable and noncontrollable fixed costs and to identify three types of responsibility centers: cost, profit, and investment.

[5] **Indicate the features of responsibility reports for cost centers.** Responsibility reports for cost centers compare actual costs with flexible budget data. The reports show only controllable costs, and no distinction is made between variable and fixed costs.

[6] **Identify the content of responsibility reports for profit centers.** Responsibility reports show contribution margin, controllable fixed costs, and controllable margin for each profit center.

[7] **Explain the basis and formula used in evaluating performance in investment centers.** The primary basis for evaluating performance in investment centers is return on investment (ROI). The formula for computing ROI for investment centers is: Controllable margin ÷ Average operating assets.

The Navigator

Glossary

Budgetary control   The use of budgets to control operations. (p. 1098).

Controllable cost   A cost over which a manager has control. (p. 1111).

Controllable margin   Contribution margin less controllable fixed costs. (p. 1115).

Cost center   A responsibility center that incurs costs but does not directly generate revenues. (p. 1112).

Decentralization Control of operations is delegated to many managers throughout the organization. (p. 1109).

Direct fixed costs Costs that relate specifically to a responsibility center and are incurred for the sole benefit of the center. (p. 1115).

Flexible budget A projection of budget data for various levels of activity. (p. 1101).

Indirect fixed costs Costs that are incurred for the benefit of more than one profit center. (p. 1115).

Investment center A responsibility center that incurs costs, generates revenues, and has control over decisions regarding the assets available for use. (p. 1112).

Management by exception The review of budget reports by top management focused entirely or primarily on differences between actual results and planned objectives. (p. 1108).

Noncontrollable costs Costs incurred indirectly and allocated to a responsibility center that are not controllable at that level. (p. 1111).

Profit center A responsibility center that incurs costs and also generates revenues. (p. 1112).

Responsibility accounting A part of management accounting that involves accumulating and reporting revenues and costs on the basis of the manager who has the authority to make the day-to-day decisions about the items. (p. 1109).

Responsibility reporting system The preparation of reports for each level of responsibility in the company's organization chart. (p. 1111).

Return on investment (ROI) A measure of management's effectiveness in utilizing assets at its disposal in an investment center. (p. 1117).

Segment An area of responsibility in decentralized operations. (p. 1110).

Static budget A projection of budget data at one level of activity. (p. 1099).

 Self-Test, Brief Exercises, Exercises, Problem Set A, and many more components are available for practice in *WileyPLUS*

Self-Test Questions

Answers are on page 1145.

(SO 1) **1.** Budgetary control involves all but one of the following:
  a. modifying future plans.
  b. analyzing differences.
  c. using static budgets.
  d. determining differences between actual and planned results.

(SO 1) **2.** Budget reports are prepared:
  a. daily.   **c.** monthly.
  b. weekly.   **d.** All of the above.

(SO 1) **3.** A production manager in a manufacturing company would most likely receive a:
  a. sales report.
  b. income statement.
  c. scrap report.
  d. shipping department overhead report.

(SO 2) **4.** A static budget is:
  a. a projection of budget data at several levels of activity within the relevant range of activity.
  b. a projection of budget data at a single level of activity.
  c. compared to a flexible budget in a budget report.
  d. never appropriate in evaluating a manager's effectiveness in controlling costs.

(SO 2) **5.** A static budget is useful in controlling costs when cost behavior is:
  a. mixed.   **c.** variable.
  b. fixed.   **d.** linear.

(SO 3) **6.** At zero direct labor hours in a flexible budget graph, the total budgeted cost line intersects the vertical axis at $30,000. At 10,000 direct labor hours, a horizontal line drawn from the total budgeted cost line intersects the vertical axis at $90,000. Fixed and variable costs may be expressed as:
  a. $30,000 fixed plus $6 per direct labor hour variable.
  b. $30,000 fixed plus $9 per direct labor hour variable.
  c. $60,000 fixed plus $3 per direct labor hour variable.
  d. $60,000 fixed plus $6 per direct labor hour variable.

(SO 3) **7.** At 9,000 direct labor hours, the flexible budget for indirect materials is $27,000. If $28,000 of indirect materials costs are incurred at 9,200 direct labor hours, the flexible budget report should show the following difference for indirect materials:
  a. $1,000 unfavorable.
  b. $1,000 favorable.
  c. $400 favorable.
  d. $400 unfavorable.

(SO 4) **8.** Under responsibility accounting, the evaluation of a manager's performance is based on matters that the manager:
  a. directly controls.
  b. directly and indirectly controls.
  c. indirectly controls.
  d. has shared responsibility for with another manager.

(SO 4) **9.** Responsibility centers include:
  a. cost centers.
  b. profit centers.
  c. investment centers.
  d. All of the above.

(SO 5) **10.** Responsibility reports for cost centers:
  a. distinguish between fixed and variable costs.
  b. use static budget data.
  c. include both controllable and noncontrollable costs.
  d. include only controllable costs.

(SO 5) **11.** The accounting department of a manufacturing company is an example of:
    a. a cost center.   **c.** an investment center.
    b. a profit center.   **d.** a contribution center.

(SO 6) **12.** To evaluate the performance of a profit center manager, upper management needs detailed information about:
    a. controllable costs.
    b. controllable revenues.
    c. controllable costs and revenues.
    d. controllable costs and revenues and average operating assets.

(SO 6) **13.** In a responsibility report for a profit center, controllable fixed costs are deducted from contribution margin to show:
    a. profit center margin.
    b. controllable margin.
    c. net income.
    d. income from operations.

(SO 7) **14.** In the formula for return on investment (ROI), the factors for controllable margin and operating assets are, respectively:
    a. controllable margin percentage and total operating assets.
    b. controllable margin dollars and average operating assets.
    c. controllable margin dollars and total assets.
    d. controllable margin percentage and average operating assets.

(SO 7) **15.** A manager of an investment center can improve ROI by:
    a. increasing average operating assets.
    b. reducing sales.
    c. increasing variable costs.
    d. reducing variable and/or controllable fixed costs.

Go to the book's companion website, **www.wiley.com/college/weygandt**, for additional Self-Test Questions.

Questions

1. **(a)** What is budgetary control?
   (b) Finn Berge is describing budgetary control. What steps should be included in Finn's description?

2. The following purposes are part of a budgetary reporting system: (a) Determine efficient use of materials. (b) Control overhead costs. (c) Determine whether income objectives are being met. For each purpose, indicate the name of the report, the frequency of the report, and the primary recipient(s) of the report.

3. How may a budget report for the second quarter differ from a budget report for the first quarter?

4. Mai Ling questions the usefulness of a master sales budget in evaluating sales performance. Is there justification for Mai's concern? Explain.

5. Under what circumstances may a static budget be an appropriate basis for evaluating a manager's effectiveness in controlling costs?

6. "A flexible budget is really a series of static budgets." Is this true? Why?

7. The static manufacturing overhead budget based on 40,000 direct labor hours shows budgeted indirect labor costs of $54,000. During March, the department incurs $65,000 of indirect labor while working 45,000 direct labor hours. Is this a favorable or unfavorable performance? Why?

8. A static overhead budget based on 40,000 direct labor hours shows Factory Insurance $6,500 as a fixed cost. At the 50,000 direct labor hours worked in March, factory insurance costs were $6,200. Is this a favorable or unfavorable performance? Why?

9. Ken Holder is confused about how a flexible budget is prepared. Identify the steps for Ken.

10. Moises Company has prepared a graph of flexible budget data. At zero direct labor hours, the total budgeted cost line intersects the vertical axis at $25,000. At 10,000 direct labor hours, the line drawn from the total budgeted cost line intersects the vertical axis at $85,000. How may the fixed and variable costs be expressed?

11. The flexible budget formula is fixed costs $40,000 plus variable costs of $4 per direct labor hour. What is the total budgeted cost at (a) 9,000 hours and (b) 12,345 hours?

12. What is management by exception? What criteria may be used in identifying exceptions?

13. What is responsibility accounting? Explain the purpose of responsibility accounting.

14. Anna Hsung is studying for an accounting examination. Describe for Anna what conditions are necessary for responsibility accounting to be used effectively.

15. Distinguish between controllable and noncontrollable costs.

16. How do responsibility reports differ from budget reports?

17. What is the relationship, if any, between a responsibility reporting system and a company's organization chart?

18. Distinguish among the three types of responsibility centers.

19. (a) What costs are included in a performance report for a cost center? (b) In the report, are variable and fixed costs identified?

20. How do direct fixed costs differ from indirect fixed costs? Are both types of fixed costs controllable?

21. Rigo Beeto is confused about controllable margin reported in an income statement for a profit center. How is this margin computed, and what is its primary purpose?

22. What is the primary basis for evaluating the performance of the manager of an investment center? Indicate the formula for this basis.

23. Explain the ways that ROI can be improved.

24. Indicate two behavioral principles that pertain to (a) the manager being evaluated and (b) top management.

Brief Exercises

Prepare static budget report.
(SO 2)

BE24-1 For the quarter ended March 31, 2012, Meine Company accumulates the following sales data for its product, Garden-Tools: $310,000 budget; $304,000 actual. Prepare a static budget report for the quarter.

Prepare static budget report for 2 quarters.
(SO 2)

BE24-2 Data for Meine Company are given in BE24-1. In the second quarter, budgeted sales were $380,000, and actual sales were $383,000. Prepare a static budget report for the second quarter and for the year to date.

Show usefulness of flexible budgets in evaluating performance.
(SO 3)

BE24-3 In Giletto Company, direct labor is $20 per hour. The company expects to operate at 10,000 direct labor hours each month. In January 2012, direct labor totaling $203,000 is incurred in working 10,400 hours. Prepare (a) a static budget report and (b) a flexible budget report. Evaluate the usefulness of each report.

Prepare a flexible budget for variable costs.
(SO 3)

BE24-4 Myles Company expects to produce 1,200,000 units of Product XX in 2012. Monthly production is expected to range from 80,000 to 120,000 units. Budgeted variable manufacturing costs per unit are: direct materials $4, direct labor $6, and overhead $8. Budgeted fixed manufacturing costs per unit for depreciation are $2 and for supervision are $1. Prepare a flexible manufacturing budget for the relevant range value using 20,000 unit increments.

Prepare flexible budget report.
(SO 3)

BE24-5 Data for Myles Company are given in BE24-4. In March 2012, the company incurs the following costs in producing 100,000 units: direct materials $425,000, direct labor $590,000, and variable overhead $805,000. Prepare a flexible budget report for March. Were costs controlled?

Prepare a responsibility report for a cost center.
(SO 5)

BE24-6 In the Assembly Department of Mantle Company, budgeted and actual manufacturing overhead costs for the month of April 2012 were as follows.

	Budget	**Actual**
Indirect materials	$15,000	$14,300
Indirect labor	20,000	20,600
Utilities	10,000	10,750
Supervision	5,000	5,000

All costs are controllable by the department manager. Prepare a responsibility report for April for the cost center.

Prepare a responsibility report for a profit center.
(SO 6)

BE24-7 Maris Manufacturing Company accumulates the following summary data for the year ending December 31, 2012, for its Water Division which it operates as a profit center: sales—$2,000,000 budget, $2,080,000 actual; variable costs—$1,000,000 budget, $1,050,000 actual; and controllable fixed costs—$300,000 budget, $310,000 actual. Prepare a responsibility report for the Water Division.

Prepare a responsibility report for an investment center.
(SO 7)

BE24-8 For the year ending December 31, 2012, Ruth Company accumulates the following data for the Plastics Division which it operates as an investment center: contribution margin—$700,000 budget, $715,000 actual; controllable fixed costs—$300,000 budget, $309,000 actual. Average operating assets for the year were $2,000,000. Prepare a responsibility report for the Plastics Division beginning with contribution margin.

Compute return on investment using the ROI formula.
(SO 7)

BE24-9 For its three investment centers, Jackson Company accumulates the following data:

	I	**II**	**III**
Sales	$2,000,000	$3,000,000	$ 4,000,000
Controllable margin	1,200,000	2,000,000	3,200,000
Average operating assets	5,000,000	8,000,000	10,000,000

Compute the return on investment (ROI) for each center.

Compute return on investment under changed conditions.
(SO 7)

BE24-10 Data for the investment centers for Jackson Company are given in BE24-9. The centers expect the following changes in the next year: (I) increase sales 15%; (II) decrease costs $200,000; (III) decrease average operating assets $400,000. Compute the expected return on investment (ROI) for each center. Assume center I has a contribution margin percentage of 75%.

Do it! Review

Do it! 24-1   In Brown Company's flexible budget graph, the fixed cost line and the total budgeted cost line intersect the vertical axis at $90,000. The total budgeted cost line is $330,000 at an activity level of 60,000 direct labor hours. Compute total budgeted costs at 70,000 direct labor hours.

Compute total budgeted costs in flexible budget.
(SO 3)

Do it! 24-2   Favre Company expects to produce 50,000 units of product IOA during the current year. Budgeted variable manufacturing costs per unit are direct materials $7, direct labor $12, and overhead $18. Annual budgeted fixed manufacturing overhead costs are $96,000 for depreciation and $45,000 for supervision.

Prepare and evaluate a flexible budget report.
(SO 3)

In the current month, Favre produced 6,000 units and incurred the following costs: direct materials $38,900, direct labor $70,200, variable overhead $116,500, depreciation $8,000, and supervision $4,000.

Prepare a flexible budget report. (*Note:* You do not need to prepare the heading.) Were costs controlled?

Do it! 24-3   The Far West Division operates as a profit center. It reports the following for the year.

Prepare a responsibility report.
(SO 6)

	Budgeted	**Actual**
Sales	$2,000,000	$1,800,000
Variable costs	800,000	750,000
Controllable fixed costs	550,000	550,000
Noncontrollable fixed costs	250,000	250,000

Prepare a responsibility report for the Far West Division at December 31, 2012.

Do it! 24-4   The service division of Brady Industries reported the following results for 2012.

Compute ROI and expected return on investments.
(SO 7)

Sales	$500,000
Variable costs	300,000
Controllable fixed costs	75,000
Average operating assets	450,000

Management is considering the following independent courses of action in 2013 in order to maximize the return on investment for this division.

1. Reduce average operating assets by $50,000, with no change in controllable margin.
2. Increase sales $100,000, with no change in the contribution margin percentage.

(a) Compute the controllable margin and the return on investment for 2012. (b) Compute the controllable margin and the expected return on investment for each proposed alternative.

Exercises

E24-1   Bruce Willis has prepared the following list of statements about budgetary control.
1. Budget reports compare actual results with planned objectives.
2. All budget reports are prepared on a weekly basis.
3. Management uses budget reports to analyze differences between actual and planned results and determine their causes.
4. As a result of analyzing budget reports, management may either take corrective action or modify future plans.
5. Budgetary control works best when a company has an informal reporting system.
6. The primary recipients of the sales report are the sales manager and the vice president of production.
7. The primary recipient of the scrap report is the production manager.
8. A static budget is a projection of budget data at one level of activity.
9. Top management's reaction to unfavorable differences is not influenced by the materiality of the difference.

Understand the concept of budgetary control.
(SO 1, 2, 3)

10. A static budget is not appropriate in evaluating a manager's effectiveness in controlling costs unless the actual activity level approximates the static budget activity level or the behavior of the costs is fixed.

Instructions
Identify each statement as true or false. If false, indicate how to correct the statement.

Prepare and evaluate static budget report.
(SO 2)

E24-2 Valenzuela Company budgeted selling expenses of $30,000 in January, $35,000 in February, and $40,000 in March. Actual selling expenses were $31,000 in January, $34,500 in February, and $47,000 in March.

Instructions
(a) Prepare a selling expense report that compares budgeted and actual amounts by month and for the year to date.
(b) What is the purpose of the report prepared in (a), and who would be the primary recipient?
(c) ◀══════ What would be the likely result of management's analysis of the report?

Prepare manufacturing flexible overhead budget.
(SO 3)

E24-3 Rooney Company uses a flexible budget for manufacturing overhead based on direct labor hours. Variable manufacturing overhead costs per direct labor hour are as follows.

Indirect labor	$1.00
Indirect materials	0.50
Utilities	0.40

Fixed overhead costs per month are: Supervision $4,000, Depreciation $1,500, and Property Taxes $800. The company believes it will normally operate in a range of 7,000–10,000 direct labor hours per month.

Instructions
Prepare a monthly manufacturing overhead flexible budget for 2012 for the expected range of activity, using increments of 1,000 direct labor hours.

Prepare flexible budget reports for manufacturing overhead costs, and comment on findings.
(SO 3)

E24-4 Using the information in E24-3, assume that in July 2012, Rooney Company incurs the following manufacturing overhead costs.

Variable Costs		**Fixed Costs**	
Indirect labor	$8,700	Supervision	$4,000
Indirect materials	4,300	Depreciation	1,500
Utilities	3,200	Property taxes	800

Instructions
(a) Prepare a flexible budget performance report, assuming that the company worked 9,000 direct labor hours during the month.
(b) Prepare a flexible budget performance report, assuming that the company worked 8,500 direct labor hours during the month.
(c) ◀══════ Comment on your findings.

Prepare flexible selling expense budget.
(SO 3)

E24-5 Russell Company uses flexible budgets to control its selling expenses. Monthly sales are expected to range from $170,000 to $200,000. Variable costs and their percentage relationship to sales are: Sales Commissions 5%, Advertising 4%, Traveling 3%, and Delivery 2%. Fixed selling expenses will consist of Sales Salaries $34,000, Depreciation on Delivery Equipment $7,000, and Insurance on Delivery Equipment $1,000.

Instructions
Prepare a monthly flexible budget for each $10,000 increment of sales within the relevant range for the year ending December 31, 2012.

Prepare flexible budget reports for selling expenses.
(SO 3)

E24-6 The actual selling expenses incurred in March 2012 by Russell Company are as follows.

Variable Expenses		**Fixed Expenses**	
Sales commissions	$9,200	Sales salaries	$34,000
Advertising	7,000	Depreciation	7,000
Travel	5,100	Insurance	1,000
Delivery	3,500		

Instructions

(a) Prepare a flexible budget performance report for March using the budget data in E24-5, assuming that March sales were $170,000. Expected and actual sales are the same.

(b) Prepare a flexible budget performance report, assuming that March sales were $180,000. Expected sales and actual sales are the same.

(c) ✏️ Comment on the importance of using flexible budgets in evaluating the performance of the sales manager.

E24-7 Byrd Company's manufacturing overhead budget for the first quarter of 2012 contained the following data.

Prepare flexible budget and responsibility report for manufacturing overhead.

(SO 3, 5)

Variable Costs		Fixed Costs	
Indirect materials	$12,000	Supervisory salaries	$36,000
Indirect labor	10,000	Depreciation	7,000
Utilities	8,000	Property taxes and insurance	8,000
Maintenance	6,000	Maintenance	5,000

Actual variable costs were: indirect materials $13,800, indirect labor $9,600, utilities $8,700, and maintenance $4,900. Actual fixed costs equaled budgeted costs except for property taxes and insurance, which were $8,200.

All costs are considered controllable by the production department manager except for depreciation, and property taxes and insurance.

Instructions

(a) Prepare a manufacturing overhead flexible budget report for the first quarter.

(b) Prepare a responsibility report for the first quarter.

E24-8 As sales manager, Magic Johnson was given the following static budget report for selling expenses in the Clothing Department of Lakers Company for the month of October.

Prepare flexible budget report, and answer question.

(SO 2, 3)

LAKERS COMPANY
Clothing Department
Selling Expense Budget Report
For the Month Ended October 31, 2012

	Budget	Actual	Difference Favorable F Unfavorable U
Sales in units	8,000	10,000	2,000 F
Variable expenses			
Sales commissions	$ 2,000	$ 2,600	$ 600 U
Advertising expense	800	850	50 U
Travel expense	3,600	4,000	400 U
Free samples given out	1,600	1,300	300 F
Total variable	8,000	8,750	750 U
Fixed expenses			
Rent	1,500	1,500	–0–
Sales salaries	1,200	1,200	–0–
Office salaries	800	800	–0–
Depreciation—autos (sales staff)	500	500	–0–
Total fixed	4,000	4,000	–0–
Total expenses	$12,000	$12,750	$ 750 U

As a result of this budget report, Magic was called into the president's office and congratulated on his fine sales performance. He was reprimanded, however, for allowing his costs to get out of control. Magic knew something was wrong with the performance report that he had been given. However, he was not sure what to do, and comes to you for advice.

Instructions

(a) Prepare a budget report based on flexible budget data to help Magic.

(b) Should Magic have been reprimanded? Explain.

*Prepare and discuss a
responsibility report.*

(SO 3, 5)

E24-9 Manning Plumbing Company is a newly formed company specializing in plumbing services for home and business. The owner, Peyton Manning, had divided the company into two segments: Home Plumbing Services and Business Plumbing Services. Each segment is run by its own supervisor, while basic selling and administrative services are shared by both segments.

Peyton has asked you to help him create a performance reporting system that will allow him to measure each segment's performance in terms of its profitability. To that end, the following information has been collected on the Home Plumbing Services segment for the first quarter of 2012.

	Budgeted	**Actual**
Service revenue	$25,000	$26,000
Allocated portion of:		
Building depreciation	11,000	11,000
Advertising	5,000	4,200
Billing	3,500	3,000
Property taxes	1,200	1,000
Material and supplies	1,500	1,200
Supervisory salaries	9,000	9,400
Insurance	4,000	3,500
Wages	3,000	3,300
Gas and oil	2,700	3,400
Equipment depreciation	1,600	1,300

Instructions

(a) Prepare a responsibility report for the first quarter of 2012 for the Home Plumbing Services segment.

(b) ✏️ Write a memo to Peyton Manning discussing the principles that should be used when preparing performance reports.

*State total budgeted cost
formulas, and prepare flexible
budget graph.*

(SO 3)

E24-10 Brees Company has two production departments, Fabricating and Assembling. At a department managers' meeting, the controller uses flexible budget graphs to explain total budgeted costs. Separate graphs based on direct labor hours are used for each department. The graphs show the following.

1. At zero direct labor hours, the total budgeted cost line and the fixed cost line intersect the vertical axis at $40,000 in the Fabricating Department and $30,000 in the Assembling Department.

2. At normal capacity of 50,000 direct labor hours, the line drawn from the total budgeted cost line intersects the vertical axis at $150,000 in the Fabricating Department, and $110,000 in the Assembling Department.

Instructions

(a) State the total budgeted cost formula for each department.

(b) Compute the total budgeted cost for each department, assuming actual direct labor hours worked were 53,000 and 47,000, in the Fabricating and Assembling Departments, respectively.

(c) Prepare the flexible budget graph for the Fabricating Department, assuming the maximum direct labor hours in the relevant range is 100,000. Use increments of 10,000 direct labor hours on the horizontal axis and increments of $50,000 on the vertical axis.

*Prepare reports in a
responsibility reporting system.*

(SO 4)

E24-11 Bush Company's organization chart includes the president; the vice president of production; three assembly plants—New Orleans, Houston, and Mobile; and two departments within each plant—Machining and Finishing. Budget and actual manufacturing cost data for July 2012 are as follows:

Finishing Department—New Orleans: Direct materials $41,500 actual, $45,000 budget; direct labor $83,000 actual, $82,000 budget; manufacturing overhead $51,000 actual, $49,200 budget.

Machining Department—New Orleans: Total manufacturing costs $220,000 actual, $216,000 budget.

Houston Plant: Total manufacturing costs $424,000 actual, $421,000 budget.

Mobile Plant: Total manufacturing costs $494,000 actual, $496,500 budget.

The New Orleans plant manager's office costs were $95,000 actual and $92,000 budget. The vice president of production's office costs were $132,000 actual and $130,000 budget. Office costs are not allocated to departments and plants.

Instructions

Using the format on page 1113, prepare the reports in a responsibility system for:

(a) The Finishing Department—New Orleans.

(b) The plant manager—New Orleans.

(c) The vice president of production.

E24-12 The Mixing Department manager of Vikings Company is able to control all overhead costs except rent, property taxes, and salaries. Budgeted monthly overhead costs for the Mixing Department, in alphabetical order, are: *Prepare a responsibility report for a cost center.*

(SO 5)

Indirect labor	$12,000	Property taxes	$ 1,000
Indirect materials	7,500	Rent	1,800
Lubricants	1,700	Salaries	10,000
Maintenance	3,500	Utilities	5,000

Actual costs incurred for January 2012 are indirect labor $12,200; indirect materials $10,200; lubricants $1,650; maintenance $3,500; property taxes $1,100; rent $1,800; salaries $10,000; and utilities $6,500.

Instructions

(a) Prepare a responsibility report for January 2012.

(b) What would be the likely result of management's analysis of the report?

E24-13 Maguire Manufacturing Inc. has three divisions which are operated as profit centers. Actual operating data for the divisions listed alphabetically are as follows. *Compute missing amounts in responsibility reports for three profit centers, and prepare a report.*

(SO 6)

Operating Data	Women's Shoes	Men's Shoes	Children's Shoes
Contribution margin	$240,000	(3)	$180,000
Controllable fixed costs	100,000	(4)	(5)
Controllable margin	(1)	$ 90,000	96,000
Sales	600,000	450,000	(6)
Variable costs	(2)	330,000	250,000

Instructions

(a) Compute the missing amounts. Show computations.

(b) Prepare a responsibility report for the Women's Shoes Division assuming (1) the data are for the month ended June 30, 2012, and (2) all data equal budget except variable costs which are $10,000 over budget.

E24-14 The Sports Equipment Division of Bob Gibson Company is operated as a profit center. Sales for the division were budgeted for 2012 at $900,000. The only variable costs budgeted for the division were cost of goods sold ($440,000) and selling and administrative ($60,000). Fixed costs were budgeted at $100,000 for cost of goods sold, $90,000 for selling and administrative, and $70,000 for noncontrollable fixed costs. Actual results for these items were: *Prepare a responsibility report for a profit center, and compute ROI.*

(SO 6, 7)

Sales	$880,000
Cost of goods sold	
Variable	409,000
Fixed	105,000
Selling and administrative	
Variable	61,000
Fixed	67,000
Noncontrollable fixed	80,000

Instructions

(a) Prepare a responsibility report for the Sports Equipment Division for 2012.

(b) Assume, instead, the division is an investment center, and average operating assets were $1,000,000. Compute ROI.

E24-15 The Red Division of Tarkington Company reported the following data for the current year. *Compute ROI for current year and for possible future changes.*

(SO 7)

Sales	$3,000,000
Variable costs	1,950,000
Controllable fixed costs	600,000
Average operating assets	5,000,000

Top management is unhappy with the investment center's return on investment (ROI). It asks the manager of the Red Division to submit plans to improve ROI in the next year. The manager believes it is feasible to consider the following independent courses of action.

1. Increase sales by $320,000 with no change in the contribution margin percentage.
2. Reduce variable costs by $100,000.
3. Reduce average operating assets by 4%.

Instructions

(a) Compute the return on investment (ROI) for the current year.

(b) Using the ROI formula, compute the ROI under each of the proposed courses of action. (Round to one decimal.)

Prepare a responsibility report for an investment center.

(SO 7)

E24-16 The Nung Dental Clinic provides both preventive and orthodontic dental services. The two owners, Chris Thao and Kim Long, operate the clinic as two separate investment centers: Preventive Services and Orthodontic Services. Each of them is in charge of one of the centers: Chris for Preventive Services and Kim for Orthodontic Services. Each month they prepare an income statement on the two centers to evaluate performance and make decisions about how to improve the operational efficiency and profitability of the clinic.

Recently, they have been concerned about the profitability of the Preventive Services operations. For several months, it has been reporting a loss. Shown below is the responsibility report for the month of May 2012.

	Actual	**Difference from Budget**
Service revenue	$40,000	$1,000 F
Variable costs:		
Filling materials	5,000	100 U
Novocain	4,000	200 U
Supplies	2,000	250 F
Dental assistant wages	2,500	–0–
Utilities	500	50 U
Total variable costs	14,000	100 U
Fixed costs:		
Allocated portion of receptionist's salary	3,000	200 U
Dentist salary	10,000	500 U
Equipment depreciation	6,000	–0–
Allocated portion of building depreciation	15,000	1,000 U
Total fixed costs	34,000	1,700 U
Operating income (loss)	$(8,000)	$ 800 U

In addition, the owners know that the investment in operating assets at the beginning of the month was $82,400, and it was $77,600 at the end of the month. They have asked for your assistance in evaluating their current performance reporting system.

Instructions

(a) Prepare a responsibility report for an investment center as illustrated in the chapter.

(b) ✏️ Write a memo to the owners discussing the deficiencies of their current reporting system.

Prepare missing amounts in responsibility reports for three investment centers.

(SO 7)

E24-17 The Panamerican Transportation Company uses a responsibility reporting system to measure the performance of its three investment centers: Planes, Taxis, and Limos. Segment performance is measured using a system of responsibility reports and return on investment calculations. The allocation of resources within the company and the segment managers' bonuses are based in part on the results shown in these reports.

Recently, the company was the victim of a computer virus that deleted portions of the company's accounting records. This was discovered when the current period's responsibility reports were being prepared. The printout of the actual operating results appeared as follows.

	Planes	Taxis	Limos
Service revenue	$?	$500,000	$?
Variable costs	5,500,000	?	320,000
Contribution margin	?	200,000	480,000
Controllable fixed costs	1,500,000	?	?
Controllable margin	?	80,000	240,000
Average operating assets	25,000,000	?	1,600,000
Return on investment	12%	10%	?

Instructions

Determine the missing pieces of information above.

Exercises: Set B

Visit the book's companion website, at **www.wiley.com/college/weygandt**, and choose the Student Companion site to access Exercise Set B.

Problems: Set A

P24-1A   Chamberlin Company estimates that 360,000 direct labor hours will be worked during the coming year, 2012, in the Packaging Department. On this basis, the following budgeted manufacturing overhead cost data are computed for the year.

Prepare flexible budget and budget report for manufacturing overhead.

(SO 3)

Fixed Overhead Costs		Variable Overhead Costs	
Supervision	$ 90,000	Indirect labor	$126,000
Depreciation	60,000	Indirect materials	90,000
Insurance	30,000	Repairs	54,000
Rent	24,000	Utilities	72,000
Property taxes	18,000	Lubricants	18,000
	$222,000		$360,000

It is estimated that direct labor hours worked each month will range from 27,000 to 36,000 hours.

During October, 27,000 direct labor hours were worked and the following overhead costs were incurred.

Fixed overhead costs: Supervision $7,500, Depreciation $5,000, Insurance $2,470, Rent $2,000, and Property taxes $1,500.

Variable overhead costs: Indirect labor $10,360, Indirect materials, $6,400, Repairs $4,000, Utilities $5,700, and Lubricants $1,640.

Instructions

(a) Prepare a monthly manufacturing overhead flexible budget for each increment of 3,000 direct labor hours over the relevant range for the year ending December 31, 2012.

(b) Prepare a flexible budget report for October.

(c) Comment on management's efficiency in controlling manufacturing overhead costs in October.

(a) Total costs: DLH 27,000, $45,500; DLH 36,000, $54,500

(b) Total $1,070 U

P24-2A   Taylor Company manufactures tablecloths. Sales have grown rapidly over the past 2 years. As a result, the president has installed a budgetary control system for 2012. The following data were used in developing the master manufacturing overhead budget for the Ironing Department, which is based on an activity index of direct labor hours.

Prepare flexible budget, budget report, and graph for manufacturing overhead.

(SO 3)

Variable costs	Rate per Direct Labor Hour	Annual Fixed Costs	
Indirect labor	$0.40	Supervision	$42,000
Indirect materials	0.50	Depreciation	18,000
Factory utilities	0.30	Insurance	12,000
Factory repairs	0.20	Rent	24,000

The master overhead budget was prepared on the expectation that 480,000 direct labor hours will be worked during the year. In June, 42,000 direct labor hours were worked. At that level of activity, actual costs were as shown below.

> *Variable—per direct labor hour:* Indirect labor $0.43, Indirect materials $0.49, Factory utilities $0.32, and Factory repairs $0.24.
> *Fixed:* same as budgeted.

Instructions

(a) Total costs: 35,000 DLH, $57,000; 50,000 DLH, $78,000
(b) Budget $66,800
Actual $70,160

(a) Prepare a monthly manufacturing overhead flexible budget for the year ending December 31, 2012, assuming production levels range from 35,000 to 50,000 direct labor hours. Use increments of 5,000 direct labor hours.

(b) Prepare a budget report for June comparing actual results with budget data based on the flexible budget.

(c) Were costs effectively controlled? Explain.

(d) State the formula for computing the total budgeted costs for Taylor Company.

(e) Prepare the flexible budget graph, showing total budgeted costs at 35,000 and 45,000 direct labor hours. Use increments of 5,000 direct labor hours on the horizontal axis and increments of $10,000 on the vertical axis.

State total budgeted cost formula, and prepare flexible budget reports for 2 time periods.

(SO 2, 3)

P24-3A Buckner Company uses budgets in controlling costs. The August 2012 budget report for the company's Assembling Department is as follows.

BUCKNER COMPANY
Budget Report
Assembling Department
For the Month Ended August 31, 2012

Manufacturing Costs	Budget	Actual	Difference Favorable F Unfavorable U
Variable costs			
Direct materials	$ 48,000	$ 47,000	$1,000 F
Direct labor	54,000	51,300	2,700 F
Indirect materials	24,000	24,200	200 U
Indirect labor	18,000	17,500	500 F
Utilities	15,000	14,900	100 F
Maintenance	9,000	9,200	200 U
Total variable	168,000	164,100	3,900 F
Fixed costs			
Rent	12,000	12,000	–0–
Supervision	17,000	17,000	–0–
Depreciation	7,000	7,000	–0–
Total fixed	36,000	36,000	–0–
Total costs	$204,000	$200,100	$3,900 F

The monthly budget amounts in the report were based on an expected production of 60,000 units per month or 720,000 units per year. The Assembling Department manager is pleased with the report and expects a raise, or at least praise for a job well done. The company president, however, is unhappy with the results for August because only 58,000 units were produced.

Instructions

(a) State the total monthly budgeted cost formula.

(b) Budget $198,400

(c) Budget $215,200
Actual $216,510

(b) Prepare a budget report for August using flexible budget data. Why does this report provide a better basis for evaluating performance than the report based on static budget data?

(c) In September, 64,000 units were produced. Prepare the budget report using flexible budget data, assuming (1) each variable cost was 10% higher than its actual cost in August, and (2) fixed costs were the same in September as in August.

Prepare responsibility report for a profit center.

(SO 6)

P24-4A Johnson Manufacturing Inc. operates the Patio Furniture Division as a profit center. Operating data for this division for the year ended December 31, 2012, are as shown on the next page.

	Budget	Difference from Budget
Sales	$2,500,000	$60,000 F
Cost of goods sold		
Variable	1,300,000	41,000 F
Controllable fixed	200,000	6,000 U
Selling and administrative		
Variable	220,000	7,000 U
Controllable fixed	50,000	2,000 U
Noncontrollable fixed costs	70,000	4,000 U

In addition, Johnson Manufacturing incurs $180,000 of indirect fixed costs that were budgeted at $175,000. Twenty percent (20%) of these costs are allocated to the Patio Furniture Division.

Instructions

(a) Prepare a responsibility report for the Patio Furniture Division for the year.

(b) ◀▬▬▬ Comment on the manager's performance in controlling revenues and costs.

(c) Identify any costs excluded from the responsibility report and explain why they were excluded.

(a) Contribution margin
$94,000 F
Controllable margin
$86,000 F

P24-5A Namath Manufacturing Company manufactures a variety of tools and industrial equipment. The company operates through three divisions. Each division is an investment center. Operating data for the Home Division for the year ended December 31, 2012, and relevant budget data are as follows.

Prepare responsibility report for an investment center, and compute ROI.
(SO 7)

	Actual	Comparison with Budget
Sales	$1,500,000	$100,000 favorable
Variable cost of goods sold	700,000	60,000 unfavorable
Variable selling and administrative expenses	125,000	25,000 unfavorable
Controllable fixed cost of goods sold	170,000	On target
Controllable fixed selling and administrative expenses	80,000	On target

Average operating assets for the year for the Home Division were $2,500,000 which was also the budgeted amount.

Instructions

(a) Prepare a responsibility report (in thousands of dollars) for the Home Division.

(b) Evaluate the manager's performance. Which items will likely be investigated by top management?

(c) Compute the expected ROI in 2013 for the Home Division, assuming the following independent changes to actual data.

(1) Variable cost of goods sold is decreased by 6%.

(2) Average operating assets are decreased by 10%.

(3) Sales are increased by $200,000, and this increase is expected to increase contribution margin by $90,000.

(a) Controllable margin:
Budget $410;
Actual $425

P24-6A Niekro Company uses a responsibility reporting system. It has divisions in Portland, Tacoma, and San Francisco. Each division has three production departments: Cutting, Shaping, and Finishing. The responsibility for each department rests with a manager who reports to the division production manager. Each division manager reports to the vice president of production. There are also vice presidents for marketing and finance. All vice presidents report to the president.

In January 2012, controllable actual and budget manufacturing overhead cost data for the departments and divisions were as shown below.

Prepare reports for cost centers under responsibility accounting, and comment on performance of managers.
(SO 4)

Manufacturing Overhead	Actual	Budget
Individual costs—Cutting Department—Tacoma		
Indirect labor	$ 73,000	$ 70,000
Indirect materials	47,700	46,000
Maintenance	20,500	18,000
Utilities	20,100	17,000
Supervision	22,000	20,000
	$183,300	$171,000

Total costs

Shaping Department—Tacoma	$158,000	$148,000
Finishing Department—Tacoma	210,000	206,000
Denver division	676,000	673,000
San Diego division	722,000	715,000

Additional overhead costs were incurred as follows: Tacoma division production manager—actual costs $52,500, budget $51,000; vice president of production—actual costs $65,000, budget $64,000; president—actual costs $76,400, budget $74,200. These expenses are not allocated.

The vice presidents who report to the president, other than the vice president of production, had the following expenses.

Vice President	Actual	Budget
Marketing	$133,600	$130,000
Finance	109,000	105,000

Instructions

(a) (1) $12,300 U
(2) $27,800 U
(3) $38,800 U
(4) $48,600 U

(a) Using the format on page 1113, prepare the following responsibility reports.
    (1) Manufacturing overhead—Cutting Department manager—Tacoma division.
    (2) Manufacturing overhead—Tacoma division manager.
    (3) Manufacturing overhead—vice president of production.
    (4) Manufacturing overhead and expenses—president.
(b) Comment on the comparative performances of:
    (1) Department managers in the Tacoma division.
    (2) Division managers.
    (3) Vice presidents.

Problems: Set B

Prepare flexible budget and budget report for manufacturing overhead.

(SO 3)

P24-1B Cobb Company estimates that 240,000 direct labor hours will be worked during 2012 in the Assembly Department. On this basis, the following budgeted manufacturing overhead data are computed.

Variable Overhead Costs		Fixed Overhead Costs	
Indirect labor	$ 72,000	Supervision	$ 75,000
Indirect materials	48,000	Depreciation	30,000
Repairs	36,000	Insurance	12,000
Utilities	26,400	Rent	9,000
Lubricants	9,600	Property taxes	6,000
	$192,000		$132,000

It is estimated that direct labor hours worked each month will range from 18,000 to 24,000 hours.

During January, 20,000 direct labor hours were worked and the following overhead costs were incurred.

Variable Overhead Costs		Fixed Overhead Costs	
Indirect labor	$ 6,200	Supervision	$ 6,250
Indirect materials	3,600	Depreciation	2,500
Repairs	2,400	Insurance	1,000
Utilities	1,700	Rent	850
Lubricants	830	Property taxes	500
	$14,730		$11,100

Instructions

(a) Total costs: 18,000 DLH,
$25,400; 24,000 DLH,
$30,200
(b) Budget $27,000
Actual, $25,830

(a) Prepare a monthly manufacturing overhead flexible budget for each increment of 2,000 direct labor hours over the relevant range for the year ending December 31, 2012.
(b) Prepare a manufacturing overhead budget report for January.
(c)   Comment on management's efficiency in controlling manufacturing overhead costs in January.

P24-2B Lombardi Manufacturing Company produces one product, Olpe. Because of wide fluctuations in demand for Olpe, the Assembly Department experiences significant variations in monthly production levels.

Prepare flexible budget, budget report, and graph for manufacturing overhead.
(SO 3)

The annual master manufacturing overhead budget is based on 300,000 direct labor hours. In July, 27,500 labor hours were worked. The master manufacturing overhead budget for the year and the actual overhead costs incurred in July are as follows.

Overhead Costs	Master Budget (annual)	Actual in July
Variable		
Indirect labor	$330,000	$29,000
Indirect materials	180,000	14,000
Utilities	90,000	8,100
Maintenance	60,000	5,400
Fixed		
Supervision	150,000	12,500
Depreciation	96,000	8,000
Insurance and taxes	60,000	5,000
Total	$966,000	$82,000

Instructions

(a) Prepare a monthly overhead flexible budget for the year ending December 31, 2012, assuming monthly production levels range from 22,500 to 30,000 direct labor hours. Use increments of 2,500 direct labor hours.

(b) Prepare a budget report for the month of July 2012 comparing actual results with budget data based on the flexible budget.

(c) ◖▬▬▬▬ Were costs effectively controlled? Explain.

(d) State the formula for computing the total monthly budgeted costs in the Lombardi Manufacturing Company.

(e) Prepare the flexible budget graph showing total budgeted costs at 25,000 and 27,500 direct labor hours. Use increments of 5,000 on the horizontal axis and increments of $10,000 on the vertical axis.

(a) Total costs: 22,500 DLH, $75,000; 30,000 DLH, $91,500

(b) Budget $86,000 Actual $82,000

P24-3B Jordan Company uses budgets in controlling costs. The May 2012 budget report for the company's Packaging Department is as follows.

State total budgeted cost formula, and prepare flexible budget reports for 2 time periods.
(SO 2, 3)

JORDAN COMPANY
Budget Report
Packaging Department
For the Month Ended May 31, 2012

Manufacturing Costs	Budget	Actual	Difference Favorable F Unfavorable U
Variable costs			
Direct materials	$ 40,000	$ 41,000	$1,000 U
Direct labor	45,000	47,000	2,000 U
Indirect materials	15,000	15,200	200 U
Indirect labor	12,500	13,000	500 U
Utilities	10,000	9,600	400 F
Maintenance	5,000	5,200	200 U
Total variable	127,500	131,000	3,500 U
Fixed costs			
Rent	10,000	10,000	–0–
Supervision	7,000	7,000	–0–
Depreciation	5,000	5,000	–0–
Total fixed	22,000	22,000	–0–
Total costs	$149,500	$153,000	$3,500 U

The monthly budget amounts in the report were based on an expected production of 50,000 units per month or 600,000 units per year.

The company president was displeased with the department manager's performance. The department manager, who thought he had done a good job, could not understand the unfavorable results. In May, 55,000 units were produced.

Instructions
(a) State the total budgeted cost formula.

(b) Budget $162,250

(b) Prepare a budget report for May using flexible budget data. Why does this report provide a better basis for evaluating performance than the report based on static budget data?

(c) Budget $124,000
Actual $126,800

(c) In June, 40,000 units were produced. Prepare the budget report using flexible budget data, assuming (1) each variable cost was 20% less in June than its actual cost in May, and (2) fixed costs were the same in the month of June as in May.

Prepare responsibility report for a profit center.
(SO 6)

P24-4B Collins Manufacturing Inc. operates the Home Appliance Division as a profit center. Operating data for this division for the year ended December 31, 2012, are shown below.

	Budget	**Difference from Budget**
Sales	$2,400,000	$100,000 U
Cost of goods sold		
Variable	1,200,000	60,000 U
Controllable fixed	200,000	8,000 F
Selling and administrative		
Variable	240,000	8,000 F
Controllable fixed	60,000	4,000 U
Noncontrollable fixed costs	50,000	2,000 U

In addition, Collins Manufacturing incurs $150,000 of indirect fixed costs that were budgeted at $155,000. Twenty percent (20%) of these costs are allocated to the Home Appliance Division. None of these costs are controllable by the division manager.

(a) Contribution margin
    $152,000 U
Controllable margin
    $148,000 U

Instructions
(a) Prepare a responsibility report for the Home Appliance Division (a profit center) for the year.
(b) ◖◖◖◖◖◖◖ Comment on the manager's performance in controlling revenues and costs.
(c) Identify any costs excluded from the responsibility report and explain why they were excluded.

Prepare responsibility report for an investment center, and compute ROI.
(SO 7)

P24-5B Ryan Manufacturing Company manufactures a variety of garden and lawn equipment. The company operates through three divisions. Each division is an investment center. Operating data for the Lawnmower Division for the year ended December 31, 2012, and relevant budget data are as follows.

	Actual	**Comparison with Budget**
Sales	$2,900,000	$120,000 unfavorable
Variable cost of goods sold	1,400,000	90,000 unfavorable
Variable selling and administrative expenses	300,000	50,000 favorable
Controllable fixed cost of goods sold	270,000	On target
Controllable fixed selling and administrative expenses	140,000	On target

Average operating assets for the year for the Lawnmower Division were $5,000,000 which was also the budgeted amount.

Instructions

(a) Controllable margin:
    Budget $950
    Actual $790

(a) Prepare a responsibility report (in thousands of dollars) for the Lawnmower Division.
(b) Evaluate the manager's performance. Which items will likely be investigated by top management?
(c) Compute the expected ROI in 2013 for the Lawnmower Division, assuming the following independent changes.
   (1) Variable cost of goods sold is decreased by 15%.
   (2) Average operating assets are decreased by 20%.
   (3) Sales are increased by $500,000 and this increase is expected to increase contribution margin by $210,000.

Problems: Set C

Waterways Continuing Problem

(*Note:* This is a continuation of the Waterways Problem from Chapters 19 through 23.)

WCP24   Waterways Corporation is continuing its budget preparations. This problem gives you static budget information as well as actual overhead costs and asks you to calculate amounts related to budgetary control and responsibility accounting.

Go to the book's companion website, **www.wiley.com/college/weygandt**, *to find the completion of this problem.*

BROADENING YOUR PERSPECTIVE

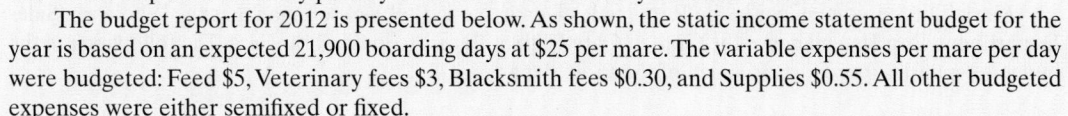

Decision Making Across the Organization

BYP24-1   Organic Pastures is a 400-acre farm on the outskirts of the Kentucky Bluegrass, specializing in the boarding of broodmares and their foals. A recent economic downturn in the thoroughbred industry has led to a decline in breeding activities, and it has made the boarding business extremely competitive. To meet the competition, Organic Pastures planned in 2012 to entertain clients, advertise more extensively, and absorb expenses formerly paid by clients such as veterinary and blacksmith fees.

The budget report for 2012 is presented below. As shown, the static income statement budget for the year is based on an expected 21,900 boarding days at $25 per mare. The variable expenses per mare per day were budgeted: Feed $5, Veterinary fees $3, Blacksmith fees $0.30, and Supplies $0.55. All other budgeted expenses were either semifixed or fixed.

During the year, management decided not to replace a worker who quit in March, but it did issue a new advertising brochure and did more entertaining of clients.[1]

ORGANIC PASTURES
Static Budget Income Statement
Year Ended December 31, 2012

	Actual	Master Budget	Difference
Number of mares per day	52	60	8*
Number of boarding days	18,980	21,900	2,920*
Sales	$379,600	$547,500	$167,900*
Less variable expenses:			
Feed	104,390	109,500	5,110
Veterinary fees	58,838	65,700	6,862
Blacksmith fees	6,074	6,570	496
Supplies	10,178	12,045	1,867
Total variable expenses	179,480	193,815	14,335
Contribution margin	200,120	353,685	153,565*
Less fixed expenses:			
Depreciation	40,000	40,000	–0–
Insurance	11,000	11,000	–0–
Utilities	12,000	14,000	2,000
Repairs and maintenance	10,000	11,000	1,000
Labor	88,000	96,000	8,000
Advertisement	12,000	8,000	4,000*
Entertainment	7,000	5,000	2,000*
Total fixed expenses	180,000	185,000	5,000
Net income	$ 20,120	$168,685	$148,565*

*Unfavorable.

---

[1]Data for this case are based on Hans Sprohge and John Talbott, "New Applications for Variance Analysis," *Journal of Accountancy* (AICPA, New York), April 1989, pp. 137–141.

Instructions

With the class divided into groups, answer the following.

(a) Based on the static budget report:

    (1) What was the primary cause(s) of the loss in net income?

    (2) Did management do a good, average, or poor job of controlling expenses?

    (3) Were management's decisions to stay competitive sound?

(b) Prepare a flexible budget report for the year based on boarding days.

(c) Based on the flexible budget report, answer the three questions in part (a) above.

(d) What course of action do you recommend for the management of Organic Pastures?

Managerial Analysis

BYP24-2 Rambis Company manufactures expensive watch cases sold as souvenirs. Three of its sales departments are: Retail Sales, Wholesale Sales, and Outlet Sales. The Retail Sales Department is a profit center. The Wholesale Sales Department is a cost center. Its managers merely take orders from customers who purchase through the company's wholesale catalog. The Outlet Sales Department is an investment center, because each manager is given full responsibility for an outlet store location. The manager can hire and discharge employees; purchase, maintain, and sell equipment; and in general is fairly independent of company control.

Maria Diego is a manager in the Retail Sales Department. Phil Jackson manages the Wholesale Sales Department. Dan Hsu manages the Golden Gate Club outlet store in San Francisco. The following are the budget responsibility reports for each of the three departments.

	Budget		
	Retail Sales	**Wholesale Sales**	**Outlet Sales**
Sales	$ 750,000	$ 400,000	$200,000
Variable costs			
Cost of goods sold	150,000	100,000	25,000
Advertising	100,000	30,000	5,000
Sales salaries	75,000	15,000	3,000
Printing	10,000	20,000	5,000
Travel	20,000	30,000	2,000
Fixed costs			
Rent	50,000	30,000	10,000
Insurance	5,000	2,000	1,000
Depreciation	75,000	100,000	40,000
Investment in assets	$1,000,000	$1,200,000	$800,000

	Actual Results		
	Retail Sales	**Wholesale Sales**	**Outlet Sales**
Sales	$ 750,000	$ 400,000	$200,000
Variable costs			
Cost of goods sold	195,000	120,000	26,250
Advertising	100,000	30,000	5,000
Sales salaries	75,000	15,000	3,000
Printing	10,000	20,000	5,000
Travel	15,000	20,000	1,500
Fixed costs			
Rent	40,000	50,000	12,000
Insurance	5,000	2,000	1,000
Depreciation	80,000	90,000	60,000
Investment in assets	$1,000,000	$1,200,000	$800,000

Instructions

(a) Determine which of the items should be included in the responsibility report for each of the three managers.

(b) Compare the actual results with the budget. Decide which results should be called to the attention of each manager.

Real-World Focus

BYP24-3 Computer Associates International, Inc., the world's leading business software company, delivers the end-to-end infrastructure to enable e-business through innovative technology, services, and education. Computer Associates has 19,000 employees worldwide and recently had revenue of over $6 billion.

    Presented below is information from the company's annual report.

Computer Associates International
Management Discussion

The Company has experienced a pattern of business whereby revenue for its third and fourth fiscal quarters reflects an increase over first- and second-quarter revenue. The Company attributes this increase to clients' increased spending at the end of their calendar year budgetary periods and the culmination of its annual sales plan. Since the Company's costs do not increase proportionately with the third- and fourth-quarters' increase in revenue, the higher revenue in these quarters results in greater profit margins and income. Fourth-quarter profitability is traditionally affected by significant new hirings, training, and education expenditures for the succeeding year.

Instructions

(a) Why don't the company's costs increase proportionately as the revenues increase in the third and fourth quarters?

(b) What type of budgeting seems appropriate for the Computer Associates situation?

On the Web

BYP24-4 There are many useful resources regarding budgeting available on websites. The following activity investigates the results of a comprehensive budgeting study.

Address:
http://www.accountingweb.com/whitepapers/centage_ioma.pdf, or go to **www.wiley.com/college/weygandt**

Instructions

Go the address above and then answer the following questions.

(a) What are cited as the two most common "pain points" of budgeting?

(b) What percentage of companies that participated in the survey said that they prepare annual budgets? Of those that prepare budgets, what percentage say that they start the budgeting process by first generating sales projections?

(c) What is the most common amount of time for the annual budgeting process?

(d) When evaluating variances from budgeted amounts, what was the most commonly defined range of acceptable tolerance levels?

(e) The study defines three types of consequences for varying from budgeted amounts. How does it describe "severe" consequences?

Communication Activity

BYP24-5 The manufacturing overhead budget for Barkley Company contains the following items.

Variable costs		Fixed costs	
Indirect materials	$24,000	Supervision	$18,000
Indirect labor	12,000	Inspection costs	1,000
Maintenance expense	10,000	Insurance expense	2,000
Manufacturing supplies	6,000	Depreciation	15,000
Total variable	$52,000	Total fixed	$36,000

The budget was based on an estimated 2,000 units being produced. During the past month, 1,500 units were produced, and the following costs incurred.

Variable costs		Fixed costs	
Indirect materials	$24,200	Supervision	$19,300
Indirect labor	13,500	Inspection costs	1,200
Maintenance expense	8,200	Insurance expense	2,200
Manufacturing supplies	5,100	Depreciation	14,700
Total variable	$51,000	Total fixed	$37,400

Instructions
(a) Determine which items would be controllable by Bart Starr, the production manager.
(b) How much should have been spent during the month for the manufacture of the 1,500 units?
(c) Prepare a manufacturing overhead flexible budget report for Mr. Starr.
(d) Prepare a responsibility report. Include only the costs that would have been controllable by Mr. Starr. Assume that the supervision cost above includes Mr. Starr's salary of $10,000, both at budget and actual. In an attached memo, describe clearly for Mr. Starr the areas in which his performance needs to be improved.

Ethics Case

BYP24-6 Continental Products Corporation participates in a highly competitive industry. In order to meet this competition and achieve profit goals, the company has chosen the decentralized form of organization. Each manager of a decentralized investment center is measured on the basis of profit contribution, market penetration, and return on investment. Failure to meet the objectives established by corporate management for these measures has not been acceptable and usually has resulted in demotion or dismissal of an investment center manager.

An anonymous survey of managers in the company revealed that the managers feel the pressure to compromise their personal ethical standards to achieve the corporate objectives. For example, at certain plant locations there was pressure to reduce quality control to a level which could not assure that all unsafe products would be rejected. Also, sales personnel were encouraged to use questionable sales tactics to obtain orders, including gifts and other incentives to purchasing agents.

The chief executive officer is disturbed by the survey findings. In his opinion, such behavior cannot be condoned by the company. He concludes that the company should do something about this problem.

Instructions
(a) Who are the stakeholders (the affected parties) in this situation?
(b) Identify the ethical implications, conflicts, or dilemmas in the above described situation.
(c) What might the company do to reduce the pressures on managers and decrease the ethical conflicts?

(CMA adapted)

"All About You" Activity

BYP24-7 It is one thing to prepare a personal budget; it is another thing to stick to it. Financial planners have suggested various mechanisms to provide support for enforcing personal budgets. One approach is called "envelope budgeting."

Instructions

Read the article provided at **http://en.wikipedia.org/wiki/Envelope_budgeting**, and answer the following questions.

(a) Summarize the process of envelope budgeting.

(b) Evaluate whether you think you would benefit from envelope budgeting. What do you think are its strengths and weaknesses relative to your situation?

Answers to Insight and Accounting Across the Organization Questions

p. 1107 Budgets and the Exotic Newcastle Disease   Q: What is the major benefit of tying a budget to the overall goals of the company? **A:** People working on a budgeting process that is clearly guided and focused by strategic goals spend less time arguing about irrelevant details and more time focusing on the items that matter.

p. 1110 Competition versus Collaboration   Q: How might managers of separate divisions be able to reduce division costs through collaboration? **A:** Division managers might reduce costs by sharing design and marketing resources or by jointly negotiating with suppliers. In addition, they can reduce the need to hire and lay off employees by sharing staff across divisions as human resource needs change.

p. 1119 Does Hollywood Look at ROI?   Q: What might be the reason that movie studios do not produce G-rated movies as often as R-rated movies? **A:** Perhaps Hollywood believes that big-name stars or large budgets, both of which are typical of R-rated movies, sell movies. However, one study recently concluded, "We can't find evidence that stars help movies, and we can't find evidence that bigger budgets increase return on investment." Some film companies are going out of their way to achieve at least a PG rating.

p. 1121 Flexible Manufacturing Requires Flexible Accounting   Q: What implications do these improvements in production capabilities have for management accounting information and performance evaluation within the organization? **A:** In order to maximize the potential of flexible manufacturing facilities, managers need to be supplied with information on a more frequent basis. In turn, the tools used to evaluate performance need to take into account what information management had at its disposal, and what decisions were made in response to this information.

Answers to Self-Test Questions

1. c **2.** d **3.** c **4.** b **5.** b **6.** a ($90,000 − $30,000) ÷ (10,000 − 0) **7.** d ($27,000 ÷ 9,000 = $3DLH); [$28,000 − (9,200 × $3)] **8.** a **9.** d **10.** d **11.** a **12.** c **13.** b **14.** b **15.** d

✔
The Navigator

✔ **Remember to go back to the Navigator box on the chapter opening page and check off your completed work.**

CHAPTER 25

Standard Costs and Balanced Scorecard

Study Objectives

After studying this chapter, you should be able to:

[1] Distinguish between a standard and a budget.

[2] Identify the advantages of standard costs.

[3] Describe how companies set standards.

[4] State the formulas for determining direct materials and direct labor variances.

[5] State the formula for determining the total manufacturing overhead variance.

[6] Discuss the reporting of variances.

[7] Prepare an income statement for management under a standard costing system.

[8] Describe the balanced scorecard approach to performance evaluation.

✔ **The Navigator**

✔ **The Navigator**

● Scan Study Objectives	○
● Read Feature Story	○
● Read Preview	○
● Read text and answer **Do it!** p. 1153 ○ p. 1157 ○ p. 1160 ○ p. 1165 ○	
● Work Comprehensive **Do it!** p. 1165	○
● Review Summary of Study Objectives	○
● Answer Self-Test Questions	○
● Complete Assignments	○
● Go to *WileyPLUS* for practice and tutorials	○

Feature Story

HIGHLIGHTING PERFORMANCE EFFICIENCY

There's a very good chance that the highlighter you're holding in your hand was made by Sanford, a maker of permanent markers and other writing instruments. Sanford, headquartered in Illinois, annually sells hundreds of millions of dollars' worth of Accent® highlighters, fine-point pens, Sharpie permanent markers, Expo dry-erase markers for overhead projectors, and other writing instruments.

Since Sanford makes literally billions of writing utensils per year, the company must keep tight control over manufacturing costs. A very important part of Sanford's manufacturing process is determining how much direct materials, labor, and overhead should cost. The company then compares these costs to actual costs to assess performance efficiency. Raw materials for Sanford's markers include a barrel, plug, cap, ink reservoir, and a nib (tip). Machines

1146

assemble these parts to produce thousands of units per hour. A major component of manufacturing overhead is machine maintenance—some fixed, some variable.

"Labor costs are associated with material handling and equipment maintenance functions. Although the assembly process is highly automated, labor is still required to move raw materials to the machine and to package the finished product. In addition, highly skilled technicians are required to service and maintain each piece of equipment," says Mike Orr, vice president, operations.

Labor rates are predictable because the hourly workers are covered by a union contract. The story is the same with the fringe benefits and some supervisory salaries. Even volume levels are fairly predictable—demand for the product is high—so fixed overhead is efficiently absorbed. Raw material standard costs are based on the previous year's actual prices plus any anticipated inflation. For the past several years, though, inflation had been so low that the company was considering any price increase in raw material to be unfavorable because its standards remained unchanged.

PreviewofCHAPTER25

Standards are a fact of life. You met the admission standards for the school you are attending. The vehicle that you drive had to meet certain governmental emissions standards. The hamburgers and salads you eat in a restaurant have to meet certain health and nutritional standards before they can be sold. As described in our Feature Story, Sanford Corp. has standards for the costs of its materials, labor, and overhead. The reason for standards in these cases is very simple: They help to ensure that overall product quality is high while keeping costs under control.

In this chapter, we continue the study of controlling costs. You will learn how to evaluate performance using standard costs and a balanced scorecard.

The content and organization of Chapter 25 are as follows.

Standard Costs and Balanced Scorecard

The Need for Standards	Setting Standard Costs	Analyzing and Reporting Variances from Standards	Balanced Scorecard
• Standards vs. budgets • Why standard costs?	• Ideal vs. normal • Case study	• Direct materials variances • Direct labor variances • Manufacturing overhead variance • Reporting variances • Statement presentation	• Financial perspective • Customer perspective • Internal process perspective • Learning and growth perspective

✔ The Navigator

The Need for Standards

Standards are common in business. Those imposed by government agencies are often called **regulations**. They include the Fair Labor Standards Act, the Equal Employment Opportunity Act, and a multitude of environmental standards. Standards established internally by a company may extend to personnel matters, such as employee absenteeism and ethical codes of conduct, quality control standards for products, and standard costs for goods and services. In managerial accounting, standard costs are predetermined unit costs, which companies use as measures of performance.

We will focus on manufacturing operations in this chapter. But you should also recognize that standard costs also apply to many types of service businesses as well. For example, a fast-food restaurant such as McDonald's knows the price it should pay for pickles, beef, buns, and other ingredients. It also knows how much time it should take an employee to flip hamburgers. If the company pays too much for pickles or if employees take too much time to prepare Big Macs, McDonald's notices the deviations and takes corrective action. Not-for-profit enterprises such as universities, charitable organizations, and governmental agencies also may use standard costs.

Study Objective [1]

Distinguish between a standard and a budget.

Distinguishing between Standards and Budgets

Both **standards** and **budgets** are predetermined costs, and both contribute to management planning and control. There is a difference, however, in the way the terms are expressed. A standard is a **unit** amount. A budget is a **total** amount. Thus, it is customary to state that the **standard cost** of direct labor for a unit of product is, say, $10. If the company produces 5,000 units of the product, the $50,000 of direct labor is the **budgeted** labor cost. A standard is the budgeted **cost per unit** of product. A standard is therefore concerned with each individual cost component that makes up the entire budget.

There are important accounting differences between budgets and standards. Except in the application of manufacturing overhead to jobs and processes, budget data are not journalized in cost accounting systems. In contrast, as we illustrate in the appendix to this chapter, standard costs may be incorporated into cost accounting systems. Also, a company may report its inventories at standard cost in its financial statements, but it would not report inventories at budgeted costs.

Why Standard Costs?

Standard costs offer a number of advantages to an organization, as shown in Illustration 25-1.

Study Objective [2]
Identify the advantages of standard costs.

Advantages of standard costs

Facilitate management planning

Promote greater economy by making employees more "cost-conscious"

Useful in setting selling prices

Contribute to management control by providing basis for evaluation of cost control

Useful in highlighting variances in management by exception

Simplify costing of inventories and reduce clerical costs

Illustration 25-1
Advantages of standard costs

The organization will realize these advantages only when standard costs are carefully established and prudently used. Using standards solely as a way to place blame can have a negative effect on managers and employees. To minimize this effect, many companies offer wage incentives to those who meet the standards.

Setting Standard Costs—A Difficult Task

Study Objective [3]
Describe how companies set standards.

The setting of standard costs to produce a unit of product is a difficult task. It requires input from all persons who have responsibility for costs and quantities. To determine the standard cost of direct materials, management consults purchasing agents, product managers, quality control engineers, and production supervisors. In setting the cost standard for direct labor, managers obtain pay rate data from the payroll department. Industrial engineers generally determine the labor time requirements. The managerial accountant provides important input for the standard-setting process by accumulating historical cost data and by knowing how costs respond to changes in activity levels.

To be effective in controlling costs, standard costs need to be current at all times. Thus, standards are under continuous review. They should change whenever managers determine that the existing standard is not a good measure of performance. Circumstances that warrant revision of a standard include changed wage rates resulting from a new union contract, a change in product specifications, or the implementation of a new manufacturing method.

Ideal versus Normal Standards

Companies set standards at one of two levels: ideal or normal. **Ideal standards** represent optimum levels of performance under perfect operating conditions. **Normal standards** represent efficient levels of performance that are attainable under expected operating conditions.

Some managers believe ideal standards will stimulate workers to ever-increasing improvement. However, most managers believe that ideal standards lower the

Ethics Note

When standards are set too high, employees sometimes feel pressure to consider unethical practices to meet these standards.

morale of the entire workforce because they are difficult, if not impossible, to meet. Very few companies use ideal standards.

Most companies that use standards set them at a normal level. Properly set, normal standards should be **rigorous but attainable**. Normal standards allow for rest periods, machine breakdowns, and other "normal" contingencies in the production process. In the remainder of this chapter we will assume that standard costs are set at a normal level.

ACCOUNTING ACROSS THE ORGANIZATION

How Do Standards Help a Business?

A number of organizations, including corporations, consultants, and governmental agencies, have agreed to share information regarding performance standards in an effort to create a standard set of measures for thousands of business processes. The group, referred to as the Open Standards Benchmarking Collaborative, includes IBM, Procter and Gamble, the U.S. Navy, and the World Bank. Companies that are interested in participating can go to the group's website and enter their information.

Source: William M. Bulkeley, "Business, Agencies to Standardize Their Benchmarks," *Wall Street Journal* (May 19, 2004).

 How will the creation of such standards help a business or organization?
(See page 1190.)

A Case Study

To establish the standard cost of producing a product, it is necessary to establish standards for each manufacturing cost element—direct materials, direct labor, and manufacturing overhead. The standard for each element is derived from the standard price to be paid and the standard quantity to be used.

To illustrate, we look at a case study of how standard costs are set. In this extended example, we assume that Xonic, Inc. wishes to use standard costs to measure performance in filling an order for 1,000 gallons of Weed-O, a liquid weed killer.

DIRECT MATERIALS

The **direct materials price standard** is the cost per unit of direct materials that should be incurred. This standard should be based on the purchasing department's best estimate of the **cost of raw materials**. This cost is frequently based on current purchase prices. The price standard also includes an amount for related costs such as receiving, storing, and handling. The materials price standard per pound of material for Xonic's weed killer is:

Item	Price
Purchase price, net of discounts	$2.70
Freight	0.20
Receiving and handling	0.10
Standard direct materials price per pound	**$3.00**

Illustration 25-2
Setting direct materials price standard

The **direct materials quantity standard** is the quantity of direct materials that should be used per unit of finished goods. This standard is expressed as a physical measure, such as pounds, barrels, or board feet. In setting the standard, management considers both the quality and quantity of materials required to manufacture the product. The standard includes allowances for unavoidable waste and normal spoilage. The standard quantity per unit for Xonic, Inc. is as follows.

Item	Quantity (Pounds)
Required materials	3.5
Allowance for waste	0.4
Allowance for spoilage	0.1
Standard direct materials quantity per unit	**4.0**

Illustration 25-3
Setting direct materials quantity standard

The standard direct materials cost per unit is the standard direct materials price times the standard direct materials quantity. For Xonic, Inc., the standard direct materials cost per gallon of Weed-O is $12.00 ($3.00 × 4.0 pounds).

DIRECT LABOR

The **direct labor price standard** is the rate per hour that should be incurred for direct labor. This standard is based on current wage rates, adjusted for anticipated changes such as cost of living adjustments (COLAs). The price standard also generally includes employer payroll taxes and fringe benefits, such as paid holidays and vacations. For Xonic, Inc., the direct labor price standard is as follows.

Alternative Terminology

The direct labor price standard is also called the *direct labor rate standard*.

Illustration 25-4
Setting direct labor price standard

Item	Price
Hourly wage rate	$ 7.50
COLA	0.25
Payroll taxes	0.75
Fringe benefits	1.50
Standard direct labor rate per hour	**$10.00**

Alternative Terminology

The direct labor quantity standard is also called the *direct labor efficiency standard*.

The **direct labor quantity standard** is the time that should be required to make one unit of the product. This standard is especially critical in labor-intensive companies. Allowances should be made in this standard for rest periods, cleanup, machine setup, and machine downtime. For Xonic, Inc., the direct labor quantity standard is as follows.

Illustration 25-5
Setting direct labor quantity standard

Item	Quantity (Hours)
Actual production time	1.5
Rest periods and cleanup	0.2
Setup and downtime	0.3
Standard direct labor hours per unit	2.0

The standard direct labor cost per unit is the standard direct labor rate times the standard direct labor hours. For Xonic, Inc., the standard direct labor cost per gallon of Weed-O is $20 ($10.00 × 2.0 hours).

MANUFACTURING OVERHEAD

For manufacturing overhead, companies use a **standard predetermined overhead rate** in setting the standard. This overhead rate is determined by dividing budgeted overhead costs by an expected standard activity index. For example, the index may be standard direct labor hours or standard machine hours.

Calculating the overhead rate

Overhead ÷ Standard activity index

As discussed in Chapter 21, many companies employ activity-based costing (ABC) to allocate overhead costs. Because ABC uses multiple activity indices to allocate overhead costs, it results in a better correlation between activities and costs incurred than do other methods. As a result, the use of ABC can significantly improve the usefulness of standard costing for management decision making.

Xonic, Inc. uses standard direct labor hours as the activity index. The company expects to produce 13,200 gallons of Weed-O during the year at normal capacity. **Normal capacity** is the average activity output that a company should experience in the long run. Since it takes 2 direct labor hours for each gallon, total standard direct labor hours are 26,400 (13,200 gallons × 2 hours).

At normal capacity of 26,400 direct labor hours, overhead costs are expected to be $132,000. Of that amount, $79,200 are variable and $52,800 are fixed. Illustration 25-6 shows computation of the standard predetermined overhead rates for Xonic, Inc.

Illustration 25-6
Computing predetermined overhead rates

Budgeted Overhead Costs	Amount	÷	Standard Direct Labor Hours	=	Overhead Rate per Direct Labor Hour
Variable	$ 79,200		26,400		$3.00
Fixed	52,800		26,400		2.00
Total	$132,000		26,400		$5.00

The standard manufacturing overhead rate per unit is the predetermined overhead rate times the activity index quantity standard. For Xonic, Inc., which uses direct labor hours as its activity index, the standard manufacturing overhead rate per gallon of Weed-O is $10 ($5 × 2 hours).

TOTAL STANDARD COST PER UNIT

After a company has established the standard quantity and price per unit of product, it can determine the total standard cost. The total standard cost per unit is the sum of the standard costs of direct materials, direct labor, and manufacturing overhead. For Xonic, Inc., the total standard cost per gallon of Weed-O is $42, as shown on the following standard cost card.

Illustration 25-7
Standard cost per gallon of Weed-O

Product: Weed-O	Unit Measure: Gallon		
Manufacturing Cost Elements	**Standard Quantity** ×	**Standard Price** =	**Standard Cost**
Direct materials	4 pounds	$ 3.00	$12.00
Direct labor	2 hours	$10.00	$20.00
Manufacturing overhead	2 hours	$ 5.00	$10.00
			$42.00

The company prepares a standard cost card for each product. This card provides the basis for determining variances from standards.

MANAGEMENT INSIGHT

How Can We Make Susan's Chili Profitable?

Setting standards can be difficult. Consider Susan's Chili Factory, which manufactures and sells chili. The cost of manufacturing Susan's chili consists of the costs of raw materials, labor to convert the basic ingredients to chili, and overhead. We will use materials cost as an example. Managers need to develop three standards: (1) What should be the formula (mix) of ingredients for one gallon of chili? (2) What should be the normal wastage (or shrinkage) for the individual ingredients? (3) What should be the standard cost for the individual ingredients that go into the chili?

Susan's Chili Factory also illustrates how managers can use standard costs in controlling costs. Suppose that summer droughts have reduced crop yields. As a result, prices have doubled for beans, onions, and peppers. In this case, actual costs will be significantly higher than standard costs, which will cause management to evaluate the situation. Similarly, assume that poor maintenance caused the onion-dicing blades to become dull. As a result, usage of onions to make a gallon of chili tripled. Because this deviation is quickly highlighted through standard costs, managers can take corrective action promptly.

Source: Adapted from David R. Beran, "Cost Reduction Through Control Reporting," *Management Accounting* (April 1982), pp. 29–33.

? How might management use this raw material cost information? (See page 1190.)

Do it!

Ridette Inc. accumulated the following standard cost data concerning product Cty31.

> Materials per unit: 1.5 pounds at $4 per pound
> Labor per unit: 0.25 hours at $13 per hour.
> Manufacturing overhead: Predetermined rate is 120% of direct labor cost.

Compute the standard cost of one unit of product Cty31.

Standard Costs

action plan
✔ Know that standard costs are predetermined unit costs.

action plan (cont.)

✔ To establish the standard cost of producing a product, establish the standard for each manufacturing cost element—direct materials, direct labor, and manufacturing overhead.

✔ Compute the standard cost for each element from the standard price to be paid and the standard quantity to be used.

Solution

Manufacturing Cost Element	Standard Quantity	×	Standard Price	=	Standard Cost
Direct materials	1.5 pounds		$4.00		$ 6.00
Direct labor	0.25 hours		$13.00		3.25
Manufacturing overhead	120%		$3.25		3.90
Total					$13.15

Related exercise material: BE25-2, E25-1, E25-2, E25-3, and **Do it!** 25-1.

The Navigator

Analyzing and Reporting Variances from Standards

Alternative Terminology

In business, the term *variance* is also used to indicate differences between total budgeted and total actual costs.

One of the major management uses of standard costs is to identify variances from standards. Variances are the differences between total actual costs and total standard costs.

To illustrate, we will assume that in producing 1,000 gallons of Weed-O in the month of June, Xonic, Inc. incurred the following costs.

Illustration 25-8
Actual production costs

Direct materials	$13,020
Direct labor	20,580
Variable overhead	6,500
Fixed overhead	4,400
Total actual costs	$44,500

Companies determine total standard costs by multiplying the units produced by the standard cost per unit. The total standard cost of Weed-O is $42,000 (1,000 gallons × $42). Thus, the total variance is $2,500, as shown below.

Illustration 25-9
Computation of total variance

Actual costs	$44,500
Less: Standard costs	42,000
Total variance	$ 2,500

Note that the variance is expressed in total dollars, and not on a per unit basis.

When actual costs exceed standard costs, the variance is **unfavorable**. The $2,500 variance in June for Weed-O is unfavorable. An unfavorable variance has a negative connotation. It suggests that the company paid too much for one or more of the manufacturing cost elements or that it used the elements inefficiently.

If actual costs are less than standard costs, the variance is **favorable**. A favorable variance has a positive connotation. It suggests efficiencies in incurring manufacturing costs and in using direct materials, direct labor, and manufacturing overhead.

However, be careful: A favorable variance could be obtained by using inferior materials. In printing wedding invitations, for example, a favorable variance could result from using an inferior grade of paper. Or, a favorable variance might be achieved in installing tires on an automobile assembly line by tightening only half of the lug bolts. A variance is not favorable if the company has sacrificed quality control standards.

Direct Materials Variances

In completing the order for 1,000 gallons of Weed-O, Xonic used 4,200 pounds of direct materials. These were purchased at a cost of $3.10 per unit. Illustration 25-10 shows the formula for the **total materials variance** and the calculation for Xonic, Inc.

Illustration 25-10
Formula for total materials variance

Actual Quantity × Actual Price (AQ) × (AP)	−	Standard Quantity × Standard Price (SQ) × (SP)	=	Total Materials Variance (TMV)
(4,200 × $3.10)	−	(4,000 × $3.00)	=	$1,020 U

Thus, for Xonic, the total materials variance is $1,020 ($13,020 − $12,000) unfavorable.

Next, the company analyzes the total variance to determine the amount attributable to price (costs) and to quantity (use). The **materials price variance** for Xonic, Inc. is computed from the following formula.[1]

Illustration 25-11
Formula for materials price variance

Actual Quantity × Actual Price (AQ) × (AP)	−	Actual Quantity × Standard Price (AQ) × (SP)	=	Materials Price Variance (MPV)
(4,200 × $3.10)	−	(4,200 × $3.00)	=	$420 U

For Xonic, the materials price variance is $420 ($13,020 − $12,600) unfavorable.

The price variance can also be computed by multiplying the actual quantity purchased by the difference between the actual and standard price per unit. The computation in this case is 4,200 × ($3.10 − $3.00) = $420 U.

Illustration 25-12 shows the formula for the **materials quantity variance** and the calculation for Xonic, Inc.

Helpful Hint
The alternative formula is:
$$\boxed{AQ} \times \boxed{AP - SP} = \boxed{MPV}$$

Illustration 25-12
Formula for materials quantity variance

Actual Quantity × Standard Price (AQ) × (SP)	−	Standard Quantity × Standard Price (SQ) × (SP)	=	Materials Quantity Variance (MQV)
(4,200 × $3.00)	−	(4,000 × $3.00)	=	$600 U

Thus, for Xonic, Inc., the materials quantity variance is $600 ($12,600 − $12,000) unfavorable.

The price variance can also be computed by applying the standard price to the difference between actual and standard quantities used. The computation in this example is $3.00 × (4,200 − 4,000) = $600 U.

The total materials variance of $1,020 U, therefore, consists of the following.

Helpful Hint
The alternative formula is:
$$\boxed{SP} \times \boxed{AQ - SQ} = \boxed{MQV}$$

Illustration 25-13
Summary of materials variances

Materials price variance	$ 420 U
Materials quantity variance	600 U
Total materials variance	**$1,020 U**

---

[1]We will assume that all materials purchased during the period are used in production and that no units remain in inventory at the end of the period.

Companies sometimes use a matrix to analyze a variance. **When the matrix is used, a company computes the formulas for each cost element first and then computes the variances.** Illustration 25-14 shows the completed matrix for the direct materials variance for Xonic, Inc. The matrix provides a convenient structure for determining each variance.

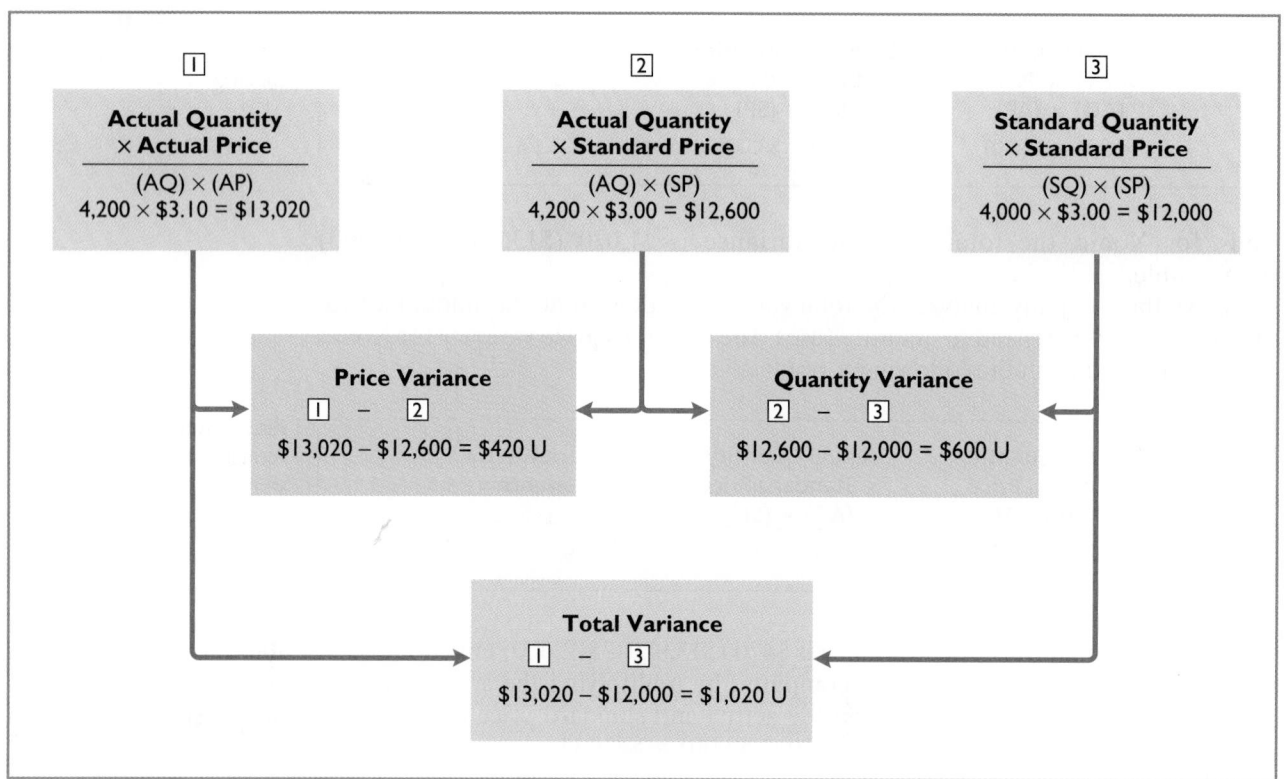

Illustration 25-14
Matrix for direct materials variances

CAUSES OF MATERIALS VARIANCES

What are the causes of a variance? The causes may relate to both internal and external factors. The investigation of a **materials price variance usually begins in the purchasing department**. Many factors affect the price paid for raw materials. These include availability of quantity and cash discounts, the quality of the materials requested, and the delivery method used. To the extent that these factors are considered in setting the price standard, the purchasing department is responsible for any variances.

However, a variance may be beyond the control of the purchasing department. Sometimes, for example, prices may rise faster than expected. Moreover, actions by groups over which the company has no control, such as the OPEC nations' oil price increases, may cause an unfavorable variance. There are also times when a production department may be responsible for the price variance. This may occur when a rush order forces the company to pay a higher price for the materials.

The starting point for determining the cause(s) of an unfavorable **materials quantity variance is in the production department**. If the variances are due to inexperienced workers, faulty machinery, or carelessness, the production department is responsible. However, if the materials obtained by the purchasing department were of inferior quality, then the purchasing department is responsible.

Do it!

Materials Variances

The standard cost of Product XX includes two units of direct materials at $8.00 per unit. During July, the company buys 22,000 units of direct materials at $7.50 and uses those materials to produce 10,000 units. Compute the total, price, and quantity variances for materials.

action plan

✔ Use the formulas for computing each of the materials variances:

Solution

Standard quantity = 10,000 × 2.
Substituting amounts into the formulas, the variances are:

Total materials variance = $(22,000 \times \$7.50) - (20,000 \times \$8.00) = \$5,000$ unfavorable.

Materials price variance = $(22,000 \times \$7.50) - (22,000 \times \$8.00) = \$11,000$ favorable.

Materials quantity variance = $(22,000 \times \$8.00) - (20,000 \times \$8.00) = \$16,000$ unfavorable.

Total materials variance = (AQ × AP) − (SQ × SP)

Materials price variance = (AQ × AP) − (AQ × SP)

Materials quantity variance = (AQ × SP) − (SQ × SP)

Related exercise material: **BE25-4, E25-5, and Do it! E25-2.**

✔
The Navigator

Direct Labor Variances

The process of determining direct labor variances is the same as for determining the direct materials variances. In completing the Weed-O order, Xonic, Inc. incurred 2,100 direct labor hours at an average hourly rate of $9.80. The standard hours allowed for the units produced were 2,000 hours (1,000 gallons × 2 hours). The standard labor rate was $10 per hour. Illustration 25-15 shows the formula for the **total labor variance** and its calculation for Xonic, Inc.

Actual Hours × Actual Rate (AH) × (AR)	−	Standard Hours × Standard Rate (SH) × (SR)	=	Total Labor Variance (TLV)
(2,100 × $9.80)	−	(2,000 × $10.00)	=	$580 U

Illustration 25-15
Formula for total labor variance

Thus, the total labor variance is $580 ($20,580 − $20,000) unfavorable.

The formula for the **labor price variance** and the calculation for Xonic, Inc. are as follows.

Actual Hours × Actual Rate (AH) × (AR)	−	Actual Hours × Standard Rate (AH) × (SR)	=	Labor Price Variance (LPV)
(2,100 × $9.80)	−	(2,100 × $10.00)	=	$420 F

Illustration 25-16
Formula for labor price variance

For Xonic, Inc., the labor price variance is $420 ($20,580 − $21,000) favorable.

The labor price variance can also be computed by multiplying actual hours worked by the difference between the actual pay rate and the standard pay rate. The computation in this example is 2,100 × ($10.00 − $9.80) = $420 F.

Illustration 25-17 (page 1158) shows the formula for the **labor quantity variance** and its calculation for Xonic, Inc.

Helpful Hint

The alternative formula is:

$\boxed{AH} \times \boxed{AR - SR} = \boxed{LPV}$

Illustration 25-17
Formula for labor quantity variance

Actual Hours × Standard Rate (AH) × (SR)	−	Standard Hours × Standard Rate (SH) × (SR)	=	Labor Quantity Variance (LQV)
(2,100 × $10.00)	−	(2,000 × $10.00)	=	$1,000 U

Thus, for Xonic, Inc., the labor quantity variance is $1,000 ($21,000 − $20,000) unfavorable.

The same result can be obtained by multiplying the standard rate by the difference between actual hours worked and standard hours allowed. In this case, the computation is $10.00 × (2,100 − 2,000) = $1,000 U.

The total direct labor variance of $580 U, therefore, consists of:

Helpful Hint

The alternative formula is:
$SR × |AH − SH| = |LQV|$

Illustration 25-18
Summary of labor variances

Labor price variance	$ 420 F
Labor quantity variance	1,000 U
Total direct labor variance	**$ 580 U**

These results can also be obtained from the matrix in Illustration 25-19.

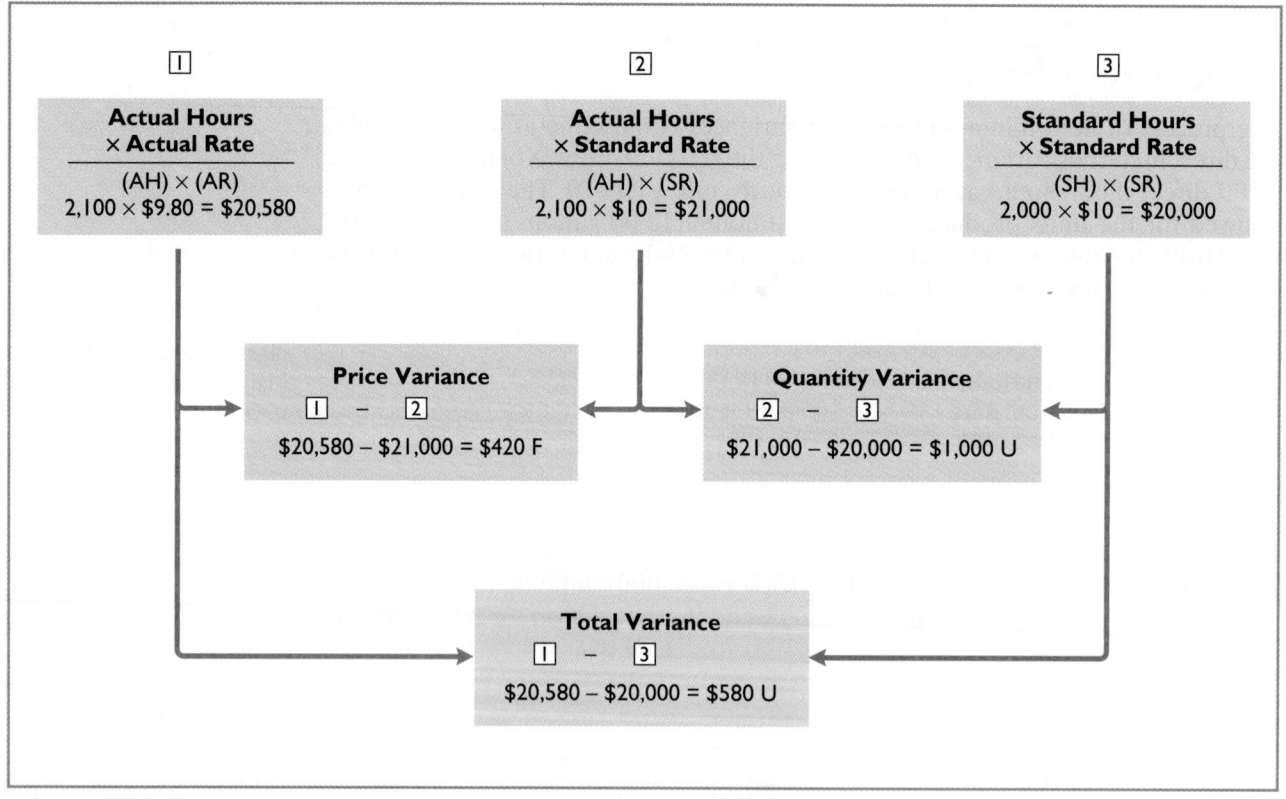

Illustration 25-19
Matrix for direct labor variances

"What caused labor price variances?"

Personnel decisions

Causes of Labor Variances

Labor price variances usually result from two factors: (1) paying workers **higher wages than expected**, and (2) **misallocation of workers**. In companies where pay rates are determined by union contracts, labor price variances should be infrequent. When workers are not unionized, there is a much higher likelihood of such variances. The responsibility for these variances rests with the manager who authorized the wage increase.

Misallocation of the workforce refers to using skilled workers in place of unskilled workers and vice versa. The use of an inexperienced worker instead of an experienced one will result in a favorable price variance because of the lower pay rate of the unskilled worker. An unfavorable price variance would result if a skilled worker were substituted for an inexperienced one. The production department generally is responsible for labor price variances resulting from misallocation of the workforce.

Labor quantity variances relate to the **efficiency of workers**. The cause of a quantity variance generally can be traced to the production department. The causes of an unfavorable variance may be poor training, worker fatigue, faulty machinery, or carelessness. These causes are the responsibility of the **production department**. However, if the excess time is due to inferior materials, the responsibility falls outside the production department.

"What caused labor quantity variances?"

Production Dept.

Manufacturing Overhead Variance

The **total overhead variance** is the difference between the actual overhead costs and overhead costs applied based on standard hours allowed. As indicated in Illustration 25-8, Xonic incurred overhead costs of $10,900 ($6,500 + $4,400) to produce 1,000 gallons of Weed-O in June. The computation of the actual overhead is comprised of a variable and a fixed component. Illustration 25-20 shows this computation.

Study Objective [5]
State the formula for determining the total manufacturing overhead variance.

Variable overhead	$ 6,500
Fixed overhead	4,400
Total actual overhead	**$10,900**

Illustration 25-20
Actual overhead costs

We then determine the overhead costs applied based on standard hours allowed times the predetermined overhead rate. **Standard hours allowed** are the hours that *should* have been worked for the units produced. Because it takes two hours of direct labor to produce one gallon of Weed-O, for the 1,000-gallon Weed-O order, the standard hours allowed are 2,000 hours (1,000 gallons × 2 hours). We then apply the predetermined overhead rate to the 2,000 standard hours allowed.

The predetermined rate for Weed-O is $5, comprised of a variable overhead rate of $3 and a fixed rate of $2. Recall from Illustration 25-6 that the amount of budgeted overhead costs at normal capacity of $132,000 was divided by normal capacity of 26,400 direct labor hours, to arrive at a predetermined overhead rate of $5 ($132,000 ÷ 26,400). The predetermined rate of $5 is then multiplied by the 2,000 standard hours allowed, to determine the overhead costs applied.

Illustration 25-21 shows the formula for the total overhead variance and the calculation for Xonic, Inc. for the month of June.

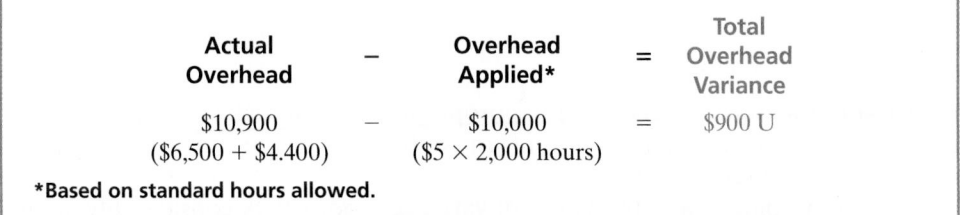

Actual Overhead	−	Overhead Applied*	=	Total Overhead Variance
$10,900	−	$10,000	=	$900 U
($6,500 + $4.400)		($5 × 2,000 hours)		

*Based on standard hours allowed.

Illustration 25-21
Formula for total overhead variance

Thus, for Xonic, Inc. the total overhead variance is $900 unfavorable.

The overhead variance is generally analyzed through a price and quantity variance. The name usually given to the price variance is the **overhead controllable variance**; the quantity variance is referred to as the **overhead volume variance**. Appendix 25B discusses how the total overhead variance can be broken down into these two variances.

CAUSES OF MANUFACTURING OVERHEAD VARIANCES

One reason for an overhead variance relates to over- or underspending on overhead items. For example, overhead may include indirect labor for which a company paid wages higher than the standard labor price allowed. Or the price of electricity to run the company's machines increased, and the company did not anticipate this additional cost. Companies should investigate any spending variances, to determine whether they will continue in the future. Generally, the responsibility for these variances rests with the production department.

The overhead variance can also result from the inefficient use of overhead. For example, because of poor maintenance, a number of the manufacturing machines are experiencing breakdowns on a consistent basis, leading to reduced production. Or the flow of materials through the production process is impeded because of a lack of skilled labor to perform the necessary production tasks, due to a lack of planning. In both of these cases, the production department is responsible for the cause of these variances. On the other hand, overhead can also be underutilized because of a lack of sales orders. When the cause is a lack of sales orders, the responsibility rests outside the production department.

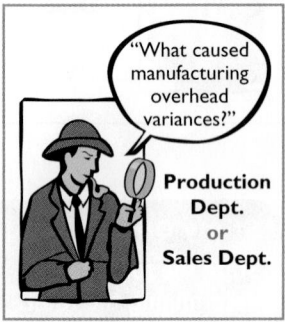

"What caused manufacturing overhead variances?"

Production Dept.
or
Sales Dept.

Do it!

Labor and Manufacturing Overhead Variances

action plan

✔ Use the formulas for computing each of the variances:

Total labor variance = (AH × AR) − (SH × SR)

Labor price variance = (AH × AR) − (AH × SR)

Labor quantity variance = (AH × SR) − (SH × SR)

Total overhead variance = Actual overhead − Overhead applied*

*Based on standard hours allowed.

The standard cost of Product YY includes 3 hours of direct labor at $12.00 per hour. The predetermined overhead rate is $20.00 per direct labor hour. During July, the company incurred 3,500 hours of direct labor at an average rate of $12.40 per hour and $71,300 of manufacturing overhead costs. It produced 1,200 units.

(a) Compute the total, price, and quantity variances for labor. **(b)** Compute the total overhead variance.

Solution

Substituting amounts into the formulas, the variances are:

Total labor variance = (3,500 × $12.40) − (3,600 × $12.00) = $200 Unfavorable

Labor price variance = (3,500 × $12.40) − (3,500 × $12.00) = $1,400 Unfavorable

Labor quantity variance = (3,500 × $12.00) − (3,600 × $12.00) = $1,200 Favorable

Total overhead variance = $71,300 − $72,000* = $700 Favorable

*3,600 hours × $20.00

Related exercise material: BE25-5, BE25-6, E25-4, E25-6, E25-7, E25-8, E25-10, E25-11, and **Do it!** 25-3.

The Navigator

Reporting Variances

Study Objective [6]
Discuss the reporting of variances.

All variances should be reported to appropriate levels of management as soon as possible. The sooner managers are informed, the sooner they can evaluate problems and take corrective action.

The form, content, and frequency of variance reports vary considerably among companies. One approach is to prepare a weekly report for each department that has primary responsibility for cost control. Under this approach, materials price variances are reported to the purchasing department, and all other variances are reported to the production department that did the work. Illustration 25-22 is a materials price variance report for Xonic, Inc., with the materials for the Weed-O order listed first.

Illustration 25-22
Materials price variance
report

Type of Materials	Quantity Purchased	Actual Price	Standard Price	Price Variance	Explanation
			Xonic, Inc. Variance Report — Purchasing Department For Week Ended June 8, 2012		
X100	4,200 lbs.	$3.10	$3.00	$420 U	Rush order
X142	1,200 units	2.75	2.80	60 F	Quantity discount
A85	600 doz.	5.20	5.10	60 U	Regular supplier on strike
Total price variance				$420 U	

The explanation column is completed after consultation with the purchasing department manager.

Variance reports facilitate the principle of "management by exception" explained in Chapter 24. For example, the vice president of purchasing can use the report shown above to evaluate the effectiveness of the purchasing department manager. Or, the vice president of production can use production department variance reports to determine how well each production manager is controlling costs. In using variance reports, top management normally looks for **significant variances**. These may be judged on the basis of some quantitative measure, such as more than 10% of the standard or more than $1,000.

Statement Presentation of Variances

In income statements **prepared for management** under a standard cost accounting system, **cost of goods sold is stated at standard cost and the variances are disclosed separately**. Illustration 25-23 shows this format. Based entirely on the production and sale of Weed-O, it assumes selling and administrative costs of $3,000. Observe that each variance is shown, as well as the total net variance. In this example, variations from standard costs reduced net income by $2,500.

Study Objective [7]
Prepare an income statement for management under a standard costing system.

Illustration 25-23
Variances in income statement for management

Xonic, Inc.
Income Statement
For the Month Ended June 30, 2012

Sales		$60,000
Cost of goods sold (at standard)		42,000
Gross profit (at standard)		18,000
Variances		
Materials price	$ 420 U	
Materials quantity	600 U	
Labor price	420 F	
Labor quantity	1,000 U	
Overhead variance	900 U	
Total variance unfavorable		2,500
Gross profit (actual)		15,500
Selling and administrative expenses		3,000
Net income		$12,500

Standard costs may be used in financial statements prepared for stockholders and other external users. The costing of inventories at standard costs is in accordance with generally accepted accounting principles when there are no significant differences between actual costs and standard costs. Hewlett-Packard and Jostens, Inc., for example, report their inventories at standard costs. However, if there are significant differences between actual and standard costs, the financial statements must report inventories and cost of goods sold at actual costs.

It is also possible to show the variances in an income statement prepared in the variable costing (CVP) format. To do so, it is necessary to analyze the overhead variances into variable and fixed components. This type of analysis is explained in cost accounting textbooks.

Balanced Scorecard

Study Objective [8]
Describe the balanced scorecard approach to performance evaluation.

Financial measures (measurement of dollars), such as variance analysis and return on investment (ROI), are useful tools for evaluating performance. However, many companies now supplement these financial measures with nonfinancial measures to better assess performance and anticipate future results. For example, airlines, like Delta, American, and United, use capacity utilization as an important measure to understand and predict future performance. Newspaper publishers, such as the *New York Times* and the *Chicago Tribune,* use circulation figures as another measure by which to assess performance. Illustration 25-24 lists some key nonfinancial measures used in various industries.

Illustration 25-24
Nonfinancial measures used in various industries

Industry	Measure
Automobiles	Capacity utilization of plants. Average age of key assets. Impact of strikes. Brand-loyalty statistics.
Computer Systems	Market profile of customer end-products. Number of new products. Employee stock ownership percentages. Number of scientists and technicians used in R&D.
Chemicals	Customer satisfaction data. Factors affecting customer product selection. Number of patents and trademarks held. Customer brand awareness.
Regional Banks	Number of ATMs by state. Number of products used by average customer. Percentage of customer service calls handled by interactive voice response units. Personnel cost per employee. Credit card retention rates.

Source: Financial Accounting Standards Board, *Business Reporting: Insights into Enhancing Voluntary Disclosures* (Norwalk, Conn.: FASB, 2001).

Most companies recognize that both financial and nonfinancial measures can provide useful insights into what is happening in the company. As a result, many companies now use a broad-based measurement approach, called the **balanced scorecard**, to evaluate performance. The balanced scorecard incorporates financial and nonfinancial measures in an integrated system that links performance measurement and a company's strategic goals. Nearly 50% of the largest companies in the United States, including Unilever, Chase, and Wal-Mart, are using the balanced scorecard approach.

The balanced scorecard evaluates company performance from a series of "perspectives." The four most commonly employed perspectives are as follows.

1. The **financial perspective** is the most traditional view of the company. It employs financial measures of performance used by most firms.

2. The **customer perspective** evaluates how well the company is performing from the viewpoint of those people who buy and use its products or services. This view measures how well the company compares to competitors in terms of price, quality, product innovation, customer service, and other dimensions.

3. The **internal process perspective** evaluates the internal operating processes critical to success. All critical aspects of the value chain—including product development, production, delivery and after-sale service—are evaluated to ensure that the company is operating effectively and efficiently.

4. The **learning and growth perspective** evaluates how well the company develops and retains its employees. This would include evaluation of such things as employee skills, employee satisfaction, training programs, and information dissemination.

Within each perspective, the balanced scorecard identifies objectives that will contribute to attainment of strategic goals. Illustration 25-25 shows examples of objectives within each perspective.

Financial perspective
 Return on assets
 Net income
 Credit rating
 Share price
 Profit per employee

Customer perspective
 Percentage of customers who would
  recommend product
 Customer retention
 Response time per customer request
 Brand recognition
 Customer service expense per customer

Internal process perspective
 Percentage of defect-free products
 Stockouts
 Labor utilization rates
 Waste reduction
 Planning accuracy

Learning and growth perspective
 Percentage of employees leaving in less than
  one year
 Number of cross-trained employees
 Ethics violations
 Training hours
 Reportable accidents

Illustration 25-25
Examples of objectives within the four perspectives of balanced scorecard

The objectives are linked across perspectives in order to tie performance measurement to company goals. The financial objectives are normally set first, and then objectives are set in the other perspectives in order to accomplish the financial objectives.

For example, within the financial perspective, a common goal is to increase profit per dollars invested as measured by ROI. In order to increase ROI, a customer-perspective objective might be to increase customer satisfaction as measured by the percentage of customers who would recommend the product to a friend.

In order to increase customer satisfaction, an internal business process perspective objective might be to increase product quality as measured by the percentage of defect-free units. Finally, in order to increase the percentage of defect-free units, the learning and growth perspective objective might be to reduce factory employee turnover as measured by the percentage of employees leaving in under one year. Illustration 25-26 illustrates this linkage across perspectives.

Illustration 25-26
Linked process across balanced scorecard perspectives

Through this linked process, the company can better understand how to achieve its goals and what measures to use to evaluate performance. In summary, the balanced scorecard does the following:

1. Employs both financial and nonfinancial measures. (For example, ROI is a financial measure; employee turnover is a nonfinancial measure.)
2. Creates linkages so that high-level corporate goals can be communicated all the way down to the shop floor.
3. Provides measurable objectives for such nonfinancial measures as product quality, rather than vague statements such as "We would like to improve quality."
4. Integrates all of the company's goals into a single performance measurement system, so that an inappropriate amount of weight will not be placed on any single goal.

SERVICE COMPANY INSIGHT

It May Be Time To Fly United Again

Many of the benefits of a balanced scorecard approach are evident in the improved operations at United Airlines. At the time it filed for bankruptcy in 2002, United had a reputation for some of the worst service in the airline business. But when Glenn Tilton took over as United's Chief Executive Officer in September 2002, he recognized that things had to change.

One thing he did was to implement an incentive program that allows all of United's 63,000 employees to earn a bonus of 2.5% or more of their wages if the company "exceeds its goals for on-time flight departures and for customer intent to fly United again." Since instituting this program, the company's on-time departures are among the best, its customer complaints have been reduced considerably, and its number of customers who say that they would fly United again is at its highest level ever. While none of these things guarantees that United will survive (given the substantial increase in oil prices), these improvements certainly increase its chances.

Source: Susan Carey, "Friendlier Skies: In Bankruptcy, United Airlines Forges a Path to Better Service," *Wall Street Journal* (June 15, 2004).

? Which of the perspectives of a balanced scorecard were the focus of United's CEO? (See page 1190.)

Do it!

Indicate which of the four perspectives in the balanced scorecard is most likely associated with the objectives that follow.

1. Percentage of repeat customers.

2. Number of suggestions for improvement from employees.

3. Contribution margin.

4. Market share.

5. Number of cross-trained employees.

6. Amount of setup time.

Solution

> **1.** Customer perspective.
>
> **2.** Learning and growth perspective.
>
> **3.** Financial perspective.
>
> **4.** Customer perspective.
>
> **5.** Learning and growth perspective.
>
> **6.** Internal process perspective.

Related exercise material: BE25-7, E25-16, and **Do it!** 25-4.

Balanced Scorecard

action plan

✔ The financial perspective employs traditional financial measures of performance.

✔ The customer perspective evaluates company performance as seen by the people who buy its products or services.

✔ The internal process perspective evaluates the internal operating processes critical to success.

✔ The learning and growth perspective evaluates how well the company develops and retains its employees.

✔ **The Navigator**

COMPREHENSIVE

Do it!

Manlow Company makes a cologne called Allure. The standard cost for one bottle of Allure is as follows.

Manufacturing Cost Elements	Standard Quantity	×	Price	=	Cost
Direct materials	6 oz.	×	$ 0.90	=	$ 5.40
Direct labor	0.5 hrs.	×	$12.00	=	6.00
Manufacturing overhead	0.5 hrs.	×	$ 4.80	=	2.40
					$13.80

During the month, the following transactions occurred in manufacturing 10,000 bottles of Allure.

1. 58,000 ounces of materials were purchased at $1.00 per ounce.

2. All the materials purchased were used to produce the 10,000 bottles of Allure.

3. 4,900 direct labor hours were worked at a total labor cost of $56,350.

4. Variable manufacturing overhead incurred was $15,000 and fixed overhead incurred was $10,400.

The manufacturing overhead rate of $4.80 is based on a normal capacity of 5,200 direct labor hours. The total budget at this capacity is $10,400 fixed and $14,560 variable.

Instructions

(a) Compute the total variance for the three cost elements, and the price and quantity variances for direct materials and direct labor.

(b) Compute the total variance for manufacturing overhead.

action plan

✔ Check to make sure the total variance and the sum of the individual variances are equal.

✔ Find the price variance first, then the quantity variance.

✔ Base overhead applied on standard hours allowed.

✔ Ignore actual hours worked in computing overhead variance.

Solution to Comprehensive Do it!

(a)

Total Variance

Actual costs incurred		
Direct materials		$ 58,000
Direct labor		56,350
Manufacturing overhead		25,400
		139,750
Standard cost (10,000 × $13.80)		138,000
Total variance		$ 1,750 U

Direct Materials Variances

Total	=	$58,000	−	$54,000	=	$4,000 U
		(58,000 × $1.00)		(60,000 × $0.90)		
Price	=	$58,000	−	$52,200	=	$5,800 U
		(58,000 × $1.00)		(58,000 × $0.90)		
Quantity	=	$52,200	−	$54,000	=	$1,800 F
		(58,000 × $0.90)		(60,000 × $0.90)		

Direct Labor Variances

Total	=	$56,350	−	$60,000	=	$3,650 F
		(4,900 × $11.50)		(5,000 × $12.00)		
Price	=	$56,350	−	$58,800	=	$2,450 F
		(4,900 × $11.50)		(4,900 × $12.00)		
Quantity	=	$58,800	−	$60,000	=	$1,200 F
		(4,900 × $12.00)		(5,000 × $12.00)		

(b)

Overhead Variance

Total	=	$25,400	−	$24,000	=	$1,400 U
		($15,000 + $10,400)		(5,000 × $4.80)		

The Navigator

Summary of Study Objectives

[1] Distinguish between a standard and a budget. Both standards and budgets are predetermined costs. The primary difference is that a standard is a unit amount, whereas a budget is a total amount. A standard may be regarded as the budgeted cost per unit of product.

[2] Identify the advantages of standard costs. Standard costs offer a number of advantages. They (a) facilitate management planning, (b) promote greater economy, (c) are useful in setting selling prices, (d) contribute to management control, (e) permit "management by exception," and (f) simplify the costing of inventories and reduce clerical costs.

[3] Describe how companies set standards. The direct materials price standard should be based on the delivered cost of raw materials plus an allowance for receiving and handling. The direct materials quantity standard should establish the required quantity plus an allowance for waste and spoilage.

The direct labor price standard should be based on current wage rates and anticipated adjustments such as COLAs. It also generally includes payroll taxes and fringe benefits. Direct labor quantity standards should be based on required production time plus an allowance for rest periods, cleanup, machine setup, and machine downtime.

For manufacturing overhead, a standard predetermined overhead rate is used. It is based on an expected standard activity index such as standard direct labor hours or standard machine hours.

[4] State the formulas for determining direct materials and direct labor variances. The formulas for the direct materials variances are:

$$\left(\begin{array}{c}\text{Actual quantity}\\ \times \text{Actual price}\end{array}\right) - \left(\begin{array}{c}\text{Standard quantity}\\ \times \text{Standard price}\end{array}\right) = \begin{array}{c}\text{Total}\\ \text{materials}\\ \text{variance}\end{array}$$

$$\left(\begin{array}{c}\text{Actual quantity}\\ \times \text{Actual price}\end{array}\right) - \left(\begin{array}{c}\text{Actual quantity}\\ \times \text{Standard price}\end{array}\right) = \begin{array}{c}\text{Materials}\\ \text{price}\\ \text{variance}\end{array}$$

$$\left(\begin{array}{c}\text{Actual quantity}\\ \times \text{Standard price}\end{array}\right) - \left(\begin{array}{c}\text{Standard quantity}\\ \times \text{Standard price}\end{array}\right) = \begin{array}{c}\text{Materials}\\ \text{quantity}\\ \text{variance}\end{array}$$

The formulas for the direct labor variances are:

$$\left(\begin{array}{c}\text{Actual hours}\\ \times \text{Actual rate}\end{array}\right) - \left(\begin{array}{c}\text{Standard hours}\\ \times \text{Standard rate}\end{array}\right) = \begin{array}{c}\text{Total}\\ \text{labor}\\ \text{variance}\end{array}$$

$$\left(\begin{array}{c}\text{Actual hours}\\ \times \text{Actual rate}\end{array}\right) - \left(\begin{array}{c}\text{Actual hours}\\ \times \text{Standard rate}\end{array}\right) = \begin{array}{c}\text{Labor}\\ \text{price}\\ \text{variance}\end{array}$$

$$\left(\begin{array}{c}\text{Actual hours}\\ \times \text{Standard rate}\end{array}\right) - \left(\begin{array}{c}\text{Standard hours}\\ \times \text{Standard rate}\end{array}\right) = \begin{array}{c}\text{Labor}\\ \text{quantity}\\ \text{variance}\end{array}$$

[5] State the formula for determining the total manufacturing overhead variance. The formula for the total manufacturing overhead variance is:

$$\left(\begin{array}{c}\text{Actual}\\ \text{overhead}\end{array}\right) - \left(\begin{array}{c}\text{Overhead}\\ \text{applied at}\\ \text{standard}\\ \text{hours}\\ \text{allowed}\end{array}\right) = \begin{array}{c}\text{Total overhead}\\ \text{variance}\end{array}$$

[6] Discuss the reporting of variances. Variances are reported to management in variance reports. The reports facilitate management by exception by highlighting significant differences.

[7] Prepare an income statement for management under a standard costing system. Under a standard costing system, an income statement prepared for management will report cost of goods sold at standard cost and then disclose each variance separately.

[8] Describe the balanced scorecard approach to performance evaluation. The balanced scorecard incorporates financial and nonfinancial measures in an integrated system that links performance measurement and a company's strategic goals. It employs four perspectives: financial, customer, internal processes, and learning and growth. Objectives are set within each of these perspectives that link to objectives within the other perspectives.

✔ **The Navigator**

Glossary

Balanced scorecard An approach that incorporates financial and nonfinancial measures in an integrated system that links performance measurement and a company's strategic goals. (p. 1163).

Customer perspective A viewpoint employed in the balanced scorecard to evaluate the company from the perspective of those people who buy and use its products or services. (p. 1163).

Direct labor price standard The rate per hour that should be incurred for direct labor. (p. 1151).

Direct labor quantity standard The time that should be required to make one unit of product. (p. 1152).

Direct materials price standard The cost per unit of direct materials that should be incurred. (p. 1151).

Direct materials quantity standard The quantity of direct materials that should be used per unit of finished goods. (p. 1151).

Financial perspective A viewpoint employed in the balanced scorecard to evaluate a company's performance using financial measures. (p. 1163).

Ideal standards Standards based on the optimum level of performance under perfect operating conditions. (p. 1150).

Internal process perspective A viewpoint employed in the balanced scorecard to evaluate the effectiveness and efficiency of a company's value chain, including product development, production, delivery, and after-sale service. (p. 1163).

Labor price variance The difference between the actual hours times the actual rate and the actual hours times the standard rate for labor. (p. 1157).

Labor quantity variance The difference between actual hours times the standard rate and standard hours times the standard rate for labor. (p. 1157).

Learning and growth perspective A viewpoint employed in the balanced scorecard to evaluate how well a company develops and retains its employees. (p. 1163).

Materials price variance The difference between the actual quantity times the actual price and the actual quantity times the standard price for materials. (p. 1155).

Materials quantity variance The difference between the actual quantity times the standard price and the standard quantity times the standard price for materials. (p. 1155).

Normal capacity The average activity output that a company should experience over the long run. (p. 1152).

Normal standards Standards based on an efficient level of performance that are attainable under expected operating conditions. (p. 1150).

Standard costs Predetermined unit costs which companies use as measures of performance. (p. 1148).

Standard hours allowed The hours that should have been worked for the units produced. (p. 1159).

Standard predetermined overhead rate An overhead rate determined by dividing budgeted overhead costs by an expected standard activity index. (p. 1152).

Total labor variance The difference between actual hours times the actual rate and standard hours times the standard rate for labor. (p. 1157).

Total materials variance The difference between the actual quantity times the actual price and the standard quantity times the standard price of materials. (p. 1155).

Total overhead variance The difference between actual overhead costs and overhead costs applied to work done. (p. 1159).

Variances The difference between total actual costs and total standard costs. (p. 1154).

APPENDIX25A
Standard Cost Accounting System

Study Objective [9]
Identify the features of a standard cost accounting system.

A **standard cost accounting system** is a double-entry system of accounting. In this system, companies use standard costs in making entries, and they formally recognize variances in the accounts. Companies may use a standard cost system with either job order or process costing.

In this appendix, we will explain and illustrate a **standard cost, job order cost accounting system**. The system is based on two important assumptions:

(1) Variances from standards are recognized at the earliest opportunity.

(2) The Work in Process account is maintained exclusively on the basis of standard costs.

In practice, there are many variations among standard cost systems. The system described here should prepare you for systems you see in the "real world."

Journal Entries

We will use the transactions of Xonic, Inc. to illustrate the journal entries. Note as you study the entries that the major difference between the entries here and those for the job order cost accounting system in Chapter 20 is the **variance accounts**.

1. Purchase raw materials on account for $13,020 when the standard cost is $12,600.

Raw Materials Inventory	12,600	
Materials Price Variance	420	
Accounts Payable		13,020
(To record purchase of materials)		

Xonic debits the inventory account for actual quantities at standard cost. This enables the perpetual materials records to show actual quantities. Xonic debits the price variance, which is unfavorable, to Materials Price Variance.

2. Incur direct labor costs of $20,580 when the standard labor cost is $21,000.

Factory Labor	21,000	
Labor Price Variance		420
Factory Wages Payable		20,580
(To record direct labor costs)		

Like the raw materials inventory account, Xonic debits Factory Labor for actual hours worked at the standard hourly rate of pay. In this case, the labor variance is favorable. Thus, Xonic credits Labor Price Variance.

3. Incur actual manufacturing overhead costs of $10,900.

Manufacturing Overhead	10,900	
Accounts Payable/Cash/Acc. Depreciation		10,900
(To record overhead incurred)		

The controllable overhead variance is not recorded at this time. It depends on standard hours applied to work in process. This amount is not known at the time overhead is incurred.

4. Issue raw materials for production at a cost of $12,600 when the standard cost is $12,000.

Work in Process Inventory	12,000	
Materials Quantity Variance	600	
Raw Materials Inventory		12,600
(To record issuance of raw materials)		

Xonic debits Work in Process Inventory for standard materials quantities used at standard prices. It debits the variance account because the variance is unfavorable. The company credits Raw Materials Inventory for actual quantities at standard prices.

5. Assign factory labor to production at a cost of $21,000 when standard cost is $20,000.

Work in Process Inventory	20,000	
Labor Quantity Variance	1,000	
Factory Labor		21,000
(To assign factory labor to jobs)		

Xonic debits Work in Process Inventory for standard labor hours at standard rates. It debits the unfavorable variance to Labor Quantity Variance. The credit to Factory Labor produces a zero balance in this account.

6. Applying manufacturing overhead to production $10,000.

Work in Process Inventory	10,000	
Manufacturing Overhead		10,000
(To assign overhead to jobs)		

Xonic debits Work in Process Inventory for standard hours allowed multiplied by the standard overhead rate.

7. Transfer completed work to finished goods $42,000.

Finished Goods Inventory	42,000	
Work in Process Inventory		42,000
(To record transfer of completed work to finished goods)		

In this example, both inventory accounts are at standard cost.

8. The 1,000 gallons of Weed-O are sold for $60,000.

Accounts Receivable	60,000	
Cost of Goods Sold	42,000	
Sales		60,000
Finished Goods Inventory		42,000
(To record sale of finished goods and the cost of goods sold)		

The company debits Cost of Goods Sold at standard cost. Gross profit, in turn, is the difference between sales and the standard cost of goods sold.

9. Recognize unfavorable total overhead variance:

Overhead Variance		900	
Manufacturing Overhead			900
(To recognize total overhead variance)			

Prior to this entry, a debit balance of $900 existed in Manufacturing Overhead. This entry therefore produces a zero balance in the Manufacturing Overhead account. The information needed for this entry is often not available until the end of the accounting period.

Ledger Accounts

Illustration 25A-1 shows the cost accounts for Xonic, Inc., after posting the entries. Note that six variance accounts are included in the ledger. The remaining accounts are the same as those illustrated for a job order cost system in Chapter 20, in which only actual costs were used.

Illustration 25A-1
Cost accounts with variances

Helpful Hint

All debit balances in variance accounts indicate unfavorable variances; all credit balances indicate favorable variances.

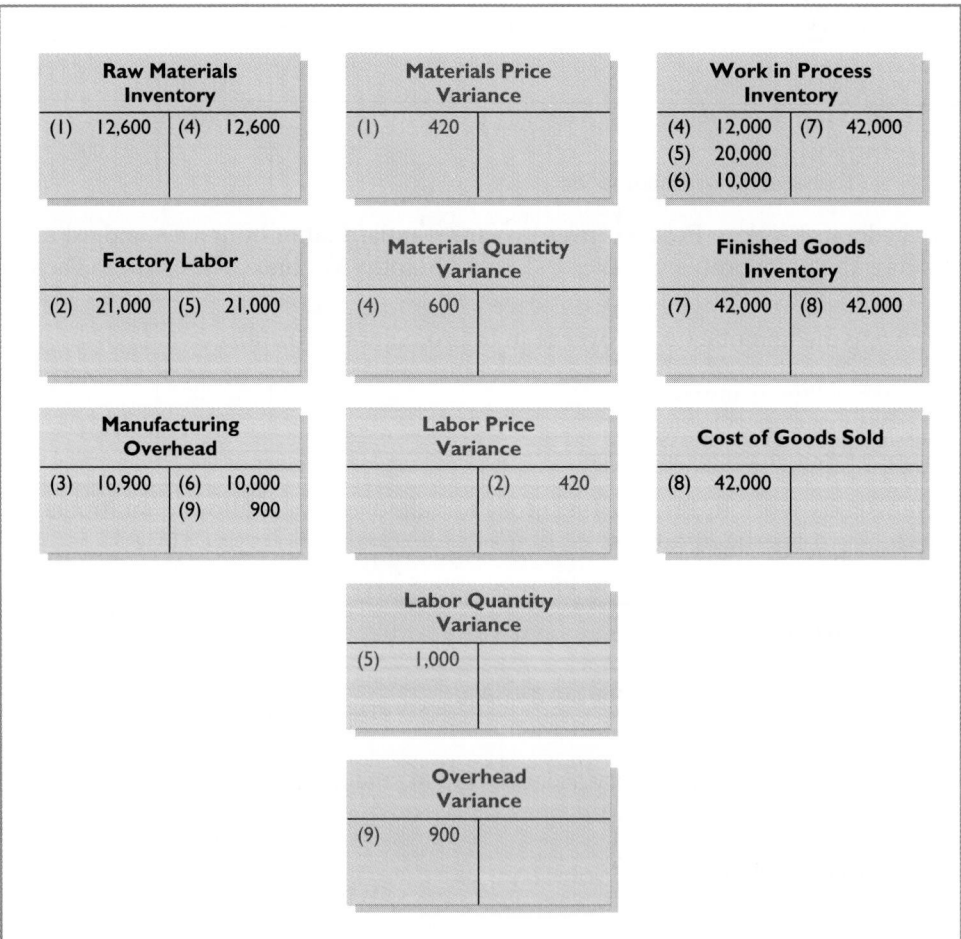

Summary of Study Objective for Appendix 25A

[9] Identify the features of a standard cost accounting system. In a standard cost accounting system, companies journalize and post standard costs, and they maintain separate variance accounts in the ledger.

Glossary for Appendix 25A

Standard cost accounting system A double-entry system of accounting in which standard costs are used in making entries and variances are recognized in the accounts. (p. 1168).

APPENDIX25B

A Closer Look at Overhead Variances

As indicated in the chapter, the total overhead variance is generally analyzed through a price variance and a quantity variance. The name usually given to the price variance is the **overhead controllable variance**; the quantity variance is referred to as the **overhead volume variance**.

Study Objective [10]
Compute overhead controllable and volume variance.

Overhead Controllable Variance

The overhead controllable variance shows whether overhead costs are effectively controlled. To compute this variance, the company compares actual overhead costs incurred with budgeted costs for the **standard hours allowed**. The budgeted costs are determined from a manufacturing overhead flexible budget. The concepts related to a flexible budget were discussed in Chapter 24.

For Xonic, Inc., the budget formula for manufacturing overhead is variable manufacturing overhead cost of $3 per hour of labor plus fixed manufacturing overhead costs of $4,400. Illustration 25B-1 shows the flexible budget for Xonic, Inc.

Illustration 25B-1
Flexible budget using standard direct labor hours

Xonic, Inc.xls					
File Edit View Insert Format Tools Data Window Help					
	A	B	C	D	E
1	XONIC, INC.				
2	Manufacturing Overhead Flexible Budget				
3	Activity Index				
4	Standard direct labor hours	1,800	2,000	2,200	2,400
5	Costs				
6	Variable costs				
7	Indirect materials	$1,800	$ 2,000	$ 2,200	$ 2,400
8	Indirect labor	2,700	3,000	3,300	3,600
9	Utilities	900	1,000	1,100	1,200
10	Total variable costs	5,400	6,000	6,600	7,200
11					
12	Fixed costs				
13	Supervision	3,000	3,000	3,000	3,000
14	Depreciation	1,400	1,400	1,400	1,400
15	Total fixed costs	4,400	4,400	4,400	4,400
16	Total costs	$9,800	$10,400	$11,000	$11,600
17					

As shown, the budgeted costs for 2,000 standard hours are $10,400 ($6,000 variable and $4,400 fixed).

Illustration 25B-2 shows the formula for the overhead controllable variance and the calculation for Xonic, Inc.

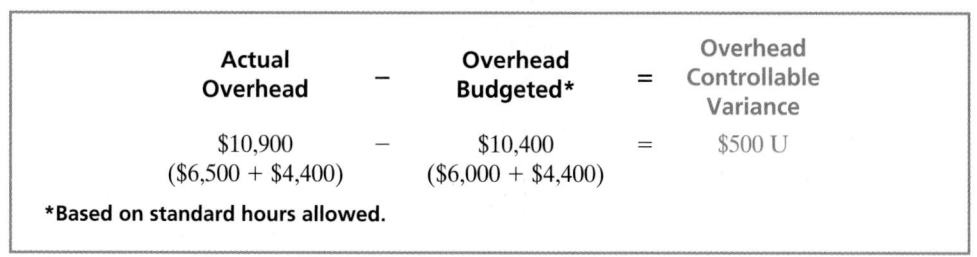

Actual Overhead	−	Overhead Budgeted*	=	Overhead Controllable Variance
$10,900	−	$10,400	=	$500 U
($6,500 + $4,400)		($6,000 + $4,400)		

*Based on standard hours allowed.

Illustration 25B-2
Formula for overhead controllable variance

The overhead controllable variance for Xonic, Inc. is $500 unfavorable.

Most controllable variances are associated with variable costs, which are controllable costs. Fixed costs are often known at the time the budget is prepared and are therefore not as likely to deviate from the budgeted amount. In Xonic's case, all of the overhead controllable variance is due to the difference between the actual variable overhead costs ($6,500) and the budgeted variable costs ($6,000).

Management can compare actual and budgeted overhead for each manufacturing overhead cost that contributes to the controllable variance. In addition, management can develop cost and quantity variances for each overhead cost, such as indirect materials and indirect labor.

Overhead Volume Variance

The **overhead volume variance** is the difference between normal capacity hours and standard hours allowed times the fixed overhead rate. The overhead volume variance relates to whether fixed costs were under- or overapplied during the year. For example, the overhead volume variance answers the question of whether Xonic, Inc. effectively used its fixed costs. If Xonic produces less Weed-O than normal capacity would allow, an unfavorable variance results. Conversely, if Xonic produces more Weed-O than what is considered normal capacity, a favorable variance results.

The formula for computing the overhead volume variance is as follows.

Illustration 25B-3
Formula for overhead volume variance

Fixed Overhead Rate	×	(Normal Capacity Hours	−	Standard Hours Allowed)	=	Overhead Volume Variance

To illustrate the fixed overhead rate computation, recall that Xonic, Inc. budgeted fixed overhead cost for the year of $52,800 (Illustration 25-6 on page 1152). At normal capacity, 26,400 standard direct labor hours are required. The fixed overhead rate is therefore $2 ($52,800 ÷ 26,400 hours).

Xonic produced 1,000 units of Weed-O in June. The standard hours allowed for the 1,000 gallons produced in June is 2,000 (1,000 gallons × 2 hours). For Xonic, standard direct labor hours for June at normal capacity is 2,200 (26,400 annual hours ÷ 12 months). The computation of the overhead volume variance in this case is as follows.

Illustration 25B-4
Computation of overhead volume variance for Xonic, Inc.

Fixed Overhead Rate	×	(Normal Capacity Hours	−	Standard Hours Allowed)	=	Overhead Volume Variance
$2	×	(2,200	−	2,000)	=	$400 U

In Xonic's case, a $400 unfavorable volume variance results. The volume variance is unfavorable because Xonic produced only 1,000 gallons rather than the normal capacity of 1,100 gallons in the month of June. As a result, it underapplied fixed overhead for that period.

In computing the overhead variances, it is important to remember the following.

1. Standard hours allowed are used in each of the variances.
2. Budgeted costs for the controllable variance are derived from the flexible budget.
3. The controllable variance generally pertains to variable costs.
4. The volume variance pertains solely to fixed costs.

Summary of Study Objective for Appendix 25B

[10] Compute overhead controllable and volume variance. The total overhead variance is generally analyzed through a price variance and a quantity variance. The name usually given to the price variance is the overhead controllable variance. The quantity variance is referred to as the overhead volume variance.

Glossary for Appendix 25B

Overhead controllable variance The difference between actual overhead incurred and overhead budgeted for the standard hours allowed. (p. 1171).

Overhead volume variance The difference between normal capacity hours and standard hours allowed times the fixed overhead rate. (p. 1172).

 Self-Test, Brief Exercises, Exercises, Problem Set A, and many more components are available for practice in *WileyPLUS*

Note: All asterisked Questions, Exercises, and Problems relate to material in the appendices to the chapter.

Self-Test Questions

Answers are on page 1190.

(SO 1) **1.** Standards differ from budgets in that:
  a. budgets but not standards may be used in valuing inventories.
  b. budgets but not standards may be journalized and posted.
  c. budgets are a total amount and standards are a unit amount.
  d. only budgets contribute to management planning and control.

(SO 1) **2.** Standard costs:
  a. are imposed by governmental agencies.
  b. are predetermined unit costs which companies use as measures of performance.
  c. can be used by manufacturing companies but not by service or not-for-profit companies.
  d. All of the above.

(SO 2) **3.** The advantages of standard costs include all of the following *except:*
  a. management by exception may be used.
  b. management planning is facilitated.
  c. they may simplify the costing of inventories.
  d. management must use a static budget.

(SO 3) **4.** Normal standards:
  a. allow for rest periods, machine breakdowns, and setup time.
  b. represent levels of performance under perfect operating conditions.
  c. are rarely used because managers believe they lower workforce morale.
  d. are more likely than ideal standards to result in unethical practices.

(SO 3) **5.** The setting of standards is:
  a. a managerial accounting decision.
  b. a management decision.
  c. a worker decision.
  d. preferably set at the ideal level of performance.

6. Each of the following formulas is correct *except:* (SO 4)
  a. Labor price variance = (Actual hours × Actual rate) − (Actual hours × Standard rate).
  b. Total materials variance = (Actual quantity × Actual price) − (Standard quantity × Standard price).
  c. Materials price variance = (Actual quantity × Actual price) − (Standard quantity × Standard price).
  d. Total labor variance = (Actual hours × Actual rate) − (Standard hours × Standard rate).

7. In producing product AA, 6,300 pounds of direct materi- (SO 4)
als were used at a cost of $1.10 per pound. The standard was 6,000 pounds at $1.00 per pound. The direct materials quantity variance is:
  a. $330 unfavorable.   **c.** $600 unfavorable.
  b. $300 unfavorable.   **d.** $630 unfavorable.

8. In producing product ZZ, 14,800 direct labor hours were (SO 4)
used at a rate of $8.20 per hour. The standard was 15,000 hours at $8.00 per hour. Based on these data, the direct labor:
  a. quantity variance is $1,600 favorable.
  b. quantity variance is $1,600 unfavorable.
  c. price variance is $2,960 favorable.
  d. price variance is $3,000 unfavorable.

9. Which of the following is *correct* about the total overhead (SO 5)
variance?
  a. Budgeted overhead and overhead applied are the same.
  b. Total actual overhead is composed of variable overhead, fixed overhead, and period costs.
  c. Standard hours actually worked are used in computing the variance.
  d. Standard hours allowed for the work done is the measure used in computing the variance.

10. The formula for computing the total overhead variance is: (SO 5)
  a. actual overhead less overhead applied.
  b. overhead budgeted less overhead applied.
  c. actual overhead less overhead budgeted.
  d. No correct answer given.

(SO 6) **11.** Which of the following is *incorrect* about variance reports?
  a. They facilitate "management by exception."
  b. They should only be sent to the top level of management.
  c. They should be prepared as soon as possible.
  d. They may vary in form, content, and frequency among companies.

(SO 6) **12.** In using variance reports to evaluate cost control, management normally looks into:
  a. all variances.
  b. favorable variances only.
  c. unfavorable variances only.
  d. both favorable and unfavorable variances that exceed a predetermined quantitative measure such as a percentage or dollar amount.

(SO 7) **13.** Generally accepted accounting principles allow a company to:
  a. report inventory at standard cost but cost of goods sold must be reported at actual cost.
  b. report cost of goods sold at standard cost but inventory must be reported at actual cost.
  c. report inventory and cost of goods sold at standard cost as long as there are no significant differences between actual and standard cost.
  d. report inventory and cost of goods sold only at actual costs; standard costing is never permitted.

(SO 8) **14.** Which of the following would *not* be an objective used in the customer perspective of the balanced scorecard approach?
  a. Percentage of customers who would recommend product to a friend.
  b. Customer retention.
  c. Brand recognition.
  d. Earnings per share.

(SO 9) ***15.** Which of the following is *incorrect* about a standard cost accounting system?
  a. It is applicable to job order costing.
  b. It is applicable to process costing.
  c. It reports only favorable variances.
  d. It keeps separate accounts for each variance.

(SO 10) ***16.** The formula to compute the overhead volume variance is:
  a. Fixed overhead rate × (Standard hours − Actual hours).
  b. Fixed overhead rate × (Normal capacity hours − Actual hours).
  c. Fixed overhead rate × (Normal capacity hours − Standard hours allowed).
  d. (Variable overhead rate + Fixed overhead rate) × (Normal capacity hours − Standard hours allowed).

Go to the book's companion website, **www.wiley.com/college/weygandt**, for additional Self-Test Questions.

 The Navigator

Questions

1. (a) "Standard costs are the expected total cost of completing a job." Is this correct? Explain.
  (b) "A standard imposed by a governmental agency is known as a regulation." Do you agree? Explain.

2. (a) Explain the similarities and differences between standards and budgets.
  (b) Contrast the accounting for standards and budgets.

3. Standard costs facilitate management planning. What are the other advantages of standard costs?

4. Contrast the roles of the management accountant and management in setting standard costs.

5. Distinguish between an ideal standard and a normal standard.

6. What factors should be considered in setting (a) the direct materials price standard and (b) the direct materials quantity standard?

7. "The objective in setting the direct labor quantity standard is to determine the aggregate time required to make one unit of product." Do you agree? What allowances should be made in setting this standard?

8. How is the predetermined overhead rate determined when standard costs are used?

9. What is the difference between a favorable cost variance and an unfavorable cost variance?

10. In each of the following formulas, supply the words that should be inserted for each number in parentheses.
  (a) (Actual quantity × (1)) − (Standard quantity × (2)) = Total materials variance
  (b) ((3) × Actual price) − (Actual quantity × (4)) = Materials price variance

  (c) (Actual quantity × (5)) − ((6) × Standard price) = Materials quantity variance

11. In the direct labor variance matrix, there are three factors: (1) Actual hours × Actual rate, (2) Actual hours × Standard rate, and (3) Standard hours × Standard rate. Using the numbers, indicate the formulas for each of the direct labor variances.

12. Nash Company's standard predetermined overhead rate is $8 per direct labor hour. For the month of June, 26,000 actual hours were worked, and 27,000 standard hours were allowed. Normal capacity hours were 28,000. How much overhead was applied?

13. How often should variances be reported to management? What principle may be used with variance reports?

14. What circumstances may cause the purchasing department to be responsible for both an unfavorable materials price variance and an unfavorable materials quantity variance?

15. What are the four perspectives used in the balanced scorecard? Discuss the nature of each, and how the perspectives are linked.

16. Ron Ely says that the balanced scorecard was created to replace financial measures as the primary mechanism for performance evaluation. He says that it uses only nonfinancial measures. Is this true?

17. What are some examples of nonfinancial measures used by companies to evaluate performance?

18. (a) How are variances reported in income statements prepared for management? **(b)** May standard costs be used in preparing financial statements for stockholders? Explain.

*19. (a) Explain the basic features of a standard cost accounting system. (b) What type of balance will exist in the variance account when (1) the materials price variance is unfavorable and (2) the labor quantity variance is favorable?

*20. If the $8 per hour overhead rate in question 12 includes $5 variable, and actual overhead costs were $218,000, what is the overhead controllable variance for June? The normal capacity hours were 28,000. Is the variance favorable or unfavorable?

*21. What is the purpose of computing the overhead volume variance? What is the basic formula for this variance?

*22. Rosie Perez does not understand why the overhead volume variance indicates that fixed overhead costs are under- or overapplied. Clarify this matter for Rosie.

*23. Rick Schroeder is attempting to outline the important points about overhead variances on a class examination. List four points that Rick should include in his outline.

Brief Exercises

BE25-1 Tijuana Company uses both standards and budgets. For the year, estimated production of Product X is 500,000 units. Total estimated cost for materials and labor are $1,200,000 and $1,600,000. Compute the estimates for (a) a standard cost and (b) a budgeted cost.

Distinguish between a standard and a budget.
(SO 1)

BE25-2 Juneau Company accumulates the following data concerning raw materials in making one gallon of finished product: (1) Price—net purchase price $2.20, freight-in $0.20, and receiving and handling $0.10. (2) Quantity—required materials 2.6 pounds, allowance for waste and spoilage 0.4 pounds. Compute the following.

Set direct materials standard.
(SO 3)

(a) Standard direct materials price per gallon.
(b) Standard direct materials quantity per gallon.
(c) Total standard materials cost per gallon.

BE25-3 Labor data for making one gallon of finished product in Juneau Company are as follows: (1) Price—hourly wage rate $12.00, payroll taxes $0.80, and fringe benefits $1.20. (2) Quantity—actual production time 1.2 hours, rest periods and clean up 0.25 hours, and setup and downtime 0.15 hours. Compute the following.

Set direct labor standard.
(SO 3)

(a) Standard direct labor rate per hour.
(b) Standard direct labor hours per gallon.
(c) Standard labor cost per gallon.

BE25-4 Brand Company's standard materials cost per unit of output is $10 (2 pounds × $5). During July, the company purchases and uses 3,200 pounds of materials costing $16,160 in making 1,500 units of finished product. Compute the total, price, and quantity materials variances.

Compute direct materials variances.
(SO 4)

BE25-5 Mersaw Company's standard labor cost per unit of output is $20 (2 hours × $10 per hour). During August, the company incurs 2,100 hours of direct labor at an hourly cost of $10.50 per hour in making 1,000 units of finished product. Compute the total, price, and quantity labor variances.

Compute direct labor variances.
(SO 4)

BE25-6 In October, McEnroe Company reports 21,000 actual direct labor hours, and it incurs $115,000 of manufacturing overhead costs. Standard hours allowed for the work done is 20,000 hours. The predetermined overhead rate is $6 per direct labor hour. Compute the total overhead variance.

Compute total overhead variance.
(SO 5)

BE25-7 The four perspectives in the balanced scorecard are (1) financial, (2) customer, (3) internal process, and (4) learning and growth. Match each of the following objectives with the perspective it is most likely associated with: (a) Plant capacity utilization. (b) Employee work days missed due to injury. (c) Return on assets. (d) Brand recognition.

Match balanced scorecard perspectives.
(SO 8)

*BE25-8** Journalize the following transactions for Bekin Manufacturing.

Journalize materials variances.
(SO 9)

(a) Purchased 6,000 units of raw materials on account for $11,100. The standard cost was $12,000.
(b) Issued 5,500 units of raw materials for production. The standard units were 5,800.

*BE25-9** Journalize the following transactions for Royer Manufacturing.

Journalize labor variances.
(SO 9)

(a) Incurred direct labor costs of $24,000 for 3,000 hours. The standard labor cost was $25,200.
(b) Assigned 3,000 direct labor hours costing $24,000 to production. Standard hours were 3,100.

*BE25-10** Some overhead data for McEnroe Company are given in BE25-6. In addition, the flexible manufacturing overhead budget shows that budgeted costs are $4 variable per direct labor hour and $50,000 fixed. Compute the overhead controllable variance.

Compute the overhead controllable variance.
(SO 10)

*BE25-11** Using the data in BE25-6 and BE25-10, compute the overhead volume variance. Normal capacity was 25,000 direct labor hours.

Compute overhead volume variance.
(SO 10)

Do it! Review

Compute standard cost.
(SO 3)

Do it! 25-1   Saito Company accumulated the following standard cost data concerning product I-Tal.

Materials per unit: 2 pounds at $5 per pound
Labor per unit: 0.2 hours at $14 per hour
Manufacturing overhead: Predetermined rate is 125% of direct labor cost

Compute the standard cost of one unit of product I-Tal.

Compute materials variance.
(SO 4)

Do it! 25-2   The standard cost of product 999 includes 2 units of direct materials at $6.00 per unit. During August, the company bought 29,000 units of materials at $6.20 and used those materials to produce 15,000 units. Compute the total, price, and quantity variances for materials.

Compute labor and manufacturing overhead variances.
(SO 4, 5)

Do it! 25-3   The standard cost of product 2525 includes 2 hours of direct labor at $14.00 per hour. The predetermined overhead rate is $21.00 per direct labor hour. During July, the company incurred 4,100 hours of direct labor at an average rate of $14.40 per hour and $81,300 of manufacturing overhead costs. It produced 2,000 units.

(a) Compute the total, price, and quantity variances for labor. (b) Compute the total overhead variance.

Match balanced scorecard perspectives and their objectives.
(SO 8)

Do it! 25-4   Indicate which of the four perspectives in the balanced scorecard is most likely associated with the objectives that follow.
1. Ethics violations.
2. Credit rating.
3. Customer retention.
4. Stockouts.
5. Reportable accidents.
6. Brand recognition.

Exercises

Compute budget and standard.
(SO 1, 2, 3)

E25-1   Horowitz Company is planning to produce 2,000 units of product in 2012. Each unit requires 3 pounds of materials at $6 per pound and a half-hour of labor at $14 per hour. The overhead rate is 70% of direct labor.

Instructions
(a) Compute the budgeted amounts for 2012 for direct materials to be used, direct labor, and applied overhead.
(b) Compute the standard cost of one unit of product.
(c) What are the potential advantages to a corporation of using standard costs?

Compute standard materials costs.
(SO 3)

E25-2   Romy Schneider manufactures and sells homemade wine, and he wants to develop a standard cost per gallon. The following are required for production of a 50-gallon batch.

    3,000 ounces of grape concentrate at $0.04 per ounce
    54 pounds of granulated sugar at $0.35 per pound
    60 lemons at $0.60 each
    50 yeast tablets at $0.25 each
    50 nutrient tablets at $0.20 each
    2,500 ounces of water at $0.004 per ounce

Romy estimates that 4% of the grape concentrate is wasted, 10% of the sugar is lost, and 20% of the lemons cannot be used.

Instructions
Compute the standard cost of the ingredients for one gallon of wine. (Carry computations to two decimal places.)

E25-3 Sergey Company has gathered the information shown below about its product.

Direct materials: Each unit of product contains 4.5 pounds of materials. The average waste and spoilage per unit produced under normal conditions is 0.5 pounds. Materials cost $4 per pound, but Sergey always takes the 2% cash discount all of its suppliers offer. Freight costs average $0.25 per pound.

Direct labor: Each unit requires 2 hours of labor. Setup, cleanup, and downtime average 0.2 hours per unit. The average hourly pay rate of Sergey's employees is $12. Payroll taxes and fringe benefits are an additional $3 per hour.

Manufacturing overhead: Overhead is applied at a rate of $6 per direct labor hour.

Compute standard cost per unit.

(SO 3)

Instructions
Compute Sergey's total standard cost per unit.

E25-4 Rush Repair Services, Inc. is trying to establish the standard labor cost of a typical oil change. The following data have been collected from time and motion studies conducted over the past month.

Compute labor quantity variance.

(SO 3, 4)

Actual time spent on the oil change	1.0 hour
Hourly wage rate	$10
Payroll taxes	10% of wage rate
Setup and downtime	10% of actual labor time
Cleanup and rest periods	30% of actual labor time
Fringe benefits	25% of wage rate

Instructions
(a) Determine the standard direct labor hours per oil change.
(b) Determine the standard direct labor hourly rate.
(c) Determine the standard direct labor cost per oil change.
(d) If an oil change took 1.5 hours at the standard hourly rate, what was the direct labor quantity variance?

E25-5 The standard cost of Product B manufactured by Sancho Company includes three units of direct materials at $5.00 per unit. During June, 28,000 units of direct materials are purchased at a cost of $4.70 per unit, and 28,000 units of direct materials are used to produce 9,000 units of Product B.

Compute materials price and quantity variances.

(SO 4)

Instructions
(a) Compute the total materials variance and the price and quantity variances.
(b) Repeat (a), assuming the purchase price is $5.20 and the quantity purchased and used is 26,200 units.

E25-6 Cherie Company's standard labor cost of producing one unit of Product DD is 4 hours at the rate of $12.00 per hour. During August, 40,800 hours of labor are incurred at a cost of $12.10 per hour to produce 10,000 units of Product DD.

Compute labor price and quantity variances.

(SO 4)

Instructions
(a) Compute the total labor variance.
(b) Compute the labor price and quantity variances.
(c) Repeat (b), assuming the standard is 4.2 hours of direct labor at $12.25 per hour.

E25-7 Injin Inc., which produces a single product, has prepared the following standard cost sheet for one unit of the product.

Compute materials and labor variances.

(SO 4)

Direct materials (8 pounds at $2.50 per pound)	$20
Direct labor (3 hours at $12.00 per hour)	$36

During the month of April, the company manufactures 230 units and incurs the following actual costs.

Direct materials purchased and used (1,900 pounds)	$4,940
Direct labor (700 hours)	$8,120

Instructions
Compute the total, price, and quantity variances for materials and labor.

Compute the materials and labor variances and list reasons for unfavorable variances.

(SO 4)

E25-8   The direct materials and direct labor data shown below pertain to the operations of Viet Manufacturing Company for the month of August.

Costs		Quantities	
Actual labor rate	$13 per hour	Actual hours incurred and used	4,200 hours
Actual materials price	$128 per ton	Actual quantity of materials purchased and used	1,225 tons
Standard labor rate	$12 per hour	Standard hours used	4,300 hours
Standard materials price	$130 per ton	Standard quantity of materials used	1,200 tons

Instructions

(a) Compute the total, price, and quantity variances for materials and labor.

(b) ◀━━━━▶ Provide two possible explanations for each of the unfavorable variances calculated above, and suggest where responsibility for the unfavorable result might be placed.

Prepare a variance report for direct labor.

(SO 4, 6)

E25-9   During March 2012, Tyson Tool & Die Company worked on four jobs. A review of direct labor costs reveals the following summary data.

Job Number	Actual		Standard		Total Variance
	Hours	Costs	Hours	Costs	
A257	220	$4,400	225	$4,500	$ 100 F
A258	450	9,900	430	8,600	1,300 U
A259	300	6,150	300	6,000	150 U
A260	115	2,070	110	2,200	130 F
Total variance					$1,220 U

Analysis reveals that Job A257 was a repeat job. Job A258 was a rush order that required overtime work at premium rates of pay. Job A259 required a more experienced replacement worker on one shift. Work on Job A260 was done for one day by a new trainee when a regular worker was absent.

Instructions

Prepare a report for the plant supervisor on direct labor cost variances for March. The report should have columns for (1) Job No., (2) Actual Hours, (3) Standard Hours, (4) Quantity Variance, (5) Actual Rate, (6) Standard Rate, (7) Price Variance, and (8) Explanation.

Compute overhead variance.

(SO 5)

E25-10   Manufacturing overhead data for the production of Product H by Garrity Company are as follows.

Overhead incurred for 52,000 actual direct labor hours worked	$213,000
Overhead rate (variable $3; fixed $1) at normal capacity of 54,000 direct labor hours	$4
Standard hours allowed for work done	51,000

Instructions

Compute the total overhead variance.

Compute overhead variance.

(SO 5)

E25-11   Bob Burgie Company produces one product, a putter called GO-Putter. Burgie uses a standard cost system and determines that it should take one hour of direct labor to produce one GO-Putter. The normal production capacity for this putter is 100,000 units per year. The total budgeted overhead at normal capacity is $800,000 comprised of $200,000 of variable costs and $600,000 of fixed costs. Burgie applies overhead on the basis of direct labor hours.

During the current year, Burgie produced 90,000 putters, worked 94,000 direct labor hours, and incurred variable overhead costs of $186,000 and fixed overhead costs of $600,000.

Instructions

(a) Compute the predetermined variable overhead rate and the predetermined fixed overhead rate.

(b) Compute the applied overhead for Burgie for the year.

(c) Compute the total overhead variance.

E25-12 Rathman Company purchased (at a cost of $10,900) and used 2,300 pounds of materials during May. Rathman's standard cost of materials per unit produced is based on 2 pounds per unit at a cost of $5 per pound. Production in May was 1,070 units.

Compute variances for materials.
(SO 4)

Instructions
(a) Compute the total, price, and quantity variances for materials.
(b) Assume Rathman also had an unfavorable labor quantity variance. What is a possible scenario that would provide one cause for the variances computed in (a) and the unfavorable labor quantity variance?

E25-13 Tovi Landscaping plants grass seed as the basic landscaping for business campuses. During a recent month, the company worked on three projects (Bose, Larkin, and Torres). The company is interested in controlling the materials costs, namely the grass seed, for these plantings projects.

Prepare a variance report.
(SO 4, 6)

In order to provide management with useful cost control information, the company uses standard costs and prepares monthly variance reports. Analysis reveals that the purchasing agent mistakenly purchased poor-quality seed for the Bose project. The Larkin project, however, received higher-than-standard-quality seed that was on sale. The Torres project received standard-quality seed; however, the price had increased and a new employee was used to spread the seed.

Shown below are quantity and cost data for each project.

Project	Actual Quantity	Actual Costs	Standard Quantity	Standard Costs	Total Variance
Bose	500 lbs.	$1,175	460 lbs.	$1,150	$ 25 U
Larkin	400	960	410	1,025	65 F
Torres	500	1,300	480	1,200	100 U
Total variance					$ 60 U

Instructions
(a) Prepare a variance report for the purchasing department with the following columns: (1) Project, (2) Actual pounds purchased, (3) Actual price, (4) Standard price, (5) Price variance, and (6) Explanation.
(b) Prepare a variance report for the production department with the following columns: (1) Project, (2) Actual pounds, (3) Standard pounds, (4) Standard price, (5) Quantity variance, and (6) Explanation.

E25-14 Figueroa Corporation prepared the following variance report.

Complete variance report.
(SO 6)

FIGUEROA CORPORATION
Variance Report—Purchasing Department
For Week Ended January 9, 2013

Type of Materials	Quantity Purchased	Actual Price	Standard Price	Price Variance	Explanation
Rogue11	? lbs.	$5.20	$5.00	$5,200 ?	Price increase
Storm17	7,000 oz.	?	3.25	1,050 U	Rush order
Beast29	22,000 units	0.45	?	440 F	Bought larger quantity

Instructions
Fill in the appropriate amounts or letters for the question marks in the report.

E25-15 Phap Company uses a standard cost accounting system. During January, the company reported the following manufacturing variances.

Prepare income statement for management.
(SO 7)

Materials price variance	$1,250 U	Labor quantity variance	$725 U
Materials quantity variance	700 F	Overhead variance	800 U
Labor price variance	525 U		

In addition, 8,000 units of product were sold at $8.00 per unit. Each unit sold had a standard cost of $6.00. Selling and administrative expenses were $6,000 for the month.

Instructions
Prepare an income statement for management for the month ended January 31, 2012.

Identify performance evaluation terminology.

(SO 3, 8)

E25-16 The following is a list of terms related to performance evaluation.

(1) Balanced scorecard
(2) Variance
(3) Learning and growth perspective
(4) Nonfinancial measures
(5) Customer perspective
(6) Internal process perspective
(7) Ideal standards
(8) Normal standards

Instructions

Match each of the following descriptions with one of the terms above.

(a) The difference between total actual costs and total standard costs.

(b) An efficient level of performance that is attainable under expected operating conditions.

(c) An approach that incorporates financial and nonfinancial measures in an integrated system that links performance measurement and a company's strategic goals.

(d) A viewpoint employed in the balanced scorecard to evaluate how well a company develops and retains its employees.

(e) An evaluation tool that is not based on dollars.

(f) A viewpoint employed in the balanced scorecard to evaluate the company from the perspective of those people who buy and use its products or services.

(g) An optimum level of performance under perfect operating conditions.

(h) A viewpoint employed in the balanced scorecard to evaluate the efficiency and effectiveness of the company's value chain.

Journalize entries in a standard cost accounting system.

(SO 9)

*E25-17 Leab Company installed a standard cost system on January 1. Selected transactions for the month of January are as follows.

1. Purchased 18,000 units of raw materials on account at a cost of $4.50 per unit. Standard cost was $4.30 per unit.
2. Issued 18,000 units of raw materials for jobs that required 17,600 standard units of raw materials.
3. Incurred 15,200 actual hours of direct labor at an actual rate of $4.80 per hour. The standard rate is $5.50 per hour. (Credit Wages Payable.)
4. Performed 15,200 hours of direct labor on jobs when standard hours were 15,400.
5. Applied overhead to jobs at the rate of 100% of direct labor cost for standard hours allowed.

Instructions

Journalize the January transactions.

Answer questions concerning missing entries and balances.

(SO 4, 5, 9)

*E25-18 Tsar Company uses a standard cost accounting system. Some of the ledger accounts have been destroyed in a fire. The controller asks your help in reconstructing some missing entries and balances.

Instructions

Answer the following questions.

(a) Materials Price Variance shows a $2,000 favorable balance. Accounts Payable shows $128,000 of raw materials purchases. What was the amount debited to Raw Materials Inventory for raw materials purchased?

(b) Materials Quantity Variance shows a $3,000 unfavorable balance. Raw Materials Inventory shows a zero balance. What was the amount debited to Work in Process Inventory for direct materials used?

(c) Labor Price Variance shows a $1,500 unfavorable balance. Factory Labor shows a debit of $140,000 for wages incurred. What was the amount credited to Wages Payable?

(d) Factory Labor shows a credit of $140,000 for direct labor used. Labor Quantity Variance shows a $900 unfavorable balance. What was the amount debited to Work in Process for direct labor used?

(e) Overhead applied to Work in Process totaled $165,000. If the total overhead variance was $1,200 unfavorable, what was the amount of overhead costs debited to Manufacturing Overhead?

Journalize entries for materials and labor variances.

(SO 9)

*E25-19 Data for Injin Inc. are given in E25-7.

Instructions

Journalize the entries to record the materials and labor variances.

Compute manufacturing overhead variances and interpret findings.

(SO 10)

*E25-20 The information shown on page 1181 was taken from the annual manufacturing overhead cost budget of Jamaica Company.

Variable manufacturing overhead costs	$33,000
Fixed manufacturing overhead costs	$19,800
Normal production level in labor hours	16,500
Normal production level in units	4,125
Standard labor hours per unit	4

During the year, 4,000 units were produced, 16,100 hours were worked, and the actual manufacturing overhead was $54,000. Actual fixed manufacturing overhead costs equaled budgeted fixed manufacturing overhead costs. Overhead is applied on the basis of direct labor hours.

Instructions
(a) Compute the total, fixed, and variable predetermined manufacturing overhead rates.
(b) Compute the total, controllable, and volume overhead variances.
(c) ◀━━━━━━ Briefly interpret the overhead controllable and volume variances computed in (b).

*E25-21 The loan department of City Bank uses standard costs to determine the overhead cost of processing loan applications. During the current month a fire occurred, and the accounting records for the department were mostly destroyed. The following data were salvaged from the ashes.

Compute overhead variances.
(SO 10)

Standard variable overhead rate per hour	$9
Standard hours per application	2
Standard hours allowed	2,000
Standard fixed overhead rate per hour	$6
Actual fixed overhead cost	$13,200
Variable overhead budget based on standard hours allowed	$18,000
Fixed overhead budget	$13,200
Overhead controllable variance	$ 1,500 U

Instructions
(a) Determine the following.
  (1) Total actual overhead cost.
  (2) Actual variable overhead cost.
  (3) Variable overhead cost applied.
  (4) Fixed overhead cost applied.
  (5) Overhead volume variance.
(b) Determine how many loans were processed.

*E25-22 Liam Company's annual overhead rate was based on estimates of $200,000 for overhead costs and 20,000 direct labor hours. Liam's standards allow 2 hours of direct labor per unit produced. Production in May was 900 units, and actual overhead incurred in May was $18,800. The overhead budgeted for 1,800 standard direct labor hours is $17,600 ($5,000 fixed and $12,600 variable).

Compute variances.
(SO 10)

Instructions
(a) Compute the total, controllable, and volume variances for overhead.
(b) What are possible causes of the variances computed in part (a)?

Exercises: Set B

Visit the book's companion website, at **www.wiley.com/college/weygandt**, and choose the Student Companion site to access Exercise Set B.

Problems: Set A

P25-1A Mifflin Corporation manufactures a single product. The standard cost per unit of product is shown below.

Compute variances.
(SO 4, 5)

Direct materials—1 pound plastic at $7.00 per pound	$ 7.00
Direct labor—1.5 hours at $12.00 per hour	18.00
Variable manufacturing overhead	11.25
Fixed manufacturing overhead	3.75
Total standard cost per unit	$40.00

The predetermined manufacturing overhead rate is $10 per direct labor hour ($15.00 ÷ 1.5). It was computed from a master manufacturing overhead budget based on normal production of 7,500 direct labor hours (5,000 units) for the month. The master budget showed total variable costs of $56,250 ($7.50 per hour) and total fixed overhead costs of $18,750 ($2.50 per hour). Actual costs for October in producing 4,900 units were as follows.

Direct materials (5,100 pounds)	$ 37,230
Direct labor (7,000 hours)	87,500
Variable overhead	56,170
Fixed overhead	19,680
Total manufacturing costs	$200,580

The purchasing department buys the quantities of raw materials that are expected to be used in production each month. Raw materials inventories, therefore, can be ignored.

Instructions
(a) Compute all of the materials and labor variances.
(b) Compute the total overhead variance.

Compute variances, and prepare income statement.
(SO 4, 5, 7)

P25-2A Simon Manufacturing Corporation accumulates the following data relative to jobs started and finished during the month of June 2012.

Costs and Production Data	Actual	Standard
Raw materials unit cost	$2.25	$2.00
Raw materials units used	10,600	10,000
Direct labor payroll	$122,400	$120,000
Direct labor hours worked	14,400	15,000
Manufacturing overhead incurred	$184,500	
Manufacturing overhead applied		$189,000
Machine hours expected to be used at normal capacity		42,500
Budgeted fixed overhead for June		$51,000
Variable overhead rate per hour		$3.00
Fixed overhead rate per hour		$1.20

Overhead is applied on the basis of standard machine hours. Three hours of machine time are required for each direct labor hour. The jobs were sold for $400,000. Selling and administrative expenses were $40,000. Assume that the amount of raw materials purchased equaled the amount used.

Instructions
(a) Compute all of the variances for (1) direct materials and (2) direct labor.
(b) Compute the total overhead variance.
(c) Prepare an income statement for management. Ignore income taxes.

Compute and identify significant variances.
(SO 4, 5, 6)

P25-3A Panache Clothiers is a small company that manufactures tall-men's suits. The company has used a standard cost accounting system. In May 2012, 11,200 suits were produced. The following standard and actual cost data applied to the month of May when normal capacity was 14,000 direct labor hours. All materials purchased were used.

Cost Element	Standard (per unit)	Actual
Direct materials	8 yards at $4.30 per yard	$371,050 for 90,500 yards ($4.10 per yard)
Direct labor	1.2 hours at $13.50 per hour	$201,630 for 14,300 hours ($14.10 per hour)
Overhead	1.2 hours at $6.00 per hour (fixed $3.50; variable $2.50)	$49,000 fixed overhead $37,000 variable overhead

Overhead is applied on the basis of direct labor hours. At normal capacity, budgeted fixed overhead costs were $49,000, and budgeted variable overhead was $35,000.

Instructions
(a) Compute the total, price, and quantity variances for (1) materials and (2) labor.
(b) Compute the total overhead variance.

(c) Which of the materials and labor variances should be investigated if management considers a variance of more than 4% from standard to be significant?

P25-4A Fuentes Manufacturing Company uses a standard cost accounting system. In 2012, the company produced 28,000 units. Each unit took several pounds of direct materials and 1½ standard hours of direct labor at a standard hourly rate of $12.00. Normal capacity was 50,000 direct labor hours. During the year, 131,000 pounds of raw materials were purchased at $0.92 per pound. All materials purchased were used during the year.

Answer questions about variances.
(SO 4, 5)

Instructions
(a) If the materials price variance was $2,620 favorable, what was the standard materials price per pound?
(b) If the materials quantity variance was $4,700 unfavorable, what was the standard materials quantity per unit?
(c) What were the standard hours allowed for the units produced?
(d) If the labor quantity variance was $7,200 unfavorable, what were the actual direct labor hours worked?
(e) If the labor price variance was $10,650 favorable, what was the actual rate per hour?
(f) If total budgeted manufacturing overhead was $350,000 at normal capacity, what was the predetermined overhead rate?
(g) What was the standard cost per unit of product?
(h) How much overhead was applied to production during the year?
(i) Using one or more answers above, what were the total costs assigned to work in process?

P25-5A Agri Labs, Inc. provides mad cow disease testing for both state and federal governmental agricultural agencies. Because the company's customers are governmental agencies, prices are strictly regulated. Therefore, Agri Labs must constantly monitor and control its testing costs. Shown below are the standard costs for a typical test.

Compute variances, prepare an income statement, and explain unfavorable variances.
(SO 4, 5, 7)

Direct materials (2 test tubes @ $1.50 per tube)	$ 3
Direct labor (1 hour @ $25 per hour)	25
Variable overhead (1 hour @ $5 per hour)	5
Fixed overhead (1 hour @ $10 per hour)	10
Total standard cost per test	$43

The lab does not maintain an inventory of test tubes. Therefore, the tubes purchased each month are used that month. Actual activity for the month of November 2012, when 1,500 tests were conducted, resulted in the following:

Direct materials (3,050 test tubes)	$ 4,270
Direct labor (1,600 hours)	36,800
Variable overhead	7,400
Fixed overhead	14,000

Monthly budgeted fixed overhead is $14,000. Revenues for the month were $75,000, and selling and administrative expenses were $4,000.

Instructions
(a) Compute the price and quantity variances for direct materials and direct labor.
(b) Compute the total overhead variance.
(c) Prepare an income statement for management.
(d) Provide possible explanations for each unfavorable variance.

*P25-6A Papillion Corporation uses standard costs with its job order cost accounting system. In January, an order (Job No. 12) for 1,900 units of Product B was received. The standard cost of one unit of Product B is as follows.

Journalize and post standard cost entries, and prepare income statement.
(SO 4, 5, 7, 9)

Direct materials	3 pounds at $1.00 per pound	$ 3.00
Direct labor	1 hour at $8.00 per hour	8.00
Overhead	2 hours (variable $4.00 per machine hour; fixed $2.25 per machine hour)	12.50
Standard cost per unit		$23.50

Normal capacity for the month was 4,200 machine hours. During January, the following transactions applicable to Job No. 12 occurred.

1. Purchased 6,250 pounds of raw materials on account at $1.06 per pound.
2. Requisitioned 6,250 pounds of raw materials for Job No. 12.
3. Incurred 2,100 hours of direct labor at a rate of $7.75 per hour.
4. Worked 2,100 hours of direct labor on Job No. 12.
5. Incurred manufacturing overhead on account $25,800.
6. Applied overhead to Job No. 12 on basis of standard machine hours allowed.
7. Completed Job No. 12.
8. Billed customer for Job No. 12 at a selling price of $70,000.

Instructions
(a) Journalize the transactions.
(b) Post to the job order cost accounts.
(c) Prepare the entry to recognize the total overhead variance.
(d) Prepare the January 2012 income statement for management. Assume selling and administrative expenses were $2,000.

Compute overhead controllable and volume variances.
(SO 10)

*P25-7A   Using the information in P25-1A, compute the overhead controllable variance and the overhead volume variance.

Compute overhead controllable and volume variances.
(SO 10)

*P25-8A   Using the information in P25-2A, compute the overhead controllable variance and the overhead volume variance.

Compute overhead controllable and volume variances.
(SO 10)

*P25-9A   Using the information in P25-3A, compute the overhead controllable variance and the overhead volume variance.

Compute overhead controllable and volume variances.
(SO 10)

*P25-10A   Using the information in P25-5A, compute the overhead controllable variance and the overhead volume variance.

Problems: Set B

Compute variances.
(SO 4, 5)

P25-1B   Lopez Corporation manufactures a single product. The standard cost per unit of product is as follows.

Direct materials—2 pounds of plastic at $5 per pound	$10
Direct labor—2 hours at $12 per hour	24
Variable manufacturing overhead	8
Fixed manufacturing overhead	6
Total standard cost per unit	$48

The master manufacturing overhead budget for the month based on normal productive capacity of 20,000 direct labor hours (10,000 units) shows total variable costs of $80,000 ($4 per labor hour) and total fixed costs of $60,000 ($3 per labor hour). Normal productive capacity is 20,000 direct labor hours. Overhead is applied on the basis of direct labor hours. Actual costs for November in producing 9,700 units were as follows.

Direct materials (20,000 pounds)	$ 98,000
Direct labor (19,600 hours)	239,120
Variable overhead	79,100
Fixed overhead	59,000
Total manufacturing costs	$475,220

The purchasing department normally buys the quantities of raw materials that are expected to be used in production each month. Raw materials inventories, therefore, can be ignored.

Instructions
(a) Compute all of the materials and labor variances.
(b) Compute the total overhead variance.

P25-2B Lopes Manufacturing Company uses a standard cost accounting system to account for the manufacture of exhaust fans. In July 2012, it accumulates the following data relative to 1,800 units started and finished.

Compute variances, and prepare income statement.
(SO 4, 5, 7)

Cost and Production Data	Actual	Standard
Raw materials		
Units purchased	21,000	
Units used	21,000	22,000
Unit cost	$3.40	$3.00
Direct labor		
Hours worked	3,450	3,600
Hourly rate	$11.80	$12.50
Manufacturing overhead		
Incurred	$101,500	
Applied		$108,000

Manufacturing overhead was applied on the basis of direct labor hours. Normal capacity for the month was 3,400 direct labor hours. At normal capacity, budgeted overhead costs were $20 per labor hour variable and $10 per labor hour fixed. Total budgeted fixed overhead costs were $34,000.

Jobs finished during the month were sold for $280,000. Selling and administrative expenses were $25,000.

Instructions
(a) Compute all of the variances for (1) direct materials and (2) direct labor.
(b) Compute the total overhead variance.
(c) Prepare an income statement for management. Ignore income taxes.

P25-3B Classy Clothiers manufactures women's business suits. The company uses a standard cost accounting system. In March 2012, 15,700 suits were made. The following standard and actual cost data applied to the month of March when normal capacity was 20,000 direct labor hours. All materials purchased were used in production.

Compute and identify significant variances.
(SO 4, 5, 6)

Cost Element	Standard (per unit)	Actual
Direct materials	5 yards at $6.80 per yard	$547,200 for 76,000 yards ($7.20 per yard)
Direct labor	1.0 hours at $11.50 per hour	$166,880 for 14,900 hours ($11.20 per hour)
Overhead	1.0 hours at $9.30 per hour (fixed $6.30; variable $3.00)	$120,000 fixed overhead $49,000 variable overhead

Overhead is applied on the basis of direct labor hours. At normal capacity, budgeted fixed overhead costs were $126,000, and budgeted variable overhead costs were $60,000.

Instructions
(a) Compute the total, price, and quantity variances for (1) materials and (2) labor.
(b) Compute the total overhead variance.
(c) ◄▬▬▬▬ Which of the materials and labor variances should be investigated if management considers a variance of more than 5% from standard to be significant?

P25-4B Quintana Manufacturing Company uses a standard cost accounting system. In 2012, 50,000 units were produced. Each unit took several pounds of direct materials and 2 standard hours of direct labor at a standard hourly rate of $12.00. Normal capacity was 96,000 direct labor hours. During the year, 200,000 pounds of raw materials were purchased at $1.00 per pound. All materials purchased were used during the year.

Answer questions about variances.
(SO 4, 5)

Instructions
(a) If the materials price variance was $8,000 unfavorable, what was the standard materials price per pound?
(b) If the materials quantity variance was $24,000 favorable, what was the standard materials quantity per unit?
(c) What were the standard hours allowed for the units produced?
(d) If the labor quantity variance was $10,800 unfavorable, what were the actual direct labor hours worked?

(e) If the labor price variance was $25,225 favorable, what was the actual rate per hour?

(f) If total budgeted manufacturing overhead was $792,000 at normal capacity, what was the predetermined overhead rate per direct labor hour?

(g) What was the standard cost per unit of product?

(h) How much overhead was applied to production during the year?

(i) Using selected answers above, what were the total costs assigned to work in process?

Compute variances, prepare an income statement, and explain unfavorable variances.

(SO 4, 5, 7)

P25-5B Private Labs performs steroid testing services to high schools, colleges, and universities. Because the company deals solely with educational institutions, the price of each test is strictly regulated. Therefore, the costs incurred must be carefully monitored and controlled. Shown below are the standard costs for a typical test.

Direct materials (1 petri dish @ $2 per dish)	$ 2.00
Direct labor (0.5 hours @ $20 per hour)	10.00
Variable overhead (0.5 hours @ $8 per hour)	4.00
Fixed overhead (0.5 hours @ $4 per hour)	2.00
Total standard cost per test	$18.00

The lab does not maintain an inventory of petri dishes. Therefore, the dishes purchased each month are used that month. Actual activity for the month of May 2012, when 2,500 tests were conducted, resulted in the following.

Direct materials (2,530 dishes)	$ 5,313
Direct labor (1,240 hours)	26,040
Variable overhead	10,100
Fixed overhead	5,700

Monthly budgeted fixed overhead is $6,000. Revenues for the month were $58,000, and selling and administrative expenses were $2,000.

Instructions

(a) Compute the price and quantity variances for direct materials and direct labor.

(b) Compute the total overhead variance.

(c) Prepare an income statement for management.

(d) Provide possible explanations for each unfavorable variance.

Journalize and post standard cost entries, and prepare income statement.

(SO 4, 5, 7, 9)

*P25-6B Uhren Manufacturing Company uses standard costs with its job order cost accounting system. In January, an order (Job No. 84) was received for 5,500 units of Product D. The standard cost of 1 unit of Product D is as follows.

Direct materials—1.4 pounds at $4.00 per pound	$ 5.60
Direct labor—1 hour at $9.00 per hour	9.00
Overhead—1 hour (variable $7.40; fixed $8.00)	15.40
Standard cost per unit	$30.00

Overhead is applied on the basis of direct labor hours. Normal capacity for the month of January was 6,000 direct labor hours. During January, the following transactions applicable to Job No. 84 occurred.

1. Purchased 8,100 pounds of raw materials on account at $3.60 per pound.

2. Requisitioned 8,100 pounds of raw materials for production.

3. Incurred 5,100 hours of direct labor at $9.25 per hour.

4. Worked 5,100 hours of direct labor on Job No. 84.

5. Incurred $87,650 of manufacturing overhead on account.

6. Applied overhead to Job No. 84 on the basis of direct labor hours.

7. Transferred Job No. 84 to finished goods.

8. Billed customer for Job No. 84 at a selling price of $280,000.

Instructions

(a) Journalize the transactions.

(b) Post to the job order cost accounts.

(c) Prepare the entry to recognize the total overhead variance.

(d) Prepare the January 2012 income statement for management. Assume selling and administrative expenses were $61,000.

*P25-7B Using the information in P25-1B, compute the overhead controllable variance and the overhead volume variance.

Compute overhead controllable and volume variances.
(SO 10)

*P25-8B Using the information in P25-2B, compute the overhead controllable variance and the overhead volume variance.

Compute overhead controllable and volume variances.
(SO 10)

*P25-9B Using the information in P25-3B, compute the overhead controllable variance and the overhead volume variance.

Compute overhead controllable and volume variances.
(SO 10)

*P25-10B Using the information in P25-5B, compute the overhead controllable variance and the overhead volume variance.

Compute overhead controllable and volume variances.
(SO 10)

Problems: Set C

Visit the book's companion website, at **www.wiley.com/college/weygandt**, and choose the Student Companion site to access Problem Set C.

Waterways Continuing Problem

(This is a continuation of the Waterways Problem from Chapters 19 through 24.)

WCP25 Waterways Corporation uses very stringent standard costs in evaluating its manufacturing efficiency. These standards are not "ideal" at this point, but management is working toward that as a goal. This problem asks you to calculate and evaluate the company's variances.

*Go to the book's companion website, **www.wiley.com/college/weygandt**, to find the remainder of this problem.*

BROADENING YOUR PERSPECTIVE

Decision Making Across the Organization

BYP25-1 Donel Professionals, a management consulting firm, specializes in strategic planning for financial institutions. Lee Dong and Geri Elton, partners in the firm, are assembling a new strategic planning model for use by clients. The model is designed for use on most personal computers and replaces a rather lengthy manual model currently marketed by the firm. To market the new model, Lee and Geri will need to provide clients with an estimate of the number of labor hours and computer time needed to operate the model. The model is currently being test-marketed at five small financial institutions. These financial institutions are listed below, along with the number of combined computer/labor hours used by each institution to run the model one time.

Financial Institutions	Computer/Labor Hours Required
Midland National	25
First State	45
Financial Federal	40
Pacific America	30
Lakeview National	30
Total	170
Average	34

Any company that purchases the new model will need to purchase user manuals for the system. User manuals will be sold to clients in cases of 20, at a cost of $300 per case. One manual must be used each time the model is run because each manual includes a nonreusable computer-accessed password for operating the system. Also required are specialized computer forms that are sold only by Donel. The specialized forms are sold in packages of 250, at a cost of $50 per package. One application of the model requires the use of 50 forms. This amount includes two forms that are generally wasted in each application due to printer alignment errors. The overall cost of the strategic planning model to clients is $12,000. Most clients will use the model four times annually.

Donel must provide its clients with estimates of ongoing costs incurred in operating the new planning model, and would like to do so in the form of standard costs.

Instructions
With the class divided into groups, answer the following.

(a) What factors should be considered in setting a standard for computer/labor hours?
(b) What alternatives for setting a standard for computer/labor hours might be used?
(c) What standard for computer/labor hours would you select? Justify your answer.
(d) Determine the standard materials cost associated with the user manuals and computer forms for each application of the strategic planning model.

Managerial Analysis

*BYP25-2   Al Ignatenko and Associates is a medium-sized company located near a large metropolitan area in the Midwest. The company manufactures cabinets of mahogany, oak, and other fine woods for use in expensive homes, restaurants, and hotels. Although some of the work is custom, many of the cabinets are a standard size.

One such non-custom model is called Luxury Base Frame. Normal production is 1,000 units. Each unit has a direct labor hour standard of 5 hours. Overhead is applied to production based on standard direct labor hours. During the most recent month, only 900 units were produced; 4,500 direct labor hours were allowed for standard production, but only 4,000 hours were used. Standard and actual overhead costs were as follows.

	Standard (1,000 units)	Actual (900 units)
Indirect materials	$ 12,000	$ 12,300
Indirect labor	43,000	51,000
(Fixed) Manufacturing supervisors salaries	22,000	22,000
(Fixed) Manufacturing office employees salaries	13,000	11,500
(Fixed) Engineering costs	27,000	25,000
Computer costs	10,000	10,000
Electricity	2,500	2,500
(Fixed) Manufacturing building depreciation	8,000	8,000
(Fixed) Machinery depreciation	3,000	3,000
(Fixed) Trucks and forklift depreciation	1,500	1,500
Small tools	700	1,400
(Fixed) Insurance	500	500
(Fixed) Property taxes	300	300
Total	$143,500	$149,000

Instructions
(a) Determine the overhead application rate.
(b) Determine how much overhead was applied to production.
(c) Calculate the controllable overhead variance and the overhead volume variance.
(d) Decide which overhead variances should be investigated.
(e) Discuss causes of the overhead variances. What can management do to improve its performance next month?

Real-World Focus

BYP25-3   Glassmaster Co. is organized as two divisions and one subsidiary. One division focuses on the manufacture of filaments such as fishing line and sewing thread; the other division manufactures antennas and specialty fiberglass products. Its subsidiary manufactures flexible steel wire controls and molded control panels.

The annual report of Glassmaster provides the following information.

| **Glassmaster Company** |
| Management Discussion |

Gross profit margins for the year improved to 20.9% of sales compared to last year's 18.5%. All operations reported improved margins due in large part to improved operating efficiencies as a result of cost reduction measures implemented during the second and third quarters of the fiscal year and increased manufacturing throughout due to higher unit volume sales. Contributing to the improved margins was a favorable materials price variance due to competitive pricing by suppliers as a result of soft demand for petrochemical-based products. This favorable variance is temporary and will begin to reverse itself as stronger worldwide demand for commodity products improves in tandem with the economy. Partially offsetting these positive effects on profit margins were competitive pressures on sales prices of certain product lines. The company responded with pricing strategies designed to maintain and/or increase market share.

Instructions

(a) Is it apparent from the information whether Glassmaster utilizes standard costs?

(b) Do you think the price variance experienced should lead to changes in standard costs for the next fiscal year?

On the Web

BYP25-4 The Balanced Scorecard Institute (**www.balancedscorecard.org**) is a great resource for information about implementing the balanced scorecard. One item of interest provided at its website is an example of a balanced scorecard for a regional airline.

Address: http://www.balancedscorecard.org/files/Regional_Airline.pdf, or go to **www.wiley.com/college/weygandt**

Instructions

Go to the address above and answer the following questions.

(a) What are the objectives identified for the airline for each perspective?

(b) What measures are used for the objective in the customer perspective?

(c) What initiatives are planned to achieve the objective in the learning perspective?

Communication Activity

BYP25-5 The setting of standards is critical to the effective use of standards in evaluating performance.

Instructions

Explain the following in a memo to your instructor.

(a) The comparative advantages and disadvantages of ideal versus normal standards.

(b) The factors that should be included in setting the price and quantity standards for direct materials, direct labor, and manufacturing overhead.

Ethics Case

BYP25-6 At Milton Manufacturing Company, production workers in the Painting Department are paid on the basis of productivity. The labor time standard for a unit of production is established through periodic time studies conducted by the Mobley Management Department. In a time study, the actual time required to complete a specific task by a worker is observed. Allowances are then made for preparation time, rest periods, and clean-up time. Tony Orlando is one of several veterans in the Painting Department.

Tony is informed by Mobley Management that he will be used in the time study for the painting of a new product. The findings will be the basis for establishing the labor time standard for the next 6 months. During the test, Tony deliberately slows his normal work pace in an effort to obtain a labor time standard that will be easy to meet. Because it is a new product, the Mobley Management representative who conducted the test is unaware that Tony did not give the test his best effort.

Instructions

(a) Who was benefited and who was harmed by Tony's actions?

(b) Was Tony ethical in the way he performed the time study test?

(c) What measure(s) might the company take to obtain valid data for setting the labor time standard?

"All About You" Activity

BYP25-7 From the time you first entered school many years ago, instructors have been measuring and evaluating you by imposing standards. In addition, many of you will pursue professions that administer professional examinations to attain recognized certification. Recently, a federal commission presented proposals suggesting all public colleges and universities should require standardized tests to measure their students' learning.

Instructions

Read the following article at **www.signonsandiego.com/uniontrib/20060811/news_1n11colleges.html**, and answer the following questions.

(a) What areas of concern did the panel's recommendations address?

(b) What are possible advantages of standard testing?

(c) What are possible disadvantages of standard testing?

(d) Would you be in favor of standardized tests?

Answers to Insight and Accounting Across the Organization Questions

p. 1150 How Do Standards Help a Business? **Q:** How will the creation of such standards help a business or organization? **A:** A business or organization may use the data to compare its performance relative to others with regard to common practices such as processing a purchase order or filling a sales order. Armed with this information, an organization can determine which areas to focus on with improvement campaigns.

p. 1153 How Can We Make Susan's Chili Profitable? **Q:** How might management use this raw material cost information? **A:** Management might decide to increase the price of its chili. Or it might revise its recipes to use cheaper ingredients. Or it might eliminate some products until ingredients are available at costs closer to standard.

p. 1164 It May Be Time to Fly United Again **Q:** Which of the perspectives of a balanced scorecard were the focus of United's CEO? **A:** Improving on-time flight departures is an objective within the internal process perspective. Customer intent to fly United again is an objective within the customer perspective.

Answers to Self-Test Questions

1. c **2.** b **3.** d **4.** a **5.** b **6.** c **7.** b $(6,300 - 6,000) \times \$1$ **8.** a $(15,000 - 14,800) \times \$8$ **9.** d **10.** a **11.** b **12.** d **13.** c **14.** d ***15.** c ***16.** c

✔ **The Navigator**

✔ **Remember to go back to the Navigator box on the chapter opening page and check off your completed work.**

CHAPTER26

Incremental Analysis and Capital Budgeting

Study Objectives

After studying this chapter, you should be able to:

[1] Identify the steps in management's decision-making process.

[2] Describe the concept of incremental analysis.

[3] Identify the relevant costs in accepting an order at a special price.

[4] Identify the relevant costs in a make-or-buy decision.

[5] Give the decision rule for whether to sell or process materials further.

[6] Identify the factors to consider in retaining or replacing equipment.

[7] Explain the relevant factors in whether to eliminate an unprofitable segment.

[8] Determine which products to make and sell when resources are limited.

[9] Contrast annual rate of return and cash payback in capital budgeting.

[10] Distinguish between the net present value and internal rate of return methods.

✔ **The Navigator**

✔ The Navigator

- Scan Study Objectives ○
- Read Feature Story ○
- Read Preview ○
- Read text and answer **Do it!** p. 1197 ○ p. 1199 ○ p. 1203 ○ p. 1209 ○ p. 1214 ○
- Work Comprehensive **Do it!** p. 1215 ○
- Review Summary of Study Objectives ○
- Answer Self-Test Questions ○
- Complete Assignments ○
- Go to *WileyPLUS* for practice and tutorials ○

Feature Story

SOUP IS GOOD FOOD

When you hear the word *Campbell*, what is the first thing that comes to mind? Soup. Campbell *is* soup. It sells 38% of all the soup—including homemade—consumed in the United States.

But can a company survive on soup alone? In an effort to expand its operations and to lessen its reliance on soup, Campbell Soup Company began searching for an additional line of business. Campbell's management believed it saw an opportunity in convenient meals that were low in fat, nutritionally rich, and had therapeutic value for heart patients and diabetics. This venture would require a huge investment—but the rewards were potentially tremendous.

The initial investment required building food labs, hiring nutritional scientists, researching prototype products, constructing new production facilities, and marketing the new products. Management predicted that with an initial investment of roughly $55 million, the company might generate sales of $200 million per year.

Four years later, the company had created 24 meals, and an extensive field-study revealed considerable health benefits from the products. Unfortunately, initial sales of the new product line, called Intelligent Quisine, were less than stellar. After three years of disappointing sales, Campbell hired a consulting firm to evaluate whether to continue the project. Product development of the new line was costing $20 million per year—a sum that some managers felt could be better spent developing new products in other divisions, or expanding overseas operations. One year later (eight years after it began), Campbell discontinued the project.

Campbell was not giving up on growth, but simply had decided to refocus its efforts on soup. The company's annual report stated management's philosophy: "Soup will be our growth engine." Campbell has sold off many of its nonsoup businesses, and in a recent year introduced 20 new soup products.

Source: Vanessa O'Connell, "Food for Thought: How Campbell Saw a Breakthrough Menu Turn into Leftovers," *Wall Street Journal* (October 6, 1998).

The Navigator

InsideCHAPTER26

Previewof**CHAPTER26**

An important purpose of management accounting is to provide relevant information for decision making. Examples of these decisions include the following: (1) Campbell Soup's decision to produce "therapeutic meals" rather than some other food product. (2) Boeing's strategic decisions to spend $5 billion to build a plane for the 21st century—the B-777—and to cancel development of a larger version of the B-747. (3) The Coca-Cola Company's decision to spend $750 million to build twelve plants in Russia.

This chapter begins with an explanation of management's decision-making process. It then considers the topics of incremental analysis and capital budgeting. The content and organization of Chapter 26 are as follows.

Incremental Analysis and Capital Budgeting	
Incremental Analysis	**Capital Budgeting**
• Management's decision-making process • Accept special-price order • Make or buy • Sell or process further • Retain or replace equipment • Eliminate unprofitable segment • Allocate limited resources	• Evaluation process • Annual rate of return • Cash payback • Discounted cash flow: NPV and IRR

✔ The Navigator

SECTION1 INCREMENTAL ANALYSIS

Management's Decision-Making Process

Study Objective [1]
Identify the steps in management's decision-making process.

Making decisions is an important management function. Management's decision-making process does not always follow a set pattern, because decisions vary significantly in their scope, urgency, and importance. It is possible, though, to identify some steps that are frequently involved in the process. These steps are shown in Illustration 26-1.

Illustration 26-1
Management's decision-making process

1. Identify the problem and assign responsibility
2. Determine and evaluate possible courses of action
3. Make a decision
4. Review results of the decision

Accounting's contribution to the decision-making process occurs primarily in Steps 2 and 4—evaluating possible courses of action, and reviewing the results. In Step 2, for each possible course of action, accounting provides relevant revenue and cost data. These show the expected overall effect on net income. In Step 4, accounting prepares internal reports that review the actual impact of the decision.

In making business decisions, management ordinarily considers both financial and nonfinancial information. *Financial information* is related to revenues and costs and their effect on the company's overall profitability. *Nonfinancial information* relates to such factors as the effect of the decision on employee turnover, the environment, or the overall image of the company in the community. Although the nonfinancial information can be as important as the financial information, we focus primarily on financial information that is relevant to the decision.

The Incremental Analysis Approach

Decisions involve a choice among alternative courses of action. Suppose that you were deciding whether to purchase or lease a computer for use in doing your accounting homework. The financial data relate to the cost of leasing versus the cost of purchasing. For example, leasing involves periodic lease payments; purchasing requires "up-front" payment of the purchase price. In other words, the financial data relevant to the decision are the data that vary among the possible alternatives. The process used to identify the financial data that change under alternative courses of action is called **incremental analysis**. In some cases, when you use incremental analysis, both costs **and** revenues will change. In other cases, only costs **or** revenues will vary.

Just as your decision to buy or lease a PC affects your future, similar decisions, on a larger scale, affect a company's future. Incremental analysis identifies the probable effects of those decisions on future earnings. Such analysis inevitably involves estimates and uncertainty. Gathering data for incremental analyses may involve market analysts, engineers, and accountants. In quantifying the data, the accountant is expected to produce the most reliable information available at the time the decision must be made.

Study Objective [2]
Describe the concept of incremental analysis.

Alternative Terminology

Incremental analysis is also called *differential analysis* because the analysis focuses on differences.

How Incremental Analysis Works

The following example illustrates the basic approach in incremental analysis.

A	B	C	D
Incremental Analysis.xls			
File Edit View Insert Format Tools Data Window Help			
	Alternative A	**Alternative B**	**Net Income Increase (Decrease)**
2 Revenues	$125,000	$110,000	$ (15,000)
3 Costs	100,000	80,000	20,000
4 Net income	$ 25,000	$ 30,000	$ 5,000
5			

Illustration 26-2
Basic approach in incremental analysis

This example compares alternative B with alternative A. The net income column shows the differences between the alternatives. In this case, incremental revenue will be $15,000 less under alternative B than under alternative A, but a $20,000 incremental cost saving will be realized.[1] Thus, alternative B will produce $5,000 more net income than alternative A.

Incremental analysis sometimes involves changes that at first glance might seem contrary to your intuition. For example, sometimes variable costs *do not change* under the alternative courses of action. Also, sometimes fixed costs *do change*. For example, direct labor, normally a variable cost, is not an incremental cost in deciding between two new factory machines if each asset requires the same amount of direct labor. In contrast, rent expense, normally a fixed cost, is an incremental cost in a decision to continue occupancy of a building or to purchase or lease a new building.

SERVICE COMPANY INSIGHT

That Letter from AmEx Might Not Be a Bill

No doubt every one of you has received an invitation from a credit card company to open a new account—some of you have probably received three in one day. But how many of you have received an offer of $300 to close out your credit card account? American Express decided to offer some of its customers $300 if they would give back their credit card. You could receive the $300 even if you hadn't paid off your balance yet, as long as you agreed to give up your credit card.

Source: Aparajita Saha-Bubna and Lauren Pollock, "AmEx Offers Some Holders $300 to Pay and Leave," *Wall Street Journal Online* (February 23, 2009).

 What are the relevant costs that American Express would need to know in order to determine to whom to make this offer? (See page 1235.)

Types of Incremental Analysis

A number of different types of decisions involve incremental analysis. The more common types of decisions are:

1. Accept an order at a special price.
2. Make or buy.
3. Sell or process further.
4. Retain or replace equipment.
5. Eliminate an unprofitable business segment.
6. Allocate limited resources.

We consider each of these types of analysis in the following pages.

Accept an Order at a Special Price

Study Objective [3]
Identify the relevant costs in accepting an order at a special price.

Sometimes, a company has an opportunity to obtain additional business if it is willing to make a major price concession to a specific customer. To illustrate, assume that Sunbelt Company produces 100,000 automatic blenders per month, which is 80% of plant capacity. Variable manufacturing costs are $8 per unit. Fixed manufacturing costs are $400,000, or $4 per unit. The blenders are normally sold directly to retailers at $20 each. Sunbelt has an offer from Mexico Co.

---

[1] Although income taxes are sometimes important in incremental analysis, they are ignored in the chapter for simplicity's sake.

(a foreign wholesaler) to purchase an additional 2,000 blenders at $11 per unit. Acceptance of the offer would not affect normal sales of the product, and the additional units can be manufactured without increasing plant capacity. What should management do?

If management makes its decision on the basis of the total cost per unit of $12 ($8 + $4), the order would be rejected, because costs ($12) would exceed revenues ($11) by $1 per unit. However, since the units can be produced within existing plant capacity, the special order **will not increase fixed costs**. The relevant data for the decision, therefore, are the variable manufacturing costs per unit of $8 and the expected revenue of $11 per unit. Thus, as shown in Illustration 26-3, Sunbelt will increase its net income by $6,000 by accepting this special order.

Illustration 26-3
Incremental analysis—accepting an order at a special price

Accepting an order at a special price.xls			
File Edit View Insert Format Tools Data Window Help			
A	B	C	D
1	Reject Order	Accept Order	Net Income Increase (Decrease)
2 Revenues	$0	$22,000	$ 22,000
3 Costs	0	16,000	(16,000)
4 Net income	$0	$ 6,000	$ 6,000
5			

Two points should be emphasized: First, we assume that sales of the product in other markets are not affected by this special order. If other sales are affected, then Sunbelt must consider the lost sales in making the decision. Second, if Sunbelt is operating at full capacity, it is likely that the special order would be rejected. Under such circumstances, the company would have to expand plant capacity. In that case, the special order would have to absorb these additional fixed manufacturing costs, as well as the variable manufacturing costs.

Do it!

Cobb Company incurs a cost of $28 per unit, of which $18 is variable, to make a product that normally sells for $42. A foreign wholesaler offers to buy 5,000 units at $25 each. Cobb will incur shipping costs of $1 per unit. Compute the increase or decrease in net income Cobb will realize by accepting the special order, assuming Cobb has excess operating capacity. Should Cobb Company accept the special order?

Special Orders

Solution

	Reject	Accept	Net Income Increase (Decrease)
Revenues	$–0–	$125,000	$125,000
Costs	–0–	95,000*	(95,000)
Net income	$–0–	$ 30,000	$ 30,000

*(5,000 × $18) + (5,000 × $1)

Given the result of the analysis, Cobb Company should accept the special order.

action plan

✔ Identify all revenues that will change as a result of accepting the order.

✔ Identify all costs that will change as a result of accepting the order, and net this amount against the change in revenues.

Related exercise material: BE26-2, BE26-3, E26-2, E26-3, and **Do it!** 26-1.

✔
The Navigator

Make or Buy

Study Objective [4]
Identify the relevant costs in a make-or-buy decision.

When a manufacturer assembles component parts in producing a finished product, management must decide whether to make or buy the components. For example, General Motors Corporation may either make or buy the batteries, tires, and radios used in its cars. Similarly, Hewlett-Packard Corporation may make or buy the electronic circuitry, cases, and printer heads for its printers. Boeing recently sold some of its commercial aircraft factories in an effort to cut production costs and focus instead on engineering and final assembly rather than manufacturing. The decision to make or buy components should be made on the basis of incremental analysis.

To illustrate the analysis, assume that Baron Company incurs the following annual costs in producing 25,000 ignition switches for motor scooters.

Illustration 26-4
Annual product cost data

Direct materials	$ 50,000
Direct labor	75,000
Variable manufacturing overhead	40,000
Fixed manufacturing overhead	60,000
Total manufacturing costs	$225,000
Total cost per unit ($225,000 ÷ 25,000)	$9.00

Or, instead of making its own switches, Baron Company might purchase the ignition switches from Ignition Inc. at a price of $8 per unit. The question again is, "What should management do?"

At first glance, it appears that management should purchase the ignition switches for $8, rather than make them at a cost of $9. However, a review of operations indicates that if Baron purchases the ignition switches from Ignition Inc., it will eliminate *all* of its variable costs but only $10,000 of its fixed manufacturing costs. Thus, $50,000 of the fixed manufacturing costs will remain if the ignition switches are purchased. The relevant costs for incremental analysis, therefore, are as follows.

Illustration 26-5
Incremental analysis—make or buy

Incremental Analysis - Make or buy.xls

File   Edit   View   Insert   Format   Tools   Data   Window   Help

	A	B	C	D
1		**Make**	**Buy**	**Net Income Increase (Decrease)**
2	Direct materials	$ 50,000	$ 0	$ 50,000
3	Direct labor	75,000	0	75,000
4	Variable manufacturing costs	40,000	0	40,000
5	Fixed manufacturing costs	60,000	50,000	10,000
6	Purchase price (25,000 × $8)	0	200,000	(200,000)
7	Total annual cost	$225,000	$250,000	$ (25,000)
8				

Ethics Note

In the make-or-buy decision, it is important for management to take into account the social impact of its choice. For instance, buying may be the most economically feasible solution, but such action could result in the closure of a manufacturing plant that employs many good workers.

This analysis indicates that Baron Company will incur $25,000 of additional costs by buying the ignition switches. Therefore, Baron should continue to make the ignition switches, even though the total manufacturing cost is $1 higher than the purchase price. The reason is that if the company purchases the ignition switches, it will still have fixed costs of $50,000 to absorb.

OPPORTUNITY COST

The foregoing make-or-buy analysis is complete only if the productive capacity used to make the ignition switches cannot be converted to another purpose. If there is an opportunity to use this productive capacity in some other manner, then this opportunity cost must be considered. **Opportunity cost** is the potential benefit that may be obtained by following an alternative course of action.

To illustrate, assume that through buying the switches, Baron Company can use the released productive capacity to generate additional income of $28,000. This lost income is an additional cost of continuing to make the switches in the make-or-buy decision. This opportunity cost therefore is added to the "Make" column, for comparison. Illustration 26-6 shows that it is now advantageous to buy the ignition switches.

Illustration 26-6
Incremental analysis—make or buy, with opportunity cost

Incremental Analysis - Make or buy with opportunity cost.xls			
File Edit View Insert Format Tools Data Window Help			
A	**B**	**C**	**D**
1	**Make**	**Buy**	**Net Income Increase (Decrease)**
2 Total annual cost	$225,000	$250,000	$(25,000)
3 Opportunity cost	28,000	0	28,000
4 Total cost	$253,000	$250,000	$ 3,000
5			

The qualitative factors in this decision include the possible loss of jobs for employees who produce the ignition switches. In addition, management must assess how long the supplier will be able to satisfy the company's quality control standards at the quoted price per unit.

Do it!

Juanita Company must decide whether to make or buy some of its components. The costs of producing 50,000 electrical cords for its floor lamps are as follows.

Make or Buy

Direct materials	$60,000	Variable overhead	$12,000
Direct labor	$30,000	Fixed overhead	$8,000

Instead of making the electrical cords at an average cost per unit of $2.20 ($110,000 ÷ 50,000), the company has an opportunity to buy the cords at $2.15 per unit. If the company purchases the cords, all variable costs and one-half of the fixed costs will be eliminated.

(a) Prepare an incremental analysis showing whether the company should make or buy the electrical cords. (b) Will your answer be different if the released productive capacity will generate additional income of $25,000?

action plan

✔ Look for the costs that change.

✔ Ignore the costs that do not change.

✔ Use the format in the chapter for your answer.

✔ Recognize that opportunity cost can make a difference.

Solution

(a)

	Make	**Buy**	**Net Income Increase (Decrease)**
Direct materials	$ 60,000	$ –0–	$ 60,000
Direct labor	30,000	–0–	30,000
Variable manufacturing costs	12,000	–0–	12,000
Fixed manufacturing costs	8,000	4,000	4,000
Purchase price	–0–	107,500	(107,500)
Total cost	$110,000	$111,500	$ (1,500)

This analysis indicates that Juanita Company will incur $1,500 of additional costs if it buys the electrical cords.

(b)

	Make	Buy	Net Income Increase (Decrease)
Total cost	$110,000	$111,500	$ (1,500)
Opportunity cost	25,000		25,000
Total cost	$135,000	$111,500	$ 23,500

Yes, the answer is different: The analysis shows that net income will be increased by $23,500 if Juanita Company purchases the electrical cords.

Related exercise material: BE26-4, E26-4, and **Do it!** 26-2.

The Navigator

ACCOUNTING ACROSS THE ORGANIZATION

These Wheels Have Miles Before Installation

Consider the make-or-buy decision faced by Superior Industries International, Inc., a big aluminum-wheel maker in Van Nuys, California. For years, president Steve Borick had ignored the possibility of Chinese manufacturing. Then, Mr. Borick started getting a blunt message from General Motors and Ford, with whom Superior does 85% of its business: Match the prices of Chinese wheel suppliers. Both auto makers said separately that if Superior could not agree to the lower prices, they would go directly to Chinese manufacturers or turn to other North American wheel-makers.

Stories like this, repeated in various industries, illustrate why manufacturers engage in overseas *off-shoring* (outsourcing). For example, compare the relative labor costs in major auto-producing nations, in dollars per hour, to see why incremental analysis often leads to outsourcing production to countries like China.

Country	Cost
Germany	$33.00
United States	$22.50
France	$22.10
Japan	$20.20
Canada	$19.40
United Kingdom	$18.60
South Korea	$8.40
Taiwan	$5.20
Mexico	$2.70
China	$0.90

Source: Norihiko Shirouzu, "Big Three's Outsourcing Plan: Make Parts Suppliers Do It," *Wall Street Journal* (June 10, 2004), p. A1.

? What are the disadvantages of outsourcing to a foreign country? (See page 1235.)

Sell or Process Further

Study Objective [5]
Give the decision rule for whether to sell or process materials further.

Many manufacturers have the option of selling products at a given point in the production cycle or continuing to process with the expectation of selling them at a higher price. For example, a bicycle manufacturer such as Schwinn could sell its 10-speed bicycles to retailers either unassembled or assembled. A furniture manufacturer such as Ethan Allen could sell its dining room sets to furniture stores either unfinished or finished. The sell-or-process-further decision should be made on the basis of incremental analysis.

The basic decision rule is: **Process further as long as the incremental revenue from such processing exceeds the incremental processing costs.**

Assume, for example, that Woodmasters Inc. makes tables. The cost to manufacture an unfinished table is $35, computed as follows.

Direct material	$15
Direct labor	10
Variable manufacturing overhead	6
Fixed manufacturing overhead	4
Manufacturing cost per unit	$35

Illustration 26-7
Per unit cost of unfinished table

The selling price per unfinished unit is $50. Woodmasters currently has unused productive capacity that is expected to continue indefinitely. Management concludes that some of this capacity can be used to finish the tables and sell them at $60 per unit. For a finished table, direct materials will increase $2 and direct labor costs will increase $4. Variable manufacturing overhead costs will increase by $2.40 (60% of direct labor). No increase is anticipated in fixed manufacturing overhead. Illustration 26-8 shows the incremental analysis on a per unit basis.

Illustration 26-8
Incremental analysis—sell or process further

Incremental Analysis - Sell or process further.xls

A	B Sell	C Process Further	D Net Income Increase (Decrease)
Sales per unit	$50.00	$60.00	$10.00
Cost per unit			
Direct materials	15.00	17.00	(2.00)
Direct labor	10.00	14.00	(4.00)
Variable manufacturing overhead	6.00	8.40	(2.40)
Fixed manufacturing overhead	4.00	4.00	0.00
Total	35.00	43.40	(8.40)
Net income per unit	$15.00	$16.60	$ 1.60

Helpful Hint

Current net income is known. Net income from processing further is an estimate. In making its decision, management could add a "risk" factor for the estimate.

It is advantageous for Woodmasters to process the tables further. The incremental revenue of $10.00 from the additional processing is $1.60 higher than the incremental processing costs of $8.40.

Retain or Replace Equipment

Management often has to decide whether to continue using an asset or replace it. To illustrate, assume that Jeffcoat Company has a factory machine with a book value of $40,000 and a remaining useful life of four years. A new machine is available that costs $120,000. It is expected to have zero salvage value at the end of its four-year useful life. If Jeffcoat acquires the new machine, variable manufacturing costs are expected to decrease from $160,000 to $125,000 annually, and the old unit will be scrapped. The incremental analysis for the **four-year period** is shown in Illustration 26-9 (page 1202).

(page 1202)

Study Objective [6]
Identify the factors to consider in retaining or replacing equipment.

Illustration 26-9
Incremental analysis—retain or replace equipment

	Incremental Analysis - Retain or replace equipment.xls						
	File　Edit　View　Insert　Format　Tools　Data　Window　Help						
	A	**B**	**C**	**D**	**E**	**F**	
1		**Retain Equipment**		**Replace Equipment**		**Net Income Increase (Decrease)**	
2	Variable manufacturing costs	$640,000	a	$500,000	b	$140,000	
3	New machine cost			120,000		(120,000)	
4	Total	$640,000		$620,000		$ 20,000	
5							
6	a(4 years × $160,000)						
7	b(4 years × $125,000)						
8							

In this case, it is advantageous to replace the equipment. The lower variable manufacturing costs related to the new equipment more than offset its purchase cost.

One other point about Jeffcoat's decision: **The book value of the old machine does not affect the decision**. Book value is a sunk cost, which is a cost that cannot be changed by any present or future decision. Sunk costs **are not relevant in incremental analysis**. In this example, if the company retains the asset, book value is depreciated over its remaining useful life. Or, if the company acquires the new unit, book value is recognized as a loss of the current period. Thus, the effect of book value on current and future earnings is the same regardless of the replacement decision. However, **any trade-in allowance or cash disposal value of the existing asset is relevant** to the decision, because the company will not realize this value if the old asset is continued in use.

Eliminate an Unprofitable Segment

Study Objective [7]

Explain the relevant factors in whether to eliminate an unprofitable segment.

Management sometimes must decide whether to eliminate an unprofitable business segment. For example, in recent years many airlines have quit servicing certain cities or have cut back on the number of flights; and Goodyear recently quit producing several brands in the low-end tire market. Again, the key is to **focus on the relevant costs—the data that change under the alternative courses of action**. To illustrate, assume that Martina Company manufactures tennis racquets in three models: Pro, Master, and Champ. Pro and Master are profitable lines. Champ (highlighted in color in Illustration 26-10) operates at a loss. Condensed income statement data for the three segments are:

Illustration 26-10
Segment income data

	Pro	Master	Champ	Total
Sales	$800,000	$300,000	$100,000	$1,200,000
Variable expenses	520,000	210,000	90,000	820,000
Contribution margin	280,000	90,000	10,000	380,000
Fixed expenses	80,000	50,000	30,000	160,000
Net income	$200,000	$ 40,000	$ (20,000)	$ 220,000

Helpful Hint

A decision to discontinue a segment based solely on the bottom line—net loss—is inappropriate.

It might be expected that total net income will increase by $20,000 to $240,000 if Martina Company eliminates the unprofitable Champ line of racquets. However, **net income may decrease if that line is discontinued**. The reason is that the other products will have to absorb the fixed expenses allocated to the Champ racquets. To illustrate, assume that the $30,000 of fixed costs applicable to the unprofitable segment are allocated ⅔ and ⅓ to the Pro and Master product lines, respectively.

Fixed expenses will increase to $100,000 ($80,000 + $20,000) in the Pro line and to $60,000 ($50,000 + $10,000) in the Master line. Illustration 26-11 shows the revised income statements.

Illustration 26-11
Income data after eliminating unprofitable product line

	Pro	Master	Total
Sales	$800,000	$300,000	$1,100,000
Variable expenses	520,000	210,000	730,000
Contribution margin	280,000	90,000	370,000
Fixed expenses	100,000	60,000	160,000
Net income	$180,000	$ 30,000	$ 210,000

Total net income has decreased $10,000 ($220,000 − $210,000). This result is also obtained in the following incremental analysis of the Champ racquets.

Illustration 26-12
Incremental analysis—eliminating an unprofitable segment

Incremental Analysis - Eliminating an unprofitable segment.xls

File   Edit   View   Insert   Format   Tools   Data   Window   Help

	A	B	C	D
		Continue	Eliminate	Net Income Increase (Decrease)
2	Sales	$100,000	$ 0	$(100,000)
3	Variable costs	90,000	0	90,000
4	Contribution margin	10,000	0	(10,000)
5	Fixed costs	30,000	30,000	0
6	Net income	$ (20,000)	$(30,000)	$ (10,000)

The loss in net income is attributable to the contribution margin ($10,000) that the company will not realize if it discontinues the segment.

In deciding on the future status of an unprofitable segment, management should consider the effect of elimination on related product lines. It may be possible for continuing product lines to obtain some or all of the sales lost by the discontinued product line. In some businesses, services or products may be linked—for example, free checking accounts at a bank, or coffee at a donut shop. In addition, management should consider the effect of eliminating the product line on employees who may have to be discharged or retrained.

Do it!

Unprofitable Segments

Lambert, Inc. manufactures several types of accessories. For the year, the knit hats and scarves line had sales of $400,000, variable expenses of $310,000, and fixed expenses of $120,000. Therefore, the knit hats and scarves line had a net loss of $30,000. If Lambert eliminates the knit hats and scarves line, $20,000 of fixed costs will remain. Prepare an analysis showing whether the company should eliminate the knit hats and scarves line.

action plan

✔ Identify the revenues that will change as a result of eliminating a product line.

✔ Identify all costs that will change as a result of eliminating a product line, and net the amount against the revenues.

Solution

	Continue	Eliminate	Net Income Increase (Decrease)
Sales	$400,000	$ 0	$(400,000)
Variable costs	310,000	0	310,000
Contribution margin	90,000	0	(90,000)
Fixed costs	120,000	20,000	100,000
Net income	$ (30,000)	$(20,000)	$ 10,000

The analysis indicates that Lambert should eliminate the knit hats and scarves line because net income will increase $10,000.

Related exercise material: BE26-7, E26-8, E26-9, and **Do it!** 26-3.

 The Navigator

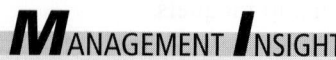 **M**ANAGEMENT **I**NSIGHT

Time to Move to a New Neighborhood?

If you have ever moved, then you know how complicated and costly it can be. Now consider what it would be like for a manufacturing company with 260 employees and a 170,000-square-foot facility to move from southern California to Idaho. That is what Buck Knives did in order to save its company from financial ruin. Electricity rates in Idaho were half those in California, workers' compensation was one-third the costs and factory wages were 20% lower. Combined, this would reduce manufacturing costs by $600,000 per year. Moving the factory would cost about $8.5 million, plus $4 million to move key employees. Offsetting these costs was the estimated $11 million selling price of the California property. Based on these estimates, the move would pay for itself in three years.

Ultimately, the company received only $7.5 million for its California property, only 58 of 75 key employees were willing to move, construction was delayed by a year which caused the new plant to increase in price by $1.5 million, and wages surged in Idaho due to low unemployment. Despite all of these complications, though, the company considers the move a great success.

Source: Chris Lydgate, "The Buck Stopped," *Inc. Magazine* (May 2006), pp. 87–95.

? What were some of the factors that complicated the company's decision to move? How should the company have incorporated such factors into its incremental analysis? (See page 1235.)

Allocate Limited Resources

Study Objective [8]

Determine which products to make and sell when resources are limited.

Companies, like individuals, face limited resources. For a retail department store, the limited resource may be floor space. For a manufacturing company, the limited resource may be raw materials, direct labor hours, or machine capacity. When a company has limited resources, management must decide which products to make and sell in order to maximize net income.

To illustrate, assume that Collins Company manufactures deluxe and standard pen and pencil sets. The limiting resource is machine capacity, which is 3,600 hours per month. Relevant data consist of the following.

Illustration 26-13
Contribution margin and machine hours

	Deluxe Sets	Standard Sets
Contribution margin per unit	$8	$6
Machine hours required	0.4	0.2

The deluxe sets may appear to be more profitable: They have a higher contribution margin ($8) than the standard sets ($6). However, the standard sets take fewer machine hours to produce than the deluxe sets. Therefore, Collins needs to find the **contribution margin per unit of limited resource**—in this case, contribution margin per machine hour. This is obtained by dividing the contribution margin per unit of each product by the number of units of the limited resource required for each product, as shown in Illustration 26-14.

Helpful Hint

CM alone is not enough in this decision. The key factor is CM per unit of limited resource.

	Deluxe Sets	Standard Sets
Contribution margin per unit (**a**)	$8	$6
Machine hours required (**b**)	0.4	0.2
Contribution margin per unit of limited resource [(a) ÷ (b)]	$20	$30

Illustration 26-14
Contribution margin per unit of limited resource

The computation shows that the standard sets have a higher contribution margin per unit of limited resource. This suggests that, given sufficient demand for standard sets, the company should shift the sales mix to standard sets or should increase machine capacity. If Collins Company is able to increase machine capacity from 3,600 hours to 4,200 hours, the additional 600 hours could be used to produce either the standard or deluxe pen and pencil sets. The total contribution margin under each alternative is found by multiplying the machine hours by the contribution margin per unit of limited resource, as shown below.

	Produce Deluxe Sets	Produce Standard Sets
Machine hours (**a**)	600	600
Contribution margin per unit of limited resource (**b**)	$20	$30
Contribution margin [(a) × (b)]	$12,000	$18,000

Illustration 26-15
Incremental analysis—computation of total contribution margin

From this analysis, we see that to maximize net income, Collins should use all of the increased capacity to make and sell the standard sets.

SECTION2 CAPITAL BUDGETING

Individuals make capital expenditures when they buy a new home, car, or television set. Similarly, businesses make capital expenditures when they modernize plant facilities or expand operations. Companies like Campbell Soup must constantly determine how to invest their resources. Other examples: Hollywood studios recently built 25 new sound stage projects to allow for additional filming in future years. Also, Union Pacific Resources Group Inc. announced that it would cut its capital budget by 19% in order to use the funds to reduce its outstanding debt.

In business, as for individuals, the amount of possible capital expenditures usually exceeds the funds available for such expenditures. Thus, the resources available must be allocated (budgeted) among the competing alternatives. The process of making capital expenditure decisions in business is known as **capital budgeting**. Capital budgeting involves choosing among various capital projects to find the one(s) that will maximize a company's return on its financial investment.

Evaluation Process

Many companies follow a standard process in capital budgeting. At least once a year, top management requests proposals for projects from each department. A capital budgeting committee screens the proposals and submits its findings to the officers of the company. The officers, in turn, select the projects they believe to be most worthy of funding. They submit this list to the board of directors. Ultimately, the directors approve the capital expenditure budget for the year. Illustration 26-16 shows this process.

   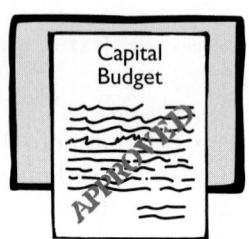

1. Project proposals are requested from departments, plants, and authorized personnel.

2. Proposals are screened by a capital budget committee.

3. Officers determine which projects are worthy of funding.

4. Board of directors approves capital budget.

Illustration 26-16
Corporate capital budget authorization process

The involvement of top management and the board of directors in the process demonstrates the importance of capital budgeting decisions. These decisions often have a significant impact on a company's future profitability. In fact, poor capital budgeting decisions have led to the bankruptcy of some companies.

Accounting data are indispensable in assessing the probable effects of capital expenditures. To provide management with relevant data for capital budgeting decisions, you should be familiar with the quantitative techniques that may be used. The three most common techniques are: (1) annual rate of return, (2) cash payback, and (3) discounted cash flow. We demonstrate each of these techniques in the following sections. To illustrate the three quantitative techniques, assume that Tappan Company is considering an investment of $130,000 in new equipment. The new equipment is expected to last 10 years. It will have zero salvage value at the end of its useful life. Tappan uses the straight-line method of depreciation for accounting purposes. The expected annual revenues and costs of the new product that will be produced from the investment are:

Illustration 26-17
Estimated annual net income from capital expenditure

Sales		$200,000
Less: Costs and expenses		
Manufacturing costs (exclusive of depreciation)	$145,000	
Depreciation expenses ($130,000 ÷ 10)	13,000	
Selling and administrative expenses	22,000	180,000
Income before income taxes		20,000
Income tax expense		7,000
Net income		$ 13,000

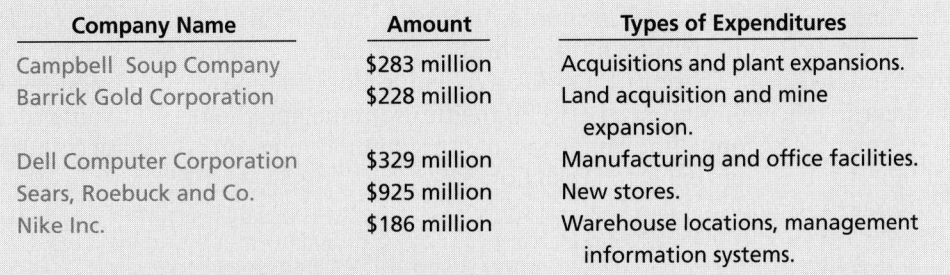

MANAGEMENT INSIGHT

Investing for the Future

Monitoring capital expenditure amounts is one way to learn about a company's growth potential. Few companies can grow if they don't make significant capital investments. Here is a list of well-known companies and the amounts and types of their capital expenditures in a recent year.

Company Name	Amount	Types of Expenditures
Campbell Soup Company	$283 million	Acquisitions and plant expansions.
Barrick Gold Corporation	$228 million	Land acquisition and mine expansion.
Dell Computer Corporation	$329 million	Manufacturing and office facilities.
Sears, Roebuck and Co.	$925 million	New stores.
Nike Inc.	$186 million	Warehouse locations, management information systems.

 Why is it important for top management to constantly monitor the nature, amount, and success of a company's capital expenditures? (See page 1235.)

Annual Rate of Return

The **annual rate of return technique** is based directly on accrual-accounting data rather than on cash flows. It indicates **the profitability of a capital expenditure** by dividing expected annual net income by the average investment. Illustration 26-18 shows the formula for computing annual rate of return.

Study Objective [9]
Contrast annual rate of return and cash payback in capital budgeting.

Expected Annual Net Income	÷	Average Investment	=	Annual Rate of Return

Illustration 26-18
Annual rate of return formula

Expected annual net income is obtained from the projected income statement. Tappan Company's expected annual net income is $13,000. Average investment is derived from the following formula.

$$\text{Average Investment} = \frac{\text{Original Investment} + \text{Value at End of Useful Life}}{2}$$

Illustration 26-19
Formula for computing average investment

The "value at the end of useful life" is the asset's salvage value, if any.

For Tappan Company, average investment is $65,000 ($130,000 + $0) ÷ 2. The expected annual rate of return for Tappan Company's investment in new equipment is therefore 20%, computed as follows.

$$\$13,000 \div \$65,000 = 20\%$$

Management then compares this annual rate of return with its **required rate of return** for investments of similar risk. The required rate of return is generally based on the company's **cost of capital**. The **cost of capital** is the rate of return that management expects to pay on all borrowed and equity funds. The cost of capital is a company-wide (or sometimes a division-wide) rate; it does not relate to the cost of funding a specific project.

Helpful Hint

A capital budgeting decision based on only one technique may be misleading. It is often wise to analyze the investment from a number of different perspectives.

The annual rate of return decision rule is: **A project is acceptable if its rate of return is greater than management's required rate of return. It is unacceptable when the reverse is true.** When companies use the rate of return technique in deciding among several acceptable projects, **the higher the rate of return for a given risk, the more attractive the investment**.

The principal advantages of this technique are simplicity of calculation and management's familiarity with the accounting terms used in the computation. A major limitation of the annual rate of return approach is that it does not consider the time value of money. For example, no consideration is given as to whether cash inflows will occur early or late in the life of the investment. As explained in Appendix D at the back of the book, recognition of the time value of money can make a significant difference between the future value and the present value of an investment. A second disadvantage is that this method relies on accrual-accounting numbers rather than expected cash flows.

Cash Payback

The **cash payback technique** identifies the time period required to recover the cost of the capital investment from the annual cash inflow produced by the investment. Illustration 26-20 presents the formula for computing the cash payback period.

Illustration 26-20
Cash payback formula

Cost of Capital Investment	÷	Net Annual Cash Flow	=	Cash Payback Period

Helpful Hint

Net annual cash flow can also be approximated by net cash provided by operating activities from the statement of cash flows.

Net annual cash flow is approximated by taking net income and adding back depreciation expense. Depreciation expense is added back because depreciation on the capital expenditure does not involve an annual outflow of cash. Accordingly, the depreciation deducted in determining net income must be added back to determine net annual cash flows.

In the Tappan Company example, net annual cash flow is $26,000, as shown below.

Illustration 26-21
Computation of net annual cash flow

Net income	$13,000
Add: Depreciation expense	13,000
Net annual cash flow	$26,000

The cash payback period in this example is therefore five years, computed as follows.

$$\$130,000 \div \$26,000 = 5 \text{ years}$$

Evaluation of the payback period is often related to the expected useful life of the asset. For example, assume that at Tappan Company a project is unacceptable if the payback period is longer than 60% of the asset's expected useful life. The five-year payback period in this case is 50% of the project's expected useful life. Thus, the project is acceptable.

It follows that when companies use the payback method to decide among acceptable alternative projects, **the shorter the payback period, the more attractive the investment**. This is true for two reasons: First, the earlier the investment is recovered, the sooner the company can use the cash funds for other purposes. Second, the risk of loss from obsolescence and changed economic conditions is less in a shorter payback period.

The preceding computation of the cash payback period assumes **equal** cash flows in each year of the investment's life. In many cases, this assumption is not valid. In the case of **uneven** cash flows, the company determines the cash payback period when the cumulative net cash flows from the investment equal the cost of the investment.

To illustrate, assume that Chen Company proposes an investment in a new website that is estimated to cost $300,000. Illustration 26-22 shows the proposed investment cost, net annual cash flows, cumulative net cash flows, and the cash payback period.

Year	Investment	Net Annual Cash Flow	Cumulative Net Cash Flow
0	$300,000		
1		$ 60,000	$ 60,000
2		90,000	150,000
3		90,000	240,000
4		120,000	360,000
5		100,000	460,000
		Cash payback period = 3.5 years	

Illustration 26-22
Net annual cash flow schedule

As Illustration 26-22 shows, at the end of year 3, cumulative cash flow of $240,000 is less than the investment cost of $300,000. However, at the end of year 4, the cumulative net cash flow of $360,000 exceeds the investment cost. The net cash flow needed in year 4 to equal the investment cost is $60,000 ($300,000 − $240,000). Assuming the net cash flow occurs evenly during year 4, we then divide this amount by the annual net cash flow in year 4 ($120,000) to determine the point during the year when the cash payback occurs. Thus, we get 0.50 ($60,000/$120,000), or half of the year, and the cash payback period is 3.5 years.

The cash payback method may be useful as an initial screening tool. It may be the most critical factor in the capital budgeting decision for a company that desires a fast turnaround of its investment because of a weak cash position. Like the annual rate of return, cash payback is relatively easy to compute and understand.

However, cash payback is not ordinarily the only basis for the capital budgeting decision because it ignores the expected profitability of the project. To illustrate, assume that Projects X and Y have the same payback period, but Project X's useful life is double the useful life of Project Y's. Project X's earning power, therefore, is twice as long as Project Y's. A further — and major — disadvantage of this technique is that it ignores the time value of money.

Do it!

Rochelle Company is considering purchasing new equipment for $250,000. The equipment has a 5-year useful life, and depreciation would be $50,000 (assuming straight-line depreciation and zero salvage value). The purchase of the equipment should increase net income by $25,000 each year for 5 years. (a) Compute the annual rate of return. (b) Compute the cash payback period.

Solution

(a) Average investment = ($250,000 + 0) ÷ 2 = $125,000
Annual rate of return = $25,000 ÷ $125,000 = 20%

(b) Net annual cash flow = $25,000 + $50,000 = $75,000
Cash payback period = $250,000 ÷ $75,000 = 3.3 years

Related exercise material: BE26-9, BE26-10, E26-11, E26-12, E26-13, and **Do it!** 26-4.

Capital Budgeting

action plan

Use appropriate formulas:

✔ Annual rate of return = Expected annual net income ÷ Average investment.

✔ Average investment = (Original investment + Value at end of useful life) ÷ 2.

✔ Cash payback period = Cost of capital investment ÷ Net annual cash flow.

✔ Net annual cash flow = Net income + Depreciation expense.

The Navigator

Discounted Cash Flow

Study Objective [10]

Distinguish between the net present value and internal rate of return methods.

The **discounted cash flow technique** is generally recognized as the best conceptual approach to making capital budgeting decisions. This technique considers both the estimated total net cash flows from the investment and the time value of money. The expected total net cash flow consists of the sum of the annual net cash flows plus the estimated liquidation proceeds when the asset is sold for salvage at the end of its useful life. But because liquidation proceeds are generally immaterial, we ignore them in subsequent discussions.

Two methods are used with the discounted cash flow technique: (1) net present value, and (2) internal rate of return. **Before we discuss the methods, we recommend that you examine Appendix D if you need a review of present value concepts.**

Net Present Value Method

The **net present value (NPV) method** involves discounting net cash flows to their present value and then comparing that present value with the capital outlay required by the investment. The difference between these two amounts is referred to as **net present value (NPV)**. Company management determines what interest rate to use in discounting the future net cash flows. This rate, often referred to as the discount rate or **required rate of return**, is discussed in a later section.

The NVP decision rule is this: **A proposal is acceptable when net present value is zero or positive.** At either of those values, the rate of return on the investment equals or exceeds the required rate of return. When net present value is negative, the project is unacceptable. Illustration 26-23 shows the net present value decision criteria.

Illustration 26-23
Net present value decision criteria

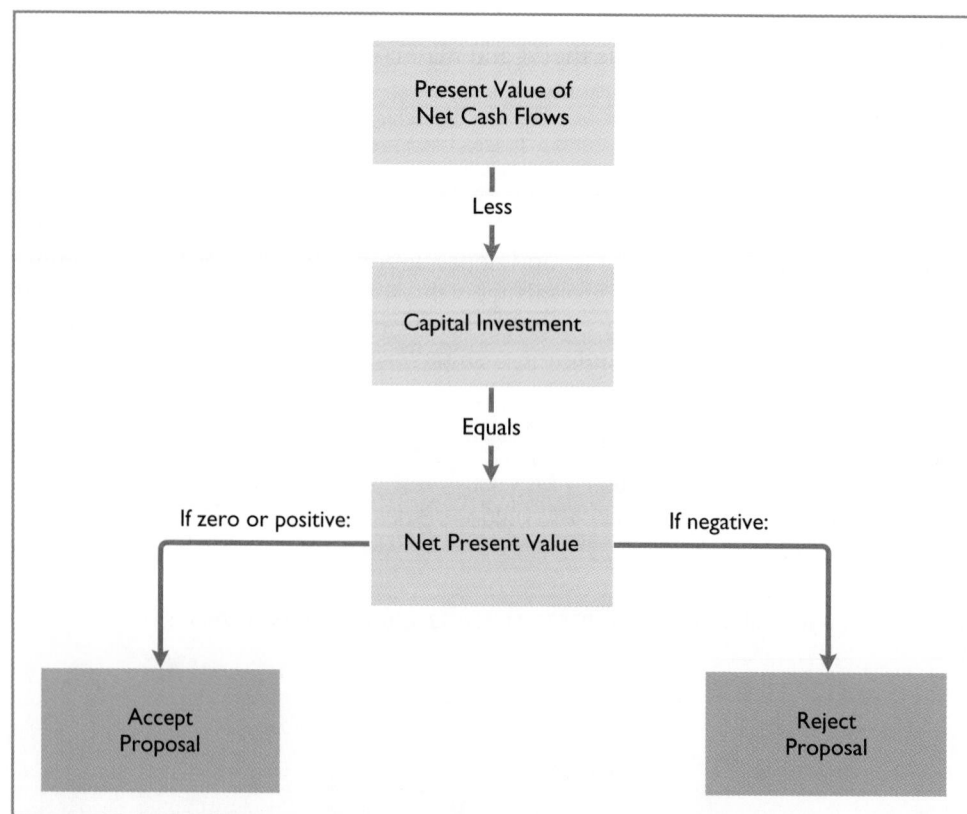

When making a selection among acceptable proposals, **the higher the positive net present value, the more attractive the investment**. The application of this method to two cases is described in the next two sections. In each case, we assume that the investment has no salvage value at the end of its useful life.

Ethics Note

Discounted future cash flows may not take into account all of the important considerations needed to make an informed capital budgeting decision. Other issues, for example, could include worker safety, product quality, and environmental impact.

EQUAL NET ANNUAL CASH FLOWS

Tappan Company's net annual cash flows are $26,000. If we assume this amount is **uniform over the asset's useful life**, we can compute the present value of the net annual cash flows by using the present value of an annuity of 1 for 10 periods (in Table 2, Appendix D). The computation at a rate of return of 12% is:

	Present Values at 12%
Discount factor for 10 periods	5.65022
Present value of net annual cash flows:	
$26,000 × 5.65022	$146,906

Illustration 26-24
Present value of net annual cash flows

The analysis of the proposal by the net present value method is as follows.

	12%
Present value of net annual cash flows	$146,906
Capital investment	130,000
Positive (negative) net present value	$ 16,906

Illustration 26-25
Computation of net present value

The proposed capital expenditure is acceptable at a required rate of return of 12% because the net present value is positive.

UNEQUAL NET ANNUAL CASH FLOWS

When net annual cash flows are unequal, we cannot use annuity tables to calculate their present value. Instead, we use tables showing the **present value of a single future amount for each net annual cash flow**.

To illustrate, assume that Tappan Company management expects the same aggregate net annual cash flow ($260,000) over the life of the investment. But because of a declining market demand for the new product over the life of the equipment, the net annual cash flows are higher in the early years and lower in the later years. The present value of the net annual cash flows is calculated as follows using Table 1 in Appendix D.

Helpful Hint

The ABC Co. expects equal cash flows over an asset's 5-year useful life.
 What discount factor should it use in determining present values if management wants (1) a 12% return or (2) a 15% return?
Answer: Using Table 2, the factors are (1) 3.60478 and (2) 3.35216.

Illustration 26-26
Computing present value of unequal annual cash flows

Year	Assumed Net Annual Cash Flows	Discount Factor 12%	Present Value 12%
	(1)	(2)	(1) × (2)
1	$ 36,000	.89286	$ 32,143
2	32,000	.79719	25,510
3	29,000	.71178	20,642
4	27,000	.63552	17,159
5	26,000	.56743	14,753
6	24,000	.50663	12,159
7	23,000	.45235	10,404
8	22,000	.40388	8,885
9	21,000	.36061	7,573
10	20,000	.32197	6,439
	$260,000		$155,667

Therefore, the analysis of the proposal by the net present value method is as follows.

Illustration 26-27
Analysis of proposal using net present value method

	12%
Present value of net annual cash flows	$155,667
Capital investment	130,000
Positive (negative) net present value	$ 25,667

In this example, the present values of the net annual cash flows are greater than the $130,000 capital investment. Thus, the project is acceptable at a 12% required rate of return. The difference between the present values using the 12% rate under equal cash flows ($146,906) and unequal net annual cash flows ($155,667) is due to the pattern of the net cash flows.

MANAGEMENT **I**NSIGHT

Seeing the Big Picture

Inaccurate trend forecasting and market positioning are more detrimental to capital investment decisions than using the wrong discount rate. Ampex patented the VCR but failed to see its market potential. Westinghouse made the same mistake with the flat-screen video display. More often, companies adopt projects or businesses only to discontinue them in response to market changes. Texas Instruments announced it would stop manufacturing computer chips, after it had made substantial capital investments that enabled it to become one of the world's leading suppliers. The company dropped out of some 12 business lines in only a few years.

Source: World Research Advisory Inc. (London, August 1998), p. 4.

 How important is the choice of discount rate in making capital budgeting decisions? (See page 1235.)

Internal Rate of Return Method

The **internal rate of return method** differs from the net present value method in that it finds the **interest yield of the potential investment**. The **internal rate of return** (IRR) is the interest rate that will cause the present value of the proposed capital expenditure to equal the present value of the expected net annual cash flows. The determination of the internal rate of return involves two steps.

Step 1. Compute the internal rate of return factor. The formula for this factor is:

Illustration 26-28
Formula for internal rate of return factor

Capital Investment	÷	Net Annual Cash flow	=	Internal Rate of Return Factor

The computation for Tappan Company, assuming equal net annual cash flows,[2] is:

$$\$130,000 \div \$26,000 = 5.0$$

---

[2]When net annual cash flows are equal, the internal rate of return factor is the same as the cash payback period.

Step 2. Use the factor and the present value of an annuity of 1 table to find the internal rate of return. Table 2 of Appendix D is used in this step. The internal rate of return is the discount factor that is closest to the internal rate of return factor for the time period covered by the net annual cash flows.

For Tappan Company, the net annual cash flows are expected to continue for 10 years. Thus, it is necessary to read across the period-10 row in Table 2 to find the discount factor. The row for 10 periods is reproduced below for your convenience.

	TABLE 2							
	PRESENT VALUE OF AN ANNUITY OF 1							
(*n*) Periods	5%	6%	8%	9%	10%	11%	12%	15%
10	7.72173	7.36009	6.71008	6.41766	6.14457	5.88923	5.65022	5.01877

In this case, the closest discount factor to 5.0 is 5.01877, which represents an interest rate of approximately 15%. The rate of return can be further determined by interpolation, but since we are using estimated net annual cash flows, such precision is seldom required.

Once managers know the internal rate of return, they compare it to the company's required rate of return (the discount rate). The IRR decision rule is as follows: **Accept the project when the internal rate of return is equal to or greater than the required rate of return. Reject the project when the internal rate of return is less than the required rate of return.** Illustration 26-29 below shows these relationships. Assuming the required rate of return is 10% for Tappan Company, the project is acceptable because the 15% internal rate of return is greater than the required rate.

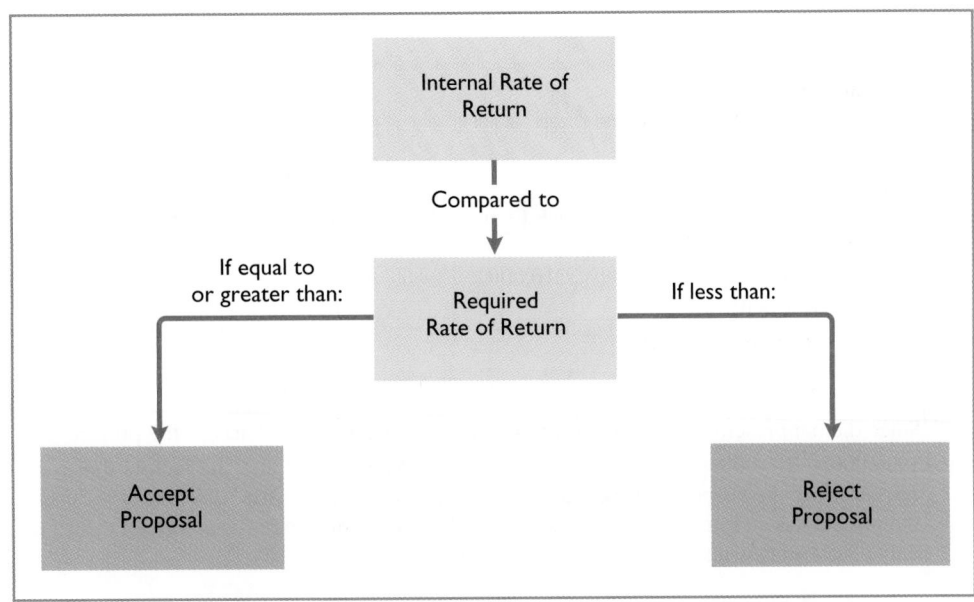

Illustration 26-29
Internal rate of return decision criteria

The IRR method is widely used in practice. Most managers find the internal rate of return easy to interpret.

Comparing Discounted Cash Flow Methods

Illustration 26-30 compares the two discounted cash flow methods—net present value and internal rate of return. When properly used, either method provides management with relevant quantitative data for making capital budgeting decisions.

Illustration 26-30
Comparison of discounted cash flow methods

Item	Net Present Value	Internal Rate of Return
1. Objective	Compute net present value (a dollar amount).	Compute internal rate of return (a percentage).
2. Decision rule	If net present value is zero or positive, accept the proposal. If net present value is negative, reject the proposal	If internal rate of return is equal to or greater than the required rate of return, accept the proposal. If internal rate of return is less than the required rate, reject the proposal.

Do it!

Discounted Cash Flow

Watertown Paper Corporation is considering adding another machine for the manufacture of corrugated cardboard. The machine would cost $900,000. It would have an estimated life of 6 years and no salvage value. The company estimates that annual cash inflows would increase by $400,000 and that annual cash outflows would increase by $190,000. Management has a required rate of return of 9%.

(a) Calculate the net present value on this project, and discuss whether it should be accepted.

(b) Calculate the internal rate of return on this project, and discuss whether it should be accepted.

action plan

✔ Compute net annual cash flow: Estimated annual cash inflows − Estimated annual cash outflows.

✔ Use the NPV technique to calculate the difference between net cash flows and the initial investment.

✔ Accept the project if the net present value is positive.

✔ Compute the IRR factor: Capital investment ÷ Net annual cash flows.

✔ Look up the factor in the present value of an annuity table to find the internal rate of return.

✔ Accept the project if the internal rate of return is equal to or greater than the required rate of return.

Solution

(a)

Estimated annual cash inflows	$400,000
Estimated annual cash outflows	190,000
Net annual cash flow	$210,000

	Cash Flow	9% Discount Factor	Present Value
Present value of net annual cash flows	$210,000	4.48592*	$942,043
Capital investment			900,000
Net present value			$ 42,043

*Table 2, Appendix D

Since the net present value is greater than zero, Watertown should accept the project.

(b) $900,000 ÷ 210,000 = 4.285714. Using Table 2 of Appendix D and the factors that correspond with the six-period row, 4.285714 is between the factors for 10% and 11%. Since the project has an internal rate that is greater than 10% and the required rate of return is only 9%, Watertown should accept the project.

Related exercise material: BE26-11, BE26-12, BE26-13, E26-12, E26-13, E26-14, E26-15, and **Do it!** 26-5.

✔
The Navigator

COMPREHENSIVE
Do it!

Sierra Company is considering a long-term capital investment project called ZIP. The project will require an investment of $120,000, and it will have a useful life of 4 years. Annual net income for ZIP is expected to be: Year 1 $12,000; Year 2 $10,000; Year 3 $8,000; and Year 4 $6,000. Depreciation is computed by the straight-line method with no salvage value. The company's cost of capital is 12%.

Instructions

(a) Compute the annual rate of return for the project.

(b) Compute the cash payback period for the project. (Round to two decimals.)

(c) Compute the net present value for the project. (Round to nearest dollar.)

(d) Should the project be accepted? Why?

action plan

✔ To compute annual rate of return, divide expected annual net income by average investment.

✔ To compute cash payback, divide cost of the investment by net annual cash flows.

✔ Recall that net annual cash flow equals annual net income plus annual depreciation expense.

✔ Be careful to use the correct discount factor in using the net present value method.

Solution to Comprehensive Do it!

(a) $9,000 ($36,000 ÷ 4) ÷ $60,000 ($120,000 ÷ 2) = 15%

(b) Depreciation expense is $120,000 ÷ 4 years = $30,000.

Net annual cash flows are:

Year 1	$12,000 + $30,000 = $42,000
Year 2	$10,000 + $30,000 = $40,000
Year 3	$8,000 + $30,000 = $38,000
Year 4	$6,000 + $30,000 = $36,000

Cumulative net cash flows would be $82,000 ($42,000 + $40,000) at the end of year 2 and $120,000 ($42,000 + $40,000 + $38,000) at the end of year 3. Since the cumulative net cash flows at the end of year 3 exactly equal the initial cash investment of $120,000, the cash payback period is 3 years.

(c)

Year	Discount Factor	Net Annual Cash Flow	Present Value
1	.89286	$42,000	$ 37,500
2	.79719	40,000	31,888
3	.71178	38,000	27,048
4	.63552	36,000	22,879
			119,315
		Capital investment	120,000
		Negative net present value	$ (685)

(d) The annual rate of return of 15% is good. However, the cash payback period is 75% of the project's useful life, and net present value is negative. The recommendation is to reject the project.

The Navigator ✔

Summary of Study Objectives

[1] Identify the steps in management's decision-making process. Management's decision-making process is: (a) identify the problem and assign responsibility, (b) determine and evaluate possible courses of action, (c) make the decision, and (d) review the results of the decision.

[2] Describe the concept of incremental analysis. Incremental analysis identifies financial data that change under alternative courses of action. These data are relevant to the decision because they will vary in the future among the possible alternatives.

[3] Identify the relevant costs in accepting an order at a special price. The relevant information in accepting an order at a special price is the difference between the variable costs to produce the special order and expected revenues.

[4] Identify the relevant costs in a make-or-buy decision. In a make-or-buy decision, the relevant costs are

(a) the manufacturing costs that will be saved, (b) the purchase price, and (c) opportunity costs.

[5] Give the decision rule for whether to sell or process materials further. The decision rule for whether to sell or process materials further is: Process further as long as the incremental revenue from processing exceeds the incremental processing costs.

[6] Identify the factors to consider in retaining or replacing equipment. The factors to consider in determining whether equipment should be retained or replaced are the effects on variable costs and the cost of the new equipment. Also, any trade-in allowance or cash disposal value of the existing asset must be considered.

[7] Explain the relevant factors in whether to eliminate an unprofitable segment. In deciding whether to eliminate an unprofitable segment, determine the contribution margin, if any, produced by the segment and the disposition of the segment's fixed expenses.

[8] Determine which products to make and sell when resources are limited. When a company has limited resources, find the contribution margin per unit of limited resource. Then multiply this amount by the units of limited resource to determine which product maximizes net income.

[9] Contrast annual rate of return and cash payback in capital budgeting. The *annual rate of return* is obtained by dividing expected annual net income by the average investment. The higher the rate of return, the more attractive the investment. The *cash payback* technique identifies the time period to recover the cost of the investment. The formula is: Cost of capital expenditure divided by estimated net annual cash flow equals cash payback period. The shorter the payback period, the more attractive the investment.

[10] Distinguish between the net present value and internal rate of return methods. Under the *net present value* method, compare the present value of future net cash flows with the capital investment to determine net present value. The NPV decision rule is: Accept the project if net present value is zero or positive. Reject the investment if net present value is negative.

Under the *internal rate of return* method, find the interest yield of the potential investment. The IRR decision rule is: Accept the project when the internal rate of return is equal to or greater than the required rate of return. Reject the project when the internal rate of return is less than the required rate.

The Navigator

Glossary

Annual rate of return technique Determines the profitability of a capital expenditure by dividing expected annual net income by the average investment. (p. 1207).

Capital budgeting The process of making capital expenditure decisions in business. (p. 1205).

Cash payback technique Identifies the time period required to recover the cost of a capital investment from the net annual cash flow produced by the investment. (p. 1208).

Cost of capital The rate of return that management expects to pay on all borrowed and equity funds. (p. 1207).

Discounted cash flow technique Considers both the estimated total net cash flows from the investment and the time value of money. (p. 1210).

Incremental analysis The process of identifying the financial data that change under alternative courses of action. (p. 1195).

Internal rate of return (IRR) The rate that will cause the present value of the proposed capital expenditure to

equal the present value of the expected net annual cash flows. (p. 1212).

Internal rate of return method Finds the interest yield of the potential investment. (p. 1212).

Net present value (NPV) The difference that results when the original capital outlay is subtracted from the discounted net cash flows. (p. 1210).

Net present value (NPV) method Discounts net cash flows to their present value and then compares that present value to the capital outlay required by the investment. (p. 1210).

Opportunity cost The potential benefit that may be obtained from following an alternative course of action. (p. 1199).

Required rate of return The rate that is generally based on the company's cost of capital. (p. 1207).

Sunk cost A cost that cannot be changed by any present or future decision. (p. 1202).

WILEY PLUS

Self-Test, Brief Exercises, Exercises, Problem Set A, and many more components are available for practice in WileyPLUS

Self-Test Questions

Answers are on page 1235.

(SO 1) **1.** Three of the steps in management's decision process are: (1) Review results of decision. (2) Identify the problem. (3) Make the decision. The steps are performed in the following order.

a. (1), (2), (3).
b. (3), (2), (1).
c. (2), (1), (3).
d. (2), (3), (1).

2. Incremental analysis is the process of identifying the (SO 2) financial data that:

a. do not change under alternative courses of action.
b. change under alternative courses of action.
c. are mixed under alternative courses of action.
d. No correct answer is given.

(SO 3) **3.** It costs a company $14 of variable costs and $6 of fixed costs to produce product A that sells for $30. A foreign buyer offers to purchase 3,000 units at $18 each. If the special offer is accepted and produced with unused capacity, net income will:
a. decrease $6,000.   **c.** increase $12,000.
b. increase $6,000.   **d.** increase $9,000.

(SO 3) **4.** Jobart Company is currently operating at full capacity. It is considering buying a part from an outside supplier rather than making it in-house. If Jobart purchases the part, it can use the released productive capacity to generate additional income of $30,000 from producing a different product. When conducting incremental analysis in this make-or-buy decision, the company should:
a. ignore the $30,000.
b. add $30,000 to other costs in the "Make" column.
c. add $30,000 to other costs in the "Buy" column.
d. subtract $30,000 from the other costs in the "Make" column.

(SO 4) **5.** In a make-or-buy decision, relevant costs are:
a manufacturing costs that will be saved.
b. the purchase price of the units.
c. opportunity costs.
d. All of the above.

(SO 5) **6.** The decision rule in a sell-or-process-further decision is: Process further as long as the incremental revenue from processing exceeds:
a. incremental processing costs.
b. variable processing costs.
c. fixed processing costs.
d. No correct answer is given.

(SO 5) **7.** Walton, Inc. makes an unassembled product that it currently sells for $55. Production costs are $20. Walton is considering assembling the product and selling it for $68. The cost to assemble the product is estimated at $12. What decision should Walton make?
a. Sell before assembly; net income per unit will be $12 greater.
b. Sell before assembly; net income per unit will be $1 greater.
c. Process further; net income per unit will be $13 greater.
d. Process further; net income per unit will be $1 greater.

(SO 6) **8.** In a decision to retain or replace equipment, the book value of the old equipment is a(n):
a. opportunity cost.   **c.** incremental cost
b. sunk cost.   **d.** marginal cost.

(SO 7) **9.** If an unprofitable segment is eliminated:

a. net income will always increase.
b. variable expenses of the eliminated segment will have to be absorbed by other segments.
c. fixed expenses allocated to the eliminated segment will have to be absorbed by other segments.
d. net income will always decrease.

10. A segment of Hazard Inc. has the following data.   (SO 7)
Sales $200,000
Variable costs $140,000
Fixed costs $100,000
If this segment is eliminated, 50% of the fixed costs will be eliminated, and the rest will be allocated to the remaining segments. What should Hazard do?
a. Eliminate the segment; net income will be $50,000 greater.
b. Eliminate the segment; net income will be $10,000 greater.
c. Keep the segment; net income will be $200,000 greater.
d. Keep the segment; net income will be $10,000 greater.

11. If the contribution margin per unit is $15 and it takes 3.0 (SO 8) machine hours to produce the unit, the contribution margin per unit of limited resource is:
a. $25.   **c.** $45.
b. $5.   **d.** No correct answer is given.

12. Which of the following is *incorrect* about the annual rate (SO 9) of return technique?
a. The calculation is simple.
b. The accounting terms used are familiar to management.
c. The timing of the net cash flows is not considered.
d. The time value of money is considered.

13. What is a weakness of the cash payback approach?   (SO 9)
a. It uses accrual-based accounting numbers.
b. It ignores the time value of money.
c. It is complicated to compute.
d. It cannot be used if a project has uneven net annual cash flows.

14. A project should be accepted if its internal rate of return (SO 10) exceeds:
a. zero.
b. the rate of return on a government bond.
c. the company's required rate of return.
d. the rate the company pays on borrowed funds.

15. A positive net present value means that the: (SO 10)
a. project's rate of return is less than the cutoff rate.
b. project's rate of return exceeds the required rate of return.
c. project's rate of return equals the required rate of return.
d. project is unacceptable.

Go to the book's companion website,
www.wiley.com/college/weygandt,
for additional Self-Test Questions.

Questions

1. What steps are frequently involved in management's decision-making process?
2. Your roommate, Dave Klein, contends that accounting contributes to most of the steps in management's

decision-making process. Is your roommate correct? Explain.
3. "Incremental analysis involves the accumulation of information concerning a single course of action." Do you agree? Why?

4. Dean Martin asks your help concerning the relevance of variable and fixed costs in incremental analysis. Help Dean with his problem.

5. What data are relevant in deciding whether to accept an order at a special price?

6. Quinones Company has an opportunity to buy parts at $7 each that currently cost $10 to make. What manufacturing costs are relevant to this make-or-buy decision?

7. Define the term "opportunity cost." How may this cost be relevant in a make-or-buy decision?

8. What is the decision rule in deciding whether to sell a product or process it further?

9. Your roommate, Sylvia Ayala, is confused about sunk costs. Explain to your roommate the meaning of sunk costs and their relevance to a decision to retain or replace equipment.

10. Beacon Inc. has one product line that is unprofitable. What circumstances may cause overall company net income to be lower if the unprofitable product line is eliminated?

11. How is the contribution margin per unit of limited resources computed?

12. Describe the process a company may use in screening and approving the capital expenditure budget.

13. Your classmate, Mindy Penland, is confused about the factors that are included in the annual rate of return technique. What is the formula for this technique?

14. Frido Ortiz is trying to understand the term "cost of capital." Define the term, and indicate its relevance to the decision rule under the annual rate of return technique.

15. Hank Snow claims the formula for the cash payback technique is the same as the formula for the annual rate of return technique. Is Hank correct? What is the formula for the cash payback technique?

16. What are the advantages and disadvantages of the cash payback technique?

17. Two types of present value tables may be used with the discounted cash flow technique. Identify the tables and the circumstance(s) when each table should be used.

18. What is the decision rule under the net present value method?

19. Identify the steps required in using the internal rate of return method.

20. Calliope Company uses the internal rate of return method. What is the decision rule for this method?

Brief Exercises

Identify the steps in management's decision-making process.
(SO 1)

BE26-1   The steps in management's decision-making process are listed in random order below. Indicate the order in which the steps should be executed.

  ＿ Make a decision.   ＿ Review results of the decision.
  ＿ Identify the problem and   ＿ Determine and evaluate
     assign responsibility.   possible courses of action.

Determine incremental changes.
(SO 2)

BE26-2   Vinh Company is considering two alternatives. Alternative A will have sales of $150,000 and costs of $100,000. Alternative B will have sales of $180,000 and costs of $120,000. Compare Alternative A to Alternative B showing incremental revenues, costs, and net income. Which alternative should you choose?

Determine whether to accept a special order.
(SO 3)

BE26-3   In Kastle Company, it costs $30 per unit ($20 variable and $10 fixed) to make a product that normally sells for $45. A foreign wholesaler offers to buy 4,000 units at $23 each. Kastle will incur special shipping costs of $1 per unit. Assuming that Kastle has excess operating capacity, prepare an incremental analysis that indicates the net income (loss) Kastle would realize by accepting the special order. Should the order be accepted?

Determine whether to make or buy a part.
(SO 4)

BE26-4   Beamer Manufacturing incurs unit costs of $8 ($5 variable and $3 fixed) in making a subassembly part for its finished product. A supplier offers to make 10,000 of the part at $5.30 per unit. If the offer is accepted, Beamer will save all variable costs but no fixed costs. Prepare an analysis showing the total cost saving, if any, Beamer will realize by buying the part. What should they do?

Determine whether to sell or process further.
(SO 5)

BE26-5   Keaton Inc. makes unfinished bookcases that it sells for $60. Production costs are $30 variable and $10 fixed. Because it has unused capacity, Keaton is considering finishing the bookcases and selling them for $72. Variable finishing costs are expected to be $8 per unit with no increase in fixed costs. Prepare an analysis on a per unit basis showing whether Keaton should sell unfinished or finished bookcases.

Determine whether to retain or replace equipment.
(SO 6)

BE26-6   Stanley Company has a factory machine with a book value of $90,000 and a remaining useful life of 4 years. A new machine is available at a cost of $200,000. This machine will have a 4-year useful life with no salvage value. The new machine will lower annual variable manufacturing costs from $600,000 to $440,000. Prepare an analysis showing whether the old machine should be retained or replaced.

BE26-7 O'Toole, Inc. manufactures golf clubs in three models. For the year, the Eagle line has a net loss of $20,000 from sales $200,000, variable expenses $180,000, and fixed expenses $40,000. If the Eagle line is eliminated, $34,000 of fixed costs will remain. Prepare an analysis showing whether the Eagle line should be eliminated.

Determine whether to eliminate an unprofitable segment.
(SO 7)

BE26-8 In Cheval Company, data concerning two products are: Contribution margin per unit—Product A $11, Product B $12; machine hours required for one unit—Product A 2, Product B 2.5. Compute the contribution margin per unit of limited resource for each product.

Show allocation of limited resources.
(SO 8)

BE26-9 Hinton Company is considering purchasing new equipment for $300,000. It is expected that the equipment will produce annual net income of $10,000 over its 10-year useful life. Annual depreciation will be $30,000. Compute the cash payback period.

Compute the cash payback period for a capital investment.
(SO 9)

BE26-10 Laura Oil Company is considering investing in a new oil well. It is expected that the oil well will increase annual revenues by $130,000 and will increase annual expenses by $80,000 including depreciation. The oil well will cost $490,000 and will have a $10,000 salvage value at the end of its 10-year useful life. Calculate the annual rate of return.

Compute annual rate of return.
(SO 9)

BE26-11 Wales Company is considering two different, mutually exclusive capital expenditure proposals. Project A will cost $395,000, has an expected useful life of 10 years, a salvage value of zero, and is expected to increase net annual cash flows by $70,000. Project B will cost $270,000, has an expected useful life of 10 years, a salvage value of zero, and is expected to increase net annual cash flows by $50,000. A discount rate of 9% is appropriate for both projects. Compute the net present value of each project. Which project should be accepted?

Compute net present value.
(SO 10)

BE26-12 Jacques Company is evaluating the purchase of a rebuilt spot-welding machine to be used in the manufacture of a new product. The machine will cost $170,000, has an estimated useful life of 7 years, a salvage value of zero, and will increase net annual cash flows by $33,740. What is its approximate internal rate of return?

Calculate internal rate of return.
(SO 10)

BE26-13 Travolta Company accumulates the following data concerning a proposed capital investment: cash cost $225,000, net annual cash flow $34,000, present value factor of cash inflows for 10 years 6.71 (rounded). Determine the net present value, and indicate whether the investment should be made.

Compute net present value of an investment.
(SO 10)

Do it! Review

Do it! 26-1 Maize Company incurs a cost of $35 per unit, of which $20 is variable, to make a product that normally sells for $58. A foreign wholesaler offers to buy 6,000 units at $31 each. Maize will incur additional costs of $2 per unit to imprint a logo and to pay for shipping. Compute the increase or decrease in net income Maize will realize by accepting the special order, assuming Maize has sufficient excess operating capacity. Should Maize Company accept the special order?

Evaluate special order.
(SO 3)

Do it! 26-2 Bert Company must decide whether to make or buy some of its components. The costs of producing 60,000 switches for its generators are as follows.

Evaluate make-or-buy opportunity.
(SO 4)

Direct materials	$30,000	Variable overhead	$45,000
Direct labor	$42,000	Fixed overhead	$60,000

Instead of making the switches at an average cost of $2.95 ($177,000 ÷ 60,000), the company has an opportunity to buy the switches at $2.75 per unit. If the company purchases the switches, all the variable costs and one-third of the fixed costs will be eliminated.

(a) Prepare an incremental analysis showing whether the company should make or buy the switches. (b) Would your answer be different if the released productive capacity will generate additional income of $30,000?

Do it! 26-3 Pantera Corporation manufactures several types of accessories. For the year, the gloves and mittens line had sales of $500,000, variable expenses of $375,000, and fixed expenses of $150,000. Therefore, the gloves and mittens line had a net loss of $25,000. If Pantera eliminates the line, $40,000 of fixed costs will remain.

Analyze whether to eliminate unprofitable segment.
(SO 7)

Prepare an analysis showing whether the company should eliminate the gloves and mittens line.

Do it! 26-4 Lumine Company is considering purchasing new equipment for $350,000. The equipment has a 5-year useful life, and depreciation would be $70,000 (assuming straight-line depreciation

Compute capital budgeting measures.
(SO 9)

and zero salvage value). The purchase of the equipment should increase net income by $40,000 each year for 5 years. (a) Compute the annual rate of return. (b) Compute the cash payback period.

Compute discounted cash flow measures.
(SO 10)

Do it! 26-5 Samantha Box Corporation is considering adding another machine for the manufacture of corrugated cardboard. The machine would cost $700,000. It would have an estimated life of 6 years and no salvage value. The company estimates that annual cash inflows would increase by $300,000 and that annual cash outflows would increase by $140,000. Management has a required rate of return of 9%.

(a) Calculate the net present value on this project, and discuss whether it should be accepted. (b) Calculate the internal rate of return on this project, and discuss whether it should be accepted.

Exercises

Analyze statements about decision making and incremental analysis.
(SO 1, 2)

E26-1 Bloom has prepared the following list of statements about decision making and incremental analysis.
1. The first step in management's decision-making process is, "Determine and evaluate possible courses of action."
2. The final step in management's decision-making process is to actually make the decision.
3. Accounting's contribution to management's decision-making process occurs primarily in evaluating possible courses of action and in reviewing the results.
4. In making business decisions, management ordinarily considers only financial information because it is objectively determined.
5. Decisions involve a choice among alternative courses of action.
6. The process used to identify the financial data that change under alternative courses of action is called incremental analysis.
7. Costs that are the same under all alternative courses of action sometimes affect the decision.
8. When using incremental analysis, some costs will always change under alternative courses of action, but revenues will not.
9. Variable costs will change under alternative courses of action, but fixed costs will not.

Instructions
Identify each statement as true or false. If false, indicate how to correct the statement.

Make incremental analysis for special order.
(SO 3)

E26-2 Billings Company manufactures toasters. For the first 8 months of 2013, the company reported the following operating results while operating at 75% of plant capacity.

Sales (400,000 units)	$4,000,000
Cost of goods sold	2,400,000
Gross profit	1,600,000
Operating expenses	900,000
Net income	$ 700,000

Cost of goods sold was 70% variable and 30% fixed. Operating expenses were 60% variable and 40% fixed.

In September, Billings Company receives a special order for 40,000 toasters at $6.00 each from Del Carpic Company of Lima, Peru. Acceptance of the order would result in $8,000 of shipping costs but no increase in fixed operating expenses.

Instructions
(a) Prepare an incremental analysis for the special order.
(b) Should Billings Company accept the special order? Why or why not?

Make incremental analysis for special-order decision.
(SO 3)

E26-3 Shank Company produces golf discs which it normally sells to retailers for $7 each. The cost of manufacturing 20,000 golf discs is:

Materials	$ 10,000
Labor	30,000
Variable overhead	20,000
Fixed overhead	40,000
Total	$100,000

Shank also incurs 5% sales commission ($0.35) on each disc sold.

Mulligan Corporation offers Shank $4.75 per disc for 5,000 discs. Mulligan would sell the discs under its own brand name in foreign markets not yet served by Shank. If Shank accepts the offer, its fixed overhead will increase from $40,000 to $45,000 due to the purchase of a new imprinting machine. No sales commission will result from the special order.

Instructions
(a) Prepare an incremental analysis for the special order.
(b) Should Shank accept the special order? Why or why not?
(c) ✏️ What assumptions underlie the decision made in part (b)?

E26-4 Nona Inc. has been manufacturing its own shades for its table lamps. The company is currently operating at 100% of capacity. Variable manufacturing overhead is charged to production at the rate of 50% of direct labor cost. The direct materials and direct labor cost per unit to make the lamp shades are $4.00 and $6.00, respectively. Normal production is 40,000 table lamps per year.

Make incremental analysis for make-or-buy decision.
(SO 4)

A supplier offers to make the lamp shades at a price of $13.50 per unit. If Nona Inc. accepts the supplier's offer, all variable manufacturing costs will be eliminated, but the $40,000 of fixed manufacturing overhead currently being charged to the lamp shades will have to be absorbed by other products.

Instructions
(a) Prepare the incremental analysis for the decision to make or buy the lamp shades.
(b) ✏️ Should Nona Inc. buy the lamp shades?
(c) ✏️ Would your answer be different in (b) if the productive capacity released by not making the lamp shades could be used to produce income of $35,000?

E26-5 Michelle Dawan recently opened her own basketweaving studio. She sells finished baskets in addition to the raw materials needed by customers to weave baskets of their own. Michelle has put together a variety of raw material kits, each including materials at various stages of completion. Unfortunately, owing to space limitations, Michelle is unable to carry all varieties of kits originally assembled and must choose between two basic packages.

Make incremental analysis for further processing of materials.
(SO 5)

The basic introductory kit includes undyed, uncut reeds (with dye included) for weaving one basket. This basic package costs Michelle $12 and sells for $27. The second kit, called Stage 2, includes cut reeds that have already been dyed. With this kit, the customer need only soak the reeds and weave the basket. Michelle is able to produce the second kit by using the basic materials included in the first kit and adding one hour of her own time (to produce two kits), which she values at $18 per hour. Because she is more efficient at cutting and dying reeds than her average customer, Michelle is able to make two kits of the dyed reeds, in one hour, from one kit of undyed reeds. The kit of dyed and cut reeds sells for $33.

Instructions
Determine whether Michelle's basketweaving shop should carry the basic introductory kit with undyed and uncut reeds, or the Stage 2 kit with reeds already dyed and cut. Prepare an incremental analysis to support your answer.

E26-6 Top Gear Bikes could sell its bicycles to retailers either assembled or unassembled. The cost of an unassembled bike is as follows.

Make incremental analysis for sell-or-process-further decision.
(SO 5)

Direct materials	$150
Direct labor	70
Variable overhead (70% of direct labor)	49
Fixed overhead (30% of direct labor)	21
Manufacturing cost per unit	$290

The unassembled bikes are sold to retailers at $400 each.

Top Gear currently has unused productive capacity that is expected to continue indefinitely; management has concluded that some of this capacity can be used to assemble the bikes and sell them at $450 each. Assembling the bikes will increase direct materials by $5 per bike, and direct labor by $20 per bike. Additional variable overhead will be incurred at the normal rates, but there will be no additional fixed overhead as a result of assembling the bikes.

Instructions
(a) Prepare an incremental analysis for the sell-or-process-further decision.
(b) Should Top Gear sell or process further? Why or why not?

Make incremental analysis for retaining or replacing equipment.
(SO 6)

E26-7 Haggis Enterprises uses a word processing computer to handle its sales invoices. Lately, business has been so good that it takes an extra 3 hours per night, plus every third Saturday, to keep up with the volume of sales invoices. Management is considering updating its computer with a faster model that would eliminate all of the overtime processing.

	Current Machine	New Machine
Original purchase cost	$15,000	$21,000
Accumulated depreciation	6,000	—
Estimated operating costs	24,000	20,000
Useful life	5 years	5 years

If sold now, the current machine would have a salvage value of $5,000. If operated for the remainder of its useful life, the current machine would have zero salvage value. The new machine is expected to have zero salvage value after 5 years.

Instructions
Should the current machine be replaced? (Ignore the time value of money.)

Make incremental analysis for elimination of division.
(SO 7)

E26-8 Gaby Rodriquez, a recent graduate of State's accounting program, evaluated the operating performance of Schultz Company's six divisions. Gaby made the following presentation to the Schultz board of directors and suggested the Ketchum Division be eliminated. "If the Ketchum Division is eliminated," she said, "our total profits would increase by $16,870."

	The Other Five Divisions	Ketchum Division	Total
Sales	$1,664,200	$ 98,200	$1,762,400
Cost of goods sold	978,520	76,470	1,054,990
Gross profit	685,680	21,730	707,410
Operating expenses	527,940	38,600	566,540
Net income	$ 157,740	$(16,870)	$ 140,870

In the Ketchum Division, cost of goods sold is $56,000 variable and $20,470 fixed, and operating expenses are $12,000 variable and $26,600 fixed. None of the Ketchum Division's fixed costs will be eliminated if the division is discontinued.

Instructions
Is Gaby right about eliminating the Ketchum Division? Prepare a schedule to support your answer.

Make incremental analysis for elimination of a product line.
(SO 7)

E26-9 Nimoy Company makes three models of phasers. Information on the three products is given below.

	Stunner	Double-Set	Mega-Power
Sales	$300,000	$500,000	$200,000
Variable expenses	150,000	200,000	140,000
Contribution margin	150,000	300,000	60,000
Fixed expenses	120,000	225,000	90,000
Net income	$ 30,000	$ 75,000	$(30,000)

Fixed expenses consist of $300,000 of common costs allocated to the three products based on relative sales, and additional fixed expenses of $30,000 (Stunner), $75,000 (Double-Set), and $30,000 (Mega-Power). The common costs will be incurred regardless of how many models are produced. The other fixed expenses would be eliminated if a model is phased out.

Mr. Spock, an executive with the company, feels the Mega-Power line should be discontinued to increase the company's net income.

Instructions
(a) Compute current net income for Nimoy Company.
(b) Compute net income by product line and in total for Nimoy Company if the company discontinues the Mega-Power product line. (*Hint:* Allocate the $300,000 common costs to the two remaining product lines based on their relative sales.)
(c) Should Nimoy eliminate the Mega-Power product line? Why or why not?

E26-10 Depp Company manufactures and sells three products. Relevant per unit data concerning each product are given below.

Compute contribution margin and determine the product to be manufactured.

(SO 8)

	Product		
	A	**B**	**C**
Selling price	$11	$12	$15
Variable costs and expenses	$4	$8	$9
Machine hours to produce	2	1	2

Instructions

(a) Compute the contribution margin per unit of the limited resource (machine hour) for each product.

(b) Assuming 3,000 additional machine hours are available, which product should be manufactured?

(c) Prepare an analysis showing the total contribution margin if the additional hours are (1) divided equally among the products, and (2) allocated entirely to the product identified in (b) above.

E26-11 Royce Service Center just purchased an automobile hoist for $15,000. The hoist has a 5-year life and an estimated salvage value of $1,080. Installation costs were $2,900, and freight charges were $820. Royce uses straight-line depreciation.

The new hoist will be used to replace mufflers and tires on automobiles. Royce estimates that the new hoist will enable his mechanics to replace four extra mufflers per week. Each muffler sells for $65 installed. The cost of a muffler is $35, and the labor cost to install a muffler is $10.

Compute cash payback period and annual rate of return.

(SO 9)

Instructions

(a) Compute the payback period for the new hoist.

(b) Compute the annual rate of return for the new hoist. (Round to one decimal.)

E26-12 Tanaka Manufacturing Company is considering three new projects, each requiring an equipment investment of $22,000. Each project will last for 3 years and produce the following cash inflows.

Compute cash payback period and net present value.

(SO 9, 10)

Year	AA	BB	CC
1	$ 7,000	$ 9,500	$13,000
2	9,000	9,500	10,000
3	15,000	9,500	9,000
Total	$31,000	$28,500	$32,000

The equipment's salvage value is zero. Tanaka uses straight-line depreciation. Tanaka will not accept any project with a payback period over 2 years. Tanaka's required rate of return is 12%.

Instructions

(a) Compute each project's payback period, indicating the most desirable project and the least desirable project using this method. (Round to two decimals.)

(b) Compute the net present value of each project. Does your evaluation change? (Round to nearest dollar.)

E26-13 Armando Company is considering a capital investment of $150,000 in additional productive facilities. The new machinery is expected to have a useful life of 5 years with no salvage value. Depreciation is by the straight-line method. During the life of the investment, annual net income and cash inflows are expected to be $18,000 and $48,000, respectively. Armando has a 12% cost of capital rate, which is the minimum acceptable rate of return on the investment.

Compute annual rate of return, cash payback period, and net present value.

(SO 9, 10)

Instructions

(Round to two decimals.)

(a) Compute (1) the annual rate of return and (2) the cash payback period on the proposed capital expenditure.

(b) Using the discounted cash flow technique, compute the net present value.

Determine internal rate of return.
(SO 10)

E26-14 Theta Company is considering three capital expenditure projects. Relevant data for the projects are as follows.

Project	Investment	Annual Income	Life of Project
22A	$240,000	$13,300	6 years
23A	270,000	21,000	9 years
24A	288,000	20,000	8 years

Annual income is constant over the life of the project. Each project is expected to have zero salvage value at the end of the project. Theta Company uses the straight-line method of depreciation.

Instructions
(a) Determine the internal rate of return for each project. Round the internal rate of return factor to three decimals.
(b) If Theta Company's required rate of return is 11%, which projects are acceptable?

Compute net present value and recommend project.
(SO 10)

E26-15 Hyung Corporation is considering investing in two different projects. It could invest in both, neither, or just one of the projects. The forecasts for the projects are as follows.

	Project A	Project B
Capital investment	$200,000	$300,000
Net annual cash flows	$50,000	$65,000
Length of project	5 years	7 years

The required rate of return acceptable to Hyung is 10%.

Instructions
(a) Compute the net present value of the two projects.
(b) What capital budgeting decision should Hyung make?
(c) Project A could be modified. By spending $20,000 more initially, the net annual cash flows could be increased by $10,000 per year. Would this change Hyung's decision?

Exercises: Set B

Visit the book's website, at **www.wiley.com/college/weygandt**, and choose the Student Companion site to access Exercise Set B.

Problems: Set A

Make incremental analysis for special order, and identify non-financial factors in decision.
(SO 3)

P26-1A Jaime Company is currently producing 16,000 units per month, which is 80% of its production capacity. Variable manufacturing costs are currently $8.00 per unit. Fixed manufacturing costs are $56,000 per month. Jaime pays a 9% sales commission to its sales people, has $30,000 in fixed administrative expenses per month, and is averaging $320,000 in sales per month.

A special order received from a foreign company would enable Jaime Company to operate at 100% capacity. The foreign company offered to pay 75% of Jaime's current selling price per unit. If the order is accepted, Jaime will have to spend an extra $2.00 per unit to package the product for overseas shipping. Also, Jaime Company would need to lease a new stamping machine to imprint the foreign company's logo on the product, at a monthly cost of $2,500. The special order would require a sales commission of $3,500.

Instructions
(a) Compute the number of units involved in the special order and the foreign company's offered price per unit.
(b) What is the manufacturing cost of producing one unit of Jaime's product for regular customers?
(c) Prepare an incremental analysis of the special order. Should management accept the order?
(d) What is the lowest price that Jaime could accept for the special order to earn net income of $1.20 per unit?
(e) What nonfinancial factors should management consider in making its decision?

P26-2A   The management of Garcon Manufacturing Company has asked for your assistance in deciding whether to continue manufacturing a part or to buy it from an outside supplier. The part, called Tropica, is a component of Garcon's finished product.

Make incremental analysis related to make or buy; consider opportunity cost, and identify nonfinancial factors.
(SO 4)

An analysis of the accounting records and the production data revealed the following information for the year ending December 31, 2012.

1. The Machinery Department produced 36,000 units of Tropica.
2. Each Tropica unit requires 10 minutes to produce. Three people in the Machinery Department work full time (2,000 hours per year) producing Tropica. Each person is paid $11.00 per hour.
3. The cost of materials per Tropica unit is $2.00.
4. Manufacturing overhead costs directly applicable to the production of Tropica are: indirect labor, $5,500; utilities, $1,300; depreciation, $1,600; property taxes and insurance, $1,000. All of the costs will be eliminated if Tropica is purchased.
5. The lowest price for a Tropica from an outside supplier is $3.90 per unit. Freight charges will be $0.30 per unit, and a part-time receiving clerk at $8,500 per year will be required.
6. If Tropica is purchased, the excess space will be used to store Garcon's finished product. Currently, Garcon rents storage space at approximately $0.60 per unit stored per year. Approximately 6,000 units per year are stored in the rented space.

Instructions
(a) Prepare an incremental analysis for the make-or-buy decision. Should Garcon make or buy the part? Why?
(b) Prepare an incremental analysis, assuming the released facilities can be used to produce $10,000 of net income in addition to the savings on the rental of storage space. What decision should now be made?
(c) ◖━━━▶ What nonfinancial factors should be considered in the decision?

P26-3A   Pierre Manufacturing Company has four operating divisions. During the first quarter of 2012, the company reported total income from operations of $61,000 and the following results for the divisions.

Compute contribution margin, and prepare incremental analysis concerning elimination of divisions.
(SO 7)

| | Division | | | |
	Denver	**Miami**	**San Diego**	**Tacoma**
Sales	$455,000	$730,000	$920,000	$515,000
Cost of goods sold	380,000	480,000	576,000	430,000
Selling and administrative expenses	120,000	207,000	246,000	120,000
Income (loss) from operations	$(45,000)	$ 43,000	$ 98,000	$(35,000)

Analysis reveals the following percentages of variable costs in each division.

	Denver	**Miami**	**San Diego**	**Tacoma**
Cost of goods sold	95%	80%	90%	90%
Selling and administrative expenses	80	60	70	60

Discontinuance of any division would save 60% of the fixed costs and expenses for that division.
Top management is deeply concerned about the unprofitable divisions (Denver and Tacoma). The consensus is that one or both of the divisions should be eliminated.

Instructions
(a) Compute the contribution margin for the two unprofitable divisions.
(b) Prepare an incremental analysis concerning the possible elimination of (1) the Denver Division and (2) the Tacoma Division. What course of action do you recommend for each division?
(c) Prepare a columnar condensed income statement using the CVP format for Pierre Manufacturing Company, assuming (1) the Denver Division is eliminated, and (2) the unavoidable fixed costs and expenses of the Denver Division are allocated 30% to Miami, 50% to San Diego, and 20% to Tacoma.
(d) Compare the total income from operations with the Denver Division ($61,000) to total income from operations without this division.

Compute gain or loss, and determine if equipment should be replaced.

(SO 6)

P26-4A   Last year (2011), Solomon Condos installed a mechanized elevator for its tenants. The owner of the company, Sam Solomon, recently returned from an industry equipment exhibition where he watched a computerized elevator demonstrated. He was impressed with the elevator's speed, comfort of ride, and cost efficiency. Upon returning from the exhibition, he asked his purchasing agent to collect price and operating cost data on the new elevator. In addition, he asked the company's accountant to provide him with cost data on the company's elevator. This information is presented below.

	Old Elevator	New Elevator
Purchase price	$120,000	$180,000
Estimated salvage value	0	0
Estimated useful life	6 years	5 years
Depreciation method	Straight-line	Straight-line
Annual operating costs other than depreciation:		
Variable	$ 35,000	$ 12,000
Fixed	23,000	8,400

Annual revenues are $240,000, and selling and administrative expenses are $29,000, regardless of which elevator is used. If the old elevator is replaced now, at the beginning of 2012, Solomon Condos will be able to sell it for $25,000.

Instructions
(a) Determine any gain or loss if the old elevator is replaced.
(b) Prepare a 5-year summarized income statement for each of the following assumptions:
    (1) The old elevator is retained.
    (2) The old elevator is replaced.
(c) Using incremental analysis, determine if the old elevator should be replaced.
(d) ✎ Write a memo to Sam Solomon explaining why any gain or loss should be ignored in the decision to replace the old elevator.

Compute annual rate of return, cash payback, and net present value.

(SO 9, 10)

P26-5A   Verdugo Corporation is considering three long-term capital investment proposals. Relevant data on each project are as follows.

	Project		
	Brown	Red	Yellow
Capital investment	$190,000	$220,000	$250,000
Annual net income:			
Year 1	25,000	20,000	26,000
2	16,000	20,000	24,000
3	13,000	20,000	23,000
4	10,000	20,000	17,000
5	8,000	20,000	20,000
Total	$ 72,000	$100,000	$110,000

Salvage value is expected to be zero at the end of each project. Depreciation is computed by the straight-line method. The company's required rate of return is the company's cost of capital which is 12%.

Instructions
(a) Compute the annual rate of return for each project. (Round to one decimal.)
(b) Compute the cash payback period for each project. (Round to two decimals.)
(c) Compute the net present value for each project. (Round to nearest dollar.)
(d) Rank the projects on each of the foregoing bases. Which project do you recommend?

Compute annual rate of return, cash payback, and net present value.

(SO 9, 10)

P26-6A   Daphne Kavier is the managing director of the Topeka Day Care Center. Topeka is currently set up as a full-time child care facility for children between the ages of 12 months and 6 years. Daphne is trying to determine whether the center should expand its facilities to incorporate a newborn care room for infants between the ages of 6 weeks and 12 months. The necessary space already exists. An investment of $25,000 would be needed, however, to purchase cribs, high chairs, etc. The equipment purchased for the room would have a 5-year useful life with zero salvage value.

The newborn nursery would be staffed to handle 12 infants on a full-time basis. The parents of each infant would be charged $200 weekly, and the facility would operate 52 weeks of the year. Staffing the nursery would require two full-time specialists and five part-time assistants at an annual cost of $103,800. Food, diapers, and other miscellaneous supplies are expected to total $14,000 annually.

Instructions
(a) Determine (1) annual net income and (2) net cash flow for the new nursery.
(b) Compute (1) the annual rate of return and (2) the cash payback period for the new nursery. (Round to two decimals.)
(c) Assuming that Topeka can borrow the money needed for expansion at 10%, compute the net present value of the new room. (Round to the nearest dollar.)
(d) ━━━━━ What should Daphne conclude from these computations?

P26-7A Aero Tech Testing is considering investing in a new testing device. It has two options: Option A would have an initial lower cost but would require a significant expenditure for rebuilding after 5 years. Option B would require no rebuilding expenditure, but its maintenance costs would be higher. Since the option B machine is of initial higher quality, it is expected to have a salvage value at the end of its useful life. The following estimates were provided. The company's cost of capital is 9%.

Compute net present value and internal rate of return.
(SO 10)

SERVICE

	Option A	Option B
Initial cost	$90,000	$170,000
Net annual cash flows	$20,000	$32,000
Cost to rebuild (end of year 5)	$26,500	$0
Salvage value	$0	$27,500
Estimated useful life	8 years	8 years

Instructions
(a) Compute the (1) net present value, and (2) internal rate of return for each option. (*Hint:* To solve for internal rate of return, experiment with alternative discount rates to arrive at a net present value of zero.)
(b) Which option should be accepted?

Problems: Set B

P26-1B Kobe Inc. manufactures basketballs for the National Basketball Association (NBA). For the first 6 months of 2013, the company reported the following operating results while operating at 90% of plant capacity.

Make incremental analysis for special order, and identify non-financial factors in decision.
(SO 3)

	Amount	Per Unit
Sales	$4,500,000	$50.00
Cost of goods sold	3,150,000	35.00
Selling and administrative expenses	360,000	4.00
Net income	$ 990,000	$11.00

Fixed costs for the period were: Cost of goods sold $900,000, and selling and administrative expenses $135,000.

In July, normally a slack manufacturing month, Kobe receives a special order for 9,000 basketballs at $32 each from the European Basketball Association (EBA). Acceptance of the order would increase variable selling and administrative expenses $0.50 per unit because of shipping costs but would not increase fixed costs and expenses.

Instructions
(a) Prepare an incremental analysis for the special order.
(b) Should Kobe Inc. accept the special order?
(c) What is the minimum selling price on the special order to produce net income of $5.00 per ball?
(d) ━━━━━ What nonfinancial factors should management consider in making its decision?

Make incremental analysis related to make or buy; consider opportunity cost, and identify nonfinancial factors.

(SO 4)

P26-2B The management of Xiao Manufacturing Company is trying to decide whether to continue manufacturing a part or to buy it from an outside supplier. The part, called BIZBE, is a component of the company's finished product.

The following information was collected from the accounting records and production data for the year ending December 31, 2012.

1. 6,000 units of BIZBE were produced in the Machining Department.
2. Variable manufacturing costs applicable to the production of each BIZBE unit were: direct materials $4.75, direct labor $4.60, indirect labor $0.45, utilities $0.35.
3. Fixed manufacturing costs applicable to the production of BIZBE were:

Cost Item	Direct	Allocated
Depreciation	$1,100	$ 900
Property taxes	500	200
Insurance	900	600
	$2,500	$1,700

All variable manufacturing and direct fixed costs will be eliminated if BIZBE is purchased. Allocated costs will have to be absorbed by other production departments.

4. The lowest quotation for 6,000 BIZBE units from a supplier is $66,000.
5. If BIZBE units are purchased, freight and inspection costs would be $0.30 per unit, and receiving costs totaling $750 per year would be incurred by the Machining Department.

Instructions

(a) Prepare an incremental analysis for BIZBE. Your analysis should have columns for (1) Make BIZBE, (2) Buy BIZBE, and (3) Net Income Increase/Decrease.

(b) Based on your analysis, what decision should management make?

(c) Would the decision be different if Xiao Company has the opportunity to produce $6,000 of net income with the facilities currently being used to manufacture BIZBE? Show computations.

(d) ◖▬▬▬▶ What nonfinancial factors should management consider in making its decision?

Compute contribution margin, and prepare incremental analysis concerning elimination of divisions.

(SO 7)

P26-3B Yacco Manufacturing Company has four operating divisions. During the first quarter of 2013, the company reported aggregate income from operations of $135,000 and the divisional results shown on the next page.

	Division			
	I	II	III	IV
Sales	$510,000	$390,000	$310,000	$170,000
Cost of goods sold	300,000	250,000	270,000	150,000
Selling and administrative expenses	60,000	80,000	65,000	70,000
Income (loss) from operations	$150,000	$ 60,000	$(25,000)	$(50,000)

Analysis reveals the following percentages of variable costs in each division.

	I	II	III	IV
Cost of goods sold	70%	80%	75%	90%
Selling and administrative expenses	40	50	60	70

Discontinuance of any division would save 50% of the fixed costs and expenses for that division.

Top management is very concerned about the unprofitable divisions (III and IV). Consensus is that one or both of the divisions should be discontinued.

Instructions

(a) Compute the contribution margin for Divisions III and IV.

(b) Prepare an incremental analysis concerning the possible discontinuance of (1) Division III and (2) Division IV. What course of action do you recommend for each division?

(c) Prepare a columnar condensed income statement for Yacco Manufacturing, assuming Division IV is eliminated. Use the CVP format. Division IV's unavoidable fixed costs are allocated equally to the continuing divisions.

(d) Reconcile the total income from operations ($135,000) with the total income from operations without Division IV.

P26-4B   Last year (2011), Bourne Company installed new factory equipment. The owner of the company, Jason Bourne, recently returned from an industry equipment exhibition where he watched computerized equipment demonstrated. He was impressed with the equipment's speed and cost efficiency. Upon returning from the exhibition, he asked his purchasing agent to collect price and operating cost data on the new equipment. In addition, he asked the company's accountant to provide him with cost data on the company's equipment. This information is presented below.

Compute gain or loss, and determine if equipment should be replaced.

(SO 6)

SERVICE

	Old Equipment	New Equipment
Purchase price	$210,000	$270,000
Estimated salvage value	0	0
Estimated useful life	6 years	5 years
Depreciation method	Straight-line	Straight-line
Annual operating cost other than depreciation:		
Variable	$50,000	$15,000
Fixed	30,000	8,000

Annual revenues are $360,000, and selling and administrative expenses are $45,000, regardless of which equipment is used. If the old equipment is replaced now, at the beginning of 2012, Bourne Company will be able to sell it for $38,000.

Instructions
(a) Determine any gain or loss if the old equipment is replaced.
(b) Prepare a 5-year summarized income statement for each of the following assumptions:
  (1) The old equipment is retained.
  (2) The old equipment is replaced.
(c) Using incremental analysis, determine if the old equipment should be replaced.
(d) ⬤━━━ Write a memo to Jason Bourne explaining why any gain or loss should be ignored in the decision to replace the old equipment.

P26-5B   Zalopa Corporation is considering three long-term capital investment proposals. Each investment has a useful life of 5 years. Relevant data on each project are as follows.

Compute annual rate of return, cash payback, and net present value.

(SO 9, 10)

	Project Ric	Project Rac	Project Roe
Capital investment	$140,000	$150,000	$180,000
Annual net income:			
Year 1	13,000	18,000	27,000
2	13,000	17,000	22,000
3	13,000	13,000	16,000
4	13,000	12,000	13,000
5	13,000	9,000	12,000
Total	$ 65,000	$ 69,000	$ 90,000

Depreciation is computed by the straight-line method with no salvage value. The company's cost of capital is 15%.

Instructions
(a) Compute the annual rate of return for each project. (Round to one decimal.)
(b) Compute the cash payback period for each project. (Round to two decimals.)
(c) Compute the net present value for each project. (Round to nearest dollar.)
(d) Rank the projects on each of the foregoing bases. Which project do you recommend?

P26-6B   Cindi Austen is an accounting major at a midwestern state university located approximately 60 miles from a major city. Many of the students attending the university are from the metropolitan area and visit their homes regularly on the weekends. Cindi, an entrepreneur at heart, realizes that few good commuting alternatives are available for students doing weekend travel. She believes that a weekend commuting service could be organized and run profitably from several suburban and downtown shopping mall locations. Cindi has gathered the following investment information.

Compute annual rate of return, cash payback, and net present value.

(SO, 9, 10)

SERVICE

1. Six used vans would cost a total of $96,000 to purchase and would have a 3-year useful life with negligible salvage value. Cindi plans to use straight-line depreciation.
2. Ten drivers would have to be employed at a total payroll expense of $70,000.

3. Other annual out-of-pocket expenses associated with running the commuter service would include gasoline $28,000, maintenance $2,800, repairs $3,500, insurance $3,200, and advertising $1,500. (Exclude interest expense.)
4. Cindi has visited several financial institutions to discuss funding for her new venture. The best interest rate she has been able to negotiate is 10%. Use this rate for cost of capital.
5. Cindi expects each van to make ten round trips weekly and carry an average of five students each trip. The service is expected to operate 30 weeks each years. Each student will be charged $16.00 for a round-trip ticket.

Instructions
(a) Determine the annual (1) net income, and (2) net cash flow for the commuter service.
(b) Compute (1) the annual rate of return, and (2) the cash payback period. (Round to two decimals.)
(c) Compute the net present value of the commuter service. (Round to the nearest dollar.)
(d) 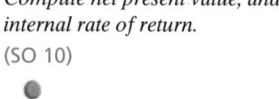 What should Cindi conclude from these computations?

Compute net present value, and internal rate of return.
(SO 10)

P26-7B   Taos Clinic is considering investing in new heart-monitoring equipment. It has two options: Option A would have an initial lower cost but would require a significant expenditure for rebuilding after 4 years. Option B would require no rebuilding expenditure, but its maintenance costs would be higher. Since the option B machine is of initial higher quality, it is expected to have a salvage value at the end of its useful life. The following estimates were made of the cash flows. The company's cost of capital is 8%.

	Option A	Option B
Initial cost	$135,000	$203,000
Net annual cash flows	$31,000	$40,000
Cost to rebuild (end of year 4)	$50,000	$0
Salvage value	$0	$10,000
Estimated useful life	8 years	8 years

Instructions
(a) Compute the (1) net present value and (2) internal rate of return for each option. (*Hint:* To solve for internal rate of return, experiment with alternative discount rates to arrive at a net present value of zero.)
(b) Which option should be accepted?

Problems: Set C

Visit the book's companion website, at **www.wiley.com/college/weygandt**, and choose the Student Companion site to access Problem Set C.

Comprehensive Problem: Chapters 19 to 26

CP26   You would like to start a business manufacturing a unique model of bicycle helmet. In preparation for an interview with the bank to discuss your financing needs, you develop answers to the following questions. A number of assumptions are required; clearly note all assumptions that you make.

Instructions
(a) Identify the types of costs that would likely be involved in making this product.
(b) Set up five columns as indicated.

	Product Costs			
Item	**Direct Materials**	**Direct Labor**	**Manufacturing Overhead**	**Period Costs**

Classify the costs you identified in (a) into the manufacturing cost classifications of product costs (direct materials, direct labor, and manufacturing overhead) and period costs.

(c) Assign hypothetical monthly dollar figures to the costs you identified in (a) and (b).

(d) Assume you have no raw materials or work in process beginning or ending inventories. Prepare a projected cost of goods manufactured schedule for the first month of operations.

(e) Project the number of helmets you expect to produce the first month of operations. Compute the cost to produce one bicycle helmet. Review the result to ensure it is reasonable; if not, return to part (c) and adjust the monthly dollar figures you assigned accordingly.

(f) What type of cost accounting system will you likely use—job order or process costing?

(g) Explain how you would assign costs in either the job order or process costing system you plan to use.

(h) Classify your costs as either variable or fixed costs. For simplicity, assign all costs to either variable or fixed, assuming there are no mixed costs, using the format shown.

Item	Variable Costs	Fixed Costs	Total Costs

(i) Compute the unit variable cost, using the production number you determined in (e).

(j) Project the number of helmets you anticipate selling the first month of operations. Set a unit selling price, and compute both the contribution margin per unit and the contribution margin ratio.

(k) Determine your break-even point in dollars and in units.

(l) Prepare projected operating budgets (sales, production, direct materials, direct labor, manufacturing overhead, selling and administrative expense, and income statement). You will need to make assumptions for each of the following:

Direct materials budget:	Quantity of direct materials required to produce one helmet; cost per unit of quantity; desired ending direct materials (assume none).
Direct labor budget:	Direct labor time required per helmet; direct labor cost per hour.
Budgeted income statement:	Income tax expense is 45% of income from operations.

(m) Prepare a cash budget for the month. Assume the percentage of sales that will be collected from customers is 75%, and the percentage of direct materials that will be paid in the current month is 75%.

(n) Determine a relevant range of activity, using the number of helmets produced as your activity index. Recast your manufacturing overhead budget into a flexible monthly budget for two additional activity levels.

(o) Identify one potential cause of materials, direct labor, and manufacturing overhead variances for your product.

(p) Assume that you wish to purchase production equipment that costs $720,000. Determine the cash payback period, utilizing the monthly cash flow that you computed in part (m) multiplied by 12 months (for simplicity).

(q) Identify any nonfinancial factors that should be considered before commencing your business venture.

Waterways Continuing Problem

(This is a continuation of the Waterways Problem from Chapters 19 through 25.)

WCP26   Waterways Corporation puts much emphasis on cash flow when it plans for capital investments. The company chose its discount rate of 8% based on the rate of return it must pay its owners and creditors. Using that rate, Waterways then uses different methods to determine the best decisions for making capital outlays. Waterways is considering buying five new backhoes to replace the backhoes it now has. This problem asks you to evaluate that decision, using various capital budgeting techniques.

Go to the book's companion website, **www.wiley.com/college/weygandt,** *to find the remainder of this problem.*

BROADENINGYOURPERSPECTIVE

Decision Making Across the Organization

BYP26-1　Bigelow Company is considering the purchase of a new machine. The invoice price of the machine is $170,000, freight charges are estimated to be $4,000, and installation costs are expected to be $6,000. Salvage value of the new equipment is expected to be zero after a useful life of 4 years. Existing equipment could be retained and used for an additional 4 years if the new machine is not purchased. At that time, the salvage value of the equipment would be zero. If the new machine is purchased now, the existing machine would be scrapped. Bigelow's accountant, Carmen Cabel, has accumulated the following data regarding annual sales and expenses with and without the new machine.

1. Without the new machine, Bigelow can sell 10,000 units of product annually at a per unit selling price of $100. If the new unit is purchased, the number of units produced and sold would increase by 20%. The selling price would remain the same.
2. The new machine is faster than the old machine, and it is more efficient in its usage of materials. With the old machine the gross profit rate will be 25% of sales. With the new machine the rate will be 28% of sales.
3. Annual selling expenses are $135,000 with the current equipment. Because the new equipment would produce a greater number of units to be sold, annual selling expenses are expected to increase by 10% if it is purchased.
4. Annual administrative expenses are expected to be $100,000 with the old machine and $113,000 with the new machine.
5. The current book value of the existing machine is $36,000. Bigelow uses straight-line depreciation.
6. Bigelow's management wants a required rate of return of 15% on its investment and a payback period of no more than 3 years.

Instructions

With the class divided into groups, answer the following. (Ignore income tax effects.)

(a) Prepare an incremental analysis for the 4 years showing whether Bigelow should keep the existing machine or buy the new machine.
(b) Calculate the annual rate of return for the new machine. (Round to two decimals.)
(c) Compute the payback period for the new machine. (Round to two decimals.)
(d) Compute the net present value of the new machine. (Round to the nearest dollar.)
(e) On the basis of the foregoing data, would you recommend that Bigelow buy the machine? Why?

Managerial Analysis

BYP26-2　Cletus Company manufactures private-label small electronic products, such as alarm clocks, calculators, kitchen timers, stopwatches, and automatic pencil sharpeners. Some of the products are sold as sets, and others are sold individually. Products are studied as to their sales potential, and then cost estimates are made. The Engineering Department develops production plans, and then production begins. The company has generally had very successful product introduction. Only two products introduced by the company have been discontinued.

One of the products currently sold is a multi-alarm clock. The clock has four alarms that can be programmed to sound at various times and for varying lengths of time. The company has experienced a great deal of difficulty in making the circuit boards for the clocks. The production process has never operated smoothly. The product is unprofitable at the present time, primarily because of warranty repairs and product recalls. Two models of the clocks were recalled, for example, because they sometimes caused an electric shock when the alarms were being shut off. The Engineering Department is attempting to revise the manufacturing process, but the revision will take another 6 months at least.

The clocks were very popular when they were introduced, and since they are private-label, the company has not suffered much from the recalls. Presently, the company has a very large order for several items from Kmart Stores. The order includes 5,000 of the multi-alarm clocks. When Cletus suggested that Kmart purchase the clocks from another manufacturer, Kmart threatened to rescind the entire order unless the clocks were included.

Cletus has therefore investigated the possibility of having another company make the clocks for them. The clocks were bid for the Kmart order, based on an estimated $5.50 cost to manufacture, as follows.

Circuit board, 1 each @ $1.00	$1.00
Plastic case, 1 each @ $0.50	0.50
Alarms, 4 @ $0.15 each	0.60
Labor, 15 minutes @ $12/hour	3.00
Overhead, $1.60 per labor hour	0.40

Cletus could purchase clocks to fill the Kmart order for $9 from Black Pearl, a Japanese manufacturer with a very good quality record. Black Pearl has offered to reduce the price to $7.50 after Cletus has been a customer for 6 months, placing an order of at least 1,000 units per month. If Cletus becomes a "preferred customer" by purchasing 15,000 units per year, the price would be reduced still further to $4.50.

Beta Products, a local manufacturer, has also offered to make clocks for Cletus. They have offered to sell 5,000 clocks for $5 each. However, Beta Products has been in business for only 6 months. It has experienced significant turnover in its labor force, and the local media have reported that the owners may soon face tax-evasion charges. The owner of Beta Products is an electronic engineer, however, and the quality of the clocks is likely to be good.

If Cletus decides to purchase the clocks from either Black Pearl or Beta, all the costs to manufacturer could be avoided, except a total of $5,000 in overhead costs for machine depreciation. The machinery is fairly new, and has no alternate use.

Instructions

(a) What is the difference in profit under each of the alternatives if the clocks are to be sold for $13.00 each to Kmart?

(b) What are the most important nonfinancial factors that Cletus should consider when making this decision?

(c) What should Cletus do in regard to the Kmart order? What should it do in regard to continuing to manufacture the multi-alarm clocks? Be prepared to defend your answer.

Real-World Focus

BYP26-3   Founded in 1983, the Beverly Hills Fan Company is located in Woodland Hills, California. With 23 employees and sales of less than $10 million, the company is relatively small. Management feels that there is potential for growth in the upscale market for ceiling fans and lighting. They are particularly optimistic about growth in Mexican and Canadian markets.

Presented below is information from the president's letter in the company's annual report.

Beverly Hills Fan Company
President's Letter

An aggressive product development program was initiated during the past year resulting in new ceiling fan models planned for introduction next year. Award winning industrial designer Ron Rezek created several new fan models for the Beverly Hills Fan and L.A. Fan lines, including a new Showroom Collection, designed specifically for the architectural and designer markets. Each of these models has received critical acclaim, and order commitments for next year have been outstanding. Additionally, our Custom Color and special order fans continued to enjoy increasing popularity and sales gains as more and more customers desire fans that match their specific interior decors. Currently, Beverly Hills Fan Company offers a product line of over 100 models of contemporary, traditional, and transitional ceiling fans.

Instructions

(a) What points did the company management need to consider before deciding to offer the special-order fans to customers?

(b) How would incremental analysis be employed to assist in this decision?

On the Web

BYP26-4   Campbell Soup Company is an international provider of soup products. Management is very interested in continuing to grow the company in its core business, while "spinning off" those businesses that are not part of its core operation.

Address: www.campbellsoups.com, or go to **www.wiley.com/college/weygandt**

Steps:

1. Go to the home page of Campbell Soup Company at the address shown above.
2. Choose **Our Company** and then **Investor Center**.
3. Choose **Financial Reports**.
4. Choose the 2007 annual report, or the current annual report if 2007 is no longer available.

Instructions

Review the financial statements and management's discussion and analysis, and answer the following questions.

(a) What was the total amount reported as "Purchases of Plant Assets" in the 2007 statement of cash flows? How does this amount compare with the previous year?

(b) What range of interest rates does the company report on its long-term liabilities in the notes to its financial statements?

(c) Assume that this year's capital expenditures are expected to increase cash flows by $45 million. What is the expected internal rate of return (IRR) for these capital expenditures? (Assume a 10-year period for the cash flows.)

Communication Activity

BYP26-5   Refer back to E26-11 to address the following.

Instructions

Prepare a memo to Billie Evans, your supervisor. Show your calculations from E26-11, parts (a) and (b). In one or two paragraphs, discuss important nonfinancial considerations. Make any assumptions you believe to be necessary. Make a recommendation, based on your analysis.

Ethics Case

BYP26-6   Forcier Company operates in a state where corporate taxes and workmen's compensation insurance rates have recently doubled. Forcier's president has assigned you the task of preparing an economic analysis and making a recommendation about whether to move the company's entire operation to Missouri. The president is slightly in favor of such a move because Missouri is his boyhood home, and he also owns a fishing lodge there.

You have just completed building your dream house, moved in, and sodded the lawn. Your children are all doing well in school and sports and, along with your spouse, want no part of a move to Missouri. If the company does move, so will you because your town is a one-industry community, and you and your spouse will have to move to have employment. Moving when everyone else does will cause you to take a big loss on the sale of your house. The same hardships will be suffered by your co-workers, and the town will be devastated.

In compiling the costs of moving versus not moving, you have latitude in the assumptions you make, the estimates you compute, and the discount rates and time periods you project. You are in a position to influence the decision singlehandedly.

Instructions

(a) Who are the stakeholders in this situation?
(b) What are the ethical issues in this situation?
(c) What would you do in this situation?

"All About You" Activity

BYP26-7   Managerial accounting techniques can be used in a wide variety of settings. As we have frequently pointed out, you can use them in many personal situations. They also can be useful in trying to find solutions for societal issues that appear to be hard to solve.

Instructions

Read the *Fortune* article "The Toughest Customers: How Hardheaded Business Metrics Can Help the Hard-core Homeless," by Cait Murphy, available at *http://money.cnn.com/magazines/fortune/fortune_archive/2006/04/03/8373067/index.htm*. Answer the following questions.

(a) How does the article define "chronic" homelessness?

(b) In what ways does homelessness cost a city money? What are the estimated costs of a chronic homeless person to various cities?

(c) What are the steps suggested to address the problem?

(d) What is the estimated cost of implementing this program in New York? What results have been seen?

(e) In terms of incremental analysis, frame the relevant costs in this situation.

Answers to Insight and Accounting Across the Organization Questions

p. 1196 That Letter from AmEx Might Not Be a Bill   Q: What are the relevant costs that American Express would need to know in order to determine to whom to make this offer? **A:** Clearly, American Express would make this offer to those customers that are most likely to default on their bills. The most important relevant cost would be the "expected loss" that an at-risk customer posed. If a customer has a high probability of defaulting, and if the expected loss exceeds the $300 cost, then American Express can probably save money by paying that customer to quit using its card so that the customer doesn't ring up an even bigger bill.

p. 1200 These Wheels Have Miles Before Installation   Q: What are the disadvantages of outsourcing to a foreign country? **A:** Possible disadvantages of outsourcing are that the supplier loses control over the quality of the product, as well as the timing of production. Also, the company exposes itself to price changes caused by changes in the value of the foreign currency. In addition, shipping large, heavy products such as tires is costly, and disruptions in shipping (due to strikes, weather, etc.) can cause delays in final assembly of vehicles. As a result of the outsourcing, the company will have to reassign, or even lay off, many skilled workers. Not only is this very disruptive to the lives of those employees, it also hurts morale of the remaining employees. As more U.S. employers begin to use robotic automation in their facilities, they are able to reduce the amount of labor required, and thus are beginning to be able to compete more favorably with foreign suppliers.

p. 1204 Time to Move to a New Neighborhood?   Q: What were some of the factors that complicated the company's decision to move? How should the company have incorporated such factors into its incremental analysis? **A:** The company received only $7.5 million for its California property, only 58 of 75 key employees were willing to move, construction was delayed by a year which caused the new plant to increase in price by $1.5 million, and wages surged in Idaho due to low unemployment. In performing incremental analysis of the decision to move, a company should perform sensitivity analysis. This would include evaluating the impact on the decision if all costs were, for example, 10% higher than expected or if cost savings were 10% lower than expected.

p. 1207 Investing for the Future   Q: Why is it important for top management to constantly monitor the nature, amount, and success of a company's capital expenditures? **A:** In order to remain competitive and to grow, companies must continually invest in new opportunities. However, not all projects will be successful, so management must continually monitor projects to ensure that continuation of the investment is in the company's best interest.

p. 1212 Seeing the Big Picture   Q: How important is the choice of discount rate in making capital budgeting decisions? **A:** The point of this discussion is that errors in implementation, as well as the accuracy of the estimated future benefits and costs as measured by cash inflows and outflows, is what matters the most when making capital expenditure decisions. While the choice of discount rates will result in incremental differences in present value calculations, "missing the big picture" has the potential to cause much bigger decision errors. Underestimating potential future cash inflows can result in missed opportunities. Underestimating future costs can result in failed investments.

Answers to Self-Test Questions

1. d   **2.** b   **3.** c [($18 − $14) × 3,000]   **4.** b   **5.** d   **6.** a   **7.** d ($68 − $32) − ($55 − $20)   **8.** b   **9.** c
10. d ($200,000 − $140,000 − $50,000)   **11.** b ($15 ÷ 3)   **12.** d   **13.** b   **14.** c   **15.** b

✔ The Navigator

✔ **Remember to go back to the Navigator box on the chapter opening page and check off your completed work.**

APPENDIXA

Specimen Financial Statements:

PepsiCo, Inc.

The Annual Report

Once each year a corporation communicates to its stockholders and other interested parties by issuing a complete set of audited financial statements. The **annual report**, as this communication is called, summarizes the financial results of the company's operations for the year and its plans for the future. Many annual reports are attractive, multicolored, glossy public relations pieces, containing pictures of corporate officers and directors as well as photos and descriptions of new products and new buildings. Yet the basic function of every annual report is to report financial information, almost all of which is a product of the corporation's accounting system.

The content and organization of corporate annual reports have become fairly standardized. Excluding the public relations part of the report (pictures, products, etc.), the following are the traditional financial portions of the annual report:

- Financial Highlights
- Letter to the Stockholders
- Management's Discussion and Analysis
- Financial Statements
- Notes to the Financial Statements
- Management's Responsibility for Financial Reporting
- Management's Report on Internal Control over Financial Reporting
- Report of Independent Registered Public Accounting Firm
- Selected Financial Data

In this appendix we illustrate current financial reporting with a comprehensive set of corporate financial statements that are prepared in accordance with generally accepted accounting principles and audited by an international independent certified public accounting firm. We are grateful for permission to use the actual financial statements and other accompanying financial information from the annual report of a large, publicly held company, PepsiCo, Inc.

Financial Highlights

Companies usually present the financial highlights section inside the front cover of the annual report or on its first two pages. This section generally reports the total or per share amounts for five to fifteen financial items for the current year and one or more previous years. Financial items from the income statement and the balance sheet that typically are presented are sales, income from continuing operations, net income, net income per share, net cash provided by operating activities, dividends per common share, and the amount of capital expenditures. The financial highlights section from PepsiCo's Annual Report is shown on page A2.

The financial information herein is reprinted with permission from the PepsiCo, Inc. 2009 Annual Report. The complete financial statements are available through a link at the book's companion website.

Financial Highlights

PepsiCo, Inc. and subsidiaries
(in millions except per share data; all per share amounts assume dilution)

	2009	2008	Chg (a)	Chg Constant Currency (a)(e)
Summary of Operations				
Total net revenue	$43,232	$43,251	–%	5%
Core division operating profit (b)	$ 8,647	$ 8,499	2%	6%
Core total operating profit (c)	$ 7,856	$ 7,848	–%	
Core net income attributable to PepsiCo (c)	$ 5,846	$ 5,887	(1)%	
Core earnings per share (c)	$ 3.71	$ 3.68	1%	6%
Other Data				
Management operating cash flow, excluding certain items (d)	$ 5,583	$ 4,831	16%	
Net cash provided by operating activities	$ 6,796	$ 6,999	(3)%	
Capital spending	$ 2,128	$ 2,446	(13)%	
Common share repurchases	$ –	$ 4,720	n/m	
Dividends paid	$ 2,732	$ 2,541	8%	
Long-term debt	$ 7,400	$ 7,858	(6)%	

(a) *Percentage changes are based on unrounded amounts.*

(b) *Excludes corporate unallocated expenses, restructuring and impairment charges and PBG and PAS merger costs. See page 91 for a reconciliation to the most directly comparable financial measure in accordance with GAAP.*

(c) *Excludes restructuring and impairment charges, PBG and PAS merger costs and the net mark-to-market impact of our commodity hedges. See pages 91 and 92 for a reconciliation to the most directly comparable financial measure in accordance with GAAP.*

(d) *Includes the impact of net capital spending, and excludes the impact of a discretionary pension contribution, cash payments for PBG and PAS merger costs and restructuring-related cash payments. See also "Our Liquidity and Capital Resources" in Management's Discussion and Analysis. See page 92 for a reconciliation to the most directly comparable financial measure in accordance with GAAP.*

(e) *Assumes constant currency exchange rates used for translation based on the rates in effect in 2008. See pages 91 and 92 for a reconciliation to the most directly comparable financial measure in accordance with GAAP.*

Core Earnings Per Share*

$3.37 $3.68 $3.71
07   08   09

*See page 92 for a reconciliation to the most directly comparable financial measure in accordance with GAAP.

Management Operating Cash Flow, Excluding Certain Items**
(in millions)

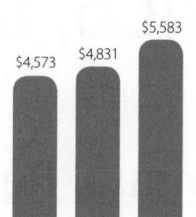

$4,573 $4,831 $5,583
07   08   09

**See page 92 for a reconciliation to the most directly comparable financial measure in accordance with GAAP.

Cumulative Total Shareholder Return

*Return on PepsiCo stock investment (including dividends), the S&P 500 and the S&P Average of Industry Groups.****

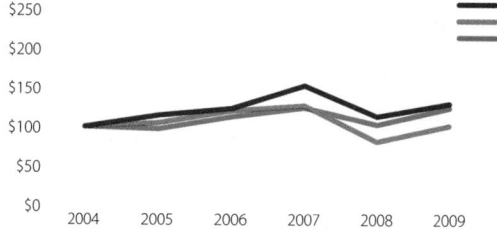

— PepsiCo, Inc.
— S&P 500®
— S&P® Average of Industry Groups***

***The S&P Average of Industry Groups is derived by weighting the returns of two applicable S&P Industry Groups (Non-Alcoholic Beverages and Food) by PepsiCo's sales in its beverage and foods businesses. The returns for PepsiCo, the S&P 500 and the S&P Average indices are calculated through December 31, 2009.

	Dec-04	Dec-05	Dec-06	Dec-07	Dec-08	Dec-09
PepsiCo, Inc.	$100	$115	$124	$154	$114	$131
S&P 500®	$100	$105	$121	$128	$ 81	$102
S&P® Avg. of Industry Groups***	$100	$ 97	$113	$125	$103	$125

PepsiCo Estimated Worldwide Retail Sales: $108 Billion

Includes estimated retail sales of all PepsiCo products, including those sold by our partners and franchised bottlers.

Net Revenues

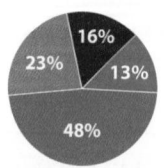

16%   13%   23%   48%

● PepsiCo Americas Foods – 48%
● PepsiCo Americas Beverages – 23%
  PepsiCo International – 29%
    ● Europe – 16%
    ● AMEA – 13%

Mix of Net Revenue

37%   63%

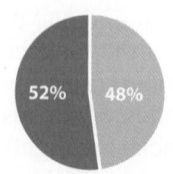

52%   48%

● Food – 63%
● Beverage – 37%

● U.S. – 52%
● Outside the U.S. – 48%

Pro Forma Revenue Percentage by Segment

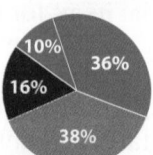

10%   36%   16%   38%

● PepsiCo Americas Foods – 36%
● PepsiCo Americas Beverages – 38%
  PepsiCo International – 26%
    ● Europe – 16%
    ● AMEA – 10%

The above pro forma 2009 revenue chart has been prepared to illustrate the effect of the PBG and PAS mergers as if the mergers had been completed as of the beginning of PepsiCo's 2009 fiscal year. The pro forma revenue presented above is not indicative of the future operating results or financial position of PBG, PAS and PepsiCo and is based upon preliminary estimates. The final amounts recorded may differ from the information presented and are subject to change.

Letter to the Shareholders

Nearly every annual report contains a letter to the shareholders from the chairman of the board or the president, or both. This letter typically discusses the company's accomplishments during the past year and highlights significant events such as mergers and acquisitions, new products, operating achievements, business philosophy, changes in officers or directors, financing commitments, expansion plans, and future prospects. The letter to the stockholders is signed by Indra Nooyi, Chairman of the Board and Chief Executive Officer, of PepsiCo.

Only a short summary of the letter is provided below. The full letter can be accessed at the book's companion website at **www.wiley.com/college/weygandt**.

Indra K. Nooyi, *Chairman and Chief Executive Officer*

Dear Fellow Shareholders,

Our commitment to the principles and values of *Performance with Purpose* has helped us earn trust and respect from our consumers and partners, and the communities in which we operate across the world. By staying true to this foundation and continuing to execute on our strategies, we are sure that PepsiCo will continue to provide long-term sustainable growth for all stakeholders.

The *Performance with Purpose* initiatives that we have chosen to showcase in this year's annual report demonstrate that what's right for society is also what's right for business. It is a belief to which we are deeply committed. It has stood the test in difficult years, and we believe it will stand the test of time to come.

INDRA K. NOOYI
Chairman and Chief Executive Officer

Management's Discussion and Analysis

The **management's discussion and analysis (MD&A)** section covers three financial aspects of a company: its results of operations, its ability to pay near-term obligations, and its ability to fund operations and expansion. Management must highlight favorable or unfavorable trends and identity significant events and uncertainties that affect these three factors. This discussion obviously involves a number of subjective estimates and opinions. In its MD&A section, PepsiCo breaks its discussion into three major headings: Our Business, Our Critical Accounting Policies, and Our Financial Results. You can access the full MD&A section at **www.wiley.com/college/weygandt**.

Financial Statements and Accompanying Notes

The standard set of financial statements consists of: (1) a comparative income statement for three years, (2) a comparative statement of cash flows for three years, (3) a comparative balance sheet for two years, (4) a statement of equity for three years, and (5) a set of accompanying notes that are considered an integral part of the financial statements. The auditor's report, unless stated otherwise, covers the financial statements and the accompanying notes. PepsiCo's financial statements and accompanying notes plus supplementary data and analyses follow.

Consolidated Statement of Income

PepsiCo, Inc. and Subsidiaries
(in millions except per share amounts)

Fiscal years ended December 26, 2009, December 27, 2008 and December 29, 2007	2009	2008	2007
Net Revenue	$43,232	$43,251	$39,474
Cost of sales	20,099	20,351	18,038
Selling, general and administrative expenses	15,026	15,877	14,196
Amortization of intangible assets	63	64	58
Operating Profit	8,044	6,959	7,182
Bottling equity income	365	374	560
Interest expense	(397)	(329)	(224)
Interest income	67	41	125
Income before Income Taxes	8,079	7,045	7,643
Provision for Income Taxes	2,100	1,879	1,973
Net Income	5,979	5,166	5,670
Less: Net income attributable to noncontrolling interests	33	24	12
Net Income Attributable to PepsiCo	$ 5,946	$ 5,142	$ 5,658
Net Income Attributable to PepsiCo per Common Share			
Basic	$ 3.81	$ 3.26	$ 3.48
Diluted	$ 3.77	$ 3.21	$ 3.41

See accompanying notes to consolidated financial statements.

Consolidated Statement of Cash Flows

PepsiCo, Inc. and Subsidiaries
(in millions)

Fiscal years ended December 26, 2009, December 27, 2008 and December 29, 2007	2009	2008	2007
Operating Activities			
Net income	$ 5,979	$ 5,166	$ 5,670
Depreciation and amortization	1,635	1,543	1,426
Stock-based compensation expense	227	238	260
Restructuring and impairment charges	36	543	102
Cash payments for restructuring charges	(196)	(180)	(22)
PBG/PAS merger costs	50	–	–
Cash payments for PBG/PAS merger costs	(49)	–	–
Excess tax benefits from share-based payment arrangements	(42)	(107)	(208)
Pension and retiree medical plan contributions	(1,299)	(219)	(310)
Pension and retiree medical plan expenses	423	459	535
Bottling equity income, net of dividends	(235)	(202)	(441)
Deferred income taxes and other tax charges and credits	284	573	118
Change in accounts and notes receivable	188	(549)	(405)
Change in inventories	17	(345)	(204)
Change in prepaid expenses and other current assets	(127)	(68)	(16)
Change in accounts payable and other current liabilities	(133)	718	522
Change in income taxes payable	319	(180)	128
Other, net	(281)	(391)	(221)
Net Cash Provided by Operating Activities	6,796	6,999	6,934
Investing Activities			
Capital spending	(2,128)	(2,446)	(2,430)
Sales of property, plant and equipment	58	98	47
Proceeds from finance assets	–	–	27
Acquisitions and investments in noncontrolled affiliates	(500)	(1,925)	(1,320)
Divestitures	99	6	–
Cash restricted for pending acquisitions	15	(40)	–
Cash proceeds from sale of PBG and PAS stock	–	358	315
Short-term investments, by original maturity			
More than three months—purchases	(29)	(156)	(83)
More than three months—maturities	71	62	113
Three months or less, net	13	1,376	(413)
Net Cash Used for Investing Activities	(2,401)	(2,667)	(3,744)
Financing Activities			
Proceeds from issuances of long-term debt	1,057	3,719	2,168
Payments of long-term debt	(226)	(649)	(579)
Short-term borrowings, by original maturity			
More than three months—proceeds	26	89	83
More than three months—payments	(81)	(269)	(133)
Three months or less, net	(963)	625	(345)
Cash dividends paid	(2,732)	(2,541)	(2,204)
Share repurchases—common	–	(4,720)	(4,300)
Share repurchases—preferred	(7)	(6)	(12)
Proceeds from exercises of stock options	413	620	1,108
Excess tax benefits from share-based payment arrangements	42	107	208
Other financing	(26)	–	–
Net Cash Used for Financing Activities	(2,497)	(3,025)	(4,006)
Effect of exchange rate changes on cash and cash equivalents	(19)	(153)	75
Net Increase/(Decrease) in Cash and Cash Equivalents	1,879	1,154	(741)
Cash and Cash Equivalents, Beginning of Year	2,064	910	1,651
Cash and Cash Equivalents, End of Year	$ 3,943	$ 2,064	$ 910

See accompanying notes to consolidated financial statements.

Consolidated Balance Sheet

PepsiCo, Inc. and Subsidiaries
(in millions except per share amounts)

December 26, 2009 and December 27, 2008	**2009**	2008
ASSETS		
Current Assets		
Cash and cash equivalents	$ 3,943	$ 2,064
Short-term investments	192	213
Accounts and notes receivable, net	4,624	4,683
Inventories	2,618	2,522
Prepaid expenses and other current assets	1,194	1,324
Total Current Assets	12,571	10,806
Property, Plant and Equipment, net	12,671	11,663
Amortizable Intangible Assets, net	841	732
Goodwill	6,534	5,124
Other nonamortizable intangible assets	1,782	1,128
Nonamortizable Intangible Assets	8,316	6,252
Investments in Noncontrolled Affiliates	4,484	3,883
Other Assets	965	2,658
Total Assets	$ 39,848	$ 35,994
LIABILITIES AND EQUITY		
Current Liabilities		
Short-term obligations	$ 464	$ 369
Accounts payable and other current liabilities	8,127	8,273
Income taxes payable	165	145
Total Current Liabilities	8,756	8,787
Long-Term Debt Obligations	7,400	7,858
Other Liabilities	5,591	6,541
Deferred Income Taxes	659	226
Total Liabilities	22,406	23,412
Commitments and Contingencies		
Preferred Stock, no par value	41	41
Repurchased Preferred Stock	(145)	(138)
PepsiCo Common Shareholders' Equity		
Common stock, par value 1 2/3¢ per share (authorized 3,600 shares, issued 1,782 shares)	30	30
Capital in excess of par value	250	351
Retained earnings	33,805	30,638
Accumulated other comprehensive loss	(3,794)	(4,694)
Repurchased common stock, at cost (217 and 229 shares, respectively)	(13,383)	(14,122)
Total PepsiCo Common Shareholders' Equity	16,908	12,203
Noncontrolling interests	638	476
Total Equity	17,442	12,582
Total Liabilities and Equity	$ 39,848	$ 35,994

See accompanying notes to consolidated financial statements.

Consolidated Statement of Equity

PepsiCo, Inc. and Subsidiaries
(in millions)

Fiscal years ended December 26, 2009, December 27, 2008 and December 29, 2007	2009 Shares	2009 Amount	2008 Shares	2008 Amount	2007 Shares	2007 Amount
Preferred Stock	0.8	$ 41	0.8	$ 41	0.8	$ 41
Repurchased Preferred Stock						
Balance, beginning of year	(0.5)	(138)	(0.5)	(132)	(0.5)	(120)
Redemptions	(0.1)	(7)	(–)	(6)	(–)	(12)
Balance, end of period	(0.6)	(145)	(0.5)	(138)	(0.5)	(132)
Common Stock	1,782	30	1,782	30	1,782	30
Capital in Excess of Par Value						
Balance, beginning of year		351		450		584
Stock-based compensation expense		227		238		260
Stock option exercises/RSUs converted(a)		(292)		(280)		(347)
Withholding tax on RSUs converted		(36)		(57)		(47)
Balance, end of year		250		351		450
Retained Earnings						
Balance, beginning of year		30,638		28,184		24,837
Adoption of guidance on accounting for uncertainty in income taxes		–		–		7
Measurement date change		–		(89)		–
Adjusted balance, beginning of year		30,638		28,095		24,844
Net income attributable to PepsiCo		5,946		5,142		5,658
Cash dividends declared—common		(2,768)		(2,589)		(2,306)
Cash dividends declared—preferred		(2)		(2)		(2)
Cash dividends declared—RSUs		(9)		(8)		(10)
Balance, end of year		33,805		30,638		28,184
Accumulated Other Comprehensive Loss						
Balance, beginning of year		(4,694)		(952)		(2,246)
Measurement date change		–		51		–
Adjusted balance, beginning of year		(4,694)		(901)		(2,246)
Currency translation adjustment		800		(2,484)		719
Cash flow hedges, net of tax:						
Net derivative (losses)/gains		(55)		16		(60)
Reclassification of losses to net income		28		5		21
Pension and retiree medical, net of tax:						
Net pension and retiree medical gains/(losses)		86		(1,376)		464
Reclassification of net losses to net income		21		73		135
Unrealized gains/(losses) on securities, net of tax		20		(21)		9
Other		–		(6)		6
Balance, end of year		(3,794)		(4,694)		(952)
Repurchased Common Stock						
Balance, beginning of year	(229)	(14,122)	(177)	(10,387)	(144)	(7,758)
Share repurchases	–	–	(68)	(4,720)	(64)	(4,300)
Stock option exercises	11	649	15	883	28	1,582
Other, primarily RSUs converted	1	90	1	102	3	89
Balance, end of year	(217)	(13,383)	(229)	(14,122)	(177)	(10,387)
Total Common Shareholders' Equity		16,908		12,203		17,325
Noncontrolling Interests						
Balance, beginning of year		476		62		45
Net income attributable to noncontrolling interests		33		24		12
Purchase of subsidiary shares from noncontrolling interests, net		150		450		9
Currency translation adjustment		(12)		(48)		2
Other		(9)		(12)		(6)
Balance, end of year		638		476		62
Total Equity		$ 17,442		$ 12,582		$ 17,296
Comprehensive Income						
Net income		$ 5,979		$ 5,166		$ 5,670
Other Comprehensive Income/(Loss)						
Currency translation adjustment		788		(2,532)		721
Cash flow hedges, net of tax		(27)		21		(39)
Pension and retiree medical, net of tax						
Net prior service (cost)/credit		(3)		55		(105)
Net gains/(losses)		110		(1,358)		704
Unrealized gains/(losses) on securities, net of tax		20		(21)		9
Other		–		(6)		6
		888		(3,841)		1,296
Comprehensive Income		6,867		1,325		6,966
Comprehensive (income)/loss attributable to noncontrolling interests		(21)		24		(14)
Comprehensive Income Attributable to PepsiCo		$ 6,846		$ 1,349		$ 6,952

(a) Includes total tax benefits of $31 million in 2009, $95 million in 2008 and $216 million in 2007.

See accompanying notes to consolidated financial statements.

Notes to Consolidated Financial Statements

Note 1 Basis of Presentation and Our Divisions

BASIS OF PRESENTATION

Our financial statements include the consolidated accounts of PepsiCo, Inc. and the affiliates that we control. In addition, we include our share of the results of certain other affiliates based on our economic ownership interest. We do not control these other affiliates, as our ownership in these other affiliates is generally less than 50%. Equity income or loss from our anchor bottlers is recorded as bottling equity income in our income statement. Bottling equity income also includes any changes in our ownership interests of our anchor bottlers. Bottling equity income includes $147 million of pre-tax gains on our sales of PBG and PAS stock in 2008 and $174 million of pre-tax gains on our sales of PBG stock in 2007. There were no sales of PBG or PAS stock in 2009. See Notes 8 and 15 for additional information on our significant noncontrolled bottling affiliates. Income or loss from other noncontrolled affiliates is recorded as a component of selling, general and administrative expenses. Intercompany balances and transactions are eliminated. Our fiscal year ends on the last Saturday of each December, resulting in an additional week of results every five or six years.

Raw materials, direct labor and plant overhead, as well as purchasing and receiving costs, costs directly related to production planning, inspection costs and raw material handling facilities, are included in cost of sales. The costs of moving, storing and delivering finished product are included in selling, general and administrative expenses.

The preparation of our consolidated financial statements in conformity with generally accepted accounting principles requires us to make estimates and assumptions that affect reported amounts of assets, liabilities, revenues, expenses and disclosure of contingent assets and liabilities. Estimates are used in determining, among other items, sales incentives accruals, tax reserves, stock-based compensation, pension and retiree medical accruals, useful lives for intangible assets, and future cash flows associated with impairment testing for perpetual brands, goodwill and other long-lived assets. We evaluate our estimates on an on-going basis using our historical experience, as well as other factors we believe appropriate under the circumstances, such as current economic conditions, and adjust or revise our estimates as circumstances change. As future events and their effect cannot be determined with precision, actual results could differ significantly from these estimates.

While the majority of our results are reported on a weekly calendar basis, most of our international operations report on a monthly calendar basis. The following chart details our quarterly reporting schedule:

Quarter	U.S. and Canada	International
First Quarter	12 weeks	January, February
Second Quarter	12 weeks	March, April and May
Third Quarter	12 weeks	June, July and August
Fourth Quarter	16 weeks	September, October, November and December

See "Our Divisions" below and for additional unaudited information on items affecting the comparability of our consolidated results, see "Items Affecting Comparability" in Management's Discussion and Analysis of Financial Condition and Results of Operations.

Tabular dollars are in millions, except per share amounts. All per share amounts reflect common per share amounts, assume dilution unless noted, and are based on unrounded amounts. Certain reclassifications were made to prior years' amounts to conform to the 2009 presentation.

OUR DIVISIONS

We manufacture or use contract manufacturers, market and sell a variety of salty, convenient, sweet and grain-based snacks, carbonated and non-carbonated beverages, and foods in over 200 countries with our largest operations in North America (United States and Canada), Mexico and the United Kingdom. Division results are based on how our Chief Executive Officer assesses the performance of and allocates resources to our divisions. For additional unaudited information on our divisions, see "Our Operations" in Management's Discussion and Analysis of Financial Condition and Results of Operations. The accounting policies for the divisions are the same as those described in Note 2, except for the following allocation methodologies:
- stock-based compensation expense,
- pension and retiree medical expense, and
- derivatives.

Stock-Based Compensation Expense

Our divisions are held accountable for stock-based compensation expense and, therefore, this expense is allocated to our divisions as an incremental employee compensation cost. The allocation of stock-based compensation expense in 2009 was approximately 27% to FLNA, 3% to QFNA, 6% to LAF, 21% to PAB, 13% to Europe, 13% to AMEA and 17% to corporate unallocated expenses. We had similar allocations of stock-based compensation expense to our divisions in 2008 and 2007. The expense allocated to our divisions excludes any impact of changes in our assumptions during the year which reflect market conditions over which division management has no control. Therefore, any variances between allocated expense and our actual expense are recognized in corporate unallocated expenses.

Pension and Retiree Medical Expense

Pension and retiree medical service costs measured at a fixed discount rate, as well as amortization of gains and losses due to demographics, including salary experience, are reflected in division results for North American employees. Division results also include interest costs, measured at a fixed discount rate, for retiree medical plans. Interest costs for the pension plans, pension asset returns and the impact of pension funding, and gains and losses other than those due to demographics, are all reflected in corporate unallocated expenses. In addition, corporate unallocated expenses include the difference between the service costs measured at a fixed discount rate (included in division results as noted above) and the total service costs determined using the Plans' discount rates as disclosed in Note 7.

Derivatives

We centrally manage commodity derivatives on behalf of our divisions. These commodity derivatives include energy, fruit and other raw materials. Certain of these commodity derivatives do not qualify for hedge accounting treatment and are marked to market

with the resulting gains and losses reflected in corporate unallocated expenses. These gains and losses are subsequently reflected in division results when the divisions take delivery of the underlying commodity. Therefore, the divisions realize the economic effects of the derivative without experiencing any resulting mark-to-market volatility, which remains in corporate unallocated expenses. These derivatives hedge underlying commodity price risk and were not entered into for speculative purposes.

In 2007, we expanded our commodity hedging program to include derivative contracts used to mitigate our exposure to price changes associated with our purchases of fruit. In addition, in 2008, we entered into additional contracts to further reduce our exposure to price fluctuations in our raw material and energy costs. The majority of these contracts do not qualify for hedge accounting treatment and are marked to market with the resulting gains and losses recognized in corporate unallocated expenses within selling, general and administrative expenses. These gains and losses are subsequently reflected in division results.

PepsiCo		
PepsiCo Americas Foods (PAF)	**PepsiCo Americas Beverages (PAB)**	**PepsiCo International (PI)**
Frito-Lay North America (FLNA)		**Europe**
Quaker Foods North America (QFNA)		**Asia, Middle East & Africa (AMEA)**
Latin America Foods (LAF)		

	2009	2008	2007	2009	2008	2007
		Net Revenue			Operating Profit[a]	
FLNA	$13,224	$12,507	$11,586	$3,258	$2,959	$2,845
QFNA	1,884	1,902	1,860	628	582	568
LAF	5,703	5,895	4,872	904	897	714
PAB	10,116	10,937	11,090	2,172	2,026	2,487
Europe	6,727	6,891	5,896	932	910	855
AMEA	5,578	5,119	4,170	716	592	466
Total division	43,232	43,251	39,474	8,610	7,966	7,935
Corporate—net impact of mark-to-market on commodity hedges	–	–	–	274	(346)	19
Corporate—PBG/PAS merger costs	–	–	–	(49)	–	–
Corporate—restructuring	–	–	–	–	(10)	–
Corporate—other	–	–	–	(791)	(651)	(772)
	$43,232	$43,251	$39,474	$8,044	$6,959	$7,182

(a) *For information on the impact of restructuring and impairment charges on our divisions, see Note 3.*

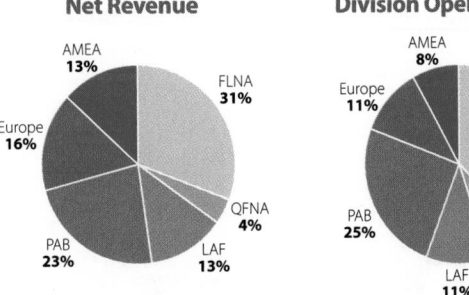

Net Revenue

AMEA 13%
FLNA 31%
Europe 16%
QFNA 4%
PAB 23%
LAF 13%

Division Operating Profit

AMEA 8%
Europe 11%
FLNA 38%
PAB 25%
QFNA 7%
LAF 11%

Notes to Consolidated Financial Statements

CORPORATE

Corporate includes costs of our corporate headquarters, centrally managed initiatives, such as our ongoing business transformation initiative and research and development projects, unallocated insurance and benefit programs, foreign exchange transaction gains and losses, certain commodity derivative gains and losses and certain other items.

OTHER DIVISION INFORMATION

	2009	2008	2007	2009	2008	2007
	Total Assets			Capital Spending		
FLNA	$ 6,337	$ 6,284	$ 6,270	$ 490	$ 553	$ 624
QFNA	997	1,035	1,002	33	43	41
LAF	3,575	3,023	3,084	310	351	326
PAB	7,670	7,673	7,780	182	344	450
Europe	9,321	8,840	7,330	357	401	369
AMEA	4,937	3,756	3,683	585	479	393
Total division	32,837	30,611	29,149	1,957	2,171	2,203
Corporate(a)	3,933	2,729	2,124	171	275	227
Investments in bottling affiliates	3,078	2,654	3,355	–	–	–
	$39,848	$35,994	$34,628	$2,128	$2,446	$2,430

(a) *Corporate assets consist principally of cash and cash equivalents, short-term investments, derivative instruments and property, plant and equipment.*

	2009	2008	2007	2009	2008	2007
	Amortization of Intangible Assets			Depreciation and Other Amortization		
FLNA	$ 7	$ 9	$ 9	$ 440	$ 441	$ 437
QFNA	–	–	–	36	34	34
LAF	5	6	4	189	194	166
PAB	18	16	16	345	334	321
Europe	22	23	20	227	210	190
AMEA	11	10	9	248	213	189
Total division	63	64	58	1,485	1,426	1,337
Corporate	–	–	–	87	53	31
	$63	$64	$58	$1,572	$1,479	$1,368

	2009	2008	2007	2009	2008	2007
	Net Revenue(a)			Long-Lived Assets(b)		
U.S.	$22,446	$22,525	$21,978	$12,496	$12,095	$12,498
Mexico	3,210	3,714	3,498	1,044	904	1,067
Canada	1,996	2,107	1,961	688	556	699
United Kingdom	1,826	2,099	1,987	1,358	1,509	2,090
All other countries	13,754	12,806	10,050	10,726	7,466	6,441
	$43,232	$43,251	$39,474	$26,312	$22,530	$22,795

(a) *Represents net revenue from businesses operating in these countries.*
(b) *Long-lived assets represent property, plant and equipment, nonamortizable intangible assets, amortizable intangible assets, and investments in noncontrolled affiliates. These assets are reported in the country where they are primarily used.*

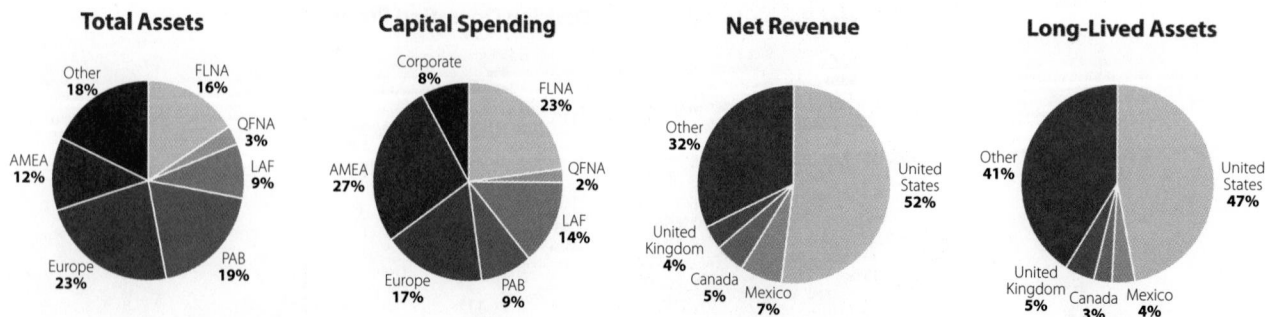

Note 2 Our Significant Accounting Policies

REVENUE RECOGNITION

We recognize revenue upon shipment or delivery to our customers based on written sales terms that do not allow for a right of return. However, our policy for DSD and certain chilled products is to remove and replace damaged and out-of-date products from store shelves to ensure that our consumers receive the product quality and freshness that they expect. Similarly, our policy for certain warehouse-distributed products is to replace damaged and out-of-date products. Based on our experience with this practice, we have reserved for anticipated damaged and out-of-date products. For additional unaudited information on our revenue recognition and related policies, including our policy on bad debts, see "Our Critical Accounting Policies" in Management's Discussion and Analysis of Financial Condition and Results of Operations. We are exposed to concentration of credit risk by our customers, Wal-Mart and PBG. In 2009, Wal-Mart (including Sam's) represented approximately 13% of our total net revenue, including concentrate sales to our bottlers which are used in finished goods sold by them to Wal-Mart; and PBG represented approximately 6%. We have not experienced credit issues with these customers.

SALES INCENTIVES AND OTHER MARKETPLACE SPENDING

We offer sales incentives and discounts through various programs to our customers and consumers. Sales incentives and discounts are accounted for as a reduction of revenue and totaled $12.9 billion in 2009, $12.5 billion in 2008 and $11.3 billion in 2007. While most of these incentive arrangements have terms of no more than one year, certain arrangements, such as fountain pouring rights, may extend beyond one year. Costs incurred to obtain these arrangements are recognized over the shorter of the economic or contractual life, as a reduction of revenue, and the remaining balances of $296 million as of December 26, 2009 and $333 million as of December 27, 2008 are included in current assets and other assets on our balance sheet. For additional unaudited information on our sales incentives, see "Our Critical Accounting Policies" in Management's Discussion and Analysis of Financial Condition and Results of Operations.

Other marketplace spending, which includes the costs of advertising and other marketing activities, totaled $2.8 billion in 2009 and $2.9 billion in both 2008 and 2007 and is reported as selling, general and administrative expenses. Included in these amounts were advertising expenses of $1.7 billion in both 2009

and 2008 and $1.8 billion in 2007. Deferred advertising costs are not expensed until the year first used and consist of:

- media and personal service prepayments,
- promotional materials in inventory, and
- production costs of future media advertising.

Deferred advertising costs of $143 million and $172 million at year-end 2009 and 2008, respectively, are classified as prepaid expenses on our balance sheet.

DISTRIBUTION COSTS

Distribution costs, including the costs of shipping and handling activities, are reported as selling, general and administrative expenses. Shipping and handling expenses were $5.6 billion in both 2009 and 2008 and $5.2 billion in 2007.

CASH EQUIVALENTS

Cash equivalents are investments with original maturities of three months or less which we do not intend to rollover beyond three months.

SOFTWARE COSTS

We capitalize certain computer software and software development costs incurred in connection with developing or obtaining computer software for internal use when both the preliminary project stage is completed and it is probable that the software will be used as intended. Capitalized software costs include only (i) external direct costs of materials and services utilized in developing or obtaining computer software, (ii) compensation and related benefits for employees who are directly associated with the software project and (iii) interest costs incurred while developing internal-use computer software. Capitalized software costs are included in property, plant and equipment on our balance sheet and amortized on a straight-line basis when placed into service over the estimated useful lives of the software, which approximate five to ten years. Software amortization totaled $119 million in 2009, $58 million in 2008 and $30 million in 2007. Net capitalized software and development costs were $1.1 billion as of December 26, 2009 and $940 million as of December 27, 2008.

COMMITMENTS AND CONTINGENCIES

We are subject to various claims and contingencies related to lawsuits, certain taxes and environmental matters, as well as commitments under contractual and other commercial obligations. We recognize liabilities for contingencies and commitments when a loss is probable and estimable. For additional information on our commitments, see Note 9.

Notes to Consolidated Financial Statements

RESEARCH AND DEVELOPMENT

We engage in a variety of research and development activities. These activities principally involve the development of new products, improvement in the quality of existing products, improvement and modernization of production processes, and the development and implementation of new technologies to enhance the quality and value of both current and proposed product lines. Consumer research is excluded from research and development costs and included in other marketing costs. Research and development costs were $414 million in 2009, $388 million in 2008 and $364 million in 2007 and are reported within selling, general and administrative expenses.

OTHER SIGNIFICANT ACCOUNTING POLICIES

Our other significant accounting policies are disclosed as follows:

- *Property, Plant and Equipment and Intangible Assets*—Note 4, and for additional unaudited information on brands and goodwill, see "Our Critical Accounting Policies" in Management's Discussion and Analysis of Financial Condition and Results of Operations.
- *Income Taxes*—Note 5, and for additional unaudited information, see "Our Critical Accounting Policies" in Management's Discussion and Analysis of Financial Condition and Results of Operations.
- *Stock-Based Compensation*—Note 6.
- *Pension, Retiree Medical and Savings Plans*—Note 7, and for additional unaudited information, see "Our Critical Accounting Policies" in Management's Discussion and Analysis of Financial Condition and Results of Operations.
- *Financial Instruments*—Note 10, and for additional unaudited information, see "Our Business Risks" in Management's Discussion and Analysis of Financial Condition and Results of Operations.

RECENT ACCOUNTING PRONOUNCEMENTS

In December 2007, the FASB amended its guidance on accounting for business combinations to improve, simplify and converge internationally the accounting for business combinations. The new accounting guidance continues the movement toward the greater use of fair value in financial reporting and increased transparency through expanded disclosures. We adopted the provisions of the new guidance as of the beginning of our 2009 fiscal year. The new accounting guidance changes how business acquisitions are accounted for and will impact financial statements both on the acquisition date and in subsequent periods. Additionally, under the new guidance, transaction costs are expensed rather than capitalized. Future adjustments made to valuation allowances on deferred taxes and acquired tax contingencies associated with acquisitions that closed prior to the beginning of our 2009 fiscal year apply the new provisions and will be evaluated based on the outcome of these matters.

In December 2007, the FASB issued new accounting and disclosure guidance on noncontrolling interests in consolidated financial statements. This guidance amends the accounting literature to establish new standards that will govern the accounting for and reporting of (1) noncontrolling interests in partially owned consolidated subsidiaries and (2) the loss of control of subsidiaries. We adopted the accounting provisions of the new guidance on a prospective basis as of the beginning of our 2009 fiscal year, and the adoption did not have a material impact on our financial statements. In addition, we adopted the presentation and disclosure requirements of the new guidance on a retrospective basis in the first quarter of 2009.

In June 2009, the FASB amended its accounting guidance on the consolidation of VIEs. Among other things, the new guidance requires a qualitative rather than a quantitative assessment to determine the primary beneficiary of a VIE based on whether the entity (1) has the power to direct matters that most significantly impact the activities of the VIE and (2) has the obligation to absorb losses or the right to receive benefits of the VIE that could potentially be significant to the VIE. In addition, the amended guidance requires an ongoing reconsideration of the primary beneficiary. The provisions of this new guidance are effective as of the beginning of our 2010 fiscal year, and we do not expect the adoption to have a material impact on our financial statements.

Note 3 Restructuring and Impairment Charges

2009 AND 2008 RESTRUCTURING AND IMPAIRMENT CHARGES

In 2009, we incurred a charge of $36 million ($29 million after-tax or $0.02 per share) in conjunction with our Productivity for Growth program that began in 2008. The program includes actions in all divisions of the business, including the closure of six plants that we believe will increase cost competitiveness across the supply chain, upgrade and streamline our product portfolio, and simplify the organization for more effective and timely decision-making. These charges were recorded in selling, general and administrative expenses. These initiatives were completed in the second quarter of 2009, and substantially all cash payments related to these charges are expected to be paid by 2010.

In 2008, we incurred a charge of $543 million ($408 million after-tax or $0.25 per share) in conjunction with our Productivity for Growth program. Approximately $455 million of the charge was recorded in selling, general and administrative expenses, with the remainder recorded in cost of sales.

A summary of the restructuring and impairment charge in 2009 is as follows:

	Severance and Other Employee Costs [a]	Other Costs	Total
FLNA	$ –	$ 2	$ 2
QFNA	–	1	1
LAF	3	–	3
PAB	6	10	16
Europe	1	–	1
AMEA	7	6	13
	$17	$19	$36

(a) Primarily reflects termination costs for approximately 410 employees.

A summary of the restructuring and impairment charge in 2008 is as follows:

	Severance and Other Employee Costs	Asset Impairments	Other Costs	Total
FLNA	$ 48	$ 38	$ 22	$108
QFNA	14	3	14	31
LAF	30	8	2	40
PAB	68	92	129	289
Europe	39	6	5	50
AMEA	11	2	2	15
Corporate	2	–	8	10
	$212	$149	$182	$543

Severance and other employee costs primarily reflect termination costs for approximately 3,500 employees. Asset impairments relate to the closure of six plants and changes to our beverage product portfolio. Other costs include contract exit costs and third-party incremental costs associated with upgrading our product portfolio and our supply chain.

A summary of our Productivity for Growth program activity is as follows:

	Severance and Other Employee Costs	Asset Impairments	Other Costs	Total
2008 restructuring and impairment charge	$ 212	$ 149	$ 182	$ 543
Cash payments	(50)	–	(109)	(159)
Non-cash charge	(27)	(149)	(9)	(185)
Currency translation	(1)	–	–	(1)
Liability as of December 27, 2008	134	–	64	198
2009 restructuring and impairment charge	17	12	7	36
Cash payments	(128)	–	(68)	(196)
Currency translation and other	(14)	(12)	25	(1)
Liability as of December 26, 2009	$ 9	$ –	$ 28	$ 37

2007 RESTRUCTURING AND IMPAIRMENT CHARGE

In 2007, we incurred a charge of $102 million ($70 million after-tax or $0.04 per share) in conjunction with restructuring actions primarily to close certain plants and rationalize other production lines across FLNA, LAF, PAB, Europe and AMEA. The charge was recorded in selling, general and administrative expenses. All cash payments related to this charge were paid by the end of 2008.

A summary of the restructuring and impairment charge is as follows:

	Severance and Other Employee Costs	Asset Impairments	Other Costs	Total
FLNA	$ –	$19	$ 9	$ 28
LAF	14	25	–	39
PAB	12	–	–	12
Europe	2	4	3	9
AMEA	5	9	–	14
	$33	$57	$12	$102

Severance and other employee costs primarily reflect termination costs for approximately 1,100 employees.

Note 4 Property, Plant and Equipment and Intangible Assets

	Average Useful Life	**2009**	2008	2007
Property, plant and equipment, net				
Land and improvements	10–34yrs.	$ **1,208**	$ 868	
Buildings and improvements	20–44	**5,080**	4,738	
Machinery and equipment, including fleet and software	5–14	**17,183**	15,173	
Construction in progress		**1,441**	1,773	
		24,912	22,552	
Accumulated depreciation		**(12,241)**	(10,889)	
		$ **12,671**	$ 11,663	
Depreciation expense		$ **1,500**	$ 1,422	$1,304
Amortizable intangible assets, net				
Brands	5–40	$ **1,465**	$ 1,411	
Other identifiable intangibles	10–24	**505**	360	
		1,970	1,771	
Accumulated amortization		**(1,129)**	(1,039)	
		$ **841**	$ 732	
Amortization expense		$ **63**	$ 64	$ 58

Property, plant and equipment is recorded at historical cost. Depreciation and amortization are recognized on a straight-line basis over an asset's estimated useful life. Land is not depreciated and construction in progress is not depreciated until ready for service. Amortization of intangible assets for each of the next five years, based on existing intangible assets as of December 26, 2009 and using average 2009 foreign exchange rates, is expected to be $65 million in both 2010 and 2011, $61 million in 2012, $58 million in 2013 and $52 million in 2014.

Notes to Consolidated Financial Statements

Depreciable and amortizable assets are only evaluated for impairment upon a significant change in the operating or macroeconomic environment. In these circumstances, if an evaluation of the undiscounted cash flows indicates impairment, the asset is written down to its estimated fair value, which is based on discounted future cash flows. Useful lives are periodically evaluated to determine whether events or circumstances have occurred which indicate the need for revision. For additional unaudited information on our amortizable brand policies, see "Our Critical Accounting Policies" in Management's Discussion and Analysis of Financial Condition and Results of Operations.

NONAMORTIZABLE INTANGIBLE ASSETS

Perpetual brands and goodwill are assessed for impairment at least annually. If the carrying amount of a perpetual brand exceeds its fair value, as determined by its discounted cash flows, an impairment loss is recognized in an amount equal to that excess. No impairment charges resulted from these impairment evaluations. The change in the book value of nonamortizable intangible assets is as follows:

	Balance, Beginning 2008	Acquisitions	Translation and Other	Balance, End of 2008	Acquisitions	Translation and Other	Balance, End of 2009
FLNA							
Goodwill	$ 311	$ –	$ (34)	$ 277	$ 6	$ 23	$ 306
Brands	–	–	–	–	26	4	30
	311	–	(34)	277	32	27	336
QFNA							
Goodwill	175	–	–	175	–	–	175
LAF							
Goodwill	147	338	(61)	424	17	38	479
Brands	22	118	(13)	127	1	8	136
	169	456	(74)	551	18	46	615
PAB							
Goodwill	2,369	–	(14)	2,355	62	14	2,431
Brands	59	–	–	59	48	5	112
	2,428	–	(14)	2,414	110	19	2,543
Europe							
Goodwill	1,642	45	(218)	1,469	1,291	(136)	2,624
Brands	1,041	14	(211)	844	572	(38)	1,378
	2,683	59	(429)	2,313	1,863	(174)	4,002
AMEA							
Goodwill	525	1	(102)	424	4	91	519
Brands	126	–	(28)	98	–	28	126
	651	1	(130)	522	4	119	645
Total goodwill	5,169	384	(429)	5,124	1,380	30	6,534
Total brands	1,248	132	(252)	1,128	647	7	1,782
	$6,417	$516	$(681)	$6,252	$2,027	$ 37	$8,316

Note 5 Income Taxes

	2009	2008	2007
Income before income taxes			
U.S.	**$4,209**	$3,274	$4,085
Foreign	**3,870**	3,771	3,558
	$8,079	$7,045	$7,643
Provision for income taxes			
Current: U.S. Federal	**$1,238**	$ 815	$1,422
Foreign	**473**	732	489
State	**124**	87	104
	1,835	1,634	2,015
Deferred: U.S. Federal	**223**	313	22
Foreign	**21**	(69)	(66)
State	**21**	1	2
	265	245	(42)
	$2,100	$1,879	$1,973
Tax rate reconciliation			
U.S. Federal statutory tax rate	**35.0%**	35.0%	35.0%
State income tax, net of U.S. Federal tax benefit	**1.2**	0.8	0.9
Lower taxes on foreign results	**(7.9)**	(8.0)	(6.6)
Tax settlements	**–**	–	(1.7)
Other, net	**(2.3)**	(1.1)	(1.8)
Annual tax rate	**26.0%**	26.7%	25.8%
Deferred tax liabilities			
Investments in noncontrolled affiliates	**$1,120**	$1,193	
Property, plant and equipment	**1,056**	881	
Intangible assets other than nondeductible goodwill	**417**	295	
Other	**68**	73	
Gross deferred tax liabilities	**2,661**	2,442	
Deferred tax assets			
Net carryforwards	**624**	682	
Stock-based compensation	**410**	410	
Retiree medical benefits	**508**	495	
Other employee-related benefits	**442**	428	
Pension benefits	**179**	345	
Deductible state tax and interest benefits	**256**	230	
Other	**560**	677	
Gross deferred tax assets	**2,979**	3,267	
Valuation allowances	**(586)**	(657)	
Deferred tax assets, net	**2,393**	2,610	
Net deferred tax liabilities/(assets)	**$ 268**	$ (168)	
Deferred taxes included within:			
Assets:			
Prepaid expenses and other current assets	**$ 391**	$ 372	$ 325
Other assets	**–**	$ 22	–
Liabilities:			
Deferred income taxes	**$ 659**	$ 226	$ 646
Analysis of valuation allowances			
Balance, beginning of year	**$ 657**	$ 695	$ 624
(Benefit)/provision	**(78)**	(5)	39
Other additions/(deductions)	**7**	(33)	32
Balance, end of year	**$ 586**	$ 657	$ 695

For additional unaudited information on our income tax policies, including our reserves for income taxes, see "Our Critical Accounting Policies" in Management's Discussion and Analysis of Financial Condition and Results of Operations.

In 2007, we recognized $129 million of non-cash tax benefits related to the favorable resolution of certain foreign tax matters.

RESERVES

A number of years may elapse before a particular matter, for which we have established a reserve, is audited and finally resolved. The number of years with open tax audits varies depending on the tax jurisdiction. Our major taxing jurisdictions and the related open tax audits are as follows:

- U.S.—continue to dispute one matter related to tax years 1998 through 2002. Our U.S. tax returns for the years 2003 through 2005 are currently under audit. In 2008, the IRS initiated its audit of our U.S. tax returns for the years 2006 through 2007;
- Mexico—audits have been substantially completed for all taxable years through 2005;
- United Kingdom—audits have been completed for all taxable years prior to 2007; and
- Canada—audits have been completed for all taxable years through 2006. The Canadian tax return for 2007 is currently under audit.

While it is often difficult to predict the final outcome or the timing of resolution of any particular tax matter, we believe that our reserves reflect the probable outcome of known tax contingencies. We adjust these reserves, as well as the related interest, in light of changing facts and circumstances. Settlement of any particular issue would usually require the use of cash. Favorable resolution would be recognized as a reduction to our annual tax rate in the year of resolution. For further unaudited information on the impact of the resolution of open tax issues, see "Other Consolidated Results."

As of December 26, 2009, the total gross amount of reserves for income taxes, reported in other liabilities, was $1.7 billion. Any prospective adjustments to these reserves will be recorded as an increase or decrease to our provision for income taxes and would impact our effective tax rate. In addition, we accrue interest related to reserves for income taxes in our provision for income taxes and any associated penalties are recorded in selling, general and administrative expenses. The gross amount of interest accrued, reported in other liabilities, was $461 million as of December 26, 2009, of which $30 million was recognized in 2009. The gross amount of interest accrued was $427 million as of December 27, 2008, of which $95 million was recognized in 2008.

Notes to Consolidated Financial Statements

A rollforward of our reserves for all federal, state and foreign tax jurisdictions, is as follows:

	2009	2008
Balance, beginning of year	$1,711	$1,461
Additions for tax positions related to the current year	238	272
Additions for tax positions from prior years	79	76
Reductions for tax positions from prior years	(236)	(14)
Settlement payments	(64)	(30)
Statute of limitations expiration	(4)	(20)
Translation and other	7	(34)
Balance, end of year	$1,731	$1,711

CARRYFORWARDS AND ALLOWANCES

Operating loss carryforwards totaling $6.4 billion at year-end 2009 are being carried forward in a number of foreign and state jurisdictions where we are permitted to use tax operating losses from prior periods to reduce future taxable income. These operating losses will expire as follows: $0.2 billion in 2010, $5.5 billion between 2011 and 2029 and $0.7 billion may be carried forward indefinitely. We establish valuation allowances for our deferred tax assets if, based on the available evidence, it is more likely than not that some portion or all of the deferred tax assets will not be realized.

UNDISTRIBUTED INTERNATIONAL EARNINGS

As of December 26, 2009, we had approximately $21.9 billion of undistributed international earnings. We intend to continue to reinvest earnings outside the U.S. for the foreseeable future and, therefore, have not recognized any U.S. tax expense on these earnings.

Note 6 Stock-Based Compensation

Our stock-based compensation program is a broad-based program designed to attract and retain employees while also aligning employees' interests with the interests of our shareholders. A majority of our employees participate in our stock-based compensation program. This program includes both our broad-based SharePower program which was established in 1989 to grant an annual award of stock options to eligible employees, based upon job level or classification and tenure (internationally), as well as our executive long-term awards program. Stock options and restricted stock units (RSU) are granted to employees under the shareholder-approved 2007 Long-Term Incentive Plan (LTIP), our only active stock-based plan. Stock-based compensation expense was $227 million in 2009, $238 million in 2008 and $260 million in 2007. Related income tax benefits recognized in earnings were $67 million in 2009, $71 million in 2008 and

$77 million in 2007. Stock-based compensation cost capitalized in connection with our ongoing business transformation initiative was $2 million in 2009, $4 million in 2008 and $3 million in 2007. At year-end 2009, 42 million shares were available for future stock-based compensation grants.

METHOD OF ACCOUNTING AND OUR ASSUMPTIONS

We account for our employee stock options, which include grants under our executive program and our broad-based SharePower program, under the fair value method of accounting using a Black-Scholes valuation model to measure stock option expense at the date of grant. All stock option grants have an exercise price equal to the fair market value of our common stock on the date of grant and generally have a 10-year term. We do not backdate, reprice or grant stock-based compensation awards retroactively. Repricing of awards would require shareholder approval under the LTIP.

The fair value of stock option grants is amortized to expense over the vesting period, generally three years. Executives who are awarded long-term incentives based on their performance are offered the choice of stock options or RSUs. Executives who elect RSUs receive one RSU for every four stock options that would have otherwise been granted. Senior officers do not have a choice and are granted 50% stock options and 50% performance-based RSUs. Vesting of RSU awards for senior officers is contingent upon the achievement of pre-established performance targets approved by the Compensation Committee of the Board of Directors. RSU expense is based on the fair value of PepsiCo stock on the date of grant and is amortized over the vesting period, generally three years. Each RSU is settled in a share of our stock after the vesting period.

Our weighted-average Black-Scholes fair value assumptions are as follows:

	2009	2008	2007
Expected life	6 yrs.	6 yrs.	6 yrs.
Risk free interest rate	2.8%	3.0%	4.8%
Expected volatility	17%	16%	15%
Expected dividend yield	3.0%	1.9%	1.9%

The expected life is the period over which our employee groups are expected to hold their options. It is based on our historical experience with similar grants. The risk free interest rate is based on the expected U.S. Treasury rate over the expected life. Volatility reflects movements in our stock price over the most recent historical period equivalent to the expected life. Dividend yield is estimated over the expected life based on our stated dividend policy and forecasts of net income, share repurchases and stock price.

A summary of our stock-based compensation activity for the year ended December 26, 2009 is presented below:

Our Stock Option Activity

	Options(a)	Average Price(b)	Average Life (years)(c)	Aggregate Intrinsic Value(d)
Outstanding at December 27, 2008	103,672	$50.42		
Granted	15,466	53.09		
Exercised	(10,546)	39.48		
Forfeited/expired	(2,581)	59.49		
Outstanding at December 26, 2009	106,011	$51.68	4.91	$1,110,793
Exercisable at December 26, 2009	68,272	$46.86	3.21	$ 965,661

(a) Options are in thousands and include options previously granted under Quaker plans. No additional options or shares may be granted under the Quaker plans.
(b) Weighted-average exercise price.
(c) Weighted-average contractual life remaining.
(d) In thousands.

Our RSU Activity

	RSUs(a)	Average Intrinsic Value(b)	Average Life (years)(c)	Aggregate Intrinsic Value(d)
Outstanding at December 27, 2008	6,151	$63.18		
Granted	2,653	53.22		
Converted	(2,232)	57.48		
Forfeited/expired	(480)	62.57		
Outstanding at December 26, 2009	6,092	$60.98	1.33	$371,364

(a) RSUs are in thousands.
(b) Weighted-average intrinsic value at grant date.
(c) Weighted-average contractual life remaining.
(d) In thousands.

OTHER STOCK-BASED COMPENSATION DATA

	2009	2008	2007
Stock Options			
Weighted-average fair value of options granted	$ 7.02	$ 11.24	$ 13.56
Total intrinsic value of options exercised(a)	$194,545	$410,152	$826,913
RSUs			
Total number of RSUs granted(a)	2,653	2,135	2,342
Weighted-average intrinsic value of RSUs granted	$ 53.22	$ 68.73	$ 65.21
Total intrinsic value of RSUs converted(a)	$124,193	$180,563	$125,514

(a) In thousands.

As of December 26, 2009, there was $227 million of total unrecognized compensation cost related to nonvested share-based compensation grants. This unrecognized compensation is expected to be recognized over a weighted-average period of 1.7 years.

Note 7 Pension, Retiree Medical and Savings Plans

Our pension plans cover full-time employees in the U.S. and certain international employees. Benefits are determined based on either years of service or a combination of years of service and earnings. U.S. and Canada retirees are also eligible for medical and life insurance benefits (retiree medical) if they meet age and service requirements. Generally, our share of retiree medical costs is capped at specified dollar amounts, which vary based upon years of service, with retirees contributing the remainder of the costs.

Gains and losses resulting from actual experience differing from our assumptions, including the difference between the actual return on plan assets and the expected return on plan assets, and from changes in our assumptions are also determined at each measurement date. If this net accumulated gain or loss exceeds 10% of the greater of the market-related value of plan assets or plan liabilities, a portion of the net gain or loss is included in expense for the following year. The cost or benefit of plan changes that increase or decrease benefits for prior employee service (prior service cost/(credit)) is included in earnings on a straight-line basis over the average remaining service period of active plan participants, which is approximately 10 years for pension expense and approximately 12 years for retiree medical expense.

Our adoption of the standard on accounting for defined benefit pension and other postretirement plans required that, no later than 2008, our assumptions used to measure our annual pension and retiree medical expense be determined as of the balance sheet date, and all plan assets and liabilities be reported as of that date. Accordingly, as of the beginning of our 2008 fiscal year, we changed the measurement date for our annual pension and retiree medical expense and all plan assets and liabilities from September 30 to our year-end balance sheet date. As a result of this change in measurement date, we recorded an after-tax $39 million decrease to 2008 opening shareholders' equity, as follows:

	Pension	Retiree Medical	Total
Retained earnings	$(63)	$(20)	$(83)
Accumulated other comprehensive loss	12	32	44
Total	$(51)	$ 12	$(39)

Notes to Consolidated Financial Statements

Selected financial information for our pension and retiree medical plans is as follows:

	Pension				Retiree Medical	
	2009	2008	2009	2008	2009	2008
	U.S.		International			
Change in projected benefit liability						
Liability at beginning of year	$ 6,217	$ 6,048	$1,270	$1,595	$ 1,370	$ 1,354
Measurement date change	–	(199)	–	113	–	(37)
Service cost	238	244	54	61	44	45
Interest cost	373	371	82	88	82	82
Plan amendments	–	(20)	–	2	–	(47)
Participant contributions	–	–	10	17	–	–
Experience loss/(gain)	70	28	221	(165)	(63)	58
Benefit payments	(296)	(277)	(50)	(51)	(80)	(70)
Settlement/curtailment loss	–	(9)	(8)	(15)	–	(2)
Special termination benefits	–	31	–	2	–	3
Foreign currency adjustment	–	–	130	(376)	6	(10)
Other	4	–	–	(1)	–	(6)
Liability at end of year	$ 6,606	$ 6,217	$1,709	$1,270	$ 1,359	$ 1,370
Change in fair value of plan assets						
Fair value at beginning of year	$ 3,974	$ 5,782	$1,165	$1,595	$ –	$ –
Measurement date change	–	(136)	–	97	–	–
Actual return on plan assets	697	(1,434)	159	(241)	2	–
Employer contributions/funding	1,041	48	167	101	91	70
Participant contributions	–	–	10	17	–	–
Benefit payments	(296)	(277)	(50)	(51)	(80)	(70)
Settlement/curtailment loss	–	(9)	(8)	(11)	–	–
Foreign currency adjustment	–	–	118	(341)	–	–
Other	4	–	–	(1)	–	–
Fair value at end of year	$ 5,420	$ 3,974	$1,561	$1,165	$ 13	$ –
Funded status	$(1,186)	$(2,243)	$ (148)	$ (105)	$(1,346)	$(1,370)
Amounts recognized						
Other assets	$ –	$ –	$ 50	$ 28	$ –	$ –
Other current liabilities	(36)	(60)	(1)	(1)	(105)	(102)
Other liabilities	(1,150)	(2,183)	(197)	(132)	(1,241)	(1,268)
Net amount recognized	$(1,186)	$(2,243)	$ (148)	$ (105)	$(1,346)	$(1,370)
Amounts included in accumulated other comprehensive loss (pre-tax)						
Net loss	$ 2,563	$ 2,826	$ 625	$ 421	$ 190	$ 266
Prior service cost/(credit)	101	112	20	20	(102)	(119)
Total	$ 2,664	$ 2,938	$ 645	$ 441	$ 88	$ 147
Components of the (decrease)/increase in net loss						
Measurement date change	$ –	$ (130)	$ –	$ 105	$ –	$ (53)
Change in discount rate	47	247	97	(219)	11	36
Employee-related assumption changes	–	(194)	70	52	(38)	6
Liability-related experience different from assumptions	23	(25)	51	(4)	(36)	10
Actual asset return different from expected return	(235)	1,850	(54)	354	(2)	–
Amortization of losses	(111)	(58)	(9)	(19)	(11)	(8)
Other, including foreign currency adjustments and 2003 Medicare Act	13	–	49	(135)	–	(1)
Total	$ (263)	$ 1,690	$ 204	$ 134	$ (76)	$ (10)
Liability at end of year for service to date	$ 5,784	$ 5,413	$1,414	$1,013		

Components of benefit expense are as follows:

	Pension						Retiree Medical		
	2009	2008	2007	2009	2008	2007	2009	2008	2007
	U.S.			International					
Components of benefit expense									
Service cost	$ 238	$ 244	$ 244	$ 54	$ 61	$ 59	$ 44	$ 45	$ 48
Interest cost	373	371	338	82	88	81	82	82	77
Expected return on plan assets	(462)	(416)	(399)	(105)	(112)	(97)	–	–	–
Amortization of prior service cost/(credit)	12	19	5	2	3	3	(17)	(13)	(13)
Amortization of net loss	110	55	136	9	19	30	11	7	18
	271	273	324	42	59	76	120	121	130
Settlement/curtailment (gain)/loss	(13)	3	–	3	3	–	–	–	–
Special termination benefits	–	31	5	–	2	–	–	3	–
Total	$ 258	$ 307	$ 329	$ 45	$ 64	$ 76	$120	$124	$130

The estimated amounts to be amortized from accumulated other comprehensive loss into benefit expense in 2010 for our pension and retiree medical plans are as follows:

	Pension		Retiree Medical
	U.S.	International	
Net loss	$108	$24	$ 5
Prior service cost/(credit)	12	2	(17)
Total	$120	$26	$(12)

The following table provides the weighted-average assumptions used to determine projected benefit liability and benefit expense for our pension and retiree medical plans:

	Pension						Retiree Medical		
	2009	2008	2007	2009	2008	2007	2009	2008	2007
	U.S.			International					
Weighted-average assumptions									
Liability discount rate	6.1%	6.2%	6.2%	5.9%	6.3%	5.8%	6.1%	6.2%	6.1%
Expense discount rate	6.2%	6.5%	5.8%	6.3%	5.6%	5.2%	6.2%	6.5%	5.8%
Expected return on plan assets	7.8%	7.8%	7.8%	7.1%	7.2%	7.3%			
Rate of salary increases	4.4%	4.6%	4.7%	4.2%	3.9%	3.9%			

The following table provides selected information about plans with liability for service to date and total benefit liability in excess of plan assets:

	Pension				Retiree Medical	
	2009	2008	2009	2008	2009	2008
	U.S.		International			
Selected information for plans with liability for service to date in excess of plan assets						
Liability for service to date	$(2,695)	$(5,411)	$ (342)	$ (49)		
Fair value of plan assets	$ 2,220	$ 3,971	$ 309	$ 30		
Selected information for plans with benefit liability in excess of plan assets						
Benefit liability	$(6,603)	$(6,217)	$(1,566)	$(1,049)	$(1,359)	$(1,370)
Fair value of plan assets	$ 5,417	$ 3,974	$ 1,368	$ 916	$ 13	$ –

Of the total projected pension benefit liability at year-end 2009, $564 million relates to plans that we do not fund because the funding of such plans does not receive favorable tax treatment.

Notes to Consolidated Financial Statements

FUTURE BENEFIT PAYMENTS AND FUNDING

Our estimated future benefit payments are as follows:

	2010	2011	2012	2013	2014	2015-19
Pension	$340	$360	$395	$415	$450	$2,825
Retiree medical[a]	$110	$120	$125	$125	$130	$ 695

(a) *Expected future benefit payments for our retiree medical plans do not reflect any estimated subsidies expected to be received under the 2003 Medicare Act. Subsidies are expected to be approximately $10 million for each of the years from 2010 through 2014 and approximately $70 million in total for 2015 through 2019.*

These future benefits to beneficiaries include payments from both funded and unfunded pension plans.

In 2010, we will make pension contributions of approximately $700 million, with up to approximately $600 million expected to be discretionary. Our net cash payments for retiree medical are estimated to be approximately $100 million in 2010.

PENSION ASSETS

Our pension plan investment strategy includes the use of actively-managed securities and is reviewed annually based upon plan liabilities, an evaluation of market conditions, tolerance for risk and cash requirements for benefit payments. Our investment objective is to ensure that funds are available to meet the plans' benefit obligations when they become due. Our overall investment strategy is to prudently invest plan assets in high-quality and diversified equity and debt securities to achieve our long-term return expectations. Our investment policy also permits the use of derivative instruments which are primarily used to reduce risk. Our expected long-term rate of return on U.S. plan assets is 7.8%, reflecting estimated long-term rates of return of 8.9% from our equity allocation and 6.3% from our fixed income allocation. Our target investment allocation is 40% for U.S. equity allocations, 20% for international equity allocations and 40% for fixed income

allocations. Actual investment allocations may vary from our target investment allocations due to prevailing market conditions. We regularly review our actual investment allocations and periodically rebalance our investments to our target allocations.

The expected return on pension plan assets is based on our pension plan investment strategy, our expectations for long-term rates of return and our historical experience. We also review current levels of interest rates and inflation to assess the reasonableness of the long-term rates. To calculate the expected return on pension plan assets, we use a market-related valuation method that recognizes investment gains or losses (the difference between the expected and actual return based on the market-related value of assets) for securities included in our equity strategies over a five-year period. This has the effect of reducing year-to-year volatility. For all other asset categories, the actual fair value is used for the market-related value of assets.

We adopted the new accounting guidance on employer's disclosures about postretirement benefit plan assets which requires that we categorize pension assets into three levels based upon the assumptions (inputs) used to price the assets. Level 1 provides the most reliable measure of fair value, whereas Level 3 generally requires significant management judgment. The three levels are defined as follows:

- Level 1: Unadjusted quoted prices in active markets for identical assets.
- Level 2: Observable inputs other than those included in Level 1. For example, quoted prices for similar assets in active markets or quoted prices for identical assets in inactive markets.
- Level 3: Unobservable inputs reflecting assumptions about the inputs used in pricing the asset.

Plan assets measured at fair value are categorized as follows:

	2009				2008
	Total	Level 1	Level 2	Level 3	Total
U.S. plan assets					
Equity securities:					
PepsiCo common stock[a]	$ 332	$ 332	$ –	$ –	$ 302
U.S. common stock[a]	229	229	–	–	103
U.S. commingled funds[b]	1,387	–	1,387	–	513
International common stock[a]	700	700	–	–	463
International commingled fund[c]	114	–	114	–	47
Preferred stock[d]	4	–	4	–	6
Fixed income securities:					
Government securities[d]	741	–	741	–	724
Corporate bonds[d]	1,214	–	1,198	16	592
Mortgage-backed securities[d]	201	–	195	6	250
Fixed income commingled fund[e]	–	–	–	–	647
Other:					
Derivative instruments	–	–	–	–	(9)
Contracts with insurance companies[f]	9	–	–	9	15
Dividends and interest receivable	32	–	–	32	19
Cash and cash equivalents	457	457	–	–	302
Total U.S. plan assets	$5,420	$1,718	$3,639	$63	$3,974
International plan assets					
Equity securities:					
U.S. commingled funds[b]	$ 180	$ –	$ 180	$ –	$ 128
International commingled funds[c]	661	–	661	–	429
Fixed income securities:					
Government securities[d]	139	–	139	–	123
Corporate bonds[d]	128	–	128	–	103
Fixed income commingled funds[e]	363	–	363	–	310
Other:					
Contracts with insurance companies[f]	29	–	–	29	26
Currency commingled funds[g]	44	–	44	–	17
Cash and cash equivalents	17	17	–	–	29
Total international plan assets	$1,561	$ 17	$1,515	$29	$1,165

(a) Based on quoted market prices in active markets.
(b) Based on the fair value of the investments owned by these funds that track various U.S. large-and mid-cap company indices. Includes one fund that represents 25% of total U.S. plan assets.
(c) Based on the fair value of the investments owned by these funds that track various non-U.S. equity indices.
(d) Based on quoted bid prices for comparable securities in the marketplace and broker/dealer quotes that are not observable.
(e) Based on the fair value of the investments owned by these funds that track various government and corporate bond indices.
(f) Based on the fair value of the contracts as determined by the insurance companies using inputs that are not observable.
(g) Based on the fair value of the investments owned by these funds. Includes managed hedge funds that invest primarily in derivatives to reduce currency exposure.

RETIREE MEDICAL COST TREND RATES

An average increase of 7.5% in the cost of covered retiree medical benefits is assumed for 2010. This average increase is then projected to decline gradually to 5% in 2014 and thereafter. These assumed health care cost trend rates have an impact on the retiree medical plan expense and liability. However, the cap on our share of retiree medical costs limits the impact. A 1-percentage-point change in the assumed health care trend rate would have the following effects:

	1% Increase	1% Decrease
2009 service and interest cost components	$ 4	$ (3)
2009 benefit liability	$30	$(26)

SAVINGS PLAN

Our U.S. employees are eligible to participate in 401(k) savings plans, which are voluntary defined contribution plans. The plans are designed to help employees accumulate additional savings for retirement. We make matching contributions on a portion of eligible pay based on years of service. In 2009 and 2008, our matching contributions were $72 million and $70 million, respectively.

For additional unaudited information on our pension and retiree medical plans and related accounting policies and assumptions, see "Our Critical Accounting Policies" in Management's Discussion and Analysis.

Note 8 Noncontrolled Bottling Affiliates

Our most significant noncontrolled bottling affiliates are PBG and PAS. Sales to PBG represented approximately 6% of our total net revenue in 2009 and 7% of our total net revenue in both 2008 and 2007.

See Note 15 for information regarding our pending mergers with PBG and PAS.

THE PEPSI BOTTLING GROUP

In addition to approximately 32% and 33% of PBG's outstanding common stock that we owned at year-end 2009 and 2008, respectively, we owned 100% of PBG's class B common stock and approximately 7% of the equity of Bottling Group, LLC, PBG's principal operating subsidiary.

PBG's summarized financial information is as follows:

	2009	2008	2007
Current assets	$ 3,412	$ 3,141	
Noncurrent assets	10,158	9,841	
Total assets	$13,570	$12,982	
Current liabilities	$ 1,965	$ 3,083	
Noncurrent liabilities	7,896	7,408	
Total liabilities	$ 9,861	$10,491	
Our investment	$ 1,775	$ 1,457	
Net revenue	$13,219	$13,796	$13,591
Gross profit	$ 5,840	$ 6,210	$ 6,221
Operating income	$ 1,048	$ 649	$ 1,071
Net income attributable to PBG	$ 612	$ 162	$ 532

Notes to Consolidated Financial Statements

Our investment in PBG, which includes the related goodwill, was $463 million and $536 million higher than our ownership interest in their net assets less noncontrolling interests at year-end 2009 and 2008, respectively. Based upon the quoted closing price of PBG shares at year-end 2009, the calculated market value of our shares in PBG exceeded our investment balance, excluding our investment in Bottling Group, LLC, by approximately $1.4 billion.

Additionally, in 2007, we formed a joint venture with PBG, comprising our concentrate and PBG's bottling businesses in Russia. PBG holds a 60% majority interest in the joint venture and consolidates the entity. We account for our interest of 40% under the equity method of accounting.

During 2008, together with PBG, we jointly acquired Russia's leading branded juice company, Lebedyansky. Lebedyansky is owned 25% and 75% by PBG and us, respectively. See Note 14 for further information on this acquisition.

PEPSIAMERICAS

At year-end 2009 and 2008, we owned approximately 43%, respectively, of the outstanding common stock of PAS.

PAS summarized financial information is as follows:

	2009	2008	2007
Current assets	$ 952	$ 906	
Noncurrent assets	4,141	4,148	
Total assets	$5,093	$5,054	
Current liabilities	$ 669	$1,048	
Noncurrent liabilities	2,493	2,175	
Total liabilities	$3,162	$3,223	
Our investment	$1,071	$ 972	
Net sales	$4,421	$4,937	$4,480
Gross profit	$1,767	$1,982	$1,823
Operating income	$ 381	$ 473	$ 436
Net income attributable to PAS	$ 181	$ 226	$ 212

Our investment in PAS, which includes the related goodwill, was $322 million and $318 million higher than our ownership interest in their net assets less noncontrolling interests at year-end 2009 and 2008, respectively. Based upon the quoted closing price of PAS shares at year-end 2009, the calculated market value of our shares in PAS exceeded our investment balance by approximately $515 million.

Additionally, in 2007, we completed the joint purchase of Sandora, LLC, a juice company in the Ukraine, with PAS. PAS holds a 60% majority interest in the joint venture and consolidates the entity. We account for our interest of 40% under the equity method of accounting.

RELATED PARTY TRANSACTIONS

Our significant related party transactions are with our noncontrolled bottling affiliates. The transactions primarily consist of (1) selling concentrate to these affiliates, which they use in the production of CSDs and non-carbonated beverages, (2) selling certain finished goods to these affiliates, (3) receiving royalties for the use of our trademarks for certain products and (4) paying these affiliates to act as our manufacturing and distribution agent for product associated with our national account fountain customers. Sales of concentrate and finished goods are reported net of bottler funding. For further unaudited information on these bottlers, see "Our Customers" in Management's Discussion and Analysis of Financial Condition and Results of Operations. These transactions with our bottling affiliates are reflected in our consolidated financial statements as follows:

	2009	2008	2007
Net revenue	$3,922	$4,049	$4,020
Cost of sales	$ 634	$ 660	$ 625
Selling, general and administrative expenses	$ 24	$ 30	$ 33
Accounts and notes receivable	$ 254	$ 248	
Accounts payable and other liabilities	$ 285	$ 198	

Such amounts are settled on terms consistent with other trade receivables and payables. See Note 9 regarding our guarantee of certain PBG debt.

We also coordinate, on an aggregate basis, the contract negotiations of sweeteners and other raw material requirements for certain of our bottlers. Once we have negotiated the contracts, the bottlers order and take delivery directly from the supplier and pay the suppliers directly. Consequently, these transactions are not reflected in our consolidated financial statements. As the contracting party, we could be liable to these suppliers in the event of any nonpayment by our bottlers, but we consider this exposure to be remote.

In addition, our joint ventures with Unilever (under the Lipton brand name) and Starbucks sell finished goods (ready-to-drink teas, coffees and water products) to our noncontrolled bottling affiliates. Consistent with accounting for equity method investments, our joint venture revenue is not included in our consolidated net revenue and therefore is not included in the above table.

Note 9 Debt Obligations and Commitments

	2009	2008
Short-term debt obligations		
Current maturities of long-term debt	$ 102	$ 273
Commercial paper (0.7%)	–	846
Other borrowings (6.7% and 10.0%)	362	509
Amounts reclassified to long-term debt	–	(1,259)
	$ 464	$ 369
Long-term debt obligations		
Short-term borrowings, reclassified	$ –	$ 1,259
Notes due 2012-2026 (4.5% and 5.8%)	7,160	6,382
Zero coupon notes, $225 million due 2010-2012 (13.3%)	192	242
Other, due 2010-2019 (8.4% and 5.3%)	150	248
	7,502	8,131
Less: current maturities of long-term debt obligations	(102)	(273)
	$7,400	$ 7,858

The interest rates in the above table reflect weighted-average rates at year-end.

In the first quarter of 2009, we issued $1.0 billion of senior unsecured notes, bearing interest at 3.75% per year and maturing in 2014. We used the proceeds from the issuance of these notes for general corporate purposes.

In the third quarter of 2009, we entered into a new 364-day unsecured revolving credit agreement which enables us to borrow up to $1.975 billion, subject to customary terms and conditions, and expires in June 2010. We may request renewal of this facility for an additional 364-day period or convert any amounts outstanding into a term loan for a period of up to one year, which would mature no later than June 2011. This agreement replaced a $1.8 billion 364-day unsecured revolving credit agreement we entered into during the fourth quarter of 2008. Funds borrowed under this agreement may be used to repay outstanding commercial paper issued by us or our subsidiaries and for other general corporate purposes, including working capital, capital investments and acquisitions. This agreement is in addition to our existing $2.0 billion unsecured revolving credit agreement which expires in 2012. Our lines of credit remain unused as of December 26, 2009.

In addition, as of December 26, 2009, $396 million of our debt related to borrowings from various lines of credit that are maintained for our international divisions. These lines of credit are subject to normal banking terms and conditions and are fully committed to the extent of our borrowings.

Subsequent to year-end 2009, we issued $4.25 billion of fixed and floating rate notes. The issuance was comprised of $1.25 billion of floating rate notes maturing in 2011 (the "2011 Floating Rates Notes"), $1.0 billion of 3.10% senior unsecured notes maturing in 2015, $1.0 billion of 4.50% senior unsecured notes maturing in 2020 and $1.0 billion of 5.50% senior unsecured notes maturing in 2040. The 2011 Floating Rate Notes bear interest at a rate equal to the three-month London Inter-Bank Offered Rate ("LIBOR") plus 3 basis points.

We intend to use the net proceeds from this offering to finance a portion of the purchase price for the mergers with PBG and PAS and to pay related fees and expenses in connection with the mergers with PBG and PAS. Pending such use we invested the net proceeds in short-term, high-quality securities. If one or both of the mergers with PBG and PAS is not completed, we intend to use the remaining net proceeds from this offering for general corporate purposes, which may include the financing of future acquisitions, capital expenditures, additions to working capital, repurchase, repayment or refinancing of debt or stock repurchases.

Concurrently with the debt issuance after year-end, we terminated the commitments from lenders to provide us with up to $4.0 billion in bridge financing to fund the mergers with PBG and PAS.

Also subsequent to year-end 2009, we entered into amendments to PBG's revolving credit facility (the Amended PBG Credit Facility) and PAS's revolving credit facility (the Amended PAS Credit Facility). Under the Amended PBG Credit Facility, subject to the satisfaction of certain conditions to effectiveness, at the closing of the merger with PBG, Metro will be able to borrow up to $1,080 million from time to time. Borrowings under the Amended PBG Credit Facility, which expires in October 2012, are guaranteed by us. Under the Amended PAS Credit Facility, subject to the satisfaction of certain conditions to effectiveness, at the closing of the merger with PAS, Metro will be able to borrow up to $540 million from time to time. Borrowings under the Amended PAS Credit Facility, which expires in June 2011, are guaranteed by us.

Notes to Consolidated Financial Statements

LONG-TERM CONTRACTUAL COMMITMENTS[a]

	Payments Due by Period				
	Total	2010	2011–2012	2013–2014	2015 and beyond
Long-term debt obligations[b]	$ 7,400	$ –	$1,332	$2,063	$4,005
Interest on debt obligations[c]	2,386	347	666	500	873
Operating leases	1,076	282	356	203	235
Purchasing commitments	2,066	801	960	260	45
Marketing commitments	793	260	314	78	141
	$13,721	$1,690	$3,628	$3,104	$5,299

(a) *Reflects non-cancelable commitments as of December 26, 2009 based on year-end foreign exchange rates and excludes any reserves for uncertain tax positions as we are unable to reasonably predict the ultimate amount or timing of settlement.*
(b) *Excludes current maturities of long-term debt obligations of $102 million. Includes $151 million of principal and accrued interest related to our zero coupon notes.*
(c) *Interest payments on floating-rate debt are estimated using interest rates effective as of December 26, 2009.*

Most long-term contractual commitments, except for our long-term debt obligations, are not recorded on our balance sheet. Non-cancelable operating leases primarily represent building leases. Non-cancelable purchasing commitments are primarily for oranges and orange juice, packaging materials and cooking oil. Non-cancelable marketing commitments are primarily for sports marketing. Bottler funding is not reflected in our long-term contractual commitments as it is negotiated on an annual basis. See Note 7 regarding our pension and retiree medical obligations and discussion below regarding our commitments to noncontrolled bottling affiliates.

OFF-BALANCE-SHEET ARRANGEMENTS

It is not our business practice to enter into off-balance-sheet arrangements, other than in the normal course of business. However, at the time of the separation of our bottling operations from us various guarantees were necessary to facilitate the transactions. We have guaranteed an aggregate of $2.3 billion of Bottling Group, LLC's long-term debt ($1.0 billion of which matures in 2012 and $1.3 billion of which matures in 2014). In the first quarter of 2009, we extended our guarantee of $1.3 billion of Bottling Group, LLC's long-term debt in connection with the refinancing of a corresponding portion of the underlying debt. The terms of our Bottling Group, LLC debt guarantee are intended to preserve the structure of PBG's separation from us and our payment obligation would be triggered if Bottling Group, LLC failed to perform under these debt obligations or the structure significantly changed. Neither the merger with PBG nor the merger with PAS will trigger our payment obligation under our guarantee of a portion of Bottling Group, LLC's debt. As of December 26, 2009, we believe it is remote that these guarantees would require any cash payment. See Note 8 regarding contracts related to certain of our bottlers.

See "Our Liquidity and Capital Resources" in Management's Discussion and Analysis of Financial Condition and Results of Operations for further unaudited information on our borrowings.

Note 10 Financial Instruments

In March 2008, the FASB issued new disclosure guidance on derivative instruments and hedging activities, which amends and expands the disclosure requirements of previously issued guidance on accounting for derivative instruments and hedging activities, to provide an enhanced understanding of the use of derivative instruments, how they are accounted for and their effect on financial position, financial performance and cash flows. We adopted the disclosure provisions of the new guidance in the first quarter of 2009.

We are exposed to market risks arising from adverse changes in:
- commodity prices, affecting the cost of our raw materials and energy,
- foreign exchange risks, and
- interest rates.

In the normal course of business, we manage these risks through a variety of strategies, including the use of derivatives. Certain derivatives are designated as either cash flow or fair value hedges and qualify for hedge accounting treatment, while others do not qualify and are marked to market through earnings. Cash flows from derivatives used to manage commodity, foreign exchange or interest risks are classified as operating activities. See "Our Business Risks" in Management's Discussion and Analysis of Financial Condition and Results of Operations for further unaudited information on our business risks.

For cash flow hedges, changes in fair value are deferred in accumulated other comprehensive loss within common shareholders' equity until the underlying hedged item is recognized in net income. For fair value hedges, changes in fair value are recognized immediately in earnings, consistent with the underlying hedged item. Hedging transactions are limited to an underlying exposure. As a result, any change in the value of our derivative instruments would be substantially offset by an opposite change in the value of the underlying hedged items. Hedging ineffectiveness and a net earnings impact occur when the change in the value of the hedge does not offset the change in the value of the underlying hedged item. Ineffectiveness of our hedges is not material. If the derivative instrument is terminated, we continue to defer the related gain or loss and then include it as a component of the cost of the underlying hedged item. Upon determination that the underlying hedged item will not be part of an actual transaction, we recognize the related gain or loss in net income immediately.

We also use derivatives that do not qualify for hedge accounting treatment. We account for such derivatives at market value with the resulting gains and losses reflected in our income statement. We do not use derivative instruments for trading or speculative purposes. We perform assessments of our counterparty credit risk regularly, including a review of credit ratings, credit default swap rates and potential nonperformance of the counterparty. Based on our most recent assessment of our counterparty credit risk, we consider this risk to be low. In addition, we enter into derivative contracts with a variety of financial institutions that we believe are creditworthy in order to reduce our concentration of credit risk and generally settle with these financial institutions on a net basis.

COMMODITY PRICES

We are subject to commodity price risk because our ability to recover increased costs through higher pricing may be limited in the competitive environment in which we operate. This risk is managed through the use of fixed-price purchase orders, pricing agreements, geographic diversity and derivatives. We use derivatives, with terms of no more than three years, to economically hedge price fluctuations related to a portion of our anticipated commodity purchases, primarily for natural gas and diesel fuel. For those derivatives that qualify for hedge accounting, any ineffectiveness is recorded immediately. We classify both the earnings and cash flow impact from these derivatives consistent with the underlying hedged item. During the next 12 months, we expect to reclassify net losses of $124 million related to these hedges from accumulated other comprehensive loss into net income. Derivatives used to hedge commodity price risk that do not qualify for hedge accounting are marked to market each period and reflected in our income statement.

Our open commodity derivative contracts that qualify for hedge accounting had a face value of $151 million as of December 26, 2009 and $303 million as of December 27, 2008. These contracts resulted in net unrealized losses of $29 million as of December 26, 2009 and $117 million as of December 27, 2008.

Our open commodity derivative contracts that do not qualify for hedge accounting had a face value of $231 million as of December 26, 2009 and $626 million as of December 27, 2008. These contracts resulted in net losses of $57 million in 2009 and $343 million in 2008.

FOREIGN EXCHANGE

Financial statements of foreign subsidiaries are translated into U.S. dollars using period-end exchange rates for assets and liabilities and weighted-average exchange rates for revenues and expenses. Adjustments resulting from translating net assets are reported as a separate component of accumulated other comprehensive loss within common shareholders' equity as currency translation adjustment.

Our operations outside of the U.S. generate 48% of our net revenue, with Mexico, Canada and the United Kingdom comprising 16% of our net revenue. As a result, we are exposed to foreign currency risks. On occasion, we may enter into derivatives, primarily forward contracts with terms of no more than two years, to manage our exposure to foreign currency transaction risk. Exchange rate gains or losses related to foreign currency transactions are recognized as transaction gains or losses in our income statement as incurred.

Our foreign currency derivatives had a total face value of $1.2 billion as of December 26, 2009 and $1.4 billion as of December 27, 2008. The contracts that qualify for hedge accounting resulted in net unrealized losses of $20 million as of December 26, 2009 and net unrealized gains of $111 million as of December 27, 2008. During the next 12 months, we expect to reclassify net losses of $20 million related to these hedges from accumulated other comprehensive loss into net income. The contracts that do not qualify for hedge accounting resulted in a net gain of $1 million in 2009 and net losses of $28 million in 2008. All losses and gains were offset by changes in the underlying hedged items, resulting in no net material impact on earnings.

INTEREST RATES

We centrally manage our debt and investment portfolios considering investment opportunities and risks, tax consequences and overall financing strategies. We use various interest rate derivative instruments including, but not limited to, interest rate swaps, cross currency interest rate swaps, Treasury locks and swap locks to

Notes to Consolidated Financial Statements

manage our overall interest expense and foreign exchange risk. These instruments effectively change the interest rate and currency of specific debt issuances. Our interest rate and cross currency swaps are generally entered into concurrently with the issuance of the debt that they modify. The notional amount, interest payment and maturity date of the interest rate and cross currency swaps match the principal, interest payment and maturity date of the related debt. Our Treasury locks and swap locks are entered into to protect against unfavorable interest rate changes relating to forecasted debt transactions.

The notional amounts of the interest rate derivative instruments outstanding as of December 26, 2009 and December 27, 2008 were $5.75 billion and $2.75 billion, respectively. For those interest rate derivative instruments that qualify for cash flow hedge accounting, any ineffectiveness is recorded immediately. We classify both the earnings and cash flow impact from these interest rate derivative instruments consistent with the underlying hedged item. During the next 12 months, we expect to reclassify net losses of $6 million related to these hedges from accumulated other comprehensive loss into net income.

Concurrently with the debt issuance after year-end, we terminated $1.5 billion of interest rate derivative instruments, and the realized loss will be amortized into interest expense over the duration of the debt term.

As of December 26, 2009, approximately 57% of total debt, after the impact of the related interest rate derivative instruments, was exposed to variable rates compared to 58% as of December 27, 2008. In addition to variable rate long-term debt, all debt with maturities of less than one year is categorized as variable for purposes of this measure.

FAIR VALUE MEASUREMENTS

In September 2006, the FASB issued new accounting guidance on fair value measurements, which defines fair value, establishes a framework for measuring fair value, and expands disclosures about fair value measurements. We adopted the new guidance as of the beginning of our 2008 fiscal year as it relates to recurring financial assets and liabilities. As of the beginning of our 2009 fiscal year, we adopted the new guidance as it relates to nonrecurring fair value measurement requirements for nonfinancial assets and

liabilities. These include goodwill, other nonamortizable intangible assets and unallocated purchase price for recent acquisitions which are included within other assets. Our adoption did not have a material impact on our financial statements. See Note 7 for the fair value framework.

The fair values of our financial assets and liabilities as of December 26, 2009 are categorized as follows:

	2009			
	Total	Level 1	Level 2	Level 3
Assets(a)				
Available-for-sale securities(b)	$ 71	$ 71	$ –	$–
Short-term investments—index funds(c)	$120	$120	$ –	$–
Derivatives designated as hedging instruments:				
Forward exchange contracts(d)	$ 11	$ –	$ 11	$–
Interest rate derivatives(e)	177	–	177	–
Prepaid forward contracts(f)	46	–	46	–
Commodity contracts—other(g)	8	–	8	–
	$242	$ –	$242	$–
Derivatives not designated as hedging instruments:				
Forward exchange contracts(d)	$ 4	$ –	$ 4	$–
Commodity contracts—other(g)	7	–	7	–
	$ 11	$ –	$ 11	$–
Total asset derivatives at fair value	$253	$ –	$253	$–
Total assets at fair value	$444	$191	$253	$–
Liabilities(a)				
Deferred compensation(h)	$461	$121	$340	$–
Derivatives designated as hedging instruments:				
Forward exchange contracts(d)	$ 31	$ –	$ 31	$–
Interest rate derivatives(e)	43	–	43	–
Commodity contracts—other(g)	5	–	5	–
Commodity contracts—futures(i)	32	32	–	–
	$111	$ 32	$ 79	$–
Derivatives not designated as hedging instruments:				
Forward exchange contracts(d)	$ 2	$ –	$ 2	$–
Commodity contracts—other(g)	60	–	60	–
Commodity contracts—futures(i)	3	3	–	–
	$ 65	$ 3	$ 62	$–
Total liability derivatives at fair value	$176	$ 35	$141	$–
Total liabilities at fair value	$637	$156	$481	$–

(a) *Financial assets are classified on our balance sheet within other assets, with the exception of short-term investments. Financial liabilities are classified on our balance sheet within other current liabilities and other liabilities.*
(b) *Based on the price of common stock.*
(c) *Based on price changes in index funds used to manage a portion of market risk arising from our deferred compensation liability.*
(d) *Based on observable market transactions of spot and forward rates.*
(e) *Based on LIBOR and recently reported transactions in the marketplace.*
(f) *Based primarily on the price of our common stock.*
(g) *Based on recently reported transactions in the marketplace, primarily swap arrangements.*
(h) *Based on the fair value of investments corresponding to employees' investment elections.*
(i) *Based on average prices on futures exchanges.*

The effective portion of the pre-tax (gains)/losses on our derivative instruments are categorized in the tables below.

	2009		
	(Gains)/Losses Recognized in Income Statement	Losses/(Gains) Recognized in Accumulated Other Comprehensive Loss	(Gains)/Losses Reclassified from Accumulated Other Comprehensive Loss into Income Statement
Fair Value/Non-designated Hedges			
Forward exchange contracts[a]	$ (29)		
Interest rate derivatives[b]	206		
Prepaid forward contracts[a]	(5)		
Commodity contracts[a]	(274)		
Total	$(102)		
Cash Flow Hedges			
Forward exchange contracts[c]		$ 75	$(64)
Commodity contracts[c]		(1)	90
Interest rate derivatives[b]		32	–
Total		$106	$ 26

(a) *Included in corporate unallocated expenses.*
(b) *Included in interest expense in our income statement.*
(c) *Included in cost of sales in our income statement.*

The fair values of our financial assets and liabilities as of December 27, 2008 are categorized as follows:

	2008			
	Total	Level 1	Level 2	Level 3
Assets[a]				
Available-for-sale securities[b]	$ 41	$ 41	$ –	$–
Short-term investments—index funds[c]	98	98	–	–
Forward exchange contracts[d]	139	–	139	–
Interest rate derivatives[e]	372	–	372	–
Prepaid forward contracts[f]	41	–	41	–
Total assets at fair value	$691	$139	$552	$–
Liabilities[a]				
Forward exchange contracts[d]	$ 56	$ –	$ 56	$–
Commodity contracts—other[g]	345	–	345	–
Commodity contracts—futures[i]	115	115	–	–
Deferred compensation[h]	447	99	348	–
Total liabilities at fair value	$963	$214	$749	$–

(a) *Financial assets are classified on our balance sheet within other assets, with the exception of short-term investments. Financial liabilities are classified on our balance sheet within other current liabilities and other liabilities.*
(b) *Based on the price of common stock.*
(c) *Based on price changes in index funds used to manage a portion of market risk arising from our deferred compensation liability.*
(d) *Based on observable market transactions of spot and forward rates.*
(e) *Based on LIBOR and recently reported transactions in the marketplace.*
(f) *Based primarily on the price of our common stock.*
(g) *Based on recently reported transactions in the marketplace, primarily swap arrangements.*
(h) *Based on the fair value of investments corresponding to employees' investment elections.*
(i) *Based on average prices on futures exchanges.*

The carrying amounts of our cash and cash equivalents and short-term investments approximate fair value due to the short-term maturity. Short-term investments consist principally of short-term time deposits and index funds of $120 million as of December 26, 2009 and $98 million as of December 27, 2008 used to manage a portion of market risk arising from our deferred compensation liability. The fair value of our debt obligations as of December 26, 2009 and December 27, 2008 was $8.6 billion and $8.8 billion, respectively, based upon prices of similar instruments in the marketplace.

The preceding table excludes guarantees, including our guarantee aggregating $2.3 billion of Bottling Group, LLC's long-term debt. The guarantee had a fair value of $20 million as of December 26, 2009 and $117 million as of December 27, 2008 based on our estimate of the cost to us of transferring the liability to an independent financial institution. See Note 9 for additional information on our guarantees.

Note 11 Net Income Attributable to PepsiCo per Common Share

Basic net income attributable to PepsiCo per common share is net income available for PepsiCo common shareholders divided by the weighted average of common shares outstanding during the period. Diluted net income attributable to PepsiCo per common share is calculated using the weighted average of common shares outstanding adjusted to include the effect that would occur if in-the-money employee stock options were exercised and RSUs and preferred shares were converted into common shares. Options to purchase 39.0 million shares in 2009, 9.8 million shares in 2008 and 2.7 million shares in 2007 were not included in the calculation of diluted earnings per common share because these options were out-of-the-money. Out-of-the-money options had average exercise prices of $61.52 in 2009, $67.59 in 2008 and $65.18 in 2007.

Notes to Consolidated Financial Statements

The computations of basic and diluted net income attributable to PepsiCo per common share are as follows:

	2009		2008		2007	
	Income	Shares[a]	Income	Shares[a]	Income	Shares[a]
Net income attributable to PepsiCo	$5,946		$5,142		$5,658	
Preferred shares:						
Dividends	(1)		(2)		(2)	
Redemption premium	(5)		(6)		(10)	
Net income available for PepsiCo common shareholders	$5,940	1,558	$5,134	1,573	$5,646	1,621
Basic net income attributable to PepsiCo per common share	$ 3.81		$ 3.26		$ 3.48	
Net income available for PepsiCo common shareholders	$5,940	1,558	$5,134	1,573	$5,646	1,621
Dilutive securities:						
Stock options and RSUs	–	17	–	27	-	35
ESOP convertible preferred stock	6	2	8	2	12	2
Diluted	$5,946	1,577	$5,142	1,602	$5,658	1,658
Diluted net income attributable to PepsiCo per common share	$ 3.77		$ 3.21		$ 3.41	

(a) *Weighted-average common shares outstanding.*

Note 12 Preferred Stock

As of December 26, 2009 and December 27, 2008, there were 3 million shares of convertible preferred stock authorized. The preferred stock was issued only for an ESOP established by Quaker and these shares are redeemable for common stock by the ESOP participants. The preferred stock accrues dividends at an annual rate of $5.46 per share. At year-end 2009 and 2008, there were 803,953 preferred shares issued and 243,553 and 266,253 shares outstanding, respectively. The outstanding preferred shares had a fair value of $73 million as of December 26, 2009 and $72 million as of December 27, 2008. Each share is convertible at the option of the holder into 4.9625 shares of common stock. The preferred shares may be called by us upon written notice at $78 per share plus accrued and unpaid dividends. Quaker made the final award to its ESOP plan in June 2001.

	2009		2008		2007	
	Shares	Amount	Shares	Amount	Shares	Amount
Preferred stock	0.8	$ 41	0.8	$ 41	0.8	$ 41
Repurchased preferred stock						
Balance, beginning of year	0.5	$138	0.5	$132	0.5	$120
Redemptions	0.1	7	–	6	–	12
Balance, end of year	0.6	$145	0.5	$138	0.5	$132

Note 13 Accumulated Other Comprehensive Loss Attributable to PepsiCo

Comprehensive income is a measure of income which includes both net income and other comprehensive income or loss. Other comprehensive income or loss results from items deferred from recognition into our income statement. Accumulated other comprehensive loss is separately presented on our balance sheet as part of common shareholders' equity. Other comprehensive income/(loss) attributable to PepsiCo was $900 million in 2009, $(3,793) million in 2008 and $1,294 million in 2007. The accumulated balances for each component of other comprehensive loss attributable to PepsiCo were as follows:

	2009	2008	2007
Currency translation adjustment	$(1,471)	$(2,271)	$ 213
Cash flow hedges, net of tax[a]	(42)	(14)	(35)
Unamortized pension and retiree medical, net of tax[b]	(2,328)	(2,435)	(1,183)
Unrealized gain on securities, net of tax	47	28	49
Other	–	(2)	4
Accumulated other comprehensive loss attributable to PepsiCo	$(3,794)	$(4,694)	$ (952)

(a) Includes $23 million after-tax gain in 2009, $17 million after-tax loss in 2008 and $3 million after-tax gain in 2007 for our share of our equity investees' accumulated derivative activity.
(b) Net of taxes of $1,211 million in 2009, $1,288 million in 2008 and $645 million in 2007. Includes $51 million decrease to the opening balance of accumulated other comprehensive loss attributable to PepsiCo in 2008 due to the change in measurement date. See Note 7.

Note 14 Supplemental Financial Information

	2009	2008	2007
Accounts receivable			
Trade receivables	$4,026	$3,784	
Other receivables	688	969	
	4,714	4,753	
Allowance, beginning of year	70	69	$64
Net amounts charged to expense	40	21	5
Deductions [a]	(21)	(16)	(7)
Other [b]	1	(4)	7
Allowance, end of year	90	70	$69
Net receivables	$4,624	$4,683	
Inventories [c]			
Raw materials	$1,274	$1,228	
Work-in-process	165	169	
Finished goods	1,179	1,125	
	$2,618	$2,522	

(a) Includes accounts written off.
(b) Includes currency translation effects and other adjustments.
(c) Inventories are valued at the lower of cost or market. Cost is determined using the average, first-in, first-out (FIFO) or last-in, first-out (LIFO) methods. Approximately 10% in 2009 and 11% in 2008 of the inventory cost was computed using the LIFO method. The differences between LIFO and FIFO methods of valuing these inventories were not material.

	2009	2008
Other assets		
Noncurrent notes and accounts receivable	$ 118	$ 115
Deferred marketplace spending	182	219
Unallocated purchase price for recent acquisitions	143	1,594
Pension plans	64	28
Other	458	702
	$ 965	$2,658
Accounts payable and other current liabilities		
Accounts payable	$2,881	$2,846
Accrued marketplace spending	1,656	1,574
Accrued compensation and benefits	1,291	1,269
Dividends payable	706	660
Other current liabilities	1,593	1,924
	$8,127	$8,273

	2009	2008	2007
Other supplemental information			
Rent expense	$ 412	$ 357	$ 303
Interest paid	$ 456	$ 359	$ 251
Income taxes paid, net of refunds	$1,498	$ 1,477	$ 1,731
Acquisitions[a]			
Fair value of assets acquired	$ 851	$ 2,907	$ 1,611
Cash paid	(466)	(1,925)	(1,320)
Liabilities and noncontrolling interests assumed	$ 385	$ 982	$ 291

(a) During 2008, together with PBG, we jointly acquired Lebedyansky, for a total purchase price of $1.8 billion. Lebedyansky is owned 25% and 75% by PBG and us, respectively.

Notes to Consolidated Financial Statements

Note 15　Acquisition of Common Stock of PBG and PAS

On August 3, 2009, we entered into the PBG Merger Agreement and the PAS Merger Agreement.

The PBG Merger Agreement provides that, upon the terms and subject to the conditions set forth in the PBG Merger Agreement, PBG will be merged with and into Metro (the PBG Merger), with Metro continuing as the surviving corporation and our wholly owned subsidiary. At the effective time of the PBG Merger, each share of PBG common stock outstanding immediately prior to the effective time not held by us or any of our subsidiaries will be converted into the right to receive either 0.6432 of a share of PepsiCo common stock or, at the election of the holder, $36.50 in cash, without interest, and in each case subject to proration procedures which provide that we will pay cash for a number of shares equal to 50% of the PBG common stock outstanding immediately prior to the effective time of the PBG Merger not held by us or any of our subsidiaries and issue shares of PepsiCo common stock for the remaining 50% of such shares. Each share of PBG common stock held by PBG as treasury stock, held by us or held by Metro, and each share of PBG Class B common stock held by us or Metro, in each case immediately prior to the effective time of the PBG Merger, will be canceled, and no payment will be made with respect thereto. Each share of PBG common stock and PBG Class B common stock owned by any subsidiary of ours other than Metro immediately prior to the effective time of the PBG Merger will automatically be converted into the right to receive 0.6432 of a share of PepsiCo common stock.

The PAS Merger Agreement provides that, upon the terms and subject to the conditions set forth in the PAS Merger Agreement, PAS will be merged with and into Metro (the PAS Merger, and together with the PBG Merger, the Mergers), with Metro continuing as the surviving corporation and our wholly owned subsidiary. At the effective time of the PAS Merger, each share of PAS common stock outstanding immediately prior to the effective time not held by us or any of our subsidiaries will be converted into the right to

receive either 0.5022 of a share of PepsiCo common stock or, at the election of the holder, $28.50 in cash, without interest, and in each case subject to proration procedures which provide that we will pay cash for a number of shares equal to 50% of the PAS common stock outstanding immediately prior to the effective time of the PAS Merger not held by us or any of our subsidiaries and issue shares of PepsiCo common stock for the remaining 50% of such shares. Each share of PAS common stock held by PAS as treasury stock, held by us or held by Metro, in each case, immediately prior to the effective time of the PAS Merger, will be canceled, and no payment will be made with respect thereto. Each share of PAS common stock owned by any subsidiary of ours other than Metro immediately prior to the effective time of the PAS Merger will automatically be converted into the right to receive 0.5022 of a share of PepsiCo common stock.

On February 17, 2010, the stockholders of PBG and PAS approved the PBG and PAS Mergers, respectively. Consummation of each of the Mergers is subject to various conditions, including the absence of legal prohibitions and the receipt of regulatory approvals. On February 17, 2010, we announced that we had refiled under the HSR Act with respect to the Mergers and signed a Consent Decree proposed by the Staff of the FTC providing for the maintenance of the confidentiality of certain information we will obtain from DPSG in connection with the manufacture and distribution of certain DPSG products after the Mergers are completed. The Consent Decree is subject to review and approval by the Commissioners of the FTC. We hope to consummate the Mergers by the end of February, 2010.

We currently plan that at the closing of the Mergers we will form a new operating unit. This new operating unit will comprise all current PBG and PAS operations in the United States, Canada and Mexico, and will account for about three-quarters of the volume of PepsiCo's North American bottling system, with independent franchisees accounting for most of the rest. This new operating unit will be included within the PAB business unit. Current PBG and PAS operations in Europe, including Russia, will be managed by the Europe division when the Mergers are completed.

Management's Responsibility for Financial Reporting

To Our Shareholders:

At PepsiCo, our actions—the actions of all our associates—are governed by our Worldwide Code of Conduct. This Code is clearly aligned with our stated values—a commitment to sustained growth, through empowered people, operating with responsibility and building trust. Both the Code and our core values enable us to operate with integrity—both within the letter and the spirit of the law. Our Code of Conduct is reinforced consistently at all levels and in all countries. We have maintained strong governance policies and practices for many years.

The management of PepsiCo is responsible for the objectivity and integrity of our consolidated financial statements. The Audit Committee of the Board of Directors has engaged independent registered public accounting firm, KPMG LLP, to audit our consolidated financial statements, and they have expressed an unqualified opinion.

We are committed to providing timely, accurate and understandable information to investors. Our commitment encompasses the following:

Maintaining strong controls over financial reporting. Our system of internal control is based on the control criteria framework of the Committee of Sponsoring Organizations of the Treadway Commission published in their report titled *Internal Control—Integrated Framework*. The system is designed to provide reasonable assurance that transactions are executed as authorized and accurately recorded; that assets are safeguarded; and that accounting records are sufficiently reliable to permit the preparation of financial statements that conform in all material respects with accounting principles generally accepted in the U.S. We maintain disclosure controls and procedures designed to ensure that information required to be disclosed in reports under the Securities Exchange Act of 1934 is recorded, processed, summarized and reported within the specified time periods. We monitor these internal controls through self-assessments and an ongoing program of internal audits. Our internal controls are reinforced through our Worldwide Code of Conduct, which sets forth our commitment to conduct business with integrity, and within both the letter and the spirit of the law.

Exerting rigorous oversight of the business. We continuously review our business results and strategies. This encompasses financial discipline in our strategic and daily business decisions. Our Executive Committee is actively involved—from understanding strategies and alternatives to reviewing key initiatives and financial performance. The intent is to ensure we remain objective in our assessments, constructively challenge our approach to potential business opportunities and issues, and monitor results and controls.

Engaging strong and effective Corporate Governance from our Board of Directors. We have an active, capable and diligent Board that meets the required standards for independence, and we welcome the Board's oversight as a representative of our shareholders. Our Audit Committee is comprised of independent directors with the financial literacy, knowledge and experience to provide appropriate oversight. We review our critical accounting policies, financial reporting and internal control matters with them and encourage their direct communication with KPMG LLP, with our General Auditor, and with our General Counsel. We also have a Compliance Department to coordinate our compliance policies and practices.

Providing investors with financial results that are complete, transparent and understandable. The consolidated financial statements and financial information included in this report are the responsibility of management. This includes preparing the financial statements in accordance with accounting principles generally accepted in the U.S., which require estimates based on management's best judgment.

PepsiCo has a strong history of doing what's right. We realize that great companies are built on trust, strong ethical standards and principles. Our financial results are delivered from that culture of accountability, and we take responsibility for the quality and accuracy of our financial reporting.

Peter A. Bridgman
Senior Vice President and Controller

Richard Goodman
Chief Financial Officer

Indra K. Nooyi
Chairman of the Board of Directors and Chief Executive Officer

Management's Report on Internal Control Over Financial Reporting

To Our Shareholders:

Our management is responsible for establishing and maintaining adequate internal control over financial reporting, as such term is defined in Rule 13a-15(f) of the Exchange Act. Under the supervision and with the participation of our management, including our Chief Executive Officer and Chief Financial Officer, we conducted an evaluation of the effectiveness of our internal control over financial reporting based upon the framework in *Internal Control—Integrated Framework* issued by the Committee of Sponsoring Organizations of the Treadway Commission. Based on that evaluation, our management concluded that our internal control over financial reporting is effective as of December 26, 2009.

KPMG LLP, an independent registered public accounting firm, has audited the consolidated financial statements included in this Annual Report on Form 10-K and, as part of their audit, has issued their report, included herein, on the effectiveness of our internal control over financial reporting.

During our fourth fiscal quarter of 2009, we continued migrating certain of our financial processing systems to SAP software. This software implementation is part of our ongoing global business transformation initiative, and we plan to continue implementing such software throughout other parts of our businesses over the course of the next few years. In connection with the SAP implementation and resulting business process

changes, we continue to enhance the design and documentation of our internal control processes to ensure suitable controls over our financial reporting.

Except as described above, there were no changes in our internal control over financial reporting during our fourth fiscal quarter of 2009 that have materially affected, or are reasonably likely to materially affect, our internal control over financial reporting.

Peter Bridgman

Peter A. Bridgman
Senior Vice President and Controller

Richard Goodman

Richard Goodman
Chief Financial Officer

Indra Nooyi

Indra K. Nooyi
Chairman of the Board of Directors and Chief Executive Officer

Report of Independent Registered Public Accounting Firm

The Board of Directors and Shareholders
PepsiCo, Inc.:

We have audited the accompanying Consolidated Balance Sheets of PepsiCo, Inc. and subsidiaries ("PepsiCo, Inc." or "the Company") as of December 26, 2009 and December 27, 2008, and the related Consolidated Statements of Income, Cash Flows and Equity for each of the fiscal years in the three-year period ended December 26, 2009. We also have audited PepsiCo, Inc.'s internal control over financial reporting as of December 26, 2009, based on criteria established in *Internal Control—Integrated Framework* issued by the Committee of Sponsoring Organizations of the Treadway Commission (COSO). PepsiCo, Inc.'s management is responsible for these consolidated financial statements, for maintaining effective internal control over financial reporting, and for its assessment of the effectiveness of internal control over financial reporting, included in the accompanying Management's Report on Internal Control over Financial Reporting. Our responsibility is to express an opinion on these consolidated financial statements and an opinion on the Company's internal control over financial reporting based on our audits.

We conducted our audits in accordance with the standards of the Public Company Accounting Oversight Board (United States). Those standards require that we plan and perform the audits to obtain reasonable assurance about whether the financial statements are free of material misstatement and whether effective internal control over financial reporting was maintained in all material respects. Our audits of the consolidated financial statements included examining, on a test basis, evidence supporting the amounts and disclosures in the financial statements, assessing the accounting principles used and significant estimates made by management, and evaluating the overall financial statement presentation. Our audit of internal control over financial reporting included obtaining an understanding of internal control over financial reporting, assessing the risk that a material weakness exists, and testing and evaluating the design and operating effectiveness of internal control based on the assessed risk. Our audits also included performing such other procedures as we considered necessary in the circumstances. We believe that our audits provide a reasonable basis for our opinions.

A company's internal control over financial reporting is a process designed to provide reasonable assurance regarding the reliability of financial reporting and the preparation of financial statements for external purposes in accordance with generally accepted accounting principles. A company's internal control over financial reporting includes those policies and procedures that (1) pertain to the maintenance of records that, in reasonable detail, accurately and fairly reflect the transactions and dispositions of the assets of the company; (2) provide reasonable assurance that transactions are recorded as necessary to permit preparation of financial statements in accordance with generally accepted accounting principles, and that receipts and expenditures of the company are being made only in accordance with authorizations of management and directors of the company; and (3) provide reasonable assurance regarding prevention or timely detection of unauthorized acquisition, use, or disposition of the company's assets that could have a material effect on the financial statements.

Because of its inherent limitations, internal control over financial reporting may not prevent or detect misstatements. Also, projections of any evaluation of effectiveness to future periods are subject to the risk that controls may become inadequate because of changes in conditions, or that the degree of compliance with the policies or procedures may deteriorate.

In our opinion, the consolidated financial statements referred to above present fairly, in all material respects, the financial position of PepsiCo, Inc. as of December 26, 2009 and December 27, 2008, and the results of its operations and its cash flows for each of the fiscal years in the three-year period ended December 26, 2009, in conformity with U.S. generally accepted accounting principles. Also in our opinion, PepsiCo, Inc. maintained, in all material respects, effective internal control over financial reporting as of December 26, 2009, based on criteria established in *Internal Control—Integrated Framework* issued by COSO.

As discussed in Note 2 to the consolidated financial statements, the Company changed its method of accounting for business combinations and noncontrolling interests in 2009.

KPMG LLP

New York, New York
February 22, 2010

Selected Financial Data

(in millions except per share amounts, unaudited)

Quarterly	First Quarter	Second Quarter	Third Quarter	Fourth Quarter
Net revenue				
2009	$8,263	$10,592	$11,080	$13,297
2008	$8,333	$10,945	$11,244	$12,729
Gross profit				
2009	$4,519	$ 5,711	$ 5,899	$ 7,004
2008	$4,499	$ 5,867	$ 5,976	$ 6,558
Restructuring and impairment charges (a)				
2009	$ 25	$ 11	–	–
2008	–	–	–	$ 543
Mark-to-market net impact (b)				
2009	$ (62)	$ (100)	$ (29)	$ (83)
2008	$ 4	$ (61)	$ 176	$ 227
PepsiCo portion of PBG restructuring and impairment charge (c)				
2008	–	–	–	$ 138
PBG/PAS merger costs (d)				
2009	–	–	$ 9	$ 52
Net income attributable to PepsiCo				
2009	$1,135	$ 1,660	$ 1,717	$ 1,434
2008	$1,148	$ 1,699	$ 1,576	$ 719
Net income attributable to PepsiCo per common share—basic				
2009	$ 0.73	$ 1.06	$ 1.10	$ 0.92
2008	$ 0.72	$ 1.07	$ 1.01	$ 0.46
Net income attributable to PepsiCo per common share—diluted				
2009	$ 0.72	$ 1.06	$ 1.09	$ 0.90
2008	$ 0.70	$ 1.05	$ 0.99	$ 0.46
Cash dividends declared per common share				
2009	$0.425	$ 0.45	$ 0.45	$ 0.45
2008	$0.375	$ 0.425	$ 0.425	$ 0.425
2009 stock price per share (e)				
High	$56.93	$ 56.95	$ 59.64	$ 64.48
Low	$43.78	$ 47.50	$ 52.11	$ 57.33
Close	$50.02	$ 53.65	$ 57.54	$ 60.96
2008 stock price per share (e)				
High	$79.79	$ 72.35	$ 70.83	$ 75.25
Low	$66.30	$ 64.69	$ 63.28	$ 49.74
Close	$71.19	$ 67.54	$ 68.92	$ 54.56

(a) The restructuring and impairment charge in 2009 was $36 million ($29 million after-tax or $0.02 per share). The restructuring and impairment charge in 2008 was $543 million ($408 million after-tax or $0.25 per share). See Note 3.
(b) In 2009, we recognized $274 million ($173 million after-tax or $0.11 per share) of mark-to-market net gains on commodity hedges in corporate unallocated expenses. In 2008, we recognized $346 million ($223 million after-tax or $0.14 per share) of mark-to-market net losses on commodity hedges in corporate unallocated expenses.
(c) In 2008, we recognized a non-cash charge of $138 million ($114 million after-tax or $0.07 per share) included in bottling equity income as part of recording our share of PBG's financial results.
(d) In 2009, we recognized $50 million of costs associated with the proposed mergers with PBG and PAS, as well as an additional $11 million of costs in bottling equity income representing our share of the respective merger costs of PBG and PAS. In total, these costs had an after-tax impact of $44 million or $0.03 per share.
(e) Represents the composite high and low sales price and quarterly closing prices for one share of PepsiCo common stock.

Five-Year Summary	2009	2008	2007
Net revenue	**$43,232**	$43,251	$39,474
Net income attributable to PepsiCo	**$ 5,946**	$ 5,142	$ 5,658
Net income attributable to PepsiCo per common share – basic	**$ 3.81**	$ 3.26	$ 3.48
Net income attributable to PepsiCo per common share – diluted	**$ 3.77**	$ 3.21	$ 3.41
Cash dividends declared per common share	**$ 1.775**	$ 1.65	$ 1.425
Total assets	**$39,848**	$35,994	$34,628
Long-term debt	**$ 7,400**	$ 7,858	$ 4,203
Return on invested capital (a)	**27.2%**	25.5%	28.9%

Five-Year Summary (continued)	2006	2005
Net revenue	$35,137	$32,562
Net income attributable to PepsiCo	$ 5,642	$ 4,078
Net income attributable to PepsiCo per common share – basic	$ 3.42	$ 2.43
Net income attributable to PepsiCo per common share – diluted	$ 3.34	$ 2.39
Cash dividends declared per common share	$ 1.16	$ 1.01
Total assets	$29,930	$31,727
Long-term debt	$ 2,550	$ 2,313
Return on invested capital (a)	30.4%	22.7%

(a) Return on invested capital is defined as adjusted net income attributable to PepsiCo divided by the sum of average common shareholders' equity and average total debt. Adjusted net income attributable to PepsiCo is defined as net income attributable to PepsiCo plus net interest expense after-tax. Net interest expense after-tax was $211 million in 2009, $184 million in 2008, $63 million in 2007, $72 million in 2006 and $62 million in 2005.

• Includes restructuring and impairment charges of:

	2009	2008	2007	2006	2005
Pre-tax	$ 36	$ 543	$ 102	$ 67	$ 83
After-tax	$ 29	$ 408	$ 70	$ 43	$ 55
Per share	$0.02	$0.25	$0.04	$0.03	$0.03

• Includes mark-to-market net (income)/expense of:

	2009	2008	2007	2006
Pre-tax	$ (274)	$ 346	$ (19)	$ 18
After-tax	$ (173)	$ 223	$ (12)	$ 12
Per share	$(0.11)	$0.14	$(0.01)	$0.01

• In 2009, we recognized $50 million of costs associated with the proposed mergers with PBG and PAS, as well as an additional $11 million of costs in bottling equity income representing our share of the respective merger costs of PBG and PAS. In total, these costs had an after-tax impact of $44 million or $0.03 per share.
• In 2008, we recognized $138 million ($114 million after-tax or $0.07 per share) of our share of PBG's restructuring and impairment charges.
• In 2007, we recognized $129 million ($0.08 per share) of non-cash tax benefits related to the favorable resolution of certain foreign tax matters. In 2006, we recognized non-cash tax benefits of $602 million ($0.36 per share) primarily in connection with the IRS's examination of our consolidated income tax returns for the years 1998 through 2002. In 2005, we recorded income tax expense of $460 million ($0.27 per share) related to our repatriation of earnings in connection with the American Job Creation Act of 2004.
• On December 30, 2006, we adopted guidance from the FASB on accounting for pension and other postretirement benefits which reduced total assets by $2,016 million, total common shareholders' equity by $1,643 million and total liabilities by $373 million.
• The 2005 fiscal year consisted of 53 weeks compared to 52 weeks in our normal fiscal year. The 53rd week increased 2005 net revenue by an estimated $418 million and net income attributable to PepsiCo by an estimated $57 million ($0.03 per share).

APPENDIX B

Specimen Financial Statements:

The Coca-Cola Company

THE COCA-COLA COMPANY AND SUBSIDIARIES
CONSOLIDATED STATEMENTS OF INCOME

Year Ended December 31,	2009	2008	2007
(In millions except per share data)			
NET OPERATING REVENUES	$ 30,990	$ 31,944	$ 28,857
Cost of goods sold	11,088	11,374	10,406
GROSS PROFIT	19,902	20,570	18,451
Selling, general and administrative expenses	11,358	11,774	10,945
Other operating charges	313	350	254
OPERATING INCOME	8,231	8,446	7,252
Interest income	249	333	236
Interest expense	355	438	456
Equity income (loss) — net	781	(874)	668
Other income (loss) — net	40	39	219
INCOME BEFORE INCOME TAXES	8,946	7,506	7,919
Income taxes	2,040	1,632	1,892
CONSOLIDATED NET INCOME	6,906	5,874	6,027
Less: Net income attributable to noncontrolling interests	82	67	46
NET INCOME ATTRIBUTABLE TO SHAREOWNERS OF THE COCA-COLA COMPANY	$ 6,824	$ 5,807	$ 5,981
BASIC NET INCOME PER SHARE[1]	$ 2.95	$ 2.51	$ 2.59
DILUTED NET INCOME PER SHARE[1]	$ 2.93	$ 2.49	$ 2.57
AVERAGE SHARES OUTSTANDING	2,314	2,315	2,313
Effect of dilutive securities	15	21	18
AVERAGE SHARES OUTSTANDING ASSUMING DILUTION	2,329	2,336	2,331

[1] Basic net income per share and diluted net income per share are calculated based on net income attributable to shareowners of The Coca-Cola Company.

Refer to Notes to Consolidated Financial Statements.

The financial information herein is reprinted with permission from The Coca-Cola Company 2009 Annual Report. The accompanying Notes are an integral part of the consolidated financial statements. The complete financial statements are available through a link at the book's companion website.

THE COCA-COLA COMPANY AND SUBSIDIARIES
CONSOLIDATED BALANCE SHEETS

December 31,	2009	2008
(In millions except par value)		
ASSETS		
CURRENT ASSETS		
Cash and cash equivalents	$ 7,021	$ 4,701
Short-term investments	2,130	—
TOTAL CASH, CASH EQUIVALENTS AND SHORT-TERM INVESTMENTS	9,151	4,701
Marketable securities	62	278
Trade accounts receivable, less allowances of $55 and $51, respectively	3,758	3,090
Inventories	2,354	2,187
Prepaid expenses and other assets	2,226	1,920
TOTAL CURRENT ASSETS	17,551	12,176
EQUITY METHOD INVESTMENTS	6,217	5,316
OTHER INVESTMENTS, PRINCIPALLY BOTTLING COMPANIES	538	463
OTHER ASSETS	1,976	1,733
PROPERTY, PLANT AND EQUIPMENT — net	9,561	8,326
TRADEMARKS WITH INDEFINITE LIVES	6,183	6,059
GOODWILL	4,224	4,029
OTHER INTANGIBLE ASSETS	2,421	2,417
TOTAL ASSETS	$ 48,671	$ 40,519
LIABILITIES AND EQUITY		
CURRENT LIABILITIES		
Accounts payable and accrued expenses	$ 6,657	$ 6,205
Loans and notes payable	6,749	6,066
Current maturities of long-term debt	51	465
Accrued income taxes	264	252
TOTAL CURRENT LIABILITIES	13,721	12,988
LONG-TERM DEBT	5,059	2,781
OTHER LIABILITIES	2,965	3,011
DEFERRED INCOME TAXES	1,580	877
THE COCA-COLA COMPANY SHAREOWNERS' EQUITY		
Common stock, $0.25 par value; Authorized — 5,600 shares;		
Issued — 3,520 and 3,519 shares, respectively	880	880
Capital surplus	8,537	7,966
Reinvested earnings	41,537	38,513
Accumulated other comprehensive income (loss)	(757)	(2,674)
Treasury stock, at cost — 1,217 and 1,207 shares, respectively	(25,398)	(24,213)
EQUITY ATTRIBUTABLE TO SHAREOWNERS OF THE COCA-COLA COMPANY	24,799	20,472
EQUITY ATTRIBUTABLE TO NONCONTROLLING INTERESTS	547	390
TOTAL EQUITY	25,346	20,862
TOTAL LIABILITIES AND EQUITY	$ 48,671	$ 40,519

Refer to Notes to Consolidated Financial Statements.

THE COCA-COLA COMPANY AND SUBSIDIARIES
CONSOLIDATED STATEMENTS OF CASH FLOWS

Year Ended December 31,	2009	2008	2007
(In millions)			
OPERATING ACTIVITIES			
Consolidated net income	$ 6,906	$ 5,874	$ 6,027
Depreciation and amortization	1,236	1,228	1,163
Stock-based compensation expense	241	266	313
Deferred income taxes	353	(360)	109
Equity income or loss, net of dividends	(359)	1,128	(452)
Foreign currency adjustments	61	(42)	9
Gains on sales of assets, including bottling interests	(43)	(130)	(244)
Other operating charges	134	209	166
Other items	221	153	99
Net change in operating assets and liabilities	(564)	(755)	(40)
Net cash provided by operating activities	8,186	7,571	7,150
INVESTING ACTIVITIES			
Acquisitions and investments, principally beverage and bottling companies and trademarks	(300)	(759)	(5,653)
Purchases of other investments	(2,152)	(240)	(99)
Proceeds from disposals of bottling companies and other investments	240	479	448
Purchases of property, plant and equipment	(1,993)	(1,968)	(1,648)
Proceeds from disposals of property, plant and equipment	104	129	239
Other investing activities	(48)	(4)	(6)
Net cash provided by (used in) investing activities	(4,149)	(2,363)	(6,719)
FINANCING ACTIVITIES			
Issuances of debt	14,689	4,337	9,979
Payments of debt	(12,326)	(4,308)	(5,638)
Issuances of stock	662	586	1,619
Purchases of stock for treasury	(1,518)	(1,079)	(1,838)
Dividends	(3,800)	(3,521)	(3,149)
Net cash provided by (used in) financing activities	(2,293)	(3,985)	973
EFFECT OF EXCHANGE RATE CHANGES ON CASH AND CASH EQUIVALENTS	576	(615)	249
CASH AND CASH EQUIVALENTS			
Net increase (decrease) during the year	2,320	608	1,653
Balance at beginning of year	4,701	4,093	2,440
Balance at end of year	$ 7,021	$ 4,701	$ 4,093

Refer to Notes to Consolidated Financial Statements.

THE COCA-COLA COMPANY AND SUBSIDIARIES
CONSOLIDATED STATEMENTS OF SHAREOWNERS' EQUITY

Year Ended December 31,	2009	2008	2007
(In millions except per share data)			
EQUITY ATTRIBUTABLE TO SHAREOWNERS OF THE COCA-COLA COMPANY			
NUMBER OF COMMON SHARES OUTSTANDING			
Balance at beginning of year	2,312	2,318	2,318
Stock issued to employees exercising stock options	—	—	8
Purchases of treasury stock	(26)	(18)	(35)
Treasury stock issued to employees exercising stock options	17	12	23
Treasury stock issued to former shareholders of glacéau	—	—	4
Balance at end of year	2,303	2,312	2,318
COMMON STOCK			
Balance at beginning of year	$ 880	$ 880	$ 878
Stock issued to employees related to stock compensation plans	—	—	2
Balance at end of year	880	880	880
CAPITAL SURPLUS			
Balance at beginning of year	7,966	7,378	5,983
Stock issued to employees related to stock compensation plans	339	324	1,001
Tax (charge) benefit from employees' stock option and restricted stock plans	(6)	(1)	(28)
Stock-based compensation	238	265	309
Stock purchased by former shareholders of glacéau	—	—	113
Balance at end of year	8,537	7,966	7,378
REINVESTED EARNINGS			
Balance at beginning of year	38,513	36,235	33,468
Cumulative effect of the adoption of new accounting guidance for pension and other postretirement plans	—	(8)	—
Cumulative effect of the adoption of new accounting guidance for uncertain tax positions	—	—	(65)
Net income attributable to shareowners of The Coca-Cola Company	6,824	5,807	5,981
Dividends (per share — $1.64, $1.52 and $1.36 in 2009, 2008 and 2007, respectively)	(3,800)	(3,521)	(3,149)
Balance at end of year	41,537	38,513	36,235
ACCUMULATED OTHER COMPREHENSIVE INCOME (LOSS)			
Balance at beginning of year	(2,674)	626	(1,291)
Net foreign currency translation adjustment	1,824	(2,285)	1,575
Net gain (loss) on derivatives	34	1	(64)
Net change in unrealized gain on available-for-sale securities	(52)	(44)	14
Net change in pension liability	111	(972)	392
Net other comprehensive income (loss)	1,917	(3,300)	1,917
Balance at end of year	(757)	(2,674)	626
TREASURY STOCK			
Balance at beginning of year	(24,213)	(23,375)	(22,118)
Stock issued to employees related to stock compensation plans	333	243	428
Stock purchased by former shareholders of glacéau	—	—	66
Purchases of treasury stock	(1,518)	(1,081)	(1,751)
Balance at end of year	(25,398)	(24,213)	(23,375)
TOTAL EQUITY ATTRIBUTABLE TO SHAREOWNERS OF THE COCA-COLA COMPANY	$ 24,799	$ 20,472	$ 21,744
EQUITY ATTRIBUTABLE TO NONCONTROLLING INTERESTS			
Balance at beginning of year	$ 390	$ 342	$ 333
Net income attributable to noncontrolling interests	82	67	46
Net foreign currency translation adjustment	49	(25)	1
Dividends paid to noncontrolling interests	(14)	(20)	(23)
Contributions by noncontrolling interests	40	31	41
Disposal of subsidiaries	—	(5)	(56)
TOTAL EQUITY ATTRIBUTABLE TO NONCONTROLLING INTERESTS	$ 547	$ 390	$ 342
COMPREHENSIVE INCOME			
Consolidated net income	$ 6,906	$ 5,874	$ 6,027
Consolidated net other comprehensive income (loss)	1,966	(3,325)	1,918
CONSOLIDATED COMPREHENSIVE INCOME	$ 8,872	$ 2,549	$ 7,945

Refer to Notes to Consolidated Financial Statements.

APPENDIX C

Specimen Financial Statements:

Zetar plc

CONSOLIDATED INCOME STATEMENT
FOR THE YEAR ENDED 30 APRIL 2009

	Note	2009 Adjusted results £'000	2009 Adjusting items £'000	2009 Total £'000	2008 Adjusted results £'000	2008 Adjusting items £'000	2008 Total £'000
Continuing operations							
Revenue	3	118,602	—	118,602	109,216	—	109,216
Cost of sales		(93,857)	—	(93,857)	(83,938)	—	(83,938)
Gross profit		24,745	—	24,745	25,278	—	25,278
Distribution costs		(4,777)	—	(4,777)	(5,013)	—	(5,013)
Administrative expenses							
– Other administrative expenses		(13,917)	—	(13,917)	(11,541)	—	(11,541)
– One-off items	4	—	(1,508)	(1,508)	—	—	—
– Amortisation of intangible assets	14	—	(456)	(456)	—	(675)	(675)
– Share-based payments	9	—	116	116	—	(377)	(377)
Operating profit		6,051	(1,848)	4,203	8,724	(1,052)	7,672
Interest income	8	47	—	47	116	—	116
Finance costs	8	(1,556)	(680)	(2,236)	(1,733)	(144)	(1,877)
Profit from continuing operations before taxation		4,542	(2,528)	2,014	7,107	(1,196)	5,911
Tax on profit from continuing activities	10	(1,241)	—	(1,241)	(2,034)	179	(1,855)
Net result from continuing operations		3,301	(2,528)	773	5,073	(1,017)	4,056
Net result from discontinued operations	11	—	(5,836)	(5,836)	—	(811)	(811)
Net result for the period		3,301	(8,364)	(5,063)	5,073	(1,828)	3,245
Basic (losses)/earnings per share (p)	12			(42.9)			29.5
Diluted (losses)/earnings per share (p)	12			(42.6)			25.9
Adjusted basic earnings per share (p)	12	28.0			46.2		
Adjusted diluted earnings per share (p)	12	27.8			40.5		

CONSOLIDATED BALANCE SHEET
AT 30 APRIL 2009

	Note	2009 £'000	2008 £'000
Non-current assets			
Goodwill	13	30,821	32,363
Other intangible assets	14	623	1,002
Property, plant and equipment	15	15,283	18,545
Deferred tax asset	21	198	167
		46,925	52,077
Current assets			
Inventories	16	14,319	13,364
Trade and other receivables	17	19,190	15,253
Derivative financial asset	30	—	72
Cash at bank	26	5,405	3,175
		38,914	31,864
Total assets		85,839	83,941
Current liabilities			
Trade and other payables	18	(23,763)	(20,337)
Performance related contingent consideration		(220)	(876)
Current tax liabilities		(252)	(687)
Obligations under finance leases	19	(214)	(470)
Derivative financial instruments	30	(607)	—
Borrowings and overdrafts	20	(15,712)	(9,289)
		(40,768)	(31,659)
Net current (liabilities)/assets		(1,854)	205
Non-current liabilities			
Performance related contingent consideration		(300)	(2,555)
Deferred tax liabilities	21	(1,575)	(1,448)
Obligations under finance leases	19	(167)	(369)
Borrowings and overdrafts	20	(4,676)	(7,609)
		(6,718)	(11,981)
Total liabilities		(47,486)	(43,640)
Net assets		38,353	40,301
Equity			
Share capital	22	1,324	1,151
Share premium account	23	28,252	26,449
Merger reserve		3,411	3,411
Equity reserve	24	2,719	1,431
Retained earnings	24	2,647	7,859
Total equity attributable to equity holders of the parent		38,353	40,301

CONSOLIDATED STATEMENT OF CHANGES IN EQUITY
FOR THE YEAR ENDED 30 APRIL 2009

| | Attributable to equity holders of the parent | | | | | |
	Share capital £'000	Share premium account £'000	Merger reserve £'000	Equity reserve £'000	Retained earnings £'000	Total £'000
Balance at 1 May 2007	1,073	22,673	3,229	621	4,914	32,510
Profit for the year	—	—	—	—	3,245	3,245
Exchange gain on translation of foreign operation	—	—	—	557	—	557
Issue of new ordinary shares	78	3,776	182	—	—	4,036
Purchase of own shares	—	—	—	—	(300)	(300)
Share-based payment charge	—	—	—	377	—	377
Deferred tax on share-based payments	—	—	—	(124)	—	(124)
Balance at 30 April 2008	1,151	26,449	3,411	1,431	7,859	40,301
Loss for the year	—	—	—	—	(5,063)	(5,063)
Exchange gain on translation of foreign operations	—	—	—	1,404	—	1,404
Issue of new ordinary shares	173	1,803	—	—	—	1,976
Purchase of own shares	—	—	—	—	(149)	(149)
Prior year share-based payment reversal	—	—	—	(116)	—	(116)
Balance at 30 April 2009	1,324	28,252	3,411	2,719	2,647	38,353

CONSOLIDATED CASH FLOW STATEMENT
FOR THE YEAR ENDED 30 APRIL 2009

	Note	2009 £'000	2008 £'000
Cash flow from operating activities			
Profit on ordinary activities before taxation		2,014	5,911
Finance costs		2,236	1,877
Interest income		(47)	(116)
Share-based payments		(116)	377
Depreciation (including trademark amortisation)	15	2,346	1,989
Loss on sale of plant and equipment		22	6
Amortisation of intangible assets		457	675
One-off items		1,388	—
Net movement in working capital		(2,469)	(1,011)
Increase in inventories		(1,299)	(2,646)
(Increase)/decrease in receivables		(4,504)	4,075
Decrease/(increase) in payables		3,334	(2,440)
Cash flow from continuing operations		5,831	9,708
Cash flow from discontinued operations		(1,002)	(1,260)
Total cash flow from operations		4,829	8,448
Net interest paid	8	(1,510)	(1,646)
Tax paid		(782)	(1,682)
Cash generated from activities in continuing operations		3,539	6,380
Cash flow generated from operating activities in discontinued operations		(1,002)	(1,260)
Total cash flow from operating activities		2,537	5,120
Cash flow from investing activities			
Purchase of property, plant and equipment		(3,847)	(3,722)
Proceeds from sale of plant and equipment		42	26
Disposal of subsidiary	11	(220)	—
Total cash impact of acquisitions		(879)	(3,733)
Acquisitions of businesses (including contingent consideration)		(879)	(2,814)
Net borrowings assumed on acquisition		—	(919)
Net cash outflow from continuing investing activities		(4,904)	(7,429)
Net cash outflow from discontinued investing activities		—	(5,244)
Net cash flow from investing activities		(4,904)	(12,673)
Cash flow from financing activities			
Net proceeds from issue of ordinary share capital		1,976	3,851
Purchase of own shares		(149)	(300)
Proceeds from new borrowings		—	5,000
Repayment of borrowings		(3,536)	(4,819)
Finance lease repayments		(457)	(472)
Minority interest dividends paid		—	—
Net cash flow from financing activities		(2,166)	3,260
Net decrease in cash and cash equivalents		(4,533)	(4,293)
Cash and cash equivalents at beginning of the year		(3,331)	917
Effect of foreign exchange rate movements		(263)	45
Cash and cash equivalents at end of the year		(8,127)	(3,331)
Cash and cash equivalents comprise:			
Cash at bank	26	5,405	3,175
Bank overdraft	26	(13,532)	(6,506)
		(8,127)	(3,331)

APPENDIX D

Time Value of Money

Study Objectives

After studying this appendix, you should be able to:

[1] Distinguish between simple and compound interest.

[2] Identify the variables fundamental to solving present value problems.

[3] Solve for present value of a single amount.

[4] Solve for present value of an annuity.

[5] Compute the present value of notes and bonds.

Would you rather receive $1,000 today or a year from now? You should prefer to receive the $1,000 today because you can invest the $1,000 and earn interest on it. As a result, you will have more than $1,000 a year from now. What this example illustrates is the concept of the **time value of money**. Everyone prefers to receive money today rather than in the future because of the interest factor.

Nature of Interest

Interest is payment for the use of another person's money. It is the difference between the amount borrowed or invested (called the principal) and the amount repaid or collected. The amount of interest to be paid or collected is usually stated as a rate over a specific period of time. The rate of interest is generally stated as an **annual rate**.

The amount of interest involved in any financing transaction is based on three elements:

1. **Principal (p):** The original amount borrowed or invested.
2. **Interest Rate (i):** An annual percentage of the principal.
3. **Time (n):** The number of years that the principal is borrowed or invested.

Simple Interest

Simple interest is computed on the principal amount only. It is the return on the principal for one period. Simple interest is usually expressed as shown in Illustration D-1 on the next page.

Study Objective [1]
Distinguish between simple and compound interest.

Illustration D-1
Interest computation

Interest	=	**Principal**	×	**Rate**	×	**Time**
		p		*i*		*n*

For example, if you borrowed $5,000 for 2 years at a simple interest rate of 12% annually, you would pay $1,200 in total interest computed as follows:

$$\text{Interest} = p \times i \times n$$
$$= \$5,000 \times .12 \times 2$$
$$= \$1,200$$

Compound Interest

Compound interest is computed on principal **and** on any interest earned that has not been paid or withdrawn. It is the return on the principal for two or more time periods. Compounding computes interest not only on the principal but also on the interest earned to date on that principal, assuming the interest is left on deposit.

To illustrate the difference between simple and compound interest, assume that you deposit $1,000 in Bank Two, where it will earn *simple interest* of 9% per year, and you deposit another $1,000 in Citizens Bank, where it will earn compound interest of 9% per year *compounded annually*. Also assume that in both cases you will not withdraw any interest until three years from the date of deposit. Illustration D-2 shows the computation of interest you will receive and the accumulated year-end balances.

Illustration D-2
Simple versus compound interest

Bank Two				**Citizens Bank**		
Simple Interest Calculation	Simple Interest	Accumulated Year-End Balance		Compound Interest Calculation	Compound Interest	Accumulated Year-End Balance
Year 1 $1,000.00 × 9%	$ 90.00	$1,090.00		Year 1 $1,000.00 × 9%	$ 90.00	$1,090.00
Year 2 $1,000.00 × 9%	90.00	$1,180.00		Year 2 $1,090.00 × 9%	98.10	$1,188.10
Year 3 $1,000.00 × 9%	90.00	$1,270.00		Year 3 $1,188.10 × 9%	106.93	$1,295.03
	$ 270.00		→ $25.03 ←		$ 295.03	
			Difference			

Note in Illustration D-2 that simple interest uses the initial principal of $1,000 to compute the interest in all three years. Compound interest uses the accumulated balance (principal plus interest to date) at each year-end to compute interest in the succeeding year—which explains why your compound interest account is larger.

Obviously, if you had a choice between investing your money at simple interest or at compound interest, you would choose compound interest, all other things—especially risk—being equal. In the example, compounding provides $25.03 of additional interest income. For practical purposes, compounding assumes that unpaid interest earned becomes a part of the principal, and the accumulated balance at the end of each year becomes the new principal on which interest is earned during the next year.

Illustration D-2 indicates that you should invest your money at the bank that compounds interest annually. Most business situations use compound interest. Simple interest is generally applicable only to short-term situations of one year or less.

Present Value Variables

The **present value** is the value now of a given amount to be paid or received in the future, assuming compound interest. The present value is based on three variables: (1) the dollar amount to be received (future amount), (2) the length of time until the amount is received (number of periods), and (3) the interest rate (the discount rate). The process of determining the present value is referred to as **discounting the future amount**.

In this textbook, we use present value computations in measuring several items. For example, Chapter 15 computed the present value of the principal and interest payments to determine the market price of a bond. In addition, determining the amount to be reported for notes payable and lease liabilities involves present value computations.

> **Study Objective [2]**
> Identify the variables fundamental to solving present value problems.

Present Value of a Single Amount

To illustrate present value, assume that you want to invest a sum of money that will yield $1,000 at the end of one year. What amount would you need to invest today to have $1,000 one year from now? Illustration D-3 shows the formula for calculating present value.

> **Study Objective [3]**
> Solve for present value of a single amount.

> **Present Value = Future Value ÷ $(1 + i)^n$**

Illustration D-3
Formula for present value

Thus, if you want a 10% rate of return, you would compute the present value of $1,000 for one year as follows:

$$PV = FV \div (1 + i)^n$$
$$= \$1{,}000 \div (1 + .10)^1$$
$$= \$1{,}000 \div 1.10$$
$$= \$909.09$$

We know the future amount ($1,000), the discount rate (10%), and the number of periods (1). These variables are depicted in the time diagram in Illustration D-4.

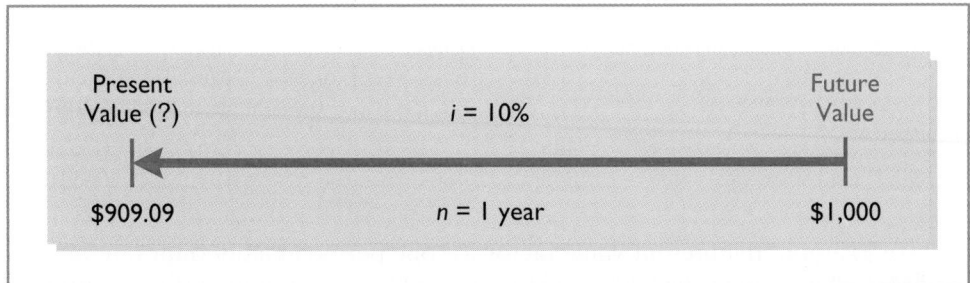

Illustration D-4
Finding present value if discounted for one period

If you receive the single amount of $1,000 **in two years**, discounted at 10% $[PV = \$1{,}000 \div (1 + .10)^2]$, the present value of your $1,000 is $826.45 [($1,000 ÷ 1.21), depicted as shown in Illustration D-5 on the next page.

Illustration D-5
Finding present value if discounted for two periods

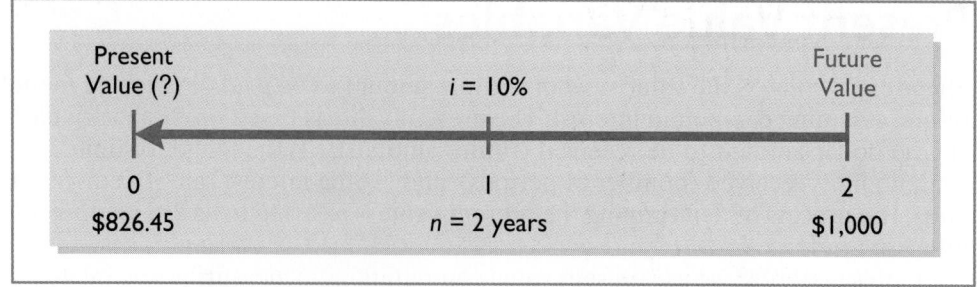

You also could find the present value of your amount through tables that show the present value of 1 for *n* periods. In Table 1, below, *n* (represented in the table's rows) is the number of discounting periods involved. The percentages (represented in the table's columns) are the periodic interest rates or discount rates. The 5-digit decimal numbers in the intersections of the rows and columns are called the **present value of 1 factors**.

When using Table 1 to determine present value, you multiply the future value by the present value factor specified at the intersection of the number of periods and the discount rate.

Table 1
Present Value of 1

(*n*) Periods	4%	5%	6%	8%	9%	10%	11%	12%	15%
1	.96154	.95238	.94340	.92593	.91743	.90909	.90090	.89286	.86957
2	.92456	.90703	.89000	.85734	.84168	.82645	.81162	.79719	.75614
3	.88900	.86384	.83962	.79383	.77218	.75132	.73119	.71178	.65752
4	.85480	.82270	.79209	.73503	.70843	.68301	.65873	.63552	.57175
5	.82193	.78353	.74726	.68058	.64993	.62092	.59345	.56743	.49718
6	.79031	.74622	.70496	.63017	.59627	.56447	.53464	.50663	.43233
7	.75992	.71068	.66506	.58349	.54703	.51316	.48166	.45235	.37594
8	.73069	.67684	.62741	.54027	.50187	.46651	.43393	.40388	.32690
9	.70259	.64461	.59190	.50025	.46043	.42410	.39092	.36061	.28426
10	.67556	.61391	.55839	.46319	.42241	.38554	.35218	.32197	.24719
11	.64958	.58468	.52679	.42888	.38753	.35049	.31728	.28748	.21494
12	.62460	.55684	.49697	.39711	.35554	.31863	.28584	.25668	.18691
13	.60057	.53032	.46884	.36770	.32618	.28966	.25751	.22917	.16253
14	.57748	.50507	.44230	.34046	.29925	.26333	.23199	.20462	.14133
15	.55526	.48102	.41727	.31524	.27454	.23939	.20900	.18270	.12289
16	.53391	.45811	.39365	.29189	.25187	.21763	.18829	.16312	.10687
17	.51337	.43630	.37136	.27027	.23107	.19785	.16963	.14564	.09293
18	.49363	.41552	.35034	.25025	.21199	.17986	.15282	.13004	.08081
19	.47464	.39573	.33051	.23171	.19449	.16351	.13768	.11611	.07027
20	.45639	.37689	.31180	.21455	.17843	.14864	.12403	.10367	.06110

For example, the present value factor for one period at a discount rate of 10% is .90909, which equals the $909.09 ($1,000 × .90909) computed in Illustration D-4. For two periods at a discount rate of 10%, the present value factor is .82645, which equals the $826.45 ($1,000 × .82645) computed previously.

Note that a higher discount rate produces a smaller present value. For example, using a 15% discount rate, the present value of $1,000 due one year from now is $869.57, versus $909.09 at 10%. Also note that the further removed from the present the future value is, the smaller the present value. For example, using the same discount rate of 10%, the present value of $1,000 due in **five years** is $620.92, versus the present value of $1,000 due in **one year**, which is $909.09.

The following two demonstration problems (Illustrations D-6 and D-7) illustrate how to use Table 1.

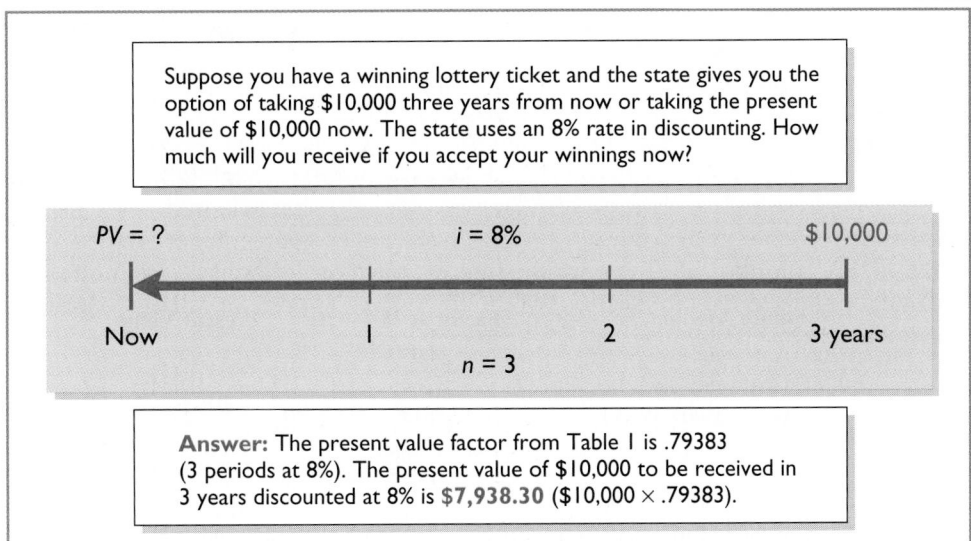

Illustration D-6
Demonstration problem—
Using Table 1 for *PV* of 1

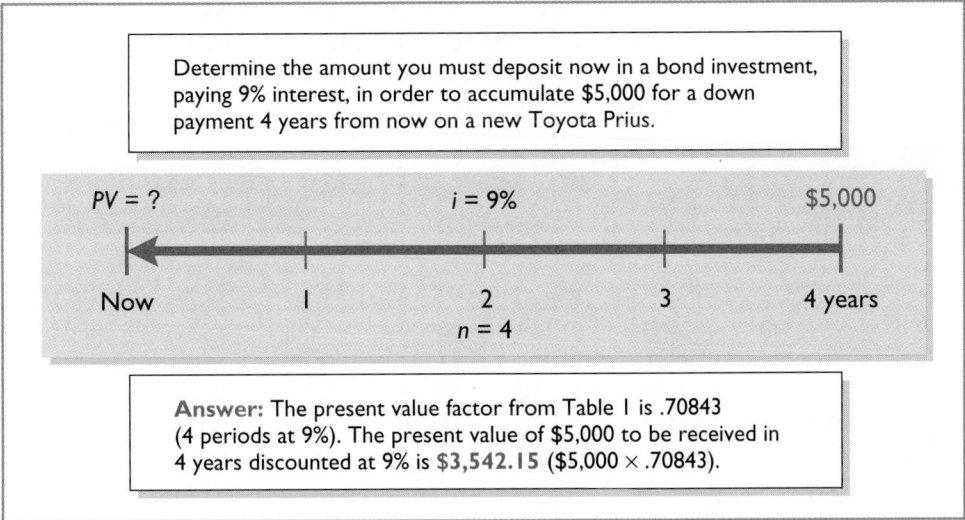

Illustration D-7
Demonstration problem—
Using Table 1 for *PV* of 1

Present Value of an Annuity

The preceding discussion involved the discounting of only a single future amount. Businesses and individuals frequently engage in transactions in which a *series* of equal dollar amounts are to be received or paid at evenly spaced time intervals (periodically). Examples of a series of periodic receipts or payments are loan agreements, installment sales, mortgage notes, lease (rental) contracts, and pension obligations. As discussed in Chapter 15, these periodic receipts or payments are **annuities**.

The **present value of an annuity** is the value now of a series of future receipts or payments, discounted assuming compound interest. In computing the present value of an annuity, you need to know: (1) the discount rate, (2) the number of discount periods, and (3) the amount of the periodic receipts or payments.

Study Objective [4]
Solve for present value of an annuity.

To illustrate how to compute the present value of an annuity, assume that you will receive $1,000 cash annually for three years at a time when the discount rate is 10%. Illustration D-8 depicts this situation, and Illustration D-9 shows the computation of its present value.

Illustration D-8
Time diagram for a three-year annuity

Illustration D-9
Present value of a series of future amounts computation

Future Amount	×	Present Value of 1 Factor at 10%	=	Present Value
$1,000 (one year away)		.90909		$ 909.09
1,000 (two years away)		.82645		826.45
1,000 (three years away)		.75132		751.32
		2.48686		$2,486.86

This method of calculation is required when the periodic cash flows are not uniform in each period. However, when the future receipts are the same in each period, there are two other ways to compute present value. First, you can multiply the annual cash flow by the sum of the three present value factors. In the previous example, $1,000 × 2.48686 equals $2,486.86. The second method is to use annuity tables. As illustrated in Table 2 below, these tables show the present value of 1 to be received periodically for a given number of periods.

				Table 2					
			Present Value of an Annuity of 1						

(*n*) Periods	4%	5%	6%	8%	9%	10%	11%	12%	15%
1	.96154	.95238	.94340	.92593	.91743	.90909	.90090	.89286	.86957
2	1.88609	1.85941	1.83339	1.78326	1.75911	1.73554	1.71252	1.69005	1.62571
3	2.77509	2.72325	2.67301	2.57710	2.53130	2.48685	2.44371	2.40183	2.28323
4	3.62990	3.54595	3.46511	3.31213	3.23972	3.16986	3.10245	3.03735	2.85498
5	4.45182	4.32948	4.21236	3.99271	3.88965	3.79079	3.69590	3.60478	3.35216
6	5.24214	5.07569	4.91732	4.62288	4.48592	4.35526	4.23054	4.11141	3.78448
7	6.00205	5.78637	5.58238	5.20637	5.03295	4.86842	4.71220	4.56376	4.16042
8	6.73274	6.46321	6.20979	5.74664	5.53482	5.33493	5.14612	4.96764	4.48732
9	7.43533	7.10782	6.80169	6.24689	5.99525	5.75902	5.53705	5.32825	4.77158
10	8.11090	7.72173	7.36009	6.71008	6.41766	6.14457	5.88923	5.65022	5.01877
11	8.76048	8.30641	7.88687	7.13896	6.80519	6.49506	6.20652	5.93770	5.23371
12	9.38507	8.86325	8.38384	7.53608	7.16073	6.81369	6.49236	6.19437	5.42062
13	9.98565	9.39357	8.85268	7.90378	7.48690	7.10336	6.74987	6.42355	5.58315
14	10.56312	9.89864	9.29498	8.24424	7.78615	7.36669	6.98187	6.62817	5.72448
15	11.11839	10.37966	9.71225	8.55948	8.06069	7.60608	7.19087	6.81086	5.84737
16	11.65230	10.83777	10.10590	8.85137	8.31256	7.82371	7.37916	6.97399	5.95424
17	12.16567	11.27407	10.47726	9.12164	8.54363	8.02155	7.54879	7.11963	6.04716
18	12.65930	11.68959	10.82760	9.37189	8.75563	8.20141	7.70162	7.24967	6.12797
19	13.13394	12.08532	11.15812	9.60360	8.95012	8.36492	7.83929	7.36578	6.19823
20	13.59033	12.46221	11.46992	9.81815	9.12855	8.51356	7.96333	7.46944	6.25933

Table 2 shows that the present value of an annuity of 1 factor for three periods at 10% is 2.48685.[1] (This present value factor is the total of the three individual present value factors, as shown in Illustration D-9.) Applying this amount to the annual cash flow of $1,000 produces a present value of $2,486.85.

The following demonstration problem (Illustration D-10) illustrates how to use Table 2.

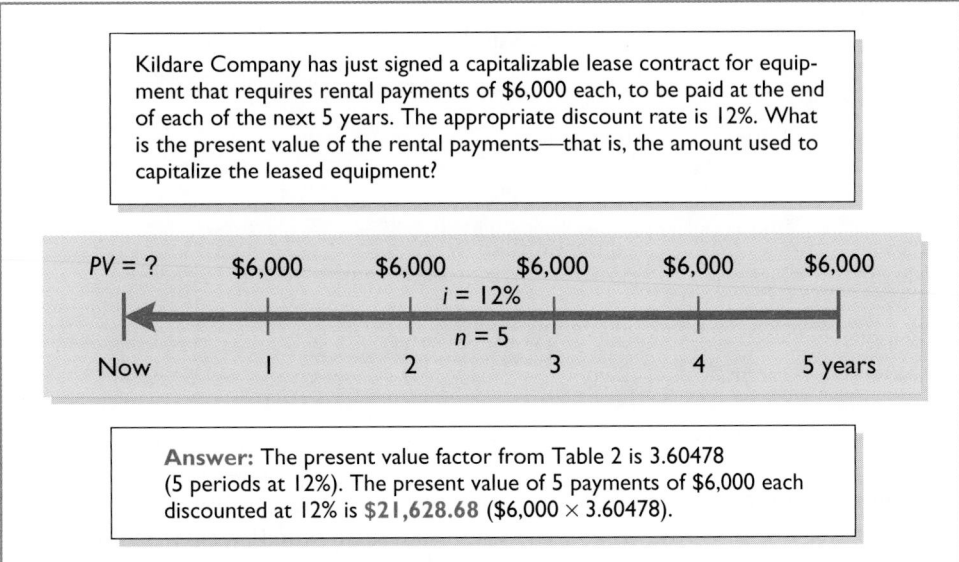

Illustration D-10
Demonstration problem—Using Table 2 for *PV* of an annuity of 1

Kildare Company has just signed a capitalizable lease contract for equipment that requires rental payments of $6,000 each, to be paid at the end of each of the next 5 years. The appropriate discount rate is 12%. What is the present value of the rental payments—that is, the amount used to capitalize the leased equipment?

Answer: The present value factor from Table 2 is 3.60478 (5 periods at 12%). The present value of 5 payments of $6,000 each discounted at 12% is **$21,628.68** ($6,000 × 3.60478).

Time Periods and Discounting

In the preceding calculations, the discounting was done on an *annual* basis using an *annual* interest rate. Discounting may also be done over shorter periods of time such as monthly, quarterly, or semiannually.

When the time frame is less than one year, you need to convert the annual interest rate to the applicable time frame. Assume, for example, that the investor in Illustration D-8 received $500 **semiannually** for three years instead of $1,000 annually. In this case, the number of periods becomes six (3 × 2), the discount rate is 5% (10% ÷ 2), the present value factor from Table 2 is 5.07569, and the present value of the future cash flows is $2,537.85 (5.07569 × $500). This amount is slightly higher than the $2,486.86 computed in Illustration D-9 because interest is paid twice during the same year; therefore interest is earned on the first half year's interest.

Computing the Present Value of a Long-Term Note or Bond

The present value (or market price) of a long-term note or bond is a function of three variables: (1) the payment amounts, (2) the length of time until the amounts are paid, and (3) the discount rate. Our illustration uses a five-year bond issue.

Study Objective [5]
Compute the present value of notes and bonds.

---

[1]The difference of .00001 between 2.48686 and 2.48685 is due to rounding.

The first variable—dollars to be paid—is made up of two elements: (1) a series of interest payments (an annuity), and (2) the principal amount (a single sum). To compute the present value of the bond, we must discount both the interest payments and the principal amount—two different computations. The time diagrams for a bond due in five years are shown in Illustration D-11.

Illustration D-11

Present value of a bond time diagram

When the investor's market interest rate is equal to the bond's contractual interest rate, the present value of the bonds will *equal* the face value of the bonds. To illustrate, assume a bond issue of 10%, five-year bonds with a face value of $100,000 with interest payable **semiannually** on January 1 and July 1. If the discount rate is the same as the contractual rate, the bonds will sell at face value. In this case, the investor will receive the following: (1) $100,000 at maturity, and (2) a series of ten $5,000 interest payments [($100,000 × 10%) ÷ 2] over the term of the bonds. The length of time is expressed in terms of interest periods—in this case—10, and the discount rate per interest period, 5%. The following time diagram (Illustration D-12) depicts the variables involved in this discounting situation.

Illustration D-12

Time diagram for present value of a 10%, five-year bond paying interest semiannually

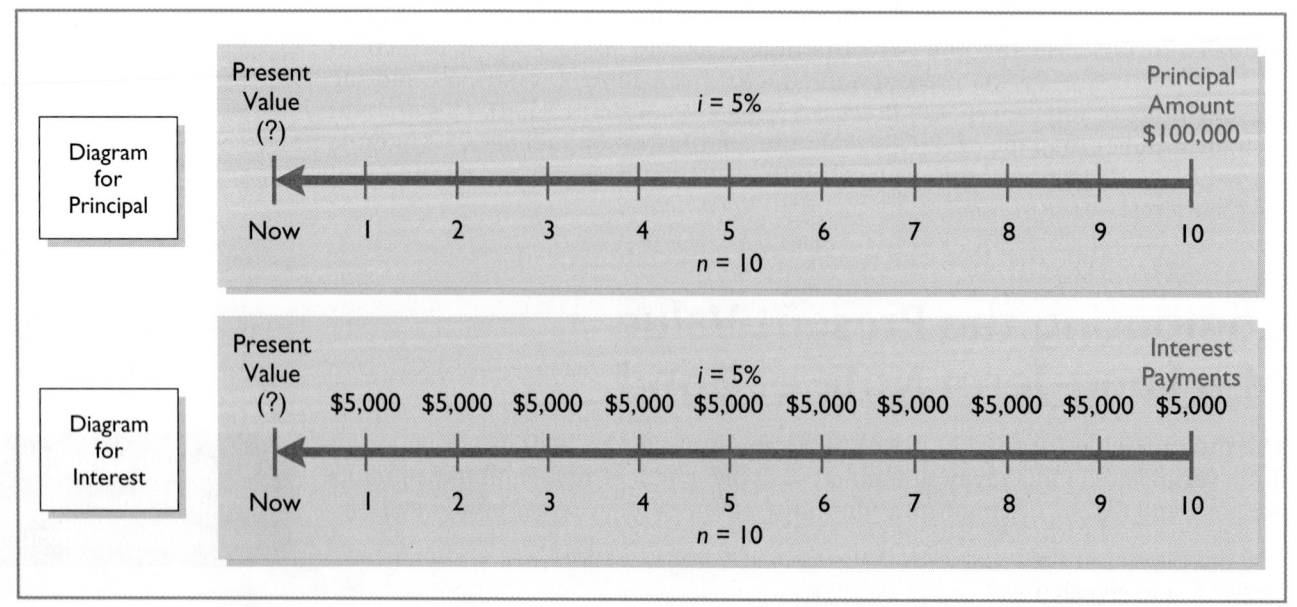

Illustration D-13 shows the computation of the present value of these bonds.

Illustration D-13
Present value of principal
and interest—face value

10% Contractual Rate—10% Discount Rate	
Present value of principal to be received at maturity	
$100,000 × PV of 1 due in 10 periods at 5%	
$100,000 × .61391 (Table 1)	$ 61,391
Present value of interest to be received periodically	
over the term of the bonds	
$5,000 × PV of 1 due periodically for 10 periods at 5%	
$5,000 × 7.72173 (Table 2)	38,609*
Present value of bonds	**$100,000**

*Rounded

Illustration D-13
Present value of principal
and interest—face value

Now assume that the investor's required rate of return is 12%, not 10%. The future amounts are again $100,000 and $5,000, respectively, but now a discount rate of 6% (12% ÷ 2) must be used. The present value of the bonds is $92,639, as computed in Illustration D-14.

10% Contractual Rate—12% Discount Rate	
Present value of principal to be received at maturity	
$100,000 × .55839 (Table 1)	$55,839
Present value of interest to be received periodically	
over the term of the bonds	
$5,000 × 7.36009 (Table 2)	36,800
Present value of bonds	**$92,639**

Illustration D-14
Present value of principal
and interest—discount

Conversely, if the discount rate is 8% and the contractual rate is 10%, the present value of the bonds is $108,111, computed as shown in Illustration D-15.

10% Contractual Rate—8% Discount Rate	
Present value of principal to be received at maturity	
$100,000 × .67556 (Table 1)	$ 67,556
Present value of interest to be received periodically	
over the term of the bonds	
$5,000 × 8.11090 (Table 2)	40,555
Present value of bonds	**$108,111**

Illustration D-15
Present value of principal
and interest—premium

The above discussion relies on present value tables in solving present value problems. Many people use spreadsheets such as Excel or financial calculators (some even on websites) to compute present values, without the use of tables. Many calculators, especially "financial calculators," have present value (PV) functions that allow you to calculate present values by merely inputting the proper amount, discount rate, and periods, and pressing the PV key. Appendix E illustrates how to use a financial calculator in various business situations.

Summary of Study Objectives

[1] Distinguish between simple and compound interest. Simple interest is computed on the principal only, while compound interest is computed on the principal and any interest earned that has not been withdrawn.

[2] Identify the variables fundamental to solving present value problems. The following three variables are fundamental to solving present value problems: (1) the future amount, (2) the number of periods, and (3) the interest rate (the discount rate).

[3] Solve for present value of a single amount. Prepare a time diagram of the problem. Identify the future amount, the number of discounting periods, and the discount (interest) rate. Using the present value of a single amount table, multiply the future amount by the present value factor specified at the intersection of the number of periods and the discount rate.

[4] Solve for present value of an annuity. Prepare a time diagram of the problem. Identify the future annuity pay-ments, the number of discounting periods, and the discount (interest) rate. Using the present value of an annuity of 1 table, multiply the amount of the annuity payments by the present value factor specified at the intersection of the number of periods and the interest rate.

[5] Compute the present value of notes and bonds. To determine the present value of the principal amount: Multiply the principal amount (a single future amount) by the present value factor (from the present value of 1 table) intersecting at the number of periods (number of interest payments) and the discount rate.

To determine the present value of the series of interest payments: Multiply the amount of the interest payment by the present value factor (from the present value of an annuity of 1 table) intersecting at the number of periods (number of interest payments) and the discount rate. Add the present value of the principal amount to the present value of the interest payments to arrive at the present value of the note or bond.

Glossary

Annuity   A series of equal dollar amounts to be paid or received at evenly spaced time intervals (periodically). (p. D5).

Compound interest   The interest computed on the principal and any interest earned that has not been paid or withdrawn. (p. D2).

Discounting the future amount(s)   The process of determining present value. (p. D3).

Interest   Payment for the use of another's money. (p. D1).

Present value   The value now of a given amount to be paid or received in the future assuming compound interest. (p. D3).

Present value of an annuity   The value now of a series of future receipts or payments, discounted assuming compound interest. (p. D5).

Principal   The amount borrowed or invested. (p. D1).

Simple interest   The interest computed on the principal only. (p. D1).

Brief Exercises

Use tables to solve exercises.

Use present value tables.

BED-1   For each of the following cases, indicate (a) to what interest rate columns, and (b) to what number of periods you would refer in looking up the discount rate.

1. In Table 1 (present value of 1):

	Annual Rate	Number of Years Involved	Compounding Per Year
(a)	12%	6	Annually
(b)	10%	15	Annually
(c)	8%	12	Semiannually

2. In Table 2 (present value of an annuity of 1):

	Annual Rate	Number of Years Involved	Number of Payments Involved	Frequency of Payments
(a)	8%	20	20	Annually
(b)	10%	5	5	Annually
(c)	12%	4	8	Semiannually

Determine present values.

BED-2   (a) What is the present value of $30,000 due 8 periods from now, discounted at 8%? (b) What is the present value of $30,000 to be received at the end of each of 6 periods, discounted at 9%?

BED-3 Ramirez Company is considering an investment that will return a lump sum of $600,000 5 years from now. What amount should Ramirez Company pay for this investment in order to earn a 10% return?

Compute the present value of a single-sum investment.

BED-4 LaRussa Company earns 9% on an investment that will return $700,000 8 years from now. What is the amount LaRussa should invest now in order to earn this rate of return?

Compute the present value of a single-sum investment.

BED-5 Polley Company sold a 5-year, zero-interest-bearing $36,000 note receivable to Valley Inc. Valley wishes to earn 10% over the remaining 4 years of the note. How much cash will Polley receive upon sale of the note?

Compute the present value of a single-sum zero-interest-bearing note.

BED-6 Marichal Company issues a 3-year, zero-interest-bearing $60,000 note. The interest rate used to discount the zero-interest-bearing note is 8%. What are the cash proceeds that Marichal Company should receive?

Compute the present value of a single-sum zero-interest-bearing note.

BED-7 Colaw Company is considering investing in an annuity contract that will return $40,000 annually at the end of each year for 15 years. What amount should Colaw Company pay for this investment if it earns a 6% return?

Compute the present value of an annuity investment.

BED-8 Sauder Enterprises earns 11% on an investment that pays back $100,000 at the end of each of the next 4 years. What is the amount Sauder Enterprises invested to earn the 11% rate of return?

Compute the present value of an annuity investment.

BED-9 Chicago Railroad Co. is about to issue $200,000 of 10-year bonds paying a 10% interest rate, with interest payable semiannually. The discount rate for such securities is 8%. How much can Chicago expect to receive for the sale of these bonds?

Compute the present value of bonds.

BED-10 Assume the same information as in BED-9 except that the discount rate is 10% instead of 8%. In this case, how much can Chicago expect to receive from the sale of these bonds?

Compute the present value of bonds.

BED-11 Berghaus Company receives a $75,000, 6-year note bearing interest of 8% (paid annually) from a customer at a time when the discount rate is 9%. What is the present value of the note received by Berghaus Company?

Compute the present value of a note.

BED-12 Troutman Enterprises issued 8%, 8-year, $1,000,000 par value bonds that pay interest semiannually on October 1 and April 1. The bonds are dated April 1, 2012, and are issued on that date. The discount rate of interest for such bonds on April 1, 2012, is 10%. What cash proceeds did Troutman receive from issuance of the bonds?

Compute the present value of bonds.

BED-13 Ricky Cleland owns a garage and is contemplating purchasing a tire retreading machine for $16,280. After estimating costs and revenues, Ricky projects a net cash flow from the retreading machine of $2,800 annually for 8 years. Ricky hopes to earn a return of 11% on such investments. What is the present value of the retreading operation? Should Ricky Cleland purchase the retreading machine?

Compute the value of a machine for purposes of making a purchase decision.

BED-14 Martinez Company issues a 10%, 6-year mortgage note on January 1, 2012, to obtain financing for new equipment. Land is used as collateral for the note. The terms provide for semi-annual installment payments of $78,978. What were the cash proceeds received from the issuance of the note?

Compute the present value of a note.

BED-15 Durler Company is considering purchasing equipment. The equipment will produce the following cash flows: Year 1, $30,000; Year 2, $40,000; Year 3, $60,000. Durler requires a minimum rate of return of 12%. What is the maximum price Durler should pay for this equipment?

Compute the maximum price to pay for a machine.

BED-16 If Carla Garcia invests $2,745 now, she will receive $10,000 at the end of 15 years. What annual rate of interest will Carla earn on her investment? (*Hint:* Use Table 1.)

Compute the interest rate on a single sum.

BED-17 Sara Altom has been offered the opportunity of investing $51,316 now. The investment will earn 10% per year and at the end of that time will return Sara $100,000. How many years must Sara wait to receive $100,000? (*Hint:* Use Table 1.)

Compute the number of periods of a single sum.

BED-18 Stacy Dains purchased an investment for $11,469.92. From this investment, she will receive $1,000 annually for the next 20 years, starting one year from now. What rate of interest will Stacy's investment be earning for her? (*Hint:* Use Table 2.)

Compute the interest rate on an annuity.

BED-19 Diana Rossi invests $8,559.48 now for a series of $1,000 annual returns, beginning one year from now. Diana will earn a return of 8% on the initial investment. How many annual payments of $1,000 will Diana receive? (*Hint:* Use Table 2.)

Compute the number of periods of an annuity.

BED-20 Minitori Company needs $10,000 on January 1, 2015. It is starting a fund on January 1, 2012.

Compute the amount to be invested.

Instructions

Compute the amount that must be invested in the fund on January 1, 2012, to produce a $10,000 balance on January 1, 2015, if:

(a) The fund earns 8% per year compounded annually.
(b) The fund earns 8% per year compounded semiannually.
(c) The fund earns 12% per year compounded annually.
(d) The fund earns 12% per year compounded semiannually.

Compute the amount to be invested.

BED-21   Venuchi Company needs $10,000 on January 1, 2017. It is starting a fund to produce that amount.

Instructions

Compute the amount that must be invested in the fund to produce a $10,000 balance on January 1, 2017, if:

(a) The initial investment is made January 1, 2012, and the fund earns 6% per year.
(b) The initial investment is made January 1, 2014, and the fund earns 6% per year.
(c) The initial investment is made January 1, 2012, and the fund earns 10% per year.
(d) The initial investment is made January 1, 2014, and the fund earns 10% per year.

Select the better payment option.

BED-22   Letterman Corporation is buying new equipment. It can pay $39,500 today (option 1), or $10,000 today and 5 yearly payments of $8,000 each, starting in one year (option 2).

Instructions

Which option should Letterman select? (Assume a discount rate of 10%.)

Compute the cost of an investment, amount received, and rate of return.

BED-23   Carmen Corporation is considering several investments.

Instructions

(a) One investment returns $10,000 per year for 5 years and provides a return of 10%. What is the cost of this investment?
(b) Another investment costs $50,000 and returns a certain amount per year for 10 years, providing an 8% return. What amount is received each year?
(c) A third investment costs $70,000 and returns $11,971 each year for 15 years. What is the rate of return on this investment?

Select the best payment option.

BED-24   You are the beneficiary of a trust fund. The fund gives you the option of receiving $5,000 per year for 10 years, $9,000 per year for 5 years, or $30,000 today.

Instructions

If the desired rate of return is 8%, which option should you select?

Compute the semiannual car payment.

BED-25   You are purchasing a car for $24,000, and you obtain financing as follows: $2,400 down payment, 12% interest, semiannual payments over 5 years.

Instructions

Compute the payment you will make every 6 months

Compute the present value of bonds.

BED-26   Contreras Corporation is considering purchasing bonds of Jose Company as an investment. The bonds have a face value of $40,000 with a 10% interest rate. The bonds mature in 4 years and pay interest semiannually.

Instructions

(a) What is the most Contreras should pay for the bonds if it desires a 12% return?
(b) What is the most Contreras should pay for the bonds if it desires an 8% return?

Compute the present value of bonds.

BED-27   Garcia Corporation is considering purchasing bonds of Fred Company as an investment. The bonds have a face value of $90,000 with a 9% interest rate. The bonds mature in 6 years and pay interest semiannually.

Instructions

(a) What is the most Garcia should pay for the bonds if it desires a 10% return?
(b) What is the most Garcia should pay for the bonds if it desires an 8% return?

APPENDIXE

Using Financial Calculators

Study Objective

After studying this appendix, you should be able to:

[1] Use a financial calculator to solve time value of money problems.

Business professionals, once they have mastered the underlying concepts in Appendix D, often use a financial (business) calculator to solve time value of money problems. In many cases, they must use calculators if interest rates or time periods do not correspond with the information provided in the compound interest tables.

To use financial calculators, you enter the time value of money variables into the calculator. Illustration E-1 shows the five most common keys used to solve time value of money problems.[1]

Study Objective [1]
Use a financial calculator to solve time value of money problems.

Illustration E-1
Financial calculator keys

where

N	=	number of periods
I	=	interest rate per period (some calculators use I/YR or i)
PV	=	present value (occurs at the beginning of the first period)
PMT	=	payment (all payments are equal, and none are skipped)
FV	=	future value (occurs at the end of the last period)

In solving time value of money problems in this appendix, you will generally be given three of four variables and will have to solve for the remaining variable. The fifth key (the key not used) is given a value of zero to ensure that this variable is not used in the computation.

Present Value of a Single Sum

To illustrate how to solve a present value problem using a financial calculator, assume that you want to know the present value of $84,253 to be received in five years, discounted at 11% compounded annually. Illustration E-2 (page E2) pictures this problem.

---

[1]On many calculators, these keys are actual buttons on the face of the calculator; on others, they appear on the display after the user accesses a present value menu.

Illustration E-2
Calculator solution for present
value of a single sum

The diagram shows you the information (inputs) to enter into the calculator: N = 5, I = 11, PMT = 0, and FV = 84,253. You then press PV for the answer: −$50,000. As indicated, the PMT key was given a value of zero because a series of payments did not occur in this problem.

Plus and Minus

The use of plus and minus signs in time value of money problems with a financial calculator can be confusing. Most financial calculators are programmed so that the positive and negative cash flows in any problem offset each other. In the present value problem above, we identified the $84,253 future value initial investment as a positive (inflow); the answer −$50,000 was shown as a negative amount, reflecting a cash outflow. If the 84,253 were entered as a negative, then the final answer would have been reported as a positive 50,000.

Hopefully, the sign convention will not cause confusion. If you understand what is required in a problem, you should be able to interpret a positive or negative amount in determining the solution to a problem.

Compounding Periods

In the problem above, we assumed that compounding occurs once a year. Some financial calculators have a default setting, which assumes that compounding occurs 12 times a year. You must determine what default period has been programmed into your calculator and change it as necessary to arrive at the proper compounding period.

Rounding

Most financial calculators store and calculate using 12 decimal places. As a result, because compound interest tables generally have factors only up to 5 decimal places, a slight difference in the final answer can result. In most time value of money problems, the final answer will not include more than two decimal points.

Present Value of an Annuity

To illustrate how to solve a present value of an annuity problem using a financial calculator, assume that you are asked to determine the present value of rental receipts of $6,000 each to be received at the end of each of the next five years, when discounted at 12%, as pictured in Illustration E-3.

Illustration E-3
Calculator solution for present
value of an annuity

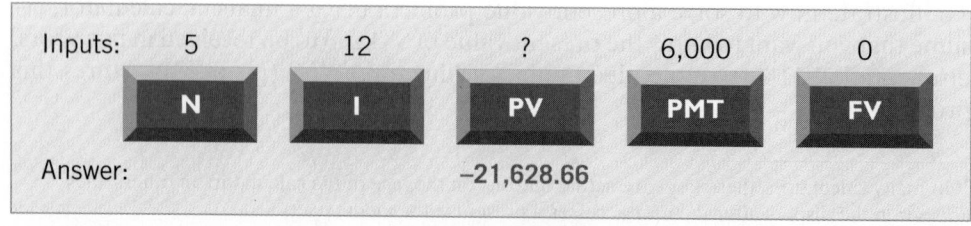

In this case, you enter N = 5, I = 12, PMT = 6,000, FV = 0, and then press PV to arrive at the answer of $21,628.66.

Useful Applications of the Financial Calculator

With a financial calculator, you can solve for any interest rate or for any number of periods in a time value of money problem. Here are some examples of these applications.

Auto Loan

Assume you are financing the purchase of a used car with a three-year loan. The loan has a 9.5% nominal annual interest rate, compounded monthly. The price of the car is $6,000, and you want to determine the monthly payments, assuming that the payments start one month after the purchase. This problem is pictured in Illustration E-4.

Illustration E-4
Calculator solution for auto loan payments

To solve this problem, you enter N = 36 (12 × 3), I = 9.5, PV = 6,000, FV = 0, and then press PMT. You will find that the monthly payments will be $192.20. Note that the payment key is usually programmed for 12 payments per year. Thus, you must change the default (compounding period) if the payments are other than monthly.

Mortgage Loan Amount

Let's say you are evaluating financing options for a loan on a house. You decide that the maximum mortgage payment you can afford is $700 per month. The annual interest rate is 8.4%. If you get a mortgage that requires you to make monthly payments over a 15-year period, what is the maximum purchase price you can afford? Illustration E-5 depicts this problem.

Illustration E-5
Calculator solution for mortgage amount

You enter N = 180 (12 × 15 years), I = 8.4, PMT = −700, FV = 0, and press PV. You find a present value of $71,509.81—the maximum house price you can afford, given that you want to keep your mortgage payments at $700. Note that by changing any of the variables, you can quickly conduct "what-if" analyses for different situations.

Summary of Learning Objective

[1] Use a financial calculator to solve time value of money problems. Financial calculators can be used to solve the same and additional problems as those solved with time value of money tables. One enters into the financial calculator the amounts for all but one of the unknown elements of a time value of money problem (periods, interest rate, payments, future or present value). Particularly useful situations involve interest rates and compounding periods not presented in the tables.

Brief Exercises

Determine interest rate.

BEE-1   Reba McEntire wishes to invest $19,000 on July 1, 2012, and have it accumulate to $49,000 by July 1, 2022.

Instructions
Use a financial calculator to determine at what exact annual rate of interest Reba must invest the $19,000.

Determine interest rate.

BEE-2   On July 17, 2012, Tim McGraw borrowed $42,000 from his grandfather to open a clothing store. Starting July 17, 2013, Tim has to make 10 equal annual payments of $6,500 each to repay the loan.

Instructions
Use a financial calculator to determine what interest rate Tim is paying.

Determine interest rate.

BEE-3   As the purchaser of a new house, Patty Loveless has signed a mortgage note to pay the Memphis National Bank and Trust Co. $14,000 every 6 months for 20 years, at the end of which time she will own the house. At the date the mortgage is signed the purchase price was $198,000, and Loveless made a down payment of $20,000. The first payment will be made 6 months after the date the mortgage is signed.

Instructions
Using a financial calculator, compute the exact rate of interest earned on the mortgage by the bank.

Various time value of money situations.

BEE-4   Using a financial calculator, solve for the unknowns in each of the following situations.

(a) On June 1, 2012, Shelley Long purchases lakefront property from her neighbor, Joey Brenner, and agrees to pay the purchase price in seven payments of $16,000 each, the first payment to be payable June 1, 2013. (Assume that interest compounded at an annual rate of 7.35% is implicit in the payments.) What is the purchase price of the property?

(b) On January 1, 2012, Cooke Corporation purchased 200 of the $1,000 face value, 8% coupon, 10-year bonds of Howe Inc. The bonds mature on January 1, 2022, and pay interest annually beginning January 1, 2013. Cooke purchased the bonds to yield 10.65%. How much did Cooke pay for the bonds?

Various time value of money situations.

BEE-5   Using a financial calculator, provide a solution to each of the following situations.

(a) Bill Schroeder owes a debt of $35,000 from the purchase of his new sport utility vehicle. The debt bears annual interest of 9.1% compounded monthly. Bill wishes to pay the debt and interest in equal monthly payments over 8 years, beginning one month hence. What equal monthly payments will pay off the debt and interest?

(b) On January 1, 2012, Sammy Sosa offers to buy Mark Grace's used snowmobile for $8,000, payable in five equal annual installments, which are to include 8.25% interest on the unpaid balance and a portion of the principal. If the first payment is to be made on December 31, 2012, how much will each payment be?

APPENDIX F

Standards of Ethical Conduct for Management Accountants

Management accountants have an obligation to the organizations they serve, their profession, the public, and themselves to maintain the highest standards of ethical conduct. In recognition of this obligation, the Institute of Management Accountants (IMA) has published and promoted the following standards of ethical conduct for management accountants.[1]

IMA Statement of Ethical Professional Practice

Members of IMA shall behave ethically. A commitment to ethical professional practice includes: overarching principles that express our values, and standards that guide our conduct.

Principles

IMA's overarching ethical principles include: Honesty, Fairness, Objectivity, and Responsibility. Members shall act in accordance with these principles and shall encourage others within their organizations to adhere to them.

Standards

A member's failure to comply with the following standards may result in disciplinary action.

I. COMPETENCE

Each member has a responsibility to:

1. Maintain an appropriate level of professional expertise by continually developing knowledge and skills.
2. Perform professional duties in accordance with relevant laws, regulations, and technical standards.
3. Provide decision support information and recommendations that are accurate, clear, concise, and timely.
4. Recognize and communicate professional limitations or other constraints that would preclude responsible judgment or successful performance of an activity.

---

[1]Reprinted by permission of the Institute of Management Accountants, *www.imanet.org/pdf/981.pdf.*

II. CONFIDENTIALITY

Each member has a responsibility to:

1. Keep information confidential except when disclosure is authorized or legally required.

2. Inform all relevant parties regarding appropriate use of confidential information. Monitor subordinates' activities to ensure compliance.

3. Refrain from using confidential information for unethical or illegal advantage.

III. INTEGRITY

Each member has a responsibility to:

1. Mitigate actual conflicts of interest. Regularly communicate with business associates to avoid apparent conflicts of interest. Advise all parties of any potential conflicts.

2. Refrain from engaging in any conduct that would prejudice carrying out duties ethically.

3. Abstain from engaging in or supporting any activity that might discredit the profession.

IV. CREDIBILITY

Each member has a responsibility to:

1. Communicate information fairly and objectively.

2. Disclose all relevant information that could reasonably be expected to influence an intended user's understanding of the reports, analyses, or recommendations.

3. Disclose delays or deficiencies in information, timeliness, processing, or internal controls in conformance with organization policy and/or applicable law.

Resolution of Ethical Conflict

In applying the Standards of Ethical Professional Practice, you may encounter problems identifying unethical behavior or resolving an ethical conflict. When faced with ethical issues, you should follow your organization's established policies on the resolution of such conflict. If these policies do not resolve the ethical conflict, you should consider the following courses of action:

1. Discuss the issue with your immediate supervisor except when it appears that the supervisor is involved. In that case, present the issue to the next level. If you cannot achieve a satisfactory resolution, submit the issue to the next management level. If your immediate superior is the chief executive officer or equivalent, the acceptable reviewing authority may be a group such as the audit committee, executive committee, board of directors, board of trustees, or owners. Contact with levels above the immediate superior should be initiated only with your superior's knowledge, assuming he or she is not involved. Communication of such problems to authorities or individuals not employed or engaged by the organization is not considered appropriate, unless you believe there is a clear violation of the law.

2. Clarify relevant ethical issues by initiating a confidential discussion with an IMA Ethics Counselor or other impartial advisor to obtain a better understanding of possible courses of action.

3. Consult your own attorney as to legal obligations and rights concerning the ethical conflict.

PHOTO CREDITS

Chapter 1   Page 3 Monica Wells/SuperStock Page 6 iStockphoto Page 8 Gemunu Amarasinghe/AP Photo Page 10 Toru Hanai/AP/Wide World Photos Page 12 Josef Volavka/iStockphoto

Chapter 2   Page 51 m63/ZUMA Press/Newscom/ NewsCom Page 55 Jonathan Daniel/Getty Images, Inc. Page 61 Sciencefaction/SuperStock Page 73 Enviromatic/ iStockphoto

Chapter 3   Page 99 James Lauritz/Digital Vision/Getty Images, Inc. Page 102 Dan Chippendale/iStockphoto Page 110 Apcuk/iStockphoto Page 114 Günay Mutlu/iStockphoto

Chapter 4   Page 153 Comstock/Getty Images, Inc. Page 165 Alex Slobodkin/iStockphoto Page 170 Christian Lagereek/ iStockphoto Page 172 Lowell Sannes/iStockphoto Page 173 Denis Vorob'yev/iStockphoto Page 174 Nikki Ward/ iStockphoto Page 175 Jorge Salcedo/iStockphoto Page 176 (top) Vladislav Gurfinkel/iStockphoto (bottom) iStockphoto

Chapter 5   Page 209 Stone/Getty Images, Inc. Page 213 Ben Blankenburg/iStockphoto Page 220 Maciej Noskowski/ iStockphoto Page 226 Heizfrosch/iStockphoto

Chapter 6   Page 261 Steve Dunning/Getty Images, Inc. Page 263 Alexey Dudoladov/iStockphoto Page 264 Yin Yang/iStockphoto Page 275 AP/Wide World Photos Page 279 Jaap Hart/iStockphoto

Chapter 7   Page 315 Terra Images/Age Fotostock America, Inc. Page 318 Sean Locke/iStockphoto Page 321 Niels Laan/ iStockphoto

Chapter 8   Page 361 Valerie Loiseleux/iStockphoto Page 371 (top) Tom Nulens/iStockphoto (bottom) Catherine Yeulet/iStockphoto Page 387 AFP Photo/Timothy A. Clary/ NewsCom

Chapter 9   Page 415 cogal/iStockphoto Page 427 Michael Braun/iStockphoto Page 430 iStockphoto Page 432 Andy Dean/iStockphoto

Chapter 10   Page 457 David Trood/Getty Images, Inc Page 461 iStockphoto Page 478 iStockphoto Page 480 Linda Steward/iStockphoto

Chapter 11   Page 509 Cary Westfall/iStockphoto Page 516 Steve Diblee/iStockphoto Page 527 Katie Nesling/iStockphoto

Chapter 12   Page 553 Charles Taylor/iStockphoto Page 556 Malcolm Romain/iStockphoto Page 559 PhotoDisc/Getty Images, Inc.

Chapter 13   Page 593 Andy Mead/YCJ/Icon SMI/ NewsCom Page 598 Paul Sakuma/AP/Wide World Photos

Page 600 Rick Bowmer/AP/Wide World Photos Page 608 Paul Vidler/Alamy

Chapter 14   Page 633 Daisy Daisy/Photographer's Choice/ Getty Images, Inc. Page 637 Alex Mathers/iStockphoto Page 641 Dietmar Klement/iStockphoto Page 643 Stephen Strathdee/iStockphoto

Chapter 15   Page 669 Corporation of London/HIP/The Image Works Page 686 Paul Fleet/Alamy

Chapter 16   Page 723 Topham/The Image Works

Chapter 17   Page 761 Justin Sullivan/Getty Images, Inc. Page 765 Darren McCollester/Getty Images, Inc. Page 773 Svetlana Tebenkova/iStockphoto Page 779 PhotoDisc, Inc./ Getty Images

Chapter 18   Page 825 Daniel Acker/Bloomberg/Getty Images, Inc. Page 836 SuperStock Page 848 Kenneth C. Zirkel/ iStockphoto

Chapter 19   Page 877 Christopher Farina/Corbis-Bettmann Page 880 Peter Kramer/Getty Images, Inc. Page 885 Glowimaes/ Getty Images, Inc. Page 894 David Joyner/iStockphoto Page 897 Octavio Campos/iStockphoto

Chapter 20   Page 923 Tim McCaig/iStockphoto Page 926 iStockphoto Page 938 Andrew Johnson/iStockphoto Page 942 Marcin Balcerzak/iStockphoto

Chapter 21   Page 965 Lou Dematteis/Reuters/Corbis Page 971 iStockphoto Page 976 MTV Games/Scripps Howard Photo Service/NewsCom

Chapter 22   Page 1011 iStockphoto Page 1014 Ugurhan Betin/iStockphoto Page 1018 Pidjoe/iStockphoto Page 1024 Digital Vision/Getty Images, Inc. Page 1028 Yael/Retna

Chapter 23   Page 1056 Thinkstock/Comstock/Getty Images, Inc. Page 1063 Vladimir Melnikov/iStockphoto Page 1067 Diane Bondareff/AP/Wide World Photos Page 1070 Wolfgang Rattya/Corbis Page 1074 AP/Wide World Photos

Chapter 24   Page 1097 Marcus Clackson/iStockphoto Page 1107 Eric Isselée/iStockphoto Page 1110 Digital Vision/ Getty Images, Inc. Page 1119 Brentmelissa/iStockphoto Page 1121 Kyodo/AP/Wide World Photos

Chapter 25   Page 1147 iStockphoto Page 1150 SpotX/ iStockphoto Page 1153 Hywit Dimyadi/iStockphoto Page 1164 Photo Disc, Inc/Getty Images, Inc.

Chapter 26   Page 1193 spxChrome/iStockphoto Page 1196 Geopaul/iStockphoto Page 1204 Max Blain/iStockphoto Page 1207 Tomislav Forgo/iStockphoto Page 1212 iStockphoto

COMPANY INDEX

Present value, 673
  of an annuity, 692–693, D5–D7, E2–E3
  and bond pricing, 690–695
  of bonds, 673
  of face value, 690–691
  of interest payments (annuities), 692–693
  of leases, 684
  of long-term notes/bonds, D7–D9
  of a single amount, D3–D5
  time periods in computing, 693–694
  using financial calculator for, E1–E2
  variables in, D3
Present value of 1 factors, D4
Price/earnings (P/E) ratio, 648n.3, 841–842
Price variances:
  labor, 1158–1159
  materials, 1156
Prior period adjustments, 644
Private accounting, 29–30. See also
  Managerial accounting
Privately held corporations, 594
Process cost flow, 969–970
Process cost system, 925–926, 966–987
  and activity-based costing, 984–985
  assigning manufacturing costs, 970–972
  equivalent units, 972–976
  example of, 976–982
  job order cost systems vs., 967–970
  and just-in-time processing, 982–984
  process cost flow, 969–970
  for service companies, 967
  uses of, 966–967
Products, sell-vs.-processing further
  decisions for, 1200–1201
Product costs, 886–887, 893–894
Production budget, 1060–1061
Production cost report, 975–976, 980
Productivity, in auto industry, 886
Product warranties, 516–517
Profitability, creditor interest in, 826
Profitability ratios, 838–842
Profit and loss statement, 23. See also
  Income statement
Profit centers, 1112, 1114–1116
Profit margin, 838–839
Pro forma income, 850
Promissory notes, 427–429. See also
  Notes receivable
Property, plant, and equipment, 173, 458,
  504–506. See also Plant assets
Proprietorships, 10–11, 176
Proving ledgers, 325, 329
Provisions, 550
"Provisions, Contingent Liabilities, and
  Contingent Assets" (IAS 37), 549, 718
Public accounting, 29
Public Company Accounting Oversight
  Board (PCAOB), 363
Publicly held corporations, 594
Pull approach to manufacturing, 982
Purchases:
  of buildings, 460
  of merchandise, recording, 213–218
  recording, 233–234
  transaction analysis for, 16–17
Purchase allowances, 216, 234
Purchase discounts, 216–217, 234
Purchase invoice, 213–214
Purchases journal, 329–331
Purchase of an interest (partnerships),
  572–573
Purchase returns, 216, 234
Push approach to manufacturing, 982

Q
Quality of earnings, 850–852
Quantity variances:
  labor, 1157–1159
  materials, 1156
Quarterly tax reports, 528
QuickBooks®, 315–317
Quick ratio, 835. See also Acid-test ratio

R
Radio frequency identification (RFID)
  technology, 279
Ratio analysis, 827, 833–844
  liquidity ratios, 835–838
  profitability ratios, 838–842
  solvency ratios, 842–843
Raw materials, 262, 885
Raw materials costs, 928, 930–931
R&D (research and development) costs,
  478–479
Real accounts, 160. See also Permanent
  accounts
Real estate taxes payable, 13
Realized gain/loss, 737–738
Reasonable assurance concept, 371
Receivables, 416–436
  accounts receivable, 417–427
  on financial statements, 433–435
  IFRS and GAAP for, 453–454
  notes receivable, 427–433
  types of, 416–417
Receivables turnover, 837
Reconciling bank accounts, 383–387
  electronic funds transfers, 387
  entries form, 385–387
  illustration of, 385–386
  procedure for, 383–385
Reconciling items, for statement of cash
  flows, 784–787
Record date (cash dividends), 635–636
Recording process, 52–76, 234
  accounts in, 52–57
  activities in, 4–5
  for contingent liabilities, 516–517
  debits and credits in, 52–56
  for employer payroll taxes, 527
  illustrated, 63–71
  for payroll, 522–524
  with periodic inventory system, 233–235
  for purchases of merchandise, 213–218
  for sales of merchandise, 218–221
  for special and general journals, 334
  steps in, 57–63
  trial balance in, 70–74
Record-keeping, segregation of physical
  custody and, 366, 373
Redeeming bonds, 679
Registered bonds, 672
Regular partnerships, 555
Regulations, government, 1148
  for corporations, 596–597
  as standards, 1148. See also Standard costs
Regulatory agencies, 7
Reimbursement requests, fraud involving,
  367
Relevance of figures, 9
Relevant range, 1014–1016, 1104
Repairs, ordinary, 470
Republic of Debtors (Bruce Mann), 669
Repurchase of shares, 608
Required rate of return, 1210
Research and development (R&D) costs,
  478–479

Reserves, 629, 630
Residual claims, 599
Residual equity, 13. See also Owner's equity
Residual value, 504
Resource allocation decisions, 1204–1205
Responsibility, establishment of, 364
Responsibility accounting, 1109–1102
  controllable vs. noncontrollable revenues/
    costs, 1111
  responsibility centers, 1112, 1114–1120
  responsibility reporting system, 1111–1113
Responsibility centers, 1112, 1114–1120
Responsibility reporting system, 1111–1113
Restricted cash, 389
Retailers, 210
Retail inventory method, 288–289
Retained earnings, 602, 642–645
  payment of cash dividends from, 634
  prior period adjustments, 644
  restrictions on, 643–644
  for statement of cash flows, 787, 795
Retained earnings statement, 645, 830–831
Retirement of plant assets, 471–472
Returns:
  purchase, 216
  sales, 219–220
Return on assets, 839–840
Return on common stockholders' equity,
  647, 840
Return on investment (ROI), 1117–1119,
  1163, 1164
Revenues, 13
  accrued, 103, 111–112
  controllable vs. noncontrollable, 1111
  in double-entry system, 55–56
  recognizing, 101–102
  for service companies, 938
  on single-step income statement, 227–228
  from stock investments, 729–730
  unearned, see Unearned revenues
Revenue expenditures, 470
Revenue recognition principle, 101–102
Reversing entries, 168, 170, 181–182
RFID technology, 279
Rifkin, Jeremy, 208
Risk assessment, 364
Risk levels of activities, 371
ROI, see Return on investment
Rolling Stones, 1028
Romania, 411
Rowlings, J.K., 475

S
Safe cash payments schedule, 566. See also
  Schedule of cash payments
Salaries, 518–519. See also Payroll accounting
  accrued, 114–116
  to partners, 562–563
Sales:
  of bonds, 725–727
  credit card, 426–427
  of equipment, loss on, 770
  of merchandise, recording, 218–221
  of notes receivable, 432
  of plant assets, 472–473
  of receivables, 425–426
  recording, 234–235
  of stocks, 728–729
Sales and administrative expense budget,
  1065
Sales budget, 1059–1060
Sales commissions, fraud involving, 368
Sales discounts, 220–221, 234–235

RAPID REVIEW
Chapter Content

ACCOUNTING EQUATION (Chapter 2)

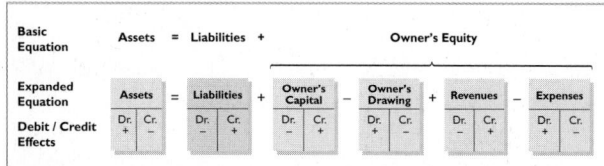

ADJUSTING ENTRIES (Chapter 3)

	Type	Adjusting Entry	
Deferrals	1. Prepaid expenses	Dr. Expenses	Cr. Assets
	2. Unearned revenues	Dr. Liabilities	Cr. Revenues
Accruals	1. Accrued revenues	Dr. Assets	Cr. Revenues
	2. Accrued expenses	Dr. Expenses	Cr. Liabilities

Note: Each adjusting entry will affect one or more income statement accounts and one or more balance sheet accounts.

Interest Computation

Interest = Face value of note × Annual interest rate × Time in terms of one year

CLOSING ENTRIES (Chapter 4)

Purpose: (1) Update the Owner's Capital account in the ledger by transferring net income (loss) and Owner's Drawing to Owner's Capital. (2) Prepare the temporary accounts (revenue, expense, Owner's Drawing) for the next period's postings by reducing their balances to zero.

Process

1. Debit each revenue account for its balance (assuming normal balances), and credit Income Summary for total revenues.
2. Debit Income Summary for total expenses, and credit each expense account for its balance (assuming normal balances).

   STOP AND CHECK: Does the balance in your Income Summary account equal the net income (loss) reported in the income statement?

3. Debit (credit) Income Summary, and credit (debit) Owner's Capital for the amount of net income (loss).
4. Debit Owner's Capital for the balance in the Owner's Drawing account and credit Owner's Drawing for the same amount.

   STOP AND CHECK: Does the balance in your Owner's Capital account equal the ending balance reported in the balance sheet and the owner's equity statement? Are all of your temporary account balances zero?

ACCOUNTING CYCLE (Chapter 4)

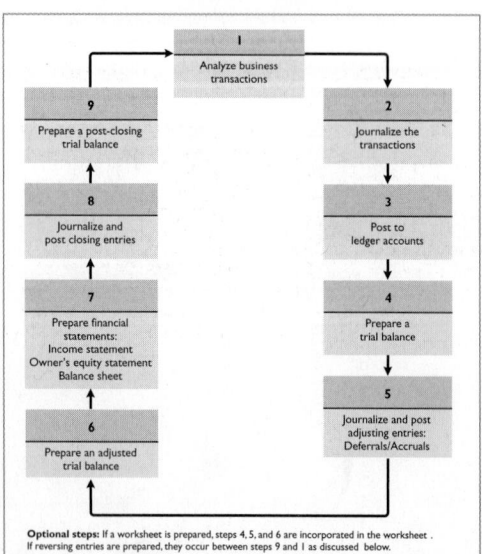

Optional steps: If a worksheet is prepared, steps 4, 5, and 6 are incorporated in the worksheet. If reversing entries are prepared, they occur between steps 9 and 1 as discussed below.

INVENTORY (Chapters 5 and 6)

Ownership

Freight Terms	Ownership of goods on public carrier resides with:	Who pays freight costs:
FOB shipping point	Buyer	Buyer
FOB destination	Seller	Seller

Perpetual vs. Periodic Journal Entries

Event	Perpetual	Periodic*
Purchase of goods	Inventory Cash (A/P)	Purchases Cash (A/P)
Freight (shipping point)	Inventory Cash	Freight-In Cash
Return of goods	Cash (or A/P) Inventory	Cash (or A/P) Purchase Returns and Allowances
Sale of goods	Cash (or A/R) Sales Cost of Goods Sold Inventory	Cash (or A/R) Sales No entry
End of period	No entry	Closing or adjusting entry required

Cost Flow Methods

- Specific identification
- First-in, first-out (FIFO)
- Weighted-average
- Last-in, first-out (LIFO)

FRAUD, INTERNAL CONTROL, AND CASH (Chapter 8)

The Fraud Triangle

Opportunity

Financial pressure

Rationalization

Principles of Internal Control Activities

- Establishment of responsibility
- Segregation of duties
- Documentation procedures
- Physical controls
- Independent internal verification
- Human resource controls

Bank Reconciliation

Bank	Books
Balance per bank statement Add: Deposit in transit	Balance per books Add: Unrecorded credit memoranda from bank statement
Deduct: Outstanding checks	Deduct: Unrecorded debit memoranda from bank statement
Adjusted cash balance	Adjusted cash balance

Note: 1. Errors should be offset (added or deducted) on the side that made the error.
2. Adjusting journal entries should only be made on the books.

STOP AND CHECK: Does the adjusted cash balance in the Cash account equal the reconciled balance?

RECEIVABLES (Chapter 9)

Methods to Account for Uncollectible Accounts

Direct write-off method	Record bad debts expense when the company determines a particular account to be uncollectible.
Allowance methods: Percentage-of-sales	At the end of each period, estimate the amount of credit sales uncollectible. Debit Bad Debts Expense and credit Allowance for Doubtful Accounts for this amount. As specific accounts become uncollectible, debit Allowance for Doubtful Accounts and credit Accounts Receivable.
Percentage-of-receivables	At the end of each period, estimate the amount of uncollectible receivables. Debit Bad Debts Expense and credit Allowance for Doubtful Accounts in an amount that results in a balance in the allowance account equal to the estimate of uncollectibles. As specific accounts become uncollectible, debit Allowance for Doubtful Accounts and credit Accounts Receivable.